Australian Master Tax Guide

Wolters Kluwer

Australian Master Tax Guide

68th Edition

2021

CCH AUSTRALIA LIMITED
GPO Box 4072, Sydney, NSW 2001
Head Office Macquarie Park
Phone: (02) 9857 1300 Fax: (02) 9857 1600
Customer Support
Phone: 1 300 300 224 Fax: 1 300 306 224
www.wolterskluwer.cch.com.au
Book Code: 10078212-0015

About Wolters Kluwer

Wolters Kluwer is a leading provider of accurate, authoritative and timely information services for professionals across the globe. We create value by combining information, deep expertise, and technology to provide our customers with solutions that contribute to the quality and effectiveness of their services. Professionals turn to us when they need actionable information to better serve their clients.

With the integrity and accuracy of over 45 years' experience in Australia and New Zealand, and over 175 years internationally, Wolters Kluwer is lifting the standard in software, knowledge, tools and education.

Wolters Kluwer — When you have to be right.

ISBN 978-1-922347-70-1

ISSN 0810-5596

Printed in Australia by McPherson's Printing Group

Foreword

We are pleased to bring you the 68th Edition of the *Australian Master Tax Guide*.

The Guide was first published in 1970 as a practical reference guide to assist in the preparation of tax returns, and to provide information relevant to the tax implications of decisions and transactions that taxpayers may face in the current financial year.

Over the course of 50+ years, the Guide has become Australia's best selling and most authoritative tax handbook. Used widely by tax agents, accountants, lawyers, financial advisers, lecturers, students and ATO officers alike, it is often the first port of call for those dealing with tax issues because of its clear and concise approach.

During this period, the Guide has grown to many times its original size, reflecting the increasing complexity of the tax environment. The Guide contains 45 chapters (including a chapter of detailed tax checklists). It also contains extra features such as an individual tax return preparation guide, tax calculators and a tax calendar. The Guide also uses shading on the side of select pages to help readers locate the most commonly used chapters, ie the income, deductions and depreciation (effective life) chapters.

Electronic versions of the Guide are available as a subscription product, updated at least 3 times a year, with all pertinent changes integrated into the relevant chapters. The online version of the Guide, in addition to having a superior searching capability via the CCH iKnow platform, provides useful links to the rulings, cases and legislation discussed in the commentary. In keeping with its role as the first point of reference in researching tax issues, the Guide contains extensive cross references to more detailed commentary in CCH's *Australian Federal Tax Reporter, Australian Federal Income Tax Reporter, Australian Superannuation Law & Practice* and *Australian GST Guide*.

The production of this Guide would not be possible without the ongoing efforts of a team of dedicated writers, subeditors and production editors who contribute in so many ways to making the Guide the Tax Practitioner's ''Bible'' — our grateful thanks go to them all.

Wolters Kluwer

January 2021

Contents

Wolters Kluwer Acknowledgments

Wolters Kluwer wishes to thank the following who contributed to and supported this publication:

Director, General Manager, Research & Learning, Wolters Kluwer Asia Pacific

Lauren Ma

Associate Director, Regional Head of Content, Wolters Kluwer Asia Pacific

Diana Winfield

Books Coordinator, Wolters Kluwer Asia Pacific

Alexandra Gonzalez

Writers

Karen Bang BCom, LLB has written for Wolters Kluwer's accounting and GST services. She has also worked as an auditor and GST consultant at a major international accounting firm.

Alan Burn BA, LLB contributes to a number of Wolters Kluwer tax publications, including the *Australian Federal Tax Reporter* and the *NSW Land Tax* services. His background covers IT, publishing and telecommunications, with technical roles at the ATO and in online tax software services.

Edwin Carr BA, LLM has worked for the ATO, and as a tax adviser in large accounting firms and financial institutions. Since then he has been a writer and editor on Australian taxation for more than 20 years, including for Wolters Kluwer.

Cindy Chan BCom, LLB, MTax is a senior content specialist at Wolters Kluwer. She also writes for Wolters Kluwer's *Australian Federal Tax Reporter*, *Australian Capital Gains Tax Planner* and *Australian Tax Week*.

Gaibrielle Cleary BEc, LLM is a Taxation Partner at Mazars. Gaibrielle practises in all areas of direct and indirect taxation. Previously, she was the in-house counsel for an ASX listed company and has practised at leading international law and accounting firms. She is one of the authors of Wolters Kluwer's *Small Business Tax Concessions Guide*, and has also written for a number of taxation publications, including Wolters Kluwer's *Australian Federal Tax Reporter*.

Linda Daniele BCom, LLB is a senior tax writer, writing mainly for the *Australian Federal Tax Reporter*. Before Wolters Kluwer, Linda worked as a legal editor at the Judicial Commission of New South Wales.

Enrico Enriquez BA, LLB writes for the Wolters Kluwer *Australian Payroll Tax Manual* and has previously written for a number of other Wolters Kluwer tax publications.

John Gaal is a very experienced and well respected tax specialist who has written for a number of Wolters Kluwer tax publications over many years. John works as a tax consultant and writer on his own account.

Ian Ross-Gowan MTax, BCom, CPA, CTA is a Director with Michael Johnson Associates (MJA). MJA is a specialised R&D tax agency and consultancy in government industry support programs. Ian is a former group taxation manager of a top 100 company and has undertaken post graduate research in taxation and accounting.

Kevin Johnson BEc, LLB, CA, CTA is a software engineer for APS developing programs for taxation and accounting professionals. Previously, he was a tax manager at a major international accounting firm. He is a registered tax agent.

Marcus Lai BA, DipLaw is a senior editor and tax writer. He has worked as the managing editor of various Wolters Kluwer tax books and is now the editor of the *Australian Master Tax Guide*. He is also a contributing writer to the Guide and a number of other Wolters Kluwer tax publications.

James Leow LLB (Hons), MTax is a superannuation and taxation consultant. He is co-author of the *Australian Master Superannuation Guide* and writes for a number of other Wolters Kluwer publications.

Amrit MacIntyre BA, LLB, CTA is a partner at Baker McKenzie.

Heidi Maguire BA, LLB (Hons), MRes is a senior tax writer at Wolters Kluwer, writing mainly for the *Australian Tax Cases* service, the *Australian Federal Tax Reporter* and *Tax Navigator for Business Activities*.

Ben Miller BCom, CA, SSA is a senior tax writer, writing and curating mainly for the online product *CCH iQ*. Ben previously worked in small and medium accounting firms as a tax, superannuation and business services manager.

Denise Mulder MCom, LLB, CA is a senior tax writer, regularly contributing to the *Australian Federal Tax Reporter* and *Australian Tax Navigator for Business Activities*. Before joining Wolters Kluwer, Denise worked for an ASX100 listed company, and a major international accounting firm.

Mary Zachariah BBus, MTax is a senior tax writer, writing mainly for the *Australian Federal Tax Reporter*. Mary has practised in both direct and indirect taxation areas and was previously a tax manager in a major international accounting firm.

Abbreviations

AAPM	*Australian Accounts Preparation Manual* (Wolters Kluwer)
AAT	Administrative Appeals Tribunal
ABN	Australian Business Number
ADF	Approved deposit fund
AMGST	*Australian Master GST Guide* (Wolters Kluwer)
AMSG	*Australian Master Superannuation Guide* (Wolters Kluwer)
APRA	Australian Prudential Regulation Authority
ASIC	Australian Securities and Investments Commission
ATC	*Australian Tax Cases* (Wolters Kluwer)
ATO	Australian Taxation Office
AWOTE	Average weekly ordinary time earnings
BAS	Business Activity Statement
CFC	Controlled foreign company
CGT	Capital gains tax
DTA	Double taxation agreement
EST	(Australian) Eastern Standard Time
ETP	Employment termination payment
FBT	Fringe benefits tax
FBTAA	*Fringe Benefits Tax Assessment Act 1986*
FBTAR	Fringe Benefits Tax Assessment Regulations 2018
FC of T	Federal Commissioner of Taxation
FIF	Foreign investment fund
FITR	*Australian Federal Income Tax Reporter* (Wolters Kluwer)
FSR	Financial Services Reform
FTA	*Fuel Tax Act 2006*
FTD	Fuel Tax Determination
FTR	*Australian Federal Tax Reporter* (Wolters Kluwer)
FTR (ch 40)	Fuel Tax Ruling
GIC	General interest charge
GST	Goods and services tax
GSTD	GST Determination
GSTG	*Australian GST Guide* (Wolters Kluwer)
GSTR	GST Ruling
HECS	Higher Education Contributions Scheme
HELP	Higher Education Loan Programme
IAS	Instalment Activity Statement
ID	ATO Interpretative Decision

IGTO ....Inspector-General of Taxation and Taxation Ombudsman
IR&D Act ....*Industry Research and Development Act 1986*
ITA ....*Australian International Tax Agreements* (Wolters Kluwer)
ITA Act ....*International Tax Agreements Act 1953*
ITAA36 ....*Income Tax Assessment Act 1936*
ITAA97 ....*Income Tax Assessment Act 1997*
ITR15 ....Income Tax Assessment (1936 Act) Regulation 2015
ITR97 ....Income Tax Assessment Regulations 1997
ITTPA ....*Income Tax (Transitional Provisions) Act 1997*
LCG ....Law Companion Guideline
MLA ....*Medicare Levy Act 1986*
MPR ....Monthly payer requirement
MRRT ....Mineral Resource Rent Tax
MT ....*Miscellaneous Tax Ruling*
NRAS.....................................National Rental Affordability Scheme
OBU ....Offshore banking unit
PAYG ....Pay As You Go
PCG..Practical Compliance Guideline
PDF ....Pooled development fund
PSI ....Personal Services Income
PS LA.....................................Practice Statement Law Administration
PST ....Pooled superannuation trust
R&D ....Research and development
RBA ....Running balance account
RBL ....Reasonable benefit limit
RSA ....Retirement savings account
SGAA.....................................*Superannuation Guarantee (Administration) Act 1992*
SGAR.....................................Superannuation Guarantee (Administration) Regulations 2018
SGC ....Superannuation Guarantee Charge
SISA ....*Superannuation Industry (Supervision) Act 1993*
SISR ....Superannuation Industry (Supervision) Regulations 1994
SLP ....*Australian Superannuation Law and Practice* (Wolters Kluwer)
SME ....Small or medium enterprise
SMSF ....Self managed superannuation fund
STP ....Single Touch Payroll
STS ....Simplified Tax System
SUMLMA ....*Superannuation (Unclaimed Money and Lost Members) Act 1999*
TAA ....*Taxation Administration Act 1953*
TAR ....Taxation Administration Regulations 2017

TASA ....*Tax Agent Services Act 2009*
TD ....Taxation Determination
TFN ....Tax file number
TOFA ....Taxation of Financial Arrangements
TR ....Taxation Ruling
TSAs ....Tax sharing agreements

Highlights of 2020 Tax Changes

¶1 HIGHLIGHTS

This edition has been fully updated to reflect developments that occurred (or remain proposed) up to **31 December 2020** unless indicated otherwise.

The highlights of the main changes included in this edition are set out below (with cross-references to where they are discussed).

CHAPTER 1 — INTRODUCTION TO AUSTRALIAN TAX SYSTEM

New laws

■ A legislative instrument has been issued to allow taxation officers to disclose protected information of a deceased person to the registered tax agent, BAS agent or legal practitioner of an executor or administrator of the deceased estate .... ¶1-220

Proposed measures

■ The government has issued its response to a parliamentary report on taxpayer engagement, agreeing to 8 of the 13 recommendations aimed at making tax obligations in Australia easier to administer and comply with .... ¶1-200, ¶1-700

Cases

■ Recent decisions on the disclosure of ''protected information'' for the purposes of the TAA *DPP & Ors v Kinghorn* (NSW Court of Appeal) and *R v Kinghorn (No 7)* (NSW Supreme Court) .... ¶1-220

CHAPTER 2 — INDIVIDUALS

New laws

■ From 1 July 2020, the top threshold of the 19% personal income tax bracket is increased from $37,000 to $45,000 and the top threshold of the 32.5% bracket is increased from $90,000 to $120,000 .... ¶2-120

■ From 1 July 2020, changes to the government-funded Paid Parental Leave (PPL) scheme allow primary carers to access parental leave pay more flexibly, particularly birth mothers and adoptive parents who are self-employed or small business owners .... ¶2-133

■ Rules have been made to assist people affected by the economic impact of the COVID-19 pandemic to be eligible for parental leave pay .... ¶2-133

■ The PPL work test period is temporarily extended from 13 months prior to the birth or adoption of a child to 20 months (600 days) for parents who have had their employment impacted by COVID-19 — applicable to births and adoptions that occur between 22 March 2020 and 31 March 2021 .... ¶2-133

■ Social security, veteran and other income support recipients (including Family Tax Benefit Part A and Family Tax Benefit Part B recipients) and eligible concession cardholders received 2 separate payments of $750 from 31 March 2020 and 13 July 2020, with a further 2 payments of $250 made progressively from 30 November 2020 to 1 March 2021 .... ¶2-133

■ Medicare levy low income thresholds and phase-in limits for 2019–20 .... ¶2-330

■ Medicare levy thresholds and phase-in limits for Senior Australians and eligible pensioners for 2019–20 .... ¶2-330

■ Study and training repayment thresholds and rates for 2020–21 .... ¶2-380, ¶2-385

CHAPTER 3 — COMPANIES

New laws

■ Eligible companies are able to carry back a tax loss from the 2019–20, 2020–21 or 2021–22 income years to offset previously taxed profits in the 2018–19 or later income years .... ¶3-080

CHAPTER 4 — DIVIDENDS • IMPUTATION SYSTEM

Proposed measures

■ A revised commencement date for the proposed Div 7A amendments has been announced ..... ¶4-200

Rulings and guidelines

■ For private companies with a regular 30 June balance date, the Div 7A benchmark interest rate for 2020–21 is 4.52% ..... ¶4-230

■ A streamlined application process has been introduced to obtain the Commissioner's exercise of the relieving discretion where the minimum repayment required for a Div 7A amalgamated loan has not been made for 2019–20 due to COVID-19 ..... ¶4-240

CHAPTER 5 — PARTNERS AND PARTNERSHIPS

Proposed measures

■ A new regime for limited partnership collective investment vehicles is proposed from 1 July 2018 ..... ¶5-030

CHAPTER 6 — TRUSTEES • BENEFICIARIES • DECEASED ESTATES

New laws

■ From 1 July 2019, the concessional tax rates available for minors receiving income from testamentary trusts are limited to income derived from assets that are transferred from the deceased estate or the proceeds of the disposal or investment of those assets ..... ¶6-105

■ The specific anti-avoidance rule that applies to closely held trusts that engage in circular trust distributions has been extended to family trusts from 1 July 2019 ..... ¶6-275

Proposed measures

■ Two new categories of collective investment vehicles are proposed, a corporate collective investment vehicle to start from 1 July 2017 (and for which draft legislation dealing with the tax law issues and the Corporations Law issues has been released) and a limited partnership collective investment vehicle to start from 1 July 2018 ..... ¶6-410, ¶41-900

Cases

■ The Full Federal Court has held that disclaimers made by default income beneficiaries under a discretionary trust deed were retrospectively effective so that the disclaiming beneficiaries' entitlements to trust income were extinguished *ab initio* (*Carter & Ors*) ..... ¶6-105

CHAPTER 7 — SMALL BUSINESS ENTITIES

New laws

■ State and territory business grants relating to recovery from COVID-19 received by small business entities and medium business entities are non-assessable, non-exempt income ..... ¶7-001

■ A range of small business concessions are available for medium business entities with aggregated turnover of $50 million over a phased-in period from 1 July 2020 to 1 July 2021 ..... ¶7-001, ¶7-050

■ Small business entities and medium business entities are eligible for the temporary full expensing of depreciating assets, including second-hand assets, acquired from 7.30 pm AEDT on 6 October 2020 until 30 June 2022 ..... ¶7-250

■ The threshold for immediate write-off for assets (also known as instant asset write-off) for small businesses has increased to $150,000 until 31 December 2020. For assets not otherwise eligible for the temporary full expensing there is an extension for first use or installation until 30 June 2021 ..... ¶7-250

■ The balance of all small business pools will be immediately deductible for income years ending after 1 July 2020 until 30 June 2022 ..... ¶7-250

■ The simplified trading stock rules will be available for medium business entities from 1 July 2021 ..... ¶7-260

Cases

■ In determining whether land is used in the course of carrying on a business for the CGT small business concessions it must have been used at some point in the course of carrying on the business. There is no requirement for the asset to have a direct functional relevance to carrying on the normal day-to-day activities of the business (*Eichmann*, Full Fed Ct) .... ¶7-145

Rulings and guidelines

■ A company carrying on business in the general sense cannot access the CGT small business concessions if its only activity is renting out an investment property (*Draft* TD 2019/D4) .... ¶7-145

CHAPTER 8 — CONSOLIDATED GROUPS

New laws

■ Tax cost setting rules are modified for depreciable assets of a joining entity that accessed the temporary full expensing rules .... ¶8-210

Rulings and guidelines

■ The ATO is reviewing arrangements involving MEC groups avoiding CGT via corporate restructures that end with the sale of an eligible tier-1 company (TA 2020/4) .... ¶8-640

CHAPTER 9 — TAX ACCOUNTING • TRADING STOCK

Rulings and guidelines

■ Standard value of goods taken from stock for private use for 2019–20 (TD 2020/1) .... ¶9-245

CHAPTER 10 — ASSESSABLE INCOME • TAX EXEMPTIONS

New laws

■ The payment period of the temporary Coronavirus Supplement was extended to 31 March 2021 .... ¶10-040

■ A JobMaker Hiring Credit is payable to employers for each additional new job they create for an eligible employee .... ¶10-040

■ The government will make 2 $250 economic support payments to eligible social security recipients and health care cardholders .... ¶10-040

■ Some state government or territory COVID-19 support payments have the character of income and are assessable .... ¶10-040

■ Cash flow boost payments for eligible businesses and not-for-profit organisations that employ staff are not subject to income tax .... ¶10-040

■ Economic Support Payments are exempt from income tax .... ¶10-040

■ The HomeBuilder grant to assist the residential construction market is not subject to income tax .... ¶10-040

■ A one-off pandemic leave disaster payment of $1,500 is available for eligible workers in participating states .... ¶10-040

■ Some small business grants by a state or territory government to relieve the effects of COVID-19 are or will be declared to be non-assessable non-exempt income .... ¶10-040

■ JobKeeper payments to employers and sole traders are included in assessable income ..... ¶10-040

■ JobSeeker and the JobSeeker Coronavirus Supplement are taxable social security payments .... ¶10-040

■ Under the JobTrainer Skills Package, eligible businesses can apply for the Supporting Apprentices and Trainees wage subsidy .... ¶10-040

■ Disaster relief payments made in relation to the 2019–20 bushfires are non-assessable non-exempt income .... ¶10-895

Proposed measures

■ The government proposes to extend the apprenticeship wage subsidy program to allow businesses of any size to claim the subsidy (2020–21 Budget) .... ¶10-040

■ It is proposed that, from 1 July 2019, all remuneration provided for the commercial exploitation of a person's fame or image will be included in the assessable income of that individual (2018–19 Budget) .... ¶10-076

■ The House of Representatives commenced an inquiry into the effectiveness of changes to the employee share schemes (ESS) regime .... ¶10-080

■ The government will amend and clarify income tax exemptions for Australian individuals engaged by the International Monetary Fund and the 3 institutions of the World Bank Group (2020–21 Budget) .... ¶10-870

Cases

■ The Full Federal Court examined the calculation of the assessable amount of non-cash business benefits under s 21A in relation to electricity connection works (*Victoria Power Networks Pty Ltd*) .... ¶10-030

■ What constitutes a "real risk" of forfeiture or loss of an ESS interest (share options) that will result in a deferred taxing point (*Gennai*) .... ¶10-089

Rulings and guidelines

■ New small businesses may seek ATO review of eligibility decisions about JobKeeper or cash flow boost payments (Inspector-General of Taxation report) .... ¶10-040

■ The ATO sets out guidance on the operation of the influence test for the purposes of the sovereign immunity tax exemption (LCR 2020/3) .... ¶10-602

■ Draft ruling on the taxation privileges and immunities of prescribed International Organisations and their staff and on who is a "person who holds an office" (*Draft* TR 2019/D1) .... ¶10-605

CHAPTERS 11 & 12 — CAPITAL GAINS TAX

New laws

■ CGT small business roll-over has been amended to allow an entity that is connected with or an affiliate of a small business entity to access the small business restructure roll-over in relation to an interest of the small business entity, even if the small business entity has aggregated turnover of between $2 million and $10 million .... ¶12-380

Proposed measures

■ Managed investment trusts (MITs) and attribution MITs (AMITs) will be prevented from applying the 50% discount at the trust level with effect from income year starting 3 months on or after assent .... ¶11-038, ¶12-660

■ The market value substitution rule will not apply to superannuation entities where the income would be non-arm's length income that exceeds the market value of the asset .... ¶11-510

■ A targeted CGT exemption is proposed to apply to the creation, variation of termination of a formal written agreement for a granny flat arrangement arising from a family relationship or personal ties with effect from the first income year after assent .... ¶11-915

Cases

■ A capital gain distributed from a non-fixed Australian resident trust to a foreign resident was not disregarded for CGT purposes (*Peter Greensill Family Co Pty Ltd (as trustee)*, Fed Ct) .... ¶11-060, ¶12-720

■ A capital gain distributed from a non-fixed Australian resident trust to a foreign resident was not disregarded for CGT purposes (*N & M Martin Holdings Pty Ltd & Anor*, Fed Ct) .... ¶11-060, ¶12-720

Rulings and guidelines

■ The Commissioner views that the capital gains of a foreign resident beneficiary from a non-fixed resident trust are not disregarded under Subdiv 855-A and neither are the additional capital gains under Subdiv 115-C (*Draft* TD 2019/D6) .... ¶11-060, ¶12-720, ¶12-735

■ The Commissioner views that the concept of "source" is not relevant for determining the amount of a trust capital gain that is assessable to a non-resident beneficiary or trustee (*Draft* TD 2019/D7) .... ¶11-060

■ The cost base of an asset for CGT purposes includes the cost of liabilities assumed in acquiring the asset to the extent that a deduction for an amount of that liability is not otherwise claimed (*Draft* TD 2019/D11) .... ¶11-550

■ The Commissioner outlines what constitutes "restructuring" for the purposes of demerger roll-over relief (TD 2020/6) .... ¶12-328

CHAPTER 13 — SUPERANNUATION FUNDS • CONTRIBUTIONS

New laws

■ A complying superannuation fund cannot claim a deduction for superannuation benefits paid because of a person's temporary inability to engage in gainful employment .... ¶13-150

■ Modifications have been made to the CGT provisions to facilitate the application of the non-arm's length income rules .... ¶13-170

■ From 2020–21, a successor fund can claim a tax offset in an income year for no-TFN contributions tax previously paid by the original superannuation provider .... ¶13-180

■ The Commissioner can make direct payments of superannuation money held by it to a KiwiSaver scheme provider .... ¶13-380

■ Employer contributions which are made during the SG amnesty period to offset the employer's SG liability under the SG amnesty are deductible .... ¶13-710

■ Contributions made by the Commissioner and employer offset contributions under the SG amnesty are not included in the calculation of an employee's low tax contributed amounts for Division 293 tax purposes .... ¶13-750

■ The age limit for making spouse contributions is increased from 69 to 74 years from 1 July 2020 .... ¶13-770

■ The Commissioner can make a determination to disregard or reallocate an employer's SG charge payment to the ATO under the SG amnesty to avoid the potential breach of an individual's contributions cap .... ¶13-785

■ Individuals aged 65 and 66 years do not have to meet the work test to make voluntary superannuation contributions (both concessional and non-concessional) from 1 July 2020 .. ¶13-825

Proposed measures

■ A Bill has proposed amendments to increase the maximum number of allowable members in an SMSF from 4 to 6 .... ¶13-060

■ Superannuation funds with interests in both the accumulation and retirement phases will be allowed to choose their preferred method of calculating the exempt current pension income exemption; no actuarial certificate will be required for the exemption where all fund members are in the retirement phase .... ¶13-140

■ A Bill has proposed amendments to extend the bring forward rule to enable individuals aged 65 and 66 years to make up to 3 years of non-concessional superannuation contributions under the bring forward rule .... ¶13-780

■ A draft determination instrument proposes to extend the SuperStream standard to rollovers and transfers to and from SMSFs requested on or after 31 March 2021 and to release authority requests issued by the Commissioner (SPR 2020/D3) .... ¶13-800

■ A Bill has proposed the closure of eligible rollover funds (ERFs) and allow the Commissioner to reunite ATO-held amounts received from ERFs with a member's active account .... ¶13-850

Cases

■ The Commissioner is not empowered to remit an amount of associated earnings as calculated on an excess non-concessional contributions determination (*Purcell*) .... ¶13-780

Rulings and guidelines

■ Guidelines on the operation of the non-arm's length income (NALI) provisions in a scheme where the parties do not deal with each other at arm's length and the superannuation entity incurs non-arm's length expenditure (*Draft* LCR 2019/D3) .... ¶13-170

■ The ATO has outlined its compliance approach where a fund incurs non-arm's length expenditure of a general nature that has a sufficient nexus to all ordinary and/or statutory income derived by the fund in the 2018–19, 2019–20 and 2020–21 income years (PCG 2020/5) .... ¶13-170

■ The ATO has outlined its compliance approach where employers claim a deduction for superannuation contributions made to the Small Business Superannuation Clearing House (SBSCH) in the year in which payment was made to the SBSCH (PCG 2020/6) .... ¶13-710

CHAPTER 14 — SUPERANNUATION BENEFITS • TERMINATION PAYMENTS

New laws

■ The minimum annual pension amount for account-based pensions and annuities, allocated pensions and annuities and market-linked pensions and annuities is reduced by 50% in the 2019–20 and 2020–21 financial years .... ¶14-125

■ The proportioning rule applies to a superannuation fund payment under the COVID-19 early release of superannuation measure; the payment is non-assessable non-exempt income ...... ¶14-130

Rulings and guidelines

■ The ATO has provided guidance on the calculation of transfer debits on the commutation of a capped defined benefit income stream, and its compliance approach on reporting commutations of market-linked pensions (CRT Alert 031/2020) .... ¶14-340

■ The ATO has clarified how superannuation funds should report death benefit rollovers, following retrospective legislative changes to the treatment of the untaxed element of death benefit superannuation lump sums .... ¶14-450

CHAPTER 15 — PERSONAL TAX OFFSETS

New laws

■ The indexed amount of the Dependant (Invalid and Carer) Tax Offset (DICTO) for the 2020–21 income year is $2,816 .... ¶15-100

■ The low income tax offset (LITO) for the 2020–21 income year is $700 .... ¶15-300

■ From the 2022–23 income year, the low income tax offset (LITO) and low and middle income tax offset (LMITO) will be merged into a new single low income tax offset .... ¶15-300

CHAPTER 16 — BUSINESS, EMPLOYMENT AND INVESTMENT DEDUCTIONS • GIFTS

New laws

■ Certain start-up capital costs for a proposed business are deductible for medium businesses from 2020–21 under the blackhole expenditure provisions .... ¶16-156

■ Wages paid to employees subsidised by JobKeeper payments are deductible .... ¶16-520

■ Community sheds added as a new category of public institutions eligible for deductible gift recipient status .... ¶16-950

Cases

■ The Full Federal Court has held that lump sum payments made to doctors by a medical centre operator were capital expenditure (*Healius Ltd*) .... ¶16-060

■ The AAT has denied a company director a deduction for settlement monies paid to avoid the legal costs of action for trading while insolvent (*Duncan*) .... ¶16-844

Rulings and guidelines

■ Simplified alternative method introduced to calculate home office expenses incurred during COVID-19 at 80 cents per hour extended to 30 June 2021 (PCG 2020/3) .... ¶16-480

■ Private and public ancillary funds incentivised to maintain annual distributions with lower minimum rates in later years .... ¶16-962

CHAPTER 17 — DEPRECIATING ASSETS

New laws

■ Eligible businesses have up to 30 June 2021 to use, or have installed ready for use, depreciating assets that access the instant asset write-off deduction which is capped at $150,000 .... ¶17-330

■ Temporary full expensing measures: for a limited period, an immediate 100% deduction is available for eligible depreciating assets of any value, including for costs of improvements .... ¶17-430

■ For a limited period, accelerated depreciation is available for new assets .... ¶17-430

CHAPTER 18 — PRIMARY PRODUCTION CONCESSIONS

Cases

■ A primary producer was not entitled to an immediate deduction for capital expenditure on fencing assets acquired as part of sheep station land (*AJ & PA McBride Ltd*, AAT) .... ¶18-090

CHAPTER 19 — MINING • INFRASTRUCTURE • ENVIRONMENTAL PROTECTION

Rulings and guidelines

■ TR 2020/2 outlines the ATO's view on deductions for expenditure on environmental protection activities .... ¶19-110

CHAPTER 20 — R&D • FILMS • CAPITAL WORKS • NRAS • INNOVATION INCENTIVES

New laws

■ The government has introduced an amended package of R&D reforms for years commencing on or after 1 July 2021 .... ¶20-160

■ The location incentive has been increased and extended until the 2026–27 income year .. ¶20-350

■ The income limits and refundable tax offset amount for the 2020–21 NRAS year have been released .... ¶20-600, ¶20-605

Proposed measures

■ The producer offset will apply at 30% for feature films and other films from 1 July 2021 .... ¶20-340

■ Thresholds and integrity amendments for the producer offset, the location offset and the PDV offset are proposed to apply from 1 July 2021 .... ¶20-340, ¶20-350, ¶20-360

Cases

■ The Federal Court has held that entitlement to the R&D tax offset is dependent on whether the taxable facts are such that the R&D claims were available to the R&D entity and not just on keeping records (*Bogiatto & Ors*) .... ¶20-170

CHAPTERS 21 & 22 — INTERNATIONAL TAXATION

New laws

■ The government has reset the monetary value thresholds for notifiable foreign investment proposals to nil .... ¶22-002

Proposed measures

■ The government proposes to amend the law to clarify the corporate residency test for foreign incorporated companies (2020–21 Budget) .... ¶21-040

■ The government has released a report by the Board of Taxation on the corporate tax residency rules .... ¶21-040

■ The government announced that it will amend the existing OBU regime to strengthen its integrity .... ¶21-080

■ The government proposes to remove the temporary nil value monetary thresholds for notifiable foreign investment proposals .... ¶22-002

Cases

■ Foreign nationals on working-holiday visas in Australia for more than 183 days in an income year were not residents of Australia (*Coelho & Ors*) .... ¶21-010

■ The Full Federal Court, by majority, rejected a legal challenge to the validity of the backpacker tax (*Addy*, on appeal to High Ct) .... ¶21-033

■ Under the CFC rules, income was attributable to an Australian resident company because subsidiary companies of its joint venture partner were associates of the Australian company (*BHP Billiton Ltd*, High Ct) .... ¶21-140, ¶21-180

■ The Full Federal Court examined the application of the transfer pricing rules in Div 13 and Subdiv 815-A to sales of copper concentrate by an Australian subsidiary of the Glencore Group (*Glencore Investment Pty Ltd*, on appeal to Full Fed Ct) .... ¶22-580

Rulings and guidelines

■ The Commissioner's view on untaxed foreign capital gains and the foreign income tax offset limit (TD 2020/7) .... ¶21-710

■ The ATO is reviewing arrangements which use offshore related entities to facilitate the avoidance of interest withholding tax (TA 2020/3) .... ¶22-020

■ The ATO will not apply compliance resources to determine whether foreign companies have a permanent establishment (PE) in Australia because of the temporary presence of employees in Australia due to COVID-19 overseas travel restrictions .... ¶22-150

■ 2020 *International Dealings Schedule* and instructions .... ¶22-630

■ Preliminary guidance on the targeted integrity rule in the hybrid mismatch rules in ITAA97 Subdiv 832-J (*Draft* LCR 2019/D1) .... ¶22-640

■ How an entity values its debt capital for the purposes of the thin capitalisation provisions (TD 2020/2) .... ¶22-700

■ Ruling on the arm's length debt test under the thin capitalisation rules as they apply to entities that are non-banks (TR 2020/4) .... ¶22-730

■ Guidelines on the ATO's compliance approach to the arm's length debt test under the thin capitalisation rules (PCG 2020/7) .... ¶22-730

CHAPTER 23 — FINANCIAL ARRANGEMENTS • TOFA

Proposed measures

■ The TOFA regime will be reformed to reduce its scope, decrease compliance costs, and increase certainty .... ¶23-020

■ The tax hedging regime will be amended to make it easier to access, encompass more types of risk management arrangements, and remove the direct link to financial accounting .... ¶23-040

■ The functional currency rules will be changed to extend the range of entities that can use a functional currency .... ¶23-070

■ Integrity provisions in the debt/equity rules will be changed to ensure multiple schemes are treated as a single scheme for the purposes of determining whether there is a debt or equity interest, where this accurately reflects the economic substance of the schemes .... ¶23-105, ¶23-115

■ It is proposed to remove, with effect from 1 July 2018, key barriers to the use of asset-backed financing arrangements, which are supported by assets, such as deferred payment arrangements, and hire purchase arrangements .... ¶23-200

CHAPTER 25 — ASSESSMENT • AUDIT • COLLECTION

New laws

■ The period of review for assessments of medium business entities will be shortened from 4 to 2 years from 1 July 2021 .... ¶25-310

Proposed measures

■ Treasury has issued a consultation paper to consider whether the ATO should be allowed to access third party information to investigate tax-related criminal offences and/or historical telecommunications data .... ¶25-220

CHAPTER 26 — PAYG WITHHOLDING

New laws

■ From 1 July 2020, voluntary reporting has been extended to include the employer withholding the child support deductions and child support garnishee amounts from salary or wages that are paid to the Child Support Registrar .... ¶26-630

Rulings and guidelines

■ Foreign employers may not need to register for PAYG withholding due to employees working temporarily in Australia due to COVID-19 travel restrictions if certain conditions are met . ¶26-600

■ *Draft* STP 2020/D4 lists the kinds of amounts that must be in the approved form for STP reporting purposes .... ¶26-630

Cases

■ The ''backpacker tax'' was found not to be contrary to Australia's DTAs (*Addy*, on appeal to High Ct) .... ¶26-277

CHAPTER 27 — PAYG INSTALMENTS

New laws

■ Entities with an aggregated turnover of up to $50 million are eligible to pay PAYG instalments using the GDP-adjusted notional tax method from 1 July 2021 .... ¶27-220

■ The GDP adjustment factor for 2020–21 is 0% .... ¶27-470

Rulings and guidelines

■ To assist businesses affected by COVID-19, the ATO will not apply penalties and interest on excessive PAYG instalment variations for the 2020–21 income year .... ¶27-320, ¶27-330

CHAPTER 28 — OBJECTIONS • APPEALS

Cases

■ The Full Federal Court has confirmed that the entitlement to interest on an RBA surplus commences 14 days from the entitlement arising, rather than when a return is filed or assessment issued (*Travelex Ltd*, on appeal to High Ct) .... ¶28-170

CHAPTER 29 — PENALTIES • OFFENCES

New laws

■ The penalty unit has been increased from $210 to $222 for offences committed on or after 1 July 2020 .... ¶29-000

Proposed measures

■ Treasury has issued a consultation paper on proposed measures relating to penalties to combat the black economy .... ¶29-000

CHAPTER 30 — TAX AVOIDANCE • ALIENATION OF INCOME • PSI

New laws

■ Measures have been enacted to target non-compliance associated with ''phoenix'' companies .... ¶30-005

■ The definition of a ''significant global entity'' has been amended from 1 July 2019 .... ¶30-200

Proposed measures

■ The government proposed a number of measures in the 2018–19 Budget to combat the black economy. It announced a review of existing criminal offences, and civil and administrative penalties for black economy activity .... ¶30-005

■ The government has sought public comment on Initial Coin Offerings (ICOs) in Australia and the application of Australia's regulatory framework, including the tax rules .... ¶30-005

■ The OECD has released non-binding rules for collection of information from digital platforms used by the sharing and gig economy .... ¶30-005

Cases

■ The Federal Court granted civil penalty orders against tax scheme promoters in 2 recent cases (*Bogiatto* and *Rowntree & Ors*) .... ¶30-300

■ The taxpayer's LinkedIn account and profile did not satisfy the PSI unrelated clients test (*Fortunatow*, on appeal to High Ct) .... ¶30-670

Rulings and guidelines

■ For the 2019–20 year, taxpayers can rely on suspended ATO guidelines on the allocation of profits within professional firms provided conditions are met (ATO website) .... ¶30-170

■ The ATO is reviewing arrangements using derivatives to access franking credits artificially (TA 2020/5) .... ¶30-195

■ The Commissioner has issued *Taxpayer Alerts* flagging reviews of cross-border schemes that potentially breach Pt IVA, the diverted profits tax (DPT) or the transfer pricing provisions (TA 2020/1, TA 2020/2) .... ¶30-205

CHAPTER 31 — TAX PLANNING • YEAR END TAX STRATEGIES

Checklists

■ Year end tax strategies checklist updated for recent developments including opportunities arising from measures to stimulate the economy in response to the COVID-19 outbreak .... ¶31-700

CHAPTER 32 — TAX AGENTS AND BAS AGENTS

New laws

■ BAS services extended to advising about entitlements under the JobKeeper Payment scheme and cash flow support for business initiatives .... ¶32-065

Reviews

■ The final report of an independent review into the effectiveness of the Tax Practitioners Board and the *Tax Agent Services Act 2009* released .... ¶32-000

CHAPTER 33 — TAX FILE NUMBERS • AUSTRALIAN BUSINESS NUMBERS • THIRD PARTY REPORTING

New laws

■ The director identification number (DIN) to combat phoenixing activity has been introduced, to commence on a day to be proclaimed .... ¶33-090

CHAPTER 34 — GOODS AND SERVICES TAX

New laws

■ From 1 April 2020, personal liability is imposed on company directors for the amount of unpaid GST liabilities of a defaulting company and the Commissioner can determine a taxpayer's GST liability on the basis of an estimate .... ¶34-150

■ From 1 July 2021, the concession available for small business entities in relation to the Commissioner's power to specify simplified accounting methods for certain industries has been extended to medium business entities .... ¶34-165

Cases

■ A company operating a sheep grazing business was liable for GST on the sales of vacant land, although the sales were unrelated to that activity (*San Remo Heights Pty Ltd*) .... ¶34-100

■ An acquisition of vacant land by a corporate trustee of a trust was not a creditable acquisition as it was not an activity that constituted the carrying on of any enterprise (*304 Wanda Street Pty Ltd*, AAT) .... ¶34-110

■ An incapacitated entity, and not its representative, was entitled to an input tax credit for an acquisition made before the representative was appointed (*Albarran & Ors as administrators of Cooper & Oxley Builders Pty Ltd*) .... ¶34-270

■ A taxpayer's supplies of gold to certain dealers constituted the "first supply of that precious metal after its refining by . . . the supplier" (*ACN 154 520 199 Pty Ltd (in liq)* 2020 ATC ¶20-772, on appeal to High Ct) .... ¶34-270

■ A taxpayer was not entitled to input tax credits for its acquisitions of gold because the AAT was not satisfied that the supplies made to the taxpayer were all taxable supplies of scrap gold (*Cash World Gold Buyers Pty Ltd*) .... ¶34-270

Rulings and guidelines

■ Guidance on how the Commissioner will administer the estimates regime that enables the Commissioner to make an estimate of certain unpaid and overdue tax-related liabilities and recover the amount of the estimates (PCG 2020/2) .... ¶34-150

■ Legislative determination has been made to ensure continued access to GST-free supplies of cars and car parts for eligible disabled people .... ¶34-220

■ The luxury car tax threshold for 2020–21 is $68,740 and the fuel-efficient car limit for 2020–21 is $75,565 .... ¶34-220

CHAPTER 35 — FRINGE BENEFITS TAX

New laws

■ Employers with an aggregated turnover of up to $50 million will be eligible for the car parking exemption from 1 April 2021 .... ¶35-254

■ The definition of a "taxi" has been amended to "a car used for taxi travel (other than a limousine)", so as to include ride share services .... ¶35-645

■ Employers with an aggregated turnover of up to $50 million will be eligible for the work-related items exemption on multiple items from 1 April 2021 .... ¶35-645

Proposed measures

■ Employer-provided retraining or reskilling expenses will be exempt from FBT, where the employee will be redeployed to a different role in the business .... ¶35-645

■ Employers will be allowed to use existing corporate records, rather than prescribed records, to comply with their FBT record-keeping obligations .... ¶35-690

Rulings and guidelines

■ The ATO will not scrutinise salary-packaged meal entertainment provided to employees of not-for-profit employers in certain situations .... ¶35-057

■ Garaging a car at an employee's home due to COVID-19 may not give rise to an FBT liability in certain situations .... ¶35-150

■ The benchmark interest rate for the FBT year commencing on 1 April 2020 is 4.80% pa .... ¶35-230, ¶35-290

■ Business use estimates may be adjusted to reflect changes in employees' driving patterns due to COVID-19 .... ¶35-240

■ The car parking threshold for the FBT year commencing on 1 April 2020 is $9.15 .... ¶35-252

■ Changes are proposed to the meaning of a commercial parking station from 1 April 2021 (*Draft* TR 2019/D5) .... ¶35-252

■ The indexation factors for valuing non-remote housing for the FBT year commencing on 1 April 2020 are available .... ¶35-420

■ The reasonable amounts for food and drink expenses for the FBT year commencing on 1 April 2020 have been released (TD 2020/4) .... ¶35-470

■ New rates are available for calculating the taxable value of a fringe benefit arising from the private use of a motor vehicle other than a car for the FBT year commencing on 1 April 2020 (TD 2020/3) .... ¶35-590

■ FBT is not payable on emergency accommodation, food, transport or other assistance provided to an employee who is, or is at risk of being, adversely affected by COVID-19 .... ¶35-645

■ FBT is not payable on temporary accommodation and meals are provided to fly-in fly-out or drive-in drive-out employees unable to return home due to COVID-19 travel restrictions ... ¶35-645

■ FBT is not payable on protective items (eg gloves, masks, sanitisers and anti-septic sprays) provided to client-facing employees and employees involved in cleaning premises .... ¶35-645

■ There is a limited FBT exemption for emergency health care provided to an employee affected by COVID-19 .... ¶35-645

■ FBT is not payable on flu vaccinations offered to all employees .... ¶35-645

■ FBT is not payable on COVID-19 testing carried out by a medical practitioner or nurse and offered to all employees .... ¶35-645

■ FBT is not payable on non-refundable costs for cancelled events employees were due to attend .... ¶35-645

■ The record-keeping exemption threshold for the FBT year commencing on 1 April 2020 is $8,853 .... ¶35-692

CHAPTER 36 — PAYROLL TAX

New laws

■ NSW: the annual threshold has increased from 1 July 2020 .... ¶36-030

■ NSW: a reduced rate of tax applies from 1 July 2020 .... ¶36-030

■ All states and territories have provided payroll tax relief for employers affected by COVID-19 .... ¶36-060

■ NT: the payroll tax exemption for hiring of resident employees is extended to 30 June 2021 .... ¶36-060

■ Tas: the payroll tax rebate scheme in relation to apprentices, trainees and youth employees is extended to 30 June 2022 .... ¶36-140

CHAPTER 37 — STAMP DUTY

New laws

■ NSW: for a 12-month period commencing 1 August 2020, stamp duty has been eliminated for newly built homes below $800,000 with the concession reducing on higher values before phasing out at $1 million .... ¶37-020

■ NSW: stamp duty brackets are indexed to CPI for transactions made on or after 1 July 2020. The first indexation occurred with effect from 1 July 2019 .... ¶37-020

Proposed measures

■ NSW: proposed measures to reform NSW state taxation include measures to replace stamp duty with an annual property tax .... ¶37-020

CHAPTER 38 — LAND TAX

COVID-19 responses

■ All states and the ACT are providing land tax relief to taxpayers in support of those affected by COVID-19 ......NSW ¶38-010; Vic ¶38-020; Qld ¶38-030; SA ¶38-040; WA ¶38-050; Tas ¶38-060; ACT ¶38-070

■ NSW: a new 25% reduction in 2021 land tax on land leased to retail tenants with annual turnover of up to $5 million where the rent is reduced over the period 1 January 2021 to 28 March 2021 .... ¶38-010

■ Vic: 2021 liability for vacancy tax has been waived for properties vacant in 2020 due to COVID-19 .... ¶38-020

■ ACT: land tax relief originally available in respect of rent reductions for residential tenancies provided over 6 months from 1 April 2020 has been extended to cover rent reductions until 30 June 2021 .... ¶38-070

New laws

■ NSW: property developers who commence construction of build-to-rent projects on or after 1 July 2020 may be eligible for a 50% reduction in land tax on the land .... ¶38-010

■ NSW: trustees of trusts which allow foreign persons to be beneficiaries must have amended the trust deed by 31 December 2020 to avoid liability for foreign owner surcharge .... ¶38-010

- Vic: from 2020 the absentee owner surcharge rate increased from 1.5% to 2% .... ¶38-020
- Vic: from 2020 vacancy tax is imposed on residential land which is left uninhabitable or derelict .... ¶38-020
- Vic: for 2021 a full exemption will replace the land tax concession for land used by non-profit clubs for activities of members .... ¶38-020
- Vic: for 2022 eligible build-to-rent developments will get a 50% land tax discount and exemption from absentee owner surcharge .... ¶38-020
- Vic: special land tax has been abolished from 16 December 2020 .... ¶38-020
- SA: changes effective for 2020–21 increase the tax-free threshold, reduce the top tax rate and aggregate land ownership for assessment. Transitional land tax relief is available to taxpayers whose liability increases above a minimum threshold as a result of land aggregation .... ¶38-040
- SA: from 1 March 2020 ex gratia relief is available to lessors who provide affordable housing through a participating community housing provider .... ¶38-040
- SA: from 2020–21 owners of land held in trust with a taxable value greater than $25,000 may be assessed at trust rates of land tax .... ¶38-040
- SA: the deadline for trustees of certain discretionary trusts to designate a beneficiary for land tax assessment has been extended to 30 June 2021 .... ¶38-040
- ACT: the maximum number of parcels of land eligible for the land tax exemption for affordable community housing has been increased to 125 .... ¶38-070

Proposed measures

- NSW: proposed reforms to NSW state taxation will allow purchasers of land to pay an annual property tax instead of stamp duty and land tax (NSW Budget 2020–21) .... ¶38-010
- WA: changes proposed for 2020–21 will ensure that residential parks with owner-occupied relocatable homes can continue to be licensed as caravan parks and eligible for land tax exemption .... ¶38-050

CHAPTER 39 — SUPERANNUATION GUARANTEE CHARGE

New laws

- Salary or wages paid to employees that do not relate to the performance of work are excluded salary or wages for SG purposes .... ¶39-030
- Employers cannot use their employees' salary sacrifice superannuation contribution obligations to reduce their own SG contributions; an employee's pre-salary sacrifice base is used when working out the employer's SG shortfall .... ¶39-250, ¶39-300
- Employers are required to offer choice of funds to employees covered by workplace determinations or enterprise agreements made on or after 1 January 2021 .... ¶39-260
- The SG amnesty for employers to self-correct historical SG non-compliance ended on 7 September 2020 .... ¶39-505
- Payments made in relation to an SG charge imposed on SG shortfalls disclosed under the SG amnesty are deductible up to the charge amount .... ¶39-550
- The Commissioner's discretion to remit a Part 7 penalty following the end of the SG amnesty is restricted in certain circumstances .... ¶39-550

Cases

- The court has provided guidance on the interpretation of SGAA s 12(3), which provides that a person working under a contract that is wholly or principally for the labour of the person is an employee of the other party to the contract (*Dental Corporation Pty Ltd v Moffet*, Full Fed Ct) .... ¶39-024
- An SG charge assessment may be amended only if there is a valid election for eligible contributions made before the assessment (*Jordyn Properties Pty Ltd*, AAT) .... ¶39-500

Rulings and guidelines

CHAPTER 40 — FUEL TAX CREDITS

New laws

¶2 CHECKLIST OF TAX CHANGES TAKING EFFECT IN 2020–21

This checklist sets out significant changes that are scheduled to operate from the 2020–21 income year (with cross-references to the commentary in the Guide where they are discussed). Note that, in some cases, implementation of these changes may be dependent on the future passage of the necessary legislation.

INDIVIDUALS

■ From 1 July 2020, the top threshold of the 19% personal income tax bracket is increased from $37,000 to $45,000 and the top threshold of the 32.5% bracket is increased from $90,000 to $120,000 .... ¶2-120

■ From 1 July 2020, changes to the government-funded Paid Parental Leave (PPL) scheme allow primary carers to access parental leave pay more flexibly, particularly birth mothers and adoptive parents who are self-employed or small business owners .... ¶2-133

■ Study and training repayment thresholds and rates for 2020–21 .... ¶2-380, ¶2-385

■ The indexed amount of the Dependant (Invalid and Carer) Tax Offset (DICTO) for the 2020–21 income year is $2,816 .... ¶15-100

■ The low income tax offset (LITO) for the 2020–21 income year is $700 .... ¶15-300

COMPANIES AND SMALL BUSINESS

■ Eligible companies are able to carry back a tax loss from the 2019–20, 2020–21 or 2021–22 income years to offset previously taxed profits in the 2018–19 or later income years .... ¶3-080

■ For private companies with a regular 30 June balance date, the Div 7A benchmark interest rate for 2020–21 is 4.52% .... ¶4-230

■ A range of small business concessions are available for medium business entities with aggregated turnover of $50 million over a phased-in period from 1 July 2020 to 1 July 2021 ..... ¶7-001, ¶7-050

■ Small business entities and medium business entities are eligible for the temporary full expensing of depreciating assets, including second-hand assets, acquired from 7.30 pm AEDT on 6 October 2020 until 30 June 2022 .... ¶7-250

■ The threshold for immediate write-off for assets (also known as instant asset write-off) for small businesses has increased to $150,000 until 31 December 2020. For assets not otherwise eligible for the temporary full expensing there is an extension for first use or installation until 30 June 2021 .... ¶7-250

■ The balance of all small business pools will be immediately deductible for income years ending after 1 July 2020 until 30 June 2022 .... ¶7-250

■ Certain start-up capital costs for a proposed business are deductible for medium businesses from 2020–21 under the blackhole expenditure provisions .... ¶16-156

SUPERANNUATION

■ From 2020–21, a successor fund can claim a tax offset in an income year for no-TFN contributions tax previously paid by the original superannuation provider .... ¶13-180

■ The age limit for making spouse contributions is increased from 69 to 74 years from 1 July 2020 .... ¶13-770

■ Individuals aged 65 and 66 years do not have to meet the work test to make voluntary superannuation contributions (both concessional and non-concessional) from 1 July 2020 .. ¶13-825

■ Employers are required to offer choice of funds to employees covered by workplace determinations or enterprise agreements made on or after 1 January 2021 .... ¶39-260

■ The SG amnesty for employers to self-correct historical SG non-compliance ended on 7 September 2020 .... ¶39-505

GOODS AND SERVICES TAX

■ The luxury car tax threshold for 2020–21 is $68,740 and the fuel-efficient car limit for 2020–21 is $75,565 .... ¶34-220

FRINGE BENEFITS TAX

■ Employers with an aggregated turnover of up to $50 million will be eligible for the car parking exemption from 1 April 2021 .... ¶35-254

■ Employers with an aggregated turnover of up to $50 million will be eligible for the work-related items exemption on multiple items from 1 April 2021 .... ¶35-645

LAND TAX

■ NSW: a new 25% reduction in 2021 land tax on land leased to retail tenants with annual turnover of up to $5 million where the rent is reduced over the period 1 January 2021 to 28 March 2021 .... ¶38-010

■ NSW: property developers who commence construction of build-to-rent projects on or after 1 July 2020 may be eligible for a 50% reduction in land tax on the land .... ¶38-010

■ NSW: trustees of trusts which allow foreign persons to be beneficiaries must have amended the trust deed by 31 December 2020 to avoid liability for foreign owner surcharge .... ¶38-010

■ Vic: 2021 liability for vacancy tax has been waived for properties vacant in 2020 due to COVID-19 .... ¶38-020

■ Vic: for 2021 a full exemption will replace the land tax concession for land used by non-profit clubs for activities of members .... ¶38-020

■ SA: changes effective for 2020–21 increase the tax-free threshold, reduce the top tax rate and aggregate land ownership for assessment. Transitional land tax relief is available to taxpayers whose liability increases above a minimum threshold as a result of land aggregation .... ¶38-040

■ SA: from 2020–21 owners of land held in trust with a taxable value greater than $25,000 may be assessed at trust rates of land tax .... ¶38-040

■ SA: the deadline for trustees of certain discretionary trusts to designate a beneficiary for land tax assessment has been extended to 30 June 2021 .... ¶38-040

■ WA: changes proposed for 2020–21 will ensure that residential parks with owner-occupied relocatable homes can continue to be licensed as caravan parks and eligible for land tax exemption .... ¶38-050

■ ACT: land tax relief originally available in respect of rent reductions for residential tenancies provided over 6 months from 1 April 2020 has been extended to cover rent reductions until 30 June 2021 .... ¶38-070

OTHER CHANGES

■ The income limits and refundable tax offset amount for the 2020–21 NRAS year have been released .... ¶20-600, ¶20-605

■ From 1 July 2020, voluntary reporting has been extended to include the employer withholding the child support deductions and child support garnishee amounts from salary or wages that are paid to the Child Support Registrar .... ¶26-630

■ To assist businesses affected by COVID-19, the ATO will not apply penalties and interest on excessive PAYG instalment variations for the 2020–21 income year .... ¶27-320, ¶27-330

■ The GDP adjustment factor for 2020–21 is 0% .... ¶27-470

■ The penalty unit has been increased from $210 to $222 for offences committed on or after 1 July 2020 .... ¶29-000

■ NSW: the annual payroll tax threshold has increased from 1 July 2020 .... ¶36-030

■ NSW: a reduced payroll tax rate applies from 1 July 2020 .... ¶36-030

■ NT: the payroll tax exemption for hiring of resident employees is extended to 30 June 2021 .... ¶36-060

■ NSW: for a 12-month period commencing 1 August 2020, stamp duty has been eliminated for newly built homes below $800,000 with the concession reducing on higher values before phasing out at $1 million .... ¶37-020

■ NSW: stamp duty brackets are indexed to CPI for transactions made on or after 1 July 2020. The first indexation occurred with effect from 1 July 2019 .... ¶37-020

■ New fuel tax credit rates are applicable from 1 July 2020 .... ¶40-210, ¶40-300

Chapter 1 Introduction to Australian Tax System

The Federal Tax Framework

¶1-010 Background to income tax in Australia

Income tax was first imposed in Australia by the States, commencing with South Australia in 1884, New South Wales and Victoria in 1895, Queensland and Tasmania in 1902 and Western Australia in 1907. The first federal income tax was levied by the Commonwealth in 1916 to finance Australia's role in World War I.

The introduction of the federal tax resulted in different tax levies by at least 2 authorities (State and federal) and, as between the States, at different rates. Accordingly, after 1916, the States and the Commonwealth endeavoured to provide a uniform tax system. In 1923, to minimise the duplication of administrative facilities, the Commonwealth and all the States except Western Australia agreed that federal income tax was to be collected by State officials. Simultaneously, certain Commonwealth officials were transferred from the Commonwealth government to the respective State departments and a joint form for State and federal income tax returns was adopted.

From 1923 to 1936 there was substantial cooperation between the Commonwealth and State governments on the levying and collection of State and federal income taxes. The object of the uniform tax system was achieved to a major degree with the enactment of the Commonwealth *Income Tax Assessment Act 1936* (ITAA36). This Act consolidated and amended the Commonwealth legislation in respect of the assessment and collection of income tax, and was adopted by the States as a model for their own income tax legislation.

Due to the varieties of special income taxes imposed by the respective States, however, significant disparities continued to exist between the States as well as between the federal and State tax systems. This position was radically changed in 1942 when, as a war-time measure, the Commonwealth suspended all agreements then existing between the Commonwealth and the States and assumed all functions connected with the imposition and collection of income tax. This has remained unchanged and, at the present time, only the Commonwealth directly imposes an income tax. However, there is no Commonwealth constitutional restriction against State income tax legislation. Indeed, in some States, the pre-1942 State legislation survives although no actual State income tax has been levied since that year.

A variation of this arrangement applies to GST collected by the Commonwealth. Revenue collected from GST is channelled back to the States and Territories in return for their agreement to abolish certain State taxes (¶37-060 and ¶37-070).

Since 1997, substantial parts of ITAA36 have been written into the *Income Tax Assessment Act 1997* (ITAA97), and the 2 Acts must now be read together to get a full understanding of the income tax system (¶1-700).

¶1-020 Constitutional basis of federal income tax

The Commonwealth Parliament derives its power to enact income tax legislation from the Constitution; at the same time, the Constitution imposes restrictions on this legislative power. The empowering provision is s 51(ii) by which the parliament has, subject to the Constitution, "power to make laws for the peace, order, and good government of the Commonwealth with respect to . . . taxation; but so as not to discriminate between States or parts of States". Other relevant provisions in the Constitution are ss 53, 55, 99, 114 and 117.

The Commonwealth law with respect to income tax has always been contained in separate Acts: one Act dealing with the subject of tax, its assessment and collection, and the other(s) imposing the tax. The convention of having separate Acts, which is followed in respect of all other Commonwealth tax laws (eg GST), is required by s 55 of the Constitution (¶1-050).

Under s 53 of the Constitution, proposed laws ''imposing taxation, shall not originate in the Senate'' and ''the Senate may not amend proposed laws imposing taxation''. Consequently, all Bills imposing tax must originate in the House of Representatives and, if the Senate wishes to amend a Bill imposing tax, it can only request that the House agree to the amendment(s).

Over the years, numerous taxpayers have attempted to argue that they are exempt from fulfilling their taxation obligations because the taxation system itself is invalid. Their endeavours to mount complex constitutional arguments based on the notion that Australia's entire legal and political systems are invalid have received short shrift from the courts, being dismissed as frivolous and disclosing no cause of action. The ATO has issued PS LA 2004/10 advising its staff on how to deal with such arguments.

The Constitution contains a number of restrictions on the federal government's powers to levy and collect income tax (¶1-040 to ¶1-090).

¶1-040 "... with respect to ... taxation"

For the valid exercise of power under s 51(ii) of the Constitution, the legislation in substance must be ''with respect to . . . taxation''.

In early cases, the High Court considered that the features of a ''tax'' were ''a compulsory exaction of money by a public authority for public purposes, enforceable by law, and which is not a payment for services rendered'' (*Matthews v The Chicory Marketing Board (Vic)*). The court also said that the features included that: (1) the payments are not penalties (*R v Barger*); (2) the exactions are not arbitrary (*Hipsleys Ltd*); and (3) the exactions should not be incontestable (*MacCormick*).

However, the High Court has taken a broader approach in later cases, holding that a compulsory payment under statutory powers could still be a tax even though it was levied by a non-public authority or for purposes that could not properly be described as public (*Air Calédonie International v Cth*). Further, it has said that the moneys need not be paid into consolidated revenue to be a tax, provided the moneys raised by the imposition form part of the Consolidated Revenue Fund from which they must be appropriated (*Northern Suburbs General Cemetery Reserve Trust v Cth*; *Australian Tape Manufacturers Association v Cth*).

The High Court confirmed that the features set out above were not an exhaustive definition of a tax in *Luton v Lessels* (¶1-050). In particular, it said that all the factors were important but that the presence or absence of any of them was not determinative; it was necessary, in every case, to consider all the features of the legislation.

The High Court upheld the validity of the superannuation guarantee charge (SGC: ¶39-000) on the basis that it was within the constitutional conception of taxation; the fact that revenue raising was secondary to the attainment of some other legislative purpose (in this case, providing superannuation benefits for employees) was no reason for treating the SGC otherwise than as a tax (*Roy Morgan*).

¶1-050 Laws imposing taxation

Section 55 of the Constitution provides that laws ''imposing taxation shall deal only with the imposition of taxation, and any provision therein dealing with any other matter shall be of no effect'' and that laws ''imposing taxation . . . shall deal with one subject of taxation only''. It is because of this provision that Australian income tax legislation consists of separate Acts: the Rating Acts, which actually impose a tax and fix the rate of tax; and ITAA36 and ITAA97, which provide for the incidence, assessment and collection of the tax and for a variety of incidental matters.

However, it is clear that a law will not necessarily be considered as imposing a tax even though it contains provisions relating to the imposition of the tax, eg if it deals with the collection and recovery of taxes and the punishment of offenders. Although these matters are necessary for the effective imposition of tax, they are not regarded as actually imposing the tax (*Re Dymond*).

Nor will a law necessarily be considered as imposing a tax merely because it creates a debt owing to the Commonwealth. In a challenge to the constitutional validity of the child support scheme contained in the *Child Support (Assessment) Act 1989* and the *Child Support (Registration and Collection) Act 1988*, the High Court held that the legislation did not amount to "laws imposing taxation" as it did not have either the purpose or effect of raising revenue for the Commonwealth; rather its purpose was to create and facilitate the enforcement of private rights and liabilities (*Luton v Lessels*).

The second paragraph of s 55 provides that laws "imposing taxation . . . shall deal with one subject of taxation only". (The second paragraph also provides that laws imposing duties of customs shall deal with duties of customs only and laws imposing duties of excise shall deal with duties of excise only.) The scope of a single subject of taxation was considered in *Resch's case*, where it was held that the taxation of both income and capital gains falls within the one subject.

¶1-070 Tax laws must not discriminate between States

Section 51(ii) of the Constitution expressly prohibits any federal tax that discriminates between States or parts of States. In addition, s 99 of the Constitution provides that the Commonwealth shall not by any law or regulation of trade, commerce or revenue, give preference to any one State or any part of it over another State or any part of it.

In *Fortescue Metals Group*, the High Court held that the former minerals resource rent tax (MRRT) was valid. The MRRT had a different practical operation in different States as those States had, by legislation, created different circumstances to which such legislation would apply. However, this did not mean that the MRRT discriminated between the States or that there was preference of one State over another. A regulation providing for the different valuation of livestock for different States was held to have violated s 51(ii) in *Cameron*, but an Act that imposed stamp duty in respect of Commonwealth places did not in *Permanent Trustee*, even though the scheme of the Act might produce differences in revenue outcomes between States.

¶1-080 Crown instrumentalities immune from tax

Section 114 of the Constitution prohibits the Commonwealth from imposing any tax on property, of any kind, belonging to a State, while ITAA97 specifically exempts from income tax the revenue from municipal corporations and other public authorities. The scope of s 114 raises a number of issues that continue to be tested in the courts, including the meaning of a "State", and whether a particular tax is a "tax on property".

In *SGH Limited* the High Court held that SGH, a building society controlled by a State instrumentality, was not the State of Queensland for tax purposes. The court said that it was relevant to consider the activities undertaken by the entity as well as the legal relationship between it and the executive government. If the entity is wholly owned by the State concerned, and must act solely in the interests of the State, the conclusion that it is the State or an emanation of the State will readily follow (*State Bank of NSW*).

In rejecting a challenge under s 114 by the State of Queensland to the imposition of FBT on States, a majority of the High Court concluded that FBT was not a tax on the property of the State but on transactions that affected that property (*State of Qld v Cth*). A challenge by South Australia succeeded in *SA v Cth*, where the High Court found that a State superannuation fund was exempt from CGT (but not from ordinary income tax) under s 114 because CGT is a tax on property.

In *Austin v Cth* the High Court declared the federal superannuation contributions surcharge legislation to be invalid in its application to a New South Wales Supreme Court judge on the ground that it placed a particular disability or burden upon the operations or activities of the State of New South Wales so as to be beyond the legislative powers of the Commonwealth. In rejecting the Commonwealth's argument that the treatment in special legislation of constitutionally protected funds was dictated by the operation of the Constitution itself, the High Court said that a federal law cannot be justified on the basis that it is an indirect means of achieving what would otherwise be prohibited by s 114.

Commonwealth bodies have had mixed results when they sought to use s 114 as protection from State taxes. In *Superannuation Fund Investment Trust v Commr of Stamps (SA)*, the High Court refused protection against South Australian stamp duty. In contrast, in *Allders International v Commr of State Revenue (Vic)*, the High Court invalidated Victorian legislation imposing stamp duty on a lease of a duty-free store in a federal airport (under s 52(i) of the Constitution, the federal government has exclusive power to legislate with respect to "Commonwealth places").

¶1-090 Territorial operation of income tax legislation

Another problem arising out of the constitutional limitations on the Commonwealth in tax matters is the territorial limitation of any Australian income tax legislation. An overriding factor here is the prefatory requirement in s 51 of the Constitution, which restricts the taxing power to legislation that is for the "peace, order, and good government of the Commonwealth". This suggests that there must be some nexus with Australia before Australian taxing legislation can have an extraterritorial effect. Before the Commonwealth can tax overseas source income, for example, the taxpayer must reside, have a presence, carry on a business or hold property within the jurisdiction.

Further, the extraterritorial operation of any statute may be a question of interpretation, as well as a question of validity, since it is presumed that a legislature intends that its legislation is restricted in its application to persons, property or events within its territory unless there is a clear intention to the contrary.

¶1-110 Revenue sharing

A necessary part of the 1942 uniform tax system (¶1-010) was the sharing of revenue by the Commonwealth with the States and Territories. In the post-war period, a complex revenue sharing system has been developed to deal with what is known as "vertical fiscal imbalance", ie the significant difference between the relative revenue and expenditure responsibilities of the Commonwealth and the States. Commonwealth funding assistance to the States takes 2 primary forms: specific purpose payments (sometimes referred to as "tied grants") and general revenue assistance.

The allocation of general revenue assistance to individual States is made on the basis of a formula recommended by an independent statutory body, the Commonwealth Grants Commission. The formula used by the Commission does not result in a simple per capita allocation. The Commission uses "horizontal fiscal equalisation" principles, which recognise that certain "donor" States (such as NSW and Victoria) have greater relative revenue capacities and/or less significant expenditure disabilities than the other States. Thus, while the Commonwealth cannot discriminate between States in levying income tax, effective discrimination may be achieved in the distribution of money under the revenue sharing arrangements (*WR Moran*).

The revenue received by the States and Territories from the Commonwealth under the revenue sharing system is insufficient to pay for their basic spending requirements. Consequently, they have traditionally relied on a variety of taxes and duties to raise additional revenue, in particular stamp duty (¶37-000), payroll tax (¶36-000) and land tax (¶38-000).

At the request of the States, the Commonwealth introduced legislation in 1998 to protect the States' tax base from any potential erosion resulting from the *Allders International* decision (¶1-080). The legislation provides for "mirroring" of stamp duty, payroll tax, financial institutions duty, bank account debits tax and any other State taxes that may become at risk, and the return to the States of any revenue collected through the mirror legislation. The validity of the *Commonwealth Places (Mirror Taxes) Act 1998* was upheld by the High Court in *Permanent Trustee*.

The commencement of GST on 1 July 2000 caused radical changes to Commonwealth/State revenue sharing. GST revenue collected by the Commonwealth is channelled to the States and Territories, in return for their agreeing to abolish certain taxes and charges (¶37-060 and ¶37-070). The distribution of GST revenue is also conditional on the States applying horizontal fiscal equalisation principles. The Commission continues to determine the equalisation formula and also proposes an equitable allocation of GST revenue. The allocation reflects the capabilities and needs of each State, as well as the fact that not all States levy the whole range of taxes to be eliminated.

Scheme of Commonwealth Tax Legislation

¶1-130 Income Tax Assessment Acts and Regulations

There are 2 principal Commonwealth Acts dealing with, but not imposing, an income tax: ITAA36 and ITAA97. By the late 1980s/early 1990s, the ITAA36 had become so complicated and unwieldy that the Tax Law Improvement Project (TLIP) was established to restructure, renumber and rewrite the income tax law. The result is ITAA97, which has replaced substantial parts of ITAA36 and can be regarded as the principal Act (¶1-700).

Just as there are now 2 Income Tax Assessment Acts, so there are now 2 sets of income tax regulations: the Income Tax Assessment (1936 Act) Regulation 2015 pursuant to ITAA36 s 266 and the Income Tax Assessment Regulations 1997 pursuant to ITAA97 s 909-1. By and large, these regulations prescribe how certain parts of ITAA36 and ITAA97 (as appropriate) are to be implemented.

¶1-150 Rating Acts

The Rating Acts impose the actual tax on taxable income as determined under ITAA36 or ITAA97. The rates are declared and imposed under a number of different Acts. The most important Acts are:

- the *Income Tax Rates Act 1986* and the *Income Tax Act 1986*, which together declare and impose income tax on all categories of taxpayers
- the *Medicare Levy Act 1986*, which imposes the Medicare levy and Medicare levy surcharge on individuals and sets out the amount of levy payable.

In addition, other Commonwealth Acts impose tax in special circumstances, eg the *Superannuation (Excess Non-Concessional Contributions Tax) Act 2007* and the *Superannuation (Excess Concessional Contributions Charge) Act 2013*.

¶1-170 Taxation Administration Act and Regulations

The *Taxation Administration Act 1953* (TAA), and the regulations made under it, contain provisions dealing with the administration of the tax laws by, and the powers of, the ATO. The TAA has become increasingly important and now contains: the PAYG withholding and instalment regimes; generic offence and prosecution provisions; generic provisions dealing with objections, reviews and appeals under various tax laws; generic provisions imposing penalties for breaches of various tax laws; generic record-keeping provisions; the payment, ABN and identification verification system; and provisions governing the public, private and oral rulings systems.

¶1-180 Other tax legislation

International tax agreements

Australia has entered into special tax treaties with over 40 countries to prevent double taxation and allow co-operation between Australia and overseas tax authorities in enforcing their respective tax laws. These treaties are generally referred to as ''double taxation agreements''. Under the Constitution, international treaties are not self-executing and must be given the force of law by an Act of parliament. This procedure is achieved under the *International Tax Agreements Act 1953* (¶22-140).

Fringe benefits tax

The *Fringe Benefits Tax Assessment Act 1986* and its associated rating Act, the *Fringe Benefits Tax Act 1986*, require employers to pay tax on the value of fringe benefits that they provide to employees or associates of employees (¶35-000).

Goods and services tax

The *A New Tax System (Goods and Services Tax) Act 1999* (GST Act) imposes a 10% indirect, broad-based consumption tax on goods, services and activities from 1 July 2000 (¶34-000), replacing the former wholesale sales tax regime.

Tax Administration

¶1-200 Australian Taxation Office

The income tax system is administered by the ATO, which is headed by the Commissioner of Taxation, several Second Commissioners and a number of First Assistant Commissioners. For details of the ATO's organisational structure, see the ATO website.

Since mid-2014, the ATO has been undertaking an organisational renewal program called ''Reinventing the ATO''. The ATO's vision under this program was for it to become a leading taxation and superannuation administration known for its contemporary service, expertise and integrity by the year 2020. The change program consists of 3 main streams: (1) transforming the client experience; (2) transforming the staff experience; and (3) changing the ATO culture.

A parliamentary committee report released in August 2018 titled *Taxpayer Engagement with the Tax System* concluded that even more should be done under Australia's self-assessment model. The committee examined the ATO's points of engagement with taxpayers and other stakeholders and reviewed its performance against advances made by revenue agencies in comparable nations. While it considered that evidence to date of the ATO's ''reinvention'' as a modern automated tax administration system gave much to be confident about, the committee was concerned that the complexity of Australia's tax system was impeding the ATO's transformation into a fully automated and intuitive service. The committee made 13 recommendations aimed at making tax obligations in Australia easier to administer and comply with, 8 of which the government has agreed to implement (see Government Response).

Each year the Commissioner presents an annual report to parliament, containing information on revenue raising, the administration of the tax Acts and the various enforcement strategies adopted by the ATO. Within the Federal Cabinet, the Assistant Treasurer oversees the ATO on administrative matters and the business tax reform process.

The Inspector-General of Taxation's office is an independent statutory office whose function is to review systemic tax administration issues and to report to the government with recommendations for improving tax administration; the Inspector-General cannot review taxation policy. The Inspector-General is also responsible for the tax investigative and complaint handling function (see below).

Review of ATO decisions

The ATO has its own internal review process. A taxpayer who has a complaint should first talk to the ATO officer who is handling the matter. If the matter is not resolved satisfactorily, the taxpayer should then talk to the officer's team leader or manager. If the matter is still unresolved, the taxpayer should make a complaint (¶28-190). The complaints officer can make recommendations but cannot overturn the original decision.

A taxpayer who is dissatisfied with an assessment or other taxation decision has the right to object to the assessment or decision (¶28-010). Subsequent review by the Administrative Appeals Tribunal (AAT: ¶28-090) or Federal Court (¶28-110) may be available. Decisions that do not relate to the assessment or calculation of tax may be subject to judicial review (¶28-180).

Taxpayers have a right to be paid compensation in certain circumstances where the ATO's actions have caused them loss. The 2 broad bases on which the ATO assesses a compensation claim are compensation for legal liability (eg negligence) and compensation for detriment caused by defective administration. Information about applying for compensation is available on the ATO website. Applicants must complete the approved form ''Applying for compensation'' (NAT 11669). If compensation is not payable, a taxpayer can apply to the Department of Finance for an act of grace payment.

A taxpayer may complain to the Inspector-General if they are dissatisfied with the administrative action taken by the ATO or the Tax Practitioners Board. Complaints may be in regard to: debt recovery actions; income tax assessment and instalment activity issues; decisions to bankrupt; conduct of audits; provision of advice; methods of handling inquiries; remission of penalties; handling of correspondence; delays in decision making; handling of private and public rulings; superannuation guarantee audits; operation of the PAYG instalment system; collection of FBT or PAYG withholding; and ATO assessments of compensation claims. Operational guidelines have been published by the Inspector-General's Office in regard to the handling of tax complaints lodged with it (*The IGTO-ATO Complaints Handling Guidelines*) and the conduct of the reviews (*The IGTO-ATO Review Operational Guidelines*).

A taxpayer who thinks that the ATO has breached the *Privacy Act 1988* and/or TAA Div 355 (¶1-220) in dealing with the taxpayer's personal information may also complain to the Privacy Commissioner.

ATO advice

The ATO provides various forms of advice to the general public and to particular entities in an effort to disseminate the Commissioner's views on, and interpretation of, the tax laws (¶24-500). Depending on the form of ATO advice, various levels of protection against primary liability, penalties and interest are afforded to those relying on the advice. The ATO also offers taxpayers the opportunity to enter into its Early Engagement Process, in order to seek preliminary advice in regard to the tax issues of complex transactions under consideration or already implemented.

¶1-205 Taxpayers' Charter

The Taxpayers' Charter (available on the ATO website) outlines the rights of taxpayers under the law, the service and other standards taxpayers can expect from the ATO, what taxpayers can do if dissatisfied with the ATO's decisions, actions or service, and the important tax obligations of taxpayers.

Broadly, the Charter states that taxpayers can expect the ATO to: treat them fairly and reasonably; treat them as being honest in their tax affairs unless they act otherwise; be accountable for what it does; offer professional service and assistance to help them understand and meet their tax obligations; give them advice and information they can rely on, and access to information it holds about them; respect their privacy and keep information confidential; explain decisions it makes about their tax affairs; respect their right to a review or to make a complaint; and help minimise their costs in complying with the tax law. The Charter, however, is not intended to create any legal rights for taxpayers.

The service standards taxpayers have the right to expect from the ATO include:

- enquiries made via automated reply email or electronic forms service will be responded to within 3 days (other written enquiries will be responded to within 28 days)
- electronic returns will be processed within 14 days of receipt and paper returns within 42 days of receipt, unless the return is incorrect or incomplete
- if a taxpayer requests a tax refund, it will be issued within 28 days of receiving all necessary information from the taxpayer
- a decision on an amendment request or objection to an assessment will generally be made within 56 days of receiving all necessary information from the taxpayer in writing (or within 28 days if the information is received electronically)
- a private ruling (and a decision on an objection to a private ruling) will generally be issued within 28 days of receiving all necessary information from the taxpayer
- phone calls to the general inquiry services will be answered within 2 minutes (5 minutes during periods of high demand, such as July to October)
- a taxpayer who visits the ATO will be attended to within 10 minutes (15 minutes during periods of high demand, such as July to October)
- a taxpayer who makes a complaint will be contacted within 3 days to resolve the issue
- a clerical or administrative error will be fixed within 14 days of receiving all necessary information from the taxpayer, and
- notification of the outcome of a tax audit will be provided within 7 days of the decision being made.

Important tax obligations of taxpayers are to:

- be truthful and co-operative in dealings with the ATO
- keep records in accordance with the law (TR 2018/2)
- take reasonable care in preparing tax returns and other documents and in keeping records
- lodge tax returns and other required information by the due date, and
- pay taxes and other amounts by the due date.

¶1-220 Confidentiality of tax information

The tax administration legislation contains a general prohibition on the unauthorised disclosure by a tax officer of "protected information", with some specific exceptions (TAA Sch 1 Subdiv 355-B). The general prohibition also applies to non-taxation officers who receive protected information whether lawfully or unlawfully (Subdivs 355-C and 355-D). Protected information is information disclosed or obtained under a taxation law (other than under TASA: ¶32-000) that relates to the affairs of a taxpayer and identifies, or is reasonably capable of identifying, a taxpayer. Tax file numbers, however, do not constitute protected information.

In relation to the secrecy provisions in ITAA36 former s 16, it was held that once the ATO comes into possession of information by whatever means, and whether due to exertions by one of its officers or not, if the information is relevant to the tax affairs of any person it becomes subject to the secrecy provisions (*Tang*).

Disclosures to certain entities are permitted, such as to the taxpayer's registered tax agent or BAS agent, legal representative for tax affairs, legal personal representative, other representative or guardian, and consolidated group or MEC group members. Other disclosures that are permitted include disclosures made in performing one's duties as a tax officer, disclosures of publicly available information, disclosures to certain government ministers, disclosures for certain other government purposes, and disclosures for law enforcement and related purposes (eg to support or enforce a proceeds of crime order). Permitted disclosures to courts and tribunals are limited to those necessary for the purpose of carrying into effect the provisions of a taxation law (*Binqld Finances Pty Ltd (in liq) & Ors v Israel Discount Bank Ltd*; *Jordan, FC of T v Second Commissioner of Taxation & Anor*; *DPP & Ors v Kinghorn; Kinghorn v DPP & Ors*) and must not be in breach of the accusatorial principle and the companion rule (*R v Leach*, as applied in *R v Kinghorn (No 7)*).

Legislation was enacted (effective 28 October 2019) to allow the ATO to disclose to Credit Reporting Bureaus the tax debt information of businesses that have not effectively engaged with the ATO to manage such debts, subject to certain conditions and safeguards being met (TAA Sch 1 ss 355-72 and 355-215; Taxation Administration (Tax Debt Information Disclosure) Declaration 2019). From 15 May 2020 onwards, tax officers can also disclose protected information of a deceased person to the registered tax agent, BAS agent or legal practitioner of an executor or administrator of the deceased estate (Taxation Administration (Remedial Power—Disclosure of Protected Information by Taxation Officers) Determination 2020).

The unauthorised disclosure of protected information is an offence punishable by a maximum penalty of 2 years' imprisonment.

Protection for whistleblowers

From 1 July 2019, a tax whistleblower protection regime is in force for individuals reporting breaches of tax laws or misconduct (TAA Pt IVD: ss 14ZZT to 14ZZZE). Key features of the regime include the kinds of disclosures that qualify for protection, who can make a protected disclosure, specific protections and immunities against victimisation, a compensation regime, and protections to maintain the confidentiality of a whistleblower's identity.

To qualify for protection, the disclosure must be made to an eligible recipient, ie the Commissioner or an auditor of the whistleblower entity, or a member of the ATO audit team; a person connected to the whistleblower entity who is likely to be able to investigate and take action in response to the disclosure; or a person or body prescribed in relation to the whistleblower entity. An individual will also be protected for a disclosure to his/her lawyer that is made for the purposes of seeking legal advice. Although the Tax Practitioners Board is not yet an eligible recipient, it is currently able to receive disclosures if the whistleblower provides consent. Note that the whistleblower protection regime is subject to statutory review 5 years from its commencement.

Public disclosures

To improve tax transparency, the Commissioner is required to publish publicly certain tax information of public corporate tax entities with a total income of $100 million or more for an income year, resident private companies with a total income of $200 million or more for the income year, and all entities that have any petroleum resource rent tax (¶19-003) payable in a given year (TAA ss 3C; 3E). The ATO released the ''Corporate tax transparency report'' for public and private corporate tax entities for the 2018–19 income year in December 2020.

Voluntary disclosures

To encourage voluntary public disclosures of tax information, the Board of Taxation (¶1-710) developed the tax transparency code (TTC). This is a set of principles and minimum standards to guide disclosure of tax information by large and medium-sized businesses. The TTC disclosure is divided into 2 parts, being Part A (improvements to disclosures of tax information in financial statements) and Part B (taxes paid).

Large businesses (ie with aggregated TTC Australian turnover of A$500 million or more) should adopt Part A and Part B, and medium businesses (ie with aggregated TTC Australian turnover of at least A$100 million but less than A$500 million) should adopt Part A only. The ATO advises that there is no prescribed timing for the release of annual TTC reports. Once a large or medium business has made its TTC report publicly available, it should notify the ATO at TTC@ato.gov.au.

[FTR ¶978-458 – ¶978-458/265]

¶1-230 The income tax process

The basic steps in the tax process are as follows.

(1) Towards the end of each financial year (30 June), the Commissioner issues a legislative instrument calling for the lodgment of annual income tax returns (¶24-010). Theoretically, every taxpayer deriving income is obliged to lodge a return although, in practice, certain low income earners are not required to do so.

(2) The appropriate tax return to be used depends on whether the taxpayer is an individual, a company, a partnership, a trustee of a trust estate or a superannuation fund, ADF or PST. Taxpayers must generally retain records for a period of 5 years in case they are required to verify or substantiate details in their returns during a subsequent audit.

(3) On receipt of the return, the Commissioner makes an ''assessment'' (¶25-100). The Commissioner ascertains the amount of taxable income and the tax payable on that taxable income. The Commissioner will then issue a notice of assessment. In the case of companies, superannuation funds, ADFs and PSTs, which are subject to a full self-assessment system, the Commissioner does not issue a formal notice of assessment — on lodgment, their return is deemed to be an assessment.

There are special provisions for the amendment of assessments at the instance of the Commissioner or a taxpayer (¶25-300), and for default assessments, which may be issued by the Commissioner when a taxpayer does not lodge a return or when the Commissioner is not satisfied with the return that has been lodged (¶25-140).

(4) Many taxpayers pay tax as they earn income, through the PAYG system (¶26-100, ¶27-100). If the tax paid through the year exceeds the tax assessed, the taxpayer will be entitled to a refund (interest may be payable by the Commissioner on the amount refunded: ¶28-170). If insufficient tax has been paid, the notice of assessment will advise the taxpayer of the additional tax payable.

(5) If the taxpayer is dissatisfied with the assessment, an objection may be lodged within the applicable time limit. An ATO officer reviews the objection and then notifies the taxpayer of the decision. A taxpayer who is dissatisfied with the decision may either apply to the AAT for a review of the decision (¶28-090) or lodge an appeal with the Federal Court (¶28-110). There may be further appeals to the Full Federal Court or, with special leave, the High Court (¶28-120).

Key Income Tax Concepts

¶1-240 Key income tax concepts

Residence and source

If a taxpayer is a resident of Australia, the taxpayer's assessable income includes all ordinary income and all statutory income from all sources, whether *in or out of Australia* (ITAA97 ss 6-5(2); 6-10(4)). However, if the taxpayer is a foreign resident, the taxpayer's assessable income includes only ordinary income and statutory income from all sources *in Australia*, plus certain other amounts that are not dependent on an Australian source (eg the capital gain on the disposal of certain assets regardless of the source of the amounts received) (ss 6-5(3); 6-10(5)). Thus, it is particularly important to determine both the residence of a taxpayer and the source of income (¶21-000).

Taxable income

The tax base on which the tax is imposed is ''taxable income'' (¶10-000). Taxable income is arrived at in the following way (ITAA97 s 4-15(1)):

taxable income = assessable income − deductions

Assessable income

Assessable income consists of income according to ordinary concepts (''ordinary income'') and other amounts that are included in assessable income under provisions of ITAA36 or ITAA97 (''statutory income'') (ITAA97 ss 6-5; 6-10: ¶10-010). Statutory income includes net capital gains (ITAA97 s 102-5). There is no definition of the word ''income'' in either ITAA36 or ITAA97 and it is therefore necessary to look to the accepted usage of this word to establish its meaning. Assessable income does not include exempt income or non-assessable non-exempt income.

Exempt income

Exempt income consists of amounts that, although received as income and otherwise taxable, are expressly or implicitly made exempt from income tax (ITAA97 s 6-20: ¶10-600).

Non-assessable non-exempt income

Non-assessable non-exempt income is ordinary or statutory income that is expressly made neither assessable income or exempt income (ITAA97 s 6-23: ¶10-895).

Deductions

There are 2 types of deduction:

(1) a *general deduction* — this is any loss or outgoing to the extent that it is incurred in gaining or producing assessable income or is necessarily incurred in carrying on a business for the purpose of gaining or producing assessable income (ITAA97 s 8-1(1): ¶16-010), and

(2) a *specific deduction* — this is an amount that is deductible under any other provision of ITAA36 or ITAA97 (ITAA97 s 8-5).

In general, personal expenses and capital expenditure are not deductible. However, there are various important exceptions, eg a deduction is allowed for depreciating assets (¶17-015) and for expenditure on capital works (¶20-470).

Offsets

In certain cases, an *offset* (ie a *credit* or a *rebate*) is available rather than a deduction for expenditure (¶15-005). An offset is an amount that is to be subtracted from the tax otherwise payable. It does not enter into the calculation of taxable income. Thus, an offset reduces a taxpayer's tax by the dollar amount of the offset, whereas a deduction only reduces tax by the amount of the deduction multiplied by the taxpayer's tax rate.

¶1-280 Proper taxpayer

It is a basic premise that tax can only be levied on the *proper taxpayer*. ITAA36 and ITAA97 require the taxpayer to pay tax (at the appropriate rates) on taxable income (ITAA97 s 4-10). Taxable income is determined by reference to assessable income (¶1-240), which must be derived by the taxpayer. Generally, an entity derives income if that entity receives it, or is entitled to receive it, or it is dealt with on behalf of or as directed by that entity. Only the entity who actually derives income should be taxed on that income — the Commissioner must find the proper taxpayer. Unless the legislation provides otherwise — and it would have to do so in specific terms — one entity is not to be taxed by reference to the income of another.

An important exception to this rule is provided by the *Fringe Benefits Tax Assessment Act 1986* where fringe benefits provided to an employee in respect of his/her employment are taxed in the hands of the employer as provider of the benefit rather than in the hands of the employee as recipient of the benefit (¶35-090).

Another exception is the foreign accruals tax system. This system, aimed at combating the sheltering of profits in low-tax countries, attributes income derived by foreign companies and trusts to controlling Australian residents and taxes the income on an accruals basis (¶21-105). See also the personal services income regime, which was introduced to counter the channelling of an individual's personal services income into a company or other business structure (¶30-600).

¶1-290 Annual accounting

Income taxes are returned, settled and litigated on an annual basis. The taxable year for most taxpayers is the 12-month period opening 1 July and closing the following 30 June. In certain circumstances, a substituted accounting period of 12 months closing on a date other than 30 June may be adopted (¶9-010). Income tax is levied for each tax year on the taxable income derived during the *income year*.

Annual accounting requires accounting rules to determine in what year income should be returned and deductions claimed. Most individual taxpayers use the *cash* (or *receipts*) method of accounting, which means that income is returned when actually or constructively received. But in the case of a business whose books are kept on the *accruals* (or *earnings*) method, that method is invariably required for calculating taxable income (¶9-030). In certain circumstances, a taxpayer can be assessable on a cash basis of accounting as well as an accruals basis in the same income year (*Dormer*; ¶9-030). Expenditure is generally deductible in the year in which it is *incurred* (¶16-040).

The annual accounting requirement can produce harsh results by causing deductions to fall in no-income or low-rate years or by causing amounts of income to be bunched together in a single year. Special relief provisions may apply to such situations, eg the carrying forward of past years' losses (¶16-880), the averaging of income for primary producers (¶18-200) and the averaging of income for artists, composers, inventors, performers, production associates, sportspersons and writers (¶2-140).

¶1-300 Companies, partnerships and trusts

Under the ‘‘classical’’ system of company tax that operated from 1940, a company was taxed as a separate legal entity and individual shareholders were taxed on dividends received without any recognition of the tax paid by the company on the profits out of which the dividends were paid. An inter-corporate rebate, however, usually effectively freed from tax dividends received by a corporate shareholder. An associated measure, to prevent private or closely held companies being used as tax shelters, imposed what was called ‘‘undistributed profits tax’’ on such companies if they failed to distribute at least a prescribed amount of their after-tax income.

The classical system of company tax was replaced in 1987 by an imputation system of company tax, which eliminated the ‘‘double taxation’’ of company profits that existed under the classical system. In broad terms, this is achieved by imputing company tax levied on resident companies to resident shareholders who are paid a dividend. Dividends received are, as previously, included in a shareholder’s assessable income, but the amount of imputed company tax is also included in assessable income with the shareholder being entitled to a tax credit for an equivalent amount (¶4-400). Certain taxpayers are entitled to a refund of any excess imputation credits (¶4-820).

The rules governing corporate earnings should be compared with those for partnerships and trust estates. A partnership is not taxed as such, but the partners are taxed individually on their shares of the net partnership income (whether distributed or not); alternatively, a partner may claim as a deduction his/her share of the partnership loss (¶5-000). The net income of trust estates is taxed to the beneficiaries who are presently entitled to the net income (and who are not under a legal disability). Any income not taxed to the beneficiaries is taxed to the trustee instead (¶6-000).

Interpretation and Application of Tax Legislation

¶1-350 The basic rule on interpreting tax legislation

Since the key thrust of tax legislation is to collect part of an entity’s earnings or profits, the courts developed a basic rule that any legislation imposing a tax was to be strictly interpreted or construed. As a result, it is also said that the legislation imposing tax must be expressed in clear and unambiguous language, precisely expressed and indicate very clearly an intention for the tax to be imposed.

Effect of the basic rule

Excluding administrative provisions, tax legislation by and large sets out 2 processes: one process deals with the gathering in of payments and transactions on which tax can be imposed; the other deals with exempting from tax certain transactions, payments and taxpayers and the allowance of deductions against assessable income. Which payments and transactions will be charged and which ones will be exempted or deductible is a matter of tax policy, but the general policy towards strict interpretation is applied equally to both types of provisions:

(1) charging provisions — if the particular payment or transaction (or category of taxpayer) is not within the strict wording of the charging provisions, no tax is payable on the payment or transaction, and

(2) exemption or deduction provisions — the strict construction rule, which works in favour of the taxpayer when the charging provisions of the taxing statute are under review, operates in favour of the ATO when applied to exemption or deduction provisions.

Ambiguity in tax legislation

Not all tax legislation is made up of precise language and clear expression. If transactions were simple and tax policy required a correspondingly simple taxing system with few benefits or special provisions, it might be possible to draft clearly written fiscal legislation. However, given the complexity and dynamic nature of modern economic and financial arrangements and the relatively static and necessarily reactive nature of law making, it is not surprising that precision has sometimes given way to ambiguity.

Where there is statutory ambiguity, there must be some attempt to make sense out of the written words. During the 1970s the High Court adopted a literal approach when interpreting tax laws. Partly in response, the federal government enacted s 15AA of the *Acts Interpretation Act 1901*, which *requires* courts to interpret Commonwealth legislation, including tax legislation, in a way that will promote the purpose of the legislation in preference to a way that will not. Further, s 15AB of that Act authorises courts to use "extrinsic" material in interpreting Commonwealth legislation — historically, courts refused to look at any document or other material outside of the legislation itself or the regulations made under it. The extrinsic material, eg official explanatory memoranda, second reading speeches, reports and so on, may now be used to confirm that the meaning of a particular provision is its ordinary meaning or to determine the meaning of a provision that is ambiguous, obscure, manifestly absurd or unreasonable.

¶1-360 Commissioner's discretion

ITAA36 and, to a lesser extent, ITAA97 empower the Commissioner to exercise a variety of discretions in making an assessment. A taxpayer who is dissatisfied with the Commissioner's exercise of an administrative discretion may challenge it *on its merits* before the AAT; the AAT "stands in the shoes of the decision-maker". It is more difficult to challenge an exercise of the Commissioner's discretion before a court as a court can only interfere with a discretion if it was not exercised in accordance with legal principles (¶28-085).

Statutory remedial power

The Commissioner has a statutory remedial power under TAA Sch 1 Subdiv 370-A to relax the taxation and superannuation laws where they lead to anomalous or unintended outcomes. The power is discretionary and allows the Commissioner to make a legislative instrument under s 370-5 to modify the law. Such a legislative instrument will apply to all entities or, if stated in the instrument, a specified class of entities or in specified circumstances. However, the modification will not apply to an entity if it would produce a less favourable result.

The power can only be exercised where the modification is consistent with the purpose or object of the relevant provision, the Commissioner considers it to be reasonable, and the revenue impact would be negligible. It is a power of last resort.

Examples of situations where the remedial power was considered but not applied are provided on the ATO website. A form is also available for stakeholders to make suggestions for the use of the Commissioner's remedial power.

¶1-380 The problem of substance versus form

Form and substance represent 2 distinct approaches to the interpretation of tax laws in Australia and elsewhere.

The form approach to the interpretation of tax law will not invalidate a transaction that is implemented in strict compliance with the specific requirements of the relevant provisions that govern it, regardless of the substantive effect of the transaction. The underlying philosophy of the form approach is that, because tax laws deprive taxpayers of their profits, taxpayers should be entitled — to the fullest extent that those laws allow — to arrange their affairs to minimise tax.

Historically, the major decision in support of the form approach is that of the House of Lords in *IRC v Duke of Westminster*; indeed the form approach is often referred to as the Duke of Westminster doctrine. In Australia, judicial adherence to a strictly formal or literal approach contributed significantly during the 1970s to the widespread emergence of schemes packaged and promoted by tax avoidance ''entrepreneurs''. It also progressively resulted in a great volume of complex tax legislation as new areas of avoidance were identified and closed off. A feature of much of that legislation was the wide discretionary powers given to the Commissioner (¶1-360).

Broadly speaking, the substance (or policy) approach does not limit its inquiries to the way in which a transaction is formally structured and documented, but goes behind the transaction to examine its substantive effects. The substance approach is regarded as being inherently revenue biased and criticised for its potential to cause unpredictable outcomes.

In addition to the use of extrinsic materials (¶1-350), there are other signs that the courts may be more inclined to look behind the form of a transaction, particularly in cases involving tax avoidance schemes. In *Spotless Services*, the High Court dismissed the Duke of Westminster doctrine as irrelevant in determining whether the general anti-avoidance provisions of ITAA36 Pt IVA (¶30-110) applied to a transaction and noted that, in such cases, the courts must consider both form and substance. The High Court ruled that the doctrine of fiscal nullity developed in the UK does *not* apply in Australia.

¶1-410 The choice principle

The income tax legislation provides taxpayers with a number of choices or options. Judicial responses to taxpayers' taking advantage of choices offered by the legislation have changed over time. In the 1980 *Westraders' case*, the High Court held that, where a taxpayer chooses to enter into a transaction in order to obtain a tax advantage and the income tax legislation specifically provides for that choice, the taxpayer is entitled to receive the tax benefits thereunder. According to Barwick CJ:

> ''Parliament having prescribed the circumstances which will attract tax, or provide occasion for its reduction or elimination, the citizen has every right to mould the transaction into which he is about to enter into a form which satisfies the requirements of the statute . . . [It cannot] matter that his choice of transaction was influenced wholly or in part by its effect upon his obligation to pay tax.''

In a 1985 decision on tax avoidance by 3 doctors who set up unit trusts to effectively split the income from their medical practices, the High Court rejected arguments by the doctors based on the choice principle. The doctors argued that by setting up the trusts, the income of which would be taxed under ITAA36, they were doing no more than choosing a course that was open to them under that Act. In rejecting the argument, Gibbs CJ stated that it was simply not right to say that ITAA36 allowed taxpayers the choice to have their income from personal exertion taxed as though it were income derived by a trust and held for the benefit of beneficiaries (*Gulland; Watson; Pincus*). The same principle would seem to apply to ITAA97.

The exercise of a choice provided by ITAA36 or ITAA97 may, in any event, be restricted by the general anti-avoidance provisions of ITAA36 Pt IVA (¶30-110). In the cases of the 3 doctors mentioned above, the High Court applied the then general anti-avoidance provision (ITAA36 former s 260) to annihilate the trust arrangements because one of their main purposes in entering into the arrangements was to avoid tax. Specific anti-avoidance rules that apply where personal services income is derived through an entity may also negate the tax advantages of entering into such a scheme (¶30-600).

[FTR ¶783-940]

Tax Rewrite and Reform

¶1-700 Rewriting and reforming the tax laws

For many years the income tax law was widely criticised for being too difficult to read and understand. The complexity of the law also increased the costs of taxpayer compliance and government administration. The Tax Law Improvement Project (TLIP) was established in 1993 following a report of a Parliamentary Committee recommending the setting up of a Task Force to rewrite the income tax law. The aim of the project was to restructure, renumber and rewrite the income tax law, rather than to reform the tax system or review tax policy.

To date, there have only been 3 formal instalments of the rewrite (dealing with core provisions and a few specific areas such as CGT), which applied from the 1997–98 and 1998–99 income years. Consequential amendments closed off the corresponding provisions in ITAA36. Since the third instalment, some sections of ITAA36 have been rewritten and relocated in ITAA97, or in the TAA, on a less formal basis. As the law currently stands, ITAA36 and ITAA97 have concurrent operation, making it necessary to work with both Acts.

Several schedules of ITAA36 have also been transferred into ITAA97 and the TAA (eg the collection and recovery provisions, the forgiveness of commercial debts provisions, leases of luxury cars provisions, the farm management deposits provisions and the general insurance provisions). Large sections of ITAA36 will also be transferred into ITAA97 as part of the ongoing tax reform process.

Relevance of cases and rulings

As TLIP's primary goal was to rewrite the provisions of ITAA36 without changing their effect, ITAA97 contains a special provision (s 1-3) designed to ensure that mere differences in drafting style should not be taken to indicate differences in meaning. Section 1-3 provides that, if ITAA36 expressed "an idea" in a particular form of words and ITAA97 "appears to have expressed the same idea in a different form of words in order to use a clearer or simpler style", then "the ideas are not taken to be different just because different forms of words are used". This provision is intended to maintain, as far as appropriate, the judicial precedents built up over many years in interpreting ITAA36.

As a corollary, TAA Sch 1 s 357-85 provides that a public or private ruling about a provision of ITAA36 is taken also to be a ruling about a corresponding provision of ITAA97 so far as the 2 provisions express the same ideas.

Future tax reform

A parliamentary committee report titled *Taxpayer Engagement with the Tax System* was released in August 2018. The committee made 13 recommendations aimed at making tax obligations easier to understand and simpler to comply with, to which the government released a response in February 2020. Notably, the first recommendation of the committee called for a complete review of the tax system by 2022 in order to reduce complexity and to make it both easier to enforce and to understand. However, due to the number of recent reviews of Australia's tax system (by the Inspector-General of Taxation, the Board of Taxation and the Productivity Commission), the government considers that a review of the entirety of the tax system is not necessary at this time. The committee's recommendations in regard to the introduction of a standard workplace expenses deduction scheme and an industry-specific ABN withholding tax system were also rejected. Other recommendations that were directed at improving the amenity of automated tax systems to assist taxpayers and reduce error were agreed to.

¶1-710 Tax design

The Department of the Treasury is responsible for assessing and advising on the general design of the tax system and its components, with input from the ATO and private sector experts, in what is known as tripartite tax law design. Treasury and the ATO have a protocol that sets out the terms of their working arrangements about tax law design. The ATO's role in the process is discussed in PS LA 2013/4. A ''collaborative'' approach is adopted and external expert involvement is encouraged.

Before a Bill containing tax measures is introduced into parliament, Treasury usually undertakes consultation on the measures and releases the proposed legislation as exposure draft legislation for public comment. Treasury's standard tax design process now incorporates a minimum 4-week consultation period although this is not always possible with urgent integrity issues and constraints around Budget decisions.

The ATO has developed a Consultation Hub on its website as a primary base for all consultation between the ATO and the public.

Board of Taxation

The Board of Taxation is an advisory body established to contribute a business and broader community perspective to the design of taxation laws and their operation. The Board has the task of advising the Treasurer on improving the general integrity and functioning of the taxation system and commissioning research and other studies on tax matters approved or referred to it by the Treasurer. However, the government is proposing to allow the Board to initiate its own reviews.

The Board maintains an online collaborative platform ''Sounding Board: Ideas for better tax regulation'' for interested parties to contribute to.

Chapter 2 Individuals

Who Must File a Return?

¶2-000 Resident individuals

The requirements for lodging annual returns are set out by the Commissioner towards the end of each financial year via Legislative Instrument (see the Australian Government Federal Register of Legislation website at www.legislation.gov.au).

For the **2020–21** income year, resident individuals whose total taxable income for the year from all sources exceeds the tax-free threshold of $18,200 are generally required to lodge a return (¶2-120 and ¶42-000). Individuals with taxable incomes below the tax-free threshold are also required to file a return in various situations (¶24-010).

Residents of Norfolk, Cocos (Keeling) and Christmas Islands are treated as residents of Australia for the purposes of assessment and payment of tax. Special provisions to exempt Norfolk Island residents from tax on Norfolk Island and ex-Australian income no longer apply from 1 July 2016 (¶10-640).

Individuals who are resident (¶21-010) for only part of the income year are required to lodge a return if their taxable income exceeds $13,464 plus $395 for each month of residence (including the month in which the person became, or ceased to be, a resident: ¶2-130).

Tax on temporary working holiday makers

Non-resident individual taxpayers that are working holiday makers (¶21-033) are taxed at 15% from their first dollar earned, up to $37,000, with ordinary marginal tax rates applying after that. However, note that the validity of the legislative provisions imposing tax on ''working holiday makers'' has been struck down by the Federal Court decision of *Addy* (appeal pending) to the extent that those provisions apply to working holiday makers who become residents of Australia. For working holiday maker rates (the ''backpacker tax'', as the measure is commonly referred to), see ¶42-018. More flexible arrangements to benefit working holiday makers and industry will be introduced, allowing an employer with premises in different regions to employ a working holiday maker for 12 months, with the working holiday maker working up to six months in each region. Further, the tax on working holiday makers' superannuation payments when they leave Australia is 65%.

[FITR ¶29-010, ¶29-130; FTR ¶3-850, ¶79-320, ¶860-480]

¶2-010 Non-resident individuals

Non-resident individuals are required to file a return if they earned *any* income from sources in Australia other than dividend, interest or royalty income subject to withholding tax (¶24-010). For the taxation of non-residents generally, see ¶22-000.

[FTR ¶79-320]

Return Forms

¶2-030 Tax returns — myTax, forms and instructions for individuals

Individual taxpayers (including sole traders and contractors) are encouraged to lodge their returns via the Internet using ''myTax''. Within myTax, there is a pre-filling service which partially completes an individual's tax return by downloading information into it using data the ATO already has from previous returns, and current year information from organisations required to report to the ATO, such as employers, banks and government agencies. An ATO app, ''myDeductions'' is also available to help taxpayers keep track of common deductions and work-related expenses. It allows taxpayers to upload their completed deductions data to the ATO, which will use this information to pre-fill myTax returns.

To lodge a tax return online, individuals will need to get a myGov account (my.gov.au) and link to the ATO as a member service. Once linked to the ATO, individuals can use their myGov account to manage tax affairs. Personal details can be updated, arrangements made to pay a debt and progress of previously lodged tax returns can be checked.

Individuals can still also lodge their returns by paper though these are no longer distributed by the ATO. The return form and the individual tax return instructions are available on the ATO website (¶44-000). There is a separate return form (Form I) for use by tax agents. For further details on the requirements relating to the lodgment of returns, see ¶24-010.

Certain information should be recorded in the individual tax return instructions or equivalent records, and taxpayers should retain the records in case the ATO requires that information to be produced at a later date. See further ''Keeping your tax records'' on the ATO website.

An individual must personally sign the return and must also complete a declaration as to the correctness of the return. Where the return contains a claim subject to the substantiation rules, the individual must also make a declaration to the effect that the relevant substantiation records are held. Where a return is prepared by a tax agent, the agent must complete the tax agent's certificate on the return.

Tax receipts

The Commissioner is required to issue a tax receipt to individual taxpayers whose total tax assessed (ITAA97 s 4-10(3)) is $100 or more for the income year (TAA Sch 1 s 70-5). The tax receipt will include information about how the total tax assessed for the year is notionally used to finance different categories of Commonwealth government expenditure.

[FTR ¶79-305, ¶79-329, ¶977-415/205]

¶2-060 Due date for lodgment of tax returns for individuals

The due date for lodgment of returns is generally 31 October. Individuals preparing and filing their own returns may, if unable to file by the due date, apply to the ATO for an extension of time (¶24-070). Reasons must be stated.

Penalties are imposed for late lodgment of returns (¶29-100) and, therefore, any application for an extension of time for filing should be made *before* the due date.

Special extension arrangements apply to returns prepared by tax agents to enable agents to spread their work over a substantial part of the year.

[FTR ¶79-310]

¶2-070 Where to lodge a tax return for individuals

For paper returns, the taxpayer must lodge the return at the address directed by the Commissioner (¶24-010).

Defence Force personnel should, unless directed otherwise by the ATO, lodge their returns at the office of the Deputy Commissioner in the state in which they are residing at the time that returns are due for lodgment.

The Northern Territory and the ACT are treated as states for return filing purposes, while Norfolk Island is treated as being in New South Wales and Cocos (Keeling) and Christmas Islands in Western Australia.

A paper return is not treated as duly lodged unless and until it is correctly completed and received, together with all the necessary annexures, at the ATO where it is required to be lodged.

[FTR ¶79-315]

¶2-080 Date of death tax returns

A return must normally be filed for a deceased taxpayer for the period from beginning of the relevant income year to the date of death of the taxpayer (TAA Sch 1 Subdiv 260-E). The return is filed by the executor or administrator of the deceased's estate and must include all assessable income derived (and all deductible losses or outgoings incurred) by the deceased in that period (¶6-030).

Date of death returns should generally be accompanied by a full and true statement of assets and liabilities valued at the date of death. However, if the deceased person was a salary or wage earner, such a statement will only be required if the Commissioner requests it. Once the assessment has been issued and tax has been paid on it, the executor or administrator can rely on the assessment notice to distribute the assets of the estate, confident that the Commissioner will not seek to reopen the assessment at a later time.

A date of death return does not have to be filed if the taxpayer would not have been obliged to file a return, eg where the deceased taxpayer was a resident whose taxable income for the period to the date of death did not exceed the tax-free threshold and there are no other circumstances requiring lodgment of a return. In such a case, the executor or administrator should instead provide the Commissioner with a non-lodgment advice. A pro forma is provided in the tax return instructions.

Note that, with limited exceptions, any capital gain or loss arising from a CGT event as a result of the death of a taxpayer is disregarded (¶12-570).

For a checklist of the tax consequences of death, see ¶44-170.

[FTR ¶977-840]

Calculation of Tax Liability

¶2-090 Calculation of tax payable: ordinary resident individual

Tax payable by an ordinary individual resident taxpayer for **2020–21** is calculated as follows (ITAA97 s 4-10).

(1) *Taxable income* is calculated. This is assessable income (eg salaries, wages, rents, interest), *less* all expenditure incurred in deriving that income (eg union dues, travel expenses, depreciation) and personal deductions (eg gifts to approved institutions, certain tax-related expenses).

(2) The *gross tax payable* is calculated by applying the general rates of tax to the taxable income.

(3) The *net tax payable* is calculated by deducting from the gross tax any *rebates/tax offsets* (eg the dependant (invalid and carer) tax offset, the zone rebate, the low income earner rebate and the medical expenses rebate).

(4) An amount for the *Medicare levy* must be added equal to 2% of the taxpayer's taxable income (exemptions and reductions may apply: ¶2-290).

(5) Where applicable, amounts must be added for Medicare levy surcharge (¶2-335) and for HELP repayments (¶2-380).

▶ Example

Jessica, an unmarried resident with no dependants, is a legal officer employed by a government department and has salary income of $80,000 for the 2020–21 income year. Jessica also received interest income of $264. Jessica was covered by private patient hospital insurance in 2020–21.

During the year, Jessica incurred the following expenses:

• subscriptions to legal periodicals	$400.00
• membership fee for professional association	40.00
• tax return expenses	50.00
• gifts to public benevolent institutions	20.00

Jessica's taxable income and tax liability are calculated as follows:

Salary		$80,000.00
Interest		264.00
Assessable income		$80,264.00
Less:		
Subscriptions	$400.00	
Membership fee	40.00	
Tax return expenses	50.00	
Gifts	20.00	510.00
Taxable income		$79,754.00
Gross tax payable at 2020–21 rates on a taxable income of $79,754 (¶42-000)		$17,467.05
Plus: Medicare levy (2% × $79,754)	$1,595.08	
2020–21 tax payable		**$19,062.13**

To arrive at the *actual tax payable/refundable*, the net tax payable will generally need to be adjusted for PAYG amounts withheld from salary or wages or from payments where an ABN or TFN has not been quoted, and/or any other credits (eg imputation credits).

Special rules for calculating tax payable apply in a number of situations. These are where: (a) the taxpayer's taxable income includes a net capital gain (Chapter 12); (b) the taxpayer is a primary producer (¶18-200); (c) the taxpayer is an author, inventor, performing artist, production associate or sportsperson (¶2-140); or (d) the taxpayer is a minor with unearned income (¶2-160). Different tax-free thresholds also apply where a taxpayer changes residency (¶2-130).

[FTR ¶860-012]

¶2-110 Quick reference chart for calculating tax liability

The following chart shows the various income and deduction items which may be taken into account in determining taxable income and rebates and credits which may reduce gross tax. The items listed, which are general, are discussed in more detail at the paragraphs indicated.

Even though fringe benefits are, in some cases, reported on a taxpayer's payment summary (¶35-055), they are not taken into account when determining taxable income.

ASSESSABLE INCOME

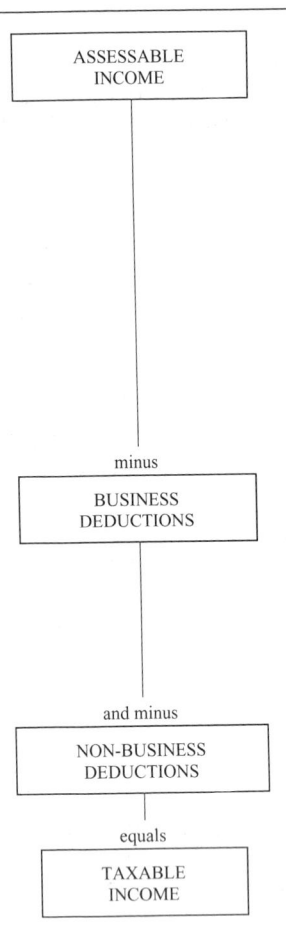

Gross business and professional receipts (¶10-110); salaries and wages (¶10-050); allowances (such as tool/clothing allowance) paid by employer (¶10-060); benefits from employer, excluding fringe benefits taxable to the employer (¶10-060); tips, gratuities and other benefits for services rendered (¶10-070); share benefits granted in relation to employment (¶10-080); lump sum payments for unused annual leave (¶14-720); lump sum payments for unused long service leave (¶14-730); certain superannuation benefit payments (¶14-220, ¶14-240, ¶14-280); certain employment termination payments (¶14-620, ¶14-680); non-exempt pensions including age pensions (¶10-190); newstart allowances/jobseeker payments and sickness allowances (¶10-190); workers compensation, insurance receipts for loss of wages, profits or trading stock (¶10-170, ¶10-180); net primary production income (¶18-030); life assurance bonuses (¶10-240); rents and royalties (¶10-620, ¶10-640); grossed-up amount of dividends (¶4-800); interest (¶10-470); liquidator's distributions (¶4-300); share in net income of partnership (¶5-130) or trust (¶6-110); net taxable capital gains (¶11-000); income from pre-CGT property acquired for profit-making by sale (¶10-430); foreign income (¶21-680); income attributable under foreign accruals measures (¶21-105); other assessable income (¶10-010).

minus

BUSINESS DEDUCTIONS

Expenses of carrying on business (¶16-015); employees' expenses (¶16-160); motor vehicle expenses (¶16-310); travel expenses (¶16-220); home office expenses (¶16-480); property and investment income expenses (¶16-650, ¶16-660, ¶16-670); depreciation (¶17-000); trade subscriptions or dues (¶16-430); special incentives for primary producers (¶18-050); cost of construction income-producing buildings (¶20-470); film industry investments (¶20-330); contributions to superannuation funds (¶13-710, ¶13-730); expenditure on environmental impact studies (¶19-060); environment protection expenditure (¶19-110).

and minus

NON-BUSINESS DEDUCTIONS

Gifts (¶16-940); tax-related expenses (¶16-850); contributions to registered political parties (¶16-950).

equals

TAXABLE INCOME

TAX LIABILITY

Tax is applied to taxable income at general rates (¶2-120): subject to special provisions for minors (¶2-160), authors, inventors, performing artists, production associates and sportspersons (¶2-140), and primary producers (¶18-210).

From the resulting tax, deduct: dependant (invalid and carer) tax offset (¶15-100), low income earners rebate (¶15-300), private health insurance offset (¶15-330), zone and overseas forces rebates (¶15-160 – ¶15-190), Senior Australians and pensioners tax offset (¶15-310), rebate in respect of employment termination payments, unused annual leave and long service leave (¶14-720, ¶14-730), rebate in respect of certain superannuation pensions and rollover annuities (¶13-160), rebate for eligible spouse superannuation contributions (¶13-770), social security beneficiary rebate (¶15-315), income arrears rebate (¶15-340), Medicare levy surcharge lump sum payment in arrears offset (¶15-350), rebate for assessable life assurance bonuses (¶10-240), tax offset for franked dividends (¶4-800), averaging rebate for primary producers where taxable income exceeds average income (¶18-210), foreign income tax offset (¶21-670).

The net tax remaining is adjusted for PAYG amounts withheld from salary or wages (¶26-150) or from payment when an ABN or TFN has not been provided (¶26-200).

An amount should be added for Medicare levy (¶2-290) and, where applicable, Medicare levy surcharge (¶2-335) and HELP repayments (¶2-380).

Rates of Tax

¶2-120 General rates of tax: individual taxpayers

In determining the rates of tax applicable to individual taxpayers, a distinction is made between residents and prescribed non-residents.

For rating purposes only, a person is treated as a resident if the person was a resident (¶21-010) at any time during the income year or was in receipt of a taxable Australian social security, military rehabilitation or veterans' entitlement pension, benefit or compensation. In any other case, the person is classed as a prescribed non-resident (*Income Tax Rates Act 1986*, s 3(1)).

Resident taxpayers are entitled to the benefit of a tax-free threshold. For **2020–21**, the threshold is $18,200. This means that the first $18,200 of taxable income derived by a resident individual is tax-free (note, however, that the low income rebate (¶15-300) may apply to effectively increase this threshold).

Taxable income in excess of the threshold is taxed at progressive rates of tax, ie the average tax rate increases as the taxable income increases. The rates scale applicable to resident individual taxpayers is set out at ¶42-000 and a ready reckoner table showing the amount of tax payable at different taxable income levels is set out at ¶42-023.

There is no tax-free threshold for individuals who qualify as prescribed non-residents. They pay tax on the very first dollar of taxable income. However, like residents, the rate of tax increases as the taxable income increases. For the rates scale applicable to prescribed non-residents, see ¶42-015.

A seven-year Personal Income Tax Plan has been implemented to progressively increase certain income tax rate thresholds in the 2018–19, 2020–21 and 2024–25 income years and to remove the 37% personal income tax bracket from the 2024–25 income year. A new low and middle income tax offset has also been introduced for the 2018–19, 2019–20, 2020–21 and 2021–22 income years (¶15-300). The Personal Income Tax Plan has been amended to further lower taxes for individuals, including changes to both the low and middle income tax offset, the low income tax offset (¶15-300) and the personal income tax rates and thresholds. From 1 July 2020, the top threshold of the 19% personal income tax bracket is increased from $37,000 to $45,000 (up from $41,000 as originally legislated under the Personal Income Tax Plan) and the top threshold of the 32.5% bracket is increased from $90,000 to $120,000. The 2020–21 Budget brought forward these changes from 1 July 2022. From 1 July 2024, the 32.5% marginal tax rate will reduce to 30%.

A tax offset is provided to individuals who run small businesses (businesses with an aggregate annual turnover of less than $5m), or who pay income tax on a share of the income of a small business. The amount of the tax offset is 8% of the income tax payable on the portion of an individual's income that is small business income. In addition to calculating the offset in this way, the maximum amount of the tax offset available to an individual in an income year is capped at $1,000 (¶7-210).

[FTR ¶860-012]

¶2-130 Reduction of tax-free threshold

The standard tax-free threshold ($18,200) is apportioned (or "pro-rated") in an income year in which a taxpayer becomes or ceases to be a resident (*Income Tax Rates Act 1986*, s 16 to 20). However, no additional threshold applies for income derived during the period the person was a non-resident. As a result, part-year residents are able to access a tax-free threshold of:

$13,464 + [$4,736 × number of months taxpayer was resident for the year ÷ 12]

▶ Example

Luc arrives in Australia on 21 November 2020 to take up permanent residence here. He earns $26,000 from 1 January 2021 to 30 June 2021. As Luc has been in Australia for eight months of the 2020–21 income year (including the month he became a resident), his reduced tax-free threshold is $13,464 + [$4,736 × 8 ÷ 12] = $16,621. The first $16,621 of Luc's taxable income is tax-free. On the basis of the rates scale at ¶42-000, the remaining $9,379 ($26,000 – $16,621) is taxed at 19%.

The threshold is not pro-rated on account of non-residency if, in the year of income, the person is in receipt of a social security or veterans' entitlement pension (other than sickness allowance, newstart allowance/jobseeker payment or special benefits) that is subject to Australian tax. Such taxpayers are entitled to the benefit of the full threshold.

Pro-rating of the threshold on account of non-residency may occur in more than one income year.

Trustees

The same pro-rating calculation applies when calculating the tax payable by the trustee of a trust estate under ITAA36 s 98 in respect of the share of trust income of a presently entitled beneficiary under a legal disability, where there is a part-year residency period in relation to the beneficiary (*Income Tax Rates Act 1986*, s 20(1A), (2)).

[FTR ¶860-480]

¶2-133 Means-tested family assistance

Family assistance, administered by the Department of Human Services, may be available to taxpayers with dependent children. These *include* Family Tax Benefit Part A, Family Tax Benefit Part B and Child Care Subsidy. From 2 July 2018, a Child Care Subsidy replaced the fee assistance provided by the Child Care Rebate and Child Care Benefit. For children born or adopted on or after 1 March 2014, a Baby Bonus is no longer available. Taxpayers may instead be eligible for Paid Parental Leave or the Newborn Upfront Payment and Newborn Supplement paid with Family Tax Benefit Part A payments.

The eligibility conditions and rates of payment of family assistance are set out in the *A New Tax System (Family Assistance) Act 1999*. The administrative, procedural and technical rules are set out in the *A New Tax System (Family Assistance) (Administration) Act 1999*.

Family assistance is received as direct fortnightly payments from the department, or as reduced child care fees. Family assistance payments are exempt from income tax (ITAA97 s 52-150).

Income test

To be eligible for family assistance, a taxpayer must pass an income test (''adjusted taxable income'') which takes into account income of the taxpayer's family. For this purpose, ''family income'' is the *sum* of the following amounts derived by the taxpayer and the taxpayer's partner:

- taxable income
- reportable superannuation contributions, ie the sum of the person's personal deductible contributions and reportable employer superannuation contributions made by the person's employer (¶13-730)
- total net investment loss, ie from financial investments (shares, interests in managed investment schemes (including forestry schemes), rights and options, and like investments), and from rental properties

- adjusted fringe benefits, ie gross rather than adjusted net value of reportable fringe benefits, except in relation to fringe benefits received by individuals working for public benevolent institutions, health promotion charities and some hospitals and public ambulance services
- income from certain tax-free pensions and benefits from the Department of Human Services or Veterans' Affairs
- target foreign income, ie any income, payment or benefit received from a foreign source that is tax exempt in Australia

minus the annual amount of any child support/child maintenance the taxpayer or the taxpayer's partner pays.

Family Tax Benefit Part A

Family Tax Benefit Part A helps with the costs of raising children and is paid per child. Eligibility is based on family income. The extent of entitlement depends on the ages and number of dependent children in the family. From 1 July 2020, family income can be $55,626 a year before the Family Tax Benefit Part A payment is reduced. The payment reduces by 20 cents for each dollar from $55,626 up to $98,988. If family income is above $98,988 a year, the base rate of Family Tax Benefit Part A ($60.90 per fortnight in 2020–21) will reduce by 30 cents for each dollar over that amount until entitlement is lost. The maximum rate of Family Tax Benefit Part A applicable from 1 July 2020 is as follows:

For each child	Maximum FTB Part A rate per fortnight
Under 13	$189.56
13–15	$246.54
16–19 who meets the study requirements	$246.54
Up to 19 in an approved care organisation	$60.90

These amounts do not include the Family Tax Benefit Part A supplement ($781.10 for **2020–21**), which may be paid after the end of the income year. An income limit of $80,000 applies on payment of the Family Tax Benefit Part A supplement.

Payment of the Family Tax Benefit Part A supplement is conditional on a child meeting the immunisation requirements. This applies to the income years in which the child turns one, two and five. The Family Tax Benefit Part A is reduced by up to $28.84 per fortnight for each child if immunisation requirements are not met.

The rate of Family Tax Benefit Part A is increased for any income year in which there is a child born into a family, the family adopts a child or a child comes into the care of the family (such as by becoming a foster child of the family), unless one of the parents receives Parental Leave Pay for the child. The amount of Newborn Upfront Payment and Newborn Supplement received depends on family income and how many children the family has. Newborn Upfront Payment is a lump sum of $570. The Newborn Supplement may be paid for up to 13 weeks from the first day of eligibility. If eligible for the whole 13 weeks, a maximum of $1,709.89 may be paid for the first child or a maximum of $570.57 for subsequent children.

Family Tax Benefit Part A is paid to families only up to the end of the calendar year in which their teenager is completing school. The 2019–20 Budget measure to extend the Family Tax Benefit (FTB) eligibility to the families of ABSTUDY secondary school students who are aged 16 years or older and are required to live away from home to attend school has been implemented. The amendments ensure that the families of ABSTUDY boarding students aged 16 to 19 are eligible for the FTB until the students complete Year 12. Youth allowance will remain available to help young people transition from school into work or post-secondary study. Exemptions will continue to apply for children who cannot work or study due to physical, psychiatric, intellectual or learning disability.

Families are only be able to receive Family Tax Benefit Part A for six weeks in a 12-month period while they are overseas. This measure aligns the portability rules for Family Tax Benefit Part A with those of Family Tax Benefit Part B and most income support payments. Family Tax Benefit recipients will still be able to take multiple trips and retain Family Tax Benefit but each trip must be less than six weeks duration.

The Family Tax Benefit Part A maximum standard, base rate and approved care organisation rate are maintained for two years at their current levels from 1 July 2017. From 1 July 2017, indexation of these amounts was paused for two years and resumed on 1 July 2019.

Family Tax Benefit Part B

Family Tax Benefit Part B is aimed at assisting single income families. It is payable where the primary earner's income or the sole parent's income is $100,000 or less for 2020–21. However, the secondary earner's income is taken into account and this person can have an income of up to $5,767 a year before payment is affected, with a reduction of 20 cents for each dollar of income over that amount.

For **2020–21**, the maximum Family Tax Benefit Part B rate is as follows:

Age of youngest child	Maximum FTB Part B rate per fortnight
Under 5	$161.14
5–18	$112.56

These amounts do not include the Family Tax Benefit Part B supplement ($379.60 per family for 2020–21), which may be paid after the end of the income year.

Family Tax Benefit Part B is no longer be paid to couple families (other than grandparents and great-grandparents) with a youngest child aged 13 or over. Single parents, grandparents and great-grandparents caring for a youngest child aged 13 to 18 will continue to have access to FTB Part B (subject to satisfying other relevant requirements).

The Family Tax Benefit Part B maximum rates were maintained for two years at their current levels from 1 July 2017. From 1 July 2017, indexation of these amounts was paused for two years and resumed on 1 July 2019.

Child Care Subsidy

From 2 July 2018, a Child Care Subsidy has been introduced to support families where both parents work. Families meeting the activity test with annual incomes up to the lower income threshold of $68,183 for 2020–21 are eligible for a subsidy of 85% of the actual fee paid, up to an hourly fee cap. The subsidy tapers to 50% for eligible families with annual incomes between $68,163 and $173,163 in 2020–21. If the combined family income is at or above the second income threshold (of $173,163), but below the third income threshold (of $252,453), the applicable percentage is 50%. If the combined family income is above the third income threshold (of $252,453) and below the fourth income threshold (of $342,453), the applicable percentage tapers down from 50% to 20%. Where the combined family income is between the fourth income threshold (of $342,453) and the upper income threshold (of $352,453), the applicable percentage is 20%. Above the upper income threshold of $352,453, no Child Care Subsidy is payable.

The effect of the formulas is to reduce the applicable percentage at a rate of 1% for every $3,000 to ensure a consistent and graduated taper. Indexation of the lower income threshold against the Consumer Price Index results in the higher threshold points shifting by the same amount. The hourly fee cap for the new Child Care Subsidy depends on the type of service providing the session of care. The hourly caps are $11.98 for care provided by centre-based day care service, $10.48 for care provided by a family day care service, $10.10 for care provided by an outside school hours care service.

On 2 April 2020, the government announced new funding arrangements for the early childhood education and care sector in response to the COVID-19 pandemic and its impact on child care enrolments and attendance. The government paid 50% of the sector's fee revenue up to the existing hourly rate cap based on a point in time before parents started withdrawing their children in large numbers, but only so long as services remained open and did not charge families for care. The new arrangements made child care services fee-free for families between 6 April and 12 July 2020, based on the number of children who were in care during the fortnight leading into 2 March 2020, whether or not they were attending services. This was extended from 28 June to 12 July 2020. The government also made payments of higher amounts available in exceptional circumstances, such as where greater funding was required to meet the needs of emergency workers or vulnerable children. The payments were made in lieu of Child Care Subsidy and Additional Child Care Subsidy payments. Child Care Subsidy started again from 13 July 2020. From then, some families affected by COVID-19 had access to more Child Care Subsidy. If families were receiving Child Care Subsidy before 6 April 2020, it automatically started again if they stayed eligible and their enrolment was current and confirmed. If families are new to child care, they should claim Child Care Subsidy as soon as possible. From 13 July 2020, families pay full fees unless they are receiving Child Care Subsidy.

Families receiving the Child Care Subsidy have until 31 March 2021 to submit their 2018–19 tax return for Child Care Subsidy purposes. Families will still be required to submit tax documents in accordance with the usual timeframes. From 13 July 2020, the Child Care Subsidy resumed operation and eligible families are expected to make a contribution towards the cost of child care. This one-off extension means that families continue to have access to the Child Care Subsidy and not be required to pay full fees, ensuring that parents can continue to access affordable care. Parents were reminded to update their details with Centrelink before 13 July 2020, especially those with reduced incomes, to ensure that they receive the correct level of subsidy they are entitled to. Under the Child Care Subsidy legislation, if families do not lodge their 2018–19 tax return by 31 March 2021, or advise Centrelink that they are not required to lodge, they will lose their entitlement to the Child Care Subsidy and will be required to pay full child care fees. Once families lodge their 2018–19 tax return, entitlement to the Child Care Subsidy can recommence. Families are encouraged to lodge their 2018–19 tax return as soon as possible, noting the extension is for Child Care Subsidy purposes only and delaying lodgment of the return could affect other benefits, such as Family Tax Benefit. Families should check the ATO website to understand the consequences for non-lodgment of tax returns by the required due date.

The Child Care Subsidy replaced child care fee assistance provided by the Child Care Rebate and Child Care Benefit.

Estimates of family income

A taxpayer who chooses to receive Family Tax Benefit fortnightly or Child Care Subsidy as a fee reduction will generally estimate family income for the current financial year. This estimate will be used by the Family Assistance Office to work out how much family assistance the taxpayer is entitled to receive.

An estimate does not need to be provided by a taxpayer who is:

- single and receiving an income support payment from either Centrelink or Veterans Affairs

- only claiming the minimum rate of Child Care Benefit and not claiming Family Tax Benefit at the same time
- claiming a lump sum payment for a previous period, or
- an approved care organisation.

Estimates given by taxpayers will be compared with their actual family income after the end of the financial year. If actual income is less than estimated income, the taxpayer could either be paid a lump sum or this amount could be offset against a tax debt. If actual income is more than estimated income, money may have to be paid back to the Department of Human Services after the end of the financial year, or the debt may be deducted from the taxpayer's tax refund.

2020 Economic Support Payments for Family Tax Benefit recipients

Schedule 4 of the *Coronavirus Economic Response Package Omnibus Act 2020* (Act No 22 of 2020), which received assent on 24 March 2020, provides for two separate $750 payments to social security, veteran and other income support recipients (including Family Tax Benefit Part A and Family Tax Benefit Part B recipients) and eligible concession cardholders.

The first payment (previously announced in the government's first economic response to COVID-19 on 12 March 2020) has been made from 31 March 2020 and is available for those who are eligible Social Security and Veterans' income support recipients, Farm Household Allowance recipients, Family Tax Benefit recipients and holders of a Pensioner Concession Card, Commonwealth Seniors Health Card or Commonwealth Gold Card at any time from 12 March 2020 to 13 April 2020 inclusive.

The second payment has been made from 13 July 2020 and is available for those who are eligible Social Security and Veterans' income support recipients, Farm Household Allowance recipients, Family Tax Benefit recipients and holders of a Pensioner Concession Card, Commonwealth Seniors Health Card or Commonwealth Gold Card on 10 July 2020, unless they are eligible to receive the Coronavirus Supplement.

Schedule 1 of the *Social Services and Other Legislation Amendment (Coronavirus and Other Measures) Act 2020* (Act No 97 of 2020) provides for the payment of 2 further Economic Support Payments of $250 to around 5 million social security and veteran and other income support recipients (including Family Tax Benefit Part A and Family Tax Benefit Part B recipients) and eligible concession cardholders in the lead up to Christmas and in the new year as part of the government's economic response to COVID-19.

The payments will be made progressively from 30 November 2020 to 1 March 2021. To be eligible, recipients must be residing in Australia and receive or hold one of the following payments or concession cards on 27 November 2020 and/or 26 February 2021: Age Pension, Disability Support Pension or Carer Payment; Carer Allowance, Double Orphan Pension or Family Tax Benefit Part A and/or Family Tax Benefit Part B (if not in receipt of a primary income support payment); Commonwealth Seniors Health Card; Pensioner Concession Card (if not in receipt of a primary income support payment); and certain Department of Veterans' Affairs payments and cards.

Centrelink will pay the Economic Support Payments straight into an individual's bank account. If an individual has a Cashless Debit Card, Centrelink will pay the Economic Support Payments into their card. If the individual is income managed, the payments are 100% income managed.

Paid Parental Leave scheme

A government-funded Paid Parental Leave (PPL) scheme applies for births and adoptions. The scheme provides 18 weeks (90 payable days) of paid postnatal leave to the child's primary carer at the federal minimum wage ($753.80 per 38-hour week or $19.84 per hour from 1 July 2020) (fathers and other partners may be eligible for two weeks' pay at the federal minimum wage). PPL has changed from 1 July 2020. The intention was to provide wider options to families who seek to access parental leave pay under the PPL scheme. The amendments in *Paid Parental Leave Amendment (Flexibility Measures) Act 2020* support women's economic independence by allowing primary carers to access parental leave pay more flexibly, particularly birth mothers and adoptive parents who are self-employed or small business owners. Instead of eligible parents only being able to receive parental leave pay in a single continuous block of up to 18 weeks and having to claim within 12 months of the birth or adoption of their child, parents (and other claimants in limited cases) are able to claim two types of parental leave pay:

- The first type is an initial period of 12 weeks called the PPL period. The rules relating to this block are the same as currently apply to the existing 18-week period — except that the period is reduced in length.
- The second type is new and takes place in the person's flexible PPL period. Days during this period are called flexible PPL days. Eligible parents (and other claimants in limited circumstances) are able to claim parental leave pay for a maximum of 30 days whenever they like during the flexible PPL period, which usually starts after the PPL period ends and finishes when the child turns two.

So, as long as an effective claim for parental leave pay in the PPL period has been made for the child, a person can claim for parental leave pay on any flexible PPL day until the child turns two. If a child's birth or adoption is on or after 1 July 2020, the child's primary carer may still receive up to 90 days PPL. However, the payment will include both a continuous PPL period of up to 12 weeks which is 60 payable days and 30 flexible PPL days. PPL can still be received in a single continuous 18-week block. To do this, a 12-week PPL period will be connected to 30 flexible PPL days. Alternatively, a shorter block of between 12 and 18 weeks can be chosen. The remaining flexible PPL days can then be taken at a later time, when it suits. Flexible PPL days must be taken before a child turns two.

To be eligible for the PPL scheme, a parent in paid work:

- must have worked continuously with one or more employers for at least 10 of the 13 months before the expected date of birth or adoption
- must have worked at least 330 hours in those 10 months (equivalent to around one full day of work each week), and
- must have an adjusted taxable income of $150,000 or less in the financial year prior to the date of birth or adoption of the child.

Rules have been made to assist the people affected by the economic impact of the COVID-19 pandemic to be eligible for parental leave pay. The Paid Parental Leave Amendment (Coronavirus Economic Response) Rules 2020 (the Amendment Rules) set out the number of hours for which a person will be taken to have performed qualifying work under the work test for parental leave pay, where the person is in a JobKeeper payment period. Under the Amendment Rules, a person will be taken to have performed:

- 7.6 hours of qualifying work for the purposes of the work test for each weekday during a period or periods of JobKeeper payment, and
- no hours of qualifying work a day for each Saturday or Sunday during a JobKeeper payment period.

Where a person performed at least one hour of paid work on:

- a weekday and the day is in the person's JobKeeper payment period, new rules provide that the person will be taken to have performed the greater of 7.6 hours or the number of hours of paid work actually performed by the person on that day, and

- a day and the day is a Saturday or Sunday that falls in a JobKeeper payment period, the person will be taken to have worked the hours actually performed on that day (instead of no hours).

The Amendment Rules also provide for similar calculations where a person takes a period of paid leave for a day that is in a JobKeeper payment period. The return to work rules are also amended for essential workers. Previously, where a person returned to work before or while they were receiving parental leave pay, or while they were receiving Dad and Partner Pay, any remaining amount of payment would be forfeited. However, under the Paid Parental Leave Act Rules, a return to work can be disregarded in a number of circumstances and is amended to include an additional circumstance to cover emergency services workers, health professionals and other essential workers who return to work in response to a state, territory or national emergency, such as the COVID-19 pandemic.

Schedule 4 of Act No 97 of 2020 introduces a revised PPL work test period for a limited time, to enable people to access parental leave pay and Dad and Partner Pay who do not meet the work test provisions because their employment has been interrupted by the COVID-19 pandemic. This will enable most individuals with a genuine work history pre-COVID-19 to qualify for payments under the PPL scheme. Amendments by the *Coronavirus Economic Response Package Omnibus (Measures No 2) Act 2020* (Act No 38 of 2020) already allow for time spent on the JobKeeper payment to count towards the PPL work test. Beyond parents receiving JobKeeper payment, some parents may have been on a pathway to maintaining a consistent work history that would have enabled them to be eligible for parental leave pay, but have not achieved a continuing work history due to the impacts of COVID-19. As a result, this cohort will have less income in the pre-birth period than originally planned, and may be relying on income support, such as the JobSeeker Payment.

The new measure temporarily extends the PPL work test period from 13 months prior to the birth or adoption of a child to 20 months (600 days) for parents who have had their employment impacted by COVID-19. This change applies to births and adoptions that occur between 22 March 2020 and 31 March 2021. Changes will allow people who meet the concessional work test to backdate the start date of their PPL period to the date of birth of their child. The retrospective nature of the measure may create overpayments where the individual or their partner have been receiving income support, Newborn Upfront Payment or Newborn Supplement for that child or Family Tax Benefit Part B for the backdated period. Existing arrangements for raising and recovery of any associated debts will continue to apply as normal. Services Australia will work with families to ensure paid parental leave eligible parents receive their payments in a way that is least likely to affect previous period payments, and will inform parents of any future debts that may arise and how these debts can be repaid. This measure commenced 14 November 2020.

Parents who are eligible for PPL are able to continue to access employer funded leave (maternity leave and recreation leave) around the time of the birth or adoption of a child. PPL is available to contractors, casual workers and the self-employed.

The government funds employers to pay their eligible employees as part of the scheme.

Parents who receive PPL will not receive the additional Family Tax Benefit Part A component that replaced the Baby Bonus (except in the case of twins or multiple births), or Family Tax Benefit Part B during the 18-week PPL period. Mothers and primary carers not in full-time paid work will continue to receive the current forms of family assistance, if they meet the relevant eligibility requirements.

Unlike other family assistance payments, PPL payments are assessable income and are included in the income test for Commonwealth income support payments (¶10-010). Compulsory superannuation contributions do not apply for PPL purposes.

[FTR ¶860-520, ¶860-523]

The Sharing Economy

¶2-135 Taxing the sharing economy

The ''sharing economy'' is a term used to describe economic activity that connects buyers (users) to sellers (providers) of goods and services through an online platform (an app or a website). Such online platforms are usually hosted by a facilitator who is neither the provider nor the consumer of those goods and services. Popular sharing economy services include:

(1) renting out a room or a whole house or unit on a short-term basis, for example Airbnb and Stayz

(2) providing ''ride sourcing'' services for a fare (considered to be taxi travel) such as Uber and GoCatch

(3) providing personal services for a fee, including creative or professional services such as graphic design and creating websites, or odd jobs such as deliveries and furniture assembly, and even pet sitting or boarding, like Airtasker and Mad Paws

(4) renting out a car parking space, for example Parkhound, Park Monkey and Spacer.

The ATO's updated guidance document *The sharing economy and tax* provides its position with respect to these four categories of participation in the sharing economy. These four categories of participation in the sharing economy are of most relevance to individual taxpayers. The challenge that the sharing economy poses in a tax context is that it brings into the market a large number of individuals who are not otherwise business taxpayers, thereby creating an administration and collection issue for income tax and GST. The sharing economy raises a range of tax issues depending on the type of transaction in question but none of those issues are particularly new or controversial. The new aspect is the scale of non-business taxpayers actually or potentially converting themselves into business taxpayers, and having to confront tax issues and levels of administration that may be unexpected.

Although the sharing economy business model differs from that of a traditional service provider, the ATO has indicated that it can only apply the tax law as it currently stands. This means that service providers within the sharing economy have the same tax obligations as traditional service providers.

The ATO guidelines reflect this view and broadly, the outcomes are as follows:

- **Income tax** — Payment for services provided is assessable income for income tax purposes (¶10-010), unless there are reasonable grounds to consider the activity of providing the services as a hobby or recreational pursuit (¶10-050). The ATO guidelines do not provide a specific example of a level of activity that would not be regarded as a business, although it is stated that if a taxpayer did jobs on an infrequent basis, ''for example one or two small paying jobs per month'', the taxpayer would not have the scale or permanency of activity that would indicate a business. From a practical point of view, the example given in the guidelines indicates that almost all sharing economy activities above the de minimus level indicated will be regarded by the Commissioner as a business. In particular, the provision of services to strangers at arm's length is said to give the activity a commercial character (¶10-105), as does the use of a sharing economy website. Consequently, unless the taxpayer provides personal services through a sharing economy platform on a very small scale, they will be required to include the amounts paid to them for the services in assessable income, and will be entitled to deduct expenses incurred in carrying on the business (¶16-015).

  Work-related expenses and deductions, and expenses relating to the use of the sharing economy platform would also be deductible under ITAA97 s 8-1 (¶16-010). In the case of renting out a room or a whole house or unit on a short-term basis, the guidelines do not contemplate a minimum level of activity in the way that they do for the provision of personal services. While it is possible that a single or small number of short-term rental arrangements might be considered de minimus, it is difficult to see how a rental arrangement might be dismissed as a hobby, or as recreational. As a general rule, income from renting out a room or whole house or unit on a short-term basis will be included in assessable income (¶10-500). Consequently, deductions will also be available under ITAA97 s 8-1 for expenses ordinarily incurred related to rental properties such as fees or commission charged by the facilitator or administrator, council rates, interest on a loan for the property, electricity and gas, property insurance, cleaning and maintenance costs (products used or hiring a commercial cleaner) (¶16-650). Where the property is the taxpayer's own residence and the rental arrangements are short-term, apportionment of those expenses will be required.

The ATO guidelines include detailed instructions on how to apportion deductions for expenses, based on the proportion of the year the house or property is rented out, the portion of the property rented out (for example, a room or the whole property), and whether the home or part of the property is used for personal use when it is not rented out.

- **GST** — If an individual is carrying on an enterprise and their annual threshold is above $75,000, they must register for GST (¶34-100).

  If an individual is carrying on an enterprise of providing ride-sourcing services, under the GST law they must be registered for GST, and must account for GST on the full amount of every fare regardless of how much is earned (¶34-220). They can also claim the business proportion of input tax credits (¶34-110). The GST registration threshold does not apply to ride-sourcing services because they are a supply, for GST purposes, of "taxi travel". The ATO also considers that the individual is running a small business as a sole trader, so they must declare all the income earned from providing ride-sourcing services and can claim the expenses related to providing the services.

  Those already registered for GST must report the income on their GST return (¶34-150).

  In the sharing economy category of renting out a room or a whole house or unit on a short-term basis, the GST position will in most cases be quite different to the issues already identified that relate to the provision of personal services for a fee, renting out a car space and the provision of "ride sourcing" services for a fare because GST does not apply to residential rent. The supply of residential premises by way of lease, hire or licence is an input taxed supply (¶34-230). Accordingly, no GST is payable with respect to rent if the property is the taxpayer's residence or a private residential investment property. However, the provision of accommodation in commercial residential premises (eg a hotel, serviced apartment, or bed and breakfast) or renting out commercial spaces like a function room or office space is generally taxable.

  There are some sharing economy rental online platforms that allow taxpayers to make commercial premises such as office space available for rent. The GST exclusion for residential rent will not apply to rent paid for these types of properties. If an individual is carrying on an enterprise and their annual threshold is above $75,000, they must register for GST (¶34-100).

- **CGT main residence exemption** — A consequence of renting out a room or a whole house or unit on a short-term basis or renting out a car parking space is that it is likely that part of the CGT exemption for a main residence will be lost. A capital gain or loss from a dwelling is disregarded if the taxpayer is an individual, the dwelling was the taxpayer's main residence throughout the ownership period and the interest did not pass to the taxpayer as a beneficiary in, or as the trustee of, the estate of a deceased person (¶11-730). If the residence is used for the purpose of producing assessable income during the ownership period, the taxpayer will lose a proportion of the exemption based on the proportion of the property made available for rent and the length of time it was rented (¶11-760).

Under ITAA97 s 118-145, the full CGT main residence exemption may still be available if the taxpayer moves out of the main residence to live in another home for a period of time (¶11-740). If the property is used for income-producing purposes, the maximum period the dwelling can be treated as the taxpayer's main residence is six years. However, the key issue in this provision extending the main residence exemption is that there must be a cessation of the property being the taxpayer's main residence. In the case where a taxpayer vacates their home for a short time to stay with friends or family in order to accommodate guests or rents out a car parking space, this is unlikely to occur.

[FITR ¶19-545; FTR ¶79-562]

Income Averaging Scheme

¶2-140 Application of the income averaging scheme

An income averaging scheme applies to certain classes of "special professionals" (authors, inventors, performing artists, production associates and sportspersons: ¶2-142). The scheme, which is contained in ITAA97 Div 405 (s 405-1 to 405-50), is designed to prevent such taxpayers from being pushed into higher tax brackets when income from their professional work in a year fluctuates above their average income from such work.

Under the scheme, the tax payable is calculated by applying to the total amount of above-average special professional income (and any capital gains) the average rate of tax which one-fifth of that amount would have borne if it had been the top slice of the taxpayer's taxable income (¶2-144).

The income averaging scheme applies in any income year in which a special professional person was a resident of Australia at any time during the year and *either*: (a) had a taxable professional income for the year which exceeded $2,500; *or* (b) was a resident at any time during a preceding income year and had a taxable professional income for that preceding year which exceeded $2,500.

[FITR ¶385-000]

¶2-142 Classes of special professionals

The classes of special professionals subject to the income averaging scheme are: authors of literary, dramatic, musical or artistic works, inventors, performing artists, production associates and sportspersons (ITAA97 s 405-25).

The expression "author" is a technical term from copyright law. Thus, a computer programmer is classified as an author for the purposes of the income averaging scheme (TD 93/65) — but see *Finlayson* below.

"Performing artist" is defined by reference to the activities which a performer undertakes as part of his/her profession. The first category of activities encompasses music, a play, dance, an entertainment, an address, a display, a promotional activity, an exhibition and similar activities. The second category comprises those activities within the performing arts field which are not always carried on in the presence of an audience. This includes the performance or appearance of a person in or on a film (including online films), tape, disc or television or radio broadcast.

"Production associate" refers to those persons who have an artistic input, as distinct from a technical input, into any of the activities mentioned in the definition of performing artist. The persons who qualify as production associates are specified in the definition of "artistic support" to be: an art director, a choreographer, a costume designer, a director, a director of photography, a film editor, a lighting designer, a musical director, a producer, a production designer, a set designer and any person who makes an artistic contribution similar to that made by any of these persons.

"Sportsperson" is any person who competes in a sporting competition in any of the ways identified in the definition of sporting competition. A "sporting competition" is a sporting activity to the extent that:

- human beings compete by riding animals, or by exercising other skills in relation to animals (eg jockeys, rodeo riders)
- human beings compete by driving, piloting or crewing motor vehicles, boats, aircraft or other modes of transport
- human beings compete with, or overcome, natural obstacles or natural forces (eg mountain climbers), or
- human beings are the sole competitors (eg footballers, golfers, athletes).

Competitors must use physical prowess, physical strength or physical stamina. Persons specifically exempt from this requirement are a navigator in a car rally, a coxswain in rowing and any competitor whose role is of a similar nature (s 405-25(8)), but not a golf caddy (*Davidson*; ID 2004/196).

Income derived from the following activities is expressly excluded from assessable professional income (ITAA97 s 405-30):

- coaching or training sportspersons
- umpiring or refereeing a sporting competition
- administering a sporting competition
- being a member of a pit crew in motor sport
- being a theatrical or sports entrepreneur
- owning or training animals.

Income from such activities will not be included in any above-average special professional income to which the averaging scheme applies.

Authors and inventors who enter into a scheme to provide services to others cannot count as assessable professional income any income derived under the scheme unless: (a) the scheme was entered into solely for the taxpayer to complete specified artistic works or inventions; and (b) the taxpayer does not provide such services to the other person or an associate under successive schemes that result in substantial continuity of the provision of such services (s 405-30). Hence persons such as journalists, draughtspersons and graphic artists who produce works as an ordinary part of their employment are not eligible for income averaging simply as a result of their ordinary employment tasks. Similarly, in *Finlayson* a computer programmer was not able to take advantage of the income averaging provisions as the ongoing requirement to improve or upgrade specific products for the one employer amounted to the provision of services under successive schemes.

[FITR ¶385-220, ¶385-230]

¶2-144 Calculation of tax under income averaging scheme

The steps involved in calculating the tax payable under the income averaging scheme are as follows.

Step 1: Divide the taxpayer's total assessable income into assessable professional income and other assessable income.

"Assessable professional income" is income derived from activities related to the taxpayer's status as a special professional (ITAA97 s 405-20). It specifically includes prizes received in connection with a taxpayer's activities as a special professional and income from endorsing products, advertising, interviews and commentating. Specifically excluded are ETPs, unused annual leave or unused long service leave payments and any net capital gain (ITAA97 s 405-30).

Step 2: Divide the taxpayer's total taxable income into taxable professional income and other taxable income.

"Taxable professional income" is the taxpayer's assessable professional income minus any deductions attributable to that income (ITAA97 s 405-45).

There are two classes of deductions: (a) those which reasonably relate to the taxpayer's assessable professional income (this class includes deductions which relate exclusively to that income, such as the cost of a sportsperson's sporting equipment, and deductions which relate in part to that income, such as the use of a car); and (b) those which have no relation to the taxpayer's assessable professional income, but which are apportionable between assessable professional income and other assessable income in the same proportion as the taxpayer's otherwise ascertainable taxable professional income bears to the aggregate of the taxable income and the apportionable deductions (eg gifts to charity).

The taxable professional income will be treated as nil where the deductions exceed the assessable professional income.

Step 3: Work out the taxpayer's average taxable professional income.

Ordinarily, "average taxable professional income" in an income year will be one-quarter of the sum of the taxable professional incomes for the preceding four years (ITAA97 s 405-50). However, there is a special rule for calculating average taxable professional income to assist taxpayers in the early stages of their careers. This rule applies where the preceding four-year period includes "professional year 1", ie the first income year in which the taxpayer was a resident for all or part of the year and had a taxable professional income of more than $2,500. In such a case, average taxable professional income is calculated as:

- in professional year 1 — nil
- in the second income year ("professional year 2") — one-third of the taxable professional income for professional year 1
- in the third income year ("professional year 3") — one-quarter of the sum of the amounts of taxable professional income for professional years 1 and 2
- in the fourth income year ("professional year 4") — one-quarter of the sum of the amounts of taxable professional income for professional years 1, 2 and 3.

A taxpayer has only one "professional year 1". For a returning former resident this may be an earlier year than the year the taxpayer returns to Australia (*Case Z6*; TD 93/33). Where the taxpayer was a foreign resident in the income year preceding professional year 1, the average taxable professional income is:

- in professional year 1 — the taxable professional income for that year (this means that there is no above-average special professional income and therefore no averaging effect in that year)
- in professional year 2 — the taxable professional income for professional year 1
- in professional year 3 — half the sum of the amounts of taxable professional income for professional years 1 and 2

- in professional year 4 — one-third of the sum of the amounts of taxable professional income for professional years 1, 2 and 3.

Step 4: Divide the taxpayer's total taxable income into above-average special professional income and normal taxable income.

"Above-average special professional income" is taxable professional income minus average taxable professional income (ITAA97 s 405-15). "Normal taxable income" is average taxable professional income plus taxable income that is not taxable professional income.

Step 5: Calculate the tax payable on the normal taxable income using ordinary individual rates (¶42-000).

Step 6: Calculate the tax payable on the normal taxable income plus one-fifth of the sum of the above-average special professional income using ordinary individual rates.

Step 7: Take the difference between the amount calculated in step 6 and the amount calculated in step 5 and multiply the difference by five. This gives the amount of tax payable on the above-average special professional income.

Step 8: Add the tax payable on the above-average special professional income (Step 7) to the tax payable on the normal taxable income (step 5) to give the total tax payable.

▶ Example

Yvonne, a jockey, is a special professional whose professional year 1 is 2018–19. She was also a resident in the previous year. She had taxable professional income of $15,000 in 2018–19 and $20,000 in 2019–20. She has a total assessable income of $60,000 in **2020–21** (professional year 3) comprising $20,000 from employment as a waitress and $40,000 from riding. Assume her only expenses are $3,000 for riding equipment. On the basis of the rates scale at ¶42-000, the tax payable on her income (disregarding Medicare levy) is calculated as follows:

1.	Assessable professional income	$40,000
	Other assessable income	$20,000
2.	Taxable professional income ($40,000 – $3,000)	$37,000
	Other taxable income	$20,000
3.	Average taxable professional income ([$15,000 + $20,000] ÷ 4)	$8,750
4.	Normal taxable income ($20,000 + $8,750)	$28,750
	Above-average special professional income ($37,000 – $8,750)	$28,250
5.	Tax on normal taxable income of $28,750	$2,004.50
6.	Tax on normal taxable income plus 1/5 of above-average special professional income (ie tax on $34,400 ($28,750 + 1/5 of $28,250))	$3,078
7.	Tax on above-average special professional income ([$3,078 – $2,004.50] × 5)	$5,367.50
8.	Total tax payable ($2,004.50 + $5,367.50)	$7,372

The total tax ordinarily payable would have been $10,072 (ie tax on $57,000). The tax saving from the averaging scheme is $10,072 – $7,372 = $2,700.

[FITR ¶385-310 – ¶385-400]

Income of Minors

¶2-160 Special tax payable by minors

Special rules apply in calculating the tax payable on income of a minor (ITAA36 Pt III Div 6AA: s 102AA to 102AGA). These rules were introduced to discourage income-splitting by diverting income to children, but they are not confined to situations where income-splitting is involved.

Under these rules, "unearned income" of minors over a certain level is taxed at the highest marginal rate of tax (45% for **2020–21**). The rules apply to income, including capital gains, derived by the minor directly or through a trust. Where the minor is a resident, the special rules do not apply if the relevant income is $416 or less.

The low income earner's rebate (¶15-300) is no longer available for the unearned income of minors.

[FTR ¶51-452 – ¶51-462]

¶2-170 Which minors are within the rules?

Persons to whom the special rules apply are called "prescribed persons". A prescribed person is any person under 18 years of age at the end of the income year *except* (ITAA36 s 102AC):

- a person who is classed as being in a "full-time occupation"
- an incapacitated child in respect of whom a carer allowance or a disability support pension was paid or would, but for eligibility tests, be payable
- a double orphan or a permanently disabled person, provided they are not dependent on a relative for support.

Full-time occupation exception

The main exception is the full-time occupation exception. A minor will be treated as being engaged in a full-time occupation if he/she was either: (a) actually engaged in a full-time occupation on the last day of the income year; or (b) engaged in a full-time occupation during the income year for at least three months (not necessarily continuously). If the minor engages in a course of full-time education after a period of full-time occupation, the period of full-time occupation is disregarded in calculating the three months (s 102AC(6), (7)).

In either case, the Commissioner must also be satisfied that, on the last day of the income year, the minor intended engaging in a full-time occupation during the whole or a substantial part of the *next* year and did not intend returning to full-time education during that next year (s 102AC(8)).

"Occupation" includes any office, employment, trade, business, profession, vocation or calling (ITAA36 s 102AA(1)). It does not include a course of education at a school, college, university or similar institution. A period during which a person is in receipt of unemployment benefits does not constitute a period of engagement in a full-time occupation.

[FTR ¶51-465, ¶51-480]

¶2-180 What income of minors is caught by special rules?

Not all types of income of a minor are caught by the special rules. The rules mainly apply to income which is sometimes called "unearned income", such as dividends, interest, rent, royalties and other income from property.

Certain categories of income are excluded from the special rules (ITAA36 s 102AE(2)). The main exclusions are for employment income and for business income (see below). The other exclusions are for income from deceased estates and income from investment of: (a) compensatory damages awards for loss of parental support, mental or physical injury, workers compensation or criminal injury compensation; (b) inherited property; (c) death benefits such as life assurance, superannuation or retirement fund payments; (d) property transferred to the minor as the result of a family breakdown (see below); (e) amounts received from public funds; (f) lottery winnings; and (g) income from reinvestment of excluded income.

As to income from trust estates, see ¶2-210.

Employment income

''Employment income'' means (ITAA36 s 102AF(1)):

- work and income support related withholding payments and benefits — these include payments to employees and payments under labour hire arrangements from which PAYG amounts must be withheld, and non-cash benefits in relation to which the provider must, under the PAYG rules, pay an amount to the Commissioner
- payments made for services rendered
- compensation, sickness or accident payments made to an individual because of that individual's or another's incapacity for work and calculated at a periodical rate.

Business income

''Business income'' means income from carrying on a business either alone or together with others, eg in a partnership. Business income also includes income from a business of providing services.

The amount of business income which can be excluded from the special rules is restricted to what the Commissioner considers ''reasonable''. In determining this question, the Commissioner has regard to: (a) the extent to which the minor participated in the business and had the real and effective conduct and control of it; (b) the extent to which the minor had the real and effective control over the disposal of income derived by him/her from the business; and (c) the extent to which capital of the business consisted of property contributed by the minor that would otherwise have produced excluded income.

These tests apply where the business is carried on by the minor either alone or in partnership with others, each of whom was under 18 on the first day of the income year. In other situations, the reasonable income from business is limited to the amount that would be a reasonable reward by way of salary or wages for any services rendered to the business by the minor, plus a reasonable return on any capital of the minor invested in the business, being capital that would normally generate excluded income in the hands of the minor.

Where a partnership derives *non-business* income, the amount of that income which will be excluded from the special rules is limited to the amount that would have been excluded if it had been derived directly by the minor.

Family breakdowns

There are two sets of circumstances in which property may be said to be transferred as the result of a ''family breakdown'' (ITAA36 s 102AGA). The first is where there is a family breakdown, ie where:

- two people cease to live with each other as spouses (a ''spouse'' includes an individual, whether of the same or different sex, who is in a registered relationship under a prescribed state or territory law with another individual, and an individual who lives with another individual as a couple: ITAA97 s 960-255 and 995-1(1)) (¶14-270)
- one of those people is the parent (a ''parent'' includes natural, adoptive and step-parents, and people who are parents because a child was the product of their relationship as a couple with another person: ITAA97 s 960-255 and 995-1(1)), or has legal guardianship of the child
- an order, determination or assessment is made as a result of the people ceasing to live together, with the effect that a person — not necessarily the parent — becomes subject to a legal obligation to maintain or benefit the child or one of the spouses. This would cover not only court orders, but also administrative assessments under the *Child Support (Assessment) Act 1989*, and is not restricted to orders, etc, made in Australia, and

- property is transferred to the minor in satisfaction of that legal obligation. Discretionary transfers are therefore excluded.

The second set of circumstances is where the parents are not living together as spouses at the time the child is born, but child support obligations exist. If property is transferred to the minor in satisfaction of a legal obligation arising under an order made as a result of the natural parents not living together, that will be classed as a transfer resulting from a family breakdown.

[FTR ¶51-498, ¶51-502, ¶51-536]

¶2-190 Anti-avoidance provisions relevant to minors

Anti-avoidance provisions are designed to ensure that the income exclusions noted at ¶2-180 are not exploited.

First, where parties were not dealing with each other at arm's length in relation to the derivation of excluded income, the excluded income is limited to the amount that would have been derived if they had been at arm's length (ITAA36 s 102AE(6)).

Second, income is not treated as excluded income if it arises from an arrangement designed at least in part to secure that the income would qualify as excluded income (s 102AE(7), (8)).

[FTR ¶51-515]

¶2-210 Trust income of minors

If a beneficiary of a trust estate is a prescribed person (¶2-170), the special rules apply to so much of the beneficiary's share of the net income as the Commissioner considers is attributable to assessable income of the trust estate that is not excepted trust income (ITAA36 s 102AG).

"Excepted trust income" is so much of the assessable income of the trust estate as is income of a deceased estate, or income of the kinds covered by the exclusions noted at ¶2-180. However, business income is not treated as excepted trust income, nor is employment income unless the relevant services are rendered by the beneficiary.

Where the excepted trust income is derived from the investment of property transferred to the trustee for the benefit of the beneficiary, it is a condition that the beneficiary must, under the terms of the trust, acquire the trust property when the trust ends. This does not apply if the property was transferred to the trustee directly from a deceased estate.

Anti-avoidance provisions corresponding to those discussed at ¶2-190 also apply in the case of trust income.

Special rules apply for determining the amount of excepted trust income of a beneficiary in a discretionary trust.

[FTR ¶51-530]

¶2-220 Calculating the tax of minors

Where a minor derives income subject to the special rules, that income (net of deductions relating to the income) is generally taxed at the top marginal rate. The net income subject to the special rules is called "eligible taxable income".

Any taxable income of the minor that is not eligible taxable income is taxed at general resident rates where the minor is a resident (or at non-resident rates where the minor is a prescribed non-resident).

For **2020–21**, the rules for calculating the tax on eligible taxable income where the minor is a resident are as follows (*Income Tax Rates Act 1986* (ITRA), s 13; Sch 11).

(1) If the eligible taxable income is $416 or less, the special rules do not apply. The whole of the taxable income is simply taxed in the normal way.

▶ Example 1

Genevieve, a minor, has a taxable income of $11,000 for 2020–21 of which $400 is eligible taxable income. As the eligible taxable income does not exceed $416, the whole of the taxable income is taxed at ordinary resident rates in the normal way. Applying 2020–21 rates (¶42-000), the tax payable by Genevieve is therefore nil. (She is not liable for the Medicare levy as her taxable income does not exceed the threshold.)

(2) If the eligible taxable income exceeds $416 but is less than $1,308, the tax on the eligible taxable income is the greater of:

(a) 66% of the excess over $416, and

(b) the difference between tax on the whole of the taxable income and tax on so much of the taxable income that does not qualify as eligible taxable income.

▶ Example 2

Nathan, a minor, has a taxable income of $20,000 for 2020–21 of which $1,200 is eligible taxable income. The tax payable on the $1,200 is the greater of:

(a) 66% × ($1,200 – $416) = $517.44, and

(b) tax on $20,000 (ie $342) less tax on ($20,000 – $1,200) (ie $114) = $228.

As (a) exceeds (b), tax payable on the $1,200 of eligible taxable income is $517.44. The total tax payable by Nathan would be $517.44 (tax on eligible taxable income) plus $114 (tax on taxable income other than eligible taxable income). The total tax payable by Nathan would be $631.44, less any rebates or credits. (He is not liable for the Medicare levy as his taxable income does not exceed the levy threshold.)

(3) Where the eligible taxable income exceeds $1,307, tax is payable on the whole of the eligible taxable income at the rate of 45%.

▶ Example 3

Rohan's only income is eligible taxable income of $40,000. Tax payable for 2020–21 (excluding Medicare levy) is $18,000 (ie 45% of $40,000) (less any rebates or credits).

▶ Example 4

Brad's income for 2020–21 consists of eligible taxable income of $15,000 and other taxable income of $10,000. The tax payable, excluding any rebates or credits, is:

Tax on $15,000 at 45%	$6,750
Tax on $10,000 at ordinary resident rates (¶42-000)	0
Tax payable (excluding Medicare levy)	$6,750

Prescribed non-residents

Where the minor is a "prescribed non-resident" (¶2-120), the $416 exemption threshold does not apply. The eligible taxable income is taxed as follows (ITRA s 15; Sch 11).

- If the eligible taxable income does not exceed $416, the tax payable on that income is the greater of: (a) 32.5% of the eligible taxable income; and (b) the difference between tax on the total taxable income and tax on the taxable income other than the eligible taxable income, using in both cases the rates applicable to non-residents.

- If the eligible taxable income exceeds $416 but does not exceed $663, the tax payable on that income is the greater of: (a) $143.52 plus 66% of the excess over $416; and (b) the difference between tax on the total taxable income and tax on the taxable income other than the eligible taxable income, using in both cases the rates applicable to non-residents.

- Where the eligible taxable income exceeds $663, tax is payable on the whole of the eligible taxable income at the rate of 45%.

[FTR ¶860-470]

¶2-250 Tax payable on income from trust estate to minor

Where a presently entitled beneficiary of a trust estate is a prescribed person (¶2-170), so much of the beneficiary's share of the net income of the trust estate as falls within the special rules is taxed to the trustee under ITAA36 s 98 at the rates that would have applied had the income been derived directly by the minor (¶2-220). Where the minor is a beneficiary in more than one trust estate and the aggregate of the amounts of eligible taxable income exceeds $416 but is less than $1,308 (or exceeds $0 but is less than $663 in the case of a non-resident beneficiary), shading-in rates do not apply but the Commissioner has a discretion to reduce the tax payable (*Income Tax Rates Act 1986*, s 13(8); Sch 11). If, in the case of a beneficiary who is a resident minor, the aggregate of the amounts does not exceed $416, no tax is payable under the special rules applying to minors.

A beneficiary who has income from other sources or from more than one trust estate is taxed on his/her share of the income of the trust estate(s) together with any other eligible income, at the special rates, with credit being allowed for the tax paid by the trustee.

[FTR ¶860-470]

Medicare Levy

¶2-290 Who is liable to pay Medicare levy?

An individual who is a resident of Australia at any time during the income year is liable to pay a Medicare levy of 2% (a proposal to increase the Medicare levy to 2.5% from 1 July 2019 did not proceed) of his/her taxable income for the year, subject to some concessions. For Medicare levy purposes, taxable income excludes the taxable component of a superannuation lump sum that attracts a tax offset under ITAA97 s 301-20, which reduces the effective tax rate on the lump sum to zero (*Kowalski*). The levy is also payable by some trustees (¶6-250).

From 1 July 2016, residents of Norfolk Island are treated as residents of Australia for the purposes of the Medicare levy and no longer exempt from it. Residents of Christmas or Cocos (Keeling) Islands are also liable for the levy.

Persons temporarily living overseas who retain Australia as their permanent place of abode are considered to be residents for tax purposes and are therefore liable for the Medicare levy. Furthermore, because of the differences in the residency tests in the income tax legislation and the health insurance legislation, a person may be liable for the Medicare levy, but not eligible for Medicare benefits and vice versa (IT 2615).

Special concessions apply to Defence Force members, veterans' entitlement beneficiaries, blind pensioners, sickness allowance recipients and foreign government representatives (¶2-340). Relief is also provided for low income earners (¶2-330).

Those on higher income without adequate private patient hospital insurance may be liable for the Medicare levy surcharge (¶2-335).

The penalty tax provisions (¶29-000) apply equally to the Medicare levy and surcharge, as the terms "income tax" and "tax" in those provisions include the Medicare levy and surcharge (ITAA36 s 251R(7)). A person who makes a false or misleading statement affecting liability to pay the levy may be guilty of an offence (¶29-700).

The legislation governing the levy is contained in ITAA36 s 251R to 251Z and in the *Medicare Levy Act 1986*.

[FTR ¶778-300]

¶2-300 Meaning of married for Medicare purposes

Income thresholds for the Medicare levy (¶2-330) and the Medicare levy surcharge (¶2-335) depend on whether the taxpayer is married but the definition is quite wide. A taxpayer's spouse may be treated as a dependant of the taxpayer for levy purposes (¶2-310).

For these purposes, an individual, whether of the same or different sex, who is in a registered relationship under a prescribed state or territory law with another individual or who lives with another individual as a couple on a genuine domestic basis, during any period, the couple will be treated as if they were married to each other and to no one else for that period (ITAA36 s 251R(2), (2A)).

A person whose spouse has died during the income year and who has not remarried will be treated as married at year's end. A couple who have separated (and remain separated at year-end) will be treated as not being married (MLA s 8(3)).

[FTR ¶778-350, ¶778-800]

¶2-310 Who is a dependant for Medicare levy purposes?

Entitlement to exemption from all or part of the Medicare levy (¶2-340) and liability to the Medicare levy surcharge (¶2-335) may depend on whether a taxpayer has dependants. For these purposes, a person is a dependant of a taxpayer if the person, whose maintenance a taxpayer contributes to, is a resident of Australia and is:

- the spouse of the taxpayer — a "spouse" includes an individual, whether of the same or different sex, who is in a registered relationship under a prescribed state or territory law with another individual (¶14-270), and an individual who lives with another individual as a couple (if either individual was legally married to another person then that relationship is disregarded)
- a child of the taxpayer under 21 — a "child" includes the individual's adopted child, stepchild, ex-nuptial child, spouse's child or a child of the individual within the meaning of the *Family Law Act 1975*, or
- a child of the taxpayer who is 21 or more but less than 25 and in receipt of full-time education at a school, college or university, provided the taxpayer is entitled to a notional dependants rebate (¶15-160 – ¶15-190) for the child (ITAA36 s 251R(3), (4)). For levy surcharge, but not levy, purposes, a student will be a dependant regardless of the level of the student's "adjusted taxable income" (¶2-133).

A spouse may be taken to be a dependant of a person who has contributed to his/her maintenance. Unless shown otherwise, a person will be taken to have contributed to the maintenance of another person during any period in which they resided together (s 251R(6)). This means, for example, that a husband and wife living together who are each in receipt of income are, for levy purposes, each treated as a person who has a dependant. Each is a dependant of the other.

It is open to persons living together to prove that they have not contributed to the maintenance of each other by providing evidence establishing that each was self-supporting. Generally, the starting point in such an exercise would be a detailed record of actual household expenses and the amounts contributed by each person. Normal domestic sharing arrangements, eg a common account to which each person contributes and which is used to meet joint expenses, is not ordinarily sufficient to establish that one person has not contributed to the maintenance of the other (TR 93/35; but see also *Thompson*).

Where the parents of a child are living separately and apart from each other and are both eligible for a specified percentage of Family Tax Benefit Part A for a child, the child is a dependant of each parent for Medicare levy exemption purposes for so much only of the shared care period as represents that percentage of the period (s 251R(5)).

▶ Example

Val and Don, although living apart, are each eligible for a 50% share of Family Tax Benefit Part A for their child Aidan. For Medicare levy exemption purposes, Aidan is a dependant of each parent for 50% of the time they share his care.

In certain circumstances, a dependant of a taxpayer who is a Defence Force member, a veterans' entitlement beneficiary, a blind pensioner or a sickness allowance recipient is not treated as being a dependant for Medicare levy purposes (¶2-340).

[FTR ¶2-395, ¶778-800]

¶2-320 Rate of Medicare levy

The basic rate of the Medicare levy is 2% of the taxpayer's taxable income for **2020–21**. A government proposal to increase the Medicare levy from 2% to 2.5% of taxable income from 1 July 2019 did not proceed. There is no ceiling on the amount of Medicare levy payable.

▶ Example

Buddy's taxable income is $40,000. The Medicare levy is calculated as 2% of $40,000 = $800. This is additional to Buddy's ordinary tax.

Note that those on higher incomes without adequate private patient hospital insurance may be liable to an additional 1% to 1.5% Medicare levy surcharge (¶2-335).

[FTR ¶860-100]

¶2-330 Relief from Medicare levy for low income earners

Relief from the Medicare levy is provided to certain low income earners. For example, no levy is payable by a person whose taxable income for **2019–20** is $22,801 or less. Where the taxable income exceeds $22,801 but does not exceed $28,502, the levy is shaded in at the rate of 10% of the excess over $22,801 (MLA s 7). The Medicare levy low income thresholds for 2020–21 are not available at the time of writing.

▶ Example 1

For 2019–20, the levy payable by a single person with a taxable income of $24,000 is $119.90 (ie 10% × ($24,000 – $22,801)).

A higher threshold applies if the taxpayer is married (¶2-300) on the last day of the income year. In these cases, no levy is payable if the family income does not exceed $38,474. That threshold amount increases by $3,533 for each dependent child or student for whom the taxpayer or the taxpayer's spouse is entitled to a notional dependants rebate for them. Where the taxpayer is not married on the last day of the year of income, the threshold amount only increases if the taxpayer is entitled to family assistance (MLA s 8(6)). In the case of a married couple (¶2-300), "family income" means the combined taxable income of both spouses. For any other taxpayer, it simply means the taxpayer's own taxable income (MLA s 8).

Where a taxpayer's family income exceeds the family income threshold by a small amount, the levy payable is shaded in, with the general effect that the levy payable cannot exceed 10% of the excess of the family income over the family income threshold (see further below). The following table shows the income thresholds for payment of the levy and the range of incomes to which a reduced rate of levy applies (as per the tax return instructions). These thresholds apply if a taxpayer does *not* qualify for the Senior Australians tax offset (see below).

2019–20 income thresholds and shading-in ranges

Category of taxpayer (col 1)	No levy payable if taxable income (or family income) does not exceed . . . (col 2)	Reduced levy payable if taxable income (or family income) is within the range (inclusive) . . . (col 3)	Ordinary rate of levy payable where taxable income (or family income) is or above . . . (col 4)
Individual taxpayer	$22,801	$22,802–$28,501	$28,502
Families* with the following children and/or students:			
0	$38,474	$38,475–$48,092	$48,093
1	$42,007	$42,008–$52,508	$52,509
2	$45,540	$45,541–$56,925	$56,926
3	$49,073	$49,074–$61,341	$61,342
4	$52,606	$52,607–$65,757	$65,758
5	$56,139	$56,140–$70,173	$70,174
6	$59,672#	$59,673#–$74,590†	$74,591

* These figures also apply to taxpayers who are entitled to a dependant (invalid and carer) tax offset and those who are notionally entitled to a rebate for a dependant child or student (including sole parents).

\# Where there are more than six dependent children and/or students, add $3,533 for each extra child or student.

† Where there are more than six dependent children and/or students, add $4,416 for each extra child or student.

Shading-in rules

The following rules apply where the family income falls within the relevant shading-in range (column 3 of the table), thereby attracting a reduced levy.

(1) Where one spouse only derives taxable income, the amount of levy payable by that spouse is 10% of the excess of the taxable income over the relevant threshold shown in column 2 of the table.

▶ Example 2

Tanya is married with two children. Her taxable income in 2019–20 is $47,000. Her husband has no income. The relevant family income threshold is $45,540 and the levy payable by Tanya is limited to 10% × ($47,000 – $45,540) = $146.00.

(2) Where each spouse has a taxable income in excess of $28,502 and the family income falls within the shading-in range, the levy payable by each represents his/her proportion of 10% of the excess of the family income over the relevant threshold. The proportion is calculated by dividing the spouse's taxable income by the family income.

▶ Example 3

For 2019–20, Adrian has a taxable income of $29,000 and his wife Jill has a taxable income of $27,000, giving a total family income of $56,000. They have four children, so the family income falls within the relevant shading-in range ($52,607 to $65,756).

The amount of levy payable by Adrian is calculated as:

$$\frac{\$29,000}{\$56,000} \times 10\% \times (\$56,000 - \$52,606)$$

$= \$175.76$

The amount of levy payable by Jill is calculated as:

$$\frac{\$27,000}{\$56,000} \times 10\% \times (\$56,000 - \$52,606)$$

$= \$163.64$

(3) Where one spouse has a taxable income in excess of $22,801 and the other spouse does not, the lower earner is not liable for any levy. The higher earner pays a levy calculated by subtracting a ''reduction amount'' from the levy otherwise payable. The reduction amount equals 2% of the relevant family income threshold minus 8% of the excess of the family income over the threshold.

▶ Example 4

Frida has a 2019–20 taxable income of $30,000 and her husband Benny has a taxable income of $17,000, giving a total family income of $47,000. They have one child, so the family income falls within the relevant shading-in range ($42,008 to $52,508).

Since Benny earns less than $22,801, he pays no levy. The levy otherwise payable by Frida is $600 (ie 2% × $30,000). This amount is reduced by the ''reduction amount'', which is calculated as:

$(2\% \times \$42,007) - (8\% \times (\$47,000 - \$42,007))$

$= \$440.70$

The amount of levy payable by Frida is, therefore, $159.30, ie $600 – $440.70.

(4) Where one spouse has a taxable income in excess of $28,502 and the other has a taxable income in excess of $22,801 but not in excess of $28,502, the ''reduction amount'' (see (3) above) is apportioned on the basis of each spouse's contribution to the family income. However, if the reduction amount as apportioned exceeds the levy otherwise payable by one spouse, the excess goes in reduction of the levy payable by the other (s 8(4)).

▶ Example 5

Bill has a taxable income of $28,000 in 2019–20 and his wife Honey has a taxable income of $23,000, giving a total family income of $51,000. They have three children, so the family income falls within the relevant shading-in range ($49,074 to $61,340).

The reduction amount is calculated as follows:

$(2\% \times \$49,074) - (8\% \times (\$51,000 - \$49,074))$

$= \$827.40$

The reduction amount is apportioned between Bill and Honey as follows:

Bill: $\frac{\$28,000}{\$51,000} \times \$827.40$ $= \$454.26$

Honey: $\frac{\$23,000}{\$51,000} \times \$827.40$ $= \$373.14$

Levy liability of Honey

The amount of levy payable by Honey equals the amount of levy otherwise payable (ie 10% × ($23,000 – $22,801) = $19.90) minus her share of the reduction amount.

ie $\$19.90 - \$373.14$

$= -\$353.24$

In other words, no levy is payable by Honey and the excess goes to reduce the amount of levy payable by Bill.

Levy liability of Bill

The amount of levy payable by Bill equals the amount of levy otherwise payable (ie 2% × $28,000 = $560) minus his share of the reduction amount and minus the excess from Honey.

ie $560.00 – $454.26 – $353.24
= –$247.50

For the thresholds relevant to trust income, see ¶6-250.

Senior Australians and pensioners

The **2019–20** Medicare levy thresholds and phase-in limits for Senior Australians and eligible pensioners (¶15-310) are as follows:

Class of people	Medicare levy low income threshold (no Medicare levy payable at or below this level)	Phase-in limit (level above which the Medicare levy is payable at the full rate)
Senior Australians and eligible pensioners	$36,056	$45,069

Medicare levy is payable at the rate of 10 cents for every dollar between those lower and upper thresholds.

The **2019–20** family income thresholds for taxpayers who qualify for the Senior Australians and Pensioners Tax Offset are as follows:

Number of dependent children or students	Medicare levy low income threshold (no Medicare levy payable at or below this level)	Phase-in limit (level above which the Medicare levy is payable at the full rate)
0	$50,191	$62,738
1	$53,724	$67,155
2	$57,257	$71,571
3	$60,790	$75,987
4	$64,323	$80,403
5	$67,856	$84,820
6	$71,389	$89,236

Note: If more than six dependent children or students, for each additional child or student, the lower income limit increases by $3,533 and the upper income limit increases by $4,416. The upper income limit includes the effect of rounding.

[FTR ¶860-100, ¶860-150]

¶2-335 Medicare levy surcharge

Individual taxpayers on higher incomes who do not have adequate private patient hospital insurance for themselves and their dependants may be liable for an additional Medicare levy surcharge (MLS), 1%, 1.25% or 1.5% of "income for surcharge purposes", depending on their income level. A taxpayer may be liable for the surcharge for a period that is less than a full year, eg where private patient hospital insurance is taken out during the year. Medicare levy surcharge is imposed on a taxpayer's taxable income by MLA s 8B to 8D and on reportable fringe benefits by the *A New Tax System (Medicare Levy Surcharge — Fringe Benefits) Act 1999.*

For **2019–20**, individual taxpayers who earn more than $90,000 for the year or, if a member of a couple, have a combined income of $180,000 and do not have private health insurance are potentially liable for the MLS. Higher thresholds apply where dependants are involved.

The tables below indicates how the MLS rules apply in conjunction with the private health insurance rebate rules (¶15-330).

2019–20 income year

	Income			
Singles	$0–$90,000	$90,001–$105,000	$105,001–$140,000	$140,001 and over
Families*	$0–$180,000	$180,001–$210,000	$210,001–$280,000	$280,001 and over
	Private health insurance rebate			
	Base Tier	**Tier 1**	**Tier 2**	**Tier 3**
Under 65 years of age	25.059% #	16.706% #	8.352% #	0%
65–69 years of age	29.236% #	20.883% #	12.529% #	0%
70 years of age and over	33.413% #	25.059% #	16.706% #	0%
	Medicare levy surcharge			
Percentage rate	0%	1%	1.25%	1.5%

* The families' threshold is increased by $1,500 for each dependent child after the first. Families include couples and single parent families.

This rebate percentage applies from 1 April 2019 to 31 March 2020.

The income thresholds that determine the tiers for the Medicare levy surcharge and the private health insurance rebate remain the same to 30 June 2021. Not adjusting the income thresholds may result in individuals with incomes just below each threshold moving into a higher income threshold sooner if their income increases.

The private health insurance rebate is indexed annually. The rebate contribution from the government is annually adjusted by a universal Rebate Adjustment Factor.

A tax offset is provided to certain taxpayers who become liable for the Medicare levy surcharge (or an increased Medicare levy surcharge) due to the receipt of a lump sum payment in arrears (¶15-350).

Private patient hospital insurance

A person is taken to be covered by an insurance policy that provides private patient hospital cover if the policy provides benefits in relation to fees and charges for hospital treatment. Ancillary cover (eg for ambulance services, medicines and drugs, hearing aids or dentures) does not constitute private patient hospital cover (MLA s 3(5), (6)).

It is not necessary that the taxpayer has personally incurred the policy premiums. The taxpayer's employer may, for example, pay the premiums under an insurance policy which provides the required cover for the taxpayer.

For the 2018–19 and later income years, taxpayers will be penalised if the private health insurance they take out has an annual excess of more than $750 for singles or more than $1,500 for families/couples. Maximum permitted excesses for private hospital insurance have been increased from $500 to $750 for singles and from $1,000 to $1,500 for families/couples. The penalty is that the high excess insurance is not treated as satisfying the definition of private health insurance for Medicare levy surcharge purposes. Insurers are able to offer products with the increased maximum voluntary excess levels that exempt the holder from the Medicare levy surcharge from 1 April 2019. This is enabled by amendments in *Private Health Insurance Legislation Amendment Act 2018*, *Medicare Levy Amendment (Excess Levels for Private Health Insurance Policies) Act 2018* and *A New Tax System (Medicare Levy Surcharge — Fringe Benefits) Amendment (Excess Levels for Private Health Insurance Policies) Act 2018*. Taxpayers have the opportunity to purchase products with a larger excess, in return for lower premiums.

The amending Acts also remove grandfathering provisions that provided the Medicare levy surcharge exemption for certain health insurance policies that pre-date the commencement of the *Private Health Insurance Act 2007*. Those individuals will need to migrate to a policy that has an excess no more than the new maximum in order to be eligible for the Medicare levy surcharge exemption.

Liability for Medicare levy surcharge

The income test for determining whether a taxpayer is liable for the Medicare levy surcharge is the taxpayer's "income for surcharge purposes". This is the *sum* of the taxpayer's taxable income (including the net amount on which family trust distribution tax has been paid), reportable fringe benefits, reportable superannuation contributions and total net investment loss (including both net financial investment losses and net rental property losses) *less* any taxed component of a superannuation lump sum received, other than a death benefit, which does not exceed the taxpayer's low rate cap (¶14-220).

Liability to the Medicare levy surcharge is also based on whether a taxpayer is a single person without dependants, is a single person with dependants or is married (two persons, whether of the same or different sex, are treated as being married if they are in a registered relationship under a prescribed state or territory law with another individual or are living together as a couple; if either individual was legally married to another person then that relationship is disregarded). A single taxpayer's surcharge liability is measured only against the taxpayer's own income for surcharge purposes. For a couple, the combined income for surcharge purposes is generally applied against the family surcharge threshold, with each member of the couple being liable if the threshold is exceeded (see below). Note that the Commissioner has no power to remit the Medicare levy surcharge imposed on a taxpayer (*McCarthy*).

The Medicare levy definition of dependant (¶2-310) is modified for levy surcharge purposes as follows (ITAA36 s 251V):

- a child in receipt of full-time education who is 21 or more but less than 25 will be a dependant regardless of the level of the dependant's adjusted taxable income (¶2-133), and

- a child whose parents are separated is potentially a dependant of each parent (ie the child may also be a dependant of the parent not in receipt of family assistance for the child).

The definitions of "dependant" and "prescribed person" (¶2-340) are also modified for levy surcharge purposes during a period where the taxpayer is: (a) a Defence Force member, or a relative or person associated with a Defence Force member, who is entitled to full free medical treatment; (b) a repatriation beneficiary entitled to full free medical treatment; or (c) a blind pensioner or a sickness allowance recipient. In this situation:

- the special rules which treat a taxpayer who would otherwise be taken to have dependants as not having dependants (¶2-340) do not apply, ie the taxpayer is taken to have dependants during the period (s 251V), and

- the special rule which treats a taxpayer as a prescribed person for one-half of the period where the taxpayer has a dependant who is not a prescribed person does not apply, ie the taxpayer is taken not to be a prescribed person during the *whole* of the period (ITAA36 s 251VA).

A single taxpayer with no dependants is liable to the surcharge if the taxpayer's income for surcharge purposes for the **2019–20** year totals more than $90,000. A taxpayer who is a member of a couple is liable to surcharge if their combined income for surcharge purposes exceeds the family surcharge threshold for **2019–20** of $180,000. If a taxpayer has dependants, the threshold above which the surcharge applies is the same for single taxpayers and members of a couple. For only one dependant, the threshold remains at $180,000. For two or more dependants, the threshold is increased by $1,500 for each dependant after the first.

Imposition of Medicare levy surcharge

Having determined whether a taxpayer is liable for the Medicare levy surcharge, the surcharge is then imposed on a taxpayer's taxable income (MLA s 8B to 8D) and reportable fringe benefits. The surcharge is also imposed on amounts derived by a taxpayer on which family trust distribution tax has been paid (MLA s 3(2A)). However, if the combined income for surcharge purposes of a couple exceeds the family surcharge threshold, but the taxable income (including the net amount on which family trust distribution tax has been paid) and reportable fringe benefits of one member of the couple does not exceed the Medicare levy low income threshold (¶2-330), that member is not liable for the surcharge.

Surcharge is calculated on a per day basis, according to the number of days in an income year that there is insufficient private health insurance. Calculations on a per day basis may also be required if a taxpayer's circumstances change during a year, eg from single to married, or from not having a dependant to having a dependant.

Where the period during which the taxpayer qualifies for levy surcharge is the *whole* of the income year, the amount of levy surcharge is 1% to 1.5% of the taxpayer's taxable income and reportable fringe benefits for the year. Where the qualifying period is a *part* only of the income year, the amount of levy surcharge attributable to that period is as follows:

$$(1\% \text{ to } 1.5\% \times \text{taxable income and reportable fringe benefits for year}) \times \frac{\text{days in period}}{\text{days in income year}}$$

▶ Example

Rod and Isabelle are married and reside together. Neither Rod nor Isabelle are prescribed persons or have private patient hospital cover in 2019–20. Rod's taxable income is $90,000 and reportable superannuation contributions of $25,000. Isabelle has taxable income of $50,000, reportable fringe benefits of $10,000 and reportable superannuation contributions of $10,000.

Because Rod and Isabelle live together, each is treated as a dependant of the other unless the contrary is established. The applicable family surcharge threshold is $180,000 and Rod and Isabelle's combined income for surcharge purposes for 2019–20 is $185,000.

Rod is liable for a levy surcharge of $900 (ie 1% × $90,000) and Isabelle is liable for levy surcharge of $600 (ie 1% × $60,000).

Where a taxpayer marries or separates during the year, the relevant threshold (ie the single surcharge threshold or the family surcharge threshold, as appropriate) applies separately for each period, but is applied only against the taxpayer's own taxable income (s 8D(4)).

Trustees liability for Medicare levy surcharge

A trustee assessed under ITAA36 s 98 in respect of a beneficiary may be liable to pay the Medicare levy surcharge (under MLA s 8E, 8F and 8G) on the beneficiary's trust income. Essentially, a trustee will be liable for the Medicare levy surcharge if the beneficiary is a high income earner without adequate private patient hospital insurance.

Specifically, Medicare levy surcharge is payable by a trustee in respect of the net income of the trust estate to which the beneficiary is presently entitled (''beneficiary's trust income'') if:

- the beneficiary on behalf of whom the trustee is assessed is not covered by an insurance policy that provides private patient hospital cover, and
- if the beneficiary is single, the amount of the beneficiary's trust income exceeds the beneficiary's singles Tier 1, Tier 2 or Tier 3 threshold for the year of income, or
- if the beneficiary is married, the sum of the beneficiary's trust income and the beneficiary's spouse's income for surcharge purposes exceeds the beneficiary's family Tier 1, Tier 2 or Tier 3 threshold for the year of income and the amount of the beneficiary's trust income exceeds the threshold amount for individuals other than certain pensioners for the year of income.

The rate of the Medicare levy surcharge will be 1%, 1.25% or 1.5%, depending on whether the Tier 1, Tier 2 or Tier 3 threshold applies. Where the relevant provisions do not apply to the beneficiary for the whole year, for example if the beneficiary is married for only part of the year, the Medicare levy surcharge is apportioned.

A beneficiary is also assessable on their share of the net income of a trust if that person is a beneficiary in more than one trust or has income from other sources (eg salary or wages, rent, interest or dividends). In such a case, the beneficiary's individual interest in the net income of the trust is aggregated with their other income (ITAA36 s 100; ¶6-120), with the result that the Medicare levy surcharge is payable by the beneficiary in their own right. This prevents a beneficiary from splitting income to potentially avoid paying the Medicare levy surcharge.

For Medicare levy surcharge purposes, any amount that is not assessable as a result of family trust distribution tax having been paid on it (¶6-268) is reinstated as part of the beneficiary's trust income (MLA s 3(2A)).

Persons with exempt overseas employment income

Taxpayers who are residents of Australia for tax purposes, and who have *both* taxable income and exempt overseas employment income (ITAA36 s 23AG; ¶10-860), are advised by the ATO to complete item M2 of the individual tax return, ie the Medicare levy surcharge item. This is because while they may not be separately liable for the Medicare levy surcharge (eg because they are under the surcharge threshold), the exempt overseas employment income is added to their taxable income to determine the average rate of tax, including Medicare levy and Medicare levy surcharge (if applicable), on their notional income. That average rate of tax is then applied to their taxable income (¶10-865).

[FITR ¶109-215; FTR ¶778-360, ¶860-100, ¶862-035]

¶2-340 Exemptions from Medicare levy for prescribed persons

Full or partial exemption from the Medicare levy is provided to a taxpayer who qualifies as a ''prescribed person'' (ITAA36 s 251T). A ''prescribed person'' is:

(1) a person entitled to full free medical treatment as a member of the Defence Forces or as a relative of, or as a person otherwise associated with, a Defence Force member

(2) a person entitled under veterans' entitlement or military rehabilitation and compensation (repatriation) legislation to full free medical treatment

(3) a blind pensioner or a sickness allowance recipient

(4) a person who is not a resident of Australia for tax purposes

(5) a person who is attached to a diplomatic mission or consular post established in Australia or a household member of the person's family, provided the person is not an Australian citizen and is not ordinarily resident in Australia

(6) a person certified by the Health Minister as not being entitled to Medicare benefits (ITAA36 s 251U(1)).

For those persons not entitled to Medicare benefits, an exemption from the Medicare levy can be claimed in their tax return. To claim the exemption, the person must have a Medicare Entitlement Statement that can be obtained from the Department of Human Services by completing the relevant application form.

Prescribed persons are **not** liable for the levy if (s 251U(2)):

- they have no "dependants" (¶2-310), or
- all of the person's dependants are themselves prescribed persons of any type.

If a prescribed person in category (1), (2) or (3) has any dependants who do not qualify as described above, that person will be treated as a prescribed person for one-half of the year, and will therefore be liable for one-half of the levy otherwise payable (¶2-360). (Prescribed persons in categories (4), (5) and (6) are fully liable for the levy if they have dependants who are not prescribed persons.)

For these purposes, prescribed persons in categories (1), (2) and (3) will be treated as *not* having dependants — and will thereby remain exempt from the levy — in certain situations (ITAA36 s 251R(6A) to (6J)). The relevant rules are as follows.

(1) Where the taxpayer has a dependant who is liable for the levy, that dependant is not treated as a dependant of the taxpayer.

▶ Example

Bruce is a blind pensioner. Bruce's spouse is a clerk liable for the levy. They have no children. Bruce's spouse is not treated as a dependant and Bruce is exempt from the levy.

(2) A child is not a dependant of the taxpayer where the taxpayer has a spouse who is liable for the levy and who contributes to the maintenance of the child.

▶ Example

Leonie is a blind pensioner. Leonie's spouse is a teacher who is liable for the levy. They have one child and they each contribute to that child's maintenance. The child is not classed as Leonie's dependant and Leonie is not liable for the levy.

(3) A child may be treated as a dependant of only one member of a married couple who are both prescribed persons (two persons, whether of the same sex or different sexes, who are in a registered relationship under a prescribed state or territory law or who lived together as a couple are treated as if they were married; if either person was legally married to another person then that latter relationship is disregarded. Further, a child of an individual includes an adopted child, stepchild, ex-nuptial child, a child of the individual's spouse and a child of the individual within the meaning of the *Family Law Act 1975*).

In these cases, only one spouse will be liable to pay half the levy on account of the child and the other spouse will be completely exempt. To qualify for this treatment, the couple must enter into a "family agreement" at or before the time of lodgment of the return of income of the person claiming the exemption. The agreement must state that, for the purposes of the levy, the child is to be treated as a dependant of only one of them and must specify which one. The tax return instructions contain a form of agreement for this purpose which can be completed by the parties. The person claiming the exemption must, depending on the complexity of their tax affairs, keep the agreement for five years, two years or any shorter period of time determined by the Commissioner (s 251R(6F)). Failure to do so causes both spouses to become liable for the levy.

[FTR ¶779-360]

¶2-360 Partial relief from Medicare levy

Where a person is a prescribed person for only part of the income year, there is a proportionate reduction in the amount of basic levy otherwise payable (MLA s 9). This also applies where such a person has dependants who are prescribed persons for only part of the relevant period.

▶ Example

Frank, who has no dependants, becomes entitled to full free medical treatment under repatriation legislation on 1 April 2020. His taxable income for 2019–20 is $30,000.

Frank was a prescribed person for 91 days in 2019–20. His levy liability is therefore:

$$(2\% \times \$30{,}000) \times \frac{(365 - 91)}{365} = \$450.41$$

[FTR ¶779-360]

¶2-370 Collection of Medicare levy and surcharge

The levy and surcharge are collected in conjunction with, and in the same way as, income tax (ITAA36 s 251R(7)). Taxpayers can elect to pay Medicare levy and surcharge through the PAYG system by giving notice to the employer to vary the PAYG amounts withheld from salary or wages (TAA Sch 1 s 15-50) (¶26-350).

[FTR ¶778-300]

Higher Education Support

¶2-380 Higher Education Loan Programme

Most students who enrol to study in award courses in higher education institutions are required to pay a contribution towards the cost of their study under the Higher Education Contribution Scheme (HECS) and the Higher Education Loan Programme (HELP). Debts deferred through the Open Learning Deferred Payment Scheme, Postgraduate Education Loan Scheme and Bridging for Overseas Trained Professionals Loan Scheme were included in an accumulated HECS debt and subject to the same repayment arrangements. The HECS-HELP program allows eligible students to defer their student contribution and repay it later through the taxation system.

Vocational education and training student loan debts (VET debts) have been separated from other forms of HELP debts and VET student loans have been established as a separate income-contingent loan, from 1 July 2019.

Students who elect to pay through the tax system will not have to make any repayments until their ''repayment income'' reaches a minimum level. Repayment income is the sum of the taxpayer's taxable income, total net investment loss, ie from financial investments (shares, interests in managed investment schemes (including forestry schemes), rights and options, and like investments), and from rental properties, reportable fringe benefits, exempt foreign employment income for the year, and reportable superannuation contributions (HESA s 154-5).

Once the minimum level of repayment income is reached, the amount of the repayment is set so that the higher the repayment income, the higher the level of repayments. From 1 January 2018, the index for amounts that are indexed annually under the *Higher Education Support Act 2003* has changed from the Higher Education Grants Index (HEGI) to the Consumer Price Index (CPI).

From 1 July 2019, repayment thresholds including minimum repayment income are indexed using the CPI rather than average weekly earnings.

Australians who have moved overseas for more than six months are required to pay back the same amount of their HELP debt as they would if they were residing in Australia. For these debtors, an obligation has been created to make repayments on their HELP debts based on their total Australian and foreign-sourced income, known as their worldwide income. From 1 January 2016, debtors going overseas for more than six months (183 days) are required to register with the ATO, while those already living overseas had until 1 July 2017 to register. Repayment obligations commenced from 1 July 2017, for income earned in the 2016–17 year.

Students may also be entitled to an income-contingent loan, the student start-up loan. There is a limit of two loans a year of $1,025 each (indexed from 2017). The loans are available on a voluntary basis, and are repayable under similar arrangements to HELP debts. Repayments of loans do not form part of deductible self-education expenses (¶16-450).

From 1 July 2019, all study and training loans will be covered by one set of thresholds and rates.

2020–21 Study and training repayment thresholds and rates

The study and training repayment income thresholds and repayment rates for the **2020–21** income year are as follows:

Income level	Rate of repayment*
Below $46,620	Nil
$46,621–$53,286	1%
$53,287–$57,055	2%
$57,056–$60,479	2.5%
$60,480–$64,108	3%
$64,109–$67,954	3.5%
$67,955–$72,031	4%
$72,032–$76,354	4.5%
$76,355–$80,395	5%
$80,396–$85,792	5.5%
$85,793–$90,939	6%
$90,940–$96,396	6.5%
$96,397–$102,179	7%
$102,180–$108,309	7.5%
$108,310–$114,707	8%
$114,708–$121,698	8.5%
$121,699–$128,999	9%
$129,000–$136,739	9.5%
$136,740 and above	10%

* The repayment rate is applied to the repayment income.

A person with a spouse and/or dependant(s) is not liable to make repayments if no Medicare levy is payable on their taxable income for that income year or if the amount of levy payable on their taxable income is reduced (HESA s 154-1(2)). The Commissioner (or the AAT) has the discretion to amend a HELP assessment so as to reduce or defer an amount payable if he is of the opinion that payment of the assessed amount has or would cause serious hardship to the person, or there are other special reasons that make it fair and reasonable to amend the assessment (HESA s 154-50; *Case 12/2004*).

Higher education contributions cannot be claimed as a tax deduction, regardless of whether they are paid by the student, a parent, an employer or some other person, unless incurred in providing a fringe benefit (ITAA97 s 26-20).

A checklist summarising other tax measures relevant to students is at ¶44-140.

[FTR ¶865-050]

¶2-385 Tertiary Student Financial Supplement Scheme

Some tertiary students were eligible to receive a voluntary financial supplement (FS) under the *Student Assistance Act 1973* or the *Social Security Act 1991*. The FS was in the form of an interest-free private sector loan paid under the former Student Financial Supplement Scheme which closed on 31 December 2003. Five years after an FS contract was entered into, the Commonwealth purchased the relevant FS debt, and the borrower became liable to repay the indexed amount of the accumulated debt through the taxation system. Existing FS debts continue to be collected through the tax system. Annual repayments calculated as a percentage of the borrower's taxable income are required once a minimum level of taxable income is reached, the repayment rate increasing as taxable income increases.

Where a person owes both a HELP debt (¶2-380) and an FS debt, the required FS debt repayment is *in addition to* any required HELP repayment. FS debt repayments cannot be claimed as a tax deduction unless incurred in providing a fringe benefit (ITAA97 s 26-20).

From 1 July 2019, all study and training loans are covered by one set of thresholds and rates (see ¶2-380).

[FTR ¶865-060]

Chapter 3 Companies

Taxation of Companies Generally

¶3-000 What is a company?

For tax purposes, a "company" is a body corporate or any other unincorporated association or body of persons, but does not include a partnership or a non-entity joint venture (ITAA97 s 995-1(1)). Although the definitions of "company" and "partnership" are mutually exclusive, most *limited partnerships* are taxed as companies (¶3-475). Most *unincorporated* clubs and associations fall outside the definition of "partnership", as they are not being conducted with a view to profit, and would thus be companies for tax purposes (¶3-800). *Incorporated* clubs and associations *are* companies within the usual concept of that term. Also, some public unit trusts are treated as if they were companies for tax purposes (¶6-310).

A company is a separate legal entity, distinct from its shareholders (*Salomon*). A company comes into existence when it is registered and is taxable in its own right (ITAA97 s 4-1).

[FITR ¶763-000, ¶766-750]

¶3-010 Australian resident and foreign resident companies

As in the case of individuals, it must be determined whether a company is a resident of Australia for tax purposes (¶21-040). This is important because:

- generally, Australian resident companies are liable to tax on total income from sources both in and out of Australia, whereas foreign resident companies are liable only on Australian source income and other income that the Act specifically includes in their assessable income (ITAA97 ss 6-5; 6-10)
- the imputation system (¶4-400) applies to dividends paid by Australian resident companies
- the consolidation regime (¶8-000) is available only to Australian resident entities
- various CGT roll-over provisions require the companies involved to be Australian residents (¶12-040)
- various anti-avoidance provisions apply depending on the residency status of the companies involved, eg thin capitalisation (¶22-700)
- special rules apply in determining income derived from foreign resident companies (¶21-110).

Australian branches of foreign resident companies

Under general law, a branch of a company is not a separate entity from the company itself and has the same residence status. However, a special tax regime provides limited separate entity treatment to Australian branches of foreign banks and foreign financial entities (ITAA36 Pt IIIB).

The tax treatment of an Australian company distribution received by the Australian branch of a non-resident company may also be different from the treatment accorded to such a distribution paid directly to the overseas company (¶4-840).

[FITR ¶18-200, ¶23-000]

¶3-015 Public and private companies

The public or private status of a company for tax purposes does not depend on its status for company law purposes. Many companies that are not private companies under the corporations law are private companies for tax law purposes. A company's status for tax purposes is determined for each separate income year.

Whether a company is a public or private company is important because certain payments, loans and debt forgivenesses made by private companies to shareholders and their associates may be treated as dividends and disallowed as deductions (¶3-240) and the Commissioner has the power to reduce otherwise deductible remunerations and other amounts that are paid to certain categories of persons where he considers the payment is excessive (¶4-220).

Public companies

A "public company" is defined (ITAA97 s 995-1(1)) as a company that is a public company, as defined in ITAA36 s 103A, for the income year. The following are public companies for tax purposes:

- a company whose shares are listed on the stock exchange in Australia or elsewhere on the last day of the income year
- a company that is a "co-operative company" (¶3-420) at all times during the income year (this may include a company that is incorporated part-way through the year: *Brookton Co-operative Society*)
- a non-profit company
- a company that is: (a) a mutual life insurance company (¶3-480); (b) a friendly society dispensary (¶3-470); (c) a government body established for public purposes or a company controlled by a government or a government body; or (d) a public company subsidiary.

Public company status may be lost

A listed company or a co-operative company may lose its public company status if *at any time* during the income year: (a) 20 or fewer persons hold, or have the right to acquire, 75% or more of the company's equity, voting or dividend-bearing shares; or (b) the voting and dividend rights in the company are capable of being varied to produce that result (s 103A(2)).

Company may be treated as public company

A company that is a public company for company law purposes, but not a public company under s 103A(2), may be treated as a public company for tax purposes. The Commissioner has the discretion to treat such a company as a public company for an income year if it is unreasonable not to do so (s 103A(5)).

In exercising this discretion, the Commissioner has regard to matters such as the number of persons controlling the company during the income year or having the beneficial ownership of its shares, and the extent of its paid-up capital. A company desiring this treatment can apply to the Commissioner and furnish the relevant information. The Commissioner can exercise the discretion without any request from the company (*Stocks & Holdings*), even if it results in the company being liable to pay more tax. The Commissioner did not exercise the discretion where a private company was wholly owned by a large superannuation fund (ID 2004/760).

If a private company is acquired by a public company, the Commissioner generally exercises his discretion to treat the private company as public for the year of acquisition.

Non-profit companies

A non-profit company is one that has never been carried on for the purpose of profit or gain to its individual members and whose constituent document prohibits any distribution to members or their relatives. It is fatal to non-profit company status if, on winding up, the shareholders have the power to distribute profits for their own benefit, eg to a company formed in their own interests (*Nadir*). A company will also be denied non-profit company status if it is stated to be carried on for the benefit of non-members but the shareholders ultimately control the distribution of profits through their power to change the terms of the constituent document (*Luceria Investments*).

Public company subsidiaries

A company is a public company if at all times during the income year it is *wholly* owned beneficially by one or more public companies (including by a company that is itself a wholly-owned public company subsidiary). A subsidiary that is not wholly publicly-owned may also qualify if it is more than 50% beneficially owned directly or indirectly by one or more *listed* public companies that satisfy the ''75%/20 persons'' test (ie 20 or fewer persons do not hold, or have the right to acquire, 75% or more of the company's equity, voting or dividend-bearing shares).

Compliance with these tests may be disregarded if the Commissioner is satisfied, having regard to certain criteria, that the subsidiary is managed or conducted in the interests of persons other than, and at the expense of, the parent company. Conversely, non-compliance may be disregarded where appropriate.

Private companies

A ''private company'' is defined (s 995-1(1)) as a company that is not a public company for the year.

[FITR ¶767-950; FTR ¶54-450 – ¶54-690]

¶3-020 Calculation of company taxable income

The taxable income of a company is worked out in much the same way as that of an individual, ie from the assessable income are deducted all ordinary business deductions, depreciation, any special incentive deductions and any relevant non-business deductions (ITAA97 s 4-15).

Companies are subject to restrictions on the deductibility of losses (¶3-060, ¶3-065, ¶3-080) and bad debts (¶3-150). Certain classes of companies receive special income tax treatment. These are co-operative companies (¶3-420), credit unions (¶3-435), copyright collecting societies (¶3-450), friendly societies (¶3-470), corporate limited partnerships (¶3-475), life insurance companies (¶3-480), RSA providers (¶3-530), and small-medium enterprises (SMEs) and PDFs (¶3-555). Special rules apply in determining income derived from foreign resident companies, or income derived by Australian resident companies from foreign sources (¶21-110, ¶21-670).

A company is eligible to claim the seafarer tax offset (a refundable tax offset linked to the concept of withholding payments paid to Australian seafarers for overseas voyages) in certain circumstances. The overseas voyage must be made by a certified vessel, and the seafarer must be employed by the company claiming the offset for at least 91 days in the income year (ITAA97 Subdiv 61-N).

[FITR ¶15-130]

¶3-030 Public officer

Every company carrying on business or deriving property income in Australia must, unless specifically exempted, at all times have a public officer (ITAA36 s 252). Failure to comply with this requirement is an offence punishable by a fine not exceeding one penalty unit (¶29-000) for each day the offence continues.

A public officer must be appointed within 3 months of the company commencing to carry on business in Australia or first deriving income in Australia. The public officer's name and address for service of notices must be given to the Commissioner at the place where the company's returns are lodged (¶24-080).

The public officer must be a natural person of at least 18 years of age who is capable of understanding the nature of the appointment. In addition, he/she must be ''ordinarily resident'' in Australia. The public officer of a company is answerable for everything that is required to be done by the company for tax-related purposes and, if in default, is liable to the same penalties (ITAA36 s 252(1)(f)). The public officer is not, however, personally liable for payment of tax due by the company. Everything done by the public officer which he is required to do in his or her capacity is deemed to have been done by the company (ITAA36 s 252(1)(g)). For a decision in which this provision was considered, see *G E Capital Finance Australasia Pty Ltd*. The Commissioner has released an impact statement on this decision.

[FTR ¶781-420]

¶3-040 Liability of directors, etc

Although there must be a public officer, a notice or process may if the Commissioner thinks fit be given to, or served on, a company by giving the notice to, or serving the process on, a director, the secretary, another officer or an attorney or agent of the company (ITAA36 s 253). Note that there are special provisions that enable the Commissioner to recover from the directors of companies unpaid amounts under, for example, the PAYG withholding system (¶25-560). See also ¶29-710.

[FTR ¶781-520]

Company Returns

¶3-045 Company return required

The requirements for lodging returns are specified annually by Legislative Instrument (ITAA36 s 161: ¶24-010, ¶24-030).

Every Australian resident company that derives Australian source income or foreign income and every foreign resident company that derives Australian source income is required to lodge a return (an Australian resident non-profit company only has to lodge a return if its taxable income is more than $416) (¶44-020). Under the group consolidation regime, corporate groups may be allowed to consolidate their tax position and lodge a single tax return (¶8-010).

Where both a receiver/manager and a liquidator of a company have been appointed, the ATO will generally look to the liquidator to lodge the return (TD 94/68). A strata title body corporate is not required to lodge a return if all its income is mutual income, but a return is required if any of its income is derived from non-mutual sources, eg bank interest.

Although companies self-assess their liability for income tax (¶25-100), they are still required to lodge returns specifying the taxable income and the amount of tax payable on that income (ITAA36 s 161). Companies (including corporate limited partnerships (¶3-475) and trustees of public trading trusts) are required to use the company return form. Records, statements and notices are generally not required to be lodged with the return, although they must be retained by taxpayers (¶24-030), and most written elections only have to be lodged when requested (¶24-040).

Companies (and partnerships and trusts) with international dealings that exceed certain thresholds must lodge additional documentation with their annual returns. This must be in the form of an International Dealings Schedule. Significant global entities (¶30-200) must also lodge annual statements of their global operations under the country-by-country (CbC) regime (¶22-630).

Reportable tax position schedule

If a company has been notified by the ATO to do so or if it is a public or foreign-owned company which meets certain total business income thresholds it must lodge a reportable tax position (RTP) schedule unless (broadly): it has already applied to the ATO for a private ruling that covers the RTP, it has reported the RTP in their company tax return or the RTP is covered by an advance pricing arrangement (APA) or an application for an APA that has been accepted into the APA program. As from the 2021–22 income year large private companies will be required to lodge an RTP schedule whether notified to do so or not.

There are various categories of RTPs. For example, a Category A RTP is a position that is about as likely to be correct as incorrect (or is less likely to be correct than incorrect) and a Category B RTP is a position in respect of which uncertainty about taxes payable or recoverable is recognised and/or disclosed in the taxpayer's or a related party's financial statements.

Due dates for lodgment of returns

For the due dates for lodgment of returns, see ¶24-060. A company that fails to lodge a return or otherwise fails to comply with a taxation law is liable for a fine or penalty tax (¶29-000).

Assessments

The Commissioner does not normally issue any formal notice of assessment to the company after lodgment of the return. Instead, the Commissioner is *deemed* to have made the assessment on the date the return is lodged, irrespective of whether the return is lodged on time, late or early (ITAA36 s 166A(2)).

[FTR ¶79-300, ¶79-310, ¶79-550]

¶3-048 Reconciliation statement

The net profit shown in a company's accounts does not necessarily correspond with its profit for tax purposes (ie its taxable income). An explanatory diagram showing the reconciliation of the net profit as per the profit and loss account with the net taxable income is given below.

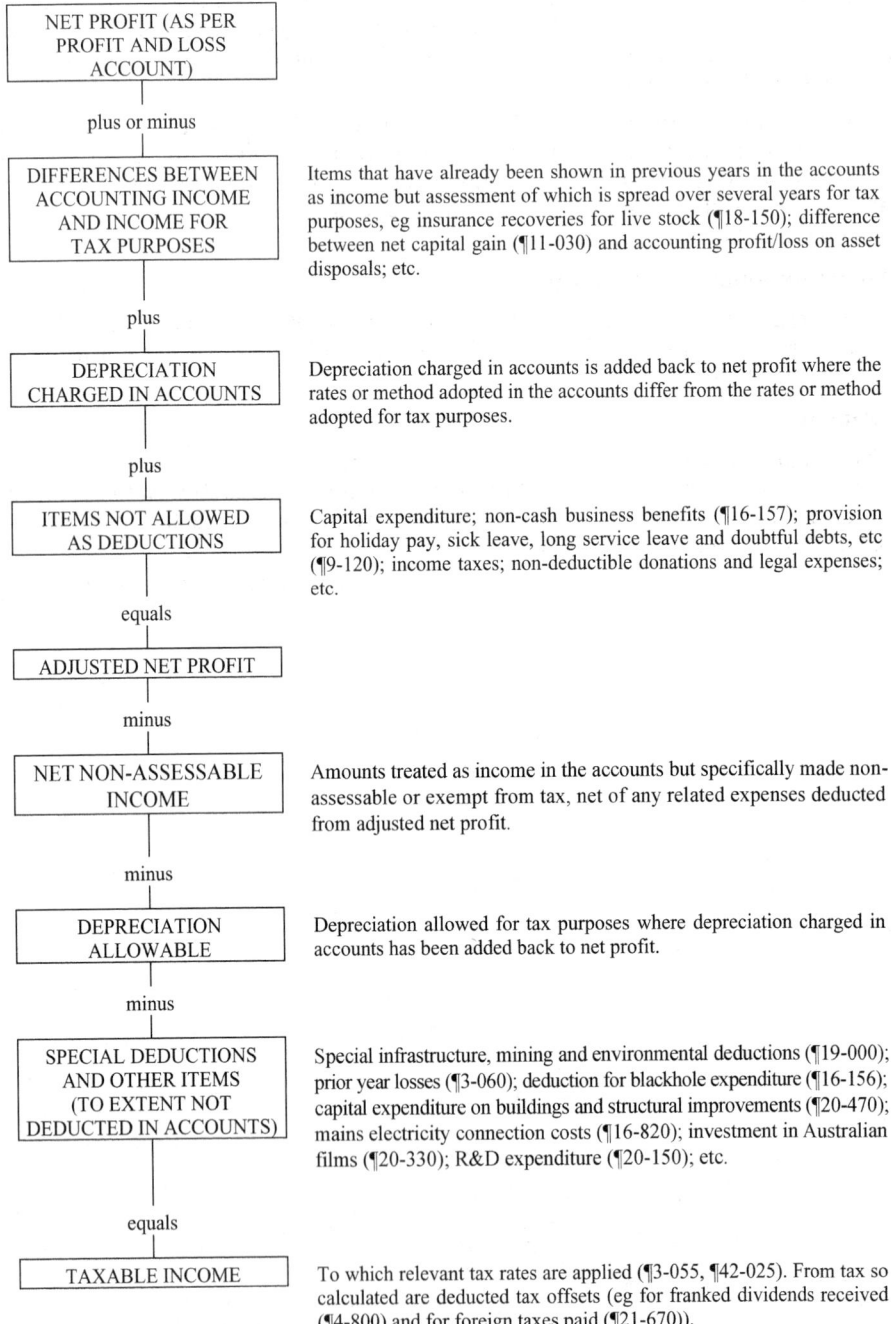

NET PROFIT (AS PER PROFIT AND LOSS ACCOUNT)	
plus or minus	
DIFFERENCES BETWEEN ACCOUNTING INCOME AND INCOME FOR TAX PURPOSES	Items that have already been shown in previous years in the accounts as income but assessment of which is spread over several years for tax purposes, eg insurance recoveries for live stock (¶18-150); difference between net capital gain (¶11-030) and accounting profit/loss on asset disposals; etc.
plus	
DEPRECIATION CHARGED IN ACCOUNTS	Depreciation charged in accounts is added back to net profit where the rates or method adopted in the accounts differ from the rates or method adopted for tax purposes.
plus	
ITEMS NOT ALLOWED AS DEDUCTIONS	Capital expenditure; non-cash business benefits (¶16-157); provision for holiday pay, sick leave, long service leave and doubtful debts, etc (¶9-120); income taxes; non-deductible donations and legal expenses; etc.
equals	
ADJUSTED NET PROFIT	
minus	
NET NON-ASSESSABLE INCOME	Amounts treated as income in the accounts but specifically made non-assessable or exempt from tax, net of any related expenses deducted from adjusted net profit.
minus	
DEPRECIATION ALLOWABLE	Depreciation allowed for tax purposes where depreciation charged in accounts has been added back to net profit.
minus	
SPECIAL DEDUCTIONS AND OTHER ITEMS (TO EXTENT NOT DEDUCTED IN ACCOUNTS)	Special infrastructure, mining and environmental deductions (¶19-000); prior year losses (¶3-060); deduction for blackhole expenditure (¶16-156); capital expenditure on buildings and structural improvements (¶20-470); mains electricity connection costs (¶16-820); investment in Australian films (¶20-330); R&D expenditure (¶20-150); etc.
equals	
TAXABLE INCOME	To which relevant tax rates are applied (¶3-055, ¶42-025). From tax so calculated are deducted tax offsets (eg for franked dividends received (¶4-800) and for foreign taxes paid (¶21-670)).

¶3-050 Short period return and accounting period change

A company that has been wound up or voluntarily dissolved must lodge a return for the short period from the start of its income year to the date of dissolution (¶9-020).

If a company is granted approval for an early-balancing substituted accounting period, it is similarly required to lodge a short period return for the first substituted period (¶9-010).

[FTR ¶6-585, ¶79-300, ¶79-340]

Company Tax Rates

¶3-055 Company rates

Companies pay a flat rate of tax without a tax-free threshold. For the 2017–18 to 2021–22 (inclusive) income years, the general company tax rate is 30%, but if the company is a base rate entity (see below), the rate is 27.5% for the first 3 of these income years and reduces to 26% for the 2020–21 income year and to 25% for the 2021–22 income year (*Income Tax Rates Act 1986* s 23).

Base rate entity

A company will be a base rate entity for an income year if:

- it meets an aggregated turnover test (¶7-050) which is less than $25 million (for 2017–18) and less than $50 million (for 2018–19 to 2021–22), and
- no more than 80% of its assessable income for the income year is ''base rate entity passive income'' (see below) (*Income Tax Rates Act 1986* s 23AA).

Note that for this purpose the aggregated turnover of a company for an income year is worked out in accordance with the definition of aggregated turnover which is set out at ¶7-050 as at the end of the income year, ie what is relevant is the actual aggregated turnover.

Base rate entity passive income

Base rate entity passive income is defined and comprises (broadly):

- dividends (other than non-portfolio dividends (as defined)) and franking credits
- interest (or a payment in the nature of interest), royalties (as defined in ITAA36 s 6(1)) (¶10-510) and rent
- non-share dividends by companies
- a gain on a qualifying security (within the meaning of ITAA36 Pt III Div 16E)
- a net capital gain
- an amount included in the assessable income of a partner in a partnership (under ITAA36 Div 5) or of a beneficiary of a trust estate (under ITAA36 Div 6) to the extent that the amount is referable (either directly or indirectly through one or more interposed partnerships or trust estates) to another amount that is base rate entity passive income under the above categories (*Income Tax Rates Act 1986* s 23AB(1)).

Interest for this purpose does not include interest to the extent that it is a return on an equity interest in a company or interest derived by certain categories of entity (for example, a financial institution) (*Income Tax Rates Act 1986* s 23AB(2)).

LCR 2019/5 deals with the base rate entity concept and the base rate entity passive income concept. The ruling makes these points in relation to base rate entity passive income:

- ''interest'' is the return, consideration, or compensation for the use or retention by one person of a sum of money belonging to, or owed to, another, and interest must be referrable to a principal. A payment in the nature of interest must have the character of return or profit to the lender for the use of money belonging to, or owed to another. Whether a payment has this character turns on its substance, no matter how it is calculated, and

- "rent" means the consideration payable by a tenant to a landlord for the exclusive possession and use of land or premises. The Commissioner's view and examples on when consideration paid for the use of land or premises will be rent for this purpose are set out in TD 2006/78.

LCR 2019/5 also considers the way the definition of base rate entity passive income operates where income passes through one or more partnerships or trusts.

Special company rates

Special tax rates apply to PDFs (¶3-555) and to certain classes of taxable income of life insurance companies (¶3-490), credit unions (¶3-435), non-profit companies (¶3-470) and RSA providers (¶3-530).

For a table of company tax rates, see ¶42-025.

Payment of tax

Companies generally pay their tax under the PAYG system in either a single lump sum or in quarterly instalments (¶27-100 and following).

[FTR ¶861-271, ¶976-700 – ¶976-825]

Company Loss Deductions

¶3-060 Deductibility of prior year losses

A company, like any other taxpayer, is entitled to carry forward losses incurred in one income year for deduction against its assessable income in subsequent years, subject to certain limitations (¶16-880). Prior year losses are deductible under ITAA97 Div 36 (ss 36-1 to 36-45). The loss company and the claiming company must be the same entity (except in limited circumstances where the loss transfer rules (¶3-090) can be applied). For example, in *Case 52/96*, a golf club with prior year losses merged with a sports and social club and the new club continued the businesses of both, as a sports and social club. The AAT held that the golf club's prior year losses could not be claimed by the new club as the golf club had ceased to exist. See also ID 2003/1118.

To claim a deduction for prior year losses, a company must satisfy either a continuity of ownership test (¶3-105) or a business continuity test (¶3-120). The need for these additional tests arises because a company is a legal entity distinct and separate from its shareholders. Without statutory safeguards, a company with unrecouped prior year losses could be sold by its shareholders to a purchaser who could use these accumulated losses to shelter income so as to reduce its exposure to tax. See also TD 2005/34, which deals with profit washing schemes that seek to utilise tax losses of an unrelated entity.

A company (or other corporate tax entity (¶4-440)) may be able to choose to carry a tax loss for 2019–20, 2020–21 or 2021–22 income year back to the 2018–19, 2019–20 or 2020–21 income year. See ¶3-080.

Company can limit its loss deduction

Corporate tax entities (¶4-440) can limit the amount of available tax losses that they utilise in an income year (s 36-17). This option can prevent wastage of tax losses and enables a corporate tax entity with prior year losses to increase the amount of franking credits that it has available to pay franked dividends.

The rules governing the amount to be deducted are as follows:

(1) if the entity has no "net exempt income" (¶16-880), it may choose the amount (if any) of the tax loss that it wishes to deduct from its (otherwise) taxable income (s 36-17(2))

(2) if the entity has net exempt income and also has taxable income (before tax loss deductions), available tax losses must be offset against net exempt income. The entity may then choose the amount (if any) of the remaining tax loss that it wishes to deduct from its (otherwise) taxable income (s 36-17(3))

(3) if the entity has net exempt income and its assessable income is more than offset by its allowable deductions (except tax losses), the excess deductions are subtracted from the net exempt income and the loss brought forward is deducted from any net exempt income that remains. There is no choice in this situation (s 36-17(4))

(4) a choice made under (1) or (2) above must not create excess franking offsets (¶3-075) for the entity, and must be nil if the entity has excess franking offsets without deducting any tax loss (s 36-17(5); ID 2004/685). The reason for this restriction is that old losses could otherwise be "refreshed" by generating excess franking offsets that in turn would be converted to new tax losses (¶3-075).

The entity must state its choice under (1) or (2) above in its income tax return for the relevant income year (s 36-17(6)). However, where there is a recalculation in the amount of an entity's tax losses, assessable income, allowable deductions or net exempt income for the year, the entity will generally be able to change its choice (or make a choice where one was not originally available). The change must be communicated by written notice to the Commissioner and is subject to the time limits in ITAA36 s 170 (¶25-300) (s 36-17(10) to (13)). Corporate tax losses brought forward must be deducted in the order in which they were incurred (s 36-17(7)).

Record retention

A taxpayer who has incurred a tax loss should retain records supporting that loss until the end of the statutory record retention period or the end of the statutory period for reviewing assessments for the income year in which the loss is fully deducted, whichever is later (TD 2007/2).

Related matters

The carry forward of *capital* losses is discussed at ¶11-080.

For the special rules applying to PDFs, see ¶3-555.

[FITR ¶85-000 – ¶85-230]

¶3-065 Deductibility of current year losses

Current year losses

The current year loss rules (ITAA97 Subdiv 165-B: ss 165-23 to 165-90) are designed to stop income derived by a company in one part of an income year when the company is owned by one set of shareholders from being offset by losses incurred by the company during another part of the income year when the company is owned by a different set of shareholders. This restricts the exploitation of current year loss companies for tax minimisation purposes.

Application of the current year loss rules

The current year loss rules are applied if:

- the company does not satisfy the continuity of ownership test (¶3-105, ¶3-130) or the business continuity test (¶3-120 – ¶3-125) for the whole income year, or

- a person begins to control, or becomes able to control, the voting power in the company where one purpose of obtaining that control is to get a tax benefit or advantage for any person (s 165-40).

Effect of the current year loss rules

If these rules apply, current year losses are *not* taken into account in working out taxable income for an income year. Instead, s 165-65 applies for the purpose of working out the taxable income of the company for the income year and a tax *loss* is worked out by applying s 165-90.

The company calculates its taxable income in the following way.

Step 1: The income year is divided into periods (s 165-45), with each change in ownership or control a dividing point between periods.

Step 2: Each period is treated as if it were an income year, and the notional loss or taxable income is worked out for that period (s 165-50).

Step 3: The taxable income for the year of change is worked out by adding up: (a) each notional taxable income; and (b) any full year amounts (ie amounts of assessable income not taken into account at Step 2), *then* subtracting any full year deductions (ie deductions not taken into account at Step 2) (s 165-65). A notional loss is *not* taken into account when calculating taxable income, but counts towards the company's tax loss.

A company's tax loss is the total of each notional loss and excess full year deductions of particular kinds (s 165-70).

The effect of the current year loss rules is that a company may be treated as having both a taxable income and a tax loss for the same income year. In some circumstances, the tax loss may be offset against the company's taxable income in later income years.

Current year deductions

Special anti-avoidance rules relating to current year deductions aim to prevent the manipulation of deductions and income to produce a favourable tax result, while denying the benefit to continuing shareholders. ITAA97 Subdiv 175-B (ss 175-20 to 175-35) covers 3 situations. These are:

(1) where income (called "injected income") is channelled into a company to get the benefit of a deduction incurred in the same income year

(2) where deductions are channelled through a company to shelter income derived by the company in the same income year

(3) where the company has entered into a scheme under which the company shelters income (because it has an "available expense") or takes the benefit of a deduction (because it has "available income") and, as a result, a person (other than the company) obtains a tax benefit.

Similar rules apply if capital gains are channelled into a company or if it has capital gains available for offset against deductions (¶11-090).

Current year deductions *may* be disallowed in any of the above situations. However, the deductions cannot be disallowed if the shareholders of the company obtain a tax benefit that is fair and reasonable, having regard to their shareholdings in the company.

Disallowed deductions may give rise to a tax loss that can be carried forward to offset against taxable income in later income years.

[FITR ¶180-500 – ¶180-680, ¶190-200 – ¶190-240]

¶3-075 Converting excess franking offsets to tax loss

A corporate tax entity's "excess franking offsets" are treated as a tax loss for the income year (ITAA97 s 36-55). As franking tax offsets are generally not refundable to corporate tax entities, these excess franking offsets could otherwise be lost.

Excess franking offsets

An entity that is a corporate tax entity at any time during an income year has "excess franking offsets" if the total non-refundable tax offsets to which it is entitled for the year under ITAA97 Div 207 (¶4-800) and Subdiv 210-H (¶3-555) exceeds the income tax that it would have to pay for that year if:

- it did not have those tax offsets, and
- it did not have any tax offsets that were subject to the tax offset carry forward rules (ITAA97 Div 65) or the refundable tax offset rules (¶15-010), but
- it had all its other tax offsets.

▶ Example 1

For the 2019–20 income year, ABC Company (which is not a base rate entity) has assessable income of $300, comprised of a fully-franked distribution of $210 and a (non-refundable) franking credit of $90. It has allowable deductions of $120, leaving taxable income of $180.

Its tax payable (ignoring the franking tax offset of $90) is $54 (ie $180 × 30%). Therefore, it has excess franking offsets of $36 (ie $90 – $54) for that year.

Amount of deemed tax loss

Excess franking offsets for the year are converted to a deemed tax loss using the method statement in s 36-55(2), as follows:

(1) work out the amount (if any) that would have been the entity's tax loss for that year, disregarding any net exempt income of the entity

(2) divide the entity's excess franking offsets for the income year by the entity's corporate tax rate for imputation purposes for that year

(3) add the results of steps (1) and (2)

(4) subtract the entity's net exempt income for the year. If the result is positive, the entity has a tax loss for the year of that amount. Otherwise, it has no tax loss for the year.

▶ Example 2

Following on from Example 1, assume that ABC Company has net exempt income of $20.

The result in step 1 is nil. The result in step 2 is $120 (ie $36 ÷ 0.30). The result in step 3 is also $120 (ie $0 + $120). The result is step 4 is $100 (ie $120 – $20).

ABC Company is therefore taken to have a tax loss of $100 for the income year.

[FITR ¶85-250]

¶3-080 Temporary loss carry back tax offset

A corporate tax entity (¶4-440) that has a tax loss (¶16-880) in any one or more of the 2019–20, 2020–21 or 2021–22 income years may (subject to qualifying conditions) choose to carry back the whole or part of the tax loss against its previously taxed profits of the 2018–19, 2019–20 or 2020–21 income years (ITAA97 Div 160).

The benefit generated by a loss carry back is received in the form of a refundable tax offset (that is allowable for the 2020–21 and/or the 2021–22 income years) and is called the loss carry back tax offset.

The choice to claim a loss carry back tax offset is an alternative to carrying the tax loss forward as a deduction for future income years. Only tax losses can be carried back; capital losses cannot be carried back.

As indicated, for an entity to be entitled to a loss carry back tax offset, it must be a corporate tax entity. Corporate tax entity status must exist for the income year for which the offset is claimed, the income year to which the loss is carried back and any intervening income year(s) (ITAA97 ss 160-5; 160-25).

In addition, for the income year in which the loss is made, the entity must be a small business entity (¶7-050) or would have been a small business entity if the aggregated turnover threshold for small business entity status was $5 billion and not $10 million (ITAA97 s 160-20).

It is also a requirement, for an entity to be entitled to a loss carry back tax offset, that the entity has lodged an income tax return for the income year in which the loss carry back tax offset is claimed and for each of the 5 immediately preceding income years (but not for an income year for which the entity was not required to lodge a return or for which the Commissioner assessed the entity's income tax liability) (ITAA97 s 160-5).

A loss carry back tax offset choice must be made in the approved form and by the time that the entity lodges its income tax return for the income year in which a loss carry back tax offset is claimed (that is the return for the 2020–21 or the 2021–22 income year), or within such further time as the Commissioner allows (ITAA97 s 160-15). It is envisaged that the approved form would be the corporate tax entity's income tax return for the 2020–21 income year (for losses made in the 2019–20 and/or 2020–21 income years) or for the 2021–22 income year (for losses made in the 2019–20, 2020–21 and/or 2021–22 income years). The choice must specify (in dollar terms) how much of a tax loss for a particular income year is to be carried back to a particular earlier income year.

Amount of the loss carry back tax offset

The amount of an entity's loss carry back tax offset for an income year (ie for the 2020–21 or the 2021–22 income year) is the *lesser* of:

- the sum of the entity's loss carry back tax offset components for the particular loss year(s), and
- the entity's franking account balance (¶4-700) at the end of the income year for which the offset is being claimed (that is, the 2020–21 or the 2021–22 income year) (ITAA97 s 160-10(1)).

Loss carry back tax offset component

An entity's loss carry back tax offset component for an income year is worked out by taking the following steps in relation to each tax loss to be carried back to a particular income year:

1. work out the amount of the tax loss that the entity is carrying back to the income year
2. reduce that amount by the net exempt income of the entity for the income year to the extent that the net exempt income has not already been utilised, and
3. convert the amount worked out under step 2 into a tax equivalent amount by multiplying the amount worked out under step 2 by the entity's corporate tax rate for the loss year (ITAA97 s 160-10(2)). For the corporate tax rates, see ¶3-055.

If an entity, in its loss carry back choice, carries back losses for 2 or 3 loss years to the income year, the entity's loss carry back tax offset component is the sum of the tax equivalent amounts worked out at step 3 above for each of those tax losses (ITAA97 s 160-10(2)).

A tax loss can only be utilised once and if a tax loss is carried back to more than one income year, the tax value of the amount carried back to each income year is limited by the available income tax liability of that income year. Each part of a tax liability can only be used once to support a loss carry back (ITAA97 s 160-10(3) and (4)).

The amount of an entity's income tax liability for an income year is the amount of income tax assessed to the entity for the year.

▶ Example

Company A (which is not a base rate entity) has at the end of the 2020–21 income year a tax loss of $900,000 for that income year and a franking account balance of $280,000.

For the 2018–19 income year Company A has an income tax liability of $120,000 and net exempt income of $5,000.

For the 2019–20 income year Company A has an income tax liability of $210,000.

Company A chooses to carry back $405,000 of its tax loss for the 2020–21 year to the 2018–19 income year and $495,000 of that loss to the 2019–20 income year.

Company A's loss carry back tax offset for the 2020–21 year is $268,500, worked out as follows:

- an offset component for the 2018–19 income year of $120,000, calculated by starting with the $405,000 carried back, reducing that at step 2 by $5,000, and multiplying the result by 30%
- an offset component for the 2019–20 income year of $148,500, calculated by starting with the $495,000 carried back and multiplying the result by 30%.

The sum of the 2 components is $268,500 (which is less than Company A's $280,000 franking account balance at the end of the 2020–21 income year). If that sum had exceeded that balance, the amount of the offset would have been limited to that balance.

Other points

A franking debit will arise in a corporate tax entity's franking account (when it gets a refund of tax as a result of the loss carry back tax offset) on the day that the refund is received (item 2 of the table at ¶4-720).

The franking account balance limit does not apply to a foreign resident entity with a permanent establishment in Australia that is not within the Australian imputation system (ITAA97 s 160-10(5)).

Any debit to the franking account of a foreign resident entity (other than a New Zealand franking company) for a refund of tax arising from a loss carry back tax offset can only reduce the account balance to nil. It cannot put the franking account into deficit (item 2A of the table at ¶4-720).

There is a specific integrity rule in the loss carry back tax offset rules (ITAA97 s 160-35). In addition, the general anti-avoidance provisions of ITAA36 Part IVA were amended so that they apply to schemes entered into with the purpose of obtaining a loss carry back tax offset.

¶3-090 Transfer of losses within a company group

As part of the introduction of the consolidation regime (¶8-000), the group loss transfer rules generally ceased to apply for income years that commence after 30 June 2003. However, group loss transfers continue to be available within company groups provided either the loss company or the income company is an Australian branch of a foreign bank or non-bank foreign financial entity.

Deductibility Tests for Losses and Bad Debts

¶3-105 Continuity of ownership test

A company cannot deduct a tax loss (ITAA97 s 165-10) unless either:

- it meets the conditions in ITAA97 s 165-12 (which is about the company maintaining the same owners), or
- it meets the conditions in ITAA97 s 165-13 (which is about the company satisfying the business continuity test) (¶3-120).

The continuity of ownership test (COT) requires that shares carrying *more than 50%* of all voting, dividend and capital rights be beneficially owned by the same persons *at all times* during the ownership test period. The ownership test period is the period from the start of the loss year to the end of the income year in which the loss is to be deducted (s 165-12(1)). The timing of a change of beneficial ownership for COT purposes may not be the same as the timing of a disposal of shares for CGT purposes (ID 2006/35).

There are 2 tests for determining whether a company has maintained the same owners. The ''primary test'' is applied unless the relevant provision requires the ''alternative test'' to be applied (ITAA97 ss 165-12; 165-37; 165-123). The alternative test applies where one or more other companies beneficially owned shares, or interests in shares, in the company *at any time* during the ownership test period.

Primary test

The primary test is satisfied at a particular time if there are persons who at that time beneficially own, between them, shares that carry:

- the right to exercise more than 50% of the voting power in the company, disregarding dual listed company voting shares (ITAA97 ss 165-150(1); 165-209)
- the right to receive more than 50% of any dividends the company may pay (ITAA97 s 165-155(1)), and
- the right to receive more than 50% of any distribution of capital of the company (ITAA97 s 165-160(1)).

Alternative test

The alternative test is satisfied at a particular time if a person or persons (none of them companies — nor trustees in the case of (1) below) collectively:

(1) are able to control more than 50% of the voting power in the company, disregarding dual listed company voting shares (ss 165-150(2); 165-209)

(2) have the right to receive for their own benefit more than 50% of any dividends that the company might pay (s 165-155(2)), and

(3) have the right to receive for their own benefit more than 50% of any distribution of capital of the company (s 165-160(2)).

The test is also satisfied where it is *reasonable to assume* that the above conditions are fulfilled. The conditions may be fulfilled either directly or through one or more interposed entities.

Under this test, indirect equity interests in the company are treated as carrying the relevant proportion of the voting power (or dividend or capital distribution rights) carried by the shares held directly or indirectly by the interposed entity in the company at all times during the ownership test period.

▶ Example

Ben holds shares in an interposed company carrying 30% of the voting power in the interposed company. The interposed company holds shares carrying 60% of the voting power in a loss company. Ben is treated as having an indirect equity interest carrying 18% (ie 30% × 60%) of the voting power in the loss company.

General rules

When applying the primary or the alternative test, a person's share in a company may be counted only if the person owns *the same interests in the same shares* throughout the relevant period (ITAA97 s 165-165). This applies to losses claimed in an income year ending on or after 21 September 1999. Previously a person did not have to beneficially own exactly the same shares for the tests to be satisfied. Splits or consolidations of shares or units are not taken as a failure to own the same shares.

The COT will not be failed merely because an external administrator or provisional liquidator is appointed to the tested company or a company interposed between it and an ultimate owner (ITAA97 s 165-208). This overcomes the High Court decision in *Linter Textiles*, where the court held that the appointment of a liquidator to the taxpayer company changed control of its voting power.

A public company is taken to have satisfied the test if it is reasonable to assume that the test is satisfied (s 165-165(7)).

Certain government bodies, statutory bodies, non-profit companies and charitable bodies are treated as if they were persons other than companies for the purposes of the COT (ITAA97 s 165-202(1)). This treatment also applies (from and including the 2011–12 income year) to a complying superannuation fund, a superannuation fund that is established in a foreign country and is regulated under a foreign law, a complying approved deposit fund, a special company or a managed investment scheme.

Shares that are beneficially owned through a charitable trust are taken to be beneficially owned by a person other than a company or trustee (ITAA97 s 165-202(2): generally applicable to losses for years commencing on or after 1 July 2002).

If a beneficial owner of shares dies, that beneficial ownership is deemed to survive as long as the shares are held by the trustee of the estate or by a beneficiary of the deceased's estate (ITAA97 s 165-205).

Non-profit companies, mutual affiliate companies and mutual insurance companies only need to establish continuity of voting power to satisfy the COT, ie they will be taken to satisfy the dividend and capital conditions (ITAA97 ss 165-12(7A); 165-37(4A); 165-115C(4A); 165-115L(5); 165-123(7A): generally applicable to losses for years commencing on or after 1 July 2002).

Part of a prior year loss may be allowed where the COT is satisfied in relation to the relevant part of the loss year under the current year loss rules (¶3-065) (ITAA97 s 165-20; ID 2003/720; ID 2004/949).

Incomplete periods

The COT can be satisfied when the tested company exists for only part of the loss year or part of the income year (ITAA97 s 165-255).

Share ownership saving provisions

Where the ownership test is failed *solely* because of the "same interests in the same shares" requirement, the failure will be disregarded if the loss company can demonstrate that less than 50% of the relevant loss or bad debt has resulted in an increased loss or reduced gain on the disposal of any direct and indirect equity interests in the company during the relevant test period (ITAA97 ss 165-12(7); 165-37(4); 165-115C(4); 165-123(7)).

Unequal rights to dividends, capital distributions or voting power

The COT has been modified for companies whose shares have unequal rights to dividends, capital distributions or voting power.

Under these modifications, if an entity is unable to work out whether a company satisfies a condition of the COT in respect of dividend or capital distributions, an entity may choose to reconsider the condition in up to 3 ways:

- the first way is to disregard debt interests (ITAA97 s 167-15)
- the second way is to disregard debt interests and certain secondary classes of shares (ITAA97 s 167-20), and
- the third way is to disregard debt interests and certain secondary classes of shares, and treat each of the remaining shares as having a specified percentage of the rights to receive dividends and capital distributions (ITAA97 s 167-25).

If a company has shares that have different voting rights or do not carry all of the voting rights in the company, then the continuity of ownership test may be applied by testing voting power solely by reference to the maximum number of votes that could be cast in a poll on:

- the election of the company's directors, or
- an amendment to the company's constitution (other than an amendment altering the rights carried by any of the company's shares or other forms of voting power in the company).

The amendments to modify the COT for companies with shares that have unequal rights to dividends, capital distributions or voting power apply from 1 July 2002. That is, the amendments apply to:

- any tax loss for an income year commencing on or after 1 July 2002
- any net capital loss for an income year commencing on or after 1 July 2002, and
- any deduction in respect of a bad debt that is claimed in an income year commencing on or after 1 July 2002.

There are other transitional and application provisions in s 167-1 of the *Income Tax (Transitional Provisions) Act 1997*.

Companies without shares

For the purposes of a test, if no shares have been issued in a company, each membership interest in the company is taken to be a share (ITAA97 s 165-203).

Change in control of voting power

The deductibility of past losses is further restricted where there has been a change in the control of the voting power and the change is associated with a purpose of gaining a tax advantage. It applies even if the company has met the conditions in s 165-12 or 165-13.

This further restriction applies where:

- for some or all of the part of the ownership test period that started at the end of the loss year, a person controlled, or was able to control, the voting power in the company
- for some or all of the loss year, that person did not control, and was not able to control, that voting power

- that person began to control, or became able to control, that voting power for the purpose (even if this is only one of a number of purposes) of getting some taxation advantage or benefit, either for that person or for someone else.

Where these conditions are met, the company cannot claim the tax loss unless it satisfies the business continuity test (¶3-120) (ITAA97 s 165-15). In this context, the company must carry on the same or a similar business throughout the income year as it did immediately before the time when the person began, or became able, to control the relevant voting power (the "test time"). The rules in s 165-15 apply equally to a listed public company (ID 2005/8).

Anti-avoidance provisions

The effectiveness of the COTs is protected by a number of anti-avoidance provisions. These basically prevent share ownership being manipulated by arrangements aimed at reducing tax liability.

- The Commissioner can disregard a person's beneficial ownership of shares if:
  - an arrangement was entered into at some time that in any way turned on: (i) the beneficial interest in the shares or the value of that interest; (ii) a right carried by, or relating to, those shares; or (iii) the exercise of such a right, *and*
  - at least one purpose of the arrangement is to eliminate or reduce a tax liability of an entity (ITAA97 s 165-180).

  The predecessor to s 165-180 (ITAA36 former s 80B(5)) was applied in *K Porter*, which involved an arrangement under which the original owners of shares agreed to retain the shares until their carry forward losses were deducted and then dispose of the shares to the new owners. In such a case, the Commissioner is empowered to treat the original owner as not continuing to beneficially own the shares.

- Shares are taken *not* to have carried particular rights during a part of the ownership test period if the Commissioner is satisfied that the shares *stopped* (or may stop) carrying those rights after the ownership test period, either because of the company's constitution (as in force at some time *during* the ownership test period) or because of an arrangement entered into before or during the ownership test period (ITAA97 s 165-185).

- Shares are taken to have carried particular rights *at all times* during a part of the ownership test period if the Commissioner is satisfied that the shares *started* (or may start) to carry those rights after the ownership test period because of the company's constitution (as in force at some time *during* the ownership test period) or because of an arrangement entered into before or during the ownership test period (ITAA97 s 165-190).

In addition to the above safeguards, ITAA97 Subdiv 175-A sets out 2 cases where the Commissioner may disallow a deduction for some or all of a prior year tax loss. However, the disallowance will not apply where the company that fails the COT test in s 165-12 meets the business continuity test in s 165-13 (ITAA97 s 175-5(2)). The 2 cases are:

- income or capital gains are injected into the company in order to take advantage of the available loss, and the Commissioner does not consider that the extent to which the continuing shareholders will benefit from the injection is fair and reasonable having regard to their respective rights and interests in the company (but if the Commissioner considers that the extent the continuing shareholders will benefit is fair and reasonable the Commissioner cannot disallow any part of the deduction for the loss) (ITAA97 s 175-10; ID 2010/49). A family trust can be a "continuing shareholder" for the purposes of s 175-10 (ID 2006/157). If the Commissioner disallows a loss under this provision, the loss may be deducted in a future income year, subject to satisfaction of the company loss rules (ID 2010/48). The Commissioner is not required to apply the ''fair and reasonable'' test to an insolvent company (ITAA97 s 175-100)

- a person other than the company obtains a tax benefit in connection with a scheme that would not have been entered into or carried out if the loss had not been available.

Special rules for widely held companies, Div 166 companies and companies owned by trusts

The COT is modified for ''widely held'' companies and ''eligible Division 166 companies'' (¶3-130). Modified COT rules also apply where certain trusts own shares in a company (¶3-110).

[FITR ¶180-100 – ¶182-163]

¶3-110 COT rules for companies owned by certain trusts

If a company is not able to pass the continuity of ownership test (COT) because interests in the company are held by non-fixed trusts, the company may still be able to deduct its losses or debts if the following alternative conditions are satisfied (ITAA97 s 165-215):

(1) at the beginning of the loss year, individuals must not have had (between them) direct or indirect beneficial fixed entitlements to more than 50% of the income or capital of the company

(2) at all times during the ownership period, fixed entitlements to all the income and capital of the company must have been held by: (a) persons; or (b) a holding entity (being a company or trust)

(3) at all times during the ownership period, non-fixed trusts (other than family trusts) must have held fixed entitlements to a 50% or greater share of the income or capital of the company (in the case of (2)(a) above) or the holding entity (in the case of (2)(b) above)

(4) the persons holding fixed entitlements to shares of the income and capital of the company or holding entity (as the case may be) in (2) above at the beginning of the loss year must have held those entitlements at all times during the ownership period, and

(5) no non-fixed trust (other than a family trust or other excepted trust: ¶6-262) that directly or indirectly held a fixed interest in the income or capital of the company during the ownership test period would have been denied the loss deduction under ITAA36 Sch 2F s 267-20 if it, rather than the company, had incurred the loss. This means that each such trust must satisfy a 50% stake test, a control test and a pattern of distributions test (¶6-264).

Current year losses

Substantially identical alternative conditions (ITAA97 s 165-220) apply in relation to current year losses except that the test period is the income year and there is a different condition (5) — for each non-fixed trust, ITAA36 Sch 2F s 267-60 does not require the trust to work out its net income and tax loss for the year under ITAA36 Sch 2F Div 268 (¶3-065, ¶6-265).

Family trusts

Shares held by a trustee of a family trust are treated as if they were owned by a notional entity so that trustee changes do not affect the COT being satisfied (ITAA97 s 165-207).

[FITR ¶181-710, ¶182-210, ¶182-220]

¶3-120 Business continuity test

A company that satisfies the business continuity test may be entitled to claim a deduction for prior year losses even if it fails the continuity of ownership test (COT) (¶3-105) (ITAA97 s 165-13). The business continuity test may also be applied in relation to a company's current year losses (¶3-065) or deductions for bad debts (¶3-150).

The term business continuity test was introduced into the ITAA97 by amendments made by the *Treasury Laws Amendment (2017 Enterprise Incentives No. 1) Act 2019*. The term effectively covers the same business test which had operated for many years and also a new similar business test which operates (subject to commencement rules) as an alternative to the same business test. Accordingly, a company can satisfy the business continuity test by carrying on either:

- the same business (¶3-123), or
- a similar business (¶3-125)

during a relevant period.

As indicated, before the amendments referred to, the same business test was the only test available where a company failed the COT. The amendments apply (broadly) in relation to:

- tax losses incurred by, and net capital losses made by companies for income years beginning on or after 1 July 2015
- working out a company's taxable income and tax loss, and net capital gain and net capital loss, in an income year beginning on or after 1 July 2015 because a change of ownership has occurred in that income year
- unrealised losses in relation to CGT assets where the income year immediately before the one in which a change of ownership or control occurred is an income year beginning on or after 1 July 2015
- debts incurred in income years beginning on or after 1 July 2015 that the company writes off as bad.

Some general points

Incomplete periods

The business continuity test can be satisfied when the tested company exists for only part of the loss year or part of the income year (ITAA97 s 165-255).

Business continuity test: "test time" for prior year tax losses

Section 165-13 provides for the following default test times to be used when applying the business continuity test in relation to prior year tax losses:

- where practicable, the test time will be the latest time that the company can show that it has satisfied the COT
- where it is not practicable for the company to show that it has satisfied the COT for any period since incurring the loss:
  - the test time is the start of the loss year if the company existed for the whole of the loss year
  - the test time is the end of the loss year if the company came into being during the loss year.

Medical defence organisations

A medical defence organisation (MDO) or its associated general insurance company will not fail the business continuity test (in relation to tax losses, net capital losses or bad debts) merely because the MDO restructured or ceased to provide medical indemnity cover before 1 July 2003 to satisfy the requirements under the *Medical Indemnity (Prudential Supervision and Product Standards) Act 2003* (ITAA97 s 165-212D).

Consolidated groups

The application of the business continuity test in the context of consolidated groups is discussed at ¶8-100 and ¶8-110.

[FITR ¶182-000]

¶3-123 Business continuity test: same business

As explained at ¶3-120, one way by which the business continuity test may be met by a company is by the company satisfying what may be called the same business test. This test is considered below.

Alternatively, subject to the commencement rules noted at ¶3-120, the business continuity test may be met by a company satisfying what may be called the similar business test which is discussed at ¶3-125.

The test

A company satisfies the same business test if it carries on the same business (see below) in the claim year as it carried on immediately before the ''test time''.

However, a company does *not* satisfy the same business test where it derives assessable income during the same business test period from:

- a business of a kind that it did not carry on before the test time (the ''new business test''), or
- a transaction of a kind that it had not entered into in the course of its business operations before the test time (the ''new transactions test'') (ITAA97 s 165-210(2)).

Where there are changes in a company's business as well as its ownership, the dates on which the changes legally occur may be critical (eg *TelePacific*). Further, an anti-avoidance measure operates where companies enter into arrangements, before a change in ownership, that are specifically designed to ensure that the same business test will be met (s 165-210(3)).

A company cannot satisfy the same business test if the business does not exist at the time the disqualifying change of ownership takes place (*Avondale Motors*).

Where a foreign resident company carries on business both in and out of Australia, the ATO has taken the view that the same business test is applied to the company's global business, not just its Australian business (ID 2006/258).

If a loss results from a company writing off a bad debt and the bad debt is deductible *only* because the company satisfies the business continuity test (there having been a change in beneficial ownership), the loss is deductible only if the company continues to satisfy the business continuity test throughout the claim year (ITAA97 s 165-132). See also ¶3-150, which deals with the bad debt provisions for companies.

Meaning of "same" business

The Commissioner's views on the meaning of ''same'' in the same business test are set out in TR 1999/9. Although ''same'' imports identity, and not merely similarity, this does not mean identical in all respects. A company can expand or contract its activities without necessarily ceasing to carry on the same business. The organic growth of a business through the adoption of new compatible operations will not ordinarily cause it to fail the same business test provided the business retains its identity. Nor would discarding, in the ordinary way, portions of its old operations. But if, through a process of evolution, a business changes its essential character, or there is a sudden and dramatic change in the business brought about by either the acquisition or the loss of activities on a considerable scale, a company may fail the test.

The following are some examples of how the same business test has been applied.

- Before a sale of its shares, a company carried on business as a dealer in motor parts and accessories. After the sale, it carried on the same kind of business but under a different name, at different places, with different directors and employees, with different stock and plant and in conjunction with a dealer having different franchises. The same business test was not satisfied (*Avondale Motors*).

- Before its takeover, a company carried on business as a wholesale spare parts dealer, and new and used car dealer. After the takeover, its business was restricted to the spare parts dealership and general administration. The same business test was not satisfied (*Case N109*).

- A change from a pastoral seed production business to that of a pastoralist or grazier meant that the taxpayer failed the same business test (*Fielder Downs*).

- A business of distributing and installing swimming pools was not the same business as manufacturing, selling and installing the pools (*Case K20*).

- A business deriving income exclusively from agricultural consulting and administration was not the same business as when the business was deriving a significant part of its income from its agricultural machinery sales agency (*Case Y45*).

- A business of selling only its own stock of telecommunications equipment failed the same business test by becoming largely a seller of Telstra stock as agent (*TelePacific*).

- Activities undertaken by a taxpayer in terminating various arrangements after selling its joint venture interest in a coal mine did not satisfy the same business test. The coal mining business was not in the process of being wound up; it was being carried on as before, but under different ownership (*Coal Developments (German Creek)*).

- Before its takeover, the taxpayer company owned a hotel which was operated and managed by another company in its group as agent for the taxpayer. Following the takeover, the taxpayer operated and managed the hotel directly. The same business test was satisfied (*Lilyvale Hotel*); the Full Federal Court held that the changes in the way in which the business was carried on did not, in this instance, make it a different business.

New transactions test

The new transactions test (mentioned above) aims to prevent the injection of income into a loss company in order to absorb its losses. It includes all transactions entered into in the course of the company's business operations. However, the test will generally not be failed by transactions of a type that are usually unmotivated by tax avoidance, ie "transactions that could have been entered into ordinarily and naturally in the course of the business operations carried on by the company before the change-over" (TR 1999/9).

[FITR ¶182-050 – ¶182-160]

¶3-125 Business continuity test: similar business

As explained at ¶3-120, amendments made by the *Treasury Laws Amendment (2017 Enterprise Incentives No 1) Act 2019* introduced a similar business test as an alternative to the same business test for the purpose of: claiming a tax loss incurred for the 2015–16 or a later income year; applying the current year loss provisions for the 2015–16 or a later income year; or claiming a deduction for the writing off of a debt incurred in the 2015–16 or a later income year as bad.

To satisfy the similar business test, a company must throughout the relevant continuity test period carry on a business that is ''similar to'' the business carried on immediately before the relevant test time (ITAA97 s 165-211).

What will constitute a ''similar'' business for this purpose will be a question of fact but s 165-211(2) provides for 4 matters that must be taken into account (along with any other considerations that are relevant in the particular situation) in ascertaining whether a company's current business is similar to its former business. In broad terms, these 4 matters are:

- the extent to which the same assets are used to generate income
- the extent to which assessable income is generated from the same activities and operations
- the identity of the current business and the identity of the former business, and
- the extent to which changes to the former business result from development or commercialisation of assets, products, etc (s 165-211(2)).

There are anti-avoidance type provisions which deal with the situations where, before the relevant test time, the company started to carry on a business that it had not previously carried on or, in the course of its business operations, entered into a transaction of a kind that it had not previously entered into, and this was done for the purpose (or a purpose) of being taken to have carried on a similar business (s 165-211(3)).

However, there is no provision equivalent to the new business or transaction prohibition that applies in the case of the same business test (¶3-123).

The Commissioner has released LCR 2019/1 which considers the operation of the similar business test. LCR 2019/1 contains a number of examples which illustrate the way the Commissioner considers the test should be applied.

[FITR ¶182-000 – ¶182-185]

¶3-130 Tracing ownership of widely held companies

Because of the difficulty widely held companies may have in tracing ownership of their shares, the tests required to be satisfied to establish continuity of ownership for the purposes of various company loss provisions (¶3-105 – ¶3-150, ¶11-090, ¶11-120) are modified for such companies (ITAA97 Div 166: ss 166-1 to 166-280). The modified rules apply to a company that is a ''widely held company'' or an ''eligible Division 166 company'', and are set out as follows:

- ITAA97 Subdiv 166-A modifies the application of ITAA97 Subdiv 165-A to deductions for prior year losses (¶3-105)
- ITAA97 Subdiv 166-B modifies the application of ITAA97 Subdiv 165-B to deductions for current year tax losses in a year of ownership change (¶3-065)
- Subdiv 166-B also modifies the application of ITAA97 Subdiv 165-CB to a net capital gain or net capital loss in a year of ownership change (¶11-090)
- ITAA97 Subdiv 166-C modifies the application of ITAA97 Subdiv 165-C to deductions for bad debts (¶3-150)
- ITAA97 Subdiv 166-CA modifies the application of ITAA97 Subdiv 165-CC for the purposes of the unrealised loss rules (¶11-120)
- Subdiv 166-CA also modifies the application of ITAA97 Subdiv 165-CD for the purposes of the inter-entity loss multiplication rules (¶3-135)

- ITAA97 Subdiv 166-D explains how the ownership conditions interact with the rules in ITAA97 Subdiv 165-D (the continuity of ownership test: ¶3-105).

Subject to transitional provisions, Div 166 applies from 1 July 2002.

Widely held companies and eligible Div 166 companies

Division 166 applies where a company is a widely held company or ''eligible Division 166 company'' at all times during the income year in which the deduction is sought. The term ''widely held company'' includes all companies that are listed on an approved stock exchange and all unlisted companies with more than 50 members where no 20 or fewer persons hold 75% or more of the voting, dividend or capital distribution rights. An ''eligible Division 166 company'' is a company (other than a widely held company) in which more than 50% of the voting power, dividend rights or capital distribution rights are beneficially owned by one or more of the following: a widely held company; a deemed beneficial owner (ie a complying superannuation fund, foreign superannuation fund, complying ADF, special company, managed investment scheme or other entity prescribed for the purposes of s 166-245); a non-profit company; or a charitable body.

Test times

Under the modified rules, companies are required to test for continuity of ownership at the start of the loss year, at the end of the income year in which the deduction is claimed, at the end of any intervening year and at the end of a ''corporate change''. A ''corporate change'' could be a takeover bid (whether or not successful), an arrangement involving 50% or more of the company's shares, an increase in the issued capital or number of shares by 20% or more, or a corporate change in a majority stakeholder (s 166-175).

Tracing rules

The tracing rules are modified so that:

- a direct stake of less than 10% is attributed to a single notional entity (s 166-225)
- an indirect stake of less than 10% is attributed to the top interposed entity (s 166-230)
- a stake of 10% to 50% (inclusive) held by a widely held company is attributed to the widely held company as an ultimate owner (s 166-240)
- a stake held by a deemed beneficial owner (ie a superannuation fund, approved deposit fund, special company or managed investment scheme) is generally attributed to that entity as an ultimate owner (s 166-245)
- an indirect stake held by way of bearer shares in a non-resident listed company is attributed to a single notional entity in certain circumstances (s 166-255)
- an indirect stake held by a depository entity through shares in a listed non-resident company is attributed to the depository entity as an ultimate owner in certain circumstances (s 166-260).

The modified COT contains a ''same share same interest rule'' comparable to that for the normal COT (¶3-105); however, it applies only to interests held by a top interposed company, a widely held company, an entity deemed to be a beneficial owner or a depository company (s 166-272).

As the tracing rules are not intended to have any detrimental effect on a company satisfying the COT, a tracing rule can be disregarded in respect of a particular stake if it would cause the company to fail the COT. A company is taken to satisfy the relevant conditions if the company believes on reasonable grounds that it would not fail the conditions if the tracing rule did not apply in respect of that stake (s 166-275).

Note that from 1 July 2018, the interposition of a holding company between the tested company and a less than 10% direct stakeholder will not, of itself, cause a failure of the COT (s 166-230(5)).

Controlled test companies rule

The controlled test companies rule (s 166-280) overrides the tracing rules in 2 circumstances.

- Where a company is sufficiently influenced by one or more controlling entities, the tracing concessions do not apply in respect of voting power or dividend or capital rights held directly or indirectly by those entities. Broadly, this will be the case where the company or its directors are obligated, accustomed or would reasonably be expected to act in accordance with the directions, instructions or wishes of the controlling entities.
- In addition, if the tested company is a widely held company, the tracing rule does not apply in relation to the voting power of the tested company where:
  - a natural person (not a trustee), together with the person's associates, holds 25% or more of the voting rights in the tested company, or
  - a trustee or company, together with its associates, holds 50% or more of the voting rights in the tested company.

In the above circumstances, the tested company must trace its ownership through to the entity that has sufficient influence or the relevant natural person, trustee or company.

[FITR ¶180-500 – ¶182-475]

¶3-135 Preventing inter-entity loss multiplication

Where a ''loss company'' (see below) experiences an alteration in its ownership or control, or its shares are declared worthless, the tax values of controlling stakeholders' equity and debt interests in the company may be reduced. Interests held by individuals are not affected. The purpose of the reductions is to prevent duplicate or multiple recognition of the company's losses up the ownership chain when inter-entity interests in the loss company are realised.

Controlling stakeholders

An entity has a ''controlling stake'' in a company if the entity and its associates between them control more than 50% of the voting power, have the right to receive more than 50% of any dividends or have the right to receive more than 50% of any distribution of capital of the company. Thus, if any entity has a controlling stake in a company, each associate of the entity also has a controlling stake (s 165-115Z).

Determining whether a company is a loss company

There are 2 different tests for determining whether a company is a ''loss company'': (a) at the first (or only) alteration time in an income year; or (b) at a subsequent alteration time in the same year.

Loss company test at the first (or only) alteration time in a year

A company is a loss company at the first (or only) alteration time in the income year if it has *any* of the following:

(1) undeducted prior year tax losses at the beginning of the year

(2) unapplied net capital losses at the beginning of the income year

(3) a tax loss for the income year

(4) a net capital loss for the income year, or

(5) an adjusted *unrealised* loss at the alteration time. In broad terms, this is the sum of the losses the company would make if it were to dispose of its CGT assets and trading stock at market value.

For the purposes of the test, the period from the beginning of the income year to the alteration time is treated as an income year.

There are double counting rules to ensure that the same losses are not taken into account more than once.

Loss company test at second or later alteration time in a year

In the case of a second or later alteration time in an income year, it is assumed that the period from the last alteration time to the current alteration time is an income year, and only items (3), (4) and (5) above are taken into account.

Relieving provisions

There are a number of relieving provisions to minimise or remove the compliance burden of calculating unrealised losses (which involves ascertaining the current values of individual assets):

- assets costing less than $10,000 are disregarded
- an item of depreciable plant costing less than $1 million can be valued at its tax written down value, providing the company can reasonably conclude that the item's market value is not less than 80% of that amount
- companies with connected net assets of $6 million or less (under the maximum net asset value test in ITAA97 s 152-15: ¶7-130) are exempted from calculating unrealised losses (ITAA97 s 165-115GC(4))
- companies without realised losses may not have to apply the loss multiplication measures where the time of alteration is not a ‘‘changeover time’’ under ITAA97 Subdiv 165-CC (¶11-120) and they are reasonably expected to be in a net unrealised gain position at that time.

The provisions deal only with the multiplication of losses by way of deductions or capital losses; they do not deal with reduced gains. Accordingly, unrealised gains are not taken into account.

"Global method" of asset valuation

In order to reduce compliance costs, companies may use a ‘‘global method’’ of valuing assets, rather than the ‘‘individual asset method’’. The choice to use the global method may be made on or before the day of lodging the income tax return for the income year in which the alteration time occurred, or a later day as the Commissioner allows (s 165-115U(1A) to (1D)).

If the global method is used and a significant equity or debt interest in the company is later realised at a loss, a special value shifting rule will apply to avoid the duplication of the unrealised loss at alteration time (ITAA97 s 165-115ZD).

Nature of the reductions

Where the measures apply, the reductions are achieved by adjusting the reduced cost bases and deduction entitlements (eg for bad debts or trading losses) in relation to ‘‘relevant equity interests’’ and ‘‘relevant debt interests’’ that controlling stakeholders hold in the loss company. A relevant equity interest is a 10% or greater direct or indirect equity interest held by a controlling stakeholder in the loss company (based upon voting power, dividend entitlements or capital entitlements). A relevant debt interest is a debt of at least $10,000 owed to a controlling stakeholder directly by the loss company or by an entity with a relevant interest in the loss company. An individual (or a partnership in which all partners are individuals) is not taken to hold a relevant interest (ss 165-115X to 165-115ZA).

Reductions are generally required only for interests held immediately before an alteration time. However, reductions may also be required where: (a) interests are disposed of within 12 months before an alteration time; or (b) interests are disposed of more than 12 months before an alteration time as part of an arrangement that *also* involves the disposal of interests at (or within 12 months before) the alteration time (ss 165-115P; 165-115Q).

Overall loss

The reductions made under Subdiv 165-CD cannot exceed the "overall loss" of the loss company. The overall loss is the sum of amounts of losses taken into account when determining that the company is a loss company (see above).

Adjustment amount

The adjustment to be applied is generally the "adjustment amount" (discussed below). However, where the cost of trading stock exceeds its market value by less than the adjustment amount, the adjustment is limited to the excess. The adjustment amount is applied to reduce the following values (s 165-115ZA):

- the reduced cost base of an equity or debt that is a CGT asset
- any deduction available in respect of equity or debt that is not trading stock
- the cost of any equity or debt that is trading stock.

The adjustment amount is calculated under s 165-115ZB, which provides a formula for straightforward situations and directional guidance for other cases.

Formula method

The formula method applies where: (a) the affected entity has a relevant equity interest consisting of directly owned shares in the loss company; (b) all the shares in the loss company are of the same class and market value; (c) if the affected entity also has a relevant debt interest, the debt consists of a single debt or 2 or more debts of the same kind; and (d) the result is reasonable in the circumstances.

The adjustment amount is the affected entity's pro rata portion of the loss company's overall loss, based on the number of shares held by the affected entity, calculated as follows (s 165-115ZB(3) to (5)):

$$\frac{\text{the number of shares in the loss company constituted by the equity immediately before the alteration time}}{\text{the total number of shares in the loss company immediately before the alteration time}} \times \text{the amount of the loss company's overall loss at the alteration time}$$

The resulting adjustment is applied first in relation to share equity (equally among all shares). The balance (if any) is applied in relation to debts (proportionately by value).

Non-formula method

Where the formula does not apply, the adjustment amount is "the amount that is appropriate" bearing in mind the object of the loss multiplication provisions and a number of other specific factors, including the amount of the overall loss and the extent to which that loss has reduced the market values of equity and debt (see, for example, ID 2006/152). The adjustment amount is to be applied "in an appropriate way" (s 165-115ZB(6), (7)).

Notice requirements

Strict notice requirements are imposed on the loss company or its controlling entity to ensure that affected stakeholders receive the information that they require (s 165-115ZC). The Commissioner may extend the notice period or waive the notice requirement in certain circumstances.

Interaction with consolidation regime

Rules to clarify the interaction of Subdiv 165-CD and the consolidation regime (¶8-000) are contained in ITAA97 ss 715-215 to 715-270.

[FITR ¶181-130, ¶181-170]

Company Bad Debt Deductions

¶3-150 Deductibility of bad debts

A company cannot claim a deduction for a bad debt unless it satisfies either:

- a continuity of ownership test (ITAA97 s 165-123), or
- a business continuity test (ITAA97 s 165-126).

The continuity of ownership test (COT) and the business continuity test for bad debts are similar to the tests laid down for company losses (¶3-105 – ¶3-120). Certain modifications to the tests apply in relation to widely held companies (¶3-130) and consolidated groups and MEC groups (¶8-020).

See also the general rules governing bad debt deductions (¶16-580 – ¶16-584).

Continuity of ownership test

Where the debt was incurred in an earlier income year, the company must satisfy the COT from the day on which the debt was incurred until the end of the income year in which it is deducted (ITAA97 ss 165-120; 165-123).

Where a debt is incurred and written off in the *same* income year, the COT must be satisfied for the whole income year (ss 165-120(2); 165-123). However, a debt that is both incurred and written off as bad *on the last day of an income year* is not deductible (s 165-120(3)).

▶ Example

A debt owing to Lauren Co, which has a 30 June year end, is created on 6 September and written off as bad on 11 March in the following calendar year. The COT must be satisfied from 1 July to 30 June (ie the whole of the income year).

In appropriate circumstances, similar to those applicable for company losses (¶3-105), a tracing of interests is made for the purposes of the COT (ITAA97 ss 165-150 to 165-160).

The COT does not apply to a debt if the Commissioner considers that, having regard to the beneficial owners of the company's shares when the debt became bad, it is unreasonable for the test to apply (s 165-120(1)(b)). The COT is safeguarded in the same way as it is in the prior year loss provisions — the provisions of ITAA97 ss 165-180 to 165-205 are invoked and anti-avoidance provisions (ITAA97 ss 175-80 to 175-90) are similar in operation to the prior year loss anti-avoidance provisions (¶3-105).

Modified COT for certain entities

ITAA97 Subdiv 166-C modifies the COT rules for widely held companies and "eligible Division 166 companies" (¶3-130).

The COT has been modified for companies whose shares have unequal rights to dividends, capital distributions or voting power (¶3-105).

Business continuity test

Where a company fails to satisfy the COT and the Commissioner does not exercise his discretion under s 165-120(1)(b), the company can still claim a deduction for a bad debt if it satisfies the business continuity test (contained in ITAA97 ss 165-210 and 165-211) at the "test time" specified in s 165-126. In broad terms, if the debt was incurred in an earlier year, the company must carry on, throughout the year in which the debt is deducted, the same or a similar business as it did before the test time. If the debt was incurred in the year in which it is deducted, the company must, throughout the remainder of that year, carry on the same or a similar business as it did immediately before the test time.

The similar business test is available in relation to debts that are incurred by a company in the 2015–16 or a later income year and which the company writes off as bad. See further ¶3-125.

Incomplete periods

The COT or business continuity test can be satisfied when the tested company exists for only part of a relevant income year (ITAA97 s 165-255).

Business continuity test: "test time" for bad debts

The business continuity test "test time" for these purposes is set out in s 165-126. It provides for the following default test times to be used when applying the business continuity test in relation to bad debts:

- where practicable, the test time for application of the business continuity test will be the latest time that the company can show that it has satisfied the COT
- where it is not practicable for the company to show that it has maintained the same owners for any period since the incurring of the bad debt:
  - if the debt was incurred before the current year or the company came into being during the current year, the test time will be the end of the day on which the debt was incurred
  - if the debt was incurred in the current year and the company existed throughout that year, the test time is the start of the current year.

Interaction with consolidation regime

In order to allow for the special characteristics of consolidated groups, the COT and business continuity test are modified for the purposes of determining whether an entity that is or has been a member of a consolidated group can deduct a bad debt (ITAA97 Subdiv 709-D: ¶8-020).

Implications for debtor

In the context of bad debts, the debtor must consider the tax implications of the commercial debt forgiveness provisions (¶16-910).

[FITR ¶31-050, ¶65-240]

Cancellation of Subsidiary's Shares

¶3-160 Share cancellations

Substantial tax advantages could arise if a holding company cancelled, for less than market value, shares in itself that were held by a subsidiary company. Special rules cover this situation by providing that:

- the tax effects of the transaction for the subsidiary are determined as if the consideration received was equal to the market value of the shares, and

- the tax consequences for the holding company on the disposal of its interests in the subsidiary are to be determined as if the subsidiary had received market value for the cancelled shares.

A corresponding provision ensures that entities interposed between the holding company and the subsidiary obtain no undue benefit (ITAA36 Pt III Div 16J).

[FTR ¶74-996]

Share Buy-backs

¶3-170 On-market and off-market buy-backs

If a company buys back shares in itself from a shareholder, the tax consequences depend on whether it is an on-market or off-market buy-back (ITAA36 Pt III Div 16K: ss 159GZZZJ to 159GZZZS). An on-market buy-back happens if the share is listed on a stock exchange and the buy-back is made in the ordinary course of business of that stock exchange, except if the transaction is described as special under the stock exchange's rules. Any other buy-back is an off-market buy-back. PS LA 2007/9 provides guidance to ATO staff on the application of various tax laws in connection with on-market and off-market buy-backs.

Off-market share buy-backs

For an off-market buy-back, the difference between the purchase price and that part of the purchase price that is debited against amounts standing to the credit of the company's share capital account (as defined) is treated as a dividend paid to the shareholder out of company profits on the day of the buy-back (s 159GZZZP). The phrase ''an account which the company keeps of its share capital'' in the definition of share capital account is not confined to that which the paid-up capital was originally credited or in which a company ordinarily kept its share capital on contribution. The phrase means an account, whether debited or credited with one or more amounts, that was either a record of a share capital transaction the company entered into or of the company's financial position in relation to its share capital (*Consolidated Media Holdings Ltd*). The ''average capital per share'' methodology is generally preferred for determining the dividend/capital split in an off-market share buy-back (PS LA 2007/9).

For general income tax and CGT purposes the disposal consideration for the share is the buy-back price (s 159GZZZQ). The CGT consequences of a share buy-back are considered at ¶12-640.

If the buy-back price is less than the market value, the market value is treated as the disposal consideration. If the buy-back price is more than the market value, any part of the buy-back price attributable to the excess over the market value is not frankable (¶4-620). TD 2004/22 sets out a methodology for determining the market value in cases involving listed shares. However, the Commissioner will not apply TD 2004/22 in cases of capital only off-market share buy-backs conducted at arm's length (PS LA 2007/9).

▶ Example

Clare owns shares in Buffalo Pty Ltd. Her cost base is $6 per share, and the current market value is $8 per share. Buffalo buys back Clare's shares for $9 per share. The buy-back consideration is debited $2 against the share capital account and $7 against accumulated profits.

The $2 per share debited to the share capital account is a non-assessable return of capital to Clare. The $7 debited to accumulated profits is treated as an assessable dividend. However, only $6 of the dividend component is frankable, because the remaining $1 represents the amount by which the buy-back consideration exceeds the market value of the share.

To prevent the deemed dividend resulting in double taxation, a reduction applies in determining the revenue gain or loss (if any) on the sale of the shares. The buy-back price is reduced by so much of the dividend as is: (a) included in the shareholder's assessable income; or (b) an eligible non-capital amount (ie an amount not debited or attributable to a share capital account or an asset revaluation reserve) (s 159GZZZQ(4)).

Various anti-avoidance provisions should be considered in relation to the terms and circumstances of an off-market buy-back, such as ITAA97 Subdiv 204-D (dividend streaming: ¶4-680); ITAA36 ss 45, 45A and 45B (capital distributions: ¶4-682); and ITAA36 s 177EA (franking credit schemes: ¶30-195).

A company contemplating an off-market share buy-back may wish to obtain a class ruling (¶24-540) setting out the implications for its shareholders. The Commissioner has issued numerous class rulings on this subject, which set out the relevant considerations.

On-market share buy-backs

In the case of an on-market buy-back, no part of the buy-back price is treated as a dividend (s 159GZZZR). The total amount received by the shareholder is, for general income tax and CGT purposes, treated as consideration in respect of the sale of the shares (s 159GZZZS).

Although there is no deemed dividend, a franking debit will arise in the company's franking account on the day of the buy-back (item 9 of the table in ITAA97 s 205-30). The franking debit will be equal to the franking debit that would have arisen if the buy-back had occurred off-market and the dividend had been franked at the entity's benchmark franking percentage (or 100% if the company did not have a benchmark franking percentage for the relevant period).

▶ Example

Jonathan owns 1,000 shares in XYZ Ltd, which he acquired as an investment 6 months earlier for $6 per share. The shares are currently trading on the ASX at $7. XYZ Ltd buys back Jonathan's shares on-market for $8 per share. The buy-back price is debited $2 against the company's share capital account and $6 against accumulated profits. XYZ Ltd's benchmark franking percentage for the period is 50%. The corporate tax rate is 30%.

No part of the $8,000 received by Jonathan would constitute a dividend. Jonathan would derive a capital gain equal to $2,000 ($8,000 – $6,000). A franking debit of $1.07 per share (ie $5 × 50% × 30/70) would arise in XYZ's franking account.

If the buy-back had occurred off-market, a deemed dividend of $6 per share would have arisen, of which $5 per share would have been frankable. (The portion of the $8 consideration that exceeded the $7 market value of the share would not have been frankable.)

Company buying back shares

Share buy-backs are tax-neutral for the company buying back its shares. In determining whether any amount is assessable or deductible (or whether a capital gain or loss has arisen) in respect of the buy-back, the buy-back is taken not to have occurred (s 159GZZZN).

The buy-back provisions apply to non-share equity interests (¶23-115), equity holders and non-share dividends (¶23-125) in the same way that they apply to shares, shareholders and dividends (ITAA36 s 159GZZZIA).

[FTR ¶75-000]

Payments to Associates

¶3-240 Advances, loans and excessive remuneration deemed to be dividends

Advances or loans made by a private company to a shareholder (or an associate of a shareholder) are automatically deemed to be dividends, unless they come within certain specified exclusions (¶4-200). The same applies to debts forgiven by the company.

A deemed dividend may also arise where a private company pays or credits the following amounts to a past or present shareholder or director, or their associate:

- remuneration for services rendered, or
- a retirement or termination allowance, gratuity or compensation (¶4-260).

[FTR ¶55-860, ¶56-000, ¶56-105 – ¶56-455]

Issuing Shares

¶3-260 Issuing shares to acquire assets or services

TR 2008/5 explains the tax consequences for a company of issuing shares for assets or services.

Loss or outgoing

When a company issues shares as consideration for assets or services, the provision of shares is neither a loss nor an outgoing of the company, and therefore no deduction arises under ITAA97 s 8-1, whatever the character or intended use of the assets or services.

However, when a company has incurred a loss or outgoing or expenditure (other than an obligation to issue its shares) to acquire assets or services and *sets off* its obligation in satisfaction of an obligation of the vendor to subscribe for shares in the company, any deductions under s 8-1 to which the company would otherwise be entitled will not be affected.

Trading stock

Where a company issues shares to acquire trading stock from a vendor in the normal course of the vendor's business, no trading stock deductions will arise for the company, as the provision of the shares will not be a loss or outgoing or expenditure of the company. ITAA97 s 70-15 specifies the year in which an outgoing incurred in connection with acquiring trading stock is deductible, but requires that it be deductible under s 8-1.

However, where a company issues shares to acquire what was trading stock of the vendor, and the disposal of the trading stock was *outside the ordinary course of the vendor's business*, the company is treated as having bought the assets for the amount included in the vendor's assessable income for the assets under ITAA97 s 70-95 (¶9-290), and therefore as having incurred expenditure of that amount. This will generally be the market value of the trading stock. The acquiring company will have a corresponding cost for the trading stock.

Cost for purposes of capital allowances

When a company issues shares for depreciating assets, the provision of shares is the provision of a non-cash benefit. Accordingly, the cost of the assets to the company for the purposes of Div 40 will be the market value of the shares at the relevant time (see items 4 and 5 of the table in ITAA97 s 40-185).

Cost for CGT purposes

When a company issues shares as consideration for assets, the provision of shares constitutes the provision of property given, or required to be given in respect of acquiring the assets. Accordingly, the market value of the shares is a component of the cost base of the assets for CGT purposes.

[FITR ¶31-180, ¶114-880]

¶3-265 Bonus shares

Where a company issues bonus shares on or after 1 July 1998 to an existing shareholder for no consideration, the cost of the original shares is generally spread across the original shares and the bonus shares (ITAA36 s 6BA). The exception is where the bonus shares are taken to be a dividend by reason of the anti-avoidance provisions in ITAA36 s 45, 45A or 45B (¶4-682).

▶ **Example**

Fred owns 100 shares in Aussie Co, for which he paid $5 per share. Aussie distributes a 1 for 1 bonus issue for no consideration. The cost of Fred's original shares will be spread across the original shares and the bonus shares, resulting in Fred holding 200 shares with a cost of $2.50 per share.

A company issues shares for no consideration if it credits its capital account with: (a) profits in connection with the issue of the shares; or (b) the amount of any dividend paid to a shareholder and the shareholder does not have a choice whether to be paid the dividend or to be issued with the shares (s 6BA(4)).

If the bonus shares are a dividend, or are taken to be a dividend, the consideration for the acquisition of the shares is so much of the dividend as is included in the taxpayer's assessable income.

In the case of dividend re-investment plans where a shareholder has a choice whether to be paid a dividend or to be issued shares, and chooses to be issued with shares:

- the dividend is taken to have been paid out of profits and credited to the shareholder
- the consideration for the acquisition of the shares is so much of the dividend as is included in the shareholder's assessable income (s 6BA(5)).

The above treatment also applies to non-share dividends (¶23-125) paid to equity holders (s 6BA(7)).

However, where a shareholder in a listed public company chooses to be issued with shares instead of franked dividends (other than certain "minimally franked dividends": ¶4-682) and the company does not credit its share capital account in connection with the issue of those shares, the shares are treated as bonus shares and, subject to the anti-avoidance rules, are not taxed as dividends (s 6BA(6)).

The cost of shares is relevant to the trading stock provisions (¶9-150). For details of the CGT treatment of bonus shares, see ¶12-600.

[FTR ¶4-990]

Co-operative Companies

¶3-420 What is a co-operative company?

To qualify as a "co-operative company" for tax purposes, a company that has share capital must limit the number of shares that any one shareholder may take and must prohibit the quotation of its shares on any stock exchange or in any other public manner (ITAA36 s 117(1)).

Regardless of whether the entity has share capital, it must be established for the purpose of carrying on a business having as one or more of its primary objects:

(1) the acquisition of commodities or goods for disposal or distribution to its members

(2) the disposal or distribution of its members' commodities or goods

(3) the storage, marketing, packing or processing of its members' commodities

(4) the rendering of services to its members

(5) the obtaining of funds from its members in order to make loans to members to enable them to acquire residential or residential/business premises.

TR 1999/14 outlines how to determine the co-operative status of a company, particularly one whose business activities include the making of loans to shareholders.

In determining if a company is a co-operative company, regard should be given to the sole or dominant purpose of the company in the relevant income year by reference to its actual activities during the year (*Brookton Co-operative Society*). A company's status may change from year to year, according to the activities it carries out in that year.

A company meeting the above requirements is deemed *not* to be a co-operative company for any year in which less than 90% of the business it carries on in the ordinary course of that business is with its members (ITAA36 s 118). A ''small'' credit union (notional taxable income under $50,000) that qualifies for exemption from tax (¶3-435) is ineligible for assessment as a co-operative company.

[FTR ¶58-705]

¶3-430 Tax treatment of co-operative companies

Companies qualifying as co-operative companies in an income year are assessable on all receipts of an income character and are specifically made assessable on all sums received, from their members or others, relating to the activities referred to in (1) and (4) at ¶3-420 (ITAA36 s 119). But for this express provision, a co-operative company's receipts from members in relation to those activities might be non-assessable under the mutuality principle (¶3-810).

Distributions from assessable income

Co-operative companies, unlike other companies, are specifically allowed deductions for amounts distributed from assessable income to members as rebates or bonuses based on business done, or as interest or dividends (ITAA36 s 120(1)).

Alternatively, co-operative companies have the option of franking distributions paid to members from assessable income (ITAA97 s 218-5).

No deduction is available for the franked part of a distribution (s 120(4)). Where the distribution is paid within 3 months after the end of the relevant income year (or such longer period allowed by the Commissioner), a co-operative company can elect (for deduction purposes) to treat the distribution as having been made on the last day of the income year (s 120(6)). The actual distribution date is used for the purposes of the imputation rules.

Distributions from other sources

Where part of an unfranked or partly franked distribution by a co-operative company is from a source other than assessable income (eg retained earnings or untaxed gains) the distribution will be apportioned to determine the deductible amount (s 120(5)). It is to be assumed that any imputation credit is attached, to the greatest extent possible, to the part of the distribution that is attributable to a source other than assessable income. This approach maximises the deductible amount.

▶ Example

ABC Co-op Ltd distributes $10 million to its shareholders in the income year. The distributions are all franked 60%. The distributions are sourced $7 million from the sale of pre-CGT land (non-assessable source) and $3 million from current year profits that were included in assessable income.

The $6 million franked portion is assumed to be attached first to the distributions from non-assessable sources, ie it is fully attributable to the $7 million from the sale of the pre-CGT land. The $4 million unfranked portion is therefore attributable $1 million to non-assessable sources and $3 million to current year assessable sources. A deduction is allowed for the part that is both unfranked and attributable to current year assessable sources, ie $3 million.

Other rules for co-operative companies

Co-operative companies are not required to provide a distribution statement for an unfranked distribution (s 218-5).

If a co-operative company breaches the benchmark rule (¶4-660), which requires that all frankable distributions made in a franking period are franked to the same extent, the normal penalties (ie a franking debit or overfranking tax: ¶4-665) apply. There is no other penalty (eg no adjustment of the deductible amount).

Distributions received are generally assessable in the hands of members but a rebate or bonus based on purchases made from the co-operative company is non-assessable unless those purchases were deductible to the member.

A mutual insurance association is treated as a company carrying on an insurance business and is specifically made assessable on insurance premiums received from its members or others (ITAA36 s 121).

Companies that qualify as co-operative companies at all times during the income year are treated as public companies (¶3-015). An incorporated co-operative that converts to a company registered under the *Corporations Act 2001* remains the same entity for ITAA purposes (ID 2004/798).

[FITR ¶217-800 – ¶217-805; FTR ¶58-900, ¶59-000]

Demutualisation

¶3-432 Tax consequences of demutualisation

Life insurance and general insurance organisations

Special provisions specify the tax treatment of transactions likely to occur in connection with the demutualisation of a life or general insurance company or an affiliate company (ITAA36 Pt III Div 9AA, ie ss 121AA to 121AT). The provisions apply to mutual insurance companies and mutual affiliate companies where the demutualisation is carried out in accordance with one of 7 specified methods. A basic requirement is that the members agree to surrender their rights in the mutual company in exchange for shares in the demutualised entity. The shares must generally be listed by ASX Limited within 2 years from the demutualisation resolution day (ie the day that the resolution to proceed with the demutualisation is passed or, where a life assurance company's life insurance business is transferred to another company under a Federal Court-approved scheme, the day on which the transfer of the whole of that business takes place). There are a number of special CGT rules that apply (¶12-650). The non-CGT consequences are broadly:

- no amount is included in a member's assessable income until the member disposes of the allotted shares (or rights to the shares or proceeds of sale)
- before listing of the shares, no ordinary net losses arise on disposal of demutualisation shares or rights to shares
- any franking account surplus of a general insurer or its subsidiaries is reduced to nil at the demutualisation resolution day. No franking credits arise in the franking account of a demutualised life or general insurance company, its mutual affiliates or its wholly-owned subsidiaries in relation to a dividend declared before the demutualisation resolution day and paid on or after that day
- where a holding company or other interposed company acquires shares in a demutualising insurance company, the deemed acquisition cost of those shares properly reflects the deemed acquisition cost of shares issued to policyholders/members.

The demutualisation concessions also apply to a friendly society that was an insurance company at the time of demutualisation and does not have capital divided into shares (s 121AB(1)(c)).

Health insurers

CGT relief applies to private health insurance policyholders when their insurer converts, by demutualising, from being a *not for profit* insurer to a *for profit* insurer (ITAA97 Div 315: ¶12-650).

Friendly societies

There is CGT relief for policyholders of friendly societies (¶3-470), including joint health and life insurers, that demutualise to become for-profit entities (¶12-650).

Non-insurance organisations

The tax consequences where mutual non-insurance organisations demutualise are set out in ITAA36 Sch 2H (ss 326-1 to 326-245). The purpose of these provisions is to remove any taxation impediments that might otherwise arise. For the CGT rules, see ¶12-650. There are provisions which ensure that franking account surpluses of the demutualising entity are retained.

Corporations Act mutual entities

The *Treasury Laws Amendment (Mutual Reforms) Act 2019* introduced a definition of a mutual entity into the *Corporations Act 2001* and made amendments that expressly permit mutual entities registered under the *Corporations Act 2001* to issue equity capital (mutual capital instruments (MCIs)) without risking their mutual structure or status. The ITAA36 and the ITAA97 were amended to clarify that the issue of MCIs by a mutual entity does not cause it to demutualise for income tax purposes (eg ITAA36 s 121AB(1)(d)). The ITAA97 was also amended to ensure that the power of a mutual entity to issue MCIs does not disturb the operation of the mutuality principle in the income tax law to the mutual entity's mutual receipts.

[FTR ¶59-120 – ¶59-226, ¶799-930 – ¶799-960]

Demergers

¶3-433 Tax relief for demergers

Tax relief is available for demergers, ie the restructuring of corporate or trust entities or groups by splitting them into 2 or more entities or groups. The relief applies to spin-offs where underlying ownership is maintained and the demerging entity divests at least 80% of its ownership interests in the demerged entity.

The measures involve CGT relief at both the shareholder and entity levels (¶12-328), and exemption of such spin-offs from dividend taxation, subject to integrity rules (¶4-160).

Credit Unions

¶3-435 Taxation of credit unions

A credit union is classified as a recognised small credit union, a recognised medium credit union or a recognised large credit union in relation to an income year as follows (ITAA36 s 6H):

Recognised classification	Notional taxable income for the relevant income year
small	less than $50,000
medium	$50,000 to less than $150,000
large	$150,000 and above

A credit union's notional taxable income for the above purposes is the amount that would be its taxable income for an income year if none of its income were exempt under ITAA36 s 23G and if it were ineligible for assessment as a co-operative company (¶3-420).

A credit union that is classified as *small* in relation to an income year, and that satisfies the Commissioner on various specified matters, is exempt from tax on interest derived from loans to members (s 23G). The exemption does not extend to rent of premises or to income from outside investments, eg interest on marketable securities. Nor does it extend to an association where membership consists solely of credit unions or a federation of such associations. A credit union that qualifies for the s 23G exemption is ineligible for assessment as a co-operative company.

Member loan interest received by a credit union is not exempt in any year when the credit union is classified as medium or large.

Large credit unions are taxed at the corporate tax rate (which from the 2017–18 income year depends on whether or not the credit union is a base rate entity) (¶3-055).

A medium credit union is subject to an effective tax rate based on a sliding scale (between nil and the large credit union rate) according to its level of taxable income.

A credit union that is classified as medium or large in the relevant year is allowed to be taxed as a co-operative company if it satisfies the requirements of ITAA36 s 117 (¶3-420). In such a case, interest received by the credit union is taken to be assessable income for the rendering of services (ITAA36 s 119(2)).

See ¶42-025 for the rates of tax applicable to credit unions.

[FTR ¶5-320, ¶11-245]

Copyright Collecting Societies

¶3-450 Taxation of copyright collecting societies

The rules governing the taxation of copyright societies are disbursed throughout the Act. The precise meaning of "copyright collecting society" is set out in ITAA97 s 995-1(1). Broadly speaking, it refers to a company that administers rights of copyright on behalf of copyright owners such as authors and composers. Copyright owners generally become members of the society. Copyright income is collected by the society. Administrative costs are recovered from that income, and the balance is held pending identification of, and allocation to, the appropriate copyright owners. After recovery of costs, copyright income is distributed to the appropriate members (copyright owners) or may be held in trust for non-member copyright owners or members who cannot be located. The statutory definition of "copyright collecting society" includes a requirement that a member (as defined) of the society cannot direct the body to pay an amount at a particular time. Other restrictions apply under the *Copyright Act 1968*, the definition of copyright collecting society in s 995-1(1) or ITR97. For example, the societies cannot pay dividends and their membership must be open to all relevant copyright owners.

Copyright collecting societies are considered to be discretionary trusts, but a special taxation regime applies to them (see particularly, ITAA97 ss 15-22 and 51-43). In summary, members are assessed on payments of copyright income and non-copyright income received from a society except to the extent that the income is or has been subject to tax in the hands of the society. So that members will know how much of a payment to include in their assessable income, the societies are required to provide notices to them setting out the relevant information (ITAA97 Div 410).

Visual artists

Analogous treatment to the above applies to royalties collected by the resale royalty collecting society which has been established in relation to visual artists royalty entitlements under the *Resale Royalty Right for Visual Artists Act 2009* (¶10-510).

[FITR ¶53-270, ¶102-585, ¶388-000]

Friendly Societies

¶3-470 Taxation of friendly societies

Taxation of friendly societies can fall under several regimes, depending on the particular society's activities.

Life insurance companies

Friendly societies that are registered under the *Life Insurance Act 1995* are categorised as life insurance companies and are taxed under the tax regime applying to such companies (¶3-480).

Income bonds

An "income bond" is a life insurance policy issued by a friendly society under which bonuses are regularly distributed (ITAA97 s 995-1(1)).

Amounts credited to income bonds are non-reversionary bonuses and are included in the bondholder's assessable income under ITAA97 s 15-75 (¶10-240).

Investment income derived by friendly societies on income bonds issued before 1 January 2003 is non-assessable non-exempt income (ITAA97 s 320-37(1)(d)).

Investment income attributable to income bonds issued on or after 1 January 2003 will be included in the friendly societies' assessable income. To prevent double taxation (at the investor and friendly society levels), friendly societies will be entitled to a deduction for investment income paid or credited to holders of income bonds issued on or after 1 January 2003.

Scholarship plans

A scholarship plan is a life insurance policy issued by a friendly society for the sole purpose of providing benefits to help in the education of nominated beneficiaries. It must not be used as security for borrowing or raising money (s 995-1(1)).

Capital and investment income in relation to scholarship plans can be divisible, ie the capital may be returned to the investor and investment income paid to the nominated student.

Investment benefits paid to or on behalf of a nominated student are included in the student's assessable income. Where the nominated student is under 18 years of age, ITAA36 Pt III Div 6AA (unearned income of minors — ¶2-160 and following) will also apply. The amount assessable to the student is calculated under ITAA97 s 15-60 where the investment income attributable to the plan is not exempt income of the friendly society. In that case, the assessable amount is the amount of the benefit reduced by any part of that benefit that reasonably relates to: (a) the premiums related to the benefit; and (b) fees and charges that have been included in the friendly society's assessable income under ITAA97 s 320-15(1)(k).

If some or all of the investment benefits accrued under a scholarship plan are returned to the investor (eg because the student does not proceed to the specified level of education), the policy will not qualify as a scholarship plan and the investment benefits will be taxed under ITAA36 s 26AH as ordinary life insurance investment policy bonuses (¶10-240).

Investment income derived by friendly societies on scholarship plans issued before 1 January 2003 is generally non-assessable non-exempt income if the friendly society that issued the plan is not carried on for profit or gain to individual members (s 320-37(1)(d)).

Friendly societies include in assessable income investment earnings attributable to scholarship plans that are not covered by the above exclusions. To prevent double taxation, they are also entitled to a deduction for investment income paid or credited on or after that date to nominated students under those scholarship plans (ITAA97 s 320-112). No deduction is allowed to the friendly society for any investment benefits accrued under the plan that are paid back to the investor (eg because the nominated student does not proceed to the specified level of education).

Funeral policies

A funeral policy is a life insurance policy issued by a friendly society for the sole purpose of providing benefits to pay for the funeral of the insured person (s 995-1(1)).

If the recipient of the proceeds of a funeral policy issued before 1 January 2003 is the trustee of the policyholder's estate, the proceeds are exempt by virtue of s 26AH(7) and ITAA97 s 118-300. Funeral policies issued on or after 1 January 2003 are specifically excluded from the operation of s 26AH; instead the trustee is assessable on the investment return under ITAA97 s 15-55 at the time of receipt. The assessable amount is the benefit paid by the friendly society, reduced by any part of that benefit that reasonably relates to: (a) the premiums paid by the policyholder; and (b) fees and charges that have been included in the friendly society's assessable income under s 320-15(k).

If the recipient of the proceeds of a funeral policy is a funeral director, the entire amount received is income according to ordinary concepts. Accordingly, the funeral director is assessable under ITAA97 s 6-5 on the whole of the proceeds of the policy (both the capital and the investment return) at the time of receipt.

Investment income derived by friendly societies on funeral policies issued before 1 January 2003 is non-assessable non-exempt (s 320-37(1)(d)).

Investment income attributable to funeral policies issued on or after 1 January 2003 is included in a friendly society's assessable income. To prevent double taxation, the friendly society is allowed a deduction for benefits paid in the income year under those policies (ITAA97 s 320-111). The amount of the deduction is the amount of the benefit reduced by any part thereof that is claimable as a deduction under ITAA97 s 320-75. This part represents the capital component of the premium paid for the policy.

▶ Example

Eduardo buys a funeral policy with Rolling Hills Friendly Society on 1 February 2013 and pays a premium of $6,000. The premium includes an entry fee of $250. Rolling Hills includes $6,000 in assessable income and can deduct $5,750 under s 320-75.

Upon Eduardo's death, Rolling Hills pays $7,900 to Eduardo's estate. Rolling Hills can claim a deduction under s 320-111 for $2,150 (ie $7,900 – $5,750).

The trustee of Eduardo's estate will include $1,900 (ie $7,900 – $6,000) in the estate's assessable income.

If Eduardo had assigned the funeral policy to a funeral director, none of the benefits would be assessable to the estate, and the funeral director would include the full $7,900 in its assessable income.

Friendly society dispensaries

A friendly society dispensary (s 995-1(1)) is taxed as a non-profit company in accordance with the mutuality principle (¶3-810). This principle excludes from tax all receipts from members, but leaves exposed to tax the profit (taxable income) arising from the following classes of receipts:

- all amounts received from the Commonwealth for the supply of pharmaceutical benefits, whether to members or non-members
- proceeds of the sale or supply of goods and services to persons who are not members of the friendly society dispensary
- investment income.

A non-profit company, such as a friendly society dispensary, pays no tax on the first $416 of taxable income. Tax is then shaded in at the rate of 55% of the excess over $416 until the tax on taxable income equals the relevant corporate tax rate (30% for the 2019–20 and 2020–21 income years but 27.5% and 26% respectively if the non-profit company is a base rate entity for the income year) (*Income Tax Rates Act 1986* s 23(6)). Where the taxable income exceeds the shade-in limit, the full taxable income is effectively taxed at the relevant company rate. See further ¶42-025.

Friendly society dispensaries are excluded from co-operative company tax status under ITAA36 s 117.

Health insurance business

Health insurance income derived by a friendly society registered under the *National Health Act 1953* is exempt (ITAA97 s 50-30).

Other friendly societies

Friendly societies that are not covered under the above categories are taxed as non-profit companies under the mutuality principle in the same manner as friendly society dispensaries. Friendly societies exclusively engaged in such businesses as aged care accommodation, hostels and retirement villages are taxed in this way.

Demutualisation of friendly societies

There is CGT relief for policyholders of friendly societies, including joint health and life insurers, that demutualise (¶12-650).

[FITR ¶18-285, ¶102-135, ¶310-040]

Corporate Limited Partnerships

¶3-475 Taxation of corporate limited partnerships

A ‘‘limited partnership’’ is:

- an association of persons (other than a company) carrying on business as partners or in receipt of ordinary income or statutory income jointly, where the liability of at least one of the persons is limited, or
- an association of persons with a separate legal personality that was formed solely for the purpose of becoming a venture capital limited partnership (VCLP), an early stage venture capital limited partnership (ESVCLP), an Australian venture capital fund of funds (AFOF) or a venture capital management partnership (VCMP): ¶5-040.

For tax purposes, most limited partnerships are *corporate limited partnerships*; ie they are effectively treated as companies that are separate taxable entities (ITAA36 s 94D; *Resource Capital Fund IV LP* (application for special leave to appeal to High Court refused)). However, a VCLP, an ESVCLP, an AFOF or a VCMP (¶5-040) cannot be a corporate limited partnership and such an entity that becomes a corporate limited partnership cannot carry back a tax loss to an income year in which it was one or other of these entities (ITAA97 s 195-72). Also, a limited partnership that is a foreign hybrid limited partnership (¶5-050) in relation to a year of income cannot be a corporate limited partnership in relation to that year (ITAA36 s 94D(5); ITAA97 s 830-10).

An association of persons who are not a partnership under the general law cannot be a corporate limited partnership; and a conclusive evidence certificate issued under state limited partnership legislation could not dictate otherwise (*D Marks Partnership*; TD 2008/15; TA 2007/5).

An unincorporated association of persons acting only in Australia who do not carry on business in common with a view to profit also cannot be a corporate limited partnership (TD 2008/15).

Modification of the tax law

Where a limited partnership is taxed as a company, the following modifications are made to the tax law:

- a reference to a company or body corporate in ITAA36 s 6 includes a reference to a limited partnership while a reference to a partnership does *not* include a reference to a limited partnership (ITAA36 ss 94J; 94K)
- a dividend includes distributions by a limited partnership to the extent that the distributions are not attributable to profits or gains of an income year in which the partnership was not taxed as a company (ITAA36 s 94L)
- drawings by partners of a limited partnership are deemed to be dividends (ITAA36 s 94M)
- subject to the operation of Div 7A (see below), a reference to a private company does not include a reference to a limited partnership (ITAA36 s 94N)
- a share includes an interest in a limited partnership and a shareholder includes a partner in such a partnership (ITAA36 ss 94P; 94Q)
- a liquidator includes a partner who winds up a limited partnership (ITAA36 s 94R)
- a change in the composition of a limited partnership does not affect the continuity of the partnership for tax purposes (ITAA36 s 94S)
- a limited partnership is a resident of Australia if it was formed in Australia, carries on business in Australia or has its central management and control in Australia (ITAA36 s 94T)
- obligations that would be imposed on a limited partnership are imposed on each of the partners but may be discharged by any one of them, ie: (a) partners are jointly and severally liable to pay any amount payable by the partnership; and (b) any tax offence committed by a limited partnership is taken to have been committed by each of the partners, although it is a defence if the partner did not aid, abet or counsel the relevant act or omission and was not knowingly involved in or party to it (ITAA36 s 94V).

The fact that a corporate limited partnership is treated as not being a private company led to arrangements utilising corporate limited partnerships to seek to avoid the operation of the Div 7A private company payment, loan and debt forgiveness rules. To overcome these arrangements, it is now provided, with effect from 1 July 2009, that a closely held corporate limited partnerships (less than 50 members or where an entity has direct or indirect beneficial interest in at least 75% of the income or capital of the partnership) is taken to be a private company for the purposes of Div 7A (ITAA36 s 109BB).

A Bermudan exempted limited partnership was a corporate limited partnership; it was not a foreign hybrid limited partnership, as Bermuda does not impose tax on income, profits, dividends or wealth (ID 2006/149).

CGT implications

The ATO considers that there is no capital gain or loss at the time of conversion of a partnership to a limited partnership (ID 2010/210). The cost base of the assumed shares in the limited partnership would be the sum of the cost bases of each partner's interests in the individual assets of the partnership and in the partnership itself.

Foreign hybrid business entities

Foreign hybrid business entities are entities (such as UK and US limited partnerships) that are treated as partnerships for foreign tax purposes and were formerly treated as companies for Australian tax purposes (ITAA97 Div 830). They are now treated as partnerships for Australian tax purposes. A UK limited partnership (UKLP) was a foreign hybrid limited partnership (ID 2006/334; ITAA97 s 830-10). For further details, see ¶5-050.

[FITR ¶632-000 – ¶632-145; FTR ¶49-650, ¶49-690]

Life Insurance Companies

¶3-480 Tax regime for life insurance companies

Life insurance companies are taxed under ITAA97 Div 320. The intent is to tax life insurance companies in a broadly comparable way to other entities that derive similar kinds of income. A "life insurance company" is a company registered under the *Life Insurance Act 1995* (ITAA97 s 995-1(1)). Companies registered under that Act include friendly societies that carry on life insurance business.

Broadly, life companies are taxed on all their profits, including:

- all management fees (except for management fees that are exempt from tax under transitional arrangements)
- underwriting profit
- profit on immediate annuity business.

A life company can segregate certain assets into "complying superannuation assets" (relating to the company's complying superannuation business) and "segregated exempt assets" (relating to immediate annuity and current pension business). Income derived from complying superannuation assets is taxed at a rate of 15%; income from segregated exempt assets is non-assessable non-exempt (¶3-505).

Division 320 also provides that the same CGT modifications that apply to complying superannuation funds also apply to the complying superannuation business of life insurance companies.

[FITR ¶310-000]

¶3-490 Classes of taxable income of life insurance companies

The taxable income of a life insurance company is divided into 2 classes:

(1) the ordinary class — which is taxed at the corporate tax rate

(2) the complying superannuation class — which is taxed at a rate of 15%.

Alternatively, the company may have a tax loss of each class, or a taxable income of one class and a tax loss of the other class (ITAA97 s 320-135). The company's tax losses of a particular class can be deducted only from its income in respect of that class (ITAA97 s 320-134).

The company's basic income tax liability (before tax offsets) is worked out separately for each class. The company's tax offsets are then deducted from the sum of these amounts to arrive at the company's income tax on its taxable income for the income year (s 320-134).

Ordinary class of taxable income

The "ordinary class" of taxable income of a life insurance company is worked out on the basis of only:

- assessable income that is not covered by ITAA97 s 320-137(2) (complying superannuation class)
- amounts (other than tax losses) that the company can deduct and are not covered by s 320-137(4) (complying superannuation class)
- tax losses that are of the ordinary class (ITAA97 s 320-139).

Tax losses of the ordinary class are worked out on the basis of the relevant assessable income and deductions (above) and net exempt income of the company that is not attributable to exempt income derived from the company's complying superannuation assets (while they were complying superannuation assets).

Tax loss adjustments under ITAA97 s 36-55 (converting excess franking offsets to tax loss: ¶3-075) affect only tax losses of the ordinary class. Similarly, a life insurance company that fails to meet the continuity of ownership and business continuity tests for deducting losses will need to recalculate the ordinary class of its taxable income and tax loss under ITAA97 Subdiv 165-B. Its complying superannuation class will not be affected (ITAA97 s 320-149).

A tax loss of the ordinary class can be deducted from: (i) net exempt income of the company that is not attributable to exempt income derived from the company's complying superannuation assets (while they were complying superannuation assets); and (ii) assessable income of the ordinary class, reduced by deductions of the ordinary class (ITAA97 s 320-143).

Any capital losses on ordinary assets (ie assets that are not complying superannuation assets or segregated exempt assets) can only be applied against capital gains from ordinary assets (ITAA97 s 320-120).

Complying superannuation class of taxable income

The "complying superannuation class" of taxable income of a life insurance company is worked out based on:

- assessable income of the types listed below
- deductions of the types listed below
- tax losses of the complying superannuation class (s 320-137).

Relevant assessable income

The items of assessable income that are attributed to the complying superannuation class of taxable income are set out in s 320-137(2) as follows:

- assessable income from the investment of the company's complying superannuation assets
- so much of the assessable life insurance premiums (item 1 of the list in ¶3-495) as is equal to the total transfer value of assets transferred to a complying superannuation asset pool in the income year under ITAA97 s 320-185(3)

- if an asset (other than money) is transferred by the company from a complying superannuation asset pool under ITAA97 s 320-180(1) or 320-185(2) or (3) — amounts that are included in the company's assessable income because ITAA97 s 320-200 deems the asset to be sold and repurchased
- amounts that are included in the company's assessable income because of ITAA97 s 320-15(db), (i) or (j) — listed in ¶3-495
- amounts that are included in the company's assessable income under ITAA97 s 115-280(4), which deals with distributions that flow indirectly from a listed investment company
- assessable income attributable to RSAs.

All other items of assessable income are attributed to the ordinary class of taxable income.

Relevant deductions

The deductions that are attributed to the complying superannuation class of taxable income are set out in s 320-137(4) as follows:

- deductions under ITAA97 s 320-55 (in respect of premiums received for policies that are transferred to complying superannuation assets, excluding amounts attributable to death and disability coverage)
- deductions (other than tax losses) in respect of investment of the company's complying superannuation assets
- deductions under ITAA97 s 320-87(1) and (3)(a) (which deal with transfers of assets from a complying superannuation asset pool)
- deductions under s 115-280(1) (for one-third of dividends received in respect of complying superannuation assets that are shares in a listed investment company)
- so much of the amounts that the company can deduct under ITAA97 s 115-215(6) as are attributable to capital gains that the company is taken to have under s 115-215(3) in respect of complying superannuation assets. This deduction ensures that a beneficiary is not taxed twice on a trust amount that is attributable to a trust estate's net capital gain.

All other deductions of the life insurance company are attributed to the ordinary class of taxable income.

Tax losses of complying superannuation class

A life insurance company's tax loss of the complying superannuation class is worked out on the basis of only the following (ITAA97 s 320-141(1)):

- assessable income covered by s 320-137(2) (see above)
- deductions covered by s 320-137(4) (see above)
- net exempt income of the company that is attributable to exempt income derived from the company's complying superannuation assets.

A tax loss of the complying superannuation class can be deducted only from: (i) net exempt income of the company that is attributable to exempt income derived from its complying superannuation assets; and (ii) assessable income attributable to the complying superannuation class, reduced by deductions attributable to that class (s 320-141(2)).

[FITR ¶310-400]

¶3-495 Assessable income of life insurance companies

The assessable income of a life insurance company includes amounts that are assessable under the general provisions of the income tax law, such as the ordinary income provisions and the CGT provisions.

In addition, because of the nature of its business, the assessable income of a life insurance company specifically includes the following items (identified below by their paragraph designations in ITAA97 s 320-15):

(a) life insurance premiums paid to the company in the income year (eg amounts paid by a policyholder for a life insurance policy or to purchase an annuity, including a deferred annuity). This includes premiums that are due but remain unpaid at the end of the year (ID 2007/41)

(b) amounts received under a contract of reinsurance to the extent that they relate to the *risk* components of claims paid under a life insurance policy. This excludes a reinsurance contract in respect of life insurance policies that are held in the complying superannuation asset pool or in segregated exempt assets of the reinsurance company (the *investment* components of claims are assessable under ITAA36 s 26AH). It also excludes a risk that is reinsured with a foreign resident (ITAA36 s 148(1))

(c) refunds (or amounts in the nature of refunds) of reinsurance premiums paid under a contract of reinsurance (excluding risks that are reinsured with foreign residents)

(ca) reinsurance commissions received or recovered by the company (excluding risks that are reinsured with foreign residents)

(d) amounts received under a profit-sharing arrangement under a contract of reinsurance

(da) the transfer values of assets transferred by the company from a complying superannuation asset pool under ITAA97 s 320-180(1) or 320-195(3)

(db) the transfer values of assets transferred by the company to a complying superannuation asset pool under s 320-180(3) or 320-185(1)

(e) the amount included in assessable income under ITAA97 s 320-200 (which deems a market value sale and repurchase) where an asset is transferred from or to a complying superannuation asset pool in various circumstances (¶3-515)

(f) the transfer values of assets transferred by the company from segregated exempt assets under ITAA97 s 320-235(1) or 320-250(2) (¶3-520)

(g) the amount included in assessable income under ITAA97 s 320-255 (which deems a market value sale and repurchase) where an asset is transferred to the segregated exempt assets in certain circumstances (¶3-520)

(h) amounts representing a decrease in the value of the net risk components of risk policy liabilities from the previous year end (see below) — not applicable to liabilities under an exempt life insurance policy, a funeral policy or a life insurance policy that provides for participating benefits or discretionary benefits

(i) amounts specified in agreements under ITAA97 s 295-260 (¶13-125), which deals with transfers of tax liabilities on assessable contributions

(j) specified roll-over amounts (ie the untaxed element of the post-June 83 component of an ETP roll-over) used to purchase a deferred annuity or an immediate annuity

(ja) premiums received by the company in respect of risk riders for ordinary investment policies where the company did not receive any life insurance premiums for those policies in that income year (s 320-15(ja)). An ordinary investment policy is one that is not: (i) a complying superannuation life insurance policy or exempt life insurance policy; (ii) a policy that provides for participating benefits or discretionary benefits; or (iii) a policy (other than a funeral policy) under which amounts are to be paid only on the death or disability of a person

(k) fees and charges imposed by the company on life insurance policies (where not otherwise taken into account in assessable income)

(l) taxable contributions made to any RSAs provided by the company that would be assessable under ITAA97 Subdiv 295-C if it applied to the company. Subdivision 295-C deals with the taxation of contributions received by superannuation entities.

Management fees included in assessable income

The assessable income of a life insurance company includes all explicit and implicit fees charged by the company. Examples are premium-based fees, establishment fees, time-based account fees, asset fees, switching fees, surrender penalties, buy/sell margins, exit fees and interest on overdue premiums. Quantifying fee income of a life insurance company can be a complex process requiring the use of actuarial models. This process is discussed in TR 2003/14.

All premium-based fees, regardless of their type, are taxed in the period the premiums are paid (this arises as a consequence of including total premiums in assessable income and allowing deductions for certain components of those premiums based on the entitlement of the policyholders).

Fees derived on life insurance policies held in a complying superannuation asset pool, or in segregated exempt assets, are included in assessable income and taxed at the corporate tax rate. This result is a consequence of provisions that relate the transfer value of segregated assets to the value of policyholder liabilities.

[FITR ¶310-070, ¶310-130]

¶3-500 Exempt income of life insurance companies

The following amounts received by a life insurance company are exempt from income tax (ITAA97 s 320-35):

- ordinary income and statutory income accrued before 1 July 1988 on assets that have become complying superannuation assets (this ensures that income derived before 1 July 1988 on assets supporting complying superannuation business is exempt from tax)
- amounts that are credited to an RSA (¶13-470) that is paying out an immediate annuity.

[FITR ¶310-150, ¶310-170]

¶3-505 Non-assessable non-exempt income of life insurance companies

The following items are ''non-assessable non-exempt income'' (¶10-890) of a life insurance company:

- ordinary income and statutory income derived on segregated exempt assets (ie assets that support immediate annuity and current pension business and business from constitutionally protected superannuation funds) (ITAA97 s 320-37(1)(a)). Franked dividends derived on such assets are eligible for tax offsets (ITAA97 s 207-110). Capital gains derived from this business are disregarded under ITAA97 s 118-315
- amounts received from the disposal of units in a PST (¶13-430: s 320-37(1)(b)). Capital gains derived from the disposal of units in a PST are disregarded under ITAA97 s 118-350

- the foreign resident portion of foreign source income derived by an Australian/overseas fund or an overseas fund that is attributable to policies issued by foreign permanent establishments (s 320-37(1)(c), (1A)). The foreign resident proportion of foreign establishment amounts is worked out using the formula in s 320-37(2)
- income derived by friendly societies that is attributable to income bonds, funeral policies, sickness policies and most scholarship plans issued before 1 January 2003 (¶3-470: s 320-37(1)(d)). Where the income consists of franked distributions, it is eligible for tax offsets (s 207-110).

[FITR ¶118-315ff, ¶154-450ff, ¶310-160]

¶3-510 Specific deductions for life insurance companies

A life insurance company is entitled to specific deductions for the following:

- certain components of life insurance premiums, as provided in ITAA97 ss 320-55 to 320-75
- the risk component of claims paid under life insurance policies, other than policies that provide participating benefits or discretionary benefits, exempt life insurance policies, FHSAs and funeral policies (ITAA97 s 320-80)
- an increase in the value of the net risk components of risk policy liabilities, other than policies that provide participating benefits or discretionary benefits, exempt life insurance policies, FHSAs and funeral policies (ITAA97 s 320-85). The net risk component is so much of the policy's risk component as is not reinsured
- reinsurance premiums paid (ITAA97 s 320-100)
- amounts relating to assets (other than money) that are transferred to or from a complying superannuation asset pool in certain circumstances (ITAA97 s 320-87; ¶3-515)
- the transfer value of assets that are transferred to segregated exempt assets in certain circumstances (ITAA97 s 320-105; ¶3-520)
- interest credited by friendly societies to holders of income bonds issued after 31 December 2002; to nominated students under scholarship plans issued after that date; and to beneficiaries of funeral policies issued after that date (ITAA97 ss 320-110 to 320-112; ¶3-470).

Amounts credited to RSAs

A life insurance company is *not* entitled to a deduction for any amounts credited to RSAs (ITAA97 s 320-115).

[FITR ¶310-200]

¶3-515 Complying superannuation asset pools

A life insurance company can create a segregated pool of assets known as a "complying superannuation asset pool", to be used for the sole purpose of discharging its complying superannuation liabilities (ITAA97 s 320-170).

Annual valuation and transfer of assets

The "transfer value" (market value less allowance for expected disposal costs: ITAA97 s 995-1(1)) of complying superannuation assets, and the amount of the company's complying superannuation liabilities, must be determined as at the end of each income year (the "valuation time") (ITAA97 s 320-175). (The time of joining or leaving a consolidated group is also a valuation time: ITAA97 s 713-525.) The valuation must be made within 60 days after each valuation time.

Once determined, the transfer value of the complying superannuation assets is compared with the sum of:

- the company's complying superannuation liabilities, and
- any reasonable provision in the company's accounts for income tax liabilities in respect of the assets.

If the value of the complying superannuation assets exceeds the above obligations, the company must (within 30 days after the day on which the valuations were completed) transfer out assets having a transfer value equal to the excess (ITAA97 s 320-180). The transfer is taken to occur at the valuation time. An administrative penalty applies where a life insurance company fails to comply with the valuation or transfer requirements (TAA Sch 1 s 288-70).

Where there is an asset shortfall at year end, the company can transfer additional assets (up to the amount of the shortfall) into the complying superannuation asset pool. This is also taken to occur at the valuation time, provided the transfer is made within 30 days after the annual valuation is performed.

Other asset transfers to a complying superannuation asset pool

Other than as mentioned above, there are only 3 circumstances in which asset transfers *to* a complying superannuation asset pool are permitted (ITAA97 s 320-185):

- to reduce or eliminate an asset shortfall at a time other than year end (determined in the same way as at year end)
- in exchange for money equal to the transfer value of the asset at the time of transfer
- an asset transfer not exceeding the value of any premiums received by the company in the income year for the purchase of complying superannuation life insurance policies.

Other asset transfers or payments from a complying superannuation asset pool

A life insurance company *must* transfer assets from or pay amounts from a complying superannuation asset pool in the following circumstances (ITAA97 s 320-195):

- to eliminate any excess where it determines that there is an excess of complying superannuation assets (determined in the same way as for the annual valuation above)
- when fees or charges are imposed by the company in respect of complying superannuation assets or complying superannuation life insurance policies other than certain policies that provide death or disability benefits
- to discharge any liabilities under its complying superannuation life insurance policies or pay any expenses incurred directly in respect of its complying superannuation assets
- to pay any unpaid PAYG instalments or income tax liabilities that are attributable to the company's complying superannuation assets.

The company can also transfer assets from its complying superannuation asset pool in exchange for an equal value of money at the time of transfer.

Consequences of transfer to or from complying superannuation assets

The consequences of transfers of assets into or from the complying superannuation asset pool (other than a transfer to segregated exempt assets: ¶3-520) are set out in ITAA97 s 320-200, the main outcomes of which are:

- for income tax purposes the asset is deemed to have been sold at market value immediately before the transfer and purchased again at market value at the time of transfer
- any resulting deduction (other than deductions in relation to depreciating assets under ITAA97 Div 40 or former Div 42) or capital loss is disregarded until the asset ceases to exist or a non-associated entity acquires a greater than 50% interest in it.

Transfer of complying superannuation assets to segregated exempt assets

Where a complying superannuation life insurance policy becomes an exempt life insurance policy (eg when a deferred annuity policy becomes an immediate annuity policy) provision is made for transferring assets from the complying superannuation asset pool to segregated exempt assets. The transfer value of the assets cannot exceed the value of the company's liabilities in respect of the policy, plus any reasonable provision made in the company's accounts for liability for income tax in respect of the assets being transferred (s 320-195(1)).

CGT treatment of complying superannuation assets

ITAA97 ss 295-85 and 295-90 apply for the purposes of working out any capital gain or capital loss that arises from a CGT event that involves a complying superannuation asset (ITAA97 s 320-45).

A discount rate of one third applies to discount capital gains by a life insurance company from a complying superannuation asset (ITAA97 s 115-100).

[FITR ¶310-180, ¶310-360, ¶310-500]

¶3-520 Segregated exempt assets of life insurance companies

A life insurance company may maintain a pool of segregated assets (known as "segregated exempt assets"). Segregated exempt assets must be used for the sole purpose of discharging the company's liabilities under exempt life insurance policies (ITAA97 s 320-225). This purpose includes the payment of fees and expenses in respect of the policies or the segregated exempt assets.

An "exempt life insurance policy" is a life insurance policy (other than an RSA) that fulfils any *one* of the following criteria (ITAA97 s 320-246):

- it is held by the trustee of a complying superannuation fund and provides solely for the discharge of liabilities for superannuation income stream benefits that are currently retirement phase superannuation income stream benefits of the fund
- it is held by the trustee of a PST and the policy provides solely for the discharge of liabilities for retirement benefit superannuation income stream benefits that are currently payable by complying superannuation funds that are unit holders of the trust
- it is held by another life insurance company as a segregated exempt asset of that other company
- it is held by the trustee of a constitutionally protected superannuation fund
- it provides for an annuity that is not an immediate annuity and is a superannuation income stream that is in the retirement phase
- it provides for an eligible immediate annuity, or
- it provides for a personal injury annuity and/or a personal injury lump sum (¶10-185), payments of which are exempt under ITAA97 Div 54.

The ordinary income and statutory income derived from the segregated exempt assets (being income relating to the segregation period) is non-assessable non-exempt under ITAA97 s 320-37(1)(a). Capital gains and capital losses made from segregated exempt assets are disregarded (ITAA97 s 118-315).

Annual valuation and transfer of assets

Within 60 days after the end of each income year, the company must calculate the "transfer value" (ie market value less allowance for expected disposal costs) of the segregated exempt assets, and the amount of the company's exempt life insurance policy liabilities, as at the end of the year (the "valuation time") (ITAA97 s 320-230). (The time of joining or leaving a consolidated group is also a valuation time: ITAA97 s 713-525.) Any excess assets above the liabilities must be transferred from the pool within 30 days of the annual valuation. The transfer is deemed to have occurred at the valuation time (ITAA97 s 320-235). An administrative penalty applies where a life insurance company fails to comply with the valuation or transfer requirements (TAA Sch 1 s 288-70).

Conversely, assets can be transferred to segregated exempt assets to offset a shortfall. Where the transfer is made within 30 days of the annual valuation, it is taken to have occurred at the valuation time.

Other transfers to segregated exempt assets

Apart from a shortfall at the annual valuation time, there are only 4 other circumstances in which assets can be transferred to segregated exempt assets:

- to partially or fully offset a shortfall of segregated exempt assets as at some date other than year end, determined in the same way as for the annual valuation (ITAA97 s 320-240(1))
- in exchange for money equal to the transfer value of the asset at the time of transfer (s 320-240(2))
- to cover life insurance premiums paid to the company in that income year for the purchase of exempt life insurance policies (s 320-240(3)), or
- where assets are transferred from complying superannuation assets to segregated exempt assets (¶3-515) to cover a complying superannuation life insurance policy that has become an exempt life insurance policy, eg a deferred annuity that has become an immediate annuity (ITAA97 s 320-195(1)).

Other transfers and payments from segregated exempt assets

Apart from the transfer of excess assets as at year end, an insurance company *must* transfer assets from or pay amounts from segregated exempt assets in the following circumstances (ITAA97 s 320-250):

- to eliminate any excess segregated exempt assets identified at any other time
- to cover any fees or charges imposed by the company in respect of the segregated exempt assets or the exempt life insurance policies supported by those assets
- to discharge any liabilities on exempt life insurance policies supported by segregated exempt assets
- to pay any expenses incurred directly by the company in respect of the segregated exempt assets.

The company can also transfer assets from its segregated exempt assets in exchange for an amount of money equal to the transfer value of the assets at the time of transfer.

From the 2017–18 income year, if a life insurance policy issued by a life insurance company becomes a complying superannuation life insurance policy and, immediately before that time, it was an "exempt life insurance policy", the company can transfer from its segregated exempt assets, to a complying superannuation asset pool, assets of any kind whose total transfer value does not exceed the company's liabilities in respect of the policy (s 320-250(1A)).

Tax consequences of transfers to or from segregated exempt assets

The tax consequences of transfers of assets to or from segregated exempt assets (other than transfers from complying superannuation asset pools) are set out in ITAA97 s 320-255, the main outcomes of which are:

- assessable income and allowable deductions, including capital gains and capital losses on transfers to segregated exempt assets, are calculated as if the asset were sold for market value consideration immediately before its transfer and repurchased at the time of transfer for the same consideration; however, any resulting deductions (including capital losses) cannot be deducted until the asset ceases to exist or a non-associated entity acquires a greater than 50% interest in it
- a company is not allowed a deduction, including a capital loss, on transfers from segregated exempt assets
- depreciable assets transferred from segregated exempt assets are treated as if they had always been used for assessable income-producing purposes. Their deemed valuation for ongoing depreciation purposes varies:
  - if the unit of plant has been a segregated exempt asset from the time it was acquired by the company or from the time the segregated pool was initially established, the lower of the unit's current market value or notional undeducted cost is used, or
  - otherwise (ie where the asset was previously transferred to segregated exempt assets other than as part of the initial transfer), the lower of the unit's current market value or its market value at the time of the previous inward transfer is used.

Deduction for transfers to segregated exempt assets

A life insurance company can deduct the transfer value of assets transferred to segregated exempt assets under s 320-235(2) or 320-240(1). In addition, if any asset (other than money) is transferred to the company's segregated exempt assets under s 320-235(2) or 320-240, the company may be entitled to a deduction because of s 320-255 (ITAA97 s 320-105). These provisions are discussed above.

[FITR ¶310-740]

¶3-525 Imputation rules for life insurance companies

The imputation rules for life insurance companies are discussed at ¶4-760.

¶3-527 Consolidation rules for life insurance companies

There are a number of special consolidation rules for life insurance companies.

The head company of a consolidated group (¶8-000) is treated as a life insurance company for an income year if one or more life insurance companies are subsidiary members of the group at any time during that year (ITAA97 s 713-505). However, this provision does not operate to give a non-insurance company access to the ITAA36 Pt III Div 9AA demutualisation regime described at ¶3-432 (ID 2007/64).

An entity cannot be a subsidiary member of the same consolidated group or consolidatable group of which a life insurance company is a member if: (a) the life insurance company owns (directly or indirectly) membership interests in the entity; and (b) some of its direct interests in the entity or an interposed entity (accounting for less than 100% of all membership interests in the entity) are complying superannuation assets or segregated exempt assets of the life insurance company (ITAA97 s 713-510).

The single entity rule (¶8-010) is disregarded to recognise intra-group transactions when determining the taxable income of consolidated groups that have life insurance company members. The rule remains valid for tax cost setting rules when a subsidiary member (ie a life insurance company) joins or leaves the consolidated group (ITAA97 s 713-510A).

There are modifications to the cost setting rules (ITAA97 s 713-515) and rules for valuing certain liabilities (ITAA97 s 713-520).

The joining time and leaving time when a life insurance company becomes or ceases to be a subsidiary member of a consolidated group are valuation times for the purposes of ITAA97 ss 320-175 (¶3-515) and 320-230 (¶3-520).

If a life insurance company leaves a consolidated group and no remaining member of the group is a life insurance company, any net capital loss from complying superannuation assets and certain other amounts are transferred to the leaving entity (ITAA97 s 713-530).

[FITR ¶546-200 – ¶546-230]

¶3-528 Transfer of life insurance business

Special rules apply where all or part of a company's life insurance business is transferred to another life insurance company after 30 June 2000 under the *Financial Sector (Transfer and Restructure) Act 1999* or in accordance with a court-approved scheme under the *Life Insurance Act 1995* Pt 9 (ITAA97 Subdiv 320-I). The provisions are designed to alleviate unintended tax consequences that might otherwise arise.

In broad terms, the rules:

- treat the consideration paid in relation to certain transferred life insurance policies as a life insurance premium
- ensure appropriate tax treatment when risk policies are transferred
- ensure, when segregated assets are transferred, that they continue to be treated as segregated assets in the hands of the transferee
- preserve the taxation character of certain pre-1 January 2003 policies issued by friendly societies and pre-10 December 1984 immediate annuity policies, where the transferee issues a substitute policy that is not materially different
- ensure that notionally segregated assets continue to be treated as separate assets after their transfer.

Where the transferor and transferee are members of the same wholly-owned group, the rules also:

- ensure that transitional provisions that apply to continuous disability policies and life insurance policies issued by the transferor before 1 July 2000 continue to apply
- allowed a CGT roll-over to apply to capital gains and capital losses that arose when the life insurance business was transferred before 30 June 2004 (ITTPA Subdivs 126-B; 170-D).

[FITR ¶310-900 – ¶310-945]

RSA Providers

¶3-530 Tax treatment of RSA business

The nature and purpose of retirement savings accounts (RSAs) is discussed at ¶13-470. They are intended to provide a simple, low-cost, low-risk vehicle for superannuation savings. An ADI, life insurance company (¶3-480) or prescribed financial institution approved by APRA can provide RSAs. An ADI (approved deposit-taking institution) is a body corporate which has an authority from APRA to carry on banking business in Australia (eg a bank, building society or credit union).

ADIs that provide RSAs

The tax treatment of ADIs that are RSA providers is governed by ITAA97 Div 295. The taxable income of an ADI that provides RSAs contains up to 3 components (s 295-555):

- the RSA component (taxed at 15%), which relates to the ADI's retirement savings account business
- the FHSA component (taxed at 15%), which relates to the ADI's first home saver accounts business (if any)
- the standard component (taxed at the relevant company tax rate (27.5% or 30%)), which represents the remaining part (if any) of the ADI's taxable income.

If the sum of the RSA component and the FHSA component exceeds the ADI's taxable income, that sum is taken to be the ADI's taxable income, and the excess is treated as a tax loss. In that situation, the standard component would be nil.

The RSA component of taxable income is worked out using the method statement in s 295-555(2) and comprises taxable contributions plus other amounts credited during the year to the provider's RSAs, less any amounts paid from those RSAs (except benefits and tax). Amounts credited to RSAs paying current pensions or annuities are exempt under s 295-410 and are not included in the provider's taxable income.

Life insurance companies that provide RSAs

The RSA business (if any) of a life insurance company is taxed under ITAA97 Div 320, which is discussed at ¶3-480 to ¶3-527. The taxable income from a life insurance company's RSA business is included in the company's complying superannuation class of taxable income, which is taxed at 15% (¶3-490). Although ITAA97 Div 295 (superannuation entities) generally does not apply to RSA providers that are life insurance companies, Subdivs 295-I and 295-J (about no-TFN contributions) do apply (ss 295-5(4); 320-155).

[FITR ¶310-000, ¶310-450]

Foreign Multinational Enterprises

¶3-540 Deduction for dividend on-paid to foreign resident owner

A deduction may be allowed for on-payments of unfranked non-portfolio dividends (including non-share dividends) by an Australian resident company to its foreign resident parent (ITAA36 s 46FA). The deduction is not available for dividends paid by or to a prescribed dual resident company. A ‘‘non-portfolio dividend'' is, broadly, a dividend paid to a company with at least a 10% voting interest in the company paying the dividend.

The deduction generally applies where:

- an Australian resident company (A) pays a non-portfolio unfranked or partly franked dividend (the ‘‘original dividend'') to another Australian resident company (B), and the unfranked part of the dividend would have been eligible for the former inter-corporate dividend rebate were it not for ITAA36 former s 46F(2)(a)(i), 46AB(1) or 46AC(2) (which denied the rebate for unfranked dividends paid outside a wholly-owned group, paid after 30 June 2003 or paid to a member of a consolidated group, respectively)

- A and B are not members of the same wholly-owned company group in the year in which the dividend is paid
- B on-pays an unfranked or partly-franked dividend (the ''flow-on dividend'') to its foreign resident parent company. The flow-on dividend can be paid in the same year as the original dividend, or in a later year
- before paying the flow-on dividend, B makes a written ''flow-on declaration'' that a percentage (up to 100%) of the unfranked amount of the flow-on dividend (the ''flow-on amount'') is an on-payment of the unfranked amount of the original dividend. The declaration cannot be revoked or varied, and
- the flow-on amount does not exceed the amount in B's unfranked non-portfolio dividend account (see below).

B must be an Australian resident company, and its foreign resident parent company must hold and beneficially own all the shares of B: (a) when B receives the original dividend from A; (b) when B makes the flow-on declaration; and (c) when B pays the dividend to its foreign resident parent. The parent company's ownership rights must not be in a position to be affected by another person (TR 2000/15).

If these conditions are met, B may claim the flow-on amount as a tax deduction, effectively freeing the unfranked non-portfolio dividend from income tax. As the distribution to the foreign resident parent is unfranked, it will usually be subject to dividend withholding tax.

Unfranked non-portfolio dividend account

In order to track the on-payment of unfranked non-portfolio dividends, the Australian resident subsidiary needs to establish an ''unfranked non-portfolio dividend account''. It may declare flow-on amounts up to the available credit balance (surplus) in the account.

The account is credited (at the time of payment) with the unfranked amount of any qualifying non-portfolio dividends that the Australian resident subsidiary receives from non-group Australian resident companies. The account is debited (at the time of declaration) with any flow-on amounts that the subsidiary validly declares to be included in the dividends it pays to its foreign resident parent (ITAA36 s 46FB). A debit balance is not permitted.

Interaction with conduit foreign income rules

There may be circumstances in which a dividend that is received and on-paid by a company potentially qualifies for both a deduction under s 46FA and treatment as non-assessable non-exempt income under the conduit foreign income rules (¶21-100). Where both concessions potentially apply, the company may choose whether to avail itself of the deduction under s 46FA or to treat the dividend as non-assessable non-exempt income under ITAA97 s 802-20. However, it is not permitted to do both (ITAA97 s 802-55).

[FTR ¶21-397/10, ¶21-397/20; FITR ¶610-255]

Strata Title Bodies Corporate

¶3-550 Strata title bodies corporate taxed as companies

Strata title bodies corporate are constituted under legislation which, on registration of a strata title scheme, operates to create a special form of legal ownership, referred to in various states as strata title, unit title, group title or cluster title. For tax purposes, they are treated as public companies (TR 2015/3) (¶3-015). They do not qualify as non-profit companies even if they include non-profit clause in their by-laws.

In determining the taxable income, mutual income (¶3-810) is excluded. No deductions are allowed for expenses relating to mutual income.

The assessable (ie non-mutual) income includes interest and dividends, and fees from third parties for giving access to records. Interest paid by a member of a body corporate for late payment of strata title levies is mutual income and not assessable. Expenses directly related to the assessable income, eg bank fees, and a proportion of other expenses may be deducted.

Returns should be prepared on the following basis in respect of common property in strata schemes:

- the income from common property is not assessable income of the strata title body in its capacity as trustee (and is assessable income of the individual proprietors)
- the strata title body is not entitled to any general deductions (under ITAA97 s 8-1) in respect of common property (and proprietors will be entitled to deductions in proportion to their lot entitlements to the extent they otherwise meet the remaining requirements of the general deduction provision), and
- the strata title body is not entitled to any deductions under ITAA97 Divs 40 and 43 in respect of common property (and proprietors will be entitled to deductions in proportion to their lot entitlements to the extent they otherwise meet the remaining requirements in those Divisions) (TR 2015/3).

A strata title body must lodge an income tax return for a year of income if required by the Commissioner. As a strata title body is a company for income tax purposes, it is required to lodge an income tax return for any year of income in which it has derived assessable income or when requested by the Commissioner. Generally, where the only income derived by a strata title body is mutual in nature, that is, consists solely of proprietors' levies or contributions, there is no assessable income, so the strata title body is not required to lodge a return. In cases where income is derived from non-mutual sources (eg interest and dividends from invested funds, fees from non-proprietors for access to books) a return is usually required to be furnished. See the Strata title body corporate tax return and instructions 2020 for instructions on how to complete the tax return. A strata title body should use a Strata title body corporate tax return or a company return form if required.

For CGT roll-over relief on strata title conversions, see ¶12-320.

[FITR ¶18-280]

Pooled Development Funds, SMEs

¶3-555 Special tax treatment of PDFs

The PDF program was closed to new registration applications from 21 June 2007. Until 20 June 2007, eligible investment companies could apply to be registered under the *Pooled Development Funds Act 1992* as pooled development funds (PDFs). PDFs provide equity capital for eligible activities to Australian resident companies with total assets not exceeding $50 million. The investee companies are referred to as small-medium enterprises (SMEs). PDFs are taxed in the same way as other companies except that they are taxed at concessional rates on certain components of income (*Income Tax Rates Act 1986* s 23(4) and (5)). A company acting in the capacity of trustee is not taxed as a PDF. Gains on the disposal of PDF shares are tax-exempt (ITAA36 s 124ZN) and are not subject to CGT (¶12-640).

Progressive replacement of PDF program

Although the PDF program has been replaced by an ''early stage venture capital limited partnership'' (ESVCLP) investment vehicle (¶5-040, ¶11-900), the program continues to operate for PDFs that were registered at the closure date of the program.

2 components of PDF income

The taxable income of a PDF is divided into 2 components:

(1) the SME income component (taxed at 15%)

(2) the unregulated investment component (taxed at 25%).

The purpose of this 2-tier rate structure is to encourage PDFs to invest their uncommitted funds in SMEs, in preference to holding interest-bearing investments for long periods.

The SME income component comprises the SME assessable income less any deductions allowable to the company for the income year (regardless of whether the deductions relate to SME investments). The SME assessable income comprises the non-CGT income derived from, or from the disposal of, the company's SME investments, plus any capital gains allocated to the SME component under ITAA36 s 124ZZB. The deductions allowable for the year include any prior year losses. If the available deductions exceed the SME assessable income, any excess deductions are taken into account in determining the unregulated investment component of taxable income.

The unregulated investment component is the difference between the taxable income of the PDF and the SME income component. Essentially, it is the income derived from lending to banks and from short-term money market deposits, *plus* capital gains allocated to this component under s 124ZZB, *less* any excess deductions that could not be absorbed against SME income. It may also include other non-SME income, such as management fees derived by the PDF.

Company registered as PDF for part of year

Where a company is registered as a PDF for only part of a year, it is taxed as an ordinary company up to the day that it becomes registered as a PDF and from that day is taxed as a PDF (see the definition of ''PDF component'' in ITAA36 s 6(1)). In such a year the company must lodge 2 tax returns, one for each period. However, where a company ceases to be a PDF, it is taxed as an ordinary company for the whole of the relevant year.

Venture capital franking rules

Under the simplified imputation regime (¶4-400), there is a special subcategory of franking applicable only to PDFs, called venture capital franking (ITAA97 Div 210). The venture capital franking rules aim to encourage superannuation funds (and other entities that deal with superannuation) to invest in PDFs. It does this by providing additional tax incentives to eligible investors, over and above the normal benefits of investing in a PDF. Venture capital franking can be ignored by investors other than eligible superannuation-related entities (see below).

Venture capital franking sub-accounts

Each PDF maintains a venture capital sub-account within its franking account (ITAA97 s 210-100). As was the case with franking account balances, venture capital franking sub-account balances were converted to a tax-paid basis (using a 30/70 factor) as at 1 July 2002 (ITTPA ss 210-1 to 210-15).

Venture capital credits

Where a PDF has a franking credit because it has paid income tax or a PAYG instalment, venture capital credits arise in the venture capital franking sub-account to the extent that payments are reasonably attributable capital gains from venture capital investments (ITAA97 s 210-105). Venture capital credits also arise where the PDF incurs a liability to pay venture capital deficit tax.

Venture capital debits

Venture capital debits arise in the sub-account in relation to: payment of a venture capital franked distribution, receipt of relevant tax refunds, failing to venture capital frank a franked distribution to the extent permitted by the surplus, certain cases of dividend streaming, or where the PDF's net venture capital credits for the income year exceed certain limits (ITAA97 ss 210-80; 210-120; 210-125).

Receipt of PDF distribution by relevant venture capital investors

A venture capital credit on a distribution is only significant to a recipient that is a complying superannuation fund or complying ADF (other than a self managed superannuation fund), a PST or a life insurance company. These entities are collectively referred to as "relevant venture capital investors" (ITAA97 s 210-170). The tax treatment of a PDF dividend received by these investors is as follows.

The entire distribution is exempt under ITAA36 s 124ZM, except to the extent that the recipient shareholder elects under s 124ZM(3) to treat a part of the franked portion as assessable (in order to obtain the normal tax offset for the franking credit). Broadly, the election is available for the part of the distribution that is franked but not venture capital franked. The election may appeal to a shareholder whose marginal tax rate is below the corporate tax rate. The election is made by the shareholder disclosing the relevant part of the dividend as income in its tax return for the relevant year.

In addition to the exemption, the investor is entitled to a tax offset under s 210-170 for the year in which the distribution is made, if:

- the recipient is not a partnership or a trustee (other than an "eligible entity": ¶13-120)
- the recipient satisfies the residency requirement (¶4-800)
- the distribution is not exempt income of the recipient (ignoring s 124ZM — discussed below)
- the recipient is a qualified person in relation to the distribution for the purposes of ITAA36 former Pt IIIAA Div 1A (the holding period and related payments rules)
- the distribution is not part of a dividend stripping operation, and
- the Commissioner has not made a determination under ITAA97 s 204-30(3)(c) (anti-streaming provisions: ¶4-680) or ITAA36 s 177EA(5)(b) (franking credit schemes: ¶30-195) that no imputation benefit is to arise.

Where the recipient is entitled to a tax offset under s 210-170, ITAA97 Div 207 (which contains the normal gross-up and tax offset rules for franked dividends) does not apply to the venture capital franked part of the distribution (ITAA97 s 210-180).

Amount of venture capital tax offset

If the recipient is not a life insurance company, the venture capital tax offset is equal to the venture capital credit on the distribution. In the case of a life insurance company, only a pro rata tax offset is available, based on the ratio of its complying superannuation class of taxable income to its total assessable income for the year (ITAA97 s 210-175).

Effect of the venture capital tax offset

The combined effect of the exempt treatment and the venture capital tax offset is that no tax is paid by the recipient, and the recipient recovers tax paid by the PDF on the underlying venture capital gains.

Excess venture capital tax offsets will generally be refundable to the recipient (¶4-820). In the case of a life insurance company, a venture capital tax offset will be refundable only to the extent that the relevant membership interest was not held by the company on behalf of its shareholders at any time during its income year up to the date of the distribution (ITAA97 s 67-25(1E)).

Receipt of PDF distribution by other entities

In the case of recipients other than relevant venture capital investors, the unfranked portion of the distribution is exempt, and the franked portion is exempt unless the recipient elects under s 124ZM(3) to treat it as assessable (as discussed above).

The exempt treatment restricts the effective tax on the underlying PDF income and gains to that paid by the PDF.

Venture capital deficit tax

Venture capital deficit tax (imposed by the *New Business Tax System (Venture Capital Deficit Tax) Act 2003*) is payable if a PDF's venture capital sub-account is in deficit at the end of the PDF's income year, or immediately before it ceases to be a PDF. A tax refund received within 3 months after the balance date is taken into account (to the relevant extent) in determining the sub-account deficit for this purpose. If an entity is liable to pay venture capital deficit tax, its liability to pay franking deficit tax (if any) is reduced accordingly. A payment of venture capital deficit tax gives rise to a franking credit and a venture capital credit (ITAA97 ss 210-135 to 210-150).

Dividend withholding tax

Dividends paid by PDFs to foreign residents are exempt from dividend withholding tax (ITAA36 s 128B(3)(ba)).

Losses

If, in a PDF's first income year, it has a taxable income in the non-PDF period and a tax loss in the PDF period, the PDF is taxed at the normal company rate (¶3-055) on the taxable income for the non-PDF period while the tax loss is carried forward to be offset against future PDF income (ITAA97 s 195-15(4)). Where the PDF incurs a tax loss in the non-PDF period and derives taxable income in the PDF period, the loss may be offset against the PDF income (s 195-15(5)). Losses are first applied against SME assessable income (ITAA36 ss 124ZU; 124ZV).

Losses incurred by PDFs are only deductible in years in which they retain PDF status (ITAA97 s 195-5). PDF losses incurred in the company's first year are recouped before non-PDF losses incurred in that year. For other years, losses are recouped in the order that they are incurred. Non-PDF losses that are not recouped before a company ceases to be a PDF continue to be deductible (s 195-15(5)).

For the purposes of the carry back of tax loss rules (¶3-080), a corporate tax entity is prevented from carrying back a tax loss that arose in an income year it ended as a PDF, unless it was a PDF throughout both the current year and the year the loss was carried back to (ITAA97 s 195-37). There is no restriction on a PDF carrying back any tax loss that arose in a year it did not end as a PDF. Nor is there any restriction on carrying back a tax loss that arose in the part of a year before the company became a PDF (ITAA97 s 195-15(5)).

A net capital loss incurred by a PDF cannot be applied against a net capital gain for a subsequent year, unless the company is a PDF throughout the last day of the later income year (ITAA97 s 195-25). A net capital loss incurred by a PDF that is a member of a company group cannot be transferred (ITAA97 s 195-30). Special rules apply where a company becomes a PDF during an income year (ITAA97 s 195-35).

[FITR ¶210-050 – ¶210-130, ¶215-200 – ¶215-380]

¶3-560 SME investments by lending institutions

Under the provisions of the former ITAA36 Div 11B the CGT provisions (rather than the revenue provisions) applied to eligible equity investments in SMEs (ie companies having a total audited asset value of $50 million or less) made by lending institutions after 30 June 1996 (ITAA36 former ss 128TG; 128TK).

An eligible equity investment was a shareholding of at least 10% of the value of the SME (including the newly issued ordinary shares). Shares acquired by a lending institution before 1 July 1996 did not count towards the 10% threshold. However, where a parcel of shares (that is less than the 10% threshold) was acquired on or after 1 July 1996 and another parcel that brought the total shareholding over the threshold was later acquired, then a deemed disposal and reacquisition at market value occurred when that second parcel of shares was acquired. Any profit or loss on the deemed disposal was brought to account under the revenue provisions in the year in which the shares were *actually* disposed of. The shares acquired under the deemed reacquisition were subject to the CGT provisions and had a cost base equal to the market value of the shares on the date of the deemed reacquisition.

These provisions were repealed by the *Treasury Laws Amendment (2018 Measures No 1) Act 2018* on the basis that the freezing of CGT indexation from 21 September 1999 meant that they no longer provided any benefit to financial institutions.

[FTR ¶69-501 – ¶69-506]

Clubs and Associations

¶3-800 Incorporated associations

All incorporated clubs, societies, organisations and associations are regarded as companies for tax purposes. Unincorporated clubs, societies, organisations and associations that cannot be categorised as partnerships (¶5-000) are also regarded as companies. These will include all social clubs, associations and societies.

Tax exemption applies, subject to certain exceptions, to the incomes of certain associations and clubs, eg trade unions, employer and employee associations and sporting and cultural associations (¶10-605).

Special tax treatment is accorded to certain co-operative societies such as credit unions, small loans societies and building societies that qualify as co-operative companies (¶3-420 – ¶3-430). For the position of friendly society dispensaries, see ¶3-470. As to the treatment of strata title bodies corporate, see ¶3-550. For the taxation issues that arise when an organisation ''demutualises'', see ¶3-432.

When an unincorporated association incorporates, it becomes a different entity. It cannot deduct a tax loss that was incurred in an earlier year prior to its incorporation (ID 2004/811).

[FITR ¶102-000]

¶3-810 Receipts from members — mutuality principle

Under longstanding ATO practice, subscriptions and contributions from members, and payments received from members for particular services provided by the club or association (eg poker machines, bar and dining room service in the case of social clubs), are generally excluded from the assessable income of that club or association. This applies to both incorporated and unincorporated entities.

The explanation for this lies in what is usually referred to as the mutuality principle which, simply, recognises that a person's income consists only of moneys derived from external sources. Where a number of persons contribute to a common fund created and controlled by them for a common purpose, any surplus arising from the use of that fund for the common purpose is not income (unless, of course, the income is derived from sources outside that group).

In the case of registered and licensed clubs, the ATO traditionally stated that the mutuality principle would apply where the club had the following general attributes:

(1) The rules of the club prohibit any distribution of surplus funds to the members.

(2) Upon dissolution of the club, the rules of the club provide that surplus funds must be donated to another club with similar interests and activities.

(3) The operations of the club fall within the ambit of state/federal laws governing clubs.

(4) The club is a member of a recognised club association.

However, the Full Federal Court has held that the mutuality principle cannot apply where an organisation is precluded from distributing to members on winding up (*Coleambally Irrigation Mutual Co-operative Ltd*). (See also *Social Credit Savings & Loan Society* and *Australian Music Traders Association*.) To ensure that not-for-profit organisations were not disadvantaged by the *Coleambally* decision, the government enacted ITAA97 s 59-35. Under s 59-35, ordinary income is treated as non-assessable non-exempt income (¶10-890) if it would have been a mutual receipt but for the entity's constituent document preventing the entity from making any distribution to its members, and it would have been assessable only because of s 6-5 (¶10-000). Section 59-35 has been amended to expressly permit mutual entities registered under the *Corporations Act 2001* to issue mutual capital instruments (MCIs) without risking their mutual structure or status.

The mutuality principle or s 59-35 would appear to apply to the sale of a club's promotional clothing to members, but not to non-mutual trading activities such as leasing of real estate to an individual member (see the ATO publication *Mutuality and taxable income guide*).

There is a statutory exemption that applies to interest derived from loans from traditional credit unions to members. However, this special tax treatment only applies to ''small'' credit unions with a notional taxable income of less than $50,000 (¶3-435).

Where volume rebates are paid to a retailer association in respect of purchases of its members, the rebates are assessable income of either the retailers or the association, depending on the facts. They are not mutual receipts (TR 2004/5).

For the operation of the mutuality principle in the case of strata title bodies, see TR 2015/3.

[FITR ¶18-255]

¶3-820 Receipts from non-members

Income from the outside investment of a club or association's funds, eg bank interest, dividends on shares and rental from property, is, of course, assessable income of the club or association (¶10-010). For example, commission income received by registered clubs from Keno licensees, the Totalisator Agency Board (TAB) or similar bodies, or from vending machine operators in respect of Keno, TAB or similar operations, is fully assessable (TD 1999/38; *North Ryde RSL*).

So also are receipts from non-members visiting the club and using its facilities, eg temporary membership fees, poker machine proceeds, bar and dining room sales. The taxable income from non-member receipts will be the gross non-member receipts minus an appropriate proportion of expenditure referable both to members *and* non-members.

[FITR ¶18-270]

¶3-830 Taxable income from non-member receipts

Where either the mutuality principle or s 59-35 (¶3-810) applies to receipts from members, it is generally very difficult to isolate from a club's total receipts those that are attributable to non-members. In practice, the Commissioner adopts a formula as a rule of thumb to determine the percentage of total receipts attributable to non-members. Clubs do not have to use the formula; the ATO will accept alternative methods that produce a reasonable and accurate measurement of a club's income. If they use the formula, individual clubs should ensure that the variables used in the formula are applicable to their own circumstances. The formula (called the *"Waratahs' formula"*) is:

$$\text{percentage of receipts attributable to non-members} = \frac{(B \times 75\%) + C}{(R \times S \times T) + A} \times \frac{100}{1}$$

where:

A = total visitors for the year of income

B = members' guests, ie visitors who are accompanied to the club by a member and signed in by that member. The formula assumes that 25% of members' guests do not contribute to the club's assessable income, ie they are non-paying guests or non-working spouses of members

C = A − B

R = average number of subscribed members for the year of income

S = the percentage of members that attend the club on a daily basis

T = the number of trading days for the year of income.

Factor A (total visitors) can be determined by summation of the visitors' and temporary/honorary members' books. Where a club does not have permanent door staff it should conduct surveys. Surveys should be conducted during periods that are likely to be representative of average trading (eg during autumn and spring months, but not during school holidays). Two one-week survey periods will be acceptable provided the surveys are performed diligently. The survey results can then be annualised to estimate total visitor attendances for the year of income. The percentage of members attending the club on a daily basis can also be determined by summation of members' daily attendance or, where there is no permanent door staff, by survey (ATO: *Mutuality and Taxable Income Guide*).

▶ Example

The X Servicemen's Club was open for 363 days (excluding Christmas Day and Good Friday) during the income year. Its financial membership for the year was 500. Approximately 15% of the members attended the club each day. The visitors' book covering the year disclosed a total attendance of 8,000 of which 4,000 were members' guests. The percentage of total receipts (from members and non-members) attributable to non-members is:

$$\frac{(75\%\text{ of members' guests}) + (\text{total visitors} - \text{members' guests})}{(15\%^{*}\text{ of membership} \times \text{number of days}) + \text{total visitors}} \times \frac{100}{1}$$

$$= \frac{(75\% \times 4{,}000) + (8{,}000 - 4{,}000)}{(15\% \times 500 \times 363) + 8{,}000} \times \frac{100}{1}$$

$$= \frac{7{,}000}{27{,}225 + 8{,}000} \times \frac{100}{1}$$

= 19.9% (the "non-member percentage")

* Percentage varies according to the individual circumstances of the club.

Where either the mutuality principle or s 59-35 (¶3-810) applies to receipts from members, the assessable income of a licensed club comprises:

- any investment income (rents, interest, etc), and
- the "non-member percentage" of gross trading income (eg gross poker machine, bar and restaurant receipts).

The allowable deductions comprise:

- expenses relating specifically to non-members (eg non-members only promotions, visitor sign-in books)
- expenses relating to wholly assessable income (eg investment expenses)
- non-apportionable deductions (eg contributions to staff superannuation, donations and costs of preparing tax returns), and
- the "non-member percentage" of the apportionable expenditure (ie the remaining expenditure, other than expenditure relating solely to members and non-allowable items such as expenditure of a capital nature).

Expenses relating specifically to members (eg members' badges, members' functions) are, of course, not allowable (TD 93/194).

Payments of annual rates and land taxes are specifically deductible to the extent that the premises are used in either or both of the following ways (ITAA97 s 25-75):

- to produce mutual receipts, amounts to which s 59-35 (¶3-810) applies, or assessable income, or
- in carrying on a business for the purpose of producing mutual receipts or amounts to which s 59-35 applies.

▶ Example

X Country Club's gross poker machine, bar and restaurant receipts for the year were $300,000. Expenses were $240,000, of which $6,000 related solely to members and $5,000 represented prescribed donations and superannuation contributions for employees. The club also earned bank interest of $9,000 and incurred expenses of $300 in earning that interest. Assuming that the percentage of trading receipts attributable to non-members (the "non-member percentage") was 10%, the club's taxable income is:

Gross trading receipts	$300,000	
amount attributable to non-members (10% of $300,000)		$30,000
Deduct: expenses	240,000	
Less: expenses relating to members	6,000	
expenses relating to interest, superannuation, donations, etc	5,300	
Net apportionable expenses	$228,700	
amount attributable to non-members (10% of $228,700)		22,870
Net (taxable) income from non-members		7,130
Add: bank interest		9,000
		16,130
Deduct: expenses relating to interest		300
superannuation, donations		5,000
Taxable income		$10,830

[FITR ¶18-270, ¶65-520]

¶3-840 Withholding PAYG amounts from payments

Clubs may be required to withhold PAYG amounts from payments made to entertainers appearing at the club where the entertainer is an employee (¶26-150) or, even if the entertainer is not an employee, if no ABN is quoted (¶26-220).

¶3-850 Rates of tax

The great majority of clubs, associations and societies would generally qualify as non-profit companies. A non-profit company generally pays no tax if its taxable income is less than $417; the tax payable is limited to 55% of the excess over $416 where the taxable income for 2020–21 does not exceed the shade-in limit of $915 ($832 for base rate entities). If the taxable income exceeds the shade-in limit, the rate of tax is a flat 30% (26% for base rate entities) on the whole of the taxable income (¶42-025). For the circumstances in which a company will be a base rate entity, see ¶3-055.

If the club, association, etc, does not qualify as a non-profit company, the whole of its taxable income will be taxed at the rate of tax applicable to companies.

[FTR ¶861-280]

Chapter 4 Dividends • Imputation System

Dividends

¶4-100 Overview: taxation of dividend recipients

Generally speaking, dividends sourced from company profits are assessable to the recipients, but the recipients are entitled to credits for Australian income tax paid by the company in earning those profits. The mechanism for achieving this outcome is called the "imputation system" (¶4-400). The aim is to prevent the income being taxed twice, ie when it is earned by the company and when the net earnings are passed on to shareholders as dividends.

An Australian resident shareholder (ie the registered holder of shares) is assessable on all dividends paid (to the shareholder) by an Australian resident or foreign resident company out of profits derived from any source (ITAA36 s 44(1)), other than dividends paid by a PDF (¶3-555). Dividends paid into an Australian resident shareholder's foreign bank account are assessable even if currency export controls prevent the funds being transferred out of the foreign country (TD 96/13). A foreign income tax offset may be available (¶21-670). A non-resident shareholder in a company is assessable on a dividend to the extent that it is paid out of profits derived by the company from sources in Australia.

Distributions on redemption, cancellation or reduction of capital and distributions out of the share capital account are, to the extent (if any) that the distributions qualify as dividends (¶4-110), deemed to have been paid out of profits (s 44(1B)). Where dividends are not paid to a shareholder but are reinvested as payment for new shares in the company, the dividends are considered to be paid to the shareholder and are therefore assessable under s 44(1) (IT 2285).

Under the imputation system (¶4-400), where a franked dividend is paid by an Australian resident company to an Australian resident shareholder, the assessable income of the shareholder includes, in addition to the amount of the dividend, the franking credit attached to the dividend, but the shareholder is entitled to a tax offset equal to the franking credit included in assessable income. Where the recipient shareholder is a company, the receipt of a franked dividend also gives rise to a franking credit (¶4-710) in the company's franking account.

Special flow-through provisions apply where a franked dividend is received by a trustee or a partnership (¶4-860).

Unfranked dividends paid by a PDF are exempt from income tax. Franked dividends paid by a PDF are also exempt unless the shareholder elects that they are to be taxed as dividends paid by an ordinary company (¶3-555).

Unfranked dividends paid to foreign residents are not usually taxed under the ordinary provisions of either ITAA97 or ITAA36 but are generally liable to flat rate withholding tax (¶22-010). However, certain foreign source dividends paid by an Australian resident company to a foreign resident shareholder are exempt from withholding tax (¶22-010). Franked dividends are also exempt from withholding tax.

If shares are sold cum dividend, the whole of the dividend subsequently paid is income of the purchaser, not the vendor. This is so even where the transfer has not yet been registered, as the vendor holds the shares as trustee for the purchaser (¶4-130).

Foreign dividend income

Where a dividend derived from foreign sources is not exempt from tax in Australia, a foreign income tax offset may be allowable (¶21-670). The recipient is assessed on the gross amount of the dividend (ie before deduction of any foreign tax).

A distribution that is declared to be conduit foreign income (¶21-100) is not assessable under s 44 (ITAA97 s 802-15).

[FTR ¶20-275]

¶4-105 Corporations law changes

The corporations law rule that dividends may only be paid out of profits of a company was replaced (from 28 June 2010) with a rule that a company must not pay a dividend unless:

- the company's assets (determined in accordance with accounting standards) exceed its liabilities (also determined in accordance with accounting standards) immediately before the dividend is declared and the excess is sufficient for the payment of the dividend
- the payment of the dividend is fair and reasonable to the company's shareholders as a whole, and
- the payment of the dividend does not materially prejudice the company's ability to pay its creditors (*Corporations Act 2001*, s 254T).

It is specifically provided that, for the purposes of ITAA36 and ITAA97, a dividend (as defined: ¶4-110) paid out of an amount other than profits is taken to be a dividend paid out of profits (ITAA36 s 44(1A)). However, the Commissioner takes the view that, for the purposes of the Corporations Act and company accounting, dividends can only be paid from profits and not from "amounts other than profits" and that Corporations Act s 254T imposes 3 specified *additional* prohibitions on the circumstances in which a dividend can be paid (TR 2012/5). See also ¶4-620.

[FTR ¶20-280]

¶4-110 What is a dividend?

For tax purposes, the expression "dividend" is defined (ITAA36 s 6(1)) to include any distribution made by a company to its shareholders whether in money or other property (including shares in that or another company) and any amount credited by a company to its shareholders as such. The term also includes any distribution by way of redemption or cancellation of a redeemable preference share, but only to the extent that the value of the distribution exceeds the amount paid-up on the share (para (e) of the definition of "dividend").

▶ Example

Where the amount paid-up on a redeemable preference share is $10 and a company redeems the share for $15, the amount taken to be a dividend is $5.

Certain payments by private companies to associated persons may be deemed to be dividends under ITAA36 Pt III Div 7A (¶4-200) or s 109 (¶4-220).

Return of capital

A distribution of capital is generally only a dividend to the extent that it exceeds the amount debited to the share capital account (para (d) of the definition of "dividend"; ID 2004/652). However, where a company raises share capital from certain shareholders and makes a tax-preferred capital distribution to other shareholders, the distribution will be treated as a dividend (s 6(4)). Capital benefits paid under a dividend substitution scheme may also be treated as dividends (ITAA36 s 45B: ¶4-682). Where property is distributed to a shareholder, the assessable dividend component of the distribution will generally be the money value of the property, reduced by the amount debited to a share capital account of the distributing company (TR 2003/8).

Additional measures apply to prevent the distribution of profits to shareholders as preferentially taxed capital rather than as dividends (¶4-682).

[FTR ¶2-655]

¶4-120 When is a dividend paid?

"Paid" in relation to a dividend or a non-share dividend includes "credited" or "distributed" (ITAA36 s 6(1)). The declaration of a dividend creates a debt owing to the shareholders and the payment, crediting or distribution of the dividend discharges that debt.

The declaration of an interim dividend by directors empowered under the company's articles of association to pay a dividend does not create a debt owing by the company to its shareholders. Consequently, the declaration of an interim dividend may be revoked before payment because it is subject to the will of the directors until it is paid, credited or distributed (*Brookton Co-operative Society*).

The posting of a dividend cheque is equivalent to payment and the dividend would be taxable in the year the cheque was posted by the company, even if it is not received or not banked until a later income year.

A dividend is "credited", so as to have been paid, provided a dividend has been declared, profits are appropriated to its payment and the shareholder's account with the company is credited in such a way that it may be drawn on as and when the shareholder desires. But mere book entries are not always sufficient. Offsetting the dividends against a debt owed to the company by a shareholder is payment, but crediting to a general "dividends payable account" is not crediting in the relevant sense. Where fully paid bonus shares are issued, a dividend need not be formally declared and the relevant amount is credited when the shares are issued, not when a book entry is made (IT 2603).

Dividends declared on shares owned by a deceased estate, but not paid over until after the production of probate, are not assessable until actually paid over.

A shareholder who, wishing to leave the amount of dividends on deposit with the company, tacitly or expressly authorises the company to retain the amounts payable as dividends remains assessable on the amount of the dividends.

[FTR ¶3-380, ¶20-310]

¶4-130 Dividends indirectly derived

Dividend income derived indirectly through a trust estate, trustee or nominee is not caught by ITAA36 s 44 because that section applies only to dividends derived by a shareholder, ie a person who is entered in the company's register of members as the holder of shares in it.

However, the beneficial owner of shares registered in the name of a nominee or trustee, or a beneficiary presently entitled to a share of trust income that consists directly or indirectly of dividends, would be assessable on such income either under ITAA97 s 6-5 or ITAA36 s 97 or, in the case of an infant beneficiary, the trustee might be assessable under ITAA36 s 98. The taxation of trust income is considered at ¶6-060; for the imputation provisions relating to trustees and beneficiaries, see ¶4-860.

Dividend income thus indirectly derived by a person (companies, partnerships, etc, as well as individuals) is deemed to be "income attributable to a dividend" (ITAA36 s 6B). The provision also applies to a "non-share dividend" (¶23-125). A foreign income tax offset may be available where an Australian resident taxpayer derives foreign income attributable to dividends (¶21-670).

[FITR ¶18-200; FTR ¶4-950, ¶50-600]

¶4-140 Profits and their source

Dividends paid to Australian resident shareholders out of *any* "profits" of the company are assessable under ITAA36 s 44. The profits need not be revenue profits or assessable profits; they may be capital profits or exempt profits. Indeed, any increase in the company's assets, including an increase resulting from a gift, is a profit (*Slater Holdings (No 2)*). In certain circumstances dividends may be *deemed* to have been paid out of profits (¶4-105, ¶4-110, ¶4-300).

Conceptually, dividends are paid out of after-tax profits, ie the dividends are not deductible in arriving at either accounting income or taxable income. There is an exception in the case of co-operative companies. Co-operatives have a choice — they can pay deductible (pre-tax) distributions, which are unfrankable, or they can make non-deductible (post-tax) distributions, which are frankable (¶3-430).

It has been suggested that, to come within s 44(1), the distribution must be made wholly out of profits and that it is not enough that there is a distribution of a mass of assets that contains profits (*Slater Holdings (No 2)*).

The assessability of dividends received by a shareholder is generally determined by whether the dividend was paid out of profits, irrespective of the Australian or foreign source of those profits. (The conduit foreign income regime (¶4-190, ¶21-100) is an exception to this general rule.)

A June 2000 distribution of shares in a foreign resident demerged entity was an assessable dividend paid wholly out of profits despite the market value of the shares being nearly 7 times the amount debited to the parent company's retained earnings in relation to the distribution (*Condell*).

A foreign resident who indirectly receives dividend income through a trust or nominee (¶4-130), and not as a shareholder, will be assessable only if the source of the dividend income is in Australia.

[FTR ¶20-275 – ¶20-395]

¶4-160 Demerger dividends

Tax relief is available for demergers, ie the restructuring of corporate or trust entities or groups (other than discretionary trusts and superannuation funds) by splitting them into 2 or more entities or groups. The relief applies to spin-offs that happen on or after 1 July 2002, where underlying ownership is maintained and the demerging entity divests at least 80% of its ownership interests in the demerged entity. The 2 main elements of this relief are CGT relief (¶12-328) and tax relief on otherwise assessable dividends (discussed below). Actual examples of the application of demerger relief are discussed in a number of class rulings.

Central to the demerger dividend relief provisions are the concepts of "demerger dividend" and "demerger allocation". A *demerger dividend* is that part of a demerger allocation that is assessable as a dividend under ITAA36 s 44(1), or would be so assessable but for s 44(3) and (4). A demerger dividend is unfrankable (¶4-620). A *demerger allocation* is the total market value of the new interests in the demerged entity that each new owner of the head entity acquires under the demerger. Depending on how the demerger is effected, the demerger allocation may consist of an otherwise assessable dividend component, a return of capital or a combination of capital and profit.

Demerger relief applies to a demerger dividend if:

- just after the demerger at least 50% (by market value) of CGT assets owned by the demerged entity or its demerger subsidiaries is used in the carrying on of a business by those entities, and
- the head entity does not elect (for all shareholders) that the relief not apply.

Where demerger relief applies, a demerger dividend is taken not to be paid out of profits and is non-assessable non-exempt income (s 44(2) to (6): ¶10-890). A withholding tax exemption is provided for the assessable dividend component of the demerger dividend received by foreign resident shareholders (ITAA36 s 128B(3D)). The ITAA36 Pt III Div 7A deemed dividend provisions (¶4-200) do not apply to deem demerger dividends of a private company to have been paid out of profits (ITAA36 s 109RA).

Integrity rules limit the relief where there is a scheme that has a purpose of obtaining the non-assessable dividend (ITAA36 ss 45B; 45BA: ¶4-682).

[FTR ¶20-400]

¶4-180 Dividends from listed investment companies

Eligible shareholders in listed investment companies (LICs) are entitled to an equivalent of a CGT discount on gains realised after 30 June 2001 by LICs on assets held for more than 12 months (¶11-038). Distribution statements provided by LICs must separately identify dividends sourced from such ''LIC capital gains''. Australian resident individuals, non-superannuation trusts and partnerships are entitled to a deduction equal to 50% of the LIC capital gain amount. A foreign resident individual is also entitled to a 50% deduction where the relevant dividend is received through the individual's permanent establishment in Australia. Resident life insurance companies (where the shares are complying superannuation assets) and complying superannuation entities are entitled to a 33 1/3% deduction. The benefit does not pass through a series of trusts or partnerships (ITAA97 s 115-280). Franking credits are available if the dividend is franked. An in-depth discussion of the rules and issues relating to LIC capital gains is provided in TR 2005/23.

A ''listed investment company'' is an Australian resident company listed on the ASX or other approved stock exchange, at least 90% of whose CGT assets consist of ''permitted investments'', being a wide range of investment and financial assets and goodwill. Direct or indirect ownership of more than 10% of another company (other than an LIC) or trust is not a permitted investment. A 100% subsidiary of an LIC that meets all the criteria except listing is also an LIC. A temporary failure to comply with the 90% requirement is not fatal if it is caused by circumstances outside the LIC's control (ITAA97 s 115-290).

[FITR ¶154-192 – ¶154-197]

¶4-190 Conduit foreign income

In general terms, conduit foreign income is foreign income that is (ultimately) received by a foreign resident through one or more interposed Australian corporate tax entities. Special rules allow conduit foreign income to flow through Australian corporate tax entities to foreign shareholders without being taxed in Australia (see ¶21-100 for details). Australian corporate tax entities that receive an unfranked distribution that is declared to be conduit foreign income will not pay Australian tax on that income if the conduit foreign income is on-paid to shareholders (net of related expenses) within a certain period. In such a case, the conduit foreign income in the unfranked distribution will be treated as non-assessable, non-exempt income of the Australian corporate tax entity. Conduit foreign income is exempt from dividend withholding tax when it is on-paid to a foreign shareholder as an unfranked distribution (¶22-010).

Deemed Dividends: Div 7A

¶4-200 Payments and loans by private companies to associated entities (Div 7A)

Under ITAA36 Pt III Div 7A (s 109B to 109ZE), amounts paid (¶4-205), lent (¶4-210) or forgiven (¶4-220) by a private company to certain associated entities (including individuals) are treated as dividends, unless they come within specified exclusions. Division 7A applies to non-share equity interests and non-share dividends (¶23-125) in the same way that it applies to shares and dividends (s 109BA). A closely held corporate limited partnership is treated as a private company for the purposes of Div 7A. There may also be a potential deemed dividend under Div 7A in some circumstances where a private company is a presently entitled beneficiary of a trust and the trust makes a payment or loan to, or forgives a debt owing by, a shareholder (or an associate of a shareholder) of the private company (¶4-246).

Putting to one side the situation where a private company is an unpaid presently entitled beneficiary of a discretionary trust, the provisions of Div 7A apply where the recipient of the payment, loan or forgiven amount is: (a) a shareholder; (b) an associate of a shareholder; or (c) a former shareholder or former associate where a reasonable person would conclude that the amount is paid, lent or forgiven because of that former status. For these purposes, ''associate'' has the meaning provided in ITAA36 s 318, which covers a broad range of entities that are associates of natural persons, companies, partnerships and trustees. For example, a discretionary object of a discretionary trust and the trustee of the trust are associates under the definition.

In the case of a former shareholder or former associate, ''because'' in the expression ''because the entity has been such a shareholder or associate at some time'' means by reason that. The reason must be a real and substantial reason for the payment, loan or debt forgiveness concerned, even if it is not the main or only reason for the transaction (TD 2008/14).

A Div 7A deemed dividend is generally taken to be paid at the end of the income year of the private company in which the amount is paid, lent or forgiven. Exceptions are an ''amalgamated loan'' (s 109E) (¶4-240) and a loan made in the course of the winding-up of a company, which is only deemed to be paid at the end of the following year if it has not been repaid by then (s 109D(1A)). To ensure that it is assessable in the associated entity's hands as a dividend (¶4-100), a Div 7A dividend is also taken to have been paid out of the company's profits, and to have been paid to the entity in the capacity of a shareholder, whether or not the entity actually was a shareholder (s 109Z).

Where the total of all Div 7A dividends paid by the private company for the year exceeds the company's ''distributable surplus'' for the year, the amount of each Div 7A dividend is proportionally reduced (¶4-249).

A shareholder, former shareholder or associate who would otherwise have a 2-year period of review (¶25-310) will have a 4-year period of review for the purposes of Div 7A if the company has a 4-year period of review (¶25-320).

A Div 7A dividend is not subject to either dividend withholding tax or PAYG withholding (s 109ZA).

Franking a deemed dividend

A Div 7A deemed dividend is assessable and is generally unfrankable (¶4-620). However, a Div 7A deemed dividend may be franked if it is taken to be paid because of a family law obligation. The recipient of the dividend need not be a shareholder (ITAA36 s 109RC).

The Commissioner also has a discretion to allow franking in certain circumstances (see Commissioner's discretions below).

Interaction with FBT

A loan or a debt forgiveness that gives rise to a deemed Div 7A dividend is not subject to FBT. Also, effective 1 April 2007, a loan that is not a deemed dividend because of a Div 7A complying written loan agreement is not a fringe benefit (¶35-070; s 109ZB). On the other hand, a payment that would otherwise fall within the FBT provisions is subject to FBT and is excluded from the operation of Div 7A. The interaction of Div 7A and FBT is one of the issues raised in the Div 7A Treasury discussion paper referred to below.

Commissioner's discretions

The Commissioner can either disregard a deemed dividend that arises under Div 7A or allow a private company to frank a deemed dividend to a shareholder that it has been taken to pay, where the failure to satisfy the requirements of Div 7A resulted from an honest mistake or inadvertent omission by the recipient, the private company or any other entity whose conduct contributed to the deemed dividend arising (ITAA36 s 109RB).

The Commissioner has issued a ruling which considers the circumstances in which the honest mistake/inadvertent omission discretion can be exercised (TR 2010/8). The ruling states that a mistake in this context is an incorrect view or opinion or misunderstanding about how Div 7A operates; about facts that are relevant to its operation; or about other matters that affect its operation. Such a mistake must be honestly made. An omission is a failure to take action that is relevant to, or affects, the operation of Div 7A. Such an omission must be inadvertent. A practice statement has been issued to provide guidance on the administration of TR 2010/8 (PS LA 2011/29). In *Case 8/2012*, the AAT exercised the honest mistake/inadvertent omission discretion in a taxpayer's favour where loan agreements did not fully comply with the Div 7A requirements.

The Commissioner is also given a discretion to extend the period during which a loan recipient may pay the minimum yearly repayment on an amalgamated loan, where the recipient is unable to make the minimum repayment due to circumstances beyond the recipient's control (ITAA36 s 109RD; ¶4-240).

Proposed amendments

A range of amendments to improve the operation and administration of the Div 7A rules were announced in the context of the 2016–17 and 2018–19 Budgets. These amendments are now to take effect in relation to income years commencing on or after the date of assent of the enabling legislation.

A Treasury discussion paper (''Targeted amendments to Division 7A'') was released on 22 October 2018 in relation to the Div 7A issues that are to be addressed by the proposed amendments. The main areas of contemplated change are:

- a self-correction mechanism for inadvertent breaches of Div 7A
- safe-harbour rules where the right to use an asset is involved
- simplified Div 7A loan arrangements
- the abolition of the distributable surplus concept
- technical adjustments to improve the operation of Div 7A, and
- clarification of the way Div 7A operates where there is an unpaid present entitlement.

The Treasury discussion paper also raises the issue whether pre-4 December 1997 loans should be brought within the operation of Div 7A.

[FTR ¶56-105]

¶4-205 Division 7A: payments

For the purposes of the Div 7A deemed dividend rules, a ''payment'' to an entity means: (a) a payment to the entity, on the entity's behalf or for the entity's benefit; (b) a credit of an amount to the entity, on the entity's behalf or for the entity's benefit; and (c) a transfer of property to the entity (the amount of the payment will be deemed to be the arm's length value of the property less any consideration given by the entity) (s 109C(3)). Payments, and amounts credited, can be apportioned where they are made, or credited, for more than one purpose. An amount that comes within the definition of a loan (¶4-210) is expressly excluded from the definition of a payment (s 109C(3A)).

A direction by a private company to a debtor to pay the debt to a shareholder is a payment by the company (*Rozman*). The release by a private company of all or part of an unpaid present entitlement that is not effectively converted to a loan constitutes a payment for the purposes of Div 7A (see (b) above) (TD 2015/20).

A payment or transfer of property made by a private company because of a maintenance order of the Family Court can be a payment for Div 7A purposes (TR 2014/5); however it can now be franked, whether the recipient is or is not a shareholder (s 109RC). The ATO takes the view that the creation of an interest in an asset (eg a leasehold interest in land) is a transfer of property and, hence, a payment.

A private company cannot be taken to have paid a dividend to another company pursuant to s 109C or 109D where the other company is the target entity under an interposed entity arrangement (TD 2001/2).

As explained at ¶4-210, a payment may be converted to a loan for the purposes of Div 7A.

Provision of asset for use

The concept of a payment to an entity for the purposes of Div 7A now extends to the provision of an asset for use by the entity (eg a licence to use a boat, car or holiday home) (s 109CA(1)). The amount of the payment is what would have been paid for the provision of the asset on an arm's length basis less any consideration in fact given. This extension to what constitutes a payment does not apply if there would otherwise be a payment (eg on the Commissioner's view, where there is a lease of real property) (s 109CA(9)).

There are the following exceptions to this deemed payment rule: minor benefits; an otherwise deductible exclusion; business residences in some circumstances; certain main residences and company title flats and home units (s 109CA(4) to (8)). The main residence exception does not apply to a dwelling acquired by a company before 1 July 2009 if a continuity of ownership test is not met by the company on and from 1 July 2009.

A payment is taken to be made (by virtue of the provision of an asset for use by an entity rule) when the entity first (a) uses the asset with the permission of the provider; or (b) has a right to use the asset (whether alone or together with other entities) when the provider does not have a right, either to use the asset or to provide the asset for use by another entity. If the use or right continues into another income year there will be a separate payment made at the start of that income year (s 109CA(2), (3)).

As noted at ¶4-200, it is proposed to introduce safe harbour rules in relation to the operation of Div 7A where there is the provision of an asset for the use of a shareholder or an associate.

For exclusions from the Div 7A payment rules, see ¶4-225.

[FTR ¶56-120 – ¶56-128]

¶4-210 Division 7A: loans

For the purposes of the Div 7A deemed dividend rules, a "loan" includes: (a) an advance of money; (b) a provision of credit or any other form of financial accommodation; (c) a payment of an amount for another entity if there is an obligation to repay the amount; and (d) a transaction that is in substance a loan (s 109D(3)). A loan is taken to be made at the time the loan is made or anything happens which is within the definition of loan (s 109D(4)). Where a loan made before 4 December 1997 is varied on or after that day by extending the term of the loan or increasing its amount, a new loan on the varied terms is deemed to be made at the time of the variation (s 109D(5)).

A payment that is made by a private company and is converted to a loan before the end of the company's lodgment day for the income year in which the payment is made will be treated as a loan made at the time of the payment (ITAA36 s 109D(4A)). This enables the recipient to repay the loan or to enter into a complying loan agreement before the company's lodgment day to avoid triggering a deemed dividend. Note that s 109D(1) and 109N(1) require the repayment to be made, or the agreement to be entered into, *before* the lodgment day (not by the end of the lodgment day). This means that the only prudent course would be to convert a payment to a loan at least one day before the lodgment day.

For the operation of the definition of loan where a private company is an unpaid presently entitled beneficiary of a trust, see ¶4-215.

For exclusions from the Div 7A loan rules, see ¶4-225. The exclusion that applies where a complying Div 7A loan agreement is put in place is discussed at ¶4-230.

As noted at ¶4-200, it is proposed to make significant changes to the operation of the Div 7A loan rules.

[FTR ¶56-130 – ¶56-135]

¶4-215 Loan issues: private company presently entitled to income

Where a private company is presently entitled to income of a trust estate there will be cases where there is in fact a loan back by the private company to the trust (so that the present entitlement is extinguished). This includes an express or implied agreement for the loan back and could be the case where the trustee, acting pursuant to a term of the trust deed, applies the trust funds for the benefit of the private company beneficiary by crediting a loan account in the company's name and assuming a corresponding obligation to repay the amount (TR 2010/3).

Where a private company's present entitlement is not extinguished, the Commissioner now takes the view that where the private company and the trust are in the same family group and there is knowledge that funds representing the unpaid present entitlement are being used for trust purposes, rather than for the private company's sole benefit without any benefit from use accruing to the trust, the non-calling for payment of the unpaid present entitlement amounts to the provision of financial accommodation and, hence, the making of a Div 7A loan. Also, in these kinds of cases the overall transaction between the private company beneficiary and the trustee includes the beneficiary's authorisation (or acquiescence with knowledge) that funds representing the unpaid present entitlement can be used for the benefit of the trust and effects, in substance, a loan of money to the trust (TR 2010/3).

There will, however, not be a Div 7A provision of financial accommodation (or in-substance) loan if the present entitlement is held on a sub-trust and the use of the funds in the main trust is on terms that entitle the private company to the sole benefit of any income generated by use of the funds.

These views on the operation of the provision of financial accommodation and in-substance loan limbs of the Div 7A definition of loan were a departure from the position previously taken by the Commissioner in public documents and only apply to unpaid present entitlements that arise on or after 16 December 2009 (the date of issue of TR 2010/3 in draft form).

PS LA 2010/4 provides guidance on the administration of TR 2010/3 (including where there will be a relevant sub-trust arrangement). Further, in June 2011 the Commissioner issued a fact sheet which addresses certain supplementary issues that arise out of TR 2010/3 and PS LA 2010/4.

For present entitlements that arise in the 2010–11 or a later income year the sub-trust must be in place by the lodgment day of the main trust for the particular income year.

By way of example of the above, if a present entitlement of a private company arose on 30 June 2020 and there is no loan back by the company within the ordinary meaning of loan, a provision of financial accommodation or in-substance loan will arise on the lodgment day of the trust for the 2019–20 income year. This will mean that the following courses of action would be open:

(1) putting the unpaid present entitlement on an acceptable subtrust arrangement by that lodgment day. This would mean that the present entitlement of the company would remain unpaid and the Div 7A trust rules would be potentially applicable to a loan by the trust, or

(2) entering into a Div 7A compliant loan agreement before the company's lodgment day for the 2019–20 income year (or paying the present entitlement out before that lodgment day). The provision of financial accommodation or in-substance loan would effectively extinguish the company's present entitlement so that there should be no scope for the Div 7A trust rules to apply.

For a sub-trust arrangement to be effective, the funds representing the private company's unpaid present entitlement must be held on the sub-trust for the sole benefit of the company. PS LA 2010/4 gives 3 options to satisfy this requirement, 2 of which involve interest-only loan backs to the main trust (for 7 years or 10 years depending on the rate of interest) and the other of which is an investment in a specific income-producing asset. The practice statement explains these options. For the Commissioner's practice where a 7-year loan matures in any of the 2016–17 to 2019–20 income years, see PCG 2017/13.

Note that where all unpaid present entitlements (UPEs) in a fixed trust were mixed with the trust fund and employed by the trustee to benefit all unit holders (by retiring trust debt) in the exact same proportion as each UPE bore to the total of all UPEs, a provision of financial accommodation loan by a corporate unitholder did not arise for the purpose of Div 7A; the unit holders had not provided and were not providing any pecuniary aid or favour to the trustee or any other taxpayer but were, instead, collectively agreeing that the funds be used for their sole benefit (ID 2012/74).

As noted at ¶4-200, it is proposed that amendments will be made that will, it would seem, effectively incorporate the Commissioner's views in relation to unpaid present entitlements into the ITAA97.

[FTR ¶56-137 – ¶56-137/20]

¶4-220 Division 7A: forgiven debts

For the purposes of the Div 7A debt forgiveness rules, generally, a debt is "forgiven" when the amount would be forgiven under the commercial debt forgiveness rules (¶16-910) (s 109F(3)). However, where "debt parking" is involved, the debt is taken to be forgiven if it is assigned by the company to another entity who is either an associate of the debtor or a party to an arrangement with the debtor about the assignment and a reasonable person would conclude that the other entity will not enforce the debt (s 109F(5)). A debt is also forgiven if, having regard to all the circumstances, it is reasonable to conclude that the private company will not insist on repayment of the debt (s 109F(6)).

The ATO considers that a loan by a private company to a shareholder or associate will become a forgiven debt if the statutory period for enforcing collection ends. However, for various reasons the Commissioner has decided to take no active compliance action to treat statute-barred private company and trustee loans made prior to 27 March 1998 as giving rise to a deemed dividend under Div 7A (PS LA 2006/2 (GA)).

A Div 7A dividend will also *not* arise if a debt owed to a private company is forgiven in any of the following circumstances (s 109G): (a) the debt is owed by another company (other than a company in the capacity of trustee); (b) the debtor has become bankrupt, or *Bankruptcy Act 1966*, Pt X applies; (c) the debt is a loan that is otherwise deemed to be a dividend under Div 7A; or (d) the Commissioner is satisfied that the reason for the forgiveness was that payment would have caused the entity undue hardship, and is satisfied that the entity had the capacity to pay the debt when it was incurred but lost that capacity as a result of circumstances beyond the entity's control.

[FTR ¶56-150]

¶4-225 Payments and loans not treated as dividends

The following payments (¶4-205) and loans (¶4-210) are *not* treated as dividends under Div 7A:

- a payment of a genuine debt (s 109J). This exclusion does not apply where a private company pays an amount (or transfers property) to an associate of a shareholder pursuant to a court order made under *Family Law Act 1975*, s 79 whether the court order is directed to the private company or to a party to the proceedings to cause the private company to make a payment (TR 2014/5). The ruling contains an administrative concession where a court order made before 30 July 2014 (the date of issue of TR 2014/5) has bound a private company to make a payment to an associate of a shareholder. In such a case, no deemed Div 7A dividend will be taken to arise. A payment or transfer of property to a shareholder would, of course, attract the ordinary dividend provisions
- a payment or loan to another company (other than a company in the capacity of trustee) (s 109K). In *3-D Scaffolding*, the Full Federal Court held that payments allegedly made to a representative of a fictitious company for scaffolding hire were in reality made to 3-D's shareholder. The payments were not deductible to 3-D and were assessable to the shareholder as deemed dividends under Div 7A
- a payment or loan that is otherwise included in the entity's assessable income or that is specifically excluded from assessable income (s 109L)
- a loan made in the ordinary course of business on ordinary commercial terms (s 109M). A failure of a shareholder or associate to repay a commercial trade debt on time will not prevent s 109M from applying (ie no deemed dividend will arise), provided the company deals with the default in the same manner in which it deals with defaults on similar loans made to parties at arm's length (TD 2008/1)
- a loan (¶4-210) made in the 2004–05 or a later income year that is repaid or put on a commercial footing before the company's ''lodgment day'' (¶4-230)
- a distribution or loan made by a liquidator in the course of winding up a private company, provided the loan is repaid by the end of the following income year (s 109NA; ID 2003/459)
- a loan by a private company solely for the purpose of enabling a shareholder or shareholder's associate to acquire an employee share scheme interest under an employee share scheme to which ITAA97 Subdiv 83A-B or Subdiv 83A-C (¶10-085) would apply (s 109NB)
- certain amalgamated loans (ss 109P; 109Q: see ¶4-240)
- a demerger dividend (¶4-160) to which ITAA36 s 45B does not apply (s 109RA).

A Div 7A loan paid out of personal services income of a company will not be assessable to the recipient where the same personal services income has been included previously in the recipient's assessable income under ITAA97 s 86-15(1) (ID 2004/967).

In *Di Lorenzo Ceramics*, loans made by a private company to the trustee of a unit trust (in which the company owned 75% of the units), were taken to be dividends assessable to the unitholders.

[FTR ¶56-250 – ¶56-305]

¶4-230 Loan with minimum rate and maximum term

A loan by a private company is *not* taken to be a Div 7A dividend in the income year if, before the company's lodgment day for that year (s 109N):

- the agreement under which the loan is made is in writing
- the interest rate payable on the loan for years of income *after* the year in which the loan is made equals or exceeds the benchmark interest rate, ie the "Indicator Lending Rates/Housing loans/Variable/Banks/Standard" rate last published by the Reserve Bank of Australia before the start of the company's income year, and
- the loan term does not exceed the specified "maximum term".

The elements of the agreement that need to be in writing for these purposes are: (a) the names of the parties; (b) the terms of the loan (ie the amount of the loan, the date that the loan amount is drawn, the requirement to repay the loan amount, the period of the loan and the interest rate payable); (c) that the parties have agreed to the terms; and (d) the date of the agreement, eg the date it was signed or executed. These essential elements may be contained in a formal written loan agreement or, for example, in an exchange of letters, emails, faxes or other means of communication, if they are dated, and provide written evidence of the terms of the loan agreement and the parties' acceptance of those terms (TD 2008/8). A number of examples are provided in the determination. A loan agreement cannot be a unilateral document (*Case 4/2009*).

When a loan agreement is being prepared after the end of the income year in which the loan was made but before the lodgment day, it is important that the agreement is drafted on the basis that there is not a new loan (to repay the original loan) but that the agreement provides the terms of the loan in fact made during the income year (ID 2012/60).

Lodgment day

The lodgment day of a company for an income year is the earlier of the actual lodgment date and the lodgment due date of the company's return for the income year in which the loan is made (s 109D(1AA)).

For the Commissioner's view on what the lodgment day is for a private company that is a subsidiary member of a consolidated group, see TD 2015/18.

Div 7A benchmark interest rates

For private companies with an income year ending on *30 June*, the benchmark interest rate is 5.45% for 2015–16 (TD 2015/15), 5.40% for 2016–17 (TD 2016/11), 5.30% for 2017–18 (TD 2017/17), 5.20% for 2018–19 (TD 2018/14), 5.37% for 2019–20 and 4.52% for 2020–21. In the case of a company with a substituted accounting period, the applicable benchmark interest rate is the "Housing loans; Banks; Variable; Standard; Owner-occupier" rate last published by the Reserve Bank of Australia before the start of the private company's substituted accounting period.

Maximum term

The maximum term is 25 years if the loan is fully secured by a registered mortgage over real property and the market value of the property at the time the loan is made (net of any other liability secured over the property) is at least 110% of the loan amount. In any other case the maximum term is 7 years.

▶ Example

In 2018–19 Private Co makes an unsecured loan of $50,000 to its majority shareholder, Henry. The loan is covered by a signed and dated agreement which is entered into before Private Co's lodgment day for 2018–19 and states that the loan is for a term of 5 years with interest calculated at the benchmark interest rate applicable to the relevant year.

As the requirements for documentation, minimum interest rate and maximum term have been fulfilled, the loan will not be treated as a deemed dividend in 2018–19.

However, the loan will form all or part of an amalgamated loan (see below) for 2018–19. If Henry fails to make the minimum yearly repayment for the amalgamated loan in 2019–20 or a later year, a deemed dividend will arise in that year (see ¶4-240).

Where a loan made during an income year is the subject of a written agreement that complies with the above conditions the loan will be or form part of what is called an amalgamated loan which is dealt with in subsequent income years under the rules described at ¶4-240.

For a decision of the AAT in which it was held that the terms of a loan agreement and the circumstances in which it was entered into established that the intention of the parties was to rescind an earlier loan agreement and replace it, see *KKQY*.

As noted at ¶4-200, it is proposed to make significant changes to the operation of the Div 7A loan rules.

[FTR ¶56-275 – ¶56-278]

¶4-235 Repayments and refinancing a private company loan

There is a provision which is designed to prevent circumvention of the Div 7A repayment requirements by a repayment and a subsequent reborrowing or by a new borrowing followed by a repayment (ITAA36 s 109R(2)).

A private company loan can be refinanced without triggering a deemed dividend under ITAA36 s 109R(2), provided the refinancing takes place because the loan becomes subordinated to another loan from another entity (eg a bank). The subordination must be beyond the control of the shareholder/associate to whom the loan was made, and the private company and the borrower must deal at arm's length with the other entity (s 109R(5)).

▶ Example

Sarah has a shareholder loan from Private Co as well as a loan from her bank. She is making the required Div 7A repayments on the company loan, but defaults on the bank loan. As a result, the bank requires the company loan to be subordinated to the bank loan. This means that Sarah must make the required repayments on the bank loan before any repayments can be made on the company loan. Under s 109R(5), Sarah could refinance the company loan to, for example, extend the term and reduce the minimum yearly repayments.

An unsecured loan (maximum term 7 years) can be converted to a loan secured by a mortgage over real property with a longer maximum term. The maximum term of the new loan is 25 years, less the period of time that the old loan has already been in place (ITAA36 ss 109N(3A), (3B); 109R(6)).

A loan secured by a mortgage over real property can be refinanced with an unsecured loan. The maximum term of the new loan will be 7 years, reduced to the extent, if any, that the old loan was already in place for more than 18 years (ITAA36 ss 109N(3C), (3D); 109R(7)).

If a private company has guaranteed a loan from a third party (eg a bank) to a shareholder/associate and the company becomes liable to make a payment to the lender, a deemed dividend will not arise under ITAA36 s 109UA if the shareholder/associate enters into a Div 7A compliant loan agreement with the company for the amount paid by the company (ITAA36 s 109UA(5)).

[FTR ¶56-300]

¶4-240 Div 7A amalgamated loans

Where a private company makes one or more loans to an entity during an income year, each of which: (a) has the same maximum term; (b) would, apart from s 109N, be treated as a Div 7A dividend in that year; and (c) is not fully repaid before the company's lodgment day for that year (s 109E(3)), the loans are brought together at the end of the year to form a single ‘‘amalgamated loan’’. The amalgamated loan is taken to have been made in the income year in which the loan(s) were in fact made (ID 2012/61). This means that there can be up to 2 amalgamated loans for each year, comprised of constituent loans that meet the criteria mentioned above for: (a) a maximum term of 7 years; or (b) a maximum term of 25 years.

For the income year in which a constituent loan or loans are made, the amalgamated loan will be the amount of the constituent loan(s) not repaid before the company's lodgment day for the income year. However, all repayments during the income year in which that lodgment day occurs count towards the minimum repayment for that income year whether the repayment occurs before or on or after the lodgment day (ID 2010/82). It is not a requirement that any repayment of a loan be made before the lodgment day of the company for the income year in which the loan is made (ID 2010/206).

An amalgamated loan is not treated as a Div 7A dividend in the year in which the amalgamation occurs (s 109P), but will give rise to a deemed dividend in a subsequent income year unless the repayments in relation to the loan during that subsequent year equal or exceed the minimum repayments specified by the formula in s 109E(6). Temporary loan repayments are generally disregarded (s 109R: ¶4-235).

▶ Example 1

A private company makes 2 unsecured loans to a shareholder on 1 July 2018. Each loan is made under a written agreement, which specifies that the rate of interest payable for all future years of income must equal or exceed that required by s 109N(1)(b). The term of one loan is 5 years; the other is 4 years. For the year ended 30 June 2019, as all the requirements of s 109N are met, the loans are not treated as dividends under Div 7A. They are treated as an amalgamated loan.

If the amount of the amalgamated loan is $100,000, the minimum yearly repayment of the amalgamated loan for the 2019–20 year of income is calculated as follows (s 109E(6)):

$$\frac{\text{amount of the loan not repaid by the end of the previous year of income} \times \text{current year's benchmark interest rate}}{1 - \left[\dfrac{1}{1 + \text{current year's benchmark interest rate}}\right]^{\text{remaining term}}}$$

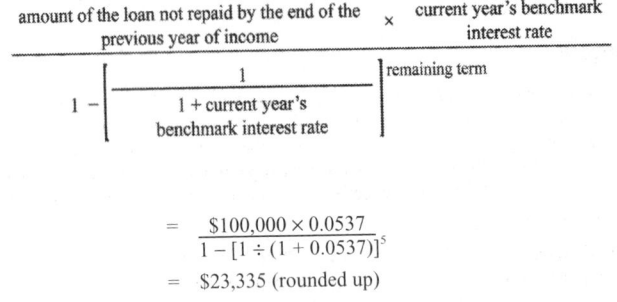

$$= \frac{\$100{,}000 \times 0.0537}{1 - [1 \div (1 + 0.0537)]^5}$$

$$= \$23{,}335 \text{ (rounded up)}$$

The ‘‘remaining term’’ is the difference between: (a) the number of years in the term of the longest constituent loan within the amalgamated loan; and (b) the number of years between the end of the company's income year in which the loan was made and the end of the income year preceding the income year for which the minimum yearly repayment is being worked out; rounded to the next higher whole number if the difference is not already a whole number (s 109E(6)).

If repayments made in the 2019–20 year of income equal or exceed the minimum yearly repayment, no amount is taken to be a dividend for the purposes of s 109E(1).

Amount of loan unpaid at end of previous year

Working out the ‘‘amount of the loan not repaid by the end of the previous year of income’’ for the purposes of the above formula sounds deceptively simple, but has proven to be controversial. It requires that the total repayments made for the year be allocated between principal and interest, so that each year the principal repayment for the current year can be deducted from the unpaid balance of the loan at the end of the previous year. Fortunately, s 109E(7) provides for interest to be calculated for this purpose at the benchmark interest rate (even if some of the constituent loans specify some higher rate). Nonetheless, issues such as simple versus compound interest and daily balances remain. It would seem that the ATO would accept the following methodology for working out the relevant amount.

▶ Example 2: Unpaid loan balance

A private company lent a shareholder $40,000 on 30 June 2019 under a written loan agreement that satisfies the requirements of s 109N. This was the only loan the company made to this particular shareholder in the 2018–19 year. During 2019–20, the shareholder made 2 repayments on the loan of $10,000 each after the company's lodgment day for the 2018–19 income year. The first payment was made on 1 January 2020 and the second was made on 30 June 2020. The benchmark interest rate is 5.37% for the 2019–20 year.

Calculations:
Interest is calculated annually in arrears by reference to the daily balance throughout the year as follows:

	Credit $	Loan balance $
Principal at 1/7/2019		40,000.00
Repayment at 1/1/2020	– 10,000.00	30,000.00
Repayment at 30/6/2020	– 10,000.00	20,000.00
Interest for 2019–20 (see below)	+ 1,879.50	21,879.50

Interest payable	=	(interest payable on $40,000 from 1/7/19 to 31/12/19) + (interest payable on $30,000 from 1/1/20 to 29/6/20) + (interest payable on $20,000 for 30/6/20)
	=	(5.37% × $40,000 × 184/366) + (5.37% × $30,000 × 181/366) + (5.37% × $20,000 × 1/366)
	=	$1,079.87 + $796.70 + $2.93
	=	$1,879.50

Of the $20,000 repayments made during the income year, $1,879.50 is taken to have been applied against the interest amount and $18,120.50 is taken to have been applied against the loan principal. This leaves $21,879.50 as the amount of the loan not repaid by the end of the income year. This figure is used in working out the minimum yearly repayment for the 2020–21 income year.

Consequences of not making minimum repayment

If the actual repayments on an amalgamated loan are less than the minimum repayment for a particular year, a deemed dividend will arise equal to the *amount of the shortfall* (ITAA36 s 109E(1), (2)). A shortfall amount that is treated as a dividend under ITAA36 s 109E will not be taxed again as a dividend if it is subsequently forgiven (s 109G). Note that the capital component of a shortfall in a repayment does not reduce the amount of the loan not repaid by the end of the previous year of income when applying the above minimum repayment formula in a subsequent income year (ID 2013/36).

▶ Example 3

Private Co makes a loan of $60,000 to its shareholder, Joshua. The minimum repayment for the year after the loan is made is $12,000, comprised of $8,000 principal and $4,000 interest. Joshua makes repayments of only $10,000 during the year. A deemed dividend of $2,000 (ie $12,000 – $10,000) would arise.

If Private Co then decides to forgive the outstanding loan balance of $54,000, the deemed dividend that arises under s 109F (as affected by s 109G) will be $52,000 (ie $54,000 – $2,000).

Commissioner's relieving discretion

Where the amount repaid in respect of an amalgamated loan is less than the minimum required to avoid a deemed dividend, the Commissioner has a discretion to treat a deemed dividend as not arising if the borrower satisfies the Commissioner that this was because of circumstances beyond the borrower's control and the borrower would suffer undue hardship if the private company was taken to pay a dividend to the entity at the end of the current year because of the loan (ITAA36 s 109Q). The application of this discretion was considered by the AAT in *VCJN*.

For a taxpayer affected by COVID-19 who was unable to make the minimum yearly repayment in respect of a Div 7A amalgamated loan by the end of the lender's 2019–20 income year, the Commissioner introduced a streamlined process to apply for an extension of time to 30 June 2021 to make the repayment.

[FTR ¶56-140 – ¶56-143]

¶4-243 Div 7A tracing rules

Special tracing rules apply where it is reasonable to conclude that there is an arrangement under which one or more entities have been interposed between the private company and the associated entity (ss 109S to 109XC).

Payments and loans through interposed entities

Under Subdiv E (ITAA36 s 109S to 109X), a private company may be taken to pay a dividend to an associated entity if an entity interposed between the private company and the target entity makes a payment or loan to the target entity under an arrangement with the private company. The rules may also operate where, for example, a private company guarantees a loan made by an interposed entity (eg a bank) to an associated entity. The Commissioner has issued a determination which sets out the factors he takes into account in determining the amount of a deemed payment or loan to a target entity (TD 2011/16). The fact that a payment or loan by a private company to the interposed entity is an ordinary commercial transaction will not preclude the tracing rules from applying (TD 2018/13).

The interaction of the Div 7A exclusion rules where there is an interposed entity is considered in TD 2012/12.

A Div 7A compliant loan agreement between a shareholder/associate and an interposed entity can be treated as being in respect of a notional loan from the private company, and repayments against the actual loan will be able to be taken as repayments of the notional loan from the private company, so that a loan from an interposed entity is treated no more strictly than a loan directly from the private company (ITAA36 ss 109W(3); 109X(2) to (4)).

[FTR ¶56-350 – ¶56-392]

¶4-246 Unpaid present entitlements

Under Subdiv EA (ITAA36 ss 109XA to 109XD), a loan (¶4-210), payment or forgiven debt is subject to the deemed dividend rules of Div 7A where:

- the trustee of a trust distributes funds to a private company's non-corporate shareholder (or shareholder's non-corporate associate) as a loan, payment or forgiven debt
- in the case of a payment, the payment is a discharge or reduction of a present entitlement of the shareholder or associate that is *attributable to an unrealised gain* of a capital or income nature (ignoring any unrealised gain to the extent that it has been or would be included in the trust's assessable income, apart from Div 7A). According to the explanatory memorandum, realisation will be taken to have occurred when a gain converts into a recoverable debt. The explanatory memorandum also states that the conversion of a beneficiary's entitlement to a loan back to the trust may be caught, and

- the company is or becomes presently entitled to an amount from the trust's net income that has not been paid to the company before the earlier of the due date for lodgment or actual date of lodgment of the trust's tax return for the income year in which the transaction took place. ''Net income'' refers to the trust's accounting income (ID 2005/58).

A deemed dividend will not arise if the loan from the trustee is repaid or put on a commercial footing before the earlier of the lodgment date or lodgment due date of the trustee's return for the income year in which the loan was made (s 109XC).

Amounts that already have been taken into account by previous applications of the rules are not to be double counted (s 109XA(4); ID 2005/299).

Under Subdiv EB (ITAA36 ss 109XE to 109XI), indirect payments and loans by a trustee are caught as are cases where the company's present entitlement is indirect. For the Commissioner's views on the operation of the indirect rules, see TD 2011/15 and examples 8 and 9 in PS LA 2010/4.

It is important to note that the circumstances in which the Div 7A trust rules in Subdiv EA may operate in practice in the case of a company and trust which are in the same family group were greatly diminished following the issue of TR 2010/3. As explained more fully at ¶4-215, where a sub-trust arrangement that complies with PS LA 2010/4 is not put in place, an in-substance or provision of financial accommodation loan from the company to the trust will arise for the purposes of Div 7A if the unpaid present entitlement is not paid. In practical terms, this will mean that the present entitlement is extinguished and the Div 7A company loan provisions will be relevant (¶4-200). If a sub-trust arrangement is put in place the Div 7A Subdiv EB trust rules will remain relevant.

Note too that where Trust B is a beneficiary of Trust A and there is an in substance loan by Trust B to Trust A (because of an unpaid present entitlement), the Div 7A trust rules may be attracted if a private company is an unpaid presently entitled beneficiary of Trust B, that present entitlement is put on an acceptable subtrust arrangement and Trust A is an associate of a shareholder of the private company.

It was announced in the 2018–19 Budget that amendments are to be made to Div 7A to ensure that unpaid present entitlements come within the scope of the Division. The amendments will ensure that the unpaid present entitlement is either required to be repaid to the private company over time as a complying loan or subject to tax as a dividend. For the proposed commencement date for this change, see ¶4-200.

[FTR ¶56-395 – ¶56-395/25]

¶4-249 Division 7A dividends limited to distributable surplus

The amount of a particular Div 7A dividend (¶4-200) is proportionately reduced if the total of all Div 7A dividends taken to be paid by the private company for the income year exceeds the ''distributable surplus'' of the company for that year. In this event, the assessable proportion is the distributable surplus divided by the total of all Div 7A dividends paid (s 109Y). See, for example, ID 2005/297.

To enable the associated entity to calculate the proportionate reduction, the private company is required to provide a written statement as soon as possible after year end setting out the company's distributable surplus and the total of all Div 7A dividends paid for that year.

Meaning of "distributable surplus"

A company's distributable surplus is represented by all realised and unrealised accumulated profits, irrespective of whether they are taxable, and is calculated using the following formula (s 109Y(2)):

Distributable surplus	=	Net assets + Div 7A amounts − Non-commercial loans − Paid-up share value − Repayments of non-commercial loans

Where:

Net assets is the amount (if any) by which a company's assets (as recorded in the company's accounting records) exceed the sum of: (a) the company's present legal obligations; and (b) the company's accounting provisions for depreciation, annual and long service leave, amortisation of intellectual property and trademarks. A "present legal obligation" for this purpose is an immediate obligation binding at law, whether payable and enforceable presently or at a future time (TD 2007/28). Provisions other than those mentioned in (b) may be prescribed under regulations. Future provisions are not included in the distributable surplus calculation except as mentioned in (b) (TD 2007/28).

The Full Federal Court has held that a company's income tax liability for an income year is a present legal obligation of the company at the end of the income year and therefore should be deducted when calculating the amount of a company's net assets and distributable surplus at the end of the income year (*H*). TD 2012/10 sets out how this decision is applied. Note that: (1) to the extent that an instalment of tax for an income year remains unpaid as at 30 June, the unpaid amount is a relevant present legal obligation; and (2) if an amended assessment is issued for an income year, the amount payable under the amended assessment is taken into account in calculating the company's distributable surplus for the income year to which the amendment relates and for each subsequent income year in which the amended assessment is not paid.

Non-commercial loans is the total of any amounts the company is deemed to have paid as dividends in earlier years of income under former s 108 or the Div 7A loan rules as are shown as assets in the company's accounting records and any amounts included in the assessable income of shareholders or associates of shareholders under the Div 7A trust provisions in earlier income years.

Paid-up share value is the paid-up share capital of the company at the end of its year of income.

Repayments of non-commercial loans is any repayments to the company of loans that have been taken to be deemed dividends, and certain amounts that have been off-set against loans that have been taken to be deemed dividends.

Division 7A amounts is the total of the dividends the company is taken to have paid in the income year as a result of payments and debt forgivenesses.

The Commissioner has a discretion to substitute a different amount where the net assets are significantly undervalued or overvalued. In exercising this discretion, the Commissioner can take into account the value of the company's assets not shown in the company's accounting records (TD 2009/5). However, this determination points out that where the company's accounting records understate the value of the company's assets because they are required to do so (eg where accounting standards require the value of internally generated goodwill to be omitted), the Commissioner will not exercise this discretion unless it is plain that the company, its shareholders and directors have acted, in making loans or other payments, in a way that treats the real and higher value of assets at their true value, that is, regardless of their value shown in the accounting records.

As pointed out at ¶4-200, it is proposed that the distributable surplus limitation will be removed.

[FTR ¶56-400 – ¶56-400/5]

¶4-252 Offset of Div 7A dividend against subsequent dividend

The situation may arise where a Div 7A dividend (eg a loan) is offset wholly or partly against a subsequent dividend. In that case, the amount of the subsequent dividend that has been set off is treated as if it were not a dividend (and is neither assessable income nor exempt income), to the extent that the subsequent dividend is unfranked (s

109ZC). The franked portion is not reduced. There is a corresponding provision which applies where a dividend is applied to repay all or part of a loan to which the Div 7A trust rules have applied (s 109ZCA).

[FTR ¶56-420 – ¶56-425]

Other Deemed Dividends

¶4-260 Excessive payments to shareholders, directors and associates

A deemed dividend can arise where a private company pays or credits the following amounts to an associated person:

- remuneration for services rendered, or
- a retirement or termination allowance, gratuity or compensation (ITAA36 s 109).

If the Commissioner considers that the amount exceeds what is reasonable, the excess is not deductible to the company and is deemed to be a dividend paid by the company on the last day of the company's income year. To ensure, where appropriate, that it is assessable in the recipient's hands as a dividend (¶4-100), it is also deemed to have been paid out of the company's profits and to have been paid to the recipient in the capacity of a shareholder, whether or not the recipient actually was a shareholder. Transfers of property are treated as if they were payments of amounts equal to the value of the property. The deemed dividend is not subject to dividend withholding tax (s 109(1)(d)) and is unfrankable (¶4-620). The provisions governing the tax treatment of ETPs (¶14-000) do not apply to that part of an amount that is deemed to be a dividend under s 109.

For the purposes of s 109, an ''associated person'' means a past or present shareholder or director, or any associate of those persons. The term ''associate'' has the same meaning as in ITAA36 s 318, which covers a broad range of entities that are associates of natural persons, companies, partnerships and trustees.

The primary test for determining the reasonableness or otherwise of the remuneration, etc, is the value of the services, but such factors as the degree of skill and responsibility of the director or employee must be weighed against the right of capital as well as management to its reward, and against the interests of the shareholders in their capacity as such. All the circumstances of the case must be taken into account. What is reasonable for the purposes of s 109 is not necessarily the same as what is justifiable under ITAA97 s 25-50 (¶16-540).

The exercise of the Commissioner's discretion under s 109 is dependent on an assessment having been issued against the payer company in which the deductibility of the payment in the hands of the company has been considered (*Case S61*).

The provisions apply to non-share equity interests, equity holders and non-share dividends in the same way that they apply to shares, shareholders and dividends (ITAA36 s 102V).

[FTR ¶56-000]

¶4-270 Entities taxed as companies

Corporate limited partnerships (¶3-475) are taxed as if they were companies. Accordingly, distributions by corporate limited partnerships are deemed to be dividends except to the extent that they are attributable to profits or gains of an income year in which the partnership was not taxed as a company (ITAA36 s 94L). Drawings by partners of a corporate limited partnership are also deemed to be dividends (ITAA36 s 94M).

Public trading trusts (¶6-310 – ¶6-330) are also taxed as companies.

[FTR ¶49-770 – ¶49-900]

¶4-280 Other deemed dividends

Certain distributions in the liquidation of a company are deemed to be dividends (¶4-300 and following), as are certain ''distribution payments'' that represent the distribution of the profits of a CFC otherwise than by a dividend (¶21-250).

Distributions in Liquidation

¶4-300 Distributions in formal liquidations

Amounts distributed to shareholders by a liquidator in the course of winding up a company, to the extent that they represent income derived by the company (whether before or during liquidation) other than income that has been properly applied to replace a loss of paid-up share capital, are deemed for tax purposes to be dividends paid by the company out of profits derived by it (ITAA36 s 47(1)).

The term ''income'' covers amounts that are of an income nature, even if exempt. The meaning of the term ''income'' has been artificially extended (by s 47(1A)) for these purposes to include:

- any amount, other than a net capital gain, that is assessable income of the company
- any net capital gain that would arise under the CGT provisions if each capital gain were calculated without regard to indexation and any capital losses were ignored.

▶ Example

During the 2019–20 income year, X Pty Ltd disposes of 4 post-CGT assets that were held for more than 12 months. The relevant details relating to the acquisition and disposal of the assets are as follows:

Asset	Cost base ($)	Cost base as indexed* ($)	Consideration for disposal ($)	Capital gain/ (loss) ($)
1	20,000	22,000	8,000	(12,000)
2	10,000	11,200	15,000	3,800
3	5,000	6,800	6,000	Nil
4	8,000	N/A	10,000	2,000

* Assumed amounts. Indexation applies only up to and including the September 1999 quarter (¶11-610).

Thus, X Pty Ltd has incurred a net capital loss of $6,200 for CGT purposes.

For the purposes of s 47(1A)(b) (ie the second bullet point above) the position is:

Asset	Deemed income ($)
1	Nil
2	5,000
3	1,000
4	2,000

Instead of a loss, X Pty Ltd is taken to have derived ''income'' of $8,000 for the purposes of s 47(1) (of course, the s 47(1) deemed dividend cannot exceed the amount of distributable funds: TD 2000/5).

By deeming distributions to be dividends paid by the company out of its profits, they are assessable in the shareholders' hands under ITAA36 s 44 (¶4-100) as though they had been received as dividends while the company was a going concern.

It is important to remember that in a final liquidation CGT event C2 (¶11-270) would apply in relation to the shares so that a capital gain or capital loss may arise to a shareholder on shares acquired on or after 20 September 1985. Where a capital gain accrues, the provisions of ITAA97 s 118-20 are designed to prevent double taxation (¶11-690; TD 2001/27).

In the case of an interim distribution by the liquidator, CGT event G1 (¶11-310) may apply to the extent that the distribution is not a deemed dividend and the company does not cease to exist within 18 months of the distribution being paid (TD 2001/27).

The distribution by a liquidator of the exempt 50% component of a capital gain that is excluded under the CGT small business CGT concessions (¶7-175) would not be deemed to be a dividend under s 47(1) (TD 2001/14). For the CGT consequences, see ¶11-270.

A deemed dividend under s 47(1) is a frankable dividend for the purposes of the imputation system (¶4-620). Therefore, care must be exercised to ensure that any distribution in the liquidation of a company, to the extent to which it is a deemed dividend, is appropriately franked.

A capital gain made by the parent company on the cancellation of its wholly owned subsidiary's shares may be reduced where, in the course of liquidating the subsidiary, the liquidator has made an *in specie* distribution involving the inter-company roll-over of a post-CGT asset (¶12-530).

The meaning of ''paid-up share capital'' and a liquidator's power to appropriate particular funds to particular distributions is discussed at ¶4-320.

[FTR ¶21-425, ¶21-441]

¶4-310 Distributions in informal liquidations

Distributions of cash or other property of a company appropriated to the shareholders, otherwise than by the company itself, in the course of an informal winding up or discontinuance of business are treated as though they were distributions by a liquidator in a formal winding up (ITAA36 s 47(2A)). This means that, to the extent that the distribution is made out of ''income'' (as defined for the purposes of s 47: ¶4-300) derived by the company, other than income properly applied to make good lost capital, it is treated as a dividend in the shareholders' hands and is usually assessable. This could occur, for example, where the company's business is discontinued and the shareholders simply appropriate the assets to themselves without making a formal application to the court for a voluntary winding up.

By way of safeguarding the revenue in these situations, s 47(2B) provides that, unless the company is dissolved within 3 years after the distribution or such further time as the Commissioner allows, the distribution is deemed to be a dividend paid by the company, as a going concern, out of its profits. In that event, any benefit to be gained through a liquidation, formal or informal, by way of cash distributions of non-assessable capital profits would be lost.

[FTR ¶21-550]

¶4-320 Liquidator's power to appropriate particular funds

A liquidator may, by a proper system of bookkeeping, so keep the accounts as to be able to make or appropriate particular distributions out of or to particular profits (*Archer Brothers*). Amounts so appropriated will represent the profits out of which the appropriation is made. A liquidator can rely on the *Archer Brothers* principle, except where a specific provision produces a different result (TD 95/10). In the absence of any such system or in the absence of a specific appropriation, the distribution will be pro-rated among the various elements in the mixed fund.

The *Archer Brothers* principle applies even where funds from an income or profit source are used to make a distribution representing a return of capital contributed by shareholders (TD 95/10).

For the *Archer Brothers* principle to apply, the ATO requires: (a) that the company accounts have been kept so that a liquidator can clearly identify a specific profit or fund in making a distribution; and (b) that the liquidator actually appropriates the specific profit or fund in making the distribution, either in the accounts or in the statement of distribution (TD 95/10). The ATO does not consider it necessary to keep separate accounts for each specific fund or profit (although the maintenance of separate accounts makes it easier to identify the source of a distribution).

"Paid-up share capital" for ITAA36 s 47 purposes expressly includes cancelled capital not previously repaid to the shareholders (s 47(3)).

[FTR ¶21-441, ¶21-475]

Simplified Imputation System

¶4-400 Summary of imputation system

The basis of the imputation system of company taxation is that shareholders who receive assessable dividends from a company are entitled to a tax offset for the tax paid by the company on its income. It is called an imputation system because the payment of company tax is imputed to shareholders. Dividends paid to shareholders may effectively become tax-free to varying extents. The company must keep records to verify the amount of tax that can be imputed to its shareholders. The simplified imputation system (ITAA97 Pt 3-6) can be briefly described as follows:

- the system applies to distributions (eg dividends: ¶4-460) paid by Australian resident corporate tax entities (¶4-440) to Australian resident members
- tax paid at the corporate level is allocated to members by way of franking credits attached to the distributions they receive. Such distributions are called franked distributions (¶4-640)
- a corporate tax entity can choose, for a particular franking period, the franking percentage for frankable distributions. There is a "benchmark rule" under which the franking percentage for the first frankable distribution made in the franking period (¶4-660) is the benchmark franking percentage for all frankable distributions made in the period
- an amount equal to the franking credits attached to franked distributions is included in the assessable income of Australian resident members, who are then entitled to a tax offset equal to the amount included in their income (¶4-800)
- tax paid and tax imputed to members is recorded in a corporate tax entity's franking account. Broadly, a credit to the entity's franking account (franking credit) arises when the entity pays income tax or receives a franked dividend (¶4-710), and a debit arises when the entity franks a dividend or receives a tax refund (¶4-720)
- where a corporate tax entity has a franking account deficit at the end of a year, it is required to pay franking deficit tax shortly after the end of the year to make good this deficit (¶4-780)
- special rules apply to franked distributions paid to a partnership or to a trustee of a trust. These rules enable the streaming of franked distributions by the trustee of a trust but otherwise ensure that the attached franking credits flow through to each partner or beneficiary (or trustee if appropriate) in proportion to their share of the net income of the trust or partnership that is attributable to franked distributions (¶4-860)
- special rules apply to prevent abuse of the imputation system (¶4-900).

Debt/equity borderline

The debt and equity provisions (¶23-100) apply to the taxation of dividends (including imputation), thin capitalisation, characterisation of payments from foreign resident entities, and the boundary between dividend and interest withholding tax. Thus, the imputation system applies to a non-share equity interest in the same way as it applies to a membership interest. It also applies to a non-member equity holder in an entity in the same way as it applies to a member of the entity (ITAA97 s 215-1).

Public trading trusts, corporate limited partnerships

The imputation system applies not only to companies but also to distributions paid by public trading trusts, which are treated as companies for tax purposes (¶6-330). Corporate limited partnerships (¶3-475) are also taxed as companies and fall within the imputation system (¶4-440).

Special rules for franking by some entities

There are special franking rules for certain entities (ITAA97 s 200-45):

- venture capital franking by a PDF (¶3-555)
- franking by life insurance companies (¶4-760)
- franking by exempting entities and former exempting entities (¶4-970)
- franking by co-operative companies (¶3-430).

Proposed integrity measure

The government has announced that a specific measure will be introduced that will prevent the distribution of franking credits where a distribution to shareholders is funded by particular capital raising activities and will address the issues raised by the ATO in TA 2015/2.

The proposed measure will apply to distributions declared by a company to its shareholders outside or additional to the company's normal dividend cycle (a special dividend), to the extent it is funded directly or indirectly by capital raising activities which result in the issue of new equity interests. Examples of capital raising activities include an underwritten dividend reinvestment plan, a placement or an underwritten rights issue. Where such arrangements are entered into, the company will be prevented from attaching franking credits to shareholder distributions.

Amendments to implement this measure (which is proposed to apply to distributions made after 12.00 pm (AEDT) on 19 December 2016) have not yet been introduced into parliament.

Note that more recently the ATO has issued a *Taxpayer Alert* TA 2020/5 relating to structured arrangements that provide imputation benefits on shares acquired where economic exposure is offset through use of derivative instruments.

[FITR ¶213-000]

¶4-405 Corporate tax rate changes for 2016–17 and onwards: imputation implications

The corporate tax rate was reduced from 30% to 28.5% for the 2015–16 income year and to 27.5% for the 2016–17 income year for corporate tax entities that were small business entities (¶7-050). The 27.5% corporate tax rate was extended to companies with an aggregated turnover of less than $25 million (for 2017–18) and less than $50 million (for 2018–19 and 2019–20) and which qualify as base rate entities (¶3-055). The corporate tax rate is reduced to 26% for the 2020–21 income year for base rate entities with an aggregated turnover of less than $50 million.

The position for the 2015–16 income year was that, although the maximum franking credit that could be allocated to a frankable distribution was usually set by the applicable company tax rate, in the case of companies that were small business entities, the franking credit cap remained at the standard corporate tax rate of 30%. However, the normal franking credit distribution provisions applied.

It was officially explained that, given the rate reductions, it was not feasible to continue to operate the imputation system at the headline corporate tax rate of 30% for all corporate tax entities.

Consequently, from the 2016–17 income year, the operation of the imputation system for corporate tax entities has been based on the company's corporate tax rate for a particular income year, worked out (broadly) having regard to the entity's position for the previous income year. This was necessary because corporate tax entities usually pay distributions to members for an income year during that income year. However, a corporate tax entity will not know its aggregated turnover for a particular income year (and therefore its corporate tax rate for that income year) until after the end of the income year.

As a result of this change, for the purposes of applying the imputation system, corporate tax entities now use what is called the ''corporate tax rate for imputation purposes''. This generally means the entity's corporate tax rate for the income year (the current income year), worked out on the assumption that the entity's aggregated turnover, base rate entity passive income and assessable income for the current income year is equal to its aggregated turnover, etc, for the previous income year. For further discussion (including an example), see ¶4-640.

[FITR ¶766-808/10]

¶4-440 Corporate tax entity and franking entity

The simplified imputation system applies to distributions made by corporate tax entities to their members. An entity is a ''corporate tax entity'' at a particular time if the entity is (ITAA97 s 960-115):

- a company at that time
- a corporate limited partnership (¶3-475) in relation to the income year in which that time occurs, or
- a public trading trust (¶6-320) in relation to the income year in which that time occurs.

These entities are taxed separately from their members, at the corporate tax rate.

Franking entity

A franking entity is any corporate tax entity other than a mutual life insurance company (ITAA97 s 202-15). However, it does not include a corporate trustee when it is acting in its capacity as trustee of a trust.

[FITR ¶213-040, ¶213-625, ¶762-220]

¶4-460 Distributions by corporate tax entities

The core of the imputation system is the attachment of tax credits to distributions paid by corporate tax entities (called ''franking'') in order to pass on to members the benefit of the tax paid at the corporate tax entity level. This eliminates double taxation (at the entity level and the investor level).

A ''distribution'' is defined in relation to the type of corporate tax entity that makes the distribution (ITAA97 s 960-120):

- a distribution by a company is a dividend, or something that is taken to be a dividend, under the Act

- a distribution by a corporate limited partnership is either: (a) a distribution made by the partnership in money or property to a partner in the partnership (excluding amounts attributable to profits or gains arising during a year of income in relation to which the partnership was not a corporate limited partnership); or (b) something that is taken to be a dividend by the partnership under the Act
- a distribution by a public trading trust (¶6-320) is a unit trust dividend, as defined in ITAA36 s 102M (¶6-330).

A corporate tax entity makes a distribution in the form of a dividend on the day on which the dividend is paid or taken to have been paid.

[FITR ¶213-045, ¶762-225]

¶4-480 Members and membership interests

The meaning of a "member" of an entity is set out in ITAA97 s 960-130. The members of various types of entities are shown in the table in ¶8-000.

Where interests or rights that give rise to membership of an entity are held jointly, each holder of the joint interest is a member of the entity.

Membership interest

A "membership interest" in an entity means each interest or set of interests in the entity, or each right or set of rights in relation to the entity, by virtue of which a person is a member of the entity (ITAA97 s 960-135).

[FITR ¶213-050]

¶4-490 Trans-Tasman triangular imputation rules

The Australian and New Zealand governments have extended their imputation systems to include companies resident in the other country. The reforms are aimed at what is known as the "triangular tax" problem, where Australian shareholders in an NZ company operating in Australia were unable to access Australian sourced franking credits, with the same problem applying in reverse for NZ shareholders in Australian companies operating in New Zealand. The Australian rules (discussed here) are contained in ITAA97 Div 220. For details of the NZ legislation, see ¶17-200 and following of the *New Zealand Master Tax Guide*.

NZ companies can elect (ie make an "NZ franking choice") to maintain an Australian franking account reflecting Australian tax paid (including income tax payments, franking credits attached to dividends received and Australian withholding tax on dividends, interest and royalties) (ITAA97 ss 220-25 to 220-50; 220-205 to 220-300). An NZ company that makes an NZ franking choice is known as a "NZ franking company".

Where a non-Tasman company is interposed between an NZ parent company and an Australian or NZ subsidiary, franking credits that would otherwise arise in the franking account of the subsidiary (the "franking donor company") are transferred to the franking account of the NZ company (the "NZ recipient company") that holds the shares in the interposed company. This rule applies only from the time that the parent company, the NZ recipient company and the franking donor company (if it is an NZ resident) have made an NZ franking choice (s 220-300).

Trans-Tasman companies that elect to do so will distribute Australian franking credits and NZ imputation credits to all shareholders in proportion to their shareholdings in the company. However, each country's credits can be claimed only by residents of that country.

▶ Example

NZ Company is owned 80% by NZ residents and 20% by Australian residents. It pays A$100,000 of Australian tax, which it fully distributes to its shareholders through franked dividends. The Australian shareholders will receive A$20,000 of franking credits (ie 20% of the total) in the form of refundable tax offsets. The remaining A$80,000 of Australian franking credits cannot be utilised as they are allocated to NZ residents.

Assume that the company also distributes NZ$200,000 of NZ imputation credits (allocated to the same dividends). Of this amount, NZ$160,000 will be received and utilised by NZ resident shareholders. The remaining 20% of the NZ imputation credits (ie NZ$40,000) will be distributed to Australian resident shareholders, who cannot utilise them.

The franking tax offset received by an Australian shareholder of an NZ company who is eligible to receive offsets for foreign tax (eg an investor with less than 10% shareholding) is reduced to the extent of the ''supplementary dividend'' (see ¶26-500 of the *New Zealand Master Tax Guide*) paid by the NZ company under NZ tax law (ITAA97 ss 220-400 to 220-410).

An NZ franking choice is made by giving notice to the Commissioner. The franking choice will generally be in force from the start of the income year in which the franking choice is made. The notice must be made at least one month before any franked distributions are made (ATO *Trans-Tasman imputation: special rules* fact sheet).

The Australian exempting company rules have been extended to include NZ companies so that they are ''looked through'' to find the ultimate effective owners. The exempting company rules have also been amended to:

- give Australian resident shareholders in an NZ listed company that is an exempting company franking benefits for franking credits attached to dividends paid by the entity
- allow a 100% owned Australian subsidiary of an NZ listed company that fails the amended exempting company rules to nevertheless pass franking credits to its parent (ITAA97 ss 220-500 to 220-700).

NZ subsidiaries of Australian companies

Imputation credits accumulated by an NZ subsidiary of an Australian company before 1 April 2003 are available to allocate to distributions by Australian companies after 1 October 2003.

Australian subsidiaries of NZ companies

Franking credits accumulated by an Australian subsidiary of an NZ company before 1 April 2003 are available to frank distributions if the subsidiary would not have been treated as an exempting company under the changes, had they applied before that date.

A company that was an exempting company immediately before 1 April 2003 can access its pre-1 April 2003 franking credits if, during the period 13 May 1997 to 1 April 2003, either: (a) the company had greater than 5% Australian effective ownership at all times; or (b) the company was a wholly-owned subsidiary of an NZ listed company (ITTPA s 220-501).

Joint and several liability

All members of a wholly-owned trans-Tasman group are jointly and severally liable for the payment of additional tax and penalties when an NZ company runs its Australian franking account into deficit and defaults on the franking deficit tax, over-franking tax or franking-related GIC or penalties payable (ITAA97 s 220-800).

Exceptions apply in sectors such as banking, funds management and insurance, where regulations prohibit entities from assuming the liabilities of others in the group.

Trans-Tasman group structures

The rules generally allow trans-Tasman group structures to pass credits through to their underlying shareholders.

Franking credits may be available to an Australian company that receives a franked distribution from an NZ franking company even where the distribution is exempt income or is non-assessable non-exempt income because it is a non-portfolio dividend or it is paid out of attributed income or attributed FIF income (ITAA97 s 220-350).

[FITR ¶218-200 – ¶218-580]

Franking Mechanism

¶4-600 Franking of distributions

An entity franks a distribution if (ITAA97 s 202-5):

- the entity is a franking entity that satisfies the residency requirement when the distribution is made
- the distribution is a frankable distribution (¶4-620), and
- the entity allocates a franking credit to the distribution (¶4-640).

A distribution franked in this way is a ''franked distribution''.

The amount of the franking credit on the distribution is generally the amount specified in the distribution statement for the distribution (¶4-640).

Residency requirement

To satisfy the residency requirement when making a distribution (ITAA97 s 202-20):

- a company or corporate limited partnership must be an Australian resident (¶3-010) at the time the distribution is made
- a public trading trust must be a resident unit trust for the income year in which the distribution is made. The term ''resident unit trust'' takes its meaning from ITAA36 s 102Q for a public trading trust (¶6-320).

[FITR ¶213-070, ¶213-610 – ¶213-630]

¶4-620 Frankable and unfrankable distributions

A distribution (including a non-share dividend) is a ''frankable distribution'' to the extent that it is not unfrankable (ITAA97 s 202-40).

The following distributions are unfrankable (ITAA97 s 202-45):

- in the case of a share buy-back that is taken to be a dividend under ITAA36 s 159GZZZP (¶3-170), the excess (if any) of the purchase price over the market value
- a distribution in respect of a non-equity share
- a distribution that is sourced, directly or indirectly, from a company's share capital account (ITAA97 s 202-45(e)). However, an exception may apply where a financial group adopts a non-operating holding company structure, an authorised deposit-taking institution (ADI) becomes a subsidiary of the holding company and a restructure instrument is in force under the *Financial Sector (Transfer and Restructure) Act 1999*. Section 202-45(e) will not cause a distribution by the holding company to be unfrankable where the distribution is sourced from profits of the ADI that would have been frankable if they had been distributed by the ADI before the restructure (ITAA97 s 202-47). Nor will s 202-45(e) cause a dividend to be unfrankable where the dividend does not breach the *Corporations Act 2001*.

(including s 254T (¶4-105)) and is paid out of profits recognised in its accounts and available for distribution (the mere fact that the company has unrecouped prior year accounting losses or has lost part of its share capital will not be relevant), or is paid out of an unrealised capital profit of a permanent character recognised in its accounts and available for distribution (provided the company's net assets exceed its share capital by at least the amount of the dividend and the dividend is paid in accordance with the company's constitution and without breaching the Corporations Act) (TR 2012/5)

- non-share dividends paid by an Australian ADI (ITAA97 s 215-10) and non-share dividends that exceed available frankable profits (ITAA97 s 215-15). A company's available frankable profits are worked out under ss 215-20 to 215-25
- distributions that are deemed to be dividends under any of the following provisions:
  - ITAA36 Pt III Div 7A (private company distributions: ¶4-200), unless ITAA36 s 109RB(6) (Commissioner's discretion to allow franking) or s 109RC(2) (dividend taken to be paid because of a family law obligation) applies
  - ITAA36 s 47A (distribution benefits — CFCs: ¶21-250)
  - ITAA36 s 109 (excessive remuneration: ¶4-220)
- an amount that is taken to be an unfranked dividend under ITAA36 ss 45 and 45C (dividend substitution arrangements: ¶4-682)
- a demerger dividend (¶4-160)
- a distribution that either ITAA97 s 152-125 (exempt payments to CGT concession stakeholders) or s 220-105 (certain distributions by an NZ franking company) says is unfrankable.

For a proposed integrity rule that will be aimed at preventing the distribution of franking credits where a distribution to shareholders is funded by particular capital raising activities, see ¶4-400.

[FITR ¶213-075, ¶213-635 – ¶213-655]

¶4-640 Allocating franking credits to distributions

A corporate tax entity evidences its intended allocation of franking credits to a frankable distribution by stating the amount of the franking credit on the distribution statement for that distribution (ID 2005/65). The amount of the franking credit on a distribution is the amount stated in the distribution statement, unless the amount stated exceeds the maximum franking credit for the distribution (ITAA97 s 202-60(1)). A public company is required to determine the extent to which it intends to frank a distribution prior to making the distribution, and the distribution statement must reflect that intention (ID 2005/65). The Commissioner will permit a distribution statement to be amended only where the amount shown on the statement was not intended. For further information regarding distribution statements, see ¶4-690.

The discussion below reflects the position as it is for the 2017–18 and later income years.

Maximum franking credit

The maximum franking credit for a distribution is equivalent to the maximum amount of income tax that the entity making the distribution could have paid on the underlying profits at the entity's corporate tax rate for imputation purposes. The maximum franking credit is worked out using the following formula (s 202-60(2)):

$$\text{Amount of the frankable distribution} \times \frac{1}{\text{Applicable gross-up rate}}$$

For this purpose, "applicable gross-up rate" means the corporate tax gross-up rate of the entity making the distribution for the income year in which the distribution is made.

The corporate tax gross-up rate of an entity for an income year is the amount worked out using the following formula (ITAA97 s 995-1):

$$\frac{100\,\% - \text{Corporate tax rate for imputation purposes of the entity for the income year}}{\text{Corporate tax rate for imputation purposes of the entity for the income year}}$$

Corporate tax rate for imputation purposes

For the 2017–18 and later income years the corporate tax rate for imputation purposes, of an entity for an income year, is the entity's corporate tax rate for the income year, worked out on the assumption that the entity's aggregated turnover, base rate entity passive income and assessable income for the income year is equal to its aggregated turnover, base rate entity passive income and assessable income for the previous income year (ITAA97 s 995-1).

The corporate tax rate for the 2017–18 to 2021–22 income years is:

- for a company that is a base rate entity (¶3-055) — 27.5% for 2017–18 to 2019–20, 26% for 2020–21 and 25% for 2021–22, and
- for all other companies — 30% (ITAA97 s 995-1).

However, if the entity did not exist in the previous income year, the corporate tax rate for imputation purposes for the income years mentioned is effectively 27.5% for 2017–18 to 2019–20, 26% for 2020–21 and 25% for 2021–22.

The upshot is that if for the 2017–18 to 2021–22 income years (inclusive), a company has a corporate tax rate for imputation purposes of:

- 27.5% — the maximum franking credit for a frankable distribution is: Amount of the frankable distribution × 27.5 / 72.5
- 26% — the maximum franking credit for a frankable distribution is: Amount of the frankable distribution × 26 / 74
- 25% — the maximum franking credit for a frankable distribution is: Amount of the frankable distribution × 25 / 75
- 30% — the maximum franking credit for a frankable distribution is: Amount of the frankable distribution × 30 / 70.

▶ Example 1

In the 2018–19 income year, Company A has an aggregated turnover of $52 million and base rate entity passive income equal to 10% of its assessable income. In the 2019–20 income year, its aggregated turnover decreased to $45 million and its base rate entity passive income increased to 15% of its assessable income.

Therefore, for the 2019–20 income year, Company A will have:

- a corporate tax rate of 27.5% (having regard to its aggregated turnover in the 2019–20 income year), and
- a corporate tax rate for imputation purposes of 30% (based on its aggregated turnover and base rate entity passive income levels in the 2018–19 income year).

As a result, if Company A makes a distribution of $100 in the 2019–20 income year, the maximum franking credit that can be attached to the distribution is $42.86, ie $100 × 30 / 70.

▶ Example 2

ABC Co, which is not a base rate entity in 2018–19, has after-tax profits of $500,000 available for distribution and decides to distribute $140,000 to its shareholders on 1 August 2019. The maximum franking credit that ABC can attach to this frankable distribution is $60,000 (ie $140,000 × 30/70).

Exceeding the maximum franking credit

If the amount of the franking credit stated in a distribution statement exceeds the maximum franking credit, it is taken to be the amount of the maximum franking credit (ITAA97 s 202-65).

▶ Example 3

Following on Example 2 above, ABC Co inadvertently states in its distribution statement that the franking credit on the distribution is $80,000. The franking credit will be taken to be $60,000, ie the maximum franking credit.

[FITR ¶213-090, ¶213-670]

¶4-660 Benchmark rule for setting franking percentage

The benchmark rule ensures that one member of a corporate tax entity is not preferred over another when the entity franks distributions. The benchmark rule requires that a corporate tax entity (except a listed public company when exempted by ITAA97 s 203-20) must frank all frankable distributions made during a ‘‘franking period’’ (generally either 6 months or 12 months: ¶4-670) at the ‘‘benchmark franking percentage’’ (ITAA97 s 203-25). The benchmark franking percentage is the same as the franking percentage for the first frankable distribution made by the entity within the franking period (ITAA97 s 203-30).

The benchmark rule allows an entity to decide what the level of franking will be for a particular franking period.

Franking percentage

The franking percentage for a frankable distribution is worked out using the formula in ITAA97 s 203-35:

$$\frac{\text{franking credit allocated to the frankable distribution}}{\text{maximum franking credit for the distribution}} \times 100$$

Where the franking percentage worked out using the formula exceeds 100%, it is taken to be 100%.

The maximum franking credit for a distribution is explained at ¶4-640.

▶ Example

On 1 August 2019, ABC Co (which is not a base rate entity) makes its first frankable distribution for its 1 July to 31 December 2019 franking period (¶4-670), amounting to $140,000. The maximum franking credit for the distribution is therefore $60,000 (see examples at ¶4-640).

As this is the first frankable distribution for the franking period, no benchmark franking percentage has been established and ABC is allowed to frank the distribution at any percentage it chooses (between 0% and 100%). ABC decides to attach a franking credit of $30,000 to the distribution. The franking percentage on the distribution is therefore 50% (ie ($30,000 ÷ $60,000) × 100).

This establishes the benchmark franking percentage for the franking period to be 50%. If ABC makes any further frankable distributions during the franking period, they should also be 50% franked.

If ABC had not franked the 1 August 2019 frankable distribution, the benchmark franking percentage for the franking period would be 0%, and ABC would not be able to frank any subsequent distributions during the franking period. If, on the other hand, the 1 August 2019 distribution was unfrankable (¶4-620), no benchmark franking percentage would be set.

Exemptions from benchmark rule

The benchmark rule does not apply to a company in a franking period if it either satisfies each of the following criteria or is a 100% subsidiary of a company that satisfies the criteria (s 203-20; ID 2004/873):

- it is a listed public company (¶3-130) at all times during the franking period
- it cannot make a distribution on one membership interest during the franking period without making a distribution under the same resolution on all other membership interests
- it cannot frank a distribution made on one membership interest during the franking period without franking distributions made on all other membership interests under the same resolution using the same franking percentage.

Membership interests that do not carry a right to receive distributions (other than winding up distributions) are ignored in determining whether the above criteria are met.

Commissioner can permit departure from benchmark rule

An entity can apply in writing to the Commissioner for a determination permitting it to frank a distribution at a franking percentage that differs from its benchmark franking percentage for the relevant period (ITAA97 s 203-55).

The Commissioner may only exercise this power in extraordinary circumstances, having regard to matters specified in s 203-55 (ID 2005/67). However, the entity, or a member of the entity, can appeal the Commissioner's determination.

The explanatory memorandum to the legislation suggests, for example, that a farming company that franked distributions in anticipation of a franking credit from a subsequent tax payment could successfully apply for permission to depart from its benchmark franking percentage if the franking credit did not eventuate due to devastation of the company's crops by flood.

[FITR ¶213-100, ¶213-800 – ¶213-870]

¶4-665 Consequences of breaching benchmark rule

If an entity makes a frankable distribution in breach of the benchmark rule:

- it is liable to pay over-franking tax (imposed by the *New Business Tax System (Over-franking Tax) Act 2002*) if the actual franking percentage *exceeds* the benchmark franking percentage for the relevant period, and
- a franking debit arises in its franking account if the actual franking percentage *is less than* its benchmark franking percentage for the relevant period. The debit arises on the day on which the frankable distribution is made.

Amount of over-franking tax or franking debit

The amount of the over-franking tax or franking debit that arises due to breaching the benchmark rule is worked out according to a formula which for the 2016–17 and later income years is (ITAA97 s 203-50(2)):

$$\text{Amount of the frankable distribution} \times \frac{\text{Franking \% differential}}{\text{Applicable gross-up rate}}$$

where:

"applicable gross-up rate" means the corporate tax gross-up rate (¶4-640) of the entity making the distribution for the income year in which the distribution is made, and "franking % differential" is the difference between the actual franking percentage and the benchmark franking percentage for the franking period in which the distribution is made. However, where the Commissioner has permitted the entity to use a different franking percentage under ITAA97 s 203-55 (¶4-660), the franking % differential is the difference between the actual franking percentage and the permitted percentage.

▶ Example

Erratic Energy makes 3 frankable distributions during a franking period. The first is franked at 50%, which becomes the benchmark franking percentage. The second distribution ($1 million) is franked at 40% and the third distribution ($2 million) is franked at 65%. It is assumed for convenience that the applicable gross-up rate is 30%.

A franking debit will arise in Erratic's franking account as a consequence of under-franking the second distribution. The amount of the debit will be $42,857 (ie 10% × $1 million × 30/70).

Erratic will also incur over-franking tax as a consequence of over-franking the third distribution. The amount of the over-franking tax will be $128,571 (ie 15% × $2 million × 30/70).

[FITR ¶213-105, ¶213-860]

¶4-670 Franking period

The franking period for an entity depends on whether the entity is a private company or not.

Franking period for private company

The franking period for a private company (¶3-015) is the same as the income year (ITAA97 s 203-45).

Franking period for all other corporate tax entities

A franking period for a corporate tax entity other than a private company is worked out under ITAA97 s 203-40. Each franking period is generally 6 months, but it cannot straddle income years. The first franking period in an income year starts at the beginning of the income year and continues for the *lesser* of 6 months or the whole of the income year. The second franking period (if any) starts immediately after the first, and also continues for the lesser of 6 months or the remainder of the income year. Where the income year is longer than 12 months, a third franking period will immediately follow the second, and will continue for the remainder of the income year.

[FITR ¶213-110, ¶213-850]

¶4-680 Anti-streaming rules

The benchmark rule (¶4-660) is supplemented by the anti-streaming rules of ITAA97 Div 204. These rules are designed to prevent such practices as circumventing the benchmark rule by exploiting the benchmark franking percentage of another entity, streaming franked distributions and tax-exempt bonus shares, or streaming imputation benefits to a member who would benefit to a greater degree than another member.

Linked distributions

A franking debit is generated under ITAA97 s 204-15 if the exercise or non-exercise of a choice by a member of one corporate tax entity results in a linked distribution being made by another corporate tax entity in substitution for a distribution by the first entity. The linked distribution must be unfranked or franked at a different rate from the first entity's benchmark franking percentage for the relevant period. The debit arises in the franking account of the entity with the higher benchmark franking percentage for the relevant period. The debit is equal to the one that would arise if the entity concerned made a distribution equal to the linked distribution and franked it at that benchmark franking percentage. The debit arises on the day on which the linked distribution is made, and is in addition to any other debit that arises in an entity's franking account because of the linked distribution.

If an entity has no benchmark franking percentage for the franking period in which the linked distribution is made, s 204-15 applies as if:

- the entity had a benchmark franking percentage of 100%, where the linked distribution has a franking percentage of less than 50%, and
- the entity had a benchmark franking percentage of 0%, where the linked distribution has a franking percentage equal to or greater than 50%.

Substituting tax-exempt bonus shares for franked distributions

A franking debit is generated in a corporate tax entity's franking account under ITAA97 s 204-25 if the exercise or non-exercise of a choice by a member of the entity determines (to any extent) that the entity issues tax-exempt bonus shares (as defined in that section), to the member or another member, in substitution for franked distributions by the entity to the member or another member.

The debit is equal to the one that would arise in the entity's franking account if the entity made a distribution, equal to the forgone distributions, franked at the entity's benchmark franking percentage for the period in which the shares are issued.

The debit arises on the day when the shares are issued.

If a company has no benchmark franking percentage for the franking period in which the tax exempt bonus shares are issued, the rule applies as if its benchmark franking percentage were 100%.

Streaming distributions

The Commissioner may apply sanctions under ITAA97 Subdiv 204-D if a corporate tax entity streams one or more distributions (with or without giving other benefits) in a period or multiple periods in such a way that:

- an imputation benefit would be received by a member of the entity (the "favoured member") and the favoured member would derive a greater benefit from franking credits than another member of the entity (the "disadvantaged member"), and
- the disadvantaged member would receive lesser (or nil) imputation benefits, but might or might not receive other benefits (such as bonus shares, return of capital, debt forgiveness or the making of a payment to, or the giving of property to, the member or another person on the member's behalf).

The remedies available to the Commissioner are debits to the franking account of the entity, and denial of imputation benefits in respect of a distribution that is made to a favoured member (ITAA97 s 204-26 to 204-55). A taxpayer to whom the remedy relates can object under TAA Pt IVC (¶28-000).

Imputation benefits

For the above purposes, any of the following would constitute an imputation benefit:

- entitlement to a tax offset in relation to franking credits under ITAA97 Div 207, or in relation to venture capital credits (¶3-555) under ITAA97 Div 210
- inclusion of an amount in the member's assessable income under ITAA97 s 207-35
- a franking credit in the member's franking account, or an exempting credit in the member's exempting account
- avoidance of withholding tax liability because of the operation of ITAA36 s 128B(3)(ga), eg because the distribution is franked.

Greater benefit from franking credits

A member of an entity derives a ''greater benefit from franking credits'' than another member if any of the following circumstances exist in relation to the other member in the income year in which the relevant distribution is made, but not in relation to the first member:

- the other member is not an Australian resident
- the other member would not be entitled to a tax offset under Div 207 because of the distribution
- the income tax that would be payable by the other member because of the distribution is less than the tax offset to which the other member would be entitled
- the other member is a corporate tax entity at the time the distribution is made, but no franking credit arises for the entity as a result of the distribution, or
- the other member is a corporate tax entity at the time the distribution is made, but cannot use franking credits received on the distribution to frank distributions to its own members either because it is not a franking entity or because it is unable to make frankable distributions.

Examples of streaming

The following examples of streaming are adapted from the explanatory memorandum to the legislation.

▶ Example 1

A foreign resident controlled company with Australian resident minority shareholders adopts a strategy of distributing all its franking credits to the minority shareholders while retaining the share of profits belonging to the controlling shareholder. It does this with a view to ultimately paying an unfranked dividend or paying some other benefit such as realising accumulated profits as a capital amount on the sale of shares.

This would constitute streaming. On the other hand, if the foreign resident majority shareholder merely deferred distributions in order to provide more equity capital for its subsidiary, but ultimately takes franked distributions, that would not be streaming.

▶ Example 2

A corporate tax entity has members with differing abilities to benefit from franking and a limited supply of franking credits. It makes a franked distribution by an off-market buy-back of shares owned by taxable Australian residents to stream the limited franking credits to those who can most benefit.

This would constitute streaming. Alternatively, where there remain sufficient franking credits to frank distributions to the remaining shareholders, streaming would not occur, unless there are other special features such as those in Example 3.

▶ Example 3

A corporate tax entity has more franking credits than it is likely to use to frank its ordinary distributions. It buys back shares off-market predominantly from members most able to benefit from franking credits because the terms of the buy-back are not attractive to the other members. The buy-back results in directing a large franked distribution to the members most able to benefit. This would constitute streaming.

Disclosure of significant change in benchmark franking percentage

An entity must notify the Commissioner if the benchmark franking percentage for the current franking period ''differs significantly'' (see below) from the benchmark franking percentage for the last franking period in which a frankable distribution was made (the ''last relevant franking period''). This will alert the Commissioner to the possibility of streaming. The notice must be in writing in the approved form, and must state the benchmark franking percentages for the current period and for the last relevant franking period. The notice must be provided with the entity's franking return for the income year in which the current period occurs or, if no franking return is required, within one month after the end of the income year (ITAA97 s 204-75(4)). The requirement does not apply to an entity to whom the benchmark rule does not apply.

Significant difference

For the above purposes, an entity's benchmark franking percentage for the current franking period differs significantly from its benchmark franking percentage for the last relevant franking period if it has increased or decreased by more than 20% *per period*, ie by more than the following amount:

number of franking periods starting immediately after the last relevant franking period and ending at the end of the current franking period	×	20 percentage points

Commissioner may require further information

Where a significant difference in benchmark franking percentages occurs, the Commissioner may request the entity to provide certain specified information and any other information that is relevant in determining whether the entity is streaming distributions (ITAA97 s 204-80). Although this provision is conditional upon there being a significant difference in benchmark franking percentages, the Commissioner has additional broad powers to obtain information under TAA Sch 1 s 353-15 (¶25-220) and 353-10 (¶25-240).

[FITR ¶213-120, ¶213-900 – ¶213-995]

¶4-682 Distributions of preferentially taxed capital

As a consequence of the abolition (from 1 July 1998) of the concepts of par value for shares, share premiums, share premium account and paid-up capital, measures were introduced to prevent the distribution of profits to shareholders as preferentially taxed capital rather than as dividends.

Streaming of shares and "minimally franked dividends"

One anti-avoidance rule applies where a company streams the provision of shares and the payment of ''minimally franked dividends'' to its shareholders in such a way that the shares are received by only some shareholders and some or all of the shareholders who do not receive the shares receive minimally franked dividends. A dividend is minimally franked if it is not franked, or is franked to less than 10% (¶4-660). In such a case, the value of the share is deemed to be an unfranked dividend paid out of profits (ITAA36 s 45).

Shareholder choice is not a precondition for s 45 to apply, and ITAA36 s 6BA(5) arrangements (where shareholders are given a choice) are excluded (¶3-265).

A company is not required to notify shareholders that the value of a share is taken to be an unfranked dividend.

Streaming of dividends and capital profits

Another anti-avoidance provision, ITAA36 s 45A, applies to capital streaming arrangements in which ''capital benefits'' are provided to some shareholders (''advantaged shareholders'') and, generally, less than fully franked dividends are provided to other shareholders. When it applies, such capital benefits are treated as unfranked dividends paid out of the profits of the company.

The crucial element in s 45A is the conclusion that the shareholders receiving the capital benefits derive a greater benefit from receiving them than the other shareholders would (ID 2004/653). Section 45A(4) gives a non-exhaustive list of circumstances in which this conclusion will automatically arise. Most of them relate to features of the CGT regime that an "advantaged" taxpayer can use to reduce or eliminate tax on capital benefits (eg having pre-CGT shares or a net capital loss for the year in which capital benefits are provided).

Section 45A does not apply if any disadvantaged shareholder receives a capital benefit. A disadvantaged shareholder is one who is not "advantaged". A shareholder is "advantaged" merely by deriving a greater benefit from capital benefits than just one other shareholder.

Schemes to provide capital benefits

Another anti-avoidance measure, ITAA36 s 45B, ensures that certain payments that are paid in substitution for dividends are treated as dividends for tax purposes. Section 45B applies where there is a "scheme" under which a person is provided with a capital benefit by the company. Under the scheme, the relevant taxpayer (who may or may not be the person provided with the capital benefit) must obtain a "tax benefit". Further, having regard to the relevant circumstances of the scheme, it must be concluded that the person, or one of the persons, who entered into the scheme or any part of the scheme did so for a purpose (whether or not the dominant purpose, but not an incidental purpose) of enabling the relevant taxpayer to obtain the tax benefit. A relevant taxpayer obtains a tax benefit if an amount of tax payable by the relevant taxpayer would, apart from the operation of s 45B, be less than the amount that would have been payable (or would be payable at a later time than it would otherwise have been payable) if the capital benefit had been a dividend. See ID 2004/654 and ID 2006/188. For guidelines on the application of s 45B to demergers (¶4-160), see PS LA 2005/21. Guidelines on the application of s 45B to a share capital reduction, including a non-share distribution to the extent to which it is a non-share capital return, are set out in PS LA 2008/10.

For the application of the provision to payments by a company to its foreign resident parent, see ID 2002/788.

Determination by Commissioner

Where the criteria in s 45A or 45B are met, the Commissioner may make a written determination in relation to the whole or part of the capital benefit, in which case the whole or part of the capital benefit is treated as an unfranked dividend paid out of profits (ITAA36 s 45C). Adjustments under ss 45A to 45C are excluded from the 2-year limit for amended assessments (¶25-320). Where the Commissioner makes a written determination under s 45B that the whole or part of the capital benefit was paid under a scheme for which a purpose (other than an incidental purpose) was to avoid franking debits, a franking debit arises on the day that notice of the determination is served on the company equal to the franking debit that would have arisen if the deemed dividend had been fully franked.

These provisions apply to non-share equity interests, equity holders and non-share dividends in the same way that they apply to shares, shareholders and dividends (ITAA36 s 43B). For the purposes of ss 45A, 45B or 45C, a non-share capital return (¶23-125) is taken to be a distribution of share capital.

[FTR ¶20-700 – ¶20-750]

¶4-690 Distribution statements

An entity that makes a frankable distribution must give the recipient a distribution statement (ITAA97 s 202-75). Entities other than private companies must provide the statement on or before the day on which the distribution is made. A private company must provide the statement within 4 months (or further time allowed by the Commissioner in writing) after the end of the income year in which the distribution is made. The extension for private companies means that a private company may retrospectively frank a distribution. However, the extension is not allowed for a franked distribution that would create or increase a liability to franking deficit tax (s 202-75(4)), or for a distribution that includes conduit foreign income (CFI) (ITAA97 s 802-15: ¶21-100).

In ID 2005/64, the Commissioner refused to exercise the discretion under TAA Sch 1 s 388-55(1) to retrospectively defer the time when a public company must issue a distribution statement, but stated that the company would be taken to have belatedly complied with its obligations under s 202-75 if it proceeded to issue the late statements. The belated statements had to reflect the franking percentage that (based on the available evidence) was intended at the time the distribution was made (ID 2005/65). In ID 2006/330, a company made a payment in respect of a security that it considered to be a debt interest but later discovered that the security was an equity interest and that the payment was a frankable distribution. In the circumstances, the company could issue a valid distribution statement after the date of payment, but it must reflect a franking percentage of zero.

A distribution statement must be in the approved form. The Commissioner accepts that a statement that contains the following information will be in the approved form:

- the name of the entity making the distribution
- the date on which the distribution is made
- the amount of the distribution
- the amount of the franking credit allocated to the distribution
- the franking percentage (¶4-660) for the distribution
- the amount of any withholding tax that has been deducted from the distribution by the entity
- the name of the shareholder
- where the distribution is unfranked — a statement to that effect
- where the distribution is franked — the franked amount and the unfranked amount of the distribution, and
- where any or all of the unfranked amount of the distribution has been declared to be conduit foreign income — the portion declared to be conduit foreign income.

If an amount of CFI is to be included in the distribution, a declaration to that effect must be made in the distribution statement (¶21-100).

It is an offence under the TAA to fail to give a distribution statement or to make a misleading statement in connection with a distribution.

Amending a distribution statement

A corporate tax entity may apply to the Commissioner to enable it to vary the franking credit allocated on a distribution by amending the distribution statement. The application must be in writing and must include all information relevant to the matters that the Commissioner is required to consider (under ITAA97 s 202-85) when making a determination.

An ATO fact sheet states that the Commissioner will generally only approve a variation if "the amount of franking credit stated on the distribution statement was not intended" (*Issuing distribution statements*). The entity or a member of the entity may object against the Commissioner's decision. Reference should also be made to PCG 2018/8.

[FITR ¶213-130, ¶213-680 – ¶213-695]

Franking Accounts

¶4-700 Franking accounts

The detailed rules for operating a franking account are contained in ITAA97 Div 205, comprising ss 205-1 to 205-50. The provisions also create a liability to pay franking deficit tax if the account is in deficit at certain times.

Every entity that is, or has been, a corporate tax entity has a franking account. Under the post-30 June 2002 simplified imputation system, franking accounts are maintained on a tax paid basis.

[FITR ¶213-140, ¶214-005]

¶4-710 Franking credits

The situations that give rise to franking credits, and the amounts and timing of the credits, are set out in a table in ITAA97 s 205-15. The following are the more significant of these situations:

Credits in the franking account

Item	If:	A credit of:	Arises:
1	the entity pays a PAYG instalment, and the entity satisfies the residency requirement for the income year in relation to which the PAYG instalment is paid, and the entity is a franking entity for the whole or part of the relevant PAYG instalment period	that part of the payment that is attributable to the period during which the entity was a franking entity less any reduction under s 205-15(4)	on the day on which the payment is made
2	the entity pays income tax, and the entity satisfies the residency requirement for the income year for which the tax is paid, and the entity is a franking entity for the whole or part of that income year	that part of the payment that is attributable to the period during which the entity was a franking entity less any reduction under s 205-15(4)	on the day on which the payment is made
3	a franked distribution is made to the entity, and the entity satisfies the residency requirement for the income year in which the distribution is made, and the entity is a franking entity when it receives the distribution, and the entity is entitled to a tax offset because of the distribution under Div 207	the franking credit on the distribution	on the day on which the distribution is made

Credits in the franking account

Item	If:	A credit of:	Arises:
4	a franked distribution flows indirectly to the entity through a partnership or the trustee of a trust, and the entity is a franking entity when the franked distribution is made, and the entity is entitled to a tax offset because of the distribution under Div 207	the entity's share of the franking credit on the distribution	at the time specified in s 205-15(2)
5	the entity incurs a liability to pay franking deficit tax under s 205-45 or s 205-50	the amount of the liability	immediately after the liability is incurred

The table in ITAA97 s 205-15 also covers the situations where:

- a franking credit arises under ITAA97 s 316-275 for the friendly society or one of its wholly owned subsidiaries because the society or subsidiary receives a refund of income tax (table item 6)
- a franking credit arises under ITAA97 s 417-50(5)(b) in relation to a deduction transferred to a corporate tax entity (table item 6A)
- a franking credit arises under ITAA97 s 417-100(1)(c) in relation to a tax loss transferred to a corporate tax entity (table item 6B)
- a franking credit arises under ITAA97 s 418-50(1) in relation to an exploration credit (table item 7), and
- the entity pays diverted profits tax; and the entity satisfies the residency requirement for the income year for which the tax is paid; and the entity is a franking entity for the whole or part of that income year (table item 8).

Clarifying rules about when an entity pays a PAYG instalment or pays income tax or diverted profits tax are contained in ITAA97 s 205-20. Note that where a debit has not been made to an entity's franking account because a refund of income tax is attributable to the refund of a tax offset which the entity is entitled to under ITAA97 Div 355 (research and development), a franking credit will not arise in respect of the payment of a PAYG instalment or income tax until these deferred franking debits are recovered (ITAA97 s 205-15).

Franking credits where tax liabilities partly paid

PS LA 2001/13 provides guidance as to how partial payments are allocated on running balance accounts in accordance with PS LA 2011/20. Where an amount of income tax remains outstanding after that allocation is made, franking credits do not arise in respect of the unpaid amount.

[FITR ¶213-150, ¶214-010 – ¶214-020]

¶4-720 Franking debits

The situations that give rise to franking debits, and the amounts and timing of the debits, are set out in a table in ITAA97 s 205-30. The following are the more significant of these situations:

Debits in the franking account

Item	If:	A debit of:	Arises:
1	the entity franks a distribution	the amount of the franking credit on the distribution	on the day on which the distribution is made
2	the entity receives a refund of income tax, and the entity satisfies the residency requirement for the income year to which the refund relates, and the entity was a franking entity during the whole or part of the income year to which the refund relates	that part of the refund that is attributable to the period during which the entity was a franking entity	on the day on which the refund is received
2A	the entity receives a tax offset refund, and the entity does not satisfy the residency requirement for the income year to which the refund relates, and the entity was a franking entity during the whole or part of the income year to which the refund relates, and the entity's franking account is in surplus on the day on which the refund is received	the lesser of: (a) that part of the refund that is attributable to the period during which the entity was a franking entity, and (b) the amount of the franking surplus	on the day on which the refund is received
3	a franking debit arises for the entity under para 203-50(1)(b) (the entity franks a distribution in contravention of the benchmark rule)	the franking debit worked out under para 203-50(2)(b)	on the day specified in s 203-50(4)
4	the entity ceases to be a franking entity, and the entity's franking account is in surplus immediately before ceasing to be a franking entity	the amount of the franking surplus	on the day on which the entity ceases to be a franking entity
5	a franking debit arises for the entity under s 204-15 (linked distributions)	the franking debit specified in s 204-15(3)	on the day specified in s 204-15(4)

Debits in the franking account

Item	If:	A debit of:	Arises:
6	a franking debit arises under s 204-25 (debit for substituting tax-exempt bonus shares for franked distributions)	the amount of the debit specified in s 204-25(2)	on the day specified in s 204-25(3)
7	the Commissioner makes a determination under para 204-30(3)(a) giving rise to a franking debit for the entity (streaming distributions)	the amount of the debit specified in the determination	on the day specified in s 204-35
7A	a franking debit arises under s 197-45(1) because an amount to which Div 197 applies is transferred to a company's share capital account	the amount of the debit specified in s 197-45(2)	at the time provided by s 197-45(1)
7B	a franking debit arises under s 197-65(2) because a company chooses to untaint its share capital account	the amount of the debit specified in s 197-65(3)	at the time provided in s 197-65(2)
8	(repealed)		
9	an on-market buy-back by a company of a membership interest in the company	an amount equal to the debit that would have arisen if: (a) the purchase of the interest were a frankable distribution equal to the one that would have arisen if the company had purchased the interest off-market, and (b) the distribution were franked at the entity's benchmark franking percentage for the franking period in which the purchase was made or, if the entity does not have a benchmark franking percentage for the period, at a franking percentage of 100%	on the day on which the interest is purchased

The table in ITAA97 s 205-30 also covers the situations where:

- a franking debit arises under ITAA97 s 316-260 for the friendly society or one of its wholly owned subsidiaries because the franking account of the society or subsidiary is in surplus (table item 10)
- a franking debit arises under ITAA97 s 316-265 for the friendly society or one of its wholly owned subsidiaries because a franking credit arises for the society or subsidiary (table item 11)
- a franking debit arises under ITAA97 s 316-270 for the friendly society or one of its wholly owned subsidiaries because a franking credit arises for the society or subsidiary (table item 12), and
- the entity receives a refund of diverted profits tax; and the entity satisfies the residency requirement for the income year to which the refund relates; and the entity was a franking entity during the whole or part of the income year to which the refund relates (table item 13).

Clarifying rules about when an entity receives a refund of income tax (including where there is a loss carry back tax offset or a research and development tax offset) or of diverted profits tax are contained in ITAA97 s 205-35.

[FITR ¶213-155, ¶214-020 – ¶214-030]

¶4-730 Franking surplus or deficit

An entity's franking account is in surplus at a particular time to the extent that the sum of the franking credits in the account exceeds the sum of the franking debits in the account at that time.

An entity's franking account is in deficit at a particular time to the extent that the sum of the franking debits in the account exceeds the sum of the franking credits in the account at that time (ITAA97 s 205-40).

[FITR ¶213-170, ¶214-035]

¶4-760 Special rules for life insurance companies

Special imputation rules are required for life insurance companies, as the 2 distinct aspects of their business require different treatment. Firstly, non-mutual life insurance companies operate a business for the benefit of their shareholders. This aspect of the business should have similar outcomes to those for other companies. However, insurance companies also invest funds on behalf of policyholders. The outcomes for such investments need to be similar to those for superannuation and other managed investments, with which they compete. A mutual life insurance company is not a franking entity (¶4-440); accordingly it cannot frank a distribution (¶4-600), and franking credits generally do not arise in its franking account.

The core imputation rules for life insurance companies are contained in ITAA97 Div 219. Rules dealing with the franking deficit tax offset entitlement (¶4-780) are contained in ITAA97 s 219-70 and 219-75. The franking deficit tax liability can only be offset against an income tax liability that is attributable to the life insurance company's shareholders. Rules about tax offsets for venture capital credits received by a life insurance company are contained in ITAA97 s 210-175 (¶3-555).

The general imputation rules (ITAA97 Pt 3-6) apply to life insurance companies in the same way as they apply to other companies, except to the extent that they are modified by Div 219 (ITAA97 s 219-10).

Franking accounts

The franking credit table in ITAA97 s 205-15 (¶4-710) does not apply to a life insurance company. The table in ITAA97 s 219-15 applies instead. Franking credits for tax paid reflect only the shareholders' share of the company's income tax liability.

Credits for PAYG instalments are initially based on the company's estimate of the shareholders' share. Upon assessment, the estimated credits are reversed and replaced by actual values.

Credits also arise when a life insurance company receives a franked distribution that is subject to the gross-up and tax offset rules under ITAA97 Div 207 (¶4-800). However, a franking credit only arises to the extent that the distribution is attributable to membership interests held on behalf of the company's shareholders.

The franking debit table in ITAA97 s 205-30 (¶4-720) *does* apply to a life insurance company, except for item 2 (tax refunds) and item 2A (tax offset refunds). It is supplemented by 2 other items: (i) the debit that arises when estimated credits are reversed; and (ii) a debit for only that portion of a tax refund that is attributable to the shareholders' share of the company's tax liability (ITAA97 s 219-30).

The special rules also contain a provision for adjusting a life insurance company's franking account where an amended assessment results in a change in the proportion of the company's tax liabilities that is attributable to the shareholders' share (ITAA97 s 219-50).

Transitional provisions (ITTPA Div 219) provide for situations where pre-1 July 2002 franking credits are reversed and replaced by franking credits calculated on a tax paid basis.

[FITR ¶218-015 – ¶218-075]

¶4-770 Example of movements in franking account

The following is an example of straightforward movements in a franking account. (For simplicity, a company rate of tax of 30% is assumed.)

		Debit ($)	Credit ($)	Balance ($)
01 Jul 2019	Opening balance	—	—	57,900
21 Jul 2019	Payment of final 2018–19 tax instalment of $60,000	—	60,000	117,900
30 Sep 2019	Fully franked dividend of $210,000 received. Credit is 30/70 × $210,000	—	90,000	207,900
28 Oct 2019	Payment of first 2019–20 PAYG instalment of $63,000	—	63,000	270,900
28 Feb 2020	Payment of second 2019–20 PAYG instalment of $65,000	—	65,000	335,900
20 Mar 2020	Refund on 2017–18 assessment of $22,500	22,500	—	313,400
28 Apr 2020	Payment of third 2019–20 PAYG instalment of $67,500	—	67,500	380,900
22 Jun 2020	Payment of fully franked dividend of $750,000. Debit is 30/70 × $750,000	321,429	—	59,471
30 Jun 2020	Closing balance (this will be the opening balance on 1 July 2020)	—	—	59,471

Franking Deficit Tax

¶4-780 Liability to franking deficit tax

Franking deficit tax (FDT) is imposed by the *New Business Tax System (Franking Deficit Tax) Act 2002* (FDT Act). A liability to FDT arises in any of the following circumstances:

- an entity's franking account is in deficit (ie its franking debits exceed its franking credits) at the end of an income year (ITAA97 s 205-45(2))

- an entity's franking account is in deficit immediately before the entity ceases to be a franking entity (s 205-45(3))
- a late balancing corporate tax entity elects (under ITTPA s 205-20) to have its FDT liability determined on 30 June, and it either:
  - has a franking deficit at the end of 30 June (ITTPA s 205-20(2)), or
  - ceases to be a franking entity and has a franking deficit immediately before that cessation (ITTPA s 205-25(3)).

The amount of FDT payable is the same as the amount of the relevant deficit (FDT Act s 5).

▶ Example 1

Cook Co's franking account has a deficit of $50,000 at the end of the 2019–20 income year. It is liable for FDT of $50,000.

Where tax refund received after year end

Where a liability (or increased liability) to FDT would otherwise be avoided, a tax refund received within 3 months after the end of the year to which it relates is treated as having been received immediately before the end of that year. A similar anti-avoidance rule applies to refunds received within 3 months after an entity ceases to be a franking entity (ITAA97 s 205-50).

▶ Example 2

Cook Co's franking account has a surplus of $10,000 at the end of the 2018–19 income year (30 June). However, Cook Co receives an income tax refund of $30,000 in August 2019. Cook Co is liable for FDT of $20,000.

The FDT is generally payable within 14 days of the day the refund is paid, unless the relevant franking return is due at a later date (ITAA97 s 214-150(4)).

Offset of FDT against income tax liability

FDT is not imposed as a penalty. It is a payment required to make good the amount imputed by a corporate tax entity to its shareholders that exceeds the amount available to be imputed.

Reflecting the fact that FDT is a prepayment of income tax prematurely imputed to its members, a corporate tax entity that meets a residency requirement may offset its FDT liability against its future income tax liabilities (ITAA97 s 205-70).

The FDT offset can be applied not only against an income tax liability arising from an original assessment but also against an increased income tax liability resulting from an amended assessment for the current year. An unapplied amount of FDT offset (including an unapplied amount from an income year when the company did not satisfy the residency requirement) can be carried forward to a future year.

The FDT offset is deducted from the entity's income tax liability after all other tax offsets (including foreign income tax offsets) have been deducted.

Penalty for excessive over-franking

Where a corporate tax entity franks a distribution during an income year and its FDT liability is more than 10% of the total franking credits arising in its franking account for the year, the entity's FD tax offset (against future company tax liabilities: see above) is reduced by 30%. The reduction applies only to the extent that the entity's FDT liability relates to franking debits that arose under the provisions specified in ITAA97 s 205-70(8). The franking debits specified in s 205-70(8) are those that arise under the following table items in s 205-30: item 1 (franking a distribution), item 3 (contravening the benchmark rule), item 5 (linked distributions) or item 6 (substituting exempt bonus shares for a franked distribution) and (if the entity has a franking debit arising under at least one of those items) item 2 (tax refund).

▶ Example 3

ABC Co has a franking deficit of $1,000 in its franking account at year end, giving rise to an FDT liability of $1,000. The franking deficit is attributable to franking debits that arose (under table item 1 in s 205-30) from ABC's making franked distributions to shareholders. During the year, $8,000 of franking credits arose in the company's franking account. As the FDT liability is greater than 10% of the total franking credits for the year, ABC's FDT offset entitlement is reduced by 30% (from $1,000 to $700). The remaining $300 of FDT operates as a penalty rather than a prepayment of tax.

The Commissioner has a discretion to allow the full FDT offset where, broadly, events that caused excessive overfranking were outside the company's control or were unanticipated, and did not involve any broader exploitation of the imputation system (s 205-70(6)).

Exception for private company's first year

Companies do not pay tax in their first taxable year of operation and therefore have no franking credits available in that year. In these circumstances, the payment of any franked distribution would automatically exceed the 10% threshold and trigger the 30% penalty. In order to facilitate the payment of franked distributions during a private company's first taxable year, the rules have been amended to allow a tax offset for the full amount of franking deficit tax paid, where certain conditions are met. To qualify for the full FDT offset, the company must have an income tax liability for the relevant year (ignoring the FDT offset), and must not have had an income tax liability for an earlier year. In addition, the amount of the income tax liability must be at least 90% of the amount of the deficit in the company's franking account at the end of the relevant year (ITAA97 s 205-70(5)).

[FITR ¶213-210, ¶214-040, ¶214-045]

Receipt of Franked Distributions

¶4-800 Effect of receiving a franked distribution

The tax consequences for a member receiving a franked distribution from an Australian corporate tax entity are set out in ITAA97 Div 207, comprising ss 207-5 to 207-160.

General rule — gross-up and tax offset

The general rule is set out in ITAA97 Subdiv 207-A. As a general rule, for the income year in which the distribution is made, the recipient of a franked distribution:

- includes in their assessable income the amount of the franking credit on the distribution. This is in addition to any other amount included in the recipient's assessable income in relation to the distribution itself (¶4-100)
- is entitled to a tax offset equal to the franking credit (s 207-20).

The general rule does not apply to situations where a distribution flows indirectly to an entity through an interposed trust or partnership. These situations are covered by ITAA97 Subdiv 207-B (¶4-860).

Medicare levy

In calculating an individual's Medicare levy, the grossed-up amount of the dividend is used, not the cash amount of the dividend (*Kellas*). The tax offset cannot be used to reduce the Medicare levy (¶15-010), but any unutilised portion will generally be refundable (¶4-820).

Residency requirements for general rule to apply

The general rule (ie gross-up and tax offset) only applies to an individual or corporate tax entity that receives a franked distribution if it meets the residency requirement. The residency requirement will be met where:

- the recipient is an individual, company or corporate limited partnership and is an Australian resident at the time the distribution is made

- the recipient is a public trading trust and is a resident unit trust for the income year in which the distribution is made (ss 207-70; 207-75), or
- the recipient is a foreign resident company or foreign resident individual and the distribution is received through the foreign resident's permanent establishment in Australia (s 207-75(2)).

▶ Example 1

Australian resident individual shareholders, Jodie and Taani, each receive a fully franked dividend of $6,400, with a franking credit of $2,743. Jodie's taxable income, apart from the dividend, is $20,000; Taani's is $90,000. Neither Jodie nor Taani has any dependants. Their 2019–20 tax liabilities (ignoring Medicare levy) are:

Jodie's tax liability

Other taxable income	$20,000
Dividend	6,400
Franking credit	2,743
Taxable income	$29,143
Tax on $29,143 (¶42-000)	2,079
Less: low income tax offset and low and middle income offset (¶15-300)	700
Less: franking tax offset	2,743
Tax refund	$1,364

Jodie pays no tax on the dividend, or on the other income of $20,000. The (non-refundable) low income and low and middle income offsets (¶15-300) are applied first. The excess franking tax offset of $1,364 is refundable.

Taani's tax liability

Other taxable income	$90,000
Dividend	6,400
Franking credit	2,743
Taxable income	$99,143
Tax on $99,143 (¶42-000)	24,179
Less: low and middle income offset	806
franking tax offset	2,743
Tax payable	$20,630

As the tax on the other income of $90,000 would have been $19,717, Taani has paid tax of only $913 on the dividend (compared with $2,560 if the dividend had been unfranked).

▶ Example 2

For 2019–20, XYZ Co, an Australian resident company (which is a base rate entity), receives a fully franked dividend of $1,400,000 from a related company (which is not a base rate entity) and has $5,000,000 of other taxable income. The taxable income and tax payable of XYZ Co are calculated as follows:

Other income	$5,000,000
Franked distribution	1,400,000
Franking credit (gross-up)	600,000
Taxable income	$7,000,000
Tax at company rate (27.5%)	1,925,000
Less: tax offset	600,000
Tax payable	$1,325,000

Exception where distribution is not taxed

Where an entity receives a franked distribution as exempt income or non-assessable non-exempt income, and the distribution does not flow through the entity to another entity, the entity will not be entitled to a tax offset (s 207-90). There are 2 exceptions to this rule (s 207-110), ie where the recipient will be eligible for a tax offset despite the distribution being untaxed:

- certain exempt income or non-assessable non-exempt income of eligible superannuation entities and life insurance companies (attributable to current pension liabilities, income bonds, funeral policies and scholarship plans)
- an exempt institution that is eligible for a refund (see below).

Exempt institution that is eligible for a refund

Certain exempt institutions, referred to in the legislation as an ''exempt institution that is eligible for a refund'' (s 207-115), are eligible for tax offsets for franking credits attached to the franked distributions that they receive. These tax offsets are refundable under ITAA97 Div 67. The eligible institutions are:

(1) an Australian resident exempt entity that is endorsed by the Commissioner and covered by item 1.1 of the table in ITAA97 s 50-5, (ie a registered charity), or item 4.1 of ITAA97 former s 50-20 (ie ancillary fund), see ¶10-605

(2) an Australian resident deductible gift recipient (ie an institution named in ITAA97 Subdiv 30-B that has an ABN or an institution endorsed under ITAA97 s 30-120(a))

(3) a public fund declared by the Treasurer to be a relief fund under ITAA97 s 30-85(2), unless the fund's eligibility is denied by regulation, or

(4) an institution prescribed by the regulations as eligible for a tax offset refund.

The residency requirement for (1) and (2) requires that, at all times during the income year in which the distribution is made, the entity has a physical presence in Australia and, to that extent, incurs its expenditure and pursues its objectives principally in Australia.

A number of anti-avoidance rules have been enacted to prevent abuse of the exception for exempt institutions that are eligible for refunds (ss 207-119 to 207-136).

Flow-through treatment of non-assessable dividends

Where a franked distribution (not covered by one of the 2 exceptions above) flows indirectly to an entity as exempt income or non-assessable non-exempt income, the entity is allowed a deduction (or reduction) to remove the franking credit from its assessable income, and the entity is not entitled to a tax offset. Also, if the distribution flows indirectly through the entity to another entity, the distribution does not receive gross-up and tax offset treatment in the hands of that other entity (s 207-95).

The only circumstances in which a franked distribution is taken to ''flow indirectly through'' an entity are set out in s 207-50(5). The concept ''flow indirectly to'' is covered by s 207-50(2) to (4) (¶4-860).

[FITR ¶214-100 – ¶214-270]

¶4-820 Refund of excess franking credits

As a general rule, taxpayers are entitled to a refund if their tax offsets for franked distributions exceed their tax liability, ignoring those offsets (ITAA97 s 67-25). Once franking credits have been used to offset any income tax liability, any excess credits will be refunded (see Example 1 at ¶4-800). Tax offsets available for distributions franked with venture capital credits (¶3-555) are also refundable.

The order for applying tax offsets, which is set out in ITAA97 Div 63, is discussed at ¶15-010. The provisions are designed to ensure that tax offsets that are refundable or can be carried forward are applied last, so that they are not wasted. Taxpayers that have a nil tax liability (before refundable tax credits are applied) will be entitled to a full refund of their refundable tax credits. Eligible taxpayers who are not required to file income tax returns can telephone the ATO or submit refund application forms to obtain their refunds.

The taxpayers entitled to the refund of excess franking credits include Australian resident: (a) individuals; (b) certain exempt institutions; (c) trustees assessed on an Australian resident beneficiary's share of trust income; (d) complying superannuation funds, complying ADFs and PSTs; and (e) life insurance companies.

Corporate tax entities are entitled to refunds only in certain limited circumstances, ie:

- the entity is an exempt institution that is eligible for a refund (¶4-800), and the entity is entitled to a tax offset under ITAA97 Div 207
- the entity is a life insurance company that is entitled to a tax offset under Div 207 or ITAA97 Subdiv 210-H (venture capital credits), and the company's membership interest (or interest in the membership interest) on which the distribution was made was not held by the company on behalf of its shareholders at any time during the company's income year, up to the time that the distribution is made (s 67-25(1C) to (1E)). Tax offsets that are attributable to the investments held on behalf of policyholders would thus qualify.

The following entities are *not* entitled to refunds:

- non-complying superannuation funds and non-complying ADFs
- a trustee, to the extent that the trustee is liable to be assessed under ITAA36 s 98 (¶6-120) or s 99A (¶6-230) in relation to the distribution
- a foreign resident that receives a franked distribution through its permanent establishment in Australia (¶4-840)
- a corporate tax entity, except as noted above.

[FITR ¶111-020, ¶112-000 – ¶112-030]

¶4-825 Franked dividends received by loss companies

Companies that have prior year losses and also receive franked dividends do not have to waste those losses by offsetting them against the franked dividends. Companies can choose the amount of prior year losses that they wish to utilise (¶3-060) and excess franking offsets will be converted to current year tax losses (¶3-075).

¶4-840 Receipt of distribution by foreign resident

If a member is a foreign resident, the tax effects of receiving a distribution are dealt with under the withholding tax provisions of ITAA36 Pt III Div 11A (¶22-010) and under ITAA97 Subdiv 207-D. As a general rule:

- the gross-up and tax offset rules do not apply
- withholding tax is payable on an unfranked distribution
- no withholding tax is payable on a franked distribution
- the distribution is non-assessable, non-exempt income (and expenses incurred in deriving that distribution income are not deductible).

Franked distributions flowing indirectly to a foreign resident

Where a franked distribution flows indirectly to a foreign resident entity, the franked portion of the distribution is non-assessable non-exempt income (ITAA36 s 128D). Assuming that the unfranked portion is subject to withholding tax, it will also be non-assessable non-exempt.

Subdivision 207-D provides for adjustments to ensure that an entity's share of the franking credit on the distribution is also excluded from its assessable income. The amount of the adjustment is worked out under ITAA97 s 207-95.

Exception for foreign-owned branches

The following treatment applies to distributions by an Australian resident company that are "attributable to" (eg paid to) an Australian permanent establishment (eg branch) of a foreign resident company or foreign resident individual (ITAA36 ss 44(1)(c); 128B(3E); ITAA97 ss 67-25(1DA); 115-280(1)(b), (ba)).

- The distribution is assessable. Relevant expenses are allowed as deductions against that assessable income.
- Withholding tax does not apply to the distribution.
- Gross-up and tax offset treatment (¶4-800) applies to the franking credit (if any) on the distribution.
- Any excess franking tax offset is not refundable under the refundable tax offset rules (¶4-820).
- Where the foreign resident is a company, excess franking tax offsets are eligible to be converted to tax losses if the relevant requirements are met (¶3-075).

The rules do not apply to dividends paid to Australian branches of foreign resident trusts.

Where the foreign resident holds interests in an Australian company independently from its Australian branch and receives distributions directly from the Australian company, the withholding tax provisions (¶22-010) will continue to apply, as the distributions will not be attributable to the branch.

Application to partnerships

Where dividends are paid by an Australian company to a partnership with a partner that is a foreign resident company or foreign resident individual, and the dividends are attributable to an Australian branch of the partnership, the foreign resident partner will be exempt from withholding tax and will be taxed on its individual interest in those dividends on a net assessment basis.

[FITR ¶214-180 – ¶214-200]

¶4-860 Distribution received through interposed trust or partnership

The general tax consequences of a franked distribution flowing indirectly through an interposed trust or partnership to members of the trust or partnership are set out in ITAA97 Subdiv 207-B, comprising ss 207-25 to 207-59. Broadly, the consequences are as follows:

- each member's share of the franking credit on the distribution is included in that member's assessable income (s 207-35)
- each member is given a tax offset equal to that share of the franking credit, provided the member is not itself an interposed trust or partnership through which the distribution flows indirectly (s 207-45)
- where the trustee is the taxpayer in relation to a share of the distribution, the trustee is given the relevant tax offset. This will be the case where the trustee is liable to be assessed under ITAA36 s 98, 99 or 99A or where the trustee is the trustee of a complying or non-complying superannuation fund, complying or non-complying ADF or PST.

Working out the entity's share of the franking credit

An entity's share of a franking credit on a franked distribution is an amount notionally allocated to the entity as its share of that credit, whether or not the entity actually receives any of that credit or distribution (s 207-57). The amount of the credit is worked out using the following formula:

$$\text{amount of the franking credit on the franked distribution} \times \frac{\text{entity's share of the franked distribution}}{\text{amount of the franked distribution}}$$

The *entity's share of the franked distribution* is determined by reference to the table in s 207-55.

Distribution flowing indirectly to an entity

The only circumstances in which a franked distribution is taken to "flow indirectly to" an entity (see below) or "flow indirectly through" an entity (¶4-800) are described in s 207-50.

Partner

A franked distribution flows indirectly to a partner in a partnership in the income year if (s 207-50(2)):

- during that income year, the distribution is made to the partnership or flows indirectly to the partnership as a beneficiary of a trust
- the partner has an individual interest in the partnership's net income or partnership loss for that year (whether or not the individual interest becomes assessable income in the hands of the partner), and
- the partner's share of the distribution under s 207-55 is a positive amount (whether or not the partner actually receives any of that share).

Beneficiary of a trust

A franked distribution flows indirectly to a beneficiary of a trust in the income year if (s 207-50(3)):

- during that income year the distribution is made to the trustee of the trust or flows indirectly to the trustee as a partner or beneficiary
- the beneficiary has one of the following amounts for the income year (the **share amount**), whether or not the share amount becomes assessable income in the hands of the beneficiary:
  - a share of the trust's net income for that income year under ITAA36 s 97(1)(a), or
  - an individual interest in the trust's net income for that income year under ITAA36 s 98A or s 100, and
- the beneficiary's share of the distribution under s 207-55 is a positive amount (whether or not the beneficiary actually receives any of that share).

Trustee of a trust

A distribution flows indirectly to a trustee of a trust in an income year if:

- a distribution is made to the trustee during the income year, or flows indirectly to the trustee as a partner or beneficiary
- the trustee is liable (or would be liable but for another provision) to be assessed in respect of an amount (the **share amount**) that is:
  - a share of the trust's net income for that income year under s 98, or
  - all or a part of the trust's net income for that income year under s 99 or s 99A

  (whether or not the share amount becomes assessable income in the hands of the trustee), and
- the trustee's share of the distribution under s 207-55 is a positive amount (whether or not the trustee actually receives any of that share).

Streaming dividend income

There are special provisions which govern the streaming of franked distributions by the trustee of a trust, providing the trust instrument confers on the trustee the necessary power.

Under these provisions, for a franked distribution to be streamed involves the trustee taking the necessary steps to make a beneficiary or beneficiaries specifically entitled to an amount of the distribution. The amount to which a beneficiary is specifically entitled is measured by reference to the beneficiary's net financial benefit that is referrable to the distribution (by taking into account for this purpose expenses that are directly relevant to the distribution) (ITAA97 s 207-58). The steps that the trustee must take include the recording of the amount, in its character as referable to the franked distribution, in the accounts or records of the trust not later than the end of the income year (ITAA97 s 207-58).

To the extent that a franked distribution is not streamed, the franked distribution flows to the beneficiaries who are presently entitled to income of the trust for the income year in the same proportions of their present entitlements to the income of the trust (adjusted to take into account the specific entitlements of other beneficiaries to franked distributions or to capital gains that are treated as income).

Where the directly relevant expenses relating to a franked distribution exceed the distribution, the benefit of the franking credit will be available to beneficiaries who are presently entitled to income of the trust providing the trust has a positive net income for tax purposes. Note that provision is made for the pooling of franked distributions which, where it is available, may overcome the difficulties of not being able to stream a franked distribution where the directly relevant expenses relating to that distribution exceed the distribution (ITAA97 s 207-59).

[FITR ¶214-125 – ¶214-158]

¶4-870 Cum dividend sales and securities lending arrangements

There are 2 situations in which a franked distribution, or a distribution franked with an exempting credit, that is made to a member of a corporate tax entity is treated as having been made to another entity. These situations are: (a) cum dividend sales; and (b) securities lending arrangements (ITAA97 Div 216).

Cum dividend sales

The first situation applies where the member is under an obligation, at the distribution closing time, to transfer their relevant membership interest to another person under a contract of sale entered into in the ordinary course of trading on an approved stock exchange. If the contract requires that the distribution be paid to the other person, it will be taken to have been made to the other person and not to the member (ITAA97 s 216-5).

Securities lending arrangements

The second situation applies where, at the time the distribution is made, the member is under an obligation (as the borrower) to pay the distribution to another person under a securities lending arrangement. If the distribution closing time occurred during the borrowing period, the distribution will be taken to have been made to the other person and not to the member (ITAA97 s 216-10).

For the above purposes, where a distribution is made to those members who were members as at a particular time (at or before the distribution is made), that time is the distribution closing time.

[FITR ¶217-600 – ¶217-630]

¶4-880 Consequences of the debt/equity rules

The imputation system applies to a non-share equity interest in the same way as it applies to a membership interest. It also applies to a non-member equity holder in an entity in the same way as it applies to a member of the entity (ITAA97 s 215-1).

[FITR ¶217-500 – ¶217-505, ¶762-748]

Imputation Integrity Measures

¶4-900 Overview of imputation integrity measures

In its basic form, the imputation system could be open to substantial abuse. Accordingly, a number of integrity measures have been put in place to ensure that the system's operation is consistent with the government's taxation policy intentions.

These measures include:

(1) anti-streaming rules (¶4-680) designed to ensure that franking benefits are not streamed mainly to members who would benefit to a greater degree than other members

(2) a general anti-avoidance rule applicable to franking credit schemes (¶30-195), which has been successfully applied in *Electricity Supply Industry Superannuation (Qld) Ltd*

(3) holding period and related payments rules (¶4-940) to prevent trading schemes in which a taxpayer might, for example, acquire shares cum dividend, collect the dividend and franking credits and then dispose of the shares at a loss

(4) rules to counteract dividend stripping (¶30-190) and distribution (dividend) washing (¶4-975)

(5) share capital tainting rules (¶4-950) to prevent companies disguising a dividend as a tax-preferred capital distribution from the share capital account

(6) debt/equity rules (¶4-880, ¶23-100) to prevent payments in the nature of interest being treated as dividends, and vice versa

(7) the "exempting entity" and "former exempting entity" rules (¶4-970).

In the case of (1) to (4) above, the gross-up and tax offset rules do not apply (¶4-920).

¶4-920 Consequences of manipulating the imputation system

Certain consequences of manipulating the imputation system are set out in ITAA97 Subdiv 207-F (ss 207-145 to 207-160). Where the relevant provisions apply, there is no gross-up of the entity's assessable income to include the relevant franking credit, and any tax offset to which the entity would otherwise have been entitled as a result of the distribution is denied. Adjustments to give effect to Subdiv 207-F are excluded from the 2-year time limit for amended assessments (¶25-320).

Direct distributions

Gross-up and tax offset treatment does not apply where an entity makes a franked distribution to another entity in one or more of the following circumstances (s 207-145):

(1) the entity is not a qualified person in relation to the distribution for the purposes of ITAA36 Div 1A of former Pt IIIAA — ie because the holding period and/or related payments rules in that Division (¶4-940) are not satisfied

(2) the Commissioner has made a determination under ITAA97 s 204-30(3)(c) (¶4-680) that no imputation benefit is to arise for the receiving entity because distributions have been streamed in a certain way

(3) the distribution is made as part of a dividend stripping operation (which includes a distribution arising out of, or in the course of, a scheme that has substantially the effect of a dividend stripping scheme: s 207-155)

(4) the Commissioner has made a determination under ITAA36 s 177EA(5)(b) (general anti-avoidance provision) that no imputation benefit is to arise (¶30-195)

(5) the distribution is one to which ITAA97 s 207-157 (which is about distribution washing) applies, or

(6) the distribution is made on or after 1 January 2019 and is one to which ITAA97 s 207-158 (which is about foreign income tax deductions) applies.

Where the Commissioner's determination in (4) above applies only to a specified part of a franked distribution, the amount included in the recipient's assessable income and the amount of the tax offset is worked out using the formula:

$$\frac{\text{franked distribution} - \text{specified part}}{\text{franked distribution}} \times \text{franking credit}$$

Indirect distributions

Gross-up and tax offset treatment also does not apply where a franked distribution flows indirectly to an entity in one or more of the following circumstances (s 207-150):

(1) the entity is not a qualified person in relation to the distribution for the purposes of ITAA36 Div 1A of former Pt IIIAA — ie because the holding period and/or related payments rules in that Division (¶4-940) are not satisfied

(2) the Commissioner has made a determination under s 204-30(3)(c) (¶4-680) that no imputation benefit is to arise for the receiving entity because distributions have been streamed in a certain way

(3) the distribution is made as part of a dividend stripping operation (which includes a distribution arising out of, or in the course of, a scheme that has substantially the effect of a dividend stripping scheme: s 207-155)

(4) the Commissioner has made a determination under s 177EA(5)(b) (general anti-avoidance provision) that no imputation benefit is to arise in respect of the distribution for the entity (¶30-195)

(5) the distribution is treated as an interest payment under s 207-160 (see below)

(6) the distribution is one to which ITAA97 s 207-157 (which is about distribution washing) applies, or

(7) the distribution is made on or after 1 January 2019 and is one to which ITAA97 s 207-158 (which is about foreign income tax deductions) applies.

Where the Commissioner's determination in (4) above applies only to a specified part of a franked distribution:

- the entity is allowed a deduction (or reduction) of an amount worked out under s 207-150(5) and (6)
- the tax offset to which the entity is entitled is worked out using the formulas in s 207-150(5) and (6).

Deemed interest payments

In certain circumstances, a franked distribution that flows indirectly to an entity is treated as an interest payment (s 207-160). This will only be the case where (broadly):

- all or part of the entity's individual interest or share amount in relation to the distribution could reasonably be regarded as the payment of interest on a loan, and
- the entity's interest in the last intermediary entity:
  - was acquired at or after 7.30 pm on 13 May 1997 by legal time in the ACT

- was acquired for a period that was extended at or after that time, or
- was acquired as part of a financing arrangement for the entity entered into at or after that time.

[FITR ¶214-240 – ¶214-270]

¶4-940 Holding period and related payments rules

As mentioned in ¶4-920, gross-up and tax offset treatment does not apply to a recipient of a franked distribution where the recipient is not a ‘‘qualified person’’ in relation to the distribution for the purposes of ITAA36 Div 1A of former Pt IIIAA — ie because the holding period rule and/or related payments rules have not been satisfied: ITAA97 ss 207-145; 207-150; TD 2007/11.

Broadly, the holding period and related payments rules contained in ITAA36 former s 160APHC to 160APHU consist of:

- a holding period rule, which (subject to certain exceptions) requires taxpayers to hold shares at risk for more than 45 days (or 90 days for preference shares) in order to qualify for a franking benefit or the former inter-corporate dividend rebate, and
- a related payments rule, which requires taxpayers who are under an obligation to make a related payment in relation to a dividend to hold the relevant shares at risk for more than 45 days (or 90 days for preference shares) during the relevant qualification period in order to qualify for a franking benefit or the former inter-corporate dividend rebate.

There is a small shareholders exemption for natural persons whose tax offset entitlement does not exceed $5,000 for the income year.

Certain ‘‘eligible taxpayers’’, such as superannuation and insurance entities and widely held trusts, could elect to have franking credit or rebate ceilings applied in accordance with a particular formula as an alternative to the holding period rule (former s 160APHR).

TD 2007/11 states that, although s 160AOAA has the effect that former Pt IIIAA does not apply to events occurring after 30 June 2002, this does not prevent the qualified person rules from having application to a franked distribution made after 30 June 2002. It would seem that the Commissioner’s view in TD 2007/11 has effectively been endorsed by the AAT in *Soubra*.

Dividend received through a discretionary trust

The rules for determining a beneficiary’s interest in shares held by a trust (former s 160APHO, 160APHL) are such that dividends received as part of a discretionary trust distribution generally will not qualify for franking credits unless:

- the beneficiary is entitled to the small shareholders exemption (above)
- the trust is a ‘‘family trust’’ (¶6-266), or
- the discretionary trust acquired the relevant shares or interests in shares before 3 pm on 31 December 1997 (eg ID 2002/604; ID 2003/1105 and ID 2003/1106; ID 2003/1108). The roll-over of a pre-20 September 1985 share for CGT purposes will not preserve its pre-31 December 1997 status for holding period purposes (ID 2006/31).

Life tenant

Similarly, a life tenant in receipt of dividends with franking credits greater than $5,000 would not qualify under the existing holding period rules in relation to shares acquired by the trust post-1997, as the shares would not be held ‘‘at risk’’ (ID 2002/122; ID 2002/604). Although the then government announced on 20 March 2006 that the rules would be amended with effect from 1 July 2002 so that beneficiaries who have a vested interest in dividend income of a testamentary trust but not the current beneficial ownership of the underlying shares (such as life tenants) would be excluded from the holding period rules, no amending legislation has been forthcoming. The exclusion was not to apply to income beneficiaries who made related payments. Trustees of affected trusts who had made family trust elections primarily for the purposes of obtaining imputation benefits were to be able to revoke those elections under ITAA36 Sch 2F s 272-80(6A)(c), subject to the rules in s 272-80(6B) to (11).

[FITR ¶214-245 – ¶214-250]

¶4-950 Tainted share capital accounts

The share capital tainting rules are designed to prevent a company transferring profits to its share capital account and then distributing those profits in the guise of a non-assessable capital distribution.

Summary of the share capital tainting rules

Briefly, the share capital tainting rules in Div 197 operate as follows:

- the tainting rules apply if an Australian resident company transfers an amount to its share capital account from another account, unless the amount transferred is share capital or another specified exception applies
- the first such transfer to an untainted share capital account taints the account. Subsequent transfers will increase the amount by which it is tainted
- if a relevant (initial or subsequent) transfer occurs, a franking debit arises in the company's franking account
- a distribution from a tainted share capital account is treated as an unfrankable distribution of profits (ITAA97 s 202-45(e))
- a company can make an irrevocable choice to untaint its share capital account. This may cause further franking debits to arise. It may also trigger a liability to untainting tax.

Further details are provided below. Note that there are proposed consequential amendments to the share capital tainting rules as a result of the changes in the corporate tax rate (¶4-405).

What is a company's share capital account?

For the purposes of ITAA97 Div 197, a share capital account is any account that the company keeps of its share capital, or any other account that was created after 30 June 1998 to which the first amount credited was an amount of share capital (ITAA97 s 975-300). If a company has more than one account fulfilling this definition, they are taken to be a single account for the purposes of the Act.

Tainting a share capital account

An untainted share capital account becomes tainted when an amount to which Div 197 applies is transferred to the share capital account of an Australian resident company.

Transferred amounts to which Div 197 applies

Division 197 applies to an amount transferred to a company's share capital account from any other account of the company, unless the transfer is excluded under Subdiv 197-A (ss 197-5; 197-50). In general terms, Div 197 does not apply to transfers of the following:

- amounts that could be identified as share capital (s 197-10)
- amounts transferred under debt/equity swaps, within certain limits (s 197-15)
- amounts transferred from the share premium account or capital redemption reserve of a non-Corporations Act company when eliminating par value shares (s 197-20)
- an amount transferred from an option premium reserve because of the exercise of options to acquire shares in the company (s 197-25)

- certain amounts transferred in connection with demutualisations or post-demutualisation transfers (ss 197-30 to 197-40).

Amounts transferred to a company's share capital account under a dividend re-investment plan will also generally not taint its share capital account, due to the specific exclusion in ITAA36 s 6BA(5) — TD 2009/4.

Tainting amount

The "tainting amount" for a company's share capital account at a particular time is the sum of: (1) the transferred amount that most recently caused the account to be tainted; and (2) any other amounts to which Div 197 applies that have been transferred since the account became tainted (s 197-50(3)).

Tainting changes nature of the account

A tainted share capital account is deemed not to be a share capital account for the purposes of the Act, other than for the purposes of the tainting rules and the CGT anti-overlap provision in ITAA97 s 118-20(6) (ITAA97 s 975-300(3)). This means that a distribution out of the account is taxed as a distribution of profits rather than a return of capital, and is unfrankable (ITAA97 s 202-45).

▶ Example 1

A company transfers $1,000 to its share capital account from another account. The transfer is not one that is excluded from the application of Div 197 under ss 197-10 to 197-40. It subsequently transfers a further $3,000 from the other account to its share capital.

The transfer of $1,000 taints the share capital account. The tainting amount at that point is $1,000. The additional transfer increases the tainting amount to $4,000.

The account remains tainted until/unless the company makes a choice to untaint it. Any distribution from the tainted account will be treated as an unfrankable distribution of profits, not a return of capital.

Franking debit arising due to relevant transfer

If an amount ("transferred amount") to which Div 197 applies is transferred to a company's share capital account, a franking debit arises in the company's franking account. This will be the case whether the amount is the first amount to which the Division applies (ie the amount that taints a hitherto untainted account under s 197-50), or an additional transfer into an already tainted account. The debit arises immediately before the end of the franking period (¶4-670) in which the transfer of the amount occurs.

Amount of the franking debit

The amount of the franking debit is calculated as follows (s 197-45):

$$\text{Transferred amount} \times \frac{\text{Applicable franking percentage}}{\text{Applicable gross-up rate}}$$

The "applicable franking percentage" is the benchmark franking percentage (¶4-660) for the franking period in which the transfer occurs, or (if no benchmark franking percentage has been set by the end of the franking period) 100%.

The "applicable tax gross-up rate" means the company's corporate tax gross up rate for the income year in which the franking debit arises. The corporate tax gross-up rate, of an entity for an income year, is the amount worked out using the following formula (ITAA97 s 995-1):

$$\frac{100\,\% - \text{Corporate tax rate for imputation purposes of the entity for the income year}}{\text{Corporate tax rate for imputation purposes of the entity for the income year}}$$

For the meaning of the corporate tax rate for imputation purposes of an entity for an income year, see ¶4-640.

▶ Example 2

Assume that the transfer of $1,000 in Example 1 takes place in August and that the transfer of $3,000 takes place in February of the same income year, which ends on 30 June. The company has 2 franking periods, ending on 31 December and 30 June. Assume that the company does not set a benchmark franking percentage for the first franking period, and that the benchmark franking percentage for the second franking period is 80%.

Assuming a corporate tax rate for imputation purposes of 30%, a franking debit of $429 (ie $1,000 × 30/70 × 100%) will arise on 31 December in relation to the first transfer. A franking debit of $1,029 (ie $3,000 × 30/70 × 80%) will arise on 30 June in relation to the second transfer.

Untainting a share capital account

Once tainted, a share capital account remains tainted until the company chooses to untaint the account. The choice can be made at any time, is irrevocable and must be made in the approved form given to the Commissioner (s 197-55). The choice to untaint the account may give rise to further franking debits and/or untainting tax.

Further franking debits due to untainting

For each transferred amount that makes up the tainting amount for the share capital account (see above), a franking debit will arise if the benchmark franking percentage for the franking period in which the transfer occurred is less than the benchmark franking percentage for the franking period in which the untainting choice is made, or (if no benchmark franking percentage has been set by the end of the franking period) 100%.

This rule is applied separately for each transferred amount (if more than one) that comprises the tainting amount.

The debits (if any) will arise at the end of the franking period in which the untainting choice is made.

Amount of each franking debit

For each transferred amount that meets the above criterion, the amount of the further franking debit will be the amount determined under the following formula *less* any franking debit that arose under s 197-45 due to the relevant transfer (s 197-65(3)):

$$\text{Transferred amount} \times \frac{\text{Applicable franking percentage}}{\text{Applicable gross-up rate}}$$

The above formula is identical to that in s 197-45. However, the "applicable franking percentage" in s 197-65(3) is the benchmark franking percentage for the franking period in which the untainting choice is made, or (if no benchmark franking percentage has been set by the end of the franking period) 100%.

▶ Example 3

The company in Example 2 subsequently decides to untaint its share capital account. Assume that the applicable franking percentage at the end of the franking period in which the untainting takes place is 90%.

In relation to the first transfer ($1,000) the franking debit of $429 that arose under s 197-45 was based on a franking percentage of 100%. Therefore, no further franking debit can arise under s 197-65 in connection with the untainting.

However, the franking debit of $1,029 that arose under s 197-45 in relation to the second transfer ($3,000) was based on a franking percentage of only 80%. Therefore, a further franking debit of $128 (ie ($3,000 × 30/70 × 90%) − $1,029) will arise under s 197-65.

Untainting tax

Untainting a share capital account may also give rise to an untainting tax liability. Conceptually, the untainting tax aims to recoup (in advance) any tax that might otherwise be inappropriately avoided by the members of the company receiving non-assessable distributions of former tainting amounts from the untainted share capital account. Untainting tax is due and payable 21 days after the end of the franking period in which the untainting choice was made, and is subject to the general interest charge if overdue more than 60 days (ss 197-70; 197-75). The amount of the untainting tax (if any) depends on whether the company is:

- a **company with only lower tax members in relation to the tainting period**, ie that was wholly-owned throughout the period by other companies, complying superannuation entities or foreign residents, or
- a **company with higher tax members in relation to the tainting period**, ie any other company.

The "tainting period" is the period from the time the account most recently became tainted until the company chooses to untaint the account.

Company with only lower tax members

A company with only lower tax members in relation to the tainting period will be liable to untainting tax only if its applicable franking percentage at the end of either the franking period in which the share capital account was tainted or the franking period in which the untainting choice was made was less than 100%. The "applicable tax rate" for such a company is the company's corporate tax rate for imputation purposes (¶4-640) for the income year in which the choice is made.

Company with higher tax members

A company with higher tax members in relation to the tainting period will always be liable to untainting tax. The "applicable tax rate" for a company with higher tax members is equal to the highest marginal personal tax rate plus Medicare levy plus Medicare levy surcharge.

Amount of untainting tax

The amount of the untainting tax (if any) is equal to the "applicable tax amount" *less* the total amount of any franking debits that arose in relation to the tainting amount under ss 197-45 and 197-65 (see above).

The **applicable tax amount** is the grossed-up tainting amount at the time of the untainting choice multiplied by the applicable tax rate (mentioned above). It can be calculated using the formulas in s 197-60(3) and (4).

It may be noted that the untainting tax levied on a company with higher tax members will result in an over-recoupment where some members are not liable to pay tax at the highest marginal tax rate. Conversely, there ultimately may be an under-recoupment from a company with only lower tax members if the membership later changes to higher tax members before a distribution is made from the untainted share capital account.

▶ Example 4

Assume that the company in Examples 1 to 3 has had only lower tax members in relation to the tainting period. Therefore, its applicable tax rate is 30%. The tainting amount is $4,000 (ie $1,000 + $3,000) and the notional franking amount is $1,714 (ie $4,000 × 30/70).

The applicable tax amount is $1,714 (ie ($4,000 + $1,714) × 30%). The untainting tax is equal to the applicable tax amount less the franking debits that have arisen under s 197-45 and 197-65. Thus, the untainting tax is $128 (ie $1,714 – $429 – $1,029 – $128).

Share capital tainting rules and consolidated groups

According to the explanatory memorandum to the Taxation Laws Amendment (2006 Measures No 3) Bill 2006, the share capital tainting rules have the following application to consolidated groups:

- if a subsidiary member of a consolidated or MEC group transfers an amount to its share capital account, only the share capital account of the *subsidiary* becomes tainted

- franking debits that arise due to tainting or untainting arise in the *head company's* franking account, as a consolidated group has only one franking account. The applicable franking percentage is the head company's franking percentage
- if a company with a tainted share capital account becomes a subsidiary member of a consolidated or MEC group, no further franking debit arises
- any untainting tax liability is calculated on the basis of the relevant *subsidiary's* position as a company with lower tax or higher tax shareholders
- if a subsidiary member with a tainted share capital account leaves a consolidated group, its share capital account remains tainted.

Tainting holiday from 1 July 2002 to 25 May 2006

Amounts transferred to a company's share capital account during the period 1 July 2002 to 25 May 2006 do not cause the account to be tainted.

Furthermore, under the transitional rules (ITTPA Div 197), if a company had a tainted share capital account under ITAA36 (as amended) as at 30 June 2002:

- the share capital account is taken to be untainted from 1 July 2002 to 25 May 2006
- no franking debit or untainting tax arises under the share capital tainting rules during that period
- any distribution from the account during that period is treated as a capital distribution
- at the start of 26 May 2006, the share capital account is taken to be tainted to the same extent under ITAA97 Div 197, but no franking debit arises as a result of the account again becoming tainted
- the company is able to untaint its share capital account under ITAA97 s 197-55.

Retrospective changes to the former tainting rules

Relevant transfers under debt/equity swaps, from option premium reserves, and in relation to demutualisations have been excluded from the operation of the former share capital tainting rules retrospective to 1 July 1998 (ITAA36 former s 160ARDM, as amended). The resulting outcomes are consistent with the current rules.

[FITR ¶211-150 – ¶211-192; FTR ¶78-365]

¶4-970 Exempting entities and former exempting entities

The exempting entity rules (ITAA97 Div 208) are designed to prevent franking credit trading schemes involving companies that are effectively owned by foreign residents or exempt entities.

Exempting entities

An exempting entity is a corporate tax entity (¶4-440) that is effectively owned by prescribed persons (ITAA97 s 208-20). It is subject to the ordinary imputation provisions and generates franking credits and debits and keeps a franking account in the usual way.

Franked distributions paid by exempting entities to Australian resident members are generally treated as unfranked distributions (ITAA97 s 208-195). There is an exception for distributions paid on shares acquired under an eligible employee share scheme (ITAA97 s 208-205).

Foreign residents in receipt of franked distributions from exempting entities are exempt from withholding tax.

Where certain conditions are met, an Australian resident exempting entity that receives a franked distribution from another exempting entity in the same effectively wholly-owned group may be entitled to a tax offset and franking credits (ITAA97 ss 208-130 to 208-140; 208-200).

Prescribed persons

Prescribed persons are essentially foreign residents and tax-exempt entities, but the term also includes interposed entities through which foreign residents and tax-exempt entities hold their interests (ITAA97 ss 208-40; 208-45).

Effectively owned by prescribed persons

An entity is effectively owned by prescribed persons at a particular time if:

- at least 95% of the accountable membership interests in the entity, or 95% of the accountable partial interests in the entity, are held by or for the benefit of prescribed persons, or
- it is reasonable to conclude that the risks and opportunities arising from the holding of those interests substantially accrue to prescribed persons (ITAA97 s 208-25 to 208-35).

Former exempting entities

A ''former exempting entity'' is a corporate tax entity that has ceased to be an exempting entity (ITAA97 s 208-50). There is an exception where an entity becomes effectively owned by prescribed persons but that status ceases within 12 months. However, if a former exempting entity becomes an exempting entity (ie effectively owned by prescribed persons) for less than 12 months, it will once again become a former exempting entity, despite the 12-month rule (*Hastie Group*; ID 2006/316).

When an exempting entity becomes a former exempting entity, its franking account is converted to an ''exempting account'', and the entity starts a new franking account. The exempting account is quarantined so that distributions franked with exempting credits only confer a franking benefit for eligible continuing substantial members (ITAA97 ss 208-240; 995-1(1)) or members holding eligible employee shares (ITAA97 s 208-235). Distributions franked with an exempting credit are exempt from dividend withholding tax, where otherwise applicable.

Consolidated groups

To determine whether a consolidated group is an exempting entity or former exempting entity, the tests in Div 208 are applied to the head company of the group, subject to additional rules contained in ITAA97 Subdiv 709-B (ss 709-150 to 709-175).

The additional rules specify, for example, that a head company that otherwise is neither an exempting entity nor a former exempting entity becomes a former exempting entity at the joining time if an exempting entity or former exempting entity joins the consolidated group.

[FITR ¶214-400 – ¶214-640]

¶4-975 Distribution (dividend) washing

Specific provisions target distribution (or dividend) washing arrangements (ITAA97 s 207-157).

Broadly, distribution (or dividend) washing is a form of scheme by which a taxpayer can obtain multiple franking credits in respect of a single economic interest by selling an interest after an entitlement to a franked distribution has accrued and then immediately purchasing an equivalent interest with a further entitlement to a corresponding franked distribution. This kind of scheme was facilitated by the fact that, for some shares, a special market for trading in shares with the attached right to the dividend (referred to as trading cum-dividend) operates for a period between the date on which the entitlement to the dividend is fixed for most interest holders (the ex-dividend date) and the final date of record for dividend entitlements. It is also possible to trade shares off market on a cum-dividend basis during this period. As a result of the amendments, franked distributions which a taxpayer receives as a result of distribution washing will not entitle the taxpayer to a tax offset or require a taxpayer to include the amount of the franking credit in their assessable income.

A distribution will be received as a result of distribution washing, where the taxpayer (or a connected entity) has also received a corresponding distribution in respect of a substantially identical interest that the taxpayer (or a connected entity) sold before acquiring the current interest (ITAA97 s 207-157(1), (3)). Where a connected entity has disposed of the substantially identical interest, the dividend washing rules will only apply if it would be concluded that either the disposal or the acquisition took place only because at least one of the entities expected or believed that the other transaction had or would occur (ITAA97 s 207-157(2)).

There is an exception to the restrictions on distribution washing for individuals who do not receive more than $5,000 in franking credits in a year (ITAA97 s 207-157(4), (5)). Note that this exception only applies to distributions made directly to an individual; it does not apply to distributions that may flow indirectly to individuals in respect of an interest held through a trust or partnership.

General anti-avoidance rule

Any arrangements by way of distribution washing that did not fall within the specific provision noted above would be potentially subject to the general anti-avoidance rules of ITAA36 Pt IVA (and s 177EA in particular: ¶30-195). TD 2014/10 sets out the operation of the general anti-avoidance rules to distribution washing schemes. Also, despite the small holding exemption, individuals who do not receive more than $5,000 in franking credits in an income year are still potentially subject to the general anti-avoidance rules.

[FITR ¶214-257]

Administrative Provisions

¶4-980 Franking returns, assessments, collection and information

Franking returns

The Commissioner may publish a general notice in the *Gazette* requiring corporate tax entities to lodge franking returns (and may notify a specific corporate tax entity in writing to lodge a franking return) within a specified time. The Commissioner may allow further time.

A franking return must be in writing in the approved form and must include:

- the entity's franking account balance at the end of the income year, or (where applicable) immediately before it ceased to be a franking entity. PDFs must also provide venture capital sub-account balances
- the amounts of any franking tax (ie franking deficit tax, over-franking tax or venture capital deficit tax) that the entity is liable to pay
- any other relevant information that the Commissioner may require.

Generally, the franking account tax return should be lodged by the end of the month following the end of the corporate tax entity's income year (eg 31 July for entities that balance on 30 June).

The franking account tax return is required to be lodged only if the entity has one of the following:

- a liability to pay franking deficit tax (¶4-780)
- a liability to pay over-franking tax (¶4-665), or
- an obligation to disclose a significant variation in benchmark franking percentages between franking periods (¶4-680).

There are special rules where a corporate tax entity receives a tax refund (including a refund of diverted profits tax) within 3 months after the end of the income year (or the time it ceased to be a franking entity), and the refund creates a liability or increased liability to franking deficit tax (¶4-780). If the entity has no outstanding franking return, it must lodge a further return within 14 days after the refund is received. If the entity has an outstanding return due within 14 days of the refund, it can account for the refund in the outstanding return or in a further return lodged within 14 days after the refund is received (ITAA97 s 214-45).

Franking assessments

The provisions for making franking assessments are contained in ITAA97 Subdiv 214-B (ss 214-60 to 214-80). An entity's first franking return for the income year is deemed to be an assessment by the Commissioner, unless the Commissioner has already made a franking assessment for the entity for the year.

If the entity is not required to lodge a franking return, but has lodged its income tax return, the Commissioner cannot make a franking assessment more than 3 years after the later of the due date or actual date for lodging the income tax return (ITAA97 s 214-60(1A)).

A corporate tax entity may object against an assessment in the usual manner (¶28-000).

Amending franking assessments

The Commissioner may amend a franking assessment at any time within 3 years after the day on which the first franking assessment for the entity for the income year was made (ITAA97 s 214-95). If the entity applies for the amendment and provides all the necessary information within the 3-year time limit, the Commissioner may amend the assessment after that time (ITAA97 s 214-110).

If the Commissioner makes an under-assessment because a corporate tax entity does not make full and true disclosure, the time limit is extended to 6 years in cases that do not involve fraud or evasion. Where the Commissioner is of the opinion that the under-assessment is due to fraud or evasion, the Commissioner may amend the assessment at any time (ITAA97 ss 214-115; 214-120).

Within 3 years after the first amendment, the Commissioner may further amend an assessment so as to reduce it (ie increase the franking surplus, reduce the franking deficit or decrease franking tax payable), where the Commissioner considers it just to do so (ITAA97 s 214-125).

Where an entity provides a further return because the entity has received a refund of tax that affects its franking deficit tax liability, that return is treated as an amended assessment (ITAA97 s 214-105).

Due date for payment of franking tax

The general rule is that franking tax (ie franking deficit tax, over-franking tax or venture capital deficit tax) is due and payable on the last day of the month immediately following the end of the relevant income year.

Franking tax due in respect of a part-year assessment is due and payable on the day specified in the notice of assessment.

An increase in franking tax resulting from an amended assessment is due and payable one month after the day on which the assessment was amended.

A liability or increased liability to franking deficit tax due to the receipt of a tax refund (including a refund of diverted profits tax) within 3 months after the end of the income year or after ceasing to be a franking entity (¶4-780) is due and payable 14 days after the day on which the refund was received unless it is accounted for in a franking return that is outstanding for the income year in which the liability arose. In the latter case, it is due on the day that the outstanding return is due (ITAA97 s 214-150).

GIC (¶29-510) applies to overdue franking tax (ITAA97 s 214-155).

Refunds of overpaid franking tax are governed by ITAA36 s 172 (¶28-160).

Records, information and tax agents

ITAA36 s 262A (record-keeping: ¶9-045) and TAA Sch 1 s 353-10 (Commissioner's access to information: ¶25-240) apply to the imputation system. Section 262A applies with appropriate modifications (ITAA97 s 214-175).

Persons giving a franking credit return or making an objection for the purposes of Pt 3-6 are covered by the *Tax Agent Services Act 2009* (¶32-010).

[FITR ¶217-000 – ¶217-185]

Chapter 5 Partners and Partnerships

Taxation of Partnerships

¶5-000 A partnership for income tax purposes

A partnership, for general law purposes, is the relationship that exists between persons carrying on business in common with a view to profit. For income tax purposes, however, the definition of "partnership" (ITAA97 s 995-1(1)) not only encompasses a partnership in that sense, but also an association of persons in receipt of income jointly, eg share farmers. Thus, the joint owners of property who share income from the property, whether as joint tenants or tenants in common, will be partners for income tax purposes, even though they may not be partners under general law (*McDonald*; *Yeung*; TR 93/32);

they will only be partners under general law if ownership of the property amounts to the carrying on of a business. The definition also expressly includes a limited partnership (¶5-030).

▶ Example

A married couple purchased an investment property as joint tenants under an arrangement in which the income was to be split 25% to the husband and 75% to the wife, with the husband carrying all losses. They were partners under tax law because they were co-owners of the investment property but they were not partners under the general law because they were not carrying on a business. The agreement under which the husband assumed liability for all losses, including the wife's losses, was therefore ineffective. Accordingly, he was only entitled to claim half of the losses in accordance with their respective interests, as joint tenants, in the properties (*McDonald*; *Cripps*).

A syndicate that may have come into existence for only a limited period or purpose may be a ''partnership'' for income tax purposes. However, a limited period joint venture between 2 entities for the construction of residential buildings, which were divided equally between the venturers after construction, was not a partnership either at general law or for income tax purposes (*ARM Constructions*). The relationship between trustees is not one of ''partnership'', although trustees are legally competent to form a partnership (*Case E39*; *Case J40*).

The parties must carry on a business in common with a view to profit, rather than merely agree to do so (*D Marks Partnership & Ors*; see also ¶5-030). Further, an association of persons not carrying on business with a view to profit (eg a club) would be a ''company'' and not a partnership (¶3-800).

Companies are specifically excluded from the definition of ''partnership'' for tax purposes (ie the 2 categories are mutually exclusive).

The general provisions for the taxation of partnerships, other than corporate limited partnerships (¶5-030), are in ITAA36 Pt III Div 5 (s 90 to 94).

Legislative references in this chapter are to ITAA36 unless otherwise specified.

[FTR ¶49-270]

¶5-010 Creation and existence of a partnership

Whether a partnership exists for income tax purposes is a question of fact to be determined in the light of *all* surrounding circumstances. The essential element in determining whether a partnership exists is mutual assent and intention to act as partners (*Jolley*). If there is no such intention, a partnership cannot exist. Evidence of the parties' intentions is often crucial as it may establish the existence of a partnership notwithstanding a lack of documentary evidence. Conversely, it may negate the existence of a partnership notwithstanding that the documents outwardly indicate a joint enterprise. For example, a marine engineer working on a fishing vessel was simply an employee even though there was a partnership agreement between himself, the skipper and the other crew members (*Case 41/93*). Similarly, no partnership existed between a married couple as their actual activities did not constitute ''carrying on business as partners'' for the purpose of the ITAA97 s 995-1(1) definition in *Case 11/2013*. In that case, the AAT held that the written partnership agreement and the couple's business plan overstated the true position that no partnership was formed.

The existence or absence of a partnership agreement, written or oral, is not conclusive evidence of an intention or lack of intention to act as partners. However, a partnership agreement will be prima facie evidence of such an intention (TR 94/8), particularly if the evidence shows that the parties have acted in accordance with the terms of the agreement. It is recommended that, at the very least, a memorandum be prepared setting out the terms under which the partnership is to operate. Thus, a taxpayer's claim that his property was owned jointly with his wife as a partnership was rejected because there was no supporting evidence (*Harbutt*).

Although intention is essential, it is not of itself sufficient to establish the existence of a partnership; the intention must be evidenced by the conduct of the parties. The following are positive factors in determining the existence of a *business* partnership, although no one factor will be decisive and the weight to be given to each factor will vary with the circumstances of each case (TR 94/8):

- joint ownership of business assets (although, in the case of a husband and wife, joint ownership may flow from their family relationship)
- entitlements to a share of the net profits (this is considered to be essential)
- the existence of a joint bank account specifically named and used as a business account, although in *Case Z7* there was no partnership despite there being a joint bank account (in the case of a husband and wife partnership, the opening of a separate business bank account is a positive factor)
- the power of the partners to operate on the partnership account
- the registration of a business name in the joint proprietorship of the partners (*Cripps*) and trading in joint names
- business records (eg books of account and minutes of partnership meetings)
- public recognition of the partnership, particularly by creditors, suppliers and customers (eg invoices, business letters and advertising in the partnership name)
- the involvement of all the parties in the particular business, although the fact that not all of them work actively in the business does not of itself preclude the conclusion that a partnership exists as between all the parties
- the sharing of contributions to assets and capital, although the fact that only one party has initially introduced capital into the business is not necessarily fatal to the existence of a partnership
- the joint leasing or ownership of business premises
- the readiness with which the parties' respective financial interests in the business may be ascertained, and
- evidence of drawings by the parties against their respective shares of the profits.

While an equal sharing of profits may point to the existence of a partnership, it may be also consistent with a corporate arrangement in which all parties hold an equal number of shares (*Ryvitch*).

A minor is not prevented at common law from entering into a partnership. However, it has been consistently found that a young child is not a partner where the child has not demonstrated consent to the partnership by signing the relevant agreement and where there are no relevant facts from which an inference of partnership can be drawn (15 TBRD *Case* Q57; 17 TBRD *Case* S21). Note that the partnership income of a minor may be taxed at the highest marginal rate (¶2-160 – ¶2-250).

A partnership cannot be created so as to operate retrospectively (*Waddington v O'Callaghan*), but if the partnership commences before the partnership agreement is executed, the agreement may recite that fact (15 CTBR *Case* 67).

Where a taxpayer who derives income from professional services enters into an arrangement with other unrelated taxpayers (as described in TA 2002/4), the Commissioner considers that these are not partnerships either at general law or for tax purposes, but are designed so that the taxpayer can split personal services income (TD 2002/24).

The ATO warns against taxpayers accessing business profits through an interposed partnership with a private company partner (TA 2015/4). It is concerned that the arrangement is being used to allow individuals to access profits at the corporate tax rate without paying additional ''top-up'' tax reflecting their higher marginal tax rate. It also warns against multinational entities using an interposed partnership structure to avoid the application of the Multinational Anti-Avoidance Law (MAAL) (TA 2016/11: ¶30-200).

[FTR ¶49-275]

¶5-030 Limited partnerships

A ''limited partnership'' is

(a) an association of persons (other than a company) carrying on business as partners or in receipt of ordinary income or statutory income jointly, where the liability of at least one of those persons is limited, or

(b) an association of persons (other than one referred to in para (a)) with legal personality separate from those persons that was formed solely for the purpose of becoming a VCLP, an ESVCLP, an AFOF or VCMP (¶5-040) and to carry on activities that are carried on by a body of that kind (ITAA97 s 995-1).

For there to be a limited partnership, a partnership must first exist at general law. Further, the requirement that liability be limited contemplates a limitation of liability of at least one partner to third parties; an agreement between the partners themselves that their liability be limited or the mere fact of registration as a limited partnership under State legislation would not suffice (*D Marks Partnership & Ors*; see also ¶5-000).

For tax purposes, most limited partnerships are ''corporate limited partnerships'', which are treated as companies under Pt III Div 5A (ss 94A to 94X) and are liable to pay income tax (*Resource Capital Fund IV LP*: see ¶3-475).

Note that limited partnerships that are commonly used as vehicles for venture capital investment (¶5-040) are *excluded* from Div 5A and treated as ordinary partnerships for tax purposes. Similarly, certain foreign hybrid business entities are also treated as partnerships rather than companies (¶5-050).

A new regime for limited partnership collective investment vehicles (CIVs) was proposed in the 2016–17 Federal Budget for income years starting on or after 1 July 2018 (¶6-410). Investors in these CIVs will generally be taxed as if they had invested directly.

[FTR ¶49-350, ¶49-400, ¶49-650]

¶5-040 Venture capital limited partnerships

Limited partnerships that are used to invest in Australian venture capital companies are treated as ordinary partnerships rather than corporate limited partnerships (¶3-475). As a consequence, the income, profits, gains and losses of the partnership flow through to the partners, who are taxed according to their tax status. For details of the exemptions applying to venture capital investments, see ¶10-845 and ¶11-900.

The ''flow-through'' tax treatment applies to the following limited partnerships through which tax-advantaged venture capital investments may be made:

- a venture capital limited partnership (VCLP) registered under the *Venture Capital Act 2002* (VCA) (ITAA97 s 118-405(2)). The Board of Taxation recommended for VCLP taxation to be simplified in 2011 (see also the 2014 Financial System Inquiry report)

- an Australian venture capital fund of funds (AFOF) registered under VCA (ITAA97 s 118-410(3))

- an early stage venture capital limited partnership (ESVCLP) registered under VCA (ITAA97 s 118-407(4)). A limited partner in an ESVCLP is entitled to a non-refundable carry-forward tax offset of up to 10% of contributions it makes to the ESVCLP during an income year from 1 July 2016. The amount of offset is reduced to the extent that the contributions are not used by the ESVCLP to make eligible venture capital investments within that income year or the first 2 months after the end of that income year (ITAA97 Subdiv 61-P: ¶20-700), and
- a venture capital management partnership (VCMP), ie a limited partnership that is a general partner of one or more VCLPs, ESVCLPs and/or AFOFs, and only carries on activities related to being a general partner (s 94D(3)).

A loss made by a non-resident venture capital entity or limited partnership on the disposal or other realisation of venture capital equity in a resident investment vehicle is not deductible if any capital gain or loss on the disposal or realisation would be disregarded for CGT purposes (ITAA97 s 26-70; ¶11-900). Further, no deduction is available to:

- a partner in a VCLP or ESVCLP for the partner's share of a loss made by the partnership from the disposal or other realisation of an eligible venture capital investment
- a partner of an AFOF for a share of a loss made by either the fund itself or a VCLP or ESVCLP of which the fund is a partner, or
- an eligible venture capital investor for a loss made on the disposal or other realisation of an eligible venture capital investment,

if the loss would be exempt from CGT under s 118-405, 118-410, or 118-415 (s 26-68: ¶10-845).

Deduction for partnership loss limited

Special rules apply to limit the losses that a limited partner may claim from a venture capital investment. The deduction allowable to the limited partner in respect of the partnership loss cannot exceed the amount of the partner's financial exposure to the loss. This amount is calculated by deducting, from the partner's contribution to the partnership, the sum of:

- any contributions that are repaid to the partner
- any deductions allowed to the partner for partnership losses incurred in previous income years, and
- any debt interests issued by the partner that are secured by the partner's interest in the partnership (s 92(2AA)).

▶ Example 1

A partner contributes $100,000 to a VCLP. The partner finances the contribution with a loan of $80,000 secured by the partner's interest in the partnership. The lender values the partner's interest in the partnership at $70,000 so the partner provides shares valued at $10,000 as security. The deduction allowable to the partner for its share of the partnership loss cannot exceed the following amount:

Partner's contribution	$100,000
Less: contribution repaid	Nil
deductions for losses in previous years	Nil
debt secured by interest in partnership	70,000
Maximum deduction for partnership loss	$30,000

The partner's share of the partnership loss for the income year is $40,000. However, the partner's deduction is limited to $30,000.

Deductions disallowed in one year (because the deduction limit is exceeded) can be carried forward and utilised in subsequent years (s 92A). A partner's unutilised carried-forward losses are referred to as the partner's "outstanding s 92(2AA) amount".

▶ Example 2

Following on from Example 1, the partner's share of the partnership loss incurred in the following income year is $5,000. During that year, the partner contributed additional capital of $20,000 which was financed from the partner's funds. There has been no change in the amount of the debt or the value of the security provided. The maximum potential deduction is calculated as follows:

Partner's contribution	$120,000
Less: contribution repaid	Nil
deductions for losses in previous years	30,000
debt secured by interest in partnership	70,000
Maximum deduction for partnership loss	20,000
Less: partner's share of current year partnership loss	5,000
	$15,000

As this amount exceeds the outstanding s 92(2AA) amount of $10,000 (see Example 1), the amount of the deduction allowable to the partner for losses in previous years is $10,000. However, if the amount worked out under this method is less than the outstanding s 92(2AA) amount, say $8,000, the amount of the deduction allowable to the partner is limited to $8,000.

[FITR ¶68-480, ¶68-490; FTR ¶49-401]

¶5-050 Foreign hybrids

Investments in foreign hybrids, ie foreign hybrid limited partnerships and foreign hybrid companies, are governed by ITAA97 Div 830.

The rules provide that foreign hybrids that would otherwise be treated as partnerships for foreign tax purposes and as companies for Australian tax purposes are treated as partnerships for Australian tax purposes. Instead of being treated as corporate limited partnerships (¶3-475), such entities are subject to the ordinary rules for partnerships and the special rules relating to foreign hybrids, except that deductions for partnership losses are limited (s 94D(5), (6)). The loss limitation rules provide that limited partners may only claim losses of the foreign hybrid to the extent of their exposure to economic loss (see below).

Other consequences that apply as a result of treating a foreign hybrid as a partnership are that:

- the CFC provisions will not apply to the entity
- distributions will not be significant for tax purposes, and
- the CGT provisions will apply only to the partners and not to the entity.

Foreign hybrids include UK limited partnerships (ID 2006/334) and US limited liability companies (ID 2006/18). A company that is a limited liability partnership for the purposes of the *Limited Liability Partnerships Act 2000* (UK) is also a foreign hybrid (ITR97 reg 830-15.01).

TD 2009/2 discusses the requirement that foreign income tax is imposed on the partners rather than the partnership in determining whether an entity is a foreign hybrid limited partnership under ITAA97 s 830-10. A partner who is not an attributable partner in a limited partnership may elect to apply partnership treatment to its interest in the limited partnership (s 830-10(2)). This election is generally not available to foreign residents, though the restriction does not apply for the purposes of calculating the net income of a partnership or trust estate, or if the foreign resident is a CFC or would be a Pt XI Australian resident under former Pt XI of ITAA36 (TD 2017/25). Where a partner is entitled to a share of the net income of a foreign hybrid, the partner is also entitled to a foreign income tax offset for foreign income tax paid in respect of that income (¶21-680), regardless of who actually paid the foreign tax (TR 2009/6).

Loss limitation rules

The loss limitation rules prevent limited partners of a foreign hybrid from claiming deductions for tax losses to which they were not exposed because of their limited liability. The rules are similar to those that apply to venture capital limited partnerships (¶5-040). They operate to limit foreign hybrid related losses that may be used by limited partners to offset against assessable income from sources other than the foreign hybrid. The limit is based on the limited partner's contributions to the foreign hybrid (the partner's loss exposure amount). If the partner's losses exceed that limit, the allowable losses are reduced so that in total they equal the partner's loss exposure amount. The loss limit is adjusted annually for additional contributions or withdrawals and for previous losses taken into account.

Limited partners may carry forward the amount by which a loss has been reduced. The unused losses may be available in future years when the partner's loss exposure amount may have increased through additional contributions to the foreign hybrid. Where the total outstanding losses are less than the partner's available loss exposure amount, the outstanding foreign hybrid net capital loss amount may be used by the partner. In that case, the partner makes a capital loss under CGT event K12 (¶11-350).

When entity becomes/ceases to be foreign hybrid

Special rules also apply where an entity becomes a foreign hybrid or where it ceases to be one. The rules ensure that there is no CGT event or any other disposal of assets at those times. The rules also provide that the partners/members of a foreign hybrid must assign an amount to their interest in each of the assets of the entity when it becomes a foreign hybrid. Similarly, when an entity ceases to be a foreign hybrid, it must assign an amount to its interest in certain assets that it continues to hold.

[FITR ¶632-000]

¶5-060 Changes in members of a partnership

Where there is a technical change in the composition of a general law partnership, eg a partner dies or retires and/or a new partner is admitted, the partnership is dissolved and a new partnership comes into existence, unless the partnership agreement provides otherwise. The ATO will treat the new general law partnership as having been reconstituted where the partnership agreement so allows and there is at least one continuing partner, there is no period where there is only one partner and there is no break in the business of the partnership. In those circumstances, the reconstituted partnership need only lodge one partnership tax return for the relevant income year but must include the distributions for every partner, including departing partners, for the whole year. The return should also provide details of the date of dissolution, the date of reconstitution, the names of all the partners, the details of all new partners (TFNs/addresses and dates of birth) and details of any changes to persons authorised to act on behalf of the partnership (where a partnership is dissolved and a new partnership is formed, the new partnership will need to get a new TFN and ABN and lodge a partnership return for the period from the date of its formation to the end of the income year; the old partnership will need to lodge a return for the period from the beginning of the income year to the date of dissolution).

It is important to note that the reorganisation of a partnership will affect the respective interests of its members in the partnership's assets. This may have important consequences for old and new members in relation to trading stock (¶9-290), depreciable property (¶17-780) and CGT (¶11-200).

Where a partnership has furnished returns on a *cash* basis and one partner dies or retires, and that partner's interest in the partnership (including book debts) is sold, it seems that that partner (or their estate) will be taxed on the proportion of the sale price attributable to that partner's share in the book debts. On the other hand, the purchaser of the share (the incoming partner) will not be taxed when the debts are realised since that share in the debts represents a capital contribution to the new partnership that has replaced the old partnership.

To avoid the complications of preparing a partnership return in which receipts are treated differently in relation to the various members of the partnership, it is advisable that, in such a case, book debts not be sold. The old partnership would then continue to exist for the purposes of collecting the book debts and generally winding up its affairs. Returns would thus continue to be lodged for the old partnership in respect of book debts collected. This method also has the important advantage of preventing the retiring partner or the estate of the deceased partner, whose interest in the partnership has been sold, from being taxed at high rates on the lump sum consideration received for those book debts.

Note that just as a partnership cannot be created retrospectively for tax purposes (¶5-010), neither can it be dissolved retrospectively (*Happ*).

[FTR ¶49-285]

Partnership Net Income or Loss

¶5-065 Partnership: return and payment of tax

A partnership (other than a corporate limited partnership: ¶3-475) is not taxable as such and does not pay tax on its income. Similarly, a net partnership loss is not deductible to the partnership as such (¶5-110). However, the members of a partnership are taxable in their individual capacities on their shares of the net partnership income (s 92), whether distributed to them or not (¶5-130).

Although a partnership does not pay tax on its income, a return of the partnership income must be lodged each year (s 91). The partnership tax return is, in one sense, simply an information return, but it provides the basis for determining the partners' respective shares of the net partnership income or net partnership loss. Each partner must then include in a personal return their individual share of the partnership income or loss, regardless of whether that share has been distributed. A corporate limited partnership is required to use the company tax return.

▶ Example

A partnership is composed of 2 partners, A and B, who share profits in the ratio of 2 to 3. In the current year, the taxable income of the business, the net partnership income, is $20,000. During the year, each partner has drawn $6,000. The partnership return will show $20,000 taxable income and $8,000 and $12,000 as the partners' shares. The partners will return their respective shares of the net partnership income in their individual returns even though the whole of such income has not been distributed.

Because a partnership does not pay tax, it does not pay PAYG instalments. Nevertheless, a partnership may have to calculate its instalment income quarterly, and notify that amount to the partners who are required to pay PAYG instalments based on their share of the partnership instalment income for the quarter (¶27-265).

The Commissioner has a long standing practice of allowing partnerships whose circumstances are out of the ordinary to adopt a substituted accounting period (SAP) (¶9-010). If all partners share the same SAP, the Commissioner will normally grant the partnership leave to adopt the same SAP. The partnership must still apply for the SAP. However, if 2 or more partners do not share common accounting periods and there is no clear control by any partner, the partnership would normally be expected to retain 30 June, in the absence of any other demonstrated business need (PS LA 2007/21).

The partnership return must be lodged by the prescribed date, unless an extension of time has been granted. For lodgment due dates and the requirements relating to the completion of returns, see ¶24-010ff.

The general obligations relating to the lodgment of partnership returns (TAA Sch 1 Subdiv 388-B) are imposed on each partner, but may be discharged by any of the partners (TAA Sch 1 s 444-30; *McGuire*). If no partner is resident in Australia, the return is to be lodged by the partnership's agent in Australia. As to who is an agent for this purpose, see ¶22-060.

The net income or loss of a partnership (other than a corporate limited partnership) is calculated as if the partnership were a *resident* taxpayer, although the CGT provisions are ignored (¶5-070). Special rules apply where a partner is a non-resident for the whole or a part of the year (¶5-150).

The distribution statement in the partnership return must be completed showing the distribution of the net Australian income or loss (other than capital gains) of the partnership. Various information must be provided in respect of each partner, including: (a) their name and TFN; (b) their share of the net Australian income or loss (including the salary or wages paid to each partner); and (c) their share of any imputation credit for franked dividends. This facilitates matching partners' individual returns to the partnership return.

Where the partnership derives income from sources outside Australia, a statement of the distribution of that income to the partners should be prepared and retained with the partnership's tax records. This statement should also show the entitlement of the partners to any credits for foreign tax paid by the partnership on its foreign source income. For details of the tax treatment of foreign source income, see ¶21-000ff.

If one of the partners in a partnership makes an incorrect statement about the income of a partnership that results in a shortfall amount, all of the partners are potentially liable to pay an administrative penalty. The amount of the penalty is in proportion to each partner's share of the net income or loss of the partnership (¶29-160).

[FITR ¶33-400; FTR ¶49-360]

¶5-070 Calculation of partnership net income or loss

Although a partnership does not itself pay tax, the net income of the partnership is calculated as if the partnership were a taxpayer in its own right. The ''net income'' of a partnership, which is ascertained at the end of the appropriate accounting period (¶5-065), means its ''assessable income'' less all ''allowable deductions'' (s 90). However, deductions for losses of previous years (¶16-880), except in the case of foreign losses (¶5-110), and deductions for superannuation contributions (¶5-140) are *not* taken into account in calculating ''allowable deductions''. Further, a number of special concessions are not available to a partnership as such but are claimable by the individual partners (eg the concession for investment in Australian film production: ¶20-330). A partnership loss arises if the ''allowable deductions'' of the partnership are greater than its ''assessable income''. Whether a partnership's income is computed on a cash or accruals basis is discussed at ¶9-030.

In calculating the net income or loss of a partnership, the partnership is treated as if it were a resident taxpayer. Accordingly, both Australian and foreign source income (and the deductions relating to that income) are taken into account (¶5-110). The CGT provisions are ignored in calculating the net income or loss of a partnership (ITAA97 s 106-5: ¶11-200). Thus, a capital gain or loss under the CGT provisions cannot arise to a partnership as such. Where a partnership asset is disposed of, any net capital gain or loss arising on the disposal is reflected in the returns of the individual partners, and not in the partnership return. Note that the commercial debt forgiveness measures also apply to partnerships (¶16-910).

Resident partners are assessable on their share of the net partnership income; similarly, they can claim a deduction for their share of the partnership loss (¶5-130). Special rules apply where a partner is a non-resident for the whole or a part of the year (¶5-150).

A partnership may also need to calculate its PAYG instalment income so that individual partners can pay PAYG instalments on their share of the partnership instalment income for that period. Instalment income is generally based only on ordinary income, and does not include statutory income (¶27-265).

Undeclared cash received by partners (a father and son) from a business of prostitution was partnership income rather than income of a company formed by the partners to receive the declared income of the business (*Interest*).

The provision of the exclusive use of plant and equipment to a partnership, at no charge, by the partners does not constitute a non-cash business benefit. Accordingly, ITAA36 s 21A (¶10-030) does not apply in the calculation of the net income of the partnership (ID 2004/955).

Work in progress payments

Payments for work in progress often occur where there is a change in the composition of a professional partnership and work has been partially completed, but not to the stage where a recoverable debt has arisen. As a result of *Crommelin* and *Coughlan* (see below), there was the possibility of double taxation of work in progress (WIP) amounts. However, to overcome the effect of those decisions, specific measures apply to remove any potential for double taxation. The measures provide for a deduction not just in the context of a professional partnership, but whenever a payment is made for a WIP amount — see ¶16-158.

The value of work in progress does not constitute assessable income unless there is a recoverable debt (*Henderson*) (¶9-050). However, a payment received by a retired partner (or by the estate of a deceased partner) on account of work in progress unbilled at the time of retirement (or death) is assessable income of the retired partner (or estate) where it reflects a calculation of the future profits the partner could have expected to receive (*Stapleton*). Work in progress payments to a retired partner will also be assessable even if, on the formation of the partnership, the partner contributed work in progress that constituted the partnership's major asset and was recorded as such by crediting the partner's capital account (*Grant*). An argument that payments to retiring partners for their share of the work in progress at the time of the dissolution of the partnership were simply repayments of their equity in the partnership, and were therefore capital, was rejected.

In *Crommelin's case*, a retiring partner was paid a lump sum of $456,000 for his one-quarter interest in the assets of the partnership. The Commissioner assessed the retiring partner for $154,000 for work in progress even though there had been no agreement by the partners that this specific amount was to be paid to the taxpayer. The Federal Court held that the amount of $154,000 was assessable income. It was not necessary that the taxpayer should have expressly agreed to receive that specific amount. In *Coughlan's case*, a new partnership purchased the business of a dissolved partnership including its work in progress. The Federal Court held that the payment made by the new partnership for the work in progress was of a capital nature and therefore not deductible by members of the new partnership.

Interest payments

Interest on a loan is deductible to a partnership where the loan is used to replace working capital used in a business carried on by the partnership to derive assessable income, including where the working capital was advanced by a partner (*Roberts and Smith*; TR 95/25). This is known as the "refinancing principle". In *Roberts and Smith*, money was borrowed by a partnership (a firm of solicitors) to allow each partner to withdraw $25,000, thereby reducing the net worth of each partner's interest in the partnership; as a result, new partners could buy into the partnership at a reduced cost. Another partner who joined the partnership at a later date was allowed a deduction in respect of her share of the interest, as she had accepted liability in respect of the interest payments as a condition of becoming a partner. Interest on borrowed funds used to replace working capital must be apportioned if the partnership business also produces exempt income or the amount borrowed is greater than the amount of working capital that is replaced (TR 95/25). Interest on money lent by a partner to the partnership is income derived by the partner as a lender and not as a partner.

Interest on a refinancing loan taken out by the joint owners of an investment property who are not partners at general law (ie they are not carrying on a business) is not deductible, even if they comprise a partnership for income tax purposes (¶5-000) (TR 95/25; *Case 12/95*).

▶ Example

A husband and wife jointly purchase a rental property using $75,000 of their own funds and a $150,000 loan. They are not carrying on a business of investing in rental properties and thus are not partners at general law. Two years later they borrow a further $75,000 to replace the funds they contributed to the purchase, using that original capital to renovate their own home. Even though the husband and wife are partners for income tax purposes, the Commissioner will not allow a deduction for the interest on the additional $75,000 loan.

On the basis of *Roberts and Smith*, interest on a loan is arguably deductible where the borrowed money is used to pay partners their share of profit distributions (except to the extent attributable to unrealised profits), to repay a loan that is being applied to income-producing purposes or to discharge a liability to a supplier of goods or services who extends trade credit to the partnership. However, the Commissioner will not allow a deduction for interest where the loan is used to replace partnership capital that is represented by internally generated goodwill or an unrealised revaluation of assets (TR 95/25).

Where one co-owner of rental property borrows funds solely for the purpose of contributing their share of the purchase price, then the interest on that borrowing would be an expense of the borrower and deductible from their share of the net rental. However, where the parties jointly incur an expense related to the property as a whole, such as interest on borrowings to fund the joint equity, that expense must be taken into account in arriving at the net income of the partnership, notwithstanding that the payment of the expense was made by one of the parties only. Thus, where a husband solely borrowed funds to repay an amount previously borrowed jointly with his wife for a rental property, the husband was not entitled to a deduction for the whole of the interest on the new borrowings as it was to fund the joint interest, not the interest of the husband alone (*Case 63/96*).

A partner is not entitled to a deduction for interest on a loan to pay personal income tax (TD 2000/24).

[FITR ¶33-400; FTR ¶49-360]

¶5-080 Elections of partnerships

Generally, elections affecting the calculation of the net partnership income or loss must be made by the partnership, rather than by the partners individually. This applies to elections as to the valuation of trading stock (¶9-180 and following), elections as to the method to be used for working out the decline in value of a depreciating asset (¶17-480) and elections available to primary producers relating to abnormal receipts (¶18-135 and following). An election made by the partnership applies to all partners.

Not all elections and notifications have to be in writing and, where they are required to be in writing, most do not have to be lodged until the Commissioner requests them (¶24-040). However, a substituted accounting period may be adopted only by seeking leave from the Commissioner (¶5-065).

[FITR ¶355-600]

¶5-090 Partners' salaries

A partnership is not a separate and distinct legal entity for income tax purposes and a partner cannot be an employee of a partnership (*Ellis v Joseph Ellis & Co*). The payment of a "salary" to a partner is simply a means of distributing partnership income and the payment is not deductible in computing the net partnership income or loss; the payment of a partnership salary cannot result in or increase a partnership loss (TR 2005/7). If a partner is entitled to a "salary" under the terms of the partnership agreement, this simply represents an entitlement to an allocation of profits before the general distribution among the partners.

▶ Example

The partnership agreement between A and B provides that A, the only active partner, is to receive a salary of $40,000 pa for managing the business and that profits and losses (computed after deducting A's salary) are to be shared equally. The year's operations result in a profit of $34,000 after A's salary is deducted. The reconciliation for the purposes of the distribution statement will be as follows:

Partnership profit (after deducting A's salary)		$34,000
Add: A's salary		40,000
Net partnership income		74,000
Distribution:		
A: salary	$40,000	
Add: 50% of balance ($34,000)	17,000	57,000
B: 50% of balance ($34,000)		17,000
Total amount distributed		$74,000

The rule that a partner's salary is not deductible in computing the net partnership income or loss was applied in *Case S75*. TR 2005/7, on the treatment of partnership salary agreements, confirms that the payment of a salary to a partner is not taken into account as an allowable deduction in calculating the net partnership income or loss under s 90. Therefore, the payment cannot result in or contribute to a partnership loss.

A partnership salary agreement varies the interests of the partners in the partnership profits and losses. However, a partnership salary amount is taken into account in determining the recipient partner's interest in the net income (or partnership loss) of the partnership under s 92(1). That partner's interest in the net income will include the partnership salary to the extent that there is available net income.

If partnership profits are not sufficient to cover the salary, it may be met from profits of subsequent years. So, if the salary drawn by a partner in a particular year exceeds that partner's interest in the net income of the partnership, the excess is not assessable income of the partner in that income year. An advance of future profits is assessable to the partner in a future year when sufficient profits are available.

The Commissioner also considers that, for a partnership salary agreement to be effective in an income year, it must be entered into before the end of that income year.

The following example, adapted from TR 2005/7, illustrates the tax treatment where there is a partnership loss after deducting salaries.

▶ Example

X and Y formed a partnership under which it was agreed that they share the profits or losses of the partnership equally. The partnership agreement also provided that X would be entitled to draw $20,000 a year for managing the business. The year's net (accounting) loss, after paying X's salary, was $10,000. Determination of the net income, for the purpose of completing the distribution statement on the partnership return, will be as follows:

Partnership net loss (after deducting salaries)	$10,000
Add: X's salary	20,000
Net income	10,000
Distribution:	
X: salary	$10,000
50% of $10,000 – $10,000	nil
Y: 50% of $10,000 – $10,000	nil
Total distribution	$10,000

Amounts treated as salaries paid to members of a family partnership involved in processing tax returns were, in reality, advance drawings by the working partners. As such, they were non-deductible and could not give rise to losses (*Scott*).

Salary, wages or other personal exertion income earned by partners in their own right outside the partnership (eg in a part-time job) are not partnership income for tax purposes, whatever the partnership agreement may provide. For example, if a partner becomes a director of a company in their individual capacity, and not in their capacity as a partner, the director's fees are income of the partner. If the fees are passed on to the partnership in accordance with the partnership agreement, the partner should be allowed a deduction for the amount passed on. Where a partner undertaking paid services outside, but associated with, the partnership business is required by the partnership agreement to obtain the approval of the other partners and to pay the remuneration into the partnership account, the remuneration should be treated as partnership income. Similarly, where the appointment as director results from the usual business practice of the partnership and the commercial contacts made by the partner in conducting this business, the director's fees will be treated as income of the partnership. See TD 97/2.

For the circumstances in which a retiring allowance paid to a partner is deductible to the partnership, see ¶16-540.

[FTR ¶49-410]

¶5-100 Partnership payments to related entities

Where a partnership makes a payment or incurs a liability (eg salary or interest) to a person who is associated with a partner (ie a related entity), and that payment or liability that otherwise qualifies as a deduction to the partnership is unreasonable in amount, the Commissioner may reduce the deduction to the partnership (ITAA97 s 26-35). The amount disallowed is not assessable to the payee unless the partner with whom the payee is associated is a private company, in which case the disallowed amount is treated as a dividend paid by the company to that person (s 65).

Whether a payment is reasonable in amount is a question of fact to be determined in the light of the particular circumstances of each case but, generally, commercial standards should be adopted.

The effect of the disallowance of such a payment will, of course, be to increase the net partnership income or reduce the net partnership loss.

The following are related entities for these purposes:

- a relative of a partner
- another partnership, a partner in which is a relative of a partner in the first partnership
- a non-partner who is or has been a shareholder or director, or the relative of a shareholder or director, of a private company that is a partner in the partnership, or
- a non-partner who is a beneficiary, or the relative of a beneficiary, of a trust estate that is a partner in the partnership.

[FITR ¶68-240; FTR ¶34-510]

¶5-110 Treatment of partnership losses

A partnership loss arises where there is an excess of allowable deductions over assessable income, calculated as if the partnership were a resident taxpayer. Income from all sources is taken into account but certain deductions are ignored (¶5-070). The partnership loss is not allowable to the partnership as such, but is distributed to the partners in the year in which it is incurred in accordance with their respective individual interests in the loss as provided by the partnership agreement (assuming the agreement is effective for tax purposes; and subject to the non-commercial loss rules: ¶16-020). It is then claimable as a deduction in the partner's individual tax return (s 92).

From the 2008–09 year, foreign losses of a partnership are no longer quarantined within the partnership and are available for distribution to the partners (¶21-800).

For the position where a partner is a non-resident for the whole or part of a year, see ¶5-150.

If a partner's share of a partnership loss is not absorbed by their other income in the year of distribution, it may be carried forward by the partner for deduction in later income years. Losses can be carried forward indefinitely until absorbed. If the partner is a company, the deductibility of the losses in later years will also depend on its satisfying either a continuity of ownership test or a business continuity test (¶3-060).

[FTR ¶49-401]

¶5-120 Partnership exempt income

The exempt income of a partnership is calculated as if the partnership were a *resident* taxpayer (s 90). This means that exempt income from sources in and out of Australia is taken into account. If there is exempt income of a partnership and there is a partnership loss (¶5-110) for the year, the loss is not offset against the partnership exempt income. In the case of resident partners, the full amount of the partnership loss and the full amount of the partnership exempt income are distributed to the partners according to their individual interests in the loss and the exempt income. The adjustment offsetting a share in the partnership loss against a share in the partnership exempt income is made in the individual returns of the partners. For the position where a partner is a non-resident for the whole or a part of the year, see ¶5-150.

The non-assessable non-exempt income of a partnership (¶10-890) is also calculated as if the partnership were a *resident* taxpayer.

[FTR ¶49-265]

Partner's Share of Income or Loss

¶5-130 Income and deductions of partner

The assessable income of a resident partner includes the partner's "individual interest" in (ie share of) the net partnership income (from all sources) as is attributable to the period when the partner was a resident (s 92(1)). The partner's share of the net partnership income will be included in their assessable income regardless of whether more or less than that share has been received, and whether received by way of "salary" (¶5-090), interest on capital or current account or other drawings. Actual drawings of partnership profits by a partner are irrelevant for tax purposes (*Case 7/2000*).

An amount a retiring partner is entitled representing their individual interest in the partnership's net income is assessable under s 92, regardless of how the payment is labelled or described and the timing of the retirement and/or payment (TD 2015/19). An amount is not so assessable, however, to the extent that it represents the partnership's net income which is attributable to both a period when the partner was not an Australian resident and sources outside of Australia.

A resident partner can claim a deduction for so much of their individual interest in any partnership loss as is attributable to the period when the partner was a resident (s 92(2)). A partnership's exempt income and "non-assessable non-exempt income" (¶10-890) is distributed to the partners on the same basis. For the position where a partner is a non-resident for the whole or a part of the year, see ¶5-150.

A partner's interest in the net partnership income or partnership loss is usually determined in accordance with the partnership agreement. However, if that is completely out of proportion to the partners' true interests in the partnership, an assessment will be made on the merits of the case (IT 2316).

The profits of the partnership cannot be allocated so that one partner receives a share of partnership income and another incurs a share of partnership loss — there is only one amount, either net income of the partnership or a partnership loss, available for distribution pursuant to s 92.

However, the partners' interests as specified in the partnership agreement may be varied. Note that such a variation may be caught by the general anti-avoidance provisions if the sole or dominant purpose of the variation is to obtain a tax benefit (¶30-120). If there is a partnership for income tax purposes only and no general law partnership (ie the partners are not carrying on a business but are earning income jointly), each partner's share of the net income or loss is determined by their respective interests in the income-earning property (eg *McDonald*) (¶5-000).

Partners do not derive their share of the net partnership income until it has been ascertained (*Galland*). This will be at the end of the relevant accounting period as accounts cannot be taken for that purpose until then. Of course, it may be necessary to take accounts at an earlier date, eg on the dissolution of the partnership.

Under PAYG, a partnership may be required to notify its "instalment income" for a quarter to a partner so that the partner can make a PAYG instalment payment based on the partner's share of the partnership instalment income (¶27-265). A partnership's instalment income is calculated using the PAYG rules and is not the same as partnership net income calculated under s 90 (¶5-070).

Each individual partner is entitled to claim a share of tax offsets (eg for franked distributions) to which the partnership is entitled. Where a partnership has derived foreign source income for which foreign tax offsets are available, each partner's share of that income and their entitlement to any foreign tax offsets will be reflected in the partner's individual return (¶21-765).

If a post-CGT asset is disposed of by the partnership, the partners must each include their share of the gain or loss in their individual personal return. Similarly, if a partner disposes of a post-CGT interest in the partnership, any gain or loss must be reflected in the partner's return (¶11-200).

Partnership income retains its character in the partner's hands and if income of different characters is derived (eg business income and dividends) it is apportioned in assessing each partner's individual return.

For the special provisions that apply to transfers of interests in trading stock associated with the formation, variation or dissolution of a partnership, see ¶9-290. Note also the application of the commercial debt forgiveness measures to partners (¶16-910).

[FTR ¶49-401, ¶49-409]

¶5-140 Life policies of partners

In accordance with general principles (¶16-550 – ¶16-570), premiums paid by a partnership for life insurance policies on the lives of the partners are not deductible for the purposes of calculating the net partnership income or partnership loss. A partner, however, may claim a deduction for insurance premiums where the proceeds of the policy would be assessable, ie where the purpose of the insurance is to fill the place of a revenue item (IT 155; IT 2503). This would presumably apply where a partner takes out a policy to insure against the sickness or disability of one or more co-partners.

The proceeds of an insurance policy will not be assessable and the premiums will not be deductible where the purpose of the insurance is to guard against a capital loss, eg where insurance is taken out to assist a partner to meet any liabilities on the death or retirement of another partner (*Wells*) or to buy out another partner's interest in the partnership. As regards CGT, no liability would arise if the proceeds are paid to the original beneficial owner of the policy or to a person who did not acquire the rights under the policy for money or other consideration (¶11-880).

Superannuation contributions

In calculating the net partnership income or loss, no account is taken of deductions allowable for personal superannuation contributions by a partner (¶13-730) (s 90). Nor will the net partnership income or loss take into account a deduction for contributions by an employer (¶13-710) on behalf of a partner because a partner is not an employee of the partnership.

¶5-150 Partnership with non-resident partner

The net income or loss of a partnership and the exempt income of a partnership are calculated by reference to income from all sources, whether Australian or ex-Australian. The calculations are made on the assumption that the partnership is a resident taxpayer (s 90: ¶5-070).

Where the partner is a resident for the whole of the year of income, no difficulty arises. The partner is assessable on their share of the net partnership income or is entitled to a deduction for their share of the partnership loss; and if there is exempt income of the partnership, the partner's exempt income includes their share of the partnership exempt income (¶5-130).

In the case of a partner who is a non-resident for the whole or a part of the year of income, special rules ensure that such a partner is not assessed on income derived from foreign sources while the partner was a non-resident (s 92).

- A partner who is a non-resident for the whole of the year is assessable only on so much of their interest in the net income of the partnership as is attributable to sources in Australia. If there is a partnership loss, the partner may claim a deduction only for their share of the loss that is attributable to Australian sources. If there is exempt income of the partnership, the exempt income includes only the partner's share of the partnership exempt income that is attributable to Australian sources.

- A partner who is a non-resident for part only of the year is assessable on: (a) so much of their share of the net income of the partnership as is attributable to Australian sources; and (b) so much of the net income as is attributable to foreign sources and to the period when the partner is a resident. Similar rules apply where there is a partnership loss or partnership exempt income.

Under the provisions of the tax law applicable to partnerships, an Australian source is attributed to certain royalties paid to non-residents and ''natural resource income'' respectively (¶21-070).

[FTR ¶49-401]

Assignment of Partnership Interests

¶5-160 Alteration of partner's profit entitlement: "Everett assignments"

By assigning an interest or part of an interest in a partnership, a partner could avoid income tax on the partnership profits attributable to the assigned interest, according to the High Court decision in *Everett's case*. The taxpayer, a partner in a firm of solicitors, assigned part of his interest in the partnership to his wife (also a qualified solicitor) in return for a payment of several thousand dollars. The deed of assignment specifically stated that she was not to become a member of the partnership by virtue of the assignment nor was she entitled to interfere with its business or affairs. The High Court held that the assignment was effective to make the wife taxable on the partnership profits attributable to the assigned interest and to relieve the taxpayer from liability to tax on that same amount.

The principle in *Everett* was taken a step further in *Galland's case* in which a solicitor in partnership with his father assigned 49% of his interest in the partnership to a discretionary family trust. The assignment was held to be effective, even though the solicitor controlled the corporate trustee of the trust and was himself a potential beneficiary under the trust. The High Court also held that, even though the assignment took place in the last few days of the income year, it was effective to assign the relevant share of partnership profits for the whole of that year, not just the profits arising after the date of the assignment. This is because a partner's assessable income can generally only be determined at the end of the income year when the net income of the partnership is ascertained.

Different considerations apply if an assignment brings about a dissolution of the partnership and its replacement by a new partnership. In *Kelly*, a retiring partner by a retirement deed was held to have assigned only a right to a share in the partnership profits that was attributable to his interest up to the date of retirement, rather than any interest in any new partnership that might form subsequently between the remaining partners.

Despite the above cases, the ATO previously said that it would consider applying Pt IVA to Everett assignments entered into on or after the 2015–16 year but before 14 December 2017, and also certain pre-1 July 2015 assignments. The ATO would rate a post-1 July 2015 assignment as ''low risk'' only if it met one of the benchmarks specified in the guidelines *Assessing the risk: allocation of profits within professional firms*. However, the ATO suspended the application of these guidelines from 14 December 2017 and said that it would be working towards providing certainty soon (¶30-170). Taxpayers who entered into relevant arrangements before 14 December 2017 can, however, continue to rely on the suspended guidelines for the year ended 30 June 2020. Taxpayers who are contemplating new arrangements or having concerns for their arrangements entered into from 14 December 2017 should engage with the ATO as soon as possible. In any event, as a general rule, the ATO would apply s 102 (¶6-240) where the deed of assignment contains a clause enabling the bare trust created by the assignment to be revoked either at the instance of the assignor or one of the other partners (IT 2501). Note the Commissioner would also treat Everett assignments as disposals (or part disposals) for CGT purposes (¶11-200).

Attempts by partners, towards the end of the year of income, to retrospectively adjust the ratios in which they share profits or losses (as distinct from altering partnership interests) were held to be ineffectual in *Case P73* and *Case Q53*. In *Nandan*, however, the Federal Court held that a dissolution agreement drawn up on the last day of an income year adjusted the partners' share of the net partnership income for that year. The court noted that the partners were aware that there would be profits for the year, but until the year ended it was not possible to say with certainty what the profits would be.

For the ATO view on changes in "no goodwill" professional partnerships, see *Administrative treatment: acquisitions and disposals of interests in "no goodwill" professional partnerships, trusts and incorporated practices.*

Professional firms as partnerships

The Commissioner warns against the use of arrangements where an individual purports to make the trustee of a discretionary trust a partner in a professional firm, but fails to account for its tax consequences (TA 2013/3: see also ¶31-570). In these arrangements, the individuals purport to alienate income attributable to their professional services to the trustee partner.

Expenses and losses claimed on assigned interests

Where a partner assigns part of a partnership interest, expenses incurred by that partner in connection with the partnership may have to be apportioned for deduction purposes in accordance with the extent of the interest assigned. For example, a partner who assigns a one-third interest in the partnership will only be entitled to a deduction for two-thirds of the interest payments under a loan used to acquire the interest in the partnership. However, expenditure that is unrelated to the partner's proportionate interest in the partnership (eg travel expenses or subscriptions) will be fully deductible (IT 2608).

Where there is a partnership loss, the share of that loss attributable to the assigned interest is deductible to the assignor partner as trustee of that interest and should be taken into account in determining the net income of the trust estate (IT 2608).

The assignment of an interest in a corporate limited partnership will be treated as if it were the transfer of a share in a company (¶3-475).

[FTR ¶49-405, ¶49-407]

Family Partnerships

¶5-170 Income-splitting device

A partnership may be an appropriate vehicle for reducing the tax liabilities of the family unit by splitting the income of the head of the household among family members as partners in a partnership formed to conduct the family business or to hold family investments (¶31-520). However, a written partnership agreement between members of a family may not be effective to create a partnership for income tax purposes (¶5-010).

¶5-180 Uncontrolled partnership income

To counteract loss of revenue through income-splitting by the use of family partnerships, a special further tax is imposed on any uncontrolled partnership income (s 94) (see ¶5-210 for the rate of the further tax).

Uncontrolled partnership income is the share of net partnership income (or part of that share) to which a partner is entitled but over which the partner does not have *real and effective control and disposal* (¶5-190, ¶5-200). A resident partner's share of the net partnership income is calculated by reference to income from all sources. For the position where a partner is a non-resident for the whole or a part of the year, see ¶5-150.

The uncontrolled partnership provisions apply to a partner who is 18 years of age or more on the last day of the partnership's income year. They also apply where a trustee/partner lacks real and effective control of the trust estate's share of partnership income and uncontrolled partnership income is included in the assessable income of the trust estate provided: (a) a beneficiary (not being a company) is over 18 years of age and is presently entitled to income of the trust estate; or (b) the income of the trust estate is income to which no beneficiary is presently entitled and which is assessed under s 99 (¶6-230).

The uncontrolled partnership income provisions do not apply where the partner or presently entitled beneficiary is under 18 years of age on the last day of the income year; the income of such persons is covered by the special rules that apply to the unearned income of minors (¶2-160).

Partnership income passing through successive trust estates retains its character for the purpose of determining the portion treated as uncontrolled partnership income in the hands of the ultimate trustee or beneficiary.

Note that s 94 has no application to partnership income derived by a company either as a partner or through a trust, the trustee of which is a partner.

[FTR ¶49-520]

¶5-190 Partner's effective control over partnership income

In determining whether a partner has real and effective control and disposal of their share of partnership income, regard should be had to:

- the terms of the partnership agreement
- the control of the partnership determined from the facts of its management and the conduct of its business, and
- the conduct of the operations of the partnership (*Robert Coldstream Partnership*).

If a partner *must* allow their share, or portion of that share, to be dealt with in a particular way so that the partner cannot deal with it in another way, the partner will lack the necessary control and disposal of that share or portion. However, neither centralisation of the power of management in one or more partners, nor the actual non-drawing of income where the partner is not *debarred* from making drawings will, of itself, mean lack of control in the relevant sense.

The Commissioner has the discretion not to apply the further tax (¶5-180) to any income of a partnership over which no real control exists where it would be unreasonable to do so (s 94(8)). The Commissioner has indicated that this discretion will generally be exercised where the partner's share of income in future years is required to pay for the acquisition of their interest in the partnership assets, provided it is a genuine arrangement. It will also be exercised where the partner's income is required to assist partnership finances, provided the same proportion of all the partners' income is similarly affected.

[FTR ¶49-540]

¶5-200 Calculation of uncontrolled partnership income

The uncontrolled partnership income of a partner is the uncontrolled portion of the net partnership income included in the partner's assessable income, as reduced by: (a) business deductions (¶16-152) exclusively relating to that income (eg interest on moneys borrowed to invest in the partnership); and (b) an appropriate proportion of other business deductions related to the derivation of that income (eg accountancy fees) and of non-business deductions (eg gifts) (s 94(10)).

▶ Example

A's taxable income of $23,090 includes $8,250 uncontrolled partnership income. In calculating the taxable income, deductions were allowed for interest on moneys borrowed to invest in the partnership ($1,690), accountancy fees (of which $260 was considered to relate to the partnership income) and gifts to eligible funds ($380). The uncontrolled partnership income liable to the special further tax is:

$$\$8{,}250 - \left(\$1{,}690 + \$260 + \frac{\$380 \times (\$8{,}250 - (\$1{,}690 + \$260))}{\$23{,}470}\right)$$

$$= \$8{,}250 - (\$1{,}950 + \$102)$$

$$= \$6{,}198$$

[FTR ¶49-550]

¶5-210 Further tax on uncontrolled partnership income

The rate of further tax on uncontrolled partnership income for 2020–21 is, with one exception (see below), 45% reduced by the average rate of ordinary tax — calculated without rebates or credits — applicable to the taxpayer's total taxable income (*Income Tax Rates Act 1986*, s 12(7)). The imposition of the further tax has the consequence that the partner pays tax on the income at the top marginal tax rate.

▶ Example

B has a taxable income of $50,000 for 2020–21, of which $10,000 is uncontrolled partnership income. B has no primary production income. Assume that there are no deductions allowable against the uncontrolled partnership income. B's tax liability is calculated as follows:

Tax payable at 2020–21 rates (¶42-000) on taxable income of $50,000		$7,797
Plus:	further tax on uncontrolled partnership income (ie $10,000 × 29.41%*)	2,941
		10,738
Plus:	Medicare levy (2% × $50,000)	1000
	Total tax payable	$11,738

* The rate of further tax is calculated as:

$$45\% - \left(\frac{\text{gross tax on taxable income}}{\text{total taxable income}} \times 100\right)\%$$

$$= 45\% - \left(\frac{\$7{,}797}{\$50{,}000} \times 100\right)\%$$

$$= 45\% - 15.59\%$$

$$= 29.41\%$$

Exception for primary producers subject to averaging

The exception is where the taxpayer is a primary producer who is subject to the averaging system. In certain situations, only part of the primary producer's income is subject to averaging (¶18-210). As 2 different rates of tax will be levied in such cases, one on income subject to averaging and another on the remaining income, it is necessary to identify separately uncontrolled partnership income that qualifies for averaging and uncontrolled partnership income that does not qualify for averaging (s 94(10A) to (10C)).

[FTR ¶864-000]

Chapter 6 Trustees • Beneficiaries • Deceased Estates

Introduction

¶6-000 Taxation of trusts

This chapter deals with the taxation treatment of the income of ordinary trusts (usually created by will or instrument of trust), deceased estates, managed investment trusts and public trading trusts. The trust income provisions are largely contained in the ITAA36, although there are CGT and imputation provisions in the ITAA97 that are relevant to trusts. Legislative references in this chapter are to the ITAA36 unless otherwise specified. Certain funds, such as ACNC registered charities, may be exempt from tax (¶10-600).

Some of the tax planning aspects relating to trusts are considered in ¶31-540 and the CGT provisions that affect trusts are considered in ¶11-290. The use of trusts to divert personal exertion income to family members is discussed at ¶30-600.

Special rules apply in calculating the tax on certain trust income of minor beneficiaries, ie persons under 18 years of age (¶2-160 and following).

The rules that apply in relation to franked distributions received through a trust are discussed at ¶4-860 and the rules that apply to capital gains received through a trust are discussed at ¶11-060.

Trusts and Trustees

¶6-010 Trusts and trustees

A trust of property or income may be described as a fiduciary obligation imposed on a person (the trustee) to hold property or income for a particular purpose or purposes, or for the benefit of other persons or classes of persons who may or may not include the trustee. The fiduciary obligation may be imposed on the trustee either by the person establishing the trust (who may be the same as the trustee), by another person, by court order or declaration, or by operation of law. Although the trustee may hold the legal title to property, etc, the trustee is compelled in equity to deal with it in accordance with the express or implied terms of the trust.

The executor or administrator of a deceased person's estate is not strictly the trustee of the estate until executorial or administrative functions are completed, but an executor or administrator is expressly made a trustee for income tax purposes by the expanded definition of "trustee" in s 6(1). A company formed by the trustee of a will in accordance with its terms to carry out some or all of the trusts is not a trustee for tax purposes. The expanded definition of "trustee" also includes a person acting in a fiduciary capacity.

The Official Receiver in Bankruptcy of an insolvent deceased estate is a trustee, as is the receiver and manager of the assets of a company appointed by the debenture holders and a mortgagee in possession.

A trust for income tax purposes is property, or an interest in property, that is vested in and under the control of a person who is a trustee, and that produces income. A deceased estate is a trust pending completion of its administration and thereafter until all the assets have been distributed to the beneficiaries. A person who has only limited powers to deal with property as an intermediary for the legal owner is not a trustee of a trust. An agent who receives moneys, etc, for a principal is not a trustee.

The following have been held to constitute a trust:

- moneys held under a court order by solicitors acting as trustees pending the outcome of proceedings to determine who was entitled to the moneys (*Harmer*)
- compensation paid into an accident compensation fund for the benefit of dependants of deceased workers (*Registrar, Accident Compensation Tribunal (Vic)*)
- moneys paid into a joint bank account "on trust" pending the determination of the parties' respective entitlements contingent upon the occurrence of future events (*Walsh Bay Developments*)
- money stolen by an employee from his employer (the money was held on constructive trust) (*Zobory*).

In *Aussiegolfa Pty Ltd (Trustee)* it was held by the Full Federal Court that, in the circumstances, an investment by a superannuation fund in units of a particular class in a managed investment scheme constituted a trust that was distinct from the managed investment scheme.

It is important to note that the provisions of Div 6, which operate to determine the circumstances in which the trustee or a beneficiary is taxed, only apply if there is income of a trust estate. That requires that the trustee must stand in relation to a proprietary right by virtue of which income of the trust arises (*Leighton*). In *Leighton*, the Full Federal Court held that the taxpayer (a non-resident individual) was not a trustee in respect of income derived on an accruals basis by 2 non-resident companies that carried on share trading activities; the proceeds of sales of shares which came to be held by the taxpayer did not represent the income of either of the companies but rather represented the realisation of the income that they had already derived.

Although a liquidator of a company is within the statutory definition of trustee a liquidator is not a trustee of a trust estate in any ordinary sense (*Australian Building Systems*).

For details of the withholding requirements relating to trust investments where no TFN or ABN is quoted, see ¶26-200.

[FTR ¶50-517, ¶50-519]

¶6-015 Amending a trust deed

There was previously considerable doubt as to whether and, if so, in what circumstances one trust estate could come to an end and a new trust estate commence. This particular issue often arose in the context of an amendment to a trust instrument and the question that was usually posed was whether the amendment would cause a ‘‘resettlement’’. Of course, if a new trust arose this could have significant income tax and CGT consequences.

In *Commercial Nominees*, the High Court (affirming a decision of the Full Federal Court) held that no new trust was created where significant changes were made to a superannuation fund trust deed, primarily because there was a continuing trust estate (ie the property of the fund). The High Court observed that the fund, both before and after the changes, was administered as a single fund, and treated that way by the regulatory authority.

More recently, the question of the continuity of a trust was considered by the Full Federal Court in *Clark*. The trust in that case was a unit trust and no amendment of the trust deed was involved. However, the Commissioner contended that there were several transactions which caused a break in the continuity of the trust. A majority of the court took the view that the indicia of continuity applied by the High Court in *Commercial Nominees* (namely, the constitution of the trust, the trust property and membership) applied generally and not only in the context of a superannuation fund.

Commissioner's views

According to TD 2012/21, as a general proposition, the approach adopted by the Full Federal Court in *Commercial Nominees* is authority for the proposition that assuming there is some continuity of property and membership of the trust, an amendment to the trust that is made in proper exercise of a power of amendment contained under the deed will not have the result of terminating the trust, irrespective of the extent of the amendments so made so long as the amendments are properly supported by the power of amendment.

Amendments validly made pursuant to a power of amendment that will not lead to the creation of a new trust include amendments adding to, or deleting, beneficiaries, the extension of the vesting day, amendments to the definition of income and amendments to permit the ‘‘streaming’’ of different classes of income. The position is the same with court sanctioned amendments or variations. But, once the vesting date of a trust has passed, it will not be able to be extended by amendment to the trust deed, even if this could have been validly done before the vesting day arrived (TR 2018/6).

However, TD 2012/21 states that even in instances where a pre-existing trust does not terminate, it may be the case that assets held originally as part of the trust property commence to be held under a separate charter of obligations as a result of a change to the terms of the trust — whether by exercise of a power under the deed (including a power to amend) or court approved variation — such as to lead to the conclusion that those assets are now held on terms of a distinct (ie different) trust. Thus, depending on the facts, the

Commissioner considers that the effect of a particular amendment might be such as to lead to the conclusion that a particular asset has been settled on terms of a different trust by reason of being made subject to a charter of rights and obligations separate from those pertaining to the remaining assets of the trust.

Vesting day issues

If a trust deed is validly amended so as to extend the vesting day of the trust, there will not be the creation of a new trust. There are, however, potential CGT and income tax issues where the vesting day of a trust passes which will mean that all of the interests in the trust as to income and capital become vested in interest and possession. These issues are considered in TR 2018/6.

Splitting a trust

A trust split constituted by an arrangement where the parties to an existing trust functionally split the operation of the trust so that some trust assets are controlled by and held for the benefit of a subset of beneficiaries, and other trust assets are controlled and held for the benefit of others, will result in the creation of a trust by declaration or settlement and CGT event E1 will happen (TD 2019/14). A trust split usually involves a discretionary trust that is part of a family group. A common reason given for splitting the trust is to allow different parts of the family group to have autonomous control of their own part of the trust fund. The determination lists features that a relevant trust split will exhibit. See also ¶11-290.

[FITR ¶151-970, ¶151-980; FTR ¶50-520, ¶50-535]

Trust Returns

¶6-020 Trust return

An annual return (often referred to as Form T) must be lodged for a trust, irrespective of the amount of income derived by the trust (¶44-060). Public trading trusts that are taxed as companies should use the company return form: ¶3-045. The trust return is to be lodged by any one of the trustees who is a resident of Australia. If there is no trustee resident in Australia, the return must be lodged by the trust's public officer (¶6-050) or, where no public officer is appointed, by the trust's agent in Australia. Trust returns are usually required to be lodged by 31 October after the end of the income year to which the return relates (¶24-060).

Under the group consolidation regime, the head company of a wholly-owned group of entities (including trusts) may lodge a single consolidated tax return (¶8-010).

The trustee of a ''transparent trust'' or a ''secured purchase trust'' is not required to lodge a return provided that, broadly speaking, the income of the trust estate is vested indefeasibly in the beneficiary (PS LA 2000/2).

The return form and the associated instructions should be checked to see what information needs to be provided with returns. Many elections available to taxpayers under the tax law are not required to be in writing or lodged with returns. Whether or not an election has been made will generally be evident from the calculation of taxable income as disclosed in the return and from the records required to be kept to verify that calculation (¶24-040).

False statements about trust income

If a trustee makes an incorrect statement about the net income of a trust estate that results in a beneficiary having a shortfall amount, the trustee is liable to pay an administrative penalty (¶29-160).

[FTR ¶79-300ff]

¶6-030 Trustee of deceased estate

For the year in which a taxpayer died, the trustee of the deceased estate is generally required to lodge an individual tax return of the deceased's income up to the date of death (¶2-030, ¶2-080). The trustee is also generally required to lodge a deceased estate trust return for the remainder of the income year for the income received or derived after death by the deceased estate.

The individual tax return of the deceased's income up to the date of death may take into account expenses incurred by the trustee in relation to the income tax affairs of the deceased (¶16-850).

PCG 2018/4 applies to smaller and less complex estates to enable the trustee to wind up the estate without concern that they may have to fund any of the deceased's pre-death liabilities from their own assets.

The trust return for the deceased estate must include income *derived* by the estate after the death of the deceased, and amounts *received* by the trustee after the death where those amounts would have been assessable to the deceased had they been received during the deceased's lifetime (¶6-180).

Generally, trust returns must continue to be lodged for each financial year until the estate is fully administered, unless the trust is non-taxable.

Note that a registered tax or BAS agent can now access a deceased person's information if they are nominated to represent a legal personal representative for a deceased estate provided that the executor or administrator has a grant of probate or letters of administration.

Rate of tax

For the first 3 income years after death, the income of a resident deceased estate is concessionally taxed at ITAA36 s 99 rates (¶42-030), ie normal individual tax rates. No Medicare levy is payable (¶42-033).

For a checklist of the tax consequences of death, see ¶44-170.

[FTR ¶977-845]

¶6-040 Personal liability of trustee

A trustee is answerable as the taxpayer for the doing of all things required by the tax law in relation to income derived by the trustee in a representative capacity (ITAA36 s 254). Under that provision, a trustee is authorised and required to retain out of that income sufficient moneys to pay taxes (including penalty tax and interest) that are or will become payable by the trustee in a representative capacity, including where the trustee holds money on trust under a court order (*Fermanis v Cheshire Holdings*). The Commissioner's view that a trustee's liability to retain does not depend on an assessment having been made was rejected by the High Court in *Australian Building Systems*. A trustee is not personally liable for tax, except to the extent of any failure to meet the retention requirements. A trustee's right of personal indemnity from a residual beneficiary in respect of proper trust expenses, including tax, was affirmed in *Balkin v Peck*, even though the beneficiary had argued that it should not be required to indemnify the trustee because the tax resulted from the trustee's failure to take the trust offshore to avoid tax.

If a trustee complies with all the requirements of the tax law and then distributes the corpus to the beneficiaries without any notice of an intention by the Commissioner to issue additional assessments, the Commissioner cannot recover taxes thereafter assessed to the trustee from the beneficiaries to whom the distributions have been made. (Trust recoupment tax, payable where there has been a ‘‘new generation’’ trust stripping scheme, is a special case: ¶6-268, ¶6-270.)

If a trustee lets trust property at a gross undervalue to a non-beneficiary tenant, this may amount to a breach of trust unless there is an intention to thereby indirectly benefit the beneficiaries. The letting at undervalue may support an inference that the property was let partly for non-income earning purposes, with the result that deductions for outgoings on the property may need to be apportioned (*Madigan*: ¶16-650; *Fletcher*: ¶16-010, ¶31-370).

[FTR ¶782-060]

¶6-050 Public officer of trust

A trust that does not have a resident trustee and that has a business in Australia or Australian source property income (except dividends, interest or royalties subject to withholding tax) is required to appoint a public officer to ensure that the trustee's taxation responsibilities are met (s 252A). The qualifications for the public officer are the same as for public officers generally (¶3-030). The Commissioner has power to exempt (conditionally or unconditionally) particular trusts from the requirement to appoint a public officer.

The appointment of a public officer must be made within 90 days after the earlier of: (a) the date on which any business was commenced to be carried on by the trust in Australia; or (b) the date on which the trust commences to derive relevant property income from Australian sources. Failure to appoint a public officer is a strict liability offence that may result in a fine not exceeding 1 penalty unit (¶29-000) for each day that an appointment is not duly made.

[FTR ¶781-600]

Method of Taxing Trust Income

¶6-060 Trust not separate taxable entity

A trust is not a separate taxable entity. This is despite the fact that a return of trust income must usually be filed by the trustee and that, in certain circumstances, the trustee may be liable to be assessed and to pay tax on the whole or part of the trust income in that representative capacity.

In general terms, it is the beneficiaries who are ultimately entitled to receive and retain the trust income (¶6-085) who are taxable on the net income as defined for income tax purposes (¶6-080). The trustee is generally taxed only on the balance (if any) of the net income as defined for tax purposes as is referrable to income to which no beneficiary is presently entitled, or to which a beneficiary *is* presently entitled but which the beneficiary cannot immediately receive because of some legal incapacity such as infancy or insanity (s 96). (Corporate unit trusts and public trading trusts are a special case: ¶6-310.)

Where the Commissioner is uncertain as to which taxpayer is liable to tax, alternative assessments may be issued in respect of the same income (¶25-100), eg one to the trustee and one to another person, provided there is no double recovery of tax (*Trustee of the Balmain Trust*).

Subject to certain qualifications relating to foreign source income, trust income is taxed in the year it is *derived by the trust*, and it is taxed either to the trustee or to the beneficiaries, or a portion of it is taxed to the trustee and a portion to the beneficiaries. Thus, the beneficiaries may be taxed on their respective shares of the net income of the trust for tax purposes even though the trustee has not physically distributed that income to them by the end of the year in which it is derived. However, it is clear that, if some or the whole of the income derived in one year is taxed to the trustee or to beneficiaries who have not yet received it, it does not again become subject to tax when it is subsequently distributed to the beneficiaries (¶6-130).

The primary provisions relating to the taxation of trust income are contained in Pt III Div 6 (ss 95AAA to 102). The primary provisions were modified, from and including the 2010–11 income year, where the trust has a net capital gain, a franked distribution or a franking credit included in its net income for tax purposes (see below).

The net income of a trust for tax purposes is taxed either to the beneficiary or trustee as follows:

- the beneficiary is assessable if the beneficiary is presently entitled to income of the trust, is not under a legal disability and is a resident at the end of the income year (¶6-110)
- the trustee is assessable on behalf of a beneficiary who is presently entitled to income of the trust but is either under a legal disability or is not a resident at the end of the income year (¶6-120), and
- the trustee is assessable on net income of the trust to the extent to which no beneficiary (or the trustee on behalf of a beneficiary) is assessed on it (¶6-230).

Undistributed foreign source income is not taxed in the year it is derived by the trust where either: (a) the beneficiary presently entitled to it is not a resident; or (b) there is no beneficiary presently entitled and, subject to special accruals measures (¶6-075), the trust is a non-resident trust. However, the income is assessable in the income year in which it is distributed to a beneficiary who is a resident at any time during that year. Where foreign source income to which no beneficiary is presently entitled is taxed to the trustee under s 99 or s 99A, because the trust is a resident trust, the distribution of that income to a non-resident beneficiary may entitle the beneficiary to a refund of the tax paid by the trustee (¶6-150).

The broad effect of the modification of the primary provisions in relation to capital gains and franked dividends is that capital gains and franked distributions are taken out of the operation of Pt III Div 6 by Div 6E and are dealt with by provisions in ITAA97 Subdiv 115-C (capital gains) and Subdiv 207-B (franked distributions). Provided the trust deed confers the necessary power, the trustee can ‘‘stream’’ capital gains and franked distributions to beneficiaries by making them ‘‘specifically entitled’’ (¶6-107).

According to the Commissioner, there has been an increase in the use of New Zealand foreign trusts by Australian residents as a vehicle for cross border tax planning. However, Australia’s right to tax the trustees of NZ foreign trusts on Australian source income under Div 6 is not affected by the treaty. For the purposes of determining residency under the treaty, the relevant person is the trustee and not the trust (TR 2005/14).

[FTR ¶50-501ff]

¶6-070 Multiple trusts

One person may create several trusts, either in the one trust instrument or by means of several separate trust instruments, in favour of the same or different beneficiaries.

With one specific exception, the incomes of separate and distinct trusts are not aggregated even though one person may be trustee of each. But, for this advantage to accrue, there must be a clear intention to create separate and distinct trusts. While it may not be necessary to keep separate bank accounts, to divide the corpus physically and to invest the funds of each trust separately, literal compliance with the terms of the trust instrument is necessary.

The exception arises where a beneficiary under 2 or more trusts is a minor whose income is taxed under the special rules discussed at ¶2-160. Where the beneficiary’s income from one trust does not exceed $416 (so that tax would not normally be payable), but the beneficiary has income under one or more other trusts and the total exceeds that amount, then the trustee must pay tax on the beneficiary's income at the rate applying to minor beneficiaries (¶2-220, ¶2-250) (*Income Tax Rates Act 1986*, s 13(4)).

[FTR ¶50-912]

¶6-075 Accumulating income of non-resident trusts

Various special measures prevent the deferral of Australian tax on trust income accumulated in a non-resident trust for the benefit of an Australian resident beneficiary of the trust (Pt III Div 6AAA). These special measures extend to trusts that do not have the derivation of trust income as an object but instead concentrate on realised capital gains at the end of a period of time.

Accruals basis of taxation The attributable income of an Australian controlled non-resident trust is required to be assessed on an accruals basis to a resident who has directly or indirectly transferred value to the trust where the transfer was made, in the case of a discretionary trust, at any time and, in the case of a non-discretionary trust, after 12 April 1989. The accruals provisions do not apply in relation to arm's length transfers or to certain post-marital or family relief trusts. See ¶21-320 for the meaning of "attributable income" and ¶21-290 for a discussion of the accruals measures.

Interest charge on distributions A distribution to an Australian beneficiary out of accumulated income of a non-resident trust that has not been taxed under the accruals measures or the ordinary trust measures bears an interest charge, measured by reference to the period from the end of the income year in which the non-resident trust derived the income to the end of the income year (of the beneficiary) in which the income is distributed (¶21-350).

[FTR ¶51-370, ¶51-398]

¶6-077 Net capital gain and franked dividends: special rules

Where the net income of a trust (¶6-080) for an income year does not include a net capital gain or a franked distribution, a beneficiary who is presently entitled to a share (ie a fraction or percentage) of the income of the trust (ie the distributable trust income as determined in accordance with trust principles and the trust deed) for the income year is taxed on that fraction or percentage of the net income of the trust for that income year as calculated for tax purposes (¶6-110, ¶6-120). The trustee is taxed on any net income that is not attributed to a beneficiary in this way.

Where the net income of a trust for tax purposes includes a net capital gain or a franked distribution then the capital gains or franked distribution that are reflected in the net income are taken outside the operation of Div 6 (by Div 6E) and are subject to the special rules in ITAA97 Subdiv 115-C (capital gains) and 207-B (franked distributions). These special rules enable the trustee to stream capital gains and franked distributions (provided the trust deed confers the necessary power on the trustee) by making beneficiaries "specifically entitled" (¶6-107) to amounts of a capital gain or a franked distribution. The way ITAA97 Subdiv 115-C and 207-B operate is described at ¶11-060 and ¶4-860.

To the extent that a capital gain or franked distribution is not attributed to a specifically entitled beneficiary then it is attributed to the beneficiaries of the trust in accordance with their adjusted Division 6 percentages. A beneficiary's adjusted Division 6 percentage is the percentage of the income of the trust (including capital gains that are treated as income and franked distributions) to which the beneficiary is presently entitled, adjusted to exclude any part of the capital gain or franked distribution to which any beneficiary is specifically entitled.

In practical terms, although capital gains and franked distribution are taken outside the operation of Div 6, capital gains and franked distributions to which no beneficiary is made specifically entitled are (broadly) taxed to the beneficiaries and/or the trustee in the same way as the other income of the trust.

Tax exempt beneficiaries

There are 2 anti-avoidance provisions which may apply where a tax exempt beneficiary is presently entitled to income of a trust. Where they apply these provisions operate to deny the present entitlement of the exempt beneficiary to income of the trust (so that the trustee is assessed on an appropriate share of the net income). See ¶6-274.

[FTR ¶50-510]

Calculation of Trust Income

¶6-080 Net income of a trust

Since a trust is not a taxable entity (¶6-060), the calculation of the "net income" of a trust is simply the first step in determining the amounts on which the trustee and/or the beneficiaries are assessable.

The net income of a trust is the total assessable income of the trust calculated as if the trustee were a resident taxpayer in respect of that income, less all allowable deductions (s 95(1)).

The calculation of the net income requires both Australian *and* foreign source income and related deductions to be taken into account. The tax treatment of net income attributable to foreign sources depends, in the case of income to which no beneficiary is presently entitled, on whether the trust is a resident trust and, in the case of a presently entitled beneficiary, on the residence of the beneficiary. Net income of a non-resident trust may be attributable in certain circumstances to a resident (¶6-075).

The character of a receipt for tax purposes (ie income or capital) is not determined by trust law or the terms of the particular trust deed. In other words, neither trust law nor the provisions of the trust deed can alter the character of a receipt for tax purposes (*ANZ Savings Bank*). Profits on the sale of capital assets would generally be an accretion to corpus for trust purposes, but may be assessable income for tax purposes, for example, under the CGT provisions (¶11-030).

In calculating the net income of a trust, a trustee carrying on a business must use generally accepted accounting principles, including accrual accounting (*Zeta Force*).

The assessable income of a trust includes the whole of the trust's interest in the net income of a partnership of which it is a member, even if that share has not been received. Whether a gain or loss from an investment is made by a trustee is on capital or income account depends on the application of the normal principles (business transaction, isolated profit-making transaction, etc) (TD 2011/21).

In general, all deductions for expenses which would be available if a resident taxpayer had derived the trust's assessable income are taken into account in calculating the net income of a trust. Where the deductions exceed the assessable income, the resulting loss is taken into account in calculating the net income of the trust for succeeding income years, ie the loss is *not* distributed among the beneficiaries or the trustee as representing corpus. However, under the trust loss measures, a trust may not be able to deduct a prior year loss or certain debt deductions (for bad debts and debt/equity swaps) unless it satisfies certain tests (¶6-262). In addition, past losses that, under trust law or the terms of the trust instrument, are required to be met out of corpus are not allowable in calculating the net income of the trust for tax purposes in relation to a life tenant or a beneficiary with no beneficial interest in the trust corpus.

▶ Example 1

For the prior income year, The Clooney Trust suffered a loss of $800. For the current income year, its net trust income for tax purposes, before taking into account the prior year loss, is $2,000. Under the terms of the trust, the loss is to be met out of corpus. One of the two beneficiaries (Andrew) is entitled to half the trust income for life but to no interest, contingent or otherwise, in corpus. The other beneficiary (Felicia) is entitled to the remaining half of the trust income and also has a contingent interest in the trust corpus. The net trust income for tax purposes for the current year is: (a) so far as Andrew is concerned, $2,000 of which his share is $1,000; and (b) so far as Felicia is concerned, $1,200 (ie $2,000 – $800) of which her share is $600 (this assumes the trust satisfies the trust loss requirements: ¶6-262).

As regards current year losses, the trust loss provisions may require a trust to work out its net income in a special way if it does not satisfy similar tests to those that apply in relation to prior year losses (¶6-262, ¶6-265).

Trust losses that are deductible in calculating the net income of the trust for tax purposes are first offset against any exempt income derived by the trust (¶16-895). If the trust's exempt income for the year exceeds the unrecouped loss, the balance is treated as exempt income of a beneficiary to the extent of the beneficiary's individual interest in that exempt income, subject to a limited exception (¶6-110). Trust losses are never available as such to reduce the other income of a beneficiary.

▶ Example 2

If, in the above example, the trust also derives $600 exempt income in the current income year, the net trust income is: (a) so far as Andrew is concerned, $1,000 (ie 50% of $2,000); and (b) so far as Felicia is concerned, $900, ie 50% of ($2,000 – ($800 – $600)). No part of the exempt income is included in Felicia's exempt income because the exempt income has been fully taken into account in calculating the net income of the trust estate (¶6-110). The amount of $300 (ie 50% of $600) is included in Andrew's exempt income.

The net income of a trust for tax purposes will not necessarily correspond with the actual net income of the trust for trust accounting purposes. The position where the net income for income tax purposes exceeds the net income for trust purposes is considered at ¶6-200. The converse situation, where the net income for trust purposes exceeds the net income for income tax purposes, is considered at ¶6-130.

Based on the "refinancing principle" recognised in *Roberts & Smith* (¶16-740), interest incurred by a trustee on a loan used to finance the payment of a returnable amount is deductible. A returnable amount arises where: (a) an individual has subscribed money for units in a unit trust, and has a right of redemption in relation to the units and the money is used by the trustee to purchase income-producing assets; and (b) a beneficiary has an unpaid present entitlement to some or all of the capital or net income of the trust estate, and the amount to which the beneficiary is entitled has been retained by the trustee and used in the gaining or producing of assessable income of the trust (TR 2005/12). For example, this would be the case if the borrowed funds are used to repay the beneficiary an amount lent by the beneficiary to the trustee who uses the amount for income-producing purposes. Amounts attributable to internally generated goodwill or the unrealised revaluation of assets are not "returnable amounts". In the absence of a returnable amount, interest is not deductible if the purpose of the loan is merely to discharge an obligation to make a distribution to a beneficiary.

Foreign trust with capital gain or loss

If a trust is a foreign trust for CGT purposes (¶12-720), a capital gain or capital loss from a CGT event happening in relation to an asset of the trust that is not taxable Australian property is disregarded under ITAA97 s 855-10, despite the fact that the trust is treated as a resident taxpayer when calculating its net income under ITAA36 s 95 (see above); also, in such circumstances the beneficiaries are not treated as having capital gains or making capital losses under ITAA97 Subdiv 115-C (TD 2017/23). Whether a distribution to a beneficiary by the trustee that is attributable to such a capital gain is assessable will largely turn on whether ITAA36 s 99B (¶6-130) is attracted. However, if s

99B is attracted, the beneficiary would not be able to offset a prior year net capital loss or a current year capital loss against the amount, and the discount capital gain concession would not be available (TD 2017/24).

PAYG instalment income of a trust

Under the PAYG system, unless a trustee is absolutely certain that no beneficiary is a quarterly PAYG instalment taxpayer, the trust must calculate the beneficiaries' instalment income quarterly. This is based on the trust's instalment income for the quarter (generally, only its ordinary income). The trustee must notify each affected beneficiary, so that PAYG instalments can be paid (¶27-270).

[FTR ¶50-545, ¶50-685]

¶6-085 The income of a trust

The income of a trust estate is an underlying concept of the trust assessing provisions of ITAA36 Div 6. It is the share of the income of a trust to which a beneficiary is presently entitled which determines the amount (share) of the net income for tax purposes on which the beneficiary (or the trustee on the beneficiary's behalf) is assessable. A beneficiary's share of the income of a trust is also the basis for determining the beneficiary's adjusted Division 6 percentage (which is relevant where the trust has a net capital gain, a franked distribution or a franking credit included in its net income for tax purposes).

The ''income'' of a trust estate is not a defined term and is simply the distributable trust income determined in accordance with trust law principles and the trust deed (*Bamford*). This means that, in determining the income of a trust for an income year any definition of income in the trust deed will be relevant, as well as any powers conferred on the trustee by the trust deed to characterise an amount as being income or capital.

''Net income'' for tax purposes is a defined term and is discussed at ¶6-080.

Commissioner's views

Draft TR 2012/D1 considers the meaning of the expression ''the income of the trust estate'' in ITAA36 Div 6. Points made in the draft ruling include:

- the ''income of the trust estate'' (ie the trust's distributable income for an income year) is measured in respect of distinct income years (being the same years in respect of which the trust's net income is calculated)
- ''income'' and ''trust estate'' are distinct concepts, income being the product of the trust estate. This means that something which formed part of the trust estate at the start of an income year cannot itself, for the purposes of ITAA36 Div 6, be treated by the trustee as income of the trust for that year
- the ''income of the trust estate'', is a reference to the income available for distribution to beneficiaries or accumulation by the trustee, (commonly referred to as ''distributable income'')
- notwithstanding how a particular trust deed may define income, the ''income of the trust estate'' must be represented by a net accretion to the trust estate for the relevant period
- if the trust's net income includes notional income amounts, those amounts cannot (except in the circumstances noted below) be taken into account in calculating the ''income of the trust estate''. Examples of amounts that may be included in calculating a trust's net income but which may not form part of the income of the trust estate are: the amount of a franking credit; so much of a share of the net income of one trust (the first trust) that is included under ITAA36 s 97 in the calculation of the net tax income of another trust, but which does not represent a distribution of income of the first trust; so much of a net capital gain that is

attributable to an increase of what would have otherwise been a relevant amount of capital proceeds for a CGT event as a result of the market value substitution rule; and an amount taken to be a dividend by ITAA36 Div 7A that is paid to the trustee of the trust.

The draft ruling states that the effect of a clause in the trust instrument (or the valid exercise of a power by the trustee) to equate the distributable income of the trust with its net income is that an amount of notional income is able to satisfy any notional expenses chargeable against trust income. However, to the extent that the total notional income amounts for an income year exceed notional expense amounts of the trust estate for that year, they cannot form part of the ''income of the trust estate'' for ITAA36 Div 6 purposes (the trust estate's ''distributable income'') for that year.

[FTR ¶50-545]

Present Entitlement

¶6-100 Meaning of presently entitled

''Present entitlement'' is a critical concept in the trust provisions. This is because the method of taxing trust income varies according to whether it is income to which a beneficiary is presently entitled or income to which no beneficiary is presently entitled. Note that, where a franked distribution or a capital gain is streamed, the relevant concept in relation to these amounts is now the statutory concept of specific entitlement which is a wider concept than the concept of present entitlement; a beneficiary who or which is presently entitled to a relevant amount will be specifically entitled, but a beneficiary may be specifically entitled without being presently entitled. For discussion of the specific entitlement concept, see ¶6-107.

The High Court has held that, for a beneficiary to be ''presently entitled'' to trust income, several conditions must be satisfied (*Whiting*; *Taylor*; *Union Fidelity Trustee Co of Australia*; *Bamford*).

First, the beneficiary must have an indefeasible, absolutely vested, beneficial interest in possession in the trust income. The interest must not be contingent but must be such that the beneficiary may demand immediate payment of that income. Or, if the beneficiary is under a legal disability such as infancy or insanity, the interest must be such that the beneficiary would have been able to demand immediate payment of the income had there been no disability or incapacity. For example, parties to a dispute concerning moneys held under a court order by solicitors acting as trustees were held not to be presently entitled beneficiaries as their interest was, at best, contingent; accordingly, the solicitors were liable to tax as trustees on the interest income earned from the investment of the disputed funds (*Harmer*). Similarly, where the funds in a joint bank account constituted a trust, the parties were neither jointly nor individually presently entitled to the interest on the funds where their respective entitlements, as set out in the constituent deed, were contingent on the occurrence of future events (*Walsh Bay Developments*).

Secondly, a beneficiary can only be presently entitled to income that is legally (ie according to trust law) available for distribution to the beneficiary, even though it may not be in the trustee's hands for distribution at the relevant time. In the case of a deceased estate, the beneficiaries will not be presently entitled to income until it is possible to ascertain the residue with certainty (after provision for debts, legacies, etc). However, it is not necessary for the estate to be wound up. Where, during the administration of the estate, it is apparent to the executor that part of the net income will not be required to pay debts, etc, and the executor pays some of the income to or on behalf of the beneficiaries, those beneficiaries will be presently entitled to the income to the extent of the amounts actually paid (IT 2622).

In *Lewski*, the Full Federal Court considered an income distribution resolution of the trustee of a discretionary trust which resolved to distribute the income of the trust for an accounting period to a named individual but went on to also resolve (in effect) that if the Commissioner made any adjustment which had the effect of increasing the income for the accounting period, the increase in the income was to be distributed to a different beneficiary. The court held that the resolution, while authorised by the trust deed, was contingent and no beneficiary was presently entitled as at 30 June to the income of the trust estate. The Commissioner has issued a decision impact statement on the *Lewski* decision. See also ¶6-110.

In *Pearson*, the trustee of a discretionary trust was not presently entitled to the net income of a unit trust where:

- there was no provision in the trust deed of the unit trust (in which the trustee held all the units) to make the trustee presently entitled, nor did the unitholders have any legal right to demand payment of undistributed net income, and
- as the sole unitholder, the trustee could have brought the unit trust to an end.

Beneficiaries may be presently entitled even if, under the terms of the trust, the entitlement is only to have money applied for their benefit and not paid directly to them (*Sacks v Gridiger*). Further, a beneficiary does not cease to be presently entitled to income merely because the income has been distributed to persons not entitled to it (*Case R32*).

Legislative extension

By way of legislative extension of the concept of present entitlement, a taxpayer is taken to be presently entitled in the following situations.

- A presently entitled beneficiary who is paid an amount of income, or for whose benefit income is applied, is to be taken as continuing to be presently entitled to that income, notwithstanding its payment or application (s 95A(1)).
- A person who is not otherwise presently entitled to the income of a trust but who has a vested and indefeasible interest in it is deemed to be presently entitled to the income (s 95A(2)) (*Estate Mortgage*). A solicitor's client was deemed under this provision to be presently entitled to interest income earned on funds held in the solicitor's name as security for costs in proceedings brought by the client (*Dwight*). Income to which a beneficiary is deemed to be presently entitled under s 95A(2) is assessed to the trustee under s 98 (¶6-120) where the beneficiary is a natural person (whether under a legal disability or not) and is not a beneficiary in the capacity of trustee of another trust.
- A beneficiary in whose favour a trustee exercises a discretion to pay or apply trust income is deemed to be presently entitled to the amount so paid or applied (s 101: ¶6-105).

In certain situations involving tax avoidance, a presently entitled beneficiary will be deemed not to be presently entitled (¶6-270, ¶6-274).

For the CGT consequences where a beneficiary is absolutely entitled to a CGT asset as against the trustee of a trust (disregarding any legal disability), see ¶11-210.

Timing of distribution

Even if the trust deed permits the distribution of income of an accounting period to be made after the end of the accounting period, to be effective for tax purposes a beneficiary must be presently entitled to income by the last day of the income year in which the income is derived by the trust (that is, on or before 30 June in the case of a trust with a regular accounting period) (*Harmer*; *Colonial First State Investments*). However, if the trust deed requires a distribution of income for an accounting period to be made at a time before the end of an accounting period the distribution must be made by the time stipulated in the deed if it is to be effective for the purposes of trust law and tax law.

Where, under the terms of a trust deed, a default income distribution clause only operates *after* the end of an income year and the clause operates in relation to an income year, the trustee (and not the default beneficiaries) will be taxed on the relevant net income (usually under s 99A) because there would have been no beneficiary who was presently entitled to the income of the trust by the end of the income year.

[FTR ¶50-565, ¶50-588, ¶50-615]

¶6-105 Discretionary trusts

Where a trustee is given a discretion to pay or apply trust income to or for the benefit of specified beneficiaries, a beneficiary in whose favour the trustee exercises the discretion is deemed to be presently entitled to the amount so paid or applied (s 101). In such a case, the beneficiary is assessable on the appropriate amount of the net income for tax purposes, except where the beneficiary is under a legal disability, in which case the trustee is assessable.

For s 101 to apply, there must be an effective exercise by the trustee of the discretion to pay or apply income for the benefit of a beneficiary before the end of the income year in which the income is derived by the trustee (or earlier date if required by the trust deed).

The fact that a discretionary trust deed may permit the trustee to make a distribution resolution after 30 June will be irrelevant for income tax purposes; for income tax purposes, the present entitlement of a beneficiary must arise by the end of the income year. If the trust deed requires that an income distribution resolution for an income year be made at a time before 30 June then to be effective for both trust law and income tax the resolution would need to be made by the earlier time.

It is essential that the way that a distribution of income is effected complies with any requirements of the trust deed and that there is appropriate evidence of what has been done (eg minutes of any meeting that was in fact held). Also, those requirements may, for instance, mean that the consent of some person, such as a guardian, is required and a failure to comply with such a requirement may result in the purported distribution being void (*Carter & Ors*). In that case the Full Federal Court considered issues that may arise where a guardian's consent is required.

Where the trustee is a company, a discretion to pay or apply trust income can be exercised without the company passing a formal resolution to that effect (*Vegners*). In that case it was held that the making of a payment involved the exercise by the trustee of a discretion as trustee within the meaning of s 101 and the effect of resolutions passed at the end of each financial year was confirmatory rather than dispositive.

Where there is an ineffective exercise by the trustee of the discretion to pay or apply income for the benefit of a beneficiary, but the trust instrument contains a vesting clause that operates before the end of the income year in default of an effective exercise of the discretion, the beneficiary or beneficiaries specified in the default vesting clause will be presently entitled to the trust income (eg *Case X40*). This has been held to be the case even where the default vesting clause may be ambiguous (*Marbray Nominees*). The Commissioner accepts this decision and has stated that, where there is ambiguity in the wording of a default vesting clause, it will generally be construed to give effect to the settlor's intention (IT 2356). For a default income clause to be effective for tax purposes it would need to be activated by the end of the particular income year.

Income is applied for the benefit of a beneficiary if the trustee takes steps that have the effect of immediately and irrevocably vesting a specific portion of the income of the year in the beneficiary, so that the beneficiary's contingent interest in the income becomes an absolute one. The following steps have been held to be sufficient to constitute an application of income for the benefit of a beneficiary:

- a resolution that income ''shall belong to'' the minor beneficiaries (*Vestey's Settlement*)
- a declaration determining that part of the income was ''to be held for the credit of'' the contingent beneficiaries (*Ward*), and
- a resolution that the income ''be set aside and apportioned for and shall belong to'' the beneficiaries (*Case E47*).

As to the position where a sole trader's trading assets are transferred to a trustee of a discretionary trust, see ¶9-290.

Disclaimer

A discretionary beneficiary may be deemed to be presently entitled notwithstanding that the beneficiary was unaware of their entitlement to trust income or even of the existence of the trust (*Vegners*). However, a beneficiary may disclaim an entitlement to trust income on it coming to their knowledge (*Cornell*) either actually or constructively (*Confidential*). Any evidence of actual dissent is sufficient and the disclaimer need not be evidenced by deed. For a disclaimer to be effective, it must be an actual disclaimer of the whole interest and not merely part of the interest. In the case of a discretionary trust, each entitlement arising as the result of the exercise of the trustee's discretion to appoint income is a separate gift, the subject matter of the gift being the income (as defined by the deed) for the relevant accounting period (*Ramsden*). Thus, the fact that a beneficiary as a discretionary object receives distributions of income in earlier years does not prevent the beneficiary from disclaiming a gift in a later income year merely because they had accepted gifts from the trustee in the past (ID 2010/85).

The interest of a default beneficiary is a separate gift arising by operation of the trust deed and relates to all accounting periods such that a disclaimer confined to one only of those accounting periods is necessarily ineffective whilst an assent in one year will prevent a disclaimer in a later year (*Ramsden*). While a disclaimer of an interest in trust income may be effective to avoid tax liability on the income, renunciation of the right to be considered as a discretionary object of the trust will not be effective to avoid liability if it is actually an attempt to ''undo the past''. In *Nguyen*, a deed of renunciation 5 years after acknowledgment of present entitlement to trust income was held to be ineffective.

Disclaimers by default income beneficiaries under a discretionary trust deed after the end of an income year were held to have retrospective effect not only for trust law purposes but also for tax law purposes (*Carter & Ors*); upon disclaimer, the general law extinguished the entitlements to trust income *ab initio*. The effect of the disclaimers was that the beneficiaries must be treated as having never been entitled to the income for the purposes of s 97 in respect of the relevant income year. A valid disclaimer in respect of a distribution of income by the trustee for an income year made in respect of that income year would, it seems, have a similar consequence for the application of s 97.

Retrospective disclaimers made by default beneficiaries were ineffective as they did not occur within a reasonable period after notice of the gift and did not constitute a rejection of their entire interests in the trust income (*Ramsden*). The effect of purported disclaimers was also considered by the Full Federal Court in *Lewski*.

Shams

Purported distributions will be treated as shams with no effect where the ''beneficiaries'' either do not exist or are never intended to receive the benefit of the trust income. The ATO has given special attention to such arrangements involving non-resident beneficiaries (*Case 46/96*). Taxpayers may be expected to provide evidence of the distribution of moneys to non-resident beneficiaries and of the fact that the beneficiaries were aware that they were entitled to the moneys. In a case where there was no evidence that 29 non-residents had any entitlements to trust income from film production totalling $565,500 or that any funds were actually paid to them, the AAT held that the purported creation of the entitlements was a sham. As a result, the wife of the film producer was liable for tax on the total amount as a default beneficiary (*Hasmid Investments*).

Disclosure of trustee beneficiaries

Trustees of closely held trusts and of discretionary trusts (with some exceptions) must disclose, in the trust's tax return, the identity of trustee beneficiaries who are entitled to any distributions made by the trust (¶6-275). Failure to disclose such beneficiaries (and the TFN of resident beneficiaries) will result in the distribution becoming taxable at the highest marginal tax rate (plus Medicare levy) in the hands of the trustee (¶6-230). For this purpose, ''closely held trusts'' are trusts that are not widely held (a ''widely held trust'' is a trust that is listed on the stock exchange or a trust where more than 20 individuals hold 75% or more of the interest in the income or capital of the trust). Also, trustees of closely held trusts including family trusts are now subject to TFN withholding rules (¶6-277).

Testamentary trusts

A testamentary trust, as its name implies, is a trust that is created by will. Typically, the terms of a testamentary trust will follow the pattern of a discretionary trust. There is no restriction on the number of testamentary trusts that can be created by a will so, for instance, there may be a separate testamentary trust created for different children of the testator. Subject to an important qualification, the taxation of the income of a testamentary trust and of the beneficiaries to whom any such income may be distributed, attracts the deceased estate taxation regime. Thus, for example, where a minor beneficiary under a testamentary trust receives a distribution of trust income, the special rules that apply to the unearned income of minors do not apply (¶2-160). Further, where the trustee is assessable on net income that is attributable to income to which no beneficiary is presently entitled, the Commissioner has a discretion to assess the trustee under s 99, rather than under s 99A. A testamentary trust is not ''the estate of a deceased person'' which means that the deceased estate rates that apply for the purposes of s 99 will not be relevant.

The important qualification is that the testamentary trust exception from the unearned income of minors rules now only applies in the case of income from property, if the property: (a) was transferred to the trustee of the trust estate as a result of the will, codicil, intestacy or varying court order; (b) represents accumulations of income or capital from such property; or (c) represents accumulations of income or capital from property that satisfies requirement (b) or requirement (c) (ITAA36 s 102AG(2) and (2AA)). These rules apply in relation to assets acquired by, or transferred to, the trustee of a trust estate on or after 1 July 2019.

[FTR ¶50-528, ¶51-025, ¶51-230ff]

Specific Entitlement

¶6-107 Meaning of specific entitlement

The way that capital gains that are reflected in the net capital gain of a trust and franked distributions received by a trust are streamed is by the trustee making a beneficiary or beneficiaries specifically entitled to an amount of the capital gain or franked distribution. The trustee must have the necessary power to do this under the trust instrument.

For a beneficiary to be specifically entitled to an amount of a capital gain or franked distribution:

(1) the beneficiary must receive, or be reasonably expected to receive, an amount equal to the ''net financial benefit'' referable to the capital gain or franked distribution in the trust, and

(2) the entitlement must be recorded in its character as such in the accounts or records of the trust no later than: (a) 2 months after the end of the income year in the case of a capital gain; and (b) the end of the income year in the case of a franked distribution. The end of the income year will also be relevant in the case of a capital gain to the extent to which it is treated as income under the trust deed.

Broadly, a beneficiary will be specifically entitled to the fraction of the (gross) tax amount that equals their fraction of the net trust amount referable to the capital gain or franked distribution. For example, a beneficiary that receives an amount specified to be half of the trust's profit from the sale of an asset will generally be specifically entitled to half of the (tax) capital gain realised on the asset (ITAA97 ss 115-228(1); 207-58(1)).

When a beneficiary has a specific entitlement to a capital gain or franked distribution, the associated tax consequences in respect of that distribution apply to that beneficiary (¶4-860, ¶11-060).

Capital gains and franked distributions to which no beneficiary is specifically entitled are attributed proportionally to beneficiaries and/or the trustee based on their ''adjusted Division 6 percentage'', that is, broadly, their share (expressed as a percentage) of the income of the trust excluding amounts of capital gains and franked distributions to which any beneficiary is specifically entitled.

To be specifically entitled, a beneficiary must receive, or reasonably be expected to receive, an amount equal to their ''share of the net financial benefit'' that is referable to the capital gain or franked distribution (see (1) above). This does not require an ''equitable tracing'' to the actual trust proceeds from the event that gave rise to a capital gain or the receipt of a franked distribution. For example, it does not matter that the proceeds from the sale of an asset or a franked distribution were re-invested during the year, provided that a beneficiary receives (or can be expected to receive) an amount equivalent to their share of the net financial benefit.

Depending on the circumstances, a beneficiary can be said to be specifically entitled to receive a share of the net financial benefit of a capital gain even if the making of the capital gain is not established until after the end of the income year (eg because of the settlement of a contract after the end of the income year) (TD 2012/11).

The entitlement can be expressed as a share of the capital gain or franked distribution. More generally, the entitlement can be expressed using a known formula even though the result of the formula is calculated later. For example, a trustee could resolve to distribute to a beneficiary:

- $50 referable to a franked distribution
- half of the ''trust gain'' realised on the sale of an asset
- the amount of a franked distribution remaining after calculating directly relevant expenses and distributing $10 to another beneficiary
- 30% of a ''net dividends account'' that includes all franked and unfranked distributions, less directly relevant expenses charged against the account (so long as their entitlement to net franked distributions can be determined), or

- the amount of (tax) capital gain included in the calculation of the trust's net tax income remaining after the application of the CGT discount concession. (In such a case the beneficiary would generally be specifically entitled to only half of the gain, and that entitlement is taken to be made up equally of the taxable and discount parts of the gain.)

A beneficiary under a deceased estate who was entitled to a remainder interest was specifically entitled to a capital gain that arose to the trustee of the deceased estate from the happening of CGT event E5 (beneficiary becoming absolutely entitled to a trust asset) on the death of the life tenant (ID 2013/33).

"Net financial benefit"

A "net financial benefit" is the "financial benefit" or actual proceeds of the trust (irrespective of how they are characterised) reduced by (trust) losses or expenses (subject to certain conditions).

"Financial benefit" is defined to mean anything of economic value (including property and services) (ITAA97 s 974-160). It includes a receipt of cash or property, an increase in the value of units in a unit trust, the forgiveness of a debt obligation of the trust or any other accretion of value to the trust. When determining a beneficiary's fraction of the net financial benefit referable to a "capital gain", the (gross) financial benefit referable to the gain is reduced by trust losses or expenses only to the extent that tax capital losses were applied in the same way. When determining a beneficiary's fraction of the net financial benefit referable to a "franked distribution", the (gross) financial benefit is reduced by directly relevant expenses only.

For further consideration of the treatment of capital gains made by trusts, see ¶11-060.

Other points

Some other points to note are:

- no beneficiary can be specifically entitled to the part of a capital gain that arises because of the market value substitution rules
- the net financial benefit referable to a franked distribution will normally equal the amount of the franked distribution after being reduced by directly relevant expenses (eg any annual borrowing expenses (such as interest) incurred in respect of the underlying shares)
- the net financial benefit referable to a capital gain will generally be the trust proceeds from the transaction or circumstances that gave rise to the CGT event, reduced by any costs incurred in relation to the relevant asset. This may be further reduced by other trust losses of a capital nature (to the extent consistent with the application of capital losses for tax purposes)
- care must be taken where a capital gain is treated under the trust deed as being partly capital and partly income as could be the case where a discount capital gain is treated as capital to the extent that it is reduced by the CGT discount concession but is otherwise treated as income
- it is not possible to stream tax amounts to beneficiaries where there is no referable net financial benefit remaining in the trust — such as when the gross benefit has been reduced to zero by losses or directly relevant expenses. However, if the trustee deals with all of the franked distributions received by the trust as a single "class" (or as part of a broader class), the provisions apply to the total franked distributions as if they were a single franked distribution (ITAA97 s 207-59), and
- it is not possible to make a beneficiary specifically entitled to franking credits, or to separately stream franked distributions and franking credits (*Thomas & Ors*).

Note that special rules allow franking credits to flow proportionally to beneficiaries that have a share of a trust's (positive) income for an income year notwithstanding that the franked distributions of the trust are entirely offset by expenses.

[FITR ¶154-190, ¶214-158]

When and How Beneficiary is Taxed

¶6-110 Beneficiary presently entitled and not under legal disability

A beneficiary who is presently entitled to a share of the income of a trust (¶6-085) and is not under a legal disability is assessable on (s 97(1)):

- that share of the net income for tax purposes (¶6-080) that is attributable to a period when the beneficiary was a resident, whatever the source of the income, and
- that share of the net income for tax purposes that is attributable to a period when the beneficiary was not a resident and that is also attributable to sources in Australia.

The reference to a beneficiary being presently entitled to a ''share'' of the income of a trust is a reference to a proportion, fraction or percentage and the reference to that share of the net income is a reference to that same fraction, proportion or percentage of the net income (*Bamford*). This is called the ''proportionate'' approach to the operation of Div 6 and its implications are considered in TD 2012/22. Just how the proportionate approach operates depends on the wording of the distribution resolution. The determination shows, by example, the effect of distribution resolutions based on fixed amounts, fixed amounts ''and the balance'' and distributions by proportions. The consequences of later amendments to the net income of a trust for tax purposes are also explained.

The ATO decision impact statement on *Lewski*, where it was held that a ''variation of income'' resolution meant that the beneficiary had a ''contingent'' present entitlement (and so was not assessable), states that the ATO is considering the changes that may need to be made to TD 2012/22 (and in particular to examples 6 and 7). The decision impact statement states that outcomes may vary depending on whether income entitlements are expressed as a percentage share or a specific amount and also whether a variation resolution seeks to deal with both decreases and increases by the Commissioner. It should be kept in mind that the examples in TD 2012/22 are part of the ruling and would be binding on the Commissioner until such time as he may vary them.

The impact statement also indicates that where a resolution is a valid exercise of a trustee's power to deal with income under the deed but operates to create an entitlement for trust purposes that is not vested and indefeasible as at year-end, there will be no scope for a default beneficiary clause to operate. The result would seem to be an assessment of the trustee usually under s 99A.

Where a trust has a net capital gain or a franked distribution, the provisions noted at ¶6-077 apply.

In the case of a deceased estate, the ATO accepts an apportionment of net income between the executor and the beneficiaries in the income year in which the estate is fully administered (IT 2622: ¶6-190).

The beneficiary's share of the net income is aggregated with other assessable income of the beneficiary subject to Australian tax and, after taking into account all deductions, the total taxable income is taxed at the rate applicable to the beneficiary. Where franked distributions are received by the trust, the beneficiary may be entitled to a franking rebate (¶4-860).

Generally, the exempt income of a beneficiary includes the beneficiary's individual interest in the exempt income of a trust. However, exempt income of the trust is not included in the beneficiary's exempt income to the extent that it is taken into account in calculating the net income of the trust (s 97(1)(b): ¶6-080). The High Court has held that exempt income is only ''taken into account'' in determining the net income of a trust estate when the trust has a loss that, in effect, absorbs the exempt income. If the trust has incurred a loss in a prior year, this must first be offset against any net exempt income of the trust; as a consequence, the beneficiary's interest in the exempt income is reduced (¶16-895). The separation of annuity income into exempt income and assessable income under s 27H (¶14-510) does not involve ''taking exempt income into account'' in calculating net income (*ANZ Savings Bank*).

The non-assessable non-exempt income of a beneficiary (¶10-890) includes the beneficiary's individual interest in the non-assessable non-exempt income of a trust.

The Commissioner takes the view that the assessable income of an investor under s 97 should include the amount of any commission paid by the investment fund to an intermediary (eg an investment adviser, accountant or solicitor) in relation to the capital of the investor where the intermediary is under an obligation to pass on the amount to the investor. The amount to be included in assessable income is reduced by deductions, such as fees charged by the intermediary for collection and administration of the commission (TR 93/36).

A distribution by the trustee of a unit trust (eg a cash management, equity, mortgage or property trust) is assessable to the unitholder in the income year in which the unitholder is presently entitled to a share of the income of the unit trust, rather than in the year in which the distribution is received by the unitholder. Unless the trust deed provides otherwise, a unitholder is entitled to a share of the income of a unit trust at the end of the period in which the income is derived (TD 94/72).

Trust income to which a resident beneficiary is deemed to be presently entitled by virtue of s 95A(2) (¶6-100) is normally assessed to the trustee under s 98, even if the beneficiary is not under a legal disability. The beneficiary continues to be assessable under s 97 where the beneficiary is a company or a beneficiary in the capacity of trustee of another trust.

Private company beneficiary

Where a private company beneficiary is presently entitled to income of a trust but the present entitlement is not paid, a loan made by the trustee to a shareholder of the company beneficiary (or to an associate of a shareholder) is treated as a loan by the company to the shareholder (or associate) and potentially subject to the deemed dividend provisions of ITAA36 Div 7A (¶4-110). The Div 7A implications of an unpaid present entitlement have, however, diminished because the Commissioner now takes the view that where a company is an unpaid presently entitled beneficiary there will be circumstances in which the company will be taken to have made a loan to the trust for the purposes of ITAA36 Div 7A on the basis that there will either be an in-substance loan by the company to the trust or a loan by the company to the trust constituted by the provision of financial accommodation (¶4-200). The practical effect of a loan by the company to the trust would be to extinguish the present entitlement and the Div 7A trust rules would not apply. However, the loan that arises from the company to the trust would potentially fall within the Div 7A company loan rules (¶4-210).

[FTR ¶50-600]

¶6-120 Beneficiary presently entitled but under legal disability

Where a beneficiary is presently entitled to a share (proportion) of the income of a trust (¶6-085) but is under a legal disability, the trustee is liable to pay tax on that share (proportion) of the net income (¶6-080) (s 98). Minors, bankrupts and insane persons are under a legal disability because they cannot give a discharge for money paid to them.

If the beneficiary is a resident for the whole of the income year, the trustee is assessable on the whole of the beneficiary's share of the net income, including net income attributable to foreign sources. If the beneficiary is a non-resident for the whole or a part of the year, the trustee is assessable on the beneficiary's share of the net income, but excluding so much of it as is attributable both to foreign sources and to a period when the beneficiary was a non-resident. The ATO will accept an apportionment of net income between executors and beneficiaries in the income year in which a deceased estate is fully administered (IT 2622: ¶6-190).

The beneficiary is also assessable on their share of the net income of the trust if that person is a beneficiary in more than one trust or has income from other sources (eg salary or wages, rent, interest or dividends). In such a case, the beneficiary's individual interest in the net income of the trust is aggregated with their other income. However, to prevent double taxation, the beneficiary is entitled to a credit against the total tax assessed for the tax paid or payable by the trustee in relation to the beneficiary's interest in the net income (s 100). The credit cannot exceed the tax otherwise payable by the beneficiary, even though the trustee assessment may have been for a greater amount. Where the trust derives franked dividend income, the tax payable by the trustee that is allowable as a credit to the beneficiary is the gross tax payable by the trustee reduced by the beneficiary's share of the trust's imputation rebate (TD 93/186).

▶ Example

Melinda, who is 17, is absolutely entitled to a one-third share of the income ($54,000) of the Beetle Trust, although she cannot actually receive it until she is 18. She is also a discretionary beneficiary of the Morris Trust. In the relevant year, the trustee of the Morris Trust pays $4,000 towards Melinda's university fees. In addition, she earns $1,800 from a holiday job. She is assessable on $23,800 ($18,000 + $4,000 + $1,800), but the tax otherwise payable is reduced by the aggregate of the tax paid by the trustees of the two trusts on her share of the net income of each trust.

Where the beneficiary is under 18 years of age and is a ''prescribed person'', special rates of tax apply to certain types of trust income to which the beneficiary is presently entitled (¶2-160 and following). A beneficiary who is presently entitled to income of a trust in the capacity of the trustee of another trust is treated as not being under a legal disability in respect of their present entitlement to that share (s 95B).

Where the only source of income of a beneficiary under a legal disability is a distribution from one trust, the beneficiary is not required to lodge a tax return (TD 92/159).

A trustee carrying on a primary production business may make farm management deposits (FMDs) on behalf of a presently entitled beneficiary who is under a legal disability (¶18-290). In such a case, the beneficiary is assessable under s 97 on their share of the trust income, regardless of whether the beneficiary is under a legal disability (s 97A). This means that the deduction for the deposit will be allowed in the beneficiary's assessment, instead of being reflected in the trustee's assessment.

The same result applies where an FMD is lodged on behalf of a beneficiary who is not under a legal disability and is deemed to be presently entitled because of their vested and indefeasible interest (¶6-100).

[FTR ¶50-600]

¶6-130 Distributions of trust income

Trust income that has been previously assessed to the trustee or the beneficiary is not assessable when received by the beneficiary. On the other hand, receipts of previously untaxed trust income may be assessable to the beneficiary. This is the case where an amount is paid to, or applied for the benefit of, a beneficiary who is a resident at any time during the income year and the amount represents trust income of a class that is taxable in Australia but which has not previously been subject to tax in the hands of the beneficiary or trustee (s 99B; *Howard* (Full Federal Court); *Campbell*; ID 2011/93).

Where, for example, an amount is paid to an Australian resident beneficiary out of foreign source income that has been accumulated in a non-resident trust (which would, therefore, not have been assessable to the trustee: ¶6-230), such an amount is assessable to the beneficiary in the year of receipt if the beneficiary is a resident *at any time* during the year (there is no requirement that the beneficiary be resident at the time of the distribution) and Pt III Div 6AAA (¶6-075) does not apply.

The beneficiary could also be assessable where an amount representing foreign source income is paid and the beneficiary, although presently entitled, is not a resident at the time the income is derived by the trust, but is a resident at some time during the year in which the amount is paid.

The amount to be included in the assessable income of the beneficiary under s 99B is the amount paid to, or applied for the benefit of, the beneficiary other than:

- amounts that would not be assessable if derived by a resident taxpayer
- amounts liable to tax in the hands of the beneficiary or the trustee, even if the amount would not actually bear tax in the hands of the beneficiary or trustee (eg because the income is below a minimum amount)
- corpus of the trust — but not to the extent that it is attributable to an amount derived by the trust that would be subject to tax if it were derived by a resident taxpayer, or
- amounts assessed under Div 6AAA (¶6-075) — such amounts are classified as non-assessable non-exempt (¶10-895).

The determination of whether an amount has been applied for the benefit of a beneficiary for the purposes of s 99B is governed by s 99C. Section 99C is expressed in extremely broad terms and has the potential to expand the scope of s 99B considerably. It is understood, however, that the Commissioner does not administer s 99C in accordance with its wide literal terms.

Interest on non-resident trust distributions

Where a resident beneficiary's assessable income includes a distribution by a non-resident trust of income of previous years that is not assessable under Pt III Div 6 or 6AAA (¶6-075), the beneficiary may be liable to pay additional tax in the nature of an interest charge in respect of that distribution (s 102AAM; *Taxation (Interest on Non-resident Trust Distributions) Act 1990*: ¶21-350). The interest charge does *not* apply to: (a) distributions from the estate of a deceased person made within 3 years after the date of death; or (b) amounts attributable to the income or profits of a public unit trust that is not a controlled foreign trust.

Income for trust purposes exceeds income for tax purposes

Where the income of a trust calculated for trust purposes *exceeds* the net income of the trust calculated for tax purposes, eg where receipts treated as income for trust purposes are treated as capital for tax purposes, the excess is not, in practice, taxed, despite the potential for the application of s 99B. For example, if 2 beneficiaries are presently entitled to 50% of trust income of $20,000, but the net income for tax purposes is only $12,000, each beneficiary will be assessed on $6,000 and not $10,000.

There have been situations where the beneficiary of a unit trust is a financial institution and holds the units as part of a financing arrangement under which the institution has effectively provided money for use by a third party. The third party may have guaranteed a particular rate of return to the institution if trust distributions do not meet an agreed rate. Because of deductions available to the trust, or because trust receipts are claimed to be capital, the income of the trust available for distribution to the institution exceeds the trust's income for tax purposes. Any distribution of the excess is income in the hands of the institution because it arises from the commercial activities of the institution (IT 2512).

[FTR ¶51-120ff]

¶6-140 Distributions out of corpus to income beneficiary

Payments made out of corpus to an annuitant or other beneficiary entitled to income, either to make up a deficiency of income or in advance on account of income, are assessable income in the hands of the recipient. For example, the fact that an annuity is paid out of capital does not affect its character as income in the hands of the annuitant.

[FTR ¶50-670]

¶6-150 Distributions to non-resident beneficiary — refund of tax

Where a trust derives foreign income to which no beneficiary is presently entitled, the trustee is assessable on that income only if the trust is a resident trust (¶6-230). The distribution of such income to a beneficiary may entitle the beneficiary to a refund of the tax paid by the trustee if the income is attributable to a period when the beneficiary was not a resident of Australia (s 99D).

An application for a refund of tax must be made to the Commissioner in writing, by or on behalf of the beneficiary, within 60 days after the date on which the payment of the trust income is made to the beneficiary or within such further period as the Commissioner allows. For a refund to be payable, the beneficiary must satisfy the Commissioner that the payment:

- is attributable to a period when the beneficiary was not a resident and to income from sources out of Australia
- was taken into account in calculating the net income of the trust, and
- is not income that is deemed not to have been paid to, or applied for the benefit of, the beneficiary or to be income to which the beneficiary is not presently entitled, by virtue of s 100A (this deals with trust stripping schemes: ¶6-270).

The Commissioner may, however, refuse to refund the tax if he considers that the whole or a part of the amount was paid to the beneficiary by the trustee for the purpose, or for purposes that included the purpose, of enabling the beneficiary to become entitled to a refund of tax under s 99D in relation to that amount.

[FTR ¶51-150]

¶6-170 Rates of tax payable by beneficiaries

Trust income assessable to a beneficiary is generally aggregated with the beneficiary's other assessable income and is taxable at whatever rate of tax is applicable to the beneficiary, ie:

- if the beneficiary is a company, at the appropriate company rate (¶42-025), or
- if the beneficiary is an individual, at the appropriate individual rates (¶42-000, ¶42-015).

Capital gains derived by a trust may be reduced by 50% in certain circumstances (¶11-033 – ¶11-038).

Distributions by trusts to a superannuation fund, other than where the fund has a fixed entitlement to the income, have been taxed at 45%. In the case of fixed entitlements to the income that are acquired under non-arm's length arrangements, any distribution to a superannuation fund in excess of an arm's length amount is also taxed at 45% (¶13-170). Distributions by trusts to a complying superannuation fund that has a fixed entitlement to the income and where the distribution is an arm's length arrangement are taxed at 15% (¶13-170).

Special rates of tax apply to certain trust income of minor beneficiaries (¶2-160).

When and How Trustee is Taxed

¶6-180 Deceased's income received after death

The trustee of the estate of a deceased taxpayer is assessed on amounts received after the death of the deceased that would have been assessable to the deceased had they been received during the deceased's lifetime — such amounts are deemed to be income to which no beneficiary is presently entitled (s 101A).

This applies to receipts by the trustee for rents or interest, etc, accrued at the date of death but only received after death (which would be corpus under trust law). It also applies to fees received after the death of a professional sole practitioner or partner whose returns were filed on a cash basis. Following the High Court's decision in *Single's case*, it seems that it affects not only fees subsequently received for completed work for which an account was rendered, but also subsequent receipts for work incomplete at the date of death.

Receipts of this kind are aggregated in the trustee's hands with other amounts of income to which no beneficiary is presently entitled and are assessed under s 99A, or under s 99 if the Commissioner is of the opinion that it would be unreasonable for s 99A to apply (¶6-230). For the applicable rates of tax, see ¶42-030. Note that an assessment of the trustee under s 99 for the income year of death and the next 2 years is at the ordinary individual rates of tax.

The deeming rules in s 101A do *not* apply to lump sum payments for unused annual or long service leave that, had they been received by the deceased, would have been assessable (IT 248). An ETP received by the trustee is treated as income to which no beneficiary is presently entitled.

A farm management deposit (¶18-290) that is repaid to a trustee of a deceased estate because of the death of the deposit owner is treated as income of the deceased owner (s 101A(4)).

For a checklist of the tax consequences of death, see ¶44-170.

[FTR ¶51-275]

¶6-190 Period of administration of deceased estate

Until the administration of a deceased estate has reached the stage where, in general terms, the residue can be ascertained with certainty, there is no trust income legally available for distribution to the beneficiaries (¶6-100).

During the period of incomplete administration, the trust income is taxed to the trustee as income to which no beneficiary is presently entitled. That income is aggregated with other income (if any) to which no beneficiary is presently entitled and is assessed under s 99.

However, if during an intermediate stage of administration of a deceased estate, part of the net income of the estate that is not required to pay debts, etc, is paid to the beneficiaries, those beneficiaries will be assessed on the basis that they are presently entitled to the income actually paid to them or paid on their behalf (IT 2622).

In the income year in which the estate is fully administered, the ATO will accept an apportionment of net income between executors and beneficiaries. Income derived during the period from the beginning of the income year to the day the administration is complete is assessed to the executors, and income derived in the period constituted by the balance of the year is assessed to the beneficiaries presently entitled to the income (or to the trustee if the beneficiary is under a legal disability) (IT 2622). There must be evidence of the income derived during these periods and apportionment of the net income of the trust estate in this manner must be requested by the taxpayers concerned (ie the executor or administrator and the beneficiaries). An apportionment of the income derived by the estate for the whole income year concerned into the 2 periods merely on a time basis is not acceptable. Of course, if an executor or administrator does in fact pay part of the income of the estate to a beneficiary before the estate is fully administered (ie during the first of the periods mentioned above), the beneficiary would be assessed on the basis that he or she was presently entitled to that income.

[FTR ¶50-600, ¶51-020]

¶6-200 Net income for tax purposes exceeds actual trust income

The actual net trust income legally (ie according to the terms of the trust or trust law) available for distribution among the income beneficiaries may be less than the net income of the trust computed for tax purposes. Situations where this may occur include:

- the incomplete administration of a deceased estate (¶6-190)
- where items that are assessable income of the trust are corpus (ie capital) according to trust law or the terms of the particular trust instrument, or
- where items that are to be met from income according to trust law or the relevant trust instrument are non-deductible for tax purposes, or are deductible but to a lesser extent, eg when depreciation may be calculated at a higher rate for trust purposes than for tax purposes.

It was held by the High Court in *Bamford* that, where the trust instrument makes an amount or class of amount "income" or permits the trustee to treat a capital receipt as income for the purposes of fixing the entitlements of beneficiaries to distributions (and the trustee does so), the amount falls within the "income of the trust estate" for the purposes of determining the amount of the net income for tax purposes on which the beneficiary is to be taxed. The Commissioner's contention that the terms of the trust instrument, either directly or indirectly through the exercise of a power by the trustee, could not alter what was the income of the trust estate for this purpose was rejected.

The Commissioner has issued a decision impact statement in relation to *Bamford's* case and has also issued PS LA 2010/1 that explains the ATO approach where deliberate attempts are made to exploit the provisions of Div 6 by the recharacterisation of an amount for trust purposes.

Where there is an "excess" of net income for tax purposes over the actual distributable trust income, the decision of the High Court in *Bamford* means that what is called the "proportionate approach" is the correct approach. The proportionate approach applies by determining the proportion or fraction of the income of the trust estate to which a beneficiary is presently entitled and it is that proportion or fraction of the net income for tax purposes that is taxed to the beneficiary. The proportionate approach applies even if the income of the trust is distributed otherwise than on a proportionate basis (eg by distributing dollar amounts and the residue).

Thus, a beneficiary who is not under a legal disability will be taxable (¶6-110) on their share of the excess of the net income for tax purposes over the actual distributable income. In the case of a beneficiary under a legal disability, the trustee would be taxable (¶6-210).

▶ Example

A trust estate's distributable income (determined in accordance with trust law as affected by the trust deed) is $60,000 and its net income for tax purposes is $90,000. The trustee distributes 30% of the distributable income to Lee and 70% to James. Under the "proportionate approach", Lee is assessed on $27,000 (ie 30% of $90,000) and James on $63,000 (ie 70% of $90,000).

In *Cajkusic*, the beneficiaries of a family trust were not presently entitled to any part of the income of the trust because there was no distributable income to which they were presently entitled (due to past losses). Accordingly, the net income of the trust was properly assessable to the trustee under s 99A.

Net capital gain

One common reason for the net income of a trust to exceed the distributable trust income is because the net income includes a net capital gain. The capital gain streaming amendments (¶6-077) have made it possible to stream the capital gain to beneficiaries by making them specifically entitled, so that they are assessable on an appropriate share of the capital gain even if they are not presently entitled to a share of the distributable trust income.

[FTR ¶50-642ff]

¶6-210 Minor beneficiaries, etc

Where a minor beneficiary (or any other beneficiary under a legal disability, such as bankruptcy or insanity) is presently entitled (¶6-100) to income of a trust estate, the income is normally assessed to the trustee, not the beneficiary. If the beneficiary is a resident for the whole of the income year, the trustee is assessable on the beneficiary's share of the net income (¶6-080). Where the beneficiary is a non-resident for all or part of the income year, the trustee is assessable on the beneficiary's share of the net income, but excluding so much of it as is attributable to foreign sources and to a period when the beneficiary was a non-resident.

The trustee is separately assessed in respect of each such beneficiary, ie it is not possible to aggregate in the trustee's hands income to which several beneficiaries under a legal disability are respectively entitled. However, income applied by the trustee in favour of a beneficiary under a legal disability in exercise of a discretionary power is deemed to be income to which that beneficiary is presently entitled (¶6-105). Such income is aggregated with any income under the same trust to which that beneficiary may otherwise be presently entitled.

Trust income to which a beneficiary under a legal disability has a present entitlement is taxed in the trustee's hands as though it were the income of an individual. However, no deductions are allowable to the trustee. Where the beneficiary is a resident, the trustee is entitled to any relevant tax offsets (¶15-000).

See ¶6-120 for the situation where the beneficiary has a beneficial interest in income from several trusts or derives income other than trust income.

[FTR ¶50-600]

¶6-220 Beneficiary non-resident at end of income year

Where a beneficiary is presently entitled to a share of trust income and is a non-resident at the *end* of the income year, the trustee is primarily liable to pay tax in respect of that share. This is so regardless of whether the beneficiary is under a legal disability. (Normally, the trustee is only liable where the beneficiary is under a legal disability.)

The trustee can also be taxed in relation to distributions where the beneficiary is a non-resident trustee at the end of the income year (in addition to where the beneficiary is a company or individual).

Tax is payable by the trustee on: (a) so much of the share of the net income (¶6-080) as is attributable to a period when the beneficiary was a resident, whatever the source of the income; and (b) so much of the share as is attributable to a period when the beneficiary was not a resident and is also attributable to Australian sources.

The tax paid by the trustee is not a final tax as a non-resident beneficiary is also taxed on the particular trust income, with a credit being allowed for the tax already paid by the trustee (s 98A). If the tax paid by the trustee exceeds the tax payable by the beneficiary, the excess is refunded to the beneficiary. Special rules apply to reverse the effect of the CGT discount in determining the amount on which a trustee pays tax (¶11-038).

The special rules imposing liability on the trustee do *not* apply where:

- the beneficiary is a tax-exempt body
- the beneficiary has made or is deemed to have made a farm management deposit (¶18-290), or
- the trustee would have been assessable under s 98 in any event.

[FTR ¶50-600]

¶6-230 No beneficiary presently entitled

To the extent to which the net income of a trust represents income to which no beneficiary is presently entitled (¶6-100) — ie accumulating income — it is taxed in the hands of the trustee.

A trustee that is liable to pay tax in respect of a beneficiary's share of the trust's net income, or the income to which no beneficiary is entitled, must pay PAYG instalments in respect of that liability. PAYG instalments are based on the beneficiary's share of the instalment income of the trust. The application of the PAYG instalments system to trust income is discussed at ¶27-270 and ¶27-500.

Where the net income is wholly or partly attributable to foreign sources, the trustee is liable to tax on the foreign source income only if the trust is a *resident* trust. A trustee of a *non-resident* trust is liable to tax only on so much of the net income as is attributable to sources in Australia (although Pt III Div 6AAA (¶6-075) may also be relevant). A trust is a *resident trust* if, at any time during the income year, either a trustee is a resident or the central management and control of the trust is in Australia (s 95(2)). In some circumstances, the distribution of foreign source income to a non-resident beneficiary by a resident trust estate will entitle the beneficiary to a refund of tax paid by the trustee (¶6-150).

The trustee of a discretionary family trust was assessable on undistributed trust income under s 99A in circumstances where the trustee had no power to appoint a particular entity as beneficiary and a default provision had not been triggered so as to entitle other beneficiaries to the income on default (*BRK (Bris)*).

Taxation at punitive rate

The tax rate applicable to the net income of a trust which represents income to which no beneficiary is presently entitled depends on whether the income is assessed under s 99 or s 99A. All such income falls initially within the ambit of s 99A.

The tax rate under s 99A is the maximum rate of personal tax, which reflects the fact that this section was originally introduced to counter tax avoidance. In a limited number of cases, the Commissioner has a discretion to assess the trustee under s 99 if the Commissioner is of the opinion that it would be unreasonable for s 99A to apply. Income taxed under s 99 is taxed at progressive rates (¶42-030). For the position in relation to Medicare levy, see ¶6-250.

The trustee of the deceased estate for his late wife included his wife's share of the proceeds from the sale of cattle in the trust return, expecting to receive the benefit of the tax-free threshold. The Commissioner exercised his discretion to assess the trustee under s 99 rather than under s 99A. However, because the wife died more than 3 years before the end of the relevant year of income, the income of the estate was subject to tax at the marginal rate of 17% (*Trustee for the Estate of EV Dukes*).

Taxation at progressive rates

The categories of trusts in respect of which the Commissioner has a discretion to assess the trustee under s 99 rather than under s 99A are limited to:

- deceased estates
- bankrupt estates administered by the Official Receiver or a registered trustee — not where a receiver and manager has been appointed *other than* under the *Bankruptcy Act 1966*, and
- trusts that consist of the following types of property as specified in s 102AG(2)(c) — damages for loss of parental support or for mental or physical injury, workers compensation or criminal injury compensation, death benefits under life insurance policies, etc, property received from a public fund for the relief of persons in necessitous circumstances, or property received in certain family breakdown situations.

In determining whether it would be unreasonable for s 99A to apply in these cases, the Commissioner is required to have regard to certain specific matters, including: (a) the manner and price at which the trust acquired its assets; (b) whether any special rights or privileges are attached to, or conferred on or in relation to, the trust property; and (c) such other matters as the Commissioner thinks fit. In the case of deceased estates, the Commissioner is to have regard, not only to the circumstances in which property and other rights were conferred on the trust itself, but also to the circumstances in which property and other rights were conferred on the deceased person.

The Commissioner will generally exercise the discretion to assess under s 99 unless there is tax avoidance involved and has advised that deceased estates of the ''ordinary and traditional'' kind will be assessed under that section. According to ATO guidelines, an estate of the ''ordinary and traditional'' kind would be one whose assets come directly from the assets of the deceased person — ordinarily the assets would be those of the deceased person, for example, a house or income-producing property, or assets purchased subsequent to the death of the deceased out of funds arising from the sale or conversion of those assets by the executor acting in the course of their duties. On the other hand, a ''$10 trust'' created by a will could not be said to be a trust of the ordinary and traditional kind.

The Commissioner is required to exercise the discretion in relation to each particular income year and the exercise of the discretion or a refusal to exercise it in one particular year does not preclude different treatment in another year.

Full details in support of a request for the exercise of the Commissioner's discretion should be filed with the trust's tax return.

Special disability trusts

A special disability trust is (broadly) a trust established to assist immediate family members to make private financial provision for the accommodation and care of a family member (called the principal beneficiary) with a severe disability. Unexpended income of a special disability trust is taxed to the trustee at the relevant beneficiary's personal income tax rates, rather than at the rate of tax under s 99A (s 95AB). This is achieved by (a) treating the principal beneficiary as being presently entitled to (and therefore taxable on) the whole of the net income of the trust (ie including any amount that was not in fact distributed by the trustee); (b) treating the beneficiary as being under a legal disability (so the trustee is assessed on the whole of the net income); and (c) entitling the beneficiary not only to a credit for the tax paid by the trustee but also to a payment by the Commissioner of any excess of the tax assessed to the trustee over the tax assessed to the beneficiary.

For the way CGT operates in relation to transfers to a special disability trust for no consideration and the operation of the CGT main residence exemption in relation to a special disability trust, see ¶11-730.

Issue of assessments

Where a trust return is lodged and shows no trustee tax liability, the Commissioner's usual practice is not to issue a nil assessment to the trustee and not to issue an original assessment on the trustee under ITAA36 s 99 or s 99A more than 4 years after the return was lodged or, if the trust is a small business entity and the income year involved is the 2013–14 or a later income year, more than 2 years after the lodgment of the return (PS LA 2015/2).

[FTR ¶50-545, ¶50-900 – ¶51-115]

¶6-240 Revocable trusts and trusts for minors

Where a person (the settlor) has created a revocable trust (ie one that can be revoked or altered so that the settlor acquires a beneficial interest in trust corpus or income), or a trust under which income is payable to, or accumulated or applicable for the benefit of, the settlor's children under the age of 18 years, the Commissioner has the discretion to tax the trustee under s 102.

This punitive tax is an amount equal to the difference between the tax actually payable by the settlor and the tax the settlor would have had to pay but for the trust. In calculating the tax, the net income of the trust is calculated without regard to so much, if any, of the net income as: (a) is derived from foreign sources and is attributable to a period when the settlor was a non-resident; or (b) is not covered by (a) and is attributable to a taxpayer under Pt III Div 6AAA (¶6-075).

This section has lost much of its sting since the High Court held that it did not apply to contingent interests in income (*Hobbs*). The High Court has also held that the payment of money to a trustee to be held on the terms of a pre-existing trust does not amount to the creation of a trust (*Truesdale*). This would seem to preclude from s 102 a typical family trust that is established by a small settlement by a person outside the family with the bulk of the trust property coming from gifts or loans made later by a person who seeks to spread income among family members.

[FTR ¶51-330ff]

¶6-250 Rates of tax payable by trustees

A summary of the rates of tax payable by trustees for the 2020–21 income year is set out at ¶42-030. Where the trustee is assessed under s 98 at individual rates, those rates reflect any pro-rated threshold that may apply to the beneficiary on the ground of non-residency during part of the year (¶2-130).

Medicare levy and Medicare levy surcharge

A summary of the Medicare levy and Medicare levy surcharge rates payable by trustees for the 2020–21 income year is set out at ¶42-033.

[FTR ¶778-350, ¶779-100]

Trust Losses

¶6-262 Restrictions on trust losses

Trusts can only deduct tax losses and certain debt deductions in limited circumstances. The restrictions, contained in Sch 2F (ss 265-5 to 272-140), apply to:

- ''tax losses'' (defined in s 272-140) of an earlier or the current income year, and
- ''debt deductions'', ie deductions for bad debts (¶16-580), and debt/equity swap deductions (¶16-586).

The trust loss measures contain provisions, including information-gathering powers, to ensure that the measures cannot be avoided where non-resident entities are concerned.

Types of trust

The particular trust loss measures that apply to a trust will depend on the type of trust. The 3 basic types of trust are:

(1) fixed trusts — these include widely held unit trusts (¶6-263)

(2) non-fixed trusts — these are any trusts that are not fixed trusts and include trusts that have both fixed and non-fixed elements (s 272-70), and

(3) excepted trusts — these are family trusts (¶6-266), complying superannuation funds, complying ADFs, PSTs, deceased estates within a reasonable administration period, ie from the date of death to the end of the income year in which the death occurred and the next full five income years (but does not include a trust, other than the deceased estate itself, established under the terms of a will or codicil), fixed unit trusts if all of the direct and indirect fixed entitlements to income and capital of the trust are held by exempt entities and designated infrastructure project entities (s 272-100).

The trust loss measures do *not* apply to a trust (other than a family trust) that, at all relevant times, is an excepted trust. For the limited application of the measures to family trusts, see ¶6-266.

The trust loss measures apply to public trading trusts.

Tests to be satisfied

Broadly, a trust (other than an excepted trust) cannot deduct current year and prior year losses and debt deductions if it fails to satisfy certain tests relating to ownership or control of the trust or if there is abnormal trading (¶6-265) in its units (Sch 2F Div 266; 267; ITAA97 s 25-35(5), item 4; 36-25 (tax losses of trusts)). Abnormal trading in units in listed and unlisted widely held trusts, unlisted very widely held trusts, or wholesale widely held trusts, may trigger the application of those tests. For current year loss purposes, if an applicable test is not satisfied, the income year is divided into periods and the net income or tax loss of the trust is calculated for each period (¶6-265). The tests to be satisfied by the various types of trust are summarised in the table below.

The tests must generally be satisfied at all times during the ''test period''. The relevant test period is generally:

- prior year loss (fixed and non-fixed trusts) — the income year in which the loss was incurred, the income year being examined and all intervening years (if any)
- current year loss (fixed and non-fixed trusts) — the income year being examined
- debt deduction (fixed and non-fixed trusts) — if the debt is incurred in an income year before the deduction arises, from the time the debt is incurred to the end of the income year in which the deduction is available. If the debt is incurred in the income year in which the deduction arises, the test period is the income year.

In the case of an unlisted very widely held trust (¶6-263), the test period does not include any start-up period of the trust (ie the period from when the trust first issued units until the earlier of the end of 2 years after that first issue or when the trust becomes an unlisted very widely held trust).

The trust loss measures also contain an income injection test that broadly applies where, in connection with a scheme, trust losses and deductions are used to shelter assessable income from tax (¶6-267).

Special rules apply to modify the tests for deducting bad debts where a trust that used to be member of a consolidated group writes off a debt that used to be owed to a member of the group (¶8-020).

PRIOR AND CURRENT YEAR LOSSES AND DEBT DEDUCTIONS: TESTS THAT APPLY TO EACH TYPE OF TRUST FOR IT TO BE ABLE TO DEDUCT A LOSS OR DEBT

Type of trust	50% stake test (¶6-264)	Business continuity test (¶6-264)	Pattern of distributions test (¶6-264)	Control test (¶6-264)	Income injection test (¶6-267)
Fixed trust other than a widely held unit trust	√(1)				√
Unlisted widely held trust	√(2)				√
Listed widely held trust	√	√(3)			√
Unlisted very widely held trust	√				√
Wholesale widely held trust	√				√
Non-fixed trust	√(4)		√(5)	√	√
Family trust					√(6)
Excepted trust (other than a family trust)					

(1) An alternate test is also available in certain cases where non-fixed trusts directly or indirectly hold fixed entitlements in the fixed trust (see below).

(2) For current year loss purposes, an unlisted widely held trust need only meet the 50% stake test when there is abnormal trading in the trust's units.

(3) This test can be applied if the 50% stake test is failed by a listed widely held trust.

(4) This test applies to a non-fixed trust where individuals have direct or indirect fixed entitlements to more than a 50% share of the income or capital of the trust. It does not apply to a discretionary trust where there are no fixed entitlements to the income or capital of the trust.

(5) This test does not apply for current year loss purposes or, in the case of a debt deduction, where the debt is incurred in the income year in which the deduction arises.

(6) The income injection test does not apply where entities and individuals within a family group inject income into a family trust with losses.

Prior year loss — alternate test for fixed trusts

As noted in the table above, an alternate test applies if the 50% stake test is not met and either: (a) a non-fixed trust or trusts (other than a family trust) hold fixed entitlements to 50% or more of the income or capital of a fixed trust; *or* (b) all the fixed entitlements to income and capital of a fixed trust are held, directly or indirectly, by another fixed trust or company *and* a non-fixed trust (other than a family trust) holds fixed entitlements to a 50% or greater share of the income or capital of the holding entity. In such circumstances, the fixed trust will be able to deduct a prior year loss if (s 266-45):

- where the fixed trust is held directly by the non-fixed trust(s), there is no change in the persons directly holding fixed entitlements to shares of the income or capital of the fixed trust nor in the percentage of those shares (where the fixed trust is held, directly or indirectly, by a holding entity, this requirement is applied to the holding entity rather than the fixed trust), and
- every non-fixed trust (other than a family trust or other excepted trust) that holds fixed entitlements in the fixed trust, directly or indirectly, satisfies the relevant tests that apply to non-fixed trusts if they stood in place of the loss trust.

Partial deduction

If a trust cannot deduct a tax loss because of a change in ownership in the loss year or because of abnormal trading in its units, it can generally deduct that part of the loss that is properly attributable to that part of the loss year occurring after the change in ownership or abnormal trading, as appropriate, providing it satisfies the relevant conditions (see above) for that part of the year (ss 266-50; 266-95; 266-130; 266-170; 267-50).

[FTR ¶799-450ff]

¶6-263 Fixed trusts

A fixed trust is a trust where *all* of the income and capital of the trust is the subject of fixed entitlements (whether held by a natural person, company, trustee or partners in a partnership) (Sch 2F s 272-65). Thus, a discretionary trust is not a fixed trust.

A beneficiary has a fixed entitlement to either income or capital of a trust where, under the trust instrument, the beneficiary has a vested and indefeasible interest in a share of the income or capital of the trust (s 272-5). The interest of a unitholder in a unit trust will not be taken to be defeasible only because units in a unit trust can be issued or redeemed (at full value). The Commissioner has a discretion to determine that an interest of a beneficiary to income or capital that is not vested and indefeasible can be treated as being vested and indefeasible.

In one case the interests of beneficiaries in a unit trust that was a managed investment scheme were defeasible because of the power of the members (under the *Corporations Act 2001*) to alter the constitution of the trust by special resolution (*Colonial First State Investments*). In a decision impact statement, the Commissioner said the decision confirmed the ATO view that very few trusts satisfy the definition of "fixed trust'' in the absence of the exercise of the Commissioner's discretion (essentially because beneficiary entitlements to income or capital are generally liable to be defeated by the exercise of a power in the deed or by a statutory power). The Commissioner has issued a compliance guideline that outlines the factors that he will consider when deciding whether to exercise the discretion to treat an entitlement as being a fixed entitlement, which would result in a trust being treated as a fixed trust (PCG 2016/16). The compliance guideline also outlines a safe harbour compliance approach for trustees of certain trusts that allows them to manage the trust's tax affairs as if the Commissioner had exercised the discretion to treat beneficiaries as having fixed entitlements to income and capital of the trust.

Interposed entities

A person will be taken to have a fixed entitlement to the income or capital of a company, partnership or trust if the person is indirectly entitled to the income or capital through fixed entitlements in a chain of one or more interposed entities (ss 272-20; 272-30). A person's entitlement to the income or capital is determined by multiplying the entitlements of the person in each successive entity.

▶ Example

Perkins Panes Pty Ltd has a 40% fixed entitlement to both the income and capital of a trust. Elizabeth holds 60% of the shares in Perkins Panes Pty Ltd, all of which are of the same class. Her fixed entitlement to the income of the trust is 60% × 40% = 24%. Elizabeth's fixed entitlement to the capital of the trust is worked out in the same way (ie also 24%), except that it is traced through her fixed entitlement to the capital of Perkins Panes Pty Ltd.

Special tracing rules apply in relation to certain interposed entities, including mutual companies, complying superannuation funds, complying ADFs, foreign superannuation funds, government bodies, credit unions, non-profit sporting clubs and trade unions (s 272-25).

Types of fixed trust

There are 5 types of fixed trust for the purpose of the trust loss measures:

(1) a fixed trust other than a widely held trust (an ''ordinary fixed trust'')

(2) an unlisted widely held trust — a widely held unit trust where the units are not listed on an approved stock exchange (s 272-110)

(3) a listed widely held trust — a widely held unit trust where the units are listed on an approved stock exchange (s 272-115)

(4) an unlisted very widely held trust — an unlisted widely held trust with at least 1,000 unitholders where the units carry the same rights (s 272-120), and

(5) a wholesale widely held trust — an unlisted widely held trust where at least 75% of the units in the trust are held by certain bodies (a listed widely held trust, an unlisted very widely held trust, a life assurance company, a registered organisation, a complying superannuation fund, a complying ADF or a PST), the initial amount subscribed for units by each particular unitholder was at least $500,000 and all the units carry the same rights (s 272-125).

An unlisted very widely held trust and a wholesale widely held trust must engage only in investment or business activities that are conducted at arm's length in accordance with the trust instrument or deed and any prospectus of the trust.

A fixed trust is a ''widely held unit trust'' if it is a unit trust and is not closely held (s 272-105). A trust is ''closely held'' if 20 or less individuals between them beneficially hold, directly or indirectly, 75% or more of the fixed entitlements to income or capital of the trust (the ''20/75 rule''). For these purposes, an individual and their relatives and nominees are treated as being one individual. A trust is also a closely held trust where no individual beneficially holds (or no individuals between them hold) entitlements to 75% or more of the income or capital of the trust. Thus, a unit trust owned by a non-fixed trust can qualify as a closely held trust.

If the fixed entitlements to income and capital of a fixed trust (other than an ordinary fixed trust or a listed widely held trust) are all held, directly or indirectly, by one or more trusts of a higher level, the subsidiary trust will be classified as a trust of the same kind as the highest level superimposed trust (s 272-127). The level of a trust is determined by the following order (lowest to highest): (a) unlisted widely held trust; (b) unlisted very widely held trust; (c) wholesale widely held trust; and (d) listed widely held trust. Note that an attribution managed investment trust is also a widely held unit trust.

A subsidiary that was collectively owned by 2 ''listed widely held trusts'' could not obtain the benefit of the higher status as it was not wholly owned by each of the trusts (*ConnectEast*, special leave to appeal to High Court refused).

[FTR ¶799-475]

¶6-264 Losses and debt deductions for trusts

The various tests that must be satisfied before a trust (other than an excepted trust) can deduct a current year or prior year loss or a debt deduction (see the table at ¶6-262) are summarised below. Those tests are set out in Sch 2F Div 269 (ss 269-5 to 269-105).

50% stake test

A trust satisfies the 50% stake test if, at all relevant times during the test period (ss 269-50 to 269-55):

- the same individuals have fixed entitlements, directly or indirectly, to more than 50% of the income of the trust, and
- the same individuals have fixed entitlements, directly or indirectly, to more than 50% of the capital of the trust (these individuals need not be the same as those who hold the fixed entitlements to income).

In the case of a widely held unit trust, the 50% stake test will be satisfied where it is reasonable to assume that the requirements of the test are met.

▶ Example 1

The Murray Trust is an ordinary fixed trust that has a loss from Year 1. The trust seeks to deduct that loss in Year 2. Throughout Year 1 and part of Year 2: (a) Ian and Valerie each have a 50% fixed entitlement to income and a 30% fixed entitlement to capital on a winding-up; and (b) Robyn and Rune each have a 20% fixed entitlement to capital on a winding-up.

During Year 2, both Ian and Valerie sell 60% of their fixed entitlements in the Murray Trust to Luc. As a result, from the time of the sale, Ian and Valerie's fixed entitlements to income and capital are each reduced to 20% and 12% respectively, while Luc has a 60% fixed entitlement to income and a 36% fixed entitlement to capital. Before the sale, Ian, Valerie, Robyn and Rune have, between them, 100% of the fixed entitlements to income and capital. After the sale, they have, between them, a fixed entitlement to income of 40% and a fixed entitlement to capital of 64%.

As the original owners of more than 50% of the fixed entitlements have not held more than 50% of the fixed entitlements to income of the Murray Trust throughout the test period, the trust fails the 50% stake test and the loss is not deductible.

Business continuity test

There are now 2 ways in which the business continuity test may be satisfied in respect of a listed widely held trust. These are by satisfying a same business test that has applied since the trust loss provisions were enacted (s 269-100) or, for tax losses for, or debts incurred in, the 2015–16 or a later income year, by satisfying a similar business test (s 269-105).

Same business

The same business test will be met if:

- at all times in the period being considered (the ''business continuity test period''), the trust carries on the same business it carried on immediately before the start of that period (the ''test time'')

- at any time in the business continuity test period, the trust does not derive assessable income from a business of a kind it did not carry on before the test time or from a business transaction of a kind it had not entered into before the test time
- before the test time, the trust does not start to carry on a business it had not previously carried on or enter into a business transaction of a kind it had not previously entered into, for the purpose (whether or not there are other purposes) of satisfying the same business test, and
- where the trust is seeking to deduct a current year loss, it does not, at any time in the same business test period, incur expenditure in carrying on a business of a kind that it did not carry on before the test time or incur expenditure as a result of a business transaction of a kind it had not entered into before the test time (this condition does not apply in relation to prior year losses and debt deductions).

Similar business

A listed widely held trust will pass the similar business test during a period (the business continuity test period) if throughout the business continuity test period it carries on a business (its current business) that is similar to the business it carried on immediately before the test time (its former business). For the purpose of determining whether a business is similar, the same 4 matters that are relevant when applying the similar business test that applies in relation to company losses are to be taken into account, along with any other relevant matters (¶3-125).

The similar business test will, however, not be passed where: (1) before the test time, the trust began to carry on a business it had not previously carried on or, in the course of its business operations, entered into a transaction of a kind that it had not previously entered into; and (2) this was done for the purpose, or for purposes including the purpose, of being taken to have carried on throughout the business continuity test period, a business that is similar to the business it carried on immediately before the test time.

Pattern of distributions test

The pattern of distributions test (which applies to non-fixed trusts only) is satisfied if, within 2 months of the end of the income year (ss 269-60 to 269-85):

- the trust has distributed, directly or indirectly, more than 50% of every ''test year distribution'' of income to the same individuals for their own benefit (ie otherwise than in the capacity of a trustee), and
- the trust has distributed, directly or indirectly, more than 50% of every ''test year distribution'' of capital to the same individuals for their own benefit (those individuals need not be the same as those to whom income is distributed).

The test is not relevant if the trust has not made relevant distributions.

The various ways income or capital may be ''distributed'' are covered in Sch 2F Subdiv 272-B (ss 272-45 to 272-63). ''Distribution'' includes paying or crediting money (including loans), reinvesting money, transferring property, allowing the use of property, dealing with money or property on behalf of a person or as the person directs, applying money or property for the benefit of a person and extinguishing, releasing or waiving a debt or other liability (but only to the extent that the amount or value exceeds any consideration given in return for the loan, payment, etc) (s 272-60). The Commissioner now takes the view that, in the case of a trust, a person who is not a beneficiary may receive a distribution as defined (TD 2017/20). The Commissioner, however, will not apply this view if a distribution transaction had begun to be carried out before 8 June 2017 (the date of issue of TD 2017/20 in draft form).

▶ Example 2

A trustee provides a beneficiary with a $1,000 interest-free loan repayable in five years. A comparable loan from a financial institution would attract a 10% interest rate and would be repayable in equal instalments. If the annual interest rate is 10%, the present value of $1,000 repayable in five years is $620. The benefit provided to the beneficiary is $1,000 – $620 = $380. That amount will be taken to be a distribution of income.

▶ Example 3 (adapted from TD 2017/20)

The Wonder Family Trust has made a family trust election and Diana Prince is the specified individual. The trust owns a holiday home which is used by Diana's friends, for no consideration, for four weeks in the year.

This transaction is not on arm's length terms nor an ordinary incident of a business being carried on by the trust. As no consideration is given in return for the use of the property, the full value of that use is a distribution within the extended meaning of ''distributes''.

A distribution will also be taken to have been made to an individual where the distribution is made to a chain of interposed entities and one of the interposed entities distributes an amount to the individual (s 272-63). The amount indirectly distributed by a trust to an individual is determined by reference to what is fair and reasonable, having regard to the actual distributions by each entity in the chain.

A ''test year distribution'' of income or capital is the total of all distributions of income or capital in a relevant period (generally an income year) made by the trust, but excluding income years beginning more than 6 years before the start of the income year in which the trust seeks to deduct the prior year loss or debt deduction (s 269-65). A ''relevant period'' is:

- the end year, ie the income year being examined and the 2 months after the end of the year
- the start year, ie the earliest of: (a) the income year in which the trust distributed income that is before the loss year but closest to the loss year; (b) the loss year if the trust distributed income in that year; and (c) the income year in which the trust distributed income that is not before the loss year but is closest to the loss year, and
- each intervening year between the start year and the end year.

There are anti-avoidance arrangements designed to ensure that persons do not enter into arrangements that ensure the pattern of distributions test is satisfied.

Control test

The control test requires that no group (ie a person and their associates, whether alone or together) begin to control the non-fixed trust, whether directly or indirectly, in the test period (¶6-262). A group is taken to control a non-fixed trust if (s 269-95):

- the group has the power to obtain, or is capable under a scheme of obtaining, the benefit of the income or capital of the trust (eg by ensuring the exercise of a trustee discretion in their favour)
- the group is able to control, directly or indirectly, or is capable under a scheme of obtaining control of, the application of the income or capital of the trust
- the trustee is accustomed, is under an obligation or might reasonably be expected, to act in accordance with the directions or wishes of the group
- the group is able to remove or appoint the trustee or any of the trustees, or
- the group gains fixed entitlements to more than 50% of the income or capital of the trust.

Control of the trust is deemed not to change where a member of the controlling group dies, separates from their spouse (including a de facto spouse) or becomes incapacitated (ie mentally or physically disabled to an extent that the person can no longer control the trust), provided the other members of the controlling group remain the same (apart from any relatives of the deceased, separated or incapacitated person) and there are no changes in the beneficiaries of the trust (apart from any relatives of the deceased, separated or incapacitated person). See, for example, ID 2007/59.

The Commissioner is given the discretion to treat a group as not beginning to control a trust where, having regard to all the circumstances, it is reasonable to do so (eg where a trustee retires but the beneficiaries do not change).

[FTR ¶799-695 – ¶799-710]

¶6-265 Current year net income/loss

If a fixed or non-fixed trust (other than an excepted trust) does not pass the current year loss tests (see the table at ¶6-262), it must work out its net income and tax loss in a special way (Sch 2F Div 268: ss 268-10 to 268-85).

(1) The trust's income year is divided into periods on the basis of when a specified event (eg a change in ownership or control) occurs. The events that result in the end of a period are summarised in the table below.

Current year losses: division of income year into periods

Type of trust	Events that result in the end of a period
Fixed trust other than widely held unit trust	Failure of 50% stake test Failure of alternate test
Unlisted widely held trust	Failure of 50% stake test (50% stake tested on abnormal trading)
Listed widely held trust	Failure of 50% stake test (unless the business continuity test is satisfied) (50% stake tested on abnormal trading)
Unlisted very widely held trust	Failure of 50% stake test (50% stake tested on abnormal trading)
Wholesale widely held trust	Failure of 50% stake test (50% stake tested on abnormal trading)
Non-fixed trust	Failure of 50% stake test Failure of continuity of control test

(2) Assessable income and deductions are allocated, where possible, to particular periods and a notional net income or notional loss is calculated for each period as if it were an income year. If there is no notional loss in any of the periods, the net income of the trust is calculated in the normal way. A notional loss incurred in the last period of an income year may be carried forward to a later year.

(3) The net income (if any) and tax loss is calculated, taking into account the notional net income and notional loss for each period and any income or deductions that cannot be allocated to particular periods.

▶ Example

The Helm Trust's income year is divided into two periods with notional net income and notional losses as follows:

Period 1	notional net income	$30,000
Period 2	notional loss	$25,000

(1) Calculation of net income

$30,000	total notional net income
+1,000	full year amount (share of net income of trust estate)
31,000	
−1,200	full year deductions (bad debts)
29,800	
− 100	other full year deductions (gifts)
−1,200	(tax losses of earlier income years)
$28,500	net income

The amount remaining ($28,500) is the trust's net income for the year. It is assessable under Pt III Div 6 (¶6-060).

(2) Calculation of tax loss

$25,000	notional loss
−3,200	net exempt income
$21,800	tax loss

The amount remaining ($21,800) is the trust's tax loss for the year. It can be carried forward for deduction in a later year.

Abnormal trading

There are 2 methods to determine whether there is abnormal trading (Sch 2F Subdiv 269-B: ss 269-10 to 269-49). "Trading" means an issue, redemption or transfer of, or other dealing in, the trust's units.

(1) A number of factors are weighed to determine whether the trading is, on balance, abnormal. The factors include:

(a) the timing of the trading when compared with the normal timing for trading in units of the trust

(b) the number of units traded by comparison with the normal number of units traded

(c) any connection between the trading and any other trading in units in the trust, and

(d) any connection between the trading and a tax loss or other deduction of the trust.

(2) Abnormal trading (other than in the case of a wholesale widely held trust) will automatically be taken to have occurred where:

(a) the trading is part of an acquisition of the trust or a merger with another trust (but only if the trustee knows or reasonably suspects this to be the case)

(b) 5% or more of the units in the trust are traded in one transaction

(c) a person and/or associates of the person have acquired and/or redeemed 5% or more of the units in the trust in 2 or more transactions (but only if the trustee knows or reasonably suspects that the acquisitions or redemptions have occurred and that they would not have been made if the trust did not have a tax loss or other deductions), or

(d) more than 20% of the units in the trust on issue at the end of any 60-day period are traded during that period (eg if ownership of more than 20% of the units changes in a 60-day period or if units are issued to new unitholders and, at the end of a 60-day period, they have more than 20% of the issued units).

In the case of a *wholesale widely held trust*, abnormal trading occurs where: (a) there is abnormal trading on balance (ie (1) above); (b) there is a merger or acquisition, or suspected merger or acquisition, of the trust (ie (2)(a) above); or (c) the trustee knows or reasonably suspects that the persons that held more than 50% of the units in the trust at the beginning of the period did not hold more than 50% of the units at the end of that period.

There are also special abnormal trading rules for a unit trust that is a *subsidiary* of another unit trust.

[FTR ¶799-545, ¶799-645 – ¶799-680, ¶799-702]

¶6-266 Family trusts

The trust loss measures, other than the income injection test (¶6-267), do not prevent a family trust from deducting current year or prior year losses or debt deductions, provided the trust is a family trust at all times in the relevant test period (Sch 2F Subdiv 272-D: ss 272-75 to 272-95).

Family trust election

A trust is a family trust where the trustee has made a family trust election. A trust cannot make a family trust election unless it passes the family control test (see below). The election must be in writing and in the approved form (s 272-80(2)).

A trustee can make a family trust election at any time in relation to an earlier income year, rather than having to include it in the tax return for the year in which the election is made. This option is only available if the specified income year is the 2004–05 or a later income year and at all times from the beginning of the specified income year until 30 June of the income year before the one in which the election is made:

- the trust passes the family control test (see below), and
- any conferral of present entitlement or any actual distributions of income or capital of the trust made by the trustee during that period have been made to the individual specified in the election or to members of that individual's family group.

The election must specify an individual as the individual whose "family group" (see below) is the subject of the election. It should also include other information required by the Commissioner, such as the name and address of the trust and the beneficiaries (s 272-80(3)). The Commissioner's view is that the individual who is specified must be alive at the time the election is made (ID 2014/3). The specified individual does not, however, need to be alive when an interposed entity election (see below) is made.

A family trust election generally cannot be revoked or varied, except in limited circumstances (s 272-80(5)).

Revocation of election

A fixed trust may revoke an election if some or all of the interests in the trust are disposed of to non-family members or if any of the persons holding the fixed entitlements cease to be family members (s 272-80(6)). However, where an election was revoked under this provision, the Commissioner determined that the trustee could not make a further election as s 272-80(11) provides that no more than one election can be made in relation to a trust (ID 2008/73).

In addition, the rules now allow an election to be revoked unless:

- tax losses have been recouped by the trust or another entity during a specified period where the losses could not have been recouped if the election had not been in force, or

- bad debt deductions or franking credits have been claimed during that period where the claim could not have been made if the election had not been in force (s 272-80(6A)).

Variation of test individual

The test individual specified in the family trust election may be varied, once only, where:

- the new test individual was a member of the original test individual's family at the election commencement time, and
- no conferrals of present entitlement to, or distributions of income or capital of, the trust (or an entity for which an interposed entity election has been made) have been made outside the new test individual's group during the period in which the election has been in force (s 272-80(5A)).

In addition, the test individual may be varied if, as a result of an obligation arising from a marriage breakdown, control of the trust passes to the new test individual or a group comprising the new individual and the members of that individual's family (s 272-80(5C)).

Family group

The family group of the individual specified in a family trust election consists of (s 272-90):

- members of the individual's family, ie the individual's spouse (¶15-120), a child, grandchild, parent, grandparent, brother, sister, nephew or niece of the individual or of the individual's spouse, and the spouse of such a child, grandchild, parent, grandparent, brother, sister, nephew or niece. In 2007, the definition of ''family'' was broadened to include lineal descendants of a nephew, niece or child of the individual or the individual's spouse. A person does not cease to be a family member merely because of the death of another family member (s 272-95)
- a person who was a spouse of the individual or of a member of his or her family (see above) before a breakdown in the marriage or relationship (including where the person is now the spouse of a person who is not within the individual's family)
- a person who was the spouse of the individual or a member of his or her family immediately before the death of the individual or the family member and who is now the spouse of a person who is not a member of the individual's family
- a person who was a child of a spouse of the individual or a member of his or her family before a breakdown of the marriage or relationship of the individual or family member
- the trust covered by the family trust election
- a trust with the same primary individual specified in its family trust election
- companies, trusts and partnerships covered by an interposed entity election (see below)
- companies, partnerships and trusts where family members and/or family trusts of those individuals have fixed entitlements to all of the income and capital of the company, partnership and trust
- certain funds, authorities or institutions in Australia to whom tax-deductible gifts may be made
- certain tax exempt bodies
- if the primary individual and all the members of their family are dead, the estate of the primary individual and the estates of family members, and
- certain interests in small and medium enterprises within the meaning of s 128TK.

Family control test

A trust cannot make a family trust election unless it satisfies the family control test. A trust will satisfy the test if it is controlled by a controlling group consisting of some or all of the following (s 272-87):

(1) the individual specified in the family trust election (the ''primary individual'') and/or one or more members of the individual's family (see above)

(2) any of the persons listed in (1) above and a professional or legal adviser to the family, or

(3) the trustees of one or more family trusts, or such trustees and any of the persons within (1) (provided the primary individual is specified in the family trust election of each of those trusts and the group has more than a 50% stake in the income or capital of the trust).

A group of any of the persons listed above is taken to control the trust if:

- the group is able to obtain, or is capable under a scheme of obtaining, the benefit (directly or indirectly) of the income or capital of the trust (eg by ensuring the exercise of a trustee discretion in their favour)
- the group is able to control (directly or indirectly), or is capable under a scheme of obtaining control of, the application of the income or capital of the trust
- the trustee is accustomed, is under an obligation or might reasonably be expected, to act in accordance with the directions or wishes of the group
- the group is able to remove or appoint the trustee
- the group has more than a 50% stake in the income or capital of the trust (this test is not available for a group described in (2) above), or
- persons in the group are the only persons who can benefit from the income and capital of the trust (this test is also not available for a group described in (2) above).

A company or partnership that proposes to make an interposed entity election (see below) satisfies the family control test at a particular time when some or all of the persons listed in (1) and (3) above (ie excluding professional or legal advisers) beneficially hold between them, directly or indirectly, fixed entitlements to more than 50% of the income or capital of the company or partnership.

Interposed entity election

A company, trust or partnership that makes an interposed entity election will be included as part of a family group (see above). An interposed entity election will be relevant where members of the primary individual's family do not have fixed entitlements to all of the income and capital of the interposed entity. If the family members do have fixed entitlements, the interposed entity is automatically part of the family group and the election is not required. An interposed entity election can be made for an income year later than the year in which the family trust election is made. The election must specify a date in the income year from which it takes effect (s 272-85).

An interposed entity election can be made at any time in relation to an earlier income year, rather than having to be included in the tax return. This option is only available if the specified income year is the 2004–05 or a later income year and if the relevant interposed entity has acted as if it were a family entity, ie where the relevant entity satisfies similar requirements to those that apply for family trust elections (see above). An interposed entity election cannot be made if the entity does not pass the family control test at the end of the income year that is specified in the election.

An interposed entity election may be revoked in certain limited circumstances:

- the election was made for an entity that was already included in the family group of the individual specified in the family trust election at the election commencement time, or

- at a later time, the entity becomes wholly-owned by members of the family group (s 272-85(5A)).

An election is automatically revoked if the family trust election to which it relates is revoked (s 272-85(5B)).

An interposed entity election cannot be made in respect of more than one family trust unless the individual specified in each family trust election is the same. So, for example, if 2 family trusts that relate to the same individual wish to make a distribution to the same interposed entity, the entity may make an interposed entity election for each family trust.

There are special information requirements if a family trust or other entity that has made an interposed entity election is a non-resident.

[FTR ¶799-790 – ¶799-845]

¶6-267 Income injection test

If a trust is involved in an income injection scheme to take advantage of losses or other deductions, it may be prevented from making full use of them under the income injection test. Under these schemes, income is injected into trusts with losses or other deductions so that the tax payable on the income is reduced or eliminated.

The income injection test (Sch 2F Div 270: ss 270-5 to 270-25) applies where:

- the trust has a deduction (including a prior year loss) in the income year being examined
- there is a scheme under which: (a) the trust derives assessable income; (b) a person not connected with the trust provides a benefit (directly or indirectly) to the trustee or a beneficiary (or their associates); and (c) a return benefit is provided to the outsider, and
- it is reasonable to conclude that the assessable income has been derived, or the benefits have been provided, wholly or partly (but not merely incidentally) because the deduction is allowable.

''Scheme'' has the same meaning as in Pt IVA (¶30-140) and ''benefit'' is broadly defined to include money or other property, services, the release or waiver of a debt and any benefit or advantage within the ordinary meaning of those words.

The income injection test also applies where a person who was an outsider before the scheme was entered into ceases, pursuant to the scheme, to be an outsider (by becoming the trustee of the trust or by receiving a fixed entitlement to a share of the income or capital of the trust) (s 270-10(2)).

The income injection test does *not* apply to excepted trusts (Sch 2F s 272-100) other than family trusts (¶6-266). In the case of family trusts, the test does not apply where benefits under an income injection scheme are provided only to one or more members of the family group (including interposed entities that have made an interposed entity election). Thus, members of the family group can inject income into the family trust to take advantage of the losses or other deductions.

If the income injection test is failed, no deduction is allowable in the income year being examined against the scheme assessable income. As a result, if the net income of the trust for that year is less than the scheme assessable income, the net income is increased to equal the full amount of the scheme assessable income. However, any deduction not related to the derivation of the scheme assessable income is still allowable to the trust (eg it can be deducted against other assessable income derived in the income year or can be deducted in a later year in the form of a tax loss) (s 270-15).

A trust loss scheme was caught under the income injection test where a trustee resolved to make a distribution equal to accumulated tax losses of the recipient. By not calling for payment of funds distributed (but not actually paid) to it, the recipient provided a benefit to that trust estate. Allowing the trust to retain use of those distributions meant that the benefit was received under a scheme, in the sense that the scheme operated to produce that effect (*Corporate Initiatives*).

[FTR ¶799-720, ¶799-820]

¶6-268 Family trust distribution tax

Family trust distribution tax is payable (under Sch 2F Div 271: ss 271-5 to 271-105) where:

- a trustee of a family trust has made a family trust election; *or* the partners in a partnership, a company or the trustee of a trust have made an interposed entity election to be included in a family group in relation to a family trust, *and*
- the trust, partnership or company makes a distribution of, or confers a present entitlement to, income or capital to a person other than the primary individual or a member of their family group (¶6-266). ''Distribution'' is defined in Sch 2F ss 272-45 to 272-63.

Family trust distribution tax is imposed by the *Family Trust Distribution Tax (Primary Liability) Act 1998* (s 4). The rate of tax for 2017–18 and subsequent years is 47% of the amount or value of the income or capital distributed or to which the entitlement relates. The tax is payable by the electing entity (ie trustee, partners or company) or, if the trustee or a partner is a company, by the directors of the company. However, a director is not liable to pay the tax in certain circumstances where it would be unreasonable (eg if the director was unaware of the decision to make the distribution or confer the entitlement, or voted against it and took reasonable steps to prevent it).

If the distribution or conferral was made before the day on which the relevant family trust or interposed entity election was made (¶6-266), family trust distribution tax is payable at the end of 21 days after the election day. In any other case, the tax is payable at the end of 21 days after the day the distribution or conferral was made. GIC may be payable if the tax remains unpaid for more than 60 days after it becomes due and payable (¶29-510). GIC would be payable on the unpaid amount for each day in the period that started at the beginning of the 60th day after the tax was due to be paid, and finished at the end of the last day the tax, or GIC on the tax, remained unpaid (s 271-80).

If a non-resident trust is liable to pay family trust distribution tax and the Commissioner is unable to recover the tax because of territorial limitations, the tax is payable by any related resident trust in which the non-resident trust has an interest. In this case, the tax is imposed by the *Family Trust Distribution Tax (Secondary Liability) Act 1998* and is equal to the amount of the unpaid family trust distribution tax. If a non-resident family trust with an interest in a resident company fails to pay the required amount of family trust distribution tax, the resident company (or its directors) is liable for the tax if the company: (a) was able to deduct a tax loss or amount in respect of a debt, or apply a net capital loss; or (b) was not required to work out its taxable income or tax loss under the current year loss rules, or the net capital gain or net capital loss rules, only because the non-resident family trust held the interest (s 271-60).

Amounts on which family trust distribution tax is paid are exempt from income tax and non-resident withholding tax (s 128B(3)(k)). One consequence is that any expenditure incurred in deriving the distributed amounts will not be deductible.

A trustee of a family trust is liable for family trust distribution tax on a payment made in respect of the redemption of units to the extent that the amount paid exceeds the value of any consideration given in return (ID 2004/162).

[FTR ¶799-740, ¶799-815]

Trust Stripping

¶6-270 Reimbursement agreements

In certain cases involving tax avoidance, a presently entitled beneficiary who would otherwise be assessed on trust income (¶6-110) will be deemed *not* to be presently entitled to income and the trustee will be assessed at a penal rate of tax (s 100A).

This measure was introduced to counter ''trust stripping'' schemes. These schemes generally involved arrangements whereby a specially introduced beneficiary was made presently entitled to income of the trust, so that the trustee was relieved of any tax liability on the income. For one reason or another, the introduced beneficiary also did not pay tax, eg because it was a tax-exempt charity. Under the arrangements, the introduced beneficiary retained only a minor portion of the trust income and another person — the true beneficiary who was actually intended to take the benefit — effectively secured enjoyment of the major portion of the trust income but in a tax-free form, eg by the settlement of a capital sum in another trust for the benefit of that person.

To combat schemes of this kind, s 100A provides that, where a beneficiary who is not under a legal disability is presently entitled to trust income (by reason either of the terms of the trust instrument or of the payment or application of income to or for their benefit) and that present entitlement is linked, directly or indirectly, to a ''reimbursement agreement'', the beneficiary is deemed not to be presently entitled to the income. Further, the trust is deemed to be a resident trust with the result that foreign source income is assessable to the trustee. The income is assessed under s 99A at the penal rate and the Commissioner has no discretion to assess under s 99 (¶6-230).

The term ''reimbursement agreement'' is defined as any agreement, arrangement or understanding providing for:

- the payment of money (including a payment by way of loan) to
- the transfer of property to, or
- the provision of services or any other benefits for,

any person other than the beneficiary, being an agreement entered into for a purpose (not necessarily the sole or principal purpose) of reducing the tax liability of *a person*. This has been interpreted as meaning an agreement, etc, entered into by any of the parties to the agreement for a purpose of reducing the tax liability of a person. The person whose tax is eliminated or reduced is not required to be the beneficiary or the trustee, nor is the money paid to that person required to find its way to entities associated with the trustee or beneficiary (*Prestige Motors*). An agreement can be a ''reimbursement agreement'' even if there is no ''reimbursement'' within the ordinary meaning of that term (*Prestige Motors*). Further, there need not be a trust in existence before the reimbursement agreement is entered into. An agreement, arrangement or understanding entered into in the course of ordinary family or commercial dealing is excluded from being a reimbursement agreement.

In the *East Finchley case*, the court commented that crediting a distribution of trust income to a loan account in a beneficiary's name in the trust's accounts constituted a ''payment'', but that s 100A would not apply where all that happens is that the trustee resolves to make a distribution to a beneficiary in circumstances where the beneficiary becomes presently entitled and thereafter enters into an arrangement with the beneficiary for a payment to be made by the latter.

In the *Prestige Motors case*, the establishment of a unit trust, the purchase by the initial trustee of the taxpayer's business, the subsequent appointment of the taxpayer as the trustee and the distribution of the bulk of the trust income to a beneficiary with large tax losses were caught by s 100A as the transactions involved reimbursement agreements that were not entered into in the course of ordinary commercial dealings.

The wide scope of s 100A was confirmed in *Idlecroft*. In that case, the taxpayers entered into joint venture agreements with a property owner under which the owner was purportedly appointed as beneficiary of discretionary trusts. As the appointment was ineffective, the question was whether the present entitlement of default beneficiaries arose out of a reimbursement agreement. The court ruled that s 100A applied where an act or circumstance — in this case the invalid appointment of income — was connected with the reimbursement agreement.

Similarly, the High Court confirmed in *Raftland* that s 100A applied to a scheme in which a trustee of a trust with considerable losses was introduced as a beneficiary in order to absorb profits arising out of a building business. In so doing, the court upheld the reasoning of the primary judge that purported distributions to the loss trust were sham transactions that should be disregarded. See also the ATO Impact Statement on the decision.

The Commissioner considers that s 100A may apply to certain arrangements that are structured so that business income passes through a chain of trusts to a loss company (TD 2005/34).

[FTR ¶51-195]

¶6-273 New generation trust stripping schemes

There is specific legislation to counter ''new generation'' trust stripping schemes that relied on s 95A(2) and that were not caught by the reimbursement agreement rules (¶6-270).

Under s 95A(2), a beneficiary having a vested and indefeasible interest in trust income is treated as being presently entitled to that income (¶6-100). In a typical new generation scheme, the income of a family trust was formally allocated for tax purposes to a tax-exempt entity, such as a charity. Although the charity was given a vested interest in the income, it was generally not entitled to payment of the income until 80 years' time. In the meantime, the charity received only a token payment, with the balance of the funds being retained for the benefit of family members. The essence of the scheme was that trust income was made to appear for tax purposes as income of an exempt body, but effective enjoyment of the income stayed with the family seeking to avoid tax.

Under the *Trust Recoupment Tax Assessment Act 1985*, a special trust recoupment tax is recoverable where a new generation trust stripping scheme is entered into. The trustee of the stripped trust is liable to trust recoupment tax on the amount of the stripped income at the top marginal tax rate. The legislation allows the beneficiaries to elect, as an alternative, to be assessed to personal income tax on the stripped income.

Sham schemes

Trust stripping schemes not covered by specific legislation have generally been treated as shams by the Commissioner (¶30-000). The general anti-avoidance provisions (¶30-120) may also be used to strike down trust stripping schemes.

[FTR ¶50-900, ¶51-195, ¶954-350]

Tax Exempt Beneficiaries

¶6-274 Present entitlement of tax exempt beneficiaries: anti-avoidance rules

There are 2 rules that may operate to deny the present entitlement of a tax exempt beneficiary to income of a trust estate (with the result that the trustee will be assessable on the relevant share of the net income under ITAA36 s 99A).

Notification of present entitlement

The first rule applies where an exempt entity which is presently entitled to income of a trust estate for an income year is not notified in writing by the trustee of its present entitlement within 2 months after the end of the income year (ITAA36 s 100AA). In that event, the beneficiary will be treated as not being presently entitled to the income to the extent that it has not been actually paid its entitlement during the 2-month period. Written notice of an exempt entity's present entitlement may take the form of a statement setting out an entitlement that is quantifiable (eg a percentage of the income of the trust estate to which the entity is presently entitled). That is, there is no requirement that the trustee provide the exempt entity with the actual dollar amount to which the entity is presently entitled.

The Commissioner does not have a discretion to extend the 2-month period but does have a discretion to disregard the trustee's failure to notify.

Disproportionate share of net income

The second rule only applies to the extent that the first rule does not apply. The second rule is intended to ensure that a tax exempt beneficiary does not have a disproportionate share of the net income of the trust attributed to it (ITAA36 s 100AB). This involves comparing the exempt entity beneficiary's adjusted Division 6 percentage of the income of the trust with the exempt entity beneficiary's ‘‘benchmark percentage’’.

The exempt beneficiary is treated as not being presently entitled to the amount of the income of the trust estate that is attributable to the percentage by which the exempt entity's adjusted Division 6 percentage exceeds the benchmark percentage.

The exempt entity's adjusted Division 6 percentage is the share of the income of the trust estate to which the exempt entity is presently entitled for the purposes of Div 6, excluding capital gains or franked distributions to which any beneficiary or trustee is specifically entitled.

The benchmark percentage against which an exempt entity's adjusted Division 6 percentage is compared is the percentage of the ‘‘adjusted net income’’ of the trust estate to which the exempt entity is presently entitled (ITAA36 s 100AB(3)). The reference to amounts to which the exempt entity is presently entitled is a reference to any amount to which the entity is presently entitled to the extent that it forms part of the trust's adjusted net income. In this context, that may include an entitlement to income or capital.

The ‘‘adjusted net income’’ of a trust is the net income (¶6-080) of the trust for the income year adjusted by the amounts set out in ITAA36 s 100AB(4). It is necessary to adjust the taxable income of the trust in this way to ensure that an entity's benchmark percentage can be properly compared to its adjusted Division 6 percentage. To arrive at the adjusted net income of a trust, the net (tax) income of the trust is adjusted in 3 ways:

(1) by reducing the amount of the net income of the trust by amounts of any capital gain or franked distribution to which a beneficiary or trustee is specifically entitled

(2) by increasing the amount of the net income of the trust by any CGT discount and small business concessions that have been claimed in relation to any remaining capital gain, and

(3) by then reducing the net income of the trust by any amounts that do not represent net accretions of value to the trust estate in the income year other than amounts included in net income under the general anti-avoidance provisions (ITAA36 Pt IVA; s 100AB(4)).

Amounts that do not represent ‘‘net accretions of value to the trust estate’’ are amounts that:

- have not been added to the trust estate during the relevant income year in terms of monetary additions, property or additions of other value, or
- represent an accretion coupled with a corresponding depletion (in cash or value) of the fund (such as a loan that is coupled with a corresponding liability for the trustee to repay that loan; or a receipt that is depleted by expenses properly chargeable for trust purposes, but which are not allowable deductions for tax purposes).

Examples of such amounts include:

- the amount of a franking credit included in the calculation of the trust's taxable income
- an amount taken to be a dividend paid to the trustee of the trust pursuant to ITAA36 s 109D(1) (loans treated as dividends under ITAA36 Div 7A)
- so much of a net capital gain that is attributable to a reduction of what would have otherwise been a relevant cost base or reduced cost base of a CGT asset as a result of the market value substitution rule, and
- so much of a net capital gain that is attributable to an increase as a result of the market value substitution rule of what would otherwise have been a relevant amount of capital proceeds for a CGT event.

The Commissioner has a discretion to not apply this anti-avoidance rule if he considers its application would be unreasonable (ITAA36 s 100AB(5)).

▶ Example

In the 2019–20 income year, the Bell Trust generated $100,000 of rental income and $70,000 of franked distributions (with $30,000 franking credits attached). The trust had no expenses. The taxable income of the trust is $200,000 (being the $100,000 rental income, $70,000 franked distributions and $30,000 franking credits).

The trust deed does not define "income" but there is a clause that allows the trustee to treat receipts as income or capital of the trust at its discretion. The trustee determines to exercise this power to treat $95,000 of the rental receipts as capital and so the income of the trust estate is $75,000.

Casey Pty Ltd, Mark and Emma are within the class of discretionary objects of the Bell Trust. Casey Pty Ltd is an exempt entity. The trustee of the Bell Trust specifically allocates all of the franked distributions to Mark and appoints all of the remaining income of the trust estate to Casey Pty Ltd ($5,000). The trustee notifies Casey Pty Ltd of its entitlement by 31 August 2020. The trustee appoints all of the capital in respect of the 2019–20 income year to Emma ($95,000).

Casey Pty Ltd's adjusted Division 6 percentage is 100% (($75,000 − $70,000/$5,000) × 100) as it is presently entitled to all of the income of the trust estate after disregarding the $70,000 of franked distributions to which Mark is specifically entitled.

However, Casey Pty Ltd's benchmark percentage is 5% (($5,000/$100,000) × 100). The franked distributions to which Mark is specifically entitled and the attached franking credits (because they do not represent net accretions of value to the trust fund) are excluded from the adjusted net income for the purpose of calculating the benchmark percentage.

Casey Pty Ltd's adjusted Division 6 percentage exceeds the benchmark percentage by 95%. The trustee of the Bell Trust is therefore assessed and liable to pay tax on $95,000 (0.95 × $100,000) under ITAA36 s 99A. Casey Pty Ltd's share of the Bell Trust's taxable income is confined to Casey Pty Ltd's entitlement of $5,000.

[FTR ¶51-185, ¶51-190]

Closely Held Trusts

¶6-275 Trustee beneficiary reporting rules

There are reporting requirements that apply to trustees of closely held trusts. The main purpose of these requirements is to ensure that the trustee of a "closely held trust" with a trustee beneficiary advises the Commissioner of the trustee beneficiaries of the net income and tax-preferred amounts of the trust. This allows the Commissioner to check whether the assessable income of the trustee beneficiaries correctly includes any required share of that net income, and whether the net assets of those beneficiaries reflect the receipt of the tax-preferred amounts.

If the trustee fails to satisfy the reporting requirements, trustee beneficiary non-disclosure tax is imposed at the highest marginal rate plus Medicare levy in respect of the untaxed part of the share of the net income. The reporting requirements are contained primarily in Pt III Div 6D (ss 102UA to 102UV).

It is also provided that, where the trustee of the closely held trust becomes presently entitled to an amount that is reasonably attributable to the whole or a part of the share of the net income of the closely held trust, tax is imposed on the amount at the highest marginal rate plus Medicare levy (s 102UM). See further below under ''Circular distributions''.

What trusts are affected?

The rules only apply to closely held trusts where a trustee beneficiary is presently entitled to a share of a tax-preferred amount in the trust, or where a share of the net income of the trust is included in the trustee beneficiary's assessable income under ITAA36 s 97 and the share comprises or includes an untaxed part. A closely held trust is:

- a trust where an individual has, or up to 20 individuals have between them, fixed entitlements to at least a 75% share of the income or capital, or
- a discretionary trust (s 102UC).

An individual and their relatives are treated as being one individual. A trustee of a discretionary trust who holds a fixed entitlement to a share of the income or capital of a fixed trust is taken to hold that fixed entitlement as an individual. A trustee beneficiary is a beneficiary of the trust in the capacity of trustee of another trust.

Certain trusts are excluded from the closely held trust measures. These are: (a) complying superannuation funds, complying ADFs and PSTs; (b) deceased estates for 5 years after the death; (c) fixed unit trusts wholly-owned by tax-exempt persons; and (d) listed unit trusts. For income years before the 2019–20 income year the following trusts were also excluded from the closely held trust measures: (i) family trusts; (ii) trusts in relation to which an interposed entity election has been made; and (iii) trusts whose income or capital is fully owned by family members and/or family trusts. Amendments made by the *Treasury Laws Amendment (2019 Tax Integrity and Other Measures No 1) Act 2019* had the effect that, from 1 July 2019, categories (i), (ii) and (iii) ceased to be excluded from the operation of the closely held trust measures. The effect of these amendments was to extend to family trusts, etc, the trustee beneficiary disclosure rules and the anti-avoidance rule that applies to other closely held trusts that undertake circular trust distributions (see under ''Circular distributions'' below).

What is the "untaxed part"?

Only ''untaxed parts'' of a share of the net income of a closely held trust are subject to the trustee reporting rules. The ''untaxed part'' of a share of the net income of a closely held trust is so much of that share as does not fall in one of the following categories (s 102UE(2)):

- the trustee of the closely held trust is assessed and liable to pay tax under s 98(4) in respect of the share
- the share is reasonably attributable to the net income of a part of another trust estate in respect of which the trustee of the other trust estate is assessed and liable to pay tax under s 98(4)
- the share is represented by, or reasonably attributable to, an amount from which an entity was required to withhold an amount under TAA Sch 1 Subdiv 12-H (regarding situations where an Australian managed fund or custodian pays amounts to non-resident trustees), or
- the share is reasonably attributable to a part of the net income of another trust estate in respect of which the trustee of the other trust estate was liable to pay trustee beneficiary non-disclosure tax.

Lodgment of trustee beneficiary statements

The trustee of a closely held trust must generally provide a correct trustee beneficiary (TB) statement by the due date for lodgment of the trust's tax return (s 102UH).

A "correct TB statement" is a written statement in the approved form by the trustee of the closely held trust which correctly sets out:

- the amount of the untaxed part of the share
- the amount of the share of the tax-preferred amount.

A correct TB statement must also contain:

- the name and tax file number of each trustee beneficiary who is resident at the end of the year of income, and
- the name and address of each trustee beneficiary who is not a resident at the end of the year of income (s 102UG).

The trustee of a closely held trust can amend an incorrect TB statement about amounts of net income outside the TB statement period where the following conditions are satisfied (s 102UK(2A)):

- the correction must be made before the trustee beneficiary non-disclosure tax becomes due and payable or within 4 years of any such tax becoming due and payable
- the trustee must have believed on reasonable grounds that the statement was correct when it was made, and
- the event that led to the need to correct the original statement could not reasonably have been foreseen by the trustee.

Trustee beneficiary non-disclosure tax

The trustee is liable to pay "trustee beneficiary non-disclosure tax" at the top marginal rate if:

- a share of the net income of a closely held trust is included in the assessable income of a trustee beneficiary under s 97
- the share comprises or includes an untaxed part
- the Commissioner has not exempted the trustee of the closely held trust from the reporting requirements
- during the TB statement period, the trustee of the closely held trust does not give to the Commissioner a correct TB statement about the share (s 102UK(1)).

Circular distributions

In order to discourage the use of circular chains of trusts to disguise the identity of the final beneficiary of trust income, trustee beneficiary non-disclosure tax is also payable on the whole or that part of the untaxed part if:

- a share of the net income of a closely held trust for a year of income is included in the assessable income of a trustee beneficiary of the trust under s 97
- the trustee of the closely held trust becomes presently entitled to an amount that is reasonably attributable to the whole or a part of the untaxed part of the share, and
- trustee beneficiary non-disclosure tax is not otherwise payable by the trustee of the closely held trust on the untaxed part (s 102UM).

For a recent decision where the general issue of circular trust distributions was considered, see *Advanced Holdings Pty Ltd as trustee for The Demian Trust & Ors* (appeal pending).

Payment of tax etc

If a trustee has a trustee beneficiary non-disclosure tax liability, the trustee must pay the tax within 21 days of the due date for lodgment of the trust return (unless the Commissioner allows further time). If the tax is outstanding 60 days after the due date for payment, GIC will be payable (¶29-510).

Trustees of closely held trusts can sue trustee beneficiaries to recover the trustee beneficiary non-disclosure tax (and any GIC) paid by them where the trustee beneficiary has received the full distribution (s 102USA). A trustee may only take recovery action if 4 conditions are satisfied:

(1) the trustee pays trustee beneficiary non-disclosure tax under s 102UK and any GIC

(2) a gross entitlement (including the amount of the trustee beneficiary non-disclosure tax) has been distributed (ie the trustee has not withheld tax from the payment)

(3) the trustee failed to make a correct TB statement because the trustee beneficiary refused or failed to give information to the trustee, or the trustee made an incorrect TB statement because the trustee was given incorrect information by the trustee beneficiary and the trustee honestly believed on reasonable grounds that the information was correct, and

(4) the person refusing or failing to provide information, or providing incorrect information, was the trustee beneficiary.

If these conditions are satisfied, the trustee can sue for the recoverable amount from the source of the incorrect information, ie the trustee beneficiary.

Tax-preferred amounts

A tax-preferred amount is any income of the trust that is not included in assessable income when calculating the trust's net income, and any capital of the trust (s 102UI). A failure by a trustee of a closely held trust to provide a TB statement in relation to the share of a tax-preferred amount constitutes an offence unless the trustee: (a) did not have all the information required to be included in the TB statement; (b) took reasonable steps to get the information; and (c) gave whatever information was available to the Commissioner (s 102UT).

[FTR ¶53-000ff]

¶6-277 TFN withholding rules

The TFN withholding arrangements now extend to closely held trusts and certain other trusts.

The trusts affected by this extension are trusts that are closely held trusts as defined in s 102UC (¶6-275), family trusts, trusts in relation to which an interposed entity election has been made and certain fixed trusts which fall within a family group under the family trust provisions.

Withholding is potentially required where there is a distribution of ordinary or statutory income to, or a present entitlement to ordinary or statutory income arises to, a beneficiary who is an Australian resident, is not exempt from tax and is not under a legal disability and the beneficiary has not quoted their TFN to the trustee. There are rules which operate where the circumstances requiring withholding overlap and distributions out of income of, or a present entitlement that arose in, the 2009–10 or an earlier income year are excluded.

No withholding is required where the trustee is required to make a correct TB statement under the rules explained at ¶6-275 or if family trust distribution tax is payable in connection with the distribution or present entitlement.

For further discussion of these TFN withholding rules, see ¶26-200.

Public Trading Trusts

¶6-310 Public trading trusts taxed as companies

Certain public unit trusts, called "public trading trusts", are treated as if they are companies for tax purposes (Pt III Div 6C: ss 102M to 102T). The trust is taxed at the company rate of tax (¶3-055) and distributions to equity holders (¶6-330) are assessable on the same basis as dividends. However, the trust loss measures (¶6-262) apply to public trading trusts and, in certain circumstances, a public trading trust must work out its net income in a special way (¶6-262, ¶6-265). The simplified imputation system applies to public trading trusts (¶4-400). Public trading trusts that elect to be taxed like companies may head consolidated groups (¶8-000). The accruals measures in Div 6AAA (¶6-075) do not apply in relation to arm's length transfers to non-resident public unit trusts (s 102AAT(1)).

[FTR ¶52-901]

¶6-320 What is a public trading trust?

A "public trading trust" is a public unit trust that is also a trading trust, and that is either a resident in the income year concerned or was a public trading trust in a previous income year (s 102R).

Whatever is encompassed by the concept of a unit trust within Div 6C there is a necessity for something which fits a description of "units" within the functional, and descriptive, notion of a unit trust. This includes a focus upon one of the core indicia of a unit, namely a beneficial interest in any of the income or property of the estate (*ElecNet*).

A unit trust is a "public unit trust" for the purposes of these provisions where (s 102P):

(1) any of the units are listed for quotation on a stock exchange

(2) any of the units were offered to the public (but not where the offer was merely to secure public status under Div 6C)

(3) the units are held by 50 or more persons, or

(4) a tax-exempt entity (ie in broad terms an entity whose ordinary and statutory income is exempt) holds a beneficial interest in 20% or more of the property or income of the trust, or during the income year concerned was paid 20% or more of the moneys paid by the trust to unitholders, or an arrangement exists whereby such an entity could have been given such a holding during the year or could have been entitled to 20% or more of any moneys paid to unitholders during the year concerned.

A unit trust that would otherwise be a public unit trust under (1), (2) or (3) above is *not* treated as a public unit trust if 20 or fewer persons hold 75% or more of the beneficial interests in the property or income of the trust, unless the Commissioner rules otherwise. Nor is it a public unit trust if 20 or fewer persons during the income year were paid 75% or more of moneys paid by the trust to unitholders, or an arrangement exists whereby such persons could have been entitled to 75% or more of any moneys paid to unitholders during the year (unless the Commissioner considers that it is not intended to implement that arrangement).

For the purpose of determining whether a unit trust is a public unit trust, a beneficiary under a trust is deemed to hold any units held by the trust of which they are a beneficiary and a person and their relatives or nominees are regarded as one. For the 2016–17 and later income years this provision does not apply where units are held by the trustee of a complying superannuation fund.

For a recent Full Federal Court decision in which the operation of Div 6C was considered, see *Trustee for the Michael Hayes Family Trust*. Note that the ultimate conclusion in this case would now be different because the facts involved an arrangement that relied on the use of a complying superannuation fund.

A unit trust is a "trading trust" if it carries on a trading business *or* controls or is able to control, directly or indirectly, a trading business carried on by another person (s 102N). A unit trust is not a trading trust if it is an interposed trust in relation to a scheme for reorganising the affairs of stapled entities in terms of the CGT roll-over under Subdiv 124-Q (¶12-440) (s 102NA).

A ''trading business'' is any business that does *not* consist wholly of ''eligible investment business'' (s 102M). Eligible investment business means any of the following:

- investment in land for rental, including investing in fixtures and certain moveable property. There is also a 25% safe harbour allowance for non-rental non-trading income from investments in land
- investment or trading in loans (secured or unsecured), securities, shares, units in a unit trust, futures contracts, forward contracts, currency swap contracts, interest rate swap contracts, forward exchange rate contracts, forward interest rate contracts, life insurance contracts, or rights or options in respect of any of these, or any similar financial instruments, or
- investing or trading in financial instruments arising under financial arrangements (other than certain leasing or property arrangements, interests in a partnership or trust estate, general insurance policies, guarantees and indemnities, superannuation and pension rights, and retirement village arrangements) (s 102MA).

The trustee of a unit trust is not treated as carrying on a trading business if not more than 2% of the gross revenue of the unit trust is not from eligible investment business and that income is not from carrying on a business that is not incidental and relevant to the eligible investment business (s 102MC).

A public unit trust carrying on a business can carry out sub-underwriting of share issues without its business becoming a trading business, provided the sub-underwriting is conducted in such a way that it is properly part of the business of ''investing in or trading in'' shares in a company, is undertaken for this purpose, and the business otherwise consists wholly of ''eligible investment business'' activities (TD 98/4).

A unit trust is a resident if, at any time during the income year:

- any property of the trust is situated in Australia *or* the trustee carries on business in Australia, *and*
- the central management and control of the trust is in Australia *or* persons who hold more than 50% of the beneficial interests in the income or property of the trust are residents (s 102Q).

[FTR ¶52-910 – ¶52-970]

¶6-330 Effect of taxing a public trading trust as a company

The consequences of treating a public unit trust as a company are listed below.

- The net income of the trust is taxed at the company rate of tax.
- Corporate trust distributions (ie ''unit trust dividends'' and ''non-unit dividends'') made to equity holders are treated in the same way as dividends paid to shareholders, ie they form part of the assessable income of the equity holder and franking credits are allowed in respect of tax paid by the unit trust. An ''equity holder'' means a unitholder or the holder of any other interest by virtue of the operation of the debt/equity rules (ss 102L; 102T). Where an equity holder is a non-resident, the dividend withholding tax provisions apply to corporate trust distributions paid to the non-resident.
- The debt/equity provisions in ITAA97 Div 974 (¶23-100 – ¶23-125) apply to public trading trusts in the same way that they apply to companies.
- The demerger relief provisions in ITAA97 Div 125 (¶12-328) apply to public trading trusts as if they were companies (s 125-230).
- The trustee of the trust pays tax under the same arrangements that apply to companies.

The specific provisions dealing with trust income are rendered inapplicable in the case of a public trading trust (s 102T), as are the primary producer averaging provisions (¶18-200).

Note, however, that a public trading trust is entitled to the benefit of the CGT discount capital gain concession (ID 2003/652, withdrawn because it was a simple restatement of the law).

[FTR ¶52-901]

Managed Funds

¶6-400 Managed investment schemes

A managed investment scheme (MIS or managed fund) is a type of collective investment vehicle such as a public unit trust. In such a trust, investors hand over money or other assets to a professional manager who manages the total funds to produce a return that is shared by the investors. As members of the scheme, investors hold units in the trust that represent a proportional beneficial entitlement to the trust assets.

MISs cover a variety of investments, including cash management trusts, property trusts and timeshare schemes. However, they do not encompass regulated superannuation funds, ADFs or term deposits. A property syndicate that is structured to comply with the MIS provisions of the *Corporations Act 2001* is taxable under the trust provisions of ITAA36 (TD 2005/28).

For the CGT rules applying to interests held by foreign residents in managed funds, see ¶12-735.

Managed investment trusts

Eligible MITs may irrevocably elect to apply the CGT provisions as the primary code for the taxation of gains and losses on disposal of certain assets (primarily shares, units and real property). If an MIT is eligible to make an election and it has not done so, then any gains or losses on the disposal of eligible assets (excluding land, an interest in land, or an option to acquire or dispose of such an asset) are treated on revenue account. See further ¶12-660.

For the purposes of the discount for qualifying affordable housing, if the ownership interest in the dwelling is owned by an MIT, the tenant must not have an interest in the MIT that passes the non-portfolio test. See further ¶11-037.

For details of the PAYG withholding rules relating to distributions from MITs to non-residents, see ¶26-267.

¶6-405 Attribution managed investment trusts

An eligible managed investment trust may elect into an attribution regime for the taxation of what are known as attribution managed investment trusts (AMITs). The relevant provisions are contained in ITAA97 Div 276.

For an election to be available, the interests of the members of the trust need to be clearly defined at all times during which the trust is in existence in the income year.

An AMIT for an income year is treated as a fixed trust and a member of the AMIT in respect of the income year is treated as having a vested and indefeasible interest in a share of the income and capital of the AMIT throughout the income year. In addition:

- amounts related to income and tax offsets of an AMIT, determined by the trustee to be of a particular tax character, are attributed to members, generally retaining that tax character

- underestimates and overestimates of amounts at the trust level are carried forward and dealt with in later years. This is done on a character-by-character basis. An underestimate in an income year of a particular character results in an under of that character. An overestimate results in an over of that character. Unders and overs arise, and are dealt with, in the income year in which they are discovered
- the trustee of an AMIT is liable to pay income tax on certain amounts reflecting under attribution of income or over attribution of tax offsets
- there are special rules that apply to a trust that ceases to be an AMIT.

For details of the PAYG withholding rules relating to distributions from AMITs to non-residents, see ¶26-268.

Other changes

A range of other MIT/AMIT related amendments have been implemented including:

- greater alignment between CGT outcomes for MITs and AMITs
- MITs with substituted accounting periods also eligible to opt into AMIT regime
- improvements to the PAYG withholding provisions
- amendments to ensure discount capital gains are properly taken into account in the AMIT "unders and overs" regime, and
- clarification in relation to operation of CGT event E10 (AMIT — cost base reduction exceeds cost base) (¶11-290).

[FITR ¶265-215ff]

¶6-410 Proposed new collective investment vehicle regimes

As part of its Ten Year Enterprise Tax Plan that was announced in the 2016–17 Federal Budget, the government will introduce a new tax and regulatory framework for 2 new types of collective investment vehicles (CIVs). CIVs allow investors to pool their funds and have them managed by a professional funds manager. The 2 new CIVs are:

- a corporate CIV (CCIV) which is to be introduced for income years starting on or after 1 July 2017, and
- a limited partnership CIV for income years starting on or after 1 July 2018.

CIVs are intended to engage in primarily passive investment activities and comply with similar eligibility criteria as MITs, such as being widely held and provide investors with tax outcomes that are generally equivalent to the tax outcomes that would have applied if they had invested directly.

Exposure draft legislation (and explanatory material) for the tax framework for the proposed CCIV regime was released by Treasury on 20 December 2017 (¶41-900).

Also, exposure draft legislation (and explanatory material) for the Treasury Laws Amendment (Corporate Collective Investment Vehicle) Bill 2018, which is to establish the regulatory framework for CIVs, has been released by Treasury in 3 tranches, the latest on 12 October 2018.

Chapter 7 Small Business Entities

Introduction

¶7-001 Concessions and tools for small business entities

The federal tax acts provide for a wide range of concessions for small businesses and their stakeholders. The potential availability of the different tax concessions generally depends upon whether the entity is a "small business entity" or a "CGT small business entity" (¶7-050). From 1 July 2020 some concessions are also available for medium business entities.

CGT Small Business Concessions available to CGT small business entities

A CGT small business entity can choose to access any one or more of the following CGT concessions, subject to satisfying applicable additional criteria:

1. CGT 15-year asset exemption (ITAA97 Subdiv 152-B: ¶7-165)
2. CGT 50% active asset reduction (ITAA97 Subdiv 152-C: ¶7-175)
3. CGT retirement exemption (ITAA97 Subdiv 152-D: ¶7-185)
4. CGT roll-over (ITAA97 Subdiv 152-E: ¶7-195).

Taxpayers that are not CGT small business entities may still qualify for the CGT small business concessions if they satisfy the maximum net asset value test of $6 million (¶7-130), the special requirements for passively held assets or the special requirements for partners in partnerships (¶7-120). While a partner in a partnership cannot (in that capacity) be a small business entity (ITAA97 s 328-110(6)), a partner in a CGT small business entity can still access concessions 1–4.

Other concessions available to small business entities and medium business entities

There are a range of concessions which are available for small business entities, and in some cases have or will be extended to be available to medium business entities, subject to satisfying any additional criteria (s 328-10(1)). The concessions and their availability for medium business entities are:

Concession	Date available to medium business entities
Special rules for prepaid expenses (ITAA36 ss 82KZM; 82KZMD: ¶16-045)	From 1 July 2020
Immediate deduction for start-up expenses (ITAA97 s 40-880(2A): ¶16-156)	From 1 July 2020
Simplified depreciation rules (ITAA97 Subdiv 328-D: ¶7-250)	Not applicable
Simplified trading stock rules (ITAA97 Subdiv 328-E: ¶7-260)	From 1 July 2021
Small business restructure roll-over (ITAA97 Subdiv 328-G: ¶12-380)	Not applicable
Annual apportionment of GST input tax credits for acquisitions and importations that are partly creditable (GSTA s 131-5: ¶34-270)	Not applicable
Accounting for GST on a cash basis (GSTA s 29-40: ¶34-130)	Not applicable
Paying GST by quarterly instalments (GSTA s 162-5: ¶34-150)	Not applicable
Simplified BAS (¶34-150)	Not applicable
A simplified accounting method for GST, if determined by the Commissioner (GSTA Div 123: ¶34-165)	From 1 July 2021
FBT car parking exemption (FBTAA s 58GA: ¶35-254)	From 1 April 2021
FBT exemption for more than one work-related portable electronic device provided to an employee a year (FBTAA s 58X(4)(b): ¶35-645)	From 1 April 2021

Concession	Date available to medium business entities
PAYG instalments based on GDP-adjusted notional tax (TAA Sch 1 s 45-130: ¶27-220)	From 1 July 2021
Standard 2-year period for amending tax assessments (ITAA97 s 328-10(2); ITAA36 s 170: ¶25-310)	Tax assessments for income years starting from 1 July 2021

An unincorporated small business tax offset is also available for a small business entity that satisfies a modified aggregated turnover test of $5 million (ITAA97 Subdiv 328-F: ¶7-210).

State and territory business grants related to recovery from COVID-19 and received in 2020–21 by a small business entity or a medium business entity are non-assessable, non-exempt income (ITAA97 s 59-97).

Companies that are base rate entities are also entitled to a concessional corporate income tax rate (see ¶3-055).

An entity that is winding up its former business and was an STS taxpayer in the income year in which it stopped carrying on that business will be able to access some of the above concessions as if it were a small business entity (ITTPA s 328-111).

ATO Guides and Tools

The ATO provides different guides and tools that are designed to assist a small business entity in applying the different rules and concessions correctly. The guides and tools are available on the ATO website at www.ato.gov.au. Two notable inclusions are:

(a) Small business benchmarks

The small business ‘‘benchmarks’’ (ie industry specific tools) provide a snapshot of what, on average, is happening in particular industries by providing a measure of various business costs in relation to turnover.

The ATO uses the benchmarks to identify businesses that may be avoiding their tax obligations by tracking performance against other businesses in the same industry. If a business is found to be falling outside the benchmarks for a particular industry, especially for a long term, it is more likely to attract ATO audit attention (*Carter*).

(b) Small business assist tool

The small business assist tool located at www.sba.ato.gov.au is designed to provide answers to questions relating to small business including questions regarding ABNs, GST obligations, lodging activity statements and employer obligations.

Small Business Entities

¶7-050 Small business entities, medium business entities & CGT small business entities

Meaning of small business entity, medium business entity & CGT small business entity

An entity is a ‘‘small business entity’’ if it:

- carries on a business, and
- satisfies the $10 million aggregated turnover test (s 328-110).

A ‘‘medium business entity’’, for an income year, is an entity that is not a small business entity for that year of income but would be small business entity if the $10 million aggregated turnover test replaced all references to $10 million with $50 million (s 328-285; ITAA36 ss 170(14); 82KZM(1A); FBTAA s 58GA(1A)).

A "CGT small business entity" is an entity that is a small business entity that also satisfies an aggregated turnover test of $2 million (s 152-10(1AA)).

No choice or election is needed to attain small business entity or CGT small business entity status.

Carrying on a business

TR 2019/1 contains the Commissioner's guidelines as to when an entity is carrying on a business for the purpose of determining whether it is a small business entity pursuant to s 328-110 (also see ¶10-105). For the purpose of the small business entity test, an entity is also taken to be carrying on a business if the entity is winding up a business that it formerly carried on and it was a small business entity for the income year in which it stopped carrying on that business (s 328-110(5)).

Satisfying the $10 million aggregated turnover test

There are 3 ways an entity can satisfy the $10 million aggregated turnover test, being:

- the entity's aggregated turnover for the previous income year was less than $10 million
- the entity's aggregated turnover for the current income year is likely to be less than $10 million, calculated as at the first day of the income year (or the first day the entity started to carry on the business, if later). This method is not available if the entity carried on business for the 2 income years before the current year and the entity's aggregated turnover for each of those income years was $10 million or more, or
- the entity's actual aggregated turnover for the current income year was less than $10 million calculated as at the end of the income year. As a practical matter, the concessions involving PAYG instalments, cash basis GST accounting, annual apportionment of GST input tax credits and GST quarterly instalments are not be available where an entity passes the test for this reason only — see the note following ITAA97 s 328-110(4).

The references to $10 million in the above tests are replaced with $50 million for determining whether an entity is a medium business entity for certain concessions (¶7-001).

Meaning of "aggregated turnover"

An entity's aggregated turnover (ITAA97 s 328-115) for an income year is the sum of:

- the entity's annual turnover for the income year
- the annual turnover of any entity that is connected with it at any time during the income year, and
- the annual turnover of any entity that is its affiliate at any time during the income year.

An entity that is an affiliate or connected entity mentioned above is referred to as a "relevant entity". In calculating the aggregated turnover the following amounts are excluded:

- amounts derived from dealings between the entity and a relevant entity, or between 2 or more relevant entities, at a time when the relevant connection or affiliation exists
- amounts derived by a relevant entity at a time when the relevant connection or affiliation does not exist (s 328-115(3)).

If the entity has no affiliates or connected entities at any time during the income year, its aggregated turnover for the income year will be the same as its annual turnover.

In determining whether the CGT small business concessions are available for a passively held CGT asset (¶7-120), the following special rules apply for calculating the aggregated turnover of the relevant business entity that is the affiliate of, or connected with, the asset owner:

- an individual's spouse or child under the age of 18 years is deemed to be the individual's affiliate where the relevant business entity is only treated as being an affiliate of, or an entity connected with, the asset owner for the CGT small business concessions because the individual's spouse or child is deemed to be that individual's affiliate pursuant to s 152-47(2) and (3)
- an entity that is an affiliate of, or connected entity with, the asset owner is treated as being an affiliate of, or connected entity with, the business entity (s 152-48(2)), and
- where the asset owner is a partner in 2 or more partnerships and the asset is used in, held ready for use in, or is inherently connected with a business carried on by at least 2 of those partnerships, each of those partnerships will be treated as being connected with the business entity (s 152-48(3)).

Meaning of "annual turnover"

An entity's annual turnover for an income year is the total ordinary income (¶10-000, ¶10-010) that the entity derives in the income year in the ordinary course of carrying on a business (ITAA97 s 328-120). The term "in the ordinary course of carrying on a business" bears its ordinary meaning (¶10-105) and can include transactions that were part of the ordinary and common flow of transactions of the business although not usually undertaken (*Doutch*). Income derived from dealings with associates (¶4-200) is to be worked out on an arm's length basis.

In working out an entity's annual turnover, the following amounts are excluded:

- GST (ie an amount that is non-assessable non-exempt income under ITAA97 s 17-5), and
- income derived from sales of retail fuel (as defined).

If an entity carries on a business for only *part of an income year*, its annual turnover is to be worked out using a reasonable estimate of what the entity's annual turnover would be if it carried on business for the whole income year (s 328-120(5)). This rule will apply to annualise the business income of a business that ceased during the year even where a different business was carried on by the same entity for the whole of that same income year (ID 2009/49).

Regulations may provide that an entity's annual turnover for an income year is to be calculated in a way that results in a lesser amount than the amount worked out under s 328-120.

Meaning of "connected with" an entity

An entity is *connected with* another entity if it controls the other entity or both entities are controlled by the same third party in a way described in ITAA97 s 328-125. The provision contains separate control tests for different entities.

Control of entity other than a discretionary trust: 40% ownership test

An entity controls another entity (other than a discretionary trust) where the first entity, its affiliates or the first entity together with its affiliates own or have the right to acquire ownership of interests in the other entity that between them give the right to receive at least 40% of any distribution of income, capital or (in the case of a partnership) net income by the other entity. For example, a partner that is receiving 40% or more of the net income of a partnership will be taken to control the partnership.

Neither the trustees nor the members of a complying superannuation fund are considered to control the fund for these purposes (TD 2006/68). Two unadministered deceased estates will not be connected with each other even where they have the same executor or beneficiaries (ID 2010/106).

Control of a company: 40% of voting rights test

An additional alternative test applies to determine whether an entity controls a company. If either the 40% ownership or 40% of voting rights test is satisfied, the entity controls the company. The 40% of voting rights test is satisfied if an entity, its affiliates or the entity together with its affiliates, between them own, or have the right to acquire ownership of, at least 40% of the voting power in the company.

Control of a discretionary trust

An entity controls a discretionary trust if *either*:

- for any of the 4 years before the current income year, at least 40% of the total amount of income or capital paid or applied by the trustee for that previous income year was paid to or for the benefit of the entity and/or its affiliates, or
- a trustee of the trust acts, or could reasonably be expected to act, in accordance with the directions or wishes of the entity, its affiliates or the entity together with its affiliates.

In applying the latter test, the sole director of the corporate trustee of a discretionary trust was held not to be a controller of the trust because: (i) no decisions were made unless they were in accordance with the wishes of sole director's father; and (ii) the appointor that had the power to remove the trustee only acted in accordance with the father's directions (*Gutteridge*). The ATO has advised that while in the particular circumstances a person could reasonably be expected to act in a certain way because they were ''accustomed to act'' in that way, this decision does not mean that the ''reasonable expectation test'' can be substituted with an accustomed to act test in all cases (*Decision Impact Statement* on *Gutteridge*).

The 40% distribution test does not apply to determine whether an exempt entity or deductible gift recipient controls a discretionary trust.

Special entities

For the purpose of applying the connected entity test, the provisions in Subdivs 106-B to 106-D (¶11-210) concerning absolutely entitled beneficiaries, bankrupt individuals, security providers and companies in liquidation apply.

Indirect control of any entity

If an entity controls another entity, and the second entity (directly or indirectly) controls a third entity, the first entity is taken to control the third entity (ITAA97 s 328-125(7)). However, this *does not* apply to:

- a company whose shares (other than shares carrying a right to a fixed dividend rate) are listed on an approved stock exchange
- a publicly traded unit trust
- a mutual insurance company
- a mutual affiliate company (ITAA36 s 121AC), or
- a 100% subsidiary company of any of the above entities.

Commissioner's discretion where control percentage below 50%

Where the control percentage is at least 40% but below 50%, the Commissioner may determine that an entity does not control the object entity if the Commissioner thinks that the other object is controlled by one or more entities that do not include the first entity or any of its affiliates (s 328-125(6)).

Deemed connected entities for passively held CGT assets

Special rules apply to treat certain entities as being connected with a business entity for the purpose of calculating the aggregated turnover of that business entity when applying the small business CGT concessions to passively held CGT assets (see "Meaning of 'aggregated turnover'" above).

Nominated controllers of certain discretionary trusts for CGT provisions

A trustee of a discretionary trust is able to make an election that nominates up to 4 beneficiaries as being controllers of the trust for an income year in which the trustee did not make a distribution of income or capital if the trust had a tax loss, or no net income, for that year. The nomination is required to be in writing and signed by the trustee and by each nominated beneficiary (s 152-78). This nomination only applies for the purpose of satisfying the basic conditions in Subdiv 152-A (¶7-120) and its related provisions being the definitions of small business entity (s 328-110), aggregated turnover (s 328-115) and connected with (s 328-125).

Meaning of "affiliate"

Only an individual or a company can be an affiliate. An individual or company will be an affiliate of another entity if the individual or company acts, or could reasonably be expected to act, in accordance with the entity's directions or wishes, or in concert with the entity, in relation to the affairs of the business of the individual or company (ITAA97 s 328-130). The test is applied in relation to the affairs of the business generally, not merely in relation to the CGT asset. A family member will not necessarily be an affiliate (*Case 2/2010*; *Altnot*).

However, an individual or company will not be an entity's affiliate merely because of the nature of the business relationship that they share. For example, a partner in a partnership would not be an affiliate of another partner merely because the first partner acts in accordance with the wishes of, or in concert with, the other partner in relation to the affairs of the partnership. Directors of the same company, trustees of the same trust, or a company and one of its directors would be in a similar position.

For the purpose of applying the CGT small business concessions to passively held CGT assets:

- an individual's spouse or child under the age of 18 years will be taken to be an affiliate of the individual for the purpose of determining whether a business entity is an affiliate of, or connected with, the asset owner (s 152-47(2))
- if an entity is an affiliate of, or connected with, another entity as a result of the above deeming rule, then that spouse or child is taken to be an affiliate of the individual for the purposes of the CGT small business concessions, and the determination of whether an entity is a small business entity (s 152-47(3))
- an entity that is an affiliate of, or connected with, the asset owner is treated as being an affiliate of, or connected with, the business entity for calculating the aggregated turnover (s 152-48(2)).

Continuing use of the STS accounting method

Small business entities that used the STS accounting method in 2006–07 may continue to use it on a transitional basis in subsequent years. However, an entity that ceases to use the STS accounting method, either by choice or because it is not a small business entity for an income year, will not be able to use it in any future year (ITTPA s 328-120). Adjustments will apply in the year that an entity ceases to use the STS accounting method (ITTPA s 328-115).

The STS accounting method and the former simplified tax system are detailed in the 2007 and earlier editions of the *Australian Master Tax Guide*.

[FITR ¶171-583, ¶313-071 – ¶313-076, ¶313-220 – ¶313-290]

CGT Small Business Concessions

¶7-110 CGT concessions for small business

There are 4 CGT small business concessions which can apply to CGT events as detailed in ITAA97 Div 152. These are:

(1) the small business 15-year exemption (¶7-165)

(2) the small business 50% reduction (¶7-175)

(3) the small business retirement exemption (¶7-185), and

(4) the small business roll-over (¶7-195).

In addition, there is a small business restructure roll-over which provides both CGT and income tax roll-over relief. The conditions for this roll-over are detailed in ¶12-380.

To qualify for the concessions in Div 152, taxpayers must satisfy a number of basic conditions (¶7-120). Further additional conditions also apply to some of the concessions.

A capital gain that qualifies for the 15-year exemption is disregarded entirely and is not taken into account in working out the taxpayer's net capital gain for the income year (¶11-030). For the other 3 concessions, taxpayers must first apply capital losses against the full capital gain and then any applicable discount percentage pursuant to Div 115 (¶11-033) before the balance of the capital gain can be reduced in accordance with the CGT small business concessions (s 102-5).

A CGT small business entity (¶7-050) can access the CGT small business concessions if it satisfies the relevant criteria. A taxpayer that is not a CGT small business entity can still qualify for CGT concessions if it satisfies either the maximum net asset value test of $6 million (¶7-130) or the requirements for passively held assets (¶7-120). A partner in a partnership that is a small business entity can also access the concessions if the relevant criteria are satisfied.

Preferential treatment for superannuation contribution purposes

Subject to a lifetime limit known as the CGT-cap, being $1,515,000 for 2019–20 or $1,565,000 for 2020–21 (indexed for inflation), certain amounts associated with the CGT small business concessions can be contributed to superannuation without being counted towards the individual's non-concessional contributions cap (¶13-780).

[FITR ¶171-500 – ¶171-950]

¶7-120 Basic conditions for CGT small business relief

The basic conditions that must be satisfied by a taxpayer to be eligible for CGT small business relief are:

(1) a CGT event happens in relation to an asset that the taxpayer owns

(2) the event would otherwise have resulted in a capital gain

(3) one or more of the following applies:

- the taxpayer satisfies the maximum net asset value test (¶7-130)
- the taxpayer is a ''CGT small business entity'' for the income year (¶7-050)
- the asset is an interest in an asset of a partnership which is a CGT small business entity for the income year, and the taxpayer is a partner in that partnership, or
- the special conditions for passively held assets in s 152-10(1A) or (1B) are satisfied in relation to the CGT asset in the income year (¶7-128)

(4) the asset satisfies the active asset test (¶7-145)

(5) if the CGT asset is a share in a company or an interest in a trust, the additional basic conditions for shares and trust interests (¶7-124), and

(6) if the CGT event involves certain rights or interests in relation to the income or capital of a partnership, an additional basic condition for partnership interests (¶7-126).

In the case of CGT event D1 (¶11-280), the first and fourth basic conditions are replaced with the condition that the right created by the taxpayer that triggers CGT event D1 must be inherently connected with a CGT asset of the taxpayer that satisfies the active asset test (s 152-12).

The CGT small business concessions do not apply to gains arising from CGT event K7 (¶11-350).

The basic conditions for the CGT small business concessions are not required to be satisfied to apply the small business retirement exemption to a capital gain from CGT event J5 or J6 (s 152-305(4); ¶11-340).

Extra conditions for specific concessions

In addition to the basic conditions detailed above, extra conditions must be satisfied in order to apply some of the CGT small business concessions (eg the 15-year exemption and the retirement exemption). There are also limitations on the availability of the concessions for CGT events J2, J5 and J6 (¶11-340).

[FITR ¶171-515]

¶7-124 Additional basic conditions for shares and trust interests under CGT small business relief

The additional basic conditions that apply for a CGT asset that is a share in a company or an interest in a trust (''object entity'') where the CGT event occurs on or after 8 February 2018 are:

(a) the relevant CGT asset must satisfy a modified active asset test (see below)

(b) if the taxpayer does not satisfy the maximum net asset test (¶7-130), the taxpayer must be carrying on a business (¶10-105) just before the CGT event

(c) the object entity must either be:

- a CGT small business entity for the income year, or
- satisfy the maximum net asset value test (¶7-130)

using a modified rule about when entities are ''connected with'' other entities, whereby (i) the only CGT assets or annual turnovers considered were those of the object entity, each affiliate of the object entity and each entity controlled by the object entity in the way described by s 328-125, (ii) each reference to 40% therein was 20%, and (iii) there was no determination under s 328-125(6) in force by which certain entities were treated as not controlling others, and

(d) just before the CGT event either:

- the taxpayer is a CGT concession stakeholder (¶7-156) in the object entity, or
- CGT concession stakeholders in the object entity have a small business participation percentage in the taxpayer of at least 90% (s 152-10(2)).

The modified active asset test for this purpose is the active asset test as prescribed in s 152-35 (¶7-145) subject to the assumption in s 152-10(2A), generally being:

- the financial instruments and cash must be inherently connected with the business and were not acquired for a purpose that included assisting an entity to satisfy this test, and
- all shares and units held by the object entity are excluded. Instead, a look-through approach will be taken with the underlying assets of the later company or trust.

¶7-126 Additional basic condition for certain partnership interests under CGT small business relief

Where the CGT event involves the creation, transfer, variation or cessation of a right or interest that entitles an entity to either:

- an amount of the income or capital of a partnership, or
- an amount calculated by reference to the partner's entitlement to an amount of income or capital of a partnership;

there is an additional basic condition that the right or interest must be a membership interest of the entity in the partnership (s 152-10(2C)). This ensures that the concessions are only available for CGT events involving a right or interest in a partnership if the right or interest would be sufficient to make the entity holding the right or interest a partner (eg the transfer of all or part of a partner's share in a partnership to another entity, making that other entity a partner or increasing their existing share in the partnership). This prevents the CGT small business concessions from being available to partners that alienate their income by creating, assigning or otherwise dealing in rights to the future income of a partnership, commonly known as Everett assignments.

¶7-128 Special conditions for passively held assets under CGT small business relief

Where a CGT event occurs in relation to a passively held CGT asset, the taxpayer will satisfy basic condition 3 of CGT small business relief (¶7-120) where it meets one of 2 alternative special conditions.

The first alternative condition requires all the following:

- an affiliate of, or an entity connected with, the taxpayer is a CGT small business entity for the income year
- the taxpayer does not carry on a business in the income year (other than in partnership)
- if the taxpayer carries on a business in a partnership — the CGT asset is not an interest in an asset of the partnership, and
- the CGT small business entity carries on the business, at a time during the income year, in relation to the CGT asset that results in the asset being an active asset (s 152-10(1A)).

The second alternative condition applies to partners in a partnership and requires all the following:

- the taxpayer is a partner in a partnership in the income year
- the partnership is a CGT small business entity for the income year
- the taxpayer does not carry on a business in the income year (other than in partnership)
- the CGT asset is not an interest in an asset of the partnership, and
- the business the taxpayer carries on as a partner in a partnership, at a time during the income year, is the business carried on in relation to the CGT asset that results in the asset being an active asset (s 152-10(1B)).

For applying the CGT concessions to such passively held assets and determining whether an entity is a CGT small business entity, special rules apply for determining entities that are affiliates of, or connected with, the taxpayer and for calculating the $2 million aggregated turnover (¶7-050).

¶7-130 Maximum net asset value (MNAV) requirements

A taxpayer satisfies the maximum net asset value (MNAV) test if, just before the time of the CGT event, the net value of the CGT assets of the taxpayer, its connected entities, its affiliates (¶7-050) and the entities connected with those affiliates does not exceed $6 million (s 152-15). The timing of the relevant CGT event is crucial for the determination of this test.

Particular care needs to be taken in determining the timing of the CGT event and therefore calculating the MNAV test, as it is not necessarily the time of signing the formal agreement. The AAT has held CGT event A1 occurred at the earlier time of execution of a Heads of Agreement (*Case 2/2013*) and on the countersigning of a letter of offer (*Scanlon & Anor*) as these documents were legally binding.

The MNAV test applies to the separate partners in a partnership rather than the partnership as a whole.

Measuring the net value of assets

The net value of the assets of an entity is the amount (whether positive, negative or nil) equal to the market value of those assets less the sum of:

- liabilities of the entity that are related to those assets, and
- provisions for annual leave, long service leave, unearned income and tax liabilities (s 152-20).

For the purpose of the test, the calculation includes the market value of both trading stock and depreciating assets even though any gains or losses from such assets are disregarded for CGT purposes.

In determining whether a foreign resident taxpayer satisfies the MNAV test, the worldwide CGT assets of the foreign resident are included (ID 2010/126).

The market value of an asset should be assessed on the basis of its "highest and best use" as recognised in the market (*Decision Impact Statement* on *Syttadel Holdings*). The arm's length selling price is generally considered to be the most relevant information for determining the market value unless there is a rational explanation for disregarding the sale price (*Excellar Pty Ltd*). The market value will be the price that is agreed between a willing but not anxious seller and a willing but not anxious buyer. A discount should not be applied to this value even if taxpayer is a minority shareholder (*Miley*). Further, the value of any restrictive covenants included in the sale is included in the value of the shares (*Miley*). See *Syttadel Holdings*.

The taxpayer bears the burden of proof in establishing that its valuation is correct or reasonable. It is not sufficient to merely disprove the Commissioner's valuation (*M & T Properties*). The ATO has warned that taxpayers that undertake their own valuations, or use valuations from people without adequate qualification, risk incorrectly reporting their tax and incurring a liability pay administrative penalties. A taxpayer that uses a qualified valuer will not generally be liable to a penalty if the valuer was provided with accurate information if the valuation ultimately proves to be deficient.

In *Breakwell*, the Federal Court held that a pre-1988 loan asset was included in the net asset calculation of a trust because the debt in South Australia would not be absolutely statute barred even if s 35(a) of the *Limitation of Actions Act 1936* (SA) applied it only bars the remedy not the cause and the limitation period could be extended. This provision is particular to South Australia, effectively providing no limitation period for debts therein. The AAT decision in *Breakwell* that the debt was not statute barred because it had been acknowledged in writing and was refreshed as a result of the debtor signing the annual financial accounts of the trust as agent for the trust was not considered.

''Liabilities'' include legally enforceable debts due for payment and presently existing legal or equitable obligations to pay either a sum certain or ascertainable sums, but does not extend to future obligations, expectancies or liabilities that are uncertain as both a theoretical and a practical matter (TD 2007/14). For example, legal fees for work done up to the date of the CGT event (but not after) are included in liabilities even where the fees are not invoiced by that time (*Byrne Hotels Qld*). For the purpose of the calculation, the GST-inclusive expenses are counted (*Excellar Pty Ltd*).

''Contingent liabilities'' are relevant for the net asset calculation where the liability is a presently existing legal or equitable obligation and the only contingency is enforcement. Where a capital gain arises from the sale of a CGT asset, any liabilities connected to the sale which only crystallise as a part of completion are taken into account in determining the net value of the CGT assets held by the taxpayer. However, a mortgage liability was not taken into account in determining the net value test where it was not in place at the time of the CGT event, even though the sale the subject of the CGT event was made dependent upon the mortgage being granted (*Phillips*). A guarantee is excluded from being a liability for the calculation where it does not relate to the guarantor's CGT assets (*Excellar Pty Ltd*). Only the value of a hire purchase debt at the time of sale can be taken into account, not all of the payments due over the life of the agreement (*Bell*).

In *Scanlon*, the AAT held an ETP to be paid to the owners of a company was not considered to be a liability taken into account due to it having the hallmarks of being a gratuitous payment and not being enforceable in law or equity against the company. Further, even if the ETP was considered a liability it was not in place immediately before the time of the CGT event. It was further considered, that even if the liability was enforceable, the ETP would be an asset of the taxpayers that could not be excluded from the test as being used solely for the personal use and enjoyment of the taxpayers.

The requirement for a liability to be related to an asset requires more than just a remote or tenuous relationship (*Tingari Village North*). In *Bell*, the Full Federal Court held that a loan taken out by a family trust to give effect to the trust's capital distribution resolution was not ''related'' to any asset of the trust and could not be taken into account for the MNAV test. In *Case 2/2015*, borrowings to fund a capital distribution by a trust were ''related to'' the CGT assets of the trust as there was no evidence the cash that represented the borrowings had been disposed of.

An individual's loan account used to purchase a main residence cannot be used to reduce the balance of the offset bank account as they were 2 separate accounts and the loan account related to the excluded main residence asset, rather than the offset account (*Bell*).

Exclusion of certain assets from test

In working out the net value of CGT assets of an entity, any shares, units or other interests (except debt) in another entity that is connected with the first entity (or with an affiliate of the first entity) are disregarded. However, any liabilities relating to such interests are included (s 152-20(2)(a)).

If the entity is an individual, the following assets are also disregarded:

- assets being used solely for the personal use and enjoyment of the individual or the individual's affiliate
- the ownership interest in the individual's main residence (including any relevant adjacent land), except where the dwelling is used to produce assessable income in which case the dwelling is only included to the extent that had interest been incurred on money borrowed to acquire the dwelling a tax deduction could have been claimed for that interest
- a right to any allowance, annuity or capital amount payable out of a superannuation fund or ADF
- a right to any asset of a superannuation fund or ADF, and
- a life insurance policy (s 152-20(2), (2A)).

In determining whether an asset is used solely for the personal use and enjoyment of an individual the use of the asset over the whole ownership period is considered, not just its use immediately before the CGT event occurs (ID 2011/37). Whether a holiday house was "being used" solely for personal use and enjoyment depends on a conglomerate of matters including the pattern of use of the owners, the amount of time it was used as a holiday house, and how the owners viewed it. Where a house is merely available for personal use, it is not sufficient to be considered to be used solely for personal use and enjoyment (*Altnot*). The use of a holiday house by non-affiliate family members or friends rent free will not of itself prevent the house from being considered to be used solely for the personal use and enjoyment of the taxpayer (ID 2011/39; ID 2011/40). However, if rent is received for its use the house will be prevented from being an asset used solely for the personal use and enjoyment of the taxpayer (ID 2011/41).

For the purpose of the calculation an individual's interest earning personal bank account (ID 2009/33) and vacant land on which a dwelling for personal use is intended to be constructed (ID 2009/34) are not assets used solely for personal use and enjoyment and therefore are not disregarded. Debts owing from related businesses are CGT assets and are included in the MNAV calculation (*Cannavo*).

In working out the net value of the assets of an affiliate (or an entity connected with such an affiliate), only include the assets of that entity that are used or held ready for use in carrying on a business by the taxpayer (or an entity connected with the taxpayer) (s 152-20(3)). However, disregard any assets used, or held ready for use, in the carrying on of a business by an entity that is connected with the taxpayer only because of the taxpayer's affiliate (s 152-20(4)). In *White*, the Federal Court applied a "but for" test in determining whether to exclude the assets of a connected entity. It held that s 152-20(3) and (4) applied to exclude the net assets of a connected entity in calculating the MNAV test where the company was only a connected entity due to shares held by the taxpayer's affiliate. Therefore, the assets of the connected company were excluded because it would not have been a connected entity "but for" the taxpayer's affiliate.

Where a beneficiary that is a connected entity of a trust has an unpaid present entitlement ("UPE") to receive income or capital from that trust, the UPE will only be included once for determining whether or not the trust satisfies the MNAV test (TR

2015/4). The way in which the value of that UPE is included varies depending on the character of the beneficiary's entitlement and the way that funds representing the UPE are held.

[FITR ¶171-520 – ¶171-535]

¶7-145 Active assets

Active asset test

A CGT asset satisfies the active asset test if the asset was an active asset of the taxpayer:

- for a total of at least half of the period from when the asset is acquired until the CGT event, or
- if the asset is owned for more than 15 years, for a total of at least seven and a half years during that period (s 152-35).

If the business ceased to be carried on in the last 12 months (or any longer period that the Commissioner allows), the period is from the acquisition date until the date the business ceases.

The date of acquisition of a CGT asset is generally the date the contract to acquire the asset is entered into (s 109-5; ¶11-440).

What is an active asset?

Generally, a CGT asset is an active asset if:

(a) the taxpayer owns the asset (whether it is tangible or intangible) and it is used, or held ready for use in the course of carrying on a business that is carried on (whether alone or in partnership) by the taxpayer, the taxpayer's affiliate or another entity that is connected with the taxpayer, or

(b) if the asset is an intangible asset — the taxpayer owns it and it is inherently connected with a business that is carried on (whether alone or in partnership) by the taxpayer, the taxpayer's affiliate or another entity that is connected with the taxpayer (s 152-40(1)).

An asset can be an active asset if it was used at some point in the course of the carrying on of an identified business. There is no requirement for the asset to be used in the course of carrying on the activities of a business that are "directed to the gaining or production of assessable income". The test does not require the use of the relevant asset to take place within the day-to-day or normal course of the carrying on of a business or a relationship of direct functional relevance between the use of an asset and the carrying on of a business (*Eichmann*). In determining if land is an active asset it is necessary to determine whether as a whole it can be considered to be used in carrying on a business. Where only a small portion of land was used in carrying on a business the land was held not to be an active asset (*Rus*). An intangible asset, such as goodwill or the benefit of a restrictive covenant, will be an active asset if it satisfies either (a) or (b).

Where a passively held CGT asset was previously used in carrying on a business by an entity that is being wound up in an income year and that asset was an active asset at a time in the income year in which the business stopped being carried on, for the purpose of determining whether the asset is an active asset under the special basic conditions (¶7-120) the following applies:

- the entity is taken to carry on the business at a time in the CGT event year, and
- either: (i) the CGT asset is taken to be used, or held ready for use, in the course of carrying on the business at that time; or (ii) if the asset is an intangible asset — the CGT asset is taken to be inherently connected with the business at that time (s 152-49).

This ensures the CGT concessions can be available for a passively held CGT asset where the CGT event happens after the business in which the asset was used has ceased.

80% test

A share in a resident company is an active asset at a given time if the taxpayer owns it and, at that time, at least 80% of the company's assets are active. The total of the following assets counts towards the 80% test:

- the market value of the company's active assets
- the market value of any of the company's financial instruments that are inherently connected with a business the company carries on, and
- any cash of the company that is inherently connected with such a business.

▶ Example

If a taxpayer holds shares in a resident company for 10 years, the company would have to satisfy the 80% test for at least 5 years during the taxpayer's period of ownership to satisfy the active asset test.

Similar rules apply to an interest in a resident trust.

A share in a company or an interest in a trust can qualify as an active asset if the company or trust owns interests in another entity that satisfies the 80% test. The "80% test" operates successively at each level in a chain of entities to determine the active asset status of the underlying interests (TD 2006/65).

The 80% test does not need to be applied on a continuous basis where it is reasonable to conclude that the test has been passed. Similarly, a share or trust interest will still be active where failure of the test is only temporary.

Where a CGT event occurs on or after 8 February 2018 and involves a share in a company or an interest in a trust, an additional modified active asset test applies for the purpose of satisfying the basic conditions (¶7-124).

Excluded assets

The following assets cannot be active assets:

- interests in a connected entity (other than those satisfying the 80% test)
- shares in companies and interests in trusts (other than those satisfying the 80% test)
- shares in widely held companies unless they are held by a CGT concession stakeholder of the company
- shares in trusts that are similar to widely held companies unless they are held by a CGT concession stakeholder of the trust or other exceptions for trusts with 20 members or less apply
- financial instruments, eg loans, debentures, bonds, promissory notes, futures contracts, forward contracts, currency swap contracts, rights and options
- an asset whose main use by the taxpayer is to derive interest, an annuity, rent, royalties or foreign exchange gains. However, such an asset can still be an active asset if it is an intangible asset that has been substantially developed, altered or improved by the taxpayer so that its market value has been substantially enhanced or its main use for deriving rent was only temporary. Even if a company is

considered to be carrying on business in the general sense as prescribed by TR 2019/1 (¶7-050) it cannot access the CGT small business concessions if its only activity is renting out an investment property (*Draft* TD 2019/D4; *Jakjoy Pty Ltd*).

▶ Example

If a company uses a house as a guesthouse, the house would be an active asset because the company would be using it to carry on a business and not to derive rent. On the other hand, if a company uses a house purely as an investment property and rents it out, the house would not be an active asset because its main (or sole) use would be to derive rent.

A key factor in determining whether the income from premises constitutes rent is whether the occupier has a right to exclusive possession and quiet enjoyment (*Tingari Village*; TD 2006/78). Where payments are rent, the premises will not constitute an active asset. However, if the arrangement allows the person only to enter and use the premises for certain purposes, the payments are unlikely to be rent. The circumstances in which premises used in a business of providing accommodation for reward will satisfy the active asset test are discussed in TD 2006/78.

An asset leased by a taxpayer to a connected entity or an affiliate for use in that entity's business is an active asset unless the use by the connected entity or affiliate is excluded, eg an asset whose main use is to derive rent (ss 152-40(4)(e); 152-40(4A); TD 2006/63).

[FITR ¶171-540 – ¶171-554]

¶7-155 Significant individual test

An entity satisfies the significant individual test if the entity had at least one significant individual just before the relevant CGT event (s 152-50). The significant individual test is relevant to the small business retirement exemption (¶7-185).

To be a significant individual of a company or trust, the individual must have a *small business participation percentage* in the company or trust of at least 20% (s 152-55; ¶7-157). The small business participation percentage is made up of direct and indirect percentages (ss 152-65 to 152-75). This means that the significant individual test can be satisfied either directly or indirectly through one or more interposed entities. All classes of shares (other than redeemable shares) are taken into account in determining if the company has a controlling individual (TD 2006/77).

Whether a taxpayer is a significant individual is also relevant for the small business 15-year exemption (¶7-165) and determining whether an individual is a CGT concession stakeholder (¶7-156).

[FITR ¶171-555 – ¶171-580]

¶7-156 CGT concession stakeholder

A CGT concession stakeholder of a company or trust is:

- a significant individual in the company or trust (¶7-155), or
- the spouse of a significant individual who has a small business participation percentage in the company or trust that is greater than zero (s 152-60).

The determination of whether an individual is a CGT concession stakeholder is relevant to the small business 15-year exemption (¶7-165) and the basic conditions for the CGT small business concessions for a CGT asset that is a share in a company or an interest in a trust (¶7-124).

[FITR ¶171-565]

¶7-157 Small business participation percentage

An entity's small business participation percentage in another entity at a time is the percentage that is the sum of the entity's direct small business participation percentage (¶7-158) and indirect small business participation percentage (¶7-159) in the other entity at that time (s 152-65).

[FITR ¶171-570]

¶7-158 Direct small business participation percentage

The determination of an entity's direct small business participation percentage in another entity depends upon the structure of the other entity.

Company

An entity's direct small business participation percentage in a company at a particular time is the following percentage that the entity has because of holding the legal and equitable interests in shares in the company:

(a) the percentage of the voting power in the company

(b) the percentage of any dividend that the company may pay

(c) the percentage of any distribution of capital that the company may make

or, if they are different, the smaller or smallest (s 152-70(1), item 1).

For the purpose of determining the percentage, any redeemable preference shares are ignored (s 152-70(2)).

Where shares are held jointly only the tests in (b) and (c) apply to enable such shareholders to have a non-zero direct small business participation percentage (s 152-70(3)).

In *Devuba Pty Ltd* it was held that the presence of a dividend access share did not diminish the dividend entitlements of the ordinary shareholders in considering "the percentage of any dividend that the company may pay". At the relevant time for determining the direct small business participation percentage in the company, the holder of the dividend access share did not carry any entitlement to a dividend as the Constitution had removed the discretionary right of the directors to declare dividends on the share until such time as the directors had first resolved that such holders were again entitled to the future exercise of a discretion to pay a dividend.

Fixed trust

A trust is a fixed trust where entities have entitlements to all the income and capital of the trust. The trustee having a power to accumulate some or all of the income of the trust for an income year does not itself prevent the beneficiaries from having entitlements to all the income and capital of the trust or the trust being a fixed trust (ID 2015/8).

An entity's direct small business participation percentage in a fixed trust at a particular time is the following percentage:

(a) the percentage of any distribution of income that the trustee may make to which the entity would be beneficially entitled

(b) the percentage of any distribution of capital that the trustee may make to which the entity would be beneficially entitled,

or, if they are different, the smaller or smallest (s 152-70(1), item 2).

Non-fixed trust

A trust is a non-fixed trust where entities do not have entitlements to all the income and capital of the trust. A trust will be a non-fixed trust where the trustee has the discretion to appoint or distribute income or capital to one or more of a class of beneficiaries (ID 2015/8).

An entity's direct small business participation percentage in a non-fixed trust (eg a discretionary trust) at a particular time is the following percentage:

(a) if the trustee makes distributions of income during the income year (the ''current year'') in which that time occurs — the percentage of the distributions to which the entity was beneficially entitled, or

(b) if the trustee makes distributions of capital during the current year — the percentage of the distributions to which the entity was beneficially entitled

or, if 2 different percentages are applicable, the smaller (s 152-70(1), item 3).

However, where a trust does not make an income or capital distribution during the income year of the CGT event and the trust has either no net income or a tax loss for that year, an entity's direct small business participation percentage in the trust is worked out based on the distributions the entity was beneficially entitled to in the last prior income year the trustee made a distribution (s 152-70(4), (5)). The entity's direct small business participation percentage in a trust will still be zero where no income or capital distribution is made during the income year of the CGT event if the trust either (s 152-70(6)):

- had net income for the income year and did not have a tax loss for that income year, or
- had never made an income or capital distribution in an earlier income year.

[FITR ¶171-575]

¶7-159 Indirect small business participation percentage

The indirect small business participation percentage that an entity (the ''holding entity'') holds at a particular time in another entity (the ''test entity'') is determined by multiplying the holding entity's direct small business participation percentage (if any) in another entity (the ''intermediate entity'') at that time by the sum of:

- the intermediate entity's direct small business participation percentage (if any) in the test entity at that time
- the intermediate entity's indirect small business participation percentage (if any) in the test entity at that time (as worked out under one or more other applications of this test) (s 152-75(1)).

This test applies to any number of intermediaries through a chain of entities. For the purpose of testing an intermediate entity's indirect small business participation percentage in another entity, the intermediate entity then becomes the holding entity.

Where there is a chain of entities, the ultimate holding entity's indirect small business participation percentage is the sum of the percentages worked out under the test in relation to each of the intermediate entities (s 152-75(2)).

[FITR ¶171-580]

¶7-160 Application of CGT concessions to deceased estates

The legal personal representative, the beneficiary of a deceased estate, a surviving joint tenant or the trustee or beneficiary of a testamentary trust can access the concessions to the extent that the deceased would have been able to access them just before he or she died (s 152-80). This only applies if the CGT event happens to the asset within 2 years (or such extended period as the Commissioner allows) of the death of the individual.

In determining whether the deceased would have been entitled to the concessions the following special rules apply:

- for the purpose of the 15-year exemption — where the deceased was not permanently incapacitated immediately prior to death, the deceased is only required to have been 55 or over (ie the CGT event is not required to happen in connection with retirement)
- for the purpose of the retirement exemption — there is no need for the CGT exempt amount to be contributed to a complying superannuation fund or an RSA (s 152-80(2)).

[FITR ¶171-585]

¶7-165 CGT 15-year exemption

A taxpayer may disregard a capital gain arising from a CGT event if the CGT asset was owned by the taxpayer for at least 15 years and satisfies the required additional conditions (ss 152-105; 152-110). Certain payments made by a trust or company to its CGT concession stakeholders that are attributable to the exempt amount are also exempt (s 152-125).

The 15-year exemption applies in the following circumstances.

- The basic conditions for CGT small business relief are satisfied (¶7-120).
- The taxpayer continuously owned the asset for the 15-year period leading up to the CGT event. The 15-year period is not broken if there is a roll-over because of a marriage or relationship breakdown, a compulsory acquisition or a small business restructure (s 152-115).
- If the taxpayer is an individual, at the time of the CGT event the individual is either: (a) over 55 and the event happened in connection with the individual's retirement; or (b) permanently incapacitated (see example below). Further, if the CGT asset is a share in a company or an interest in a trust, the company or trust had a significant individual for periods totalling at least 15 years during which the individual owned the CGT asset. There is no requirement for the same person to be a significant individual over the 15 years (s 152-105).
- If the taxpayer is a company or trust, the taxpayer has a significant individual for periods totalling at least 15 years during which the entity owned the CGT asset (even if it was not always the same significant individual during the 15 years). The individual who was the significant individual just before the CGT event must be either: (a) over 55 at the time of the CGT event and the event happened in connection with their retirement; or (b) permanently incapacitated at that time (s 152-110).

The term permanent incapacity is not defined in ITAA97 but based on the definition in retirement and superannuation law, an indicative description is ill health (whether physical or mental), where it is reasonable to consider that the person is unlikely, because of ill health, to engage again in gainful employment for which the person is reasonably qualified by education, training or experience. The incapacity does not necessarily need to be permanent in the sense of everlasting.

▶ Example

Johnny had been carrying on an accounting business continuously for 16 years when he was diagnosed with early on-set Alzheimer's disease. The condition deteriorated to the extent he was no longer able to effectively carry on the business and therefore he sold the business. At the time of the sale he was 51 years old and he obtained from his doctor a written statement that his condition meant he was unlikely to be able to engage in gainful employment again.

Johnny would be considered to be permanent incapacitated at the time the business was sold and, subject to satisfying the other conditions, the small business 15-year exemption will be available even though he is under age 55 at the time of the CGT event.

▶ Planning point

If a CGT asset has been held for close to 15 years, there may be benefits in delaying the sale of goodwill or other business CGT assets until they have been held for 15 years to obtain the benefit of the 15-year exemption.

If a capital gain of a company or trust qualifies for the 15-year exemption, any payment of the exempt amount (whether directly or indirectly through one or more interposed entities) to a CGT concession stakeholder (¶7-156) will be exempt if it is made before the later of:

- 2 years after the CGT event, or
- if the relevant CGT event occurred because of the disposal of a CGT asset — 6 months after the latest time a possible financial benefit becomes or could become due under a look-through earnout right relating to that CGT asset and the disposal (s 152-125(1)).

However, the exemption in this case is limited to the percentage interest that the CGT concession stakeholder has in the company or trust. In the case of a discretionary trust, a CGT concession stakeholder's participation percentage is 100% divided by the number of such stakeholders in the trust (ie 100% if there is only one CGT concession stakeholder, 50% each if there are 2 CGT concession stakeholders etc) (s 152-125(2)).

Where a CGT asset was acquired prior to 20 September 1985 but is treated as a post-CGT asset because of a change in the majority underlying ownership (¶12-870), the 15-year exemption will apply such that the period of ownership will start from the time of actual acquisition, not the time the asset is deemed to have been acquired under s 149-30 (s 152-110(1A)). Similarly, any change in majority underlying interest in an asset is ignored for testing whether the entity had a significant individual for at least 15 years.

In calculating the CGT exempt amount the capital gain is calculated using the original cost base of the asset, not the deemed cost base of the asset at the time of the change in majority underlying interest (s 152-125(1)(a)(iv)). This ensures the full capital gain on the asset is exempt and is able to be distributed to CGT concession stakeholders tax-free.

[FITR ¶171-610 – ¶171-640]

¶7-175 CGT 50% reduction

A capital gain that arises from a CGT event happening to an active asset may be reduced by 50% (s 152-205). To qualify for the 50% reduction, the basic conditions for small business relief must be satisfied (¶7-120).

If the capital gain has already been reduced by 50% under the general discount (¶11-033), the 50% reduction applies to that reduced gain, so that only 25% of the original capital gain remains taxable. The capital gain may be further reduced by the small business retirement exemption (¶7-185), the small business roll-over (¶7-195), or both, in the order that the taxpayer chooses (s 152-210). None of these rules apply if the 15-year asset exemption (¶7-165) applies to the capital gain, because the full capital gain would have been disregarded (s 152-215).

A taxpayer may choose not to apply the 50% reduction.

▶ Planning point

Choosing not to apply the 50% reduction may be beneficial in circumstances where a company or trust could make larger tax-free payments for its CGT concession stakeholders utilising the small business retirement exemption. It may also allow an individual taxpayer to make payments into superannuation beyond the normal non-concessional contributions cap.

The automatic application of the 50% active asset exemption does not constitute the making of a choice for the CGT small business concessions by the taxpayer. Therefore, it would not prevent the taxpayer from applying the retirement exemption to the whole of the gain where the Commissioner allows further time to make that choice.

[FITR ¶171-710 – ¶171-735]

¶7-185 CGT retirement exemption

A taxpayer can choose to disregard a capital gain from a CGT event happening to an asset of a small business if the capital proceeds from the event are used in connection with retirement. There is a lifetime limit of $500,000 in respect of any one individual. The small business 50% reduction applies before the small business retirement exemption unless the taxpayer chooses not to apply the 50% reduction (¶7-175). The CGT retirement exemption may be utilised before or after the small business roll-over (¶7-195).

Individuals

The CGT retirement exemption is available to an individual if the basic conditions for small business relief are satisfied (¶7-120) and if the individual is under 55 just before making the choice, the individual contributes an amount equal to the asset's CGT exempt amount to a complying superannuation fund or RSA (s 152-305(1)). It is the taxpayer's age at the time of making the choice (ie lodging the relevant tax return) which is relevant for these purposes, not their age at the time of the CGT event. The contribution may be satisfied by transferring real property instead of money to the complying superannuation fund or RSA (ID 2010/217). Where the capital proceeds from a CGT event are received by an individual in instalments (including financial benefits received under a look-through earnout right (¶11-675)) the contributions are required to be made into a complying superannuation fund or RSA by the later of the time of the choice and the receipt of the instalment (up to the CGT exempt amount) (s 152-305(1B)).

▶ Planning point

Where a taxpayer is aged either 53 or 54 years old at the time of lodgment of the tax return for the CGT event and does not want to contribute an amount into superannuation, the taxpayer may utilise the small business roll-over to delay the taxation on the capital gain for 2 years and then apply the CGT retirement exemption at the end of that period when aged 55. This prevents the CGT exempt amount from being required to be contributed into a superannuation fund.

Where the gain arises from CGT event J5 or J6 (ie failure to acquire a replacement asset or to incur sufficient expenditure thereon) the taxpayer does not need to satisfy the basic conditions to apply the CGT retirement exemption (s 152-305(4)).

Companies and trusts

The CGT retirement exemption is available to companies and trusts if the basic conditions are satisfied (¶7-120), the entity satisfies the significant individual test (¶7-155) and the ‘‘company or trust’’ conditions are satisfied (ss 152-305(2); 152-325).

The ‘‘company or trust’’ conditions require the entity to make payments of the CGT exempt amount to at least one of its CGT concession stakeholders upon: (a) making the choice to apply the exemption if the relevant event is CGT event J2, J5 or J6; or (b) in any other case, the entity receiving an amount of capital proceeds from a CGT event for which it chooses to disregard a capital gain under the CGT retirement exemption (s 152-325(1)). If the company or trust receives the capital proceeds in instalments (including financial benefits received under a look-through earnout right (¶11-675)), payments must be made from each instalment in succession up to the CGT exempt amount.

The payment or payments must meet the requirements of s 152-325, which are:

(1) Where the payment is made to more than one CGT concession stakeholder the amount of each payment is worked out by reference to the individual's percentage entitlement to the relevant CGT exempt amount.

(2) The percentage entitlement for each CGT concession stakeholder is the amount specified in the written choice to apply the exemption. The percentage can range from nil to 100%, but the total of the percentages must add up to 100%.

(3) If the CGT concession stakeholder is an employee of the entity, the payment must not be of a kind mentioned in s 82-135, which specifies certain types of payments that are not employment termination payments, including a payment that is deemed to be a dividend.

(4) The payment must be made by the later of 7 days after (a) the choice to apply the retirement exemption is made or (b) the entity receives the capital proceeds. However, if CGT event J2, J5 or J6 applies the payment must be made within 7 days of the choice to apply the retirement exemption.

(5) The amount of the payment, or sum of the amounts of the payments, must be equal to the lesser of the capital proceeds received and the relevant CGT exempt amount.

(6) If a CGT concession stakeholder is under the age of 55 just before receiving the payment, the payment must be made into a complying superannuation fund on behalf of the CGT concession stakeholder. The payment may be made by way of the transfer of property instead of money to the complying superannuation fund (ID 2010/217). The CGT concession stakeholder is not able to claim a deduction for the contribution (s 290-150(4)(a)).

Payments may be made indirectly through one or more interposed entities (s 152-325(1)).

The CGT retirement exemption will only apply where the company or the trustee of the trust chooses to apply the exemption. The CGT concession stakeholders of the company or trust are not able to make the choice (*Davies & Anor*).

A payment that satisfies the company or trust conditions is excluded from being a dividend or frankable distribution, including for the purpose of the deemed dividend provisions in ITAA36 Div 7A (¶4-200) and s 109 (¶4-220) (s 152-325(9) to (11)).

Consequences of CGT retirement exemption

If the individual, company or trust claims the CGT retirement exemption, the part of the capital gain equal to its CGT exempt amount is disregarded (s 152-310).

Any payment that the company or trust makes to comply with the above "company or trust" conditions cannot be deducted from the company's or trust's assessable income and constitutes non-assessable, non-exempt income of the CGT concession stakeholder to whom it is made (s 152-310(2)(a)). The classification as non-assessable, non-exempt income prevents CGT event E4 from applying to a payment received from a trust (¶11-290) or CGT event G1 from applying to a payment received from a company (¶11-310).

Choosing the CGT exempt amount

The CGT exempt amount is all or part of the capital gain chosen by the taxpayer. Where the taxpayer is an individual the amount chosen cannot exceed the taxpayer's CGT retirement exemption. Where the taxpayer is a company or trust, the amount chosen cannot exceed the CGT retirement exemption limit of each individual for whom the choice is made (s 152-315). The CGT retirement exemption limit is a lifetime limit of $500,000 and is reduced by any previous amounts disregarded under the small business retirement exemption. If an individual is one of at least 2 CGT concession stakeholders of a company or trust, and the company or trust made a choice for the individual, only the individual's percentage of the asset's CGT exempt amount counts towards that individual's CGT retirement exemption limit (s 152-320).

The CGT exempt amount must be specified in writing in the choice to apply the retirement exemption (s 152-315(4)). The way in which the tax return is prepared is not sufficient evidence of the choice. If a company or trust is making the choice and it has more than one CGT concession stakeholder, it must specify in writing the percentage of each CGT asset's CGT exempt amount that is attributable to each of those stakeholders (s 152-315(5)). One of the percentages may be nil, but they must add up to 100%. The choice must be made by the date of lodgment of the tax return for the income year in which the CGT event occurs, or such further time as the Commissioner allows (s 103-25). If an eligible individual taxpayer dies before lodgment, the executor can make the choice when lodging the deceased's tax return (ID 2012/39).

▶ Example

Daryl is a significant individual in a company. The company specifies 90% for Daryl. This means that the percentage specified for the other stakeholder must be 10%. Daryl's retirement exemption limit is $500,000. To work out whether the limit is exceeded, Daryl would take 90% of the asset's CGT exempt amount, add that to CGT exempt amounts previously claimed in relation to him and see whether the total exceeds $500,000. If the $500,000 limit would be exceeded, the company should consider reducing the percentage attributable to Daryl so as to achieve an overall better result.

[FITR ¶171-815 – ¶171-850]

¶7-195 CGT roll-over

The small business roll-over allows a taxpayer to choose to defer the making of a capital gain from a CGT event happening in relation to one or more active assets if the basic conditions for small business relief are satisfied (s 152-410; ¶7-120). The 50% active asset concession applies before the roll-over (¶7-175). The roll-over may be utilised before or after the CGT retirement exemption (¶7-185). This roll-over is distinguished from the CGT small business restructure roll-over available for small business entities (¶12-380).

There is no specific requirement to acquire a replacement asset or incur improvement expenditure in order to obtain the roll-over. However, the following CGT events need to be considered (¶11-340):

- CGT event J5 happens if, by the end of the replacement asset period, the taxpayer does not acquire a replacement asset or incur the improvement expenditure
- CGT event J6 happens if, by the end of the replacement asset period, the cost of the replacement asset or the amount of improvement expenditure incurred (or both) is less than the amount of the capital gain the taxpayer disregarded
- CGT event J2 happens if the taxpayer has acquired a replacement asset or incurred improvement expenditure but there is a change in relation to the replacement asset after the end of the replacement asset period.

Unless modified or extended (s 104-190), the "replacement asset period" starts one year before and ends 2 years after the last CGT event in the income year for which the taxpayer obtains the roll-over (s 104-185). However, where a CGT event involves a look-through earnout right, the end of the replacement asset period is extended to be 6 months after the expiration of the right (s 104-190(1A); ¶11-675).

A taxpayer that chooses the roll-over can disregard all or part of the gain (s 152-415).

▶ Planning point

A taxpayer can utilise the small business roll-over to delay taxation on the whole or a part of an eligible capital gain for 2 years. This can be particularly beneficial where the taxpayer is expected to be on a lower marginal tax rate in 2 years.

Special rules ensure that a CGT event is not triggered only because the holder of a replacement asset dies (s 152-420).

Where the taxpayer satisfies the conditions for applying both a replacement-asset roll-over pursuant to Subdiv 124-B and the small business roll-over pursuant to Subdiv 152-E, the taxpayer may choose which roll-over to apply (ID 2009/147).

[FITR ¶171-920 – ¶171-955]

Income Tax Concessions

¶7-210 Small business income tax offset

Individuals that receive business income from a small business entity other than via a company, are entitled to a discount on the income tax payable pursuant to the "small business income tax offset" (Subdiv 328-F). For the purpose of this offset, the definition of a "small business entity" (¶7-050) is modified to apply a reduced aggregated turnover threshold of $5 million (s 328-357).

The discount on the income tax payable up to a $1,000 cap per individual per year is as follows:

Income year	Discount rate
2019–20	8%
2020–21	13%
2021–22	16%

An individual is entitled to the small business tax offset for an income year where either:

- the individual is a small business tax entity for the income year, or
- has assessable income for the income year that includes a share of the net income of a small business entity that is not a corporate tax entity (s 328-355).

The offset applies to the income tax payable on:

- the taxable income derived by a sole trader from his/her small business
- the business income derived by an individual partner of a partnership that is a small business entity
- the business income received as an individual beneficiary of a trust that is a small business entity.

The amount of the offset for 2020–21 is equal to 13% of the following (s 328-360):

$$\frac{\text{The individual's total net small business income for the income year}}{\text{The individual's taxable income for the income year}} \times \text{The individual's basic income tax liability for the income year}$$

For these purposes, the individual's total net small business income for the income year means so much of the sum of the following that does not exceed the individual's taxable income for the income year:

- where the individual is a small business entity — the individual's net small business income for the income year, and
- the individual's share of a small business entity's net small business income for the income year that is included in assessable income (excluding that of a corporate tax entity) less relevant attributable deductions to that share (s 328-360(1)).

The calculation of the total net small business income for an income year is modified if the individual is a "prescribed person" (¶2-170) (s 328-375).

The amount of the offset is limited to $1,000 per individual, per income year (s 328-360(2)).

An entity's "net small business income" is the result of:

- the entity's assessable income for the income year that relates to the entity carrying on a business disregarding any net capital gain and any personal services income not produced from conducting a personal services business
- LESS: the entity's relevant attributable deductions attributable to that share of assessable income (s 328-365).

If the result is less than zero, the net small business income is nil.

Relevant attributable deductions are deductions attributable to the assessable income other than tax-related expenses under s 25-5, gifts and contributions under Div 30 or personal superannuation contributions under Subdiv 290-C (s 328-370).

▶ Example

Pat Train was carrying on a restaurant business as a sole trader. For the 2019–20 income year, the business was a small business entity with less than $5 million aggregated annual turnover. The business had assessable income of $300,000 and deductions of $230,000 including a personal superannuation contribution of $30,000. Pat had other taxable income of $40,000.

Pat's net small business income for the year is $100,000. Pat's taxable income for the year is $110,000.

The percentage of Pat's taxable income that was "total net small business income" was 90.9% (being $100,000 ÷ $110,000). The basic income tax liability is $28,197. The result of the tax offset formula is $2,050 (being 8% × 90.9% × $28,197). As this result exceeds $1,000, the small business income tax offset is $1,000.

The effect of the offset is to reduce the income tax payable to $27,197 (excluding Medicare levy and low and middle income tax offset).

¶7-250 Simplified depreciation for small business

Small business entities can choose to deduct amounts for most of their depreciating assets under a special depreciation regime ("small business depreciation").

Small business depreciation

The simplified regime for calculating capital allowances on depreciating assets is contained in ITAA97 Subdiv 328-D. Small business entities that choose to use this regime are not subject to the provisions of ITAA97 Div 40 (ITAA97 s 328-175). Under the simplified regime, small business entities have access to an immediate write-off for low-cost depreciating assets and a simple pooling facility for other depreciating assets (ITAA97 s 328-180). Simplified methods are also provided for balancing adjustments relating to the disposal of assets and for dealing with assets that are only partly used for business purposes. Depreciating assets that are not deductible under Div 40, including those excluded by ITAA97 s 40-45 (capital works, pre-21 September 1999 IRUs and Australian films) and 40-27 (second-hand assets in residential premises), are also excluded from small business depreciation (¶17-030, ¶17-012), as are assets for which a deduction was available under the R&D provisions.

The small business provisions are subject to the operation of the limited recourse finance provisions (¶23-260). See also the special provisions for hire purchase agreements (¶23-250).

Small business entities that are subject to the personal services income rules in ss 85-10 and 86-60 (¶30-620, ¶30-630) can deduct amounts for depreciating assets under the small business depreciation regime (s 328-235). However, the restrictions on car deductions imposed by ss 86-60 and 86-70 apply (¶30-630).

Immediate write-off/instant asset write-off

An immediate deduction is available to small business entities that use simplified depreciation for a low-cost asset in the income year in which it was first used, or installed ready for use, for a taxable purpose. This is also referred to as the instant asset write-off.

Assets costing less than the relevant instant asset write-off threshold are written off in the year they are first used, or installed ready for use. The applicable threshold depends upon the date the asset is acquired and first used, or installed ready for use. The relevant dates and thresholds are:

Date range	Asset threshold
Prior to 7.30 pm (AEST) 12 May 2015	$1,000
7.30pm (AEST) 12 May 2015 to 28 January 2019	$20,000
29 January 2019 to before 7.30 pm (AEDT) 2 April 2019	$25,000
7.30 pm (AEDT) 2 April 2019 to 11 March 2020	$30,000
12 March 2020 to 31 December 2020 purchased (with extension for first use or installed ready for use to 30 June 2021)	$150,000
7.30 pm (AEDT) 6 October 2020 to 30 June 2022 (full expensing — see below)	Unlimited

The above rules are subject to the temporary full expensing of depreciating assets provisions (ITTPA s 328-181). For small business entities choosing to apply the simplified depreciation rules the provisions allow for full expensing of the cost of an asset where the taxpayer both (i) started to hold the asset and (ii) started to use, or have the asset installed ready for use, for a taxable purpose, during the period from 7.30 pm (AEDT) 6 October 2020 until 30 June 2022. This is available for the purchase of new or second-hand assets.

For the acquisition of a car, the deduction under the instant asset write-off or the temporary full expensing provision is subject to the car cost depreciation limit, being $57,581 for 2019–20 and $59,136 for 2020–21.

From 1 July 2022 the threshold will reduce back to $1,000 (s 328-180(1)).

The instant asset write-off (¶17-330) and the temporary full expensing provisions (¶17-430) are also available to other businesses.

The deduction is limited to the taxable purpose proportion (see below) of the asset's cost. For example, if an asset that is newly acquired for $800 is to be used 60% for business purposes, the deduction will be $480. However, if it is to be used only for business purposes, the deduction will be $800. Unpooled low-cost assets that were held before the taxpayer chose to apply small business depreciation do not qualify for the immediate deduction but may be pooled.

Where a taxpayer claimed an immediate deduction for a low-cost asset in an income year and in a subsequent income year while still a small business entity first incurs a second element cost on the asset, the taxpayer can claim an immediate deduction for the second element cost where the cost was incurred at the time when it is less than the relevant threshold detailed above.

Where the second element cost equals or exceeds the relevant threshold for immediate deduction, or the taxpayer was previously entitled to a deduction for a second element cost on the asset, the cost is included in the pool (s 328-180(3)). For these purposes, the second element of the cost is treated as the asset's adjustable value (s 328-180(4)). The asset is included in the pool even if the cost addition occurs during an income year in which the taxpayer is not a small business entity or does choose to apply simplified depreciation (s 328-180(5)). Full expensing is also available for second element expenditure incurred during the period from 7.30 pm (AEDT) 6 October 2020 (ITTPA s 328-181).

Small business depreciation pools

Subject to limited exceptions, depreciating assets (other than buildings) that are not entitled to an immediate deduction are automatically pooled in a single depreciating pool (ITAA97 s 328-185).

Buildings are specifically excluded from the pooling arrangements unless the building would qualify for deduction under Div 40 (¶17-015).

Where a depreciating asset with an effective life that is greater than 25 years has been used or installed ready for use for a taxable purpose before 1 July 2001, the taxpayer may choose to claim deductions under Div 40 instead of pooling the asset. The choice must be made for the first income year in which the taxpayer uses small business depreciation and cannot be changed for later years.

Assets are allocated to a small business pool at their GST-exclusive cost if the taxpayer is eligible for input tax credits (ITAA97 s 27-100). The opening pool balance may be reduced by any decreasing adjustment or increased by increasing adjustment.

Taxpayers who are subject to the alienation of personal services income provisions (¶30-600) cannot allocate more than one vehicle with a private use component to a small business pool (ITAA97 ss 86-70; 328-235).

Business and private use

Under small business depreciation, taxpayers are required to estimate the extent that they will use a depreciating asset for assessable income-producing purposes. This business use percentage (the ''taxable purpose proportion''), multiplied by the asset's cost (or adjustable value, where appropriate) represents the amount that is available for inclusion in a pool. The example in s 328-205(4) illustrates the taxable purpose proportion concept.

Where a taxpayer's latest estimate of an asset's business use percentage changes by more than 10 percentage points, an adjustment to the opening balance of the pool is required (ITAA97 s 328-225). Adjustments are optional if the asset has been pooled for at least 3 income years after the income year it was allocated.

Deductions for pooled assets

The annual depreciation deduction for a pool is calculated under ITAA97 s 328-190 by multiplying the pool's opening balance by the depreciation rate of 30%. Further, subject to special rules for accelerated depreciation detailed below, deductions of 15% are allowed for the taxable purpose proportions of:

- assets added to the pool during the year, regardless of when in the year the assets were acquired, and
- additional depreciable expenditure (''cost addition amounts'') incurred during the year on existing pooled assets.

Where the relevant asset added to the pool is eligible for accelerated depreciation in ITTPA s 40-125 (¶17-430) and its cost is equal to or more than $150,000 then the deduction claimed is increased to 57.5% in the year that the asset is first used or installed ready for use (ITTPA s 328-182).

A deduction for the entire balance of the small business depreciation pool can be claimed in an income year, where the balance of the pool prior to the calculation of the depreciation for that income year is less than the applicable threshold for an income year ending in the relevant date range above (ITAA97 s 328-210; ITTPA ss 328-180(6), 328-181(5)). For the year ended 30 June 2020 this applies where the balance of the pool prior to depreciation is less than $150,000. For income years ending after 7.30 pm AEDT on 6 October 2020 until 30 June 2022, the full balance of the pool can be deducted irrespective of its balance.

Opening pool balance

The initial opening balance of a pool is the sum of the taxable purpose components of all the depreciating assets that are automatically allocated to the pool as at the beginning of the taxpayer's first year within the small business depreciation regime. This does not include assets acquired during that year. For a later income year, a pool's opening balance is its prior year closing balance, adjusted for changes in current year business use estimates.

▶ Example

Gerard uses all his assets 100% for business purposes. The closing value of Gerard's small business pool for 2018–19 was $200,000.

Therefore, the opening balance of his general small business pool for 2019–20 is $200,000.

During 2019–20 the following occurred:

- acquired a single depreciating asset used 100% for business purposes — $25,000
- cost addition amounts for assets in the pool in January 2020 — $35,000
- proceeds from disposal of pooled assets (used 100% for business) — $5,500.

An immediate deduction is available for the single depreciating asset of $25,000. The closing value of the small business pool for 2019–20 is calculated as follows:

Opening balance	$200,000
Plus: additions	-
Plus: cost addition amounts (January 2020)	$35,000
Less: depreciation at 30% on opening balance — s 328-190	($60,000)
Less: depreciation at 15% on additions — s 328-190	($5,250)
Less: disposal proceeds (termination values)	($5,500)
Closing balance of small business pool for 2019–20	$164,250

In 2020–21 the balance of this pool will be available for immediate deduction.

Disposal of depreciating asset

A "balancing adjustment event" occurs when the taxpayer disposes of a depreciating asset. If the asset is a low-value asset for which an immediate deduction was obtained, the taxable purpose proportion of the "termination value" (broadly, the disposal proceeds) is included in the taxpayer's assessable income. If it is a pooled asset, the taxable purpose proportion of the asset's termination value is subtracted from the pool. For the meaning of "termination value", see ¶17-640.

Where a pooled asset's business use estimate has been adjusted, the taxpayer is required to use an average of the asset's current and previous business use estimates to work out the taxable purpose proportion of the termination value.

Where the year-end pool balance would otherwise be less than zero (due to balancing adjustment events), the negative amount is added to assessable income and the pool's closing balance then becomes zero.

Unless the conditions of CGT event K7 are satisfied, any capital gain or loss arising from the disposal of an asset is disregarded if the taxpayer has deducted an amount for the asset under the small business depreciation provisions during the year of the balancing adjustment event (ITAA97 s 104-235; ¶11-350).

Roll-over relief

Optional roll-over relief applies for changes in partnership interests and in the constitution of a partnership, ie where the entities before and after the change are partnerships (¶17-780) (ITAA97 ss 328-243 to 328-257).

Optional roll-over relief also applies where:

- there is a change in the holding of, or the interests of entities in, an asset
- at least one of the entities that had an interest in the asset before the change has an interest in it after the change
- the asset was a partnership asset either before the change or becomes one as a result of the change (s 328-243).

This means that roll-over relief would apply if a sole trader takes on a new partner, or if a partner leaves a partnership and the remaining partner carries on as a sole trader. However, roll-over relief is not available if all the assets that were allocated to the partnership's general small business pool are disposed of to the former partners and, just after the disposals, no single former partner has an interest in each of the assets that were allocated to the pool (ID 2011/99).

The roll-over must be used for all assets in the pool. If there has been roll-over relief, any deduction (or assessable amount) is split between the transferor and the transferee equally (unless the asset is first used or installed ready for use by the transferee). If more than one roll-over has occurred, any deduction (or assessable amount) is split equally between all entities concerned. This also applies to cost addition amounts incurred by the transferor (but amounts incurred by the transferee are deductible to the transferee). Assets eligible for roll-over relief continue to be allocated to a small business pool even if the transferee is not a small business entity.

Optional roll-over relief also applies where: (a) a small business sole trader, trustee or a partnership disposes of all of the assets in its small business pool to a wholly owned company; or (b) a small business pool is transferred as a result of a court order upon a marriage or relationship breakdown if a joint election is made by transferor and transferee.

Primary producers

A primary producer who applies small business depreciation for the year is able to make a one-time choice (in relation to each depreciating asset) whether to claim deductions under the primary production capital allowance provisions (¶16-820, ¶18-060 – ¶18-100) or the small business depreciation provisions. However, the cost of grapevines and horticultural plants can only be deducted under the capital allowance provisions (¶18-000).

Leased assets

Leased assets (including assets that are reasonably expected to be predominantly leased in future) are excluded from the small business depreciation regime to prevent the benefits of small business treatment from being transferred to larger taxpayers. The exclusion applies to an asset that will be let more than 50% of the time but does not apply to short-term hire and hire purchase arrangements.

Existing assets in non-small business pools

Deductions are not available under the small business depreciation regime for assets that were allocated to a low-value pool before the taxpayer started using small business depreciation (¶17-810) or a software development pool (¶17-370). Deductions for these assets continue to be covered by Div 40.

Ceasing to apply small business depreciation

If a taxpayer ceases to apply the small business depreciation for an income year, the small business depreciation rules continue to apply to the taxpayer's existing small business depreciation pools for that year and later years, including the write-off of a pool balance less than the relevant threshold. This applies even if the entity has ceased to hold the asset or to carry on business, provided the taxpayer continues to exist. However, assets cannot be added to a small business pool while the taxpayer is not using the small business depreciation regime, subject to the rule for second element costs detailed above.

Where a taxpayer stops using small business depreciation and then starts to use it again, depreciating business assets that the taxpayer acquired while not using small business depreciation are automatically allocated to the relevant pool, unless the taxpayer (eg a primary producer) can choose to claim deductions for the asset under other capital allowance provisions. A business use percentage estimate must be made for each of these assets.

The general rule is that a taxpayer who chooses to use small depreciation in one income year and (although eligible to do so) does not choose to use it in a later income year cannot choose to use small depreciation again until at least 5 years after the income year in which they were eligible but chose not to use it (ITAA97 s 328-175(10)). However, this lock-out rule does not apply to income years if any day in the year occurs during the period 12 May 2015 to 30 June 2022 (ITTPA s 328-180).

[FITR ¶313-000 – ¶313-178]

¶7-260 Simplified trading stock rules

A simplified trading stock regime is available for small business entities (¶7-050). This concession will also be available for income years starting on or after 1 July 2021 for medium business entities (s 328-285).

The simplified rules provide that, where the difference between the value of trading stock on hand at the start of an income year and the reasonably estimated value at the end of the year is $5,000 or less, a small business entity can choose *not* to:

- value each item of trading stock on hand at the end of the income year
- account for any change in the value of trading stock on hand (ITAA97 Subdiv 328-E: ss 328-280 to 328-295).

If the choice is made, the closing value of the trading stock for tax purposes will be the same as the opening value for that year (ITAA97 s 328-295(2)). This will also be the opening value for the following year: ITAA97 s 70-40.

A reasonable estimate will be an approximation of the value by the taxpayer that is reasonable in all of the circumstances.

▶ Example

For the 2019–20 income year, Debra is a small business entity using the accruals accounting method. Debra had 15,500 units of trading stock on hand at the end of the 2018–19 income year, which she valued for tax purposes at a cost of $1 per unit ($15,500). This value becomes the value of trading stock on hand at the start of the 2019–20 income year (s 70-40).

Debra purchases 15,000 units of trading stock at a cost of $1 per unit. She sells 19,000 units at $3 per unit.

Debra estimates that her trading stock has declined in value by $4,000. This estimate is based on the difference between units purchased (15,000) and units sold (19,000) in the year. This estimate is reasonable because Debra maintains accurate records of her trading stock.

Having estimated that the change in value of trading stock does not exceed $5,000, Debra chooses not to account for the change. She is therefore not required to value each item of trading stock on hand at the end of the year for income tax purposes.

The value of trading stock on hand at the end of the 2019–20 year is deemed to equal the value of trading stock on hand at the start of the year, ie $15,500.

In calculating taxable income for 2019–20, Debra includes $57,000 in assessable income for sales (ie 19,000 × $3) and deducts $15,000 for purchases.

A small business entity may, of course, decide to do a stocktake and account for changes in the value of trading stock in any income year. This may be due to a preference by the taxpayer to adjust assessable income in annual increments rather than in one larger amount when the change in value of trading stock exceeds $5,000.

Where the difference between the value of trading stock on hand at the start of the year and the reasonably estimated value at the end of the year is greater than $5,000, a small business entity must value each item of trading stock on hand at the end of the year and account for the change in value in the normal way under ITAA97 s 70-45.

[FITR ¶313-180 – ¶313-214]

Chapter 8 Consolidated Groups

Introduction

¶8-000 Overview of the group consolidation regime

The group consolidation regime allows wholly-owned groups of companies (together with eligible trusts and partnerships) to consolidate as a single entity for income tax purposes. The main features of the regime (comprising ITAA97 Pt 3-90) are:

- the "head company" of a wholly-owned group of entities can make an irrevocable choice to consolidate with its wholly-owned Australian subsidiaries for income tax purposes. If the choice is made, all of the wholly-owned subsidiaries become "subsidiary members" of the consolidated group and, together with the head company, constitute the "members" of the group, and
- the group of entities that is a consolidated group is treated as a single entity, ie a single taxpayer during the period of consolidation (¶8-010).

Non-income tax matters (eg FBT and GST) are not included within the consolidation regime and continue to be the responsibility of the individual entities in the group. The GST grouping provisions (¶34-180) operate independently of the consolidation regime, with substantially different rules. A withholding obligation of a subsidiary also falls outside the consolidation regime as it relates to income tax payable by a third party.

Australian resident wholly-owned subsidiaries of a common foreign holding company may be able to form a multiple entry consolidated (MEC) group (ITAA97 Div 719: ¶8-610).

A group of entities consolidated for income tax purposes either as a consolidated group or a MEC group may choose to also consolidate for purposes of the petroleum resource rent tax under *Petroleum Resource Rent Tax 1987*, Div 8 (¶19-003).

Consolidatable group

A consolidatable group consists of a head company and *all* of the subsidiary members of the group.

Head company

The head company is the peak holding company in a consolidatable or consolidated group. To be a "head company", a company:

- must be an Australian resident (but not a prescribed dual resident: ¶21-040)
- must have some or all of its income (if any) taxed at the corporate tax rate (or equivalent)
- must not be an excluded entity under ITAA97 s 703-20 (see below), and
- must not be a wholly-owned subsidiary of another entity that meets the above requirements or, if it is, it must not be a subsidiary member of a consolidatable group or consolidated group.

Certain public trading trusts that elect to be taxed like companies are able to head consolidated groups (¶8-550).

Subsidiary member

The subsidiary members of a consolidatable group or consolidated group are wholly-owned (directly or indirectly) by the head company. An entity is a subsidiary member of a consolidatable group or consolidated group if (ITAA97 s 703-15):

- it is:
  - an Australian resident company (but not a prescribed dual resident) that has all or some of its taxable income taxable at the corporate tax rate. To determine whether the residence requirements are met, it is not considered to be part of the single entity that is the consolidated group (ID 2009/8)
  - a partnership (rare), or
  - an Australian resident trust (including, in rare situations, a non-fixed trust)
- it is a wholly-owned subsidiary of the head company of the group, and

- where there are any interposed entities between it and the head company, each of the interposed entities is either a subsidiary member of the group or holds its interests as a nominee for other members of the group (ITAA97 s 703-45).

Certain transitional measures applicable only to groups that consolidated before 1 July 2004 allow certain foreign resident entities to be interposed between members of the group (ITTPA ss 701C-10; 701C-15). ITTPA s 701C-10(8) does not prevent a company from becoming a subsidiary member of a consolidated or MEC group when it is directly acquired by members of the group including one or more such transitional foreign-held subsidiary members (ID 2008/33).

A consolidatable group can exist where a subsidiary member holds some membership interests in the head company (ID 2008/32).

A United States limited liability company that is a foreign hybrid company (and treated as a partnership under ITAA97 s 830-20) is regarded as a member of a consolidated group if it is a wholly-owned subsidiary of the head company (ID 2009/149).

Wholly-owned subsidiary

A company, trust or partnership will be a ''wholly-owned subsidiary'' of the head company if all of the membership interests in that company, trust or partnership are beneficially owned by the head company and/or one or more other wholly-owned subsidiaries of the head company (ITAA97 s 703-30). For these purposes, the members of various entity types are:

Entity	**Member**
Company	A member of a company or a stockholder in the company
Partnership	A partner in the partnership
Public trading trust	A unitholder of the trust
Other trusts	A beneficiary, unitholder or object of the trust

The beneficial ownership of an entity does not change merely because it is under external administration, ie the entity is not prevented from being a member of a consolidated group (ITAA97 s 703-30(3)).

In determining whether an entity is a wholly-owned subsidiary, shares acquired under employee share schemes eligible for deferred taxation (Subdiv 83A-C: ¶10-089) totalling not more than 1% of the ordinary shares in the entity or an interposed company are disregarded (ITAA97 ss 703-35; 719-30). Membership interests acquired under an employee share scheme eligible for deferred taxation that form part of stapled securities are also disregarded if they account for not more than 1% of such interests in the company. Apart from this concession, the rules exclude individuals from holding any membership interest in a subsidiary member of a consolidated group or MEC group. Transitional rules ensure that the above consolidation provisions continue to apply to shares and membership interests acquired under the former employee share scheme rules (ITAA36 Div 13A) for both consolidated groups and MEC groups.

Subsidiary members that are authorised deposit-taking institutions (ADIs) can issue certain preference shares to non-group members without losing their member status. Preference shares that qualify for the exception will be ignored for the purposes of the consolidation rules (other than those applying to MEC groups). This will assist financial groups containing ADIs to adopt a non-operating holding company structure (ITAA97 s 703-37).

Finance shares that are debt interests (¶23-105) are disregarded in determining whether an entity is a wholly-owned subsidiary of another entity.

An entity held through a non-fixed trust may also be treated as a wholly-owned subsidiary in certain circumstances (ITAA97 s 703-40).

Excluded entities

The following entities cannot be members of a consolidatable or consolidated group (ITAA97 s 703-20):

- an entity whose total ordinary income and statutory income is exempt under ITAA97 Div 50 (exempt entities: ¶10-604)
- a recognised medium credit union (¶3-435)
- an approved credit union under ITAA36 s 23G that is not a recognised large credit union
- a pooled development fund (¶3-555)
- a complying superannuation entity, non-complying ADF or non-complying superannuation fund
- certain subsidiaries of life insurance companies (¶3-527)
- a corporate collective investment vehicle (¶6-410).

Forming a consolidated group

A consolidated group is established by the head company making a choice that a consolidatable group is consolidated on and after a specified day, provided it was also the head company on that day. The choice takes effect from the earliest point in time that a consolidatable group exists on that day (TD 2006/74; ID 2005/63). There must be at least one subsidiary member in existence at the time that the choice is made. Once made, the choice is irrevocable and the specified date cannot be changed (ITAA97 s 703-50(2)).

The choice must be made in writing no later than the day the head company lodges the first consolidated tax return or, if a return is not required, the day it would otherwise have been due. The head company must notify the Commissioner of the choice made in the approved form within the same time frame (ITAA97 s 703-58). No extension of time can be sought under TAA Sch 1 s 388-55 to make the choice (*MW McIntosh*). However, an extension of time for notifying the Commissioner of the choice may be sought. A technical defect in the notice to the Commissioner does not invalidate the choice made.

▶ Example: Forming a consolidated group

Assume that all members of a consolidatable group have the standard 30 June tax year and that the head company wishing to consolidate with effect from 1 October 2018, lodges its consolidated return for the income year ended 30 June 2019 on 2 December 2019. In that case, the head company must make its choice to consolidate from 1 October 2018 in writing, and also notify the Commissioner of this choice in the approved form no later than 2 December 2019.

Under the ''one in, all in'' principle, all members of the consolidatable group (other than a transitional foreign loss maker: ¶8-600) are consolidated (TD 2005/40). Every newly acquired eligible subsidiary of the head company automatically becomes a subsidiary member of the consolidated group. Any subsidiary member that ceases to be a wholly-owned Australian resident subsidiary of the head company automatically leaves the consolidated group.

The same consolidated group will continue to exist when subsidiary members leave the group, or new subsidiary members join the group, so long as the head company remains a head company. This will be the case even if all subsidiary members become ineligible, leaving only the head company. However, if a head company ceases to be eligible to be a head company, a consolidated group will cease to exist. In limited circumstances, a new head company can be interposed between the original head company and its shareholders without disbanding the consolidated group (¶8-500).

▶ Planning points: forming a consolidated group

- There may be scope for including/excluding certain entities from the group by acquiring minority interests or selling part-interests before the consolidation date. However, this should be examined in the context of the ITAA36 Pt IVA general anti-avoidance provisions (¶8-950).
- Consolidating on the first day of the tax year is not essential, but if a group consolidates part-way through the year, each member will need to file a return for the non-membership period (see below). If the head company is a public trading trust, the consolidation must take place on the first day of the trust's income year (¶8-550).

Tax liability in transitional income years

Where an entity becomes (or ceases to be) a member of a consolidated group during an income year, or ceases to be the head company of one consolidated group and simultaneously becomes a subsidiary member of another consolidated group, each part of the income year in which a different consolidation status applied will be treated separately.

Income and deductions attributable to the period where the entity was a member of a consolidated group are included in the head company's consolidated return. However, the entity will be responsible for self-assessing its tax liability for periods during which it was not part of a consolidated group, ie before joining a group and/or after leaving a group (ITAA97 s 701-30). It lodges a full-year return but includes only the income and deductions attributable to the period(s) when it was not a member of a consolidated group. The due date for the subsidiary member's return is the same as it would have been if it had not joined a group.

Where, just before the joining time, there is an arrangement in force for the supply of goods or services between a joining entity and the head company or another joining entity, ITAA97 s 701-70 may adjust the assessable income or deductions of the parties to the arrangement (the ''combining entities''). The purpose of the adjustment is to align the tax positions of the combining entities before they lose their separate identities. (See PS LA 2006/15 for the application of penalties and remission of interest charges in this context.)

Tax debts and tax sharing agreements

Subject to provisions concerning tax sharing agreements, the head company will be liable for the income tax debts of the consolidated group that are applicable to the period of consolidation. However, income tax debts may be recovered from subsidiary members in certain circumstances (ITAA97 Div 721; see also PS LA 2013/5). An exclusion applies to a subsidiary member that is legally prohibited from subjecting itself to such a liability (ITAA97 s 721-15(2); TR 2004/12).

The head company can enter into a tax sharing agreement (TSA) with one or more subsidiary members (TSA contributing members). Providing the TSA meets the requirements of ITAA97 s 721-25 (eg each TSA contributing member's contribution amount can be determined and represents a reasonable allocation, and the arrangement was not entered into to prejudice recovery by the Commissioner), each TSA contributing member is liable to pay the Commonwealth an amount equal to its contribution amount under the agreement (ITAA97 s 721-30). A TSA contributing member generally can leave the group clear of its liability by paying the head company the actual or estimated amount of its liability before the leaving time (ITAA97 s 721-35; PS LA 2013/5).

Entities with substituted accounting periods

When a consolidated group is formed, the head company will continue to use its existing tax accounting period. Thus, if the head company has a substituted accounting period (SAP), the consolidated group will use the same SAP.

In the case of a MEC group (¶8-610), if there is a change in head company, the new head company of the MEC group must use the same accounting period as the former head company.

Life insurance companies

Special consolidation rules are provided for groups that include one or more life insurance companies in order to ensure that the special regime for taxation of life insurance companies (¶3-480) applies appropriately to such groups (¶3-527).

Financial reporting and tax consolidation

Accounting Standard AASB 112 *Income Taxes* prescribes the accounting treatment for income taxes in financial reports of Australian entities (¶9-000). However, various issues have arisen concerning the appropriate application of AASB 112 by a tax consolidated group and its individual entities. The Australian Accounting Standards Board has provided authoritative guidance on these issues in Urgent Issues Group Interpretation 1052 *Tax Consolidation Accounting*, which is available for download at www.aasb.gov.au.

¶8-010 Single entity rule

Where a group of corporate tax entities is a consolidated group, the group is treated as a single taxpayer (the "single entity rule": s 701-1) and:

- lodges a single annual tax return
- pays consolidated income tax instalments, after being given an instalment rate worked out by the Commissioner from its first consolidated assessment. Before that time, the members of the newly consolidated group continue to pay their own PAYG instalments. The head company is entitled to franking credits for PAYG payments made by subsidiary members in relation to post-consolidation periods
- maintains a single franking account (¶8-300)
- pools losses (¶8-100), franking credits (¶8-300) and foreign income tax offsets (¶8-600)
- effectively maintains a common tax accounting period for all its member entities.

Intra-group transactions (such as dividends, loans and transfer of assets) between members of a consolidated group are ignored for income tax purposes. Assets can therefore be transferred between members without tax consequences. A member company can be liquidated without triggering a deemed dividend or a capital gain or loss.

The actions and transactions of a subsidiary member with someone outside the consolidated group are treated as undertaken by the head company for income tax purposes (TD 2004/36; TD 2004/76). Thus, all the assessable income and deductions of the group are attributable to the head company (after eliminating intra-group transactions). An offshore branch of a subsidiary member is also treated as if it were a branch of the head company (ID 2009/161). The head company is treated as the responsible taxpayer for most purposes.

The head company is taken to acquire any CGT assets that a member entity acquires while a member of the group, and to hold any CGT assets for so long as they are held by a member entity. Any CGT events (¶11-240) happening in relation to CGT assets held by an entity while it is a member of the consolidated group are taken to happen in relation to the asset while being held by the head company (TD 2004/82; TD 2004/40).

However, obligations or rights that relate to income tax assessments of a subsidiary member before it joined a consolidated group remain with the subsidiary (TD 2004/79).

The single entity rule applies for the purposes of determining the head company's and the subsidiary members' income tax liability or tax loss for an income year. It does not apply for other purposes or to an entity outside the consolidated group (TD 2004/68; *Draft* TD 2007/D5; TD 2004/42; TD 2004/47; TD 2004/50; TD 2004/51). The meaning and application of the single entity rule is also discussed in detail in TR 2004/11.

The thin capitalisation rules (¶8-600, ¶22-700) treat a consolidated group as a single entity. There are also special rules for foreign banks and non-bank foreign financial entities (¶8-600).

▶ Planning points: single entity rule

- While consolidation may initially involve considerable compliance costs in modifying accounting systems and procedures, valuing assets and analysing the effects on losses, after consolidation there should be some cost benefits and additional flexibility as intra-group transactions generally have no income tax implications.
- Consolidation removes the potential for duplication of gains and losses (within a subsidiary and on disposal of interests in the subsidiary) and removes the need to deal with complex loss integrity and value shifting provisions of the Act.
- A consolidated group is treated as a single entity under the thin capitalisation rules and may be able to better utilise foreign income tax offsets or pre-commencement excess foreign income tax (¶21-670, ¶21-760).

The ATO is also reviewing arrangements where a consolidated group has a subsidiary using an offshore PE that has intra-group transactions. The effect of the arrangement is a double non-taxation of income because income is sheltered from tax in the foreign jurisdiction which allows for the intra-group expense, and the intra-group receipt is ignored in Australia because of the single entity rule. The ATO is concerned that such consolidated groups are not reporting sufficient Australian assessable income or are treating excessive amounts of income connected to the PE as non-assessable non-exempt income (TA 2016/7).

[FITR ¶540-160]

¶8-020 Inherited history rules

The so-called ‘‘inherited history rules’’ govern the extent to which the past tax history of an entity is taken into account after it joins or leaves a consolidated group. These rules are necessary as subsidiary members lose their identities upon joining a consolidated group.

Entry history rule

The ‘‘entry history rule’’ (ITAA97 s 701-5) states that everything that happened to an entity before it became a subsidiary member is taken to have happened in relation to the head company for ‘‘head company core purposes’’, ie for the purposes of working out the head company's liability for income tax or its losses after the entity becomes a member (ITAA97 s 701-1).

For example, the head company may be entitled to deductions in relation to a subsidiary's pre-joining expenditure on borrowing expenses, gifts (where the deduction is spread over multiple periods), water facilities (ID 2007/37), power or telephone connection costs, and costs allocated to a project pool. The head company may also be entitled to bad debt deductions where accounts and loans receivable of the joining entity become uncollectable (ITAA97 s 716-400; ID 2004/3). The head company may also need to include assessable income due to events that took place before an entity joined the group. For example, due to a prepayment received by a subsidiary or the recoupment of expenditure made by a subsidiary before it joined the group.

The entry history rule preserves the pre-CGT status of assets brought into the group, subject to the rules concerning a change in majority underlying interests (¶12-870).

The head company will be taken to acquire the assets of a joining entity at the time those assets were acquired by the joining entity (rather than at the joining time) for the purposes of qualifying for changes in depreciation rates, effective 8 May 2007. This will ensure, for example, that the head company cannot apply the 200% diminishing value uplift to assets that were acquired by the joining entity before 10 May 2006.

If a finance subsidiary had entered into borrowings to finance its group companies in the ordinary course of its business prior to consolidation of the group, the head company is taken to have done the same under the entry history rule (ID 2010/100).

The Explanatory Memorandum to the New Business Tax System (Consolidation) Bill (No 1) 2002 confirms that private binding rulings (¶24-560) issued to the entity before the joining time will apply to the head company insofar as the relevant facts have not changed, either by reason of consolidation or otherwise.

History that is not related to working out the head company's income tax liability or losses is not inherited. Examples include franking credits (¶8-300) and foreign income tax offsets (¶8-600), for which there are separate rules.

For the purposes of the business continuity test in the loss recoupment rules, the entry history rule does not operate when an entity joins a group. This means that a head company's business will not include the business of a joining entity before it became a member of the group when determining if the head company satisfies the business continuity test (ITAA97 s 165-212E).

The entry history rule is affected by the cost setting rules for assets brought into the group (¶8-200) and the rules for transferring and utilising losses (¶8-100). This is because the operation of the core rules is subject to any contrary provisions in ITAA97 Pt 3-90 or another part of the income tax law (ITAA97 s 701-85).

Exit history rule

When a subsidiary member leaves a consolidated group, taking with it any asset, liability or business, the entity inherits the tax history associated with that asset, liability or business (ITAA97 s 701-40). This "exit history rule" applies for the purposes of working out the leaving entity's income tax liability or loss for any period after it leaves the group (ie for "entity core purposes"). The history in relation to a business might, for example, extend to whether the business qualifies for tax treatment that applies to specific types of business such as primary production or exploration or prospecting for minerals.

The exit history rule is also relevant to pre-CGT assets and private binding rulings (see above).

As in the case of the entry history rule, the exit history rule is affected by contrary provisions, such as the cost setting rules for assets taken from the group and the rules that result in losses and foreign income tax offsets remaining in the group (ITAA97 ss 701-85; 707-410; 717-10).

Treatment for irrevocable entity-wide elections

When an entity joins a consolidated group either at its formation time or a later date, it will not always be appropriate for the head entity to be bound by irrevocable elections ("choices") that the joining entity has made. Similarly, it will not always be appropriate for a leaving entity to be bound by irrevocable choices made by the head entity. Accordingly, separate rules may apply to override the entry history rule and exit history rule in relation to such choices (ITAA97 Subdiv 715-J; 715-K; ITTPA Subdiv 715-J; 715-K). There are 3 lists of choices, each with a distinct method of treatment.

Resettable choices treatment

Some choices are eligible for resettable choices treatment. This treatment allows the head company to decide whether or not to reset a joining entity's irrevocable choices at the joining/consolidation time according to the head company's preferences. It will not be bound by earlier choices made by the joining entity. Such choices are effective from the consolidation time or joining time (ITAA97 s 715-660). A similar decision is available to a leaving entity at the leaving time (ITAA97 s 715-700). The head company (or leaving entity) generally has 90 days after the joining time (or leaving time) in which to make its new choice.

The list of choices that are subject to resettable choices treatment comprises choices made under:

- a provision of ITAA36 Pt X — attribution of income in respect of controlled foreign companies
- a provision of ITAA97 Subdiv 420-D — choosing a valuation method for a registered emissions unit
- item 1 in the table in ITAA97 s 960-60(1) — choosing to use a functional currency (¶8-600)
- ITAA97 ss 230-210, 230-255, 230-315 and 230-395 — choice about the treatment of gains and losses from Div 230 financial arrangements
- any other matter prescribed by regulations.

Limited resettable choices to overcome inconsistencies

The second treatment category permits the head company or leaving entity to reset choices only where there would otherwise be inconsistency of treatment among joining entities, between a joining entity and the group, or between the head company's choice status and the choice status that a leaving entity had before joining the group (ITAA97 s 715-665; 715-705). The head company (or leaving entity) generally has 90 days after the joining time (or leaving time) in which to make its new choice. This treatment is applicable to irrevocable choices made in respect of:

- ITAA36 s 148 — reinsurance with foreign residents. However, the reset applies only to new reinsurance contracts entered into with foreign residents at or after the consolidation/joining time (or leaving time)
- ITAA97 ss 230-210, 230-255, 230-315 and 230-395 — choice about the treatment of gains and losses from Div 230 financial arrangements
- ITAA97 s 775-80 — forex realisation gains and losses
- any other matter prescribed by regulations.

Choices with ongoing effect

The third treatment category ensures that a choice that affects certain assets, liabilities or transactions will continue to have ongoing effect when the relevant entity joins a consolidated group (ITAA97 s 715-670). Consistent with this approach, a leaving entity will simply inherit the choice status of the head company under the exit history rule.

This treatment applies to a choice made under ITAA97 s 775-150 to disregard certain forex realisation gains and losses. However, a s 775-150 election made by an entity when it is already a subsidiary member of a consolidated group is not taken to be a valid election by the head company of the consolidated group (ID 2006/201).

Bad debts and swap losses

Special bad debt rules ensure that an entity can deduct a bad debt that for a period has been owed to a member of a consolidated group, and for another period has been owed to an entity that was not a member of that group (ITAA97 Subdiv 709-D). The provisions modify the continuity of ownership test (COT) and business continuity test for deducting bad debts by companies (¶3-150), and the tests for deducting bad debts by trusts (¶6-262). Broadly, the claimant can deduct a bad debt if each entity to whom the debt has been owed could (under the modified rules) have deducted the debt if it had been written off as bad at the end of its holding period. For example, a deduction might be available under the modified rules where a debt was first owed to a trust; the trust later joined a consolidated group (so that the debt was deemed to be owed to the head company); the debt then left the group as an asset of a company leaving the group; and the debt was then written off by that company.

The consolidation bad debt rules override the inherited history rules in identifying the relevant test period. However, the inherited history rules still operate to treat a debt as having been included in the claimant's assessable income (ITAA97 s 716-400; ¶8-580).

The modifications in Subdiv 709-D also apply to determine whether consolidated groups can deduct swap losses (¶16-586), as defined in ITAA36 s 63E (ITAA97 s 709-220).

In relation to MEC groups, further modifications to the bad debt/swap loss rules are contained in ITAA97 Subdiv 719-I. Notably, these modifications apply the COT to the *top company* of the MEC group (¶8-610), whereas the business continuity test is applied to the head company of the group.

[FITR ¶540-165, ¶540-200, ¶540-245, ¶543-805]

Losses

¶8-100 Transferring losses to joined group

When an entity first becomes a member of a consolidated group (as either a subsidiary member or head company), any losses it made in an income year before joining the group are tested to determine whether they can be transferred to the group. Any such losses that fail the transfer tests are permanently lost.

The following realised losses can potentially be transferred:

- tax losses (¶3-060), including film losses
- net capital losses (¶11-080)
- foreign losses (¶21-800).

Losses that meet the relevant tests are automatically transferred to the head company of the joined group under ITAA97 s 707-120 unless the head company makes an irrevocable choice to cancel the transfer under ITAA97 s 707-145. The cancellation can be made on a loss by loss basis (ID 2004/939).

Loss transfer tests

Broadly, a loss can be transferred by an entity (''joining entity'') upon joining a consolidated group only if the joining entity could have used the loss outside the group. The transfer tests are, therefore, essentially the existing company loss (¶3-060, ¶3-065) and trust loss (¶6-262) utilisation provisions, modified to account for the fact that the joining entity is absorbed into the consolidated group and that the losses are thereafter identified with the head company as head of the consolidated group. For example, the ownership tests are applied as though the entity had sought to claim the loss for an income year (''trial year'') generally starting 12 months before, and ending immediately after, the entity joined the group.

Trial year

The trial year is the period ending *immediately after* the joining time and starting at the latest of the following times:

- the time 12 months before the joining time
- the time the joining entity came into existence
- the time the joining entity last ceased to be a subsidiary member of a consolidated group (if applicable) (ITAA97 s 707-120(2)).

For loss years starting before 1 July 1999, the same business test will be satisfied for loss transfer purposes if the joining entity carried on the same business: (a) just before the ownership or control tests were first failed (¶3-105); and (b) throughout the trial year. For loss years starting after 30 June 1999, the business continuity test will be satisfied for loss transfer purposes if the joining entity carried on the same or similar business: (a) just before the end of the loss year; (b) throughout the income year in which the joining entity first failed the ownership or control tests; and (c) throughout the trial year.

▶ Planning point: loss transfers

Before forming a consolidated group including loss companies, or before an existing consolidated group wholly acquires a loss company, it should be considered whether the loss company's losses are transferable. The fact that a loss passes the tests to be utilised by the loss company does not automatically mean that the losses will be transferable to the group when it consolidates. Modification of the loss tests for the purposes of loss transfer discussed above may cause the transfer tests to be failed.

Tax losses of a designated infrastructure project entity (ITAA97 Div 415) are not subject to the loss transfer tests. The limits on utilisation of transferred losses (¶8-110) also do not apply if the head company is a designated infrastructure project entity after the losses are transferred.

Effects of loss transfer

A loss that meets the required transfer tests is transferred to the head company and is taken to have been made by the head company for the income year in which the loss is transferred. It is no longer taken to have been made by the joining entity (ITAA97 s 707-140).

For example, if a widely held joining entity, for purposes of meeting the loss transfer test, were to opt not to apply certain modifications which would otherwise apply, that choice does not affect a head company's ability to apply those modifications when it seeks to utilise that loss in a future year (ID 2013/7).

COT transfers

The transfer of a loss by a joining *company* to the head company is a "COT transfer" if the loss is transferred because the joining company satisfies the modified continuity of ownership test and does not fail the control tests in ITAA97 s 165-15(1) (ITAA97 s 707-210(1A)). Losses transferred under a COT transfer may be eligible to be utilised in accordance with the concessional loss utilisation rules (¶8-120).

In determining whether the head company can utilise such a loss, pre-consolidation changes of ownership of the loss company are recognised. The transfer of a part-year loss under ITAA97 s 707-120 because the loss could have been utilised by the transferor under ITAA97 s 165-20 cannot be a COT transfer (TD 2006/75). A modified pattern of distributions test (ITAA97 s 707-130) applies to test whether a subsidiary satisfies the COT to transfer a loss where non-fixed trusts hold fixed entitlements to 50% or more of a head company's income or capital (ID 2004/959; ID 2004/960).

Transfers that satisfy the business continuity test

A loss that has been transferred because the joining entity satisfied the modified business continuity test is not tested again under this test unless the consolidated group fails the continuity of ownership or control test (ITAA97 s 707-210).

Loss bundles

Transferred losses (other than transferred concessional losses — see ¶8-110 below) are kept in bundles. All of the losses that are transferred at the joining time by the entity that actually made them constitute a single bundle. If the losses are transferred again, they stay in the original bundle. However, if the entity that made the losses leaves the group and later rejoins, any losses transferred at the second joining time would constitute a new bundle.

A loss bundle will cease to exist if the losses in it can no longer be used by any entity, eg they have been fully deducted or no longer pass the utilisation tests.

A bundle of losses has an "available fraction" that determines the maximum proportion of the head company's relevant income or gain for a year that can be offset by the losses in that bundle (¶8-120). The available fraction is the same for all losses in that particular bundle.

[FITR ¶542-702 – ¶542-750]

¶8-110 Utilisation of losses by joined group

Like other companies, the head company of a consolidated or MEC group must pass the continuity of ownership test (COT: ¶3-105) or the business continuity test (¶3-120) in order to utilise its tax losses. This is the case whether the losses have been generated by or transferred to the group.

Business continuity test

The business continuity test is applied to the one overall business carried on by the head company (including its subsidiaries). It is irrelevant whether a business carried on by one entity of the group continues to be carried on by the same entity or a different entity within the group. The entry history rule (¶8-020) does *not* operate to deem the business of the head company to include the business of a joining entity before it became a member of the group (ITAA97 s 165-212E). When applying the test, the head company's business is established considering the activities of all subsidiary members including inter-group activities (TR 2007/2).

Order of utilising losses

Losses generated by the consolidated group ("group losses") must effectively be used before transferred losses of the same sort (ITAA97 s 707-310(3)(b)).

There are no requirements that one bundle of transferred losses must be utilised before another bundle.

Annual limits on use of transferred losses

The use of transferred losses is generally limited by the "available fraction method" (¶8-120). The available fraction for a bundle of losses is determined and then multiplied by the head company's pre-loss taxable income to determine the maximum taxable income that the head company can offset against that loss bundle in a year. This approach follows the basic policy intent that transferred losses should be utilised at a rate that approximates the rate at which they could have been utilised if the group had not consolidated.

Two transitional options were available which may simplify the calculations and/or increase the rate at which transferred losses can be utilised:

- if the group consolidated before 1 July 2004, it may have been able to increase the available fraction under transitional rules where multiple companies joined the group at the same time and the loss company would have been able to transfer the losses to one or more of those companies under the group loss transfer rules. Referred to here as the "transitional available fraction method", this alternative provided a faster utilisation rate than the basic available fraction method, and

- certain losses transferred under a COT transfer before 1 July 2004 (called "concessional losses") can be utilised at the rate of 1/3 per year. The concessional method was the simplest method to apply. Depending on the facts, losses may be utilised faster or slower under this alternative than under the other methods.

These transitional options are discussed at ¶8-130 and ¶8-140 of the *2017 Australian Master Tax Guide* (62nd edition).

MEC groups

Modifications to the loss transfer and loss utilisation rules are made by ITAA97 Subdiv 719-F (ITAA97 ss 719-250 to 719-325) to ensure that they apply appropriately to MEC groups (¶8-610). The modifications mainly affect: (a) rules about maintaining the same ownership to be able to utilise a loss; and (b) rules for working out how much of a loss can be utilised using the available fraction method.

▶ Planning point: utilising losses

The annual utilisation of a subsidiary's losses by a consolidated group may be limited. By accelerating income and deferring deductible expenditure, it may be possible to increase the taxable income of a loss company in the period before consolidation, thus utilising or reducing some of its pre-consolidation losses. Although such measures may result in increased losses in the subsequent period, post-consolidation losses can be fully offset against group income.

[FITR ¶542-910, ¶551-552 – ¶551-625]

¶8-120 Utilising losses: available fraction method

The use of transferred losses (which are not "concessional losses" (¶8-110)) is restricted, with the intent that the losses are able to be used by the group at approximately the same rate that they would have been used by the joining entity had it remained outside the group. This is achieved by limiting the rate at which a head company can deduct or apply transferred losses by reference to their "available fraction". The available fraction is basically the proportion that the joining entity's market value (at the time of joining) bears to the value of the whole group (including the joining entity) at that time (ITAA97 s 707-320).

The available fraction for a bundle of losses is calculated using the formula:

$$\frac{\text{modified market value of the real loss-maker at the initial transfer time}}{\text{transferee's adjusted market value at the initial transfer time}}$$

The result is rounded to 3 decimal places. However, where rounding would result in a "nil" available fraction, the result is rounded to the first non-zero digit (ITAA97 s 707-320(4)).

Explanation of numerator

In general terms, the "modified market value" of a joining entity (in this case, the real loss-maker) is its market value, *ignoring any interests it has in other members of the group* and assuming that:

- it has no losses and the balance of its franking account is nil, and
- the subsidiary members of the group at the joining time are separate entities and not divisions or parts of the head company (ITAA97 s 707-325).

The "real loss-maker" is the entity that makes the initial transfer of the loss upon joining a group. The "initial transfer time" is when the bundle comes into existence, ie the time when a loss is first transferred to any group under ITAA97 Subdiv 707-A.

Preventing artificial inflation of modified market value

There are special rules in ITAA97 s 707-325 to prevent artificial inflation of the modified market value through injections of capital or non-arm's length transactions in the 4 years prior to consolidation. The term "injection of capital" has its ordinary meaning for the purposes of ITAA97 s 707-325 (TR 2004/9). The purpose of the capital injection or transaction is irrelevant (ID 2004/182). Under a publicly listed share offer, an injection of capital occurs when the company issues shares to the applicants (TD 2006/18).

Explanation of denominator

The "transferee's adjusted market value at the initial transfer time" means the market value of the transferee at the initial transfer time, assuming that (at that time) the transferee had no losses in earlier years and its franking account was nil. The transferee is the head company to which the losses in the bundle were transferred at the initial transfer time.

▶ Planning point: available fraction

A loss company that is heavily leveraged (funded by debt) is likely to have a low or nil market value, resulting in a very low or even nil available fraction such that its transferred losses cannot be utilised (unless the group consolidated before 1 July 2004 and the transitional loss provisions apply). In such instances, the loss subsidiary may be able to utilise its losses faster than the group. This may influence the head company to delay forming a consolidated group or to defer the loss company joining the consolidated group by selling part of its ownership to an outside party. In the latter case, the potential application of the ITAA36 Pt IVA general avoidance provisions (¶30-000) should be considered (¶8-950). Note however, losses of an insolvent entity may be utilised in certain circumstances if ITAA97 s 707-415 applies (see below).

Adjustment of available fraction

The available fraction for a bundle is adjusted or maintained (never increased) when one of the 5 adjustment events set out in the table in ITAA97 s 707-320(2) occurs. The adjusted available fraction is worked out by multiplying the existing available fraction for the bundle by the factor set out in the table. The adjustment events and relevant factors can be summarised as follows:

Available fraction adjustments

Item no	Adjustment event	Factor
1	Previously transferred loss bundles are transferred to a new head company.	The lesser of one and this fraction: $\frac{\text{market value of the old group}}{\text{market value of the new joined group}}$
2	Previously transferred loss bundles are transferred to a new head company and, at the same time, the old group also transfers its group losses to the new head company.	$\frac{\text{the lesser of the available fraction for group losses and 1}}{\text{the total of available fractions for all bundles being transferred}}$
3	Existing group with transferred losses acquires new loss bundles.	$1 - \left\{\text{the total of the available fractions for all new loss bundles that have been transferred to the head company}\right.$
4	There is an increase in the market value of the group as a result of an injection of capital or a non-arm's length transaction.	$\frac{\text{market value of the group just before the event}}{\text{market value of the group just before the event + amount of the increase}}$
5	Available fractions total more than one.	$\frac{1}{\text{total of available fractions}}$

Source: Explanatory Memorandum to the New Business Tax System (Consolidation) Bill (No 1) 2002.

Applying the available fraction to utilise transferred losses

Once the available fraction is determined for a bundle of losses, the maximum application of the losses in the bundle for a particular year is determined by applying the available fraction to the head company's income or gains of each relevant type for the income year. This is a 3-step process.

Step 1

Work out the amount of each income or gain category from column 2 of the table in ITAA97 s 707-310(3). This is the group's total income or gains for each category, reduced by applicable deductions and grossed-up franking offsets. The deductions include group losses (ie losses generated by the group) as well as transferred concessional losses, but not losses otherwise transferred (eg losses limited by their available fraction).

The categories of income or gains covered by the table are:

- capital gains
- exempt film income
- assessable film income
- other exempt income
- other assessable income.

Step 2

Multiply each amount from step 1 by the bundle's available fraction. The result is treated as if it were the head company's only income or gains of that category.

Step 3

Based on the income or gains determined under step 2, work out a notional taxable income for the head company (this involves deducting amounts of each sort of loss in the bundle from the relevant type of income or gains). The amount of the losses of each sort that is applied in working out that notional taxable income can then be utilised in working out the head company's actual taxable income. In other words, the head company cannot use any more losses from the bundle than it could have used had the results in step 2 been the only income and gains of the relevant type.

▶ Example 1

Headco has a single loss bundle with an available fraction of 0.145, containing unused net capital losses of $80 and unused ordinary tax losses of $2,000. There are no group losses or concessional losses. For the year of income, Headco has capital gains of $1,000 (after deducting any capital losses) and taxable income of $9,000 (after deductions but before applying the bundled losses) (step 1).

Headco can offset a maximum of $145 (ie $1,000 × 0.145) of its capital gain and $1,305 (ie $9,000 × 0.145) of its other assessable income by the losses in the bundle (step 2).

Headco can offset $145 of capital gains by the $80 capital loss in the bundle and the remainder by $65 ($145 – $80) of ordinary losses in the bundle. It can also offset $1,305 of ordinary income by the remaining ordinary losses in the bundle (step 3). Therefore, the total losses that Headco can utilise from the bundle for the year are the $80 capital loss and $1,370 of ordinary losses, leaving $630 of ordinary losses.

Special rule for deducting transferred losses from exempt income

The available fraction is applied to all income (including exempt income) in calculating the amount of losses that may be utilised in a particular year. However, this amount can then be applied proportionately between exempt income and non-exempt income, ie the losses that are available for utilisation need only be applied against a portion of exempt income (rather than total exempt income). The balance can be applied against a portion of taxable income (ITAA97 s 707-340).

▶ Example 2

Assume Headco has a bundle containing $40,000 of ordinary tax losses with an available fraction of 0.300. Headco has exempt income (after relevant deductions) of $10,000 and taxable income (after relevant deductions but before applying losses) of $90,000. The maximum losses that Headco can apply is $30,000 (ie $100,000 × 0.300). Of this amount, $3,000 is to be applied against exempt income and $27,000 against taxable income.

Loss transferred by head company to itself

Where the head company transferred losses to itself on forming a consolidated group part way through an income year, its use of its own prior year losses is unrestricted in relation to income attributable to the pre-consolidation period (ITAA97 s 707-335(3)(e)). In relation to income attributable to the post-consolidation period, utilisation of its own transferred losses is governed by the available fraction applicable to that bundle.

Part years

Use of transferred losses is apportioned, ie limited to what is reasonable, where their available fraction applied for only part of the year (ITAA97 s 707-335). This can occur where: (a) the losses were transferred part way through the head company's income year; or (b) the value of the available fraction for the bundle changes during the period. The second circumstance may occur where another loss bundle is transferred to the head company, or there has been a capital injection or a non-arm's length transaction (see table above).

Available fraction where head company joins a new group

Where the head company of a consolidated group (the "old group") becomes a subsidiary member of another group (the "bigger group") and transfers losses to the bigger group, the ex-head company's modified market value or market value is worked out as if each subsidiary member of the old group were part of the ex-head company (ITAA97 s 707-330).

Losses of an insolvent joining entity

If an entity's liabilities exceed its assets at the joining time (ie it is insolvent), losses transferred to the head company will have a nil available fraction. In absence of transitional concessions, such losses cannot be utilised. However, such losses can be utilised in the following situations under ITAA97 s 707-415:

- where the losses are wholly or partly attributable to a debt owed by the joining entity to a party outside the group and the debt is forgiven after the joining entity joins the consolidated group. The losses can reduce the total net forgiven amount of the debt under the commercial debt forgiveness rules (ITAA97 Div 245) up to the gross forgiven amount of the debt (ITAA97 s 245-75) (¶16-910)

- where the losses are a result of a debt terminated after the joining entity joins the group subjecting the head company to the limited recourse debt rules (ITAA97 Div 243). The losses can be used to reduce a capital allowance under the limited recourse debt rules (ITAA97 s 243-35(1); ¶23-260)

- the losses can be used to reduce the head company's CGT event L5 capital gain when a joining entity subsequently leaves the group if the entity's liabilities are the same as they were on joining.

[FITR ¶542-920 – ¶542-945]

Assets

¶8-200 Accounting for assets brought into a consolidated group

Under the single entity rule (¶8-010), all of the assets of a consolidated group are treated as being owned by a single entity, being the head company. Intra-group assets and liabilities (such as membership interests in subsidiaries) are ignored. When an entity joins a consolidated group, it is therefore necessary to set the head company's tax cost for the assets brought into the group by the joining entity, and to eliminate the tax cost of the membership interests that the head entity holds in the joining entity. A detailed set of rules known as the ''tax cost setting rules'' are provided for this purpose.

The tax cost setting rules are set out in 5 subdivisions of ITAA97 Div 705, as follows:

- basic case: a single entity joining an existing consolidated group (ITAA97 Subdiv 705-A: ¶8-210)
- case of group formation (ITAA97 Subdiv 705-B: ¶8-220)
- case where a consolidated group is acquired by another (ITAA97 Subdiv 705-C: ¶8-230)
- case where multiple entities linked by membership interests join a consolidated group (ITAA97 Subdiv 705-D: ¶8-240)
- adjustments for errors (ITAA97 Subdiv 705-E: ¶8-250).

[FITR ¶541-200 – ¶541-205]

¶8-210 Where single entity joins existing consolidated group

When an entity joins an existing consolidated group, the tax cost of each asset brought into the group is set at the asset's ''tax cost setting amount'' (ITAA97 s 701-10). The relevant tax cost setting amounts are worked out by allocating the consolidated group's ''allocable cost amount'' (ACA) for the joining entity to the joining entity's assets. The ACA is broadly representative of the cost of equity in the joining entity and its liabilities. Depending on the type of asset, its original tax cost may either be retained or changed by resetting it to either a higher or lower amount.

Use of tax cost setting amount

An asset's tax cost setting amount is used by the head company when applying relevant provisions of the income tax law depending on the type of asset. Under ITAA97 s 701-55, specific provisions deal with the use of the tax cost setting amount of depreciating assets, trading stock, registered emissions units (¶19-130), qualifying securities, assets taxed under CGT provisions, assets which are ITAA97 Div 230 financial arrangements (¶23-030), work-in-progress (WIP) amount assets (¶8-580) and consumable stores. For example:

- to work out the decline in value of a depreciating asset, the head company is taken to have acquired a joining entity's asset at the joining time and for a cost equal to its tax cost setting amount (ITAA97 s 701-55(2))
- trading stock of a joining entity is treated as the head company's trading stock on hand at the start of the relevant income year whose deemed value is equal to its tax cost setting amount (ITAA97 s 701-55(3))
- the CGT provisions apply such that the asset's cost base or reduced cost base is its tax cost setting amount (ITAA97 s 701-55(5))

- for the purposes of applying ITAA97 Div 230, a head company is deemed to have acquired a Div 230 financial arrangement at the joining time for a payment equal to the asset's tax cost setting amount if the accruals, realisation or hedging methods apply. If the fair value, financial reports or retranslation methods apply, the cost of the asset is its ‘‘Div 230 starting value’’ at the joining time (ITAA97 s 701-55(5A) and (5B)). Any excess of the Div 230 starting value over the tax cost setting amount is included in the head company's assessable income and a shortfall is allowed as a deduction, over 4 years (ITAA97 s 701-61). Any prior history for the financial arrangement or inherited transitional balancing adjustment amounts are disregarded for purposes of applying ITAA97 Div 230 (ID 2012/41; ID 2012/42)
- for the purposes of applying ITAA97 s 25-95, the head company is treated as having paid a WIP amount equal to the tax cost setting amount of the joining entity's WIP amount asset (ITAA97 s 701-55(5C)) as it generally applies to entities joining a consolidated group after 30 March 2011. ITAA97 s 25-95 applies to determine if the WIP amount is then deductible
- when an entity joins a consolidated group holding an asset that is consumable stores, for the purposes of a ITAA97 s 8-1 deduction, the head company is taken to have incurred an outgoing to acquire the asset at the joining time equal to its tax cost setting amount (ITAA97 s 701-55(5D)).

Other assets are dealt with by the ‘‘residual tax cost setting rule’’ (ITAA97 s 701-55(6)) which allows the asset's tax cost setting amount to be used when applying other provisions of the income tax law. Under this rule, the head company is taken to have incurred expenditure to acquire a joining entity's assets equal to their tax cost setting amount at the joining time. Broadly, for entities joining a consolidated group after 30 March 2011, the head company is also taken to have acquired these assets of the joining entity as part of acquiring the joining entity's business as a going concern. This means that the revenue or capital nature of the asset depends on the asset's character in the hands of the head company and not the joining entity, making the entry history rules irrelevant for the purpose of determining the treatment of these assets (ITAA97 s 701-56). The assets will therefore generally be taken to be on capital account and their tax costs only recognised when a CGT event happens and no immediate revenue deductions are available. Certain capital expenditure is excluded from ITAA97 s 701-55(6). In such cases, future deductions continue to be based on the original capital expenditure (eg primary production depreciation assets, Div 43 capital works assets).

Scope of assets

The tax cost setting rules apply only to CGT assets, revenue assets, depreciating assets, trading stock and assets which are or are part of Div 230 financial arrangements (ITAA97 s 701-67). Only assets of a joining entity that are recognised for tax purposes will have their tax cost set so excluding intangible assets such as customer relationships, customer lists, unregistered trademarks and trade names, information databases and trade secrets. Section 701-67 broadly applies only to entities that join a consolidated group *after* 30 March 2011. Refer to ¶8-210 of the *2011 Australian Master Tax Guide* (49th edition) for further information on the pre-2011 rules.

Amendments in *Tax Laws Amendment (2012 Measures No 2) Act 2012* (Act No 99 of 2012) introduced ITAA97 s 701-63 as it broadly applies retrospectively to entities that joined a consolidated group *before* 31 March 2011. It treats customer relationship assets, know-how assets and other accounting intangible assets as part of the joining entity's goodwill asset. This includes customer lists, unregistered trademarks and trade names, information databases and trade secrets. No shortfall interest or administrative penalty, or interest on over-payment of taxes will be payable as a result of shortfalls or over-payments of tax arising from assessments amended due to these retrospective changes to the tax cost setting rules (*Tax Laws Amendment (2012 Measures No 4) Act 2012* (Act No 142 of 2012)).

Where the goodwill of a joining entity is identified and its tax cost setting amount determined according to ITAA97 s 705-35(3), it can be split from and merged with goodwill of the other entities in the group in accordance with changes to the management, organisation and structure of the business of the group. However, the goodwill of the entity (which will be taken by the leaving entity on leaving the group) will retain its character as a separate identifiable CGT asset with a cost base or reduced cost base, as the case may be for the purpose of ITAA97 s 711-25(2) (TD 2007/27).

Working out tax costs for joining member's assets

The steps for working out the tax cost setting amounts (head company's tax costs) for a joining member's assets are as follows (ITAA97 s 705-20 to 705-55).

(1) Work out the ACA for the joining member.

(2) Reduce the ACA by the total of the tax cost setting amounts for the retained cost base assets.

(3) Apportion the remainder of the ACA over the reset cost base assets in proportion to their market values, subject to any adjustment in respect of assets held on revenue account.

(4) If required, adjust the amounts allocated for accelerated depreciation assets and certain privatised assets.

Working out the allocable cost amount

The steps for working out the group's ACA for a joining entity are set out in the table in ITAA97 s 705-60. For an outright acquisition of 100% of the entity that results in the entity joining the consolidated group, only steps 1 and 2 are relevant. Steps 3 to 8 are relevant for a progressive or staggered acquisition (where a consolidated group held some interest in the entity before acquiring the remaining interests enabling it to join the consolidated group), or in a formation scenario (see ¶8-220). The steps are as follows:

Step 1:

Start with the cost of membership interests in the joining entity held by members of the group, worked out under ITAA97 s 705-65. This includes non-membership equity interests in the joining entity, eg convertible notes or rights to acquire membership interests.

Step 2:

Add the value of all the joining entity's liabilities, worked out in accordance with ITAA97 s 705-70.

The liabilities must be established in accordance with accounting principles the joining entity would use if it were to prepare financial statements just before the joining time (*Envestra Limited*). However, certain liabilities are excluded, namely, deferred tax liabilities (for entities joining on or after 15 February 2018), securitisation liabilities and liabilities that will be deductible to the head company if it makes a payment to discharge the liabilities (for entities joining on or after 1 July 2016). Deductible liabilities are, however, not excluded if they are accounting liabilities held by insurance companies and relate to policy holders, Div 230 financial arrangements or relate to certain retirement village contracts.

The value of liabilities that are included at step 2 is adjusted to account for the following (ITAA97 s 705-75 to 705-85; TD 2004/70):

(a) future deductions obtained by the head company for liabilities that were not excluded above

(b) recognising liabilities (or gains or losses from changes in liabilities) for tax purposes at the same time as for accounting purposes

(c) amounts in excess of a corresponding asset's cost base (only applicable to intra-group liabilities)

(d) employee share interests disregarded under s 703-35, and

(e) non-membership equity interests issued to members outside the consolidated group.

A life insurance company's liabilities are to be valued in accordance with ITAA97 s 713-520 (TD 2005/17).

Various other issues arising under step 2 are also discussed in TD 2004/72, TD 2004/74 and TD 2004/79. See also TR 2006/6 for additional guidance.

Step 3:

Add the value of undistributed, frankable pre-joining time profits accruing to the joined group before the joining time, in accordance with ITAA97 s 705-90. Accounting losses that did not accrue to the joined group (ie that were incurred before the joining entity was acquired) are to be ignored (ITAA97 s 705-90(2A)). It is acceptable, but not mandatory, to assume that profits have been distributed on a last-in first-out basis and that untaxed profits were paid out as unfranked distributions before taxed profits (ITAA97 s 705-90(10)). Deductible liabilities excluded at step 2 are also to be ignored in working out the step 3 amount, meaning the profits are increased by these liabilities that otherwise reduced the profits. Various issues arising under step 3 are discussed in TD 2004/53, TD 2004/55 and TD 2004/62.

Steps 3A to 8:

(3A) Make an adjustment (as provided in ITAA97 s 705-93; 705-147; 705-227) in limited circumstances where the joining entity holds a CGT asset (other than a pre-CGT asset) that has a deferred roll-over gain or loss. If the result after step 3A is a negative amount, the head company makes a capital gain of that amount (CGT event L2 (¶11-360): ITAA97 s 104-505). This step is relevant in a scenario of the formation of consolidated group (¶8-220).

(4) Subtract the amount of pre-joining time distributions out of certain profits, worked out under ITAA97 s 705-95. Various issues arising under step 4 are discussed in TD 2004/57, TD 2004/58 and TD 2004/60.

(5) Subtract the amount of certain losses accruing to the joined group before the joining time, worked out under ITAA97 s 705-100. Where the loss already reduces the step 3 amount it is not also included under step 5 (TD 2004/59).

(6) Subtract the remainder of the losses that the joining entity transferred to the head company, worked out under ITAA97 s 705-110.

(7) Subtract certain deductions to which the head company is entitled (ITAA97 s 705-115).

(8) If the remaining amount is positive, it is the joined group's ACA. Otherwise, the ACA is nil.

If a particular amount is reduced from the ACA in more than one step (eg step 5, step 3 and/or from the cost base of membership interests in step 1), the head company can make a choice in writing as to which step will include the particular amount to prevent double counting (ITAA97 s 705-62).

The ACA is then reduced by allocating costs to the assets of the joining entity to which the tax cost setting rules apply (ITAA97 s 701-67).

Tax cost setting amount for retained cost base assets

The ACA is first reduced by the tax cost setting amount of an entity's retained cost base assets. A retained cost base asset is (ITAA97 s 705-25):

(a) Australian currency (other than trading stock or collectables of the joining entity)

(b) a right to receive a specified amount of Australian currency (other than a marketable security) eg debts or bank deposits (TR 2005/10)

(c) a unit in a cash management trust expressed in Australian dollars whose redemption value cannot increase

(d) qualifying securities (¶23-320)

(e) (broadly) entitlements to prepaid services

(f) certain depreciating assets used in petroleum activities transitioned from Australia to Timor-Leste to which special rules apply under ITAA97 Div 417

(g) financial arrangements under ITAA97 Subdiv 250-E, and

(h) a right to future income other than a WIP amount asset (¶8-580).

The tax cost setting amount of a joining entity's retained cost base asset falling under either (a), (b) or (c) above is set at the amount of Australian currency concerned (ie face value). For a qualifying security under (d) above, the tax cost setting amount is the joining entity's "terminating value" for the security, ie the amount at which the joining entity, just before joining, could dispose of the security without affecting its taxable income under ITAA36 s 159GS (ITAA97 s 705-25; 705-30). The tax cost setting amount for a prepaid entitlement under (e) above is the amount of deductions to which the head company is entitled in respect of the prepaid expenditure. The tax cost setting amount for a financial arrangement under Subdiv 250-E is also the joining entity's terminating value. The terminating value is the amount of consideration that the joining entity would need to receive if it were to dispose of the financial arrangement just before the leaving time without an amount being included in assessable income, or being allowed as a deduction, under Subdiv 250-E. The tax cost setting amount is also the joining entity's terminating value for assets falling under (f) and (h).

Where a group consolidated before 1 July 2004, the cost bases of other assets could also be retained under several transitional rules (see ¶8-220 of the *2017 Australian Master Tax Guide* (62nd edition)). If an entity joining a consolidated group has the same majority owners from 27 June 2002 up to the joining time, the trading stock of the joining entity is treated as a retained cost base asset. The tax cost to the head company will therefore be the joining entity's closing value for its trading stock (ITTPA s 701A-5(1), (2)).

If the total amount to be treated as payment for retained cost base assets (ie ACA allocated to retained cost base assets) exceeds the joined group's ACA for the joining entity, the head company makes a capital gain equal to the excess (CGT event L3 (¶11-360): ITAA97 s 104-510). From 10 February 2010, if the market value of a debt is lower than its face value (say, if the debt is impaired), its tax cost setting amount is reduced from its face value by the amount of the CGT Event L3 capital gain. As a result, the CGT event L3 capital gain is also reduced by the same amount (ITAA97 s 705-27). This rule is applicable from 1 July 2002 if the head company made a choice to that effect by 30 June 2011 (or within a further time as allowed by the Commissioner).

Tax cost for reset cost base assets

The amount of allocable cost remaining (if any) after valuing the retained cost base assets is allocated to the reset cost base assets in proportion to their market values (ITAA97 s 705-35). A reset cost base asset is any asset of a joining entity that is not a retained cost base asset.

If there are no reset cost base assets, the amount of ACA remaining is treated as a capital loss of the head company (CGT event L4 (¶11-360): ITAA97 s 104-515). Where the value of the reset cost base assets is trifling, they can be ignored (TD 2005/54).

Goodwill associated with the joining entity is a reset cost base asset. Although the goodwill may include synergistic goodwill that the head company has as a result of its ownership and control of the joining entity, it is deemed to be an asset brought into the group by the joining entity. Generally, the market value of the total goodwill can be taken as the amount of any excess of the market value of the joining entity at the joining time over the market value of the net identifiable assets of the joining entity. As in the case of other reset cost base assets, the tax cost of the goodwill may be set higher or lower than its market value when the ACA is allocated. For further assistance in identifying and setting the tax cost of goodwill, see TR 2005/17 and TD 2007/1. ITAA97 s 701-63 (as it applies to entities joining a consolidated group before 31 March 2011) treats goodwill as a single asset and deems certain intangible assets as forming part of the joining entity's goodwill asset.

In the case of a reset cost base asset that is *held on revenue account* (ie trading stock, a depreciating asset or a ''revenue asset''), the deemed payment for the asset must not exceed the greater of: (a) its market value; or (b) the joining entity's terminating value for the asset. Any excess is reallocated on an iterative basis among the other reset cost base assets until the full amount is allocated. If any excess cannot be reallocated (because all the reset cost base assets are valued at their limits), any remaining excess is treated as a capital loss of the head company (ITAA97 s 705-40; CGT event L8: ITAA97 s 104-535). A ''revenue asset'' is any CGT asset (except trading stock and depreciating assets) where any profit or loss on realisation would be reflected in the joining entity's taxable income, otherwise than solely as a capital gain or capital loss (ITAA97 s 977-50; TD 2007/18). PS LA 2004/12 describes the procedures that may be applied in resetting the cost base of depreciating assets, including acceptable short cuts.

For depreciating assets to which the temporary full expensing or accelerated depreciation rules (ITTPA97 Subdivs 40-BB and BA: ¶17-430) or the instant asset write-off for medium-sized businesses (ITAA97 s 40-82; ¶17-330) applied before the joining time, the deemed payment for the asset is capped at the joining entity's terminating value for the asset (ITAA97 s 705-45(2)). This is to prevent an uplift in the tax cost of such assets where the joining entity has benefited from these incentives. However, in the case of assets to which accelerated depreciation under former ITAA97 Div 42 applied — due to pre-21 September 1999 acquisition or roll-over — the accelerated depreciation rates will automatically apply if the deemed payment for the asset does not exceed the joining entity's terminating value for the asset (ITAA97 s 701-80). Where the deemed payment exceeds this limit, the head company can voluntarily reduce it under ITAA97 s 705-45(1) and continue to apply the accelerated rates. Unlike the adjustments for assets held on revenue account in s 705-40, any reduction under both s 705-45(1) or (2) is lost. It is not reallocated to other assets.

Where a tax exempt (or previously exempt) entity joins a consolidated group, the tax cost for depreciating assets (privatised assets) of the entity is capped (s 705-47) unless certain exceptions apply (*Australian Pipeline Limited*).

The head company may choose the order in which it applies ss 705-40; 705-45 and 705-47. If it does not choose, they apply in sequential order (ITAA97 s 705-55).

▶ Planning point: tax cost setting

Consolidation may provide an opportunity to step up the tax value of some assets brought into the group. This can result in increased depreciation deductions or reduced capital gains.

Special rules for certain assets

Special rules apply to:

- finance leases (ITAA97 s 705-56; ID 2009/153)
- certain mining, quarrying and exploration expenditure (ITAA97 s 716-300; ITTPA Subdiv 705-E; 712-E)
- low-value pools and software development pools (ITAA97 Subdiv 716-G; ITTPA Subdiv 716-G)
- rights to future income other than WIP amount assets and consumable stores (¶8-580)
- non-taxable Australian property of a joining entity that was owned by a foreign entity (ITAA97 s 716-440; LCR 2019/2).

Note that a transitional foreign-held subsidiary (ITTPA s 701C-10) was also treated as part of the head company and its assets retained their existing tax values for pre-1 July 2004 consolidations (ITTPA s 701C-30; TD 2005/41 to TD 2005/44).

Restructures involving scrip for scrip roll-overs

The scrip for scrip CGT roll-over provisions prevent an acquiring entity from obtaining a market value cost base for qualifying interests that it acquires in the original entity, where the arrangement is taken to be a restructure (¶12-325). If the original entity becomes a member of a consolidated group or MEC group under the arrangement, the head company of the group can elect to retain the tax costs of the original entity's assets rather than apply the consolidation tax cost setting rules to reset the costs of the original entity's assets (ITAA97 Subdiv 715-W).

Linked assets and liabilities

The consolidation cost setting rules are modified for a set of linked assets and liabilities. A set of "linked assets and liabilities" is one or more of an entity's assets and liabilities that are netted-off and presented as a net amount in the entity's balance sheet according to accounting principles the entity would use if it were to prepare its financial statements just before the joining time. In such cases, a special netting-off treatment will also apply to the linked assets and liabilities under the cost setting rules. The value of retained cost base assets is not affected by the modifications (ITAA97 s 705-59).

Pre-CGT assets

Pre-CGT assets of a joining entity will retain their pre-CGT status in the consolidated group. Pre-CGT assets taken from the group by a leaving entity retain their pre-CGT status in the leaving entity's hands.

Pre-CGT membership interests

If any of the membership interests in the joining entity is a pre-CGT asset of the group, a mechanism for preserving the pre-CGT status of those interests involves determining a "pre-CGT proportion" of the membership interests in a joining entity (ITAA97 s 705-125).

The pre-CGT proportion is calculated by dividing:

(1) the market value of the pre-CGT membership interests in the joining entity held by a member of the group at the joining time, by

(2) the market value of all membership interests in the joining entity held by a member of the group at the joining time.

If the joining entity is a trust, a discretionary interest (ie a membership interest that is neither a unit nor an interest in the trust) is ignored in the above calculation.

When an entity leaves the group, the entity's pre-CGT proportion is applied to the number of membership interests held by members of the group to calculate the proportion of the membership interests held by the group at the leaving time that should be treated as pre-CGT interests. The head company chooses which particular membership interests are pre-CGT assets. If more than one class of shares is involved, a proportion is determined separately for each class of shares and the head company chooses which membership interests within a class of shares are pre-CGT (ITAA97 s 711-65). Again, a discretionary interest is ignored (ITAA97 s 711-65(8)).

▶ Example: Pre-CGT proportion

Until 30 June 2019, Headco, the head company of a consolidated group, holds 900 shares in Subco. All of Headco's shares in Subco are pre-CGT assets. On 1 July 2019, Headco acquires the remaining 100 shares in Subco, which becomes a subsidiary member of the consolidated group. At 1 July 2019, the market value of Subco is $5,000. Each share has a market value of $5.

The pre-CGT proportion of Headco's membership interests in Subco is 90% calculated as:

$$\frac{\$5 \times 900}{\$5 \times 1{,}000} = 90\%$$

On 1 July 2020, Headco chooses to sell 600 pre-CGT shares to a third party and Subco leaves the consolidated group. Of the 500 shares Headco continues to hold in Subco, 100 are post-CGT shares and 300 are pre-CGT shares.

An integrity rule applies if any assets brought into the consolidated group by a leaving entity stopped being pre-CGT assets under ITAA97 Div 149 while being held by the head company. In such cases, the pre-CGT proportion of the leaving entity at the leaving time is taken to be nil and an adjustment may be made to the group's ACA for the leaving entity (ITAA97 s 711-70) (¶8-400). An integrity rule may also modify the operation of CGT event K6 (¶11-350) under ITAA97 s 711-75.

Former pre-CGT membership interests

There may also be circumstances where a pre-CGT membership interest in the joining entity held by a member of the joined group at the joining time had at some previous time been converted to a post-CGT asset by the operation of ITAA97 Div 149, with the result that the cost base of the membership interest was restated at market value (¶12-870). Subject to certain control tests for value shifting purposes, the loss of pre-CGT status may have occurred when the interest was not held by the member.

Under the tax cost setting rules, the increased cost base of the membership interest may result in the tax cost setting amount for an asset that is trading stock, a depreciating asset or a revenue asset (revenue, etc, asset) being set at greater than its terminating value, with a resulting increase in tax deductions. To overcome this risk to the revenue, the tax cost setting amount for revenue, etc, assets is reduced where applicable (but not below the asset's terminating value) to eliminate the effect of "loss of pre-CGT status adjustments" on the cost bases of membership interests (ITAA97 s 705-57). Section 705-57 is modified by ITAA97 s 705-163 to work out the adjustment where the entity joins at the formation time.

An amount equal to the resultant reductions is allowed as a capital loss (CGT event L1: ¶11-360). The capital loss is available to be offset against capital gains over a period of 5 years at the rate of 1/5 each year on a cumulative basis (ITAA97 s 104-500).

If the entity leaves the group before the fifth year, the 1/5 per year restriction is removed where: (a) members of the consolidated group held all of the membership interests in the entity from the end of 30 June 2002 until it became a subsidiary member of the consolidated group; and (b) during the period of consolidation the head company did not dispose of the entity's assets, other than minor assets disposed of in the ordinary course of business (ITTPA s 701B-1).

Partner or partnership joins consolidated group

Refinements to the cost setting rules operate to determine the tax cost setting amount of certain partnership-related assets where either:

(1) a partner in a partnership joins a consolidated group, but the partnership does not, or

(2) a partnership joins a consolidated group, because all the partners have joined the group (ITAA97 s 713-200 to 713-240).

Broadly, in case (1) above, the partner's individual shares in the assets of the partnership (or in other assets that relate to the partnership) are recognised (described as "partnership cost setting interests"). However, underlying partnership assets and the partner's membership interests in the partnership itself are not recognised.

In case (2), the underlying assets of the partnership are recognised. The partners' membership interests in the partnership and their individual shares in the assets of the partnership are not recognised.

[FITR ¶541-210 – ¶541-335]

¶8-220 Cost setting at formation time

When a consolidated group is formed, the cost values of the assets of the head company remain unchanged. However, any debt interests or membership interests held by the head company in the subsidiary members are ignored for tax purposes.

Each entity becoming a subsidiary member of the consolidated group at the time it is formed is treated in the same way as an entity joining an existing consolidated group, subject to the following modifications to working out the allocable cost amount (ACA) for the entity.

- Where an entity (the "first level entity") holds membership interests (including non-membership equity interests) in another entity that becomes a subsidiary member at the formation time, the tax cost setting amounts for the entities' assets are worked out "from the top down". First, the tax costs for the first level entity's assets are set according to the usual rules for a joining entity, including setting the cost base of the first level entity's membership interests in the other entity. That cost base is then used in step 1 in working out the ACA for the other entity and the tax costs for its assets (ITAA97 s 705-145).
- The step 3A amount (ie the deferred rollover gain or loss) is apportioned among the entity and any "first level entities" interposed between the entity and the head company (ITAA97 s 705-147).
- The reduction under step 4 for pre-formation distributions is only made for profits that have been effectively distributed to the head company in respect of its direct interests in the joining entities (ITAA97 s 705-155).
- For the purposes of apportioning the entity's ACA over its reset cost base assets, the market value of its membership interests in another entity that becomes a subsidiary member at the formation time is increased by the first entity's interest in any loss of the other entity that reduces its ACA under step 5 (or increased by its interest in any profit that increases its ACA under step 3) (ITAA97 s 705-160). The intention is to prevent a distortion in the apportionment of the first entity's ACA.

For transitional rules applicable to consolidated groups that came into existence before 1 July 2004, see ¶8-220 (*2017 Australian Master Tax Guide* (62nd edition)).

[FITR ¶541-340 – ¶541-385]

¶8-230 Consolidated group acquired by another

Special rules apply where an existing consolidated group is acquired by another consolidated group (ITAA97 Subdiv 705-C, comprising s 705-175 to 705-200; modified by s 719-170 for MEC groups). The core rules and cost setting rules will apply in this circumstance as if the joining group were a single entity. See, for example, ID 2007/127. Modifications to the cost setting rules are made where certain non-membership equity interests have been issued by subsidiary members of the acquired group to members of the acquiring group or to third parties, or there are employee shares or certain ADI restructure preference share interests in a subsidiary member of the acquired group.

Where a single entity that is not a member of a consolidated group or MEC group acquires all the membership interests in, respectively, a consolidated group or the eligible tier-1 companies of a MEC group and then makes the choice to form a consolidated group, the tax cost setting modifications will not apply (ID 2009/160; ID 2010/40). In such a scenario, the consolidated group or MEC group will deconsolidate and the exit cost setting rules will apply (¶8-400) and entry cost setting rules apply upon formation of the new consolidated group or MEC group. ITAA97 s 705-175(1) applies only where an *existing consolidated group* acquires all the membership interests in the acquired group. The words ''become members of another consolidated group'' indicate that there must be an existing consolidated group as the acquiring group. (Where a MEC group is acquired by another MEC group or a consolidated group, the MEC cost setting rules in ITAA97 Subdiv 719-C are modified to align with Subdiv 705-C.)

[FITR ¶541-400 – ¶541-440]

¶8-240 Multiple joining entities linked by membership interests

Special rules apply where the combined membership interests of an existing consolidated group and an acquired entity result in additional entities becoming subsidiary members of the group (ITAA97 Subdiv 705-D, comprising s 705-215 to 705-240). This includes the situation where an acquired entity has a wholly-owned subsidiary (linked entities).

The cost setting rules applicable to a single joining entity are applied, subject to certain modifications. The modifications are made for:

- specifying the order in which tax cost setting amounts are worked out
- working out the step 3A amount of the allocated cost amount to take into account membership interests held by linked entities in other linked entities
- working out step 4 of the allocated cost amount for successive distributions of certain profits
- taking into account owned profits or losses of certain linked entities
- making adjustments to the tax cost setting amount for certain assets where there has been a loss of pre-CGT status of membership interests in the linked entity.

[FITR ¶541-450 – ¶541-490]

¶8-250 Adjustments of cost-setting errors

Under ITAA97 Subdiv 705-E (ss 705-305 to 705-320), a head company may be able to reverse unintentional errors affecting tax costs of reset cost base assets by realising an immediate capital gain or capital loss (CGT event L6: ¶11-360). Subject to certain conditions being satisfied, the tax costs that are affected by the errors are taken to be correct for most purposes. This approach is intended to avoid the time and expense involved in correcting the errors. It is available where it would be unreasonable to require a recalculation of the amounts involved, having regard to the relative size of the errors, the number and difficulty of the calculations required, the number of adjustments in assessments and tax returns and the difficulty in obtaining any necessary information.

The Commissioner must be notified of the amount by which the tax cost setting amount was overstated or understated as soon as practical after the error is discovered. The notification must be in the approved form. The rules for adjusting unintentional errors are explained in TR 2007/7.

[FITR ¶541-550 – ¶541-575]

¶8-280 Market valuation for tax consolidation

One of the most challenging aspects of consolidating a group will be the need to develop and document defendable market valuation data in the following circumstances:

- to establish the basis for revaluing the reset cost base assets brought into the group by a joining entity where the allocable cost amount (ACA) method is used (¶8-210)
- to ensure that revenue assets are not valued higher than their market value where the ACA method is used (¶8-210)
- to calculate the pre-CGT proportion arising from pre-CGT membership interests in a joining entity (¶8-210)
- to calculate an adjustment to the result of step 3 in the ACA calculation for an entity where the joining entity holds a CGT asset with a deferred roll-over gain or loss
- to calculate the ACA for subsidiary members that have not been chosen to have the transitional method of valuing assets apply
- to establish the available fraction attached to losses transferred to the consolidated group, other than concessional losses (¶8-120).

In calculating market values for the above purposes, taxpayers will need to balance the costs of determining and documenting market values of particular assets or asset groups against the risks of incurring additional tax, penalties and compliance costs if the taxpayer assigns values that cannot be defended or prove to be substantially wrong.

▶ Planning points: market valuation

- Determining market values, as required under the ACA method (and also required to establish pre-CGT proportions relevant to pre-CGT membership interests and available fractions relevant to transferred losses), can be costly and complex and can introduce substantial tax risks. The costs and risks may be mitigated by concentrating valuation resources on the most significant and sensitive asset areas.
- Costs incurred in obtaining market valuations required under the consolidation regime are deductible under ITAA97 s 25-5 as a tax-related expense. If the valuation is obtained for multiple purposes, the deduction may need to be apportioned (TD 2003/10; TD 2003/11). The costs are not deductible under ITAA97 s 8-1 (TR 2004/2).

The Commissioner has released general guidelines on *Market valuation for tax purposes* (¶17-050). Selected issues covered in the guidelines are discussed below.

The tax cost setting process involves allocating the ACA to underlying assets on the basis of proportionate market value. The values should be allocated on a reasonable basis, which includes the residual value method to allocate any remaining value to goodwill. The guidelines detail the allocation process and also provide 5 valuation shortcut options that may be used to value certain assets:

Valuation short cut	Type of asset	Valuation option
1	Depreciating assets (not including intangible assets) that *have not* been depreciated on an accelerated basis whose individual adjustable values are 1% or less of the joining subsidiary's allocable cost amount (ACA)	*Adjustable value* (which can be revised to ignore any balancing adjustment amount that had the effect of reducing the adjustable value) can be used as market value
2	Depreciating assets (not including intangible assets) that *have* been depreciated on an accelerated basis whose individual adjustable values are 1% or less of the joining subsidiary's allocable cost amount (ACA)	Adjustable value, revised to ignore the effect of accelerated depreciation (and which can be revised to ignore any balancing adjustment amount that had the effect of reducing the adjustable value), can be used as market value
3	Trading stock (other than live stock and growing crops) that is not a retained cost base asset	Terminating value at the joining time may be used as market value except in certain circumstances
4	Employee share scheme shares	Existing market valuation updated if appropriate
5	Unlisted shares	Existing market valuation updated if appropriate

However, the following constraints apply to the use of the valuation short cut options.

- The taxpayer must have adequate supporting documentation that demonstrates that the asset satisfies the eligibility requirements of the particular short cut.
- With one exception, the decision to use a particular short cut must apply to all of an entity's assets that are eligible for that short cut. The exception is that a taxpayer may generally opt to use short cuts 1 and 2 for a joining entity's eligible depreciating assets, while obtaining new market values for the assets (including those eligible for the short cut) that make up a single large functioning unit of integrated plant, such as integrated plant within an oil refinery, an oil rig facility, a communications cable and integrated plant within a factory production line.
- Short cuts other than short cut 3 (trading stock) are not available where there is a specific intention at the joining time that the joining entity, all or part of the underlying business of the joining entity or the asset itself will be sold following consolidation.
- Short cuts are not available as a means of calculating the joining entity's market value for the purpose of calculating an available fraction to be applied to transferred losses.
- Where short cuts have been adopted for certain assets, the short cut values should be used in determining the market value of the entity's goodwill (given that goodwill is determined as the excess of the market value of the entity over the market value of its net identifiable assets).

Records supporting market valuations must be kept for at least the statutory 5-year period that applies to other tax records (¶9-045). In the context of consolidation, the relevant transaction for record-keeping purposes would be the eventual disposal of the asset by the consolidated group. The particular records that need to be kept are based on the generic documentation requirements of the Act, of which ITAA36 s 262A (¶9-045) and ITAA97 s 121-20 (¶11-920) are most relevant. Taxpayers will need to exercise commercial judgment as to the extent of documentation which they should retain. Relevant factors include the complexity of the valuations, the value of the assets relative to the total assets of the business and the degree of subjectivity inherent in the valuation process. The guidelines also include the ATO's minimum requirements for a market valuation report.

Imputation Aspects of Consolidation

¶8-300 Consolidation: franking accounts and franking deficit tax offsets

The head company of a consolidated group will operate a single franking account on behalf of the group and the imputation rules will operate as if the group were a single entity.

When an entity joins a consolidated group any franking account surplus that it has at that time is transferred to the head company's franking account. If the entity has a franking account deficit just before joining, it must pay the appropriate amount of franking deficit tax. The joining entity's franking account balance becomes nil and the franking account remains dormant during the period of consolidation.

Events that would normally cause a franking debit or credit to arise in the franking account of a subsidiary member of the group will instead arise in the franking account of the head company. This includes a subsidiary member that is a trust receiving a franked distribution from outside the group, provided the head company is entitled to a tax offset under Div 207 (TD 2014/8; ¶4-800). The rules also apply where, after the leaving time, a former subsidiary member pays tax (or receives a refund) that relates to the time when it was a member of the group (ITAA97 s 709-95; 709-100).

Only the head company may allocate franking credits to frankable distributions made by a subsidiary member of the group, such as distributions in relation to employee share acquisition scheme shares or non-share equity interests. Intra-group dividends, like other intra-group transactions, are disregarded.

▶ Planning points: Franking credits

- The pooling of franking credits may free up blocked franking credits from subsidiaries and increase the amount of franked dividends that the head company can pay to its shareholders.
- Where dividends are paid on employee shares in subsidiaries, the franking percentage may increase or decrease due to pooling (depending on the availability of group credits and timing of the dividends).

Franking deficit tax offsets

When an entity joins a consolidated group any unapplied franking deficit tax offsets (¶4-780) that it has at that time are transferred to the head company (ITAA97 Subdiv 709-C). However, when an entity ceases to be a subsidiary member of a consolidated group, it does *not* take any franking deficit tax offsets with it.

The Commissioner has the discretion to allow the full franking deficit tax offset against an income tax liability where the events that caused the deficit were outside the company's control (¶4-780). This includes situations where a consolidated group's franking account is in deficit because it receives tax refunds for earlier years due to retrospective changes in the consolidation legislation. At the time of allocating franking credits to a distribution, the group must have had no reasonable expectation that its franking account would be in deficit due to these changes.

[FITR ¶214-050, ¶543-640 – ¶543-790]

Leaving Consolidated Group

¶8-400 Leaving a consolidated group

Membership interests in leaving entity

Immediately before an entity leaves a consolidated group, the head company is deemed to have acquired the membership interests (including non-membership equity interests) in the leaving entity at a cost equal to the group's cost for the net assets of the leaving entity, as set out in ITAA97 Div 711. This involves calculating the group's allocable cost amount for the leaving entity (the "exit ACA") which is allocated to the membership interests in the leaving entity, ie the asset that emerges as a result of the entity leaving the consolidated group (ITAA97 s 711-15).

Calculating the exit ACA

The 5 steps for working out the group's exit ACA for a leaving entity are set out in the table in ITAA97 s 711-20.

(1) Start with the terminating values of the leaving entity's assets held just before the leaving time (ITAA97 s 711-25; TD 2006/19; TD 2006/53; TD 2007/27).

(2) Add the value of certain deductions (multiplied by the general company tax rate) the leaving entity is entitled to as a result of leaving the group which are not reflected in the above step 1 amount (ITAA97 s 711-35).

(3) Add the sum of the tax cost setting amounts of the leaving entity's assets corresponding to liabilities owed to it by other members of the group at the leaving time (ITAA97 s 711-40). These are commercial or business liabilities and corresponding assets that would be matched under generally accepted Australian valuation principles (TD 2005/45). The tax cost setting amount will depend on the nature of the corresponding asset. If it is a debt owing to the leaving entity, the tax cost setting amount is the market value of the asset at the leaving time; otherwise, it is an amount that reflects the cost of the asset (ITAA97 s 701-60A, applicable to arrangements commencing on or after 7.30 pm AEST 14 May 2013).

(4) Subtract certain liabilities of the leaving entity held just before the leaving time (*Handbury Holdings*). These are amounts which will be treated as liabilities according to accounting principles the group would use if it were to prepare financial statements just before the leaving time (ITAA97 s 711-45). This step 4 amount is subject to various adjustments to account for among others, disregarded employee share interests, the leaving entity's future entitlement to deductions, intra-group liabilities, unrealised gains or losses (including special rules for liabilities of a retirement village operator (PCG 2019/4)) and if a different amount was adopted for the liability when calculating the entry ACA. The liabilities covered in step 4 include those which are extinguished by the transaction which caused the entity to leave the group in the first place, ie issue of shares in leaving entity to an entity outside the group (ID 2007/118). Adjustments relating to deferred tax liabilities are also excluded for entities joining on or after 15 February 2018.

(5) If the remaining amount is positive, it is the exit ACA. If it is negative, the head company's cost to acquire the leaving entity's membership interests is nil.

Where the result is negative, the head company will make a capital gain equal to that amount (CGT event L5 (¶11-360): ITAA97 s 104-520; see also ID 2006/170 and ID 2006/171). The capital gain under CGT event L5 is reduced in certain circumstances if the leaving entity transferred losses with a nil available fraction when it joined the group (¶8-120: ITAA97 s 707-415).

Based on the deemed cost of its membership interests in the leaving entity, the head company may realise a capital gain or capital loss on the disposal of those interests at or after the leaving time. Where the disposal gives rise to a prima facie capital loss, the deemed cost of the membership interests may need to be recalculated to reset the terminating value of certain CGT assets at their reduced cost base rather than their cost base to determine the amount of the capital loss, if any (ITAA97 s 711-20).

Where the leaving entity holds membership interests in other subsidiary members of the group, those entities will be ineligible to remain in the group. The cost of any membership interests that one leaving entity holds in another is treated in a similar way to the head company's membership interests (s 711-5(4)).

The application of the pre-CGT proportion to an entity's shares allows any pre-CGT status of its shares to be maintained at the same percentage when it enters and exits consolidation.

Deregistered subsidiary

A subsidiary company that is deregistered ceases to be a member of the group and is treated as a leaving entity (TD 2006/58). Other implications of the deregistration of a subsidiary member are considered in TD 2006/59, TD 2007/12 and TD 2007/13. A deregistered company that is reinstated under *Corporations Act 2001*, s 601AH is taken to have continued in existence as if it had not been deregistered (TD 2007/15).

Partnership leaves group

Special cost setting rules apply where a partnership leaves a consolidated group (ITAA97 s 713-250 to 713-265).

Other implications of leaving group

Other implications of an entity leaving the group are as follows.

- The tax cost to the head company of liabilities owed to it by the leaving entity is set at market value (ITAA97 ss 701-20; 701-60; TD 2005/46; ¶8-210).
- The leaving entity is treated as having acquired its trading stock and registered emissions unit upon leaving the group for an amount reflecting its "tax-neutral" treatment in the hands of the head company (ITAA97 s 701-25).
- Under the exit history rule (¶8-020), the CGT assets that the leaving entity takes with it are deemed to have been acquired by the leaving entity at the time that the head company was recognised as having acquired them (ID 2006/130).
- The leaving entity's franking account becomes active again, starting with a nil balance.
- Where, just before the leaving time, there is an arrangement in force for the supply of goods or services between the leaving entity and the head company or another leaving entity, ITAA97 s 701-75 may adjust the assessable income or deductions of the parties to the arrangement, in order to align their tax positions.
- All losses remain in the head company (ITAA97 s 707-410).

The treatment of foreign income tax offsets, CFC attribution surpluses and post FIF abolition surpluses is discussed at ¶8-600.

Where subsidiary member acquired by another consolidated group

Where all the shares of a subsidiary member of a consolidated group are acquired at a single point in time by another consolidated group, the asset cost setting rules in ITAA97 Div 701; 705 and 711 apply. In such cases, ITAA97 s 45-15, which deals with the disposal of shares in a subsidiary that leases plant (¶23-230) does not apply (ID 2006/338).

▶ Planning point: Acquisition of group member

A prospective purchaser of a company that is a subsidiary member of a consolidated group should ensure that the head company will provide full details of the tax cost of the subsidiary's assets. The purchaser might also seek warranties in the event the costs are incorrect.

Where consolidated group ceases to exist

Where a consolidated group ceases to exist because the head company is no longer eligible, the subsidiary members of the group are deemed to leave the group immediately before it ceases to exist. There is an exception, however, where a consolidated group is acquired by another consolidated group (¶8-230). In such a case, the tax cost setting rules in ITAA97 Div 711 do not apply to subsidiary members of the consolidated group (TD 2006/38).

Incidental costs

Incidental costs incurred by a head company in acquiring or disposing shares in a subsidiary member are not deductible under ITAA97 s 40-880(2) by virtue of ITAA97 s 40-880(5)(f) if they are incurred when the subsidiary is not part of the consolidated group (TD 2011/8; TD 2011/10). A deduction is not prevented by ITAA97 s 40-880(5)(f) if the head company incurs the incidental costs when the subsidiary is part of the consolidated group (TD 2010/1; TD 2011/9). The incidental costs are described in s 110-35(2) and include legal and accounting fees but not remuneration to a member of the group.

[FITR ¶544-900 – ¶544-970]

Special Consolidation Rules

¶8-500 Interposing a shelf head company

Special provisions enable a shelf company to be interposed between the head company of a consolidated group (the "original company") and its shareholders without disbanding the consolidated group (ITAA97 s 615-30(2); 703-70). For this to happen, the interposition of the new company must be achieved through an exchange of shares in accordance with the conditions set out in ITAA97 Div 615 (¶12-370).

If, immediately after the completion time (for Div 615 purposes), the interposed company is the head company of a consolidatable group consisting only of itself and the members of the consolidated group immediately before the completion time, then the interposed company must choose for the consolidated group to continue in existence. The choice must be made within 28 days after the completion time, or such further time as the Commissioner allows (ITAA97 s 615-30(3)).

The effects of the choice on the consolidated group are set out in ITAA97 ss 703-65 to 703-80. Broadly, the interposed company is taken to have become the head company and the original company is taken to have become a subsidiary member of the group. However, the rules that apply when a subsidiary member joins a consolidated group do not apply when the original company becomes a subsidiary member, subject to any specific exceptions (s 703-70(3)). The interposed company is treated as substituted for the original company at all times before the completion time, and is taken to be the head company of the consolidated group for the income year that ends after the completion time. The group will not fail the continuity of ownership test for recoupment of company losses (¶3-105) merely because of the interposition of the new head company (ID 2007/106; ID 2007/107).

There is compulsory deferral of capital gains or capital losses on disposal, cancellation or redemption of shares in the original company until the replacement shares of the interposed company are disposed of. Where some of the original shares were trading stock or revenue assets of the shareholder, (broadly) the cost of the shares is included in the shareholder's assessable income, and a like amount is taken to have been paid for the relevant replacement shares (ITAA97 s 615-50; 615-55).

[FITR ¶540-675]

¶8-550 Consolidation and particular kinds of entities

ITAA97 Div 713 contains rules for particular kinds of entities.

Discretionary trusts

There are special rules for working out the allocable cost amount (ACA) of a discretionary trust that joins a consolidated group (ITAA97 Subdiv 713-A). Where a membership interest in a trust is neither a unit nor an interest in the trust, has no cost base and only began to be owned because something was settled on the trust, the ACA will be increased to properly reflect the settled capital that would have been distributed tax free to the group if the trust had ended when it joined the group (ITAA97 s 713-20 to 713-50).

Unit trusts

Certain public trading trusts (PTTs) that elect to be taxed like companies are able to head consolidated groups. Such a trust has the benefit of income it receives; it does not receive the income as a trustee but as the head of a consolidated group (*Intoll Management*). The consolidation must take effect on the first day of the trust's income year (ITAA97 s 713-130; ID 2006/206). Once a trust chooses to head a consolidated group, it continues to be taxed like a company, even if the group it heads deconsolidates or it fails the definitional requirements of a PTT (ITAA97 Subdiv 713-C).

Partnerships

Special rules (ITAA97 Subdiv 713-E) apply where a partner or partnership joins a consolidated group (¶8-210), or a partnership leaves a consolidated group (¶8-400).

Life insurance companies

For the special rules for life insurance companies, see ¶3-527.

General insurance companies

ITAA97 Subdiv 713-M sets out special rules for a general insurance company becoming or ceasing to be a subsidiary member of a consolidated group.

[FITR ¶545-700 – ¶546-440]

¶8-580 Miscellaneous special consolidation rules

Miscellaneous special rules, including provisions for spreading assessable income, deductions and fully-deductible capital expenditure over more than one membership or non-membership period, are set out in ITAA97 Div 716.

Assessable income spread over 2 or more income years

Special rules apply where the tax law requires an entity to recognise an amount of assessable income over 2 or more years, and the entity is a member of a consolidated group for part but not all of one of those years. In that case, that part of the amount that was to be recognised as assessable income in the relevant year will be split between the entity and the head company of the consolidated group. The proportion attributable to the head company is determined by *dividing*: (a) the number of days when the entity was a member of the group that are in both the income year and the spreading period *by* (b) the total number of days that are in both the income year and the spreading period (ITAA97 s 716-15). The remaining proportion will of course be attributable to the entity's non-membership period and will be allocated to the entity itself.

▶ Example 1

Get Fit Co sells a 5-year gym membership on 1 March 2020 for $3,000 (ie $50 per month). On 1 June 2020 Get Fit joins a consolidated group.

Of the $3,000, $200 (4 months) is assessable in 2019–20. The spreading period is 1 March 2020 to 28 February 2025, and the period falling within both the spreading period and the income year (ie 1 March 2020 to 30 June 2020) consists of 122 days. Of those 122 days, Get Fit was a member of the consolidated group for 30 days and a non-member for 92 days.

Get Fit will include $150.82 (ie $200 × 92/122) in its assessable income, and the head company will include the remaining $49.18 (ie $200 × 30/122) in its assessable income for 2019–20.

Deductions spread over 2 or more income years

A similar allocation mechanism operates where an amount incurred by an entity is deductible over 2 or more income years and the entity is a member of a consolidated group for only part of a relevant income year (ITAA97 s 716-25).

▶ Example 2

Continuing from Example 1, Get Fit Co had incurred $5,000 of borrowing expenses on 1 August 2016. The expenses were deductible over 5 years (the spreading period), with $1,000 deductible in 2019–20.

As 366 days of the spreading period fall within 2019–20, and Get Fit is a member of the consolidated group for 30 of those days, the head company will deduct $81.97 (ie $1,000 × 30/366) and Get Fit will deduct $918.03 (ie $1,000 × 336/366) for 2019–20.

Exception for depreciation

This provision does not apply to deductions for the decline in value of a depreciating asset. The reason for the exclusion is that the tax value of assets is reset at the time an entity joins a consolidated group, so that the basis of the deductions changes. Furthermore, the existing depreciation rules enable the head company and the joining or leaving entity to each work out their own depreciation deduction for the part of the year that the asset is theirs.

Immediately deductible capital expenditure

Certain capital expenditure is deductible in the year that it is incurred rather than being spread over a period of years. Where the entity incurring the expenditure joins or leaves a consolidated group later in the income year after the entitlement to a deduction arises, the deduction is split between the entity and the head company. The allocation formula is essentially the same as for splitting assessable income (above). The spreading period in this case is the period from the time that an entity would become entitled to deduct the amount until the end of the income year (ITAA97 s 716-70).

▶ Example 3

Farm Co spends $20,000 on a landcare operation (¶18-100) on primary production land on 1 October 2019. It joins a consolidated group headed by MegaFarm Co on 1 January 2020. The deduction will be spread over the period 1 October 2019 to 30 June 2020 (274 days). Farm Co will be entitled to deduct $6,715 (ie $20,000 × 92/274) and MegaFarm Co will be entitled to deduct $13,285 (ie $20,000 × 182/274).

Capital expenditure deductible over 5 years

Certain types of business-related capital expenditures are deductible over 5 years under ITAA97 s 40-880 (¶16-156) provided they cannot be taken into account under some other provision and are not specifically made non-deductible. The capital expenditure should be related to the overall business of the head company or a particular aspect of its overall business which was formerly undertaken or is proposed to be undertaken (TR 2011/6). Before the enactment of s 40-880, these expenditures were "blackhole expenditures" that were ignored for tax purposes. This provision ensures that capital expenditures incurred in connection with intra-group assets of a consolidated group are able to qualify for deduction over 5 years even though the asset itself may not be recognised due to the single entity rule. This measure also applies to MEC groups.

▶ Example 4

The head company of a consolidated group incurs capital expenditure to incorporate a new subsidiary company, which automatically becomes part of the consolidated group. The capital expenditure cannot form part of the cost base of the head company's interest in the subsidiary, as that interest is ignored under the single entity rule. Instead, the expenditure is deductible over 5 years under ITAA97 s 40-880.

Partnership and trust amounts

A similar set of rules applies where a partner in a partnership or a beneficiary of a trust is a subsidiary member of a consolidated group for only part of an income year (ITAA97 ss 716-75 to 716-100). These provisions attribute the partner's or beneficiary's shares of the underlying partnership or trust income or deductions of each non-membership period to the partner or beneficiary; and for each membership period to the group's head company. The partner's or beneficiary's shares of income or deductions that cannot reasonably be attributed to a particular period in the year are apportioned between the entity (partner or beneficiary) and the head company based on the number of membership and non-membership days.

Different income years

Joining or leaving a consolidated group does not affect the income year of the individual entity. Therefore the joining or leaving entity may have a different income year from the consolidated group.

Rather than introducing complex rules to deal with this circumstance, ITAA97 s 716-800 requires amounts to be apportioned between periods in the most appropriate way, having regard to the other apportionment rules and to the objects of the consolidation rules. In particular, an item is to be recognised only once for a particular purpose.

Grossing up threshold amounts for periods of less than 365 days

Certain provisions of the income tax law operate on the basis of whether some threshold is met. In working out how such a provision operates for an entity's non-membership period, the amount applicable to the non-membership period is worked out in relation to a "reference period" starting at the start of the income year and ending at the end of the non-membership period. That amount is then annualised up by multiplying it by 365 and dividing it by the number of days in the reference period (ITAA97 s 716-850).

Assets giving rise to bad debts

A debt included in a joining entity's assessable income before it joins a consolidated group is taken to have been included in the head company's assessable income at the debt's tax cost setting amount (ITAA97 s 716-400). This facilitates the head company's bad debt deduction under ITAA97 s 25-35 in the event the debt goes bad. Similar provisions ensure debts arising from a money lending business have the same treatment. See also ¶8-020 for special bad debt rules for debts of a consolidated group.

Rights to future income

There are special rules on rights to future income assets held by an entity when it joins a consolidated group. A right to future income is a valuable right to receive an amount that forms part of a contract, has a market value greater than nil, is not a Div 230 financial arrangement or a part of one, and it is reasonable to expect the amount will be included in an entity's future assessable income (ITAA97 s 701-63).

Broadly, the rules apply differently to: (1) entities that join before 12 May 2010 ("pre-rules"); (2) entities that join between 12 May 2010 and 30 March 2011 (inclusive) ("interim rules"); and (3) entities that join after 30 March 2011 ("prospective rules").

Under the "prospective rules", rights to future income that are WIP amount assets or consumable stores are allowed a revenue deduction (ITAA97 s 701-55(5C), (5D)). WIP amount assets are assets of work partially performed but not yet completed to a stage where a recoverable debt has arisen (ITAA97 s 701-63(6)). All other rights to future income are treated as retained cost base assets (ITAA97 s 705-25). Due to the application of ITAA97 s 701-67, some rights to future income assets are excluded from the tax cost setting process completely (¶8-210).

For a discussion on the pre-rules and interim rules, see ¶8-580 of the *2018 Australian Master Tax Guide* (63rd edition).

[FITR ¶540-215, ¶540-223 – ¶540-223/2, ¶548-911]

Research & development activities

Special rules ensure that the R&D tax incentive provisions interact properly with the consolidation provisions (ITAA97 Subdiv 716-V: ¶20-150).

R&D expenditure incurred by a subsidiary member is taken to be incurred by the head company. R&D activities carried out by or on behalf of a subsidiary member of a consolidated group are considered to be carried out by or on behalf of the head company of the group under the single entity rule. If a subsidiary member is bound by an agreement to conduct R&D activities for a foreign entity, its head company is treated as bound by the same agreement. To be eligible for the R&D tax incentive, the head company must be the registered R&D entity because any joining entity's R&D status is not imputed to the head company. A failure to have the appropriate head entity apply for the R&D tax incentive led to unsuccessful outcomes for the taxpayers in *DZXP & Ors v Innovation and Science Australia* as any purported registration by the subsidiary members were of no effect. Furthermore, the AAT did not have the power to vary deemed decisions of the Innovation and Science Australia to have them apply to different entities.

Other

Other special rules apply to:

- certain mining, quarrying and exploration expenditure (ITAA97 s 716-300)
- low-value pools and software development pools (ITAA97 Subdiv 716-G; ITTPA Subdiv 716-G).

[FITR ¶548-400 – ¶549-255]

International Aspects

¶8-600 International aspects of consolidated groups

There are special rules dealing with the transfer of pre-commencement excess foreign income tax (¶21-760) and transferring of surpluses for CFCs and FIFs. There are also implications under the thin capitalisation rules. Various measures targeting multinationals including hybrid mismatch rules (¶22-640) and penalties for significant global entities (¶30-200) also have special modifications for consolidated groups and multiple entry consolidated (MEC) groups.

Functional currency

The head company of a consolidated group can make a choice to use the "applicable functional currency" (¶23-070) under ITAA97 s 960-60 (TD 2006/7). The applicable functional currency is determined by looking at the accounts of all the members of the group (TD 2007/24). Such a choice is eligible for resettable choices treatment (¶8-020). The choice is applicable to all subsidiary members of the group (ID 2011/85).

Foreign income tax offsets

Companies joining or forming a consolidated group will be able to transfer any pre-commencement excess foreign income tax balances (¶21-760) to the head company. The head company will pool these according to the income year in which they arose.

Unexpired pre-commencement excess foreign income tax balances will remain with the head company whether or not the transferring entity remains in the consolidated group (ITAA97 s 717-1 to 717-10).

On an ongoing basis, foreign income tax offsets (FITOs) that would otherwise have become available to a subsidiary member of the group will become available to the head company (ITAA97 s 717-10).

CFC and FIF surpluses

Where a joining entity holds interests in a CFC or FIF, it will be able to transfer any attribution surpluses of the CFC and post-FIF abolition surpluses to the head company at the formation or joining time (ITAA97 Subdiv 717-D).

If a subsidiary member leaves the group, taking with it interests in a CFC or FIF, it will also be able to take a proportion of the head company's attribution surplus in relation to the CFC and/or post-FIF abolition surplus (ITAA97 Subdiv 717-E).

Additional rules about deferred attribution credits are contained in ITAA97 s 717-227 and 717-262.

Conduit foreign income

The effects of consolidation on conduit foreign income (¶21-100) are dealt with in ITAA97 Subdiv 715-U (ITAA97 ss 715-875 to 715-880). The single entity rule and entry history rule have effect for all the purposes of ITAA97 Subdiv 802-A (about conduit foreign income). However, despite ITAA97 s 701-40 (the exit history rule), a subsidiary member of a consolidated group has no conduit foreign income at the time it ceases to be a subsidiary member of the group.

Thin capitalisation

Consistent with the single entity rule, a consolidated group is treated as a single entity under the thin capitalisation rules (¶22-700). Any intra-group debt and equity interests are ignored. Only external loans to the group and external equity in the head company are relevant.

The thin capitalisation rules can apply separately to different parts of a year, where the thin capitalisation classification (ie inward/outward investing entity; general/financial; ADI/non-ADI) or consolidation status of a company changes (ITAA97 Subdiv 820-FA).

The thin capitalisation grouping rules generally ceased to operate from 1 July 2003. However, a head company or single Australian resident company can elect to treat an Australian branch of a foreign bank or financial entity (within the same wholly-owned group) as part of itself for thin capitalisation purposes (ITAA97 Subdiv 820-FB). There are a number of other special rules for foreign-owned banks.

Offshore banking units

When a subsidiary member of a consolidated group is an offshore banking unit (OBU), the head company is treated as an OBU (¶21-080) for the purposes of determining its income tax liability (ITAA97 Subdiv 717-O). This treatment does not apply for the purposes of determining whether a foreign resident lender to the group is entitled to a withholding tax exemption on interest received.

ITAA36 s 121EH, which is aimed at preventing the excessive use of non-OB money to fund OB activities, will apply to the consolidated group as a whole rather than only to actual OBUs within the group (Explanatory Memorandum to the *New Business Tax System (Consolidation and Other Measures) Act 2003*).

Transitional foreign loss makers

Under transitional provisions, a subsidiary that had an unrecouped foreign loss was able to be excluded from a consolidated group for up to 3 years, subject to certain conditions. A subsidiary that was excluded on this basis was called a ''transitional foreign loss maker''. The consolidated group had to exist before 1 July 2004 (ITTPA Div 701D).

[FITR ¶549-600ff]

¶8-610 MEC groups

Australian resident wholly-owned subsidiaries of a common foreign holding company may be able to form multiple entry consolidated (MEC) groups that would not qualify as consolidated groups under ITAA97 Div 701. The modified requirements for MEC groups are provided by ITAA97 Div 719. A MEC group generally comprises 2 or more wholly-owned first tier Australian resident subsidiaries of a foreign resident ultimate parent company (''top company''), together with their wholly-owned lower tier Australian resident subsidiaries.

The consolidation regime (other than ITAA97 Div 703; 719) applies to a MEC group and its members in essentially the same way that it applies to a consolidated group and its members, subject to necessary modifications (ITAA97 s 719-2; ITTPA s 719-2).

Terminology

Top company

A company is a ''top company'' if it is a foreign resident and is not a wholly-owned subsidiary of another company (other than a dual resident or an Australian resident that fails the income tax treatment requirements for a tier-1 company) (ITAA97 s 719-20).

Tier-1 company

A ''tier-1 company'' of a top company:

- must be an Australian resident (but not a prescribed dual resident)
- must be a wholly-owned subsidiary of the top company
- must *not* be a wholly-owned subsidiary of an Australian resident company (other than a company that is a prescribed dual resident or fails to meet the income tax treatment requirements, eg because some or all of its taxable income is not taxed at the corporate tax rate) (s 719-20).

If 2 or more wholly-owned subsidiaries of the top company own a company, and these subsidiaries are tier-1 companies, the company is treated as a wholly-owned subsidiary of one of these tier-1 companies and is therefore not a tier-1 company.

Eligible tier-1 company

A tier-1 company of a top company is an eligible tier-1 company *unless* there is an entity interposed between it and the top company that satisfies *all 3* of the conditions in ITAA97 s 719-15(3) (TD 2005/39). The 3 conditions are:

(1) the interposed entity is any of the following:

  (a) a company that is a foreign resident or prescribed dual resident

  (b) a foreign resident trust

  (c) an Australian resident trust that is not a wholly-owned subsidiary of another tier-1 company of the top company

  (d) an entity of a type that is specifically excluded from being a member of a consolidated group (¶8-000)

(e) a non-profit company that is a wholly-owned subsidiary of another tier-1 company of the top company

(f) an Australian resident company that has none of its taxable income taxed at the corporate tax rate

(2) the interposed entity does not hold membership interests only as a nominee of one or more entities, each of which is:

(a) another tier-1 company of the top company, or

(b) a wholly-owned subsidiary of such a tier-1 company, and

(3) a membership interest in the interposed entity is beneficially held by, or as nominee for:

(a) another tier-1 company of the top company, or

(b) a wholly-owned subsidiary of such a tier-1 company.

The insertion of a partnership, all the partners of which are foreign resident wholly-owned subsidiary companies of the top company, between the top company and an eligible tier-1 company member of the MEC group will not cause the eligible tier-1 company to cease to be an eligible tier-1 company of the top company (ID 2009/44). This is essentially due to the partnership being a wholly-owned subsidiary of the top company, which is conditional upon the partners beneficially owning their interests in the partnership. As the partners and the partnership are wholly-owned subsidiaries of the top company, the eligible tier-1 company continues to be a wholly-owned subsidiary of the top company, and an eligible tier-1 company member of the MEC group.

Potential MEC group

It is important to identify all the members of a potential MEC group ''derived from'' one or more tier-1 companies, as the membership of a MEC group at a particular time will comprise all the members of the potential MEC group derived from the eligible tier-1 companies who are members of the MEC group at that time.

Broadly, the membership of a potential MEC group derived from one or more eligible tier-1 companies of a top company consists of:

(1) those tier-1 companies

(2) all the entities that qualify under certain standard membership tests, ie

(a) all the wholly-owned subsidiary companies of the tier-1 companies in (1) that are Australian resident companies (but not prescribed dual residents or non-profit companies) and have at least part of their income taxed at the general company rate

(b) all the wholly-owned subsidiary Australian resident trusts of the tier-1 companies in (1) that are not of a type that is specifically excluded from being a member of a consolidated group, and

(c) all the partnerships that are wholly-owned subsidiaries of the tier-1 companies in (1)

(3) all the entities that qualify under certain interposed foreign resident entity tests set out in ITTPA ss 701C-10 and 701C-15. These tests differ for companies, trusts and partnerships. The interposed foreign resident entities themselves are not part of the potential MEC group but the tests effectively allow them to be disregarded for the purposes of determining who is a member of the potential MEC group.

Only MEC groups that consolidated before 1 July 2004 are eligible to have any foreign resident entities interposed between members of the group. If the tests in ITTPA ss 701C-10 and 701C-15 are not satisfied at any time, an entity that qualified under the tests will no longer be eligible to be a member of the MEC group.

Forming a MEC group

A MEC group is formed where any 2 or more eligible tier-1 companies of a top company choose to consolidate and that choice takes effect (ITAA97 s 719-5; 719-50; 719-55). The MEC group will come into existence from the beginning of the day specified in the choice (TD 2006/26) and the choice cannot be revoked. It is not necessary for all eligible tier-1 companies to join the MEC group (TD 2005/38).

The choice must be made in writing by the time the first consolidated tax return is lodged or, if a return is not required, the date it would otherwise have been due. The written choice must specify the date when consolidation is to commence, identify the top company and include an appointment of an eligible tier-1 company to be the provisional head company of the MEC group. While the choice itself need not be given to the Commissioner, notification of the choice made must be provided to the Commissioner in the approved form within the same time frame (s 719-76). The Commissioner has a discretion to extend the deadline for notification under TAA Sch 1 s 388-55.

An eligible tier-1 company may be taken to have made the choice to consolidate even though it ceases to exist before the head company lodges its first consolidated income tax return or if no return is required, the last day by which such a return would otherwise have been due (ITAA97 s 719-50(4); ID 2005/60).

The provisional head company cannot have any of its membership interests beneficially owned by another member of the MEC group.

A MEC group is also formed when an ordinary consolidated group headed by a tier-1 subsidiary of a top company converts to a MEC group as a result of a ‘‘special conversion event’’ (¶8-640).

▶ Example 1

Top Co, a foreign resident company, has 2 directly-owned subsidiaries incorporated in Australia (A Co and B Co), each of which in turn wholly owns 2 additional Australian subsidiaries (tier-2 companies). The 2 tier-2 companies owned by A Co each own 50% of the same tier-3 company.

A Co and B Co can form a MEC group and appoint either A Co or B Co as provisional head company. The MEC group must include all the eligible subsidiaries of A Co and B Co.

Provisional head company and head company

As a mechanism to ensure that the same company is treated as the head company of a MEC group for the whole of an income year (or that part when it is in existence), the head of the group is technically referred to as a ‘‘provisional head company’’ throughout the year. The provisional head company of the MEC group at the end of an income year is treated as head company of the MEC group for the whole of the income year (or that part when the MEC group existed) even though it may have been appointed provisional head company part way through the year.

Change of provisional head company

The provisional head company of a MEC group retains that status until it ceases to be eligible, eg it ceases to be a wholly-owned subsidiary of the ultimate foreign resident parent. Where a provisional head company ceases to be eligible, the MEC group will continue to exist, provided the remaining tier-1 companies appoint a new provisional head company from their ranks by making a choice in writing. A notice of the choice made must be given to the Commissioner within 28 days of the change. The losses, franking credits, etc, of the group will be transferred from the outgoing head company to the new head company. The group will retain its existing income year. Where only one eligible tier-1 company remains, it can appoint itself as the provisional head company (ID 2007/165).

Expansion of a MEC group

An existing MEC group can expand its membership by the provisional head company making a choice in writing to admit a new eligible tier-1 company of the top company. All wholly-owned subsidiaries of the new eligible tier-1 company (or those that become wholly-owned by the expanded group) must also join, eg in some cases a consolidated group could be absorbed into a MEC group.

The choice must be made by the time the MEC group's income tax return for the year in which the change occurs is lodged (or, if a return is not required, the time when it otherwise would have been due). The provisional head company must also notify the Commissioner of the change in membership within the same time frame. The Commissioner has a discretion to extend the notification deadline.

The choice must take effect from the time the joining company becomes an eligible tier-1 company of the top company; there is no provision for it to join at a later date. Accordingly, in *GE Capital Finance Australasia*, the Federal Court held that a valid choice to admit an eligible tier-1 company existed despite the omission of the joining date from the choice.

If the joining tier-1 company is already part of a MEC group, then the choice must include all the members of that MEC group that have become eligible tier-1 companies of the top company at the same time.

Leaving a MEC group

Members of a MEC group will leave the group when they are no longer eligible to be members.

MEC group ceases to exist

A MEC group will cease to exist when:

- the group no longer has a provisional head company
- there are no eligible tier-1 members left in the group, or
- all the members of the MEC group become members of another MEC group following a change in the identity of the top company (see ''Expansion of a MEC group'' above).

▶ Example 2

Top Co, a foreign resident company, has 2 directly-owned subsidiaries incorporated in Australia (A Co and B Co), each of which wholly owns 2 Australian subsidiaries (tier-2 companies).

Assume that A Co and B Co form a MEC group, nominating B Co as the provisional head company. Two years later, Top Co sells a 49% interest in B Co.

B Co and its 2 tier-2 subsidiaries will leave the group. The MEC group will continue to exist if, within 28 days, A Co is appointed as the replacement provisional head company by making a choice in writing. Otherwise, the MEC group will cease to exist. Notification of the appointment must be given to the Commissioner within 28 days of B Co leaving the group.

Change of top company

Where there is a change in the identity of the top company of a potential MEC group but no change in the eligible tier-1 companies that are members of the group, the change does not affect the continuity of the group or the companies' status as eligible tier-1 companies of the top company (ITAA97 s 719-10(8)).

Franking credits

A MEC group will have a single franking account, operated by the head company. Any distributions made by a subsidiary member of the group to an entity outside the group will be taken to be made by the head company for franking purposes (TD 2006/21). The benchmark rule (ITAA97 s 203-25) also applies to the provisional head company (TD 2006/20).

Membership interests in tier-1 companies

The cost of all membership interests in tier-1 companies that are not held by members of the group will be recalculated when a tier-1 company ceases to be a member of the group or a CGT event (¶11-240) happens in relation to a membership interest in a tier-1 company.

Interest on funds borrowed by a member of a MEC group from outside the group to purchase (from the top company) shares in an existing eligible tier-1 company of the group may be deductible under the refinancing principle (TD 2006/47).

It is the Commissioner's opinion that a "non-eligible tier-1 company" subsidiary member of a MEC group will not cease to be a member of the group, if, at a particular time, membership interests in it are transferred to a foreign resident member of the same wholly-owned group, and at that time it becomes an eligible tier-1 company of the top company and a member of the MEC group (ID 2010/141).

Application events

An "application event" may occur where either: (i) an eligible tier-1 company becomes a member of an existing MEC group, or (ii) a consolidated group is converted to a MEC group by a special conversion event (ITAA97 s 719-300; ¶8-640). This may cause ITAA97 ss 719-305 to 719-325 to operate, limiting the rate at which prior group losses of the head company may be utilised (TD 2006/50).

[FITR ¶551-300 – ¶551-870]

¶8-620 Options and constraints for tier-1 companies

In order to meet the differing needs of international groups, tier-1 companies have been given substantial flexibility. If, eg, a foreign top company has 10 tier-1 companies in Australia:

- any 2 or more of the tier-1 companies can form a MEC group, ie there could be up to 5 MEC groups formed in this case
- any or all of the tier-1 companies can remain unconsolidated
- any of the tier-1 companies can form a consolidated group consisting of itself and all its wholly-owned subsidiaries, or
- there can be a mixture of the above outcomes.

While an eligible tier-1 company remains unconsolidated, it continues to have the option of consolidating at a later date by forming a new consolidated group with its eligible subsidiaries or forming a new MEC group with one or more other unconsolidated eligible tier-1 companies (assuming the normal requirements are met). Constraints are generally imposed after a choice is made. For example:

- An eligible tier-1 company that chooses not to join a MEC group when it is formed cannot join that group at a later date. However, it can (at that time or later) form a consolidated group or a different MEC group.
- If an existing MEC group does not take in a new eligible tier-1 company when it becomes eligible to join the group, it cannot do so later.

- If a consolidated group headed by an eligible tier-1 company does not form a MEC group with a new eligible tier-1 company when it is first able to do so, it cannot form a MEC group with that company at a later date.

¶8-640 Restructures involving MEC groups

Creating a consolidated group from a MEC group

A consolidated group is created from a MEC group if the cessation of the MEC group happens because the entity that is the sole eligible tier-1 company in the MEC group fails the conditions for being an eligible tier-1 company and, immediately after that time, it meets the conditions for being a head company of a consolidated group (ITAA97 ss 703-5(1)(b); 703-55(1)).

Conversion of consolidated group to MEC group

A consolidated group converts to a MEC group (referred to as a ‘‘special conversion event’’) if:

- an eligible tier-1 company of a top company is the head company of a consolidated group
- another company becomes a tier-1 company of the top company, and
- the head company of the consolidated group makes a choice in writing that a MEC group is to come into existence, specifying the eligible tier-1 companies (ITAA97 s 719-40). The choice must be made by the time the head company lodges its income tax return for the year in which the other company became an eligible tier-1 company of the top company. If the choice is not made within the applicable period, the consolidated group will continue unchanged. Notice of the choice made must be given to the Commissioner in the approved form within the same time frame. The Commissioner has a discretion to extend the deadline for notification under TAA Sch 1 s 388-55.

The head company of the consolidated group must be eligible to be the provisional head company of the MEC group. The MEC group will include the former consolidated group, the newly eligible tier-1 company and any other eligible subsidiaries of the tier-1 companies in the MEC group. The choice takes effect from the time that the other company becomes an eligible tier-1 company of the top company.

▶ Example

Top Brass, a foreign resident company, owns 100% of C Co (an Australian resident company). C Co has a wholly-owned subsidiary, S Co, and elected to consolidate from 1 July 2007. On 1 September 2019, Top Brass acquires all the shares of another Australian resident company, D Co (which has no subsidiaries).

The consolidated group headed by C Co is eligible to convert to a MEC group, consisting of C Co, S Co and D Co, effective 1 September 2019. This will happen if C Co makes this choice before it lodges its tax return for 2019–20. C Co will be the provisional head company of the MEC group.

It is possible that the new eligible tier-1 company will also be the head of a consolidated group. In that case, the entire consolidated group will be brought into the new MEC group.

If multiple companies become eligible tier-1 companies of the top company at the same time, the new MEC group can include one or more of these, as specified in the notice by the head company of the consolidated group. However, where any of these are already members of a MEC group, then a choice to include one of the eligible tier-1 companies from that MEC group must include all the other eligible members of that MEC group.

When a special conversion event happens in relation to a consolidated group, the consolidated group ceases to exist and a MEC group comes into existence (ID 2006/145 and ID 2006/146). A special conversion event cannot happen to the potential MEC group when both the head company of the consolidated group and the other eligible tier-1 company become eligible tier-1 companies of another top company at the same time (ID 2010/4).

Impact on ongoing members

Whether a consolidated group is created from a MEC group or vice versa, ITAA97 Subdiv 719-BA ensures that the tax consequences to any ongoing members (ie members of the old group and the new group) are minimal. Specifically:

- the new group's head company retains the history of the old group's head company, including everything that happened to the old group because of applying the single entity rule (¶8-010) and the entry history rule (¶8-020)
- the tax cost setting rules (ITAA97 Div 705; 711) do not apply when an entity leaves the old group and joins the new group. An exception applies if the ongoing member becomes an eligible tier-1 company of a new MEC group (ITAA97 s 719-130), and
- losses transferred from an entity of the old group to its head company are taken to be transferred to the new group's head company.

The ATO is scrutinising restructures that involve the creation of a MEC group, where ownership of underlying CGT assets is transferred to a newly incorporated eligible tier-1 company before it is sold by the top company. The concern is that these groups may be avoiding CGT, otherwise payable by a head company or other resident company of the group, via complex restructures that have unnecessary additional steps (TA 2020/4). See also TA 2019/1.

Other Issues

¶8-920 Consolidation and CGT

A special category of CGT events deal with specific events and transactions in relation to consolidated groups. These CGT events (CGT events L1 to L8) are listed at ¶12-360 and are referred to as appropriate within this chapter.

A number of other CGT issues have arisen in relation to consolidated groups, eg:

- Where, because of an intra-group transaction, a head company incurs third party expenditure in relation to a CGT asset that it holds, the expenditure can be included in the second element of the cost base and reduced cost base of the asset (ITAA97 s 110-35(10)). Where the head company does not ''hold'' the asset, eg because it is an intra-group asset that is not recognised in consolidation, the cost may nonetheless be deductible over 5 years under the ''blackhole'' expenditure provisions (ITAA97 s 40-880; ¶8-580).
- Incidental costs incurred by a head company of a consolidated group in acquiring or disposing of shares in a subsidiary member to a non-group entity prior to the subsidiary leaving the consolidated group are not prohibited from the deduction provided under s 40-880(2) by s 40-880(5)(f). Section 40-880(5)(f) prohibits the deduction under s 40-880(2) to the extent that the expenditure would be included in the calculation of a capital gain or loss of a CGT event under the CGT rules. Such incidental costs would not be included in the cost base of the head company or the reduced cost base of the shares. Thus they would not be included in the calculation of the capital gain or loss under the CGT rules, especially as they also do not fit the description of costs in any other CGT event (TD 2010/1; TD 2011/9). Conversely, incidental costs incurred when the subsidiary is *not* part of the consolidated group can be included in the cost base or reduced cost base of the shares as the shares are a recognised asset held by the head company at the time (ie not an intra-group asset) (TD 2011/8 and TD 2011/10).

- Where a debt is created within a consolidated group and later transferred to a non-group entity, no CGT event happens, as it effectively represents the borrowing of money or obtaining of credit from the third party (TD 2004/33). However, the ATO may scrutinise arrangements that it considers seek to avoid CGT via the sale of an eligible tier-1 company holding intra-group debt (TA 2019/1)

- Where an option granted within a consolidated group is later transferred to a non-group entity, CGT event A1 (¶11-250) happens (TD 2004/34).

- Where a licence granted within a consolidated group is later transferred to a non-group entity for no capital proceeds, CGT event A1 (¶11-250) happens (TD 2004/35).

- If an entity contracts to sell a CGT asset and the contract settles after the entity becomes, or ceases to be, a member of a consolidated group, the ''CGT contract rules'' (¶11-250, ¶11-440) are modified such that the CGT event happens at the time of the settlement and not when the contract was entered into (ITAA97 s 716-860). The CGT contract rules continue to operate normally for the entity acquiring the CGT asset.

- If an entity has contracted to buy a CGT asset from another taxpayer and the contract is not completed at the time it joins or leaves a consolidated group, the asset is not an asset of the entity at that time (TD 2008/30). If an entity has contracted to sell a CGT asset to another taxpayer and the contract is not completed at the time it joins or leaves a consolidated group, the asset is an asset of the entity at that time (TD 2008/31).

- A small business entity that makes a capital gain before becoming a subsidiary member of a consolidated group can apply the small business replacement asset roll-over (¶7-195) under ITAA97 Subdiv 152-E if it acquires a replacement asset after joining the consolidated group. The single entity rule (¶8-010) does not apply because the decision to apply the roll-over affects the pre-joining tax liability of the entity (TD 2004/79).

- The small business 15-year exemption (¶7-165) can apply to a payment made by the head company to a CGT concession stakeholder in respect of the disposal of an asset legally owned by a subsidiary member of the consolidated group (TD 2004/82).

- Certain aspects of the ITAA97 Subdiv 170-D deferred loss rules for linked company groups (¶11-120) are considered in TD 2004/80 and TD 2004/81.

- The principal asset test for purposes of determining a foreign resident's CGT liability (¶12-725) will exclude the market value of certain assets arising from intercompany dealings within a consolidated group for CGT events occurring after 7.30 pm (AEST) 14 May 2013 (ITAA97 s 855-32).

- Where a pre-CGT asset is rolled over under Subdiv 126-B (¶12-490), the recipient company is taken to have inherited the originating company's cost base and reduced cost base for the purposes of determining the joining entity's ACA and the cost base of assets under the tax cost setting provisions in Div 705 (s 716-855). However, a similar rule does not exist for a pre-CGT asset rolled over under Subdiv 122-A (¶12-040). In such a scenario, the asset's cost base for the purposes of the tax cost setting provisions is the consideration paid for it at the time of the roll-over (*Financial Synergy*, ATO *Decision Impact Statement*).

¶8-950 Consolidation and Pt IVA

A scheme involving consolidation may attract the application of ITAA36 Pt IVA, where there is a sole or dominant purpose of obtaining a tax benefit (¶30-170). Virtually any decision to consolidate will generate tax benefits (¶30-160) for both the head company (eg deductions that would otherwise have been allowed to a subsidiary) and for subsidiaries (eg diversion of assessable income from the subsidiary to the head company), but for the exclusions in ITAA36 s 177C(2). Section 177C(2) provides that a tax benefit is not obtained by the mere making of a choice, election, selection, etc, provided for in the Act, unless the relevant scheme was carried out for the sole or dominant purpose of creating the circumstances necessary to enable the making of the choice, etc.

If a scheme involved the formation of a consolidated group where the Commissioner's counterfactual scenario was that a subsidiary member would have not joined the consolidated group, the relevant taxpayer for purposes of Pt IVA could be the subsidiary member (*Channel Pastoral*). In that case, the Full Federal Court held that the Commissioner could give effect to an ITAA36 s 177F determination (¶30-180) in respect of the subsidiary member by issuing an assessment to the subsidiary member as a stand-alone taxpayer. In such circumstances, it was held not possible to issue the assessment to the head company because of the counterfactual. The Commissioner will take this approach to schemes identified that include a taxpayer becoming a member of a tax consolidated group (Appendix 1 to TR 2004/11).

The Commissioner's opinion on the potential application of Pt IVA to consolidation is set out in the *ATO Consolidation Reference Manual* (C9-1-220).

In the Commissioner's view, if a scheme is found to have a dominant purpose of enabling an election to be made, then it is still necessary to undertake the analysis required by ITAA36 s 177D to see if the scheme was entered into or carried out for the dominant purpose of obtaining the tax benefit. The reorganisation of a group that exhibits a purpose of permitting an election to consolidate may still be explicable by purposes other than the purpose of obtaining tax benefits.

If a company is already the head company in a consolidatable group, a scheme that merely increases or decreases the number of subsidiaries affected by the election to consolidate would not seem to be one that could be entered into for the purpose of enabling a consolidation election to be made. However, a number of schemes and scenarios are listed in the paper that might potentially attract the operation of Pt IVA. These include:

- a scheme to turn a subsidiary into a head company
- a scheme to split a consolidatable group into a number of such groups
- the acquisition of a subsidiary by a company that has no subsidiaries, predominantly to enable the company to consolidate
- a company arranging for itself to be acquired by another company to enable the latter company to elect to consolidate
- a head company of a consolidatable group acquiring a loss company and then electing to consolidate in order to utilise the losses
- the interposition of an entity resulting in the formation of a consolidatable group
- the leaving out of an entity from a consolidatable group prior to the group consolidating
- the shifting of value out of an entity in a consolidatable group prior to the group consolidating
- the disposal of an interest in a group company prior to the group consolidating

- the post-consolidation dissolution of a company
- the purchase of a minority interest in a group company prior to consolidation
- the use by a consolidatable group of a special purpose vehicle to issue preference shares to unrelated investors while maintaining 100% ownership of its subsidiaries
- the use by a consolidatable group of non-share equity interests to maintain economic control over a related party.

Part IVA may or may not apply in the above circumstances, depending upon the facts and dominant purposes. Specific examples of the above scenarios are discussed in detail in the reference manual.

Where Pt IVA does apply, the Commissioner will generally seek to disallow only the actual tax advantage (net benefit) gained by the relevant taxpayer (eg the head company), rather than the entire tax benefit. However, where the net benefit cannot be readily determined, the Commissioner may disallow the entire tax benefit and then consider making compensating adjustments requested by the taxpayer under ITAA36 s 177F(3) where the taxpayer is able to demonstrate a fair and reasonable basis for such an adjustment.

Chapter 9 Tax Accounting • Trading Stock

Tax Accounting

¶9-000 Tax accounting

Tax accounting refers to the accounting methodology and practices required for the purposes of taxation law. Although the accounting requirements of taxation law sometimes reflect financial accounting principles, taxation accounting requirements are distinct and include fundamental differences from financial accounting (see below). Taxation accounting rules may affect the *treatment* and *timing* [of recognition] of an item or transaction.

Rules dealing with the translation of foreign currency amounts into Australian currency are discussed at ¶23-070.

Accounting profits vs taxable income

The net profit (or loss) shown in a taxpayer's financial accounts is generally not the same as taxable income. This is because the basis for recognising income and expenditure, assets and liabilities is determined by accounting standards (the requirements of which are incorporated into the Corporations legislation by reference) applicable to financial reporting which differ from the requirements of the taxation legislation. Treatment of these differences is referred to as tax-effect accounting. Notwithstanding, an entity reporting significant accounting profit in comparison to taxable income is likely to attract ATO attention. Specific issues arise for trusts (¶6-085).

Tax-effect accounting

For tax-effect accounting purposes the differences that give rise to a difference between net profit and taxable income can be broadly categorised as temporary (or timing) differences — those where the difference between the tax and accounting treatment is one of timing, such that when multiple periods are aggregated there is no net difference in the treatment; and permanent differences — where this "reversal" does not occur. Examples include:

- certain capital expenditure for which an immediate deduction or deduction over a certain period, for tax purposes is allowable, may be required to be amortised or capitalised for accounting purposes
- trading stock may be valued in the accounts on a basis different from that adopted for tax purposes (¶9-180), particularly in relation to obsolescence
- provisions such as those for doubtful debts, annual and long service leave, are generally expensed for accounting purposes based on a "matching principle" which does not equate to being "incurred" for tax purposes (¶9-120)
- different depreciation rates used for tax and accounting purposes should generate a timing difference, although any accelerated (over 100%) depreciation component for certain expenses for tax purposes would be a permanent difference
- the prohibition against claiming tax deductions for fines and penalties (permanent difference)
- sale of capital assets may give rise to timing (revenue recognition) and permanent (capital gains discount) differences.

The following pronouncements of the Australian Accounting Standards Board (AASB) apply to the determination of tax balances in financial reports:

- AASB 112: *Income taxes* prescribes the accounting treatment for income taxes in financial reports of for-profit Australian entities, adopting a balance sheet approach incorporating International Accounting Standard IAS 12
- UIG Interpretation 125: Changes in the Tax Status of an Entity or its Shareholders
- UIG Interpretation 1052: Tax Consolidation Accounting.

[AAPM ¶7-752]

Accounting Period

¶9-005 The financial year and the income year

The "financial year" is the 12-month period starting on 1 July and ending on the following 30 June. Income tax is levied for each financial year by reference to a taxpayer's taxable income for an "income year" (ITAA97 s 4-10). The income year is generally the same as the financial year, subject to 2 exceptions in s 4-10(2), the most common of which being where a taxpayer has an adopted accounting period (or substituted accounting period) ending on a date other than 30 June (¶9-010). The exception in s 4-10(2)(a) is of limited practical significance since the introduction of the PAYG system in TAA Sch 1 Pt 2-5 (¶27-220).

[FITR ¶15-120]

¶9-010 Substituted accounting period

Generally, tax returns must be prepared on the basis of an income year ending on 30 June (¶9-005). However, with the Commissioner's permission, a taxpayer may adopt an alternate accounting period, often referred to as a substituted accounting period (SAP), ending on a date other than 30 June (ITAA36 s 18).

The Commissioner's guidelines for approval of SAPs, set out in PS LA 2007/21, reflect the decision in *MLC Investments Ltd*.

When deciding whether to grant leave to adopt an SAP each case is considered on its merits taking into account all relevant facts. The Commissioner seeks to balance convenience to the taxpayer with the efficient administration of the taxation law; consideration of the business needs relevant to the efficient administration of the taxpayer's business in their market, other taxpayers in similar situations, and the aggregate effect of grants of SAPs. Leave will generally be granted to adopt an SAP where it can be demonstrated that the circumstances of the case are out of the ordinary. Applications for SAPs must be in writing and lodged in a timely fashion with regard to when the circumstances which form the basis of the SAP application first arise. An application form (NAT 5087) is available from the ATO website.

Where leave to adopt a SAP ending on any date between 1 July and 30 November is granted, the SAP is in lieu of the income year ended on the *preceding* 30 June, ie the taxpayer is a late balancer. For example, for an SAP ending on 31 October 2021, the period 1 November 2020 to 31 October 2021 is in lieu of the income year ending on 30 June 2021. Where an SAP ends between 1 December and 30 June, the SAP is in lieu of the income year ending on the *following* 30 June, ie the taxpayer is an early balancer. For example, for an SAP ending on 31 March 2021, the period 1 April 2020 to 31 March 2021 is in lieu of the income year ending on 30 June 2021.

In the year an entity first adopts an SAP, it normally lodges a return for a transitional period shorter or greater than 12 months. For example, where leave is granted to an existing business to adopt an accounting period ending between 1 July and 30 November in lieu of the preceding 30 June, the first assessment for the new accounting period is based on its income for the period from 1 July in one year to the last day of the SAP in the following year, even though this exceeds 12 months. PS LA 2007/21 provides a table that sets out the length of transitional accounting periods. Where a newly registered entity is granted an SAP, its first year will be the period starting on its date of incorporation (or commencement of trading) and ending on the next succeeding balance date of their requested SAP, ie it will not exceed 12 months.

Consolidated groups

When a consolidated group is formed, the head company continues to use its existing tax accounting period. Its payment, reporting and lodgment obligations (as head company of the group) will be based on this period. A subsidiary member retains its own balance date when entering or exiting the group, unless it had applied and been granted a different balance date. See further ¶9-020.

[FTR ¶6-585]

¶9-020 Short period returns

Ordinarily, no return is allowed for a period of more than 12 months, except in certain cases where there is a change to or from a substituted accounting period (¶9-010). Returns for a period of less than 12 months are more frequently required, for example:

- a return for a deceased taxpayer is lodged for the period from the first day of the income year to the date of death (¶6-030)
- the estate (of a deceased person) lodges a separate return in respect of the income from the date of death to the close of the estate's income year
- new taxpayers lodge a return for the period from the date on which income commenced to be derived to the last day of the income year
- a dissolved company lodges a return from the first day of the income year to the date of dissolution
- where there is any variation in the membership of a partnership, a return may need to be lodged for the partnership as originally constituted from the first day of the income year to the date of the variation, with a separate return being lodged for the reconstituted partnership from that date to the end of the income year (¶5-060)
- where a trust is created or terminated, a return must be lodged for the period from its creation to the end of the income year, or from the first day of the income year to the trust's dissolution.

A subsidiary that joins or leaves a consolidated group during the subsidiary's income year *does not* lodge a part-year return, but rather lodges a return for the whole income year, at the normal lodgment time, including only income and deductions properly attributable to the non-membership period(s) (¶8-000).

[FTR ¶79-300]

Accounting Method

¶9-030 Cash versus accruals basis

Taxable income must be calculated not only on the basis of a fixed accounting period, but also in accordance with the *method* of accounting that correctly reflects the true income (*CT v Executor & Trustee Agency Co of South Australia* (*Carden's case*)). There are currently 2 methods of determining income for tax purposes:

Cash or receipts basis. This method is used by most individuals. Income is returned in the year when it is actually or constructively received, either in the form of cash or its equivalent, or other property.

Accruals or earnings basis. Generally used by business taxpayers. Income is brought to account when the right to receive it comes into being, ie when all the events that determine the right have occurred. It is not actual receipt but the *right to receive* that is critical.

Deductions under both bases of income recognition are claimed in accordance with the rules allowing the deduction. For deductions claimed under ITAA97 s 8-1, this is in the year the expenses are *incurred* (TR 97/7; ¶16-040); deductions allowable under special provisions (eg film investments) are deductible in accordance with that provision.

The method that truly reflects the income of the particular taxpayer in accordance with the taxation law is a question the final adjudication of which, lies with the courts (*Henderson*, see below) not a choice of the taxpayer from year to year. Accordingly, the method first applied by the taxpayer to determine taxable income is generally adhered to strictly. Notwithstanding, certain circumstances (see ¶31-120) may support a change of method. Changes of method in bringing income to account for tax purposes are rare, as it results in double taxation of income when moving from accrual to cash, and an amount not subject to tax when moving from cash to accrual (see below).

Generally, the mere act of consolidation will not affect the choice of income recognition method for business activities carried out by a consolidated group (TD 2005/3) (see below).

Guidelines for choice of tax accounting method

Guidelines for choosing which method of tax accounting is likely to provide a substantially correct reflex of income in a given income year are set out in TR 98/1. A cash basis is likely to be appropriate for income derived as an employee, for *non-business* income derived from providing knowledge or skill, and for income derived from investments. The ruling includes exceptions to the general rule in respect of interest income (¶9-050).

The cash basis may also be appropriate for *business* income derived from providing knowledge or skill. However, the presence of the following factors, to a significant extent, may result in the accruals basis being more appropriate:

- the taxpayer's activities involve the sale of trading stock
- the taxpayer's outgoings in the day-to-day conduct of the business relate directly to income derived
- the taxpayer relies on circulating capital or consumables to produce income, or
- the taxpayer relies on staff or equipment to produce income.

The accruals basis is usually appropriate for trading or manufacturing businesses. Although, a separate determination should be made of the appropriate method for accounting for the income from each different business activity, unless the differences between the various business activities are significant different methods need not be adopted. In most cases the same method is likely to be appropriate for income from all business activities.

Professional practices

It is not always clear which accounting basis (ie accruals or cash) a professional practice should use to return income. In *Henderson*, it was held, for a large firm of accountants, the accruals basis was appropriate to reflect its income and the Commissioner could not insist the firm continue with the cash basis. Moreover, in the year of changeover, there was no basis for bringing to account any amount for fees earned but uncollected at the end of the immediately preceding year. A similar decision was reached in *Barratt*.

For a solicitor or accountant in sole practice, the cash basis is the correct method of tax accounting (*Firstenberg*, *Dunn*).

Henderson and *Firstenberg* represent the extremes between which most professional practices lie. Unfortunately, they do not provide any principles with which to identify the taxpayers to which each method is most appropriate.

In *Dormer*, an accountant was assessable on a cash receipts basis on income received from his former sole practice and on an accruals basis on income derived from a new partnership in the same income year. The full Federal Court distinguished the case from *Henderson* on the basis that the new partnership was a different business from the sole practice.

[FITR ¶27-000ff, ¶27-030ff]

Timing of Income and Deductions

¶9-035 Timing of income and deductions

Determining taxable income involves applying tax accounting principles to identify all items of assessable income (¶10-000) and all allowable deductions (¶16-000) for a particular period. Whether an item is relevant to a particular period is a *timing* issue.

The main issue relating to when income is assessable is the time it is *derived* (ITAA97 s 6-5; ¶9-050).

If expenditure has been incurred (but not actually paid), a deduction is only allowable to the extent that the expenditure is properly referable to the income year, ie to the extent that the benefit derived is put to profitable advantage or used in the taxpayer's income-producing activities in the relevant income year (*Coles Myer Finance*, ; TR 94/26, TR 97/7; ¶16-040). Notwithstanding specific deduction provisions may not rely on the concept of ''incurred'' (relevant for claiming deductions under s 8-1) (eg s 70B ITAA36 which allows a deduction for certain traditional securities in the year of disposal) it remains generally relevant.

Judicial interpretation of *derivation* of income and *incurring* deductible expenditure have evolved on a largely separate basis, and should not be viewed as different aspects of the same timing issue.

[FITR ¶18-200, ¶27-000]

¶9-045 Record-keeping

Every taxpayer carrying on a business must keep records, irrespective of whether any of these documents are required to be lodged with a tax return, that record and explain all transactions and other acts engaged in by the taxpayer that are relevant for tax purposes, in such a way as to enable the person's tax liability to be readily ascertained, including:

- any documents that are relevant for the purpose of ascertaining the taxpayer's income and expenditure
- documents containing particulars of any election, choice, estimate, determination or calculation made by the taxpayer and the basis on which any such calculation was made (ITAA36 s 262A(2); ¶24-040).

Records must be accessible, capable of being extracted and converted into a standard data format; kept in writing (or capable of being easily converted) in the English language. The occupier of a building or place must provide an authorised taxation officer with all reasonable facilities and assistance for the effective exercise of powers under TAA Sch 1 s 353-15 (¶25-220).

Records are normally required to be retained for 5 years from the date on which the record was prepared or obtained, or from the time the relevant transaction or act was completed, whichever is the later. If the period within which the Commissioner can amend a taxpayer's assessment is extended (¶25-300), the retention period for the records is similarly extended. A taxpayer who has incurred a tax loss should retain records supporting that loss until the end of the statutory record retention period or the end of the statutory period for reviewing assessments for the income year in which the loss is fully deducted, whichever is later (TD 2007/2).

Statutory provisions under other legislation may require retention of business records for a longer period than that specified in s 262A, eg *Corporations Act 2001*, s 286 requires a company to retain accounting records for a period of 7 years after completion of the transaction to which they relate. Special record-keeping requirements are contained in the substantiation rules (¶16-210), the CGT provisions (¶11-920), the transfer pricing provisions (¶22-630) and the FBT legislation (¶35-690).

The maximum penalty under s 262A is a fine of 30 penalty units (¶29-000).

A checklist of the main types of tax records that need to be kept by individual taxpayers is provided at ¶44-100.

Electronic records

The record keeping requirements were drafted with respect to written records but apply equally to electronic records (TR 96/7, TR 2018/2). In this context "reasonable facilities and assistance" includes the provision of login codes, keys (including encryption keys) and passwords, and documentation. It is generally not necessary to retain a hard copy of the information contained in an electronic record unless hard copies are specifically required by a particular law or regulation.

Electronic records must:

- not be altered or manipulated, and stored so as to restrict alteration or manipulation
- be capable of being retrieved and read, supported by system documentation, encryption keys, and data manipulation tools made available to taxation officers at their request. The documentation requirements in relation to off-the-shelf software packages are outlined in PS LA 2008/14. Taxation officers can accept that taxpayers using commercial off-the-shelf software packages are maintaining appropriate system documentation where:
  - the software name and version is recorded
  - a record is made of the components of the software package that have been installed and the date of installation
  - a chronological record is kept of all system changes or upgrades
  - a record is made of the options that have been enabled or disabled, and
  - any manuals or instructions provided with the software package are kept.

[FTR ¶785-080]

When Income is Derived

¶9-050 Timing of income

An annual basis of taxation involves the computation of income derived during a particular income period (ITAA97 s 6-5), accordingly it is necessary to consider whether an item is *income* and whether it has been *derived*.

The question of when income is derived depends on the nature of the income and, in some cases, on the nature of the income-earning activities of the taxpayer who derived the income. Constructive receipt of income is considered at ¶9-080 and prepaid income is discussed at ¶9-090.

Trading income

Trading income is generally derived when the right to receive it arises as a debt due and owing (*Case 39/96*). Income from the sale of goods for a specified sum is generally derived when the goods are delivered.

Bona fide dispute. In *BHP Billiton* the full Federal Court unanimously held where part of the consideration for a supply was subject to a bona fide dispute and *not paid on invoice*, the disputed income was derived when the dispute was settled and not when the commodity was supplied. However, the court also observed that, where consideration received is under dispute, income may be derived at the time of receipt.

Commission income. The derivation of commission by an insurance agent or broker is a question of fact, a significant consideration of which being the terms of the contract as between agent or broker, and the insurance company. Timing of derivation of commission income by travel agents is considered in TD 93/149 and real estate agent commissions in TR 97/5.

Conditional contracts. Under a conditional contract, income is assessable to the seller on accepting the purchase order and a deduction is allowable if the goods are subsequently returned under the terms of the contract (TR 97/15).

Insurance premium income. See IT 2663 for the Commissioner's views on treatment of premiums arising from general insurance contracts that straddle income years.

Lay-by. See TR 95/7. Although less common than in the past, in the absence of specific ATO guidance, the ruling may offer some guidance regarding treatment of more contemporary ''post-pay'' arrangements.

Manufacturers' credits on aircraft purchases. See TR 96/6.

Motor vehicle dealers. For guidelines on the point in time when holdback receipts and warranty indemnities are derived by motor vehicle dealers, see IT 2648.

Pharmacists. Where a pharmacist returns income on an accruals basis, income from the supply of products under the Pharmaceutical Benefits Scheme (PBS) is assessable in the year in which it is derived — the time the product is dispensed to the customer (TR 96/19).

Primary production income. Where a primary producer delivers produce for disposal under a marketing scheme such as a co-operative pool, income is derived when a debt for an ascertainable sum arises (¶18-030). For the Commissioner's views on when the proceeds of wheat and grain sales are assessable, see TR 2001/1 and TR 2001/5 (¶18-030).

Trading stock discounts. Where trading stock is sold under an arrangement that provides for a prompt payment discount (eg 5% discount on invoice price if paid within 30 days), income is assessable to the seller at the time of sale for the full invoice price. If the discount is subsequently accepted, then the difference between the invoice price and the discounted price is deductible at the time payment is received. Where the discount is taken up at the time of sale, such as cash discounts, trade discounts and quantity or bulk discounts, only the discounted price is assessable at that time (TR 96/20). This treatment of trading stock discount still applies where the discount is dealt with at the buyer's instruction (TD 96/45). The High Court decision in *Ballarat Brewing* suggests that only the discounted price should be recognised at the time of sale where receipt of the discount is virtually certain.

Salary and wages

Salary and wages are generally derived when received, whether the amount is payment for current or past services. Back pay, arrears of pay that accrue during a period of suspension, retrospective award increases, lump sum workers compensation arrears and special bonuses are all assessable in the year of receipt (but a special rebate operates to limit the tax payable on such payments: ¶15-350).

An employee cannot apportion a lump sum leave payment between the 2 financial years straddled by the leave period (*Hannavy*), nor can derivation of back pay be deferred to a later financial year by an employee refusing the tender of a cheque (*Case D62*). A former employee in *Blank* derived amounts for relinquishing claims with respect to an employee profit participation plan as and when they are paid to him or applied on his behalf.

Where an employee agrees to forgo a portion of normal annual salary in return for paid leave in a later period, the deferred salary component is not assessable until received, except where the amount is applied, accumulated or invested beforehand for the benefit of the employee (TD 93/242). See also ¶9-080.

Professional fees

A professional person returning income on the accruals basis (¶9-030) derives fee income where a recoverable debt is created and the taxpayer is not obliged to take any further steps before becoming entitled to payment (*Henderson*). Subject to the terms of the contract or arrangement with the client, the same is generally true for disbursements on-charged to clients (TR 97/6). Most commonly, a recoverable debt is created when the taxpayer invoices the client, even if the invoice allows time for payment. Fees paid in advance are derived in the year the person completes the work to which the fees relate (¶9-090). A statutory impediment to a professional person commencing legal proceedings for the recovery of professional fees does not defer the time when income is derived (*Barratt*; TR 93/11). A professional person assessed on a cash basis derives fees and recouped disbursements at the time they are received.

This means, a professional person using the accruals basis need not bring anything into account as assessable income in respect of incomplete work or work in progress unless the contract provides for periodical accounts to be rendered for partially completed work. For the tax treatment of payments for work in progress where a professional partnership is reconstituted, see ¶5-070.

Doctors' fees collected from patients by a hospital as agent for the doctor are derived in the year they are paid by the patient, notwithstanding that they are not actually received by the doctor until a later year (*Case T44*).

Management/service fees

Management/service fees are derived when a recoverable debt is created, which can be several years after the relevant costs have been incurred (*Lee McKeand*).

In *Business Research Management*, management fees were "paid" to the taxpayer in a "round robin" series of paper transactions. The transactions involved limited recourse loans from a related party of the taxpayer to investors. Corresponding amounts were on-paid to the taxpayer as management fees and paid back to the related party by the taxpayer as deposits. To the extent that the related party did not recover the limited recourse portions of the loans, the taxpayer would not recover its deposits, as the related party had no other funds. The taxpayer was held to have derived the entire amount of the management fees referable to the year in question at the time of the round robin transactions, notwithstanding failure of the project and the investors never repaying the limited recourse portions of the loans.

Interest

Interest is generally not derived until it has been received or the debt for interest has in some way been discharged. Subject to the following exceptions, TR 98/1 espouses the cash basis as appropriate for determining income derived from investments:

Money lending business. In *News Australia Holdings Pty Ltd*, the accruals basis was also appropriate although the taxpayer did not carry on a business of money lending, it had income earning activities which included lending money to, among others, its parent company on commercial terms for reward.

Interest on overdue customer accounts. Where the provision of credit is a regular feature of the business activities and the interest is charged on an accruals basis. The interest owing at the end of a year is considered to be derived during that income year, not when the interest is received.

Investors in fixed or variable interest securities cum interest. Where the principal and interest components are not marketed separately and the taxpayer's other income is calculated on an accruals basis.

Cash on deposit. Where a business actively manages its funds on deposit in the ordinary course of carrying on that business, and the business income is properly assessable on an accruals basis.

Banks and other financial institutions generally derive interest income as it accrues (*Australian Guarantee Corporation*; *Alliance Holdings*). See further TR 94/32 (non-accrual loans), TR 93/27 (assessment of interest derived and incurred by financial institutions), TR 93/28 (assessment of income derived from securities purchased and sold cum interest) and TR 1999/11 (assessment of interest paid in advance and received in advance by financial institutions).

A finance company entering into a debt defeasance arrangement is assessable on the difference between the face value of the debt and the amount paid to assign the debt only at the time when the debt matures and not at the time of entering the arrangement (*Unilever*)

See also ¶23-030 on the taxation of various types of financial arrangements; TR 93/6 (¶10-470) regarding interest offset arrangements.

Income from long-term construction projects

The ascertainment of taxable income is an annual exercise. A long-term construction project straddles more than one income year (although it need not be more than 12-months in duration). The only acceptable methods (TR 2018/3) for bringing income from long-term constructions projects to account are:

Basic method. Bringing of all progress and final payments (including upfront payments or advance progress payments) received in a year into assessable income and the claiming of deductions for losses and outgoings as they are incurred (*Grollo Nominees*), or

Estimated profits method. Permits the spreading of ultimate profit or loss on a long-term project over the years taken to complete the contract. Tender costs and unspecified expenses set aside as a management reserve cannot be taken into account.

Where an amount under a contract is retained under a retention clause such that the taxpayer is not entitled to receive the payment, the income is not derived until the taxpayer receives or is entitled to receive the payment. Outgoings are deductible as they are incurred, also meaning that amounts retained by a taxpayer from a subcontractor are not deductible until due to the subcontractor (TR 2018/3).

Neither the *completed contracts basis* (under which the bringing of profits or losses into account is deferred until completion of the contract) nor the *emerging profits basis* are acceptable methods of tax accounting for long-term construction contracts (*Grollo Nominees*; TR 2018/3).

Rent

Rent is generally derived for tax purposes when it is received. Where "rent" for a whole term is payable in advance, reference is required to be made to the lease agreement (and any other relevant factors) to determine whether it is derived when received, or week-by-week over the term of the lease.

Taxable income from chattel leases. Should be calculated in accordance with the asset method, ie gross rentals less deductions by way of depreciation and balancing adjustment on disposal (IT 2594). Use of the finance method to return income from leasing luxury cars (thereby avoiding the car depreciation limit) was rejected in *Citibank.*

Income from transfer of land

Generally, if the income from the transfer of land is of a revenue nature it will be treated as derived when the income is received. In *Tagget*, the full Federal Court upheld the assessment of market value income from an agreement to transfer land as not derived until the actual transfer (in 2005 when the market value was $1,200,000) rather than when a deed of agreement to transfer the land was entered into (7 years previously when the market value was $450,000).

Income from proprietary software licences or hosting

Income from the granting of a proprietary licence for software, or a software hosting arrangement (including bundled additional services) is derived when the obligation is fully performed or the contingency of repayment, namely a contractual or commercial obligation to make a refund; or a contractual exposure for damages, otherwise lapses (TR 2014/1). Income from such software arrangements is deferred where the contingency of repayment is active.

[FITR ¶18-200, ¶27-000]

¶9-080 Constructive receipt

Income that normally needs to have been received before it can be said to be derived may sometimes be deemed to have been received (ITAA97 ss 6-5(4), 6-10(3)).

Constructive receipt is when income is credited without restriction and made available to the taxpayer. The income must be finally earmarked for the taxpayer. Mere crediting in an employer's books of amounts such as salaries, directors' fees, retiring allowances, that are not able to be withdrawn at will, are assessable only when they are actually received or made available.

Common examples of constructive receipt include interest credited on fixed-term deposits and added to capital, interest credited on savings bank deposits even though not noted in the depositor's passbook or statement, and dividends absolutely credited and made subject to a shareholder's demand (such as a DRP), or unpaid due to failure to provide banking details. Income reinvested, accumulated, capitalised, carried to any reserve or sinking fund, or otherwise dealt with *on the taxpayer's behalf or as the taxpayer directs*, is constructively received (see also TR 2018/7). Proceeds from the sale of mining tenements by a taxpayer that were not received by the taxpayer but by associated entities at the direction of the taxpayer were still derived by the taxpayer because the taxpayer had directed the sales proceeds to be paid to those entities (*Kirkby*).

The gross amount of an employee's wages (before PAYG withholding and deductions such as employee superannuation contributions, health fund contributions, workplace giving) is assessable. However, benefits received under an effective "salary sacrifice" arrangement are not assessable to the employee, but may be subject to fringe benefits tax (¶31-120; see also TR 2018/7 from para 30). Dividends credited to a shareholder and, at the shareholder's direction, retained by the company as an advance are constructively received when credited. Cheques are generally regarded as payment when received and not when presented.

A share in uncollected book debts sold as part of a retiring partner's interest in a partnership (that lodges returns on a cash basis) is capitalised on sale of the interest and assessed to the retiring partner. The purchaser is not assessed on subsequent collections of those debts (¶5-060).

An amount is not taken to *be dealt with on a taxpayer's behalf* (and therefore constructively received) when a debtor refrains from making a payment otherwise due to a taxpayer, at the request of a creditor (*Brent*). It is so dealt with once the amount is paid to the creditor on the taxpayer's behalf (*Blank*).

See TR 93/6 (¶10-470) for the Commissioner's views on interest offset arrangements. For a discussion on the transfer of rights to receive income, see ¶30-900.

[FITR ¶18-200, ¶28-000; FTR ¶6-700]

¶9-090 Prepaid or estimated income

Where advance amounts are received for a specific number of discrete services (eg dance, sport lessons) and such payments are *brought to account as income in the taxpayer's accounts only when earned*, they are treated as unearned income not assessable for tax purposes until they are earned (*Arthur Murray*).

This rule has been applied to prepaid magazine subscriptions (*Country Magazine*) and to an advance payment for a fixed-term maintenance and service contract (*Case C86*). The Commissioner applies the same principle to: (a) advance deposits for goods to be manufactured and delivered later at the buyer's request; (b) goods acquired under take or pay contracts, eg in the natural resource industry (TR 96/5); and (c) other cases where services are to be rendered over a fixed period of time (eg television servicing contracts).

To be able to apply the *Arthur Murray* principle it is necessary that the taxpayer's financial accounts are prepared on the basis that advance payments are kept in a suspense or unearned income account and not treated as income until earned, or where the advance payments are credited to gross revenue account in the books but a balance date adjustment is made at the close of the income year to exclude unearned income from the profit and loss account.

Once an up-front payment is brought to account as assessable income under one apportionment method using the *Arthur Murray* principle, a different apportionment method cannot later be adopted in relation to that payment (*Commercial Union*).

The Commissioner does not accept that Arthur Murray is authority for the proposition that where a vehicle is sold subject to a warranty (whether a sale by a manufacturer or distributor to a dealer, or a sale of a new or used car by a dealer to a retail customer), a portion of the sale price relates to the warranty and is not derived at the time of the sale. The Commissioner treats the whole of the sale proceeds as derived by the manufacturer, distributor or dealer at the time of sale (IT 2648). This view should be contrasted with the decision in *Mitsubishi Motors*.

Income received but never earned, as such, cannot escape tax altogether. Adjustments are made so that receipts are treated as income after a reasonable time has passed and there is no longer any likelihood that the taxpayer will be called upon to *earn* the income.

See ¶18-030 for the derivation of income by primary producers under pool contracts.

Schemes under which income is deferred to a later year are specifically countered (¶16-110).

[FITR ¶18-200, ¶27-000]

Timing of Deductions

¶9-100 Prepaid expenses, deferred charges and other timing considerations

The main issues governing when a deduction is allowable are the *time* when expenditure is incurred and the *period* to which it is properly referable (ITAA97 s 8-1: ¶16-040) (*Coles Myer Finance*).

If either a cash or accruals taxpayer pays for supplies that will not be fully used until a future year, the taxpayer is generally entitled to a deduction in the year of payment, ie the year in which the expenditure is incurred.

If the liability incurred or payment made creates an asset having a useful life that extends substantially beyond the end of the income year in which it is paid or incurred, the expense or outgoing may be capital in nature and either not deductible at all or only partly deductible in that year. If payment is made or a liability is incurred for a depreciating asset or other capital expenditure, a depreciation deduction (¶17-005) or special write-off may be available (¶18-000, ¶19-000, ¶20-000).

Conditional contracts. The buyer is allowed a deduction at the time the purchase order is accepted but is assessable on the cost of any goods returned under the terms of the contract (TR 97/15).

Gold forward fees. See *Case 5/98*; TR 92/5; ¶16-045 (deductions for prepayments spread over time).

Prepayments for franchise/renewal fees. Deductible over the eligible service period under the prepayment provisions in ITAA36 Subdiv H of Div 3 (¶16-045; *Inglewood & Districts Community Enterprises Limited*).

Prepayments for services provided over long term. Special rules affect the timing of deductions for expenditure incurred in advance of the provision of services (¶16-045). Deductions for otherwise allowable expenses may also be deferred or denied altogether where the expenses have been incurred under certain types of tax avoidance schemes (¶9-110).

Prepayments for trading stock. ITAA97 s 70-15 prevents expenditure incurred in acquiring trading stock from being claimed as a deduction until the income year in which the stock is on hand (¶9-170, ¶16-040).

Trading stock discounts. Where trading stock is purchased under an arrangement that provides for a prompt payment discount (eg 5% discount on invoice price if paid within 30 days), a deduction is allowable to the purchaser at the time of purchase for the full invoice price. If the discount is subsequently accepted, then the difference between the invoice price and the discounted price is assessable at the time of payment. The High Court decision in *Ballarat Brewing* suggests that only the discounted price should be recognised at the time of purchase where receipt of the discount is virtually certain. For the deductibility of trading stock generally, see ¶16-040. Where the discount is taken up at the time of purchase, such as cash discounts, trade discounts and quantity or bulk discounts only the discounted price is deductible (TR 96/20). This treatment of trading stock discount still applies where the discount is dealt with at the buyer's instruction (TD 96/45).

Solicitor disbursements. A deduction is generally allowable to a solicitor for disbursements on behalf of a client at the time the amount is incurred, whether or when the amount is recovered from the client is not relevant (TR 97/6).

[FTR ¶47-500 – ¶47-550; FITR ¶114-410]

¶9-110 Prepayment and tax deferral schemes

Special provisions apply to counter schemes involving the prepayment of certain deductible expenses, such as interest, rent and expenditure in acquiring trading stock, etc, where the taxpayer (or associate) receives a compensatory benefit in return for the prepayment. Special provisions also apply to counter schemes between associated parties under which taxation of an amount passing between the parties is deferred to a later year (¶16-045, ¶16-110).

[FTR ¶46-801 – ¶47-216]

¶9-120 Deductions for provisions for estimated expenses

Accounting provisions or reserves established for anticipated future outgoings such as advertising, legal expenses, doubtful debts are not allowable deductions as they are not incurred. Although provisions established in respect of incurred expenses may be deductible, in most cases, a presently existing pecuniary liability at the end of the relevant income year is necessary for accrued expense to be incurred (¶16-040) and deductible (TR 94/26). Accordingly, the expenses and losses for which the provision was created are usually only deductible in the income year in which they are actually incurred or paid.

Income tax is not an allowable deduction, and accordingly neither are provisions for income tax.

Although doubtful debt provisions are not deductible, bad debts may be deductible when incurred (¶16-580). Provisions for accrued audit fees in respect of work yet to be undertaken by the auditor at balance date are not considered deductible. A deduction is only allowable in the year the fees are actually incurred (IT 2625).

Employers are not entitled to deductions for accounting provisions to cover commitments for annual, long service and other leave. The deduction is allowable only when the relevant amount is paid (ITAA97 s 26-10; ¶16-040). For the deductibility of payments for the transferred accrued leave entitlements of employees transferred between employers, see ¶16-155.

Provision made by a general insurer for claims outstanding at the end of a year (including claims incurred but not yet reported) is an allowable deduction (*RACV Insurance*, *Commercial Union*; ¶16-040). The Commissioner accepts that the expense is incurred, although not quantifiable and is generally prepared to accept the calculation made by an actuary (or other competent person) of the amount of the insurer's income that needs to be set aside to pay the outstanding claims in the future (IT 2663; ¶16-040) as the deductible amount.

Accumulated jackpot amounts displayed on gaming machines are not allowable deductions by gaming machine operators (including casinos, registered clubs and hotels) until a player actually wins the jackpot (TD 96/12).

[FITR ¶31-050, ¶68-140]

Trading Stock

¶9-150 Identifying trading stock

"Trading stock" is defined as including anything produced, manufactured or acquired that is held for the purposes of manufacture, sale or exchange in the ordinary course of business (ITAA97 s 70-10(1)). It excludes Div 230 financial arrangements (¶23-020), shares in a PDF (¶3-555), registered emissions units (¶19-135) and certain shares, units and land owned by superannuation entities (ITAA97 ss 70-10(2), 70-12).

The statutory definition of trading stock is not exhaustive. Anything that is included in the ordinary meaning of trading stock is also included unless specifically excluded. The work in progress of a manufacturer is trading stock, but work in progress under a long-term construction project is not trading stock of the builder (TR 2018/3). For the treatment of the work in progress of a *professional* in a partnership, see ¶5-070. See also TR 98/2 (trading stock in the mining industry) and TR 93/3 (trading stock of gold miners).

Live stock

"Trading stock" specifically includes live stock. Animals used as beasts of burden or working beasts in a non-primary production business are specifically excluded from being "live stock" (ITAA97 s 995-1(1)). Animals, such as racehorses, used as working beasts in a business other than primary production are plant (ie depreciating assets). For trading stock issues specific to the horse industry, see TR 93/26; and TR 2008/2 relating generally to the horse industry including whether horse related activities amount to the carrying on of a business. If a taxpayer's horse related activities do not amount to the carrying on of a business, the horse will be a depreciating asset and will not be trading stock of any business of the taxpayer.

Domestic pets are not live stock. Freshwater crayfish kept and bred on farms or in hatcheries for sale, and live pearl oysters used in a business of pearl culture (a business of primary production) are live stock (TD 2017/7; *Case 32/95*). Bees kept for the purposes of honey production are also live stock (TD 2008/26; PS LA 2008/4 (GA)).

Crops, trees and nursery stock

Trading stock does not cover standing or growing crops, timber (TR 95/6) or fruit. Crops, timber and fruit become trading stock only when severed from the land; although standing timber purchased with the intention of taking the timber within a reasonably short period after acquiring the interest may be trading stock (*Case 42/95*). A deduction may be available under ITAA97 s 70-120 if a taxpayer acquires land carrying trees or a right to fell trees on another's land where the amount paid took the trees into account (¶18-120). Wool becomes trading stock once shorn from the sheep.

Various measures which deal with assessable income arising from disposals of trading stock outside the ordinary course of business (¶9-245, ¶9-290, ¶9-295, ¶9-300) apply to standing or growing crops, crop-stools or trees planted and tended for sale as if they were trading stock (ITAA97 s 70-85).

Stocks of plants in pots (greenstock) at varying stages of maturity, but not plants growing in the ground, are trading stock for nurseries (IT 33).

Containers, labels, packaging materials, spare parts, etc

Packaging materials fall within the ordinary meaning of trading stock on hand if:

- the taxpayer is in business, trading in "core" goods
- the materials are closely associated with the core goods in the sense that they either:
  - form part of the core goods, or
  - bring the core goods into the form, state or condition in which they are sold, or intended to be sold, to the customer, and
- the materials are disposed of by the taxpayer (ie property in them passes) in conjunction with the sale of the core goods (TR 98/7).

Returnable packaging items are not trading stock, but may be depreciating assets if they are held by a taxpayer who is, or will be, engaged in business trading in "core" goods but who does not dispose of, or pass property in, the items to its customers.

If a type of packaging item, material or spare part has mixed uses, a determination based on a realistic estimate of past (or current) use of similar items is an acceptable means of calculating the extent of the trading stock component (TR 98/7).

A service provider (eg a tradesperson or repairer) who obtains materials, spare parts and packaging items for supply to customers as part of the provision of services is generally considered to hold those items as trading stock (unless the supply of the goods is only a minor and incidental aspect of the provision of the service). This is the case where property in a separately identifiable item passes in connection with the provision of services and the item retains its individual character or nature after it has been supplied, eg building, electrical and plumbing parts (TR 98/8).

Consumable stores are not trading stock and are generally deductible when purchased (IT 333). Computer spare parts of a computer supplier are generally trading stock (TR 93/20).

Computer software

Computer software produced or developed for sale by a software manufacturer or developer, or acquired for sale by a distributor, in the course of business is trading stock. Software produced or developed for licence rather than for sale is trading stock where the developer or supplier carries on a business of trading in software licences (TR 93/12).

Motor vehicles

Demonstration vehicles and ''drive cars'' are generally trading stock of a motor vehicle dealer (IT 2648). Where cars are held as trading stock and then cease being so held (but continue to be owned by the taxpayer), the change is treated as a deemed disposal and reacquisition at cost (¶9-245).

Cars subject to a floor plan arrangement were held to be trading stock of a wholesale car dealer even though the dealer did not own the vehicles, had no legal obligation to buy them, had incurred no financial commitment for them, and merely held them as bailee for the manufacturer (*Suttons Motors*). See also IT 2325 in relation to floor plans.

Goods on consignment

Where goods on consignment are delivered to an agent for sale by the agent on behalf of the consignor as principal, the goods remain trading stock of the consignor. However, if the goods are delivered to the consignee on approval, or on sale or return, and the consignment involves a sale of the goods to the consignee, the goods are included in trading stock on hand of the consignee and deductions are allowed to the consignee for the cost of the goods as at the date of delivery (IT 2472).

Land

Land is capable of being trading stock in the hands of a land dealer, notwithstanding that it may not be in the condition in which it is intended to be sold (*St Hubert's Island*, *R & D Holdings*).

To be trading stock, the land must be held for resale and a business activity that involves dealing in land must have commenced. The acquisition of land does not have to be repetitive. Land from a single acquisition of land for the purpose of development, subdivision and sale by a business commenced for that purpose can be trading stock (TD 92/124).

Trading stock must be acquired for the purpose of manufacture, sale or exchange (s 70-10), accordingly where a taxpayer acquires a right to a proportion of the proceeds from the sale of land, if the right was not acquired for the purpose of resale the acquisition cost of the interest in the land is not an allowable trading stock deduction (*Case 12/2009*).

If a taxpayer initially acquires land as a capital asset but later ventures it into a property development business, then, if the land becomes trading stock, the change is treated as a disposal and reacquisition of the land at cost or market value. Conversely, if a land development and subdivision project is abandoned, and the land stops being held as trading stock, the change is accounted for at cost (¶9-245).

Where land is acquired as trading stock, expenses such as interest, council rates and land tax incurred on or after the acquisition of the land do not form part of its cost price (TD 92/132).

In the case of land purchased by a developer for subdivision and sale, it is only when the individual lots of the subdivision become marketable that each lot is an item of trading stock in its own right (*Barina*). However, the whole area of the land (excluding infrastructure land) may be trading stock before subdivision (*Kurts Development*). In *Gasparin* land ceased to be trading stock of a developer upon settlement of contracts for the sale of the land and not when the contracts became unconditional at some time after the exchange of contracts. In *Starco* where a block of strata title units was built partly for family members and partly for sale, the units transferred to family members were not trading stock.

Retirement villages

Where a property developer develops a retirement village for the purpose of sale to a village operator, the land and buildings are trading stock of the developer (TR 2002/14).

Shares, property trust units, futures contracts

Shares and units can be trading stock in the hands of a dealer or trader (*Investment & Merchant Finance*; *Wong*). Whether a taxpayer is carrying on a trading business is a question of fact (*Case 10/2011*, *Hartley*). Where a part of the taxpayer's business consists of the investment of funds (eg a bank or insurance company) but the investments are not held for profit-making by sale, the taxpayer would not be regarded as a dealer.

Shares held by a taxpayer who is in the business of trading options can be trading stock (ID 2009/59), however shares yet to be acquired by year end by a taxpayer in the business of entering short sale transactions (ie who is obliged to provide shares to close out a short sale) cannot be regarded as trading stock (ID 2007/198). Bonus shares may be trading stock even if the dominant purpose for acquiring them is to obtain a tax advantage (*John*).

Futures contracts held by futures traders are not trading stock (IT 2228 (partially withdrawn)).

See ¶9-200 regarding valuing shares held as trading stock.

Bitcoin — digital currency

The Commissioner regards bitcoin to be property for tax purposes, rather than money, currency or foreign currency: TD 2014/25. Bitcoin held for the purpose of sale or exchange in the ordinary course of business is trading stock (TD 2014/27).

¶9-160 Deduction for cost of trading stock

Established commercial and accounting principles calculate the gross profit from business operations by deducting the cost of goods sold from receipts. There are a number of acceptable methods of calculating the cost of goods sold to clearly reflect the income of a single accounting period.

For tax purposes gross trading receipts are brought to account as assessable income (rather than gross profit or gain), and a taxpayer carrying on a business may claim a deduction for the cost of acquiring trading stock under the general deduction provision (ITAA97 s 8-1). In addition, an adjustment is required for the difference between all trading stock *on hand* (¶9-170) at the start of the income year and all trading stock on hand at the end of that year to arrive at the taxpayer's taxable income (ITAA97 s 70-35).

Where the value of closing stock exceeds the value of opening stock, the amount of the excess is assessable (s 70-35(2)). Where the value of opening stock exceeds the value of closing stock, the amount of the excess is deductible (s 70-35(3)). Where a business is commenced after the beginning of an income year, the value of stock on hand at the end of the first year is assessable despite there being no opening value.

Broadly, speaking this methodology approximates the accounting method of determining cost of goods sold (by resellers) by adding to the opening stock on hand at the start of the year the cost of goods purchased or produced during the year, and deducting from this total the closing stock on hand at the end of the year.

▶ Example: Calculating cost of goods sold

Adam Co buys old boilers and rebuilds and sells them. For the year ended 30 June, it had an opening stock of $40,000 and a closing stock of $50,000. It had sales of $105,000, paid $20,000 for old boilers, $26,000 for labour in renovating them and $5,000 for new parts. Its trading account is as follows:

[Gross sales		$105,000]
Less: Cost of goods sold:		
Opening stock	$40,000	
Add: purchases	$20,000	
labour	$26,000	
parts used	$5,000	
	$91,000	
Deduct: closing stock	$50,000	
Cost of goods sold		$41,000
[Gross profit		$64,000]

Unless a taxpayer records purchases and sales of trading stock in such a way as to create a continuous record of stock on hand, supported by stocktaking throughout the year such that each line of stock is counted at least once, an annual physical stocktake is required at the end of the financial year (TD 93/125). An adjustment is required for goods taken out of trading stock and used for private purposes. For this purpose, the goods are brought to account at cost (¶9-245). Small business entities may apply simplified rules (¶7-260).

[FITR ¶114-020]

¶9-170 When is trading stock on hand?

As noted in ¶9-160, while the cost of acquiring trading stock is deductible under the general deduction provision (ITAA97 s 8-1), the deduction is not allowable until the stock is actually on hand, or until an amount has been included in the taxpayer's assessable income in connection with the disposal of the item (ITAA97 s 70-15; TD 93/138). This deferral provision does not apply to expenditure incurred in bringing trading stock into existence through manufacturing or production by the taxpayer, except where it relates to the acquisition of inputs to the manufacturing or production processes that are themselves trading stock (TR 93/9; ¶9-150).

Trading stock is on hand if the taxpayer has the power to dispose of the stock (IT 2670). Generally, the power of disposal lies with the person who owns the stock. See further ¶9-150. Stock may also be on hand even though the taxpayer does not have physical possession of it, eg trading stock in transit at year end, where property has passed to the taxpayer, is trading stock on hand of that taxpayer (*All States Frozen Foods*).

Conversely, goods cease to be trading stock on hand once the trader no longer has the power of disposition of the goods (TR 94/13). When produce sold by a grower to a packing house is pooled with produce from other growers it ceases to be trading stock on hand of the grower (*Farnsworth*). See TR 2001/1 and TR 2001/5 in relation to when wheat or grain ceases to be trading stock. See TR 97/9 for when property in shorn wool passes to the buyer (ceasing to be trading stock of the grower) under various modes of sale.

Lay-bys, conditional contracts and demonstrators

Goods in the possession of a seller that are subject to a lay-by sale agreement are trading stock on hand of the seller (TR 95/7). See also ¶9-050 recognition of income.

Goods delivered under a conditional contract and held by the buyer are trading stock on hand of the buyer. If the buyer returns goods to the seller before the end of the income year, those goods are trading stock of the seller at year end (TR 97/15).

Demonstrator computers lent by a wholesaler to a prospective purchaser (excluding retailers) on the basis of approval, exchange or return; or to a retailer for display purposes only, remain trading stock on hand of the wholesaler until the prospective purchaser enters into a contract to buy the demonstrator; or the demonstrator continues to be held by the retailer for display purposes only (TD 95/48).

[FITR ¶114-310, ¶114-410, ¶114-450]

Valuation of Trading Stock

¶9-180 Valuation of trading stock

For tax purposes a taxpayer may value trading stock, including live stock (see further ¶9-250), at cost (¶9-190), market selling value (¶9-220), or replacement value (¶9-225) (ITAA97 s 70-45). A different basis may be adopted for a class of stock, or for each individual *item* of stock. A different basis may be adopted for any one item or class of items each year end.

Accordingly, the closing value adopted for an item of trading stock at the end of one income year automatically becomes its opening value at the beginning of the next income year (ITAA97 s 70-40). If a valuation basis has been adopted (either expressly or implicitly) and the taxpayer is assessed on that basis, the taxpayer cannot subsequently vary it by objecting to the assessment or requesting an amendment (TD 94/10). Similarly, s 70-40 does not appear to allow the opening value of a taxpayer's trading stock to be amended to reflect the closing value that *should have been* taken into account at the end of the previous year where the time for amendment of the previous year's assessment has expired (*Energy Resources*).

If no assessment was made for a preceding income year the value of an item of trading stock at the start of the income year is nil (*Bywater Investments Ltd & Ors*), on the basis that the item was not taken into account under Div 70 or Subdiv 328-E at the end of the previous income year (s 70-40(2)).

The closing value of trading stock excludes the amount of GST for which the taxpayer is entitled to claim an input tax credit (s 70-45(1A); ¶34-100).

See ¶31-270 for tax planning aspects of trading stock valuation.

Trade incentives

The effects of trade incentives on assessable income and allowable deductions are outlined in ¶9-050 and ¶9-100 respectively.

Trade incentives or other payments that are not directly connected to the buyer's purchase of trading stock do not reduce the cost or sale proceeds of the trading stock for the buyer or seller (eg a promotional rebate paid to a buyer for keeping a prominent display of the seller's range of products in its store). Such trade incentives are treated as ordinary income of the buyer, and as a business expense of the seller.

Where there is more than one purpose for the trade incentive, each purpose should be considered in determining the extent to which the payment reduces the cost of the trading stock. If this cannot be determined, the trade incentive should not be treated as if it is directly connected to the purchase of trading stock (TR 2009/5).

Translation of foreign currency amounts

Standardised rules are used to translate foreign currency amounts into Australian dollars for taxation purposes (¶23-070). Where trading stock is valued at cost, the foreign currency value is translated at the rate applicable at the time when the item became "on hand" (¶9-170). Where trading stock is valued at market selling value or replacement value, the foreign currency amount is translated at the rate applicable at the end of the income year (ITAA97 s 960-50(6)).

[FITR ¶114-450, ¶114-460, ¶114-465]

¶9-190 Cost of trading stock

"Cost" refers to the full absorption cost of an item of trading stock (*Philip Morris*). This is not just the invoice or purchase price but also appropriate costs associated with bringing the stock into its existing condition and location. A number of rulings applicable to specific industries have been issued.

Retail and wholesale industries. Full absorption cost of trading stock purchased ready for sale is the purchase price plus a suitable proportion of costs such as freight, insurance, customs and excise duties, purchasing, warehousing and distribution (PS LA 2003/13; AASB 102; IAS 2; TR 2006/8). Taxpayers with a gross operating turnover of less than $10 million may make an appropriate estimate of the additional costs to be absorbed (TR 2006/8).

Work in progress and manufactured goods. Full absorption cost includes the cost of labour and materials, plus an appropriate proportion of variable and fixed factory overheads, eg power, rent, rates and factory administration costs (IT 2350, IT 2402). The direct cost method is not acceptable for work in progress and manufactured goods as it does not reflect the full absorption cost (*Philip Morris*).

Land developers. The cost of infrastructure land (eg parks and roads), associated infrastructure costs and other external costs (ie the cost of meeting the conditions for approval of a subdivision) form part of the cost of the land that is being developed and sold, notwithstanding the infrastructure land vests in the Crown upon subdivision (*Kurts Development*).

Traded-in motor vehicles. See TR 93/29. Notional cost is not acceptable.

Banana growers. See TD 93/47, cost valuations can be based solely on harvesting and processing expenses.

Beekeepers. See PS LA 2008/4 (GA). The unit of valuation is a live hive (ie a queen bee and an indeterminate number of worker and drone bees) excluding the value of the hive structure box and frame. An average cost of $20 per live hive can be used.

Mining industry. See TR 98/2.

Special valuation provisions apply where trading stock is purchased at an excessive price and the parties are not acting at arm's length (¶9-210).

The tax consequences of a company issuing shares to acquire trading stock are discussed in TR 2008/5 (¶3-260).

[FITR ¶114-470]

¶9-200 Methods used to work out the cost of trading stock

It is often impossible or impracticable for the actual cost of each item of trading stock on hand to be ascertained, particularly where there have been a number of purchases of trading stock at varying prices and part, but not the whole, of the purchases remains as trading stock on hand at the end of the year. In such circumstances the following methods, that consistently produce a valuation reasonably approximating full absorption cost, are acceptable for the purpose of valuing trading stock on hand at year end:

FIFO (first-in-first-out). Assumes that trading stock is disposed of in the order in which it was acquired. The cost of trading stock on hand at the end of the year is the cost of the items most recently acquired

Average cost. The cost of each item of a particular type on hand at the end of the year is the weighted average of the cost of all such items that were on hand at the beginning of the year and all those acquired during the year. The Commissioner accepts this method where the actual cost of stock cannot be ascertained (IT 2289)

Standard cost. A predetermined standard cost per unit is used. This is acceptable if standards are reviewed regularly to equate with current prices

Retail inventory. Goods in stock are marked at their retail selling prices, the marked prices are added together in the course of stocktaking and this figure is then reduced by the amount of the mark-up to arrive at the cost of the goods on hand. This is acceptable if old stock is not marked down as it falls in value.

The following valuation methods are *not* acceptable:

LIFO (last-in-first-out). Assumes that the most recently acquired items of trading stock are disposed of first. The items on hand at the end of the year is the cost of the same number of items first acquired. In an inflationary environment the cost of goods sold will be higher than other methods.

Base stock. This assumes the need for a minimum or basic amount of stock for the operation of business. The base stock is valued at cost as at the date of the manufacturing process to which it relates and quantities in excess of the base stock are valued by some other method.

Shares. Where *equity interests* held as revenue assets by a taxpayer can be *specifically identified* using appropriately detailed records, actual cost is used for the purposes of valuing closing stock. Where shares cannot be specifically identified, taxpayers must normally use the FIFO method to value closing stock (TR 96/4).

[FITR ¶114-475]

¶9-210 Purchase of stock not at arm's length

Normally, cost is calculated on the basis of actual purchase price. However, market value applies to both the buyer and the seller if a taxpayer buys trading stock for more than its market value and the taxpayer and the seller did not deal with each other at arm's length (ITAA97 s 70-20). The same applies to any outgoing that is directly attributable to buying or obtaining delivery of trading stock.

As this treatment applies only to amounts attributable to buying or obtaining delivery of trading stock, it does not affect the cost of manufactured trading stock. In the case of manufactured stock, the profit from the sale of the stock can effectively be spread among more than one company of a group by, for example, the manufacturing company hiring machines from an associated company. The deductibility of the hiring charges is governed by the principles discussed at ¶16-070, and the effect of consolidation (¶8-000).

[FITR ¶114-320]

¶9-220 Market selling value of stock

The market selling value of stock is based on a sale in the ordinary course of the taxpayer's business and not a forced sale or break-up (*Australasian Jam*).

It is the current selling value of the stock in the particular taxpayer's *own selling market*. For a wholesaler, this is the current wholesale value of comparable items; for a retailer, the current retail value. An anticipated fall in market price cannot be taken into account.

Where special circumstances exist (¶9-240), such as trading stock that consists of unusual new and used machinery for which there is demand only from specialised purchasers, and may remain "on hand" years prior to sale, market value is not an appropriate valuation method. Where there is no way of calculating the real market selling value of such machinery, the stock can be valued on a reasonable basis, eg scrap value (*Case W110*). See further ¶9-240.

See IT 33 for the valuation of nursery greenstock.

[FITR ¶114-495]

¶9-225 Replacement value of stock

The replacement value of trading stock is the amount that the taxpayer would have to pay in its normal buying market on the last day of the income year to obtain an item substantially identical and available in the market (TD 92/198).

Motor vehicle dealers. See IT 2648 for the application of replacement value to demonstration vehicles on hand at year end. The price at auction or the arm's length wholesale price at which a comparable vehicle could be purchased from another dealer is acceptable. Trade-in prices are not a suitable basis of valuation, nor are values listed in various used car guides. See TR 93/29 for use of replacement value of traded-in motor vehicles, for which a dealer must use an independent valuation; or a recognised industry guide which must be used for all trade-ins valued at replacement value for that income year.

[FITR ¶114-500]

¶9-240 Special value in case of obsolescence

The value of trading stock may be less than its cost, market selling value or replacement value due to obsolescence or other special circumstances particular to the relevant trading stock, eg the discontinuation of a product line or a fickle market. In such cases, the taxpayer may adopt a lower value for the stock, provided that value is reasonable (ITAA97 s 70-50).

In determining the value to be adopted, the following might be taken into account: (a) the quantity of closing stock on hand; (b) the quantity of stock sold, exchanged or used in manufacture since the end of the income year; (c) the prospect of future sales, exchange or use in manufacture; and (d) the quantity of the same kind of trading stock sold, exchanged or used in manufacture by the taxpayer during the income year and preceding years. See also ¶9-220.

The Commissioner has issued general guidelines for trading stock valuations where obsolescence or other special circumstances exist (TR 93/23). Specific guidelines for winemakers where there has been an adverse grape harvest are contained in IT 2001.

[FITR ¶114-600]

¶9-245 Transfer of property to or from trading stock

Property that later becomes trading stock

Where an asset of the taxpayer that is not held as trading stock becomes trading stock, the change is treated as a disposal and reacquisition at cost or market value, at the taxpayer's election (ITAA97 s 70-30). Accordingly, the cost or market value of the property (whichever is chosen by the taxpayer) is its cost for trading stock purposes. A deduction is available under ITAA97 s 8-1 at the time of the change as if the property had been acquired as trading stock from a third party. The amount chosen is also taken to be the proceeds on disposal of the property for the purpose of working out the tax consequences of the notional disposal of the property. For example, the amount (cost or market value) is also used to work out balancing adjustments, eg under the depreciation provisions (¶17-630), or any CGT event K4 capital gain or capital loss (¶11-350). This treatment does *not* apply, where items of property are sold as part of the sale of the taxpayer's business (¶9-290). See TR 2008/2 for the application of these provisions to race horses.

Crops. A notional disposal and reacquisition does not happen when standing or growing crops, crop-stools or trees planted and tended for sale become trading stock on being severed from the land (s 70-30(5)).

Land. Where land originally acquired as a capital asset is later ventured into a property development business and becomes trading stock of the taxpayer, its market value is determined having regard to the ''highest and best use'' that can be made of it (TD 97/1). Due weight must be given to the land's potential utility and to the likelihood of approval being obtained for that potential use.

Property that stops being held as trading stock

Where an item trading stock ceases to be trading stock, but continues to be owned by the taxpayer, it is treated as if it had been sold to someone else so that the cost of the item is included in the taxpayer's assessable income. At the same time, the item is taken to have been immediately reacquired by the taxpayer at cost (ITAA97 s 70-110). Examples include: (a) where a farmer takes an item of trading stock for personal consumption; and (b) where an item of trading stock starts being used in the taxpayer's business as plant (ie a depreciating asset) and is no longer for sale, eg if a computer supplier takes a computer from trading stock for use in its business. The provision also applies to standing or growing crops, crop-stools or trees planted and tended for sale (ITAA97 s 70-85).

The Commissioner releases standard values each year for goods taken from trading stock for private use for some businesses where difficulties typically arise in keeping appropriate records. The values are based on an amount per person aged over 16, and for children 4 to 16 years who comprise a household, as set out in the table below. The listed values exclude GST.

Value of goods taken from trading stock for private use 2019–20 (*TD 2020/1*)		
Type of business	**Amount for adult/ child over 16 years ($)**	**Amount for child 4 to 16 years ($)**
Bakery	1,350	675
Butcher	850	425
Restaurant/cafe (licensed)	4,640	1,750
Restaurant/cafe (unlicensed)	3,500	1,750
Caterer	3,790	1,895
Delicatessen	3,500	1,750
Fruiterer/greengrocer	880	440
Takeaway food shop	3,440	1,720
Mixed business (includes milk bar, general store and convenience store)	4,260	2,130

Taxpayers are not restricted to the values in the table, they may use higher or lower values if they are appropriate and justifiable.

In some circumstances the supply of trading stock for private use may be treated as a taxable supply for GST purposes (GSTD 2009/2).

[FITR ¶114-340, ¶115-020]

¶9-247 Value shifting involving trading stock

The general value shifting regime (from ¶12-800) although applying mainly in the CGT context, can also apply to trading stock and revenue assets. For example, equity or loan interests to which the value shifting regime may apply, may be held as trading stock. Value shifting may also occur by creating rights in respect of non-depreciating assets that are held as trading stock, or the rights created may themselves be trading stock.

In addition, special rules in ITAA97 Divs 723, 725 and 727 deal with direct value shifts and indirect value shifts involving revenue assets and assets that are held as trading stock.

Live Stock

¶9-250 Valuation of live stock

The bases of measuring the closing value of trading stock (¶9-180) apply to determining the closing value for live stock, including horse breeding stock (ITAA97 s 70-45, subject to closing value options in ss 70-60 and 70-65).

Although, the basis of live stock valuation can be changed from year-to-year and can be varied on an item-by-item basis, where the cost basis is used for valuing live stock, the valuation is typically based on average cost. For horse breeding stock per unit per year valuation may be more appropriate.

▶ Example: Valuing live stock

		Number	*Value*
Opening stock (sheep)		1,000	$12,000
Purchases		300	4,500
Natural increase at selected value of $4 (¶9-260)		350	1,400
		1,650	$17,900
Average cost ($17,900 ÷ 1,650)	$10.85		

See ¶9-220 for market selling value. For the valuation of property transferred to or from trading stock, see ¶9-245. For the Commissioner's guidelines on the valuation of horses as live stock, see TR 2008/2.

[FITR ¶114-650]

¶9-260 Valuation of live stock natural increase

Livestock acquired by natural increase may be valued at cost, market selling value or replacement value (¶9-180). If live stock is valued at cost, the taxpayer can use actual cost or the cost prescribed by the regulations, regardless of which is lower (ITAA97 s 70-55). Actual cost is the full cost of bringing the live stock into its current state and location, including expenses such as veterinary fees, feed, fencing. The prescribed costs (ITR97 reg 70-55.01) are:

Class of live stock	Cost ($)
Cattle	20.00
Deer	20.00

Class of live stock	Cost ($)
Emus	8.00
Goats	4.00
Horses	20.00
Pigs	12.00
Poultry	0.35
Sheep	4.00

Live stock acquired by natural increase may be valued per item per year on different bases. A horse acquired by natural increase that is on hand at the end of an income year cannot be valued a less than the service fees incurred in breeding the horse (s 70-55(2)).

[FITR ¶114-620]

Disposals not in Ordinary Course of Business

¶9-290 Stock disposed of outside ordinary course of business

When trading stock is sold in the ordinary course of trading, gross sales less the cost of goods sold are brought to account in accordance with the tax accounting rules applicable to trading stock (¶9-160).

However, where an item of trading stock (with or without other business assets) is disposed of outside the ordinary course of a taxpayer's business, the taxpayer is required to bring to account as assessable income the *market value* of that stock on the date of disposal. The person acquiring the trading stock is, for tax accounting purposes, deemed to have purchased the trading stock at that value (ITAA97 ss 70-90, 70-95).

Accounting for disposals of trading stock in this manner applies to every disposal of trading stock outside the ordinary course of business, whether by sale, gift or otherwise, in circumstances other than those incidental to the normal business practice of the particular business. A transfer in specie to the sole beneficial shareholder of a company in liquidation is a disposal by that company for purposes of s 70-90 (*St Hubert's Island*). A disposal also occurs where 2 existing entities are amalgamated into a single new entity. While inter-company sales at below market value may occur in the ordinary course of business, caution is required. A sale at well below market value (at a time when the seller knew the buyer had already negotiated resale to an unrelated party at a much higher price) was not in the ordinary course of business in *Pastoral & Development*; *Case R85*.

Where the disposal of property by way of gift occurs and a valuation has been obtained from the Commissioner under ITAA97 s 30-212 within 90 days of the disposal (s 70-90(1A)) the market value may be replaced with the value of the property so determined. See further ¶16-970 regarding concessional deductions for certain gifts of trading stock.

The value attributed to trading stock in a contract of sale of a business (ie its *sale* price) is not necessarily its *market* value. Nor is *market* value necessarily the same as *market selling* value.

In applying s 70-90, the transaction must be viewed as a whole to determine whether there is a disposal of the entire ownership in the trading stock (*Rose*); and may also apply to a transaction in which the disposal of the entire ownership is carried out by successive disposals of part of that ownership (*Benwerrin*). Section 70-90 does not apply where a sole trader who owns trading stock declares himself/herself the trustee of a discretionary trust holding that trading stock (TD 96/2).

Sections 70-90 and 70-95 also apply to disposals of standing or growing crops, crop-stools or trees planted and tended for sale.

Special elections are available to permit the deferral of assessment of profit where there is a forced disposal of live stock by a primary producer (¶18-160).

Profits from the disposal of trading stock may be deferred if the conditions for a business restructure roll-over under ITAA97 Div 615 are satisfied (¶12-370). Roll-over relief is also available for gains from the transfer of trading stock of a small business entity that changes its legal structure without changing the asset's ultimate economic ownership under ITAA97 Subdiv 328-G (¶12-380).

[FITR ¶114-830]

¶9-295 Partial change in ownership of stock

A partial change in the ownership of trading stock is treated as a notional disposal of the trading stock by all the old owners to all the new owners (ITAA97 s 70-100). The provision also applies to standing or growing crops, crop-stools or trees planted and tended for sale (ITAA97 s 70-85). A partial change of ownership occurs if, after the change, a new owner and at least one of the old owners has an ownership interest in the trading stock (eg where a partnership is formed, varied or dissolved). For planning aspects, see ¶31-270.

▶ Example: Sole trader becomes a partnership

Heidi, the sole proprietor of a business, decides to sell an undivided half-interest in the business to Anton. There is a deemed disposal of the trading stock on hand *from* Heidi *to* Heidi and Anton at market value.

▶ Example: Reconstruction of partnership

The partnership of Nick, Sarah and Laura is treated for tax purposes as dissolved when Laura retires, selling her undivided interest to Adam. There is a deemed disposal of the trading stock *from* Nick, Sarah and Laura *to* Nick, Sarah and Adam at market value.

Agreement between old and new owners

The old and new owners may agree to adopt the tax value of the trading stock as its disposal value, rather than market value (s 70-100(4)). The tax value of the trading stock is what would have been its value in the hands of the transferor at the end of the income year if the income year had ended on the date of the change. The agreement must be made in writing before 1 September following the end of the financial year in which the change occurred or within any extended period allowed (s 70-100(7)).

The option to adopt the tax value is available where:

- the item becomes an asset of the business carried on by the new owners
- after the notional disposal, the old owners retain at least a 25% interest in the item, and
- the market value of the item as at the date of disposal is greater than the value that would have been taken into account at the end of the income year if the income year had ended on the date of the change of ownership.

▶ Example: Agreement to dispose of stock at tax value

On 30 June, Mel and Liz, equal partners in a manufacturing business, admit Nina as a full partner, *each* selling 1/3 of their interest in the total partnership assets to Nina. As at 30 June, the closing value at cost of the partnership's stock on hand was $3,000, its market value $5,000. As there is a 66 2/3% continuity of interest of Mel and Liz in the new partnership of Mel, Liz and Nina, they may make an agreement under s 70-100(4).

If no agreement is made, for tax purposes the old partnership is deemed to have sold, and the new partnership to have purchased, the trading stock for its market value (¶9-290) of $5,000. Mel and Liz, as the partners in the old partnership, are assessed on the profit of $2,000 (ie $5,000 – $3,000).

If an agreement *is* made, for tax purposes the old partnership is deemed to have sold, and the new partnership to have purchased, the trading stock for its closing value of $3,000 (cost), and there is no assessable profit on the transaction. The assessment of profit is deferred until the stock is sold in the ordinary course of the new partnership business.

The provisions of s 70-100(4) do *not* apply in the following situations:

- where the transaction occurs outside the course of ordinary family or commercial dealing and the consideration receivable in connection with the partial change of ownership substantially exceeds the amount that might reasonably be expected to have been receivable if the item was valued at its tax value (s 70-100(10))
- where the item is a thing in action (ie a chose in action, or legally enforceable right), eg shares or debentures (s 70-100(6)(d)), or
- where trading stock is distributed to a deceased estate (ID 2002/625).

Section 70-100 does not require that the item transferred become trading stock in the hands of the new owners. Nor does s 70-100 necessarily apply only to transactions outside the ordinary course of business (*Westraders*). There is no notional trading stock disposal under s 70-100 if a newly admitted partner does not purchase any part of the old partners' interests in the partnership trading stock.

Granting an option to purchase the taxpayer's interest in trading stock does not amount to a change in ownership of the stock for the purposes of s 70-100 (*Glenfield Estates*).

Application to trusts

The Commissioner has issued a number of taxation determinations dealing with the application of s 70-100 in situations involving trusts (former s 36A(2)). According to the Commissioner, s 70-100 can apply if a partnership transfers trading stock to the trustee of a unit trust in which the former partners of the partnership hold at least 25% of the units, provided the trust deed specifies that unitholders have a proprietary interest in the underlying assets of the trust (TD 96/4). Section 70-100 can also apply where a sole trader transfers trading stock to a partnership comprising the sole trader and the trustee of a discretionary trust, and that partnership in turn transfers the trading stock to the trustee of the discretionary trust. Such an arrangement should expect to be scrutinised, particularly if it appears to be contrived to exploit tax benefits arising from the application of s 70-100 (TD 96/3).

Section 70-100, does *not* apply where a sole trader transfers trading stock to the trustee of a discretionary trust (TD 96/1); or where a sole trader owning trading stock declares himself/herself the trustee of a discretionary trust holding that trading stock (TD 96/2).

[FITR ¶114-900]

¶9-300 Trading stock on death of owner

When due to the death of a person, trading stock, standing or growing crops, crop-stools or trees planted and tended for sale, pass to the executor or administrator of the deceased estate, the market value of that trading stock, etc, may have to be included in the deceased's assessable income up to the date of death. In this event, the estate is deemed to have purchased the trading stock, etc, at that market value (ITAA97 s 70-105). Unless: (a) the executor or administrator of the estate continues to carry on the deceased's business (b) the trading stock continues to be held as trading stock of the business (or, in the case of crops, etc, continues to be held as an asset of the business), and (c) the executor or administrator of the estate makes the appropriate election. In such a case, the trading stock, etc, is treated as if there was no death, ie the business is treated as a continuing one although a return must still be lodged for the deceased up to the date of death and a separate return must be lodged for the estate as from the following day. In the estate's return, the closing values of trading stock adopted in the deceased's return to the date of death must be the opening values in the estate's first return (s 70-105(6)). The executor or administrator of the estate may elect to treat crops, etc, as having a nil value at the time of death.

The above treatment does *not* apply on the death of a partner in a partnership notwithstanding that the death results in the dissolution of the partnership (at least) for tax purposes. There results a partial change in ownership of the trading stock. See ¶9-295 for the nature of the choice that may be available in such circumstances.

[FITR ¶115-000]

Chapter 10 Assessable Income • Tax Exemptions

Para

What is "Assessable Income"?

¶10-000 Overview of assessable income

Tax is levied on the taxable income of the taxpayer derived during the income year. Taxable income is calculated by deducting from the taxpayer's assessable income all allowable deductions. "Assessable income" consists of ordinary income and statutory income (ITAA97 s 6-1(1)). However, an amount of ordinary income or statutory income will not be assessable income if the amount is made exempt or is otherwise excluded from assessable income.

"Ordinary income" is defined to mean income according to ordinary concepts (ITAA97 s 6-5(1)). The legislation does not provide any specific guidance on what is meant by "income according to ordinary concepts". However, a substantial body of case law has evolved to identify various factors that indicate whether an amount is income according to ordinary concepts (¶10-010).

In certain situations, an amount of ordinary income may also be included in assessable income under a specific provision of ITAA97 or ITAA36. In this event, the amount is assessable under the specific provision only, unless the provision provides otherwise (ITAA97 s 6-25). For example, an annuity is income according to ordinary concepts but may be included in assessable income by a specific provision such as ITAA97 s 301-25 if it is paid by a superannuation fund (¶14-220).

An amount is "statutory income" if the amount is: (a) *not* ordinary income; and (b) included in assessable income by a specific provision of ITAA97 or ITAA36 (ITAA97 s 6-10(2)). An example of statutory income is a royalty which is not ordinary income under s 6-5 but which is included in assessable income under ITAA97 s 15-20 (¶10-510).

Where the disposal of an asset causes an amount to be included in assessable income and also results in a capital gain for CGT purposes, the full amount is included in assessable income and the capital gain is reduced by that amount (ITAA97 s 118-20).

Taxable income

Taxable income is generally defined as assessable income minus all general and specific deductions (ITAA97 s 4-15). Such deductions will include all normal business expenses, ie expenses connected with the production of *assessable* income (excluding capital or private expenses), certain special deductions for expenditure of a capital nature and personal deductions. Taxable income is the amount to which the tax rates are applied. Tax offsets, eg credits for foreign taxes or rebates for medical expenses or dependants, are deducted not from the assessable or taxable income but from the computed tax to determine the final tax payable (ITAA97 s 4-10).

Source and residence

The assessable income of a resident (¶21-010) of Australia includes ordinary income derived (¶9-050) directly or indirectly from all sources *in or out of Australia* (s 6-5(2)). Statutory income from all sources in or out of Australia is also included (s 6-10(4)). By contrast, a non-resident's assessable income includes only (ss 6-5(3); 6-10(5)):

- ordinary income and statutory income from all sources (¶21-060) *in Australia*, and
- other ordinary and statutory income that a provision includes in assessable income on some basis other than having an Australian source.

Exempt income

An amount of ordinary income or statutory income is not included in assessable income if the amount is "exempt income", ie if the amount is expressly *made exempt* from income tax by a provision of ITAA97, ITAA36 or another Commonwealth law (ITAA97 ss 6-15(2); 6-20(1)).

Ordinary income is also "exempt income" if it is *excluded* from being assessable income (s 6-20(2)). By contrast, an amount which falls within a statutory income provision but which is excluded from being assessable income is not "exempt income" unless it is made exempt by a provision apart from ss 6-1 to 6-25 or another Commonwealth law (s 6-20(3)). This means that the amount is treated as if it had never been included as statutory income. The distinction between exempt income and an amount which never became statutory income in the first place is important because of the special way that exempt income is treated (eg under the tax loss carry-forward rules). The categories of exempt income are discussed at ¶10-600 onwards.

Non-assessable non-exempt income

Some ordinary income and statutory income is neither assessable income nor exempt income (s 6-1(4)). An amount of ordinary or statutory income is "non-assessable non-exempt income" if a provision in ITAA97, ITAA36 or any other Commonwealth law states that it is not assessable income and is not exempt income (s 6-23). For details, see ¶10-890.

Effect of GST

Generally, GST is disregarded when working out assessable income (ITAA97 Div 17). The GST payable on "taxable supplies" (¶34-100), as well as any increasing adjustment relating to a supply (¶34-140), are expressly excluded from assessable and exempt income and so are non-assessable non-exempt income. If the recoupment of an amount paid to acquire something is included in assessable income, the GST effect of that recoupment is also excluded. However, the amount of a decreasing adjustment under *A New Tax System (Goods and Services Tax) Act 1999* (GST Act) Div 129 is included in assessable income. This will be the case, for example, when something acquired for use in making input taxed supplies is instead applied in making taxable supplies.

Decreasing adjustments under GST Act Div 132 (ie where something acquired for private purposes or for the purpose of making financial supplies is later sold as part of a taxable supply or as part of a GST-free disposal of a business) are also included in assessable income.

For the interaction of GST and the uniform capital allowance system, see ¶17-090.

Summary

The following analysis may be applied in determining whether an amount is included in assessable income:

- are the residency and source of income requirements satisfied?
- is the amount ordinary income?
- is the amount statutory income under a provision apart from the CGT provisions?
- is the amount exempt income?
- is the amount non-assessable non-exempt income?
- is the amount statutory income under the CGT provisions?

[FITR ¶15-120, ¶15-130, ¶18-200, ¶23-000]

¶10-005 Checklist of taxable and non-taxable items

This checklist shows the *general* taxation status of a wide range of income items and where they are dealt with in Chapter 10 or elsewhere (as indicated in the **Source** column) *except for*:

- the taxation of social security payments (¶10-195)
- the taxation of veterans' pensions and similar benefits (¶10-200), and

- the taxation of superannuation benefits and termination of employment payments (¶42-250 and following).

Item	**Taxable (T)/Non-taxable (NT)**	**Source**
ADF income	T	¶13-410
Austudy or ABSTUDY scheme payments	T	¶10-700
Accrued leave entitlements, payment received for transferring employee	T	¶10-110
Advance rent, royalties	T	¶10-500, ¶10-510
Advances kept in suspense account	NT	¶9-090
Agency cancellation payments	T	¶10-114
Allowances connected with employment	T	¶10-060
Allowances paid to visiting fellow	T	¶10-070
Annual honorarium	NT	¶10-070
Apprentices training bonuses	NT	¶10-700
Assets sterilisation, compensation for	NT	¶10-115
Attendant allowance	NT	¶10-200
Back pay	T	¶10-050
Bad debt recoveries where deduction previously allowed	T	¶10-270
Balancing adjustments (unless roll-over relief available):		
Depreciating assets	T	¶17-630 – ¶17-660
Barter/countertrade (business) transactions	T	¶10-030
Bitcoin (business) transactions	T	¶10-030
Benefits for veterans and dependants	NT	¶10-200
Benefits (non-cash) connected with employment	NT	¶10-060, ¶35-000
Benefits (non-cash) provided to business taxpayers	T	¶10-030
Bequests and devises	NT	¶10-840
Bereavement payments for disabled veterans	NT	¶10-200
Betting or gambling wins of a taxpayer who is carrying on a business of betting, etc	T	¶10-430
Board of employee (meals)	NT	¶35-630
Body corporate levies	NT	¶3-550
Bonus shares	T	¶4-110
Bonuses including cash bonuses on insurance policies	T	¶10-240
Book debts, sale of	T	¶9-080
Bounty in carrying on business	T	¶10-160
Business proceeds	T	¶10-110, ¶10-112
Cancellation of contract of service	T	¶10-072
Capital gains (net)	T	¶11-030
Car, employee's private use	NT	¶35-150
Cash flow boost payments (COVID-19)	NT	¶10-040
Cash insurance bonuses	NT	¶13-140
Charitable organisations' income	NT	¶10-605

Item	Taxable (T)/Non-taxable (NT)	Source
Child care benefit	NT	¶10-197
Child support payments	NT	¶10-855
Children with autism payments	NT	¶10-200
Clean energy payments	NT	¶10-200
Clothing allowance	NT	¶10-200
Clothing allowance from employer	T	¶10-060
Clubs, receipts from members	NT	¶3-810
Continence aids payments	NT	¶10-200
Clubs, receipts from non-members	T	¶3-820, ¶3-830
''Combat zone'' pay	NT	¶10-780
Commissions	T	¶10-050, ¶10-110
Commonwealth education or training payments	T	¶10-700
Commonwealth securities:		
Accrued interest on Special Bonds	T	¶23-400
Profit on sale or redemption of securities acquired at a discount after 30 June 1982	T	¶10-885
Surplus on redemption, sale, etc, of non-interest bearing Treasury Notes, etc	T	¶23-410
Community service organisations' income	NT	¶10-605
Company loss transfer payments	NT	¶3-090
Compensation:		
Accident or disability policy payments	T	¶10-210
Cancellation, etc, ordinary contracts	T	¶10-114
Defamation	T	¶10-170
Interruption to business	T	¶10-170
Live stock loss, death, etc	T	¶18-150 – ¶18-160
National redress scheme payments	NT	¶10-010
Reduction in salary (compensation)	T	¶10-072
Standing timber	T	¶18-150
Tax liability	T	¶10-010
Trading stock losses	T	¶10-170
Workers compensation	T	¶10-180
Conference delegates (visiting)	NT	¶22-100
Contract adjustments for rates, land tax, etc	T	¶10-270
Contributions by employer to super fund	NT	¶10-050
Credit unions (small), interest on loans	NT	¶3-435
Cryptocurrencies	T	¶10-030
Damages:		
Compensation for loss of income	T	¶10-175
Personal injuries lump sums	NT	¶10-185
Debt defeasance arrangements	T	¶23-325

Item	Taxable (T)/Non-taxable (NT)	Source
Decoration allowance	NT	¶10-200
Defence Force members' pay and allowances	T	¶10-750 – ¶10-780
Defence Force Reserves	NT	¶10-770
Defence Force retirement pension	T	¶10-202
Depreciable plant: broadly excess of sale price over written down value	T	¶17-630, ¶17-710
Diesel Fuel Rebate Scheme payments	T	¶10-260
Disability pensions (war or social services)	NT	¶10-200 – ¶10-202
Disabled persons, open employment incentive bonus	NT	¶10-197
Disaster relief payments	NT	¶10-195
Disaster subsidies and grants	NT	¶10-197
Discount employee share scheme shares	T	¶10-085
Discount on prepaid school fees	NT	¶10-010
Dividends and deemed dividends subject to imputation system and inter-corporate dividend rebate	T	¶4-100, ¶4-400
Dividends paid by PDFs	NT	¶3-555
Dividends paid to non-residents	T	¶22-010
Double orphan pension	NT	¶10-195
Early completion bonuses	NT	¶10-440
Economic security payments	NT	¶10-195
Economic support payments (COVID-19)	NT	¶10-040
Education allowance (full-time)	NT	¶10-740
Education entry payments	T	¶10-700
Electoral expenses reimbursed	T	¶10-270
Emergency Reserve Forces	NT	¶10-770
Employment entry payment	NT	¶10-195
Endowment policies, lump sum proceeds	NT	¶10-230
Entertainment allowance from employer	T	¶10-060
Exceptional circumstances relief payments	T	¶10-195
Exempt organisations and funds	NT	¶10-604
Expenses of employee paid by employer	NT	¶35-330
Experts (visiting), remuneration of	NT	¶22-100
Film, disposal of copyright	T	¶20-330
Financial arrangements	T	¶23-070
Footballer, restrictive covenant payment	NT	¶10-076
Foreign currency exchange gains	T	¶23-075
Foreign government representatives, salaries	NT	¶22-080
Foreign income of residents:		
CFC income	T	¶21-190
Employment income of charity/government workers	NT	¶10-860
Non-resident trust estate income	T	¶21-310

Item	Taxable (T)/Non-taxable (NT)	Source
Foreign income of residents from approved overseas development projects	NT	¶10-870, ¶10-880
Foreign military personnel in Australia	NT	¶10-780
Franked dividends paid to non-residents	NT	¶4-840, ¶22-010
Frequent flyer/fly buys/consumer loyalty programs	NT	¶10-030
Friendly society education fund payments	T	¶10-740
Fringe benefits provided by employers	NT	¶10-060, ¶35-000
Funeral benefits for veterans	NT	¶10-200
Gifts, when personal to recipient	NT	¶10-070
Grants for research	T	¶10-010, ¶10-740
Gratuities	T	¶10-010, ¶10-060
Hire charges	T	¶10-110, ¶10-500
Hobby proceeds	NT	¶10-050, ¶10-430
Holiday pay	T	¶10-050
HomeBuilder grant	NT	¶10-040
Housekeeping allowance	NT	¶10-070
Housing allowance	T	¶10-060
Housing, subsidised or free, for employee	NT	¶35-380
Illegal transactions	T	¶10-450
Incentive payments	T	¶10-030, ¶10-050
Income:		
Arrears, subject to possible tax offset	T	¶15-350
Capital asset sold for income	T	¶10-020
Interest in income under will, settlement	T	¶6-130
Periodical payments	T	¶10-010, ¶10-072, ¶10-180
Income support bonus	NT	¶10-780
Income tax refunds	NT	¶10-270
Industrial dispute settlement payments	T	¶10-074
Industrial property (copyright, patent, etc) profit on exploitation	T	¶10-510
Inheritances, other than income	NT	¶10-840
Interest:		¶10-470
Non-accrual loans	T	¶9-050
Interest derived by body corporate	T	¶3-550
Interest offset arrangements	NT	¶10-470
Interest on early payments of tax	T	¶10-470, ¶25-440
Interest on overpayments of tax	T	¶10-470, ¶28-170
Interest on overseas borrowings	NT	¶22-020
Interest on personal injury damages award	NT	¶10-185
Interest on unclaimed moneys	NT	¶10-470, ¶13-850
Interest paid to non-residents	T	¶22-020

Item	Taxable (T)/Non-taxable (NT)	Source
Investment products, refunds of non-tax-deductible service fees and commissions	NT	¶23-350
Investment income from life policy	T	¶10-230
Investment income	T	¶13-120, ¶13-410, ¶13-440
Investments, profits where acquired for profit-making by sale or in course of business	T	¶10-112, ¶10-340, ¶23-340, ¶23-350
Isolated children's scheme payments	NT	¶10-700
JobKeeper payment	T	¶10-040
JobMaker Hiring Credit	T	¶10-040
JobSeeker Payment (including Coronavirus Supplement)	T	¶10-040
Jury attendance fees	T	¶10-050
Know-how, payments for sale or supply of	T	¶10-110
Land sale or exchange profits	T	¶10-112, ¶10-120, ¶10-340
Lay-by sales	T	¶9-050, ¶10-110
Lease incentives	T	¶10-116
Lease income from "sale and leaseback"	T	¶23-240
Lease premiums	NT	¶10-500
Leased cars and other equipment, profit on disposal	T	¶10-380 – ¶10-422
Leave payments	T	¶10-050, ¶10-110
Legacy	NT	¶10-840
Lessee's improvements	NT	¶10-505
Licence in patents, copyrights, designs, etc:		
Payment for grant of	T	¶10-510
Payment for use of	T	¶10-510
Life insurance proceeds	NT	¶10-230
Liquidation distributions otherwise than from income	NT	¶4-300
Liquidation distributions out of "income"	T	¶4-300, ¶4-310
Living-away-from-home allowance	NT	¶35-460
Living quarters	NT	¶35-380
Loan procuration fee	T	¶10-110
Loans, from employer	NT	¶35-270, ¶35-300
Loans to private company shareholders	T	¶4-110
Location allowance to employee	T	¶10-060
Long service leave payment	T	¶10-050, ¶14-730
Loss of earnings allowance	NT	¶10-200
Loss of future income-earning capacity	NT	¶10-072, ¶10-180
Lottery wins	NT	¶10-440
Lump sum damages or out-of-court settlement for loss of income	T	¶10-175
Lump sum for lost earnings	T	¶10-072

Item	Taxable (T)/Non-taxable (NT)	Source
Luxury car lease notional finance charges	T	¶17-220
Luxury car lease notional loan principal	NT	¶17-220
Maintenance payments	NT	¶10-855
Meal allowances	T	¶10-060
Mobility allowance	NT	¶10-195
Motor vehicle allowance	T	¶10-060
Motor vehicle, employee's private use	NT	¶35-150
Municipal corporations' income	NT	¶10-605
Mutual income	NT	¶3-810
National disability insurance scheme payments	NT	¶10-197
Native title payments	NT	¶10-187
Natural resource payments to non-residents	T	¶21-070
Net capital gain	T	¶11-030
Newstart Allowance	T	¶10-195
No-TFN contributions income	T	¶13-180
Non-cash benefits	T	¶10-030
Overtime pay	T	¶10-050, ¶10-060
Paid parental leave	T	¶2-133
Pandemic leave disaster payment	T	¶10-040
Parenting payment	NT	¶10-195
Partnership, share of net income	T	¶5-130
Payments to volunteer respite carers	NT	¶10-010
Pensions, social security	T	¶10-190
Pensions, social security — supplementary amount	NT	¶10-195
Periodical receipts	T	¶10-010, ¶10-072
Pharmaceutical allowance	NT	¶10-195, ¶10-200
Premium, non-refundable, received on issue of debt securities	T	¶10-110
Press members (visiting), remuneration of	NT	¶22-100
Prizes or awards (business connection)	T	¶10-440
Procurement fees	T	¶10-050
Profit from business of trading in futures	T	¶23-370
Profit on mere realisation of capital assets	NT	¶10-120, ¶10-340, ¶23-350
Profits from isolated business or commercial transaction where profit-making purpose	T	¶10-112
Profits on sale, exchange or other realisation of shares, land, houses, businesses	T	¶10-112, ¶10-120, ¶10-340, ¶23-350
Profit on disposal of car which taxpayer or an associate has previously leased	T	¶10-380
Profit on sale of other leased equipment	T	¶10-422
Property provided by employer	NT	¶35-490

Item	Taxable (T)/Non-taxable (NT)	Source
Public educational institutions' income	NT	¶10-605
Public hospitals' income	NT	¶10-605
Quiz prizes generally	NT	¶10-440
Racehorse winnings including betting wins and prize money, where racing activities part of business	T	¶10-430
Rates, adjustment to vendor on sale	T	¶10-270
Recreation transport allowance	NT	¶10-200
Re-engagement bounty (Defence)	NT	¶10-760
Refunds of rates, taxes and other items	T	¶10-270
Reimbursements for certain expenses	NT	¶10-060, ¶35-330
Rents, including hire charges for plant, etc	T	¶10-500
Repayment of share capital on cancellation, reduction or redemption	NT	¶4-100, ¶4-110
Repayments of FMD amounts	T	¶18-310
Resale royalties for visual artists	NT	¶3-450, ¶10-510
Research grants	T	¶10-740
Restart income support	NT	¶10-195
Return to work payments	T	¶10-074
Reversionary bonus on life policy	NT	¶10-240
Rewards for services rendered	T	¶10-050
Royalties	T	¶10-510
Royalties paid to non-residents	T	¶22-030
Salaries	T	¶10-050
Scholarships:		
Australian/US Educational Foundation grants	NT	¶10-700
Endeavour Awards scholarships	NT	¶10-700
Foreign students and trainees from Commonwealth	NT	¶10-700
Non-bonded scholarships and allowances	NT	¶10-740
Secondary education assistance	NT	¶10-700
Scientific institutions' income	NT	¶10-605
Securities gains on disposal or redemption	T	¶23-320
Securities acquired after 10.5.89, gains on disposal or redemption	T	¶23-340
Services provided by employer (residual fringe benefits)	NT	¶35-570
Sex Discrimination Act, compensation	NT	¶10-072
Shares, profits on disposal	T	¶10-112, ¶10-340, ¶23-350
Shipping income	NT	¶10-883
Sickness benefits	T	¶10-190, ¶10-195
Sickness benefits (refunded)	NT	¶10-190

Item	Taxable (T)/Non-taxable (NT)	Source
Sickness payments under disability policy, workers compensation	T	¶10-180, ¶10-210
Social security payments	T	¶10-195
Sovereign entities	T	¶10-602
Sporting clubs' income	NT	¶10-605
Sportspersons, signing-on fees	T	¶10-076
Subsidies for carrying on business	T	¶10-160
Subsidies (for inflation on pensions)	T	¶10-010
Subvention payments	NT	¶3-090
Superannuation contributions by employer	NT	¶10-050
Superannuation contributions deducted from salary or wages	T	¶10-050
Superannuation fund income	T	¶13-125, ¶13-170, ¶13-200 – ¶13-300
Superannuation fund payments to employer-sponsor if contributions deductible	T	¶10-270, ¶13-150
Superannuation funds, members' non-deductible contributions	NT	¶13-125, ¶13-220
Telephone allowance	NT	¶10-195, ¶10-200
Temporary incapacity allowance	NT	¶10-200
Tips	T	¶10-010
Tobacco leaf stored by grower awaiting sale	NT	¶9-150
Trade tie, in nature of restrictive covenant, payment for	NT	¶10-115
Trauma insurance policy, payments under	NT	¶10-210
Travel allowance to employee	T	¶10-060
Travel expenses for veterans' health	NT	¶10-200
Travel provided or paid for by employer	NT	¶35-520, ¶35-570, ¶35-580, ¶35-645
Trust income, adult beneficiary's share	T	¶6-110
Tuition allowance received from employer	T	¶10-740
Unemployment benefits	T	¶10-195
Uniform allowance to employee	T	¶10-060
Vehicle Assistance Scheme payments	NT	¶10-200
Veterans' entitlement pensions (as specified)	—	See table at ¶10-200
Victoria Cross allowance	NT	¶10-200
Wages	T	¶10-050
Waiver of debt owed to employer	NT	¶35-310
War pensions (some)	NT	¶10-200 – ¶10-204
Wine producer rebate	T	¶10-160
Work in progress payments:		
Generally	T	¶10-110, ¶16-158
Retiring partner	T	¶5-070

Item	Taxable (T)/Non-taxable (NT)	Source
Workers compensation	T	¶10-180
Youth Allowance	T	¶10-195

¶10-010 Income according to ordinary concepts

The courts have identified a number of factors which indicate whether an amount has the character of income according to ordinary concepts.

A frequent characteristic of income receipts is an element of periodicity, recurrence or regularity, even if the receipts are not directly attributable to employment or services rendered. For example, weekly payments to a soldier from his former employer to make up the difference between his civil and military pay (*Dixon*) and regular subsidies paid by a bank to selected former employees in order to counter the eroding effects of inflation on the real value of their pensions (*Blake*) have been held to be income according to ordinary concepts. Periodicity was a relevant factor in determining that the gross receipts from "leasing" motor vehicles to a taxpayer's customers were income (*Citibank*). On the same basis, the government-funded parental leave payment (¶2-133) is regarded as income because it is regular, expected and able to be relied upon.

Periodicity, recurrence or regularity is not always essential, however, for an amount to be income. The proceeds of an isolated transaction, even if received as a lump sum, may be income (eg ¶10-112), while instalments of a capital sum, even though received regularly from the one source, are not income. An unsolicited lump sum payment which is unlikely to be repeated is generally not income according to ordinary concepts (eg *Harris* — a gratuitous payment by a former employer to supplement the taxpayer's pension). However, a lump sum lease incentive payment (to induce a business taxpayer to move to new rented premises) is likely to be income in the hands of the recipient (¶10-116). Lump sum damages will be assessable where they are compensation for losses of an income nature only (¶10-175).

Personal earnings from the performance of services, whether as an employee or otherwise, are clearly income even if the services are performed, and the rewards received, irregularly (¶10-050). The payment by another person of a taxpayer's tax liability, or a payment to compensate a taxpayer for his/her tax liability, will have the character of income for the taxpayer (eg *Case Y53*). Where the tax liability is paid by an employer, FBT may be payable (*Case 13/98*). An amount of deferred compensation paid to a taxpayer for service rendered as an employee was assessable as ordinary income (*Blank*; ¶14-610).

Workers compensation payments are generally income receipts (¶10-180).

Amounts received as a result of carrying on a business (¶10-110), but not a pastime or hobby (¶10-050), are income. The concept of carrying on a business is discussed at ¶10-105. The proceeds arising from an isolated transaction outside the ordinary course of business may also be income according to ordinary concepts if the purpose of the transaction is to make a profit (¶10-112). If the proceeds of the sale of a dwelling are income according to ordinary concepts (eg where the sale is part of the vendor's business or is an isolated profit-making transaction), the CGT main residence exemption is irrelevant (TD 92/135).

Receipts in the nature of a return on capital invested, such as interest (¶10-470), dividends (¶4-100) and rents (¶10-500), are income according to ordinary concepts and will be assessable unless expressly excluded or exempted.

The proceeds of illegal activities may also be income receipts; the tests for determining whether an amount is income according to ordinary concepts are the same whether it is received from legal or illegal activities (¶10-450).

The consideration from a barter or countertrade transaction is likely to be income according to ordinary concepts, except where the transaction is a domestic or social arrangement (IT 2668) (¶10-030).

Amounts which are not income

Some items by their very nature are *not* income according to ordinary concepts (eg a loan). A reimbursement of capital, such as the repayment of an advance, is not income unless the advance was a revenue outgoing incurred in the course of a business and the debt, having turned bad, has been allowed as a deduction (¶10-270). In one case, a payment under an industry assistance scheme was held to be a conditional loan which was progressively converted into income in the form of a non-refundable grant as, over a number of years, the conditions of the scheme were complied with (*Case 22/94*). Certain education and training grants may be exempt (¶10-700 – ¶10-740). Discounts allowed on prepayments of school fees are not income (TD 2004/5).

Increases in the value of property, without any realisation through conversion into money or other property, cannot give rise to income, except in the case of trading stock. The proceeds of a mere realisation of property or the book gains on changes of investments are generally not income (¶10-120, ¶23-350), though the CGT rules may apply.

A gift will not generally be regarded as income in the hands of the recipient (¶10-070). By contrast, a tip given to a waiter or taxi driver is income in the hands of the recipient because it is a product of the services which have been rendered.

Medals or trophies awarded to sportspersons are not assessable as they are given and received on purely personal grounds (TR 1999/17; ¶10-070). Payments received under the *National Redress Scheme for Institutional Child Sexual Abuse Act 2018* are not income (TD 2018/16).

Money that is not received from external sources is not income, because of the mutuality principle (¶3-810). This includes, for example, amounts received by a strata title body by way of levies imposed on proprietors (TR 2015/3).

Payments to a volunteer respite carer to cover expenses of providing respite care for a disabled person are not assessable income (TD 2004/75). Likewise, certain payments to a volunteer foster carer to provide foster care are not assessable (TD 2006/62).

The fact that an amount is not income according to ordinary concepts does not necessarily mean that it is tax-free. For example, if an asset acquired on or after 20 September 1985 is disposed of, a capital gain within the CGT provisions may arise (¶11-000). In addition, there are other provisions (eg ITAA97 Subdiv 20-B: ¶10-380) which bring into assessable income amounts which are not income according to ordinary concepts.

[FITR ¶18-210, ¶18-245]

¶10-020 Income vs capital receipts

Not every receipt is ordinary income in the recipient's hands. Capital gains are not ordinary income and thus are not assessable under ITAA97 s 6-5 (although they may be assessable as statutory income under another provision). This fundamental distinction between ordinary income and capital gains remains important because:

- CGT does not catch all capital gains (eg gains on the disposal of a main residence are exempt), and
- the amount of tax payable on income and capital profits may differ depending on whether it is taxed under the income tax regime or the CGT regime (eg a CGT discount may apply) (¶11-000).

The CGT provisions potentially apply to every disposal of an asset acquired or deemed to have been acquired on or after 20 September 1985, regardless of whether the gain would normally be treated as a capital gain. If the gain is also assessable as ordinary income, the amount of the capital gain is reduced accordingly (¶11-690).

The income/capital distinction also remains relevant in relation to assets acquired before 20 September 1985 as the CGT provisions do not apply to the disposal of such assets. If a taxpayer acquired property before 20 September 1985 as a genuine investment, eg real estate for rental purposes, any profit on the subsequent disposal of the property would be capital in nature and tax-free (¶10-120). In some cases, the profit on the realisation of a capital asset acquired before 20 September 1985 may be caught by some specific provision such as ITAA97 s 15-15 if sold at a profit from 1997–98 (¶10-340).

The traditional approach to distinguishing income from capital is to liken capital to a tree and income to the fruit of the tree (see, for example, comments of the High Court in *DP Smith's case* where payments under a disability insurance policy were held to be income). Obvious examples of income in the nature of a return on capital (ie the fruit of the tree) are interest (¶10-470) and rents (¶10-500).

Although some items are clearly income (eg wages: ¶10-050) and others are clearly capital (eg a lump sum legacy), it is not always easy to determine whether a receipt is income or capital. Ultimately, it depends on the facts and circumstances of each particular case (*Northumberland Development*; *Haig*).

Character of receipt

It is the character of the receipt(s) in the hands of the recipient which has to be determined; how the amount would be characterised in another context is irrelevant (*Federal Coke*; *Liftronic*). The nature of a payment may sometimes be determined by the character of the matter in respect of which the moneys are received (eg *JB Chandler Investment* — procurement fees were income; *MIM Holdings* — payments for ensuring subsidiary supplied electricity were income; *Murdoch* — a payment in settlement of an action for breach of trust was capital). Thus if a capital asset not acquired for profit-making by sale and not used in a business or other profit-making undertaking or scheme is sold, the consideration is usually a receipt of capital (¶10-120), even if payable by instalments. In contrast, a lump sum received in exchange for a future income stream is likely to be income (*Myer Emporium*, discussed below). In some cases, the form which a receipt takes is an important factor as, generally speaking, periodical payments (¶10-010) are more likely to be income (although see below).

The character of a receipt is not determined by the character of its proposed expenditure by the recipient. For example, in *GP International Pipecoaters* the taxpayer company, which was incorporated for the sole purpose of performing a contract to coat natural gas pipes, received "establishment costs" to pay for the construction of a plant to carry out the pipe-coating work. The High Court held that the "establishment costs" were income in the taxpayer's hands, even if they were received for the purpose of expenditure on the construction of the plant.

Lump sum payments made by healthcare centre operators to healthcare practitioners as an inducement for the practitioner to enter into agreements to provide healthcare services from the healthcare centre are generally assessable as ordinary income (ATO website, 15 March 2017).

Converting income and capital

A capital asset may be exchanged for income, eg an annuity or pension. If payments take the form of periodical payments, the question is often whether those payments are truly instalments of a fixed capital sum or are truly in the nature of income (eg as in the case of "annuities"). For example, a capital asset may be sold for cash consideration payable in instalments which would generally be capital provided the instalments were calculated by reference to a fixed purchase price (*IR Commissioners v Ramsay*). However, if an employee agreed to the cancellation of a service contract for monetary compensation, the payment would be capital if received by the employee in a lump sum or instalments. If the employee agreed to take regular payments spread over the unexpired term of the service contract, the payments would normally be of an income nature and fully assessable under s 6-5.

In certain circumstances, it may be possible to convert what would otherwise be income into a capital receipt. For example, a pension or annuity may be wholly or partly commuted to a lump sum which would not be ordinary income, although the superannuation lump sum rules would generally be attracted (¶14-000). On the other hand, a lump sum received as consideration for the assignment to a finance company of the taxpayer's right to receive interest under an $80 million loan to a subsidiary (at commercial rates of interest) was income according to ordinary concepts (*Myer Emporium*).

A lump sum payment received from a financial institution as consideration for the taxpayer assigning its rights to receive annual royalties under a licence agreement was held to be income according to ordinary concepts (under the agreement the taxpayer licensed 2 trade competitors to use labels and trade marks previously used by the taxpayer and a subsidiary) (*Henry Jones (IXL)*). Similarly, a lump sum received by the trustee of a discretionary family trust for the assignment, for a period of almost 8 years, of the trust's entitlement to so much of certain royalties as did not exceed a specific threshold was of an income nature (*SP Investments*). In another case, monthly payments received by a milk producer for assigning its right to a source of future income were held to be on revenue account (*Moneymen*).

[FITR ¶18-300, ¶19-065]

¶10-030 Convertibility into money

Under general principles, a benefit is not income within the ordinary meaning of that term unless it consists of money or is capable of being converted into money.

Thus, in *Cooke & Sherden*, in which home delivery soft drink retailers were provided with free non-transferable overseas holidays under a sales incentive scheme run by their supplier, it was held that the benefit in the form of the holidays was not income because it was not convertible into money. However, the court recognised that a benefit may be assessable even though it is not *directly* convertible into money.

The value of shares issued by a company to an independent contractor as consideration for performing services in relation to research and development activities undertaken by the company is assessable income of the recipient; the amount of assessable income is the market value of the shares at the time they are issued (TD 93/234).

Non-cash business benefits

The principle that a benefit is not assessable as income if it is not convertible into money has been substantially altered by special statutory rules enacted to overcome practices which became widespread following *Cooke & Sherden*.

The rules apply to non-cash business benefits (ITAA36 s 21A). In this context, a "non-cash business benefit" means property or services provided to a business taxpayer wholly or partly in connection with a business relationship (s 21A(5)). An interest-free loan from a principal to an independent contractor will generally qualify as a non-cash business benefit (*Case 7/97*). Similarly, the transfer of plant and equipment from another business will also constitute a non-cash business benefit (*Case 4/2010*).

The effect of the rules is as follows:

- a non-cash business benefit may be treated as income according to ordinary concepts even if it is not convertible into cash, provided it is otherwise of an income nature (s 21A(1)), and

- where a non-cash business benefit (whether convertible to cash or not) is in the nature of income, the recipient is required to include in his/her assessable income the arm's length value of the benefit, less any unreimbursed amount contributed by the recipient in acquiring the benefit (a deduction for depreciation may be available if the benefit represents plant which is used to produce assessable income). If the benefit is not convertible into cash, any conditions which prevent or restrict the conversion of the benefit to cash are disregarded in determining the arm's length value (s 21A(2)).

The Full Federal Court examined the valuation of electricity connection works in calculating the assessable amount of a non-cash business benefit of the taxpayer under s 21A (*Victoria Power Networks Pty Ltd*).

The statutory rules do *not* apply in the following situations:

- where the benefit is used in circumstances such that, if the recipient had incurred its cost, the recipient would have been entitled to a once-only deduction (the "otherwise deductible" rule), eg where an interest-free or low interest loan is used for business purposes (s 21A(3)) (where the recipient would only have been entitled to a partial deduction, the assessable amount of the benefit is proportionately reduced)
- where the cost of the benefit is non-deductible entertainment expenditure (¶16-390) to the provider (eg the provision of free holidays as in *Cooke & Sherden*) (s 21A(4)), and
- where the total assessable value of non-cash business benefits received by the taxpayer in the income year does not exceed $300 (ITAA36 s 23L(2)).

▶ Example

A building contractor engages a plumbing sub-contractor to assist at a construction site. As reward for the sub-contractor's services, the contractor agrees: (a) to pay the sub-contractor $4,500; and (b) to take out a non-transferable 12-month pay TV subscription in the sub-contractor's name. The subscription has an arm's length value of $500 disregarding the non-transferability condition.

The subscription is a non-cash business benefit as it represents services provided in respect of a business relationship. In determining whether the subscription is ordinary income of the sub-contractor, the non-transferability condition is disregarded. The subscription represents income of the sub-contractor as it is received in the ordinary course of business and is taken to be convertible to cash by virtue of s 21A.

The arm's length value of the subscription is $500. However, the arm's length value is reduced to nil as the subscription is non-deductible entertainment expenditure of the contractor. No amount is included in the sub-contractor's assessable income in the relevant income year for the subscription.

Special deductibility rules apply where a non-cash business benefit is provided as an inducement to taxpayers to purchase particular items of plant or equipment or to receive particular services (¶16-157).

The benefit received by an insurance agent who is provided with an interest-free or low interest loan by an insurer is also likely to be a non-cash business benefit (TR 93/38). If the agent uses the loan (or part of it) for income-producing purposes, the "otherwise deductible" rule will apply to reduce the assessable amount. The "otherwise deductible" rule is also likely to apply where an interest-free or low interest loan from an insurer to an insurance agency is on-lent to an employee (or an associate of an employee) for use for private purposes (TD 95/5).

The assessability of non-cash lease incentives is considered at ¶10-116.

Barter/countertrade transactions

The consideration received from a barter or countertrade transaction (either in terms of cash, credit units, goods or services) represents assessable income under s 21A where the transaction is a business one (IT 2668). The ATO will accept a fair market value as adequately reflecting the money value or arm's length value of the consideration. In the case of business-oriented countertrade organisations, the ATO will deem the fair market value of each of their credit units to equal one Australian dollar, unless it can be shown that the credit units are being traded consistently at a different value (IT 2668).

Cryptocurrency/bitcoin transactions

Business transactions using cryptocurrencies, especially bitcoins, are akin to barter transactions, with similar tax consequences. Where taxpayers receive bitcoin for goods or services provided as part of their business, they will need to record the value of the bitcoin in Australian dollars and return it as assessable income. The value in Australian dollars will be the fair market value which can be obtained from a reputable bitcoin exchange.

Frequent flyer and consumer loyalty programs

Benefits received by employees under frequent flyer programs as a result of employer-paid expenditure are not assessable income (TR 1999/6; *Payne*).

"Flight rewards" (eg free flights or accommodation) received under consumer loyalty programs arise as a result of a personal (ie non-employment/non-business) contractual relationship between the recipient and the provider. In the case of employees, this means that flight rewards received as a result of employer-paid expenditure are neither income according to ordinary concepts nor assessable under ITAA97 s 15-2. In the case of business taxpayers, s 21A will not apply as the rewards are not provided in respect of a business relationship. The exceptions are where a person renders a service on the basis that an entitlement to a flight reward will arise (eg a person enters into a secretarial service contract with an understanding that a flight reward will be received) or, in a business context, where the activities associated with the obtaining of the benefits amount in themselves to a business activity (TR 1999/6). For details of the FBT treatment of flight rewards, see ¶35-120. As to deductions for rewards providers, see ¶16-040.

Rewards received under consumer loyalty programs will be taxable where the reward is received as part of an income-earning activity and:

- there is a business relationship between the recipient of the reward and the reward provider, and
- the benefit is convertible directly or indirectly to money's worth, or
- the taxpayer is carrying on a business, and s 21A operates to include the reasonable value of the non-cash business benefit in the taxpayer's assessable income.

Similarly, where the activities associated with the obtaining of a reward amount to a business or commercial activity and the reward is a non-cash business benefit in terms of s 21A, the reward will be assessable (PS LA 2004/4 (GA)).

Rewards received under a consumer loyalty program that result from private expenditure are also not assessable (TD 1999/34).

Non-cash fringe benefits provided to employees

Where a non-cash benefit arises out of an *employment* relationship, as distinct from a business relationship, the value of the benefit will generally be subject to FBT payable by the employer (¶35-000), regardless of whether the benefit is convertible into money.

Product promotion arrangements

Where a distributor is given a non-cash business benefit by a manufacturer under a product promotion arrangement, the Commissioner considers that:

- if the distributor chooses to keep the benefit, the value of the benefit is assessable to the distributor under s 21A

- if, at the time the benefit is provided, the distributor chooses to pass on the benefit to its employees, the value of the benefit that would otherwise be included in the distributor's assessable income is reduced by the value of the benefit passed on to its employees if the ''otherwise deductible'' rule (see under ''Non-cash business benefits'' above) applies. The distributor is also liable for FBT on the taxable value of the benefit (determined in the same way as for general property fringe benefits: ¶35-530)

- if the decision to keep or pass on the benefit is not made at the time the benefit is provided to the distributor, the value of the benefit must be included in the distributor's assessable income at the time the benefit is given (the ''otherwise deductible'' rule does not apply). If the distributor later chooses to pass on the benefit, the value of the benefit passed on is deductible under ITAA97 s 8-1 at the time it is passed on, but the distributor is liable for FBT on the taxable value of the benefit

- if the arrangement requires the distributor to pass on the benefit to its employees, the distributor is liable for FBT on the taxable value of the benefit (TD 93/6).

[FITR ¶18-210, ¶18-245; FTR ¶7-130, ¶11-295]

COVID-19 Stimulus Measures

¶10-040 COVID-19 income support and economic stimulus

The federal government introduced a range of measures as part of its economic response to the Coronavirus (COVID-19) pandemic. The measures were designed to provide income support for employees and households, boost cash flow for employers, provide new or enhanced tax breaks for business investment (¶7-250, ¶17-330) and support businesses financially. The government has amended COVID-19 stimulus measures to adapt to changing circumstances.

The income support and cash flow boosting measures included:

Economic support payments

The government is providing 2 separate $250 economic support payments to recipients of specified social security and veterans' payments and concession cardholders, with the first payment made from 30 November 2020 and the second from 1 March 2021. To be eligible, recipients must reside in Australia and receive one of the specified payments or hold one of the concession cards on 27 November 2020 and/or 26 February 2021, as applicable.

The payments are exempt from tax and do not count as income support for the purposes of any income support payment.

Pandemic leave disaster payments

A one-off payment of $1,500 is available to eligible workers in all Australian states. The payment assists eligible individuals who are unable to work and earn income while under a direction to self-isolate, quarantine or who are caring for someone who has tested positive to COVID-19.

JobKeeper

The JobKeeper Payment scheme is a temporary subsidy for businesses and other entities significantly affected by COVID-19. JobKeeper payments are made to qualifying entities in respect of their eligible employees, business participants or religious practitioners. The payments are being made over a twelve-month period from 30 March 2020 to 28 March 2021.

In the period from 30 March 2020 to 27 September 2020, eligible employers, sole traders and other entities could apply to receive $1,500 per eligible employee per fortnight. The employer must make monthly business declarations to the ATO, starting in June, to receive reimbursements for payments made in the previous month.

In the period from 28 September 2020 until 3 January 2021, the JobKeeper payment was reduced to $1,200 (from $1,500) and a lower rate of $750 will be paid for employees and business participants working less than 20 hours a week. Those amounts will be further reduced in the period from 4 January 2021 to 28 March 2021 ($1,000 and $650, respectively). From 28 September 2020, employers were required to meet additional decline in turnover tests.

The JobKeeper scheme is administered by the ATO. Find comprehensive information about the eligibility requirements on the ATO website.

Employers treat JobKeeper receipts as assessable income and claim deductions for wages paid. Employers withhold PAYG from payments to employees. Sole traders must include JobKeeper payments as assessable income of the business. For employees, salary or wages supplemented by JobKeeper is assessable income.

The ATO has power to recoup JobKeeper payments in circumstances where eligibility conditions have not been met. For ATO guidelines about schemes that potentially breach the integrity rules, see PCG 2020/4.

New small businesses that the ATO considered not to be eligible for JobKeeper or cash flow boost payments because they had no sale or supply before 12 March 2020 may still be eligible and may seek a review of the decision. For more information about reviewing ATO decisions and relevant time limits see ¶28-000 and the ATO website.

[FTR ¶855-100]

JobSeeker expanded — Coronavirus Supplement

The government temporarily expanded eligibility to claim the JobSeeker Payment and the Youth Allowance and introduced a new, time-limited Coronavirus Supplement. JobSeeker and the JobSeeker Coronavirus Supplement are taxable social security payments.

The Coronavirus Supplement and expanded access for some social security payments commenced on 27 April 2020. The amount of the supplement was $550 per fortnight in the period ending 24 September 2020. The supplement was reduced to $250 per fortnight in the period from 25 September 2020 to 31 December 2020. The supplement is $150 per fortnight between 1 January and 31 March 2021.

[FTR ¶856-100, ¶857-100]

Apprentices and trainees wage subsidy

Under the government's JobTrainer Skills Package, eligible small businesses that had an apprentice or trainee in place on 1 March 2020 can apply for a wage subsidy (the Supporting Apprentices and Trainees wage subsidy) of 50% of an eligible apprentice or trainee's wages.

The government announced that the wage subsidy will be extended and expanded to include medium-sized businesses that had an apprentice in place on 1 July 2020. The subsidy will apply to all eligible businesses paying wages from 1 July 2020 to 31 March 2021. Legislation to implement the announced changes has not been enacted. Small and medium-sized businesses may make claims for payment. Final claims must be lodged by 30 June 2021.

The government proposes to further extend the apprenticeship wage subsidy program to allow businesses of any size to claim the subsidy, from 5 October 2020 to 30 September 2021. Eligible businesses that employ apprentices or trainees will receive up to a 50% wage subsidy, up to $7,000 per quarter, capped at 100,000 places (2020–21 Budget Paper No 2, p 229).

JobMaker Hiring Credit

A JobMaker Hiring Credit is payable to employers for each additional new job they create for an eligible employee from 7 October 2020 to 6 October 2021. The JobMaker Hiring Credit will be available from the date of employment for up to 12 months and capped at $10,400 for each additional new position created. Eligible employers who can demonstrate that the new employee will increase overall employee headcount and payroll will receive $200 per week if they hire an eligible employee aged 16 to 29 years, or $100 per week if the employee is aged 30 to 35 years.

The employee must have worked at least 20 hours per week, averaged over one quarter, and be in receipt of the JobSeeker Payment, Youth Allowance (Other) or Parenting Payment for at least one month out of the 3 months before they were hired.

HomeBuilder grant

The HomeBuilder grant is available to eligible owner-occupiers building a new home or substantially renovating an existing home. Applications for the grant must be received no later than 14 April 2021.

For new build contracts signed by eligible owner-occupiers between 4 June and 31 December 2020 inclusive, a grant of $25,000 is available. To be eligible, the value of renovations must be within the price range of $150,000 and $750,000, the total value of the existing house and land must not exceed $1.5 million, and construction must commence within 6 months of the contract date.

For new build contracts signed between 1 January and 31 March 2021 inclusive, eligible owner-occupiers will receive a $15,000 grant. However, the property price cap will be increased to $950,000 for New South Wales, $850,000 for Victoria and it will remain at $750,000 in all other states and territories. The total value of the existing house and land must not exceed $1.5 million, and construction must commence within 6 months of the contract date.

The grant is administered by the relevant state or territory authority and is not subject to income tax, consistent with existing state and territory First Home Owner Grant (FHOG) programs.

Cash flow boost payments

Eligible businesses and not-for-profit (NFP) organisations that employed staff received between $20,000 to $100,000 in cash flow boost amounts by lodging their business activity statements up to the month or quarter of September 2020. The cash flow boosts were delivered as credits against PAYG withholding tax paid in the activity statement system.

An additional cash flow boost applied when activity statements for each monthly or quarterly period from June to September 2020 were lodged. The credits equalled the total boosts credited for March–June 2020.

Cash flow boosts are non-assessable non-exempt income and not subject to GST.

Economic support payments

The federal government provided 2 separate payments of $750 to social security, veteran and other income support recipients and eligible concession cardholders. Eligibility for each payment, made from 31 March 2020 and from 13 July 2020, depended on the claimants' income support or cardholder status at 12 March 2020 and 10 July 2020 respectively. The payments are exempt from income tax.

[FTR ¶858-100]

State government COVID-19 payments

A number of state government COVID-19 support payments have the character of income and are assessable. The Tax Essentials page of the ATO's website lists some common payments made in the different states that must be included in the income of a business or an individual.

Small business grants tax exempt

Payments received by eligible businesses under certain grant programs administered by a state or territory government (or a state or territory authority) are non-assessable non-exempt income in the 2020–21 income year and later income years. To qualify, the payment must be made under a grant program that is declared to be eligible and is, in effect, responding to the economic impacts of COVID-19. For example, the government has declared a number of grant programs administered by the Victorian government as eligible for the relevant exemption.

Earnings for Personal Services

¶10-050 Remuneration and rewards for services

All remuneration and rewards for personal services, whether received in the capacity of employee or otherwise in connection with employment or personal services, are income according to ordinary concepts.

Assessable earnings for personal services include salary, wages, consultants' fees, overtime payments, commissions, retrospective award increases, back pay, long service leave pay, holiday pay, directors' fees, payments for services based on a percentage of profits and procurement fees. A one-off payment made to a taxpayer by a holding company to ensure he remained in employment with its subsidiary for a further 12 months, refundable on a pro rata basis if the taxpayer resigned before completing the 12 months' service, was income in the form of salary and wages (*Dean*). In one case, a payment of $8 million was so closely associated with the services performed by the taxpayer that the payment was assessable income even though it was not made pursuant to a contract for his services (*Reuter*). In another case, the managing director of a company was assessable on amounts paid by the company to a Hong Kong entity (via a supplier) for investment at his direction as the amounts were effectively paid in consideration for his services (*Case 39/94*). Further, a payment made by an employer to an employee share trust for the taxpayer's benefit, in lieu of bonuses, was assessable income (*Sent (No 2)*).

Earnings from irregular work, eg random weekend or after hours ''jobs'', are just as much income as earnings from regular employment. A payment for participation in a product market research session is also assessable (ID 2002/822).

A commission paid to a taxpayer for acting as the executor of a deceased estate is assessable (ID 2014/44). Similarly, jury attendance fees are assessable unless reimbursed to the juror's employer.

Payments and prizes received by sportspersons who earn income from services are assessable, unless received in the pursuit of a pastime or hobby (*Stone*; TR 1999/17). In *Stone*, the High Court held that the athletic activities of a police officer in full-time employment constituted the conduct of a business. As a result the taxpayer was assessable in respect of prize money and grants she received (¶10-070). Sponsorship and appearance fees are assessable whether or not a business is being carried on. For signing-on fees, see ¶10-076.

A lump sum representing wages not paid during a period of suspension from duty and paid after the suspension is lifted is assessable (*Case X55*). Allowances may be assessable under ITAA97 s 15-2 (¶10-060).

The wife of a train robber was held to have derived assessable income, and not a capital payment, when she received money for telling her life story to a newspaper for its exclusive publication (*Brent*).

PAYG amounts withheld from gross salary or wages, an employee's superannuation contributions and any other payments which the employee may have directed or authorised the employer to make on his/her behalf (eg health insurance premiums and loan repayments) are normally included as income; the *employer's* contributions to a superannuation fund for the benefit of the employee are not assessable to the employee. However, an employee's assessable income may be reduced by an effective salary sacrifice arrangement, ie where the gross salary entitlement is reduced in exchange for a lower salary together with a benefit from the employer (¶31-120). Ineffective salary sacrifice arrangements and arrangements that are caught by the general anti-avoidance provisions of ITAA36 Pt IVA (¶30-130) would result in the amounts being treated as assessable income (*Yip*).

A contribution to an employee remuneration trust is assessable income of an employee under ITAA97 s 6-5 where it has the character of ordinary income, is applied or dealt with on the employee's behalf or as the employee directs, and is not excluded from the operation of s 6-5 (TR 2018/7).

The tax treatment of lump sum payments received on leaving a job, whether voluntarily or otherwise, or on retiring from the workforce, including severance pay and unused leave payments, is considered in Chapter 14. The tax treatment of annuities and superannuation income streams is also discussed in Chapter 14.

Earnings for personal services are assessable in the year of receipt (or constructive receipt: ¶9-080) and not in the year earned, except where the services are rendered in the course of a business or professional practice which is subject to an accruals basis of accounting (¶9-030).

▶ Example 1

An employee who receives a lump sum representing an underpayment of wages (accidental or otherwise) in August 2020, for services rendered in the 2019–20 and/or earlier income years, is taxed on that lump sum in the 2020–21 income year. (Note, however, that the employee may be eligible for the income arrears rebate: ¶15-350.)

▶ Example 2

An employee, who commences annual and long service leave on 20 June 2020 and resumes work on 15 August 2020, receives a payment for the period of leave on 16 June 2020. The whole of the payment is assessable in the 2019–20 income year.

▶ Example 3

Commissions received in September 2020 for sales made in the 2019–20 income year must be included in the 2020–21 return.

The timing of the derivation of real estate agents' commission income assessable on an accruals basis is discussed at ¶9-050.

In certain circumstances, a tax offset is available to limit the tax payable on arrears of salary or wages, etc, paid in a lump sum and which accrued before the year of receipt (¶15-350).

Amounts mistakenly paid to an employee (whether as salary or wages, income support or workers compensation) but to which the employee is not beneficially entitled and is obliged to repay are not income (TD 2008/9).

Amounts received as a result of carrying on a pastime or hobby are not income (eg *Case C18* — prize money from motor racing activities which constituted a hobby only was not assessable: TR 1999/17). Betting and gambling winnings are usually considered to be the proceeds of a hobby (¶10-430). See also ¶10-440 (assessability of prizes and awards).

[FITR ¶19-005]

¶10-060 Allowances and fringe benefits

Non-cash fringe benefits which are provided to an employee by an employer are generally subject to FBT which is a tax imposed on the employer. A benefit which is subject to FBT is neither assessable income nor exempt income of the employee or other recipient (ITAA36 s 23L).

ITAA97 s 15-2 provides for the inclusion in a taxpayer's assessable income of all allowances, gratuities, compensations, benefits, bonuses and premiums provided to the taxpayer which relate directly or indirectly to the taxpayer's employment or to services rendered by the taxpayer. Workers compensation payments are not caught by the section (*Inkster*), although they are generally assessable as ordinary income (¶10-180).

Section 15-2 has only a residual operation because it does *not* apply to a benefit that is a fringe benefit under the FBT legislation. Section 15-2 also does not apply to an amount that is assessable as ordinary income under s 6-5 (s 15-2(3)(d)).

Guidelines on the difference between an allowance and a reimbursement for the purposes of determining whether a payment is a fringe benefit or assessable income are set out in TR 92/15. In general, a payment is considered to be a ''reimbursement'' when the recipient is compensated exactly for an expense already incurred (in certain circumstances, a payment in advance of expenditure may also be treated as a reimbursement), whereas a payment is considered to be an ''allowance'' when an employee is paid a definite predetermined amount to cover an estimated expense, regardless of whether the employee incurs that expense (TR 92/15).

Flight rewards (eg free flights or accommodation) received by employees from employer-paid expenditure are not assessable under s 15-2 (TR 1999/6: ¶10-030). The ATO also accepts that strike fund payments made by trade unions to striking members are not assessable under s 15-2 (TR 2002/8).

A camping allowance paid to employees required to camp at a work site was considered not to be a fringe benefit in *Roads and Traffic Authority of NSW* (and thus the allowance would be assessable income), although the Commissioner considers that a camping allowance will usually be an assessable fringe benefit and thus not assessable in the employee's hands (TD 93/230).

A living-away-from-home allowance (LAFHA) is treated as a fringe benefit and thus is not assessable in the hands of the employee (FBTAA s 30(1); *Hancox*). However, a hardlying allowance paid to employees for the hardship of living on an off-shore drilling rig was an assessable allowance, not a LAFHA (¶35-460).

The taxation of benefits associated with the acquisition of shares, rights to acquire shares and stapled securities under an employee share scheme is governed by ITAA97 (Div 83A) and the CGT provisions (¶12-630).

If an employee is reimbursed on a per kilometre basis for the cost of using a car (whether owned or leased), such a benefit, with certain exceptions, is an exempt fringe benefit (¶35-340) and the amount of the reimbursement is assessable income of the employee (ITAA97 s 15-70).

[FTR ¶11-290, FITR ¶53-020]

¶10-070 Voluntary payments or gifts

A voluntary payment or gift which is properly characterised, in the hands of the recipient, as a product or incident of employment or a reward for services (including for past services), is assessable income, even if paid or given by a third party (*Moorhouse v Dooland*; *Mews*). However, a voluntary payment or gift that is not related in any way to personal exertion will not be assessable (*Hayes* — a gift of shares after employment relationship ended was not assessable).

The motive of the donor and the periodicity or recurrence of the payment are relevant but not decisive factors (eg *Dixon*, noted at ¶10-010). These principles are reflected in IT 2674 which deals with the assessability of gifts to ministers of religion, missionaries and other church workers. A gift made to a church or missionary society as an agent for a church worker is assessable to the worker at the time it is received by the church. A gift made to a church with the wish it be passed on to a church worker is assessable to the worker to the extent the church passes on the gift or deals with it on the worker's behalf.

A gratuitous payment to an employee in needy circumstances may be regarded as a non-assessable gift. However, it is often extremely difficult to determine whether a voluntary payment is made because of the person's personal qualities or circumstances, or in recognition of, or incidental to, services performed by the person.

Ex gratia payments for honorary services, unsolicited donations received by an evangelist and an award received as best and fairest footballer have all been held to be assessable. The ''gift'' of a home unit in lieu of a $1 million commission was also assessable (*Brown*). However, in one case a $100 annual honorarium paid to a friendly society's district officer was not assessable, as payment of the honorarium depended on the goodwill of the friendly society's members (*Case Z16*). In another case, an ex gratia lump sum payment by the state government as reimbursement of costs incurred by a local government employee in connection with an inquiry into his performance was not assessable (*Rowe*: ¶10-260).

The Commissioner considers that grants received by sportspersons are assessable where there is an element of periodicity, recurrence or regularity to the payments. An ''occasional'' voluntary payment is assessable if it is paid in respect of employment, the provision of services, or a business (TR 1999/17). In *Stone*, the High Court held that the athletic activities of a taxpayer constituted the conduct of a business. Accordingly, the taxpayer was assessable in respect of grants she received.

Gifts to an individual, whether because of that person's personal qualities or needs (eg the recipient's dire financial circumstances) or as a token of gratitude for past personal advice or friendship, are not income. For example, the ATO accepts that one-off voluntary payments made by a trade union to members in financial hardship during industrial action are not assessable (TR 2002/8).

One-off disaster relief money received by a taxpayer carrying on a business from charity as part of community assistance is not assessable under either ITAA97 s 6-5 or 15-10 (TD 2006/22).

Accommodation, meals and a research allowance provided under a fellowship to a distinguished visiting scholar by the host university were non-assessable gratuities that were conferred on her because of her personal qualities as a scholar and not because of any services rendered to the university (*Case V135*). The Commissioner, however, considers that the decision is wrong and has said that he will not follow it (IT 2612). The assessability of prizes and awards is considered further at ¶10-440.

Gifts to a child on special occasions (such as birthdays and religious festivals) and gifts by a parent to a child out of natural love are not income, although any interest earned on monetary gifts may be assessable under ITAA36 Pt III Div 6AA (¶2-160). Similarly, a housekeeping allowance paid to the payer's spouse is not income.

Where the activities of the recipient of a gift are of such a nature and extent that the recipient is carrying on a business (eg in the case of a church worker — a business of evangelism), the gift is assessable (IT 2674). Gifts may also be included as assessable income under ITAA97 s 15-2 (¶10-060).

Where a voluntary payment takes the form of a non-cash business benefit, the special rules explained at ¶10-030 need to be taken into account.

[FITR ¶19-005]

¶10-072 Loss or restriction of right to earn income

A payment received by a person in consideration of restrictions on his/her *future* income-earning capacity (ie negative covenants), provided it is received in the form of a lump sum or as instalments of a fixed sum, is generally capital and not income (*Higgs v Olivier*; *Dickenson*). This will be so whether the payment is received before or after the termination of the current services (whether as employee or otherwise), provided it is received for a restriction on the taxpayer's activities *after* the termination. If the payment is made pursuant to a post-19 September 1985 agreement, the CGT provisions may apply (¶11-280).

An amount received as compensation for the cancellation, termination or surrender of rights under a contract of service or for the surrender or commutation of pension rights is also generally capital and not ordinary income. However, if the amount is paid in consequence of the termination of the taxpayer's employment (including the holding of any office), it is taxable under the special rules applicable to employment termination payments (¶14-600). If the amount is paid in respect of the cancellation, termination or surrender of rights under a post-CGT contract, a capital gain may arise (¶11-280).

If a taxpayer receives a lump sum for agreeing, during the currency of the taxpayer's service agreement or employment, to a reduction in salary, that sum is fully assessable as remuneration for services rendered. A payment received by a person to prevent his/her resignation is also fully assessable.

If an employee whose service contract has been cancelled receives similar amounts at similar intervals over the same period, the amounts are of an income nature (*Phillips*;). The amounts, however, may be taxed as employment termination payments.

Compensation for unfair dismissal would normally be exempt from CGT (ITAA97 s 118-37; ¶11-650). However, it may be taxed as an employment termination payment (¶14-610).

Other types of compensation received under equal opportunity or sex discrimination laws for lost earnings or in substitution for income which would otherwise be earned are assessable as ordinary income. But, a payment to compensate for personal injury, injury to feelings, humiliation, etc, is neither assessable as ordinary income nor as a taxable capital gain (ITAA97 s 118-37; ¶11-650).

[FITR ¶19-265]

¶10-074 Return to work payments

Amounts paid to induce a person to return to work are assessable, regardless of how the payments are described or paid, or by whom they are paid (ITAA97 s 15-3). Likewise, an amount paid to induce a person to commence employment is assessable (*Pickford*).

Ordinarily, payments made by an employer to an employee to take up or resume work (eg as part of the settlement of an industrial dispute) would qualify as ordinary income. Section 15-3 is designed to ensure that such payments are not free of tax because, for example, they are designated as representing compensation for hardship suffered as a result of dismissal or are not paid by the employer concerned.

[FITR ¶53-030]

¶10-076 Signing-on and similar fees received by sportspersons

Broadly, sportspersons who are carrying on a business or who earn income from services provided in relation to a sport are assessable on income connected with those activities (TR 1999/17). However, money and other benefits received from the pursuit of a pastime or hobby are not assessable (¶10-050).

Lump sum signing-on fees received by sportspersons, such as professional footballers, are generally treated as ordinary income (IT 2307). However, this will not be so where the fee is consideration for a restrictive covenant, eg to play only for a certain club if the taxpayer were to join another league (*Woite*) (although the fee would probably be income if the taxpayer actually played for that club). In *Case R123*, a lump sum received by a successful professional runner on joining a football club was not income where it was received in return for giving up his career as a runner, although the Commissioner treats this decision as being confined to its own particular facts (IT 2307).

In some cases, it has been held that the payment is really for services to be rendered in the taxpayer's employment and, on this basis, the payment has been held to be income (eg *Riley v Coglan*; *Case R107*). In one case, a payment received by a professional footballer from the Queensland Rugby League as an inducement to play in Queensland rather than in New South Wales (where he could have earned more money) was income (*Case Y53*) (¶10-050). So were payments made to a football player through a sham trust structure which had been designed to avoid salary cap restrictions (*Oliver*).

The ATO states that, for the period up to 1 July 2020, it will not seek to apply compliance resources to review an arrangement entered into before 24 August 2018 (the date of withdrawal of *Draft* PCG 2017/D11), where that arrangement complies with the terms of the withdrawn guideline. *Draft* PCG 2017/D11 considered the tax treatment of payments for use and exploitation of a professional sportsperson's ‘‘public fame’’ or ‘‘image’’.

High-profile taxpayers and rights assignments

The government proposed that from 1 July 2019, all remuneration provided for the commercial exploitation of a person's fame or image would be included in the assessable income of the individual. High-profile individuals would no longer be able to take advantage of income splitting and lower tax rates by licensing their fame or image to another entity. In December 2018, the government released a consultation paper on its proposed approach to implement this 2018–19 Budget measure.

Note the income averaging scheme applicable to sportspersons (¶2-140 – ¶2-144).

Where amounts are not income, consideration needs to be given to the application of the CGT provisions (¶11-280).

[FITR ¶19-520]

Employee Share Schemes

¶10-080 Employee share schemes

Special rules apply to the taxation of benefits in the form of discounts on shares and rights acquired under employee share schemes (ITAA97 Div 83A). There are also employee share scheme withholding tax provisions (TAA Sch 1 Subdiv 14-C) and employee share scheme reporting requirements (TAA Sch 1 Div 392) (¶10-090).

For guidance about the ATO's view on the criteria to be met by an employee share trust (EST) in order for the EST, its beneficiaries and the employer company to qualify for certain capital gains tax (CGT) and FBT concessions, see TD 2019/13.

In February 2020, the House of Representatives Committee on Tax and Revenue commenced an inquiry into the effectiveness of changes to the employee share schemes (ESS) regime made in 2015.

¶10-085 Division 83A employee share schemes

Generally, Div 83A applies where an employee acquires an ESS interest under an employee share scheme at a discount from 1 July 2009 (s 83A-20). However, the provisions purport to cover not only employees but also those in employee-like relationships, such as directors, office holders and independent contractors (s 83A-325).

An ESS interest is defined as: (a) a beneficial interest in a share in a company; or (b) a right to acquire a beneficial interest in a share in a company (s 83A-10). Where one of the components of a stapled security is a share in a company, the stapled security is treated as a share (s 83A-335).

An ''employee share scheme'' is defined as a scheme under which ESS interests in a company are provided to employees or associates of employees (including past or prospective employees) of: (a) the company; or (b) subsidiaries of the company, in relation to the employees' employment.

Generally Div 83A taxes discounts on ESS interests upfront, ie at acquisition (s 83A-25). However, an employee may be entitled to have:

(a) the amount included in assessable income reduced (¶10-087), or

(b) the income year in which it is included deferred (¶10-089).

An employee will be entitled to have the amount included in assessable income reduced if the employee meets the conditions set out in s 83A-33 (start-up companies) or 83A-35 (other cases).

An employee will be able to defer taxation of the discount where the ESS interest obtained under the employee share scheme is at real risk of forfeiture or is obtained under a salary sacrifice arrangement. Deferral of taxation can also apply to a right if the employee share scheme restricted the employee immediately disposing of the right.

With effect from 1 July 2015, there is a specific concession available to employees of certain small start-up companies (¶10-090).

For Div 83A purposes, the date of acquisition of the ESS interest is important because the market value of listed shares can fluctuate.

Where discounts on ESS interests are taxed under Div 83A, they are exempt from being taxed as a fringe benefit (s 83A-5; FBTAA s 136(1) definition of ''fringe benefit'' para (h) and (ha)) or under the CGT provisions (s 130-75).

However, once an ESS interest has been taxed under Div 83A, any subsequent gain or loss is taxed in the same way as other capital assets (eg under the CGT regime (¶12-660)) but possibly under other regimes (eg the trading stock rules).

Application of Div 83A

As noted above, Div 83A applies to ESS interests acquired from 1 July 2009; former Div 13A (and former s 26AAC) will continue to apply to shares and rights acquired under those rules which are not transitioned to Div 83A. For more information on the application and transitional rules, see the 67th edition of the *Australian Master Tax Guide* and earlier editions.

[FITR ¶131-000]

¶10-087 Upfront taxation of discount on ESS interest

Generally, a discount received by an employee on an ESS interest under an employee share scheme is taxed on acquisition, ie upfront. However, provided certain conditions are met, an employee can reduce their taxable discount income by up to $1,000 (see below). Deferred taxation is available where the ESS interest obtained under the employee share scheme is at real risk of forfeiture or is obtained under a salary sacrifice arrangement or is a right subject to disposal restrictions (¶10-089).

The discount — being the market value of the ESS interest less any consideration paid by the employee — is assessable in the year of receipt (Subdiv 83A-B; s 83A-25(1)). ''Market value'' is given its ordinary meaning but the regulations set out an amount that can be used instead of market value for valuing unlisted rights (ITR97 regs 83A-315.01 to 83A-315.09). The Commissioner can also, by legislative instrument, approve optional safe harbour valuation methodologies which will be binding on the Commissioner (s 960-412; see *Income Tax Assessment (Methods for Valuing Unlisted Shares) Approval 2015*).

▶ Example 1

Bob is employed by Hugh's Skips Pty Ltd. Under an employee share scheme, he acquires Hugh's Skips shares with a market value of $100,000 in return for a payment of $50,000. He has, therefore, received a discount of $50,000 which he will have to include in his assessable income on acquisition of the ESS interests.

For these purposes, a discount on an ESS interest relating to employment outside Australia is taken to be from a foreign source (s 83A-25(2)).

$1,000 exemption

Where an employee is assessable on a discount received on an ESS interest upfront, a $1,000 exemption applies where the following conditions are satisfied at the time of acquisition (ss 83A-35; 83A-45):

- the *sum* of the taxpayer's taxable income, reportable fringe benefits total, reportable superannuation contributions and total investment loss (¶2-133) for the income year is $180,000 or less (including the discount but disregarding the upfront exemption: s 83A-35)
- the employee is employed by the company offering the employee share scheme, or one of its subsidiaries
- the scheme is only offered in a non-discriminatory way to at least 75% of Australian resident permanent employees of the company with 3 or more years service
- the shares or rights provided are *not* at real risk of forfeiture (¶10-089)
- the ESS interests offered under the scheme relate to ordinary shares. An interest in a corporate limited partnership is treated as an ordinary share (ID 2010/62)
- the shares or rights are required to be held by the employee for 3 years (or less if the Commissioner allows) or until the employee ceases employment (''minimum holding period rule''). For the meaning of ceasing employment, see ¶10-096
- the employee does not receive more than 10% ownership of the company, or control more than 10% of the voting rights in the company, as a result of participating in the scheme. For ESS interests acquired before 1 July 2015, the relevant percentage for ownership and voting rights was 5%.

In addition, an integrity rule about share trading and investment companies must also be satisfied (¶10-091).

▶ Example 2

Dave is employed by Walters Bank. Under the bank's employee share scheme, he acquires shares in Walters Bank at a $1,500 discount (to their market value). The shares provided under the scheme are not at risk and, therefore, the discount on the ESS interests acquired under the scheme is not eligible for deferral.

The sum of Dave's taxable income, reportable fringe benefits, reportable superannuation contributions and total net investment loss is $80,000 (including the discount but disregarding the upfront exemption).

If Dave and Walters Bank's scheme meet the other conditions, Dave will be eligible for the upfront exemption — he can reduce the amount of the discount to be included in his assessable income by $1,000 but will still need to include the remaining $500.

[FITR ¶131-030 – ¶131-040]

¶10-089 Deferred taxation and ESS

Deferred taxation (under Subdiv 83A-C) can apply to:

- a share, right or stapled security acquired at a discount under an employee share scheme where the share, right or security is subject to a real risk of forfeiture
- a share or stapled security acquired under salary sacrifice arrangements provided the employee receives no more than $5,000 worth of shares under those arrangements in an income year, and
- a right, if the employee share scheme restricted the employee immediately disposing of the right and the scheme rules expressly state that the scheme is subject to Subdiv 83A-C (s 83A-100).

In order to qualify for deferred taxation, the ESS and the employee must meet all the following general conditions:

- the ESS interest acquired by the employee must be in their employer or a holding company of the employer
- when an employee acquires the interest, all the ESS interests available for acquisition under the employee share scheme must relate to ordinary shares
- the employee does not receive more than 10% ownership of the company, or control more than 10% of the voting rights in the company, as a result of participating in the scheme. For ESS interests acquired before 1 July 2015, the relevant percentage for ownership and voting rights was 5% (s 83A-105(1)).

A further condition is that at the time of acquisition of the ESS interest at least 75% of the Australian-resident permanent employees with at least 3 years service are, or at some earlier time had been, entitled to acquire ESS interests in their employer or a holding company under an employee share scheme (s 83A-105(2)). An integrity rule about share trading and investment companies must also be satisfied (¶10-091).

Real risk of forfeiture schemes

An ESS interest is at real risk of forfeiture if a reasonable person would consider that there is a real risk under the conditions of the scheme that the employee would:

(1) in the case of shares, forfeit or lose the interest (other than by disposing of it)

(2) in the case of rights, forfeit or lose the interest (other than by disposing of it, exercising it, letting it lapse or through the market value of the ESS interest falling to nil) (s 83A-105(3)).

In relation to rights, there is a real risk of forfeiture where the conditions of the scheme provide for a minimum term of employment. For example, the conditions may:

- provide for a staged vesting of the rights (in the form of shares) at various periods of time after the date of grant (eg at one year, 2 years and 3 years), or
- contain "good leaver" provisions which provide that an employee who ceases employment because of death, invalidity, bona fide redundancy or retirement 6 months after the date of grant will retain the vesting rights (eg ID 2010/61).

The risk that an employee could lose their job amounted to a "real risk" that they would forfeit or lose an ESS interest (share options), resulting in a deferred taxing point (*Gennai*).

Salary sacrifice schemes

For deferred taxation to apply to ESS interests acquired under a salary sacrifice arrangement:

- the ESS interests must relate to shares (not rights)
- the employee must receive the shares for no consideration (ie the discount per share provided through the arrangement is equal to the market value of the share)
- the employee must receive no more than $5,000 worth of shares (valued at market value) per income year, and
- the governing rules of the employee share scheme must state that deferred taxation applies to the scheme (s 83A-105(4)).

Disposal of rights restricted

Deferred taxation can apply to rights if:

- the employee share scheme is a scheme in which employees can access ESS interests that are rights
- the scheme genuinely restricts the employee immediately disposing of those rights, and
- the scheme rules expressly state that the scheme is subject to deferred taxation under Subdiv 83A-C (s 83A-105(6)).

Section 83A-105(6) only applies in relation to ESS interests acquired on or after 1 July 2015.

Deferred taxing point

When tax on the acquisition of an ESS interest is deferred, it is delayed until when the earliest ESS taxing point occurs. These points are set out below. However, where the employee disposes of the interest within 30 days of the original deferred taxing point, the date of disposal is taken to the deferred taxing point (“30-day rule”: ss 83A-115(3); 83A-120(3)).

Subject to the 30-day rule, the deferred taxing point for *shares* is the earliest of:

- when there is no real risk that the employee will forfeit or lose the share(s) (other than by disposal), and there are no genuine restrictions preventing disposal
- when the employee ceases the employment for which they acquired the share(s) (¶10-096)
- 15 years after the employee acquired the share(s). For ESS interests acquired before 1 July 2015 the time period was 7 years (s 83A-115).

Subject to the 30-day rule, the deferred taxing point for *rights* is the earliest of:

- when the employee ceases the employment for which they acquired the right(s) (¶10-096)
- 15 years after the employee acquired the right(s). For ESS interests acquired before 1 July 2015 the time period was 7 years
- when there is no real risk of forfeiture of the rights and any restrictions on the sale of the rights are lifted, or
- when the employee exercises the right, and after exercising the right there is no real risk of forfeiture of the underlying share and the restrictions on sale of the share are lifted. For ESS interests acquired before 1 July 2015, the requirement was when there was no real risk of forfeiture of the benefits and any restrictions on the sale or exercise were lifted (s 83A-120).

Roll-over relief for corporate restructures

Where employees have a deferred tax liability on a discount on an ESS interest and a takeover or corporate restructure of their employer occurs triggering a disposal or breaking the employment relationship, roll-over relief may be available.

In particular, where:

- an arrangement is entered into that results in the original company becoming the subsidiary of another company, or
- there is a change in the ownership of the existing company that results in any ESS interests in the old company being replaced, whole or partly, by ESS interests in one or more other companies,

the new interests are treated as continuations of the old interests (s 83A-130).

However, the new interests must be ordinary shares or rights over ordinary shares and must reasonably be regarded as matching the old interests (s 83A-130(4), (5)).

Further, the roll-over relief is only available to employees who, at the time of acquisition of the new interests, do not hold a beneficial interest in more than 10% of the shares in the new company, and are not in a position to cast more than 10% of the maximum number of votes at a general meeting. For ESS interests acquired before 1 July 2015, the relevant percentage for ownership and voting rights was 5%.

Any consideration paid by the employee for the ESS interests is spread among the matching ESS interests in proportion to their market values immediately after the corporate restructure. This allows the apportionment of the cost base and the calculation of the discount for tax purposes for those ESS interests that are not subject to the roll-over and those that will.

Assessable amount

Under deferred taxation, the amount to be included in assessable income for the income year in which the deferred taxation point occurs is the market value of the ESS interest (at the deferred taxing point) reduced by the cost base of the ESS interest (s 83A-110(1)).

As noted above, ''market value'' takes it ordinary meaning but the Commissioner can, by legislative instrument, approve optional safe harbour valuation methodologies which will be binding on the Commissioner (s 960-412; see *Income Tax Assessment (Methods for Valuing Unlisted Shares) Approval 2015*). The ''cost base'' takes into account consideration paid, expenses such as interest and brokerage fees, or events such as value shifting, a return of capital or other expenses incurred in holding the asset in the same way as for CGT purposes (¶11-550). However, the cost base does not include a payment made by the employee to the ESS trustee to retain the shares in the ESS beyond a 3-year restriction period (*Munnery*).

The market value substitution rules in ITAA97 ss 112-20 (¶11-570) and 116-30 (¶11-510) are ignored for these purposes.

▶ Example

Jake acquires ESS interests in his employer, Beanstalk Co, through an employee share scheme, which meets the conditions for deferred taxation. He purchases the ESS interests at a 50% discount to their market value of $2,000, ie for $1,000. Beanstalk Co passes on brokerage fees of $50 to Jake. The cost base of Jake's ESS interests is $1,050.

Further, for these purposes, a discount on an ESS interest relating to foreign service is taken to be from a foreign source (s 83A-110(1)).

[FITR ¶131-050 – ¶131-095]

¶10-090 Start-up companies and ESS

A specific concession applies to employees of certain small start-up companies when acquiring shares or rights in their employer or a holding company of their employer on or after 1 July 2015 (s 83A-33). Broadly, the concession provides an income tax exemption for the discount received on certain shares and the deferral of the income tax on the discount received on certain rights which are instead taxed under the capital gains tax rules (ss 83A-33(1); 115-30(1)).

In relation to shares, the discount is not subject to income tax and the share, once acquired, is then subject to the capital gains tax system with a cost base reset at market value. In relation to rights, the discount is not subject to upfront taxation and the right is then subject to capital gains tax with a cost base equal to the employee's cost of acquiring the right (ss 83A-30(2); 130-80(4)).

To access the concession, no equity interests in the company in which the ESS interest is in can be listed on an approved stock or securities exchange. Further, the ESS interests need to be in a company that had been incorporated less than 10 years at the end of the most recent income year before the ESS interest was acquired. In relation to this requirement, it is the company's income year that is the relevant income year (s 83A-33(2), (3)). In addition, the ESS interests need to be in a company that has an aggregated turnover not exceeding $50 million for the income year prior to the income year in which the ESS was acquired (s 83A-33(4)). Also, the employing company (which may or may not be the company issuing the ESS interest) must be an Australian resident taxpayer. If the ESS interests are not in the employing company, only the employing company needs to be an Australian resident taxpayer (s 83A-33(6)). Moreover, the ESS interest must:

- in the case of a share — be acquired with a discount of not more than 15% of the market value of the share when acquired, and
- in the case of a right — have an exercise price (or strike price) that is greater than or equal to the market value of an ordinary share in the issuing company at the time the right is acquired (s 83A-33(5)).

In addition to satisfying the above specific conditions in s 83A-33(2) to (6), the ESS interest must also satisfy the general conditions in s 83A-45 and, in relation to shares, the broad availability rule in s 83A-105(2) (s 83A-33(1)).

The start-up concession applies to the exclusion of all other ESS taxation rules. That is, those eligible for the small start-up concession cannot access either the $1,000 up-front concession (¶10-087) or the deferred taxation concession (¶10-089; ss 83A-35(2)(c); 83A-105(1)(ab)).

[FITR ¶131-036 – ¶131-038]

¶10-091 ESS integrity rules

Division 83A contains a number of integrity rules, including new employer reporting requirements and new tax file number (TFN) withholding tax provisions. These are discussed below.

Employer reporting

A company which provides ESS interests to an employee under an employee share scheme ("provider") during an income year must, at the end of the income year (and in certain cases, at the end of a later year) give a statement to the Commissioner and to the employee if:

- the provider provided interests to the employee during the year which were taxed under Subdiv 83A-B (upfront taxation) or 83A-C (deferred taxation), or
- the provider has provided deferred tax interests to the employee (during that income year or a previous income year), and the ESS deferred taxing point for the interests occurred during the year (TAA Sch 1 s 392-5(1)).

The statement must be in the approved form and may require certain information, eg the provider's ABN, the employee's details, information about the ESS interests provided, the provider's estimate of the market value of the interests at the time of acquisition, the amount paid towards the acquisition and the amount of "TFN withholding tax (ESS)" (see below) paid or payable by the provider in respect of the interests.

Further, the statements must be given by the provider to the employee no later than 14 July after the end of the year, and to the Commissioner no later than 14 August after the end of the year (TAA Sch 1 s 392-5(5), (7)), although the Commissioner may defer the deadlines. For these purposes, the year is the financial year in which the ESS deferred taxing point occurs.

The provider may disregard the 30-day rule for the ESS deferred taxing point for reporting purposes, if they are not aware of when or whether the employee disposed of the ESS interest within 30 days of the ESS deferred taxing point (TAA Sch 1 s 392-5(6)).

An administrative penalty applies to providers who fail to provide the statement (TAA Sch 1 s 286-75(2BA)).

TFN withholding (ESS)

A TFN withholding tax is payable in the rare cases where the provider provides an ESS interest under an employee share scheme, an amount is taxed under Div 83A in an income year and the employee has not quoted their TFN or their ABN to the provider by the end of that income year (TAA Sch 1 s 14-155; ¶26-320). The rate of withholding tax for the 2018–19 year is 47%.

Other integrity rules

Further integrity measures are as follows:

- ESS interests provided to associates of employees (other than employee share trusts), in relation to an employee's employment, are treated as though the interests are acquired by the employee (s 83A-305)
- employees with a beneficial interest in an employee share trust are taxed as though they are the legal owners of those shares (s 83A-10). To overcome trust law restrictions, shares or rights to acquire shares in a trust are treated as though they were beneficially owned by particular employees (s 83A-320)
- an employee is not eligible for the upfront concession or deferred taxation if: (1) the employee is employed by a company whose predominant business is the acquisition, sale or holding of shares, securities or other investments; and (2) the employee is also employed by a subsidiary, a holding company or an subsidiary of the holding company of that company (ss 83A-45(3); 83A-105(1)(b)).

[FITR ¶131-115; FTR ¶978-910]

¶10-092 Refund for forfeited shares

A refund is available for tax paid on ESS interests where the employee had no choice but to forfeit the interest (other than a choice to cease employment or a choice not to exercise a right or to let a right be cancelled), and where the conditions of the scheme were not constructed to protect the employee from market risk (s 83A-310).

In particular, Div 83A is taken never to have applied in relation to an ESS interest (thereby resulting in a refund of income tax paid) where:

- an amount is included the employee's assessable income under Div 83A in relation to an ESS interest
- the employee has either forfeited the ESS interest or, in the case of a right, the employee has lost the right without having disposed of or exercised it

- the forfeiture or loss is neither the result of a choice made by the individual (other than a choice by the employee to cease that particular employment or, for ESS interests acquired on or after 1 July 2015, a choice not to exercise a right or allow the right to be cancelled) nor of a condition of the scheme that has the direct effect of wholly or partly protecting the employee from a fall in the market value of the ESS interest.

Where these conditions are satisfied, the taxpayer can request that the Commissioner amend the assessment to remove an amount which has previously been assessed under Div 83A. There is no time limit on amending an assessment to exclude an amount for a share interest which is forfeited or a right which was lost without being exercised (ITAA36 s 170(10AA), item 28).

[FITR ¶131-120]

¶10-094 Deduction for employers for ESS

A limited, specific deduction is available to employers that provide discounts on ESS interests to employees under an employee share scheme. However, the employee must be eligible for the upfront exemption disregarding the income test (ss 83A-200; 83A-205(1)).

The amount of the deduction for the employer is an amount equal to the discount on the ESS interest which the employee would not have to include in their assessable income (by operation of the upfront exemption but disregarding the income test); a maximum deduction of $1,000 is available (s 83A-205(2), (3)).

Where 2 or more employers jointly provide the ESS interest, the deduction must be apportioned between them on a reasonable basis (s 83A-205(4)).

Arrangements

An employer may provide an amount of money or property to another entity under an indirect arrangement (eg an employee share trust) for the purpose of providing ESS interests to its employees under an employee share scheme. In these cases, the deduction for the employer is delayed until such time as the employee acquires an ESS interest (s 83A-210).

[FITR ¶131-100 – ¶131-110]

¶10-096 Miscellaneous ESS matters

Indeterminate rights

In some cases, it is unclear at the time of acquisition whether a right to a benefit will result in the receipt of an ESS interest, or it may be that the exact number of ESS interests to be received is unknown. If and when it becomes clear that a right to the benefit will result in the receipt of a definite ESS interest or a definite number of ESS interests, the right will be treated as an ESS interest from the time that the original right was acquired (s 83A-340; *Davies* and ATO *Decision Impact Statement*). For the circumstances when a contractual right, which is subject to the satisfaction of a condition, becomes a right to acquire a beneficial interest in a share, see TD 2016/17.

For the purposes of taxing a benefit which becomes an ESS interest, the Commissioner has the power to amend an assessment at anytime (ITAA36 s 170(10AA)).

Ceasing employment

For the purposes of Div 83A, an employee is considered to have ceased employment when he/she is no longer employed either by his/her employer, a holding company or subsidiary of their employer, or a subsidiary of a holding company (s 83A-330).

Entities treated like companies

Division 83A purports to apply to interests in corporate limited partnerships and public trading trusts acquired in the same way as it applies to shares and rights in companies.

Dividend equivalent payments

A dividend equivalent payment is assessable to an employee as remuneration (and therefore ordinary income) when the employee receives such a payment for, or in respect of, services they provide as an employee, or similarly, where the payment has a sufficient connection with their employment (TD 2017/26). TD 2017/26 explains when a dividend equivalent payment is for services provided as an employee and sets out the Commissioner's practical administrative approach. It applies to employee share scheme interests granted on or after 1 January 2018.

[FITR ¶131-140, ¶164-157]

Business Income

¶10-105 Carrying on a business

The question whether ''a business is being carried on'' is fundamental to determining whether the earnings or proceeds of a business are to be included in assessable income and, conversely, whether deductions are allowable for all revenue expenses incurred in the course of deriving that income (¶16-015).

Whether or not a taxpayer's activities amount to carrying on a business is ''a question of fact and degree'' and is ultimately determined by a weighing up of the taxpayer's individual facts and circumstances.

Under the definition in s 995-1, a ''business'' includes any profession, trade, vocation or calling. In most cases, it is obvious whether a business is being carried on. Where it is not obvious, in particular where the relevant activity is subsidiary to a person's main income-producing activity, eg where the person engages in share transactions or vigorously pursues a hobby, the most important factors in determining whether a business is being carried on appear to be:

- *Profitability* — the fact that a profit is being made is a strong indication that a business is being carried on. However, the lack of profit does not necessarily mean that there is no business.

- *Size* — the bigger the operations, the more likely it is that there is a business being carried on.

- *Effort* — if the activities involve a substantial and regular effort over a period of time, they are more likely to constitute a business. However, it is possible to carry on a business as a part-time sideline to the taxpayer's main activities. Similarly, a single transaction can amount to the carrying on of a business if it results from a concerted effort, especially if it is connected in some way with the taxpayer's normal business activities. Apart from this, however, the mere realisation of capital assets would not normally constitute a business.

- *Business records* — if detailed business records are kept, this is a strong pointer to the existence of a business. The lack of records is a common weakness in cases presented by persons seeking to obtain deductions for losses incurred from their alleged business activities.

A more detailed list of the factors involved is given below.

Positive factors	Negative factors
More likely to be a business if . . .	*Less likely to be a business if . . .*
Large scale operations	Small scale operations
Involves employees	One person operation
Frequent acts/transactions	Infrequent acts/transactions
Conducted with a view to profit	Conducted as mere hobby
Profitable	Non-profitable
Conducted over long period	Short-term
Conducted continuously and systematically	Spasmodic
In commercial premises	At home
Involves items typically dealt with commercially	Involves items not ordinarily dealt with commercially
Involves exercise of specialised knowledge	Involves little knowledge or skills
Significant capital investment	Little or no capital investment
Business records kept	Records not kept, or inadequate
Full-time	Part-time
Market research done	No market research
Associated with other commercial activities of taxpayer	No other commercial activities
Existence of business organisation, business name	Conducted personally/privately
Advertising	No advertising
Active	Inactive or preliminary

For the Commissioner's views, see TR 2019/1 (when a company carries on a business for the purposes of the definition of a "small business entity": ¶7-050), TR 97/11 (business of primary production), TR 2005/1 (business as a professional artist), and TR 2008/2 (horse industry). See also *Gilbert* (motorcycle sidecar racing), *Block* (horse and sheep breeding), *Kennedy* (film-making business), *Phippen* and *Hattrick* (boat-chartering business: ¶16-420), *Peerless Marine* (boat-building), *Pedley* and *Case 4/2005* (professional artist); and *Leggett* (financial services franchise).

Whether a person is carrying on a business of betting or gambling (in which case losses would be deductible) is considered at ¶10-430. The concept of carrying on a business of primary production, or carrying on business under afforestation, live stock leasing or similar schemes, is considered at ¶18-020.

[FITR ¶31-581]

¶10-110 Business income

Australian tax law generally requires the gross *earnings or proceeds* of a business, and not the gross *profit*, to be included in assessable income.

Receipts derived by a business which are capital in nature are only assessable if and to the extent that the CGT provisions or some other express statutory provision make them assessable.

Amounts received from transactions carried out in the ordinary course of business are income (*California Copper Syndicate Ltd v Harris*). On this basis, payments received by a company for the costs of establishing a plant in which the company was contracted to carry out pipe-coating work for the payer were held to be income (*GP International Pipecoaters*). Similarly, payments received by a taxpayer as compensation for the non-return by customers of scaffolding equipment hired from the taxpayer in the course of its business were income (*GKN Kwikform Services*) (a contrasting case is *Hyteco Hiring*, noted at ¶10-112). An amount received by a company which carried on petroleum exploration operations in Bass Strait from a joint venture partner for contributing deep water mining technology to the joint venture was held to be income as the entry into the joint venture was part of or incidental to the ordinary course of the company's business (*Esso Australia Resources*). Lease incentives received in relation to business premises may constitute assessable income (¶10-116). Profits or gains arising from debt defeasance arrangements may be assessable as income according to ordinary concepts or under the CGT provisions (¶23-325). Further, the profit made by a private equity entity from the disposal of shares in an Australian public company for the purpose of profit-making by sale in a commercial transaction (eg such as in a leveraged buyout) will constitute ordinary income (TD 2010/21).

A profit or gain made in an isolated transaction entered into otherwise than in the ordinary course of carrying on a business may also be income (¶10-112). The assessability of compensation payments is considered at ¶10-170 and following.

Amounts received for the sale of know-how or secret processes, etc, even if not "royalties" as such (¶10-510), will generally be assessable as normal trading receipts unless a discontinuance or disposal of a business is involved (ID 2007/68). Much the same principle applies in the case of lump sum receipts for the sale or grant of exclusive distribution rights (*Borg*) and licences to use, patents, designs, etc. If the taxpayer's business involves the acquisition, exploitation, sale or otherwise turning to account of such assets, the receipts will be assessable as income.

The proceeds from the sale of trading stock of a business are ordinary income and stock on hand at the beginning and end of the income year is required to be brought to account as trading stock (¶9-150). Shares can be trading stock where the taxpayer's purchases and sales are sufficient to amount to the conduct of a business. This also applies to land dealings. Even if property is not trading stock, its disposal may give rise to income if the disposal occurs in the course of the carrying on of the taxpayer's business (*Memorex*). The treatment of gains realised on the sale of depreciated equipment forming part of the ordinary course of the taxpayer's business is discussed at ¶17-630.

Partly-manufactured goods are normally treated as trading stock. Amounts received for other types of work in progress are specifically made assessable (ITAA97 s 15-50; ¶16-158).

A payment in respect of accrued leave entitlements of an employee transferred from one employer to another is assessable income of the employer who receives the payment where the payment is made under: (a) a Commonwealth, state or territory law; or (b) an award, order, determination or industrial agreement under any such law (ITAA97 s 15-5).

Fees or commissions for procuring a loan of money are generally ordinary income (*National Mortgage*). A fee for guaranteeing the repayment of a loan may also be assessable as ordinary income or under ITAA97 s 15-2 (¶10-060) (*Case W26*).

Interest, non-refundable premiums, etc, received by banks and finance companies are assessable income. All amounts received from an insured in connection with the writing of general insurance contracts, including stamp duty, fire brigade charges and reinsurance commissions, are assessable income of the insurer. Special rules govern how and when insurance premiums are assessed (¶9-050). The taxation of life assurance companies is considered at ¶3-480 and following.

For the tax treatment of sale and leaseback arrangements, see ¶23-240.

The question of *when* income is derived can depend on the nature of the income and the income-earning activities of the taxpayer. The timing of the derivation of income arising from a range of transactions and income-earning activities is examined at ¶9-050.

[FITR ¶18-300, ¶19-210, ¶19-400, ¶53-050]

¶10-112 Isolated transactions: *Myer* principle

The profit arising from an isolated business or commercial transaction will be ordinary income if the taxpayer's purpose or intention in entering into the transaction was to make a profit, notwithstanding that the transaction was not part of the taxpayer's daily business activities (*Myer Emporium*). This is called the *Myer* principle. In *Myer Emporium*, the taxpayer company lent $80 million to a subsidiary (at commercial rates of interest) as part of an extensive plan to diversify its operations. A few days later, the taxpayer assigned to a finance company for a lump sum of $45 million its right to receive interest under the loan to the subsidiary. The High Court held that the $45 million was received as part of a profit-making scheme and was, therefore, ordinary income (¶10-020). An important factor in this decision was that the 2 transactions were integral elements in the plan to diversify (the taxpayer would not have made the loan if the finance company had not agreed to take the assignment of the right to interest).

Compensation received for the compulsory acquisition of land acquired by a taxpayer for sandmining and eventual subdivision was assessable pursuant to the *Myer* principle (*Moana Sand*). A gain realised on the disposal of land by a taxpayer who carried on a building and project management business was also assessable as the land had been acquired to prevent the former owner opposing the rezoning of a site which was the subject of a development project to be coordinated by the taxpayer (*Richardson*). A payment to a solicitor to vacate leased office premises, one year after exercising an option to renew the lease for a further 3-year term, was held to be income (*Case 57/94*).

For the *Myer* principle to apply, profit-making must be a significant (but not necessarily the sole or dominant) purpose or intention (TR 92/3). Although the taxpayer's purpose or intention is usually to be ascertained from an objective consideration of the circumstances of each case, the taxpayer's subjective purpose or intention may be the determining factor (*Westfield*). The Commissioner considers that it does not matter if the profit is obtained by a means which was not specifically contemplated when the taxpayer entered into the transaction (TR 92/3), but there are statements in *Myer Emporium* and *Westfield* which suggest otherwise. The factors which the Commissioner considers to be relevant in determining whether an isolated transaction amounts to a business or commercial transaction are set out in TR 92/3.

The *Myer Emporium* decision does not mean that every profit made by a taxpayer in the course of a business activity is income. For example, in *Westfield*, the profit made by a shopping centre developer from the sale of land acquired for a shopping centre it planned to build and manage itself, but which it eventually built for another company, was capital and not income. The resale of land was not part of the taxpayer's ordinary business activities and, at the time the land was acquired, the taxpayer intended to develop the land itself and not to realise a profit by resale. In the *Hyteco Hiring case*, a taxpayer which carried on a business of hiring out forklifts was not assessable on the profits from the sale of forklifts which were no longer suitable for hire as the profits were not an ordinary incident of its business. Of course, a capital receipt may be assessable under the CGT provisions.

On the basis of *Myer*, indemnification amounts paid to a non-resident lender by a borrower against the liability for interest withholding tax will normally be income of the lender. Those amounts will therefore be assessable if their source (¶21-070) is in Australia (TR 2002/4).

[FITR ¶18-235, ¶18-300]

¶10-114 Cancellation or variation of business contracts

Ordinarily, amounts received in connection with the variation, cancellation or breach of ordinary commercial contracts are income in nature (eg *Heavy Minerals*; *Toyota Manufacturing*). In one case, however, compensation for the variation of a long-term supply contract paid to a wholly-owned subsidiary, where the subsidiary had given no consideration for the payment and the payment was not a product of any business or revenue-producing activity carried on by it, was not assessable in the hands of the subsidiary (*Federal Coke*). If the compensation had been paid to the supplier itself, it would have been assessable. (The CGT provisions would be relevant if the case were heard today.)

Where compensation is received for the cancellation, assignment, variation or breach of an agency agreement, and the agency is one of several held by the taxpayer so that its cancellation, etc, may be regarded as a normal trading risk in the course of carrying on the business, the receipt will be treated as ordinary income. For example, a payment received as compensation for termination of an agency agreement relating to the distribution of a particular product was held to be income where the agency constituted only one section of the taxpayer's many business activities — the taxpayer had not parted with a substantial part of its business undertaking and the payment was essentially designed to compensate the taxpayer for the loss of profits anticipated to flow from the agency agreement (*Allied Mills Industries*).

On the other hand, where the agency or other agreement in question is the source of the whole or the greater part of the business earnings, so that the cancellation of the agreement constitutes a destruction of the taxpayer's profit-making structure, the receipt will be capital. See, for example, *Case Y24* where a company whose sole business was to deliver newspapers and magazines received a payment on the cancellation of the delivery contract. In those circumstances, the payment will be assessable only to the extent that the CGT provisions apply. In *Co-operative Motors*, a company's long-standing motor vehicle distributorship was effectively terminated. The company had no right to compensation, but it did receive a $500,000 ex gratia payment from the vehicle manufacturer in recognition of its past services. The company argued that the payment was a gift, but the Federal Court ruled that it was a product of the company's income-earning activities and, accordingly, was assessable income.

The assessability of an ex gratia compensation payment arising from a government decision prohibiting or restricting the commercial operations of a business will be determined in accordance with the principles outlined above. If the business is forced to close down completely, the payment is likely to be capital but may be assessable under the CGT provisions.

[FITR ¶19-250, ¶19-255]

¶10-115 Amounts received for restrictive covenants/sterilisation of assets

Amounts received in consideration of a restrictive covenant, where the recipient undertakes not to use specified assets or to trade only with the other party to the agreement, are of a capital nature (*Dickenson*). They are therefore only assessable to the extent that the CGT provisions apply (¶11-280). Nevertheless, in some circumstances, an amount received for limiting or restricting the operations of the recipient may be of a revenue nature, eg where it is in the nature of an amount intended to replace profits which would otherwise have been made.

Amounts received for the sterilisation of assets are capital receipts (eg a lump sum payment as consideration for surrendering valuable stock options: *McArdle's case*), except where the asset is merely rendered partially inoperative for a limited period. If the asset was acquired on or after 20 September 1985, the CGT provisions may apply, although in some limited circumstances roll-over relief may be available. A lump sum or instalments of a lump sum received by a service station proprietor for exclusive trade ties to an oil company are generally regarded as capital.

A lump sum payment received as compensation for the forfeiture to the Crown of a beneficial interest in coal mines and seams was held to be a capital sum in *Northumberland Development*.

[FITR ¶18-300, ¶19-097]

¶10-116 Lease incentives

In general, a cash incentive paid to a business taxpayer to enter into a lease of business premises is assessable income (*Montgomery*; *Cooling*; *O'Connell*). In *Montgomery*, the High Court held that payments received by a law firm as an incentive to enter into a lease of premises were assessable income, even though they were not received by the firm in the ordinary course of its business. The court considered that the firm used or exploited its capital (whether taken to be the entering into the lease agreement or the firm's goodwill) to obtain the incentive payments.

A lease surrender payment received by a service company for a large firm of solicitors was assessable as ordinary income (*Rotherwood*). In TR 2005/6, the Commissioner states that a lease surrender receipt would constitute assessable income under ITAA97 s 6-5 if received:

(1) (a) *in the case of a lessee*, in the ordinary course of carrying on a business of trading in leases; or (b) *in the case of a lessor*, in the ordinary course of carrying on a business of granting and surrendering leases

(2) as an ordinary incident of business activity (even though it was unusual or extraordinary compared to the usual transactions of the business), or

(3) as a profit or gain from an isolated business operation or commercial transaction entered into by the lessee or lessor (otherwise than in the ordinary course of carrying on a business), with the intention or purpose of making the relevant profit or gain.

A lease surrender receipt of a lessor is otherwise of a capital nature. A lease surrender receipt of a lessee is of a capital nature when received for the surrender of a lease that formed part of the profit-yielding structure of the business of the lessee. For details of the CGT treatment of lease surrender receipts, see ¶11-270 and ¶12-680.

An amount paid to a business tenant to vary a lease to take up extra space or to relocate within the same building, or to encourage the tenant to remain in the same leased premises, is also assessable. However, an incentive paid to a taxpayer entering into a lease to commence an entirely new business is unlikely to be ordinary income although it would constitute an assessable capital gain under the CGT provisions (IT 2631; ¶11-300).

Non-cash lease incentives

Non-cash lease incentives which are convertible to cash (eg vehicles, boats, paintings or computer equipment), and which are received by business taxpayers in relation to business premises, have an income character, either inherently or by virtue of ITAA36 s 21A (¶10-030), and are taxable at their full monetary value. If the incentive qualifies as depreciable plant or equipment and is used for income-producing purposes, the taxpayer is entitled to a depreciation deduction (¶17-010).

Non-cash lease incentives which are not convertible to cash are assessable by virtue of s 21A except where the "otherwise deductible" rule applies or where it is non-deductible entertainment expenditure (¶10-030). The application of s 21A to non-cash lease incentives can be summarised as follows (IT 2631):

- rent-free period — effectively tax-free
- interest-free loan — effectively tax-free, provided it is a genuine business loan and not a disguised cash payment
- free fit-out:
  - if owned by the landlord — effectively tax-free
  - if owned by the tenant — assessable but a deduction will be allowed for depreciation to the extent that the fit-out qualifies as depreciable plant or articles

- free holiday — a complete holiday package comprising travel, accommodation, meals and recreation will be effectively tax-free to the tenant, as the cost will not be deductible to the landlord
- payment of removal costs — fully taxable except to the extent that the costs relate to revenue items such as trading stock
- payment of surrender value of existing lease — fully taxable.

Where s 21A applies, the ‘‘arm’s length value’’ of the incentive is assessable (¶10-030).

[FITR ¶19-210; FTR ¶7-175]

Realisation of Real Property and Securities

¶10-120 Realisation of real property

The proceeds from the mere realisation of a capital asset or from the change of an investment do not give rise to income according to ordinary concepts or to a profit arising from a profit-making undertaking or plan within the meaning of ITAA97 s 15-15 (for property acquired before 19 September 1985) (¶10-340), even if the realisation or change is carried out in the most advantageous manner — these being an affair of capital. Of course, the CGT provisions may apply in relation to property acquired on or after 20 September 1985.

In the *NF Williams case*, the High Court commented that an owner of land who holds it until the price of land has risen and then subdivides and sells it is not thereby engaging in an adventure in the nature of trade or carrying out a profit-making scheme, even if the landowner seeks and acts on the advice of experts as to the best method of subdivision and sale or carries out work such as grading, levelling, road building and the provision of water and power. More examples of the principle that the proceeds from the mere realisation of a capital asset are not assessable as ordinary income are *Statham* (profits realised on the sale of subdivided farming land); *Ashgrove* (receipts under agreements for the sale of timber growing on the taxpayers’ land); *Casimaty* (progressive sale of farming property); and *McCorkell* (profits from the sale of a subdivided orchard).

The distinction between the mere realisation of an asset and a business venture is not always clear and, in some cases, the development of land may be so extensive that the taxpayer is in fact engaged in a business venture (ultimately it is a question of fact). In *Whitfords Beach*, the taxpayer company acquired 1,584 acres of land for non-commercial purposes. Thirteen years later, the original shareholders sold out and the company, under its new ownership, adopted an entirely new set of articles; it then embarked on a long and complex course of activity which involved the land being rezoned and developed as a residential subdivision. Vacant lots were sold over a period of many years for a substantial profit. The High Court held that the taxpayer’s activities amounted to more than the mere realisation of a capital asset and constituted the carrying on of an actual business of subdividing and selling land. See also *Stevenson*, *Abeles* and *August*. Similarly, where properties are sold by a property investment company as part of its normal business operations, the profits will be assessable as ordinary income (*CMI Services*).

In the following circumstances, the net profit on the sale of land is assessable as ordinary income, although each case must be determined on its facts:

- where land is acquired in an isolated commercial transaction for the purpose of development, subdivision and sale, but the development and subdivision do not proceed and the land is subsequently sold (TD 92/126)
- where land is acquired for development, subdivision and sale but the development is abandoned and the land is sold in a partly developed state (TD 92/127)

- where land is acquired for development, subdivision and sale but, after some initial development, the project ceases and is recommenced in a later income year (TD 92/128).

The valuation of subdivided farm land is discussed in TD 97/1.

Land can be trading stock in the hands of a land dealer (¶9-150) in which case the net profit is assessable income at the time of settlement, not when the contract was entered into (*Benwerrin*; *Gasparin*).

If a gain is not assessable as ordinary income or under ITAA97 s 15-15, it may be assessable under the CGT provisions (¶11-000). Where a capital gain arises under the CGT provisions (CGT event A1), the gain is assessable at the time the contract was entered into, not at the time of settlement (¶11-250).

[FITR ¶18-300, ¶19-525]

¶10-130 Realisation of securities

The basic rules governing the tax treatment of gains from the realisation of shares or other securities are the same as for other property. For further discussion, see ¶23-350. Special rules apply to the disposal or redemption of "traditional securities" (¶23-340) and the conversion of semi-government securities (¶23-355).

[FTR ¶16-260]

¶10-140 Foreign exchange and futures transactions

For details of the tax treatment of foreign exchange gains and losses, see ¶23-075. For investments and speculation in futures contracts, see ¶23-370.

Bounties and Subsidies

¶10-160 Treatment of bounties and subsidies

Ordinarily, bounties and subsidies received in relation to carrying on a business are assessable as ordinary income. Such items are included in assessable income on an accruals basis where the items represent trading income of the taxpayer (¶9-030).

Bounties and subsidies received in relation to carrying on a business which are not assessable as ordinary income (ie receipts of a capital nature) are expressly included in assessable income by ITAA97 s 15-10. In this situation, the amount is included in assessable income in the year of receipt, unless the amount has been prepaid.

The following payments have been held to be ordinary income:

- distributions by a Totalisator Agency Board to racing clubs (the distributions were also held to be subsidies) (*Brisbane Amateur Turf Club*; *Case K48*)
- an R&D grant made to a manufacturing company to reimburse the company for expenditure of a revenue nature (the grant was also held to be a bounty or subsidy) (*Reckitt and Colman*).

Guidelines on the tax treatment of government payments to industry to assist entities to commence, continue or cease business are set out in TR 2006/3.

A payment by a state government to a building society following the winding up of a compulsory contingency fund was assessable under s 15-10 as a subsidy (*First Provincial Building Society*), as was a grant received by a taxpayer under the Dairy Regional Assistance Program (*Plant*). Grants under the First Home Owner Grant Scheme are not assessable. The wine producer rebate is assessable as ordinary income (ATO Fact Sheet "Wine Equalisation Tax — new wine producer rebate" (NAT 11779)).

Grant payments received under the Sustainable Rural Water Use and Infrastructure Program are usually assessable as ordinary income or under s 15-10 to the extent that they are not consideration for the surrender of water rights. However, taxpayers may choose to make the payments non-assessable non-exempt income (and to disregard any capital gain or loss from transferring water rights) in which case the expenditure that is made from the payments will not be deductible (and will not form part of the cost base of the asset) (¶18-080).

For details of the tax treatment of various government payments, see ¶10-197. A payment from a fund comprised of public donations is characterised as a gift (¶10-070).

[FITR ¶53-100]

Compensation Payments

¶10-170 Compensation for loss of trading stock and profits

Insurance payments or other receipts in respect of lost trading stock, eg by fire, compulsory takeover or destruction, etc, and amounts received for loss of profits or income due to an interruption to business, eg caused by fire, rain, etc, are assessable either as ordinary income under ITAA97 s 6-5 or statutory income under ITAA97 s 15-30 or 70-115. So, for example, the following payments have been held to be assessable:

- compensation paid to a poultry farmer for loss of income suffered when many of the farmer's hens died or became sick because of excessive amounts of pesticide in their feed (*Gill v Australian Wheat Board*)
- damages awarded to a landlord against a tenant remaining unlawfully in occupation, and which represented the difference between the rent paid by the tenant and the rent obtainable on the open market (*Raja's Commercial College v Gian Singh & Co*)
- damages for lost profits awarded to a lift installation and maintenance company against a manufacturer which supplied it with defective lift equipment (*Liftronic*)
- compensation received by tax agents from the ATO under the Scheme for Detriment Caused by Defective Administration (*Pope*).

For special provisions relating to insurance recoveries for live stock and timber losses, see ¶18-150. A right under an insurance policy may be an asset for CGT purposes and an insurance recovery may give rise to a capital gain (¶11-880). In addition, a right to recover damages would be an asset for CGT purposes (¶11-380) and an award of damages may give rise to a capital gain (¶11-650). Further, balancing adjustments must usually be made where assets for which depreciation or other similar deductions have been allowed are lost, destroyed, etc (¶17-630).

Compensation payments for injury to business reputation are usually capital, even if assessed by reference to lost profits (*Sydney Refractive Surgery Centre*).

[FITR ¶19-070, ¶19-087, ¶53-300]

¶10-175 Damages paid in undissected lump sum

Lump sum damages, or a lump sum out-of-court settlement, representing compensation for losses of an income nature only, will be assessable income in accordance with ordinary principles (¶10-010; TD 93/58).

Where the relevant payment can be dissected into its income and capital components, the income components (such as interest on the principal sum: ¶10-185) will be assessable income. A lump sum settlement received from an insurer was assessable to the extent that it related to a salary continuance benefit payable to the taxpayer but not assessable to the extent that it related to a superannuation continuance benefit (*YCNM*).

However, where lump sum damages are a lesser amount received in settlement of an unliquidated claim covering both income and capital elements but cannot be dissected into those elements, the whole amount is treated as capital (*McLaurin*; *Allsop*; *CSR*; *Kort* (AAT)).

This treatment of undissected amounts was clearly favourable to taxpayers before the advent of CGT. However, the CGT provisions now treat the right to sue for damages (or the right to give up the right to sue) as an asset (¶11-380) which can be disposed of by obtaining an award of damages or by accepting a settlement. Generally there will be a better CGT outcome if the amount received can be attributed at least partly to an ''underlying asset'' (eg damaged property) rather than solely to the asset embodied in the right to sue. If the amount is an undissected amount and the taxpayer cannot make a reasonable estimate of the income and capital components, the whole amount will be taken to relate to the disposal of the taxpayer's right to sue (TR 95/35; ¶11-650).

[FITR ¶19-095]

¶10-180 Workers compensation

Weekly or other periodical workers compensation payments (or periodical payments under other legislation) received as compensation for loss of wages (whole or partial) are fully assessable as ordinary income (they are not assessable under ITAA97 s 15-2: ¶10-060) (*Inkster*; *Case Y47*; *Maher*). The same generally applies to a lump sum paid in lieu of the right to receive weekly payments of income or for loss of employment (*Coward*; *Brackenreg*; *Riley*; *Edwards*; *Gupta*; TD 2016/18). However, if the commutation to a lump sum can only be made under certain circumstances, and its calculation requires consideration of other factors, it may possibly be capital (*Barnett*). A lump sum commutation referable to the period after the taxpayer reached the age of 65 years has also been held to be capital (*Coward*).

A fixed sum workers compensation award for loss of a limb, eye, finger, etc, is not assessable, nor is a payment for medical, etc, expenses. Likewise, a fixed sum awarded in full satisfaction of an employee's workers compensation claim against an employer, even though it represents in part unpaid periodical payments as well as compensation for loss of a limb, etc, and loss of earning capacity. For guidelines on when the receipt of a lump sum compensation/settlement amount is assessable, see TD 93/58.

In *Rayner,* it was held that a taxpayer who had to repay workers compensation payments after receiving a lump sum settlement was not entitled to have a previous assessment amended to exclude the compensation payments. In *Reiter*, workers compensation payments received by a taxpayer after he had recovered damages were not assessable income as they were required to be repaid under Victorian ''double dipping'' legislation.

In *Cooper*, a lump sum payment representing arrears of invalidity benefits was assessable in the year of receipt. The same applies to arrears of workers compensation paid as a lump sum (*Vargiemezis*) and a lump sum compensation payment received by a Reserve Force member in respect of lost civilian income.

[FITR ¶19-110, ¶53-358]

¶10-185 Personal injury compensation

The general position is that lump sum compensation payments for personal injury (including any pre-judgment interest component) are not assessable as ordinary income or statutory income (ITAA97 s 51-57). They are also exempt under the CGT provisions (¶11-650), although a component of a lump sum that is identifiable as compensation for loss of earnings is taxable. A lump sum awarded to the spouse of the injured person in recognition of the care the spouse provides may be non-assessable. However, where the personal injury component of an undissected lump sum termination settlement could not be separately identified, no part of the payment was exempt as personal injury compensation (TR 95/35; *Dibb*).

Compensation payments that provide the victim with an income stream are generally assessable. Deferred lump sums may also be assessable under ITAA36 Div 16E if they fall within the definition of a qualifying security (¶23-320).

Normally, if an annuity is purchased out of a lump sum tax-free payment, it may be assessable to the extent that the annuity payments include a component related to the investment earnings on the underlying lump sum (ITAA36 s 27H).

In *Brackenreg*, a lump sum settlement, which had been commuted from a weekly compensation payment, was assessable income. In *Maher*, weekly compensation payments under the *Safety, Rehabilitation and Compensation Act 1988* were assessable income. In *Case 9/2006*, weekly workers compensation paid in arrears as part of a clearly dissected lump sum was assessable income.

Division 54 exemption for structured settlements and orders

ITAA97 Div 54 provides an exemption for certain annuities and lump sums provided to personal injury victims under structured settlements or structured orders.

A *structured settlement* is one that meets all of the following 5 conditions:

(1) The claim must be for compensation or damages for personal injury suffered by a person and the claim must be made by the injured person or by his/her legal personal representative.

(2) The claim must be based on the commission of a wrong or on a right created by statute.

(3) The claim cannot be an action against a defendant in his/her capacity as an employer, or an associate of an employer, or a claim made under workers compensation law, or a claim that could instead be made under workers compensation law.

(4) The settlement must be in a written agreement between the parties to the claim. This applies whether or not the agreement is approved by an order of a court or is in a consent order made by a court.

(5) The terms of the settlement must provide for some or all of a lump sum award of compensation or damages to be used by the defendant or the defendant's insurer to purchase from one or more life insurance companies or state insurers:

- an annuity or group of annuities to be paid to the injured person (or his/her trustee), or
- an annuity or group of annuities combined with one or more deferred lump sums to be paid to the injured person (or his/her trustee).

A *structured order* is essentially an order of a court that satisfies conditions (1), (2), (3) and (5) above but is not an order approving or endorsing an agreement as mentioned in (4) above.

Exempt personal injury annuities

A personal injury annuity is an annuity purchased under the terms of a structured settlement or structured order. A personal injury annuity will be eligible for exemption (ITAA97 s 54-15) if (broadly) the following conditions are met:

- The compensation payment or damages, if paid in the form of a lump sum at the date of settlement or order, would not have to be included in the assessable income of the injured person (eg it is not compensation for lost earnings) (ITAA97 s 54-20).

- The annuity instrument only allows for payments of the annuity to be made to the injured person, his/her trustee, a reversionary beneficiary or the injured person's estate and contains a statement to the effect that the annuity cannot be assigned and cannot be commuted except by a reversionary beneficiary (ITAA97 s 54-25).

- The annuity instrument provides that the payments of the annuity are to be made at least annually over a period of at least 10 years during the life of the injured person or for the life of the injured person. Annuity payments may be guaranteed up to 10 years after the date of settlement. In the event the injured person dies during the guarantee period, the remaining payments may be made to either the injured person's estate or a reversionary beneficiary (ITAA97 ss 54-30; 54-35).

- The annuity or annuities in total provide a minimum monthly level of support over the annuitant's life (ITAA97 s 54-40).

Exempt personal annuity lump sums

Structured settlements and structured orders may include non-annual lump sum payments that are made to claimants at regular intervals to fund expected purchases, eg a payment every 5 years to replace a wheelchair. A personal injury lump sum is a lump sum that is purchased under the terms of a structured settlement or structured order. Personal injury lump sums will be exempt from income tax if all of the following conditions are met (ITAA97 ss 54-45 to 54-60):

- There is at least one personal injury annuity provided under the same structured settlement or structured order that satisfies the eligibility conditions described above.

- The lump sum would not have been taxable if it had been paid as a lump sum at the time of settlement.

- The annuity instrument identifies the structured settlement or structured order under which the personal injury lump sum is provided and only allows for payments of the annuity to be made to the injured person or his/her trustee, or contains a statement to the effect that the right to receive the lump sum cannot be assigned or commuted/cashed out.

- The contract specifies the date and amount of the payment of the lump sum. The lump sum can only be increased through appropriate indexation or by a specified percentage.

Payments to reversionary beneficiaries

A reversionary beneficiary will be exempt from income tax on the periodic payments or the lump sum payment if the payment(s) would have been exempt from income tax in the hands of the injured person (ITAA97 s 54-65).

Payments to/from trustee

Broadly, structured payments that would have been exempt if paid directly to the injured person or reversionary beneficiary will be exempt when received by a trustee for the injured person or reversionary beneficiary, and when paid out by the trust (ITAA97 s 54-70). The exemption does not extend to investment earnings of the trust.

A payment of a lump sum to an injured person's estate or testamentary trust will also be exempt (s 54-70(3)).

[FITR ¶102-620, ¶104-000]

¶10-187 Native title payments

An amount or benefit that an indigenous person or indigenous holding entity receives directly from entering into an agreement or as compensation under the *Native Title Act 1993* (ie a native title benefit) is non-assessable non-exempt income (ITAA97 s 59-50). An indigenous holding entity includes distributing bodies, trusts and registered charities (ITAA97 s 59-50(6)).

[FITR ¶108-087]

Social Security, etc, Pensions

¶10-190 Overview of social security, etc, pensions

Most pensions paid under the social security and the veterans' entitlements legislation to persons of pension age (¶10-195) and to wives of men of pension age are assessable. Some of these pensions are assessable *irrespective* of the age of the recipient. For details of the treatment of pensions, benefits and allowances, see ¶10-195 – ¶10-204.

Where sickness allowances are repaid by a taxpayer on receipt of a lump sum settlement, the assessments for the years in which the allowances were received may be amended so as to exclude the allowances from the assessable income of those years (ITAA97 s 59-30; ¶10-895). However, this provision does not apply to amounts repaid because a taxpayer received a lump sum as compensation or damages for a wrong or injury suffered in their occupation.

Where Australia has concluded a tax treaty with another country, pensions received from that country are generally assessable only in Australia (¶22-150).

In certain circumstances, tax offsets are available to reduce or eliminate tax on assessable pensions and benefits (¶15-310 – ¶15-315).

¶10-195 Assessability of social security payments

Most social security payments are assessable, with a portion of the payment being exempt (ITAA97 ss 52-5 to 52-40). However, special rebates are allowable for recipients of some types of social security payments.

Pension age

In some cases, some or all of a social security pension may be exempt if the recipient is of "pension age". That is the age when the person may first apply for an age pension. From 1 July 2019, the pension age for men and women is 66 years.

Stepped increase in pension age

In the period from:	The "pension age" is or will be:
1 July 2017 to 30 June 2019	65 years and 6 months
1 July 2019 to 30 June 2021	66 years
1 July 2021 to 30 June 2023	66 years and 6 months
1 July 2023	67 years

Pensions and other benefits under Social Security Act

The table below shows the status of pensions, benefits and allowances payable under the *Social Security Act 1991*.

Pension, benefit or allowance	Basic amount	Supplementary amount
2020 Economic support payments	Exempt	N/A
Advance pharmaceutical supplement	Exempt	N/A
Age pension	Assessable	Exempt[1]
Australian Government Disaster Recovery Payment	Exempt	N/A
Australian Victim of Terrorism Overseas Payment	Exempt	N/A
Austudy payment	Assessable	Exempt[1]
Bereavement allowance (ceased 20 March 2020)	Assessable	Exempt[1]
Carer allowance	Exempt	N/A
Carer payment:		
– carer or care receiver is pension age or over	Assessable	Exempt[1]
– carer and care receiver under pension age (or care receiver deceased)	Exempt	Exempt[1]
– one-off payments (carer payment related)	Exempt	N/A
Carer supplement	Exempt	N/A
Child disability assistance	Exempt	N/A
Crisis payment	Exempt	N/A
Disability support pension:		
– over pension age	Assessable	Exempt[2]
– under pension age	Exempt	Exempt[2]
Double orphan pension	Exempt	N/A
Economic support payments (COVID-19)	Exempt	N/A
Education entry payment supplement	Exempt	N/A
Energy supplement	Exempt	N/A
Fares allowance	Exempt	N/A
JobSeeker Payment	Exempt	N/A
JobSeeker Coronavirus Supplement	Exempt	N/A
Mature age allowance	Assessable	Exempt
Mature age partner allowance	Assessable	Exempt[1]
Mobility allowance	Exempt	N/A
Newstart Allowance (ceased 20 March 2020)	Assessable	Exempt[3]
Parenting payment:		
– benefit PP (partnered)	Assessable	Exempt[3]
– pension PP (single)	Assessable	Exempt[3]
Partner allowance	Assessable	Exempt[3]
Pension education supplement	Exempt	N/A
Quarterly pension supplement	Exempt	N/A
Sickness allowance (ceased 20 March 2020)	Assessable	Exempt[1]
Special benefit	Assessable	Exempt[1]
Special needs age pension	Assessable	Exempt[1]
Special needs disability support pension:		
– pension age or over	Assessable	Exempt[1]
– under pension age	Exempt	Exempt[1]
Special needs widow B pension (ceased 20 March 2020)	Assessable	Exempt[1]

Pension, benefit or allowance	Basic amount	Supplementary amount
Special needs wife pension:		
– taxpayer or partner pension age or over	Assessable	Exempt[1]
– taxpayer and partner under pension age (or partner deceased)	Exempt	Exempt[1]
Telephone allowance	Exempt	N/A
Utilities allowance	Exempt	N/A
Widow allowance	Assessable	Exempt[3]
Widow B pension (ceased 20 March 2020)	Assessable	Exempt[1]
Wife pension (ceased 20 March 2020):		
– taxpayer or partner pension age or over	Assessable	Exempt[1]
– taxpayer and partner under pension age (or partner deceased)	Exempt	Exempt[1]
Youth Allowance	Assessable	Exempt[3]
Bereavement payments:		
– special provisions apply where a lump sum social security payment is made because of the death of the taxpayer's partner and the payment is an age pension, carer pension, disability support pension, mature age (pre-1 July 1996) allowance, mature age partner allowance, special needs age pension, special needs disability support pension, special needs wife pension or wife pension.		

(1) Increased amounts by way of: rent assistance; remote area allowance; pharmaceutical allowance; and incentive allowance.

(2) Increased amounts by way of: rent assistance; remote area allowance; pharmaceutical allowance; incentive allowance; language, literacy and numeracy supplement; pension supplement; and clean energy supplement.

(3) Increased amounts by way of: rent assistance; remote area allowance; pharmaceutical allowance; language, literacy and numeracy supplement; pension supplement; and clean energy supplement.

Changes to benefits

From 20 March 2020, the JobSeeker Payment replaced the Newstart Allowance as the main payment for people of working age. JobSeeker also replaced the widow B pension, wife pension, bereavement allowance and sickness allowance on the same date. The widow allowance closed to new entrants from 1 January 2018 and will cease on 1 January 2022, when all recipients have moved to the age pension. The partner allowance will cease from 1 January 2022.

[FITR ¶103-000, ¶103-510]

¶10-197 Other exempt government payments

In addition to the social security and veterans affairs payments listed at ¶10-195 and ¶10-200, the federal government also makes a range of other payments. These include the following exempt payments (special conditions may apply):

- cash flow boost payments (ITAA97 s 59-90)
- family tax benefit (ITAA97 s 52-150)
- child care benefit and child care rebate (ITAA97 s 52-150)

- single income family bonus and single income family supplement (ITAA97 s 52-150)
- Commonwealth education or training supplementary payment (ITAA97 s 52-140)
- economic security strategy payment (ITAA97 ss 52-150; 52-160)
- HomeBuilder grant (¶10-040)
- clean energy payments under the *Social Security Act 1991* (ITAA97 s 52-10)
- disability services payment made under the Commonwealth Rehabilitation Work Training Scheme (ITAA97 s 53-10, item 2)
- disaster recovery payments to special category visa (subclass 444) holders (ITAA97 s 51-30)
- payments from the Thalidomide Australian Fixed Trust (ITAA97 s 51-30)
- tobacco industry exit grant (ITAA97 s 53-10)
- Outer regional and remote payment under the Helping Children with Autism scheme (ITAA97 s 52-170)
- Outer regional and remote payment under the Better Start for Children with Disability initiative (ITAA97 s 52-172)
- payment under the Continence Aids Payment Scheme (ITAA97 s 52-175)
- National Disability Insurance Scheme (NDIS) payment (ITAA97 s 52-180)
- Prime Minister's Prizes for Australian History and Science (ITAA97 s 51-60)
- Prime Minister's Literary Awards (ITAA97 s 51-60).

[FITR ¶40-340, ¶102-560]

¶10-200 Veterans' pensions and similar benefits

The table below shows the status of pensions, benefits and allowances payable under the *Veterans' Entitlements Act 1986* (ITAA97 ss 52-60 to 52-110). Payments made because of a person's death are exempt (ITAA97 s 52-65(4)). In the case of non-exempt service pensions, a special rebate may be allowable to the recipient (¶15-310).

Pension, benefit or allowance	Basic amount	Supplementary amount
Age service pension	Assessable	Exempt[1]
Attendant allowance	Exempt	N/A
Carer service pension:		
– both taxpayer and partner are under pension age and partner receiving an invalidity service pension	Exempt	Exempt[1]
– taxpayer under pension age and invalidity service pensioner partner deceased	Exempt	Exempt[1]
– other	Assessable	Exempt[1]
Clean energy payment	Exempt	N/A
Clean energy payment under Veterans' Children Education Scheme	Exempt	N/A
Clothing allowance	Exempt	N/A
Decoration allowance	Exempt	N/A

Pension, benefit or allowance	Basic amount	Supplementary amount
Defence Force income support allowance:		
– where the whole of the underlying social security payment for which the allowance is paid is exempt	Exempt	N/A
Energy supplement	Exempt	N/A
Funeral benefit (veterans)	Exempt	N/A
Funeral benefit (dependants of deceased veterans)	Exempt	N/A
Income support supplement:		
– taxpayer under pension age and permanently incapacitated for work	Exempt	Exempt[1]
– both taxpayer and severely handicapped person constantly cared for under pension age	Exempt	Exempt
– both taxpayer and invalidity service pensioner or disability support pensioner partner under pension age	Exempt	Exempt
– both taxpayer and permanently incapacitated partner under pension age	Exempt	Exempt
– other	Assessable	Exempt[1]
Invalidity service pension:		
– pension age or over	Assessable	Exempt[1]
– under pension age	Exempt	Exempt[1]
Loss of earnings allowance	Exempt	N/A
Partner service pension:		
– both taxpayer and invalidity service pensioner partner under pension age	Exempt	Exempt[1]
– taxpayer under pension age and invalidity service pensioner partner deceased	Exempt	Exempt[1]
– other	Assessable	Exempt[1]
Pension for defence-caused death or incapacity	Exempt	N/A
Pension for war-caused death or incapacity	Exempt	N/A
Quarterly pension supplement	Exempt	N/A
Recreation transport allowance	Exempt	N/A
Special assistance	Exempt	N/A
Travelling expenses	Exempt	N/A
Vehicle Assistance Scheme	Exempt	N/A
Veterans supplement	Exempt	N/A
Victoria Cross allowance	Exempt	N/A
Bereavement payment:		
– payments made after the death of a person for a number of the above pensions, benefits and allowances are exempt		

(1) Increased amounts because of: rent assistance; dependent children; remote area allowance; pension supplement; and clean energy supplement.

Continuing payments under former Repatriation Acts

Pensions, attendants' allowances and similar payments under former Repatriation Acts — the *Repatriation Act 1920*, the *Repatriation (Far East Strategic Reserve) Act 1956*, the *Repatriation (Special Overseas Service) Act 1962* and the *Interim Forces Benefits Act 1947* — which continued to be paid under the *Veterans' Entitlements (Transitional Provisions and Consequential Amendments) Act 1986*, are generally exempt except for the part of a pension that is:

- an alternative to a widow's pension paid to the mother of a deceased member of the Forces, or
- an alternative to a social security pension paid to a parent of a deceased member of the Forces where the parent is of pension age (s 52-105).

[FITR ¶103-060, ¶103-090]

¶10-202 Pensions similar to veterans' pensions

Payments by the Australian and United Kingdom governments that are of a similar nature to exempt payments listed in ¶10-200 are also exempt (ITAA97 s 53-20). However, the exemption does not extend to ordinary Commonwealth Public Service or Defence Force superannuation or retirement payments (ITAA97 s 55-5).

An amount paid to a former soldier under the *Safety, Rehabilitation and Compensation Act 1988* was not exempt, as it was in the nature of workers compensation and was not similar to an income support pension payable to war widows and widowers under the *Veterans' Entitlements Act 1986* (*Davy*).

Certain service-related wounds and disability pensions that are of a kind specified in *Income and Corporation Taxes Act 1988* (UK) s 315(2) *and* similar to a payment of the kind discussed in ¶10-195 or ¶10-197 are exempt (ITAA97 s 53-10, item 5). The UK legislation exempts wounds pensions granted to members of the armed forces of "the Crown" and disablement or disability pensions granted to members, other than commissioned officers, of the armed forces on account of medical unfitness attributable to or aggravated by military service. The Commissioner accepts that the exemption applies to relevant pensions payable by "any Government" (IT 2586). The exemption applies to pensions paid to the person who suffered the wounds or disability but not to pensions paid to a surviving spouse (*Case T2*).

[FITR ¶103-510, ¶103-520, ¶104-510]

¶10-204 War-time compensation payments

A payment to an Australian resident person from a source in a foreign country is exempt from income tax if it is in connection with:

- any wrong or injury
- any loss of, or damage to, property, or
- any other detriment,

that the recipient, or another individual, suffered as a result of:

- persecution by the National Socialist regime of Germany during the National Socialist period
- persecution by any other enemy of the Commonwealth or by an enemy-associated regime during the Second World War
- flight from such persecution

- participation in a resistance movement during the Second World War against forces of the National Socialist regime of Germany or against forces of any other enemy of the Commonwealth (ITAA97 s 768-105).

The exemption extends to the legal personal representative of an individual, and to the trustee of a trust established by the will of a deceased individual, in the same way as it would apply to the individual. It also extends to compensation received in relation to an injury or wrong suffered by another person. However, for the exemption to apply, the payment must not be received from an ‘‘associate’’ (¶4-200) of the recipient. A similar exemption is provided by s 118-37 for a capital gain or loss made by an Australian resident individual as a result of receiving such compensation (¶11-650).

[FITR ¶585-210]

Insurance Proceeds — Accident/Disability/Life

¶10-210 Accident and disability policies

Periodical payments received by a taxpayer during a period of total or partial disability under a personal accident, income protection or disability insurance policy taken out by the taxpayer are assessable on the same principle as workers compensation (¶10-180), ie they are assessable where they are paid to fill the place of lost earnings (see, for example, *DP Smith*). This also applies to lump sums paid to settle all outstanding claims under the policy (*Sommer*).

An amount payable under a trauma insurance policy to an employee or self-employed person does not replace earnings lost by the taxpayer and is therefore not assessable income (and may also be exempt from CGT).

As to the deductibility of premiums paid on accident and disability policies, see ¶16-560.

¶10-220 Insurance on directors and employees

Amounts received by an employer under an *accident* (or term) policy taken out in respect of its directors and other employees are assessable as ordinary income if the purpose of the insurance is to fill the place of a revenue item (eg to replace profits lost through the loss of the employee’s services). This principle applies equally where the insured receiving the proceeds is not the actual employer but is a holding company which takes out accident insurance in relation to its subsidiary’s employees (*Carapark Holdings*).

The proceeds of these policies will not be assessable as income if the purpose of the insurance is to guard against a capital loss. This would apply where, for example, insurance is taken out by a company in respect of a director for the purpose of providing, in the event of the director’s death by accident, funds for the payment to the estate of a debt owing to the director.

The proceeds of a *life* (or endowment) policy taken out by an employer in respect of employees or a director are not assessable as income (IT 155).

The above rules also apply where insurance is taken out by a partner in respect of another partner or by a taxpayer in respect of a ‘‘key’’ business associate, even though the person is not an employee (eg a supplier).

For the application of the CGT provisions to insurance recoveries, see ¶11-880.

[FITR ¶53-358]

¶10-230 Life assurance and endowment policies

The lump sum proceeds of a life assurance or endowment policy are capital and not assessable as income even though they may be received in more than one instalment of the fixed capital sum. Similarly, an amount received on the surrender of such a policy is capital.

If, however, the policy provides for the payment of a pension or annuity and not a fixed sum, or allows the beneficiary the choice between a fixed sum and a pension, the pension payments are wholly or partly assessable. See further ¶14-220.

Where the holder of a life insurance policy has control over the investment of the funds paid over as life insurance premiums, the income credited to the investor's account is assessable income of the investor derived at the time of crediting (TD 92/166). This does not apply where the investor merely has the right to direct that the investment be placed in a particular class of investment operated by the insurer for investors generally.

For the application of the CGT provisions in relation to life insurance, see ¶11-880.

[FITR ¶53-358]

¶10-240 Bonuses on insurance policies

There are difference types of bonuses payable on life insurance policies: (1) annual bonuses; and (2) reversionary bonuses paid on maturity, forfeiture or surrender of a life policy.

Annual bonuses are assessable (ITAA97 s 15-75). However, the assessable income of a complying superannuation fund does not include a non-reversionary bonus on a life assurance policy (ITAA97 s 295-335, item 1; ¶13-140).

Reversionary bonuses received under short-term life policies taken out after 28 August 1982 are subject to the following special tax treatment if the risk commenced after 7 December 1983 (ITAA36 s 26AH):

(i) if received, reinvested or otherwise dealt with on the taxpayer's behalf or as he/she directs in the first 10 years, tax is phased in as follows: within 8 years of the commencement of risk — assessable in full; in the ninth year, assessable as to two-thirds; in the tenth year, assessable as to one-third (s 26AH(6)), unless the Commissioner gives a discretionary reduction (where the policy is forfeited or surrendered early and it would be unreasonable to include the full amount (s 26AH(8))). However, a tax offset of 30% is available (ITAA36 s 160AAB)

▶ Example

On 1 January 2015, A takes out a life policy. Six years later he surrenders the policy and receives a bonus of $1,200. The whole of the $1,200 forms part of A's assessable income in 2020–21. However, he is entitled to a tax offset under s 160AAB. The amount of the tax offset is calculated by applying the standard rate of tax to $1,200.

(ii) if received after 10 years, not assessable.

Exemptions

Exemptions also apply to:

- bonuses paid on pre-28 August 1982 policies
- amounts received as a result of death, accident, illness or other disability
- amounts received under a policy held by a superannuation fund or ADF (whether complying or not), PST or RSA provider, or effected for the purposes of a complying or non-complying superannuation scheme

- amounts received on the forfeiture, surrender or other termination of a policy in circumstances arising out of serious financial difficulties of the taxpayer (s 26AH(7)). This last exclusion does not apply where the policy was taken out or purchased with a view to it maturing or being terminated within 10 years.

Anti-avoidance

There are various anti-avoidance provisions in s 26AH designed to catch disguised bonuses (eg a low interest or interest-free loan received in relation to an eligible policy) (s 26AH(9), (13)).

[FITR ¶53-550, ¶270-380; FTR ¶15-975, ¶75-545]

Recoupments and Repayments

¶10-260 Assessability of recoupments as ordinary income

There is no general principle which establishes that a payment made as reimbursement of, or compensation for, an expense previously deducted is inherently income (*HR Sinclair*; *Rowe*), although there are specific statutory provisions dealing with recoupment (¶10-270).

It is the character of the receipt, not the fact of the reimbursement, that has to be considered. If the receipt is of an income character, it is assessable. For example, if deductible expenditure is incurred in the course of carrying on a business, a reimbursement in respect of that expenditure is similarly derived in the course of business and is properly treated as part of its proceeds (*Warner Music Australia*).

Disbursements incurred by a solicitor in respect of clients otherwise than as an agent are deductible and any amounts recovered are assessable as ordinary income (TR 97/6). A rebate paid under the Diesel Fuel Rebate Scheme will be assessable as ordinary income if paid as a consequence of the recipient's income-producing activities (TD 97/25). Statutory electoral funding provided to political parties is not assessable (ID 2006/72).

Note that a legally enforceable right to a recovery is an asset for CGT purposes. However, the CGT rules would not apply where a compensation payment is made where there was no right to recover and no other CGT asset is involved. In such a case, its assessability will depend on the application of ordinary income tax principles. For the special CGT provisions relating to insurance recoveries, see ¶11-880.

[FITR ¶18-225]

¶10-270 Statutory provisions dealing with recoupment

Special provisions operate to include in assessable income amounts received as recoupment for certain previously deducted losses or outgoings. The provisions are contained in ITAA97 Subdiv 20-A (ss 20-10 to 20-65). Subdivision 20-A does not apply, however, to amounts that are ordinary income or that are included in assessable income by any other provision.

For Subdiv 20-A to operate, there must be an ''assessable recoupment'' (s 20-20). ''Recoupment'' of a loss or outgoing is broadly defined to include any kind of reimbursement, refund, insurance, indemnity or recovery, or a grant in respect of the loss or outgoing (s 20-25(1)). An amount received as reimbursement of deductible legal expenses incurred in disputes concerning termination of employment was an assessable recoupment, not an eligible employment payment (TR 2012/8; *Falk*). A Commonwealth grant received for the establishment of windfarms was an assessable recoupment of an outgoing, even if the payment was treated as being on capital account (*Denmark Community Windfarm*). However, an amount received in settlement of a dispute concerning a failed retirement village development was not an assessable recoupment (*Batchelor*).

The concept of "indemnity" covers an adjustment in the vendor's favour for council and water rates and land taxes in a contract for the sale of a business or of real property (*Goldsbrough Mort & Co*). A taxpayer is also taken to receive a recoupment if another entity pays an amount on the taxpayer's behalf, or if the taxpayer receives an amount for disposing of the right to receive a recoupment (s 20-25(2), (3)).

An "assessable recoupment" is: (a) an amount received *by way of insurance or indemnity* as recoupment of a loss or outgoing deducted under any provision of ITAA97; or (b) an amount received as recoupment (*except* by way of insurance or indemnity) of a loss or outgoing deducted under any of the provisions of ITAA97 listed below:

Expenditure	**ITAA97 deduction**	**Reference**
Rates or taxes	8-1; 25-75	¶16-870
Bad debts	8-1; 25-35	¶16-580
Tax-related matters	25-5	¶16-850
Capital allowances	Div 40	¶17-000
Work in progress amounts	25-95	¶16-158
Contributions to fund-raising events	30-15 (items 7 and 8)	¶16-977
Mains electricity connection	Former Subdiv 387-E	¶16-820
Embezzlement by employee	25-47	¶16-590
R&D	Div 355	¶20-150
Election expenses	25-60; 25-65	¶16-500
Water conservation or conveyance	Former Subdiv 387-B	¶18-080
Land degradation prevention	Former Subdiv 387-A	¶18-100
Environmental impact study	Former Subdiv 400-A	
Environmental protection	Former Subdiv 400-B	¶19-110
Forex realisation loss	775-30	¶23-075
Registered emissions unit	420-15	¶19-130
Mining and quarrying	Former 330-80	¶19-010, ¶19-050
Transport of minerals and quarry materials	Former 330-370	¶19-090
Exploring, prospecting and mining	Former 330-15	¶19-010
Balancing adjustment — mining or quarrying	Former 330-485	¶17-630
Rehabilitating mining, quarrying and petroleum sites	Former 330-435	¶19-100
Horticultural plant establishment	Former Subdiv 387-C	¶18-070
Drought mitigation	—	¶18-000
Spectrum licences	Former Subdiv 380-A; 380-C	¶17-630
Software	Former Subdiv 46-B; 46-C; 46-D	¶17-490
GST plant	Former 25-80	
Petroleum resource rent tax	Former 330-350	¶19-003

Subdivision 20-A applies to recoupments of deductible rates and taxes, eg payroll tax, sales tax or FBT. It does not, however, apply to recoupments of income tax (¶16-856) or higher education contributions (except where incurred in providing a fringe benefit) (¶16-452) as these are not deductible.

A government rebate received by a rental property owner is an assessable recoupment where the owner is not carrying on a property rental business and receives the rebate for the purchase of a depreciating asset (eg an energy-saving appliance) for use in the rental property (TD 2006/31). However, an amount received as compensation for the estimated loss in value of depreciating assets is not an assessable recoupment (TR 2006/3).

Amount included in assessable income

Where the loss or outgoing was deducted in a single year, the assessable recoupment is included in assessable income in the year of receipt to the extent of the amount of the loss or outgoing. An assessable recoupment received in advance of the year in which the loss or outgoing is deducted is treated as having been received in the deduction year (s 20-35).

▶ Example 1

Retail Co writes off as bad in 2019–20 a trade debt of $1,000 previously included in assessable income and claims a deduction of $1,000 under ITAA97 s 25-35. In the 2020–21 year Retail Co recovers $700 from the debtor. The $700 receipt is an assessable recoupment and is included in Retail Co's assessable income in 2020–21.

In 2021–22 Retail Co receives a further payment of $400 from the debtor in respect of the same debt. The $400 receipt is also an assessable recoupment. Only $300 of this amount is included in Retail Co's assessable income in 2021–22. The balance of $100 is not assessable. (It is assumed in this example that the receipts of $700 and $400 are not ordinary income or statutory income because of a provision outside Subdiv 20-A.)

Where the loss or outgoing is deductible over several income years, the amount of assessable recoupment included in assessable income in the year of receipt is limited to the total amount deducted to date (including deductions in the year of receipt). Amounts may also be included in assessable income in subsequent income years to the extent deductions for the loss or outgoing are available in those years. The total amount of assessable recoupment included in assessable income over all income years cannot, however, exceed the loss or outgoing (s 20-40).

▶ Example 2

Manufacturing Co incurs $10 million in 2019–20 for the acquisition of plant which it commences to use in 2019–20. Its expenditure on the plant is deductible on a prime cost basis over 10 years commencing in 2019–20.

In 2020–21 Manufacturing Co receives a $5 million grant from the state government in respect of its plant expenditure. The $5 million receipt is an assessable recoupment and is included in assessable income as follows:

Income year	Deduction ($m)	Assessable recoupment ($m)	Assessable income ($m)
2019–20	1	—	—
2020–21	1	—	—
2021–22	1	5	3
2022–23	1	—	1
2023–24	1	—	1
2024–25	1	—	—
2025–26	1	—	—
2026–27	1	—	—
2027–28	1	—	—
2028–29	1	—	—
Total	10	5	5

Where the assessable recoupment relates to property for which a balancing charge has been included in assessable income in the current year or in an earlier year, the total amount deducted in respect of the property is taken to be reduced for recoupment purposes by the balancing charge (s 20-45).

▶ Example 3

Assume that in the previous example: (a) Manufacturing Co sells the plant at the end of 2020–21 for $9 million so that a balancing charge of $1 million is recognised in that year; and (b) Manufacturing Co still receives a $5 million grant in 2021–22. The amount of assessable recoupment included in Manufacturing Co's assessable income (in 2021–22) is still limited to the total of amounts deducted for the plant. However, this total ($2 million) is taken to be reduced by the balancing charge ($1 million) so that the amount included in assessable income under Subdiv 20-A is limited to $1 million.

In the case of *partly* deductible losses or outgoings, the amount of the assessable recoupment is taken to be correspondingly reduced and the amount of the loss or outgoing itself is taken for recoupment purposes to be only the *deductible* portion (s 20-50).

▶ Example 4

Heidi owns a rental property that is used 75% for income-producing purposes in 2020–21. She incurs expenditure of $800 on local council rates. In June 2021, Heidi receives a payment of $200 by way of reimbursement for this expenditure.

Heidi is taken to have received an assessable recoupment of $150 (ie 75% × $200). The expenditure incurred by her for Subdiv 20-A purposes is taken to be $600 (ie 75% × $800). As the deemed assessable recoupment of $150 does not exceed the deemed outgoing of $600, an amount of $150 is included in Heidi's assessable income in 2020–21.

Special rules apply where a taxpayer entitled to deductions in respect of an outgoing did not incur it, and the recoupment is received by the entity who incurred the outgoing. If the outgoing is deductible only to the taxpayer, Subdiv 20-A will apply as if the taxpayer had incurred the outgoing and received the recoupment (s 20-60). If the outgoing is deductible to 2 or more taxpayers (which may include the entity who incurred the outgoing), each taxpayer will be taken to have incurred the outgoing and to have received the recoupment to the extent to which deductions have been claimed by that taxpayer (deductions will be recouped in the order in which they were claimed) (s 20-65).

Superannuation contributions

Payments from a superannuation fund to an employer-sponsor which has been allowed a deduction for contributions to the fund are assessable (ITAA97 s 290-100).

[FITR ¶60-200]

¶10-280 Repayments of previously assessable income

The converse of a recoupment is where income derived during an income year is repaid in a later income year. In this situation, the taxpayer may be able to have the original assessment amended to exclude the amount repaid as non-assessable non-exempt income (ITAA97 s 59-30).

Under this provision, an amount received by a taxpayer is not assessable income for an income year if: (a) the taxpayer is required to repay it and does so in a later income year; and (b) the repayment is not deductible in any income year. The assessment for the earlier income year may therefore be amended, irrespective of whether the normal time for amendment of assessments has expired (ITAA36 s 170(10AA) item 22). It is irrelevant whether the amount repaid had originally been received as part of a larger amount, or whether the obligation to repay arose before or after the amount was received.

This provision may apply, for example, where a Defence Force member who has received a lump sum retention bonus is later required to make a pro rata repayment on early resignation. However, it does not apply where a taxpayer who has received instalments of workers compensation or sickness allowance has to repay them after receiving a lump sum payment of compensation or damages for a wrong or injury suffered in his/her occupation (ITAA97 s 59-30(3)).

An amount received by a taxpayer which is subject to a repayment arrangement, but has not yet been repaid, is not treated as "not assessable income" under s 59-30 (ID 2004/274).

The requirement that the repayment not be deductible means that the provision would not apply if a repayment is made as part of carrying on a business (¶16-010).

[FITR ¶108-070]

Isolated Property Transactions

¶10-340 Profits from sale of property

The question of when an isolated transaction or venture produces assessable income has always given rise to difficulties. In addition to general concepts of what constitutes ordinary income (¶10-010), there are a number of specific provisions which are relevant, including the CGT provisions.

The proceeds of a *mere* realisation or change of investment or from an enhancement of capital are not ordinary income (¶10-120 – ¶10-130). However, an isolated business transaction entered into with a view to making a profit may give rise to income according to ordinary concepts (¶10-112); this may also be the case if a capital asset is ventured in an undertaking or scheme which involves more than the mere realisation of the asset (¶10-120).

The disposal of property acquired after 19 September 1985, even if acquired as a long-term investment, may give rise to a capital gain within the meaning of the CGT provisions. If the disposal also gives rise to ordinary income, the capital gain will be reduced or eliminated to prevent double taxation (¶11-690). The Commissioner may, in fact, seek to assess the gain as ordinary income and not under the CGT provisions as the amount of tax recoverable may be greater (eg because of a CGT discount: ¶11-000).

Pre-CGT acquisitions

If property was acquired for the purpose of profit-making by sale before 20 September 1985, the profit arising is assessable under ITAA36 s 25A if sold at a profit before 1997–98 and under ITAA97 s 15-15 if sold at a profit in the 1997–98 or later income year. However, these sections do not apply if the relevant profit-making by sale of a pre-CGT property is assessable as ordinary income, eg as in *Whitfords Beach* (ITAA97 s 15-15(2); ¶10-120; ¶10-130).

[FITR ¶53-150; FTR ¶12-400, ¶12-510]

Profit on Sale of Leased Equipment

¶10-380 Profit on sale of leased cars

Where a leased car used for income-producing purposes is subsequently purchased by the lessee or an associate who then disposes of it, any profit made on the disposal is assessable in the hands of the lessee or associate, as the case may be, under ITAA97 Subdiv 20-B (ss 20-100 to 20-160). The profit is taxable on a basis which recoups the deductions claimed for the lease payments.

For the sale of leased property, other than a car, at a profit, see ¶10-422.

[FITR ¶60-410]

¶10-390 Conditions for application: Subdiv 20-B (disposal of leased car)

ITAA97 Subdiv 20-B applies to a taxpayer where:

- a car is leased to the taxpayer or to an associate of the taxpayer (a "lease" for these purposes does not include a hire purchase agreement or an agreement for the hiring of a car on a temporary or casual basis: ITAA97 s 20-155)
- the lease payments are wholly or partly deductible
- the taxpayer or associate (or an entity including the taxpayer or associate) acquires the car from the lessor, or another entity acquires the car from the lessor under an arrangement that enables the taxpayer or associate to acquire the car, and
- at any later time, the taxpayer disposes of the car for a profit, ie the consideration receivable for the disposal exceeds the sum of the cost to the taxpayer of acquiring the car plus any capital expenditure incurred by the taxpayer on the car after acquiring it (ITAA97 ss 20-110(1); 20-125(1)).

A "car" for Subdiv 20-B purposes is any motor-powered road vehicle (including a 4-wheel drive vehicle) designed mainly for carrying passengers.

"Consideration receivable" means:

- where the car is sold for a specific price — the sale price less the sale expenses (eg costs of advertising the vehicle for sale, sales commissions)
- where the car is sold with other property and no specific price is allocated to the car — the price reasonably attributable to the car less expenses
- where the car is traded in to buy another car — the value of the trade-in plus any other consideration received (eg a reduction in lease payments under a new lease: TR 98/15), or
- where the car is disposed of to an insurer because it is lost or destroyed — the amount or value received under the insurance policy (ITAA97 s 20-115(2)).

However, if the disposal of the car is a taxable supply, the consideration receivable does not include an amount equal to the GST payable on the supply (s 20-115(3)).

An "associate" is defined broadly for these purposes (ITAA97 s 995-1(1)).

Subdivision 20-B does not apply where the person selling the car inherited it (ITAA97 s 20-145).

[FITR ¶60-430 — ¶60-450, ¶766-350]

¶10-400 Amount assessable under Subdiv 20-B (disposal of leased car)

Where there is a profit (¶10-390) on the disposal of the car, the amount included in assessable income cannot exceed the lowest of:

- the amount of notional depreciation attributed to the lessee in respect of the lease period (¶10-410)
- the amount of deductible lease payments paid under the lease, or
- in a case where the disposal is not the first disposal after the acquisition of the car from the lessor — the amount by which the consideration receivable exceeds the cost of the car to the entity who acquired it from the lessor (including any capital expenditure incurred on the car by that entity) (ITAA97 ss 20-110(2); 20-125(2)).

The assessable profit is also reduced by any amount included in assessable income under any other provision apart from the depreciation balancing charge provisions, eg where the profit is income according to ordinary concepts (¶10-112) (ITAA97 s 20-150).

Where a car has been the subject of more than one lease to the taxpayer or an associate, the amount of profit included in assessable income is worked out by reference to the aggregated first and second limits for each lease (ITAA97 ss 20-110(3); 20-125(3); 20-130).

Where there is a sequence of disposals involving the lessee and associates, the maximum amount assessable in respect of any disposal after the first one is determined by reference to the 3 limits noted above, as further reduced by any amount(s) included in assessable income by virtue of any previous operation of ITAA97 Subdiv 20-B or another provision apart from the depreciation balancing charge provisions (ITAA97 s 20-140). Once a vehicle is disposed of by a lessee or an associate for a consideration that is not less than market value, Subdiv 20-B does not apply in relation to any subsequent disposal (ITAA97 s 20-135). Special rules apply where there is a disposal of only a part-interest in a car (ITAA97 s 20-160).

[FITR ¶60-440 — ¶60-490]

¶10-410 Calculation of notional depreciation under Subdiv 20-B (disposal of leased car)

One of the ceilings imposed on the profit which is assessable under ITAA97 Subdiv 20-B is the amount of notional depreciation attributed to the lessee for the lease period (¶10-400). This is a notional calculation; no depreciation would in fact have been allowed because the lessee was not the owner of the car.

The amount of notional depreciation is calculated by comparing the car's cost to the lessor for depreciation purposes as worked out under Div 40 (¶17-080) with the car's termination value (¶17-640), in accordance with the following formula (ITAA97 s 20-120):

$$\text{notional depreciation} = (\text{cost} - \text{termination value}) \times \frac{\text{number of days in lease period}}{\text{number of days lessor owned car}}$$

Where the termination value equals or exceeds the cost, the notional depreciation is zero.

▶ Example

Lease Co purchases a car for $30,000 on 1 July 2020 and, on 1 September 2020, leases the car to Mary for 2 years. The lease expires on 31 August 2022 and Mary purchases the car from Lease Co for $22,000. The notional depreciation is calculated as follows:

$$\text{notional depreciation} = \$(30{,}000 - 22{,}000) \times \frac{731}{793}$$
$$= \$7{,}374.52$$

If the car is subject to the car (depreciation) limit (¶17-200), both the cost and the termination value will be adjusted for the purposes of the notional depreciation calculation. See the example at ¶10-420.

[FITR ¶60-460]

¶10-420 Example of calculation under Subdiv 20-B (disposal of leased car)

The following example illustrates how the amount assessable under ITAA97 Subdiv 20-B on sale is calculated.

▶ Example

Assume that:

(1) on 1 March 2018, Cindy leases a BMW for a period of 36 months

(2) the lease payments are $1,600 per month

(3) use of the car by Cindy is 70% business and 30% private

(4) Cindy acquires the BMW from the lessor, Car Leasing Services, on expiry of the lease (ie 28 February 2021) for $40,000, its residual value

(5) Cindy sells the car in April 2021 for $60,000, and

(6) Car Leasing Services acquired the car on 15 February 2018 for a cost of $80,000 but it is subject to the car depreciation limit ($57,581 for the 2017–18 year) for the purpose of calculating the notional depreciation (¶17-200).

Cindy's actual profit on the acquisition and sale is $20,000 (ie $60,000 − $40,000). However, the amount included in Cindy's assessable income under Subdiv 20-B cannot exceed the lesser of:

- the amount of notional depreciation for the lease (see below), and
- the deductible lease payments of $40,320 (ie $1,600 × 36 × 70%).

Calculation of notional depreciation

The cost of the car to Car Leasing Services is limited to $57,466. The termination value for Car Leasing Services is adjusted as follows:

$$\text{termination value} = \$40{,}000 \times \frac{\$57{,}581}{\$80{,}000}$$

$$= \$28{,}790$$

The notional depreciation is calculated as follows:

$$\text{notional depreciation} = \$(57{,}581 - 28{,}790) \times \frac{1{,}096}{1{,}110}$$

$$= \$29{,}154$$

Since the actual profit ($20,000) is less than the amount of the notional depreciation ($29,154) and also the amount of the deductible lease charges ($40,320), the amount to be included in Cindy's assessable income in 2020–21 is $20,000.

¶10-422 Profit on sale of other leased equipment

An amount received by a taxpayer as a result of the sale, at a profit, of plant or equipment previously leased by the taxpayer (including a car, in which case special provisions also apply: ¶10-380) and used in the conduct of its business may be assessable as ordinary income; alternatively, the CGT provisions may apply (the CGT provisions do not apply to cars). Similarly, where a previously leased asset is traded in and the trade-in credit reduces the cost of a replacement asset or the lease payments under a lease for the new asset, all or part of the trade-in credit may be assessable under the depreciation provisions (if depreciation was allowed before the trade-in and the trade-in credit exceeds the written down value), or as ordinary income or under the CGT provisions (TR 98/15).

The assessability as ordinary income of gains realised on the sale of leased equipment is illustrated by *Reynolds*, where a log haulier sold a leased truck with the approval of the lessor. The surplus of the sale price over the amount required to pay out the lease was held to be income according to ordinary concepts because its receipt was closely related to the taxpayer's business. See also *Case X57*, where the profit arising on the trade-in of a leased truck for a new leased truck was assessable.

For the position where leases are assigned, see ¶23-230.

[FITR ¶19-225]

Gambling Wins • Prizes • Awards

¶10-430 Betting and gambling wins

Betting and gambling wins are not assessable (and losses not deductible) unless the taxpayer is carrying on a business of betting or gambling. The principal criteria for determining whether such a business is being carried on were summarised in *Brajkovich's case* as follows:

- whether the betting or gambling is conducted in a systematic, organised and businesslike way — betting activities did not amount to a business where the taxpayer did not maintain an office, employ staff, use a computer or keep detailed records (*Evans*; *Babka*)
- the volume and size of the betting or gambling — these factors of themselves are seemingly not conclusive (*Evans*). In *Case 49/96*, the taxpayer played blackjack at a casino for 30 hours a week using a card counting system. The AAT ruled that, even if his technique did turn the odds more in his favour, the modest size of his bets meant that it was simply not a business proposition
- whether the betting or gambling is related to, or part of, other activities of a businesslike character, such as bookmaking or training or breeding racehorses (eg *Trautwein*). In *Shepherd's case*, however, a taxpayer with a ''passion for horses'' who looked after the few racehorses she owned was not assessable on her betting wins and prize winnings (whether horse-breeding, training and/or racing activities constitute a business is considered in TR 2008/2)
- whether the form of betting or gambling is likely to reward skill and judgment or depends largely on chance — in the latter case, eg roulette or two-up, gambling is unlikely to ever constitute a business
- whether the taxpayer is betting or gambling principally for profit or for pleasure — merely indulging in a passion or satisfying an addiction will not constitute a business (eg *Martin*) and a pastime does not become a business merely because a person devotes considerable time to it (*Babka*).

The Commissioner will apply the above criteria in determining whether a business is being carried on, although ultimately each case depends on its own facts. However, there appears to be no Australian case in which the winnings of a mere punter or gambler have been held to be assessable (or the losses deductible). As stated in *Babka's case*, ''the intrusion of chance into the activity as a predominant ingredient'' will usually preclude such a finding (IT 2655).

Winnings from betting or other forms of gambling do not give rise to a capital gain under the CGT provisions (¶11-660), although the disposal of an asset constituting such winnings may give rise to a capital gain (or a capital loss) (¶11-660).

[FITR ¶19-310]

¶10-440 Prizes and awards

Windfall gains resulting from winning a prize in a lottery or in a competition are generally non-assessable. However, where a taxpayer makes regular appearances on radio or television programs, the rewards for appearing, whether appearance fees or prizes in cash or kind, may be assessable (IT 167).

The value of any prize under an investment-related lottery is assessable (ITAA36 s 26AJ). An investment-related lottery is one where the chance to win the prize arises because the taxpayer holds an investment with an investment body such as a bank. The section will not apply if the chance to win the prize or the prize itself is otherwise taxable. The time when the prize is taxed and the value at which it will be taxed depend on whether the prize is in the form of cash, a loan or other property or services. The taxpayer will be assessed even if the prize is provided to an associate or to another person under an arrangement to which the taxpayer or associate is a party. The section does not affect ordinary lotteries, games such as Lotto and Tattslotto, art unions and raffles, nor does it apply to loans provided by the Starr-Bowkett building societies.

Prizes or awards won as an incident of the taxpayer's income-producing or business activities will be assessable, eg an author's literary competition prize, the ''Farmer of the Year'' award, and prizes and awards made to a taxpayer carrying on a business as a sportsperson (¶10-050). On this basis, the cash proceeds of the sale of a car won by a newsagent in a newspaper's sales competition were assessable (*Case V6*).

BHP Awards for the Pursuit of Excellence are not assessable in the hands of recipients. Although they are sometimes made for achievements directly connected to the winner's vocation or business, the Commissioner accepts that they are personal windfalls which are tax-free (IT 2145).

Prizes or winnings from a lottery, game or competition do not give rise to a capital gain under the CGT provisions, although the disposal of an asset constituting such a prize or winnings may give rise to a capital gain (or a capital loss) (¶11-660).

[FITR ¶19-300; FTR ¶15-980]

¶10-450 Illegal gains

The tests for determining whether the proceeds from illegal activities or transactions (such as drug dealing, prostitution, SP bookmaking, insider trading or theft) are income according to ordinary concepts are the same as for receipts from legal activities or transactions (TR 93/25). For example, if illegal activities are such as to constitute a business, the proceeds will be income in nature (¶10-110).

Amounts received from an illegal activity or transaction which are later repaid or recovered are not deductible, but relevant assessments may be amended, subject to the appropriate time limits (¶25-300), to exclude such amounts from assessable income. See also ¶16-010.

Penalties and fines in relation to illegal activities are not deductible from any assessable income (¶16-845).

[FITR ¶31-587]

Distributions from Unit Trusts

¶10-460 Distributions to unit trust holders

Whether moneys distributed to unitholders in a unit trust (¶31-560) are taxable depends on the character of the moneys in the hands of the trustee prior to distribution (*Charles*). A distribution to unitholders out of income (but not exempt income) would be assessable income of the unitholders, but a distribution out of capital receipts would only be taxable in the hands of the unitholder to the extent that it represents an amount of assessable income of the trust estate, eg a net capital gain that accrues by reason of the CGT provisions. As to when a distribution is assessable, see ¶6-110 – ¶6-170.

Where the trustees are engaged in a business of buying and selling properties, the proceeds of sale would be of an income nature and distributions to unitholders would be assessable. Otherwise, profits from the disposal of properties acquired on or after 20 September 1985 would usually fall within the CGT provisions.

¶10-465 Financing unit trust arrangements

According to the Commissioner, the principle that the character of the money in the hands of the trustee determines its character in the hands of the unitholder (¶10-460) does not apply to what are known as "financing unit trust" arrangements. Under these arrangements, a financier provides funds for a project such as a property investment or development by subscribing for units in a unit trust, rather than by making a straight-out loan to the developer. The financier receives distributions from the trust instead of interest income.

The distributions are not assessable under the trust provisions, but are assessable in the hands of the financier because they arise from the commercial activities of the financier (IT 2512). This is so even if the distribution is of an amount that is capital in the hands of the trustee.

[FTR ¶50-510]

Interest

¶10-470 Assessability of interest income

Interest received by or accrued to a resident is usually assessable income whatever its source or the form of payment, eg as a lump sum (*Case W40*). Interest paid on the amount of compensation determined by a court or tribunal for the compulsory acquisition of property is assessable (*Haig*; *Case 2/2005*). The lump sum consideration received for the assignment by a lender of its right to interest under a loan was held to be assessable in *Myer Emporium* (¶10-020). The ATO has confirmed that pensioners do not have to pay tax on interest notionally assessed for social security purposes on amounts held in cash or low interest accounts.

Pre-judgment interest awarded in a settlement for underpayment of wages is assessable (ID 2003/404). However, neither the pre-judgment nor the post-judgment interest components of damages awarded by a court for a taxpayer's personal injuries are assessable (¶10-185).

Interest income on a joint bank account is assessable to the account holders in proportion to their beneficial ownership of the money in the account. Unless there is evidence to the contrary, it is presumed that joint account holders beneficially own the money in equal shares (TD 2017/11). In *Tanumihardjo*, the taxpayer argued that she was not assessable on interest accruing on an account jointly held with her mother because she was the nominee of her mother who was not resident in Australia. However, there is a "presumption of advancement", which the taxpayer was unable to rebut, that an investment, made by a parent in the name of a child, is owned beneficially by the child. Accordingly, one-half of the interest was assessable to the taxpayer.

Where an employee misappropriates funds belonging to an employer, a constructive trust arises for the employer and any interest accruing on those funds is income of the employer as beneficiary (*Zobory*).

Interest derived by a resident from sources outside Australia is subject to Australian tax, but a tax offset is allowed against the Australian tax for any foreign tax paid on that income (¶21-680). Interest on loans raised in Australia by advertisement, prospectus or otherwise by any foreign government or semi-government body is deemed to have an Australian source in the hands of an Australian resident lender (ITAA36 s 27).

Generally speaking, interest received by a non-resident which is an outgoing of an Australian business is not included in assessable income but is subject to a flat rate withholding tax of 10%. Where, however, the non-resident carries on business in Australia through a permanent establishment, withholding tax does not apply and the interest is assessable by the normal assessment process — but only, of course, to the extent that it has an Australian source. Interest on *certain* foreign loans is exempt from withholding tax and indeed from all Australian taxation (¶22-020). Payments made by a borrower to indemnify a non-resident lender against liability for interest withholding tax are not themselves interest (*Century Yuasa Batteries Pty Ltd*), but may be assessable as business income (¶10-112). The source of interest payments is considered at ¶21-070.

Interest is usually taxed as and when received except in the case of a money-lending business which uses the accruals basis of accounting (¶9-030). Interest may, however, be constructively received without actual receipt if it is made available to the lender's use or is capitalised or otherwise dealt with on behalf of or at the direction of the lender (¶9-080). An accruals basis of accounting is imposed for interest relating to certain discounted and other deferred interest securities (¶23-320).

Interest offset arrangements, under which a bank or other financial institution allows a customer to use savings to offset borrowings, eg a home mortgage, are generally structured so that no interest is derived by the customer and therefore there is no tax liability in respect of the benefit arising from the account. TR 93/6 explains which interest offset arrangements are acceptable to the Commissioner. If the arrangement involves a single account and there is an entitlement to interest on credit balances, any interest credited is assessable and the account may only qualify as an acceptable arrangement when it is in debit. If the arrangement involves dual accounts (ie a loan account and a deposit account), it will not be acceptable unless the customer has no legal or equitable entitlement to receive interest on the amounts credited to the deposit account. One person's deposit account cannot be linked to another person's offset arrangement except in limited circumstances, for example where a husband and wife's mortgage account is linked to the wife's deposit account. In addition, the Commissioner will not accept an arrangement which attempts to link an existing deposit account with a loan account which might be taken out in the future. A customer is advised to seek approval for a particular arrangement by requesting a private ruling (¶24-560).

The ''principle of mutuality'' (¶3-810) extends to interest received by a body corporate in respect of late levies paid by proprietors, ie such interest is not assessable income of the body corporate (TR 2015/3).

Where a taxpayer deposits funds in an insurance bond account and the insurer invests the funds and uses the resulting interest to discount the premiums otherwise payable by the taxpayer, the interest is earned by the taxpayer and not the insurer (IT 2546).

Interest on government and semi-government securities is assessable in the same way as other interest. See also ¶23-400 and ¶23-410. For the sale of securities cum interest, see ¶23-430.

Interest payable by the Commissioner under the *Taxation (Interest on Overpayments and Early Payments) Act 1983* (¶25-440, ¶28-170) is assessable under ITAA97 s 15-35 in the year in which it is received or otherwise applied against any tax liability of the taxpayer.

Interest paid by the Commonwealth from 1 July 2013 on unclaimed moneys reclaimed (bank accounts, corporate property and life insurance amounts) is exempt (s 51-120). For the treatment of interest on unclaimed superannuation moneys reclaimed, see ¶13-850.

For rules distinguishing interest paid to a company creditor from returns on equity in the company, see ¶23-100.

[FITR ¶19-035, ¶53-400]

¶10-480 Interest from children's savings accounts

Interest earned on a child's savings account may in some circumstances be treated as income of the parent, rather than the child. The Commissioner's views are set out in TD 2017/11 as follows:

- if the money in the account really belongs to the parent, in the sense that the parent provided the money and may spend it as he/she likes, then it will be treated as belonging to the parent and the interest should be included in the parent's return. If the money belongs to the child and the child's total income (excluding wages and other payments for work personally performed) for 2017–18 is less than $416 (¶2-160), no tax is payable and a tax return will not be required (a return will be required if the child receives wages from which PAYG instalments have been withheld: ¶24-010)
- where a parent operates an account on behalf of a child, but the Commissioner is satisfied that the child beneficially owns the money in the account, the parent can nonetheless show the interest in a tax return lodged for a child. The lodgment of a trust tax return will not be necessary
- where interest income on a bank account is assessable to a child under 18, that income may be subject to higher rates of tax under the rules in ITAA36 Pt III Div 6AA that apply to the income of certain children (¶2-160).

[FITR ¶28-090]

Dividends and Distributions

¶10-490 Dividends and distributions

For details of the tax treatment of dividends, see ¶4-100. For the treatment of *deemed* dividends, see ¶4-200.

Rents and Royalties

¶10-500 Rents and premiums

Rents under a lease and hiring charges (eg for the use of plant or machinery) are assessable as ordinary income. They are generally assessable on a receipts basis (¶9-050). Rental income earned by co-owners of a property must generally be shared according to their legal interests except where they can establish that their equitable interests are different; a partnership agreement varying profit and loss entitlements only has effect where there is also a partnership at general law, ie where ownership constitutes a business (TR 93/32) (¶5-000). Amounts received from a lessee, whether as damages or otherwise, for non-compliance with a lease obligation to repair business premises are specifically assessable under ITAA97 s 15-25 to the extent that they are not of an income nature.

Payments which are not in a true sense rental but are premiums received for the grant, assignment or surrender of a lease, or amounts received for the lessor's consent to such action, are generally capital receipts. However under ITAA36 s 26AB, a premium (or a payment in the nature of a premium) received in respect of the assignment (or assent to the assignment) of a lease of property granted before 20 September 1985 which, at the time of the assignment, was not intended by the assignee (or some other person) to be used for income-producing purposes is, with certain exceptions (eg a mining lease), assessable. If part of the property was, at the relevant date, intended to be used for income-producing purposes, only a portion of the premium will be assessable (s 26AB(3)). A premium received in respect of the assignment (or assent to the assignment) of a lease granted on or after 20 September 1985 may be assessable under the CGT provisions (¶11-320). The CGT implications of granting a lease are discussed at ¶11-300.

A lump sum payment received for granting a life time right for a relative to reside in an investment property is assessable where the tenant has a right to a pro rata refund on vacating the property (ID 2003/526).

There are no tax consequences where the owner of a residence permits persons to share it on the basis that all the occupants, including the owner, bear an appropriate proportion of the costs actually incurred on food, electricity, etc (IT 2167). Amounts received by host families under educational ''homestay'' arrangements would normally be treated as non-commercial and not assessable (ID 2001/381).

The taxation of cash and non-cash lease incentives is considered at ¶10-116. For the treatment of rental income received through the sharing economy, see ¶2-135.

[FITR ¶53-300; FTR ¶15-750]

¶10-505 Improvements by lessee

The value of improvements effected on leasehold land by a lessee, which, on termination of the lease, by effluxion of time or otherwise, eventually benefit the lessor, are generally capital and not assessable to the lessor as ordinary income. The relevant CGT provisions are considered at ¶12-680.

[FITR ¶165-040]

¶10-510 Royalties

The word ''royalty'' is used in 2 senses for income tax purposes: its ordinary meaning and the extended statutory definition in ITAA36 s 6(1) — see below. Royalties in the ordinary sense of the word are assessable under ITAA97 s 6-5 if they are of an income nature, and are assessable under ITAA97 s 15-20 if they are capital in nature. Payments which are *not* royalties within the ordinary meaning of the word, but which fall within the extended statutory definition in s 6(1), are assessable under s 6-5 provided they are of an income nature. Payments falling within the extended definition which are not royalties in the ordinary sense and which are capital in nature may be taxable under the CGT provisions. *Case U33* (noted below), which pre-dated the commencement of the CGT provisions, provides an example of a royalty which fell within the statutory definition but was not assessable because it was a capital receipt.

Royalties are generally assessable only when actually or constructively received. But note that advance payments on account of royalties, if they are truly advances and are not intended to be repaid, are assessable.

In the case of royalties derived from overseas, if withholding tax is deducted at source before the royalties are paid, the taxpayer remains assessable on the gross amount of the royalties, not just the net amount actually received (*Case V122*), although the taxpayer may be entitled to a foreign income tax offset (¶21-680). A withholding tax applies to royalties paid or credited to non-residents (¶22-030).

Ordinary meaning of royalty

The ordinary meaning (ie dictionary definition) of ''royalty'' for income tax purposes encompasses the following types of payment:

- a payment to a land-owner by the lessee of a mine in return for the privilege of working it
- a payment to the owner of a patent for the use of it
- a payment to an author, editor, or composer for each copy of a book, piece of music, etc, sold by the publisher, or for the representation of a play.

Thus the word royalty, in its ordinary sense, has been used to describe payments made to a singer in respect of recordings made of his songs, sums paid for a right to cut timber where based on the quantity cut and payments for removing furnace slag from land.

Payments for the provision of ‘‘know-how’’ have been held not to be royalties within the ordinary meaning of the word (*Sherritt Gordon Mines*), although they would now be caught by the extended statutory definition. A payment to a taxpayer for sharing its knowledge of how to maintain the purity of uncontaminated breeding stock was also not a royalty within the ordinary meaning of the term, although it fell within the statutory definition of royalty (see below). The payment was not of a capital nature as the taxpayer was entitled to continue to use its know-how; the payment was therefore assessable as ordinary income (*Case W10*).

Monthly payments received by a milk producer for assigning its right to a source of future income were held not to be royalties within the ordinary meaning of the term as they did not relate to the frequency, value or volume of milk supplied, although they were assessable as ordinary income (*Moneymen*). On appeal, the Full Federal Court upheld the decision that the payments were assessable as ordinary income (¶10-020) and did not need to consider whether they were assessable as royalties.

A lump sum will be a royalty if it is a pre-estimate or after the event recognition of the amount of use made of the privilege or right. However, in one case, a lump sum characterised in the agreement under which it was payable as an advance payment in respect of royalties was held, on the proper construction of the agreement, to be consideration for the grant of an exclusive licence to ‘‘make, have made, use and sell’’ the relevant item. Accordingly, the lump sum was not a royalty within the ordinary meaning of the term and also was not income (*Case U33*). Note that the CGT provisions may now apply in a case of this kind. In contrast, in the *Henry Jones (IXL) case* a lump sum payment received from a financial institution as consideration for the taxpayer assigning its rights to receive annual royalties under a licence agreement was held to be assessable income (¶10-020).

Extended definition of royalty

The extended definition of ‘‘royalty’’ in s 6(1) includes any amount paid or credited, however described or computed, and whether the payment is periodical or not, to the extent to which it is paid or credited as consideration for:

(1) the use of, or the right to use, any copyright, patent, design or model, plan, secret formula or process, trade mark, or other like property or right (eg payments to an author for the use of the author’s copyright in an article: TD 2006/10)

(2) the use of, or the right to use, any industrial, commercial or scientific equipment (‘‘equipment’’ does not have a narrow meaning and includes things such as machinery and apparatus: IT 2660)

(3) the supply (presumably by any means whatsoever and including indirectly through an agent or employee: IT 2660) of scientific, technical, industrial or commercial knowledge or information (eg the knowledge shared in *Case W10* — see above)

(4) the supply of any assistance that is ancillary and subsidiary to, and is furnished as a means of enabling the application or enjoyment of, any property, right, equipment, knowledge or information mentioned in (1) to (3)

(5) the use of, or the right to use, motion picture films, films or video tapes for use in connection with television, or tapes for use in connection with radio broadcasting

(6) the reception of, or the right to receive, visual images and/or sounds transmitted to the public by satellite, cable, optic fibre or other similar technology

(7) the use of, or the right to use, in connection with television or radio broadcasting visual images and/or sounds transmitted by satellite, cable, optic fibre or other similar technology

(8) the use of, or right to use, part of the spectrum specified in a spectrum licence, and

(9) a total or partial forbearance in relation to any property, right, equipment, knowledge, information, assistance, etc, specified in (1) to (8) (this would cover, for example, a payment to the owner of technology not to make the technology available to any other person).

IT 2660 states that the extended definition of "royalty" encompasses a payment for the use of, or the right to use, a right, property, knowledge, etc, even though it is not used physically by the person making the payment or is not supplied directly by the person to whom the payment is made (eg a payment by a film distributor to a non-resident for the distributor's right to exploit a film by allowing cinema owners to exhibit it). Guidelines on when amounts paid as consideration for the assignment of copyright are royalties under the extended definition are set out in TR 2008/7.

IT 2660 also deals with the distinction between royalty payments and payments for services. Payments for services are not royalties, unless they are ancillary to, or part and parcel of, enabling relevant technology, information, know-how, copyright, machinery or equipment to be transferred or used. Whether a payment is a royalty payment or a payment for services depends on the nature and purpose of the arrangement having regard to the circumstances of the particular case. A contract for the supply or use of a "product" which is already in existence (or substantially in existence) is more likely to be a contract for the supply of know-how, payments under which will be royalties. In the Commissioner's view, a contract for services is likely to involve a much greater level of expenditure. If both know-how and services are supplied under the same contract, an apportionment of the 2 elements may be necessary.

As regards payments in relation to computer software, a payment is considered to be a royalty (including under the statutory definition) where it is consideration for: (a) the granting of a licence to reproduce or modify a computer program in a manner that would, without such a licence, constitute an infringement of copyright (eg payments for the right to manufacture copies of a program from a master copy for distribution and for the right to modify or adapt a program); or (b) the supply of know-how (eg payments for the supply of the source code or algorithms of a program) (TR 93/12). However, the following are *not* considered to be royalties for income tax purposes: (a) payments for the transfer of all rights relating to copyright in the program; (b) payments for the granting of a licence which allows only simple use of the software; (c) payments for the provision of services in the modification or creation of software; and (d) the proceeds from a sale of goods (eg where hardware and software are sold without being unbundled) (TR 93/12). Payments for the exclusive right to use a broadcasting licence and an apparatus licence are not royalties (ID 2006/307), nor are payments for the surrender of data licensing rights (ID 2007/4).

The expanded definition of royalty is particularly relevant in the case of non-residents whose liability to Australian tax is limited to Australian source assessable receipts. ITAA36 s 6C deems royalties paid or credited to non-residents which are an outgoing of an Australian business to have an Australian source (¶22-030). Note that if there is a conflict between the definition of royalty in s 6(1) and the definition in a double taxation agreement, the latter definition will override s 6(1). In *Seven Network*, it was held that payments made for the broadcasting rights to the Olympic Games were not "royalties" as defined in the Australia and Switzerland DTA (¶22-030).

Resale royalty payments

Under the *Resale Royalty Right for Visual Artists Act 2009*, visual artists are entitled to a royalty payment on the sale price of any commercial resale of their original works of art over $1,000 for works acquired after 9 June 2010. The resale royalty is 5% of the sale price.

Copyright Agency Limited is responsible for collecting resale royalty payments and distributing them to the visual artists. Royalty payments received by Copyright Agency Limited are exempt income, as is other income derived by the society to the extent it does not exceed the lesser of $5 million and 5% of its total income for the income year (ITAA97 s 51-43; ¶3-450). In turn, royalty payments received by an artist from Copyright Agency Limited, except to the extent that any amount of the payment is assessable to the collecting society, are assessable income of the artist (ITAA97 s 15-23).

[FITR ¶53-250; FTR ¶3-880]

¶10-520 Payments for mining, quarrying or prospecting information

An amount received by a taxpayer for providing mining, quarrying or prospecting information to another entity is assessable, provided that the taxpayer continues to retain economic ownership of the information (ITAA97 s 15-40). However, if the taxpayer started to hold the information before 1 July 2001, the assessable amount is reduced by so much of the pre-1 July 2001 capital cost of acquiring the information as was deductible.

This rule, which is associated with the introduction of the uniform capital allowance system (¶17-000), does not apply if the amount received is assessable in any event as ordinary income.

[FITR ¶53-420]

Exempt Income

¶10-600 Classes of exempt income

Exempt income can be divided into the 2 main classes listed in ITAA97 s 11-1:

(1) income of particular entities that are exempt from income tax (¶10-604 and following), no matter what kind of ordinary or statutory income they have (see the listing in s 11-5)

(2) income of a particular type that is exempt, including income that is exempt only if it is derived by certain entities (see the listing in s 11-15).

Some exemptions and exclusions are discussed in other chapters and these are noted at ¶10-885. Miscellaneous exemptions which are more or less self-explanatory are also listed at ¶10-885. Exemption from withholding tax is discussed at ¶22-010 – ¶22-030. For a list of non-taxable items, see the checklist at ¶10-005.

[FITR ¶25-000, ¶40-300]

¶10-602 Sovereign immunity

The sovereign immunity tax exemption is governed by ITAA97 Div 880 which commenced on 1 July 2019. Before 1 July 2019, under a longstanding administrative arrangement, the ATO provided a tax exemption for foreign government investors on income from "non-commercial" investments. The ATO generally exempted a sovereign investor from interest and dividend withholding taxes, capital gains tax and tax on trust distributions where the investor was not acting in a commercial capacity and did not influence the decision-making of an entity. Transitional rules apply to protect existing arrangements from the impact of Div 880.

From 1 July 2019, the sovereign immunity tax exemption applies to situations where sovereign investors have an ownership interest of less than 10% and do not have influence over the entity's key decision making. Tax applies to active business income earned through a trust.

A "sovereign entity" is any of the following:

- a body politic of a foreign country or a part of a foreign country
- a foreign government agency, including a foreign government or government authority or

- a foreign resident entity which is wholly owned by a body politic of a foreign country or a part of a foreign country, or a foreign government agency.

A sovereign entity is liable to pay tax on its taxable income. However, an amount of ordinary income or statutory income of a sovereign entity will be non-assessable non-exempt (NANE) income if, broadly:

- the amount is a return on a portfolio-like membership interest, debt interest or non-share equity interest in an Australian company or MIT and
- no member of the sovereign entity group has influence (either directly or indirectly) over decisions that comprise the control and direction of the operations of the Australian company or MIT. The views of the ATO on the influence test are found in LCR 2020/3.

An amount of ordinary income or statutory income that is NANE income of a sovereign entity will also be exempt from withholding tax.

Generally, a sovereign entity will be liable to pay income tax on its taxable income at a rate of 30%.

[FITR ¶660-000]

Exempt Organisations, Funds and Persons

¶10-604 Exempt entities: general rules

The definition of ‘‘exempt entity’’ includes an entity whose whole ordinary and statutory income is exempt from income tax under ITAA97 or any other Commonwealth law, and all untaxable Commonwealth entities.

An organisation or fund that is not operated for profit, or for the individual gain of its members or promoters, is not automatically exempt from paying income tax. However, the income of the various organisations and funds listed in ¶10-605 is exempt. The exemption may be denied if a tax avoidance agreement is involved (¶10-620). The application of the mutuality principle or s 59-35 should also be considered (¶3-810).

To be classified as ‘‘non profit’’ or ‘‘not-for-profit’’, an organisation’s governing documents or rules must prohibit the distribution of profits to its members and provide for the distribution of any assets remaining on a winding up to another non-profit organisation (*Cancer and Bowel Research Association*).

The main exemptions are found in ITAA97 Div 50 (ss 50-1 to 50-75).

Companies controlled by exempt entities

A non-profit company will not be exempt merely because it is controlled by an entity or entities that are exempt under Div 50. The company must itself be covered by the tables in that Division (TR 2005/22).

General rules for certain categories

Some general rules apply for income derived by certain categories of organisations to be exempt. The organisations affected are those under the headings of: charity, education and science; community service; employment; finance; health; and sports, culture, film and recreation.

In general, for its income to be exempt, the organisation must:

- have a physical presence in Australia, and incur its expenditure and pursue its objects principally in Australia. In *Word Investments*, the High Court held that a company that distributed its funds to a charitable institution which used the funds overseas satisfied this requirement
- be listed in one of the deductible gift tables (¶16-952)

- distribute solely to:
  - charities located in Australia that incur their expenditure principally in Australia and pursue their charitable purposes solely in Australia, and/or
  - deductible gift recipients (DGRs) (including non-charity DGRs such as public universities, public museums and public art galleries), or
- be a prescribed organisation either:
  - located outside Australia and exempt in the country of residence, or
  - with a physical presence in Australia but which incurs its expenditure and pursues its objects principally outside Australia.

TR 2019/6 sets out the ATO's view on what the phrase ''in Australia'' means for the purpose of working out whether certain funds, authorities and institutions are eligible to be deductible gift recipients (DGRs) and whether the income of certain charities and not-for-profit entities is tax exempt. For example, an entity will meet the ''in Australia'' condition if it is established or legally recognised in Australia and it operates in Australia. An entity satisfies the Div 50 ''in Australia'' condition where it has a physical presence in Australia and, to that extent, incurs its expenditure and pursues its objectives principally in Australia.

In determining whether an institution, etc, incurs its expenditure or pursues its objects principally in Australia, distributions of an amount received by way of gift or government grant or from a gift-deductible fund that it operates are disregarded (s 50-75).

Prescribed organisations and institutions can be found in the Income Tax Assessment Regulations 1997 (ITR97) regs 50-50.01 and 50-50.02.

[FITR ¶102-002]

¶10-605 Exempt entities: listing

A checklist of ''entities that are exempt no matter what kind of ordinary or statutory income they have'' is set out in ITAA97 s 11-5, together with the provision of the tax law under which each exemption is granted. Those exemptions are discussed below under the same category headings that appear in the checklist. The final category of exemptions discussed below (international organisations and office holders) is not listed in s 11-5, as those exemptions are granted by different legislation.

Charity, education and science

Entities that qualify for exemption under this category include: charitable, scientific and public educational institutions; a fund established by will or instrument of trust for public charitable purposes; a fund established to enable scientific research to be conducted by or in conjunction with a public university or public hospital; and a non-profit society, association or club established for the encouragement of science (ITAA97 s 50-5). Religious institutions would normally qualify as charities.

It should be noted that special conditions apply as follows:

- a registered charity must satisfy the special conditions in ITAA97 s 50-50 — these include that the fund comply with all the substantive requirements of its governing rules and apply its income and assets solely for the purpose for which it was established (TR 2015/1). Further, the charity must be endorsed by the Commissioner as exempt (¶10-610)
- scientific institutions and public educational institutions must satisfy the requirements in ITAA97 s 50-55
- scientific research funds must satisfy the requirements in ITAA97 s 50-65
- bodies established for the encouragement of science must satisfy the requirements in ITAA97 s 50-70.

"Institution"

"Institution" has its ordinary meaning and does not encompass a mere trust (*Douglas*). An organisation is not an "institution" where it is controlled by family members and friends, and the fact that an organisation is incorporated does not necessarily mean it is an institution (*Pamas Foundation*).

"Charitable"

"Charitable" has been used in ITAA97 in its common law technical, legal sense. From 1 January 2014 it has changed as a result of the enactment of a statutory definition in the *Charities Act 2013* (see further below).

At common law, there are 4 recognised heads of charity: (1) the advancement of education; (2) the relief of poverty; (3) the advancement of religion; and (4) other purposes beneficial to the community. Generally, the charitable purpose must also be directed to the benefit of the community; the Commissioner considers that a public benefit may be presumed under the first 3 heads but that it needs to be established under the fourth head (TR 2011/4).

A body that presented views on vocational training was a charitable institution under the advancement of education head (*Property Services Industry Training Advisory Board*). A foundation promoting innovation and entrepreneurship was held to be exempt on the basis that its objects and operations were for purposes beneficial to the community (*Triton Foundation*). A company established to assist Tasmanian business to adopt electronic commerce and to compete in the electronic marketplace was a charitable institution (*Tasmanian Electronic Commerce Centre*). An association incorporated for the advancement of women in the legal profession was charitable because its purposes were beneficial to the community (*Victorian Women Lawyers' Association*). A division of medical practitioners was a charitable organisation despite the fact that most of its funding was provided by a Commonwealth department under project grants and outcomes-based funding agreements (*Central Bayside*). Further, a cycling promotion association was entitled to endorsement as a charitable organisation because its purpose was to benefit the community (*Bicycle Victoria*).

Significantly, the High Court has found that a company which raised funds exclusively for supporting exempt charities was itself charitable; the fact that the company raised funds through a commercial enterprise did not preclude it from being a charity (*Word Investments Ltd*).

An institution which monitored, researched and campaigned to government about the delivery of overseas aid with the objective of promoting aid programs that were environmentally sound and effectively delivered was held to be charitable under the fourth head (other purposes beneficial to the community); the High Court held that there was no general rule excluding "political objects" from charitable purposes (*Aid/Watch Incorporated*).

TR 2011/4 describes the circumstances in which an institution or fund will be considered charitable. TR 2004/8 includes a less comprehensive discussion of the subject. Registration as a charity under state or territory law does not mean the institution is automatically exempt.

The common law meaning of a "charity" is extended by the *Extension of Charitable Purpose Act 2004* to include:

- organisations providing child care to the public on a non-profit basis
- self-help bodies with open and non-discriminatory membership
- closed or contemplative religious orders that offer prayerful intervention for the public.

The statutory definition

As indicated above, a statutory definition of charity applies for the purposes of the Commonwealth taxation laws from 1 January 2014. The statutory definition generally preserves the common law principles by introducing a statutory framework based on those principles but incorporating minor modifications to modernise and provide greater clarity and certainty about the meaning of charity and charitable purpose. Some points to note in relation to the definition are as follows:

- the purpose of preventing and relieving sickness, disease or human suffering, the purpose of advancing education, the purpose of relieving the poverty, distress or disadvantage of individuals or families, the purpose of caring for and supporting the aged or people with disabilities, and the purpose of advancing religion are presumed as being for the public benefit, unless there is evidence to the contrary
- an entity that directs benefits to persons who are related may fail the public benefit test. However, where the purpose of an entity that has land rights related assets would fail a public benefit test solely because the entity directs benefits to Indigenous Australians who are related, the purpose is treated as being for the public benefit
- the public benefit test does not apply to open and non-discriminatory self help groups, closed or contemplative religious orders or where the purpose is directed to one or more individuals in necessitous circumstances, as described in ITAA97
- a purpose of engaging in, or promoting, activities which are unlawful or contrary to public policy is disqualifying. Public policy refers to such matters as the rule of law and system of government. It does not refer to government policies
- a purpose of promoting or opposing a political party or candidate is disqualifying
- categories of charitable purposes are: advancing health; advancing education; advancing social or public welfare; advancing religion; advancing culture; promoting reconciliation, mutual respect and tolerance between groups of individuals that are in Australia; promoting or protecting human rights; advancing the security or safety of Australia or the Australian public; preventing or relieving the suffering of animals; advancing the natural environment; and any other purpose beneficial to the general public that may reasonably be regarded as analogous to, or within the spirit of, these purposes
- promoting or opposing a change to any matter established by law, policy or practice in the Commonwealth, a state, a territory or another country, in furtherance or protection of one or more of the above purposes
- charitable purpose extends beyond the relief of individual distress after a disaster to include assisting with the rebuilding of a community within specified limits, and
- funding charity-like government entities does not prevent a contributing fund from being charitable for the purposes of Commonwealth law.

"Scientific"

The "scientific" category includes associations for professionals in a scientific field, eg the Royal Australasian College of Surgeons, but only if their main purpose is scientific. (See *Australian Dental Association (NSW Branch)*, in which the Association was held to be of a professional nature and not exempt.)

"Educational"

A public educational institution must be available to the public or a section of it. A national association of surveyors was not a public educational institution as it merely had a co-ordinating role, not an educational one (*Case 46/94*). A taxpayers' organisation was not an educational institution as it had outsourced virtually all of its activities, and its journals, seminars and telephone help-line were purely informational (*The Taxpayers' Association of NSW*).

Community service

A non-profit society, association or club established for community service purposes, excluding political or lobbying purposes, is exempt (s 50-10).

The expression "community service purposes" has a wide meaning and encompasses traditional service clubs (eg Apex, Rotary, Lions, Zonta and Quota) and community service organisations (eg Country Women's Associations) (TD 93/190). Age pensioner and senior citizens' associations (that do not conduct significant political or lobbying activities), non-profit child care centres and nursing homes, refuge and crisis centres, refugee and migrant welfare centres and associations of playgroups are also exempt. A council with the predominant purpose of co-ordinating community service work and providing information on women's issues was also exempt (*National Council of Women of Tasmania*), as was an entity established to facilitate face-to-face banking services in a rural town without those services (*Wentworth District Capital*).

However, military service unit organisations, clubs providing a social forum for retired business people (eg Probus) or expatriates of a particular country, masonic clubs, debating clubs, model railway clubs and philatelic societies are not exempt (TD 93/190; TD 94/30). Providing a meeting hall for use by certain groups is not an activity for community service purposes (*Douglas*).

Employment

Employee or employer associations, registered under a Commonwealth, state or territory law relating to the settlement of industrial disputes, and trade unions are exempt (s 50-15). "Trade union" has its dictionary meaning of an association formed to protect and further the interests of its members in respect of their conditions of employment. Therefore, an unregistered employees' association was not a trade union as it had been formed to provide financial assistance to members (*Norseman*). See also ID 2005/348.

The High Court has held that an association of news agents was not an "employer association", even though it was party to an award and certain industrial agreements. The members were not required to be employers and were not associated in their capacity as employers, but as newsagents (*Associated Newsagents Co-operative Ltd*). The ATO determined that an association of contractors was also not an employer association (ID 2006/155).

Film

The Australian Film Finance Corporation Pty Ltd is exempt (s 50-45, item 9.3).

Ancillary funds

A public or private ancillary fund established by will or instrument of trust solely for the purpose of contributing to another fund that is a DGR is exempt (former s 50-20, item 4.1). The exemption was terminated with effect from 1 January 2014 and replaced by a specific provision in the *Charities Act 2013*. Funds exempted under former s 50-20 before 1 January 2014 continue to enjoy exempt status by virtue of transitional rules.

Government

Municipal corporations, local government bodies (including those in Norfolk, Cocos (Keeling) or Christmas Islands) and public authorities constituted under an Australian law are exempt (s 50-25).

A company established by a local council to run a building complex was not itself a municipal corporation or local government body (ID 2004/757).

In order to be a ''public authority'', a body must perform a function of government (*Coal Mining Industry Long Service Leave (Funding) Corporation*). Delegation of the tax collecting function is a powerful indication that a body is performing such a function. The Western Australian and Sydney Turf Clubs were not public authorities (*Western Australian Turf Club*; *Case K48*) as the private activities and characteristics of the clubs took precedence over their public functions. A statutory office holder whose functions are mainly administrative is seemingly not a public authority for these purposes (*Registrar, Accident Compensation Tribunal (Vic)*).

Wholly-owned state, territory and local government trading enterprises (STBs), other than those specified in the Income Tax (Excluded STBs) Regulations, are also exempt (ITAA36 ss 24AK to 24AZ).

Health

Public hospitals and non-profit hospitals operated by a society or association are exempt, as are non-profit hospital, medical or health benefits organisations registered under the *National Health Act 1953* (Cth) (s 50-30).

Information and communications technology

Not-for-profit organisations established to promote the development of information and communications technology resources in Australia are exempt (s 50-40, item 8.3).

Primary and secondary resources, and tourism

Non-profit societies or associations established for the purpose of promoting the development of aviation or tourism, or of the agricultural, horticultural, industrial, manufacturing, pastoral, viticultural, aquacultural or fishing resources of Australia, Australian information and communications technology services, or Global Infrastructure Hub Ltd are exempt (s 50-40, items 8.1 to 8.4). The surveying profession (*Case 46/94*) and the insurance industry (*Australian Insurance Association*) are not industrial resources of Australia. However, a grain handling cooperative did promote the development of Australian agricultural resources (*Cooperative Bulk Handling*). The terms ''promoting the development of'' and ''industrial resources'' are also discussed in IT 2415.

Sports, culture and recreation

A non-profit society, association or club established for musical purposes or for the encouragement of animal races, art, a game or sport, literature or music is exempt (s 50-45). A non-profit society, etc, located outside Australia that promotes cultural activities and provides performances at Australian cultural events is not exempt unless it is prescribed in ITR97 or the income is protected by a double taxation agreement (¶22-140) (TD 1999/7).

This category includes amateur theatrical and musical groups, but not philatelic societies (TD 94/30). The terms ''sport'' and ''game'' are used in their ordinary sense; thus, bridge and chess clubs may be exempt but model railway clubs (*Case 10/93*) and social dancing clubs (TR 97/22) are not.

A society, etc, will not be exempt unless its main purpose (ascertained annually) is the encouragement of a sport or game (TR 97/22). However, the provision of social facilities will not disqualify the society, etc, from the exemption provided that this is merely an incidental activity and is not its predominant function or an independent purpose. Thus, a club will not be exempt where its main purpose is the provision of social amenities for members, rather than the promotion or encouragement of sport (*Cronulla Sutherland Leagues Club*; *''The Waratahs'' Rugby Union Football Club*; *North Suburban Club Inc*; *South Sydney Junior Rugby League Club*). However, where the social and gambling facilities are subordinate to the encouragement and promotion of the sport, the club will qualify for the exemption (*St Marys Rugby League Club*). Factors that the Commissioner takes into account in determining the main purpose of a club are set out in TR 97/22.

A club may have a predominantly sporting purpose even though most of its income or expenses relate to non-sporting activities. The following have been held to be exempt: a golf/tennis club (*Case X25*); bowls clubs (*Case W114*; *Tweed Heads Bowls Club*); and a country club (*Terranora Lakes Country Club*).

The Australian Sports Drug Agency is exempt under *Australian Sports Drug Agency Act 1990*, s 65A. However, regulations may provide that the exemption does not apply in relation to specified taxes.

The ICC Business Corporation FZ-LLC (IBC) is exempt from income tax and from interest, dividend and royalty withholding tax liability for amounts paid to it from 1 July 2018 to 30 June 2023.

International organisations and office holders

In addition to the entities listed in s 11-5, certain international organisations and persons who hold an office in them may be exempt from specified taxes in accordance with regulations under the *International Organisations (Privileges and Immunities) Act 1963* (IOPI Act). A ‘‘person who holds an office’’ includes an employee of an international organisation but is not: (a) a person who is locally engaged and paid at an hourly rate; or (b) a person engaged as an expert or consultant. In *Jayasinghe*, the High Court held that a civil engineer engaged by the United Nations Office for Project Services as a contractor in Sudan did not hold an ‘‘an office in an international organisation’’ under s 6(1)(d) of the IOPI Act and was not entitled to an exemption from tax.

Draft TR 2019/D1 updates ATO views on the taxation privileges and immunities of prescribed International Organisations and their staff (expressed in former TR 92/14) and on who is a ‘‘person who holds an office’’ as specified in various regulations made under the IOPI Act (covered previously by former TD 92/153) and incorporates the High Court’s decisions in *Macoun* and *Jayasinghe*.

[FITR ¶102-000, ¶102-195; FTR ¶11-357]

¶10-610 Obtaining exemption

Charitable entities seeking to claim exempt status are required to obtain an Australian Business Number (¶33-100) and be registered with the Australian Charities and Not-for-profits Commission (ACNC) Commissioner, the Commonwealth level regulator for charities. An online register of charities is available on the ACNC website.

Generally, entities that were endorsed by the ATO before the commencement of the ACNC regime are automatically transferred to the new regime. However, entities should check that their registration has been transferred.

Applications for registration may be made to the ACNC Commissioner in the approved form (ACNC Act s 30-10). Registration also allows entities to access other concessions such as refundable imputation credits, FBT rebate and GST concessions. To be registered and to maintain registration, entities must also:

- be a NFP entity (¶10-604)
- comply with governance and external conduct standards, and record keeping and reporting requirements (ACNC Act Pt 3-1)
- must not be characterised as engaged in or supporting terrorist or other criminal activities.

The ACNC Commissioner may revoke an entity’s registration in certain circumstances (ACNC Act s 35-10). There are rights of review or appeal against decisions of the ACNC Commissioner, including decisions to refuse or revoke registration (ACNC Act Pt 7-2).

While the registration of charities is the responsibility of the ACNC, whether any special conditions that must be met for a tax concession to apply are in fact met is decided by the ATO.

[FITR ¶102-172, ¶102-200, ¶102-255]

¶10-620 Tax avoidance agreements involving exempt entities

Entities that would otherwise be tax exempt are specifically made liable to pay tax on income that is diverted to them as part of a tax avoidance agreement, eg where a person with a right to receive an amount on which he/she would be liable to pay tax assigns that right to an exempt entity for a lesser or non-taxable amount (ITAA36 Pt III Div 9C: ss 121F to 121L). The entity is taxed on the diverted income at the maximum personal rate of tax applicable (including Medicare levy) for the relevant year (*Income Tax (Diverted Income) Act 1981*), ie 47% for 2017–18. The exempt entities affected are: those listed at ¶10-605; life assurance companies (income derived on segregated exempt assets; ITAA97 s 320-37(1)(a)); income of a state/territory body (STB) other than an excluded STB (ITAA36 s 24AM); and any other entity exempt from income tax under any other Commonwealth legislation.

Tax is imposed where:

- an exempt entity derives income from property that it has acquired in the capacity of trustee or otherwise as part of a tax avoidance agreement. It is not necessary that tax avoidance be the sole purpose, nor that all parties share that purpose; however, the arrangement will not be caught if tax avoidance is merely an incidental purpose
- the income so derived would not otherwise attract income tax, and
- the consideration provided by the entity for the acquisition of the property substantially exceeds the amount that it might reasonably be expected to have provided if it were liable to be taxed on the income arising from the property at the company tax rate.

In calculating the diverted income liable for tax, no deductions are allowable for losses or outgoings incurred under or in connection with a tax avoidance agreement.

The general anti-avoidance provisions should also be considered (¶30-000).

[FTR ¶60-601]

¶10-630 When a tax-exempt entity becomes taxable

Special rules deal with the transitional issues that arise when a tax-exempt entity becomes taxable (ITAA36 Sch 2D: ss 57-1 to 57-130). These rules ensure that all (and only) the income, deductions, gains and losses that relate to the period after the entity becomes taxable are taken into account in determining its tax position. The rules apply only if *all* of the income of an entity is fully exempt from income tax and, immediately afterwards, *any* of its income becomes assessable to any extent. It applies to both government exempt entities that become privatised, either by legislation or by sale to private interests, and non-government exempt entities that cease to be exempt.

As a result, income derived or expenditure incurred during the post-exemption period in respect of services rendered or goods supplied during the exemption period is treated as having been derived or incurred during the exemption period. Correspondingly, income derived or expenditure incurred during the exemption period in respect of services rendered or goods supplied during the post-exemption period is treated as having been derived during the post-exemption period. In addition, the rules:

- value the entity's assets and liabilities at their adjusted market value as at the date of transition (ie market value less income received or receivable at or after that time that is not included in assessable income, plus income received or receivable before that time that is so included)

- deny deductions for superannuation payments, bad debts, R&D expenditure, eligible termination payments and employee leave entitlements to the extent that they relate to the period when the entity was exempt. A deduction is, however, allowed for a surplus in a defined benefit superannuation scheme at the time of transition. Further, the amount of bad debt deductions disallowed is reduced where such a debt is sold at or after the transition time
- ensure changes in the value of trading stock are calculated from the time the entity becomes taxable
- ensure that expenditure that provides an enduring benefit (eg the cost of a depreciable asset and mining deductible capital expenditure) is notionally written down during the exemption period
- cancel the franking surplus of a wholly-owned subsidiary of a tax-exempt entity when that entity becomes subject to tax, and cancel the franking surplus when a taxable subsidiary ceases to be effectively wholly-owned by a tax-exempt entity (ITAA97 s 208-145).

[FTR ¶799-040]

¶10-640 Norfolk Island residents

From 1 July 2016 the Australian taxation system applies in Norfolk Island in the same way it applies in mainland Australia with the exception of indirect taxes, including GST. As a result, Norfolk Island resident individuals, companies and trustees are taxed on their Norfolk Island sourced income and their foreign-sourced income. For the CGT rules applicable to Norfolk Island residents, see ¶11-670.

Prior to 1 July 2016, special exemptions were granted to ''genuine'' residents of Norfolk Island (former ITAA36 ss 24B to 24P).

[FTR ¶5-726, ¶11-360]

Education

¶10-700 Education, training and apprenticeships

Commonwealth education or training payments

''Commonwealth education or training payments'' are generally liable to tax. These are payments by the Commonwealth to or on behalf of:

- a participant in a ''Commonwealth labour market program'', or
- a student — in respect of a period commencing when the student was at least 16 years old — under the following schemes: ABSTUDY; Assistance for Isolated Children; Veterans' Children Education; Youth Allowance; Austudy payment; the education and training scheme under the *Military Rehabilitation and Compensation Act 2004*, s 258.

The ''supplementary amount'' of a Commonwealth education or training payment is exempt. The supplementary amount generally comprises so much of the payment as is included to assist with, or reimburse, the cost of: rent; living in a remote area; commencing employment; travelling to or participating in courses, interviews, education or training; a child or children dependent on the taxpayer; telephone bills; living away from the taxpayer's usual residence and maintaining that usual residence; travel to that residence while undertaking education or training away from the residence; accommodation, books or equipment; discharging a HEC assessment debt or the compulsory repayment amount of an accumulated HELP debt (¶2-380); acquiring any special equipment, services or transport to assist with a disability; pharmaceuticals; and anything that would prevent the taxpayer from undertaking any education or training (ITAA97 ss 52-140; 52-145).

A ''Commonwealth Trade Learning Scholarship'' is exempt from income tax (ITAA97 s 51-10, item 2.3).

Commonwealth secondary education and isolated children's payments

Payments to, or in respect of, a student under a Commonwealth scheme providing assistance for secondary education or in connection with the education of isolated children are exempt (s 51-10, item 2.1B). However, Commonwealth education or training payments and education entry payments to sole parent pensioners are *not* exempt under this provision (s 51-40).

International scholarships

Scholarships, bursaries or other educational allowances that are provided by the Commonwealth to foreign students and trainees who are in Australia solely for study or training are exempt (ITAA97 s 842-105, item 7). The exemption applies whether or not the study or training is pursued as a full-time course and whether or not the student or trainee has part-time employment related or unrelated to the studies.

Payments received under a grant from the Australian-American Educational Foundation (ie Fulbright Scholarships) are exempt (s 51-10, item 2.1).

Research fellowships under the Endeavour Awards and the Endeavour Executive Award, in which recipients are not required to be in full-time study, are also exempt from income tax.

Apprentice payments

The first $1,000 of a bonus paid by a state or territory government to apprentices for the early completion of their apprenticeships is exempt. Payments made under the Skills for Sustainability for Australian Apprentices and under the Australian Apprenticeships Incentives Program for Tools For Your Trade (5 payments over the apprenticeship) are also exempt (ITAA97 s 51-10, items 2.7, 2.8).

A checklist summarising other tax measures relevant to students is at ¶44-140.

[FITR ¶102-530, ¶103-185]

¶10-740 Other scholarships, grants, etc

There is a general exemption for other scholarships, bursaries or other educational allowances derived by a student (of any age) receiving full-time education at a school, college or university (ITAA97 s 51-10, item 2.1A). ''Full-time education'' in this context means a full-time course as opposed to a part-time course and does not preclude the student from holding a part-time job.

The Commissioner has issued TA 2007/6 warning taxpayers to be cautious of arrangements that seek to reduce tax through education or scholarship trusts for a student who may be a family member of the person contributing to the trust.

Exclusions from exemption

A number of exclusions from the item 2.1A exemption are listed in s 51-35.

Payments received by a student ''on the condition'' that the student will (or will if required) become, or continue to be, an employee of the payer or enter into, or continue to be, a party to a contract for labour with the payer are excluded from the exemption. Whether such a condition exists is determined at the time the scholarship is granted (*Polla-Mounter*).

In *Polla-Mounter*, the fact that, at the time the scholarship was granted, it was a condition that the student was a playing member of the rugby club was not sufficient to exclude the scholarship from the exemption — there also had to be a condition that the student ''will'' render or ''continue'' to render those services. However, the exclusion applied to an arrangement under which a student rendered services under a contract entered into with someone other than the scholarship provider (*Hall*).

The words ''on the condition'' do not require there to be a contract between the payer and the recipient or any other form of legal relationship between the parties (*Ranson*). The exclusion would clearly apply where the student is bonded to serve his/her benefactor at the time of receiving payments or in the future, whether the bond is to the government (eg in the case of teacher trainees) or to a private employer. However, fees paid directly to the educational institution by the employer or other benefactor would not be in the nature of income and could only be assessable, if at all, as an allowance in relation to employment (¶10-060).

The mere fact that a scholarship holder has to lodge an annual progress report to the scholarship provider does not constitute a requirement to render services (IT 2581). On this basis, payments under National Health and Medical Research Council (NHMRC) scholarships will generally be exempt. However, NHMRC *fellowships* are not exempt as the conditions attached to the fellowships amount to a requirement to render services. Wholly CSIRO funded studentships and scholarships are exempt where received by full-time university students (CR 2003/26).

Also excluded are payments under a scholarship that is not provided *principally* for educational purposes. It does not matter whether the provider is motivated by purely educational purposes or has in mind some collateral advantage, but at least one of the purposes for which the grant is made must be the education of the recipient (*Hall*). Payments received in the capacity of an employee (*Case J58*) or company executive (*Case N28*), rather than as a student, will not qualify.

Remuneration received by a trainee for services rendered during the period of training is assessable. Research grants would usually be assessable — for example, a grant to a doctor of medicine to carry out special research, which he did at a university but not under its control or direction, was assessable as ordinary income (16 TBRD *Case* R10). Amounts paid under a postgraduate research scholarship granted to a PhD student by a university out of funds provided by the Asthma Foundation were also not exempt as the Foundation financed the scholarship on the condition that the student would analyse, collate and prepare for publication the findings of a respiratory survey conducted on behalf of the Foundation (*Hall*).

Where a friendly society education fund (¶3-470) pays education costs to or for the benefit of a student undertaking full-time education at a school, college or university, such a payment will not be exempt because it does not qualify as a scholarship, bursary or other educational allowance or assistance (TR 93/39).

In *Muir*, an anaesthetist who received a $120,000 fellowship for 2 years of full-time training in pain management did not qualify for the exemption. The training was at a hospital, not a university. Although the hospital was associated with a university, this association was not relevant to a significant part of the training.

[FITR ¶102-530, ¶102-570]

Defence

¶10-750 Defence Force income generally

Generally, persons serving with the Defence Forces and Reserves include the same items in income as do civilians. Hence, amounts based on periods of service or special duty and comparable allowances are fully included in assessable income in the absence of specific statutory exclusions.

Similarly, the same deductions and rebates are available to service personnel as to civilians. The interaction between the rebate and exemption provisions for Defence Force personnel is discussed in TR 97/2. The estates of deceased service personnel are released from so much of any unpaid tax liability as is applicable to Defence Force pay and allowances (ITAA36 s 265A).

[FTR ¶786-160]

¶10-760 Defence Force pay and allowances

The pay and allowances received by military, naval and air force personnel are assessable as ordinary income. However, the payments and allowances below are expressly exempt (ITAA97 s 51-5, items 1.1, 1.2 and 1.6):

- the following allowances or reimbursements payable to, or in respect of, a Defence Force member (ITR97 reg 51-5.01). The Determination refers to *Defence Determination* 2005/15, made under the *Defence Act 1903*, effective 31 May 2005:
  - a deployment allowance paid under Div 1 of Pt 9 of Ch 17 of the Determination
  - a disturbance allowance paid under Div 2 of Pt 1 of Ch 6 of the Determination
  - a reimbursement of education costs for a child while the member is resident in Australia paid under Pt 4 of Ch 8 of the Determination
  - a reimbursement of education costs for a child educated at the location of a member's long-term posting overseas paid under Pt 6 of Ch 15 of the Determination
  - a reimbursement of education costs for a child educated in Australia while the member is on a long-term posting overseas paid under Pt 6 of Ch 15 of the Determination
  - a reimbursement in place of a child's scholarship paid under Div 3 of Pt 4 of Ch 8 of the Determination
  - a separation allowance paid under Div 1 of Pt 1 of Ch 6 of the Determination
  - a transfer allowance paid under Div 3 of Pt 3 of Ch 14 of the Determination
  - a rent allowance paid under Pt 6 of Ch 7 of the Determination to a member without dependants or a member with dependants (separated) within the meaning of the Determination
- the value of rations and quarters supplied without charge to a member of the Defence Force
- F-111 deseal/reseal ex-gratia lump sum payments.

Note that the value of allowances given or granted to Defence Force members in respect of their service as such is assessable in full, whether received in cash or some other form. Fringe benefits that are either assessable or expressly exempt under the *Fringe Benefits Tax Assessment Act 1986* (¶35-000) are excluded.

[FITR ¶102-520]

¶10-770 Part-time members of reserves

Pay and allowances of part-time members of the Defence Force Reserves are exempt (ITAA97 s 51-5, item 1.4). The exemption applies only to pay and allowances for *part-time service*, including pay for part-time training. It does not apply where a member of the Reserves has volunteered or been called up for full-time duty. Cash prizes under the Military Skills Awards program to members of the Army Reserve are also exempt (IT 2474).

Part-time defence reservists that leave the Reserve Defence Forces due to injury or disease sustained while performing employment for a Reserve Defence Force may receive compensation under the *Safety, Rehabilitation and Compensation Act 1988* or the *Military Rehabilitation and Compensation Act 2004* for loss of pay and allowances. That compensation is generally exempt (ITAA97 s 51-5, item 1.5; 51-33).

[FITR ¶102-520]

¶10-780 Other military exemptions

Exemptions relating to military service also apply to the following forms of income:

- pay and allowances earned by an ADF member where a certificate is in force to the effect that the person is on eligible service with a specified organisation in a specified area outside Australia other than duty as, or under, an attaché at an Australian embassy or legation (ITAA36 s 23AD; ITR15 reg 6): duty with the United Nations Assistance Mission in Afghanistan on Operation Palate II from 27 June 2005 to 31 December 2016; duty with the Australian Defence Force on Operation Accordion from 1 July 2014; duty on Operation Augury from 4 July 2014; duty on Operation Highroad from 1 January 2015; duty on Operation Manitou from 15 May 2015; duty on Operation OKRA from 10 September 2015; duty on Operation Steadfast after 9 September 2018
- compensation received by an ADF member on eligible service who is repatriated to Australia due to a service-related injury or disease under the *Safety, Rehabilitation and Compensation (Defence-related Claims) Act 1988* or compensation under the *Military Rehabilitation and Compensation Act 2004* for loss of pay for warlike service or for loss of an allowance (ITAA97 ss 51-5 item 1.1A; 51-32)
- pay and allowances earned in Australia by persons enlisted in or appointed to the military forces of any foreign country unless they are paid by the Australian government (ITAA97 s 842-105, item 5)
- compensation paid in respect of death, impairment or incapacity resulting from the service of civilian personnel contributed by Australia to an armed force of the United Nations (UN) overseas. Relief from unpaid tax in respect of pay and allowances is accorded to the estate of a deceased civilian who has performed UN service, and living allowances paid during periods of UN service are assessable only as to $2 per week. This applied to members of the UN peace-keeping force in Cyprus and the United Nations Integrated Mission in Timor-Leste (ITAA36 s 23AB(5), (6), (10); ITR15 reg 5).

US domestic corporations, and US residents and citizens are effectively exempt from Australian tax in respect of profits or remuneration derived as contractors, sub-contractors or employees from the performance of US government contracts relating to the establishment, operation or maintenance of the North West Cape naval communications station, the Sparta project, the Joint Defence Space Research Facility and the Joint Defence Space Communications Station (ITAA36 s 23AA). The exemption is dependent on the income being taxable in the US, and is achieved by deeming the taxpayers to be non-residents and the income to be from sources outside Australia. Certain dependants, US government employees and accompanying civilians are also covered.

Reparation payments made under the Defence Abuse Reparation Payment Scheme are exempt from 1 July 2013 (ITAA97 s 51-5, item 1.7). Payments made to a recipient from the Commonwealth on the recommendation of the Defence Force Ombudsman in relation to abuse by ADF personnel are exempt from income tax from 1 July 2017.

Payments under Military Rehabilitation and Compensation Act

A compensation scheme covering all injuries or conditions arising from service in the Australian Defence Force is provided for under the *Military Rehabilitation and Compensation Act 2004* (MRC Act). The exemptions applicable to compensation payments made under the scheme are listed in ITAA97 s 52-114 as follows (section references are to the relevant payment provisions):

- alterations to aids and appliances relating to rehabilitation (s 57) — exempt[1]
- compensation for journey and accommodation costs (ss 47; 290; 291; 297; 328(4)) — exempt[1]
- compensation for permanent impairment (ss 68; 71; 75; 80) — exempt[1, 2]
- compensation for financial and legal advice (ss 81; 205; 239) — exempt[1] (see ITAA97 s 52-114)
- compensation for incapacity for Permanent Forces member or continuous full-time Reservist (s 85) — exempt[2] (see ITAA97 s 51-32 regarding ordinary payments)
- compensation for incapacity for part-time Reservist (s 86) — exempt[2] (see ITAA97 s 51-33 regarding ordinary payments)
- compensation by way of Special Rate Disability Pension (s 200) — exempt[1]
- compensation under the motor vehicle compensation scheme (s 212) — exempt[1]
- compensation for household services and attendant care services (ss 214; 217) — exempt[1]
- MRCA supplement (ss 221; 245; 300) — exempt[1]
- compensation for loss or damage to medical aids (s 226) — exempt[1]
- compensation for a wholly dependent partner for a member's death (s 233) — exempt[2]
- continuing permanent impairment and incapacity, etc, compensation for a wholly dependent partner (s 242(1)(a)(i), (iii)) — exempt[2]
- compensation for eligible young dependants of deceased member (s 253) — exempt[2]
- continuing permanent impairment and incapacity, etc, compensation for eligible young persons (s 255(1)(c)(i), (iii)) — exempt[2]
- education and training, or a payment under the education scheme for certain eligible young persons (s 258) — exempt[2] (ordinary payment also exempt if for/to a person under 16)
- income support bonus under the education scheme for certain eligible young persons (s 258) — exempt[1]

- compensation for other dependants of deceased member (s 262) — exempt[2]
- compensation for cost of a funeral (s 266) — exempt[2]
- compensation for treatment costs (ss 271; 272; 273) — exempt[1]
- special assistance (s 424) — exempt[1, 2]
- clean energy payment (ss 83A; 209A; 238A and Pt 5A of Chap 11) — exempt[1].

Note 1: Ordinary payment is exempt.

Note 2: Payment because of a person's death is exempt.

[FTR ¶9-350, ¶9-575, ¶9-700, ¶9-730, ¶9-820]

Bequests and Windfall Gains

¶10-840 Interest in capital or income under a will or settlement

Assets or money acquired in satisfaction of an interest in *capital* under a will, intestacy or settlement are not income and, except for capital gains tax (CGT), are not assessable. Apart from CGT, a specific bequest of an asset or a sum of money is equally non-assessable unless it is received by the executor for the performance of his/her executive duties. As a general rule, property acquired under these circumstances cannot be regarded as acquired for profit-making by sale and any surplus on a straight-out sale of such property over its value at the date of acquisition is not assessable under the ordinary income tax provisions. However, property acquired under such circumstances may be ventured in a business or profit-making scheme and, in that event, any surplus may be assessable (¶10-120).

Beneficial interests in *income* under a will, settlement, etc, are taxed in accordance with Pt III Div 6 (¶6-060).

[FITR ¶18-300]

¶10-842 Non-assessability of windfall gains

Windfall gains such as gambling and lottery wins and competition prizes that are not won as a part of the taxpayer's income-producing activities or business are generally not income and are therefore non-assessable (¶10-440). They are also ignored for CGT purposes under ITAA97 s 118-37(1)(c) (¶11-660).

[FITR ¶19-300, ¶154-560]

Investments

¶10-845 Venture capital investments

Certain foreign resident investors can disregard capital gains and capital losses from CGT events that relate to venture capital investments (¶11-900). There are corresponding rules in ITAA97 Div 51 to ensure that an exemption will also be available where the same circumstances apply but the gain or profit is on revenue account rather than capital account.

Profits on venture capital investment

Income tax exemptions that correspond to the CGT exemptions in ITAA97 Subdiv 118-F, are contained in ITAA97 s 51-54. These exemptions relate to gains or profits derived or losses incurred after 30 June 2002 from certain venture capital investments by foreign residents from a number of specified countries. In particular:

- an eligible non-resident partner in a venture capital limited partnership (VCLP: ¶5-040) is exempt from income tax on the partner's share of a gain or profit made by the VCLP from the disposal or other realisation by the VCLP of an eligible venture capital investment (s 51-54(1)). The VCLP must be unconditionally registered under the *Venture Capital Act 2002*, and the circumstances must be such that the disposal or realisation would qualify for the CGT exemption under s 118-405 (¶11-900) if it were a disposal of a CGT asset. This requires, for example, that the investment was held at risk and owned by the VCLP for at least 12 months. Any loss on the investment is not deductible (ITAA97 s 26-68(1)). A partner in an early stage venture capital limited partnership (ESVCLP: ¶5-040) is similarly exempt

- an eligible venture capital partner in an Australian venture capital fund of funds (AFOF: ¶5-040) is exempt from income tax on the partner's share of a profit or gain made by either the AFOF itself or a VCLP in which the AFOF is a partner. The AFOF and VCLP must be unconditionally registered under the *Venture Capital Act 2002*, and the circumstances must be such that the disposal or realisation would qualify for the CGT exemption under s 118-410 (¶11-900) if it were a disposal of a CGT asset. This requires, for example, that the investment was held at risk and owned by the AFOF or VCLP for at least 12 months. Any loss on the investment is not deductible (ITAA97 s 26-68(2)). A profit or gain by an ESVCLP in which the AFOF is a partner also qualifies for exemption

- an eligible venture capital investor is exempt from income tax on any profit or gain from the disposal or other realisation of an eligible venture capital investment, where the circumstances such that the disposal or realisation would qualify for the CGT exemption under s 118-415 (¶11-900) if it were a disposal of a CGT asset. This requires, for example, that the investment was held at risk and owned by the investor for at least 12 months. Any loss on the investment is not deductible (ITAA97 s 26-68(3)).

The venture capital tax concessions are available for investments in financial technology businesses (''fintech'') made on or after 1 July 2018 (¶20-700).

Investment by foreign pension funds

Income tax exemptions that correspond to the CGT exemptions in Subdiv 118-G are contained in s 51-55. The exemption applies to a venture capital investment by a foreign resident tax-exempt pension fund that invests in an Australian company or fixed trust (a resident investment vehicle). Any gain or profit made from the disposal or other realisation of the investment is exempt from income tax if it is made by a venture capital entity or limited partnership (referred to in s 118-515(2)) and the circumstances are such that the disposal etc would qualify for the CGT exemption under Subdiv 118-G (¶11-900) if it were a disposal of a CGT asset. This requires, for example, that the investment was held at risk and owned by the investor for at least 12 months.

[FITR ¶102-605, ¶102-610]

¶10-850 Other investment-related exemptions

A number of other investment-related exemptions are discussed in other chapters. These include:

- interest or dividends from Australia derived by a **foreign superannuation fund** (¶13-250)

- certain income from **pooled development fund (PDF) shares** including dividends paid while a company is a PDF and income from the sale of PDF shares. A capital gain realised by a PDF on a qualifying SME investment is also effectively exempt to the extent that it is distributed to a complying superannuation fund (or similar entity) other than a self managed superannuation fund. This result is achieved through a ''venture capital franking rebate'' to the superannuation entity (¶3-555)

- interest and gains during the exemption period in respect of **tax-exempt infrastructure borrowings**, unless the taxpayer elects otherwise (this concession was abolished with effect from 21 February 2018)
- income derived by complying superannuation funds and insurance companies on **assets used to fund current pensions and annuities** (¶3-500, ¶13-140).

Maintenance

¶10-855 Family maintenance payments

Periodic maintenance payments received by a taxpayer are exempt if the taxpayer is:

- a spouse or former spouse (including a de facto spouse) of the payer
- a child (including an adopted child, step-child or ex-nuptial child) or a former child of the payer, or
- a child (as above) who is or was connected to the payer through a marriage or de facto relationship of a parent (ITAA97 s 51-50).

Maintenance payments that are attributable to payments made by such a payer (eg where they are paid through a child support trust account or the Child Support Agency) are also exempt.

The exemption does not apply where the maintenance payer has effectively diverted income from himself/herself, or divested himself/herself of income-producing assets to cover those payments. Payments made from the relevant payer's deceased estate, or from some other source organised by the payer, will also not generally be exempt under s 51-50 as they would not be (or be attributable to) payments by the payer.

No deduction or rebate is available to a maintenance payer in respect of the maintenance payments.

[FITR ¶102-560]

Exemption for Overseas Employment Income

¶10-860 Earnings from foreign service

Foreign earnings derived by an Australian resident taxpayer from at least 91 days' continuous foreign service may be exempt (ITAA36 s 23AG). The exemption only applies to foreign earnings: (1) as an aid or charitable worker employed by an approved developing country relief fund, a public disaster relief fund or a prescribed charitable institution that is exempt from Australian income tax; (2) as a worker delivering Australian official development assistance (except if the worker's employer is an Australian government agency); or (3) as a government employee deployed as a member of a disciplined force (ITAA36 s 23AG(1AA); TR 2013/7). In this context, disciplined force refers to the Australian Defence Force, the Australian Federal Police, and the state and territory police forces (TR 2013/7).

To be eligible for the exemption, the taxpayer must be classified as an Australian resident at the time the earnings are derived (¶21-010).

The exemption from Australian tax will *not* apply where the income is exempt from income tax in the foreign country *only* because of one or more of the following (ITAA36 s 23AG(2)):

- the income is exempt under a double taxation agreement (DTA) or a law of a country that gives effect to a DTA
- the foreign country exempts from income tax, or does not provide for the imposition of income tax on, income derived in the capacity of an employee, income from personal services or similar income
- a law or international agreement, to which Australia is a party, dealing with privileges and immunities of diplomats or consuls or of persons connected with international organisations applies.

Where the earnings would also have been exempt in the foreign country for another reason (eg because of the operation of a DTA *and* a specific agreement), the exemption will still apply (TD 2005/15; *Grant*, *Coventry*). Australian Defence Force personnel engaged in UN peacekeeping operations will generally qualify for the exemption (TD 2005/37).

▶ Example

An Australian resident volunteer aid worker has earnings in Fiji that are exempt in that country because of Art 21 of the Australia/Fiji DTA and also because of a Memorandum of Understanding with the Fijian government relating to aid workers. Those earnings will qualify for exemption because they are not exempt from tax in Fiji *only* because of the DTA.

Foreign earnings

"Foreign earnings" means income consisting of wages, salary, commissions, bonuses and allowances. The source of remuneration under a normal contract of employment is generally the place where the duties or services are performed (¶21-060). Accordingly, a salary supplement paid by the Australian government to a customs officer while he served overseas was held to be foreign earnings (*Case 11/94*). The term does *not* include pensions, annuities or superannuation payments of a recurring or pension nature, lump sum superannuation payments paid by a foreign-based superannuation fund and lump sum termination payments paid by an employer. Other foreign earnings exclusions are: (a) the tax-free amount of a bona fide redundancy payment (or of an approved retirement scheme payment); (b) payments made by way of an advance or loan; (c) restraint of trade payments or payments for personal injury; and (d) transfers between superannuation funds.

Income assessed under ITAA97 Div 83A employee share scheme provisions (¶10-085) that is attributable to foreign service qualifies for exemption as foreign employment income (s 23AG(7) definition of "foreign earnings").

Foreign earnings derived by defence force members from leave following an accident or illness while deployed as a member of a disciplined force are also exempt under s 23AG (TD 2013/18).

Foreign service

"Foreign service" means service in a foreign country as the holder of an office or in the capacity of an employee, including a person employed by a government or an authority of a government or by an international organisation. This involves taxpayers actually on the job performing the service in a particular foreign country (*Overseas Aircrew Basing*). Foreign earnings from independent personal services are not covered (*Lopez*). Service on a ship predominantly in international waters does not constitute "foreign service" (*Chaudhri*).

A person who dies before attaining 91 days of foreign service may qualify for the exemption (s 23AG(1A)).

Temporary absences

Where a taxpayer is absent from work due to accident or illness or is on recreation leave that is wholly attributable to that foreign service (other than leave without pay or on reduced pay, or long service type leave), the absence is included in a taxpayer's period of foreign service (s 23AG(6)).

In addition, the continuity of foreign service will not be broken by other types of temporary absence, provided the time away does not exceed one-sixth of the total number of days of foreign service (s 23AG(6A)). TD 2012/8 provides that temporary absences for recreational leave attributable to the period of foreign service, accident or illness, and work-related trips will not break the continuity of foreign service. However, absences for recreational leave not attributable to foreign service, long service leave, purchased leave, leave without pay, furlough, extended leave and maternity/parental leave will.

▶ Example

Tina, an Australian resident, engages in foreign service for 55 days, then takes off 5 days for illness in accordance with the terms and conditions of her foreign service, then takes 15 days holiday, then works for a further 50 days. The 15 days of holidays are not part of her foreign service because they accrued in relation to employment in Australia.

There are 60 days (ie 55 + 5) of foreign service in the first period, followed by 15 days absence, 15/60 = one-fourth. As this is more than one-sixth, the next period of foreign service may not be added to the first period. Tina's first (60-day) period of foreign service will never qualify for the exemption. When she recommences work for 50 days, she will start a new period of foreign service and will need to extend that period to 91 days before any of the earnings for the second period are exempt.

[FTR ¶9-920 – ¶9-935]

¶10-865 Calculation of tax on other income

Foreign earnings exempt under ITAA36 s 23AG are taken into account in calculating the tax payable on other income derived by the taxpayer. This method of calculation — referred to as ''exemption with progression'' — prevents the exempt income from reducing the Australian tax payable on the other income.

Tax on the non-exempt income is calculated by applying to that income the notional average rate of tax payable on the sum of exempt income and non-exempt income. The amount of tax payable on the non-exempt income is calculated using the following formula:

$$\frac{\text{notional gross tax}}{\text{notional gross taxable income}} \times \text{other taxable income}$$

where:

notional gross tax is the tax (in whole dollars) that would be assessed (including the Medicare levy and Medicare levy surcharge (ITAA36 s 251R(7)), but excluding any rebates and tax offsets) on the amount that would be the total taxable income if the exempt amount was assessable income (including any exempt resident foreign termination payments: ¶14-740)

notional gross taxable income is the amount (in whole dollars) that would be the total taxable income if the exempt amount was assessable income (ie total income from all sources less all deductions). Accordingly, any deductions that relate to the exempt income are allowed as if the exempt income was assessable income (eg employment-related expenses are deducted from the exempt employment income)

other taxable income is the amount remaining after deducting from assessable income any allowable deductions that relate exclusively or appropriately to that assessable income. These deductions include a proportion of deductions (''apportionable deductions'') that are allowed without having any connection with the production of assessable income (eg gifts). Deductions for superannuation contributions and tax agents' fees are not apportionable and are to be applied solely against the taxpayer's other taxable income (TD 2000/12). As the Commissioner had previously taken the opposite view, taxpayers may wish to seek amended assessments where relevant.

The formula for calculating the apportionment of the deductions is:

$$\text{apportionable deductions} \times \frac{\text{other taxable income calculated without regard to apportionable deductions}}{\text{apportionable deductions + notional gross taxable income}}$$

▶ Example

During the 2019–20 income year, Karen received gross exempt foreign income of $26,000 and incurred deductions relating to that income of $2,000. She also earned assessable income of $35,400 and incurred expenses of $4,400 to derive that income.

In addition, she made a deductible contribution of $3,000 to a complying superannuation fund, paid $400 for tax agent fees for the preparation of her Australian tax return and made a donation of $1,000.

Notional gross taxable income:

Gross exempt foreign income		$26,000
Less: Deductions		2,000
Exempt foreign income		$24,000
Gross assessable income		$35,400
Less: Expenses related to that income	$4,400	
Superannuation contributions	3,000	
Tax agent fees	400	7,800
Other taxable income before apportionable deductions		$27,600
Exempt foreign income		$24,000
Other taxable income before apportionable deductions		27,600
Less: Apportionable deductions (donation)		1,000
Notional gross taxable income		$50,600

Apportionment of deductions:

The calculation of the apportionment of the deduction claimed for the donation is:

$$\$1,000 \times \frac{\$27,600}{\$1,000 + \$50,600}$$

$$= \$534.88$$

Other taxable income:

Karen's other taxable income is therefore:

Gross assessable income		$35,400
Less: Expenses related to that income	$4,400	
Superannuation contributions	3,000	
Tax agent fees	400	
Apportioned deductions	534	8,334
Other taxable income		$27,066

Tax payable on non-exempt income:

The tax payable on Karen's "other taxable income", ie her non-exempt income, is calculated as follows:

Notional gross tax on $50,600 (including Medicare levy) = $9,004

Therefore, tax payable on other taxable income of $27,066 equals:

$$\frac{\$9{,}004}{\$50{,}600} \times \$27{,}066 = \$4{,}817$$

The exemption with progression rule does not apply where the foreign earnings are exempt under another provision. This means that if a taxpayer's foreign earnings satisfy the foreign earnings exemption but are also exempt under other specific provisions, such as those for pay and allowances of Defence Force members, for pay from international organisations or by virtue of a double taxation agreement, tax on a taxpayer's non-exempt income is not calculated on an exemption with progression basis (TD 94/58).

[FTR ¶9-927]

Approved Overseas Projects

¶10-870 Exemption of income derived on approved overseas projects

Income derived by an Australian resident taxpayer from at least 91 days' continuous employment (¶10-875) on an approved overseas project (¶10-880) is exempt from tax (ITAA36 s 23AF). The taxpayer must be an Australian resident at the time the foreign remuneration is derived. Taxpayers who may be entitled to this exemption need to lodge annual returns in Australia as usual.

The services must be performed for an Australian resident, an Australian government or authority (Commonwealth, state or territory), the government or an authority of an overseas country, or a designated international body such as the World Bank or the Asian Development Bank.

Income directly attributable to qualifying service by the taxpayer on an approved project, eg salary, wages, commission, bonuses, allowances, contractual payments and payments for recreation leave entitlements that accrue during the relevant period, is eligible for the exemption. The following amounts are excluded:

- payments in lieu of long service leave and superannuation and pension payments
- certain lump sum payments, including lump sum superannuation payments paid by a foreign-based superannuation fund (¶14-420) and lump sum employment termination payments (¶14-610)
- the tax-free amount of a bona fide redundancy payment (or of an approved retirement scheme payment)
- payments made by way of advance or loan
- restraint of trade payments or payments for personal injury
- transfers between superannuation funds
- income that is exempt from tax in the source country solely because of a double taxation agreement
- exempt foreign earnings (¶10-860).

Income assessed under the ITAA97 Div 83A employee share scheme provisions (¶10-085) that is attributable to qualifying service is eligible for the exemption as foreign employment income (s 23AF(18) definition of "eligible foreign remuneration").

Approved overseas project income is taken into account in calculating Australian tax payable on other income derived by the taxpayer. Tax on the non-exempt income is calculated by applying a notional average rate of tax payable on the sum of the exempt income and non-exempt income using the same formula as in ¶10-865.

The income tax exemptions for Australian individuals engaged by the International Monetary Fund and the 3 institutions of the World Bank Group will be clarified (2020–21 Budget Paper No 2, p 22).

[FTR ¶9-890]

¶10-875 Continuous period of qualifying service

The approved overseas project exemption applies where the qualifying service is for a continuous period of at least 91 days. Broadly, this comprises days performing personal services abroad on the project and reasonable time spent travelling between Australia and the project site. It also includes: weekends and equivalent time off; and periods of absence from work due to illness or accident and holidays taken — during or at the end of the assignment to the project and whether in Australia or overseas — that accrued during the relevant period. Note that a person is deemed to have taken leave in the most advantageous order.

Provision is made for cases where, during assignment to a project, the taxpayer returns to Australia on non-qualifying service for short periods of time, in effect breaking the continuity on the project into 2 or more periods. Provided that the number of intervening days spent in Australia does not exceed one-sixth of the number of days engaged on qualifying service on the approved project, the service period will not be regarded as broken. However, the number of the intervening days spent in Australia will not count as days of qualifying service on the project.

Where, because of unforeseen circumstances (such as ill-health or death in the family), a person does not complete the period of service, the proportion of eligible income exempted will be based on the number of days in the planned period of the assignment. The qualifying period for a person engaged to complete the original person's assignment will be based on the combined periods spent on the project by that person and the person originally assigned.

A safeguarding provision is designed to counter arrangements that seek to take advantage of the exemption by inflating the amount of income that is attributable to qualifying service. Income will not be exempt to the extent that it exceeds an amount that the Commissioner considers would be reasonable remuneration for the services.

[FTR ¶9-890]

¶10-880 Approved overseas projects

The taxpayer must perform personal services overseas in connection with an ‘‘approved project’’. Applications for approved project status should be made to AUSTRADE (the Australian Trade Commission).

In *Wilson*, the AAT held that income received by a taxpayer from working as a contractor for the US Army overseas was not exempt from tax in Australia under ITAA36 s 23AF because the taxpayer did not work on an ‘‘approved project’’. It said there was no evidence that the Trade Minister or his delegate either determined that the projects were in the national interest, or exercised their discretion to approve them in a written and signed document. See also IT 2064.

[FTR ¶9-907]

Shipping

¶10-883 Exemption for shipping income

Ordinary and statutory income from qualifying shipping activities using an eligible vessel is exempt from income tax (ITAA97 s 51-100). An eligible vessel is one which has a shipping exempt income certificate issued by the Minister for Infrastructure and Transport for it.

The exemption applies to all the income from core shipping activities relating to the vessel, ie activities directly involved in operating a qualifying vessel to carry shipping cargo or shipping passengers such as demurrage or cleaning charges. Core shipping activities include:

- carrying the shipping cargo or shipping passengers on the vessel
- crewing the vessel
- carrying goods on board for the operation of the vessel (including for the enjoyment of shipping passengers)
- providing the containers that carry shipping cargo on the vessel
- loading shipping cargo onto, and unloading it from, the vessel.

The exemption also applies to income from incidental shipping activities to the extent that the total incidental shipping income does not exceed 0.25% of the total core shipping income in the income year; if the total incidental shipping income exceeds 0.25% of the total core shipping income in the year then none of the income from incidental shipping activities will be exempt.

Miscellaneous Exemptions

¶10-885 Miscellaneous tax exemptions

In addition to items discussed above, the following are exempt from tax:

- remuneration of **certain visitors to Australia**, subject to limitations (¶22-080 – ¶22-100)
- certain **mining-related income** including the income of the British Phosphate Commissioners Banaba Contingency Fund (ITAA97 s 50-35)
- **foreign source income of foreign residents** (¶22-000)
- income exempted under **double taxation agreements**, eg *Ardia* (¶22-140 – ¶22-160). This includes salaries paid to certain foreign residents (French, German, Italian and Japanese) employed as assistant teachers in Australian schools, where the relevant **visiting teacher** criteria (¶22-150) are met (TD 2001/21 to TD 2001/24)
- interest derived by **"small" credit unions** from loans to members (¶3-435)
- most income of **copyright collecting societies** (¶3-450, ¶10-510)
- **exempt fringe benefits** (ITAA36 s 23L(1A)) and **non-cash business benefits** less than $300 (¶10-030). Most fringe benefits are non-assessable non-exempt (¶10-895)
- **reversionary bonuses on a life assurance policy** in limited circumstances (¶10-240)
- income from a trust estate where the trustee is an **offshore banking unit** and the beneficiaries are foreign residents (¶21-090).

Exclusions from Income

¶10-890 Non-assessable income

Ordinary income and statutory income are divided into subcategories:

- assessable income (which is taken into account in working out a taxpayer's taxable income)
- exempt income (which is excluded from taxable income but is taken into account in working out a taxpayer's loss for an income year or how much of a prior year tax loss is deductible in an income year: ¶16-880)
- non-assessable non-exempt income (which is both excluded from taxable income and ignored when working out a taxpayer's available losses: ¶10-895).

General rules for income categories

To ensure that there is no overlap or confusion between the above income categories, the following general rules apply (ITAA97 s 6-1 and following).

- An amount of ordinary income or statutory income can have only one status: assessable income, exempt income or non-assessable non-exempt income.
- An amount that is not ordinary income or statutory income cannot be assessable income, exempt income or non-assessable non-exempt income.
- An amount that is ordinary income or statutory income is assessable income unless it is exempt income or non-assessable non-exempt income.
- An amount of ordinary income or statutory income is exempt income if a Commonwealth law says that it is exempt income; or it is ordinary income and ITAA97 or ITAA36 excludes it (expressly or by implication) from being assessable income.
- An amount of ordinary income or statutory income is non-assessable non-exempt income if a Commonwealth law says that it is not assessable income and not exempt income.

ITAA97 Div 59 contains the operative provisions for miscellaneous items of non-assessable non-exempt income that are not dealt with as part of a larger legislative regime.

[FITR ¶85-110, ¶85-120]

¶10-895 Checklist of non-assessable non-exempt income

ITAA97 Subdiv 11-B contains a checklist of non-assessable non-exempt income provisions. The following provisions specify some of the amounts that are non-assessable non-exempt income (ITAA97 s 11-55).

Alienated personal services income

- ITAA97 s 85-20(3): non-deductible payment or obligation to associate (¶30-620)
- ITAA97 s 86-30: amounts that are personal services income of a personal services entity but are assessable to an individual (¶30-610)
- ITAA97 s 86-35(1): payments by a personal services entity or associate of personal services income already assessable to an individual (¶30-610)
- s 86-35(2): entitlements to a share of net income that is personal services income already assessable to an individual (¶30-610)

COVID-19 economic stimulus payments

- ITAA97 s 59-90: cash flow boost payments (¶10-040)
- ITAA97 s 59-95: COVID-19 economic response payments (¶10-040)

Disaster relief payments

- ITAA97 s 59-55: 2019–20 bushfires — payments for volunteer work with fire services (¶10-070)
- ITAA97 s 59-60: 2019–20 bushfires — disaster relief payments and non-cash benefits
- ITAA97 s 59-85: 2019 floods — recovery grants
- ITAA97 s 59-86: 2019 floods — on-farm grant program

Dividends

- ITAA36 s 44(4): demerger dividends (¶4-160)
- ITAA36 s 109ZC(3): a later dividend set off against an amount taken to be a dividend under ITAA36 Div 7A (¶4-200)

Foreign aspects of income taxation

- ITAA97 s 802-20: distributions of conduit foreign income (¶21-100)
- ITAA36 s 23AH: foreign branch profits of Australian companies (¶21-098)
- ITAA36 s 23AI: attributed controlled foreign company income (¶21-097, ¶21-210)
- ITAA36 s 128B(3)(jb): dividend and interest income of a foreign superannuation fund, if that income is exempt in the fund's country of residence
- ITAA36 s 128D: dividend, interest and royalty income payable to foreign residents that is subject to **withholding tax** (¶26-250), or would be subject to withholding tax but for certain exceptions (¶22-040)
- ITAA97 s 768-5: non-portfolio dividend from a CFC to an Australian resident company (¶21-095)
- ITAA97 s 768-910: foreign income derived by temporary residents (¶22-125)
- ITAA97 s 768-980: certain interest paid to foreign residents by temporary residents (¶22-125)

GST

- ITAA97 s 17-5(a): GST payable on a taxable supply (¶34-360)
- ITAA97 s 17-5(b), (c): increasing adjustments

Mining

- ITAA97 s 59-15: payments to Aboriginal people and distributing bodies subject to withholding tax. However, payments received by way of remuneration or for services rendered are assessable, eg payments received as salary by staff of the distributing body, or by persons making ordinary commercial contracts with it

Mutual receipts

- ITAA97 s 59-35: amounts that would be mutual receipts but for a prohibition on distributions to members (¶3-810)

National Rental Affordability Scheme payments

- ITAA97 s 380-35: state and territory assistance under the National Rental Affordability Scheme (ITAA97 s 380-35; ¶20-600)

Non-cash benefits

- ITAA36 s 23L(1): fringe benefits (¶10-060, ¶35-000). However, *exempt fringe benefits* (s 23L(1A)) and *non-cash business benefits* less than $300 (¶10-030) are exempt (¶10-885)

Notional sale and loan

- ITAA97 s 240-40: arrangement payments a notional seller receives or is entitled to receive (¶23-250)
- ITAA97 Div 242: luxury car lease payments that the lessor receives or is entitled to receive (¶17-220)

Related entities

- ITAA97 s 26-35(4): amounts received from related entities, to the extent that the entity's deduction is reduced (¶16-530)

Repayable amounts

- ITAA97 s 59-30: amounts received that must be and are repaid in a later year, where the repayment is not deductible (¶10-280)

Small business assets

- ITAA97 s 152-110(2): income arising from a CGT event where company or trust owned asset continuously for 15 years (¶7-165)

Tax loss transfers

- ITAA97 s 170-25(1): consideration received by loss company from income company (¶3-090)
- ITAA97 s 170-125(1): consideration received by loss company from income company for transfer of net capital loss (¶11-110)

Trading stock

- ITAA97 s 70-90(2): amounts received on disposal of trading stock outside the ordinary course of business (¶9-290)

Trusts

- ITAA36 s 99B: amounts representing attributable income (¶6-130, ¶21-290 – ¶21-350)
- ITAA36 Sch 2F s 271-105(3): amounts subject to family trust distribution tax (¶6-268).

[FITR ¶40-350 – ¶40-360]

Chapter 11 Capital Gains Tax • General Topics

Introduction

¶11-000 Overview of the capital gains tax provisions

A comprehensive capital gains tax (CGT) regime generally applies to CGT events that happen to CGT assets acquired by a taxpayer after 19 September 1985.

The CGT provisions are found in ITAA97 Pts 3-1 and 3-3. This chapter outlines the *general CGT rules* under Pt 3-1. It also outlines certain rules applying to companies only (under ITAA97 Pt 3-5) (¶11-080 – ¶11-120). The *special CGT rules* under Pt 3-3 and the value shifting rules are dealt with in ¶12-000ff. The CGT small business concessions are covered from ¶7-110. Note that all section references in this chapter are to ITAA97 unless otherwise indicated.

The CGT provisions are *catch-all* provisions. They apply to all gains that arise as a result of a CGT event happening (whether or not the gains are of a capital nature), subject to certain exemptions and exceptions, and to territorial and temporal limitations. However, where a capital gain arises from a CGT event and an amount is also assessable under some other (non-CGT) provision, double taxation is avoided by reducing or eliminating the amount of the capital gain.

The characterisation of a gain or loss on capital or revenue account is determined based on all surrounding circumstances. A gain or loss made on an investment by a trustee of a trust does not necessarily result in only CGT treatment (TD 2011/21).

Assessable income includes net capital gain

The CGT rules affect a taxpayer's income tax liability because assessable income includes a *net capital gain* for the income year. A net capital gain is the total of a taxpayer's capital gains for an income year, reduced by certain capital losses made by the taxpayer. A capital loss cannot be deducted from a taxpayer's assessable income, but it can reduce a capital gain in the current income year or a later income year.

The amount of a capital gain is generally discounted by 50% for a resident individual or trust, or 33$^{1}/3$% for certain superannuation funds and for life insurance companies from CGT assets that are complying superannuation assets. The general 50% discount percentage available for an individual taxpayer is reduced for any periods in which the taxpayer is either a foreign resident or a temporary resident during the period of ownership from 9 May 2012 (¶11-060). No discount is allowed if the capital gain is made by a company generally or by a life insurance company from its non-complying superannuation assets.

A company can only offset a net capital loss against a capital gain if it passes either the continuity of ownership test or the same business test in relation to both the capital loss year, the capital gain year and any intervening years. If it fails both the continuity of ownership test and the same business test in an income year, the company must work out net capital gains and losses in a special way (¶11-090).

A net capital loss of any taxpayer may be reduced if it has a commercial debt forgiven.

Capital gain or loss only if CGT event happens

A taxpayer can only make a capital gain or loss if a *CGT event* happens. The specific time when a CGT event happens is important for various reasons. In particular, the timing is relevant for working out whether a capital gain or loss from the event affects the taxpayer's income tax for the current income year or the CGT discount applies. If a CGT event involves a contract, the time of the event is usually when the contract is executed.

Most CGT events involve a *CGT asset*. However, some CGT events are concerned directly with capital receipts and do not involve a CGT asset. Many CGT assets are easily recognisable, eg land and buildings, shares, units in a unit trust, collectables and personal use assets. Other CGT assets are not so well recognised, eg the family home (which is usually exempt from CGT), contractual rights and goodwill.

▶ Planning point

Unforeseen tax problems can easily arise in the CGT context. Some of the potential pitfalls include:

- ascertaining which, if any, CGT event has occurred (as this affects the calculation and timing of any assessable gain)
- the loss of an asset's pre-CGT status where the underlying beneficial interests change
- the diminution of the value of pre-CGT assets
- non-assessable amounts which give rise to CGT consequences (such as CGT event E4 (¶11-290))
- value shifts that give rise to a deemed capital gain or reduce the cost base of the relevant asset (¶12-800)
- the immediate assessability of the consideration, even where paid by instalments (¶11-500)
- the taxpayer incurring non-deductible expenditure in relation to an asset where the expenditure does not form part of the cost base of the asset
- disposals involving multiple taxpayers (eg there may be ordinary income to one taxpayer and a capital gain to another), and
- a taxable CGT event (¶11-240) arising in relation to a pre-CGT asset.

Great care should be taken to ensure that an asset-rich individual preparing a will is aware of the likely CGT consequences of creating interests such as life estates where the final distribution of the assets is effectively postponed (¶12-580). In the Commissioner's view, the transfer of an asset from the trustee of a testamentary trust, established by will after administration, to a remainderman following the death of a life tenant is not eligible for roll-over. Nor is the passing of an asset from a trustee of a testamentary trust to a beneficiary, where the asset is a substitute for an asset held by the deceased at the date of death.

Working out capital gains and losses

For most CGT events, a *capital gain* arises if a taxpayer receives amounts from the CGT event which exceed the taxpayer's costs associated with that event. Conversely, a *capital loss* arises if the taxpayer's costs associated with the CGT event exceed the amounts received from it.

The amounts received from a CGT event are generally called the *capital proceeds*. The taxpayer's total costs associated with a CGT event are usually worked out in 2 different ways. For the purpose of working out a capital gain, those costs are called the *cost base* of the CGT asset. For the purpose of working out a capital loss, those costs are called the *reduced cost base* of the asset.

Where the taxpayer is an individual, a superannuation fund, a trust or a life insurance company (in respect of its complying superannuation assets), the capital gain may be discounted if the asset has been owned for at least 12 months.

To work out a capital gain, the cost base for the CGT asset is subtracted from the capital proceeds. If the capital proceeds exceed the cost base, the difference is a capital gain. If there is no capital gain, the capital proceeds are subtracted from the reduced cost base of the asset. If the reduced cost base exceeds the capital proceeds, the difference is a capital loss. If the capital proceeds are less than the cost base but more than the reduced cost base, there is neither a capital gain nor a capital loss.

If a taxpayer's total capital gains for an income year are more than the sum of the taxpayer's total capital losses for the income year and unapplied net capital losses from previous years, the taxpayer has a net capital gain for the income year equal to the difference.

Alternatively, if the taxpayer's total capital losses for the income year are more than the taxpayer's total capital gains for the income year, the taxpayer has a net capital loss for the income year equal to the difference.

Exceptions, exemptions and roll-overs

Where a capital gain or loss arises from a CGT event, an exception or exemption could apply to reduce or eliminate that gain or loss. Most of the exceptions are in Div 104 while the exemptions are in Div 118. The small business concessions are in Div 152.

If a roll-over is available, a capital gain or loss from a CGT event can be deferred or disregarded. Taxpayers must choose to apply some roll-overs while some apply automatically. There are 2 types of roll-overs: (1) a replacement-asset roll-over which allows a capital gain or loss to be deferred from one CGT event until a later CGT event if a CGT asset is replaced with another CGT asset; and (2) a same-asset roll-over which allows a capital gain or loss to be disregarded in a case where the same CGT asset is involved.

Keeping CGT records

Taxpayers are required to keep records of all matters that could result in them making a capital gain or loss. Those records must be kept for 5 years after the relevant CGT event has happened (s 100-70).

¶11-005 Checklist of CGT taxable and non-taxable events

This checklist shows whether a wide range of items and events are generally subject to CGT implications and where they are dealt with (as indicated in the Source column). Please note that the checklist does not address:

(a) the taxpayer's ability to roll-over a capital gain (see ¶7-195 and from ¶12-040), or

(b) the application of the CGT small business concessions (see ¶7-110).

The paragraph shown in the Source column should be referred to for the particular circumstances under which the relevant item under which the CGT event or exemption applies.

Item/Event	CGT (Y) / No CGT (N)	Source
Assignment of expectancy	Y	¶11-280
Bankrupt pays amount in relation to debt	Y	¶11-350
Bankruptcy trustee, transfer of asset to	N	¶11-210
Beneficiary becomes absolutely entitled to trust asset where		
– beneficiary paid consideration for trust interest	Y	¶11-290
– beneficiary paid no consideration for trust interest	N	¶11-290
Bitcoin, sale or use in a transaction	Y	¶11-380
Cancellation of intangible asset	Y	¶11-270
Capital payment in relation to a share	Y	¶11-310
Carried interest, entitlement to receive payment of	Y	¶11-350
Cessation of Australian tax residency	Y	¶11-330
Collectables, sale of		
– costing less than $500	N	¶11-640

Item/Event	CGT (Y) / No CGT (N)	Source
– others	Y	¶11-390
Company ceases to be a member of wholly owned group after intercompany group roll-over	Y	¶11-340
Compensation or damages for personal injuries	N	¶11-650
Compensation or damages for non-personal injuries	Y	¶11-650
Contract terminated or voided before completion	N	¶11-250
Confiscation of asset	Y	¶11-270
Conservation covenant over land granted	Y	¶11-280
Consideration received for variation of share rights	Y	¶11-320
Consolidated groups		
– error discovered in cost setting amount for joining entity asset	Y	¶11-360
– excess net allocable cost base on joining with no reset cost base assets	Y	¶11-360
– leaving ACA is negative	Y	¶11-360
– negative ACA on entity joining	Y	¶11-360
– tax cost setting amount for retained cost base asset exceed ACA on joining	Y	¶11-360
– reduction in tax cost setting amounts for reset cost base assets cannot be allocated	Y	¶11-360
Conversion of convertible note into shares or units	N	¶12-620
Converting trust to a unit trust	Y	¶11-290
Creating a trust over future property	Y	¶11-290
Damages for libel, slander or defamation	N	¶11-650
Death of asset owner		
– asset passes to beneficiary pursuant to will or intestacy	N	¶12-570
– asset passes to complying superannuation fund	Y	¶11-350
– asset passes to non-resident beneficiary	Y	¶11-350
Declaration of bare trust over asset	N	¶11-290
Declaration of new fixed trust over asset by trustee of fixed trust that has same beneficiaries	N	¶12-552
Declaration of trust over asset	Y	¶11-290
Decoration of valor	N	¶11-640
Deferred purchase agreement warrant comes to an end	Y	¶11-270
Destruction of asset	Y	¶11-270
Depreciating asset sale		
– asset used wholly for income-producing purposes	N	¶11-640
– asset not used for wholly income purposes	Y	¶11-350

Item/Event	CGT (Y) / No CGT (N)	Source
Direct value shift	Y	¶11-350
Discharge from intangible asset	Y	¶11-270
Disposal by beneficiary of capital interest in trust	Y	¶11-290
Dissolution of company, effect on shareholders	Y	¶11-270
Distribution of non-assessable income by discretionary trust to beneficiary	N	¶11-290
Distribution of non-assessable income by fixed trust to beneficiary	Y	¶11-290
Earnout arrangement, grant of	N	¶11-675
Easement, grant of	Y	¶11-280
Exchange traded option closed-out	Y	¶11-270
Exclusive trade tie agreement entered	Y	¶11-280
Exercise of option	N	¶12-700
Exercise of right or option to acquire shares or units	N	¶12-610
Expiry of lease, not used mainly for income-producing purposes	N	¶11-670
Expiry of lease, used mainly for income-producing purposes	Y	¶11-270
Expiry of option without exercise	Y	¶11-270
Expiry of right	Y	¶11-270
Financial contract for differences maturity or close	Y	¶11-270
Foreign currency hedging contract	N	¶11-670
Forfeiture of deposit on house sale	Y	¶11-320
Forfeiture of property	Y	¶11-250
Gifting an asset	Y	¶11-250
Granny flat in family arrangements (proposed)	N	¶11-915
Grant of right to use trademark	Y	¶11-280
Granting a lease	Y	¶11-300
Granting a long-term lease	Y	¶11-300
Granting a right to income from mining entitlement	Y	¶11-280
Granting an option	Y	¶11-280
Guarantees		
– to debtor on full payment by guarantor	N	¶11-270
– to guarantor if does not recover from indemnity	Y	¶11-270
– to creditor if both debtor and guarantor default	Y	¶11-270
Information and know-how		
– licence to use	Y	¶11-280, ¶11-380
– right to disclose	Y	¶11-280, ¶11-380
– transfer of	N	¶11-380

Item/Event	CGT (Y) / No CGT (N)	Source
Insurance moneys under personal accident policy	N	¶11-650
Instalment trust/warrants, final payment on	N	¶11-210
Joint tenancy converting to tenants in common	N	¶11-250
Leasehold fixture left at end of lease	Y	¶11-250
Lessee receives payment from lessor to vary lease	Y	¶11-300
Lessor incurs expenditure in getting lessee to vary lease	Y	¶11-300
Liquidator declares financial instrument worthless	Y	¶11-310
Liquidator declares shares worthless	Y	¶11-310
Liquidator's interim distribution received more than 18 months before liquidation	Y	¶11-310
Liquidator's final distribution received	Y	¶11-270
Liquidator acquires assets of company pursuant to liquidation	N	¶11-210
Loss of asset	Y	¶11-270
Main residence sale		
– resident	N	¶11-730
– non-resident	Y	¶11-730
Merging of assets	N	¶11-250
Motor cycle sale	N	¶11-640
Motor vehicle sale	N	¶11-640
Native title transfers	N	¶11-670
Nominee, transfer to or from absolutely entitled beneficiary	N	¶11-210
Non-competition contract	Y	¶11-280
Partnership		
– admission of partner	Y	¶11-200
– assignment of partnership interest	Y	¶11-200
– conversion to limited partnership	N	¶11-250
– retirement of partner	Y	¶11-200
Personal use asset, sale of		
– acquired for more than $10,000	Y	¶11-400
– acquired for $10,000 or less	N	¶11-400
Pre-CGT asset disposal	N	¶11-250
Pre-CGT shares or trust interest disposal		
– post-CGT assets of trust or company exceed 75% of net value	Y	¶11-350
– otherwise	N	¶11-250
Post-CGT building on pre-CGT land	Y	¶11-410
Premium rebate under policy of insurance	Y	¶11-320
Redemption of units	Y	¶11-270
Relationship breakdown settlement	N	¶11-670
Release of debt, creditor	Y	¶11-270

Item/Event	CGT (Y) / No CGT (N)	Source
Release of debt, debtor	N	¶11-270
Release from contract	Y	¶11-270
Renewal or extension of a lease	Y	¶11-300
Renewal or extension of an option	Y	¶11-280
Restrictive covenant entered into	Y	¶11-280
Retail premium paid to non-participating shareholder	Y	¶11-270
Right to reside in property for period granted	Y	¶11-280
Shares in a PDF sold	N	¶11-640
Short-term forex realisation gains and losses	Y	¶11-350
Small business roll-over		
– failure to acquire replacement asset with value to cover disregarded capital gain from roll-over	Y	¶11-340
– failure to acquire replacement asset within required period	Y	¶11-340
– replacement asset becomes trading stock	Y	¶11-340
– replacement asset ceases to be an active asset	Y	¶11-340
Strata title conversion	N	¶11-670
Trading stock, asset starts to be held as	Y	¶11-350
Trading stock sale	Y	¶11-640
Transfer of asset to a trust	Y	¶11-290
Trust fails to cease to exist within 6 months after trust roll-over	Y	¶11-340
Trustee transfers asset to beneficiary to end beneficiary's capital right	Y	¶11-290
Trustee transfers asset to beneficiary to end beneficiary's income right	Y	¶11-290
Sale of asset	Y	¶11-250
Security holder, transfer asset as security	N	¶11-210
Settlement of damages claim for negligence	Y	¶11-270
Shares on wind-up of company	Y	¶11-270
Splitting asset	N	¶11-570
Surrender of lease	Y	¶11-270
Use and enjoyment right prior to title	Y	¶11-260
Vary terms of trust in accordance with trust power	N	¶11-290

Net Capital Gains and Losses

¶11-030 Net capital gain assessable

A taxpayer's assessable income includes any net capital gain made by the taxpayer for the income year (s 102-5). Net capital gain is worked out using the following 5 steps.

Step 1: Capital gains made during the income year are reduced by any capital losses made during the income year. The taxpayer can choose the order in which the capital gains are reduced. Some provisions permit or require a taxpayer to disregard certain capital gains or losses when working out net capital gain. For instance, a small business taxpayer may be allowed, under Subdiv 152-B (¶7-165), to disregard a capital gain on an asset held for at least 15 years.

Step 2: If the capital gains are more than the capital losses, the difference is further reduced by any unapplied net capital losses carried forward from earlier income years. Again, the taxpayer can choose the order in which the capital gains are reduced.

Step 3: Each amount of a discount capital gain (¶11-033) remaining after Step 2 is reduced by the discount percentage (¶11-036).

Step 4: If any of the taxpayer's capital gains (whether or not they are discount capital gains) qualify for any of the small business concessions in Div 152 (¶7-110), those concessions, as appropriate, are applied to each capital gain.

Step 5: Add up the amounts of capital gains remaining after Step 4. The sum is the taxpayer's net capital gain for the income year.

Applying other exemptions

Certain CGT events require a taxpayer to disregard a capital gain or loss (eg if CGT event A1 happens to a CGT asset acquired by the taxpayer before 20 September 1985). In other cases, certain exemption provisions apply to reduce or disregard the capital gain or loss arising from a CGT event. In calculating the capital gain that is subject to the discount (Step 3), the taxpayer takes these general exemption provisions into account before applying any available capital losses or the CGT discount.

▶ Example 1

Rohan bought a beachfront house in December 2010 for $280,000. After renting it out for 4 years, Rohan moved into the house in December 2014 and it became his main residence for the next 6 years. He sold the house in December 2020 for $600,000. Rohan has carried forward prior year net capital losses of $4,000 and current year capital losses of $6,000. He has been a tax resident for the whole period of ownership. Rohan will apply the partial main residence exemption first to reduce the capital gain received on disposal of the house.

Capital proceeds ($600,000) – cost base ($280,000) = capital gain ($320,000)

$320,000 reduced by 6/10 (partial main residence exemption) = $128,000

Rohan will then apply his capital losses:

$128,000 – current year losses ($6,000) – prior year losses ($4,000) = $118,000

Rohan can then apply the CGT discount to calculate his net capital gain:

$118,000 × 50% = $59,000

Applying capital losses

A taxpayer may choose to apply capital losses against capital gains in any order. In most cases, the best outcome will be achieved if capital losses are applied against capital gains in the following order:

- to capital gains that are not entitled to indexation of cost base (¶11-610), the CGT discount or any benefit of the CGT small business concessions
- to capital gains calculated with the asset's indexed cost base

- to discount capital gains that are not eligible for the CGT small business concessions
- to capital gains that are eligible for the CGT small business concessions but are not discount capital gains
- to discount capital gains that are eligible for the CGT small business concessions.

If the taxpayer chooses to use frozen indexation (¶11-038), capital losses will be applied against the capital gain arising after deducting the cost base, including any indexed elements, from the capital proceeds. Where the gain is a discount capital gain, the capital loss is applied against the full capital gain, calculated by deducting the non-indexed cost base from the capital proceeds, and then applying the relevant discount to the balance.

Net capital losses from previous income years must be applied in the order in which they were made. Subject to this rule, the taxpayer can choose to apply any prior year net capital losses against capital gains for the income year in any order. Any prior year net capital losses will be applied against the current year capital gains before applying the CGT discount (Step 2 above). A beneficiary cannot apply a capital loss against an amount included in their assessable income under s 99B(1) (¶6-130) that had its origins in a capital gain from non-taxable Australian property of a foreign trust for CGT purposes (TD 2017/24).

If a capital gain remains after applying all available capital losses, the remaining capital gain is reduced by the appropriate CGT discount (if available) (Step 3 above). If any of the capital gains qualify for small business concessions in Div 152, those concessions are then applied against each qualifying capital gain (Step 4 above). The remaining amount is the taxpayer's net capital gain for the year.

▶ Example 2

Brad acquired shares in a listed public company in June 1998 and units in a listed unit trust in May 2001. He has a carried forward net capital loss of $12,000 from 2015–16 and incurred a further capital loss of $6,000 in August 2020.

Brad sold the shares in July 2020 and made a capital gain of $4,000 (on choosing the indexation method). When he sold the units in October 2020, Brad chose the CGT discount rather than the indexation option, and made a pre-discount capital gain of $22,000.

Brad may choose to apply his capital losses in any order, but they must be applied against discount gains prior to reduction by the discount. Brad chooses to apply the $6,000 current year loss first against the $4,000 gain realised in July 2020. The remaining $2,000 current year loss balance and the prior year loss of $12,000 are applied against the discount gain of $22,000, resulting in a nominal gain after losses of $8,000.

The nominal gain is reduced by the CGT discount (50% for resident individuals), leaving a net capital gain of $4,000 for 2020–21.

Effect of bankruptcy on net capital losses

If a taxpayer becomes bankrupt or is released from debts under a law relating to bankruptcy, the taxpayer's net capital losses carried forward from previous income years can no longer be used to offset capital gains made by the taxpayer. This rule applies even if the bankruptcy is annulled under a composition or scheme of arrangement and the taxpayer was, will be or may be released from debts which would have been released if the taxpayer became a discharged bankrupt.

If there is a subsequent repayment of any debt which was taken into account in calculating a net capital loss that was disallowed because of bankruptcy, that repayment gives rise to a capital loss (¶11-350).

[FITR ¶151-400]

¶11-033 Discount capital gains

A discount capital gain is a capital gain that satisfies the requirements of Subdiv 115-A (ss 115-5 to 115-50). To be a discount capital gain, a capital gain must:

- be made by an individual, a complying superannuation entity (ie a complying superannuation fund, a complying ADF or a PST: s 995-1(1)), a trust, or by a life insurance company from a CGT event in respect of a CGT asset that is a complying superannuation asset
- be worked out without the cost base being indexed, and
- result from a CGT event happening to a CGT asset owned by the taxpayer for at least 12 months.

A life insurance company can only segregate assets for its complying superannuation business in a complying superannuation asset pool (¶3-480, ¶3-515).

Asset owned by the taxpayer for at least 12 months

The discount is generally only available where the CGT asset has been owned by the taxpayer for at least 12 months. The ATO considers this 12-month requirement means that a period of 365 days (or 366 in a leap year) must elapse between the day on which the CGT asset was acquired and the day on which the CGT event happens. For example, if the asset was acquired on 2 February 2018, the discount would not apply if the CGT event occurred before 3 February 2019 (TD 2002/10).

Notwithstanding the general rule, the CGT discount may be available where an asset has been held by a taxpayer for less than 12 months. This can apply where the taxpayer is deemed to have acquired the asset at an earlier time under the special acquisition rules in s 115-30. The rules include the following:

- an asset acquired under the same-asset (¶12-450) or replacement-asset (¶12-150) roll-over provisions is treated as being acquired when the previous owner acquired the asset
- an asset acquired as a beneficiary or legal personal representative of a deceased person (¶12-580) is treated as being acquired:
  - if the asset was a pre-CGT asset of the deceased — when the deceased died
  - if the asset was a post-CGT asset of the deceased — when the deceased acquired the asset
- a share acquired through exercising an ESS interest that is a right eligible for the start-up company concession in s 83A-33 is treated as being acquired on the date the right was issued (¶12-630).

For the purpose of applying the CGT discount in relation to a retail premium being received in connection with renounceable rights offers, the right is treated as being acquired on the date the original shares were acquired (TR 2017/4).

The following CGT events do not qualify for the CGT discount: D1 to D3, E9, F1, F2, F5, H2, J2, J5, J6 and K10 (s 115-25(3)). For details of these events, see the table in ¶11-240.

What are not discount capital gains?

A capital gain from a CGT event is specifically stated not to be a discount capital gain in 2 cases.

(1) Agreement entered into within 12 months of the CGT event

The first case is where the taxpayer makes a capital gain from a CGT event happening to a CGT asset under an agreement made within 12 months of acquiring the asset (s 115-40). This applies even if the gain otherwise meets the discount capital gain requirements.

(2) Changes to equity interests in a company or trust

The second case is aimed at stopping taxpayers from obtaining the benefit of discounted capital gains by purchasing assets through an existing company or trust and effectively selling that asset within the 12-month period through a sale of the shares in the company or trust interests which have been held for at least 12 months (s 115-45).

Accordingly, a capital gain is not a discount capital gain if:

- just before the CGT event happened to the shares or trust interest, the taxpayer and associates beneficially owned: (i) at least 10% by value of the shares in the company (except shares having only limited income and capital rights); or (ii) at least 10% of the trust voting interests, issued units or other fixed interests in the trust

- the total of the cost bases of CGT assets that the company or trust owned at the time of the CGT event and had acquired less than 12 months before then is more than half of the total of the cost bases of the CGT assets the company or trust owned at the time of the event, and

- had the company or trust disposed of the assets it had held for less than 12 months at the time of the CGT event happening in relation to the shares or trust interests, the net capital gain from those assets would have been more than half of the net capital gain that the company or trust would have made if it disposed of all of its assets at that time. For the purpose of these calculations, it must be assumed that all disposals are for market value and that the company or trust does not have any net capital losses which can be offset against capital gains.

This second rule does not stop a capital gain from being a discount capital gain if the shares are in a company with at least 300 members, or the interests are in a fixed trust with at least 300 beneficiaries, unless there is ''concentrated ownership'' of the company or trust (s 115-50). A fixed trust for these purposes is a trust in which persons have fixed entitlements to all of the income and corpus (s 995-1(1)).

There is ''concentrated ownership'' if an individual owns, or up to 20 individuals own between them, directly or indirectly, shares in the company or interests in the trust with fixed entitlements to at least 75% of the income or capital, or at least 75% of the voting rights. For this purpose, one individual together with associates, and any nominees of the individual or of the individual's associates, are counted as one individual. The test also considers whether it is reasonable to conclude that the rights attaching to any of the shares or interests can be varied or abrogated in such a way that ownership would be concentrated. This would involve looking, for example, at the company or trust's constituent document and any agreements under which a person had a power to acquire shares or interests (s 115-50(7)). It is irrelevant whether the rights are actually varied or abrogated.

An amount included in a beneficiary's assessable income under s 99B(1) (¶6-130) that had its origins in a capital gain from non-taxable Australian property of a foreign trust for CGT purposes will not be a discount capital gain (TD 2017/24).

[FITR ¶154-125 – ¶154-170]

¶11-036 Discount percentage

A discount capital gain remaining after applying any current year or prior year capital losses is reduced by the discount percentage when working out a taxpayer's net capital gain (¶11-030). The discount percentage is:

- generally, 50% if the gain is made by a resident individual, but is reduced for periods in which a taxpayer is a foreign resident or a temporary resident during the ownership period from 9 May 2012 (see below)
- 50% if the gain is made by a trust, or
- 33 1/3% if the gain is made by a complying superannuation entity.

A 60% discount is available for a resident individual making a capital gain from investing in qualifying affordable housing, including through a trust (¶11-037).

The discount percentage is not available to other entities, such as companies generally or life insurance companies in respect of assets that are not complying superannuation assets. For special rules applying to listed investment companies, see ¶11-038.

Reduction of discount for foreign and temporary resident individuals

The 50% discount percentage available to individual taxpayers is reduced for any periods in which the taxpayer has been a foreign resident or a temporary resident during the period of ownership, subject to transitional rules for assets held as at 9 May 2012 (s 115-105). The reduction applies irrespective of whether the taxpayer makes the capital gain for an asset owned directly or a discount capital gain received through a trust (ss 115-105; 115-110).

The calculation of the reduced discount percentage depends on the circumstances, including date of acquisition and the taxpayer's residency status on 8 May 2012 where the asset was held on that date (s 115-115). The relevant formulas for calculating the discount percentage are detailed below applying the following terms:

"*Excess*" the amount equal to the market value of the asset as at 8 May 2012 less its cost base

"*Shortfall*" means the amount that the Excess is less than the discount capital gain

"*apportionable day*" means a day, after 8 May 2012, during the discount testing period

"*discount testing period*" generally means the period starting from the date of acquisition of the asset (or if the taxpayer is a beneficiary of a trust, the date taxpayer last became a beneficiary of the trust, if this is later) and ending on the day of the CGT event

"*eligible resident*" means an Australian resident that is not a temporary resident.

The date of acquisition and days of being an eligible resident may be affected where the individual taxpayer directly holds the asset but is treated as having acquired the asset on an earlier date pursuant to s 115-30 (s 115-105(3)).

Asset acquired after 8 May 2012

Where the asset was acquired by the taxpayer after 8 May 2012 the discount percentage is calculated using the following formula (s 115-115(2)):

$$\frac{\text{Number of days during discount testing period that you were an Australian resident (but not a *temporary resident)}}{2 \times \text{Number of days in discount testing period}}$$

▶ Example 1

Tyler acquired a property on 9 May 2017 while he was a resident (but not temporary resident) for $900,000. On 9 November 2018, Tyler ceased to be a resident but continued to own the property. On 14 March 2020, Tyler sells the property for $980,000.

In this case, the number of days in the testing period is 1,041 and the days Tyler was an Australian resident was 549. Accordingly, Tyler's discount percentage is 26.37%.

Where the taxpayer is a foreign resident or temporary resident for the whole of the ownership period, the discount percentage will be 0%. Where the taxpayer is a resident (other than a temporary resident) at all times during the ownership period the discount percentage is 50%.

Asset held when taxpayer was a resident as at 8 May 2012

Where the asset was acquired by the taxpayer on or before 8 May 2012 and the taxpayer was a resident (other than a temporary resident) as at that date, the discount percentage is calculated using the following formula (s 115-115(3)):

$$\frac{\text{Number of days in discount testing period} - \text{Number of apportionable days that you were a foreign resident or }^{*}\text{temporary resident}}{2 \times \text{Number of days in discount testing period}}$$

▶ Example 2

Chad acquired shares in Nickel Co Pty Ltd on 11 October 2010 for $100,000 when he was a resident of Australia. On 12 November 2018, Chad ceased to be a resident and made the election under s 104-165 to disregard the capital gain from CGT event I1. As a result of the election the shares became taxable Australian property. On 1 April 2020, Chad sells the shares for $600,000.

In the circumstances, the days in the testing period is 3,461 and the days he was a foreign resident is 507. The discount percentage in these circumstances is 42.68%.

Where the taxpayer is a resident at all times during the ownership period the discount percentage is 50%.

Asset held when taxpayer a foreign resident or temporary resident as at 8 May 2012

Where the taxpayer is either a foreign resident or a temporary resident as at 8 May 2012, the individual taxpayer can choose to apply the 50% CGT discount to the portion of the capital gain that accrued as at 8 May 2012 *provided* the taxpayer acquires a valuation of the relevant asset as at that date (s 115-115(4)). That is, an effective discount of 50% is potentially available for the amount equal to the market value of the asset as at 8 May 2012 less its cost base (ie the "Excess"). In these circumstances, where the Excess is equal to or more than the discount capital gain calculated at the time of the CGT event (ie the value of the asset fell since 8 May 2012), the discount percentage applying to the discount capital gain will be 50%. If the discount capital gain is more than the Excess the discount percentage is calculated using the following formula (s 115-115(5)):

$$\frac{\text{Excess} + \left(\text{Shortfall} \times \dfrac{\text{Number of apportionable days that you were an eligible resident}}{\text{Number of apportionable days}}\right)}{2 \times \text{Amount of the }^{*}\text{discount capital gain}}$$

▶ Example 3

Gwen acquired a house in Sydney on 8 April 2011 for $500,000 while a temporary resident. She became a full resident on 2 January 2016. On 30 March 2020, Gwen sold the house for $750,000. She obtained a valuation which provided the market value of the house as at 8 May 2012 was $680,000.

In these circumstances, where Gwen chooses to use the market value method in s 115-115(5) the Excess is $180,000, the discount capital gain is $250,000, the shortfall is $70,000, the number of apportionable days is 2,883 and the apportionable days she was an eligible resident is 1,550. Accordingly, the applicable discount is 44.62%.

If a valuation is not obtained for an asset held at that date, the taxpayer will effectively not receive any discount for capital gains accrued prior to that date even if the taxpayer subsequently becomes a resident (other than a temporary resident). In this case, the discount is calculated using the following formula (s 115-115(6)):

$$\frac{\text{Number of apportionable days that you were an Australian resident (but not a *temporary resident)}}{2 \times \text{Number of days in discount testing period}}$$

▶ Example 4

Using the same facts as in Example 3 except that Gwen did not obtain a market valuation of the property as at 8 May 2012.

In these circumstances, the number of apportionable days Gwen was an Australia resident is 1,550 and the number of days in the discount testing period is 3,280. Accordingly, the applicable discount is 23.63%.

Where a valuation is not obtained as at 8 May 2012 and the taxpayer is a foreign resident or temporary resident at all times since that date the discount percentage is nil.

▶ Planning point

Taxpayers that are foreign residents or temporary residents holding taxable Australian property as at 8 May 2012 with unrealised gains should obtain a valuation of that property as at that date to be able maximise the discount capital gain.

[FITR ¶154-175 – ¶154-179/10]

¶11-037 Discount for qualifying affordable housing

With effect from 1 January 2018, the CGT discount is increased from 50% to 60% for capital gains made by a resident individual from a dwelling used to provide affordable housing for at least 1,095 days (which may be aggregated over different periods) during the ownership period. The additional discount is available to capital gains made by a resident individual or distributed/attributed to a resident individual by a trust (other than a public unit trust or a superannuation fund), a managed investment trust or a partnership (s 115-125).

The CGT discount is calculated as the sum of the following:

(a) The CGT discount percentage that applies under ordinary rules (¶11-036)

(b) The amount calculated as:

$$\frac{\text{Discount percentage that would ordinarily apply to the capital gain}}{5} \times \frac{\text{Affordable housing days}}{\text{Total ownership days}}$$

Where:

- ***Affordable housing days*** means the number of days the dwelling was used to provide affordable housing during its ownership period less the number of days when the individual receiving the affordable housing capital gains discount was a foreign or temporary resident
- ***Total ownership days*** means the number of days during the ownership period of the dwelling less the number of days after 8 May 2012 during that ownership period that the individual was either a foreign resident or a temporary resident.

For these purposes, a dwelling is used to provide affordable housing if the following conditions are satisfied:

- residential premises condition — the dwelling is residential premises that is not commercial residential premises
- property management condition — the tenancy of the dwelling or its occupancy is exclusively managed by an eligible community housing provider
- providing affordable housing certification condition — the eligible community housing provider has given each entity that holds an ownership interest in the dwelling certification that the dwelling was used to provide affordable housing
- National Rental Affordability Scheme (NRAS) condition — no entity that has an ownership interest in the dwelling is entitled to receive an NRAS incentive for the NRAS year (¶20-600), and
- MIT membership condition — if the ownership interest in the dwelling is owned by an MIT, the tenant does not have an interest in the MIT that passes the non-portfolio test (s 980-5).

[FITR ¶154-179/20]

¶11-038 Application of the discount to particular taxpayers

Individuals

If an individual makes a capital gain from a CGT asset held for at least 12 months prior to the CGT event, the taxable capital gain is calculated by applying the discount percentage to the capital gain (calculated without indexation of the cost base) remaining after the application of any current year or prior year capital losses (s 102-5).

If the CGT asset was acquired before 21 September 1999 the individual can instead choose to calculate the taxable capital gain by using the indexed cost base frozen as at 30 September 1999, without any discount (ss 110-36(2); 114-5; 115-25(1)).

▶ Planning point

A taxpayer needs to work out the results of each method to determine which method is preferable in any particular case. In general, the discounted basis is more attractive as time goes on, particularly if the gain is large. However, the frozen indexation option may be preferable if the pre-1 October 1999 inflation component of the gain is substantial.

▶ Example

Holly (a resident at all times) acquired shares in a listed public company in August 1994 for $20 each and sold the shares in July 2020 for $38 each. At the date of sale, the indexed cost base would be $22, based on indexation frozen at 30 September 1999. Holly can choose to calculate the capital gain for each share in either of the following ways:

- the excess of disposal proceeds ($38) over indexed cost base ($22), giving a capital gain of $16, or
- half of the realised nominal gain, being the excess of the capital proceeds ($38) over the cost base without any indexation ($20), the nominal gain being $18 and half of that gain being $9.

Given this outcome, Holly can choose to claim the CGT discount.

If Holly had capital losses (or net capital losses), indexation could produce a better result, eg if Holly had capital losses of $16, then the indexation method would give a net capital gain of nil while applying the discount method would give a net capital gain of $1.

Complying superannuation entities

If a complying superannuation entity (ie a complying superannuation fund, a complying ADF or a PST) makes a capital gain from a CGT event happening to a CGT asset held for at least 12 months prior to the CGT event, the entity will be taxed on two-thirds of the gain, without any indexation applying to the cost base.

Note, however, that where a non-complying superannuation fund that is constituted as a trust makes a capital gain, the gain may be reduced by 50%, ie the discount percentage that applies for a trust.

If the CGT asset was acquired before 21 September 1999 the entity can instead choose to include in its assessable income 100% of the capital gain (without discount) calculated with the indexed cost base frozen from 30 September 1999.

Life insurance companies

If a life insurance company makes a capital gain from a CGT event happening to a CGT asset that is a complying superannuation fund asset (¶3-515) and has been held for at least 12 months prior to the CGT event, the company will be taxed on two-thirds of the gain, without any indexation applying to the cost base.

Trusts

If a trust makes a capital gain from a CGT event happening to a CGT asset that has been held for at least 12 months prior to the CGT event, the trust is entitled to the 50% discount percentage on the capital gain calculated without the benefit of indexation.

If the CGT asset was acquired before 21 September 1999 the trust can instead choose to calculate the capital gain with an indexed cost base frozen as at 30 September 1999 but with no discount (ss 110-36(2); 114-5; 115-25(1)).

Special rules apply for determining the taxable income of a beneficiary of a trust that is either specifically entitled or presently entitled to trust income that includes a net capital gain. The rules are detailed in ¶11-060.

Managed investment trusts (MITs) and attribution MITs (AMITs) are proposed to be prevented from applying the 50% discount at the trust level with effect to payments made in income years commencing on or after 3 months after the date of assent. MITs and AMITs that derive a capital gain will still be able to distribute this income as a capital gain that can be discounted in the hands of the beneficiary (*2018–19 Budget Paper* No 2, p 44).

Listed investment companies

Normally, a shareholder receiving a distribution of a capital gain as a dividend does not benefit from any CGT discount that may have been available if the shareholder had made the capital gain directly. However, there is an exception to this rule in the case of dividends from listed investment companies (LICs). This exception enables resident shareholders in LICs to benefit from the CGT discount on assets realised by the LIC, provided that the assets have been held for more than 12 months. In effect, those LIC shareholders who receive a dividend that is attributable to a capital gain will be allowed a deduction that reflects the CGT discount the shareholder could have claimed if they had made the capital gain directly. For example, in the case of a resident individual shareholder, the deduction will be equal to 50% of the attributable part, but if the shareholder is a complying superannuation entity, an FHSA trust or a life insurance company, the deduction will be 33$^{1}/_{3}$%. An LIC will be required to maintain records so that it can advise shareholders of the attributable part included in each dividend it pays.

The effect of this measure (Subdiv 115-D) is that LIC dividends have a broadly similar tax outcome to distributions made to members of managed funds. The Commissioner's views on the operation of this measure are set out in TR 2005/23.

A foreign resident individual may access the deduction where a dividend is received through the individual's permanent establishment in Australia.

[FITR ¶151-400, ¶154-125 – ¶154-197]

¶11-040 Net capital losses

A net capital loss is worked out by subtracting capital gains for the income year from capital losses for the income year. If the resulting amount is more than nil, it is the taxpayer's net capital loss for the income year (s 102-10).

A net capital loss is not deductible from a taxpayer's assessable income. However, it can generally be offset against capital gains made by the taxpayer in later income years (¶11-030).

To the extent that a net capital loss cannot be used to offset capital gains in an income year, it can be carried forward to a later income year.

[FITR ¶151-410]

¶11-050 Exceptions and modifications to general CGT rules

In some circumstances, the general rules for calculating net capital gains and losses are varied (s 102-30).

- Companies can only offset a net capital loss against a capital gain if they pass either the continuity of ownership test or the same business test in relation to the capital loss year, the capital gain year and any intervening years (¶11-080).
- Companies must work out net capital gains and losses in a special way if they fail both the continuity of ownership test and the same business test in an income year (¶11-090).
- Companies may have to work out a net capital loss in a special way and the Commissioner can disallow their net capital losses or current year capital losses if: (a) a capital gain or loss is injected into the company; (b) a tax benefit is obtained from available net capital losses or current year capital losses; or (c) a tax benefit is obtained because of available capital gains (¶11-120).
- Net capital losses may be reduced if a taxpayer's commercial debts are forgiven (¶16-910).
- Capital losses from collectables can only be offset against capital gains from collectables (¶11-390).
- Capital losses from personal use assets are disregarded (¶11-400).
- Beneficiaries of a trust whose net income from the trust includes a net capital gain are treated as making additional capital gains (¶11-060).
- The capital gain or loss a company makes from a CGT event that happened to a share in a company that is a foreign resident may be reduced (¶12-745).
- Special rules also apply to life insurance companies (¶3-480), head companies of consolidated groups or multiple entry consolidated groups (¶8-210), and PDFs (¶3-555).
- Special rules apply to Managed Investment Trusts (MITs) (¶12-660).

[FITR ¶151-470]

Capital Gains of Trusts

¶11-060 Net capital gains of trusts

Special interim rules apply in determining the taxation treatment of trusts and their beneficiaries where the trust derives a net capital gain during an income year (Subdiv 115-C).

The manner in which beneficiaries and/or trustees of a trust are taxed on trust income is outlined in ¶6-077. From a CGT perspective, the effect of the provisions is to directly tax the beneficiaries on their ''specific entitlements'' (¶6-107) to, and their share of other, capital gains made by the trust solely under the CGT provisions.

A trust, where permitted by its trust deed, is able to stream capital gains to particular beneficiaries. The beneficiaries are considered to be ''specifically entitled'' to such capital gains provided the beneficiary receives, or can reasonably be expected to receive, an amount equal to the net financial benefit referable to that capital gain and the entitlement is recorded as such in the accounts or records of the trust (s 115-228). A beneficiary can be reasonably expected to receive the net financial benefit from a capital gain even though the capital gain will not be established until after year end (TD 2012/11). However, a beneficiary cannot be made specifically entitled to a capital gain calculated by using the market value substitution rule or that has been reduced to nil as a result of losses. The beneficiary's fraction of the net financial benefit referable to a capital gain is reduced by trust losses or expenses applied to those gains (s 115-228(1)). Where a trustee makes a capital gain pursuant to CGT event E5 as a result of a beneficiary becoming absolutely entitled to an asset as a remainder beneficiary under a will, the beneficiary can be specifically entitled to the gain, as the financial benefit is the asset transferred and the will which created the trust recorded the absolute entitlement (ID 2013/33). The Commissioner has issued a warning against using artificial capital gains tax streaming arrangements to create a mismatch between amounts beneficiaries are entitled to receive from a trust and the amounts they are taxed on (TA 2013/1).

A trustee can be made specifically entitled to an amount of a capital gain by choosing to be assessed on it provided it is permitted under the trust deed and no trust property representing the capital gain is paid to or applied for the benefit of a beneficiary of the trust by the end of 2 months after the end of the income year (s 115-230).

Any capital gain remaining after the specific entitlements have been determined will flow proportionately to the beneficiaries (and/or trustee) based on their share of the income of the trust, excluding the amounts to which beneficiaries/trustee are specifically entitled. The proportionate interest is known as the beneficiary's ''adjusted Division 6 percentage'' (s 115-227).

Where a beneficiary has an entitlement to a capital gain made by the trust, whether due to a specific entitlement or otherwise, the beneficiary is treated as having made an extra capital gain for CGT purposes which is determined by the following 4-step process:

1. Determine the beneficiary's share of the capital gain of the trust, being the total of the capital gain to which the beneficiary is specifically entitled plus the beneficiary's adjusted Division 6 percentage of capital gains to which no beneficiary is specifically entitled.
2. Divide that amount by the total capital gain to provide the beneficiary's fraction of the capital gain.
3. Provided the total of the net capital gains and franked distributions (after being reduced by deductions directly relevant to them) is less than the trust's net income (ignoring franking credits), multiply the fraction in step 2 by the taxable income of the trust that relates to the capital gain. This generally gives the ''attributable gain'' (s 115-225(1)).

4. Gross up the result of step 3 based on any CGT concessions which were applied as follows:

- if either, but not both, of the CGT general discount or the small business 50% reduction (¶7-110) applied to the capital gain — double the step 3 amount
- if both the 50% discount and the small business 50% reduction applied to the capital gain — quadruple the step 3 amount
- if no discounts or concessions applied — the step 3 amount (ie no gross up) (s 115-215).

The beneficiary's extra capital gain is equal to the amount resulting from step 4. This process allows the beneficiary to apply any of its current year or prior year capital losses against the gain and then reapply any CGT discount (at its discount percentage) and/or small business 50% reduction, as appropriate. The 4-step process applies on a gain by gain basis for each capital gain of the trust.

▶ Example 1

On 3 May 2020, the Blonde Discretionary Trust made a capital gain of $10,000 when it disposed of a CGT asset that it acquired on 2 April 2012. The trustee applies the 50% CGT discount (small business relief is not available), resulting in a discounted capital gain of $5,000. The trust has no capital losses or income losses. The trust makes also $2,000 of net rental income.

In accordance with the trust deed, the trustee resolves to distribute 50% of the gain from the sale of the asset to resident beneficiary Deborah, thereby making her specifically entitled to 50% of the capital gain. The other income is resolved to be distributed between Deborah as to 40% and DH Pty Ltd as to 60%.

In accordance with the 4-step process, the additional capital gain to Deborah is calculated as follows:

1. Share of the capital gain = $2,500 (being the specific entitlement) + $1,000 (being the adjusted Division 6 percentage of 40% of the balance of the capital gain) = $3,500
2. Beneficiary Fraction = $3,500 / $5,000 (being the capital gain) = 70%
3. Attributable gain = 70% × $5,000 = $3,500
4. Double the step 3 amount (as 50% discount applied) = $7,000.

Deborah has an additional capital gain of $7,000 in 2019–20. Deborah has a separate $1,000 capital loss in this year. After applying the capital loss to the additional capital gain and applying the 50% discount, Deborah has a capital gain of $3,000. Note she also has trust income of $800.

The additional capital gain for DH Pty Ltd is calculated as follows:

1. Share of the capital gain = $1,500 (being the adjusted Division 6 percentage of 60% of the capital gain remaining after specific entitlements excluded)
2. Beneficiary Fraction = $1,500 / $5,000 (being the capital gain) = 30%
3. Attributable gain = 30% × $5,000 = $1,500
4. Double the step 3 amount (as 50% discount applied) = $3,000.

DH Pty Ltd has an additional capital gain of $3,000 in 2019–20. As DH Pty Ltd is a company it is not entitled to reapply the 50% discount. Note DH Pty Ltd will also have trust income of $1,200 for the year.

Where the total of the trust's net capital gains and franked distributions (after being reduced by deductions directly relevant to them) exceeds the trust's net income (ignoring franking credits), the attributable gain in step 3 is calculated by undertaking the rateable reduction in the following formula (s 115-225):

$$\text{Attributable gain} = \text{Taxable amount of capital gain} \times \frac{\text{Taxable income of the trust (excluding franking credits)}}{\text{net capital gain of the trust + net franked distributions}}$$

▶ Example 2

During 2019–20, the Woodley Trust made a capital gain of $3 million. The capital gain was eligible for the general discount at 50%, the 50% small business discount and applied the CGT retirement exemption in relation to $500,000. The net capital gain was reduced to $250,000. The Woodley Trust also derived $35,000 of franked distributions, $15,000 of franking credits and had a net rental loss of $100,000. The taxable income of the trust for 2019–20 was $200,000 (being $185,000 excluding franking credits).

Trustee exercised its discretion to make Frank specifically entitled to the capital gain and distribute all other income of the trust to Frank.

In accordance with the 4-step process, the additional capital gain to Frank is calculated as follows:

1. Share of the capital gain = $250,000 (being the specific entitlement)
2. Beneficiary Fraction = $250,000 / $250,000 (being the capital gain) = 100%
3. Attributable gain = $250,000 × $185,000 / ($250,000 + $35,000) = $162,281.
4. Four times step 3 amount (as both 50% general and 50% small business discounts applied) = $649,124.

Frank has a personal current year capital loss of $20,000 and derived no other income. As a result, the net capital gain in Frank's hands is $157,281 (being ($649,124 – $20,000)/4) plus the reduced franked distributions $22,719 plus franking credits of $15,000 giving taxable income of $195,000. Frank will be entitled to a franking offset of $15,000 against tax payable.

A foreign resident or temporary resident beneficiary of a fixed trust may be able to disregard the extra capital gain made if it relates to a CGT asset of the trust that is not taxable Australian property (ss 855-40; 768-915; ¶22-125). This exemption does not apply to a non-resident beneficiary of a non-fixed resident trust (*Draft* TD 2019/D6; *Peter Greensill Family Co Pty Ltd (as trustee)*; *N & M Martin Holdings Pty Ltd & Anor*).

To avoid double taxation on the capital gain in the beneficiary's hands, ITAA36 Div 6E generally adjusts the amount assessable to the beneficiary under Div 6 by assuming the trust has no capital gains (¶6-077). However, the trustee of the trust may be liable under ITAA36 s 98 on such an amount (eg where beneficiary is a foreign resident or beneficiary under a legal disability) or s 99 or 99A. In such cases similar grossing up rules will apply (ss 115-220; 115-222). However, the CGT discount is not allowed for a trustee assessed under ITAA36 s 98(3)(b), (4) (¶6-220) or 99A (¶6-230) (ss 115-220; 115-222).

Where a foreign trust has a CGT event in relation to a CGT asset that is not taxable Australian real property, the following will apply:

- the trustee disregards any capital gain (or capital loss) from that event in calculating the net income of the trust under ITAA36 s 95(1)
- the trust's beneficiaries are not treated as having made capital gains for the purposes of Subdiv 115-C in respect of the event, and
- if the amount is paid to a resident beneficiary it will be included in the beneficiary's assessable income pursuant to ITAA36 s 99B(1) and the beneficiary is not entitled to apply any capital loss or the CGT discount to such an amount (TD 2017/24).

The source of income is not relevant in determining whether an amount of trust capital gain is assessable to a non-resident beneficiary or trustee pursuant to Subdiv 115-C (*Draft* TD 2019/D7). The same view applies in relation to a non-resident beneficiary's share of "taxable Australian property" gains of a non-resident trust and a trustee's share of a capital gain to which s 115-222 applies.

A complying superannuation entity that is a trust is only affected by these rules if it is a beneficiary of a trust. In such a case, the entity is affected as a beneficiary, but not as a trust (s 115-210(2)).

A public trading trust (¶6-310) is a "trust" for the purposes of the CGT discount.

In general, the distribution of a non-assessable amount to a beneficiary with a fixed interest in a trust will trigger CGT event E4 (¶11-290).

[FITR ¶151-180 – ¶154-230]

Capital Gains and Losses of Companies

¶11-080 Prior year net capital losses of companies

A company cannot apply a prior year net capital loss against a capital gain in a later year unless:

- the same people had majority ownership of the company in the period from the start of the capital loss year to the end of the capital gain year, *and*
- no person controlled the company's voting power at any time during the capital gain year who did not also control it during the whole of the capital loss year,

or the company has carried on the same business and commenced no additional business or new transactions, or by carrying on a similar business (Subdiv 165-CA).

These tests correspond to the continuity of ownership test (¶3-105) which apply in relation to prior year revenue losses being carried forward by companies. The business continuity test comprises of the same business test (¶3-123) or the alternative similar business test (¶3-125). Also note the anti-avoidance rules in Subdiv 175-CA (¶11-120).

[FITR ¶180-800 – ¶180-820]

¶11-090 Current year capital losses of companies

Special rules stop capital gains made by a company in one part of an income year when it was owned by one set of shareholders from being offset by capital losses made by the company during another part of the income year when it was owned by a different set of shareholders (¶3-065).

Where, in respect of an income year, a company fails both the continuity of ownership test (¶3-105) and the business continuity test (¶3-120), comprising of the same business test (¶3-123) or the alternative similar business test (¶3-125), it is required to work out its net capital gain or loss for that year under Subdiv 165-CB rather than under the usual rules.

Broadly, the company must divide the income year into periods. A new period begins when persons holding more than a 50% stake in the company during that period no longer hold more than a 50% stake or when a person starts controlling the voting power in the company. The notional net capital gain or loss for each period is then calculated as if each period were an income year.

In a case where there is no notional net capital loss for any of the periods, the company's net capital gain is calculated as normal.

In other cases, the company is taken to have made a net capital gain equal to the sum of the company's notional net capital gains for each period reduced by any prior year net capital losses that can be applied (¶11-080), and to have incurred a net capital loss equal to the sum of the company's notional net capital losses for each period.

A net capital loss which is not able to be offset in the current income year may be able to be offset against capital gains in future years if it satisfies the tests for being carried forward (¶11-080).

[FITR ¶181-000 – ¶181-120]

¶11-110 Transfer of net capital losses within company groups

A company (the loss company) can transfer surplus net capital losses to another company (the gain company) in the same wholly-owned group, so that the gain company can offset those losses against capital gains it has made provided one of the companies is an Australian branch of a foreign bank (¶3-090) and the other company is either: (a) the head company of a consolidated group or MEC group; or (b) is not a member of a consolidatable group (Subdiv 170-B).

The net capital loss transferred cannot be more than the amount of the loss company's net capital loss that, apart from the transfer, the loss company could carry forward to the income year after the transfer year (s 170-145).

▶ Example

In the transfer year, a loss company has: (i) a prior year net capital loss of $39,000; (ii) current year capital losses totalling $3,000; and (iii) current year capital gains totalling $14,000. Of the $39,000 prior year net capital loss, the loss company can transfer to the gain company no more than $28,000, ie:

$39,000 – ($14,000 – $3,000)

[FITR ¶185-350 – ¶185-505]

¶11-120 Anti-avoidance: capital gains and losses of companies

A number of anti-avoidance measures potentially affect the availability of net capital losses to a company, or of certain deductible amounts.

Capital gains and losses injected into company

If: (i) a capital gain or loss is injected into a company; (ii) a tax benefit is obtained from a company's available net capital losses or current year capital losses; or (iii) a tax benefit is obtained because of a company's available capital gains, the Commissioner can disallow the net capital losses and/or current year capital losses of the company (Subdivs 175-CA; 175-CB).

Group company loss transfers

Where a tax loss is transferred between wholly-owned group companies involving an Australian branch of a foreign company under Subdiv 170-A, the cost base and reduced cost base of equity and debt interests in the loss company may be reduced (Subdiv 170-C). Further, the cost base and reduced cost base of debt or equity interests in the income company may be increased. The adjustments are required to neutralise loss duplication and loss cascading occurring on transfers of losses between wholly-owned companies.

The transfer of net capital losses between group companies under Subdiv 170-B (¶11-110) triggers an identical cost base and reduced cost base adjustment mechanism.

Linked company groups

The right to utilise certain capital losses or tax deductions is deferred where there is a transfer of an asset between companies in a linked company group (Subdiv 170-D). The deferred capital loss or deduction only becomes available, broadly, where the company that has disposed of the asset, or the asset itself, ceases to belong to the linked group.

The deferral also applies to losses realised on the happening of other CGT events including the creation of certain rights or options in a company in the same linked group as the creator company, and similar transactions involving trusts or individuals connected with a linked group company.

Two companies are linked to each other if one of them has a controlling stake in the other, or the same entity has a controlling stake in each of them. A capital loss or deduction that has become available may be disallowed if the asset is later reacquired, or the entity owning the asset is acquired, by a member of the linked group.

Limits on unrealised losses of companies

When the ownership of a company changes so that it fails the continuity of ownership test (¶3-105), it may be denied the right to utilise capital losses that were *unrealised* at the time of the ownership change (Subdiv 165-CC). Certain "unrealised deductions", such as balancing adjustments on depreciable assets owned at the ownership change, may also be disallowed.

When assets that are owned at the ownership change are later disposed of, the same business test (¶3-123) must be applied to determine whether losses will be disallowed.

The maximum amount of capital losses or deductions denied is limited to the company's "unrealised net loss" at the time of the ownership change. This is the amount of the net loss, if any, that the company would make if it sold all of its assets for market value on the day of the change. It requires a calculation of all relevant net capital and revenue gains and losses.

A company may use a "global method" of valuing assets in calculating its unrealised net loss. The choice to use the global method must be made on or before the day the company lodges its income tax return for the income year in which the ownership change occurred, unless the Commissioner allows a later day.

Inter-entity loss multiplication

The multiple recognition of realised and unrealised losses is prevented in circumstances where a company has an "alteration" (Subdiv 165-CD). An alteration happens when: (i) there is a change in ownership or control in the company; or (ii) a liquidator makes a declaration that the company's shares are worthless. For further details, see ¶3-135.

[FITR ¶181-130, ¶181-170, ¶185-800, ¶190-250]

Capital Gains and Losses

¶11-170 Making a capital gain or loss

A taxpayer can only make a capital gain or loss if a CGT event happens (s 102-20). The provisions dealing with each CGT event identify whether a taxpayer makes a capital gain or loss from that CGT event.

There are no CGT consequences arising from a particular CGT event if the capital gain and loss calculations for that CGT event result in neither a capital gain nor a capital loss arising.

[FITR ¶151-430]

¶11-180 Amount of capital gain or loss

The amount of a capital gain or loss arising from a CGT event is worked out by reference to the provisions dealing with each particular CGT event (¶11-240). For most CGT events, the amount of a capital gain or loss is the difference between the 2 amounts referred to in the section dealing with the relevant CGT event (s 102-22). For example, for many CGT events, a capital gain is the excess of the capital proceeds over the cost base of the CGT asset. In some cases, the capital gain or loss is determined by considering just one amount, eg CGT event G3. The general rule for working out a capital gain or loss can be represented as follows.

Capital gain

Capital proceeds from CGT event	LESS	Cost base of asset	EQUALS	Capital gain

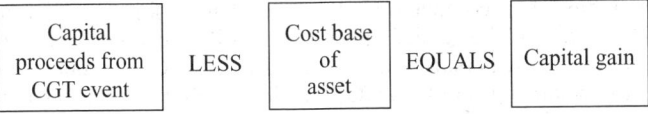

Capital loss

Reduced cost base of asset	LESS	Capital proceeds from CGT event	EQUALS	Capital loss

[FITR ¶151-440]

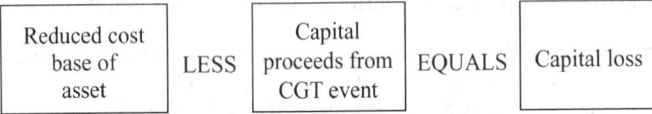

¶11-190 Some general CGT rules

Property or money given or received

Several CGT provisions say that a payment, cost or expenditure can include giving property, eg CGT event C3. Where this happens, the market value of the property is used in working out the amount of the payment, cost or expenditure (s 103-5).

If money or other property has been applied for a taxpayer's benefit in relation to a CGT event (including the discharge of all or part of a debt) or has been applied at the direction of the taxpayer, the CGT provisions apply as if that money or other property has actually been received by the taxpayer (s 103-10). In addition, in relation to a CGT event, if a taxpayer is entitled to have money or other property so applied, or if the money or other property will not be received until a later time or is payable by instalments, the CGT provisions apply as if the taxpayer is immediately entitled to receive the money or other property.

If, in relation to a transaction that is relevant for CGT purposes, a taxpayer does not have to pay money or give property until a later time or money is payable by instalments, the CGT provisions apply as if the taxpayer is immediately required to pay the money or give the other property (s 103-15).

Foreign currency

If a transaction or event involving an amount of money or the market value of other property is relevant for CGT purposes and the money or market value is expressed in a foreign currency, the amount or value is to be converted into the equivalent amount of Australian currency at the time of the transaction or event (s 960-50, table item 5). This requirement means conversion at the time of *each* transaction or event. Note that the Commissioner does not consider bitcoin to be foreign currency (TD 2014/25).

Choices

Where a taxpayer can make a choice (or election) under the CGT provisions, it must be made by the day the taxpayer lodges the tax return for the income year in which the relevant CGT event happened or within such further time as the Commissioner allows (s 103-25). The way the taxpayer and any other entity that is involved prepare their tax returns is usually sufficient evidence of a choice being made. However, there are exceptions which require a choice to be made earlier (¶12-370) or in writing (¶7-185) (s 103-25(3)). A choice may be varied where financial benefits are provided or received under a look-through earnout right (¶11-520).

[FITR ¶151-600 – ¶151-640]

¶11-200 Special CGT rules for partnerships

A capital gain or loss arising from a CGT event that happens in relation to a partnership or to one of its assets is made by the partners individually, not the partnership (s 106-5). A partnership cannot make a capital gain or loss. This means that any capital gain or loss which arises belongs proportionately to each individual partner. Each partner's capital gain or loss is worked out in proportion to each partner's interest in the partnership by reference to the partnership agreement or, if there is no such agreement, to partnership law.

For example, where a partnership asset is sold to a third party, each partner disposes of their fractional interest in the asset and the capital gain or loss, if any, arises directly to the relevant partner. The outcome for each partner varies according to the timing and costs involved in the acquisition of the particular partner's fractional interest.

Each partner has a separate cost base and reduced cost base for the partner's interest in each asset of the partnership. Special rules ensure that a partner's cost base and reduced cost base are decreased if an amount is deductible to the partnership or a non-assessable recoupment of expenditure is received by the partnership.

There is an exception to this treatment if the CGT event happens in relation to a depreciating asset under the uniform capital allowance rules (eg CGT event K7: ¶11-350). In this case, the partnership is treated as owning the asset.

Roll-over relief is available for the transfer of a partnership asset to a company which is wholly-owned by the partners (¶12-090).

Admission and retirement of partners

If a new partner is admitted to a partnership, the new partner acquires a part of each partnership asset. The relevant proportion is worked out in accordance with the partnership agreement or, if there is no such agreement, under partnership law. In addition, the existing partners are treated as having disposed of part of their interest in each partnership asset to the extent that the new partner has acquired it. The amount received by the continuing partners must be broken down into separate amounts. This enables the continuing partners to work out the amounts of any capital gains or losses arising from the disposal of those fractional interests.

If a partner leaves a partnership, the capital proceeds received by the outgoing partner must be broken down into separate amounts, representing the partner's fractional interest in each partnership asset. This enables the outgoing partner to determine the amounts of any capital gains or losses arising from the disposal of those fractional interests. To the extent, if any, that the capital proceeds cannot be attributed to fractional interests in partnership assets (including goodwill), or to work in progress, etc, that amount is brought to account for CGT purposes in relation to the disposal of a residual asset, being the outgoing partner's interest in the partnership itself (s 108-5(2)(d)).

At the same time, each continuing partner acquires a separate CGT asset to the extent that he/she acquires a part of the outgoing partner's interest in a partnership asset. The amount paid by the continuing partners to acquire their additional interests in the partnership must be broken down into separate amounts, representing additional fractional interests in each underlying partnership asset. However, the continuing partners are not affected if the leaving partner sells their interest to an entity that was not a partner.

In the case of large partnerships, the Commissioner generally accepts that the partners are dealing with each other at arm's length and that any consideration paid or received is the consideration relevant for CGT purposes. This means that if, for example, the partnership arrangement is such that no amount is payable for the acquisition or disposal of goodwill, the value of the goodwill is nil for CGT purposes. This is also the case if the partners in a smaller partnership deal with each other at arm's length in an ordinary commercial context. For the ATO view on changes in ''no goodwill'' professional partnerships, see Administrative treatment: acquisitions and disposals of interests in ''no goodwill'' professional partnerships, trusts and incorporated practices.

A payment to a retiring partner for work in progress is usually assessable as ordinary income if the amount is identifiable or discrete (¶5-070), but is otherwise capital. Specific measures apply to prevent double taxation of payments for work in progress (¶16-158). In the case of partnerships providing professional services, such as legal or accounting services, work in progress is usually a CGT asset (*Case 41/96*) but not always (TR 1999/16).

Changes in interests of existing partners

The interests of an individual partner in an asset may have changed since the asset was originally acquired, eg by the admission or retirement of other partners. Generally speaking, an incoming partner acquires part of each existing partner's interests in partnership assets, so that there is a part disposal by each existing partner. Similarly, when a partner retires, each remaining partner acquires a pro rata portion of that partner's interests in each partnership asset.

Even if the asset was physically acquired by the partnership before 20 September 1985 (pre-CGT), if there have been admissions to, or retirements from, the partnership since that time, a continuing partner's fractional interest in the asset will have changed and a proportion of that interest will have an acquisition date on or after 20 September 1985 (s 106-5).

Where a partner has interests in partnership assets that were acquired both before and after 20 September 1985 and there is a subsequent disposal of a part of those interests that cannot be specifically identified, it is open to the partner to decide which of those interests (ie which pre-CGT or post-CGT interests) in the partnership assets were disposed of.

Where there has been a change in the interests of the individual partners in an asset since its acquisition, the onus rests on each partner to determine any capital gain or loss on the disposal of the partner's interest in that asset (IT 2540).

Everett assignments

In the case of an Everett assignment (ie where a partner assigns his or her interest, or part of that interest, in a partnership) the assigning partner disposes of his or her interest (or part thereof) for CGT purposes, even though the assignee only has an equitable interest in the assignor's partnership interest and legal title to the partnership assets continue to vest in the partners to the exclusion of the assignee (¶5-160). Such an assignment is treated as a part disposal of the partner's interest in the partnership assets (IT 2540).

As an Everett assignment is unlikely to be made on an arm's length basis, the capital proceeds from the disposal of the assigning partner's interests in partnership assets is, generally, their market value.

For the rules affecting pre-admission Everett assignments, see ¶11-290. The CGT small business concessions are not available for Everett assignments (¶7-110).

Limited partnerships

A limited partnership is a partnership in which the liability of at least one partner is limited. Corporate limited partnerships are treated as companies for tax and CGT purposes (¶3-475). However, limited partnerships used for venture capital investment (¶5-040) and certain foreign hybrid entities (¶5-050) are treated as ordinary partnerships rather than companies.

[FITR ¶152-600]

¶11-210 Different entity makes capital gain or loss

There are special rules which apply to ensure that the CGT provisions look through certain nominee owners to the underlying owners of the CGT asset. The provisions apply to bankrupt individuals, companies in liquidation, absolutely entitled beneficiaries, security providers, instalment warrants and similar arrangements.

Bankruptcy and liquidation

For CGT purposes, and for determining whether an entity is a small business entity, the vesting of an individual's CGT assets in a trustee under the *Bankruptcy Act 1966* or under a similar foreign law is disregarded (s 106-30). In such circumstances, the provisions apply to an act done by a trustee in relation to an individual's CGT assets as if it had been done by the individual.

This applies to acts of: (i) the Official Trustee in Bankruptcy or a registered trustee, or the holder of a similar office under a foreign law; (ii) a trustee under a personal insolvency agreement made under Pt X of the *Bankruptcy Act 1966*, or under a similar instrument under a foreign law; and (iii) a trustee as a result of an arrangement with creditors under the *Bankruptcy Act 1966* or a similar foreign law. Therefore, any capital gain or loss which arises belongs to the individual, not the trustee.

Similarly, the vesting of a company's CGT assets in a liquidator, or holder of similar office under a foreign law, is disregarded for the purposes of CGT and the determination of a small business entity (s 106-35). The provisions apply to treat an act done by a liquidator of a company, or the holder of a similar office under a foreign law, as if the act had been done instead by the company (s 106-35). Therefore, any capital gain or loss that arises belongs to the company, not the liquidator.

Absolutely entitled beneficiaries

If a taxpayer is absolutely entitled to a CGT asset as against the trustee of a trust (disregarding any legal disability, eg infancy or mental incapacity), for CGT purposes and for determining whether an entity is a small business entity, the asset is treated as being an asset of the taxpayer (instead of the trust). In this manner, the CGT provisions apply to an act done, in relation to the asset, by the trustee as if the taxpayer had done it (s 106-50). This means that any capital gain or loss that arises belongs to the taxpayer, not the trustee. The concept of absolute entitlement is addressed in *Draft* TR 2004/D25 and the *Decision Impact Statement* on *Kafataris*.

The effect of this rule is illustrated by the following example.

▶ Example

The taxpayer, an overseas resident, asked an Australian friend to purchase a property on his behalf. Because of the lender's requirements, the property had to be registered in the friend's name. They agreed that the friend was to hold the property on trust for the taxpayer. The property was purchased before 1985 but legal title in the property was not transferred to the taxpayer until 1993.

The taxpayer was absolutely entitled to the property as against the trustee. Therefore, the property is treated being an asset of the taxpayer since prior to 1985, rather than when legal title was obtained in 1993. The property is a pre-CGT in the hands of the taxpayer.

The onus is on the legal owner to prove that the asset is held as trustee for another party. In *Bottazzi*, the legal owner was not able to prove a CGT asset was held on trust for another party and therefore the capital gain from CGT event A1 arose to the legal owner. In *Mingos* an individual failed to prove he had absolute entitlement to a property.

Security holders

For CGT purposes and for determining whether an entity is a small business entity, the vesting in an entity of a CGT asset over which the entity holds a security, charge or encumbrance is ignored, and during the period of holding such security, charge or encumbrance, any acts done by the agent in relation to the CGT asset are treated as being done by the person who provided the security. However, the CGT asset is treated as vesting in the entity if, while continuing to hold the asset, it ceases to hold a security, charge or encumbrance over the asset (s 106-60).

This means that any capital gain or loss that arises belongs to the person who provided the security, not the entity which accepted the security. For example, if a lender sells property under a power of sale after the failure of the owner of the property to make payments on the loan, any capital gain or loss is made by the owner of the property, not the lender.

Instalment trusts

Look-through treatment applies to instalment trusts (Div 235). For these purposes, instalment trusts include instalment warrants, instalment receipts and limited recourse borrowings by superannuation funds (s 235-825). Look-through treatment applies by treating an asset held in an instalment trust as an asset of the investor instead of the trust. In this manner, an act of the trustee is treated as being an act of the investor. The investor is treated as having the investment trust asset in the same circumstances as the investor has the interest in the instalment trust (s 235-820). The treatment ensures CGT event E5 does not apply to the trustee on the payment of the final instalment (¶11-290). Neither of the absolutely entitled beneficiaries provisions, nor the security holder provisions, apply to instalment trusts (s 235-845).

[FITR ¶152-630 – ¶152-660]

CGT Events

¶11-240 Overview of the CGT events

A capital gain or loss can only arise if a CGT event happens (s 102-20). The following table lists all of the CGT events, the time when each CGT event happens and how to work out any capital gain or loss that arises from those CGT events (s 104-5). Each of the CGT events is considered in more detail after the table.

When deciding if a CGT event has happened in relation to a taxpayer, each such occurrence must be considered in light of all of the possible CGT events. Even though an occurrence does not give rise to one CGT event, it may still give rise to another. Additionally, if an occurrence does give rise to a CGT event, it is still necessary to consider if it also gives rise to another CGT event.

Order for applying CGT events

The general rule is that, if more than one CGT event happens (except CGT events D1 and H2), the one that applies is the one that is most specific to the taxpayer's situation (s 102-25). For example, CGT event E2 applies in preference to CGT event A1 where there is a transfer of an asset to an existing trust (*Healey*). However, if circumstances that gave rise to CGT event J2 also constitute another CGT event, CGT event J2 applies in addition to the other event. Similarly, if CGT event K5 happens, it applies in addition to whichever of CGT events A1, C2 and E8 triggered it.

CGT event K12 happens in addition to the individual CGT events that ultimately gave rise to a foreign hybrid net capital loss amount (¶5-050).

CGT events D1 and H2 can only apply if no other CGT event happens in the circumstances. If both CGT events D1 and H2 happen in such circumstances, CGT event D1 applies in preference to CGT event H2.

CGT event number and description	*Time of event is:*	*Capital gain is:*	*Capital loss is:*
A1 Disposal of a CGT asset (s 104-10)	when disposal contract is entered into or, if none, when entity stops being asset's owner	capital proceeds from disposal *less* asset's cost base	asset's reduced cost base *less* capital proceeds
B1 Use and enjoyment before title passes (s 104-15)	when use of CGT asset passes	capital proceeds *less* asset's cost base	asset's reduced cost base *less* capital proceeds
C1 Loss or destruction of a CGT asset (s 104-20)	when compensation is first received or, if none, when loss discovered or destruction occurred	capital proceeds *less* asset's cost base	asset's reduced cost base *less* capital proceeds
C2 Cancellation, surrender and similar endings (s 104-25)	when contract ending asset is entered into or, if none, when asset ends	capital proceeds from ending *less* asset's cost base	asset's reduced cost base *less* capital proceeds
C3 End of option to acquire shares, etc (s 104-30)	when option ends	capital proceeds from granting option *less* expenditure in granting it	expenditure in granting option *less* capital proceeds
D1 Creating contractual or other rights (s 104-35)	when contract is entered into or right is created	capital proceeds from creating right *less* incidental costs of creating it	incidental costs of creating right *less* capital proceeds
D2 Granting an option (s 104-40)	when option is granted	capital proceeds from grant *less* expenditure to grant it	expenditure to grant option *less* capital proceeds
D3 Granting a right to income from mining (s 104-45)	when contract is entered into or, if none, when right is granted	capital proceeds from grant of right *less* expenditure to grant it	expenditure to grant right *less* capital proceeds
D4 Entering into a conservation covenant (s 104-47)	when covenant is entered into	capital proceeds from covenant *less* cost base apportioned to the covenant	reduced cost base apportioned to the covenant *less* capital proceeds from covenant
E1 Creating a trust over a CGT asset (s 104-55)	when trust is created	capital proceeds from creating trust *less* asset's cost base	asset's reduced cost base *less* capital proceeds

CGT event number and description	*Time of event is:*	*Capital gain is:*	*Capital loss is:*
E2 Transferring a CGT asset to a trust (s 104-60)	when asset transferred	capital proceeds from transfer *less* asset's cost base	asset's reduced cost base *less* capital proceeds
E3 Converting a trust to a unit trust (s 104-65)	when trust is converted	market value of asset at that time *less* its cost base	asset's reduced cost base *less* that market value
E4 Capital payment for trust interest (s 104-70)	when trustee makes payment	non-assessable part of the payment *less* cost base of the trust interest	*no capital loss*
E5 Beneficiary becoming entitled to a trust asset (s 104-75)	when beneficiary becomes absolutely entitled	for trustee — market value of CGT asset at that time *less* its cost base; for beneficiary — that market value *less* cost base of beneficiary's capital interest	for trustee — reduced cost base of CGT asset at that time *less* that market value; for beneficiary — reduced cost base of beneficiary's capital interest *less* that market value
E6 Disposal to beneficiary to end income right (s 104-80)	the time of the disposal	for trustee — market value of CGT asset at that time *less* its cost base; for beneficiary — that market value *less* cost base of beneficiary's right to income	for trustee — reduced cost base of CGT asset at that time *less* that market value; for beneficiary — reduced cost base of beneficiary's right to income *less* that market value
E7 Disposal to beneficiary to end capital interest (s 104-85)	the time of the disposal	for trustee — market value of CGT asset at that time *less* its cost base; for beneficiary — that market value *less* cost base of beneficiary's capital interest	for trustee — reduced cost base of CGT asset at that time *less* that market value; for beneficiary — reduced cost base of beneficiary's capital interest *less* that market value
E8 Disposal by beneficiary of capital interest (s 104-90)	when disposal contract entered into or, if none, when beneficiary ceases to own CGT asset	capital proceeds *less* appropriate proportion of the trust's net assets	appropriate proportion of the trust's net assets *less* capital proceeds

CGT event number and description	*Time of event is:*	*Capital gain is:*	*Capital loss is:*
E9 Creating a trust over future property (s 104-105)	when entity makes agreement	market value of the property (as if it existed when agreement made) *less* incidental costs in making agreement	incidental costs in making agreement *less* market value of the property (as if it existed when agreement made)
E10 Annual cost base reduction exceeds cost base of interest in AMIT (s 104-107A)	when reduction happens	excess of cost base reduction over cost base	*no capital loss*
F1 Granting a lease (s 104-110)	for grant of lease — when entity enters into lease contract or, if none, at start of lease; for lease renewal or extension — at start of renewal or extension	capital proceeds *less* expenditure on grant, renewal or extension	expenditure on grant, renewal or extension *less* capital proceeds
F2 Granting a long-term lease (s 104-115)	for grant of lease — when lessor grants lease; for lease renewal or extension — at start of renewal or extension	capital proceeds from grant, renewal or extension *less* cost base of leased property	reduced cost base of leased property *less* capital proceeds from grant, renewal or extension
F3 Lessor pays lessee to get lease changed (s 104-120)	when lease term is varied or waived	*no capital gain*	amount of expenditure to get lessee's agreement
F4 Lessee receives payment for changing lease (s 104-125)	when lease term is varied or waived	capital proceeds *less* cost base of lease	*no capital loss*
F5 Lessor receives payment for changing lease (s 104-130)	when lease term is varied or waived	capital proceeds *less* expenditure in relation to variation or waiver	expenditure in relation to variation or waiver *less* capital proceeds
G1 Capital payment for shares (s 104-135)	when company pays non-assessable amount	payment *less* cost base of shares	*no capital loss*
G3 Liquidator declares shares worthless (s 104-145)	when liquidator makes declaration	*no capital gain*	shares' reduced cost base

CGT event number and description	*Time of event is:*	*Capital gain is:*	*Capital loss is:*
H1 Forfeiture of a deposit (s 104-150)	when deposit is forfeited	deposit *less* expenditure in connection with prospective sale	expenditure in connection with prospective sale *less* deposit
H2 Receipt for event relating to a CGT asset (s 104-155)	when act, transaction or event occurred	capital proceeds *less* incidental costs	incidental costs *less* capital proceeds
I1 Individual or company stops being a resident (s 104-160)	when individual or company stops being Australian resident	for each CGT asset the person owns, its market value *less* its cost base	for each CGT asset the person owns, its reduced cost base *less* its market value
I2 Trust stops being a resident trust (s 104-170)	when trust ceases to be resident trust for CGT purposes	for each CGT asset the trustee owns, its market value *less* its cost base	for each CGT asset the trustee owns, its reduced cost base *less* its market value
J1 Company stops being member of wholly-owned group after roll-over (s 104-175)	when the company stops being a member of group	market value of the rolled-over asset at time of event *less* its cost base	reduced cost base of the rolled-over asset *less* that market value
J2 Change in relation to replacement asset or improved asset after a roll-over under Subdiv 152-E happens (s 104-185)	when the change happens	the amount mentioned in s 104-185(5)	*no capital loss*
J4 Trust fails to cease to exist after a roll-over under Subdiv 124-N (s 104-195)	when the failure happens	market value of asset *less* its cost base	reduced cost base of asset *less* its market value
J5 Failure to acquire replacement asset and to incur fourth element expenditure after a roll-over under Subdiv 152-E (s 104-197)	at the end of the replacement asset period	the amount of the capital gain disregarded under Subdiv 152-E	*no capital loss*

CGT event number and description	*Time of event is:*	*Capital gain is:*	*Capital loss is:*
J6 Cost of acquisition of replacement asset or amount of fourth element expenditure, or both, not sufficient to cover disregarded capital gain (s 104-198)	at the end of the replacement asset period	the amount mentioned in s 104-198(3)	*no capital loss*
K1 An incoming international transfer of a Kyoto unit or an Australian carbon credit unit from your foreign account or your nominee's foreign account, you start to hold the unit as a registered emissions unit (s 104-205)	when you start to hold the unit as a registered emissions unit	market value of unit *less* its cost base	Reduced cost base of unit *less* its market value
K2 Bankrupt pays amount in relation to debt (s 104-210)	when payment is made	*no capital gain*	so much of payment as relates to denied part of a net capital loss
K3 Asset passing to tax-advantaged entity (s 104-215)	when individual dies	market value of asset at death *less* its cost base	reduced cost base of asset *less* that market value
K4 CGT asset starts being trading stock (s 104-220)	when asset starts being trading stock	market value of asset *less* its cost base	reduced cost base of asset *less* its market value
K5 Special capital loss from collectable that has fallen in market value (s 104-225)	when CGT event A1, C2 or E8 happens to shares in the company, or an interest in the trust, that owns the collectable	*no capital gain*	market value of the shares or interest (as if the collectable had not fallen in market value) *less* the capital proceeds from CGT event A1, C2 or E8
K6 Pre-CGT shares or trust interest (s 104-230)	when another CGT event involving the shares or interest happens	capital proceeds from the shares or trust interest (so far as attributable to post-CGT assets owned by the company or trust) *less* the assets' cost bases	*no capital loss*

CGT event number and description	*Time of event is:*	*Capital gain is:*	*Capital loss is:*
K7 Balancing adjustment occurs for a depreciating asset used for purposes other than taxable purposes (s 104-235)	when balancing adjustment event occurs	termination value *less* cost times fraction	cost *less* termination value times fraction
K8 Direct value shifts affecting equity or loan interests in a company or trust (s 104-250; Div 725)	the decrease time for the interests	the gain worked out under s 725-365	*no capital loss*
K9 Entitlement to receive payment of a carried interest (s 104-255)	when the entitlement arises	capital proceeds from entitlement	*no capital loss*
K10 Forex realisation gain covered by item 1 of the table in s 775-70(1) (s 104-260)	when the forex realisation event happens	the forex realisation gain	*no capital loss*
K11 Forex realisation loss covered by item 1 of the table in s 775-75(1) (s 104-265)	when the forex realisation event happens	*no capital gain*	the forex realisation loss
K12 Foreign hybrid loss exposure adjustment (s 104-270)	just before the end of the income year	*no capital gain*	the amount stated in s 104-270(3)
L1 Reduction under s 705-57 in tax cost setting amount of assets of entity becoming subsidiary member of consolidated group (s 104-500)	just after entity becomes subsidiary member	*no capital gain*	amount of reduction
L2 Amount remaining after step 3A, etc, of joining allocable cost amount is negative (s 104-505)	just after entity becomes subsidiary member	amount remaining	*no capital loss*

CGT event number and description	*Time of event is:*	*Capital gain is:*	*Capital loss is:*
L3 Tax cost setting amounts for retained cost base assets exceed joining allocable cost amount (s 104-510)	just after entity becomes subsidiary member	amount of excess	*no capital loss*
L4 No reset cost base assets against which to apply excess of net allocable cost amount on joining (s 104-515)	just after entity becomes subsidiary member	*no capital gain*	amount of excess
L5 Amount remaining after step 4 of leaving allocable cost amount is negative (s 104-520)	when entity ceases to be subsidiary member	amount remaining	*no capital loss*
L6 Error in calculation of tax cost setting amount for joining entity's assets (s 104-525)	start of the income year when the Commissioner becomes aware of the errors	the net overstated amount resulting from the errors, or a portion of that amount	the net understated amount resulting from the errors, or a portion of that amount
L8 Reduction in tax cost setting amount for reset cost base assets on joining cannot be allocated (s 104-535)	just after entity becomes subsidiary member	*no capital gain*	amount of reduction that cannot be allocated

[FITR ¶151-430, ¶151-460, ¶151-740]

¶11-250 CGT event from disposal of CGT asset

CGT event A1 — Disposal of a CGT asset

CGT event A1 happens if a taxpayer disposes of a CGT asset (s 104-10). The disposal of a CGT asset takes place if a change of ownership occurs from the taxpayer to another entity, whether because of some act or event or by operation of law.

Change of ownership

A change of ownership does not occur merely because there is a change of trustee or if a taxpayer stops being the legal owner of an asset but continues to be its beneficial owner.

While the most common example of CGT event A1 is the sale of an asset, it will also occur where:

- an asset is transferred from one person to another by way of gift
- a taxpayer ceases to hold an asset as trustee of a trust and commences to hold the asset in its own capacity (ID 2010/72)

- an asset is vested in a statutory trustee for the purpose of sale (ID 2009/129).

There will not be a change of ownership, or CGT event A1, where:

- a CGT asset is split or changed (¶11-570)
- the asset is disposed of to provide or redeem a security
- an asset vests in a trustee in bankruptcy or in a liquidator of a company
- there is a transfer of the legal title of a CGT asset from the asset's legal owner to the person that is absolutely entitled to the CGT asset as against its legal owner (s 106-50)
- the assets of a person vest in a trustee as a result of the person becoming mentally incapacitated
- a bare trust is created by transferring an asset to a trustee
- the conversion of a property holding from a joint tenancy to a tenancy in common in equal shares
- the conversion of a co-operative into an unlisted public company (CR 2008/68)
- 2 or more CGT assets are merged into a single asset (TD 2000/10)
- a partnership converts into a limited partnership (ID 2010/210)
- a contract falls through before completion, or if, after completion, a contract is rendered void from the start, eg due to fraud (TR 94/29).

▶ Planning point

When considering a sale of a business, the CGT consequences of selling the business assets as distinct from the sale of the shares in the company should be analysed to determine the best outcome (¶31-100).

When selling the assets of the business, the CGT consequences of each asset being sold, and any concessions available, needs to be considered (¶31-610).

Where a taxpayer owns assets which are identical and were acquired at different times, it may not be possible to identify which particular assets are being disposed of, eg shares, trust units, coins and stamps. In these circumstances, a taxpayer may adopt the first-in first-out (FIFO) basis or specifically select which assets are being disposed of (TD 33). Alternatively, average cost may be used for shares which are in the same company, are acquired on the same day, and involve identical rights and obligations. However, any shares which have a market value cost because of the market value substitution rule must be excluded from the average cost calculation (TD 33). Where shares are held as revenue assets by banks or insurance companies, the FIFO method must be used if the individual shares are not sufficiently identifiable. As an alternative to FIFO, average cost may be used on the same conditions as above (TR 96/4).

Where shares are proposed to be sold under a ''wash sale'' the potential application of the distribution washing provisions in s 207-157 and the general anti-avoidance provisions in ITAA36 Pt IVA need to be considered (TR 2008/1; TD 2014/10; ¶30-195).

Before considering a wash sale, a taxpayer should find out if the liquidator is in a position to declare the shares worthless so as to crystallise a capital loss under CGT event G3 (¶11-310).

The CGT consequences arising in relation to certain arrangements are considered by the Commissioner as follows:

- disposing of insurance registers — TR 2000/1
- immediate and deferred transfer farm out arrangements — MT 2012/1 and MT 2012/2

- Prepaid Forward Purchase Agreements which attempt to reduce the assessable income of an Australian resident taxpayer — TA 2009/2.

Leasehold fixtures and improvements

For CGT purposes, a lessee continues to own an asset which the lessee has affixed to the lessor's land if: (i) the lessee is taken to be the owner of the asset within the terms of IT 175 (¶17-020); or (ii) a relevant state or territory law provides for the ownership of the asset to remain with the lessee (TD 46). In these circumstances, there is no disposal of the asset by the lessee to lessor when it is affixed to the land during the period of the lease.

The owner of the land will become the owner of a fixture that is taken to be owned by a lessee during the period of a lease if it remains affixed to the land at the end of the lease (TD 47). As a result, CGT event A1 happens to the fixture at the end of the lease giving rise to a capital gain or loss by the lessee.

Similar rules apply to capital expenditure made by a lessee on leasehold improvements, ie if a lessee continues to own the improvements during the period of the lease, the cost base of the improvements includes the capital expenditure incurred in making them. If the improvements remain affixed to the land on expiry or termination of the lease, CGT event A1 happens to the improvements and a capital gain or loss is worked out accordingly. If the parties are not dealing at arm's length or no capital proceeds are received on disposal, the market substitution rule applies (TD 98/23).

If a fixture installed by a lessee is regarded as no longer owned by the lessee, the lessee has disposed of the asset in terms of CGT event A1 and the owner of the land is treated as having acquired it, usually at the time the asset is affixed to the land (TD 48). However, there are also circumstances where ownership of the asset immediately vests in the lessor and ownership is not transmitted as such (eg where the asset is constructed on the leasehold land). In those cases, the asset is taken to be acquired by the lessor immediately without ever having been owned by the lessee.

Time of CGT event A1

If the asset is disposed of under a contract, the time of CGT event A1 is when the taxpayer enters into the contract. For this purpose, a contract may be an oral contract, provided it has all attributes required by common law, eg an intention for the parties to be immediately bound. In this manner, CGT event A1 has been held to occur on the countersigning of a letter of offer (*Scanlon & Anor*) and the signing of a heads of agreement despite the express statement it was "subject to and conditional upon" signing of formal agreement (*Case 2/2013*). Similarly, CGT event A1 was held to occur on the signing of the contract even though the terms of the contract were subsequently varied (*Case 7/2014*). Under NSW conveyancing practice, a binding contract for the sale of land would not normally be entered into until there is an exchange of written contracts (*McDonald*). However, a contract for the sale of land in Victoria was accepted as having occurred at the time a written offer and a written acceptance had been made, even though formal contracts were not entered into until over 2 months later (*Gardiner*).

If there is no contract for disposal of the asset, CGT event A1 happens when the change of ownership in the asset occurs. In cases where an asset is acquired from a taxpayer under a power of compulsory acquisition, CGT event A1 happens at the earliest of when: (i) compensation is received; (ii) the change of ownership happens; (iii) the acquiring entity enters upon the asset; or (iv) the acquiring entity takes possession.

So, for example, the timing of CGT event A1 may be when: (i) an instrument evidencing a transaction is executed; (ii) a transaction is otherwise entered into; (iii) an asset is transmitted by operation of law; or (iv) the asset is delivered.

A taxpayer is not required to report any capital gain or loss from CGT event A1 until an actual change of ownership occurs, eg at settlement. This means that when the change in ownership takes place in a later year, an earlier assessment for the year in which the contract was made may have to be amended. In such cases, late payment interest is generally waived if an amendment is sought within one month after settlement (TD 94/89). If a contract is subject to a condition (such as obtaining approval for finance), it does not affect the time the contract was made unless it is a condition precedent to the formation of the contract (*Case 24/94*).

▶ Planning point

As a capital gain (or loss) arises in the income year in which the disposal of an asset occurs (ie regardless of whether any of the proceeds for the disposal have been received) the terms for payment of the proceeds should be carefully considered. This is particularly relevant in circumstances involving vendor finance to the purchaser as the vendor may be liable for taxation prior to the receipt of the proceeds.

Where a business is being sold the use of look-through earnout rights may delay the point of taxation of the earnout payment: see ¶11-675.

If there are 2 or more contracts that affect the rights and obligations of parties to a disposal of assets, it is necessary to determine which contract is the source of the obligation to effect the disposal (*Sara Lee*).

If an option is exercised, the time of CGT event A1 in relation to the asset which is the subject of the option, is the date of the transaction entered into as a result of the exercise of the option (TD 16). The date the option was granted is not relevant (*Van*; ¶12-700). Similarly, if an unexercised option is assigned, the time of CGT event A1 is the date of the assignment with the acquisition date being when the option was granted.

Time of acquisition as a result of CGT event A1

If an asset is acquired by a taxpayer as a result of CGT event A1, it is acquired at the time of that CGT event.

Capital gains and losses

A taxpayer makes a capital gain from CGT event A1 if the capital proceeds from the disposal of the asset are more than its cost base. If the capital proceeds are less than the reduced cost base of the CGT asset, a capital loss is made.

If a taxpayer disposes of an asset because another entity exercises an option granted in relation to the asset, the capital proceeds from the disposal include any payment received for granting the option. If an option granted by the taxpayer requires the taxpayer to both acquire and dispose of an asset, the option is treated as 2 separate options and half of the capital proceeds from the granting of the option is attributed to each option (¶11-280).

If a previously leased asset is traded in, the credit for the trade-in must be taken into account when working out if there is a capital gain or loss (TR 98/15).

A capital loss that a lessee makes from the assignment of a lease (other than a lease granted for 99 years or more) is disregarded if the lessee did not use the lease mainly for income-producing purposes (¶11-670).

Exception for pre-CGT assets

A capital gain or loss from CGT event A1 is disregarded if the asset was acquired before 20 September 1985. If the asset is a lease, the capital gain or loss is disregarded if it was granted before 20 September 1985 or, if it has been renewed or extended, the start of the last renewal or extension occurred before 20 September 1985.

[FITR ¶151-770]

¶11-260 CGT event from use and enjoyment

CGT event B1 — Use and enjoyment before title passes

CGT event B1 happens if a taxpayer enters into an agreement with another entity under which the right to the use and enjoyment of a CGT asset owned by the taxpayer passes to the other entity and title in the asset will or may pass to the other entity at or before the end of the agreement, eg under a hire purchase arrangement (s 104-15).

CGT event B1 does not happen in situations where equipment is taken under a normal commercial lease. In such a case, if the lessee buys the equipment at its residual value at the end of the lease, the equipment is taken to be acquired when the lessee acquires the lessor's interest (CGT event A1), not when the equipment was taken on lease (*Case X81*).

CGT event B1 may also happen where there is an agreement for the use and enjoyment of a property for a specified period, after which title to the property passes to the other entity, but not where title may pass at an unspecified time in the future (*CGT events affecting real estate*).

The time of CGT event B1 is when the other entity first obtains the use and enjoyment of the asset. If an asset is acquired by a taxpayer as a result of CGT event B1, it is acquired at the time of that CGT event. If title to the asset does not actually pass under the agreement, eg because some of the payments are not made, any capital gain or loss which initially arises when the use and enjoyment of the asset passes is disregarded. In such a case, if a previous income tax assessment of the lessor was affected by a capital gain or loss made from CGT event B1, it must be amended.

A taxpayer makes a capital gain from CGT event B1 if the capital proceeds from the agreement are more than the cost base of the asset. If the capital proceeds are less than the reduced cost base of the asset, a capital loss is made.

A capital gain or loss from CGT event B1 is disregarded if the asset was acquired before 20 September 1985.

▶ Example

A father agreed to obtain a loan so that his children could purchase a property. The loan required that the property be registered in the father's name. Under the agreement, the children had full use of the property, they agreed to meet all outgoings including loan repayments and title to the property would be transferred to them in 5 years' time.

CGT event B1 applied in this case as it was the most specific event. This meant that any CGT liability would be based on the market value of the property at the time of the agreement, not at the time of the transfer. If title to the property does not pass to the children, any capital gain or loss the father made from CGT event B1 would be disregarded (based on ID 2005/216).

[FITR ¶151-810]

¶11-270 CGT events from ending a CGT asset

CGT event C1 — Loss or destruction of a CGT asset

CGT event C1 happens if a CGT asset owned by a taxpayer is lost or destroyed (s 104-20). An asset cannot be lost voluntarily, but may be lost by confiscation. However, in a confiscation situation, it may be more appropriate to consider whether there has been a change of ownership or forfeiture of the asset. An asset may be destroyed through deliberate or involuntary destruction. CGT event C1 may apply to intangible assets (TD 1999/79). CGT event C1 arises where shares are sold without the owner's consent (ID 2010/116; ID 2010/124).

If the taxpayer receives compensation for the loss or destruction of the asset, the time of CGT event C1 is when the compensation is first received. If the taxpayer does not receive any compensation, CGT event C1 happens when the loss is discovered or the destruction occurred. Roll-over may be available in such a case (¶12-260).

A taxpayer makes a capital gain from CGT event C1 if the capital proceeds from the loss or destruction of the asset are more than its cost base. If the capital proceeds are less than the reduced cost base of the asset, a capital loss is made.

A capital gain or loss from CGT event C1 is disregarded if the asset was acquired before 20 September 1985.

CGT event C2 — Cancellation, surrender and similar endings

CGT event C2 happens if a taxpayer's ownership of an intangible CGT asset ends because it is redeemed, cancelled, released, discharged, satisfied, abandoned, surrendered, forfeited or expired (s 104-25). For this purpose, a lease is taken to have expired even if it is extended or renewed. If an option is exercised or a convertible note or interest is converted, CGT event C2 happens at that time.

As an asset comes to an end when CGT event C2 happens, there is no acquisition of the asset by another person at that time.

An asset can expire by effluxion or lapse of time but not as a result of a voluntary termination (TD 1999/76). This means that, for example, the market value substitution rule (¶11-510) can apply to capital proceeds on the voluntary termination of a lease, but not where the lease goes to term and has no value at that time.

Some examples of when CGT event C2 happens are:

- on a redemption of units in a unit trust (TD 40)
- to shares held in a company where the company is wound up
- when an option expires without being exercised
- on the maturity or close-out of a financial contract for differences (TR 2005/15)
- when an investor's ownership of contractual rights under an investment product known as a Deferred Purchase Agreement warrant comes to an end upon delivery of the delivery assets (TD 2008/22)
- on the close-out of an exchange-traded option (ID 2005/164)
- when a retail premium is paid to a non-participating shareholder (TR 2017/4; TR 2012/1)
- on settlement of a damages claim for negligence and breach of contract (*Coshott*).

However, CGT event C2 did not happen on maturity of an unsecured note when the company that issued the note defaulted on repayment (ID 2008/58).

The rights which a company acquired against an assumption party under a debenture liability agreement were an asset for CGT purposes in *Orica*. Further, the performance by the assumption party of its obligations under the agreement, and the discharge in part of those obligations by performance, was a disposal of an asset under the former provisions corresponding to CGT event C2. This decision is also discussed at ¶23-325.

If a commercial debt is forgiven, the debtor's unrecouped prior year net capital losses may be reduced (¶16-910). Depending on the market value of the debt, the creditor may incur a capital loss from CGT event C2 (TD 2), except where the debt is a personal use asset (¶11-400).

A payment made by a guarantor in relation to a debt guarantee following a debtor's default has no CGT consequences for the debtor (TR 96/23). If the guarantor pays the debt in full, the creditor's capital gain from the guarantee is offset by the capital loss from the debt. If both the debtor and the guarantor default, the creditor makes a capital loss on the debt from CGT event C2, and if the guarantor is insolvent no capital gain arises from the guarantee. A capital loss is incurred by the guarantor if there is a shortfall in the amount repaid by the debtor under the guarantor's right of indemnity. Irrespective, a capital loss cannot be claimed if the debt is a personal use asset (¶11-400).

Timing of CGT event C2

If the taxpayer enters into a contract that results in the asset ending, the time of CGT event C2 is when the taxpayer enters into that contract. If there is no such contract, CGT event C2 happens when the asset comes to an end.

In the fact situation of *Orica* (see above), disposals were constituted by the progressive discharge of the debt. Elsewhere a taxpayer unsuccessfully argued that the disposals should be taken to have occurred at the time the agreement was originally made (*Dulux Holdings*).

When a company is dissolved, CGT event C2 happens to the shares at the time of dissolution (TD 2000/7). Under the relevant provisions in *Corporations Act 2001*, the time of dissolution is:

- where the company is wound up by an order of a court and the liquidator has obtained from the court an order that the company be dissolved — the date of the order
- where the company is wound up voluntarily — 3 months after the lodging of the return of the final meeting of members and/or creditors, or on such other date as the court may order, or
- where a defunct company's registration is cancelled — on the date of the *Government Gazette* in which notice of the deregistration is published.

However, the timing of a capital gain or loss in such circumstances could be accelerated by the liquidator making a declaration in accordance with the requirements of CGT event G3 (¶11-310).

Capital gains and losses

A taxpayer makes a capital gain from CGT event C2 if the capital proceeds from the asset ending are more than its cost base. If the capital proceeds are less than the reduced cost base of the asset, a capital loss is made.

To the extent that a liquidator's distribution is assessable (¶4-300), relief from double taxation (¶11-690) is available (TD 2001/27). However, the amount of the capital gain is not reduced by any imputation credit (s 118-20(1B)).

Where there is an in-specie distribution of an asset which has been subjected to an inter-company roll-over (¶12-490), a capital gain or loss arising on the cancellation of the liquidated company's shares may be adjusted to account for the notional gain or loss in respect of the distributed asset (¶12-530).

On the surrender of a lease by the lessee, CGT event C2 happens when the lessor receives an amount for the discharge of its rights under the agreement (TR 2005/6). If the agreement to end the lease is made more than 12 months after the lease was granted, the 12-month rule for a discount capital gain (¶11-033) will be satisfied.

If expenditure by a lessee on leasehold improvements which become owned by the lessor enhances the value of the lease, it is included in the cost base of the lease to the lessee and is considered when working out a capital gain or loss on expiry or termination of the lease. If any part of the expenditure is recouped, eg from the lessor on termination of the lease, it cannot be included in the cost base of the lease (TD 98/23).

The renunciation by a beneficiary of an interest in a discretionary trust would give rise to CGT event C2, but no capital gain is likely to arise unless the beneficiary has a pre-existing interest in either the assets or the income of the trust. The renunciation would not normally have any CGT consequences for the trustee or the trust (TD 2001/26).

Capital proceeds

A liquidator's final distribution made in relation to the winding up of a company forms part of the capital proceeds from CGT event C2 happening to the share (TD 2001/27). This also applies where an interim distribution is made within 18 months before the company ceases to exist. However, if the company ceases to exist more than 18 months after the payment, CGT event G1 will apply instead (¶11-310). If the taxpayer acts on an incorrect assumption that the company will be dissolved within 18 months, any underpayment arising from failing to apply CGT event G1 should normally be corrected within a month after the 18 months expires, otherwise the general interest charge may be imposed. Conversely, the taxpayer may be entitled to interest on any overpayment if it applies CGT event G1 on the basis of a wrong assumption that the dissolution will not occur within 18 months (TD 2001/27).

The final distribution of the exempt component of a capital gain that arose on the earlier disposal of the goodwill of a company forms part of the capital proceeds from CGT event C2 on winding up the company (TD 2001/14). Accordingly, the benefit of the CGT small business concessions may be lost on winding up because the active asset test cannot be passed in relation to the shares (¶7-145). However, the CGT discount would generally still apply to the cancellation of the shares (except where the shareholder is a company) (¶11-033).

The capital proceeds from the expiry, surrender or forfeiture of a lease under CGT event C2 include any payment made by the lessor to the lessee once the lease has ended for expenditure of a capital nature incurred by the lessee in making improvements to the leased property.

Special rules apply to calculate the capital proceeds from the expiry of an exploration benefit provided under a farm-in, farm-out arrangement (¶11-520).

Exception for pre-CGT assets

A capital gain or loss from CGT event C2 is disregarded if the asset was acquired before 20 September 1985. If the asset is a lease, the capital gain or loss is disregarded if it was granted before 20 September 1985 or, if it has been renewed or extended, the start of the last renewal or extension occurred before 20 September 1985. No CGT will be payable where consideration is received by a lessee for the surrender of a lease granted before 20 September 1985 (IT 2363).

Other exceptions

There are some other exceptions relating to CGT event C2, ie where a lease expires and the taxpayer did not use it mainly to produce assessable income (¶11-670), where rights to acquire shares or units are exercised (¶12-610), where shares or units are acquired by converting a convertible interest (¶12-620), where an option is exercised (¶12-700) and the cessation of a look-through earnout right (¶11-675). In addition, a company can agree to forgo any capital loss it makes from forgiving a commercial debt owed to it by a group company (¶16-910).

CGT event C3 — End of option to acquire shares, etc

CGT event C3 happens if an entity is granted an option by a company or the trustee of a unit trust to acquire shares or debentures of the company or units or debentures of the unit trust and the option ends because it is: (a) not exercised before it expires; or (b) cancelled, released or abandoned (s 104-30).

An option to convert debt to shares in a convertible note is covered by CGT event C3 only if part of the consideration received for the note is in respect of the option, eg where the issuing company is required to repay only part of the amount received on issue of the note (TD 38).

The time of CGT event C3 is when the option ends.

A company or the trustee of a unit trust makes a capital gain from CGT event C3 if the capital proceeds from the grant of the option are more than the expenditure incurred in granting it. If the capital proceeds are less than the incurred expenditure, a capital loss is made.

The expenditure incurred in granting the option can include giving property (¶11-190). However, the incurred expenditure does not include any non-assessable recoupment of that expenditure.

A capital gain or loss from CGT event C3 is disregarded if the option was granted before 20 September 1985.

[FITR ¶151-840 – ¶151-870]

¶11-280 CGT events involving bringing a CGT asset into existence

CGT event D1 — Creating contractual or other rights

CGT event D1 happens if a taxpayer creates a contractual right or other legal or equitable right in another entity, eg a restrictive covenant (s 104-35). However, CGT event D1 does not happen in any of the following circumstances:

(i) the taxpayer created the right by borrowing money or obtaining credit from another entity

(ii) the right requires the taxpayer to do something which gives rise to another CGT event for the taxpayer

(iii) a company issues or allots equity interests such as shares

(iv) a company grants an option to acquire equity interests or debentures in the company

(v) the trustee of a unit trust issues units in the trust

(vi) the trustee of a unit trust grants an option to acquire units or debentures in the trust, or

(vii) a right created by creating in another entity a right to receive an exploration benefit under a farm-in, farm-out arrangement.

For example, CGT event D1 may happen if:

- a person agrees not to compete with another person for a specified period or within a specified area
- a person agrees to enter into an exclusive trade tie agreement with another person
- a person agrees to play sport only with a particular club or to play only a particular sport
- a property owner grants management rights over the property
- a person agrees to endorse the use of particular goods and services
- a person agrees not to take any legal action in relation to the cessation of an allowance
- there is a grant of a right to use a trade mark
- there is an agreement for the supply of mining information in the possession of the taxpayer
- there is an agreement to vary a contract, where the variation does not amount to a disposal of the whole or part of the rights under the contract

- there is an agreement for the assignment of an expectancy or of a right which is yet to come into existence, such as an agreement to assign interest which may accrue in future on an existing loan repayable without notice
- a taxpayer receives money or property for withdrawing an objection against a proposed land development and the receipt is not for permanent damage or reduction in value caused to the taxpayer's property by the development (TD 1999/80)
- a right to reside in a property for life (or a term of years) is granted other than pursuant to a mere family or social arrangement (TR 2006/14).

CGT event D1 will occur at the time of a breach of contract. As no consideration is generally paid at this time, there will be no capital gain or capital loss. However, where instalment moneys (other than deposits) are lawfully applied in satisfaction of damages for breach of contract, a capital gain normally arises because of either a disposal of the asset created by CGT event D1 or CGT event H2 happens (TR 94/29).

The Commonwealth, a state or a territory is an entity which can create rights for the purposes of CGT event D1, ie it is a body politic for purposes of the definition of "entity" (TD 1999/77). However, a court is not an entity for these purposes (TD 1999/81).

The capital gain or loss from CGT event D1 happening from a look-through earnout right being created in another entity is disregarded (s 118-575; ¶11-675).

Subsequent expiry

In many of the above examples the asset created will eventually expire or otherwise be extinguished. When this occurs, CGT event C2 (¶11-270) happens in relation to the asset acquired as a result of CGT event D1.

Easements, profits à prendre, licences

CGT event D1 happens if a taxpayer grants an easement, profit à prendre or licence over an asset (TD 2018/15). In cases where the sale of standing timber is associated with a right of the purchaser to remove timber in the future, the agreement must be considered to see if what is involved is the creation of a new interest in land (a profit à prendre subject to CGT) or the sale of timber which forms part of the realty (exempt if the land is pre-CGT) (*Ashgrove*; TR 95/6; TD 2018/15).

Sale of knowledge, know-how, information

Difficulties may arise where an agreement is made to provide knowledge, know-how, information, etc. Knowledge is not property (*United Aircraft Corporation*). Being neither property nor a right, it is not a CGT asset (¶11-380). However, a right to require the supply of information or knowledge is a CGT asset. Where such a right is created, CGT event D1 may happen.

Restrictive covenants and trade ties

CGT event D1 happens if there is a transaction involving an amount (whether property or money) being received for entering into any restrictive covenant, including an exclusive trade tie, an exclusive dealing contract and an agreement not to compete in trade (TR 95/3). Where a restrictive covenant relates both to a current period of employment and to a period after the end of that employment, any part of the capital proceeds which relates to the period of employment is also assessable as ordinary income, and the capital gain is reduced accordingly under the anti-overlap provisions (¶11-690). For the treatment of covenants entered into under accredited land conservation programs, see CGT event D4 below.

A question may arise as to whether a particular amount is paid for a restrictive covenant, or as a payment for business goodwill eligible for concessional treatment or roll-over relief. If the parties are at arm's length and reasonably attribute an amount to the restrictive covenant, that allocation is accepted. In such a case, if a nil amount is allocated to the restrictive covenant, the giving of the restrictive covenant is treated as being ancillary to the disposal of the goodwill of the business and no part of the capital proceeds needs to be attributed to the grant of the restrictive covenant (TR 1999/16).

A restrictive covenant may have a measurable benefit in its own right where the vendor has significant personal goodwill in the form of a loyal clientele, but not where the covenant is given merely as a matter of form by a vendor who is retiring from a particular business and does not wish to compete further. If a vendor has been fully remunerated for goodwill, based on normal industry valuation methods, any further amount must reasonably relate to the restrictive covenant. If a vendor of a business who is also an employee of that business receives a payment for a restrictive covenant on the sale of the business, the amount may be characterised as a component of the intangible elements that comprise goodwill (TR 95/3).

The person entitled to the benefit of a restrictive covenant normally incurs a capital loss when it expires (¶11-270). If, however, the covenant is part of business goodwill, there are no CGT consequences until a CGT event happens to that goodwill (TD 95/54).

Timing of CGT event D1

The time of CGT event D1 is when the taxpayer enters into the contract or creates the other right. If a contractual or other right is acquired by a taxpayer as a result of CGT event D1, it is acquired at the time of that CGT event.

Capital gains and losses

A taxpayer makes a capital gain from CGT event D1 if the capital proceeds from creating the right are more than the incidental costs incurred in creating it. If the capital proceeds are less than the incidental costs, a capital loss is made. A capital gain from CGT event D1 cannot be a discount capital gain (¶11-033).

The market value substitution rule does not apply to capital proceeds received from CGT event D1.

The expenditure incurred in creating the right can include giving property. However, the incidental costs do not include any non-assessable recoupment of those costs nor any part of those costs that is deductible.

CGT event D2 — Granting an option

CGT event D2 happens if a taxpayer grants an option to an entity, or renews or extends a previously granted option (s 104-40). CGT event D2 does not happen if CGT event C3 (¶11-270) applies to the situation. CGT event D2 also does not happen if an option relates to a collectable or personal use asset.

In some cases, the grantor of an option may not, at the time of granting it, own the property in respect of which the option is granted and in fact may never own that property if the option expires, or is cancelled, released or abandoned. Similarly, the option may bind the grantor to acquire property which, because the option expires or is cancelled, released or abandoned, is not acquired. Nevertheless, CGT event D2 includes the granting of such an option.

The time of CGT event D2 is when the taxpayer grants, renews or extends the option. If an option is granted to a taxpayer and CGT event D2 applies to the grantor in relation to that option, the taxpayer acquires the option at the time of that CGT event. If CGT event D2 applies to the grantor of an option because it is renewed or extended, the option is still taken to have been acquired by the grantee when it was originally granted.

A taxpayer makes a capital gain from CGT event D2 if the capital proceeds from granting, renewing or extending the option are more than the expenditure incurred in making the grant, renewal or extension. If the capital proceeds are less than the incurred expenditure, a capital loss is made. A capital gain from CGT event D2 cannot be a discount capital gain (¶11-033).

The expenditure incurred in granting, renewing or extending the option can include giving property. However, the incurred expenditure does not include any non-assessable recoupment of the expenditure nor any part of the expenditure that is deductible.

A capital gain or loss from CGT event D2 is disregarded if the option is exercised. For the consequences of an option being exercised, see ¶12-700.

There is no exception to CGT event D2 if an option is granted on or after 20 September 1985 in relation to property acquired by the grantor before that date. This is because the relevant CGT asset is the option and not the original property from which the option was derived.

The happening of CGT event D2 from a deferred transfer farm out arrangement is considered in MT 2012/2.

CGT event D3 — Granting a right to income from mining

CGT event D3 happens if a taxpayer owns a prospecting or mining entitlement, or an interest in one, and grants another entity a right to receive income from operations carried on under the entitlement (s 104-45). If CGT event D3 happens, there is no disposal of the entitlement so CGT event A1 (¶11-250) does not happen.

If the right to the income is granted to the other entity under a contract, the time of CGT event D3 is when the taxpayer enters into the contract. If there is no such contract, the time of CGT event D3 is when the right to the income is granted. If a right to receive income from mining is acquired by a taxpayer as a result of CGT event D3, it is acquired at the time of that CGT event.

A taxpayer makes a capital gain from CGT event D3 if the capital proceeds from granting the right to the income are more than the expenditure incurred in granting that right. If the capital proceeds are less than the incurred expenditure, a capital loss is made. A capital gain from CGT event D3 cannot be a discount capital gain (¶11-033).

The expenditure incurred in granting the right to the income can include giving property. However, the incurred expenditure does not include any non-assessable recoupment of the expenditure nor any part of the expenditure that is deductible.

Special income tax arrangements apply to taxpayers who carry on mining operations (¶19-010) or who incur mining transport capital expenditure (¶19-090). In line with these arrangements, assets that fall within the various capital expenditure categories which attract income tax deductions and balancing adjustments on disposal are treated as separate assets for CGT purposes (¶11-410). Where such assets are not treated as separate assets, they are included in the cost base of the prospecting permit or mining right.

CGT event D4 — Conservation covenants

CGT event D4 happens if a taxpayer enters into a conservation covenant over land that it owns (s 104-47). The time of the event is when the taxpayer enters into the covenant. For the definition of a conservation covenant, see ¶16-972.

If the capital proceeds from entering into the covenant are more than the part of the cost base of the land that is attributed to the covenant, the taxpayer makes a capital gain. If the capital proceeds are less than the part of the reduced cost base of the land attributable to the covenant, the taxpayer makes a capital loss. Where the taxpayer enters into the covenant for no material benefit and is entitled to a deduction under s 31-5 (¶16-972), the capital proceeds are the amount of that deduction (s 116-105). If there are no capital proceeds and no deduction, CGT event D1 will apply instead of CGT event D4. There will be no capital gain or loss in any event if the taxpayer acquired the land before 20 September 1985.

The part of the cost base of the land that is attributed to the covenant is:

$$\text{cost base of land} \times \frac{\text{capital proceeds from entering into the covenant}}{\text{those capital proceeds plus the market value of the land just after the taxpayer enters into the covenant}}$$

▶ Example

The cost base of land owned by the taxpayer is $200,000. The taxpayer received $10,000 for entering into a conservation covenant covering part of the land. The market value of the land just after the covenant was entered into is $285,000. The part of the cost base of the land that is attributed to the covenant is:

$$\frac{\$200{,}000 \times \$10{,}000}{\$10{,}000 + \$285{,}000} = \$6{,}780$$

The taxpayer, therefore, makes a capital gain of ($10,000 – $6,780) = $3,220.

[FITR ¶151-900 – ¶151-935]

¶11-290 CGT events involving trusts

CGT event E1 — Creating a trust over a CGT asset

CGT event E1 happens if a taxpayer creates a trust over a CGT asset by declaration or settlement (s 104-55). However, CGT event E1 does not happen if the trust is not a unit trust and the taxpayer is the sole beneficiary absolutely entitled to the CGT asset as against the trustee (ignoring any legal disability), eg where a bare trust is created (s 104-55(5)). The mere change of trustee of trust will not trigger CGT event E1 (note to s 104-55(1)).

The term ''settlement'' is not defined in ITAA97 and therefore takes its common law meaning. The meaning of settlement was addressed in *Taras Nominees* which held CGT event E1 arose because a trust was created by settlement as a result of land being transferred by the taxpayer to a trustee to hold on trust for the benefit of others pursuant to a joint venture development. The arrangement could not be excluded under s 104-55(5) as the taxpayer was not the sole beneficiary of trust and/or was not absolutely entitled to the land as against the trustee.

In accordance with *Kafataris* the term ''declaration'' takes its ordinary meaning. A trust is created by ''declaration'' when it is created by the holder of an undivided legal interest in property using words or actions which sufficiently evidence an intention to create a trust over that property. In that case, the transfer of a jointly owned property by a husband and wife to a wholly-owned company created a trust over the property by declaration or settlement and therefore gave rise to CGT event E1 (as opposed to CGT event A1). This is because the contracts used the express language of trust, with the offer being to acquire ''an equitable interest'' and once accepted, the husband and wife were ''bound to hold the property in trust'' for the purchaser.

The time of CGT event E1 is when the trust over the asset is created. If an asset is acquired by a trustee as a result of CGT event E1, it is acquired at the time of that CGT event.

A taxpayer makes a capital gain from CGT event E1 if the capital proceeds from creating the trust are more than the cost base of the asset. If the capital proceeds are less than the reduced cost base of the asset, a capital loss is made.

If the taxpayer is the trustee of the trust and no beneficiary is absolutely entitled to the asset as against the taxpayer, the first element of the asset's cost base and reduced cost base in the taxpayer's hands is its market value when the trust is created.

Where a trustee resolved to appoint company shares for the absolute benefit of certain named beneficiaries, it was both a declaration of trust and a settlement and, therefore, CGT event E1 arose. However, CGT event E5 did not apply as the interest was defeasible (*Oswal*).

CGT event E1 will occur where there is a specified "trust split" (TD 2019/14). A "trust split" generally refers to an arrangement where the parties to an existing trust functionally split the operation of the trust so that some trust assets are controlled by and held for the benefit of one class of beneficiaries, and other trust assets are controlled and held for the benefit of others.

CGT event E1 happens if a shareholder in a company in voluntary administration declares a trust over their shares for the benefit of a purchaser. In these circumstances, the shareholder will make a capital loss on the share if, at the time the trust is created, the market value of the share is less than its reduced cost base. However, the shareholder will not make a capital loss if the general anti-avoidance provisions of ITAA36 Pt IVA apply (TD 2004/13).

A limited CGT roll-over is available where a trustee of a fixed trust creates a new fixed trust over the asset and both trusts have the same beneficiaries with the same entitlements and no material discretionary elements (Subdiv 126-G; ¶12-552).

CGT event E1 will occur where a new trust is created. *Clark* held that the same trust continued where there was a continuum of property and membership in a trust that could be identified at any time from an unamended trust deed. The vesting of a trust in itself will not cause a new trust to arise or CGT event E1 to occur (TR 2018/6).

Pursuant to TD 2012/21 CGT event E1 does not happen if, pursuant to a valid exercise of a power contained within the trust's constituent document or as varied with the approval of the court, the terms of the trust are changed. However, CGT event E1 will happen if the amendment causes the trust to terminate for trust law purposes, or the effect of the amendment is to lead to a particular asset being subject to a separate charter of rights and obligations such as to give rise to the conclusion that that asset has been settled on terms of a different trust. Where permitted by the trust deed pursuant to a power of amendment or varied with court approval, CGT event E1 will not arise as a result of the addition of new entities to a class of objects, an expansion of the power of investment, an extension of the vesting date, an amendment to the definition of income or the power to stream income. A trustee may rely on a broad variation power to extend the vesting date (*Andtrust v Andreatta*). However, it is the Commissioner's view that once a vesting date has passed, a trust has vested and varying the vesting date retrospectively is not possible. Upon vesting the interests of the "takers on vesting" become fixed at law and the result cannot be avoided by the parties continuing to carry on as though the trust has not vested or by an exercise of power to vary the deed. The continued behaviour by a trustee and beneficiaries in a way that is consistent with the terms of the trust that existed before vesting is not enough to extend the vesting date (TR 2018/6).

For the CGT consequences of creating life and remainder interests in property and subsequent dealings in those interests see TR 2006/14.

A capital gain or loss from CGT event E1 is disregarded if the asset was acquired before 20 September 1985.

CGT event E2 — Transferring a CGT asset to a trust

CGT event E2 happens if a taxpayer transfers a CGT asset to an existing trust (s 104-60). However, CGT event E2 does not happen if the trust is not a unit trust and the taxpayer is the sole beneficiary absolutely entitled to the asset as against the trustee (ignoring any legal disability), eg where the trust acquiring the asset is a bare trust. A mere change of trustee of a trust does not trigger CGT event E2 (note to s 104-60(1)).

For the CGT consequences of creating life and remainder interests in property and subsequent dealings in those interests see TR 2006/14. CGT event E2 will not arise as a result of a change in the terms of the trust pursuant to a valid exercise of a power contained within the trust's constituent document (TD 2012/21; see above).

The time of CGT event E2 is when the CGT asset is transferred. If an asset is acquired by a trustee as a result of CGT event E2, it is acquired at the time of that CGT event.

A taxpayer makes a capital gain from CGT event E2 if the capital proceeds from the transfer are more than the cost base of the asset. If the capital proceeds are less than the reduced cost base of the asset, a capital loss is made.

If the taxpayer is the trustee of the trust and no beneficiary is absolutely entitled to the asset as against the taxpayer, the first element of the asset's cost base and reduced cost base in the taxpayer's hands is its market value when the asset is transferred (s 112-20).

A capital gain or loss from CGT event E2 is disregarded if the asset was acquired before 20 September 1985. There is also an exception for employee share trusts (¶12-630).

A limited CGT roll-over is available where an asset is transferred between fixed trusts that have the same beneficiaries with the same entitlements and no material discretionary elements (Subdiv 126-G; ¶12-552).

CGT event E3 — Converting a trust to a unit trust

CGT event E3 happens if a trust (that is not a unit trust) over a CGT asset is converted to a unit trust and, just before the conversion, a beneficiary under the trust was absolutely entitled to the asset as against the trustee (s 104-65).

The time of CGT event E3 is when the trust is converted to a unit trust. If an asset is acquired by a trustee as a result of CGT event E3, it is acquired at the time of that CGT event.

The beneficiary makes a capital gain from CGT event E3 if the market value of the asset when the trust is converted is more than the cost base of the asset. If that market value is less than the reduced cost base of the asset, a capital loss is made.

A capital gain or loss from CGT event E3 is disregarded if the asset was acquired before 20 September 1985.

CGT event E4 — Capital payment for trust interest

CGT event E4 happens if the trustee of a trust makes a payment to the taxpayer in respect of the taxpayer's unit or interest in the trust, and some or all of the payment is not assessable (s 104-70). A payment includes giving property, eg where there is a distribution of property in specie. CGT event E4 will arise where a unit holder receives a distribution of trust income for an income year which exceeds the trust's net income for that year even where the difference results from an expense being deductible for taxation purposes in that year which was properly charged against income for trust law purposes (ID 2012/63).

The taxpayer makes a capital gain from this event if the total non-assessable part of the payment made by the trustee during the income year is more than the cost base of the taxpayer's unit or interest. In such a case, the capital gain is equal to the excess and the cost base and reduced cost base of the unit or interest is reduced to nil. If the non-assessable part is not more than the cost base, there is no capital gain, but the cost base and the reduced cost base are reduced accordingly; for guidelines, see TD 93/170 and TD 93/171. CGT event E4 cannot produce a capital loss, and any capital gain will be disregarded if the taxpayer acquired the unit or interest before 20 September 1985. CGT event E4 does not happen to the extent that the payment is reasonably attributable to a "LIC capital gain" made by a listed investment company (¶11-038).

CGT event E4 also does not happen if the payment involves CGT event A1 (¶11-250), C2 (¶11-270), E1, E2, E6 or E7 happening in relation to the trust unit or interest. CGT event E4 does not occur in relation to a unit or an interest in an AMIT as CGT event E10 will apply (see below). However, for distributions made in relation to 2017–18, investors in MITs will be required to adjust the cost base of their units in the MIT when it distributes a CGT concession amount. Further, CGT event E4 does not happen where the payment is to a beneficiary of a discretionary trust (or a default beneficiary whose interest was not acquired for consideration or by way of assignment) (TD 2003/28).

▶ Planning point

When deciding whether to structure an investment using a fixed trust or unit trust as opposed to a discretionary trust, the potential application of CGT event E4 needs to be considered (¶31-560).

There is also an exception to CGT event E4 for distributions from the trustee of a trust to a foreign resident beneficiary. CGT event E4 does not happen to the extent that the payment is reasonably attributable to income that is not Australian sourced. However, this exception does not apply if the trust is a public trading trust (¶6-310). For details of related measures that apply to foreign residents who make a capital gain or loss in respect of interests in managed funds, see ¶12-735.

The time of the event is generally just before the end of the income year in which the trustee makes the payment. However, if some other type of CGT event happens to the unit or interest after the payment, but before the end of the income year, the time of CGT event E4 is just before that other event. For example, this would happen if a trust unit was sold during the income year after a non-assessable distribution had been made.

Calculating the non-assessable part

The non-assessable part to which CGT event E4 applies includes amounts associated with the small business 50% reduction (¶7-175), frozen indexation, building allowance and accounting differences in income.

However, the non-assessable part does not include:

(i) non-assessable non-exempt income (¶10-890)

(ii) payments from an amount that has been assessed to the trustee

(iii) assessable personal services income (¶30-600)

(iv) amounts repaid by the taxpayer

(v) compensation paid by the taxpayer that can reasonably be regarded as a repayment

(vi) amounts exempt under the small business 15-year exemption (¶7-165)

(vii) compensation or damages the trust receives for:

  (a) any wrong or injury suffered in the taxpayer's occupation, or

  (b) any wrong, injury or illness the taxpayer or taxpayer's relative suffers personally

(viii) amounts exempt or disregarded under the ESVCLP tax concession in ss 51-54 and 118-407 (¶11-900), and

(ix) tax-free payments pursuant to s 360-50(4) under the early stage innovation company provisions (¶11-910).

The non-assessable part is not reduced by any part of the payment that is deductible to the taxpayer. A payment of the CGT exempt amount to a CGT concession stakeholder of a trust under the small business retirement exemption is non-assessable non-exempt income and therefore will not give rise to CGT event E4 (¶7-185).

The non-assessable part is also adjusted to exclude any part attributable to:

(i) amounts that are exempt income arising from shares in a PDF

(ii) exempt payments related to infrastructure borrowings, and

(iii) proceeds from a CGT event that happens in relation to shares in a PDF.

However, these exclusions do not apply in calculating the reduction to the reduced cost base in situations where there is no capital gain (s 104-71).

If the non-assessable part reflects a discount capital gain (¶11-033), the non-assessable part is reduced to reflect the amount of the CGT discount allowed to the trustee. This measure enables a payment of the CGT discount amount without triggering CGT event E4 and is designed to ensure that persons investing through managed funds receive a similar CGT outcome to those investing directly. Corresponding rules apply where the payment of a CGT discount flows through a chain of trusts (s 104-71). CGT event E4 may apply to a payment of other tax deferred amounts to each trustee in a chain of trusts. However, in the case of the small business 50% reduction amount, this will not generate a capital gain (s 104-72).

Other adjustments to the non-assessable part are necessary where CGT concessions allowed to a beneficiary are less than those allowed to the trustee, eg where capital losses are involved or the beneficiary is not entitled to claim the full benefit of the CGT discount claimed by the trustee (s 104-71).

CGT event E5 — Beneficiary becoming entitled to a trust asset

CGT event E5 happens if a beneficiary becomes absolutely entitled to a CGT asset of a trust as against the trustee, ignoring any legal disability of the beneficiary (s 104-75). *Draft* TR 2004/D25 outlines the concept of absolute entitlement in this context. Absolute entitlement will not arise where an interest in an asset is absolute but defeasible (*Oswal*). For the CGT consequences of creating life and remainder interests in property and subsequent dealings in those interests see TR 2006/14.

CGT event E5 does *not* happen if the trust is a unit trust or a deceased estate.

The time of CGT event E5 is when the beneficiary becomes absolutely entitled to the asset. If an asset is acquired by a trust beneficiary as a result of CGT event E5, it is acquired at the time of that CGT event. CGT event E5 can arise when a trust vests and the ‘‘takers on vesting’’ become absolutely entitled as against the trustee to CGT assets (TR 2018/6).

A trustee of a trust makes a capital gain from CGT event E5 if the market value of the asset at the time of the event is more than its cost base. If that market value is less than the reduced cost base of the asset, a capital loss is made.

A beneficiary makes a capital gain from CGT event E5 if the market value of the asset at the time of the event is more than the cost base of the beneficiary’s interest in the trust capital to the extent it relates to the asset. If that market value is less than the reduced cost base of that interest, a capital loss is made.

Exceptions

A capital gain or loss made from CGT event E5 by a trustee is disregarded if the asset was acquired before 20 September 1985. There is also an exception for employee share trusts (¶12-630).

A capital gain or loss made from CGT event E5 by a beneficiary is disregarded if:

- the trust interest was acquired for no expenditure (except where it was assigned from another entity)
- the trust interest was acquired before 20 September 1985, or

- the gain or loss made by the trustee was disregarded under the main residence exemption, eg due to being a special disability trust (s 104-75(6); ¶11-730, ¶11-770).

CGT event E5 does not arise on the payment of the final instalment of an instalment warrant (s 235-820; ¶11-210).

CGT event E6 — Disposal to beneficiary to end income right

CGT event E6 happens if the trustee of a trust disposes of a CGT asset of the trust to a beneficiary to satisfy all or part of the beneficiary's right to trust income (s 104-80). However, CGT event E6 does not happen if the trust is a unit trust or a deceased estate. For the CGT consequences of creating life and remainder interests in property and subsequent dealings in those interests see TR 2006/14.

The time of CGT event E6 is when the disposal occurs. If an asset is acquired by a trust beneficiary as a result of CGT event E6, it is acquired at the time of that CGT event.

A trustee of a trust makes a capital gain from CGT event E6 if the market value of the asset at the time of the disposal is more than its cost base. If that market value is less than the reduced cost base of the asset, a capital loss is made.

A beneficiary makes a capital gain from CGT event E6 if the market value of the asset at the time of the disposal is more than the cost base of the beneficiary's right to trust income. If that market value is less than the reduced cost base of that right, a capital loss is made. In working out the cost base and reduced cost base of the right to trust income, the market value substitution rule (¶11-570) does not apply if the beneficiary did not pay anything for the right.

A capital gain or loss made from CGT event E6 by a trustee is disregarded if the asset was acquired before 20 September 1985. Similarly, a capital gain or loss made from CGT event E6 by a beneficiary is disregarded if the right to trust income was acquired before 20 September 1985.

CGT event E7 — Disposal to beneficiary to end capital right

CGT event E7 happens if the trustee of a trust disposes of a CGT asset of the trust to a beneficiary to satisfy all or part of the beneficiary's interest in trust capital (s 104-85). However, CGT event E7 does not happen if the trust is a unit trust or a deceased estate. CGT event E7 can arise where there is a distribution of a trust asset to a beneficiary after vesting (TR 2018/6). For the CGT consequences of creating life and remainder interests in property and subsequent dealings in those interests see TR 2006/14.

The time of CGT event E7 is when the disposal occurs. If an asset is acquired by a trust beneficiary as a result of CGT event E7, it is acquired at the time of that CGT event.

A trustee of a trust makes a capital gain from CGT event E7 if the market value of the asset at the time of the disposal is more than its cost base. If that market value is less than the reduced cost base of the asset, a capital loss is made.

A beneficiary makes a capital gain from CGT event E7 if the market value of the asset at the time of the disposal is more than the cost base of the beneficiary's interest in trust capital. If that market value is less than the reduced cost base of that interest, a capital loss is made.

A capital gain or loss made from CGT event E7 by a beneficiary is disregarded if:

- the trust interest was acquired for no expenditure (except where it was assigned from another entity)
- the trust interest was acquired before 20 September 1985, or
- the gain or loss made by the trustee was disregarded under the main residence exemption, eg due to being a special disability trust (s 104-85(6); ¶11-730, ¶11-770).

CGT event E8 — Disposal by beneficiary of capital interest

CGT event E8 happens if the beneficiary of a trust:

(i) disposes of all or part of the beneficiary's interest in trust capital to someone other than the trustee of the trust

(ii) did not acquire the interest by assignment, and

(iii) did not give any money or property to acquire that interest (s 104-90).

However, CGT event E8 does not happen if the trust is a unit trust or a deceased estate. For the CGT consequences of creating life and remainder interests in property and subsequent dealings in those interests, see TR 2006/14.

To be an interest in trust capital for these purposes, the interest must be a vested and indefeasible interest in a share of trust capital. In this regard, a taker in default does not have the required interest in the trust capital (TD 2009/19).

If the trust interest is disposed of under a contract, the time of CGT event E8 is when the beneficiary enters into the contract. If there is no contract for disposal of the trust interest, CGT event E8 happens when the beneficiary stops owning the relevant trust interest. If a trust interest is acquired by a taxpayer as a result of CGT event E8, it is acquired at the time of that CGT event.

Where the taxpayer is the only beneficiary with an interest in the trust capital, a capital gain arises from CGT event E8 if the capital proceeds from the disposal are more than the net asset amount (s 104-95). The net asset amount is found by adding:

- the sum of the cost bases of the trust's CGT assets acquired on or after 20 September 1985
- the sum of the market values of the trust's CGT assets acquired before 20 September 1985, and
- the amount of money that formed part of the trust capital at the time of disposal

and subtracting any liabilities of the trust at that time. For this purpose, a special indexation rule applies to the cost base calculation (¶11-610).

A capital loss arises from CGT event E8 if the capital proceeds from the disposal are less than the reduced net asset amount. The reduced net asset amount is worked out in the same way as the net asset amount, except that the reduced cost bases of the trust's post-CGT assets are taken into account rather than their cost bases.

Where there is more than one beneficiary having an interest in the trust capital or a beneficiary is disposing of only a part of such an interest, capital gains and losses from CGT event E8 are worked out in the same way, except that the net asset amount and reduced asset amount are reduced by reference to the proportion of the trust interest being disposed of.

A capital gain or loss from CGT event E8 is disregarded if the trust interest was acquired before 20 September 1985.

CGT event E9 — Creating a trust over future property

CGT event E9 happens if the taxpayer agrees for consideration that when property comes into existence it will be held in trust (s 104-105). However, for CGT event E9 to happen, it must also be that, at the time of the agreement, no potential beneficiary of the trust has a beneficial interest in the rights created by the agreement.

CGT event E9 may happen where a person creates a trust over an asset and the trust beneficiaries have no beneficial interest in the asset, eg a discretionary trust. The principal (but not sole) intention of CGT event E9 is to ensure that, where a prospective interest in a partnership is assigned (ie a pre-admission Everett assignment), it is subject to CGT. Under such an assignment, the prospective partner agrees that, upon becoming a partner, he/she will hold a share of the partnership interest on trust for another person, or will assign that share to the person. The effect, if consideration is given, is that the prospective partner becomes a trustee of the assigned property as soon as that property comes into existence, ie when the prospective partner is admitted to the partnership (*Norman*). If the assignment is made to a particular person, the beneficial interest in the partnership share vests in that person and CGT event D1 (¶11-280) happens. If, on the other hand, the partner holds the partnership share as trustee for a discretionary trust, the partnership share is not vested in another person and CGT event E9 happens.

The time of CGT event E9 is when the agreement is made. If an asset is acquired by a trustee as a result of CGT event E9, it is acquired at the time of that CGT event.

The taxpayer makes a capital gain from CGT event E9 if the market value the property would have if it existed at the time of the agreement is more than any incidental costs (¶11-550) incurred in relation to the event. If that market value is less than those incidental costs, a capital loss is made.

The incidental costs can include giving property. However, they do not include any non-assessable recoupment of the expenditure nor any part of the expenditure that is deductible.

CGT event E10 — Annual cost base reduction exceeds cost base of interest in AMIT

CGT event E10 happens to a taxpayer that (i) holds a CGT asset that is a unit or interest in an AMIT, (ii) either the cost base of that CGT asset is reduced due to tax deferred distributions (per s 104-107B) or the cost base is nil at the start of the income year and (iii) ‘‘AMIT cost base net amount’’ for the income year of the reduction exceeds the cost base of the asset (s 104-107A). The time of the CGT event is the time of the reduction. The capital gain is equal to the excess. When the cost base of the asset is nil at the start of the year the capital gain will be the cost base net amount.

A capital gain is disregarded where the taxpayer acquired the CGT asset that is the unit or interest prior to 20 September 1985 (s 104-107A(4)).

Where a taxpayer holds a CGT asset that is a unit or an interest in an AMIT, there is an annual adjustment to the cost base of the asset. The provisions in ss 104-107A to 104-107H provide for annual upward and downward adjustments to the cost base.

The annual adjustment is made just before the end of the income year unless a CGT event happens in relation to the asset before the end of the income year in which case the adjustment is made just before that CGT event (s 104-107B(4)). Broadly, the cost base will either be:

(a) increased where and to the extent that the ‘‘AMIT cost base increase amount’’ (as defined in s 104-107E) exceeds the ‘‘AMIT cost base reduction amount’’ (as defined in s 104-107D)

(b) decreased, but not below zero, where and to the extent that the ‘‘AMIT cost base reduction amount’’ exceeds the ‘‘AMIT cost base increase amount’’.

The increase or decrease amount is known as the ‘‘AMIT cost base net amount’’ (s 104-107C).

The AMIT cost base reduction amount for the income year is, to the extent that it is reasonably attributable to the CGT asset that is the membership interest, the total of:

- any money and the market value of any property that the member starts to have a right to receive from the AMIT in the income year, where that right is indefeasible or is reasonable likely not to be defeated
- all amounts of tax offset that the member has a right to receive from the AMIT in the income year (s 104-107D(1)).

The AMIT cost base increase amount for the income year is, to the extent that they are reasonably attributable to the CGT asset that is the membership interest, the sum of:

- all amounts (disregarding the AMIT's net capital gain for the income year) included in the member's assessable income or non-assessable non-exempt income (either because of s 276-80 or because of another provision in the income tax law) for the income year, worked out on the assumption that the member is an Australian resident, and

- the amount of the member's determined member components of a character relating to a capital gain that the member has for the income year in respect of the AMIT that is taken into account under s 276-80, worked out on the assumption that the member is an Australian resident — in the case of a discount capital gain, this amount includes the discount component of the discount capital gain (s 104-107E).

A tax deferred or tax-free distribution or entitlement will arise in relation to a membership interest that is held by an entity that is a member of an AMIT in respect of an income year if:

- the member starts to have a right to receive any money or any property from the trustee of an AMIT in the income year

- the right is indefeasible or is reasonably likely not to be defeated

- the right is not remuneration or consideration for the member providing finance, services, goods or property to the trustee of the AMIT or to another person

- the right is reasonably attributable to a CGT asset that is a membership interest in the AMIT

- the CGT asset is not trading stock or a TOFA financial arrangement, and

- as a result of the member starting to have the right, the CGT asset's AMIT cost base reduction amount for the income year is increased because of the operation of s 104-107D (s 104-107F).

The tax-deferred or tax-free distribution or entitlement derived from the membership interest in these circumstances is not included in the member's assessable income under provisions outside of the rules for AMITs (s 104-107F(2), (3)).

Where the AMIT unit or membership interest is a revenue asset the cost base will be adjusted in accordance with s 104-107G with an amount being included in revenue in accordance with s 104-107H.

[FITR ¶151-960 – ¶152-070]

¶11-300 CGT events involving leases

CGT event F1 — Granting a lease

CGT event F1 happens if a lessor grants, renews or extends a lease (s 104-110). However, CGT event F1 does not happen if the lessor can and chooses for CGT event F2 (see below) to apply. Additional special rules may also apply to some lease transactions (¶12-680).

Where a lease is granted, the time of CGT event F1 is when the contract for the lease is entered into or, if there is no such contract, at the start of the lease. This means that a capital gain can arise to a lessor on the grant of a lease even if the property being leased was acquired before 20 September 1985.

Where a lease is renewed or extended, the time of CGT event F1 is at the start of the renewal or extension. Therefore, if a lease granted before 20 September 1985 is renewed or extended on or after that date, the new lease attracts CGT (s 109-5(2)). If a lease is granted to a lessee, or is renewed or extended, as a result of CGT event F1, it is acquired at the time of that CGT event.

A lessor makes a capital gain from CGT event F1 if the capital proceeds, eg a lease premium, from the grant, renewal or extension are more than the expenditure incurred in relation to it. If the capital proceeds are less than the incurred expenditure, a capital loss is made. A capital gain from CGT event F1 cannot be a discount capital gain (¶11-033).

A capital loss that a lessee makes from the expiry, surrender or forfeiture of a lease (¶11-270), or from the assignment of a lease (¶11-250), is disregarded if the lessee did not use the lease solely or mainly for income-producing purposes (¶11-670).

The expenditure incurred can include giving property. However, the incurred expenditure does not include any non-assessable recoupment of the expenditure nor any part of the expenditure that is deductible.

Lease premiums versus goodwill

Lease premiums must be distinguished from payments for goodwill, which may attract concessional CGT treatment. In *Krakos Investments*, a case involving the sale of a hotel business on a leasehold basis, it was found that the parties' bona fide allocation of $420,000 of the sale price to goodwill was effective for tax purposes. There was no suggestion that the agreement was a sham, or that the rent was below market value. This conclusion was supported by a provision in the contract which obliged the vendor to buy back the goodwill, if required to do so by the purchaser, at the original price (see TR 96/24).

Lease inducements

It has been held that a cash lease inducement paid to a partnership of solicitors on the taking up of a lease of premises by the partnership's service company was assessable as ordinary income (¶10-116) (*Cooling*; *Montgomery*). Such a payment also gives rise to a capital gain from CGT event D1 (¶11-280). However, in such circumstances, the capital gain is reduced to prevent double taxation (¶11-690).

CGT event F2 — Granting a long-term lease

CGT event F2 happens if a lessor grants, renews or extends a lease over land that is for a period of at least 50 years and the lessor chooses for CGT event F2 to happen instead of CGT event F1 which deals with ordinary leases (s 104-115). Additional special rules may also apply to some lease transactions (¶12-680).

The time of CGT event F2 is when the lease is granted, renewed or extended. If a lease is granted to a lessee, or is renewed or extended, as a result of CGT event F2, it is acquired at the time of that CGT event.

A lessor makes a capital gain from CGT event F2 if the capital proceeds from the grant, renewal or extension are more than the cost base of the lessor's interest in the land. If the capital proceeds are less than that cost base, a capital loss is made. A capital gain from CGT event F2 cannot be a discount capital gain (¶11-033).

A capital gain or loss from CGT event F2 is disregarded if the land, or the lease to the lessor, was granted before 20 September 1985. This is also the case if the lease to the lessor was last renewed or extended before 20 September 1985.

CGT event F3 — Lessor pays lessee to get lease changed

CGT event F3 happens if a lessor incurs expenditure to get the lessee's agreement to vary or waive a term of the lease (s 104-120). However, CGT event F3 does not happen if the lessor can and does choose for CGT event F2 (see above) to apply. The expenditure can include giving property. For consequences relating to lease surrender payments, see ¶12-680 and ¶16-640.

The time of CGT event F3 is when the lease term is varied or waived.

A lessor makes a capital loss from CGT event F3 equal to the amount of expenditure it incurred in getting the lessee's agreement to the lease variation. A capital gain cannot be made from CGT event F3.

CGT event F4 — Lessee receives payment for changing lease

CGT event F4 happens if a lessee receives a payment from the lessor for agreeing to vary or waive a term of the lease (s 104-125). The payment can include giving property. For consequences relating to lease surrender payments, see ¶12-680 and ¶16-640.

The time of CGT event F4 is when the lease term is varied or waived.

A lessee makes a capital gain from CGT event F4 if the capital proceeds from the event are more than the lease's cost base. A capital loss cannot be made from CGT event F4.

The cost base of the lease to the lessee is reduced to nil if the lessee makes a capital gain. If the capital proceeds are less than the cost base, the cost base of the lease to the lessee is reduced by the capital proceeds.

A capital gain from CGT event F4 is disregarded if the lease was granted before 20 September 1985 or was last renewed or extended before that date.

CGT event F5 — Lessor receives payment for changing lease

CGT event F5 happens if a lessor receives a payment from the lessee for agreeing to vary or waive a term of the lease (s 104-130). The payment can include giving property. For consequences relating to lease surrender payments, see ¶12-680 and ¶16-640.

The time of CGT event F5 is when the lease term is varied or waived.

A lessor makes a capital gain from CGT event F5 if the capital proceeds from the event are more than the expenditure incurred in relation to the variation or waiver. If the capital proceeds are less than the incurred expenditure, a capital loss is made.

Where CGT event F5 happens, the payment made by the lessee is capital expenditure incurred to enhance the value of the lease and is included in the fourth element of the lessee's cost base and reduced cost base for the lease.

The expenditure incurred can include giving property. However, the incurred expenditure does not include any non-assessable recoupment of that expenditure.

A capital gain or loss from CGT event F5 is disregarded if the lease was granted before 20 September 1985 or was last renewed or extended before that date.

[FITR ¶152-100 – ¶152-150]

¶11-310 CGT events involving shares

CGT event G1 — Capital payment for shares

CGT event G1 happens if:

(i) a company makes a payment to a taxpayer in relation to a share the taxpayer owns in the company

(ii) some or all of the payment (the non-assessable part) is not a dividend or a liquidator's distribution that is taken to be a dividend, and

(iii) the payment is not included in the taxpayer's assessable income (s 104-135).

The payment can include giving property, eg the distribution of an asset in specie.

Any part of the payment that is:

(i) non-assessable non-exempt income (¶10-890)

(ii) repaid by the taxpayer

(iii) compensation the taxpayer provided that can reasonably be regarded as a repayment of all or part of the payment, or

(iv) an amount referred to in s 152-125 (¶7-165) as an exempt amount, is disregarded when working out the non-assessable part.

However, the non-assessable part is not reduced by such amounts that are deductible to the taxpayer.

CGT event G1 does not apply to bonus shares issued out of a share capital account (TD 2000/2; ¶12-600) or to a payment made in relation to CGT event A1 (¶11-250) or C2 (¶11-270) happening to the share.

CGT event G1 may arise where a company makes a distribution to its' shareholders that constitutes an unauthorised reduction and return of share capital due to the distribution not complying with the requirements in the *Corporations Act 2001*, s 254T or Pt 2J.1 for the payment of a dividend or a reduction of capital (TR 2012/5).

CGT event G1 potentially applies where a liquidator's interim distribution is made more than 18 months before the company ceases to exist, but for other liquidators' distributions CGT event C2 will apply (TD 2001/27). See ¶11-270.

The time of CGT event G1 is when the company makes the payment.

Capital gains and losses

A taxpayer makes a capital gain from CGT event G1 if the non-assessable part is more than the share's cost base. A capital loss cannot be made from CGT event G1.

The exempt component of a capital gain that arose on the earlier disposal of an asset of the company, eg goodwill, forms a non-assessable part of a payment where CGT event G1 applies to a liquidator's interim distribution on winding up (TD 2001/14).

A capital gain from CGT event G1 is disregarded if the share was acquired before 20 September 1985.

Cost base and reduced cost base adjustments

The cost base and reduced cost base of a share are reduced to nil if the taxpayer makes a capital gain from CGT event G1. However, if the non-assessable part is not more than the cost base, the cost base and reduced cost base are reduced by the non-assessable part.

CGT event G3 — Liquidator declares shares or financial instruments worthless

CGT event G3 happens if a taxpayer owns shares in, or financial instruments issued or created by, a company and the company's liquidator or administrator declares in writing that he/she believes:

- for shares — there to be no likelihood of shareholders (or shareholders of a particular class of shares) receiving further distributions
- for financial instruments — the instruments (or a particular class of instruments), have no or only a negligible value (s 104-145).

This mechanism allows taxpayers to accelerate the crystallisation of a capital loss without the need to dispose of the shares or financial instruments by a "wash sale" (¶11-250). There cannot be a capital gain from CGT event G3.

Liquidators and administrators may notify the shareholders or creditors of the declaration in any way they choose (TD 92/101).

A declaration in relation to shares can state that distributions are not expected to be made to shareholders generally or can be limited to holders of particular classes of shares (TD 92/102). If a liquidator declares that it is expected that a distribution, however small, will be made during winding up, an election is precluded (TD 2000/52).

Timing of CGT event G3

The time of CGT event G3 is when the liquidator makes the declaration.

Capital losses

A taxpayer can choose to make a capital loss equal to the reduced cost base of the taxpayer's shares or financial instrument at the time of the declaration. A capital gain cannot be made from CGT event G3.

If the taxpayer chooses to make a capital loss from CGT event G3, the cost base and reduced cost base of the relevant shares or financial instruments are reduced to nil just after the liquidator makes the declaration. These continue to be relevant for working out if the taxpayer makes a capital gain or loss from any later CGT event that happens in relation to the shares or financial instruments.

▶ **Example**

In 2000, Jennie purchased shares in Tooth & Co Ltd. On 24 June 2020 the liquidators of the company made a declaration that they had reasonable grounds to believe that there was no likelihood that the shareholders would receive any distribution on a winding up. Jennie opted to make a capital loss equal to the reduced cost base of her shares as at 24 June 2020. This reduced the cost base and reduced cost base of her shares to nil.

A taxpayer cannot choose to make a capital loss from shares or financial instruments acquired before 20 September 1985 or where such assets were revenue assets at time the declaration was made.

[FITR ¶152-170 – ¶152-200]

¶11-320 CGT events from special capital receipts

CGT event H1 — Forfeiture of a deposit

CGT event H1 happens if a deposit paid to the taxpayer is forfeited because a prospective sale or other transaction does not proceed (s 104-150). The payment can include giving property.

The most common example of CGT event H1 is where a deposit is forfeited under a contract for the sale of land (*Brooks*).

CGT event H1 applies where a forfeited deposit arises in relation to the sale of land in circumstances where there is no "continuum of events" constituting a later sale of the land. If there is a continuum of events, the forfeited deposit will be treated as part of the capital proceeds from disposal of the land (TR 1999/19).

Where instalment moneys (other than deposits) are lawfully applied in satisfaction of damages for breach of contract, a capital gain normally arises either because of a disposal of the right created by CGT event D1 (¶11-280) or CGT event H2 (see below) happens (TR 94/29).

As to the application of the main residence exemption to forfeited deposits, see ¶11-730.

The time of CGT event H1 is when the deposit is forfeited, ie when the cancellation or termination of the prospective purchase or other transaction takes place (*Case 32/94*).

A taxpayer makes a capital gain from CGT event H1 if the deposit is more than the expenditure incurred in connection with the prospective sale or other transaction. If the deposit is less than the incurred expenditure, a capital loss is made.

The expenditure incurred can include giving property. However, the incurred expenditure does not include any non-assessable recoupment of that expenditure.

CGT event H2 — Receipt for event relating to a CGT asset

CGT event H2 happens if an act, transaction or event occurs in relation to a CGT asset the taxpayer owns and the act, transaction or event does not result in the cost base or reduced cost base of the asset being adjusted (s 104-155). However, CGT event H2 does not happen if:

(i) the act, transaction or event is the borrowing of money or the obtaining of credit from another entity

(ii) the act, transaction or event requires the taxpayer to do something that involves another CGT event happening to the taxpayer

(iii) a company issues or allots equity interests such as shares

(iv) the trustee of a unit trust issues units

(v) a company grants an option to acquire equity interests or debentures

(vi) a company grants an option to dispose of shares in the company to the company

(vii) the trustee of a unit trust grants an option to acquire units or debentures, or

(viii) a company or trust that is a member of a demerger group issues new ownership interests under a demerger (¶12-328).

CGT event H2 is a residual CGT event and only applies if no other CGT event happens.

Where instalment moneys (other than deposits) are lawfully applied in satisfaction of damages for breach of contract, a capital gain normally arises because CGT event D1 (¶11-280) or H2 happens (TR 94/29).

CGT event H2 may happen if there is a variation in share rights, eg an alteration in voting rights, a change in dividend entitlements or conversion of a share from one class to another. However, in such a situation, CGT event H2 does not apply if CGT event G2 also happens. In the usual case, a share remains in existence following a variation in share rights. A variation in share rights does not result in the part disposal of a share under CGT event A1 or the creation of new rights under CGT event D1 (TR 94/30). However, if the variation results in a cancellation or redemption of the original share, CGT event C2 happens. A conversion of a co-operative into an unlisted public company and the issue of new share certificates do not give rise to CGT event A1 for its members (CR 2008/68).

A resolution by an insurer to allow a premium rebate under a policy of insurance gave rise to CGT event H2 in respect of the policy holder's bundle of rights under the policy (ID 2006/222).

The time of CGT event H2 is when the act, transaction or event occurs.

A taxpayer makes a capital gain from CGT event H2 if the capital proceeds received are more than the incidental costs incurred in relation to the event. If the capital proceeds are less than those incidental costs, a capital loss is made. The incidental costs can include giving property. However, the incidental costs do not include any non-assessable recoupment of that expenditure.

The market value substitution rule does not apply to capital proceeds received from CGT event H2.

[FITR ¶152-230 – ¶152-238]

¶11-330 CGT events from Australian residency ending

CGT event I1 — Individual or company stops being resident

CGT event I1 happens if an individual or company stops being an Australian resident (s 104-160). Special rules apply to individuals and companies (including CFCs) when they become residents (¶12-740).

The time of CGT event I1 is when the individual or company stops being a resident.

If CGT event I1 happens to a taxpayer, the taxpayer must look at each CGT asset (other than certain taxable Australian property (¶12-725) excluding indirect interests) that the taxpayer owned just before Australian residency ended and see if a capital gain or loss has been made on it.

A taxpayer makes a capital gain from CGT event I1 in relation to a particular asset if the market value of the asset is more than its cost base. If the market value of the asset is less than its reduced cost base, a capital loss is made.

Exceptions

A capital gain or loss from CGT event I1 is disregarded if the asset was acquired before 20 September 1985.

An individual can also choose to disregard the capital gains and losses from *all* CGT assets caught by CGT event I1. If this choice is made, each of those assets is taken to be taxable Australian property (¶12-725) until the earlier of: (i) when another CGT event happens to the asset, possibly crystallising a capital gain or loss at that time; or (ii) when the taxpayer again becomes a resident, at which time it again becomes an ordinary asset within the CGT net (s 104-165).

▶ Planning point

In determining whether to make this election or not, the taxpayer needs to consider any expected increases in value of the asset and the potential reduction of the general discount for the period of non-residency which may increase the assessable gain against paying taxation prior to actual disposal.

A capital gain or loss arising from CGT event I1 in relation to a share or right held by the taxpayer that is an ESS interest which has not been subject to income tax pursuant to Div 83A will be disregarded (s 130-80; ¶10-085, ¶12-630).

A capital gain or loss from CGT event I1 is also disregarded if the taxpayer was a temporary resident immediately before the relevant CGT event (¶12-760).

With effect from 9 May 2017, subject to transitional rules to 30 June 2020, the main residence exemption is not available for CGT event I1 (¶11-730).

CGT event I2 — Trust stops being a resident trust

CGT event I2 happens if a trust stops being an Australian resident trust (s 104-170). Special rules apply to trusts when they become resident trusts for CGT purposes (¶12-740).

The time of CGT event I2 is when the trust stops being a resident trust for CGT purposes (¶12-720).

If CGT event I2 happens to a trust, the trustee must look at each CGT asset (other than certain taxable Australian property (¶12-725) excluding indirect interests) that it owned as trustee of the trust just before Australian residency ended and see if a capital gain or loss has been made on it.

A taxpayer makes a capital gain from CGT event I2 in relation to a particular asset if the market value of the asset is more than its cost base. If the market value of the asset is less than its reduced cost base, a capital loss is made.

A capital gain or loss from CGT event I2 is disregarded if the asset was acquired before 20 September 1985.

With effect from 9 May 2017, subject to transitional rules to 30 June 2020, the main residence exemption is not available for CGT event I2 (¶11-730).

[FITR ¶152-270 – ¶152-278]

¶11-340 CGT events relating to roll-overs

CGT event J1 — Company ceasing to be member of wholly-owned group after roll-over

CGT event J1 happens if:

(i) a CGT asset is rolled over between companies in the same wholly-owned group

(ii) the recipient company stops being a wholly-owned subsidiary of the group's ultimate holding company (¶3-090), and

(iii) at the time of the roll-over, the recipient company was a wholly-owned subsidiary of the other company involved in the roll-over event (the originating company) or of another member of the same wholly-owned group (s 104-175).

Following the introduction of the group consolidation regime (¶8-000), CGT event J1 has lost much of its relevance. However, it may still apply where transfers of assets involving foreign resident companies occur (¶12-490).

Unless the break-up exceptions (see below) apply, CGT event J1 happens if:

- shares of the company holding the rolled-over asset are issued or disposed of outside the company group in which the ultimate holding company remains
- shares of a company which is in the direct ownership chain between the ultimate holding company and the company holding the rolled-over asset are issued or disposed of outside the company group, or
- the ultimate holding company is dissolved.

Neither the issue or transfer of shares of the ultimate holding company itself nor the transfer of shares between group companies causes CGT event J1 to happen. CGT event J1 does not apply where a partnership is interposed between the ultimate holding company of the wholly owned group and the subsidiary that received the assets pursuant to the roll-over, if the partners in the partnership are also members of the wholly owned group (ID 2009/43).

Once CGT event J1 happens, any roll-overs of the asset before the break-up time are no longer relevant. CGT event J1 then only has to be considered in relation to a subsequent roll-over or series of roll-overs, and in relation to the company which is the ultimate holding company when the first such subsequent roll-over occurs.

Timing of CGT event J1

The time of CGT event J1 is the break-up time. This is when the recipient company stops being a wholly-owned subsidiary of the group's ultimate holding company.

Capital gains and losses

A company makes a capital gain from CGT event J1 if the market value of the roll-over asset at the break-up time is more than its cost base. If the market value of the roll-over asset is less than its reduced cost base, a capital loss is made.

A capital gain or loss from CGT event J1 is disregarded if the roll-over asset is taken to have been acquired before 20 September 1985 under the roll-over provisions, ie if the originating company acquired the roll-over asset, or is taken to have acquired it, before that date. However, this exclusion does not apply if the roll-over asset has stopped being a pre-CGT asset, eg because of Div 149 (¶12-870).

CGT event J1 does not happen to a demerged entity or a member of a demerger group if CGT event A1 or C2 happens to a demerging entity under a demerger (¶12-328).

Acquisition rules

Once CGT event J1 has happened to an asset, it is taken to have been acquired by the recipient company at the break-up time. In addition, for purposes of later CGT events, the first element of the recipient company's cost base and reduced cost base is its market value at the break-up time.

Sub-group break-up exception

CGT event J1 does not happen if a sub-group break-up occurs so that the asset remains within the same sub-group even if it is no longer a wholly-owned subsidiary of the ultimate holding company (s 104-180).

Consolidated group break-up

CGT event J1 does not happen if the recipient company ceases to be a member of a consolidated group at the break-up time (s 104-182).

CGT event J2 — Change in relation to replacement asset or improved asset after a roll-over under Subdiv 152-E

CGT event J2 happens if a taxpayer has chosen the CGT small business roll-over (¶7-195), the taxpayer acquires a replacement asset meeting certain conditions and a specified change happens after the end of the replacement asset period (s 104-185). The conditions the replacement asset must meet are:

(1) the replacement asset is acquired or improved in the replacement asset period (see below)

(2) the replacement asset is active at the end of that period

(3) if the replacement asset is a share in a company or an interest in a trust, at the end of the replacement asset period:

- the taxpayer, or an entity connected with the taxpayer, is a CGT concession stakeholder (¶7-155) in the company or trust, or
- CGT concession stakeholders in the company or trust have a small business participation percentage (¶7-155) in the taxpayer of at least 90%.

Note that if these conditions are not satisfied, CGT event J5 will occur at the end of the replacement asset period (see below).

The specified changes that will result in CGT event J2 happening are:

(a) the replacement asset:

(i) stops being the taxpayer's active asset (eg a disposal of the asset)

(ii) becomes trading stock, or

(iii) starts being used solely to produce exempt income or non-assessable non-exempt income, or

(b) if the replacement asset is a share in a company or an interest in a trust:

(i) CGT event G3 or I1 happens, or

(ii) the relevant condition in (3) above ceases to be satisfied.

There can be one or more replacement assets. If there is only one replacement asset, or if a change happens to all of the replacement assets, the capital gain is the amount that was originally rolled over.

If there is more than one replacement asset and a change happens to less than all of the replacement assets, the capital gain is the difference between the amount that was originally rolled over and the relevant expenditure on the remaining replacement assets that satisfied relevant conditions.

The capital gain may be reduced where CGT events J5, J6 or both have previously happened in relation to the roll-over.

The small business retirement exemption and the CGT small business roll-over may potentially apply to reduce the capital gain from CGT event J2 (s 152-10(4)). However, none of the CGT discount, the small business 15-year exemption or the small business 50% reduction can apply to the capital gain from CGT event J2 (ss 115-25; 152-10(4)).

Replacement asset period

The replacement asset period is generally the period starting one year before, and ending 2 years after, the last CGT event in the income year for which a taxpayer obtained roll-over relief (s 104-185). However, the replacement asset period may be modified in certain circumstances or extended by the Commissioner (s 104-190).

CGT event J4 — Trust fails to cease to exist after roll-over under Subdiv 124-N

CGT event J4 happens where:

- a roll-over in Subdiv 124-N (¶12-395) is chosen for an asset disposed of to a company during the trust restructuring period
- the trust fails to cease to exist within a certain timeframe (generally 6 months after the first asset transfer), and
- the company owns the asset when the failure happens.

As a result, the effect of the roll-over is reversed.

CGT event J4 is also triggered where:

- a Subdiv 124-N roll-over is chosen by a beneficiary of the trust in respect of an interest in the trust that was exchanged for a share under a trust restructure
- the trust fails to cease to exist within the required time, and
- the beneficiary still owns the share in the company.

The effect of the roll-over will also be reversed for the beneficiary.

CGT event J5 — Failure to acquire replacement asset and to incur fourth element expenditure after a roll-over under Subdiv 152-E

CGT event J5 happens where a taxpayer has chosen the small business roll-over (¶7-195) and by the end of the replacement asset period the taxpayer has not acquired a replacement asset and has not incurred expenditure to improve the asset (*''replacement asset''*), or the replacement asset does not satisfy certain conditions (s 104-197). The conditions are:

- the replacement asset must be the taxpayer's active asset
- if the replacement asset is a share in a company or an interest in a trust
  - the taxpayer, or an entity connected with the taxpayer, must be a CGT concession stakeholder (¶7-155) in the company or trust, or
  - CGT concession stakeholders in the company or trust must have a small business participation percentage (¶7-155) in the taxpayer of at least 90%.

The capital gain is the amount of the capital gain that was previously rolled over.

The small business retirement exemption may potentially apply to reduce the capital gain from CGT event J5 (s 152-10(4)). In such a case the taxpayer will not be required to satisfy the basic conditions in Subdiv 152-A in order to apply the exemption (s 152-305(4)). However, none of the other CGT small business concessions, nor the CGT discount, can apply to reduce the capital gain (ss 115-25; 152-10(4)).

CGT event J6 — Cost of acquisition of replacement asset or amount of fourth element expenditure, or both, not sufficient to cover disregarded capital gain

CGT event J6 happens where the taxpayer has chosen the small business roll-over (¶7-195) and by the end of the replacement asset period the taxpayer has incurred expenditure on acquiring a replacement asset and/or improving an asset (*''replacement asset''*) meeting certain conditions but that expenditure is less than the amount of the capital gain that was disregarded under the small business roll-over (s 104-198). The conditions are the same as detailed above for CGT event J5.

The relevant expenditure consists of:

- costs that would be included in the first element of the asset's cost base
- incidental costs of acquisition of the asset, and
- costs that would be included in the fourth element of the asset's cost base (¶11-550).

The capital gain is the difference between the amount of the capital gain that was rolled over and the amount of expenditure incurred.

The small business retirement exemption may potentially apply to reduce the capital gain from CGT event J6 (s 152-10(4)). In such a case the taxpayer will not be required to satisfy the basic conditions in Subdiv 152-A in order to apply the exemption (s 152-305(4)). However, none of the other CGT small business concessions, nor the CGT discount, can apply to reduce the capital gain (ss 115-25; 152-10(4)).

[FITR ¶152-300 – ¶152-330]

¶11-350 Other CGT events

CGT event K1 — Incoming international transfers of emissions unit

CGT event K1 will happen if:

(i) there is an international transfer of a Kyoto unit or an Australian carbon credit unit

(ii) as a result of the transfer the taxpayer holds the unit as a registered emissions unit, and

(iii) just before the transfer, the unit was neither trading stock nor a revenue asset of the taxpayer (s 104-205).

A capital gain will arise if the unit's market value just before it started to be held as a registered emissions unit is more than its cost base. A capital loss would arise if the market value is less than its reduced cost base.

CGT event K2 — Bankrupt pays amount in relation to debt

CGT event K2 happens if:

(i) the taxpayer makes a net capital loss for an income year that cannot be offset against capital gains because the taxpayer became bankrupt or was released from debts under a bankruptcy law

(ii) the taxpayer later makes a payment in respect of a debt that was taken into account in working out that net capital loss, and

(iii) the denied part of the net capital loss would otherwise have been able to be offset against capital gains in the payment year (s 104-210).

The payment can include giving property. However, the payment does not include any non-assessable recoupment of the payment.

The time of CGT event K2 is when the payment is made.

A taxpayer makes a capital loss from CGT event K2 equal to the smallest of:

(i) the amount paid

(ii) that part of the payment that was taken into account in working out the denied part of the net capital loss, or

(iii) the denied part of the net capital loss reduced by the sum of capital losses made from CGT event K2 as a result of previous payments made in respect of the debt.

A capital gain cannot be made from CGT event K2.

CGT event K3 — Asset passing to tax-advantaged entity

CGT event K3 happens if a taxpayer dies and a CGT asset passes to a beneficiary that is an exempt entity, is the trustee of a complying superannuation fund, a complying ADF or a PST or is not an Australian resident (s 104-215). However, if the asset passes to a beneficiary that is not a resident, CGT event K3 happens only if the taxpayer was a resident and the asset (in the hands of the beneficiary) is not taxable Australian property (¶12-725).

The time of CGT event K3 is just before the taxpayer dies. If an asset is acquired by a tax-advantaged entity as a result of CGT event K3, it is acquired at the time of that CGT event.

A taxpayer makes a capital gain from CGT event K3 if the market value of the asset on the day the taxpayer dies is more than its cost base. If the market value of the asset is less than its reduced cost base, a capital loss is made.

A capital gain or loss from CGT event K3 is disregarded if the asset was acquired before 20 September 1985. Capital gains or losses are also disregarded if they are from a testamentary gift that would have been deductible under the normal rules if made during the taxpayer's lifetime (s 118-60).

CGT event K4 — CGT asset starts being trading stock

CGT event K4 happens if a taxpayer starts holding as trading stock a CGT asset already owned by the taxpayer but not held as trading stock and the taxpayer elects to be treated as having sold the asset for its market value (¶9-245) (s 104-220). If the taxpayer elects the cost of the asset, CGT event K4 does not apply and any capital gain or capital loss is disregarded (¶11-700).

The time of CGT event K4 is when the taxpayer starts holding the asset as trading stock.

A taxpayer makes a capital gain from CGT event K4 if the market value of the asset just before it becomes trading stock is more than its cost base. If the market value of the asset is less than its reduced cost base, a capital loss is made.

A capital gain or loss from CGT event K4 is disregarded if the asset was acquired before 20 September 1985.

CGT event K5 — Special collectable losses

CGT event K5 happens if:

(i) there is a fall in the market value of a collectable (¶11-390) of a company or trust

(ii) CGT event A1 (¶11-250), C2 (¶11-270) or E8 (¶11-290) happens to shares that the taxpayer owns in the company (or in a company that is a member of the same wholly-owned group) or an interest the taxpayer has in the trust, and there is no roll-over for that CGT event, and

(iii) as a result of the capital proceeds from that event being replaced under a special rule (¶11-520), the taxpayer makes a capital gain that would not otherwise be made, does not make a capital loss that would otherwise be made or makes a capital loss that is less than would otherwise be made (s 104-225).

The time of CGT event K5 is when the triggering CGT event A1, C2 or E8 happens.

A taxpayer makes a capital loss from a collectable under CGT event K5 equal to the market value of the shares or trust interest, worked out at the time of the triggering CGT event (A1, C2 or E8) as if the fall in market value of the collectable had not occurred, less the actual capital proceeds from CGT event A1, C2 or E8. A capital gain cannot be made from CGT event K5.

CGT event K6 — Pre-CGT shares or trust interest

CGT event K6 is designed to stop the potential avoidance of CGT where, instead of an entity disposing of an asset it acquired on or after 20 September 1985, the owners of pre-CGT interests in the interposed entity dispose of those interests. Both direct and indirect interests are caught.

More specifically, for CGT event K6 to happen:

(i) the taxpayer must own shares in a company or an interest in a trust acquired before 20 September 1985

(ii) one of CGT events A1, C2, E1, E2, E3, E5, E6, E7, E8, J1 and K3 must happen in relation to the shares or trust interest, and

(iii) there must not be a roll-over for the other (non-K6) CGT event (s 104-230).

However, CGT event K6 only happens if just before the other (non-K6) CGT event happened, the market value of post-CGT property (other than trading stock) of the company or trust *or* the market value of interests the company or trust owned through interposed companies or trusts in post-CGT property (other than trading stock) is at least 75% of the net value of the company or trust. The 2 amounts cannot be added together to determine if the 75% test is satisfied (TR 2004/18).

Property that is taken to be acquired before 20 September 1985, eg under a roll-over provision, is not post-CGT property for these purposes. However, an exception applies where the CGT asset is treated as having been acquired post-CGT because of the operation of Div 149 (¶12-870) (TR 2004/18).

The market value of post-CGT property or of an interest in such property is determined by reference to market value without regard to liabilities. In the case of leased equipment, the market value of the lease (not the equipment) is used (TD 54).

The net value of a company or trust is the amount by which the sum of the market values of the assets of the company or trust exceeds the sum of its liabilities. However, in working out this net value, the discharge or release of any liabilities and the market value of any CGT assets acquired are disregarded if the discharge, release or acquisition was done for a purpose that included ensuring that the "75% of net value" test would not trigger CGT event K6.

For the purposes of working out the net value of a company, assets mean the property and other economic resources owned by the company that can be turned to account. On the other hand, liabilities do not include contingent liabilities (TR 2004/18).

CGT event K6 does not happen if the company which owns the relevant post-CGT property has had some of its shares listed on an Australian or foreign stock exchange for the 5 years before the other (non-K6) CGT event happened. The same exception applies if the trust which owns the relevant post-CGT property is a unit trust and has had some of its units so listed, or ordinarily available to the public for subscription or purchase, for that period. Where there is a disposal of new interests in a demerged entity under a demerger (¶12-328), CGT event K6 does not apply if the combined period that the head entity and the demerged entity have been continuously listed on the stock exchange is at least 5 years.

A capital gain or loss made by a demerging entity from CGT event A1, C2 or K6 happening as a result of demerger is also disregarded (¶12-328).

CGT event K6 also does not happen if the taxpayer is a foreign resident and the pre-CGT shares or trust interest being disposed of is not subject to CGT (*Case 42/96*). This is so even if the post-CGT property of the company or trust is taxable Australian property (¶12-725).

Timing of CGT event K6

The time of CGT event K6 is when the other (non-K6) CGT event happens. If a share or a trust interest is acquired by a taxpayer as a result of CGT event K6, it is acquired at the time of that CGT event.

Capital gains

A taxpayer makes a capital gain from CGT event K6 equal to that part of the capital proceeds from the shares or trust interest that is reasonably attributable to the amount by which the market value of the relevant post-CGT property is more than the sum of the cost bases of that property. Indexation can be applied in working out the cost base of property provided it was acquired at or before 11.45 am on 21 September 1999 (TR 2004/18). A capital loss cannot be made from CGT event K6.

The capital proceeds may be affected by the market value substitution rule (s 116-25; ¶11-510). The Commissioner has provided a formula and examples of calculating a capital gain from CGT event K6 (TR 2004/18).

The CGT discount and small business CGT relief can apply to capital gains made from CGT event K6 (TR 2004/18).

CGT event K7 — Balancing adjustments for depreciating assets

CGT event K7 happens where a balancing adjustment event happens to a depreciating asset that has been used, or installed ready for use, wholly or partly for a non-taxable purpose (s 104-235). In broad terms, a taxable purpose is a business purpose (s 40-25).

CGT event K7 also happens where a balancing adjustment event occurs for a depreciating asset held by a taxpayer that is an R&D entity, when the asset was held the taxpayer could deduct an amount under s 40-25 for the asset and the taxpayer either:

(i) used the asset other than for a taxable purpose or for carrying on R&D activities, or

(ii) had it installed ready for use other than for a taxable purpose (s 104-235(1B)).

CGT event K7 will not apply where:

- the depreciating asset is used in carrying on R&D activities

- there is roll-over relief for the balancing adjustment event under s 40-340 (¶17-710), or
- the asset is covered by Subdiv 40-F or Subdiv 40-G (s 104-235(1A)).

To ensure consistency of treatment between the capital allowance rules and the CGT rules, a capital gain or loss under CGT event K7 is calculated on the basis of the asset's cost and termination value, instead of on the usual CGT basis of cost base and capital proceeds. The gain or loss is also treated as arising at the same time as any balancing adjustment.

If the use was 100% taxable, CGT event K7 does not apply, but there will be a balancing adjustment under the capital allowances system (¶17-670). If the use is 100% *non*-taxable, there will be a capital gain/loss under CGT event K7 based on the difference between the asset's termination value and its cost (s 104-240); in such a case, there will be no balancing adjustment. If there is a mixed use (eg partly taxable and partly non-taxable), there may be both a balancing adjustment and a capital gain/loss. That capital gain/loss will be based on the difference between the termination value and the cost, apportioned to reflect the taxable component of the decline in value (s 104-240). Special rules apply to depreciating assets that have been allocated to a low-value pool (s 104-245).

If CGT event K7 happens to a depreciating asset (or a pooled asset), the termination value of the asset is reduced by any amount misappropriated by an employee or agent and increased by any amount received as a recoupment of an amount so misappropriated. An assessment can be amended within 4 years, starting immediately after a taxpayer discovers a misappropriation or receives an amount as recoupment.

CGT event K7 is disregarded if the asset was acquired before 20 September 1985 or the taxpayer could deduct an amount under the simplified depreciation rules for small business in Div 328 for the income year in which the balancing adjustment occurred (s 104-235(4)). If the private use of the asset is such that it falls within the personal use asset rules, capital gains are exempt if the asset was acquired for $10,000 or less and capital losses are disregarded (¶11-400).

A capital gain made as a result of CGT event K7 can be a discount capital gain but is not eligible for the CGT small business concessions (¶7-120).

CGT event K8 — Direct value shifts

CGT event K8 happens where a taxing event generates a gain for a ''down interest'' under s 725-245 pursuant to the direct value shifting rules in Div 725 (s 104-250).

The time of CGT event K8 is the decrease time for the down interest, ie the time when the decrease in market value happens.

A capital gain is disregarded if the down interest was acquired prior to 20 September 1985.

CGT event K9 — Carried interests

CGT event K9 happens where an entitlement to receive a payment of a ''carried interest'' arises. A carried interest can be held by:

- a general partner in a venture capital limited partnership or an Australian venture capital fund or funds (¶5-040), or
- a limited partner in a venture capital management partnership (s 104-255).

In broad terms, a carried interest is the partner's entitlement to a distribution from the partnership to the extent that the distribution is contingent upon the attainment of profits for the partners. The amount of any capital gain when CGT event K9 happens is the amount of the capital proceeds (¶11-500). The taxpayer cannot make a capital loss.

The time of CGT event K9 is when the entitlement to receive the payment arises. Anti-overlap provisions provide that the payment of a carried interest is not treated as income (¶11-700).

CGT event K10 — Certain short-term forex realisation gains

CGT event K10 happens if:

- an entity makes a forex realisation gain as a result of forex realisation event 2, and
- item 1 of the table in s 775-70(1) applies (s 104-260).

The time of the event is when the forex realisation event happens. Only a capital gain can arise from CGT event K10.

CGT event K11 — Certain short-term forex realisation losses

CGT event K11 happens if:

- an entity makes a forex realisation loss as a result of forex realisation event 2, and
- item 1 of the table in s 775-75(1) applies (s 104-265).

The time of the event is when the forex realisation event happens. Only a capital loss can arise from CGT event K11.

CGT event K12 — Foreign hybrid loss exposure adjustment

CGT event K12 happens where a limited partner makes a capital loss equal to an outstanding foreign hybrid net capital loss amount (s 830-70). CGT event K12 allows the limited partner to use this capital loss in calculating its net capital gain or loss for the income year. However, loss limitation rules apply to a limited partner's net capital losses in relation to a foreign hybrid (¶5-050).

The time of the event is just before the end of the income year (s 104-270).

[FITR ¶152-360 – ¶152-400]

¶11-360 CGT and consolidated groups

CGT event L1 — Loss of pre-CGT status of membership interests in entity becoming subsidiary member

CGT event L1 happens where, under s 705-57 (¶8-210), there is a reduction in the tax cost setting amount of assets of an entity that becomes a subsidiary member of a consolidated group (s 104-500). A capital loss equal to the reduction is allowed to the head company.

The time of CGT event L1 is just after the entity becomes a subsidiary member of the group. For further details, see ¶8-210.

CGT event L2 — Where pre-formation intra-group roll-over reduction results in negative allocable cost amount

CGT event L2 happens where an entity becomes a subsidiary member of a consolidated group and a pre-formation intra-group roll-over reduction results in negative allocable cost amount (s 104-505).

The time of CGT event L2 is just after the entity becomes a subsidiary member of the group. For further details, see ¶8-220.

CGT event L3 — Where tax cost setting amounts for retained cost base assets exceed joining allocable cost amount

CGT event L3 happens where an entity becomes a subsidiary member of a consolidated group and the sum of the tax cost setting amounts for all of the retained cost base assets that become those of the head entity exceeds the group's allocable cost amount for the entity (s 104-510). The capital gain that arises under CGT event L3 is reduced where a joining entity has impaired debts at the joining time (s 705-27).

The time of CGT event L3 is just after the entity becomes a subsidiary member of the group. For further details, see ¶8-210.

CGT event L4 — Where no reset cost base assets and excess of net allocable cost amount on joining

CGT event L4 happens where an entity becomes a subsidiary member of a consolidated group and there are no reset cost base assets against which to apply the excess of net allocable cost amount on joining (s 104-515).

The time of CGT event L4 is just after the entity becomes a subsidiary member of the group. For further details, see ¶8-210.

CGT event L5 — Where amount remaining after step 4 of leaving allocable cost amount is negative

CGT event L5 happens where an entity ceases to be a subsidiary member of a consolidated group and, in working out the group's allocable cost amount for the entity, the amount remaining after applying step 4 of the table in s 711-20 is negative (s 104-520). The entity's net assets are assessed just before the moment of deconsolidation (*Handbury Holdings Pty Ltd*).

The time of CGT event L5 is when the entity ceases to be a subsidiary member of the group. For further details, see ¶8-400.

CGT event L6 — Error in calculation of cost setting amount for joining entity's assets

CGT event L6 happens where the head company of a consolidated group has a net overstated amount or a net understated amount for the subsidiary member (s 104-525).

The time of CGT event L6 is the start of the income year in which the Commissioner becomes aware of the errors. For further details, see ¶8-250.

CGT event L8 — Where reduction in tax cost setting amounts for reset cost base assets cannot be allocated

CGT event L8 happens where there is an excess of allocable cost amount on joining that cannot be allocated to reset cost base assets because of the restriction under s 705-40 (¶8-210) on the cost that can be allocated to reset cost base assets that are held on revenue account (s 104-535).

The time of the event is just after the entity becomes a subsidiary member of the group.

Where there is an excess of allocable cost amount remaining after the operation of the restriction, the head company makes a capital loss equal to the unallocated amount. A capital gain cannot arise from CGT event L8.

[FITR ¶152-440 – ¶152-461]

CGT Assets

¶11-380 What is a CGT asset?

A CGT asset is any kind of property, or a legal or equitable right that is not property (s 108-5). CGT assets include:

(i) part of, or an interest in, property or a legal or equitable right that is not property

(ii) goodwill or an interest in it

(iii) an interest in a partnership asset, and

(iv) an interest in a partnership that is not an interest in a partnership asset.

Examples of CGT assets include land and buildings, shares in a company, units in a unit trust, options, debts owed to a taxpayer, a right to enforce a contractual obligation and foreign currency, but not Australian currency when it is used as legal tender (TD 2002/25). Bitcoin is neither money nor a foreign currency, but it does constitute a CGT asset for which the disposal will give rise to a CGT event (TD 2014/25; TD 2014/26). An individual using bitcoin with a cost base of less than A$10,000 for personal purposes will not have any CGT consequences due to the exclusion for personal use assets (¶11-400). A car (including an antique or vintage car) is a CGT asset, but any capital gain made from it is exempt (¶11-640). An athlete's entitlement to receive a dAIS sports grant is a CGT asset, but any capital gain or capital loss resulting from the receipt of a payment is disregarded. A payment received under the Perth Voluntary Taxi Plate Buyback Scheme from the Western Australian state government is subject to CGT (ATO Fact Sheet).

Where a taxpayer owns an interest in an asset and then acquires a further interest, the interests remain separate assets. This means that the interests have separate cost bases and the capital proceeds arising from a CGT event happening to the total interests would have to be apportioned (TD 2000/31).

In the case of stapled securities, the individual securities that are stapled are separate assets. For example, if a share in a company and a unit in a unit trust are stapled, the share is a separate asset from the unit. To work out the cost base of each asset, the amount paid to acquire the security must be apportioned between the separate assets.

A unitholder does not have an interest in the underlying property of a unit trust for CGT purposes. The unit in the unit trust is the relevant CGT asset (TD 2000/32).

Property or a right can be a CGT asset even if it does not have a market value, ie there is no condition in the definition of a CGT asset requiring a market value before a CGT asset can be said to exist (TD 2000/34).

Property and rights

If, before 26 June 1992, a taxpayer became the owner of something that is not a form of property, eg a legal or equitable right that is not property, it is not a CGT asset. For this CGT exception to apply, the asset must have commenced to be constructed or created before that date.

This means that a right created *before* 26 June 1992 is subject to the CGT rules only if it is property. Property is generally regarded as something that is capable of assignment or transmission. The kinds of rights which are not capable of assignment but which are CGT assets if created *on or after* 26 June 1992 include:

- rights under a contract for personal services
- rights of a party to a restrictive covenant or exclusive trade tie agreement
- rights of a sporting club under an agreement that requires a sportsperson to play for that club.

A cause of action claiming damages for negligence and breach of contract is a CGT asset as it is either a kind of property for the purposes of s 108-5(1)(a) or, legal or equitable rights that is not property for the purposes of s 108-5(1)(b) (*Coshott*). The argument that a payment of damages per se could not give rise to a profit or gain was dismissed.

Personal rights such as the right to work are not CGT assets (*Hepples*). Personal liberties and freedoms are not legal or equitable rights (recognised and protected by law) and are therefore not CGT assets. However, amounts received in relation to personal liberties and freedoms may be subject to CGT provisions where legal or equitable rights are created (¶11-280).

Mere information is not a CGT asset because it is neither property nor a right. For example, ''know-how'' is not a CGT asset because it is not a form of property nor a legal or equitable right (TD 2000/33). However, a right to require information to be supplied is an asset. For example, a contractual right to require the disclosure of know-how is a CGT asset. Likewise, a licence to use know-how is a CGT asset. Seismic data is not a CGT asset (TR 2019/4).

A CGT asset, being a right, comes into existence when a non-participating shareholder becomes entitled to a retail premium (TR 2010/1).

Assets of joint tenants

Individuals who own a CGT asset as joint tenants are treated as if they each owned a separate CGT asset constituted by an equal interest in the asset and as if each of them held that interest as a tenant in common (s 108-7). This applies even if the party was on the title deed solely to protect the property from being sold on a whim, where there was no evidence of a trust relationship (*Gerbic*). The conversion of a joint tenancy to a tenancy in common (or vice versa) has no CGT consequences. However, the transfer of a 50% interest in jointly-owned shares by 2 brothers to each other was subject to CGT as the restructuring constituted a disposal (*Johnson*). Further, the transfer of the registration of a share from a single name to be owned jointly with a spouse results in a disposal of 50% of the interest (*Murphy*).

Joint trustees of one trust estate who own property are treated as a single person.

Assets subject to special rules

Particular CGT provisions govern the treatment of some kinds of assets, eg collectables (¶11-390), personal use assets (¶11-400), certain investments (¶12-600 – ¶12-650), leases (¶12-680) and options (¶12-700).

[FITR ¶152-810 – ¶152-870]

¶11-390 Collectables

A collectable is an artwork, an item of jewellery, an antique, a coin, a medallion, a rare folio, a rare manuscript, a rare book, a postage stamp or a first day cover that is used or kept mainly for personal use or enjoyment (s 108-10). Collectables also include an interest in any of the above items, a debt that arises from those items, or an option or right to acquire any of those items. An artwork held as a long-term investment in the expectation of capital appreciation is a collectable. However, collectables acquired for $500 or less are CGT exempt (¶11-640).

An antique is considered to be an object of artistic and historical significance that is over 100 years old. For this purpose, the age of an item is worked out as at the time of the relevant CGT event, eg an item which is not an antique because it is acquired when it is 95 years old is an antique if it is over 100 years old when disposed of (TD 1999/40).

If collectables that comprise a set and would ordinarily be disposed of as a set are disposed of in one or more transactions for the purpose of trying to obtain the exemption for collectables under $500, the set of collectables is itself taken to be a single collectable and each disposal is taken to be a disposal of part of that collectable (s 108-15). This rule does not apply to collectables acquired before 16 December 1995.

The third element of the cost base (which involves the non-capital costs of ownership: ¶11-550) is not counted for collectables (s 108-17).

Capital gains and losses from collectables

In working out a net capital gain or loss, capital losses from collectables can only be used to offset capital gains from collectables (s 108-10). A capital gain from a collectable can qualify as a discount capital gain. The taxpayer can choose the order in which the capital gain from collectables is reduced by capital losses from collectables. If some or all of a capital loss from a collectable cannot be applied in an income year, the unapplied amount (a net capital loss from collectables) can be applied in the next income year for which the taxpayer has capital gains from collectables that exceed capital losses from collectables. A net listed personal-use asset loss for 1997–98 (which includes such losses for earlier years) is taken to be a net capital loss from collectables for that income year (collectables were referred to as listed personal-use assets under ITAA36).

An ordinary capital loss cannot generally be made from the disposal of shares in a company or an interest in a trust that owns a personal use asset which has declined in value (¶11-520).

▶ Example

A taxpayer sells 5 collectables over a 2-year period as follows:

Collectable	Income year of disposal	Cost base and reduced cost base	Cost base (indexed)	Capital proceeds	Collectable gain (loss)
A	Year 1	$1,500	$1,520	$1,800	$280
B	Year 1	$1,000	$1,020	$680	($320)
C	Year 2	$2,020	$2,070	$3,000	$930
D	Year 2	$4,000	$4,080	$3,860	($140)
E	Year 2	$600	$650	$475	($125)

For the first income year, the taxpayer has a net collectable loss of $40, ie $320 (Asset B) – $280 (Asset A). For the second income year, the taxpayer (using the indexation method) makes a capital gain of $625, calculated as follows:

$930 (Asset C) – $140 (Asset D) – $125 (Asset E) – $40 (Year 1 collectable loss) = $625

Note: In the second year, this taxpayer would be better off using the discount method. On this basis, the net capital gain would be:

50% × ($980 (Asset C) – $140 (Asset D) – $125 (Asset E) – $40 (Year 1 collectable loss)) = $337.50

[FITR ¶152-875 – ¶152-915]

¶11-400 Personal use assets

A personal use asset is a CGT asset, other than a collectable, that is used or kept mainly for the personal use or enjoyment of the taxpayer (or associate: ¶10-390). It includes an option or right to acquire such an asset, a debt arising from a CGT event relating to such an asset, and a debt arising other than from income-producing activities or carrying on a business, eg where a parent lends money to a child to help buy a house (s 108-20). A capital gain from a personal use asset is CGT exempt if it is acquired for $10,000 or less (¶11-640).

Land, strata title units, and buildings and structures that are taken to be separate CGT assets (¶11-410) are not personal use assets. The exclusion of land and buildings means that, while houseboats and caravans that are not fixed to land can be personal use assets, holiday houses erected on land cannot. Other examples of personal use assets include clothing, white goods, furniture, sporting equipment, cameras and boats.

Where a director/shareholder is required to make a payment under a guarantee of a company's debt, the resulting debt owing to the shareholder by the company is not a personal use asset if the objectively determined primary purpose of the guarantee payment was assisting the business so as to promote the future flow of dividends to the shareholder, provided the amount of expected dividends is not completely disproportionate to the amount of the liability under the guarantee (TR 96/23).

A horse acquired by a taxpayer who races horses as a hobby (ie who is not carrying on a business of racing horses) is a personal use asset (TR 93/26).

If personal use assets that comprise a set and would ordinarily be disposed of as a set are disposed of in one or more transactions in order to meet the $10,000 exemption threshold, the set is treated as a single personal use asset (s 108-25).

The third element of the cost base (which involves the non-capital costs of ownership: ¶11-550) is not counted for personal use assets (s 108-30).

Capital gains and losses from personal use assets

In working out a net capital gain or loss, capital losses from personal use assets are disregarded (s 108-20). A capital loss cannot be made from the disposal of shares in a company or an interest in a trust that owns a personal use asset which has declined in value (¶11-520).

[FITR ¶152-920 – ¶152-955]

¶11-410 Separate CGT assets

For CGT purposes, there are exceptions to the common law principle that what is attached to land is part of the land. Special rules apply about buildings and adjacent land and when a capital improvement is treated as a separate CGT asset.

Buildings and structures

A building or structure on land acquired on or after 20 September 1985 (post-CGT) is treated as a separate CGT asset from the land if a balancing adjustment can apply to the building or structure under the provisions for depreciating assets and R&D (s 108-55). Buildings and structures for which only a capital works deduction (¶20-470) is available are not treated as separate assets from post-CGT land.

A building or structure that is constructed on land acquired before 20 September 1985 (pre-CGT) is treated as a separate CGT asset from the land if the construction contract was entered into post-CGT or, if there is no contract, construction started post-CGT (s 108-55(2)).

Where a pre-CGT building is relocated to post-CGT land, the relocation costs may be included in the cost base of the land. Once the building is affixed to the land, there is a single post-CGT asset that comprises both the land and the building. A post-CGT building relocated to pre-CGT land is a separate post-CGT asset *constructed* on that land (TD 93/182 to TD 93/184). A depreciating asset that forms part of a building or structure is treated as a separate CGT asset from the building or structure (s 108-60).

Adjacent land

Post-CGT land that is adjacent to pre-CGT land is treated as a separate CGT asset from the pre-CGT land if it and the pre-CGT land are amalgamated into one title (s 108-65). Where pre-CGT land is owned by 2 tenants in common, a buy-out by one of the parties will result in that party owning 2 assets consisting of: (i) a pre-CGT interest in the land; and (ii) a post-CGT interest (TD 2000/31).

Capital improvements

A capital improvement to land is treated as a separate CGT asset from the land if a balancing adjustment can apply to the improvement under the provisions for depreciating assets and R&D (s 108-70).

A capital improvement to a pre-CGT asset is also treated as a separate CGT asset if its cost base — indexed, if appropriate — when a CGT event happens in relation to the pre-CGT asset is: (i) more than the improvement threshold for the income year in which the event happened; and (ii) more than 5% of the capital proceeds from the event. The improvement thresholds are set out at ¶42-230. Note that the thresholds are only relevant for capital improvements that are not buildings or structures.

Similarly, capital improvements to a pre-CGT asset that are related to each other are treated as a separate CGT asset if the total of their cost bases when a CGT event happens in relation to the pre-CGT asset is:

(i) more than the improvement threshold for the income year in which the event happened, and

(ii) more than 5% of the capital proceeds from the event.

In deciding whether capital improvements are related to each other, the factors to be considered include:

(a) the nature of the CGT asset to which the improvements are made

(b) the nature, location, size, value, quality, composition and utility of each improvement

(c) whether an improvement depends in a physical, economic, commercial or practical sense on another improvement

(d) whether the improvements are part of an overall project

(e) whether the improvements are of the same kind, and

(f) in terms of time, how closely together the improvements are made (s 108-80).

In determining whether the improvement threshold test and the 5% of capital proceeds test are met, renovations and refurbishments that are part of *one plan of improvement* are aggregated (*Case 38/94*).

A capital improvement may include an improvement of a non-tangible nature (such as council approval to rezone and subdivide land) (TD 2017/1).

If a person makes a post-CGT improvement to a pre-CGT asset and it is transferred to a spouse under a court order following marriage breakdown, the roll-over of the asset (¶12-460) means that a capital gain or loss does not arise. However, if the improvement exceeds the improvement threshold and 5% of the capital proceeds, then, for purposes of any subsequent disposal by the spouse, the original pre-CGT asset and the post-CGT improvement retain their status as such in the spouse's hands (TD 96/19). Where a taxpayer makes a post-CGT improvement to a pre-CGT asset and the improved asset is inherited by a beneficiary on the taxpayer's subsequent death, the improvement and the asset are treated as one asset when acquired by the beneficiary (TD 96/18).

An improvement to a main residence which is a separate asset can qualify for the main residence exemption (¶11-730) (TD 96/21).

A capital improvement is not a separate CGT asset if it arose from a pre-CGT contract or, if there was no contract, it had a pre-CGT start date. Capital improvements consisting of repairs to, or restoration of, a pre-CGT asset are not treated as separate CGT assets if there is a CGT roll-over because the asset was compulsorily acquired, lost or destroyed.

Special rules may apply where the CGT asset is a depreciating asset, a Crown lease, a statutory licence or a prospecting or mining entitlement and a roll-over is involved (ss 108-70(5); 108-75).

Apportionment of capital proceeds

If an asset that is made up of 2 or more separate CGT assets is disposed of, the capital proceeds are apportioned between the separate CGT assets. Taxpayers are not required to get an independent valuation to justify the apportionment, but must take adequate steps in working out the proper value of the particular asset (TD 9). Taxpayers who make their own estimates must be able to justify them. The written-down value of depreciable assets does not necessarily represent market value. An independent valuation is a good idea, especially where a variation (within the likely range of estimated values) would materially alter the tax liability. If an asset is disposed of under a contract, it is preferable that the parties allocate the overall proceeds in the contract. Later agreements allocating the capital proceeds are also acceptable if an allocation was not made in the original contract for sale and the parties are dealing at arm's length (TD 98/24).

Split, changed or merged assets

Special provisions govern the determination of the cost base and reduced cost base of an asset where, without any change in beneficial ownership, 2 or more assets have merged, an asset has been divided into 2 or more assets, or an asset has been changed (in whole or in part) into an asset of a different nature (¶11-570).

[FITR ¶152-960 – ¶153-005]

Acquisition of CGT Assets

¶11-440 General CGT acquisition rules

The time when a CGT asset is acquired is crucial to the CGT consequences which can arise in relation to the asset. Firstly, if an asset was acquired before 20 September 1985, there is generally no CGT liability which can arise from a CGT event happening in relation to the asset. Secondly, the time of acquisition is relevant for determining whether the CGT discount is available (¶11-033). Thirdly, the time of acquisition determines whether the cost base of the asset is able to be indexed up to 30 September 1999 and the extent of that indexation (¶11-610).

In accordance with the general acquisition rule, a taxpayer acquires a CGT asset at the time when the taxpayer becomes its owner (s 109-5). For example, this rule applies if a person constructs or creates a building, painting, statue or other physical object for another person. Where the asset is constructed or created otherwise than under a contract, the time of acquisition depends on the operation of the general law; eg where a person constructs a building on another person's pre-CGT land, the other person acquires the building when the construction commences because the building is a fixture to the land acquired by the land-owner as soon as it is attached.

Where an entity carrying on an existing business acquires an additional business, the goodwill of the businesses coalesce and are treated as having been acquired at the same time as the original business goodwill (ID 2010/208; TR 1999/16).

A property was acquired before 20 September 1985 (pre-CGT) when the taxpayer became entitled to claim title to the property by adverse possession even though the taxpayer did not make that claim or become the registered owner, until after that date (ID 2004/731).

Specific rules apply as to when a taxpayer acquires an asset as a result of a CGT event happening. These rules are considered in the context of each CGT event (¶11-240 – ¶11-350).

Special rules about the time of acquisition for CGT discount purposes are set out in s 115-30 (¶11-033).

[FITR ¶153-175]

¶11-450 Acquisitions without a CGT event

There are also some specific rules for the circumstances in which, and the time at which, a CGT asset is acquired independently of a CGT event happening (s 109-10).

If a taxpayer constructs or creates a CGT asset and owns it when the construction is finished or the asset is created, it is acquired when the construction, or the work that resulted in the creation, started. It makes no difference if the asset is a physical asset or an intangible asset. This rule applies, for example, to the creation of a sculpture by an artist, the construction of a unit of machinery by a manufacturer, the creation of a patented process by a chemist and the building of goodwill by a shopkeeper. Goodwill is acquired when a business commences, even where the business is a new business or there is no purchased goodwill. This is so even if the sources of the goodwill of a business vary during the life of the business or if there are fluctuations in the goodwill during the life of the business, provided the business does not change so much that it can no longer be considered to be the same business (TR 1999/16). Similarly, a patent is acquired when the R&D work expected to result in the granting of the patent commences (IT 2484).

The identification of the relevant asset may be critical to the outcome. For example, in one case where a pre-CGT management services agreement had been repudiated, a taxpayer received money as part of a settlement arrangement in which the taxpayer agreed not to sue for damages. The taxpayer was found to have disposed of a pre-CGT right to receive management fees rather than a post-CGT right to sue for damages. Accordingly, the payment was not subject to CGT although it was treated as assessable income (*Case Z21*).

If a company issues or allots equity interests (such as shares) to a taxpayer, they are acquired when the contract to acquire the shares is entered into or, if there is no contract, when the shares are issued or allotted. There is no disposal of the shares by the company.

If the trustee of a unit trust issues units in the trust to a taxpayer, they are acquired when the contract to acquire the units is entered into or, if there is no contract, when the units are issued. There is no disposal of the units by the unit trust.

A taxpayer does not acquire a CGT asset if it was disposed of to provide or redeem a security (s 106-60). Nor does a taxpayer acquire a CGT asset because it vests in a trustee under the *Bankruptcy Act 1966* (or under a similar foreign law) or because it vests in a liquidator of a company (or the holder of a similar office under a foreign law) (ss 106-30, 106-35). In such circumstances, the CGT rules operate as if the taxpayer that held the asset before bankruptcy or liquidation continues to hold the asset (¶11-210).

[FITR ¶153-180]

¶11-460 Specific CGT acquisition rules

There are many other CGT acquisition rules which apply in specific situations and which are dealt with by specific provisions covering those situations (s 109-55). These situations are where:

- an asset devolves to a legal personal representative or a beneficiary because someone dies (¶12-580)
- a taxpayer gets only a partial main residence exemption on a dwelling but would have got a full exemption if a CGT event happened to it just before the first time it became income-producing (¶11-760)
- the trustee of a deceased estate acquires a dwelling under a will for a taxpayer to occupy it and the taxpayer obtains an interest in it (¶12-580)
- a replacement-asset roll-over happens for a pre-CGT asset (¶12-150)
- a replacement-asset roll-over happens for a Crown lease (¶12-400), or for a prospecting or mining entitlement (¶12-420), that is renewed or replaced where part of the new entitlement relates to a part of a pre-CGT entitlement
- the taxpayer obtains a same-asset roll-over for a pre-CGT asset (¶12-450)
- there is a same-asset roll-over for a post-CGT asset because the trust deed of a complying superannuation fund or ADF is changed (¶12-550)
- there is a same-asset roll-over for a CGT event that happens to a CGT asset (¶12-450)
- the taxpayer obtains a replacement-asset roll-over for replacing a CGT asset (¶12-150)
- a surviving joint tenant acquires a deceased joint tenant's interest in a CGT asset (¶12-580)
- a company or unit trust issues bonus equities to a taxpayer and no amount is included in the taxpayer's assessable income (¶12-600)
- a taxpayer owns shares in a company or units in a unit trust and exercises rights to acquire new equities in the company or trust (¶12-610)
- a taxpayer acquires shares in a company or units in a unit trust by converting a convertible interest (¶12-620)
- a taxpayer acquires shares in a company in exchange for the disposal or redemption of an exchangeable interest (¶12-625)
- a taxpayer acquires a share or right under an employee share scheme from an employee share trust (¶12-630)
- a lessee of land acquires the reversionary interest of the lessor and there is no roll-over for the acquisition (¶12-690)
- the taxpayer owns a pre-CGT asset and there has been a change in the majority underlying interests in the asset (¶12-870)
- the taxpayer becomes a resident while owning a post-CGT asset that was not taxable Australian property (¶12-725)
- the taxpayer ceases to be a temporary resident (but remains, at that time, a resident) while owning a post-CGT asset that was not taxable Australian property
- an asset is rolled over between companies in the same wholly-owned group and the recipient company stops being a wholly-owned subsidiary of the group (¶11-340).

[FITR ¶153-220]

¶11-470 Other acquisition rules

There are several other acquisition rules which apply for non-CGT situations (s 109-60) but which also apply for CGT purposes:

- a taxpayer stops holding an item as trading stock (¶9-245)
- a trust ceases to be a resident trust and there is an attributable taxpayer (¶21-290)
- a CGT event happens to an asset in connection with the demutualisation of an insurance company (¶12-650)
- a CGT event happens to a pre-1 July 1988 asset of a complying superannuation fund, a complying ADF or a PST (¶13-130)
- a CFC owned an asset on its commencing day (¶21-200)
- an asset is owned by a tax-exempt entity that becomes taxable (¶10-630).

[FITR ¶153-230]

Capital Proceeds

¶11-500 General rules for capital proceeds

The amount of the capital proceeds from a CGT event is generally the sum of the money received or receivable and the market value of any other property received or receivable as a result of the CGT event (s 116-20). If the CGT event is a "supply" for GST purposes, the GST on the supply is excluded when working out the capital proceeds.

The capital proceeds from a CGT event are defined by reference to money and property that a taxpayer has received *or is entitled to receive*, but a capital gain or loss arises in the income year in which the CGT event happens. Accordingly, where a CGT event happens in relation to an asset, the whole of the capital gain or loss is brought to account in the year of the CGT event, even though part or all of the capital proceeds from it are received in a later year.

If the capital proceeds originally agreed to are renegotiated before settlement, the amount of the capital proceeds is the renegotiated amount (s 116-20). A mechanism for payment by direction of consideration for a sale of an asset did not have the effect of extinguishing a taxpayer's entitlement to receive an amount and therefore did not reduce the capital proceeds from the CGT event (*Quality Publications Australia*).

A capital gain on the sale of shares under a forward purchase agreement was assessed only by reference to the capital proceeds from the share sale, and not by reference to any dividends that were received from the date of contract until the date of completion 4 years later (*Lend Lease*).

A dividend will form part of the capital proceeds of CGT event A1 in relation to a sale of share where the receipt of the dividend forms part of the sale arrangement (TR 2010/4).

A payment of an ETP approved by the directors of a Company to its shareholders around the time of the sale of the shares was included in the capital proceeds for the sale of the shares as they formed part of the consideration which moved the sale (*Scanlon & Anor*).

General rules modified for many CGT events

The general rules for capital proceeds are modified for many CGT events (¶11-510). Other more specific rules also apply in some cases (¶11-520).

Special rules for some CGT events

Special rules apply to work out the amount of the capital proceeds when CGT event F1, F2 (¶11-300), H2 (¶11-320) or K9 (¶11-350) happens (s 116-20(2)). For CGT event F1, the capital proceeds are any premium paid or payable for the grant, renewal or extension of the lease. For CGT event F2, the capital proceeds are the greatest of:

(i) the market value of the freehold estate or head lease

(ii) what that market value would have been but for the lease being granted, renewed or extended, and

(iii) any premium paid or payable for the grant, renewal or extension of the lease.

For CGT event H2, the capital proceeds are the money or other consideration received, or entitled to be received, for the relevant act, transaction or event. For CGT event K9, the capital proceeds are the amount of the payment, to the extent that it is a payment of the carried interest (¶11-350).

For the purposes of CGT event F2, when working out the market value of the property that is the subject of the grant, renewal or extension of a long-term lease, the market value of any building, part of a building, structure or improvement that is treated as a separate CGT asset from the property must be included. However, for these purposes, the lessor's depreciating assets must be disregarded. Further, when working out the amount of any premium paid or payable to the lessor for the grant, renewal or extension of a long-term lease, any part of the premium that is attributable to depreciating assets must also be disregarded for these purposes.

[FITR ¶154-220]

¶11-510 Modifications to rules for capital proceeds

There are 6 modifications to the general capital proceeds rules that may be relevant to a CGT event. A table in s 116-25 sets out the CGT event for which the general rules about capital proceeds are relevant, the modifications that can apply to that event and the special rules (if any) that apply to that event. CGT events not referred to in the table have capital gains and losses worked out without reference to capital proceeds.

First modification: market value substitution rule

If a taxpayer does not receive any capital proceeds from a CGT event, the market value of the relevant CGT asset is taken to be the amount of the capital proceeds (s 116-30). This market value is worked out as at the time of the CGT event. However, this rule does not apply if the expiry of a CGT asset or the cancellation of a statutory licence happens under CGT event C2 (¶11-270) or if CGT event D1 (¶11-280) happens. Expiry is limited to expiration by effluxion or lapse of time and does not include voluntary termination of an interest in an asset (TD 1999/76). The Commissioner accepts that shares in a "no goodwill" incorporated practice have a nil market value for the purpose of applying the market value substitution rule to an individual practitioner shareholder's admission to or exit from the practice for no consideration in specified circumstances (Administrative treatment: acquisitions and disposals of interests in "no goodwill" professional partnerships, trusts and incorporated practices).

The capital proceeds from a CGT event are also replaced with the market value of the relevant CGT asset if some or all of those proceeds cannot be valued. This rule does not apply if it is merely difficult, costly or inconvenient to obtain a valuation (TD 1999/84). Similarly, if the capital proceeds are more or less than the market value of the asset and:

(i) the parties to the CGT event are not dealing with each other at arm's length, or

(ii) the CGT event is CGT event C2, the capital proceeds are replaced with the market value of the CGT asset.

The market value substitution rule does not apply where CGT event C2 (¶11-270) occurs in relation to certain interests in widely held entities. An interest in a widely held entity refers to a share in a company or a unit in a unit trust where the company has at least 300 members or the trust has at least 300 unit holders and neither has concentrated ownership.

In exposure draft legislation it is proposed that the market value replacement rule will not apply where:

- the taxpayer is a complying superannuation fund, a complying approved deposit fund or a pooled superannuation trust
- the capital proceeds from the CGT event exceed the market value of the CGT asset, and
- the capital proceeds would be non-arm's length income pursuant to Subdiv 295-H (proposed s 116-30(2C)).

This is proposed to apply from the income year starting on or after the date of assent.

Second modification: apportionment rule

If payments are received in connection with a transaction that relates to more than one CGT event or to a CGT event and something else, the capital proceeds for the respective CGT events are so much of the payments as are reasonably attributable to each CGT event (s 116-40).

Third modification: non-receipt rule

The capital proceeds from a CGT event are reduced if it is unlikely that the taxpayer will receive some or all of those proceeds (s 116-45). However, this rule only applies if the non-receipt did not arise because of anything the taxpayer did or did not do and all reasonable steps were taken to enforce payment of the unpaid amount. The amount of the reduction is the unpaid amount.

The non-receipt rule does not apply where part or all of the capital proceeds from a CGT event are in the form of property and the value of the property falls before it is received (s 116-20(1)).

If the capital proceeds are reduced by the unpaid amount and all or part of that amount is later received, the capital proceeds are increased by that amount.

There is an entitlement to receive money or other property if a taxpayer is entitled to have the money or other property applied for the benefit, or in accordance with the directions, of the taxpayer.

If the capital proceeds are expressed in a foreign currency, the Australian equivalent at the time of the CGT event is taken into account.

Fourth modification: repaid rule

The capital proceeds from a CGT event are reduced by any part of them that is repaid by the taxpayer and by any compensation paid by the taxpayer that can reasonably be regarded as a repayment of part of them (s 116-50). However, the capital proceeds are not reduced by any part of the payment that is deductible. The payment can include giving property.

A capital gain was reduced where the taxpayer subsequently reimbursed the purchaser for certain liabilities in accordance with the original sale agreements (*Case 2/2006*).

Fifth modification: assumption of liability rule

The capital proceeds from a CGT event are increased if the entity acquiring the relevant CGT asset acquires it subject to a liability by way of security over the asset (s 116-55). In such a case, the capital proceeds are increased by the amount of the liability that the acquiring entity assumes.

Sixth modification: misappropriation rule

The sixth modification provides that the capital proceeds from a CGT event are reduced if an employee or agent misappropriates all or part of those proceeds. If the taxpayer later receives an amount as recoupment of all or part of the misappropriated amount, the capital proceeds are increased by the amount received (s 116-60).

[FITR ¶154-225 – ¶154-260]

¶11-520 Specific rules for capital proceeds

Exercised options

A special rule applies where there is a grant, renewal or extension of an option in relation to a CGT asset, another entity exercises the option and, because of the exercise of that option, the taxpayer creates (including grants or issues) or disposes of the asset. In that case, the capital proceeds from the creation (including grant or issue) or disposal include any payment received for granting, renewing or extending the option (s 116-65).

Another rule applies where an option is granted, renewed or extended which requires the taxpayer to acquire a CGT asset and create (including grant or issue) or dispose of the same asset. In that case, the option is treated as 2 separate options and half of the capital proceeds from the grant, renewal or extension is attributed to each option (s 116-70).

CGT event happening to a lease

The capital proceeds from the expiry, surrender or forfeiture of a lease include any payment made by the lessor to the lessee as a result of the lease ending to compensate for expenditure of a capital nature incurred by the lessee in making improvements to the leased property (s 116-75).

Disposal of interest where entity owns collectables or personal use assets

Specific rules apply for working out the capital proceeds where there is a fall in the market value of a personal use asset (other than a car, motor cycle or similar vehicle) or a collectable of a company or trust and a CGT event happens to the shares in the company or an interest in the trust owned by the taxpayer (s 116-80). In such a case, the capital proceeds are replaced with the market value of the shares or trust interest. In working out that market value, the fall in the market value of the personal use asset or collectable is disregarded. In this situation, a loss from a collectable may be made under CGT event K5 (¶11-350).

Certain cases where CFC rules involved

Specific rules may also apply to work out the capital proceeds from a CGT event where ITAA36 s 47A applies to a rolled-over asset or where a CGT event happens to a CGT asset of a CFC which had previously stopped being a resident of an unlisted country and had become a resident of a listed country (ss 116-85; 116-95).

Gifts of property

Where a taxpayer donates property for which a valuation is required in order to obtain a gift deduction under Div 30 (¶16-942), the taxpayer may choose that the capital proceeds from the event are replaced with the value of the property, provided the valuation was made no more than 90 days before or after the CGT event (s 116-100).

Farm-out arrangements

Where CGT event A1 arises as a result of disposal of part of an interest in a mining, quarrying or prospecting right pursuant to farm-in, farm-out arrangement and the taxpayer receives exploration benefit in respect of the event happening, for calculating the capital proceeds the market value of the exploration benefit is treated as zero (s 116-115(1)).

Where CGT event C2 arises as a result of an exploration benefit being provided to a taxpayer under a farm-in, farm-out arrangement, for calculating the capital proceeds for the event the market value of the exploration benefit is treated as zero (s 116-115(2)).

Look-though earnout rights

Where a sale of business assets involves a ''look-through earnout right'' (¶11-675) the capital proceeds that the seller receives for those assets:

- excludes the value of the right
- is increased by any financial benefits received by the seller under the right, and
- is reduced by any financial benefit the seller provides under the right (s 116-120).

As financial benefits under a look-through earnout right may be provided or received for up to 4 years after the acquisition, the amendment period for an assessment involving such a right is 4 years after the expiry of the right. Further, a taxpayer is allowed to vary a CGT choice affected by financial benefit provided or received under the right. The variation must be made by the time the taxpayer is required to lodge the tax return for the income year in which the financial benefit is provided or received (s 116-120).

[FITR ¶154-265 – ¶154-300]

Cost Base and Reduced Cost Base

¶11-550 Cost base

The cost base of a CGT asset is often relevant in finding out if a capital gain has been made from a CGT event which happens in relation to that asset. However, for some CGT events, cost base is not relevant. In such cases, the provisions dealing with the relevant CGT event explain the amounts which are instead used for working out if there is a capital gain.

The cost base of a CGT asset acquired prior to 11.45 am EST on 21 September 1999 may be indexed for inflation up to 30 September 1999 (when indexation was frozen). However, where such an asset is owned by an individual, a complying superannuation entity or a trust, the taxpayer can essentially choose to either calculate the capital gain using this indexed cost base or calculate the capital gain without indexation but apply the CGT discount (¶11-033).

In determining the cost base of an asset, any amount incurred in a foreign currency is included at its Australian currency equivalent (¶11-190).

If it is necessary to calculate the cost base of a CGT asset where there is no CGT event, the taxpayer must assume that a CGT event has occurred in relation to that asset.

Elements of cost base

The cost base of a CGT asset has 5 elements (s 110-25). The cost base is reduced by net input tax credits (see below).

The cost base of a CGT asset acquired before 11.45 am EST on 21 September 1999 also includes indexation of the elements of the cost base (except the third element) if the requirements of Div 114 (¶11-610) are met, unless the taxpayer qualifies for, and chooses to apply, the CGT discount rules (s 110-36). Deductible amounts and non-assessable recoupments are excluded from an asset's cost base (see below).

First element: acquisition cost

The *first element* is the total of:

- the money paid, or required to be paid, in respect of acquiring the CGT asset, and
- the market value of any other property given, or required to be given, in respect of acquiring the CGT asset (s 110-25(2)).

The money paid or property given ''in respect of acquiring'' the asset does not necessarily have to be paid or given to the taxpayer that disposed of the CGT asset. It may be paid or given to an entity nominated by the taxpayer and still be included in the first element of the asset's cost base (TD 2003/1). Money paid may also include the amount of a liability extinguished under the doctrine of set-off (TD 2005/52). The cost base of an asset for CGT purposes includes the cost of liabilities assumed in acquiring the asset, but only to the extent that a deduction for an amount of that liability is not otherwise claimed when it is later discharged (*Draft* TD 2019/D11).

The value of a taxpayer's own labour cannot be included in the cost base of an asset (TD 60). For money to be required to be paid, there must be a requirement for either an actual payment or, at least, a present obligation to pay a specific amount at some future date. It is not enough that an amount might become payable in the future upon the happening of some contingency (*Dingwall*).

The costs incurred by an initial shareholder in the formation of the company are not incurred in respect of the acquisition of the initial shares in that company and therefore are not included in the cost base of the shares held by the initial shareholder (ID 2009/1).

If a shareholder acquires a share under a dividend reinvestment plan, the first element of the cost base of that share includes the amount of the dividend applied by the shareholder to acquire the share (TD 2000/3). Where a purchaser acquires shares under an agreement for which a dividend was to be paid to the vendor, while the dividend will be included in the capital proceeds for CGT event A1, the dividend does not form part of the cost base of the shares in the hands of the purchaser (TR 2010/4).

In a takeover or merger, where a shareholder in the target company exchanges its shares for shares in the bidder company, the first element of the cost base of the bidder company shares is the market value of the target company shares at the time the offer is accepted. The ATO considers that this normally applies even if the contract is subject to a condition such as the bidder company acquiring 90% of the shares. These conditions operate as conditions precedent to the performance of the contract and do not prevent the contract coming into existence. However, if there is a condition precedent to the creation of the contract, the date of acquisition of the bidder company shares is the later of the date that the condition is met or the offer is accepted. If the bidder company shares are acquired under a scheme of arrangement, the acquisition cost of the shares is determined based on the market value of the target company shares on the date the scheme of arrangement becomes effective (TD 2002/4). Special rules apply to the calculation of the cost base of shares acquired where the shareholder chooses to obtain a scrip for scrip roll-over (¶12-325).

When a company issues shares for acquiring CGT assets, the market value of the shares is a component of the cost base of the assets so acquired (TR 2008/5). See also ¶3-260.

Second element: incidental costs

The *second element* consists of various specified incidental costs incurred by the taxpayer (s 110-25(3)). There are a number of incidental costs that may be incurred (s 110-35). These are:

- remuneration for the services of a surveyor, valuer, auctioneer, accountant, broker, agent, consultant or legal adviser, including costs incurred after the time of a CGT event, eg solicitor's fees and agent's commission in relation to the sale of real estate that are incurred after the exchange of contracts (TD 2017/10). Remuneration paid to a legal adviser as a result of an action for damages brought by the purchaser in connection with the consideration for the sale of an asset may be included (ID 2006/179). Remuneration paid for tax advice is not included unless it is provided by a recognised tax adviser and incurred after 30 June 1989
- costs of the transfer
- stamp duty or other similar duty
- in relation to the acquisition of a CGT asset, the costs of advertising to find a seller and, in relation to a CGT event, the costs of advertising to find a buyer
- costs relating to the making of any valuation or apportionment
- penalty interest (TR 2019/2)
- marketing expenses
- search fees relating to a CGT asset
- the cost of a conveyancing kit (or a similar cost)
- borrowing expenses (such as loan application fees and mortgage discharge fees)
- certain expenses incurred by the head company of a consolidated group or MEC group (¶8-920)
- termination and other similar fees incurred as a direct result of a CGT asset ending.

Third element: ownership costs

The *third element* is the costs of owning an asset (but only if the asset was acquired after 20 August 1991) (s 110-25(4)). However, there is no third element for collectables or personal use assets.

Costs of owning an asset consist of any expenditure incurred by a taxpayer to the extent to which it is incurred in connection with the continuing ownership of the asset. These costs include interest on money borrowed to acquire an asset, costs of maintaining, repairing and insuring an asset, rates and land tax, interest on money borrowed to refinance the money borrowed to acquire an asset, and interest on any money borrowed to finance capital expenditure incurred to increase an asset's value.

The cost of obtaining a loan is not part of the cost base of the asset acquired, ie it is a cost which relates to the borrowing, not the asset financed by the borrowing (TD 93/1).

Costs of ownership that are disallowed under ITAA36 Pt IVA (¶30-000) do not form part of the cost base of an asset unless the Commissioner makes a compensating adjustment to that effect. A compensating adjustment is not available in the case of split loan arrangements of the type discussed in TR 98/22 (TD 2005/33).

Fourth element: enhancement costs

The *fourth element* is capital expenditure incurred to increase or preserve the value of the CGT asset (s 110-25(5)). The fourth element includes capital expenditure that relates to installing or moving the asset. However, it does not apply to capital expenditure incurred in relation to goodwill.

TD 98/23 details the inclusion of expenditure incurred by a lessee on capital improvements to a leased property. The cost of non-deductible initial repairs (¶16-700) incurred after the acquisition of an asset may be included in the fourth element of the cost base of an asset (TD 98/19).

Fifth element: title costs

The *fifth element* is capital expenditure incurred to establish, preserve or defend the taxpayer's title to the asset (s 110-25(6)). An amount of damages paid by a taxpayer to a potential purchaser upon the acceptance of the termination of contract to sell the asset following repudiation of the contract by the taxpayer may be included in the fifth element of the cost base of that asset (ID 2008/147).

Amounts not included in cost base

Assets acquired after 7.30 pm on 13 May 1997

Expenditure does not form part of the cost base of an asset to the extent that the taxpayer can deduct it, eg interest, or to the extent that a non-assessable recoupment is received in respect of it (s 110-45). An amount received pursuant to the First Home Owners Grant for building a home is excluded from the cost base of the property. Where a taxpayer has omitted to claim a deduction and the amendment period for claiming the deduction has expired, the cost base of the asset will not be reduced by the deduction that was previously available (TD 2005/47).

Capital expenditure incurred by another entity, such as a previous owner, in respect of the asset which the taxpayer can deduct, eg under the capital works provisions of Div 43 (¶20-470), reduces the cost base of that asset. In certain circumstances the Commissioner will accept that the taxpayer cannot deduct an amount under Div 43 and is therefore not required to reduce the asset's cost base (PS LA 2006/1 (GA)).

Expenditure does not form part of the cost base to the extent that heritage conservation expenditure or landcare and water facilities expenditure incurred after 12 November 1998 gives rise to a tax offset. Where the benefit of a deduction is effectively reversed by a balancing adjustment, the relevant expenditure is increased. Similar rules apply to a partnership in which the taxpayer is a partner where expenditure is deductible or a recoupment is not assessable (s 110-50).

For this purpose, compensation received for permanent damage to an asset is treated as a non-assessable recoupment. To the extent that the compensation exceeds the unindexed costs of an asset, no CGT implications arise (TR 95/35). Where a taxpayer purchases an asset using a limited recourse loan and the taxpayer defaults on the loan resulting in the asset being transferred to the lender in full satisfaction of the loan at a time when its market value is less than the balance of the outstanding loan, the shortfall is a recoupment and accordingly excluded from the cost base of the asset (ID 2013/64).

These rules also apply to expenditure incurred after 30 June 1999 on land and buildings acquired before 13 May 1997 where the expenditure forms part of the fourth element (ie enhancement costs) of the cost base of the land or building.

▶ Example

John bought a building on 1 December 2011 for $200,000. The building qualifies for capital works deductions at the rate of 2.5% a year. If the building was sold on 30 November 2020, then, for the purpose of working out the capital gain on disposal, the cost base (indexed where relevant) is reduced by $45,000 to account for the capital works deductions available to John in the 9 years leading up to 30 November 2020.

Assets acquired before 7.30 pm on 13 May 1997

Where assets were acquired before 7.30 pm EST on 13 May 1997, expenditure is not included in the second and third elements of the cost base if it is deductible nor in any element if a non-assessable recoupment is receivable in respect of the expenditure (s 110-40). Similar rules apply where expenditure was deductible, or a recoupment was not assessable, to a partnership in which the taxpayer was a partner (s 110-43).

Other exclusions

Expenditure does not form part of any element of the cost base of an asset to the extent that it (s 110-38):

- relates to illegal activities for which a deduction is denied under s 26-54 (¶16-105)
- is a bribe to a public official or foreign public official
- is in respect of entertainment
- is a penalty that is excluded from deduction under s 26-5 (¶16-845)
- is for the excess of boat expenditure over boat income that is excluded from deduction under s 26-47 (¶16-420)
- is for political contributions and gifts that are excluded from deduction (s 110-38(6)).
- travel expenditure related to the use of residential premises for rental for which a deduction is denied pursuant to the s 26-31 (s 110-38(4A)).

GST net input tax credits are excluded from all elements of the cost base and reduced cost base of a CGT asset (s 103-30).

General rules modified for many CGT assets

The general cost base rules are modified for most CGT assets (¶11-570). Other more specific rules also apply in many cases (¶11-580). Modifications to the general cost base rules are also required where an asset is affected by a roll-over.

[FITR ¶153-370 – ¶153-404]

¶11-560 Reduced cost base

The reduced cost base of a CGT asset is often relevant in finding out if a capital loss has been made from a CGT event which happens in relation to that asset. However, for some CGT events, the reduced cost base is not relevant in determining this. In such cases, the provisions dealing with the relevant CGT event explain the amounts which are instead used for working out if there is a capital loss.

Elements of reduced cost base

The reduced cost base of a CGT asset has 5 elements (s 110-55). These elements are *not* indexed in any event.

All of the elements of the reduced cost base of a CGT asset are the same as those for the cost base (¶11-550), except the third one. The third element is instead any amount that is assessable because of a balancing adjustment (eg ¶17-630) for the asset, or would be assessable if certain balancing adjustment relief (eg ¶17-710) was not available.

Amounts not included in the reduced cost base

Expenditure is not included in any element of the reduced cost base if it is deductible or if a non-assessable recoupment is receivable in respect of the expenditure (s 110-55(4), (6)). A taxpayer who has omitted to claim a deduction because the amendment period for the deduction has expired can, provided the amendment period for the tax consequences of the CGT event has not expired, ensure that this amount does not reduce the reduced cost base of the asset (TD 2005/47). In certain circumstances where an amount cannot be deducted under Div 43 (¶20-470) it is not required to reduce the asset's reduced cost base (PS LA 2006/1 (GA)).

Compensation received for permanent damage to an asset is treated as a non-assessable recoupment (TR 95/35). Similar rules apply where expenditure is deductible, or a recoupment is not assessable, to a partnership in which the taxpayer is a partner (s 110-60). Where a taxpayer purchases an asset using a limited recourse loan and the taxpayer defaults on the loan resulting in the asset being transferred to the lender in full satisfaction of the loan at a time when its market value is less than the balance of the outstanding loan, the shortfall is a recoupment and accordingly excluded from the reduced cost base of the asset (ID 2013/64).

Deductible amounts excluded from the reduced cost base include amounts that are deductible because of available balancing adjustments. Those excluded amounts also include any eligible heritage conservation works expenditure for which a capital works deduction (¶20-470) would have been available if it was not specifically prevented (¶20-510).

Where an asset is used partly for income-producing purposes, only a proportionate depreciation deduction is available. However, in working out the reduced cost base of the asset, the whole of the potential deduction is treated as if it were deductible (s 110-55(5)).

Expenditure does not form part of the reduced cost base of an asset to the extent that it:

- relates to illegal activities for which a deduction is denied under s 26-54 (¶16-105)
- is a bribe to a public official or foreign public official
- is in respect of entertainment
- is a penalty that is excluded from deduction under s 26-5 (¶16-845)
- is for the excess of boat expenditure over boat income that is excluded from deduction under s 26-47 (¶16-420)
- is for political contributions and gifts excluded from deduction under s 26-22.

If it is necessary to calculate the reduced cost base of a CGT asset where there is no CGT event, the taxpayer must assume that a CGT event has occurred in relation to that asset (s 110-55(10)).

Dividend adjustment

If the CGT asset is a share in a company, its reduced cost base is decreased if:

(i) the taxpayer is a corporate tax entity (¶4-440)

(ii) the company makes a distribution under an arrangement

(iii) the distribution is attributable to profits derived by the company before the share was acquired (the attributable amount), including a deemed acquisition under Div 149 (TD 2001/13)

(iv) the taxpayer is entitled to a tax offset under Div 207 (¶4-800) on the distribution, and

(v) the taxpayer was a controller (¶12-810) of the company or an associate of such a controller when the arrangement was made or carried out (s 110-55(7)).

The amount of the reduction to the reduced cost base of the share is:

$$\text{attributable amount} \times \frac{\text{amount of tax offset}}{\text{dividend amount} \times \text{corporate tax rate}}$$

The High Court has held that unrealised pre-merger profits of a company's subsidiary should be taken into account when calculating the reduced cost base of the company's shares in its subsidiary. This meant that the capital loss attributable to the shares, which was transferred by the company to the subsidiary, had to be reduced (*Sun Alliance*).

General rules modified for many CGT assets

The general reduced cost base rules are modified for most CGT assets (¶11-570). Other more specific rules also apply in many cases (¶11-580). Modifications to the general reduced cost base rules are also required where an asset is affected by a roll-over.

[FITR ¶153-405 – ¶153-415]

¶11-570 General modifications to cost base and reduced cost base

The general rules for working out the cost base and reduced cost base of a CGT asset often have to be modified. Modifications can be required at any time from when a CGT asset is acquired to when a CGT event happens in relation to that CGT asset (s 112-5). Most modifications replace the first element of the cost base and reduced cost base of a CGT asset, ie the amount paid for the CGT asset (s 112-15).

If a cost base modification replaces an element of the cost base of a CGT asset with a different amount, the CGT provisions apply as if that other amount was paid.

Market value substitution rule

The first element of the cost base and reduced cost base of a CGT asset acquired from another entity is its ''market value'' (¶17-050) at the time of acquisition if:

(i) the taxpayer did not incur expenditure to acquire it (except where the acquisition of the asset resulted from CGT event D1 happening or from another entity doing something that did not constitute a CGT event happening)

(ii) some or all of the expenditure incurred to acquire it cannot be valued, or

(iii) the taxpayer did not ''deal at arm's length'' (¶17-045) with the other entity in connection with the acquisition (s 112-20).

A taxpayer seeking to rely on the market value substitution rule must provide sufficient evidence to prove the transaction was not at arm's length (*Healey*). The cost base of a debt can be reduced below face value to market value in accordance with the market value substitution rule if parties entered into debt on non-arm's length terms (*QFL Photographics Pty Ltd*).

However, if the taxpayer did not deal at arm's length with the other entity and the taxpayer's acquisition of the CGT asset resulted from another entity doing something that did not constitute a CGT event happening, eg if the asset is a share in a company that was issued or allotted to the taxpayer by the company, then the market value is substituted only if the amount paid for the CGT asset is more than its market value at the time of acquisition.

Additionally, the market value substitution rule does not generally apply to a CGT asset that is:

(i) a right to income from a trust (other than a unit trust or deceased estate) that is acquired for no consideration

(ii) a decoration awarded for valour or brave conduct that is acquired for no consideration

(iii) a contractual or other legal or equitable right resulting from CGT event D1 happening that is acquired for no consideration

(iv) a right to acquire shares or options in a company or units or options in a unit trust that is acquired for no consideration and is exercised

(v) a share in a company (or a right to acquire a share or debenture in a company) issued to the taxpayer by the company for no consideration

(vi) a unit in a unit trust (or a right to acquire a unit or debenture in a unit trust) issued to the taxpayer by the unit trust for no consideration, and

(vii) a right to dispose of a share in a company if the right was issued by the company and it was exercised either by the shareholder or by another entity who became the owner of the right.

However, if a share in a company or a unit in a unit trust is acquired in a non-arm's length situation before 16 August 1989 and the taxpayer paid less than the market value for the share or unit, the market value substitution rule still applies.

A lessee who acquired leased equipment at its residual value under the terms of a standard commercial lease was held to have acquired the equipment at arm's length. As the market value substitution rule did not apply, the lessee was not able to claim the higher market value of the equipment as its cost base (*Granby*).

The market value substitution rule will not apply to replace the cost base of an asset acquired by exercising an option where the exercise price is different to the market value at the time of the exercise where the terms of the option were in accordance with market value conditions as at the time the option was granted (ID 2009/18).

Split or changed assets

Special cost base rules apply if a CGT asset is split into 2 or more assets or if it changes in whole or in part into an asset of a different nature, but only if the taxpayer remains the beneficial owner of the new assets after the change (s 112-25).

If a CGT asset is split or changed, the split or change is not a CGT event (TD 2000/10). In addition, the cost base and reduced cost base of each new asset are calculated by working out each element of the cost base and reduced cost base of the original asset at the time of the split or change and apportioning them in a reasonable way.

One example of an asset being split is where a block of flats owned by a taxpayer under one title is converted by the taxpayer into strata title. The cost base and reduced cost base of each flat is a proportionate share of the cost base or reduced cost base of the original asset at the time when the original asset was converted to strata title. The cost base of each flat is indexed in the usual way as if it was acquired at the time when the original asset was acquired, considering its share of any cost base adjustments which happened up until the time of the split and the whole of any cost base adjustments in respect of that flat after the split. Similarly, the reduced cost base of each flat is worked out having regard to its share of any cost base reductions before the split and the whole of any cost base reductions in respect of the flat after the split. Note also the optional roll-over relief for strata title conversions (¶12-320).

Another example is where a taxpayer owns a house and adjacent land on the same title. If the taxpayer subsequently obtains a separate title for some of the adjacent land, the cost base and reduced cost base of the house and the land on which it is situated are reduced by the proportionate amount of the cost base or reduced cost base attributed to the adjacent land for which the separate title was obtained.

Further examples of asset division are considered in TD 7 and TD 93/180 to TD 93/183.

Merged assets

If 2 or more CGT assets are merged into a single asset, the merger is not a CGT event and each element of the cost base and reduced cost base of the new asset (at the time of merging) is the sum of the corresponding elements of each original asset (s 112-25(4)) (TD 2000/10).

Apportionment rules on acquisition or disposal of part

If only part of the expenditure incurred in relation to a CGT asset relates to the asset, the relevant element of the cost base and reduced cost base of the asset only includes that part of the expenditure that is reasonably attributable to the acquisition of the asset (s 112-30).

If a CGT event happens to some part of a CGT asset but not to the remainder of it, the cost base and reduced cost base of that part are generally worked out as follows:

$$\text{cost base or reduced cost base of the asset} \times \frac{\text{capital proceeds for the CGT event happening to the part}}{\text{those capital proceeds plus the market value of the remainder of the asset}}$$

The remainder of the cost base and reduced cost base of the asset is attributed to the part of the asset that remains.

However, if an amount of the cost base and reduced cost base (or part of it) is wholly identifiable with the part of the asset to which the CGT event happened or to the remaining part, no apportionment is made. In such a case, the amount is allocated wholly to the relevant part of the asset.

The apportionment rule applies where, for example, a taxpayer disposes of 3 of 10 acres of land. Other examples include situations where a taxpayer who owns a 30% interest in an asset disposes of a 20% interest or where the owner of an asset disposes of an interest (eg by contributing the asset to a partnership).

In *Kneebones Service Station*, the original land upon which a service station was located fronted onto the main highway. The site was later extended and redeveloped by the acquisition of adjacent land. The taxpayer argued that, on sale, the pre-CGT land should be allocated a greater proportion of the proceeds because historically it was the more valuable part (due to its proximity to the highway compared to the later acquisitions). However, the AAT decided that once the land was sold as a single consolidated site, the historical use values of the respective pre-CGT and post-CGT sites were irrelevant. The land was sold as one site for one price, and there was no basis for saying that any particular part of it deserved to have a higher valuation than that attributed to another. As a result, the only reasonable basis for valuation was on a pro rata area basis for the whole site.

The totality of rights arising under a contract are generally treated as a single asset, and the assignment of one of those rights is treated as the disposal of a separate asset requiring apportionment. However, this treatment may vary depending on the particular facts (TD 93/86).

The sale of standing timber on land owned by the taxpayer is a disposal requiring the apportionment of the cost base between the timber and the land (*Ashgrove*; TD 2018/15).

The disposal of a subdivided block of land requires an apportionment of the cost base of the original parcel of land. The Commissioner accepts any basis of attribution which is appropriate in the circumstances, eg on the basis of area or relative market value (TD 97/3).

▶ Example

Trevor subdivides his post-CGT land into 2 blocks (A and B) with the intention of selling A and retaining B. The subdivision costs of survey fees, legal fees, and subdivision application fees must be apportioned over both blocks (usually on an area or relative market value basis). The cost of connecting electricity and water to Block A relate only to that block and therefore it is reasonable to attribute these costs solely to that block.

Where joint owners of land subdivide the land into 2 smaller blocks and each owner takes ownership of a separate block, each owner is taken to have disposed of their 50% interest in the block retained by the other owner (TD 92/148). However, if they continue to jointly own each subdivided block, no disposal occurs (TD 7).

Where part of an asset is compulsorily resumed, the capital proceeds for that CGT event will include any part of the compensation that reflects the reduction in value of the remaining part of the asset caused by the resumption (TD 2001/9).

Compensation can be received by a landowner from a public authority for the acquisition of an easement either:

(i) compulsorily, under the authority's statutory powers, or

(ii) by an agreement which avoids the necessity for the authority to exercise its statutory powers.

In either case, TR 97/3 says that the capital proceeds are treated as having been received in respect of the disposal of part of the underlying asset (ie the land) and *not* in respect of the disposal by the landowner of the right to compensation within the terms of TR 95/35 (¶11-650). The Commissioner regards the easement as having being created by operation of the relevant statute and *not* by the landowner (as required for CGT event D1: ¶11-280).

Assumption of liability rule

If a CGT asset is acquired from another entity and it is subject to a liability, the first element of the cost base and reduced cost base of the asset includes the amount of the assumed liability (s 112-35).

Look-through earnout rights

Where an acquisition of business assets involves a "look-through earnout right" (¶11-675) entered into on or after 24 April 2015 the buyer's cost base or reduced cost base of those assets:

- excludes the value of the right
- is increased by any financial benefits provided by the buyer under the right, and
- is reduced by any financial benefit the buyer receives under the right (s 112-36).

As financial benefits under a look-through earnout right may be provided or received for up to 4 years after the acquisition, the amendment period for an assessment involving such a right is 4 years after the expiry of the right. Further, a taxpayer is allowed to vary a CGT choice affected by financial benefit provided or received under the right. The variation must be made by the time the taxpayer is required to lodge the tax return for the income year in which the financial benefit is provided or received (s 112-36).

Cost base of put options

If a company issues tradable put options to a shareholder, the market value of the options at the time of issue is included in the shareholder's assessable income (*McNeil*; ¶10-110).

This amount is not taxed again if the shareholder makes a capital gain or loss when a subsequent CGT event happens to the rights or the shares disposed of as a result of the exercise of the rights (applicable to rights issued on or after 1 July 2001). The first element of the cost base and reduced cost base of a right to dispose of a share in a company that a taxpayer acquires as a result of CGT event D2 happening is the sum of:

- the amount included in the taxpayer's assessable income as ordinary income as a result of acquiring the right, and
- the amount (if any) paid by the taxpayer to acquire the right (s 112-37).

[FITR ¶153-550 – ¶153-597]

¶11-580 Specific rules for modifying cost base and reduced cost base

There are many other specific situations that *may* require the cost base and reduced cost base of a CGT asset to be modified under the CGT provisions (ss 112-40 to 112-97). These are:

- when CGT event D4, E1, E4, F4, G1, G3, J4 or K8 happens in relation to a CGT asset
- when a capital gain or loss is made from certain gifts (¶11-670)
- when the CGT asset is a main residence (¶11-730)
- when scrip for scrip roll-over relief applies (¶12-325)
- when a demerger occurs (¶12-328)
- when a taxpayer dies (¶12-570)
- when the CGT asset is a bonus share or unit (¶12-600)
- when the CGT asset is a right in relation to a share in a company or a unit in a unit trust (¶12-610)
- when the CGT asset is a convertible interest (¶12-620)
- when the CGT asset is a share or right acquired at a discount under an employee share scheme (¶12-630)
- when the CGT asset is an exchangeable interest (¶12-625)
- when the CGT asset relates to a lease (¶12-680)
- when the CGT asset relates to an option (¶12-700)
- when an individual, company or trust becomes an Australian resident for tax purposes (¶12-740)
- when a temporary resident ceases to be a temporary resident (but remains, at that time, an Australian resident) (¶12-760)
- when the CGT asset stops being a pre-CGT asset (¶12-870)
- when a CGT event happens in relation to the demutualisation of certain mutual entities (¶12-650), and
- when net capital losses are transferred within a wholly-owned group of companies (¶11-110).

Special cost base and reduced cost base modifications may also be required by provisions other than the CGT provisions (including non-CGT provisions in ITAA36), where:

- an item stops being held as trading stock (¶9-245)
- a commercial debt is forgiven (¶16-910)
- a tax-exempt entity becomes taxable (¶10-630)
- a CGT event happens to an asset of a complying superannuation fund, ADF or PST (¶13-130)
- a CGT asset is taken into account in calculating the attributable income of a CFC (¶21-200)
- shares in a holding company are cancelled (¶3-160), or
- where under a farm-in, farm-out arrangement, the taxpayer receives an exploration benefit or an entitlement to an exploration benefit (ss 40-1120; 40-1125).

[FITR ¶153-600 – ¶153-662]

¶11-590 Replacement-asset roll-over modifications

A replacement-asset roll-over (¶12-150) allows a taxpayer to defer the making of a capital gain or loss from one CGT event until a later CGT event happens (s 112-105). It involves the taxpayer's ownership of one CGT asset ending and the acquisition of a replacement asset.

If the original CGT asset was a post-CGT asset, the first element of the replacement asset's cost base and reduced cost base is replaced by the original asset's cost base and reduced cost base at the time the taxpayer acquired the replacement asset (s 112-110). In addition, some replacement-asset roll-overs involve other rules that affect the cost base or reduced cost base of a replacement asset (¶12-160). If the original CGT asset was a pre-CGT asset, the replacement asset is also taken to be a pre-CGT asset (¶12-160).

[FITR ¶153-670 – ¶153-685]

¶11-600 Same-asset roll-over modifications

A same-asset roll-over (¶12-450) allows one entity (the transferor) to ignore a capital gain or loss it makes from disposing of a CGT asset to, or from creating a CGT asset in, another entity (the transferee). Any capital gain or loss is deferred until another CGT event happens in relation to the asset in the hands of the transferee (s 112-140).

If the CGT asset was a post-CGT asset in the hands of the transferor, the first element of the asset's cost base and reduced cost base in the hands of the transferee is replaced by the asset's cost base and reduced cost base in the hands of the transferor at the time the transferee acquired it (s 112-145). If the asset was a pre-CGT asset in the hands of the transferor, it continues to be a pre-CGT asset in the hands of the transferee.

[FITR ¶153-705 – ¶153-725]

¶11-610 Indexation of cost base

The indexed cost base may be used for calculating a capital gain from a CGT event happening in relation to a CGT asset that was acquired at or before 11.45 am EST on 21 September 1999. While indexation is available for all taxpayers, since 30 September 1999 it has had limited importance for the following reasons:

- indexation has been frozen from that date (s 960-275), and
- individuals, complying superannuation entities and trusts can only use an indexed cost base where they choose not to apply the CGT discount in Div 115 (ss 115-20; ¶11-033).

Where an asset was acquired at or before 11.45 am EST on 21 September 1999, each of the 5 elements of cost base (except for the third element being non-capital costs) that were incurred at or before that time may be indexed for inflation (ss 114-1; 960-275(4)). Indexation is not relevant to expenditure incurred after 11.45 am EST on 21 September 1999.

The indexed cost base is only relevant for working out the cost base of a CGT asset in relation to a CGT event (s 114-5). The elements of the cost base are indexed in accordance with s 960-275. The elements of a reduced cost base of a CGT asset are not indexed and therefore are not relevant for calculating a capital loss.

How indexation works

Generally, expenditure is indexed from when it is incurred, even if some or all of the expenditure is not actually paid until a later time, eg under a contract to purchase an asset by instalments (*Dolby*; IT 2362). However, when there is an acquisition that did not result from a CGT event, the first element of the cost base of the CGT asset is indexed from when the expenditure was paid.

A cost included as a relevant element of cost base is indexed by multiplying it by the relevant indexation factor, provided that indexation factor exceeds 1 (s 960-270).

The indexation factor for a relevant cost is generally determined by applying the following formula:

$$\frac{\text{the index number for the quarter ending on 30 September 1999 (being 68.7)}}{\text{the index number for the quarter in which the expenditure was incurred}}$$

However, where the relevant asset is a share in a company or a unit in a unit trust, the indexation factor applied to an amount included in the first element of cost base that was paid to the company or trust at a time after it was acquired is determined as follows:

$$\frac{\text{the index number for the quarter ending on 30 September 1999 (being 68.7)}}{\text{the index number for the quarter in which the amount was paid}}$$

The indexation factor is rounded to 3 decimal places, with rounding up if the fourth decimal point is 5 or more (s 960-275(5)).

▶ Example 1

If an asset was purchased in June 1991 and sold in September 2019, the indexation factor is 1.164 (ie September 1999 index number of 68.7 ÷ June 1991 index number of 59.0, rounded to 3 decimal places).

The index number for a quarter is the All Groups Consumer Price Index number (''CPI'') first published by the Australian Statistician for the quarter (s 960-280) and are listed in ¶42-225.

▶ Example 2

Gene bought an asset on 22 September 1989 for $10,000 and sold it on 25 July 2020 for $17,000. She incurred capital expenditure of $3,000 to enhance the value of the asset in March 1994. The cost base of the asset (as indexed) is:

(10,000 × 68.7/54.2) + ($3000 × 68.7/61.5)
= ($10,000 × 1.267) + ($3,000 × 1.117)
= $12,670 + $3,351
= $16,021

Where a taxpayer made an ''off the plan'' purchase (eg entered into an agreement to purchase a property subject to a condition precedent such as the erection of a building), the deposit paid on entering into the contract is indexed from that time, with the balance of the purchase price being indexed from the date the condition precedent was satisfied (TD 18).

Where a taxpayer entered into a set fee construction contract which provided for payment by instalments corresponding to the value of work done by the builder as per an architect's certificate, each progress payment is indexed from the quarter in which the architect's certificate in relation to that payment was issued (TD 19).

Effect of cost base modifications on indexation

The general rule is that, if a cost base modification replaces an element of the cost base of a CGT asset, the element is indexed from the quarter when the modification occurred (s 114-15). If the modification only adds an amount to the existing amount of the element, only the amount of the modification is indexed from that quarter.

However, if a cost base modification reduces the *total* cost base of a CGT asset, the total of all the elements as reduced forms a new first element which is then indexed from the quarter when the modification occurred.

Amounts paid for options or convertible notes and amounts paid for the exercise of options or the conversion of convertible notes are indexed only from the quarter in which the liabilities to pay the amounts were incurred.

When expenditure is incurred for roll-overs

If there is a replacement-asset roll-over (¶12-150) in relation to a CGT asset and the first element of its cost base is the whole of the cost base of the original asset, the amount of that element (including indexation) at the time of the CGT event giving rise to the roll-over is indexed from the quarter in which the CGT event happened to the original asset (s 114-20).

If there is a same-asset roll-over (¶12-450) in relation to a CGT asset and the first element of its cost base is the whole of the cost base, the amount of that element (including indexation) at the time of the CGT event giving rise to the roll-over is indexed from the quarter in which the CGT event happened (s 114-20).

Indexation will only be relevant where the roll-over took place prior to 21 September 1999.

Choosing indexation or CGT discount

Where an individual, trust or complying superannuation entity makes a capital gain from a CGT event happening in relation to a CGT asset acquired prior to 21 September 1999, the taxpayer can choose to utilise the indexed cost base instead of applying the CGT discount in Div 115 to calculate the taxable capital gain (¶11-033). The indexed cost base would only be chosen where the net taxable capital gain from the CGT event would be lower.

▶ Example 3

Bradley bought vacant land on 14 November 1985 for $1 million. The land was sold in December 2020. The indexation factor for the property is 1.696 (being the index number for the September 1999 of 68.7 ÷ the index number for December 1985 of 40.5). The indexed cost base of the property is $1,696,000.

Where Bradley does not have any current year or carried forward prior year capital losses, he would generally only choose to use the indexed cost base method, as opposed to the CGT discount under Div 115, where the capital proceeds from the sale was less than $2,392,000. Bradley would be indifferent between the methods where the consideration from the sale was $2,392,000 as the taxable capital gain would be $696,000 under either method as follows:

- Indexation method: Taxable capital gain = $2,392,000 – $1,696,000 = $696,000
- Discount method: Taxable capital gain = ($2,392,000 – $1,000,000) × 50% = $696,000.

The 50% CGT discount would give Bradley a lower taxable capital gain where the capital proceeds exceeded $2,392,000.

In determining which method is preferable to a taxpayer eligible for the CGT discount, any current year or carried forward prior year capital losses should also be taken into account. This would impact upon which method should be chosen.

▶ Example 4

Using the facts from Example 3, Bradley sold the land for $2,500,000 but in the same income year also made a capital loss of $200,000 from a separate CGT event, No other capital gains or losses were made in that year. The taxable capital gain under each method would be calculated as follows:

- Indexation method: Taxable capital gain = $2,500,000 – $1,696,000 – $200,000 = $604,000
- Discount method: Taxable capital gain = ($2,500,000 – $1,000,000 – $200,000) × 50% = $650,000.

In such a case, Bradley would have a lower tax payable if he used the indexed cost base method.

The way in which the taxpayer prepares the tax return is sufficient evidence of the choice being made (s 103-25(2)).

[FITR ¶154-000 – ¶154-100, ¶762-420]

General CGT Exemptions

¶11-640 Assets exempt from CGT

Cars and motor cycles

A capital gain is exempt from CGT and a capital loss is disregarded if it is made in relation to a car, motor cycle or similar vehicle (s 118-5). A car is a motor vehicle (but does not include a motor cycle or similar vehicle) designed to carry a load of less than one tonne and less than 9 passengers (including the driver: *Case J63*). A motor vehicle is any motor-powered road vehicle (including a 4-wheel drive vehicle).

The designed load-carrying capacity of a vehicle is determined by reference to the Australian Design Rules (*Case J63*). On this basis the designed load of a vehicle is calculated as:

> maximum loaded vehicle weight, ie gross weight (as indicated on the compliance plate)
>
> less
>
> unladen weight, ie the weight of the vehicle with a full capacity of lubricating oil, coolant and fuel, but without goods, occupants or options other than options which are essential to the test for which unladen weight is specified.

Motor vehicles in the one tonne range, fitted with a normal timber and steel tray, are generally not cars that are exempt for CGT purposes.

Station wagons, panel vans and utility trucks are usually cars that are exempt for CGT purposes. For this purpose, a panel van is a passenger car derivative having the same body configuration as a car forward of the windscreen, eg a Ford Falcon panel van. By way of contrast, Ford Transit vans and Toyota Hi-Ace vans are not panel vans. A utility truck is a vehicle which is a derivative of a car and does not cover vehicles which are made along the same lines as a truck, ie which incorporate a chassis to which a variety of goods-carrying sections can be fitted (*Case M10*).

A stretch limousine is a car (*Case Z25*), but a hearse is not (TD 2006/39). Any capital gain or loss made from an antique or vintage car is disregarded (TD 2000/35).

No CGT consequences arise when compensation is received (by way of an insurance payment or otherwise) wholly for the loss or destruction of, or permanent damage to, a car which is exempt for CGT purposes (TD 97/5).

Decorations for valour

A capital gain or loss from a decoration awarded for valour or brave conduct is disregarded unless it was purchased by the taxpayer (s 118-5).

Collectables costing $500 or less

A capital gain or loss from a collectable (¶11-390) is disregarded for CGT purposes if the first element of its cost base, or the first element of its cost if it is a depreciating asset, is $500 or less (excluding any input tax credit for the acquisition: ¶34-100) (s

118-10(1)). Where the collectable is an *interest* in artwork, jewellery, an antique, a coin or medallion, a rare folio, manuscript or book, or a postage stamp or first day cover, it is the market value of the asset itself (and not of the interest) which determines whether the exemption applies, eg if a 20% interest in a collectable is acquired for $400, the exemption does not apply because the asset is worth $2,000. However, this rule about interests in collectables does not apply to interests acquired before 16 December 1995. As a result, a capital gain or loss from such an interest is disregarded if the cost of the interest was $500 or less.

Certain personal use assets

A capital gain from a personal use asset (¶11-400), or part of the asset, is disregarded if the first element of its cost base, or the first element of its cost if it is a depreciating asset, is $10,000 or less (excluding any input tax credit for the acquisition: ¶34-100) (s 118-10(3)). A taxpayer cannot make a capital loss from a personal use asset. A capital loss from the disposal of shares in a company or an interest in a trust does not result in a capital loss to the extent that the loss relates to the decline in value of a personal use asset owned by the company or trust (s 116-80).

Asset used to produce exempt income

A capital gain or loss from a CGT asset used *solely* to produce exempt income or non-assessable non-exempt income (¶10-890) is disregarded (s 118-12). However, the exemption does not apply if the asset was used to gain or produce non-assessable non-exempt income because of certain provisions that apply to prevent such amounts from being double taxed.

Shares in a PDF

A capital gain or loss from a CGT event happening in relation to shares in a PDF is disregarded (s 118-13).

[FITR ¶154-460 – ¶154-510]

¶11-650 CGT implications for compensation or damages for wrong or injury

The CGT implications depend upon whether the compensation or damages is received in relation to personal injuries or not.

Compensation or damages for personal injuries

For CGT purposes, any gains or losses made from a CGT event relating to any of the following are disregarded:

(a) compensation or damages received for any wrong, injury or illness suffered personally by the taxpayer or a relative, or for any wrong or injury suffered by a taxpayer at work (s 118-37(1)(a))

(b) compensation or damages a trustee (other than a trustee of a complying superannuation entity) receives for a wrong or injury a beneficiary suffers in their occupation, or a wrong, injury or illness a beneficiary or their relative suffers personally (s 118-37(1)(b))

(c) a CGT asset that is received as a beneficiary of a trust, from the trustee of the trust to the extent that it is attributable to an amount the trustee receives pursuant to (b) (s 118-37(1)(ba)).

Damages for personal injuries (including psychological damage or mental injury) or for libel, slander or defamation and insurance moneys received under personal accident policies fall into this category. Damages for the death of a spouse or for the negligence of a solicitor failing to institute a personal injuries action also fall within the exemption, as do amounts received under a trauma insurance policy by the person insured under the policy or the spouse of that person.

The exemption extends to property other than money received as compensation, although the disposal by the taxpayer of property received as compensation or damages may give rise to a capital gain. The exemption is not available for lump sum damages for such a personal wrong or injury where it is not possible to dissect the portion of the payment attributable to that part of the taxpayer's claim (*Kort*).

Compensation for non-personal wrong or injury

The CGT consequences of compensation payments for wrongs or injuries which are not of a personal nature are generally as follows (TR 95/35):

- The CGT consequences of an award of damages depend on whether there is an underlying asset to which the damages have a direct and substantial link. Such a link may be established if there is a CGT asset which has been disposed of, permanently damaged or reduced in value by the circumstances which generated the right to compensation.
- If a CGT event has happened to the underlying asset, the compensation is treated as capital proceeds. So, if the asset was a pre-CGT asset, or is otherwise exempt, the compensation generally has no CGT consequences. If the asset was a post-CGT asset, a capital gain or loss may arise from the CGT event.
- If a CGT event does not happen to the asset, but it has been permanently damaged or reduced in value, the compensation is treated as a recoupment of all or part of the total acquisition costs of the asset. So, if the asset was a pre-CGT asset, or was otherwise exempt, the compensation has no CGT consequences. If it is a post-CGT asset, its cost base and reduced cost base are decreased by the amount of the recoupment.
- If there is no underlying asset, the compensation is generally treated as capital proceeds from a CGT event which happens in relation to an asset, being the right to seek compensation.
- In the rare case where the compensation does not relate either to an underlying asset or the disposal of a right to seek compensation, CGT event H2 (¶11-320) may happen in relation to the amount received as compensation.
- If the compensation amount relates to a number of heads of claim and cannot be allocated on any reasonable basis between those heads of claim, the whole amount is taken to relate to the disposal of the taxpayer's right to seek compensation. If one of the undissected components relates to, say, a personal injury of the taxpayer, the exemption which may otherwise be available (see above) does not apply.

This compensation issue has also been considered by the courts on a number of occasions with several views being expressed.

In *Tuite v Exelby*, the court awarded damages for a reduction in the value of certain shares against defendants who had violated a restrictive covenant. The court concluded that the award was likely to be assessable under the former provisions corresponding to CGT event H2 (¶11-320) and increased the award to cover the likely tax liability.

In *Carborundum Realty v RAIA Archicentre*, the plaintiff had earlier been awarded damages of $75,000 for the defendant's negligence in failing to detect and report certain defects in connection with the inspection of a residential property. The plaintiff sought leave to amend its statement of claim to cover anticipated CGT liability on that amount, based upon a private ruling from the ATO. Leave was refused for a variety of reasons. Harper J said that damages extracted by a court did not give rise to a real gain in the hands of the plaintiff and parliament did not intend to impose CGT on transactions in such cases, ie where the compensation merely put the plaintiff back in the position he was in before the defendant intervened. The Federal Court also declined to adjust (for potential CGT liability) a damages award relating to breach of copyright (*Namol*).

Where damages are awarded for non-performance of obligations under a contract for the sale of property, a capital gain normally arises, either on the disposal of the right to sue (CGT event A1: ¶11-250) or because CGT event H2 (¶11-320) happens (TR 94/29). In *Rabelais v Cameron*, the court suggested that the cost base of the asset disposed of is normally no less than the capital component of the damages. In *Provan v HCL Real Estate*, a plaintiff was held to be entitled to an indemnity from a defendant against any CGT which might subsequently be found to be payable on damages from an aborted property sale. The right of indemnity in such a case would itself be a CGT asset with potential CGT implications (¶11-380).

Where the compensation is closely connected to the disposal of a main residence, the compensation may be exempt from CGT under the main residence exemption (¶11-730; *Guy*).

[FITR ¶154-560 – ¶154-572]

¶11-660 Other receipts disregarded for CGT purposes

Any gains or losses arising from receipt of the following are disregarded for CGT purposes (s 118-37):

- compensation received under the firearms surrender arrangements
- a re-establishment grant or a dairy exit payment under the *Farm Household Support Act 1992*
- winnings or losses from gambling, a game or a competition with prizes. This exempts winnings from, for example, race bets, Tattslotto, Lotto, raffles and quiz shows. An asset won is taken to be acquired at its market value and a subsequent CGT event may give rise to a capital gain or loss (IT 2584)
- a tobacco industry exit grant received under the Tobacco Growers Adjustment Assistance Programme 2006. This exemption only applies if, as a condition of receiving the grant, the recipient agreed not to become the owner or operator of any agricultural enterprise within 5 years after receiving the grant
- a right or entitlement to a tax offset, deduction, or other similar benefit
- payments or property received in connection with persecution or property lost during the Second World War
- payments received as reimbursement or payment of expenses under a scheme established by an Australian government agency, a local governing body or a foreign government agency under an enactment or an instrument of a legislative character
- payments received as reimbursement or payment of expenses under the General Practice Rural Incentives Program, the Rural and Remote General Practice Program, the Sydney Aircraft Noise Insulation Project, the M4/M5 Cashback Scheme, the Unlawful Termination Assistance Scheme or the Alternative Dispute Resolution Assistance Scheme
- a water entitlement, to the extent that the CGT event happens because an entity derives a Sustainable Rural Water Use and Infrastructure Program payment that is non-assessable, non-exempt under s 59-65
- a Sustainable Rural Water Use and Infrastructure Program payment derived that is non-assessable, non-exempt under s 59-65.

[FITR ¶154-560]

¶11-670 CGT exempt or capital loss-denying transactions

Leases not used for income-producing purposes

A capital loss a lessee makes from the expiry, surrender, forfeiture or assignment of a lease (except one granted for 99 years or more) is disregarded if the lessee did not use the lease solely or mainly for income-producing purposes (s 118-40).

Strata title conversions

If a taxpayer owns land on which there is a building, the building is subdivided into stratum units and each unit is transferred to the entity having the right to occupy it just before the subdivision, a capital gain or loss made by the taxpayer from transferring the units is disregarded (s 118-42).

In such situations, a roll-over is also available for the occupiers of the building in relation to the change in the nature of their rights of occupation (¶12-320).

Mining rights of genuine prospectors

A capital gain or loss from the sale, transfer or assignment of rights to mine in certain areas of Australia is disregarded if the income from the sale, transfer or assignment is exempt because of former s 330-60 (about genuine prospectors) (s 118-45).

Foreign currency hedging contracts

A capital gain or loss from a hedging contract entered into solely to reduce the risk of financial loss from currency exchange rate fluctuations is disregarded (s 118-55).

Gifts of property

A capital gain or loss from a testamentary gift of property is disregarded (s 118-60) if it arises from a testamentary gift that would have been deductible under s 30-15 (¶16-942) if it had not been a testamentary gift. As an anti-avoidance measure, if a testamentary gift is reacquired for less than market value by either the estate of the deceased person or an associate of the deceased person's estate, the rules relating to the effect of death on CGT assets will apply (¶12-580).

Relationship breakdown settlements

Capital gains and losses arising from relationship breakdown settlements are generally disregarded.

A capital gain or loss that is made as a result of CGT event C2 happening to a right (¶11-270) is disregarded if:

- that gain or loss is made in relation to a right that directly relates to the breakdown of a relationship between spouses, and
- at the time of the trigger event, the spouses involved are separated and there is no reasonable likelihood of cohabitation being resumed (s 118-75).

See ¶14-270 for the definition of a ''spouse'', which includes same-sex couples.

Native title and rights to native title benefits

A capital gain or loss made by a taxpayer that is either an indigenous person or an indigenous holding entity is disregarded where the gain or loss happens in relation to a CGT asset that is either a native title or the right to be provided with a native title benefit, and the gain or loss happens because of one of the following:

- the taxpayer transfers the CGT asset to one or more entities that are either indigenous persons or indigenous holding entities
- the taxpayer creates a trust that is an indigenous holding entity, over the CGT asset
- the taxpayer's ownership of the CGT asset ends (eg by cancellation or surrender), resulting in CGT event C2 happening in relation to the CGT asset (s 118-77).

Norfolk Island Residents

Norfolk Island residents are fully subject to Australia's income tax and CGT (see ¶10-640). However, capital gains or losses on CGT assets held by Norfolk Island residents before 24 October 2015 are disregarded if the Norfolk Island resident would have been entitled to an exemption on those gains under the law that existed before 1 July 2016. This is implemented by treating such assets as if they were acquired prior to 20 September 1985 (ITTPA s 102-25(2)).

Other exemptions

An exemption may also apply in relation to foreign branch gains and losses of companies (¶21-098), external territories (¶10-640), securities lending arrangements (¶12-430), ETPs (¶14-000), life insurance companies (¶3-480), demutualisation of insurance companies (¶12-650), offshore banking units (¶21-080), cancellation and buy-back of shares (¶3-160, ¶3-170), superannuation and related businesses (¶13-130), calculating the attributable income of a CFC (¶21-200), assets transferred for no consideration to a special disability trust or a trust that becomes a special disability trust as soon as practicable after transfer (s 118-85) and a capital gain or loss made from a registered emissions unit or a right to receive an Australian carbon credit unit (s 118-15).

[FITR ¶154-575 – ¶154-614/20]

¶11-675 Look-through earnout arrangements

Look through CGT treatment applies to a ''look-through earnout right'' entered into on or after 24 April 2015 by:

- disregarding any capital gain or loss relating to the creation of the right
- for the buyer — treating financial benefits provided (or received) under the right as forming part of (or reducing) the cost base of the business asset acquired (¶11-570)
- for the seller — treating financial benefits received (or provided) under the right as increasing (or decreasing) the capital proceeds of the business asset sold (¶11-510).

For these purposes, a ''financial benefit'' means anything of economic value and includes property and services (s 974-160).

A taxpayer disregards the capital gain or loss relating to the creation of the right arising from:

- CGT event C2 (¶11-270) in relation to a right received, or
- CGT event D1 (¶11-280) for a right created in another entity (s 118-575).

A right will be a ''look-through earnout right'' where the following conditions are satisfied:

(a) the right is a right to future financial benefits that are not reasonably ascertainable at the time the right is created

(b) the right is created under an arrangement that involves the disposal of a CGT asset

(c) the disposal causes CGT event A1 to happen

(d) just before the CGT event, the CGT asset was an ''active asset'' of the seller

(e) all of the financial benefits that can be provided under the right must be provided no later than 5 years after the end of the income year of the CGT event

(f) the financial benefits are contingent on the performance of the CGT asset or a business that the CGT asset is expected to be an active asset for the period of the right

(g) the value of the financial benefits reasonably relate to the economic performance, and

(h) the parties to the arrangement are dealing at arm's length (s 118-565(1)).

The 5-year requirement in (e) is treated as having never been satisfied where the arrangement includes an option to extend or renew that arrangement, the parties vary the arrangement or the parties enter into another arrangement over the CGT asset so that a party could receive financial benefits over a period ending later than 5 years after the end of the income year in which the CGT event happens (s 118-565(2)).

A CGT asset owned by an entity is an active asset for the purposes of requirement (d) where it meets the definition in s 152-40 (¶7-145) or it satisfies all of the following:

- is a share in an Australian company or an interest in a resident trust
- the holder of the share or interest is either (i) an individual that is a CGT concession stakeholder (¶7-156) of the company or trust or (ii) not an individual but has a small business participation percentage (¶7-156) in the company or trust of at least 20%
- the company or trust is carrying on a business and has carried it on since the start of the prior income year
- in the prior income year the assessable income of the company or trust was more than nil and at least 80% of it was from the carrying on of a business or businesses and was not from an asset used to derive interest, annuities, rent, royalties or foreign exchange gains (s 118-570).

A look-through right also includes a right to receive future financial benefits that are for ending such a defined look-through right, provided the arrangement does not result in a breach of the 5-year limitation (s 118-565(3)).

Temporarily disregard capital loss

Where a taxpayer makes a capital loss from disposing of a CGT asset which may be reduced as a result of the receiving financial benefits under a look-through earnout right, a portion of the capital loss must be temporarily disregarded. The portion of the capital loss that is temporarily disregarded is:

- where the maximum financial benefits cannot exceed a certain maximum amount — so much of the capital loss that equals that maximum amount
- otherwise — the whole capital loss.

The capital loss is only disregarded until and to the extent that the loss becomes reasonably certain (s 118-580).

CGT small business concessions

The CGT small business concessions effectively apply to a sale of assets involving a look-through earnout right by extending both the time to choose to apply the concessions and the replacement asset period. The CGT small business concessions are detailed from ¶7-145. The time to make superannuation contributions pursuant to the CGT cap is also extended (¶13-780).

Board of Taxation

The Board of Taxation has released a report providing for various recommendations around the operation of the CGT look-through earnout provisions having identified difficulties arising where the rules fail to align tax consequences with the commercial outcomes of transactions.

[FITR ¶155-260 – ¶155-272]

¶11-680 Taxpayers exempt from CGT

If the income of a taxpayer for an income year is exempt, any capital gains are also exempt. A capital loss made by an entity is disregarded if it was an exempt entity *at the time* that it made the loss despite not being an exempt entity at all times during the year (s 118-70). Exempt entities are detailed in ¶10-604, which include entities exempt from taxation pursuant to Div 50 such as charitable, educational, scientific or religious institutions.

All income of constitutionally protected funds is exempt (¶13-300).

[FITR ¶154-613]

¶11-690 General relief from double taxation

A capital gain is reduced if, because of the CGT event giving rise to it, a tax provision (other than a CGT provision) includes an amount in the taxpayer's assessable income (including an ETP) or exempt income or, if the taxpayer is a partner in a partnership, in the assessable or exempt income of the partnership (s 118-20). Any capital gain that a non-participating shareholder makes from the receipt of a retail premium is reduced to the extent that the amount is otherwise included in assessable income or is non-assessable non-exempt income (TR 2012/1). A capital gain is also reduced if an amount is specifically treated as being neither assessable nor exempt, eg ITAA36 s 121EG, which deals with offshore banking units (¶21-080). The capital gain is reduced to zero if it is not more than the assessable amount included in the taxpayer's income because of the non-CGT provision. However, a capital gain cannot be reduced below nil so as to create a capital loss. If the capital gain is more than that assessable amount, it is reduced by that assessable amount.

However, a capital gain is not reduced if an amount is included in assessable income because of a balancing adjustment. The capital gain is also not reduced in some circumstances where an amount is included in non-assessable non-exempt income under ITAA36 s former 23AJ; ITAA97 s 768-5 (about exempting certain non-portfolio dividends paid by foreign residents: ¶21-095).

This rule against double taxation does not apply to an amount under a share buy-back that is taken to be a dividend (¶3-170) nor to an assessable imputation gross-up amount attached to a franked distribution (¶4-800).

Special rules also apply to a superannuation fund that becomes a resident (¶13-270) or becomes non-complying (¶13-200) if the asset's market value was taken into account in working out the net previous income of the fund.

These rules ensure that an amount which is taxed under another provision of ITAA97 or ITAA36, or which is specifically granted concessional tax treatment under another provision, is not inappropriately taxed under the CGT provisions.

▶ Example

MiaCo bought a vacant block of land with the intention of building a factory on it and then selling it at a profit. MiaCo is not carrying on a business of dealing in land and the land is not trading stock. Any profit arising from the venture is assessable as ordinary income.

Section 6-5		
Proceeds of sale		$600,000
Less: Cost of land	$150,000	
Cost of construction, etc	200,000	
Holding and financing costs	80,000	
Incidental costs	10,000	440,000
Assessable profit		$160,000
Unreduced capital gain		
Capital proceeds		$600,000
Cost base (indexed)		480,000
		$120,000

The capital gain of $120,000 is reduced by the amount assessable as ordinary income. As the amount assessable as ordinary income is $160,000, the capital gain is reduced to nil.

[FITR ¶154-530 – ¶154-538]

¶11-700 Other CGT anti-overlap provisions

In addition to general relief from double taxation, a number of other specific exemptions ensure that there is no overlap of taxation in relation to CGT and specific provisions dealing with a particular area.

Carried interests

A venture capital manager's entitlement to receive payment of a carried interest that is CGT event K9 (¶11-350) is taxed as a capital gain. The carried interest is not ordinary income of the venture capital manager and a deduction is not allowable to the limited partnership for the payment (s 118-21).

Depreciating asset exemptions

A capital gain or loss may be disregarded if it arises from a CGT event (that is also a balancing adjustment event) that happens to a depreciating asset (s 118-24). There are exceptions to this rule where the capital gain or loss arises under CGT events J2 (¶11-340) and K7 (¶11-350), or where the CGT event is not equivalent to a balancing adjustment event, eg where rights are created over a depreciating asset. Exceptions also apply to various primary production assets for which amounts are deductible under Subdiv 40-F (water facilities, horticultural plants and grapevines) or 40-G (landcare operations, electricity connections and telephone lines). For further details, see ¶17-670.

Trading stock exemption

A capital gain or loss from trading stock is disregarded (s 118-25) (¶9-150). A capital gain or loss is also disregarded if the taxpayer starts holding as trading stock a CGT asset it already owns but did not previously hold as trading stock, provided the taxpayer elects for the asset to be treated as having been sold for its cost. If, in such circumstances, the taxpayer elects to treat the asset as being sold for market value, CGT event K4 (¶11-350) happens.

To ensure that CGT is the primary taxing code for complying superannuation funds, "eligible assets" acquired by a complying superannuation on or after 10 May 2011 are excluded from being trading stock (s 70-10(2); ¶13-130). Eligible assets are primarily shares, units in a trust and land (s 275-105; ¶12-660).

Taxation of financial arrangements

Generally, a capital gain or loss a taxpayer makes from a CGT asset, in creating a CGT asset or from the discharge of a liability will be disregarded if it was part of a Div 230 financial arrangement (¶23-020) and there is an assessable gain or deductible loss pursuant to Div 230 (s 118-27). The capital gain or loss will not be disregarded where:

- the financial arrangement is a hedging financial arrangement and the gain/loss arising on the arrangement is treated as a capital gain/loss
- a loss of a capital nature arises on ceasing to have a financial arrangement
- the capital gain or loss is not assessable/deductible under Div 230.

Film copyright exemption

A capital gain or loss from a CGT event relating to an interest in the copyright of a film is disregarded if an amount is assessable under ITAA36 s 26AG because of the CGT event (s 118-30).

R&D exemption

A capital gain or loss from a CGT event is disregarded purposes if an amount is assessable under specified R&D provisions because of that CGT event (s 118-35).

[FITR ¶154-539 – ¶154-555]

Main Residence Exemption

¶11-730 Basic concepts of main residence exemption

A capital gain or loss from a dwelling is disregarded if the taxpayer is an individual, the dwelling was the taxpayer's main residence throughout the ownership period and the interest did not pass to the taxpayer as a beneficiary in, or as the trustee of, the estate of a deceased person (s 118-110). With effect from 7.30 pm (AEST) on 9 May 2017, the main residence exemption is not available to a taxpayer that is either:

(a) an ''excluded foreign resident'' — being a foreign resident that has been a foreign resident for a continuous period of more than 6 years, or

(b) a foreign resident that does not satisfy the ''life events test'' (s 118-110(3), (4)).

A taxpayer will satisfy the life events test in (b) if the taxpayer has been a foreign resident for 6 years or less and satisfies one of the following:

- the taxpayer or taxpayer's spouse or child under 18 years has had a terminal medical condition during that period of foreign residency
- the death of either the taxpayer's spouse or child under 18 years at the time of death during that period of foreign residency
- the CGT event happens because of the taxpayer's divorce or separation (s 118-110(5)).

The main residence exemption does not apply to CGT events I1 or I2.

A property held by a foreign resident prior to 9 May 2017 is still eligible for the exemption for a CGT event occurring on or before 30 June 2020 under transitional provisions.

If the conditions for main residence exemption are satisfied, a taxpayer cannot choose not to apply the exemption, eg where a capital loss was made. However, a capital gain or loss may still arise if the dwelling was also used for income-producing purposes, including room rentals through Airbnb (¶11-760). A separate rule applies for beneficiaries and trustees of deceased estates (¶11-770).

The main residence exemption also applies to a residence that is owned by a special disability trust (¶6-230) and used by the relevant beneficiary as their main residence (s 118-218).

Scope of exemption

For the purpose of the main residence exemption, a dwelling includes a unit of accommodation that is a building, or is contained in a building, and consists wholly or mainly of residential accommodation, a unit of accommodation that is a caravan, houseboat or other mobile home, and any land immediately under the unit of accommodation (s 118-115). A dwelling can include more than one unit of accommodation, provided those units are used together as one place of residence or abode (TD 1999/69).

Factors that are taken into account in deciding if a dwelling is a taxpayer's main residence include:

(i) the length of time the taxpayer has lived in the dwelling

(ii) the place of residence of the taxpayer's family

(iii) whether the taxpayer's personal belongings have been moved into the dwelling

(iv) the address to which the taxpayer's mail is delivered

(v) the taxpayer's address on the electoral roll

(vi) the connection of services such as telephone, gas and electricity, and

(vii) the taxpayer's intention in occupying the dwelling.

In addition, it is relevant whether the taxpayer freely chooses or is obliged to spend time at one residence or another (*Case 26/93*).

A dwelling can only be the main residence of the taxpayer if the taxpayer actually occupies the dwelling. The mere intention of a taxpayer to occupy the dwelling as a main residence is insufficient to obtain the exemption (*Couch*). The exemption is not available to a taxpayer who did not reside on the property even if the property was the co-owner's main residence (*Gerbic*).

An improvement to a main residence which is a separate CGT asset (¶11-410) can qualify for the exemption (TD 96/21).

The main residence exemption can apply to moneys received from a forfeited deposit if a contract for its disposal falls through where the deposit is forfeited as part of a continuum of events for selling the dwelling, ie the dwelling must be put straight back onto the market and be subsequently resold (s 118-110(2); *Guy*; TR 1999/19). The exemption also applies to damages received from a defaulting purchaser to compensate for any loss from reselling the dwelling in a falling market, provided the necessary continuum of events exists.

The main residence exemption does not apply to moneys received from the grant of an easement or profit à prendre over adjacent land (TD 2018/15).

The main residence exemption is available for CGT purposes only. If the sale of a dwelling gives rise to ordinary income, eg because the sale is part of a business or a profit-making transaction, the income is assessable under s 6-5. For example, if a builder builds a "spec" home for the purpose of resale, but resides in it while building a second "spec" home, the profit from the sale of the first home is assessable even if it is exempt from CGT (TD 92/135).

Adjacent land

The main residence exemption is available for a dwelling's adjacent land. A dwelling's adjacent land is land adjacent to a dwelling to the extent that the land was used primarily for private or domestic purposes in association with the dwelling (s 118-120). The maximum area of adjacent land for the exemption is generally 2 hectares less the area of land immediately under the dwelling. The taxpayer can choose which 2 hectares the main residence exemption is to apply to (TD 1999/67). The cost base of land exceeding 2 hectares can be apportioned on a pro rata basis (ID 2002/691). Land does not have to touch or connect with the main residence dwelling to be adjacent for these purposes. It only has to be close to the dwelling so that it can be used in association with the dwelling (TD 1999/68).

In the event that the taxpayer has previously claimed the main residence exemption in relation to a compulsory acquisition of part of a dwelling's adjacent land, or ownership in it, separate from the dwelling, the exemption will only apply to the dwelling's adjacent land in relation to the maximum exempt area (s 118-120(4)). The maximum exempt area for the CGT event and the dwelling is 2 hectares less any area previously claimed as exempt pursuant to a compulsory acquisition (s 118-255).

The main residence exemption applies to an adjacent structure of a flat or home unit (if the same CGT event happens to that structure or the taxpayer's ownership interest in it) as if it were a dwelling (s 118-120(5)). For a flat or home unit, a dwelling also includes a garage, storeroom or other structure that is associated with it (s 118-120(6)).

It does not matter if the adjacent land was acquired after the dwelling (TD 92/171). Adjacent land used for agistment during most of the relevant period is not eligible for exemption. If the adjacent land is used primarily for private or domestic purposes in association with the dwelling for some of the period, a part exemption (¶11-760) is available to that extent (TD 2000/15).

Generally, if any part of a dwelling's adjacent land or an associated garage, storeroom or other structure is disposed of separately from the rest of the dwelling, the main residence exemption does not apply to that disposal (¶11-750). However, the CGT main residence exemption applies to compulsory acquisitions (and certain other involuntary events) of adjacent land or buildings to a dwelling that are used as the taxpayer's main residence (ss 118-245; 118-250; ¶11-740).

Ownership period

For the purpose of the main residence exemption, the taxpayer's ownership period for a dwelling is the period on or after 20 September 1985 when the taxpayer had an ownership interest in the dwelling or in land (acquired on or after 20 September 1985) on which the dwelling is later built (s 118-125). Where land or a dwelling is acquired or disposed of under a contract and legal ownership passes at a later date, eg upon settlement, the ownership period is worked out on the basis of legal ownership. However, if the purchaser has a contractual right to occupy before legal ownership passes, the ownership period commences when the right begins.

A taxpayer has an ownership interest in land or a dwelling if:

- for land, the taxpayer has a legal or equitable interest in the land or a right to occupy it
- for a dwelling that is not a flat or home unit, the taxpayer has a legal or equitable interest in the land on which the dwelling is erected, or a licence or right to occupy the land; eg a leasehold interest is an ownership interest, as is a licence arrangement in relation to, say, a retirement village, or
- for a flat or home unit, the taxpayer has a legal or equitable interest in a stratum unit in it, a licence or right to occupy it, or a share in a company that owns a legal or equitable interest in the land on which the flat or home unit is erected that gives the taxpayer a right to occupy it (s 118-130).

A dwelling owned by the trustee of a deceased estate or a special disability trust may qualify for exemption (¶11-770). The only other circumstance in which a dwelling owned by a trustee may qualify for exemption is if the beneficiary is absolutely entitled to the dwelling as against the trustee (¶11-210). A dwelling owned by a family company is not eligible for the exemption (s 118-110(1)), nor is one owned by an individual in a trustee capacity.

For a checklist of the tax aspects of a family home, see ¶44-108.

[FITR ¶154-630 – ¶154-670]

¶11-740 Rules extending main residence exemption

Moving into a main residence

If a dwelling becomes a taxpayer's main residence by the time it was first practicable for the taxpayer to move into it after it was acquired, the dwelling is treated as the taxpayer's main residence from when it was acquired until it actually became the taxpayer's main residence (s 118-135).

A taxpayer who rents out a property for a period prior to moving in is only eligible for a partial exemption as the taxpayer does not move in as soon as practicable (*Chapman*; *Caller*).

This extension of the main residence exemption will not apply in the situation where a taxpayer purchases a property with the intention of occupying it as their main residence but never actually occupies the property (*Couch*).

Changing main residences

If a taxpayer acquires a dwelling that is to become the taxpayer's main residence and the taxpayer still owns an existing main residence, both dwellings are treated as the taxpayer's main residence for up to 6 months (s 118-140). However, this rule only applies if the taxpayer's existing main residence was the taxpayer's main residence for a continuous period of at least 3 months in the 12 months before it was disposed of and it was not used for income-producing purposes in any part of that 12-month period when it was not the taxpayer's main residence.

This concession applies even if the taxpayer has made a choice under s 118-145 or 118-150 that only one of the dwellings is to be treated as a main residence (TD 1999/43).

Where a taxpayer subdivides land on which a main residence is built and constructs a new main residence on the vacant part of the land, the main residence exemption is not available for both dwellings for the full period of ownership. However, both dwellings may be exempt for up to 6 months (TD 2000/13; TD 2000/14).

Dwelling stops being main residence

If a dwelling that was a taxpayer's main residence stops being the taxpayer's main residence, the taxpayer may choose to continue to treat it as a main residence (s 118-145). If the dwelling is not used for income-producing purposes during the taxpayer's absence this choice can apply indefinitely. However, if the property is used for income-producing purposes, the maximum period the dwelling can be treated as the taxpayer's main residence is 6 years.

▶ Example 1

Sharon lives in her own house for 2 years. She is posted overseas for 4 years, during which period she rents the house. On her return, she lives in the house for 2 years and is then again posted overseas for 5 years (again renting out her house). She then returns to Australia and while a resident she sells the house. Sharon can choose to treat her house as her main residence during both absences because each absence is less than 6 years (in this case, no other house can be treated as her main residence, unless s 118-140 applies). She can do this by not including any capital gain or loss in her income tax return for the year in which the house is sold.

For examples of the interaction between the 6-year extended exemption and the special rule where the first use of a main residence to produce income occurs after 20 August 1996, see ¶11-760.

The absence exemption can apply to a main residence that the taxpayer owned overseas before becoming a resident of Australia (TD 95/7).

The 6-year period in relation to income-producing use need not be continuous. If there are intermittent periods of income-producing use during the one period of absence, those intermittent periods are aggregated in calculating whether the 6-year limitation has been exceeded. However, if a dwelling stops being a taxpayer's main residence more than once during the ownership period, the 6-year limitation applies separately for each period of absence (s 118-145(2)).

The application of the temporary absence provision may be applied where a taxpayer rents out the whole of their main residence for a period of time through Airbnb or other property sharing arrangements. For example, where the whole property is rented out for a total period of no more than 6 continuous years at a time, the owner re-establishes the property as their main residence within that period and does not claim any other property as a main residence, the full main residence exemption may still be available. Note that the temporary absence rule is not relevant for the rental of only part of the property (eg one room) under Airbnb (¶11-760).

▶ Example 2

Bowie purchases a property in April 2008 and uses it as his main residence for the period of ownership except for 6 weeks over December/January each year where he goes on an overseas holiday and rents the house out through Airbnb. In April 2020, he sells the property. At no time during the ownership period did he own any other property. Bowie is entitled to the full main residence exemption on the sale of the property due to the temporary absence provision applying to the rental period each year.

Building, renovating or repairing a main residence

In some circumstances, the main residence exemption can be applied to land owned by a taxpayer for an additional period of up to 4 years if the taxpayer builds a dwelling on the land or repairs, renovates or finishes building a dwelling on the land (s 118-150). In such a case, the exemption applies from the time the land is acquired. However, if the land was acquired more than 4 years before the dwelling became the taxpayer's main residence, the exemption period starts 4 years before the dwelling became the taxpayer's main residence. The Commissioner has a discretion to extend the 4-year period (s 118-150(4)(a)). The discretion should be exercised in the following non-exhaustive special circumstances:

- the taxpayer is unable to build, repair or renovate the dwelling within this time period due to either circumstances outside their control or unforeseen circumstances arising, or
- building, repairing or renovating the dwelling within the 4 years would impose a severe financial burden on the taxpayer.

For the exemption to apply, the dwelling on the land that is constructed, repaired or renovated must become the taxpayer's main residence as soon as practicable after the work is finished (TD 92/147) and must continue to be so for at least 3 months (*Case 2/2003*). Taxpayers were not entitled to the exemption because they either could not prove the property was their main residence as soon as practicable after building completed or that it was used as their main residence for at least 3 months (*Erdelyi*; *Keep*). In *Summers*, a taxpayer who lived in a 2-room builder's shed on a property for approximately 4 months was entitled to a partial exemption. However, the taxpayer was unable to claim the additional 4-year exemption as she had not moved in as soon as practicable after completion of the building.

Special rules allow for the additional 4-year exemption to still be available if the taxpayer dies before being able to move into the dwelling (s 118-155). With effect from 9 May 2017 this rule is not available to a foreign resident, subject to transitional provisions to 30 June 2020 (s 118-155(5)). More generous relief is available if a dwelling stops being a taxpayer's main residence (see above), provided the taxpayer moves into the dwelling for a period before carrying out the repairs or renovations.

Where a dwelling is built on or after 20 September 1985 on pre-CGT land and is treated as a separate CGT asset (¶11-410), the choice must be made to apply the exemption to the period prior to becoming the taxpayer's main residence (TD 2017/13).

If the death of a taxpayer activates the concession, the dwelling is the taxpayer's main residence for the lesser of: (i) the period from the date of the acquisition of the land and ending at the taxpayer's death; or (ii) the period of 4 years immediately before the taxpayer's death. If the dwelling straddles 2 post-CGT blocks, the period commences (subject to the 4-year limit) when the earlier block was acquired (TD 92/129).

A taxpayer who makes use of the additional 4-year exemption cannot claim a main residence exemption for any other dwelling during that period (s 118-150(6); TD 1999/43), except for the 6-month double exemption allowed when changing main residences (see above).

Main residence accidentally destroyed

If a dwelling that is the taxpayer's main residence is accidentally destroyed and another dwelling is not built on the land, the taxpayer can choose to apply the main residence exemption to the land as if, from the time of the destruction until the time of disposal, the dwelling had not been destroyed and continued to be the taxpayer's main residence (s 118-160). However, no other dwelling can be treated as the taxpayer's main residence during this period.

Compulsory acquisitions related to a main residence

The main residence exemption applies to disregard a capital gain or loss if it arises from any of the following circumstances:

- compulsory acquisition of part of a taxpayer's main residence
- compulsory ending of an ownership right over a taxpayer's main residence
- compulsory creation of a right over a taxpayer's main residence
- relevant negotiated agreements made in connection with such a compulsory transaction (ss 118-245; 118-250).

A reference to part of the main residence includes adjacent land to the dwelling and structures built thereon. This exemption applies despite the application of s 118-165 (¶11-750).

Where there is a compulsory acquisition or other involuntary event that affects part of a property larger than 2 hectares, the taxpayer will have the choice of whether to apply the exemption to some or all of the affected area (up to 2 hectares) (s 118-245(2)). With effect from 9 May 2017, the exemption is not available where the taxpayer is an excluded foreign resident or a foreign resident who does not satisfy the life events test (¶11-730), subject to transitional rules up to 30 June 2020 (s 118-245(3)).

A capital gain or loss from such an event will only be disregarded to the extent that the taxpayer would have been entitled to the main residence had the entire main residence been disposed of just before the compulsory transaction.

Replacement dwellings

The main residence exemption can apply to a replacement dwelling where the original dwelling is destroyed or compulsorily acquired at a time when the original dwelling was no longer the taxpayer's actual main residence but was still being treated as such under the temporary absence provision. The taxpayer can treat the replacement dwelling as the main residence despite having never lived in the replacement dwelling provided the replacement dwelling (or the land on which it is built) is acquired no later than one year after (or such further time as the Commissioner allows) the end of the income year in which the original dwelling was destroyed or compulsorily acquired (s 118-147).

Where the taxpayer acquires vacant land within the one-year period, the main residence status will only transfer to a replacement dwelling built thereon if it is built within 4 years after the original dwelling was destroyed or compulsorily acquired (or after the land for the replacement dwelling was acquired if that was later) (s 118-147(2)).

If the taxpayer transfers the main residence status to a replacement dwelling, it is treated as being the main residence from when the replacement dwelling was acquired (or from a year before the original dwelling was destroyed or compulsorily acquired if that is later) (s 118-147(2)).

The time limits in relation to the temporary absence rule in s 118-145 apply. Therefore, the exemption applies indefinitely if the replacement dwelling is not used to produce assessable income (s 118-147(5)). However, where the replacement dwelling is used for producing assessable income the maximum period for which the main residence exemption can apply to the replacement dwelling is 6 years, or where the original property was used for an income-producing purpose immediately before the compulsory acquisition or destruction, the balance of the 6-year period remaining on the original dwelling (s 118-147(4)). The exemption only applies where no other property is treated as the taxpayer's main residence during the period (s 118-147(6)).

[FITR ¶154-680 – ¶154-730, ¶154-865 – ¶154-870]

¶11-750 Rules limiting main residence exemption

CGT event happens to adjacent land or related structure only

The main residence exemption does not generally apply to a CGT event that happens in relation to adjacent land or a garage, storeroom or other structure if that CGT event does not also happen in relation to the dwelling upon which the exemption relies (s 118-165). For example, land under a unit of accommodation will not benefit from the main residence exemption if the taxpayer sells that unit of accommodation separately from the land (TD 1999/73).

However, the main residence exemption is available where that adjacent land or structure is disposed of pursuant to a compulsory acquisition or certain other involuntary events (¶11-740).

Spouses with different residences

If, during a period, a dwelling is the taxpayer's main residence and another dwelling is the main residence of the taxpayer's spouse (including a de facto spouse but not a spouse living permanently separate and apart from the taxpayer — see definition at ¶14-270), only one of the dwellings can be treated as the main residence of both the taxpayer and spouse for that period (s 118-170). It does not matter if one of the dwellings is a pre-CGT dwelling (TD 92/172). The taxpayer and the taxpayer's spouse do not have to have an interest in each dwelling, ie a taxpayer may nominate a dwelling owned by the taxpayer's spouse.

Alternatively, both dwellings can be treated as main residences for the period. If this happens, the exemption is split. If the taxpayer's interest in his or her dwelling is not more than half of the total interests held by all persons in the dwelling, it is taken to be a main residence during the whole of the period. Otherwise, the dwelling is taken to be a main residence for only half of the period. Similar rules apply for the spouse's dwelling.

A nominated dwelling may be one which is treated as a main residence during a taxpayer's absence (TD 92/174; ¶11-740).

In the case of jointly owned property to which the above rules do not apply, any joint owner who uses the dwelling as a main residence is eligible for the exemption (IT 2485).

Taxpayer and dependant with different residences

If, at a particular time, a dwelling is the taxpayer's main residence and another dwelling is the main residence of an economically dependent child of the taxpayer who is under 18, only one of those main residences can be treated as a main residence for the purpose of the exemption (s 118-175). Unlike the situation for spouses with different residences, there is no facility for splitting the exemption.

Marriage or relationship breakdown roll-overs

Where a marriage or relationship breakdown roll-over (¶12-460) is available to the transferor spouse, eligibility for the main residence exemption is based on the way in which both the transferor and transferee spouses used the dwelling during their combined period of ownership (s 118-178).

▶ Example

Kate (the transferor spouse) was the 100% owner of a dwelling that she used only as a rental property for 2 years before transferring it to Sam (the transferee spouse). Sam used the dwelling only as a main residence for 2 years before selling it. Having regard to how both spouses used the dwelling, Sam will be eligible for only a 50% main residence exemption.

Dwelling transferred from company or trustee after marriage or relationship breakdown

The CGT provisions apply to a taxpayer as if he/she owned land or a dwelling during a period when it was actually owned by a company or trustee if: (i) it was acquired from the company or trustee; (ii) it was a post-CGT asset in the hands of the company or trustee; and (iii) a marriage or relationship breakdown roll-over (¶12-470) was available to the company or trustee on its disposal. A taxpayer who has acquired land or a dwelling in such a way cannot treat it as a main residence during the period it was owned by the company or trustee (s 118-180).

[FITR ¶154-740 – ¶154-770]

¶11-760 Partial CGT main residence exemption

Main residence for part of ownership period

Only a partial main residence exemption is available in respect of a dwelling if it was the taxpayer's main residence for part only of the ownership period and it did not pass to the taxpayer as a beneficiary in, or as a trustee of, a deceased estate (s 118-185). The full exemption is proportionately reduced by reference to the period for which the dwelling was not the taxpayer's main residence (subject to the temporary absence rule).

▶ Example 1

Lisa acquired a dwelling on 18 October 2015 which she let out to tenants until 19 October 2018, from which date she used the dwelling as her main residence. Lisa eventually sold the dwelling on 5 September 2020 and made a capital gain of $40,000, calculated without regard to the exemption provisions. The capital gain is reduced pro rata by reference to the period Lisa used the dwelling as her main residence. The reduced capital gain is:

$$\$40{,}000 \times \frac{1{,}098 \text{ (number of days from 18 October 2015 to 19 October 2018)}}{1{,}785 \text{ (number of days of Lisa's ownership)}}$$

= $24,605

With effect from 9 May 2017, the partial main residence exemption is not available where at the time of the CGT event the taxpayer is an excluded foreign resident or a foreign resident that does not satisfy the life events test, subject to transitional rules to 30 June 2020 (s 118-185(3)).

Main residence used for income-producing purposes

Only a partial main residence exemption is available if the dwelling was used for income-producing purposes during all or a part of the ownership period and, if interest was incurred on money borrowed to acquire the dwelling, it would be deductible (s 118-190). This interest deductibility test is a hypothetical test which assumes that the taxpayer had borrowed money to acquire the dwelling and had incurred interest on the money borrowed. The capital gain or loss that would have arisen is increased by an amount that is reasonable having regard to the extent to which that interest would be deductible. However, the exemption is not reduced if part of a taxpayer's dwelling is used by someone else, eg another family member, for an income-producing purpose (TD 1999/71).

For this purpose, if a dwelling was acquired by a taxpayer as the trustee or beneficiary of a deceased estate, any use of the dwelling by the deceased for income-producing purposes is disregarded if the dwelling was the main residence of the deceased just before death and it was not being used for income-producing purposes at that time.

Some of a taxpayer's main residence exemption may be lost if a person lets out part of a main residence. For example, in *Walter*, the taxpayer was assessable on part of a capital gain because she had shared her home unit with other people, even though those people only paid about half the market rental.

The partial main residence exemption will be relevant where the owner rents out a part of his/her main residence through property sharing arrangements such as Airbnb. This is because part of the property will be used for income-producing purposes and the full main residence will not be available.

▶ Example 2

Tom acquired a 2-bedroom unit in April 2016 as his main residence. As a way of paying the mortgage, he immediately begins renting the spare bedroom through Airbnb until the property was sold in April 2020. At all times while renting the room he also resided in the unit. Tom will only be entitled to a partial main residence exemption.

Part of a dwelling is taken to be used for income-producing purposes only if it has the character of a place of business (IT 2673). Whether a part of a dwelling has the character of a place of business is a question of fact, but the broad test is whether a particular part of the dwelling: (i) is set aside exclusively as a place of business; (ii) is clearly identifiable as a place of business; and (iii) is not readily suitable or adaptable for use for private or domestic purposes in association with the dwelling generally.

This test is not satisfied, for example, if music lessons are provided or tuition is given from a study in a home, nor if an insurance agent uses a study in his or her residence for personal and family purposes but also uses it to interview prospective clients and to store business papers. Income from such activities is nevertheless assessable and some deductions may be allowable for electricity and other running expenses (¶16-480).

The general rule for apportioning the main residence exemption is to make adjustments on the basis of floor area in a way similar to the calculation of proportionate interest or rent deductions, but also taking into account the period of income-producing use. However in some cases, a more appropriate basis for apportionment may be available (TD 1999/66).

Main residence first becomes income-producing

There is a special rule where a main residence is first used for producing income after 7.30 pm EST on 20 August 1996. The rule applies if only a partial main residence exemption would be available because the dwelling was used for income-producing purposes during the ownership period and a full main residence exemption would have been available if a CGT event happened just before the first time (the income time) it was used for income-producing purposes during that period (s 118-192). In such a case, the dwelling is taken to have been acquired at the income time for its market value at that time. This means that a taxpayer does not have to keep records of expenditure on a dwelling which is solely a main residence until the income time. Further specific rules apply if the dwelling passed to the taxpayer as a trustee or beneficiary of a deceased estate.

If, as a result of the application of this rule, the taxpayer is taken to have acquired a dwelling less than 12 months before a CGT event gave rise to a gain, it will not be a discount capital gain (¶11-033).

The rule in s 118-192 does not apply where, by making a choice under s 118-145 (¶11-740), a taxpayer is entitled to a full exemption. However, a choice can be made under s 118-145 (to treat a dwelling as a main residence for up to 6 years) even though the rule in 118-192 applies (*Treating a dwelling as your main residence after you move out*). The following examples illustrate the application of these rules without regard to eligibility for indexation (¶11-610) or a discount capital gain (¶11-033).

▶ Example 3: Dwelling first used to produce income after 20 August 1996

On 1 July 1995 Bev paid $250,000 for a house that she used as her main residence until 1 July 2010, at which time its market value was $350,000.

If Bev then rented the house until she sold it at any time before 1 July 2016, she would still be able to claim a full exemption by relying on the 6-year extended exemption under s 118-145 provided she did not claim any other property as her main residence during the period.

However, if Bev continued to rent the house before selling it for $700,000 on 1 July 2020, ie 11 years after its first income use, she could only claim a partial exemption. In that case, the market value of the house at the time of its first income use ($350,000) is used to determine the capital gain (ie $700,000 – $350,000 = $350,000). The taxable capital gain would be worked out (ignoring leap years in accordance with the example in s 118-185) as follows:

$$\$350{,}000 \times \frac{1{,}825 \text{ days}}{4{,}015\text{days}} \quad \begin{matrix}\text{(non-main residence days)}\\ \text{(days in deemed ownership period)}\end{matrix}$$

= $159,091

▶ Example 4: Dwelling first used to produce income before 20 August 1996

Assume the same initial facts as in Example 3 except that Bev first ceases to use the house as her main residence on 1 July 1996. She then recommences using the property as her main residence on 1 July 2002 and then recommenced renting the property out from 1 July 2009 until the time of sale.

Where Bev sold the property on 1 July 2015 she would be able to claim a full exemption by relying on 2 applications of the 6-year extended exemption under s 118-145 available due to the recommencement of using the property as her main residence.

However, where she sold the property for $700,000 on 1 July 2020 she could only claim a partial exemption. In that case, the market value of the house at the time of its first income use is not relevant and the capital gain is determined on the basis of the original cost base, ie $700,000 – $250,000 = $450,000. The taxable capital gain would be worked out (ignoring leap years) as follows:

$$\$450{,}000 \times \frac{1{,}825 \text{ days}}{8{,}760 \text{ days}} \quad \begin{matrix}\text{(non-main residence days)}\\ \text{(days in actual ownership period)}\end{matrix}$$

= $93,750

[FITR ¶154-780 – ¶154-800]

¶11-770 Dwellings acquired from deceased estates

A capital gain or loss from a CGT event that happens in relation to a dwelling, or the ownership interest in it, is disregarded if the taxpayer is an individual and the interest passed to the taxpayer as a beneficiary in a deceased estate, or the taxpayer owned the dwelling as the trustee of a deceased estate and the following conditions are satisfied:

1. either:

   (a) the deceased acquired the ownership interest on or after 20 September 1985 and the dwelling was the deceased's main residence just before death and was not then being used for incomes-producing purposes, or

   (b) the deceased acquired the ownership interest before 20 September 1985, and

2. either:

   (a) the ownership interest ends within 2 years of the deceased's death, or within such longer period allowed by the Commissioner, or

(b) the dwelling was, from the deceased's death until the taxpayer's ownership interest ends, the main residence of one or more of the following persons:

(i) the spouse of the deceased immediately before the death

(ii) an individual who had a right to occupy the dwelling under the deceased's will, or

(iii) if the CGT event was brought about by the individual to whom the ownership interest passed as a beneficiary — that individual (s 118-195(1)).

For this purpose, a taxpayer who acquires a dwelling as a surviving joint tenant is treated as acquiring the dwelling as a beneficiary of a deceased estate (s 118-197).

With effect from 9 May 2017 this exemption is not available where at the time of death the deceased was an excluded foreign resident (s 118-195(1)(c)). A transitional rule allows the exemption to apply to a property acquired prior to 9 May 2017 where the deceased died on or before 30 June 2020. Further, items (2)(a) and (b) do not apply where the deceased was an excluded foreign resident (¶11-730) just before death (s 118-195(1A)(a)). Item (2)(b)(iii) does not apply where the individual is an excluded foreign resident (s 118-195(1A)(b)). The main residence exemption can still apply where the beneficiary, or trustee of the deceased estate, uses the property for income-producing purposes after the death of the deceased (TD 1999/70).

The terms of this exemption are strictly interpreted. The exemption will only apply where the ownership interest disposed of by the taxpayer is the same as the ownership interest that the deceased held at the time of death. In *Estate of Jack Reginald Cawthen (Deceased)*, the exemption was not available on the sale of a 50% interest in a dwelling by the trustee of a deceased estate because at the time of death the deceased only had a right to occupy the dwelling. This applied even though at the time of death the dwelling was owned by a company that was 50% owned by the deceased and the 50% interest in the dwelling was ultimately distributed to the trustee of the deceased estate as the company's 50% shareholder on the liquidation of the company.

A full exemption was not available where an individual was granted a right of occupancy under the will for only part of the period from the time of the deceased's death until the dwelling was sold (ID 2004/882). See also ID 2006/34. A full exemption is available where an individual is granted a right to occupancy under a will, but only occupies the dwelling from the time probate of the estate was granted until it was sold by the trustee (ATO publication *CGT exemptions for inherited dwellings*).

For a post-CGT dwelling of the deceased that was acquired before 7.30 pm EST on 20 August 1996 by the trustee of the deceased's estate, or passed to a beneficiary of the deceased before that time, the full exemption is only available if the dwelling was the main residence of the deceased for the deceased's whole ownership period. In addition, in such cases the trustee or beneficiary cannot take advantage of the rule for main residences which become income-producing for the first time (¶11-760) and must take into account the use of the dwelling by the deceased during the ownership period of the deceased for the purpose of working out any partial exemption.

Partial exemption

Where the taxpayer is an individual and the interest passed to the taxpayer as a beneficiary in a deceased estate, or the taxpayer owned the dwelling as the trustee of a deceased estate and the conditions for a full exemption are not satisfied, either a partial exemption or no exemption will be available (s 118-200(1)). The amount of the capital gain or loss is apportioned by working out the number of non-main residence days as compared to the total ownership days that are relevant for main residence exemption purposes (s 118-200(2)). The apportionment formula is adjusted where a dwelling is inherited from someone who had previously acquired the dwelling by inheritance (s

118-205). With effect from 9 May 2017, where the property was acquired by the deceased on or after 2 September 1985 the non-main residence days will also include days where the property was the main residence of an excluded foreign resident (s 118-205(4)).

Special rules also apply where, under a deceased person's will, the trustee of the deceased estate acquires an ownership interest in a dwelling for occupation by an individual (s 118-210). Such an acquisition may be in pursuance of the will or under its authority but does not have to be by force of the will nor in strict conformity with it. However, if a trustee acquires an ownership interest in a dwelling in the course of the administration of an intestacy, the trustee does not acquire the interest under the deceased's will because there is no will (TD 1999/74). If a CGT event happens to the interest in relation to the individual and the trustee receives no money or property for it (typically, where the dwelling is distributed in specie to the individual): (i) no capital gain or loss arises to the trustee; (ii) the first element of the dwelling's cost base (and reduced cost base) in the hands of the individual is its cost base (and reduced cost base) in the trustee's hands at the time of the event; and (iii) the individual is taken to have acquired the dwelling when the trustee acquired it.

Alternatively, if the trustee does receive money or property as a result of the CGT event happening, or the event happens in relation to another entity, and the dwelling was the main residence of the individual from the time the trustee acquired it until the time of the event, no capital gain or loss arises for the trustee. However, if the dwelling was the main residence of the individual during only part of that period, a capital gain or loss arises. In such a case, the amount of the capital gain or loss is apportioned by working out the number of non-main residence days as compared to the total ownership days that are relevant for main residence exemption purposes. With effect from 9 May 2017 (subject to transitional rules to 30 June 2020 for properties held prior to 9 May 2017) this does not apply if the deceased was an excluded foreign resident just before death (s 118-210(6)).

Extension of 2-year period

PCG 2019/5 provides details of the factors considered in exercising the Commissioner's discretion to extend the 2-year period with a safe harbour to treat the discretion as being exercised. In this regard, the discretion can be treated as being exercised where the following 5 conditions are satisfied:

- in the first 2 years, more than 12 months was spent addressing certain circumstances. These include (i) a challenge to a will or ownership of the dwelling, (ii) a life or other equitable interest delayed the disposal, (iii) complexity of the estate delayed administration, or (iv) settlement of a sale contract was delayed due to circumstances outside the taxpayer's control

- the dwelling is listed for sale as soon as practically possible after the above circumstances are resolved

- the sale is completed within 12 months of the dwelling being listed for sale

- no adverse factors exist eg activities undertaken to improve the sale price of the dwelling, and

- the longer period for the discretion to be exercised is not more than 18 months.

Special disability trust

The main residence exemption is available in the event of the death of the principal beneficiary of a special disability trust where the intended recipient of the residence disposed of the dwelling within 2 years of the death and the dwelling was not used to produce assessable income (s 118-222). A partial exemption may be available to the trustee in the event the property was used to produce assessable income prior to the principal beneficiary's death.

[FITR ¶154-810 – ¶154-840]

Other Exemptions

¶11-880 CGT: insurance and superannuation exemptions

Insurance policies and annuity instruments

The insurance policy exemption comes into play when a CGT event affects an insurance policy so as to give rise to a capital gain or loss. This happens, for example, when an insurance policy is paid out, when an asset is transferred to the policy owner in accordance with the policy or when the surrender value of the policy is paid.

All insurance policies and annuity instruments

If a CGT event happens to a general insurance policy, a life insurance policy or an annuity instrument, a capital gain or loss made from it by the insurer or the entity that issued the annuity instrument is disregarded (s 118-300).

General insurance policies

If a CGT event happens to a general insurance policy taken out in respect of property that is exempt from CGT, a capital gain or loss made from it by the insured person is disregarded. For example, the general insurance exemption applies to the disposal of the rights of an insured person under a policy of insurance relating to a pre-CGT asset, a car, trading stock or a main residence.

Where an asset, or part of an asset, is lost or destroyed, any insurance proceeds received by the taxpayer are taken to relate to that asset and not to the insurance policy (s 118-300(1), example 1). This means that, if a general insurance policy relates to property that is not exempt from CGT, the CGT consequences of receiving any insurance proceeds are the same as where compensation is received in relation to an asset (¶11-650).

Life insurance policies and annuity instruments

If a CGT event happens to a policy of insurance on the life of an individual or an annuity instrument, a capital gain or loss made from it by:

(a) the original owner of the policy or instrument

(b) an entity that acquired the interest in the policy for no consideration

(c) a beneficiary (including a legal personal representative) on a subsequent payment made by the trustee that is attributable to such policy or instrument

(d) a trustee of a complying superannuation fund, ADF or PST from a CGT event happening to a policy of insurance against an individual suffering an illness or injury,

is disregarded (s 118-300).

A ''policy of insurance on the life of an individual'' is not limited to a life insurance policy within the common law meaning of that term. It also includes other life insurance policies (as defined in s 995-1(1)), but only to the extent that those policies provide for a payment to be made if an event happens that results in the death of an individual (TD 2007/4). The exemption for life insurance policies may not apply to life insurance bonds issued from a tax haven (TA 2009/17).

Rights arising from superannuation

A capital gain or loss is also disregarded if a CGT event happens in relation to a right to an allowance, annuity or capital amount payable out of a superannuation fund or ADF, a right to an asset of such a fund or a right to any part of such an allowance, annuity, capital amount or asset (s 118-305). However, this exemption is not available if the taxpayer is the trustee of the fund and a CGT event happens in relation to a CGT asset of the fund. Similarly, this exemption is not available if an entity receives a payment or property where the entity was not a member of the fund and the entity acquired the right to the payment or property for consideration.

For specific modifications of the CGT provisions in relation to superannuation funds, see ¶13-130. For the CGT roll-over relief available for a change to a trust deed, see ¶12-550.

Superannuation and marriage breakdown

Special CGT rules apply in relation to the division of superannuation on a marriage breakdown. The effects of these rules are:

- capital gains or losses that may arise from the creation or forgoing of rights when spouses enter into a binding superannuation agreement or where the agreement comes to an end are disregarded (s 118-313)
- the exemption under s 118-305 for payments made from a superannuation fund or ADF (see above) applies to non-member spouses, and
- roll-over relief applies to in specie transfers between funds with fewer than 5 members (¶12-480).

Rights arising from an RSA

A capital gain or loss from a CGT event happening in relation to a right to, or any part of, an RSA is also disregarded (s 118-310).

Demutualisation of insurance companies

The operation of the CGT rules is modified in situations where there is a demutualisation of a life or general insurance company or an affiliate company (¶12-650).

[FITR ¶155-000 – ¶155-033]

¶11-890 CGT: exemption for PST units

A capital gain is exempt from CGT and a capital loss is disregarded if it is made in relation to units in a PST and the entity is:

- the trustee of a complying superannuation fund, a complying ADF or a PST
- a life insurance entity and, just before the event happened, the unit was included in a tax-advantaged insurance fund of the entity, or
- a registered organisation and, just before the event happened, the unit was owned by the entity solely for carrying on a tax-advantaged business of the entity (s 118-350).

[FITR ¶155-110]

¶11-895 CGT: entitlements under the financial claims scheme

A capital gain or loss arising from a payment made by APRA, or by a liquidator, under the financial claims scheme will be disregarded (Subdiv 253-A). Pursuant to the financial claims scheme, APRA is allowed to pay eligible depositors in failed ADIs some part of their deposit using government funds.

There are 2 rights arising from the scheme in relation to ADI deposits to which the CGT rules can apply being:

(1) the right of the depositor to receive a payment from the scheme administrator, and

(2) the right to a portion of the funds in the ADI deposit (being part of the original deposit debt) that is transferred to the scheme administrator following payment by the scheme administrator to the depositor.

A capital gain or loss from the disposal of either of these rights will be disregarded (s 253-10).

The cost base of an entitlement under the scheme is equal to the payment under the scheme. The cost base of the remainder of an entitlement following a payment from the scheme is equal to the cost base of the entitlement reduced by the amount that has been paid under the scheme (s 253-15).

[FITR ¶250-000 – ¶250-040]

¶11-900 CGT: venture capital exemption

Certain investors can disregard capital gains and capital losses from CGT events that relate to venture capital investments (Subdiv 118-F: ss 118-400 to 118-445). Unless the investments are made through early stage venture capital limited partnerships (see below), the exemption is only available to foreign residents.

For corresponding revenue exemptions relating to venture capital investments, see ¶10-845.

Exemption for profits on venture capital investments

The exemption is available for venture capital investments in Australian companies (and in some cases foreign holding companies) and unit trusts made by:

- certain foreign residents holding less than 10% of the equity in a venture capital limited partnership (VCLP) (s 118-405)
- foreign resident investors through an Australian venture capital fund of funds (AFOF) (s 118-410)
- tax-exempt foreign residents (s 118-415), and
- Australian and foreign residents in early stage venture capital activities through an early stage venture capital limited partnership (ESVCLP) (s 118-407).

To qualify as an eligible venture capital investment, the investment must:

- be at risk, ie the investor must not be a party to any arrangement to support the value of the shares or any earnings or returns from the shares
- at the time of the CGT event, be owned by the investor and have been owned for at least 12 months, and
- consist of shares in a company or units in a unit trust, options (including warrants) to acquire shares in a company or units in a unit trust, or convertible notes (other than debt interests) issued by a company or unit trust, provided the company or unit trust meets certain requirements. One of the requirements is that more than 75% of the activities of the company, trust or group, having regard to certain attributes, must not relate to specified activities. Ineligible activities consist of property development or land ownership; certain finance activities; insurance; construction or acquisition of infrastructure facilities; or making investments designed to generate interest, rents, dividends, royalties or lease payments (ss 118-425; 118-427).

In addition, the total amount invested by the partnership in all the debt and equity interests held in the company or unit trust, and any of its connected entities must not exceed 30% of the partnership's committed capital.

Eligibility for the exemption also applies to investments in the holding company of a corporate group that satisfy certain requirements. The requirements vary according to whether the investment is being made into a new company or an existing holding company.

An eligible venture capital investment cannot be made into an entity whose asset value, together with that of any connected entity, exceeds $50 million (in the case of an ESVCLP) or $250 million (in any other case) immediately before the investment is made. However, an investment in an entity that is acquired from a group whose asset value is greater than the relevant amount will qualify for the concession if, after the investment is made, the entity will not be connected to the group (s 118-440).

ESVCLPs are not required to divest a company when its value exceeds $250 million (¶20-700). However, if an ESVCLP does not dispose of an investment in an entity within 6 months after the end of an income year in which the investee's market value exceeds $250 million, then the ESVCLP will only be entitled to a partial CGT exemption equal to the amount of the exempt capital gain that would have arisen had the investment been sold at the end of 6 months after the income year in which the $250 million threshold was first exceeded (s 118-408).

Exemption for foreign resident pension funds

A foreign resident tax-exempt pension fund that invests in venture capital in an Australian company or fixed trust (a resident investment vehicle) can disregard a capital gain or capital loss it makes from a CGT event that happens to the shares or trust interests if: (i) the entity is registered under the *Pooled Development Funds Act 1992*; and (ii) the entity owned the shares or interests for at least 12 months (Subdiv 118-G: ss 118-500 to 118-525).

A capital gain or loss is disregarded if it is made from a CGT event happening to "venture capital equity" that was acquired by a "venture capital entity" and that, at the time of the CGT event, was owned by that entity and had been owned by that entity for at least 12 months (s 118-505).

An entity is a "venture capital entity" if:

- it is a foreign resident
- it is a foreign superannuation fund (as defined in s 118-520)
- it is not a prescribed dual resident (¶21-040)
- it is a resident of Canada, France, Germany, Japan, the United Kingdom, the United States or some other foreign country prescribed by the regulations, and
- its income is exempt, or effectively exempt, from taxation in its country of residence (s 118-515(1)).

A partner in a partnership of venture capital entities is eligible for the exemption if the venture capital equity in a resident investment vehicle is provided through the partnership. In the case of a limited partnership, the concession is available to the partners if: (i) all the partners, other than the general partner or managing partner, are venture capital entities; and (ii) the general or managing partner's interest in the partnership is less than 10% of the value of the total assets of the partnership (s 118-515(2)).

A CGT asset is ‘‘venture capital equity’’ if it is a share in a company or an interest in a trust where:

- the company or trust is a ‘‘resident investment vehicle’’, ie an Australian resident which does not have total assets exceeding $50 million at the time of the new investment (including the new investment) and does not at any time have property development or ownership in land as its primary activity (s 118-510)
- the share or interest was issued or allotted to the entity by the company or trust, and
- the entity was at risk in owning the share or interest (s 118-525(1)).

However, a share or interest is not venture capital equity if it is connected to the issue or allotment of a share or interest in a resident investment vehicle to a venture capital entity and:

- a share or interest in that resident investment vehicle that was acquired by another entity before the issue or allotment is cancelled or redeemed
- there is a return of capital in that vehicle that was acquired before the issue or allotment, or
- value is shifted out of a share or interest in that vehicle acquired before that issue or allotment (s 118-525(2)).

[FITR ¶155-150 – ¶155-230]

¶11-910 CGT: exemption for start-up investments

A CGT exemption applies for investments made, whether directly or indirectly, in a start-up known as an Early Stage Innovation Company (‘‘ESIC’’).

ESIC

Generally, a company qualifies as an ESIC if it is at an early stage of its development and it is developing new or significantly improved innovations with the purpose of commercialisation to generate an economic return.

The following tests must be satisfied to be an ESIC:

1. At the time of the investment the company was:
   a. incorporated in Australia within the last 3 income years
   b. incorporated in Australia within the last 6 income years and across the last 3 of those income years it and its 100% subsidiaries (if any) incurred total expenses of $1 million or less, or
   c. registered with the Australian Business Register within the last 3 income years
2. the company and its subsidiaries (if any) incurred expenses of $1 million or less in the immediately preceding income year
3. the company and its subsidiaries (if any) derived no more than $200,000 assessable income in the immediately preceding income year
4. none of the company’s equity interests are listed on any stock exchange, and
5. the company is undertaking an ‘‘eligible business’’ (s 360-40(1)).

An eligible business will be a business that has at least 100 points under the test in s 360-45, or is a company genuinely focused on developing its new or significantly improved innovation (in the form of products, processes, services or marketing or organisational methods) for the purpose of commercialisation and shows that the business relating to that innovation:

- has the potential for high growth
- has scalability
- can address a broader than local market, and
- has competitive advantages (s 360-40(1)(e)).

CGT Concessions

An entity that is issued a share in an ESIC and is entitled to the tax offset under Subdiv 360 (¶20-700), whether received or not, will be taken to hold the shares on capital account and be subject to the CGT provisions (s 360-50(1), (2)).

The CGT provisions in relation to such shares acquired from issue in an ESIC are:

- any capital gain made in relation to a share held for a continuous period of less than 12 months will be subject to CGT under the ordinary rules
- any capital gain made in relation to a share held for a continuous period of at least 12 months but less than 10 years may be disregarded
- any capital loss made in relation to a share held for a continuous period of less than 10 years is disregarded
- where the entity has held the share continuously for 10 years, the first element of the cost base, or reduced cost base, will be the market value of the share on the 10th anniversary of issue in order to preserve the tax-free status of any unrealised capital gain to that date (s 360-50).

Special provisions apply to ensure a partner in a partnership is treated as an entity for these purposes (s 360-55). CGT event E4 will not arise where a trust receives a tax-free capital gain under these concessions (¶11-290).

To the extent that a share in an ESIC is the subject of a same asset roll-over or a replacement asset roll-over (excluding the scrip for scrip roll-over in Subdiv 124-M or the newly incorporated company roll-over in Div 122), the acquiring entity is treated as acquiring the shares as at the date of the original investor (ss 360-60; 360-65).

Integrity measures ensure any scheme or arrangement to obtain CGT concessions under these provisions is within Pt IVA.

[FITR ¶336-000 – ¶336-065]

¶11-915 CGT: proposed exemption for granny flat arrangements

A targeted CGT exemption is proposed for granny flat arrangements where there is a formal written agreement. The CGT exemption will be available for the creation, variation or termination of a granny flat arrangement where there is a formal written agreement in place. The exemption will apply to arrangements with older Australians or those with a disability. The CGT exemption will only apply to agreements that are entered into because of ‘‘family relationships or other personal ties’’ and will not apply to commercial rental arrangements.

The measure will have effect from the first income year after the date of assent, expected to be from 1 July 2021 (2020–21 Budget Paper No 2, p 23).

Record-keeping for CGT Purposes

¶11-920 What CGT records must be kept?

Taxpayers must keep records of matters that affect the capital gains and losses that they make. More specifically, taxpayers must keep records of every act, transaction, event or circumstance that can reasonably be expected to be relevant to working out whether they have made a capital gain or loss from a CGT event (s 121-20). For examples of the types of records that must be kept, see the tax records checklist at ¶44-100.

Records do not have to be kept if the capital gain or loss that might be made in relation to a CGT asset or a CGT event is to be disregarded (s 121-30). However, records must still be kept if such a capital gain or loss would only be disregarded because of a roll-over.

If a taxpayer was retaining records under the former CGT provisions, they must continue to be retained in accordance with those rules.

The records must be in English, or be readily accessible and convertible into English. They must show the nature of the act, transaction, event or circumstance, the day when it happened or arose and, in the case of an act, who did it, and in the case of a transaction, who were the parties to it. The records must also show details (including relevant amounts) of how the act, transaction, event or circumstance is relevant (or can reasonably be expected to be relevant) to working out whether a capital gain or loss has been made from a CGT event. If the necessary records do not already exist, they must be reconstructed.

CGT records must be retained for 5 years after it becomes certain that no CGT event can happen for which those records could reasonably be expected to be relevant in working out a capital gain or loss (s 121-25). However, records do not have to be retained for the required 5-year period if the Commissioner decides it is not necessary or if a company has finally ceased to exist. The maximum penalty for failing to keep CGT records as required is 30 penalty units ($3,300).

A taxpayer who has made a net capital loss should retain relevant records until the end of the statutory retention period under s 121-25 or the end of the statutory period of review (¶25-300) for the income year in which the loss is fully deducted, whichever is later (TD 2007/2).

Asset registers

As an alternative to keeping full records for CGT purposes, taxpayers can instead choose to transfer some or all of those records to an asset register (s 121-35). An entry made on an asset register is only valid if it is certified by a registered tax agent or other approved person. The register entry must be in English and contain the same information as the relevant document. For the Commissioner's views about how asset registers work, see TR 2002/10.

The taxpayer is required to retain the document(s) to which an asset register entry relates for 5 years after the date on which the entry is certified. An asset register entry must itself be retained for 5 years after the occurrence of a CGT event for which the entry is relevant.

[FITR ¶155-300 – ¶155-320]

Chapter 12 Capital Gains Tax • Special Topics

Introduction

¶12-000 Overview of the special CGT topics

This chapter deals with *special CGT rules* under ITAA97 Pt 3-3 that may apply in relation to the calculation of capital gains and losses. *General CGT rules* under Pt 3-1, together with special rules that apply for companies only, are discussed in ¶11-000ff. The CGT concessions for small business are outlined below (¶12-005), with detailed coverage at ¶7-001ff. Section references in this chapter are to ITAA97 unless otherwise indicated. The topics covered are outlined below.

Roll-overs

The effect of a roll-over is that any capital gain or loss made because a CGT event happens to a CGT asset is disregarded. However, a capital gain or loss may later arise when a CGT event happens to the same asset or a replacement asset in respect of which the roll-over is made.

Effect of death

Special CGT rules apply when a taxpayer dies and an asset owned by the taxpayer just before death passes to the taxpayer's deceased estate or to a beneficiary of that estate. There are other special CGT rules about what happens when a joint tenant dies.

Investments

There are special CGT rules which apply in relation to bonus shares and units, rights, convertible notes, exchangeable interests and shares acquired under an employee share scheme. Most of these rules are about modifying the cost base and reduced cost base of an asset.

Leases

Leases are subject to special CGT rules. Most of these rules are about modifying the cost base and reduced cost base of an asset. Other rules look at the timing of when land is acquired by a lessee in particular situations.

Options

Special CGT rules apply in relation to options. These rules explain what happens to the cost base and reduced cost base of an option when it is exercised. The rules are relevant for both the taxpayer that granted the option and the taxpayer that exercised it.

Foreign residents

A foreign resident makes a capital gain or loss only if a CGT event happens to an asset of the taxpayer that is taxable Australian property. Other CGT rules explain the CGT consequences for a foreign resident who becomes a resident.

Value shifting

Where value is shifted between interests, generally to take advantage of the difference between the tax value and the market value of the interests, there are rules designed to prevent related entities from obtaining a tax advantage from the value shift. The rules are contained in the general value shifting regime. The regime applies to arrangements and dealings involving entities that are not part of the same consolidated group, but are related in some other way.

Change in majority underlying interests in pre-CGT asset

Where there is a change in the majority underlying interests in a pre-CGT asset, the asset is taken to have been acquired for CGT purposes at the time of the change. The first element of the cost base and reduced cost base of the post-CGT asset is the market value of the asset at that time.

Special rules apply to determine whether there has been a change in the majority underlying interests in an asset of a public entity.

¶12-005 CGT concessions for small business

There are 4 CGT concessions for CGT small business entities available under Div 152. For details of the CGT concessions see ¶7-110 onwards. There is also a CGT small business restructure roll-over available for small business entities undertaking a change in legal structure without a change of beneficial ownership (¶12-380).

[FITR ¶171-500 – ¶171-955]

Roll-overs Generally

¶12-035 Types and effect of CGT roll-over of asset

The effect of a roll-over is that any capital gain or loss made because a CGT event happens to a CGT asset is disregarded. However, a capital gain or loss may later arise when a CGT event happens to the same asset or a replacement asset in respect of which the roll-over is made.

When a roll-over happens, the asset held by a taxpayer after the roll-over carries the same CGT characteristics as the asset held before the roll-over. In other words, when a pre-CGT asset is rolled over, the asset held after the roll-over remains a pre-CGT asset. When a post-CGT asset is rolled over, the asset held after the roll-over carries the same cost base or reduced cost base as the asset held before the roll-over.

Generally, a taxpayer must choose for a roll-over to happen. However, in some cases, roll-overs are compulsory.

There are 2 types of roll-overs, being replacement-asset roll-overs (¶12-150) and same-asset roll-overs (¶12-450).

The Board of Taxation is exploring opportunities to rationalise the existing CGT rollovers and associated provisions into a simplified set that have a substantially similar practical effect but are easier to use and interpret. It is considering 2 categories of rollovers, firstly where there is no underlying change in the economic ownership after the CGT event, and secondly, for involuntary disposals.

The Board of Taxation has also issued a report recommending the introduction of an optional asset merger roll-over relief that would defer the tax liability arising from the disposal of a company's interests in assets in a merger with interests in assets of another company, and for asset for scrip mergers between companies. The government is yet to formally respond to this recommendation.

[FITR ¶153-665 – ¶153-725]

Roll-over to Company by Individual or Trustee

¶12-040 When CGT roll-over is available

Disposal or creation of assets in a wholly-owned company

A taxpayer who is an individual or a trustee may be able to choose to obtain a roll-over if a *trigger event* happens to a CGT asset of the taxpayer (s 122-15). The trigger event must involve the taxpayer disposing of an asset to a company or creating an asset in it. Balancing adjustment relief is also available for depreciation purposes (¶17-710).

The most common trigger event is CGT event A1 which happens when an asset is disposed of. CGT events D1, D2, D3 and F1 are also trigger events.

Consideration for trigger event

For the roll-over to be available, the only consideration the taxpayer can receive as a result of the trigger event is non-redeemable shares in the transferee company (s 122-20). However, if there is a disposal of an asset or of all the assets of a business, the consideration may be non-redeemable shares in the company *and* the company assuming one or more liabilities in respect of the asset or assets of the business.

The market value of the shares the taxpayer receives as a result of the disposal must be substantially the same as the market value of the asset or assets disposed of, reduced by any liabilities assumed by the company in respect of the asset or assets. Any contingent liability inherent in a transferred asset (eg a contingent tax liability for an unrealised capital gain) is ignored in comparing the market values of the asset or assets disposed of and the shares received, as those contingent liabilities will be reflected in the market value of the shares (s 122-20(4)).

Where an asset is created in the company, the market value of the shares the taxpayer receives must be substantially the same as the market value of the newly-created asset.

Taxpayer must own shares after trigger event

For the roll-over to be available, the taxpayer must also own all the shares in the company just after the time of the trigger event (s 122-25). These shares must be owned immediately after the trigger event in the same capacity as the taxpayer owned or created the assets that the company now owns.

Residency requirements for obtaining roll-over

If both the transferor individual or trustee and the transferee company are residents at the time of the trigger event, the roll-over is available for any CGT asset. Otherwise both of the following requirements must be satisfied (s 122-25):

- each asset must be taxable Australian property (¶12-725) at that time
- the shares in the transferee company must be taxable Australian property just after that time.

Assets for which roll-over not available

The roll-over is not available for collectables, personal use assets, a decoration awarded for valour or brave conduct (unless the taxpayer paid money or gave other property for it), precluded assets or an asset that becomes either trading stock of the company or a registered emissions unit held by the company just after the trigger event (s 122-25).

However, where the taxpayer disposes of all the assets of a business to the company, an asset that becomes either trading stock of the company or a registered emissions unit held just after the trigger event can be rolled over if it was the taxpayer's trading stock or registered emissions unit when the taxpayer disposed of it to the company. Similarly, precluded assets can be rolled over where they are included in the disposal of all of the assets of a business to the company. A *precluded asset* is a depreciating asset, trading stock, an interest in the copyright of a CGT-exempt film or a registered emissions unit (s 122-25(3)).

Income of company cannot be exempt

For the roll-over to be available, the ordinary and statutory income of the company must not be tax-exempt for the income year of the trigger event (s 122-25).

Where company assumes liability in respect of asset

Where a taxpayer disposes of an asset and the company assumes one or more liabilities in respect of it, the roll-over is only available if the amount of the liabilities that the company assumes is limited (s 122-35). For a post-CGT asset, the assumed liabilities cannot be more than the asset's cost base at the time of the disposal. For a pre-CGT asset, the assumed liabilities cannot be more than the market value of the asset at the time of the disposal.

Where a taxpayer disposes of all the assets of a business and the company assumes one or more liabilities in respect of those assets, the roll-over is similarly only available if the amount of the liabilities that the company assumes is limited. If all the assets are post-CGT assets, the assumed liabilities cannot be more than the sum of the market values of the precluded assets (see above) and the cost bases of the other assets at the time of the disposal. If all the assets are pre-CGT assets, the assumed liabilities cannot be more than the sum of the market values of the assets at the time of the disposal.

Where the assets of the business are a mixture of post-CGT and pre-CGT assets, the liabilities assumed in respect of post-CGT assets cannot be more than the sum of the market values of the precluded assets and the cost bases of the other post-CGT assets. Likewise, the liabilities assumed in respect of pre-CGT assets cannot be more than the sum of the market values of those assets.

Liability in respect of an asset

A liability incurred for the purposes of a business that is not a liability in respect of a specific asset or assets of the business is taken to be a liability in respect of all the assets of the business, eg a bank overdraft (s 122-37). If a liability is in respect of 2 or more assets, including a liability in respect of all the assets of a business, the proportion of the liability that is in respect of any one of those assets is:

$$\frac{\text{the market value of the asset}}{\text{the total of the market values of all the assets that the liability is in respect of}}$$

[FITR ¶160-006 – ¶160-014]

¶12-050 CGT roll-over for an individual or trustee disposing of an asset

If a taxpayer chooses (¶11-190) to take advantage of roll-over relief in relation to the disposal of an asset to a wholly-owned company, a capital gain or loss the taxpayer makes from the disposal is disregarded (s 122-40). The roll-over is a replacement-asset roll-over because the taxpayer replaces the asset disposed of with shares in the company.

If a post-CGT asset is rolled over, the first element of the cost base of each share in the company is the asset's cost base when the taxpayer disposed of it (less any liabilities the company assumes in respect of it), divided by the number of shares. The first element of each share's reduced cost base is worked out in a similar way.

If a pre-CGT asset is rolled over, the shares in the company are also taken to be pre-CGT assets.

[FITR ¶160-016]

¶12-060 CGT roll-over for an individual or trustee disposing of all assets of a business

If a taxpayer chooses to take advantage of roll-over relief in relation to the disposal of all the assets of a business to a wholly-owned company, a capital gain or loss the taxpayer makes from the disposal of each of the assets is disregarded (s 122-45). The roll-over is a replacement-asset roll-over because the taxpayer replaces the assets disposed of with shares in the company.

Cost base and reduced cost base if all assets post-CGT

If all the assets of the business that are being rolled over are post-CGT assets, the first element of each share's cost base is the sum of the market values of the precluded assets at the time of the disposal and the cost bases of the other assets (less any liabilities the company assumes in respect of all those assets) at that time, divided by the number of shares (s 122-50). The first element of each share's reduced cost base is worked out in a similar way.

▶ Example 1

Lucie is a small trader. She wants to incorporate her business. She disposes of all its assets to a company and receives 10,000 shares in return. All the assets of the business are post-CGT.

The market value of the items of trading stock (a precluded asset: ¶12-040) when Lucie disposes of them is $15,000. The cost bases of the other assets when she disposes of them are: pre-1 July 2001 plant and equipment ($57,000) and buildings ($130,000). Lucie also has a business overdraft of $18,000. It is taken to be a liability in respect of all the assets of her business.

The first element of the cost base of the 10,000 shares is $184,000 (ie $15,000 + $57,000 + $130,000 – $18,000). As a result, the cost base of each share is $18.40 (ie $184,000/10,000).

Cost base and reduced cost base if all assets pre-CGT

If all the assets of the business that are being rolled over are pre-CGT assets, the shares in the company are also usually taken to be pre-CGT assets (s 122-55).

However, if at least one of the assets is a precluded asset (¶12-040), not all of the shares are taken to be pre-CGT assets. The number of shares that are taken to be pre-CGT assets is the greatest possible number that (when expressed as a percentage of all the shares) is not more than:

- the total of the market values (at the time of the disposal) of the assets that are not precluded assets, reduced by any liabilities the company assumes in respect of those assets,

expressed as a percentage of:

- the total of the market values of all the assets at the time of the disposal, reduced by any liabilities the company assumes in respect of those assets.

The remaining shares that are not pre-CGT assets are taken to be post-CGT assets.

The first element of the cost base and reduced cost base of each share that is taken to be a post-CGT share is the total of the market values of the precluded assets at the time of the disposal (less any liabilities the company assumes in respect of those assets), divided by the number of those post-CGT shares.

▶ Example 2

Assume the same facts as in Example 1, except that all the assets are instead pre-CGT assets. In addition, the market values of the assets of the business (other than trading stock) at the time of the disposal are plant and equipment ($39,000) and buildings ($170,000).

The number of pre-CGT shares is worked out as:

$$10{,}000 \times \left(\frac{\$39{,}000 + \$170{,}000 - \$16{,}795^{*}}{\$15{,}000 + \$39{,}000 + \$170{,}000 - \$18{,}000} \right)$$

= 9,330 shares (rounded)

* The assumed liability of $18,000 is apportioned as follows:

$$\$18{,}000 \times \left(\frac{\$39{,}000 + \$170{,}000}{\$39{,}000 + \$170{,}000 + \$15{,}000} \right)$$

= $16,795 (rounded)

The first element of the cost base of the other 670 post-CGT shares is $13,795 (ie $15,000 – $1,205**). As a result, the cost base of each post-CGT share is $20.59 (ie $13,795/670).

** The amount of $1,205 is the assumed liability of $18,000 reduced by the $16,795 attributable to non-precluded assets (see above).

Cost base and reduced cost base if a mix of pre-CGT and post-CGT assets

If the business assets that are being rolled over are a mix of pre-CGT and post-CGT assets, only some of the shares in the company are taken to be pre-CGT assets (s 122-60).

The number of shares that are taken to be pre-CGT assets is the greatest possible number that (when expressed as a percentage of all the shares) is not more than:

- the total of the market values (at the time of the disposal) of the pre-CGT assets that are not precluded assets, reduced by any liabilities the company assumes in respect of those assets, expressed as a percentage of:

- the total of the market values of all the assets at the time of the disposal, reduced by any liabilities the company assumes in respect of those assets.

The remaining shares that are not pre-CGT assets are taken to be post-CGT assets.

The first element of the cost base (or reduced cost base) of each share that is taken to be a post-CGT share is the sum of the market values of the precluded assets and the cost bases (or reduced cost bases) of any other post-CGT assets at the time of the disposal (less any liabilities the company assumes in respect of those assets), divided by the number of those post-CGT shares.

[FITR ¶160-018]

¶12-070 Consequences of company acquiring disposed of asset under CGT roll-over

If a taxpayer chooses to take advantage of roll-over relief in relation to the disposal of assets to a wholly-owned company, there are CGT consequences for the company acquiring those assets (s 122-70). Those consequences are relevant for each asset, other than a precluded asset (¶12-040), that is rolled over to the company. A capital gain or loss from a precluded asset is disregarded. The roll-over is a same-asset roll-over (s 112-150).

If a post-CGT asset is rolled over, the first element of the asset's cost base in the hands of the company is its cost base when the taxpayer disposed of it. Similarly, the first element of the asset's reduced cost base in the hands of the company is its reduced cost base when the taxpayer disposed of it.

If a pre-CGT asset is rolled over, it is also taken to be a pre-CGT asset in the hands of the company. The cost base of such a pre-CGT asset acquired by the company is taken to be the market value of the shares issued as consideration for the acquisition determined as at the date of the roll-over (*Financial Synergy Holdings*; ATO Decision Impact Statement).

[FITR ¶160-022]

¶12-080 CGT roll-over where an individual or trustee creates asset in company

Consequences for taxpayer

If a taxpayer chooses to take advantage of roll-over relief in relation to the creation of an asset in a wholly-owned company, a capital gain or loss the taxpayer makes from the trigger event is disregarded (s 122-65). The roll-over is a replacement-asset roll-over (s 112-115). The shares acquired pursuant to the roll-over are post-CGT assets.

The first element of the cost base and reduced cost base of each share in the company is:

- if the asset is created as a result of CGT event D1, the incidental costs incurred by the taxpayer in relation to that event
- if the asset is created as a result of CGT event D2, the expenditure incurred by the taxpayer in granting the option
- if the asset is created as a result of CGT event D3, the expenditure incurred by the taxpayer in granting the right, or
- if the asset is created as a result of CGT event F1, the expenditure incurred by the taxpayer on the grant, renewal or extension of the lease,

divided by the number of shares.

▶ Example 1

Greg grants a licence (CGT event D1) to Bostonco (a company wholly-owned by him). The company issues him with 100 additional shares. He incurs legal expenses of $1,500 in granting the licence. Greg's cost base or reduced cost base for those 100 shares is $15 each.

Consequences for company

If a taxpayer chooses to take advantage of roll-over relief in relation to the creation of an asset in a wholly-owned company, there are CGT consequences for the company acquiring the asset (s 122-75). The roll-over is a same-asset roll-over (s 112-150).

The first element of the asset's cost base and reduced cost base in the hands of the company is the same as the cost base or reduced cost base of all the shares in the company issued to the taxpayer in relation to the created asset (see above), eg if the asset is created as a result of CGT event D2, the cost base of the option is the expenditure incurred by the taxpayer in granting the option.

▶ Example 2

Continuing the above example, the cost base or reduced cost base of the licence in Bostonco's hands is $1,500.

[FITR ¶160-020 – ¶160-022]

¶12-090 CGT roll-over to company by partners

Disposal or creation of assets in a wholly-owned company

The partners in a partnership may be able to choose to obtain a roll-over if a *trigger event* happens to a CGT asset of the partners (s 122-125). The trigger event must involve each partner disposing of his/her interest in an asset of the partnership to a company or creating an asset in that company.

The roll-over is only available if *all* the partners choose to obtain roll-over relief.

The most common trigger event is CGT event A1, which happens when an asset is disposed of. CGT events D1, D2, D3 and F1 are also trigger events.

A partnership for these purposes includes a tax law partnership (¶5-000), ie the roll-over may apply to joint owners of income-producing property.

Consideration for trigger event

For the roll-over to be available, the only consideration the partners can receive as a result of the trigger event is non-redeemable shares in the transferee company (s 122-130). However, if there is a disposal of their interests in an asset or in all the assets of a business, the consideration may be non-redeemable shares in the company *and* the company assuming one or more liabilities in respect of their interests.

The market value of the shares each partner receives as a result of the disposal must be substantially the same as the market value of the interests in the asset or assets the partner disposed of, reduced by any liabilities assumed by the company in respect of the interests in the asset or assets. Where an asset is created in the company, the market value of the shares each partner receives must be substantially the same as the market value of what would have been the partner's interest in the newly-created asset if it were an asset of the partnership.

In working out the market value of shares in the case of a disposal, if the market value of the shares is different to what it would otherwise be only because of the possibility of liabilities attaching to the asset or assets, that difference is ignored. For example, the company may have to pay tax if an amount is assessable to it because of a CGT event happening to an asset the taxpayer disposed of, or it may have a liability because of accrued leave entitlements of employees. In such situations, the market value of the shares should reflect those contingent liabilities.

Partners must own all the company's shares after trigger event

For the roll-over to be available, the partners must also own all the shares in the company just after the time of the trigger event (s 122-135). These shares must be owned by the partners immediately after the trigger event in the same capacity as they owned their interests in the assets of the partnership or participated in the creation of the asset in the company. This is satisfied even where the disposal contract provides the shares are not issued until completion (ID 2010/114).

Other conditions and consequences

The remaining conditions and consequences relating to the roll-over of assets from a partnership to a company are similar to those for individuals making a roll-over to a company (¶12-040). In particular, there are similar requirements in relation to: (a) residency; (b) assets for which the roll-over is not available; (c) exempt companies; and (d) the assumption of liabilities in respect of assets rolled over (ss 122-135 to 122-145).

In addition, similar rules apply as for individuals, depending on whether only particular assets are rolled over to the company or whether all the assets of a business are rolled over (ss 122-150 to 122-195; ¶12-050, ¶12-060).

The consequences for the company acquiring the disposed of assets from the partners or the assets created in the company by the partners are also similar to those where an individual disposes of the assets to, or creates the assets in, the company (ss 122-200; 122-205; ¶11-080, ¶12-070).

[FITR ¶160-030 – ¶160-046]

Replacement-asset Roll-overs

¶12-150 When replacement-asset CGT roll-over available

A replacement-asset roll-over allows taxpayers to defer the making of a capital gain or loss from one CGT event until a later CGT event happens. It involves a CGT event happening in relation to an asset which the taxpayer no longer owns after the roll-over. Instead, the taxpayer owns a different asset (ie the replacement asset) after the roll-over. Any capital gain or loss arising from the CGT event which gave rise to the roll-over is deferred until a later time when a CGT event happens to the replacement asset. The CGT characteristics of the original asset are transferred to the replacement asset. Any CGT liability remains with the taxpayer, even though that liability arises in relation to a different asset.

To find out if there is a replacement-asset roll-over in the event of a taxpayer's ownership of one or more CGT assets ending, taxpayers need to consider if an appropriate replacement asset is acquired. The replacement asset roll-overs are listed in s 112-115.

Taxpayers then need to consider both the general consequences of making a replacement-asset roll-over and any special rules relevant to the particular roll-over. Finally, if a taxpayer is satisfied that an optional roll-over is desirable in relation to a particular CGT event, the taxpayer can choose for the roll-over to happen, provided all the necessary conditions are met. If a compulsory roll-over is undesirable, a taxpayer may consider structuring its affairs to stop the conditions for the roll-over being met.

[FITR ¶161-000]

¶12-160 General rules for replacement-asset CGT roll-overs

Where ownership of one asset ends

If a taxpayer chooses for a replacement-asset roll-over to happen in relation to an asset, any capital gain or loss the taxpayer makes from the original asset is disregarded (s 124-10). However, a car, motor cycle or similar vehicle cannot be a replacement asset.

Post-CGT assets

If the original asset is a post-CGT asset, the first element of each replacement asset's cost base (or reduced cost base) is:

$$\frac{\text{the original asset's cost base (or reduced cost base)}}{\text{number of replacement assets}}$$

For this purpose, the cost base and reduced cost base of the original asset are worked out when the taxpayer's ownership of it ends.

▶ Example 1

Eric's commercial fishing licence expires and a new one is obtained. The cost base of the expired licence is $4,000. This becomes the first element of the cost base for the replacement licence.

In some cases, if a taxpayer also pays an amount to acquire the replacement asset, that amount also forms part of the first element.

Pre-CGT assets

If the original asset is a pre-CGT asset, the replacement asset is also taken to be a pre-CGT asset.

Where ownership of 2 or more assets ends

If a taxpayer chooses for a replacement-asset roll-over to happen in relation to 2 or more assets at the same time, any capital gain or loss the taxpayer makes from each original asset is disregarded (s 124-15). However, a car, motor cycle or similar vehicle cannot be a replacement asset.

Post-CGT assets

If each original asset is a post-CGT asset, the first element of each replacement asset's cost base (or reduced cost base) is:

$$\frac{\text{the total of the cost bases (or reduced cost bases) of all the original assets}}{\text{number of replacement assets}}$$

For this purpose, the cost base and reduced cost base of the original asset are worked out when the taxpayer's ownership of it ended.

Pre-CGT assets

If each original asset is a pre-CGT asset, each replacement asset is also taken to be a pre-CGT asset.

Mix of pre-CGT and post-CGT assets

If the original assets are a mix of pre-CGT and post-CGT assets, a number of replacement assets are also taken to be pre-CGT assets. That number is the maximum possible that does not exceed:

$$\text{number of replacement assets} \times \frac{\text{number of original pre-CGT assets}}{\text{total number of original assets}}$$

If the result is less than one, none of the replacement assets are taken to be pre-CGT assets. The replacement assets that are not taken to be pre-CGT assets are taken to be post-CGT assets.

▶ Example 2

Geraldine owns 100 shares in a company. The company cancels these shares and issues Geraldine with 10 shares in return. If 48 of Geraldine's 100 original shares are pre-CGT assets, the number of replacement shares that are taken to be pre-CGT is 4 (ie 10 × (48/100) rounded down).

The first element of the cost base of the post-CGT assets is:

$$\frac{\text{total of cost bases (or reduced cost bases) of all the post-CGT original assets}}{\text{number of post-CGT replacement assets}}$$

▶ Example 3

Continuing Example 2, if the total of the cost bases of Geraldine's 52 post-CGT shares is $300, the first element of the cost base of each of her 6 post-CGT replacement shares is $50 (ie $300/6).

Share and interest sale facilities

Subject to certain conditions, a foreign taxpayer's ability to apply the following replacement roll-overs is preserved where a share sale facility is used under a restructure:

- Change of incorporation — Subdiv 124-I (¶12-390)
- Disposal of assets by a trust to a company — Subdiv 124-N (¶12-395)
- Exchange of stapled ownership interests for ownership interests in a unit trust — Subdiv 124-Q (¶12-440)
- Exchange of shares in a company or units in a unit trust for shares in another company pursuant to the business restructure roll-over — Div 615 (¶12-370).

This is achieved by treating the foreign interest holder as owning the roll-over interest, rather than the share sale facility which actually owns the interest (s 124-20).

[FITR ¶161-000 – ¶161-022]

Involuntary Disposal of Asset

¶12-260 CGT roll-over for asset compulsorily acquired, lost or destroyed

A replacement-asset roll-over may be available to a taxpayer if an involuntary disposal happens to an asset owned by the taxpayer because (s 124-70):

- it is compulsorily acquired by an Australian government agency
- it is compulsorily acquired by a private acquirer under a statutory power of compulsory acquisition other than a compulsory acquisition of minority interest under company law
- the asset, or part of it, is lost or destroyed
- the taxpayer disposes of the asset to an entity (other than a foreign government agency) after a notice was served by or on behalf of the entity inviting negotiations with a view to the entity acquiring the asset by agreement where, if those negotiations were unsuccessful, the asset would be compulsorily acquired by the entity under a statutory power (as above)
- the taxpayer disposes of land (and any depreciating asset fixed to the land) to an entity, other than a foreign government agency, where a mining lease was compulsorily granted over the land and the lease significantly affected the taxpayer's use of the land, or
- the taxpayer disposes of land (and any depreciating asset fixed to the land) to an entity, other than a foreign government agency, where a mining lease would have been compulsorily granted if the taxpayer had not disposed of the land and the lease would have significantly affected the taxpayer's use of the land.

A roll-over was not available where an easement was created over a landowner's property as the easement was considered to be a new asset (ID 2010/34). The main residence exemption will apply where there is a compulsory acquisition of a part of a taxpayer's main residence (¶11-740).

For the roll-over to be available, the entity acquiring the asset must be the Commonwealth, a state, a territory or an authority thereof and not merely an entity which is given authority under a Commonwealth, state or territory Act to acquire the asset. The roll-over does not apply if the entity acquiring the asset is merely authorised to do so by a Commonwealth, state or territory authority (TD 2000/36).

An asset acquired by a taxpayer before an Australian government agency has given formal notice of an intention to compulsorily acquire the asset can be a replacement asset provided it is acquired no earlier than one year before (or such longer period as allowed by the Commissioner) the original asset is compulsorily acquired (TD 2000/37).

Where a taxpayer satisfies the conditions for applying both the replacement-asset roll-over in Subdiv 124-B and the small business roll-over pursuant to Subdiv 152-E, the taxpayer may choose which roll-over to apply (ID 2009/147).

Capital proceeds must be compensation or insurance proceeds

The roll-over is only available if the taxpayer receives money or another asset (except a car, motor cycle or similar vehicle), or both, as compensation for the CGT event happening or under an insurance policy against the risk of loss or destruction of the asset.

Asset must be taxable Australian property if taxpayer foreign resident

If the taxpayer is a foreign resident or is the trustee of a foreign trust, the roll-over is only available if the original asset is taxable Australian property (¶12-725) just before the CGT event happens and the replacement asset is taxable Australian property just after the taxpayer acquires it.

[FITR ¶161-030]

¶12-270 Conditions for CGT roll-over where money received from involuntary event

If a taxpayer receives money for the event happening (due to the compulsory acquisition, loss or destruction of an asset), the roll-over is only available if (s 124-75):

- the taxpayer incurs expenditure in acquiring another asset or, if part of the original asset is lost or destroyed, incurs expenditure of a capital nature in repairing or restoring it. For these purposes, ''incur'' has the same meaning as it has under the general deduction provision of s 8-1(1) (TD 2000/39), and
- *some* of that expenditure is incurred no earlier than one year before the CGT event happens and no later than one year after the end of the income year in which the CGT event happens. The Commissioner may extend these limits in special circumstances. What are special circumstances depends on the facts of each particular case (TD 2000/40).

Roll-over relief is not available on the loss or destruction of an asset if the asset is only damaged. However, a roll-over is available if the damage done to the asset is so extensive that the asset or a part of the asset can be considered lost or destroyed (TD 2000/38).

Where the taxpayer acquires another asset, the roll-over is only available if, just before the CGT event happened to the original asset, it was used in the taxpayer's business (or was installed ready for such use) and the new asset is used in the business (or installed ready for such use) for a reasonable time after the taxpayer acquires it. If the original asset was not so used in a business, the roll-over is only available if the new asset is used for a similar purpose to that for which the original asset was used just before the CGT event happened. Whether an asset is used for a similar purpose as another asset is a question of fact and degree to be determined in the particular circumstances of each case (TD 2000/42).

▶ **Example**

A rental house that has been treated as a separate asset is destroyed by fire. There is a replacement asset if the insurance proceeds are used: (a) to build a block of rental units on the same site; (b) to build a house for rental purposes on a different site; or (c) to acquire an existing house and land for rental purposes. However, if the insurance proceeds are used to acquire shares in a public company for income-producing purposes there is no replacement asset.

The new asset cannot be a depreciating asset whose decline in value is worked out under Div 40 (¶17-015). The roll-over is also not available if the new asset becomes trading stock of the taxpayer or a registered emissions unit just after it is acquired (s 124-75(5), (6)).

There is no restriction on the number of assets that may be treated as replacements for an original asset. An improvement to an existing asset is not a replacement asset unless it is taken to be a separate asset. However, it may still qualify for roll-over relief if it represents a restoration of the original asset.

If an asset is owned by the partners in a partnership, the replacement asset tests apply at the partner level and not at the level of the partnership. Each individual partner needs to satisfy the tests for his/her particular interest in each partnership asset to qualify for the roll-over (TD 2000/43).

[FITR ¶161-035]

¶12-280 Conditions for CGT roll-over where asset received from involuntary event

If the taxpayer receives a new asset for the event happening (due to the compulsory acquisition, loss or destruction of an asset), the roll-over is only available if (s 124-80):

- the market value of the new asset at the time of acquisition is more than the cost base (as indexed) of the original asset just before the CGT event happened, and
- the new asset is not a depreciating asset whose decline in value is worked out under Div 40 (¶17-015). In addition, the new asset cannot become trading stock of the taxpayer just after it is acquired.

[FITR ¶161-040]

¶12-290 Consequences of CGT roll-over where only money received from involuntary event

If a taxpayer only receives money for the event happening (due to the compulsory acquisition, loss or destruction of an asset) and chooses to take advantage of the roll-over, there are different consequences depending on whether the original asset is a pre-CGT or a post-CGT asset (s 124-85).

Original asset is a post-CGT asset

Where the original asset is a post-CGT asset, and both the money received from a CGT event is more than the expenditure incurred to acquire another asset (or to repair or restore the original asset) and the capital gain is greater than that excess, then: (a) the capital gain is reduced to the amount of the excess; and (b) the expenditure (for cost base purposes) is reduced by the amount by which the gain (before it is reduced) exceeds the excess. If the capital gain is not more than the amount of the excess, the capital gain is not reduced (TD 93/178).

On the other hand, if the money received from a CGT event is not more than the expenditure incurred to acquire another asset (or to repair or restore the original asset), any capital gain from the CGT event is disregarded and the expenditure (for cost base purposes) is reduced by the amount of the capital gain.

▶ Example

Last year, Inga bought a small factory. This year, a fire destroyed part of it and she received $80,000 under an insurance policy.

The factory's cost base at the time of the fire is $50,000 and the market value of the part that is not destroyed is $120,000. The cost base of the part that is destroyed is:

$$\$50,000 \times \frac{\$80,000}{\$80,000 + \$120,000}$$

$$= \$20,000$$

Accordingly, the capital gain is $60,000 (ie $80,000 – $20,000).

If Inga spends $65,000 on repairing the factory, the money she received under the insurance policy is more than the repair cost by $15,000. The capital gain exceeds that by $45,000. As a result, the capital gain is reduced to $15,000 and the $65,000 she spends on repairs is reduced to $20,000.

If Inga instead spends $10,000 on repairs, the money she received under the insurance policy is more than the repair cost by $70,000. This is greater than the capital gain she made. As a result, the capital gain is unaffected by the roll-over and the $10,000 she spends on repairs becomes part of the factory's cost base.

If Inga spends $100,000 on repairs, the capital gain is disregarded and the $100,000 is reduced to $40,000.

Where a taxpayer receives compensation for the compulsory acquisition of part of an asset, the compensation, to the extent to which it is attributable to the reduction in value of the remainder of the asset which was compulsorily acquired, forms part of the capital proceeds for the part of the asset compulsorily acquired (TD 2001/9).

Original asset is a pre-CGT asset

Where the original asset is a pre-CGT asset and the taxpayer buys another asset in its place, the new asset is taken to be a pre-CGT asset if the expenditure is not more than 120% of the market value (at the time of the CGT event) of the original asset. This 120% of market value test does not have to be satisfied if a natural disaster happens so that the original asset, or part of it, is lost or destroyed and it is reasonable to treat the other asset as substantially the same as the original asset. Natural disasters include such things as bushfires, cyclones, earthquakes, floods and storms.

Whether it is reasonable to treat an asset as substantially the same as another is an objective question and the answer depends on the facts of each particular case. Consideration needs to be given to such matters as the nature of the replacement asset, the use to which it is put, its location, size, value, quality and composition, compared with those attributes of the original asset (TD 2000/45).

Similarly, if the original asset is a pre-CGT asset and the taxpayer incurs expenditure of a capital nature in repairing or restoring it, the original asset (as repaired or restored) is also taken to be a pre-CGT asset.

[FITR ¶161-045]

¶12-300 Consequences of CGT roll-over where asset received from involuntary event

If the taxpayer *only* receives another asset (or assets) for the event happening (due to the compulsory acquisition, loss or destruction of an asset) and chooses to take advantage of the roll-over, a capital gain made from the original asset is disregarded (s 124-90). If the original asset is a post-CGT asset, the first element of the new asset's cost base (and reduced cost base) is the same as the original asset's cost base (and reduced cost base) at the time of the CGT event. On the other hand, if the original asset is a pre-CGT asset, the new asset is also taken to be a pre-CGT asset.

▶ **Example**

Roberto bought land for $180,000. The following year, the government compulsorily acquired it and gave him some different land in return. Any capital gain Roberto makes from the original land is disregarded. If the cost base of the original land when it is compulsorily acquired is $190,000, the first element of the new land's cost base is $190,000.

There is no restriction on the number of replacement assets (TD 94/77).

Consequences of roll-over where both money and asset received

If a taxpayer receives both money and at least one asset from a CGT event and chooses to take advantage of the roll-over, there are different consequences for each part of the compensation attributable to the original asset, having regard to the amount of money and the market value of the asset acquired (s 124-95). This requires a proportional attribution of the cost base of the original asset. Once apportioned, the rules that apply when only money is received (s 124-85) or when only an asset is received (s 124-90) can then be applied to the respective proportionate amounts. However, there is an additional condition requiring that, for the roll-over to be available in such situations, the market value of the new asset (at the time it is acquired) must be more than the part of the cost base of the original asset that is attributable to the new asset.

[FITR ¶161-050 – ¶161-055]

Other Replacement-asset Roll-overs

¶12-310 CGT roll-over for statutory licences

Automatic roll-over relief applies in certain circumstances where one or more statutory licences are issued in consequence of the ending of one or more licences (s 124-140).

The roll-over applies when a statutory licence ends, CGT event C2 happens (¶11-270), and one or more new licences which authorise activity that is substantially similar to that authorised by the original licence, are issued for the original licence. Where there are multiple licences, all of the original licences must end as part of a single arrangement and the new licence or licences must be issued as part of that arrangement.

What is a statutory licence?

A statutory licence is an authority, licence, permit or quota (other than a lease or a mining or prospecting entitlement) granted by an Australian or foreign government agency. Examples include radio and television broadcasting licences, marine radio licences, taxi licences, import and export quotas, fishing permits or quotas, oyster farming licences, milk quotas, wool quotas and liquor licences.

Consequences of roll-over

The consequences of the roll-over are that any capital gain or loss arising from the ending of the original licence is disregarded (s 124-145). The cost base rules vary according to whether the original licence was acquired before or on or after 20 September 1985, ie pre-CGT or post-CGT.

Where the original licence was post-CGT, its cost base becomes the first element of the cost base of the new post-CGT licence. Where more than one licence ends or more than one new licence is received, the cost base of each new licence must be determined on a reasonable basis, having regard to the number, market value and character of the original and new licences (s 124-155).

Where the original licence was pre-CGT, the new licence is also taken to be pre-CGT (s 124-160). Where some original licences were pre-CGT and others were post-CGT, each new licence is taken to be 2 separate assets, one pre-CGT and the other post-CGT. The cost base of each of those assets is determined by allocating the total of the cost bases of the original post-CGT licences between the new licences in proportion to their market values (s 124-165).

Partial roll-over

Where a taxpayer receives non-licence capital proceeds (eg cash) in addition to a new licence, a partial roll-over is available. In that case, the roll-over applies only to the extent of the receipt of the new licence; any capital gain or loss arising from non-licence capital proceeds cannot be rolled over (s 124-150).

[FITR ¶161-070 – ¶161-079]

¶12-320 CGT roll-over for strata title conversion

A taxpayer can choose to obtain a roll-over if (s 124-190):

- the taxpayer owns property that gives him/her a right to occupy a unit in a building
- the building's owner subdivides it into stratum units, and
- the owner transfers to the taxpayer the stratum unit that corresponds to the unit the taxpayer had the right to occupy just before the subdivision.

In such situations, the building's owner is also entitled to a CGT exemption in relation to the disposal of the stratum units (¶11-670).

A stratum unit is a lot or unit (however described in an Australian or foreign law relating to strata title or similar title) and any accompanying common property.

Consequences of roll-over

The consequences of the roll-over are those that generally apply for replacement-asset roll-overs (¶12-160). The first element of the cost base and reduced cost base of the stratum unit is worked out under those general rules. In addition, the first element of the cost base and reduced cost base of the new stratum unit includes any amount the taxpayer paid to get it.

TR 97/4 considers strata title conversion roll-overs in relation to home unit companies, long-term leases of 99 years or more and tenancies in common.

[FITR ¶161-080]

¶12-325 Scrip for scrip CGT roll-over

A taxpayer can choose to obtain ''scrip for scrip'' roll-over when interests held in one entity (''original entity'') are exchanged for replacement interests in another entity (''acquiring entity''), typically as a result of a takeover offer or merger (Subdiv 124-M: ss 124-775 to 124-810).

Scrip for scrip roll-over relief is available where all of the following are satisfied:

1. an entity exchanges an ''original interest'' in a company or trust for a ''replacement interest'' in the company or trust
2. the exchange is in consequence of a ''single arrangement''
3. a capital gain would have arisen but for the roll-over
4. the required choice and notifications are made to apply the roll-over
5. the special rules for non-arm's length transactions are satisfied
6. the arrangement is not excluded from roll-over relief
7. the acquiring entity does not breach the rules regarding new debt and equity.

The requirements to satisfy these conditions are outlined separately below. Note that TR 2005/19 examines certain tax avoidance schemes which seek to utilise the scrip for scrip roll-over to obtain the benefit of a capital gain without paying CGT.

Exchange of original interests for replacement interests

Roll-over relief is available for the exchange of post-CGT:

(a) shares in a company

(b) units, or other interests, in a trust in which entities have fixed entitlements to all the income and capital of the trust, or

(c) options, rights or similar interests to such interests in a company or trust, (referred to as the ''original interest''),

for an equivalent interest in another company or trust (referred to as the ''replacement interest'') (ss 124-780; 124-781).

For example, a taxpayer can exchange an option to acquire a share in A Co (the original company) for an option to acquire a share in X Co (the acquiring company), but cannot exchange an A Co option for an X Co share. Similarly, an interest in a company cannot be exchanged for an interest in a trust, or vice versa. However, the exchange of an interest (not being a unit) in a trust for a unit in a unit trust will constitute an equivalent interest (TD 2002/22).

Where the exchange relates to an original interest in a company, the replacement interest must be an equivalent interest in either the acquiring company, or where the acquiring company is a member of a wholly-owned group, the ultimate holding company of the wholly-owned group.

The rights which attach to a replacement interest do not have to be the same as those which attached to the original interest (unless the exchange is between non-arm's length parties: see below). For example, a taxpayer can choose roll-over relief where redeemable preference shares in one company, which constitute ''debt interests'' under the debt/equity rules (¶23-105), are exchanged for ordinary shares in another company (ID 2003/893).

A share in a company includes an interest in a limited partnership that is a corporate limited partnership pursuant to ITAA36 s 94D scrip for scrip (ID 2010/9).

Exchange in consequence of a single arrangement

There are separate requirements for the exchange of original interests in companies and trusts.

Where the exchange involves original interests in a company, the exchange must be in consequence of a single arrangement pursuant to which the acquiring company must become the owner of at least 80% of the voting shares in the original company (s 124-780(2)). If the acquiring company holds more than 80% of the shares in the original company before acquisition the arrangement must increase the acquiring entity's percentage ownership of the original company (TD 2000/50).

The exchange of an original interest must also be in consequence of an arrangement that satisfies one of the following:

- an arrangement in which all owners of voting shares in the original company (apart from the acquiring company) could participate on substantially the same terms. It is not necessary that the acquiring company have any shares in the original company before launching a takeover bid (TD 2000/51)
- an arrangement that is or includes a takeover bid within the meaning of the *Corporations Act 2001*, Ch 6 for the original interests by the acquiring entity that is not carried out in contravention of the provisions in s 612(a) to (g) of that Act (which generally regulates takeovers of companies and managed investment schemes that are either listed or have more than 50 members)
- an arrangement that is or includes a compromise or scheme of arrangement within the meaning of *Corporations Act 2001*, s 411 (s 124-780(2), (2A)).

In determining whether an exchange is made as a consequence of a single arrangement on substantially the same terms, the terms of the contract need to be considered. A shareholder's indifference as to the allocation of purchase price cannot be taken into consideration (*Fabig*).

Shares will be considered to be exchanged in consequence of a single arrangement where remaining interests are compulsorily acquired under the *Corporations Act 2001* on the expiry of a successful takeover offer and exchanged for interests in the acquiring entity (CR 2008/66).

In the case of a trust, the exchange must be in consequence of a single arrangement pursuant to which the acquiring trust obtains 80% of the original trust's voting interests or if there are none, 80% or more of the units or other interests in the original entity (s 124-781(2)).

The exchange of interests in a trust must also be an arrangement in which at least all of the owners of voting interests (or of units or other interests) in the original entity (apart from the acquiring entity) could participate on substantially the same terms (s 124-781(2)).

Anything received as part of the exchange which is additional to the replacement interest (eg cash) is treated as "ineligible proceeds" and does not qualify for roll-over (see "Partial roll-over" below).

Where capital gain would have arisen

Roll-over relief is only available if a capital gain would have arisen on the exchange of the original interest but for the roll-over (ss 124-780(3); 124-781(3)). Roll-over relief is not available where a capital loss would arise.

Additionally, roll-over relief is generally only available where the original interest is a post-CGT interest. However, where CGT event K6 would arise on the disposal of a pre-CGT original interest, the capital gain will be disregarded if the original interest holder could have chosen the roll-over for the gain if it had been a post-CGT interest (s 104-230(10)).

Choice and notification for roll-over

Roll-over relief will only be available where:

- if the original interest holder is a significant stakeholder or a common stakeholder for the arrangement:
  - the original interest holder and the replacement entity jointly choose to obtain roll-over relief, and
  - the original interest holder informs the replacement entity in writing of the cost base of its original interest worked out immediately before the CGT event happened
- in any other case — the original holder chooses to obtain roll-over relief (ss 124-780(3); 124-781(3)).

An original interest holder will be a significant stakeholder for an arrangement if, together with its associates, it has 30% or more of the voting rights, rights to dividends or rights to capital distributions in both the original entity before the exchange and the acquiring entity after the exchange. An original interest holder will be a common stakeholder if, together with other entities, it had at least 80% of the voting rights, rights to dividends or rights to capital distributions in both the original entity before the exchange, and the acquiring entity after the exchange (s 124-783).

The significant and common stakeholder tests take into account any entitlement to acquire "stake interests" (eg voting rights), including any entitlement arising under a right, option, share or other interest ("stake option"). This is achieved by treating any entitlement to acquire relevant interests as being realised (s 124-783A). This does not apply where an entitlement may diminish its holding (eg a put option) or the stake option cannot be realised within 5 years.

Special rules for non-arm's length exchanges

Additional conditions must be satisfied where the original interest holder and the acquiring entity did not deal with each other at arm's length and either of the following apply (ss 124-780(4), (5); 124-781(4)):

(1) The original entity or the acquiring entity had less than 300 members (for a company) or 300 beneficiaries (for a trust) immediately before the original interest was exchanged. A company will be treated as having less than 300 members if, broadly:

   (a) there is a 75% concentration of ownership of shares in the hands of up to 20 individuals. For these purposes, an individual, associates of the individual and nominees of the individual will be counted as one individual, or

   (b) the concentration of ownership referred to in (a) is, on an objective basis, capable of arising because of a range of possible eventualities including changes to rights attaching to any of the shares in the company, the conversion, cancellation, redemption or acquisition of those shares and the exercise by a person of any power or authority in relation to rights attaching to the shares.

   A similar set of tests applies in relation to the beneficiary threshold for a trust.

(2) The taxpayer, the original entity and the acquiring entity were all members of the same "linked group" immediately before the taxpayer exchanged the relevant interest. This will be the case when one of the entities has a controlling stake in each of the others or another entity has a controlling stake in each of them.

In these situations, roll-over will be available only where the following additional conditions are also satisfied:

- the market value of the capital proceeds for the exchange is at least substantially the same as the market value of the original interests
- the replacement interest carries the same rights and obligations as those attached to the original interests (eg see ID 2004/498).

A party is able to frame an offer in terms that it knows will attract the other party and still be considered to have dealt with each other at arm's length (*AXA Asia Pacific Holdings Ltd*).

Roll-over exclusions

Roll-over is not available where (s 124-795):

- just before the exchange, the taxpayer is a foreign resident unless the replacement interest is taxable Australian property (¶12-725)
- any capital gain that may arise from the replacement asset would not be subject to CGT (other than because of a roll-over). In this context, a roll-over includes any provision that has the effect of deferring tax recognition of a capital gain and providing for a cost base/reduced cost base transfer (TD 2006/9)
- just before the exchange, the taxpayer and the acquiring entity are members of the same wholly-owned group and the acquiring entity is a foreign resident (¶12-490)
- a roll-over from an individual, trustee or partnership to a company is available (¶12-040 – ¶12-090)
- an interposed entity roll-over is available, or
- the replacement entity chooses not to apply the roll-over and the taxpayer is notified in writing of this choice prior to the exchange.

Debt and equity restrictions

Where the acquiring entity is a member of a wholly-owned group, there is a requirement that no member of the group issues equity (other than a replacement interest), or owes new debt, under the arrangement:

- to an entity that is not a member of the group, and
- in relation to the issuing of the replacement interest (s 124-780(3)(f)).

The debt or equity will be "in relation to the issue of replacement interests" where it is new debt owed or equity issued, directly or indirectly, to compensate the issuer of the replacement interests for that issue.

This condition does not apply to:

- the issue of replacement interests themselves
- new debt owed or equity issued to an external financier or investor to fund the purchase of original interests under the arrangement, or
- new debt owed or equity (including equity other than replacement interests) issued to the original interest holders as consideration for their original interests.

Consequences of roll-over

Where the roll-over applies, the capital gain arising to the taxpayer from the exchange of the original interest is disregarded (s 124-785). The first element of the cost base of the replacement interest is calculated on the basis of a reasonable apportionment of the cost base of the original interest. The reduced cost base is worked out on a similar basis.

▶ Example 1

Ian owns 5,000 shares in Noprofitsyet, each having a cost base of $2. An investment company called Buyanything! makes a takeover offer which results in Ian receiving 20,000 shares in Buyanything!. The first element of the cost base of each of the replacement shares will be $0.50.

Variation: Ian receives 5,000 ordinary shares (market value $5 per share) and 5,000 preference shares (market value $3 per share). The cost base of the replacement shares is determined as follows:

(1) ordinary shares ($5 × $2)/$8 = $1.25

(2) preference shares ($3 × $2)/$8 = $0.75.

When an exchange of interests involves something other than just replacement interests (see below), the cost base of the original interests (immediately before the exchange) must be reduced by so much of the cost base as is attributable to an ineligible part.

For the acquiring entity, the cost base of the interests acquired will generally be determined under the ordinary cost base rules (¶11-550). However, where the original holder is either a significant stakeholder or a common stakeholder for the arrangement the first element of the cost base of the interest acquired will be the original interest holder's cost base in that original interest (s 124-782(1)). Similarly, there is a transfer of the cost base based on a reasonable allocation where there is a cancellation of the original interests (s 124-782).

Other special cost base rules apply where:

- the arrangement constitutes a restructure (see below) (ss 124-784A to 124-784C)
- where the replacement interests are issued to any member of the wholly-owned group (s 124-784).

Partial roll-over

A taxpayer may choose to apply the roll-over to only some of the interests exchanged under an arrangement, ie there is no requirement that all such interests must be chosen.

Where the exchange involves interests in shares or trusts plus other consideration (eg cash), the other consideration is treated as "ineligible proceeds" and roll-over is denied for the portion of the original interests which the other consideration is attributable. The cost base of the ineligible part is the cost base of the original interest that is reasonably attributable to it.

▶ Example 2

Ralph owns 1,000 shares in A Co (with a cost base of $6). He exchanges those shares for 1,000 B Co shares (market value $10) plus $5 cash for each A Co share. Ralph has ineligible proceeds of $5,000. The cost base of Ralph's A Co shares which is attributable to the cash component can be calculated as follows:

$$\frac{1{,}000 \times \$6 \times \$5{,}000}{\$15{,}000} = \$2{,}000 \text{ (\$2 per share)}$$

This means that in respect of his A Co shares Ralph makes a capital gain of: $5,000 (ineligible proceeds) – $2,000 (cost base of ineligible part) = $3,000 and the cost base of each of his B Co shares is $4.

Exchange of pre-CGT interests

When pre-CGT interests are included in an exchange for which a roll-over is available, the first element of the cost base and reduced cost base of any interests in the replacement entity acquired in relation to those pre-CGT interests is their market value at the time of the exchange (s 124-800; TD 2002/4). However, the cost base will be reduced to the extent that a capital gain arising from CGT event K6 (¶11-350) was disregarded because the taxpayer would have been able to apply the roll-over had the interest been acquired on or after 20 September 1985 (ss 124-800(2); 104-230(10)).

Restructures

Special cost base rules apply to scrip for scrip roll-overs that are restructures of companies or trust. An arrangement will be a restructure where:

- the replacement entity reasonably knows, or reasonable expects, that a scrip for scrip roll-over has been, or will be, obtained in relation to the arrangement
- there is a common stakeholder for the arrangement
- just after the completion time the market value of the issued replacement interests under the arrangement is more than 80% of the market value of all the shares, trust interests, options, rights and similar interests issued by the replacement entity (s 124-784A).

Where the arrangement is a restructure, the cost base for the qualifying interests that the acquiring entity acquires in the original entity will be determined pursuant to a method statement that reflects the cost bases of the underlying net assets of the original entity, as opposed to the market value of the original entity (s 124-784B).

This cost base is used in determining the value of the target entity's assets in consolidation if the target entity subsequently joins the acquiring entity's consolidated group (ss 715-910; 715-920).

[FITR ¶161-400 – ¶161-435]

¶12-328 Demerger CGT roll-over relief

Demerger relief is available where a company or trust group restructures under a demerger by splitting into 2 or more entities or groups. The relief applies where a demerger group divests itself of at least 80% of its interests in a demerger subsidiary to the interest owners of the head entity.

There are 3 elements of demerger relief: (a) a CGT roll-over for owners of interests in the head entity of a demerger group; (b) a CGT exemption for members of a demerger group; and (c) a dividend exemption for the owners of the head entity (¶4-160). The CGT roll-over and exemption are discussed below.

Roll-over for interest owners

In broad terms, the owners of interests in a company or trust can choose a roll-over if a CGT event happens to their interests because of the demerger of an entity from the group of which the company or trust is the head entity (Subdiv 125-B). This ensures that the pre-CGT status of interests in the head entity carries over to new interests in the demerged entity.

To qualify for the roll-over, the following conditions must be met (s 125-70):

- there is a restructuring of the demerger group (see TD 2020/6 for what constitutes ''restructuring'')
- at least 80% of the demerger group's ownership interests in the demerged entity are acquired by the owners of the group's head entity
- a CGT event happens to the owners of the original interests in the head entity, or the owners simply acquire a new interest (and nothing else)
- the acquisition by owners of new interests happens only because those owners held original interests in the head entity — this condition is still satisfied if head entity shareholders give consideration for the shares they receive in the demerged entity (ID 2004/455)
- all of the owners receive the same proportion, or as nearly as practicable the same proportion, of new interests in the demerged entity (which may be allocated to a nominee in certain circumstances) as they had in the head entity just before the demerger
- the proportionate market values of the interests in the demerger group as a whole are maintained before and after the demerger
- the new interests are of a similar kind as the original interests.

A foreign interest holder is treated as owning an interest in the relevant entity at the time the share sale facility owns that interest under a restructure subject to certain conditions (s 125-235).

A restructure where the owners of original interests in the head entity receive new interests in the demerged entity that are not in the same proportion as their original interests is not a demerger.

Dual listed companies

Demerger roll-over is only available in relation to a dual listed company voting share in a head entity where there are more than 5 dual listed company voting shares in that company (s 126-60(2)). A ''dual listed company voting share'' is a company share:

- issued as part of a dual listed company arrangement and mainly for the purpose of ensuring that shareholders of both companies involved in the arrangement vote as a single decision-making body on matters affecting them, and
- that does not carry rights to financial entitlements (except the return of the amount paid up on the share and a dividend that is the equivalent of a dividend paid on an ordinary share) (s 125-60(3)).

The definition of a ''dual listed company arrangement'' refers to an arrangement under which 2 publicly listed companies, while maintaining their separate legal entity status, shareholdings and listings, align their strategic directions and the economic interests of their respective shareholders by meeting the requirements in s 125-60(4).

Demerger group

A demerger group comprises the head entity of a group of companies or trusts and at least one demerger subsidiary. A company or trust is the head entity of a demerger group if no other member of the group has ownership interests in the company or trust (s

125-65). Discretionary trusts and superannuation funds cannot be members of a demerger group. However, where such an entity is the owner of ownership interests in the head entity of the group, either one may choose the roll-over.

A corporation sole and a complying superannuation entity are excluded from a demerger group (s 125-65(2A)). This exclusion allows an entity owned by a corporation sole or a complying superannuation entity to qualify as the head entity of a demerger group.

A listed public company or listed widely-held trust may choose that an entity be excluded from a demerger group if that entity owns, either alone or together with another entity, between 20% and 80% of the interests in the company or trust.

A company or trust is a demerger subsidiary where another company or trust has a holding of more than 20% in the subsidiary. In the case of a company, this means the right to receive more than 20% of income or capital, or the right to exercise, or control the exercise of, more than 20% of the voting power of the company. In the case of a trust, it simply means the right to receive more than 20% of any distribution of income or capital by the trustee.

When roll-over does not apply

The demerger roll-over is not available where:

- the interest owner is a foreign resident and the new interest acquired under the demerger is not taxable Australian property just after it is acquired
- the interest owner can obtain another CGT roll-over for the CGT event that happened, eg scrip for scrip roll-over (¶12-325)
- the ownership interests acquired under the demerger are not of a similar kind to the original ownership interests
- certain owners of interests in the head entity are excluded from participating in the demerger, or
- an interest owner receives something other than new interests in the demerged entity, such as cash, even if the owner also receives a new interest in the demerged entity.

Consequences of roll-over

The effect of the roll-over is to defer the making of a capital gain or capital loss. If an owner of the interests in the head entity chooses the roll-over, the capital gain or capital loss from a CGT event that happens to an original interest is disregarded (s 125-80).

If the roll-over is chosen, the sum of the cost bases of all the owner's post-CGT interests in the head entity just before the demerger must be apportioned across their post-CGT new interests in the demerged entity and any remaining original interests. The apportionment must be done on the basis of the market values, or an anticipated reasonable approximation of the market values, of the ownership interests. The Commissioner considers that the apportionment will be reasonable if the owner calculates the new cost base of each post-demerger interest in accordance with the market value of that interest relative to the total market value of all of their post-demerger interests. However, there may be more than one method of allocating the cost bases of ownership interests that results in a reasonable apportionment (TD 2006/73).

If *all* the owner's original interests are pre-CGT interests, all the owner's new interests in the demerged entity will be treated as pre-CGT interests. If *some* of the owner's original interests in the head entity are pre-CGT interests, the number of pre-CGT new interests in the demerged entity is based on the proportion of pre-CGT original interests, having regard to the relative market values of the interests before and after the demerger. If a proportion of the owner's original interests, some of which were acquired pre-CGT, ends under the demerger, the same proportion of pre-CGT interests also ends.

▶ Example 1

Bert owned 100 shares in a company of which 50 were acquired pre-CGT. Under a demerger, 20 of Bert's 100 shares were cancelled in exchange for new interests. As 20% of his shares were cancelled, 10 of his pre-CGT shares are taken to have been cancelled.

If there is a demerger, but no CGT event happens to the owner's original interests or the roll-over is not chosen, the cost base and reduced cost base of those interests must be adjusted to reflect the change in value caused by the demerger. If such adjustments are made, no other adjustment can be made because of the demerger (ss 125-85 to 125-95). Note that the cost base adjustment rules in s 125-90(2) do not apply to a new interest received in respect of an original interest that was acquired pre-CGT if no CGT event happens to that original interest under a demerger. Also, in these circumstances, a new interest acquired in a demerged entity is not treated as a pre-CGT interest.

Where the roll-over is not chosen, s 125-85 does not apply to deem any of the new interests acquired to have a pre-CGT status if the original interests were acquired pre-CGT (ID 2003/875). Despite not choosing the roll-over, however, a taxpayer may be able to adopt an earlier date of acquisition in order to claim the CGT discount (ID 2003/1031).

Exemption for members of demerger group

The other element of CGT demerger relief is that certain capital gains or capital losses made by a demerging entity are disregarded (Subdiv 125-C). This exemption automatically applies, ie the members of a demerger group cannot choose that it does not apply.

One consequence is that any gain or loss made by a demerging entity from CGT event A1, C2, C3 or K6 happening to its ownership interests in a demerged entity under a demerger is disregarded (s 125-155).

▶ Example 2

The taxpayer is the ultimate holding company of a large group and proposes to restructure its group via a demerger arrangement. Under the proposed arrangement, the taxpayer will dispose of its shares in a wholly-owned subsidiary (the "demerged company") to its shareholders. As a preliminary step to the disposal, certain subsidiaries of the taxpayer will be transferred to the demerged company. The taxpayer will then undertake a notional "cash" distribution to the shareholders equal to the purchase price of the demerged company. This distribution will partly be a return of capital and partly a dividend. The shareholders will agree to purchase the shares in the demerged company and will be obliged to apply the notional "cash" amount to acquire those shares.

When the taxpayer (a demerging entity) disposes of its ownership interests in the demerged company (the demerged entity) to the taxpayer's shareholders under the proposed demerger arrangement, any capital gain or capital loss that it would make will be disregarded.

Another consequence is that CGT event J1 (¶11-340) does not happen to the demerged entity or any other member of the demerger group (s 125-160).

▶ Example 3

Assume the same facts as in the previous example, except that the taxpayer is a member of the group that proposes to restructure.

When the holding company disposes of its ownership interests in the taxpayer to its shareholders under the proposed demerger arrangement, they will no longer be members of the same wholly-owned group. As a result, CGT event J1 would normally be triggered but for the exception in s 125-160.

Accordingly, CGT event J1 will not happen to the taxpayer (being the demerged entity) at the time of the proposed demerger with respect to the subsidiaries proposed to be rolled over by the holding company.

In addition to the consequences outlined above, a capital loss made because of a value shift under a demerger may be reduced to the extent that the loss is reasonably attributable to a reduction in the market value of the asset (s 125-165). Also, if the value of the asset is reduced and the asset is subject to roll-over after the demerger, the reduced cost base of an asset may be reduced by the decrease in value (s 125-170).

The rules governing the operation of CGT event K6 (¶11-350) ensure the preservation of the pre-CGT treatment of interests received as a result of a demerger.

[FITR ¶161-900 – ¶162-100]

¶12-330 CGT roll-over for exchange of shares in same company

A taxpayer can choose to obtain a roll-over if (s 124-240):

- the taxpayer owns shares of a certain class in a company
- the company redeems or cancels all shares of that class
- the company issues the taxpayer with new shares (and the taxpayer receives nothing else) in substitution for the original shares
- the market value of the new shares just after they were issued is at least equal to the market value of the original shares just before they were redeemed or cancelled
- the paid-up share capital of the company just after the new shares were issued is the same as just before the original shares were redeemed or cancelled, and
- the taxpayer is a resident at the time of the redemption or cancellation or, if the taxpayer is a foreign resident, the original shares were taxable Australian property (¶12-725) just before that time and the new shares are taxable Australian property when they are issued.

A CGT event does not happen when a company splits or consolidates its share capital. Accordingly, if there is no cancellation or redemption of the original shares and no change in total capital amounts or proportions of equity, there is no need for roll-over relief (TD 2000/10).

The consequences of the roll-over are those that generally apply for replacement-asset roll-overs (¶12-160). The first element of the cost base and reduced cost base of the new shares is worked out under those general rules.

[FITR ¶161-090]

¶12-340 CGT roll-over for exchange of units in same unit trust

A taxpayer can choose to obtain a roll-over if (s 124-245):

- the taxpayer owns units of a certain class in a unit trust
- the trustee of the unit trust redeems or cancels all units of that class
- the trustee of the unit trust issues the taxpayer with new units (and the taxpayer receives nothing else) in substitution for the original units
- the market value of the new units just after they were issued is at least equal to the market value of the original units just before they were redeemed or cancelled, and
- the taxpayer is a resident at the time of the redemption or cancellation or, if the taxpayer is a foreign resident, the original units were taxable Australian property (¶12-725) just before that time and the new units are taxable Australian property when they are issued.

The consequences of the roll-over are those that generally apply for replacement-asset roll-overs (¶12-160). The first element of the cost base and reduced cost base of the new units is worked out under those general rules.

[FITR ¶161-095]

¶12-350 CGT roll-over for exchange of rights or option of company

A taxpayer can choose to obtain a roll-over if (s 124-295):

- the taxpayer owns: (a) rights to acquire shares in a company; (b) rights to acquire an option to acquire shares in a company; or (c) an option to acquire shares in a company

- the shares are: (a) consolidated and divided into new shares of a larger amount; or (b) subdivided into new shares of a smaller amount
- the company cancels the original rights or option because of the consolidation or subdivision
- the company issues the taxpayer with new rights or option relating to the new shares in substitution for the original rights or option
- the taxpayer receives nothing else in substitution for the original rights or option
- the market value of the new rights or option just after they were issued is at least equal to the market value of the original rights or option just before they were cancelled, and
- the taxpayer is a resident at the time of the cancellation or, if the taxpayer is a foreign resident, the original rights or option were taxable Australian property (¶12-725) just before that time and the new rights or option are taxable Australian property when they are issued.

The consequences of the roll-over are those that generally apply for replacement-asset roll-overs (¶12-160). The first element of the cost base and reduced cost base of the new rights or option is worked out under those general rules.

[FITR ¶161-110]

¶12-360 CGT roll-over for exchange of rights or option of unit trust

A taxpayer can choose to obtain a roll-over if (s 124-300):

- the taxpayer owns: (a) rights to acquire units in a unit trust; (b) rights to acquire an option to acquire units in a unit trust; or (c) an option to acquire units in a unit trust
- the units are: (a) consolidated and divided into new units of a larger amount; or (b) subdivided into new units of a smaller amount
- the trustee of the unit trust cancels the original rights or option because of the consolidation or subdivision
- the trustee of the unit trust issues the taxpayer with new rights or option relating to the new units in substitution for the original rights or option
- the taxpayer receives nothing else in substitution for the original rights or option
- the market value of the new rights or option just after they were issued is at least equal to the market value of the original rights or option just before they were cancelled, and
- the taxpayer is a resident at the time of the cancellation or, if the taxpayer is a foreign resident, the original rights or option were taxable Australian property (¶12-725) just before that time and the new rights or option are taxable Australian property when they are issued.

The consequences of the roll-over are those that generally apply for replacement-asset roll-overs (¶12-160). The first element of the cost base and reduced cost base of the new rights or option is worked out under those general rules.

[FITR ¶161-115]

¶12-370 CGT roll-over for business restructures

The general roll-over for business restructures is available pursuant to Div 615. The roll-over is available where interests, being shares or units in a unit trust, are disposed of, redeemed or cancelled, for shares in a company.

Disposal of interests for shares in a company

A taxpayer is able to choose the roll-over in the disposal case where:

(a) the taxpayer is a member of a company or a unit trust (**original entity**)

(b) the taxpayer and at least one other entity (**exchanging members**) own all the shares or units in the original entity

(c) under a scheme for reorganising its affairs, the exchanging members dispose of all their shares or units in it to a company (**interposed company**) in exchange for shares in the interposed company (and nothing else), and

(d) the additional conditions for roll-over, as detailed in 1 – 8 below, are satisfied (s 615-5(1)).

The roll-over applies automatically where the original company was the head company of a consolidated group immediately before the disposal (s 615-5(2)).

Redeeming or cancelling interests for shares in a company

A taxpayer can choose the roll-over in the redemption or cancellation case where the taxpayer is a member of a company or a unit trust (**original entity**), and under a scheme for reorganising its affairs:

(a) a company (**interposed company**) acquires no more than 5 shares or units in the original entity

(b) these are the first shares or units that the interposed company acquires in the original entity

(c) the taxpayer and at least one other entity (**exchanging members**) own all the remaining shares or units in the original entity

(d) those remaining shares or units are redeemed or cancelled

(e) each exchanging member receives shares (and nothing else) in the interposed company in return for their shares or units in the original entity being redeemed or cancelled, and

(f) the additional conditions for roll-over, as detailed in 1–8 below, are satisfied (s 615-10(1)).

The original entity, or its trustee if it is a trust, can issue shares or units to the interposed entity as part of the scheme (s 615-10(3)).

The roll-over automatically applies where the original company was the head company of a consolidated group immediately before the cancellation or redemption of the shares under the scheme (s 615-10(2)).

Additional conditions for roll-over

The additional conditions that must be satisfied in order for roll-over to be available are:

1. the interposed entity must own all the share or units in the original entity immediately after the time the exchanging members' shares are transferred, cancelled or redeemed under the scheme (referred to as the **completion time**) (s 615-15)
2. immediately after the completion time, each exchanging member must own a whole number of shares in the interposed company and those shares as a percentage of the total shares issued to exchanging members is equal to the percentage of shares or units that the member held in the original entity before the completion time (s 615-20(1))
3. the following ratios are equal:
   - the ratio of the market value of each exchanging member's shares in the interposed company to the market value of the shares in the interposed company issued to all the exchanging members (worked out immediately after the completion time)

  - the ratio of the market value of that member's shares or units in the original entity that were disposed of, redeemed or cancelled under the scheme to the market value of all the shares or units in the original entity that were disposed of, redeemed or cancelled under the scheme (worked out immediately before the first disposal, redemption or cancellation) (s 615-20(2))

4. either:
   - the taxpayer is an Australian resident at the time of the disposal, redemption or cancellation, or
   - the taxpayer's shares or units in the original entity are taxable Australian property immediately before that time and their shares in the interposed entity are taxable Australian property immediately after the completion time (s 615-20(3))
5. the shares in the interposed company are not redeemable shares (s 615-25(1))
6. each exchanging member who is issued shares in the interposed company must own the shares from the time they are issued until at least the completion time (s 615-25(2))
7. immediately after the completion time either:
   - the exchanging members must own all the shares in the interposed company, or
   - entities other than the exchanging members must own no more than 5 shares in the interposed company, and the market value of those shares expressed as a percentage of the market value of all the shares in the interposed company must be such that it is reasonable to treat the exchanging members as owning all the shares (s 615-20(3)), and
8. either:
   - where immediately before the completion time, a consolidated group consisted of the original entity as head company and one or more other members (**other group members**) and immediately after the completion time, the interposed company is the head company of a consolidatable group consisting only of itself and the other group members — the interposed company must choose within 28 days of the completion time (or such further time as the Commissioner allows) that a consolidated group continues in existence at and after the completion time with the interposed company as its head company
   - in any other case, the interposed entity must choose within 2 months of the completion time (or such further time as the Commissioner allows) to apply the consequences of the roll-over detailed in s 615-65 (s 615-30).

For the purpose of condition 3, where a taxpayer holds any shares in the interposed company before the reorganisation and, after the reorganisation, continues to hold those shares along with the replacement shares, the proportionality requirements for the roll-over are not achievable (TR 97/18).

If the taxpayer satisfies all the conditions, the roll-over relief will apply regardless of the character of the asset.

Where the original entity is an ADI, certain preference shares can be disregarded for the purpose of applying the conditions (s 615-35).

CGT Consequences of applying roll-over

For CGT purposes, where the conditions for roll-over relief are satisfied, the general rules for replacement asset roll-overs in Subdiv 124-A as detailed in ¶12-160 apply (s 615-40). Accordingly, the first element of the cost base and reduced cost base of the shares in the interposed company are worked out under those rules.

Roll-over for trading stock and revenue assets

A taxpayer can choose to defer a profit or loss arising in relation to the shares or units in the original entity that were held as trading stock or revenue assets where the taxpayer chooses to apply the CGT roll-over and the shares in the interposed entity acquired in exchange for those shares or units have the same character (s 615-45).

An automatic deferral of the profit or loss on a disposal of shares or units in the original entity held as trading stock or revenue assets applies where the CGT roll-over relief automatically applies due to the restructure relating to the head company of a consolidated group (s 615-45).

To enable the election to apply effectively, the CGT exemption for trading stock in s 118-25 is disregarded for the purpose of applying the roll-over (s 615-60).

Where the shares or units in the original entity are held as trading stock and roll-over relief applies, the taxpayer who exchanges its shares or units is taken to have received an amount equal to either:

- the cost of the trading stock at the time of the restructure, or
- if the trading stock was held at the start of the income year, the value of the trading stock at the start of the income year plus any subsequent increase in cost (s 615-50(1)).

The new shares received in the interposed entity are treated as being acquired for the amount that has been included in the taxpayer's assessable income for the disposal of the shares or units in the original entity divided by the number of new shares that are trading stock (s 615-50(2)).

To prevent the market value trading stock provisions in Div 70 from applying (¶9-210, ¶9-290) the transaction is treated as arm's length transaction undertaken in the ordinary course of business (s 615-50(3)).

Where the shares or units in the original entity are held as revenue assets, the taxpayer is taken to have realised their interests for an amount that would result in them not making a profit or loss on the realisation of those shares or units (s 615-55(1)). Generally, this will be the price at which the taxpayer acquired the shares or units.

For the purpose of calculating any future profit or loss on the shares acquired in the interposed entity, the taxpayer is treated as having acquired each share for the total amount they were taken to have received in respect of their shares or units in the original entity for divided by the total number of new shares in the interposed entity that are revenue assets (s 615-55(2)).

Consequences for the interposed entity

Where the interposed entity chooses to apply the roll-over pursuant to s 615-30(1) (ie in condition 8) and any of the original entity's assets at the completion time are pre-CGT assets, the interposed entity is taken to have pre-CGT shares or units in the original entity (s 615-65(2)). The number of pre-CGT shares or units in the original entity is the greatest possible whole number that (when expressed as a percentage of all the shares or units) does not exceed the market value of the original entity's pre-CGT assets less its liabilities (if any) in respect of those assets expressed as a percentage of the market value of all the original entity's assets less all of its liabilities (s 615-65(3)). The remainder of the shares or units in the original entity are taken to be post-CGT units.

The first element of the cost base of the interposed company's post-CGT shares or units in the original entity is the total of the cost bases (at the completion time) of the original entity's post-CGT assets less its liabilities (if any) in respect of those assets. The first element of the reduced cost base of the interposed company's shares or units in the original entity is worked out in a similar way (s 615-65(4)).

A liability of the original entity that is not a liability in respect of a specific asset or assets of the entity is taken to be a liability in respect of all the assets of the original entity, eg a bank overdraft (s 615-65(5)). If a liability is in respect of 2 or more assets, the proportion of the liability that is in respect of any one of those assets is (s 615-65(6))::

$$\frac{\text{The market value of the asset}}{\text{Total market value of all assets that liability is in respect of}}$$

[FITR ¶425-000 – ¶425-050]

¶12-380 CGT small business restructure roll-over

Optional roll-over relief is available for the transfer of assets as part of a change of legal structure without a change in the ultimate legal ownership of the assets pursuant to Subdiv 328-G. The roll-over relief is available for gains and losses that arise on the transfer of CGT assets, trading stock, revenue assets and depreciating assets.

The roll-over is available where the 6 conditions in s 328-430, as detailed below, are satisfied.

1. Genuine Restructure

The transaction is, or is part of, a genuine restructure of an ongoing business (s 328-430(1)(a)). The meaning of the term ‘‘genuine restructure of an ongoing business’’ is explained in LCR 2016/3. The determination of whether there is a genuine restructure will be a question of fact determined by all surrounding circumstances. The following features may indicate the transaction is part of a genuine restructure:

- It is a bona fide commercial arrangement undertaken in a real and honest sense to facilitate growth, innovation and diversification, adapt to changed conditions, or reduce administrative burdens, compliance costs and/or cash flow impediments.
- It is authentically restructuring the way in which the business is conducted as opposed to a ‘‘divestment’’ or preliminary step to facilitate the economic realisation of assets.
- The economic ownership of the business and its restructured assets is maintained.
- The small business owners continue to operate the business through a different legal structure.
- It results in a structure likely to have been adopted had the small business owners obtained appropriate professional advice when setting up the business.

Without limiting the above, there is a safe harbour rule that provides the transaction will be a genuine restructure where in the 3-year period after the transaction takes effect:

(a) there is no change in ultimate economic ownership of any of the significant assets of the business (other than trading stock) that were transferred under the transaction

(b) those significant assets continue to be active assets, and

(c) there is no significant or material use of those significant assets for private purposes (s 328-435).

2. Parties to transaction are eligible entities

The roll-over is only available where each party to the transfer is an entity that satisfies one or more of the following for the income year of the transfer:

(a) it is a small business entity (¶7-050)

(b) it has an affiliate that is a small business entity

(c) it is connected with an entity that is a small business entity

(d) it is a partner in a partnership that is a small business entity (s 328-430(1)(b)).

However, neither the transferor nor transferee can be an exempt entity or a complying superannuation fund (s 328-430(2)).

3. Ultimate economic ownership of the assets must be maintained

The transaction cannot have the effect of materially changing:

(a) the individual(s) which have the ultimate economic ownership of the asset

(b) where there is more than one individual, the individual's share of that ultimate economic ownership (s 328-430(1)(c)).

Where a discretionary trust is involved, this condition will be considered to be satisfied where:

- immediately before and/or after the transaction took effect, the asset was included in the property of a non-fixed trust that was a family trust (¶6-266), and
- every individual who, just before and just after the transfer took effect, had ultimate economic ownership of the asset was a member of the family group of that family trust (s 328-440).

4. The asset transferred is an eligible asset that satisfies the active asset test

The asset being transferred is a CGT asset (other than a depreciating asset) and at the time of transfer is:

(a) where the party to the transfer is a small business entity — an active asset

(b) where the party to the transfer is entity that has an affiliate or connected entity that is a small business entity — an active asset that satisfies the conditions for a passively held asset in s 152-10(1A) or would satisfy if the test allowed the entity to have a turnover threshold of less than $10 million (¶7-120)

(c) where the party to the transfer is a partner in a partnership — an active asset and an interest in an asset of that partnership (s 328-430(1)(d)).

While a depreciating asset is excluded from being an eligible asset, roll-over relief is effectively provided for such assets under item 8 of the table in s 40-340(1). A determination has been issued to ensure there is no direct income tax consequences from the depreciating assets as a part of the transaction (¶17-710; *Taxation Administration (Remedial power — Small Business Restructure Roll-over) Determination 2017*). This active asset requirement effectively prevents the transfer of loans to shareholders to avoid the application of Div 7A.

5. The parties to the transfer satisfy the residency requirement

The transferor and the transferee to the transaction must be resident of Australia as follows:

(a) an individual or company that is an Australian resident (¶21-010, ¶21-040)

(b) a resident trust for CGT purposes

(c) a corporate limited partnership that is a resident for tax purposes under s 94T of ITAA36

(d) if the entity is a partnership (other than a corporate limited partnership) — at least one of the partners is an Australian resident (ss 328-430(1)(e); 328-445).

6. The choice is made

The transferor and the transferee must choose the roll-over to apply (s 328-430(1)(f)).

Consequences of roll-over

The intention of the roll-over is to be tax neutral such that there will be no direct income tax consequences arising from the transfer of asset pursuant to the roll-over (s 328-450). This includes the potential application of Div 7A where the transfer may otherwise have been treated as a deemed dividend (see example to s 328-450). However, this will not prevent a potential application of GST, stamp duty or Pt IVA.

The CGT effect of applying the roll-over is as follows:

(a) the CGT asset is treated as being transferred for an amount equal to the transferor's cost base of the asset just before the transfer, thereby preventing any capital gain or loss from arising (s 328-455(2)(a))

(b) any pre-CGT asset transferred maintains its pre-CGT status (s 328-460)

(c) for the purpose of determining whether there will be a discount capital gain in the future, the transferee will be treated as having acquired the CGT asset at the time of the transfer. Unlike other roll-overs, there is no deemed acquisition back to the date of original acquisition by the transferor.

For details on the consequences of the roll-over and examples, see LCR 2016/2.

Effective roll-over relief also applies to the trading stock, revenue assets and depreciating assets (ss 328-455; 40-340). *Taxation Administration (Remedial Power — Small Business Restructure Roll-over) Determination 2017)* ensures that where the depreciating assets are transferred under this roll-over from 1 December 2017 balancing adjustment roll-over relief will automatically apply pursuant to s 40-340.

Where membership interests are issued in consideration for the transfer of a roll-over asset or assets, the cost base and reduced cost base of those new membership interests is worked out based on the sum of the roll-over costs and adjustable values of the roll-over assets, less any liabilities that the transferee undertakes to discharge in respect of those assets, divided by the number of new membership interests (s 328-465).

A capital loss that is made on any direct or indirect membership in the transferor or the transferee to which the roll-over has occurred will be disregarded except to the extent that the entity can demonstrate that the capital loss is attributable to a matter other than the transfer (s 328-470).

Effect on other CGT small business concessions

Where an asset that was subject to the small business roll-over in Subdiv 152-E (¶7-195) is transferred under the roll-over, the transferee will be treated as if it made the choice to apply the roll-over for the purposes of CGT event J2, J5 and J6 (s 328-475).

For the purpose of applying the 15-year exemption in Subdiv 152-B (¶7-165), the transferee is taken as having acquired the asset when the transferor acquired it (s 152-115(3)).

[FITR ¶313-500 – ¶313-555]

¶12-390 CGT roll-over for conversion of body to incorporated company

A taxpayer can choose to obtain a replacement-asset roll-over if (s 124-520):

(a) the taxpayer is a member of a body that is incorporated under either:

- a law other than the *Corporations Act 2001* or a similar law relating to foreign companies
- a law other than the *Corporations (Aboriginal and Torres Strait Islander) Act 2006* ("CATSI Act")

(b) the body is converted into a company incorporated under the *Corporations Act 2001*, a similar law relating to foreign companies, or the CATSI Act (without creating a new legal entity)

(c) the company issues the taxpayer with shares (and nothing else) in substitution for the taxpayer's interest in the body just before the conversion

(d) there is no significant difference in ownership before and after the conversion or in the mix of ownership before and after the conversion, and

(e) the taxpayer is a resident at the time of the conversion or, if the taxpayer is a foreign resident, the taxpayer's interest in the body was taxable Australian property (¶12-725) just before that time and the shares are taxable Australian property when they are issued.

The roll-over is also available where members of an incorporated body in (a) are wound up and then subsequently reincorporated as a company detailed in (b) provided the same interests in the entities are maintained (s 124-525). In such a case, roll-over relief applies to gains and losses realised by the original entity as a result of becoming assets of the newly incorporated entity pursuant to the reincorporation (s 620-20).

A taxpayer is allowed to receive shares on incorporation that reflect all of the interests and rights they held in the body prior to the incorporation or transfer of incorporation.

Consequences of roll-over

The consequences of the roll-over are those that generally apply for replacement-asset roll-overs (¶12-160). The first element of the cost base and reduced cost base of the shares in the company is worked out under those general rules.

[FITR ¶161-214 – ¶161-218]

¶12-395 CGT roll-over for trust restructures

An optional roll-over is available where a trust disposes of all of its assets to a company and the beneficiaries' interests in the trust are exchanged for shares in the company (Subdiv 124-N: ss 124-850 to 124-875). Both the trust and its beneficiaries can access the roll-over.

The benefits of the roll-over will be reversed by CGT event J4 (¶11-340) if the trust does not cease to exist within 6 months from the disposal of the first asset to the company (or longer if the reasons for the delay are beyond the trustee's control). However, CGT event J4 cannot happen to a roll-over asset that is sold by the company during the trust restructuring period.

Requirements for roll-over

The roll-over is generally available where a trust, or 2 or more trusts, restructure into a single company. CGT event E4 (¶11-290) must be capable of applying to all of the interests in the trust. Accordingly, the roll-over is not available for a restructure undertaken by a discretionary trust (ID 2002/955). In addition, the following requirements must be met:

- all of the CGT assets of the trust (or trusts) must be disposed of to the company during the trust restructuring period apart from assets retained to pay existing or expected debts of the trust (s 124-860(1))
- the company is generally a shelf company at the time the asset disposals commence (see below)
- all the beneficiaries must own shares in the company in the same proportion as they owned interests in the trust, and the market value of the interests before and after the restructure must be at least substantially the same (s 124-860(6))
- the entities involved choose the roll-over (s 124-865).

The roll-over is not available for a CGT asset if it is trading stock of the trust or it becomes trading stock of the company on its acquisition.

Trust restructuring period

All of the CGT assets of the trust must be disposed of to the company during the trust restructuring period. Assets disposed of before the start of the trust restructuring period are not taken into account.

This requirement does not include assets retained in the trust to pay existing or expected debts (ID 2003/340; ID 2003/341). However, the value of the retained assets is taken into account in determining whether the market value of the assets is maintained after the restructure (see below).

The trust restructuring period starts just before the first asset is disposed of to the company under a trust restructure. The restructuring period ends when the last CGT asset is disposed of to the company (after which time all the interests in the trust will have been exchanged for shares in the company).

Characteristics of the company

The company (which could be a shelf company) must:

- not be an exempt entity
- never have carried on commercial activities
- have no CGT assets other than (i) small amounts of cash or debt; and/or (ii) rights under an arrangement which only facilitate the transfer of the assets from the transferor to it, and
- have no losses of any kind (s 124-860(3), (4)).

The last 3 requirements do not apply to a transferee that is the trustee of the transferor (s 124-860(5)).

If the company is a foreign resident, the roll-over only applies to an asset that is taxable Australian property (¶12-725) just after the company acquires it under the trust restructure (s 124-875(6)).

Maintaining proportionate interests

Just after the trust restructuring period, the shareholders must own shares in the company in the same proportions that they owned interests in the trust. In addition, the market value of the shares just after the restructure must be at least substantially the same as the market value of the interests in the trust just before the start of the restructuring period.

In determining proportionate interests, ignore any shares in the company that: (a) just before the restructure period were owned by entities that held no more than 5 shares; and (b) just after the restructure period represented such a low percentage of market value that it is reasonable to treat other entities as if they owned all the shares in the company (s 124-860(7)).

▶ Example

A solicitor owns 2 shares in a shelf company before the trust restructure. Immediately after the restructure, the 2 beneficiaries of the trust each receive 5,000 shares of equal value in the company. The beneficiaries will be treated as if they owned all the shares in the company.

Choosing the roll-over

The roll-over is only available for the trust and company under the trust restructure if they both choose to obtain it (s 124-865). However, the beneficiaries of the trust may choose the roll-over irrespective of whether the trust and company choose to obtain it. The choice must be made on an asset-by-asset basis (s 124-870).

A foreign resident beneficiary cannot choose the roll-over unless the replacement shares received in exchange for the beneficiary's interests in the trust are taxable Australian property (¶12-725).

Consequences of roll-over

Where the requirements for the roll-over are met, the trust can disregard the capital gain or loss where CGT event A1 (¶11-250) happens on the disposal of an asset to the company. The cost base and reduced cost base of the CGT asset for the trust becomes the first element of the cost base or reduced cost base of the asset for the company. If the original asset acquired by the trust is a pre-CGT asset, the asset acquired by the company will be treated as a pre-CGT asset.

The consequences of the roll-over for beneficiaries are those that generally apply for replacement asset roll-overs (¶12-160).

[FITR ¶161-440 – ¶161-455]

¶12-400 CGT roll-over for crown leases

Compulsory roll-over

A compulsory replacement-asset roll-over happens if (s 124-575):

- a taxpayer holds a Crown lease over land
- the taxpayer surrenders the Crown lease or it expires, and
- the taxpayer is granted an estate in fee simple or a new Crown lease over the land (or both).

For this purpose, a Crown lease is a lease of land granted by the Crown under an Australian law (other than the common law) or a similar lease granted under a foreign law.

Further conditions for roll-over

In addition, for the roll-over to happen, the estate in fee simple or new Crown lease must be granted by:

- renewing or extending the term of the original Crown lease, mainly because the taxpayer held the original Crown lease
- changing the purpose for which the land to which the original Crown lease related can be used
- converting the original Crown lease to a Crown lease in perpetuity
- converting the original Crown lease to an estate in fee simple
- consolidating, or consolidating and dividing, the original Crown lease
- subdividing the original Crown lease
- excising or relinquishing a part of the land to which the Crown lease related, or
- expanding the area of the land (s 124-575(2)).

Renewal may occur even if lessor changes

A lease of land (whether or not it is a Crown lease) granted to a taxpayer is treated as being a renewal of the taxpayer's original lease if (s 124-605):

- after the grant of the original lease, the land to which it related became vested in an Australian government agency (other than the one that granted the original lease)
- the second agency granted the fresh lease over the original land, over the original land less an excised area or over the original land and other land, and
- the fresh lease was granted under an Australian law (other than the common law).

This rule applies even if there is a period between the end of the original lease and the grant of the fresh lease, provided the taxpayer continues to occupy the original land during that period under a permission, licence or authority granted by the second agency.

Roll-over where land not the same

Even if the estate in fee simple or new Crown lease relates to different land to that to which the original Crown lease related, the Crown lease roll-over still happens if: (a) the difference in area is not significant; (b) the difference in market value is not significant; (c) the estate in fee simple or Crown lease corrects errors in or omissions from the original Crown lease; (d) the estate in fee simple or new Crown lease relates to a significantly different area of land but reasonable efforts were made to ensure that the area was the same; or (e) it is otherwise reasonable for the roll-over to apply (s 124-585).

Exception where part of land excised

Only a partial roll-over applies if the original Crown lease is a post-CGT asset and the land to which the estate in fee simple or new Crown lease relates is different in area to the land the subject of the original Crown lease because a part of the land to which the original Crown lease related was relinquished by the taxpayer for consideration (s 124-590). This consideration can include property. If so, the market value of the property is used when working out the amount of the payment.

There is no roll-over for the excised part. Because the excision of part of the Crown lease involves the end of an asset, a capital gain or loss may be made on the excised part from CGT event C2 happening in relation to it. For this purpose, the cost base (and reduced cost base) of the excised part is so much of the cost base (or reduced cost base) of the relevant Crown lease as is attributable to the excised part.

Parts of estate in fee simple and new Crown lease as separate assets

Each part of a taxpayer's estate in fee simple or new Crown lease after the roll-over has been made is divided into separate assets for CGT purposes by reference to the extent to which the original Crown lease relates to pre-CGT Crown leased land, to post-CGT Crown leased land and to other land (s 124-595). For this purpose, where a separate asset relates to pre-CGT Crown leased land, the separate asset is also treated as a pre-CGT asset.

Consequences of roll-over

The consequences of the roll-over are those that generally apply for replacement-asset roll-overs (s 124-600) (¶12-160). The first element of the cost base and reduced cost base of the new Crown lease or estate in fee simple is worked out under those general rules.

However, slightly different rules apply to work out the cost base and reduced cost base of a post-CGT estate in fee simple or new Crown lease if part of the land is excised (see above) or if separate assets arise (see above).

If part of the land is excised, the first element of the cost base of a post-CGT estate in fee simple or new Crown lease is reduced by the part of the cost base that is attributable to that excised part.

If separate assets arise, the first element of the cost base for each separate post-CGT asset is:

$$\text{cost base of post-CGT original Crown lease} \times \frac{\text{market value of separate asset}}{\text{market value of all the separate assets}}$$

The first element of the reduced cost base of each of those assets is worked out in a similar way.

[FITR ¶161-235 – ¶161-265]

¶12-410 CGT roll-over for depreciating assets held by quasi-owner

A compulsory replacement-asset roll-over of depreciating assets (¶17-015), happens if:

- the asset is attached to land which the taxpayer holds under a quasi-ownership right (¶17-020)
- the quasi-ownership right is surrendered by the taxpayer, expires or is terminated
- the taxpayer is granted a new quasi-ownership right or an estate in fee simple in relation to the land, and
- a Crown lease roll-over (¶12-400) or a prospecting and mining entitlements roll-over (¶12-420) does not happen (s 124-655).

The depreciating assets roll-over only happens in the limited circumstances where a Crown lease roll-over does not happen because a quasi-ownership right over land covers more than just Crown leases, eg an easement over land.

Consequences of roll-over

The consequences of the roll-over are those that generally apply for replacement-asset roll-overs (¶12-160). The first element of the cost base and reduced cost base of the new asset is worked out under those general rules.

Right granted to associate

If the quasi-ownership right or estate in fee simple is instead granted to the taxpayer's associate or an associated government entity, there is no roll-over. In addition, the reduced cost base of the depreciating asset in the taxpayer's hands is decreased by the adjustable value of the asset (¶17-640) just before the original quasi-ownership right expired or was surrendered or terminated (s 124-660). The adjustable value was formerly described as the ''undeducted cost''.

[FITR ¶161-285]

¶12-420 CGT roll-over for prospecting and mining entitlements

Compulsory roll-over

A compulsory replacement-asset roll-over happens if (s 124-705):

- a taxpayer holds a prospecting or mining entitlement
- the taxpayer surrenders the entitlement or it expires, and
- the taxpayer is granted a new entitlement which relates to the same land as the original entitlement.

Prospecting and mining entitlements

A prospecting entitlement is an authority, licence, permit or entitlement under an Australian or foreign law to prospect or explore for minerals in an area. It also includes a lease of land that allows the lessee to prospect or explore for minerals on the land. An interest in such an entitlement is also a prospecting entitlement (s 124-710).

A mining entitlement is a similar authority, licence, permit, entitlement, lease or interest relating to the actual mining of minerals.

Further conditions for roll-over

In addition, for the roll-over to happen, the new entitlement must be granted by:

- renewing or extending the term of the original entitlement, mainly because the taxpayer held the original entitlement
- consolidating, or consolidating and dividing, the original entitlement
- subdividing the original entitlement
- converting a prospecting entitlement to a mining entitlement or vice versa

- excising or relinquishing a part of the land to which the original entitlement related, or
- expanding the area of the land.

Roll-over where land not the same

Even if the new entitlement relates to different land to that to which the original entitlement related, the prospecting or mining right roll-over still happens if: (a) the difference in area is not significant; (b) the difference in market value is not significant; (c) the new entitlement corrects errors in or omissions from the original entitlement; or (d) it is otherwise reasonable for the roll-over to apply (s 124-715).

Exception where part of land excised

Only a partial roll-over applies if the original entitlement is a post-CGT asset and the land to which the new entitlement relates is different in area to the land the subject of the original entitlement because a part of the land to which the original entitlement related was relinquished by the taxpayer for consideration (s 124-720).

There is no roll-over for the excised part. Because the excision of part of the entitlement involves the end of an asset, a capital gain or loss may be made on the excised part from CGT event C2 happening in relation to it. For this purpose, the cost base (and reduced cost base) of the excised part is so much of the cost base (or reduced cost base) of the relevant entitlement as is attributable to the excised part.

Parts of new entitlement may be treated as separate assets

Each part of a prospecting or mining entitlement that exists after the roll-over has been made is divided into separate assets for CGT purposes by reference to the extent to which it relates to land covered by a pre-CGT original entitlement, to land covered by a post-CGT original entitlement and to other land (s 124-725). For this purpose, where a separate asset relates to land covered by a pre-CGT original entitlement, the separate asset is also treated as a pre-CGT asset.

Consequences of roll-over

The consequences of the roll-over are those that generally apply for replacement-asset roll-overs (s 124-730) (¶12-160). The first element of the cost base and reduced cost base of the new entitlement is worked out under those general rules.

However, slightly different rules apply to work out the cost base and reduced cost base of a post-CGT entitlement if part of the land is excised or if separate assets arise (see above).

If part of the land is excised, the first element of the cost base of a post-CGT entitlement is reduced by the part of the cost base that is attributable to that excised part.

If separate assets arise, the first element of the cost base for each separate post-CGT asset is:

$$\text{cost base of post-CGT original entitlement} \times \frac{\text{market value of separate asset}}{\text{market value of all the separate assets}}$$

The first element of the reduced cost base of each of those assets is worked out in a similar way.

[FITR ¶161-310 – ¶161-335]

¶12-430 CGT roll-over for securities lending arrangements

Automatic roll-over relief is available to taxpayers engaging in eligible securities lending arrangements (ITAA36 s 26BC). Securities lending arrangements are typically entered into where a seller of securities does not have enough securities available to complete the sale to the buyer. To cover the sale, the seller obtains from a third person (the "lender") the securities needed to complete the sale. After completion of the sale, the seller returns replacement securities to the lender, who is also paid a fee for the use of the securities. Both before and after the transaction, the lender holds the same number and type of securities. The arrangements have the essential characteristics of loan transactions because the lender receives back the equivalent of what was lent.

The broad effect of extending roll-over relief to securities lending arrangements is as follows:

- if the original securities are pre-CGT assets in the hands of the lender, the replacement securities are also taken to be pre-CGT assets in the hands of the lender
- if the original securities are post-CGT assets in the hands of the lender, the cost base (as indexed) and reduced cost base to the lender of the replacement securities are the same as that of the original securities at the time of the loan.

Securities eligible for the roll-over relief are:

- shares, bonds, debentures, convertible notes, rights or options issued by a public company
- units, bonds, debentures, convertible notes, rights or options that are issued by a publicly listed unit trust or are ordinarily available for subscription or purchase by the public
- bonds, debentures or similar securities which are issued by a government (or government authority) in Australia or elsewhere.

The conditions that must be met for roll-over relief to apply to a securities lending arrangement are:

- the securities lending arrangement must be in writing
- the replacement securities must be the same securities as those originally lent (or identical securities) and the reacquisition of the replacement securities by the lender must be within 12 months of the original disposal
- the borrower and the lender must have been dealing with each other at arm's length in relation to the transaction.

Special provision is made where, during the subsistence of the securities lending arrangement, a distribution (eg a dividend, interest, bonus shares or bonus units) is made in respect of the borrowed securities, a right or option is issued in respect of the borrowed securities or, if the borrowed securities are rights or an option, the rights are, or the option is, exercised.

Eligible securities lending transactions do not give rise to income being assessable as ordinary income or under the rules dealing with traditional securities (¶23-340). However, this exclusion does not apply to the fee payable to the lender for the use of the original securities.

[FTR ¶16-300]

¶12-435 CGT roll-over for medical defence organisations

A roll-over is available for the exchange of membership interests in medical defence organisations (MDOs) (Subdiv 124-P).

A member of an MDO can choose the roll-over when a post-CGT membership interest in an MDO is replaced with a similar membership interest in another MDO. For the roll-over to apply, both MDOs must be companies limited by guarantee and the exchange must be in consequence of a single arrangement. The roll-over is not available to defer the making of a capital loss (s 124-980).

A partial roll-over is available to the extent that a member receives something other than a replacement interest, eg cash, in exchange for their original interest (s 124-990).

Consequences of roll-over

If a member chooses the roll-over:

- a capital gain made from the original interest is disregarded, and
- the first element of the cost base of the replacement interest is the cost base of the original interest that was exchanged for it (s 124-985).

If a member exchanges a pre-CGT membership interest for a replacement interest, the first element of the cost base of the replacement interest is zero (s 124-995).

[FITR ¶161-555 – ¶161-575]

¶12-440 CGT roll-over for exchange of stapled securities

A roll-over is available where there is an exchange of ownership interests under a scheme for reorganising the affairs of stapled entities (Subdiv 124-Q).

Stapled entities are a group of entities that may consist of 2 or more trusts, or one or more companies and one or more trusts, whose ownership interests are stapled together to form stapled securities.

Requirements for roll-over

The roll-over is available to the holders of ownership interests of the stapled entities where, under a scheme for reorganising the affairs of the entities, they dispose of their interests in the entities in exchange for a proportionate number of ownership interests in an interposed public unit trust. The roll-over is only available where the stapled entities include at least one entity that is taxed like a company and at least one that is not (s 124-1045).

The exchanging member must be an Australian resident at the completion time or, if the member is a foreign resident:

- some or all of their ownership interests in the stapled entities must have been taxable Australian property (¶12-725) just before that time, and
- their ownership interests in the interposed trust must be taxable Australian property just after that time (s 124-1050).

Consequences of roll-over

The CGT consequences for exchanging members are set out in s 124-1055. The CGT consequences for the interposed trust in relation to the ownership interests in each of the stapled securities that the trustee of the interposed trust acquires under the scheme are set out in s 124-1060.

[FITR ¶161-600 – ¶161-630]

¶12-445 CGT roll-over for transformation of water rights

CGT roll-over relief applies to capital gains or losses arising from the ending of one or more water entitlements and the issue of one or more replacement water entitlements (including transformations) (Subdiv 124-R). For these purposes a water entitlement is a legal or equitable right that an entity owns that relates to water, including a right to receive water, take water from a water resource, have water delivered or deliver water (s 124-1105(4)).

Automatic roll-over relief applies where a taxpayer replaces a single water entitlement with one or more new water entitlements (replacement roll-over) (s 124-1105(1)). A taxpayer can choose to apply roll-over relief on a bundled basis where the taxpayer holds more than one water entitlements and replaces the entitlements with one or more different water entitlements (s 124-1105(2)).

A water entitlement that is a statutory licence and that qualifies for the roll-over in Subdiv 124-C will not qualify for the water entitlement roll-over (s 124-1105(3)). Where roll-over relief applies the following consequences apply:

- the capital gain or loss arising to both the taxpayer and the operator from the transformation of the water rights is disregarded (s 124-1110)
- where the water right was a pre-CGT asset, the water entitlement (comprising of the statutory licence and any other assets received) is treated as a pre-CGT asset (s 124-1125)
- where the water right was a post-CGT asset, the first element of the cost base of the water access entitlement is equal to the cost base of the water right immediately before the transformation (s 124-1120).

The roll-over applies to the extent that the relevant taxpayer receives one or more replacement water entitlements or allocations. A taxpayer is entitled to partial roll-over relief where something else (eg cash) is received (s 124-1115).

The roll-over applies irrespective of whether the replacement water entitlements or allocations were issued by the same entity that issued the original entitlements or allocations to the taxpayer or another entity. The roll-over is available in situations when a taxpayer's ownership of one or more water entitlements end and, in substance, their remaining water entitlements became their replacement entitlements (s 124-1135).

A taxpayer that has a CGT event happen to any asset they own as a direct result of circumstances that qualify for the replacement roll-over will qualify for the variation roll-over if they continue to own the asset (s 124-1155).

[FITR ¶161-701 – ¶161-770]

¶12-447 CGT roll-over for mining, quarrying and prospecting rights

CGT roll-over applies in relation to mining, quarrying or prospecting rights acquired prior to 1 July 2001 and disposed of under an interest realignment arrangement (s 124-1225). Without the roll-over a capital gain or loss may arise under CGT event A1. An interest realignment arrangement occurs where the parties to a joint venture exchange interests in mining, quarrying or prospecting rights to pursue a single development project, with a view to aligning the ownership of individual rights with the ownership of the overall venture (s 40-363(5)). A partial roll-over is available where the capital proceeds include something other than an interest or a new interest in a mining, quarrying or prospecting right (s 124-1230).

The roll-over consequences depend upon whether:

- all original interests were post-CGT and were acquired before 1 July 2001 (''pre-UCA'') (s 124-1235)
- all original interests were pre-CGT (s 124-1240)
- original interests were of mixed CGT status but all were pre-UCA (s 124-1245)
- some original interests were pre-UCA (s 124-1250).

[FITR ¶161-805 – ¶161-820]

Same-asset Roll-overs

¶12-450 When same-asset CGT roll-over available

A same-asset roll-over allows a taxpayer to ignore the making of a capital gain or loss from a CGT event. It involves a CGT event happening in relation to an asset which changes hands from one taxpayer to another, with the roll-over attaching to the asset in the hands of the transferee taxpayer. Any capital gain or loss arising in the hands of the transferor taxpayer from a CGT event is disregarded. Any capital gain or loss which later arises from another CGT event happening to the asset is only relevant for the transferee taxpayer. The CGT characteristics of the roll-over asset are transferred with the asset from the transferor taxpayer to the transferee taxpayer.

To find out if a same-asset roll-over is available for a CGT event, taxpayers need to consider if the CGT event meets the conditions for a roll-over to be available. A list of the same-asset roll-overs is contained in s 112-150.

Taxpayers then need to consider the consequences of making a same-asset roll-over in the relevant circumstances. If a taxpayer is satisfied that an optional roll-over is desirable in relation to a particular CGT event, the taxpayer can choose for the roll-over to happen, provided all the necessary conditions are met. If a compulsory roll-over is undesirable, a taxpayer may consider structuring its affairs to stop the conditions for the roll-over being met.

[FITR ¶162-295 – ¶162-300]

Marriage and Relationship Breakdown Roll-overs

¶12-460 CGT roll-over between spouses on relationship breakdown

Roll-over relief automatically applies in certain cases involving the transfer of assets as a result of the breakdown of a marriage or a relationship. A compulsory same-asset roll-over happens if a CGT event involves an individual taxpayer disposing of an asset to, or creating an asset in, his or her spouse (or former spouse) because of:

(1) a court order under the *Family Law Act 1975*, a state law, territory law or foreign law relating to breakdown of relationships between spouses

(2) a court-approved maintenance agreement or a similar agreement under a foreign law

(3) a binding financial agreement under Pt VIIIA of the *Family Law Act 1975* or a corresponding written agreement that is binding because of a corresponding foreign law

(4) an arbitral award under the *Family Law Act 1975* or a corresponding arbitral award under a corresponding state, territory or foreign law

(5) a written agreement that is binding because of a state, territory or foreign law relating to breakdowns of relationships between spouses where the agreement cannot be overridden by a court order except to avoid injustice, or

(6) a Pt VIIIAB financial agreement under the *Family Law Act 1975* or corresponding written agreement that is binding because of a corresponding foreign law (s 126-5).

In the case of (3), (5) and (6), the roll-over applies only if, at the time of the CGT event:

- the spouses are separated and there is no reasonable likelihood of cohabitation being resumed, and
- the CGT event happened because of reasons directly connected with the breakdown of the relationship between the spouses or former spouses (s 126-25).

However, roll-over relief is not available where the asset is transferred to a corporate trustee, even if the asset is transferred for the benefit of, or at the direction of, the former spouse (*Sandini Pty Ltd & Ors*).

Where the roll-over applies, balancing adjustment relief is also available for depreciation purposes (¶17-710).

A marriage or relationship breakdown roll-over can only happen if an asset is disposed of because CGT event A1 or B1 happens or if an asset is created because CGT event D1, D2, D3 or F1 happens.

However, there is no marriage or relationship breakdown roll-over if the asset involved is trading stock of the transferor spouse or, in the case of CGT event B1, title in the asset does not pass to the transferee spouse when the agreement ends.

The various aspects of marriage breakdown roll-overs are dealt with in TD 1999/47 to TD 1999/61.

Capital gain or loss of transferor spouse disregarded

If a marriage or relationship breakdown roll-over happens, any capital gain or loss from the CGT event made by the transferor spouse is disregarded.

Consequences for transferee spouse in disposal situation

If a post-CGT asset of the transferor spouse is disposed of to the transferee spouse and there is a marriage or relationship breakdown roll-over, the first element of the asset's cost base (or reduced cost base) in the hands of the transferee is the asset's cost base (or reduced cost base) in the hands of the transferor at the time the transferee acquires it.

▶ Example

Jen transfers land to her former spouse, Alf, because of a court order under the *Family Law Act 1975*. Any capital gain or loss Jen makes from the disposal is disregarded. If the cost base of the land to Jen at the time Alf acquired it is $100,000, the first element of the land's cost base in Alf's hands is $100,000.

If a pre-CGT asset of the transferor is disposed of to the transferee, it is also taken to be a pre-CGT asset in the hands of the transferee.

If a collectable or a personal use asset is disposed of by the transferor, it retains the same character in the hands of the transferee.

Consequences for transferee spouse in creation situation

If the transferor spouse creates an asset in the transferee spouse and there is a marriage or relationship breakdown roll-over, the first element of the asset's cost base (or reduced cost base) in the hands of the transferee is:

- if the asset is created as a result of CGT event D1, the incidental costs incurred by the transferor in relation to that event
- if the asset is created as a result of CGT event D2, the expenditure incurred by the transferor in granting the option
- if the asset is created as a result of CGT event D3, the expenditure incurred by the transferor in granting the right, or
- if the asset is created as a result of CGT event F1, the expenditure incurred by the transferor on the grant, renewal or extension of the lease.

Associated provisions

For the calculation of the main residence exemption where a marriage or relationship breakdown roll-over is available, see ¶11-750. For the exemption relating to marriage or relationship breakdown settlements, see ¶11-670.

[FITR ¶162-310 – ¶162-330]

¶12-470 CGT roll-over involving company or trustee on relationship breakdown

A compulsory marriage or relationship breakdown roll-over also happens under s 126-15 if the conditions outlined at ¶12-460 are met and a company or trustee of a trust (the transferor) disposes of, or creates an asset in, the spouse or former spouse of an individual (the transferee).

In such a situation, a capital gain or loss made from the CGT event by the transferor is disregarded. Similarly, the same roll-over consequences (as set out in ¶12-460) apply to the transferee.

In such cases, balancing adjustment relief is also available for depreciation purposes (¶17-710).

There are some additional consequences if a CGT event happens to a particular post-CGT asset that, just before the time of the transfer, was directly or indirectly owned by a taxpayer (including the transferee). Where the transferor is a company, the relevant post-CGT asset is a share in, or a loan to, the company. Where the transferor is the trustee of a trust, the relevant post-CGT asset is an interest or unit in the trust or a loan to the trustee.

▶ Example

Arnold owns all the shares in Altico, a company that owns land. As a result of Arnold's marriage breakdown, the Family Court orders the company to transfer some of the land it owns to Arnold's ex-wife, Megan. When Arnold sells the shares, the additional consequences are relevant.

One of the additional consequences is that the cost base and reduced cost base of the asset (eg a share in the company) are decreased by an amount that reasonably reflects the fall in its market value because of the transfer of assets (eg land) by the company or trust to the transferee. The reduction occurs at the time of this transfer. Further, if the taxpayer owning the asset (the share referred to above) is also the transferee, the cost base and reduced cost base of that asset are then increased by any amount that is included in the spouse's assessable income for any income year because of the transfer, ie because of a subsequent capital gain on a transferred asset (eg the land referred to above). See TR 2004/5 for the application of the roll-over for transfers of property pursuant to a marriage breakdown in compliance with an order pursuant to s 79 of the *Family Law Act 1975*.

Special rules apply to marriage or relationship breakdown roll-overs involving CFCs and certain non-resident trusts (s 126-20).

[FITR ¶162-320 – ¶162-325]

¶12-480 CGT roll-over for small superannuation funds on relationship breakdown

A marriage or relationship breakdown roll-over is available for certain transfers of any CGT asset reflecting the personal interest of either spouse (but not both) in a small superannuation fund (ie a fund with fewer than 5 members) to another complying superannuation fund (s 126-140).

Under the roll-over, any capital gain or loss arising to the trustee of a small superannuation fund from the transfer of the assets will be deferred in certain circumstances. The roll-over automatically applies where:

- there is a payment split under the *Family Law Act 1975* resulting in the transfer of an asset from a small superannuation fund to another complying superannuation fund in which a non-member spouse is a member
- as a result of a request from a non-member spouse under the Superannuation Industry (Supervision) Regulations 1994, the trustee of a small superannuation fund transfers an asset to another complying superannuation fund for the benefit of the non-member spouse, or
- as a result of a marriage or relationship breakdown there is a transfer of a CGT asset that reflects the personal interest of either spouse (but not both) in a small superannuation fund to another complying superannuation fund.

To be eligible, the transfer must be in accordance with:

(1) an award made in an arbitration of property settlement proceedings under the *Family Law Act 1975* or a corresponding award under a corresponding state, territory or foreign law

(2) a court order made under the *Family Law Act 1975* altering property interests of, or binding some other person to effect a division of property between, an individual and their spouse or former spouse

(3) a court order made under a state, territory or foreign law relating to de facto marriage breakdowns that corresponds to an order made under (2)

(4) a binding financial agreement under the *Family Law Act 1975* or a corresponding written agreement that is binding because of a corresponding foreign law

(5) a written agreement that is binding under a state, territory or foreign law relating to de facto marriage breakdowns that, because of such a law, prevents a court making an order about matters to which the agreement applies, or that is inconsistent with the terms of the agreement in relation to those matters, unless the agreement is varied or set aside

(6) a court order made under s 90SM of the *Family Law Act 1975* altering the property interests of, or binding some other person to effect a division of property between, parties to a de facto relationship (including same-sex relationship)

(7) a Pt VIIIAB financial agreement under the *Family Law Act 1975* between parties to a de facto relationship (including same-sex relationship) that is binding pursuant to s 90UJ of the *Family Law Act 1975* (s 126-140(2B)).

The roll-over is not available unless:

- the spouses (including de facto partners) involved are separated and there is no reasonable likelihood of cohabitation being resumed, and
- the transfer happened because of reasons directly connected with the breakdown of the marriage or de facto marriage (s 126-140(2C)).

Consequences of roll-over

If a roll-over happens, the consequences are:

- a capital gain or loss made by the trustee on transfer of the asset is disregarded until a later CGT event such as a sale by the trustee who acquired it
- the first element of the asset's cost base (or reduced cost base) for the trustee who acquired the asset on transfer is the same as it was for the trustee who transferred the asset
- if the asset is a pre-CGT asset of the trustee who transferred it, the asset will be a pre-CGT asset of the trustee who acquired it.

For exemptions relating to the division of superannuation interests on marriage breakdown, see ¶11-880.

[FITR ¶162-455]

Inter-company Roll-overs

¶12-490 Conditions for inter-company CGT roll-overs

Same-asset roll-over relief is available under Subdiv 126-B in certain cases where a company transfers a CGT asset to, or creates a CGT asset in, another company that is a member of the same wholly-owned group. The roll-over is only available where one of the companies is a non-resident.

There is an inter-company roll-over if either:

- the trigger event would have resulted in the originating company making a capital gain, or making no capital loss and not being entitled to a deduction, or
- the roll-over asset is a pre-CGT asset.

In addition, both the originating company and the recipient company must choose to obtain the roll-over (s 126-55).

The roll-over can only take place if an asset is disposed of because CGT event A1 or B1 happens or if an asset is created because CGT event D1, D2, D3 or F1 happens (s 126-45). However, the roll-over does not happen in the case of CGT event B1 if title in the asset does not pass to the recipient company at or before the end of the hire purchase or other agreement.

Where the conditions for roll-over relief are satisfied, balancing adjustment roll-over relief is also available (¶17-710).

Where assets are transferred between companies under common ownership, the value shifting provisions (¶12-800) may apply.

The roll-over is not available for an asset that is either trading stock or a registered emissions unit of the recipient company just after the trigger event. In addition, if the roll-over asset is a right, option, convertible interest or exchangeable interest and the recipient company acquires another asset by exercising that right or option, or by converting the convertible interest, or in exchange for the disposal or redemption of the exchangeable interest, the other asset cannot become trading stock of the recipient company just after it is acquired. If it does, the roll-over will not be available.

For the roll-over to be available, the ordinary and statutory income of the company must not be tax-exempt for the income year of the trigger event.

At the time of the trigger event, either the recipient company or the originating company must be a foreign resident.

If the originating company is a non-resident and the asset has already been rolled over to that non-resident by a resident company, a subsequent roll-over is not available. However, if the asset is merely transferred back to the resident company by the non-resident, the roll-over is available for the subsequent re-transfer. The roll-over is also available where the asset is transferred from the head company of a MEC group (¶8-610) to its non-resident parent, then subsequently transferred back to the head company of the same MEC group (s 126-50). See also ID 2004/459.

Interaction with Subdiv 170-D

Subdivision 170-D (¶11-120) provides for deferral of capital losses or deductions which would otherwise be realised where a CGT asset is disposed of or created within a wholly-owned group. As Subdiv 126-B has no application where Subdiv 170-D applies, this effectively confines the roll-over to situations where the originating company:

- would otherwise make a capital gain
- would otherwise make no capital loss or not be entitled to a deduction, or
- acquired the roll-over asset before 20 September 1985.

Subdivision 126-B thus provides a standard roll-over concession allowing for the retention of the pre-CGT status of assets (including on ''loss assets'' otherwise subject to deferral) and for the roll-over of gain assets. If the asset would have generated a capital loss or deduction, it cannot be rolled over under Subdiv 126-B unless it is a pre-CGT asset, in which case the effect of the roll-over is to preserve that pre-CGT status.

[FITR ¶162-345 – ¶162-395, ¶185-800 – ¶185-870]

¶12-510 Consequences of inter-company CGT roll-over

Consequences for originating company

In all cases, if there is an inter-company roll-over, a capital gain made from the trigger event by the originating company is disregarded (s 126-60).

Consequences for recipient company in disposal situation

If a post-CGT asset of the originating company is disposed of and an inter-company roll-over takes place, the first element of the asset's cost base (and reduced cost base) in the hands of the recipient company is the asset's cost base (or reduced cost base) in the hands of the originating company at the time of the trigger event.

If a pre-CGT asset of the originating company is disposed of and an inter-company roll-over takes place, the asset is also taken to be a pre-CGT asset in the hands of the recipient company.

If a personal use asset of the originating company is disposed of and an inter-company roll-over takes place, the asset is also taken to be a personal use asset in the hands of the recipient company.

Consequences for recipient company in creation situation

If an asset is created in the recipient company by the originating company and an inter-company roll-over takes place, the first element of the asset's cost base (and reduced cost base) in the hands of the recipient company is:

- if the asset is created as a result of CGT event D1, the incidental costs incurred by the originating company in relation to that event
- if the asset is created as a result of CGT event D2, the expenditure incurred by the originating company in granting the option
- if the asset is created as a result of CGT event D3, the expenditure incurred by the originating company in granting the right, or
- if the asset is created as a result of CGT event F1, the expenditure incurred by the originating company on the grant, renewal or extension of the lease.

In addition, CGT event J1 happens to the rolled-over asset if, at a later time, the recipient company still owns the asset and stops being a member of the same wholly-owned group.

[FITR ¶162-370]

¶12-530 Effect of CGT roll-over where wholly-owned subsidiary liquidated

A capital gain on shares made by a holding company as a result of the liquidation of its wholly-owned subsidiary is reduced if:

- there was an inter-company roll-over for at least one post-CGT asset being disposed of by the subsidiary to the holding company in the course of the liquidation of the subsidiary
- the disposals were either part of an interim liquidator's distribution occurring within 18 months of the subsidiary's dissolution or part of the liquidator's final distribution in the course of the liquidation
- the holding company beneficially owned all the shares in the subsidiary from when the roll-over asset was disposed of to the holding company until the cancellation of the shares
- the market value of the roll-over asset or assets comprised at least part of the capital proceeds for the cancellation of the shares in the subsidiary that were beneficially owned by the holding company, and
- one or more of the cancelled shares was a post-CGT share (s 126-85).

Reducing the capital gain

The capital gain on shares made by a holding company as a result of the liquidation of its wholly-owned subsidiary is calculated using the steps below.

Step 1. Work out the capital gains and the capital losses the holding company would make on the cancellation of its subsidiary's shares.

Step 2. Work out the capital gains and the capital losses the subsidiary would make on the disposal of its roll-over assets to the holding company in the course of the liquidation, assuming the capital proceeds were the assets' market values at the time of the disposal.

Step 3. An adjustment is necessary if, after subtracting the capital losses from the capital gains, there is an overall capital gain from step 1 and an overall capital gain from step 2. Otherwise there is no adjustment.

Step 4. Express the number of post-CGT shares as a fraction of the total number of shares the holding company owned in the subsidiary.

Step 5. Multiply the overall capital gain from step 2 by the fraction from step 4.

Step 6. Reduce the overall capital gain from step 1 by the amount from step 5. The result is the capital gain the holding company makes from the cancellation of its shares in the subsidiary.

▶ Example

Wilco owns all the shares in Banco. The shares have a cost base of $100 and a market value of $1,000. Banco owns one asset with a cost base of $100 and a market value of $1,000. An inter-company roll-over is made and, on final distribution by the liquidator, the asset is distributed in specie to Wilco and the shares are cancelled. The capital proceeds are $1,000 (ie the market value of the transferred asset). The overall actual gain on the cancellation of the shares ($900) is reduced by the notional gain on the transferred asset ($900). The end result is that there is no capital gain.

[FITR ¶162-395]

Other Same-asset Roll-overs

¶12-545 CGT roll-over for merger of complying superannuation funds

An optional roll-over is available for capital losses and net capital losses that arise on the merger of superannuation entities. For details on the CGT roll-over relief see ¶13-130.

[*FITR* ¶299-000]

¶12-550 CGT roll-over for changes to trust deed of fund or ADF

There is a compulsory same-asset roll-over where CGT event E1 or E2 happens in relation to a CGT asset because the trust deed of a complying superannuation fund or a complying ADF is amended or replaced. However, the roll-over only happens if the amendment or replacement is done for the purpose of complying with the *Superannuation Industry (Supervision) Act 1993* or enabling a complying ADF to become a complying superannuation fund. It is also necessary that the assets and members of the fund do not change as a consequence of the amendment or replacement.

The roll-over is also available for a fund that amends or replaces its trust deed in order to have the fund approved as an approved worker entitlement fund (¶35-645).

Consequences of roll-over

If a roll-over happens, a capital gain or loss made by the transferor superannuation fund or ADF is disregarded (s 126-135).

If a roll-over asset is a pre-CGT asset of the transferor fund, it is also a pre-CGT asset of the transferee fund.

If a roll-over asset is a post-CGT asset of the transferor fund, the transferee fund is taken to have acquired the asset at the time of the CGT event. In addition, the first element of the asset's cost base (and reduced cost base) to the transferee fund is the same as it was in the hands of the transferor fund.

[FITR ¶162-435]

¶12-552 CGT roll-over for assets between fixed trusts

A limited CGT roll-over is available for assets transferred between fixed trusts that have the same beneficiaries with the same entitlements and no material discretionary elements (Subdiv 126-G). The roll-over is available where all of the following are satisfied:

- the trustee of a fixed trust either creates a trust (''receiving trust'') over a CGT asset or transfers a CGT asset to an existing trust (also ''receiving trust'') at a particular time (''transfer time'')
- immediately before the transfer time, the receiving trust has no CGT assets other than (i) small amounts of cash or debt; and/or (ii) rights under an arrangement which only facilitate the transfer of the assets to it from the transferring trust

- CGT event E4 is capable of happening to all of the units or interests in each of the trusts at the transfer time
- just after the transfer time all of the following are satisfied:
  - both trusts have the same beneficiaries with effectively the same interests
  - the market value of each beneficiary's interest in both trusts is the same as the beneficiary's interest in the transferor trust before the transfer time
  - there is no power to materially alter a beneficiary's interest in either trust
  - there is no power to issue or redeem membership interests in either trust at a discount of more than 10% of their market value
- the trustees of both trusts choose to apply roll-over relief (ss 126-225; 126-230).

If the receiving trust is a foreign trust for the income year in which the transfer time occurs the roll-over is only available if the asset is taxable Australian property just after the transfer time (s 126-235(1)). The roll-over is not available where the trust is a public trading trust (s 126-235(2)). The roll-over is generally only available if both trusts have the same tax choices or elections in force after the transfer time (s 126-235(3)). For example, the election is not available if the transferor makes a family trust election but the transferee did not. See TA 2019/2 for details of arrangements the Commissioner may apply Pt IVA to.

[FITR ¶162-815 – ¶162-825]

¶12-555 CGT roll-over following demutualisation of insurance company

A same-asset roll-over is available where, following the demutualisation of an insurance company:

- a trust is established to hold shares on behalf of policyholders/members (eg those who cannot be located at the time of the demutualisation)
- the demutualisation shares are exchanged for replacement shares under a scrip for scrip roll-over (¶12-325) before the trustee transfers the shares to policyholders/ members, and
- the policyholders/members later become absolutely entitled to the shares held on trust once they have been identified and verified (s 126-190).

In these circumstances, any capital gain or loss made by the trustee will be disregarded. In addition, the first element of the cost base and reduced cost base of the new shares to the policyholder/member will equal the cost base and reduced cost base of those shares to the trustee just before the relevant CGT event happened (s 126-195).

This roll-over is not available for the demutualisation of either private health insurers (s 315-160) or friendly societies (s 316-180). For the roll-over relief available for lost policy holders on the demutualisation of a private health insurer, see Subdiv 315-C (¶12-650).

[FITR ¶162-505 – ¶162-520]

CGT Consequences of Death

¶12-570 CGT consequences for deceased taxpayer

The general rule is that, when a taxpayer dies, a capital gain or loss from a CGT event relating to a CGT asset the taxpayer owned just before death is disregarded (s 128-10). However, a capital gain or loss can still arise from CGT event K3 if the asset passes to a beneficiary that is a non-resident, an exempt entity or the trustee of a complying superannuation fund, complying ADF or PST (¶11-350).

A capital loss of a deceased taxpayer may be offset against any capital gain of the taxpayer in the final individual tax return. Any unrecouped net capital losses lapse altogether on death (TD 95/47).

For a checklist of the tax consequences of death, see ¶44-170.

[FITR ¶163-000 – ¶163-010]

¶12-580 CGT consequences for beneficiary or legal personal representative

Special rules apply in relation to CGT assets that are owned by a taxpayer just before dying which pass to the taxpayer's legal personal representative or a beneficiary of the taxpayer's estate as a result of the taxpayer's death (s 128-15).

Different rules apply if the asset passes to a beneficiary of the taxpayer's estate that is an exempt entity (¶10-605), a non-resident or the trustee of a complying superannuation fund, complying ADF or PST. In such a case, CGT event K3 will arise unless the beneficiary is a non-resident and the asset that passes is taxable Australian property (¶11-350).

Acquisition rules

When a taxpayer dies, assets that pass to the legal personal representative or a beneficiary of the taxpayer's estate are taken to be acquired by them on the day the taxpayer died. Where a non-resident person bequeaths a CGT asset which is not subject to CGT (¶12-720) to a resident beneficiary, the beneficiary makes a capital gain or loss if a CGT event later happens to the asset (TD 2000/6).

Asset passing from legal personal representative to beneficiary

For assets that initially pass to the taxpayer's legal personal representative on the taxpayer's death, any capital gain or loss that the legal personal representative makes when those assets pass from it to a beneficiary of the taxpayer's estate is disregarded. The ATO has a longstanding practice of treating the trustee of a testamentary trust in the same way as a legal personal representative (PS LA 2003/12; TR 2006/14). In this manner the cost base and reduced cost base of the asset in the hands of the ultimate beneficiary will be determined by reference to the cost base and reduced cost base of the asset in the hands of the legal personal representative (PS LA 2003/12, para 4).

Cost base rules for assets acquired

When a taxpayer's legal personal representative or a beneficiary of the taxpayer's estate acquires an asset as a result of the taxpayer's death, the cost base and reduced cost base of the asset in the hands of the legal personal representative or beneficiary are modified under s 128-15(4).

Where the asset is a pre-CGT asset in the hands of the deceased taxpayer, the first element of the cost base (and reduced cost base) to the taxpayer's legal personal representative or beneficiary at the time of acquisition by them is the market value of the asset on the day of the taxpayer's death.

Where the asset is a post-CGT asset in the hands of the deceased taxpayer, the general rule is that the first element of the cost base (and reduced cost base) to the taxpayer's legal personal representative or beneficiary at the time of acquisition by them is the deceased taxpayer's cost base (or reduced cost base) on the day of death. However, if the asset is a dwelling that was the deceased taxpayer's main residence before he/she died and was not used for income-producing purposes at that time, the cost base (and reduced cost base) to the taxpayer's legal personal representative or beneficiary is the market value of the dwelling on the day of the taxpayer's death. If the asset was trading stock of the deceased taxpayer just before death, the first element of the cost base (and reduced cost base) is the amount worked out under s 70-105 (¶9-300).

Specific cost base rules apply to assets of a deceased foreign resident that form part of the estate and are not taxable Australian property (¶12-725). Such assets are treated as being acquired by the deceased's legal personal representative or beneficiary for their market value on the day the deceased died.

The 12-month rule relating to application of the CGT discount and cost base indexation is modified for assets acquired from deceased estates (¶11-033, ¶11-610).

Where an asset passes from a legal personal representative to a beneficiary, the beneficiary can include in the cost base (or reduced cost base) of the asset any expenditure that the legal personal representative would have been able to include at the time the asset passes to the beneficiary. The beneficiary is taken to have incurred that cost base expenditure when the representative incurred it.

▶ Example 1

Bob dies on 1 May 2020 owning land. On 15 June 2020, his executor pays council rates of $500 for the land. On 31 July 2020, the executor transfers the land to Bob's daughter, Anne, in accordance with Bob's will. Anne is taken to have acquired the land on 1 May 2020 and can include the $500 paid by the executor in the third element of the cost base of the land. It is included on 15 June 2020.

A deceased taxpayer's legal personal representative or beneficiary is taken to have acquired a collectable or a personal use asset if the asset was a post-CGT collectable or personal use asset (as appropriate) of the deceased taxpayer at the time of death.

Acquisition of asset after death of deceased

The rules in Div 128 (about the CGT consequences of death) do not apply to an asset acquired by a legal personal representative after the death of a person because the asset is not owned by the deceased at the time of death. For instance, the ordinary CGT rules apply to bonus shares issued after the date of death (TD 2000/11).

Where asset passes to remainder beneficiary on death of life tenant

Where an asset which formed part of a deceased person's estate passes to a remainder beneficiary on the subsequent death of a life tenant, the remainder beneficiary is taken to have acquired the asset when the deceased owner died (not when the life tenant died) (TR 2006/14).

Cost base rules for joint tenants

Special cost base rules apply where a surviving joint tenant acquires the interest of a deceased joint tenant in an asset (s 128-50). In such cases, rules similar to those above apply, except that the cost base and reduced cost base of the deceased taxpayer's interest acquired by the surviving tenants are divided between them equally. For a post-CGT interest of the deceased taxpayer, the cost base at the time of death is equally divided between the surviving joint tenants. For a pre-CGT interest of the deceased taxpayer, the market value at the time of death is equally divided between the surviving tenants.

▶ Example 2

In 2001, Mick and Jerry buy land for $80,000 as joint tenants. They are each taken to have a 50% interest in it. On 1 August 2020, Mick dies. Jerry is taken to have acquired Mick's interest on 1 August 2020. If the cost base of Mick's interest on that day is $45,000, Jerry is taken to have acquired his interest for that amount.

The 12-month rule relating to application of the CGT discount and cost base indexation is modified for assets acquired by surviving joint tenants (¶11-033, ¶11-610).

Cost base rules where beneficiary is a superannuation fund, ADF or PST

Special cost base rules also apply where the beneficiary is the trustee of a complying superannuation fund, a complying ADF or PST (s 128-25). In such cases, a capital gain or loss may be made by the deceased taxpayer from CGT event K3. In addition, the beneficiary is taken to have acquired the asset on the day the deceased taxpayer died, and the first element of the cost base and reduced cost base of the asset to the beneficiary is its market value on that day.

[FITR ¶163-000 – ¶163-050]

¶12-590 When asset passes to a beneficiary of a deceased estate for CGT purposes

Generally, when a taxpayer dies a capital gain or loss from a CGT event relating to a CGT asset the taxpayer owned just before death is disregarded.

A CGT asset passes to a beneficiary of a deceased taxpayer's estate if the beneficiary becomes the owner of the asset:

- under the taxpayer's will, or that will as varied by a court order
- by operation of an intestacy law, or such a law as varied by a court order
- because it is appropriated to the beneficiary by the deceased taxpayer's legal personal representative in satisfaction of a pecuniary legacy or some other interest or share in the estate, or
- under a deed of arrangement, where the beneficiary entered into the deed to settle a claim to participate in the distribution of the estate and any consideration given by the beneficiary for the asset consisted only of the variation or waiver of a claim to an asset of the estate (s 128-20).

It does not matter whether the asset is transmitted directly to the beneficiary or is transferred to the beneficiary by the deceased taxpayer's legal personal representative.

The Commissioner also considers that an asset can pass to a beneficiary of a deceased estate prior to transfer of legal ownership if the beneficiary becomes absolutely entitled to the asset as against the trustee. This applies regardless of whether the asset is later transferred to the beneficiary (TD 2004/3).

However, an asset does not pass to a beneficiary of the deceased taxpayer's estate in circumstances where the beneficiary becomes the owner of the asset because the deceased taxpayer's legal personal representative transfers it under a power of sale. This is so even if such a sale happens because the beneficiary exercises an option granted by the deceased's will.

The CGT consequences where a legal personal representative uses funds from a deceased estate to purchase an asset for a beneficiary in satisfaction of a general legacy are the same as if the beneficiary had received the money and purchased the asset directly (TD 93/36).

[FITR ¶163-030]

CGT Rules for Certain Investments

¶12-600 CGT consequences of bonus shares and units

Special acquisition and cost base rules apply for bonus shares issued by a company and bonus units issued by the trustee of a unit trust (s 130-20). These rules do not apply to a public trading trust.

Where bonus issue assessable

For bonus shares, the first element of the taxpayer's cost base and reduced cost base includes any part of the bonus shares that is a dividend (¶4-110) or is taken to be a dividend because of a capital streaming or dividend substitution arrangement (¶4-680, ¶4-900). For bonus units, the first element of the taxpayer's cost base and reduced cost base includes any part of the bonus units that is assessable. The amount of calls paid on partly paid bonus shares or units also forms part of the first element of their cost base and reduced cost base.

Where bonus issue not assessable

Where a bonus issue is not assessable and the original equities are post-CGT assets, the taxpayer is taken to have acquired the bonus equities when the original equities were acquired. In addition, the first element of the cost base and reduced cost base of the original equities is apportioned in a reasonable way between the original and bonus equities.

Where a bonus issue is not assessable, the original equities are pre-CGT assets and an amount must be paid for the bonus equities, the taxpayer is taken to have acquired the bonus equities when the liability to pay the amount arose. In addition, the first element of the cost base and reduced cost base of the bonus equities includes their market value just before that time.

Where an issue of fully paid bonus equities is not assessable and the original equities are pre-CGT assets, the bonus equities are also taken to be pre-CGT assets. As a result, any capital gain or loss the taxpayer makes from the bonus equities is disregarded.

Where an issue of partly paid bonus equities is not assessable, the original equities are pre-CGT assets and no amount has been paid since the issue of the bonus equities, the bonus equities are also taken to be pre-CGT assets. As a result, any capital gain or loss the taxpayer makes from the bonus equities is disregarded.

Where bonus issue partly assessable

Where an issue of bonus shares is partly assessable, the taxpayer apportions the first element of the cost base and reduced cost base of the original shares in a reasonable way between both the original shares and the bonus shares.

Dividend reinvestment arrangements

For the tax implications of dividend reinvestment arrangements, see IT 2603 and TD 2000/3.

[FITR ¶164-020 – ¶164-030]

¶12-610 CGT consequences of exercise of rights

Special rules may apply if a taxpayer exercises rights to acquire shares (or options to acquire shares) in a company or to acquire units (or options to acquire units) in a unit trust (s 130-40). Options are treated as rights for these rules (s 130-50). Different rules apply to the exercise of rights acquired under employee share schemes (¶10-080).

When the special rules apply

The special rules will apply where the taxpayer did not pay for the rights and at the time the taxpayer was issued with the right, the taxpayer already owned:

- shares in, or convertible interests issued by, the company or a company that is a member of the same wholly owned group, or
- units in, or convertible interest issued by the trustee of, the unit trust (provided the right was issued after 28 January 1988).

For this purpose, a company that is a member of the same wholly-owned group includes a company that ceases to be a member of that group by the exercise of the rights.

The special rules also apply if the taxpayer acquired the rights from an entity that already owned shares, units or convertible interests (as applicable) of the kind referred to in the above bullet points.

Capital gain or loss disregarded

In accordance with the special rules, a capital gain or loss made from the exercise of a right, ie because CGT event C2 happens to it, is disregarded.

Special acquisition rules

Where rights are acquired from the issuing company or trustee without payment, a taxpayer is taken to have acquired the rights when the original shares, units or interests were acquired (s 130-45). If the existing shares consist of both pre-CGT and post-CGT shares, the rights are apportioned as pre-CGT and post-CGT assets (TD 93/80). In addition, where shares, units or options are acquired by exercising rights, a taxpayer is taken to have acquired the new shares, units or options when the rights were exercised.

Cost base modifications

In addition, the general rules for working out the cost base and reduced cost base of the shares, units or options are modified (s 130-40(6)). The cost base modifications apply where:

- rights issued by a company or trustee to a taxpayer are exercised
- rights acquired by a taxpayer from another entity are exercised
- a taxpayer exercises rights issued to it by a company or trustee and those rights are taken to be pre-CGT rights because they were issued in respect of pre-CGT shares.

In each of these situations, the first element of the taxpayer's cost base and reduced cost base for the shares, units or options is the sum of:

- the cost base of the rights at the time of exercise
- any amount paid to exercise the rights, and
- any amount by which the capital gain from the right has been reduced under s 118-20 (¶11-690).

[FITR ¶164-100 – ¶164-110]

¶12-620 CGT consequences of turning convertible interests into shares/units

Special rules apply if a taxpayer acquires shares in a company or units in a unit trust by converting a convertible interest (s 130-60).

Capital gain or loss disregarded

One of the special rules is that a capital gain or loss made from converting a convertible interest, ie because CGT event C2 happens to it, is disregarded.

Special acquisition rules

A taxpayer is taken to have acquired the shares or units as a result of the conversion at the time that the conversion happened.

Cost base modifications

In addition, the general rules for working out the cost base and reduced cost base of the share or unit are modified (s 130-60(1)). The cost base modifications apply where:

- shares in a company or units in a trust are acquired by converting a convertible interest that is a traditional security (¶23-340)
- shares in a company are acquired by converting a convertible interest that is *not* a traditional security, and
- units in a trust are acquired by converting a convertible interest (not being a traditional security) that was issued by the trustee of the unit trust after 28 January 1988.

In each of these situations, the first element of the taxpayer's cost base and reduced cost base for the shares or units is the sum of:

- the cost base of the convertible interest at the time of conversion
- any amount paid to convert the convertible interest, and
- any amount by which the capital gain from the convertible interest has been reduced under s 118-20 (¶11-690).

A payment to convert a convertible interest can include giving property (s 130-60(1B)).

[FITR ¶164-130]

¶12-625 CGT implications for exchangeable interests

Special rules apply if a taxpayer acquires shares in a company in exchange for the disposal or redemption of an exchangeable interest (Subdiv 130-E).

An exchangeable interest is a traditional security that is issued on or after 1 July 2001 on the basis that it will or may be redeemed or disposed of to the issuer in exchange for shares in a company that is not the issuer (or a connected entity of the issuer) (s 130-100).

Capital gain or loss disregarded

Any capital gain or loss arising from the disposal or redemption of the exchangeable interest is disregarded.

Special acquisition rules

A taxpayer is taken to have acquired the shares when the disposal or redemption of the exchangeable interest happened.

Cost base modifications

The general rules for working out the cost base and reduced cost base of the share are modified (s 130-105(1)).

When an exchangeable interest is disposed of or redeemed, the first element of the taxpayer's cost base and reduced cost base of the share is the sum of:

- the cost base of the exchangeable interest at the time of the disposal or redemption
- any other amount paid for the exchange, and
- any amount by which the capital gain from the exchange has been reduced under s 118-20 (¶11-690).

A payment for the exchange of an exchangeable interest can include giving property (s 130-105(3)).

[FITR ¶164-200]

¶12-630 CGT consequences of employee share schemes

Special rules apply if a taxpayer acquires shares in a company under an employee share scheme. The rules which apply to shares and rights issued under an employee share scheme on or after 1 July 2009 are summarised below (¶10-080). For the operation of shares and options issued prior to 1 July 2009, see the 2009 *Australian Master Tax Guide* (45th Edition) or earlier editions.

For the CGT treatment that applies to an employee remuneration trust or ERT, see TR 2018/7.

Shares or rights acquired under employee share scheme

The basic rule is that a discount received on a share or rights under an employee share scheme (an ''ESS interest'') will be taxed primarily under the income tax rules pursuant to Div 83A unless it qualifies for the small start-up concessions (see below). The taxation on a discount received on an ESS interest will only be deferred in the limited circumstances where there was a genuine risk of forfeiture or a salary sacrifice arrangement has been entered into. Accordingly, CGT will not generally apply to an ESS interest until an amount has first been included in assessable income pursuant to Div 83A (s 130-75).

A capital gain or loss arising from a CGT event (other than CGT event E4, G1 or K8) that happens to an ESS interest will be disregarded to the extent that an amount will be, but has not yet been, included in the taxpayer's assessable income (s 130-80(1)).

Where the discount received on the ESS interest is included in the employee's assessable income in the income year of acquisition, the first element of the cost base of an ESS interest will be its market value (ss 83A-30; 130-80(4)). Where the taxing point of the ESS interest is deferred, for CGT purposes the recipient will be treated as having acquired the ESS interest at the ESS deferred taxing point for its then market value (ss 83A-125; 130-80(3)).

Shares or rights entitled to small start-up concessions

Special rules apply for ESS interests acquired from 1 July 2015 in small start-up companies that meet the conditions in s 83A-33 (¶10-090).

Where the ESS interest acquired is a share, the discount is not subject to income tax and the cost base of the share for CGT purposes is its market value as at the date of issue.

Where the ESS interest acquired is a right, there is no income tax on acquisition and the cost base for CGT purposes is equal to the employee's cost of acquiring the right (ss 83A-30(2); 130-80(4)). There is no CGT on the exercise of the right and the cost base of the share is equal to the cost base of the right plus the exercise price of the right. However, for the purpose of determining whether a capital gain is a discount gain, a share acquired as a result of exercising such a right is treated being acquired on the date the right was acquired, rather than the date of exercise (s 115-30, item 9A; ¶11-033).

Shares or rights acquired under employee share scheme involving associate

For the purpose of determining whether to exclude the capital gain or loss under s 130-80(1) an ESS interest acquired by an associate is treated as having been acquired by the employee and any actions of the associate are treated as having been done by the employee (ss 83A-305; 130-85(3)).

Shares or rights acquired under employee share trusts

Where a taxpayer acquires an ESS interest as a result of an interest held in an employee share trust, the taxpayer is treated as if the taxpayer was absolutely entitled to the share or right under the ESS and CGT provisions (s 130-85).

In general, the capital gain or capital loss from either CGT event E5 or E7 to an employee share trust, or a beneficiary of the trust, will be disregarded to the extent it arises due to the disposal of a share acquired by the trust from the exercise of a right that was an ESS interest (s 130-90). Further any capital gain or loss made by an employee share trust is disregarded where it arises as a result of a beneficiary of the trust becoming absolutely entitled to an employee share scheme share, or as a result of a disposal of an employee share scheme share or right to a beneficiary (s 130-90(1A)).

Stapled securities

The ESS provisions apply to stapled securities in the same way they apply to a share in a company provided at least one of the ownership interests in the stapled security is a share in a company (s 83A-335).

Temporary residents

Capital gains and losses realised on ESS interests acquired under an employee share scheme are eligible for the temporary residents CGT exemption in a similar manner as other CGT assets provided the income taxing point has occurred under the income tax provisions of Div 83A (¶12-760).

The exemption for temporary residents does not apply to ESS interests that constitute taxable Australian property.

[FITR ¶131-035, ¶131-090, ¶131-145, ¶164-135 – ¶164-157]

¶12-640 CGT consequences of share buy-backs

Special provisions, some of which have CGT implications, govern the tax treatment of situations where a company buys back its own shares or non-share equity interests (ITAA36 Pt III Div 16K).

In the case of *off-market* share buy-backs, the capital proceeds on disposal of the shares exclude the assessable dividend component of the buy-back price. In the case of *on-market* share buy-backs, the capital proceeds include the total amount received.

So far as the company is concerned, the buy-back is taken not to have occurred, so no capital gain or loss arises to it.

For further details of the tax treatment of share buy-backs, see ¶3-170. The ATO has Fact Sheets on share buy-backs by community banks.

[FTR ¶75-000 – ¶75-028]

¶12-650 CGT implications for demutualisation of mutual entities

Special provisions specify the tax treatment of transactions likely to occur in connection with the demutualisation of:

- a life or general insurance company or an affiliate company (ITAA36 ss 121AA to 121AT)
- mutual non-insurance entities (ITAA36 Sch 2H Div 326)
- private health insurance entities (ITAA97 Div 315)
- friendly societies, including joint health and life insurers (ITAA97 Div 316).

For details regarding the general taxation consequences from demutualisation, see ¶3-432. For the specific roll-over allowed for replacement shares in a scrip for scrip transaction, see ¶12-325.

Life or general insurance organisations

The special provisions apply to the demutualisation of life or general insurance companies and mutual affiliate companies that existed at 7.30 pm EST on 9 May 1995, where the demutualisation is carried out in accordance with one of 7 specified methods in ss 121AF to 121AL. A basic requirement for the provisions is that the members agree to surrender their rights in the mutual company in exchange for shares in the demutualised entity. The shares must generally be listed by ASX Limited within 2 years from the demutualisation resolution day (ie the day that the resolution to proceed with the demutualisation is passed or, where a life assurance company's life insurance business is transferred to another company under a Federal Court-approved scheme, the day on which the transfer of the whole of that business takes place).

The modifications of the CGT rules that apply in connection with a demutualisation are detailed in Table 1 of s 121AS. Broadly, the main CGT consequences are:

- any capital gain or loss from the surrender of the membership interests in the mutual insurance company or mutual affiliate company is disregarded
- a capital gain is only realised when the member disposes of the allotted shares (or rights to the shares or proceeds of sale)
- the shares in the new entity are treated as post-CGT shares
- before listing, the CGT cost base of the former members' shares is set by reference to the actuarially determined embedded value of a life office, or the net tangible assets of a general insurance office. After listing, the cost base is the lower of this amount and the closing price on the first day of trading. To the extent that indexing applies, the cost base is indexed from the demutualisation resolution day
- before the listing of the shares, capital losses do not arise on disposal of demutualisation shares or rights to shares
- where a holding company or other interposed company acquires shares in a demutualising insurance company, the deemed acquisition cost of those shares properly reflects the deemed acquisition cost of shares issued to policyholders/ members.

Mutual non-insurance entities

Special provisions in ITAA36 Sch 2E Div 326 apply to the demutualisation of a resident mutual entity that is not an insurance organisation, a health insurer, a friendly health society or a life insurer (s 326-10(1)).

The special provisions apply where the demutualisation is carried out in accordance with one of 4 specified methods in ss 326-45 to 326-55 and the continuity of beneficial interest test is satisfied (s 326-60). The shares must generally be listed by ASX Limited within 2 years from the demutualisation resolution day.

Broadly, the CGT consequences that apply in connection with the demutualisation are:

- any capital gain or loss from the extinguishment of the membership rights in the mutual entity is disregarded
- the amount paid for the acquisition of shares in the demutualised entity allotted to a former member is determined according to when the original membership interest was acquired
- the amount paid for the acquisition of shares in the demutualised entity allotted to a former member is determined according to when the original membership interest was acquired. For a pre-CGT member, the amount paid is determined by reference to the member's share of the market value of the demutualising entity determined immediately before demutualisation (reduced by the member's share of any franking surplus). For a post-CGT member, the amount paid is determined by reference to the costs incurred by the member in acquiring and maintaining their rights of membership (eg joining fees) to the extent that such costs are not deductible.

Private health insurance entities

CGT relief is available to private health insurance policyholders when their insurer converts, by demutualising, from being a *not for profit* to a *for profit* insurer under the special provisions in ITAA97 Div 315. For the provisions to apply, the demutualising insurer must not be registered under the *Life Insurance Act 1995*, or have capital divided into shares, and must convert in accordance with a conversion scheme approved under the *Private Health Insurance Act 2007* (s 315-15).

Broadly, the CGT consequences from the demutualisation are:

- any capital gain arising in relation to the shares, rights or cash payments received by policyholders on the private health insurer's demutualisation are disregarded (s 315-5). Corresponding exemptions apply to legal personal representatives of policy holders (ss 315-10; 315-310)
- a CGT exemption applies to capital gains or losses arising from the demutualisation to the insurer (s 315-25) or interposed entities (s 315-30)
- for CGT purposes, any shares or rights received from the demutualisation are treated as if they had been acquired for market value on the date of issue (s 315-80). These "demutualisation assets", which must all be distributed at the same time, must consist of shares in the demutualising insurer, or its holding company, or rights to acquire such shares (s 315-85). They must be issued to "participating policy holders", ie policy holders, former policy holders, or other persons who are or were insured (s 315-90), in connection with the variation or cancellation of their pre-existing rights. A corresponding exemption applies where the participating policy holder dies before the shares or rights are issued (s 315-260). The method of determining market value is varied if the shares or rights relate to a holding company that owns other assets in addition to its shares in the demutualising insurer (s 315-210).

Special rules apply to cover the tax position of ''lost policy holders'' trusts (which do not need to exist under a court approved scheme) that are set up for the purpose of holding share or trust entitlements on behalf of policy holders whose entitlements have not been verified, or who are living overseas (s 315-140). The trustee is treated as having acquired the demutualisation assets at market value at the time they are issued (s 315-145). Assets held by these trusts are given roll-over relief when they are transferred to the lost policy holder, or that holder becomes absolutely entitled (s 315-150). Otherwise, the trustee will be taxable on the beneficiary's share of the net capital gain (s 315-155).

Friendly societies

CGT relief is available to policyholders of friendly societies, including joint health and life insurers, which demutualise to *for profit* entities (Div 316).

The special provisions apply in connection with the demutualisation of a friendly society that: (a) provides health insurance or life insurance, or has a wholly owned subsidiary that provides such insurance; (b) does not have its capital divided into shares; and (c) after the demutualisation is to be carried on for profit (s 316-5).

Broadly, the CGT consequences from the demutualisation are:

- any capital gain or loss arising to a member or insured entity of the friendly society under its demutualisation is disregarded except where the member or insured entity receives an amount of money (s 316-55)
- where the member or insured entity receives an amount of money, a capital gain or loss may be realised through special adjustment rules to the cost base of the interest affected by the demutualisation (s 316-60; Subdivs 316-B; 316-C). The adjustments ensure that the same treatment applies as if the entity received the allocation of shares and immediately disposed of them
- the cost base for shares issued to members and insured entities is based on (a) the market value of the friendly society's health insurance business; and (b) the embedded value of the life insurance business and any other business of the friendly society (Subdiv 316-C)
- corresponding treatment applies to legal personal representatives and beneficiaries of deceased policy holders. A capital gain or loss arising from the shares passing from the legal personal representative to the beneficiary is disregarded (s 316-200)
- capital gains or losses arising from the demutualisation to the friendly society are disregarded (s 316-75)
- where an entity is established solely for the purpose of participating in the friendly society's demutualisation which is not a lost policy holders trust and the entity makes capital gains or losses connected to the allocation or distribution of the friendly society's accumulated mutual surplus which arise prior to, or at the time, the surplus is allocated or distributed, those capital gains or losses are disregarded (s 316-80).

Special rules apply to cover the tax position of ''lost policy holders'' trusts that are set up for the purpose of holding share or trust entitlements on behalf of members and insured entities whose entitlements have not been verified, or who are living overseas (Subdiv 316-D). Such shares or rights may be held on trust and transferred to the policyholder without CGT consequences to the trustee. The policyholder receives the shares or rights with the same CGT attributes as if they had received them directly.

[FTR ¶59-120 – ¶59-226, ¶799-932 – ¶799-960; FITR ¶306-000 – ¶307-550]

¶12-660 CGT consequences for managed investment trusts

Managed Investment Trusts (MITs) are allowed to make an irrevocable election to treat gains and losses on eligible investments on capital account for taxation purposes. The election makes the CGT provisions the primary code for taxing gains and losses on the disposal of eligible investments by MITs that make the election, subject to integrity rules.

CGT treatment applies to gains and losses made by a MIT where all the following conditions are satisfied:

- the entity is an eligible MIT
- the asset is an eligible asset
- the gain or loss arises on the disposal or other realisation of an eligible asset
- the trustee of the MIT makes or has made an irrevocable election to apply the CGT provisions as the primary code for eligible assets (Subdiv 275-B).

This enables investors in MITs to obtain the benefit of any CGT tax concessions on distributions of capital gains. Where an eligible entity does not make the election it will forever be subject to revenue treatment on such gains and losses.

It is proposed that managed investment trusts (MITs) and attribution MITs (AMITs) will be prevented from applying the 50% discount at the trust level but will still be able to distribute such income as a capital gain that can be discounted in the hands of the beneficiary, with effect from the income year starting on or after 3 months after the date of assent of the enabling legislation (2018–19 Budget Paper No 2, p 44).

An eligible asset is a share or non-share equity interest in a company, a unit in a unit trust, land or a right or option to acquire or dispose of any of the preceding assets, but excludes an asset that is a Div 230 financial arrangement or a debt interest (s 275-105).

Eligible MIT

A trust is an eligible MIT for an income year, where it is a MIT. A trading trust cannot be an MIT (ss 275-100; 275-110). A unit trust is a MIT in relation to an income year where:

- at the time of the first fund payment in relation to the income year, the trustee of the trust was an Australian resident or the central management and control of the trust was in Australia
- the trust is not a trading trust, nor carrying on a trading business, in relation to the income year
- a substantial portion of the investment management activities carried out in relation to the trust in respect of all of its Australian connected assets (ie assets situated in Australia, taxation Australian property and shares, units or interests listed for quotation on an approved stock exchange in Australia) throughout the income year are carried out in Australia
- the trust has MIS status under s 9 of the *Corporations Act 2001*
- the trust is either a wholesale managed investment trust which satisfies the licensing requirements or is a registered MIS pursuant to s 601EB of the *Corporation Act 2001*
- the trust satisfies the relevant widely-held requirements
- the trust satisfies the relevant closely-held restrictions
- the trust satisfies the relevant licensing requirements (s 275-10).

A trust is treated as satisfying the widely-held and closely-held requirements for an income year if it was created in the period starting 12 months before the start of the income year and ending at the end of the income year or if a trust ceases to exist during an income year but was a MIT in the previous income year (s 275-10(6)).

The extended definition of a MIT broadly includes each of the following:

(a) a trust that is an Australian resident trust and every member of the trust is a MIT (or treated as a MIT) in relation to the income year (s 275-45)

(b) a trust that is not a MIT because a fund payment was not made in relation to the income year but had a fund payment been made on both the first day and the last day of the income year it would have been a MIT (s 275-50)

(c) the trust would be a MIT but for a circumstance that is temporary and arose outside the control of the trustee and it is fair and reasonable to treat the trust as a MIT (s 275-55).

Election

The election is irrevocable and must be made in the approved form by the relevant time. In general, the election needs to be made on or before the time it is required to lodge its income tax return for the income year in which it became a MIT and will have effect from the time it came into existence.

Where the election is made, the CGT provisions are the primary code for taxing eligible assets (s 275-100). A MIT is treated as owning an asset to the extent that the MIT has an interest in the asset as a limited partner in a VCLP or ESVCLP, thereby making CGT the primary code for such investments (s 275-100(1A)). However, where a MIT is eligible to make the election but does not make it, a gain or loss on an eligible asset (other than land, an interest in land or an option to acquire or dispose of such an asset) will forever be treated as being on revenue account (s 275-120).

Carried interests

The CGT provisions generally do not apply to ''carried interests'' in a MIT. Instead the holder of a ''carried interest'' in a MIT, is required to include in their assessable income:

- any amount received as a distribution from the MIT in relation to the carried interest
- the proceeds from the disposal of a carried interest (s 275-200).

For these purposes, a carried interest refers to a CGT asset that was acquired because of services to be provided to the MIT by the holder of the CGT asset or an associate, as a manager of the MIT, an employee of a manager or an associate of such an employee or manager.

[*FITR* ¶265-045 – ¶265-065]

Leases

¶12-680 CGT cost base modifications for leases

Several CGT events deal specifically with leases (¶11-300). In addition, Div 132 specifically provides for cost base modifications for leases. These are considered below.

Cost to lessee of varying lease

If the lessee of property incurs expenditure in obtaining the consent of the lessor to vary or waive a term of the lease, the fourth element of the lessee's cost base and reduced cost base for the lease includes the amount of that expenditure (s 132-1).

Leasehold improvements

The fourth element of the cost base and reduced cost base of property that was subject to a lease includes any payment (because of the lease expiring or being surrendered or forfeited) by the lessor to the lessee for expenditure of a capital nature incurred by the lessee in making improvements to the lease property (s 132-5).

The CGT consequences of a lessee incurring expenditure of a capital nature on making improvements to leased property depend on whether the lessee or the lessor is the owner of the improvements (TD 98/23). If the lessee owns the improvements, the cost base of the improvements includes the amount of capital expenditure incurred in making the improvements. If the lessee does not own the improvements but the capital expenditure is incurred to increase or preserve the value of the lease, the expenditure is included in the cost base of the lease to the lessee (s 110-25(5)). If any part of the lessee's expenditure is recouped, and the amount of the recoupment received is not included in the lessee's assessable income, the recouped amount cannot form part of the cost base of the lease.

Effect on lessor granting long-term lease

The general cost base rules are modified for a lessor who chooses that CGT event F2 happens in respect of a long-term lease it has granted (s 132-10).

Firstly, the cost base and reduced cost base of the land (or the lessor's lease of it) for the purposes of any later CGT event that happens to it excludes: (a) any expenditure incurred before CGT event F2 happens; and (b) the cost of any depreciating asset for which the lessor can claim depreciation. This modification also applies to the cost base and reduced cost base of any building, part of a building, structure or improvement that is treated as a separate CGT asset (¶11-410).

Secondly, the fourth element of the property's cost base and reduced cost base to the lessor includes any payment by the lessor to the lessee to vary or waive a term of the lease or for the forfeiture or surrender of the lease.

Lease surrender payments

Where a lessor makes a lease surrender payment to obtain a permanent advantage, the payment is of a capital nature and can be included in the cost base of the asset (ie the lease) acquired. However, where a lessee makes a lease surrender payment, eg to dispose of an onerous lease, the amount of the payment cannot be included in the cost base of the lease disposed of because it is not an incidental cost as defined (TR 2005/6). A lease surrender payment may also give rise to a capital gain or loss (¶11-270). For the general tax treatment of lease surrender receipts and payments, see ¶10-116 and ¶16-640.

Acquisition of reversionary interest in chattel

In the case of the lease of a chattel, the acquisition of a lessor's reversionary interest by a lessee takes place at the time the agreement for the acquisition is entered into (*Case X81*; TD 11).

[FITR ¶165-000 – ¶165-070]

¶12-690 CGT where lessee acquires reversionary interest in land

Special acquisition and cost base rules apply where a lessee of land acquires a lessor's reversionary interest and a Crown lease roll-over does not apply to the acquisition (s 132-15).

Lease granted for 99 years or more

Where the lease was originally granted for 99 years or more and a lessee of land acquires the lessor's reversionary interest in it without a roll-over, the lessee is taken to acquire the land when the lease was granted or assigned to the lessee. In addition, the cost of the land to the lessee is taken to be the premium paid by the lessee for the grant or assignment of the lease (if any) plus the amount paid to acquire the reversionary interest.

Lease granted for less than 99 years

Where the lease was originally granted for less than 99 years and a lessee of land acquires the lessor's reversionary interest in it without a roll-over, the lessee is taken to acquire the land when it acquires the reversionary interest. In addition, if the lease is a post-CGT lease of the lessee, the cost of the land to the lessee is taken to be the premium paid by the lessee for the grant or assignment of the lease (if any) plus the amount paid to acquire the reversionary interest. However, if the lease is a pre-CGT lease of the lessee, the cost of the land to the lessee is taken to be the market value of the land when the lessee acquired it.

Indexing of premium

Any premium paid is indexed from the time the lessee acquired the reversionary interest (¶11-610).

[FITR ¶165-100]

Options

¶12-700 CGT consequences of exercise of options

When an option is exercised, the usual CGT rules are modified (s 134-1). However, these modifications do not apply where the special CGT rules dealing with certain rights and options issued by a company or trust are involved (¶12-610).

The rules apply to an option for the disposal, creation (including grant or issue) or acquisition of a CGT asset. The rules also apply to the renewal or extension of an option in the same way. For example, the rules apply to an option to grant a lease or easement or an option to issue units in a unit trust.

Capital gain or loss disregarded when option exercised

A capital gain or loss the grantee of an option makes from exercising the option is disregarded. Similarly, a capital gain or loss the grantor of an option makes if the grantee exercises it is also disregarded (s 104-40(5)).

Cost base modifications when option exercised

When an option is exercised, the cost base and reduced cost base of the option is modified for both the grantor of the option and the grantee of the option (ie the taxpayer that exercises the option).

In the case of a call option, ie where the option binds the grantor to dispose of, or create (including grant or issue), an asset, the first element of the grantee's cost base and reduced cost base for the asset acquired is what the grantee paid for the option (or to renew or extend it) plus any amount paid by the grantee to exercise that option. In addition, the grantor's capital proceeds from the relevant CGT event are worked out in the same way. If the option was granted pre-CGT and exercised post-CGT, the first element of the cost base and reduced cost base of the acquired asset includes the market value of the option at the time of exercise. However, this rule does not apply to an option last renewed or extended after 19 September 1985.

In the case of a put option, ie where the option binds the grantor to acquire an asset, the first element of the grantor's cost base and reduced cost base for the asset acquired is the amount the grantee paid for the asset it was required to purchase because the grantee exercised the option, reduced by the amount received by the grantor for the grant of the option (or to renew or extend it). In addition, the second element of the grantee's cost base and reduced cost base for the asset acquired by the grantor includes any payment the grantee made to acquire the option (or to renew or extend it).

▶ Example 1

Elaine gives Jerry an option to buy her boat for $50,000. Jerry pays $10,000 for the option and later exercises it. The first element of his cost base and reduced cost base for the boat includes the $10,000 he paid for the option. Accordingly, the first element of his cost base and reduced cost base for the boat is $60,000 (ie $50,000 + $10,000).

▶ Example 2

Herman owns 5,000 shares in Munsterco. Lily gives Herman an option which, if exercised, would require her to buy the shares for $1 each. Herman pays Lily 30 cents per share for the option. Herman exercises the option and Lily pays $5,000 for the shares. The first element of Lily's cost base and reduced cost base for the shares is $3,500 (ie $5,000 – $1,500). In working out whether Herman makes a capital gain or loss on the sale of the shares, the second element of his cost base and reduced cost base includes the $1,500 he paid for the option.

If a payment made to exercise an option is indexed (¶11-610), indexation applies from when that payment was incurred (TD 17). If an option is exercised, the date of the acquisition of the asset subject to the option is the date of the transaction that arises from the exercise of the option (TD 16). In *Van*, shares were acquired under an option agreement when the option was exercised, ie the date on which the taxpayer applied for and was allotted the shares, not when the option was granted. See also ID 2003/128.

[FITR ¶166-020]

International Tax Rules

¶12-720 CGT rules for foreign residents

Foreign residents will only recognise a capital gain or loss where the CGT event happens in relation to certain specified assets known as taxable Australian property (ITAA97 Div 855; ¶12-725). Taxable Australian property broadly includes direct or indirect interests in Australian real property and the business assets (other than Australian real property) of an Australian permanent establishment. Capital gains or losses made from other CGT assets will be disregarded (s 855-10). However, this will not apply to exempt the additional gain under Subdiv 115-C (¶11-060) in relation to a capital gain distributed to a foreign resident or temporary resident from a non-fixed trust (*Draft* TD 2019/D6; *Peter Greensill Family Co Pty Ltd (as trustee)*; *N & M Martin Holdings Pty Ltd & Anor*). These rules also apply to a trustee of a foreign trust for CGT purposes (see below).

Foreign trust for CGT purposes

A foreign trust for CGT purposes means a trust that is *not* a resident trust for CGT purposes. A trust is a resident trust for CGT purposes for an income year where, at any time during the year:

- if the trust is *not a unit trust*, either the trustee is a resident or the central management and control of the trust is in Australia, or
- if the trust is a *unit trust*: (a) either any property of the trust is situated in Australia or the trustee carries on business in Australia; and (b) either the central management and control of the unit trust is in Australia or residents held more than 50% of the beneficial interests in the income or property of the trust (s 995-1(1)).

In calculating a capital gain or loss made by a foreign trust for CGT purposes, the residency assumption (¶6-080) in ITAA36 s 95(1) does not apply. Therefore, the trustee will disregard any capital gain or loss made from a CGT event that happens to an asset that is not taxable Australian property and any beneficiaries receiving a distribution from this amount are not treated as having capital gains (TD 2017/23).

[FITR ¶649-000]

¶12-725 Taxable Australian property for CGT purposes

A foreign resident's liability for CGT is based on whether the relevant asset is taxable Australian property.

The following assets are taxable Australian property (s 855-15):

(1) taxable Australian real property

(2) an indirect interest in Australian real property

(3) a business asset of a permanent establishment in Australia

(4) an option or right to acquire any of the CGT assets in items 1 to 3, or

(5) a CGT asset that is deemed to be Australian taxable property where a taxpayer, on ceasing to be an Australian resident, makes an election under s 104-165 (¶11-330).

A non-final withholding tax applies on the sale of taxable Australian property to increase the recovery of CGT from foreign residents (¶26-269).

Taxable Australian real property

Taxable Australian real property not only includes real property situated in Australia, it also extends to a lease of Australian land and mining, quarrying or prospecting rights where the materials are situated in Australia (s 855-20; TD 2009/18). *Resource Capital Fund IV LP* provides detailed analysis of the meaning of ‘‘mining, quarrying or prospecting rights’’. In that decision the Full Court considered that the term ‘‘real property’’ included ‘‘rights to exploit or to explore for natural resources’’, hence the relevant shares and interests sold by the taxpayers were a mining, quarrying or prospecting right and constituted taxable Australian real property. However, mining information obtained through exploration expenditure is not taxable Australian real property (ID 2012/13).

Indirect real property interest

Taxable Australian property also includes an interest in Australian real property that is held indirectly through a chain of interposed entities. An indirect Australian real property interest exists where a foreign resident has a membership interest in an entity and that interest passes 2 tests (s 855-25):

- the non-portfolio interest test, and
- the principal asset test.

Non-portfolio interest test

An interest held by an entity (the holding entity) in another entity (the test entity) passes the non-portfolio interest test if the sum of the direct participation interests held by the holding entity and its associates in the test entity is 10% or more (s 960-195).

A direct participation interest is the total interest that an entity directly holds in another entity (s 960-190).

The test is satisfied if the interest passes the test either:

- at that time (generally the time of the CGT event), or
- throughout a 12-month period that began no earlier than 24 months before that time and ended no later than that time.

Principal asset test

A membership interest must also pass the principal asset test to be an indirect Australian real property interest. The principal asset test is used to determine when an entity’s underlying value is principally derived from Australian real property. The Full Federal Court has held that, for the purposes of the principal asset test, the values of the relevant entity’s individual assets should be determined as if there was an assumed simultaneous sale of assets to the same hypothetical purchaser (*Resource Capital Fund III LP*).

A membership interest held by a foreign resident (the holding entity) in another entity (the test entity) passes the principal asset test if more than 50% of the value of the test entity’s assets is attributable to Australian real property (s 855-30). For these purposes an ‘‘asset’’ of an entity is anything recognised in commerce and business as having economic value to the entity at the time of the relevant CGT event for which a purchaser of the entity’s membership interests would be willing to pay (ID 2012/14). The principal asset test is applied on an associate inclusive basis for foreign tax residents with indirect interests in Australian real property (s 855-30(4A)).

The principal asset test was considered in detail in *Resource Capital Fund IV LP* (overturned on appeal), where it was held that the preferred method for valuation of ore before its further processing was a netback method, rather than the market approach. On appeal, the Full Court did not specifically consider the principal asset test. However, it is unlikely that the lower court's findings on such remain valid given that the Full Court, after concluding that the relevant assets were taxable Australian real property, appeared to reject the expert evidence of the taxpayer in favour of that of the Commissioner as to valuation.

Where the assets of 2 or more entities are included in the principal asset test, the test is amended to disregard the market value of non-taxable Australian real property assets arising from transactions between those 2 or more entities created before the CGT event (s 855-32). This is to ensure that non-taxable Australian real property assets cannot be counted multiple times to dilute the true asset value of the group.

TA 2008/19 and TA 2008/20 warn against foreign residents entering into certain arrangements attempting to avoid Australian CGT on the sale of indirect holdings in Australian real property. The alerts cover arrangements that attempt to circumvent indirect holding rules through staggered sell down arrangements or the manipulation of the value of assets.

Permanent establishment in Australia

Taxable Australian property also includes assets that a foreign resident has used at any time in carrying on a business through a permanent establishment in Australia as defined under the relevant tax treaty, or if no treaty exists, the definition in ITAA36 s 6(1) (s 855-15).

A capital gain or loss made from an asset that was used in carrying on a business through a permanent establishment in Australia is proportionately reduced if it was used in this way for only part of the period from when the taxpayer acquired it to when the CGT event happened (s 855-35).

▶ Example

A foreign resident acquired an asset on 1 January 2018 for $21,000. On 1 October 2018, it was first used by the taxpayer in carrying on a business at the taxpayer's permanent establishment in Australia. The taxpayer sold the asset on 10 January 2020 for $10,000. The period of qualifying use is 467 days (ie 1 October 2018 to 10 January 2020). The ownership period is 740 days (ie 1 January 2018 to 10 January 2020). The capital loss is therefore $11,000 × 467/740 = $6,942.

[FITR ¶649-010 – ¶649-045]

¶12-735 CGT exemption for foreign resident interests in fixed trusts

A CGT exemption is available under s 855-40 where a foreign resident makes a capital gain or loss on an interest in a fixed trust (including a managed fund) and that interest is *not* taxable Australian property (¶12-725).

The object of the rule is to provide comparable tax treatment between indirect ownership of interests in fixed trusts and direct ownership of such interests.

The exemption applies where:

- the gain is attributable to a CGT event happening to a CGT asset of a trust (the CGT event trust) that is:
  - (i) the fixed trust, or
  - (ii) another fixed trust in which that trust has an interest (directly, or indirectly through a chain of fixed trusts), and
- either:
  - (i) the asset is not taxable Australian property for the CGT event trust at the time of the CGT event, or

(ii) the asset is an interest in a fixed trust which is taxable Australian property ("first trust") and either of the following are satisfied:

(A) at least 90% (by market value) of the underlying assets of the trust must not be taxable Australian property, or

(B) at least 90% (by market value) of the assets held by other fixed trusts in which the first trust has an interest (directly or indirectly through a chain of fixed trusts) must not be taxable Australian property.

This exemption does not apply to the capital gain of a foreign resident beneficiary from a non-fixed resident trust, even if the gain is made in relation to non-taxable Australian property of the trust (*Draft* TD 2019/D6; *Peter Greensill Family Co Pty Ltd (as trustee)*).

CGT event I2 which arises when a trust stops being an Australian resident trust (¶11-330) will constitute a CGT event happening to a CGT asset of a trust for these purposes (ID 2010/102).

A trustee will not be liable to tax on an amount that is disregarded for a beneficiary.

A distribution of foreign source income by the trustee of a trust to a foreign resident beneficiary will not trigger CGT event E4 (¶11-290).

[FITR ¶649-050]

¶12-740 CGT implications of becoming an Australian resident

If an individual or company becomes an Australian resident or a trust becomes a resident for CGT purposes, special cost base and acquisition rules apply in respect of each CGT asset owned by the taxpayer just before becoming a resident (ss 855-45; 855-50). However, these rules do not apply to pre-CGT assets or assets that are taxable Australian property (¶12-725).

The first element of the cost base and reduced cost base of an asset held at the time the taxpayer becomes a resident is its market value at that time. The taxpayer is treated as having acquired the asset at the time of becoming a resident. As a result, the taxpayer will only be eligible for the CGT discount (¶11-033) if the asset is held for at least 12 months from the time of becoming a resident, even though it was actually owned before that time. Where a taxpayer was previously an Australian resident and made the election under s 104-165(2) to treat an asset as being taxable Australian property, the date of acquisition of the asset will be its original date of acquisition, not the date of recommencing Australian residency (ID 2009/148).

Special rules may apply where an inbound resident owns employee shares or rights (see below).

Exception for CFCs and controlled foreign trusts

These rules do not apply to a trust that became a resident trust for CGT purposes if, just before it did so, it was a controlled foreign trust because a controller had previously transferred property or services to it (¶21-290).

Different rules apply for a CFC that becomes a resident (s 855-55).

Inbound residents holding employee shares or rights

Where the taxation of the discount under an employee share scheme ("ESS") interest is deferred and the ESS deferred taxing point for that interest has not arisen, the ESS interest is treated as having been acquired for its market value at the ESS deferred taxing point (ss 855-45(4); 83A-115; 83A-120).

In all other cases, the first element of the cost base and reduced cost base of the share or right will be its market value at the time the taxpayer becomes a resident.

[FITR ¶649-070 – ¶649-085]

¶12-745 Reduction in CGT for interests in active foreign companies

A capital gain or loss made by an Australian company where certain CGT events happen to interests held in a foreign company will be reduced to the extent that the foreign company has an underlying active business (Subdiv 768-G). This concession is also known as the participation exemption.

A corresponding reduction will also apply to the attributable income arising where the specified CGT events happen to shares owned by a CFC in a foreign company.

This concession applies to CGT events A1, B1, C2, E1, E2, G3, J1, K4, K6, K10 and K11. However, it does not apply to holdings of shares that are equivalent to debt rather than equity, ie eligible finance shares or widely distributed finance shares in the foreign company.

To be eligible for the reduction, the taxpayer company must have held a direct voting percentage in the foreign company of at least 10%, for a continuous period of at least 12 months, in the 2 years before the CGT event.

The extent to which the foreign company carries on an active business is determined by calculating an active foreign business asset percentage for the company. Subject to special rules and thresholds, this percentage is the value of active foreign business assets held by the foreign company as a percentage of the value of all of its assets. The valuation may be done by a market value method or a book value method. If the taxpayer company does not make this valuation, the default rule is that the full capital gain is taxable and any capital loss is reduced to nil (s 768-510).

Where the active foreign business asset percentage is less than 10%, any capital gain will be taxable and any loss will be available to be deducted or carried forward. Conversely, where the active foreign business asset percentage is 90% or more, any capital gain or loss will be disregarded.

An asset is defined as an active foreign business asset if it is: (i) an asset used, or held ready for use, by the company in the course of carrying on a business; (ii) goodwill; or (iii) a share. Assets that are specifically excluded from this definition include: (i) an asset that is taxable Australian property (¶12-725); (ii) a financial instrument; (iii) an interest in a trust or partnership; (iv) a life insurance policy; (v) cash; and (vi) an asset used to derive passive investment income. The active assets of a partnership in which a foreign company is a partner are also excluded (TD 2008/23).

Conduit foreign income

Tax relief is available for conduit foreign income, ie foreign income received by a foreign resident through an Australian corporate tax entity. A capital gain that is reduced under this concession (eg as a result of the sale of shares in a foreign company with an underlying active business) will increase the amount of conduit foreign income. A capital loss that is reduced under this concession will decrease the amount of conduit foreign income. For further details of this measure, see ¶21-100.

[FITR ¶585-600 – ¶585-675]

¶12-760 CGT implications for temporary residents

Capital gains or capital losses that a temporary resident makes from a CGT event are disregarded in certain circumstances. The exemption applies where the capital gain or capital loss would not have been made if the temporary resident had been a foreign resident when or immediately before the CGT event happened.

Ignoring shares or rights acquired under an ESS (¶12-630), the tax treatment of capital gains or capital losses realised by a temporary resident is determined as if the temporary resident were a foreign resident (s 768-915). However, this only applies to capital gains and losses made by a temporary resident in their personal capacity, not in their capacity as trustee of a trust (ID 2009/88).

Individual becoming an Australian resident

Normally, when a foreign resident becomes an Australian resident, a market value cost base applies for certain assets held by that person (¶12-740). This rule will not apply where the person is a temporary resident immediately after becoming an Australian resident (s 768-950).

Australian resident ceasing to be a temporary resident

Where a temporary resident ceases to be a temporary resident but remains an Australian resident (eg becomes a permanent resident), it will be necessary to establish a cost base and a nominal acquisition date for any CGT assets that are brought within the CGT net by virtue of the change of residency status.

The first element of the cost base or reduced cost base of each such CGT asset will be deemed to be its market value at the time that the person ceased to be a temporary resident. The CGT provisions will apply to the asset as if it had been acquired at that time (s 768-955).

For further details of the concessions available to temporary residents, see ¶22-125.

[FITR ¶587-100 – ¶587-440]

¶12-780 Double taxation relief for CGT

Where a resident derives a capital gain from sources outside Australia, and the gain is subject to tax in the other country, double taxation relief is available. Statutory relief is provided by the foreign income tax offset (FITO) system (¶21-670). Where the 50% discount is applied to a foreign capital gain only 50% of the foreign tax paid on the gain is available (*Burton*; Decision Impact Statement; ID 2010/175).

[FITR ¶588-000]

¶12-785 Double taxation agreements and CGT

The articles of a double taxation agreement (DTA) that are of particular interest in a CGT context are the articles dealing with business profits and the alienation of property (¶22-150).

Business profits

The broad effect of the business profits articles is that the business profits of an enterprise of one of the Contracting States is exempt from tax in the other Contracting State unless the enterprise carries on trade or business in the other Contracting State through a permanent establishment. A reference to the profits of a business or activity should be read, where the context so permits, as a reference to taxable income derived from that business or activity (*International Tax Agreements Act 1953*, s 3(2)). In this context, an isolated adventure in the nature of trade may constitute an enterprise carried on for the purposes of Art 7 of the Swiss Agreement (*Thiel*). However, *Thiel* supports a view that only business profits are exempted, and that profits not in the nature of trade (ie from a purely passive investment) are not covered.

Alienation of property

Not all agreements contain an alienation of property article and the articles in the various agreements differ in scope. For example, some agreements deal only with the alienation of land and interests in land, while others also deal with the alienation of other forms of property. Some of the more recent DTAs contain a ''sweep up'' provision (eg Art 13.5 of the Thai Agreement) which preserves the application of a law of a Contracting State relating to the taxation of gains of a capital nature derived from the alienation of property which is not specifically covered elsewhere in the agreement. Strictly, these provisions require an actual alienation of property and relate only to property. As a result, capital gains arising from all the CGT events may not be covered.

Application of CGT where not covered by pre-CGT DTAs

Where a DTA was negotiated before the enactment of the CGT provisions (generally applicable to CGT events happening on or after 20 September 1985), Australia's right to tax capital gains in Australia exclusively under the CGT regime is limited by the DTA. In *Virgin Holdings SA*, the court held that the Swiss DTA operated to deny Australia the right to impose CGT on a capital gain made by a Swiss resident company on the sale of shares in an Australian company. This decision was confirmed in relation to a sale of shares in Australian companies by companies resident in the United Kingdom and the Netherlands pursuant to the pre-CGT DTAs for the United Kingdom and Netherlands in *Undershaft No 1 Ltd; Undershaft No 2 BV*.

[ITA ¶9-040, ¶28-125]

¶12-790 Foreign income accruals system and CGT

In broad terms, the CFC provisions (¶21-110) and the transferor trust provisions (¶21-290) require the inclusion of attributable income derived by certain non-resident companies and trusts wholly or partly in the assessable income of an Australian entity (the attributable taxpayer) in relation to the company or trust. Certain aspects of the CGT provisions are modified when determining attributable income (¶21-200).

[FTR ¶51-426, ¶51-428, ¶796-370 – ¶796-560]

Value Shifting Rules

¶12-800 Overview of general value shifting regime

Value shifts are subject to a general value shifting regime. In broad terms, a value shift occurs when something is done that results in the value of one asset decreasing and the value of another increasing (or being issued at a discount).

The general value shifting regime mainly affects interests in companies and trusts that meet control or common ownership tests. Entities dealing at arm's length or on market value terms are not subject to the value shifting rules. The rules have no impact on value shifts between members of a consolidated group (¶8-000) or a multiple entry consolidated (''MEC'') group (¶8-610).

There are 3 main areas covered by the value shifting rules:

(1) direct value shifting involving equity or loan interests in both companies and trusts — Div 725 (¶12-810)

(2) direct value shifting creating rights in respect of non-depreciating assets — Div 723 (¶12-830)

(3) indirect value shifting involving non-arm's length dealings — Div 727 (¶12-840).

In most cases the consequence will be an adjustment of cost bases (or adjustable values), but in some cases it may also result in taxable income or a taxable gain.

The value shifting rules only apply to ''affected owners'' (controllers, associates or active participants in the scheme). If interests are held by entities who are not affected owners, the regime has no implications.

The following transactions could be subject to the rules:

- issue of interests in a company or trust at a discount to market value
- alteration of rights attaching to existing equity or loan interests in a company or trust
- restructure of group financing arrangements
- restructures of a group of entities involving transfer of assets and/or the issue/cancellation of interests
- debt forgiveness

- creation of rights over non-depreciating assets which are then sold at a loss, or
- service arrangements made on a non-arm's length basis.

If one event triggers the operation of both the direct value shifting rules and the indirect value shifting rules, the direct value shifting rules will take precedence.

General purpose of rules

The value shifting rules are designed to prevent related entities from obtaining tax advantages from value shifting arrangements. For example, by shifting value out of assets that are due to be realised in the short term and into assets that are not due to be realised until sometime later, taxpayers are able to bring forward losses and defer gains.

The regime may apply to value shifting schemes even if there is no tax avoidance purpose. The general anti-avoidance provisions of ITAA36 Pt IVA may still apply to a value shift.

General exclusions

The value shifting rules do not apply where:

- interests (equity or loans) are issued at market value, or at a premium
- rights are created over non-depreciating assets for full market value consideration, or
- entities provide benefits to each other at market value or otherwise deal at arm's length.

Small value exclusions also ensure that the regime is targeted at substantial value shifts. The following *de minimis* thresholds apply:

- direct value shifts involving equity or loan interests must total at least $150,000 in respect of the overall scheme
- shortfalls (ie excesses of market value over taxed value) must be more than $50,000 where rights are created over non-depreciating assets
- indirect value shifts must be greater than $50,000.

[FITR ¶555-000]

¶12-810 Direct value shifting: interests in companies or trusts

Direct value shifting rules apply if, under a scheme, value is shifted from equity or loan interests in a company or trust to other equity or loan interests in the same company or trust (Div 725). A direct value shift may result from issuing new shares or trust units at a discount, buying back shares at less than market value or changing the voting rights attached to shares.

The rules are designed to prevent losses or gains from arising on realisation of the interests by:

- adjusting the value of those interests for income tax purposes to take account of material changes in market value that are attributable to the value shift
- treating the value shift as a partial realisation to the extent that value is shifted either between interests held by different owners, from post-CGT to pre-CGT assets or between interests of different characters.

The rules only apply to value shifts involving direct equity or loan interests in companies or trusts that are controlled. If the value shift is only partly caused by what is done under the scheme, the rules operate to that extent only.

The key features of the direct value shifting rules in Div 725 are that they:

- apply to target entities, ie companies, fixed trusts and some non-fixed trusts
- apply not only to controllers of such entities but also to active participants in a scheme who hold interests, but only in closely held entities that are controlled

- apply to both debt and equity interests
- only apply where there is a material decrease ($150,000 on a scheme basis)
- provide for special relief where a value shift under a scheme reverses on its own terms
- contain no materiality requirement for uplifts — taxpayers may choose to calculate small uplifts (but there must still be a material decrease for the rules to apply)
- deal with revenue consequences for interests held as trading stock or revenue assets
- allow uplifts for shifts from pre-CGT interests
- allow uplifts for off-market buy-backs at undervalue, and
- exclude the interest holder from *gain* treatment where a value shift is *neutral* for that holder, even if it is not neutral for other affected holders.

What is a direct value shift?

There is a direct value shift under a scheme involving equity or loan interests in a target entity if (s 725-145):

- there is a decrease in market value of one or more equity or loan interests in the target entity that is reasonably attributable to one or more things done under the scheme and occurs at or after the time when that thing, or the first of those things, is done — a ‘‘down interest’’, and
- one or more equity or loan interests in the target entity increases in market value or is issued at a discount, and the increase, or issue, is reasonably attributable to the thing, or one or more of those things done, and occurs at or after the time the thing, or the first of those things, is done — an ‘‘up interest’’.

▶ Example

Mum and Dad run a family business through a company. They each hold one share that originally issued for $2. The market value of each share is $300,000 (representing the value of the assets of the company less its liabilities). The company issues one more share to Bob (Mum and Dad's son) for nothing. Caution is needed in such a situation because 1/3 of the company's value is shifted to Bob, ie Mum and Dad are each taken to make a capital gain of $100,000. No such liability would arise if the share had been issued for the market value of a share in the company at that time, ie $300,000.

The direct value shifting rules do not apply to shares issued at a premium to market value because no interests in the company decrease in value as a consequence (ID 2003/890).

Scheme

‘‘Scheme’’ is defined very broadly as any arrangement, agreement, understanding, promise or undertaking, whether express or implied, and whether or not enforceable by legal proceedings; or any scheme, plan, proposal, action or course of conduct, whether unilateral or otherwise. A tax avoidance purpose in respect of a scheme is not required.

A series of events or transactions may form part of one scheme. If, for example, a share value shift proceeds over a long period, each decrease in value of a share may be attributed to a single scheme.

Conditions for a direct value shift

A direct value shift under a scheme involving equity or loan interests in a ‘‘target entity’’ will only have consequences for a taxpayer with such interests if (s 725-50):

- the target entity is a company or trust at some time during the scheme period
- the controlling entity test is satisfied
- the value shift is reasonably attributable to what is done under the scheme
- the entity is an affected owner of a down interest or an up interest or both, and
- the value shift is not reversed.

In addition, the rules will not apply unless the shift involves a material decrease, ie the sum of the decreases in the market value of all down interests because of direct value shifts under the same scheme is at least $150,000. A special rule applies to prevent taxpayers from using different schemes in order to benefit from this threshold (s 725-70).

Controlling entity test

The direct value shifting rules will not apply unless an entity (not necessarily the taxpayer) controls the target entity for value shifting purposes at some time during the scheme period, ie from the time the scheme is entered into until it has been carried out (s 725-55). There are separate control tests for companies, fixed trusts and non-fixed trusts.

Companies

An entity is a controller of a company for value shifting purposes if, in broad terms, it meets one of the following tests (s 727-355):

- the **50% stake test** — where the entity, either alone or together with its associates, has at least 50% of voting, dividend or capital rights in the company, either directly or indirectly
- the **40% stake test** — where the entity only has 40% of the rights (as under the 50% stake test), that will be sufficient unless another entity, either alone or together with its associates, in fact controls the company, or
- the **actual control test** — where the entity actually controls the company.

Fixed trusts

An entity is a controller of a fixed trust for value shifting purposes if, in broad terms, it meets one of the following tests (s 727-360):

- the **40% stake test** — where the entity, either alone or together with its associates, has the right to receive (either directly or indirectly through interposed entities) at least 40% of any distribution of trust income or trust capital to beneficiaries of the trust, or
- **other control tests** — where the entity is able to obtain or control the trust's income or capital, to remove or appoint the trustee, or to generally cause the trustee to act according to its directions.

Non-fixed trusts

An entity is a controller of a non-fixed trust for value shifting purposes if, in broad terms, it meets one of the following tests (s 727-365):

- **trustee tests** — where the entity is able to remove or appoint the trustee, or to generally cause the trustee to act according to its directions, or
- **tests based on control of trust income or capital** — where the entity is able to obtain or control the trust's income or capital, to benefit under the trust other than because of a fixed entitlement to the trust's income or capital, or to have the right to receive at least 40% of any distribution of the trust's income or capital.

Cause of value shift

For the direct value shifting rules to apply, there must be a nexus between the scheme and the decrease in value of the down interest or the increase in value of the up interest. If the value shift is only partly caused by what is done under the scheme, the rules operate to that extent only (s 725-165).

An equity or loan interest is a "down interest" if there is a decrease in its market value which is reasonably attributable to one or more things done under a value shifting scheme and the decrease occurs at or after the time that the first of those things is done. An equity or loan interest is an "up interest" if it is issued at a discount or there is an increase in its market value which is reasonably attributable to the things done under a value shifting scheme. The increase in market value or the issue at a discount must occur at or after the time of the doing of the first thing under the scheme (s 725-155).

The direct value shifting rules only have consequences for affected owners of a down interest or an up interest. The value shift must be caused by something that the target entity, the controller, an associate of the controller or an active participant in the scheme, either alone or together, did under the scheme to decrease the market value of down interests and increase the market value of up interests. To be an active participant in a scheme, the entity must have actively participated in, or directly facilitated, the entering into or carrying out of the scheme (s 725-65).

A director who was issued shares at a discount was considered to be an active participant in a scheme as the director had direct knowledge of the scheme and was involved in the decision to issue additional shares even though they were issued at the instigation of the majority shareholder (ID 2004/210).

Reversal of value shift

A special rule applies so that there will be no consequences for a direct value shift if, more likely than not, it will be reversed within 4 years. An example is where voting rights to a class of shares are changed but, under the company's constitution, the change is to last for only 3 years (s 725-90).

[FITR ¶555-010 – ¶555-015, ¶556-000 – ¶556-125]

¶12-820 Consequences of a direct value shift

A direct value shift can result in a taxing event that generates a gain (**disposal treatment**) or changes to adjustable values of assets (**roll-over treatment**). In some cases, both a taxing event and a change of adjustable value may occur for a particular interest. There is no taxing event to allow a loss on a direct value shift.

The consequences of a direct value shift will depend on whether the interests affected by value shifting:

- have increased or decreased in value (or been issued at a discount to market value)
- are held on capital account (and whether they are pre-CGT or post-CGT assets)
- are held as revenue assets
- are held as trading stock, and/or
- could have, prior to the value shift, realised a gain or loss for income tax purposes.

The consequences only apply where value is shifted between down interests and up interests that are owned by affected owners. In the usual case where interests are held on capital account, the CGT consequences are set out in Subdiv 725-D. In the less common situation where the interests of an affected owner are held as trading stock or revenue assets, separate rules apply (Subdiv 725-E).

Where an amount is otherwise included in the cost base or reduced cost base of an up interest as a result of a direct value shift, the uplift in the adjustable value of that interest will be reduced by that amount in order to prevent double counting (ss 725-250(3); 725-335(4)).

Roll-over treatment

Where a direct value shift occurs between interests of the same tax character owned by the same person, the rules operate to change the adjustable values of each down interest and up interest of an affected owner to take account of the market value increases and decreases. This ensures that inappropriate gains and losses do not arise when these interests are later realised.

Changes are made to the adjustable values of interests regardless of when they were acquired by the affected owner, ie whether they are pre-CGT or post-CGT interests. In this case there are no taxing events generating a gain.

The amount of any uplift is limited for a CGT asset to the extent that the amount of the uplift is still reflected in the market value of the interest when a later CGT event happens to the interest (s 725-240(5)). A similar rule exists for trading stock and for revenue assets.

Disposal treatment

If the shift is from post-CGT to pre-CGT interests (that are not trading stock or revenue assets) of the same person, or between a person's interests of a different tax character (ie capital account, revenue account or trading stock), a taxing event as well as a realignment of adjustable value may occur.

Where a shift has the same economic effect as a part disposal of an asset to another person (eg a transfer of value to an associate), it is broadly treated as if it were a part disposal. A proportionate part of the adjustable value of the interest (eg its cost base) is compared with the amount of value shifted (equivalent to a disposal price).

A tax liability is triggered where value is shifted from:

- post-CGT interests (with pre-shift gains) to pre-CGT interests
- a down interest (with pre-shift gains) of a taxpayer to an up interest owned by another affected owner
- a down interest (with pre-shift gains) that is not trading stock or a revenue asset to an up interest that is trading stock or a revenue asset
- a down interest (with pre-shift gains) that is a revenue asset or trading stock to an up interest of a different kind such as a CGT asset, a revenue asset or trading stock (s 725-245).

▶ Example

Larry owns all one million A class shares in a company, which have a market value of $20 each, and Brad owns one million B class shares in the same company, which have a market value of $10 each.

Larry and Brad agree to vary the rights attaching to both classes of shares, resulting in the market value of the A class shares decreasing by $10 each and the market value of the B class shares increasing, also by $10 each.

The total market value of Larry's A class shares has fallen by $10 million and the total market value of Brad's B class shares has increased correspondingly by $10 million. Thus, there has been a direct value shift from Larry to Brad of $10 million.

This has the same economic effect as if Larry disposed of half of his shareholding to Brad. Assuming the total cost base for all Larry's shares is $5 million, Larry makes capital gains of $7.5 million and his total cost bases for the A class shares is reduced to $2.5 million.

Brad must make cost base uplifts to avoid double taxation. Assuming his shares had cost bases of $4 million, his cost bases in total are increased to $14 million.

Where a debt decreases in value under a scheme, and immediately before the decrease time its market value is equal to its cost base and reduced cost base, it has a pre-shift loss for each of those adjustable values. As a result, there will be consequences for the adjustable value of the debt (ATO Publication, *Guide to the general value shifting regime*).

If there is a taxing event generating a gain on a down interest, CGT event K8 happens (¶11-350). However, any capital gain made under CGT event K8 is disregarded if the down interest is trading stock or a pre-CGT asset.

Special cases

There is a special rule covering neutral value shifts (s 725-220). An example of a neutral value shift is where options to acquire additional shares were issued to a shareholder at less than market value and the effect was to reduce the market value of existing shares by an equivalent amount (ID 2003/892). Where a value shift is neutral for a taxpayer, the gain is worked out under s 725-365, taking into account only those interests that are owned by the taxpayer.

If bonus shares or units are issued at a discount, the consequences are varied in accordance with s 725-225.

A special rule also applies to alter the consequences of a direct value shift in the event of an off-market share buy-back for less than market value (s 725-230).

[FITR ¶555-020, ¶556-200 – ¶556-330]

¶12-830 Direct value shifting: created rights

Direct value shifting rules in Div 723 may apply where value is shifted out of a non-depreciating asset over which a right has been created. The rules generally apply where a lease, licence, option, covenant or similar right is granted to an associate for less than its market value. As a result of the creation of the right, the market value of the underlying asset is decreased.

Subject to a $50,000 threshold, the rules in Div 723 apply where the underlying asset realised at a loss is held on capital account, or is an item of trading stock or a revenue asset. The rules apply to reduce the loss that would otherwise be realised in respect of the underlying asset.

There are special rules to reduce or remove the impact of the rules where the right has been realised and a capital gain or assessable income accrues to an associate. There are also special rules to deal with situations where the underlying asset is rolled over, including where replacement interests for a roll-over are involved.

The rules do not apply to depreciating assets, conservation covenants or testamentary estates where a right is created on the death of the owner of the asset.

Broadly, Div 723 will apply where:

- value is shifted from an underlying asset to an asset held by an associate by the creation of a right
- the market value of the right (when created) exceeds the consideration for tax purposes by more than $50,000
- the underlying asset is realised at a loss by the entity that created the right, and
- just before the time of realisation of the underlying asset, it is still subject to the right held by an associate of the entity realising the underlying asset.

The rules do not apply where:

- a market value substitution rule, such as s 116-30 (¶11-510), applies to the creation of the right, as there is no shortfall (ie no difference between capital proceeds and market value), and
- the creation of the right results in a partial disposal or realisation of the underlying asset, or where a specific provision of the tax law treats the granting of the right as a disposal of the underlying asset.

Consequences under Div 723

Division 723 only has consequences when a "realisation event" has occurred and, but for the rules, a loss would have been realised for tax purposes. Division 977 identifies when a realisation event happens.

The overall effect of the rules is to deny the loss realised by the entity to the extent it is attributable to the value shifted out of the underlying asset by the creation of the right. Comparable adjustments are also made to ensure that the loss cannot be realised on replacement interests if the underlying asset has been rolled over.

The rules address the effect of the value shift by reducing the amount of any loss on realisation of the underlying asset. The amount of the reduction is the lesser of the shortfall on creating the right (market value less capital proceeds) and the deficit on realisation.

The amount of the reduction is itself reduced by the amount of any gain made on the realisation of the right before, at or within 4 years after the realisation event for the underlying asset. The realisation must be by the owner of the right, who is (or was) an associate of the owner of the underlying asset.

Where there is only a partial realisation of the underlying asset, the amount by which the loss is reduced is calculated on a proportionate basis (s 723-25).

If the underlying asset has been transferred to an associate under a replacement asset roll-over, the tax consequences (that would have occurred in the underlying asset under these rules) will apply to the replacement asset by decreasing its reduced cost base (s 723-105).

The following example is adapted from the explanatory memorandum to the amending Bill.

▶ Example

X Co owns land with a reduced cost base of $40 million and a market value of $45 million. X Co grants a 6-year lease to Y Trust, an associate, for no premium and no rental is to be paid under the lease. The market value of the land decreases by $10 million to $35 million as a result of the creation of this right.

X Co then disposes of its reversionary interest in the land to a third party in an arm's length dealing for $35 million.

This ensures X Co and its associate retain rent-free use of the land for the 6 years, and that a capital loss of $5 million would, but for the value shifting rules, be realised. However, economically, no loss has been suffered.

The direct value shifting rules in Div 723 operate to deny X Co the $5 million capital loss.

If X Co did not sell the land until after the 6-year period had expired, there would be no reduction to any capital loss made on its realisation because the right no longer affects its market value.

[FITR ¶555-030 – ¶555-040, ¶555-300 – ¶555-370]

¶12-840 Indirect value shifting

An indirect value shift arises where there is a net shift of value from one related entity to another, eg transferring assets or providing services for less than or more than market value. It involves a reduction in the value of equity or loan interests in one entity (the losing entity) and a corresponding increase in the value of interests in another entity (the gaining entity).

Indirect value shifting rules deal with the consequential effects on the values of interests that are held directly or indirectly by the entities involved (Div 727). The rules prevent a loss or gain from arising because of the value shift when the interests are realised.

The key features of the rules indirect value shifting in Div 727 are that they:

- apply to companies and trusts where control or common ownership tests are satisfied (the common ownership test applies only to closely held entities)
- cover equity and loan interests on capital account, trading stock or revenue account
- apply to the full range of value shifting by way of provision of economic benefits, not only to asset transfers and creations, and debt forgiveness
- apply not only to transfers or creations at less than their market value, but also to overvalue transfers
- have a consistent treatment of creation of rights depending on economic substance rather than legal form
- include *de minimis* exclusions

- contain an exclusion for distributions
- include an arm's length exclusion, and
- incorporate extensive safe-harbours, particularly for value shifts involving the provision of services.

Application of rules

An indirect value shift will have consequences under these rules where:

- economic benefits are provided by one entity to another in connection with a scheme (as defined in s 995-1(1))
- the entities are not dealing at arm's length
- the market value of the economic benefits provided by the losing entity to the gaining entity exceeds the market value of the benefits provided by the gaining entity in connection with the scheme
- the losing entity must be either a company or a trust (excluding certain superannuation entities), and
- the gaining entity can be any kind of entity, including an individual, but is usually a company or trust.

▶ Example

Eddie owns all of the shares in Down Co and all the interests in Up Trust. Down Co transfers an asset with a market value of $100,000 to Up Trust in return for a single cash payment of $75,000.

As a consequence, the market value of Eddie's shares in Down Co has declined by $25,000 and the market value of his interests in Up Trust has increased by $25,000. There has been an indirect value shift of $25,000 from Down Co (the losing entity) to Up Trust (the gaining entity).

Exclusions

The scope of the indirect value shifting rules is limited because:

- arm's length dealings and economic benefits provided at market value are excluded
- the interests of small business entities (¶7-050), and entities that meet the maximum net asset value test (¶7-130), are excluded
- only entities that satisfy one of the following tests are affected:
  - *an ultimate controller test* — ie one entity must control the other or both must be controlled by the same entity, or
  - *a common ownership nexus test* — ie both the losing and gaining entities must be closely held and there must be at least 80% common ownership between the entities
- a wide range of transactions and dealings are excluded including:
  - value shifts of $50,000 or less (s 727-215)
  - property transferred for at least the greater of its cost or cost base, provided no affected owner acquired its interest in the losing entity after the property was acquired by it (s 727-220). This exclusion does not apply when land is transferred at cost and the cost is more than the market value of the land (ID 2003/891)
  - services provided for at least their direct cost or for no more than a commercially realistic price, provided the service component of the benefits is at least 95% on a market value basis (ss 727-230 to 727-245)

- distributions to members and beneficiaries that have consequences under other provisions (s 727-250)
- most cases where value is shifted to a wholly-owned subsidiary of the losing entity (s 727-260).

[FITR ¶555-045 – ¶555-060]

¶12-850 Consequences of an indirect value shift

The indirect value shifting rules in Div 727 do not give rise to assessable gains or losses. Instead, adjustments are made for the consequential or indirect effects of the value shift. The consequences are limited to either reducing losses or gains that would otherwise arise when the interests are realised or, where a choice is made, varying the adjustable values of interests held by affected owners. Special rules apply for interests held as trading stock or revenue assets.

To work out the consequences of an indirect value shift, the ‘‘realisation time method’’ applies unless a choice is made to use the ‘‘adjustable value method’’ (s 727-455).

An indirect value shift only has consequences if the losing entity and gaining entity satisfy an ultimate controller test or, if both entities are closely held, a common ownership test. There are only consequences for an affected owner of certain equity or loan interests in the losing entity or gaining entity.

Realisation time method

Under the realisation time method, adjustments are made in relation to interests held by affected owners when the interests are disposed of or realised in some other way. This method provides for:

- losses on realisation of affected interests in the losing entity to be reduced
- gains on realisation of affected interests in the gaining entity to be reduced
- certain 95% services indirect value shifts to be disregarded (s 727-600).

The advantage of the realisation time method is that adjustments are only required to be made if interests in the losing entity are realised at a loss. The method does not apply where the value shift means that losses that would otherwise be made on interests in the gaining entity are reduced.

Adjustable value method

As the realisation time method can limit relief for interests realised in the gaining entity, a choice may be made to make adjustments to the adjustable values of interests in both the losing and gaining entity as at the time of the value shift. Under the adjustable value method:

- the adjustable values of affected interests in the losing entity are reduced
- the adjustable values of affected interests in the gaining entity are uplifted, within limits worked out by having regard to the adjustable values of affected interests in the losing entity (s 727-750).

The consequences for the affected interest depend on its character. For CGT assets, the cost base and reduced cost base of the interests are reduced or uplifted (or both). If the interests are also trading stock or revenue assets, there are additional consequences in respect of their character as such.

The choice to use the adjustable value method does not have to be made until an affected interest in the losing or gaining entity is first realised after the time of the indirect value shift. Once the first realisation occurs, the choice must be made within 2 years from that time.

[FITR ¶555-065]

Change in Majority Underlying Interests

¶12-870 General rule for when asset stops being pre-CGT

An asset stops being a pre-CGT asset when majority underlying interests in the asset were not held by the same ultimate owners who held those interests in the asset immediately before 20 September 1985. In addition, the CGT provisions apply to the asset as if the taxpayer had acquired it at the time when the majority underlying interests changed (s 149-30). However, for the purpose of determining the period of ownership in applying the 15-year exemption (¶7-165), the date of actual acquisition is used (s 152-110(1A)).

For this purpose, if a person holds an interest in an asset because it was transferred to him/her by way of a marriage or relationship breakdown roll-over or because of the death of a person, the person is taken to have acquired that interest when the former owner did (s 152-115).

▶ Planning point

If additional funds are being injected into a company that has pre-CGT assets, care should be taken to prevent any pre-CGT assets becoming post-CGT assets.

Special rules apply for certain public entities (¶12-880). Further, if a non-public entity is partly owned by a public entity, the non-public entity should take into account all available results of the public entity's tracing of underlying interests in pre-CGT assets at its most recent test day (TD 2000/8).

If the Commissioner is satisfied, or thinks it reasonable to assume, that, at all times on and after 20 September 1985 and before a particular time, majority underlying interests in the asset were held by the same ultimate owners who held majority underlying interests in the asset immediately before that day, the asset continues to be a pre-CGT asset. Where partners in a partnership roll-over a pre-CGT asset into a company pursuant to Subdiv 122-B, the ultimate owners are those pre-CGT partners who can trace their interests back to that pre-CGT asset (ID 2010/228). Where a company's shares carry discretionary rights to dividends the majority underlying ownership will be maintained where there is no change in the ultimate owners since 19 September 1985 (ID 2011/101), but it will not be maintained if any new shareholder is admitted after that date (ID 2011/107).

An ultimate owner includes an individual or a company whose constitution prevents it from making any distribution to its members (s 149-15). Accordingly, where an incorporated association's constitution prevented it from making a distribution to members, the pre-CGT status of assets was maintained when the association was registered as a company with similar restrictions in its constitution (ID 2004/978). However, a company is not an ultimate owner if at that time its constitution provides that rights to surplus assets on a subsequent winding-up are to be determined under legislation that does not prevent a distribution to members (ID 2010/98).

Cost base of assets that become post-CGT assets

If an asset stops being a pre-CGT asset, the first element of its cost base and reduced cost base is the asset's market value at the time it becomes a post-CGT asset (s 149-35). However, for the purpose of determining the CGT exempt amount able to be distributed to CGT concession stakeholders under the 15-year exemption, the original cost base of the asset, not the deemed cost base, is used (s 152-125(1)(a)(iv)).

Where there is a change in the majority underlying interests of a company carrying on a business with pre-CGT goodwill at a time when the contract for the acquisition of the assets of a new business has not been completed, the acquisition date and cost base consequences referred to in ss 149-30(1A) and 149-35(2) are applied to the goodwill of the business then conducted by the company. When the acquired business is later subsumed, the coalesced goodwill assets will have an acquisition date after 20 September 1985 (ID 2010/208).

[FITR ¶169-000 – ¶169-014]

¶12-880 Assets ceasing to be pre-CGT assets — public entity rules

Special rules apply for publicly listed companies, publicly traded unit trusts, mutual insurance companies and mutual affiliate companies (s 149-50). The rules extend to entities which are beneficially owned, whether directly or indirectly, by such entities.

Within 6 months of each test day, the entity must give the Commissioner written evidence about the majority underlying interests in its pre-CGT assets at the end of the test day (s 149-55). However, the Commissioner may extend the period for doing so. The evidence must be given in a form that makes the information about those interests readily apparent.

Test days

Each of these days is a test day:

- 30 June 1999
- a day that is 5 years (or a multiple of 5 years) after 30 June 1999
- for a company, a day on which there is abnormal trading in the company's shares
- for a publicly traded unit trust, a day on which there is abnormal trading in units in the trust
- for 100% beneficially owned companies, a day on which there is abnormal trading in the shares or units of its beneficial owner.

Abnormal trading

A trading in shares in a company happens if there is an issue, redemption or transfer of those shares or any other dealing in those shares, but only if it changes the respective proportions in which the ultimate owners of the shares have underlying interests in assets of the company. A similar rule applies to the trading of units in a unit trust.

An *abnormal trading* in shares in a company, or in units in a unit trust, happens if a trading in the shares or units is abnormal having regard to all relevant factors, including:

- the timing of the trading, when compared with the normal timing for trading in the company's shares or in the trust's units
- the number of shares or units traded, when compared with the normal number of the company's shares or the trust's units traded
- any connection between the trading and any other trading in the company's shares or in the trust's units
- any connection between the trading and a tax loss or other deduction of the company or trust (Subdiv 960-H).

In addition, an *abnormal trading* in the shares of a company or in units of a unit trust is specifically stated to happen if:

- 5% or more of the shares or units are traded in one transaction
- a trading in those shares or units happens and the company or trustee (of the unit trust) knows or reasonably suspects that the trading is part of an acquisition or merger of the company with another company or of the trust with another trust, or
- more than 20% of the shares or units are traded during a 60-day period.

Evidence of majority underlying interests

On the basis solely of the evidence about majority underlying interests given to him, the Commissioner must be satisfied that, at the end of the test day, majority underlying interests in the pre-CGT asset being considered were held by ultimate owners who also held majority underlying interests in the asset at the end of 19 September 1985 or a day between 1 July 1985 and 30 June 1986 that gives a reasonable approximation of the ultimate owners who held underlying interests in the assets of the entity at the end of 19 September 1985 (s 149-60). TR 2004/7 clarifies the rules for tracing underlying ownership of assets and the information used by the Commissioner to decide whether ownership has changed for CGT purposes.

For this purpose, to the extent that it is not possible to identify who held the underlying interests in the assets of the entity at the end of the starting day (19 September 1985 or a day chosen by the company between 1 July 1985 and 30 June 1986), the evidence must be treated on the assumption that those interests were then held by ultimate owners who did not have underlying interests in the asset at the end of the test day. Further, if a person holds an interest in an asset because it was transferred to him/her by way of a marriage breakdown roll-over or because of the death of a person, the person is taken to have held the interests held by the former owner over the years.

Effects if majority underlying interests have changed

The pre-CGT assets of an entity become post-CGT assets if, on the evidence, the Commissioner is not satisfied that, at the end of the test day, majority underlying interests in those assets were held by the ultimate owners who held them at the end of the starting day (s 149-70). In such a case, the CGT provisions apply to those assets as if the entity had acquired them at the end of the test day.

Special rules for test days before 30 June 1999

When a public entity fails the majority underlying interests test in relation to a test day before 30 June 1999 and, before that day, was not required to test under the terms of either IT 2361 or IT 2530, the asset is taken to have been acquired by the entity on that day for its market value on that day. In broad terms, these rulings required a public entity to test only when there had been abnormal trading in shares or units, ie trading outside the conduct of normal stock market trading, such as trading associated with a take-over or merger (TR 1999/4).

When a public entity fails the test at the first test time and, before that time, was required to test under the terms of either IT 2361 or IT 2530, the asset is taken to have been acquired on the day on which the entity was required to test or the day on which it failed the test, whichever happened earlier. If neither of these days is applicable, the asset is taken to have been acquired on 20 January 1997. The earliest date on which a public entity was required to test under the terms of the above rulings is 4 May 1989 (TR 1999/4).

TR 1999/4 also makes some important points about the application of the test in this context:

- the former rules for tracing interests of less than 1% can be used, but not if the notional holder would be taken to hold more than a 20% interest or it is reasonable to assume that there had been a change in majority underlying interests. Where the notional holder has a 20% interest or less, the notional holder rules can be used, unless there is clear evidence that there has been a change
- the former rules for tracing interests through interposed superannuation funds, ADFs, special companies and government bodies can be used
- public entities do not have to apply the abnormal trading principles in IT 2361 and IT 2530 to determine whether testing was required under those rulings. As a concession, the Commissioner allows public entities to retrospectively use the more flexible abnormal trading rules in the legislation (see above).

The rules for tracing underlying ownership of assets and the information used by the Commissioner to decide whether ownership has changed for CGT purposes are explained in TR 2004/7.

Cost base of assets that become post-CGT assets

If an asset stops being a pre-CGT asset, the first element of its cost base and reduced cost base is the asset's market value at the time it becomes a post-CGT asset (s 149-75).

Determinations not required for post-CGT assets

Once an asset stops being a pre-CGT asset because the Commissioner is satisfied that its majority underlying interests have changed, the entity need not give any more evidence to the Commissioner about its underlying interests (s 149-80).

[FITR ¶169-016 – ¶169-026, ¶762-300 – ¶762-330]

¶12-910 Assets ceasing to be pre-CGT assets — demutualised entities

When working out the majority underlying interests in publicly listed companies, 100% beneficially owned companies and publicly traded unit trusts, simplified rules apply if the entity is a mutual insurance company or a mutual affiliate company that has demutualised since the starting day (19 September 1985 or a day chosen by the company between 1 July 1985 and 1 July 1986) (s 149-165). However, these rules only apply if, when the company demutualised, it had more than 50 members.

In such a case, the entity may require the Commissioner to treat its evidence on the assumption that an ultimate owner who:

- immediately before the demutualisation time was a member of the entity, and
- immediately after the demutualisation time held an underlying interest in the asset,

held the interest at all times from and including the end of the starting day until immediately after the demutualisation time.

Similar rules apply if there is an interposed company that has demutualised since the starting day (s 149-170).

[FITR ¶169-036, ¶169-038]

Chapter 13 Superannuation Funds • Contributions

Understanding Australian Superannuation

¶13-010 Superannuation taxation overview

This chapter covers the taxation rules for superannuation funds, the tax concessions for superannuation contributions and limits on the concessional treatment of contributions under the Tax Acts, and the supervisory regime under the superannuation industry supervision (SIS) legislation. The taxation rules for superannuation fund benefits and employment termination benefits are discussed in ¶14-000ff. The superannuation guarantee scheme is discussed in ¶39-000ff.

This chapter also outlines the taxation rules for other entities which make up the Australian superannuation system such as approved deposit funds, pooled superannuation trusts and providers of retirement savings accounts.

The main stages of superannuation taxation are as follows:

(1) contributions received by complying superannuation funds are taxed in the fund at 15% if they are concessional contributions and are not taxed if they are non-concessional contributions (¶13-125). Various concessions (such as a tax deduction, tax offset or government co-contribution) are available for contributions made to complying superannuation funds if certain conditions are met (¶13-700).

Excess contributions charge or tax is payable by individuals on concessional and non-concessional contributions which exceed annual limits (¶13-775, ¶13-780)

Additional tax (Division 293 tax) is payable by individuals whose income and concessionally taxed superannuation contributions exceed an annual threshold (¶13-750)

(2) complying superannuation funds are taxed on their earnings and concessional contributions received by them during the accumulation stage at 15%, while their non-arm's length income (NALI) (if any) is taxed at 45% (¶13-170). The earnings derived from assets in complying funds which are supporting income streams in the retirement phase, and the capital gains on the disposal of those assets, are tax-exempt (¶13-140)

(3) lump sum and income stream payments received by individuals from complying superannuation funds, and lump sum employment termination payments and related payments, are concessionally taxed under special rules, by way of concessional tax rates and tax offsets (¶14-000ff)

(4) an individual's ''total superannuation balance'' (¶14-050) must be below a certain amount to be eligible for certain tax concessions, eg the unused concessional contributions cap carry forward, non-concessional contributions cap and bring forward cap, government co-contributions or spouse contributions tax offset

(5) the amount that an individual is able to transfer to the retirement phase of superannuation (ie to enable a superannuation fund to pay income stream benefits to the individual) is subject to a transfer balance cap (¶14-320) and excess transfer balance tax is payable for exceeding the cap (¶14-360). Where defined benefit income streams (which are generally not commutable) are payable to individuals, these income streams are subject to a defined benefit income cap each year and additional tax consequences apply if the cap is exceeded (¶14-370).

Australian non-complying superannuation funds are taxed on all of their taxable income at 45% (¶13-220), and special taxation rules apply to foreign superannuation funds (¶13-250).

Wolters Kluwer provides additional coverage on superannuation taxation and regulation for trustees and superannuation professionals in the *Australian Master Superannuation Guide 2020/21* and other superannuation services, such as the WK *Superannuation Law & Practice* and *Practical Guide to SMSFs*.

COVID-19 — superannuation relief measures

A summary of the COVID-19 superannuation tax and regulatory relief measures and Regulators' guidelines may be found in ¶13-810.

¶13-015 Making superannuation contributions

Superannuation contributions made by employers or individuals can be compulsory and/or voluntary, or may be prohibited, depending on the circumstances. In addition, special rules govern the making of contributions under the First Home Savers Superannuation Scheme (¶13-790), or of downsizer contributions (see below).

The ability to make superannuation contributions is also indirectly affected by the SISR rules on acceptance of contributions by regulated superannuation funds (¶13-825). Contributions which breach the rules must be returned.

Employer contributions

Employers are required to make mandatory superannuation contributions under the superannuation guarantee (SG) scheme in each financial year for their employees with some exceptions (see ¶39-000ff). Some employers also make mandated contributions for their employees under an industrial award, or make additional contributions under an employment contract (non-mandated contributions) or salary sacrifice arrangement.

Employers are generally entitled to a deduction with no limit for their superannuation contributions for employees, where certain conditions are met (¶13-710). Employer contributions (and deductible personal contributions, see below) are ‘‘concessional contributions’’ under ITAA97, and are subject to additional tax rules where they exceed certain limits in a year (see ‘‘Consequences of having excessive concessional and non-concessional contributions’’ below).

Personal contributions

Where certain conditions are met, an individual may be entitled to tax concessions for making personal contributions, such as a tax deduction (¶13-730), a government co-contribution or a low income superannuation tax offset (¶13-760).

An individual may also make superannuation contributions for his/her spouse and is entitled to a tax offset where certain conditions are met (¶13-770).

Consequences of having excessive concessional and non-concessional contributions

An individual’s deductible personal contributions and an employer’s contributions for employees are ‘‘concessional contributions’’ under ITAA97 (¶13-775).

Where the concessional contributions made for or by an individual exceed an annual cap, the excess contributions are included in the individual’s assessable income and are taxed at marginal tax rates. The individual is liable to pay excess contributions charge on the excess concessional contributions and, as part of the assessment process, the individual receives a non-refundable tax offset of 15% of the excess contributions (¶13-775). To avoid the charge, an individual may elect to release up to 85% of excess concessional contributions from his/her superannuation fund. The released amount is not assessable income and not exempt income (¶13-777).

High income individuals may also be liable to pay Division 293 tax if their income and certain concessionally taxed superannuation contributions exceed an annual threshold (¶13-750).

An individual’s non-deductible contributions are ‘‘non-concessional contributions’’ under ITAA97. An individual who has excess non-concessional contributions may elect to release an amount equal to the excess contributions plus 85% of an associated earnings amount on those contributions from his/her superannuation fund. The associated earnings amount is included in the individual’s assessable income in the year the excess contribution arose and is taxed at the individual’s marginal tax rate. The individual is entitled to a non-refundable tax-offset equal to 15% of the associated earnings amount included in assessable income (¶13-780).

Superannuation funds receiving contributions are liable to pay contributions tax

Concessional contributions (and certain other amounts) received by a complying superannuation fund are included in the fund’s assessable income and are taxed at 15% (this is commonly referred to as ‘‘contributions tax’’). Non-concessional contributions received are not subject to contributions tax (¶13-125). The tax rate on all of a non-complying fund’s taxable income is 45% (¶13-220).

Complying and non-complying funds must also pay tax on no-TFN contributions income, if any. A tax offset is available if the member’s TFN is subsequently received (¶13-180).

Total superannuation balance

An individual’s ‘‘total superannuation balance’’ is used to determine the individual’s eligibility for deductions and certain tax concessions in relation to contributions (¶14-050).

Making downsizer contributions

Where certain conditions are met, an individual who is 65 years old or older can choose to make downsizer contributions to a superannuation fund of up to $300,000 from the proceeds of selling the individual's main residence (¶13-795). Downsizer contributions interact with other contributions rules and caps as follows:

(i) A downsizer contribution is not a non-concessional contribution and does not count towards the individual's contribution caps (see above).

(ii) A downsizer contribution does not affect an individual's total superannuation balance until the balance is re-calculated to include all contributions made, including the downsizer contributions, on 30 June at the end of the financial year (¶14-050).

(iii) A downsizer contribution when subsequently paid as a retirement income stream benefit is counted towards the individual's transfer balance cap (¶14-320).

¶13-025 Accessing superannuation benefits

A member's benefits in a superannuation fund may be paid as one or more lump sums or pensions, or both, if permitted by the fund's governing rules and the SISR payment rules are complied with.

Preservation rules in the SISR ensure that the member's entitlements are retained in the superannuation fund for their stated purpose (ie to provide superannuation and retirement/death benefits) and they cannot be accessed unless the member satisfies a ''condition of release'' as specified in the SISR (eg attaining age 65, retirement, incapacity, and so on). The conditions of release also provide for early access to benefits in certain circumstances. For example, members who have reached their preservation age (¶13-800) may access their superannuation entitlements as non-commutable income streams without having to ''retire'', and early release of benefits is allowed in hardship cases or on compassionate grounds, or under an ATO release authority, or for temporary resident members who are departing or have left Australia.

The SISR also impose rules on the form in which member benefits may be cashed from regulated superannuation funds, as well as restrictions on payment of death benefits as income streams (¶13-800). Benefits are portable (ie transferable from fund to fund without loss of tax concessions) where permitted by the governing rules of the transferor and transferee funds and the SISR.

The taxation of superannuation benefits is discussed at ¶14-000ff.

Superannuation Entities

¶13-050 Superannuation funds

A ''superannuation fund'' is a scheme for the payment of superannuation benefits upon retirement or death, or a superannuation fund as defined in *Superannuation Industry (Supervision) Act 1993* (SISA), s 10 (ITAA36 s 6(1); ITAA97 s 995-1(1)).

Under SISA, a ''superannuation fund'' is: (a) an indefinitely continuing fund that is a provident, benefit, superannuation or retirement fund; or (b) a public sector superannuation scheme, ie a scheme for the payment of superannuation, retirement or death benefits established by a Commonwealth, state or territory law, or under the authority of the Commonwealth, state or territory government or a municipal corporation, local government or public authority.

The expressions ''indefinitely continuing fund'' and ''provident, benefit, superannuation or retirement fund'' in the SISA definition of ''superannuation fund'' are not defined but have been considered in a number of court decisions (see *Cameron Brae Pty Ltd*; *Baker*; *Case 3/2018*; *Scott (No 2)*; *Mahoney*).

Categorisation of superannuation funds

In the superannuation industry, funds are referred to by generic terms, such as corporate or employer-sponsored funds, industry funds, retail funds and public offer funds, public sector funds, small APRA funds (SAFs) and self managed superannuation funds (SMSFs). This classification is primarily for regulatory purposes under the SIS legislation (see below) and generally does not affect their taxation (¶13-060).

Prudential regulation of funds

The regulatory regime for superannuation entities under the SISA and related legislation is outlined in ¶13-800. The Australian Prudential Regulation Authority (APRA) is the Regulator of superannuation funds that are not SMSFs while the ATO is the Regulator of SMSFs.

The fund-type categorisation allows for different prudential regulation of funds under the SISA or their governing Act. For tax purposes, superannuation funds are generally subject to the same treatment except for the special treatment of exempt public sector superannuation schemes and constitutionally protected funds (¶13-300).

In the SISA, a ''public sector fund'' is a superannuation fund that is part of a public sector superannuation scheme (see above). Any other superannuation fund is a ''private sector fund''. Public sector funds (except for exempt public sector superannuation schemes: ¶13-300) and private sector funds are generally required to comply with the same regulatory conditions under the SIS legislation or their enabling Act to qualify for concessional tax treatment as complying superannuation funds.

Less onerous, and sometimes different forms of, prudential regulation under SISA may apply to SMSFs and small APRA funds compared to other regulated superannuation funds.

A regulated superannuation fund (other than an SMSF), an ADF or a PST is called a ''registrable superannuation entity'' (RSE) in SISA. Trustees of RSEs must be licensed under SISA and are subject to additional obligations. RSE licensees that are authorised by APRA can offer MySuper products (these are special classes of cost-effective accounts within a superannuation fund) and can operate a regulated superannuation fund as an eligible rollover fund (¶13-850).

[AMSG ¶3-010]

¶13-060 Self managed superannuation funds

A ''self managed superannuation fund'' (SMSF) is a ''superannuation fund'' (¶13-050) with a maximum of 4 members that satisfies the conditions in SISA s 17A. Funds with fewer than 5 members that do not meet the s 17A conditions are not SMSFs, but are known as ''small APRA funds''.

An SMSF can be a single member fund or have 2 to 4 members, and can have individuals as trustees or a corporate trustee. The s 17A conditions ensure that each member is an individual trustee or a director of the corporate trustee, no member is an employee of another member unless they are relatives, and trustee remuneration is prohibited subject to certain exceptions (SISA s 17B).

All members are trustees

Any individual who is not a disqualified person can be a ''member'' of a regulated superannuation fund, including a minor. A member also includes a person who receives a pension from the fund or who has deferred his/her entitlement to receive a benefit from the fund.

▶ Example

An SMSF has 4 members comprising Allan, his 2 daughters and a son-in-law. Allan has retired and is being paid a pension from the fund. If Allan's 12-year-old grandson were to become a member, the fund would no longer be an SMSF as it would then have 5 members. A minor counts as a member of the fund.

Relative of a member

A ''relative'', in relation to an individual, means:

(a) a parent, child, grandparent, grandchild, sibling, aunt, uncle, great-aunt, great-uncle, niece, nephew, first cousin or second cousin of the individual or of his/her spouse or former spouse, or

(b) a spouse or former spouse of the individual, or of an individual referred to in (a) (s 17A(9)).

A ''child'', in relation to a person, includes an adopted child, a stepchild or an ex-nuptial child of the person, a child of the person's spouse, and someone who is a child of the person within the meaning of the *Family Law Act 1975* (SISA s 10(1); ID 2011/77: former stepchild, child and dependant).

For the purposes of para (a) of the definition of ''relative'', if an individual is the ''child'' (as defined) of another individual, relationships traced to, from or through the individual are to be determined in the same way as if the individual were the natural child of the other individual (s 17A(9A)).

A ''spouse'' of a person is defined to include another person (whether of the same or different sex) with whom the person is in a relationship that is registered under a law of a state or territory prescribed for the purposes of s 2E of the *Acts Interpretation Act 1901*, or another person who, although not legally married to the person, lives with the person on a genuine domestic basis in a relationship as a couple (s 10(1); ¶14-270).

Meaning of employee

The term ''employee'' in the SISA has its common law meaning and the extended meaning in s 15A. For the purposes of the SMSF definition, a member of a fund, who is an employee of an employer-sponsor is also deemed to be an employee of another person in certain circumstances, or a person can be deemed not to be an employee (s 17A(6)–(8); SISR reg 1.04AA).

Other rules governing SMSFs and their trustees

In the circumstances set out in s 17A(3), another person (eg the legal personal representative of a member who has died or is under a legal disability, the parent of a minor member, or a person holding an enduring power of attorney) may be appointed as a trustee or director of the corporate trustee of an SMSF in place of a member. The ATO's guidelines on trustee appointments for holders of an enduring power of attorney under s 17A(3)(b)(ii) are set out in SMSFR 2010/2.

A ''disqualified person'' (as defined in SISA) cannot be a superannuation fund trustee, and a person in the capacity of legal personal representative of a disqualified person also cannot be the trustee of an SMSF (s 17A(10)).

Proposed changes — increase in SMSF membership to 6

Amendments have been proposed to the SISA to increase the maximum number of allowable members in SMSFs and small APRA funds from 4 to 6 from the start of the first quarter that begins after the day the Act receives assent (Treasury Laws Amendment (Self Managed Superannuation Funds) Bill 2020: ¶41-200).

[AMSG ¶5-200; SLP ¶6-150 – ¶6-250]

¶13-070 ADFs, PSTs and RSAs

Approved deposit funds (ADFs), pooled superannuation trusts (PSTs), and providers of retirement savings accounts (RSAs) that are not life insurance companies, are taxed under the rules set out in ITAA97 Div 295 (¶13-120). To qualify, these entities must come within the definition of those terms in SISA (for ADFs and PSTs) and in the *Retirement Savings Accounts Act 1997* (RSAA) (for RSA providers) and comply with the prudential requirements under SISA or RSAA.

The nature and taxation of ADFs, PSTs and RSAs are discussed at ¶13-400, ¶13-430, ¶13-470 respectively. The taxation of the superannuation business of RSA providers that are life insurance companies is discussed in ¶3-480.

[AMSG ¶3-650 – ¶3-730; SLP ¶3-290 – ¶3-376, ¶60-300ff]

Taxation of Superannuation Funds

¶13-100 Complying and regulated fund status

A superannuation fund must be a "complying superannuation fund" to be eligible for concessional tax treatment under ITAA97 Div 295. This requires the fund to have received a notice under SISA from APRA (or the Commissioner) stating that it is a complying superannuation fund. A fund remains a complying superannuation fund for tax purposes until it is notified that its complying status has changed.

By virtue of its status, an exempt public sector superannuation scheme (¶13-300) is a complying superannuation fund.

Main requirements for complying fund status

To obtain a complying fund notice under SISA:

- a fund must be "regulated superannuation fund" that is an "Australian superannuation fund" at all times during the year of income that it was in existence (or be a resident ADF for part of the year), and
- it must comply with the regulatory provisions in SISA or, if it contravened the regulatory provisions, it must not fail the "culpability test" set out in SISA s 42(1A) or, in the case of an SMSF, the "compliance test" set out in SISA s 42A(5).

A "regulatory provision" means a provision of the SIS legislation and *Financial Sector (Collection of Data) Act 2001*, certain provisions in the *Corporations Act 2001* and, for an SMSF, certain provisions in TAA Sch 1 (SISA s 38A).

Regulated superannuation fund

A fund is a "regulated superannuation fund" if the fund has a trustee and:

- the governing rules of the fund either require an Australian corporate trustee (the "corporations route") or provide that the sole or primary purpose of the fund is to provide old-age pensions (the "pensions route"), and
- the trustee irrevocably elects for SISA to apply to the fund by lodging the election in the approved form with APRA (or other person prescribed by the regulations) within 60 days of setting up the fund (SISA s 19; SISR reg 1.04A).

The above requirements and election process form part of the fund's registration in the tax and superannuation systems, such as applying for an ABN, a TFN and GST. The ATO is responsible for receiving and processing the election to become a regulated superannuation fund (reg 1.04A). After registration, the ATO will retain the election and fund information for SMSFs and provide APRA with the information in the case of APRA-regulated superannuation entities. An ATO system enables online registration and allows superannuation entities to change their registration details.

The government's Super Fund Lookup website (www.superfundlookup.gov.au) contains publicly available information about superannuation funds that have an ABN.

Australian superannuation fund

A fund is an "Australian superannuation fund" at a time, and for the income year in which that time occurs, if:

- the fund was established in Australia, or any asset of the fund is situated in Australia at that time
- at that time, the central management and control (CMC) of the fund is ordinarily in Australia
- at that time, either the fund had no active member, or active members who are Australian residents hold at least 50% of the following:
  (i) the total market value of the fund's assets attributable to superannuation interests held by active members, or
  (ii) the sum of the amounts that would be payable to or in respect of active members if they voluntarily ceased to be members (ITAA97 s 295-95(2)).

The central management and control of a superannuation fund is ordinarily in Australia at a time even if that central management and control is temporarily outside Australia for a period of not more than 2 years (s 295-95(4); *CBNP Superannuation Fund*). A member is an "active member" at a particular time if they contribute to the fund at that time, or is an individual for whom contributions have been made. However, a member is not an active member at the relevant time if they are foreign residents and are not contributors at that time and the only contributions made to the fund for the member since becoming a foreign resident were made in respect of a time when they were Australian residents (s 295-95(3)).

Guidelines on the 3 tests to be an Australian superannuation fund are set out in TR 2008/9. For guidelines on the CMC test of company residency, see ITAA36 s 6(1), TR 2018/5 and PCG 2018/9.

Loss of complying fund status

A superannuation fund automatically loses its complying fund status if it is not an Australian superannuation fund (*CBNP Superannuation Fund*).

A fund may lose its complying fund status if it breaches one or more regulatory provisions in a year and fails the culpability test in SISA s 42(1A) or, for an SMSF, the compliance test in SISA s 42A(5) (*Case 7/2009*; *Re JNVQ*; *ZDDD*; *Sutherland v Woods*; *Triway*; *Shail*; *Montgomery Wools*; *Re-Ali*).

When determining a fund's complying status, a contravention of a regulatory provision is ignored unless the contravention is an offence, a contravention of a civil penalty provision, or a contravention of certain TAA provisions (applicable to SMSFs only) (SISA s 39).

PS LA 2006/19 outlines the factors the Commissioner will consider when deciding whether a notice of non-compliance should be given to an SMSF which has breached the regulatory provisions (*XPMX*; *Decision Impact Statement* VRN 3265 of 2007, 3633 of 2007: alternative options available to the ATO for breaches). The Commissioner's decision to issue a notice of non-compliance to a fund was set aside in *Pabian Park*. According to the AAT, the case was "finely balanced" and "weighing up all the factors", it would not be inconsistent with the objects of SISA to exercise the discretion in favour of the fund. The ATO accepted that it was open to the AAT to reach its decision on the facts but noted that, in doing so, the AAT has accepted and followed the general approach taken in PS LA 2006/19 (*Decision Impact Statement* VRN 2004 of 2010).

In certain circumstances, the Commissioner may accept an enforceable undertaking from fund trustees to rectify contraventions (PS LA 2006/18). The court's powers to grant orders in relation to enforceable undertakings under s 262A(4)(d) of the SISA include deeming a fund to be complying in an appropriate case (*Interhealth Energies*).

A regulated superannuation fund that fails to qualify as a complying superannuation fund remains regulated under the SISA at all times. That is, while the fund is taxed as a non-complying fund (¶13-220), it continues to be subject to all the regulatory provisions applicable to it, including the SISA penalty regime.

If a complying fund notice is revoked, or the decision to give the notice is set aside, the fund is treated as a non-complying fund for each of the years of income covered by that notice. Where a complying fund becomes non-complying, the tax concessions that the fund previously enjoyed are recouped (¶13-200).

The decision under SISA to give a notice that a fund is or is not a complying superannuation fund, or refusal to give such a notice, is a ''reviewable decision'' under SISA.

[AMSG ¶2-130; SLP ¶2-160]

¶13-120 Taxation of complying superannuation entities

ITAA97 Div 295 provides the special rules for the taxation of the following superannuation entities, whether they are established by an Australian law, by a public authority constituted under such a law or in some other way:

- a complying superannuation fund or non-complying superannuation fund
- a complying ADF or non-complying ADF (¶13-400), and
- a PST (¶13-430) (ITAA97 s 295-5).

Division 295 also applies to public sector superannuation schemes, although constitutionally protected funds are exempt from tax (¶13-300).

The Division also provides for the taxation of the RSA business of an RSA provider that is not a life insurance company (¶13-480). The taxation of life office RSA providers is governed by ITAA97 Div 320 (¶3-530).

A complying fund or PST is an entity that satisfies the prescribed conditions in SISA for complying superannuation funds, complying ADFs and PSTs, while a non-complying fund is an entity that fails, for whatever reason, to comply with those conditions (¶13-100, ¶13-400, ¶13-430). An entity that does not comply with the SISA conditions prescribed for PSTs is not taxed under Div 295. Such entities are taxed under the appropriate provisions of ITAA36 or ITAA97, eg as a trust or a managed investment scheme (see ¶6-000ff).

Taxable income and tax payable — method statement

The tax payable by a superannuation fund, ADF or PST is worked out using the steps below:

Step 1. For a superannuation fund, work out the no-TFN contributions income and apply the applicable rates set out in the *Income Tax Rates Act 1986* (ITRA) to that income (¶13-180).

Step 2. Work out the entity's assessable income and deductions taking account of the special rules in Div 295 (these rules modify some ITAA97 provisions, include certain amounts in assessable income, and provide for certain deductions and exemptions: ¶13-125 – ¶13-170).

Step 3. Work out the entity's taxable income as if its trustee were an Australian resident or, in the case of a non-complying superannuation fund that is a foreign superannuation fund (¶13-250), not an Australian resident.

Step 4. Work out the entity's low tax component and non-arm's length component of the taxable income (¶13-170).

Step 5. Apply the applicable rates in the ITRA to the components, or to the taxable income of a non-complying superannuation fund or non-complying ADF.

Step 6. Subtract the entity's tax offsets from the step 5 amount or, for a superannuation fund, from the sum of the fund's step 1 and step 5 amounts (ITAA97 s 295-10(1)).

The taxable income of a complying superannuation fund, complying ADF or PST is made up of 2 components — a low tax component which is taxed at 15% and a non-arm's length component which is taxed at 45%. The non-arm's length component for an income year is the entity's non-arm's length income for the year less any deduction attributable to that income (¶13-170), while the low tax component is any remaining part of the entity's taxable income for the income year (ITAA97 s 295-545). The no-TFN contributions income (if any) of a superannuation fund (see Step 1) is taxed at different rates (¶13-180).

Complying funds and PSTs are eligible for a one-third discount on the capital gains that are included in assessable income or, in certain cases, a choice of the CGT discount or calculation of the cost base of assets with indexation frozen at 30 September 1999 (¶13-130).

By contrast, the whole taxable income of a non-complying superannuation fund or non-complying ADF is taxed at 45% and none of the special concessions applicable to complying funds is available (¶13-220). A special tax regime applies to complying superannuation funds which become non-complying or non-resident superannuation funds which become resident, in the year in which the fund's complying or residency status changes (¶13-200, ¶13-270).

Like other taxpayers under the CGT regime, a superannuation fund's unrealised capital losses (eg due to changes in the market value of the fund's investments) are not deductible in calculating its net taxable income for the year (see Step 2 in the method statement). However, any realised capital losses incurred (eg sale of the fund's CGT assets) can be offset against its realised capital gains from other CGT assets (if any) in the same year. If the fund's capital loss exceeds its capital gain for the income year, this net capital loss cannot be deducted from the fund's net income but is carried forward and applied against future capital gains.

If a fund has not received a notice under SISA about its complying status, the Commissioner can assess the fund as a complying fund or PST in anticipation that its status will be determined as such (ITAA97 s 295-25). Such an assessment is not allowed if the Commissioner is satisfied that the notice will not be given, or APRA does not receive an audit report on the fund (as required under the SISA prudential standards) before the end of 12 months after the assessment is made.

In each year, a superannuation fund is required to lodge an income tax return with the ATO (¶13-350), as well as a regulatory return with APRA. SMSFs lodge a combined tax and regulatory return with the ATO each year.

The PAYG system as it applies to superannuation funds is discussed in ¶26-100ff and ¶27-100ff.

Look-through tax treatment for assets acquired under limited recourse borrowing arrangements

Regulated superannuation funds which enter into a limited recourse borrowing arrangement (LRBA) to acquire assets with a trust holding the assets (in accordance with SISA s 67A or former s 67(4A)) are subject to a look-through tax treatment which ensures that most of the income tax consequences associated with the underlying asset of the trust flow through to the fund as if it had invested in the asset directly. The holding trust under the LRBA is effectively ignored and anything that happens to or results from being the owner of the asset (such as receiving franked dividends) affects the trustee of the superannuation fund, and not the trustee of the holding trust.

The look-through tax treatment, which applies to assets acquired in the 2007–08 or later income years, confirms the long-standing ATO and industry practice which has been to ignore the existence of the trust for CGT purposes (¶11-210) (ITAA97 Subdiv 235-I, ss 235-810 to 235-845).

ATO tax governance guidelines

The ATO has released guidelines to assist SMSF trustees and professionals to develop an effective governance framework and identify ways to improve existing governance practices within their SMSF (Fact Sheet *SMSFs*).

Taxpayer Alert TA 2016/6 covers arrangements where individuals (typically SMSF members at or approaching retirement age) purport to divert income earned from their personal services to an SMSF. The ATO is concerned that, in order to avoid paying tax at their personal marginal rate, individuals enter into these arrangements in an attempt to divert personal services income (PSI) to an SMSF where the income is concessionally taxed or treated as exempt current pension income.

[AMSG ¶7-000; FITR ¶270-010; SLP ¶45-100]

¶13-125 Assessable income of superannuation funds and contributions

The assessable income of a superannuation fund in a year of income includes contributions or payments received by it in the income year (s 295-160) (¶13-120). These contributions are taxed at 15% in the year that they are received by the fund (commonly referred to as "contributions tax") (¶13-120).

TR 2010/1 sets out the ordinary meaning of contribution, how a contribution can be made and when a contribution is made for the purposes of ITAA97 (¶13-705). Funds can only accept contributions in accordance with the SISR (¶13-825).

Subject to certain additions and exceptions, the 3 main types of assessable contributions of a complying superannuation fund are:

- contributions made by a contributor (eg an employer) on behalf of someone else (eg an employee)
- personal contributions for which the contributor is entitled to a deduction, and
- amounts transferred from a foreign superannuation fund.

A complying superannuation fund may transfer its tax liability on assessable contributions to an eligible entity (eg a PST). Where applicable, a complying fund may also use its pre-1 July 1988 funding credits to exclude otherwise assessable contributions (see below).

Apart from contributions tax, a superannuation fund is also liable to pay tax for no-TFN contributions income received by it in each year (¶13-120, ¶13-180).

Superannuation contributions made to a fund for or by an individual are "concessional contributions" or "non-concessional contributions" under the ITAA97. Under the excess concessional contributions charge and excess non-concessional contributions tax regimes in ITAA97 Div 291 and Div 292, individuals are liable to pay a charge or tax if their contributions exceed the concessional or non-concessional contributions cap for the year (¶13-775, ¶13-780).

Contributions made on behalf of an individual

The assessable income of a complying superannuation fund for a year of income includes the following:

- contributions to provide superannuation benefits for someone else, except a "roll-over superannuation benefit" (see below) and certain contributions expressly excluded (see "Contributions that are not assessable contributions" below)

- payments under s 65 of the SGAA (these are payments of the shortfall component of a superannuation guarantee charge to the fund: ¶39-600)
- payments under s 61 or 61A of the *Small Superannuation Accounts Act 1995* (these are amounts transferred to the fund from a person's individual account in the Superannuation Holding Accounts Special Account: ¶39-650) (ITAA97 s 295-160, table items 1, 3, 4).

Employers are generally required to make superannuation contributions for their employees under the SGAA (¶39-000). In addition, some employers make contributions for employees under an award or contractual obligation. These contributions are assessable income of the fund, regardless of whether the employer has claimed a tax deduction for the contributions (¶13-710).

A ''roll-over superannuation benefit'' is a lump sum superannuation member benefit that can be paid from, and to, a complying superannuation plan, or is paid to an entity to purchase a superannuation annuity (see below). A person may have more than one superannuation plan with a superannuation provider. A superannuation benefit may be rolled over from one plan to another plan held by the same provider. A plan may also contain more than one superannuation interest. If an amount is transferred from a superannuation interest in a plan to another interest in the same plan, the transfer is treated as a payment in determining whether it is a superannuation benefit or a roll-over superannuation benefit (s 307-5(8); TD 2013/10: using deceased member's benefits in a fund to start a pension for a beneficiary is not a transfer of an amount between superannuation interests in that fund).

A roll-over superannuation benefit is not assessable contributions of a complying fund under s 295-160, but is assessable income under s 295-190 in certain circumstances (see ''Personal contributions and roll-over amounts'' below).

Contributions that are not assessable contributions

The following contributions or payments received by a superannuation fund are not assessable contributions:

- contributions made on behalf of a spouse (¶13-770)
- government co-contributions (¶13-760)
- contributions for a person under 18 (¶13-775) that are not employer contributions
- contributions made out of the complying superannuation assets or segregated exempt assets of a life insurance company, or contributions made by a complying superannuation fund, a complying ADF or a PST when the contribution was made
- a member's contributions for a non-member spouse in satisfaction of the non-member spouse's entitlement to a superannuation interest in the fund under the family law
- a contribution made to a public sector superannuation scheme to the extent that the trustee chooses, with the agreement of the contributor, not to be included in assessable income (note that the choice cannot exceed the amount covered by notices given by the scheme under ITAA97 s 307-285. Making this choice effectively shifts the liability to pay the tax on those contributions to the recipient of the benefit when it is paid by the scheme)
- contributions to a non-complying fund that is a foreign superannuation fund for a person who is a temporary resident of Australia at the end of the income year to which the contribution relates (ss 295-165; 295-170; 295-173; 295-175; 295-180; 295-185).

Amounts transferred from KiwiSaver schemes to a complying superannuation fund are also not included as assessable income of the fund (¶13-380).

Personal contributions and roll-over amounts

The assessable income of a complying superannuation fund includes the following amounts as assessable contributions:

- personal contributions for which the contributor has given the fund a valid notice of intent to claim a deduction for the contributions (see ''Member contributions'' below)
- a roll-over superannuation benefit that a person is taken to receive under s 307-15 to the extent that it consists of an element untaxed in the fund and is not an excess untaxed roll-over amount for that person (see ''Assessable roll-over superannuation benefits'' below) (s 295-190(1)).

Member contributions

A complying superannuation fund will include a member's personal contributions in its assessable income if the member has given the fund a notice under ITAA97 s 290-170 (before the fund lodges its tax return for the year that the contributions are made) that a tax deduction would be claimed for the contributions (s 295-190(2)). Tax deductions for personal contributions are discussed at ¶13-730. If the notice is received after lodgment of its return, the fund will include the contributions covered by the notice as assessable contributions in the year in which the notice is received (s 295-190(3)).

If a member's contributions have been included as assessable contributions by the fund before its tax return for the year is lodged, and the fund receives a later notice from the member reducing the amount covered by the earlier notice, the fund can reduce its assessable contributions for the year accordingly (ITAA97 s 295-195(1)).

If the fund is notified of the reduction after it has lodged its return, the fund is entitled to a deduction in the income year in which it is notified (s 295-490(1), table item 2). Alternatively, the fund has the option to amend that tax return to exclude the reduction amount, but only if that would result in a greater reduction in tax for that year than the reduction that would occur for the income year in which the notice is received (s 295-195(3)).

Assessable roll-over superannuation benefits

A ''roll-over superannuation benefit'' is a lump sum superannuation member benefit (¶14-120) that can be paid to or from a complying superannuation fund (see ''Contributions on behalf of a person'' above) (ITAA97 s 306-10: ¶14-450).

A person is taken to have received a superannuation benefit when a payment is made for the person's benefit, or payment has been made to another person at the person's direction or request (ITAA97 s 307-15).

A roll-over superannuation benefit taken to be received is not assessable income and not exempt income of the person for whom the roll-over is made. However, the roll-over benefit is assessable contributions of the roll-over fund in the income year in which the roll-over occurs to the extent that: (a) the benefit consists of an element untaxed in the fund (other than an element untaxed in the fund under ITAA97 s 307-290(4): ¶14-450), that is an untaxed roll-over amount, and (b) the benefit is not an ''excess untaxed roll-over amount'' for that person (s 295-190(1), item 2).

An excess untaxed roll-over amount arises if the untaxed roll-over amount exceeds the person's untaxed plan cap amount ($1.565 million in 2020–21: ¶42-250). Tax is payable by the person on the excess amount at 47% (ITAA97 s 306-15: ¶14-450). The overall effect is that the untaxed roll-over amount is taxed at 15% as assessable contributions in the roll-over fund while the excess amount which has already been subject to tax, as noted above, is not subject to further tax in the fund. When the person's entitlements are subsequently paid as a benefit from the fund, the excess amount remains tax-free (¶14-140).

A roll-over superannuation benefit taken to be received by an individual under ITAA97 s 307-15 is also assessable contributions of the recipient roll-over fund in the income year in which the roll-over occurs to the extent that the fund is a successor fund or continuing fund under ITAA97 s 311-10(3) and the benefit relates to a contribution in the circumstances set out in item 2A in s 295-190(1).

A roll-over superannuation benefit that is a departing Australia superannuation payment made under s 20H(2), (2AA) or (2A) of the *Superannuation (Unclaimed Money and Lost Members) Act 1999* (¶14-390) is not assessable contributions of the recipient fund (s 295-190(1A)).

Pre-1 July 1988 funding credits

Certain employer contributions that would otherwise be assessable contributions in the hands of a complying superannuation fund are excluded from assessable income if they are made in respect of unfunded liabilities for member benefits accrued up to 30 June 1988. This exemption is available to funds that were exempt from tax up to 30 June 1988. A fund may apply for approval of a pre-1 July 1988 funding credit as provided by s 342 of the SISA.

A superannuation fund with approved pre-1 July 1988 funding credits may choose to apply an amount of the credits (subject to limits) each year to reduce the fund's assessable contributions relating to the unfunded liabilities (ITAA97 s 295-265). The trustees must make a choice before the fund's tax return for the relevant year is lodged, subject to any extension of time by the Commissioner.

A complying superannuation fund can also reduce the contributions otherwise included in its assessable income in anticipation of APRA confirming the amount of credits available as at 1 July 1988. However, the credits will not be considered available for the income year to the extent that the notice received differs from the amount anticipated (ITAA97 s 295-270).

Transfer of assessable contributions

A complying superannuation fund or a complying ADF (transferor) that has investments in the form of superannuation policies with a life assurance company or units in a PST may transfer its tax liability on assessable contributions to that entity (transferee) by written agreement between the transferor and transferee. The agreement, which is irrevocable, must be made on or before lodgment of the fund's tax return for the year to which the agreement relates (ITAA97 s 295-260). The transferor may make one agreement only for an income year with a particular transferee. The effect of the transfer is that the relevant contributions are excluded from the transferor's assessable income and included in the transferee's assessable income for the relevant year.

The total amount of contributions covered by the agreements cannot exceed the total amount otherwise included as assessable contributions of the transferor for the income year. The amount covered by an agreement with a particular transferee is limited to the amount calculated by dividing the greatest equity value of the transferor's investments in the transferee in the income year by the transferor's low tax component tax rate for the income year.

Transfers from foreign superannuation funds

The following amounts transferred from a foreign superannuation fund (¶13-250) are assessable income of the transferee fund in the income year in which the transfer happens (ITAA97 s 295-200):

- where the transferee is an Australian superannuation fund — an amount transferred in relation to a member of the foreign fund to the extent that the amount exceeds amounts vested in the member at the time of the transfer, or

- where the transferee is a complying superannuation fund — so much of the amount transferred as specified in a choice made by a former member of the foreign fund under ITAA97 s 305-80 (¶14-420; ID 2012/27: choice is binding and cannot be revoked or varied) (*Baker*: IRA not a foreign superannuation fund).

The above treatment also applies to transfers from a superannuation scheme that is not, and has never been, an Australian superannuation fund or foreign superannuation fund, was not established in Australia, and is not centrally managed or controlled in Australia (s 295-200(4)). However, amounts transferred from KiwiSaver schemes to a complying superannuation fund are not included as assessable income of the fund (¶13-380).

[AMSG ¶7-120; FITR ¶270-010ff; SLP ¶45-140ff]

¶13-130 Superannuation funds — capital gains or losses

The CGT provisions in ITAA97 Pt 3-1 and 3-3 (see ¶11-000ff and ¶12-000ff) apply to a complying superannuation fund in the same way as any other taxpayer, subject to the modifications in ITAA97 s 295-85 (see ''CGT primary code'' below) and s 295-90 (see ''30 June 1988 asset and cost base'' below). The modifications do not apply to non-complying superannuation funds or non-complying ADFs.

A look-through tax treatment applies where superannuation funds acquire an asset under a limited recourse borrowing arrangement as permitted by the SISA (¶13-120).

CGT primary code

If a CGT event happens involving a CGT asset owned by a complying superannuation fund (or a complying ADF or a PST), the provisions below do not apply to the CGT event:

- ITAA97 ss 6-5 (about ordinary income), 8-1 (about amounts that are deductible), and 15-15 and 25-40 (about profit-making undertakings or plans)
- ITAA97 s 230-15 (about financial arrangements)
- ITAA36 ss 25A and 52 (about profit-making undertakings or schemes) (s 295-85(2)).

The modifications in s 295-85(2) do not apply to the CGT event if:

- a capital gain or loss from the event is attributable to currency exchange rate fluctuations, or
- the CGT asset is a debenture stock, bond, debenture, promissory note, certificate of entitlement, bill of exchange, promissory note or other security, a bank deposit or a loan (secured or not), or other loan contract (s 295-85(3)).

The modifications can also apply to the CGT event if a capital gain or loss is disregarded because of certain ITAA97 provisions (eg for cars, shares in a pooled development fund, collectables, trading stock, insurance policies, etc) (s 295-85(4)).

The above modifications have the effect that the CGT provisions are the primary code for determining the capital gain or capital loss arising from a CGT event happening to a CGT asset of a complying superannuation fund except for the CGT assets and transactions specified in s 295-85(3). For example, the capital loss realised by a superannuation fund from its investment activities is determined under the CGT provisions, not as a deduction under s 8-1 (ID 2009/92: a share does not come within the meaning of ''security'' (see 2nd dot point above); ID 2009/110, ID 2009/111: exchange traded options, treatment of premiums payable and receivable; ID 2010/7: futures contracts).

The s 295-85(2) modifications can apply to a venture capital limited partnership when a complying superannuation fund is a partner in the partnership such that gains flowing to the fund by reason of being a partner are taxed as capital gains (ID 2011/7).

Trading stock

For CGT assets owned by a fund on or after 7.30 pm on 10 May 2011, the trading stock exception provided in s 295-85(4) item 5 is not available in relation to assets covered by ITAA97 s 275-105 (ie shares, units in a trust, and land) (ITAA97 s 70-10(2)(b)). Complying superannuation entities may only access the trading stock exception to the CGT primary code rule for assets other than those covered by s 275-105 where such assets can appropriately be treated as trading stock.

▶ Example

An SMSF buys and sells shares during a year pursuant to the fund's investment objectives and strategy.

The fund must determine whether a capital gain or a capital loss arises for each share transaction during the year under the normal CGT rules.

The fund does not need to consider whether the buying and selling of shares would qualify as being in the business of share trading, or whether the shares bought and sold during the year would be trading stock. The normal CGT consequences will apply to the fund's share transactions.

Insurance policies

A capital gain or capital loss is disregarded when a CGT event happens to an interest in a policy of insurance for an individual's illness or injury if it is made by the trustee of a complying superannuation entity for the income year in which the CGT event happened (ITAA97 s 118-300(1), item 7).

▶ Example

The ABC Superannuation Fund holds total and permanent disability insurance cover for its members, through Safe Insurance Co. Samantha, a fund member, is injured at work and applies to be paid a total and permanent incapacity benefit from the Fund. Safe Insurance Co is satisfied it must pay the insured amount to the Fund in respect of Samantha's injury.

Any capital gain made by the Fund on the payment from Safe Insurance Co is disregarded under the insurance CGT exemption in s 118-300(1).

For the Fund, the disregarded capital gain is governed by the CGT primary code rule in s 295-85(2) and is not subject to treatment on revenue account.

30 June 1988 asset and cost base

An asset owned by a complying superannuation fund at the end of 30 June 1988 is taken, for CGT purposes, to have been acquired by the fund on that date (a "30 June 1988 asset"), and not the actual date of acquisition (ITAA97 s 295-90). The CGT provisions can therefore apply to an asset of the fund even though it was acquired before 20 September 1985, unlike other taxpayers where a potential CGT liability only arises if an asset is acquired after 19 September 1985.

The cost base of each 30 June 1988 asset of a complying fund is the *greater* of the asset's market value and cost base at the end of 30 June 1988. The reduced cost base of each 30 June 1988 asset is the *lesser* of the asset's market value and its cost base at the end of 30 June 1988. This means that the cost base or reduced cost base of each 30 June 1988 asset is whichever of the cost base or the market value at 30 June 1988 yields the lower gain or loss. Where indexation applies, the cost base is indexed from 30 June 1988 (ITTPA Subdiv 295-B). Cost base indexation is not available for assets acquired on or after 21 September 1999 (¶11-610).

The market value of assets at 30 June 1988 is ascertained according to general valuation principles. Special rules deal with a return of capital on company shares, and with the valuation of options, rights and assets acquired under options or rights that were held at 30 June 1988 (TD 44).

Funds with assets at 30 June 1988 which have difficulty in accurately identifying the cost of specific assets disposed of after that date may substitute average cost for actual cost where the asset is part of an identical group of assets held at 30 June 1988 (IT 2548). For assets acquired after that date, actual cost should be used.

CGT roll-over relief involving superannuation entities

The transfer of assets from one superannuation fund to another fund will typically trigger CGT event A1 (ITAA97 s 104-10: disposal of a CGT asset), or may trigger CGT event E2 (ITAA97 s 104-60: transferring a CGT asset to a trust). For the transferor fund, the transfer represents a change in ownership of the assets and a consequential realisation of capital gains and/or capital losses.

However, CGT event A1 does not happen merely because of a change of fund trustees if there is no change in the underlying beneficial ownership of the fund assets even though there may be a change in the legal ownership (¶11-250).

Division 310 merging superannuation funds relief

When superannuation funds merge and a merging (transferor) fund is wound up following its asset transfers and transfers of members' accounts to the transferee fund, the transferor fund's capital losses that would otherwise be available to offset present and future capital gains are lost. Similarly, revenue losses (eg foreign exchange losses) that would otherwise be available to offset against current year income, or carried forward, are also extinguished.

A fund merger may therefore lead to a reduction in the value of members' superannuation interests and have a negative impact on their benefits where the tax benefits of unrealised net capital losses or revenue losses have been included in the valuation of the superannuation interests of the transferor fund's members.

To address the above, ITAA97 Div 310 allows complying superannuation funds (other than SMSFs) which merge to choose optional loss transfer or same asset roll-over relief, or a combination of both (ITAA97 s 310-10(1)).

Eligibility for the asset roll-over is conditional on an entity being eligible for the loss transfer, but does not depend on the entity actually choosing the loss transfer. This will permit superannuation fund mergers to occur in the following ways:

- the transfer of cash only following the disposal of all the transferring entity's assets
- the transfer of other assets only, or
- a combination of cash and other asset transfers.

Capital losses and revenue losses realised before the merger that may be transferred are:

- net capital losses for earlier income years than the transfer year to the extent that they were not utilised before the completion time
- net capital losses for the transfer year, worked out as if the transfer year ended at the completion time
- tax losses for earlier income years than the transfer year to the extent that they were not utilised before the completion time, and
- tax losses incurred for the transfer year, worked out as if the transfer year ended at the completion time (ITAA97 s 310-30).

The effect of transferring a capital loss is that the previously realised net capital loss for an income year that is not the transfer year will be taken, if it is transferred, not to have been made by the transferring entity for that earlier income year and an amount equal to the transferred loss will be taken to have been made by the receiving entity in the transfer year (s 310-35(1)(b)). A receiving entity is therefore able to utilise the transferred capital losses against capital gains only in the income year that the losses are transferred or in future income years.

As with capital losses, an earlier year's tax loss can be transferred to a receiving entity so that the transferring entity will be taken not to have incurred the loss for that earlier income year. For the purposes of ITAA97 s 36-15 (deduction of tax losses), an amount equal to the transferred loss will be taken to have been made by the receiving entity in the income year immediately prior to the transfer year (s 310-40(1)(b)). For all other tax purposes, an amount equal to the transferred loss is taken to be incurred by the receiving entity in the transfer year (s 310-40(1)). This means that the receiving entity will be able to utilise the transferred tax losses against income only in the income year that the losses are transferred or in future income years.

Roll-over of assets

Superannuation funds, ADFs, PSTs and life insurance companies that meet the eligibility conditions for the loss transfer may also choose a roll-over for assets from the transferring entity to the receiving entity where additional conditions are met (ITAA97 Subdiv 310-D; s 310-45).

An entity may choose between 2 methods for executing the roll-over, regardless of the entity's net position with respect to the transferred assets — the global asset approach or individual asset approach. An entity must make a choice of the form of the roll-over that is to apply to its CGT assets and revenue assets (ss 310-50(1), 310-60, 310-70). Only one method can be chosen; an entity cannot use the individual asset approach in relation to some transferred assets and the global asset approach in relation to the remaining transferred assets. However, one method may be chosen for assets that are revenue assets and the other method for CGT assets (s 310-50, note).

Other CGT roll-over relief for superannuation fund asset transfers

Where a complying superannuation fund amends or replaces its trust deed to comply with the SISA, CGT roll-over relief is available for disposals of assets from CGT event E1 or E2 happening, provided the fund assets and members do not change as a consequence (¶12-550).

When a marriage or relationship breaks down, CGT roll-over relief is available for certain asset transfers of assets of a party (eg a former spouse) between small superannuation funds (¶12-480).

CGT exemption for funds paying current pensions

A superannuation fund paying current pensions is entitled to a tax exemption for the normal assessable income derived from the assets of the fund supporting its current pension liabilities (¶13-140).

Any capital gain or loss that a complying superannuation fund makes from a CGT event happening to a "segregated current pension asset" (¶13-140) is disregarded (ITAA97 s 118-320). In addition, when a CGT event happens to assets used solely to produce exempt current pension income, any capital gain or capital loss is disregarded (ITAA97 s 118-12).

Avoiding double taxation

The capital gain calculated under the CGT provisions may be reduced or extinguished if the trustee of a superannuation fund disposes of an asset (and makes a notional capital gain) and the market value of the asset has been taken into account in determining the fund's net previous income in respect of previous years of income under ITAA97 s 295-325 (where a complying fund becomes non-complying: ¶13-200) or ITAA97 s 295-330 (where a non-resident fund becomes a resident fund: ¶13-270).

If the notional capital gain exceeds the amount that would have been included in assessable income as a capital gain if the asset had been disposed of for its market value at the time of calculating the fund's net previous income, the excess is assessable under the CGT provisions. If the notional capital gain does not exceed that amount, no amount is included in assessable income under the CGT provisions (ITAA97 s 118-20(4A)).

ATO guidelines on propagation arrangements

Practical Compliance Guideline PCG 2018/2 provides guidance on the use of propagation arrangements (a tax parcel selection process) to select assets for disposal where registrable superannuation entities (RSEs) have contracted with custodians to provide custodial and investment administration services for the RSE's assets. RSEs are regulated superannuation funds (other than SMSFs), ADFs and PSTs. The guideline explains the Commissioner's compliance approach to propagation arrangements which satisfy the asset identification principles and record-keeping methodologies described in TD 33, TR 96/4 and TR 96/7, the circumstances where propagation is considered appropriate, and when the ITAA36 Pt IVA anti-avoidance provisions may apply.

[AMSG ¶7-130 – ¶7-140; FITR ¶151-500ff, ¶270-100ff; SLP ¶45-160]

¶13-140 Superannuation funds providing pensions

A complying superannuation fund is entitled to an exemption for so much of its ordinary or statutory income that is derived from assets which enables the fund to discharge its liability in respect of certain superannuation income stream benefits where the conditions in ITAA97 s 295-385 or 295-390 are met. The exempt income is generally referred to as "exempt current pension income" (ECPI).

There are 2 methods of determining the exempt income amount — the segregated current pension assets method (s 295-385) and the attributable proportion method (s 295-390) — either, or both, of which may apply.

Exempt current pension income exemption

The income exemption under both the segregated current pension assets method and attributable proportion method applies only to ordinary income or statutory income derived by the fund, and not assessable contributions (¶13-125) or "non-arm's length income" (NALI: ¶13-170) of the fund (*SCCASP Holdings as trustee for the H&R Super Fund*: meaning of arm's length income).

The exemption generally does not continue when a superannuation income stream benefit has ceased to be payable, eg the pension is fully commuted, or the SISR or RSAR pension standards are breached (TR 2013/5 explains when a pension ceases: ¶14-120). An exception is where the cessation is because of the death of the original pension recipient in which case the exemption continues to apply for a limited period (see "Exception — exempt current pension income when pensioner dies" below).

Operation of exemption provisions and key terms in ss 295-385 and 295-390

For 2017–18 and later years, the ECPI provisions refer to fund assets "invested, held in reserve ... to enable the fund to discharge its liabilities in respect of 'RP superannuation income stream benefits'" (see below), rather than to assets supporting "superannuation income stream benefits that are payable at the time" as was the case previously (ss 295-385(3)(a), (4)(a), (5); 295-390(7); 295-395(3)).

A "superannuation income stream benefit" is a benefit specified in the regulations that is paid from a "superannuation income stream".

The regulations provide that a ''superannuation income stream benefit'' is:

- a payment from an interest that supports a superannuation income stream, and
- for the purposes of ITAA97 ss 295-385, 295-390, 295-395, 320-246 and 320-247, includes an amount taken to be the amount of a superannuation income stream benefit under reg 995-1.01(3) or (4) (these subregulations provide an expanded meaning of superannuation income stream benefit so that funds paying death benefits continue to qualify for the current pension income exemption for a limited period: see ''Exception — exempt current pension income when pensioner dies'' below).

A ''superannuation income stream'' under the regulations means:

(a) an income stream that is taken to be an annuity of a pension for the purposes of the SISA in accordance with reg 1.05(1) or reg 1.06(1) of the SIS Regulations, or a pension for the purposes of the RSA Act in accordance with reg 1.07 of the RSA Regulations

(b) an income stream that is an annuity or pension within the meaning of the SISA and that commenced before 20 September 2007, or

(c) a deferred superannuation income stream that is taken to be an annuity or pension under the SISA because they meet the standards in reg 1.06A(2) of the SIS Regulations (ITAA97 s 307-70(2); ITR97 reg 995-1.01).

RP superannuation income stream benefits

The concept of ''RP superannuation income stream benefits'' is used in s 295-385(3)(a) and 295-385(4) (which set out the meaning of ''segregated current pension assets'': see below) and in s 295-390(3) (which contains the formula for determining the attributable proportion of the value of current pension liabilities: see below).

A superannuation income stream benefit is a ''retirement phase superannuation income stream benefit'' (or RP superannuation income stream benefit) of a superannuation fund at a time if:

- if it is payable by the fund from a superannuation income stream that is in the *retirement phase* (see below) at that time, or
- if it is payable by the fund *after* that time from a superannuation income stream that is a deferred superannuation income stream and is in the retirement phase at that time (ITAA97 s 307-75).

A superannuation income stream is in the ''retirement phase'' at a time if:

- a superannuation income stream benefit is payable from it at the time, or
- it is a deferred superannuation income stream, and a superannuation income stream benefit will be payable from it to a person after that time and the person has satisfied (whether at or before that time) a condition of release under SISR Sch 1 items 101, 102A, 103, 106 (because of retirement, terminal medical condition, permanent incapacity or attaining age 65) (ITAA97 s 307-80(1), (2)).

A superannuation income stream from which a superannuation income stream benefit is payable is *not* in the retirement phase at a time if:

- it is any of the following:
  - a transition to retirement income stream (TRIS) within the meaning in SISR Pt 6 or RSAR Pt 4
  - a non-commutable allocated annuity or non-commutable allocated pension (within the meaning of those regulations)

- the person to whom the benefit is payable is *not* a reversionary beneficiary, and
- at or before that time, the person to whom the benefit is payable:
  - has not satisfied a condition of release specified in s 307-80(2)(c) (see above), or
  - has satisfied a condition of release relating to retirement, terminal medical condition or permanent disability, but has not notified the income stream provider of that fact (s 307-80(3)) (see ‘‘TRIS and reversionary beneficiaries’’ below).

A superannuation income stream is also *not* in the retirement phase in an income year if:

- the income stream is specified in an ATO commutation authority to a superannuation provider in respect of a member's excess transfer balance amount
- the provider is required by TAA Sch 1 s 136-80 to pay a superannuation lump sum but fails to do so within the 60-day period mentioned in that section, and
- the income year is the income year in which the 60-day period ended, or a later income year (¶14-350) (s 307-80(4)).

TRIS and reversionary beneficiaries

A TRIS is not in the retirement phase unless a superannuation income stream benefit is currently payable from it and the recipient:

- is 65 years old or older, or
- has met a relevant condition of release with a nil cashing restriction and has notified the TRIS provider of that fact, or
- is receiving the TRIS as a reversionary beneficiary.

A TRIS is not in the retirement phase but will move into the retirement phase when the member meets one of the following conditions of release specified in s 307-80(2)(c), ie retirement, terminal medical condition, permanent incapacity or attaining age 65 years (see above).

The move into the retirement phase happens as soon as the member reaches age 65 years, or if a reversionary income stream starts to be paid to a reversionary beneficiary after the member's death. With the retirement, terminal medical condition, permanent incapacity conditions of release, the TRIS will move into the retirement phase at the time the TRIS provider is notified.

A member does not need to commute and restart a TRIS for it to move into the retirement phase.

A TRIS does not convert into any other form of superannuation income stream when it moves into the retirement phase. That is, it will continue to satisfy the definition of a TRIS, but it will be ‘‘converted’’ to another kind of superannuation income stream if the TRIS has ceased and a new superannuation income stream is commenced.

Essentially, once a member meets one of the specified conditions of release, the restrictions particular to the TRIS (the 10% maximum annual payment and commutation restrictions) fall away automatically, subject to the governing rules of the fund and/or the agreement or standards under which the TRIS is provided. Once those limitations are gone, the TRIS has the same restrictions and requirements as any other account-based superannuation income stream.

A reversionary TRIS can always be paid to a reversionary beneficiary, regardless of whether the beneficiary has satisfied a condition of release, for the purpose of meeting the requirement of being an income stream in the retirement phase (s 307-80(3)(aa)). For that purpose, a TRIS paid to a reversionary beneficiary is only subject to the general retirement phase definition in s 307-80(1) (which requires that a superannuation benefit is paid). This is consistent with the treatment of other superannuation income streams which do not require the reversionary beneficiary to satisfy a condition of release.

ATO *Guidance Note* GN 2019/1 provides further guidelines on TRISs and reversionary beneficiaries.

2 forms of "segregated current pension assets"

A superannuation fund's assets are ''segregated current pension assets'' if they come within the meaning given in s 295-385(3) or s 295-385(4) to (6) and they are not ''disregarded small fund assets'' (see below).

Segregated current pension assets under s 295-385(3)

The assets of a complying superannuation fund are segregated current pension assets under s 295-385(3) at a time if:

(a) the assets are invested, held in reserve or otherwise being dealt with at that time for the sole purpose of enabling the fund to discharge all or part of its liabilities (contingent or not) as they become due, in respect of RP superannuation income stream benefits (see above) of the fund at that time, and

(b) the trustee of the fund obtains an actuary's certificate before the date for lodgment of the fund's income tax return for the income year to the effect that the assets and the earnings that the actuary expects will be made from them would provide the amount required to discharge in full those liabilities, or that part of those liabilities, as they fall due.

Segregated current pension assets under s 295-385(4)

The assets of a complying superannuation fund are segregated current pension assets under s 295-385(4) at a time if the assets are invested, held in reserve or otherwise being dealt with at that time for the sole purpose of enabling the fund to discharge all or part of its liabilities (contingent or not), as they become due, in respect of superannuation income stream benefits:

- that are RP superannuation income stream benefits of the fund at that time, and
- prescribed by the regulations for the purposes of this section (see below).

Regulation 295-385.01 has prescribed the following superannuation income stream benefits:

(a) an RP superannuation income stream benefit of a superannuation fund payable from an allocated pension, a market-linked pension or an account-based pension (within the meaning of the SIS Regulations)

(b) an amount taken to be the amount of a superannuation income stream benefit under reg 995-1.01(3) or (4), where the superannuation income stream that was payable to the deceased mentioned in that subregulation was a pension mentioned in (a) of which the deceased was a retirement phase recipient.

Points to note about segregated current pension assets

The sole purpose requirement in ss 295-385(3) and (4) means that the asset must only be invested, held or otherwise dealt with for the relevant purpose, and not partly for any other purpose.

As some bank accounts are used for a range of different purposes, TD 2014/7 sets out the circumstances in which a bank account (or sub-account) of a complying superannuation fund is a segregated current pension asset for the purposes of s 295-385(3) or (4).

A notable difference between the above provisions is that an actuary's certificate is not required for segregated current pension assets under s 295-385(4). That is:

- s 295-385(3) applies where the trustee obtains an actuary's certificate before the date of lodgment of the fund's tax return for the income year to the effect that the assets and the earnings expected to be made from them would provide the amount required to discharge in full all or part of the fund's liabilities (contingent or not) in respect of RP superannuation income stream benefits payable by the fund as they fall due, and
- s 295-385(4) applies in respect of RP superannuation income stream benefits prescribed in ITR97 (ie allocated pensions, market-linked pensions, and account-based pensions).

Note that s 295-385(4) does not apply unless, at all times during the income year, the liabilities of the fund (contingent or not) to pay RP superannuation income stream benefits are liabilities in respect of the prescribed income stream benefits above. Also, the assets supporting a prescribed income stream benefit are not segregated current pension assets to the extent that the market value of the assets exceeds the account balance supporting the benefit (s 295-385(5), (6)).

Disregarded small fund assets

SMSFs and small APRA funds cannot use the segregated current pension assets method to determine their earnings tax exemption for an income year if:

- at a time during the income year, there is at least one superannuation interest in the fund that is in the "retirement phase" (see above)
- just before the start of the income year:
  - a person has a total superannuation balance (¶14-050) that exceeds $1.6 million, and
  - the person is the retirement phase recipient of a superannuation income stream (whether or not the fund is the provider of the income stream), and
- at a time during the income year this member has a superannuation interest (in accumulation or in retirement phase) in the fund (ss 294-20; 295-385(7); 295-387).

The fund assets covered by s 295-387 (known as "disregarded small fund assets") cannot be segregated current pension assets for the purposes of s 295-385 or segregated non-current assets for the purposes of s 295-395.

This means that funds in those circumstances cannot use the segregated current pension assets method in s 295-385 for their ECPI calculation and must use the attributable proportion method in s 295-390. This is the case even if the fund's only member interests are retirement phase superannuation income streams where an actuarial certificate will enable the fund to claim a 100% pension income exemption (see "Actuary's certificates" below).

Proposed changes — ECPI calculation

The government has announced that:

- superannuation funds with interests in both the accumulation and retirement phases during an income year will be allowed to choose their preferred method of calculating their ECPI, and
- the redundant requirement for superannuation funds to obtain an actuarial certificate when calculating ECPI using the proportionate method, where all members of the fund are fully in the retirement phase for all of the income year, will be removed (2019–20 Budget Paper No 2, p 23).

The start date of the proposed measures has been revised from 1 July 2020 to 1 July 2021 (Assistant Treasurer's media release, 30 June 2020).

Exception — exempt current pension income when pensioner dies

The ECPI exemption does not continue when a superannuation income stream benefit has ceased to be payable because a pensioner has died, subject to a limited exception as noted below.

To provide tax certainty for deceased estates, the term ''superannuation income stream benefit'' for the purposes of the exemption has an expanded meaning (ITR97 reg 295-385.01(b)):

- where a fund member (pensioner) was receiving a superannuation income stream immediately before his/her death, and
- that income stream is not reversionary (ie it does not automatically revert to another person on the pensioner's death).

In that case, an amount that is either paid as a death benefit lump sum using only an amount from the superannuation interest that was supporting the deceased pensioner's income stream immediately before death, or that is applied from that interest to commence a new income stream, is taken to be a superannuation income stream benefit payable by the fund for a specified period. The specified period is from the pensioner's death until as soon as it was practicable to pay the death benefit lump sum or commence the new income stream. This effectively allows the fund to continue to be entitled to the current pension income exemption in relation to such an amount during that period.

The deemed superannuation income stream benefit is reduced by any amount, other than investment earnings, that was added to the superannuation interest on or after the pensioner's death. ''Investment earnings'' does not include an amount paid under a policy of insurance on the life of the deceased or an amount arising from self-insurance. This ensures that the exemption amount for the relevant after-death period is no greater than it was before the pensioner's death (allowing only for the post-death investment earnings).

Method 1 — segregated current pension assets

Under the segregated current pension assets method, the fund segregates its assets as specifically relating to its current pension liabilities in respect of the fund's RP superannuation income stream benefits (s 295-385). In this case, the exempt income is that part of the fund's income that is derived from the segregated current pension assets.

As noted above, the term ''superannuation income stream benefit'' has an expanded meaning in relation to a deceased estate where a person who was receiving an income stream dies and there is no reversionary interest.

Section 295-385 only requires the segregation of current pension assets as a whole from the other assets of the fund. There is no requirement to segregate assets in respect of each individual member who is receiving a superannuation income stream benefit although funds may choose to do so where permitted by their trust deed.

Method 2 — attributable proportion of assets to meet current pension liabilities

Under the attributable proportion method, the exemption is based on the proportion of unsegregated current pension liabilities of the fund to its total unsegregated superannuation liabilities in respect of RP superannuation income stream benefits of the fund at any time in the year (s 295-390).

That calculated proportion of the fund's income (other than income exempt under s 295-385, income derived from assets that are segregated non-current pension assets, NALI or assessable contributions of the fund) is exempt from tax.

The ''average value of current pension liabilities'' is the average value of the fund's current liabilities (contingent or not) in respect of RP superannuation income stream benefits of the fund at any time in that year (other than liabilities for which segregated current pension assets are held). The ''average value of superannuation liabilities'' is the average value for the income year of the fund's current and future liabilities (contingent or not) in respect of superannuation income stream benefits in respect of which contributions have, or were liable to have, been made (other than liabilities for which segregated current pension assets or segregated non-current assets are held).

A superannuation fund's ''segregated non-current pension assets'' are assets relating to the fund's superannuation liabilities *other than* current pension liabilities (as certified by an actuary), ie assets invested or held by the fund for its non-current pension liabilities (s 295-390). No tax exemption is available for income derived from segregated non-current pension assets.

Actuary's certificates

An actuary's certificate is not required in order to claim the current pension income exemption if a superannuation fund is using the segregated current pension assets method and is only paying allocated pensions, market-linked pensions or account-based pensions (ITAA97 s 295-385(4); ITR97 reg 295-385.01). A fund that uses the segregated assets method and pays other types of pensions will need to obtain a certificate covering all pensions that the fund pays.

All funds using the proportional (unsegregated assets) method to claim the current pension income exemption will need an actuarial certificate for each year that it claims an exemption, regardless of the type of pension being paid (s 295-390(4) to (7)) (see ''Proposed changes — ECPI calculation'' above).

Funds paying pensions may also require additional actuarial certifications for financial management purposes as part of the SISA prudential requirements (SISR Pt 9).

ATO guidelines — powers of general administration

The ATO has provided guidelines for funds claiming the ECPI, the actuarial certificate requirements, the annual return requirements for a fund in both the pension and accumulation phase, the effect of tax losses or capital gains and losses on a fund's claim for ECPI, and the reporting labels in an SMSF's tax return (Fact Sheet *Self-managed super funds and tax exemptions on pension assets*).

In certain circumstances (eg honest mistakes and matters beyond the fund trustee's control), the Commissioner may exercise the general powers of administration to allow funds to claim ECPI even though the SISR minimum pension standards (¶14-120) have not been met (www.ato.gov.au/Super/Self-managed-super-funds/In-detail/SMSF-resources/SMSF-technical/SMSFs--Minimum-pension-payment-requirements---frequently-asked-questions).

ATO guidelines — superannuation funds which provide a pension tax bonus to members

PCG 2019/7 states that, where certain conditions are met, the ATO will not allocate compliance resources to review the calculation of a superannuation fund's ECPI under Subdiv 295-F as a result of the fund not incorporating the value of the pension tax bonus into the member's pension account balance when calculating the required minimum pension payments.

[AMSG ¶6-470, ¶7-150ff; FITR ¶270-390; SLP ¶38-665, ¶45-200]

¶13-150 Superannuation funds — allowable deductions

The deductibility of expenditure incurred by a complying superannuation fund is determined under the general deduction provision in ITAA97 s 8-1 (¶16-000), unless a specific provision applies (eg under ITAA97 s 25-5 as a tax-related expense).

A checklist of deductions may be found in ¶16-005. Expenditure must be "incurred" in order to qualify for a deduction (¶16-040).

General and specific deductions

TR 93/17 explains the general principles governing deductibility of expenditure for superannuation funds, ADFs and PSTs (superannuation entity) under s 8-1 and other specific provisions.

Subject to the need for apportionment, expenses that are ordinarily deductible under s 8-1 include: (a) actuarial costs (except those incurred in complying with, or managing, the fund's income tax affairs which are ordinarily deductible under s 25-5); (b) accountancy fees (except those incurred in complying with, or managing, the fund's income tax affairs which are ordinarily deductible under s 25-5); (c) audit fees; (d) non-capital costs of complying with a "regulatory provision" (as defined in SISA s 38A) or relevant legislation; (e) trustee fees and premiums under an indemnity insurance policy; (f) costs in connection with the calculation and payment of benefits to members (but not the cost of the benefit itself), eg interest on money borrowed to secure temporary finance for the payment of benefits and medical costs in assessing invalidity benefit claims; (g) investment adviser fees and costs in providing pre-retirement services to members; (h) membership subscriptions paid to professional associations; and (i) other administrative costs incurred in managing the fund (TD 2004/1: costs of subscriptions to share market information services and journals).

Some other expenses which are commonly incurred by superannuation funds, such as levies, legal expenses and trust deed expenses, are also deductible as discussed below.

Fees paid to a commercial superannuation provider in respect of a product purchased by the superannuation fund (eg investment or administration charges levied by a life assurance company or PST) are generally not deductible. Investment-related expenses (eg commissions and ongoing management fees) would ordinarily be deductible, but up-front fees incurred in investing money are of a capital nature and are not deductible (TD 95/60 at ¶16-660; ID 2004/968: management fees and allocated pension fund).

Costs incurred in amending a superannuation fund's trust deed are deductible if they are not of a capital nature. An example is where the deed amendments are necessitated by changes in government regulations and are made to ensure that the fund's day-to-day operations continue to satisfy the requirements for a complying superannuation fund, or where the amendments make administration of the fund more efficient and do not amount to a restructuring of the fund (IT 2672; TR 93/17, para 23). In contrast, amendment costs incurred by an employer-sponsor of a superannuation fund are deductible, regardless of whether the amendments are necessitated by changes in government regulations.

A complying superannuation fund can claim a deduction under ITAA36 s 70B for the full amount of a loss it incurs on the disposal or redemption of a "traditional security" (as defined in ITAA36 s 26BB: ¶23-340) which is not a segregated current pension asset (where ITAA97 s 295-390 applies to exempt some of the income of the fund: ¶13-140) (ID 2014/26: loss on redemption of traditional security).

The deductibility of legal expenses depends on whether the expenses are of a capital or revenue nature, but certain legal expenses are specifically made deductible (¶16-830).

Capital expenditure incurred in establishing a structure for a regulated superannuation fund (eg purchase of a trust deed) is not deductible under ITAA97 s 40-880(2A) (¶16-156).

A deduction was not available under ITAA97 s 25-45 (loss by theft) for misappropriation by the trustee of an SMSF as the loss was not caused by the misappropriation of an employee or agent (*Shail*).

Apportionment of expenditure

Expenditure that is only incurred in gaining or producing non-assessable income is not deductible under s 8-1. However, expenditure (eg a fund's general administrative and management expenses) which is incurred partly in producing assessable income and partly in gaining non-assessable income must be apportioned to determine the amount that is deductible under s 8-1.

Apportionment ensures that expenditure is deductible only to the extent to which it is incurred in producing assessable income (the first limb in s 8-1(1)(a)), or it has the character of an operating or working expense of a business or is an essential part of the cost of the fund's business operations (the second limb in s 8-1(1)(b)).

Expenditure that is deductible under s 25-5 does not need to be apportioned to the extent the fund gains or produces non-assessable income. Apportionment is also not required for non-capital expenditure incurred solely in gaining contributions made to the fund (see ''Cost of collecting contributions'' below).

TR 93/17 explains the correct method for apportioning expenditure between assessable income and non-assessable income depending on the particular circumstances of the case. The Ruling also sets out 2 generally accepted apportionment methods, but other methods are acceptable provided they give a fair and reasonable assessment of the extent to which the outlay relates to assessable income. For apportionment purposes, the exempt income of a fund includes non-reversionary bonuses and exempt current pension income (¶13-140).

ATO guidelines — tax treatment of penalty interest

''Penalty interest'' is an amount payable by a borrower under a loan agreement in consideration for the lender agreeing to an early repayment of the loan. The amount payable is commonly calculated by reference to a number of months of interest payments that would have been received but for the early repayment.

TR 2019/2 explains when penalty interest is deductible under ITAA97 s 8-1, 25-25, 25-30, 25-90 or 40-880. The Ruling also considers whether penalty interest is included in the cost base or reduced cost base of a CGT asset as an incidental cost under ITAA97 s 110-35(9) or 110-55(2), or in the cost of a depreciating asset under s 40-190(2)(b).

Taxpayer alert — non-arm's length borrowings and transactions

TA 2008/3 and TA 2008/4 set out the ATO's concerns about non-arm's length arrangements under which a fund uses borrowed fund's to acquire an interest in an investment vehicle, and certain non-arm's length arrangements under which a superannuation fund derives income through a direct or indirect interest in a closely held trust. The concerns include the deductibility of expenses, and whether income derived by the fund from the trust is NALI (¶13-170).

Cost of collecting contributions

In determining deductions under s 8-1, a contribution made to a complying superannuation fund is taken to be assessable income, whether or not it is an assessable contribution (ITAA97 s 295-95; TR 93/17). That is, the receipt of non-assessable contributions does not reduce the extent to which a fund can deduct expenditure incurred in obtaining contributions. Accordingly, complying funds can claim a deduction for expenses incurred in obtaining contributions whether or not the full amount of those contributions is included in the fund's assessable income (¶13-125). The non-capital expenditure of a fund in obtaining contributions do not need to be apportioned for s 8-1 purposes where it is incurred in obtaining both assessable and non-assessable contributions (including a single contribution that has both an assessable and non-assessable portion). This modification also applies to a non-complying superannuation fund that is an Australian superannuation fund, a complying or non-complying ADF, and an RSA provider.

A roll-over superannuation benefit (¶13-125) to a fund is a ''contribution'' for s 295-95(1) purposes. For example, the whole roll-over amount is treated as if it were included in the fund's assessable income when working out the deductible portion of an administrative fee under s 8-1. This is consistent with the policy intention underpinning s 295-95(1) that a fund can deduct losses and outgoings incurred in obtaining a roll-over superannuation benefit in its entirety (not just the assessable part).

Cost of insurance premiums for death or disability benefits

A complying superannuation fund which provides death and disability benefits that are specified in ITAA97 s 295-460 can claim a deduction related to the cost of providing these benefits. The quantum of the deduction is calculated either on a premiums basis or by using a formula based on actual costs under ITAA97 s 295-465. Alternatively, the fund may choose not to claim deductions under s 295-465 for an income year and to deduct amounts instead under ITAA97 s 295-470 based on the fund's future liability to pay the benefits (see ''Deduction based on actual cost of providing benefits'' below) (s 295-465(4)). An RSA provider can claim a deduction relating to the provision of these benefits on a premiums basis (ITAA97 s 295-475).

Section 295-460 covers superannuation death benefits, disability superannuation benefits, temporary income protection benefits and terminal medical condition benefits (see below). A ''superannuation death benefit'' means a lump sum or pension benefit paid after the death of a member (¶14-270). A ''disability superannuation benefit'' means a lump sum or pension benefit paid to an individual because they suffer from ill-health (whether physical or mental) and 2 legally qualified medical practitioners have certified that, because of the ill-health, it is unlikely that the individual can ever be gainfully employed in a capacity for which the individual is reasonably qualified because of education, experience or training (ITAA97 s 995-1(1)). A superannuation lump sum can be a disability superannuation benefit even if it is not paid under the SISR ''permanent incapacity'' condition of release (ID 2009/109).

An income protection benefit is an income stream payable due to a person's temporary incapacity to engage in gainful employment and is payable for no longer than 2 years, or such longer period as allowed by APRA or the Commissioner (see TD 2007/3 below).

A s 295-465 deduction (see below) is available for premiums on insurance policies where the income payments under the policy are made to members during periods of temporary incapacity which last longer than 2 years, provided the benefits payable under the policy comply with the SISA requirements. The provision of temporary disability benefits is an approved ancillary purpose under the sole purpose test in the SISA and such benefits may potentially be paid for a period of more than 2 years but not exceeding the period of incapacity (TD 2007/3).

If a fund receives a rebate or refund of premiums paid for which a deduction has previously been allowed, that amount is included in the fund's assessable income for the year in which it is received (ITAA97 s 295-320, item 4).

Deduction on premiums basis

The deduction for insurance premiums under s 295-465(1) is as follows:

(1) 30% of the premium for a whole of life policy — a ''whole of life policy'' is an insurance policy that satisfies the following conditions: (a) the policy includes an investment component; (b) the premium is not dissected; and (c) the proceeds are payable only on death or on attaining an age of 85 years or more (deduction not allowed where the premium is dissected between an entry fee and the investment component of the policy: see ID 2009/100)

(2) 10% of the premium for an endowment policy — an "endowment policy" is an insurance policy that satisfies the following conditions: (a) the policy is not a whole of life policy; (b) the policy includes an investment component; (c) the premium is not dissected; and (d) the proceeds are payable only on death or on attaining an age specified in the policy

(3) 30% of that part of the premium for a non-whole of life policy that is specified in the policy as being for a distinct part of the policy, if that part would have been a whole of life policy had it been a separate policy

(4) 10% of that part of the premium for a non-endowment policy that is specified in the policy as being for a distinct part of the policy, if that part would have been an endowment policy had it been a separate policy

(5) that part of the premium as specified in the policy as being wholly for the liability to provide the benefits referred to in s 295-460

(6) so much of other insurance policy premiums as are attributable to provide the benefits referred to in s 295-460 (supported by an actuary's certificate) (s 295-465(1) items 1–6, (3)).

For item (6), the deductible proportion of premiums for certain prescribed TPD policies that are treated as being attributable to a liability to provide the benefits is set out in ITR97 reg 295-465.01. Funds may deduct the specified proportion of the premium in reg 295-465.01(1) provided those policies are more restrictive or have substantially the same meaning as the conditions specified in reg 295-465.01(5). In such cases, an actuary's certificate is not required (s 295-465(1B), (3A)). A fund can still deduct an amount under item (6) without recourse to the regulations, but will need to obtain an actuary's certificate in that case.

A deduction can be claimed under item (6) for the remaining part of an insurance premium for which a partial deduction has been claimed under item (5) (because part of the premium is specified in the policy as being wholly for the liability to provide benefits referred to in s 295-460). For example, if only part of an insurance premium is specified in the policy as being wholly for the liability to provide superannuation death benefits (s 295-460), the fund may be able to claim a deduction under item (6) for the part of the remainder of the premium attributable to a liability to provide benefits referred to in s 295-460 by reference to reg 295-465.01 or by obtaining an actuary's certificate (s 295-465(1A)).

Self-insuring funds

Superannuation funds which self-insure their liability to provide the benefits referred to in s 295-460 may deduct the amount the fund could reasonably be expected to pay in an arm's length transaction to obtain insurance to cover the liability. An actuary's certificate is required to claim the deduction (s 295-465(2), (3)).

Self-insuring funds may determine the deductible amount under s 295-465(2) using the percentages in reg 295-465.01, for example, where an actuary has calculated the arm's length cost of an insurance policy which covers a broader class of benefits than is referred to in s 295-460 and the policy is of a kind specified in reg 295-465.01 (s 295-465(2A), (2B), (3)).

Deduction based on actual cost of providing benefits

A fund that elects under s 295-465(4) not to claim deductions on the premiums basis may claim a deduction based on the actual cost of providing the death or disability benefits which arise each year under s 295-470. The election must be made by the fund's tax return lodgment date for the year in which the election is to apply. Once made, the election also applies for all later years unless the Commissioner decides otherwise (s 295-465(5)). An election is not required to be in writing or lodged with the Commissioner. The deductible amount is the future service element of the lump sum or pension death or disability benefits during the year, as calculated using the formula in s 295-470(2). A choice can be made under s 295-465(4) to claim a deduction under s 295-470 before or after the death of an insured fund member (ID 2015/17).

Terminal medical condition benefits

A terminal medical condition (TMC) exists in relation to a person at a particular time if the following circumstances exist:

- 2 registered medical practitioners have certified, jointly or separately, that the person suffers from an illness, or has incurred an injury, that is likely to result in the death of the person within a period (the certification period) that ends not more than 24 months after the date of the certification
- at least one of the registered medical practitioners is a specialist practising in an area related to the illness or injury suffered by the person, and
- for each of the certificates, the certification period has not ended (ITR97 reg 303-10.01).

A complying superannuation fund that provides TMC benefits to its members can claim a deduction for a specified amount that is part of a premium which is wholly for the liability to provide TMC benefits, or for so much of the premium as is attributable to the liability to provide TMC benefits (ss 295-460(aa); 295-465(1), table items 5 and 6). The deduction applies in relation to a current or contingent liability of the fund to provide TMC benefits.

▶ Example

The ABC Superannuation Fund takes out insurance in relation to its members for death cover and terminal illness cover. The fund's trust deed specifies that the fund has a liability to pay TMC benefits to members.

The insurance premium paid by the fund is deductible under item 5 or 6 of s 295-465(1), as the premium relates partly to a liability of the fund to provide TMC benefits to members under s 295-460(aa) and partly to a liability to provide death benefits under s 295-460(a).

If there is no insurance coverage, the fund can claim a deduction for an amount it could reasonably be expected to pay in an arm's length transaction to obtain an insurance policy to cover that part of its current or contingent liabilities to provide TMC benefits (s 295-465(2)). An actuary's certificate is required in order to apportion premiums under s 295-465(1) item 6 or the amount under s 295-465(2). Alternatively, self-insuring funds may choose to deduct an amount for a future liability to pay TMC benefits using a formula based on the actual cost of providing the benefits which arise each year (s 295-470).

The taxation of TMC benefits is discussed in ¶14-310.

ATO guidelines on deductions for TPD cover

TR 2012/6 provides guidelines on how s 295-465(1), (1A) and (1B) together with s 295-460(b) apply to premiums paid by a complying superannuation fund for insurance policies which provide TPD cover for members, the relationship between deductibility of premiums and the SISR rules on provision of benefits to members, and the interaction of the ITAA97 provisions with ITR97 reg 295-465.01.

Taxpayer alert — life insurance bonds issued by tax haven entities

TA 2009/17 dealing with life insurance bonds issued from tax haven entities warns that Australian residents investors (including SMSFs) in these types of bonds may not be eligible for concessional tax treatment, such as a deduction of 30% of the insurance premium under s 295-465 (or ITAA36 former s 279), the CGT exemption and special rules applicable to reversionary bonus paid from life insurance bonds.

Expenses relating to investments in PSTs or life policies

A complying superannuation fund (or a complying ADF) may claim a deduction for non-capital expenses incurred in relation to investments in PSTs, in life assurance policies issued by life assurance companies or in custodian trusts under such policies (ITAA97 s 295-100; TD 1999/6). Investment or administration charges levied by a PST or life office that are generally of a capital nature are not normally deductible (TR 93/17, para 23(d)). Except where deductible under s 295-465 (see "Cost of insurance premiums for death or disability benefits" above), fees and charges incurred in respect of complying superannuation life insurance policies, exempt life insurance policies or exempt units in a PST are not deductible (s 295-100).

Payment to employer-sponsor

If a superannuation fund pays an amount or a benefit (eg a return of surplus) to an employer-sponsor who has been allowed a deduction for contributions made to the fund (¶13-710), the value of the amount or benefit is assessable income of the employer (ITAA97 s 290-100). Similarly, if the fund or a successor fund provides to any person a payment or benefit that reasonably represents a return of deductible employer contributions (or earnings thereon), the value of the payment or benefit is included in the recipient's assessable income. The payer superannuation fund is *not* entitled to a deduction for the amounts paid.

Payment of benefits

A complying superannuation fund cannot claim a deduction for superannuation benefits paid, including payments under an income stream because of a person's temporary inability to engage in gainful employment (ITAA97 s 295-495, items 1 and 6).

Levies

The superannuation supervisory levy and the financial assistance funding levy paid by a superannuation fund are deductible, but not associated penalties (¶13-870).

A grant of financial assistance under SISA Pt 23 is exempt income to the recipient fund and any repayment of financial assistance by a fund is not an allowable deduction (¶13-870).

Deductions relating to holding vacant land

Expenses related to holding vacant land, residential rental property under construction or a completed property not available for rent, are not deductible, except in certain circumstances (ITAA97 s 26-102). Superannuation plans (other than SMSFs) are not covered by the restriction on such deductions (¶16-650).

[AMSG ¶7-150ff; FITR ¶31-050ff, ¶270-460; SLP ¶45-200ff]

¶13-160 Superannuation funds — offsets, losses and other concessions

Other tax offsets (rebates and credits) and taxation concessions which may be relevant to superannuation entities are outlined below.

Franking credits

The imputation system is discussed in detail in ¶4-100 and ¶4-400 onwards.

A complying superannuation fund that receives franked distributions will have its assessable income grossed up to include the amount of franking credits attached (ie reflecting the company tax paid attributable to the distributions) in the same manner as other recipients of franked distributions (¶4-800). Distributions where no tax has been paid by the resident payer entities are treated as unfranked distributions.

A complying superannuation fund is entitled to a franking tax offset of the full amount of franking credits, even though its primary tax rate as a complying fund is 15% or its income is exempt (such as income relating to current pension liabilities), except on dividends paid as part of a dividend stripping operation. The offset may be set off against tax on other fund income.

A venture capital franking tax offset is similarly available if the fund receives a venture capital franked dividend paid by a pooled development fund (PDF) even though the dividend is exempt.

A superannuation fund must therefore include the total franked and unfranked amount of distributions received, as well as the franking credits attached, to determine its net income or loss.

To the extent that family trust distribution tax has been paid on a distribution that was paid or credited to a superannuation fund by a company that has made an interposed entity election, the distribution is excluded from the fund's assessable income (ITAA36 Sch 2F s 271-105). Any loss or outgoing incurred in deriving such excluded distributions is not deductible and the fund cannot claim a credit or tax offset for any franking credit attached to the whole or a portion of the exempt income.

Refund of excess franking credits

A complying superannuation fund (or a complying ADF or PST) is entitled to a refund of excess franking credits which exceed the fund's tax liability after taking into account other tax offsets to which the fund is entitled (ITAA97 ss 63-10(1), item 40; 67-25; ¶4-820). A claim for excess franking credits is made as part of the assessment process in the fund's tax return.

Integrity measures — distribution washing

The operation of the imputation system is supported by many integrity measures, such as the anti-streaming rules, the holding period and related payments rules, and the ITAA36 Pt IVA general anti-avoidance provisions. The consequences of manipulating the imputation system (eg the loss of gross-up and tax offset treatment) are discussed in ¶4-900 onwards.

An entity's ability to obtain the benefits of additional franking credits received as a result of ''distribution washing'' is restricted (ITAA97 s 207-157) (¶4-975). The AAT has held that the ITAA36 Pt IVA determination process and anti-avoidance rule in s 177EA (¶30-195) could apply to certain benefits arising from dividend washing transactions entered into before 1 July 2013, ie before s 207-157 was operative (*The Trustees of the WT and A Norman Superannuation Fund*). The ATO states that the AAT's reasoning was consistent with its view in TD 2014/10 on the law relating to ''dividend washing'' transactions. The commencement of s 207-157 has removed the need for the Commissioner to make determinations under s 177EA to deny imputation benefits arising under dividend washing transactions for distributions which are made on or after 1 July 2013 (*Decision Impact Statement* VRN 6023 of 2014 and 6090 of 2014).

In *Lynton ATF the David Lynton Superannuation Fund*, the AAT affirmed the Commissioner's decision that s 177EA applied to dividend washing trades so that no imputation benefit arose in respect of distributions made as a result of the scheme. The Commissioner had correctly applied s 207-145(1)(f) to those parts of the dividend washing trades in the 2012 and 2013 income years where the shares were held for less than 45 days. Accordingly, the superannuation fund was not entitled to a tax offset in respect of the shares for those years.

Contrived dividend arrangements involving SMSFs

TA 2015/1 covers arrangements where a private company with accumulated profits channels franked dividends to an SMSF instead of the company's original shareholders. As a result, the original shareholders escape tax on the dividends and the original shareholders or individuals associated with the original shareholders benefit as members of the SMSF from franking credit refunds to the SMSF.

The ATO is concerned that contrived arrangements are entered into by individuals (typically SMSF members approaching retirement) so that dividends subsequently flow to, and are purportedly treated as exempt from income tax in, the SMSF because the relevant shares are supporting pensions. The intention is for the original shareholders of the private company and/or their associates to avoid ''top-up'' income tax on the dividend income; and for the SMSF to receive a refund of the unused franking credit tax offset, which is available for tax-free distribution to its members. Such an arrangement has features of dividend stripping which could lead to the ATO cancelling any tax benefit for the transferring shareholder and/or denying the SMSF the franking credit tax offset.

The ATO had also issued private rulings on arrangements with features similar to those described in TA 2015/1 and applied the anti-avoidance provisions to determine whether:

- franked dividends received by the SMSF may be part of a dividend stripping operation under ITAA97 s 207-145(1)(d) (¶4-920)
- an arrangement may be a scheme by way of, or in the nature of, or have substantially the effect of, dividend stripping to which ITAA36 s 177E applies (¶30-190)
- the arrangement may be a scheme to obtain imputation benefits to which ITAA36 s 177EA applies (¶30-195).

The ATO has applied the NALI provisions for arrangements of the type described in TA 2015/1 (see TR 2006/7: ¶13-170). Affected SMSFs may also have other compliance issues, including: (i) CGT consequences (eg for transfers below market value); (ii) ordinary dividend or deemed dividend consequences; (iii) superannuation regulatory issues, including non-arm's length dealings between members or associates and the SMSF; and/or (iv) excess contributions tax consequences.

Investments in PSTs, life assurance policies

If a complying superannuation fund invests in a PST or a life assurance policy:

- the income derived and capital gains realised by the PST or life assurance company are not taxable to the investing fund, and
- the gains on disposal or redemption of units in the PST or of the life assurance policy are not taxable under the CGT provisions and realised losses cannot be used to offset other capital gains (ITAA97 ss 118-300; 118-350).

A non-reversionary bonus (ie cash bonus) received by a complying superannuation fund on its investment in a life assurance policy is excluded from assessable income as the relevant income would have already been taxed in the hands of the life assurance company (ITAA97 s 295-335, item 1).

Complying superannuation funds may claim a deduction for expenses relating to investments in PSTs and in life assurance policies (¶13-150).

Reversionary bonus rebate

A complying superannuation fund is entitled to a rebate of tax under ITAA36 s 160AAB(5A) where an ''eligible 26AH amount'' is included in its assessable income under ITAA36 s 26AH (¶10-240). These amounts are reversionary bonuses (ie bonuses paid on maturity, forfeiture or surrender of a life assurance policy) received under short-term life assurance policies issued by a life office whose investment income was not tax-exempt, or by a friendly society. The rebate can be offset against tax payable from any source (IT 2499), but excess rebates are not refundable. For the ATO's warnings on investments in life insurance bonds issued by tax haven entities, see TA 2009/17 (¶13-150).

Trust loss restrictions

The trust loss and debt deduction measures in ITAA36 Sch 2F Divs 266 and 267 (¶6-262) do *not* apply to complying superannuation funds as they are "excepted trusts". A superannuation fund was held to be entitled to use carry-forward losses (prior to the enactment of the trust loss restrictions) despite undergoing major changes, including converting from a defined benefits to an accumulation fund, having new classes of members and allowing unrelated employers to participate (*Commercial Nominees of Australia*: ¶6-015).

Taxation of financial arrangements

Superannuation funds with assets of $100 million or more in value must comply with the taxation of financial arrangements rules in ITAA97 Div 230 (see ¶23-020).

International taxation

Superannuation funds with foreign operations are subject to the accrual taxation system on their share of income derived by certain foreign entities which has not been comparably taxed offshore and are entitled to a tax offset for foreign tax paid on amounts included in their assessable income under the foreign income tax offset system (¶21-670).

[AMSG ¶7-155ff; SLP ¶45-250]

¶13-170 Superannuation funds — non-arm's length income

The "non-arm's length component" of a complying superannuation fund (or a complying ADF or PST) for an income year is the amount of the fund's "non-arm's length income" (NALI) less any deductions to the extent that they are attributable to that income (ITAA97 s 295-545(2)).

The "low tax component" of the fund's taxable income is the amount of the fund's taxable income remaining after deducting the non-arm's length component from its total taxable income (ITAA97 s 295-545).

The low tax component is taxed at 15% while the non-arm's length component (if any) is taxed at 45% (ITRA ss 26(1)(b); 35). The 45% rate ensures that income derived from a transaction that is not on unrelated party, commercial terms does not receive concessional treatment in the superannuation fund.

NALI — what are the NALI rules?

ITAA97 s 295-550 provides the meaning of NALI and how NALI arises for a complying superannuation entity (see below). The purpose of the NALI provisions is to prevent superannuation entities from inflating their earnings through non-arm's length dealings, including via schemes involving non-commercial arrangements that stream income to the entity.

An amount of ordinary income or statutory income is NALI if it is derived by an entity in the circumstances below:

- the amount of ordinary or statutory income is derived from a scheme where the parties are not dealing with each other at arm's length and one of the following applies:
  - (i) the amount of the income is greater than what the entity might have been expected to derive if those parties had been dealing at arm's length in relation to the scheme — see "Income from non-arm's length dealings" below

(ii) in gaining or producing the income, the entity incurs a loss, outgoing or expenditure of an amount that is less than the amount that the entity might have been expected to incur if those parties had been dealing with each other at arm's length in relation to the scheme — see ''Expenses in non-arm's length dealings'' below

(iii) in gaining or producing the income, the entity does not incur a loss, outgoing or expenditure that the entity might have been expected to incur if those parties had been dealing with each other at arm's length in relation to the scheme — see ''Expenses in non-arm's length dealings'' below

- the amount is a dividend paid to the entity by a private company or is reasonably attributable to such a dividend, unless the amount is consistent with an arm's length dealing — see ''Private company dividends'' below
- the amount is derived by the entity from a discretionary trust or from a trust through holding a fixed entitlement — see ''Trust distributions'' below (ITAA97 s 295-550).

Guidelines on NALI are set out in TR 2006/7 (which deals with ''special income'' under ITAA36 former s 273, the equivalent to s 295-550 in pre-2007–08 years). The ruling states that to the extent that it addresses issues in s 295-550 that are the same as were in s 273, the references to ''special income'' should be read as ''NALI'' (para 1C).

Statutory income for the purposes of s 295-550 includes amounts obtained as a refund of franking credits and net capital gains (see *Allen & Anor* below), and trust distributions covers amounts included in assessable income under ITAA36 Pt III Div 6 (para 10, 11).

An amount of income either has the character of being special income or it does not. When an amount of income is special income, the whole amount is special income. An amount of income that is characterised as special income cannot be divided between an amount that is special income and an amount that is not. The amount that is special income is not only the amount by which an amount of income is greater than the amount that might have been derived if the parties had been dealing at arm's length, but the whole amount of income derived (TR 2006/7, para 12).

Additional ATO guidelines deal specifically with NALI arising from non-arm's length expenditure and under a limited recourse borrowing arrangement (LRBA) (see below).

The CGT provisions also contain modifications to ensure the proper application of the NALI rules (see ''Interaction of certain CGT rules and NALI'' below).

Income from non-arm's length dealings

Income (other than dividends or trust distributions) derived by a superannuation fund from a scheme is NALI if the parties to the scheme are not dealing at arm's length and that income is greater than might have been expected had the parties been dealing at arm's length in relation to the scheme (s 295-550(1); TR 2006/7 para 71).

For the NALI rules to apply to a scheme, it is necessary that the parties to the scheme were not dealing with each other at arm's length. The term ''scheme'' is defined (ITAA97 s 995-1(1)). The concept of ''non-arm's length'' takes its ordinary meaning. In determining whether parties deal at ''arm's length'', consider any connection between them and any other relevant circumstance (ITAA97 s 995-1(1); *AXA Asia Pacific Holdings Ltd*).

The proviso that the parties to the scheme are not dealing with each other at arm's length means that the NALI rules do not apply in respect of a superannuation entity's arrangements that are purely internal. This is because the internal functions are not undertaken with another party on any terms, non-arm's length or otherwise. For example, where an SMSF trustee undertakes book-keeping activities for no charge in performing their trustee duties, the NALI rules do not apply to the internal arrangements as they do not constitute a scheme between parties dealing with one another on a non-arm's length basis.

The test of NALI of this type is a question of fact, and all of the circumstances in a relationship will be relevant when determining whether the parties are dealing at arm's length.

In determining whether the quantum of income derived from a scheme is greater than might have been expected to have been derived had the parties been dealing at arm's length, the Commissioner will take into account all relevant matters, such as the commercial risks undertaken by the fund. If the income derived is greater than might have been expected, the fund will have to establish that unusual circumstances exist before the Commissioner will accept that the income is not NALI.

Expenses in non-arm's length dealings

From the 2018–19 income year, a superannuation entity's NALI includes income where expenditure incurred in gaining or producing it was not an arm's length expense. This includes where no expense was incurred (but might be expected to have been incurred if the transaction were on arm's length terms) (s 295-550(1)). This ensures that superannuation entities cannot circumvent the NALI rules by entering into schemes involving non-arm's length expenditure, regardless of whether the scheme was entered into before 1 July 2018, and applies to outgoings or expenditure whether of a revenue or capital nature (s 295-550(7)).

A similar integrity measure applies when a superannuation entity holds a fixed entitlement to the income of a trust and derives income as a beneficiary of that trust and non-arm's length expenses are incurred in acquiring the entitlement or in gaining or producing the income (s 295-550(7)) (see ''Trust distributions'' below).

In some circumstances, non-arm's length capital expenditure can result in a superannuation entity earning non-arm's length income. Where a fund acquires an asset for less than market value through non-arm's length dealings, the revenue generated by that asset may be NALI, as well as any statutory income (ie net capital gains) resulting from the disposal of that asset (s 295-550(1)(b), 295-550(7)), This ensures that trustees of funds do not have an incentive to acquire assets at less than market value for the purpose of generating potentially significant ongoing amounts of income which would be sheltered from marginal rates of tax. It further ensures that such income cannot escape taxation entirely where the assets are held in the retirement phase (ie the income would no longer be treated as exempt current pension income).

Private company dividends

An amount of ordinary income or statutory income is NALI if it is a dividend paid by a private company, or is reasonably attributable to such a dividend, unless the amount is consistent with an arm's length dealing (s 295-550(2)). Section 295-550 applies to a non-share equity interest in the same way as it applies to a share, and to an equity holder in a company in the same way as it applies to a shareholder in the company, and to a non-share dividend in the same way as it applies to a dividend (s 295-550(6)).

In determining if an amount is consistent with an arm's length dealing, the Commissioner must have regard to the following factors in s 295-550(3): (a) the value of the shares held by the fund in the company; (b) the cost to the fund of the shares on which the dividends were paid; (c) the dividend rate on those shares; (d) whether dividends have been paid on other shares in the company and the dividend rate; (e) whether the company has issued shares in lieu of dividends to the fund and the circumstances of the issue; and (f) any other relevant matters. In *Darrelen (as trustee of Henfam Superannuation Fund)*, the Full Federal Court examined whether a determination not to treat the dividends as special income should have been made having regard to the factors in para (a) to (f) of former s 273(2)) and held that the discretion in s 273(2) should not be exercised. The ATO has accepted the court's view in that case that s 273(2)(c) (rate of the dividend paid) did not permit consideration of the rate of return on the investment, or yield, but such a consideration was permissible under para (f) (any other matters). Accordingly, TR 2006/7 was amended to take account of the court's decision and observations about para (c) (*Decision Impact Statement* VRN 1079 of 2009). Note that although s 295-550(3) sets out the same factors as in former s 273(2), it does not impose a discretion on the Commissioner; rather, it has an objective test requiring the amount received to be consistent with an arm's length dealing.

In *GYBW* , the AAT rejected the argument that s 295-550(2) was only concerned with the relative amount of the dividend paid to the SMSF in the case, as compared to dividends on other shares of the company; rather, the provision extended to whether the amounts paid were sourced in an arm's length transaction. The non-arm's length transaction on the acquisition of the relevant shares in the case had the effect that income was diverted from a non-concessional taxpayer to the SMSF through its shareholding. Accordingly, the dividends and franking credits received by the SMSF were NALI.

Trust distributions

Trust distributions are NALI of a complying superannuation entity if they are:

- discretionary distributions, ie where the entity does not have a fixed entitlement to income from the trust, and
- distributions where the entity has a fixed entitlement to income from the trust.

Discretionary distributions

NALI under this category is income derived by a fund as a beneficiary of a trust other than because of holding a fixed entitlement to the income. That is, the fund is a beneficiary or unitholder that is dependent upon the trustee of the trust or unit trust exercising a discretion to distribute the income to the fund (s 295-550(4)).

▶ Example

A husband and wife are principals of a business conducted using a discretionary trust. The beneficiaries of the trust are the principals, other family members and a superannuation fund in which the principals are members. The trustee of both the discretionary trust and the superannuation fund is a corporate trustee, which is 100% owned by the principals. This ensures that the husband or wife has effective control over the activities of both the discretionary trust and the superannuation fund.

The trustee of the trust exercises its discretion to distribute an amount of trust income to the trustee of the superannuation fund in preference to the other beneficiaries who would otherwise be taxable on the income at their applicable marginal tax rates. The distributions are NALI.

In a case dealing with trust distributions (*SCCASP Holdings as trustee for the H&R Super Fund,*), the court held that the superannuation fund had derived "special income" under ITAA36 former s 273(6) (the equivalent to s 295-550(4)) in its capacity as a beneficiary of the trust. The court said that the term "derived" must accommodate how a particular type of assessable income (which can form part of the net income of the trust estate) is included in the assessable income of a beneficiary, and the "income derived" concept in s 273(6) must bear a meaning which accommodates how a particular type of assessable income which can form a component of the net income of the trust estate, namely a net capital gain, is included in the assessable income of a beneficiary. That is, "derived" for the purposes of s 273(6) must bear a meaning which extends to include "attributed to" or "imputed to". It would make no sense to construe the word "derived" in s 273 in a way that included some types of assessable income but excluded others (see also *Allen's* case below).

TA 2008/4 describes a non-arm's length arrangement under which a superannuation fund derives income through a direct or indirect interest in a closely held trust or other arrangements. The ATO considers that these arrangements may give rise to taxation issues, including whether income derived by the fund from the trust is NALI as well as other taxation consequences for the individual or other family members as discussed in TA 2008/3.

Distributions to a fund by virtue of fixed entitlement

Income derived by a fund through holding a fixed entitlement to the income of a trust is NALI if, as a result of a scheme the parties to which were not dealing with each other at arm's length in relation to the scheme, one or more of the following applies:

(a) the amount of the income is more than the amount that the fund might have been expected to derive if those parties had been dealing with each other at arm's length in relation to the scheme

(b) in acquiring the entitlement or in gaining or producing the income, the fund incurs a loss, outgoing or expenditure of an amount that is less than the amount that it might have been expected to incur if those parties had been dealing with each other at arm's length in relation to the scheme

(c) in acquiring the entitlement or in gaining or producing the income, the fund does not incur a loss, outgoing or expenditure that it might have been expected to incur if those parties had been dealing with each other at arm's length in relation to the scheme (s 295-550(5)).

NALI arising under items (b) and (c) apply in relation to income derived in the 2018–19 income year and later income years, regardless of whether the scheme was entered into before 1 July 2018. This applies to outgoings or expenditure whether or not it is of capital or of a capital nature (s 295-550(7)). The measures ensure consistency between the general non-arm's length income rules for income directly derived by a superannuation entity and where the entity derives income through its fixed entitlement to the income of a trust.

▶ Example (adapted from the EM to Act No 78 of 2019)

A superannuation fund which acquires units in a unit trust (as a beneficiary with a fixed entitlement) pays a substantially lower amount for the units than stated in the promotional material for the unit trust due to a scheme the fund entered into with the broker.

In acquiring the entitlement to a share of the unit trust's earnings, the fund did not incur expenditure it might have been expected to incur if dealing at arm's length with the broker in purchasing the units.

The income derived from the units would have been the same whether or not they were acquired under an arm's length transaction.

The amount earned is NALI of the superannuation fund. Any net capital gain made on disposal of the units may also be NALI under 295-550(1).

In *Trustee for MH Ghali Superannuation Fund*, the AAT found that income derived by the fund was special income under the test in ITAA36 former s 273(7) (ie a fixed entitlement or income derived under an arrangement where the parties were not dealing with each other at arm's length and the income derived was greater than might have been expected). The AAT considered that "fixed entitlement" in s 273 takes the meaning provided in ITAA36 Sch 2F s 272-5. This was contrary to, and would be less favourable to taxpayers than, the Commissioner's approach set out in TR 2006/7 that a superannuation fund has a fixed entitlement to income if "...entitlement to the distribution does not depend upon the exercise of the trustee's or any other person's discretion" (TR 2006/7, para 102). The ATO has confirmed that the s 272-5 test does not apply for the purposes of s 273 and ITAA97 s 295-550. Rather the "fixed entitlement" test operates in the manner described in TR 2006/7 as noted above (*Decision Impact Statement* VRN 1079 of 2009).

The Full Federal Court has held that "income derived" in s 273(7) (the equivalent to ITAA97 s 295-550(5)) was not limited to income according to ordinary concepts (ITAA97 s 6-5). It included statutory income (ITAA97 s 6-10), and therefore net capital gains. A distribution of a capital gain from a hybrid trust to a fixed trust, which in turn distributed it to a superannuation fund under an arrangement involving one or more parties not dealing with each other at arm's length was held to be ''special income'' under former s 273(7). The taxpayer's leave to appeal to the High Court was refused (*Allen & Anor*; *Decision Impact Statement* VRN QUD 82 of 2008).

ATO guidelines — non-arm's length expenditure and LRBAs

Non-arm's length expenditure and ATO's transitional compliance approach

Draft LCR 2019/D3 clarifies how s 295-550 operates in a scheme where the parties do not deal with each other at arm's length and the trustee of a complying superannuation entity incurs non-arm's length expenditure (or where expenditure is not incurred) in gaining or producing ordinary or statutory income derived in the 2018–19 income year and later income years, regardless of whether the scheme was entered into before 1 July 2018. The Commissioner's preliminary view is that certain non-arm's length expenditure incurred may have a sufficient nexus to all ordinary and/or statutory income derived by the fund for that income to be NALI (eg fees for accounting services). This can be contrasted to non-arm's length expenditure that has a more direct nexus to particular ordinary or statutory income derived by the fund (eg expenditure relating to the acquisition of an income-producing asset).

Pending the finalisation of *Draft* LCR 2019/D3, the ATO's transitional compliance approach is that it will not allocate compliance resources to determine whether the NALI provisions apply to a complying superannuation fund for the 2018–19, 2019–20 and 2020–21 income years where the fund incurred non-arm's length expenditure (as described in paras 9 to 12 of *Draft* LCR 2019/D3) of a general nature that has a sufficient nexus to all ordinary and/or statutory income derived by the fund in those respective income years (eg non-arm's length expenditure on accounting services). This transitional compliance approach does not apply where the fund incurred non-arm's length expenditure that directly related to the fund deriving particular ordinary or statutory income (PCG 2020/5).

Determining NALI under LRBAs

When parties to a scheme that include a trustee of an SMSF enter into a LRBA on terms which are not at arm's length, it is necessary to consider whether the SMSF has derived more ordinary or statutory income under the scheme than might have been expected if the parties had been dealing with each other at arm's length (see s 295-550(1)(b)). NALI will only arise where the answer to this question is affirmative.

For this purpose, TD 2016/16 states that it is necessary to first identify both the steps of the relevant scheme and the parties dealing with each other under those steps, and then determine the amount of ordinary or statutory income that the SMSF might have been expected to derive if the same parties had been dealing with each other on an arm's length basis under each identified step of the scheme. That is:

1. identify what the terms of the borrowing arrangement may have been if the parties were dealing with each other at arms' length (''the hypothetical borrowing arrangement''), and

2. establish whether it is reasonable to conclude that the SMSF could have and would have entered into the hypothetical borrowing arrangement.

Where it is reasonable to conclude that the SMSF could not, or would not, have entered into the hypothetical borrowing arrangement, the SMSF will have derived more ordinary or statutory income under the scheme than it might have been expected to derive. In this instance, the ordinary or statutory income derived under the scheme is NALI.

Where the SMSF can objectively establish with evidence that it could and would have entered into the hypothetical borrowing arrangement, a comparison can then be made of the SMSF's ordinary or statutory income from the scheme and the income under the hypothetical borrowing arrangement.

The terms of the borrowing arrangement to be considered include (but are not limited to) the interest rate, whether the interest rate is fixed or variable, the term of the loan and the loan to market value ratio (LVR).

Safe harbours in LRBAs

PCG 2016/5 sets out safe harbours for SMSFs which have entered into LRBAs to acquire certain assets in accordance with SISA s 67A (or former s 67(4A)), regardless of when the arrangement commenced. The safe harbours specify the LRBA characteristics (such as the interest rate, fixed or variable, the term of the loan, its valuation ratio and loan security, and the nature and frequency of repayments) which will be accepted as being consistent with an arm's length dealing.

Taxpayer alerts on NALI

TA 2003/1 warns about taxpayers establishing a fixed trust to distribute business profits to the taxpayer's superannuation fund under arrangements where the fund members are the owners of the business and other family members. Other ATO warnings involving trust arrangements and NALI may be found in TA 2008/3, TA 2008/4 and TA 2010/3.

Interaction of certain CGT rules and NALI

The CGT provisions below provide modifications in relation to their application to certain superannuation operations:

- ITAA97 s 116-30(2C) provides that the capital proceeds from a CGT event are not replaced with the market value of a CGT asset under the market value substitution rule in s 116-30(2) (¶11-570) if the proceeds from the CGT event exceed the market value and are not received at arm's length.

  This ensures that where merging superannuation funds transfer assets and losses under Div 310 (¶13-130), the NALI rules will not apply if the circumstances of the transaction are consistent with an arm's length dealing, even if the merger is between funds with the same trustee and the assets are transferred at a value or cost base that is different from market value.

- Subsection (2) to ITAA97 s 118-320 (about disregarding capital gains or losses when a CGT event happens to a segregated current pension asset: ¶13-125) provides that non-arm's length capital gains are not disregarded.

  This ensures that these gains remain statutory income and are subject to the NALI rules so as to discourage shifting of amounts into the superannuation environment through non-arm's length transactions.

[AMSG ¶7-170; FITR ¶270-570; SLP ¶45-300]

¶13-180 Tax on no-TFN contributions income

The provision of a person's tax file number (TFN) for tax purposes is discussed in ¶33-000ff (for TFNs and superannuation see ¶33-025). The SIS and RSA legislation provides for the extended use of the TFNs of members of superannuation entities and RSA providers for general superannuation administration purposes.

A complying or non-complying superannuation fund and an RSA provider (superannuation provider) is required to include no-TFN contributions income (if any) in its taxable income in each income year (¶13-120, ¶13-480). A no-TFN contributions tax is payable on such income at the rates imposed by the *Income Tax Rates Act 1986*

(ITAA97 s 295-605). A tax offset is available to superannuation providers that had paid no-TFN contributions tax if a TFN is later provided (see below). From 2020-21, a successor fund can also claim the tax offset for the tax paid by the original provider.

No-TFN contributions income

Superannuation contributions made to a superannuation provider are no-TFN contributions income in a year of income if:

- the contributions are included in the provider's assessable income under Subdiv 295-C for the income year (¶13-125)
- the contributions are made to provide superannuation benefits for an individual, and
- by the end of the income year, the individual has not quoted (for superannuation purposes) a TFN to the provider (ITAA97 s 295-610(1)).

A superannuation provider cannot reduce its no-TFN contributions income by transferring the contributions to another entity or by using pre-1 July 1988 funding credits (¶13-125) (ITAA97 s 295-620).

An individual is taken to have "quoted (for superannuation purposes)" a TFN under s 295-610 to a superannuation provider (entity) if:

- the individual quotes his/her TFN to the entity
- the individual is taken by the SISA or the RSA Act to quote his/her TFN to the entity in connection with the operation of the Superannuation Acts (as defined in SISA s 299W) or the RSA Act, or
- the Commissioner gives notice of the individual's TFN to the entity (s 295-615).

An individual making a TFN declaration to an employer that makes a superannuation contribution for the individual is taken to have authorised the employer to inform the entity of the individual's TFN (ITAA36 s 202DHA). An employer who fails to pass on the TFN to the entity is guilty of an offence (SISA s 299C).

No-TFN contributions tax offset — TFN is quoted later

A superannuation provider is entitled to a tax offset for tax on no-TFN contributions income if the individual in respect of whom the contributions were made (ie a fund member or RSA holder) quotes a TFN within 4 years of the no-TFN contributions tax being payable (s 295-675).

The tax offset is the amount of no-TFN contributions tax that was paid in the 3 income years preceding the income year in which the individual first quotes their TFN to the superannuation provider.

In pre-2020-21 years, a TFN that is quoted to a successor fund does not entitle the successor fund to a tax offset for the no-TFN contributions tax paid by the original fund (ID 2008/161) (see "Successor funds entitled to tax offset from 2020-21" below).

Interest may be payable to a superannuation fund where a person's quotation of a TFN results in the fund receiving a tax offset (*Taxation (Interest on Overpayments and Early Payments) Act 1983*, ss 8ZD; 8ZE; 8ZF) (see PS LA 2011/23). Interest is only payable if an individual has quoted a TFN to the employer and the employer has failed to pass on the TFN to the superannuation fund to which the contributions were made.

As noted above, where the Commissioner gives notice of an individual's TFN to a superannuation or RSA provider, it is taken to have been quoted by the individual (SISA s 299SA; RSA Act s 140A).

Successor funds entitled to tax offset from 2020–21

From 2020–21, a successor fund can claim a tax offset in an income year for no-TFN contributions tax previously paid by the original provider. This applies where the original provider paid tax in any of the previous 3 income years (or relevant part-years) on an individual's no-TFN contributions income and the individual had never quoted their TFN to the original provider and has quoted it to the successor fund for the first time in the income year (ITAA97 s 295-675(4) and (5)).

Where the income years of the original provider and successor fund are not aligned, the tax offset is available for the no-TFN contributions tax that was payable by the original provider in the income years starting or ending in the income year of the successor fund in which the TFN is provided. This ensures there is no part-year gap in which a no-TFN contributions tax was payable but an offset was not available because a successor fund transfer occurred.

Successor funds that have a TFN quoted for the first time in the 2020–21 income year are able to claim the tax offset for tax paid by an original provider from the 2017–18 income year.

No PAYG on no-TFN contributions income

Superannuation funds and RSA providers are not required to take account of their no-TFN contributions income when working out their PAYG instalments. Any tax attributable to no-TFN contributions income and tax offsets for no-TFN contributions income are ignored when working out the entity's PAYG notional tax or benchmark tax (TAA ss 45-325(1A); 45-365(1A)). This ensures that any extra tax that a superannuation or RSA provider has to pay or any tax offset it can claim because of no-TFN contributions income is taken into account in the entity's income tax assessment, not in its PAYG instalments.

Tax rate on no-TFN contributions income

The rate of tax on no-TFN contributions income is set out below (*Income Tax Rates Act 1986*, s 29; 35).

2017–18 and later years

Entity	**Tax rate on assessable contributions**	**Tax rate on no-TFN contributions income**	**Overall tax rate**
Complying superannuation fund	15%	32%	47%
Non-complying superannuation fund	45%	2%	47%
RSA provider: – life insurance company – company (not a life insurance company)	15%	32%	47%

[AMSG ¶7-200; FITR ¶270-590; SLP ¶45-320]

¶13-200 Taxation of previously complying funds

If a complying superannuation fund in relation to one year becomes a non-complying superannuation fund in relation to the year immediately following, the fund's assessable income in the year in which its status changed will include its ordinary income and statutory income from previous years as calculated using the formula below (ITAA97 s 295-320, item 2):

asset values *less* undeducted contributions and contributions segment

where:

- "asset values" means the sum of the market values of the fund's assets just before the start of the income year, ie the year in which the fund becomes non-complying, and

- "undeducted contributions and contributions segment" means the sum of the part of the "crystallised undeducted contributions" that relates to the period after 30 June 1983 and the "contributions segment" (as defined in ITAA97 ss 307-220 and 307-225: ¶14-140) for current members at that time so far as they have not been, and cannot be, deducted (ITAA97 s 295-325).

The effect of the above is that the tax concessions applicable to the fund when it was a complying fund are effectively recouped.

Generally, a fund will only lose its complying status if it ceases to be an Australian superannuation fund, or if it contravenes a regulatory provision and fails the *culpability test* or *compliance test* (¶13-100).

The amount as calculated under s 295-325 is included in the fund's assessable income for the year that it is a non-complying fund and is taxed at 45%.

ITAA97 s 118-20(4A) prevents double taxation under the CGT provisions on a subsequent disposal of the relevant assets by the fund (¶13-130).

[AMSG ¶7-250; FITR ¶270-360; SLP ¶45-350]

¶13-220 Taxation of non-complying funds

A non-complying superannuation fund means a "superannuation fund" (¶13-050) that is a fund and is not a complying superannuation fund. That is, the fund is an indefinitely continuing fund and a provident, benefit, superannuation or retirement fund or a public sector superannuation scheme (ITAA97 s 995-1(1)).

The taxable income of a non-complying fund is taxed at 45% (ITRA ss 26(2); 35(1)).

A non-complying fund may be a resident fund or a foreign superannuation fund (¶13-250). Examples of non-complying funds include:

- a superannuation fund, other than an exempt public sector superannuation scheme, that does not elect to become a regulated superannuation fund under the SISA
- a foreign superannuation fund, whether or not a regulated superannuation fund
- a regulated superannuation fund that has contravened a regulatory provision and failed the culpability test or compliance test, or
- a previously complying superannuation fund that has received a notice under the SISA stating that it is a non-complying superannuation fund (¶13-100).

The taxable income of a non-complying superannuation fund is determined as if the trustee were a taxpayer and a resident in the case of a resident fund, or a non-resident in the case of a non-resident fund (ITAA97 s 295-10). A non-resident fund that is a foreign superannuation fund is entitled to special exemptions (¶13-250).

A non-complying fund is *not* eligible for the following tax concessions available to a complying fund (as discussed at ¶13-120 – ¶13-160):

- tax at the lower 15% rate on its taxable income (other than NALI: ¶13-170)
- special CGT rules and the 33 1/3% CGT discount (see "Capital gains" below)
- death or disability insurance deductions
- exemption of income related to current pension liabilities
- ability to transfer contributions tax liability
- ability to exclude "last minute" employer contributions from fund income
- ability to invest with PSTs

- exemption of income accrued prior to 1 July 1988
- exemption of non-reversionary or cash bonuses on a policy of life assurance
- exemption as an excepted trust under the trust loss provisions
- concessional tracing rules for the purposes of applying the trust loss rules to another trust.

Other tax matters

Other tax matters relating to non-complying funds include the following:

- member contributions to a non-complying fund are not tax-deductible (¶13-730); neither is the contributor entitled to a tax offset (¶13-770)
- employer contributions for employees to a non-complying fund cannot satisfy the employer's obligations for superannuation guarantee purposes (¶39-000)
- non-complying funds may have a tax liability for amounts transferred from certain superannuation funds (see "Assessable contributions" below)
- individuals who have an account balance in the Superannuation Holding Accounts Special Account (SHASA) cannot transfer the account balance to a non-complying fund (¶39-650).

In addition, a non-complying fund cannot deduct current year or prior year losses, or claim debt deductions, unless it satisfies the tests relating to ownership or control of the trust (¶6-262).

Previous tax concessions are recouped if a superannuation fund changes from complying to non-complying (¶13-200).

A non-complying fund that is a regulated superannuation fund must comply with all the regulatory provisions applicable to it under the SISA and related Acts (¶13-800), including the lodgment of an annual return.

A non-complying fund is also required to lodge an income tax return and other regulatory returns annually (¶13-350) and is subject to the PAYG withholding (¶26-100ff) and instalment (¶27-100ff) systems.

Assessable contributions

The taxable income of a non-complying fund includes "assessable contributions" received by the fund during the year, based on whether the fund is an Australian superannuation fund or a foreign superannuation fund for the income year in which the contributions were made (ITAA97 s 295-160).

An Australian superannuation fund that is a non-complying fund is allowed a deduction for the cost of collecting contributions as if all contributions made to it were included in assessable income (ITAA97 s 295-95).

Deductions and other concessions

As a general rule, the deductibility of expenditure incurred by a non-complying superannuation fund is determined under ITAA97 s 8-1, unless a specific provision applies (eg ITAA97 s 25-5). TR 93/17 sets out the principles governing deductibility of expenditure incurred by superannuation funds, including non-complying funds (¶13-150).

Payment to employer-sponsor

If a non-complying fund pays an amount (eg a return of surplus) to an employer-sponsor who has been allowed a deduction for contributions previously made to the fund, that amount is assessable income of the employer (ITAA97 s 290-100). Similarly, if the fund or a successor fund provides to any person a payment or benefit that reasonably represents a return of deductible employer contributions (or earnings thereon), the value of the payment or benefit is included in the recipient's assessable income (¶10-270). A non-complying fund that pays an amount to which s 290-100 applies is allowed a deduction for the amount paid if it is a continuously non-complying fund, ie it has never been entitled to exemption from tax or other concessional tax treatment (ITAA97 s 295-490, item 4).

Capital gains

A non-complying fund is liable for tax on realised capital gains in the same manner as other taxpayers under the CGT provisions in ITAA97 (¶11-000, ¶12-000).

A non-complying fund is not entitled to the 33$^{1}/_{3}$% CGT discount for complying superannuation entities but, as a trust, may be entitled to a 50% CGT discount under ITAA97 s 115-100(a)(ii) (former ID 2003/48).

To avoid double taxation, ITAA97 s 118-20(4A) may apply to reduce or extinguish any capital gain that would arise under the CGT provisions on the disposal of an asset whose market value was taken into account in determining the fund's net previous income in respect of previous income years (¶13-200).

Franking credits

The imputation system, as it applies to complying superannuation funds (¶13-160), is also applicable to non-complying funds. However, a non-complying fund (or a non-complying ADF) cannot claim a refund of excess franking credits. Although non-complying funds would rarely be in a position to claim a refund of excess franking credits, the measure prevents funds from entering into artificial schemes so as to produce surplus franking credits.

Levies

Payments of the supervisory levy or financial assistance funding levy by a non-complying fund are deductible expenses (ITAA97 ss 25-5; 295-490(1), item 3). Any late lodgment amount or late payment penalty is not deductible (ITAA97 ss 26-5; 26-90).

Payment of benefits

No deduction is allowed for superannuation benefits paid by a non-complying fund except as provided by items 2 and 6 of ITAA97 s 295-495.

[AMSG ¶7-300 – ¶7-350; FITR ¶270-010; SLP ¶45-370]

¶13-250 Taxation of foreign superannuation funds

A superannuation fund may be an Australian superannuation fund or a foreign superannuation fund. Only Australian superannuation funds (¶13-100) can be complying funds and be entitled to the tax concessions in ITAA97 Div 295 (¶13-120). A foreign superannuation fund is taxed as a non-complying fund (¶13-220), but may be entitled to certain concessions (see below).

A special tax regime applies to a foreign superannuation fund that becomes an Australian superannuation fund during an income year (¶13-270).

Foreign superannuation fund

A superannuation fund is a "foreign superannuation fund":

- at a time if the fund is not an Australian superannuation fund at that time, and
- for an income year if the fund is not an Australian superannuation fund for the income year (ITAA97 s 995-1(1)).

An Individual Retirement Account in the US is not a "foreign superannuation fund" (or a scheme payment "in the nature of superannuation") for the purposes of concessional tax treatment under ITAA97 s 305-80 (¶14-420).

A foreign superannuation fund is exempt from ordinary income tax in respect of all interest derived from Australia and dividends from Australian resident companies. Provided the fund is exempt from tax in its own country, it is also exempt from withholding tax on such income.

A non-resident that derives dividends and interest paid by Australian residents is generally subject to withholding tax on the payments (see ¶22-010 and ¶22-020). A withholding exemption applies to interest and dividend (including non-share dividend) income derived by a non-resident that is a ''superannuation fund for foreign residents'' as defined in ITAA97 s 118-520 (ID 2009/67: foreign retirement plan) (ITAA36 ss 128B(1); 128B(3)(jb)).

From 1 July 2019, the withholding tax exemption for superannuation funds for foreign residents under s 128B(3)(jb) is restricted to income derived from portfolio-like investments, subject to a 7-year transitional rule for assets acquired by funds on or before 27 March 2018 (s 128B(3CA) to (3CE)) (LCR 2020/3).

Under ITAA36 s 128D, income upon which withholding tax would be payable but for certain provisions, including s 128B(3)(jb), is not assessable income and is not exempt income (ID 2009/77 to ID 2009/79: non-share dividends and interest is income).

The venture capital CGT exemption for superannuation funds for foreign residents is discussed in ¶11-900.

[AMSG ¶7-400ff; SLP ¶45-400]

¶13-270 Former foreign superannuation funds

If a foreign superannuation fund becomes an Australian superannuation fund (¶13-100) during a year of income, its assessable income in the year it changes its status will include its ordinary income and statutory income from previous years as calculated using the formula below (ITAA97 s 295-320, item 3):

asset values *less* member contributions

where:

- ''asset values'' is the sum of the market values of the fund's assets just before the start of the year of income, and
- ''member contributions'' is the amount in the fund at that time representing contributions made by current members of the fund (ITAA97 s 295-330).

[AMSG ¶7-450; FITR ¶270-370; SLP ¶45-420]

¶13-300 Government and semi-government funds

Superannuation funds for the benefit of employees of the Commonwealth, state and territory governments or of a government and semi-government authority (is public sector funds or schemes) have been subject to tax since 1 July 1988 (ITAA97 s 295-1).

To qualify for taxation as complying superannuation funds, public sector funds are required to satisfy the same requirements as private sector funds under the SISA. However, a public sector fund or scheme that is prescribed as an ''exempt public sector superannuation scheme'' (as specified in SISR Sch 1AA) is exempt from the SIS legislation and is, instead, subject to regulation under its own enabling Act.

The anti-avoidance provisions in ITAA36 Pt IVA apply to the streaming of franking credits by a Queensland Government master superannuation fund to a member fund (*Electricity Supply Industry Superannuation (Qld) Ltd*: ¶30-195).

Limit on Commonwealth's taxing power

The taxation of public sector funds only applies as far as the Commonwealth's taxing power extends. If any imposition of tax would be a tax on the property of a state (prohibited by s 114 of the Constitution), that tax does not apply (ITAA97 s 295-15). The constitutional power of the Commonwealth to tax a state superannuation fund was considered in *South Australia v The Commonwealth*, where the High Court held that: (a) the fund was exempt from tax on capital gains under s 114 of the Constitution because a tax on capital gains was a tax on property; but (b) the fund was not exempt from tax on interest income.

Constitutionally protected superannuation funds

Funds that are constitutionally protected superannuation funds are prescribed in ITR97 reg 995-1.04 and Sch 4. Income derived by constitutionally protected funds is specifically exempt from tax (ITAA97 s 50-25).

[AMSG ¶7-500; FITR ¶270-010; SLP ¶45-430]

¶13-350 Superannuation fund tax returns and assessments

With certain exceptions, the trustee of a superannuation fund, ADF, or PST is required to lodge an income tax return in the approved form with the Commissioner if it is:

- an Australian resident, or
- a non-resident and it derived income (including capital gains) that is taxable in Australia (other than dividend, interest or royalty income and payments from managed investment trusts that are subject to withholding tax).

The exceptions apply to the trustees of exempt state or territory funds and corporate trustees which are subsidiary members of a consolidated or MEC group with respect to their consolidated activities.

Superannuation entities are subject to self-assessment and their assessments are deemed to be made on the day they lodge their tax return with the ATO in each year. The self-assessment system and tax return lodgment requirements are discussed in detail at ¶24-000, ¶24-060 and following.

Superannuation entities are also required to lodge annual returns with the ATO or APRA under the SISA, and are liable to pay a supervisory levy each year (¶13-870).

[AMSG ¶11-000ff]

Trans-Tasman Portability of Superannuation

¶13-380 Transfers between KiwiSaver schemes and Australian funds

The *Arrangement between the Government of Australia and the Government of New Zealand on Trans-Tasman Retirement Savings Portability* (Arrangement) 2009 established a scheme under which Australians and New Zealanders can transfer their retirement savings when they move between Australia and New Zealand, while preserving the integrity of the retirement savings systems of both countries. The key features of the Arrangement are:

- individuals may transfer their retirement savings between Australian complying superannuation funds and New Zealand KiwiSaver schemes
- retirement savings from an Australian untaxed source, or an Australian defined benefit scheme, cannot be transferred to a KiwiSaver scheme
- the transfer of retirement savings is voluntary for members, and it is voluntary for funds to accept the transferred savings (SISR regs 12A.07(3); 12A.08(4))
- retirement savings are to be transferred with minimal compliance and administration costs

- the transferred savings are generally subject to the superannuation and tax rules of the host country, with limited and specified exceptions
- the transferred savings must be separately identifiable within the account established in the host country to allow the application of certain source country rules (SISR regs 12A.06(3); 12A.07(4); 12A.08(3))
- any decrements are first applied to host country retirement savings, before being applied to retirement savings transferred from the source country (SISR regs 12A.06(2); 12A.07(7)), and
- New Zealand-sourced retirement savings transferred to Australia are subject to the non-concessional contributions cap arrangements on their initial entry into the Australian superannuation system.

ITAA97 Div 312 provides for the tax treatment of transactions under the Arrangement, covering:

- amounts transferred from KiwiSaver schemes to complying superannuation funds
- superannuation benefits paid to KiwiSaver scheme providers by complying superannuation funds, and by the ATO, and
- the disclosure of information requirements.

A ''KiwiSaver scheme'' has the meaning given by s 4 of the *KiwiSaver Act 2006* of New Zealand, and a ''KiwiSaver scheme provider'' means a provider within that Act (ITAA97 s 995-1(1)).

An ''Australian-sourced amount'' is an amount first held in a complying superannuation fund, which is subsequently paid to a KiwiSaver scheme and identified as such by the receiving KiwiSaver scheme. Likewise, a ''New Zealand-sourced amount'' is an amount first held in a KiwiSaver scheme, which is subsequently paid to a complying superannuation fund and identified as such by the receiving fund's trustee (SISR reg 12A.02). The separate identification of source country amounts in the host country fund or scheme is required by the Arrangement to allow the source country's rules to be applied to the amounts that are transferred to the host country in certain circumstances (see below).

Australian-sourced amounts held in KiwiSaver schemes:

- may not be withdrawn to purchase a first home
- may be accessed when the individual reaches age 60 and satisfies the ''retirement'' definition in the SISR at that age, and
- may not be transferred to a third country.

New Zealand-sourced amounts held in Australian superannuation funds:

- may only be transferred to and held in APRA-regulated complying superannuation funds
- may not be transferred to or held in SMSFs (SISR reg 12A.07(2))
- may not be transferred to a third country, and
- may be accessed when the member reaches the age of retirement as defined in the *New Zealand Superannuation and Retirement Income Act 2001* (currently 65).

A ''returning New Zealand-sourced amount'' is a New Zealand-sourced amount that was paid from a complying superannuation fund to a KiwiSaver scheme, and subsequently received by a complying superannuation fund. The returning New Zealand-sourced amount may be received by the same fund which held the New Zealand-sourced amount originally or by a different fund which is receiving the returning New Zealand-sourced amount for the first time (SISR reg 12A.02). A returning New Zealand-sourced amount is therefore always a New Zealand-sourced amount as defined, and a New Zealand-sourced amount becomes a returning New Zealand-sourced amount when it re-enters the Australian superannuation system for the second (or subsequent) time.

Superannuation entities, payments and interests covered by SISR Pt 12A

Part 12A sets out the rules for New Zealand-sourced amounts in a complying superannuation fund to be subject to the SISR (as modified) in relation to various matters, namely SISR Pt 1 (preliminary matters), Pt 6 (benefit protection standards), Pt 7 (payments standards) and Pt 8 (contribution and benefit accrual standards).

The scheme in Pt 12A applies to:

- payments made between an Australian complying superannuation fund and a New Zealand KiwiSaver scheme
- payments made between complying superannuation funds under the portability provisions (SISR Div 6.5) where the payment includes a New Zealand-sourced amount, and
- cases where the member's interest includes a New Zealand-sourced amount but the payment to another complying superannuation fund does not include the New Zealand-sourced amount (SISR reg 12A.03(1)(a) to (c)).

Part 12A does not apply to:

- payments from KiwiSaver schemes to Australian superannuation entities that are not complying superannuation funds (such as RSA and ADFs) or to payments from Australian complying superannuation funds to NZ retirement savings entities that are not KiwiSaver schemes.
- a defined benefit interest in a defined benefit fund
- an unfunded public sector superannuation scheme, or an SMSF
- payments that contain an element untaxed in the fund or benefits that are being paid as a pension (SISR reg 12A.03(2), (3)).

Fund members, or members with interests that are excluded from the Pt 12A scheme, who wish to move their retirement savings to a KiwiSaver scheme, can therefore roll over or transfer their benefits to a complying superannuation fund covered by Pt 12A (subject to the fund rules) or commute their pension interests before moving them to a KiwiSaver scheme.

Contribution to complying superannuation fund from KiwiSaver schemes

An amount transferred from a KiwiSaver scheme to an Australian complying superannuation fund is treated as a personal contribution of the person for whom the transfer is made (ITAA97 s 312-10(1)). The tax and regulatory consequences are summarised below.

Not assessable contribution of Australian superannuation fund

An amount transferred from a KiwiSaver scheme to an Australian complying superannuation fund as a contribution is not assessable income of the fund. This means that the contribution is not subject to the tax arrangements for transfers from foreign superannuation funds under ITAA97 s 295-200 (¶13-125) and Subdiv 305-B (¶14-420) (s 312-10(1) Note 1, (2)).

Non-concessional contribution

Except for certain amounts, an amount transferred from a KiwiSaver scheme to an Australian complying superannuation fund (the contribution) is treated as a non-concessional contribution on initial entry into the Australian superannuation system and is subject to the non-concessional contributions cap arrangements in ITAA97 Subdiv 292-C (¶13-780).

Transferred amounts which are excluded as non-concessional contributions are the ''Australian-sourced amount'' (an amount that was originally contributed to an Australian superannuation fund before its transfer to a KiwiSaver scheme) and a ''returning New Zealand-sourced amount'' (an amount that was originally contributed to a KiwiSaver scheme before its initial transfer to an Australian superannuation fund) of the contribution. These amounts are excluded as they have already been counted towards the non-concessional contributions cap in the year in which they were first contributed to an Australian superannuation fund (s 312-10(3)).

Information about amounts previously contributed to an Australian superannuation fund is provided to the KiwiSaver scheme provider and to the member on the statement about benefits paid to KiwiSaver schemes (see below). This information will assist the KiwiSaver scheme provider or the member to provide evidence of the returning amounts' status to the receiving fund, so that the amounts are not subject to the contributions cap again.

Acceptance of contributions rules — amounts received from KiwiSaver scheme

For SISR purposes (¶13-825), an amount received by a complying superannuation fund from a KiwiSaver scheme is treated as a contribution, and a ''member contribution'' (SISR reg 12A.08(5)).

Non-assessable income and CGT treatment

The contribution is non-assessable non-exempt income of the member (consistent with the treatment of roll-over superannuation benefits between Australian superannuation funds under ITAA97 s 306-5: see ''Assessable roll-over superannuation benefits'' in ¶13-125) (ITAA97 s 312-10(4)).

As with other superannuation contributions, the contribution is not subject to CGT on entry into the Australian superannuation system. Also, ITAA97 s 118-305 (about disregarding capital gain or capital loss) applies in relation to the amount transferred as if the KiwiSaver scheme were a superannuation fund (¶11-880) (ITAA97 s 312-10(5)).

Components of superannuation interest

A ''tax free component of an Australian-sourced amount'' is an Australian-sourced amount that previously formed part of the tax free component of the member's former superannuation benefits in a complying superannuation fund before being paid to a KiwiSaver scheme (SISR reg 12A.02).

When an amount is transferred from a KiwiSaver scheme to an Australian complying superannuation fund (the contribution), a New Zealand-sourced amount and any tax free component of an Australian-sourced amount of the contribution are included in the contributions segment of the member's superannuation interest in the fund (¶14-140) (s 312-10(6)(a), (b)).

This means that those amounts (if any) form part of the tax free component of the member's interest in the Australian superannuation fund while the balance of the contribution will be part of the taxable component (as the tax free component is used to work out the components of any benefits subsequently paid from the member's interest: ¶14-150).

The receiving Australian fund must be advised of the New Zealand-sourced amount and any tax free component of an Australian-sourced amount of the contribution for those amounts to be included in the contributions segment. Information about the tax free and taxable components of the member's former interest in an Australian superannuation fund is provided to KiwiSaver scheme providers and members on the statement about benefits paid to KiwiSaver schemes. This information enables the KiwiSaver scheme provider or member to provide evidence of any tax free component of an Australian-sourced amount to a receiving Australian superannuation fund so the tax free component maintains its status in the member's current interest in the fund (see below).

No deduction or tax offset for amounts transferred from KiwiSaver scheme

ITAA97 Div 290 (about tax concessions for personal superannuation contributions) does not apply to an amount transferred from a KiwiSaver scheme to a complying superannuation fund (s 312-10(2)).

Consequently, the contribution is not a deductible personal contribution under ITAA97 Subdiv 290-C (¶13-730) and is not eligible for the spouse contribution offset under ITAA97 Subdiv 290-D (¶13-770).

An amount transferred from a KiwiSaver scheme to a complying superannuation fund under s 312-10 is not an eligible personal superannuation contribution for the purposes of entitlement to the government co-contribution (¶13-760). This is consistent with the treatment of lump sums paid from foreign superannuation funds.

Payment of benefits to KiwiSaver schemes by Australian funds or the Commissioner

A superannuation benefit paid to a KiwiSaver scheme provider by a complying superannuation fund in respect of a member is non-assessable non-exempt income of the member (ITAA97 s 312-15). This is consistent with the income tax treatment of roll-over superannuation benefits between Australian superannuation funds and the CGT treatment superannuation fund benefit payments (see "Non-assessable income and CGT treatment" above).

The Commissioner can make direct payments of superannuation money held by it to a KiwiSaver scheme provider, instead of via a complying superannuation fund, under the *Superannuation (Unclaimed Money and Lost Members) Act 1999* (¶13-850).

Providing statements about benefits paid to KiwiSaver schemes

The trustee of a complying superannuation fund which pays a member's superannuation benefit to a KiwiSaver scheme provider must provide a statement in the approved form to the provider and to the member in respect of the member's benefits paid to the KiwiSaver scheme (TAA Sch 1 s 390-12).

The information given in the statements will enable the KiwiSaver scheme provider or member to provide evidence of the tax status of any returning amounts to a receiving Australian fund if these amounts re-enter the Australian superannuation system as noted above (eg to determine whether the amounts were previously counted towards the non-concessional contributions cap and/or were included in the taxable or tax free components of the member's superannuation interest).

Departing Australian superannuation payments

An amount transferred from an Australian complying superannuation fund to a KiwiSaver scheme is not taxed on its exit from the Australian superannuation system. The departing Australia superannuation payment regime does not apply to Australian and New Zealand citizens and permanent residents (¶14-390).

Approved Deposit Funds

¶13-400 The nature and purpose of ADFs

Approved deposit funds (ADFs) function as roll-over vehicles so as to enable an individual's superannuation benefits to be retained in the superannuation system until they are paid from the ADF.

An ADF can accept superannuation benefits which are rolled over to it for the benefit of an individual and ATO payments of the shortfall component of a superannuation guarantee charge for the benefit of the individual (¶39-600), but cannot accept superannuation contributions directly from employers or individuals. An ADF can only pay lump sum superannuation benefits to its members, not pensions.

Moneys deposited in an ADF are invested to generate income which is taxed at 15% for a complying ADF and at 45% for a non-complying ADF (¶13-410). Deposits and accumulated earnings withdrawn from an ADF are taxable at that time as superannuation benefits in the hands of the recipients (¶14-000ff).

The SISA and related Acts provide for the prudential regulation of ADFs (¶13-800).

[SLP ¶2-220, ¶2-800]

¶13-410 Taxation of ADFs

The taxation of ADFs is governed by Div 295 of ITAA97 and other ITAA36 and ITAA97 provisions.

An entity is eligible for concessional tax treatment as a complying ADF under Div 295 if:

- it is an ''approved deposit fund'' (ie an indefinitely continuing fund that is maintained by a body corporate registrable superannuation entity (RSE) licensee solely for approved purposes (¶13-400))
- it is resident in Australia (SISA s 20A)
- it has complied with all regulatory provisions applicable to it (or contraventions are disregarded by APRA), and
- it has received a notice from APRA stating that it is a complying ADF, and has not received a later non-complying ADF notice (SISA ss 43; 47).

An ADF that does not satisfy the conditions to be a complying ADF is taxed as a non-complying ADF under Div 295.

The taxable income of an ADF is worked out using the method statement in s 295-10 (¶13-120) as if the trustee were a taxpayer and a resident.

The taxable income of a complying ADF is split into a non-arm's length component and a low tax component. The non-arm's length component for an income year is the fund's ''non-arm's length income'' (NALI: ¶13-170) for that year less any deductions to the extent that they are attributable to that income. The low tax component is any remaining part of its taxable income for the income year (ITAA97 ss 295-545; 295-550).

For a complying ADF, the low tax component is taxed at 15% and the non-arm's length component is taxed at 45%. By contrast, the whole of the taxable income of a non-complying ADF is taxed at 45% (ITRA ss 27(1)(b), (2); 35(1)).

The ITAA97 provisions governing deductions for superannuation funds similarly apply to ADFs (¶13-150).

Other tax rules for ADFs

A complying ADF is subject to the following taxation treatment (like complying superannuation funds):

- certain roll-over superannuation benefits (¶13-125) and payments of the shortfall component of the superannuation guarantee charge to a complying ADF are assessable contributions (ITAA97 ss 295-160; 295-190)
- liability on assessable contributions may be transferred (ITAA97 s 295-260)
- complying ADFs are subject to modified CGT rules and are entitled to the CGT discount (¶13-130)
- the imputation system and entitlement to claim unused franking credits apply to complying ADFs (¶13-160)
- complying ADFs are entitled to special treatment for their investments in PSTs and life policies, and for the expenses relating to these investments (¶13-140)
- complying ADFs are entitled to the special deduction rules in relation to contributions and payment of levies (¶13-150)
- complying ADFs are exempted from the trust loss and debt reduction provisions, being "excepted trusts" (¶6-262).

A continuously complying fixed interest ADF's income that is attributable to deposits of certain eligible depositors held in the fund at 25 May 1988 may be exempt from tax (ITTPA s 295-390). Stringent conditions and restrictions apply, such as the nature of the fund's investments, the age of depositors (who must be at least 50 years at 25 May 1988) and the source of the deposits.

A non-complying ADF is not entitled to the tax concessions available to complying ADFs as noted above.

[AMSG ¶7-600, ¶7-650; FITR ¶270-010; SLP ¶45-450, ¶45-460]

Pooled Superannuation Trusts

¶13-430 The nature and purpose of PSTs

A pooled superannuation trust (PST) is a resident unit trust that complies with the definition of PST in the SISA and is used only for investing assets of a regulated superannuation fund, an ADF or another PST, or the complying superannuation assets or segregated exempt assets of a life insurance company. The trustee of a unit trust that wishes to be a PST must give APRA a confirmation of its intention to be a PST (SISR reg 1.04(5)).

A "unit trust" generally means any trust estate, whether or not the interests in it are unitised. The general rules in ITAA97 apply to determine a unit trust's residency status.

The SISA and related Acts provide for the prudential regulation of PSTs (¶13-800).

[SLP ¶2-250]

¶13-440 Taxation of PSTs

The taxation of PSTs is governed by Div 295 of ITAA97 and other ITAA36 and ITAA97 provisions.

A unit trust is taxed as a PST under Div 295 only if it has received a notice from APRA under SISA s 48 stating that it is a PST. A trust that fails to qualify as a PST is taxed under the general trust provisions in ITAA36 (¶13-120).

The taxable income of a PST is worked out using the method statement in s 295-10 (¶13-120).

The taxable income of a PST is split into a non-arm's length component and a low tax component. The non-arm's length component for an income year is the PST's "non-arm's length income" (NALI: ¶13-170) for that year less any deductions to the extent that they are attributable to that income. The low tax component is any remaining part of its taxable income for the income year (ITAA97 ss 295-545; 295-550).

The low tax component is taxed at 15% and the non-arm's length component is taxed at 45% (ITRA ss 27A(b); 35(1)).

Capital gains

The modifications to the CGT rules for complying superannuation funds and entitlement to the CGT discount similarly apply to PSTs (¶13-130).

Investments by superannuation funds and ADFs

A complying superannuation fund or complying ADF, with the agreement of a PST, may transfer its liability on contributions (except no-TFN contributions: ¶13-120) to the PST (¶13-125).

Complying superannuation funds or complying ADFs that invest in PSTs are not themselves liable for tax on the income derived by the PST, or on capital gains on the realisation or redemption of units in the PST (ITAA97 s 118-350).

Non-reversionary bonus

Any non-reversionary bonus (ie cash bonus) received by a PST on a life assurance policy is excluded from assessable income (ITAA97 s 295-335, item 1).

Exemption for current pension liabilities

A PST is entitled to a tax exemption on that part of its assessable income that is attributable to the current pension liabilities of a complying superannuation fund that is a unitholder (ITAA97 s 295-400). The exempt income is the PST's normal assessable income for the year multiplied by the proportion of the investing fund's unit holdings (that are segregated current pension assets) to the average total units in the PST. Alternatively, the PST may elect to have the exemption based on the percentage of its assessable income that would have been exempt under ITAA97 s 295-385 or 295-390 if that income had been derived directly by the investing fund. An election must be lodged with the Commissioner.

Deductions and other concessions

The general principles governing deductions (¶13-150) and the imputation system (¶13-160) as they apply to superannuation funds similarly apply to PSTs.

A PST, being an excepted trust, is not subject to the trust loss or debt deduction measures (¶6-262).

[AMSG ¶7-700; FITR ¶270-010; SLP ¶45-470]

Retirement Savings Accounts

¶13-470 The nature and purpose of RSAs

Retirement savings accounts (RSAs) are provided to the general public by approved RSA institutions (eg banks, credit unions and cooperatives) as a simple, low-cost and low-risk savings product that employers may use as an alternative to making contributions to superannuation funds for their employees, and which individuals may use for making personal superannuation contributions or spouse contributions.

Where offered by a financial institution, an RSA will be an account (similar to a deposit account) on the balance sheet of the RSA provider and, where offered by a life insurance company, an RSA will be a policy provided through a statutory fund. An RSA may be held only by individuals and must be maintained for the purpose of providing retirement benefits to the RSA holder or death benefits to the RSA holder's dependants.

RSA providers and RSA business are subject to a prudential supervision regime under the RSA legislation and related Acts in a broadly similar manner as superannuation entities and their products (¶13-800).

[AMSG ¶10-030; SLP ¶60-100]

¶13-480 Taxation of RSA business

The taxation of the RSA business of a bank or other financial institution (financial institution) is governed by ITAA97 Div 295. The taxation of the RSA business of a life assurance company (life office) is governed by ITAA97 Div 320 (¶3-530).

The method statement in ITAA97 s 295-10 is used to work out the taxable income of a financial institution RSA provider for its RSA business, namely:

- its no-TFN contributions income (¶13-180)
- the specific amounts to be included in assessable income (eg assessable contributions and other amounts credited to RSAs not paying current pensions or immediate annuities)
- the specific amounts that are exempt from tax (eg amounts credited to RSAs paying current pensions or immediate annuities) or are non-assessable non-exempt income
- the specific deductions available (eg premiums for providing death and disability benefits to RSA holders, but not amounts credited to RSAs and benefits paid from RSAs).

Once the total taxable income of a financial institution RSA provider is determined (ie from its RSA business), it is divided into an RSA component which is taxed at 15% and a standard component which is taxed at the general company tax rate.

Taxpayers making contributions to RSAs are eligible for tax concessions in the same way as for contributions made to complying superannuation funds (¶13-700 and following). Benefit payments from RSAs are also subject to an equivalent taxation regime as that applying to superannuation fund payments and benefits (¶14-000ff).

The RSA regime is discussed in detail in the *Australian Master Superannuation Guide 2020/21*.

[AMSG ¶10-030; SLP ¶60-100]

Superannuation Contributions

¶13-700 Tax treatment of superannuation contributions

Employers are required under the SGAA to make mandatory superannuation guarantee (SG) contributions for their employees with some exceptions (¶39-000), or may make additional superannuation contributions for their employees under an employment contract or industrial agreement. Individual taxpayers may make personal superannuation contributions, either from after-tax income or under salary sacrifice arrangements, as their own superannuation savings. Generally, where certain conditions are met:

- employers are entitled to a deduction for superannuation contributions made for employees, regardless of whether they are mandatory or additional contributions (¶13-710)

- individuals are entitled to a deduction for their personal superannuation contributions (¶13-730)

- individuals (including self-employed persons) are entitled to government co-contributions for their non-deductible personal contributions, and to a low income superannuation tax offset for concessional contributions (¶13-760)

- individuals who make superannuation contributions for or on behalf of a spouse who earns little or no income are entitled to a tax offset (¶13-770)

- employer contributions and deductible personal contributions are "concessional contributions", while non-deductible personal contributions and other contributions are "non-concessional contributions" under ITAA97 and are subject to additional tax rules (see "Tax payable by individuals, superannuation funds and employers" below)

- the Commissioner may exercise a discretion to disregard or reallocate contributions to another income year in "special circumstances" under the concessional and non-concessional contributions regime (¶13-785).

The SIS Regulations and RSA Regulations impose rules on the acceptance of contributions by superannuation funds and RSA providers (conversely, the rules govern who can make contributions to a fund or RSA), and contributions made in breach of the rules must be returned (¶13-825).

Tax payable by individuals, superannuation funds and employers

In each financial year, excess concessional contributions charge and excess non-concessional contributions tax is payable by an individual if the individual's concessional contributions (generally assessable contributions in the recipient funds) or non-concessional contributions (generally non-assessable contributions) exceed the cap amounts for the year (¶13-775, ¶13-780).

Concessional contributions (and certain other amounts) received by a superannuation fund are included in the fund's assessable income and are subject to contributions tax at 15% (for complying funds) or at 45% (for non-complying funds). Non-concessional contributions received are not subject to tax (¶13-125).

Additional tax of 15% (Division 293 tax) may be payable by individuals whose income and relevant concessionally taxed superannuation contributions exceed a prescribed income threshold ($250,000 in 2017–18 and later years). The tax, which is imposed on the concessionally taxed contributions which exceed the threshold, has the effect of reducing the tax concessions enjoyed by these individuals on their concessional contributions (¶13-750).

A tax is also payable by complying and non-complying funds on any no-TFN contributions income received by them. A tax offset is available if the individual's TFN is subsequently received (¶13-180).

In all states and territories, pay-roll tax is payable on employer superannuation contributions as they are "wages" under pay-roll tax legislation (¶36-140).

Employer superannuation contributions for employees are not fringe benefits if they are made to a complying superannuation fund or an RSA, or to a non-resident superannuation fund for an employee who is a temporary resident of Australia. Other employer contributions may be fringe benefits and be subject to FBT, eg those made for an associate of an employee (¶35-070).

[AMSG ¶6-000ff; FITR ¶268-302; SLP ¶36-050, ¶36-460]

¶13-705 Meaning of "contribution" to a superannuation fund

The term "contribution" is not defined in ITAA97 although it is used in many provisions relating to superannuation operations. It is therefore necessary to ascertain the meaning of "contribution" to a superannuation fund having regard to the context and underlying purpose of the legislative provisions in which the term appears.

TR 2010/1 discusses the ordinary meaning of "contribution" as used in relation to a superannuation fund (or ADF and RSA) in ITAA97. A "contribution" in the superannuation context is anything of value that increases the capital of a superannuation fund which is provided by a person whose purpose is to benefit one or more particular fund members or all members in general. Generally, a person will be taken to intend the natural and probable consequences of their acts and, likewise, their purpose may be inferred from their acts. This is a determination of a person's objective (not subjective) purpose.

A superannuation fund's capital is most commonly increased by transferring funds to it. A contribution can be made in money, money equivalent or in specie, or by increasing the value of an existing fund asset (whether by way of an improvement to the asset or by shifting the value of interests in the asset), or meeting or reducing an existing liability of a fund, paying expenses on behalf of the fund, and rendering services to the fund (to the extent that those services are not remunerated at fair market value). An increase in the fund's capital due to income, profits and gains arising from the use of the fund's existing capital will not, generally, be derived from someone whose purpose is to benefit one or more particular members of the fund (TR 2010/1, para 133).

With specie contributions, the amount of the contribution is or includes the market value of the property, reduced by the value of any consideration given for the transfer of the property (ITAA97 s 285-5).

A contribution by cheque or promissory note (other than an investment-related promissory note) is made when received by the fund, unless it is subsequently dishonoured (*Peaker*). In the case of an electronic funds transfer between bank accounts, a contribution is not made to a superannuation fund until the funds are credited to the superannuation fund's account in the recipient bank (*Chantrell*).

A contribution of property is received when either legal or beneficial ownership of the property passes to the fund. If there is no formal registration process which evidences ownership, ownership passes when the fund acquires possession of the property or on execution of a deed of transfer of the property. Otherwise (eg with shares in a publicly listed company or Torrens title land), ownership passes when the fund is registered as the property's owner or when the fund acquires beneficial ownership of the property (eg possession of the requisite transfer forms, a properly completed off-market share transfer form).

A contribution by way of debt forgiveness is taken to occur when the lender executes a deed of release that relieves a superannuation fund from its obligation to repay the loan.

Where a person pays an amount to a third party to satisfy a superannuation fund's liability, the fund is taken to have constructively received the payment made to the third party. That payment increases the capital of the fund because the person's payment has extinguished the fund's liability. The Commissioner recognises that it is common for expenses incurred by a superannuation fund to be paid by an employer or individual on the fund's behalf and for these payments to be later journalised as employer or member superannuation contributions to the fund. The Commissioner's preferred approach is for all superannuation fund expenses to be paid directly out of the fund itself and for superannuation contributions to be made directly to the fund (TR 2010/1, para 173–174).

Where a member of an unfunded defined benefits fund makes a payment under s 16(7) of the *Superannuation Contributions Tax (Assessment and Collection) Act 1997* (SCTA) to reduce the amount by which the member's surcharge debt account in the fund is in debit, the payment is not a contribution by the member for the purpose of obtaining superannuation benefits (ID 2014/27).

Contributions for an income or financial year

The ''financial year'' is the 12-month period starting on 1 July and ending on the following 30 June, while the ''income year'' is the same as the financial year except in 2 cases (¶9-005). Correctly identifying the financial year or income year in which a superannuation contribution is made is important as different expressions are used in the tax law provisions dealing with contributions which give rise to a tax concession or tax liability. For example:

- employers can deduct a contribution made for employees under ITAA97 s 290-60 (¶13-710), and individuals can claim a deduction for personal contributions under ITAA97 s 290-150 (¶13-730), only for the income year in which they made the contribution (see also ''Timing of contributions and contributions made through a clearing house'' in ¶13-710)
- a superannuation fund is required under ITAA97 s 295-160 to include in its assessable income contributions for the income year in which the contributions are received (¶13-125)
- the Commissioner must make an assessment under ITAA97 s 292-230 of a person's liability to excess contributions tax if the person has excess non-concessional contributions for a financial year (¶13-780)
- a co-contribution is payable under s 6 of the *Superannuation (Government Co-contributions for Low Income Earners) Act 2003* if a person makes one or more eligible personal superannuation contributions during the income year (¶13-760).

Under s 36(2) of the *Acts Interpretation Act 1901*, if an Act requires or allow a thing to be done, and the last day for doing the thing is a Saturday, a Sunday or a holiday, then the thing may be done on the next day that is not a Saturday, a Sunday or a holiday. In respect of years when 30 June falls on a weekend or holiday, the issue is whether contributions received by a superannuation fund on 1 or 2 July of a year should be treated as having been received in the preceding income year. The ATO notes that the above provisions do not ''require or allow'' a contribution to be made or received by the last day of a particular year; rather, they provide for a particular outcome should a contribution be made or received on or before the last day of a particular year. Therefore, s 36(2) does not apply to extend the income or financial year for the purposes of the above provisions regardless of whether the last day of the year falls on a Saturday, a Sunday or a holiday (*Chantrell*: electronic funds transfer made on 30 June (a Saturday) was not credited by the bank to a superannuation fund account until 2 July (a Monday)).

Provision of information to ATO

Superannuation providers are required to provide the ATO with information about contributions received and roll-over superannuation benefits each year (¶39-530). The ATO uses the information received for various purposes such as administration of the SG, co-contribution and concessional and non-concessional contributions cap regimes.

¶13-710 Deduction — contributions by employers

An employer may claim a deduction for all contributions made to a complying superannuation fund or an RSA for the purpose of providing superannuation benefits for an employee if the conditions in ITAA97 Subdiv 290-B are satisfied (ITAA97 s 290-60(1)).

If the employer's contributions for the employee (and other ''concessional contributions'' of the employee, if any) exceed the concessional contributions cap for the year, the excess is included as assessable income and is taxed at the employee's marginal tax rates. In addition, an excess contributions charge is payable by the employee (¶13-777).

Subdivision 290-B does not apply to a contribution that is:

- a roll-over superannuation benefit (¶13-125)
- a superannuation lump sum that is paid from a foreign superannuation fund (¶13-250)
- an amount transferred from a scheme for the payment of superannuation upon retirement or death that:
  - (i) is not, and never has been, an Australian superannuation fund or a foreign superannuation fund
  - (ii) was not established in Australia, and
  - (iii) is not centrally managed or controlled in Australia.

An employer cannot deduct an amount paid as contributions to a complying superannuation fund or RSA except as provided by Subdiv 290-B (ITAA97 s 290-10).

In certain circumstances, an employer's deduction may be reduced, increased or denied under other provisions of the income tax law (eg ITAA97 ss 85-25 and 86-75: see ''Personal services income rules may deny deduction'' below) (ITAA97 s 290-60(1) Note).

A deduction is allowable only for the year in which the contribution is made (see ''Timing of contributions and contributions made through a clearing house'' below) (s 290-60(3)).

TR 2010/1 sets out guidelines on the meaning of superannuation contribution (¶13-705), and on particular aspects of deductibility of employer contributions for employees under Subdiv 290-B.

Eligibility conditions

An employer's superannuation contribution is deductible under Subdiv 290-B if:

- the contribution is made to a superannuation fund or an RSA for the purpose of providing superannuation benefits *for another person* who is an ''employee'' of the employer when the contribution is made (regardless of whether the benefits are paid to a ''SIS dependant'' of the employee if the employee dies before or after becoming entitled to receive the benefits), and
- the employee activity condition, complying fund condition and age-related condition (see below) are met (ITAA97 ss 290-60; 290-70; 290-75; 290-80).

The employer contribution must be made *for another person* so that this person cannot be the same person as the entity claiming the deduction. If an individual is an ''employee'' of an entity under SGAA s 12 at the relevant time (eg former employees, see below), Subdiv 290-B applies as if the individual were an employee of the entity. A partner who makes a contribution for an employee of the partnership can deduct the contribution against his/her own income, even though the partner is not strictly the employer. This does not limit the ability of the partnership to claim a tax deduction when it makes a superannuation contribution on behalf of the same employee, but a partner and the partnership cannot claim a tax deduction in respect of the same contribution (s 290-65(2)).

The eligibility conditions are modified for contributions made for former employees and controlling interest deductions.

An employer is not entitled to a deduction for contributions under s 290-60(1) if:

- the contribution is made under the *Family Law Act 1975* to a superannuation fund to satisfy the entitlement of a former spouse who may also be an employee (s 290-60(4))
- the employer has elected under SGAA s 23A for the contribution to offset the employer's liability to pay a superannuation guarantee (SG) charge liability (¶39-400) (s 290-95(1)). An exception applies under the SG amnesty, see below.

An employer is allowed a deduction for offset contributions that are made during the amnesty period to the extent that the contributions relate to a SG shortfall for which employer qualified for the SG amnesty (s 290-95(2)). The SG amnesty is discussed in ¶39-505.

Employee activity condition

For a contribution to be deductible, the person for whom the contribution is made must be:

- an employee (within the expanded meaning of "employee" given by SGAA s 12) of the employer), or
- engaged in producing assessable income of the employer, or
- an Australian resident who is engaged in the employer's business (s 290-70).

An employer can therefore claim a deduction for contributions made on behalf of its SG employees who are neither engaged in producing the assessable income of the business nor engaged in the business of the employer (eg a person who works under a contract that is wholly or principally for the labour of the person, or a person who does work of a domestic or private nature and is an SG employee). For a list of SG employees covered by s 12, see ¶39-020.

A taxpayer was denied a deduction for salary and wages, and for contributions made for his spouse for administrative work in connection with the taxpayer's rental property as there was no genuine employment relationship in the circumstances (*France*; *Brown*; *VN Railway*: family members of a trading trust were not "eligible employees" under ITAA36 former s 82AAC).

Superannuation contributions made for the directors of a passive investment company are deductible in circumstances where the company derived its assessable income from its passive investments, provided the directors were entitled to payment for their services (ID 2007/144). In *Kelly*, the Full Federal Court held that a contribution for a director of the trustee company of family trust was not deductible as the director was not an employee. Without a company resolution, the director was not entitled to payment for duties performed as a director, and not an "employee". This was the case whether or not the payment was made, as SGAA s 12(2) clearly required that an entitlement to payment must have existed (¶39-020). The ATO states that the court's decision is consistent with its view in para 243 of TR 2010/1 that a superannuation contribution for the director of a corporate trustee can only be deducted from the income of the trust if the director was a common law employee of the trust engaged in producing assessable income of the trust or its business (*Decision Impact Statement* VRN QUD 361 of 2012).

Former employees and SG contributions

An employer can claim a deduction for a contribution made for a former employee if:

- the contribution reduces the employer's superannuation guarantee charge percentage in respect of the former employee under the special rules in SGAA s 15B dealing with former employees (¶39-020), or

- the contribution is a one-off payment in lieu of salary or wages that relate to a period of service during which the person was an employee (ITAA97 s 290-85(1)).

The contributions covered by s 290-85 include those made under salary sacrifice arrangements and contributions made by a contributor on behalf of an employer where the other person was never an employee of the contributor (see examples below) (s 290-85(1A)).

▶ Example 1 — salary sacrifice

Andrew entered into a salary sacrifice arrangement during his employment under which 20% of his salary was contributed to superannuation.

Andrew resigns from his job on 1 December when he is age 50. His final pay period ends on 20 December.

The 20% of Andrew's final pay that is contributed to a complying superannuation fund on 20 December is an allowable deduction to his former employer.

▶ Example 2 — contribution on employer's behalf

John terminates employment with his employer, ABC Pty Ltd, on 28 January.

ABC Pty Ltd pays John his final salary on 15 February and consequently there is an SG obligation on this final salary payment.

XYZ Pty Ltd, which holds a 50% shareholding in ABC Pty Ltd, makes a contribution to satisfy ABC Pty Ltd's SG obligation for John.

The contribution made by XYZ Pty Ltd is deductible, even though John was never an employee of XYZ Pty Ltd (s 290-85(1A)).

Contributions made for a former employee are also deductible where they are made:

- within 4 months of the employee ceasing employment (employers may make SG contributions within 28 days of the end of each quarter under the SGAA: ¶39-240), or
- to fund a defined benefit interest which accrued when the member was an employee (regardless of when the contributions are made), the employer was at arm's length with the former employee in relation to the contribution and an actuarial certificate verifies that the additional contributions are required (s 290-85(1AA), (1AB)).

Controlling interest in employer

Where superannuation contributions are made by an entity other than an employer, a deduction may be available to an entity with a controlling interest in the employer. Such a situation arises where the entity makes a contribution in respect of another person at a time, and at that time:

(a) the other person is an employee of a company in which the entity has a controlling interest, or

(b) the entity (eg a shareholder of a company) is connected to the other person in the way prescribed in s 290-90(5), or

(c) the entity is a company that is connected to the other person in the way prescribed in s 290-90(6) (ITAA97 s 290-90(1)).

In that situation, the other person is treated as the entity's employee at that time for the purposes of s 290-60(1) in the circumstances prescribed in s 290-90.

The term ''controlling interest'' is not defined and will take its common law meaning. A shareholder will have a controlling interest in a company if the shareholder has a bare majority (more than 50%) of the voting power or has the power, by the exercise of voting rights, to carry a resolution at a general meeting of the company. If 2 directors hold equal shares of 50%, neither has a controlling interest (TR 2010/1, para 48–51).

Making provision for superannuation benefits

Employer superannuation contributions for an employee are deductible under s 290-60(1) only if the contributions are made for the purpose of providing superannuation benefits for the employee. This requirement will be satisfied even if these benefits are payable to dependants of the employee (or their legal personal representative) after the death of the employee. For contributions made in respect of an employee who has died, see ‘‘Former employees and SG contributions’’ above.

The purpose of the taxpayer is the key factor when determining if contributions are made for the purpose of making provision for superannuation benefits for another person. It does not matter that a taxpayer takes account of the incidental consequences of making a contribution, such as obtaining a tax deduction (TR 2010/1, para 41). Employer contributions to an employer-sponsored fund have been held to be not deductible where the main purpose was to generate tax-deductible payments which could be returned to the employer (eg as low-interest loans) (*Raymor Contractors*). The facts of each case are relevant to determine the taxpayer's purpose and, if required, may look beyond the terms of the trust deed to establish the purpose. Relevant considerations include the trustee's use of the trust funds, the extent to which the employees actually receive benefits from the fund, and the extent to which the funds are used to benefit persons who are not employees (*Case 25/93*).

Age-related condition

An employer's contribution is deductible under s 290-60(1) subject to the following rules (ITAA97 s 290-80(1)):

- the employer must have made the contribution within 28 days after the end of the month in which the employee turned 75 — in this case, the whole contribution is deductible
- the employer was required to make the contribution by an industrial award, determination or notional agreement preserving state awards (within the meaning of the *Fair Work (Transitional Provisions and Consequential Amendments) Act 2009*) that is in force under an Australian law — in this case, no age limit applies but the deduction is limited to the amount required by the award, determination or agreement (s 290-80(2)), or
- for contributions made after 30 June 2013, the contribution reduces the employer's SG charge percentage under the SGAA in respect of the employee — in this case, no age limit applies but the deduction is limited to the amount that reduces the charge percentage (s 290-80(2A)).

The SGAA requires employers to make SG contributions for employees regardless of their age, except those who are ‘‘exempted’’ from SG coverage (¶39-030). If a contribution is covered by both the second and third dot points (and not the first), the deductible amount is the greater of the amounts permitted (s 290-80(2B)).

An award or determination does not include an industrial agreement, such as enterprise agreement or a similar agreement made under a state law (s 290-80(2)). This is because a person can otherwise enter into such agreements thus enabling the employer to meet the age-related condition and claim a deduction for contributions made under the agreement.

Complying superannuation fund condition

Employer superannuation contributions are deductible under s 290-60 only if they are made to a complying superannuation fund or an RSA. For contribution made to a superannuation fund, one of the following conditions must be satisfied:

1. the fund was a complying superannuation fund for the income year of the fund in which the employer made the contribution

2. at the time of the contribution, the employer had reasonable grounds to believe that the fund was a complying superannuation fund for that income year, or

3. before making the contribution, the employer obtained a written statement from the fund that it was a "resident regulated superannuation fund" and was not prohibited from accepting employer contributions under SISA s 63 (s 290-75(1)).

Points 2 and 3 cannot be satisfied if, when the contribution was made:

- the employer was the trustee or the manager of the fund (or associate of the trustee or the manager of the fund), and
- the employer had reasonable grounds to believe that the fund was not a resident regulated superannuation fund or was operating in contravention of a regulatory provision under the SISA (s 290-75(2)).

Timing of contributions and contributions made through a clearing house

Employer superannuation contributions in a financial year are deductible only for the year in which the contribution is made (s 290-60(3)).

The general rule is contributions are made to a complying superannuation fund (or RSA) when the payment is received by the fund (*Liwszyc*; TR 2010/1 para 182–210; see also "Contributions for an income or financial year" in ¶13-705).

Where contributions are made using a clearing house, there may be a period of time before the complying fund or RSA actually receives the contribution. This means that employer contributions made towards the end of an income year may not be received by the fund in the same income year and this may impact on the year in which the employer is entitled to a deduction for the contribution.

ATO's compliance approach for payments to SBSCH

Under the SGAA, employer payments made to the Small Business Superannuation Clearing House (SBSCH) are taken to be contributions made on the day they are accepted by the SBSCH. This is only for the purpose of determining whether an employer is liable for the SG charge and does not extend to determining when an employer is entitled to claim a tax deduction (SGAA s 23B) (¶39-240).

PCG 2020/6 states that the ATO will not apply compliance resources to consider whether employer contributions via the SBSCH were received by the complying superannuation fund or RSA in the same income year in which payment was made provided payment to the SBSCH was made before close of business on the last business day on or before 30 June. Also, at the time of making the payment, the employer must have provided all relevant information to enable the SBSCH to process the payment to the employees' superannuation fund accounts or RSA and the SBSCH has accepted the payment in accordance with the SBSCH terms and conditions (¶39-240).

This compliance approach means that where the PCG 2020/6 requirements are met, an employer does not need to check with the employees' superannuation funds to determine in which income year the contributions were received from the SBSCH prior to claiming a tax deduction in the income year the payment was made to the SBSCH. This approach does not apply where the employer payment is made through a clearing house other than the SBSCH (a commercial clearing house).

Personal services income rules may deny deduction

In certain circumstances, an individual or a personal services entity may be denied a tax deduction for superannuation contributions under the personal services income regime in ITAA97 Div 86 (¶30-600). A "personal services entity" is a company, trust or partnership whose assessable income includes the personal services income of one or more individuals (ITAA97 s 86-15). Personal services income (PSI) is income that is gained mainly as a reward for the personal efforts or skills of an individual (ITAA97 s

84-5; TD 2015/1: PSI includes payments received by a personal services entity from a service acquirer during a period the service provider is not providing services to the acquirer until further called upon).

The restrictions on the deduction for superannuation contributions do not apply if the individual or the personal services entity is conducting a ‘‘personal services business’’ (ie one of the personal services business tests is met: ¶30-660) (ITAA97 s 87-1).

Contributions by individuals

An individual cannot deduct a contribution made to a superannuation fund or RSA to provide for superannuation benefits for the individual’s associate (eg a spouse) to the extent that the associate’s work relates to gaining or producing the individual’s personal services income (ITAA97 s 85-25(1)).

A deduction, however, may be allowed to the extent that the associate performs work which forms part of the ‘‘principal work’’ for which the individual gains or produces personal services income (s 85-25(2); *Taneja*). Principal work is work that is central to meeting the individual’s obligations under agreements between the individual or a personal services entity and the acquirer of the personal services. Generally, principal work does not include work which is ancillary (eg helping or aiding the work of the test individual), unless this directly contributes to the generation of the relevant personal services income. Work associated with administration or other clerical work is ancillary and is not principal work unless the work to be performed for the service acquirer includes that administrative work (TR 2001/8, para 59).

If the associate is engaged in providing part of the individual’s principal work, superannuation contributions that are related to that engagement may be deductible, but the deduction is limited to the minimum amount required to be contributed by the individual on behalf of the associate to comply with the SG obligations (¶39-000). The minimum contribution is calculated as if the associate’s ordinary time earnings for SG purposes is the amount paid to the associate to perform the principal work (s 86-75).

Contributions by personal services entity

A personal services entity is entitled to deduct certain contributions it makes to a superannuation fund or RSA on behalf of an individual whose personal services income is included in its income (ITAA97 s 86-75). This applies, for instance, if an individual provides personal services and the personal services income from providing those services is paid to a personal services entity (eg a company, trust or partnership) rather than to the individual.

If a contribution is made on behalf of an associate of an individual whose personal services income is included in the entity’s income, and the associate performs less than ‘‘20% (by market value)’’ (TR 2001/8, para 60 to 65) of the entity’s principal work, the deduction is limited to the amount required to be contributed to avoid an individual SG shortfall (s 86-75(2)). The required minimum contribution is calculated as if the associate’s ordinary time earnings for SG purposes are the amount paid to the associate to perform the principal work (s 86-75(3)).

In TR 2003/10, the Commissioner accepts that the interpretation of s 86-75(2) is ‘‘not without difficulties’’ (para 58). However, having regard to the overall context of the provisions and their intended purpose, the Commissioner considers that the provision has an effect where an associate of the test individual performs less than 20% by market value of the entity’s principal work, including where the associate’s work that is entirely non-principal work. The deduction allowed to the personal services entity is capped (or in the case of entirely non-principal work it is not allowed at all) at the amount necessary to avoid an individual superannuation guarantee shortfall. The cap is therefore calculated by reference to the salary or wages attributable to the principal work performed by the associate plus any salary or wages paid to the associate for work performed in gaining or producing other income (ie non-personal services income) of the entity.

In a practical sense, this means the deduction is limited to the *lesser* of the amount contributed by the entity to the superannuation fund or RSA, the age-based deduction limit under ITAA36 former s 82AAC (not relevant from the 2007–08 year onwards), and the deduction limit set by s 86-75(2). The provision does not cap a deduction for superannuation contributions made in respect of an associate of the test individual where the contribution is in respect of work performed by the associate that is 20% or more (by market value) of the principal work of the entity. However, in such a case, the personal services entity would generally satisfy the employment test and not be subject to ITAA97 Div 86 (para 59, 60).

▶ Example 3

Monacoy, a personal services entity, receives $200,000 for personal services performed by John. Monacoy has no other income. Monacoy pays John's son, Peter, $10,000 to carry out certain tasks, comprising 10% (by market value) of the principal work that generates the personal services income. Peter is also paid $30,000 for miscellaneous administrative support. The maximum deduction to which Monacoy is entitled for superannuation contributions made for Peter is:

$$9.5\% \times \$10{,}000 = \$950$$

Contributions in excess of $950 are not deductible.

Returned contributions are assessable income

Contributions that are returned to an employer (or to a contributor on behalf of an employer), and earnings on those contributions, are assessable income to the recipient if the contributions have previously been deductible to the employer under Subdiv 290-B, unless they are received as a superannuation benefit (ITAA97 s 290-100).

Returned contributions cover direct and indirect returns. An example of an indirect return of a contribution is where the fund to which it was made transfers to another fund assets that include the contribution, and the other fund returns the contribution to the person who made it.

Salary sacrifice arrangements

Employees may enter into an *effective* salary sacrifice arrangement (SSA) with their employer under which the employee can "sacrifice" a future entitlement to salary or wages in return for the employer making superannuation contributions (or providing other fringe benefits) of an equivalent value for the employee. Superannuation contributions for employees under an effective SSA are treated as employer contributions and are deductible where the Subdiv 290-B eligibility conditions discussed above are met. The ATO guidelines on effective and ineffective SSAs and their tax consequences are set out in TR 2001/10 (¶31-120).

Related tax matters

Employer superannuation contributions for employees are assessable contributions of the recipient superannuation funds (¶13-125) or RSA providers (¶13-480), and are concessional contributions in ITAA97 (¶13-775).

Financing costs (eg interest expenditure on borrowings) to the extent that they relate to obtaining finance to make the employer superannuation contributions for employees are tax-deductible provided the contributions themselves are deductible under Subdiv 290-B (ITAA97 s 26-80).

[AMSG ¶6-100 – ¶6-260; FITR ¶268-325ff; SLP ¶36-050]

¶13-730 Deduction — personal superannuation contributions

An individual taxpayer is entitled to a deduction for personal superannuation contributions if the conditions in ITAA97 Subdiv 290-C are satisfied.

A taxpayer's deductible contributions (called "concessional contributions" in ITAA97) are included as assessable contributions and subject to 15% contributions tax in the hands of the recipient fund (¶13-125). If the taxpayer's concessional contributions (plus other "concessional contributions" made for the taxpayer, if any, such as employer contributions) exceed the concessional contributions cap for the year, the excess is included in the taxpayer's assessable income and is taxed at marginal tax rates. In addition, the taxpayer is liable to pay an excess contributions charge (¶13-775).

A refund of excess contributions (¶13-775) is not used to reassess whether an individual is entitled to deduct personal superannuation contributions.

Subdivision 290-C does not apply to a contribution that is a roll-over superannuation benefit (¶13-125) or a superannuation lump sum that is paid from a foreign superannuation fund or an amount transferred from a scheme that has never been an Australian superannuation fund or from a foreign superannuation fund (ITAA97 s 290-5).

An individual cannot deduct personal contributions, except as provided by Subdiv 290-C (ITAA97 s 290-10).

No deduction is allowed for an individual's contribution that is covered under ITAA97 s 292-102 (downsizer contributions: ¶13-795) (s 290-167), or the individual has notified the Commissioner that the contribution is made under ITAA97 s 313-50 (recontributing amounts that were previously released under the FHSS Scheme: ¶13-790) (s 290-168).

In certain circumstances, a taxpayer's deduction may be limited, reduced or denied under other provisions of the income tax law (eg ITAA97 s 26-55: see "Related tax matters" below).

TR 2010/1 sets out guidelines on the meaning of superannuation contribution (¶13-705), and on particular aspects of deductibility of personal contributions for under Subdiv 290-C. The SISR rules on the acceptance of contributions are summarised at ¶13-825.

Transfers from a KiwiSaver scheme to a complying superannuation fund are not deductible personal contributions (¶13-380).

Eligibility conditions

An individual taxpayer's personal superannuation contributions are deductible if the contributions are made to a complying superannuation fund or RSA for the purpose of providing superannuation benefits for the taxpayer, even if the benefits are payable to the taxpayer's "SIS dependants" (within the meaning of the SISA) on the taxpayer's death (ITAA97 s 290-150).

A deduction is allowed only for the year in which the contribution is made (ITAA97 s 290-150(3)).

If a contribution is the CGT exempt amount arising from the disposal of active assets of a small business and the contributor is under age 55 (¶7-185), the contribution is not deductible to the extent that it is attributable to the exempt amount (s 290-150(4)).

Where applicable, the following conditions must also be met:

- the complying fund is not:
  - a Commonwealth public sector superannuation scheme in which the taxpayer has a defined benefit interest
  - a constitutionally protected fund (CPF) or other untaxed fund that would not include the taxpayer's contribution in its assessable income under s 295-190, or

  - a superannuation fund that has notified the ATO in the approved form of its election to treat all member contributions to the fund as non-deductible (see below), or the defined benefit interest within the fund as non-deductible, before the start of the income year (s 290-155; ITR97 regs 290-155.01; 290-155.05) (ATO factsheet *How to elect to be non-deductible (or revoke election)*).

- if the taxpayer is under age 18 at end of the income year in which the contribution is made, the taxpayer must have derived income in the year from carrying on a business or from employment-related activities (see "Age-related condition" below)

- the taxpayer must notify the fund trustee or RSA provider in writing that they intend to claim the deduction, and the trustee or RSA provider must acknowledge receipt of the notice (see "Notice requirements" below).

When determining if a fund is an untaxed fund in respect of a contribution (see the first dot point above), amounts that are excluded from the fund's assessable income because of ITAA97 Subdiv 295-D (ie transferring the liability for contributions to a life insurer or PST) are disregarded (s 290-155(2)).

Age-related condition

An individual must satisfy the age-related condition below to qualify for a deduction under s 290-150 for personal superannuation contributions:

- if the person is under 18 years of age at the end of the income year in which the contributions were made — the person must have derived income from the carrying on of a business, or is an employee under the SGAA (see below), and

- in any other case — the person made the contributions before the 28th day after the end of the month in which they turned 75 (ITAA97 s 290-165).

An employee under the SGAA is a common law employee or a person under the extended meaning of employee in the SGAA, such as a person receiving payments for performing functions and duties, or engaging in work and holding an office or appointment), including those doing work of a private or domestic nature for not more than 30 hours per week who would not be employees under the SGAA.

Notice requirements

To qualify for a deduction for the whole or a part of personal contributions, a taxpayer must give a notice in the approved form to the superannuation fund trustee or RSA provider stating his/her intention to claim a deduction for the whole or a part of the contributions covered by the notice, and the trustee must have given the taxpayer an acknowledgment of the notice (ITAA97 ss 290-170(1), 290-175) (ATO approved form).

The notice must be given:

- if the taxpayer has lodged an income tax return for the income year in which the contribution was made on a day before the end of the next income year — before the end of that day, or

- otherwise — before the end of the next income year (*Ariss*; *Johnston*).

Validity of notice and acknowledgment

A notice is not valid in any of the circumstances specified in s 290-170(2) (eg the contribution is covered by an earlier notice or contributions-splitting application).

A trustee or RSA provider is required to acknowledge receipt of a valid notice without delay (normally within 30 days of receipt or by 30 June of the financial year in which the contribution is made) (s 290-170(3)).

The trustee or RSA provider may refuse to acknowledge receipt of a valid notice if the value of the superannuation interest to which the notice relates when the trustee or RSA provider received the notice is less than the tax that would be payable in respect of the contribution (or part of the contribution) if the trustee or provider were to acknowledge receipt of the notice (ITAA97 s 290-170(4)).

Revocation and variation of notice

A taxpayer cannot revoke or withdraw a valid notice in relation to the contribution or a part of the contribution (ITAA97 s 290-180).

A taxpayer can vary a valid notice, but only so as to reduce the amount stated in relation to the contribution (including to nil) (ATO approved form).

A taxpayer cannot vary a valid notice in certain cases, but this restriction does not apply if:

- the taxpayer claimed a deduction for the contribution (or a part of the contribution) and the deduction is not allowable (in whole or in part), and
- the variation reduces the amount stated in relation to the contribution by the amount not allowable as a deduction (s 290-180(3), (4)).

A variation notice is not effective if, when it is made, the taxpayer has ceased to be a member, the fund no longer holds the contribution or has commenced to pay a pension based in whole or in part on the contribution (s 290-180(3A)).

If a fund no longer holds a contribution, or a part of it, because the member has rolled over a part of the superannuation interest held in the fund, a valid deduction notice will be limited to a proportion of the tax free component of the interest that remains in the fund after the roll-over. That proportion is the value of the relevant contribution divided by the tax free component of the interest immediately before the roll-over. An income stream is based in whole or part on the contribution if it is commenced from the superannuation interest to which the contribution was made (TR 2010/1, para 71, 72, 94–102).

▶ Example

Lisa makes a $50,000 personal contribution increasing her interest in her superannuation fund to $200,000.

If she were to commence a pension from the fund using $180,000 of her $200,000 interest before lodging a s 290-170 deduction notice, her fund would have commenced to pay a superannuation income stream based in whole or in part of the contribution. Any deduction notice that Lisa later gives to her fund will be invalid. This is so even if, after contributing the $50,000, Lisa were to commence a pension of only $140,000 leaving the value of her interest in excess of the amount she intended to deduct.

Notices to a successor fund

An individual may give a deduction or variation notice to a successor fund for contributions made to the original superannuation fund (s 290-170(5)). If an individual's account in a superannuation fund is mandatorily transferred to a MySuper product in another complying fund under the SISA, the notice may be given to the transferee fund for the contribution that was made to original fund (s 290-170(6)).

Related tax matters

A deduction for personal superannuation contributions under Subdiv 290-C is limited to an individual's adjusted assessable income for the year (before taking into account the contribution deduction) (ITAA97 s 26-55(2); *Sutton*). The deduction cannot create or increase a loss to be carried forward.

An individual's deductible superannuation contributions are assessable contributions in the hands of the recipient superannuation fund (¶13-125) or RSA provider (¶13-480), and are ''concessional contributions'' under ITAA97 (¶13-775). An individual's concessional contribution that is not allowable as a deduction under Subdiv 290-C is a non-concessional contribution for the year (ITAA97 s 292-90: ¶13-780).

A deduction is personal and is not taken into account in calculating the loss or profit of any partnership of which the individual is a member (ITAA36 s 90).

No deduction is allowed for financing costs (eg interest) incurred on borrowings to finance personal superannuation contributions (ITAA97 s 26-80: ¶16-740).

[AMSG ¶6-300 – ¶6-380; FITR ¶268-420ff; SLP ¶36-460]

¶13-750 Division 293 tax on excess concessional contributions

An individual whose income and relevant concessionally taxed superannuation contributions exceed a prescribed threshold in an income year is liable to pay Division 293 tax at 15% on the excess (ITAA97 Div 293; *Superannuation (Sustaining the Superannuation Contribution Concession) Imposition Act 2012*). Where the tax applies, the individual's concessional contributions exceeding the income threshold are therefore subject to a total tax of 30% (ie 15% contributions tax in the hands of the recipient superannuation fund (¶13-125) plus 15% Division 293 tax in the hands of the individual).

Liability to Division 293 tax

A Division 293 tax liability arises if an individual has taxable contributions for an income year. An individual has ''taxable contributions'' if the sum of the amounts below exceeds the prescribed threshold (see below):

- the individual's ''income for surcharge purposes'' (*less* reportable superannuation contributions) for an income year, and
- the individual's ''low tax contributions'' for the corresponding financial year (these are concessionally taxed contributions: see below).

Where the threshold is exceeded, the individual's taxable contributions are the *lesser* of:

- the amount of the low tax contributions, and
- the amount of the excess over the threshold amount (s 293-20(1)).

The above calculation to determine liability means that an individual who has income exceeding prescribed threshold but does not have low tax contributions is not liable to Division 293 tax.

Division 293 tax threshold

The threshold for liability to Division 293 tax is $250,000 (2017–18 and later years).

Income for surcharge purposes

A broad based concept of income applies to ensure that various forms of income are included in the prescribed threshold and that the tax cannot be reduced or avoided, for example, by entering into salary packaging arrangements.

''Income for surcharge purposes'' is the concept of income used for determining whether an individual is liable to pay Medicare levy surcharge (¶2-335). It comprises the individual's taxable income (disregarding the person's assessable FHSS released amount for the income year but including the net amount on which family trust distribution tax has been paid), reportable superannuation contributions, reportable fringe benefits (¶35-055), and total net investment loss (including both net financial investment loss and net rental property loss), *less* the taxed element of the taxable component of a superannuation lump sum benefit (other than a death benefit) up to the ''low rate cap amount'' (¶14-220) (ITAA97 s 995-1(1)).

The accepted tax treatment is that employment income is derived when the income is actually received irrespective of the period for which the payment occurs (*Blank*; *Re-Tong*). In *DHDF*, where the taxpayer derived employment income in relation to services performed over 4 different income years, the AAT held that the whole of the income received by the taxpayer in 2013–14 was taxable income in that year because it was received in that year even though the amounts related to services performed in previous years.

For the purpose of the Division 293 tax threshold, an individual's income for surcharge purposes is reduced by reportable superannuation contributions to avoid double counting as these contributions are already included in low tax contributions (see below). Reportable superannuation contributions are reportable employer superannuation contributions (¶13-760) and personal superannuation contributions of self-employed persons and other eligible individuals for which a tax deduction is claimed.

Working out low tax contributions

An individual's "low tax contributions" for a financial year is worked out as provided in ITAA97 s 293-30 (the general method), or as modified by the special rules in Subdivs 293-D to 293-F (see below).

The general method applies in the majority of cases, where contributions or allocated amounts are made to accumulation interests in the individual's superannuation fund. Under the general method, an individual's low tax contributions for a financial year are the "low tax contributed amounts" (see below) for the financial year *less* excess concessional contributions for the financial year (if any) (s 293-25).

Special rules modify the general method in respect of:

- individuals with defined benefit interests — for these taxpayers, the individual's low tax contributions are low tax contributed amounts to any accumulation interests, *plus* any defined benefit contributions (see below), *less* any excess concessional contributions (ITAA97 Subdiv 293-D)

- certain State higher level office holders — for these taxpayers, the low tax contributions are low tax contributed amounts *plus* defined benefit contributions (reduced by contributions in respect of constitutionally protected funds that are not made as part of a salary package arrangement), *less* any excess concessional contributions (ITAA97 Subdiv 293-E), and

- certain Commonwealth justices and judges — for these taxpayers, the low tax contributions are low tax contributed amounts *plus* defined benefit contributions (except defined benefit contributions for a defined benefit interest in a superannuation fund established under the *Judges' Pensions Act 1968*), *less* any excess concessional contributions (ITAA97 Subdiv 293-F).

The inclusion of defined benefit contributions in the above cases ensures that individuals with defined benefit interests are treated in a similar way to individuals with accumulation interests. As the actual value of benefits received by an individual from a defined benefit interest is known only when the benefit is paid, the value of the employer financed benefits accruing in a financial year for the interest is an estimate (notional employer contributions) which is used by the Commissioner to assess the individual's liability to Division 293 tax each year. The above rules also ensure that Division 293 tax is not payable by:

- constitutionally protected State higher level office holders in respect of contributions to constitutionally protected funds unless they are salary packaged contributions (as defined in s 293-160) (s 293-145(1)), and

- Commonwealth justices and judges in respect of contributions to a defined benefit interest established under the *Judges' Pensions Act 1968* (s 293-190(1)) (*Watson*: no exemption for Presidential Member of the AIRC, as s 63(2) of the *Workplace Relations Act 1996* does not equate the position of a AIRC Presidential Member with that of a judge of the Federal Court).

An individual's "defined benefit contributions" in a financial year in respect of a defined benefit interest has the meaning given by regulation (ITAA97 ss 293-115(1); 293-150; 293-195).

The methods to determine the defined benefit contributions for an individual with a defined benefit interest for the purposes of s 293-115(1) are prescribed by ITR97 Subdiv 293-DA (regs 293-115.05 to 293-115.20; Sch 1AA) based on:

- whether the individual is an "accruing member" or "non-accruing member" (as defined in reg 293-115.05(2)) of a superannuation fund, and
- in the case of an accruing member, whether the individual's defined benefit interest is a "funded benefit interest" (as defined in reg 293-115.15(2)) (see table below).

Defined benefit interests in most private sector funds are fully funded and, therefore, are funded benefit interests.

For the financial year, the individual is:	Defined benefit contributions in respect of the individual's defined benefit interest in the fund is:
• a non-accruing member (reg 293-115.10)	• nil (reg 293-115.10(2))
• an accruing member with funded benefit interests (reg 293-115.15)	• the individual's notional taxed contributions for the year in respect of the interest (reg 293-115.15(3)) (for notional taxed contributions, see ITAA97 s 291-170 and ITR97 Subdiv 292-D and Sch 1A, disregarding ITTPA Subdiv 291-C)
• an accruing member with other interests (reg 293-115.20)	• the amount worked out using the method in Sch 1AA of the ITR97 (reg 293-115.20(2))

The Division 293 tax threshold ($250,000 from 2017–18 onwards) also applies to members of defined benefits schemes and constitutionally protected funds who are subject to Division 293 tax. Also, the notional (estimated) and actual employer contributions are included in the concessional contributions cap for members of unfunded defined benefits schemes and constitutionally protected funds, and these members can enter into salary sacrifice arrangements like members of accumulation funds. Grandfathering arrangements (¶13-775) apply to determine the concessional contributions for defined benefit interests of individuals who were members of a funded defined benefits scheme as at 12 May 2009.

Low tax contributed amounts

"Low tax contributed amounts" are broadly concessional contributions (as defined in ITAA97 s 291-25: ¶13-775). They include contributions to tax-exempt constitutionally protected funds that would otherwise be concessional contributions, but not notional taxed contributions for defined benefit interests (s 293-30).

For an individual who only has contributions to accumulation interests (none of which is in a constitutionally protected fund), the individual's low tax contributed amounts for a financial year is the amount of concessional contributions for the financial year (eg employer contributions, including compulsory SG contributions and salary sacrificed amounts, and the individual's deductible personal contributions).

To ensure that employees are not disadvantaged where employers benefit from the SG amnesty (¶39-505), any contributions made by the Commissioner and employer offset contributions for the purposes of the SG amnesty are not included in the calculation of an employee's low tax contributed amounts and therefore will not attract Division 293 tax (s 293-30(4)(d)).

Steps to calculate an individual's Division 293 tax liability

1. Add the individual's income for surcharge purposes and low tax contributions (ie low tax contributed amounts *less* excess concessional contributions, if any).
2. Compare the amount from Step 1 to the prescribed threshold to determine the excess above the threshold.
3. Compare the low tax contributions amount to the amount from Step 2 — the *lesser* of the 2 amounts is the individual's taxable contributions.
4. The Division 293 tax payable is 15% of the taxable contributions amount.

▶ Example

In 2020–21, Anna has income for surcharge purposes of $293,000 and low tax contributions of $25,000. The sum of these 2 amounts is $318,000.

When the $318,000 is compared to the $250,000 threshold in 2020–21 (see Step 2), there is an excess of $68,000.

Anna's low tax contributions ($25,000) is compared to the excess amount ($68,000). The *lesser* amount of $25,000 is Anna's taxable contributions (see Step 3).

For 2020–21, Anna is liable to pay Division 293 tax of $3,750 (ie $25,000 × 0.15).

Assessment of Division 293 tax

Division 293 tax is not subject to the self-assessment regime (TAA Sch 1 s 155-15(1)).

In each year of income, the Commissioner makes assessments of Division 293 tax for the year (TAA Sch 1 s 155-5), based on an individual's tax return and information provided by superannuation providers under the TAA (¶39-530). The Commissioner will also make a determination in relation to assessed Division 293 tax that specifies how much of the tax is attributable to a defined benefit interest and is deferred to a debt account (see below).

An individual's assessed Division 293 tax is:

- due and payable within 21 days after the notice of assessment is issued, to the extent the tax relates to an accumulation superannuation interest (ITAA97 s 293-65), or
- deferred to a debt account maintained by the Commissioner for later payment to the extent the tax relates to a defined benefit interest (see below).

Assessed Division 293 tax deferred to a debt account

The Commissioner must make a determination specifying the amount ascertained as being the extent to which an individual's assessed Division 293 tax for an income year is defined benefit tax attributable to a superannuation interest (TAA Sch 1 s 133-10). The "defined benefit tax" for an income year is worked out in accordance with the formula in s 131-15. For individuals with more than one defined benefit interest, the defined benefit tax for the year is attributable to each such interest in proportion to the defined benefit contributions for the interest for the financial year (s 133-20).

The Commissioner keeps a debt account for individuals whose assessed Division 293 tax is deferred to a debt account for the superannuation interest, and debits the debt account for the amount of assessed Division 293 tax that is deferred.

An individual may make voluntary payments for the purpose of reducing the amount by which a debt account for a superannuation interest is in debit (s 133-70). The ATO must inform a superannuation fund if the ATO starts to keep a debt account for members with a superannuation interest in the fund (s 133-75).

When is a debt account discharge liability payable?

An individual is liable to pay the amount of their debt account discharge liability for a superannuation interest if the "end benefit" (as defined in s 133-130) for the interest becomes payable. The liability arises at the time the end benefit becomes payable or, if the end benefit is a superannuation death benefit, just before the individual dies (s 133-105).

The amount of an individual's debt account discharge liability for a superannuation interest is due and payable at the end of 21 days, after the day on which the end benefit for the superannuation interest is paid (s 133-110). The "debt account discharge liability" is the amount by which the debt account is in debit at the time the end benefit for the superannuation interest becomes payable (s 133-120).

Releasing superannuation money to pay Division 293 tax

Different TAA rules apply for releasing money from an individual's superannuation interest as below:

- TAA Sch 1 Div 131 – which allows an individual who has received a Division 293 tax assessment to request the Commissioner to release an amount from the individual's superannuation interests (¶13-755), and
- TAA Sch 1 Div 135 – which allows the Commissioner to issue an individual with a release authority for money to be released from a superannuation plan to pay an individual's debt account discharge liability (ie a liability concerning a defined benefit superannuation interest for which a debt account is kept and an end benefit has become payable from that superannuation interest, see above).

The amount of a Div 315 release entitlement is the "debt account discharge liability" (see above) (TAA Sch 1 s 135-10).

An individual may only give a release authority issued for a debt account discharge liability to the superannuation provider that holds the defined benefit interest to which the debt relates. This may be given within 120 days after the date of the release authority (TAA Sch 1 s 135-40). A provider that receives a release authority must pay the release amount (as specified in s 135-85) to the Commissioner within 30 days of receiving the release authority (TAA Sch 1 ss 135-75, 135-95).

Tax treatment of payments under a release authority

An amount paid to the Commissioner in accordance with a release authority is non-assessable non-exempt income to the extent that the amount released does not exceed the release entitlement amount (ITAA97 s 303-20). Any excess amount released is assessable income (ITAA97 304-20).

The proportioning rule (¶14-130) does not apply to a payment made under an ATO release authority, ie the provider is not required to calculate either the tax free component or taxable component of the superannuation benefit (TAA Sch 1 s 135-100).

Related tax matters

Payments of Division 293 tax are not deductible for income tax purposes (ITAA97 s 26-98).

General interest charge (GIC) is payable on an amount of Division 293 tax that remains unpaid after its due date for each day the unpaid amount remains outstanding (ITAA97 ss 293-65; 293-70; 293-75). The Commissioner may remit the GIC under the existing remission guidelines. GIC is discussed further in ¶29-510.

SIC does not apply to an amount of Division 293 tax arising as a result of an amended assessment that is deferred to a debt account as the amount has not become due and payable (s 280-102B(2)).

The Commissioner may remit the SIC under the existing remission guidelines. The SIC is discussed further in ¶25-450.

Former temporary residents who receive a departing Australia superannuation payment (DASP) are entitled to a refund of Division 293 tax that they have paid (ITAA97 Subdiv 293-G). This treatment reflects that any concessional tax treatment of their superannuation contributions has been removed by the final withholding tax on DASPs (¶14-390). A refund is not available for assessed Division 293 tax for a period when an individual is an Australian resident (but not a temporary resident) (ITAA97 s 293-235(3)).

[AMSG ¶6-400ff; FITR ¶269-500ff, ¶977-455, ¶977-457; SLP ¶36-480ff]

¶13-755 Releasing superannuation money under Div 131 release authority

From 1 July 2018, TAA Sch 1 Div 131 ss 131-5 to 131-75 provide for the release of an individual's superannuation interests under an ATO release authority where the individual has received any of the following:

- a notice of assessment for Division 293 tax (¶13-750)
- an excess concessional contributions (ECC) determination (¶13-777)
- an excess non-concessional contributions determination (ENCC) (¶13-780), or
- an FHSS determination under the First Home Super Saver (FHSS) Scheme (¶13-790).

The Div 131 regime replaced the different processes for releasing superannuation money under an ATO authority previously provided by TAA Sch 1 former Div 96 (for ECC and ENCC determinations) and by Div 135 (for Division 293 tax assessments), subject to certain application provisions (Treasury Laws Amendment (Fair and Sustainable Superannuation) Act 2016 (Act No 81 of 2016), Sch 10 Pt 1 Div 3 items 40 to 54). The Div 131 regime does not affect the rules for releasing superannuation money under an ATO release authority in relation to Division 293 debt account discharge liabilities under Div 135 (¶13-750).

Division 131 release authority process

The release authority process is summarised below.

- Request for issue of a release authority — Individuals who receive an ECC or ENCC determination or a notice of assessment for Division 293 tax or an FHSS determination may request the Commissioner, in the approved form, to release certain amounts from their superannuation.

  This request must be made within 60 days of the issue of the determination or notice (or such further time as the Commissioner may allow) (s 131-5).

  The total amount that an individual can request to be released is:

  - the amount of the assessed Division 293 tax liability
  - up to 85% of the contributions stated in the ECC determination
  - the ''total release amount'' stated in the ENCC determination (ie the full amount of the excess contributions plus 85% of associated earnings, or nil (TAA Sch 1 s 97-25(1)(c)), or
  - the FHSS maximum release amount stated in the FHSS determination (s 131-10).

- Commissioner's obligations — Upon receiving a valid request, the Commissioner must issue a release authority to each superannuation provider that holds a superannuation interest identified in the request (s 131-15).

  The Commissioner *may* issue a release authority to a superannuation provider without a request from an individual in the following cases:

  – the individual is liable for ENCC tax

  – the individual is liable for assessed Division 293 tax and has neither paid the tax nor released the amount of the tax from superannuation within 60 days of the issue of the notice, or

  – the individual has been issued with an ENCC determination and has not made a request under s 131-5 to the Commissioner within 60 days of the issue of the determination (or allowed more time by the Commissioner) (s 131-15(2)-(4)).

- Superannuation provider's obligations — A superannuation provider issued with a release authority under s 131-15 must pay the *lesser* of the amount stated in the release authority and the sum of the "maximum available release amount" (s 131-45) for each of the superannuation interest held by the provider for the individual (except defined benefit interests) (s 131-35). An administrative penalty applies for non-compliance (TAA Sch 1 s 288-95(3)).

  A superannuation provider may choose to voluntarily comply with a release authority with respect to defined benefit interests if this is practical in the circumstances and is consistent with the fund rules (s 131-40).

  A superannuation provider must pay the Commissioner within 10 business days of the issue of the release authority (or such further time as the Commissioner may allow) (see "Temporary timeframe extension" below).

  The provider must also notify the Commissioner in the approved form of the payment (or non-payment) in the same timeframe (s 131-50). An administrative penalty applies for non-compliance (TAA Sch 1 s 286-75(1)).

  The Commissioner must notify an individual of any payment made or non-payment by a provider in relation to the release authority within the required time (s 131-55).

- Character of amounts received under a release authority — An amount released from superannuation because of a release authority is generally non-assessable non-exempt income (ITAA97 s 303-15). The payment is exempt from the proportioning rule (TAA Sch 1 s 131-75).

  Amounts released to the Commissioner are generally credited against an individual's tax liability and any excess is refunded to the individual. Interest is payable for any undue delay in making a refund (PS LA 2011/23) .

  Amounts released in relation to Division 293 tax liabilities that are deferred to a debt account are treated as a voluntary payment towards the debt account (TAA Sch 1 s 131-65(3), 131-70).

Temporary timeframe extension

The timeframe for the return of and payment under streamlined release authorities has been temporarily extended from 10 to 20 business days, effective from 1 July 2018 (Release authorities). The extension applies to release authorities for excess contributions and Division 293 tax liabilities, not for FHSS determinations which need to be actioned within 10 business days.

The extension applies until the ATO digitises its release authority process (ie via SuperStream: ¶13-800) after which the timeframe will return to the legislated 10 business days.

ATO guidelines on release authorities

ATO information on the various kinds of release authorities and interest payments may be found in Fact Sheet *Release authorities* and in PS LA 2011/23.

¶13-760 Government co-contributions

The government makes co-contributions to match the personal superannuation contributions made by eligible individual taxpayers to complying superannuation funds and RSAs (*Superannuation (Government Co-contribution for Low Income Earners) Act 2003* (CCA) and Regulations (CCR)).

The maximum co-contribution payable in a year of income is $500 for taxpayers whose total income is below a lower income threshold. The maximum co-contribution amount is reduced by 3.333 cents for each dollar by which the taxpayer's income for the income year exceeds the lower income threshold so that the co-contribution is fully phased out when the taxpayer's income reaches or exceeds an upper income threshold (see "Lower and higher income thresholds" and "Calculation of government co-contribution" below) (CCA s 10(1C)).

Eligibility for government co-contribution

A person is entitled to government co-contribution for an income year if the following conditions in CCA s 6(1) are met:

- the person makes one or more eligible personal superannuation contributions (see below) during the income year
- 10% or more of the person's total income (see "10% total income test" below) for the income year is attributable to either or both of the following:
  - (i) the person engaging in activities covered by CCA s 6(2) (eg holding an office or appointment, engaging in work, or doing acts or things) that result in the person being treated as an employee under SGAA (including certain workers who are non-SGAA employees, see below), or
  - (ii) the person carrying on a business
- the person's *total income* for the income year is less than the higher income threshold for the year (see "Co-contribution payable — total income threshold test" below)
- an income tax return for the person for the income year is lodged
- the person's non-concessional contributions for the financial year corresponding to the income year do not exceed the non-concessional contributions cap for the year ($100,000 in 2017–18 to 2020–21: ¶13-780)
- immediately before the start of the financial year, the person's total superannuation balance (¶14-050) is less than the general transfer balance cap for the year ($1.6 million in 2017–18 to 2020–21: ¶14-320) (CCA s 6(1)(da), (db)).
- the person is less than 71 years old at the end of the income year, and
- the person:
  - is not the holder of a temporary visa under the *Migration Act 1958* at any time in the income year, or
  - at all times when holding such a temporary visa during the income year, is a New Zealand citizen or the holder of a visa prescribed for the purposes of s 20AA(2) of the *Superannuation (Unclaimed Money and Lost Members) Act 1999*.

For the purposes of the employee activity test (see the second dot point above), a person who is engaged in the specified activities in s 6(2)(a) is taken to be an employee, even though the person is not an employee under the SGAA because they are paid to do work wholly or principally of a domestic or private nature for not more than 30 hours a week (CCA s 6(2)(b); ¶39-020).

A person is not required to apply for co-contribution. The Commissioner is responsible for determining if co-contribution is payable based on the person's income tax return, information about contributions provided by superannuation funds to the ATO and other information as requested by the Commissioner (CCA ss 13; 14). Any co-contribution due will be paid for the benefit of the person in accordance with CCA s 15(1) and CCR reg 5.

Eligible personal superannuation contributions

A contribution made by a person is an "eligible personal superannuation contribution" if it is made to a complying superannuation fund or RSA to obtain superannuation benefits for the person (or in the event of the person's death, for dependants of the person), to the extent that it is not a deductible personal contributions (CCA s 7(2)). Certain personal contributions cannot be an eligible contribution. These include a roll-over superannuation benefit (¶14-450), an amount transferred from a KiwiSaver scheme (¶13-380), a superannuation lump sum paid from a foreign superannuation fund (¶14-420) or an amount transferred from a scheme mentioned in ITAA97 s 290-5(c) (these are schemes which are not and never have been Australian superannuation funds or foreign superannuation funds) (CCA s 7(1)(c)).

Other contributions which are not eligible for the co-contribution include employer contributions and salary sacrifice contributions, being employer contributions (¶13-710), and contributions made for a spouse (¶13-770).

10% total income test

A person's "total income" in a year of income means the sum of the person's:

- assessable income for the income year (disregarding the person's assessable FHSS released amount for the year: ¶13-790), and
- reportable fringe benefits total and, from the 2009–10 year of income onwards, the total of the person's reportable employer superannuation contributions (see below) (CCA s 8(1)).

For the above purposes, any excess concessional contributions that are included in the person's assessable income under ITAA97 s 291-15(a) (¶13-777) for the income year are disregarded (s 8(1A)).

When determining whether 10% or more of a person's total income is earned from employment or carrying on a business, or both, the total income is not reduced by the deductions that result from carrying on a business (s 8(3)) (see example below). The gross total income concept is used to ensure that self-employed individuals with low incomes or low profit margins are not disadvantaged by arbitrarily failing the test.

For the purposes of s 6(1)(b)(ii) (see above), a beneficiary's share of the net income of a trust estate that carries on a business is not included in the beneficiary's total income from carrying on a business (ID 2007/195). The beneficiaries of a trust that carries on a business are not themselves carrying on a business, even if the beneficiary is also one of the trustees of trust (*Doherty*).

Reportable fringe benefits total and reportable employer superannuation contributions

A "reportable fringe benefits total" refers to the amount that an employer reports on an employee's payment summary as the grossed-up taxable value of certain fringe benefits provided to the employee during the FBT year (other than excluded fringe benefits such as employer superannuation contributions), where the value of the benefits provided exceeds $2,000 (¶35-055).

A "reportable employer superannuation contribution" for an individual in an income year refers to an amount that has been, is, or will be, contributed in respect of the income year by the individual's employer (or an associate of the employer) to a superannuation fund or an RSA for the individual's benefit as specified by TAA Sch 1 s 16-182.

Additional contributions to cover the cost of premiums for insurance cover for an employee who has chosen, by default or otherwise, a superannuation fund to which the employer must contribute under the SGAA choice of fund rules (¶39-260) are reportable employer superannuation contributions (ID 2010/112).

Co-contribution payable — "total income" threshold test

The definition of "total income" (see above) is used for determining whether an amount of co-contribution is payable. For this purpose, the person's total income is reduced by amounts for which the person is entitled to a deduction as a result of carrying on a business (s 8(2)). These deductions do not include work-related employee deductions or deductions that are available to eligible individuals (including the self-employed) for their personal superannuation contributions. That is, a net income concept is used for individuals who carry on a business. The use of the net income concept is to ensure that self-employed individuals with high gross business receipts do not arbitrarily exceed the co-contribution income threshold.

▶ Example

Joan, a self-employed person in 2020–21, has gross business receipts of $43,000, business deductions of $41,500, and other personal investment income of $15,000.

She is entitled to a government co-contribution for her personal contributions because the percentage of gross income from employment or carrying on a business is 74% of her gross total income (ie $43,000 / ($43,000 + $15,000)), and the net income for co-contribution threshold purposes is $16,500 (ie $43,000 + $15,000 – $41,500) which is below the 2020–21 lower income threshold (see ¶42-330).

Lower and higher income thresholds

The income thresholds for eligibility to co-contribution are set out in ¶42-330. They are indexed annually (CCA s 10A(2), (3)).

Calculation of government co-contribution

The matching rate of government co-contribution is 50% of the amount of a taxpayer's eligible personal superannuation contributions made during the year (CCA s 9(1)(d)).

An income test and maximum amount applies so that the co-contribution amount payable cannot not exceed the maximum amount worked out using the table below (s 10(1C)).

Person's total income for the income year is:	Maximum co-contribution amount is:
the lower income threshold or less	$500
more than the lower income threshold but less than the higher income threshold	$500 reduced by 3.333 cents for each dollar by which the person's total income exceeds the lower income threshold
more than the higher income threshold	$0

▶ Example

In 2020–21, Alison who has an employment income of $45,000 makes eligible personal contributions of $2,000 to a complying superannuation fund. As her income of $45,000 exceeds the 2020–21 lower income threshold of $39,837 by $5,163, the maximum co-contribution amount is reduced by the income test to $328, as calculated below:

$500 – [($45,000 – $39,837) × 3.333%] = $500 – [$5,163 × 0.03333] = $500 – $172 = $328

The amount of co-contribution payable may be subject to adjustments as applicable (CCA s 10(2)).

(1) *Minimum government co-contribution.* If the co-contribution amount for an income year is less than $20, this amount is increased to $20 (CCA s 11).

(2) *Interest for late payment.* If the Commissioner does not pay the co-contribution in full on or before the co-contribution payment date, the co-contribution amount is increased by interest (CCA s 12). The interest forms part of the actual co-contribution and is treated for all purposes in the same manner.

(3) *Interest for underpayment.* If the Commissioner does not pay an underpaid amount of co-contributions in full on or before the payment date for the underpaid amount, or an underpayment arose because of an administrative error, the co-contribution amount is increased by interest (CCA ss 21; 22). For an underpayment that is less than $5, the co-contribution amount is increased by the difference between $5 and the underpaid amount (CCA s 23).

The rate of interest to be applied to late payments or underpayments of co-contributions is the base interest rate worked out under TAA s 8AAD (CCA s 12(2)) (¶28-170).

Tax treatment of co-contribution

Government co-contributions are not subject to tax when received by the superannuation fund or RSA (ie they are not assessable contributions: ¶13-125). They are also not non-concessional contributions (¶13-780). They form part of the contributions segment of the tax free component when paid as a superannuation benefit (¶14-140) and are tax-free. Earnings on co-contribution amounts are taxed like any other earnings in the superannuation fund or RSA, ie they form part of the taxable component of a superannuation benefit (¶14-150).

Co-contributions are preserved benefits in the fund or RSA like other contributions under the SIS or RSA Regulations.

[AMSG ¶6-700]

¶13-765 Low income superannuation tax offset

An individual who has an adjusted taxable income below $37,000 in a year may be entitled to a low income superannuation tax offset (LISTO) for their concessional contributions which are made to a complying superannuation fund or RSA (*Superannuation (Government Co-contribution for Low Income Earners) Act 2003*, Pt 2A ss 12B to 12G).

The LISTO amount is 15% of the individual's concessional contributions for the year up to a maximum of $500, and is non-refundable.

The purpose of the LISTO is to compensate low income individuals for the 15% contributions tax on the individual's concessional contributions (eg employer contributions and deductible personal contributions: ¶13-125) as the contributions tax can otherwise mean that low income individuals are taxed at a higher rate on concessional contributions than if they had received the contributions as salary or wages.

The ATO determines an individual's entitlement to the LISTO, based on information provided by superannuation providers and other tax information available to the ATO on the individual.

The general administrative machinery provisions applicable to government co-contributions (¶13-760) also apply to the LISTO (CCA s 12B). For example, the ATO may pay the LISTO to a superannuation fund, an RSA, an individual or an individual's legal personal representative, or a Superannuation Holding Accounts Special Account in a similar manner as for co-contribution payments.

LISTO eligibility conditions

An individual is entitled to the LISTO in an income year if the following conditions in CCA s 12C(1) are met:

- the person's *concessional* contributions for the financial year that corresponds to the income year are for a financial year on or after 1 July 2017
- the person's adjusted taxable income for the year (see below) does not exceed $37,000
- 10% or more of the person's total income for the income year is attributable to the person's employment activities or the person carrying on a business, or both (this condition is the same as that for government co-contribution under s 6(1)(b): see "10% total income test" in ¶13-760)
- the person is not the holder of a temporary visa under the *Migration Act 1958* at any time in the income year or, when holding such a temporary visa, is a New Zealand citizen or the holder of a visa prescribed for the purposes of s 20AA(2) of the *Superannuation (Unclaimed Money and Lost Members) Act 1999* (this condition is the same as that for government co-contribution under s 6(1)(f): ¶13-760).

There is no age test for the LISTO eligibility, unlike the government co-contribution which is restricted to individuals under age 71 years (¶13-760).

A person's "adjusted taxable income" (ATI) in an income year means sum of taxable income, adjusted fringe benefits total (as defined in ITAA36 s 6(1), this is the taxable value of fringe benefits provided to the individual during the FBT year), foreign income that is not taxable in Australia, total net investment loss (as defined in ITAA97 s 995-1(1), this is the amount by which deductions attributable to financial investments and rental property exceed the gross income from financial investments and rental property), tax-free pensions or benefits (not including superannuation income stream benefits that are tax-free), and reportable superannuation contributions (as defined in ITAA97 s 995-1(1): ¶13-760), *less* any deductible child maintenance expenditure for that year (s 12C(1)(b)).

Commissioner may use estimates to determine eligibility

An estimation process is used by the Commissioner to determine a person's LISTO eligibility in an income year where, 12 months after the end of the income year, the Commissioner reasonably believes there is insufficient information to decide whether the person has met all the eligibility conditions in s 12C(1) (see above) (s 12C(2)). For example, this process may be used to determine the LISTO entitlement for eligible low income earners who did not lodge a tax return for the year (eg because their taxable income is below the tax-free threshold).

What is considered insufficient information is at the discretion of the Commissioner, subject to the rules below:

- when estimating whether an individual's ATI exceeds $37,000, the Commissioner may treat the individual as having total deductions of $300 for the relevant income year (unless it has information to the contrary), and

- when deciding if an individual is engaged in employment-related activities, the Commissioner is not required to determine that the individual engaged in those activities during the relevant income year in which the contribution was made, unlike under the co-contribution eligibility determination process (s 12C(2)–(5)).

Concessional contributions

A person's concessional contributions include employer contribution, deductible personal contributions, salary sacrifice contributions, allocations from a fund's reserves, and notional taxed contributions for individuals with a defined benefit interest (CCA s 12C(1)(a)) (¶13-775). The LISTO may therefore be payable in relation to an amount that is not an actual contribution made.

In relation to defined benefit schemes:

- LISTO is payable to eligible members of funded defined schemes to the extent that the member receives concessional contributions (''notional taxed contributions'') in the year, and
- LISTO is not payable where there has been no ''taxed'' concessional contribution made (eg for members of fully unfunded defined benefit schemes or constitutionally protected funds as the member contributions in these funds are taxed at the benefit phase, rather than at the contribution phase).

LISTO amount

The LISTO amount payable in a year is based on 15% of the person's concessional contributions for the year, subject to a maximum amount of $500 and a minimum amount of $10 (an entitlement of less than $10 is rounded up to $10) (s 12E(2)). For this purpose, the following are disregarded:

- contributions to a constitutionally protected fund, and
- the amounts by which a person's defined benefit contributions for the financial year in respect of a defined benefit interest exceed notional taxed contributions (ITAA97 ss 291-370(1)(a) and (c)); 12E(3)).

The overpayments rule in s 24 and underpayments rule in s 19 do not apply for amounts under $10 (s 12E(3), (4)).

Related tax matters

The LISTO is not included in the assessable income of the superannuation provider to which it is paid (¶13-125).

When a superannuation benefit is paid to a person, the LISTO forms part of the contributions segment (tax free component) of the benefit (¶14-140) and is tax-free.

[AMSG ¶6-770]

¶13-770 Tax offset — contributions for spouse

An individual taxpayer is entitled to a tax offset in each year of income for contributions made to a complying superannuation fund or RSA for the purpose of providing superannuation benefits for his/her spouse (or the spouse's SIS dependants in the event of the spouse's death) if:

- the taxpayer and the spouse were Australian residents at the time the contributions were made
- the taxpayer has not deducted and cannot deduct an amount for the contributions under ITAA97 s 290-60 (¶13-710), and

- the total of the spouse's assessable income, disregarding the spouse's assessable FHSS released amount for the income year (¶13-790), reportable fringe benefits total and reportable employer superannuation contributions for the income year is less than $40,000 for 2017–18 and later years (ITAA97 s 290-230(1), (2)).

The spouse contributions tax offset is not available in certain circumstances (see "Compliance with other caps" and "Additional conditions relating to taxpayer's spouse" below).

Certain amounts that are rolled over or transferred to a superannuation fund as a contribution, including a transfer from a KiwiSaver scheme (¶13-380), do not qualify for the tax offset (ITAA97 s 290-5; ITTPA s 290-10).

The meaning of "reportable fringe benefits total" and "reportable employer superannuation contributions" is discussed in ¶13-760.

The contributing spouse is not subject to a work or age test. If the spouse for whom the contributions are made is under age 65, spouse contributions may be accepted by the superannuation fund or RSA without restrictions. If the spouse is between age 65 and 70 (or 74 for contributions made from 1 July 2020), the spouse must satisfy a work test for spouse contributions to be accepted and if the spouse is not under age 70 (or 75 for contributions made from 1 July 2020), spouse contributions cannot be accepted (¶13-825).

If a taxpayer is entitled to the tax offset, the taxpayer may, with the consent of the spouse, quote the spouse's TFN to the superannuation fund or RSA provider to which the contributions are made (ITAA97 s 290-240).

Compliance with other caps

A taxpayer is not entitled to a spouse contributions tax offset in an income year if:

- the taxpayer's spouse has exceeded his/her non-concessional contributions cap for the year (¶13-780), or

- before the start of the year, the taxpayer's spouse has a total superannuation balance (¶14-050) that is equal to or exceeds the general transfer balance cap for the year (¶14-320) (s 290-230(4A)).

Additional conditions relating to taxpayer's spouse

A taxpayer is not entitled to a spouse contributions tax offset if:

- the taxpayer is living separately and apart from his/her spouse on a permanent basis at the time of contribution (s 290-230(3)), or

- the contribution is made for the benefit of a non-member spouse in satisfaction of his/her entitlement of a superannuation interest in the fund under the family law (s 290-230(4)).

A "spouse" of a person includes another person (whether of the same sex or a different sex) with whom the person is in a registered relationship (prescribed for the purposes of s 2E of the *Acts Interpretation Act 1901*), or another person who, although not legally married to the person, lives with the person on a genuine domestic basis in a relationship as a couple (ITAA97 s 995-1(1) definition of "spouse": ¶14-270).

A taxpayer who is the employer of his/her spouse may be entitled to claim a deduction for the contributions under s 290-60 (¶13-710), in which case the taxpayer is not entitled to the tax offset.

Calculating amount of tax offset

An individual's tax offset amount in a year for making spouse contributions is calculated as 18% of the *lesser* of:

- $3,000 *reduced* by the amount (if any) by which total income of the individual's spouse exceeds $37,000, and
- the sum of the spouse contributions made by the individual in the income year (ITAA97 s 290-235(1)(a)).

More than one spouse

If a taxpayer satisfies the eligibility conditions in relation to more than one spouse in a year, the offset is the *lesser* of: (a) the sum of the offset entitlements for each spouse; and (b) $540 (s 290-235(2)).

Related tax matters

A taxpayer's tax offset for spouse contributions (including the sum of other tax offsets) can only reduce the amount of income tax otherwise payable by the taxpayer to nil. A refund of excess tax offset for spouse contributions is not allowed (ITAA97 s 4-10(3)).

Spouse contributions which qualify for the offset are not assessable contributions of the recipient fund (¶13-125, ¶13-480), and are counted as the spouse's non-concessional contributions (¶13-780).

[AMSG ¶6-800; FITR ¶268-490ff; SLP ¶36-880]

¶13-775 Excess concessional contributions

An excess concessional contributions charge regime applies to an individual's concessional contributions in each financial year (ITAA97 Div 291; TAA Sch 1 Div 96).

An individual's excess concessional contributions are included in assessable income and are taxed at marginal tax rates, with a tax offset equal to 15% of the excess contributions. An individual is also liable to pay excess concessional contributions charge for having excess concessional contributions for the year (¶13-777).

Concessional contributions are generally contributions which are included in the assessable income of the recipient superannuation funds and are subject to "contributions tax" in the fund (see below).

Excess concessional contributions arise in a financial year if the amount of an individual's concessional contributions for the year exceeds the concessional contributions cap for the year (ITAA97 s 291-20(1)).

The concessional contributions cap amount from 2017–18 onwards is $25,000 for all individuals, regardless of their age. Individuals who have unused cap amounts from previous years are permitted to make "catch-up" contributions (see below) from 1 July 2018.

Eligible individuals with SG contributions from multiple employers may apply to the Commissioner to opt-out of the SG regime in respect of one or more employers so as to avoid unintentionally breaching the annual concessional contributions cap (¶39-030).

What are concessional contributions?

An individual's concessional contributions for a financial year in relation to an accumulation interest in a superannuation fund is the sum of:

- contributions made in the financial year to a complying superannuation in respect of the individual, where the contributions are included in the assessable income of the recipient superannuation fund or, by way of a roll-over superannuation benefit, in the assessable income of a complying superannuation fund in the circumstances mentioned in s 290-170(5) (about transfers to a successor fund) or s 290-170(6) (about transfers to a MySuper product in another fund) (subject to certain exceptions and modification, see "Assessable contributions" below) (s 291-25(2)), and

- an amount allocated for the individual in accordance with the conditions specified in the regulations, with some exceptions (see "Reserve allocations treated as concessional contributions and exceptions" below) (s 291-25(3)).

The meaning of concessional contributions is modified for defined benefit interests (see below).

Assessable contributions

The types of contributions that are included in a superannuation fund's assessable income under s 291-25(2) (see the first dot point above) are generally employer contributions, deductible personal contributions, roll-over superannuation benefits under ITAA97 Subdiv 295-C (¶13-125).

Also, for the purposes of s 291-25(2), certain contributions which are otherwise not assessable contributions of the recipient fund, as below, are specifically included as concessional contributions in respect of the individual (s 291-25(4)):

(i) contributions received by a superannuation fund which are transferred to an investment vehicle (eg a life insurance company or a PST), and

(ii) contributions which are reduced by the application of pre-1 July 88 funding credits or anticipated funding credits (ITAA97 ss 295-260 to 295-270; ¶13-125).

Where there are special circumstances, an individual may apply to the Commissioner to disregard or reallocate to another year all or a part of the individual's concessional contributions (and/or non-concessional contributions) in a year (ITAA97 s 291-465) (¶13-785).

Transfers from a family trust to a superannuation fund were held to be concessional contributions in the absence of clear evidence that they were the beneficiary's personal contributions (*Jendahl Investments Pty Ltd (as trustee for the Jensen Superannuation Fund)*).

Reserve allocations treated as concessional contributions and exceptions

Subject to an exception, an amount which is allocated by a superannuation fund under SISR Div 7.2, and which is assessable income of the fund under ITAA97 Subdiv 295-C, is a concessional contribution (ITR97 reg 291-25.01(2)). Under SISR Div 7.2, a fund that receives a contribution in a month in relation to an accumulation interest must allocate the contribution to a fund member within 28 days after the end of the month, or within such longer period as is reasonable in the circumstances (SISR reg 7.08(2)). The exception is where the contribution is made to a constitutionally protected fund, or the amount is assessable contributions because it is a roll-over superannuation benefit or a transfer from a foreign superannuation fund (s 291-25(2)(c); reg 291-25.01(3)).

A contribution made in one financial year (year 1), which is allocated under SISR Div 7.2 to an accumulation interest of a fund member with effect from a date in the subsequent financial year (year 2) is included in the member's concessional contributions for year 2 as an amount covered under s 291-25(3). In such a case, the amount is not also included in the member's concessional contributions for year 1 as a contribution covered under s 291-25(2) (TD 2013/22). This is to avoid double counting of the concessional contribution — once under s 291-25(2) when received by the fund, and a second time under s 291-25(3) when allocated to the member.

▶ Example

Harry, a member of a retail superannuation fund.

He makes a personal contribution of $20,000 which is received by his fund on 30 June 2020. The fund trustees apply this amount to an unallocated contributions account established in accordance with the governing rules of the fund. On 2 July 2020, the trustees allocate the amount of $20,000 to Harry's member account in the fund with effect from that date.

Harry's contribution is covered by a valid and acknowledged notice under ITAA97 s 290-170 of his intention to deduct the amount of the contribution.

The $20,000 contribution is included in the amount of Harry's concessional contributions for the 2020–21 financial year as an amount covered under s 291-25(3).

An amount allocated from a reserve to a member is treated as a concessional contribution of the member except:

- an amount allocated on a fair and reasonable basis to all fund members, or to a class of members to which the reserve relates, where the allocated amount for the financial year is less than 5% of the member's interest at the time of allocation, or
- an amount allocated from a reserve used solely for the purpose of discharging superannuation income stream liabilities that are currently payable, and any of the following applies:
  - the amount has been allocated to satisfy a pension liability paid during the financial year
  - on the commutation of the income stream (except as a result of the death of the primary beneficiary), the amount is allocated to the recipient of the income stream, to commence another income stream, as soon as practicable
  - on the commutation of the income stream as a result of the death of the primary beneficiary, the amount is allocated to a death benefits dependant to discharge liabilities for a superannuation income stream benefit that is payable by the plan as a result of the death, or is paid as a superannuation lump sum as a superannuation death benefit, as soon as practicable (reg 291-25.01(4), (5); ID 2015/22: commutation of a lifetime pension and commencement of a market linked pension or account-based pension using the lifetime pension account and pension reserve).

If a superannuation fund allocates an amount from a reserve to a member as a substitute for an actual employer contribution for the member and the amount allocated is net of tax (ie contributions tax has been paid on that contribution), the allocated amount is grossed up by 1.176 so that the gross contribution amount represented by the allocation from the reserve is counted as concessional contributions (reg 291-25.01(6)).

▶ Example

An employer is required to contribute $1,000 to a superannuation fund for an employee. Instead, the trustee of the fund allocates $850 to the member's account, being what would have been the post-tax amount if the employer had made the contribution. The $850 is grossed up by 1.176 ($850 × 1.176 = $1,000) to work out the amount that is taken to be allocated.

ATO guidance on reserves and concerns about the use of reserves by SMSFs

There is no definition of "reserve" in the ITAA97 or ITR97. The Commissioner considers that "reserve" as used in reg 291-25.01 has a wider meaning for the purposes of determining excess concessional contributions than its meaning for SISA purposes (SMSFRB 2018/1) (ID 2015/21: allocation from a fund's self-insurance reserve; ID 2015/22: allocation from a pension reserve account supporting a complying lifetime pension; APRA's Prudential Practice Guide SPG 222 on management of reserves).

SMSF Regulator's Bulletin SMSFRB 2018/1 states that any need to maintain reserves in SMSFs is distinct from the need to maintain reserves in APRA-regulated funds. SMSFs should use reserves only in limited circumstances and only for specific and legitimate purposes. The ATO will scrutinise arrangements where an SMSF purports to hold an amount in a reserve rather than allocate it to a member's account outside of these circumstances, and consider the potential application of the SISA sole purpose test and the ITAA36 Pt IVA anti-avoidance provisions.

The ATO is also concerned that SMSFs may implement strategies utilising reserves or other accounts to circumvent restrictions under the tax law. These include the intentional use of reserves to reduce:

- a member's total superannuation balance so as to make non-concessional contributions without breaching the non-concessional contributions' cap, or reduce the balance below $500,000 to access the catch-up concessional contributions arrangements, or reduce the balance below $1.6 million to allow the SMSF to use the segregated assets method to calculate its exempt current pension income, and
- a member's transfer balance account below the transfer balance cap to allow the member to allocate a greater amount to the retirement phase and thereby have a greater amount of fund earnings being treated as exempt current pension income.

Defined benefit interests — concessional contributions

The meaning of concessional contributions is modified for defined benefit interests (Subdiv 291-C: ss 291-155 to 291-175).

A defined benefit interest exists where all or part of the superannuation benefits payable to a person are defined by reference to the person's salary, a specified amount or specified conversion factors. The concessional contributions amount for a defined benefit interest is the sum of the contributions covered by s 291-25(2) and (3) (see above) to the extent that they do not relate to the defined benefit interest and the ''notional taxed contributions'' for the person for the financial year in respect of the defined benefit interests (ss 291-165; 291-170). The calculation of notional taxed contributions for a financial year in various circumstances (eg for a fund with 5 or more defined benefit members or where notional taxed contributions are taken to be at the maximum level of the contributions cap for the year) is prescribed by regulations (ID 2008/89: non-accruing member; ID 2008/97: choice by member; ID 2008/98: superannuation salary increase; ID 2008/162: productivity notional taxed contributions to PSS) (ITR97 regs 292-170.01 to 292-170.06) (note that these regulations have effect for s 291-170 under savings provisions: see Act No 118 of 2013 Sch 1 Pt 7).

Under grandfathering arrangements, members with a defined benefit interest on 5 September 2006 with notional taxed contributions in excess of the concessional contributions cap are taken to have the notional taxed contributions as their concessional contributions cap (ITTPA s 291-170(2)). In addition, grandfathering rules ensure that members who held a defined benefit interest on 12 May 2009 with notional taxed contributions exceeding the reduced cap amounts (which came into effect from the 2009–10 year) are taken to have their concessional contributions for that defined benefit interest deemed as their concessional contributions cap (ITR97 regs 292-170.07; 292-170.08). These transitional arrangements cease to apply if the rules of the scheme change to increase the member's benefit. However, defined benefit schemes may amend their rules to meet other legislative requirements without their members losing access to the transitional arrangements.

Concessional contributions — constitutionally protected funds and defined benefit schemes

Contributions and certain other amounts relating to constitutionally protected funds and unfunded defined benefit schemes are concessional contributions and are counted towards an individual's concessional contributions cap.

LCR 2016/11 provides guidelines on the calculation of concessional contributions and amounts allocated by superannuation providers for financial years commencing on or after 1 July 2017.

Concessional contributions cap amount

The concessional contributions cap amount is $25,000 in 2017–18 to 2020–21 for all individuals, regardless of their age (s 291-20). The cap amount is indexed annually to AWOTE, in increments of $5,000 rounded down (ITAA97 ss 960-265; 960-285; see ¶42-320 for the cap amount in earlier years).

Making catch-up concessional contributions

An individual who has a total superannuation balance (¶14-050) of less than $500,000 on 30 June of the previous financial year is entitled to contribute more than the general concessional contributions cap amount for the year by making additional concessional contributions for any unused concessional contributions cap amounts of earlier years.

The first year of entitlement to the carry forward unused amounts is the 2019–20 financial year. Unused cap amounts are available for a maximum of 5 years and cannot be carried forward after this period. For the operation of the carry forward cap, see ¶42-320.

¶13-777 Excess concessional contributions — assessment and charge

An individual's assessable income from the 2013–14 year of income includes the individual's excess concessional contributions for the corresponding financial year (ITAA97 s 291-15).

In addition, the individual is liable to pay excess concessional contributions charge on the increase in the tax liability as a result of having excess concessional contributions for the relevant financial year. This charge is imposed by the *Superannuation (Excess Concessional Contributions Charge) Act 2013*. Shortfall interest charge (SIC) and general interest charge (GIC) apply to the charge in the same way as the income tax liability to which the charge relates.

An individual can elect to release excess concessional contributions from his/her superannuation fund in accordance with TAA Sch 1 Div 96 (see below).

In special circumstances, an individual can apply for an exercise of the Commissioner's discretion to disregard or reallocate excess concessional contributions made in a financial year and can object to the Commissioner's decision on the exercise of the discretion under TAA Pt IVC (¶13-785) (ITAA97 ss 291-465; 292-465).

Tax offset

An individual is entitled to a tax offset for 15% of excess concessional contributions that has been included in assessable income (see above) for the financial year corresponding to the income year. The offset reduces the individual's tax liability for the contributions tax that has been paid by the superannuation fund (¶13-125) in respect of the excess concessional contributions (¶13-125). The tax offset cannot be refunded, carried forward or transferred (ITAA97 ss 63-10(1), table item 20; 291-15).

Excess concessional contributions charge

Certain individuals may derive a tax advantage by having their excess concessional contributions included in their assessable income and taxed at marginal rates. For example, making excess concessional contributions ensures that this income is not taken into account under the PAYG rules and allows the earnings from the contributions to be retained in the concessionally taxed superannuation environment, thus increasing the amount held in superannuation funds.

Peter has 60 days to take up the option to withdraw some of his excess concessional contributions from one of his superannuation funds to pay his tax debt.

He decides to release $4,250 (the maximum amount of 85% of the excess contributions of $5,000) by making a request in the approved form to the ATO under s 131-5(3).

On receipt of Peter's request, the ATO will issue a release authority to Peter's nominated superannuation fund to release $4,250 to the ATO. When received, the ATO will offset the amount against any tax debt that Peter may have before refunding any balance to him.

Non-concessional contributions and excess concessional contributions

An individual's non-concessional contributions (¶13-780) in a financial year includes the individual's excess concessional contributions.

However, if an individual elects to release an amount of excess concessional contributions, the amount of the individual's excess concessional contributions is reduced for the purpose of determining the individual's non-concessional contributions (ITAA97 s 292-90(1A)). The amount of the reduction is a gross-up amount equal to 100/85 of the amount released (ie the amount released divided by 85%).

This means that if an individual chooses to release the full 85% of an excess concessional contributions amount for a financial year, the released excess concessional contributions have no impact upon the individual's non-concessional contributions. An individual will, therefore, always have the option of avoiding being in a position where his/her excess concessional contributions result in having excess non-concessional contributions. In addition, the release may prevent the automatic bring forward provisions in ITAA97 for eligible taxpayers in certain circumstances.

▶ Example (adapted from the EM)

Lucy has excess concessional contributions of $10,000 in 2020–21. Assume that when these excess concessional contributions are included as non-concessional contributions, Lucy's total non-concessional contributions for the financial year will amount to $105,000. As the 2020–21 non-concessional contributions cap is $100,000, Lucy will have excess non-concessional contributions of $5,000 as a result.

If Lucy elects to release $7,000 of her excess concessional contributions from her superannuation fund, this will reduce her non-concessional contributions by a gross-up amount as calculated below:

$$\$7,000 \div 85\% = 100 \times \$7,000/85 = \$8,235$$

This means that Lucy's non-concessional contributions in 2020–21 will be reduced to $96,765 ($105,000 – $8,235), and she will not have excess non-concessional contributions for the year.

[AMSG ¶6-500ff; FITR ¶268-600ff; SLP ¶37-400ff]

¶13-780 Excess non-concessional contributions tax

The rules on excess non-concessional contributions tax are set out in ITAA97 Subdiv 292-C (ss 292-75 to 292-105).

An individual taxpayer whose non-concessional contributions in a year exceed the non-concessional contributions cap for the year is liable to pay excess contributions tax on the excess at 47% (*Superannuation (Excess Non-concessional Contributions Tax) Act 2007*, ss 5; 6).

An individual with excess non-concessional contributions may elect to withdraw the excess contributions plus 85% of the associated earnings on those contributions from his/her superannuation fund (see "Electing to release excess non-concessional contributions" below).

An individual's non-concessional cap amount in 2017–18 to 2020–21 is $100,000, but is nil if, before the start of the year, the individual's "total superannuation balance" is equal to or more than the general transfer balance cap for the year (see "Non-concessional contributions cap" and "Cap under a bring forward rule" below).

What are non-concessional contributions?

Non-concessional contributions are generally contributions made in a financial year for or by a person that are not included in the assessable income of a superannuation fund (other than certain amounts: see ''Amounts excluded'' below), certain allocations from reserves, and the amount of the person's excess concessional contributions (if any) for the year (s 292-90(1)).

If a person has contributed to more than one fund, the non-concessional contributions made to all the funds during the period are added together and counted for the purposes of the cap.

A person's non-concessional contributions for a financial year include:

- personal contributions for which an income tax deduction is not claimed (including contributions made to a constitutionally protected fund)
- contributions made for the person by the person's spouse
- contributions in excess of the person's capital gains tax (CGT) cap amount (see below)
- amounts transferred from foreign superannuation funds (excluding amounts included in the fund's assessable income)
- contributions made for the benefit of a person under 18 years of age that are not employer contributions for the person
- an amount in a superannuation fund that is not assessable income of the fund and is allocated for a member in accordance with the conditions in ITR97 reg 292-90.01 and SISR Div 7.2
- the amount of a contribution that is covered by a valid and acknowledged notice under s 290-170 (¶13-730) to the extent that the contributor is not entitled to a deduction
- the person's excess concessional contributions (if any) for the financial year (see *Sutton's case* below) (ITAA97 s 292-90).

If a person has elected to release excess concessional contributions under TAA Sch 1 Div 131 (or former Div 96), the released contributions are excluded when determining the person's excess non-concessional contributions (ITAA97 s 292-90(1A)) (¶13-777).

An amount transferred from a KiwiSaver scheme to an Australian complying superannuation fund is treated as a non-concessional contribution on initial entry into the Australian superannuation system, with some exceptions (¶13-380).

Where a person's intention to make a contribution is clear, the ATO will include the full amount of the person's contribution as non-concessional contributions even though part of it has been returned by the recipient fund purportedly under the law of restitution (ID 2010/104).

Contributions that are not non-concessional contributions

The following contributions (which are not included in the assessable income of a superannuation fund) are not non-concessional contributions:

- government co-contributions (¶13-760)
- contributions arising from certain structured settlements or orders for personal injuries (see below)
- contributions arising from the small business CGT concessions which are within the person's CGT cap amount (see below)
- downsizer contributions (¶13-795)

- contributions made to a constitutionally protected fund that are not included in the contributions segment of the person's superannuation interest in the fund
- contributions not included in the assessable income of a public sector superannuation scheme under an ITAA97 s 295-180 election (¶13-125), and
- roll-overs or transfers between complying superannuation funds (other than certain amounts transferred from foreign superannuation funds) (s 292-90(2)(c)).

A contribution by a taxpayer to a superannuation fund, which arose from an eligible termination payment made to the taxpayer from a superannuation fund, was held to be a non-concessional contribution, not a roll-over superannuation benefit (¶14-450) (*Player*).

Contributions — personal injuries and CGT exemptions

As noted in bold dot point 2 above, superannuation contributions in the circumstances below are not non-concessional contributions (s 292-90(2)(c)(ii), (iii)):

- contributions relating to personal injury payments. The contribution must arise from a personal injury structured settlement, court-ordered payment or lump sum workers' compensation payment, and must be made to a superannuation fund within 90 days of receiving payment or structured settlement or order coming into effect (whichever is later), and other medical certification and notification requirements are also met (ITAA97 s 292-95), and
- contributions arising from the disposal of assets that qualify for the small business 15-year asset exemption or retirement exemption up to a person's lifetime "CGT cap" amount (see below).

Counting non-concessional contributions against the CGT cap

Contributions made to a superannuation fund for or by an individual arising from certain small business CGT concessions are counted against a CGT cap, rather than the annual non-concessional contributions cap. The CGT cap amount (which is a lifetime limit for each individual) is $1.565 million in 2020–21 (ITAA97 s 292-105). The CGT cap amount is indexed annually to AWOTE, in increments of $5,000 rounded down (ITAA97 ss 960-265; 960-285) (see ¶42-325 for the cap amount in earlier years). The contributions covered by the CGT cap are:

- the CGT exempt amount (of up to $500,000) under the retirement exemption provided in ITAA97 Subdiv 152-D (¶7-185)
- the *capital proceeds* from the disposal of active assets that qualify for the 15-year asset exemption under Subdiv 152-B (¶7-165), and
- the *capital proceeds* from the disposal of assets that would have qualified for the 15-year asset exemption but for:
  - the disposal of the asset resulting in no capital gain or a capital loss
  - the asset being a pre-CGT asset, or
  - the asset being disposed of before the required 15-year holding period had elapsed because of the permanent incapacity of the person which occurred after the asset was purchased (ITAA97 s 292-100).

For the above purposes, a pre-CGT asset is treated as a post-CGT asset (s 292-100(5)).

For contributions in a financial year to be counted in the CGT cap, they must be paid to the superannuation fund in the manner and by the time set out in s 292-100 (based on the CGT concessions involved). The election to use the CGT cap must be made in the approved form ("Capital gains tax cap election" form) and be given to the superannuation fund on or before the time the contribution is made (s 292-100(9)). This gives an individual the choice as to whether all or part of a contribution is counted against the non-concessional contributions cap or CGT cap.

A "CGT concession stakeholder" (¶7-155) of a small business entity (eg a company or a trust) that has a capital gain which is disregarded under the 15-year asset exemption or retirement exemption can also use the CGT cap provided the entity makes a payment to or on behalf of the stakeholder as required by s 292-100(4) and (8).

An individual claiming the Div 152-D retirement exemption who is under 55 years of age must contribute an amount equal to the CGT exempt amount to a complying superannuation fund or RSA (ITAA97 s 152-305(1)(b)). Likewise, where a company or trust chooses the retirement exemption and a CGT concession stakeholder is under 55 just before a payment is made in relation to them, the company or trust must contribute the CGT exempt amount to a complying superannuation fund or an RSA (ITAA97 ss 152-325(7)(a); ¶7-185). Contributions for this purpose may be made in specie, provided the relevant SISA provisions governing such transfers are met (ID 2010/217).

Non-concessional contributions cap

An individual's non-concessional contributions cap is:

- $100,000 (is based on 4 times the concessional contribution cap amount for the year), or
- nil — if the individual's total superannuation balance (¶14-050) equals or exceeds the general transfer balance cap for the year ($1.6 million in 2020–21: ¶14-320) (ITAA97 s 292-85(2)).

An individual who has a total superannuation balance of $1.6 million or more therefore cannot make non-concessional contributions for the year without being subject to excess non-concessional contributions tax. A bring forward cap may be available for certain individuals (see below).

If an individual has more than one fund, the non-concessional contributions made to all the funds in a financial year are added together and counted towards the cap for the year.

Non-concessional contributions cap under a bring forward rule

A special rule allows an individual who is under 65 years of age in an income year (or under 67 years of age for contributions from 1 July 2020, see "Proposed changes — extending the bring forward rule" below) to "bring forward" the cap amount of 2 later years as the individual's non-concessional contributions cap over a 3-year period, including that income year (s 292-85(3)).

In conjunction with the transfer balance cap and total superannuation balance restrictions from 2017–18 (¶14-050, ¶14-320), the application of the bring forward cap from 1 July 2017 depends on the individual's total superannuation balance on the day before the financial year that the non-concessional contributions triggered the bring forward (see below).

The bring forward rule applies to individuals who meet the eligibility criteria below:

- the individual's non-concessional contributions for the first year exceed the general non-concessional contributions cap for that year ($100,000 for 2017–18 to 2020–21: see above)
- the individual's total superannuation balance (¶14-050) as at 30 June of the previous year is *less* than the general transfer balance cap for the year ($1.6 million for 2017–18 to 2020–21: ¶14-320)
- the individual is under 65 years at any time in the year (see "Proposed changes — age cut-off under the bring forward rule" below)
- a bring-forward period is not currently in operation in respect of the year because of an earlier application of the bring forward rule, and

- the difference between the general transfer balance cap for the first year and the individual's total superannuation balance before the start of the first year (the "first year cap space") is *greater* than the general non-concessional contributions cap for the first year (s 292-85(3)).

If an individual satisfies the eligibility criteria, and triggers the bring forward rule (effectively by making contributions that exceed the general non-concessional contributions cap in the first year: see the first dot point above), the cap amount for first, second and third year in the "bring forward period" is calculated in accordance with ss 292-85(4)–(7).

Proposed changes — age cut-off under the bring forward rule

Amendments have been proposed to increase the cut-off age in s 292-85(3)(c) for access to the bring forward non-concessional contributions cap from 65 to 67 years, applicable to non-concessional contributions on or after 1 July 2020 (Treasury Laws Amendment (More Flexible Superannuation) Bill 2020: ¶41-150).

Electing to release excess non-concessional contributions

An individual whose non-concessional contributions for a financial year exceed the non-concessional contributions cap may elect to have an amount equal to the excess contributions plus 85% of an associated earnings amount released from his/her superannuation fund in accordance with a release authority issued by the Commissioner.

The released amount of excess contributions is non-assessable non-exempt income, but an amount corresponding to the associated earnings on the excess contributions is included in the individual's assessable income and is taxed at marginal tax rates. The individual is entitled to a non-refundable tax-offset equal to 15% of the associated earnings amount included in assessable income (see below).

Excess non-concessional contributions tax is imposed on excess non-concessional contributions that are not released from a superannuation interest where the remaining value of all the individual's superannuation interests is not nil.

Excess non-concessional contributions determination

If an individual has non-concessional contributions which exceed the non-concessional contributions cap for a financial year, the Commissioner must make and give a written notice of the determination to the individual, stating:

- the amount of the excess contributions
- the amount of the associated earnings for those contributions (see below), and
- the total release amount (ie the amount of the excess contributions plus 85% of the associated earnings amount) (TAA Sch 1 s 97-25).

The associated earnings amount is worked out using an average of the GIC rate for each of the quarters of the financial year in which the excess contributions were made, and compounds on a daily basis. The period for which the associated earnings amount is calculated commences on 1 July of the financial year in which the excess contributions occurred (contributions year) and ends on the day that the Commissioner makes the first determination of excess non-concessional contributions for the relevant contributions year (this is similar to the period used for calculating the excess concessional contributions charge for excess concessional contributions) (TAA Sch 1 s 97-30). Sections 97-25 and 97-30 are not penalty provisions, and the Commissioner is not empowered under the TAA to remit an amount of associated earnings as calculated (*Purcell*).

The rules for the release of superannuation money under an ATO release authority following the issue of an excess concessional or non-concessional contributions determination, or an assessment of Division 293 tax or an FHSS determination by the Commissioner under TAA Sch 1 Div 131, are discussed in ¶13-755.

Release of associated earnings amount and offset

An amount paid on behalf of an individual by a superannuation provider in accordance with a ATO release authority is a superannuation lump sum benefit of the individual, but the payment does not have income tax consequences for the individual as it is non-assessable non-exempt income (¶14-310) (ITAA97 s 303-17).

Only 85% of the associated earnings amount can be released as the superannuation fund may have already included the earnings on investments made with the excess contributions in its assessable income and would have been taxed on those earnings at a rate of up to 15%.

When an excess contributions amount is released or where the Commissioner determines that the value of an individual's superannuation interests is nil, the associated earnings amount is included in the individual's assessable income. This removes a taxation benefit that would otherwise be obtained by making excessive non-concessional contributions despite their release. However, if no amount is released and the individual has a superannuation interest or interests with a value greater than nil, no associated earnings amount is included in individual's assessable income and excess non-concessional contributions tax will apply (ss 292-20; 292-25; 292-30; 292-85).

The Commissioner will include the whole of the associated earnings amount in the individual's assessable income in the year corresponding to the financial year the individual had excess non-concessional contributions. This amount is taxed at the individual's marginal tax rate and the individual is entitled to a non-refundable tax-offset equal to 15% of the associated earnings amount included in assessable income, reflecting the tax liability of the superannuation fund on the earnings (¶14-300).

Related tax matters

The proportioning rule in ITAA97 s 307-125 which requires superannuation benefits to be treated as made from particular components of a superannuation interest in proportion to the overall composition of the interest (¶14-130) does not apply to release amounts.

Assessment of excess non-concessional contributions tax and review rights

An individual who has excess non-concessional contributions in a financial year will receive an excess non-concessional contributions tax assessment from the Commissioner stating the amount of the excess and the excess non-concessional contributions tax payable for the year (ITAA97 s 292-230).

An individual who is dissatisfied with the assessment may object in accordance with Pt IVC of the TAA 1953 (ITAA97 s 292-245).

An individual who is dissatisfied with a decision of the Commissioner in relation to the matters below can also object as set out in Pt IVC:

- an excess non-concessional contributions determination
- an assessment to include an offset or to include associated earnings in the individual's assessable income (or both)
- a decision not to make a direction under s 292-467 that an individual's superannuation interest is nil, and
- a decision to exercise a discretion to disregard an individual's non-concessional contributions or re-allocate the contributions to another year, or a decision not to exercise the discretion (¶13-785) (TAA Sch 1 s 97-35; ITAA97 s 292-467(4)).

If an individual who makes one of the objections above on a particular ground also makes, or could have made, another one or more of the objections on the same ground, the taxation decisions to which the objections are made are treated as a single taxation decision for the purposes of Pt IVC (TAA s 14ZVC).

Taxpayer Alert on arrangements to avoid excess contributions tax

The Commissioner has warned about:

- arrangements which allow a member of a superannuation fund to circumvent the excess contributions tax and related rules (TA 2008/12), and
- certain limited-recourse borrowings arrangements entered into by superannuation funds, where money is advanced by a member or related party at zero or less than a commercial rate of interest, as this can be characterised as a contribution and may result in the member having to pay excess non-concessional contributions tax (TA 2008/5).

[AMSG ¶6-540; FITR ¶268-900ff; SLP ¶37-290ff]

¶13-785 Commissioner's discretion to disregard or re-allocate excess contributions

An individual can apply to the Commissioner in the approved form for a determination that all or a part of the individual's concessional contributions and/or non-concessional contributions for a financial year are to be disregarded or reallocated instead to another financial year (ss 291-465(1); 292-465(1); www.ato.gov.au/Forms/Application---excess-contributions-determination) (NAT 71333).

An exception to an individual having to apply to the Commissioner to make a determination arises where the Commissioner has made contributions on behalf of the individual and the contributions represent amounts recovered from the individual's employer under the SG amnesty (see below).

The Commissioner may make the determination only if he considers that there are ''special circumstances'' and making the determination is consistent with the object of ITAA97 Div 291 or 292. The second part of this test is to ensure that the amount of concessionally taxed superannuation benefits that a person receives results from contributions that have been made gradually over the course of the person's life (ss 291-465(2); 292-465(3)).

To ensure that employees are not disadvantaged where employers benefit from the SG amnesty (as discussed in ¶39-505), the Commissioner can make a determination to disregard or reallocate employer payments of the SG charge to the ATO under the SG amnesty (s 291-465(2A)). This does not apply where the employer has made the contributions directly to an employee's fund to offset the employer's SG charge liability because the potential breach of an individual's contributions cap would have been due to the employer. In such cases, individuals who are affected can still apply to the Commissioner to exercise the discretion under s 291-465(1).

Each application for the exercise of the s 291-465 or 292-465 discretion is considered by the Commissioner on its merits. This will involve an examination of evidence of the contributions made, the extent of the individual's control over the amount and timing of a particular contribution, and the extent to which an excess is foreseeable (*Decision Impact Statements Hamad* (2012/0487), *Longcake* (2012/0354), *Bornstein* (2011/5143)).

In making a determination, the Commissioner must have regard to the matters set out in s 291-465(3) or 292-465(4) to (6) and any other relevant matters. *Practice Statement* PS LA 2008/1 sets out the factors that the Commissioner will take into account when exercising a discretion (see further below).

Whether an individual's circumstances are special will vary from case to case. In the following cases, it was found that there were no ''special circumstances'': *Schuurmans-Stekhoven*; *Tran*; *Peaker*; *Leckie*; *Naude*; *Kuyper*; *Chantrell*; *Rawson*; *Paget*; *The Applicant*; *Lynton*; *Davenport*; *Verschuer*; *Confidential*; *Dowling*; *McLennan*; *KBFC*; *Liwszyc*; *Thompson*; *Sisely, Hope & Anor*; *Brady* (¶13-780); *Azer*; *Mills* and *Moore*.

For cases where special circumstances were found to exist so as to warrant an exercise of the Commissioner's discretion, see *Bornstein*, *Longcake*, *Hamad* and *Dowling*.

In *Dowling*, the ATO considers that the AAT's approach was consistent with the principles stated by the Federal Court, both in that case and in *Liwszyc*, as to the correct approach to applying the discretion to disregard or reallocate contributions to another financial year under s 292-465 (*Decision Impact Statement* on *Dowling's case* VRN 2727 of 2012 and 2728 of 2012). In *Ward*, the Full Federal Court held that the AAT erred in concluding that because the imposition of the tax was a natural and foreseeable consequence of the taxpayer's decisions, it was necessarily outside the scope of ''special circumstances''. The AAT erred in law by taking too narrow a view of what may constitute ''special circumstances''. On remittal of the case, the AAT subsequently found that special circumstances existed in Mr Ward's situation, but it was bound by *Dowling's case* to find that the test in s 292-465(3)(b) had not been met. Accordingly, the AAT affirmed the Commissioner's decision not to make a determination under s 292-465(1) to disregard the excess contribution (*Ward*).

ATO guidelines where employers make remedial SG contributions

Some employers make remedial SG contributions where they have not paid enough SG contributions on time for their current or former employees in the past (¶39-500). Even though these remedial SG contributions may relate to an earlier period of time, they are treated as a concessional contribution in the year they are made to the employee's chosen superannuation fund. As a result, SG remedial contributions may cause employees to exceed their concessional contributions cap and result in an additional tax and excess concessional contributions charge liability (¶13-777).

An employee may apply to the Commissioner for a determination to have remedial SG contributions disregarded or allocated to another year and not count towards their concessional contributions cap in the year they are made by using the *Application – excess-contributions-determination form*. This form cannot be used where the employee considers that the ATO has relied on incorrect information or has applied the law incorrectly. In these cases, the employee should contact the information provider or object against the tax assessment or ATO determination.

Additional information on the exercise of the Commissioner's discretion to disregard or reallocate remedial SG contributions may be found in ATO Fact Sheet *Exercising the Commissioner's discretion* and PS LA 2008/1.

Objection against assessments

A taxpayer who is dissatisfied with the Commissioner's determination or decision not to make a determination may object in the manner set out in TAA Pt IVC. The Commissioner's determination is a decision which forms part of a tax assessment process for the purposes of the *Administrative Decisions (Judicial Review) Act 1977* (ss 291-465(7), (8); 292-465(9); *McMennemin*; *AAT* and *Decision Impact Statement* (VID 738 of 2010), 17 June 2011 and *Ward* and *Decision Impact Statement* VRN 3760 of 2013).

[AMSG ¶6-665; FITR ¶269-480, ¶268-690ff; SLP ¶37-340ff]

¶13-790 First home savers superannuation scheme

Individuals can make voluntary contributions to their superannuation account under the First Home Super Saver (FHSS) Scheme from 1 July 2017 (ITAA97 Div 313; TAA Sch 1 Div 138). The Scheme enables individuals to save for their first home and take advantage of the concessional taxation arrangements that apply in the superannuation system. An FHSS tax is payable if the individuals do not purchase their first home within a specified period or recontribute an amount into superannuation.

The key features of the FHSS Scheme are as follows:

- To be eligible to benefit from the FHSS Scheme, an individual must be at least 18 years, must have never used the FHSS Scheme before, and must have never owned real property unless specific financial hardship circumstances apply (see below).
- The maximum voluntary contributions under the Scheme is $15,000 a year, and $30,000 in total. Voluntary contributions can be non-concessional or concessional contributions and are subject to the contributions caps (¶13-777, ¶13-780).
- An individual may apply to the ATO to withdraw up to their ''FHSS maximum release amount'', which is the sum of eligible contributions of up to $30,000 and associated deemed earnings, to use as a deposit on a home.
- To initiate the withdrawal, the individual must request a ''first home super saver determination'' (FHSS determination) from the Commissioner.
- In making an FHSS determination, the Commissioner must identify a ''maximum release amount'' based on the individual's past contributions and associated earnings.
- An individual who receives an FHSS determination can request the Commissioner to issue a release authority in respect of their superannuation interests under TAA Sch 1 Div 131 (see ¶13-755).
- The maximum FHSS releasable contributions amount is the amount of the associated earnings plus 85% of concessional contributions and 100% of non-concessional contributions.
- The individual's superannuation fund must pay the amount to be released to the Commissioner, who will withhold an amount for the tax payable and pay the balance to the individual. The amount withheld will reflect the best estimate of the tax payable or, if such an estimate cannot be made, 17% of the amount released (FHSS released amount).
- An FHSS released amount is subject to concessional tax treatment. Concessional contributions and earnings that are withdrawn will be included in the individual's assessable income and benefit from a non-refundable 30% tax offset. For released amounts of non-concessional contributions, only the associated earnings will be taxed, with a 30% tax offset.
- An individual can enter into a contract to purchase or construct their home provided they have applied for and received an FHSS determination, and have made a valid request for release under that determination within 14 days of entering into the contract. The individual does not have to wait for the administrative release process to finalise or receive their released amount before entering into a contract to purchase or construct their home.
- An individual will generally have 12 months after money is released from superannuation to sign a contract to purchase a home or construct a home. The premises must be occupied as soon as practicable and for at least 6 months of the first year after it is practicable to do so.
- If a home is not purchased, the individual is required to re-contribute an amount into superannuation or pay 20% FHSS tax on the FHSS released amount to unwind the concessional tax treatment when it was released.
- The FHSS tax is imposed by the *First Home Super Saver Tax Act 2017*.

ATO guidelines on the operation of the FHSS Scheme are set out in LCR 2018/5 and *Guidance Note* GN 2018/1.

Eligible person for FHSS Scheme

Generally, an individual must have never held an ownership or similar interest in Australian real property (eg a home, an investment property or vacant land) to be eligible to use the FHSS Scheme (see above). An individual who previously held such an interest is still eligible if the Commissioner determines that the individual had suffered a ''financial hardship'' that resulted in the individual ceasing to hold such property interest held at the time of the hardship and the individual had not held any other such property interests since that time (TAR reg 61A).

Treatment of amounts released under the FHSS Scheme

The general tax treatment of superannuation benefits (which include lump sums paid out of superannuation) is governed by ITAA97 Div 301, based on the status of the recipient and the ''components'' of the benefit (¶14-200).

The tax rules below apply to amounts which are released to an individual from their superannuation interests under a release authority issued in relation to an FHSS determination (¶13-755):

- any amount calculated by reference to an individual's FHSS eligible *non-concessional contributions* is treated as non-assessable non-exempt (NANE), and
- any amount related to the individual's FHSS eligible *concessional contributions*, and the total associated earnings calculated in respect of *any* contributions, are included in the individual's assessable income (referred to as an individual's ''assessable FHSS released amount'') and taxed at the individual's marginal rates, with a tax offset of 30% available.

Assessable FHSS released amounts are calculated independent of the general tax treatment that applies to superannuation benefits. The proportioning rule (¶14-130) does not apply to FHSS released amounts.

Using the amount specified in an FHSS determination works appropriately where the total amounts that are released from superannuation are equal to the FHSS maximum release amount specified in the determination. If an individual has elected to have a lesser amount released, or the amount available for release is less than the release amount requested, the amount that is included in an individual's assessable income is reduced by any difference between the total amount that was actually released and the FHSS maximum release amount specified in the relevant determination. The amount included in an individual's assessable income cannot be reduced to less than nil. This ensures that where an individual's FHSS maximum release amount includes amounts related to non-concessional contributions, the difference between the FHSS maximum release amount and the actual release amount is first taken from the amounts that are included in assessable income.

Tax offset for amounts included in assessable income

The tax offset is equal to 30% of the individual's assessable FHSS released amount so that the individual is taxed on the assessable amounts released at their marginal tax rate *less* 30%. The tax offset is not refundable and cannot be carried forward.

Withholding on FHSS Scheme amounts

The Commissioner is required to withhold an amount from assessable FHSS released amounts that are paid in respect of an individual based on an estimate of the tax that will be payable in relation to the individual's assessable FHSS released amount, as calculated in accordance with the TAR reg 53A(1)(a). The Commissioner will withhold an amount at the individual's expected marginal rate less 30% offset.

If the Commissioner is unable to make an estimate of an individual's marginal tax rate, 17% of the individual's assessable FHSS released amount must be withheld (TAR reg 53A(1)(b)). This default rate is based on the maximum amount of tax that an individual would be expected to pay on an FHSS released amount if they were on the top marginal rate and received the full benefit of the 30% offset. In the event that an individual is not on the top marginal tax rate, the difference in the amount withheld and the actual tax liability will be refunded through the assessment process.

Obligations on individuals after amounts are released

As the FHSS Scheme is designed to assist individuals in saving for a deposit for their first home, a post-release compliance approach applies to ensure that individuals have access to the amount saved under the Scheme before they are required to pay their deposit. That is, instead of requiring individuals to provide evidence that they have entered into a home-purchase contract, they are simply required to purchase their first home within a specified period after the amounts are released.

An individual who fails to purchase a home within this period of time has the option of recontributing an amount back into superannuation or paying an amount of tax that will broadly neutralise the tax concessions received from accessing the FHSS Scheme.

Entering into contract to purchase home or recontributing to superannuation

Individuals are required to notify the Commissioner that they have purchased their home or recontributed the required amount into superannuation as below.

Purchase requirements

An individual can notify the Commissioner of compliance with the purchase requirements if:

- the individual enters into a contract to purchase or construct a CGT asset that is a residential premises within 12 months of the time that the first amount is released under the FHSS Scheme
- the price for the purchase or construction of the premises is at least equal to the sum of the amounts that were released
- the individual has occupied the premises, or intends to occupy it as soon as practicable, and
- the individual intends to occupy the premises for at least 6 of the first 12 months that it is practicable to occupy the premises.

Recontributing amounts into superannuation requirements

An individual who does not satisfy the purchase requirements may instead notify the Commissioner, in the approved form, of compliance with the superannuation re-contribution requirements if:

- the individual makes one or more non-concessional contributions during the period available for entering into a contract to purchase or construct a first home (or any longer period allowed by the Commissioner), and
- the total amount of the non-concessional contributions must be at least equal to their assessable FHSS released amount *less* any amounts that were withheld by the Commissioner.

The recontribution must be made by non-concessional contributions to ensure that the individual does not receive a further benefit from claiming another deduction in recontributing the necessary amount into superannuation (see below). In addition, any recontribution must be within the individual's non-concessional contribution cap.

The reduction of the recontribution amount by an amount withheld by the Commissioner recognises that for individuals who were required to pay tax on their assessable FHSS released amount, a recontribution of the full assessable FHSS released amount would have to be partially funded from other sources. Individuals who will be affected in this way are those whose marginal tax rate is greater than 30% (being the amount of the tax offset).

No deduction allowed for recontribution

Individuals who notify the Commissioner that they have made non-concessional contributions as recontributions are denied a deduction for the contributions covered by the notification (ITAA97 s 290-168: ¶13-730). An individual therefore cannot report a recontribution as a non-concessional contribution, and later claim a deduction for it. This rule does not require the tracing of specific contributions and deductions. It applies where an individual's non-concessional contributions for a financial year are less than the contributions notified to the Commissioner. In such circumstances, any deduction that the individual claims for other contributions will be reduced to the extent of the difference.

First home super saver tax

Individuals are liable to pay first home super saver tax (FHSS tax) if they do not:

- enter into a contract to purchase or construct their first home or recontribute the required amount into superannuation, or
- notify the Commissioner that they have purchased a home or recontributed the required amount into superannuation.

FHSS tax is imposed by the *First Home Super Saver Tax Act 2017*, and is equal to 20% of an individual's assessable FHSS released amounts (a flat rate of tax which is unrelated to the personal income tax system or an individual's marginal tax rate).

While the rate of the tax provides an incentive for individuals to take one of the actions necessary to avoid liability to the tax, the government states that the rate does not unfairly impact individuals who are subject to the tax as they would have received a tax offset equal to 30% of their assessable FHSS released amounts and have benefited from the concessions that apply to the contributions and earnings within the superannuation system.

Assessment and payment of FHSS tax

The self-assessment regime does not apply to FHSS tax. Instead, the general assessment provisions in TAA Sch 1 Div 155 are used for assessments of FHSS tax (this Division contains the general rules for making, amending and reviewing assessments which are also used in respect of Division 293 tax and excess transfer balance tax).

The Commissioner is required to provide a notice of assessment to an individual as soon as practicable after an assessment is made showing an assessable amount.

An individual's assessed FHSS tax is due and payable at the end of 21 days after the Commissioner gives the individual a notice of the assessment of the tax.

Where an individual's assessment is amended by the Commissioner, any extra assessed FHSS tax is due and payable at the end of 21 days after the Commissioner gives the individual a notice of the amended assessment.

If an individual fails to pay an amount of assessed FHSS tax by its due date, general interest charge is imposed for each day in the period that the tax is due and unpaid in accordance with TAA Pt IIA.

¶13-795 Making downsizer contributions

An individual who is aged 65 or over may make "downsizer contributions" from the proceeds of the sale of a dwelling that was the person's main residence, applicable to the proceeds from contracts entered into on or after 1 July 2018. Proceeds arising from an exchange of contracts occurring before 1 July 2018 cannot be made as a downsizer contribution, even if the settlement of the contracts occurs on or after 1 July 2018.

The total amount that can be treated as downsizer contributions for an individual is the *lesser* of $300,000 and the individual's share of the sale proceeds from the sale of a main residence (see "Cap on downsizer contributions and multiple contributions" below). Further downsizer contributions cannot be made in the future in relation to the sale of another main residence.

Guidelines on downsizer contributions and how they interact with other tax and superannuation concepts (eg contribution caps, CGT, acceptance of contributions rules) are set out in LCR 2018/9 and *Guidance Note* GN 2018/2.

Qualifying as a downsizer contribution

A contribution is a downsizer contribution in respect of an individual if the following conditions are satisfied:

- the individual is aged 65 years or older at the time the contribution is made
- the contribution must be in respect of the proceeds of the sale of a qualifying dwelling in Australia
- the 10-year ownership condition is met
- a gain or loss on the disposal of the dwelling must have qualified (or would have qualified) for the main residence CGT exemption in whole or part
- the contribution must be made within 90 days of the disposal of the dwelling, or such longer time as allowed by the Commissioner
- the individual must choose to treat the contribution as a downsizer contribution, and notify their superannuation provider in the approved form of this choice before or at the time the contribution is made
- the individual does not have downsizer contributions in relation to an earlier disposal of a main residence (ITAA97 s 292-102(1)(i), (3)).

A contribution must be made in respect of an individual, but there is no specific requirement about who must actually make the contribution so long as the individual is the one who makes the choice to treat the contribution as a downsizer contribution (s 292-102(1)(a), (h)).

Cap on downsizer contributions and multiple contributions

The total amount of downsizer contributions that can be made in respect of an individual is the *lesser* of $300,000 and the total proceeds that the individual and their spouse receive from disposing of their ownership interests in the dwelling (s 292-102(3)).

Subject to the cap, an individual can make more than one downsizer contributions provided the contributions are made from the proceeds of one sale of a dwelling (s 292-102(1)(h), (i), (3)). Also, as multiple contributions can be made, individuals can make contributions to different superannuation providers.

The maximum cap amount is reduced by any earlier contributions that have already been made by either spouse in respect of the proceeds from the disposal of their interests in the same property (s 292-102(3)(b)). This reduction ensures that the total amount that is contributed between both spouses does not exceed the total proceeds that they receive from the disposal of their ownership interests in the same property.

While an individual can have contributions made from the proceeds of both their own interest and their spouse's ownership interest in a dwelling, any such ownership interests must have been disposed of under the same contract (s 292-102(1)(b), (c), (i)).

An individual can make a downsizer contribution in respect of the proceeds from a property that was held by their spouse where the property is a pre-CGT asset that would have been subject to the main residence exemption if it had been acquired after 1 September 1985 (s 292-102(1)(d)(ii)). In addition, in working out the maximum amount of downsizer contributions that an individual can make, the market value substitution rule in ITAA97 s 116-30 (dealing with capital proceeds: ¶11-570) cannot increase the amount of capital proceeds from the disposal of their ownership interests in a dwelling (s 292-102(3A)).

Amounts over $300,000 need to be assessed as to whether they are eligible to remain in the fund under the non-concessional contribution cap (see below). If not, they are to be refunded to the member. If they are left in the fund, the member may be subject to excess non-concessional contributions tax (s 292-102(3)).

Contribution must be made within 90 days

A contribution must be made within 90 days of the change in ownership that occurs as a result of the disposal of the relevant ownership interest, or such longer time as the Commissioner allows. The change of ownership is usually the contract settlement date, when the purchaser pays the balance of the purchase price under the contract to the vendor (s 292-102(1)(g)).

Choosing to treat a contribution as a downsizer contribution

An individual must choose to treat a contribution as a downsizer contribution in the approved form, which must be given to the superannuation fund (or RSA) to which the contribution is made before or at the time of contribution (s 292-102(1)(h), (8)). A contribution that does not comply will be treated as a personal contribution and counted towards the individual's non-concessional contributions cap (see below).

Commissioner may determine that a contribution is not a downsizer contribution

If a contribution does not satisfy the requirements for a downsizer contribution, the Commissioner may request additional or further information from the individual in respect of whom the contribution was made. There is no review opportunity (other than under the *Administrative Decisions (Judicial Review) Act 1977*) at this stage of the process.

If the Commissioner remains of the view that a contribution that an individual has elected to treat as a downsizer contribution does not satisfy all the requirements, the Commissioner must notify the recipient superannuation fund of this. Once notified, the fund may assess whether it could otherwise have accepted the contribution based on the individual's age or working status under the acceptance of contributions rules (¶13-825). In such cases, the contribution will also count towards the individual's contributions cap, generally as a non-concessional contribution.

Interaction with contribution cap and total superannuation balance

A downsizer contribution is excluded from being a non-concessional contribution and does not count towards an individual's non-concessional contributions cap (¶13-780) (ITAA97 s 292-90(2)(c)(iiia)).

A contribution that does not meet the downsizer contribution requirements is counted against the non-concessional contribution cap unless the superannuation fund has returned the contribution under the acceptance of contributions rules (¶13-825). This is consistent with the treatment for other kinds of contributions.

The total superannuation balance test (which applies to determine an individual's eligibility for various tax concessions, including the non-concessional contributions cap: ¶14-050) does not restrict an individual's ability to make downsizer contributions. However, a downsizer contribution will increase the individual's total superannuation balance when this is re-calculated to include all contributions made, including the downsizer contributions, on 30 June at the end of the financial year for the purposes of that test.

If a downsizer contribution amount is later transferred to the pension phase in a fund, that amount is counted towards the individual's transfer balance cap ($1.6 million in 2020–21: ¶14-320).

Downsizer contributions are not tax-deductible

Individuals cannot claim a deduction for any contribution that they choose to treat as a downsizer contribution (ITAA97 s 290-167: ¶13-730).

Regulatory Regime — Superannuation Entities

¶13-800 Regulation of superannuation entities

The SIS legislation, together with the *Financial Sector (Collection of Data) Act 2001* (FSCODA), the *Corporations Act 2001* and TAA, constitute the principal legislation governing the prudential supervision of superannuation funds, ADFs and PSTs. Compliance with the SISA and other regulatory Acts, insofar as is applicable, is mandatory for an entity to qualify as a complying superannuation fund, complying ADF or PST for tax purposes (¶13-100, ¶13-410, ¶13-440).

The generic term ''regulatory provision'' is used in SISA to refer to the principal prudential standards and obligations that apply to an entity under the above Acts (SISA s 38A). Where a regulatory provision is contravened, various forms of penalties may be imposed under the SISA and regulatory Acts, in addition to the potential loss of the entity's complying status and entitlement to concessional tax treatment under the tax laws.

Service providers to superannuation entities (such as auditors and actuaries) are also subject to the SIS prudential regime with respect to provision of services and certain duties to the entities. Superannuation fund auditors and actuaries are generally required to report contraventions of a regulatory provision to the ATO.

The prudential supervision regime for superannuation entities and their service providers is complex with diverse rules for different types of superannuation entities. Trustees and superannuation professionals responsible for compliance management may refer to other Wolters Kluwer products such as the *Australian Master Superannuation Guide 2020/21*, *Superannuation Law & Practice* and *Practical Guide to SMSFS* for more comprehensive coverage.

The preservation and payment of superannuation benefits under the SIS regulations, and certain prudential requirements covering the operation of superannuation funds, are briefly outlined below. The acceptance of contributions rules for superannuation funds are summarised at ¶13-825.

Preservation, payment and portability of benefits

Under the SISR, a member's benefits in a superannuation fund are categorised as preserved benefits, restricted non-preserved benefits and unrestricted non-preserved benefits for the purposes of the payment standards prescribed under the SIS Act (ie the SISR preservation and payment of benefit rules). This categorisation is not the same as the division of superannuation benefits into its tax free and taxable components under ITAA97 for taxation purposes, as discussed in ¶14-000ff. However, superannuation benefits that are paid in breach of the SIS payment standards do not receive concessional tax treatment as superannuation benefits but are taxed as ordinary income at marginal tax rates (¶14-300).

Briefly, the SISR preservation rules provide that a member's preserved benefits and restricted non-preserved benefits can only be accessed if the member satisfies a condition of release in SISR Sch 1 (subject to a cashing restriction on the form and payment amount in certain cases). The conditions of release cover a range of situations such as retirement on or after preservation age (see below), attaining age 65, death, permanent or temporary incapacity, severe financial hardship or compassionate grounds, payment under an ATO release authority or to temporary residents departing Australia. Not all conditions of release are applicable to all members.

Penalties may be imposed if a person promotes an illegal early release scheme of superannuation benefits which does not comply with the SISR payment rules (SISA s 68B).

Briefly, under the SISR payment rules, the payment (cashing) of a member's benefits can be *voluntary* (generally by satisfying a condition of release and cashing restriction (if any), see above), or *compulsory* (ie when the member dies). With *compulsory* cashing, a member's benefits in a regulated superannuation fund must be cashed, or rolled over for immediate cashing *as soon as practicable* after the member dies (reg 6.21(1), (3)). This rule effectively allows fund members to keep their superannuation entitlements in the fund until their death.

The payment rules also govern the manner, time and extent to which a member's benefits in a regulated superannuation fund must be paid, and the persons to whom the benefits are paid. The rules require fund trustees to have regard to their SISA covenants, a member's death benefit nomination and any other duty that may arise in a particular case, such as giving or seeking information or restrictions under the family law (SISR regs 6.17A; 6.17AA; 6.17B; 6.17C).

Lump sum and income stream payments

A member's benefits may be cashed as a lump sum, or as one or more income stream benefits each of which is a superannuation income stream that is in the retirement phase, subject to reg 6.21(2A) and (2B) which impose additional conditions for payment of a death benefit as an income stream (see below) (reg 6.21(2)).

A superannuation provider is allowed to pay a death benefit as a superannuation income stream (rather than a lump sum), or to purchase an annuity only, if the entitled recipient (beneficiary):

- is a dependant of the member, and
- in the case of a child of the member:
  - is less than 18 years of age
  - being 18 or more years of age, is either financially dependent on the member and less than 25 years of age, or has a disability of the kind described in s 8(1) of the *Disability Services Act 1986* (reg 6.21(2A)).

In addition, if death benefits are being paid to a child of the deceased member as a pension (or annuity) under reg 6.21(2A), the benefits must be cashed as a lump sum on the earlier of:

(a) the day on which the pension is commuted, or the term of the pension expires (unless the benefit is rolled over to commence a new annuity or pension), and

(b) the day on which the child attains 25 years of age, unless the child has a disability of the kind described in s 8(1) of the Disability Services Act on the day that would otherwise be applicable under item (a) or (b) (reg 6.21(2B)).

Portability of benefits

Member benefits paid as a lump sum (but not as income streams) may be made in specie, provided the SISR investment provisions and the fund's trust deed are satisfied (reg 6.01(2), definition of "lump sum") (SMSFD 2011/1).

The SISR and RSAR also prescribe rules for the portability of superannuation which allow fund and RSA members to move their superannuation interests by way of transfers or roll-overs. Individuals may request the consolidation of their superannuation accounts using the ATO electronic portability scheme or via myTax and myGov (SISA s 34A; SISR regs 6.33; 6.33A; Pt 6A; RSAA s 138A; RSAR regs 4.35C to 4.35P, Pt 4AA). Special rules govern the transfers and management of unclaimed superannuation, including allowing the ATO to consolidate member accounts proactively in certain circumstances (¶13-850).

Superannuation data and payment standards — SuperStream

Trustees of superannuation entities and employers are required to comply with the superannuation data and payment standards made under SISA Pt 3B and the related superannuation roll-over and transfer standards and procedures in SISR Pt 6 Div 6.5 (collectively known as SuperStream standards). Briefly, the SuperStream standards require:

- employers, when making superannuation contributions on behalf of their employees, to provide the payments and associated data to superannuation funds in a specific electronic format, and
- superannuation funds, including SMSFs, to receive contributions electronically and process roll-overs in accordance with standards, and
- superannuation funds (and SMSFs from 31 March 2021) to provide data to regulators and transfer payments between funds using the SuperStream electronic payment and data verification system.

The ATO's SuperStream checklists for employers and superannuation funds (including a SuperStream decision tool and FAQs) may be found at www.ato.gov.au/super/superstream/employers/employer-checklist--a-step-by-step-guide and www.ato.gov.au/uploadedFiles/Content/SPR/downloads/Superstream_Decision_tree.pdf.

The electronic SuperStream Rollover Standard used for the transfer of information and money between employers, superannuation funds and the ATO will be expanded from 31 March 2021 to enable the ATO to send electronic requests to superannuation funds to release money under a number of arrangements (2019–20 Budget Paper No 2, p 169).

A draft instrument proposes amendments to extend the SuperStream standard to rollovers and transfers to and from SMSFs requested on or after 31 March 2021, and to release authority requests issued by the Commissioner under TAA Sch 1 Div 131 on or after 31 March 2021 (Draft Superannuation Data and Payment Standards (Release Authorities, and SMSF Rollovers) Amendment 2020 (SPR 2020/D3)).

Superannuation events-based reporting

Reporting to the ATO by APRA-regulated superannuation funds is made through 3 reporting services — Member Account Attribute Service (MAAS), Member Account Transaction Service (MATS) and SuperStream rollover message for unclaimed super money (USM) (www.ato.gov.au/super/superstream/apra-regulated-funds/reporting-obligations). These services supplement other superannuation reporting requirements (such as transfer balance account reporting: see ¶14-340), as well as replaced the former reporting systems using the member contributions statement (¶39-530), lost member statement and USM statement (¶13-850).

Taxpayer Alerts and guidelines on superannuation fund operations

The ATO has raised various tax and regulatory concerns over the years on particular superannuation fund operations, for example, non-cash contributions (TA 2008/12); dividend stripping arrangements involving transfers of private company shares to an SMSF (TA 2015/1); diverting personal services income to SMSFs (TA 2016/6) (available on the ATO legal database).

The ATO's legal database also contains Law Companion Rulings and Practical Compliance Guidelines on a range of superannuation topics such as the transfer balance cap: ¶14-320; total superannuation balance: ¶14-050; first home savers superannuation: ¶13-790; and downsizer contributions: ¶13-795, as well as law administration guidelines, eg PS LA 2020/3 dealing with administrative penalties imposed on SMSF trustees under SISA s 166(1).

Retirement Income Review and other superannuation reforms

The government has released the final report of the 2019 review into the retirement income system and exposure draft legislation for the *Your Future, Your Super* package of reforms announced in the 2020–21 Budget (¶41-900).

The *Financial Sector Reform (Hayne Royal Commission Response) Act 2020* has made amendments to implement several of the superannuation regulatory reform measures recommended by the Royal Commission into Misconduct in the Banking, Superannuation and Financial Services Industry.

The Wolters Kluwer *Australian Master Superannuation Guide 2020/21* provides further information on the review as well as other superannuation reform proposals.

[AMSG ¶3-000ff, ¶3-280, ¶3-286, ¶17-600; SLP ¶2-100ff]

¶13-810 COVID-19 — superannuation relief measures

Below is a summary of the relief measures affecting superannuation taxation which were introduced as a consequence of the COVID-19 pandemic. Other tax relief measures and concessions are discussed in various chapters of the Guide (see ''COVID-19'' in the Index section). Relief measures dealing with superannuation regulation and related matters are covered in the Wolters Kluwer *Australian Master Superannuation Guide 2020/21.*

Minimum annual pension payment limits halved

The minimum annual payment amount required for account-based pensions and annuities, allocated pensions and annuities, and market-linked pensions and annuities (also called term allocated pensions) is reduced by 50% in the 2019–20 and 2020–21 financial years (¶14-125).

Superannuation pension and annuity providers are required to calculate the minimum annual payment amount based on the account balance of the member or annuitant as at 1 July of each year and the 50% reduction will apply to the calculated minimum annual payment.

Early release of superannuation

Superannuation fund members and RSA holders who satisfy the eligibility rules set out in SISR reg 6.19B (or RSAR reg 4.22B) may apply for early release of their preserved or restricted non-preserved benefits in a regulated superannuation fund or RSA.

Eligible individuals must apply to the ATO online using myGov to access an amount of up to $10,000 of their superannuation in 2019–20 (for applications made before 1 July 2020) and a further amount of up to $10,000 in 2020–21 (for applications made from 1 July 2020 until 31 December 2020). Temporary residents are only entitled to make a single application during the 2019–20 financial year.

The ATO will follow up on compliance issues (if any) directly with the individual applicants. The application process and compliance checks are set out in the ATO's Fact Sheet *Design and implementation information.*

Tax treatment of fund payments under COVID-19 early access arrangements

- Any amount withdrawn is non-assessable non-exempt income (NANE); it will not affect Centrelink or Veterans' Affairs payments.
- The payment is not a ''withholding payment'' (as defined in ITAA97 s 995-1(1)); no tax withholding applies as the payment is NANE (TAA Sch 1 s 12-1(1A)).
- Funds are not required to issue PAYG statements showing a proportion of the payment to be taxable component — untaxed element.
- The payment is subject to the proportioning rules (¶14-130).

ATO FAQs and guidelines

The ATO's guidelines and compliance approach dealing with the SIS and tax obligations faced by superannuation funds and FAQs relating to COVID-19 relief measures are available at ATO FAQs.

¶13-825 Acceptance of contributions and benefit accruals

The rules governing whether a regulated superannuation fund can accept contributions, or grant benefit accruals in the case of defined benefit funds, are set out in Pt 7 of the SISR (regs 7.01–7.11). Broadly similar contributions rules apply to RSA providers under the RSAR.

A ''contribution'' in relation to a fund or an accrual of benefit does not include benefits that have been ''rolled-over'' or ''transferred'' to the fund (ie payments within the superannuation system (SISR regs 1.03(1); 5.01(1); 7.01(1)). The contributions rules also do not apply to proceeds from an insurance policy (eg for a claim paid in respect of a member's life or disability insurance policy) or to superannuation interests subject to a payment split as provided for under SISR Pt 7A. By contrast, certain transfers or roll-overs from *outside* the superannuation system are subject to the contributions rules, such as, funds transferred from an overseas superannuation fund (¶14-420) and payments of a CGT exempt amount to the fund (¶13-780).

It must be noted that the governing rules of a fund may have more restrictive contribution provisions than the SISR rules. Also, subject to its governing rules, a fund may accept in specie contributions provided these rules and the relevant SISA restrictions on the acquisition of assets are also complied with.

An exception to the SISR contributions rules applies for contributions of the proceeds from the sale of a business involving earnout rights to which certain small business CGT concessions apply (see ''Exception: contributions related to earnout rights'' below).

A fund which receives a contribution in a manner that is inconsistent with the SISR rules is generally required to return the contribution to the contributor (see below).

For APRA guidelines to RSE licensees on the contributions rules, covering risk management associated with the processing of contributions (including contributions made in error) and administration (eg establishing, monitoring and reviewing policies and procedures regarding the acceptance, classification and allocation of contributions), see *Prudential Practice Guide SPG 270 — Contribution and Benefit Accrual Standards.*

Rule 1: Age of member and work test

A regulated superannuation fund may accept contributions only in accordance with reg 7.04(1) (see the table below, applicable in relation to contributions made in 2020–21 and later financial years). Where applicable, reg 7.04(2) (see Rule 2 below), reg 7.04(4) (see ''Returning contributions made in breach of rules'' below) and reg 7.04(6) (as discussed below) must also be complied with.

Member's age	The fund may accept ...
1. Member is under 65	all contributions made in respect of the member
1A. Member is not under 65, but is under 67	contributions made in respect of the member that are: (a) ''mandated employer contributions'' (see below) (b) employer contributions (except mandated employer contributions) (c) member contributions, or (d) downsizer contributions

Member's age	The fund may accept ...
2. Member is not under 67, but is under 70	contributions made in respect of the member that are: (a) ''mandated employer contributions'' (b) if the member has been gainfully employed on at least a part-time basis during the financial year in which the contributions are made (this is commonly referred to as the ''work test'': see below): (i) employer contributions (except mandated employer contributions), or (ii) member contributions (c) downsizer contributions, or (d) if the member has not satisfied the work test during the financial year in which the contributions are made, but satisfies the requirements in reg 7.04(1A): (i) employer contributions (except mandated employer contributions), or (ii) member contributions (see ''Work test exemption for members with low balances'': below)
3. Member is not under 70, but is under 75	contributions made in respect of the member that are: (a) mandated employer contributions (b) if the member has been gainfully employed on at least a part-time basis during the financial year in which the contributions are made — contributions received on or before the 28th day after the end of the month in which the member turns 75 that are: (i) employer contributions (except mandated employer contributions), or (ii) member contributions (c) downsizer contributions, or (d) if the member has not satisfied the work test during the financial year in which the contributions are made, but satisfies the requirements in reg 7.04(1A) — contributions received on or before the 28th day after the end of the month on which the member turns 75 that are: (i) employer contributions (except mandated employer contributions), or (ii) member contributions (see ''Work test exemption for members with low balances'': below).
4. Member is not under 75	mandated employer contributions

Note that in any of the above circumstances, a fund may also accept contributions in respect of a member if it is reasonably satisfied that the contribution is in respect of a period during which the fund may accept the contribution, even though the contribution is actually made after that period (reg 7.04(6)).

An exception to the reg 7.04(1) restrictions applies for amounts relating to some CGT small business concessions (see ''Exception: contributions related to earnout rights'' below).

Employer contributions and member contributions

''Employer contributions'' are contributions by or on behalf of an employer-sponsor of the fund, and ''member contributions'' are contributions by or on behalf of a member other than employer contributions, eg personal contributions, spouse contributions and government co-contributions (SISR regs 1.03(1); 5.01(1)).

''Mandated employer contributions'' are:

- superannuation guarantee (SG) contributions, ie contributions made by or on behalf of an employer to reduce the employer's potential liability to the SG charge (¶39-240)
- payments of SG shortfall components, ie ATO payments of the shortfall component of the SG charge (¶39-600)
- award contributions made by or on behalf of an employer in satisfaction of the employer's obligations under an industrial agreement or award
- payments from the Superannuation Holding Accounts Special Account (¶39-650) (SISR reg 5.01(1), (2)).

Employer contributions include contributions made under an effective salary sacrifice arrangement. However, only those contributions to the required SG support level (9.5% in 2019–20 and 2020–21: ¶39-100), or contributions under an industrial award or agreement (if higher than the SG support level), are mandated employer contributions. Any excess over these levels may be accepted only if the relevant rules for non-mandated employer contributions in the above table are satisfied.

Work test

The trustee of a superannuation fund can only accept a contribution for an individual who has turned 67 (but is under 75) if the person is ''gainfully employed on at least a part-time basis'' in the year the contribution is made (the work test).

A person is ''gainfully employed on a part-time basis'' during a financial year if the person was gainfully employed at least 40 hours in a period of not more than 30 consecutive days in that financial year (SISR reg 7.01(3)). For example, a person who works 40 hours in a fortnight can make superannuation contributions for the rest of the financial year.

''Gainfully employed'' means being employed or self-employed for gain or reward in any business, trade, profession, vocation, calling, occupation or employment. ''Gain or reward'' is the receipt of remuneration such as wages, business income, bonuses and commissions, in return for personal exertion in these activities. It does not include the passive receipt of income, eg receipt of rent or dividends (SISR reg 1.03(1)).

APRA's view is that where an employer is receiving the JobKeeper wage subsidy for an individual, RSE licensees should consider the individual to be ''gainfully employed'' for the purpose of the work test, even if that individual has been fully stood down and is not actually performing work. In APRA's view, this approach is appropriate because the individual is still employed and is obtaining a valuable benefit from his/her employer.

Work test exemption for members with low balances

A work test exemption enables superannuation funds to accept voluntary superannuation contributions (both concessional and non-concessional contributions) for individuals who are aged 67 to 74 years and who have a total superannuation balance of less than $300,000 (see para (d) in items 2 and 3 in the table above) for 12 months from the end of the financial year in which they last met the work test if the following requirements are met:

- the member has *not* been gainfully employed on either a full-time or part-time basis during the financial year in which the contributions are made (ie the member does not satisfy the work test in the contribution year), but satisfied the work test in the previous financial year
- the member has a total superannuation balance (¶14-050) below $300,000 on 30 June of the previous financial year, and

- the member has not previously relied on the work test exemption in relation to a previous financial year (reg 7.04(1A)).

The work test exemption does not apply to defined benefit funds. This does not prevent a member of a defined benefit fund from opening an accumulation superannuation account in order to make voluntary contributions utilising the work test exemption.

Downsizer contributions

The downsizer contributions scheme is discussed in ¶13-795. The term "downsizer contribution" takes its meaning from ITAA97 s 292-102.

A contribution is only a downsizer contribution to the extent that it is from an individual's share of the proceeds of the sale of a dwelling under a contract entered into on or after 1 July 2018. The maximum amount that an individual can contribute from the proceeds of such a sale is $300,000. This can be done as a single contribution or as multiple contributions.

If a superannuation fund becomes aware that a contribution is an ineligible downsizer contribution, in whole or in part, (eg it exceeds the $300,000 limit or the fund is notified of that fact by the Commissioner), the fund must re-assess whether it can otherwise accept the contribution under a different rule based on the member's age or work test status. If they can then be accepted, these contributions will count towards the individual's applicable contribution caps like other contributions.

Downsizer contributions are treated in the same way as other contributions that a superannuation fund is permitted to accept. That is, fund trustees that generally have discretion regarding contributions made to the fund are not obligated to accept downsizer contributions' However, the superannuation providers must accept the contribution in accordance with SISA s 29TC(1)(f) where downsizer contributions are made into a MySuper product.

Exception: contributions related to earnout rights

A regulated superannuation fund may accept a contribution of an amount from the proceeds of the sale of a business to which the small business's 15-year asset exemption and retirement exemption apply, if the sale involved an earnout right and the contribution would not have been affected by the contribution restrictions had it been made during the financial year in which the business was sold.

Specifically, despite reg 7.04(1), a fund may accept, as a contribution, an amount to the extent that the amount does not exceed the member's CGT cap amount (¶13-775) if:

(a) the amount to be accepted as a contribution could be covered under ITAA97 s 292-100 (certain CGT-related payments) in relation to a CGT event referred to in that section

(b) the capital proceeds from the CGT event were or could have been affected by one or more financial benefits received under a look-through earnout right (¶11-675), and

(c) reg 7.04(1) would not have prevented the fund from accepting the amount as a contribution had it been made to the fund in the financial year in which the CGT event happened (reg 7.04(6A)).

The relevant CGT event is the one referred to in whichever of s 292-100(2), (4), (7) and (8) that could cause the amount to be covered under that subsection (reg 7.04(6A) note). In reg 7.04(6A), the terms "capital proceeds", "CGT cap amount", "CGT event", "financial benefit" and "look-through earnout right" have the same meaning as in the ITAA97 (reg 7.04(7)).

Rule 2: Member contributions where no TFN is provided

In addition to Rule 1, a regulated superannuation fund must not accept any *member contributions* if the member's TFN has not been quoted for superannuation purposes (¶13-180) to the trustee of the fund (SISR reg 7.04(2)).

Returning contributions made in breach of rules

If a fund receives a contribution in a manner that is inconsistent with Rules 1 or 2, the fund is required to return the contribution to the entity or person that paid the amount within 30 days of becoming aware of the inconsistency unless, in the case of Rule 2, a TFN number has been provided to the fund within the 30-day period (reg 7.04(4)(a)).

Where a contribution is returned, the fund is also authorised to take certain actions under reg 7.04(4)(b) to the extent permitted by the rules of the fund. For example, a fund may return an amount that reflects investment outcomes such as gains or losses that the fund made after the contribution was accepted and that is net of reasonable administration and transaction costs.

[AMSG ¶3-220; SLP ¶2-982]

¶13-840 TFN approvals

The TFN rules under the tax laws are discussed in ¶33-000 to ¶33-085.

In addition, SISA Pt 25A contains specific TFN provisions for trustees of eligible superannuation entities and regulated exempt public sector superannuation schemes (superannuation providers) and their members (SISA ss 299A–299Z).

APRA has made Superannuation Industry (Supervision) Tax File Number approval No 1 of 2017 (F2017L01262) which sets out the "approved manner" in which a TFN can be collected, reported, quoted, dealt with and used. The 2017 approval also reflects the current Privacy (Tax File Number) Rule 2015 (2015 TFN Rule) issued by the Privacy Commissioner under s 17 of the *Privacy Act 1988*.

The RSAA 1997 contains TFN provisions equivalent to SISA Pt 25A (RSAA Pt 11). APRA has made a similar TFN approval which outlines the approved manner in which a TFN can be collected, reported, quoted, dealt with and used by RSA providers and RSA holders under RSAA ss 134, 135(1), 136(1), 138(2), 142(1) and 139(a) (Retirement Savings Accounts Tax File Number approval No 1 of 2017 (F2017L01270)).

¶13-850 Unclaimed superannuation money

Under the *Superannuation (Unclaimed Money and Lost Members) Act 1999* (SUMLMA) and Superannuation (Unclaimed Money and Lost Members) Regulations 2019 (SUMLMR), superannuation funds, ADFs and RSA providers are required to provide "lost members" information and pay members' unclaimed superannuation money (USM) to the ATO in various circumstances, including:

- "unclaimed money" and USM of "former temporary residents"
- "lost member accounts", ie accounts of lost members with balances below the threshold amount of $6,000 or inactive accounts of unidentifiable lost members where the fund has not received an amount for the member within the last 12 months (SUMLMA ss 12; 14; 20AA; 24B(1)(b); (2)(b)).

The unclaimed money provisions do not apply to defined benefit interests. Prescribed state and territory public sector superannuation schemes are permitted, but not required, to pay unclaimed money, lost member accounts and former temporary resident's unclaimed moneys to the Commissioner (SUMLMA ss 18AA; 20JA).

Superannuation providers are required to report lost member information to the Commissioner in accordance with its events-based reporting obligations under TAA Sch 1 s 390-5(9) (see below).

Reporting member information and USM

When reporting lost members to the ATO and updating members' status, superannuation entities and RSA providers must comply with the events-based reporting obligations under TAA Sch 1 s 399-5 using the Member Account Attribute Service (MAAS) (¶39-530).

Superannuation funds are required to report USM using the SuperStream data standard roll-over message (¶13-800).

The ATO also issues notices under SUMLMA s 20C (Section 20C notices) to notify funds of former temporary residents using the roll-over message.

Reporting USM and payment obligations apply twice a year; however, funds may under the roll-over message system voluntarily report USM or respond to Section 20C notices sooner.

Transferring inactive low-balance accounts to ATO

Superannuation funds and RSA providers with members who have inactive low-balance accounts are required to report these accounts, and pay their account balances, to the Commissioner in accordance with SUMLMA Part 3B.

An ''inactive low balance account'' (ILBA) is an account that relates to a MySuper product or choice product where the account balance is less than $6,000 and the provider has not received an amount for crediting to that account in the last 16 months (SUMLMA s 20QA). Some member accounts are not ILBAs by definition, eg accounts in an SMSF or small APRA fund, accounts related to a defined benefit interest, and accounts where the member has elected to have or maintain insurance cover under SISA s 68AAB(2) or 68AAC(2) (s 20QA(1)(a)(i), (vii), (viii), (ix)).

An account is also not an ILBA if the member has met one of the conditions of release specified in SUMLMR ss 10 to 12. This recognises that there are some circumstances where a member may no longer be making contributions but has chosen to leave the balance in the account.

From 22 June 2020, members must make an election directly to their fund for their account to not be treated as an ILBA (previously, members made this election to ATO). A member's election is valid for 16 months, and fund trustees must maintain appropriate evidence of the election. If a fund receives the election after the ILBA has been reported and paid to the ATO, the fund should advise the member accordingly (Fact Sheet *Member ILBA election requirements*).

The requirement to report and pay an amount to the Commissioner does not apply to a trustee of a state or territory public sector superannuation scheme which reports and makes payments to a state or territory authority under SUMLMA s 18 (SUMLMA ss 20QG, 20QH). Where an ILBA also meets the SUMLMA definition of ''unclaimed money'', ''temporary resident''' or ''lost member'', the member's account will be paid to the Commissioner under the appropriate SUMLMA requirements as a priority order (s 20QD(5)).

Repayments of USM by the ATO

The Commissioner must pay USM held by the ATO in respect of an individual to a complying superannuation fund nominated by the individual if satisfied that it is possible to do so.

Also, the Commissioner may pay USM held by it directly to an individual who has reached eligibility age or has a terminal medical condition, or the amount is below $200, or to the beneficiaries or legal personal representative of a deceased individual (SUMLMA ss 17(2), 20H, 24G).

New Zealand residents who have USM held by the ATO in respect of them under the SUMLMA are currently unable to have the money paid directly to their KiwiSaver scheme account, but must transfer the USM from the ATO to a complying superannuation fund and then request the fund to transfer the money to a KiwiSaver scheme provider. Amendments have been made to the SUMLMA to allow individuals to direct the Commissioner to pay USM directly to KiwiSaver scheme providers, effective on a date to be proclaimed or within 12 months of assent to the *Treasury Laws Amendment (2020 Measures No 5) Act 2020*.

Tax treatment of USM repayments by the ATO

The Commissioner's payments under ss 17(2), 20H or 24G are treated as if they are paid from a complying superannuation fund and are taxed as superannuation benefits (¶14-100, ¶14-130), except the following:

- an amount of less than $200 is non-assessable non-exempt income (¶14-310), and
- an amount repaid under s 20H that is a departing Australia superannuation payment (DASP) is non-assessable non-exempt income but is subject to final withholding tax (¶14-390).

Payments made from complying superannuation funds (or by the Commissioner to a KiwiSaver scheme provider, see above) under the SUMLMA are non-assessable non-exempt income of the individual in respect whom the payment was made (ITAA97 ss 11-55, 312-1, 312-5, 312-20).

Interest on repayments of unclaimed money held by the ATO

The Commissioner must pay interest worked out in accordance with the SUMLMR:

- on USM payments under s 24G(2) (s 24G(3A) or 24G(3B)), and
- on general unclaimed money payments under s 17(2) or on USM payments for former temporary residents under s 20H(2) (ss 17(2AB), 17(2AC), 20H(2AA)) (PSLA 2011/23).

The tax treatment of the interest paid is as follows:

- interest paid, other than interest paid on the USM of former temporary residents, is a tax free component of a superannuation benefit (¶14-140)
- interest paid on the return of USM to former temporary residents is subject to DASP tax (¶14-390)
- interest paid to current residents of Australia is tax-free, and
- interest paid in respect of unclaimed First Home Saver Accounts is exempt from tax (ITAA97 former ss 51-120(c), (d); 307-142(3B), (3C)).

Proactive consolidation of accounts held by the ATO

The Commissioner is empowered to proactively consolidate ATO-held superannuation (unclaimed money, ILBAs and lost member accounts) into an active superannuation account for a person (SUMLMA Part 4B). The Commissioner must pay the ATO-held amounts into a superannuation fund that has received contributions for the person where the consolidated account balance will be equal to or greater than $6,000 (ss 24NA, 24NB).

Eligible rollover funds

An eligible rollover fund (ERF) is a regulated superannuation approved by APRA to operate as an ERF in accordance with SISA Pt 24.

ERFs operate as temporary repositories for small superannuation account balances or accounts belonging to persons who cannot continue to be a member of a fund. An ERF can transfer accounts to another superannuation fund where the member has an account with that fund and that fund has received a contribution for the member in the last 12 months or through a successor fund transfer. Like other superannuation funds, an ERF is also required to transfer amounts to the ATO as provided in SUMLMA, eg where the amount is unclaimed, a lost member account, an inactive low-balance account, or a DASP of a former temporary resident (see above).

Amendments have been proposed to SUMLMA, SISA and RSAA:

- to require all accounts with balances of less than $6,000 that are held by ERFs on 1 June 2020 to be transferred to the ATO by 30 June 2020 (to be extended to 30 June 2021, see below) and all remaining accounts to be transferred by 30 June 2021 (to be extended to 31 January 2022, see below), unless the ERF has ceased to hold the accounts earlier
- to allow amounts paid to the ATO from ERFs to be included in the amounts that the Commissioner can proactively reunite with a member's active superannuation account, and
- to prevent superannuation funds and RSA providers from transferring new amounts to ERFs from the later of 7 days after assent or 1 May 2020 (Treasury Laws Amendment (Reuniting More Superannuation) Bill 2020: ¶41-100).

The government proposes to amend the above Bill to defer:

- the date by which ERFs are required to transfer accounts to the ATO to 30 June 2021 (for accounts with balances below $6,000), and to 31 January 2022 (for all other accounts), and
- by 12 months the start date of the measure preventing transfers of new amounts to ERFs by superannuation funds (*Economic and Fiscal Update*, July 2020).

¶13-870 Superannuation levies

All superannuation entities are liable to pay a superannuation supervisory levy each year to recover the cost of their supervision by APRA and the Commissioner, and superannuation entities (other than SMSFs) may also be liable to pay a financial assistance funding levy (see below).

The supervisory levy is determined annually while the financial assistance levy is determined from time to time as required (Non-SMSFs: *Superannuation Supervisory Levy Imposition Act 1998*, *Superannuation (Financial Assistance Funding) Levy Act 1993*, *Financial Institutions Supervisory Levies Collection Act 1998*; SMSFs: *Superannuation (Self Managed Superannuation Funds) Supervisory Levy Imposition Act 1991*, *Superannuation (Self Managed Superannuation Funds) Taxation Act 1987;* Australian Prudential Regulation Authority Supervisory Levies Determination 2020: F2020L00855).

There is also a separate levy which is imposed on ASIC-regulated entities to recover ASIC's regulatory costs in each financial year (*ASIC Supervisory Cost Recovery Levy Act 2017 and Regulations, ASIC Supervisory Cost Recovery Levy (Collection) Act 2017*). Leviable entities include superannuation trustees and certain Australian financial services licensees (www.asic.gov.au).

Superannuation supervisory levy

The supervisory levy amount payable by the different superannuation entity types (ie SMSFs, small APRA funds, single member ADFs, PSTs and all other superannuation entities) may be found in ¶18-650 of the *Australian Master Superannuation Guide 2020/21*.

The levy is deductible as a tax-related expense (ITAA97 s 25-5). Late lodgment charges and payments by way of or as a penalty are not deductible (ITAA97 ss 26-5; 26-90).

Financial assistance funding levy

The *Superannuation (Financial Assistance Funding) Levy Act 1993* (Levy Act) imposes a levy on regulated superannuation funds and ADFs (other than a levy-exempt fund or an SMSF or SMADF) to recoup the financial assistance given to superannuation entities which suffer losses due to fraudulent conduct or theft (SISA Pt 23). The levy rate, amount and entities subject to the levy are set out in determinations made under the Levy Act.

The levy is deductible when incurred (ITAA97 ss 295-490, item 3; 290-490(2)). A grant of financial assistance is exempt from income tax in the hands of the recipient superannuation entity (ITAA97 s 295-405, item 1). A repayment of a grant of financial assistance by the entity is not deductible (s 295-495, item 5).

[AMSG ¶3-900ff; SLP ¶4-900ff]

Chapter 14 Superannuation Benefits • Termination Payments

Superannuation Benefits Tax

¶14-000 Taxation of superannuation and termination payments

This chapter covers the concessional taxation of employment termination payments and superannuation lump sum and income stream benefits and related payments under ITAA97 Pt 2-40 and Pt 3-30 (¶14-100ff, ¶14-600ff).

The PAYG withholding and reporting obligations for these payments and benefits are discussed in ¶26-100ff.

The payment process of superannuation benefits is closely linked to the operating standards for superannuation entities which are prescribed by the SISA and RSAA and their regulations, such as the rules for the preservation, portability and payment of benefits, including paying superannuation death benefits as income streams (¶13-800), and the minimum standards for income streams (¶14-125). Payments of benefits paid in breach of certain prescribed rules do not qualify for concessional taxation as superannuation benefits (¶14-300).

[AMSG ¶8-000ff; FITR ¶290-000ff; SLP ¶38-000ff]

¶14-050 Total superannuation balance

The concept of "total superannuation balance" in ITAA97 s 307-230 is used as the method to value an individual's total superannuation interests for tax purposes. A superannuation interest is an interest in a superannuation fund, an ADF or a superannuation annuity (¶14-130).

An individual's total superannuation balance is relevant to determine eligibility for:

- the unused concessional contributions cap carry forward in a financial year — an individual whose total superannuation balance is less than $500,000 *just before* the start of the financial year may increase his/her concessional contributions cap using any unused concessional contributions cap amounts of one or more of the previous 5 years (ITAA97 s 291-20(3)(b), (c)) (¶13-775)
- the non-concessional contributions cap and bring forward of the non-concessional contributions cap — an individual whose total superannuation balance *immediately before* the start of a financial year is below the general transfer balance cap ($1.6 million in 2020–21: ¶14-320) is eligible for a non-concessional contributions cap for the year of 4 times the concessional contributions cap (not taking into account increases under the concessional cap carry forward measure) (ITAA97 s 292-85(2)(a)). Under a bring forward arrangement, the individual may also be eligible for a non-concessional contributions cap of up to 3 times the annual non-concessional cap amount over a 3-year period (s 292-85(3) to (7)) (¶13-780).
- government co-contribution — an individual is eligible for government co-contribution in an income year if:

  (i) the individual's non-concessional contributions for the financial year do not exceed the non-concessional contributions cap for the financial year, and

  (ii) *immediately before* the start of that financial year, the individuals' total superannuation balance is less than the general transfer balance cap for that financial year (SGCLIEA s 6(1)(da), (db)) (¶13-760).
- spouse contributions tax offset — an individual is not entitled to the tax offset if:

  (i) the spouse's non-concessional contributions for the financial year exceeds the non-concessional contributions cap for the financial year, or

  (ii) *immediately before* the start of the financial year, the spouse's total superannuation balance equals or exceeds the general transfer balance cap for the financial year (ITAA97 s 290-230(4A)) (¶13-770).

The total superannuation balance of an individual (a fund member) is also used to determine whether an SMSF or small APRA fund is eligible to use the segregated assets method to calculate its exempt current pension income (see ''Disregarded small fund assets'' in ¶13-140).

LCR 2016/12 and GN 2017/8 Total superannuation balance provide guidelines and examples on how an individual's total superannuation balance is calculated.

An individual's total superannuation balance can generally be measured at any time, but the balance is only relevant for tax purposes at the end of a particular income year. The terms ''immediately before'' and ''just before'' the start of the financial or income year as the relevant time for calculating a total superannuation balance refer to the end of 30 June of the previous financial or income year (LCR 2016/12 para 4).

What is an individual's total superannuation balance at a particular time

An individual's total superannuation balance at a particular time is the *sum* of the components below, *reduced* by the sum of any structured settlement contributions (if any):

> Component 1 — the accumulation phase value of the individual's superannuation interests that are *not* in the retirement phase (ss 307-205(2); 307-230(1)(a)). This component is the accumulation phase value as set out in regulations made for the purposes of ITAA97 s 307-205(2)(a), or the total amount of superannuation interests that would become payable if the individual had voluntarily ceased the interest at that time (ITR97 reg 307-205.02C)

Component 2 — the individual's "transfer balance" (¶14-320 and LCR 2016/9) or "modified transfer balance" (but not less than nil), if the individual has a "superannuation income stream in the retirement phase" (see below). The transfer balance is modified for an individual who receives certain account-based income streams in the retirement phase and/or has made structured settlement contributions (see "Individual's transfer balance or modified transfer balance" below) (s 307-230(1)(b), (4)), and

Component 3 — any roll-over superannuation benefit (¶14-450) not already reflected in the individual's accumulation phase value of superannuation interests or transfer balance (ie under the first and second components). This ensures that roll-overs just before the end of a financial year are included in the individual's total superannuation balance which is calculated on 30 June of the financial year (s 307-230(1)(c)).

In certain circumstances, an individual's total superannuation balance may have a fourth component (see "Total superannuation balance may include an individual's share of an LRBA balance" below).

Meaning of superannuation income stream in the retirement phase

A superannuation income stream is "in the retirement phase" at a time if:

- a superannuation income stream benefit is payable from it at that time (this is the general definition: see "Exceptions — income streams not in the retirement phase" below), or

- it is a deferred superannuation income stream (within the meaning in SISR reg 1.03(1)) and income stream benefits will be payable from it to a person after that time, and the person has satisfied (whether at or before that time) the condition of release (dealing with retirement, terminal medical condition, permanent incapacity, or attaining age 65) (s 307-80(1); (2)).

Exceptions — income streams not in the retirement phase

Certain income streams are not in the retirement phase by operation of the law, either because the law specifically excludes them from being in the retirement phase, or they do not comply with the definition of "superannuation income stream in the retirement phase". Examples of these are:

1. a deferred superannuation income stream that has not yet become payable to a person or the person has not yet met a relevant condition of release (see above)

2. a transition to retirement income stream (TRIS), transition to retirement income pension or non-commutable allocated annuity or non-commutable allocated pension (within the meaning in SISR Pt 6 or RSAR Pt 4) where the person to whom the benefit is payable is *not* a reversionary beneficiary and the person:

   - has not satisfied a condition of release specified in s 307-80(2)(c) (see above), or

   - has satisfied a condition of release relating to retirement, terminal medical condition or permanent disability, but has not notified the income stream provider of that fact (s 307-80(3))

3. an income stream that is specified in an ATO commutation authority to a superannuation provider in respect of a member's excess transfer balance amount , and:

   - the provider is required by TAA Sch 1 s 136-80 to pay a superannuation lump sum but fails to do so within the 60-day period mentioned in that section, and

- the income year is the income year in which the 60-day period ended, or a later income year (¶14-350) (s 307-80(4)).

A TRIS that is paid to a reversionary beneficiary qualifies as an income stream in the retirement phase by operation of the general definition in s 307-80(1), ie a superannuation income stream benefit is payable from it at that time (see above).

The expression "superannuation income stream in the retirement" is also used in ITAA97 for the purpose of determining a superannuation fund's current pension income exemption (¶13-140).

Individual's transfer balance or modified transfer balance

The second component of an individual's total superannuation balance is the individual's "transfer balance" if the individual has a "transfer balance account" (¶14-340). These are individuals who have a superannuation income stream in the retirement phase.

The transfer balance or modified transfer balance in Component 2 cannot be less than nil (this requirement is determined after the modifications in s 307-230(2) and (3) (where applicable), as discussed below, have been made).

Modifications of transfer balance for account-based income streams

An individual's transfer balance is modified if a credit has arisen in the individual's transfer balance account in relation to superannuation income streams in the retirement phase that are allocated annuities or pensions, account-based annuities or pensions, or market-linked annuities or pensions as defined in SISR or RSAR (generally called "account-based income streams") (s 307-230(3), (4)).

The modification is to disregard the debits and credits below which have arisen in the transfer balance account:

- credits from the individual becoming a retirement phase recipient of the prescribed account-based superannuation income streams (see above) (s 294-25(1) table items 1 and 2)
- debits from:
  - commutations of the prescribed account-based superannuation income stream in the retirement phase (s 294-80(1) table item 1)
  - an event that results in the superannuation interest that supports the prescribed account-based superannuation income stream being reduced (eg fraud or dishonesty; bankruptcy) (s 294-80(1) table item 3)
  - a payment split that applies to the prescribed account-based superannuation income stream (eg divorce or relationship breakdown) (s 294-80(1) table item 4)
  - a superannuation income stream provider failing to comply with a commutation authority in respect of the prescribed account-based superannuation income stream (s 294-80(1) table item 5)
  - a prescribed account-based superannuation income stream that fails to comply with the relevant pension or annuity standards (s 294-80(1) table item 6).

Disregarding credits and debits simply means that the credits are subtracted from, and the debits are added back to, an individual's transfer balance.

The following credit and debits in an individual's transfer balance account are *not* disregarded:

- credits from excess transfer balance earnings (s 294-25(1) table item 3)
- debits from:

- structured settlement contributions (s 294-25(1) table item 2) (the debit is applied instead by the modification to the transfer balance for such contributions — see ''Modifications of transfer balance for structured settlement contributions'' below).
- a notice issued under s 136-70 of Sch 1 to the *Taxation Administration Act 1953* of a non-commutable excess transfer balance (s 294-25(1) table item 7).

Modifications of transfer balance for structured settlement contributions

A structured settlement contribution arises where the compensation or damages received by an individual from a personal injury settlement or court order are contributed to a complying superannuation plan and this results in a debit to the individual's transfer balance account (s 294-80(1) table item 2).

If an individual has made a ''structured settlement contribution'', a modification applies to the individual's transfer balance by disregarding the debit that has arisen in respect of the structured settlement contribution (ie the debit amount is added back to the individual's transfer balance). This modification applies to both account-based and non-account-based income streams (s 307-230(2)(b)(i)). This modification has the effect of negating the provision that debits that have arisen because of structured settlement contributions are not disregarded for account-based income streams as noted earlier (see ''Modifications of transfer balance for account-based income streams'' above and Examples 5 and 6 in LCR 2016/12).

In summary, when determining the total superannuation balance for an individual who has structured settlement contributions, the sum of the individual's accumulation phase value of superannuation interests, transfer balance or modified transfer balance and roll-over superannuation benefits (components 1, 2 and 3, see above) which has been calculated is reduced by the settlement contribution amounts (s 307-230(2)(a), (b)(ii)).

Total superannuation balance may include an individual's share of LRBA balance

An individual's total superannuation balance may include an additional amount (ie a fourth component) if an asset that supports one or more of the individual's superannuation interest is subject to a limited recourse borrowing arrangement (LRBA) entered into by an SMSF or a small APRA fund on or after 1 July 2018 (ITAA97 s 307-231; ITTPA s 307-231). This applies only in respect of LRBAs where:

- the individual (whose superannuation interests are supported by assets to which the LRBA relate) has satisfied a condition of release specified in ITAA97 s 307-80(2)(c) (ie a condition of release in the SISR with a nil cashing restriction), or
- the LRBA is between the fund and one of its associates (see Examples 4A and 4B in LCR 2016/12).

The fourth component amount is equal to a proportion of the outstanding balance of the LRBA as at the end of the income year, based on the individual's share of the total superannuation interests that are supported by the asset subject to the LRBA (s 307-231(2) and (3)). Including a proportion of the outstanding balance prevents double counting from occurring where more than one member has an interest supported by an asset that was acquired through the LRBA. Therefore, if only one member's interest is supported by the asset, the proportion is equal to 1, so that the whole outstanding LRBA amount is added to the member's total superannuation balance.

It should be noted that artificially manipulating the allocation of assets that are subject to LRBAs against particular superannuation interests may be subject to the general anti-avoidance rules in ITAA36 Pt IVA where such allocations formed part of a scheme for the dominant purpose of obtaining a tax benefit.

Practitioner articles

Articles on ''Strategies to reduce your total superannuation balance'' are available in Wolters Kluwer's *Australian Tax Week* (see ''2018 Tax Week'': ¶426, ¶484 and ¶637). They examine a range of issues, including the various components of a person's total superannuation balance, the effects of making pension and/or lump sum payments and paying arm's length expenses to reduce the balance, and tax effect accounting and contribution splitting.

Superannuation Benefits

¶14-100 What is a superannuation benefit?

A ''superannuation benefit'' is defined in ITAA97 s 307-5(1). It covers a superannuation member benefit or a superannuation death benefit such as:

- a superannuation fund payment to a fund member or to another person after the fund member's death
- an RSA payment to an RSA holder or to another person after the RSA holder's death
- an ADF payment to a depositor or to another person after the death of the depositor
- a small superannuation account payment to a person under ss 63, 64, 65, 65A, 66, 67, 67A or 76(6) of the *Small Superannuation Accounts Act 1995* (SSAA), or a payment to the legal personal representative of the deceased under SSAA s 68 or 76(7) (a payment from the SHASA by the ATO: ¶39-650)
- an ''unclaimed money payment'' to a person or the person's legal personal representative under ss 17(1), (2), (2AB), (2AC), 20F(1), 20H(2), (2AA), (2A), (3), 24E, 24G(2), (3A) or (3B) of the *Superannuation (Unclaimed Money and Lost Members) Act 1999*, or a payment to or by a state or territory as mentioned in s 18(4) or (5) of that Act (¶13-850)
- a superannuation co-contribution benefit payment to a person or the person's legal personal representative under s 15(1)(c) or (d) of the *Superannuation (Government Co-contribution for Low Income Earners) Act 2003* (see ''Government co-contributions: ¶13-760)
- a superannuation guarantee payment under s 65A of the *Superannuation Guarantee (Administration) Act 1992* to a person who is aged 65 or over, or under s 66 to a person who has retired because of incapacity or invalidity, or under s 66A to a person who has a terminal medical condition, or a payment under s 67 of that Act to the legal personal representative of a deceased person (see ''Distribution of shortfall component'': ¶39-600)
- a superannuation annuity payment to the annuitant from a superannuation annuity or arising from the commutation of a superannuation annuity, or a payment to another person after the death of the annuitant. A ''superannuation annuity'' is an income stream purchased from a life insurance company or a similar provider that complies with prescribed standards (ITR97 reg 995-1.01).

Certain payments are specifically stated not to be superannuation benefits (see below).

Superannuation member benefit and superannuation death benefit

A superannuation benefit can be either:

- a "superannuation member benefit", ie one of the above payments to a fund member, RSA holder, ADF depositor or beneficiary (as described in column 2 of the table in s 307-5(1), and extended by s 307-5(5) to (7)), or
- a "superannuation death benefit", ie one of the above payments to a person because of the death of another person (as described in column 3 of the table in s 307-5(1)) (s 307-5(2), (4)).

A superannuation death benefit is included in the meaning of "roll-over superannuation benefit" in ITAA97 s 307 (¶14-450) from 1 July 2017. This is to facilitate the payment and roll over of death benefit income streams for eligible beneficiaries and ensure that rolled-over death benefits receive the same tax treatment as rolled-over member benefits. That is, the roll-over benefit is not treated as a superannuation contribution (¶13-825), and is considered as non-assessable non-exempt income (ITAA97 s 306-5).

When determining if a superannuation fund has made a death benefit payment for the purpose of s 307-5(1), journal entries are insufficient as actual payment needs to be made (ID 2015/23). The SISR rules for the payment (cashing) of a deceased member's benefits are discussed in ¶13-800.

Contributions-splitting superannuation benefit

Eligible members of superannuation funds and exempt public sector superannuation scheme (EPSSS) and RSA holders can split their personal and employer contributions with their spouse by way of a "contributions-splitting superannuation benefit". This is effectively a roll-over, transfer or allotment of an amount of a member's benefit to his/her spouse in accordance with SISR Div 6.7 or RSAR Div 4.5.

A contributions-splitting superannuation benefit payment is not a superannuation benefit of the member spouse originally entitled, but a benefit of the receiving spouse (s 307-5(6)).

Family law superannuation payment

A "family law superannuation payment" is a payment of any of the following kinds and which satisfies the requirements (if any) specified:

- a payment in accordance with Pt VIIIB of the *Family Law Act 1975* or the Family Law (Superannuation) Regulations 2001
- a payment in accordance with Pt 7A of the SISR or Pt 4A of the RSAR (superannuation interests subject to family law payment splits), or
- a payment specified in the ITR97 (s 307-5(7)).

These are payments from a member spouse's entitlement in a superannuation fund for the benefit of a non-member spouse. A family law superannuation payment is not a superannuation benefit of the member spouse originally entitled but a benefit of the non-member spouse (s 307-5(5) to (7)).

Payments that are not superannuation benefits

The following are not superannuation benefits (ITAA97 s 307-10):

- Payments under an income stream because a person is temporarily unable to engage in gainful employment. These payments are considered to be replacement of regular income and are taxable at marginal rates.

- A benefit to which ITAA36 s 26AF(1) or 26AFA(1) applies. These are benefits paid in breach of the payment standards in the SISR and are taxable at marginal rates (¶14-300).
- An amount required by the *Bankruptcy Act 1966* to be paid to a trustee in bankruptcy. These amounts are not subject to tax.
- Payments received from a commutation of a pension from a constitutionally protected fund or a superannuation provider and wholly applied to pay a superannuation contributions surcharge liability. These payments are tax-free.
- Pension or annuity payments from a foreign superannuation fund. These may be taxable in Australia, subject to any applicable DTA (¶14-510).

[AMSG ¶8-130; FITR ¶296-000ff; SLP ¶38-050ff]

¶14-120 Superannuation lump sums and income streams

A superannuation benefit can be a superannuation member benefit or a superannuation death benefit (¶14-100), and can be either a lump sum or an income stream benefit.

A superannuation lump sum means a superannuation benefit that is not a superannuation income stream benefit (ITAA97 s 307-65). The meaning of "superannuation income stream benefit" (as defined in ITAA97 s 307-70(1)) and the minimum standards that income stream payments from a superannuation interest must comply with so as to qualify as a superannuation income stream for tax purposes are discussed in ¶14-125.

The Federal Court has provided guidance on the interpretation of ss 307-65 (meaning of superannuation lump sum) and 307-70 (meaning of superannuation income stream and superannuation income stream benefit) in 3 test cases (*Burns*, *Walker* and *Douglas*: see ¶14-130).

Superannuation member benefits taxation

The taxation of superannuation member benefits (lump sums and income streams) received from a complying superannuation plan is governed by Div 301 and is discussed in ¶14-200. Generally, superannuation benefit taxation is based on the amount of the payment, whether the benefit is a lump sum or income stream benefit, the recipient's age and whether the payer is a taxed or untaxed source (¶14-220, ¶14-240). For the taxation of benefits received from a non-complying plan, including foreign superannuation funds, see ¶14-400 and ¶14-420.

Superannuation death benefits taxation

A superannuation benefit is a "superannuation death benefit" if it is paid to a taxpayer (eg a dependant or non-dependant or the trustee of a deceased estate) because of the death of the person originally entitled to the benefit (the fund member) (s 307-5(1), Table column 3).

The taxation of superannuation death benefits (lump sums and income streams) from a complying plan is governed by Div 302 and is discussed at ¶14-270 and ¶14-280.

Special taxation rules for certain benefit payments

Special taxation rules override the tax treatment in Divs 301 and 302 for payments from complying superannuation plans that are in breach of prescribed legislative requirements or are made in particular circumstances (¶14-300, ¶14-310), or are departing Australia superannuation payments (¶14-390).

Transfer balance tax and additional tax consequences for certain income streams

The amount of an individual's total income stream benefits in the retirement phase (¶13-140) is limited by a transfer balance cap (¶14-320) and an individual is liable to pay excess transfer balance tax if the cap is exceeded (¶14-360). Special rules apply to capped defined benefit income stream benefits under the transfer balance tax regime, with additional tax consequences if the benefits exceed a defined benefit income cap in a year (¶14-370).

[AMSG ¶8-130ff; FITR ¶290-000; SLP ¶38-050ff]

¶14-125 Superannuation income stream benefits and minimum standards

Superannuation funds and life insurance companies providing certain superannuation income streams which meet the SISR and RSAR pension and annuity standards (generally referred to as ''minimum standards'') receive an earnings tax exemption on the income derived from assets they hold to support these income streams (¶13-140). In addition, income streams which comply with the standards are pensions and annuities for the purposes of SISA and RSAA, and are ''superannuation income streams'' and ''superannuation income stream benefits'' under ITAA97 (¶14-100) which qualify for concessional tax treatment (¶14-200 – ¶14-240).

Superannuation income stream benefits

A ''superannuation income stream benefit'' is a payment from a superannuation interest that supports a superannuation income stream (ITAA97 s 307-70(1); ITR97 reg 995-1.01, definition of ''superannuation income stream benefit'').

A ''superannuation income stream benefit'' in s 307-70(1) has 2 limbs — the first requires that the benefit be a ''superannuation benefit specified in the regulations'', and the second requires that the benefit be paid from a ''superannuation income stream''.

The SISR and RSAR standards set out rules on various matters with which each type of superannuation income stream must comply at all times, such as commutation restrictions, maximum annual pension payment limit (where applicable), as well as the minimum annual pension payment requirements (see ''Income streams must meet minimum standards'' below).

A ''superannuation income stream benefit'' thus covers the various types of income stream payments from annuity providers and pension providers (superannuation funds and RSA providers) which have complied with the applicable standards, based on the date the benefit first commenced to be paid and whether the benefit is account-based or non-account-based (eg allocated pensions, transition to retirement pensions, lifetime pensions, market-linked (term allocated) pensions).

A superannuation fund is taken to be paying 2 distinct superannuation income streams if the product provides for an agreed level of payments (supported by an investment in a life insurance policy) in the event the assets (other than the life insurance policy) supporting the member's pension are exhausted (ID 2009/151: superannuation product income streams). Amounts paid by a trustee to a fund member are superannuation income stream benefits where the amounts are attributable to an account balance of the member and the trustee has agreed to protect part of the member's account balance for an agreed period of time (ID 2014/5).

An income stream payment to a deceased estate from an exempt public sector superannuation scheme as a result of a Family Court order is not a superannuation income stream but is treated as a superannuation lump sum death benefit (ID 2014/2: ¶14-280).

Death benefit payments

A lump sum death benefit or new income stream benefit is also a ''superannuation income stream benefit'' if it is payable from the time that a person who was receiving an income stream dies until as soon as it was practicable to pay the lump sum or new income stream benefit (reg 995-1.01(2) to (5)). This extended definition allows the earnings tax exemption to continue until the deceased member's benefits have been paid from a complying superannuation fund (¶13-140).

From 1 July 2017, a lump sum payment arising from a partial commutation of a superannuation income stream is generally treated as a superannuation lump sum but is treated as a superannuation income stream benefit for the purposes of the earnings tax exemption provisions (s 307-65(2)).

Income streams must meet minimum standards

As noted above, an income stream that is paid by a superannuation fund or RSA provider from a superannuation interest must ensure that the income stream complies with the relevant SISR or RSAR minimum standards in order for it to qualify as a superannuation income stream benefit for taxation purposes.

Where the standards impose a minimum annual pension payment requirement, the minimum pension amount in a year is worked out using the applicable Schedules in the Regulations, based on the type of pension and its commencement date, the pensioner's age and the account balance as at 1 July of that year (SISR Sch 1A cl 3A, 3B; Sch 1AAB cl 3A, 3B; Sch 6 cl 10, 11; Sch 7 cl 4A, 4B; RSAR Sch 1 cl 3A, 3B; Sch 1A, cl 3A, 3B; Sch 4 cl 10, 11).

A payment by way of commutation of a pension is excluded from being counted towards the minimum annual payment amount required to be paid from the pension account (SISR reg 1.06(9A)(a)).

Minimum pension payment amount halved for 2019–20 and 2020–21

The minimum annual pension amount for account-based pensions and annuities, allocated pensions and annuities and market-linked pensions and annuities is reduced by 50% in the 2019–20 and 2020–21 financial years.

Pension payments in excess of the reduced minimum drawdown limit for the financial year which have been received cannot be re-categorised. That is, they remain as superannuation income stream benefits, and are not superannuation lump sums.

The reduced minimum pension amount for a financial year is calculated based on a member's pension account balance as at 1 July of the year (or a later pension commencement date during the year) and cannot be recalculated at another point in time during the year (eg based on a member's smaller account balance due to losses incurred by the fund during the year).

A member who has received more than the reduced minimum annual pension amount can make a re-contribution to an accumulation account (in the same or another superannuation fund) provided the member is eligible to make contributions (¶13-825) and other rules or limits such as the contributions caps are met (¶13-775, ¶13-780).

Standards for innovative income stream products

Innovative income stream products which meet the standards in SISR reg 1.06A are also pensions and annuities under SISA and are superannuation income stream benefits for tax purposes. The reg 1.06A standards cover lifetime products that do not meet the annuity and pension standards in SISR regs 1.05(11A) and 1.06(9A) (eg deferred superannuation income streams, pooled investment pensions and pooled investment annuities).

Briefly, these innovative income streams are required to be payable for a beneficiary's lifetime, with payments guaranteed in whole or part by the income stream provider, or determined in whole or part through returns on a collective pool of assets or the mortality experience of the beneficiaries of the asset pool. They may also have a deferral period for annual payments and are permitted to be commuted subject to a declining capital access schedule and preservation rules (see reg 1.06A(3) for the 4 key elements).

When an income stream commences and ceases

The time of commencement and cessation of a superannuation income is important to determine the taxation consequences for both the superannuation fund (¶13-130, ¶13-140) and the member in relation to superannuation income stream benefit paid (¶14-220).

TR 2013/5 clarifies when a ''superannuation income stream'' (within the meaning in ITR97 reg 995-1.01(a)(ii)) commences and ceases. These are income streams which meet the standards in SISR reg 1.06(1) and 1.06(9A)(a) (commonly called account-based pensions, including transition to retirement income streams).

A superannuation income stream commences on the first day of the period to which the first payment of the income stream relates, as determined by reference to the terms and conditions of the income stream agreed by the trustee and member, the fund rules and the SISR standards. Once an income stream commences, it is payable (ie there is an obligation to pay the benefits under that superannuation income stream) until such time as that income stream ceases.

An income stream ceases when there is no longer a member who is entitled, or a dependent beneficiary who is automatically entitled, to be paid an income stream benefit from the superannuation interest supporting the income stream, as determined by reference to the fund's trust deed, the SISR standards and the particular facts and circumstances for payment of the benefits. Examples of these circumstances include:

- the failure to comply with the minimum payment standards in an income year
- when the capital supporting the income stream has been reduced to nil
- when the member's entitlements to future income stream benefits have been *fully* commuted into a lump sum entitlement (a partial commutation does not result in the cessation of the income stream), and
- when the member receiving the income stream dies, unless a reversionary income stream takes effect at that time (ie a dependent beneficiary is automatically entitled under the fund's deed or rules to receive an income stream).

¶14-130 Components of a superannuation benefit

A superannuation benefit, whether a lump sum or an income stream, may comprise 2 components — the tax free component and the taxable component (s 307-120(1)).

The proportioning rule in s 307-125 (see below) applies to work out these components, except for superannuation benefits where the rules to work out the components are specified by s 307-120(2)(b) to (e) as follows:

- a ''superannuation guarantee payment'' (¶14-100) or a ''contributions-splitting superannuation benefit'' (¶14-120) — the tax free component is nil and the taxable component is the amount of the benefit (ss 307-130; 307-140)
- a ''superannuation co-contribution benefit payment'' (¶14-100) — the tax free component is the whole amount of the benefit and the taxable component is nil (s 307-135)
- a payment by the Commissioner under s 17(2), (2AB), (2AC), 20H(2), (2AA), (2A), (3), 20QF(2), (5) or (6) or 24G(2), (3A) or (3B) of the *Superannuation (Unclaimed Money and Lost Members) Act 1999,* or by a state or territory authority as mentioned in s 18(5) of that Act (¶13-850) — the tax free component and taxable component are worked out as provided in s 307-142.

For a disability superannuation benefit, the components are worked out under s 307-145 (see ‘‘Modification for disability benefits’’), and for superannuation lump sum benefits with an element untaxed in the fund, the components are worked out under s 307-150 (see ‘‘Modification for lump sums with an element untaxed in the fund’’ below).

The taxable component of the superannuation benefit may consist of an element taxed in the fund or an element untaxed in the fund, or both. The determination of the taxed and untaxed elements is specified by ITAA97 Subdiv 307-E (¶14-150).

A superannuation fund payment as a result of an ATO determination under the COVID-19 early release of superannuation measure (¶13-810) is non-assessable non-exempt income (ie tax-free), but is subject to the proportioning rule to determine the components of the superannuation interest from which it is paid.

Proportioning rule

The proportioning rule provides for the tax free component and the taxable component of a superannuation benefit to be calculated by:

Step 1 — determining the proportions of the value of the superannuation interest that those components represent, and

Step 2 — applying those proportions to the benefit (s 307-125(1)).

The purpose of the proportioning rule is to remove an individual’s capacity to reduce a potential tax liability by manipulating the tax components of a superannuation benefit when it is paid from a superannuation plan, including by way of a roll-over of the superannuation benefit. The rule ensures that the tax free and taxable components of the benefit bear the same proportion that they have to the ‘‘value of the superannuation interest’’ (s 307-125(2)). Each benefit payment to an individual will therefore consist of the same proportion of the tax free and taxable component and the individual cannot choose to have the benefit paid from only a particular component.

▶ Example

A lump sum benefit of $100 is payable by a superannuation fund to a member. Just before the benefit is paid, the value of the member’s superannuation interest in the fund is $1,000, of which $200 is the tax free component and $800 is the taxable component.

For the $100 lump sum benefit that is to be paid to the member, the tax free component is $20 and the taxable component is $80.

The proportioning rule in s 307-125(2) does not apply to a superannuation benefit if:

- the regulations specify an alternative method for determining those components of the benefit (eg a benefit paid after the death of a recipient of a superannuation income stream)
- the Commissioner has determined, by legislative instrument, one or more alternative methods for determining those components of a superannuation benefit, or
- the Commissioner consents in writing to the use of another method for determining those components of the benefit (s 307-125(4), (5)).

In the above circumstances, the alternative method as prescribed, determined or approved is used to determine the tax free and taxable components (see ‘‘Alternative methods to calculate components’’ below).

Where a fund member fully commutes a current pension with an ‘‘internal roll-over’’ of the remaining balance of the pension account to the accumulation phase, the fund must recalculate (in accordance with s 307-125) the tax free component and taxable component of any new benefit subsequently paid from the fund.

▶ Example

Amy commenced an account-based pension from her SMSF with her superannuation interest in the fund totalling $100,000. The interest is made up of 50% tax free component (TFC) and 50% taxable component (TC).

On 30 June 2020, Amy commutes the pension and the commutation lump sum was returned to the accumulation phase in the fund on that day.

Assume that the pension account balance was $60,000 on 30 June 2020, reflecting pension payments of $20,000 and negative investment returns of $20,000 in 2019–20. The TFC and TC of the commutation lump sum would be $30,000 for each component in accordance with s 307-125(3)(c).

On 1 December 2020, Amy decides to commence a new account-based pension with the full amount of her accumulation interest which amounted to $75,000, comprising the $60,000 commutation amount from the first pension and $15,000 investment returns up to 30 November 2020.

At the time just before the new pension is commenced, the percentage of the TFC of Amy's accumulation interest is 40% ($30,000 ÷ $75,000) and the percentage of the TC of the interest is 60% (100% – 40%). Amy's new account-based pension will have a TFC percentage of 40% and a TC percentage of 60%.

Other circumstances where the proportioning rule does not apply

The proportioning rule does not apply to a payment from a superannuation fund under an ATO release authority:

- for refunded excess concessional contributions pursuant to a request under TAA Sch 1 s 131-5) (¶13-755, ¶13-775) (TAA Sch 1 s 131-75)
- for the release of excess concessional contributions which are included in a taxpayer's assessable income (¶13-775) (TAA Sch 1 s 131-75)
- for refunded excess non-concessional contributions and 85% of any associated earnings which are included in a taxpayer's assessable income (¶13-780) (TAA Sch 1 s 131-75, ITAA97 former s 292-410, former s 292-415)
- to pay assessed Division 293 tax (¶13-750) (TAA Sch 1 s 135-100).

Amounts paid under a release authority are superannuation benefit payments but are not assessable income and not exempt income, except where the payment exceeds the release entitlements (ITAA97 ss 303-15; 303-17; 303-20) (¶14-310).

A superannuation provider is not required to reduce either the tax free component or taxable component of a superannuation interest which is not providing an income stream. These components do not have to be calculated until the provider pays a superannuation benefit that requires the calculation of each of the components.

Superannuation interest

A "superannuation interest" is an interest in a superannuation fund, an ADF, an RSA or a superannuation annuity (s 995-1(1)) (see "Step 1. The superannuation interest" below). The "value of a superannuation interest" is the value determined by a method specified in the regulations or, if there is no such value, the total amount of all superannuation lump sums that could be paid to the person from the interest at that time (s 307-205).

A superannuation benefit that is an unclaimed money payment or a small superannuation account payment is treated as a superannuation benefit paid from a superannuation interest, and the amount of the benefit is the value of that interest just before the benefit is paid (s 307-125(6)).

There are 2 steps when determining the value of a superannuation interest:

Step 1 — work out what the superannuation interest is, and

Step 2 — work out what the value of the superannuation interest is.

Step 1. The superannuation interest

A superannuation interest may be treated as 2 or more interests, or 2 or more interests may be treated as one interest (s 307-200). Based on the nature of the superannuation interest, the following rules apply:

- Every amount, benefit or entitlement that a member holds in an SMSF comprise one superannuation interest unless provided otherwise by ITR97 Subdiv 307-D (ITR97 reg 307-200.02).
- A superannuation interest within a public sector superannuation scheme is to be treated as more than one interest where different amounts are subject to different benefit payment rules and administrative rules prevent them being treated as a single interest. This means that every amount, benefit or entitlement within a public sector scheme is able to be treated as a separate interest, eg an amount sourced from contributions or earnings into the scheme can be treated as a separate interest to ensure that funded amounts within a public sector scheme are treated separately from unfunded amounts (reg 307-200.03).
- If a superannuation income stream is payable (or will be payable and it is a deferred superannuation income stream), an amount held in the fund supporting the income stream is treated as a separate superannuation interest (reg 307-200.05).

For tax purposes, a superannuation income stream means an income stream that is taken to be an annuity or pension because the income stream is provided under the rules of a superannuation fund or a contract of an insurance company which meet the pension and annuity standards in the SISR or RSAR (¶14-120). A superannuation income stream includes a deferred superannuation income stream (ITR97 reg 995-1.01(1)(c)).

Step 2. Value of the superannuation interest

The value of a superannuation interest is the total amount of all superannuation lump sums that could be payable from the superannuation interest at that time (s 307-205), subject to the regulations specifying another method for determining the value, as below.

- When determining the pre-July 83 amount of the crystallised segment of a tax free component, the value of a superannuation interest must be calculated using the method in ITR97 reg 307-205.01. The method applies for both accumulation and defined benefit interests, but is not used to calculate the tax free component of a superannuation interest supporting an income stream already being paid at 1 July 2007 which is covered by the transitional rule in ITTPA s 307-125 (see below).
- The method for determining the value of a superannuation interest *at a particular time* allows interests which support an income stream to be valued for the purposes of the proportioning rule (ITR97 reg 307-205.02). The value of the superannuation income streams to which the regulation applies is calculated using the factors in ITR97 Sch 1B. Income streams are excluded from the valuation methodology where the benefits are directly related on an ongoing basis to an ascertainable amount in the member's account, eg an allocated pension.

The value of a superannuation interest, and the amount of each of the components of the interest, is determined at whichever of the following time applicable:

(a) if the benefit is a superannuation income stream benefit — when the benefit commences

(b) if the benefit is a superannuation lump sum — just before the benefit is paid

(c) despite (a) and (b), if the benefit arises from the commutation of a superannuation income stream — when that income stream first commenced or, if the income stream is a deferred superannuation income stream that had not commenced before the time the commutation happened, just before the time the commutation happened, and

(d) despite (a) and (b), if the benefit is an involuntary roll-over superannuation benefit paid from a superannuation interest that was supporting an income stream — when the income stream commenced (s 307-125(3)).

▶ Example 4

Assume that Peter, age 56, has a superannuation interest with a value of $400,000, made up of a tax free component of $100,000 and a taxable component of $300,000. Peter used all of his superannuation interest to purchase an income stream in January 2020.

The tax free percentage of Peter's superannuation interest when the superannuation income stream commenced would be:

$$\frac{\text{tax free component}}{\text{value of the interest}} = \frac{\$100{,}000}{\$400{,}000} = 25\%$$

The taxable percentage of Peter's superannuation interest would therefore be 75%.

Assume that Peter receives a superannuation income stream benefit of $20,000 in 2020–21. The tax free component of this superannuation benefit would be $5,000, ie $20,000 × 25%.

The taxable component of this superannuation benefit would therefore be $15,000 ($20,000 – $5,000).

Value of an interest in deferred income streams and pooled investment income streams

The value of a deferred or pooled investment income stream is specified by ITR97 regs 307-205.02C, 307-205.02D and 307-205.02E.

A "deferred superannuation income stream" means a benefit supported by a superannuation interest where the fund rules or contract governing the income stream provide for benefit payments to start *more than* 12 months after the interest is acquired and, thereafter, to be made at least annually (SISR reg 1.03(1)).

A pooled investment pension (PIP) means an income stream that continues for the remainder of an individual's life where the payments are determined having regard to the age, life expectancy or other factors relevant to the mortality of each individual who has that kind of interest in the fund and the collective asset pool held for the benefit of those individuals (ITR97 reg 307-205.02D(2)). A pooled investment annuity (PIA) is a comparable product to a PIP that is provided by a life insurance company (ITR97 reg 307-205.02E(2)).

To ensure that there is no overlap of the valuation rules, a deferred superannuation income stream must not be a PIP or PIA.

The value of these products is also the value that is credited to the individual's transfer balance account (¶14-340) when the interest holder enters the retirement phase.

Alternative methods to calculate components

A member of the Military Superannuation and Benefits Scheme who is below preservation age (¶14-220) and is receiving a benefit that comprises an amount that accrued before 1 July 1999 can choose (subject to certain limits) the proportions of the amount that are the tax free and taxable components (s 307-125(4)(a); ITR97 reg 307-125.01).

For benefits paid on or after 4 June 2013, reg 307-125.02 specifies an alternative method to determine the tax free and taxable components where there is no reversionary income stream on the death of the original beneficiary, and a superannuation death benefit lump sum (and/or an income stream) is paid using only an amount from the relevant superannuation interest after the beneficiary's death.

Where the death benefit lump sum or new income stream benefit is not to any extent attributable to an anti-detriment increase or an insurance-related amount paid or arising on or after the deceased's death, the benefit has the same proportions of tax free and taxable components as the income stream benefit that was paid to the deceased. Otherwise, the general proportioning rule in s 307-125 applies to the amount of the benefit as reduced by the extent to which it may be so attributable. The anti-detriment increase and the insurance-related amount are effectively included in the taxable component of the benefit (ITR97 reg 307-125.02).

▶ Example 5

John was receiving a superannuation pension before his death on 1 February 2020. When the pension first commenced, the value of the superannuation interest from which the pension was paid (the relevant interest) was $100,000, of which the tax free component was $20,000 (20% of the value) and the taxable component was $80,000 (80% of the value).

John's pension was non-reversionary and no amount was added to his superannuation interest on or after his death. The fund trustee decided to pay the entire value of the John's superannuation interest in the fund (valued at $75,000 at the time of John's death) as a single lump sum to Mary (John's adult child).

The lump sum death benefit ($75,000) was paid on 20 July 2020 using only the amount from the relevant interest, ie the benefit was not increased to any extent attributable to an insurance-related amount arising from John's death.

In this case, the lump sum death benefit of $75,000 will comprise a tax free component of $15,000 (20% of the amount of the benefit) and a taxable component of $60,000 (the remainder of the benefit).

Deductible amount for pre-1 July 2007 superannuation income streams

The "deductible amount" of a superannuation income stream which first commenced before 1 July 2007 (as calculated under ITAA36 s 27H(1): ¶14-510) constitutes the tax free component of the benefit until a trigger event (see below) occurs (ITTPA s 307-125).

The annual deductible amount (as calculated under s 27H(1)) is applied proportionately to each income stream benefit received in the income year as the tax free component, and the balance of the benefit (ie the income stream amount reduced by its tax free component) constitutes the taxable component of the benefit.

▶ Example 6

Assume that Michael, age 57, is receiving a superannuation pension which first commenced before 1 July 2007. The annual deductible amount for the pension is $6,000 (as calculated when the pension first commenced to be paid) and Michael receives monthly pension payments of $1,000 (ie $12,000 pa). The annual deductible amount is apportioned to each pension benefit made to him and this apportioned amount is the tax free component of the pension benefit received by him for an income year.

The tax free component of each $1,000 pension benefit is calculated as follows:

> Step 1 — Calculate the proportion of the pension benefit to the total pension benefit received in the year, ie $1,000/($12,000) = 8.33%
>
> Step 2 — Multiply the annual deductible amount by the percentage calculated in Step 1, ie $6,000 × 8.33% = $500

The tax free component of each pension benefit is $500 and the taxable component is $500 ($1,000 – $500).

Trigger events

Four events trigger the recalculation of the tax free and taxable components of a superannuation income stream that first commenced to be paid *before* 1 July 2007 for continuing payments of the income stream after the events. The trigger events are the holder of the income stream was 60 years of age or over at 1 July 2007, the holder turns 60 years old or has died, or the income stream has been partially or wholly commuted (ITTPA s 307-125(3)).

The recalculation is made at the *earliest* of the events in accordance with the methods set out in s 307-125(4) to (7).

Modification for disability benefits

If an individual receives a superannuation lump sum that is a ''disability superannuation benefit'' (¶14-220), the tax free component of the benefit is the sum of the tax free component of the benefit and the amount worked out using the formula in s 307-145(3), as below:

$$\text{Amount of benefit} \times \frac{\text{Days to retirement}}{\text{Service days} + \text{Days to retirement}}$$

In the formula, ''Days to retirement'' is the number of days from the day on which the person stopped being capable of being gainfully employed to his/her last retirement day, and ''Service days'' is the number of days in the service period for the lump sum.

The tax free component cannot exceed the amount of the benefit. The balance of the superannuation benefit is the taxable component of the benefit.

If a fund member's benefits are transferred from an accumulation sub-fund to a pension sub-fund to facilitate the commencement of an account-based pension, the transfer is not the payment of a superannuation lump sum and s 307-145 cannot be applied to increase the tax free component of that superannuation lump sum (ID 2009/125).

The Federal Court has provided guidance on the meaning of ''superannuation lump sum'', superannuation income stream and ''superannuation income stream benefit'' (in ITAA97 ss 307-65 and 307-70: ¶14-120) in 3 test cases brought by the Commissioner against AAT decisions concerning the taxation of invalidity benefits received pursuant to the *Military Superannuation and Benefits Act 1991* (*Burns*, *Walker*) and the *Defence Force Retirement and Death Benefits Act 1973* (*Douglas*). The AAT had accepted that the invalidity benefits in each of the cases were a superannuation lump sum within the meaning of s 307-65 because the payments received were not a superannuation income stream benefit within the meaning of s 307-70(1).

The Federal Court said that there are 2 limbs to the meaning of ''superannuation income stream benefit'' in s 307-70(1) — the first requires that the benefit be a ''superannuation benefit specified in the regulations'', and the second requires that the benefit be paid from a ''superannuation income stream''. The Court disagreed with the Tribunal's conclusion that ITR97 reg 995-1.01 failed to provide the requisite specification for the purposes of s 307-70(1). The Court's decision was important to the taxpayers as the tax concession is greater if the invalidity benefits they each received were superannuation lump sums rather than superannuation income stream benefits.

Modification for lump sums with an element untaxed in the fund

Under the proportioning rule, the tax free component and the taxable component of a superannuation lump sum (being a superannuation benefit) are calculated to reflect the same proportions that those components make up the superannuation interest from which the lump sum is paid, unless otherwise excluded.

A modification applies for superannuation lump sums that have not been subject to contributions or earnings tax in the fund, ie they contain an element untaxed in the fund (ITAA97 s 307-150). The modification, which only applies to benefits to the extent that they are attributable to a pre-1 July 2007 superannuation interest, has the following effect:

- the tax free component of the benefit is increased by the *lesser* of the amount worked out under the formula in s 307-150(4) and the amount of the element untaxed in the fund (ignoring the effect of s 307-150), and
- the element untaxed in the fund is reduced by the amount by which the tax free component is increased (s 307-150(3)).

For the purposes of the formula in s 307-150(4), if the superannuation benefit is in part attributable to a ''crystallised pre-July 83 amount'' (¶14-140), the amount of the benefit that is attributable to the crystallised segment of the superannuation interest from which the benefit is paid is disregarded in working out the tax free component of the benefit.

If a member of an untaxed superannuation scheme makes a contribution to the scheme before a superannuation lump sum benefit is paid, the contribution does not reduce the element untaxed in the fund of the benefit paid to the member (for an example, see ID 2011/64).

[AMSG ¶8-160; FITR ¶290-000; SLP ¶38-070ff]

¶14-140 Tax free component of a superannuation benefit

The tax free component of a ''superannuation interest'' (¶14-130) is so much of the value of the interest consisting of the contributions segment and the crystallised segment (ITAA97 s 307-210(1)). If a superannuation benefit is paid from the superannuation interest:

- the crystallised segment of the interest is reduced (but not below zero) by an amount equal to the tax free component of the benefit, and
- the contributions segment is reduced (but not below zero) by that remaining amount, thereby reducing tax free component of the interest by the amount of the benefit's tax free component (s 307-210(2)).

Contributions segment

The ''contributions segment'' is made up of contributions made from 1 July 2007 that have *not* been included in the assessable income of the superannuation fund in which the superannuation interest is held (s 307-220(1)). These are generally non-concessional contributions (¶13-780).

In determining whether contributions are included in the contributions segment under s 307-220(1):

- disregard the taxable component of a roll-over superannuation benefit paid into the interest (any excess untaxed roll-over amount of the roll-over benefit is treated as part of the tax free component — see ''Roll-over superannuation benefit paid into a superannuation interest'' below)
- treat a superannuation plan that is a constitutionally protected superannuation fund as if it were not such a fund
- disregard the tax free component of an involuntary roll-over superannuation benefit paid from another interest (the earlier interest), other than an earlier interest that was supporting a superannuation income stream immediately before the roll-over (for the amount included as a contribution, see ''Determining components under involuntary roll-over superannuation benefit'' below) (s 307-220(2)(a)).

Certain non-assessable contributions

The contributions segment does not include contributions that would otherwise be assessable contributions but have been excluded because of s 295-180 (ie contributions to a public sector fund excluded by agreement between the fund and member) or Subdiv 295-D (ie contributions transferred to a PST or a life insurance company or covered by pre-1 July 1988 funding credits) (¶13-125) (s 307-220(2)(b)).

Roll-over superannuation benefit paid into a superannuation interest

Roll-over superannuation benefits (other than those from an untaxed source to a taxed superannuation scheme) are not included in the recipient fund's assessable income (¶13-125) and are disregarded when determining whether they are included in the contributions segment. However, if the roll-over benefit includes amounts which exceed the untaxed plan cap amount ($1.565 million in 2020–21: ¶14-240) and have been subject to excess untaxed roll-over tax (¶14-450), the excess untaxed roll-over amount of the roll-over benefit is treated as part of the tax free component, instead of the taxable component, of the benefit (s 307-220(2)(a)(i), (3)).

Roll-over benefit is a departing Australia superannuation payment

The rule in s 307-220(2)(a)(i) does not apply to a roll-over superannuation benefit that is a departing Australia superannuation payment (DASP) under s 20H(2), 20H(2AA) or 20H(2A) of the *Superannuation (Unclaimed Money and Lost Members) Act 1999* (¶14-390). In this case, the whole DASP is included in the contributions segment of the superannuation interest (ie as part of the tax free component) as the payment has never been included as assessable contributions (ITAA97 s 295-190(1A): ¶13-125). This treatment ensures that the amount of the payment which has been subject to DASP withholding tax (¶14-390) is not subject to further tax when paid as a superannuation benefit from the superannuation interest (s 307-220(4)).

KiwiSaver scheme transfers

An amount transferred from a KiwiSaver scheme to an Australian complying superannuation fund is included in the contributions segment of the member's superannuation interest in the fund if the amount is a New Zealand-sourced amount or the tax free component of an Australian-sourced amount (ITAA97 s 312-10(6)) (¶13-380).

The New Zealand-sourced amount and any tax-free Australian-sourced amount therefore form part of the tax free component while the balance of the transferred amount is included in the taxable component of a superannuation interest.

Determining components under involuntary roll-over superannuation benefit

Transfers of an individual member's superannuation interest between superannuation plans without an individual's specific request or consent (''involuntary transfer'') are payments of superannuation benefits, and are also ''roll-over superannuation benefits'' if the transfer is between complying superannuation plans (¶14-450).

A roll-over superannuation benefit is an ''involuntary roll-over superannuation benefit'' if it is an involuntary transfer of an individual's interest under a successor fund arrangement, or a compulsory transfer of an individual's accrued default amount to a MySuper product in another complying superannuation plan, or a transfer to an eligible rollover fund (ITAA97 s 306-12).

Where an involuntary roll-over of an individual's superannuation interest is made, the following rules apply to ensure that the individual remains in the same taxation position as if the transfer had not occurred:

- if the interest in the original plan was *not* supporting an income stream — the contributions segment in the new plan includes an amount equal to the sum of the contributions and crystallised segments of the interest in the original plan (or a proportion thereof)
- if the interest in the original plan was supporting an income stream that began to be paid on or after 1 July 2007 — the proportions of the tax free and taxable components of the income stream commenced in the new plan will be the same as the income stream in the original plan, and
- if the interest in the original plan was supporting an income stream that began to be paid before 1 July 2007 — the income stream commenced in the new plan is treated in the same way as the income stream in the original plan (s 307-220(5); ITTPA ss 307-125; 307-127).

Crystallised segment

The "crystallised segment" of a superannuation interest is calculated by assuming that an eligible termination payment (ETP) representing the full value of the superannuation interest is paid just before 1 July 2007 (s 307-225). This crystallised segment is a fixed amount which does not change when a superannuation benefit is paid after 1 July 2007, ie it will form a fixed part of the tax free component of the benefit at that time.

Calculation of crystallised segment

The crystallised segment of the superannuation interest is the total amount of the following components (within the meaning in ITAA36 former s 27A(1)) of the ETP:

- the concessional component
- the post-June 1994 invalidity component
- the undeducted contributions component
- the CGT exempt component, and
- the pre-July 83 component.

Briefly, the concessional component of an ETP is so much of the ETP that consists of, or is attributable to, a bona fide redundancy payment, an approved early retirement scheme payment or an invalidity payment made before 1 July 1994.

The post-June 1994 invalidity component is the part of the ETP that consists of, or is attributable to, an invalidity payment made on or after 1 July 1994.

The undeducted contributions component of an ETP is that part of the ETP consisting of contributions paid by the taxpayer, or by a person other than an employer of the taxpayer, to a superannuation fund where no deduction has been allowed for the contributions.

The CGT exempt component of an ETP refers to the exempt amount which was contributed to the superannuation fund under the small business retirement exemption in ITAA97 Subdiv 152-D. The amount of the CGT exempt component is:

- for a s 27A(1) para (a) ETP where the whole or a part of the ETP is taken to consist solely of a CGT exempt component — the amount of that component, or
- for a s 27A(1) para (jaa) ETP — the amount of the ETP.

The pre-July 83 component of an ETP arises where the eligible service period relating to the payment commenced before 1 July 1983. This component is calculated using the formula in ITAA36 former s 27AA(1)(d)(i) or (ii).

The value of these components is crystallised on 30 June 2007 based on the amount of the superannuation interest attributable to the component on that date. The ATO's ''Superannuation crystallisation calculator'' is available at www.ato.gov.au/Calculators-and-tools/Superannuation-crystallisation-calculator.

Separate arrangements reflecting the pre-1 July 2007 tax regime apply to superannuation benefits which have not been subject to contributions tax within the fund (s 307-150). In such a case, the pre-July 83 segment for an element untaxed in the fund is only calculated when a lump sum superannuation benefit is withdrawn from a superannuation plan or rolled over into a taxed superannuation scheme.

Tax free component of pre-1 July 2007 superannuation income streams

With some exceptions, ITTPA s 307-125 provides for the recipients of superannuation income streams existing as at 30 June 2007 to retain the pre-1 July 2007 tax-free deductible amount of their superannuation income stream as the tax free component of the benefit from 1 July 2007. The taxable component is the remainder of the benefit. The deductible amount is calculated under ITAA36 s 27H(2) (¶14-510). A recalculation of the tax free and taxable components will need to be made only when a trigger event happens (¶14-130).

[AMSG ¶8-170; FITR ¶290-000; SLP ¶38-150ff]

¶14-150 Taxable component of a superannuation benefit

The taxable component of a ''superannuation interest'' (¶14-130) is the total value of the interest less the tax free component (s 307-215).

The taxable component may consist of an element taxed in the fund or an element untaxed in the fund, or both (s 307-275(1)).

Element taxed in the fund

The taxable component will consist wholly of an element taxed in the fund except where specified by a provision in ITAA97 Subdiv 307-E (s 307-275(2)) (see ''Element untaxed in the fund'' below)

For a taxed superannuation fund (generally private sector superannuation funds), the element taxed in the fund would normally be the total value of the superannuation interest *less* the tax free component.

Element untaxed in the fund

The taxable component of a superannuation benefit that is a ''small superannuation account payment'' or a ''superannuation guarantee payment'' (¶14-100) contains wholly of an element untaxed in the fund (s 307-275(3)). These superannuation payments are made by the ATO directly and have not been subject to tax in the fund.

The taxable component of the superannuation benefits below have an element untaxed and/or an element taxed in the fund as specified in Subdiv 307-E:

- benefits paid from a constitutionally protected fund. As these funds are exempt from tax on contributions or earnings, the taxable component will consist wholly of an element untaxed in the fund (s 307-280). The exception is where the benefit is a lump sum and is attributable to one or more roll-over superannuation benefits that contain or include an element taxed in the fund, in which case the taxable component will have a taxed element equal to the total of those taxed elements. If an income stream benefit is paid from a constitutionally protected fund at the time the income stream commenced, the taxable component will consist wholly of an element untaxed in the fund
- benefits paid from a public sector superannuation fund (not a constitutionally protected fund). If the benefit paid is not sourced to any extent from contributions made into a superannuation fund (or earnings on such contributions), the taxable

component consists wholly of an element untaxed in the fund (s 307-295). If the benefit is partly sourced from contributions or earnings on contributions, the element taxed and the element untaxed in the fund of the taxable component are worked using the method statement in s 307-295(3). The regulations may specify additional circumstances in which the benefit paid from a public sector superannuation scheme will consist of an untaxed element (s 307-297)

- benefits paid from a public sector superannuation scheme which came into operation before 6 September 2006 where the trustee has given the member a written notice specifying an amount as an element untaxed (s 307-285). In this case, the taxable component consists of an element untaxed in the fund equal to the specified amount

- death benefit payments from a superannuation fund that has claimed a tax deduction for insurance premiums under ITAA97 s 295-465 or 295-470. In this case, the elements taxed and untaxed of a lump sum superannuation death benefit are worked out using the formula in s 307-290. The untaxed element reflects the insurance component of the benefit as the deductibility of the insurance premiums results in no contributions or earnings tax having been paid on this component of the death benefit (see below)

- unclaimed money payments. These are payments made by the Commissioner under s 17(2), 20H(2), (2AA), (2A) or (3), 20QF(2) or 24G(2) of the *Superannuation (Unclaimed Money and Lost Members) Act 1999* (SUMLMA) (¶13-850). For these benefits, the elements taxed and untaxed in the fund of the taxable component are worked out as provided by s 307-300(2) to (4). As these payments are treated and taxed as if they are paid from a superannuation fund, the amount of the elements essentially reflect the amount of elements when they were paid to the ATO as unclaimed superannuation by the original superannuation funds (to the extent they are included in the Commissioner's payment) (s 307-300)).

If a superannuation benefit paid by the Commissioner under SUMLMA s 17(2AB), (2AC), 24G(3A), (3B) or (3C), or under s 20H(2AA) in respect of a person who is not a former temporary resident, the taxable component of the benefit is nil (s 307-142(3B), (4)). The element taxed in the fund is nil, if the superannuation benefit is paid under s 20H(2AA), ie interest on unclaimed money paid as a superannuation benefit (see below).

Section 307-290 applies to create an untaxed element in a superannuation lump sum death benefit by providing the formula to work out the taxed and untaxed element in the fund where the payer superannuation fund has claimed or will claim deductions for costs arising from certain insurance policies (or its future liability to pay death or disability benefits) that relate to the deceased fund member and the deductions relate to the superannuation lump sum. For the purposes of s 307-290, a deduction need not have been made in every income year for the life insurance linked to the member's superannuation interest. Nor is it necessary for a deduction to be, or have been, claimed for the particular year that the death benefit is payable. It is sufficient that a deduction for insurance premiums has been, or is to be claimed, in relation to the death benefit in any year of income (ID 2010/76). Also, a deduction claimed under ITAA36 former s 279 or 279B is treated as a deduction under ITAA97 s 295-465 or 295-470 respectively (ITTPA s 307-290). Deductions for insurance premiums are discussed in ¶13-150.

The circumstances where there may be a sufficient relationship between the payment of the lump sum and the deductions include cases where the payer superannuation fund is either the fund that claimed the deductions in relation to the member or is a successor fund to the fund that claimed the deductions for the member. The Commissioner's guidelines on the application of s 307-290 where death benefits are rolled over are discussed in ¶14-450.

Interest on unclaimed money

Interest paid by the Commonwealth in respect of unclaimed superannuation is a tax free component of a superannuation benefit (except in relation to the unclaimed money of a former temporary resident) (ITAA97 ss 307-142(2), (3B); 307-300(2), (3A)). As a consequence, the interest payment is non-assessable non-exempt income (ITAA97 s 301-30).

Departing Australia superannuation payments (DASPs) are taxed under special withholding tax arrangements. From 1 July 2013, interest on the unclaimed money of former temporary residents is a taxable component of a superannuation benefit that is untaxed in the fund (ITAA97 ss 307-142(3C); 307-300(2), (3A)). This ensures that the interest payment is subject to DASP withholding tax as part of the element untaxed in the fund (¶14-390).

[AMSG ¶8-170; FITR ¶290-000; SLP ¶38-080ff]

Taxation of Superannuation Member Benefits

¶14-200 Payments from a complying plan

The taxation treatment of a superannuation member benefit paid from a complying superannuation plan (other than those paid after the death of the member) is based on:

- the age of the benefit recipient
- whether the benefit is a lump sum or an income stream
- whether the benefit comprises a tax free component and/or a taxable component (¶14-140, ¶14-150), and
- whether the taxable component of the benefit includes an ''element taxed in the fund'' and/or an ''element untaxed in the fund'' (¶14-150).

The general rule is that a superannuation benefit paid to a person aged 60 and over as a superannuation lump sum or income stream benefit is not assessable income and not exempt income if the payer is a taxed source, ie the benefit does not have any element untaxed in the fund (¶14-220).

If the person is under 60 years of age, all of the above factors will be relevant to determine the tax treatment of the benefit. Superannuation lump sums are subject to an effective tax rate cap. This is given effect through a tax offset mechanism which reduces the ordinary tax rates as they are applied to that income so that the applicable effective marginal rate does not exceed a specified fixed tax rate (¶14-220, ¶14-240).

A ''complying superannuation plan'' means a complying superannuation fund, a public sector superannuation scheme that is a ''regulated superannuation fund'' or ''an exempt public sector superannuation scheme'' (as defined in the SISA), a complying ADF, or an RSA (ITAA97 s 995-1(1)).

Separate tax rules apply to superannuation death benefits paid from a complying plan (¶14-270), and to payments from non-complying plans (¶14-400, ¶14-420).

Under the constructive receipt rule, a superannuation benefit is treated as being made to, or received by, a person if it is made for the person's benefit, or is made to another person or entity at the person's direction or request (s 307-15).

Transfer balance tax and additional tax consequences for certain income streams

The amount of an individual's total income stream benefits in the retirement phase (¶13-140) is limited by a transfer balance cap (¶14-320) and an individual is liable to pay excess transfer balance tax if the cap is exceeded (¶14-360). Special rules apply to capped defined benefit income stream benefits under the transfer balance tax regime, with additional tax consequences if the benefits exceed a defined benefit income cap in a year (¶14-370).

Interaction with CGT and other tax rules

A payment from a superannuation fund (or an ADF or RSA) is the disposal of a right to an allowance, annuity or capital amount, or a right to an asset. Any capital gain or capital loss arising is disregarded, ie there are no CGT consequences for the member or RSA holder (ITAA97 ss 118-305; 118-310: ¶11-880). For example, a superannuation lump sum payment made to a member from an employer superannuation fund (CGT event C2 happening and the member's right to receive the payment ending) will have no CGT consequences for the member. The member is also not entitled to a tax deduction if the member's benefit amount paid on withdrawal from the superannuation fund is less than the amount invested or contributed as the loss is capital in nature.

The CGT exemption is not available to a non-member who had previously paid to acquire the right or the payer superannuation fund, ADF or RSA, but is available to a legal personal representative of a deceased member or if a payment split under the family law happens to the member's benefit and a payment is made to the non-member spouse as a result (¶11-880).

A non-resident who receives a payment from an Australian superannuation fund is assessable in Australia on that income (ITAA97 s 6-10(5): ¶21-000).

Medicare levy is levied and payable by an individual who is a resident of Australia at any time during the income year based on the individual's taxable income for the year, but no levy is payable on any portion of a superannuation benefit that is included in the individual's assessable income in respect of which a tax offset has reduced the primary rate of tax to 0% (ITAA36 s 251S(1A)).

[AMSG ¶8-200ff; FITR ¶290-000ff; SLP ¶38-150ff]

¶14-220 Taxation of benefits from a taxed source

The tax treatment of a superannuation benefit paid from a taxed source (ie where the benefit is an element taxed in the fund) depends on the age of the recipient (member), the amount of the payment (see "Low rate cap amount"), whether the benefit is paid as a lump sum or as an income stream, and whether the benefit contains a tax free and/or a taxable component (¶14-140, ¶14-150).

Medicare levy is added to whichever rate of tax (other than 0%) is applicable (ITAA36 s 251S(1A)).

Low rate cap amount

A benefit payment is compared to a low rate cap amount to determine its tax treatment.

The low rate cap amount is $215,000 in 2020–21 (ITAA97 s 307-345: see ¶42-250 for the cap amount in earlier years).

A member's low rate cap amount is a lifetime cap which is reduced for all superannuation lump sum payments received by the member (but not below zero) and is increased annually by the indexation amount (in increments of $5,000 rounded down) at the start of each income year (ITAA97 ss 960-265 to 960-285).

Member aged 60 or over

If the member is 60 years or over when the superannuation benefit is received, the benefit is not assessable income and not exempt income (s 301-10). This applies to both superannuation lump sums and income streams.

Member over preservation age and under 60

If the member is under age 60 but has reached his/her "preservation age" (see below) when the benefit (whether a lump sum or an income stream) is received, the tax free component of the benefit is not assessable income and not exempt income (s 301-15).

Superannuation lump sum

The taxable component of a superannuation lump sum is assessable income (s 301-20(1)).

The member is entitled to a tax offset which ensures that the tax rate on the taxable component of the lump sum which is included in assessable income up to the low rate cap amount does not exceed 0%, and the tax rate on the amount exceeding the low rate cap amount does not exceed 15% (s 301-20(2) to (5)).

Superannuation income stream

The taxable component of a superannuation income stream benefit is assessable income and is taxed at marginal tax rates.

The member is entitled to a tax offset equal to 15% of the taxable component of the benefit (s 301-25).

Member below preservation age

If the member is under preservation age when the superannuation benefit is received, the tax free component of the benefit, whether a lump sum or an income stream, is not assessable income and not exempt income (s 301-30).

Superannuation lump sum

The taxable component of a superannuation lump sum is assessable income.

The member is entitled to a tax offset which ensures that the tax rate on the taxable component of the lump sum included in assessable income does not exceed 20% (s 301-35).

Superannuation income stream

The taxable component of a superannuation income stream is assessable income and is taxed at marginal tax rates.

If an income stream is also a disability superannuation benefit, the member is entitled to a tax offset equal to 15% of the taxable component (s 301-40).

Disability superannuation benefits

A superannuation benefit is a "disability superannuation benefit" if:

(a) the benefit is paid to a person because he/she suffers from ill-health (whether physical or mental), and

(b) 2 legally qualified medical practitioners have certified that, because of the ill-health, it is unlikely that the person can ever be gainfully employed in a capacity for which he/she is reasonably qualified because of education, experience or training (s 995-1(1)).

The term "legally qualified medical practitioners" in the definition of disability superannuation benefit is not a defined term. The Commissioner relies on its ordinary meaning and takes the view that legally qualified medical practitioners are persons who have general or specialist registration with the Medical Board of Australia (ID 2015/11).

A medical certificate supplied by a person for a particular superannuation lump sum can satisfy the requirements of paragraph (b) of the definition (see above) and be used for later lump sums paid to the person by the same superannuation fund provided the superannuation lump sums are paid over a short period of time and there is no evidence to suggest that the person's circumstances have changed in some relevant way (ID 2015/19: disability superannuation benefit medical certificate).

The tax free component of a disability superannuation benefit received as a lump sum may be increased to reflect the period where the member could have been expected to have been gainfully employed (s 307-145).

Transfer balance tax and additional tax consequences for certain income streams

The amount of an individual's total income stream benefits in the retirement phase (¶13-140) is limited by a transfer balance cap (¶14-320) and an individual is liable to pay excess transfer balance tax if the cap is exceeded (¶14-360). Special rules apply to capped defined benefit income stream benefits under the transfer balance tax regime, with additional tax consequences if the benefits exceed a defined benefit income cap in a year (¶14-370).

Preservation age

A person's preservation age (as defined in the SISR) is based on the person's date of birth — see ¶42-250.

Other rules affecting superannuation benefits

Special rules apply where a superannuation member benefit is paid in breach of rules or is less than $200, or it arises from the commutation of an income stream by a dependant, or the recipient has a terminal medical condition, or the benefit is paid under an ATO release authority (¶14-300, ¶14-310).

¶14-240 Taxation of benefits from an untaxed source

The tax treatment of a superannuation benefit paid from an untaxed source (eg a public sector fund where the benefit includes an element taxed in the fund) depends on the age of the recipient (member), the payment amount (see ''Untaxed plan cap amount''), whether the benefit is paid as a lump sum or as an income stream and whether the benefit contains a tax free or taxable component (¶14-140, ¶14-150).

Medicare levy is added to whichever rate of tax (other than 0%) is applicable (ITAA36 s 251S(1A)).

If a member receives a superannuation benefit that includes an element untaxed in the fund, the tax free component (if any) of the benefit is not assessable income and not exempt income (s 301-90). The element taxed in the fund (if any) of the benefit is taxed as discussed in ¶14-220 and the element untaxed in the fund is taxed as discussed below.

Untaxed plan cap amount

A benefit payment is compared to an untaxed plan cap amount to determine its tax treatment.

The untaxed plan cap amount is $1.565 million in 2020–21 (ITAA97 s 307-350: see ¶42-250 for the cap amount in earlier years).

A member's untaxed plan cap amount is a lifetime cap which is reduced for previous superannuation lump sum payments received by the member (but not below zero) and increased annually by the indexation amount (in increments of $5,000 rounded down) at the start of each income year (ITAA97 ss 960-265 to 960-285).

A separate untaxed plan cap amount applies for each superannuation plan that pays a member a lump sum benefit that includes an element untaxed in the fund. If a member receives one or more superannuation member benefit that includes an element untaxed in the fund from a superannuation plan at a time, the untaxed plan cap amount is reduced after that time as follows:

(i) by the untaxed element amount of the lump sum benefit or benefits — if the total of the elements untaxed in the fund is below the member's untaxed plan cap amount at that time, or

(ii) to nil — in other cases (s 307-350(2)).

Member aged 60 or over — lump sum benefit

If the member is 60 years or over when receiving a superannuation lump sum benefit that contains an element untaxed in the fund, that amount is assessable income (s 301-95).

The member is entitled to a tax offset which ensures that the tax rate applicable to the element untaxed in the fund, up to the untaxed plan cap amount, does not exceed 15%. The remainder of the element untaxed in the fund is taxed at the top marginal rate (45%).

▶ Example 1

Janet, a member of a public sector superannuation fund, receives a superannuation lump sum of $500,000 from the fund when she is 60 years old. The lump sum comprises a tax free component of $100,000 and a taxable component made up of an element taxed in the fund of $100,000 and an element untaxed in the fund of $300,000.

The tax free component and the element taxed in the fund of the lump sum benefit are not subject to tax (as Janet is 60 years of age: ¶14-220).

The element untaxed in the fund of the benefit is included in Janet's assessable income. As the untaxed plan cap amount is not exceeded, the untaxed element is taxed at her marginal tax rates up to a maximum rate of 15% (plus the Medicare levy).

Member aged 60 or over — income stream benefit

If a member is 60 years or over when receiving a superannuation income stream benefit, the element untaxed in the fund of the benefit is assessable income and subject to marginal tax rates. The member is entitled to a tax offset equal to 10% of the element untaxed in the fund of the benefit (s 301-100).

▶ Example 2

Tina, who is 62 years of age, receives a superannuation income stream of $56,000 a year.

The income stream, which had commenced before 1 July 2007, comprised a deductible (tax-free) amount of $6,000 for contributions made from post-tax income and a taxable component made up of an element untaxed in the fund of $50,000.

Tina will continue to receive the deductible amount of $6,000 as the tax free component, but is assessed on the remaining taxable component of $50,000 at marginal rates (plus Medicare levy). A tax offset of 10% of $50,000 (ie $5,000) is available to Tina.

Member over preservation age and under 60 — lump sum

If a member has reached his/her "preservation age" (¶14-220) but is below age 60 when receiving a superannuation lump sum benefit, the element untaxed in the fund is assessable income and is subject to tax at the following rates (s 301-105):

- on the amount up to the low rate cap amount ($215,000 in 2020–21: ¶14-220) — up to a maximum rate of 15%
- on the amount up to the untaxed plan cap amount for each superannuation plan (excluding any low rate cap amount) — up to a maximum rate of 30%, and
- on the amount exceeding the untaxed plan cap amount — the top marginal tax rate.

▶ Example 3

In 2020–21, Nick (age 56) receives a superannuation lump sum of $220,000 made up of an element untaxed in the fund. He has not previously received a superannuation lump sum.

The amount up to Nick's low rate cap amount of $215,000 in 2020–21 is taxed at a maximum rate of 15% and the remaining $5,000 is taxed at marginal tax rates up to a maximum rate of 30%.

Member over preservation age and under 60 — income stream

If a member has reached his/her preservation age but is below age 60 when receiving a superannuation income stream benefit, the element untaxed in the fund is assessable income and is taxed at marginal tax rates, plus Medicare levy (s 301-110).

Member below preservation age — lump sum

If a member is below his/her preservation when receiving a superannuation lump sum benefit, the element untaxed in the fund is assessable income (s 301-115).

The member is entitled to a tax offset on the element untaxed in the fund up to the untaxed plan cap amount for the plan which ensures that the tax rate does not exceed 30%. The remainder of the element untaxed in the fund is taxed at the top marginal tax rate. Medicare levy is added to whichever rate is applicable.

Member below preservation age — income stream

If a member is below his/her preservation age when receiving a superannuation income stream benefit, the element untaxed in the fund is assessable income and is taxed at marginal tax rates (plus Medicare levy), with no tax offset available (s 301-120).

Transfer balance tax and additional tax consequences for certain income streams

The amount of an individual's total income stream benefits in the retirement phase (¶13-140) is limited by a transfer balance cap (¶14-320) and an individual is liable to pay excess transfer balance tax if the cap is exceeded (¶14-360). Special rules apply to capped defined benefit income stream benefits under the transfer balance tax regime, with additional tax consequences if the benefits exceed a defined benefit income cap in a year (¶14-370).

Preservation age

A person's preservation age is based on the person's date of birth — see ¶42-250.

Other tax rules affecting superannuation benefits

Special rules apply where a superannuation member benefit is paid in breach of rules or is less than $200 or it arises from the commutation of an income stream by a dependant, or the recipient has a terminal medical condition, or the benefit is paid under an ATO release authority (¶14-300, ¶14-310).

Taxation of Superannuation Death Benefits

¶14-270 Superannuation death benefits

Superannuation death benefits cover benefit payments to a taxpayer after the death of another person, for example, a benefit payment from a superannuation fund to a dependant, non-dependant or legal personal representative, of a deceased fund member (¶14-100).

ITAA97 Div 302 provides for the taxation of superannuation death benefits based on:

- whether the recipient of the death benefit is a death benefits dependant or non-dependant of the deceased, and
- whether the amount is paid as a lump sum or an income stream.

Death benefits dependant, spouse and child

A "death benefits dependant" of a person who has died is:

(1) the deceased person's spouse or former spouse

(2) the deceased person's child, aged below age 18

(3) any other person with whom the deceased person had an "interdependency relationship" (see below) just before he/she died, or

(4) any other person who was financially dependent on the deceased person just before he/she died (s 302-195(1)).

Whether a person satisfies the test in (1) and (2) is determined just before the deceased person died, consistent with the test in (3) and (4) (TD 2013/12: deceased person's child).

Spouse

A "spouse" of an individual includes:

- another individual (whether of the same sex or a different sex) with whom the individual is in a relationship that is registered under a state or territory law prescribed for the purposes of s 2E of the *Acts Interpretation Act 1901* (AIA 1901) as a kind of relationship prescribed for the purposes of that section (see below), and
- another individual who, although not legally married to the individual, lives with the individual on a genuine domestic basis in a relationship as a couple (ITAA97 s 995-1(1); ITTPA s 302-195A; SISA s 10(1)).

A taxpayer who lived with a deceased fund member on a genuine domestic basis in a relationship as a same-sex couple is a "former spouse" of the deceased under s 302-195(1)(a) (ID 2011/83).

The following kinds of relationships are prescribed for s 2E of the AIA 1901:

- a registered domestic relationship as defined in s 3 of the *Relationships Act 2008* (Vic)
- a significant relationship as defined in s 4 of the *Relationships Act 2003* (Tas)
- a civil union as described in s 6(1) of the *Civil Unions Act 2012* (ACT)
- a relationship as a couple between 2 adult persons who meet the eligibility criteria for entering into a civil partnership mentioned in s 37C of the *Domestic Relationships Act 1994* (ACT)
- a registered relationship as defined in s 4 of the *Relationships Register Act 2010* (NSW)
- a relationship as a couple between 2 adults who meet the eligibility criteria mentioned in s 5 of the *Relationships Act 2011* (Qld) for entry into a registered relationship
- a relationship as a couple between 2 adults who meet the eligibility criteria mentioned in s 5 of the *Relationships Register Act 2016* (SA) (Acts Interpretation (Registered Relationships) Regulations 2008, reg 3).

Child

A death benefits dependant of a person who has died includes a child who is aged less than 18 of the deceased person (s 302-195(1)(b)). Each of the following is a "child" of an individual:

- the individual's adopted child, stepchild or ex-nuptial child
- a child of the individual's spouse, and
- a child of the individual within the meaning of the *Family Law Act 1975* (FLA) (ITAA97 s 995-1(1); SISA s 10(1)).

A person ceases to be a "stepchild" for the purposes of being a "dependant" of a superannuation fund member under SISR reg 6.22 when the legal marriage of their natural parent to the member ends (ID 2011/77: former stepchild).

A "child" under the Family Law Act has its ordinary meaning and includes:

- a person born to a woman as the result of an artificial conception procedure while that woman was married to or was a de facto partner of another person (whether of the same or opposite sex) (FLA s 60HB), and

- a person who is a child of a person because of a state or territory court order made under a state or territory law prescribed for the purposes of s 60HB giving effect to a surrogacy agreement.

The above definitions mean that a same-sex partner of an individual and the children of a same-sex couple can be a death benefits dependant, regardless of whether he/she satisfies the interdependency criteria (see below). For example, this will enable the surviving member of the couple to receive the deceased member's superannuation benefits as a reversionary pension, or alternatively receive a superannuation lump sum death benefit tax-free. Similarly, when an individual in a same-sex relationship dies, a child of that relationship who is under 18 years of age can be a death benefits dependant and will be taxed concessionally on any superannuation death benefits received (¶14-280).

Two principles under ITAA97 Subdiv 960-J apply to clarify family relationships. The first ensures that the same tax consequences, as from a marriage, flow from the relationship between 2 people who are an unmarried couple (whether of the same or different sex), provided their relationship is registered under particular state or territory laws (see above) or they live together on a genuine domestic basis in a relationship as a couple. The second ensures that anyone who is an individual's child (as defined for tax purposes) is treated in the same way as if he/she were the individual's natural child (ITAA97 s 960-252). Both principles extend to tracing other family relationships beyond the couple, their children and parents, eg to determine if a person is a relative (ITAA97 s 960-255).

▶ Example

George and Mandy are not legally married, but live together on a genuine domestic basis in a relationship as a couple. The income tax Acts treat them as part of each other's family.

Mandy's stepfather Frank has a sister Angela. The income tax Acts apply as if Angela were Mandy's aunt because Mandy is defined to be Frank's child. That is, Mandy's relationship to Angela is determined on the basis that Mandy is Frank's natural child.

Interdependency relationship

Two persons (whether or not related by family) have an ''interdependency relationship'' if they have a close personal relationship, live together, and one or each of them provides the other with financial support and domestic support and personal care (ITAA97 s 302-200(1)). Examples of these relationships are where 2 elderly sisters reside together and provide financial and other support for each other, an adult child who resides with and cares for an elderly parent, and same-sex couples who reside together (ID 2005/143: mother of deceased taxpayer interdependency relationship).

Two persons who have a close personal relationship (whether or not related by family), but do not satisfy the other requirements above because either or both of them suffer from a physical, intellectual or psychiatric disability (eg a person with a disability who lives in an institution), also have an interdependency relationship (s 302-200(2)).

ITR97 reg 302-200.02 specifies the matters that are, or are not, to be taken into account in determining under s 302-200(1) or (2) whether 2 persons have an interdependency relationship or had an interdependency relationship immediately before the death of one of them.

Two people do not have an interdependency relationship if one of them provides domestic support and personal care to the other under an employment contract or a contract for services, or on behalf of another person or organisation such as a government agency, a body corporate or a benevolent or charitable organisation (reg 302-200.02(5)). This does not affect people who otherwise meet the definition of ''interdependency relationship'' but who receive a carer's allowance or similar payment from a government or other organisation.

Financial dependant of a deceased person

A person who is financially dependent on a deceased person is a death benefits dependant (s 302-195(1)(d)).

The determination of financial dependence is a question of fact. The financial contribution by the deceased must be examined to determine whether it is ''necessary and relied on'' by a person to maintain a normal standard of living, and that the financial contribution does not necessarily have to be more than 50% to be considered as substantial support by the deceased (*Malek*: significant financial support received in the form of mortgage repayments, maintenance and other home expenses; *Case 2/2016*: parent and deceased child and interdependency relationship).

An adult taxpayer who was living at home and was receiving Youth Allowance payments from Centrelink at the time of his parent's death was held to be a death benefits dependant. The Youth Allowance payments received were calculated at a lower ''at home'' rate as opposed to the higher ''independent'' rate, which indicated that the taxpayer was substantially financially dependent on the parent (ID 2014/6).

Other death benefits dependants

An individual who receives a superannuation lump sum because of the death of another person who ''died in the line of duty'' as a Defence Force member, an Australian federal, state or territory police force member or a protective service officer is treated as a death benefits dependant of the deceased person (ITAA97 s 302-195(2)). The circumstances in which a person has ''died in the line of duty'' are set out in ITR97 regs 302-195 and 302-195A.

[AMSG ¶8-300ff; FITR ¶291-000; SLP ¶38-260ff]

¶14-280 Taxation of superannuation death benefits

The taxation treatment of a superannuation death benefit (¶14-120) depends on whether it is a lump sum or an income stream and whether payment is made to a death benefits dependant (¶14-270) of the deceased.

Payments to a dependant — lump sum

A superannuation lump sum death benefit paid to a death benefits dependant of the deceased is not assessable income and not exempt income (s 302-60).

Also, a superannuation lump sum from the commutation of a superannuation income stream is not assessable income and not exempt income in certain circumstances (s 303-5: ¶14-310).

Payments to a dependant — income stream

A superannuation income stream benefit (¶14-120) paid to a dependant is not assessable income and not exempt income if either or both the deceased was aged 60 or more at the time of death and the dependant was aged 60 or more at the time of receiving the benefit (s 302-65).

A superannuation income stream benefit is taxed as follows if both the dependant and the deceased are under age 60 at the time of the death:

- the tax free component (¶14-140) of the income stream is not assessable income and not exempt income (s 302-70)
- the element taxed in the fund of the taxable component (¶14-150) is assessable income, but the dependant is entitled to a tax offset equal to 15% of the element taxed in the fund (s 302-75), and
- when the recipient turns 60, the income stream becomes not assessable income and not exempt income (s 302-65).

Element untaxed in the fund

Where the taxable component of a superannuation income stream benefit includes an element untaxed in the fund (¶14-150):

- the tax free component is not assessable income and not exempt income
- the element taxed in the fund is treated in the same way as the taxable component of a superannuation income stream benefit under s 302-65 (ie not assessable income and not exempt income if either the deceased or the dependant is aged 60 or more, see above), or under s 302-75 (ie as assessable income but with a tax offset equal to 15% of the taxable component, see above), and
- the element untaxed in the fund is treated, depending on the age of the deceased and the dependant, as follows:
  (i) if either the deceased was aged at least 60 at the time of death or the dependant was aged at least 60 at the time of receiving the benefit, the dependant is entitled to a tax offset of 10% of the element untaxed in the fund, or
  (ii) if neither was age 60, the element untaxed in the fund is included in the dependant's assessable income, and the dependant will receive a tax offset of 10% only when he/she attains age 60 (ss 302-80; 302-85; 302-90).

Payments to a non-dependant — lump sum

The tax free component of a superannuation lump sum paid to a non-dependant is not assessable income and not exempt income (s 302-140). The taxable component of the lump sum is included in assessable income and taxed at marginal rates. A tax offset applies to ensure that the tax rate on the element taxed in the fund does not exceed 15% and the tax rate on the element untaxed in the fund does not exceed 30% (s 302-145).

A person who is not a dependant of the deceased can only receive a superannuation lump sum, not a superannuation income stream benefit (SISR reg 6.21(2A): ¶13-800).

A recipient of a death benefit income stream which commenced before 1 July 2007 is taxed in the same way as payments made to dependants (see above).

Payments to the trustee of deceased estate

A superannuation death benefit paid to the trustee of a deceased estate in that capacity is subject to tax in the following manner:

- to the extent that one or more beneficiaries of the estate who were death benefits dependants of the deceased have benefited, or may be expected to benefit, from the superannuation death benefit — the benefit is treated as if it were paid to a death benefits dependant of the deceased
- to the extent that one or more beneficiaries of the estate who were not death benefits dependants of the deceased have benefited, or may be expected to benefit, from the superannuation death benefit — the benefit is treated as if it were paid to a non-dependant of the deceased, and
- the benefit is taken to be income to which no beneficiary is presently entitled (s 302-10).

The trustee of the deceased estate may, therefore, be liable to tax on the above basis and will be required to withhold any tax payable from the superannuation death benefit received (ITAA36 s 101A(3); *Fyffe v Fyffe*).

An income stream, arising from a family law payment split, that is paid to a deceased estate from an exempt public sector superannuation scheme (EPSSS) is treated as a superannuation lump sum death benefit under ITAA97 s 307-65, and a family law superannuation payment under ITAA97 s 307-5(7) (¶14-120). As an EPSSS is not a regulated superannuation fund, the income stream payments from the EPSSS cannot be superannuation income stream benefits because the SISR pension standards as discussed in ¶14-125 are not met. An EPSSS is nevertheless a complying superannuation plan for income tax purposes (ITAA97 s 995-1(1): definition of "complying superannuation plan") and the income stream payments to the deceased estate are subject to tax in the hands of the trust estate under s 302-10 as noted above (ID 2014/2).

Transfer balance tax and additional tax consequences for certain income streams

The amount of an individual's total income stream benefits in the retirement phase (¶13-140) is limited by a transfer balance cap (¶14-320) and an individual is liable to pay excess transfer balance tax if the cap is exceeded (¶14-360). Special rules apply to capped defined benefit income stream benefits under the transfer balance tax regime, with additional tax consequences if the benefits exceed a defined benefit income cap in a year (¶14-370).

[AMSG ¶8-300ff; FITR ¶291-000; SLP ¶38-270ff]

Other Superannuation Benefits

¶14-300 Benefits paid in breach of rules

The concessional taxation rules for superannuation member benefits and death benefits in Div 301 and 302 (¶14-200, ¶14-280) do not apply to the receipt of superannuation benefits in breach of certain legislative requirements. These cases arise where a person receives a benefit from a complying superannuation fund or previously complying fund, an ADF or an RSA and:

- the fund has not complied with the sole purpose test in s 62 of the SISA, or
- the person received the benefit otherwise than in accordance with the payment standards prescribed under the SISR or RSA Regulations (ITAA97 ss 304-5; 304-10).

In these cases, the benefit received is included in assessable income and is taxed at the recipient's marginal tax rates.

The Commissioner has a discretion to exclude an amount from a person's assessable income, and have the amount treated as a superannuation benefit, to the extent that he is satisfied that it would be unreasonable not to do so having regard to the nature of the superannuation fund and other matters that the Commissioner considers relevant (s 304-10(4)). In *Smith*, the Commissioner's discretion was held not to encompass the facts of the case where the members had accessed their superannuation benefits for the purpose of preserving their personal business. The AAT agreed with the Commissioner's submission that the apparently unfettered discretion under s 304-10(4) must be constrained by the context in which it appears in ITAA97. The meaning of "unreasonable" in s 304-10(4) was considered in *Mason*, where the AAT said that it may be "unreasonable" to include a superannuation benefit paid in breach of the legislative requirements in a person's assessable income (with the result that it is taxed at marginal tax rates) in circumstances where, for example:

- this would be in addition to other taxation consequences which flow from the breach (eg the superannuation fund no longer gets the benefit of an exemption or becomes non-compliant for the relevant tax year), and/or
- the benefit arose in circumstances beyond the recipient's effective control.

The AAT has held that a payment made by a superannuation fund to a fund member in the course of a real property transaction that was not completed should not have been included in the member's assessable income as it was "unreasonable" to do so, and that the Commissioner should have exercised his discretion under s 304-10(4) to exclude that payment from the member's assessable income (*Wainwright & Anor*). The AAT had identified a series of factors, including some events which occurred *after* the relevant superannuation benefit was paid, but did not refer to the weight or degree of relevance it had given or applied to those events. The ATO view is that little weight should be given to events that occur after the superannuation benefits have been provided when deciding on the exercise of the s 304-10(4) discretion but, being a highly factual case, the AAT's decision was open to it on the facts and evidence (*Wainright* decision impact statement).

In *Brazil*, the taxpayer transferred money in a fraudulent enterprise operated by others from his superannuation fund to another SMSF (which was found to be merely a vehicle in the enterprise for early access to superannuation) which then made a superannuation benefit payment to the taxpayer. The AAT held that as the taxpayer suspected (or should have suspected) that the SMSF was not a bone fide superannuation fund but made no effort to find out about the fund or obtain documentation that tax had been deducted and remitted, the ATO was right not to exercise the s 304-10(4) discretion in favour of the taxpayer or remit the penalty imposed (*Sinclair*: mere financial difficulties did not warrant exercise of discretion, but penalty remitted; *Yrorita*: taxpayer failed to make appropriate inquiries, but penalty remitted; *Vuong*: early superannuation payout, of which the taxpayer received only a part from a fraudulent bank account, formed part of assessable income, but penalty remitted as the taxpayer acted with honest, albeit naive, intent at all times).

Excess payments from an ATO release authority

The tax treatment of benefit payments by a superannuation provider under an ATO release authority in various circumstances is discussed in ¶14-310.

[AMSG ¶8-500; FITR ¶293-000; SLP ¶39-040]

¶14-310 Benefits paid in particular circumstances

The taxation rules for superannuation benefits and death benefits in Divs 301 and 302 (as discussed in ¶14-200, ¶14-280) do not apply to certain superannuation payments as below, which are subject to different tax rules:

- superannuation lump sum benefits of less than $200 covered by ITAA97 Subdiv 301-E
- superannuation benefits covered by ITAA97 Div 303 — certain commutation payments, payments to persons with a terminal medical condition, certain payments under an ATO release authority, and
- unclaimed money payments under the constructive receipt rule.

Departing Australia superannuation payments covered by ITAA97 Subdiv 301-D are also not subject to the other tax rules within Div 301 or the rules in 302. They are not assessable income and not exempt income (ITAA97 s 301-175), and are subject to withholding tax (¶14-390).

Small benefit payments under $200

A superannuation lump sum member benefit which is less than $200 in value and is the member's entire superannuation interest, and which meets the requirements specified in ITR97 reg 301-225.01, is not assessable income and not exempt income (ITAA97 s 301-225(1)).

Also, a superannuation lump sum benefit of less than $200 in value received from the Commissioner under s 24G(2)(d) of the *Superannuation (Unclaimed Money and Lost Members) Act 1999* (being the repayment of lost members' money which had previously been paid to the ATO by a superannuation provider that Act: ¶13-850) is not assessable income and not exempt income (ITAA97 s 301-225(2)).

The small benefit rules do not apply to benefits which are departing Australia superannuation payments (DASPs). All DASPs, including those that are less than $200, are subject to DASP withholding tax (¶14-390).

Commutation of income streams by dependants

A superannuation lump sum received by a taxpayer from a complying superannuation plan that arises from the commutation of a superannuation income stream is not assessable income and not exempt income if:

- any of conditions below are met:
  - the taxpayer is under age 25 at the time of receiving the lump sum
  - the commutation takes place because the taxpayer attains age 25, or
  - the taxpayer is permanently disabled at the time of receiving the lump sum, and
- the taxpayer had received one or more superannuation income stream benefits from the income stream before the commutation because of the death of a person of whom the taxpayer was a "death benefits dependant" (¶14-270) (ITAA97 s 303-5).

A deceased person's child aged less than 18 just before the deceased person died is a "death benefits dependant" for the above purpose. Consequently, a superannuation lump sum arising from the commutation of an income stream is covered by s 303-5 (ie it is not assessable income and not exempt income), even if the child is aged 18 or more when they receive the superannuation lump sum (TD 2013/12).

A child under age 25 who is receiving a death benefit superannuation income stream is required to commute the benefit to a lump sum by age 25 unless the child has a disability of the kind described in s 8(1) of the *Disability Services Act 1986* (SISR reg 6.21(2B)). The fund trustee must determine whether the child has a disability of the kind described in s 8(1) on the day the child turns 25 (or an earlier date, if applicable under 6.21(2B)(a)) (SMSFD 2013/1).

Persons with terminal medical condition

A superannuation benefit paid to a person having a "terminal medical condition" as defined in ITR97 is non-assessable and non-exempt income (ITAA97 s 303-10; ITR97 reg 303-10.01). The benefit must be a lump sum superannuation member benefit which is:

- paid from a complying superannuation plan, or
- a superannuation guarantee payment, a small superannuation account payment, an unclaimed money payment, a superannuation co-contribution benefit payment or a superannuation annuity payment (¶14-100).

The tax exemption applies if a terminal medical condition exists when the person receives the lump sum or within 90 days after receiving it (ITTPA s 303-10(2)).

Payments under an ATO release authority

A superannuation provider may make certain superannuation payments under an ATO release authority pursuant to TAA Sch 1 Div 131 and the conditions of release of superannuation benefits in SISR Sch 1. The Div 131 regime replaced the former provisions dealing with releasing superannuation money under the ITAA97 and TAA Sch 1 former Div 96 and Div 135.

A payment made in accordance with an ATO release authority is a "superannuation benefit" (¶14-100). The tax treatment of these payments is summarised below:

- a release of excess concessional contributions is not assessable income and not exempt income (ITAA97 s 303-15). These are payments under a request or election made by a person pursuant to TAA Sch 1 s 131-5 (or TAA Sch 1 former s 96-5) (¶13-777)
- a payment to an individual under ITAA97 former s 292-410 of excess non-concessional contributions tax assessment (¶13-777) is not assessable income and not exempt income to the extent that it does not exceed the amount specified in the release authority (ITAA97 s 304-15(2)). Any excess is included as assessable income and is subject to tax at marginal rates (see below)
- a payment to an individual under TAA Sch 1 former s 96-12 of excess non-concessional contributions (¶13-780) is not assessable income and not exempt income (ITAA97 former s 303-17). Any associated earnings amount released is included in assessable income and is subject to tax at marginal rates (ITAA97 ss 292-20; 292-25)
- a payment under a release authority given to an individual for the purpose of paying a Division 293 tax liability (¶13-750) is not assessable income and not exempt income to the extent that it does not exceed the entitlement amount specified in the release authority (ITAA97 s 303-20). Any excess is included as assessable income and is subject to tax at marginal rates (see below).

Excess payments under a release authority

A superannuation benefit payment to or on behalf of an individual under an ATO release authority which *exceeds* the release entitlement specified in the release authority is included in assessable income of the individual and is subject to tax at marginal tax rates. These cover:

- payments received under a release authority given to an individual pursuant to ITAA97 former s 292-410 to release an amount to pay an excess non-concessional contributions tax assessment (¶13-780) (ITAA97 former s 304-15(4)), and
- payments from an individual's superannuation fund to pay a Division 293 tax liability (¶13-750) (ITAA97 ss 303-20; 304-20).

An amount of associated earnings which is released together with a refund of excess non-concessional contributions under a request pursuant to TAA Sch 1 s 131-5 is also assessable income of the individual and is subject to tax at marginal tax rates (¶13-755) (ITAA97 ss 292-20; 292-25). A non-refundable tax offset of 15% of the amount included in assessable income under s 292-25 is available (ITAA97 s 292-30).

Unclaimed money payment

An unclaimed money payment that a superannuation fund member is taken to receive under the constructive receipt rule in s 307-15, because it is paid in accordance with the *Superannuation (Unclaimed Money and Lost Members) Act 1999* (SUMLMA) to the Commissioner or a state or territory authority is not assessable income and is not exempt income (ITAA97 s 306-20). The unclaimed money payment may be taxed as a superannuation benefit or superannuation death benefit when it is subsequently paid by the Commissioner or the authority (¶14-100).

[AMSG ¶8-500; FITR ¶292-000; SLP ¶39-040]

Superannuation Transfer Balance Cap

¶14-320 Transfer balance cap regime

A transfer balance cap applies from 1 July 2017 to limit the total amount of superannuation that an individual can transfer into the retirement phase of superannuation, where earnings from the income streams are exempt from taxation

(ITAA97 Div 294 ss 294-5 to 294-250). The cap also effectively limits the amount of exempt income from assets supporting the income stream accounts in the hands of the income stream provider. The meaning of "retirement phase" and "retirement phase superannuation income streams" is discussed in ¶13-140.

The ATO keeps a transfer balance account for individuals who have income streams in the retirement phase (¶14-340).

If an individual's transfer balance account balance (including excess transfer balance earnings) exceeds the transfer balance cap, the Commissioner will direct the individual's income stream provider to commute the individual's retirement phase interests held with the provider by the excess amount so as to rectify the breach (ITAA97 s 294-230).

In addition, the individual will be liable to pay excess transfer balance tax on the excess transfer balance earnings in the transfer balance account to neutralise the benefit received from having excess capital in the tax exempt retirement phase. The tax rate on excess transfer balance earnings is 15% for a first breach and 30% for the second and subsequent breaches in the year (¶14-360).

General transfer balance cap and an individual's personal transfer balance cap

The general transfer balance cap is $1.6 million for the 2017–18 to 2020–21 financial years. The cap is subject to indexation in $100,000 increments on an annual basis in line with the CPI (ss 294-35(3); 960-285).

An individual's transfer balance comprises the value of the individual's superannuation interests supporting retirement phase superannuation income streams as at 30 June 2017, together with the commencement value of new superannuation income streams starting after that date (see (¶14-340).

An individual's personal transfer balance cap begins as the general transfer balance cap at the time the individual first begins to have a transfer balance. This means that at the time an individual first commences a retirement phase superannuation income stream, the individual's transfer balance cap will be equal to the general transfer balance cap for that financial year. In later years, the personal transfer balance cap amount is modified by the proportional indexation (see below).

Proportional indexation of the personal transfer balance cap

If an individual with a transfer balance account has not used the full amount of their cap, proportional indexation in line with increases in the general transfer balance cap applies to the individual's personal transfer balance cap (s 294-35(1), (2)).

Proportional indexation is intended to hold constant the proportion of an individual's used and unused cap space as the general cap increases. The indexation is only applied to an individual's unused cap percentage. This is worked out by comparing the individual's highest transfer balance at the end of a day at an earlier point in time to the individual's personal transfer balance cap on that day, and expressing the unused cap space as a percentage (ITAA97 s 294-40).

Modifications for child death benefit recipients

The transfer balance cap that applies to child dependants in receipt of a death benefit income stream from a deceased parent is subject to modifications which generally allow the child to receive their share of the deceased's retirement phase interest (¶14-330).

Modifications for capped defined benefit income streams

Defined benefit lifetime pensions and other superannuation income streams with commutation restrictions (called capped defined benefit income streams) are not subject to excess transfer balance tax but are subject to a different tax treatment (¶14-370).

ATO guidelines

LCR 2016/9 provides guidelines on how the transfer balance cap operates for *account-based superannuation income stream products*, covering:

- how the excess transfer balance tax is calculated
- when the Commissioner will issue an excess transfer balance determination, and
- the effect of transfers and/or commutations on the individual's transfer balance.

Special rules and guidelines apply to *capped defined benefit income streams* (see LCR 2016/10 Capped defined benefit income streams — non commutable lifetime pensions and lifetime annuities and LCR 2017/1 Capped defined benefit income streams — pensions or annuities paid from non-commutable life expectancy or market-linked products).

Other ATO guidance on various aspects of the transfer balance cap and related laws include the following:

- LCR 2016/8 Transfer balance cap and transition-to-retirement reforms: transitional CGT relief for superannuation funds
- LCR 2016/11 Concessional contributions — defined benefit interests and constitutionally protected funds
- LCR 2016/12 Total superannuation balance
- LCR 2017/3 Superannuation death benefits and the transfer balance cap
- PCG 2017/3 Income tax — supporting the implementation of changes to the taxation of transition to retirement income streams
- PCG 2017/5 and PCG 2017/6 dealing with commutations of income streams before 1 July 2017
- Super Guidance Notes (listed under ''ATO law aids'' in the ATO's database).

[AMSG ¶6-420; FITR ¶269-560ff; SLP ¶38-600ff]

¶14-330 Modifications for child benefit recipients

A child who receives a death benefit income stream is entitled to a modified transfer balance cap which is generally set by reference to the child's portion of the deceased parent's retirement phase interests (ITAA97 ss 294-170; 294-175).

A child benefit recipient is a deceased person's dependent child who is:

- under the age of 25
- between 18 and 25 and financially dependent on the deceased, or
- has a permanent disability (SISR reg 6.21(2A)).

A child benefit recipient is required to commute any death benefit income stream benefits and remove the capital from the superannuation system on attaining age 25 unless the child has a permanent disability (SISR reg 6.21(2B)). This means that a child's transfer balance account and modified transfer balance cap will generally cease when all death benefit income streams are commuted at age 25, or when the funds supporting the income streams are exhausted (see ''When does a child recipient's transfer balance account cease'' below), unless the child also has other superannuation income streams (see ''When a child already has a transfer balance account'' below).

Child transfer balance cap

A child who is only receiving death benefit income streams as a child benefit recipient does not have a personal transfer balance cap (¶14-320). Instead, the child's transfer balance cap is generally determined by reference to the value of the deceased's retirement phase interests that the child receives through a series of transfer balance cap increments (see below) that has accrued to the child (s 294-185(1)).

If the child recipient receives other superannuation income streams in addition to the death benefit income stream, the child's transfer balance cap is the total of:

- the child's personal transfer balance cap (worked out according to the general rules: ¶14-320), and
- the total amount of transfer balance cap increments (see below) the child receives as a child recipient (s 294-185(2)).

Transfer balance cap increments

The amount of a child's transfer balance cap increments is based on:

- whether the child started to receive death benefit income streams before 1 July 2017 (s 294-190), or
- if the child started to receive them on or after 1 July 2017 — whether the deceased had a transfer balance account just before the time of death (s 294-195), and
- if deceased had a transfer balance account just before the time of death — whether the deceased had an excess transfer balance in the retirement phase just before the time of death (s 294-200).

The examples below are given in or adapted from the explanatory memorandum to Act No 81 of 2016.

▶ Example: Child's transfer balance cap increment where deceased parent does not have a transfer balance account — single beneficiary

Joseph dies on 15 November 2020, aged 56, with accumulation assets worth $2 million. His 12-year-old daughter Eliza is the sole beneficiary of his estate.

As Joseph has not yet retired, he does not have a transfer balance account.

As there are no other beneficiaries, the cap increment for Eliza is the general transfer balance cap.

Eliza can receive $1.6 million of the $2 million as a death benefit income stream. The remaining $400,000 would need to be paid to Eliza as a death benefit lump sum and removed from the superannuation system where it would most likely be managed by a guardian or held in trust.

▶ Example: Child's transfer balance cap increment where deceased parent does not have a transfer balance account — multiple beneficiaries

Emma died on 6 June 2021, aged 55, with accumulation interests worth $2 million.

Emma's 2 daughters, Sana and Chloe, are the beneficiaries of her superannuation interests. Emma had a binding nomination that her superannuation interests are to be shared equally between Sana and Chloe.

As Emma did not have a transfer balance account before her death, her beneficiaries are entitled to their proportion of the general transfer balance cap as corresponds with their share of Emma's superannuation interest. Sana and Chloe will each receive a transfer balance cap increment of $800,000 (50% of the 2020–21 general transfer balance cap).

Sana and Chloe may each receive a death benefit income stream of $800,000. The remaining $200,000 that each child receives would need to be taken as a death benefit lump sum and cashed out of the superannuation system.

▶ Example: Death benefit wholly sourced from deceased parent's retirement phase interests

At the time of her death, Esther was being paid a superannuation income stream and had $150,000 in an accumulation phase interest. The value of the superannuation interest supporting the income stream at that time was $750,000.

Esther left 2 dependants, her child Tiffany (aged 12) and her husband Matthew. The trustee of Esther's superannuation fund decided to pay a $750,000 death benefit income stream to Tiffany from the Esther's income stream interest and a $150,000 death benefit lump sum to Matthew from Esther's accumulation phase interest.

Matthew elected to receive a death benefit lump sum as he had already started a superannuation income stream to the full value of his transfer balance cap.

As the death benefit income stream paid to Tiffany is solely sourced from Esther's retirement phase interest, the amount of Tiffany's transfer balance cap increment is equal to her death benefit income stream — $750,000.

If a child's death benefit income stream is wholly sourced from the deceased parent's accumulation phase interests, the transfer balance cap increment for the child's cap is nil (s 294-200(3)).

▶ Example: Death benefit wholly sourced from deceased parent's accumulation phase interests

Edmond dies on 24 November 2020. He had $500,000 in an accumulation phase interest just before he died.

Edmond's daughter, Arwen, is advised that if she was to request a death benefit income stream, her transfer balance cap increment would be nil because it would be solely sourced from Edmond's accumulation phase interest, thus making the whole amount in excess of her transfer balance cap. Therefore, Arwen instead requests that the $500,000 be paid to her as a death benefit lump sum.

Similarly, if a child's death benefit income stream is only *partly sourced* from the deceased parent's retirement phase interests, the amount of the child's cap increment will be equal to only that part. The part of the death benefit income stream paid to a child that is sourced from the deceased parent's accumulation phase interest will exceed the child's transfer balance cap (unless the child also has a cap increment because of the death of another parent, or the child also has a personal transfer balance cap because of a separate non-death benefit income stream) (s 294-200(4)).

▶ Example: Death benefit partly sourced from deceased parent's retirement phase interest and partly from accumulation phase interest

At the time of his death, Sam was being paid a superannuation income stream and had $350,000 in an accumulation phase interest. The value of the superannuation interest supporting the income stream at that time was $750,000.

Sam left 2 dependants, his child Jackson, aged 5, and his wife, Sybil.

Sybil seeks financial advice in respect of Sam's superannuation interest as she wants to maximise the amount of any death benefit income stream paid to Jackson as a child beneficiary. She is advised that if the whole of Sam's superannuation interest were paid as a death benefit income stream to Jackson, it would exceed the transfer balance cap increment that he would receive as it would be partly sourced from Sam's accumulation phase interest.

Sybil requests that a death benefit income stream of $750,000 from Sam's retirement phase interest be paid to Jackson and a death benefit income stream of $350,000 be paid to herself from Sam's accumulation phase.

As the death benefit income stream paid to Jackson is solely sourced from Sam's retirement phase interest, the amount of Jackson's transfer balance cap increment is equal to his death benefit income stream — $750,000.

As Sybil had not previously been paid a superannuation income stream, the $350,000 death benefit income stream she will receive from Sam's accumulation interest does not exceed her transfer balance cap.

Earnings form part of deceased person's retirement phase interest

Earnings that accrue on a deceased person's retirement phase interest after their death but before the commencement of a death benefit income stream are considered to be part of the deceased person's retirement phase interest. To the extent that the accrued earnings are included in a death benefit income stream payable to a child, the earnings are therefore considered to be sourced from the deceased parent's retirement phase interest and will be included in the child's transfer balance cap increment for the death benefit income stream.

However, accrued earnings do not include an amount paid from a life insurance policy or from a reserve. The amounts are considered to form part of the deceased parent's accumulation phase interest (s 294-200(7)).

▶ Example: Child's cap increment where deceased parent has a transfer balance account — multiple beneficiaries

Damien dies at age 70, with retirement phase interests worth $1.3 million and accumulation phase interests of $400,000 in his superannuation fund. Damien's 2 children, Alyssa, 15, and Zali, 13, are his sole superannuation beneficiaries.

Damien's binding death benefit nomination with his superannuation fund provided for his superannuation interests are to be evenly divided between his 2 children.

Accordingly, the trustee of the fund pays:

- Damien's retirement phase interests to Alyssa and Zali, as a $650,000 death benefit income stream to each of them, and
- Damien's accumulation phase interests to Alyssa and Zali as a $200,000 death benefit lump sum to each of them, to be cashed out of the superannuation system.

As the death benefit income streams payable to Alyssa and Zali are sourced solely from Damien's retirement phase interest, each child receives a transfer balance cap increment of $650,000.

▶ Example: Inclusion of investment earnings in transfer balance cap increment

Further to the example above, assume that earnings of $4,000 accrued to Damien's retirement phase interest from the date of his death up to the time of the payment of the death benefit income streams to Alyssa and Zali.

In that case, each child could start a $652,000 death benefit income stream that is accommodated under a transfer balance cap increment.

Child's transfer balance cap increment — where the deceased parent has an excess transfer balance

A child's transfer balance cap increment is reduced if the deceased parent had an excess transfer balance just before death by the child's proportionate share of the excess transfer balance. However, the cap increment is not reduced to the extent that the child's entitlement to the deceased's retirement phase interests is paid as a death benefit lump sum and not as a death benefit income stream (s 294-200(5)).

▶ Example: Parent's excess transfer balance

Jonathan commenced a pension worth $1.8 million. He has a personal transfer balance cap of $1.6 million and his transfer balance is $1.8 million, ie he has an excess transfer balance of $200,000. Jonathan passed away shortly after commencing his pension.

The superannuation interest that supported Jonathan's pension at the time of his death is $1.7 million (it has reduced in value due to pension payments to Jonathan before his death).

Jonathan's son, Callum, aged 16, is his sole beneficiary. If Callum were to commence a $1.7 million death benefit income stream, his transfer balance cap increment would be reduced from $1.7 million to $1.5 million because of the application of his father's excess transfer balance. This would result in a $200,000 excess transfer balance for Callum.

Instead, Callum starts a $1.5 million death benefit income stream and takes the remaining $200,000 as a death benefit lump sum which is cashed out of the superannuation system.

A credit of $1.5 million arises in Callum's transfer balance account. Callum receives a transfer balance cap increment of $1.5 million and this is not reduced because the death benefit lump sum that Callum receives from Jonathan's retirement phase interests equals the amount of Jonathan's excess transfer balance.

▶ Example: Parent's excess transfer balance — reversionary superannuation income stream

Thomas commenced a reversionary pension worth $1.8 million. He has a personal transfer balance cap of $1.6 million and his transfer balance is $1.8 million, ie he has an excess transfer balance of $200,000.

Thomas passed away in February 2020, shortly after commencing his pension.

On Thomas' death, a reversionary pension became payable to his son, Bruce, aged 16. The superannuation interest that supported Thomas' pension at the time of his death is $1.7 million (it has reduced due to investment losses).

A credit for $1.7 million will arise in February 2021, 12 months after the pension reverts to Bruce.

A transfer balance cap increment of $1.5 million (the value of the $1.7 million pension *less* Thomas' $200,000 excess transfer balance) will also arise for Bruce in February 2021. If Bruce does nothing, he will have a $200,000 excess transfer balance in February 2021.

To avoid having an excess transfer balance, Bruce will need to partially commute his reversionary pension and take the excess transfer balance as a death benefit lump sum of $200,000 out of the superannuation system.

Child's transfer balance cap — where both parents die

Where both parents of a child die, the child's transfer balance cap is the sum of amounts worked out in relation to each parent.

Child's transfer balance cap — where child already has a transfer balance account

A child may have a transfer balance account and a personal transfer balance cap either, before or after, the child starts to receive death benefit income streams as a child recipient. In such a case, the child's transfer balance cap is increased by the sum of cap increments discussed above.

To ensure that the credits and debits which a child recipient receives in relation to transfer balance cap increments do not affect the indexation of the child recipient's personal transfer balance cap, these amounts are disregarded for the purpose of calculating the child recipient's transfer balance cap, including access to proportional indexation (s 294-185(2)(b)).

▶ Example: Increasing an existing transfer balance cap

On 1 August 2020, Barbara received a structured settlement of $5 million as a result of a debilitating injury she suffered.

On 1 September 2020, Barbara contributes the settlement amount into her superannuation and, combined with her existing $400,000 of accumulation phase interests, starts a superannuation income stream worth $5.4 million.

Barbara starts to have a transfer balance account and transfer balance cap on 1 September 2020. Her transfer balance cap is $1.6 million. Her transfer balance account is credited $5.4 million for the new superannuation income stream and is debited by $5 million for the structured settlement contribution. At the end of 1 September 2020, her transfer balance is $400,000 and she has $1.2 million of available cap space.

On 1 January 2021, Barbara's father, Jim, dies. Jim had a $1.8 million superannuation interest that was supporting a pension paid to him (Jim's superannuation interest had grown due to investment earnings — he was not in excess of his transfer balance cap at the time of his death). The pension was not a reversionary pension and it ceased on Jim's death. Barbara, Jim's sole beneficiary, was paid a new $1.8 million death benefit income stream from Jim's retirement phase interest.

On 1 January 2021, Barbara's transfer balance cap is increased to $3.4 million (her $1.6 million transfer balance cap plus the $1.8 million cap increment from the value of Jim's retirement phase interests). A credit of $1.8 million arises in her transfer balance account. Barbara's transfer balance is now $2.2 million while her available cap space is still $1.2 million.

For the purposes of proportional indexation, Barbara's highest transfer balance is $400,000 (her credit of $1.8 million for the death benefit income stream is disregarded). Assuming no further changes, she will be entitled to 75% any future indexation of the general transfer balance cap.

When does a child recipient's transfer balance account cease

A child recipient's transfer balance account ceases:

- where the child attains age 25 and is required under the SISR compulsory cashing rule (¶13-800) to commute an income stream death benefit into a lump sum, or the child's death benefit income streams (that they receive as a child recipient) have been exhausted before that time, or
- where the child has a permanent disability and is not required to cash out death benefit income streams at the age of 25, when the relevant death benefit income streams are exhausted or have otherwise ceased.

Once a child recipient's transfer balance account has ceased, a new transfer balance account and transfer balance cap will arise when the child subsequently has income streams which are covered by the transfer balance cap regime, based on the general transfer balance cap at that time (s 294-180).

A child recipient's transfer balance account does not cease if they have received any superannuation income streams other than as a child recipient at any time before they cease to be a child recipient (whether they were a child recipient at that earlier time or not) (s 294-180(1)(c)).

¶14-340 Transfer balance account — credits and debits

ITAA97 Subdiv 294-B and 294-C contain the rules governing an individual's transfer balance account, what are transfer balance credits and debits and when they arise in the transfer balance account, and the circumstances which modify when transfer balance credits and debits arise (ss 294-15–294-95).

An individual has a transfer balance account if he/she is or has at any time been a ''retirement phase recipient'' of a superannuation income stream, ie the income stream is in the retirement phase and the superannuation income stream benefits from that income stream are payable to the individual at that time, or the income stream is a deferred superannuation income stream and an income stream benefit will be payable to the individual from the income stream after that time (¶14-050).

The transfer balance account starts on the later of 1 July 2017 and the day the individual starts to be a retirement phase recipient of a superannuation income stream (ITAA97 ss 295-15; 294-20).

For individuals who are receiving retirement phase superannuation income streams on 1 July 2017, their transfer balance account begins on that date. For individuals with deferred superannuation income streams, it is not necessary that benefits be currently payable provided income stream benefits will become payable to the individual later and the deferred superannuation income stream is in the retirement phase (s 294-20(2)).

An individual's transfer balance account is a lifetime account which ceases on the individual's death (ITAA97 s 294-45).

For the purposes of working out if an individual has a transfer balance account, and the transfer balance in the account at a particular time, there is an assumption that an income stream complies with the pension and annuity standards under it is provided, based on the facts and circumstances that exist at that time (ITAA97 s 294-50). These assumptions ensure that the creation of a transfer balance account and a transfer balance credit are not invalidated because of subsequent events which result in a superannuation income stream no longer being in the retirement phase.

Transfer balance accounts are maintained by the ATO, using information provided by superannuation providers under an event-based reporting regime (see below) in conjunction with the other reporting requirements under the TAA (¶39-530).

Operation of transfer balance account

An individual's transfer balance account effectively records the net amounts the individual has in the retirement phase according to the transfer balance credits and debits made to the account. A credit reduces the amount of available transfer balance cap space an individual has, while a debit reduces the value of the individual's retirement phase interests.

An individual has an excess transfer balance at a particular time if, at that time, the transfer balance in the individual's transfer balance account exceeds the individual's transfer balance cap at that time. The excess transfer balance is the amount of the excess (ITAA97 s 294-30).

After a superannuation income stream has commenced, changes in the value of its supporting interest are not counted as credits or debits. That is, any increase in the interest supporting the income stream because of investment earnings does not count towards the cap. Similarly, reductions in the superannuation interest due to investment losses or income stream drawdowns are not reflected in the individual's transfer balance account.

Modifications to the transfer balance credit and debit rules for defined benefit income streams are provided by Subdiv 294-D (see "Credit and debit amounts arising from capped defined benefit income streams" below) (ss 294-125 to 294-145).

Transfer balance credits

The situations that give rise to transfer balance credits in an individual's transfer balance account, the amount of the credit and when it arises are set out in the table in ITAA97 s 294-25(1), as follows:

Credits in the transfer balance account

Item	If:	A credit of:	Arises:
1	just before 1 July 2017, you are the retirement phase recipient of a superannuation income stream	the value, just before 1 July 2017, of the superannuation interest that supports the superannuation income stream	on the later of: (a) 1 July 2017, and (b) if you are a reversionary beneficiary — the last day of the period of 12 months beginning on the day a superannuation income stream benefit first becomes payable from the income stream
2	on a day (the ***starting day***) on or after 1 July 2017, you start to be the retirement phase recipient of a superannuation income stream	the value on the starting day of the superannuation interest that supports the superannuation income stream	(a) on the starting day, unless para (b) applies, or (b) if you are a reversionary beneficiary — at the end of the period of 12 months beginning on the starting day

Credits in the transfer balance account			
Item	**If:**	**A credit of:**	**Arises:**
3	you have excess transfer balance at the end of a day	your excess transfer balance earnings for that day	at the start of the next day
4	a transfer balance credit arises under s 294-55 because of the repayment of a limited recourse borrowing arrangement	the amount of the credit specified in s 294-55	at the time provided by s 294-55
5	a transfer balance credit arises under regulations made for the purposes of this item	the amount of the credit worked out in accordance with the regulations	at the time specified in the regulations

Note 1: Special rules govern the calculation of the transfer balance credit amount for certain capped defined benefit income streams in particular circumstances (see "Credit and debit amounts arising from capped defined benefit income streams" below) and for deferred superannuation income streams (see "Innovative income streams" below).

Note 2: The meaning of ***excess transfer balance earnings*** is provided by s 294-235 (¶14-360).

Note 3: If a payment split applies to payments from the superannuation income stream, a debit arises under s 294-90.

No credit will arise in an individual's transfer balance account under item 3 because of an excess transfer balance if the Commissioner has made an excess transfer balance determination (¶14-350) in respect of the individual (s 294-25(2)).

The regulations may provide that an item of the table for credits and debits to a transfer balance account does not apply to a class of superannuation income streams (ss 294-25(3); 294-80(3)) (see below under transfer balance debits).

Transfer balance credit for LRBA repayments

An integrity measure prevents value shifting from accumulation assets into pension accounts to avoid the application of the transfer balance cap rules. This measure applies where an individual is a member of a complying superannuation fund that is an SMSF or a small APRA fund (ie a fund with fewer than 5 members) which has a borrowing under a limited recourse borrowing arrangement (LRBA) (as permitted by SISA ss 67A and 67B) under contracts entered into on or after 1 July 2017.

In the above circumstances, a transfer balance credit will arise for the individual where the fund makes a payment in respect of the LRBA that increases the value of a superannuation interest supporting a retirement phase superannuation income stream (ss 294-25(1) table item 4; 294-55). This credit ensures that the transfer balance cap captures the shift of value that occurs if liabilities arising from the LRBA are paid using accumulation phase assets. This is consistent with the way transfers from assets that do not support a superannuation income stream (accumulation phase assets) are treated when a superannuation income stream is commenced.

The transfer balance credit arises at the time of the payment, and the credit amount is the amount by which the individual's superannuation income stream increased in value because of the payment (s 294-55(2), (3)). A transfer balance credit will therefore only arise where the payments in respect of the LRBA supporting a retirement phase superannuation income stream are *sourced from assets that do not support the same income stream*. For example, where such a payment is sourced from assets supporting the retirement phase interest, the payment does not affect the value of the interest because the reduction in the LRBA liability is offset by a corresponding reduction in assets supporting the retirement phase interest. By contrast, where the payment of the LRBA's liability is sourced from assets that support accumulation phase interests, the payment will increase the value of the individual's retirement phase superannuation interest and trigger a transfer balance credit as there is no offsetting decrease in the value of assets supporting that retirement phase interest.

▶ Example: no assets supporting superannuation interest

Eddy is the sole member of his SMSF and his superannuation interests are valued at $1.6 million.

The SMSF acquires an investment property for $0.5 million, property, using $0.2 million of the SMSF's cash and $0.3 million in borrowings under an LRBA.

Eddy then commences a superannuation income stream, supported by his $1.6 million superannuation interest (which is backed, in part, by the property).

The SMSF uses rental income from the property and its other cash resources to repay the LRBA over time. As the repayments are sourced from assets that support Eddy' retirement phase interests, the repayments do not increase the value of Eddy' superannuation interest supporting his income stream and no transfer balance credit will arise for the LRBA repayment. Any other increase in value of Eddy' superannuation interest (eg from capital growth or income generated by fund assets) will also not trigger a credit.

▶ Example: repayment for assets solely supporting retirement interests

Michael is the sole member of his SMSF and his superannuation interests are valued at $3 million.

The SMSF acquires an investment property for $1.5 million, using $0.5 million of the SMSF's cash and $1.0 million in borrowings under an LRBA.

Michael then commences an account-based superannuation income stream. The superannuation interest that supports this superannuation income stream is backed by the property which has a net value of $0.5 million (ie $1.5 million less the $1 million LRBA liability). Michael therefore has a transfer balance credit of $0.5 million in his transfer balance account in respect of the superannuation income stream.

The SMSF makes monthly repayments of $10,000. Half of each repayment amount comes from the rental income from the property and the other half from the cash that supports Michael's other accumulation interests. At the time of each repayment, Michael receives a transfer balance credit of $5,000, representing the increase in value of the superannuation interest that supports his superannuation income stream. The repayments that are sourced from the rental income that the SMSF receives do not give rise to a transfer balance credit because they do not result in a net increase in the value of the superannuation interest that supports his superannuation income stream.

Purchase of deferred superannuation income stream by instalments

A deferred superannuation income stream is a benefit supported by a superannuation interest where the contract or rules governing the benefit provide for payments of the benefit to start more than 12 months after the interest is acquired and for payments to be made at least annually afterwards (ITAA97 s 995-1(1); SISR reg 1.03(1)).

The method for determining the value of an individual's superannuation interest that supports a deferred superannuation income stream at a particular point in time is prescribed in ITR97 reg 307-205.02C(1). This will be the value credited to the individual's transfer balance account when the interest holder enters the retirement phase, and also the value for the purposes of applying the proportioning rule in ITAA97 when benefit payments are made (¶14-130).

The value of such an interest at a particular time is the greater of:

- the sum of each amount of consideration paid for the income stream, and a notional earnings amount on each amount of consideration (as worked out under ITR97 reg 307-205.02C(2)), or
- the amount of superannuation benefits payable from the interest if the holder voluntarily caused the interest to cease at that time.

This method recognises the current value of the consideration paid for a deferred superannuation income stream interest which is purchased with a single amount, or through instalment amounts, before the retirement phase start day. Consideration may be paid by way of superannuation roll-over amounts or by making contributions to the superannuation fund providing a deferred superannuation income stream.

Credits arising from death benefit income streams

Superannuation funds are allowed to pay a superannuation death benefit as an income stream in accordance with the SISR payment standards. In summary, when an individual who has a superannuation interest dies, the fund trustees are required under the payment standards to cash the deceased's remaining superannuation interest (accumulation and retirement phase interests) from the superannuation system as soon as practicable. This remaining interest is usually paid as a death benefit lump sum to a beneficiary of the deceased (ie cashed out of the superannuation system), or is paid as a death benefit income stream to a beneficiary who is a dependant of the deceased (¶13-800).

The value of a death benefit income stream that is paid to a dependant is a credit to the dependant's transfer balance account. This value may include investment gains that accrued to the deceased's superannuation interest between the time of death and when death benefit income streams become payable to the beneficiary.

A death benefit income stream payment to an individual beneficiary, together with the individual's own superannuation income stream benefits (if any), may result in a beneficiary exceeding the transfer balance cap. In such a case, the beneficiary will need to decide which superannuation income stream to commute so as to comply with the transfer balance cap rules. The superannuation death benefit cannot remain as an accumulation interest in the fund for the benefit of the beneficiary as the SISR standards require death benefits to be cashed out of the system as soon as practicable (¶13-800). The examples below (adapted from the explanatory memorandum to Act No 81 of 2016) show the options available in these circumstances.

▶ Example

Henry has a $500,000 superannuation income stream and a transfer balance of $500,000.

Sally (Henry's wife) who has superannuation interests of $288,000 died on 30 June 2020 and her superannuation fund informed Henry in July 2020 that he was the sole beneficiary of Sally's' superannuation interest.

The superannuation fund pays the death benefit (now worth $290,000) in the form of a death benefit income stream to Henry from 1 August 2020. This increases Henry's transfer balance account to $790,000 on that date. As this is still below Henry's transfer balance cap, he does not need to take any further action.

▶ Example: Death benefit income stream where beneficiary spouse has not used all their transfer balance cap

Louise and her husband (Greg) both receive non-reversionary superannuation income streams from their superannuation fund (Fund), with each having a superannuation interest and transfer balance of $1 million.

Greg died in December 2020 leaving $800,000 in superannuation interests.

On 15 January 2021, the Fund informed Louise that she was Greg's death benefit dependant and was eligible to receive a death benefit income stream from Greg's superannuation interests of $800,000 from the Fund.

If Louise were to receive the $800,000 death benefit income stream in addition to her own $1 million income stream, she would exceed her transfer balance cap by $200,000. Louise may either:

- receive from Greg's superannuation interest a $600,000 death benefit income stream and a $200,000 death benefit lump sum — the $200,000 death benefit lump sum must be cashed out of the superannuation system, or

- receive from Greg's superannuation interest an $800,000 death benefit income stream and partially commute her own superannuation income stream by $200,000 — the $200,000 commutation lump sum may be retained in superannuation in an accumulation interest.

Under either option, Louise will have a transfer balance account with a balance of $1.6 million, fully exhausting her transfer balance cap.

▶ Example: Death benefit income stream where beneficiary has no transfer balance account

Mary and her husband (David) have both retired. David has commenced a superannuation income stream with $1 million. Mary has no superannuation interests.

On David's death, his superannuation fund pays his $800,000 superannuation income stream to Mary as a death benefit income stream. At that time, Mary will have a transfer balance account with a credit balance of $800,000.

▶ Example: Death benefit income stream where beneficiary spouse has used all their transfer balance cap

Mabel and her husband Kenny both commenced a superannuation income stream in 2019, Mabel with $1 million and Kenny with $1.6 million using up his transfer balance cap.

When Mabel died in June 2020, her superannuation interests were worth $800,000 and Kenny was her sole beneficiary. At this time, the superannuation interest that supports Kenny's superannuation income stream has a value of $1.4 million. (The value of both their individual superannuation interests have been reduced since commencement by payments of superannuation income stream benefits.)

As Kenny had started his superannuation income stream with the full value of his transfer balance cap, he cannot transfer further amounts into the retirement phase without reducing his transfer balance first.

Kenny may take Mabel's superannuation interest of $800,000 as a death benefit lump sum, which must be cashed out of the superannuation system.

Alternatively, he could partially commute $800,000 of his superannuation income stream and retain the commutation lump sum in the accumulation phase, and take a new death benefit income stream of $800,000. In this way, Kenny would still have his original superannuation income stream in the retirement phase (now supported by a superannuation interest of $600,000 after the partial commutation) and would also have $800,000 in accumulation interests. If Kenny chooses this option, he would not need to cash any of Mabel's superannuation interest out of the superannuation system as a death benefit lump sum.

Modifications for reversionary superannuation income streams

Reversionary superannuation income streams are different from other death benefit income streams because they revert to the reversionary beneficiary immediately (and automatically) on the death of the primary pensioner fund member, rather than being paid at the discretion of the fund trustee.

For a reversionary income stream benefit, the credit that arises in the beneficiary's transfer balance account is the value of the supporting superannuation interest at the time it becomes payable to the beneficiary consistent with the general rules outlined above. However, a modification applies to defer the time the credit arises in the beneficiary's transfer balance account in respect of the reversionary income stream for 12 months after the benefit first becomes payable to the beneficiary, or 12 months after the income stream benefits became payable to that beneficiary (s 294-25(1) items 1 and 2: see the table above). This is to give reversionary beneficiaries time to manage their tax affairs before any consequences arise (eg a breach of the transfer balance cap).

Death benefit income streams must also be in the retirement phase

The SISR compulsory cashing rules allow for the payment of death benefit income streams to eligible beneficiaries provided they are also income streams in the retirement phase (¶13-140, ¶13-800).

As death benefits cannot remain in the accumulation phase, any amount that cannot be used to pay a death benefit income stream in the retirement phase must be cashed out as a death benefit lump sum. This ensures that the income stream provider does not contravene the SISR rules as well as limit the value of a death benefit income stream to the amount available under the beneficiary's transfer balance cap.

A death benefit income stream ceases to be in the retirement phase if the income stream provider is required to comply with a commutation authority but has failed to do so (¶14-050). Where this happens, a **debit** will arise in the individual member's transfer balance account because the death benefit income stream has ceased to be in the retirement phase (see item 5 in the table below).

Transfer balance debits

The situations that give rise to transfer balance debits in an individual's transfer balance account, the amount of the debit and when it arises are set out in the table in ITAA97 s 294-80(1), as follows:

Debits in the transfer balance account

Item	If:	A debit of:	Arises:
1	you receive a superannuation lump sum because a superannuation income stream of which you are a retirement phase recipient is commuted, in full or in part	the amount of the superannuation lump sum	at the time you receive the superannuation lump sum
2	a structured settlement contribution is made in respect of you (for an alternative debit for contributions before 1 July 2017, see below)	the amount of the contribution	at the later of: (a) the time the contribution is made, and (b) the start of the day you first start to have a transfer balance account
3	a transfer balance debit arises under s 294-85 because of an event that results in reduced superannuation	the amount of the debit specified in s 294-85	at the time provided by s 294-85
4	a transfer balance debit arises under s 294-90 because of a payment split	the amount of the debit specified in s 294-90	at the time provided by s 294-90
5	a superannuation income stream of which you are a retirement phase recipient stops being in the retirement phase under s 307-80(4)	the value of the superannuation interest that supports the superannuation income stream at the end of the period within which the commutation authority mentioned in that subsection was required to be complied with	at the end of the period within which the commutation authority mentioned in that subsection was required to be complied with

Debits in the transfer balance account

Item	If:	A debit of:	Arises:
6	a superannuation income stream of which you were a retirement phase recipient stops being a superannuation income stream that is in the retirement phase at a time (the ***stop time***), but items 1 and 5 do not apply	the value of the superannuation interest that supported the income stream just before the stop time	at the stop time
7	the Commissioner gives you a notice under s 136-70 in Sch 1 to the *Taxation Administration Act 1953* (about non-commutable excess transfer balance)	the amount of the excess transfer balance stated in the notice	at the time the Commissioner issues the notice
8	a transfer balance debit arises under the regulations made for the purposes of this item	the amount of the debit worked out in accordance with the regulations	at the time specified in the regulations

Special rules govern the calculation of the transfer balance debit amount for certain capped defined benefit income streams in particular circumstances (see ''Credit and debit amounts arising from capped defined benefit income streams'' below) and for deferred superannuation income streams (see ''Innovative income streams'' below).

Alternative transfer balance debit for structured settlement contributions made before 1 July 2017

An alternative transfer balance debit applies where an individual would have otherwise received a debit under s 294-80(1) table item 2 (see above) for contributing the proceeds of a structured settlement into superannuation *before* 1 July 2017 but the amount of that debit would be less than the combined values of the retirement phase superannuation interests that the individual had at that time. In such cases, the individual has a debit equal to the combined values of all transfer balance credits that he/she received for those retirement phase superannuation interests instead of a debit for the amount of the contributions (ITTPA s 294-80).

The alternative debit only applies where the sum of all transfer balance credits is greater than the structured settlement contribution. Where it applies, an individual's transfer balance in their transfer balance account on 1 July 2017 is equal to nil, and this will allow the individual to commence new superannuation income streams up to the amount of the general transfer balance cap.

Credits and debits — regulations may provide for exceptions

The regulations may provide that an item of the table for credits and debits to a transfer balance account does not apply to a class of superannuation income streams (ss 294-25(3); 294-80(3)).

This is to ensure that the transfer balance credit and debit rules can be modified so as to apply appropriately in respect of particular superannuation income stream products (eg innovative income stream products), or to address unforeseen issues arising under the transfer balance rules.

In addition to prescribing additional transfer balance credit and debit categories, the regulations may exclude particular items in the credit and debit tables to a class of superannuation income streams. Such exclusions may be required to prevent a superannuation income stream from being covered by multiple credit and debit categories as that would otherwise result in inappropriate double counting.

Replenishment debits

An individual may lose some or all of his/her superannuation interests where certain events arise, such as losses or reductions in the individual's superannuation account due to fraud, dishonesty, void payments under s 139ZQ of the *Bankruptcy Act 1966*, and family law payment splits (ITAA97 ss 294-85 to 294-95).

An individual affected by such an event can notify the Commissioner in the approved form of the happening of the event and receive a replenishment debit to his/her transfer balance account. There is no time limit within which the Commissioner is to be notified.

Capped defined benefit income streams — credits and debits

Capped defined benefit income streams are lifetime pensions and annuities, life expectancy pensions and annuities, and market-linked pensions and annuities (as prescribed in ITAA97 s 294-130(1) table items 1 to 7 or by ITR97: see table below). With the exception of lifetime pensions (Item 1 products), the pension or annuity must be in "retirement phase" (¶14-050) just before 1 July 2017 to satisfy the definition of a capped defined benefit income stream.

Superannuation income streams are also capped defined benefit income streams if ITR97 reg 294-130.01(2), (3), (3A), (3B) or (4) applies to the income stream (see table below).

Subdivision 294-D provides modifications to the general transfer balance cap rules for a superannuation income stream that meets the definition of a capped defined benefit income stream so that:

- an individual will have a "capped defined benefit balance" which reflects the credits and debits in the individual's transfer balance account that relate to the capped defined benefit income stream(s), and
- the "special value" of the defined benefit income streams (ie the credit or debit value that counts in relation to the income stream) is determined as summarised in the table below.

Capped defined benefit income stream product (ITAA97 s 294-130(1) Table items)	**Calculation of credit value (special value)**	**Calculation of debit value**
Item 1 Lifetime pension (SISR reg 1.06(2)) *Item 2* Lifetime annuity (SISR reg 1.05(2))	Annual entitlement of income stream × 16 (s 294-135(2); ITR97 reg 294-135.01)	Starting special value *less* previous debits — this represent the residual of the income stream's special value, after taking into account previous associated debit amounts (other than debits for payment splits). This calculation ensures that the total debits that an individual receives in

Capped defined benefit income stream product (ITAA97 s 294-130(1) Table items)	Calculation of credit value (special value)	Calculation of debit value
		relation to a fully commuted lifetime pension or annuity is equal to the amount of credits associated with the income stream (s 294-145(5); ITR97 reg 294-145.01) (see also ATO guidelines below).
Items 3 and 4 Life expectancy annuity or pension (SISR reg 1.05(9); 1.06(7)) *Items 5 and 6* Market-linked annuity or pension (SISR reg 1.05(10); 1.06(8)) *Item 7* Market-linked pension (RSA) (RSAR reg 1.07(3A))	Annual entitlement × remaining term (rounded to the nearest whole number) (s 294-135(3))	Special value at the relevant time – this represents the income stream's special value at the relevant time, based on the remaining term of the product at that time. This calculation will incorporate the ordinary decline in value of a term product, regardless of whether associated debits have previously arisen (s 294-145(6)) (see also ATO guidelines below).
Products prescribed in ITR97 reg 294-130.01 cover: ● certain lifetime pensions that may be commuted in limited circumstances or where payments are ceased or varied for a child beneficiary, pensions paid from a successor fund, and disability pensions paid under a public sector superannuation scheme, and ● lifetime pensions, life expectancy pensions and market-linked pensions that start to be in the retirement phase on or **after 1 July 2017** and arise as a direct result of the payment of an involuntary roll-over superannuation benefit to a successor fund (see further ¶14-370).	Annual entitlement of income stream × 16 (ITR97 reg 294-135.01)	As calculated under ITR97 reg 294-145.01.

▶ Example 1: Credit value of lifetime pension

Sarah is the recipient of a lifetime pension. Under the terms of the pension, Sarah is entitled to receive $2,000 every fortnight (a 14-day period). Her annual entitlement is worked out as follows:

$2,000/14 × 365 = $52,142.86

Applying the multiplication factor of 16, Sarah's pension has a special value of $834,285.71.

A credit arises in Sarah's transfer balance account for this amount.

▶ Example 2: Debit value of a lifetime pension

Mark starts a lifetime pension that has a special value of $1 million (ie the debit value of the pension at this time is $1 million).

If a debit of $300,000 were to arise subsequently in relation to the pension, the debit value of the pension will be $700,000 from that time.

▶ Example 3: Debit value of a term product

Grant purchased a market-linked pension in January 2020 with a 5-year term.

On 30 June 2020, the pension has an annual entitlement of $100,000 and a remaining term which is rounded up to 5 years. Grant's pension has a special value of $500,000.

On 30 June 2021, Grant's pension has an annual entitlement of $90,000. The remaining term of the pension is 4 years. The pension has a debit value of $360,000 on 30 June 2021.

Reduction in value of lifetime benefits and annuities

Generally, the reduction in value of a superannuation income stream that is not attributable to losses or regular pension payments is attributable to a commutation or partial commutation of the income stream (which gives rise to a transfer balance debit under item 1 of the table in s 294-80(1): see above).

However, the value of certain defined benefit superannuation income streams can be reduced in circumstances that are not captured by the debits by s 294-80(1). This can arise under the rules of the fund or scheme where the calculation of the income stream benefit is varied due to a change in the circumstances of the individual recipient, rather than from a commutation of the defined benefit income stream (mainly in respect of public sector superannuation schemes). Examples of where these reductions can occur include:

- a reversionary defined benefit pension paid to a surviving spouse or a beneficiary. In some cases, the first payment is the full amount of the payment that was made to the deceased, whereas the second and all subsequent payments are a proportion of the full entitlement. As a result, the annualised payment is based on an inflated figure, and
- a reversionary defined benefit pension paid to a surviving spouse that is calculated by reference to the deceased's dependent children. In such cases, the surviving spouse's entitlement can be reduced as the children cease being dependent (generally at 18 or 25 years depending on their circumstances).

To ensure consistent treatment between reductions in the value of lifetime defined benefit income streams, a transfer balance debit arises for individuals in the circumstances prescribed in ITR97 reg 294-80.01, namely individuals (retirement phase income stream recipients) receiving a lifetime pension or annuity (or a similar superannuation income stream prescribed under reg 204-130.01) and the income stream benefit is subsequently reduced where the reduction is not attributable to either:

- circumstances that give rise to another transfer balance debit (either under items 1 to 7 of the table in s 294-80(1) or another regulation made under item 8 in that table), or
- a Consumer Price Index adjustment.

This ensures that the individual's transfer balance account reflects the decrease in the value of the individual's annual entitlement to superannuation income stream benefits. The amount of the debit arising in the individual's transfer balance account is the special value of the superannuation interest supporting the income stream just before the earlier time, *less* the special value of the superannuation interest supporting the income stream just before the later time. The special value of a lifetime pension or annuity at a particular time is the member's annual entitlement to superannuation income stream benefits multiplied by 16 (see above).

Debit value — innovative income streams

These are income streams that do not immediately pay a superannuation income stream benefit but are still superannuation income streams that are in the retirement phase if an individual to whom the income stream benefit will be payable has met a specified condition of release (s 307-80(2): ¶13-140, ¶14-125).

ITR97 reg 294-80.02 provides the rule for working out the transfer balance account debit where a deferred superannuation income stream ceases to be in the retirement stage, and reg 294-80.03 provides that items 5 and 6 of the table in s 294-80(1) (see above) do not apply to deferred income streams that are covered by the rule. This means that the value of the transfer balance account debit that arises at the time of cessation is simply the amount that the individual would be entitled to if they voluntarily ceased to hold the superannuation interest, and the indexed consideration paid for the interest is not relevant (see ITR97 reg 307-205.02C).

Successor fund transfers

A successor fund transfer occurs where a fund (the original fund), as part of a superannuation fund merger or acquisition, transfers its members' interests to a successor fund. Where an original fund is paying a capped defined benefit income stream as set out in the table in s 294-130(1) (see above) to an individual, the successor fund transfer will result in the original fund ceasing the income stream and the successor fund commencing to pay an equivalent income stream to the individual.

Under ITAA97 s 294-130(1)(b), a superannuation income stream covered by items 2 to 7 of the table is not a capped defined benefit income stream where the income stream commences to be in retirement phase on or after 1 July 2017. Accordingly, where the successor fund transfer occurs on or after 1 July 2017, the income stream paid to the member by the successor fund will not be a capped defined benefit income stream for the purposes of the transfer balance cap.

To address unintended adverse consequences that may potentially arise, ITR97 prescribes a superannuation income stream to be a capped defined benefit income stream under s 294-130(2) where it would be a capped defined benefit income stream if it had started on or before 1 July 2017 and it arises as a direct result of the payment of an involuntary roll-over superannuation fund to a successor fund (reg 294-130.01).

For successor fund transfers that occur on or after 1 July 2017, the special value is:

- for a lifetime annuity started under a successor fund transfer — the individual's annual entitlement to superannuation income stream benefits multiplied by 16, and
- for other superannuation income streams — life expectancy or market-linked pensions or annuities created under a successor fund transfer — the individual's annual entitlement to superannuation income stream benefits multiplied by the remaining term of the income stream (ITR97 reg 294-135.01).

The debit value of other superannuation income streams (life expectancy or market-linked pensions or annuities) created as a result of a successor fund transfer is the debit value of the superannuation interests under ITAA97 s 294-145 (6A) and ITR97 reg 294-145.01(6).

Debit value — commutation of certain capped defined benefit income streams

Where there is a full commutation of a capped defined benefit income stream covered by items 3 to 7 of the table in s 294-130(1), the value of the transfer balance debit is the debit value of the superannuation interest that supported the superannuation income stream just before the commutation takes place. The debit value is calculated as provided in s 294-145(1)(b)(ii) and 294-145(1B). This applies from 1 July 2017 to ensure that individuals who had previously received a nil debit value from a commutation will retrospectively receive the correct debit value as calculated in accordance with provisions above.

The ATO has reviewed its previous advice that it would not take compliance action if a fund did not report the required transfer balance account events of the commutation and has restarted a market-linked pension, or has reported a commutation amount other than nil to the ATO (SMSF News Alert 2018/3; CRT Alerts 066/2018 and 031/2020). The revised ATO guidelines and information on the income streams that are affected and how the debit value is calculated may be found in ATO factsheets ''Updated guidance – market linked pensions'' and ''Timeframe for reviewing reporting of commutations of market linked pensions''.

Proposed changes — amendments to commutation rules for certain income stream products

Amendments have been proposed to ITAA97 to ensure that retirees who have commuted and restarted certain market-linked pensions, life expectancy pensions and similar products are treated appropriately under the transfer balance cap.

The measure will enable retirees with these products who have been unable to commute amounts in excess of their transfer balance cap to undertake the necessary partial commutation, and ensure appropriate tax outcomes for these retirees given their prior inability to comply with the transfer balance cap rules.

These amendments will take effect from the date of assent to the amending legislation (2020–21 Mid-Year Economic and Fiscal Outlook, Appendix A: Policy decisions taken since the 2020–21 Budget, p 138).

TBAR — transfer balance events-based reporting

Superannuation funds are required to report transactions (or events) associated with their members' retirement phase accounts in the approved form (Transfer Balance Account Report (TBAR)) to enable the ATO to determine whether an individual's transfer balance account has exceeded the transfer balance cap and to take appropriate action. The TBAR and ATO instructions are available at www.ato.gov.au/forms/super-transfer-balance-account-report-instructions.

Reporting transfer balance events by APRA-regulated superannuation funds

APRA-regulated superannuation funds are required to report on a monthly basis by lodging a TBAR with the ATO within 10 working days of the end of each month in which the transfer balance account reporting event occurred, or such later date as the Commissioner may allow (F2017L01273; www.ato.gov.au/super/apra-regulated-funds/reporting-and-administrative-obligations/reporting-and-administrative-obligations-for-the-transfer-balance-cap).

The TBAR reporting operates in conjunction with MAAS and MATS reporting (¶39-530).

Reporting transfer balance events by SMSFs

SMSFs must report events that affect their members' transfer balances as below:

- where all members have a total superannuation balance of less than $1 million — the SMSF can report annually at the time it lodges its annual return, or
- where any member has a total superannuation balance of $1 million or more — the SMSF must report quarterly using the TBAR, within 28 days after the end of the quarter in which the event occurs (www.ato.gov.au/super/self-managed-super-funds/administering-and-reporting/new-reporting-obligations-for-smsfs/ and www.ato.gov.au/forms/super-transfer-balance-account-report-instructions/).

¶14-350 Excess transfer balance determination and commutation authority

The Commissioner must issue determinations and commutation authorities for excess transfer balance tax purposes under a 2-stage process in accordance with TAA Sch 1 Div 136 (TAA Sch 1 s 136-1 to 136-90).

Stage 1 — excess transfer balance determination

The first stage in managing breaches of the transfer balance cap by an individual is where the Commissioner makes an *excess transfer balance determination* (determination) in relation to the individual's excess transfer balance in their transfer balance account (s 136-10(1)). This determination is to advise the individual of the excess transfer balance, and to crystallise the amount of the excess (see below) as excess transfer balance earnings that accrue after issuing the determination are *not* credited towards the individual's transfer balance account.

If an individual has already taken steps to rectify a breach of the transfer balance cap by commuting an excess transfer balance amount, a determination is not issued if the Commissioner is aware that the individual no longer has an excess transfer balance. However, the individual is still liable for excess transfer balance tax even if no determination is issued (s 136-10(1) Note).

The amount of excess transfer balance stated in a determination is called the **crystallised reduction amount**). This is the sum of:

- transfer balance credits relating to the individual's superannuation income streams in the retirement phase, and
- excess transfer balance earnings that remain in excess of the individual's transfer balance cap at the date of the determination (s 136-10(3)).

The crystallised reduction amount is the value by which the individual's superannuation income streams must be commuted to bring the transfer balance within the transfer balance cap.

A determination by the Commissioner under s 136-10(1) must include a notice (**default commutation notice**):

- stating that the Commissioner will issue one or more commutation authorities if the individual does not make an election under s 136-20 within the period specified in the section (see below), and
- specifying the income stream providers to whom a commutation authority will be issued, the income stream(s) the provider will be obliged to commute (in full or in part), the amount to be stated in each commutation authority or the method the Commissioner will use to work out the amount to be stated (s 136-10(6), (7)).

Election by taxpayer under s 136-20

An individual with more than one superannuation income stream who receives a s 136-10 determination (and default commutation notice) may elect the income stream or streams to be commuted or partially commuted. The total amount of the commutations specified in the individual's election must equal the crystallised reduction amount (s 136-20).

An election must be made in the approved form to the Commissioner within 60 days from the date the determination was issued (or such further time as the Commissioner allows) (s 136-20(4)).

An election is irrevocable and the Commissioner will issue commutation authorities in accordance with the election (s 136-20(5)).

An individual is not required to make an election if the superannuation income stream to be commuted is the income stream specified in the default commutation notice.

Notifying the Commissioner of transfer balance debits

An individual may notify the Commissioner of a debit that has arisen in their transfer balance account after receiving an excess transfer balance determination (eg the individual's income stream has been fully or partially commuted after the determination was issued).

This notification allows the Commissioner to determine whether the individual still has an excess transfer balance and whether there is a requirement to issue a commutation authority (s 136-25).

The individual must notify the Commissioner in the approved form that the debit has arisen before the individual makes an election and before the end of the 60-day period in which to make the election.

Commissioner may amend or revoke determination

The Commissioner may amend or revoke a determination at any time to take into account additional information before issuing a commutation authority under TAA Sch 1 s 136-55 (see below) relating to the determination (s 136-10(4)).

Objection against determinations

An individual who is dissatisfied with an excess transfer balance determination issued under s 136-10 may object against the determination in accordance with TAA Pt IVC within 60 days of the date of service of the determination (TAA s 14ZW(1)(c)).

An individual may wish to lodge an objection if the Commissioner did not know about or take into account certain debits that arose before the Commissioner issued the determination or otherwise made an error in making the determination (s 136-15(1)).

A default commutation notice included with the determination does not form part of the taxation decision to which an individual can object (s 136-15(2)). This is because the default commutation notice is only intended to inform the individual of the superannuation income stream(s) in respect of which the Commissioner intends to issue a commutation authority if the individual does not make an election under s 136-20 (see above).

The Pt IVC objection regime is considered to provide the appropriate review and remedy process for individuals affected by the Commissioner's transfer balance decisions. The *Administrative Decisions (Judicial Review) Act 1977* does not apply to excess transfer balance determinations and other decisions the Commissioner makes in relation to the transfer balance cap (*Administrative Decisions (Judicial Review) Act 1977*, Sch 1(gab)).

The AAT has affirmed an assessment for excess transfer balance tax on a taxpayer's notional earnings on an excess transfer balance (¶14-360). The taxpayer claimed that poor language on the ATO website (www.ato.gov.au) had misled him to an erroneous belief that his pension drawdowns together with a transfer from his income stream account would bring his transfer balance below the transfer balance cap. The AAT held that it had no jurisdiction to entertain or determine an application against the Commissioner for misleading and deceptive conduct, as it was not a court (as defined under any Commonwealth or state consumer protection statutes) and did not have any analogous general law jurisdiction. Neither the TAA nor *Administrative Appeals Tribunal Act 1975* gave it the jurisdiction to inquire into, or adjudicate upon, an allegation that a taxpayer had been led into error because the Commissioner had engaged in misleading or deceptive conduct (*Lacey*).

The AAT has held that the determination period upon which an excess transfer balance tax liability is based was not determined by reference to when the taxpayer was first informed of an excess transfer balance. Also, a taxpayer cannot avoid a tax liability by complying with a request to commute funds out of his superannuation income streams (*Vernik*). In *Vernik*, the AAT stated that the Commissioner had acted in a timely manner by making the excess transfer balance determination soon after being informed by the superannuation funds of the relevant amounts. Furthermore, there was no "special circumstances" provision applicable to a liability arising under Div 294 and the Commissioner had no discretion to waive the tax payable. Also, the taxpayer was not entitled to transitional relief as the excess transfer balance was greater than $100,000 and was still in existence as at 1 January 2018 (ITTPA s 294-30).

Stage 2 — ATO commutation authority to reduce an excess transfer balance

The second stage in managing breaches of the transfer balance cap by an individual is where the Commissioner issues a commutation authority to one or more of the individual's superannuation income stream providers so as to effect a reduction in the individual's transfer balance (ss 136-50; 136-55).

The Commissioner must issue a commutation authority if an excess transfer balance determination (see above) has been issued to an individual and the individual has not notified the Commissioner that they have subsequently received debits equal to the crystallised reduction amount stated in the determination (the **commutable amount**) (s 136-55(1)).

If the individual has made a valid election for a superannuation income stream (other than the income stream specified in the default commutation notice, see above) to be commuted, the Commissioner must issue the commutation authority in accordance with the individual's election (s 136-55(2)).

If the individual's election would not result in the commutable amount being commuted because it applied to a lesser amount, the Commissioner must issue *additional* commutation authorities (s 136-55(3)).

Where the individual has not made an election to commute a different superannuation income stream, the Commissioner will issue commutation authorities consistent with the default commutation notice (s 136-55(5)).

The Commissioner is also required to issue a commutation authority to the superannuation income stream provider specified in the default commutation notice if the amount the individual elects to have commuted falls short of the commutable amount (s 136-55(4)).

Each commutation authority issued by the Commissioner must contain:

- the superannuation income stream that the income stream provider is required to fully or partially commute
- the amount by which the income stream is to be commuted (the **reduction amount**)
- its issue date, and
- any other relevant information (s 136-55(5)).

The total of all reduction amounts stated in all commutation authorities must not exceed the commutable amount (s 136-55(6)).

Commissioner may vary or revoke commutation authority

The Commissioner may vary or revoke a commutation authority at any time before the Commissioner receives a response from the superannuation income stream provider (s 136-60).

The Commissioner may also issue further commutation authorities where the initial authority was insufficient to achieve the required reduction or the superannuation income stream provider has not complied with the original commutation authority (s 136-65).

Complying with an ATO commutation authority

A superannuation income stream provider is required to comply with a commutation authority issued to it by commuting the identified income stream by the reduction amount stated in the authority (s 136-80).

Where the maximum available release amount of the identified superannuation income stream is *less* than the reduction amount stated in the commutation authority, the superannuation income stream provider is required to commute the superannuation income stream in full.

The **"maximum available release amount"** (defined in s 131-45) means the total amount of all superannuation lump sums that could be paid from the superannuation interest at that time.

The superannuation income stream provider is required to reduce the superannuation income stream within 60 days of when the commutation authority is issued.

Income stream provider to consult with individuals

A superannuation income stream provider should make reasonable efforts to consult with individuals whose superannuation income streams are covered by a commutation authority on whether they wish the amount by which the income stream is commuted (whether fully or partially) to remain within superannuation or, for individuals who have met a relevant condition of release, whether they wish the commutation amount to be paid to them as a superannuation lump sum.

A commutation amount that remains in the superannuation system is no longer in the retirement phase and the income stream provider may need to create an accumulation interest for the individual, if required.

An income stream provider that transfers a commutation into an accumulation interest for an individual when complying with a commutation authority is subject to the requirement to disclose significant events in s 1017B of the *Corporations Act 2001*.

A commutation amount paid to an individual is superannuation lump sum benefit and may have tax consequences for the individual (¶14-220).

When an income stream provider is not required to comply with commutation authority

A superannuation income stream provider is not required to comply with a commutation authority if:

- the superannuation income stream is a capped defined benefit income stream (¶14-370)
- the individual for whom the excess transfer balance determination was issued has died (s 136-80(2), (3)).

Notifying Commissioner and member when a commutation authority is received

An income stream provider that is issued with a commutation authority must notify the Commissioner and the individual in the approved form of:

- the amount by which the superannuation income stream has been commuted, or
- that the income stream provider has not complied with the commutation authority because the income stream is a capped defined benefit income stream (ss 136-85; 136-90).

The Commissioner must also be notified if non-compliance with the commutation authority is because of an individual's death (s 136-85(2)).

The notices must be given within 60 days after the commutation authority was issued (ss 136-85(3); 136-90(2)).

Commissioner to notify members of non-commutable excess transfer balance

The Commissioner is required to notify an individual of a non-commutable excess transfer balance where an individual has an excess transfer balance and has no remaining account-based superannuation income stream to be commuted (s 136-70).

Where the Commissioner issues a notice in this situation, a debit for the remaining excess balance identified in the notice is applied to the individual's transfer balance account. This is to recognise that, although the individual still has an excess transfer balance, the individual no longer has any superannuation income stream or the only remaining superannuation interests are non-commutable.

This will effectively write off the remainder of the excess so that excess transfer balance earnings do not continue to accrue (ITAA97 s 294-80(1) table item 7).

Consequences of not complying with a commutation authority

Where a commutation authority is issued in respect of a superannuation income stream and the superannuation income stream provider fails to comply with the authority, the income stream will cease to be in the retirement phase (ITAA97 s 307-80(4)). The consequence of not being in the retirement phase is that the income stream provider no longer qualifies for the earnings tax exemption discussed in ¶13-140.

The superannuation income stream will cease to be in the retirement phase from the start of the financial year in which the income stream provider fails to comply with the commutation authority and all later financial years.

In the above circumstances, a debit arises in the individual's transfer balance account for the value of the superannuation interest that supports the income stream that has ceased to be in the retirement phase because of non-compliance with the commutation authority. The debit arises at the end of the period in which the income stream provider was required to comply with the commutation authority. Generally, this will mean that the individual no longer has an excess transfer balance at this time (ITAA97 s 294-80(1)).

There may be additional regulatory and taxation consequences for SMSFs as the requirement to comply with a commutation authority is also a "regulatory provision" (SISA s 38A(ab)(iii): see ¶13-100).

An individual who wishes to again have a superannuation income stream in the retirement phase (and for it qualify for the earnings tax exemption) will need to commute the superannuation income stream in full and start a new superannuation income stream. The individual does not get a debit for this commutation as the superannuation income stream will not be in the retirement phase at this time and a debit has already arisen with respect to the income stream.

A superannuation income stream provider does *not* fail to comply with a commutation authority if:

- it commuted the superannuation income stream by the maximum available release amount, or

- it was not required to comply with the commutation authority because the identified superannuation income stream was a capped defined benefit income stream or because the relevant individual had died.

A similar situation may arise if the death benefit income stream ceases to be a superannuation income stream because it has failed to comply with the rules or standards under which it is provided.

ATO guidelines on transfer balance cap and Commissioner's commutation authority

Additional information and guidelines are available from the ATO webpage *Transfer balance cap – Commissioner's commutation authority* (www.ato.gov.au/Super/APRA-regulated-funds/Reporting-and-administrative-obligations/Reporting-and-administrative-obligations-for-the-Transfer-balance-cap/).

¶14-360 Excess transfer balance tax

An individual who has an excess transfer balance period for his/her transfer balance account (¶14-320) is liable to pay excess transfer balance tax imposed by the *Superannuation (Excess Transfer Balance Tax) Imposition Act 2016* (SETBTIA) for the period (ITAA97 s 294-230(1)).

The tax is based on the notional earnings of capital moved into a retirement phase superannuation account that is in excess of the $1.6 million transfer balance cap (¶14-320).

''Notional earnings'' means the sum worked out under ITAA97 s 294-230(3) for the excess transfer balance period.

The ''excess transfer balance period'' for a transfer balance account is the continuous period of one or more days for which there is excess transfer balance in the account at the end of each day (s 294-230(2)).

An individual's excess transfer balance tax is worked out by reference to the sum of:

- the individual's excess transfer balance earnings for each day (see below) in the excess transfer balance period, and
- for each day in the excess transfer balance period that is also a day in the determination period mentioned in s 294-25(2) — the amount worked out by multiplying the rate mentioned in s 294-235(2) for the day by the sum of the individual's excess transfer balance earnings for each previous day in the determination period (s 294-230(3)).

An individual's ''excess transfer balance earnings for a day'' is worked out by multiplying the rate for that day by the amount of the individual's excess transfer balance at the end of that day. This rate is the *lower* of:

- the rate worked out under TAA s 8AAD(1) for the day, and
- the rate for a day as prescribed by legislative instrument (s 294-235).

Excess transfer balance earnings generally compound daily while the individual has an excess transfer balance. However, once the Commissioner issues a determination to the individual, notional earnings are no longer credited to the individual's transfer balance account (¶14-320). This allows the Commissioner's determination to identify a fixed excess transfer balance that must be removed from the retirement phase. However, excess transfer balance earnings will start to be credited to a transfer balance account again if an individual receives another credit in their transfer balance account (for starting a new superannuation income stream) (s 294-25(2)).

Rate of excess transfer balance tax

The excess transfer balance tax rate is 15% for the first breach of the transfer balance cap in the year, and 30% for the second and subsequent breaches. The 15% tax rate is intended to neutralise the advantage that an individual has received from the superannuation provider's earnings tax exemption (¶13-140), even though the tax is based on a notional earnings rate rather than actual earnings. This reflects that, but for the individual's breach, the excess amount on which excess transfer balance earnings is calculated would have been in the accumulation phase where the earnings would have been taxed at 15% (SETBTIA s 5(1)(b)).

The higher 30% tax rate for additional excess transfer balance tax assessments is intended to be a deterrent for individuals who would otherwise continue to exceed their transfer balance cap after receiving an earlier assessment if the actual earnings on the ''excess amount'' is greater than the standard 15% tax rate (SETBTIA s 5(1)(a)).

Assessments and payment of excess transfer balance tax payable

The provisions dealing with assessments of excess transfer balance tax are set out in TAA Sch 1 Div 155.

Excess transfer balance tax is payable by an individual as below:

- for original assessments — the tax is due and payable at the end of 21 days after the Commissioner gives the individual notice of the assessment of the amount of the excess transfer balance tax
- amended assessments — any extra assessed excess transfer balance tax resulting from an amended assessment is due and payable 21 days after the day the Commissioner gives the individual notice of the amended assessment (ITAA97 ss 294-240; 294-245).

If an amount of assessed excess transfer balance tax remains unpaid after the time by which it is due to be paid, an individual is liable to pay the general interest charge on the unpaid amount as determined under ITAA97 s 294-250 in accordance with Pt IIA of the *Taxation Administration Act 1953*.

The Commissioner does not have a discretion to waive a taxpayer's liability to excess transfer balance tax (*Vernik*: ¶14-350; *Jacobs*).

An individual who is dissatisfied with an excess transfer balance assessment may object under TAA Pt IVC (TAA Sch 1 s 155-90) (*Lacey* and *Vernik*: ¶14-350).

¶14-370 Defined benefit income cap — modified tax rules on excessive payments

The transfer balance cap regime applies to limit the amount that an individual can have as retirement phase income stream accounts in a superannuation fund. Excess transfer balance tax is payable for exceeding the cap in a financial year (¶14-320).

However, an individual's **capped defined benefit income streams** (as defined in ITAA97 s 294-130: see ¶14-340) do not cause an individual to breach the transfer balance cap. Instead, a separate "defined benefit income cap" applies, and if the individual's capped defined benefit payments exceed the cap amount for the year, additional tax consequences apply in respect of the capped defined benefit income received by the individual for the year to the extent of the excess. The reason for the different treatment of capped defined benefit income streams is because these income streams generally cannot be commuted as a lump sum so as to address an excess of the transfer balance like other superannuation income streams.

Modifications to tax treatment for capped defined benefit income streams

Firstly, a statutory formula is used to work out the value of an individual's superannuation interest that supports a capped defined benefit income stream (called the "special value"), which gives rise to the credits and debits in the individual's transfer balance account.

An individual will have a "capped defined benefit balance" which reflects the credits and debits in the individual's transfer balance account relating to the capped defined benefit income stream(s) (s 294-135) (see "Capped defined benefit income streams — credits and debits" in ¶14-340).

Secondly, an individual's capped defined benefit income streams in a year are subject to a defined benefit income cap and there are tax consequences for exceeding the cap (see below).

Defined benefit income cap

The defined benefit income cap is relevant where an individual is:

- 60 years of age or over, or
- under 60 years of age and a death benefits dependant, where the deceased died at 60 years of age or over.

In the above circumstances, the defined benefit income cap applies if the individual receives one or more superannuation income stream benefits that are defined benefit income to which "concessional tax treatment" applies (see below). The defined benefit income cap does not have taxation consequences outside of these circumstances.

An individual's **defined benefit income cap** for a financial year is equal to the general transfer balance cap amount *divided by 16* (ITAA97 s 303-4) (¶42-265).

Reduction of cap

An individual's defined benefit income cap amount is subject to proportional reduction if the individual:

- first becomes entitled to concessional tax treatment in respect of defined benefit income part-way through a financial year (eg turning age 60 during the year), or
- is entitled to other defined benefit income that is *not* subject to concessional tax treatment under ITAA97 ss 301-10, 301-100, 302-65 and 302-85 (eg the individual receives death benefits and member benefits in certain circumstances) (s 303-4(3)) (see "Tax consequences of exceeding defined benefit income cap" below).

Defined benefit income to which concessional tax treatment applies

Concessional tax treatment applies to defined benefit income stream benefits as summarised below:

- the tax free component of a superannuation income stream benefit that is defined benefit income is *non-assessable non-exempt income* if the individual is:
  - 60 years of age or over (ss 301-10; 302-65) (¶14-220, ¶14-240), or
  - under 60 years of age and in receipt of a death benefit, where the deceased died at 60 years of age or over (¶14-280) (s 302-65)
- the taxed element of a superannuation income stream benefit that is defined benefit income is *non-assessable non-exempt income* if the individual is:
  - 60 years of age or over (ss 301-10; 302-65) (¶14-220), or
  - under 60 years of age and in receipt of a death benefit, where the deceased died at 60 years of age or over (s 302-65) (¶14-280)
- the untaxed element of a superannuation income stream benefit that is defined benefit income is included in the individual's assessable income.

  An individual is entitled to a tax offset equal to 10% of the untaxed element if the individual is:
  - 60 years of age or over (ss 301-100; 302-85) (¶14-240), or
  - under 60 years of age and in receipt of a death benefit, where the deceased died at 60 years of age or over (¶14-280) (s 302-85).

Tax consequences if defined benefit income cap is exceeded

The general rules for the tax treatment of superannuation income stream and death benefit income stream benefits are discussed in ¶14-220, ¶14-240 and ¶14-280.

Where the defined benefit income cap is exceeded, an individual's defined benefit income that is otherwise non-assessable non-exempt income is included in assessable income and any tax offset that is otherwise available for the untaxed element of defined benefit income is reduced, as summarised below:

- **additional assessable income** — where the sum of the tax free component and taxed element of benefits that are defined benefit income and non-assessable non-exempt income exceeds the individual's defined benefit income cap, 50% of the excess is assessable income (to which no tax offset applies) (s 303-2)

- **reduced tax offset** — where:
  - the individual is entitled to tax offset(s) in respect of the untaxed element of a defined benefit income stream, and
  - the sum of the non-assessable non-exempt income amounts and assessable amounts exceeds the individual's defined benefit income cap for a financial year,

  the sum of those tax offsets for the year is reduced by 10% of that excess (the tax offsets cannot be reduced below zero).

Departing Australia Superannuation Payments

¶14-390 Superannuation payments to former temporary residents

Taxpayers who have entered Australia temporarily on certain classes of visa and are departing or have departed Australia permanently are eligible to receive their superannuation entitlements as a departing Australia superannuation payment (DASP). A DASP is not taxed as a superannuation lump sum benefit (¶14-200) but is subject to tax under a final withholding tax arrangement.

A superannuation lump sum is a ''DASP'' if it is paid to a person who has departed Australia in accordance with:

- SISR reg 6.20A, 6.20B or 6.24A, or RSAR reg 4.23A, or the equivalent rules of an exempt public sector superannuation scheme, or
- s 67A of the *Small Superannuation Accounts Act 1995* (ITAA97 s 301-170; ITR97 reg 301-170.01).

To qualify for a DASP, the former member or RSA holder must be a temporary resident who is not an Australian citizen, New Zealand citizen or permanent resident, who has left Australia and whose visa has ceased to be in effect. The payment process and visa verification requirements are set out in the above regulations.

A ''temporary resident'' means a holder of a temporary visa under the *Migration Act 1958* (SISR reg 6.01(2)). A temporary visa is one that enables a person to remain in Australia during a specified period, or until a specified event occurs, or while the holder has a special status. The SISR definition of ''temporary resident'' is the same as para (a) of the definition of ''temporary resident'' in ITAA97 s 995-1(1): see ¶22-125. A New Zealand citizen who was present in Australia as the holder of a Special Category Visa and who has departed Australia will still ''hold a temporary visa'' for the purposes of para (a) of the ''temporary resident'' definition in ITAA97 (TD 2012/18).

A superannuation lump sum that is paid under s 20H of the *Superannuation (Unclaimed Money and Lost Members) Act 1999* (SUMLMA) is also a DASP *except:*

- if, when it is paid, the Commissioner is satisfied that the person has not held a temporary visa, or at least a continuous period of 6 months has not passed since the person's temporary visa ceased to be in effect and the person leaving Australia, or
- the payment is prescribed by the Regulations not to be a DASP (s 301-170(2) to (4)).

The scheme for dealing with the unclaimed superannuation of former temporary residents under SUMLMA Pt 3A (s 20A to 20P) is outlined below.

- The Commissioner must give a superannuation fund (or ADF or RSA provider) a notice if the Commissioner is satisfied that a ''former temporary resident'' (as defined in s 20AA) has a superannuation interest in the fund.

No notice is required to be given if the superannuation provider is a state or territory public sector superannuation scheme or an unfunded public sector superannuation schemes (s 20C(3)).

- If the Commissioner gives such a notice, the fund must:
  (a) give the Commissioner a statement in the approved form about the member's superannuation interest by 31 October and 30 April, and
  (b) pay to the Commissioner the amount that would have been payable to the member if he/she had requested payment in connection with departing Australia, reduced by amounts already paid or payable from the fund for the member (ss 20E; 20F).
- When a superannuation fund makes payment to the Commissioner under s 20F, the fund ceases to be liable for the amount paid (s 20G).
- The Commissioner on his own initiative, or on application by a person in the approved form, must pay the amount received from a fund under s 20F to the member, to a complying superannuation fund identified by the member or, if the member has died, to the member's legal personal representative (s 20H).

DASP withholding tax

A payer's obligations under the PAYG rules are discussed at ¶26-260.

A superannuation benefit that is a DASP is not assessable income and not exempt income when received by a person (ITAA97 s 301-175). Instead, final withholding tax is imposed by the *Superannuation (Departing Australia Superannuation Payments Tax) Act 2007* (DASP Act) (¶42-125).

A nil withholding tax rate applies to the tax free component and a withholdings rate of 35% and 45% applies to the taxed element and untaxed element, respectively, of the taxable component of a DASP. Where the DASP is a roll-over superannuation benefit, a nil withholding tax rate also applies to the amount of the untaxed element of the taxable component that is an excess untaxed roll-over amount (as imposing tax would result in double taxation otherwise) and a withholding rate of 45% applies to the amount that is not an excess untaxed roll-over amount (DASP Act s 5).

DASP tax rate for working holiday makers

Where a DASP to a person includes amounts attributable to superannuation contributions made while the person was a "working holiday maker" (¶26-277), withholding tax is imposed at the rates below:

- on the tax free component — nil
- on the element taxed in the fund — 65%
- on the element untaxed in the fund — 65%
- on the amount (if any) of the element that is not an excess untaxed roll-over amount — 65%, and
- on the amount (if any) of the element that is an excess untaxed roll-over amount — nil (DASP Act s 5(3)).

The DASP tax for working holiday makers was introduced at the same time as the "backpacker tax" specified in Pt III of Sch 7 to the *Income Tax Rates Act 1986* (under which taxpayers on working holiday visas in Australia were subject to a higher rate of tax than an Australian national performing the same work in Australia: ¶21-033). The Full Federal Court held in a test case that the imposition of a tax at a higher rate on the holders of specific visas did not discriminate against the holder solely on the basis of nationality and did not offend Art 25(1) of the Australia–UK Double Taxation Agreement (*Addy*).

[AMSG ¶8-400; SLP ¶40-185]

Payments from Non-Complying Funds

¶14-400 Benefits from Australian superannuation funds

Special rules apply to the taxation of superannuation benefits received from a non-complying superannuation fund that is an Australian superannuation fund (¶13-100) for the income year in which the benefit is paid.

A ''non-complying superannuation fund'' is a superannuation fund that is not a complying fund (s 995-1(1)).

A superannuation benefit received from a non-complying superannuation fund that is an Australian superannuation fund is exempt income if:

- the fund has *never* been a complying superannuation fund (¶13-100), or last stopped being a complying superannuation fund for the income year in which 1 July 1995 occurred or a later year, and
- the fund has *never* been a foreign superannuation fund (¶14-420), or last stopped being a foreign superannuation fund for the income year in which 1 July 1995 occurred or a later income year (ITAA97 s 305-5).

[AMSG ¶8-350; FITR ¶294-000; SLP ¶39-050]

¶14-420 Benefits from foreign superannuation funds

A ''foreign superannuation fund'' (¶13-250) is a fund that is not an ''Australian superannuation fund'', ie a fund that is not established in Australia and is not centrally managed or controlled in Australia (¶13-100).

If an individual receives a superannuation lump sum from a foreign superannuation fund, the tax treatment depends on whether it is received within 6 months or later than 6 months after the individual becomes an Australian resident or terminated foreign employment, as provided in ITAA97 Subdiv 305-B.

The transfers of benefits from KiwiSaver schemes for an individual as a contribution to an Australian superannuation fund are not subject to the rules in Subdiv 305-B (ITAA97 s 312-10(2): ¶13-380).

An Individual Retirement Account (IRA) that is maintained for the benefit of an individual in the USA is not a ''superannuation fund'' within the meaning in ITAA97, and is also not a foreign superannuation fund within the meaning of ITAA97 s 305-80(1) (*Baker*). An IRA does not qualify as one ''for the payment of benefits in the nature of superannuation upon retirement or death'' within the meaning of ITAA97 s 305-55(2). In *Baker*, the taxpayer had sought a ruling for the purposes of making a choice under ITAA97 s 305-80 to have a payment from the IRA paid to an Australian complying fund (see ''Payments received after six months'' below).

Payment received within 6 months

A superannuation lump sum received by a person from a foreign superannuation fund is not assessable income and not exempt income if:

- it is received within 6 months after the person became an Australian resident, and it relates only to a period:
  - when the person was not an Australian resident, or
  - starting after the person became an Australian resident and ending before the payment is received, and
- it does not exceed the amount in the fund that was vested in the person when he/she received the payment (ITAA97 s 305-60).

A superannuation lump sum received by an individual is also not assessable income and not exempt income if:

- it is received by a person in consequence of the termination of the person's employment as an employee, or as the holder of an office, in a foreign country or the termination of the person's engagement on qualifying service on an approved project (within the meaning of ITAA36 s 23AF) relating to a foreign country
- it relates only to the period of that employment, etc
- the person was an Australian resident during the period of the employment, etc
- the person received the lump sum within 6 months after the termination
- the lump sum is not exempt from taxation under the law of the foreign country, and
- the foreign earnings from the employment, etc, are exempt from income tax under ITAA36 s 23AF or 23AG, as appropriate (ITAA97 s 305-65) (¶14-740).

Payments received after 6 months

If a person receives a superannuation lump sum from a foreign superannuation fund more than 6 months after becoming an Australian resident or termination of foreign employment:

- the lump sum benefit is included in the person's assessable income for so much of the lump sum attributable to the "applicable fund earnings" as worked out under ITAA97 s 305-75, and
- the remainder of the lump sum is not assessable income and not exempt income (ITAA97 s 305-70).

A person may choose under s 305-80(2) to pay all or a part of the assessable lump sum covered by s 305-75 to a complying superannuation fund instead, in which case that amount becomes assessable contribution of the fund, rather than the person's assessable income (s 305-70(2)(b)) (see "Choice to contribute assessable amount to a fund" below).

Any part of the lump sum that is paid to another foreign superannuation fund is not assessable income and not exempt income (s 305-70(4)). The person's applicable fund earnings in relation to a later lump sum payment out of the other foreign superannuation fund may include an amount (previously exempt fund earnings) attributable to the lump sum.

The "applicable fund earnings" amount is generally the earnings that have accrued to the person in the foreign superannuation fund since the person became an Australian resident. This amount is worked out in accordance with s 305-75(2) or (3) based on whether the person was an Australian resident at all times and whether the person had received previous lump sums from the fund or previously exempt fund earnings (ID 2009/124: relevant period for calculation).

▶ Example

Abby (a non-resident) joined a foreign superannuation fund on 2.1.10. She moved to Australia and became an Australian resident on 1.7.17.

The value of Abby's account with the foreign superannuation fund just before the day she first became an Australian resident was $5,500. She left Australia and ceased to be an Australian resident on 1.1.18. Abby then returned to Australia and became an Australian resident again on 1.7.18.

Abby was paid a lump sum of $6,500 by her foreign superannuation fund on 30.6.19. Since moving to Australia on 1.7.17, there has been no contribution made to the foreign superannuation fund, and no amount has been transferred into the foreign superannuation fund from other sources.

In this case, "the period to which the lump sum relates", for the purposes of s 305-75(3), is from 2.1.10 to 30.6.19. However, "the period", for the purposes of s 305-75(3)(c), is from 1.7.17 to 30.6.19 (ie 730 days). During "the period", the superannuation lump sum increased by $1,000.

Abby's Australian residency days are from 1.7.17 to 1.1.18 (184 days) and 1.7.18 to 30.6.19 (365 days), a total of 549 days.

Therefore, the applicable fund earnings are: $1,000 × 549/730 = $752.05

Abby will have to include $752.05 in her assessable income.

When working out applicable fund earnings in relation to a superannuation lump sum, the correct rule for translating foreign currency into Australian dollars (AUD) is the rule described in Item 11A of the table in ITAA97 s 960-50(6) (ITR97 reg 960-50.01(1); ID 2015/7: translation at the exchange rate applicable at the time of receipt of superannuation lump sum) (¶23-070).

Where an individual receives a superannuation lump sum from a foreign superannuation fund in circumstances where an annuity may be paid subsequently from that fund, a proportionate approach is not used to calculate the applicable fund earnings under s 305-75(3), unless an annuity is commenced from the foreign superannuation fund at the same time (ID 2018/48, ID 2012/49).

Choice to contribute assessable amount to a fund

A person may choose to pay all or a part of the assessable lump sum paid from a foreign superannuation fund that is covered by s 305-70 (see above) to a complying superannuation fund in which case the fund will include the assessable amount in its assessable income as assessable contributions (¶13-125). A choice can only be made if all of the lump sum is paid into the complying superannuation fund and immediately after that time the person no longer has a superannuation interest in the foreign superannuation fund (s 305-80). The choice must be made in writing and comply with regulations (if any). A person's choice under s 305-80 is binding and cannot be revoked or varied once it is made (ID 2012/27).

If a choice is made, the amount transferred from the foreign superannuation fund will not be subject to double taxation on distribution where the amount has been subject to tax under the attribution rules in the former FIF provisions (ITTPA s 305-80).

Uncommercial offshore superannuation trusts

TA 2009/19 warns about arrangements that use offshore trust structures (purported to be superannuation funds) in an attempt to shift funds into Australia in a concessionally taxed manner or substantially defer the time at which such amounts are subject to tax in Australia.

Among other things, the ATO's concerns are whether these arrangements give rise to regulatory and tax issues, including whether the offshore trust fund is a superannuation fund under ITAA97 (¶13-050), whether employer contributions to the fund are deductible under ITAA97 s 290-60 (¶13-710), the potential application of the concessional/non-concessional caps and excess contributions tax under ITAA97 Div 292 (¶13-775), the trust fund's liability to pay tax under ITAA97 s 295-5(2) (¶13-120), and whether lump sum payments may be non-assessable and non-exempt under s 305-60 and 305-65 and the payments received may be ''applicable fund earnings'' and assessable under s 305-70 (see above).

Income streams from foreign superannuation fund

A superannuation income stream received by a taxpayer from a foreign superannuation fund is taxable in Australia, subject to any applicable double taxation agreement (¶22-150). The amount of the income stream payments received, reduced by a deductible amount (if any), is included in the taxpayer's assessable income and taxed at marginal rates (¶14-510).

[AMSG ¶8-370; FITR ¶294-000; SLP ¶39-050]

Roll-over Superannuation Benefits

¶14-450 Treatment of superannuation roll-overs

A superannuation benefit (¶14-100) is a ''roll-over superannuation benefit'' if:

- it is a superannuation lump sum and a superannuation benefit (TD 2013/11: pre-1 July 2017 death benefit)
- it is not a superannuation benefit of a kind specified in ITR97 reg 306-10.01 (see below)
- it is paid from a complying superannuation plan or is an unclaimed money payment, or it arises from the commutation of a superannuation annuity (¶14-100), and
- the benefit satisfies either of the conditions below:
  - the benefit is paid to a complying superannuation plan
  - the benefit is paid to an entity to purchase a superannuation annuity from the entity (ITAA97 s 306-10).

A superannuation lump sum death benefit that is rolled over is also a roll-over superannuation benefit from 1 July 2017 (see ''Death benefit roll-overs'' below).

A ''complying superannuation plan'' means a complying superannuation fund, an ADF or an RSA, a public sector fund that is a regulated superannuation fund or an exempt public sector superannuation scheme or a complying ADF (ITAA97 s 995-1(1)).

A superannuation benefit may be paid from one superannuation plan of a superannuation provider to another plan of the same provider. If an amount is transferred from one superannuation interest in a superannuation plan to another interest in the same plan, the transfer is treated as a payment in determining whether the transfer of the amount is a superannuation benefit or a roll-over superannuation benefit (ITAA97 s 307-5(8)).

A superannuation benefit received by a taxpayer, and accounted for as such, but which was immediately paid to another superannuation fund was held not to be a roll-over superannuation benefit under s 306-10; rather, it is treated as the taxpayer's contribution to the fund (¶13-780) (*Player*). In that case, the ATO considered that s 306-10 will be satisfied only if a payment is made directly by a complying superannuation plan to a complying superannuation plan, so that if the amount is first deposited to a different account before being on-paid the requirements of the section are not met.

An SMSF that was used as a ''vehicle'' in a fraudulent enterprise to access superannuation benefits was held not to be a superannuation fund. A payment of benefits from a superannuation fund to that vehicle was not a roll-over superannuation benefit (*Brazil*: ¶14-400).

Tax treatment of a roll-over superannuation benefit

A roll-over superannuation benefit that a person is taken to have received under the constructive receipt rule in s 307-15 is not assessable income and not exempt income of the person (ITAA97 s 306-5). A cap applies where the roll-over superannuation benefit consists wholly or partly of an amount paid from an element untaxed in the fund (see ''Taxation of roll-over superannuation benefits from untaxed schemes'' below).

Under the constructive receipt rule, a person is taken to receive a benefit under s 307-15 when it is made for the person's benefit or is made to another person or to an entity at the person's direction or request. Subject to special rules for roll-overs from untaxed schemes (see below), the tax treatment of the rolled-over benefit will arise at the time when it is subsequently paid from rolled-over fund (¶14-200ff).

Superannuation death benefits specified in reg 306-10.01

Superannuation death benefits are prevented from being a superannuation roll-over benefit unless the death benefit is paid to a person covered by SISR reg 6.21(2A) or RSAR reg 4.24(3A) (ITR97 reg 306-10.01(a)). The SIS and RSA regulations ensure that death benefit income stream payments can only be made to a deceased's dependants, including a spouse or child of the deceased (¶13-800). The effect of reg 306-10.01(a) is that where a death benefit beneficiary is not eligible to receive a death benefit income stream, the death benefit is excluded from being a roll-over superannuation benefit and the beneficiary must be paid a death benefit lump sum which must be cashed out of the superannuation system.

Terminal medical condition superannuation benefits specified in reg 306-10.01

A superannuation lump sum benefit paid to a member having a terminal medical condition is not a roll-over superannuation benefit (ITTPA s 303-10(2); ITR97 reg 306-10.01(b)). The commencement of an account-based pension using the entire balance of a member's accumulation amount in a superannuation fund is not treated as a payment for the purposes of ITAA97 s 307-5(8) and, accordingly, there is no roll-over superannuation benefit (ID 2009/125) (TD 2013/10: using a deceased member's benefits to commence a pension is not a transfer of superannuation interests).

Death benefit roll-overs

From 1 July 2017, a superannuation death benefit for dependants can be a ''roll-over superannuation benefit'' (the definition in s 306-10 previously covered only superannuation member benefits). This change from 1 July 2017 allows dependants to roll over their superannuation lump sum death benefits to a fund of their choice and receive the same taxation treatment as member benefits that are rolled over, namely, the rolled-over benefit is not treated as a superannuation contribution and is non-assessable non-exempt income.

The circumstances in which a lump sum death benefit paid by a superannuation fund may have an untaxed element is discussed in ¶14-150. According to the ATO, a transferring fund is still required to apply s 307-290 to determine if there is an untaxed element in the lump sum being rolled over where the fund has claimed, or will claim in relation to the benefit, deductions for superannuation premiums.

However, where a dependant beneficiary rolls over a death benefit, the Commissioner's view is that there is insufficient connection between any deductions claimed by the transferring fund and any lump sum benefits paid by the receiving fund from the dependant beneficiary's new pension interest for s 307-290 to apply to any of those subsequent payments. That is, where the receiving fund does not claim any deductions for any death and disability insurance offered to the dependant beneficiary as part of their new pension interest in the receiving fund, s 307-290 will not apply to any lump sums paid from that interest.

ATO Fact Sheet *Clarification on reporting and paying death benefit rollovers* provides guidelines on how funds should report death benefit roll-overs and pay death benefits from an interest where a fund reported an untaxed element on or after 1 July 2017 (see ''Reporting rollovers and other PAYG obligations'' below).

Taxation of roll-over superannuation benefits from untaxed schemes

If a roll-over superannuation benefit consists wholly or partly of an amount paid from an element untaxed in the fund (an ''untaxed roll-over amount''), the untaxed roll-over amount is not assessable income and not exempt income of the person for whom the roll-over is made up to the person's untaxed plan cap amount ($1.565 million in 2020–21: ¶14-240) (ss 306-5; 306-15). The cap amount is indexed annually (see ¶42-250 for the cap amount in earlier years) (ITAA97 s 307-350).

The untaxed roll-over amount up to the untaxed plan cap amount is assessable contributions in the superannuation fund to which the roll-over is made (ITAA97 s 295-190(1) item 2: ¶13-125).

Any excess untaxed roll-over amount (ie the amount exceeding the untaxed plan cap amount) is subject to tax at 47% (ITAA97 s 306-15(3)). The tax is imposed by the *Superannuation (Excess Untaxed Roll-over Amounts Tax) Act 2007*. Tax is levied on the person for whom the roll-over is made and must be withheld by the entity making the roll-over (TAA Sch 1 ss 12-312; 12-313).

The tax on excess untaxed roll-over amounts does not apply to a roll-over superannuation benefit that is transferred from one superannuation interest in a superannuation plan to another interest in the same plan (s 306-15(1A)).

Related tax rules

The related tax rules below deal with roll-over superannuation benefits in various circumstances:

- a deduction cannot be claimed for a contribution that is a roll-over superannuation benefit (s 290-5(a))
- the part of a roll-over superannuation benefit that is included in a fund's assessable income under s 295-190(1) (item 2) is not a concessional contribution (s 291-25(2)(c)(ii))
- a contribution that is a roll-over superannuation benefit is not a non-concessional contribution (s 292-90(2)(c)(vi))
- a contribution that is a roll-over superannuation benefit is not assessable income of the fund (s 295-160, items 1 and 2); however, it is a contribution to the fund to which that roll-over is made for the purposes of s 295-95(1) (this allows the roll-over fund to claim a deduction for expenses incurred in obtaining contributions, regardless of whether the full amount of the contributions is included in the fund's assessable income: ¶13-150)
- the taxable component of a roll-over superannuation benefit paid into a superannuation interest is disregarded when determining the contributions that are included in the contributions segment of an interest (s 307-220(2)(a)(i)).

Reporting rollovers and other PAYG obligations

A superannuation fund that pays a roll-over superannuation benefit must comply with reporting obligations (TAA Sch 1 s 390-10(1), (2)).

The PAYG withholding and reporting obligations in relation to the excess untaxed roll-over amount of a roll-over superannuation benefit are discussed in ¶26-262.

The Commissioner has provided guidelines on death benefit roll-overs covering the following:

- reporting death benefit roll-overs from a fully taxed superannuation fund and roll-overs from an untaxed or hybrid fund
- paying death benefits from a fully taxed fund after receiving a roll-over, and

- paying a death benefit from an interest where a fund reported an untaxed element on or after 1 July 2017 (Fact Sheet *Clarification on reporting and paying death benefit rollovers*).

[AMSG ¶8-600; FITR ¶295-000; SLP ¶39-055]

Annuities and Foreign Fund Pensions

¶14-510 Taxation of non-superannuation annuities and foreign pensions

Section 27H of ITAA36 provides for the taxation of an annuity or pension paid from a foreign superannuation fund or source, or a pension paid from a scheme that is not, and has never been, an Australian superannuation fund (within the meaning in ITAA97 s 290-5(c)), *other than*:

- an annuity that is a qualifying security for the purposes of ITAA36 Pt III Div 16E, or
- a ''superannuation income stream'' as discussed in ¶14-120 (s 27H(4)).

Under s 27H, the taxpayer's assessable income in a year of income includes the amount of any annuity or pension received during the year of income after excluding, in the case of a purchased annuity or pension, the ''deductible amount'' (see below) for that year of income. Any supplement to the annuity or pension, whether voluntary or not, is also included in assessable income.

The calculated deductible amount is apportioned according to the number of days the pension or annuity is payable for a pension or annuity that commences or ceases during an income year (TD 2006/17).

The s 27H deductible amount method previously applied to all annuities and superannuation pensions. That ceased from 1 July 2007 and the tax treatment of Australian-sourced superannuation income streams (including the calculation of their tax free component) is governed by ITAA97 from that date (¶14-220, ¶14-240), subject to ITTPA s 307-125 which preserves the calculation of the deductible amount for superannuation pensions which first commenced before 1 July 2007 (¶14-140).

The taxation of Australian social security pensions and other payments is discussed at ¶10-190.

Calculation of non-assessable portion

The ''deductible amount'' of an annuity or pension (ie the amount of the undeducted purchase price excluded each year from assessable income) is calculated using the formula below (s 27H(2)):

$$\frac{\mathbf{A\,(B - C)}}{\mathbf{D}}$$

Component A: relevant share — ''A'' is the relevant share of the annuity received by the taxpayer. Where the taxpayer receives the entire annuity, this component will be 1. Where the annuity is payable jointly to more than one person, the component A for each annuitant will reflect their respective share in the whole annuity, eg if the taxpayer has a half share in the annuity, component A will be 0.5.

Component B: undeducted purchase price — ''B'' is the undeducted purchase price of the annuity.

Component C: residual capital value — "C" is the residual capital value (if any) on termination of the annuity, eg on death or on the expiration of a given period (with the usual type of life annuity there is no value). This value must be either specified in the annuity agreement or ascertainable from the agreement at the time when the annuity is first derived.

Component D: relevant number — "D" is the relevant number, as specified in s 27H(4). For an annuity payable for a specified period of years, component D will be that number of years. For an annuity payable only during the lifetime of a nominated person (whether the recipient or not), component D is the "life expectation factor" (see below) of that person. In any other case, component D is the number that the Commissioner considers appropriate (see "Component D: reversionary annuities and other cases" below).

Life expectation factor — component D

A person's life expectation factor for the purposes of component D is determined from the Australian Life Tables (prepared by the Australian Government Actuary) that are most recently published before the year in which the annuity first commences to be payable (ITR15 reg 7). The life expectation factor is based on the person's age when the annuity (or pension) first commenced to be paid. For an annuity which first commenced to be paid on or after 1 January 2020, the relevant tables are the 2015–17 Life Tables.

A taxpayer suffering a medical condition cannot use a reduced life expectation factor (ID 2001/618).

Calculation of deductible amount — Commissioner's discretion

If the Commissioner considers that the deductible amount as determined under s 27H(2) is inappropriate, he may substitute another amount. For the circumstances and manner in which the Commissioner will exercise this discretion, see s 27H(3) or (3A) (if there is a partial commutation of an annuity) and IT 2157.

The Commissioner's views on the calculation of the deductible amount in respect of particular foreign pensions may be found in TR 93/13: British National Insurance Scheme (BNIS); IT 2554: Italian pensions; TR 2002/17: Austrian superannuation insurance fund pensions; ID 2001/3: non-BNIS UK pensions; TD 2000/46: Netherlands Social Insurance system pensions; TD 2006/54: lifetime pension from overseas retirement fund; ID 2003/140: Belgian pension; and ID 2003/180: non-military insurance Swiss pension.

An Australian-sourced annuity or a pension paid to a non-resident taxpayer or a foreign-sourced pension that is not a superannuation income stream paid to a resident taxpayer is included in the taxpayer's assessable income, subject to any applicable DTA (ITAA97 ss 6-5(2), (3); 10-5; ID 2007/22: allocated pension paid to Sri Lankan resident; ID 2010/119: Swedish government service pension and social security pension; ID 2010/153: Malaysian government service pension; ID 2010/154: Netherlands government service pension and social security pension).

[AMSG ¶8-370; FTR ¶16-940; SLP ¶39-092]

Employment Termination Payments

¶14-600 Payments on termination of employment

Payments on termination of employment are of 2 types — a "superannuation lump sum benefit" which covers payments from superannuation entities, and an "employment termination payment" which covers payments in consequence of a person's termination of employment. A payment from a superannuation provider in the form of an income stream is taxed as a "superannuation income stream benefit" under ITAA97 (¶14-120).

ITAA97 Pt 2-40 provides for the taxation of termination payments from an employer and for the taxation of accrued annual leave and long service leave payments on termination of employment. An employment termination payment can be:

- a "life benefit termination payment", which is received by a person in consequence of the termination of that person's employment (¶14-620), and
- a "death benefit termination payment", which is received by a person in consequence of the termination of employment (death) of another person (¶14-680).

A termination payment paid by an employer cannot be rolled over to a superannuation fund (¶14-610).

Section 15-2 of ITAA97 includes as assessable income of the taxpayer all allowances, gratuities, compensation, benefits, bonuses and premiums provided in respect of, or for or in relation directly or indirectly to, any employment of or services rendered by the taxpayer, but not a superannuation lump sum or an employment termination payment which are taxed under specific rules in ITAA97 (s 15-2(3)) (*Purvis*, where a benefit received was not a fringe benefit as it was an ETP: ¶14-610).

[AMSG ¶8-800ff; FITR ¶130-000ff; SLP ¶39-060ff]

¶14-610 What is an employment termination payment?

An employment termination payment is subject to concessional tax treatment under ITAA97 Pt 2-40 Div 82 (¶14-620, ¶14-680).

A payment to a person is an "employment termination payment" if the following conditions are met:

- the payment is received in consequence of the termination of the person's employment or, after another person's death, in consequence of the termination of the other person's employment
- the payment is received no later than 12 months after the termination (see "Exceptions to the 12-month rule" below), and
- the payment is not excluded as an employment termination payment by ITAA97 s 82-135 (see "Payments that are not employment termination payments" below) (ITAA97 s 82-130(1)).

"Employment" includes the holding of an office (ITAA97 s 80-5). A termination of employment includes the cessation of employment by retirement or death (ITAA97 s 80-10).

An employment termination payment can include a transfer of property. The value of such a payment is the market value of the property less any consideration given for the transfer of the property (ITAA97 s 80-15).

An employment termination payment is not included in the assessable income of a foreign resident unless it has an Australian source (see "Payments to non-residents" in ¶14-620).

Examples of employment termination payments include a gratuity or "golden handshake", payments made for unused sick leave or unused rostered days off, payments in lieu of notice, compensation for loss of job or wrongful dismissal, invalidity payments, and genuine redundancy payments or early retirement scheme payments which exceed the tax-free threshold (¶14-700, ¶14-710). The concessional taxation rules which apply to genuine redundancy payments or early retirement scheme payments and other termination of employment payments such as unused annual leave or long service leave payments are discussed in ¶14-700 to ¶14-730.

Meaning of "in consequence of"

The phrase "in consequence of" is not defined and the question of whether a payment is made in consequence of the termination of employment is determined by the relevant facts and circumstances of each case. Generally, there must be a causal connection between the termination and the payment, although the termination need not be the dominant cause of the payment. The Commissioner's view is that a payment is made in consequence of the termination of employment if the payment "follows as an effect or result of" the termination. That is, but for the termination of employment, the payment would not have been made to the taxpayer (*Reseck*; *McIntosh*; *Le Grand*; *Forrest*; *Case 7/2010*; *Purvis*; *VGDW*) (TR 2003/13).

An amount received in relation to a termination of employment dispute is not an employment termination payment if the amount is capable of being identified as relating specifically to the reimbursement of legal costs. If a deduction for legal costs is available under ITAA97 s 8-1, a settlement or award in respect of legal costs will be included in the recipient's assessable income as an assessable recoupment under ITAA97 Subdiv 20-A. Where the amount of a settlement or court award received is a lump sum and the component that relates to legal costs has not been and cannot be determined, the whole amount is treated as being received in consequence of termination of employment (TR 2012/8).

The court has held that a deferred compensation amount paid to a taxpayer as a reward for service rendered as an employee was assessable ordinary income under ITAA97 s 6-5 as the payment was neither made in consequence of the termination of employment nor was it exempt income under ITAA36 s 23AG. The fact that the amount was paid after termination of the contract of service, by a person other than the employer, and separately to ordinary wages, salary or bonuses, did not detract from this characterisation. The court also dismissed the taxpayer's contention that his associated rights under the agreements were assets of a proprietary nature, analogous to options (*Blank*; ATO decision impact statement).

A lump sum settlement paid to an employee who was made redundant under a deed of release was held to be assessable as a life benefit termination payment. The payment was not a transitional termination payment as there was no basis to apportion all or part of the lump sum settlement received to a pre-10 May 2006 contractual entitlement (*Case 5/2014*).

Exceptions to 12-month rule

The 12-month rule in s 82-130(1)(b) is intended to prevent abuse of the tax concession for employment termination payments by making a series of payments over a number of income years.

A payment that fails the 12-month rule, or is not covered by an exception to the rule, is assessable income of the recipient and is taxed at marginal rates (ITAA97 s 83-295).

The 12-month rule does not apply if:

- the payment is a genuine redundancy payment (¶14-700) or an early retirement scheme payment (¶14-710) (s 82-130(4)(b))
- the Commissioner determines in writing under s 82-130(5) that the time between the termination and the payment is reasonable, having regard to the circumstances of the termination (including any dispute in relation to the termination, the circumstances of the payment and of the payer, and any other relevant circumstances), or
- the payment is a class of payments, or is made to a class of recipients, as specified in a determination made under s 82-130(7).

The third dot point (ie under s 82-130(7) determinations) cover payments which are received more than 12 months after termination of employment under the legal action exception and the redundancy trust exception, as summarised below.

The legal action exception is where:

- legal action was commenced about either or both the person's entitlement to the payment and the amount of the entitlement within 12 months of the person's termination of employment, or
- the payment was made by a liquidator, receiver or trustee in bankruptcy of an entity that is otherwise liable to make the payment, where that liquidator, receiver or trustee is appointed no later than 12 months after the termination of employment (Income Tax Employment Termination Payments (12 month rule) Determination 2018 (F2018L00431), applicable to payments after 28 March 2018.

Legal action covers any court, tribunal and other proceedings of a judicial or quasi-judicial nature which may result in the payment of an amount in consequence of the termination of a person's employment.

▶ Example: legal action exception

Angela lodges a valid application to the Fair Work Commission for unfair dismissal and she receives a settlement offer from her former employer before a determination is made by the Commission. Angela accepts the settlement offer, of which two-thirds of the settlement amount is in consequence of the termination. She signs a settlement deed and receives the settlement amount 14 months after termination of employment.

The two-thirds of the settlement payment paid in consequence of Angela's termination does not meet the 12-month requirement in s 82-130(1)(b), but will qualify as an employment termination payment by operation of the legal action exception.

The redundancy trust exception is where:

- a person who was a member of a redundancy trust has applied to the trustee of the redundancy trust within 12 months of becoming entitled to the payment under the trust deed of the redundancy trust, and
- payment was made by the trustee as soon as practicable after receipt of the application, or no later than 2 years after the termination of the person's employment that led to the entitlement, whichever occurs earlier (Employment Termination Payments Redundancy Trusts (12 month rule) Determination 2019 (F2019L00409)).

A ''redundancy trust'' means a fund endorsed as an approved worker entitlement fund under FBTAA s 58PB(3), or the entity operating the fund is endorsed for the operation of the fund under s 58PB(3A), or a fund that, just before 28 June 2011, was an approved worker entitlement fund under s 58PB(2). A ''member of a redundancy trust'' means a person entitled to payments under the terms of the redundancy trust's deed due to termination of employment. The person must be a member of the redundancy trust at the time the application for the payment is lodged with the trustee, or have been a member at the time of death in the case of a death benefit payment.

▶ Example: redundancy trust exception

Albert is a member of a redundancy trust and his employment was terminated on 1 August 2019. Under the redundancy trust, Albert does not become entitled to payment of a benefit from the redundancy trust until 52 weeks after the termination. Albert applied to the trustee of the redundancy trust for payment of the benefit on 1 September 2020 and was paid on 1 October 2020.

The payment made on 1 October 2020, while paid in consequence of termination of employment, does not meet the definition of ''employment termination payment'' as the 12-month rule is not met. However, the redundancy trust exception applies as Albert's application for payment was lodged with the trustee of the redundancy trust within 12 months of becoming entitled to the payment under the terms of the trust deed and payment was made less than 2 years after the termination of employment.

A life benefit termination payment may be made up of 2 components — the tax free component and the taxable component.

The tax free component is not assessable income and is not exempt income. The taxable component is assessable income, but a tax offset that puts a ceiling on the tax rate is applicable depending on the person's age and the amount of the payments received in the year or in consequence of the same termination (see "Taxable component and tax offset" below).

Tax free component

The tax free component of a life benefit termination payment is so much of the payment as consists of:

(i) the invalidity segment of the payment, and

(ii) the pre-July 83 segment of the payment (s 82-140).

The invalidity segment is the portion of the payment that compensates the taxpayer for termination of employment due to invalidity and is calculated as the portion of the payment that represents the period between termination and the last retirement day (¶14-640). The pre-July 83 segment is the portion of the payment that is attributable to the taxpayer's service period before 1 July 1983 (¶14-630).

The tax free component is not assessable income and not exempt income (s 82-10(1)).

Taxable component and tax offset

The taxable component is the whole termination payment amount reduced by the tax free component after that has been calculated (s 82-145).

The taxable component is included in an individual's assessable income (s 82-10(2)). A tax offset is available to ensure that:

- if the individual has reached his/her preservation age (ie age 55 to 60, based on the person's date of birth: ¶14-220) or will do so in the income year in which the payment is received — the taxable component that is within the ETP cap amount or whole-of-income cap amount is taxed at a maximum tax rate of 15%, and the remainder of the taxable component is taxed at the top marginal rate, and
- if the individual is below his/her preservation age throughout the income year — the taxable component that is within the ETP cap amount or whole-of-income cap amount is taxed at a maximum tax rate of 30%, and the *remainder of the taxable component* (see below) is taxed at the top marginal rate (s 82-10(3), (4); *Income Tax Rates Act 1986* (ITRA 1986), Sch 7 cl 1(aa)).

Medicare levy is added to whichever rate of tax applies (ITAA36 s 251S(1A)).

A $180,000 whole-of-income cap applies in conjunction with the normal ETP cap amount on certain employment termination payments (see "ETP cap and whole-of-income cap" below).

The "remainder of the taxable component" which does not benefit from the tax offset is referred to as the "employment termination remainder" (ETR) in s 3(1) of the ITRA 1986. The ETR is therefore "so much of the taxable income" as is included in assessable income under a maximum tax rate provision in ITAA97 Div 82 (see above) that does not give rise to an entitlement to tax offset under that maximum tax rate provision. The Federal Court has held that the qualifying words "so much of the taxable income" in the ETR definition places a cap or ceiling on the amount that can be ETR and that cap or ceiling is the taxable income. The ETR cannot be greater than the taxable income in a particular case. Where a taxpayer has both an ETP cap amount and an ETR as assessable income and allowable deductions, the allocation of deductions against different classes of the taxpayer's assessable income does not enter into the equation to calculate the ETR because such deductions have already been taken into account in calculating taxable income (*Boyn*; *Decision Impact Statement* DIS NSD 1651 of 2012).

ETP cap and whole-of-income cap

The ETP cap amount is $215,000 in 2020–21. The cap amount is increased by indexation annually, in increments of $5,000 rounded down (ITAA97 s 82-160: see ¶42-270 for the cap amount in earlier years).

A whole-of-income cap amount of $180,000 (non-indexed) applies in conjunction with the indexed ETP cap amount for employment termination payments that are not "excluded payments" (see below). For these payments, the applicable cap which is used to determine entitlement to the ETP tax offset is the *lesser* of:

- the ETP cap amount (as indexed), or
- the amount worked out under the whole-of-income cap (see below) (s 82-10(4)).

Examples of payments that are not excluded payments and are measured against the *lesser* cap are golden handshakes, gratuities, unused sick leave payments made in consequence of termination of employment (¶14-610). For excluded payments, the applicable cap to determine entitlement to the ETP tax offset is the indexed ETP cap amount for the year.

The applicable cap for a year is reduced (but not below zero) for each life benefit termination payment already received in that income year, or received for the same termination either in that or an earlier year. For example, if the applicable cap amount has been exceeded because of one or more earlier termination payments, any further termination payment in the same year is taxed at the top marginal rate. This ensures that no more than the applicable cap amount can be received at concessional tax rates in respect of any one termination and that individuals cannot seek to pay less tax by having their termination payments paid in instalments (s 82-10(4), (8)).

Excluded payments

The following employment termination payments are "excluded payments" (and are measured only against the indexed ETP cap):

- genuine redundancy payments and early retirement scheme payments (only the amounts exceeding the tax-free amounts are ETPs: ¶14-700, ¶14-710)
- invalidity payments
- compensation received due to a genuine employment-related dispute relating to personal injury, unfair dismissal, harassment, discrimination, or any other matter prescribed by the regulations (s 82-10(6)).

If a person receives multiple termination payments at different times where only some payments are excluded payments, the applicable cap amount is applied separately to the excluded and non-excluded payments. This ensures that a person who receives a non-excluded payment earlier in the year, which is affected by the whole-of-income cap, does not exhaust the ETP cap on the non-excluded payment (which may not be eligible for an ETP tax offset) at the expense of a later excluded payment the person may receive. To summarise:

- excluded payments will benefit from the ETP tax offset in the first instance, as the ETP cap amount will be reduced only by prior excluded payments received
- non-excluded payments will benefit from the ETP tax offset in the second instance, as the ETP cap amount will be reduced by any prior termination payments received, whether or not they are excluded or non-excluded payments (s 82-10(4)(a)(i), (b)(i))

- the total amount of termination payments (whether excluded or not) that can receive the ETP offset is limited to the amount of all termination payments that fall under either the ETP cap amount or the whole-of-income cap, and which in aggregate does not exceed the ETP cap amount (s 82-10(8)).

If a person's single termination payment includes both an excluded payment part and a non-excluded payment part (where both parts are received at the same time), then the amount of the payment eligible for the ETP tax offset (as calculated in s 82-10(4)) is the amount worked out as if the part of the payment that is an excluded payment was received first (s 82-10(7)). For example, a person who receives a compensation ETP is only excluded from the whole-of-income cap to the extent that that payment is in excess of what the person would have been eligible for voluntary termination of employment (eg retirement or resignation). The component of the payment for which the person would have been eligible on voluntary termination is not an excluded payment, while the amount in excess of this is an excluded payment (s 82-10(6)(d)(iii)).

Working out the whole-of-income cap amount

The applicable whole-of-income cap is worked out by subtracting the person's taxable income for the income year in which the ETP is made (eg salary and wage income or other income) from $180,000 (but not below zero). Taxable income, for this purpose, *excludes* the ETP in question or any ETP received later in the income year (s 82-10(4), (5)). Tax losses are also *not* taken into account in working out the whole-of-income cap. The effect of this is that the sum of the ETP amount and the individual's other taxable income which is equal to or below the whole-of-income cap of $180,000 continues to be eligible for the ETP tax offset, while any amount of the ETP that takes the individual's total taxable income over whole-of-income cap amount of $180,000 is taxed at marginal rates.

▶ Example 1 — whole-of-income cap

Adrian's taxable income (from wages and investments) is $100,000 in 2020–21. He retired from employment in December 2020 and received a gratuity (an employment termination payment (ETP)) of $50,000. The payment is not an excluded payment so that the *lesser* of the ETP cap and whole-of-income cap applies for the purposes of determining the ETP tax offset.

The whole-of-income cap of $180,000 is reduced by Adrian's taxable income for the income year (disregarding the termination payment received) as below:

- the $180,000 whole-of-income cap is reduced to $80,000 ($180,000 – $100,000) because Adrian had taxable income of $100,000 in that income year
- as Adrian's calculated whole-of-income cap of $80,000 is less than the applicable ETP cap of $215,000 in 2020–21, the calculated whole-of-income cap is used to determine his eligibility to the ETP tax offset.

As Adrian's ETP ($50,000) is *less* than his calculated whole-of-income cap ($80,000), the whole ETP is eligible for the ETP tax offset.

▶ Example 2

Sally retires on 31 July 2020 and receives an employment termination payment (ETP) of $200,000 (not an excluded payment). In 2020–21, she has a tax loss of $20,000 from her share investments and a nil taxable income (disregarding the ETP).

Under the whole-of-income cap rules in s 82-10(4)(c), Sally reduces the whole-of-income cap amount of $180,000 by $0, which is her non-ETP taxable income for the year (ie tax losses are disregarded). Sally's calculated whole-of-income cap is therefore $180,000. Of the $200,000 ETP amount, $180,000 falls within the whole-of-income cap.

As the ETP amount eligible for the ETP tax offset is the *smaller* of the whole-of-income cap ($180,000) and the ETP cap ($215,000 in 2020–21), Sally is only eligible for the ETP offset on $180,000 of her ETP.

▶ Example 3 — ETP cap

John (age 61) retired from his job on 31 July 2020.

His employer paid him a termination payment (an ETP, but not an excluded payment) of $50,000 in the form of a gratuity on his retirement. He has no other non-ETP taxable income and has not received any salary or wage income as he retired at the start of the income year.

As the ETP is a not an excluded payment, the *lesser* of the ETP cap and whole-of-income cap applies to determine the amount eligible for the ETP tax offset.

John's whole-of-income cap remains at $180,000 because he had no other taxable income in 2020–21.

As John's ETP cap ($215,000 in 2020–21) is more than his calculated whole-of-income cap, the smaller whole-of-income cap applies to the ETP.

As John's ETP amount ($50,000) is less than the whole-of-income cap amount ($180,000), the whole ETP amount qualifies for the ETP tax offset.

Termination payments made more than 12 months after termination

A payment that would have been an employment termination payment had it been made within 12 months of termination of employment is assessable income and subject to tax at marginal tax rates if it is paid after the 12-month period and is not exempted from the 12-month rule (as discussed in ¶14-610) (s 83-295).

Payments to non-residents

The assessable income of a foreign resident includes statutory income from all Australian sources (ITAA97 s 6-10(5)(a)). The taxable component of an employment termination payment paid to a foreign resident is therefore included in the person's assessable income if the payment has an Australian source (s 82-10(2)) (ID 2010/111). The source of a payment is based on the facts in each case (*Nathan*).

In each case, it is also necessary to consider if a tax treaty may be applicable to determine a liability to tax on Australian sourced income received by a foreign resident. Tax treaties are discussed in ¶22-140.

[AMSG ¶8-820; FITR ¶130-300ff; SLP ¶39-060]

¶14-630 Pre-July 83 segment

The pre-July 83 segment is one of the 2 segments that make up the tax free component of an employment termination payment (¶14-620). The other segment is the invalidity segment (¶14-640).

An employment termination payment includes a "pre-July 83 segment" if any of the employment to which the payment relates occurred before 1 July 1983 (s 82-155(1)).

The amount of the pre-July 83 segment is worked out using the method statement in s 82-155(2) as below:

Step 1 — Subtract the invalidity segment (¶14-640) from the employment termination payment.

Step 2 — Multiply the amount at Step 1 by the fraction:

$$\frac{\text{Number of days of employment to which the payment relates that occurred before 1 July 1983}}{\text{Total number of days of employment to which the payment relates}}$$

[AMSG ¶8-860; FITR ¶130-370; SLP ¶39-060]

¶14-640 Invalidity segment

The invalidity segment is one of the 2 segments that make up the tax free component of an employment termination payment (¶14-620). The other segment is the pre-July 83 segment (¶14-630).

An employment termination payment includes an invalidity segment if:

- the payment was made to a person who stopped being gainfully employed because he/she suffered from ill-health (whether physical or mental)
- the gainful employment stopped before the person's last retirement day, and
- 2 legally qualified medical practitioners have certified that, because of the ill-health, it is unlikely that the person can ever be gainfully employed in a capacity for which he/she is reasonably qualified because of education, experience or training (ITAA97 s 82-150(1)).

"Gainfully employed" means employed or self-employed for gain or reward in any business, trade, profession, vocation, calling, occupation or employment (ITAA97 s 995-1(1)). As one of the requirements to qualify as an employment termination payment is that the payment is received in consequence of the termination of employment (¶14-610), self-employed persons and partners in a partnership cannot receive an employment termination payment or a tax-free invalidity payment.

The "last retirement day" means:

- if an individual's employment or office would have terminated on reaching a particular age or completing a particular period of service — the day the individual would reach the age or complete the period of service (as the case may be), or
- in any other case — the day on which the individual would turn age 65 (ITAA97 s 995-1(1)).

In *Pitcher*, a lump sum paid in redemption of the taxpayer's weekly compensation entitlements was held to be an ETP that was made in consequence of the termination of employment. The court said the time that the certificates must have been issued was not when the termination payment was made but when it fell to be characterised as an invalidity payment in relation to the taxpayer. There was a possibility that the taxpayer had, at that time, by training or education undertaken after the former employment was terminated, qualified himself or herself for employment in a capacity in which such employment was not available when the earlier termination occurred.

The medical certification test of disability to the required standard reposes in the medical practitioners, not the Commissioner. However, it remains a question of fact for the Commissioner or the Tribunal whether the 2 medical certificates have properly met the test as required (*Pitcher*; *Sills*). In *Sills' case*, the AAT held that 2 lump sum payments received by a taxpayer were eligible termination payments under ITAA36 (as the invalidity component under former s 27G) as the taxpayer had tendered 2 medical certificates which sufficiently informed that he was unlikely ever to be gainfully employed in a relevant capacity for which he was reasonably qualified because of his education, experience or training. The ATO accepted that the decision was open to the AAT on the particular facts of the case (ATO *Decision Impact Statement* VRN 2940–2941 of 2009). This view confirms that the AAT would generally not look behind the conclusion expressed in a medical certificate where the medical practitioner has properly answered the test of disability in s 82-150(1)(d).

Calculation of invalidity segment

The invalidity segment is worked out using the following formula in s 82-150(2):

$$\text{Amount of employment termination payment} \times \frac{\text{Days to retirement}}{\text{Employment days} + \text{Days to retirement}}$$

where:

days to retirement is the number of days from the day on which the person's employment was terminated to the last retirement day, and

employment days is the number of days of employment to which the payment relates.

[AMSG ¶8-850; FITR ¶130-360; SLP ¶39-060]

¶14-680 Death benefit termination payments

A death benefit termination payment is an employment termination payment (¶14-610) received by a person after another person's death in consequence of termination of the other person's employment (ITAA97 s 82-130(1)(a)(ii)).

As with other employment termination payments, the payment must be received no later than 12 months after the termination unless the Commissioner determines that a longer period is appropriate (¶14-610).

A death benefit termination payment may comprise 2 components — the tax free component and the taxable component.

The tax free component is so much of the payment as consists of the invalidity segment (¶14-640) and the pre-July 83 segment (¶14-630) (s 82-140). The tax free component is not assessable income and not exempt income (ss 82-65(1); 82-70(1)).

The taxable component is the amount of the payment less the tax free component (s 82-145).

Taxation of taxable component

The tax treatment of the taxable component depends on whether the recipient is a "death benefits dependant" of the deceased (¶14-270) and the amount received in consequence of the same termination in relation to the ETP cap amount.

Payments to a death benefits dependant

If a dependant receives a death benefit termination payment:

- the amount of the taxable component of the payment up to the ETP cap amount (see below) is not assessable income and not exempt income, and
- the remainder of the payment (being the amount exceeding the ETP cap amount) is taxed at the top marginal rate (45%) (s 82-65(2)).

▶ Example 1

Angela is a full-time student who lives at home with her mother (Susan) and is financially dependent on her mother who supported her throughout her studies. When Susan died in 2020–21, her employer made a death benefit termination payment of $250,000 to Angela.

As Angela is a death benefits dependant, she is not taxed on the first $215,000 of the payment and will pay tax at the top marginal rate on the remaining $35,000.

Payments to a non-death benefits dependant

If a non-dependant receives a death benefit termination payment, the amount of the taxable component of the payment is included in the recipient's assessable income and taxed as follows:

- a tax offset applies so that the amount up to the ETP cap amount (see below) is taxed at a maximum tax rate of 30%, and
- the amount exceeding the ETP cap amount is taxed at the top marginal tax rate (45%) (s 82-70(2) to (4)).

Payments to the trustee of a deceased estate

A death benefit termination payment to the trustee of a deceased estate in that capacity is subject to tax in the hands of the trustee as below:

- to the extent that one or more beneficiaries of the estate who were death benefits dependants of the deceased have benefited, or may be expected to benefit, from the payment — the payment is treated as if it had been made to a death benefits dependant
- to the extent that one or more beneficiaries of the estate who were not death benefits dependants of the deceased have benefited, or may be expected to benefit, from the payment — the payment is treated as if it had been made to a non-death benefits dependant, and
- the payment is taken to be income to which no beneficiary is presently entitled (s 82-75).

The "presently entitled" condition means that the tax payable (if any) is imposed on the trustee, rather than the beneficiaries of the estate. The trustee must withhold sufficient funds to meet the tax liability before making distributions to beneficiaries (*Fyffe v Fyffe*).

▶ Example 2

Michael appointed Jane as the trustee of his estate in his will. The will provided for his estate to be distributed equally between his daughter (a death benefits dependant) and his nephew (not a death benefits dependant) when he dies.

When Michael died in September 2020, Jane (as the trustee of Michael's estate) received a death benefit termination payment of $150,000 (of which there is no tax free component) from Michael's former employer.

Half of the payment ($75,000) will be treated as if it had been paid directly to Michael's daughter, and no tax is payable by the trustee of the estate on that amount.

The remaining $75,000 will be treated as if it had been paid directly to Michael's nephew, and the trustee of the estate will be liable to tax at 30% on this amount as it is below the ETP cap amount ($215,000) for 2020–21.

▶ Example 3

Justin appointed Matthew as the trustee of his estate in his will. The will provided for his estate to be distributed equally to his son, Ricky (a death benefits dependant) and his 3 friends, Glenn, Shane and Adam, who are not dependants.

When Justin died in August 2020, Matthew (as the trustee of Justin's estate) received a death benefit termination payment of $400,000 (of which there is no tax free component) from Justin's former employer. One quarter of the payment ($100,000) will be treated as if it had been paid directly to Justin's son Ricky. As this amount is less than the ETP cap amount for the year ($215,000), the trustee of the estate is not liable to tax on the $100,000.

The remaining $300,000 is treated as if it were paid to non-death benefits dependants. The trustee of the estate will be liable to tax at 30% on $215,000 and at the top marginal tax rate on $85,000.

ETP cap amount and operation of cap

The "ETP cap amount" is $215,000 in 2020–21 (ITAA97 s 82-160). This amount is increased by indexation annually, in increments of $5,000 rounded down (ITAA97 s 960-285: see ¶42-270 for the cap amount in earlier years).

The ETP cap amount is reduced by the amount of any death benefit termination payment received in consequence of the same termination, whether in that year or an earlier income year (s 82-65(4)). The ETP cap amount is not reduced because of the receipt of a life benefit termination payment in the same year (¶14-620).

[AMSG ¶8-840; FITR ¶130-310; SLP ¶39-070]

Other Termination Payments

¶14-700 Genuine redundancy payments

A genuine redundancy payment is so much of a lump sum payment received by an employee who is dismissed from employment because the employee's position is genuinely redundant as exceeds the amount that could reasonably be expected to be received by the employee in consequence of the voluntary termination of employment at the time of the dismissal (ITAA97 s 83-175(1)).

A payment cannot be both a genuine redundancy payment and an early retirement scheme payment (¶14-710) because of the nature of each of these types of payment (ITAA97 s 83-170).

Conditions to be met

A genuine redundancy payment must satisfy the following conditions:

- the employee is dismissed before the *earlier* of the following:
  - the day the employee reached ''pension age'' (within the meaning given by s 23(1) of the *Social Security Act 1991*: ¶10-195), or
  - if the employee's employment would have terminated on reaching a particular age or completing a particular period of service — the day the employee would reach the age or complete the period of service (as the case may be)
- if the dismissal was not at arm's length — the payment does not exceed the amount that could reasonably be expected to be made if the dismissal were at arm's length, and
- at the time of the dismissal, there was no arrangement between the employee and the employer, or between the employer and another person, to employ the employee after the dismissal (s 83-175(2)).

A genuine redundancy payment does not include any part of a payment that was received by the employee in lieu of superannuation benefits to which the employee may have become entitled at the time the payment was received or at a later time (s 83-175(3)).

A payment is not a genuine redundancy payment if it is excluded by s 82-135 as an employment termination payment (s 83-175(4): ¶14-610).

TR 2009/2 provides guidelines on the conditions to be met for a payment to qualify as a genuine redundancy payment.

Whether a redundancy is ''genuine'' is determined on an objective basis. The fact that an employer and employee have an understanding that a payment on termination is caused by redundancy or that the employer treats the payment as a redundancy payment for tax purposes does not of itself establish genuine redundancy.

The loss of a particular position with an employer is not a dismissal unless all employment with the employer is severed. The exception to this general principle is where the person holds an office with the employer at the same time as having a common law employment relationship with the same employer. In this case, dismissal from either will qualify as a dismissal under s 83-175, eg a person who is both a director of the employer company and a common law employee of the company who is terminated from one of these 2 capacities.

''Dismissal'' is a particular mode of termination of employment at the initiative of the employer without the consent of the employee, in contrast to a termination of employment at the employee's initiative (eg resignation or retirement). Consent in this context refers to the employee choosing to agree to or approve the act or decision to terminate employment in circumstances where the employee has the capacity to make such a choice. A dismissal can occur even where an employee has indicated that he/she would be interested in a termination, provided that the final decision to terminate employment remains solely with the employer (eg where expressions of interest are sought from employees in receiving a redundancy package as part of an employer structured process).

Dismissal also includes the notion of ''constructive dismissal'', eg where an employer places an employee in a position in which the employee has little option but to resign (*Case 12/98*).

In *Marriott*, the taxpayer's employment was terminated under an ATO reorganisation arrangement. Although the relevant clause under which the taxpayer's employment was terminated referred to an employee's services no longer being able to be utilised, the AAT was satisfied that this was done as part of an arrangement that would allow the taxpayer to be paid a package. In the circumstances, the taxpayer's termination of employment resulted from a course of action that he initiated and directed and, accordingly, the termination was not a ''dismissal'' because it was voluntary on his part (*Case 1/2015*: employee's resignation as part of performance management process).

''Redundancy'' refers to the situation where an employer no longer requires employees to carry out work of a particular kind or work of a particular kind at the same location. An employee's position is redundant when an employer determines that it is superfluous to the employer's needs and the employer does not want the position to be occupied by anyone (*Dibb*). The situation where a job effectively disappears must be distinguished from the situation in which the employer no longer wants a job done by the (former) employee in question. In the latter case, there is no genuine redundancy (*Weeks*).

It is fundamentally the employer's decision that a position is redundant, even if the decision may be unavoidable due to the circumstances surrounding the employer's operations. Redundancy generally arises in a situation where the dismissal is not caused by any consideration peculiar to the employee. It will therefore not extend to the dismissal of an employee for personal or disciplinary reasons or because the employee has been inefficient (*Hollows*).

A redundancy of an employee is regarded as a dismissal in the sense that it is a non-consensual separation. In *Long*, the taxpayer was an acting director of a company and also held a management administrative role. On winding up of the company, the taxpayer was regarded as having been dismissed as she had not consented, as a director, to her own termination of employment. In *Coker*, the taxpayer was paid for his part time services as a director of a credit union, but was neither in a management role nor an employee. A termination payment received by him when he was aged 76 was held not to be a redundancy payment as the age 65 or employee conditions in s 83-175 were not met (see above).

A lump sum payment to an employee under a Deed of Separation and Release with the employer in relation to the termination of employment was held not be genuine redundancy payment under s 83-175(1). The employee's position was not made redundant and the termination took place within a performance management process. Accordingly, the full amount of the payment is assessable as an employment termination payment under s 82-130(1) (¶14-600) (*Case 1/2015*).

When a director of a private company makes a decision to end the company's existence or to cease trading, the director cannot be said to have been involuntarily dismissed from employment. Also, a redundancy would not arise where the duties of the position of director will continue to exist after the services of a particular director are terminated or, in a private company reorganisation, provision has been made for others to perform the directors' duties upon their departure from the company by appointing new directors (TR 2009/2).

Taxation of genuine redundancy payments

A genuine redundancy payment comprises a tax-free amount and an assessable amount (s 83-170). The tax-free amount is non-assessable non-exempt income. The amount in excess of the tax-free amount is assessable as an employment termination payment if it qualifies as such a payment under s 82-130 (¶14-610).

The tax-free amount is worked out by the formula:

Base amount + (service amount × years of service)

where:

base amount is $10,989 and **service amount** is $5,496 in 2020–21.

The base amount and the service amount are indexed annually (Subdiv 960-M) (see ¶42-270 for the amounts in earlier years).

[AMSG ¶8-880; FITR ¶130-530; SLP ¶39-080]

¶14-710 Early retirement scheme payments

An early retirement scheme payment is so much of a payment received by an employee because the employee retires under an early retirement scheme as exceeds the amount that could reasonably be expected to be received by the employee in consequence of the voluntary termination of employment at the time of the retirement (ITAA97 s 83-180(1)).

A payment cannot be both a genuine redundancy payment (¶14-700) and an early retirement scheme payment, because of the nature of each of these types of payment (s 83-170).

Conditions to be met

An early retirement scheme payment must satisfy the following conditions:

- the employee retires before the earlier of:
  - the day the employee reached ''pension age'' (within the meaning given by s 23(1) of the *Social Security Act 1991*: ¶10-195), or
  - if the employee's employment would have terminated on reaching a particular age or completing a particular period of service — the day the employee would reach the age or complete the period of service (as the case may be)
- if the retirement is not at arm's length — the payment does not exceed the amount that could reasonably be expected to be made if the retirement were at arm's length, and
- at the time of the retirement, there was no arrangement between the employee and the employer, or between the employer and another person, to employ the employee after the retirement (s 83-180(2)).

The conditions to be met to qualify as an ''early retirement scheme'' are set out in s 83-180(3) and (4). Even where the conditions are not satisfied, the Commissioner may treat a scheme as an early retirement scheme where special circumstances exist, eg where a scheme is implemented due to a delay in processing an application for its approval or is implemented without approval because the employer had not realised the tax implications (s 83-180(5)). Particular cases of approval of early retirement schemes are set out in class rulings issued by the ATO (eg CR 2020/71: University of Melbourne scheme).

Taxation of early retirement scheme payments

An early retirement scheme payment comprises a tax-free amount and an assessable amount (s 83-170).

The tax-free amount is non-assessable non-exempt income. The amount in excess of the tax-free amount is assessable as an employment termination payment if it qualifies as such a payment under s 82-130 (¶14-610).

The tax-free amount is worked out by the formula:

Base amount + (service amount × years of service)

where:

base amount is $10,989 and **service amount** is $5,496 in 2020–21.

The base amount and the service amount are indexed annually (Subdiv 960-M) (see ¶42-270 for the amounts in earlier years).

[AMSG ¶8-870; FITR ¶130-560; SLP ¶39-080]

¶14-720 Unused annual leave payments

A payment made to an employee in consequence of the termination of employment for unused annual leave is not taxed as an employment termination payment (¶14-620). Instead, certain parts of the unused annual leave payment may be taxed concessionally under ITAA97 Subdiv 83-A (ss 83-10 to 83-15).

The meaning of "in consequence of" the termination of employment as discussed in ¶14-610 is also relevant for the above purposes (s 83-10). Where there is no termination of employment, the payment is not covered by Subdiv 83-A.

Subdivision 83-A covers payments made for accrued leave of the following types (whether they are made available as an entitlement or as a privilege):

- leave ordinarily known as annual leave, including recreational leave and annual holidays, and
- any other leave made available in circumstances similar to those in which the leave mentioned above is ordinarily made available (s 83-10(1)).

A pro rata payment of annual leave entitlements to employees who retire or terminate their employment before becoming fully entitled may also be covered by Subdiv 83-A (ITAA97 s 83-10(3)(c)).

▶ Example

Anita, who is covered by an industrial award, resigned after completing only 8 months of the 12 months' service that would have given her an entitlement to 4 weeks of annual leave (worth $2,000). Under the award, she becomes entitled to a pro rata payment of 8/12 of the 12-month entitlement, ie $1,333. This amount will be taxed as an unused annual leave payment, regardless of how the entitlement is described, as long as the description recognises that the qualifying period for the annual leave had been partially served by Anita at the date of resignation.

A payment that is received in consequence of the termination of a person's employment is an "unused annual leave payment" if it is a payment, bonus or additional payment for annual leave that the person has not used (s 83-10(3)). An unused annual leave payment cannot include a transfer of property (s 80-15).

A taxpayer is assessed on the amount actually received in a particular year even if the amount, or part of the amount, related to a payment in substitution of wages that would normally have been payable in the next financial year (*Hannavy*).

The AAT has affirmed the Commissioner's decision that a lump sum received by a taxpayer in respect of accrued annual leave and long service leave entitlements were properly assessable under ss 83-10 and 83-80. The applicant resigned from employment and received a lump sum payment for accrued annual leave and long service leave. During his employment, the applicant had entered into a salary sacrifice arrangement (SSA) to forgo part of his salary (but not leave entitlements) for superannuation contributions. Subsequent to receiving the lump sum payment, the taxpayer sought a ruling from the Commissioner as to whether part of the accrued leave payment could be treated for taxation purposes as if it had been paid into his superannuation fund under the SSA. The Tribunal concluded that the taxpayer had in fact received payment for the unused leave entitlements and that ss 83-10 and 83-80 applied at that time (*Heinrich*).

Taxation of unused annual leave payments

A lump sum payment for unused annual leave is included in a taxpayer's assessable income for the year that it is received and taxed at marginal rates (ITAA97 s 83-10(2)).

A tax offset applies so that the rate of tax applicable to the amount of the unused annual leave payment is limited to 30% to the extent that:

- the payment was made in respect of employment before 18 August 1993, or
- the payment was made in conjunction with a payment that consists of or includes a genuine redundancy payment (¶14-700), an early retirement scheme payment (¶14-710) or an invalidity segment of an employment termination payment or superannuation benefit (¶14-640) (ITAA97 s 83-15).

The portion of the unused annual leave payment that accrued in respect of service before 18 August 1993 can be calculated as follows:

$$\textbf{payment} \times \frac{\textbf{number of days in the accrual period that occurred before 18 August 1993}}{\textbf{number of days in the accrual period}}$$

where the **accrual period** is the number of whole days over which the unused annual leave accrued, assuming that the leave accrues in accordance with the employee's ordinary conditions of employment and that it relates to the last period of service (TD 94/8).

Medicare levy and, if applicable, levy surcharge is payable on the amount of unused annual leave payment included in assessable income.

Payments for unused annual leave made on the death of an employee to the deceased's beneficiaries or the trustee of the deceased's estate are exempt from tax (ITAA36 s 101A(2)).

The PAYG obligations for a payer of accrued leave payments are discussed in ¶26-180.

[AMSG ¶8-890, ¶8-900; FITR ¶130-420ff; SLP ¶39-085]

¶14-730 Unused long service leave payments

A payment to an employee in consequence of the termination of employment for unused long service leave is not taxed as an employment termination payment (¶14-610). Instead, certain parts of the payment are concessionally taxed under ITAA97 Subdiv 83-B (ss 83-65 to 83-115).

The concessional taxation rules apply to lump sum payments to a taxpayer in consequence of retirement from, or termination of, an office or employment after 15 August 1978. For these purposes, the meaning of "in consequence of" the termination of employment discussed at ¶14-610 is also relevant. An unused long service leave payment cannot include a transfer of property (s 80-15).

Amount included in assessable income

A taxpayer's assessable income in the year that an unused long service leave payment is made includes:

- 5% of that part of the payment — to the extent that the payment is attributable to the pre-16/8/78 period
- 100% of that part of the payment — to the extent that the payment is attributable to the pre-18/8/93 period, and
- 100% of that part of the payment — to the extent that the payment is attributable to the post-17/8/93 period (s 83-80(1)).

The remainder of that part (if any) of an unused long service leave payment that is attributable to the pre-16/8/78 period is not assessable income and is not exempt income (s 83-80(2)).

The amount included in the taxpayer's assessable income under s 83-80(1) is taxed at the taxpayer's marginal rates. A tax offset applies to ensure that the rate of tax on assessable income is limited to a maximum rate of 30%:

- to the extent that it is attributable to the pre-18/8/93 period, and
- to the extent that it is attributable to the post-17/8/93 period and the payment was made in connection with a payment that includes, or consists of, any of the following:
  - a genuine redundancy payment (¶14-700) or an early retirement scheme payment (¶14-710), or
  - an invalidity segment of an employment termination payment or a superannuation benefit (s 83-85; ¶14-640).

Medicare levy and, if applicable, levy surcharge is payable on the amount of unused annual leave payment included in assessable income.

The apportionment of assessable income into the various components attributable to the pre-16/8/78 period, pre-18/8/93 period and post-17/8/93 period is based on the employment period in relation to the unused long service leave (s 83-90). This is worked out using the method and formula provided in s 83-95. A taxpayer is assessed on the amount actually received in a particular year even if the amount, or part of the amount, could be said to relate to a payment that would normally have been payable in the next financial year (*Hannavy*). The AAT has held that a lump sum payment for accrued long service and annual leave already received by a taxpayer was properly assessable under ss 83-10 and 83-80 at that time (*Heinrich*: ¶14-720).

Payments for unused long service leave made on the death of an employee to the deceased's beneficiaries or the trustee of the deceased's estate are exempt from tax (ITAA36 s 101A(2)).

The PAYG obligations for a payer of accrued leave payments are discussed in ¶26-180.

What is long service leave and unused leave?

For the purposes of Subdiv 83-B, "long service leave" means long service leave, long leave, furlough, extended leave or leave of a similar kind (however described) to which a person is entitled by law, award or contract. It also covers leave made available to a taxpayer as a privilege, rather than as an entitlement, where the availability of the leave is determined by reference to similar criteria (s 83-70).

Some State Acts provide that an employer may be exempted from the laws relating to the provision of long service leave benefits for employees if they operate schemes which provide certain other benefits. Where such an exemption exists, leave benefits provided under the alternative scheme are also treated as long service leave, except where they are annual leave (¶14-720).

A payment that a person receives in consequence of the termination of employment is an unused long service leave payment if:

- it is for long service leave the person has not used, or
- it is for long service leave to which the person was not entitled just before the employment termination, but that would have been made available to the person at a later time if it were not for the employment termination (s 83-75).

Pro rata payments of long service leave entitlements of taxpayers who retire or terminate employment before becoming fully entitled are also covered.

▶ Example 1

John, who is covered by an industrial award, retired after completing 10 of the 15 years' service that would have given him an entitlement to 3 months' long service leave (worth $6,000). Under the award, he becomes entitled to a pro rata payment of 10/15 of the full 15-year entitlement, ie $4,000. This amount will be taxed as an unused long service leave payment, regardless of how the entitlement is described, provided the description recognises that the qualifying period has been partially served by John at retirement time.

If an industrial award covering long service leave entitlements is varied after 15 August 1978 (eg by increasing an employee's entitlement after 15 years' service), this does not mean that the whole increase is to be treated as attributable to post-15 August 1978 service. The entitlement, as increased, should simply be apportioned in the usual way (IT 2097).

Service partly full-time, partly part-time

Where a taxpayer's service is partly full-time and partly part-time, separate calculations must be made for each type of service. In these calculations the amount of the lump sum, the period of leave and the period of employment must all be apportioned between the full-time and the part-time service (s 83-110).

Long service leave where leave is taken at less than full pay

If a taxpayer used days of long service leave at a rate of pay that is less than the rate to which the taxpayer is entitled, the number of days of long service leave that the taxpayer is taken to have used is calculated based on the proportion of rate of pay at which leave was actually taken to the rate of pay to which the taxpayer was entitled when taking leave (s 83-115).

▶ Example 2

Assume that John took 100 actual days of long service leave at a rate of pay of $30 per hour, when the rate of pay to which John was entitled when taking leave was $40 per hour.

John is taken to have used 75 days of long service leave, ie 100 actual days of long service leave × 30/40.

[AMSG ¶8-900; FITR ¶130-455ff; SLP ¶39-085]

¶14-740 Foreign termination payments

ITAA97 Subdiv 83-D provides for the tax treatment of termination payments arising out of foreign employment. These payments are not employment termination payments (¶14-610) and are not assessable income and not exempt income except for amounts worked out under the Subdivision.

Two types of foreign termination payments are covered by Subdiv 83-D:

- termination payments relating to a period when the taxpayer was not an Australian resident, and
- termination payments relating to a period when the taxpayer was an Australian resident.

Termination payments — foreign resident period

A payment received by a taxpayer in respect of a foreign resident period is not assessable income and is not exempt income if:

- it was received in consequence of the termination of the taxpayer's employment in a foreign country
- it is not a superannuation benefit (ie it is not a superannuation fund payment: ¶14-100)
- it is not a payment of a pension or an annuity (whether or not the payment is a superannuation benefit — this ensures that only lump sum payments are covered), and
- it relates only to a period of employment when the taxpayer was not an Australian resident (ITAA97 s 83-235; *Branson*: exempt non-resident foreign termination payment).

A payment that relates to a period of employment during which the recipient was variously a resident and not a resident of Australia, does not relate only to a period of employment when the person was not a resident. Such a payment will not be tax-free under s 83-235, either in whole or in part (ID 2009/123; *Case 16/2000*; *Branson*).

Termination payments — Australian resident period

A payment received by a taxpayer is not assessable income and is not exempt income if it was received in consequence of:

- the termination of the taxpayer's employment in a foreign country, or
- the termination of the taxpayer's engagement on qualifying service on an approved project (within the meaning of ITAA36 s 23AF) in relation to a foreign country (ITAA97 s 83-240).

"Termination" for the above purposes includes retirement from the engagement and cessation of the engagement because of the death.

For the payment to be non-assessable non-exempt income, the following conditions must also be met:

- the payment relates only to the period of that employment or engagement
- the payment is not a superannuation benefit
- the payment is not a payment of a pension or an annuity (whether or not the payment is a superannuation benefit)
- the taxpayer was an Australian resident during the period of the employment or engagement
- the payment is not exempt from income tax under the law of the foreign country
- for a period of employment — the taxpayer's foreign earnings from the employment are exempt from income tax under ITAA36 s 23AG (¶10-860) (*Blank*: exempt foreign earnings must be derived exclusively from foreign service; *Lochtenberg*: not exempt as foreign earnings lacked the requisite connection with the taxpayer's foreign service), and
- for a period of engagement — the taxpayer's eligible foreign remuneration from the service is exempt from income tax under s 23AF.

[AMSG ¶8-910; FITR ¶130-600ff; SLP ¶40-192]

Chapter 15 Personal Tax Offsets

Personal Tax Offsets

¶15-000 What is a personal tax offset?

This chapter discusses the personal tax offsets that are available to individual taxpayers, namely those that, in general terms, relate to the taxpayer's personal circumstances. Tax offsets are subtracted from the tax calculated on taxable income (ITAA97 s 4-10). Subject to few exceptions (¶15-010), the sum of all tax offsets allowable to a taxpayer cannot exceed the amount of tax otherwise payable, and any unused offsets cannot be carried forward to be set off against tax payable in future years. In contrast, a deduction is subtracted from assessable income in calculating the taxable income (or loss) after which any tax payable is calculated.

▶ Example:

Carrie-anne has a 2020–21 assessable income of $37,500 and deductions of $500. Her taxable income is therefore $37,000 and her gross tax $3,572. She is entitled to the full low income earners rebate of $445 (¶15-300). Her net tax is therefore $3,572 – $445 = $3,127.

The ITAA97 uses the generic term ''tax offset'' to describe what the ITAA36 called ''rebates'' and the ATO refers virtually exclusively to ''tax offsets''. In this text, however, the terms are used interchangeably generally based on whether the particular entitlement arose under the ITAA36 or ITAA97.

Types and amount of offsets

The amount of personal tax offsets available in **2020–21** are set out in the table at ¶42-165. See ¶15-005 for a comprehensive list of the tax offsets/rebates available to individual taxpayers dealt with elsewhere.

[FITR ¶40-500, ¶40-510]

¶15-005 Tax offset finding table

Use this table to find detailed information for specific tax offsets.

Offset/rebate	Location
ABSTUDY allowances	¶15-315
AIC allowances	¶15-315
Austudy allowances	¶15-315
Annuities	¶14-510
Beneficiaries	¶15-315
Bonuses under short-term life policies	¶10-240
Child care	¶2-133
Conservation tillage refundable tax offset	¶19-135
Defence Force members	¶15-180
Dental expenses — see Medical expenses	
Dependant (Invalid and Carer) Tax Offset (DICTO)	¶15-100
Dividends, franked, received by resident individuals, eligible superannuation funds, ADFs, PSTs, registered organisations	¶4-800
Dividends received by life insurance companies	¶4-760
Doctors' bills — see Medical expenses	
Drought relief payment	¶15-315
Education allowances	¶15-315
Exceptional circumstances relief payment	¶15-315
Exploration development incentive *see* Junior Minerals Exploration Incentive (JMEI)	¶19-010
Farm household support (grant of financial assistance)	¶15-315
FBT, non-profit employers only	¶35-642
Film production offset	¶20-330
Health insurance premiums	¶15-330
Hospital expenses — see Medical expenses	
Income arrears received in a lump sum	¶15-340
Income streams provided by superannuation funds:	
from a taxed source	¶14-220

Offset/rebate	Location
from an untaxed source	¶14-240
Invalid relative, contributions to maintenance	¶15-100
Junior Minerals Exploration Incentive (JMEI) (formerly Exploration development incentive (EDI))	¶19-010
Leave payments, unused annual or long service leave	¶14-720
Life benefit termination payment	¶14-620
Limited partners in early stage venture capital limited partnerships (ESVCLPs)	¶5-040
Low and middle income earners (LMITO)	¶15-300
Low income earners (LITO)	¶15-300
Low income aged persons (SAPTO)	¶15-310
Lump sums paid by superannuation funds:	
from a taxed source	¶14-220
from an untaxed source	¶14-240
Mature age allowance	¶15-315
National Rental Affordability Scheme	¶20-600
Newstart allowance/JobSeeker Payment	¶15-315
Nursing home fees — see Medical expenses	
Optical expenses — see Medical expenses	
Parenting payment	¶15-315
Partner allowance	¶15-315
Pensions paid by taxed superannuation funds	¶14-240
Pensions paid in arrears	¶15-340
Pensioners (SAPTO)	¶15-310
Primary producer's income (averaging provisions)	¶18-210
Research and development tax incentive	¶20-150
Seafarer's tax offset	¶3-020
Self-funded retirees of pension age	¶15-315
Senior Australians and pensioners tax offset (SAPTO)	¶15-310
Sickness allowance	¶15-315
Small business income tax offset	¶7-210
Special benefit	¶15-315
Superannuation contributions for low income/non-working spouse	¶13-770
United Nations service overseas	¶15-190
VCES allowances	¶15-315
Widow allowance	¶15-315
Youth allowance	¶15-315
Zone rebates for taxpayers in remote areas	¶15-190

¶15-010 Personal tax offsets priority rules

Under s 63-10(1), the order in which personal tax offsets are applied is as follows:

- senior Australians and pensioners tax offset (SAPTO), also known as the low income aged persons offset (¶15-310)
- low income aged persons offset for trustee (¶15-310)

- beneficiary offset (¶15-315)
- low, and low and middle, income rebate (¶15-300)
- any offset not covered by another item in the list, eg the dependant (invalid and carer) tax offset (¶15-100); and the zone/overseas service rebates (¶15-160, ¶15-180, ¶15-190)
- foreign income tax offset (¶21-670), and
- refundable tax offsets, eg the private health insurance offset (¶15-330).

Section 63-10(1) also specifies what happens to any excess or unused amount of any tax offset. The unused portion of only a limited number of tax offsets may be transferred to one's spouse, refunded or carried forward to future income years.

[FITR ¶110-510, ¶112-000]

Income Test for Certain Tax Offsets

¶15-025 Income test for certain tax offsets

Certain tax offsets/rebates are subject to an income test and limit, ie the dependant (invalid and carer) tax offset (DICTO) (¶15-100) and the zone/overseas service rebates (¶15-160, ¶15-180, ¶15-190).

For **2020–21**, the "adjusted taxable income for offsets" limit is $100,000.

"Adjusted taxable income for offsets" is defined as meaning "adjusted taxable income for rebates" in s 6(1) ITAA36 which takes the meaning of "adjusted taxable income" in the *A New Tax System (Family Assistance) Act 1999*, disregarding cl 3 and 3A of Sch 3 to that Act.

The adjusted taxable income for offsets/rebates is the *total* of the following amounts:

- taxable income
- reportable superannuation contributions, ie the sum of the person's personal deductible contributions and reportable employer superannuation contributions made by the person's employer (¶13-730)
- total net investment loss, ie from financial investments (shares, interests in managed investment schemes (including forestry schemes), rights and options, and like investments), and net loss from rental properties
- adjusted fringe benefits, ie gross rather than adjusted net value of reportable fringe benefits, except in relation to fringe benefits received by individuals working for public benevolent institutions, health promotion charities and some hospitals and public ambulance services
- income from certain tax-free pensions and benefits from Department of Human Services or Veterans' Affairs
- target foreign income, ie any income, payment or benefit received from a foreign source that is tax exempt in Australia,

less the annual amount of any child support/child maintenance the taxpayer pays.

Dependant (Invalid and Carer) Tax Offset

¶15-100 Dependant (Invalid and Carer) Tax Offset

The Dependant (Invalid and Carer) Tax Offset (DICTO) in Subdiv 61-D ITAA97 is available to taxpayers maintaining certain classes of dependants who are genuinely unable to work due to invalidity or carer obligations (s 61-5).

The indexed amount of the DICTO for the **2020–21** income year is $2,816.

Where the taxpayer claims the DICTO for a spouse, the income test is based on the ATIO of the taxpayer; for any other kind of dependant (eg a parent, child, brother or sister, etc), the income test is based on the combined ATIO of the taxpayer and the taxpayer's spouse.

The amount of the DICTO is indexed annually and is reduced by $1 for every $4 by which the dependant's adjusted taxable income for offsets (''ATIO'') exceeds $282. The DICTO is not available to a taxpayer whose ATIO exceeds the income limit, of $100,000, for family assistance purposes (s 61-20(1); ¶15-025).

Eligiblity for DICTO

Taxpayers will be eligible for DICTO if:

(1) they contribute to the maintenance of an eligible dependant

(2) the eligible dependant receives an eligible pension or payment

(3) they do not receive a disqualifying payment, and

(4) they do not exceed the relevant ATIO.

Maintenance of an eligible dependant

Taxpayers are eligible for DICTO if they contribute to the maintenance of an eligible dependant who is unable to work due to invalidity or care obligations. Eligible dependants are:

- spouses
- parents and spouse's parents
- children, brothers, sisters, spouse's child and spouse's brothers and sisters over 16 years of age.

These terms are explained at ¶15-120. Taxpayers can claim for their spouse as an invalid or carer, not both, and claims can only be made for specific dependants. The eligible dependant must be an ''Australian resident'' or deemed to be one (s 61-10(1)(c); ¶15-120).

The term ''maintenance'' is neither defined nor limited. A taxpayer will be considered to maintain another person if they reside together.

Dependant for part year only

In addition to the ATIO limit above which individuals are ineligible for DICTO (see above), where a person is dependant for only part of the year, the DICTO allowable to the taxpayer is the amount which the Commissioner considers to be reasonable in the circumstances (ss 61-20; 61-40). In practice, the DICTO is apportioned on a time basis. In apportioning the DICTO, only ATIO of the dependant during the part of the year when they were a dependant is taken into account.

The same principles apply where a dependant is resident for only part of the year.

2 or more contributing to maintenance

Where 2 or more persons contribute to the maintenance of a person who is a dependant of one or more of those contributing, a partial rebate will be allowed of such amount as, in the Commissioner's opinion, is reasonable (ITAA97 s 61-40). This is the case for the remaining contributor/s even if one (or more) of the contributors is not entitled to a rebate in regard to his/her contributions.

Eligible invalidity and care payments

Taxpayers can only receive DICTO if the dependant receives an eligible payment of pension. These are limited to the following:

- a disability support pension or a special needs disability support pension under the *Social Security Act 1991*
- an invalidity service pension under the *Veterans' Entitlements Act 1986*
- a carer allowance under the *Social Security Act 1991* in the case of a spouse, parent or parent-in-law, or
- a carer payment under the *Social Security Act 1991* in relation to caring for a child, brother, sister, brother-in-law or sister-in-law who is aged 16 or older.

Disqualifying payments

Taxpayers are not eligible for DICTO if they are eligible to receive Family Tax Benefit Part B (or if their spouse is also eligible to receive this benefit) in respect of the dependant (s 61-25).

Income limits and part year issues

When their ATIO, and that of their partner exceeds the $100,000 ATIO limit (ITAA97 s 61-20) for 2020–21 — see the income tests at ¶15-025.

If an individual has a spouse for part of the year then only their spouses's ATIO for the period that they were spouses is taken into account (ITAA97 s 61-20(3)). The definition of "spouse" is broad, and includes de facto couples (¶15-120). This means that a couple who live together on a permanent basis and who get married during the year could be treated as being spouses for the entire year.

▶ Example

Ashton's daughter Meg lives with him and he receives a carer allowance for her. On 18 March 2021, Ashton marries Mila. Mila has an ATIO of $95,000 and Ashton has income of $8,000. Ashton therefore has to include Mila's ATIO for 105 days (18 March to 30 June 2021), ie (105 ÷ 365) × $95,000 = $27,328 (ignore cents as per the *Individual tax return instructions*). Their combined ATIO is $35,328, ie $27,328 plus $8,000 and, therefore, Ashton can claim for the DICTO for the 2020–21 year.

More than one DICTO

Taxpayers may be eligible for more than one DICTO in an income year if they had more than one dependant during the income year (none of whom are their spouses) or if they had different spouses during the year. For example, if the taxpayer divorced a spouse during an income year and remarried later that year, he/she could claim an amount of DICTO for each spouse (for each part of the year).

If a taxpayer maintained 2 or more spouses for whom he/she may be eligible to claim the DICTO, a claim exists only for the spouse with whom the taxpayer resided (s 61-15(1)). If the taxpayer did not reside with any of the spouses or if he/she resided with more than one, the taxpayer's DICTO is limited to one amount, being the smallest offset that could be claimed in respect of one of the spouses (s 61-15(2)).

Interaction with other rebates

The amount of DICTO to which a taxpayer is entitled will be increased where the taxpayer is also entitled to a zone rebate (¶15-160).

[FITR ¶108-540 – ¶108-595]

¶15-120 Definitions of dependant for DICTO

DICTO may be claimed in respect of the following dependants (s 61-10(1)(a)):

Brother means the brother of the taxpayer or their spouse. Using the reasoning containing in ITAA97 s 960-255(2), brother would seem to include stepbrothers because the stepfather or stepmother is deemed to be the natural child of both children for the purposes of the ITAA36 and ITAA97 (however, this could be affected if the parent's relationship ended).

Child is defined in s 995-1(1) to include an adopted child, a step-child or an ex-nuptial child of a person or their spouse or a child within the meaning of the *Family Law Act 1975*.

Parent of taxpayer or taxpayer's spouse. An individual is the parent of anyone who is the individual's child (ITAA97 s 995-1(1)). It includes the parents of the taxpayer and the parents of the taxpayer's (legal or de facto) spouse, but does not include a grandparent (*Case D67*).

Australian resident is defined in s 995-1(1) to mean ''resident'' as defined by ITAA36 s 6(1) (¶21-010). However, a foreign resident spouse or child is effectively deemed to be a resident and an eligible dependant if the taxpayer has a domicile in Australia for the purpose of the DICTO under ITAA97 s 61-10. If a migrant taxpayer's spouse and children are overseas waiting to join the taxpayer, the migrant may claim the dependent spouse rebate for a period of up to 5 years after arriving in Australia, provided arrangements have been made for the spouse and children to migrate to Australia as soon as possible and the other requirements for entitlement are met. In such a case, the ATO may require the following information to be provided: (i) the date of the taxpayer's arrival in Australia; (ii) the reason why the dependants are overseas; (iii) evidence of the arrangements that have been made for the dependants to come to Australia; and (iv) the expected date of the dependants' arrival in Australia.

A rebate may also be claimed in respect of a dependant who is temporarily overseas. In such a case, the ATO may require the taxpayer to provide a statement outlining the circumstances of the dependant's temporary absence from Australia and the expected date of his/her return to Australia. A proportionate rebate may be claimed in respect of a dependant who is a resident for only part of the year.

Sister is defined in equivalent terms to ''brother'' outlined above.

Spouse is defined inclusively in ITAA97 s 995-1(1), and includes a spouse if they are in a registered relationship with another individual (including same-sex relationships) under a state or territory law for the purposes of *Acts Interpretation Act 1901*, s 2E; and a person, who although not married, is in a relationship with another individual and they live with the other individual on a genuine domestic basis in a relationship as a couple.

[FTR ¶75-072]

Zone/Overseas Service Rebates

¶15-160 Zone rebate for residents of isolated areas

A rebate of tax is available to individuals who are residents of specified remote areas of Australia. The rebate is calculated as the sum of a ''basic amount'', plus a percentage of the ''relevant rebate amount'', being the total of the rebates for the income year for DICTO (¶15-100) and certain other notional tax offsets to which the taxpayer is entitled.

The remote areas generally in the west and north of mainland Australia and Tasmania, as well as central Australia, in respect of which the rebate is available are divided into Zone A and Zone B (ITAA36 s 79A) areas. In general, Zone A comprises those areas where the factors of isolation, uncongenial climate and the high cost of living are more pronounced and Zone B comprises of areas less affected by those factors. Accordingly, the rebate for ordinary Zone A residents is higher than the rebate for ordinary Zone B residents. In addition, a special category of zone allowances is available to taxpayers residing in particularly isolated areas (''special areas'') within either zone. Special areas of Zone A include Macquarie Island, Norfolk Island, Cocos (Keeling) Islands, Christmas Island, Heard Island, McDonald Islands, Lord Howe Island and the Australian Antarctic Territory. Zone B also covers islands forming part of Australia that are adjacent to the coastline of the portions of the mainland and Tasmania. Special areas of Zone B include King Island (Tas) and the Furneaux Group of Islands (Tas). Where a taxpayer satisfies the residency tests for more than one area, the taxpayer is entitled to the greater rebate for which he/she qualifies (TR 94/27).

From 1 July 2015, the zone rebate excludes ''fly-in fly-out'' (FIFO) and ''drive-in drive-out'' workers where their normal residence is not within a ''zone''. FIFO workers who spend more than 183 days in a particular zone, but whose normal residence is not in that zone, will not qualify for the zone tax offset for that zone and will instead be taken to be a resident of the area incorporating their normal residence.

An Australian zone list of towns falling in Zones A and B, as well as the special areas in the zones, is available from the ATO website at www.ato.gov.au/calculators-and-tools/australian-zone-list. A non-exhaustive list is normally contained in the *Individual tax return instructions supplement*. For general guidelines on eligibility for the zone rebate, see TR 94/27.

Meaning of resident of zone area

To be eligible for the zone rebate, a taxpayer must satisfy one of the following residency tests (s 79A(3B)):

(1) the taxpayer had his/her usual place of residence in a zone area for more than half of the income year, ie for at least 183 days (a day includes a fraction of a day: TR 94/27)

(2) the taxpayer died and, at the date of death, had his/her usual place of residence in a zone area

(3) in 2 consecutive income years, the taxpayer had his/her usual place of residence in a zone area for one half or less of the income year in each year but, taken together, the period in the zone area was more than 182 days. The taxpayer is taken to be a resident of a zone area in the second year. This test only applies if the taxpayer was not eligible for a zone rebate in the first income year. The time period in the zone in the first year excludes any days taken into account in determining rebate entitlements under s 79B (Australian Defence Force personnel serving overseas: ¶15-180) or ITAA36 s 23AB (overseas service with UN forces: ¶15-190)

(4) in the income year concerned (the ''last income year''), the taxpayer had his/her usual place of residence in a zone area for less than 183 days. That residency was at the end of a continuous period of residency in a zone area that spanned earlier years of income. In the first year of that continuous period (called the ''relevant preceding year of income''), the taxpayer was a resident in the zone for less than 183 days. The sum of the periods of residence in the zone in the first year and the last year was more than 183 days. The continuous period of residence for this purpose can start in any of the 4 income years preceding the year before the last income year. However, the taxpayer's period of residence in a zone area in the first

income year excludes any days taken into account in determining rebate entitlements under s 79B or 23AB, and the taxpayer must not have qualified for a zone rebate in that income year.

▶ Example: Period of residence in Zone straddles financial years

Josh has lived in Perth all his life. He moves to a zone area on 1 February 2019 and has his usual place of residence there until 31 October 2020. He qualifies as a zone resident in the 2019–20 income year as he has spent more than 182 days in a zone area over a period of 2 consecutive income years.

▶ Example: Broken period of residence in a Zone

Assume the same facts as in the previous example. Josh moves back into a zone area and has his usual place of residence there for 4 months in the 2020–21 income year. He qualified for a zone rebate in the 2019–20 income year. He cannot use the period of residence in a zone in that income year to qualify as a zone resident in 2020–21.

A taxpayer will qualify as a resident of a ''special area'' in a zone if he/she meets the residency tests set out above in relation to the special area itself, eg the taxpayer must have had his/her usual place of residence in the special area for more than half the income year. Even where these tests are not satisfied, the taxpayer will nevertheless benefit from any time spent in the special area in calculating the amount of the rebate allowable.

▶ Example: Special area

Kate has her usual place of residence in Zone A for the whole of the 2020–21 income year and has her usual place of residence in a special area in the zone from 1 November 2020 to 30 June 2021. Kate qualifies as a resident of the special area as she has had her usual place of residence in the special area for more than half the income year.

▶ Example: Pro rata of special area amount

In the 2020–21 income year, Tara has her usual place of residence in Zone B for 200 days. Of that 200 days she spends 100 days in the special area in the zone. Tara qualifies as a resident of Zone B, but not as a resident of the special area as she has spent less than half the income year in the special area. However, she will benefit from the time spent in the special area in calculating the amount of the rebate allowable.

The factors taken into account by the Commissioner in determining whether a person ''resided'' in a zone area include the intended and actual length of stay in the area, the establishment of a home in the area and the existence of a residence outside the area (TR 94/27). A mine worker living in barracks at a mine site in Zone A was held to be resident in that zone, notwithstanding that he continued to maintain a family home in Perth where his wife and children lived and where he returned for periods of leave (*Case W96*).

Amount of zone rebate

The zone rebate is calculated as the sum of:

(1) a fixed amount, which is higher for Zone A than for Zone B and higher still for special areas, *plus*

(2) a percentage (either 50% or 20%) of the sum of the following offsets to which the taxpayer is entitled (if any):

  (a) the dependant (invalid and carer) tax offset (DICTO) (¶15-100) to which the taxpayer is entitled under ITAA97 Subdiv 61-A the indexed amount of which is $2,816 for **2020–21**

  (b) any notional tax offset to which the taxpayer is entitled under ITAA97 Subdiv 961-B (the dependant (non-student child under 21 or student) notional tax offset), unchanged at $1,607 for **2020–21**, and

(c) any notional tax offset to which the taxpayer is entitled under ITAA97 Subdiv 961-A (the dependant (sole parent of a non-student child under 21 or student) notional tax offset), unchanged at $376 for **2020–21** cutting out when the dependant's adjusted taxable income for offsets (ATIO) exceeds $1,786 (s 79A(2)).

The zone rebate is *in addition to* any of these other rebates. However, the sum of these rebates cannot exceed the tax otherwise payable (¶15-010).

The zone rebate otherwise allowable is reduced by: (a) the amount of any remote area allowance paid during the income year to the taxpayer under the *Social Security Act 1991* or the *Veterans' Entitlements Act 1986*; or (b) that part of an exceptional circumstances relief payment or a payment of restart income support, under the *Farm Household Support Act 1992* equivalent to a remote area allowance (s 79A(2A), (4)).

The zone rebate levels for **2020–21** are set out below.

Resident of special area in Zone A or special area in Zone B

A taxpayer who is a resident of the special area in either Zone A or Zone B in the year of income is entitled to a rebate of:

$1,173 + 50% of the relevant rebate amount (ie DICTO and notional tax offsets covering children, students and sole parents)

Resident of ordinary Zone A

A taxpayer who is a resident of Zone A in the year of income but has not resided or actually been in the special area in Zone A or Zone B during any part of the income year is entitled to a rebate of:

$338 + 50% of the relevant rebate amount (ie DICTO and notional tax offsets covering children, students and sole parents)

Resident of ordinary Zone B

A taxpayer who is a resident of Zone B in the year of income but has not resided or actually been in Zone A (including the special area in Zone A) or in the special area in Zone B during any part of the income year is entitled to a rebate of:

$57 + 20% of the relevant rebate amount (ie DICTO and notional tax offsets covering children, students and sole parents)

▶ Example: Calculating zone rebate — dependents living apart

Michael had his usual place of residence in Zone A for 210 days in 2020–21. His dependent, invalid spouse Stephanie and 2 sons attending high-school, lived in Fremantle. Stephanie's ATIO for the year was $6,500. Their sons had no ATIO. Michael and Stephanie's combined ATIO was less than $100,000. Michael is entitled to claim DICTO for Stephanie.

Michael is entitled to the Zone A rebate in 2020–21 because he lived in Zone A for more than 182 days. The rebate is $1,251, calculated as follows:

(1) The first component is the fixed amount for Zone A: $338.

(2) The second component is 50% of Michael's ''relevant rebate amount''. Michael is entitled to a DICTO of $1,212 ($2,766 – [($6,500 – $282)/4]) and the notional dependents offset for 2 student children: $752 ($376 × 2), totalling $1,964. 50% of the relevant rebate amount is $982.

▶ Example: Calculating zone rebate — dependents living together

Rob was working for an accounting firm in Brisbane when he was seconded to a branch office in Townsville, Queensland from 22 April 2020 until 31 October 2020. Rob's partner Kerry and their daughter aged 4 lived with him. In the 2020–21 year, Kerry's ATIO was $7,900. Rob and Kerry's combined ATIO for the 2020–21 year was less than $100,000.

Townsville is in Zone B. Rob cannot claim the zone rebate in 2019–20. He lived there only for 70 days. He is entitled to the Zone B rebate in 2020–21 because he satisfied the 2-year test in s 79A(3B)(d). That is, although he lived in the zone for only 70 days in 2019–20, the combined period in 2019–20 and 2020–21 was more than 182 days. Rob's Zone B rebate is $132, calculated as follows:

(1) The first component is the fixed amount for Zone B: $57.

(2) The second component is 20% of Rob's ''relevant rebate amount'', being the notional dependents offset for one child: $376. 20% of the notional offset is $75.

Other situations

Where a taxpayer resides in a zone area but does not fall into any of the categories listed above, the Commissioner may determine the amount of the rebate that is reasonable (s 79A(2)(f)). However, any discretion exercised by the Commissioner for the zone rebate will be made with reference to the taxpayer's usual place of residence. For example, if a taxpayer is a resident of Zone A for zone rebate purposes but has actually been in the special area of Zone A either for work or a holiday for part of the income year (but less than 182 days), the taxpayer is still able to claim the Zone A rebate, as his/her usual place of residence is in Zone A, but he/she will not be able to access the special area Zone A rebate via the Commissioner's discretion. Where the discretion *is* exercised, the rebate cannot exceed the maximum rebate allowable to a resident of the special area in Zone A or Zone B, or be less than the rebate allowable to a resident of ordinary Zone B.

[FTR ¶38-700 – ¶38-725]

¶15-180 Overseas defence forces rebate

A special rebate is available to a taxpayer who serves in a qualifying overseas locality as a member of the Australian Defence Forces (ADF) (ITAA36 s 79B).

If the total period of service in qualifying overseas localities is more than half the income year, *or* if the taxpayer dies while on service in a qualifying overseas locality, the maximum rebate allowable is $338 plus 50% of any rebates or notional rebates to which the taxpayer is entitled for the income year for:

- dependants who are genuinely unable to work due to invalidity or carer obligations (DICTO) (¶15-100) the indexed amount of which is $2,816 for **2020–21** (s 61-30)
- sole parent, unchanged at $1,607 for **2020–21** (s 961-60), and
- child or student, unchanged at $376 for **2020–21** (s 961-10) cutting out when the dependant's ATIO exceeds $1,786 (s 79A(2)).

If less than half of the income year is spent in qualifying overseas localities (and the taxpayer does not die in such a locality), the rebate is apportioned on a time basis in accordance with the formula (TR 97/2):

$$\frac{A}{183 \text{ days}} \times \text{full allowable rebate}$$

where: A = the number of days served in an overseas locality (including any period in the year during which the taxpayer served in an area comprised in Zone A or Zone B, as defined for the purposes of s 79A).

The total period of service in qualifying overseas localities includes any period during which the taxpayer served as an ADF member in Zone A or Zone B (¶15-160), but does not include any period of service which entitles the taxpayer to an exemption under ITAA36 s 23AD. Section 23AD exempts the salary and allowances of ADF personnel serving with certain United Nations forces or other organisations outside Australia (¶10-780).

Periods of overseas service cannot qualify for both the overseas defence forces rebate and the tax exemption for foreign source earnings under ITAA36 s 23AG (¶10-860).

▶ Example: Calculation of combined rebate for ADF

Colonel Piddle serves as a member of the ADF at a qualifying overseas locality (see below) for 8 months of the 2020–21 income year. He has a dependant who is unable to work due to invalidity and 2 dependent children who are at school. The notional dependants rebates to which he is entitled are:

Dependant (invalid and carer) tax offset (DICTO)	$2,816
Notional rebate for 2 children	$752
	$3,568

Colonel Priddle is entitled to the full s 79B rebate for the 2020–21 income year calculated as follows:

$$\$338 + (50\% \times \$3{,}568) = \$2{,}122$$

▶ Example: Calculation of Defence rebate

Sergeant Paine serves as a member of the ADF at a qualifying overseas locality (see below) from 1 March 2021 to 26 June 2021 (118 days). She is not entitled to any rebates (including notional rebates) for the 2020–21 income year. She is entitled to a proportionate s 79B rebate calculated as follows:

$$\frac{118}{183} \times \$338 = \$218$$

Qualifying overseas localities

The overseas defence forces rebate is available where ADF personnel serve in an overseas locality specified in a declaration made by the Federal Treasurer. A list of these localities is set out in TR 97/2, last updated in 1998, although a more current list can be found on the ATO website at www.ato.gov.au/Individuals/Income-and-deductions/In-detail/Defence-forces-or-Australian-Federal-Police-overseas-service/Overseas-forces-tax-offset---specified-localities.

The overseas defence forces rebate is not available in relation to service as or under an attaché at an Australian Embassy or Legation in an overseas locality which is specified as such for this purpose (s 79B(1A), (5A)). Nor is it available to civilians employed by the Department of Defence (*Case T39*).

Eligibility for zone rebate

If the taxpayer is also eligible for a zone rebate (¶15-160) and the amount of that zone rebate exceeds the maximum allowable under s 79B (eg because the taxpayer is entitled to a special area zone rebate), the taxpayer can claim the zone rebate but not the s 79B rebate (s 79B(4A)). The taxpayer can claim the higher of the 2 rebates. Otherwise, the maximum rebate allowable to a taxpayer who is entitled to both a s 79B rebate and a zone rebate or a rebate for overseas service with UN forces (¶15-190) is the maximum rebate allowable under s 79B (s 79B(4)). Together with other offsets to which the taxpayer may be entitled, this rebate is non-refundable (¶15-010).

[FTR ¶38-750]

¶15-190 Civilians serving with UN forces

A special rebate is available to civilian personnel, prescribed by regulation, contributed by Australia to an armed force of the United Nations overseas (ITAA36 s 23AB(7)), currently members of the Australian Federal Police who are members of the UN peacekeeping force in Cyprus (ITR15 reg 5).

The full rebate is $338 plus 50% of the rebates or notional rebates to which the taxpayer is entitled for the income year for:

- dependants who are genuinely unable to work due to invalidity or carer obligations (DICTO) (¶15-100), indexed to $2,816 for **2020–21**, and
- child or student, unchanged at $376 for **2020–21** (s 961-10) cutting out when the dependant's ATIO exceeds $1,786 (s 79A(2)).

The full rebate is available where the taxpayer's UN service overseas exceeds half the income year or if the taxpayer dies while performing that service. Where the taxpayer's period of service is less than half the year (and the taxpayer does not die while performing that service) the rebate allowable is the amount the Commissioner considers reasonable, generally apportioned on a time basis.

A taxpayer's period of UN service overseas includes periods of service in a zone area (¶15-160) (s 23AB(8)). Periods of overseas service cannot qualify for both the UN forces rebate and the tax exemption for foreign source earnings under ITAA36 s 23AG (¶10-860).

A taxpayer who also qualifies for a zone rebate is only entitled to the rebate that provides the greater amount (s 23AB(9) to (9B)). Together with other offsets to which the taxpayer may be entitled, this rebate is non-refundable (¶15-010).

[FTR ¶9-575, ¶9-589]

Low and Middle Income Tax Offsets

¶15-300 Offsets for low and middle income taxpayers

"Low income" resident individuals are entitled to a rebate (ITAA36 ss 159H; 159N) referred to as the low income tax offset, or LITO. From 1 July 2020, the amount of the rebate is $700 (s 159N(2)) which applies to taxable incomes of up to $37,500. Above this amount, LITO is tapered off at 2 different levels. Individuals with taxable incomes between:

- $37,500 and $45,000 are tapered off at 5 cents per dollar, and
- $45,000 and $66,667 are tapered off at 1.5 cents per dollar.

The ATO automatically applies the rebate to eligible taxpayers on assessment, the offset does not apply to reduce Medicare levy and can only reduce tax liability to zero (¶15-010).

▶ Example: Full LITO

Kelly's taxable income for 2020–21 is $24,540. As her taxable income does not exceed $37,500, she is entitled to the maximum low income rebate of $700.

▶ Example: Partial LITO

John's taxpayer's taxable income for 2020–21 is $39,500. As his taxable income exceeds $37,500, John can claim a rebate as follows:

Maximum low income rebate	$700
Reduction in rebate ($39,500 – $37,500) × 0.05	$100
Rebate allowable	$600

The rebate may not be applied against "unearned" income (¶2-160) of minors, but is available in respect of income from employment.

Low and middle income tax offset

From the 2018–19 income year Australian resident individuals (and certain trustees) are entitled to an additional low and middle income tax offset (LMITO). Entitlement to the LMITO is in addition to the existing LITO. Like LITO, the ATO automatically applies the LMITO on assessment to eligible taxpayers.

The minimum LMITO is $255 for taxable income up to $37,000, increasing to a maximum of $1,080 with relevant income up to $126,000 on the following scale:

- for taxpayers with income exceeding $37,000 but not exceeding $48,000 — $255 plus 7.5% of the amount of the income that exceeds $37,000

- for taxpayers with income exceeding $48,000 but not exceeding $90,000 — $1,080, and
- for taxpayers with income exceeding $90,000 — $1,080 less 3% of the amount of the income that exceeds $90,000.

It is intended that from the 2022–23 income year, the LITO and LMITO will be merged into a new single (higher) low income tax offset (s 61-110). Consistent with the LITO, individuals (as well as certain trustees taxed on behalf of individuals) with taxable income that does not exceed $66,667 will be entitled to the low income tax offset of $700 from the 2022–23 income year, reduced by 5% of the amount by which the taxpayer's relevant income exceeds $37,500 but does not exceed $45,000; and by 1.5% of the amount by which the taxpayer's relevant income exceeds $45,000.

[FTR ¶75-123; FITR ¶108-900 – ¶108-920]

Senior Australians and Pensioners Tax Offset

¶15-310 Senior Australians and pensioners tax offset

Certain low income aged persons, both pensioners and "self-funded retirees", are entitled to a special additional low income aged persons and pensioner's rebate (ITAA36 s 160AAAA) generally referred to as the seniors and pensioners tax offset (SAPTO).

The classes of person eligible to claim the offset are as follows:

- a taxpayer who, at some point during the income year: (a) is eligible for a pension, allowance or benefit under the *Veterans' Entitlements Act 1986*; (b) has reached veteran pension age under that Act; and (c) is not in gaol
- a taxpayer who, at some point during the income year: (a) is qualified for an age pension under the *Social Security Act 1991*; and (b) is not in gaol, or
- a taxpayer whose assessable income includes an amount of: (a) social security pension or education entry payment under the Social Security Act; or (b) service pension, carer service pension, income support supplement or Defence Force Income Support Allowance or a like payment under the Veterans' Entitlements Act; and the taxpayer is not in gaol.

This therefore includes: (a) persons who were eligible for a veterans pension, allowance or benefit but did not receive it, eg because of the assets or income tests; and (b) persons who did not satisfy the residency criteria for an age pension but were eligible for that pension on alternative grounds.

Rebate income

The SAPTO is calculated based on a taxpayer's "rebate income" which is defined in ITAA36 s 6 as the sum of the following amounts of an individual for a year of income:

- taxable income
- reportable superannuation contributions
- total net investment loss, and
- adjusted fringe benefits total.

Calculation of offset

To be eligible for the offset, the person must have rebate income below a certain cut-out threshold. The maximum amount of the offset, and the cut-off threshold, vary according to the taxpayer's marital status (ITR15 regs 9; 10; 11). The levels for **2020–21** are unchanged at:

- for single persons the maximum offset is $2,230. Combined with the LITO (¶15-300), no tax is payable on a rebate income of $32,279 or less. The maximum offset is reduced by 12.5 cents for each dollar of rebate income in excess of $32,279 — the shade-out threshold. This means that once the person's rebate income reaches $50,119, known as the cut-out threshold, no part of the offset is available
- for each partner of a couple, the maximum offset is $1,602. Combined with the LITO, no tax is payable by a partner with a rebate income of $28,974 or less. The maximum offset is reduced by 12.5 cents for each dollar of rebate income in excess of $28,974. This means that once the partner's rebate income reaches $41,790, no part of the offset is available to that partner, and
- for each partner of an illness-separated couple, the maximum offset is $2,040. Combined with the LITO, no tax is payable by a partner with a rebate income of $31,279 or less. The maximum offset is reduced by 12.5 cents for each dollar of rebate income in excess of $31,279. This means that once the partner's rebate income reaches $47,599, no part of the offset is available to that partner.

The shade-out and cut-out thresholds for SAPTO have been amended to ensure that they match the thresholds for the low income tax rebate. For the purpose of determining whether a taxpayer who has a spouse satisfies the cut-off threshold, the taxpayer's rebate income is taken to be half the couple's combined taxable incomes. Accordingly, for **2020–21**, for couples, the combined rebate income threshold is $83,580 and, for illness separated couples, it is $95,198. However, the taxpayer's *actual* rebate income is used in calculating the amount of the offset.

▶ Example

James and Katie are a married couple. For 2020–21, James has a rebate income of $38,000 and Katie $22,000. Their combined rebate income is therefore $60,000. For the purpose of determining whether they satisfy the cut-off threshold, each is taken to have rebate income of 1/2 × $60,000 = $30,000. As this is less than the relevant cut-off threshold ($41,790), each is eligible for the offset.

As James' actual rebate income ($38,000) exceeds $28,974, his offset is shaded-in as follows:

$1,602 – 1/8 × ($38,000 – $28,974) = $473

As Katie's actual rebate income ($22,000) is less than $28,974, she is entitled to the maximum offset of $1,602.

A person who was married for only part of the year can claim on whatever basis gives the bigger rebate entitlement.

The LMITO (¶15-300) may also be available where SAPTO does not eliminate tax altogether.

The offset is also available where a person who satisfies the above conditions is a presently entitled beneficiary of a trust estate but is under a legal disability (ITAA36 s 160AAAB). The trustee is entitled to the offset if the beneficiary would be entitled to the offset under s 160AAAA if the trust income were taken to be the only income of the beneficiary.

The offset is available on assessment. However taxpayers entitled to the offset are exempt from paying PAYG instalments and can apply to the Commissioner for a reduction in amounts withheld from salary, wages, pensions, etc, under the PAYG withholding system.

Transfers of unused offsets

In accordance with the general rule, the offset is limited to the amount of tax otherwise payable (¶15-010). A person can therefore have some "unused" offset if their tax is very low. The benefit of this is normally lost. However, if a partnered person is eligible for the offset, and their spouse is eligible for the offset, there is provision for some or all of the unused offset/rebate to be transferred to the other person, in reduction of their tax (ITR15 reg 12). In determining the amount of unused offset/rebate, no other offsets or credits are taken into account.

[FTR ¶75-530]

Beneficiary Rebate

¶15-315 Recipients of social security benefits and allowances

Taxpayers whose assessable income includes certain benefits are entitled to a rebate of tax known as the ‘‘beneficiary rebate’’ (ITAA36 s 160AAA(1), (3)). The various payments that entitle a taxpayer to the beneficiary rebate are:

- certain Australian social security payments — ie Newstart allowance/JobSeeker Payment, sickness allowance, special benefit, partner allowance, mature age allowance and widow allowance
- the parenting payment (partnered) to the extent that it is not exempt
- disaster recovery allowance, exceptional circumstances relief payments or payments of restart income support (formerly called drought relief payments)
- amounts paid as wages or supplements to participants in Community Development Employment Projects
- farm household support paid by way of a grant of financial assistance
- Commonwealth education or training payments — ie youth allowance; allowances paid under Austudy, ABSTUDY, the Veterans' Children Education Scheme and the Assistance for Isolated Children Scheme; education and training scheme payments made under the *Military Rehabilitation and Compensation Act 2004*; and payments to or on behalf of a participant in a Commonwealth labour market program (ITAA97 s 52-145(1)). However, such payments will *not* qualify for the beneficiary rebate if the recipient, or the individual on whose behalf the payment is received, is an employee of a person who is entitled to a related Commonwealth employment subsidy, and
- interim income support payments made to farmers and small business owners affected by Cyclone Larry or Cyclone Monica, and
- Equine Workers Hardship Wage Supplement Payment.

A taxpayer is entitled to the beneficiary rebate even if exempt foreign employment income is derived in addition to assessable income that includes Newstart allowance (TD 93/84).

The beneficiary rebate is calculated in accordance with ITR15 reg 13. The rebate is calculated on the amount of rebatable benefit received during the year, and is intended to ensure that a person who receives a full rate rebatable benefit for the whole year and has no other taxable income will pay no tax for the year.

Where the amount of the rebatable benefit is $37,000 or less (the upper threshold for the lowest marginal tax rate in **2020–21**), the formula is:

$$[A - \$6{,}000] \times 0.15$$

where A is the amount of rebatable benefit received by the taxpayer during the year rounded to the nearest dollar.

This effectively means that the rebate is 15% of the excess of the rebatable benefit over $6,000 (up to $37,000).

Where the amount of the rebatable benefit is more than $37,000 (the upper threshold for the lowest marginal tax rate in **2020–21**), the formula is:

$$[A - \$6{,}000] \times 0.15 + [A - \$37{,}000] \times 0.15$$

where A is the amount of rebatable benefit received by the taxpayer during the year rounded to the nearest dollar.

This effectively means that the rebate is the same as for rebatable benefits up to $37,000 but is increased to 30% for that portion of the rebatable benefit above $37,000.

▶ **Example**

In the 2020–21 income year, Gary receives rebatable benefits of $39,000. He is entitled to a rebate of: [$39,000 – $6,000] × 0.15 + [$39,000 – $37,000] × 0.15 = $5,250.

If a taxpayer is potentially entitled to both the beneficiary rebate and SAPTO (¶15-310) and the rebates are the same, only one will be allowed (if the rebates are not the same, the greater one will be allowed) (s 160AAA(4)). Together with other offsets to which the taxpayer may be entitled, this rebate is non-refundable (¶15-010).

[FTR ¶75-540]

Private Health Insurance Offset

¶15-330 Offset for private health insurance

A tax offset is available for certain taxpayers for the cost of private health insurance premiums (ITAA97 Subdiv 61-G (ss 61-200–61-215)). The taxpayer may opt for the offset to be delivered as reduced health insurance premiums (under the *Private Health Insurance Act 2007*). A taxpayer cannot benefit from both reduced premiums and the offset (s 61-210(2)–(5)).

The private health insurance offset is means tested, ie the level of offset available is dependent on the taxpayer's "income for surcharge purposes" or if a member of a couple, the family income for surcharge purposes — ¶2-335.

Generally, 2 conditions must be satisfied for an individual to be eligible for the tax offset. First, the individual (or the individual's employer if providing a fringe benefit) must pay a premium in respect of a "complying health insurance policy". Secondly, the premium must be paid in the same income year that it is claimed as an offset, although premiums may in some cases be paid in advance.

A "complying health insurance policy" is generally a policy which provides hospital cover, ancillary cover or combined cover. A complying policy also requires each person and their dependent children to be eligible to claim benefits under Medicare (*Private Health Insurance Act 2007*, s 63-10). For the purposes of this definition a "dependent child" is either a person aged 18 or older but less than 25 years of age who does not have a partner or a person defined as a dependent child for the purposes of the policy (*Private Health Insurance Act 2007*, Sch 1).

The tax offset is available to individual taxpayers and is a refundable offset (¶15-010). The offset is also available to trustees assessed under ITAA36 s 98 on trust income to which a beneficiary under a legal disability is presently entitled (¶6-210), if that beneficiary would have been entitled to the offset. However, in this situation, any refund will be available only to the beneficiary, so as to avoid the possibility of double refunds.

The offset cannot be claimed by individuals in their capacity as an employer. Where an employer pays for private health insurance on behalf of an employee as a fringe benefit, it is the employee who is entitled to claim the offset. Entitlement to the offset is determined in accordance with the *Health Insurance Act 1973* and Subdiv 61-G.

Private health insurance tiers

The private health insurance tax offset applies "tiers" (¶2-335) based on a combination of income for surcharge purposes and age to determine the offset is available and the percentage. For the purpose of applying the tiers, family refers to a person married on the last day of the tax year or a person who contributes in a substantial way to the maintenance of a dependent child (including siblings).

[FITR ¶109-200]

Income Arrears Rebate

¶15-340 Income received in arrears

Individual taxpayers who receive certain income in a lump sum payment containing an amount that accrued in earlier income years may be entitled to a rebate of tax (ITAA36 ss 159ZR to 159ZRD).

The rebate is intended to address more tax being payable in the year in which the lump sum is received than would have been payable if the lump sum had been taxed in each of the years in which it accrued. The rebate is calculated as the difference between the extra amount of tax payable in the year of receipt of the lump sum and the amount of tax that would have been payable if the lump sum had been taxed as it accrued. The rebate is not available to a person in his/her capacity as a trustee (ITAA36 s 159ZRA(2)). Together with other offsets to which the taxpayer may be entitled, this rebate is non-refundable (¶15-010).

The following income is eligible for the rebate (ITAA36 s 159ZR):

- salary or wages to the extent to which they accrued during a period ending more than 12 months before the date on which they were paid
- salary or wages paid to a person after reinstatement to duty following a period of suspension to the extent to which the salary or wages accrued during the period of suspension
- superannuation income streams or annuities paid to individuals subject to TAA s 12-80 or 12-120 Sch 1
- a Commonwealth education or training payment, eg an Austudy or ABSTUDY allowance (¶15-315)
- income by way of compensation or sickness or accident pay in respect of an incapacity for work which is covered by ITAA97 Div 52, 53 or 55 but which is not exempt income under those divisions, and
- assessable pensions, benefits and allowances under the *Social Security Act 1991* or the *Veterans' Entitlements Act 1986*, or similar payments made under a law of a foreign country, state or province.

For the purposes of the rebate, "salary or wages" includes payments to persons as employees or company directors (other than associates of the company), payments to members of parliament or eligible local governing bodies and payments to persons holding or performing the duties of a statutory office or otherwise in the service of the Commonwealth, a state or a territory.

"Normal taxable income" is the amount that would be taxable if certain specified items of income, which are generally of a non-recurrent nature, were excluded. Namely:

- amounts included in assessable income under ITAA97 Div 82 (employment termination payments), ss 83-10 (unused annual leave payments), 83-80 (unused long service leave payments), Div 301 (superannuation member benefits), Div 302 (superannuation death benefits) or ITTPA Div 82 (transitional termination payments)
- any above-average special professional income included in taxable income under ITAA97 s 405-15, and
- net capital gains included in assessable income under ITAA97 s 102-5.

BSWAT payment amount

"BSWAT payment amount" is defined in s 159ZR(1) to be an amount paid to a person under the *Business Services Wage Assessment Tool Payment Scheme Act 2015* (BSWATPS Act). The Business Services Wage Assessment Tool (BSWAT) is a method of assessing the productivity and competence of some individuals with intellectual impairment that were employed by Australian Disability Enterprises in Commonwealth-supported positions, to calculate a reduced wage for the individuals. In *Nojin v Commonwealth*, the Full Federal Court found that the use of the tool to determine wages for 2 particular individuals was discriminatory. The BSWATPS Act implemented a scheme whereby individuals who had their wages assessed using the BSWAT could register to receive payments from the Commonwealth in relation to those wages. The scheme was administered by the Department of Social Services. To receive payments, individuals must have registered for the scheme before 1 May 2017 and must have applied for that payment by 30 November 2017. Section 159ZR(2) provides that a BSWAT payment amount is to be treated as an eligible lump sum accrued wholly in an earlier year or years of income (ie the years in which the relevant wages were paid). This ensures that recipients are eligible for a tax rebate under s 159ZRA in the same way as recipients of lump sum payments of salary or wages earned in previous income years. The BSWAT payment scheme started on 1 July 2015 and ended on 31 December 2018. Depending on when an individual applied, they may have received the payment in one of these financial years: 2016–17, 2017–18 or 2018–19.

Calculation of rebate

To be eligible for the rebate, the amount of the eligible lump sum which accrued before the year of receipt must not be less than 10% of the taxable income of the year of receipt after deducting the amount of the eligible lump sum that accrued in earlier years, abnormal income, net capital gains, ETPs and lump sum payments on termination of employment in lieu of annual leave or long service leave (ITAA36 s 159ZRA). A year in which any part of the eligible lump sum accrued is called an "accrual year".

Where the eligibility test is satisfied, the rebate is calculated according to the formula:

tax on arrears *less* notional tax on arrears

where:

tax on arrears is the amount of tax (excluding Medicare levy) payable in the year of receipt attributable to the amount of the eligible lump sum that accrued in earlier years. Tax offsets under ITAA97 Div 82 (employment termination payments), Div 83 (other payments on termination of employment), Div 301 (superannuation member benefits) or Div 302 (superannuation death benefits), s 392-35(2) (which allows some primary producers tax offsets) or ITTPA Div 82 (transitional termination payments) are taken into account (ITAA36 ss 159ZR(1), definition of "rebated tax"; 159ZRB).

notional tax on arrears is basically the amount representing the tax that would have been payable on the amount of the lump sum that accrued before the year of receipt if that amount had been taxed in the year in which it accrued.

The notional tax on arrears equals the sum of:

(1) the notional tax on the amount of the eligible lump sum that accrued in the 2 most recent accrual years before the year in which the lump sum was received (these are called ‘‘recent accrual years’’), and

(2) the notional tax on the amount of the eligible lump sum that accrued in accrual years (if any) before the recent accrual years (these are called ‘‘distant accrual years’’).

Years in which no part of the eligible lump sum accrued are ignored for the purposes of calculating the rebate.

The notional tax for recent accrual years is the extra tax that would have been payable if the amount that accrued in those years had been taxed as income in those years (ITAA36 s 159ZRC). Medicare levy is disregarded for this purpose (subject to a separate rebate, see ¶15-350), but allowance is made for any tax offsets under ITAA97 Div 82 (employment termination payments), Div 83 (other payments on termination of employment), Div 301 (superannuation member benefits) or Div 302 (superannuation death benefits), s 392-35(2) (which allows some primary producers tax offsets) or ITTPA Div 82 (transitional termination payments).

The notional tax for distant accrual years is the amount of the lump sum that accrued in those years multiplied by the average rate of tax on the amount that accrued in the recent accrual years (ITAA36 s 159ZRD). The average rate can generally be worked out by dividing the notional tax on arrears for the recent accrual years by the amount of arrears that accrued in those years. However, if the taxable income of a recent accrual year included an ETP, a payment for unused leave received on termination of employment, abnormal income or a net capital gain, the average rate is calculated without regard to those amounts.

▶ Example

During the 2020–21 income year, Paul received a lump sum payment of $10,000 representing a back payment of workers compensation. The lump sum accrued as follows:

$1,500 in 2017–18	(‘‘distant accrual’’ year)
$3,200 in 2018–19 $2,800 in 2019–20	(‘‘recent accrual’’ years)
$2,500 in 2020–21	(year of receipt)

Paul’s taxable incomes were $15,000 in 2017–18, $18,000 in 2018–19, $28,000 in 2019–20 and $65,000 (including the lump sum of $10,000) in 2020–21. Assume that Paul is not entitled to any other rebates for those years.

Eligibility for rebate

The method for determining whether Paul meets the 10% eligibility test for the rebate is calculated as follows:

(a) Amount of lump sum accrued before year of receipt $7,500

(b) Taxable income of year of receipt reduced by amount of lump sum accrued before year of receipt ($65,000 – $7,500) $57,500

As (a) exceeds 10% of (b), Paul is entitled to the rebate.

Calculation of rebate

The rebate is equal to the amount calculated as:

tax on arrears *less* notional tax on arrears.

The steps for calculating the rebate are as follows:

Step 1: Calculate the tax on arrears

Gross tax on 2020–21 taxable income ($65,000) (¶42-000)	$12,672
Less: gross tax on 2020–21 taxable income, excluding amounts that accrued in earlier years (ie tax on $57,500)	$10,235
Gross 2019–20 tax attributable to lump sum in arrears	$2,437

Step 2: Calculate notional tax for recent accrual years

2018–19 year		
Gross tax at 2018–19 rates on 2018–19 adjusted income ($18,000 + $3,200)	$570	
Less: gross tax on actual 2018–19 income ($18,000)	$0	$570
2019–20 year		
Gross tax at 2019–20 rates on 2019–20 adjusted income ($28,000 + $2,800)	$2,394	
Less: gross tax on actual 2019–20 income ($28,000)	$1,862	$532
Notional tax for recent accrual years		$1,102

Step 3: Calculate notional tax for distant accrual year

The notional tax for the only distant accrual year (2017–18) is calculated by multiplying the amount of the arrears which accrued in that year ($1,500) by the average rate of tax on the arrears that accrued in the years.

The average rate is (rounded to 3 decimal places):

(570/3200) + (532/2800) divided by 2

= 0.184

Notional tax amount for distant accrual years (1,500 × 0.184) $276

Step 4: Calculation of rebate amount

Tax on arrears (Step 1)	$2,437.00
Less: notional tax on arrears (Steps 2 and 3) (ie $1,102 + $276)	$1,378
Amount of income arrears rebate allowable in 2020–21	$1,059

Note: If no amount of the lump sum accrued in 2019–20, the recent accrual years would be 2017–18 and 2018–19 (there would be no distant accrual year).

[FTR ¶75-492 – ¶75-496, ¶75-498 – ¶75-499]

Medicare Levy Surcharge Lump Sum Arrears Offset

¶15-350 Medicare levy surcharge lump sum arrears offset

The Medicare levy surcharge lump sum payment in arrears offset (ITAA97 ss 61-580 to 61-590) is available to a taxpayer, and in some cases the taxpayer's spouse, for a Medicare levy surcharge (¶2-335) that arose or increased because the taxpayer received an eligible lump sum payment in arrears in the year of income. Broadly, this offset is equivalent for Medicare levy surcharge purposes to the income arrears offset for income tax purposes.

Eligible lump sum payments in arrears for Medicare levy surcharge offset purposes consist of: (1) eligible income for the purposes of the lump sum in arrears tax offset (¶15-340) which is received in the relevant income year; and (2) a lump sum payment in arrears of ''exempt foreign employment income'' (¶10-860) for the relevant year but which accrued for a period more than 12 months before the date on which it was paid.

Also, consistent with the income arrears offset, a lump sum payment in arrears will only be eligible for the Medicare levy surcharge lump sum arrears offset if the lump sum represents *one-eleventh or more* of the taxpayer's:

- taxable income in the relevant year (under ITAA36 s 159ZR)
- exempt foreign employment income for the current year
- reportable fringe benefits total for the current year
- amounts that would be included in assessable income if family trust distribution tax was ignored (ITAA36 Sch 2F s 271-105(1))
- reportable employer superannuation contributions for the current year, and
- total net investment loss for the current year.

Amount of the offset

Where a lump sum payment in arrears meets the criteria, the offset is equal to the amount of Medicare levy surcharge liability attributable to that lump sum. The offset is available where the Medicare levy surcharge liability arose entirely as a result of the receipt of the lump sum payment in arrears, as well as where an existing Medicare levy surcharge liability is increased by the payment of an eligible lump sum.

The amount of the offset is calculated as follows.

Total Medicare levy surcharge – Total non-arrears Medicare levy surcharge

The offset is non-refundable, ie it cannot exceed the amount of the Medicare levy surcharge liability.

Offset for spouses

Because a family's Medicare levy surcharge liability is determined by adding both spouses' incomes to see whether the family Medicare levy surcharge threshold has been reached, a lump sum payment in arrears received by a spouse may affect their Medicare levy surcharge liability as well as that of their spouse. (Once the Medicare levy surcharge family threshold has been reached, the Medicare levy surcharge payable by each spouse is calculated on the basis of their own taxable income.) Accordingly, if a lump sum payment in arrears results in a Medicare levy surcharge liability for the taxpayer's spouse, then the spouse will receive an offset equal to the amount of that Medicare levy surcharge liability. However, the spouse is not entitled to the offset unless the taxpayer receiving the lump sum is also entitled.

Where a lump sum payment in arrears is received by a taxpayer, and both the taxpayer and his/her spouse are already liable for the Medicare levy surcharge (eg because their non-lump sum payment in arrears income exceeds the family threshold), the offset will only be available to the taxpayer.

[FITR ¶110-215 – ¶110-225]

Chapter 16 Business, Employment and Investment Deductions • Gifts

What are Income-related Deductions?

¶16-000 Scope of this deductions chapter

Income tax is calculated on the basis of the taxpayer's taxable income. The taxable income is calculated by deducting "general" and "specific" deductions for the income year from the total assessable income for that year. A "general" deduction under ITAA97 s 8-1 is a loss or outgoing that has the relevant connection with income or business activities, and that is not of a capital, private or domestic nature. A "specific" deduction, on the other hand, is an amount that a provision other than the general deduction provision allows as a deduction (ITAA97 s 8-5).

▶ Planning points

- Increasing allowable deductions reduces your tax liability. ''Accelerating'' deductions so as to incur them in the current year is particularly beneficial, especially if a higher marginal tax rate applies in the current year (subject to the rules for prepayments: ¶16-045).
- Deductions against salary (¶26-130) or non-salary (¶27-280) income reduces current year tax and possibly the PAYG withholding/instalment rate for the following year.
- If the general deduction provision is not satisfied (eg capital outgoings), check whether the outgoing is recognised under other provisions.

This chapter gives an outline of the principles to be applied in determining whether a loss or outgoing is a general deduction and then discusses some of the common deductions that arise from activities directed towards the production of income by all types of taxpayers, ie business taxpayers, salary and wage earners and investors. While these deductions are usually general deductions, some specific deductions are also relevant, eg repairs and past years' losses. Income-related deductions may be contrasted with personal deductions that are not related to income-earning activities: see gifts (¶16-940) and tax-related expenses (¶16-850).

There is a checklist of deductible and non-deductible items at ¶16-005, including cross-references to the paragraph(s) at which the item is discussed.

[FITR ¶15-000ff, ¶31-000ff]

¶16-005 Deductions checklist

This checklist shows the *general* deductibility status of a wide range of expenses and where they are dealt with (as indicated in the **Source** column).

Item	**Deductible (D)/Non-deductible (ND)**	**Source**
Accident insurance premiums	D	¶16-560
Accountant's fees for preparing returns	D	¶16-850, ¶16-858
Accrued leave entitlements, transferred employee payments	D	¶16-154
Accumulated jackpot payments	ND	¶9-120
Advertising expenses	D	¶16-152
Airport lounge memberships (paid by an employer)	D	¶16-270
Alterations to plant or premises (¶16-700) not deductible outright but may be subject to depreciation (¶17-000) or capital works deduction (¶20-470)	ND	
Appeal costs relating to tax disputes	D	¶16-850
Audit costs, including ATO audit	D	¶16-850
Bad debts	D	¶16-580
Bank charges, business	D	¶16-152
Bills of exchange, discount factor	D	¶23-330
''Blackhole'' (business capital) expenses	D	¶16-156
Borrowing expenses	D	¶16-800
Bribes	ND	¶16-152
Briefcases	D	¶16-170
Broker's commission on borrowed moneys	D	¶16-800

Item	Deductible (D)/Non-deductible (ND)	Source
Buildings and structural improvements	D	¶20-470
Business, cost of purchasing	ND	¶16-154
Business operating expenses	D	¶16-152
Business subscriptions	D	¶16-430
Business trips, expenses of	D	¶16-220
Capital loss (net)	ND	¶11-040
Car expenses (non-business)	ND	¶16-310
Car expenses (business)	D	¶16-310
Carbon pricing	D	¶19-130
Child minding expenses	ND	¶16-175
Clothing (corporate wardrobes and uniforms, occupation-specific clothing, protective clothing)	D	¶16-180
Clothing generally	ND	¶16-180
Club fees (not a fringe benefit)	ND	¶16-410
Commercial websites	D	¶16-725
Commission	D	¶16-650
Commuting to and from place of work	ND	¶16-230
Company loss transfer payments	ND	¶3-090
Competition, payment to avert	ND*	¶16-060, ¶16-156, ¶16-840
Computer software	D	¶16-725, ¶17-370
Consolidation valuation expenses	D	¶16-850
Convention expenses	D	¶16-260
Copyrights, patents and registered designs: registration fees and amortisation of development cost or purchase price	D	¶17-015
Corporate wardrobes and uniforms	D	¶16-180
Credit card (personal) used for work-related purposes	D	¶16-440
Death or disability benefits provided by superannuation fund	D	¶13-150
Debt/equity swaps resulting in a loss	D	¶16-586
Depreciation of business assets	D	¶17-000
Discontinuance of business, expenses associated with	ND*	¶16-155, ¶16-156
Discounts or rebates on sales income	D	¶9-050
Distributions by co-operative to members	D	¶3-430
Dividends paid by companies (including deemed dividends under Div 7A)	ND	¶4-200; ¶23-115
Division 293 tax	ND	¶16-858
Domain name registration	D	¶16-725
Donations — see Gifts		
Driver's licence	ND	¶16-310

Item	Deductible (D)/Non-deductible (ND)	Source
Dues: union, professional or business associations	D	¶16-430
Education expenses	D	¶16-450
Election expenses: local government	D	¶16-510
Election expenses: parliamentary	D	¶16-500
Electricity connection costs	D	¶16-820
Emissions units	D	¶19-130
Employer's costs of share scheme	D	¶10-085
Employment agreement expenses of:		
employer	D	¶16-152
employee	D	¶16-200
Employee's expenses:		¶16-160ff
Self-education	D	
Special clothing, purchase and laundering	D	
Technical and trade journals	D	
Tools of trade	D	
Travel, but generally excluding to and from work	D	
Professional indemnity insurance (not reimbursed by employer)	D	¶16-550
Entertainment expenses related to business (limited)	D	¶16-390
Entertainment expenses generally	ND	¶16-390
Environmental impact study expenses:		
general	D	
mining	D	¶19-060
Environmental protection expenditure:		
general	D	¶19-110
mining	D	¶19-100
Equipment (work-related)	D	¶16-170
Eviction proceedings against tenant	ND	¶16-844
Excess concessional contributions charge	ND	¶13-777
Excess non-concessional contributions tax	ND	¶16-858
Excess transfer balance tax	ND	¶16-858
Exchange loss	D	¶23-075
Farmers — see Primary producers		
FBT payments	D	¶16-858
FEE/HELP	ND	¶16-452
Feasibility study expenses for new business	ND	¶16-154
Feasibility study expenses for new project	D	¶19-060
Film (Australian) investment	D	¶20-330
Financial arrangements losses	D	¶23-020
Fines	ND	¶16-845
Fitness expenses (related to job or profession)	D	¶16-190

Item	Deductible (D)/Non-deductible (ND)	Source
Fixed capital assets, cost of protecting	ND	¶16-060
Food, personal or family requirements	ND	¶16-175
Forestry expenses	D	¶18-125
Fruit and nut trees, costs of (unless part of new horticultural plantation)	ND	¶18-020 ¶18-070
Geosequestration expenditure	D	¶16-152
GIC	D	¶16-850
Gifts: advertising or public relations	D	¶16-440
Gifts: made to current or former business clients	D	¶16-015
Gifts: valuation fees under the Cultural Program	D	¶16-965
Gifts: works of art and heritage items	D	¶16-965, ¶16-967
Gifts: $2 or more to prescribed recipients	D	¶16-942ff
Glasses (anti-glare)	D	¶16-170
Gratuities to employees	D	¶16-520
Grooming costs	ND	¶16-175
GST payments	ND	¶16-860
Guarantee payments	ND	¶16-152
HELP payments	ND	¶16-452
Higher qualification expenses	D	¶16-450
Hobby losses	ND	¶16-015
Home office expenses, unless home is used for income-producing purposes	ND	¶16-480
Home office expenses where home is used as business premises	D	¶16-480
Home office expenses (working from home during COVID-19)	D	¶16-480
Illegal activities, expenses relating to	ND	¶16-105
Income tax	ND	¶16-856
Insurance company, unreported claims	D	¶16-040
Insurance premiums (business related)	D	¶16-550
Insurance premiums under key-person life or endowment policy	ND	¶16-570
Intellectual property	D	¶16-727
Interest on borrowings for employer superannuation contributions	D	¶16-740
Interest on borrowings to finance life premiums	ND	¶16-740
Interest on borrowings to finance personal superannuation contributions	ND	¶16-740
Interest on borrowings to pay income tax	D	¶16-856
Interest on late lodgments	D	¶16-856
Interest on late payments of tax	D	¶16-856
Interest on money used for assessable income production or purchase of income-producing assets	D	¶16-740
Interest on money used to pay HELP	D	¶16-452
Interest on partner's capital	ND	¶5-090

Item	Deductible (D)/Non-deductible (ND)	Source
Interest on underpaid tax where assessment amended	D	¶16-856, ¶29-550
Interest referable to home office where home used as business premises	D	¶16-480
Interest withholding tax	D	¶16-740, ¶26-250
Internet expenses if work-related	D	¶16-400
Investment losses	D	¶16-665
Investment portfolio, expenses of servicing	D	¶16-660
Land holding costs (vacant land)	ND	¶16-650
Land tax on business premises	D	¶16-870
Late payment penalty interest	D	¶16-856
Lease incentive payment	D	¶16-650
Lease premiums	ND	¶16-640
Lease preparation expenses	D	¶16-640
Lease surrender payments	ND	¶16-640, ¶16-650
Lease termination payments (business)	D	¶16-159
Leasehold improvements	ND	¶16-640
Leave accrued but unpaid	ND	¶16-040
Leave payments made by employer	D	¶16-040, ¶16-155
Legal expenses:		
Proceedings affecting future income-earning	D	¶16-840, ¶16-842
Relating to borrowing or mortgage discharge	D	¶16-800
Tax advice costs	D	¶16-850
Legal expenses, capital	ND	¶16-156, ¶16-840
Legal expenses, personal:		
Custody application	ND	¶16-840
Obtaining divorce	ND	¶16-840
Will preparation	ND	¶16-840
Leisure facility expenditure	ND	¶16-420
Lessee's legal expenses in defending lessor's attempted termination of lease	ND	¶16-640
Lessor's or lessee's payment to secure early termination of non-business lease	ND	¶16-060
Lessor's or lessee's payment to secure early termination of business lease	D	¶16-159
Living-away-from-home allowance expenses	D	¶16-240
Loss on sale of property acquired before 20.9.85	D	¶16-680
Losses of certain former bankrupts	ND	¶16-895

Item	Deductible (D)/Non-deductible (ND)	Source
Losses (company) of current year	D	¶3-065
Losses (trust) of current year	D	¶6-262
Losses on isolated business transactions	D	¶16-010
Losses: previous years	D	¶3-060, ¶16-880
Losses (foreign)	D	¶21-800
Losses (trust) of previous years	D	¶6-080, ¶6-262
Losses through theft or misappropriation	D	¶16-590
Losses, transferred from group company	D	¶3-090
Low-cost items	D	¶16-153, ¶17-810
Luxury car lease expenses	D	¶17-220
Luxury car lease notional loan principal	ND	¶17-220
Mains electricity connection	D	¶16-820
Maintenance payments	ND	¶10-855
Management expenses, investor	D	¶16-660
Meal costs	ND	¶16-175
Mining expenditure	D	¶19-000
Modernisation of premises or plant	ND	¶16-700
Mortgage discharge expenses	D	¶16-800
Motor vehicle dealers: warranty repair costs	D	¶16-040
Municipal rates on business premises	D	¶16-870
National Disability Insurance Scheme expenditure	ND	¶16-107
Natural disasters recovery expenses	D	¶44-130
Net capital loss	ND	¶11-040
Newspapers and magazines	D	¶16-440, ¶16-660
Overtime meal allowance expenses	D	¶16-210
Parking fees	D	¶16-310
Partner's salary	ND	¶5-090
Partnership, interest on loans	ND	¶5-070
Partnership, share of net losses	D	¶5-110
Patent, design, copyright registration costs	D	¶17-015
Penalties and fines	ND	¶16-845
Penalty tax	ND	¶16-845, ¶16-850
Petroleum resource rent tax	D	¶19-003
Plant demolition costs	ND	¶16-060
Plant (installed), cost of bringing to full operation	D	¶16-060, ¶17-100

Item	Deductible (D)/Non-deductible (ND)	Source
Political parties, contributions and gifts by non-business individuals	D	¶16-950, ¶16-170
Political parties, contributions by business	ND	¶16-152
Primary producers:		
Agistment fees	D	
Breeding service fees	D	
Depreciation	D	¶17-000
Droving expenses	D	
Electricity connection costs	D	¶16-820
Farm management deposits	D	¶18-295
Fencing assets (primary production)	D	¶18-090; ¶18-100
Fertiliser	D	
Fodder storage	D	¶18-085
Food for employees	D	
Grapevine establishment costs	D	¶18-070
Hire of farm implements	D	
Horticultural plantation establishment	D	¶18-070
Insecticides, weedkillers, rabbit fumigant	D	
Insurance premiums	D	
Landcare expenditure	D	¶18-100
Lease preparation expenses	D	¶16-640, ¶16-650
Low-cost items	D	¶16-153, ¶17-810
Mains electricity connections	D	¶16-820
Marketing and delivery expenses	D	
Motor vehicle expenses	D	¶16-310
Newspaper (rural) expenses	D	
Payment to co-ops for business services	D	
Payroll tax	D	¶16-858
Power, fuel, light	D	
Printing, stationery	D	
Rates and land taxes	D	¶16-870
Rent on farm property	D	
Rent on residence used by employees	D	
Repairs	D	¶16-700
Salaries and wages	D	
Seeds	D	
Shearing expenses	D	
Subscriptions to producers' organisations	D	¶16-430
Telephone expenses in business	D	

Item	Deductible (D)/Non-deductible (ND)	Source
Telephone line expenses	D	¶18-060
Timber felling deduction	D	¶18-120
Vaccination against Q fever	D	¶16-175
Veterinary fees	D	
Water facility expenditure	D	¶18-080
Wool levy	D	
Workers compensation premiums	D	
Private or domestic expenditure	ND	¶16-010
Professional journals: subscriptions	D	¶16-440
Professional qualifications	D	¶16-450
Project infrastructure costs	D	¶19-050
Promissory notes, discount factor	D	¶23-330
Protective clothing	D	¶16-180
Provisions and reserves	ND	¶16-040
Relocation expenses incurred by employee	ND	¶16-200
Relocation expenses incurred by employer	D	¶16-152
Rent collection, commission on	D	¶16-650
Rent for business premises	D	¶16-640
Rent referable to home office (business)	D	¶16-480
Repair costs under warranty	D	¶16-700
Repairs to family residence	ND	¶16-700
Repairs to income-producing property	D	¶16-700
Repayments of travel agents' commission	D	¶16-152
Repayments from illegal activities	ND	¶16-010
R&D expenses (notional deductions only)	ND	¶17-420, ¶20-150
Reserves and provisions	ND	¶9-120, ¶16-040
Restrictive covenants	ND	¶16-540
Retiring allowances	D	¶16-540
Salaries paid in business	D	¶16-520
Salaries (excessive remuneration to relatives or associated persons)	ND	¶16-530
Salaries (undeclared cash in hand wages)	ND	¶16-520
Self-education expenses	D	¶16-450
Self-insurers' provisions for workers compensation	D	¶16-040
Service fees	D	¶16-070
Shortfall interest charge	D	¶16-850
Sickness/accident premiums	D	¶16-560
Software expenses	D	¶16-725
Solicitor disbursements	D	¶9-100, ¶16-152

Item	Deductible (D)/Non-deductible (ND)	Source
Spare parts	D	¶16-730
Sponsorship fees	D	¶16-152
Start-up costs	D	¶16-156
Structural improvements (post-26.2.92)	D	¶20-470
Student financial supplement scheme: debt repayments	ND	¶16-452
Subvention payments	ND	¶3-090
Superannuation contributions:		
By employer	D	¶13-710, ¶16-575
By individuals including self-employed persons and employees	D	¶13-730, ¶16-575
Re-contribution under First Home Super Saver Scheme	ND	¶13-790
Downsizer contributions	ND	¶13-795
Superannuation funds expenses	D	¶13-150, ¶13-220, ¶13-870
Superannuation guarantee charge	ND	¶16-858
Superannuation supervisory levy	D	¶13-870
Superannuation trust deed, amendments	ND	¶13-150
Takeover defence costs	D	¶16-156
Tax advice costs	D	¶16-850
Tax agents' fees	D	¶16-850
Tax return lodgment costs	D	¶16-850
Technical qualifications	D	¶16-450
Telephone expenses if work-related	D	¶16-400
Telephone lines on primary production land	D	¶18-060
Telephone ''silent'' number fee	ND	¶16-400
Tender costs	D	¶16-152
Timber depletion	D	¶18-120
Tools, depreciation and cost of transporting and insuring	D	¶16-170
Trade qualification	ND	¶16-450
Trade union dues	D	¶16-430
Trading stock	D	¶16-040
Trading stock taken to new premises	D	¶16-060
Travel costs of accompanying relative	ND	¶16-280
Travel (relocation) costs paid by employer	D	¶16-152
Travel expenses:		
commuting to and from work	ND	¶16-220, ¶16-230
in search of employment	ND	¶16-200
spouse accompanying taxpayer on business trip	ND	¶16-280
in connection with residential investment property	ND	¶16-650

Item	Deductible (D)/Non-deductible (ND)	Source
related to business	D	¶16-220
Traveller accommodation buildings	D	¶20-470
Trees, carbon sink forests	D	¶19-120
Trees, purchased in immature forest or plantation and sold standing	D	¶18-120
Uniforms, special clothing for employees	D	¶16-180
Union officials' election fund levies	ND	¶16-430
Vaccinations	ND	¶16-175
Volunteer worker's expenses	ND	¶16-010
Water facilities	D	¶18-080
Water rates on business premises	D	¶16-870
Website maintenance or modifications	D	¶16-725
Work clothes, suitable for use outside work	ND	¶16-180
Workers compensation repayments	ND	¶16-160
Work in progress payment	D	¶16-158

* *Certain capital expenses qualify for a write-off (¶16-156).*

¶16-010 General allowable deductions

The general deduction provision in ITAA97 s 8-1 allows a deduction for a loss or outgoing *to the extent* it is:

(1) incurred in gaining or producing the taxpayer's assessable income (the ''first limb''), or

(2) necessarily incurred in carrying on a business for the purpose of gaining or producing the taxpayer's assessable income (the ''second limb'').

However, even if the first or second limb is satisfied, a deduction is not permitted under s 8-1 *to the extent* the loss or outgoing is:

(1) capital, or of a capital nature

(2) private or domestic in nature

(3) incurred in gaining or producing the taxpayer's exempt income or non-assessable non-exempt (NANE) income, or

(4) otherwise prevented from being deducted by a specific provision of the ITAA97 or ITAA36.

This means that a particular item of expenditure may have to be apportioned into its deductible and non-deductible components, eg where expenditure is incurred in deriving both assessable income and exempt income (¶16-070) or where travel expenses are incurred partly for assessable income-producing purposes and partly for private purposes (¶16-290; eg an employee's relocation expenses in *Waters*). In this context, assessable income includes employment, business, royalty and other types of income. However, the inclusion in assessable income of a net capital gain (¶11-030) does not give rise to an allowable deduction (ITAA36 s 51AAA: eg IT 2589; TD 2004/1).

The anti-avoidance provisions and the substantiation provisions are examples of specific provisions that can prevent expenses from being deductible (¶16-110, ¶16-210, ¶16-300, ¶16-320).

The term ''outgoing'' encompasses all types of expenditure, while the term ''loss'' ensures that losses where no payment is involved (eg theft) and involuntary payments are potentially covered. A net amount (eg the excess of interest expenses on borrowings to fund an asset over the income derived from the asset) cannot be a loss or outgoing unless, if the net amount were instead a profit, such net amount would be income according to ordinary concepts (ID 2012/91).

To be deductible in a particular year, a loss or outgoing must generally have been incurred in that year. The principles to be applied in determining when a loss or outgoing is incurred are discussed at ¶16-040. The amount of the deduction is the nominal value of the loss or outgoing at the time it is incurred and not its ''actual'' or ''present'' value (*Burrill*; *Mercantile Mutual Insurance*; *City Link*). A legislative exception to this rule applies in the case of insurance companies (¶16-040).

Where a taxpayer has claimed a deduction for a loss arising from the realisation of an asset that is also a CGT asset, the reduced cost base of the asset is reduced by the amount of the deduction (¶11-560). An item of expenditure should either be deductible or included in the cost base of a CGT asset, but not both (TD 2019/D11).

While barter and countertrade transactions give rise to deductions to the same extent as other cash or credit transactions, amounts paid in such transactions need to reflect the real commercial value of the goods or services being purchased (IT 2668). The ATO has published fact sheets about bartering generally and record keeping for barter transactions.

Losses or outgoings of capital or of a capital nature

Capital losses or outgoings and losses or outgoings of a capital nature, even though they are incurred in the course of producing assessable income, are not deductible under s 8-1. For example, the cost of buildings, alterations and additions to buildings, of shares not held for resale and of other capital assets is a capital outgoing. The dividing line between capital and revenue expenses is often difficult to draw (¶16-060).

However, certain capital costs may be deductible either outright or by way of depreciation or amortisation under other specific provisions of the tax law. Other capital costs, such as the costs of establishing a business structure, may also be deductible under special ''blackhole'' expenditure provisions (¶16-156). As to the treatment of capital losses for the purposes of the CGT provisions, see ¶11-040.

"Essential character" test

The first limb of s 8-1 is available to all taxpayers, whether in business or not. The second limb applies only where the taxpayer is carrying on a business (¶16-015, ¶10-105). The 2 limbs are not mutually exclusive and a business expense is frequently deductible under either.

To be deductible under the first limb, a loss or outgoing must be incidental and relevant to gaining or producing assessable income (*Ronpibon Tin NL*). To be deductible under the second limb, a loss or outgoing must be part of the cost of trading operations to produce income (*John Fairfax & Sons*). The expenditure must have the character of a working or operating expense of the business or be an essential part of the cost of its business operations (TR 2004/2).

These statements are reflected in the ''essential character'' test, namely, that to be deductible under the section a loss or outgoing must have the essential character of a business or income-producing expense (*Lunney*; *Fletcher*). In practical terms, that test is not always helpful and it is ultimately a question of fact and degree whether a particular loss or outgoing is deductible.

Relevance of taxpayer's purpose

The taxpayer's subjective purpose in incurring a loss or outgoing is normally irrelevant in the case of a voluntary loss or outgoing, particularly where the outgoing gives rise to the receipt of a larger amount of assessable income. However, the taxpayer's and the taxpayer's advisers' intentions may be relevant, and in some cases the decisive factor, if no income is produced or the relevant assessable income is less than the amount of the outgoing (*Magna Alloys & Research*), or if the connection between the loss or outgoing and the production of income is not objectively clear (*Fletcher*; IT 2606; TR 95/33).

If, after weighing all the circumstances in a commonsense and practical manner, including the direct and indirect objectives and advantages, it can be concluded that the expenditure is genuinely used in an assessable income-producing activity, the Commissioner will accept that a deduction is allowable. If it is concluded that the disproportion between the outgoing and the relevant assessable income is essentially to be explained by reference to the independent pursuit of some other objective (eg to derive exempt income or obtain a tax deduction), then the outgoing must be apportioned between the pursuit of assessable income and the other objective (TR 95/33).

The taxpayer's purpose in incurring the loss or outgoing is irrelevant where it is incurred involuntarily, eg business takings stolen (*Charles Moore & Co (WA)*). In any event, it seems from *Fletcher's case* that an outgoing will at least be deductible to the extent of any income which is derived, ie to the extent necessary to produce a nil result for taxation purposes. Ultimately, the Commissioner believes that the method of apportionment must be "fair and reasonable" (TR 95/33).

A deduction is not necessarily disallowed because it is part of a tax minimisation scheme; see, for example, cases involving deductions for interest payments (¶16-740). Expenditure may be deductible so long as, objectively, the outgoing is reasonably capable of being seen as directed towards the gaining of assessable income (and was so seen by the taxpayer), despite the taxpayer's subjective purpose of reducing tax (*Service*; *Cooke*). This is subject, of course, to the application of the general anti-avoidance provisions (¶30-000).

▶ Planning points

A high rate taxpayer can pay deductible amounts to an associated low rate taxpayer as a way of diverting income (eg secretarial fees: ¶16-170). However the effect of *Fletcher's case* may be to limit the use of such planning methods to situations where the payment to the low rate taxpayer is commercially justified and the overall tax savings are merely an incidental benefit. In addition, specific anti-avoidance provisions (¶16-045, ¶16-110) may apply.

Employing family members is another method for diverting income (eg the spouse or older children may act as receptionists, gardeners, secretaries etc) subject to the rules discussed at ¶16-530. If family members are employed, consider the effect on other forms of government assistance (eg family assistance), keep records of the duties performed by the family employee, and have regard to the market rates for work of a similar type. In determining the salary payable to a low rate taxpayer by a family company, consider the deemed dividend provisions (¶4-220). Where the taxpayer is a child under the age of 18, the special tax rate for minors might apply (¶2-160).

Employee benefit trust arrangements

Employer contributions to employee benefit trusts, which were purportedly made to retain employees, but which had significant elements of tax minimisation, were held not to be deductible (*Essenbourne*; *Kajewski*; *Cajkusic*; *Cameron Brae*; *Benstead Services*; *Wensemius*: ¶30-170). On the other hand, subject to the anti-avoidance rules: ¶30-160, a deduction was available for payments made to an Employee Welfare Fund under a contractual obligation arising out of the employment agreements (*Trail Bros*), and to a redundancy fund (CR 2012/28). For the FBT implications of such payments, see ¶35-080.

The Commissioner's view is that irrevocable cash contributions made by an employer to an employee benefit trust primarily to enable remuneration benefits to be directly provided to employees within a relatively short period are deductible. There must be a reasonable expectation that the business will benefit via an improvement in employee performance, morale, efficiency and loyalty, and importantly, the contribution must not be made for the benefit of an owner, controller or shareholder. The contribution is not deductible to the extent it secures a capital advantage, unless such an advantage is trifling. The amount of the deduction may need to be spread over an "eligible service period" under the prepayment rules (¶16-045) unless the contribution is an amount paid in satisfaction of a liability arising under a contract of service between the employer and the employee (TR 2018/7; ¶16-060, ¶16-070).

Losses from isolated transactions

A loss from an isolated transaction is generally deductible where: (a) in entering into the transaction, the taxpayer intended or expected to derive a profit that would have been assessable income; and (b) the transaction was entered into, and the loss was made, in the course of carrying on a business or in carrying out a business operation or commercial transaction (TR 92/4; *Myer Emporium*: ¶10-112). Such losses are deductible on completion of the transaction rather than in the year in which the outgoings are incurred (*Commercial and General Acceptance*). In *Visy*, deductions for losses incurred relating to events that culminated in the disposal of shares by 3 companies in the same corporate group were permitted as the taxpayers had a relevant profit-making intention in entering into the isolated transactions. A senior business executive with a "sophisticated" profit-making strategy was allowed a deduction for losses on shares in a company that went into administration; the profit-making intention and the systematic acquisition of shares by a business person, using his business knowledge and experience reinforced the business or commercial nature of the transaction (*Greig*). In *Elvy*, a loss incurred by a taxpayer resulting from an investment in a company running a local basketball team was not deductible because the arrangement lacked commerciality and there was no objective basis for inferring that the taxpayer had profit-making intentions.

Connection with income of the taxpayer

A loss or outgoing need not actually produce assessable income to give rise to a deduction, so long as it would be expected to produce assessable income. In any event, it is the assessable income of the person who incurred the loss or outgoing that is relevant. Thus, where a company takes out a loan, the fact that an associated company will derive assessable income as a result is not of itself sufficient to allow a deduction for the interest on the borrowed moneys (*Hooker Rex*).

In determining whether assessable income is produced, the court may look beyond the immediate transaction in which the outgoing was incurred. For example, in *Total Holdings* a deduction was allowed for money that was on-lent interest-free to a subsidiary. Even though the loan was interest-free, it was intended to render the subsidiary more profitable, thus ensuring the possibility of assessable dividends being derived by the parent company. It has also been held that rent paid in respect of plant leased by a parent company, but used rent-free by its subsidiaries, was deductible to the parent company (*EA Marr & Sons (Sales)*). Although the Commissioner accepts that the decision in *Total Holdings* is correct and will allow a deduction in a substantially similar case (IT 2606), both that decision and the *Marr* decision should not be taken too far. In the case of an intermediate holding company, it is also necessary to consider whether the taxpayer is carrying on a business (*Spassked*).

For example, a taxpayer was not allowed a deduction for interest on a loan taken out to alleviate the indebtedness of his company because there was no prospect of the company reaching profitability and the taxpayer deriving income from it (*Case 48/97*). See also *Case 51/97*; *Daff* and *Riha*. See ¶16-152 for the deductibility of payments made under guarantees, including guarantees in respect of subsidiaries. See also CR 2009/40 (Medicare Teen Dental Plan payments). A specific rule may deny a deduction for expenses related to vacant land where there is no prospect of deriving income (¶16-650).

Connection with income of earlier or later years

It is not necessary that the expenditure in question should produce assessable income in the same year in which the expenditure is incurred, particularly in the case of a continuing enterprise or activity; it may have been relevant to income of an earlier or a later year or may have been expedient to reduce current or future expenses (¶16-740). Further, the courts have held that a revenue loss (eg a bad debt) or outgoing (eg damages) arising out of an income-earning activity of a prior year may be deductible in a subsequent year even though no continuing business is then being carried on, provided the occasion of the business loss or outgoing is found in the business operations directed towards the gaining or producing of assessable income generally (*AGC (Advances)*; *Placer Pacific Management*; *Case 5/95*; ID 2002/1092). However, expenditure must not have been incurred at a ''point too soon'' (¶16-154, ¶16-200; ID 2004/375).

This principle has been applied to guarantee payments (*Evenden*), legal expenses (¶16-840), lease expenses (ID 2002/1091) and interest (¶16-740) incurred after the cessation of the business.

Commercial and accountancy practice

Commercial and accountancy practice may assist in ascertaining the true nature of an outgoing as a step towards determining whether it answers the test laid down by s 8-1, but it cannot be substituted for that test. Accounting principles and practice are particularly relevant in determining the year to which an incurred loss or outgoing is properly referable (¶16-040).

Connection required with assessable income

No deduction is available in the following circumstances because the expenditure is not incurred in gaining assessable income:

- expenditure relating to voluntary work (*Case Z16*; TR 2005/13; CR 2010/5; ATO fact sheet: *Australian Government funded volunteers abroad*) or to a hobby or pastime such as football or tennis refereeing (CR 2009/42; CR 2009/55; CR 2011/65; CR 2011/103; CR 2012/23; CR 2012/35)
- personal care payments under the NSW Lifetime Care and Support Scheme (CR 2011/85)
- joining fees or annual fees paid for a consumer loyalty program (except when paid by an employer as a cost of employing a person or when forming part of a business activity) (TD 1999/35)
- the value of an airline ticket acquired by redeeming privately accrued consumer loyalty points (ID 2004/847)
- management fees debited to a retiree's allocated pension account (ID 2004/968)
- interest and bank charges incurred for the (apparent) assumption of a debt owed by an associated company to a foreign bank, in exchange for non-interest bearing receivables from associated companies (*Fitzroy Services*; ¶16-740)
- where payment was made on behalf of another person on the basis that the taxpayer would be reimbursed by that other person (*Sheil*)
- contributions made by a bankrupt taxpayer towards the bankrupt estate (*Case 8/99*)

- where a taxpayer was issued with a PAYG director penalty notice in respect of his paid role as a (former) director of a liquidated company which ultimately resulted in legal and accounting expenses being incurred in bankruptcy annulment and proof of debt proceedings (*Healy*)
- amounts forfeited to the Commonwealth under the *Proceeds of Crime Act 1987* (TR 93/25). Losses and outgoings incurred in relation to illegal activities are not deductible (¶16-105) nor are amounts obtained from illegal activities that are later repaid or recovered for whatever reason (however, such amounts may be excluded from the assessable income of the income year in which they were derived) (TR 93/25)
- loan repayments made by a solicitor to his client in circumstances where the solicitor had invested the borrowed money on his client's behalf (*Thorpe*)
- amounts contributed to an offshore "employee welfare fund" (*Allan J Heasman Pty Ltd*)
- costs incurred by a strata corporation in deriving its mutual receipts are not deductible because such receipts (eg proprietor contributions to an administrative or sinking fund) are not assessable income (¶3-810; TR 2015/3).

Natural disaster recovery expenses

For the deductibility of natural disaster recovery expenses, see the ATO guidance at *Rental properties and business premises after a disaster* (¶44-130).

[FITR ¶31-050, ¶31-100, ¶31-110, ¶31-370, ¶31-400, ¶31-480, ¶31-500, ¶31-720; FTR ¶23-003]

¶16-015 Expenses incurred in carrying on a business

Expenses necessarily incurred in carrying on a business are deductible under ITAA97 s 8-1 (¶16-010). For a discussion of whether a business is being carried on, see ¶10-105; for a "primary production business", see ¶18-020 and for a business of betting or gambling, see ¶10-430. Even where a taxpayer is considered to be carrying on a business, losses from the business cannot be claimed against other income unless the tests outlined at ¶16-020 are satisfied.

For a discussion of whether particular items of business expenditure are deductible, see ¶16-152. See also the checklist at ¶16-005.

For further details of the Commissioner's views, see TR 2005/1 (business as a professional artist) and TR 2008/2 (horse industry). See also *Gilbert* (motorcycle sidecar racing); *Block* (horse and sheep breeding); *Kennedy* (film-making business); *Phippen* and *Hattrick* (boat-chartering business: ¶16-420); *Peerless Marine* (boat-building); *Pedley* and *Case 4/2005* (professional artist); *Leggett* (financial services franchise); *Hartley* (share trading); and *Case 1/2014* (rental properties).

Gifts provided by a business taxpayer to current or former clients for the purpose of generating future assessable income are deductible, unless they constitute the provision of entertainment (¶16-390) or are bribes to a foreign or public official (¶16-152): TD 2016/14.

Outgoing "necessarily incurred"

The following principles apply in determining whether an outgoing is necessarily incurred in carrying on a business to produce assessable income.

- The word "necessarily" does not mean that the outgoing must be unavoidable or logically necessary. What it means is that the outgoing must be "clearly appropriate or adapted for" the ends of the business. For practical purposes, it is for the person carrying on the business to be the judge of what outgoings are necessarily to be incurred. It is not for the Commissioner to instruct a taxpayer as to the nature and extent or manner of conduct of his or her business activities (*Tweddle*).

- Where the outgoing is voluntary, the controlling factor is that objectively the outgoing must be reasonably capable of being seen as desirable or appropriate from the point of view of the pursuit of the business ends of the business (*Magna Alloys & Research*). Where there is no obvious commercial connection between the loss or outgoing and the carrying on of the taxpayer's business, or where the expenditure did not achieve its intended result, it may be necessary to have regard to the taxpayer's subjective purpose (TR 95/33).
- In many cases, the legitimate ends of a business will encompass what is in the personal interests of the directors and employees. The fact that the dominant motive in incurring an expense is to provide a benefit to directors does not, of itself, prevent the outgoing from being necessarily incurred in carrying on the taxpayer's business (*Magna Alloys & Research*).
- The economic results achieved by a transaction may be examined to cast some light on whether the outgoings are capable of being regarded as desirable or appropriate from the point of view of the business ends of the business (*Gwynvill Properties*).
- If trading has commenced and the activities reveal a discernible trading pattern, the motive for undertaking the activities or a particular transaction cannot serve to characterise the person engaged in those activities as a non-trader or as a non-trader in relation to the particular transaction (*John*).
- Expenses associated with the purchase or establishment of a business are generally incurred at a point too soon to be regarded as being deductible business expenses (¶16-154). However, certain capital expenses involved in establishing a business may qualify for a write-off (¶16-156).

Personal services businesses

Where the taxpayer is rendering personal services, special tests apply in determining whether a business is being carried on. Where these tests are not satisfied, there are restrictions placed on the types of deduction that can be claimed (¶30-620).

[FITR ¶31-520, ¶31-580, ¶766-550]

¶16-020 Limit on losses from non-commercial business activities

Special measures apply to prevent a loss from a non-commercial *business* activity carried on by an individual taxpayer (alone, or in a general law partnership) being offset against other assessable income in the year in which the loss is incurred (ITAA97 Div 35). The measures also apply to certain pre-business and post-business capital expenditure that is otherwise deductible under s 40-880 (see below).

Under these measures, a loss cannot be offset against other income in the year in which it arises (ie the loss is quarantined). Instead, the loss may be carried forward and offset against assessable income from the business in the next year that the business is carried on (future year). If a loss also arises in the future year, the loss may be offset against other income if one of 4 tests is satisfied, or the Commissioner exercises his discretion, or an exception applies (see below). Additional restrictions may apply if the taxpayer has unutilised net exempt income or becomes bankrupt (see below). For a general discussion of losses, see ¶16-880.

In quantifying a non-commercial loss (under s 35-10(2)), assessable income must be "from" the business activity and amounts that could otherwise be deducted must be "attributable to" the business activity. For example, periodic partial disability payments received under an income protection insurance policy were not "from" a taxpayer's business activity as a financial planner (*Watson*). Also, assessable income may arise when a farm management deposit is withdrawn. Where the deposit was funded by the primary production business activity, and the withdrawal occurs while the same business activity is conducted, then the assessable income will be "from" the business activity (TR 2001/14).

Tests for deductibility

A taxpayer can deduct a loss from a non-commercial activity against other income if their "adjusted taxable income" for the income year is less than $250,000 and one of the 4 tests below is satisfied for the year. If one of the 4 tests is not satisfied, such taxpayers may offset a non-commercial loss against other assessable income if the Commissioner's discretion is exercised or an exception applies for the year.

In comparison, if a taxpayer has an adjusted taxable income of $250,000 or more for an income year, then any loss from a non-commercial activity is quarantined (ITAA97 s 35-10), unless the Commissioner exercises the discretion or an exception applies for the year.

"Adjusted taxable income" for an income year is the sum of taxable income (disregarding any of the taxpayer's deductible non-commercial losses for the year), reportable fringe benefits, reportable superannuation contributions and total net investment losses for the year (s 35-10(2E)). When applying the FBT otherwise deductible rule, an employee's adjusted taxable income is increased by third party expenditure that is reimbursed to the employee pursuant to a salary sacrifice arrangement (where the expenditure is notionally subject to Div 35) (TD 2013/20; TR 2013/6; ¶35-360).

The 4 tests are as follows:

1. *Assessable income test:* the assessable income (including capital gains) for that year from the activity must be at least $20,000 (ITAA97 s 35-30). If the business activity started or ceased during the year, this test is based on the taxpayer's "reasonable estimate" of the amount that would have been the assessable income if the activity had been carried on for the whole year. This may involve consideration of factors such as the cyclical nature of the business, any orders received or forward contracts, and industry trends. If a taxpayer lodges their return on the basis of a correctly made reasonable estimate, there is nothing in the ITAA 97 that allows the taxpayer to later revoke the estimate (TR 2001/14).

2. *Profits test:* the particular activity must have resulted in taxable profit in at least 3 out of the last 5 income years, including the current year. Deferred non-commercial loss deductions, and deferred s 40-880 blackhole expense deductions related to a period when the business was proposed to be carried on, are disregarded when calculating the taxable profit. In the case of a partnership, an individual partner's share of the assessable income and deductions of a general law partnership is included when calculating a profit, in addition to any assessable income and deductions of the individual attributable to the partnership activity outside the partnership (ITAA97 s 35-35). The test does not require the business activity to be carried on for 5 years (eg a profit in 3 out of 4 years is sufficient). Taxable profits made by a previous owner before a change of ownership can be counted in some circumstances (TR 2001/14).

3. *Real property test:* the total reduced cost bases of real property or interests in real property used on a continuing basis in carrying on the activity (other than privately used dwellings and tenant's fixtures) must be at least $500,000 (ITAA97 s 35-40). Real property or interests in real property may be valued at the greater of the reduced cost base or market value, or

4. *Other assets test:* the total value of other assets (other than motor vehicles) used on a continuing basis in the activity must be at least $100,000 (ITAA97 s 35-45). This comprises the written down value of depreciated assets, the tax value of trading stock and leased assets, and the reduced cost base of trade marks, patents, copyrights and similar rights.

▶ Planning point

The assessable income test includes balancing adjustments from the sale of assets in the normal course of business (where the small business entity depreciation rules are not applied). For example an individual in business with $18,000 of sales who realises a $2,500 balancing adjustment gain from the sale of a business motor vehicle will satisfy the $20,000 threshold for the assessable income test (see CCH *Tax Week* at ¶580 (2012)).

Where a business activity is carried on by an individual in partnership with an entity, only that part which is attributable to the interests of the *individuals* in the partnership is taken into account for the purposes of the assessable income test, the real property test and other assets test. Further, assessable income and assets of an individual partner on his/her own account, outside the partnership, are also taken into account by that partner in considering these tests (ITAA97 s 35-25).

In applying the rules, business activities of a similar kind *may* be grouped together (s 35-10). Such business activities need not be identical (TR 2001/14). The application of these rules to partnerships is discussed in TR 2003/3.

Commissioner's discretion

A taxpayer may apply in the approved form for an exercise of the Commissioner's discretion to allow a non-commercial loss to be offset against other assessable income (ITAA97 s 35-55). The approved form is a private ruling application, see ¶24-560 and the ATO website at *Private ruling form (non-commercial losses)*. For guidelines on the exercise of the Commissioner's discretion, see TR 2007/6 and the ATO website at *Non-commercial losses: Commissioner's discretion*.

The Commissioner may exercise the discretion for one or more income years (excluded year(s)), if it would be unreasonable not to do so in any of the following 3 situations.

1. Special circumstances

The discretion is available if the business activity is affected by ''special circumstances'' outside the control of the taxpayer (eg drought, flood, bushfire or other natural disasters such as earthquakes, pest plagues, hailstorms or diseases destroying live stock or crops). It is intended to provide for business activities that would have satisfied one of the 4 tests (see above) had the special circumstances not occurred.

For taxpayers with adjusted taxable incomes greater than or equal to $250,000 in an income year, the ATO's view is that the special circumstances discretion may be available if the taxpayer can prove, on the balance of probabilities, that the business activity would have produced a taxable income if the special circumstances had not occurred (TR 2007/6, paras 13A and 41D). This ''principle'' is supported by the AAT's reasons in *Heaney*.

In comparison, the AAT considered that the discretion should be exercised in favour of the taxpayer in *Bentivoglio* because his olive growing and production business was affected by bug infestations, adverse weather events, and other special circumstances outside his control. The AAT said that it often assists taxpayers with adjusted taxable incomes of $250,000 or more to prove that their business activity would have produced a taxable income had the special circumstances not occurred. However, the AAT held that this was only a relevant consideration and not a requirement for the favourable exercise of the discretion for such taxpayers, and thereby disagreed with the AAT's view in *Heaney*. Despite this, the ATO prefers the AAT's view in *Heaney* on this point and so it does not intend to amend TR 2007/6 (*Decision Impact Statement*: *Bentivoglio*).

The Commissioner also has a discretion to allow a deduction for blackhole expenditure (¶16-156) if it is unreasonable to defer a deduction because special circumstances have prevented a proposed business activity from starting (s 35-55(2)).

For examples of when the Commissioner refused to exercise the discretion under the special circumstances limb, see *Delandro*; and *Delacy*.

2. Business expected to be commercial — adjusted taxable income < $250,000

The discretion is available where: (i) the taxpayer's adjusted taxable income is less than $250,000 for the most recent income year before an application is made; (ii) the business activity has started to be carried on; (iii) none of the 4 tests is satisfied for the excluded years because of the nature of the activity; and (iv) for the excluded years, there is an objective expectation (based on evidence from appropriate independent sources, if available) that the activity will either meet one of the 4 tests or will produce a taxable income for an income year within a period that is commercially viable for the industry concerned. This may apply, for example, where there is necessarily a long lead-up time between the commencement of the activity and the production of assessable income. The discretion is available even though losses are made in a year after one of the tests has already been met or taxable income produced (eg where there has been a thinning operation in a viable forestry plantation).

As noted in condition (iii) above, the business activity must not have satisfied any of the 4 tests ''because of its nature'' (ie having regard to some inherent feature in the activity rather than to the peculiar way in which the taxpayer runs it) (*Eskandari*; *Kennedy*; *Hall*; *Case 1/2013*). In *Case 13/2011*, the making of losses over 2 decades was not ''in the nature of'' a beef cattle production activity. Instead, the losses were due to the taxpayer's idiosyncratic, managerial choices, and the discretion was not exercised in the taxpayer's favour.

3. Business expected to be commercial — adjusted taxable income ≥ $250,000

The discretion is also available where: (i) the taxpayer's adjusted taxable income is $250,000 or more for the most recent income year before an application is made; (ii) the business activity has started to be carried on; (iii) a taxable income from the business activity will not be produced for the excluded years because of the nature of the activity; and (iv) for the excluded years, there is an objective expectation (based on evidence from appropriate independent sources, if available) that the activity will produce a taxable income for an income year within a period that is commercially viable for the industry concerned. Note that a taxpayer can not lengthen the commercial viability period for their industry based on circumstances that are special to them (*Bentivoglio*).

The discretion was not exercised in the following cases involving taxpayers with adjusted taxable incomes greater than $250,000 because:

- the losses incurred were attributed to the taxpayer's decision to take a gradual approach to planting vines which, although commercially prudent and common practice, was not due to the nature of the taxpayer's vineyard business (*Case 1/2013*)
- there was nothing in the nature of the taxpayer's cattle stud business that prevented it from becoming profitable in the period under review, including the taxpayer's debt financing costs which were normally associated with such businesses (*Hefner*)
- the taxpayer's beef production activity would not have produced taxable income within a commercially viable period for the industry because the taxpayer had limited financial resources available to service his high debt level. There was also no evidence that the taxpayer had the necessary resources to substantially increase his stock of cattle to generate a taxable income from the activity without incurring further borrowing (*Heaney*).

The Commissioner is prepared to exercise the discretion in relation to the software timber project in PR 2014/18, provided certain conditions are satisfied. Also see PR 2015/5 to PR 2015/7.

Review of the Commissioner's discretion

If the Commissioner makes the ruling, the details of the scheme must be set out in the body of the ruling. A taxpayer can object if dissatisfied with the ruling, or if the Commissioner declines to make the ruling (¶24-560). Any review by the Federal Court or AAT must be based on the scheme identified by the Commissioner in the ruling (*McMahon*; *Case 4/2015*). For example, in *Case 7/2012*, the AAT did not allow additional evidence to be admitted which would have resulted in a material change to the description of the scheme contained in the private ruling. The result was that the taxpayer could not offset losses from his cattle breeding activities against other income.

Exceptions

The prohibition against claiming losses from non-commercial business activities against other income does *not* apply to:

- an individual carrying on a primary production business (¶18-020) or a professional arts business (ie as author of a literary, dramatic, musical or artistic work, or performing artist or production associate: ¶2-142; *Farnan*) if the income from other sources (excluding net capital gains) is less than $40,000 (s 35-10). For the meaning of ''carrying on a professional arts business'', see TR 2005/1 (¶16-015).
- activities that do not constitute a business (eg a hobby, or the receipt of income from passive investments such as rent from negatively geared property, dividends from shares and interest on infrastructure bonds, or where a business has ceased).

▶ Example — operation of the loss deferral rule

Matthew is employed as a software engineer. In his spare time, he conducts a small, internet marketing business. In Income Years 1 to 3, Matthew is required to defer losses from his marketing business under Div 35. Matthew passes the assessable income test in Income Year 4. The information below illustrates how Div 35 applies to Matthew's business.

Income Year	**Assessable income (1)**	**Deductions (2)**	**Deferred deduction from previous year (3)**	**Total current year deductions (4) [ie (2) + (3)]**	**Current year taxable profit/ (loss) (1) – (4)**	**Deferred deduction for current year**
1	$5,000	$7,000	Nil	$7,000	($2,000)	$2,000
2	$10,000	$13,000	$2,000	$15,000	($5,000)	$5,000
3	$9,000	$8,000	$5,000	$13,000	($4,000)	$4,000
4	$22,000	$19,000	$4,000	$23,000	($1,000)	Nil

The example shows that a deferred non-commercial loss from a prior year is absorbed into the current year calculation. This is different from the treatment of ordinary tax losses, which retain a connection to the loss year. Matthew's $1,000 loss for Year 4 can be offset against his other assessable income because he satisfies the assessable income test in Year 4.

Exempt income, bankruptcy

A loss from a non-commercial business activity that is to be deferred to the next year that the activity is carried on (future year), is reduced by the amount of any net exempt income derived in the current year that has not already been offset against ordinary losses in the year (unutilised net exempt income) (¶16-880). In the future year, if the taxpayer does not satisfy any of the Div 35 tests or exclusions, any deferred loss from the previous year that the activity was carried on must first be reduced by the taxpayer's unutilsed net exempt income for the future year. This reduction is made before any remaining deferred loss from the previous year is used as a deduction in the future year. Note that these conditions also apply if the taxpayer has an overall taxable profit from the business in the future year, and none of the Div 35 tests or exclusions are satisfied. If a non-commercial loss also arises in the future year, it is further reduced by any unutilised net exempt income that remains (ITAA97 s 35-15). These principles are illustrated in the following example.

▶ Example

Jane is employed as a sales assistant and also runs a mobile dog-washing business in her spare time. In Income Years 1 to 3, Jane is required to defer losses from her dog-washing business under Div 35. Jane passes the assessable income test in Income Year 4. The following information is relevant to calculating Jane's tax position under Div 35.

Income Year	Assessable income	Unutilised net exempt income	Deductions (excluding deferred deductions)	Deferred deduction for current year
1	$11,000	Nil	$16,000	$5,000
2	$9,000	$3,000	$8,000	$1,000
3	$2,000	$3,000	$8,000	$4,000
4	$23,000	$6,000	$26,000	Nil

In Year 2, the $5,000 deferred loss from Year 1 is reduced by the net exempt income in Year 2. The remaining $2,000 deferred loss from Year 1 is then added to the other Year 2 deductions ($8,000) to produce total deductions for Year 2 of $10,000. The result is that Jane has a deferred loss deduction for Year 2 of $1,000.

In Year 3, the $1,000 deferred loss from Year 2 is reduced to nil after it is applied against the net exempt income in Year 3. The $6,000 loss in Year 3 is then reduced by the $2,000 of remaining net exempt income in Year 3. The result is that Jane has a deferred loss deduction for Year 3 of $4,000.

In Year 4, both the deferred deduction from Year 3 and the Year 4 loss are not reduced by the net exempt income in Year 4 because Jane passes the assessable income test. Jane's total deductions in Year 4 are $30,000 ($26,000 + $4,000), and her $7,000 business loss in Year 4 is not deferred and can be offset against her other assessable income.

Where a taxpayer has a loss from a non-commercial business activity that has been carried forward and then becomes bankrupt, the loss incurred prior to the date of bankruptcy cannot be deducted after the date of bankruptcy (ITAA97 s 35-20).

Pre-business and post-business expenditures

The non-commercial loss provisions also apply to pre-business or post-business capital expenditure that is deductible under s 40-880 (¶16-156; TR 2011/6), unless one of the exceptions noted further above about primary production or professional arts businesses applies.

An individual cannot deduct s 40-880 capital expenditure incurred on a business they *propose* to carry on (either alone or in partnership) before the income year in which the business starts. Instead, the s 40-880 deduction is deferred and can only be claimed against assessable income from the business activity in the year the business commences (s 35-10(2B) to (2D)). This restriction also applies to the immediate deduction for small business from the 2015–16 income year for some proposed business expenses (under s 40-880(2A)) where the taxpayer is an individual. It also applies to deductions for capital costs incurred by individuals in connection with a business that another entity proposes to conduct (under s 40-880(4)). If the deduction is deferred to the commencement year and the business has a loss in that year, then the loss may be quarantined unless the Div 35 tests described further above allow the claim. However, an individual may apply for an exercise of the Commissioner's discretion to allow a s 40-880 deduction in an income year before the proposed business starts. The Commissioner may allow the s 40-880 deduction if special circumstances prevented the business from starting and it would be unreasonable to deny the deduction (s 35-55(2)).

Individuals (either alone or in partnership) can not deduct s 40-880 capital costs related to a *former* business unless an exception applies. The first exception is where the taxpayer had an adjusted taxable income below $250,000, and satisfied one of the 4 Div 35 tests set out further above, for the year the business ceased or an earlier year. The second is where the Commissioner exercised the discretion to allow the taxpayer to deduct a loss that would otherwise have been denied by Div 35, for the cessation year or an earlier year. The third is where the taxpayer satisfies the exclusion for primary production or professional arts business (s 35-10(2A)). The rules for former business expenses are modified if the taxpayer becomes bankrupt (see above; s 35-20).

▶ Examples

1. Nerida incurs $1,000 of capital expenditure during Year 1 for the purpose of establishing a supermarket business in Year 3. Assume the expenditure qualifies for a deduction over 5 years under s 40-880. Nerida cannot deduct the amounts arising from the pre-business expenditure prior to the business commencing, unless the Commissioner exercises the discretion. The $200 amounts that were otherwise deductible in each of Years 1 and 2 are quarantined and are claimed against the income from the supermarket in Year 3.

2. Josh incurs $1,000 in Year 1 for the purpose of establishing a website development business in Year 2. Apart from Div 35, assume Josh is entitled to s 40-880 deductions of $200 in each of Years 1 to 5. The business ceases at the end of Year 3. If the business did not pass any of the Div 35 tests and the Commissioner's discretion was not exercised, Josh cannot deduct any amount in Years 4 and 5.

[FITR ¶83-000]

Timing Issues

¶16-040 When is a loss or outgoing incurred?

To be deductible in a particular year, the expenditure must generally have been incurred in that year (ITAA97 s 8-1). Special rules apply to prepayments (¶16-045).

Taxpayers must be "definitively committed"

For a liability to have been incurred, it is not necessary that a disbursement has actually been made. If, in the relevant year, the taxpayer is definitively committed, or has completely subjected itself, to the expenditure, it will be deductible (*James Flood*; *New Zealand Flax*). A taxpayer can be said to be completely subjected to a liability, notwithstanding that the amount of the liability cannot be precisely determined, provided that it is capable of reasonable estimation. The amount of a liability is capable of reasonable estimation if it is capable of approximate calculation based on probabilities. If that approximation later proves incorrect, the necessary adjustments should be made in the income year the liability is actually paid.

In *Case 1/2012*, despite a lack of satisfactory evidence of payment, deductions were allowable because there was evidence that software licence fees had been incurred. In *Case S28* it was held that where a separate legal entity accepts a liability by recording it in its books of account, and shows the other party as creditor, it is "definitively committed" to the payment and has therefore incurred it.

A scriptwriter was denied a deduction for marketing fees owed to an overseas agent under an arrangement in which the agent agreed to deduct the fees from the proceeds of any subsequent sales (*Brown*). In *Kelly's Office Furniture*, deductions were denied for amounts described as "accrued expenses", management fees, and salary and wages, as the taxpayers failed to establish with sufficient evidence that they were "definitely committed" to the alleged expenses.

In *Sanctuary Lakes*, expenditure in respect of: (i) obligations to undertake development works; and (ii) obligations under planning and environmental legislation, that were associated with a residential resort, golf course and club house development were not incurred in the income year in question. This was because no liability or obligation to make the payments had come into existence under the relevant agreements.

The taxpayer in *Desalination Technology Pty Ltd* did not incur R&D expenditure because no obligation came into existence when invoices were rendered. This was because of contingencies attached to a running account to which the R&D expenditure was debited. The contingencies included that the taxpayer had funds and that it thought it was prudent to make repayments. Even if there was an obligation, the court held that it was so affected by these contingencies that the taxpayer was not definitely committed to the obligation. The Commissioner considers that the general anti-avoidance provisions (in ITAA36 Pt IVA) may apply to contrived invoicing arrangements like those in this case (*Decision Impact Statement*: *Desalination Technology*).

Interest expenses claimed as a deduction in *Sandbach* were not incurred. This was because the taxpayer was no longer definitely committed or completely subjected to any interest outgoings on entering into a settlement arrangement related to the relevant loans.

An amount provided as security to a bank to obtain a bank guarantee is not "incurred" until the amount is actually withdrawn (ID 2004/178).

However, a presently existing liability is not necessary where the taxpayer makes a purely voluntary payment or a prepayment (TR 94/26, outlining the Commissioner's views on the meaning of "incurred").

Liability may be defeasible

A taxpayer may completely subject itself to a liability, notwithstanding that the liability is defeasible. Thus, it has been held that royalties paid under protest for bauxite mined in a previous year were allowable deductions in calculating a company's income for that earlier year (*Commonwealth Aluminium Corporation*). Similarly, payroll tax was found to have been incurred in the year in which the wages were paid, even though the employer lodged no return and paid no payroll tax until a default assessment was issued some years later (*Layala Enterprises*: ¶16-858). An outgoing was incurred where the taxpayer was subject to an immediate obligation to pay the sum, notwithstanding that payment was not in fact made in the year in question (*De Simone*). If in a later income year the liability is divested or destroyed, the amount of the liability should be included in the taxpayer's assessable income for that year, provided the amount can be properly characterised as assessable income of that year.

On the other hand, a loss is not incurred if it is no more than impending, threatened or expected (*James Flood*). This depends on the contractual arrangements between the parties. On this basis, a balance day adjustment in respect of a contingent liability is not deductible (TD 93/188). Conditions affecting the timing of discharge of a liability (but not the creation of the liability) do not render the liability contingent (*City Link*).

The obligation to pay the residue of the purchase price under a contract for the sale of land, which was agreed to be on revenue account, was not incurred in the year of income in which contracts were exchanged, but rather on settlement (*Malouf*).

"Properly referable" to the income year

In *Coles Myer Finance*, the High Court said that it was not enough to establish the existence of a loss or outgoing actually incurred (ie a presently existing liability). It must be "properly referable" to the income year in question (for an application of this principle, see *City Link*). The Commissioner has noted that these requirements will generally apply to financing transactions, or a liability accruing daily or periodically, or other cases where it is necessary to determine whether a loss or outgoing is properly referable to a particular income year. The Commissioner regards "properly referable" as being concerned with the period of time during which the benefit from incurring the loss or outgoing is put to profitable advantage (TR 94/26). Accounting principles may be relevant in determining the year to which the amount is properly referable (TR 97/7).

Cash or earnings basis of returning income

The above principles apply whether the taxpayer returns income on the ''cash'' or ''earnings'' basis (¶9-030). Thus, a taxpayer who uses the cash basis of returning income need not necessarily have paid or borne a loss or outgoing before claiming a deduction for it. However, deductions claimed on a cash paid basis by taxpayers who return income on a cash basis will be allowed, provided no deduction is also claimed in the year the loss or outgoing is incurred but not paid (TR 97/7). A taxpayer using the cash basis wanting to claim an outgoing incurred but not claimed in a prior year may seek amendment of the prior year's assessment, subject to the limitations in the amendment provisions (¶25-300). The ''incurred'' basis of claiming deductions must then continue to be used. Voluntary payments (ie payments not necessitated by a liability, such as gifts, insurance premiums, licence renewals and motor vehicle registration fees) are incurred when paid (TR 97/7). See also IT 2613.

Some specific cases

The following are specific examples of when particular losses or outgoings have been incurred:

- interest payments (¶16-748)
- real estate agents' commissions that have been included in the assessable income of a real estate agent on an accruals basis, and which are either repaid or never collected because of industry practice (eg where a sale falls through), are deductible in the year in which they are repaid or in the year in which the decision is made not to collect (TR 97/5)
- audit fees (IT 2625)
- lease payments, including balloon payments, prepayments, down payments and deposits (TR 98/15)
- losses on forward sales contracts (ID 2003/835) and payments relating to certain options (ID 2009/54; ID 2009/55; ID 2009/58)
- where a principal acts through an agent, the principal is entitled to a deduction when the agent incurs the liability on the principal's behalf, rather than at the earlier time when the principal contributed money to the agent (TR 2004/5: retailers' volume rebates). However, expenditure is not incurred by a principal if there is insufficient evidence of an agency relationship, or if there is no evidence that a taxpayer is under a presently existing legal obligation to reimburse another entity for expenses paid on the taxpayer's behalf (*Healy*)
- where a trader offers customers a ''prompt payment'' discount for settling their credit accounts promptly, the customer should claim a deduction for the full invoice price at the time of purchase. The discount is then deductible to the trader when the liability is satisfied. However, in the case of a cash discount, a trade discount and a quantity or bulk discount, the discounted price is deductible to the customer (TR 96/20; ¶9-100)
- when a company issues shares as consideration for assets or services, no loss or outgoing arises, regardless of the character of the assets or services or their intended use (TR 2008/5)
- losses from specified financial arrangements (¶23-020)
- forward deductions for mine site rehabilitation payments (TA 2009/3)

- GIC accruing over 6 income years is incurred when the taxpayer is served with a notice of assessment triggering the liability to pay the income tax to which the GIC relates (*Nash*)

- shortfall interest charge (TD 2012/2).

Trading stock

Expenditure incurred in acquiring trading stock is deductible under s 8-1. However, the deduction is not allowable until the income year in which the taxpayer has taken the trading stock into account as stock on hand, or, if earlier, the year in which the taxpayer includes an amount in assessable income in connection with the disposal of the stock (ITAA97 s 70-15; ¶9-170; TD 93/138). An example of the latter situation may be where a taxpayer incurs expenditure in respect of goods on order from a manufacturer and agrees to sell the goods before they are manufactured. The cost of trading stock is reduced by any trade incentives that relate directly to the purchase (TR 2009/5).

The deduction for the cost of stock may be spread over more than one income year. Where some part of the stock has become trading stock on hand, a deduction will be allowed in that income year for the expenditure attributable to that part. If, for example, the balance of the stock is on hand by the end of the next income year, a deduction relating to the balance will be allowable in that year. The cost of bar shouts and in-house competition prizes of cash and liquor supplied by hoteliers to encourage patronage is allowable as the cost of trading stock (TD 94/60).

Section 70-15 cannot apply to expenditure incurred on bringing trading stock into existence through the taxpayer's manufacturing or production processes unless it relates to the acquisition of inputs that are themselves trading stock (TR 93/9). Thus, s 70-15 does not apply to expenditure incurred by a primary producer on seed for planting or semen for the artificial insemination of live stock, or to part of the purchase price of an orchard that is attributable to a growing crop. Nor does it apply to a primary producer's participation in a live stock breeding arrangement that forms part of a live stock breeding business of the taxpayer.

A simplified trading stock regime applies to small business entities (¶7-260).

Reserves, provisions, conditional contracts

Amounts set aside at the end of the income year to provide for liabilities that are expected to occur in the future are generally not deductible (*Flood's case*), even though business expediency and accounting practice may require that the potential liability be reflected in the taxpayer's accounts (¶9-120). On this basis, motor vehicle dealers cannot claim deductions for amounts representing a reasonable estimate of warranty repair costs expected to be attributable to the year of income; warranty repair costs are only deductible when actually incurred (IT 2648; ID 2004/403). See also TD 96/12 (provisions for accumulated jackpot amounts by gaming machine operators). The Commissioner has warned taxpayers about arrangements under which deductions are claimed for contributions made to an Employee Entitlement Fund purportedly established, in Australia or in a foreign country, to meet entitlements that may arise in the future for employees (TA 2007/2).

Where goods are sold under a conditional contract, no deduction is allowed to the seller in respect of anticipated returns, but a deduction may be allowed when the goods are actually returned (TR 97/15) (¶9-100). Similarly, where there is a consumer loyalty program (¶10-030), a deduction is allowable to the reward provider when the reward is actually redeemed and supplied, not at the earlier time when the points are simply credited to the member nor when the required number of points is reached by the member (TD 2003/20).

Insurance companies

At the end of each year of income, an insurance company will normally have outstanding claims, ie claims communicated to the company but not yet paid in full, and claims incurred but not reported. The company is entitled to a deduction for any annual increase in these claims (*RACV Insurance*; *Commercial Union*; IT 2663). A similar principle has also been applied to a reinsurer's outstanding claims provision (TR 95/5) and to self-insurers in relation to their estimated workers compensation liabilities (*ANZ Banking Group Ltd*; TD 97/14).

A provision by an insurance company for unreported claims may give rise to a deduction even where there were time limits on the making of claims and in many cases these had expired (*Commercial Union*). The court said that it was long-established practice and policy to pay claims notwithstanding that they had not been notified in time. Payment was a ''commercial necessity'' and was not subject to any contingency that would be regarded as such in the world of ordinary business affairs. The company had ''completely subjected'' itself to the payments and could therefore be said to have incurred the outgoings.

The deduction is calculated on a discounted or ''present value'' basis. This means that the deduction is equal to the annual increase in the amount that the company reasonably estimates is appropriate to set aside and invest in order to provide sufficient funds to pay the liabilities and associated direct settlement costs (ITAA97 Div 321).

Captive insurers

Premiums paid by a tobacco products' manufacturer and distributor to a captive insurance company (ie a wholly-owned company) for coverage that was unavailable from other insurers were allowed as a deduction (*WD & HO Wills*). Similarly, payments made to a mutual entity offering risk coverage were deductible (ID 2004/494). PS LA 2007/8 contains the ATO guidelines on the deductibility of insurance premiums paid to non-resident captive insurer, ie an insurance entity where the parent company is not primarily engaged in the business of insurance.

Long service leave, annual leave

Employers are not entitled to claim deductions for provisions in their accounts to cover employees' entitlements to annual leave, long service leave or other kinds of leave. An employer can claim a deduction for leave payments in the year in which payment is made to the employee or, if the employee is deceased, to a dependant or personal representative (ITAA97 s 26-10(1)). The terms of this provision should be carefully observed. In one case, for example, no deduction was available where payment was made to a family company associated with a deceased employee (*Case Q103*). A deduction is also available to one employer for accrued leave payments paid to another employer for transferred employees in certain circumstances (¶16-155).

Directors' fees, employee bonuses

A company is not entitled to deductions for directors' fees, bonuses or similar payments until the income year in which it has definitively committed itself to the payment, eg by passing a properly authorised resolution (IT 2534) or incurring a quantifiable legal liability to pay a bonus (*Merrill Lynch International*). Thus, the practice adopted by some companies of bringing to account in one income year directors' fees, etc, actually determined and authorised to be paid after the close of the income year is not acceptable for income tax purposes. If a company passes a resolution creating an unconditional commitment to pay the fees and the payment occurs within a reasonable time period in the following year of income, the amount is deductible. However, the Commissioner has warned companies about claiming deductions where amounts remain unpaid by the end of the following income year (TA 2011/4; *ATO media release No 2011/31*, 2 June 2011).

Prepayments

Subject to the prepayment rules discussed at ¶16-045, a prepayment of a revenue nature is deductible in full in the year in which the payment is made (TR 94/25).

[FITR ¶31-280 – ¶31-320, ¶68-140, ¶114-310]

¶16-045 Advance payments for services

Where expenditure qualifies for deduction under ITAA97 s 8-1, the deduction is generally allowable in full in the year the expenditure is incurred (TR 94/25: ¶16-040). However, special prepayment rules affect the timing of deductions for certain types of advance payments (ITAA36 ss 82KZL to 82KZO).

These prepayment rules potentially apply where a taxpayer incurs expenditure for something to be done — in whole or in part — in a later income year. Where these rules apply, the deduction for the expenditure is spread (or ''apportioned'') over the period covered by those services, up to a maximum of 10 years.

The prepayment rules do *not* apply to the following (''excluded expenditure''):

- amounts less than $1,000 (excluding input tax credits: ID 2004/398). However, if 2 or more payments of less than $1,000 are made to avoid the prepayment rules, the anti-avoidance rules of ITAA36 Pt IVA may apply (TD 93/118)
- amounts required to be paid by law or by a court order (eg a registration fee for a business vehicle but not audit fees: ID 2006/218)
- payments of salary or wages, ie payments under a contract of service
- amounts that are capital, private or domestic (s 82KZL)
- certain non-deductible R&D amounts (¶20-150), or
- certain amounts incurred by a general insurer in connection with the issue of policies or the payment of reinsurance premiums.

The prepayment rules also do not apply to certain prepayments under timber plantation managed investment schemes (¶18-125) or to financial arrangements that are subject to ITAA97 Subdiv 250-E or the TOFA rules (ITAA36 s 82KZLA; ¶23-020, ¶23-210). For anti-avoidance measures directed at certain prepayment schemes, see ¶16-110.

The prepayment provisions may apply to payments made by a mining company under arrangements aimed at bringing forward deductions for mine site rehabilitation expenditure (TA 2009/3).

The prepayment rules also apply to work out the amount of notional deductions for R&D expenditure (s 355-110; ¶20-150).

Small business entities and non-business expenditure of individuals

A prepayment rule may apply where:

- the taxpayer is a ''small business entity'' (¶7-050) and does not choose to apportion the expenditure under s 82KZMD (see below)
- the taxpayer is an individual and the expenditure is not incurred in carrying on a business (eg work expenses, or expenses on a passive investment property), or
- the obligation to make the prepayment arose before 21 September 1999 (a ''pre-RBT obligation'') (ITAA36 s 82KZM).

Where the prepayment rule applies, the deduction for expenditure deductible under ITAA97 s 8-1 or the notional deduction under the R&D provisions (¶20-150) is apportioned on a time basis over the income years covered by the eligible service period. Apportionment is only required where the ''eligible service period'' is:

- more than 12 months (eg ID 2003/1073), or
- 12 months or shorter, but ends after the end of the income year *following* the income year in which the expenditure is incurred (the ''expenditure year'').

Thus expenses paid by a small business entity or a non-business individual are deductible in the year of payment if the eligible service period is not longer than 12 months and ends before the end of the income year following the expenditure year. No apportionment is required for ''excluded expenditure''.

The ''eligible service period'' generally begins on the day the thing under the agreement commences to be done, or on the day the expenditure is incurred, whichever is later. It continues until the end of the last day the thing under the agreement ceases to be done. The eligible service period is, however, always limited to 10 years (ITAA36 s 82KZL).

For prepayments of interest, rent, lease payments and insurance premiums, the eligible service period is as follows:

- the period to which the interest relates, not the period of the loan. For the application of the prepayment rules to interest paid in advance by a financial institution, see TR 1999/11
- the period to which the rent or lease payments relate, not the period of the lease
- the period during which the insurance cover is provided, even though the insurer may actually pay out under the policy at a later time.

▶ Example 1: Eligible service period more than 12 months

On 1 November Year 1, a small business entity takes advantage of an early payment discount by paying $20,000 in advance for computer services over a 3-year period from 1 December Year 1 to 30 November Year 4 (ie a period of 1,095 days, comprising 212 days in Year 1, 365 days in Year 2, 365 days in Year 3, and 153 days in Year 4). As the eligible service period is more than 12 months, the deduction for the $20,000 must be apportioned as follows:

Income year	**Amount of deduction**				
Year 1	212/1,095	×	$20,000	=	$3,872.14
Year 2	365/1,095	×	$20,000	=	$6,666.67
Year 3	365/1,095	×	$20,000	=	$6,666.67
Year 4	153/1,095	×	$20,000	=	$2,794.52

▶ Example 2: Eligible service period less than 12 months but ending after expenditure year

On 30 June 2018, a small business entity takes advantage of an early payment discount by paying $10,000 in advance for business services to be provided from 1 August 2018 to 31 July 2019 (ie 365 days, consisting of 334 days in 2018–19 and 31 days in 2019–20). The eligible service period is therefore not more than 12 months, but ends after the end of the income year following the expenditure year (ie it ends after the end of 2018–19). The deduction for the $10,000 must therefore be apportioned as follows:

Income year	**Amount of deduction**				
2017–18			Nil		
2018–19	334/365	×	$10,000	=	$9,151
2019–20	31/365	×	$10,000	=	$849

Business taxpayers and non-business non-individuals

An apportionment is also required where taxpayers carrying on a business and non-individuals that do not carry on a business incur expenditure for services that are not to be wholly provided within the income year in which the expenditure is incurred (the ''expenditure year'') (ITAA36 ss 82KZMA; 82KZMD). Small business entities may also choose to apply these rules. The apportionment rules apply to expenses that would otherwise be deductible under either ITAA97 s 8-1 or the R&D provisions (¶20-150) to: (a) a non-business taxpayer who is not an individual; or (b) a business taxpayer. No apportionment is required for ''excluded expenditure'' or expenditure meeting a pre-RBT obligation.

Where these rules apply, the deduction for the expenditure is apportioned on a time basis over the income years covered by the eligible service period. This apportionment is carried out in the same way as in Example 1 above.

Special situations

Special rules apply where, at the end of a year of income, a taxpayer no longer has any rights under the prepaid agreement (ITAA36 s 82KZN), where a partnership is formed, reconstituted or dissolved (ITAA36 s 82KZO), to ''balloon'' payments (s 82KZM; TD 93/119; TR 98/15). Section 82KZM applies to fees paid for the arrangement of an interest rate swap contract but not to swap payments made in advance (IT 2682).

Where a commercial debt is forgiven, amounts deductible to the debtor under the prepayment rules may be reduced under the rules discussed at ¶16-910.

Prepayments under "tax-shelter" arrangements

Prepaid expenditure incurred in relation to tax-shelter arrangements is required to be spread over the period in which the services are provided if the payment is made for the doing of a thing that is not to be wholly done within the expenditure year (ITAA36 s 82KZME). The period over which the services are to be provided is the ''eligible service period''. The rules apply if:

- the taxpayer's allowable deductions under an arrangement for the income year in which the expenditure is incurred exceed the assessable income under the arrangement for that year
- all significant aspects of the day-to-day management of the arrangement during that income year are conducted by people other than the taxpayer (eg in the case of a passive investment: TD 2005/26), and
- either more than one taxpayer participates in the arrangement or the manager (or an associate) also manages similar arrangements on behalf of others.

The rules do *not* apply if (a) the prepayment is for buildings, contents or rent protection insurance, or for interest on funds borrowed to acquire real property (or interests in real property), publicly listed shares or units in a widely held unit trust (eg ID 2003/1119); (b) under the arrangement, the taxpayer has obtained or is reasonably expected to obtain rent from real property, dividends or distributions from a unit trust, and no other income (except capital gains or an insurance receipt); and (c) all aspects of the arrangement are conducted at arm's length.

[FTR ¶47-500]

Limits and Exclusions

¶16-060 Revenue vs capital outgoings and losses

Often there is no problem in distinguishing between non-deductible capital expenditure and revenue expenditure that is deductible under s 8-1. For example, the cost of purchasing business premises is capital expenditure, while rent paid for business premises is revenue expenditure (¶16-640); the cost of alterations, additions or renovations that add to the value or useful life of an asset is capital expenditure, while the cost of repairs is revenue expenditure (¶16-700). In other cases, it is often difficult to determine whether expenditure is of a revenue or capital character.

In some cases involving low-cost tangible assets, the Commissioner accepts the use of statistical sampling (¶16-153).

Certain business capital expenditure (''blackhole expenditure'') is deductible immediately or over 5 years under s 40-880 (¶16-156).

There is no presumption that mining or petroleum exploration expenditure has a capital nature and characterisation depends on the facts and circumstances (see TR 2017/1 for examples). However, certain expenditure incurred by seismic surveyors to collect and process seismic data is capital nature and may be depreciated over 15 years (TR 2019/4; ¶17-350).

Tests of capital losses or outgoings

The guidelines for distinguishing between capital and revenue outgoings were laid down in the *Sun Newspapers case*. There it was pointed out that expenditure in establishing, replacing and enlarging the profit-yielding (ie business) *structure* itself is capital and is to be contrasted with working or operating expenses. The test laid down in the *Sun Newspapers case;* involved 3 elements, although none is in itself decisive:

(1) the nature of the advantage sought by making the payment(s)

(2) the way it is to be used or enjoyed

(3) the means adopted to get it.

As regards the first 2 elements, the lasting or recurrent character of the advantage and the expenditure is important. Thus the courts have held that, in the absence of special circumstances, expenditure is capital in nature where it is made with a view to bringing into existence an asset or an advantage (tangible or intangible) for the enduring benefit of the business (*British Insulated & Helsby Cables v Atherton*). In addition, it is the nature of the advantage sought by the *taxpayer* that is relevant. Thus payments for ''rent'' on business premises were fully deductible, even though part of the payments were liable to be credited against the purchase price for the premises under an option held by an associated company (*South Australian Battery Makers*; ITAA36 s 82KL: ¶16-110).

The third element involves a consideration of whether the outlay is a periodic one covering the use of the asset or advantage during each period, or whether the outlay is calculated as a single final provision for the future use or enjoyment of the asset or advantage.

Expenditure to increase sales and expand business, takeover defence costs

The courts have tended to regard expenditure incurred in the continual competitive battle for business, or to obtain sales or expand business, as being of a revenue nature even though the particular expenditure could, in a sense, be said to produce an advantage for the enduring benefit of the trade. Much depends on the nature of the advantage obtained in the context of the particular business or class of business.

Costs incurred by a target company in defending itself against a takeover attempt are outgoings of capital or of a capital nature. These would include legal costs and the costs of acquiring shares in the offeror company (a reverse takeover), although interest paid on loans used to buy shares in the offeror company would be of a revenue nature (IT 2656; ¶16-840). Capital costs of defending or attempting a takeover may nevertheless be deductible over 5 years (¶16-156).

Characterisation of the expenditure

In determining the true nature of a payment it may be necessary to go behind the description of the payment that is given in the relevant documentation. For example, the fact that payments are called rent and are made periodically would not necessarily prevent them from being, in part, an outgoing of a capital nature. The question of what the payment is for must be determined by reference to the legal obligations or rights under which it was paid, ie by reference to the agreement that operated to create the obligation to pay (but in some cases it is necessary to go outside the legally binding agreement: *BHP*; *Star City*; *Carioti*; *Mussalli & Ors*, appeal pending).

However, the characterisation of an expense does not depend on its effectiveness, either economically (in the sense that it earned a profit) or legally. Thus, rent payments may be deductible even though the lease under which they are made is invalid (*Emmakell*).

Cost of trading stock is not capital

The cost of trading stock is specifically treated as non-capital expenditure (ITAA97 s 70-25). The fact that the cost of acquiring trading stock is treated as revenue led to a land developer obtaining a deduction for the payment of the tax debts of its land-owning subsidiaries. The land developer had undertaken to meet the debts in order to get the Commissioner's approval to the subsidiaries being wound up and their assets (ie the land) distributed to the developer. The payments were held to be deductible outgoings because they were effectively part of the cost to the developer of acquiring its trading stock (*Hooker Rex*).

Demolition costs

Costs incurred by a mining company in demolishing 2 obsolete and dangerous structures on one of its mining sites were held to be capital costs (*Mount Isa Mines*). The High Court remarked that, in some situations, the demolition of structures and plant which have a very short life may be capable of being treated as a matter of maintenance or upkeep or as an incident in the day-to-day conduct of a business (and therefore the expenditure may be stamped with a revenue character). Here, however, the purpose of the demolition was to confer a positive and enduring advantage on the taxpayer's business premises by removing a disadvantageous asset. Costs incurred in demolishing plant and in clearing a site to make way for new plant are of a capital nature (IT 2197). Once new plant is installed and in an operational state, the cost of bringing that plant into full operation, but not the cost of additions or modifications, is of a revenue nature (TD 93/126). See also ¶17-105.

Costs incurred by a mining company in dismantling, removing and storing a combined dredge and concentrator were held to be deductible because the nature of sand mining (which required moving to successive sites as deposits were exhausted) meant that expenses of relocation and temporary storage were an inevitable part of the regular cost of the conduct of the business (*Associated Minerals*).

Lease, hire and rental payments

Recurrent rental payments to secure the hire of an income-producing asset are usually of a revenue nature, but one-off payments to secure the use of an asset for an extended period of time or to reduce subsequent payments are of a capital nature. See generally IT 28 (¶16-310).

For the deductibility of lease payments (in particular balloon payments, prepayments, deposits or down payments), see TR 98/15.

Hire purchase transactions are treated as a sale of property by a financier to a buyer, financed by a loan from the financier to the buyer (ITAA97 Div 240). As the hire purchaser is treated as the owner, it can claim depreciation (¶23-250) or, if the property is trading stock, a deduction for the cost.

Losses from financial arrangements and currency fluctuations

The TOFA provisions treat losses from specified financial arrangements as being on revenue account and also deal with the timing of deductions (¶23-020). The deductibility of losses arising from foreign currency fluctuations is governed by the rules set out at ¶23-075.

Examples: capital expenditure

The losses or outgoings identified below have been held to be capital and thus *non-deductible* under the general deduction provision (although they may be deductible under a specific deduction provision):

- newspaper's payment to prevent threatened competition (*Sun Newspapers Ltd & Associated Newspapers Ltd*)
- expenditure in protecting, preserving or defending fixed capital assets (*John Fairfax & Sons*)
- damages for breach of contract, the result of the breach being the taxpayer's freedom to reorganise its trading structure (*Foley Bros*)
- cost of obtaining an initial business licence (*Case B31*)
- cost of acquiring an insurance register (except in limited circumstances) (TR 2000/1) or a subscriber list (ID 2004/656) or the cost incurred by a service provider to install cables in order to expand its customer base (ID 2008/91)
- losses on sale of golf club memberships and forgiven debts associated with the development of a residential resort, golf course and club house development (*Sanctuary Lakes*)
- support payments made by a parent company to its loss-making subsidiary, or to its subsidiary that is not sufficiently profitable (TD 2014/14; ¶16-156)
- costs incurred by a retirement village operator in developing or acquiring a village to conduct the business of granting occupancy rights to residents (TR 2002/14; see also *Case 12/2009*). However, payments made by the proprietor of a retirement village to its residents for a share of the capital appreciation in a resident's unit transferred to a new resident were deductible (*Case 4/2011*; *Case 12/2013*; associated *Decision Impact Statements*; PCG 2016/15; and ¶16-060)
- amount paid out of surplus profits to an employee benefit trust (*Essenbourne*; *Walstern*; *Benstead Services*)
- employer contributions to employee remuneration trusts that enable the trustee to provide finance to employees (eg loans) or to acquire a direct interest in the employer (eg shares), creating an investment fund with no intention of permanently or entirely dissipating the fund by remunerating employees (TR 2018/7)
- employer contributions to employee remuneration trusts that are applied to remunerating employees wholly engaged in affairs of capital of the business, eg projects that construct or upgrade depreciating assets (TR 2018/7)
- remuneration to employees engaged in the construction of depreciating assets (eg a distribution network) and running costs of vehicles used in such construction (ID 2011/42; ID 2011/43; ID 2011/44)
- remuneration to employees and other labour costs for performing functions that relate to the construction or creation of capital assets (*Draft* TR 2019/D6)

- cost of preparing new premises and of installing plant and equipment (*Lister Blackstone*; eg the cost of installing a GPS in a car: ID 2004/614). The cost of a shop fit-out by a tenant was non-deductible even though the tenant had received a lease incentive in respect of the fit-out (*Lees & Leech*) (¶10-116)
- payments by a lessor to bring to an end an uneconomic lease (*Kennedy Holdings and Property Management*; but see ¶16-159)
- compensation paid by a business tenant to the landlord for failing to carry out covenanted repairs, where the payment was a precondition to the landlord's consent to an assignment of the lease (*Peyton*)
- accountant's guarantee of the performance of a transaction by a finance company client of his firm (*Case B3*). See also TR 96/23 at ¶16-152
- business profits paid to a bank under a loan contract, to the extent that they represented repayment of the loan principal (*Case 50/96*)
- payment to prevent a possible investigation into a taxpayer's business practices (*Case V64*)
- compulsory contribution to a local town planning development scheme that involved improvement of sewerage, drainage and roads in the area where the taxpayer's business premises were situated (*Case V37*)
- expenditure incurred by a gold mining company in relocating a highway, thus allowing mining operations to continue (*Pine Creek Goldfields*)
- cost of constructing a tailings dam, dyke, mudlake and other industrial residue or waste disposal facility (TR 1999/2)
- payment by the buyer of a mine to reimburse the seller for the cost of work in progress (¶16-158) where such payment was part of the purchase price of the mine (*QCT Resources*)
- service station operator's one-off payment to a petroleum company to participate in the company's marketing program (*Labrilda*)
- statutory charge payable by the owner of an uninsured building for the fire brigade's attendance (*Case X5*)
- establishment expenses incurred by a company preparatory to listing its shares on an Australian or foreign stock exchange (TD 92/143; now deductible under the provisions at ¶16-156)
- mailing costs incurred by a trustee in seeking contributions from beneficiaries to finance litigation (*Trustees of the Estate Mortgage Fighting Fund Trust*)
- cost of acquiring a profit à prendre, eg right to remove timber (*Nizich*; *Case 42/95*)
- investments in certain primary production schemes (¶18-020), a franchise (*Taylor*; *Leggett*; *Player*; ¶16-660), certain life insurance policies (TA 2009/17), a retirement village (*Case 12/2009*) and a base metals exploration and prospecting project (*Case 4/2007*, affirmed in *Narbey*)
- margin payments made in respect of exchange-traded option and futures contracts (TD 2006/25)
- maintenance costs of plants (other than plants replacing dead or diseased stock) held by a seller/nursery before delivery to a taxpayer who is carrying on a horticulture business (TD 2006/46: ¶18-070)

- lump sum payments to doctors by the operator of a chain of medical centres for their promise to conduct their practice as an independent contractor exclusively from its medical centre for 5 years (*Healius Ltd*; appeal pending)
- franchise fees paid by an electricity supplier to the state government as "monopoly rent" (*United Energy*)
- imposts paid to the State Treasurer (Vic) by the licensee of an electricity transmission business were capital because they were part of the acquisition price of the business (*Ausnet Transmission Group Pty Ltd*)
- franchise establishment fees paid to operate a Bendigo Bank branch under a community bank model (*Inglewood and Districts Community Enterprises*)
- "capacity charges" paid to a state-owned corporation by a private energy provider because they were part of the acquisition of rights to trade in the electricity output of public generators, rather than for an annual supply of electricity to be resold (*Origin Energy Ltd*)
- "special rental" payments made by a casino operator to a government for the exclusive right to operate a casino (*Jupiters Ltd*; *Star City Pty Ltd*)
- gaming machine entitlements paid to the State of Victoria by a gaming venue operator with a pre-existing business generating gaming revenues (*Sharpcan*)
- the cost of leasing taxi licences for a 50-year period (ID 2005/147)
- an amount described as "interest" and paid as part of the purchase price of shares (*BHP Co Ltd*)
- amounts lent by a life insurer to an insurance agent and subsequently written off (TR 2001/9)
- the cost of training a guard dog used to provide security for business premises (ID 2011/18)
- establishment costs connected with the sale and leaseback of a capital asset (TD 2003/15)
- the cost of pools of unpaid loans (eg credit card and personal) and billing receivables by a taxpayer who subsequently seeks to collect the debts contained within the pools (ID 2012/26).

Examples: non-capital expenditure

On the other hand, the following losses or outgoings have been held not to be capital and to be *deductible* under the general deduction provision:

- payments to secure a competitor's agreement not to use trade marks or names similar to those used by the taxpayer (*Duro Travel Goods*)
- oil company's payments to retailers to secure exclusive trade ties (but not where by lease/re-lease arrangement) (*BP Aust*) and payments made to independent contractors for the assignment of security monitoring service agreements (*Tyco Australia*)
- bank's payment to the Commonwealth Government for the exclusive right to make subsidised loans to Defence Force staff (*National Australia Bank*)
- brewery's contribution to a trade association for a Sunday opening campaign (*Cooper v Rhymney Breweries Ltd*)
- payment for cancellation of agreement whereby the taxpayer was to be supplied with know-how for several years in return for royalties (*J Gadsden & Co Ltd*)

- cost of award variation application for after-hours trading (*Case B74*)
- cost of moving trading stock from old premises to new (*Lister Blackstone*)
- lump sum paid for release of onerous loan obligations (*Metals Exploration*)
- expenditure incurred by a lessee in installing leased equipment (IT 2197)
- trust establishment costs incurred by a company that carried on a business of establishing, managing and administering secondary mortgage trusts (*Fanmac*)
- costs incurred by a quarry operator in renewing planning permission to operate a quarry, where the permission was only short-term and conferred no enduring benefit (*Chapman*)
- certain costs of removing and disposing of mining overburden (TR 1999/2; ¶19-050)
- compensation paid by a mining company to an Aboriginal community for deprivation of possession of land the subject of a mining lease, calculated as a percentage of gross sales (*Cape Flattery Silica Mines*)
- costs incurred by a state forestry management body in planting and maintaining forests (ID 2004/718; ID 2004/768)
- cost of a licence for a pistol obtained by a solicitor on police advice (*Case X74*)
- expenditure incurred in acquiring television program licences (IT 2646)
- expenditure incurred by a legal services agency in purchasing those services under a prepaid warrant arrangement (*Lamont*; however see TA 2005/2 and TD 2003/9)
- annual concession fees paid by a private road provider for the right to operate the road system and collect tolls (*City Link*)
- certain annual business fees (ID 2004/648), franchise investment fees (*Miniello*; see also ¶16-660) and franchise renewal fees paid to renew a community bank franchise for 5 years (*Inglewood and Districts Community Enterprises*)
- payments made to persuade a defaulting purchaser under an instalment sales contract to vacate the property (ID 2004/29)
- additional interest paid by a building society to its depositors during the 3 years following the society's conversion into a bank (*NMRSB Ltd*)
- payments made by a retirement village operator to outgoing residents (or their representatives), which represented an agreed share of the unrealised capital growth in village units while the outgoing residents had resided there (*Case 12/2013* and related *Decision Impact Statement*). The ATO issued an addendum to update its view that such payments are deductible (TR 2002/14A2: *Case 12/2013*). Retirement village operators who treated these payments as capital before TR 2002/14A2 was issued (on 26 November 2014) may continue to do so, and also include them in the CGT cost base of the relevant apartment. If they do not make this choice, the pre-26 November 2014 payments are deductible (under s 8-1), and the operator can request an amended assessment or object against their original assessment: PCG 2016/15.

Reference should also be made to the checklist at ¶16-005 for the deductibility status of a wide range of expenditure. See also ¶16-840 for discussion of the distinction between revenue and capital outgoings in relation to legal expenses. As to the treatment of capital outgoings under the CGT rules, see ¶11-550.

[FITR ¶31-050, ¶31-920, ¶114-020, ¶114-310]

¶16-070 Apportionment and dual-purpose expenditure

Losses and outgoings are allowable under ITAA97 s 8-1 *to the extent* to which they are incurred in the course of gaining assessable income, and are not allowable *to the extent* that they are of a capital, private or domestic nature, or are incurred in the gaining of exempt or non-assessable non-exempt income. This means that a particular item of expenditure may have to be apportioned into its deductible and non-deductible components. Apportionment is a question of fact and involves a determination of the proportion of the expenditure that is attributable to deductible purposes. The Commissioner believes that the method of apportionment must be ''fair and reasonable'' in all the circumstances. In *Fletcher*, this resulted in the interest deduction being limited to the amount of assessable income actually received (TR 95/33). See also *Ure* discussed at ¶16-740.

Once it is established that the outgoing was incurred for the relevant purpose, the Commissioner cannot apportion the outgoing (reduce the deduction) simply because it is greater than the amount which would normally have been incurred by a prudent business person. ''It is not for the Court or the Commissioner to say how much a taxpayer ought to spend in obtaining his income but only how much he has spent'' (*Ronpibon Tin NL*; also *Cecil Bros Pty Ltd*). However, payments of inflated amounts under a scheme designed to create artificial deductions were not deductible (*Hargraves & Stoten*).

On the other hand, the fact that a payment is commercially realistic may be relevant in determining whether it is deductible. In *Phillips*, the Federal Court held that amounts paid by a partnership of chartered accountants to a service trust (¶31-180) set up to carry on the non-professional activities of the partnership were wholly deductible. A crucial factor supporting the full deductibility of the expenditure was that the rates charged by the service trust were commercially realistic (see ¶16-152 for the Commissioner's views on this issue). This raised the presumption that the expenditure was outlaid for the purpose of obtaining assessable income. In *Lau*, the fact that the parties were at arm's length and the transactions were negotiated in a genuine commercial setting was relevant to the conclusion that no part of the payment could be attributed to some ''private'' purpose.

A deduction for an outgoing incurred in deriving income from a taxable supply does not need to be apportioned just because some of the income relates to the GST payable on the supply and is non-assessable non-exempt income (TD 2005/35).

Where employer contributions are made to employee remuneration trusts to secure ''very small'' or ''trifling'' capital advantages, an amount need not be apportioned to the capital advantage. For example, if within a relatively short period of making the contribution (which secures the capital advantage), it is permanently and entirely dissipated in remunerating employees (TR 2018/7).

Anti-avoidance provisions

The Commissioner may reduce the amount of a deduction otherwise allowable under s 8-1 where a tax avoidance scheme is involved (¶16-110, ¶30-120). The Commissioner may also reduce the amount of a deduction where trading stock is sold at excessive prices in a non-arm's length sale (¶9-210), where excessive payments are made to related entities (¶16-530) or by a private company to shareholders (¶4-220), or where private benefits are provided as an inducement to a business taxpayer to purchase particular goods or services (¶16-157).

In the case of transactions with an international element, the Commissioner has the power under the transfer pricing provisions (¶22-580) and the various double taxation agreements to impose arm's length standards in determining allowable deductions.

[FITR ¶31-200 – ¶31-260]

¶16-100 Double deductions

In many instances, an item of expenditure may appear to qualify for deduction under 2 or more provisions or by more than one method. For example, a bad debt written off during the year of income may in some circumstances qualify for deduction under ITAA97 s 8-1 as well as falling within the special provisions of ITAA97 s 25-35 (¶16-580).

However, there is a general prohibition against double deductions, ie expenditure cannot be deducted under more than one provision by the same taxpayer, whether in the same or different years. A taxpayer can only deduct the amount under the provision that is most appropriate (ITAA97 s 8-10). A deduction may be available even though the amount is also subject to a rebate/tax offset (*Frisch*).

Deductible expenditure incurred on an income-producing property cannot be deducted in ascertaining the assessable profit or loss on the sale of that property (ITAA36 s 82). However, this may not apply where the original deduction was provided as a specific incentive (*MLC Limited*: ¶20-530).

A taxpayer cannot claim a deduction and a capital loss for the same economic loss if a CGT event happens to a CGT asset (¶11-560).

[FITR ¶36-100]

¶16-105 Deductions and illegal activities

No deduction is available for losses and outgoings to the extent that they are incurred in the furtherance of, or directly in relation to, activities in respect of which the taxpayer has been convicted of an indictable offence (ITAA97 s 26-54). Such losses and outgoings are also excluded from the cost base or reduced cost base of a CGT asset for capital gains purposes.

Deductions are denied for all expenditure where the activities are wholly illegal (eg drug dealing or people smuggling). There may be cases where the taxpayer is undertaking a lawful business but is convicted of an illegal activity while carrying out that business. In these cases, deductions are only denied where the expenditure directly relates to entering into and carrying out the actual illegal activity. However, a deduction is allowed for the expenditure if it would have been incurred in any case, regardless of the illegal activity.

[FITR ¶68-380]

¶16-107 Other exclusions from deductibility

As well as the general exclusions detailed above, there are a number of provisions limiting or prohibiting the deductibility of particular types of expenditure, for example penalties (¶16-845), excessive remuneration to relatives (¶16-530), and expenditure subject to the anti-avoidance provisions discussed at ¶16-110 and ¶16-151. The hybrid mismatch rules in ITAA97 Div 832 may operate to deny certain deductions in order to neutralise the effect of arrangements taking advantage of different tax treatments in 2 or more jurisdictions. The rules apply from 1 January 2019 and generally target multinational groups.

No deductions against certain government assistance payments

No deduction is available against rebatable government assistance payments such as the Austudy and ABSTUDY living allowance, Newstart allowance/JobSeeker Payment and Youth allowance (ITAA97 s 26-19 overcoming the effect of *Anstis*; ¶16-450).

A participant of the National Disability Insurance Scheme (NDIS) can not claim a deduction for expenses incurred to the extent they are funded by certain amounts derived under their NDIS plan (s 26-97).

Anti-avoidance Measures

¶16-110 Tax deferral schemes, prepayment schemes, etc

Deductions for otherwise allowable expenses may be deferred or denied altogether where the expenses have been incurred under specific types of tax avoidance schemes.

Tax deferral schemes

Tax deferral schemes involve arrangements between associated parties to defer tax. Under a typical scheme, the taxpayer makes a payment in advance for goods or services to be provided by the associate in the future. The taxpayer claims a deduction for the amount paid while the associate seeks to spread the income over the years in which the goods or services are provided. The effect of special anti-avoidance measures is to deny the taxpayer a deduction in this situation until the income year in which the goods or services are supplied (ITAA36 s 82KK(3)).

Under another type of deferral scheme, the taxpayer incurs a loss or outgoing in the current income year for goods or services to be wholly provided by an associate in the current year. The taxpayer claims a deduction in the current year, even though the whole amount is not actually paid to the associate in that year. The associate claims that it is not taxable on the entire amount, or a part of it, until a later year (eg because the associate recognises the receipt on a cash basis and the entire amount is not yet received). In this situation, the taxpayer can only claim a deduction for the expenditure in the income year(s) they actually pay for the goods or services, and only to the extent of any payment made (s 82KK(2); ID 2014/34).

Prepayment schemes

The effect of prepayment schemes is that the taxpayer prepays interest, rent or some other revenue expense with the aim of reducing the non-deductible capital amount payable for the acquisition of property by the taxpayer or an associate. In such circumstances, deductions for the prepayments may be denied (ITAA36 s 82KJ). However, this provision does not apply if the amount was no more than what might reasonably be expected to have been paid under an arm's length transaction (see, for example, *Cooke*).

Even without this express provision, the Federal Court has struck down a prepaid interest scheme, holding that the interest was not deductible under the general deduction provisions (*Ilbery*; ¶16-746). For other prepayment rules, see ¶16-045. Prepayments in one income year for trading stock to be delivered in the following year will not be deductible until the income year in which the stock is on hand (¶16-040).

Expenditure recoupment schemes

Under an expenditure recoupment scheme, the taxpayer incurs an otherwise deductible loss or outgoing but receives a compensatory benefit that, together with the expected tax saving, effectively recoups the expenditure for the taxpayer so that no real deductible loss or outgoing is suffered. The deduction will be denied altogether in these circumstances (ITAA36 s 82KL).

Leasing arrangements

For anti-avoidance measures directed at certain leasing arrangements, see ¶23-210 and ¶23-240.

[FTR ¶46-801]

¶16-151 Personal services income deductions

Where an individual generates personal services income as a contractor, but is not carrying on a personal services business, the deductions relating to that income are generally restricted to those that would have been available if the individual had been an employee (¶30-600).

Business Deductions

¶16-152 Business expenses

Ordinary recurring operating expenses of a business are deductible under ITAA97 s 8-1 and a useful checklist may be found at ¶16-005. The record-keeping requirements for business taxpayers are discussed at ¶9-045.

▶ Planning point

Tax planning raises different considerations for businesses, partly due to the fact that businesses are subject to non-tax regulations and other considerations (eg industrial awards etc). Non-compliance with regulatory requirements may give rise to a non-deductible penalty (¶16-845, ¶16-858).

Salaries, wages and directors' fees and fringe benefits are discussed at ¶16-520.

Most advertising expenses are clearly deductible, eg where incurred for the purpose of selling trading stock, letting rental properties, hiring employees, obtaining publicity for a business name, or recouping lost sales. A levy paid by a tobacco manufacturer to an industry association to fight proposed legislation that would have restricted the advertising and sale of tobacco products and the sponsorship of sporting events was deductible (*Rothmans of Pall Mall (Australia)*; TR 95/1). Sponsorship fees (ID 2005/284; ID 2003/922; ID 2003/923), and the cost of gifts to clients (TD 2016/14) are deductible.

Consolidation valuation expenses incurred by a head company of a consolidated group or by an entity that may become a subsidiary member of such group are deductible as tax-related expenses (¶16-850) rather than as ordinary business expenses (TR 2004/2).

Expenditure on entertainment for promotional or advertising purposes may be deductible provided it is made available to the public generally. Where this is not the case, it is necessary to dissect the expenditure into its (deductible) advertising and (non-deductible) entertainment elements (¶16-390). Fees paid under internet marketing schemes are not deductible (TD 2002/23).

Tender costs are deductible to a business taxpayer (even if the tender is unsuccessful) provided the tender costs are an ordinary incident of that business (TD 93/32). In one case, review, evaluation and bidding costs in relation to the mining of coal, oil shale and mineral deposits were not deductible as they were not incurred as part of the taxpayer's business of producing and selling oil and gas, and the taxpayer was not in the business of exploration (*Esso*).

Where a seller, who is on the accruals rather than the cash basis of returning income (¶9-030), enters into a lay-by sale agreement and the agreement is subsequently terminated, payments refunded to the buyer and payments not received by the seller are not deductible to the seller as these amounts have not been previously included in assessable income. However, a deduction is allowable if the seller decides to refund a non-refundable deposit as this amount would have been included in assessable income (TR 95/7). Commissions repaid by a travel agent to a service provider, which have previously been returned as assessable income, are deductible (TD 93/149).

Where an employer pays travel costs in relation to the relocation of an employee, the costs are deductible, regardless of whether the employee is an existing employee or a new employee (IT 2566). Where an employer incurs costs associated with employment agreements, those costs are deductible to the employer in relation to an existing business but not a new business (TR 2000/5). The payment or reimbursement by an employer of an employee's costs associated with an employment agreement gives rise to a fringe benefit (TR 2000/5; ¶35-330).

Disbursements such as counsel fees, court fees, photocopying and travel made by solicitors in the performance of legal services are deductible outgoings when incurred. However, no amount is deductible if the solicitor is acting as the client's agent or if the solicitor is making a loan to the client (TR 97/6).

Management fees paid by 2 professional footballers to management companies for negotiating playing contracts were deductible because the footballers were conducting a business and the fees were of a revenue nature (*Spriggs; Riddell*).

In some cases, deductible business expenses will include royalty payments. However, no deduction is available for such amounts unless the taxpayer has complied with the PAYG withholding requirements (¶26-250) for royalty payments to non-residents (ITAA97 s 26-25; ID 2007/188).

Contributions (including membership fees) and gifts made by business taxpayers to political parties, members of parliament and candidates on or after 1 July 2008 are not deductible (s 26-22; ¶16-950). Arrangements under which the taxpayer makes a cash deposit for a vendor to purchase pharmaceuticals from a low cost overseas supplier which are then valued at a much higher cost for gifting to an overseas charity may be ineffective (TA 2010/8).

Expenditure on geological sequestration may be deductible as an ordinary business expense or under the mine site rehabilitation (¶19-100) or environmental protection (¶19-110) provisions (TR 2008/6).

Exploration expenditure to investigate a new mineral a miner has not previously mined may not be immediately deductible under the general deduction provision (s 8-1). However, non-capital expenditure to investigate a new opportunity to mine a substance that a taxpayer has previously mined may qualify for a general deduction (TR 2017/1).

Service fees

In *Phillips' case*, amounts paid by a partnership of chartered accountants to a service trust set up to carry on the non-professional activities of the partnership were wholly deductible. The Commissioner accepted the decision because the service fees charged by the trust were realistic and not in excess of commercial rates (IT 276; ¶16-070). There were sound commercial reasons for the arrangement quite apart from the tax savings. However, if a payment for services was grossly excessive, the presumption would arise that it was made for some other purpose.

Service fees calculated using the particular mark-up adopted in *Phillips' case* are not necessarily deductible. If the services provided are obviously connected to the conduct of the taxpayer's income-earning activities or business, and the service fees are commercially realistic, then the Commissioner will presume that the entire expense is a real and genuine cost of earning the taxpayer's income (TR 2006/2; ATO publications *Your service entity arrangements* and *FAQs on service entity arrangements*). Where these objective commercial connections do not exist, the Commissioner may examine the circumstances surrounding the arrangement (including the taxpayer's intention) to determine the character of the expense. Service arrangements involving the prepayment of service fees from a trading entity to an associated service entity aimed at securing a deduction in the year of payment rather than in the year any services are provided are not effective (TA 2008/10). See also CCH *Tax Week* ¶674 (2005) and ¶1 (2006).

▶ Planning point

Self-employed professional persons, whether sole practitioners or in partnership, can set up administration companies provided the company is established only for the purpose of providing employer-sponsored superannuation benefits (IT 2494; IT 2503). For discussion of the FBT consequences, see TD 95/57 and TD 95/34.

Payment of fees by a professional partnership to an entity in return for the provision of premises, plant, equipment and administrative services may be beneficial if the entity is owned by family members of the partnership on lower marginal tax rates than the partners. To avoid the application of the general anti-avoidance provisions (¶30-120), partnerships using a service entity should: (i) enter into a written agreement setting out the nature of the services and the fees to be charged; (ii) ensure that those fees are at commercial rates; (iii) ensure that the service entity invoices the business regularly for the services performed; (iv) separate the administration of the service entity from the rest of the business; (v) ensure that employees know who their employer is (ie the service entity or the partnership); and (vi) review the operation of the service entity from time to time, including the fees charged.

In *BCD Technologies*, a deduction was allowed for management fees paid by the taxpayer to a related entity in respect of management services provided. The amount of the payment had been calculated with reference to the expenses of the company in the preceding year with a 15% mark-up. See also *Case 15/2006*.

Fees paid to a trustee by a non-working partner for services to satisfy the partnership's outsourcing requirements are deductible to the partner (under s 8-1; ¶16-010), provided the fees represent a commercial arm's length fee for the actual services provided (CR 2013/64).

Bribery and corporate crime

No deduction is available for bribes paid to public officials nor do such bribes form part of the cost base of any relevant asset for CGT purposes (ITAA97 ss 26-52; 26-53). A "bribe" is an amount incurred in providing a benefit (ie any advantage) that is not legitimately due to another person, where the amount is incurred with the intention of influencing the public official in the exercise of the official's duties in order to obtain or retain business or a business advantage.

An amount paid to *foreign* public officials is not a bribe if either: (a) the written law of the foreign country requires or permits the provision of the benefit; or (b) the amount is incurred for the sole or dominant purpose of expediting or securing the performance of routine government actions of a minor nature and the benefit is of a minor nature.

The ATO has issued *Guidelines for dealing with bribery of public officials* to assist businesses manage their tax obligations in relation to bribes and facilitation payments (available on ATO website).

No deduction will be available for a loss or outgoing incurred by an entity under terms of a Deferred Prosecution Agreement entered into under the *Commonwealth Deferred Prosecution Agreement Scheme* proposed in the Crimes Legislation Amendment (Combatting Corporate Crime) Bill 2019. The scheme will allow prosecutors to invite certain entities that engaged in serious corporate crime to negotiate compliance with specific conditions in order to not be prosecuted.

Native title claims deductions

Expenses incurred in implementing the *Native Title Act 1993* (including payments for the temporary impairment or extinguishment of native title) are deductible to the extent that they are incurred as part of the ongoing operation of the business of the taxpayer (s 8-1; *Cape Flattery Silica Mines*). However, expenditure incurred to protect the capital assets of the business is not deductible under s 8-1 but may be deductible as project expenditure (¶19-050) or be included in the cost base of the asset.

Guarantee and indemnity payments

Payments made under guarantee are capital in nature unless the provision of guarantees and the losses or outgoings arising under the guarantees are normal incidents of the taxpayer's income earning activities. A payment under a guarantee is deductible if the giving of the guarantee, the guarantor's payment and the incurring of the loss or outgoing have an income-producing purpose. This would be the case if: (a) the guarantor is engaged in the business of giving guarantees for reward; (b) the giving of guarantees is a regular and normal incident of the taxpayer's earning activities; or (c) the guarantee is provided to customers, including customers of the guarantor's subsidiary (TR 96/23; ID 2010/37).

However, no deduction is allowable for payments made under guarantee by shareholders or directors in respect of the company, or by a parent company in respect of a subsidiary (TR 96/23; for the CGT consequences, see ¶11-270); by a shareholder with a minority interest in a business partner (a private company) (*Bell & Moir*); by a landlord in respect of the tenant's default to make certain payments under an overdraft facility (*Case 38/96*). Similarly, no deduction was available for indemnity payments made to the purchaser of the taxpayer's subsidiary because the immediate advantage to the taxpayer, ie the sale of the shares at the maximum price possible, related to the taxpayer's dividend yielding structure rather than the process by which dividends were earned (*Email Ltd*; ID 2004/657).

On the other hand, an indemnity fee connected to a forward exchange contract entered into to mitigate potential deductible losses was akin to a payment for insurance (¶16-550) and was deductible (*Visy Industries USA*). The ATO accepts that once it was concluded that the taxpayer in *Visy Industries USA* entered into the forward exchange contract within the scope of its business (although not within the ordinary course), it was open to conclude that the not insignificant purpose of profit making attributed to the contract led to the same tax consequences as a transaction entered into in the ordinary course of the taxpayer's business (*Decision Impact Statement* on *Visy Industries USA*).

[FITR ¶32-610 – ¶32-740]

¶16-153 Low-cost business expenditure and statistical sampling

The Commissioner accepts that certain expenditure incurred by a *business* taxpayer on low-cost tangible or intangible assets is of a revenue nature and is immediately deductible *(the threshold rule)*. The Commissioner also accepts the use of sampling methods *(the sampling rule)* when estimating the revenue expenditure component of bulk purchases (PS LA 2003/8). The ATO has released a number of fact sheets dealing with the rules.

Expenditure on any of the following is ineligible for the threshold or sampling rules:

- establishing a business or business venture or building up a significant store or stockpile of assets
- assets held by the taxpayer under a lease, hire purchase or similar arrangement
- assets leased or hired to another entity
- assets included in an asset register
- any asset that forms part of a collection of assets, or
- trading stock or spare parts.

Further, the threshold or sampling rules do not apply: (i) to component parts of composite assets (eg scaffolding clamps) as those items are not normally separate assets; or (ii) to taxpayers using the small business capital allowance regime in Div 328 (¶7-250).

Threshold rule

Taxpayers may immediately deduct expenditure to acquire a business asset with a GST-inclusive cost of up to $100. The ATO treats such costs as revenue expenses, although no deduction is available to the extent the taxpayer claimed an input tax credit or decreasing adjustment for the expense (¶16-860).

Sampling rule

The Commissioner accepts that a *business* taxpayer with a low-value pool (¶17-810) may use statistical sampling to determine the proportion of the total purchases on low-cost assets that are revenue expenditure. The purchases eligible for sampling are those that are not excluded as outlined above and which cost less than $1,000 (GST exclusive). The sampling results can only be applied against eligible purchases: the revenue component is immediately deductible and the capital component, to the extent that it relates to depreciating assets, is allocated to the low-value pool.

Statistical sampling is not acceptable where current business systems result in reliable individual identification and accounting of low-cost items (PS LA 2003/8). The sampling results must be statistically valid and result in objective, reliable and conservative estimates. The statistical sample continues to be valid for a maximum of 3 income years (including the income year in which the sampling takes place) so long as it remains representative.

Temporary rules allow business taxpayers to fully write off the cost of eligible depreciating assets but assets allocated to a low-value pool do not qualify (¶17-430).

[FITR ¶87-800 – ¶87-815]

¶16-154 Expenses on commencement of business

Expenses associated with the purchase or establishment of a business are generally incurred at a point too soon to be regarded as being incurred in carrying on the business, although certain start-up costs may be written off as ‘‘blackhole expenditure’’ (¶16-156).

Preliminary expenses on feasibility studies and tests in connection with establishing a paper production mill were held not to be deductible in the *Softwood Pulp & Paper case.* Similarly, expenses incurred by a coal mining company in assessing the feasibility of participating in a project to construct an aluminium smelter were not deductible as they were part of the cost of establishing a new source of income (*Griffin Coal Mining*; *Balestra*). A similar result was reached in *Case 62/94*, but the mining company was allowed a deduction for permanent employees’ salary and wages costs that had been allocated to the project. Expenditure on feasibility studies may, of course, qualify for a general deduction if they are a normal part of a taxpayer’s existing business (eg a taxpayer already in the mining industry; TR 2017/1).

In cases where it is necessary to discern between the activity constituting the carrying on of a business and an activity that is preliminary to the carrying on or recommencement of a business, it is the element of commitment to the relevant income-producing activity that establishes the requisite connection between the expenditure and the business said to be carried on for income-producing purposes (*Esso*: ¶16-152, ¶16-740; *Case 4/2007*). For example, deductions have been disallowed where the activity amounted only to the carrying out of a preliminary R&D project and the expenditure was incurred prior to carrying on the business (*Goodman Fielder Wattie*; *Howland-Rose*; *Brody*).

Costs of trips to secure export markets as a preliminary to the establishment of a business would not normally be deductible (¶16-270). No deduction is available to an employer for the cost of drawing up employment agreements for a new business (TR 2000/5).

Expenses incurred during the early years of a business before any income commences to be derived may be deductible where this is a normal characteristic of the type of business — as in mining operations and primary production (IT 2208). This is subject to the special rules regarding losses from non-commercial business activities outlined at ¶16-020 if the expenses are incurred by an individual (alone or in partnership).

Certain project infrastructure costs and feasibility study costs may be deductible under special provisions (¶19-050).

[FITR ¶31-550, ¶31-560, ¶32-610, ¶32-630]

¶16-155 Expenses on cessation of business

Payments incurred in closing down a business, as distinct from carrying it on, would not normally be deductible under the ordinary deduction provisions. For this reason, retirement payments made as compensation on the closing down of a business would not be allowed under ITAA97 s 8-1, although they may qualify for deduction under the retiring allowances provisions (¶16-540). Payments to creditors by liquidators following lodgment of proofs of debt were deductible where they were made when the company was still solvent, the unsecured creditors were paid 100 cents in the dollar and some staff and assets were retained (*EA Marr & Sons (Sales)*).

For the deductibility of expenses incurred as a result of business activities that have since ceased, see ¶16-010 and ¶16-740.

Certain types of business-related capital expenditures related to ceasing business are specifically made deductible under s 40-880, including costs incurred to stop the business or to liquidate a company that carried on a business (¶16-156).

Accrued leave entitlements

Where a business is sold and the purchaser assumes liability for making payments in respect of accrued leave entitlements of employees, the purchaser can claim a deduction for these payments at the time payment is made to the employee. A payment made by the former employer to the new employer in respect of accrued leave entitlements of transferred employees may be deductible under ITAA97 s 26-10 if the payment is made under an Australian law, or an award, order, determination or industrial agreement under an Australian law (¶16-040). However no deduction is available under s 26-10 if the payment by the old employer to the buyer of the business (the new employer) is simply made as a result of a contractual obligation. The amount is also not deductible under s 8-1 (ID 2003/827).

[FITR ¶31-570, ¶68-140]

¶16-156 Write-off for ("blackhole") business capital expenditure

Except for small and medium businesses (see below), capital expenditure that is not otherwise deductible and that relates to a business that is, was or is proposed to be carried on for a taxable purpose is deductible over 5 years provided the deduction is not denied by some other provision (''blackhole expenditure'') (ITAA97 s 40-880). The deduction is available at the rate of 20%, starting in the year in which the expenditure is incurred and for the next 4 years. For expenditure to be related to a business, there must be a sufficient and relevant connection between expenditure and the business (TR 2011/6). For the meaning of ''capital'', see ¶16-060.

Thus, a taxpayer can deduct capital expenditure they incur in relation to their current business; or a business that used to be, or is proposed to be, carried on. A deduction is also available for expenditure incurred to liquidate or deregister a company of which the taxpayer was a member, to wind up a partnership of which the taxpayer was a partner or to wind up a trust of which the taxpayer was a beneficiary, if the company, partnership or trust carried on a business.

In relation to the *taxpayer's* business, a deduction is only available to the extent that the business is carried on, was carried on or is proposed to be carried on for a taxable purpose. However, no deduction is available if the taxpayer ceases to exist, eg it is wound up. A ''taxable purpose'' is the purpose of producing assessable income, the purpose of exploration or prospecting, the purpose of mining site rehabilitation, or environmental protection activities. Further, the deduction may be reduced under the tax-preferred leasing provisions in s 250-150 (¶23-210).

Expenditure relating to *another entity's* business is deductible only to the extent that such business was carried on, or is proposed to be carried on, for a taxable purpose. Furthermore, the expenditure must relate to the assessable income derived by the taxpayer from the business and to the business that was carried on or is proposed to be carried on.

▶ Planning point

The expenditure must relate to the business of the entity. For example, if the income of the business was from retail trading, the expenditure must be incurred in relation to that business and not for other purposes (eg to purchase shares for investment purposes).

Where a business is proposed to be carried on, it must be reasonable, having regard to any relevant circumstances, to conclude that the business is proposed to be carried on within a reasonable time.

If expenditure on a single thing or service serves more than one purpose, it may be apportioned on a fair and reasonable basis. If the business is carried on for both taxable and non-taxable purposes, a fair and reasonable apportionment may be made on the basis of the proportion of exempt income to total income. However this may be inappropriate if for instance an integral part of the business activities did not have a taxable purpose (TR 2011/6).

An apportionment must be made to exclude from deduction under s 40-880 certain expenditure including where:

(a) it forms part of the cost of a depreciating asset that the taxpayer holds, used to hold or will hold, or

(b) it is otherwise deductible or it would be taken into account in working out an assessable profit, deductible loss, or capital gain or capital loss (TD 2010/1, TD 2011/8 to TD 2011/10 dealing with consolidated groups), excluding expenditure incurred to preserve the value of goodwill, or

(c) it forms part of the cost of land, or

(d) it is in relation to a lease or other legal or equitable right, eg a profit à prendre, easement or right of access to land, franchise rights (*Inglewood and Districts Community Enterprises*), excluding expenditure incurred to preserve the value of goodwill, or

(e) another provision would expressly make the expenditure non-deductible (eg entertainment expenditure), or

(f) the expenditure is of a private or domestic nature, or relates to gaining or producing exempt income or non-assessable non-exempt income.

Support payments made by a parent company to its loss-making subsidiary, or to its subsidiary that is not sufficiently profitable, are not deductible under s 40-880 because they are taken into account when calculating a capital gain or capital loss on CGT events happening to the parent company's direct or indirect investment in the subsidiary (ie fourth element expenditure; ¶11-550) (TD 2014/14). In this context, support payments are those that provide financial assistance to a subsidiary in a start-up period, or in times of adverse business conditions or financial stress.

Furthermore, no deduction is available for repayments (unless the amount was included in assessable income), returns in respect of a debt or equity interest (ID 2011/78; ID 2011/79), or amounts excluded from the cost of a depreciating asset or the cost base or reduced cost base of a CGT asset because of a market value substitution rule.

Section 40-880 is intended to provide a deduction for business capital expenditure that falls outside the positive business limb of s 8-1. However, the mere fact that the expenditure fails the positive business limb of s 8-1 does not necessarily bring it into s 40-880. Furthermore non-business expenditure (eg expenditure relating to employment or passive investment) is not subject to s 40-880.

Where expenditure is incurred in relation to an asset, the expenditure is appropriately included in the cost of the depreciating asset (for the purposes of the capital allowance rules in Div 40, where the expenditure is incurred on or after 1 July 2005) or the cost base of the CGT asset (for CGT events that happen on or after 1 July 2005) (¶17-100, ¶17-105).

The non-commercial loss provisions in Div 35 apply to business expenditure by individuals (either alone or in partnership) that is deductible under s 40-880 (¶16-020). A person who is not taken to be conducting a personal services business is prevented from deducting any amount (including under s 40-880) that an employee could not deduct in relation to personal services income (s 85-10).

If the taxpayer incurred the expenses under an arrangement with someone who was not at arm's length, and the expenses are higher than market value, the eligible expenditure is limited to the market value (ITAA97 s 40-885; ¶17-045, ¶17-050).

Some costs involved in either accepting a government payment to industry or finalising business obligations may be deductible under s 40-880, if they are costs incurred to stop carrying on a business and are not otherwise deductible (TR 2006/3).

Start-up costs for entrepreneurs, small and medium businesses

Small business entities, medium business entities and taxpayers not yet carrying on a business may be able to immediately deduct certain start-up capital expenses incurred for a business they propose to carry on (s 40-880(2A)).

To qualify, the capital expenditure must relate to a proposed business. It needs to be incurred in obtaining advice or services for the proposed structure or operation of the business. Alternatively, it must be a fee, tax or charge paid to an Australian government agency relating to the set up or operating structure of the business.

The taxpayer must either be a small business entity (deductible from 2015–16) or a medium business entity (deductible from 2020–21) for the income year the expense was incurred. Alternatively, for the year the expense was incurred, the taxpayer must neither: (i) carry on a business; nor (ii) be connected or affiliated with a non-small business entity or non-medium business entity that carries on a business (ss 328-125; 328-130; ¶7-050).

Note that the non-commercial loss rules may operate to defer the deduction for a proposed business activity until the income year the proposed business starts, if the taxpayer is an individual (¶16-020).

[FITR ¶88-783 – ¶88-790]

¶16-157 Non-deductible non-cash business benefits

A deduction allowable to a business taxpayer may be reduced where non-cash business benefits are provided to induce the taxpayer to purchase particular items of plant or equipment or to receive particular services (ITAA36 s 51AK).

If the benefit is a private benefit, ie is not to be used exclusively for the purpose of deriving assessable income, then:

- the taxpayer will be treated as having paid the full arm's length price for the benefit
- the cost of the main item is reduced accordingly.

▶ Example

A taxpayer purchases a computer for business purposes for a total expenditure of $10,000 and as a ''free bonus'' receives from the supplier a watch worth $500 for the taxpayer's private use. The taxpayer will be treated as having paid $9,500 for the computer and $500 for the watch. Depreciation on the computer will therefore be based on a cost of $9,500. The deemed $500 payment for the watch is not deductible under ITAA97 s 8-1 because it is not incurred for the purpose of gaining or producing assessable income, nor does the watch qualify for depreciation because it is not a business asset.

This provision is not specifically limited to the purchase of plant or equipment or the provision of services. It applies wherever: (a) a taxpayer incurs expenditure under an agreement that calls for a non-cash business benefit to be provided to the taxpayer or another person; and (b) the benefit is not to be used exclusively for the purpose of gaining the taxpayer's assessable income.

A ''non-cash business benefit'' means property or services provided wholly or partly in connection with a business relationship (ITAA36 ss 21A; 51AK(4)).

For the assessability of the arm's length value of a non-cash business benefit provided to a taxpayer, see ¶10-030.

[FTR ¶7-130, ¶26-660]

¶16-158 Work in progress payments

Payments made to acquire work in progress in the form of partly-manufactured goods would normally be treated as payments for trading stock (¶9-150).

In the case of a professional practice or service business, work in progress means work that has been performed but has not yet been completed to a stage where a recoverable debt has arisen. Where a business is purchased and an amount is paid as part of the purchase price for work in progress, an amount that can be identified as being for work in progress (other than goods) is assessable to the seller (ITAA97 s 15-50) and deductible to the buyer (ITAA97 s 25-95). In the absence of the specific deduction for the buyer, there would have been double taxation because the buyer would also have been assessable on the proceeds of the work in progress when it subsequently billed clients.

The deduction is available in the income year in which the payment is made, provided that at the end of that income year a recoverable debt has arisen for the work or is reasonably expected to arise within 12 months after payment. To the extent that this does not apply, the deduction will be available in the income year following the year of payment.

▶ Example

On 1 December Income Year 1, Sally, a sole trader, sells her business to Snowy Partners. The sale price includes $10,000 for work in progress. As at 30 June Income Year 1, $3,000 of the work in progress has been billed to clients. It is also reasonable to expect that a further $5,000 will be billed to clients by 1 December Income Year 2. This means that a total of $8,000 is deductible to Snowy Partners in Income Year 1. The balance ($2,000) will be deductible in Income Year 2.

Although this issue will commonly arise in the context of partners retiring from professional partnerships (¶5-070), these provisions apply generally and are not limited to partnership situations.

[FITR ¶65-560]

¶16-159 Lease/licence termination payments

Lease surrender payments made by a lessee are generally of a capital nature, except where the lessee carries on a business of entering into and surrendering leases (TR 2005/6). Similarly, lease surrender payments made by a lessor are generally not deductible under s 8-1, even though the payment is made in order to re-let the property at a higher rent (such expenditure may form part of the cost base of an asset for the purposes of the CGT rules: ¶11-550). However, such payments may be deductible if the lessor carries on a business that involves granting and surrendering leases as a normal incident of it, or that involves incurring recurrent outlays to obtain lease surrenders as part of the constant demand of its business which have to be met out of circulating capital (TR 2005/6).

Capital expenditure incurred to terminate a lease or licence (including an authority, permit or quota) is deductible at the rate of 20% from the income year in which the lease or licence is terminated and for each of the next 4 income years (s 25-110). The deduction is only available if the expenditure is incurred in the course of carrying on a business or in connection with ceasing to carry on a business. This means that the deduction is not available if the taxpayer is not carrying on a business, eg in the case of a lessor of one or 2 residential rental properties (IT 2423; TR 93/32). It is available to a lessee, lessor, licensee, licensor, and also to any third party making a payment to obtain the termination of the lease or licence. If the payment is made by instalments, no deduction is available until the lease is terminated.

Such deduction is not available in respect of a finance lease (ie a lease that transfers substantially all the risks and rewards incidental to ownership of an asset) or if, after the termination, the taxpayer or an associate enters into another lease or licence of the same kind with the same party or an associate of that party. In addition, no deduction is available to the extent that the expenditure is for the granting or receipt of another lease or licence in relation to the asset that was the subject of the original lease or licence.

If the parties did not deal at arm's length, the deduction is limited to the market value of what the expenditure was for (assuming the termination did not occur and was never proposed to occur).

[FITR ¶65-640]

Employee Expenses

¶16-160 Expenses incidental and relevant to employment

In accordance with general principles, an employee is entitled to a deduction for expenditure incurred in gaining or producing assessable income, but cannot claim for expenditure that is of a capital, private or domestic nature.

To qualify for a deduction, it is not necessary for the employee to show that the claimed expenditure is incurred as an express or implied condition of employment (*Wilkinson*). Even so, it will normally strengthen a taxpayer's case if the taxpayer is able to provide some evidence that the employer considers that the type of expenditure in question falls within the scope of the employment. However, the mere fact that the employee incurs the expense at the direction of the employer does not mean that the amount is necessarily deductible (TR 97/12). The requirement for deduction is satisfied "if the subject of the claim . . . is something that might ordinarily be expected to occur in carrying out the duties of the employment" (IT 2198).

No deduction is available for repayments of workers compensation payments out of an award for damages (*Rayner*).

Where an amount received must be and is repaid in a later year and the repayment is not deductible, the amount is non-assessable and non-exempt (ITAA97 s 59-30; ¶10-280). See also TD 2008/9 for amounts mistakenly paid as salary or wages to employees (or as income support payments or worker's compensation amounts), to which they are not beneficially entitled, and which they are obliged to repay.

Special rules generally require the *substantiation* of employment-related expenses such as for meals, accommodation, tools, protective clothing, trade journals, subscriptions, repairs and election expenses (¶16-210).

The ATO has issued an *Employees guide for work expenses* setting out deductibility rules for common expenses and related substantiation requirements and TR 2020/1 to explain the Commissioner's view on the fundamental general deductibility principles.

Where an expense allowance is received

While an expense allowance received by an employee is generally assessable to the employee (¶10-060), the Commissioner may not allow expenses incurred over and above the amount of the allowance as a deduction. However, if expenses are incidental and relevant to the employment and are not of a capital, private or domestic nature, and if an itemised list of outgoings can be substantiated, the outgoings are clearly deductible, irrespective of whether they exceed the allowance. Where the deductible expenditure is less than the allowance, the whole allowance may remain assessable. Where the allowance is not assessable because it is subject to FBT (as in the case of a living-away-from-home allowance: ¶35-460), no deduction is available to the employee for expenses covered by the allowance (TR 98/14).

The receipt of a site or height allowance, or an allowance to compensate for inconvenience, isolation or discomfort suffered during the course of employment, does not entitle the employee to an offsetting deduction (TD 93/49). Similarly, where an employee in receipt of an allowance for depreciation of personal and/or household effects as a result of relocation in employment uses the allowance to purchase personal and/or household effects, the expenditure is not deductible (IT 2614). The receipt of a clothing, uniform or laundry allowance does not make the expenditure on buying (or washing or maintaining) conventional clothing (¶16-180) necessarily deductible (TR 98/5; TR 97/12).

Expense paid or reimbursed by employer

If an employee incurs an expense that is paid directly by the employer, the payment by the employer gives rise to a fringe benefit on which the employer may be liable for FBT (¶35-330). The same applies if the employee is reimbursed for the expense by the employer. In such cases, the amount paid is not assessable to the employee. Correspondingly, the employee's entitlement to a deduction for the expense is generally either reduced or disallowed altogether (ITAA36 s 51AH) but depreciation deductions may still be available (¶17-010). For the assessability of recoupments generally, see ¶10-260 and ¶10-270.

Where an employee makes a contribution towards the cost of certain types of fringe benefits provided by the employer, the employee is not entitled to a deduction for the contribution to the extent that the contribution is, in effect, a payment for the private element of the benefit (ITAA36 s 51AJ). This provision applies to board benefits, loan benefits, property benefits, airline transport benefits and residual benefits.

Providers of personal services

Where an individual generates personal services income as a contractor but is not carrying on a personal services business, the deductions relating to that income are generally restricted to those that would have been available if the individual had been an employee. For details see ¶30-600.

Specific deductions

For specific deductions allowable to employees, see ¶16-170 and following as well as the list at ¶16-005. For a list of rulings issued by the Commissioner on the types of deductions that can be claimed by taxpayers in specific occupations, see ¶16-635.

[FITR ¶34-130, ¶37-000; FTR ¶26-640, ¶26-650]

¶16-170 Employee expenses: deductible items

An employee is entitled, under the general deduction provision of ITAA97 s 8-1, to deductions for the following items (see also the rulings referred to at ¶16-635).

• *Tools of trade* — Expenditure in insuring and repairing tools of trade in certain vocations is deductible. A deduction is available for the decline in value of tools (¶17-010). In some circumstances, an outright deduction for low-cost tools is available (¶17-330), or alternatively low-cost assets may be pooled (¶17-810). For example, building workers or carpenters may claim for hand tools and hairdressers may claim for combs, curlers, razors, etc, which they themselves supply. Similarly, tools or instruments may be deductible to engineers, electricians, painters, metal trade workers, waterside workers, doctors and so on.

• *Equipment* — Employees are also entitled to claim deductions for the cost of insuring and repairing various items of their own equipment (eg calculators, computers, mobile telephones, answering machines, electronic work organisers and pagers) that they use for work-related purposes. Generally, the cost of equipment is depreciable (see ¶17-010 and ¶17-810 for the provisions dealing with the decline in value of assets and pooling of low value assets). Low-cost items may be immediately deductible (¶17-330). Teachers may claim for teaching aids (TR 95/14, but see *Jones*), and shearers for shearers' slings (*Gaydon*). The cost of maintaining a watch may be deductible to taxpayers such as nurses for a nurse's fob watch (TR 95/15), physical education teachers for a dedicated stopwatch (TR 95/14), and police officers in the diving squad for a scuba diving watch (TR 95/13). Personal paging units may be deductible to employees on call, such as nurses and doctors. The cost of larger items of equipment, such as television sets, computers and voice recorders, briefcases, kitbags, suitcases, etc, which are used as an integral part of employment, may also be claimed under the depreciation provisions (TR 95/19; ¶17-010, ¶17-330). The treatment of software is outlined at ¶16-725. For the treatment of protective sunglasses and anti-glare glasses, see ¶16-180.

• *Technical and trade books, journals* — These are allowable where reasonably necessary to discharge the duties of employment efficiently and sufficiently (eg in the case of an architect, engineer, real estate agent, etc). As to the deductibility of trade, business and professional subscriptions, see ¶16-430 and ¶16-440.

• *Gifts, advertising* — Real estate industry employees who earn commission income are entitled to a deduction for the cost of advertising, gifts and greeting cards, property presentation costs and referral expenses (TR 98/6). A contribution (including membership fees) or gift made by an individual to political parties, members and candidates, that is related to the individual's employment income may be deductible (s 26-22; ¶16-950).

• *Travel expenses, self-education expenses, home office expenses* (¶16-220, ¶16-310, ¶16-450, ¶16-480).

• *Entertainment expenses* — To a limited extent (¶16-390).

• *Telephone expenses* (¶16-400).

• *Premiums for sickness/accident insurance* (¶16-560).

• *Tax-related expenses* (¶16-850).

• *Secretarial services fees* — For example *Wells*; including when incurred by a taxpayer in order to overcome physical disability (*Frisch*, but not under a purely domestic relationship: *France*; *Brown*). See also ¶16-520.

[FITR ¶37-000]

¶16-175 Employee expenses: non-deductible items

The following expenses are *not* deductible to employees, subject to limited exceptions.

Meal and accommodation expenses

The cost of meals or accommodation is generally a non-deductible private expense (*Cooper*) unless the occasion of the outgoing gives the expenditure the essential character of a working expense, as in the case of work-related entertainment (¶16-390) or expenditure incurred while away from home (*Roads and Traffic Authority*; ¶16-220). See also CR 2004/30 (costs incurred by shoppers while carrying out assignments for Shoppers Anonymous). Expenditure on meals consumed by truck drivers (TR 95/18) or members of parliament (TR 1999/10) in the normal course of a working day will not have sufficient connection with the income-producing activities and is in any case a private expense. A truck driver who worked up to 18 hours a day was denied a deduction for meal expenses (other than award overtime meal allowance expenses) (*Carlaw*). No deduction is available for the cost of a meal purchased between jobs (TD 93/26). Wine purchased by a beverage analyst was not deductible (ID 2002/319).

A deduction for the cost of meals and accommodation is available where the employee's work activity required them to travel, required them to sleep away from home overnight, they have a permanent home elsewhere and the cost is not incurred for the employee to relocate or live away from home (*Draft* TR 2017/D6). In *Re Pollak Partners*, the AAT stated that, had the cost of lunch consumed during computer training courses been incurred by the computer trainers (rather than by their employer), such cost would have been allowable because the trainers were required to consume lunch with the course participants and to perform work duties while eating lunch. See also ¶16-450 about the deductibility of meal expenses incurred in relation to self-education. Contributions by a shearing industry employee towards the cost of meals provided by their employer are deductible if the employee is paid at the ''not found'' rate, the taxpayer is travelling away from home overnight in the course of their duties as a shearing industry employee and the substantiation requirements are met (ID 2010/187).

Child care expenses

An employee's expenses in having someone care for a child during working hours are not deductible (*Martin*), including in one case where the child care was necessary to enable a taxpayer to undertake tertiary studies that were instrumental in obtaining job promotions (*Jayatilake*). If, in addition to providing child care services, the child carer carries out duties related to the taxpayer's income-producing activities, it seems that some part of the expenses of hiring the child carer may be allowable (*Case V39*).

Grooming expenses

Expenditure incurred by taxpayers on grooming (hairdressing and cosmetics) is generally not deductible even though the taxpayer may be required to maintain a high standard of appearance (*Case 72/96*; TR 96/18) — see also taxation rulings on: shop assistants (TR 95/10), flight attendants (TR 95/19), hospitality industry employees (TR 95/11), hairdressers (TR 95/16), employee journalists (TR 98/14) and real estate industry employees (TR 98/6). Similarly, hairdressing costs are not deductible to members of the Australian Defence Forces even though the expense is incurred to comply with military regulations (TR 95/17). However, a deduction is allowable to performing artists for the cost of make-up and for the cost of maintaining a particular style or length of hair for the purposes of a performance (but not for the cost of products to relieve skin conditions) (TR 95/20).

In most cases (including where the taxpayer travels for work on aircraft as a passenger) expenditure on moisturizers, make-up, hairdressing and conditioners is not deductible. However such expenditure is allowable to flight attendants if there are harsh working conditions and the employer requires the taxpayer to be well groomed (*Mansfield*; TR 95/19). Moisturisers and conditioners may be deductible to a hydrotherapy assistant who is constantly exposed to chlorinated water (TR 2003/16). The cost of hairdressing and make-up was not allowed to a television newsreader in *Case 72/96*.

Health-related expenses

A deduction is normally not allowable for the cost of vaccinations as a precaution against diseases that may be contracted in the course of the taxpayer's income-producing activities (eg for nurses TR 95/15 or cleaners TR 95/8). However, the cost of vaccination against Q fever may be deductible for a taxpayer whose business involves regular contact with potentially infected cattle (ID 2002/775). The cost (including travel costs) of medical examinations required for the renewal of a licence required for employment (eg by an airline employee) is also allowable (TR 95/19). Travel and accommodation related expenses to obtain a medical certificate are deductible where the certificate is required to be provided to a paying authority to ensure the continued receipt of workers compensation. The expenses are incurred to maintain entitlement to income by satisfying the specific requirements of the workers compensation legislation and are therefore incurred in gaining or producing the assessable workers compensation payments. No deduction was available for the cost of travelling to medical and other health practitioners for treatment (*Rossitto*) or for the cost of psychotherapy sought for work-related stress (*Case 9/2005*) or for contributions to a private health fund, even if it is a condition of employment that the person take out the insurance (TD 93/22). For the treatment of sun protection items, see ¶16-180. See ¶16-190 for fitness expenses.

[FITR ¶32-020 – ¶32-050, ¶33-235, ¶34-130, ¶34-210]

¶16-180 Occupational clothing and protective gear

To be deductible, expenditure on clothing and its maintenance must have the ''essential character'' of an outgoing incurred in gaining or producing assessable income, ie an income-producing expense. Clothing expenditure is generally private expenditure and is not deductible. In some circumstances, however, expenditure on certain types of occupational clothing gives rise to a deduction. The deduction would cover the cost of buying, renting, laundering, dry-cleaning, repairing and replacing the clothing. For the Commissioner's views on the deductibility of clothing expenditure generally, see TR 97/12. Clothing expenditure incurred in earning exempt income (eg on Army Reserve uniforms) is not deductible.

Conventional clothing

While there is no universal rule that conventional clothing can never be deductible, in most cases expenditure on conventional clothing will not be deductible (TR 94/22; TR 97/12). One example of a successful claim was by the personal secretary to the wife of a state governor, who was allowed a deduction for expenditure incurred on additional daily changes of clothing, including hats, gloves and formal wear (*Edwards*). The fact that expenditure is on additional clothing (ie over and above the taxpayer's personal requirements of modesty, decency and warmth) is not sufficient to establish deductibility if the income-earning activities do not turn on the wearing of the additional clothes and the clothes are not specific and suited only for the income-earning activity (TR 97/12).

A flight attendant was allowed a deduction for shoes she wore on board the aircraft. Besides matching her uniform, the cabin shoes had to be a half size too large for ordinary use because of swelling caused by the pressurised cabin conditions, and the nature of the job resulted in regular scuffing of the shoes (*Mansfield*). The cost of shoes, socks and stockings is not deductible unless the items form an integral part of a compulsory and distinctive uniform, the components of which are set out by the employer in its expressed uniform policy or guidelines (TR 96/16; see also taxation rulings on shop assistants (TR 95/10), police officers (TR 95/13), nursing industry employees (TR 95/15), hairdressers (TR 95/16), Defence Force members (TR 95/17) and airline industry employees (TR 95/19)).

The following are examples where expenditure on conventional clothing would be deductible: (a) a professional actor who buys clothing to wear on stage as a costume in a particular production (TR 95/20); (b) police officers who are required as part of their law enforcement activities to wear clothing of a kind they do not normally wear that enables them to pose as criminals (TR 95/13); and (c) a television game show host who buys evening and formal wear to complement the sets and prizes (TR 95/20).

Some examples of claims that have *not* been allowed include: a solicitor's dark suit, taxi-driver's white shirt and nurse's stockings; sports clothes worn by sports teachers (eg T-shirts, shorts, socks and running/aerobic shoes) and fitness instructors (*Staker*; TR 95/14; TR 97/12); formal black dinner suits, tails and other items of conventional clothing (eg evening dresses, shirts, black trousers, shoes and bow ties) worn by members of an orchestra (TD 93/111); swimsuit of a swimming instructor. The CEO and director of a company was not entitled to a deduction of about $38,800 (out of a total amount of approximately $81,800) for abnormal work-related clothing expenses because the clothing items were conventional in nature (*Case 3/2006*).

The fact that an employer requires a taxpayer to dress in a particular way for work will not in itself be sufficient to allow a deduction. Deductions have been disallowed, for example, to a female shop assistant required to wear an ordinary black dress to work (*Case H2*) and to another required to wear a black skirt and white blouse (*Case U95*). Expenditure incurred by an employee on an employer's range of brand name conventional clothing, which is required to be worn as a condition of employment, is not deductible (TR 94/22). This is to be contrasted with the decision in *Case U85* where the manager of a footwear retailer who was required, as part of the terms of her employment, to purchase and wear a large number of very fashionable and expensive shoes was allowed a deduction for the amount over and above what she would otherwise have spent on shoes.

Compulsory uniforms

Compulsory uniforms (ie non-conventional clothing that the employee is compelled to wear) such as those worn by police and airline pilots will generally be deductible (TR 96/16; TD 1999/62). A ''uniform'' is a collection of inter-related items of clothing and accessories (including stockings and footwear) that is distinctive to a particular organisation (TR 97/12).

Non-compulsory uniforms

Deductions are specifically denied for non-compulsory uniforms unless the design of the uniform is entered on the Register of Approved Occupational Clothing at the time the expense is incurred (ITAA97 Div 34), in which case a deduction is available for the rental, purchase or maintenance of the non-compulsory uniform. The Register is kept by the Industry Secretary who can register a design only if it meets certain criteria set out in guidelines formulated by the Treasurer. The *Approved Occupational Clothing Guidelines 2017* were registered on the Register of Legislative Instruments on 11 August 2017 (*Legislative Instrument* F2017L01012). It is the employer's responsibility to apply for registration of the design. This restriction on deductions in respect of non-compulsory uniforms does not apply to occupation-specific clothing or protective clothing.

A ''uniform'' is a set of one or more items of clothing that distinctively identify the wearer as a person associated with the employee's employer or a group consisting of that employer and one or more of its associates (ITAA97 s 34-15). A uniform is ''non-compulsory'' where the employer does not have an express policy that prohibits employees substituting items of ordinary clothing for an item of clothing included in the set or, if the employer has such a policy, it is not consistently enforced.

Collections of conventional clothing are not automatically excluded from registration because they lack a particular or peculiar design, provided the uniform has a sufficiently distinctive look and a cohesive and obvious identity. Thus, the clothing design of a heavy engineering company that adopted a colour-coded system for clothing worn by employees in different departments should have been included in the Register. The clothing consisted of standard King Gee catalogue items acquired in the relevant colours with the employer identifier, a woven badge, sewn on (*Walkers*).

Occupation-specific clothing

A deduction will generally be allowed for occupation-specific clothing. This is clothing that distinctively identifies a person as a member of a specific profession, trade, vocation, occupation or calling.

For example, the cost of purchasing and maintaining a female nurse's traditional uniform (eg cap, white uniform, cardigan and special non-slip shoes, but not stockings or hose unless they are part of a compulsory uniform) is deductible (TR 95/15; TR 97/12). Other examples of deductible occupation-specific clothing are a religious cleric's ceremonial robes, a chef's chequered pants and a barrister's robes; but the cost of long-lasting clothing such as judges' robes, barristers' silk robes and wigs worn by employee lawyers for court appearances is depreciable (TR 95/9; TR 97/12).

Clothing that could belong to a number of occupations would not fall within the definition of occupation-specific clothing (eg a white coat worn with white trousers). However, a white coat worn by, for example, a dentist or laboratory technician would probably qualify for a deduction if worn as protective clothing.

Glasses, sunhats and sunscreen

Expenditure on sunglasses, sunscreen and sunhats has been held to be deductible for a range of taxpayers who were required, as part of their duties, to work outside in the open air exposed to sunlight (*Morris*). The taxpayers in this test case were a farm manager, a master of a game fishing vessel, a maritime studies teacher, a surveyor, a site construction supervisor, a self-employed builder, a physical education teacher, an electrical fitter and mechanic, a tennis umpire and a tax auditor with outdoor duties. Cosmetic products that happen to also provide sun protection would be regarded as a private expense; sun protection should be the primary purpose of the product. The cost of this expenditure must be apportioned to account for any private use.

The Commissioner has accepted that this decision applies to taxpayers who are required to work in the sun for sustained periods for all or part of the day, eg people involved in building and construction; delivery and courier services; farming, agriculture and horticulture; fishing; forestry and logging; landscaping and gardening; open-air minerals, oil and gas exploration and extraction; outdoor sports; and other outdoor services. However, it would not apply where an office worker is simply required to take a short walk between office premises (TR 2003/16).

The Commissioner has also accepted that deductions were available for items such as:

- special anti-glare glasses used by the operator of a video display unit (*Case U124*) or by pilots and flight engineers (TR 95/19)
- wrap-around sunglasses used by a police motor cycle patrol officer, where the safety features protected against more than just glare and ultra-violet radiation (*Case 10/94*)
- tinted contact lenses to alter a performing artist's eye colour or special spectacle frames required for a particular role (TR 95/20).

Other protective clothing and safety footwear

The cost of protective clothing or safety footwear is deductible. ''Protective clothing'' is clothing that is specifically designed to protect: (a) the taxpayer from personal work injury, disease or death (eg steel cap boots, safety helmets, goggles, safety glasses, breathing masks, fire-resistant clothing, rubber boots of a concreter, non-slip nurse's shoes, special gym shoes of an aerobic instructor conducting ''high impact'' classes); or (b) the taxpayer's conventional clothing or artificial limb or other aid from the hazards of the work environment (eg overalls or aprons).

Wet weather gear is deductible where it has a distinct occupational character (TR 2003/16). An example of this was *Case V79*, where the cost of a waterproof jacket, woollen jumper and thick socks acquired exclusively for use at work in the rigorous climate of the Snowy Mountains was allowed.

Based on *Morris* (above), expenditure on a protective item will have a sufficient connection with the earning of assessable income where:

- the taxpayer is exposed to the risk of illness or injury in the course of carrying out his/her income-earning activities
- the risk is not remote or negligible, ie it would be a real risk to anyone who worked where the taxpayer is required to work
- the protective item is of a kind that provides protection from that risk and would reasonably be expected to be used in the circumstances
- the taxpayer uses the item in the course of carrying out his/her income-earning activities (TR 2003/16).

Otherwise-private items may have additional features that indicate that they are not of a private or domestic nature (TR 2003/16).

The Commissioner has issued rulings on the circumstances in which protective clothing expenditure will be deductible to various categories of employees including shearers (TR 2003/16), building workers, shop assistants, hospitality industry employees, machine operators and hairdressers (¶16-635).

If the expenditure is of a capital nature (eg the cost of an X-ray technician's lead apron), a deduction is available for the item's decline in value (¶17-000).

Laundry and dry-cleaning expenses

A deduction is available for the cost of cleaning and maintaining clothing and footwear if the items are used for income-producing purposes and the expense is occasioned by the performance of income-producing duties (TR 97/12). In effect, the deduction is only allowed in relation to the laundering of protective clothing, occupation-specific clothing, compulsory and non-compulsory uniforms specified above, as well as conventional clothing in limited circumstances (TR 98/5). "Abnormal expenditure" incurred in dry-cleaning conventional work clothing was allowed in *Westcott* (note, however, that the Commissioner generally does not accept the deductibility of abnormal expenditure on conventional clothing: TR 98/14).

Clothing and laundry expenses are a key focus area for ATO audits.

[FITR ¶34-140, ¶82-050]

¶16-190 Fitness expenses

An employee required to have a high degree of physical fitness to carry out a job may be entitled to deduct expenses associated with keeping fit — eg a police academy physical training instructor (TD 93/114; TR 95/13) or a performing artist such as a circus trapeze artist (TR 95/20). However, teachers, even physical education teachers, are not entitled to such a deduction (TR 95/14). Similarly, fitness expenses incurred by Defence Force members are not deductible except in special circumstances requiring a fitness level well above the general standard (TR 95/17). Sport expenses incurred by sportspersons are not deductible against voluntary payments such as awards, prizes and grants (TR 1999/17).

A professional footballer contractually obliged to keep fit and obey training instructions and who was instructed by his coach to play squash for sharpening his reflexes was allowed the cost of doing so (*Case J3*; see also IT 54). A dancer employed by a professional dance company was allowed a deduction for massage treatment to keep her in good shape and injury-free — her physical well-being was so basic to her occupation that it was an implied condition of her employment that she maintain a very high level of physical fitness (*Case P90*). On the other hand, a pilot who undertook a fitness course to help him lose weight was denied a deduction for the cost of the course even though, had he failed his regular 6-monthly medical examination because he was overweight, he would have lost his pilot's licence (*Case N72*; *Case P17*; TD 93/112).

Where allowed, deductions may include transport costs, depreciation of equipment, fitness course costs, gym membership fees and protective sport footwear, but generally not the cost of conventional clothing (TD 93/114).

[FITR ¶34-240, ¶37-420]

¶16-200 Expenses of getting, changing or maintaining a job

Expenses incurred by an employee in getting a job or in changing jobs (eg travel expenses, moving expenses or costs associated with an employment agreement unrelated to the employee's business) are not deductible because the expenses come at a point in time too early to be regarded as being incurred in gaining assessable income (*Maddalena*; TR 2000/5; IT 2406; *Draft* TR 2017/D6; *Draft* TR 2019/D7). Similarly, expenditure that is a prerequisite to obtaining the particular employment (eg the cost of obtaining a police clearance certificate) is not deductible (TR 98/6). On the other hand, a public service accountant was successful in a claim for the travelling and incidental costs of arranging job interviews as part of a 12-month ''interchange'' program with private industry (*Case R40*). The cost of travelling to meet a new employer once the job has been secured may also be deductible (*Scott (No 5)*).

No deduction is available for expenses (and depreciation of assets) incurred in gaining or producing certain rebatable government assistance payments such as Newstart/ JobSeeker, Austudy, ABSTUDY, and Youth allowance (ITAA97 s 26-19: overcoming the effect of *Anstis*; ¶16-450).

Expenses incurred in travelling overseas to gain experience or qualifications to further the taxpayer's career in Australia have been characterised as expenses to obtain new employment and thus were not deductible (*MI Roberts*). In another case, however, a taxpayer who was re-employed by his former employer on returning to Australia after working overseas was allowed a deduction for the overseas travel costs (*Kropp*). The Commissioner considers that the decision in *Kropp's case* is incorrect (TR 98/9). See also ¶16-450.

A teacher who requested a transfer from one locality to another was allowed a deduction for her relocation expenses in *Case T92*. The Commissioner does not accept that the decision was correct (IT 2481) and, in a subsequent case, a taxpayer who was required by his employer to relocate or face possible retrenchment was denied a deduction for his moving expenses (*Fullerton*).

Costs associated with extending, varying, renegotiating or renewing an employment agreement or drawing up a replacement agreement with an existing employer are deductible to an employee if the agreement allowed for such changes (TR 2000/5).

Expenses incurred in applying for a promotion are deductible provided they objectively lead to, or are likely to lead to, an increase in the taxpayer's assessable income without a change in the taxpayer's income-earning activities (TD 93/175).

Commissions paid by employee performing artists to theatrical agents are an allowable deduction, but up-front joining or search fees or the cost of attending auditions are not deductible (TR 95/20). Similarly, a deduction is allowable to an agency nurse for fees paid by the nurse to the agency (but not for up-front fees, joining fees or search fees) (TR 95/15). Management fees paid by 2 professional footballers to management companies for services performed in negotiating playing contracts were deductible because the footballers were conducting a business and the fees were of a revenue nature (*Spriggs; Riddell* discussed in CCH *Tax Week* ¶728 (2009)).

[FITR ¶34-230]

¶16-210 Substantiation of work expenses

The key principle underlying substantiation is that to deduct work expenses, the taxpayer (whether an individual or a partnership including at least one individual) needs to substantiate them by obtaining written evidence of the expense (ITAA97 Div 900: ss 900-1 to 900-250).

The substantiation rules are explained below. Many of the concepts are the same as those contained in the car expenses substantiation rules (¶16-320) and appropriate cross-references to further explanation have been provided to avoid unnecessary duplication.

- Written evidence (paper or electronic) is a document obtained from the supplier of the goods or services that contains certain information (¶16-340).
- The requirement to obtain a document from the supplier does *not* apply if the expense is $10 or less and the total of all such expenses is $200 or less. In such cases, the taxpayer may instead make a record of the expense.
- The taxpayer's record of the expense (eg in a diary or on a travel itinerary) will also be sufficient if it would be unreasonable to insist on the supplier's document. Such expense may be more than $10 and does not count towards the $200 limit. Examples of expenses for which the taxpayer's record is acceptable are: toll bridge fees, parking meter fees, cash payments to informants and entrance fees to shows where entry tickets must be handed in on entry (TR 97/24).
- Annual payment summaries (¶26-640) can be used as evidence of certain expenses, including where expenses of the same nature are shown on the summary as a total (eg the total amount of union fees paid during the year).
- The written evidence must be retained by the taxpayer and be made available to the Commissioner on request. It is not required to be lodged with annual tax returns.
- Records need to be kept for a period of 5 years from the date of lodgment of the return in which the claims are made. This period is extended if, at the end of the 5 years, the taxpayer is involved in a tax dispute with the Commissioner.
- The substantiation requirements do *not* apply where an employee's claims for work expenses (including laundry expenses) total $300 or less. If the total amount of the claims exceeds $300 the total amount must be substantiated. Expenses relating to allowances covered by special rules (ie overtime meal allowances, travel allowances and award transport payments: see below) and car expenses are not taken into account in determining whether this limit has been reached.
- Special rules apply if records are lost or destroyed (¶16-340).
- The Commissioner has a discretion in certain circumstances not to apply the substantiation requirements (see below).

Even where the substantiation requirements do not apply (as in the case of certain overtime meal expenses — see below) the taxpayer must still be able to show that the expense was incurred for deductible purposes and that the basis for determining the amount of the claim is reasonable (TR 2004/6).

Work expenses

"Work expenses" are expenses that are incurred by a taxpayer in producing salary, wages or certain PAYG withholding payments (ie payments to employees, company directors and office holders, return to work payments, retirement payments, employment termination payments and annuities, benefit and compensation payments) (¶26-120) (s 900-12). Common examples of work expenses include the cost of tools, protective clothing, periodical subscriptions to trade, business or professional associations, repairs, payments associated with the leasing of property used in the job, and interest and borrowing costs associated with loans used to produce salary or wages. Depreciation of property used to produce the salary or wages (and other withholding payments) is expressly included in work expenses (s 900-30).

Work expenses include travel allowance expenses and meal allowance expenses. Most motor vehicle expenses are not included in work expenses — however, they may be covered by the car expenses substantiation rules (¶16-320).

Local government councillors who receive an allowance or other remuneration and incur expenses while performing council business are not required to substantiate work expenses unless the council has passed a unanimous resolution that it be subject to PAYG withholding and has notified the Commissioner (TAA 1953 Sch 1 s 446-5).

Laundry expenses

If the total amount of work expenses exceeds $300 and laundry expenses exceed $150, the whole amount must be substantiated by written evidence (eg a one-month diary, evidence of average power consumption for household appliances and receipts). However, the taxpayer is not required to maintain written evidence for: (a) laundry expenses exceeding $150, provided total work expenses are less than $300; or (b) laundry expenses of up to $150 (whether or not total work expenses exceed $300). Where written evidence is not required, the Commissioner will accept claims of $1 per load (if work clothing only is being laundered), or 50 cents per load (if both work and other clothing is being laundered) (TR 98/5). Laundry expenses include the cost of washing, drying or ironing clothing, but not dry-cleaning. Laundry expenses are a key focus area for ATO audits.

Overtime meal allowances

The general rule is that no deduction is allowable for expenses incurred by an employee on food and drink for which a meal allowance is paid unless written evidence for the expense is obtained. However, an important exception to this rule applies if the taxpayer receives an overtime meal allowance under an industrial instrument and the Commissioner considers the total of the expenses claimed to be reasonable. In such a case, the cost of the overtime meals may be deductible without the requirement for written evidence. If the claim exceeds the reasonable amount specified by the Commissioner, the whole claim must be substantiated, not just the excess over the reasonable amount. For the 2019–20 income year, the reasonable amount is $31.25 per overtime meal (TD 2019/11) and for the 2020–21 income year it is $31.95 per overtime meal (TD 2020/5). An allowance up to that amount need not be included in the taxpayer's return provided the allowance was not included in the payment summary and was fully expended and no deduction is claimed (TR 2004/6; ¶16-240).

An ‘‘overtime meal allowance’’ is one that is paid under a law or industrial award or agreement for the purpose of enabling an employee to buy food or drink in connection with overtime. It does not include allowances negotiated privately between an employer and an employee or amounts folded in as part of normal salary and wages.

Travel allowances

No deduction is generally allowable for expenses incurred by an employee for the cost of food, drink, accommodation and incidentals for which a travel allowance is paid, unless written evidence of the expenditure is obtained and travel records (such as a travel diary) are kept containing particulars of each activity undertaken on the relevant travel (¶16-300). There are 2 exceptions to this rule. Note that a taxpayer relying on the 2 exceptions may still be required to show the basis for determining the amount of the claim and the connection between the taxpayer's work and the expense. In relation to accommodation, the domestic travel exception only applies if the taxpayer has used commercial accommodation establishments (TR 2004/6). See ¶16-240.

Travel in Australia

The first exception applies where the taxpayer receives a travel allowance relating to *travel in Australia*. If the Commissioner considers the amount of the expenses claimed for travel covered by the allowance to be reasonable, the travel expenses specified above may be deductible without written evidence or a diary (s 900-50). Domestic travel allowance expense claims are considered reasonable if they do not exceed the daily rates set out in TD 2019/11 for the 2019–20 income year and TD 2020/5 for the 2020–21 income year. For office holders covered by the Remuneration Tribunal, the daily travel allowances set by the Remuneration Tribunal for the particular office holder are regarded as reasonable. If the taxpayer claims an amount greater than the amount considered reasonable, the whole claim, not just the excess, must be substantiated. In *McIntosh*, the mere fact that a construction worker received a travel allowance did not entitle him to make an unsubstantiated claim for the maximum amount considered reasonable. However, the worker was entitled to claim $60 a day for unsubstantiated meal and accommodation expenses actually incurred, even though his actual travel allowance was only $39 a day.

Employee long distance truck drivers

The reasonable amounts for the 2019–20 income year for meal expenses of *employee long distance truck drivers* who receive travel allowances and sleep away from home are $25.20 for breakfast, $28.75 for lunch and $49.60 for dinner (TD 2019/11). These amounts for the 2020–21 income year are $25.75, $29.35 and $50.65 respectively (TD 2020/5). These separate amounts cannot be aggregated into a single daily amount, and cannot be moved from one meal to another.

The following claims by employee truck drivers must be substantiated in full: (a) claims exceeding the above rates by drivers who received a travel allowance and slept away from home; (b) accommodation expenses, even if an allowance has been received; and (c) claims by drivers who did not receive a travel allowance. Expenses, such as for meals, incurred by drivers who did not sleep away from home are not considered to be in respect of travel and are not deductible, even if a travel allowance has been received. TR 95/18 contains detailed information on the written evidence and travel records required to substantiate travel expenses for employee truck drivers. As owner drivers do not receive a travel allowance, travel records and written evidence are required to substantiate their accommodation, meal and other travel expenses.

Upon review or audit, employee truck drivers will be required to show how they calculated the amount they claimed, including evidence that they travelled for work on the relevant days and were required to sleep or take their major rest break away from home. They will also be required to show that they received a travel allowance for the relevant days, and correctly returned this allowance as income in their tax return.

In *Fardell*, an amount paid to truck drivers who drove over 500 km in a 24-hour period was a "loading", rather than a travel allowance, and meal expenses had to be substantiated in full. The employee truck driver in *Gleeson* established that he had incurred travel allowance expenses despite not having kept receipts or other records of his expenses. The driver was entitled to a deduction for his travel allowance expenses because they were based on the Commissioner's reasonable rates, or, alternatively, because he had a reasonable expectation that he need not comply with certain substantiation requirements (under s 900-200). The ATO has reminded employee truck drivers that they must actually incur their travel expenses to claim a deduction, and they must be able to show how their deduction claims are calculated (*Decision Impact Statement*: *Gleeson*). If the number of days away from home used by the employee to assert that their daily travel allowance expense is within the reasonable rates is not accepted (say because the employer provides a lesser number of days), the Commissioner can apply this lesser number to the total expenses claimed which can result in the daily expense exceeding the reasonable rates. The deductions will then require substantiation with receipts or records. The absence of such adequate records and the exercise of the Commissioner's discretion (see below) resulted in partial disallowance of travel allowance expenses for the truck driver in *Tyl*.

Travel outside Australia

The second exception relates to food, drink and incidentals, but not accommodation. It applies where the taxpayer receives an allowance for *travel outside Australia*. If the Commissioner considers that the total of the expenses claimed for travel covered by the allowance is reasonable, then those expenses may be deductible notwithstanding the absence of written evidence. Under this exception, accommodation expenses will still need to be substantiated by written evidence. If the taxpayer is absent for 6 or more nights in a row, travel records must be kept. However, where an overseas travel allowance is received by a taxpayer as a member of the crew of an international flight, and the claim does not exceed the amount of the allowance received, the travel records requirement is also removed. For the 2019–20 income year, overseas travel allowance expense claims are considered reasonable if they do not exceed the overseas travel allowance amount (for meals and incidentals) set out in TD 2019/11 (TD 2020/5 for 2020–21).

If the taxpayer claims more than the amount considered reasonable, the whole claim, not just the excess, must be substantiated.

The ATO has also clarified that if the above exceptions involving reasonable amounts are relied upon, and the ATO checks a taxpayer's return, taxpayers will still be required to show that they spent money in performing their work duties, how the claim was determined, that they spent the money and were not reimbursed, and that the allowance was correctly declared as income in their tax return.

When the travel allowance exceptions do not apply

The travel allowance exception does not apply to part-day travel allowances paid to employees for travel not involving an overnight absence — therefore, such allowances are fully assessable and any deductions are subject to the ordinary substantiation requirements discussed at ¶16-300 (TR 2004/6). Further, the exception only applies in relation to an allowance paid to cover expenses of work-related travel and would not apply, for example, where a set travel allowance is paid for the year regardless of whether or how often travel is undertaken. The allowance must be a bona fide amount reasonably expected to cover travel costs (TR 2004/6).

The ATO considers that the travel allowance exception does not apply to claims for living expenses of academics on sabbatical leave and that such claims must be substantiated in full.

Award transport payments

Unless the taxpayer elects otherwise, the substantiation provisions do not apply to claims within the limits of payments to employees for fares, car expenses or other transport costs, where the payment (either by way of allowance or reimbursement) does not exceed the amount payable under the relevant award as at *29 October 1986*. See ATO publication *Claiming a deduction for car expenses — award transport payments* and ¶16-326.

Commissioner's discretion to disregard substantiation rules

The Commissioner has a limited discretion not to apply the substantiation rules to an expense where the rules would otherwise affect the taxpayer's right to a deduction for the expense. The substantiation rules will not apply where the nature and quality of the evidence the taxpayer has to substantiate the claim satisfies the Commissioner that the taxpayer: (a) incurred the expense; and (b) is entitled to deduct the amount claimed. For an example of a case in which the AAT found that the Commissioner's discretion should have been exercised, see *Chaudri*. For the Commissioner's views on the exercise of the discretion, see TR 97/24, PS LA 2005/7 and PS LA 2011/25 (¶16-340).

▶ Planning point

Ensure you keep required documentation. If substantiation requirements cannot be satisfied, check whether the Commissioner's discretion may be exercised.

[FITR ¶33-270, ¶680-100]

Travel Expenses

¶16-220 Deductibility of travel expenses: general principles

Travel expenses incidental and relevant to a taxpayer's derivation of assessable income, including salary and wages, are deductible under the ordinary provisions of ITAA97 s 8-1, but subject to the limitations of that section. A simple example of deductible travel expenses would be car expenses incurred by a commercial traveller in carrying out work-related duties. Certain taxpayers' deductions for travel expenses in connection with residential rental properties are denied (¶16-650).

The Commissioner has stated that an employee's travel expenses are deductible where the travel is undertaken in performing the employee's work activities (*Draft* TR 2017/D6) or occurs on work time (*Draft* TR 2019/D7). The factors he considers relevant to determine this are: whether the work activities require the employee to undertake the travel or whether the travel fits within the duties of employment; whether the employee is paid, directly or indirectly, to undertake the travel; whether the employee is subject to the direction and control of their employer for the period of the travel; whether the travel is relevant to the practical demands of carrying out the work duties, and whether the above factors have been contrived to give a private journey the appearance of work travel.

Travel expenses could cover not only transportation costs but also the cost of meals, accommodation and travel between the accommodation and the place or places of business visited while away (TR 2017/D6). While the costs of maintaining a second home in a place the taxpayer regularly visits on business are unlikely to be deductible (*Case X4*), the Commissioner has stated a preliminary view that additional property expenses an employee incurs to finance, hold and maintain residential property they have purchased or leased where they travel away from home for work and stays at the property may be claimed. This is provided that the employee's work activity requires them to travel, sleep away from home overnight, they have a permanent home elsewhere and are not relocating or living away from home (TR 2017/D6).

For the deductibility of travel expenses incurred in relation to self-education, see ¶16-450. For travel claims by investors, see ¶16-660. The deductibility of motor vehicle expenses is considered at ¶16-310.

Special substantiation rules apply to overseas and domestic travel (¶16-300) and to domestic car travel (¶16-320).

Travel between places of work or business

The costs of travel between 2 places of employment as part of the same job are deductible on the basis that the travel is undertaken in performing an employee's work activities (TR 2017/D6). The employment must be the occasion for the travel expenses (TR 2019/D7). The costs of travel between one place of business and another for the purposes of the one business are also deductible as are the costs of travelling between 2 unrelated workplaces, eg in *Kaley*, an architect was allowed a deduction for the cost of travelling between 2 unrelated places of employment.

A specific deduction is available for revenue expenses for travel directly between unrelated workplaces, ie travel between a place where the taxpayer is engaged in income-producing activities or business activities and a second place if: (a) the purpose of travel to the second workplace is to engage in income-producing activities or business activities; and (b) the taxpayer did engage in such activities (ITAA97 s 25-100). However, the deduction is not available if: (i) the taxpayer resides at one of the 2 workplaces (including a holiday home, shared accommodation and a second residence); or (ii) at the time of the travel, the arrangement by which the assessable income was gained or produced, or the business in which the taxpayer engaged in the activities at the first workplace, has ceased permanently.

Where part of an amount which is otherwise deductible as a transport expense for travel between workplaces (one of which is a business) under s 25-100 is attributable to a business activity which is subject to the non-commercial loss provisions in Div 35 (¶16-020), an apportionment must be made on a ''fair and reasonable'' basis, generally 50% to each activity (TD 2006/61).

The specific deduction was introduced to overcome the effect of the High Court decision in *Payne*. In that case, a pilot claimed a deduction for the costs of travelling between his income-producing deer farm and his place of employment at an airport. In rejecting the claim, the court said that the travel was neither part of the taxpayer's job as an employee, nor part of his business as a farmer — instead, it related to the intervals *between* those 2 types of income-earning activity. It was therefore not sufficiently connected with either income-producing activity and the costs should not be allowable.

Although *Payne* involved the additional factor that the deer farm was also the taxpayer's home, the High Court's view did not seem to be limited to that situation. To this extent, it seemed to be more restrictive than earlier views. For example, the Commissioner had previously drawn a distinction in these cases according to whether the home was involved (IT 2199). Where the home is not involved, the Commissioner evidently considered that travel directly between 2 places of employment or business was deductible if the travel was undertaken *for the purpose of enabling* the taxpayer to engage in income-producing activities. Where the home was involved, it appeared to be necessary to show that the travel was part and parcel of the income-producing activities. For example, a doctor who conducted a home surgery would be allowed a deduction for travel from home to a hospital to carry out medical duties, but a house painter operating from home would not be allowed a deduction for travel from home to a part-time bar job.

The earlier case of *Garrett* involved a doctor who lived in a country centre where he carried on both a farming business and a medical practice. He used an aircraft to travel to various other medical practices that he ran and to transport vaccines. His claim for the leasing costs of the aircraft was allowed. The Commissioner accepted the decision but expressed the view that travel between a taxpayer's home at which a business of primary production is conducted and the taxpayer's other business or employment is generally not deductible unless: (a) some significant activity related to the primary production business is undertaken on the trip (eg carrying feed or stock to market); or (b) the employment circumstances warrant deductibility (eg the employment is itinerant or the home constitutes a base of the other business or employment activities) (TD 96/42). Even after *Payne*, it may be that *Garrett* is still supportable on the ground that the medical practices were related or that the transport of the vaccines was a significant part of the taxpayer's business.

[FITR ¶33-120 – ¶33-270]

¶16-230 Deductibility of travel between home and work

Expenses of commuting between home and place of work are generally not deductible, ie where the travel is to start work or depart after work is completed (*Lunney*), even where a travel allowance is received (*Draft* TR 2017/D6; IT 2543), incidental tasks are performed en route, the travel is outside normal working hours or the travel involves a second or subsequent trip. This also extends to where the employee travels to work from another location, eg a café or holiday location, or travels from home to a different location that is more convenient as a work location, ie the travel is not explained by their employment duties but their personal choice: *Draft* TR 2019/D7.

However, a deduction may be allowed in certain exceptional circumstances — eg where the taxpayer's job is itinerant, where the taxpayer is required to carry bulky tools or equipment to work, where the taxpayer is on call or stand by, or where the taxpayer is required to attend a business trip on the way to or from work (¶16-220). Even though the taxpayer is required to carry bulky equipment to work, no deduction is allowable if a secure storage area is provided at the workplace (*Crestani*; TR 95/8; *Brandon*; *Rafferty*).

The ATO has stated its view in TR 2017/D6 that travel expenses are deductible where the travel is undertaken in performing an employee's work activities. This can include travel described as ''special demands travel'' which involves travel between home and a work location where the journey, or part of it, is included in the activities for which the employee is paid under the terms of their employment, meaning there may be another location treated as the ''point of hire''. Whether or not an employee is subject to the direction and control of the employer for the period of the travel is one of the relevant factors to determine whether such travel is undertaken in performing an employee's work activities. It may also include travel between home and an alternative work location where an employee is required to work in more than one location (''coexisting work locations travel'').

A similar concept is described as the ''transit point'' in TR 2019/D7 from which point an employee travels to reach the place where their substantive duties are carried out. The cost of travel between home and the transit point would not be deductible, but travel between the transit point and the second place will be deductible, on the basis that it is the point from which the employee commences their duties. The form and substance of the arrangement and the need for the transit point must fit within the reasonable expectations of the particular duties of employment, eg the remoteness of a location as in *John Holland Group Pty Ltd*. Here, air fare costs incurred by an employer to fly employees from Perth to Geraldton (WA) for a rail upgrade project (along with the return trip), were otherwise deductible to the employees for FBT purposes (¶35-680). This was because the employees were travelling in the course of their employment at their employer's direction from the time they arrived at Perth airport, and they were paid to do so. This situation subsisted until they returned to Perth at the end of their rostered-on time (also see *Decision Impact Statement*: *John Holland*).

Examples of deductible home to work travel

Academic living in semi-retirement was allowed a deduction for the cost of travel from his home to the city some 180 km away where he lectured 2 days a week. The claim was allowed on the ground that he used his home as a base for extensive work in preparing lectures and marking exam papers. He was also allowed a deduction for accommodation costs on the nights he had to stay in the city (*Case W4*). Note that somewhat similar claims have been disallowed in earlier cases, so the position is not clear. A taxpayer's home may not be regarded as an alternative work location (as described in *Draft* TR 2017/D6) to enable the travel between home to work to be deductible as ''co-existing work locations travel'' as in the Commissioner's view, this category is attributable to an employee having to work in more than one place, rather than their choice about where to live. Living a significant distance from work does not make the transport expense deductible, unless the travel is not attributable to the employee's choice of where to live, but due to the requirement of their employment duties (TR 2019/D7).

Computer consultant on call 24 hours a day was allowed the costs of travel between home and the office outside the normal daily journey since her home could be regarded as another place of work (*Collings*; TR 2019/D7).

Employed carpenter was allowed a deduction for car expenses in travelling between home and work because he had to transport heavy tools to work (*Case U29*; *Crestani*). However, an aircraft maintenance engineer was denied a deduction for expenses in transporting his tools by car each day where this was done purely for convenience and not for reasons of practical necessity (*Case Z22*).

Employed dentist who had to transport sensitive, valuable and potentially embarrassing items between one surgery and another was entitled to deductions for car expenses even though most of the journeys involved travel from his home (*Scott (No 3)*). The Commissioner had previously stated that a deduction should not be allowed simply on the ground that the items that are required to be transported are valuable (TR 95/20).

"Itinerant" teacher engaged in a special scheme, which involved teaching at 5 schools each day and using her home as a base for preparing lessons and keeping materials, was allowed her car travelling expenses between schools and between home and school (*Wiener*; *Kerry*). See TR 95/34 for a list of factors that indicate itinerancy.

Plumber working for a construction company who is assigned to work at different sites every day can claim a deduction for the cost of home to work travel (ATO *Plumber employees — claiming work-related expenses*).

Professional footballer was allowed a deduction for car expenses in travelling: (a) from his place of full-time work to training sessions and then home; and (b) from home to various matches (both "home" and "away") and back home again (*Ballesty*).

Professional musician who worked at various clubs and had to transport bulky musical equipment was allowed a deduction for car travel between home and his places of work (*Vogt*). The cost of preparing for and attending an audition is not deductible to employee performing artists (TR 95/20).

Self-employed shearers can claim expenses (including accommodation and meals) incurred in travelling between home and places where they exercise their trade or between home and a place of assembly for a shearing tour (IT 2273; *Gaydon*). For the deductibility of expenses of *employee* shearers, see TR 95/34.

Examples of non-deductible home to work travel

Casual nurse whose jobs were arranged through an agency, usually at short notice, and involved her working at a number of different hospitals each week (*Genys*). Thus, working on a casual basis for a different employer each day and often being called at short notice may not be enough to support a deduction for the cost of travelling between the home and the place where the taxpayer works on a particular day. See also *Draft* TR 2019/D7.

Employee building worker even if the worker is required to have a car available at work or if it is impracticable to use public transport (TR 95/22; TR 95/34).

Labourer who held a number of short-term jobs in regional locations and lived in a motorhome so he could be close to his work, was not an itinerant worker. Accordingly, he could not rely on TR 95/34 to claim car or travel expenses related to travelling to and from work (*Hill*; see also *Walker*).

Pilot who claimed he was obliged to drive his car from home to the airport when flying because of the weight of documents and equipment he was required to carry (*Yeates*). The pilot was not entitled to deductions for his home to work travel expenses because his employer provided most of the documents and equipment he required when flying.

Radiographer who, despite being on call, did not commence the income-producing duties until arrival at the hospital (*Pitcher*). The mere fact that a taxpayer, such as an airline pilot, is on stand-by duty at home is not sufficient to justify the deductibility of home/work travel.

Sheet metal worker who transported bulky tools to and from work because he did not believe his workplace storage lockers to be secure. The taxpayer's associated transport costs were not deductible because he was not required to transport his bulky tools to work each day, but rather did so out of a personal choice based on unfounded security concerns (*Reaney*).

Teachers travelling between their home and their regular school to attend parent-teacher meetings and other school functions even when the trip is made outside school hours or is a second or subsequent trip (*Draft* TR 2017/D6).

Tugboat crewman, despite the lack of public transport, the erratic hours and times of his job, the receipt of an out-of-hours travel allowance and the on-call nature of the job (*Case U156*).

Travel to client's premises

The total journey from an employee's home to a client's premises and then on to the office will be accepted as deductible business travel (MT 2027) where:

- the employee has a regular place of employment and travels to it habitually
- in the performance of the duties as an employee, travel is undertaken to an alternative destination that is not itself a regular place of employment (ie this would not apply, for example, to a plant operator who ordinarily travels directly to the job site rather than calling first at the depot, or to an employee of a consultancy firm who is placed on assignment for a period with a client firm)
- the journey is undertaken to a location at which the employee performs substantial employment duties.

These principles apply equally to cases where an employee makes a business call in the afternoon and travels from there to home, rather than returning to the office.

Personal service providers

Home/work travel expenses that are not allowable to employees are also not available where they relate to personal services rendered by individual contractors who are not conducting a personal services business (¶30-600).

[FITR ¶33-140 – ¶33-200]

¶16-240 Deductibility when travel allowances received

Payment of a travel allowance indicating official recognition by an employer may indicate that travel is a necessary element of the employment. Payment of an allowance must be considered together with the other characteristics of the employee's work in determining the deductibility of the travel expense. Thus, receipt of an allowance does not automatically entitle the employee to a deduction (TR 95/34). Equally, absence of an allowance does not necessarily prevent the travel expenditure from being deductible. It is the nature of the expense and its connection to the income-producing activities that determines whether it is deductible (*Draft* TR 2017/D6).

For the assessability of travel allowances and of reimbursements of car expenses on a cents per kilometre basis, see ¶10-060.

All allowances must be shown as assessable income in the employee's tax return, except where all the following conditions are satisfied:

- the allowance is not shown on the employee's payment summary
- the allowance received is a bona fide overtime meal allowance or a bona fide travel allowance
- the allowance received does not exceed the reasonable amount, and
- the allowance has been fully expended on deductible expenses.

Where the allowance is not required to be shown as assessable income in the employee's tax return, and is not shown, a deduction for the expense cannot be claimed in the tax return (TR 2004/6).

In general, car expenses are not deductible unless written evidence is kept (¶16-320). A corresponding rule applies to overseas and domestic travel (¶16-300). See ¶16-210 for the rules that apply where an employee receives a domestic or overseas travel allowance.

[FITR ¶33-210]

¶16-260 Deducting travel expenses: attending a convention

Deductible travel expenses include those incurred by the taxpayer in attending a convention relating to the taxpayer's business or employment (ITAA97 s 8-1). The fact that vacation or leave time is utilised in attending such conferences, or that attendance is voluntary, will not necessarily preclude a deduction. Where only part of the purpose of the trip was attendance at the convention, the expenses may be apportioned (¶16-290). See ¶16-450 for the deductibility of convention expenses as self-education expenses.

[FITR ¶33-220]

¶16-270 Overseas travel expenses

The deductibility of overseas travelling expenses depends on the same principles as the deductibility of ordinary travelling expenses (ITAA97 s 8-1), whether the expenses are incurred, reimbursed or allowed for by an employer, or are incurred by an employee or self-employed person on their own account. See also *Draft* TR 2019/D7 and *Draft* TR 2017/D6 for the Commissioner's preliminary views on claiming travel expenses.

In the case of a business taxpayer, fares to Australia of a new employee whose duties are related to the production of business income are deductible (but not if the employee is needed to set up the business structure). The cost of overseas travel to obtain a new employee would also be deductible, but not the costs of hiring a partner (*Case T36*).

In general, travel expenses aimed at obtaining new agencies or assets, or otherwise expanding the business structure, are non-deductible, while travel expenses in seeking new marketing or manufacturing trends, ie in keeping abreast or ahead, are deductible. The cost of an importing company's first overseas buying trip would be deductible if it had previously secured firm provisional orders (*Case T46*).

It seems that travelling expenses in connection with overseas agencies are deductible where the purpose of the trip is to maintain and improve relations in regard to existing agencies, but not where its purpose is to obtain new agencies. On the other hand, as long as the gaining or losing of agencies is merely an incident in the taxpayer's business so that compensation received for an agency cancellation would be assessable (¶10-114), travel and other expenses in seeking or gaining an agency should equally be deductible as a revenue outgoing.

Similarly, in the case of professional persons and academics, whether in private practice or employment, expenses of overseas travel undertaken to keep aware of new developments, attend conferences and conventions are deductible (*Finn*; ¶16-450).

The travel costs of an employee's spouse who accompanied him as a personal carer when travelling overseas to attend work-related conferences were not deductible to the taxpayer on the basis that the costs were incurred in relation to the taxpayer putting himself in a position where he was able to engage in employment. The expenses were in connection with gaining or producing assessable income but were not in the course of gaining or producing that assessable income (*Case 8/2016*).

There have been some remarkable successes in relation to overseas travel claims. For example, 2 junior police officers (a husband and wife) won a claim to deduct $25,000 incurred on an overseas trip, during which they made pre-arranged visits to numerous police stations to gain knowledge of new police methods (*Case W73*).

Many cases have involved schoolteachers or other persons associated with education whose travel overseas is associated, to varying degrees, with their professional interests. The question here is principally whether the necessary connection can be found between the travel and the teacher's income-producing activities (¶16-450). Although many of these claims fail, there have been a number of cases in which deductions have been allowed, for example: an academic's trip to India to conduct a project while on sabbatical (*Chaudri*); an ancient history teacher's trip to Italy and Greece (*Case Q104*) and to historic sites and museums (*Case W75*); a curriculum research officer's trip to the USA and Canada (*Case Q114*); a history teacher's trip to China (*Case R20*); an Indian history teacher's trip to Burma, Nepal and Thailand (*Case T65*); a music teacher's trip to Europe to take up a specialist music scholarship (*Case V1*); an outdoor education teacher's canoeing expedition in Canada (*Case V74*); a teacher's trip to Canada to participate in a teacher exchange program (*Case V82*; ID 2001/329) and a Studies of Society and the Environment (SOSE) teacher's trip to Asia, the UK and Europe (*Lenten*). It may be that teachers qualifying as "master" teachers are more likely to succeed in such claims (*Case R73*). It is not necessary that there be an express direction from the school to take the trip (*Case S1*).

Employers are allowed a general deduction for annual fees incurred on airport lounge memberships for employees (eg Qantas Club memberships): TD 2016/15. No deduction is permitted, if such fees are incurred to produce the employer's exempt or non-assessable non-exempt income. The deduction is available, even if an employee uses the membership substantially for private purposes (eg when they are on holidays). An FBT exemption may be available (FBTAA s 58Y; ¶35-645). The cost of travel insurance, visas and passport fees are not deductible (*Waters*; ID 2001/615; CR 2003/65).

Travel expenses incurred by travel agents in attending conferences, seminars, training courses and industry promotions are usually deductible (see *Travel agent employees — income and work-related deductions* on the ATO website). In *Sanchez*, a travel agent's expenses on travelling overseas were found to have the required connection with his job.

[FITR ¶33-240 – ¶33-270, ¶37-480]

¶16-280 Travel expenses: accompanying relatives

Special rules apply in certain circumstances to deny deductions for expenses attributable to an accompanying relative (ITAA97 s 26-30). These rules, which apply to employees as well as to recipients of certain PAYG withholding payments (payments to directors and office holders, return to work payments, benefit training and compensation payments: ¶26-120), apply where the taxpayer is undertaking travel as an employee or in the course of carrying on a business and is accompanied by a relative, unless:

- during the trip, the relative performs substantial duties as employee of the taxpayer or of the taxpayer's employer, and
- it is reasonable to conclude that the relative would still have gone on the trip even in the absence of the personal relationship with the taxpayer.

Expenses attributable to a wife who accompanied a taxpayer as his personal carer while he undertook travel as an employee were held not deductible under s 26-30. If a relative was employed by a taxpayer to be a carer, it was considered possible to satisfy the first requirement above but whether the second condition as to reasonably concluding that a relative would have still gone on the trip in the absence of a personal relationship with the taxpayer was considered more difficult to satisfy (*Case 8/2016*).

Where the expenses are incurred in providing a fringe benefit, the general prohibition on deductibility does not apply.

Apportionment of travel costs

Where the taxpayer's own travel is accepted as deductible, but the travel of an accompanying person is not, the question may arise as to how the travel costs are to be apportioned. The Commissioner normally applies a 50/50 apportionment but, in one case, apportionment was made on a "marginal cost" basis and the taxpayer was allowed a deduction for 92% of his total accommodation costs on the ground that there was only an 8% difference between single and double room rates at the particular hotel where he and his wife were staying (*Case R2*; see also *Case V39*). However, neither method of apportionment has universal application in arriving at the proportion of the overall costs that can fairly and properly be attributed to the derivation of the taxpayer's assessable income (*Case V15*). In *Case V15*, which involved a claim by a professor on sabbatical leave, it was held that: (a) the cost of the professor's and his wife's overnight stay at a city hotel prior to departure overseas was deductible on the marginal cost basis; (b) the cost of their taxi fare to the airport was fully deductible; and (c) the cost of renting a campus apartment for 10 months was deductible on a 50/50 basis.

If a person who is required to incur accommodation expenses for work can demonstrate that their choice of accommodation was not influenced by the fact that they were accompanied by another person(s), and the expense incurred is not affected by having that company, they will not be required to apportion the accommodation costs as, on the facts, the expense is solely related to their travel for work (*Draft* TR 2017/D6, example 7).

[FITR ¶31-260, ¶68-220]

¶16-290 Travel expenses: trips partly for pleasure

Difficulty may arise where a trip is a business one, but part of the time overseas is devoted to non-business pursuits. The Commissioner's view appears to be that, where the main purpose of the trip was the gaining or producing of income, the related expenses will be fully deductible under ITAA97 s 8-1 notwithstanding the existence of an incidental private purpose. If, however, the gaining or producing of income was merely incidental to the private purpose, apportionment of the expenses is necessary and only the expenses directly attributable to the income-earning purpose will be allowable. Where both purposes are equal, 50% of the expenses incurred for both purposes (ie other than those directly attributable to income-earning purposes) will be deductible (TR 98/9). Where an employee's trip has a private element that is not merely incidental, the expense must also be apportioned to that extent. The ATO has illustrated in examples in *Draft* TR 2017/D6 that in some scenarios, it may be necessary to consider transport expenses separately from accommodation, meal and incidental expenses for this purpose.

A particularly striking example of apportionment where a trip was substantially for non-business purposes is provided by *Cunliffe's case*, where a restaurateur's $46,493 claim for the costs of a 16-month overseas gastronomic tour by himself, his future wife and various others was reduced to $15,730.

Apportionment on the basis of *time* spent on each activity was found to be a "totally inappropriate method; the proper method is to determine the degree of predominance to be attached to the objects or purposes in the pursuit of which the taxpayer incurred the particular expenditure which is to be the subject of apportionment" (*Case R13*). In that case a dentist was allowed a deduction for one-half of his return airfares, notwithstanding that only 5 out of 40 days overseas were spent on business.

[FITR ¶31-260]

¶16-300 Substantiation of overseas and domestic travel

Special substantiation rules apply to expenses in relation to overseas and domestic travel (ITAA97 Div 900: ss 900-1 to 900-250). The rules apply to expenses incurred by the taxpayer on his/her *own* travel, whether as a recipient of certain PAYG withholding payments (ie payments to employees, company directors and office holders, return to work payments, retirement payments, employment termination payments and annuities, and benefit and compensation payments: ¶26-120), an employer, self-employed person, or a partnership that includes at least one individual. They do *not* apply to expenses incurred by a company or a trust.

The effect of the substantiation rules is that domestic and overseas travel expenses are not deductible unless the following 2 conditions are satisfied:

(1) Written evidence (¶16-340) must be obtained by the taxpayer in respect of expenses relating to travel, regardless of length of absence from home. In the case of a *business* travel expense (ie a travel expense incurred in producing income other than salary or wages), written evidence need only be kept if the travel involved at least one night away from home.

(2) Travel records (ie a travel diary or similar document) must be kept by a taxpayer where the taxpayer was away from the ordinary place of residence for 6 or more consecutive nights. The records must contain particulars of each business activity undertaken during the relevant travel. Entries must be made before the activity ends or as soon as possible afterwards, setting out: (a) the nature of the activity; (b) the day and approximate time when it began; (c) how long it lasted; and (d) where the activity took place.

The requirements for retention and production of these records are similar to those applying to car expenses (¶16-320).

These rules extend to car expenses incurred in respect of overseas travel and taxi expenses, but not to other motor vehicle expenses — car expenses are subject to their own substantiation rules (¶16-320). Taxpayers are exempt from the substantiation rules in any year in which their claim for work expenses, including travel expenses, does not exceed $300 (¶16-210). Expenses relating to allowances covered by special rules (ie overtime meal allowances, travel allowances and award transport payments: ¶16-210) are not taken into account in determining whether this limit applies.

Owner-drivers of long distance trucks who are required to sleep away from home are required to substantiate accommodation, meal and other travel expenses (if the driver does not sleep away from home, those expenses are not considered to be deductible as travel expenses). The Commissioner considers that it is reasonable to obtain receipts for meal expenses in roadhouses or other similar food outlets (food and drink purchases from vending machines or roadside caravans may be substantiated by an entry in a diary or other record). A diary must be kept for absences of 6 or more nights in a row (TR 2004/6).

[FITR ¶680-220, ¶680-495, ¶680-760]

Motor Vehicle Expenses

¶16-310 Deductible motor vehicle expenses

Motor vehicle expenses incurred in the course of deriving assessable income or in carrying on business are allowable deductions (ITAA97 s 8-1). Such expenses include petrol, oil, repairs, servicing, new tyres, lease charges, interest on a car loan and car washes and polishes. The Commissioner's preliminary view in *Draft* TR 2017/D6 on the deductibility of travel expenses also applies in the context of determining whether car expenses are deductible.

The cost of a driver's licence is not an allowable deduction (*Case R49*), even if the holding of the licence is a condition of employment, but any premium on top of the cost of a standard licence would be allowable (TD 93/108). Bridge or road tolls, car registration, third party insurance, insurance excess (ID 2004/393), comprehensive insurance and annual fees for membership in motorists' associations also form part of deductible motor vehicle expenses (but parking fines are not deductible).

The calculation of car expense deductions where a car is jointly owned, jointly leased or jointly hired under a hire purchase agreement is discussed in PS LA 1999/2.

Taxpayers who choose to use their own private car for work purposes, even though they could have free use of a company vehicle, are still entitled to claim a deduction for the costs of business travel in the car (*Case V112*). These may include damages or compensation paid for damage caused to a third party vehicle involved in an accident where an employee used their own car in the course of employment (*Car expenses*, ATO website).

For the special substantiation rules that apply to car expenses, see ¶16-320.

Car parking expenses

Generally, a deduction is allowable for parking fees incurred while travelling in circumstances where the travel expenses are deductible (¶16-230) (TR 98/14). However, deductions are not allowable for parking fees incurred by an employee where the car is used to commute from home to work and is parked at or near the employee's main workplace for more than 4 hours during the day between the hours of 7 am and 7 pm (ITAA36 s 51AGA; ID 2005/246). A deduction for car parking expenses is not denied if the employee is the driver of, or a passenger in, the car and is entitled under state or territory law to use a disabled person's parking space and a valid disabled person's car parking permit is displayed on the car (ITR15 reg 8).

Depreciation

A deduction may be available for depreciation of a vehicle owned by the taxpayer (¶17-010). Depreciation may also be claimed on radios, air conditioners, etc, attached to a vehicle at the time of purchase. Car phones qualify for depreciation whether installed before or after delivery. Special rules apply if the vehicle is being acquired under a hire purchase agreement (¶23-250).

Leasing charges

Rentals under car and truck leases are deductible as rent only to the extent that they meet the usual requirements of revenue outgoings under the general deduction provisions, so that any part of the rentals that represents private use or partial payment towards the ultimate purchase is not deductible (see generally IT 28). This is also the case for any other plant, machinery or equipment leasing arrangements. In particular, IT 28 contains the Commissioner's views about acceptable leases and minimum residual values (as updated in TD 93/142 and ID 2002/1004).

No deduction is allowed to an employee for lease payments made by an employer to a finance company in a partial novation under a motor vehicle lease novation arrangement (TR 1999/15; *Jones*). In a full novation, the employer is entitled to a deduction for lease expenses where the vehicle is used in the business or provided as part of a salary package (there are no income tax consequences for the employee). In the case of a luxury car, the deduction is based on an accrual amount and depreciation, subject to the car depreciation limit (¶17-200, ¶17-220). See ¶35-150 for the FBT consequences.

Entitlement to private use

If an employer provides a car for the exclusive use of an employee or the employee's relatives in circumstances where the employee or relatives are entitled to use the car for private purposes, expenses incurred in connection with the car by the employee are not deductible (ITAA36 s 51AF). The section applies to both the provision of a leased vehicle (the lease terms of which are paid for by the employee) and the provision of a vehicle at will by the employer for use in specified duties (*Pierce*). However, it does not apply where, under a partial novation entered into after 17 June 1998, the lease payments are incurred by the employer, rather than by the employee (TR 1999/15; *Jones*). Expenses such as parking fees and bridge tolls that are linked to a car but are not involved in its direct operation, and are not otherwise factored into an FBT valuation, are not caught by s 51AF and thus are deductible (*Case Y43*; ID 2004/613). Note that parking fees may be disallowed where s 51AGA applies — see above.

[FTR ¶26-600, ¶26-630]

¶16-320 Substantiation rules for car expenses

Special substantiation rules apply to claims for car expenses incurred in relation to travel within Australia (ITAA97 Div 28: ss 28-1 to 28-185). These rules apply to employees as well as to other recipients of withholding payments (¶26-120), self-employed persons and partnerships including at least one individual taxpayer, but *not* to companies or trusts. The rules do not apply unless the taxpayer owns or hires under a hire purchase agreement or leases the car. A taxpayer who does not own the car cannot use the special methods but can claim deductions for fuel, oil and other actual costs. See ¶16-324 for the types of vehicles to which the rules apply.

There are 2 methods for claiming car expense deductions that can satisfy the substantiation rules. They are the logbook method and the cents per kilometre method. Where the substantiation rules are not met, no deduction is allowable for the expenses. Unlike employees' work expenses, which are subject to a $300 threshold, there is no substantiation-free threshold for car expenses.

If a taxpayer wishes to claim car expenses by reference to actual expenses apportioned between income-producing use and private use of a car, the expenses must be substantiated under the logbook method. Under this method, claims must be supported by written evidence, logbook records and odometer records (ITAA97 ss 900-70; 900-75).

▶ Example

A taxpayer's total car expenses, including depreciation, for the income year amount to $9,000 and the business proportion of these expenses is 70%. Where the requirements of the logbook method are satisfied, the taxpayer's deduction for car expenses would be calculated as 70% × $9,000 = $6,300.

Taxpayers can get full or partial exemption from the substantiation rules by electing to make their claim on an arbitrary basis. From the 2015–16 year, this is achieved by using the cents per kilometre method because this calculation does not directly relate to the taxpayer's actual expenditure on business usage. Note that the one-third of actual expenses method and the 12% of original value method cease to apply from the 2015–16 income year, and details of these former, arbitrary methods can be found in the *Australian Master Tax Guide* (57th and earlier editions).

The 2 available methods are shown below. For guidance as to which method will provide the greatest deduction in particular circumstances, see ¶16-375.

Method	Extent of substantiation required
Logbook method	Logbooks required to be kept for at least 12 weeks in the first year and then every 5 years (¶16-350). Odometer records required (¶16-360). Written evidence of expenses (receipts, etc) required (¶16-340).

Method	Extent of substantiation required
	Fuel and oil expenses may be substantiated by odometer records (¶16-340, ¶16-360).
Cents per kilometre method (if business use is 5,000 km or less, or a claim is limited to 5,000 km)	Substantiation records not relevant. Number of business kilometres based on reasonable estimate (¶16-370).

''Business kilometres'' are a reasonable estimate of the kilometres the car travelled in the course of producing assessable income or travelling between workplaces, and include kilometres travelled by a taxpayer to consult with a tax agent (ID 2010/195). Under the logbook method, the estimate takes into account logbooks, odometer records, variations in patterns of a car's use, changes in the number of cars used to produce income, and any other relevant matters (s 28-90(5)).

Taxpayers are not required to lodge their supporting records with their returns. However, they must produce them if required to do so by the Commissioner (ITAA97 ss 900-75; 900-160 to 900-185).

Records must be kept for 5 years after the relevant return is lodged or until the relevant dispute is settled (ss 900-165; 900-170). Where the logbook method is used, the retention period applies from the date of lodgment of the last return in which a claim is based on those records. The Commissioner has a limited discretion to disregard a failure to comply with the retention requirements applying in respect of logbooks and odometer records. The substantiation rules will not apply where the nature and quality of the evidence the taxpayer has to substantiate the expenses (under the logbook method) satisfies the Commissioner that the taxpayer: (a) incurred the expense; and (b) is entitled to deduct the amount claimed (ITAA97 s 900-195; 900-200). For the rules applicable where records are lost or destroyed, see ¶16-340.

For situations in which car expenses need not be calculated using the logbook or cents per kilometre methods, see ¶16-324.

[FITR ¶70-000ff, ¶680-380, ¶680-875, ¶681-095]

¶16-324 What motor vehicles are covered by the substantiation rules?

The car expense substantiation rules apply to any motor-powered road vehicle (including 4-wheel drive vehicles) designed to carry a load of less than one tonne and fewer than 9 passengers (thus including station wagons, panel vans and utility trucks designed to carry less than one tonne). They do not apply to motor cycles or similar vehicles or taxis. Hired motor vehicles are only subject to the rules if hired on a regular basis (ITAA97 ss 28-12; 28-165; 995-1(1)).

Exceptions

For certain types of cars used in particular ways, it is not compulsory for a taxpayer to use the logbook or cents per kilometre methods. Instead, the taxpayer can *choose* to: (i) use one of those methods; or (ii) calculate their claim using general deduction principles (eg s 8-1), including the apportionment rules for private expenses (¶16-070) and the depreciation provisions (ss 28-170; 28-175).

This choice applies where the car is a panel van, utility truck, taxi or any road vehicle designed to carry less than one tonne (excluding any vehicle designed principally to carry passengers) which is used *only* in one or more of the following ways:

- for travel undertaken in the course of, or which is incidental to, producing the taxpayer's assessable income
- for travel between the taxpayer's residence and the place where the car is used in the course of producing the taxpayer's assessable income

- for travel by some other person who was given the car to travel between their residence and where the car is used in the course of producing the taxpayer's assessable income, or
- for private travel, by the taxpayer or some other person, that was minor, infrequent and irregular.

The choice may also be made for all types of cars in any of the following circumstances:

- the car is provided for the exclusive use of employees or their relatives and any of them was entitled to use it for private purposes
- the car is hired or leased in the course of carrying on a business of hiring or leasing cars
- the car is part of the trading stock of a business of selling cars and is used in the course of that business
- the car is unregistered and used principally in producing assessable income
- the car is trading stock of the taxpayer's business of selling cars and is not used by the taxpayer at any time during the year, or
- the expense is related to repairs or other work on the car and is incurred in a business of doing repairs or other work on cars.

[FITR ¶70-015, ¶70-165 – ¶70-175]

¶16-326 What car expenses are affected by the substantiation rules?

Car expenses affected by the substantiation rules are any losses or outgoings to do with a car, or to do with operating a car (eg fuel, oil, servicing and interest) and depreciation (ITAA97 s 28-13). In the case of depreciation, the substantiation rules are relevant to establishing the cost of the vehicle.

Car expenses do not include taxi fares or similar losses or outgoings, or expenses on travel outside Australia — these may be subject to the substantiation rules relating to work expenses (¶16-210) or to business travel expenses (¶16-300).

Intermittent hire car expenses are not subject to the provisions of ITAA97 Div 28. However, if they relate to travel outside Australia, they may be treated as work expenses (¶16-210) or business travel expenses (¶16-300). Expenses incurred in hiring cars on a long-term basis are subject to the car expenses substantiation rules (ITAA97 s 28-165).

If car expenses related to award transport payments (¶16-210) are deducted without written evidence, and without using the logbook or cents per kilometre methods (2 methods), a taxpayer's use of those methods is affected. This is especially relevant to a taxpayer whose car expenses are not incurred solely to derive award transport payments. The taxpayer may use either of the 2 methods for their non-award car expenses. However, the kilometres related to the award transport payments are not counted as business kilometres when using either method, and, in the case of the logbook method, the logbook requirements must be satisfied for all car expenses (including the expenses related to the award payments) (ITAA97 ss 28-180; 900-250).

[FITR ¶70-015, ¶70-020, ¶681-255]

¶16-340 The logbook method and obtaining written evidence of car expenses

The logbook method requires a taxpayer to multiply each car expense by the business use percentage. The car expenses must qualify for a general or specific deduction under normal deduction rules. If only part of a car expense qualifies for a deduction, then only that part is multiplied by the business use percentage (s 28-90).

Where a taxpayer claims car expenses using the logbook method (¶16-320), the expenses must be verified by written evidence such as a document from the supplier of the goods or services (ITAA97 Div 900: ss 900-1 to 900-250). While generally there is no time limit for getting written evidence of an expense, the taxpayer is not entitled to a deduction until they have obtained the written evidence. However, the deduction may be claimed, even in the absence of the written evidence, if the taxpayer has good reason to expect to obtain the evidence within a reasonable time. If written evidence of an expense is obtained after the end of an income year, the expense remains deductible for the year to which it relates, and not the year the evidence is obtained (s 900-110).

The supplier's document (eg a receipt, invoice, certificate or statement) must set out the name of the supplier, the amount of the expense, the nature of the goods or services supplied, the date the expense was incurred and the date of the document. This is subject to 2 exceptions: (a) if the supplier's document does not show the day the expense was incurred, the taxpayer may use other independent evidence such as a bank statement to show when the expense was paid; and (b) if the supplier's document does not specify the nature of the goods or services (eg a credit card receipt), the taxpayer may add that information to the document before lodging the income tax return (s 900-115).

The Commissioner will accept a document containing the necessary information, whether issued by the supplier or a third party (eg a bank statement evidencing a BPAY or internet banking transaction). Such record is not required to show when the document was produced, provided the date of the payment is shown. Electronic records and electronic copies of records are also acceptable (PS LA 2005/7).

Depreciation

In relation to claims for depreciation, the supplier's document must record the name of the supplier, the cost of the property to the taxpayer, the nature of the property, the date on which the property was acquired by the taxpayer, and the date on which the document was made out (s 900-120). If the supplier's document does not specify the nature of the property, the taxpayer may write in the missing details. If the taxpayer does not get the supplier's document in time, eg because he/she only decided to use the property for income-producing purposes several years after acquiring it, the deduction may still be available (see below under "Special situations").

Fuel and oil expenses

A taxpayer using the logbook method is not required to obtain written evidence of fuel and oil expenses (s 900-70(3)). This is because odometer records are required under the logbook method, and the Commissioner accepts a reasonable estimate of fuel and oil costs based on business kilometres travelled, average fuel and oil costs, and average fuel and oil consumption (TD 97/19).

Small claims

The requirement to obtain written evidence does *not* apply where the taxpayer makes a claim for expenses which individually do not exceed $10 and which in total do not exceed $200 for the income year. Nor does it apply if it would be unreasonable to expect the taxpayer to obtain written evidence of the expense (even if the expense is more than $10 or the $200 limit is exceeded). In such cases, it will be sufficient for the taxpayer to record all the relevant details of the expense in a document (such as a diary) as soon as possible after incurring the expense (ss 900-125; 900-130).

The taxpayer's own document must contain all the information that would have been required to be contained in the supplier's document (diary entries simply showing where the taxpayer was on certain days without details of goods and services purchased would be insufficient). A series of cheque butts containing the required information (supplier's name, amount, nature of the goods or services, date) would seem sufficient to satisfy this requirement. In the case of depreciation, the taxpayer's document must record, as soon as possible after the end of the income year, the nature of the property, the amount of depreciation, the day the record is made and who made the record.

Special situations

Relief from the substantiation requirements may be granted by the Commissioner if the nature and quality of the evidence the taxpayer can produce satisfies the Commissioner that the taxpayer incurred the expense and is entitled to deduct the amount claimed (s 900-195). A bona fide attempt to comply with the requirements is likely to prompt the exercise of the discretion, but unsupported estimates and the taxpayer's unsupported statements will not. The discretion is unlikely to be exercised in the absence of supporting documentation or factual material evidencing the expense (TR 97/24; *Snaidr*; *Case 12/99*), even where it is reasonable to assume that the taxpayer did incur some work-related expenses (*Case 15/2000*).

In addition, the right to a deduction is not affected by the failure to follow the substantiation rules if the *only* reason for such failure was that the taxpayer had a genuine and reasonable expectation that he/she would not need to comply with those rules (s 900-200). An example is the taxpayer's reasonable expectation, at the time the expense was incurred, that the expense would be in an exception category (eg the expectation that work expenses totalling less than $300 would be incurred during the year). While ignorance of the law, recklessness or carelessness will not attract the discretion, a reasonable expectation created by ATO advice or conduct may (TR 97/24).

Where documents are lost or destroyed, the following rules apply (s 900-205). Complete copies of documents are treated as the original document (however, a deduction claim will fail if the original document would not have complied with the substantiation rules: *Turner*). If no complete copy existed and the Commissioner is satisfied that the taxpayer took reasonable precautions to prevent the loss or destruction (ie there was no recklessness or carelessness), then: (a) the deduction is not affected if the lost or destroyed document was not written evidence, ie it was a logbook, odometer records or a travel record; or (b) if the document was written evidence, substitute written evidence (eg a substitute receipt) will suffice. If it is not reasonably possible to obtain substitute written evidence (ie if a bona fide attempt to obtain a copy is made or it is reasonable to believe that such an attempt would be unsuccessful), the deduction is not affected by the loss or destruction of the document (TR 97/24).

For the Commissioner's approach to the reissue and reconstruction of records which have been lost or destroyed as a result of a natural disaster, see the ATO website at *Dealing with disasters* (¶44-130).

[FITR ¶680-380, ¶680-620, ¶680-650, ¶680-660, ¶681-095, ¶681-110]

¶16-350 Logbook requirements

In addition to written evidence (¶16-340) to substantiate car expenses, taxpayers using the logbook method must support their claim by appropriate logbook records (ITAA97 ss 28-105; 28-130) and odometer records (ITAA97 ss 28-135; 28-140).

For the first year in which car expenses are claimed using the logbook method, a logbook recording each business journey must be kept for a minimum continuous period of at least 12 weeks at any time in the year. The 12-week period may overlap the start of an income year. To use the logbook method for 2 cars, the logbook for each car must cover the same period. Odometer records must also be kept showing the odometer reading of the car at the beginning and end of the 12-week period (¶16-360).

The logbook must include for each business trip: (a) the date the trip began and ended; (b) odometer readings at the start and end of the trip; (c) kilometres travelled on the journey; and (d) the purpose of the trip. The record must be made at the end of the trip or as soon as possible afterwards. Where 2 or more business journeys are made consecutively during the one day, only one logbook entry for that day is required. Where the logbook was unreliable and did not appear to have been completed progressively or after each trip, or with sufficient description, it could not be accepted as an accurate record of business kilometres (*Latif*).

In addition, the logbook must contain the following information: (a) when the 12-week period began and ended; (b) odometer readings at the beginning and end of the period; (c) total number of kilometres travelled during the period; (d) total number of business kilometres travelled during the period on trips recorded in the logbook; and (e) percentage of business kilometres to total kilometres.

Once the extent of business use of the vehicle during the 12-week period has been established, the taxpayer can make a reasonable estimate of the number of business kilometres travelled during the income year. This estimate must take into account all relevant matters including the logbook, odometer or other records, any variation in the pattern of use of the car (eg for holiday or seasonal factors) and any changes in the number of cars used for income-producing purposes during the year. The proportion of the estimated number of business kilometres to the total number of kilometres travelled while it was owned or leased during the income year is then applied to the substantiated car expenses to calculate the amount of deductible car expenses.

Essentially, a new logbook will not have to be kept until 5 years have passed, unless specific rules require a logbook to be kept earlier. For example, if a logbook was kept in 2012–13, a new logbook will generally not be required to be kept until 2017–18. In the 4 years following the first year, the logbook is relevant for determining the reasonable estimate of business kilometres travelled during the income year. Logbooks do not have to be kept in those years, but the taxpayer must keep odometer records (¶16-360) to establish total kilometres travelled in the car during each year, as well as record the estimate of business kilometres and the business use percentage for the year.

Having kept the logbook for one income year, the taxpayer is not required to keep one for the next 4 income years unless:

- the Commissioner sends the taxpayer a notice before the income year directing the taxpayer to keep a logbook for that year, or
- during the income year, the taxpayer gets one or more additional cars for which the taxpayer wants to use the logbook method in that year.

A taxpayer may choose to keep a logbook in an income year, even in the absence of a requirement to do so (eg to establish higher business usage). If the car is replaced with another, the taxpayer is treated as having continuously held the one car, even though there may be a period when the taxpayer held both cars or neither car, and the business use percentage established by the logbook may be relied on for the replacement car. The taxpayer must nominate in writing the replacement car and specify the date from which the replacement is to take effect. The nomination document is subject to the same retention period as the logbook for the original car.

Where a car is held for less than 12 weeks, a logbook must be kept for the entire period for which the taxpayer held the car.

There is no discretion in the Commissioner to disregard a failure to comply with the logbook or odometer requirements, other than the retention requirements. However, the Commissioner has a discretion to disregard a failure to comply with the substantiation rules that apply to written evidence. Special rules apply if a logbook or odometer records are lost. See further ¶16-340.

CR 2013/85 sets out the conditions by which an electronically-created, car logbook system satisfies the logbook requirements in circumstances where reports are generated based on information exported from calendar applications as well as manually entered information. Other electronic systems that satisfy logbook requirements are outlined in CR 2016/44 and CR 2016/47.

[FITR ¶70-090ff, ¶70-109ff, ¶70-149ff]

¶16-360 Odometer records

The logbook method of claiming car expenses (¶16-320) requires odometer records to be kept in each year in which the method is used (ITAA97 ss 28-135; 28-140). Entries containing odometer readings at the beginning and end of the relevant period (ie the period when the taxpayer held the car during the income year and, if a logbook must be kept in the income year, the logbook period) must be made at or as soon as possible after the start or end of the specified period. Odometer records must also contain details of the make, model, registration number and engine capacity of the car — these entries must be made before lodging the income tax return. Where a car has been replaced (¶16-350), the odometer records must contain the above details in respect of both the original and the replacement cars. A device or information system that is used to calculate odometer readings at the start and end of a journey, other than the car's own odometer, may be acceptable to calculate odometer readings provided it is of sufficient integrity (CR 2012/48; CR 2013/85).

[FITR ¶70-139ff]

¶16-370 Cents per kilometre method for substantiating car expenses

If a car travelled 5,000 km or less during the year on ''business'' (or the claim is limited to 5,000 km), a taxpayer is not required to maintain substantiation documents if the taxpayer opts to claim a deduction using the cents per kilometre method in lieu of a deduction based on actual expenditure and business usage (ITAA97 ss 28-25 to 28-35). The option is available if the car travels more than 5,000 km, provided the deduction claim is limited to the first 5,000 km only (that is, no deduction is available for the business kilometres over 5,000 km). Where this option is exercised, the deduction is based on a reasonable estimate of business kilometres. In *Latif*, the unreliability of the logbook data in relation to business kilometres meant that both the cents per kilometre and the logbook methods were equally inappropriate.

Although written evidence is not required, the ATO expects a taxpayer making the claim to be able to demonstrate the car travelled on business and how the amounts of the claims were determined. The ATO uses enhanced technology and data analytics to closely examine claims based on the cents per kilometre method to identify unusual claims.

The cents per kilometre rate is 68 cents for the 2019–20 income year and 72 cents for the 2020–21 income year. These rates apply to all cars (¶42-170).

Special rules apply for the purposes of calculating depreciation balancing adjustments on the loss or disposal of a car where the cents per kilometre method has been used (¶17-665).

[FITR ¶70-038ff, ¶70-054ff, ¶70-074ff, ¶680-380ff]

¶16-375 Switching car substantiation methods

A different method of substantiation (logbook method or cents per kilometre method) can be used for each car held by the taxpayer for income-producing purposes. The taxpayer can also switch from one method to another year by year (ITAA97 s 28-20). While a taxpayer can only use one method for all car expenses for one car in a particular income year, that choice may be changed (eg if during the Commissioner's audit, the taxpayer decides to adopt a different method).

The logbook method is often the preferred method where the business use percentage and car expenses are high. It may also be favoured by taxpayers whose business kilometres far exceed 5,000. However, in considering the appropriateness of the logbook method, particularly where more than 5,000 business kilometres are travelled, the size of the deduction must also be balanced against the reduced record-keeping requirements that the cents per kilometre method offers. Where business kilometres are close to 5,000 (under or over), it is prudent to check both methods (assuming logbook requirements are satisfied).

▶ Example

The taxpayer travelled 30,000 km in a leased car during the income year and incurred the following expenses:

	$
Insurance (comprehensive)	1,540
Lease payments	6,200
Petrol and oil	5,000
Registration and third party insurance	1,100
Repairs	1,400
Total	$15,240

The following table shows the method that gives the preferred result in 2 situations.

Method of deduction	Deduction if 6,000 km are for income-producing purposes ($)	Deduction if 8,000 km are for income-producing purposes ($)
Logbook	3,048	4,064 (preferred)
Cents per km (2020–21 rate is 72 cents/km)	3,600 (preferred)	3,600

[FITR ¶70-002, ¶70-004]

Entertainment Expenses

¶16-390 Limited deduction for entertainment expenses

Entertainment expenses are not deductible except in very limited circumstances (ITAA97 Div 32: ss 32-1 to 32-90). This prohibition extends to entertainment in the form of food, drink or recreation. Recreation includes amusement, sport and similar leisure-time pursuits and would include recreation and amusement in vehicles, vessels or aircraft (eg joyflights, sightseeing tours; ID 2009/45). Common examples of entertainment are business lunches, cocktail parties, tickets to sporting or theatrical events, sightseeing and so on. Entertainment also covers accommodation or travel associated with any of these items, and incidental items such as "entertainment allowances". In general, the prohibition applies no matter who the recipients of the entertainment are and irrespective of whether there is a genuine connection with business activities.

The provision of an item of property is the provision of entertainment where the usefulness of the item of property expires after consumption or the item is returned at the completion of use and the entertainment arises from the use of the property. The provision of items such as bottled spirits, games, TV sets, VCRs, computers, crockery, swimming pools and gardening equipment will not generally constitute the provision of entertainment because such items have an enduring character and only an indirect nexus to any immediate entertainment (TD 94/55).

The prohibition also applies to prevent claims (such as depreciation and repairs) for plant and equipment to the extent that it is used for the provision of non-deductible entertainment. It also prevents a deduction for a lease incentive payment in the form of a complete holiday package (IT 2631).

The cost to an employer of providing staff social functions is a non-deductible entertainment expense. So is the cost of providing Christmas gifts to employees where the gift provides entertainment by way of food, drink or recreation (eg a holiday, tickets to sporting events, the theatre or cinema or the cost of a night out at a restaurant). However, the cost of relatively inexpensive Christmas gifts (eg a bottle of whisky or wine or a food hamper) that will be consumed by an employee at home will not be treated as entertainment (TR 2007/12). Nor will morning and afternoon teas and light lunches provided by an employer during the working day to employees and their associates (IT 2675). Airport lounge membership fees incurred by an employer are not entertainment expenses (TD 2016/15; ¶16-270).

The factors to be taken into account in determining whether the provision of food and drink constitutes entertainment are set out in TR 97/17. The ruling contains a detailed table summarising the FBT and income tax outcomes for various circumstances in which food and drink is provided to employees and their associates, as well as a number of examples. The following questions need to be considered to determine whether or not the provision of food and drink constitutes the provision of entertainment.

- Why is the food and drink provided? — Where provided for the purposes of refreshment, it will generally not be entertainment. Where provided in a social situation, it will generally be entertainment.

- What food and drink is being provided? — The more elaborate the meal, the more likely it will be entertainment.

- When is the food and drink being provided? — If provided during work time, overtime or while travelling, it is less likely to be entertainment as it will usually be for a work-related purpose. However, a social function held during work time will still be entertainment.

- Where is the food and drink being provided? — Where provided on the employer's business premises or at the usual workplace of the employee, it is less likely to be entertainment. Where provided in a function room, hotel, restaurant or consumed with other forms of entertainment, it is likely to be entertainment.

Where an employee travelling in the course of performing employment duties consumes food and drink, including alcohol (whether alone, with other employees or with clients who are also travelling, or with a spouse), the food and drink provided to the employee without any supplementary entertainment (eg a floor show) do not have the character of entertainment. If the provision of food and drink does not amount to entertainment, the expenditure may be deductible under the general deduction provisions, whether or not it is subject to FBT (TR 97/17). For example a deduction is available to journalists who, as part of their work, are required to report on a particular social function (TR 98/14). Meals taken while travelling overnight on business, meals of a restaurant reviewer or tickets of a theatre critic do not constitute entertainment.

Whether food and drink constitutes entertainment is a matter of characterisation and is not to be determined by reference to subjective matters such as the purpose of a person. Rather, it depends on all relevant circumstances such as the venue, quality of food and drink, the occasion, cost and nature. Therefore, a gala dinner at a leadership seminar held at a luxurious location was entertainment, but the provision of sandwiches and coffee during a working session would not be (*Amway of Australia*; CR 2005/89).

There are a number of exceptions to the general prohibition on the deductibility of entertainment expenses that are explained below. The fact that a particular expenditure is excepted does not necessarily mean that it is deductible: the expenditure must still satisfy the usual requirements for deductibility under ITAA97 s 8-1.

Deductible where fringe benefit

Where entertainment expenses are incurred in providing a fringe benefit (¶35-617), the general prohibition on deductibility does not apply. However, where the taxable value of the fringe benefit is reduced in respect of entertainment expenses incurred by an employee on a person other than the employee or an associate, the amount of that reduction will not be deductible. Similarly, where an employer elects to use the 50/50 split method or the 12-week register method for determining the taxable value of meal entertainment fringe benefits (¶35-617), only a corresponding proportion of the meal entertainment expenditure is deductible (ITAA36 ss 51AEA to 51AEC).

In-house dining facilities

The general prohibition does not prevent a deduction being claimed for the cost of providing food and drink on working days to the taxpayer's employees (including directors) in an "in-house dining facility". This also applies to employees and directors of related companies. However, no deduction is allowed for costs incurred on parties (including Christmas parties), receptions or other social functions (although there are exceptions — see above).

An in-house dining facility means a canteen, dining room or similar facility that is:

- on property occupied by the taxpayer or by a related company. This would extend to vessels (eg boats) or floating structures (eg oil drilling platforms)
- operated mainly for providing food or drink to employees or directors of the taxpayer or of a related company, and
- not open to the public.

A boardroom or meeting room with kitchen facilities is not an in-house dining facility (IT 2675).

The cost of providing food and drink to non-employees (eg clients) in an in-house dining facility is also deductible on the condition that an amount of $30 is included in the taxpayer's assessable income for each meal provided. If the taxpayer elects not to include the amounts in assessable income, the cost is not deductible. An election must be made on or before the date the tax return for the relevant year is lodged, or before such later date as the Commissioner allows. A separate election can be made for each in-house dining facility. An election is not required to be in writing.

Taxpayers in business of entertainment

Where the taxpayer's business consists of providing entertainment to paying clients or customers (eg theatres, restaurants), the cost of providing that entertainment in the ordinary course of business is deductible. This also applies where the provision of entertainment for payment forms only a part of the taxpayer's business (eg the cost to an airline of providing meals to passengers), as well as to the cost incurred by employees working for such businesses in providing entertainment (eg uniform laundry expenses of a restaurant waiter or theatre usher).

The cost of meals provided by a restaurant or other dining facility to the employees who work there may be a deductible expense. A corresponding rule applies where the employer operates an accommodation, recreation or travel facility. For example, a hotel, motel, resort or theatre that contains dining facilities may claim a deduction for meals provided for their staff at those facilities. This is so whether the staff work in the dining facilities or not. For these purposes, a dining facility is a canteen, dining room, cafe or restaurant, or similar facility. It must be located on the employer's premises (this includes vessels) or on premises of a related company. No deduction is allowed for food or drink provided at a party, reception or other social function.

Seminars

The general prohibition does not apply to the cost of food, drink, accommodation and travel that is reasonably incidental to a person's attendance at a "seminar" lasting at least 4 hours (TD 93/195). Meals, rest or recreation breaks do not affect the continuity of a seminar and are not taken into account in determining its duration.

A seminar includes a conference, convention, lecture, meeting, award presentation, speech, question-and-answer session, training session or educational course. An expense is not deductible, however, if: (a) the seminar is a "business meeting"; or (b) the main purpose of the seminar is the promotion or advertising of a business or of its goods or services or the provision of entertainment. A seminar is a business meeting if its main purpose is to enable discussion of the affairs of a particular business between persons associated with that business.

Deductibility is not denied, however, if the seminar is:

- organised by or on behalf of the employer solely for training employees, partners and/or directors in matters relevant to the company's business, and/or enabling employees, partners and/or directors to discuss general policy issues relevant to the internal management of the employer's business, and
- conducted in conference facilities operated by a person whose business includes organising seminars or making property available for conducting seminars.

The cost of recreation provided in connection with a seminar is not deductible. For example, if a seminar fee includes a meal plus a visit to a local tourist attraction, then, assuming that the fee is otherwise deductible, the part relating to the visit would be denied deductibility. In *Re Pollak Partners*, lunch provided to the taxpayer's training staff at computer training courses did not constitute "recreation" because the trainers were required to attend lunch with the course participants and to perform their duties while eating lunch.

Promotion, advertising

The prohibition on entertainment expense deductions does not apply where the expense is incurred to promote or advertise to the public the taxpayer's business or its goods or services, and:

- the taxpayer provides entertainment to an individual as part of a contract for the supply of goods or services in the ordinary course of the taxpayer's business, eg a taxpayer offers a free holiday as an incentive to customers to purchase its goods
- the taxpayer provides discounted or free entertainment as part of its business, eg a restaurant provides a complimentary meal, or a cinema chain provides free movie passes
- the taxpayer incurs costs in exhibiting the goods and services of its business (this applies only to direct costs, not to associated entertainment), or
- the taxpayer provides entertainment that is made available generally to ordinary members of the public; consequently, expenses are not deductible if special access to the entertainment is provided to special classes of people such as clients, customers, suppliers and employees.

▶ Example

A deduction could be allowed for promotional shows at a shopping mall, but not for food and drink provided at an invitation-only film premiere or product launch restricted to selected guests.

Overtime meals

The general prohibition does not apply to the cost of providing overtime food or drink to an employee under an "industrial instrument", ie an industrial award, order, determination or agreement in force under Commonwealth, state or territory law or to the cost incurred by an employee in buying overtime food or drink where an overtime meal allowance under an industrial agreement has been received.

Thus, if the employee receives an overtime meal allowance under an industrial instrument, the allowance is deductible to the employer and assessable to the employee, although the employee can claim a deduction for costs actually incurred on overtime meals (¶16-210).

In-house recreational facilities

The general prohibition does not prevent a deduction being claimed for the costs of operating certain recreational facilities. The recreational facility must be located on property occupied by the taxpayer and must be operated mainly for use by employees (including directors) of the taxpayer or of a related company.

To qualify as "recreational", the facility must be for amusement, sport or similar leisure-time pursuits. Accommodation facilities are excluded and so are dining and drinking facilities. However, food and drink vending machines will qualify.

Charitable entertainment

The general prohibition does not prevent a deduction being claimed for the cost of gratuitous entertainment provided to members of the public who are sick, disabled, poor or otherwise disadvantaged, eg where a company sponsors a Christmas party in a children's hospital.

Entertainment allowances

An entertainment allowance provided to an employee of the taxpayer may be deductible, provided that the allowance is included in the employee's assessable income and it satisfies the requirements of the general deduction provisions. However, entertainment expenditure incurred by the employee is generally not deductible, in accordance with the rules explained above.

An amount must be deducted under the PAYG withholding system (¶26-120) from employees' entertainment allowances or other allowances having a substantial entertainment purpose. The same applies to overtime meal allowances not made under an industrial award (IT 2229).

Safeguarding measures

The Commissioner is authorised to look behind the terms of an agreement to determine how much of an outgoing is, in reality, connected with the provision of non-deductible entertaining. For example, a taxpayer who sponsors a sporting event may, under a collateral arrangement, also be provided with a hospitality tent or viewing box. In such a case, the Commissioner will estimate how much the sponsorship costs are related to that entertainment component and disallow them accordingly. Where advertising signs are provided in conjunction with a corporate box, the Commissioner generally accepts that 5% of the total cost represents the (deductible) portion applicable to advertising and 95% is in respect of (non-deductible) entertainment (TD 92/162).

[FITR ¶78-000ff; FTR ¶26-588]

Telephone and Internet Expenses

¶16-400 Some telephone and internet expenses deductible

For an employee, the cost of installing a landline at home that is used for work-related purposes is a non-deductible capital expense (*Case N84*; TR 98/14). However, a proportion of landline *rental* costs may be allowed to employees who are on call, or who are required to telephone their employer (or clients: TR 98/6) on a regular basis (ITAA97 s 8-1).

The work-related portion of the cost of portable electronic telecommunication devices (such as smartphones and tablets) may be deductible upfront by an employee (s 40-80(2); ¶17-330), or depreciated (¶17-480), depending on the circumstances.

An employee may also deduct the unreimbursed cost of telephone calls and home internet use, to the extent these costs relate to the course of their employment. Evidence that an employer requires an employee to work from home, or to make work calls, supports a deduction claim.

An employee normally determines the work-related percentage of their phone and internet costs by establishing a pattern of use over a 4-week representative period. This is achieved by keeping diary records of work calls and work-internet use. The pattern-of-use percentage is then applied on a reasonable basis to the yearly costs, noting that leave periods are excluded (PS LA 2001/6). Itemised bills assist in the calculation and should be used if provided. Specifically, a pattern of work-call use may be determined by comparing both the number of work calls (incoming and outgoing) and the time spent on such calls, with the total over the representative period. For internet use, an itemised bill in conjunction with diary records help establish the data downloads for work over the representative period. The amount is compared with the total household downloads on the taxpayer's account to establish a work-use percentage (data basis). The time a taxpayer spends on their home internet for work over the representative period, compared with the total household time on the taxpayer's internet account, may also establish a work-use percentage (time basis). The data basis and time basis might need to be considered together in some situations to determine a reasonable percentage.

For bundled phone and internet services, an employee can claim the work-related cost of each component service, which is separately determined using the methods just mentioned. If an employee's phone use is merely incidental to their employment and their total claim is $50 or less for a year, they may claim: 25¢ per work call on a landline, 75¢ per work call on a mobile, and 10¢ per work-related text message (see ATO website *Claiming mobile phone, internet and home phone expenses*).

For an example of how a smartphone app can assist in calculating the work-related portion of a taxpayer's mobile phone costs, see CR 2015/106.

Reported examples of successful claims for telephone expenses include those made by a computer consultant whose employment required her to be on call 24 hours a day (*Collings*), an employed farm manager who was also on call 24 hours a day and who had a second telephone for his non-business calls (*Case M94*), a car salesman who was required to make and receive work-related phone calls at his home (*Case N57*) and an airline employee who took business calls out of hours (*Case R113*). An on-call radiographer was allowed a deduction for 50% of the cost of a mobile phone and monthly access fees as the dominant purpose of the purchase was to enable her to contact the hospital in case of delay (*Pitcher*).

Deductions have been refused in the case of a specialist ambulance officer who was always contacted by telephone if he was needed to work overtime (*Case N5*) and a TV cameraman whose employer expected to be able to contact him at home to instruct him to go to the scene of a news story (*Case N84*), despite claims in both cases that the availability of the phone enabled the employee to derive extra income. It is difficult to reconcile all the cases in this area.

The cost of maintaining a ''silent'' telephone number for privacy (eg to protect a police officer's home and family members) is a non-deductible private expense (TD 93/115).

Casual employees are not regarded as ''at call'' employees and as they do not derive assessable income until they commence work, their telephone rental expenses are not deductible (*Claiming mobile phone, internet and home phone expenses*, ATO website).

Self-employed persons and business taxpayers

A self-employed person may claim a deduction for rental and cost of calls referable to a business telephone. Where a taxpayer carries on business from home and maintains only one telephone there, the claim should be apportioned between private and business use. If the taxpayer has 2 telephones at home, one of which is used exclusively for business purposes, then the expenses referable to that phone are fully deductible.

A medical specialist was allowed a deduction for 80% of the telephone rental on a telephone installed in her investment/holiday home on the basis that it was essential for the purposes of her job that she be contactable at all times (*Case R118*).

The cost of installing a business phone would form part of the total capital cost of the phone and a capital allowance may be permitted. In IT 2197, the Commissioner accepted that a deduction for lease rental and initial connection fees was available to a taxpayer who had leased from the telephone company data transmission lines for the operation of new computer facilities.

Taxpayers working from home during COVID-19 have an option of a simpler method to claim phone and internet expenses (¶16-480).

[FITR ¶33-650]

Club Fees and Leisure Facilities

¶16-410 Fees paid to social and sporting clubs

Membership fees for a social or sporting club (whether incorporated or not) are generally not deductible, regardless of the business use made of the club by the member (ITAA97 s 26-45). This is so whether the fees are paid by the member or by another person, such as the member's employer, and whether the fees relate to full membership or something less than full membership, such as provisional membership. The general prohibition on deductibility does not apply, however, where the fees are incurred in providing a fringe benefit.

Membership fees paid by police officers to Australian Federal Police pistol clubs are deductible to the extent that they are incurred for work-related purposes (TR 95/13). Airport lounge clubs are not recreational clubs: TD 2016/15 (see ¶16-270).

[FITR ¶68-280]

¶16-420 Expenditure relating to leisure facilities and boats

The cost of a leisure facility is generally not deductible unless the facility is used for specified business purposes (ITAA97 s 26-50). The restriction extends to all charges and expenses of the ownership, retention, use, operation, maintenance and repair of a leisure facility. If the leisure facility is used for a specified purpose for only part of the year, a reasonable amount may be deducted. Deductions for depreciation of leisure facilities are similarly restricted (¶17-010).

A ''leisure facility'' is land or a building, part of a building or other structure used, or held for use, for holidays or sport, amusement or similar leisure-time pursuits (eg tennis courts, bowling greens, golf courses, holiday cottages, swimming pools and associated amenity buildings).

The prohibition on deductibility does *not* apply where, at all times in the income year, the taxpayer's use of the leisure facility is for one of the following specified business purposes:

- for sale in the ordinary course of the taxpayer's business of selling leisure facilities
- in the ordinary course of the taxpayer's business of providing leisure facilities for payment or to produce assessable rents, lease premiums, licence fees or similar charges (eg squash courts regularly let on hire, a beach house regularly let to tenants), or
- mainly for the taxpayer's employees to use (other than directors or shareholders, if the taxpayer is a company), or for the care of children of those employees (eg a swimming pool in the vicinity of a factory that may be used by employees in general).

The general prohibition on deductibility does not apply where expenditure on leisure facilities is incurred in providing a fringe benefit or, in the case of depreciation, where the use of the facility constitutes a fringe benefit (¶17-010).

Boat expenses

A deduction may be available under the ordinary deduction provisions for boat expenses that are incurred in carrying on a business. TR 2003/4 deals with when the taxpayer's activity amounts to the carrying on of a business in relation to a boat. In *Athineos*, a taxpayer who hired out 2 yachts was not carrying on a business.

In addition, taxpayers who cannot demonstrate that they are carrying on a business using a boat can:

- deduct expenditure relating to their boating activity up to the level of income generated in that year from their boating activity. This will apply to ''amounts relating to using or holding boats'', ie both expenditure and decline in value (depreciation) deductions, and
- carry forward any excess deductions and deduct them against income from that boating activity in future years (s 26-47).

Any carry forward amount is applied in the following order: (i) to reduce a boating capital gain a taxpayer has for the year (s 118-80) — quarantined amounts are not included in the asset's cost base; (ii) against boating business profits; (iii) against any exempt income derived in the current year that has not already been offset against carry-forward amounts from ITAA97 Div 35 (non-commercial losses) or Div 36 (general tax losses).

Expenditure in providing a fringe benefit will remain deductible regardless of the employer's boating income. A quarantined amount arising before bankruptcy cannot be deducted afterwards.

The cap on the boat expenses does not apply if the amount is attributable to:

- holding a boat as trading stock
- using a boat (or holding it) mainly for letting it on hire in the ordinary course of a business that the taxpayer carries on (eg rowing boats for hire). In *Lee Group Charters Pty Ltd & Anor*, luxury yachts were used exclusively for letting on hire in the ordinary course of the taxpayers' business (also see the related ATO *Decision Impact Statement*). If a yacht is leased by the taxpayers to a boat charterer (which in

turn uses the boat in its charter business) the business of hiring out boats is not being carried on by the taxpayer (*Ell*). A different conclusion was reached in *Case 19/2006* but the Commissioner considers that the case turned on its particular facts.

- using a boat (or holding it) mainly for transporting the public or goods (eg ferries and cargo ships) for payment in the ordinary course of a business that the taxpayer carries on, or
- using a boat for a purpose that is essential to the efficient conduct of a business that the taxpayer carries on (eg a fishing boat, a boat used for transport to an oil rig, a luxury catamaran used for demonstration purposes: *Peerless Marine*). The equivalent requirement in the former provisions was not satisfied in *Case R63* (boat used to entertain clients or prospective clients); *Sinclair* (boat used primarily as a residence that was also helpful for business demonstration purposes) or *Hattrick* (catamaran used for private recreation purposes).

[FITR ¶68-300]

Trade, Business and Professional Subscriptions

¶16-430 Payments to associations

Union dues and other periodical subscriptions (including, in some cases, life membership fees: TD 1999/45) to trade, business or professional associations are generally deductible provided the association's services have a direct nexus with the derivation of the taxpayer's assessable income (ITAA97 s 8-1). However, no deduction is available under the general deduction provision for initial joining or professional registration fees, or to the extent to which the subscription relates to a person's activities which produce exempt or non-assessable non-exempt income (TR 98/6; TR 2000/7) or to entertainment (CR 2007/71).

In addition, there is a specific deduction for payments for *membership* of a trade, business or professional association, including initial joining fees, up to $42 for each association (ITAA97 s 25-55). This deduction is not limited to persons who actively exercise the trade, business or profession and can be claimed by persons such as retired members who would not be entitled to a deduction under s 8-1 (TR 2000/7). Additional levies or contributions that are not made for membership are not deductible under s 25-55 nor are contributions to pensioner or retiree associations.

Section 25-55 is not an exclusive provision and the deductibility of payments to a relevant association should also be considered under s 8-1. If s 8-1 applies, the payment may be fully deductible under that section and the $42 deduction limit will not apply. Nor in such a case will the payment count towards the $42 deduction limit, leaving the whole amount available for a deduction for other payments to that association that are not deductible under s 8-1 (eg for initial joining fees).

Examples of general deduction

The cost of a subscription to associations by pensioners or self-funded retirees is deductible under s 8-1 if the activities of the association can be shown to be related to the gaining of the member's assessable income (eg where it primarily provides investment or taxation information to members). However, payments to an association set up primarily to lobby politicians or to influence public opinion on matters unconnected with the derivation of its members' assessable income (eg environmental issues) would not be deductible (TR 2000/7).

Periodical subscriptions to an association primarily engaged in protecting its members' interests, improving their working conditions and remuneration, or in disseminating information designed to keep members abreast of current developments in their employment field are deductible. Payments made to an Industrial Registrar in lieu of annual union dues by a person whose conscientious beliefs prevent him/her from joining a union are also deductible if the person would be entitled to a deduction for the annual union dues (TD 2000/17). Payments made by ambulance officers to a legal defence fund were deductible in CR 2007/82 as was contributions to a litigation fund to pay for legal advice and representation for ATO employees (CR 2018/8).

A levy or contribution paid to enable a trade union or professional association to acquire or construct new premises in which to conduct its activities, to refurbish existing premises or to acquire plant and equipment would be deductible. However, a deduction is not allowed for levies and contributions paid to assist a political party to provide overseas relief. Nor are payments by salaried elected union officials into a fund for the election of union officials deductible (TR 2000/7). Levies or contributions paid to a fund to provide financial relief for union members during a strike or lay-off are not deductible, unless the strike fund is used solely to maintain or improve the contributor's pay (TR 2002/7).

[FITR ¶33-100, ¶65-440]

¶16-440 Deductibility of other subscriptions

Subscriptions to technical, scientific, trade, business or professional journals, information services, newspapers and magazines are deductible, provided the subscriptions relate to the production of the taxpayer's assessable income (ITAA97 s 8-1). This applies to employees as well as other taxpayers. The cost of newspapers, Internet use and pay TV access may be deductible to the extent of work-related use: see, for example, TR 98/14 (journalist researching a particular topic), TR 1999/10 (members of parliament), TR 98/6 (real estate industry employees using the property section of a newspaper), *Lenten* (teacher) and ID 2002/484 (subscription paid by accountant for accredited professional education channel). Internet installation and initial connection costs are of a non-deductible capital nature.

In the case of taxpayers carrying on a business, subscriptions and donations of various kinds to organisations that are paid for purely business purposes (eg as a form of advertising) may also be claimed in full.

Credit card subscriptions may in some circumstances be deductible. For example, a public servant was allowed a deduction for the cost (joining fee and annual fee) of acquiring a credit card that he used to meet unexpected expenses while on an overseas business trip (*Case P77*).

The cost of the *Australian Master Tax Guide* was allowed by the Commissioner as a deduction to a public service auditor in *Case R70*.

[FITR ¶33-630]

Self-education Expenses

¶16-450 Deductions for self-education expenses

In general terms, self-education expenses are deductible under ITAA97 s 8-1 where the expenses have the necessary connection with the production of the taxpayer's assessable income. However, a deduction is not available in respect of the first $250 of certain kinds of self-education expenses (¶16-460).

According to TR 98/9, the following principles govern deductibility of self-education expenses:

(1) The cost of improving knowledge or skills is not an outgoing of capital (*Finn*).

(2) Expenses incurred in keeping up to date or to better enable the taxpayer to discharge existing duties or to earn present income may be deductible (*Finn*).

(3) Where (2) does not apply and a new or further qualification is sought, there must be at least a high degree of probability that it will lead to an increase of earnings if the cost is to be deductible (*Hatchett*). However, the qualification need not necessarily have to give rise to an increase in salary (*Smith*). It will not be sufficient simply to establish that the employer has encouraged the employee to undertake the self-education. If the taxpayer is not currently occupied or employed in an area that makes the study necessary or desirable, it seems that the cost is not deductible.

(4) No deduction is allowable for self-education expenses where the study is to enable a taxpayer to get employment, to obtain new employment or to open up a new income-earning activity (even in the taxpayer's present employment). The expenses are incurred at a point too soon to be regarded as incurred in gaining or producing assessable income. In *Roberts' case*, a mining engineer was denied a deduction for the costs incurred in undertaking an overseas MBA course after he was retrenched from his job as a mine manager. Before completing the course, the taxpayer accepted an offer of employment as a mine manager with another company. The costs of the course were held to have been incurred for the purpose of obtaining new employment. See also *Cheung*; *Southwell-Keely*; *Yan*; and *Vakiloroaya*. A Treasury discussion paper considers expanding allowable deductions to self-education expenses that are not related to an individual's current employment to support retraining and reskilling in the job market.

For the above principles to be relevant, the expenses themselves should be properly identifiable as self-education expenses. Costs incurred by a post-graduate researcher to construct a test chamber for experimentation and costs related to filing patent applications to protect intellectual property were found not to be "self-education" expenses (*Vakiloroaya*).

The Commissioner has indicated (TR 98/9, and the non-withdrawn paragraphs of TR 92/8) that, where the requirements for deductibility are otherwise met, the following expenses qualify as self-education expenses:

- tuition or course fees (including student union fees) related to attending an educational institution or work-related conferences or seminars (eg TD 93/195). The deduction is available even if the student subsequently cancels his or her enrolment (ID 2005/69)

- the cost of textbooks, professional and trade journals and photocopying

- fares incurred on overseas study tours or in attending work-related conferences or seminars or an educational institution (¶16-270). Accommodation and meal expenses are allowable where the taxpayer is required to be away from home overnight, but not where the taxpayer establishes a new home base. In *Mandikos*, the AAT rejected this "home base" test, preferring to disallow a claim for living expenses on the separate ground that their essential character was private

- motor vehicle expenses incurred in travelling between: (a) home and an educational institution (including a library for research) and back again; and (b) the place of work and the educational institution and back again. If a taxpayer travels from home to an educational institution and then on to his/her place of work and returns home by the same route, only the costs of the first leg of each journey are deductible. If the taxpayer carries out income-earning activities at the institution, only the cost of travel between the institution and the taxpayer's place of work is deductible (TR 92/8 — paras 11(d) and 13(c), which remain operative despite the Ruling being withdrawn)

- interest on moneys borrowed to pay for the expenses listed above. The relevant connection between the interest and the relevant activities must exist in each year in which the interest is claimed (thus a change in employment may mean that the connection no longer exists). This view should now be seen in the light of the decisions in *Brown* and *Jones* (¶16-740).

Depreciation may be claimed on professional libraries and other items used in connection with self-education (such as computers, filing cabinets and desks) (¶17-010). Interest on moneys borrowed to purchase such items is deductible under the general deduction provision (TR 98/9).

According to the Commissioner, the intention or purpose of a taxpayer in incurring the self-education expenses can be an element in determining deductibility. This could be relevant where, for example, a study tour had both a private purpose and a purpose of gaining or producing assessable income. See ¶16-290 for a discussion of an equivalent situation in the context of travel expenses.

The Commissioner is reviewing the deductibility of expenses incurred under arrangements involving the purchase of self-study training programs which may be undertaken at a holiday destination of the taxpayer's choice, self-study training programs, seminars on board a cruise ship, and wealth creation seminars undertaken while travelling (TA 2011/3).

Deductibility does not extend to the cost of meals purchased by a taxpayer while attending a course at an educational institution unless the taxpayer is required to sleep away from home (eg no deduction would be allowable for meals purchased by a taxpayer living in Sydney and attending an institution within the metropolitan area). No deduction is allowable for expenditure on accommodation and meals where a taxpayer has travelled to another location for self-education purposes but is considered to have established a new home there (eg to do a 2-year course) (TR 98/9; *Case 5/2009*). The costs of attending a graduation ceremony (including the cost of hiring an academic gown) are not deductible (*Berrett*).

Student contributions and debt repayments under the tertiary student financial supplement scheme (¶2-380, ¶2-385) are not deductible by the student or any other person who makes the payments on behalf of the student, unless incurred in providing a fringe benefit (ITAA97 s 26-20; ID 2005/27; ID 2002/463). Debt repayments related to trade support loans, student start up loans, or ABSTUDY student start-up loans, are also denied deductibility. Interest paid on moneys borrowed for the purpose of making such payments may be deductible under the general deduction provisions where the education costs would themselves be deductible. Course fees relating to current income-earning activities are deductible even if the taxpayer has obtained a loan for the course fees under the HELP programme (see ID 2005/26; and the ATO website at *Education and study*). Also see ¶2-380 for details of the current student assistance scheme.

Payments made to reduce a liability to the overseas debtors repayment levy are not deductible (ITAA97 s 26-20). This levy allows HELP and trade support loan debts to be recovered from debtors residing overseas.

Self-education expenses and government assistance payments

No deduction is available for expenses (and depreciation of assets) incurred in gaining or producing rebatable government assistance payments (eg Newstart/JobSeeker, Austudy, ABSTUDY and Youth allowance), thus overcoming the effect of the decision in *Anstis* in which self-education expenses were allowed against Youth allowance income (ITAA97 s 26-19).

[FITR ¶32-980 – ¶33-090]

¶16-452 Examples of self-education claims

Successful self-education claims involving attendance at overseas conferences or courses include: a medical technologist's trip to an immunology conference in Paris (*Case R75*); an architecture student's trip to a European design conference (*Case R87*); a dentist's trip to a Dental Congress in Paris (*Case R13*); a French teacher's trip to France for a professional development course (*Case T47*); and an actress' trip to attend a BBC radio drama course (*Case V32*). A claim by a locum professional for the cost of a refresher course was disallowed in *Case T10*, but allowed in *Case T90*.

A music teacher was allowed a deduction for the cost of attending musical performances and functions (*Brimo*). The actress in *Case V32* was allowed a deduction for the costs of a one-week side-trip in Russia attending plays and talking to producers. See TR 95/20 for the deductibility of a performing artist's costs of coaching lessons and of researching a role or character.

The cost of taking French lessons was allowed to a public servant who was about to go to an important international seminar in France (*Case V31*). An economic analyst was allowed a deduction for expenses incurred in attending Swedish language courses in Sweden to enable him to read Scandinavian language journals provided by his employer and relevant to his employment (*Case 41/95*).

Self-improvement or personal development courses are non-deductible unless the course is directly related to the production of income (TR 98/9; ID 2003/84; ID 2003/614). For example, the features editor of a newspaper was allowed a deduction for the cost of a speech therapy course undertaken to enable him to better present himself to people in work situations (*Case Z42*). The taxpayer in *Case V31* was allowed a deduction for the costs of a management course that he had taken in order to cope with increased managerial responsibilities. An air force manager was allowed the costs of ''Mastery University'' courses designed to enhance leadership, management capabilities and decision-making processes, but not courses relating to personal financial planning skills (*Naglost*). The cost of necessary first aid training is deductible for a person designated to assist in emergency situations in the workplace (see the rulings referred to in ¶16-635). The costs of a heavy vehicle training course may be deductible for a mechanic responsible for road testing those vehicles (ID 2002/517).

In *Case S21*, a director of a building society was allowed a deduction for expenses associated with a graduate diploma course in professional accounting. A Human Services course was considered to assist a taxpayer in her current employment as a health insurance officer and help her achieve her career aspirations with her current employer, even though no salary advancement was attributable to the course (*Davis*).

However, a legal officer with the public service was denied a deduction for the costs of a 6-month pre-admission course at the College of Law and for the costs of being admitted as a solicitor (*Case Z1*). A high school teacher of mathematics and science, who studied a postgraduate business management degree, was denied a deduction for course expenses related to financial accounting and marketing subjects (*Ting*). A former bank director could not deduct MBA course fees incurred after he was made redundant because the nexus to his employment was lost (*Thomas*).

Costs of specialist courses

A deduction may be allowed for expenses incurred in obtaining a higher degree or qualification relevant to the taxpayer's profession. In *Highfield's case*, a dentist in general practice was allowed a deduction for air fares, university fees and meals and accommodation costs incurred in studying overseas for a specialist degree. It was accepted that he had taken the specialist degree (in periodontics) so that he could expand that aspect of his work, and charge higher fees, in his general practice (as distinct from becoming a specialist periodontist). A similar claim was allowed in *Mandikos*. The costs of a trip were not deductible, however, in *Case T73*, where the taxpayer had ceased his employment as a medical registrar and travelled to the UK to undertake specialised research. On his return he commenced practice on his own account. The AAT distinguished *Highfield's case* on the ground that it involved a self-employed taxpayer who was already in practice before taking the trip.

Where a general medical practitioner undertakes further study in order to set up practice as a specialist dermatologist, the expenses related to the study are not deductible since the study is designed to open up a new income-earning activity (TR 98/9).

A law clerk, already admitted to the bar, who travelled to the UK to attend a post-graduate course in international law, which it was claimed would assist him in earning his future income as a barrister, was allowed a deduction for air fares, course fees and living costs (*Case T78*). However, the correctness of this decision was questioned in *Case U186*, where travel claims were disallowed to a taxpayer who had resigned his position as an employee lawyer before going overseas (TR 95/9). A clinical nurse was entitled to a deduction for the costs of a postgraduate course in adult education (*Maclean*) but a professional investor was not allowed a deduction for the cost of attaining Masters degrees in subjects in which he did not have prior qualifications (*Elder*).

Flying lessons

Costs incurred on flying lessons by air traffic controllers may be deductible where the lessons are undertaken for the purpose of improving the taxpayer's efficiency in the performance of an air traffic controller's duties, thereby enhancing the prospects of promotion (*Wilkinson*). A Qantas flight engineer was allowed a deduction for flying lessons as they would enable him to do his job better, irrespective of whether the lessons would help him obtain promotion (*Studdert*). No deduction was available to a solicitor specialising in building and construction law, but wishing to expand his practice into aviation law, for the expenses of obtaining an Australian pilot licence and aviation training (*Case 5/2011*).

Costs incurred by existing pilots in obtaining more specialised licences will also normally be deductible. A deduction has also been allowed to a doctor who took flying lessons so that he would be accepted as a Designated Medical Examiner for airline personnel (*Case R50*), but not to an adviser on a potentially dangerous cloud-seeding project (*Case S32*).

[FITR ¶33-020, ¶33-030, ¶68-180]

¶16-460 Limit on self-education expenses deduction

The amount deductible for self-education expenses under ITAA97 s 8-1 cannot be greater than the excess of the net amount of "expenses of self-education" (see below) over $250 (ITAA36 s 82A).

In calculating the deduction limit (ie the net amount of expenses of self-education *minus* $250), expenses of self-education are not restricted to amounts that are deductible under s 8-1 but do not include depreciation (TR 98/9). Furthermore, deductions for expenses that do not come within the definition of "expenses of self-education" are not affected by the limit (eg for the costs of short-term refresher courses), nor are deductions under other specific deduction provisions (eg for computer repairs).

▶ Example

Karen is studying a postgraduate university course to improve her knowledge and skills in her current employment. She incurs the following expenses related to her studies: tuition fees ($6,000), bus fares for travel directly from home to university and return ($400), child care fees ($600) and computer repairs ($300). Depreciation on her computer amounts to $200. The "expenses of self-education" comprise the tuition fees, bus fares, child care fees, and computer repair expenses (totalling $7,300).

The effect of the $250 rule is that the maximum amount allowable under s 8-1 is $7,050 (ie $7,300 – $250). However, Karen's claim under s 8-1 is only $6,400 (tuition fees and bus fares) and the $250 rule will not limit her claim. Karen will still be entitled to specific deductions for the computer repair expenses and depreciation (to the extent they relate to producing her assessable income).

Where the first $250 of expenses of self-education is excluded, the taxpayer is not required to substantiate that $250 (TD 93/97).

The expression ''expenses of self-education'' is defined, for these purposes, to mean all expenses (other than student contributions and debt repayments under the tertiary student financial supplement scheme: ¶2-380 and ¶2-385) necessarily incurred by a taxpayer in connection with a prescribed course of education — ie one provided by a school, college, university or other place of education and undertaken by the taxpayer to gain qualifications for use in the carrying on of a profession, business, trade or in the course of any employment. ''Necessarily incurred'' means compulsory and unavoidable expenses, as well as those for which a need may be shown (eg fees, fares, books, child care costs, capital cost of equipment), but not those which are merely useful. Debt repayments related to trade support loans, student start up loans, or ABSTUDY student start-up loans, as well as payments to reduce a liability to the overseas debtors repayment levy, are not ''expenses of self-education''.

A ''prescribed course of education'' is a full-time or part-time organised course of study provided by an institution or organisation whose primary function is the provision of systematic instruction, training or schooling in a subject, skill or trade (including sport). Such institutions have been held to cover a trade school which provided a course for apprentice butchers who attended 3 times a week for 6 weeks in each year (*Case P95*), a flying school that provided courses of instruction for commercial pilots (*Case P17*), the Law Extension Committee of Sydney University that ran Barristers' Admission Board courses (*Case T34*), a correspondence school that provided hotel management courses (*Case S95*) and an institution providing speed reading courses (TR 98/9).

''Course of education'' requires an element of continuity and of ongoing instruction and training. Short-term refresher courses, in-service activities or short-term development courses do not qualify (TR 98/9).

Where a taxpayer is entitled to be reimbursed for education expenses and the reimbursement does not fall into assessable income, it must be subtracted in determining the ''net amount of expenses of self-education'' before the excess over $250 is calculated.

Treasury has issued a discussion paper considering the removal of the $250 reduction, as part of expanding deductions for self-education expenses.

[FITR ¶32-990; FTR ¶42-790]

Home Office Expenses

¶16-480 Deductions for home office expenses

A taxpayer who carries on part or all of their business or employment activities at home may be entitled to a deduction for part of their outgoings related to the home. The deductions that may be claimed depend on whether the taxpayer's home is used as a place of business (eg a doctor's surgery), or as the sole base for their income earning activity (eg where no other work location is provided to an employee). Alternatively, they depend on whether the home office is simply used for personal convenience (eg a consultant's study space used when they work from home as their employer provides for this flexibility, or a teacher's home study that is used for lesson preparation and marking), noting that the deductions available in the personal convenience situation are fewer.

Depending on the circumstances, there are 2 broad types of home office expenses that might be claimed: (i) occupancy expenses (or costs of occupying the office — eg mortgage interest, rent, council and water rates, land taxes, building insurance premiums, etc); and (ii) running expenses (or costs of running the office — eg office heating/ cooling, lighting, and cleaning expenses; costs of repairing office equipment or furniture; equipment leasing costs; office depreciation charges, etc).

Home office as a place of business or income earning base

Examples of taxpayers using their home as a place of business or sole base of income earning operations include:

- a doctor or dentist who has a surgery, consulting or waiting room(s) at home
- a tradesperson who has a workshop at home
- a self-employed scriptwriter who conducts writing activities from a room in their apartment (*Swinford*)
- a territory manager who is not provided with office accommodation by their employer and so sets aside a room in their home to attend to job-related matters (*Case T48*)
- a sales representative who is required by their employer to maintain a home office to carry out work duties (*Case U65*)
- a bank's IT employee required to perform duties during after-hours and weekends who works from home using equipment supplied by the employer (*McAteer*)
- an employee architect who is also allowed to conduct a small private practice from home (*Case F53*).

In determining whether an area set aside qualifies as a place of business or income earning base, the Commissioner considers whether the area is (TR 93/30):

- clearly identifiable as a place of business or income earning base
- not readily suitable or adaptable for use for private or domestic purposes in association with the home generally
- used exclusively, or almost exclusively, for business purposes
- used regularly for visits by clients or customers.

These factors along with the essential character of the area, the nature of the taxpayer's income earning activity, and any other relevant factors are used to make a balanced assessment of whether the taxpayer's activity constitutes a place of business or income earning base. See also ATO publication *Deductions for home-based business expenses*.

The fact that a taxpayer no longer resides in the house will, of course, substantially assist a claim. For example, a taxpayer who used a room in his ex-wife's home as a study for work purposes and continued to make the mortgage payments on that home was allowed a deduction for the proportion of mortgage interest referable to the study (*Case V69*).

Where a home is also used as a place of business or income earning base, a taxpayer can claim deductions for both occupancy and running expenses to the extent they relate to their income producing activity (often under s 8-1, but specific provisions such as s 25-10 and Div 40 are also relevant). Occupancy expenses will be apportioned based on the floor area of the home used for the income earning activity as follows:

$$\frac{\text{Floor area related to the income earning activity}}{\text{Total floor area}} \times \text{Relevant expenditure}$$

In determining the ''total floor area'' (denominator in the above formula), it was not possible to exclude certain areas that were not used for income earning activities (*Case 10/2016*).

Home office occupancy expenses incurred in relation to a jointly owned building must also be apportioned on a floor area basis by reference to the area used as a home office, rather than on the basis of ownership (*Case 7/2007*).

In addition to the floor areas basis, an apportionment on a time basis may be required if the home office is used to produce income for only part of the income year. Some further details about the running expenses that may be claimed where the home office is a place of business or income earning base include:

- *heating, lighting* — additional expenditure incurred to provide heating and lighting while engaged exclusively in income-producing activities can be claimed. These claims are generally small and reasonable estimates would normally be accepted (TR 93/30; in *Ovens*, the taxpayer's basis of apportionment was rejected)
- *depreciation, insurance, repairs* — these claims are permitted if they relate to office equipment, desks, chairs, bookshelves, curtains, floor coverings, fluorescent lighting systems, etc
- *cleaning costs, pest control* — such costs are normally calculated on a floor area basis
- *repairs, maintenance* — these claims are allowed if referable to the part of the home that is a place of business or income earning base, and are subject to apportionment for any private use (¶16-700)
- *decorating* — an example is painting or wallpapering the place of business or income earning base, and such expenses can be claimed, subject to apportionment for any private use
- *telephone, internet* — see ¶16-400.

The administrative concession in PS LA 2001/6 (see below) may also assist in easing the compliance burden when claiming running expenses.

Where an area of the home is a place of business or income earning base and the home is sold, the CGT provisions treat a capital gain or loss as having accrued to the extent to which the home disposed of was also used for the purpose of gaining or producing assessable income during the period of ownership (TR 93/30; ¶11-760).

Home office for personal convenience

More difficult issues arise where taxpayers (self-employed or employed) simply maintain an office or study in their home in which they undertake income-producing work which is not convenient to carry out at their normal place of work. In such cases, although the area in question is used for income-producing activities, it will not normally qualify as a place of business or income earning base in the way described above (IT 2673; TR 93/30; ¶11-760).

The High Court decisions in *Handley's case* and *Forsyth's case* have established that taxpayers in this position cannot claim deductions under the general deduction provision for occupancy expenses such as mortgage interest, rent (*Bradshaw*), house insurance, council and water rates, or certain repairs (*Geekie*). Both cases involved barristers claiming occupancy expenses for home studies that were used almost exclusively for professional purposes. There was no physical separation of the studies from their homes and they were adjacent to the taxpayers' living rooms. The barristers also maintained chambers at different locations from their homes. In both cases, a majority of the High Court held that the taxpayers were not entitled to the deductions claimed. The home studies in each case remained an integral part of the taxpayers' home and were not, in a real sense, a place of business and the expenses were essentially domestic in character.

The employee pilot in *Yeates* was not entitled to deductions for home office occupancy costs as his employer did not expect pilots to perform any duties at home, and office-type facilities were provided by the employer at the airport to enable pilots to perform their duties.

However, deductions may be allowed for work or business-related home office running expenses, such as heating/cooling, lighting expenses, cleaning costs, and depreciation on a professional library or equipment, repairs to furniture and equipment (TR 93/30). The deduction applies only to costs that are additional to those that would have been incurred in any event. For example, if a taxpayer undertakes a work activity in a room where other family members are watching television, there may be no additional cost of heating, cooling or lighting occasioned by that work activity, but there may be computer, phone or internet expenses that are work related, so only deductions for those would be appropriate. If a taxpayer works at home but has no dedicated work area, deductions are also limited to work-related telephone and internet costs (see ¶16-400) and depreciation on equipment.

The Commissioner will accept itemised supplier records showing a work use proportion, or a diary covering a 4-week representative period as establishing an individual's pattern of use for the whole year, or where the claim is small, by providing a reasonable estimate (PS LA 2001/6).

Once the relevant period of work or business-related use has been established, the Commissioner will accept a claim based on 52 cents an hour (from 1 July 2018; previously 45 cents) to cover heating/cooling, lighting, repairs and depreciation on furniture (PS LA 2001/6). A separate calculation must be made for phone and internet expenses, depreciation on equipment, such as a computer, laptop or printer. This should be based on a bona fide estimate of the percentage of work or business use, which may be based on the 4-week representative diary. A taxpayer of course retains the option of establishing actual costs as the basis of their claim.

Working from home during COVID-19

A temporary option available to taxpayers working from home during the COVID-19 pandemic is to claim 80 cents an hour for every hour worked at home. This is in place of claiming any additional running expenses, phone or internet expenses, depreciation of furniture and equipment, consumables or stationery (PCG 2020/3). The option is available for hours worked at home from 1 March 2020 to 30 June 2020 for the 2019–20 income year, and for the whole 2020–21 income year. A record of hours worked should be maintained, eg a timesheet. If this method is used, no other expenses for working from home can be claimed for that period. An amount claimed using this method should be included under the "other work-related expenses" question in the tax return with the description "COVID-hourly rate".

Personal service providers

For restrictions applying to individual contractors who provide personal services, but who do not conduct personal services businesses, see ¶30-600.

[FITR ¶32-780, ¶32-790]

Election Expenses

¶16-500 Parliamentary election expenses

Expenses incurred by a taxpayer in contesting elections for membership of the federal or a state parliament or the ACT or Northern Territory Legislative Assembly are deductible under ITAA97 s 25-60 irrespective of the candidate's success or failure. Recoupments of such expenses may be included in assessable income (¶10-270).

Regardless of when the expenses are incurred, there must be a sufficient connection between the particular expenditure and the contesting of an election for a deduction to be allowable. However, the deduction is not restricted to expenses incurred after the election process has been formally initiated by the issue of writs. For example, the deduction has been held to apply to expenses incurred by a candidate up to 2 years before the election was actually held (*Wilcox*). In practice, expenditure will be deductible if it is of "a type that would be incurred by a candidate to further his/her chances of being elected" (TR 1999/10).

Expenses incurred by a taxpayer in gaining preselection as his/her party's candidate for a forthcoming election are not deductible (*Case L32*; *Flegg*).

A comprehensive list of deductible expenditure — ranging from the cost of car stickers to ex gratia payments to volunteer workers — is contained in TR 1999/10.

Entertainment expenses generally do not qualify for deduction as election expenses (ITAA97 s 25-70). The exceptions are: (a) entertainment that is available to the public generally; or (b) food and drink that does not involve the entertainment of another person. This means, for example, that the cost of a candidate's food and drink while travelling away from home in the course of a campaign may still qualify for deduction as does the cost of providing light refreshments such as morning and afternoon tea for staff and visitors.

In addition to the costs of contesting elections, members of parliament can claim a deduction under ITAA97 s 8-1 for expenses incurred in carrying out their official duties. A detailed list of typical deductions is given in TR 1999/10.

Electoral expenses must be fully substantiated as work expenses (¶16-210). If the Commissioner considers as reasonable the amount of the expenses claimed for travel covered by a domestic travel allowance, the expenses may be deductible notwithstanding the absence of written evidence; see further TR 2004/6. A member of parliament may choose not to claim a deduction for expenses incurred that are equal to or greater than a reasonable travel allowance and not to include the allowance in assessable income (TR 1999/10 (the ATO intends to clarify this ruling); TR 2004/6). Where it is impractical to obtain receipts, eg for modest cash handouts for needy callers, it is sufficient to record the expense in a petty cash diary.

[FITR ¶65-460, ¶65-500]

¶16-510 Local government elections

A deduction of up to $1,000 is allowed for expenses incurred in seeking election to a local government body (s 25-65; former ITAA36 s 74A). The $1,000 limit applies to each election contested, whether successfully or not, and whether the expenditure is incurred in one or more years of income. However, no deduction is allowable in respect of entertainment expenses, except in the limited circumstances covered at ¶16-500 (s 25-70). For the type of expenses that may be deductible, see TR 1999/10.

A taxpayer was denied a deduction under the general deduction provision for the excess of his local council election expenses over $1,000, primarily on the basis that he performed an honorary function for which he received no remuneration (*Case 47/95*) or because the expenditure was not incurred in carrying on a business (*Vance*).

Where deductible election expenditure is reimbursed to a taxpayer (eg by a political organisation), the amount of the reimbursement may be included in the taxpayer's assessable income (¶10-260, ¶10-270).

The amount of this reimbursement or payment is treated as having effectively reduced the deduction for the purposes of calculating whether the $1,000 limit has been exceeded.

▶ Example

In Year 1 John incurs expenditure of $1,200 in contesting the local council election, of which he deducts $1,000. In Year 2, he receives $360 as a recoupment of the expenditure. Of this amount, $300 is included in assessable income by s 20-35 as extended by s 20-50 (¶10-270).

Because of the assessable recoupment, $300 of the expenditure is disregarded in applying the $1,000 limit, and as a result, John's deductions are treated as being only $700. While the original deduction for Year 1 is not affected, the previously undeducted $200 can be deducted for Year 2. This triggers a further application of s 20-35 (as extended by s 20-50) to include the remaining $60 of the assessable recoupment in John's assessable income for Year 2. Total deductions (net of assessed recoupment) are $840, equalling original expenditure (net of recoupment).

Election expenses are subject to substantiation requirements (¶16-210).

[FITR ¶65-480]

Remuneration and Other Compensation Paid

¶16-520 Salaries, wages, directors' fees, fringe benefits

Salary or wages, bonuses, gratuities, allowances (and, in the case of a company, directors' fees) or other compensation or rewards for personal services paid by a taxpayer engaged in the production of assessable income are deductible to the extent to which they are incurred in producing the taxpayer's assessable income (ITAA97 s 8-1). This includes parental leave pay provided to employees and wages paid that are supported by the JobKeeper Payment scheme. However, remuneration paid to persons for the specific purpose of carrying out an affair of capital (eg employees engaged in the construction of depreciating assets: ID 2011/42; ID 2011/43), or the construction of other tangible or intangible capital assets (*Draft* TR 2019/D6) is of a capital nature and, therefore, not deductible (*Goodman Fielder Wattie*; see also temporary full expensing allowed for depreciating assets at ¶17-430). Amounts paid to partners are not salary and are not deductible to the partnership (¶5-090). See ¶16-040 for the deductibility of directors' fees.

Payments made (or non-cash benefits provided) on or after 1 July 2019 to employees, directors and contractors, or in relation to a supply of goods or services, are not deductible if a payer fails to comply with the applicable PAYG withholding obligations (see ¶26-150 and ¶26-300).

Where fringe benefits are provided by an employer, the amount deductible for the cost of the fringe benefits will be (TR 2001/2):

- the GST exclusive value — where a GST input tax credit was available in respect of the acquisition of the fringe benefits, or
- the full amount paid or incurred on the relevant acquisition — if no GST input tax credit was available in respect of the acquisition of the fringe benefit (¶34-100, ¶35-000).

A deduction is allowable where real estate salespersons who only earn commission pay wages to other persons providing services and assistance related to the salesperson's income (TR 98/6). Similarly, a deduction may be allowable to a member of parliament for wages paid in limited circumstances (TR 1999/10) and to a bank officer for a fee paid for secretarial services (*Wells*: ¶16-170), but not under a purely domestic relationship (*France*; *Brown*). Special rules apply to remuneration paid to relatives (¶16-530).

The deduction for fees paid by a professional practice to a non-arm's length administration entity will be limited to an amount that reasonably reflects the level of services provided by the entity (IT 2630; ¶16-070, ¶16-152). The deductibility of the fees will not be affected by the proportion of the fee that represents salary or superannuation contributions.

Payments to employees are deductible where they are made in the regular course of a continuing business and are likely to promote harmony, efficiency or economy in working relations or operations (eg a Christmas bonus or a payment to the surviving spouse on the death of an employee or director). A deduction may be available for expenses incurred by an employer in sending a director to work-related stress counselling (ID 2001/748). Certain retiring allowances are deductible (¶16-540).

The compensation paid must relate to the assessable income of the taxpayer paying it. For example, if an employee of one taxpayer performs services for another taxpayer and the first taxpayer does not charge the second for the employee's services, generally the first taxpayer will not be able to claim deductions for the salary, etc, it pays its employee for the period when the employee is engaged in performing services for the other taxpayer.

Contributions to employee benefits trusts were not deductible in *Essenbourne*; *Kajewski*; *Walstern*; *Cajkusic* and *Cameron Brae* (¶13-710, ¶16-010, ¶35-080). The contributions were disallowed under the general anti-avoidance provisions in *Pridecraft*. Premiums on shares allocated to employees' accounts were deductible in *Experienced Tours*, but see the Commissioner's *Decision Impact Statement*.

Leave and redundancy contributions to worker entitlement funds (¶35-645) are deductible (ID 2004/489; CR 2006/46; CR 2006/50; CR 2012/94) as are contributions to industry welfare funds (CR 2004/76).

No deduction is available for the cost of maintaining a spouse or child under 16 years, eg where a farmer provides food and lodgings to a child in return for the work the child performs on the farm (s 26-40). This exclusion does not apply to a spouse permanently living both separately and apart from the taxpayer, although such a taxpayer would still be required to satisfy the general deduction requirements (s 8-1; ¶16-010).

The ATO has warned about the use of arrangements that attempt to artificially create up-front tax deductions for employment costs through the issue of discretionary options (TA 2009/18).

Interests under employee share schemes

A limited, specific deduction is available to employers that provide employee share scheme interests (or money or property) to employees through employee share schemes or arrangements but these are subject to the special rules relating to employee share schemes (¶10-094). Operating costs incurred to implement and administer an employee share scheme are deductible under the general deduction provision (s 8-1; ¶16-010) when incurred because they represent ordinary employee remuneration costs (ID 2014/42).

Personal service providers

Deductions for payments made to associates may be restricted where they are made by individual contractors who provide personal services but are not conducting a personal services business (¶30-600).

[FITR ¶32-940, ¶32-960]

¶16-530 Excessive remuneration to relatives

Although salary or wages paid by a taxpayer to a relative or by a company to a shareholder or director who is also an employee may qualify for deduction, the Commissioner can disallow the deduction to the extent that he considers the remuneration to be in excess of a reasonable amount (ITAA97 s 26-35; ITAA36 s 109).

For a discussion of this power in relation to payments made by a partnership, see ¶5-100 and, in relation to those made by a company, see ¶4-220. So far as an individual taxpayer is concerned, this restriction potentially applies where amounts are paid or liabilities incurred by the taxpayer to:

- a relative, ie a parent, grandparent, brother, sister, uncle, aunt, niece, nephew, lineal descendant (child, grandchild) or adopted child of either the taxpayer or his/her (legal or de facto) spouse; or the (legal or de facto) spouse of the taxpayer or of any of the previously specified persons, or

- a partnership, a partner in which is a relative of the taxpayer.

What is a reasonable salary must be decided on the facts of each case, but a ''commercial standards'' test has been applied in the past. This test assumes, in effect, that the amount that would be reasonable when paid for those services as performed by an outsider does not cease to be reasonable when paid to a relative performing the same services under the same or similar conditions (TR 1999/10 provides an example regarding members of parliament).

[FITR ¶68-240; FTR ¶56-000]

¶16-540 Deductions for retiring allowances

A retiring allowance, whether in lump sum or pension form and whether paid to an employee or director or to a spouse, widow, widower, etc, is deductible under ITAA97 s 8-1 only if its payment can be shown to be in the future interests of the business. Such payments would include amounts paid to an employee or director or to his/her dependants on cancellation of a contract of service, payments to induce unsatisfactory employees to retire, compensation for redundancy, etc.

On the other hand, payments solely in consideration of past services and payments by way of compensation to employees on the closing down of business would not be deductible (subject to the rules noted at ¶16-156). Payments in consideration of a retiring employee not competing with the business are also not deductible (*Riba Foods*).

There is a special deduction provision for certain retiring and death benefits or gratuities that would not otherwise be deductible (ITAA97 s 25-50). Pensions, gratuities or retiring allowances paid during the income year to employees or former employees or to their dependants are deductible to the extent that they are paid in good faith in consideration of the employee's past services in any business carried on by the taxpayer for the purposes of producing assessable income. Such amounts are deductible whether paid by way of lump sum or pension. For example, payments made to ex-directors some months after a corporate reorganisation would not be deductible under s 8-1 (because they were made at a time when the company had ceased business) but might still be deductible under s 25-50.

To be deductible under s 25-50, the amounts must be paid in relation to the past services of an *employee*: the deduction will be allowed for payments to working directors or their dependants where those payments relate to the director's services as an employee but not when they relate to his/her services as a director. Moreover, payment to a deceased employee's estate will not qualify. The fact that the payment may not be assessable in the hands of the recipient under the ETP provisions does not prevent it from being deductible under s 25-50. Although a partner is neither an employee of the partnership nor of his/her co-partners, so that retiring allowances paid to a partner or his/her dependants cannot strictly qualify under s 25-50, in practice a deduction is allowed in relation to the retirement of a working partner who was formerly an employee.

The question whether a relevant payment was made in good faith is to be determined on an objective basis, but still involves an assessment of the taxpayer's subjective state of mind (for factors relevant to this issue, see IT 2152 and IT 2621). This is separate and distinct from the opinion to be formed by the Commissioner as to the reasonableness of the amount of a retiring allowance paid by a private company (¶4-220).

The deduction under s 25-50 applies to sums which are paid by the taxpayer during the year of income. The setting off of one liability against another may be regarded as a sum paid in certain circumstances (*Spargo's case*). On the other hand, it has been held that, where there is no pre-existing liability to be set off, a conveyance of land could not be treated as a sum paid for the relevant purposes (*Case K4*).

Unlike s 8-1 deductions, amounts that are deductible under s 25-50 cannot produce or increase a tax loss (¶16-880).

[FITR ¶31-570, ¶32-960, ¶65-380ff]

Insurance Premiums and Superannuation Contributions

¶16-550 Deductions for insurance premiums

Premiums paid by an employer for workers compensation insurance and premiums paid to insure the employer against death or disablement of its employees through accident are usually deductible (ITAA97 s 8-1). It seems that premiums for accident insurance effected by a parent company in respect of employees of its subsidiary may also be deductible if the purpose of the insurance was to compensate the parent company for the loss of dividends that might result due to the subsidiary's loss of its employees' services.

The Commissioner accepts that premiums paid by a business for fire, burglary, professional indemnity, public risk, motor vehicle or loss of profits insurance are deductible, even where the loss insured against is a capital loss (eg fire or motor vehicle insurance). Premiums paid by a hotel operator for insurance against the possibility of exchange losses arising under an overseas loan to finance the building of a casino were held to be deductible, notwithstanding that the exchange gains would themselves be on capital account (*Australian National Hotels*).

Premiums paid by a company director for professional liability insurance to cover him in his capacity as director were necessarily incurred in carrying on business as a director of a number of companies and therefore deductible (*Adler*). The cost of professional indemnity insurance taken out by an employee lawyer is deductible (TR 95/9).

Premiums paid for insurance to indemnify an employer against its liability to pay an employee a lump sum on retirement were held to be deductible in *Case W62*. That decision was distinguished in *Case X51*, where premiums were held not to be deductible on the basis that the amounts payable under the policies were inadequate to meet the taxpayer's liability; the premiums were characterised as payments made on savings investment policies and were therefore of a capital nature.

In *Gandy Timbers*, premiums for insurance bonds held by the employees' family trusts to provide lump sum payments to employee directors were not deductible to the employer, as nothing in the arrangements advanced the business ends of the employer and the premium outgoings were investments on capital account.

As to the position in relation to partners' insurances of themselves or their co-partners, see ¶5-140. Amounts set aside by self-insured employers to cover expected workers compensation liability may be deductible in the circumstances outlined in TD 97/14 (¶16-040). Businesses should be wary of arrangements that attempt to create inflated deductions for uncommercial insurance premiums, paid to a related tax haven entity, which are excessive in relation to the coverage provided and feature no significant transfer of insurance risk (TA 2009/15).

United Medical Protection Limited support payments are deductible under ITAA97 s 25-105 if they are not otherwise deductible (eg if the taxpayer has retired or left the profession).

[FITR ¶32-820 – ¶32-850]

¶16-560 Deductions for personal sickness/accident premiums

A self-employed taxpayer is entitled to a deduction under ITAA97 s 8-1 for sickness/accident premiums paid under an insurance policy providing the taxpayer with benefits of an income nature during a period of disablement (commonly called an income protection policy). This deduction is also available to employees (*DP Smith*). Deductions are not allowed where premiums are paid under arrangements that are not legally enforceable or to which the general anti-avoidance provisions apply (IT 2460).

Where the benefits under the policy take the form solely of a (capital) lump sum payment for, say, loss of a limb or death, no part of the premium is deductible. No deduction is available to a policy owner for premiums incurred for life cover, total and permanent disability cover, and/or trauma cover, even if the benefits under these policies are payable in instalments (eg PR 2014/13; PR 2014/14; PR 2015/9; PR 2016/6).

Where a policy provides for both income and capital benefits, the part of the premium that is referable to the income benefits is deductible, provided that evidence as to what that part is can be adduced (PR 2015/11). Failure to adduce such evidence caused the taxpayer to lose in *Case J45*, but in *Case R100* a partial deduction was allowed even though the part of the premium referable to the income benefits could not be determined with actuarial precision.

The premium payable by a self-employed person or an employee on a trauma insurance policy that provides a capital amount on the suffering of a specified medical condition is not deductible (TD 95/41). However, such a premium may be deductible by an employer if: (a) the premium is paid for a revenue purpose; (b) the purpose of the policy is to advance the business ends of the employer; (c) the policy is owned by the employer; and (d) the employer is the beneficiary under the policy (TD 95/42; CR 2005/103).

Premiums paid by employees for travel insurance would not normally be deductible even if the travel is work-related (*Case T78*).

[FITR ¶32-840]

¶16-570 Deductions for "key-person" insurance premiums

The Commissioner treats premiums paid under ''key-person'' life and endowment policies as non-deductible under ITAA97 s 8-1. For key-person accident or term policies, however, premiums are deductible where the purpose of the insurance is to fill the place of a revenue item (IT 155). It would follow that, if the purpose is to insure against the possibility of a capital loss, the premiums will normally be treated as non-deductible (eg where insurance is taken out by a company for the purpose of providing, in the event of a director's death by accident, funds for the payment to the director's estate of a debt owing to him/her). Evidence of purpose would include minutes and book entries, the use to which the proceeds are actually put and advance declarations of the taxpayer's intentions.

Where a life policy is issued with a term accident and/or sickness rider, the Commissioner treats the premiums as being wholly for life assurance (and not deductible) unless they are readily divisible. No part of a premium paid by an employer under a ''split purpose'' insurance arrangement is deductible (TD 94/40).

For the tax consequences of ''split dollar'' insurance arrangements entered into by an employer and a key employee, see IT 2434.

[FITR ¶32-830]

¶16-575 Deductions for superannuation contributions

Superannuation contributions by an employer or associated person in respect of an employee are deductible (¶13-710). A contribution to a superannuation fund or RSA by an individual taxpayer for themselves may also qualify for deduction (¶13-730). As to the position in relation to superannuation contributions by partnerships, see ¶5-140. For the deductibility of interest on funds borrowed to finance superannuation contributions, see ¶16-740. See also ¶13-760 (government co-contribution), ¶13-770 (rebates), ¶13-777 (excess concessional contributions charge), ¶13-790 (re-contribution under First Home Super Saver scheme) and ¶13-795 (downsizer contributions).

Bad Debts, Theft and Misappropriation

¶16-580 Deductions for bad debts

Reserves or provisions for doubtful debts are not deductible. Before a deduction is allowable, the debt must be bad. That is a question of fact, dependent on the circumstances of each case, but generally a debt is bad in any of the following circumstances (TR 92/18):

- the debtor has died without leaving assets or is insolvent
- the debt is statute-barred and the debtor relies on this as a defence for non-payment
- the debtor and the debtor's assets cannot be traced
- in the case of a corporate debtor, the company is in liquidation and there are insufficient funds to pay the debt, or
- on an objective view, there is little or no likelihood of the debt being recovered.

A bad debt deduction may be claimed under ITAA97 s 25-35 (¶16-582) or, alternatively, under ITAA97 s 8-1 (¶16-584). Companies and trusts wishing to claim bad debt deductions under either provision must meet stringent preconditions (¶3-150; ¶6-262).

To be deductible, the debt must be in existence at the time it is treated as a bad debt and claimed as such. A release of a debt extinguishes it, leaving nothing to be incurred within the meaning of s 8-1, nor to be written off as bad under s 25-35 (*Point*). This is also the case wherever a debt is released, compromised or otherwise extinguished by the voluntary or acquiescent act of the creditor (*GE Crane Sales*). Where a commercial debt is forgiven, the debtor may be affected by the debt forgiveness provisions (¶16-910). In addition, a deemed dividend may arise where a private company forgives a debt owed by a shareholder (¶4-200).

For the tax position where there is a sale of property held as security against a debt, or property is taken in satisfaction of the debt, see TR 92/18. For the position where a life insurance company forgives an agency development loan made to an insurance agent, see TR 2001/9.

No deduction is allowable for the bad debts of a foreign branch of a moneylender where assessable income has not been derived from those debts because the branch income is exempt from Australian tax (¶21-098). Where some of the income derived from such a debt is assessable to Australian tax, the deduction will be apportioned (ITAA36 s 63D). Losses arising on the non-recovery of a debt that qualifies as a traditional security will not give rise to a loss in certain circumstances (¶23-340).

There is a limit on the amount a taxpayer may deduct for a bad debt relating to lease payments for the lease of a luxury car (¶17-220). Lease payments written off as bad debts by the lessor may only be deducted up to the amount of the finance charge reduced by the amounts of earlier deductions.

A deduction for a bad debt may, in certain circumstances, be denied if a tax avoidance scheme is involved (¶16-110). The recoupment of an amount deductible in respect of a debt written off as bad gives rise to an assessable amount (¶10-270).

Special provisions apply for bad debts in relation to consolidated groups (¶8-020).

[FITR ¶33-740 – ¶33-790, ¶65-240ff]

¶16-582 Deductibility of bad debts under s 25-35

To qualify for a bad debt deduction under ITAA97 s 25-35, the debt or part of a debt must not only be objectively bad (*Case X9*) but must satisfy the 2 conditions set out below.

(1) The debt must be written off as bad during the year of income in which the deduction is claimed. There must be a physical writing off of the debt — not necessarily a book entry but something in writing to indicate that the creditor has treated the debt as bad. It is not sufficient that the debt is written off when the accounts are completed after the close of the income year (in conformity with usual accounting practice) and merely relates back to the income year just closed (*Point*).

(2) Except in the case of taxpayers in the business of lending money, the debt must have been brought to account by the taxpayer as assessable income (eg *Case 7/2000*). This requirement will not be satisfied by a taxpayer who lodges returns on a cash basis because those debts will not have been brought to account as assessable income (*Case P78*). Thus, an employee who is paid by a dishonoured cheque cannot claim a bad debt deduction (TD 92/201).

It appears the Commissioner will generally require a taxpayer to have taken the appropriate steps in an attempt to recover a debt, including the obtaining and enforcement of a judgment against the debtor and valuation of any securities held against the debt (TR 92/18).

A beneficiary of a trust is not entitled to a bad debt deduction under s 25-35 for unpaid present entitlement amounts that have been written off as bad debts (TD 2016/19). Also, in *Pope*, a trustee had the power to create a present entitlement to trust income by setting it aside in a loan account for a beneficiary. A beneficiary subsequently wrote off their outstanding loan balance as bad, and a s 25-35 bad debt deduction was denied. This was because there was no continuing identity between the amount included in the taxpayer's assessable income (being a trust distribution to which he was presently entitled), and the subsequently written off debt (being an investment the beneficiary had made in the trust's business).

Moneylending business

A bad debt in respect of money lent in the ordinary course of a moneylending business carried on by the taxpayer is deductible even though it has not previously been brought to account as assessable income. The taxpayer must be in the business of moneylending at the time the loan is made, but not necessarily at the time the debt is written off (TR 92/18).

Whether a taxpayer is carrying on a business of lending money is a question of fact, as determined by reference to the context in which the business is carried on, rather than by reference to the way in which a major bank might carry on its business. For example, a subsidiary which in the course of the business of lending money, made loans to other subsidiaries of the parent company could deduct certain bad debts (*BHP Billiton Finance Ltd*; *Ashwick Qld*). It is not necessary for each loan to be motivated by the profit-making purpose to be regarded as part of the continuing business (*BHP Billiton Finance*).

Moneylending need not be the only or principal business of the taxpayer. Nevertheless, it must be established that moneylending is a distinct business as opposed to a subordinate activity carried on as an adjunct to the taxpayer's main business. To qualify as carrying on a business of lending money, the taxpayer does not have to be ready and willing to lend to all and sundry — it is sufficient if the taxpayer lends money to a certain class of borrowers, provided it does so in a businesslike manner with a view to yielding a profit (TR 92/18).

Further, the loan must have been made in the *ordinary* course of the moneylending business. Thus, an inter-company loan between 2 moneylending companies would not necessarily qualify, although the High Court has held that a transaction different from the usual moneylending transactions of the business at the time may nevertheless be *in the ordinary course* of a moneylending business and that only transactions not entered into for business purposes are excluded (*Fairway Estates*). Moreover, said the court, a business may be found to exist although there is no more than an *intention* and one sole transaction in pursuance of it. This ''ordinary course of business'' requirement does not exist, as such, in an alternative claim under the general deduction provision (¶16-584).

A deduction is also available where the bad debt was bought by the taxpayer in the ordinary course of the taxpayer's moneylending business. In this case, the deduction cannot exceed the amount incurred in buying the debt. If only part of the debt is written off, only the amount incurred in buying the debt less the amount which has not been written off can be claimed.

The head company of a consolidated group can obtain a deduction for a debt that is written off as bad by a subsidiary member where the debt is in respect of money lent by the subsidiary in the ordinary course of its business of lending money before consolidation (TD 2005/23).

[FITR ¶65-240]

¶16-584 Deductibility of bad debts under s 8-1

A bad debt that, for one reason or another, is not deductible under ITAA97 s 25-35 (¶16-582) may, nevertheless, be deductible under ITAA97 s 8-1.

To be deductible under s 8-1, the bad debt must have been *incurred* and must be a loss (or non-receipt) relating to the production of the taxpayer's assessable income. It will not qualify for deduction if it is a loss of capital or a loss of a private or domestic nature. However, the debt need not be brought to account as assessable income. Normal business loans may be deductible as bad debts under the general deduction provision, but advances of capital made to salvage or protect an investment threatening to go bad are not.

In the case of company taxpayers (¶3-150) and trusts (¶6-262) there must be a physical writing off of the debt before a deduction will be allowed.

Factoring discount fees may be deductible under s 8-1. Debt factoring arrangements may be acceptable for tax purposes where the arrangement is explicable by reference to ordinary business or commercial standards. The parties to a debt factoring arrangement do not need to be at arm's length but, where they are not, the arrangement will be examined to determine whether it is commercially realistic (IT 2538; TD 93/83).

[FITR ¶33-740 – ¶33-780]

¶16-586 Debt/equity swaps

A deduction is allowable for losses incurred where a debt is extinguished as part of a debt/equity swap (ITAA36 s 63E). Debt/equity swap deductions are subject to the rules in ITAA36 s 63D (¶16-580). Companies (¶3-150) and trusts (¶6-262) wishing to claim such deductions must meet stringent preconditions (s 63E(5A)).

A debt/equity swap occurs where, under an arrangement, a taxpayer discharges, releases or otherwise extinguishes a debt in return for equity in the form of shares or units in the debtor. For the rules to apply, the debt must have been brought into account by the taxpayer as assessable income in an income year or the debt was in respect of money loaned in the ordinary course of the taxpayer's business of lending money. The deductible loss is the amount by which the book value of the extinguished debt exceeds the value of the equity received in return for extinguishing the debt. The value of the equity is the greater of the market value of the shares or units and their value shown in the taxpayer's accounts at the time they were issued to the taxpayer. A swap loss deduction is reduced to the extent that it has previously been allowed under other provisions of the tax law, or under s 63E itself (ITAA36 s 63F).

Profits or losses realised on a subsequent disposal, cancellation or redemption of equity acquired in a debt/equity swap are assessable income or allowable deductions, as the case requires. See generally TR 92/18.

[FTR ¶34-142, ¶34-146]

¶16-590 Deductibility of losses through theft or misappropriation

A loss of money caused by theft, stealing, embezzlement, larceny, etc, by an employee or agent of the taxpayer is deductible in the year in which it is discovered if the money was included in the taxpayer's assessable income of that or an earlier year (ITAA97 s 25-45). The deduction is not available where the loss was caused by the actions of persons acting in a private capacity (eg a non-employee spouse; *Case 15/2004*). The requirement that the wrongdoing be committed by an employee or agent may not be satisfied where the wrongdoing is by directors who were acting as the mind and will of the company taxpayer (*EHL Burgess*), or possibly by partners in the firm.

Once money received as income is deployed by the taxpayer, personally or by way of an agent, for expenditure or investment, the characterisation as income is no longer appropriate and the loss cannot be said to have been incurred in respect of the money included in assessable income (*Lean*). In other words, the money must be traceable (*EHL Burgess*; *Grima*).

The deduction is further limited in that the offences covered by the provisions have technical meanings and limited scope. However, a loss incurred through robbery, theft or misappropriation may qualify for deduction under ITAA97 s 8-1 provided it is a loss of such a character as to be the kind of casualty, mischance or misfortune that is a natural or recognised incident of the taxpayer's operations (*Charles Moore*).

Under s 25-47, a deduction is also allowable for amounts or non-cash benefits that are misappropriated (by theft, embezzlement, larceny or otherwise) by an employee or agent and that have been included in the termination value of a depreciating asset under the balancing adjustment provisions referred to at ¶17-640. The deduction is available in the year in which the misappropriation occurs. The amount that can be deducted is reduced to reflect any use of the asset for a non-taxable purpose and for certain taxpayers and second-hand assets, use in a residential rental property. If a misappropriation is discovered in a later year of income, the taxpayer may request an amendment within 4 years, starting immediately after the taxpayer discovers the misappropriation. Any subsequent recoupment of the misappropriated amount is assessable in the year of the recoupment.

Capital proceeds from a CGT event are reduced in the case of misappropriation by an employee or agent (¶11-510). The recoupment of an amount deductible under s 25-45 or s 25-47 gives rise to an assessable amount (¶10-270).

Deductions under s 8-1 were available in respect of:

- losses, through armed robbery, of the day's takings (*Charles Moore*; *Gold Band Services*)
- cheques forged by an employee (*Case H114*) and reimbursement to a trust for stolen trust funds held for clients of a real estate agency (ID 2010/207)

- a solicitor having to make good a loss to clients' funds caused by an employee's fraudulent misrepresentation (*Webber*) or by a former partner's misappropriation (*Sweetman*) (although a different result was reached in *Ash*).

No deductions are available for losses relating to income gained from illegal activities (¶16-105).

An employee, such as a flight attendant, who deals with customers' money can claim a deduction for any cash shortages that they are required to repay (TR 95/19). An investor's legal costs of seeking to recover investment funds that had been misappropriated were not deductible (ID 2001/42).

The theft of a depreciating asset would be treated as an involuntary disposal, entitling the owner to a balancing adjustment offset (¶17-720).

[FITR ¶33-785, ¶65-360]

Special Occupations

¶16-635 Deductions for taxpayers in special occupations

The Commissioner has released many rulings and other guidelines about the types of deductions that can be claimed by taxpayers in particular occupations and these can be used as a handy reference. They include airline industry employees (TR 95/19); Australian Defence Force members (TR 95/17); civil marriage celebrants (IT 2409); employee building workers (TR 95/22); employee cleaners (TR 95/8); employee factory workers (TR 95/12); employee journalists and radio and television presenters (TR 98/14); employee lawyers (TR 95/9); employee performing artists (TR 95/20); employee shop assistants (TR 95/10); hairdressers (TR 95/16); hospitality industry employees (TR 95/11); itinerant employees (TR 95/34); members of parliament (TR 1999/10); nurses (TR 95/15); officers of military cadets (TD 1999/63); police officers (TR 95/13); real estate industry employees (TR 98/6); teachers (TR 95/14); and truck drivers (TR 95/18). See also ATO Fact Sheet *Adult industry workers — claiming work-related expenses*. Appendix 1 to TR 2020/1 also contains a convenient list of all ATO guidance on the deductibility of various work-related expenses incurred by employees.

[FITR ¶37-000ff]

Landlord and Tenant Expenses

¶16-640 Tenant's or lessee's expenses

Rent for business premises, repairs to such premises, rates, taxes and other outgoings incurred by the tenant under the lease are deductible (ITAA97 s 8-1).

Amounts paid for failure to comply with a lease obligation to make repairs to premises that the taxpayer uses, or has used, for income-producing purposes are deductible under ITAA97 s 25-15.

Rent is *incurred* when it becomes legally due so that it may be claimed as a deduction, although not paid. Moreover if, under the terms of the lease, rent is required to be paid weekly, monthly or annually in advance, it is deductible in full when legally due. Where rent is paid in advance, the deduction will generally be spread over the period to which the payment relates (¶16-045). See also ¶16-110 for measures designed to counter tax avoidance schemes involving prepayment of rent.

In some cases, so-called rent payments have been disallowed as deductions because in reality they represent part of the capital cost of acquiring an asset. On this basis, the following amounts have been disallowed: (a) a lump sum payment that was made for the renewal and extension of a Crown lease and calculated as 9 times the current annual rent for the land (*Case V55*); (b) a lump sum paid for the right to occupy a time share holiday investment unit at specified times each year for 40 years (*Case V29*); and (c) a prepayment of ‘‘rent’’ under a 20-year lease of a pine plantation which in fact represented the payment for an interest in the timber (*Case 42/95*).

Premiums paid for the grant or assignment of a lease are capital payments not ordinarily qualifying for deduction. The same is the case for leasehold improvements. Lease surrender payments made by a lessee are generally of a capital nature, but may be deductible under the rules set out in ¶16-159. A rental bond paid on business premises is not deductible (ID 2002/919).

The cost of a shop fit-out was not allowable to a tenant even though, under the lease, the receipt of a lease incentive payment from the landlord was conditional on the fit-out being carried out (*Lees & Leech*).

Any outgoings incurred by a lessee or lessor of a business property for the preparation, registration or stamping of a lease, or an assignment or surrender of a lease, are deductible (ITAA97 s 25-20). This would also apply to amounts of such expenditure reimbursed by the lessee to the lessor. Where the property is used only partly for income-producing purposes, the deduction is allowable to the extent of the income-producing use (eg ID 2012/36). A lease includes a Crown lease for a definite period.

A lessee’s legal expenses in defending a lessor’s attempts to terminate a lease are not deductible (TD 93/141).

As to depreciation claims by lessees, see ¶17-020.

[FITR ¶32-920, ¶65-160, ¶65-180]

¶16-650 Rental property — landlord or lessor expenses

In general, the cost of purchasing a rental property is capital and not deductible under s 8-1, though it may form part of the cost base for CGT purposes. The same would apply to other acquisition and disposal costs of the property, eg conveyancing costs. Travel expenses incurred in connection with the purchase are neither deductible under s 8-1 nor do they form part of the cost base of the property according to ATO guidance. Certain capital construction costs may qualify for a special write-off (¶20-470). Costs related to holding vacant land, including land on which a residential rental property is under construction may also not be deductible (see below). For a useful checklist, see ¶44-107.

Generally, deductions may be claimed under ITAA97 s 8-1 for expenses relevant and incidental to the production of rental income derived by a landlord/lessor. These would normally be claimable from the time the property is listed for rental with an estate agent. Deductions may also be allowable under other specific provisions. Rental property deductions are a key focus area for ATO audits.

If property is let furnished or equipped, the lessor may claim depreciation of plant, equipment and articles installed by the lessor, although limitations apply to investors in residential properties from 1 July 2017 (¶17-020, ¶17-040; see TD 2006/31 for the assessability of rebates received for the purchase of depreciating assets). The Commissioner’s depreciation tables reproduced at ¶43-000 provide a checklist of items that qualify for depreciation and their depreciation rates. The temporary rules allowing full expensing of the cost of depreciating assets are only available to taxpayers carrying on a business (¶17-430).

Travel expenses incurred in collecting rent, to visit a property manager, or in connection with maintenance and repair, for a residential rental property held as an investment, are not deductible from 1 July 2017 (ITAA97 s 26-31). Exceptions to this rule are where the expense is incurred in the course of carrying on a business (LCR 2018/7), or is incurred by companies or institutional investors such as MITs. The restriction affects individuals, SMSFs and other closely held entities. Such travel expenses also cannot form part of the cost base of the residential property (ITAA97 s 110-38(4A)).

Deductible expenses may include (¶44-107):

- rent paid (eg where the lessor rents the property and subleases it to a tenant)
- telephone (¶16-400), stamps, stationery
- agent's commission for rent collection and other management fees
- repairs and ongoing maintenance (¶16-700)
- environmental protection expenses (¶19-110)
- annual power guarantee payment made on a remote rental property (ID 2002/573)
- fee for the use of a safe deposit box to hold title documents
- secretarial and bookkeeping expenses
- audit fees where reasonably necessary (IT 2625)
- tax advice costs, tax return preparation expenses and expenses in objecting or appealing against an assessment (¶16-850)
- costs of attending a property investment seminar, to the extent that they related to operating, or maximising the return from, current investment properties (ATO publication *Rental properties 2020*; ¶16-660)
- payment of rates and land tax (¶16-870)
- strata title body corporate fees for ongoing administration and general maintenance (ATO publication *Rental properties 2020*), but not special levies for capital improvements
- insurance premiums (¶16-550)
- legal expenses in recovering arrears of rent or ejecting a tenant for non-payment (¶16-842)
- borrowing and mortgage discharge expenses (¶16-800)
- interest on moneys borrowed to purchase or refinance the property (¶16-740) or to effect repairs (¶16-700)
- advertising
- expenses of preparation, registration and stamping of leases, assignments and surrenders in respect of rented premises (¶16-640). This includes stamp duty, and preparation and registration costs in respect of the "acquisition" of a rental property situated in the ACT
- servicing expenses.

In the case of a residential rental property, the deductible amount includes any GST component of the outgoing relating to the rent (¶16-860).

The provision of lease incentives will usually give rise to a deduction for the lessor, except where the true purpose of providing the incentive is not to induce the entering into of the lease (eg to benefit an associate or to shift income to an associate with carry-forward losses). Where the incentive takes the form of a rent-free or reduced rent period, the lessor will not be allowed a deduction for the rent forgone.

Lease surrender payments made by a lessor are generally not deductible, except under the special rules set out in ¶16-159.

Where a landlord undertook to meet the tenants' indebtedness to a bank in the case of the tenants' default, amounts paid by the landlord under the undertaking were not sufficiently connected with rental income and were not deductible (*Case 38/96*).

An employee who leases their private residence to their employer and then salary sacrifices rent is not entitled to deductions for property expenses of the residence (TD 2004/26).

A landlord's claims will need to be apportioned where only part of the property is let, the property is let for only part of the year or the property is let for a mixture of commercial and non-commercial purposes. Where only part of the property is let and the rest is used for private purposes, the claim is normally apportioned on a floor-area basis.

Where rent is received from a short-term commercial letting of a holiday house, the losses and outgoings are normally apportioned on a time basis according to the period that the property is actually let (*Case R118*). Any period that the property was available for letting may also be taken into account in making the apportionment, provided it can be shown that active and bona fide efforts were made to obtain tenants during that time (IT 2167; see also *Case V133* and *Bonaccordo*). In *Case 3/2012*, a taxpayer was allowed deductions for lawn mowing, insurance, electricity and advertising. The ATO has issued a *Decision Impact Statement* on the case stating that it had a narrow application and would not impact the ATO's view on the deductibility of these expenses generally.

From 1 July 2019, expenses related to holding vacant land, including land on which a residential rental property is either under construction or being substantially renovated, or which has a completed residential property that is not available for rent, are not deductible, regardless of when the land was purchased (ITAA97 s 26-102). This includes interest expenses or other ongoing borrowing costs to acquire the land, land taxes, council rates or maintenance costs. The restriction applies to individuals, SMSFs and closely held partnerships and trusts, but not to companies and institutional investors, such as other superannuation funds and MITs. However, various exclusions apply including where the expenses are incurred in connection with carrying on a business, eg property development, or a primary production business. The expenses are also deductible if vacant land is leased out by a primary producer, or under an arm's length arrangement to another entity carrying on a business, provided the land does not contain residential premises, and residential premises are not being constructed on the land. Also, a property that was rented out which becomes vacant due to a natural disaster, building defect or other exceptional circumstances beyond the taxpayer's control (such that it is uninhabitable) is also excluded, with deductions allowed for up to 3 years. Expenses denied under these rules can be included in the CGT cost base of the property.

These amendments mean that an intention of deriving rental income at the time of purchase of a property may no longer be sufficient to claim a deduction for interest and other expenses where no income can be derived because the property is either not able to be occupied or not available for rent (as was permitted in *Ormiston*; ¶16-740). Previously, such taxpayers were asked to demonstrate this intention existed and that they had continued to hold it for that purpose (*Dram Nominees* and *Fogarty*).

The cost of moving furniture to a new main residence in order to lease a previous main residence is a private or domestic expense and is not deductible (*Wray-McCann*).

Where a landlord is the sole owner of a mortgaged rental property, but the mortgage is held in joint names with a spouse, the landlord can nevertheless claim the full amount of the mortgage interest paid (TR 93/32). A taxpayer's share of rental property expenses may be claimed against rental income received from their co-owner who lives in the property (ATO publication *Rental properties 2020*).

For the appropriate exchange rate to be used to translate foreign currency rental deductions into Australian dollars for tax purposes where an average rate of exchange has not been used, see the ATO website at *Translation of foreign currency rental expenses* (¶23-070).

Non-arm's length leases

Leasing a house to a relative for a low rental has often been seen as a way of conferring a benefit on the relative while still retaining the tax advantages of being a landlord, ie by disclosing the rental as income and claiming a relatively substantial deduction for outgoings. In extreme cases, eg where the rental is only a token amount, the Commissioner may treat such a "lease" as a domestic arrangement with no tax consequences (*Groser*). Alternatively, where the transaction has both business and private elements, apportionment may be appropriate (*Kowal*). For example, where a property was rented to a relative at 25% of market rental, it was appropriate to allow 25% of the deductions claimed or an amount equal to the rental income returned (*Madigan*).

However, where the property is let to relatives on a normal commercial basis, the landlord will be treated in the same way as any other owner in a comparable arm's length situation (IT 2167). In *Bocaz*, the AAT held that the rental agreement that a taxpayer entered into with her son was commercial where the rent received was higher than the median rent figure submitted by the Commissioner. The taxpayer also received rent that was close to the median rent figure from a property leased to her ex-husband with whom she had an arrangement to undertake renovation work. The taxpayer was able to deduct interest and other expenses incurred in respect of the rental properties to reflect her share and period of ownership.

In cases involving non-commercial elements, the Commissioner may also seek to limit the deduction for outgoings to the amount of income received if insufficient evidence to justify a higher claim is provided (IT 2167). See further ¶16-740.

[FITR ¶33-995]

Investment Income Expenses and Losses

¶16-660 Expenses in deriving investment income

A taxpayer who derives assessable income from investments (ie dividends and interest) may deduct certain expenditure incurred in connection with that income (eg collection expenses, bookkeeping and secretarial expenses, interest, borrowing expenses and audit fees where an audit is reasonably necessary). Appropriate documentation should be maintained (*Sobel Investments*).

A fee paid to a financial planner or adviser for drawing up a new financial plan (eg for a statement of advice) is not deductible, even if some of the investor's existing investments are included in the plan. In contrast, ongoing management fees or retainers paid to advisers, or costs of servicing and managing an investment portfolio, are deductible (IT 39; TD 95/60). The cost of advice to change the mix of investments, whether by the original or a new adviser, is treated as part of the cost of managing a portfolio and is deductible, provided it does not amount to a new financial plan (TD 95/60). However, if the advice covers other matters, or relates in part to investments that do not produce assessable income, only a proportion of the fee is deductible. No deduction is available for management fees debited to a retiree's allocated pension account (ID 2004/968).

A deduction is allowable for travel costs of consulting with interstate brokers and attending interstate stock exchanges as part of servicing an investment portfolio (IT 39). This may also cover travel costs genuinely attributable to attending an annual general meeting of a company in which the investor holds shares (*Elder*). The cost of overseas travel has been held to be deductible to the extent that it was incurred to consult financial advisers in connection with the management of the taxpayer's investment portfolio and properties (*Case T8*).

A deduction is allowable for the cost of subscriptions to share market information services and investment journals (including periodicals such as the *Financial Review*) to the extent that they relate to the gaining or producing of interest and dividends from a share or bond portfolio and that they are not a capital cost of setting up the investment. A share investor is more likely to show the required connection with the income (being interest and dividends, rather than simply capital gains) if he/she is actively involved in managing an investment portfolio (TD 2004/1; *Case T96*). Depreciation on share trading software may also be claimed (¶17-370). In *Petrovic*, investment seminar fees were an investment of capital made to prepare the taxpayer for the future commencement of a property investment business and were therefore not deductible.

As a general rule, interest on moneys borrowed to acquire investments (eg shares) is deductible where it is expected that income (eg dividends) will be derived (¶16-742). Bank charges and borrowing expenses may also be deductible (¶16-800), as may certain legal expenses (¶16-830). However, a once-only payment for service fees incurred in the acquisition of units in a property trust was held not to be deductible (*Case U53*; IT 2428). For the deductibility of scrip loan fees and call option payments made where a taxpayer borrows ''cum dividend'' shares, see TD 2003/32.

Where taxpayers were involved in a previous tax avoidance scheme, no deduction may be available for debts relating to that scheme that have been forgiven or for repayments of the debt that have been refunded (TA 2008/6).

Managed investment schemes (MIS)

For the deductibility of expenses incurred under MIS, see ¶18-020 (non-forestry), ¶18-125 (forestry) and ¶30-170 (anti-avoidance provisions). Investors' contributions to an agricultural MIS which are incurred in the course of carrying on a business and are of a revenue nature are deductible (*Decision Impact Statement* on *Hance*). Where failure to plant all the trees intended to be established under a forestry MIS results in no deduction being allowable under the special forestry MIS rules (¶18-125) in respect of a participant's initial contribution to the scheme, a deduction may be available under s 8-1 if the conduct of the MIS constitutes the carrying on of a business (TD 2010/15). See also TD 2010/14. The disposal or termination of an interest in a non-forestry MIS arising out of circumstances outside the taxpayer's control does not result in the denial of previously allowed deductions (TD 2010/8).

The Commissioner has issued a number of product rulings dealing with the application of the deduction provisions and the anti-avoidance provisions to specified investment projects (generally afforestation and primary production projects) (¶24-540).

▶ Planning point

Many tax shelters marketed towards the end of each income year involve tax-deferral through the investment of borrowed funds (ie the creation of deductions are generated in the early years of the transaction), with assessable income being generated in later years. This can be of benefit in the case of a high income earner and generate significant cash flow advantages. If tempted to invest in tax shelters, seek independent professional advice, check any product rulings, and refer to the ATO publication *Tax planning*. The ATO has issued practice instructions to ATO staff on the treatment of aggressive tax planning (PS LA 2008/15).

[FITR ¶33-300]

¶16-665 Investment losses

Losses made on investments such as shares and other securities are deductible under ITAA97 s 8-1 if the taxpayer is carrying on a business of investing for profit or of trading in investments. Whether a taxpayer is carrying on such a business is often difficult to determine and depends on the facts of the particular case (¶16-015, ¶10-105). Relevant factors include the frequency, volume and scale of transactions and whether they are carried out in a businesslike way (*Radnor*; *Firth*; *Wong*). The taxpayer's purpose in entering into the transactions may also be relevant. In one case, a deduction was allowed for a loss made on reselling the first 2 houses purchased by a taxpayer in the business of buying and selling houses for profit, even though the taxpayer did not purchase other houses due to a slump in property prices (*Case 15/98*). Similarly, a taxpayer who bought more and sold less shares during the year due to the global financial crisis was considered to be carrying on a share trading business in that year, even though he had decided to hold on to the shares instead of making a short term loss (*Case 10/2011*). See also *Price Street Professional Centre*.

A mere speculator in shares is not accepted as a share trader (*AC Williams*) nor is an investor (*Case 9/94*). A taxpayer who worked full time for an international bank and conducted various buying and selling transactions in shares on his own account, was not carrying on a business as share trader as he did not exhibit a discernible pattern of trading and held the relevant shares for periods longer than a share trader would, and did not take profits as they arose (*Smith*; see also *Case 15/2004* and *Case X86*). However, a taxpayer involved in systematic arbitrage operations was found to be carrying on a business, albeit for a short time only (*Shields*). Similarly, in *Mehta*, the activities amounted to the carrying on of a business as the taxpayer had intended his activities to constitute a business, had applied his mind to the carrying on of that business and had followed expert advice. Where a taxpayer is carrying on a business of a share trader, the shares, etc, are trading stock (¶9-150).

The mere fact that a loss from an investment is made by an entity in its capacity as trustee of a trust is not conclusive as to whether the loss is on revenue or capital account. The loss is on revenue account if no provision specifically treats it as being on capital account and, after consideration of all of the relevant factors, it is determined that the loss was from a normal operation in the course of carrying on a business of investment, an extraordinary operation by reference to the ordinary course of that business but one entered into with the intention of making a profit or gain, or a one-off or isolated transaction where the investment was acquired in a business operation or commercial transaction for the purpose of profit-making (TD 2011/21).

The ATO has warned taxpayers about arrangements whereby: (a) a taxpayer's shareholding status is changed from that of a long term capital investor to a trader in shares in order to re-characterise capital losses as revenue losses (TA 2009/12); and (b) a purported partnership is inserted into an investment in an afforestation, agricultural or horticultural Managed Investment Scheme in order to generate deductions for the newly inserted partners (TA 2009/13).

Losses incurred in investing in a commodity futures trading trust (*Case X38*) and on the surrender of an insurance bond were not deductible (*Case Y36*) but a deduction was allowed to a building company for the loss it suffered when a finance company with which it had funds on short-term deposit collapsed (*Marshall and Brougham*).

Where shares (and similar assets, such as units in unit trusts, that are listed and traded on the stock exchange) are held by a taxpayer as revenue assets but not as trading stock (eg shares held by an insurance company or a bank), any loss on disposal is ascertained in accordance with the principles set out in TR 96/4.

Losses incurred by a taxpayer in buying and selling stapled securities (consisting of a note and a preference share) in the ordinary course of business are deductible (TA 2008/1). Land impairment trust arrangements (involving land being sold at a loss) associated with forestry managed investment schemes give rise to taxation issues including whether the sale of land to a related party is at an impaired value and, if so, whether it gives rise to a revenue or capital loss (TA 2008/11).

Where an allowable deduction is obtained in connection with a wash sale, the anti-avoidance provisions may apply in particular circumstances, except in the case of a "genuine disposal" at market value (TR 2008/1; TA 2008/7; *ATO Media Release*

2008/20). Under a wash sale arrangement, assets (generally shares) are disposed of with the intention of generating a capital loss. Subsequently, the same or substantially the same asset is acquired.

For details of the provisions that deny deductions for losses arising from the disposal of venture capital investments (ITAA97 s 26-68) or venture capital equity (ITAA97 s 26-70), see ¶5-040.

For the treatment of losses from futures transactions, see ¶23-370.

[FITR ¶33-340, ¶114-150]

Land and Share Transactions

¶16-670 Deductible expenses — pre-20 September 1985 land and share acquisitions

Where the profit arising from the carrying out of a profit-making undertaking involving land or shares (or other property) acquired before 20 September 1985 is assessable under ITAA97 s 15-15, certain expenditure is taken into account in arriving at the assessable profit although it may not have been deductible when incurred. Such expenditure is also taken into account in calculating profits arising from the *sale of property* acquired before 20 September 1985 for the purpose of profit-making by sale (ITAA36 s 25A).

As to the treatment of expenses where property acquired after 19 September 1985 is disposed of and the CGT provisions apply, see ¶11-550.

[FITR ¶53-150]

¶16-680 Losses arising from pre-20 September 1985 acquisitions

A loss arising from the carrying out of a profit-making undertaking or plan (other than a loss arising in respect of the sale of post-19 September 1985 property) is deductible under ITAA97 s 25-40 but only where, if there had been profits rather than losses, the profits would have been assessable under ITAA97 s 15-15 (¶16-670). A loss arising on the *sale of property* acquired before 20 September 1985 for profit-making by sale may be deductible under ITAA36 s 52 if any profits would have been assessable under ITAA36 s 25A (¶16-670). The CGT provisions apply to a loss arising on the sale of property acquired after 19 September 1985 (¶11-250).

[FITR ¶65-340]

¶16-690 Losses from share trading schemes

A number of provisions in the tax law are designed to counter tax avoidance schemes under which taxpayers aim to secure deductions for losses on the disposal of shares or other securities.

One measure seeks to overcome schemes which rely on the manufacture of artificial share trading losses by using the general deduction provisions or the provisions governing losses incurred on property acquired for profit-making (ITAA36 s 52A).

A second measure is designed to overcome so-called *Curran schemes* by providing that non-assessable bonus shares are to be treated as having no independent cost to the taxpayer. Thus, in calculating the deductible loss on the sale of such shares, the amount paid for the original shares in relation to which the bonus issue was made is to be spread over those original shares and the bonus shares (ITAA36 s 6BA: ¶3-265). For the CGT implications, see ¶12-600.

[FTR ¶4-990, ¶26-925]

Repairs

¶16-700 Deductions for repairs

Non-capital expenditure incurred on repairs to plant or to premises held or used for the production of assessable income is specifically made deductible under ITAA97 s 25-10. There is no requirement for the taxpayer to own the property or item that is repaired. A lessee who repairs the leased property may therefore be entitled to a deduction. However, repairs actually made by a lessor are deductible to the lessor, even where the lease requires the lessee to make the repairs.

If expenditure is on improvements or ''initial repairs'' it is capital expenditure and is not deductible (see below). If work done constitutes capital improvements, no amount can be allowed for ''notional'' repairs (ie an estimate of what it would have cost the taxpayer if the premises, plant, etc, had merely been repaired). Expenditure of a capital nature should be considered under the depreciation provisions (¶17-000), the capital works provisions (¶20-470) or as part of the cost base for CGT purposes (¶11-550).

A ''cash basis'' for claiming repair expenses applies on a transitional basis for certain small businesses that were in the former Simplified Tax System before 1 July 2005 and elected to continue using the STS accounting method (¶7-050).

Asset held or used for income-producing purposes

Expenditure on repairs to premises or plant used only partly for income-producing purposes is deductible only to the extent to which the asset is used for income-producing purposes (TR 97/23). Where a part of premises is used entirely for income-producing purposes (eg a house that contains a separate surgery or office), repairs to the income-producing part are deductible in full (TR 93/30).

Expenditure on repairs is deductible if incurred when the taxpayer used or held the property wholly for income-producing purposes, even where: (a) some or all of the damage or deterioration giving rise to the repairs is attributable to a period when the property was used by the taxpayer for non-income-producing purposes; or (b) the expenditure is incurred *before* income has been derived (TR 97/23).

The cost of repairs carried out *after* premises have ceased to be used for income-producing purposes may be deductible, provided that: (a) the necessity for the repairs can be related to the period of time during which the premises were producing assessable income; and (b) the premises have been used for the production of assessable income during the year in which the expenditure is incurred (IT 180; TR 97/23).

What is a repair?

A repair involves a restoration of a thing to a condition it formerly had without changing its character. What is significant is the restoration of efficiency in function rather than the exact repetition of form and substance. Repair involves restoration by replacement or renewal of a worn-out or dilapidated part of something but not reconstruction of the whole thing, ie the entirety. But determining what is the entirety is a question of fact in each case and often causes difficulty. In a case involving a claim for general repairs to a building, it was said that the question was not whether the roof or floor or some other part of the building, looked at in isolation, was repaired, as distinct from wholly reconstructed, but whether what was done to the floor or the roof, etc, was a repair to the building (*W Thomas & Co*). Thus the replacement of bricks that lined the inside of the bake furnace in an aluminium smelter, and refurbishment and upgrade of the fume scrubber (including waste gas ductwork) in the furnace was a repair and not renewal (*Alcoa*). The taxpayer's depreciation for accounting purposes of individual components on a ''line by line'' basis was not determinative of whether the bake furnace was or was not an entirety. On the other hand, in a case involving the demolition and reconstruction of a slipway, the slipway was held to be an entirety in itself. For tests to identify an entirety, see TR 97/23. For instance, a stove, a refrigerator, a complete fence or a building is an entirety.

Painting, conditioning gutters, maintaining plumbing, repairing electrical appliances, mending leaks, replacing broken parts of fences and windows and repairing machinery would generally constitute deductible repairs. See also ID 2002/291 and ID 2002/292 (partial rebuilding of an external protective wall was repair but complete rebuilding was not), and ID 2004/796 (repeat hydraulic fracture stimulation).

Improvement versus repair

Repairs generally improve the condition of the property and a minor or incidental degree of improvement may be done and still constitute a repair. However, substantial improvements, additions, alterations, modernisations and reconstructions are not repairs. While reconstructions are not repairs, a progressive restoration over a period of time may involve a series of deductible repairs. The Commissioner accepts that the character of a repair does not necessarily change because it is carried out at the same time as an improvement. If individual parts of an extensive renovation or restoration project combining repairs and improvements can be characterised as repairs, and if their cost can be segregated and accurately quantified, those items are repairs (TR 97/23).

Some of the factors pointing to an improvement rather than a repair are whether:

- the modification work has effected an improvement to the asset
- there is greater efficiency of function of the property
- there is an increase in the value of the asset
- the expenditure reduces the likelihood of future repairs.

The following are considered to be improvements, not repairs:

- the replacement of a dilapidated ceiling with an entirely new and better ceiling (*Western Suburbs Cinemas*)
- the replacement of canvas awnings on the balconies of holiday flats with sound-resistant double glazed partitions to prevent noise pollution (*Case M60*)
- the replacement of a rotten wooden floor in a block of flats with a better, longer-lasting and more moisture resistant concrete floor (*Case N61*)
- the replacement of cupboards as part of the refurbishment of the whole kitchen (*Case 6/99*)
- landscaping or insulating a house or adding another room (ATO publication *Rental properties 2020*).

Use of different material, however, does not necessarily prevent the work from being a repair, provided the work merely restores a previous function to the property or restores the efficiency of the previous function (TR 97/23). For example, the following work constituted deductible repairs:

- replacing rotten timbers in a wall and cladding the wall with "Celluform" instead of painting it (*Case R102*)
- removing worn carpets and polishing the existing floorboards in a rental property (ID 2002/330)
- re-paving a container terminal even though the new bitumen was of a better quality and was laid more thickly and over a better foundation (*Case W93*).

Repairs are not limited to rectifying defects that have already become serious. The Commissioner accepts that repairs include work done to remedy defects, damage or deterioration even though the work is partly (and even largely) done to prevent or anticipate defects or damage, or to rectify defects in their very early stages. However, the costs incurred by an oil refinery in encasing wooden piles on a wharf in concrete to stop marine organisms from further damaging the piles was considered to be an improvement, not a repair, since the work involved something more than the restoration of something lost or damaged (*BP Oil Refinery (Bulwer Island)*).

Maintenance work such as oiling or cleaning something that is in good working condition in order to prevent future defects is not a repair (but may be deductible under the general deduction provisions). It follows that preventative measures to control future health risks (eg asbestos and chlorofluorocarbon gases removal) will not qualify as a repair unless the work remedies a defect, damage or deterioration to property. Where such work does not qualify as a repair, the expense may be deductible under the general deduction provisions or as environmental protection expenditure (¶19-110). Work done to meet the requirements of regulatory bodies is only deductible as a repair if it is done to remedy defects, damage or deterioration to the property (TR 97/23).

No deduction is allowed for the cost of repairs to plant or equipment to the extent that it is used for the provision of non-deductible entertainment (¶16-390). For the types of repairs allowable to taxpayers in specific occupations, see the taxation rulings referred to at ¶16-635.

For the deductibility of natural disasters recovery expenses including repair costs, see ¶44-130.

"Initial repairs"

If an asset was in disrepair at the time of its acquisition, the cost of "initial repairs" to remedy those defects is of a capital nature and non-deductible (*Law Shipping*). This also applies in relation to property acquired by inheritance, and in relation to a purchaser who knew nothing of the defects until after the purchase. An apportionment on a time basis may be made to allow a deduction where the initial repairs remedy deterioration arising from the holding of the property for income purposes after its acquisition (TR 97/23). The cost of initial repairs is included in the cost base of the asset for CGT purposes (¶11-550) or depreciable cost of the asset (¶17-000).

▶ Planning point

If property requiring repairs is to be transferred, effect the repairs *before* the transfer (with an appropriate adjustment to the purchase price).

Deductibility of warranty/maintenance repair costs

Costs (eg on labour and parts) incurred in carrying out repairs under a warranty or maintenance agreement are deductible under the general deduction provision in the year in which they are incurred. This may apply even though the business has ceased since the warranted goods were sold (¶16-010; TR 2004/4). Estimated repair costs are not deductible if there is no presently existing liability (TR 93/20) (¶16-040).

[FITR ¶65-120ff]

Computer Hardware and Software

¶16-725 Deductions for computer hardware and software

Computer hardware costs

Computer hardware is normally a depreciating asset whose cost may be written off as an ordinary capital allowance (Div 40; ¶17-330, ¶17-480), or as a small business capital allowance (Div 328; ¶7-250).

Computer software

Computer software is the digital system comprised of the programs, data and associated documentation, that instructs other parts of a computer, and may include website content. A general deduction is available for revenue expenditure on computer software used for income producing purposes (s 8-1; ¶16-010).

A capital allowance is available for ''in-house software'' used for an income producing purpose (Div 40) or the small business capital allowance regime may apply (Div 328; ¶7-250). Sometimes, an immediate deduction may instead be available for capital expenditure on in-house software (¶17-370).

To the extent that software costs are not general deductions (s 8-1; ¶16-010), or are not in-house software, the costs may be recognised in the CGT cost base of a CGT asset (typically, the first or fourth elements; s 110-25). Otherwise, as a last resort, the costs might be recognised as blackhole expenses (s 40-880; ¶16-156).

Deductions for expenditure on intellectual property and related expenditure are discussed at ¶16-727.

Commercial website costs

Business taxpayers will often incur expenditure on acquiring, developing, maintaining or modifying a website used in the business (commercial website expenses). The following table summarises the Commissioner's views (in TR 2016/3) about the characterisation of common commercial website expenses as deductible revenue expenses, or as capital expenses for which a capital allowance may be available (¶17-370):

Type of commercial website expense	Deductible revenue expense	Capital expense
Labour costs (eg employee or contractor costs)	• Website labour costs for operational matters	• Website labour costs that enhance a business's profit-yielding structure
Off-the-shelf software costs	• Periodic licence fees • Periodic payments to lease a commercial website from a web developer, provided the lessee does not have a right to become the website's owner	• Costs to acquire off-the-shelf products that enhance a business's profit-yielding structure
Usage fees	• Periodic operating or registration fees	*****
Website acquisition or development costs	*****	• Costs of acquiring or developing a website for a new or existing business (note: such expenditure might be for in-house software)

Type of commercial website expense	Deductible revenue expense	Capital expense
Website maintenance/ modification costs (*)	● Costs to make changes that add minor functionality or enhancements to an existing website ● Costs to remedy software faults ● Periodic costs to upgrade existing website software so webpages appear correctly on new mobile devices, browsers and operating systems ● Costs to make routine or piecemeal modifications (eg ID 2003/931) ● Costs to preserve the useful life of a website	● Costs to make changes that add new functionality (back-end or front-end), or that materially expand existing functionality, and which provide a structural advantage (see below) ● Costs to replace a material part of a website ● Modification costs related to a work program that significantly upgrades or improves a website ● Costs to extend the useful life of a website
Content migration costs	● Content migration costs involved in upgrading an existing website, that do not significantly enhance or replace the website	● Content migration costs involved in establishing a new website
Social media costs	● Costs of maintaining a social media presence (eg updating social media content)	● Costs of establishing a presence on a social media site
(*) Some website maintenance activity requires no modifications (eg website monitoring). Other maintenance requires modifications, such as: updating content, embedding (plug-in) applications and security software, bug fixes, search engine optimisation (SEO), and data restoration after a power surge.		

The factors used to determine whether a modification represents a structural advantage to a business include: the website's role in the business; the nature of the modification to the website; the degree of planning and amount of resources employed in effecting the modification; the level of approval required for the modification; and the expected useful life of the modification.

Commercial website costs of a capital nature may be incurred before a business commences (eg as part of a hobby). If such costs form part of the cost of a depreciating asset (namely, the website), then the decline in value and adjustable value of the website is calculated from the time it is held (s 40-60; ¶17-480). The private-use component of the decline in value will obviously not be deductible.

Domain names

The Commissioner's view is that domain name usage rights (along with computer hardware, and website content with an independent value to a business) are not considered part of a commercial website. Domain name registration costs and server hosting fees that relate to a taxpayer's business are usually deductible revenue expenses (s 8-1).

A domain name can not be owned; but, a right to use a domain name can be owned and sold separately from a website's software. Such a right is a CGT asset, which can lapse if registration is not maintained.

The right to use a commercially desirable domain name can have considerable market value which does not diminish over time. A one-off payment to secure the right to use a domain name (eg through a public auction) is likely to be capital expenditure, and included in the first element of the right's CGT cost base. Where a right to use a new domain name is not secured by payment and has no market value, but is acquired only in conjunction with paying a registration fee for the initial period, the CGT cost base of the right would be nil (TR 2016/3).

[FITR ¶32-675; ¶86-915]

Intellectual Property

¶16-727 Deductions for intellectual property and related expenditure

Intellectual property (IP) is defined for tax purposes (tax IP) as the rights an entity has as the owner or licensee of a patent, registered design or copyright (or equivalent rights under a foreign law): s 995-1. Although narrower than the legal concept of IP, the tax IP concept is mainly relevant to the deductibility of expenditure under the capital allowance regime (see below) where it is not held as trading stock. The tax IP definition excludes, eg rights under trademarks and plant breeder's rights. Rights relating to intangible assets such as goodwill, unregistered trademarks, domain name rights and business name rights are also excluded. The principles set out below apply to expenditure on both tax IP and expenditure on related intangible assets and rights, unless specific reference is made to tax IP.

IP expenditure is deductible when incurred provided the necessary connection exists between the expenditure and the assessable income producing activity, and the expense is of a revenue nature (s 8-1; ¶16-010). For example, patent renewal fees, salary or wage costs incurred to maintain software, and costs of acquiring IP held as trading stock on hand are deductible under s 8-1 if the necessary connection exists. Royalties paid periodically for the use of another entity's IP in the ordinary course of the taxpayer's business are deductible under s 8-1, provided withholding tax is paid if the recipient is a non-resident: s 26-25 (¶22-030). Revenue costs incurred to enable a licensee to use the taxpayer's IP are deductible under s 8-1, if the amounts received for granting the right (eg royalties) are assessable income (¶10-510).

IP expenditure of a capital nature is not deductible under s 8-1 and the tests outlined in ¶16-060 are used to characterise the expense.

Capital allowance (or depreciation) deductions are available for items of tax IP (not held as trading stock), in-house software (¶17-370), and other intangible assets included in the s 40-30 ''depreciating asset'' definition (¶17-015), to the extent they are used for an income producing purpose. An explanation of the costs which may be included when depreciating tax IP commences at ¶17-080. The effective life of IP-related depreciating assets is set out in s 40-95(7) (¶17-280). The prime cost method (¶17-490) is used to calculate the decline in value of tax IP. An immediate deduction is available in limited situations where the cost does not exceed $300 (¶17-330) or $100 for business taxpayers (¶16-153). In some cases, pooling rules may apply to low-cost tax IP assets (¶17-810) and expenditure on in-house software may be allocated to a software development pool (¶17-370). Capital costs incurred in seeking to obtain a right to tax IP may qualify as a project amount (s 40-840(2); ¶19-060) with a deduction potentially available under the project pool expenditure rules (¶19-050).

The disposal of tax IP on capital account, which was held for an income producing purpose, will trigger a balancing adjustment event with a deduction available if the termination value (¶17-640) is less than the adjustable value (¶17-485) (and an assessable income inclusion arising in the converse situation): s 40-285 (¶17-630). The disposal of tax IP on capital account, which was held partly for an income producing purpose, may result in a capital gain or loss under CGT event K7 (¶11-350).

Small business entities can choose to take advantage of the capital allowance rules discussed at ¶7-250 when depreciating and disposing of tax IP on capital account. Temporary rules allow business taxpayers to fully write off the cost of depreciating assets, including intangible assets that qualify (¶17-430).

The grant or assignment of an interest in tax IP (eg by way of a licence) on capital account results in: (i) the original tax IP asset being split into 2 parts; (ii) a disposal of the part that is the subject of the grant or assignment; and (iii) a balancing adjustment event occurring for the disposed part, which may give rise to a deduction (or an assessable income inclusion) depending on the calculation (s 40-115(3); ¶17-630). The grant or assignment of interests in CGT assets that are not tax IP (on capital account) might result in a capital gain or loss from CGT event D1 (¶11-280). If so, only non-deductible incidental costs (¶11-550) relating to the creation of the relevant rights are included to reduce the capital gain or increase the capital loss: s 104-35.

Companies that incur IP expenditure related to eligible research and development activities may qualify for a tax offset rather than a deduction (¶20-150).

A deduction for the decline in value of film copyright acquired from 1 July 2004 is generally available over its effective life using the prime cost method (¶17-490) or diminishing value method (¶17-500). The cost of the copyright may be reduced if the ''producer offset'' is available (¶20-340). Other concessions related to films are outlined at ¶20-330.

The cost of tax IP and other related assets might be reset when transferred into a consolidated group by a joining entity, which can affect the head company's capital allowance deductions and CGT exposure on any subsequent disposal: s 701-55 (¶8-210; ¶8-220). The tax cost of IP and other related assets that a subsidiary takes with it when exiting a consolidated group is explained at ¶8-400.

Goodwill, trademarks, domain name rights and business name rights are CGT assets and IP expenditure that satisfies the cost base (or reduced cost base) elements (¶11-550) is recognised in calculating the capital gain or loss on their disposal to the extent the costs have not already been deducted. The CGT discount (¶11-033) or small business CGT concessions (¶7-110) might be available for the disposal of such CGT assets.

If IP-related capital costs are not deductible elsewhere and are not included in the cost base (or reduced cost base) of a CGT asset (eg capital expenditure to acquire or develop trade secrets or know-how), then they might be deductible as a business-related capital cost under s 40-880 (¶16-156).

Non-arm's length amounts paid by an Australian enterprise to a foreign associate for IP-related expenditure might be adjusted under the transfer pricing rules thereby affecting the deductibility of the expenditure (¶22-580). Incorrectly characterising payments to a non-resident for use of IP as for goods or services may also affect the deductibilty of such payments (TA 2018/2). The receipt of a royalty from a non-resident might give rise to a foreign income tax offset (and not a deduction) for foreign royalty withholding tax (¶21-670).

[FITR ¶86-910]

Spare Parts

¶16-730 Deductions for spare parts

Expenditure on spare parts and consumable stores is deductible as an ordinary business expense (ITAA97 s 8-1). The deduction may be claimed on an ''expenditure incurred'' basis (ie in the year of purchase) where the intention is simply to ensure continuity of production. Where, however, a store of spare parts is being built up, the Commissioner considers that the deduction is more properly claimable on a ''usage'' basis — ie in the year in which the particular item is used (IT 333). For the deductibility of spares purchased with plant, see ¶17-015.

As to whether spare parts are included in *trading stock*, see ¶9-150. As to deductions for large-scale purchases of low-cost items, see ¶16-153, ¶17-330, ¶17-810 and ¶7-250.

[FITR ¶33-640]

Interest

¶16-740 Deductions for interest expenses

Interest is deductible to the extent to which it is incurred in gaining or producing assessable income or in carrying on a business for that purpose and is not of a capital, private or domestic nature (ITAA97 s 8-1). Interest is not normally a capital outgoing because it is a recurrent expense which does not secure an ''enduring advantage''; rather, it simply secures the use of borrowed money during the term of the loan. Generally, this applies even where the borrowed funds are used to purchase a capital asset (*Steele*) although some exceptions apply to vacant land (see below). Interest paid to secure a capital sum or keep it in circulation was on revenue account (*Ashwick (Qld)*). However, no deduction is available for interest on borrowings relating to the production of exempt income (*Case Y5*; *Case Z33*).

The same principles apply to determine the deductibility of both ordinary interest and compound interest as both are simply the cost of borrowed funds (*Hart*; *R & D Holdings*). The deductibility of compound interest is not necessarily determined by the use to which the original loan funds were put (TD 2008/27).

The "use" and "purpose" test

In determining the deductibility of interest, the courts and tribunals have looked at the purpose of the borrowing and the use to which the borrowed moneys have been put (TR 2004/4). For example, interest on borrowed moneys may be deductible where the moneys are used to acquire income-producing assets (eg property for rental, shares for dividends: IT 2606, but not options: TR 2004/4), to finance business operations (eg as working capital) or to meet current business expenses (eg overdraft moneys used to pay business outgoings such as wages, purchase of trading stock or materials). The security given for the borrowed money is totally irrelevant (TD 93/13). Penalty interest for early repayment of a loan will generally be deductible if the payment is made to rid the taxpayer of a recurring obligation to pay interest on the loan where the interest would itself have been deductible if incurred (TR 2019/2). For the deductibility of interest on funds borrowed to pay tax, see ¶16-856.

Debenture interest payments made by a bank to a subsidiary were of a capital nature because the predominant purpose of the payments was to enable it to comply with the capital adequacy requirements thus securing a structural advantage (*St George Bank*; see also *Macquarie Finance Ltd*). Such payment would now be subject to the rules referred to at ¶23-100 and ¶23-020.

In PR 2010/16 and PR 2010/17 (Investments in Macquarie Flexi 100 Trust June 2010 Offer), the Commissioner accepted the deductibility of interest under full recourse and limited recourse borrowings.

Relevance of other factors and "negative gearing"

While the main test is the ''use'' test, it may also be necessary to consider other factors in particular circumstances, eg where the interest on the borrowings exceeds the return on the investment. In *Fletcher's case*, which involved a complex and highly artificial annuity scheme, the income derived from the annuity was less than one-eighth of the deduction claimed for interest. The High Court accepted that the interest was deductible to the extent of the income derived. However, beyond that point, the deductibility of the interest had to be determined by weighing up the whole set of circumstances, including the direct and indirect objects and advantages that the taxpayer sought in making the outgoing. The court took the view that if, on consideration of all those factors, the whole of the interest could be characterised as ''genuinely and not colourably incurred in gaining or producing assessable income'', the interest would be fully deductible. If only part of the outgoing could be so characterised, apportionment between the pursuit of assessable income and of other objectives was necessary. See also *Spassked*. In TR 95/33, the Commissioner accepts the effectiveness of commonly encountered negative gearing arrangements (¶31-170). It is important to note that the relevant factual considerations can change over the term of the loan so that the facts relevant to the criteria for deductibility in one year will not necessarily mirror those in another year (*Spassked*; TD 2008/27).

Where the taxpayer had no intention or expectation to derive assessable income by reason of its borrowings and continued, deliberately, not to derive dividend income, the occasion of the incurrence of the interest was the creation of the deduction in a non-income earning company which was in a position to transfer the resulting losses to other group companies, and therefore no interest was deductible (*IEL Finance*).

If funds are borrowed for income-producing purposes as part of a larger loan, the interest is deductible if the taxpayer is able to trace the original borrowing to the funds on which the interest accrues (*Case 14/2000*).

▶ Planning point

An outgoing may be deductible in a year of income although the assessable income motivating the outgoing is not generated until a subsequent year of income. Where deductions associated with an investment exceed the assessable income derived from the investment in a particular income year, the excess can be used to reduce the tax payable on other assessable income of the investing taxpayer. Therefore, negative gearing can be particularly useful to taxpayers on high incomes.

Deductions are not available from 1 July 2019 for costs related to holding vacant land, or land on which there is either a residential property under construction or a residential property not available for rent. Such costs include interest on borrowing to acquire the land. The deductions are only available once the residential property can be lawfully occupied, and is rented out or at least available for rent (¶16-650).

Where borrowed funds are on-lent

A similar approach to that in *Fletcher's case* was taken in *Ure's case* where the taxpayer borrowed money at commercial rates of interest (up to 12.5%) and on-lent it to his wife and a family company at 1% interest — they in turn used the money for non-business purposes. The deduction for interest was limited to the 1% interest returned as assessable income. In *Tanti*, no deduction was available for interest paid by the sole shareholder and director on funds borrowed and on-lent interest-free to an unprofitable company as there was no prospect of deriving any income from the company, whether as dividends or interest (*Case 26/94*; *Brian Reilly Freighters*). Similarly, interest incurred on funds borrowed and on-lent to a company by a joint shareholder and director was not deductible as there was no connection between the interest and the gaining or deriving of assessable interest or dividends by the taxpayer (*Knox*).

On the other hand, in the case of a continuing business, the fact that a low rate of interest or no interest at all is charged by the taxpayer for borrowed moneys on-lent to an associated entity may not necessarily preclude a deduction for the whole of the interest. This is illustrated by the *Total Holdings case* where money was on-lent interest-free to a subsidiary with the intention that, once the subsidiary became profitable, the profits would be remitted to the parent company by way of dividends and interest. The Commissioner has said that a deduction will be allowed in a substantially similar case (IT 2606). Thus in *Economedes*, a deduction was allowed for interest on borrowed funds which were on-lent by the taxpayer to a company controlled by him and his wife, on the basis that the loan was intended to render the company profitable as soon as possible.

Interest and bank expenses incurred on money borrowed from a foreign bank, which the taxpayer on-lent immediately on receipt to associated companies by way of interest-free loans, were not connected with the production of any assessable income and could not be deducted (*Fitzroy Services*; ¶16-010). In *Rawson Finances Pty Ltd*, the taxpayer established that funds received from a foreign bank were loans (and not income as alleged by the Commissioner), as this reflected the intended and enforceable reality of the transactions. It followed that interest payments on the contentious loans were deductible because they were incurred in deriving income from related entities to which the taxpayer had on-loaned the funds.

For further examples involving company groups, see *Metropolitan Oil Distributors (Sydney)*; *Rocca* and TD 2004/36.

Preservation of income-producing assets

Interest on borrowings applied to private purposes (eg the purchase of a residence) is not deductible, even though the borrowing enables the taxpayer to use other funds or existing investments to produce assessable income, eg by renting out a former residence or by keeping other funds on high interest-bearing deposit (*Case Z18*). Similarly, interest on money borrowed to satisfy a Supreme Court order under testator family maintenance provisions was not deductible, even though the loan enabled the executor to retain the income-producing assets of the estate without encumbrance (*Hayden*).

Linked or split loans, redraw or credit line facilities

A typical ''linked'' or ''split'' loan facility involves 2 or more loans or sub-accounts. One is for private purposes and the other(s) for business purposes. Repayments are allocated to the private account and the unpaid interest on the business account is capitalised. This maximises the potential interest deduction by creating interest on interest. However, in *Hart*, the High Court ruled that the arrangement triggered the general anti-avoidance provisions of ITAA36 Pt IVA and that the additional interest was not deductible (¶31-170). The general anti-avoidance provisions could apply to ''investment loan interest payment arrangements'' despite the taxpayer's purpose of ''paying their home loan off sooner'' (TD 2012/1). See also TR 98/22.

In contrast, interest incurred under a refinanced investment loan of the kind set out in PR 2013/22 or PR 2014/7, which is part of a scheme designed to accelerate the repayment of a refinanced home loan, is deductible. Some distinguishing features of these schemes is that they do not involve: (i) the capitalisation of any interest or a line of credit for the investment loan; (ii) a linked or split loan facility as set out in TR 98/22; or (iii) an ''investment loan interest payment arrangement'' as described in TD 2012/1.

Non-capital costs of ownership that are disallowed under ITAA36 Pt IVA do not form part of the cost base of an asset unless the Commissioner makes a compensating adjustment to that effect. However, in the case of split loan arrangements, a compensating adjustment is not available (TD 2005/33).

The Commissioner adopts the same approach to certain line of credit facilities that involve capitalisation of interest (TD 1999/42). Where no capitalisation of interest is involved, and funds drawn down on a line of credit facility or a redraw facility are used only partly for income-producing purposes, interest on the funds is apportioned between the income-producing and the other purposes in accordance with the principles set out in TR 2000/2. The deductibility of interest on a further borrowing of money under a redraw or line of credit facility depends upon the use to which the funds redrawn or drawn down are put, regardless of the purpose of the original borrowing. See also *Domjan*.

The Commissioner has questioned the deductibility of interest under ''mortgage management'' arrangements in which the taxpayer refinances a home loan and establishes purported investment loans to fund the purchase of shares in companies controlled by the promoter of the arrangement (TA 2009/20).

"Refinancing" principle

Interest on money borrowed by a partnership to repay money advanced by a partner, which was used as working capital, is deductible (*Roberts & Smith*). This "substitution of partnership capital principle" or "refinancing principle" applies to allow companies a deduction for interest on borrowings to fund a declared dividend or a repayment of share capital, where the payment is made out of a realised profit reserve or out of capital or working capital employed in the company's income-producing business (TR 95/25). For the application of the refinancing principle to trusts and to partnerships, see ¶6-080 and ¶5-070 respectively.

Connection with income of earlier years

In accordance with general principles (¶16-010), interest on funds used to purchase a business remains deductible if the occasion of the outgoing is found in the taxpayer's income-producing business operations, even if the interest is incurred in a year later than the year in which the income was derived, or the business has ceased to exist or the assets representing those funds have been lost to the taxpayer.

For example, in *Brown*, a deduction was allowed for interest on a loan used to purchase a business where the interest was incurred during a period after the business had been sold. Similarly, in *Jones*, interest on a loan taken out to purchase equipment for a partnership business was held to be deductible for some time after the business ceased on the death of one of the partners. The deduction continues to be available even after the loan has been re-financed and even though the taxpayer has the legal right to repay the loan early, thus preventing further interest accruing. However, in the case of a "roll-over" business loan facility, as distinct from a loan that runs for an agreed term unless the taxpayer decides to repay early, the deduction may cease to be available if a taxpayer with the resources to pay out such a roll-over loan decides not to do so, and rolls the loan over instead (*Brown*; *Jones*).

In TR 2004/4, the Commissioner accepts that interest incurred after the cessation of the business activities may be deductible even though the loan is not for a fixed term, the taxpayer has the legal entitlement to repay the loan before maturity, with or without penalty, or the original loan is refinanced. However, no deduction is available if: (a) the loan is kept on foot for reasons unassociated with the former income-earning activities; or (b) the taxpayer makes a conscious decision to extend the loan for a commercial advantage unassociated with the former income-earning activities. Legal or economic inability to repay suggests that the loan was not kept on foot for purposes other than income-producing purposes. The same principles apply to non-business activities (eg passive investments).

In *Davies*, the amount of time that elapsed between when the loan was first taken out and when the taxpayer accepted liability to make payments on the loan, and the taxpayer's refusal to make payments on the loan, indicated that the connection between the payments and the income-producing activities no longer existed (*Riverside Road Lodge*; *Brown*; *Steele*). On the other hand, in *Guest* and *R & D Holdings* the connection was present despite a significant time period having elapsed. In *Willersdorf-Greene*, interest on a loan used to satisfy a guarantee which had been integral to the income-producing activities was deductible, even though the loan was taken out after the relevant income producing activities had ceased.

Interest incurred on a loan to acquire an asset after the asset has been disposed of, will only be deductible if the sale proceeds are used for income-producing purposes (TD 95/27).

Connection with income of later years

Case authority have established that interest on funds used to purchase a property (eg land) on which the taxpayer intends to build an income-producing asset (eg a motel) may be deductible from the time of the acquisition of the property (*Steele*). It is not necessary to show that the interest was incurred in producing income of a particular year, though a large gap may indicate that the necessary connection does not exist or that the expense was entirely preliminary (¶16-154). Further, interest that is otherwise deductible is not excluded from deductibility as a capital expense simply because no assessable income was derived in the relevant year.

The Commissioner limits the operation of *Steele's case* to circumstances where:

- the interest is not preliminary to the income-earning activities. In other words, it is not incurred too soon
- the interest is not of a private or domestic nature
- the period prior to the derivation of income is not so long that the required connection between the outgoings and income is lost
- the interest is incurred with one end in view, namely the gaining or producing of assessable income
- continuing efforts are undertaken in pursuit of that end. While this does not require constant on-site development activity, the requirement is not satisfied if the venture becomes truly dormant and the holding of the asset is passive, even if there is an intention to revive the venture at some time in the future (TR 2004/4).

Specific rules that apply from 1 July 2019 deny a deduction for interest on borrowings to acquire vacant land or land where a residential property is under construction or not available for rent, except if in relation to carrying on a business, eg property development (¶16-650).

Interest on money borrowed to fund the renovation of property was not deductible where the future use of the property — whether for income production or otherwise — was entirely undecided (*Anovoy*; *Temelli*; *Sinclair*). However, in *Ormiston*, interest was deductible where the taxpayer purchased the property with the intention of deriving rental income, even though no income was ever derived (the application of this case may be diminished for taxpayers caught within s 26-102: ¶16-650).

Borrowings to finance life premiums

Deductions for interest and expenses associated with money borrowed to pay life insurance premiums can only be claimed if the risk component of the premium received by the insurer is the entire amount of the premium and amounts the insurer is liable to pay under the policy would be included in the person's assessable income if paid (ITAA97 s 26-85). See also IT 2504 and *Rydell*.

Borrowings to finance superannuation contributions

Deductions for interest and borrowing costs connected with a contribution can only be claimed if a deduction can be claimed for the contribution under Subdiv 290-B, ie by an employer (ITAA97 s 26-80).

Debt and equity rules, financial products

The special rules that apply to distinguish debt (eg loans) and equity (eg shares) are outlined at ¶23-100 and following.

A return that an entity pays or provides on a "debt interest" is not prevented from being deductible under s 8-1 merely because (ITAA97 s 25-85):

(1) the return is contingent on the economic performance of the entity (or a part of the entity's activities) or of a connected entity (or a part of the activities of a connected entity), or

(2) the return secures a permanent or enduring benefit for the entity or a connected entity of the entity.

If the return is a dividend, the entity can deduct the return to the extent to which it would have been deductible under s 8-1 and it satisfies the following tests:

- the payment of the return is the incurring by the entity of a liability to pay the same amount as interest
- the interest was incurred in respect of the finance raised by the entity and in respect of which the return was paid or provided, and
- the debt interest retained its character as a debt interest.

The above rules do not apply to a return to the extent that it would be deductible under s 8-1, apart from s 25-85 or to the extent that the rate of return exceeds a specified limit. No deduction for the return is available to the extent to which the annually compounded internal rate of return exceeds the benchmark rate of return for the interest increased by 150 basis points (s 25-85(5); ID 2006/102; ID 2006/319).

An Australian entity can also deduct a loss or outgoing incurred in deriving certain types of non-assessable non-exempt income (eg exempt foreign source income) (not necessarily in the same year: TD 2009/21) if the amount is a cost relating to a debt interest (s 25-90). From 17 October 2014, non-portfolio foreign equity distributions that flow through certain interposed trusts and partnerships to Australian resident corporate beneficiaries or partners may be regarded as non-assessable non-exempt income (s 768-5(2)). Debt financing costs incurred to derive such distributions may be deductible under s 25-90 (s 768-5(3)).

However, certain debt interest costs that are interest (or have such a nature), or which are calculated using the time value of money, are not deductible under s 25-90. This deduction denial applies where the costs are incurred in earning income that satisfies both the foreign branch income exemption (in s 23AH; ¶21-098), and the foreign equity distribution exemption (in s 768-5; ¶21-095) (TD 2016/6).

In *Noza Holdings*, there was no presently existing liability to pay dividends on redeemable preference shares until the dividends were declared. The declaration of the dividend gave rise to a debt, notwithstanding that the payer had insufficient profits to fund the dividend. TA 2009/9 describes certain contrived cross-border financing arrangements with no or little commercial or economic purpose which seek to generate debt deductions under s 25-90 for costs incurred in deriving non-assessable non-exempt income.

The meaning of a debt interest is determined generally in accordance with the tests in the debt/equity rules. Those rules determine whether returns on an interest may be frankable and non-deductible (like a dividend) or may be deductible but not frankable (like interest).

Where a debt interest is also a ''financial arrangement'', the TOFA rules outlined at ¶23-020 prevail over ss 25-85 and 25-90.

The deductibility of the discount on bills of exchange and promissory notes is considered at ¶23-330.

"Grossing up" or tax indemnification payments

Indemnification amounts paid to a non-resident lender by a borrower against the liability for interest withholding tax are normally deductible to the borrower if the borrowed funds are used for business purposes (TR 2002/4).

Limitations on deductibility of interest

Interest on borrowings to pay income tax, PAYG withholding amounts, or PAYG installments, is not deductible under s 25-5. No deduction is available for an amount of interest (including an amount in the form of a non-cash benefit) unless the taxpayer has complied with the withholding requirements of the PAYG system (¶26-250) for payments to non-residents (ITAA97 s 26-25; ID 2004/848; ID 2005/356; ID 2007/187).

Debt deductions arising from debt used to finance the Australian operations of certain multinational investors may be limited under the "thin capitalisation" rules (¶22-700) and the transfer pricing rules (¶22-580). For the interaction of those rules, see TR 2010/7. The interaction of the apportionment provisions of s 8-1 and the thin capitalisation provisions in the context of branch funding for multinational banks is discussed in TR 2005/11.

Consolidated entities

The head company of a multiple entry consolidated group can claim a deduction for interest paid on funds borrowed from outside the group by it or a subsidiary member to buy shares in an existing eligible tier-1 company of the group (TD 2006/47) and in another subsidiary member of the group (TD 2006/48).

[FITR ¶31-480 – ¶31-500, ¶31-630 – ¶31-700, ¶33-350 – ¶33-590, ¶68-200]

¶16-742 Interest on borrowings to acquire investments

As a general rule, interest on moneys borrowed to acquire shares will be deductible where it is reasonably expected that assessable dividends will be derived from the investment (ITAA97 s 8-1; ID 2005/42). Interest will not be deductible where the shares are acquired solely for the purpose of making a capital profit on their resale and the proceeds on sale are not assessable as ordinary income (IT 2606), but may be included in the cost base of the asset for CGT purposes.

For the consequences of negative gearing arrangements, see TR 95/33 (¶16-740). For the method of calculating deductions for interest on fixed-term loans or hire purchase agreements, see TR 93/16 and ITAA97 Div 240 (¶23-250).

Capital protected loans

Under ITAA97 Div 247 (introduced to reverse the effect of *Firth*), where the expense on a capital protected borrowing (CPB) exceeds a benchmark rate, part of the expense is attributed to the cost of the capital protection feature. The amount of the excess is treated as being: (a) not interest (rather as the cost of the capital protection feature); and (b) not deductible, if this cost is capital in nature. The capital protection feature is treated in the same way irrespective of whether it is provided explicitly (eg by an actual put option) or implicitly through the term of the arrangement.

A CPB is an arrangement under which there is a borrowing or a provision of credit where the borrower is, wholly or partly, protected against a fall in the market value of a thing to the extent that the borrower uses the amount borrowed or credit provided to acquire the protected thing or uses the protected thing as security for the borrowing or provision of credit, eg instalment warrants and capital protected equity loans (s 247-10).

Division 247 applies to CPBs entered into from 1 July 2007, where the "protected thing" is: a share, or a unit in a unit trust, that is listed on an approved stock exchange; or a stapled security where the issuer is listed. It also applies to shares, units and stapled securities that are not listed on an approved stock exchange, but where the issuer is widely-held. In addition, Div 247 applies to CPBs entered into in the interim period (16 April 2003 to 30 June 2007), where the protected thing is a listed share, unit in a unit trust, or a stapled security. Such CPBs entered into in either time period are also covered where the protected thing is held by the borrower through an interposed entity (eg a trust). However, the provisions do not apply to CPBs relating to interests under employee share schemes (s 247-15). For recent examples of the application of Div 247, see PR 2014/9, PR 2015/3, PR 2016/2 and PR 2016/7.

From 1 July 2013, the benchmark rate is the RBA indicator lending rate for standard variable housing loans (investor), plus 100 basis points (ITAA97 s 247-20(5); ITTPA s 247-80(4); TD 2016/10).

Interest on a full recourse loan will not be denied deductibility by Div 247 where that loan is used to prepay interest on another loan which is a CPB (TD 2013/1).

Linked bonds

For the deductibility of interest and other expenditure incurred in respect of linked bonds and notes paying fixed interest on maturity and a bonus return linked to the performance of a preselected equity, interest rate or exchange rate, see *ATO media releases* NAT 99/21, 99/84, 02/14 and *Young*. Generally, the ATO will allow a deduction for the cash outlay on interest charged on the notes. Money borrowed from the note issuer to "prepay" the balance of interest charged would not be allowed as a deduction.

Investing in trusts

No deduction for interest on borrowings is available to beneficiaries against distributions from discretionary trusts because the beneficiary has a mere expectancy of receiving income from the trust and is not presently entitled to the income of the trust when the expenditure was incurred (*Antonopoulos*; *Lambert*; *Chadbourne*). Even with present entitlement, the interest expense must also have a nexus with that income. Being presently entitled to income in future years is insufficient nexus to warrant a deduction for a current year's interest expense in the ATO's view (TD 2018/9). On the other hand, interest payments on loans taken to purchase units in a hybrid trust under which income was to be held on a fixed trust and capital gains on a discretionary trust were deductible (*Forrest*; ATO *Decision Impact Statement*). In PR 2014/15, interest incurred on borrowings used to invest in a unit trust, which only conferred benefits on unit holders, qualified as general deductions (s 8-1).

Interest on money borrowed to acquire units in a split property unit trust is generally fully deductible, even where the trust distribution consists of both assessable and non-assessable amounts. The interest deduction may be limited where the expected return from the units, both income and capital growth, does not provide an obvious commercial explanation for incurring the interest, especially if the expected amount of assessable income is disproportionately less than the interest. Interest on borrowings to acquire growth units in a split property trust that are expected to produce only negligible income is deductible only to the extent of the assessable income actually received (IT 2684). See also ID 2004/175.

For the Commissioner's views on certain home loan unit trust arrangements involving claims for interest deductions, see TR 2002/18 (¶30-170).

Interest is not deductible to the extent that the borrowed moneys are settled by the borrower on trust to benefit persons other than the taxpayer (TD 2009/17; TA 2008/3; TA 2008/4), eg other general beneficiaries or remainder beneficiaries (PR 2011/15).

Investment and related parties

A family trust was able to deduct the whole of the interest on borrowings to purchase a residence leased to a beneficiary of the trust at a commercial rent, even though the interest substantially exceeded the rental income (*Janmor Nominees*; distinguished in *Tabone*).

[FITR ¶33-350 – ¶33-600; ¶235-000]

¶16-744 Apportionment of interest deductions

Where a loan is taken out for 2 purposes, one business and one non-business, only a proportion of the interest will generally be deductible under ITAA97 s 8-1 (TR 95/33).

However, in *Carberry's case*, a married couple were allowed a deduction for the full amount of interest on a loan used to purchase a combined dwelling/child-minding business, where it was shown that the whole of the loan related to the purchase of the business and the dwelling was purchased with the proceeds from the sale of their previous home. The Commissioner accepts this approach where an asset can be notionally divided into a part acquired for business purposes and a part acquired for non-business purposes, and the loan can be attributed to the notional business part. If an asset cannot be notionally divided (eg most motor vehicles and machines), the interest is deductible to the extent to which the asset is used for income-producing or business purposes (IT 2661).

The income or loss from a rental property must be shared according to the legal interests of the owners, whether they are joint owners or tenants in common, except in those very limited circumstances where there is sufficient evidence to establish that the equitable interests are different from the legal interests (¶5-000, ¶5-130; TR 93/32). Where taxpayers are related, eg, husband and wife, it is assumed that the equitable right is exactly the same as the legal title. Any capital gain or loss is also apportioned on the same basis as the rental income or loss.

In one case, the fact that a loan taken out in the joint names of the taxpayer and his wife was used to purchase a business in the wife's name only did not disentitle the taxpayer to a deduction for one-half of the interest (*Reed*). Conversely, a joint owner of a rental property was not allowed a deduction for the whole of the interest paid on a loan used to finance the rental property, whether the loan was in joint names (*Case 6/97*) or in only one name (*Case 63/96*).

[FITR ¶31-200 – ¶31-260]

¶16-746 Prepayments of interest

The fact that interest has been prepaid may preclude a deduction in certain circumstances, particularly where the taxpayer's dominant purpose in making the prepayment was to gain a tax advantage.

For example, in *Ilbery's case*, the taxpayer was denied a deduction for a prepayment of interest on a loan that was subsequently used to purchase an income-producing property. The prepayment was made solely to reduce tax and there was no legal obligation on the taxpayer to make the payment in order to obtain the loan. In addition, at the time the prepayment was made, the property had not yet been acquired and the income-producing activity had not begun.

In relation to prepayment schemes, reference should be made to the specific anti-avoidance provisions noted at ¶16-110. Special rules also affect the *timing* of otherwise allowable deductions for prepaid interest (¶16-045).

[FITR ¶33-520]

¶16-748 When is interest "incurred"?

Interest is deductible under ITAA97 s 8-1 when it is "incurred" (¶16-040). This will usually be when the interest becomes due and payable. In *Case 14/97*, interest on funds borrowed to invest in an employee share scheme was deductible when the employee was committed to pay, even though no payment was in fact ever made and the liability was subsequently waived.

Interest expenditure is incurred by financial institutions on a daily accruals basis, except where the terms and conditions of the loan agreement displace the ordinary rule that interest accrues day by day (TR 93/27; TR 1999/11; *Alliance Holdings*; *Australian Guarantee Corporation*; ID 2006/217).

Special statutory rules apply to ensure that the issuer of a discounted or deferred interest security is entitled to claim deductions on the accruals basis for the discount or deferred interest component of the security — correspondingly, the holder of the security is taxed on the income on the accruals basis (¶23-320). The TOFA rules that apply to specified financial arrangements are outlined at ¶23-020.

[FITR ¶33-520]

Borrowing Expenses

¶16-800 Borrowing and mortgage discharge expenses

Expenditure incurred in borrowing money or in the discharge of a mortgage is normally non-deductible capital expenditure. However, ITAA97 s 25-25 specifically allows a deduction for certain borrowing expenses and ITAA97 s 25-30 allows a deduction for certain mortgage discharge expenses.

Borrowing expenses

Borrowing expenses (such as procuration fees, loan establishment fees, mortgage protection insurance, legal expenses, stamp duty, valuation and survey fees, broker's commission, underwriter's fees, prospectuses, advertising, printing and other expenses relating to debenture issues) are deductible to the extent that the borrowed moneys are used for the purpose of producing assessable income (s 25-25). As is the case with interest (*Steele*: ¶16-740), it is not necessary that the expenses should actually produce assessable income in the same year in which they are incurred (although some limitations apply from 1 July 2019 in relation to vacant land: ¶16-650). However, where the loan does not proceed, the borrowing expenses are not deductible. See also ID 2009/51 and ID 2010/160 (credit card payment fee).

Provided the borrowed money is used *by the taxpayer* solely for income-producing purposes, borrowing expenses are fully deductible even if the funds are on-lent to persons who use the money for non-income-producing purposes (*Ure*; *Case 11/99*; ID 2009/51).

The expenses are deductible over the period of the loan specified in the contract, or the actual loan period (eg if the loan is repaid early), or 5 years, whichever is the shorter period, beginning with the year in which they were incurred. The amount deductible each year is obtained by dividing the undeducted expenditure by the number of days remaining in the loan period and multiplying the result by the number of days in the loan period that are in the income year. If borrowing expenses incurred in any year are $100 or less, they are deductible in that year.

▶ Example

On 2 January Year 1, Louisa obtained a 4-year loan of $10,000, which she used solely for income-producing purposes throughout the period of the loan. Borrowing expenses incurred in relation to the loan in Year 1 amounted to $200. The total period of the loan was 4 years, ie 1,461 days. The period applicable to Year 1 (a leap year) was 181 days. The borrowing expenses ($200) would be allowed as follows:

Year 1: $24.77 (ie $\frac{\$200}{1{,}461} \times 181$)

($200 − $24.77 = $175.23)

Year 2: $49.96 (ie $\frac{\$175.23}{1{,}280} \times 365$)

($175.23 − $49.96 = $125.27)

Year 3: $49.97 (ie $\frac{\$125.27}{915} \times 365$)

($125.27 − $49.97 = $75.30)

Year 4: $49.97 (ie $\frac{\$75.30}{550} \times 365$)

($75.30 − $49.97 = $25.33)

Year 5: $25.33 (ie $\frac{\$25.33}{185} \times 185$)

If the loan was repaid early, on 31 December of Year 4, the deduction in Year 4 would be:

$75.30 (ie $\frac{\$75.30}{184} \times 184$)

Neither expenses in relation to the issue of redeemable preference shares (*Case J57*), nor premiums paid on a life policy used as security for a loan (*Case Y21*), are borrowing expenses, but expenses of issuing convertible notes are. Bonuses paid either on maturity or by instalments during the currency of a loan would also not be within the scope of the deduction. For the costs of raising equity, see ¶16-156.

Expenditure otherwise deductible under s 25-25 will be disallowed where it is incurred as part of an ‘‘expenditure recoupment’’ tax avoidance scheme (¶16-110). Where a commercial debt is forgiven, the debtor’s deduction for borrowing expenses may be reduced under the rules discussed at ¶16-910.

Expenses of discharging a mortgage

Expenses incurred to discharge a mortgage given as security for the repayment of money borrowed, or for the payment of the whole or part of the purchase price of property, are deductible in the year incurred, but only to the extent that the money or the property was used for producing assessable income (s 25-30). Deductible expenses incurred in the discharge of a mortgage include penalty interest for early repayment of the loan (TR 2019/2).

Expenditure otherwise deductible under s 25-30 will be disallowed where it is incurred as part of an ‘‘expenditure recoupment’’ tax avoidance scheme (¶16-110).

[FITR ¶65-200, ¶65-220]

Mains Electricity Connections

¶16-820 Deductions for connection costs

A deduction is available for capital expenditure incurred in connecting mains electricity to land on which a business is carried on or in upgrading an existing connection to such land (ITAA97 ss 40-645 to 40-665). The deduction is allowable in equal instalments over 10 years, ie one-tenth of the expenditure is deductible in the income year in which the expenditure is incurred, one-tenth in the next year and so on.

The person incurring the expenditure must have an interest in the land, eg as the owner or tenant, or be a sharefarmer who is carrying on a business on the land.

Where the expenditure is incurred by a partnership, it is not taken into account in determining the partnership’s net income or loss. Instead, each partner claims a proportionate deduction (or the agreed amount borne by the partner) in his/her own return.

The deduction is available only where some or all of the electricity to be supplied is intended by the taxpayer or another person to be used in carrying on business for the purpose of producing assessable income, exploration or prospecting, mining site rehabilitation or environmental protection. The deduction will be withdrawn if, during the 12 months after the electricity is first supplied, it is not used for any of those purposes.

Expenditure qualifying for the deduction covers:

- connection of mains electricity cables to a metering point *on* the taxpayer’s land, whether or not the point from which the cable is connected is on the land
- provision or installation of the metering equipment or other equipment for use directly in connection with the supply of electricity to the metering point
- work undertaken to increase the amount of electricity supplied to a metering point
- work to modify or replace metering equipment or equipment used directly in connection with the supply of electricity, if the modification or replacement results from increasing the amount of electricity supplied

- work carried out as a result of a contribution to the cost of a project consisting of the connection of mains electricity facilities to the land or other land.

The deduction takes the place of any depreciation or other deduction that might otherwise have been available.

The deduction does not extend to work undertaken, or cables or equipment installed, in the course of replacing or relocating any existing cables or equipment, otherwise than in the course of increasing the amount of electricity that can be supplied to a metering point on the land.

Where a commercial debt is forgiven, the debtor's deduction for mains electricity connection costs may be reduced under the rules discussed at ¶16-910. Recoupments of mains electricity connection costs may give rise to assessable income (¶10-270).

[FITR ¶88-325ff]

Legal Expenses

¶16-830 Legal expenses deductible under special provisions

Certain kinds of legal expenses are specifically made deductible, even though they might not be deductible under the general deduction provisions because of their capital, private or domestic nature. These are legal expenses associated with:

- certain borrowings of money (¶16-800)
- the discharging of certain mortgages (¶16-800)
- the preparation of leases (¶16-640, ¶16-650), or
- the preparation of an income tax return, the disputing of a tax assessment and the obtaining of professional tax advice (¶16-850).

Certain capital legal expenses of a business may also qualify for a 5-year write-off (¶16-156).

[FITR ¶33-810]

¶16-840 Legal expenses deductible under general provisions

Apart from their deductibility under specific provisions of the tax law (¶16-830), the deductibility of legal expenses, like other business expenses, is to be considered under ITAA97 s 8-1. In determining whether the costs of legal proceedings are deductible, it is irrelevant whether the taxpayer is successful in those proceedings. The character of legal expenses follows the purpose of incurring the expense (*Hallstroms*; *Cape Flattery Silica Mines*). The essential character of the advantage sought in undertaking the proceedings determines whether the expenses are on revenue or capital account (TD 93/29).

Some legal expenses are clearly of a capital nature (eg conveyancing costs in connection with the purchase of real estate, legal fees in connection with the purchase or establishment of a business or other capital asset for use in a business) and some are clearly of a revenue nature (eg legal costs of recovering business debts). Others are clearly of a non-deductible private nature (eg costs of conducting typical Family Court proceedings). But the borderline area of legal expenses has given rise to much litigation. For examples of deductible legal expenses, see ¶16-842; for examples of non-revenue legal expenses, see ¶16-844.

Deductible legal expenses do not lose their deductibility simply because they are paid after the business has ceased, provided they relate to business activities conducted before the cessation (¶16-010).

Eliminating or preventing competition

Legal expenses incurred in attempting to eliminate or prevent competition, even for a short period of time, are generally capital expenses. Thus, legal costs incurred by a cinema proprietor in opposing the granting of a cinema licence to an intending competitor were disallowed (*Broken Hill Theatres*). So too were legal costs incurred by an AM radio station in obtaining an FM licence to prevent a potential competitor obtaining the licence (*Sunraysia Broadcasters*). On the other hand, deductions have been allowed for the costs of opposing an application by a trade competitor to extend a patent (*Hallstroms*) and in preventing a competitor using a name similar to the taxpayer's (*Duro Travel Goods*).

Defending the taxpayer's business methods

Legal costs incurred in defending the taxpayer's business methods are considered to be deductible. For example, a taxpayer's expenses in defending criminal charges brought against its directors and agents in relation to marketing practices adopted in selling the taxpayer's products were allowed (*Magna Alloys & Research*). Similarly, costs incurred by a company in defending, before a Royal Commission, allegations of overcharging and unfair business practices were held to be deductible (*Snowden & Willson*).

Defending right to practise a profession or employment

Costs incurred in defending the right to practise a profession may not be deductible. Thus, legal expenses incurred by a pharmacist (*Case N65*) and a doctor (*Case X84*) in defending deregistration proceedings have been held not to be deductible (ID 2004/367). Contrast *Case U4*, where costs incurred by a doctor in defending charges brought by the Health Insurance Commission were held to be deductible, and *Inglis* where the costs of proceedings brought by a public servant against her employer to protect work conditions were allowed (her actual employment was not under threat).

Decisions allowing deductions for legal costs incurred in opposing an application to be struck off the roll of barristers (referred to in *Case V49*), and in securing continued employment under a new contract (*Case X42*), are questionable.

Legal costs are generally deductible if they are incurred or the claim is encountered because of the very act of performing the work by which the taxpayer earns assessable income (*Rowe*; *Elberg*; *Schokker*).

However the legal proceedings need not relate to the activities of one's employment for the related legal expenses to be deductible and the dichotomy between conduct undertaken in performance of the tasks for which the taxpayer was employed and improper conduct in breach of his duties was rejected by the High Court in *Day* as a test for deductibility. The relevant question was: what was productive of assessable income in a particular case, taking account of any number of positive and negative duties to be performed or observed by an employee or other salary earner. In that case, the taxpayer's duties as an officer of the public service, and the possible consequences to him of internal disciplinary proceedings and action with respect to the continuation or termination of his service, formed part of what was productive of his assessable income in that capacity. As the occasion of the legal expenses was to be found in his position, the expenses were deductible. For analysis of the decision, see the practitioner article at CCH *Tax Week* ¶85 (2009). Where the terms of employment do not oblige a taxpayer to observe certain standards of conduct, legal expenses incurred by an employee to defend a charge because it may result in his or her dismissal may not be deductible. In addition, the costs of defending criminal proceedings will rarely, if ever, be deductible under s 8-1 (ATO *Decision Impact Statement* on *Day*).

See TR 2012/8 for the assessability of amounts received in respect of deductible legal costs incurred in disputes concerning termination of employment.

Costs relating to employment agreements

Costs associated with securing an employment agreement with a new employer are not deductible to the employee, but costs incurred in altering or extending an existing agreement are deductible provided the existing agreement allows for such changes. Costs incurred in settling disputes arising out of employment agreements are deductible to both employer and employee (TR 2000/5). However fees incurred to negotiate employment contracts are deductible where the employment activities form part of the carrying on of a business (*Spriggs and Riddell*).

Defence against prosecutions

Generally, deductions will not be allowed for legal expenses incurred by a taxpayer in defending itself or its employees from prosecutions for breaches committed in the course of carrying on its business. However, there may be marginal cases in which a deduction may be available to taxpayers who are necessarily exposed to the risk of occasional prosecution through the action of an employee (eg breaches of food laws by a restaurant). No deduction is available to taxpayers such as transport operators who, as a calculated risk, incur fines regularly in the interests of the efficient operation of their business (IT 149).

Protecting or preserving a business

While expenditure incurred in protecting or preserving a business would generally be non-deductible capital expenditure, it has been held that legal expenses incurred by an agricultural chemical manufacturing company in protecting trade secrets were deductible on the basis that they were outgoings that the nature of the business required as part of prudent management (*Consolidated Fertilizers*).

Legal expenses incurred by a target company in defending itself against a takeover attempt are not deductible as revenue expenses, as they relate to either the structure of the business or the ownership of the business structure (IT 2656; *Re GHI*). However, they may be deductible over 5 years under the special provisions outlined at ¶16-156.

Annual retainers to solicitors

Taxpayers carrying on a business sometimes pay an annual retainer to a solicitor. In such cases it is often claimed in practice that the whole amount is deductible without attempting to allocate it to the various services performed, some of which may relate to capital items. However, if an actual bill of costs for specific work performed relates to work done for both deductible and non-deductible items or purposes, the taxpayer bears the onus of providing sufficient proof for calculating the deductible portion. As a retainer guarantees the availability of legal services should a future need arise, the ATO regards the expense as capital in nature (withdrawal notice of ATO ID 2002/935).

[FITR ¶33-810 – ¶34-030]

¶16-842 Examples of deductible legal expenses

In addition to the expenses noted at ¶16-840, the following are examples of legal expenses that have been held to be deductible under ITAA97 s 8-1:

- costs of defending proceedings for the unauthorised use of a trademark (*Pech*)
- costs of patent infringement action ((1963) 13 TBRD *Case* N78)
- costs of defending an employee against corruption charges ((1953) 3 TBRD *Case* C85), assault charges (*Case 9/97*)
- costs of recovering a payment in lieu of a termination notice period of 12 months (*Romanin*; ID 2010/131)
- costs incurred by an employee to prevent defamatory statements being made by a colleague (ID 2001/549)

- costs of defending misrepresentation suit in connection with sale of goods (*Reo Motors*)
- costs and damages of an employer in an employee's personal injuries claim against the employer (5 TBRD *Case* E14)
- legal expenses of pursuing an assessable workers compensation claim (ID 2010/209) or income entitlements under an employment contract (TR 2012/8)
- costs of a landlord in ejectment proceedings against a rent-defaulting tenant (15 TBRD *Case* Q49), but not costs of evicting tenant to obtain virtually indefinite occupancy of whole of premises for business purposes (5 TBRD *Case* E6)
- costs of opinion as to whether goods could be sold in another state ((1950) 1 TBRD *Case* 50)
- damages and costs of a newspaper in defending a libel action (*Herald and Weekly Times*)
- costs incurred by a company in supporting an application by an ex-director for leave to resume his activities as a director notwithstanding a prior conviction (*Magna Alloys & Research*)
- costs of defending an action for wrongful dismissal brought by a former director (*Case P16*), but see TR 2012/8
- costs incurred by a director in defending a defamation action brought against the board of directors by a dismissed executive (*Case V116*)
- cost of arbitration to settle a dispute between a solicitor and his partners as to his share of the profits and his subsequent purported expulsion from the partnership (*Creer*)
- costs of recovering a misappropriated bank deposit but only to the extent that the costs related to recovery of interest accrued on the deposit from the date of the misappropriation (*Case V123*)
- costs of opposing a neighbourhood development that would cause excessive dust and damage to the taxpayer's plant nursery (*Case W30*)
- costs of an accountant/trustee in defending a charge of conspiring with the debtor of an insolvent estate to defraud the Commonwealth (*Putnin*)
- cost of maintaining the amount of trust income to which the taxpayer was entitled under a will (ID 2004/214)
- costs incurred by a trustee company in defence of a writ served on a director of the trustee company (ID 2003/145)
- legal expenses incurred by an employee in recovering wages paid by a dishonoured cheque (TD 93/29) and travel and incidental expenses relating to a legal action to recover unpaid wages (ID 2004/659).

[FITR ¶33-810]

¶16-844 Examples of non-revenue legal expenses

In addition to the examples given at ¶16-840, the following are examples of legal expenses that have been held not to be deductible under the general provisions of ITAA97 s 8-1. Note, however, that some may be deductible under the more specific provisions noted at ¶16-830:

- where a taxpayer was issued with a PAYG director penalty notice in respect of his paid role as a (former) director of a liquidated company which ultimately resulted in legal and accounting expenses being incurred in bankruptcy annulment and proof of debt proceedings (*Healy*)
- reimbursement to a competitor of trade mark application expenses on agreeing to withdraw (10 CTBR *Case* 38; (1957) 8 TBRD *Case* H108)
- costs of settlement of breach of contract action, the result being that the taxpayer was free to reorganise its trading structure and method (*Foley Bros*)
- costs of settlement of legal action against a company director for trading while insolvent (*Duncan*), distinguished from *Day* as advantage sought was unrelated to maintaining employment (¶16-840)
- costs incurred in administering a class action settlement fund even though funds for distribution were held in an interest-bearing account (*Watson as trustee for the Murrindindi Bushfire Class Action Settlement Fund*)
- costs of defending the legal validity of a contract on the basis of which the viability of the taxpayer's business depended (*PBL Marketing Pty Ltd*)
- costs of defending a driving charge where the taxpayer's employment was conditional on holding a driver's licence (*Case Q99*)
- trustee's expenses of unsuccessful opposition to an action for the trustee's removal (3 TBRD *Case* C107)
- costs of eviction proceedings against a tenant whose term had expired (5 TBRD *Case* E50; *Case K7*)
- costs of action for damage done to a rent-producing property (2 TBRD *Case* B3)
- legal expenses incurred in seeking to regain employment by a policeman who was dismissed following a Police Integrity Commission inquiry (*Museth*) and costs of action for damages for wrongful dismissal (TD 93/29; TR 2012/8)
- costs of a company in resisting winding-up action by a dissident shareholder (14 TBRD *Case* P55) or dissident directors (8 TBRD *Case* H60)
- costs of a newspaper in defending acquisition of an interest in another newspaper (*John Fairfax and Sons*)
- costs of resisting land resumption and disputing the compensation amount (*Pye*)
- payments made by a solicitor suspended from practice to cover legal and investigation costs incurred by the Law Society where the payment was a prerequisite to resumption of practice (*Case V140*)
- costs incurred by a salesman in obtaining a restricted driver's licence to enable him to drive for business purposes during specified hours while his driver's licence was cancelled (*Case P54*)
- costs incurred by a public servant in connection with disciplinary and demotion proceedings that arose from his gambling activities (*Case W94*)
- costs incurred by an accountant convicted of stealing money from his employer (*Sobczuk*)
- employee's costs of defending an allegation of sexual harassment at work (ID 2002/664)
- an investor's expenses incurred in challenging the redemption of units he held in an investment fund (*Cachia*) or to stop a further share issue (ID 2007/136)

- legal expenses in relation to an ASIC investigation incurred by a company director who did not receive any director's fees or share of profits (ID 2003/801)
- costs incurred in seeking registration as a tax agent (*Case Y49*)
- professional footballer's legal costs in obtaining a release from his home league (*Kemp*)
- pharmaceutical company's legal costs incurred in trying to prevent competitors from gaining approval to market competing products (*Smithkline Beecham Laboratories (Australia)*)
- costs incurred by the owner of a shopping centre in seeking to overturn the rezoning of nearby land that would have allowed a larger shopping centre to be built (*Case 37/97*)
- costs of defending an action for misrepresentation of the value of goodwill of the business sold by the taxpayer (ID 2010/91).

[FITR ¶33-810]

¶16-845 Deductions for fines and breaches of law

Penalties or fines imposed, eg tax shortfall penalties, as a result of breaches of the law are specifically excluded from deduction (ITAA97 s 26-5). Even in the absence of this special rule, the courts have consistently held that penalties and fines are not deductible, either on the grounds of public policy or because their very nature severs them from the expenses of trading (*Herald and Weekly Times*; *Madad*; *Mayne Nickless*).

ATO guidance indicates professional footballers may deduct fines or penalties for on-field conduct and related legal expenses that result from their performance as a player and part of a football game. However, fines for off-field breaches of conduct are not deductible.

Fees for the late lodgment of documents by corporations under the corporations regulations and penalties for prescribed offences imposed under the Corporations law are ''penalties'' and therefore not deductible (TD 94/84). As to late payment of rates and land tax, see ¶16-870.

[FITR ¶68-120]

Tax-related Expenses

¶16-850 Deductions for tax-related expenses

A taxpayer can deduct expenditure to the extent it is incurred for: managing the taxpayer's income tax affairs; complying with an obligation imposed by a Commonwealth law in relation to the income tax affairs of an entity; the GIC, shortfall interest charge (SIC), or a GST instalment underestimation penalty; the major bank levy under the *Major Bank Levy Act 2017*; or obtaining valuations from the Commissioner for either gifts of property under Div 30 (¶16-940) or for market valuations of land that are subject to conservation covenants under Div 31 (¶16-972) (ITAA97 s 25-5). (The deduction is allowable in the income year in which the expenditure is incurred (¶16-040) and is available to all types of taxpayers, whether business taxpayers, salary or wage earners or investors. Recoupments of such expenses may be assessable (¶10-270).)

Examples of tax-related expenses that qualify for deduction are those incurred in connection with:

- having an income tax return, a BAS or an IAS prepared (which could include the cost of travelling to a recognised tax adviser for this purpose and other incidental costs such as the cost of accommodation, meals, taxi fares and travel insurance: TD 2017/8)
- obtaining tax advice and management of the taxpayer's tax affairs and compliance (*Falcetta*)
- lodging an income tax return electronically (TD 93/63)
- attending to an ATO audit
- objecting or appealing against an assessment or a determination of the Commissioner (eg court or tribunal fees)
- preparing a financial statement to support an application for an extension of time to pay tax
- the cost of attending a tax return preparation course (ID 2003/955)
- obtaining an exchange rate (ID 2004/856)
- obtaining valuations for various purposes under the consolidated group tax rules (TD 2003/10; TD 2003/11; TR 2004/2), or
- the superannuation supervisory levy payable by a superannuation fund, approved deposit fund or pooled superannuation trust. This is because it relates to the management or administration of the fund's tax affairs (TR 93/17).

Income tax affairs are matters relating to all income taxes and thus extend to PAYG withholding and PAYG instalments, as well as interest on overpayments, franking deficit tax and GIC (but not FBT, GST, trust recoupment tax or state taxes).

Fees or commissions paid for professional advice on income tax matters are deductible under s 25-5 only if the advice is provided by a recognised tax adviser (ie a registered tax agent, BAS agent, or tax (financial) adviser; or an enrolled legal practitioner).

Where a fixed fee of $250,000 was payable for the totality of services provided to the taxpayer in relation to the establishment of a superannuation fund and was neither calculated on a time basis nor as a percentage of the amount contributed to the fund, it was impossible to apportion the fee for tax advice provided and no part of the fee was deductible (*Harvey*).

The cost of obtaining income tax advice concerning the day-to-day running of a taxpayer's business may be deductible as an ordinary business expense. Thus, a deduction has been allowed for the cost of legal advice relating to liability for deducting withholding tax from payments made in the course of the taxpayer's business (*Cliffs International Inc*). There is no restriction in ITAA97 s 8-1, as there is in s 25-5, that the advice must be provided by a recognised tax adviser. For the deductibility of advice relating to business taxes such as FBT and GST, see ¶16-858.

The deduction under s 25-5 specifically extends to expenditure incurred in complying with an obligation imposed on the taxpayer in relation to the income tax affairs of *another* entity (eg costs incurred in complying with a request by the Commissioner for information concerning the income tax affairs of another taxpayer, or incurred as a public officer of a company or trust estate). The deduction would, therefore, apply to costs incurred by a taxpayer in relation to amounts subject to the PAYG withholding system and costs incurred in complying with a PAYG director penalty notice (¶26-100; *Falcetta*). The legal and accounting expenses in *Healy* were not incurred by the taxpayer and even if they were, they would not have been deductible because they related to the taxpayer's bankruptcy and proof of debt proceedings, and not a PAYG director penalty notice issued to him as a former director of a liquidated company.

In the case of a trust, only the trustee may claim a deduction for expenditure incurred in relation to the management or administration of the trust. However, any taxpayer (including a beneficiary or director of a corporate trustee) who incurs expenditure on complying with an obligation imposed on the taxpayer in relation to the affairs of the trust will be allowed a deduction for such expenditure (TD 94/91).

In some circumstances, payments made to a ''fighting fund'' for the purpose of funding litigation, negotiating a settlement outcome or otherwise managing an income tax dispute arising from an investment or scheme are deductible under s 25-5 (TD 2002/1).

Judgment debt interest imposed on a judgment debt for outstanding income tax liabilities is not deductible.

Although GIC and SIC are deductible under s 25-5, the tax shortfall and other administrative penalties are not deductible. A taxpayer does not ''incur'' a GIC liability on unpaid income tax debts until they are served with a notice of assessment triggering the liability to pay the income tax to which the GIC relates (*Nash*; see also ATO *Decision Impact Statement*). GIC accruing after the issue date of an income tax assessment is deductible on a daily basis. SIC is incurred in the income year in which the Commissioner gives a taxpayer a notice of amended assessment. This is the case even if the SIC liability is notified separately from the notice of amended assessment, or if the SIC is unpaid at the end of that year of income (eg because the due date for payment of the SIC falls in the next year of income) (TD 2012/2).

The use of a capital asset for managing a taxpayer's income tax affairs, or for complying with an obligation imposed by a Commonwealth law regarding the income tax affairs of an entity, is treated as being for the purpose of producing assessable income, unless a provision provides otherwise. This means, for example, that a taxpayer may be able to claim depreciation on their computer to the extent that it is used to prepare their income tax return (¶17-005).

Exclusions

The deduction under s 25-5 is *not* available in relation to:

- expenditure of a capital nature (¶16-854; *Healy*)
- payments of the tax itself (including payments under the PAYG system) or interest payments or borrowing costs incurred to finance such payments (¶16-856)
- penalties payable under a local or foreign law or amounts payable on conviction for an offence against such a law
- expenditure relating to the commission of an offence against a local or foreign law, eg costs incurred in the investigation of, or in defending a prosecution for, a tax-related offence, or
- expenditure which, by virtue of a provision of the tax law other than s 8-1, is not deductible under s 8-1 (eg entertainment expenditure).

Tax affairs of a deceased taxpayer

Expenditure incurred by a trustee in relation to the income tax affairs of a deceased taxpayer is deductible against the deceased's income in the return to the date of death (s 25-5(8)).

[FITR ¶34-050, ¶65-080ff]

¶16-854 Treatment of tax-related capital expenditure

Tax-related expenditure that is capital in nature (eg the cost of a computer to be used in complying with the taxpayer's tax obligations; cost of establishing a superannuation fund: *Drummond*) is not deductible (ITAA97 s 25-5). Such capital expenditure may be included in the cost base of an asset for CGT purposes (¶11-550).

Expenditure will not be taken to be expenditure of a capital nature merely because the income tax affairs to which the expenditure relates are of a capital nature (s 25-5(4)). Examples of the kind of expenditure to which this exclusion might apply are: expenditure incurred in applying for a private ruling on whether an item of property is depreciable; the costs of disputing whether expenditure associated with the establishment of a business are deductible; and fees paid for professional tax advice relating to the application of CGT to an asset.

Expenditure on acquiring property for use in the management of the taxpayer's income tax affairs is not deductible under s 25-5. However, any use made of property by a taxpayer for an income tax-related matter will be taken to be for the purpose of producing assessable income. This will enable depreciation to be claimed on property such as a computer used by a taxpayer in ascertaining or meeting his/her income tax obligations or, for example, a deduction to be claimed for the borrowing costs associated with the acquisition of an item of property used for a tax-related matter.

[FITR ¶65-080ff]

¶16-856 Deductions for payments of income tax

Payments of income tax are not deductible under ITAA97 s 25-5, nor are interest or borrowing costs incurred to finance such payments (ID 2010/160).

It has generally been accepted that interest on a loan taken out to pay personal income tax is not deductible under ITAA97 s 8-1 (eg *Case V48*). However, where a business taxpayer uses an overdraft to pay income tax or pays the tax out of a larger loan taken out to meet general business expenses, the ATO will not disallow that part of the interest on the overdraft or loan that is attributable to the payment of tax. Further, the Commissioner accepts that, where a business taxpayer borrows money to pay income tax, the interest incurred on those borrowings is deductible provided the borrowings are connected with the carrying on of the business (IT 2582; *Case 14/98*). Partners are not entitled to a deduction for interest on borrowings to pay personal income tax (TD 2000/24).

The shortfall interest charge and the GIC (¶29-510) payable in respect of late lodgments, late payments and underpayments, as well as for failure to make deductions under the PAYG system, are deductible under s 25-5. No deduction is available under either s 25-5 or s 8-1 for judgment debt interest levied in respect of the taxpayer's outstanding income tax liability under legislation governing the local court.

Where GIC that applies to an RBA deficit debt (¶24-300) is deductible, no deduction is also available for the corresponding GIC on tax debts that have been allocated to the RBA.

[FITR ¶65-080]

¶16-858 Deductibility of other taxes and related costs

Where a taxpayer is carrying on a business, the cost of preparing a payroll tax or land tax return is deductible under ITAA97 s 8-1. The cost of objecting or appealing against any resulting assessment is also deductible. The cost of obtaining professional advice on matters relating to these taxes would generally also be deductible. For example, in one case, a retail motor trader was allowed a deduction of nearly $500,000 in fees paid for advice and administrative work in connection with a sales tax minimisation scheme (*Jezareed*).

Payroll tax and other business taxes are allowable as business deductions where the requirements of s 8-1 are satisfied (¶16-010). For the deductibility of GST payments, see ¶16-860. Where, under the Western Australian payroll tax legislation, the tax became payable when the wages were paid, payroll tax was incurred as a deduction in that year, despite the fact that no payroll tax return was lodged or payroll tax paid until a default assessment was issued some years later (*Layala Enterprises*).

Where the requirements of s 8-1 are satisfied (¶16-010), a deduction is also available for taxes and levies incurred in carrying on a business such as excise duty (ID 2004/277; ID 2004/278); wine equalisation tax, and luxury car tax incurred by a car dealer (ID 2005/99); and stamp duty associated with revenue transactions; land tax (¶16-870). A deduction is available to mining companies for state royalties, crude oil excise, resource rent royalties, the petroleum resource rent tax (¶19-003).

Payments of FBT are also deductible. FBT is incurred by an employer at the end of the FBT year and FBT instalments are incurred when the liability to pay them arises (¶35-000, ¶35-050). For the 2019–20 income tax year, most employers can claim a deduction for:

- the amount of the actual FBT liability for the FBT year ending 31 March 2020, *plus*
- the June 2020 quarter FBT instalment, *less*
- the June 2019 quarter FBT instalment.

A monthly pro rata basis applies in the case of employers with substituted accounting periods (TR 95/24). The ATO accepts that where a taxpayer is carrying on a business, the cost of preparing an FBT return is deductible, as is the cost of providing the fringe benefits (¶16-520).

The superannuation supervisory levy is deductible as a tax-related expense (¶16-850) but late lodgment charges and late payment penalties are not deductible (ITAA97 ss 26-5; 26-90; ¶13-870). Deductions are not allowable in respect of a charge imposed under the superannuation guarantee scheme although a temporary amnesty permits certain deductions (ITAA97 s 26-95; ¶39-500). Deductions are also not allowable in respect of the excess non-concessional contribution tax (ITAA97 s 26-75), Division 293 tax (ITAA97 s 26-95) or excess transfer balance tax (ITAA97 s 26-99).

[FITR ¶34-060, ¶34-070]

¶16-860 Effect of GST on deductions

The special provisions dealing with the interaction of the GST and the calculation of deductions (¶34-000) have the following effect (ITAA97 ss 27-1 to 27-35).

(1) No deduction is available for the GST component of a loss or outgoing to the extent that the taxpayer is entitled to an input tax credit for the acquisition or to a decreasing adjustment of GST to allow a greater input tax credit for the acquisition.

▶ Example 1

In June, Ron acquires materials for $11,000 solely for use in his business, and not for use in making input taxed supplies. The supply of materials to Ron is a taxable supply. He is entitled to an input tax credit of $1,000. His deduction in Year 1 for the cost of the materials is $10,000 (not $11,000). If the price increases to $11,550 in July due to late payment, the additional consideration of $550 is deductible in Year 2. The correct input tax credit is $1,050 (ie 1/11th of $11,550). Ron therefore has a decreasing adjustment of $50. His deduction in Year 2 is $500.

(2) A deduction is available for increasing adjustments of GST (ie reductions in input tax credits) that are due to changes in the creditable purpose of the acquisition (other than for adjustments relating to an increased use of the item for private or domestic purposes).

▶ Example 2

Ron buys an asset to be used to the extent of 40% for private purposes and 60% for business purposes. The asset costs $6,600, including $600 GST. He is entitled to an input tax credit of 60% of $600, ie $360. His deductions for the asset are reduced by $360. If he actually uses the asset 50% privately, the input tax credit should have been 50% of $600, ie $300. The increasing adjustment is $60. However, as the increasing adjustment is attributable to an increased private or domestic use of the asset, there is no deduction for the increasing adjustment.

(3) A deduction is available for increasing adjustments of GST on cessation of the entity's GST registration provided the asset is held, immediately after the cancellation, for income-producing purposes.

▶ **Example 3**

If Ron cancels his GST registration and the GST inclusive market value of his materials is now $5,500, the amount of the increasing adjustment is 1/11th of $5,500, ie $500. Because the asset has lost value, the deduction is less than the original reduction in deductions on account of the input tax credit (under (1) above).

(4) GST is excluded from amounts taken into account in calculating deductions (eg where a deductible amount is calculated by subtracting amounts received or receivable from amounts paid or payable). GST payable and increasing adjustments are excluded from amounts received or receivable, and amounts corresponding to input tax credits and decreasing adjustments are excluded from amounts paid or payable.

▶ **Example 4**

As part of his business of buying and selling residential and commercial properties, Joseph buys an office block for $330,000. GST payable is $30,000 and his input tax credit is $30,000. He sells the office block for $308,000 and the GST payable on the sale is $28,000. Joseph is entitled to a loss on the sale of $20,000, ie $300,000 (purchase price excluding input tax credit) – $280,000 (sale price excluding GST).

(5) No deduction is available for payments to the Commonwealth of the net amount of GST payable for a tax period on the taxpayer's taxable supplies (other than for wine equalisation tax or luxury car tax included in a net amount) or of the GST payable on the taxpayer's taxable importations, to the extent that the taxpayer is entitled to an input tax credit for the importation.

[FITR ¶69-000ff]

Rates and Land Tax

¶16-870 Deductions for rates and land tax

Rates and taxes incurred in respect of income-producing premises or land may be deductible as a normal business expense under ITAA97 s 8-1. If the land or premises is used partly for income-producing purposes and partly for other purposes, the deduction must be apportioned. Where part of the home is used as a place of business (and not merely as a "study"), a deduction for rates and taxes in respect of that part may be allowed (¶16-480). The deduction applies to municipal, city council and shire rates, water, sewerage and drainage rates, and land tax. Recoupments of rates and taxes may be assessable (¶10-270).

Land tax is imposed according to the use of the premises at a particular date (eg 31 December), and so may be fully deductible even though the premises later cease to be income-producing part-way through the year. The deduction applies in the income year in which the rates or land tax are "incurred" (eg when the liability to pay them arises: ¶16-040), even if they are not actually paid during that year. Interest paid on the late payment of council rates may be deductible as it is an administrative charge rather than a penalty (ATO publication *Rental properties 2020*). However, the penalty on land tax arrears is not deductible (ITAA97 s 26-5).

As is the case with interest (*Steele*: ¶16-740), it is not necessary that the expenses should actually produce assessable income in the same year in which they are incurred.

A similar argument may suggest that a vacancy levy imposed on foreign owners of vacant residential property may be deductible under ITAA97 s 8-1. However, the ATO may take a view that as the levy is imposed for a property that is vacant or not genuinely available for rent, it is not incurred in gaining or producing assessable income or is capital in nature.

The High Court has held that an adjustment paid by the purchaser to the vendor on settlement of the purchase of a block of rent-producing flats representing the unexpired portion of municipal and water rates was deductible (*Morgan*).

For the deductibility of annual rates and land taxes to entities receiving mutual income (eg clubs or professional associations), see ¶3-830 and TR 2015/3.

[FITR ¶34-080, ¶34-110]

Losses

¶16-880 What is a tax loss?

A tax loss incurred in one income year may be carried forward and deducted in arriving at the taxpayer's taxable income of succeeding income years.

Domestic losses incurred in 1989–90 and later years may be carried forward indefinitely until absorbed (ITAA97 Div 36: ss 36-1 to 36-55; ¶16-895). From 1 July 2008, foreign losses are no longer quarantined into separate classes or from domestic assessable income. As such, deductions and prior-year losses that are applied to reduce a taxpayer's assessable income may include both a foreign and domestic component (¶21-800). TA 2008/18 deals with arrangements to shift foreign business losses into Australian branches or resident entities.

For the special rules that apply to losses from non-commercial business activities, see ¶16-020.

Calculation of loss

A loss is incurred in any income year if the taxpayer's allowable deductions — other than any unrecouped losses brought forward from an earlier year — exceed the assessable income and the net exempt income (if any) of the year. The amount of the loss is the amount of the excess (s 36-10). Allowable deductions cover business deductions, tax-related expenses (¶16-850) and most special incentive deductions, but not the deductions noted below.

▶ Example 1

In Year 1, Jo incurred a loss of $1,000. In Year 2, her assessable income was $5,000. She had no exempt income. Her allowable deductions amounted to $7,500. Her tax loss for Year 2 is $2,500 (ie $5,000 – $7,500). The loss of $1,000 incurred in Year 1 is not taken into account in determining the extent of the loss incurred in Year 2.

Where a company has excess franking offsets for an income year, they are treated as tax losses to be utilised in future years (s 36-55; ¶3-075).

"Net exempt income"

''Net exempt income'' in relation to a resident taxpayer is the excess of exempt income from all sources, whether in or out of Australia, over the sum of: (a) non-capital expenses incurred in deriving that income; and (b) any foreign tax on that income (s 36-20).

In the case of a non-resident, net exempt income means the excess of: (a) the exempt income derived from Australian sources and film income exempt under ITAA36 s 26AG; over (b) the non-capital expenditure incurred in gaining that income and foreign taxes on the film income.

''Exempt income'' (¶10-600) does not include amounts of ''non-assessable non-exempt income'' that are listed at ¶10-895.

If a taxpayer has a net exempt loss for a year of income, that loss cannot be carried forward to a future year but is lost (*The Trustee for the Payne Superannuation Fund*).

Certain deductions disregarded in calculating loss

A tax loss cannot be produced or increased by the deductions allowable under the following provisions (ITAA97 s 26-55):

- ITAA97 Divs 30 and 31 — gifts and conservation covenants (¶16-940 and following)
- ITAA97 s 25-50 — pensions, gratuities or retiring allowances (¶16-540)
- ITAA97 s 290-150 — personal contributions to superannuation funds (¶13-730).

If an amount that is deductible under one of those provisions is also allowable under another provision (eg ITAA97 s 8-1), assuming that the no double deduction provisions of ITAA97 s 8-10 did not apply, that amount can contribute to a carry-forward loss. If the taxpayer already has prior year losses, then the specified deductions must be taken into account first (IT 2422).

▶ Example 2

Assessable income	$10,000
Business deductions	9,900
	100
Gifts $250 but deduction limited under s 26-55 to	100
Balance	nil

Taxable income is nil and there is no loss to be carried forward.

If, instead of business deductions of $9,900, the taxpayer had a prior year loss of $9,900, the gift deduction of $250 would be allowable in full. The amount of $9,750 (ie $10,000 – $250) of the $9,900 prior year loss would be deductible, leaving the remaining unrecouped prior year loss of $150 to be carried forward to subsequent years.

[FITR ¶68-400, ¶85-000ff]

¶16-895 Carrying forward prior year losses

In general, the procedures for carrying forward a loss are automatic and do not allow a taxpayer to elect the year or years in which to deduct a prior year loss; losses must be carried forward one year at a time until exhausted (*Case W52*). However, *companies* can choose the amount of prior year losses they utilise in an income year (¶3-060).

In general, prior year losses are personal to the taxpayer who incurs them and are neither lost, for example by sale of the taxpayer's business, nor transferable to another (*Case 52/96*). For example, if a sole trader who has past tax losses from a bakery business sells that business, the purchaser cannot utilise the vendor's losses but the vendor can continue to claim them. The pre-incorporation losses of an association cannot be claimed after it is incorporated as the unincorporated association and the company are different entities (ID 2004/811). Special rules apply to company groups under the consolidation rules (¶8-100) and under the group loss transfer rules that apply in limited circumstances (¶3-090).

Where a loss is brought forward, it must first be offset against any "net exempt income" (¶16-880) and then against any assessable income remaining after all current year deductions are allowed (ITAA97 Div 36: ss 36-1 to 36-55). If, in the year of recoupment, the deductions exceed the total assessable income, that excess is subtracted from the net exempt income and the tax loss is deducted from any net exempt income which remains.

▶ Example 1

Ian incurred a loss of $7,000 in Year 1. In Year 2 he has assessable business income ($18,000), allowable business deductions ($13,000) and net exempt income ($300). His Year 1 loss brought forward is offset as to $300 against the net exempt income and as to $5,000 against the taxable income of $5,000 ($18,000 – $13,000). The Year 1 loss unrecouped as at the end of Year 2 ($7,000 – $5,300), ie $1,700, may be carried forward for deduction against income of Year 3 and so on.

▶ Example 2

In Year 1, Lisa incurs a loss of $7,000. In Year 2, Lisa has assessable income ($20,000), allowable business deductions ($23,000) and net exempt income ($15,000). The excess of deductions over assessable income ($3,000) is subtracted from net exempt income, resulting in a balance of $12,000. The tax loss from Year 1 is deducted from that balance, reducing it to $5,000. The tax loss is now exhausted. See also ID 2004/810.

If, in the year of recoupment, there is no net exempt income, the tax loss carried forward from a previous year is simply deducted from the excess of assessable income over the current year deductions.

▶ Example 3

Lee has a loss of $25,000 in Year 1. In Year 2, his total assessable income is $20,000 and deductions (other than for the tax loss) are $3,000, thus resulting in an excess of $17,000. As there is no net exempt income in Year 2, the $25,000 is carried forward so as to reduce the amount of $17,000 to nil. The balance of the loss ($8,000) is available to be carried forward to Year 3 or subsequent income years.

If there are 2 or more losses, they are deductible in the order in which they were incurred (s 36-15(5)).

Where a commercial debt is forgiven, the debtor's losses may be reduced under the rules discussed at ¶16-910.

Other special loss rules

A company cannot carry forward losses unless it satisfies either the ''continuity of ownership'' test or the ''business continuity'' test (¶3-105, ¶3-120). Companies can temporarily carry back losses against previously taxed profits (¶3-080). When calculating a qualifying shipping company's losses, 90% of the net exempt income is disregarded (ITAA97 ss 36-10(5); 36-17(4A)).

Strict rules apply to trust losses (¶6-262) and partnership losses are deductible to the partners (¶5-110). Primary production losses are treated as general losses and governed by ITAA97 Div 36 (¶16-880), although pre-1989–90 losses may be carried forward until absorbed (ITTPA s 36-110). Special rules apply for capital losses (¶11-040) and tax-exempt entities that become taxable (¶10-630).

Effects of bankruptcy

Losses incurred before a taxpayer's bankruptcy or release from debts cannot be carried forward (s 36-30; *Case 36/97*), although they may be recouped to a certain extent if debts taken into account in calculating such a loss are voluntarily paid (ss 36-40; 36-45; TD 93/10).

Where a taxpayer's bankruptcy is annulled under *Bankruptcy Act 1966*, s 74 because the creditors have accepted a proposal for a composition or scheme of arrangement and the taxpayer has been, or can be, released from certain debts from which he/she would have been released on discharge of the bankruptcy, then the taxpayer will be denied deductions for revenue losses incurred before becoming bankrupt (s 36-35). The deduction is only denied in years after the income year in which the taxpayer became bankrupt. These provisions do not apply where the annulment is due to the payment of debts in full.

[FITR ¶85-000ff]

Commercial Debt Forgiveness

¶16-910 Commercial debt forgiveness

The commercial debt forgiveness rules broadly apply where a creditor forgives a commercial debt owing by a debtor (ITAA97 Div 245 comprising ss 245-1 to 245-265 which replaced the pre-2010/11 rules in former ITAA36 Sch 2C Div 245). These special rules apply to remedy the effective duplication of tax deductions that would otherwise arise from the forgiveness of commercial debt. Duplication could occur because, while a creditor may be entitled to a tax deduction or a capital loss when a debt is forgiven, the debtor, though relieved of the liability to repay the debt, is not assessed on any gain and could continue to claim deductions for accumulated revenue and capital losses and other undeducted expenditure. Division 245 of ITAA97 treats the ''net forgiven amount'' of a commercial debt as having been used to generate the deductions that would otherwise be available to the debtor. Duplication of deductions is eliminated by applying the net forgiven amount to reduce the deductions in the following order:

(1) deductible revenue losses (s 245-115)

(2) deductible net capital losses of the income years before the forgiveness year (s 245-130)

(3) a wide range of deductible expenditure, such as expenditure relating to depreciating assets, R&D, Australian films and capital works (s 245-145). Special rules apply to the reduction of deductible expenditure (see below), and

(4) the cost bases of certain CGT assets (ss 245-175 to 245-190).

Within each of the above 4 classes of deductible amounts, the debtor can choose the relevant loss, item of expenditure or asset against which the net forgiven amount is to be applied and the amount to be applied, but the net forgiven amount must be applied to the maximum extent possible within each class. Any part of the net forgiven amount which remains after being applied against all available deductible amounts is disregarded, except where the debtor is a partnership, in which case the residual amount is applied against the reducible amounts of the partners (ss 245-195; 245-215). A debtor under Div 245 includes a person acting in the capacity of a trustee of a trust estate in respect of the trust estate's debts.

What constitutes a ''debt'' is not affected by the debt/equity rules (ID 2004/377).

Division 245 applies to more than the conventional release or waiver type of forgiveness; it extends to a number of specific circumstances (such as debt parking and some debt-for-equity swaps) in which a forgiveness will be deemed to have occurred (ss 245-35 to 245-45). On the other hand, a forgiveness effected under a bankruptcy law, by will, or for reasons of love and affection (if creditor is a natural person: *Draft* TD 2019/D9), is excluded (s 245-40). The payment of a debt by a guarantor does not constitute the forgiveness of the debt (TD 2004/17).

The waiver of a debt constituting a fringe benefit (¶35-270) is disregarded for the purposes of the Division (s 245-40) as is a debt that is included in a taxpayer's assessable income, for example as a deemed dividend (¶4-200).

For the application of the provisions to the forgiveness by a life insurance company of an agency development loan made to an insurance agent, see TR 2001/9.

For the interaction of the commercial debt forgiveness rules and the company loss rules, see ID 2004/981, ID 2005/12, ID 2005/13, and ID 2005/30. The application of the debt forgiveness rules to an entity leaving a consolidated group is considered in ID 2005/244.

Commercial debt

A debt falls within the rules in Div 245 if the whole or any part of the interest payable on the debt is, was, or will be an allowable deduction to the debtor (eg ID 2007/137). Division 245 also catches debts in respect of which interest would have been deductible except for the operation of a provision — other than ITAA97 s 8-1 — which prevents a deduction that would otherwise be allowable (s 245-10). The thin capitalisation rules (¶22-700) and ITAA97 s 26-26 (distribution on a non-share equity interest) are examples of such a provision.

Where interest is not payable on a debt, the debt will be subject to the rules where, had interest been charged, it would have been deductible. Shares will be treated as a commercial debt of the issuing company if dividends payable on the shares are equivalent to interest on a loan (s 245-15). See also ID 2012/25.

Net forgiven amount

The amount that a debtor must apply against its deductible amounts is called the ‘‘net forgiven amount’’. To determine this amount a debtor must:

- calculate the value of the debt. The generally applicable rules for doing this are contained in s 245-55 (eg see *Tasman Group Services*; ID 2011/22); separate rules apply when the debt forgiven is a non-recourse debt (s 245-60; ID 2007/167; ID 2007/168) or parked debt (s 245-61)

- calculate what (if any) consideration was given for the forgiveness (s 245-65). Again, different rules apply to different kinds of debt

- subtract the consideration from the value of the debt to arrive at the gross forgiven amount of the debt. If the value is equal to or less than the consideration, Div 245 will not apply (s 245-75), and

- finally, reduce the gross forgiven amount by certain amounts that, as a result of the forgiveness, will be taken into account in arriving at the debtor's taxable income. For example, a forgiveness could result in the cost base of an asset being reduced (s 245-85). However, if a creditor forgives a commercial debt under a settlement agreement, and also pays the debtor an additional amount under that agreement which is included in the debtor's assessable income, the additional amount does not reduced the gross forgiven amount (ID 2014/33).

Where there is a forgiveness of an intra-group debt, ie a debt owed by one company to another company under common ownership, the debtor company can avoid the reduction of its own reducible amounts if the creditor company agrees to forgo an equivalent amount of its entitlement to a capital loss or bad debt deduction (s 245-90).

Method of reduction of deductible expenditure

The manner in which an item of deductible expenditure is reduced by a net forgiven amount depends on whether the prime cost or diminishing value method is used to calculate deductions in relation to the relevant expenditure (ss 245-155; 245-157; ¶17-510, ¶17-640, ¶17-670).

Where the expenditure reduced by a net forgiven amount is incurred under a provision that disallows previous deductions where the expenditure is recouped, the reduction amount is included in the debtor's assessable income in the recoupment year (s 245-160).

Record-keeping

Division 245 contains record-keeping obligations in relation to information relevant to a taxpayer incurring a commercial debt, and in the case of a company, the cessation of common ownership (s 245-265).

Gifts

¶16-940 Concessional deduction for gifts

Gifts made as part of a business, eg for publicity purposes, may qualify for deduction as normal business expenses in certain circumstances (¶16-440). Gifts provided by a business taxpayer to current or former clients for the purpose of generating future assessable income are deductible, unless they constitute the provision of entertainment (¶16-390) or are bribes to a foreign or public official (¶16-152): TD 2016/14.

Alternatively, a concessional, or ''personal'', deduction is allowed for certain gifts that do not necessarily have any connection with a business or income-earning activities.

In the following commentary on the concessional gifts deduction, all legislative references are to ITAA97 unless otherwise indicated.

¶16-942 Gifts of $2 or more deductible

Every person, whether an individual, the trustee of a trust estate or superannuation fund, a partnership or a company, and whether a resident or non-resident of Australia, is entitled to a deduction from assessable income for individual gifts of money or property of $2 or more made during the year to nominated funds (including private ancillary funds), authorities, institutions or bodies or classes of them, or specified persons (Div 30: ss 30-1 to 30-320). A deduction is also allowed for gifts of publicly listed shares that have been held for at least 12 months and which are valued at $5,000 or less. However, a deduction is generally not available unless the recipient is registered with the ACNC Commissioner or specifically listed by name in ITAA97 or its regulations (see below).

The deduction is subject to the following conditions:

(1) the gift must not be made by will (however, testamentary gifts of property are exempt from CGT: ¶11-670)

(2) each gift must be of $2 or more. The gift may be of money, or property other than money, eg shares, land or personal property

(3) if property other than money is given, the property must either have been purchased by the person making the gift during the 12 months before the gift is made or be valued by the Commissioner at more than $5,000, and

(4) the recipient of the gift must normally be in Australia (including Norfolk, Cocos (Keeling) and Christmas Islands). For an exception, see ¶16-955.

The general conditions above no longer apply to gifts or contributions to political parties, see ¶16-950.

For the rules applying to gifts of works of art, gifts of national heritage properties or gifts of trading stock, see ¶16-965 and following.

The deduction may be withdrawn where the gift is made under certain types of schemes designed to exploit the gift deduction provisions (¶16-975).

There are 2 main categories of recipients: those that fall within the approved general categories (¶16-950), including overseas aid funds, cultural organisations and environmental organisations; and those that are specifically identified in ITAA97 (¶16-952), including funds which are private ancillary funds (¶16-962).

Value of gifts of property

Where the gift is property purchased within the previous 12 months, the amount deductible is the lesser of the cost price of the property and its market value at the time it is given. Where the property was not purchased within the previous 12 months and is valued at more than $5,000, the amount deductible is the value of the property as determined by the Commissioner. Requests for valuation must be made in writing on a form approved by the Commissioner and lodged with the Australian Valuation Office. The valuation fee is tax-deductible (s 25-5).

Spreading of deductions

In general, deductions for gifts cannot give rise to a tax loss (s 26-55; ¶16-880). However, deductions for certain gifts can be spread, in instalments chosen by the taxpayer, over a period of up to 5 years. This applies to gifts to cultural organisations (¶16-965), gifts to environmental organisations (¶16-960), gifts to heritage organisations (¶16-967), gifts of property valued by the Commissioner at over $5,000 (see above), grants of conservation covenants (¶16-972) and gifts of cash to deductible gift recipients.

Registration of recipients

A taxpayer cannot obtain a tax deduction for a gift to a fund, authority or institution covered by item 1, 2 or 4 of the table in s 30-15, unless the recipient is: (i) registered by the Australian Charities and Not-for-profit Commission (ACNC) (¶10-610) and endorsed by the Commissioner under Subdiv 30-BA (s 30-120); or (ii) is specifically listed by name in the ITAA97 or its regulations as eligible to receive deductible gifts (s 30-17). The ACNC Register is available on the ACNC website (www.acnc.gov.au), and the procedural rules relating to endorsement (including the Commissioner's power to revoke an endorsement) commence at TAA 1953 Sch 1 s 426-15.

To be endorsed under Subdiv 30-BA, the recipient must have an Australian Business Number (¶33-100) and meet certain conditions set out in s 30-125. For example, in *Cancer and Bowel Research Association Inc*, the AAT held that a deductible gift recipient's endorsement should be retrospectively revoked because its trust deed did not comply with the s 30-125(6) condition requiring surplus assets to be transferred to another eligible recipient if it were wound up or disendorsed. The Full Federal Court held that the Commissioner's power to retrospectively revoke an entity's endorsement (in TAA 1953 Sch 1 s 426-55) was dependent on the entity not being entitled to endorsement on the date the revocation decision was made (*Cancer and Bowel Research Association Inc* (Full Fed Ct)).

Substantiation

Gifts are not subject to the formal substantiation requirements (¶16-210), but donors must be able to produce supporting evidence, if required. Typically, this will consist of a receipt. If a deductible gift recipient (DGR) issues a receipt, its name, ABN, and the fact that the contribution was a gift or related to certain fund-raising events, must be specified (s 30-228). The Commissioner may revoke a DGR's endorsement if receipts are issued that do not comply with these requirements (TAA 1953 Sch 1 s 426-55).

Where there is a workplace-giving program, the employee-donors will need to receive confirmation from the employer of the details of the gift. This may be a written or electronic communication or, where the gift deduction has been reflected in PAYG deductions, in the PAYG Payment Summary (PS LA 2002/15).

The Commissioner may accept itemised mobile phone invoices to substantiate deduction claims for certain gifts via SMS to the United Nation's Children Fund (CR 2014/5), the World Wide Fund for Nature (CR 2014/13), and Vision Australia Ltd (CR 2014/15); evidence on a bank or credit card statement of gifts made using a Donation Point Tap EFTPOS terminal is also acceptable to substantiate a deduction (CR 2017/14).

[FITR ¶74-000]

¶16-945 What constitutes a "gift"?

A transfer of property will constitute a ''gift'' if the property was transferred voluntarily and no advantage of a material character was received by the taxpayer in return (TR 2005/13). Thus, a payment by a parent to a school building fund, pursuant to an arrangement whereby the parent received a reduction in the amount of fees to be paid in respect of the child attending the school, was not a gift (*McPhail*). A contribution to an overseas aid fund that enabled the taxpayer to participate in an aid project and which funded his airfare and accommodation was also not a gift (*Hodges*). The cost of attending a fundraising function is not deductible if a material benefit, such as a meal, is received (but see also ¶16-977). However, it will be deductible if only something of insubstantial value, such as a plastic lapel badge or a sticker, is received. In the *Individual tax return instructions*, the Commissioner states that a deduction cannot be claimed for a donation if something was received for it, such as a pen, raffle ticket, dinner or reduction in your child's school fees.

A gift must also be voluntary. In *Cyprus Mines Corporation*, a mining company, under the terms of an agreement with a state government, was permitted to make a donation to a prescribed authority within the gift provisions instead of paying mining royalties to that state. It was held that the donation was not deductible as a gift since it could not be said that the payment was voluntary or that no advantage of a material character had been received by the company in return for it. It was also held that the donation was not allowable as a business deduction. Similarly, in *Case 3/2000* a payment to a charity by an associate of the purchaser of land was not a gift as: (i) the payment was made pursuant to a contractual obligation; and (ii) the purchaser obtained the benefit of being relieved of the obligation to make the payment itself.

Donations to a football club or any other third party will not be made tax-deductible simply by channelling them through the Australian Sports Foundation (ASF) (a specified recipient). Where the donor insists, or the ASF guarantees, that a donation will necessarily be applied to a particular beneficiary, then the donation will not be tax-deductible (*Klopper*).

A gift of services is not deductible under Div 30. Expenditure incurred by a taxpayer in undertaking unpaid work for a charitable organisation is not deductible as a gift. Thus, no deduction was allowed for the cost of travel and postage incurred by a taxpayer while engaged in fundraising and associated activities for a charitable association (*Case S43*).

A motive of benefaction on the part of the donor is also an essential element of a gift (*Leary*). This does not have to be the sole motive — the fact that the donor is also motivated by the desire to obtain a tax deduction cannot, of itself, disentitle the donor to the deduction (*Coppleson*).

[FITR ¶74-002]

¶16-950 General categories of gift recipients

Gifts of $2 or more to the organisations, institutions, funds, etc, listed below are deductible, subject to the qualifications mentioned at ¶16-942 and, particularly, the requirement that the recipient of the gift be a charity, fund, organisation or authority in Australia. This normally requires that the institution be established and operated in Australia (TR 2019/6; ¶10-604).

A gift may be used by the recipient for any purpose within the scope of the objects for which it is established, except where there is an express requirement or limitation as to the use to which a gift may be put (TR 95/27). The meaning of ''charity'' has been extended by legislation (¶10-605).

Eligible recipients

(1) Public or non-profit **hospitals** (s 30-20).

(2) **Public benevolent institutions** (PBIs) (s 30-45), ie a charitable institution with a main purpose of providing benevolent relief targeted to people in need, and not to the broader general community. Detailed guidelines are in the ACNC Commissioner's Interpretation Statement on the meaning of a PBI (CIS 2016/03).

An organisation whose principal activity was to raise funds to be used by other members of a worldwide project aimed at relieving hunger was a public benevolent institution. There was no requirement that a PBI needs to engage directly in the activities making up the object of its benevolence (*The Hunger Project Australia*).

An organisation that provides general advice, information, research and advocacy services to a whole or part of a community is unlikely to be a PBI but may be so where the benevolence is targeted at a community where the vast majority are people in need, eg a community nutritional advice organisation (*Vibrational Individuation Programme*). A government entity (CIS 2016/01) cannot be a registered PBI as it is not a ''charity''. However, a land council set up under legislation to manage Aboriginal lands, with only very limited ministerial control, was a PBI (*Northern Land Council*). Mere funds are not ''institutions'' and therefore cannot qualify under this head, though they may qualify under other heads set out below (*Trustees of the Indigenous Barristers' Trust*). Donations of $2 or more made by landlords to an endorsed PBI participating in the affordable housing initiative noted in CR 2016/42 are deductible.

(3) Public funds established before 23 October 1963 to **provide money for hospitals or institutions** in (1) or (2), or public funds established to **relieve the necessitous circumstances** of one or more individuals in Australia (ss 30-20; 30-45). For the Commissioner's views on necessitous circumstances funds, see TR 2000/9. In *Trustees of the Indigenous Barristers' Trust*, it was held that necessitous circumstances were not restricted to poverty and extended to the special disadvantages suffered by indigenous people, but the ATO does not accept that interpretation.

(4) Public funds providing money to approved voluntary **marriage guidance** organisations (s 30-70).

(5) Public authorities or institutions engaged in research into the **cause, prevention or cure of disease** in human beings, animals or plants; and charitable institutions whose principal activity is to promote the prevention or control of human diseases (s 30-20; ACNC *Commissioner's Interpretation Statement* CIS 2015/01). In *Study and Prevention of Psychological Diseases Foundation*, an organisation unsuccessfully claimed that it undertook research, and tried and tested its research findings by conducting programs to promote psychological disease prevention. Instead, the organisation's activities were conducted for the members' personal benefit and it was not a charitable institution. A similar outcome befell a foundation whose stated activities focused on dissemination and funding of research into adverse health consequences of exposure to excessive noise and vibration but was found to be primarily responding to requests from people claiming to be affected by noise exposure (*Waubra Foundation*).

(6) Public funds or institutions maintained for the comfort, recreation or welfare of British Commonwealth or Allied **Armed Forces** (s 30-50).

(7) Public funds providing money for buildings used or to be used as government, semi-government or private non-profit **schools or colleges** (s 30-25). This has been held not to cover a fund to raise money to improve and equip a school oval (*Cobb & Co Ltd*). However, the ATO may accept that enclosed buildings, which are used for sporting or gymnasium purposes (including swimming pools), may be treated as part of a school building complex where it has been shown that a comprehensive physical education program forms an integral part of the school's curriculum. A ''voluntary'' donation to a school building fund as an alternative to an increase in school fees will not be allowable as a gift deduction (*McPhail*, noted at ¶16-945). Similarly, compulsory school enrolment fees paid or transferred to a school building fund and payments to a school building fund that result in a benefit to the payer are considered not to be deductible (TD 93/57; TD 2004/7).

To qualify for deductible gift recipient status, the school building fund should be established by trust deed or other written declaration of trust (ID 2013/60; ID 2013/61; ID 2013/62). Detailed guidelines on the requirements that the Commissioner considers must be satisfied in order for a fund to qualify as a school building fund are set out in TR 2013/2.

(8) **Public universities** or public funds for the establishment of public universities (s 30-25).

(9) **Residential educational institutions** affiliated with a public university or established by the Commonwealth (s 30-25).

(10) **Public libraries, public museums and public art galleries** or an institution consisting of any 2 of these categories (s 30-100). A public library, public museum or public art gallery is expected to have the following features: (a) it is an institution whose collection is made available to the public; (b) it is owned or controlled by a government or quasi-government authority, or by persons or an institution having a degree of responsibility to the public; and (c) it is constituted and recognised as a library, museum or art gallery and it conducts itself in ways that are consistent with such a character (TR 2000/10).

(11) Approved **scientific research** institutes (s 30-40).

(12) The Commonwealth or a state, where the gift is for **defence** purposes (s 30-50).

(13) **Environmental organisations** entered on the Register of Environmental Organisations (s 30-55; ¶16-960).

(14) Institutions certified by the Education Minister as **technical and further education institutions**, where the gift is made for purposes or facilities (including residential accommodation) that have been certified as relating to tertiary education (s 30-30).

(15) **Higher education institutions** and affiliated residential educational institutions (s 30-25).

(16) Public funds established and maintained exclusively for the purpose of providing **religious instruction** in government schools in Australia. Deductions are also available for gifts to the Council for Christian Education in Schools, the Council for Jewish Education in Schools and to public funds established and maintained by a Roman Catholic archdiocesan or diocesan authority exclusively for the purpose of providing religious instruction in government schools in Australia. Public funds established and maintained solely for the purpose of providing ethics education in Australian government schools as an alternative to religious instruction may also qualify as eligible recipients (s 30-25).

(17) Non-profit public building funds for hostels that provide residential **accommodation for school students** from rural areas (ss 30-25; 30-35).

(18) Certain **overseas aid funds** (s 30-80; ¶16-955).

(19) **Cultural organisations** entered on the Register of Cultural Organisations (s 30-100; ¶16-957).

(20) Public funds (and prescribed private funds) established by **will or trust instrument** devoted exclusively to providing money, property or benefits to or for any of the funds, authorities or institutions referred to above, or to establishing any of those funds, authorities or institutions (s 30-15).

(21) Contributions of money (or property purchased in the 12 months before the contribution was made), including membership subscriptions (TD 92/114), made by individuals (not in the course of carrying on a business) to a registered **political party** under Pt XI of the *Commonwealth Electoral Act 1918* up to a maximum of

$1,500 in a year of income (ss 30-242; 30-243(3)) and to an **independent candidate** for a state or territory election or to an **independent member** of a parliament or legislative assembly, also up to a maximum of $1,500 in a year of income.

(22) Registered tax-exempt **harm prevention** charities whose principal activity is ''the promotion of the prevention or the control of behaviour that is harmful or abusive to human beings'' (s 30-45). This behaviour may be emotional, sexual, substance or physical abuse, suicide, self-harm or harmful gambling.

(23) **Public ambulance services** and public funds established and maintained for the purpose of providing money for the provision of public ambulance services (s 30-20).

(24) State and territory **coordinating bodies for fire and emergency services** (s 30-102). This has been extended to volunteer fire services.

(25) Government schools providing **special education for students with permanent disabilities** (s 30-25).

(26) Public funds established and maintained for the reconstruction or critical repair of a **damaged war memorial**.

(27) Public funds established and maintained by a public benevolent institution solely to provide money to assist persons in distress, or to re-establish communities as a result of **declared natural or man-made disasters** in a developed country (including Australia).

(28) Charitable institutions with a principal activity of providing **short-term direct care to animals** that are lost, mistreated, without owners and/or are rehabilitating those animals if they are orphaned, sick or injured. The taxpayer in *Sea Shepherd Australia* was not an eligible recipient because its campaigns to protect marine wildlife did not amount to providing short-term direct care to animals in the sense required by s 30-45. The Commissioner considers that wild animals are not ordinarily expected to have an owner and so do not come within this category. In addition, for an institution to qualify based on activities related to animals without owners, the animals are required to need care because of the misfortune of being without an owner (ATO *Decision Impact Statement*: *Sea Shepherd*).

(29) **Charitable institutions that would be a public benevolent institution** except that they also undertake activities that would fall under the existing recipient categories of a health promotion charity and/or a harm prevention charity.

(30) Public funds that are established for charitable purposes solely to provide money for **scholarships, bursaries or prizes to promote education** where entry is open to persons at a national, state, territory or regional level.

(31) Public institutions that qualify as **community sheds** established to advance mental health and relieve social isolation (s 30-20).

[FITR ¶74-025 – ¶74-115]

¶16-952 Specific recipients of tax-deductible gifts

In addition to the above general categories of funds, authorities, institutions and organisations, gifts of $2 or more made to deductible gift recipients (DGRs) specified in ss 30-15 to 30-100 are deductible.

A complete list of deductible gift recipients is available at abn.business.gov.au/Tools/DgrListing.

[FITR ¶74-025 – ¶74-115]

¶16-955 Gifts to overseas aid funds

Under the Overseas Aid Gift Deduction Scheme, gifts of $2 or more to eligible overseas aid funds to provide relief for persons in developing countries qualify for deduction (ss 30-15; 30-80; 30-85). Guidelines on the requirements that must be satisfied for a fund to be admitted to the scheme, to change its name or to leave the scheme, are set out in TR 95/2.

Laws in some developing countries prevent expatriates from transferring money to Australia. Expatriates of such countries who have become residents of Australia may make deductible gifts to eligible overseas aid funds by transferring money from their blocked accounts to accounts held by the aid funds in those countries.

[FITR ¶74-095]

¶16-957 Gifts to cultural organisations

Gifts of $2 or more made to the public gift fund of a cultural organisation will be tax-deductible if the gift was made on or after the date the organisation was admitted to the Register of Cultural Organisations maintained by the Arts Minister and the Treasurer (ss 30-15; 30-100; 30-290 to 30-310).

[FITR ¶74-115, ¶74-360ff]

¶16-960 Gifts to environmental organisations

Gifts of $2 or more (whether of money or property) made to the gift fund of an environmental organisation entered on the Register of Environmental Organisations will be tax-deductible if the organisation is on the Register when the gift is made (an organisation can be removed from the Register) (ss 30-15; 30-55; 30-250 to 30-285).

The criteria to be satisfied for an organisation to be entered on the Register of Environmental Organisations include:

- the organisation's principal purpose must be the protection and enhancement of the environment (whether in Australia or elsewhere) or a significant aspect of the environment, or the provision of information or education, or the carrying on of research about, the environment or a significant aspect of the environment (''environment'' for these purposes refers to the natural environment and includes all aspects of the natural surroundings of humans). The organisation must use gifts made to its gift fund for its principal purpose
- the organisation must not give any of its profits, financial surplus or property to its members, shareholders, controllers, etc
- in the event of a winding up, any surplus assets or funds of the organisation are to be transferred to another fund entered on the Register
- the organisation must have a policy of not acting as a mere conduit, or umbrella organisation, for other organisations or persons, and
- the organisation must agree to provide to the Department of the Environment, statistical data about gifts to its gift fund and to comply with any relevant rules made by the Environment Minister and the Treasurer.

Deduction may be spread over 5 years

Deductions for gifts of property to certain environmental organisations may be spread over a period of up to 5 income years at the election of the taxpayer. To qualify, the property must be valued by the Commissioner at more than $5,000.

The election must be in writing and be made before the taxpayer lodges an income tax return for the income year in which the gift is made. The election must specify the percentage, if any, to be deducted in each income year. A copy of the election must be given to the Secretary of the Department that administers the *Environment Protection and Biodiversity Conservation Act 1999* before lodging an income tax return for the year in which the gift is made. The election may be varied at any time, although the variation will only apply to the percentage of the original deduction that is to be claimed in income years for which an income tax return has not yet been lodged (Subdiv 30-DB: ss 30-247 to 30-249D).

Conservation covenants

For details of the deduction available to landowners entering into perpetual conservation covenants, see ¶16-972.

[FITR ¶74-310ff]

¶16-962 Gifts to ancillary funds

Gifts of $2 or more made to certain types of public or private ancillary funds are deductible (s 30-15, item 2). An ‘‘ancillary fund’’ is a fund that collects tax deductible donations which they on-distribute to deductible gift recipients. Only public ancillary funds can accept tax deductible donations from the public.

To qualify as a deductible gift recipient, an ancillary fund must be established and maintained under a will or trust instrument solely: (i) to provide money, property or benefits to a recipient listed at ¶16-950; or (ii) to establish such a recipient, for any of its purposes.

An ancillary fund is a ‘‘public ancillary fund’’ for the purposes of the gift provisions where it is the intention of the founders or promoters of the fund that the public will contribute to the fund and the public, or a significant part of it, does in fact contribute to the fund (*Bray*; *Case X13*). The Commissioner’s requirements for a fund to qualify as a public ancillary fund are set out in TR 95/27. Where the trustee of a public fund has an obligation to apply funds in accordance with the requests of a donor, a separate private ancillary fund is created (TD 2004/23). Private ancillary funds are designed to promote philanthropy among private groups by providing them with greater flexibility when establishing trust funds for philanthropic purposes. Only trusts with corporate trustees can be approved private ancillary funds.

The *Public Ancillary Fund Guidelines 2011* and *Taxation Administration (Private Ancillary Fund) Guidelines 2019* outline rules that an ancillary fund must comply with to remain endorsed as a deductible gift recipient, including minimum annual distribution rates. Penalties may be imposed on trustees who fail to comply with these guidelines and the Commissioner may suspend or remove trustees for breaching their obligations (TAA 1953 Sch 1 Subdiv 426-D; PS LA 2014/1). To encourage funds to continue giving despite the circumstances of COVID-19, if a fund makes distributions above the minimum rates in 2019–20 and 2020–21, it will receive a credit that can reduce its minimum annual distributions for later years.

[FITR ¶74-025]

¶16-965 Gifts of works of art

Under the Cultural Gifts Program, certain gifts of works of art and comparable property qualify for deduction on a more liberal basis than other gifts (s 30-15, items 4 and 5). Such gifts are also exempt from CGT (s 118-60(2)).

The program applies to gifts of property with a value of $2 or more for inclusion in the collections maintained by the Australiana Fund, a public art gallery, public library or public museum, or Artbank. Gifts by will and gifts of money are excluded. Companies, as well as individuals, are entitled to a deduction under the program (TD 93/28), although the making of a gift does not create or increase a carry-forward loss (¶16-880) (TD 92/195).

Within certain limits, the program allows a deduction for a qualifying gift to be based on the GST inclusive market value of the gift rather than its cost. It also dispenses with the requirement for other gifts (¶16-942) that the gifted property must have been purchased by the taxpayer within 12 months of the gift being made or be valued by the Commissioner at more than $5,000. A taxpayer must, of course, own the gifted property to claim a deduction (eg *Case Y22*, where a deduction for the value of donated excess film footage in which the taxpayer did not own the copyright was denied). A proportionate deduction is allowed where property is owned and gifted by 2 or more persons (s 30-225).

The deduction for qualifying gifts is generally based on the GST inclusive market value of the gift at the time it was made, determined by reference to the average of *2 or more* valuations obtained from approved valuers. Valuations must be in writing and must state the estimated GST inclusive market value of the property at the time the gift was made or, provided the valuation is made within 90 days before or after the time the gift is made, the GST inclusive value of the property at the time of valuation (s 30-200). The general rule is that the average of the GST inclusive market values specified in the valuations will be treated as the value of the property. However, in some cases an adjustment may be necessary for any input tax credit entitlement (ss 30-15(3); 30-215(4)).

The valuation method should determine what price a willing, but not anxious, vendor and a willing, but not anxious, purchaser could reasonably be expected to agree on for the transfer of the property (TR 96/1). The ATO does not accept the decision in *Case X12*, that the value of opals donated to a museum was the average of 2 retail valuations supplied by the taxpayer's valuers, as authority for a contrary view. The cost of such valuations is deductible as a tax-related expense (TD 93/92).

A person making a gift should send the written valuations to the recipient institution which should then forward them, together with any further documentation required, to the Committee on Cultural Gifts Program. If the Committee accepts that the values and other aspects of the gift conform with the relevant requirements, it will endorse the valuations and return them to the taxpayer. The taxpayer need only produce the valuation documents to the ATO when requested to do so (TR 96/1).

There are important exceptions to the rule that the deduction for eligible art gifts is based on market value for *recent or prearranged acquisitions* (s 30-215(3); (4)) and *artists, art dealers, etc.* (ss 30-205; 30-215(3)). In any other case, if the average of the valuations does not fairly represent market value, the deductible amount is the market value of the property on the day the gift was made.

Deduction may be reduced

The deduction may be reduced by a ''reasonable'' amount where the recipient does not obtain the right to immediate custody and control of the property or full legal and equitable title to the property (s 30-220). This is also the case where the custody, control or use of the property by the recipient is affected by any agreement entered into in connection with the gift.

For example, assume that a gift worth $10,000 is made on condition that the taxpayer retains full rights of possession and enjoyment for the next 10 years. The appropriate discounting factor could be 10%. Using this factor, the present value of the $10,000 gift would be $3,885 and that would be the amount of the reduced deduction allowable (IT 295).

Deduction may be spread over 5 years

Deductions for gifts made under the Cultural Gifts Program may be spread over a period of up to 5 income years at the election of the taxpayer.

The election must be in writing and be made before the taxpayer lodges an income tax return for the income year in which the gift is made. The election must specify the percentage, if any, to be deducted in each income year. A copy of the election must be given to the Secretary of the Department administering the *National Gallery Act 1975* before lodging an income tax return for the year in which the gift is made. The election may be varied at any time, although the variation will only apply to the percentage of the original deduction that is to be claimed in income years for which an income tax return has not yet been lodged (Subdiv 30-DB: ss 30-246 to 30-248).

[FITR ¶74-025, ¶74-250ff]

¶16-967 Gifts of national heritage significance

Gifts of property of national heritage significance made to National Trust bodies (other than gifts by will) qualify for deduction on the same liberal basis as gifts of works of art (s 30-15, item 6). The deduction will normally be based on a market valuation determined by reference to at least 2 valuations by approved valuers (¶16-965).

For this concessional treatment to apply, the property must be listed in the National Heritage List, the Commonwealth Heritage List or the Register of the National Estate at the time the gift is made, and be accepted by the National Trust for the purpose of preserving the property for the benefit of the public.

Deduction may be spread over 5 years

Deductions for gifts of property made to certain heritage organisations may be spread over a period of up to 5 income years at the election of the taxpayer. To qualify, the gift must be valued by the Commissioner at more than $5,000.

The election must be in writing and be made before the taxpayer lodges an income tax return for the income year in which the gift is made. The election must specify the percentage, if any, to be deducted in each income year. A copy of the election must be given to the Secretary of the Department that administers the *Australian Heritage Council Act 2003* before lodging an income tax return for the year in which the gift is made. The election may be varied at any time, although the variation will only apply to the percentage of the original deduction that is to be claimed in income years for which an income tax return has not yet been lodged (Subdiv 30-DB: ss 30-247 to 30-249D).

[FITR ¶74-025]

¶16-970 Gifts of trading stock

Gifts of trading stock made to eligible recipients (¶16-950, ¶16-955) are not subject to the normal restrictions that apply to most other gifts.

Gifts of trading stock disposed of outside the ordinary course of business are deductible regardless of when the stock was acquired by the taxpayer (s 30-15). The amount of the deduction is taken to be the market value of the stock on the day the gift was made. For other taxation consequences of the disposal for the donor, see ¶9-290.

No deduction is allowed if the gifted property is made the subject of an election to claim concessional treatment on the basis of a forced disposal under Subdiv 385-E (¶18-160).

[FITR ¶74-025]

¶16-972 Conservation covenants

A deduction can be claimed where a taxpayer enters into a perpetual conservation covenant with an authorised body or a government body for no consideration (s 31-5).

For these purposes, an authorised body is a fund, authority or institution that qualifies as an eligible gift recipient (s 31-10). If the fund, etc, is not listed specifically in Subdiv 30-B, it must be in Australia and must either be registered (¶16-942) or be a prescribed private fund.

A government body is the Commonwealth, a state, a territory or local governing body or an authority of the Commonwealth, a state or a territory.

The covenant must: (i) be over land owned by the taxpayer; (ii) be permanent; (iii) restrict or prohibit certain activities on the land that could degrade its environmental value; (iv) be registered on the title to the land (if registration is possible); and (v) be approved by the Environment Minister.

The taxpayer must not receive any money, property or other material benefit for entering into the covenant. In addition, as a result of entering into the covenant, the market value of the land must decrease. If the taxpayer entered into a contract to acquire the land more than 12 months before entering into the covenant, this decrease must be of more than $5,000.

The amount of the deduction is equal to the difference between the market value of the land just before and just after the covenant is entered into, to the extent that this is attributable to the covenant. This difference must be valued by the Commissioner (s 31-15). The valuation fee is tax deductible (s 25-5). Like other gift-type deductions, the deduction cannot create a tax loss (¶16-880). However, to avoid this, it may be spread, in instalments chosen by the taxpayer, over 5 years (s 30-248). For associated CGT measures, see ¶11-280.

[FITR ¶77-020]

¶16-975 Anti-avoidance measures for gifts

A deduction cannot be claimed for a gift unless a bona fide benefit is conferred on the charity, fund or institution (TR 2005/13). This is the effect of a special anti-avoidance measure (ITAA36 s 78A) that denies any deduction under Div 30 for a gift where, by reason of the making of the gift or under any agreement or scheme associated with the gift:

- the amount or value of the benefit derived by the charity, fund or institution as a consequence of the gift is, or may reasonably be expected to be, less than the amount or value of the property comprising the gift at the time it was made. A deduction will not be denied where the reduction in benefit is caused only by reasonable expenses having been incurred in obtaining or soliciting the gift
- a fund, authority or institution, other than the donee, becomes liable to make a payment or transfer property, or becomes liable to suffer some detriment, disadvantage, liability or obligation
- the taxpayer or an associate obtains, or may reasonably be expected to obtain, any benefit, advantage, right or privilege other than the benefit of a tax saving, or
- the charity, fund or institution is to acquire property (other than the gift) from the taxpayer or an associate.

This does not affect the (reduced) deduction that may apply where eligible art gifts (¶16-965) or heritage gifts (¶16-967) are made subject to benefits being reserved to the taxpayer making the gift.

[FTR ¶38-512]

¶16-977 Contributions to fundraising events

A deduction is available to an individual for:

- a contribution of cash exceeding $150, or property with a value exceeding $150, which is made for the right to attend or participate in a fundraising event conducted by a deductible gift recipient (DGR). The deduction is reduced by the GST-inclusive value of any minor benefit received in return. The minor benefit must not exceed the lower of $150, or 20% of the contribution (s 30-15, item 7), and/or
- a contribution of cash exceeding $150 for the purchase of goods or services resulting from a successful bid at a fundraising auction conducted by a DGR. The deduction is reduced by the GST-inclusive market value of the goods or services on the day the contribution is made, and the market value must not exceed the lower of $150, or 20% of the contribution (s 30-15, item 8).

The deduction for contributions for the right to participate in a fundraising event is limited to 2 contributions for the same event. However, there is no limit to the number of deductions for successful bids for goods or services at a fundraising auction.

Eligible fundraising events

Eligible fundraising events are limited to one-off events conducted by DGRs in Australia, eg fetes, balls, gala shows, performances and similar events, and even golf games. The DGR must use the funds raised at the event/auction for the same purpose that enables them to qualify as a DGR.

Eligible contributions of property

Where the contribution is property provided in exchange for a right to attend or participate in a fundraising event, it must be valued at more than $150 if purchased within 12 months of the contribution being made. For this purpose, the property's value is the lower of its market value on the day the contribution is made and the amount the contributor paid for the property.

There is a special rule for contributions consisting of shares listed on an Australian stock exchange that were not purchased within 12 months of the fundraising contribution. Such shares are valued at their market value on the day of the contribution, provided that value exceeds $150 but is less than or equal to $5,000.

In all other circumstances where the property was not purchased within 12 months of the contribution being made, the property's value is determined by the Commissioner. To qualify, the Commissioner's valuation must exceed $5,000, and the GST-inclusive value of the right to attend or participate in the fundraising event must not exceed $150.

The deduction for contributions of property is limited to those for the right to attend or participate in a fundraising event. Gifts of goods or services for fundraising auctions are not deductible under these rules, but may qualify under the general rules commencing at ¶16-950.

DGR to assess minor benefit

The DGR is responsible for determining the market value of the minor benefit given in return for a contribution. Where the DGR issues a receipt to a contributor, it must state either the GST-inclusive market value of the right to participate in the fundraising event or, where a successful bid at a fundraising auction has been made, the GST-inclusive market value of the goods or services purchased by the contributor.

Chapter 17 Depreciating Assets

Introduction

¶17-000 Overview of uniform capital allowance system

Deductions for the decline in value of depreciating assets are available under the uniform capital allowance system (ITAA97 Div 40). It also contains rules that provide deductions for certain other capital expenditure including primary production assets (¶18-050) and for mining and quarrying operations (¶19-000).

The write-off for (''blackhole'') business capital costs is outlined at ¶16-156 and the deduction for mains electricity supply is at ¶16-820.

A separate regime (ITAA97 Div 43) applies to capital works expenditure on buildings and structural improvements (¶20-470).

Small business entities can choose simplified depreciation arrangements (¶7-250).

¶17-005 Deduction for depreciating assets

The cost of a depreciating asset is generally of a capital nature and is therefore not immediately deductible as an ordinary business expense (¶16-060). However, deductions may be available for the decline in value of a depreciating asset to the extent that the asset is used for a taxable purpose (ITAA97 Div 40). The decline in value is usually calculated by spreading the cost of the asset over its effective life and using either the prime cost or the diminishing value method. Effective life is either self-assessed or determined by the Commissioner although a statutory effective life applies in limited cases (¶17-270). Balancing adjustments may be required if a balancing adjustment event occurs (¶17-630) and any CGT consequences must also be considered. In some cases, roll-over relief is available.

Certain expenditure on software development (¶17-370) or low-cost depreciating assets (¶17-810) may be grouped into a ''pool'' and deductions allowed for the decline in value of the pool. An immediate write-off or accelerated depreciation is temporarily available for assets purchased by a business and also for non-business assets costing $300 or less (¶17-430 and ¶17-330).

The deductions for the decline in value of depreciating assets may be subject to a number of anti-avoidance provisions. In particular, the provisions dealing with hire purchase arrangements (¶23-250), tax-preferred asset financing (¶23-210) and limited recourse financing (¶23-260). The effectiveness of sale and leaseback arrangements is discussed at ¶23-240.

As the cost of an entity's depreciating assets is reset when it joins a consolidated group (¶8-210), the head company and the joining or leaving entity work out their own depreciation for the part of the year that the asset is theirs (ITAA97 s 716-25; ITTPA s 701A-10). Special rules apply for low-value and software pools (ITAA97 Subdiv 716-G).

For the consequences of acquiring depreciating assets in foreign currency transactions, see ¶23-070.

[FITR ¶86-801]

Requirements for Deduction

¶17-010 Assets used for taxable purposes

A deduction is available for the decline in value of a ''depreciating asset'' (¶17-015) that is held by the taxpayer for any time during the year. The deduction is reduced to reflect the extent to which the asset was used during the income year for a purpose other than a ''taxable purpose'' (eg private or domestic purposes or to produce exempt income) (ITAA97 s 40-25). Further reductions apply for second-hand assets in residential rental properties (¶17-012).

''Use'' requires the employment of the asset so that it can reasonably be expected to decline in value (TD 2007/5; ID 2006/151).

A depreciating asset may be used for a taxable purpose even though it does not, of itself, generate assessable income. The provider of a fibre optic cable network was entitled to a deduction for the entire decline in value of the cable network even though only 8 of the 12 fibre optic strands gave rise to an assessable licence fee (*Reef Networks*). A taxpayer granting to a partnership, of which he was a partner, the exclusive use of an asset to enable the partnership to provide a service to the taxpayer was considered to have been used for a taxable purpose (ID 2004/958).

▶ Planning point

As no decline in value deduction is available if income-producing operations have not commenced (TD 2007/5), assets should start being used after such operations have commenced.

''Held in reserve''

A deduction is also available for the decline in value of a depreciating asset that is not actually used for a taxable purpose during the year but is installed ready for use for a taxable purpose and held in reserve. An asset is held in reserve if it is on hand and in such a state that it is ready to perform its function, its use being contingent on some future event occurring in a taxpayer's existing income-producing activities (ID 2006/151; ID 2004/146).

Decline in value deductions and employees

An employee may be entitled to a deduction for the decline in value of assets that the employee holds and uses in relation to a job even if such use is not a condition of employment. It is enough for the use of the asset to be within the scope of the particular duties of employment (IT 2198). Where an employee claims a deduction for the decline in value of an asset, the substantiation requirements must be considered (¶16-210).

Despite being reimbursed for the cost of a depreciating asset acquired on or after 1 July 2008, an employee is entitled to the deduction (ITAA36 s 51AH(3)). Employees cannot claim depreciation deductions for FBT eligible work-related items (under FBTAA 1986 s 58X) acquired after 13 May 2008 which were provided as expense payment of property fringe benefits (s 40-45(1)).

Even items intrinsically private in nature may qualify for deduction in appropriate circumstances (¶16-170), eg the decline in value of TVs may be deductible to journalists, entertainers and football coaches if the necessary connection with the job can be shown (*Case R113*; *Case T17*). Teachers may claim deductions for the decline in value of items such as calculators, voice recorders and computers. Deductions may be allowed for briefcases, carry-bags, kit bags, suitcases, etc, that are used as an integral part of employment (*Case P56*; *Case R89*). Such claims are reduced to reflect the degree of private use.

Taxpayers with physical disabilities are not entitled to deductions for the decline in value of medical appliances such as wheelchairs, hearing aids, artificial limbs, spectacles, etc, even though without them the taxpayer could not do their job (IT 2217).

Taxable purpose

The deduction for the decline in value of a depreciating asset is reduced to the extent that the asset was used or installed ready for use for a purpose other than a taxable purpose (eg furniture in a private home). ‘‘Taxable purpose’’ (s 40-25(7)) is the purpose of producing assessable income (¶16-010; *Case 9/2009*; ID 2009/137), exploration or prospecting (¶19-040), mining site rehabilitation (¶19-100) or environmental protection activities (¶19-110). If the asset is used partly for private purposes and partly for producing income, the deduction must be apportioned (¶17-570).

If the tax-preferred leasing provisions (¶23-210) apply to an asset, the taxpayer is taken not to be using the asset for a taxable purpose (except to the extent that the use of the asset is not a tax-preferred use or a private use, or that financial benefits are not to be provided to the taxpayer by tax-preferred entities).

Leisure facilities and boats

A deduction is generally not available for the decline in value of a leisure facility, except to the extent that the use of the asset constitutes a fringe benefit for FBT purposes, or occurs in the course of the taxpayer's business or for the taxpayer's employees, (s 40-25(3), (4): ¶16-420).

For the rules that apply to deductions for boat expenses (including the decline in value), see ¶16-420.

[FITR ¶86-880]

¶17-012 Second-hand depreciating assets in residential premises

The deduction for the decline in value of depreciating assets (¶17-015) used or installed in residential rental property is reduced to the extent the assets were previously used by another entity (other than as trading stock) (ITAA97 s 40-27(2)). The effect of this rule is that the deduction for decline in value for depreciating assets used to generate income from residential premises is only available to assets acquired new for that purpose, and not for second-hand assets.

The restriction affects not only investors in residential property containing existing depreciating assets but also owner-occupiers where their home is subsequently rented out. Where assets in the home were previously used, or installed ready for use, by the landlord (ie not for a taxable purpose), and not in a way that was "occasional", the deduction for the decline in value is not available to the landlord for such depreciating assets.

The restriction applies to income years starting on or after 1 July 2017. It applies to assets acquired at or after 7.30 pm (AEST) on 9 May 2017 unless the asset was acquired under a contract entered into before this time. Depreciating assets acquired before this time which are moved from a taxpayer's home into a rental property are also subject to this rule.

Exceptions

The reduction in s 40-27(2) does not apply if the income is produced in the course of carrying on a business.

It also does not apply to reduce the deduction for depreciating assets allocated to a low-value pool. However, when first allocating an asset to a low-value pool, the extent of the asset's value attributable to its use in a residential rental property (and so affected by s 40-27) cannot be placed in the pool (¶17-810).

The reduction importantly does not apply to corporate tax entities (ITAA97 s 960-115), a superannuation plan that is not an SMSF, a managed investment trust (¶6-405), a public unit trust (¶6-320) or a unit trust or partnership where each member is one of the above. The rule therefore generally applies to individuals, SMSFs and closely held partnerships and trusts.

The restriction also do not apply to those depreciating assets used in a residential premises to generate income other than from providing residential accommodation, eg income from the sale of electricity from solar panels, or agistment fees from a horse stable that forms part of the residential premises.

An exception is also available for assets in new residential premises (¶34-230). Where a developer acquires and installs depreciating assets in a new or substantially renovated premises, the investor may not be affected by this rule and is therefore able to claim the decline in value. This is provided that no entity has been previously entitled to the decline in value for those depreciating assets, and either no one resided in the premises before it was held by the investor, or the premises was supplied to the investor within 6 months of it becoming new residential premises and where the asset has not been previously used or installed in a residence.

[FITR ¶86-887]

¶17-015 Depreciating assets

A "depreciating asset" is defined as an asset that has a limited effective life and that is reasonably expected to decline in value over the time it is used (ITAA97 s 40-30; see, for example, ID 2003/820 and ID 2004/721). An asset is something that is capable of being put to use in the business of the holder and, for example, extends to an open pit mine site improvement (TR 2012/7). Land and items of trading stock are specifically excluded, as are intangible assets (such as licences and permits: ID 2002/755). However, the following intangible assets are included:

- mining, quarrying or prospecting rights (¶19-010; ID 2010/45)
- mining, quarrying or prospecting information (¶19-010)
- geothermal-exploration rights or information (between 1 July 2012 and 30 June 2014)
- items of intellectual property (see below)
- in-house software (¶17-370)

- indefeasible rights to use a telecommunications cable system (IRU)
- spectrum licences
- datacasting transmitter licences, and
- telecommunications site access rights acquired by licensed telecommunications carriers (incurred on or after 12 May 2004) which are rights to share or install a facility or to enter premises for such a purpose. A facility is any part of the infrastructure of a telecommunications network or anything used in connection with such network.

Temporary full expensing or accelerated depreciation may be available for depreciating assets meeting the relevant eligibility requirements (¶17-430).

The definition of a depreciating asset includes items of plant (¶17-040) as well as other assets that are wasting in nature. Depreciating assets are not limited to assets that lose value steadily over their effective lives, nor are they limited to things that only ever decline in value. All that is required is for the asset to lose its value overall (other than scrap value) by the end of its effective life, even though the asset may hold or even increase its value for a time. Forestry roads and timber mill buildings are depreciating assets and subject to ITAA97 Div 40.

The Commissioner's effective life tables (commencing at ¶43-000) provide a practical checklist of what constitutes a depreciating asset.

Improvements to land and fixtures on land are treated as separate assets for purposes of determining if they are a depreciating asset, whether or not they can be removed from the land (s 40-30(3)). An open pit mine site improvement that enhances the use of the land to the miner constitutes an improvement to land (TR 2012/7); a gully dam constructed on land as an improvement to land is a separate depreciating asset (ID 2008/50). An accommodation unit (such as those used in a caravan/tourist park) may be a chattel where it merely rests on land or is affixed in such a way that facilitates easy removal, or where the purpose and mode of affixing are for the more complete enjoyment of the unit as a chattel. An accommodation unit fixed to the ground may lose its identity as a chattel and become a fixture on land (TD 97/24).

The renewal or extension of a right is treated as the continuation of the original right, rather than as a separate depreciating asset (s 40-30(5)). Conversions of a mining, quarrying or prospecting right are taken to be a continuation of the original right if that right ends and the new right relates to the same area. The Full Federal Court ruled that separate rights to explore and recover petroleum were the same depreciable asset in *Mitsui & Co.*

Certain assets may qualify as depreciating assets but may be specifically excluded from the application of the uniform capital allowance system (¶17-030).

Items of trading stock (¶9-150) are not depreciating assets. Spare parts held for maintenance and repair purposes are depreciating assets. Spare parts are otherwise deductible on either an incurred basis or a usage basis (IT 333: ¶16-730) or, in some situations, may be treated as trading stock (¶9-150).

Composite assets

Whether a particular item (rather than its components) is a depreciating asset is a question of fact and degree to be determined in the light of all the circumstances of the case (s 40-30(4)). For example, a car is one depreciating asset (rather than its individual components), but a portable GPS device installed in the car is a separate asset. On the other hand, the separate assets constituting a floating restaurant (eg the ship, cutlery, crockery, furniture, stoves and refrigerators) are treated as separate depreciating assets.

A component or a group of components of a composite asset is a depreciating asset in its own right if its commercial or economic value can be separately identified or recognised, using its purpose or function as a guide (TR 2017/D1). The function of the composite asset should be considered against its components, in the circumstances in which they are used. TR 2017/D1 outlines the guiding principles for this purpose and a number of examples to illustrate them. The test is similar to the "functionality test" used to identify a "unit of plant" under the former depreciation rules (TR 94/11; ID 2003/491; ID 2004/271; ID 2007/88; ID 2009/130).

Buildings and foundations

Although a building is a depreciating asset, expenditure on buildings is generally deductible under the capital works provisions (Div 43; ¶20-470) and not under the uniform capital allowance system (¶17-030). However, expenditure on "plant" is not subject to the capital works provisions (¶20-510).

Generally, a deduction is not allowed under the depreciating assets provisions (Div 40) for buildings used to house a depreciating asset. However, the Commissioner allows depreciation on the whole or part of a building where plant and building become so integrated that plant includes the whole or part of the building (TR 2007/9). Components such as air conditioning systems, lifts and escalators are plant. A building forms an integral part of plant to the extent that it is absolutely essential to the support of the working plant (IT 31). An electrical switchboard, mains, submains cables, gas and telephone installations, security items and vehicle control equipment are not plant, but rather form part of the structure of the building (*Woodward*).

For the distinction between plant and premises, including residential rental property, see ¶17-040.

Where the whole of a building is plant, the concrete foundations or footings in which the uprights of the structure are embedded also qualify as plant. The cost of excavating for foundations is accepted as part of the depreciable cost, but not general site preparation.

If only part of a building is plant, the cost of the building is apportioned. Indirect construction costs having a link to both the plant and non-plant components of a building may be allocated in proportion to direct costs.

Intellectual property

Depreciating assets include certain items of intellectual property, namely the rights that a person has under Commonwealth or foreign law (ID 2006/169) as patentee, or as owner of a registered design or a copyright, or as licensee of any of those items. The decline in value of such items is calculated over the statutory effective life (¶17-280) and using the prime cost method (¶17-490). Trademarks and other items of intellectual property are not depreciating assets: ID 2004/858.

The cost of registering or extending a patent, registered design or copyright is included in the "cost" of the relevant asset and is deductible over the effective life of the asset (ID 2002/810 and ID 2002/811).

Under transitional provisions, unrecouped pre-1 July 2001 expenditure on items of intellectual property that were amortised under the former provisions continues to be written off under Div 40, on the prime cost basis, using the same cost and effective life.

A company that purchased and operated medical and dental practices was not entitled to depreciation deductions in respect of patient records because copyright did not subsist in the patient records and lists of the practices that the taxpayer purchased. Even if copyright had passed to the taxpayer under the sale agreements it would not have been depreciable as no amount of the purchase price was allocated to copyright (*Primary Health Care*; TD 2005/1).

A deduction for the decline in value of film copyright acquired on or after 1 July 2004 is available over the effective life of the copyright (either self-assessed or determined by the Commissioner), using either the prime cost or diminishing value method (¶17-280), provided no deduction was claimed under the former film concessions in ITAA36 Pt III Divs 10B and 10BA. The cost of the copyright is reduced by the amount of any ''producer offset'' available under the rules discussed at ¶20-340.

See also TR 2002/19 (licence arrangements) and ID 2004/982 (integrating purchased software and an algorithm into a computer program).

Spectrum licences

The decline in value of a spectrum licence is calculated over the term of the licence (¶17-280) and using the prime cost method (¶17-490). There are special rules dealing with replacement spectrum licences (ITAA97 s 40-120). Unrecouped pre-1 July 2001 expenditure on licences for which a deduction was available under the former provisions continues to be amortised under Div 40, on the prime cost basis, using the same cost and effective life.

[FITR ¶86-804, ¶86-890 – ¶86-931]

¶17-020 Holder of depreciating asset entitled to deduction

A deduction for the decline in value of a depreciating asset for an income year can only be claimed by a person who ''held'' the asset at any time during the income year. The general rule is that the owner (or the legal owner, if there is both a legal and an equitable owner) holds the asset (ITAA97 s 40-40, item 10). Proprietors in strata schemes registered under state or territory legislation can claim capital allowance deductions on the basis that they hold the legal and beneficial ownership of common property (TR 2015/3, and see below).

Additional rules specify who is taken to hold the depreciating asset in different circumstances (ITAA97 s 40-40, items 1 to 9). These specific rules apply in preference to Item 10, ie the holder is the owner of the asset only if none of the special circumstances apply (ID 2004/957).

(1) A luxury car in respect of which a lease is granted (¶17-220) is held by the lessee, while the lessee has the right to use the car, and *not* by the lessor (Item 1). Where the lease ends or is terminated early and the lessee becomes the holder under Item 10, no balancing adjustment occurs (ID 2003/756).

(2) A depreciating asset that is fixed to land that is subject to a quasi-ownership right (or an extension or renewal of the right) is held by the owner of the right, while the owner has the right to remove the asset (Item 2). A ''quasi-ownership right'' is a lease of the land, an easement in connection with the land, or any other right, power or privilege over or connected with the land, eg a sublease (ITAA97 s 995-1(1); ID 2009/156). For Div 40 purposes, a fixture on land, whether removable or not, is an asset separate from the land (ITAA97 s 40-30(3)). See TR 2006/13 (assets held under sale and leaseback arrangements) and ID 2012/9 (right to remove asset).

▶ Example

Lessee leases land from Lessor and affixes a depreciating asset to it. Although Lessor now legally owns the asset, Lessee has the right to remove the asset while the lease subsists and for a reasonable time afterwards. Lessee is the holder of the asset while the right to remove the asset remains. If both Lessor and Lessee contribute to the cost of the fixture, Lessee is a holder under Item 2 and Lessor is a holder under Item 10. They are each entitled to a deduction for the decline in value of the asset based on the cost of the asset to each of them.

(3) An improvement (whether a fixture or not) to land subject to a quasi-ownership right (or an extension or renewal of the right), made or improved by any owner of the right for the owner's own use, where the owner has no right to remove the asset, is held by the owner of the quasi-ownership right (while it exists) (Item 3). An improvement to land, whether removable or not, is an asset separate from the land (s 40-30(3)).

▶ Example

Lessee leases land and a building from Lessor and carries on a business in the building. Lessee installs an in-ground watering system on the land at its expense and for the benefit of its business. Under the lease, Lessee is not permitted to remove fixtures from the land. Lessee is the holder of the watering system while the lease exists.

(4) A depreciating asset that is subject to a lease where the asset is fixed to land and the lessor has the right to recover the asset is held by the lessor (while the right to recover exists) (Item 4). See TR 2006/13 for assets held under sale and leaseback arrangements.

▶ Example

Damian leases equipment to Simone, which Simone attaches to land she owns. Under the lease, Damian has a right to recover the equipment at the end of the lease. Damian is the holder of the equipment while the right to recover the equipment exists. Simone is also the holder of the equipment under Item 10 (and may be able to deduct her costs, eg installation and modification costs).

(5) A *right* that an entity legally owns, but that another entity (the economic owner) exercises or has the right to exercise immediately, is held by the economic owner if the economic owner has a right to become its legal owner and it is reasonable to expect: (i) that the economic owner will become the legal owner; or (ii) that the right will be disposed of at the direction and for the benefit of the economic owner (Item 5). Such asset is *not* held by the legal owner. An economic owner may lack legal title because the asset is subject to a legal mortgage, a hire purchase agreement, a product financing agreement, a reservation of title arrangement, or a bare trust.

▶ Example

Joe borrows money from Financier and secures the loan by granting a mortgage over a patent he has. Under the mortgage agreement, legal title to the patent is assigned to Financier but Financier grants Joe a licence to continue to use the patent in his business. Joe is the holder of the patent because he exercises the rights over the subject matter of the patent, has the right to become the legal owner of the patent and it is reasonable to expect that he will.

(6) Item 6 deals with the case where an entity (the former holder) would be taken to hold an asset, and another entity (the economic owner) possesses the asset (or has a right against the former holder to possess the asset immediately) and has a right against the former holder to become the holder (under these rules). In this case, if it is reasonable to expect that the economic owner will exercise that right or that the asset will be disposed of at the direction, and for the benefit, of the economic owner, the asset is held by the economic owner. It is *not* held by the former holder. Item 6 would apply to hire purchase agreements under which the hirer has an option to purchase the asset after paying the final instalment under the agreement (in this case, the legal owner of the asset is *not* the holder). For the interaction of this Item and the provisions of ITAA97 Div 240 (¶23-250), see TR 2005/20. For examples of the application of this rule, see ID 2007/170, ID 2007/171, ID 2011/71 and ID 2012/80. For sale and leaseback arrangements generally, see ¶23-240.

▶ Example

In order to acquire additional finance for her business, Emma sells an asset to a financier and agrees to repurchase it for a price equal to the original sale price plus a finance charge. Emma remains in possession of the asset and continues to use it and the financier is the legal owner. She is the holder of the asset because she has the right to possess the asset, the right to become its legal owner and it is reasonable to expect that she will.

(7) A partnership asset is held by the partnership (Item 7). It is *not* held by any particular partner (eg ID 2002/1037; ID 2002/1083; ID 2009/135).

(8) Mining, quarrying or prospecting information (whether or not generally available) is held by the entity that has the information, provided it is relevant to mining operations carried on or proposed to be carried on by the entity or it is relevant to the business carried on by the entity that includes exploration or prospecting for minerals or quarry materials (Item 8).

(9) Any other mining, quarrying or prospecting information is held by the entity that has it, provided the information is not generally available (Item 9).

If, under any of the above rules, the holder ceases to hold the asset, a balancing adjustment event arises (¶17-630).

Jointly held assets

Where 2 (or more) taxpayers are considered to hold the asset (eg a lessor under the general rule in Item 10 and a lessee under Item 3), they are considered to hold the asset jointly. In such case, each taxpayer is entitled to a deduction for the decline in value of the asset, calculated on the basis of the cost of the asset to each taxpayer, and as if the taxpayer's *interest in* the underlying asset was the asset (ITAA97 s 40-35). A composite asset (¶17-015) that is a single depreciating asset is also considered to be jointly held even if 2 or more taxpayers own discrete parts of the asset (TR 2017/D1).

The deduction is therefore in relation to the decline in value of the interest, and not the underlying asset. The interest takes the characteristics of the underlying asset (eg its decline in value is calculated on the basis of the effective life of the underlying asset). If the underlying asset starts to be or ceases to be jointly held, there is no balancing adjustment, but rather the asset is taken to be split or merged (¶17-630).

Capital allowance deductions (under ITAA97 Div 40) that are attributable to the derivation of income from strata scheme common property, are allowed to the proprietors (and not the owners corporation) in proportion to their lot entitlements and to the extent of the income producing use of their individual lots. However, proprietors and strata schemes that previously relied on withdrawn IT 2505 may elect to continue to treat common property as being held on trust for the proprietors (TR 2015/3, including para 98).

The rules also apply where both lessor and lessee contribute to the cost of the asset, and where there are multiple interests in the same land or depreciating asset and more than one holder of the asset contributes to the cost of the asset (eg joint lessees). The joint holding rules do not lead to a duplication of deductions because the deduction to which each of the joint holders is entitled is based on the cost to that holder.

"Owner"

"Owner" is not defined in ITAA97 and, accordingly, has its ordinary meaning. To qualify for a deduction as the holder of a depreciating asset, the taxpayer does not have to personally use it in carrying on a trade or business, provided it is used for a taxable purpose. For example, if the asset is leased by the taxpayer to someone else, it is the taxpayer owner who generally gets the deduction. Thus, if furnished premises are leased, it is the lessor and not the lessee who claims deductions for the decline in value of furniture, fittings and other equipment owned by the lessor (under the general rule in Item 10). However, if the lessee installs an asset in the premises and owns and uses it for income-producing purposes, the lessee can generally claim deductions for the decline in value of that asset (under Item 2 or 3).

Motor vehicle lease novation arrangements

The taxation consequences of certain motor vehicle lease novation arrangements are set out in TR 1999/15 (see also *Jones* and ¶16-310). These arrangements involve the novation (or transfer) by an employee to an employer of some of the obligations under a motor vehicle lease. The ruling applies to both luxury and non-luxury cars. Under such arrangements, the employer/lessee is the holder of the car (if either Item 1 or 6 applies).

On early termination or expiry of the lease, the employee becomes the holder and a balancing adjustment must be made (ID 2003/759 to ID 2003/762). The FBT implications of such arrangements are outlined at ¶35-150.

[FITR ¶86-935, ¶86-945 – ¶87-000]

¶17-030 Excluded assets for capital allowances

The following assets are specifically excluded from the operation of the uniform capital allowance system (ITAA97 s 40-45; ITTPA s 40-47):

- capital works for which an amount is deductible under ITAA97 Div 43 (¶20-470) or would have been deductible, had the expenditure not been incurred before a particular day or had the works been used for the required purpose (¶20-480). Assets for which an amount is not deductible under Div 43 for any other reason are not excluded (ID 2005/21). As capital works that are ''plant'' (¶17-040) are excluded from Div 43, deductions for the decline in value of plant are available under ITAA97 Div 40 (¶17-015)
- certain assets provided by an employer as expense payment benefits or property benefits that are exempt from FBT under *Fringe Benefits Tax Assessment Act 1986*, s 58X (¶35-645)
- an asset for which the taxpayer could deduct an amount under the former film concession provisions in ITAA36 Divs 10B; 10BA of Pt III.

Other limitations include:

- no deduction for the decline in value of an R&D depreciating asset if expenditure on the asset has given rise to an R&D tax offset (ITAA97 s 355-715; ¶17-420)
- no deduction for the decline in value of cars if car expense deductions are calculated using the cents per kilometre method (ITAA97 s 40-55; ¶16-370)
- special provisions for software pools apply, rather than the general rules dealing with the decline in value of individual assets, where expenditure on in-house software is pooled (¶17-370)
- special provisions dealing with horticultural plants (¶18-070), water facilities (¶18-080), fodder storage assets (¶18-085), fencing assets (¶18-090), landcare operations (¶18-100), electricity connections (¶16-820) or telephone lines (¶18-060) apply, rather than the general rules (including those dealing with balancing adjustments). Capital repairs, alterations, additions or extensions to water facilities, fodder storage assets, fencing assets, and landcare operations are treated as a separate depreciating asset (s 40-53).

Small business entities can choose to calculate depreciating assets deductions under Div 328, instead of Div 40 (¶7-250).

[FITR ¶87-010 – ¶87-030]

¶17-040 Plant subject to capital allowances

The cost of ''plant'' (defined in ITAA97 s 45-40) is excluded from expenditure deductible under the capital works provisions (¶20-510) and is therefore subject to the uniform capital allowance system (¶17-030). The concept of ''plant'' is also relevant to the landcare operations provisions (¶18-100), the lease assignment provisions (¶23-230) and the water conservation provisions (¶18-080).

The primary factor in determining whether an item qualifies as plant is its function (TR 94/11). If the function is to provide the setting or environment within which income-producing activities are conducted, an item does not qualify as plant (eg an office building, a rock wall: ID 2007/160; demountable car park: IT 2130). Conversely, if the function is essentially the permanent means or apparatus used to produce the income (eg machines or manufacturing equipment) the item qualifies as plant, whether it is fixed or movable. Breakwaters installed by a port authority, used to keep vessels in place while inspections and repairs were carried out, were plant but a retaining wall, whose primary function was to protect reclaimed land, the cliffs and a factory, was not (*Port of Portland*).

An item used to create a particular atmosphere or ambience for premises used in a cafe, restaurant, licensed club, hotel, motel or retail shopping business performs a function that is so related to that business to warrant the item being held to come within the ordinary meaning of plant. This is because the atmosphere or ambience is intended to attract customers and is a definable element in the service which the business provides and for which its customers are prepared to pay (TR 2007/9). The item will only come within the ordinary meaning of plant if it does not form part of the premises. Describing an item as decor does not of itself mean that the item comes within the ordinary meaning of plant.

In addition to the kinds of property that fall within its ordinary meaning, ''plant'' also includes (s 45-40):

- articles, machinery, tools and rolling stock
- animals used as working beasts in a business other than a primary production business, eg racehorses
- plumbing fixtures and fittings, including wall and floor tiling, provided principally for the personal use of employees (or their children) in the taxpayer's business
- fences, dams and other structural improvements on land used for agricultural or pastoral pursuits and structural improvements on land used for forest operations (in either case whether the land is so used by its owner or another person), and structural improvements used wholly and exclusively for pearling or similar operations (provided they are situated at or near a port or harbour from which those operations are conducted) *other than*:
  - structural improvements used for domestic or residential purposes except as accommodation for employees (not necessarily of the taxpayer), tenants or share-farmers engaged in those pursuits or operations, and
  - forestry roads.

Residential rental premises or plant (TR 2004/16)

In deciding whether an item is part of residential rental premises or plant, the following matters are relevant:

- whether the item appears visually to retain a separate identity
- the degree of permanence with which it has been attached
- the incompleteness of the structure without it, and
- the extent to which it was intended to be permanent or whether it was likely to be replaced within a relatively short period.

Where an item neither forms part of the premises nor falls within the above extended definition of ''plant'', it will come within the ordinary meaning of plant. This will only occur where the function performed by the item is so related to the particular taxpayer's income-earning activities, or the function of the item is so special, that it warrants the item held to be plant. Such an occasion is likely to be rare in the context of a residential rental property.

An item cannot be an article if: (a) it is a structure erected or built on, or into, land; or (b) it forms part of the premises. However, an item may be an article even though it is attached to the premises. Carpet, curtains, desks and bookshelves are articles.

Machinery is plant whether or not it forms an integral part of a building or is a part of the setting of the landlord's rent-producing activities. The process of determining whether something is machinery involves: (a) identifying the relevant thing (unit) or things (units) based on a consideration of functionality; and (b) deciding whether that thing or each of those things satisfies the ordinary meaning of machinery.

The ordinary meaning of machinery includes devices, such as computers and microprocessors, which utilise in various processes minute amounts of energy in the form of electrical impulses. It also includes heating appliances, such as stoves, cooktops, ovens and hot water services. However, it does not include anything that is merely a reservoir or conduit, such as ducting, piping or wiring, although connected with something that is machinery. In other words, if the ducting, piping or wiring forms part of a unit that is a machine then it is machinery. Conversely, if it is merely connected to, but not part of, a unit that is a machine, then it is not machinery.

It follows that built-in kitchen cupboards, fences, insulation batts, built-in wardrobes and ducted vacuum system tubing are not plant (but the power unit, hose and brush elements of the vacuum system are plant). For the Commissioner's determination of the effective lives of items that are used by residential property operators, see ¶43-000.

The depreciation deduction for plant in a residential rental premises held as an investment is limited for certain taxpayers to new assets and is not available for previously used assets (¶17-012).

[FITR ¶99-600]

¶17-045 Non-arm's length dealings and capital allowances

If a taxpayer is not dealing at arm's length and incurs expenditure that is greater than the market value of what the expenditure is for, the amount paid is taken to be the "market value" (¶17-050). This applies in determining both the first and the second element of cost of the depreciating asset (¶17-100, ¶17-105). This stops the taxpayer from claiming a higher capital allowance deduction based on an artificially inflated purchase price.

Similarly, if a taxpayer is not dealing at arm's length and disposes of property for an amount that is less than market value, the amount received is taken to be the market value (¶17-640). This stops the taxpayer from obtaining a more favourable tax result by calculating its balancing adjustment on disposal of the asset on the basis of an artificially reduced disposal price.

The non-arm's length rule also applies to the deductions for certain primary production expenditure (¶18-050) and to the mining, project infrastructure and environmental protection deductions outlined at ¶19-000.

Dealing at arm's length

Parties are generally "at arm's length" if they are unrelated and neither party is effectively controlled by the other. In an arm's length situation, each party normally stands upon their rights and conducts their business in a formal manner without trusting the other's control or overmastering influence.

In determining whether parties are "dealing with each other at arm's length", an assessment must be made of whether the parties deal with each other as arm's length parties normally do, so that the outcome of their dealing is a matter of real bargaining (*Furse*).

A connection between the parties to a transaction is not conclusive evidence that they are not dealing with each other at arm's length, but is merely a factor to be taken into account. There may be transactions between related parties where the parties do deal with each other at arm's length. This may happen even if there is a close relationship between the parties or if one party has the power to control the other. It is not enough to look only at the relationship between the parties without examining the nature of the particular dealing between them (*Barnsdall*).

Parties at arm's length are not *dealing with each other* at arm's length if they collude to achieve a particular result or one party submits the exercise of its will to the dictation of the other (*Granby*). If more than one item of property is transferred as part of one transaction and one of the parties is indifferent to the apportionment of the consideration between the various items of property, the parties are considered not to be dealing with each other at arm's length because the acceding party has submitted the exercise of its will to the wishes of the other party (*Collis*).

[FITR ¶88-550]

¶17-050 Definition of market value

"Market value" is defined (ITAA97 s 995-1(1)) as having a meaning affected by ITAA97 Subdiv 960-S. Subdivision 960-S contains special rules for working out the market value of assets and non-cash benefits. For an asset, its market value is reduced by any input tax credits (¶34-100) to which the taxpayer would be entitled if it had acquired the asset solely for a creditable purpose. In working out the market value of a non-cash benefit, anything that would prevent or restrict the conversion of the benefit into money is to be disregarded. The Commissioner may approve valuation methods to establish the market value of assets or non-cash benefits. If a taxpayer uses an approved valuation method for an asset or non-cash benefit, the calculation is binding on the Commissioner. For an item that is not an asset or a non-cash benefit, the ordinary meaning of "market value" applies. The ordinary meaning of "market value" is the price that a willing but not anxious buyer would have to pay to a willing but not anxious seller for the item (*Spencer*). This test was later adopted in *Abrahams* where the market value was said to be "the price which a willing but not anxious vendor could reasonably expect to obtain and a hypothetical willing but not anxious purchaser could reasonably expect to have to pay . . . if the vendor and purchaser had got together and agreed on a price in friendly negotiation".

Market value has also been described as the best price that may reasonably be obtained for property if sold in the general market. If there is no general market, eg as in the case of shares in a private company, such a market is to be assumed. In addition, all possible buyers should be taken into account, even a buyer who, for his/her own reasons, is prepared to pay an excessive price (*Brisbane Water County Council*). The existence of a potential liability due to providing a guarantee can affect the value of shares, regardless of whether the likelihood of the guarantee being called upon can be established. The relevant question is what value will a prospective purchaser attribute to shares in the circumstances (*SDRQ*).

If shares are listed on a stock exchange, the most appropriate market to use for determining value is normally the stock exchange market (*Clifford*). The price bid for an item of property at auction may also provide a measure of market value (*Collis*). A market value determined on the basis of a trade-in price is not appropriate if this is not the price obtainable in the best available market (14 CTBR *Case* 29).

If considerable amounts are involved, a taxpayer would be prudent to obtain the services of a qualified valuer if there is any doubt about the fair market value, so that the taxpayer has a contemporaneous and expert record that enables the ready ascertainment of the market value of the property at a particular date. The Commissioner will apply the guidelines contained in *Market valuation for tax purposes*.

[FITR ¶767-590]

Cost of Depreciating Assets

¶17-080 Cost as initial basis for calculating decline in value

The decline in value of a depreciating asset is calculated on the basis of the ''cost'' of the asset to the particular taxpayer (¶17-480). Cost is also relevant in calculating any capital gain or loss if a balancing adjustment event happens for the asset (¶17-670). The cost of a depreciating asset held by the taxpayer consists of the first element of cost (generally the consideration provided by the taxpayer to hold the asset) and the second element of cost (generally the consideration provided by the taxpayer to bring the asset to its present condition and location from time to time) (ITAA97 s 40-175). While the first element of cost (¶17-100) applies to almost every asset, the second element (¶17-105) only applies to some assets. The cost rules apply regardless of whether the asset is acquired new or secondhand. An incorrectly calculated cost amount may be rectified.

Special rules deal with split assets and merged assets (¶17-100) and assets of consolidated groups (¶8-200, ¶8-580). In some cases the cost of an asset is modified (¶17-090).

[FITR ¶87-270 – ¶87-440]

¶17-090 Adjustments to cost of depreciating asset

Certain amounts are excluded from the cost of a depreciating asset:

- amounts that are not of a capital nature (ITAA97 s 40-220), whether or not deductible (eg whether or not deductible under the general deductions provisions: ¶16-000). Once plant has been installed and handed over to its owner in an operational state, the cost of bringing the plant into full operation is revenue expenditure and immediately deductible (TD 93/126).
- where an offset has been available in respect of expenditure on an R&D asset, the expenditure is not also allowable under the capital allowance provisions (ITAA97 s 355-715; ¶17-420).
- for depreciating assets that are not plant, amounts incurred before 1 July 2001 or under a contract entered into before that date (ITAA97 s 40-200). Any amounts incurred on plant before that date may form part of the cost of a depreciating asset under transitional provisions.

Once the cost of a depreciating asset has been established under the rules at ¶17-100 and ¶17-105, it may have to be further adjusted as follows:

- the cost of a car exceeding the car limit may be reduced to that limit (¶17-200)
- the cost of a car acquired at a discount under a scheme to avoid the car limit may be increased by the discount (¶17-210)
- the cost of a copyright in a film is reduced by the amount of the producer offset available under the rules discussed at ¶20-340 (ITAA97 s 40-45)
- each element of the asset's cost is reduced to the extent that any part of the cost is deductible under a provision other than the uniform capital allowance provisions or the special provisions for small business taxpayers (ITAA97 s 40-215)

- cost may be reduced if a commercial debt is forgiven (¶17-510)
- cost of an asset may be reduced if the asset it replaces has been disposed of involuntarily (¶17-720), or
- cost of an asset does not include an amount that is denied deductibility (under ITAA97 s 26-97) because it is funded by certain amounts derived by participants of the National Disability Insurance Scheme (ITAA97 s 40-235).

The foreign currency denominated cost of a depreciating asset is converted at the exchange rate applicable when the taxpayer began to hold the asset or when satisfying the liability to pay for it, whichever occurs first (¶23-070). See also the foreign exchange gains and losses rules (¶23-075).

The TOFA rules (¶23-020) may affect the calculation of the cost of a depreciating asset where a financial arrangement is used as consideration for acquiring the asset.

GST and depreciating assets

The cost of a depreciating asset (and, in a year after the first year of use, the opening adjustable value) is reduced by any input tax credits relating to the acquisition of the asset or to second element costs of the asset, and by certain decreasing adjustments relating to the asset. If the decreasing adjustment is due to a change in planned use, it is included in assessable income (ITAA97 Subdiv 27-B). If the cost is taken to be market value, that is also a GST-exclusive value.

The cost of the asset (and, in a year later than the first year of use, the opening adjustable value) may be increased by certain increasing adjustments relating directly or indirectly to the asset. If the increasing adjustment is due to a change in planned use, it is deducted. For detailed explanation of increasing and decreasing adjustments, see the *Australian Master GST Guide*.

▶ Example

George, who is registered for GST, buys a ladder for $550 that will be used 80% of the time in his plumbing business. The remaining 20% usage is for non-taxable purposes. The cost of the asset is taken to be the purchase price reduced by $40, ie $510 (calculated as $550 – [(1/11 × $550) × 80%]). If the decline in value is $110 over 2 years, the opening adjustable value at the start of Year 3 is $400.

If the usage changes at the commencement of Year 3 to a 100% taxable purpose, there will be an assessable decreasing adjustment of $10 (ie [1/11 × $550] – $40).

If, instead, the usage changed to a 50% taxable purpose, there would be a deductible increasing adjustment of $15 (calculated as $40 – [1/11 × $550] × 50%).

[FITR ¶69-150 – ¶69-240, ¶87-400, ¶87-420, ¶87-425]

¶17-100 First element of cost of depreciating asset

The first element of cost of a depreciating asset generally represents the amount the taxpayer has paid or is taken to have paid in order to hold the asset, and is worked out when the taxpayer begins to hold the asset (ITAA97 s 40-180).

The first element of cost is subject to certain exclusions and modifications and is GST-exclusive (¶17-090).

If an amount is paid for 2 or more things including one depreciating asset, the amount is apportioned on a reasonable basis between those things, generally based on relative market values (ITAA97 s 40-195). That is not necessarily the adjustable value of the asset (ID 2002/818).

The first element of cost includes an amount paid or taken to be paid in relation to starting to hold the asset, if that amount is directly connected with holding the asset. It does not include an amount that forms part of the second element of cost of another depreciating asset.

The first element of the cost of a mining, quarrying or prospecting right may be reduced by the market value of exploration benefits received under farm-in farm-out arrangements (s 40-1130; ¶19-010).

A lessor's deduction for decline in value of an asset subject to a sale and leaseback arrangement is based on the cost of the asset to the lessor, not the cost to the lessee (TR 2006/13).

The amount the taxpayer is taken to have paid

The cost rules specify the amount that the taxpayer is taken to have paid to hold a depreciating asset (ie first element of cost) or to bring it to its current location and condition (ie the second element of cost). The taxpayer is taken to have paid the greater of the following 2 amounts (ITAA97 s 40-185):

(1) the consideration given, ie the sum of the following:

(a) any amount paid to buy or create the asset (eg labour and materials) or to bring the asset to its current location and condition. This would cover incidental costs (eg stamp duty) and if the taxpayer makes a prepayment, it is the amount of the prepayment. It includes amounts that the taxpayer *is taken to have paid*, such as the price of the notional purchase made when trading stock is converted to a depreciating asset (¶9-245), the cost of an asset held under a hire purchase arrangement under ITAA97 s 240-25 (¶23-250), and a lessor's deemed purchase price when a luxury car lease ends (ITAA97 s 242-90: ¶17-220; ID 2005/197). If the asset is a Div 230 financial arrangement or a Div 230 financial arrangement is involved in the consideration, ITAA97 s 230-505 applies (¶23-020)

(b) the amount of a liability to pay money. Only the part of the liability that has not been satisfied is taken into account

(c) where there is a reduction in a right to receive money (eg a debt is waived), the amount of the liability when it is terminated

(d) the market value of a non-cash benefit provided by the taxpayer. A non-cash benefit is any property or services that are not money (ITAA97 s 995-1(1)). Where a company issues shares for depreciating assets, TR 2008/5 applies (¶3-260).

(e) the market value of a non-cash benefit that the taxpayer becomes liable to provide. Only the part of the liability that has not been satisfied is taken into account, and

(f) where the liability to provide a non-cash benefit to the taxpayer is terminated, the market value of the benefit when the liability is terminated, and

(2) amounts included in assessable income because a taxpayer started to hold the asset (ie where an amount is assessable under ITAA36 s 21A (¶10-030) for receiving the depreciating asset as a non-cash benefit) or gave something to start holding it (this would be the case where the taxpayer exchanges a depreciating asset for another and as a result a balancing adjustment amount is assessable). In the case of second element costs, the relevant amount is the amount included in assessable income because the taxpayer received the benefit or gave something to receive the benefit (ie the benefit that brought the asset to its current condition and location, eg the modification to a truck). In determining the amount included in assessable income, the value of anything provided by the taxpayer that reduced the amount actually included in assessable income must be ignored.

For examples of the application of the above cost rules, see ID 2003/1085, ID 2004/116 and ID 2008/93.

▶ Example 1: Amount included in assessable income under s 21A

If Aco provides medals (with a market value of $20,000) and a payment of $75,000 to Bco in return for a stamping machine (with an arm's length value of $100,000), Aco will include $25,000 (ie $100,000 – $75,000) in its assessable income. The first element of cost of the machine for Aco is the greater of: (a) the sum of the amount paid ($75,000) and the market value of the medals provided ($20,000), ie $95,000; and (b) the amount that would have been included in assessable income, if one ignored the contribution of $75,000 made by Aco, ie $100,000. This produces a first element of cost of $100,000.

▶ Example 2: Assessable balancing adjustment amount

Mary exchanges a tractor with an adjustable value (¶17-485) to her of $10,000 in return for a plough with a market value of $15,000. The termination value of the tractor is the market value of the plough, ie $15,000 (¶17-640). The assessable balancing adjustment to be made as a result of disposing of the tractor is $5,000 (ie $15,000 – $10,000). The first element of cost of the plough is the greater of: (a) the market value of the tractor she provided; and (b) the amount that was assessable for giving the tractor in order to start holding the plough (ie $15,000), ignoring the value of the tractor.

If the plough had a market value of $5,000, the deductible balancing adjustment would be $5,000 (ie $10,000 – $5,000). In this case, the first element of cost of the plough would be the greater of: (a) the market value of the tractor; and (b) the amount that would have been assessable (ie $5,000), ignoring the adjustable value of the tractor.

▶ Example 3: Consideration provided by taxpayer

Fiona, a house painter, buys a panel van from Andrew in exchange for: painting his home (market value of painting services is $4,000), terminating a $1,000 debt owed to her by him, undertaking to repaint his home in 10 years (market value of the painting services that she is under a liability to provide is $1,500), and incurring a liability to pay him $1,000. The first element of cost of the panel van is $7,500 (ie the sum of $4,000 + $1,000 + $1,500 + $1,000).

Specified amounts of first element of cost

In the following cases, the first element of cost is specified in s 40-180, rather than being the amount that the taxpayer is taken to have paid to hold the asset under the above rules (cases 1 to 13 do not apply to determine the second element of cost). If more than one item covers the asset, the last applicable item applies.

(1) If a depreciating asset is split into 2 or more assets, the first element of cost of each new asset is a reasonable proportion of the sum of the adjustable value (¶17-485) of the original asset before the split and of the splitting costs (the splitting costs are calculated under the above rules for determining the amount that a taxpayer is taken to have paid) (ITAA97 s 40-205). Such reasonable proportion may be based on the relative market values of the new assets. See also ¶17-630.

(2) If a depreciating asset or assets is or are merged into another depreciating asset, the first element of cost of the new asset is a reasonable proportion of the sum of the adjustable value or values of the original asset or assets just before the merger and of the merger costs (the merger costs are calculated under the above rules for determining the amount that a taxpayer is taken to have paid) (ITAA97 s 40-210). See also ¶17-630.

(3) If the taxpayer stops using a depreciating asset for any purpose expecting never to use it again (thus triggering a balancing adjustment event: ¶17-630), but continues to hold it, the first element of cost of the asset is the termination value (¶17-640) of the asset at the time of the event.

(4) If the taxpayer has not used a depreciating asset and expects never to use it (thus triggering a balancing adjustment event: ¶17-630), but continues to hold it, the first element of cost of the asset is its termination value (¶17-640) at the time of the event.

(5) If a partnership asset was held, just before becoming a partnership asset, by one or more partners, the first element of cost of the asset to the partnership is the market value (¶17-050) of the asset when the partnership started to hold it.

If a balancing adjustment event happens to a depreciating asset because there is a change in the holding of, or interests in, an asset and one of the entities that held the asset before the change has an interest in it after the change (¶17-780), and the asset was a partnership asset before the change or becomes one as a result of the change, the first element of cost of the asset is the market value of the asset when the change occurred.

(6) If a balancing adjustment event happens to a depreciating asset but roll-over relief (¶17-710) applies, the first element of cost of the asset for the transferee is the adjustable value (¶17-485) of the asset to the transferor just before the event occurred.

(7) If the taxpayer is the legal owner of an asset hired under a hire purchase agreement, the hirer (the economic owner) is the holder of the asset as long as it has the right to become the legal owner of the asset. If the hirer does *not* become the legal owner (eg because it does not exercise the option to purchase the asset), the legal owner is taken to start ''holding'' the asset and the first element of cost of the asset is its market value at that time.

(8) If the taxpayer starts to hold the asset under a non-arm's length dealing for a cost exceeding its market value, the first element of cost of the asset is taken to be its market value (¶17-045, ¶17-050) at that time.

(9) If the taxpayer starts to hold the asset under a private or domestic arrangement (eg as a gift or under a consumer loyalty program by redeeming reward points: ID 2002/915), the first element of cost of the asset is its market value (¶17-050) at that time.

(10) If the Minister for Finance has determined a cost under *Airports (Transitional) Act 1996*, ss 49A, 49B, 50A, 50B, 51A or 51B, the first element of cost of the asset is that amount.

(11) The first element of cost of an asset that was previously owned by an exempt entity (and to which ITAA97 Div 58 applies: ¶17-130) is the notional written down value of the asset or the undeducted pre-existing audited book value of the asset, plus any acquisition costs (ITAA97 s 58-70(3), (5)).

(12) If the asset has devolved to the taxpayer as the legal personal representative of a deceased person, the first element of cost of the asset is its adjustable value (¶17-485) at the time of death. If the asset was allocated to a low-value pool, the cost is so much of the closing pool balance for the year of death as is attributable to that asset.

(13) If, as a result of a person's death, the asset has passed to the taxpayer as the beneficiary or joint tenant, the first element of cost of the asset is its market value when the taxpayer started holding it, less any capital gain that was disregarded by the deceased or by the legal personal representative.

(14) If a balancing adjustment occurs in relation to a mining, quarrying or prospecting right, the first element of cost is the amount that would be the asset's adjustable value on the day the balancing adjustment event occurs (ignoring ITAA97 s 40-285(3), which would otherwise deem the adjustable value to be nil).

[FITR ¶87-290 – ¶87-370]

¶17-105 Second element of cost of depreciating asset

The cost of a depreciating asset (which is relevant to calculating the decline in value of the asset) comprises a first element (¶17-100) and a second element of cost. The second element is the amount the taxpayer is taken to have paid to bring the asset to its present condition and location from time to time (ITAA97 s 40-190). For example, the second element of cost would include the cost of modifications, alterations or improvements made to the asset by the taxpayer during the relevant income year. It also includes the cost of transporting the asset to its current location such as freight, import duties, installation costs and legal costs (eg ID 2003/514 to ID 2003/516; ID 2009/74). It does not include expenses that are not capital or capital in nature, eg repairs, annual registration and compulsory third party insurance costs of a car.

If the cost of bringing the asset to its present condition or location is incurred in a non-arm's length dealing for a cost exceeding the market value of the benefit (eg a service), or in a private or domestic arrangement, the second element of cost is the market value of that benefit. For example, if an associate of the taxpayer provides modifications to the taxpayer's panel van for $6,000, but the modifications have a market value of $3,000, the second element of cost of the van is $3,000.

In any other circumstances, the second element of cost is calculated as the amount the taxpayer is taken to have paid under the rules discussed at ¶17-100 to bring the asset to its present condition and location.

If the taxpayer has paid an amount for 2 or more things including bringing a depreciating asset to its present condition and location, the amount is apportioned on a reasonable basis (generally based on relative market values) (ITAA97 s 40-195).

Certain amounts cannot form part of the second element of cost of an asset and generally, cost is the GST-exclusive amount (¶17-090).

The second element of cost also includes all costs reasonably attributable to a balancing adjustment event (eg demolition costs: ID 2006/275).

Installation, dismantling and transport costs

Generally, installation costs do *not* include the cost of *structural* alterations to the building in which plant is to be housed and that may be necessary for its efficient integration into the operations, eg extensions to a building to make room for new plant are not part of the cost of installing that plant (9 TBRD *Case* J65; IT 2197). However, the Commissioner's depreciating asset effective life tables (commencing at ¶43-000) show certain special factory buildings and foundations forming an integral part of plant as qualifying for deduction, but usually with longer effective lives than the plant or machinery itself.

Alterations and additions to depreciating assets and dismantling, transporting and re-erecting costs (eg on removal to new premises) would constitute second element costs. However, the cost of *minor* removals and rearrangements of depreciating assets within existing premises is claimable as an outright deduction in the year incurred. Likewise, maintenance, repairs and similar recurrent revenue expenditure are deductible outright and not added to cost for capital allowances purposes. Furthermore, expenditure incurred by a taxpayer in installing *leased* plant may be deductible under ITAA97 s 8-1 in the same way as normal lease payments (IT 2197).

Expenditure on temporary buildings and facilities directly related to the construction of plant may, in some circumstances, be part of the depreciable cost of that plant (IT 2618).

[FITR ¶87-380]

¶17-130 Depreciating assets and tax-exempt entities

There is a limit to the deductions for the decline in value of depreciating assets that can be claimed by: (i) tax-exempt entities that become taxable; and (ii) taxable entities that acquire the depreciating assets of tax-exempt entities in connection with the acquisition of a business. Taxable entities are only allowed to claim deductions for the decline in value of a depreciating asset based on either: (i) the depreciating asset's notional written down value; or (ii) the asset's undeducted pre-existing audited book value recorded in the tax-exempt entity's audited annual accounts before 4 August 1997 (ITAA97 Div 58; ¶17-100). Under Div 58, taxpayers use the ordinary Div 40 rules with some minor modifications for all privatised depreciating assets (ID 2007/84 to ID 2007/86). In particular, a transition entity in an entity sale situation (where the income of an exempt entity becomes, to any extent, taxable) is obliged to make a choice, after the transition time, to determine the effective life of the depreciating asset it holds at the transition time and may later recalculate such effective life (ID 2006/287 to ID 2006/289). Division 58 (rather than ITAA36 Sch 2D Div 57: ¶10-630) applies to all depreciating assets, including non-plant assets.

[FITR ¶87-350, ¶106-500]

Car Limit

¶17-200 Depreciating cars: cost price limit

A limit is placed on the first element (¶17-100) of the cost of cars over a certain price (ITAA97 s 40-230). The limit for cars first held in 2019–20 is $57,581. The limit is $59,136 for the 2020–21 income year as determined by the Commissioner (ATO website *Buying and using assets*).

For example, if a car is bought in December 2019 for $60,000, the deduction for the decline in value of the car is calculated as if the first element of cost were only $57,581. The cost of a car includes a radio, air conditioner etc, attached to the vehicle at the time of purchase, but not a radar detector (IT 2611). The limit applies regardless of whether the vehicle is new or secondhand.

The car limit is indexed each year for inflation. For the limits in previous years, see ¶43-110. The particular car limit that applies to a car is the limit for the financial year (not the income year) in which the car is first held by the taxpayer.

"Car" is defined to mean a motor vehicle (other than a motorcycle) designed to carry a load of less than one tonne and fewer than 9 passengers. Furthermore, the car limit only applies to cars designed mainly for carrying passengers. It applies independently of the luxury car tax provisions.

The car limit applies both to cars used by their owners and to cars owned by leasing companies. In *Citibank*, a lessor who used the finance method of accounting for direct financing leases to record income from luxury car leases (¶17-220) failed to avoid the effect of the car limit. The gross rental receipts were held to be income from which allowable deductions, including depreciation, were to be deducted to arrive at taxable income. For the application of the car limit to novated car leases, see ID 2005/197.

Stretched limousines may be subject to the car limit, but only to the extent of the first element of cost (subsequent modifications to "stretch" the original vehicle are included in the second element of cost). Hearses are not subject to the car limit (TD 2006/39). Vehicles fitted out for transporting disabled persons seated in wheelchairs for profit, eg modified taxis, are excluded from the car limit, as are cars whose first element of cost exceeds the car limit only because of modifications made to enable an individual with a disability to use the car for a taxable purpose (eg in a disabled taxpayer's courier business).

The car limit applies after the discount provisions (¶17-210) have applied and after the cost of the car has been reduced by any GST input tax credits (TD 2006/40). If a car is held by 2 or more entities, the car limit is applied to the cost of the car and not to the cost of each entity's interest in the car.

Special rules apply when the car is disposed of (¶17-640).

[FITR ¶87-435]

¶17-210 Car limit applies for trade-ins on cars

An anti-avoidance measure counters avoidance of the car limit where an asset (including a car) is traded in on the purchase of a car by adjusting the purchase price of the car upwards (ITAA97 s 40-225).

The measure applies if: (i) it is reasonable to conclude that a car was able to be purchased at a discount and that the discount was referable to the taxpayer or another entity selling another asset for less than its market value; (ii) an amount was deducted for the other asset; and (iii) the pre-discount price exceeds the car limit for the financial year in which the taxpayer used the new car for any purpose. In such a case, the amount of the discount is added to the discounted purchase price of the new car. The measure does not apply to cars that are modified for disabled persons. Special rules apply when the car is disposed of (¶17-640).

[FITR ¶87-430]

¶17-220 Luxury car leases

Luxury car leases (including subleases), other than genuine short-term hire arrangements and hire purchase agreements, are treated as sale (by the lessor to the lessee) and loan transactions. The lessee (and not the lessor) is treated as the owner of the car until the lease ends or the lessee enters a sublease (ITAA97 Div 242; ¶17-020). This treatment applies where the cost of a car (whether new or secondhand) is more than the car limit applying for the income year in which the lease commenced, ensuring that the limit applies equally to *leased* luxury cars and purchased or otherwise financed cars.

The market value of the car at the start of the lease (or a specified amount in the case of a sublease) is taken to be the first element of cost for the car for depreciation purposes (¶17-100; s 242-20). Such market value, less any amount actually paid by the lessee to the lessor is also taken to be the amount that the lessee has borrowed from the lessor (s 242-25). Lease payments are divided into notional loan principal and interest components.

Taxation treatment of lessor

The lessor is assessable on the interest component of the lease payment, ie the return on funds lent by the lessor. Such assessable income is calculated by multiplying the outstanding notional loan principal at the start of the lease payment period by the implicit interest rate for the period (s 242-35). The implicit interest rate is the rate under the lease for a payment period (maximum 6 months), taking into account the total lease payments payable under the lease and any termination payments. The lessor is not entitled to deductions for the decline in value of the car.

Taxation treatment of lessee

The lessee is entitled to: (i) a deduction equal to the interest component which is assessable to the lessor, calculated for each payment period and apportioned to reflect any private use (ss 242-45 to 242-55); and (ii) deductions for the decline in value of the car based on the market value of the car, reduced according to the car limit applicable in the income year, and by any private use. The lessee is not entitled to a deduction for the capital component of lease payments.

Lease extension, renewal, termination or expiry

If the lease is extended, renewed or ends, and the sum of the lease payments and any termination amounts paid to the lessor exceeds the sum of the notional principal and interest, the excess is assessable to the lessor and deductible to the lessee. If the sum of the lease payments and any termination amounts paid to the lessor is less than the sum of the notional principal and interest, the difference is deductible to the lessor and assessable to the lessee (ss 242-65; 242-70).

When the lease expires or is terminated, and is then extended or renewed, the original loan is treated as having been repaid and the lessor is treated as having made a new loan in the amount of the car's market value at the time of the extension or renewal (s 242-80). The notional loan is treated as a termination amount and the lessee continues to be the owner of the car.

If at the end of the lease (renewal or extension) the lessee acquires the car from the lessor, the transfer and termination payments to acquire the car are ignored for tax purposes and the lessee continues to own the car and therefore the amount paid by the lessee is not assessable to the lessor or deductible to the lessee (s 242-85).

If the lessee's right to use the car ends, and no amount is paid to the lessor by the lessee to acquire the car, the lessee is treated as having sold the car back to the lessor for its market value at the end of the lease (s 242-90).

[FITR ¶229-000]

Effective Life of Depreciating Assets

¶17-270 Effective life of depreciating asset

The decline in value of a depreciating asset is calculated on the basis of the effective life of the asset (¶17-490, ¶17-500). Taxpayers can work out their own estimate of the effective life of a depreciating asset or rely on the Commissioner's determination (ITAA97 s 40-95). The Commissioner's determination is contained in TR 2020/3, which replaces TR 2019/5 from 1 July 2020. The choice must be made for the year in which the asset is first used, or installed ready for use, by the taxpayer for any purpose. In some circumstances, no choice can be made and a statutory effective life applies (¶17-280).

The ATO periodically reviews the effective lives of some assets in its published determinations. Details of the assets currently under review are updated in the ATO document *Reviews in progress*.

The effective life of a depreciating asset generally does not need to be worked out if the temporary full expensing rules apply, unless the asset's opening adjustable value needs to be determined (¶17-430).

Taxpayer's estimate of effective life

The effective life adopted by a taxpayer must relate to the total estimated period the asset can be used by *any* entity for the purpose of producing income (assessable, exempt or non-assessable non-exempt), exploration or prospecting, mining site rehabilitation or environmental protection activities, or conducting R&D activities (ITAA97 s 40-105). Therefore even if the taxpayer expects to dispose of the asset before its effective income-producing life is over, the effective life does not end at this earlier time, unless it is likely to be scrapped.

In determining effective life, the task is to find the period of time over which the asset can be used by any entity for the specified purposes, having regard to the wear and tear reasonably expected from the taxpayer's circumstances of use and assuming that the asset will be maintained in reasonably good order and condition. A determination is expected to take into account the factors outlined in TR 2020/3.

Where plant is acquired *secondhand* its secondhand condition may be taken into account in estimating its effective life.

If the taxpayer concludes that the asset is likely to be scrapped, sold for no more than scrap value or abandoned at a specific point in time (earlier than what would otherwise be its effective life), its effective life ends at that earlier time. That conclusion may be on the basis of experience in the particular industry in relation to the scrapping of assets (eg an asset may be scrapped where, because of the need to keep up with technology, it is no longer useful for income-producing purposes). An asset may also be scrapped because the goods it produces have gone out of production or the production process has changed. However, the technical risk arising from conducting R&D activities is ignored in making the assessment (s 40-105).

Where a depreciating asset is acquired for a particular project, a balancing adjustment event occurs for that asset at the completion of the project if the taxpayer stops using the asset, or having it installed ready for use, for any purpose and expects never to use it (TD 2006/33). Note that an asset cannot be treated as scrapped simply because its use is discontinued or the asset is stored (4 CTBR *Case* 31). However, an asset may be treated as destroyed if rendered useless and left in place (*BP Oil*).

The effective life is calculated at the time when the asset is first used by the taxpayer for any purpose or is installed ready for use for any purpose and held in reserve.

Re-estimation of effective life

The effective life of an asset *must* be recalculated if during the relevant income year the cost of the asset is increased by at least 10%, even though the taxpayer may conclude that the effective life is the same. This rule is intended to ensure that second element costs incurred during the year are deducted over the life of the asset if they relate to future activities over a substantial period.

The recalculated effective life is used for the future write-off of the balance of the amount yet to be deducted.

The following examples illustrate the method of calculating effective life.

▶ Example 1

According to a manufacturer's specifications, a new photocopier is capable of producing one million copies before needing to be replaced. When purchased new, Copy Co expects that, as used in its business, it will produce half a million copies in 2 years. It is therefore reasonable to conclude that the copier has an effective life of 4 years, even if Copy Co's intention is to sell the copier after 2 years to someone else who may use it more or less heavily.

▶ Example 2

The operators of a luxury hotel chain refurbish every 5 years. Carpets and curtains are scrapped. TVs are sold at auction. If the TVs had continued to be used by the hotel chain instead of being sold, they would have required replacement after another 2 years. The effective life of the carpets and curtains is 5 years and the effective life of the TVs is 7 years.

▶ Example 3

A company that uses specialist machinery has a policy of continuous plant development and improvement. Experience demands new generation machines every 5 years and older machines are then obsolete. The effective life of the machines is 5 years.

▶ Example 4

A mining company purchases mining equipment to use in a remote locality. The expected life of the mine is 10 years at the end of which the equipment will be abandoned, although it is still physically capable of operation. The effective life of the equipment is 10 years. If it was expected that the equipment could reasonably be transferred to, and used at, another mine site, the effective life could not be limited to the life of the first mine.

▶ Example 5

A company purchases machines for use in its business. Environmental legislation will outlaw the use of the particular type of machine throughout Australia within 5 years. The effective life of the machines could not be more than 5 years.

Mining, quarrying and prospecting rights or information

A taxpayer self-assesses the effective life of rights or information related to mining, quarrying or prospecting activities where an immediate deduction is unavailable. They do this by estimating the life of the existing or proposed mine, petroleum field, or quarry. Where the right or information relates to more than one mine, field or quarry, a taxpayer uses the activity with the longest estimated life (s 40-95(10)).

The effective life is to be reasonably estimated from the time the taxpayer first uses the rights or information for any purpose. In doing so, the taxpayer must only refer to the time over which the mining, petroleum or quarrying reserves are expected to be extracted using an accepted industry practice (s 40-95(11)). This enables a taxpayer to take a prior owner's use of the rights or information into account in calculating the remaining effective life.

A taxpayer may recalculate the effective life if it is no longer accurate because of changed circumstances related to the existing or proposed mine, field or quarry (ss 40-110(3B); 40-110(4)). For example, the asset may be written off at the taxpayer's choice if the exploration is unsuccessful.

If rights or information do not relate to an existing or proposed mine, petroleum field, or quarry, their effective life is 15 years (s 40-95(12)). An example of such information is seismic data held by an entity that licenses it on a non-exclusive basis to multiple clients (TR 2019/4).

Either the prime cost or the diminishing value methods may be used to calculate the decline in value of the rights or information.

The conditions for claiming an immediate deduction for expenditure on rights or information related to mining, quarrying or prospecting activities under s 40-80 are discussed at ¶17-350 and ¶19-010. Special rules apply where mining, quarrying or prospecting rights are exchanged for exploration benefits under a farm-in farm out arrangement. Special rules also apply where joint venture parties exchange post-30 June 2001 rights to pursue a single development under an interest realignment arrangement (¶19-010).

A production licence granted under the *Petroleum (Submerged Lands) Act 1967* (Cth) which included both a right to explore and a right to produce petroleum constituted a single depreciating asset, rather than 2 assets depreciable over different time periods (*Mitsui & Co Ltd*).

Commissioner's determination of effective life

The Commissioner publishes recommended periods of effective life which taxpayers may optionally adopt as a safe harbour estimate for a depreciating asset (ITAA97 s 40-100). For the Commissioner's latest determinations of effective life see ¶43-000 (TR 2020/3).

The appropriate determination to be applied to determine the effective life of a depreciating asset is that in force (s 40-95):

- when the taxpayer entered into a contract to acquire the asset
- when the taxpayer otherwise acquired the asset, or
- when the taxpayer started to construct the asset (eg ID 2002/180),

provided the asset started to be used (or was installed ready for use) for any purpose within 5 years of that time. Otherwise, it is the determination in force when the asset starts being used (or is installed ready for use) for any purpose.

However, if the taxpayer acquired plant or started to construct plant or entered into a contract to acquire plant before 11.45 am on 21 September 1999, the appropriate effective life is that contained in IT 2685. There is no restriction on the period within which the plant must first be used or held ready for use.

There is a "statutory cap" on the effective lives of specified assets where the taxpayer has chosen the effective life determined by the Commissioner (¶17-280).

Re-estimation of effective life

If the effective life based on the Commissioner's determination is no longer accurate because of changed circumstances relating to the nature of the use of the asset, the taxpayer *may* recalculate the effective life of the asset (s 40-110). The taxpayer *must* recalculate the effective life if using the Commissioner's determination of effective life and the prime cost method (¶17-490), and the cost of the asset during the income year is increased by at least 10%. The taxpayer may conclude that the effective life is unchanged. For example, the effective life of an asset must be recalculated if the cost of modifications to an asset done during an income year after the year of acquisition increases the total cost of the asset by at least 10%. This is because the cost of improvements may extend the life of the asset.

[FITR ¶87-110 – ¶87-160]

¶17-280 Statutory effective life of depreciating asset

Generally, the effective life of an asset is either self-assessed by the taxpayer or as determined by the Commissioner (¶17-270). In the following circumstances, however, a statutory effective life applies for the asset.

Temporary full expensing or accelerated depreciation may be available for assets meeting the relevant eligibility requirements although there are specific conditions for larger taxpayers in relation to second-hand assets and intangible assets (¶17-430).

Asset acquired from associate

If the taxpayer acquired the depreciating asset from an associate who used the diminishing value method, the effective life of the asset for the taxpayer is the same as that used by the associate (ITAA97 s 40-95(4)). If the associate used the prime cost method, the taxpayer must use the remaining effective life of the asset. The taxpayer may request the associate to give it the information about the method and effective life it used for the asset, within 60 days (ITAA97 s 40-140). There are special rules if the ‘‘statutory cap’’ (see below) applies.

If either in the year of the acquisition or in a later year the cost of the asset increases by at least 10%, the effective life *must* be recalculated (ITAA97 s 40-110(2), (3)).

Holder changes but user is the same or is an associate of former user

This rule deals with the case where the taxpayer acquires the asset from the former holder but the user of the asset (while the taxpayer is the holder of the asset) is the same as, or is an associate of, the user of the asset while the asset was held by the former holder (s 40-95(5)). In this case, if the former holder used the diminishing value method, the taxpayer must use the same effective life that was used by the former holder (eg not an accelerated depreciation rate under the former law: ID 2003/754). If the former holder was using the prime cost method, the taxpayer must use the remaining effective life. If either the former holder did not use an effective life or the taxpayer does not know and cannot readily find out the effective life used by the former holder, the taxpayer must use the effective life determined by the Commissioner. There are special rules if the ‘‘statutory cap’’ (see below) applies.

If either in the year of the acquisition or in a later year the cost of the asset increases by at least 10%, the effective life *must* be recalculated (s 40-110(2), (3)).

Intangible depreciating assets

The effective life of an intangible depreciating asset mentioned in the table below is the period applicable to the asset under the table and cannot be recalculated (s 40-95(7)).

Asset	Effective life
Standard patent	20 years
Innovation patent	8 years
Petty patent	6 years
Registered design	15 years

Asset	Effective life
Copyright (other than film copyright)	The shorter of: (a) 25 years from acquisition of copyright; and (b) the period until the copyright ends
A licence (not relating to a copyright or in-house software)	The term of the licence
A licence relating to copyright (except copyright in a film)	The shorter of: (a) 25 years from when the taxpayer became licensee; and (b) the period until the licence ends
In-house software	5 years if first used, or installed ready for use, from 1 July 2015; otherwise 4 years
Spectrum licence	The term of the licence
Datacasting transmitter licence	15 years
Telecommunications site access right	The term of the right

Film copyright (and exclusive licences relating to copyright in a film) acquired on or after 1 July 2004 is specifically excluded from the treatment of ordinary copyright. Deductions may be available for the decline in value of film copyright on the basis of its effective life (self-assessed, or determined by the Commissioner), using either the prime cost or diminishing value methods (¶17-015).

The effective life of an **indefeasible right to use** a telecommunications cable system is the effective life of the cable over which the right is granted. For expenditure incurred from 12 May 2004, this applies to both domestic and international IRUs (¶17-015). Such effective life can be self-assessed by the taxpayer or determined by the Commissioner.

The effective life of any other intangible depreciating asset (other than mining, petroleum or quarrying rights: ¶17-270) cannot be longer than the term of the asset as extended by any reasonably assured extension or renewal of that term.

Statutory caps on effective life of specified assets

A statutory ''capped'' life applies for specified assets if the taxpayer has chosen the effective life determined by the Commissioner (¶43-000) and the capped life is shorter than the life determined by the Commissioner (ITAA97 s 40-102). Taxpayers will continue to be able to self-assess the effective life of the asset based on their own circumstances (if they do not wish to adopt the capped life or the life determined by the Commissioner). For details of the statutory caps, see ¶43-105.

[FITR ¶87-110, ¶87-115, ¶87-160]

Special Rates of Decline in Value

¶17-325 Small business simplified depreciation rules

A simplified regime for calculating capital allowances on depreciating assets is contained in ITAA97 Subdiv 328-D. Small business entities that choose to use this regime are not subject to the provisions of ITAA97 Div 40 (ITAA97 s 328-175). For full details see ¶7-250.

[FITR ¶313-085 – ¶313-095]

¶17-330 Low-cost assets: instant asset write-offs

Medium-sized business entities

An immediate 100% deduction for certain depreciating assets used by a ''medium-sized business'' for a taxable purpose is available for a limited period. A medium-sized business is an entity that is not a small business entity (¶7-050) but would qualify as a small business entity if the threshold of the aggregated turnover test was either of the prescribed higher thresholds in ITAA97 s 40-82 instead of the $10 million in ITAA97 s 328-110. A medium-sized business would not be able to access the simplified depreciation regime available to small business (¶7-250).

If an entity satisfies the aggregated turnover test assuming the threshold is $50 million, an immediate deduction is available:

- for depreciating assets costing less than $30,000 first acquired between 7.30 pm (AEDT) on 2 April 2019 and 11 March 2020. The taxpayer must have started to use the asset or had it installed ready for use before 12 March 2020, and
- for depreciating assets costing less than $150,000 first acquired between 7.30 pm (AEDT) on 2 April 2019 and 31 December 2020. The taxpayer must have started to use the asset or had it installed ready for use between 12 March 2020 and 30 June 2021.

The deduction is available in an income year that ends on or after 2 April 2019.

An entity also qualifies as a medium-sized business for purposes of the immediate deduction if it satisfies the aggregated turnover test assuming the threshold is $500 million and starts to use the depreciating asset or has it installed ready for use between 12 March 2020 and 30 June 2021. The immediate deduction is available for assets costing less than $150,000 first acquired between 7.30 pm (AEDT) on 2 April 2019 and 31 December 2020. The deduction is available in an income year that ends on or after 12 March 2020.

The deduction is limited to the taxable purpose proportion of the asset's cost (¶17-570). For the income year in which the entity first used the asset or installed it ready for use for any taxable purpose, the amount of the deduction is the asset's cost. For any other income year (eg where the asset was first used for a non-taxable purpose), the deduction is equal to the sum of the asset's opening adjustable value (¶17-485) and any amount included in the second element of its cost for that year.

Where the medium-sized business has claimed the immediate deduction for an asset in an income year under s 40-82, an immediate deduction is also available for any second element cost on the asset incurred in a later year. The second element cost amount must be less than the cost threshold that applied to the asset, and be incurred within the applicable time period (ie either before 12 March 2020 or between 12 March 2020 and 31 December 2020).

The immediate deductions under s 40-82 are not available for assets that are acquired, started to be used or installed ready for use, or included as second element costs, outside of the above prescribed periods. The rule also does not override specific rules for deductions elsewhere in Div 40 or ITAA97, eg special rules for horticultural plants (¶18-070). Temporary full expensing of depreciating assets of any value is also available, although specific exclusions or conditions that apply under those rules (eg exclusion of second-hand assets or the asset's location must be Australia) do not apply under s 40-82 (¶17-430).

Deriving non-business income

An immediate 100% deduction applies for depreciating assets costing $300 or less and used by taxpayers predominantly in deriving non-business assessable income provided: (a) the asset was not part of a set of assets acquired during the year where the total cost of the set exceeded $300; and (b) the total cost of the asset and any identical or substantially identical item that the taxpayer started to hold in that year did not exceed $300 (ITAA97 s 40-80(2)). For the meaning of "identical", see ID 2003/80. The deduction is available for the cost of the asset, reduced by any input tax credits which the taxpayer may be entitled to claim. An apportionment is required if the asset is only partly used for taxable purposes. However, no reduction is made for part-year use of an asset. Such expenditure cannot be allocated to a low-value pool (¶17-810).

[FITR ¶87-081, ¶87-083]

¶17-350 Depreciation of exploration or prospecting assets

Immediate deduction for exploration or prospecting assets

An immediate deduction may be available for the cost of depreciating assets that are first ‘‘used’’ for exploration or prospecting for either minerals or quarry materials (s 40-80(1); ¶19-010). The materials must be obtainable by mining and quarrying operations.

Depreciating assets that are mining, quarrying or prospecting rights are taken to be ‘‘used’’ when something is done that is permitted or authorised by such rights, meaning the terms of a right are relevant. This is whether the something is done by the holder of the right or an entity authorised by the holder. The mere holding of the right or satisfying conditions to hold or retain the right would not constitute ‘‘use’’ in the ATO’s view. For designing an exploration plan to be able to hold a mining right is not ‘‘use’’ of the right, neither would carrying out an aerial survey of land, for which no such right had to be held. However, exploratory drilling on the tenement constitutes ‘‘use’’ (TD 2019/1).

Expenditure on mining, quarrying or prospecting rights or information first held after 7.30 pm EST on 14 May 2013 must have been acquired from an Australian government authority to qualify for the immediate deduction. Alternatively, if the asset is information, the taxpayer must have: (i) acquired a geophysical or geological data package from a recognised mining provider; (ii) created the information, or contributed to the cost of its creation; or (iii) caused, or contributed to the cost of, the information being created by a recognised mining provider. A recognised mining provider is an entity whose predominant business involves providing information to those involved in mining and quarrying operations (s 40-80(1AA)). If the only reason that a taxpayer does not qualify for the immediate deduction is because the rights or information fail to meet any of these particular conditions, then the asset is depreciated over the shorter of 15 years or its effective life. However, in some cases it may be written off at the taxpayer’s choice (s 40-95(10A)).

Similar criteria apply to the immediate deductibility of second element exploration or prospecting costs (s 40-80(1AB)). If second element expenditure on improving mining, quarrying or prospecting information satisfies the conditions in the previous paragraph, then it may qualify for an immediate deduction regardless of how the original information was acquired.

Expenditure incurred to collect and process seismic data that is licensed to clients on a non-exclusive basis does not come within the immediate deduction under s 40-80 but the costs of such data is to be depreciated over 15 years (s 40-95(12); ¶17-270).

Deduction over time for exploration or prospecting assets

If an immediate deduction is not available for an exploration or prospecting depreciating asset, then a deduction may be claimed over the asset’s effective life using the prime cost or diminishing value method (¶17-270).

Other exploration expenditure

An immediate deduction may be available for capital expenditure incurred on exploring or prospecting for minerals, or quarry materials, unrelated to a depreciating asset. To qualify, the materials must be obtainable by, and the taxpayer’s business must involve, mining and quarrying operations (s 40-730; ¶19-040).

The Commissioner's views on the deductibility of mining or petroleum exploration expenditure under the general deduction provision (s 8-1; ¶16-010), or under s 40-730, are in TR 2017/1. PCG 2016/17 sets out how the ATO will administer the law and the ruling to assure deductions claimed for exploration expenditure.

In addition, certain mining project and related transport expenditure of a capital nature that does not form part of a depreciating asset's cost may be deductible over the estimated life of the project (ss 40-830 to 40-885; ¶19-050).

[FITR ¶87-080]

¶17-370 Depreciation of computer hardware and software

Computer hardware

Computer hardware (eg laptops, screens, backup drives, routers, modems, and scanners) are normally depreciating assets, or parts of depreciating assets. Their cost may be written off as an ordinary capital allowance (Div 40; ¶17-330; ¶17-430; ¶17-480), or as a small business capital allowance (Div 328; ¶7-250).

Computer software

Computer software is the digital system comprised of the programs, data and associated documentation, that instructs other parts of a computer, and may include website content. A capital allowance is available for "in-house software" (s 40-30(2)(d)) used for an income producing purpose usually over 5 years, or as part of a software development or low value pool (Div 40). Alternatively, the small business capital allowance regime may apply (Div 328; ¶7-250). Sometimes, an immediate deduction may instead be available for capital expenditure on in-house software (see below).

To the extent that software costs are not general deductions (s 8-1; ¶16-010), or are not in-house software, the costs may be recognised in the CGT cost base of a CGT asset (typically, the first or fourth elements; s 110-25). Otherwise, as a last resort, the costs might be recognised as blackhole expenditure (s 40-880; ¶16-156).

Deductions for expenditure on intellectual property and related expenditure are discussed at ¶16-727.

"In-house software" defined

"In-house software" is defined as computer software (or a right to use computer software), that a "taxpayer" acquires, develops or commissions and that is "mainly" used by them in performing the functions for which the software was developed (ie not mainly for sale; s 995-1(1)). Also, the expenditure must not be deductible outside the ordinary capital allowance regime (in Div 40; ¶17-480) and the rules for small business taxpayers (in Div 328; ¶7-250) (eg ID 2010/14). For example, if expenditure qualifies for a general deduction, it will not be in-house software; instead it may have the character of maintenance expenditure. Software developed for conjunctive use within a taxpayer's corporate group was in-house software in ID 2014/16.

The definition requires the software to be used by the "taxpayer" in performing the functions for which it was developed. For example, a taxpayer's website might provide access to software that: (i) is installed on a user's device for offline use independent of the taxpayer's business; or (ii) is provided mainly for the user's benefit and not to enable further interactions with the taxpayer. The Commissioner's view is that such software is not in-house software for the taxpayer because it is not used by them to perform the functions for which it was developed. Also, content that is incidental to a website, which does not have value separate from the website, is not in-house software (TR 2016/3).

The use of the word "mainly" in the definition covers dual-purpose situations. For example, if a taxpayer develops software for their own use, but they also license it to other businesses, then the taxpayer's "main" use of the software will be a question of fact in establishing if it is in-house software.

Prime-cost capital allowances

Deductions are available for the decline in value of a depreciating asset that is ''in-house software'' held for a taxable purpose. The decline in value is calculated using the prime cost method. The effective life is 5 years if the in-house software is first used, or installed ready for use, from 1 July 2015; otherwise it is 4 years (¶17-010, ¶17-280).

If in-house software stops being used and the taxpayer expects never to use it again, or if the taxpayer has never used the software and decides never to use it, a balancing adjustment event occurs (¶17-630) and the termination value of the software is zero (¶17-640).

A deduction is available for in-house software expenditure (other than software pool expenditure), if the taxpayer intends to use the software for a taxable purpose, but, before being able to use it (or install it ready for use), they decide never to use or install it (s 40-335). The amount deductible is the total expenditure incurred on the software reduced by any consideration derived for the software (up to the amount of the expenditure), reduced by the non-taxable use proportion. Any recoupments of the expenditure are included in assessable income (¶10-270).

Software development and low-value pool regimes

Taxpayers may include expenditure on developing or commissioning (but not acquiring) in-house software in a software development pool if the software is intended to be used *solely* for a taxable purpose (ie the purpose of producing assessable income, of exploration or prospecting, of mining site rehabilitation or environmental protection activities) (ITAA97 s 40-450). A separate software development pool must be created for each income year in which expenditure on such software is incurred. Amounts allocated to a software development pool are reduced by any available input tax credits, and the pool value is reduced by decreasing adjustments and increased by increasing adjustments (¶34-100) to which the taxpayer is entitled for the acquisition of the asset (ITAA97 s 27-100).

Software development pool expenditure incurred in the 2015–16 or a later income year is deducted over 5 years. No amount is deducted for the income year the expenditure is incurred (Year 1). The taxpayer calculates the total amount incurred on developing or commissioning in-house software in Year 1, and deducts 30% of that amount for each of income Years 2, 3 and 4 and the remaining 10% for income Year 5 (s 40-455).

Expenditure incurred before the 2015–16 income year is deducted over 4 years. No amount is deducted for Year 1; 40% of the Year 1 total is deducted for each of income Years 2 and 3, with the remaining 20% being deducted for income Year 4.

The deduction is available even if the software is not used or installed until later (or ever). After the pool is created in an income year, all software development expenditure incurred in that year or a later year must be allocated to a software development pool.

Consideration derived in relation to pooled software (eg for the disposal, grant, licence or loss of the software) is assessable, except where roll-over relief is elected (¶17-710; s 40-460). The balancing adjustment provisions (¶17-630) do not apply.

The low-value pool regime (in Subdiv 40-E; ¶17-810) may also apply to a depreciating asset that is in-house software, but not if expenditure has already been recognised in a software development pool. Assets allocated to the low-value pool or software development pool do not qualify for temporary full expensing.

Small business capital allowance regime

If the entity incurring in-house software expenditure is a small business entity (SBE) (under Div 328), then they may qualify for an immediate deduction if the software's cost is below any applicable low-cost asset threshold (s 328-180; ¶7-250). If the asset's cost is at or above that threshold, the asset can be allocated to the general small business pool. A deduction applies only to the extent the software is used for a taxable purpose. Also, the expenditure must not have been allocated to a software development pool (s 328-175(7)).

Immediate deduction for other taxpayers

Businesses who do not use the small business capital allowance regime in Div 328 may be able to access an immediate deduction for in-house software under the temporary instant asset write-off or full expensing rules, to the extent used for a taxable purpose (¶17-330; ¶17-430) where not allocated to a software development pool. Alternatively, they may immediately deduct in-house software with a GST-inclusive cost of up to $100 (PS LA 2003/8; ¶16-153). The ATO regards such expenditure to have a revenue nature and to be deductible, provided all general deduction requirements are satisfied (s 8-1; ¶16-010).

An immediate deduction for capital expenditure on in-house software costing $300 or less may also be available, provided the software is not used predominantly to produce business income (s 40-80(2); ¶17-330).

Commercial website development and maintenance expenditure of a revenue nature may be deductible as a general business expense (TR 2016/3; ¶16-725), or give rise to an R&D offset (¶17-420). Monthly enhancement and support fees for in-house software are immediately deductible under s 8-1 (ID 2003/931).

[FITR ¶32-675, ¶86-915, ¶87-675, ¶87-865 – ¶87-885]

¶17-420 Depreciation of R&D assets

An entity is entitled to a tax offset if it qualifies for a *notional* R&D deduction for the decline in value of a tangible depreciating asset (and capital works, other than buildings) used for R&D purposes (Div 355; s 355-305; ¶20-150ff). The entity must satisfy both the R&D and the depreciating assets provisions. The provisions do not apply to pooled assets and conversely, R&D assets cannot be pooled.

No actual deduction is available under the depreciating assets rules in respect of expenditure on the basis of which an R&D tax offset has been claimed. However, the offset is treated as a deduction for the purposes of other tax provisions such as the prepayment, debt forgiveness and anti-avoidance rules. Furthermore, if an asset is used for both R&D and other taxable purposes, an actual Division 40 deduction may be available in respect of the non-R&D use (eg if the asset is used in carrying on a business for the purpose of producing assessable income) (ss 355-310; 355-715). Special rules apply to the R&D assets of partnerships (ss 355-520; 355-525).

The rules apply to the use of depreciating assets in an income year commencing on or after 1 July 2011, regardless of when the assets were acquired. If an asset was held before that date, the same method and effective life must be used and the previously depreciated asset cannot be pooled. Transitional rules apply where a balancing adjustment event happens after 1 July 2011 to an asset held before that date.

In working out the notional Division 40 deduction, the purpose of conducting one or more R&D activities is treated as a taxable purpose. The effective life of the asset is calculated under the rules at ¶17-270, by estimating the period that the asset can be used by an entity for a taxable purpose, the purpose of producing exempt income or non-assessable non-exempt income, or the purpose of conducting R&D activities. In having regard to the period within which the asset is likely to be scrapped or abandoned, reasons attributable to technical risk in conducting R&D activities are to be disregarded.

The temporary full expensing and accelerated depreciation rules may be applied to calculating the notional deduction (¶17-430).

Design expenditure is tested for its inclusion in the cost of a depreciating asset at the time the entity begins to hold the asset. The expenditure is included in the asset's cost to the extent it relates to the final shape or features of the asset. Design expenditure will not be notionally deductible as R&D expenditure (under s 355-205; ¶20-170) where it is included in the cost of a tangible depreciating asset under Div 40 (TD 2014/15).

Either the prime cost or diminishing value method (¶17-480) may be used but if actual deductions have previously been worked out, the same method must be used to work out notional deductions, and vice versa (s 40-65(6), (7)).

Where a balancing adjustment event happens in relation to a depreciating asset which has been used *solely* for R&D activities, and in respect of which R&D decline in value deductions have been available, a balancing adjustment is required. This results in either a further notional R&D deduction (included in the calculation of the R&D offset) or an uplifted amount being included in assessable income (s 355-315). The amount of the uplift is equal to one third of the assessable balancing adjustment calculated under s 40-285 (up to the total decline in value).

If the asset was used *partly* for R&D activities and partly for another taxable purpose, use for the R&D purpose is taken to be a taxable purpose (s 40-292). If a balancing deduction arises under s 40-285, the amount of the balancing deduction is increased by half if the R&D entity's aggregated turnover is less than $20 million and one third in other cases. If an assessable balancing amount arises under s 40-285, the amount assessable (up to the asset's total decline in value) is increased by one third. Section 40-293 deals with balancing adjustments for partnership R&D assets.

The balancing adjustment calculations will be more accurate from 1 July 2021, whether assets are solely or partly used for R&D activities and regardless of size of the R&D entity. The increase in or deduction from assessable income will be based on the grossed-up value of the incentive component of the associated R&D tax offset amounts. Transitional rules and those for R&D partnerships will also be amended.

[FITR ¶335-100 – ¶335-300]

¶17-430 Temporary full expensing and accelerated depreciation for assets

Temporary full expensing of depreciable assets

An immediate 100% deduction is available for the cost of eligible depreciating assets of any value (¶17-080) for a limited period. The asset must be first held and first used or installed ready for use for a taxable purpose (¶17-010) between 7.30 pm (AEDT) on 6 October 2020 (2020 Budget time) and 30 June 2022 (ITTPA97 Subdiv 40-BB). The asset must be located in Australia and used principally in Australia for carrying on a business. The cost of improvements (¶17-105) to these assets and to existing depreciable assets made during this period can also be fully deducted. The deductions are automatic unless a taxpayer chooses to opt-out for a particular asset, and apply the normal Div 40 rules (this choice is irrevocable).

The assets must be on hand in the year the full cost is deducted, ie no balancing adjustment event happened in the year of deduction. The deduction is limited to the taxable purpose proportion of the asset's cost (¶17-570). For the income year in which the entity first used the asset or installed it ready for use for any taxable purpose, the amount of the deduction is the asset's cost. For any other income year (eg where the asset was first used for a non-taxable purpose), the deduction is equal to the sum of the asset's opening adjustable value (¶17-485) and any amount included in the second element of its cost for that year.

The deduction is available to entities that satisfy the aggregated turnover test in s 328-110 assuming a turnover threshold of $5 billion. The usual exclusions apply for certain depreciating assets (¶17-030), pooled assets (¶17-370) and Subdiv 40-F primary production assets (¶18-000). Additional exclusions apply for entities with an aggregated turnover of $50 million or more:

- second-hand assets (special rules apply to certain intangible assets)
- assets the entity already committed to purchase before the 2020 Budget time, eg by entering a contract
- assets for which an entity has already claimed depreciation deductions, including under the instant write-off rules (¶17-330), and split or merged assets (¶17-100)
- assets previously held by a consolidated group.

The rules also allow a full deduction of the second element of cost of these excluded assets, provided it is incurred between 2020 Budget time and 30 June 2022.

Corporate groups that fail the $5 billion aggregated turnover test can still access the rules if they satisfy an alternative test allowing them to exclude certain income of foreign affiliated or connected entities, provided they can demonstrate substantial historical asset investments in Australia. Specific rules also ensure that for these groups, the write off is not available for intangible assets previously held by an associate where the asset can be used by a non-resident.

Where assets deducted under this temporary measure are sold or scrapped, the balancing adjustment provisions in ITAA97 Subdiv 40-D apply, as if the decline in value was claimed under ITAA97 Subdiv 40-B (ITTPA97 s 40-180(3)). A balancing adjustment event also arises if the asset stops being used in Australia for carrying on a business, the asset is relocated outside Australia, or the asset was never relocated to Australia although this was the original intention, on which basis the full cost was deducted. This is regardless of whether the asset is still held by the taxpayer. If this occurs, the balancing adjustment or deduction is calculated as if the taxpayer stopped using the asset, or stopped having it installed ready for use for any purpose and it will not be used or ready for use again (¶17-630; ¶17-640). In such an instance, temporary full expensing that may otherwise be available, will not be available in a later income year. However, if relevant conditions are satisfied, normal depreciation rules under Div 40 are available. The first element of cost of the asset for this purpose is equal to the termination value at the time of the balancing adjustment event (ITTPA97 s 40-185: ¶17-100).

For the temporary full expensing rules for small business entities see ¶7-250.

Temporary accelerated depreciation

Certain medium-sized businesses are eligible to deduct 50% of a depreciating asset's cost in the year the asset is first used or installed ready for use for a taxable purpose under temporary accelerated depreciation rules (ITTPA97 Subdiv 40-BA). The remaining 50% of the cost is deducted under ordinary Div 40 rules, assuming it is the asset's cost. The total amount deducted for decline in value of the asset cannot exceed its original cost in the taxpayer's hands. A special deduction rate is also available for new assets added to a small business depreciation pool (¶7-250).

The incentive is only available for assets acquired between 12 March 2020 and 30 June 2021, by entities that satisfy the aggregated turnover test in s 328-110 assuming a turnover threshold of $500 million. It can only be claimed in one year (either 2019–20 or 2020–21) with ordinary Div 40 rules applying in later years.

Certain assets specifically excluded from the incentive are (ITTPA97 ss 40-120, 40-125):

- second-hand assets (special rules apply to certain intangible assets)
- assets the entity already committed to purchase before 12 March 2020, eg by entering a contract
- assets for which an entity has already claimed depreciation deductions, including under the instant write-off rules (¶17-330), and split or merged assets (¶17-100)
- assets previously held by a consolidated group
- assets where depreciation is worked out under low-value or software pools (¶17-370)
- primary production assets depreciated under Subdiv 40-F and excluded assets (¶17-030), and
- assets not located in Australia.

Where assets deducted under this temporary measure are sold or scrapped, the balancing adjustment provisions in ITAA97 Subdiv 40-D apply, as if the decline in value was claimed under ITAA97 Subdiv 40-B (ITTPA97 s 40-135(4)).

If an asset either qualifies only for full expensing or both full expensing and accelerated depreciation, and no opt-out election is made for the asset, full expensing applies automatically. If an asset is eligible only for accelerated depreciation but not full expensing, the accelerated deduction is also automatic unless the irrevocable opt-out election is made for the asset.

[FITR ¶86-803, ¶86-804]

Calculating Decline in Value

¶17-480 Choice of method to calculate decline in value

A depreciating asset starts to decline in value from its ‘‘start time’’, ie from when the taxpayer first uses it or has it installed ready for use for *any* purpose (ITAA97 s 40-60). However, deductions for the decline in value of the asset are only available in respect of the taxpayer's use of the asset for taxable purposes (¶17-010). A tangible depreciating asset does not start to decline if it is held in anticipation of being used in a business that has not commenced to be carried on (TD 2007/5).

There are 2 methods of calculating the decline in value of a depreciating asset (ITAA97 s 40-65): the prime cost (or straight line) method (¶17-490) and the diminishing value (or reducing balance) method (¶17-500). The use of either method may not be relevant where special temporary rules apply to fully deduct the cost of the asset (¶17-330; ¶17-430).

The taxpayer must choose which method is to be used before lodging the income tax return for the income year to which the choice relates (ITAA97 s 40-130). The choice does not have to be made formally or in writing and is normally self-evident from the taxpayer's capital allowances schedule (¶17-880). The choice is exercised on an asset-by-asset basis and on a year-by-year basis. This means, eg, that a choice made for a depreciating asset that is *first* held in the 2019–20 year does not affect the choice for any other depreciating asset that is first held in that income year. Nor does it affect the choice for any depreciating asset that is first held in a later income year, ie a separate choice is made for each depreciating asset that is first held in a particular year.

However, the choice of method for a particular asset applies for that income year and all later years in which the taxpayer claims a deduction for the decline in value of that asset (s 40-130).

No choice of method is made in the following circumstances:

- where a depreciating asset is acquired by the taxpayer from an associate, the taxpayer must use the same method that the associate was using in calculating its deductions for the decline in value of the asset. The taxpayer may request the associate to give information about the method it was using
- if the taxpayer acquires a depreciating asset from the former holder and the user of the asset while the taxpayer holds the asset is the same as, or is an associate of, the user of the asset while the asset was held by the former holder, the taxpayer must use the same method as that used by the former holder. Examples of cases where this might apply are sale and leaseback arrangements. If the former holder did not use a method, or if the taxpayer cannot readily find out the method used by the former holder, the taxpayer must use the *diminishing value method*
- if the depreciating asset is in a low-value pool, the decline in value is calculated in accordance with the rules outlined at ¶17-810
- if the depreciating asset was used for certain exploration or prospecting purposes (¶17-350) or if an asset costing $300 or less is used for non-business income-producing purposes (¶17-330), the decline in value is the cost of the asset
- if the cost of the depreciating asset is the decline in value (¶17-330), or
- the decline in value of an asset that was used for R&D and which is subject to the R&D offset provisions (¶17-420), must be calculated using the same method that was used to calculate the R&D notional deduction, and vice versa (s 40-65).

Regardless of which method is used, the decline in value of an asset cannot exceed its adjustable value (¶17-485). This ensures that the total amount allowed for the decline in value of a depreciating asset cannot exceed its original cost in the taxpayer's hands. Special rules apply to assets held by tax-exempt entities that became taxable (¶10-630, ¶17-130).

[FITR ¶87-050]

¶17-485 Adjustable value of depreciating asset

The concepts of ''adjustable value'' and ''opening adjustable value'' (ITAA97 s 40-85) are relevant to the calculation of the decline in value of a depreciating asset (¶17-490, ¶17-500) and balancing adjustments for the asset (¶17-630).

The opening adjustable value for an income year is the adjustable value of the asset at the end of the previous income year, ie the closing adjustable value from the previous income year.

The adjustable value of an asset at a particular time is the opening adjustable value for that year plus any second elements of cost for the year, less its decline in value for the year up to that time. Generally, this includes capital expenditure relating to the asset which is not deductible, such as improvements or enhancements. If the asset has not yet been used or installed ready for use, the adjustable value of the asset is its cost. In the income year in which the asset is first used or installed ready for use for any purpose, the adjustable value of an asset at a particular time is its cost less its decline in value up to that time.

If an understatement in the first element of cost of an asset is discovered, the opening adjustable value of the asset is recalculated for each income year from that time, using the correct cost of the asset.

After a balancing adjustment event occurs, the adjustable value of the asset is zero. However, if: (a) the event happens because the taxpayer expects never to use the asset again; (b) either the taxpayer stops using the asset for any purpose or never used the asset; and (c) the taxpayer continues to hold the asset, the opening adjustable value for the year after the event is the termination value at the time of the event, plus any second element costs incurred in the event year, after the event (s 40-285(3), (4)).

Generally, the opening adjustable value of an asset is reduced by any input tax credits and decreasing adjustments relating to the acquisition of the asset or to second element costs of the asset (¶17-090). It may also be reduced if a commercial debt has been forgiven (¶17-510), if there has been an involuntary disposal of an asset (¶17-720) or if the short-term forex realisation rules have applied (ITAA97 ss 775-70; 775-75).

If the tax-preferred leasing provisions (¶23-210) have applied in respect of an asset and the arrangement period for the asset ends, the adjustable value of the asset at the end of the period is the "end value" (s 250-180) of the asset. If only some of the capital allowances were disallowed during the period of the arrangement (ie s 250-150 has applied to apportion the deductions), the adjustable value is modified under s 250-285.

Where the initial owner of a mining, quarrying or prospecting right transfers part of the right under a farm-in farm-out arrangement, the right is taken to be split into 2 depreciating assets immediately before the disposal (s 40-115). The entire adjustable value is allocated to the retained part (s 40-1110; ¶19-010).

[FITR ¶87-090]

¶17-490 Prime cost method

Under the prime cost method, the annual decline in value of a depreciating asset is calculated by allocating the cost of the asset over its effective life in accordance with the formula (ITAA97 s 40-75):

$$\frac{\text{cost}}{\text{effective life}} \times \frac{\text{days held}}{365}$$

Cost includes the first element and the second element of cost of the asset (¶17-080). This method assumes that an asset declines in value uniformly throughout its life. The use of this method is not relevant where the special temporary rules apply to fully deduct the cost of the asset (¶17-330; ¶17-430), unless the asset's opening adjustable value needs to be determined (see below).

If the taxpayer holds the asset for the entire year in a leap year, the "days held" will be 366. The denominator in the formula remains at 365.

The decline in value of the asset cannot exceed its opening adjustable value plus second element costs for the year (or its cost, in the year in which it is first used or installed ready for use).

▶ Example

Paul purchases a depreciating asset on 1 July 20X1 for $60,750 and commences to use it in his business on that day. The effective life of the asset is 4.5 years. Using the prime cost method, Paul is entitled to a deduction for the decline in value of the asset of $13,500 [($60,750/4.5) × (365/365)] in 20X1–X2, 20X3–X4 and 20X4–X5. In the 20X2–X3 year, he is entitled to a deduction of $13,537 [assuming 20X3 is a leap year ($60,750/4.5) × (366/365)]. In the 20X5–X6 year, he is entitled to deduct the balance of $6,713 (ie $60,750 – $13,537 – ($13,500 × 3)).

Apportionment

Where a depreciating asset is used (or is installed ready for use) for only part of the year, the decline in value of the asset is calculated on a pro rata basis (¶17-560). The deduction for the decline in value is reduced to reflect the extent of any use for non-taxable purposes (¶17-010, ¶17-570).

When opening adjustable value (rather than cost) is used

In the following circumstances, the prime cost method is applied by spreading the ''opening adjustable value'' (¶17-485) of the asset plus any second element costs for the year (instead of cost) over the period of the effective life that is yet to elapse as at the start of the relevant year (s 40-75(2)):

- if the effective life of the asset is recalculated during the year (¶17-270)
- if second element costs (¶17-105) are incurred in an income year after the year in which the asset was first used or installed ready for use for any purpose
- if the debt forgiveness provisions have applied to reduce the asset's opening adjustable value (¶17-510)
- if there was roll-over relief for an involuntary disposal (¶17-720)
- if certain GST adjustments were made (eg if the opening adjustable value was reduced by GST input tax credits for second element costs for the year, or by a decreasing adjustment, or was increased by an increasing adjustment: ¶17-090)
- if the opening adjustable value was increased or reduced under the short-term forex realisation gains and losses provisions (ITAA97 ss 775-70; 775-75), or
- if the cost of the asset was deducted under the temporary accelerated depreciation or full expensing rules in ITTPA97 Subdiv 40-BA or 40-BB in the previous income year (¶17-430).

Intangible assets

The decline in value of in-house software, intellectual property (other than film copyright), spectrum licences, datacasting transmitter licences and telecommunications site access rights must be calculated using the prime cost method (¶17-280).

If a patent (whether standard, innovation or petty patent), registered design, licence (other than one relating to a copyright or in-house software), spectrum licence or datacasting transmitter licence is acquired from a former holder, the cost of the asset is spread over the number of years remaining in the effective life of the asset as at the start of the income year in which the taxpayer acquires the asset (s 40-75(5)). The cost of copyrights (other than film copyright), licences relating to copyrights and in-house software acquired from a previous holder is spread over the statutory effective life applied as from the time of acquisition.

[FITR ¶87-070]

¶17-500 Diminishing value method

Under the diminishing value method, the decline in value of a depreciating asset is assumed to be greatest in the first year and smaller in each succeeding year. For assets that start to be held on or after 10 May 2006, the diminishing value rate is 200%. For pre-10 May 2006 assets, the rate is 150%. Anti-avoidance provisions ensure that expenditure on pre-10 May 2006 assets cannot be ''freshened up'' to attract the higher rate. The decline in value of the asset is calculated in accordance with the formula (ITAA97 ss 40-70; 40-72):

$$\frac{\text{base value}}{\text{effective life}} \times \frac{\text{days held}}{365} \times 200\% \text{ (or } 150\%\text{)}$$

In the first year in which the asset is used or installed ready for use, the base value is the cost of the asset. In following years, the base value is the sum of the opening adjustable value (¶17-485) for that year plus any second elements of cost (¶17-105) for that year. The decline in value of the asset in any year cannot exceed the base value for the year. A depreciating asset whose opening adjustable value has been reduced to less than $1,000 can be allocated to a low-value pool (¶17-810).

If the taxpayer holds the asset for the entire year in a leap year, the ''days held'' will be 366.

▶ Example

A depreciating asset costing $20,000 acquired on the first day of Year 1 has an effective life of 4 years. As the asset was acquired after 10 May 2006, the 200% rate applies. The following table shows the annual decline in value and adjustable values under the prime cost (PC) and diminishing value (DV) methods for comparison (ignoring leap years):

	PC	DV
Cost	$20,000	$20,000
Year 1 decline in value	5,000	10,000
Opening adjustable value	15,000	10,000
Year 2 decline in value	5,000	5,000
Opening adjustable value	10,000	5,000
Year 3 decline in value	5,000	2,500
Opening adjustable value	5,000	2,500
Year 4 decline in value	5,000	1,250
Adjustable value	nil	$1,250

Under the diminishing value method there is a balance of $1,250 (the adjustable value at the end of Year 4) which has not been written off. This amount can be further depreciated. If the asset is scrapped, the adjustable value can be claimed as a deduction. A balance less than $1,000 can be allocated to the taxpayer's low-value pool (¶17-810).

Where an asset is used or is installed ready for use for only part of the year, the decline in value is calculated on a pro rata basis (¶17-560). The deduction is also reduced to reflect any use for non-taxable purposes (¶17-010, ¶17-570).

The diminishing value method cannot be used to calculate the decline in value of in-house software, intellectual property (other than film copyright), spectrum licences, datacasting transmitter licences and telecommunications site access rights.

The use of this method is not relevant where special temporary rules apply to fully deduct the cost of an asset (¶17-330; ¶17-430), unless the asset's opening adjustable value needs to be determined.

[FITR ¶87-060, ¶87-062]

¶17-510 Calculating depreciation where commercial debt forgiven

Where commercial debts are forgiven (¶16-910), a taxpayer (the debtor) may be required to reduce the base amount used in calculating the deduction for the decline in value of a depreciating asset. In such case, the cost and the opening adjustable value of an asset is reduced by the amount forgiven (ITAA97 s 40-90). This affects both the calculation of the decline in value of the asset, any balancing adjustments for the asset (¶17-640) and any capital gains and losses (¶17-670).

If the prime cost method is being used, the asset's opening adjustable value (rather than its cost), as reduced by the forgiven amount, is spread over the remaining effective life of the asset (¶17-490).

▶ Example 1: Prime cost method

An asset costing $10,000 is being depreciated over 5 years and a debt of $2,000 is forgiven in Year 2. The annual deduction in Years 2, 3, 4 and 5 is reduced from $2,000 (ie $10,000/5) to $1,500 (ie (Year 2 opening adjustable value of $8,000 – $2,000 reduction from amount forgiven)/4).

If the diminishing value method is being used, the opening adjustable value is reduced by the forgiven amount.

▶ Example 2: Diminishing value method

A post-10 May 2006 asset costing $10,000 and having an opening adjustable value of $6,000 is being depreciated over 5 years and a debt of $2,000 is forgiven in Year 2. The opening adjustable value is reduced to $4,000 so that the deduction for the decline in value of the asset in the year the debt is forgiven is $1,600 (ie $4,000/5 × 200%) rather than $2,400 (ie $6,000/5 × 200%).

[FITR ¶87-105]

Pro-rating Rules

¶17-560 Part-year use of depreciating asset

Where a depreciating asset is held and used (or is installed ready for use) for only part of the income year, then the full year's decline in value is automatically reduced (ITAA97 ss 40-70; 40-75). This is because the calculation formulae for both the prime cost and diminishing value methods include the number of days that the asset is held and used or installed ready for use *for any purpose* by the taxpayer during an income year.

▶ Example

An asset with an effective life of 10 years is acquired at a cost of $50,000. Using the prime cost method, the full-year decline in value is $5,000 but as the taxpayer acquired the asset on 21 April 2017, the actual decline in value would be only $973 (ie $5,000 × 71/365).

Whether the asset is used for taxable or non-taxable purposes affects the amount of the deductions available for the decline in value (¶17-570) but does not affect the amount by which the asset declines in value.

The number of days the asset was held and used is calculated from the start time of the asset, ie from the time when the asset was first used or installed ready for use for any purpose (this may differ from the time when the taxpayer started holding the asset).

[FITR ¶87-060 – ¶87-070]

¶17-570 Depreciating asset only partly used for business

Where a depreciating asset is used during an income year partly for a taxable purpose and partly for another purpose (eg for private purposes or to produce exempt income), the deduction for the decline in value of the asset is reduced by the part of the decline in value that is attributable to the use, or the asset being installed ready for use, for the non-taxable purpose (ITAA97 s 40-25(2)). A "taxable purpose" is the purpose of producing assessable income, of exploration or prospecting, of mining site rehabilitation or environmental protection activities (s 40-25(7)).

For example, if a car is used 40% for private purposes and the logbook method of claiming expenses is used (ITAA97 ss 40-25; 40-55), only 60% of the car's decline in value is deductible.

However, the adjustable value (¶17-485) of the asset for the purpose of calculating the decline in value of the asset in subsequent years is calculated by taking into account the full amount of the decline in value.

▶ Example 1

In Year 1, the income producing use of a car was 55%. The car was acquired on 1 July Year 1 for $32,000 and the 200% rate applies. The car has an effective life of 8 years. The actual decline in value for Year 1 using the diminishing value method, and the adjustable value for the purpose of calculating its decline in value for Year 2, are:

Cost of car	$32,000
Less: decline in value for 12 months (assuming Year 1 consists of 366 days due to a leap year)	8,022
Adjustable value at end of Year 1 and opening adjustable value for Year 2	23,978
Actual depreciation allowed for Year 1 (55% × $8,022)	$4,412

▶ Example 2

A car with an effective life of 8 years is used 60% for income producing purposes. The cost of the car purchased on 1 July Year 1 was $16,000. The prime cost decline in value for Year 3 is worked out as follows:

Cost of car	$16,000
Less: decline in value for 2 years	4,000
Adjustable value at end of Year 2 and opening adjustable value for Year 3	$12,000
Decline in value for Year 3	$2,000
Actual deduction allowed Year 3 (60% × $2,000)	$1,200

For the method of calculating balancing adjustments on disposal of a depreciating asset that has been used only partly for taxable purposes, see ¶17-660.

[FITR ¶86-880, ¶86-885]

¶17-580 Deductions for decline in value where prior non-business use

Where a depreciating asset is used by a taxpayer solely for private purposes and/or for producing exempt income, the asset declines in value and the adjustable value (¶17-485) of the asset is reduced (even though the decline is not deductible). If the asset later commences to be used by the taxpayer (wholly or partly) for "taxable purposes" (¶17-570), the deduction for the decline in value of the asset is limited to the asset's opening adjustable value for the year in which it started being used for income-producing purposes and any second element costs for that year. Prime cost method deductions are still based on the cost of the asset, while diminishing value method deductions are based on the opening adjustable value of the asset.

▶ Example

At the start of Year 2, Grace, a doctor, commences to use part of her home as a surgery. The furniture in the waiting room was bought for private purposes on 1 July Year 1 at a cost of $4,000. The furniture is depreciated using the diminishing value method and has an effective life of 5 years. The deduction for the decline in value of the furniture for Year 2 is $960, calculated as follows:

Year 1	
Cost price (opening value) at start of year 1	$4,000
Less: Decline in value $\left(\text{ie } \frac{\$4{,}000}{5} \times 200\%\right)$	1,600
Adjustable value at end of Year 1	$2,400
Year 2	
Opening adjustable value at start of Year 2	$2,400
Less: Deduction for decline in value	960
Adjustable value at end of Year 2	$1,440

The decline in value in Year 2 is $960 (ie $2,400/5 × 200%). The total amount deductible in that and following years cannot exceed $2,400. (The rate of 200% applies to assets that start being held on or after 10 May 2006.)

If the prime cost method had been used, the opening adjustable value for Year 2 would be $3,200 (ie $4,000 – $4,000/5). The annual deductions for the decline in value for Years 2, 3, 4 and 5 would be $800, up to a total of $3,200.

[FITR ¶87-060 – ¶87-070]

Balancing Adjustment Events

¶17-630 Assessable or deductible balancing adjustments

When is a balancing adjustment required

A balancing adjustment either increases or decreases assessable income. It arises when a ''balancing adjustment event'' occurs (ITAA97 s 40-295), which happens when a taxpayer stops ''holding'' (¶17-020) a depreciating asset, or part of it (ITAA97 s 40-115). This generally occurs when an asset is sold, scrapped, destroyed, lost, given away or otherwise disposed of, starts to be held as trading stock or, in the case of a right, ceases or expires, or the taxpayer dies.

Balancing adjustments are also required where:

- a taxpayer stops using the asset (or stops having it installed ready for use) for any purpose and expects never to use (or install) it again (eg ID 2003/825; TD 2006/33)
- a taxpayer has not used the asset and stops having it installed ready for use (if it was so installed) and decides never to use it (eg ID 2003/185; ID 2003/186; ID 2005/190)
- there is a partial change in the ownership of the asset (¶17-780). For partnership assets, the balancing adjustment event happens for the partnership and not for the individual partners
- an existing vessel is disposed of, but in the second income year after the year of disposal (ITAA97 s 40-285(5))
- a taxpayer makes a choice in relation to certain mining rights or information first used for exploration or prospecting purposes that were not immediately deductible (¶17-350; s 40-295(1A)). This applies if they started to hold the asset after 7.30 pm EST on 14 May 2013. A further balancing adjustment event happens if the exploration or prospecting subsequently becomes successful (s 40-295(1B)).

See also ID 2002/997 (call and put options), ID 2003/110 to ID 2003/112 (theft of depreciating asset), ID 2003/218 to ID 2003/221 (amalgamation of 2 incorporated associations), ID 2003/756 (car leases), ID 2004/261 (demolition and dismantlement), ID 2005/197 (termination of novated car lease), ID 2006/168 (grant of a licence to exploit patent), ID 2008/92 (uncompleted work).

Where the tax-preferred leasing provisions have applied to an asset and an event happens that would constitute a balancing adjustment event under the above rules, the event is treated as a balancing adjustment event and a balancing adjustment is made under Subdiv 40-D, based on the adjustable value of the asset (s 250-290; ¶23-210). Sections 40-290 (¶17-660) and 40-292 (see below), dealing with reductions to the balancing adjustment amount to reflect non-taxable use of the asset, as well as s 40-291 dealing with reductions to the balancing adjustment to reflect use as a second-hand asset in a residential rental property, do not apply.

Balancing adjustment events do not occur for:

- a mere change of use of the asset (eg ID 2003/625) except where temporary full expensing applied (¶17-430)
- the merging of assets ie an asset held by a taxpayer is merged into another depreciating asset. The taxpayer is treated as having stopped holding the original assets and started holding the merged asset (ITAA97 s 40-125). For the cost of the merged assets, see ¶17-100
- the splitting of an asset into 2 or more assets. The taxpayer is treated as having stopped holding the original asset and started holding the new split assets (ITAA97 s 40-115). If however, the taxpayer stops holding part of a depreciating asset, the original asset is taken to have been split into the part the taxpayer stopped holding (for which there is a balancing adjustment event) and the rest of the asset. If the taxpayer grants or assigns an interest in an item of intellectual property, the taxpayer is treated as having stopped holding part of the asset. When a taxpayer enters into an IRU agreement (¶17-015) giving indefeasible rights to the use of a telecommunications cable system, the depreciating assets (eg each segment of the cable system) that are held by the taxpayer and that form the cable system are not split into 2 or more separate assets (ID 2012/38). For the cost of the split assets, see ¶17-100
- pooled in-house software (¶17-370)
- primary producers' assets (¶18-050)
- a ''government payment to industry'' (GPI) that is calculated having regard to some effect on a depreciating asset but the asset continues to be held for current or future use (TR 2006/3).

The disposal of depreciated plant for a consideration in excess of its cost may, in appropriate circumstances, give rise to income, eg where the taxpayer trades in that kind of property and the disposal in fact occurs as part of the conduct of the business (*Memorex*; ¶10-110). In such a case, the termination value, in working out the assessable or deductible balancing adjustment amount, does not include an amount included in assessable income under ITAA97 s 6-5 or 6-10 (s 40-300(3)). However, if the property sold is the very equipment with which the taxpayer conducts its business, the proceeds may be of a capital nature (eg *Hyteco Hiring*: ¶10-112).

For the consequences of the loss of a business asset in a natural disaster, see ¶44-130.

Effects of balancing adjustment event

An assessable or deductible balancing adjustment is required if the taxpayer worked out (or is treated as having worked out) the decline in value of the asset under Subdiv 40-B, or would have worked out such decline if it had used the asset (s 40-285).

The adjustable value of an asset after a balancing adjustment event is zero. However, where the event happened because: (a) the taxpayer stopped using the asset expecting never to use it again; or (b) the taxpayer had not used and expected never to use it, the adjustable value is the termination value plus any second element costs.

The balancing adjustment rules of the uniform capital allowance system apply to assets that start being held on or after 1 July 2001 as well as assets that were held on that date, where the balancing adjustment event occurs on or after that date. Where relevant, amounts deductible under the former depreciation provisions are taken into account in making balancing adjustment calculations (ITTPA s 40-285). For an example, see ID 2003/461 (pre-CGT asset).

For the CGT consequences of disposing a depreciating asset, see ¶17-670.

R&D depreciating assets

If a depreciating asset has been used for R&D as well as other taxable purposes, with the result that a notional deduction has been available under the R&D provisions (¶17-420) and an actual deduction under ITAA97 Div 40, the balancing adjustment amount is the difference between the termination value and the adjustable value of the asset. In calculating the balancing adjustment amount, the R&D use is treated as use for a taxable purpose. In addition, an adjustment is made to reflect the extent of R&D use of the asset over its life (ITAA97 s 40-292: ¶17-420).

Deductible balancing adjustment

If the ''termination value'' (¶17-640) of a depreciating asset (usually its selling price on disposal) is *less* than its adjustable value just before the balancing adjustment event occurred (¶17-485), the difference is deductible in the year of the event (ITAA97 s 40-285(2)), subject to the application of roll-over relief.

▶ Example 1

A depreciating asset purchased on 1 July Year 1 for $3,000 was scrapped on 31 March Year 4 when its residual scrap value at market price was $600. Its decline in value was calculated using the prime cost method over 5 years.

Cost	$3,000
Less: full decline in value for Year 1, Year 2, Year 3 and nine months for Year 4	2,250
Adjustable value at 31 March Year 4	750
Less: scrap value	600
Balancing deduction	$150

Thus, in Year 4, the taxpayer can claim a total deduction of $600, ie 9 months decline in value ($450) and a balancing deduction ($150).

Assessable balancing adjustment

If the termination value of a depreciating asset is *more* than its adjustable value just before the balancing adjustment event occurred (¶17-485), the excess is assessable in the year of the event (s 40-285(1)) unless balancing adjustment roll-over relief (¶17-710, ¶17-720) is used to defer or offset the adjustment.

▶ Example 2

A post-10 May 2006 depreciating asset purchased on 1 July Year 1 for $5,000 was sold for $2,600 on 31 October Year 4. Its decline in value was calculated under the diminishing value method over 5 years.

Cost	$5,000
Less: Year 1 decline in value	2,000
Opening adjustable value Year 2	3,000
Less: Year 2 decline in value	1,200
Opening adjustable value Year 3	1,800
Less: Year 3 decline in value	720
Opening adjustable value Year 4	1,080
Less: Decline in value for 4 months to 31 October Year 4	144
Adjustable value at 31 October Year 4	$936

Thus, in Year 4, a deduction of $144 is allowed for the decline in value of the asset and a balancing adjustment of $1,664 (ie $2,600 – $936) is assessable.

If the termination value is later repaid, any assessable balancing adjustment is not treated as non-assessable non-exempt income under ITAA97 s 59-30 but may be treated as the cost of the reacquired asset (ID 2011/94).

[FITR ¶87-170, ¶87-180, ¶87-510, ¶87-540]

¶17-640 Termination value of depreciating assets

When a balancing adjustment event happens for a depreciating asset (eg the asset is disposed of) (¶17-630), the balancing adjustment is calculated by comparing the termination value and the adjustable value (¶17-485) of the asset. The termination value of an asset excludes any GST component (see below). Selling expenses do not reduce the termination value of an asset, but rather are included in the second element of cost of the asset (¶17-105).

The termination value for a depreciating asset is either the amount that the taxpayer has received, or is taken to have received, under the balancing adjustment event or, in certain circumstances, the amount attributed under the termination value table in ITAA97 s 40-300. Termination value does not include amounts of ordinary or statutory income. The termination value of the part of a mining, quarrying or prospecting right transferred under a farm-in farm-out arrangement is reduced by the value of the exploration benefit received (s 40-1105; ¶19-010).

If the taxpayer receives an amount for 2 or more things, including for a balancing adjustment event for an asset, the amount is apportioned on a reasonable basis (ITAA97 s 40-310).

The TOFA rules (¶23-020) may affect the calculation of an asset's termination value where a financial arrangement is used as consideration for ceasing to hold a depreciating asset.

Amount taxpayer taken to have received for the balancing adjustment event

The general rule is that the termination value of the asset is the amount the taxpayer is taken to have received for the balancing adjustment event (ITAA97 s 40-305; eg ID 2006/167). This amount is the greater of:

(1) the consideration received under the balancing adjustment event, being the sum of any of the following:

(a) any amount that the taxpayer has received or is deemed to have received. This includes the price of the notional sale taken to have occurred when a depreciating asset is converted to trading stock (¶9-245), the consideration for an asset held under a hire purchase arrangement under ITAA97 s 240-25 (¶23-250), or a lessee's deemed receipt when a luxury car lease ends under ITAA97 s 242-90 (¶17-220). If the asset is a Div 230 financial arrangement or a Div 230 financial arrangement is involved in the consideration, ITAA97 s 230-505 applies

(b) the amount of any liability of the taxpayer to pay an amount that has been terminated (eg ID 2002/1016; ID 2002/1017; ID 2004/160)

(c) the amount of any right to receive an amount that has been granted to the taxpayer (or the increase in such amount), to the extent that the right has not been satisfied

(d) the market value of any "non-cash benefit" received by the taxpayer. "Non-cash benefits" (ITAA97 s 995-1(1)) are all property and services that are not money

(e) the market value of any "non-cash benefit" that the taxpayer is granted a right to receive (or an increase in such non-cash benefit), to the extent that the right has not been satisfied

(f) the market value of a non-cash benefit that the taxpayer is no longer required to provide, and

(2) the sum of amounts deductible or deducted, or taken into account in working out deductions, as a result of the balancing adjustment event, and any amount by which the amount deductible was reduced because of an amount of consideration calculated under (1).

▶ Example 1: Consideration taken to have been received (from the Explanatory Memorandum)

Andrew sells a panel van to Fiona, a house painter, in return for: painting Andrew's home (this non-cash benefit has a market value of $4,000); terminating a $1,000 debt owed to her by Andrew; undertaking to repaint Andrew's home in 10 years (this non-cash benefit has a market value of $1,500) and undertaking to pay Andrew $1,000. The termination value of the panel van is $7,500.

▶ Example 2: Amount deductible (from the Explanatory Memorandum)

ShopCo gives a depreciating asset to one of its customers. If the market value of the asset is a deductible outgoing under ITAA97 s 8-1, it will also be the termination value of the asset.

Specified termination value

The following rules for determining the termination value of an asset (as set out in s 40-300) apply in preference to the general rules described above. If more than one of the listed cases apply, the last applicable amount is the termination value of the asset. For the meaning of "market value", see ¶17-050.

(1) If the taxpayer stops using the depreciating asset or having it installed ready for use for any purpose and expects never to use it again (but still holds it), the termination value is the market value of the asset when the taxpayer stops using it or having it installed ready for use.

(2) If the taxpayer decides never to use an asset that the taxpayer has not used (but still holds it), the termination value is the market value at the time of making that decision.

(3) If the taxpayer stops using in-house software for any purpose and expects never to use it again (but still holds it), the termination value is zero (therefore, the whole adjustable value is deductible).

(4) If the taxpayer decides never to use in-house software that the taxpayer has not used (but still holds), the termination value is zero (therefore, the whole adjustable value is deductible).

(5) If one or more partners stops holding a depreciating asset when it becomes a partnership asset, the termination value is the market value of the asset when the partnership started holding it. If there is a partial change of ownership (¶17-780), the termination value is the market value of the asset at the time of the change.

(6) If the taxpayer stopped holding the asset under a non-arm's length dealing (¶17-045) for less than its market value, the termination value is its market value just before the taxpayer stopped holding it.

(7) If the taxpayer stopped holding a depreciating asset under a private or domestic arrangement (eg gave it as a gift), the termination value is the market value of the asset just before the taxpayer stopped holding it.

(8) The termination value of an asset that is lost (including stolen: ID 2003/111) or destroyed is the amount or value received or receivable under an insurance policy or otherwise for the loss or destruction.

(9) The termination value of an asset held by a deceased taxpayer and that starts being held by the legal personal representative as a result of the death, is the adjustable value of the asset at the time of the death.

(10) The termination value of an asset held by a deceased taxpayer and that passes directly to a beneficiary or joint tenant is the market value of the asset on the day of the death. The termination value of an asset allocated to a low-value pool is so much of the closing pool balance for the year of the death as is reasonably attributable to the asset.

(11) The termination value of an asset for which the Minister for Finance has determined an amount under *Airports (Transitional) Act 1996*, s 52A is that amount.

(12) If a balancing adjustment event occurs under ITAA97 s 40-295(1A), which applies to mining, quarrying or prospecting rights or information, where exploration or prospecting on a related tenement has ceased, the termination value is zero.

(13) If a balancing adjustment event occurs under ITAA97 s 40-295(1B), where exploration or prospecting recommences after ceasing, the termination value is the asset's adjustable value on the day the balancing adjustment event occurs (ignoring ITAA97 s 40-285(3) — which would otherwise deem the adjustable value to be nil).

GST implications

The termination value of a depreciating asset is reduced by any GST payable in respect of the balancing adjustment event (ITAA97 s 27-95). If the termination value of an asset is its market value, such market value is defined to be the GST exclusive market value of the asset (s 995-1(1)). The termination value is increased by any decreasing adjustments and reduced by any increasing adjustments (¶34-140) made in the same income year as the balancing adjustment event (s 27-95). Any decreasing or increasing adjustments made in later years are assessable and deductible respectively.

▶ Example 3

If Jonesco sells a depreciating asset for $880, including GST of $80, and the adjustable value of the asset before the sale was $900, the deductible balancing adjustment amount is $100 [ie $900 – ($880 – $80)].

Fixtures attached to realty

The termination value rules apply to an improvement to land, or a fixture on land, whether the improvement or fixture is removable or not, as if it were an asset separate from the land (ITAA97 s 40-30(3)). Where a separate value has been allocated by parties dealing at arm's length, the Commissioner accepts that value (TD 98/24).

Trade-ins

The termination value of an asset that is traded-in is generally the amount of the trade-in allowance. However, where there is a non-arm's length distortion in the trade-in allowance and purchase price of the new asset, the market value rules under ITAA97 s 40-300(2) item 6 above would apply.

Cars subject to car limit

Where a balancing adjustment event happens for a car subject to the car limit (¶17-200) (eg the car is disposed of), the termination value for the purpose of calculating any balancing adjustment is adjusted (ITAA97 s 40-325) by multiplying it by the fraction worked out under the following formula:

$$\frac{\text{car limit} + \text{second element costs}}{\text{total cost of car}}$$

The "car limit" is the car limit for the financial year in which the taxpayer first used the car for any purpose. "Total cost" of the car is the actual (GST-exclusive) cost of the car and includes both first and second elements of the cost of the car. The termination value is reduced by any GST payable on the supply (eg ID 2002/933).

The excess of the loss on sale of such cars over the allowable balancing deduction cannot be claimed as a deduction under s 8-1 (*ANZ Banking Group*).

Where the cost of a car was adjusted under the rules dealing with cars acquired at a discount (¶17-210), the termination value of the car must be increased by the "discount portion" for the car (ITAA97 s 40-320).

▶ Example 4: Termination value less than adjustable value

On 10 October 2020, Taani buys a car for $70,000, which she uses solely for business purposes. She sells the car on 18 July 2021 for $60,000. Taani calculated the decline in value of the car over 8 years using the prime cost method. As the car limit for the 2020–21 year during which the car was used was $59,136, the annual decline in value is calculated as if the car cost $59,136, not $70,000. The deduction for the decline in value is as follows:

Year 1

Decline in value: $\frac{\$59{,}136}{8} \times \frac{263^*}{365}$ $5,326

Year 2

Decline in value: $\frac{\$59{,}136}{8} \times \frac{18^*}{365}$ $365

Deduction for decline in value to date of sale $5,691

Adjustable value at date of sale ($59,136 – $5,691) = $53,445

In calculating the balancing adjustment on sale, the actual sale price of the car ($60,000) is reduced as follows:

$$\text{sale price} \times \frac{\text{car limit}}{\text{actual cost of vehicle}}$$

$$\text{ie } \$60{,}000 \times \frac{\$59{,}136}{\$70{,}000}$$

adjusted sale price = $50,688

* Pro rata depreciation applies (¶17-560).

As the termination value is less than the adjustable value (¶17-485) of the car, Taani is entitled to a balancing deduction of $2,757 (ie $53,445 – $50,688) in the 2021–22 year. This is in addition to the deduction of $365 for the decline in value of the car in that year.

▶ Example 5: Termination value more than adjustable value

Assume the same facts as in Example 1 except that Taani sells the car for $65,000. The adjusted sale price is:

$$\$65{,}000 \times \frac{\$59{,}136}{\$70{,}000}$$

$$= \$54{,}912$$

In 2021–22, Taani is entitled to a pro rata annual deduction of $365, but a balancing charge of $1,467 (ie $54,912 – $53,445) must be included in her assessable income.

Commercial debt forgiveness

Where commercial debts are forgiven (¶16-910), a taxpayer (the debtor) may be required to reduce the amount used in calculating the deduction for the decline in value for a depreciating asset (¶17-510). In working out any balancing charge or deduction, the opening adjustable value of the depreciating asset is reduced by the debt forgiveness amount.

▶ Example 6

If the opening adjustable value of an asset costing $10,000 (but subject to the application of a $2,000 forgiven debt) is $4,400 and the asset is sold for $9,500, the assessable balancing amount is $7,100 (ie $9,500 – $2,400). If the asset is instead sold for $2,000, the balancing deduction is $400 (ie $2,400 – $2,000).

[FITR ¶69-210, ¶87-105, ¶87-550 – ¶87-665]

¶17-660 Reduction to balancing adjustment

Balancing adjustment where part business use

If the deduction for the decline in value of a depreciating asset held by a taxpayer is reduced because the asset was used for non-taxable purposes or because the asset was a boat or leisure facility that did not satisfy certain conditions (¶17-010, ¶17-570), any balancing adjustment amount that would otherwise be assessable or deductible (¶17-630) is reduced by the fraction (ITAA97 s 40-290; ID 2007/69):

$$\frac{\text{sum of reductions}}{\text{total decline}}$$

The sum of reductions is the sum of the amount by which the deductions for the decline in value of the asset were reduced in the hands of the taxpayer under ITAA97 s 40-25, or an earlier transferor (if there has been roll-over relief: ¶17-710), or a deceased taxpayer (if the asset is now held by the legal personal representative of the deceased taxpayer). Total decline refers to the sum of the decline in value of the asset while being held by the taxpayer, or an earlier transferor or a deceased taxpayer.

In addition, the balancing adjustment amount relating to a split or a merged asset (¶17-100) must be reduced to a reasonable extent to reflect any non-taxable use of the asset from which the current asset was split or with which it was merged.

The reduction does not apply to geothermal exploration, mining, quarrying or prospecting information (noting that such assets are no longer depreciable if they start being held from 1 July 2014).

▶ Example

Fran acquires a computer for $2,000 and uses it for income-producing purposes to the extent of 60% in Years 1 to 3. Assuming an effective life of 4 years and using the 200% diminishing value method rate for post-9 May 2006 assets (¶17-500), the decline in value of the asset and the deductions for such decline are:

			Deduction	Reduction
Cost		$2,000		
Less: Year 1 decline in value	$\frac{\$2,000}{4} \times 200\%$	$1,000	$600	$400
Adjustable value end of Year 1		$1,000		
Less: Year 2 decline in value	$\frac{\$1,000}{4} \times 200\%$	$500	$300	$200
Adjustable value end of Year 2		$500		
Less: Year 3 decline in value	$\frac{\$500}{4} \times 200\%$	$250	$150	$100
Adjustable value end of Year 3		$250		

The total decline in value is $1,750 (ie $1,000 + $500 + $250).

The sum of the reductions is $700 (ie $400 + $200 + $100).

Therefore, the balancing adjustment amount must be reduced by 40% $\left(\text{ie } \frac{\$700}{\$1,750}\right)$

Fran sells the computer on 1 July of Year 4. The possible balancing adjustment and CGT outcomes (¶17-670) are as follows, depending on the proceeds from the sale.

- If the computer is sold for $1,000, the assessable balancing amount is $450, ie [($1,000 – $250) – (40% × $750)]. There is also a capital loss of $400 (ie [$2,000 – $1,000] × 40%).
- If the computer is sold for $200, the deductible balancing amount is $30, ie [($250 – $200) – (40% × $50)]. There is also a capital loss of $720 (ie [$2,000 – $200] × 40%).
- If the computer is sold for $2,500, the assessable balancing amount is $1,350, ie [($2,500 – $250) – (40% × $2,250)]. There is also a capital gain of $200 (ie [$2,500 – $2,000] × 40%).

Balancing adjustment where asset in residential rental property

A similar reduction to a balancing adjustment applies if the deduction for the decline in value of a depreciating asset held by certain taxpayers is reduced because the asset was a second-hand asset in a residential rental property (¶17-012). The balancing adjustment amount that would otherwise be assessable or deductible (¶17-630) is reduced by the fraction (ITAA97 s 40-291):

$$\frac{\text{sum of s 40-27 reductions}}{\text{total decline}}$$

The sum of reductions is the sum of the amount by which the deductions for the decline in value of the asset were reduced in the hands of the taxpayer under ITAA97 s 40-27, or an earlier transferor (if there has been roll-over relief: ¶17-710), or a deceased taxpayer (if the asset is now held by the legal personal representative of the deceased taxpayer). Total decline refers to the sum of the decline in value of the asset while being held by the taxpayer, or an earlier transferor or a deceased taxpayer.

In addition, the balancing adjustment amount relating to a split or a merged asset (¶17-100) must be reduced to a reasonable extent to reflect the use of the asset in a residential rental property.

For the CGT consequences of the above reductions, see ¶17-670.

[FITR ¶87-530]

¶17-665 Special balancing adjustment rules for certain cars

Special balancing adjustment rules may apply to cars for which car expenses have been substantiated using the cents per kilometre method or the 12% of original value method for one or more income years (¶16-320). Although taxpayers cannot substantiate their car expenses using the 12% method from the 2015–16 year, the balancing adjustment rules below relating to that former method continue to apply for taxpayers who chose the 12% method for any year(s) before the 2015–16 year.

The one-third of actual expenses method for substantiating car expenses also ceased to apply from the 2015–16 year. This means that for balancing adjustment events occurring from 1 July 2015, taxpayers could not have *solely* used the 12% method or the one-third of actual expenses method to substantiate their car expenses.

If car expense deductions have been calculated using *only* the cents per kilometre method (¶16-320), no balancing adjustment amount or capital gain or loss arises if a disposal or other balancing adjustment event occurs for the car (¶17-030).

If the deductions have *only* been calculated using the logbook method (¶16-320), any balancing adjustment amount is calculated on the basis of the ordinary balancing adjustment rules. Where the logbook method was used, the percentage of the balancing adjustment equal to the non-business use is excluded.

The special balancing adjustment rules apply to a car for which the taxpayer had used multiple methods over the life of the car: either the 12% of original value method (before the 2015–16 year) or the cents per kilometre method to calculate their car expenses for an income year(s), as well as the one-third of actual expenses method (before the 2015–16 year) or the logbook method in other years (ITAA97 s 40-370; TD 2006/49). In calculating the reduction in deductions using the methodology shown in ¶17-660, such a car is assumed to have been used one-third for income purposes during a year in which the former 12% method was used, and one-fifth for income purposes during a year in which the cents per kilometre method was used. Further, the adjustable value of the car is calculated as if the decline in value for the years in which the cents per kilometre method or former 12% method applied, was calculated on the same basis as when the logbook method or the former one-third of actual expenses method were used.

The resulting balancing charge or deduction calculated according to the above methodology is then reduced to exclude the proportion of the ownership period during which the cents per kilometre method or former 12% method was used.

▶ Example 1

Jones buys a car for $30,000 and uses it for business purposes to the extent of 80%. He uses the logbook method for the full year in which he first uses the car (Year 1). In Year 2, he uses the one-third of actual expenses method (as it could still be chosen for this year), and in Year 3 he uses the cents per kilometre method. He sells the car at the end of Year 3 for $17,000.

Year 1

The logbook method was used for deducting car expenses. The decline in value of the car was calculated using the prime cost method and an effective life of 5 years. Decline in value was $6,000 (ie $30,000 ÷ 5) producing an adjustable value of $24,000 (ie $30,000 – $6,000). There was a reduction for non-taxable purpose use of $1,200 (ie $6,000 × 20%). The deduction for the decline in value was $4,800 (ie $6,000 – $1,200).

Year 2

The one-third of actual expenses method was used for deducting car expenses. The decline in value of the car must be calculated using the same method and effective life as in Year 1 (ie the prime cost method and an effective life of 5 years). Decline in value was $6,000 (ie $30,000 ÷ 5) producing an adjustable value of $18,000 (ie $24,000 – $6,000). Under ITAA97 s 40-25(6), there was a reduction for non-taxable purpose use of $4,000 (ie $6,000 × 2/3). The deduction for the decline in value was $2,000 (ie $6,000 – $4,000).

Year 3

The cents per kilometre method was used for deducting car expenses. No decline in value of the car was calculated under Div 40 but adjustable value was calculated on the same basis as in Years 1 and 2 (ie using the prime cost method and an effective life of 5 years). Deemed decline in value was $6,000 (ie $30,000 ÷ 5), producing an adjustable value of $12,000 (ie $18,000 – $6,000). Under s 40-370(4)(c), it is assumed that the car was used for taxable purposes to the extent of 20%. Therefore, there was a reduction for non-taxable purpose use of $4,800 (ie $6,000 × 80%). The deduction for the decline in value was $1,200 (ie $6,000 – $4,800).

Step 1

The step 1 amount is $5,000, ie the termination value ($17,000) less the adjustable value of the car just before the balancing adjustment event ($12,000).

Step 2

The sum of the reductions is $10,000 (ie $1,200 + $4,000 + $4,800). The total decline of the car while held by Jones was $18,000 (ie $6,000 × 3). The non-taxable use portion is calculated using the formula:

$$\frac{\$10,000}{\$18,000} \times \$5,000 = \$2,777$$

The step 1 amount ($5,000) is reduced by the non-taxable use portion ($2,777) resulting in a step 2 amount of $2,223.

Step 3

The step 2 amount is multiplied by the number of days when Div 40 deductions were available (ie an actual expense method, which was used in Years 1 and 2) and divided by the total number of days when the taxpayer held the car (3 years), ie:

$$\frac{730 \text{ days}}{1{,}095 \text{ days}} \times \$2{,}223 = \$1{,}482$$

As this is a positive number, this amount is included in assessable income.

▶ Example 2

Assume that in the example above the facts remained the same except that Jones sold his car for $10,000.

Step 1

The step 1 amount is ($2,000), ie $10,000 less $12,000.

Step 2

The sum of the reductions is $10,000 and the total decline of the car while held by Jones was $18,000 (as in Example 1). The non-taxable use portion is calculated using the formula:

$$\frac{\$10{,}000}{\$18{,}000} \times (\$2{,}000) = (\$1{,}111)$$

The step 1 amount, ie $2,000, is reduced by the non-taxable use portion ($1,111) resulting in a step 2 amount of ($889).

Step 3

The step 2 amount is multiplied by the number of days when Div 40 deductions were available (ie in Years 1 and 2) and divided by the total number of days when the taxpayer held the car (3 years), ie:

$$\frac{730 \text{ days}}{1{,}095 \text{ days}} \times (\$889) = (\$592)$$

As this is a negative number, this amount is deductible.

[FITR ¶87-740]

¶17-670 Balancing adjustments and CGT

Whether a balancing adjustment event for a depreciating asset held by a taxpayer triggers a balancing adjustment amount (¶17-630), a capital gain/loss (¶11-000), or both, depends on the extent of the use of the asset for "taxable purposes" (¶17-010) or, for certain taxpayers, as a second-hand asset in a residential rental property (¶17-012).

In the case of R&D assets, use for R&D purposes is treated in the same manner as a taxable purpose and the percentage of business use is calculated on the basis of notional ITAA97 Div 40 deductions (¶17-420).

If a depreciating asset is *wholly* used for taxable purposes, a balancing adjustment amount may arise and no capital gain or loss arises (ITAA97 ss 40-285; 118-24).

If the asset was *wholly* used for non-taxable purposes or as a second-hand asset in a residential rental property, the balancing adjustment amount is reduced to nil to reflect such use (¶17-660). If the asset was used *partly* for either of these purposes, the balancing adjustment amount is reduced by the proportion of such use of the asset (¶17-660). In either case, CGT event K7 (¶11-350) also arises provided the depreciating asset is not a pre-CGT asset, a collectable, personal use asset, or an asset for which a deduction could be claimed in the year of the balancing adjustment event under the rules for small business taxpayers (¶7-250). The CGT event occurs at the time of the balancing adjustment event (ITAA97 s 104-235).

Under CGT event K7, if the *cost* of the asset exceeds its termination value, the excess, multiplied by the percentage of non-business and residential property use, constitutes a capital loss (ITAA97 s 104-240; ¶11-350; ID 2006/200). If the termination value of the asset exceeds its *cost*, the excess, multiplied by this percentage, constitutes a capital gain. This is subject to the following rules:

- if an amount (eg the sale proceeds) is misappropriated by an employee or agent, the termination value of the asset is reduced by that amount and increased by any amount recouped (¶16-590)
- if a commercial debt of the taxpayer is forgiven, the cost of the depreciating asset is reduced by the forgiven amount (¶16-910; ITAA97 s 40-90; ¶17-090, ¶17-510)
- cost is adjusted for any GST input tax credit, or increasing or decreasing adjustment
- the CGT discount provisions may apply (¶11-033), but the small business CGT concessions do not (¶7-110)
- any capital gain or loss from a CGT event happening to an asset of a partnership arises for the partnership, rather than for the individual partners (s 118-24).

Primary producers' assets under ITAA97 Subdivs 40-F and 40-G (¶18-000) are subject to the ordinary CGT rules, and not to CGT event K7.

CGT event K7 does not apply when there is roll-over relief (¶17-710) for the balancing adjustment event. See also ID 2003/461 (pre-CGT asset).

[FITR ¶152-380 – ¶152-384, ¶154-543]

Balancing Adjustment Relief

¶17-710 Balancing adjustment roll-over relief

Balancing adjustments arising from changes in ownership interests in depreciating assets (¶17-630) may be rolled over in certain circumstances under ITAA97 s 40-340. The consequences of roll-over relief are that (ITAA97 s 40-345):

- no balancing adjustments arise for the transferor under ITAA97 s 40-285, and
- the transferee stands in the transferor's shoes with regard to the amount and timing of future deductions and the amount of a potential balancing adjustment on subsequent disposal. In particular, the transferee must use the same method and effective life (or remaining effective life, if using the prime cost method) that the transferor was using. The transferee acquires the asset at the transferor's adjustable value (¶17-485) for the asset. For an example, see TD 2005/1.

Special provisions apply where an interest in a leased asset or the lease itself has been transferred (¶23-230).

Roll-over relief does not apply if ITAA97 Subdiv 170-D (dealing with certain transactions by companies within linked groups) applies to the disposal of the asset or change in interests in the asset.

When an existing shipping vessel is disposed of, a balancing adjustment amount is included in the second income year after the income year of disposal. Balancing adjustment roll-over relief applies if another vessel is held on the second anniversary of the disposal of the original vessel and, in such case, a balancing adjustment amount is included only to the extent that the balancing adjustment exceeds the cost of the new vessel (ITAA97 s 40-362).

A balancing adjustment roll-over may be chosen where mining, quarrying or prospecting rights are disposed of under an interest realignment arrangement entered into after 7.30 pm EST on 14 May 2013 (s 40-363). Such arrangements arise where joint venture parties exchange post-30 June 2001 rights to pursue a single development project. Their goal is to align the ownership of individual rights with that of the overall venture. However, any non-realignment amounts received under the arrangement are assessable income, with the payer including an equivalent amount in the cost of the rights they acquire. After an interest realignment arrangement takes effect, new information may make it apparent that one of the parties originally made an inadequate contribution. The arrangement may provide for adjustments and a party receiving an adjustment includes the amount in their assessable income. The party paying the adjustment includes the amount in the second element of the cost of the rights they acquired under the realignment (s 40-364). Roll-over relief is also available for taxpayers entering into eligible farm-in farm-out arrangements after 7.30 pm EST on 14 May 2013 (¶19-010).

Automatic roll-over

Balancing adjustment roll-over relief is automatic (ie mandatory) in some situations. It is assumed that Div 118 (CGT exemptions), and also ss 122-25(3) and 124-870(5) (which exclude certain assets from some CGT roll-overs) do not apply. Based on these assumptions, CGT roll-over relief would be obtained for:

- transfer of an asset as a result of marriage breakdown (¶12-460, ¶12-470)
- disposal of an asset to a wholly-owned company (¶12-040)
- transfer of an asset of a fixed trust to a company under a trust restructure (¶12-395) or of an asset between fixed trusts (¶12-552)
- disposal of partnership property to a company that is wholly owned by the partners (¶12-090)
- disposal of an asset within a wholly-owned group (¶12-490). As a consequence of the consolidation regime (¶8-000), such roll-over relief is limited
- disposal of an asset as part of a superannuation fund merger (if the transferor chooses Subdiv 310-D roll-over), or as part of a transfer to a MySuper product (if the transferor chooses Subdiv 311-B roll-over), or
- depreciating asset transfers from 1 July 2016 under the small business restructure roll-over (¶12-380).

Roll-over is not available in respect of other disposals, eg a disposal from a discretionary trust to a unit trust.

Balancing adjustment roll-over relief is specifically extended to motor vehicles and other exempt assets as if they were assets to which the CGT roll-over provisions applied. Roll-over relief may also apply to a succession of transfers of a single depreciating asset.

The transferor must provide sufficient information to enable the transferee to calculate the transferee's deductions (ITAA97 s 40-360).

Optional roll-over

Optional balancing adjustment roll-over relief is available if a *joint election* for roll-over relief is made by the transferor *and* the transferee in relation to a partial change in ownership interests in a partnership asset, eg where there is a variation in the constitution of the partnership or in interests of the partners (s 40-340; ¶17-780). Where the change in interests occurs due to the death of a partner, the trustee of the deceased partner's estate may be a party to a joint election. The election must be in writing and must contain such information as the transferee requires in order to work out how the capital allowance provisions apply to the transferee's holding of the depreciating asset.

[FITR ¶87-685 – ¶87-720]

¶17-720 Offsetting balancing charge for involuntary disposals

A balancing adjustment offset is available for certain involuntary disposals. An involuntary disposal arises where plant is lost or destroyed (including stolen: ID 2002/782), or an Australian government agency acquires it compulsorily or by forced negotiation (ITAA97 former ss 42-293(2); 40-365).

In addition, the offset is available: (a) where a private acquirer compulsorily acquires an asset through recourse to a statutory power other than a compulsory acquisition of minority interests under company law; or (b) where a landowner whose land is compulsorily subject to a mining lease (or is subject to a mining lease in the shadow of compulsion) sells the land to the lessee and acquires a replacement asset, if the lease would significantly affect the landowner's use of the land. This concession does not extend to initial exploration licences or retention licences.

Under the offset rules, the balancing adjustment amount is not included in assessable income and is instead applied to reduce the cost (¶17-080) and the opening adjustable value (¶17-485) of the replacement asset (in years later than the year in which the replacement asset is first used or installed ready for use for any purpose).

The expenditure on the replacement asset must be incurred no earlier than one year before the time of the disposal of the asset and no later than one year after the end of the income year in which the disposal occurred. The Commissioner can agree to extend the time limit. At the end of the year in which the taxpayer starts holding the replacement asset or incurs the expenditure, the replacement asset must be used wholly for taxable purposes (¶17-010). Where there are 2 or more replacement assets, the offset amount must be apportioned between those items on the basis of their cost for capital allowance purposes.

The balancing adjustment offset for replacement plant for disposals that are not involuntary no longer applies (ITAA97 former s 42-290; ITTPA s 40-295).

[FITR ¶87-730]

Partial Change of Ownership

¶17-780 Disposal taken to occur on partial change of ownership

If there is a partial change in the holding of, or in interests of entities in, a partnership asset or in an asset that becomes a partnership asset (eg where a partnership is created, varied or dissolved), an adjustment may be required under the balancing adjustment rules (ITAA97 ss 40-285; 40-295(2)). This applies where at least one entity that had an interest in the asset before the change, has an interest in it after the change.

Unless a joint election for roll-over relief (¶17-710) is made by both the transferor(s) and the transferee(s), the termination value (¶17-640) of the asset for balancing adjustment purposes and the cost (¶17-100) to the transferee is the market value of the asset at the time of the change (ITAA97 ss 40-180; 40-300).

▶ Example

Mel and Liz, who have carried on a partnership together, admit John as a third partner, selling John 50% each of their interests in the partnership assets including depreciating assets. The partnership agreement indicates that the value attributed to the depreciating assets is $1,800 which is also the market value. If the cost of those assets to Mel and Liz was $2,000 and the decline in value of the assets up to the date of the new agreement was $1,600, there is an assessable balancing adjustment of $1,400 (ie the termination value of $1,800 less the adjustable value of $400) for the partnership of Mel and Liz, and further deductions for the decline in value of the assets of the partnership of Mel, Liz and John are based on a cost of $1,800 (assuming a joint election for roll-over relief is not made).

[FITR ¶87-540]

Pooling of Depreciating Assets

¶17-810 Low-value depreciating asset pools

Taxpayers may elect to claim deductions for the decline in value of depreciating assets (''low-cost assets'') costing less than $1,000 through a low-value pool (ITAA97 ss 40-420 to 40-445). An asset (''low-value asset'') whose decline in value was calculated using the diminishing value method can also be pooled where its adjustable value (¶17-485) is less than $1,000. An immediate write-off for low-cost depreciating assets and pooling of other depreciating assets is available under the special rules for small business entities (¶7-250). Temporary rules allow an immediate write-off for certain depreciating assets by medium-sized business entities in which instance they cannot be pooled (¶17-330). Assets allocated to a low-value pool also do not qualify for temporary accelerated depreciation or full expensing (¶17-430).

Pooling low-cost and low-value assets

The main rules for pooling of low-cost and low-value depreciating assets are as follows:

- a low-cost depreciating asset (ie an asset whose cost at the end of the income year in which it starts being used or installed ready for use for a taxable purpose is less than $1,000) can be allocated to a low-value pool for the income year in which the taxpayer starts to use it, or has it installed ready for use, for a taxable purpose. For jointly held assets, the $1,000 limit applies to each holder's interest in the asset
- a taxpayer that pools a low-cost depreciating asset must pool all low-cost depreciating assets acquired during that year and all subsequent years
- the following assets cannot be allocated to a low-value pool: assets whose costs are immediately deductible (¶17-330); horticultural plants (¶18-070); depreciating assets subject to the rules for small business taxpayers (¶7-250); assets subject to the R&D offset rules (¶17-420)
- non-business assets costing $300 or less each but that are identical and, therefore, not immediately deductible (¶17-330) may be allocated to a low-value pool even if their overall cost exceeds $1,000 (ID 2003/946)
- an asset whose decline in value was calculated using the diminishing value method for a previous income year can be allocated to a low-value pool if its opening adjustable value (¶17-485) at the start of the current income year is less than $1,000. This decision can be made on an item-by-item basis
- once allocated to a low-value pool, an item must remain in the pool
- first and second element costs (¶17-080) are allocated to a low-value pool exclusive of input tax credits relating to the acquisition of the asset allocated to the pool or to second element costs for such an asset (ITAA97 s 27-100)
- low-cost items may continue to be allocated to a pre-1 July 2001 pool. The decline in value of such pools continues to be calculated under the above rules on the basis of the closing pool balance at the end of the 2000–01 income year (ITTPA s 40-420)
- special cost setting rules apply for consolidated groups (ITAA97 Subdiv 716-G).

The Commissioner accepts the use of sampling methods to estimate the revenue/capital expenditure component of bulk purchases (¶16-153): the revenue component is immediately deductible while the capital component may be pooled (if it relates to depreciating assets).

Expected private or exempt use

When allocating an asset to a low-value pool, the taxpayer must estimate the percentage (if any) of the asset's usage (including past use) that will be for non-taxable purposes (¶17-010), ie generally purposes other than producing assessable income. The estimate must take into account the usage over the effective life (for a low-cost asset) or the remaining effective life (for a low-value asset). The cost that would otherwise have been allocated to the pool must be reduced by that percentage (s 40-435). Such percentage cannot be varied later to reflect actual usage (see ATO publication *Guide to depreciating assets 2020*).

▶ Example 1

Zoe, a computer programmer, acquires a printer for $600. She has elected to create a low-value pool, and estimates that the printer will be used 85% for income-producing purposes and 15% for private purposes. The amount to be allocated to the pool is $510, ie 85% of $600.

In allocating assets to a low-value pool, a non-taxable purpose includes the use of assets in a residential rental property for certain taxpayers affected by s 40-27 (¶17-012).

Decline in value of a low-value pool

The decline in value of a low-value pool for an income year is the sum of 37.5% of:

- the closing pool balance for the previous income year, and
- the taxable use percentage of the opening adjustable value of low-value assets allocated to the pool for that year.

Further deductions of half that rate (ie 18.75%) are allowed for the taxable use percentage of:

- the first and second element costs (¶17-080) of low-cost assets allocated to the pool during the year, and
- the second element costs of: (a) assets allocated to the pool in previous years; and (b) low-value assets allocated to the pool in the current year.

"Closing pool balance"

The closing pool balance for an income year is calculated by adding up:

- the closing pool balance for the previous income year
- the taxable use percentage of the first and second element costs of low-cost assets allocated to the pool during the current year
- the taxable use percentage of the adjustable value of low-value assets allocated to the pool during the year, as at the start of the year
- the taxable use percentage of second element costs incurred during the year in respect of low-value assets allocated during the year and of *any* assets allocated in earlier years

and then subtracting

- the decline in value of the pooled assets for the current year (as worked out under the above rules).

▶ Example 2

ABC Co pools 50 low-cost depreciating assets with a total purchase price of $25,000 in an income year (Year 1). Second element costs incurred during the year in relation to these low-cost assets total $5,000. As at the beginning of the year, ABC Co also allocates to the pool 29 items with a diminishing value, opening adjustable value (less than $1,000 each) totalling $19,600 (no second element costs are incurred for these assets). No private or exempt use is expected. The closing pool balance for the previous income year (Year 0) was nil. The Year 1 decline in value and the closing pool balance are calculated as follows:

			$
(a) Closing pool balance at end of Year 0			nil
(b) Low-cost assets pooled during Year 1			30,000
(c) Low-value assets pooled during Year 1			19,600
(d) Decline in value:			
On (a): 37.5% × nil	=	nil	
On (b): 18.75% × $30,000	=	$5,625	
On (c): 37.5% × $19,600	=	$7,350	
Total			(12,975)
(e) Closing pool balance at end of Year 1			$36,625

Note: If no assets are allocated to the pool and no second element costs are incurred in the next income year (Year 2), the decline in value of the pool for that year will be 37.5% of the Year 1 closing pool balance (ie $13,734).

Disposal of pooled assets

If a balancing adjustment event happens (eg the pooled asset is sold, scrapped, destroyed, lost, given away or otherwise disposed of), the closing pool balance for the year is reduced by the relevant termination value (¶17-640), eg the disposal proceeds (s 40-445). Where a percentage of the cost or opening adjustable value of an asset (representing expected private or exempt use) was originally excluded from the pool, a corresponding percentage of its termination value is ignored for these purposes. Where the termination value exceeds the closing pool balance for that year, the excess is included in the taxpayer's assessable income. No roll-over relief applies (eg ID 2003/1133).

The balancing adjustment event may also trigger CGT event K7 (¶17-670). In such case, the non-taxable use percentage (see above) of the excess of the termination value of the asset over its cost is a capital gain and the non-taxable use percentage of the excess of cost over termination value is a capital loss (ITAA97 s 104-245).

A taxpayer can continue to deduct the pool balance attributable to the asset, even though the taxpayer no longer holds the asset, eg if the termination value is less than the amount still to be written off (s 40-25(5)).

▶ Example 3

Zoe sells the printer that she pooled in Example 1 above. The disposal proceeds (termination value) are $200. The closing pool balance should be reduced by $170 (ie 85% of $200). There is a capital loss of $60 (ie 15% × [$600 – $200]).

[FITR ¶87-800 – ¶87-855, ¶152-384]

Records and Accounting

¶17-880 Schedules and records for capital allowances

Taxpayers claiming capital allowance deductions need to include the total amount on their tax return. A capital allowance schedule is no longer included with tax returns. To assist taxpayers with their calculations, the ATO has provided a worksheet in its publication *Guide to depreciating assets 2020*.

Documentation of purchase details must be obtained from the supplier (¶16-210, ¶16-340). Generally, records must be retained for 5 years (ITAA36 s 262A(4)(a)). For a useful records checklist, see ¶44-100.

Taxpayers will have a hard time proving depreciation deductions where inadequate records are kept and may be subject to penalties (*Rigoli*; ATO *Decision Impact Statement*).

[FTR ¶785-080 – ¶785-120]

Chapter 18 Primary Production Concessions

Concessions for Primary Producers

¶18-000 Summary of primary production concessions

The rules for calculating deductions and writing off capital expenditure incurred in primary production are contained in the uniform capital allowance system (ITAA97 ss 40-510 to 40-675). This chapter covers additional tax concessions for taxpayers engaged in a primary production business (''primary producers'').

The cost of planting annual crops is deductible under the general deduction provisions in the income year in which the expenditure is incurred. On the other hand, expenditure on planting trees, shrubs and similar long-lived plants is generally capital and non-deductible (¶18-020). A special write-off is available for capital expenditure incurred in establishing horticultural plants, including grapevines.

Primary producers may, of course, qualify for the deductions allowable to taxpayers generally, for example, the 10-year write-off for electricity connection costs (¶16-820) and the deduction for repairs (¶16-700) and for the decline in value of depreciating assets (¶17-000). For a list of the usual deductions allowable to primary producers, see the checklist at ¶16-005.

Non-residential buildings used in the primary production, forestry and pearling industries are treated as depreciating assets (¶43-100) as are employee amenities (eg sanitary ware, etc, forming part of toilet accommodation or washing facilities). Improvements to or fixtures on land, whether removable or not, are treated as assets separate from the land (s 40-30; ¶17-020).

There is a special deduction for entering into a permanent conservation covenant over land with certain deductible gift recipients (¶16-972). Primary production losses may be carried forward indefinitely (¶16-895). The measures that prevent a loss from non-commercial business activities being offset against other assessable income in the year in which the loss is incurred do not apply to an individual carrying on a primary production business if the income from other sources is less than $40,000 (¶16-020).

Where an amount is derived or incurred in a foreign currency, the foreign currency conversion rules (¶23-070) and foreign exchange gains and losses provisions (¶23-075) may need to be considered.

Trading stock

As with other taxpayers, primary producers are not entitled to a deduction for the cost of trading stock until the stock is on hand (ITAA97 s 70-15; ¶16-040). For the application of this rule to expenditure incurred under live stock breeding arrangements and to certain other expenditure, such as the cost of seed for planting, see TR 93/9 noted at ¶16-040. The trading stock provisions, including the special valuation provisions for livestock are outlined at ¶9-150 to ¶9-300.

Small business entities (SBE)

Primary producers who are small business entities (ITAA97 s 328-110) with an aggregated turnover of less than $10 million may choose, on a asset-by-asset basis, whether to claim deductions under the primary production provisions or the SBE provisions (ITAA97 s 328-175(3)). However, deductions for horticultural plants (including grapevines) are only available under the relevant primary production provisions (¶18-070), not under the SBE rules (ITAA97 s 328-175(5)). For a general outline of the SBE provisions, see ¶7-001.

Capital works deductions

Where capital expenditure on a fodder storage asset (¶18-085), water facility (¶18-080) or fencing asset (¶18-090) is deductible under both capital works expenditure (ITAA97 Div 43; ¶20-470) and primary production concessions (ITAA97 Subdiv 40-F), or would be deductible under Subdiv 40-F if the asset were used for the purpose of producing assessable income, Div 43 does not apply (ITAA97 s 43-70(2)(f)(i)).

GST and primary production deductions

The cost of a depreciating asset and other primary production expenditure deductible under ITAA97 Div 40 (other than on a depreciating asset) is reduced by any GST input tax credits relating to the acquisition of the asset or to the expenditure (ITAA97 Subdiv 27-B). Adjustments are also required if a decreasing or an increasing adjustment is made.

Natural disasters

The Commissioner has issued information dealing with the concessions available for small business owners affected by natural disasters. Information is also available on the ATO website about how primary producers affected by certain natural disasters can access farm management deposits (*Farm management deposits scheme*). Refer to the Natural Disasters Checklist at ¶44-130.

¶18-010 Meaning of "primary production business"

Many of the primary production concessions dealt with in this chapter are only available to taxpayers carrying on a primary production business. Thus, a shareholder in a primary production company, a salaried manager of an agricultural or pastoral property, or the owner of such a property who has leased it and/or the business to another, will not qualify as a primary producer for the purposes of the averaging provisions (¶18-200). On the other hand, the city-dwelling owner of a primary production business would qualify as a primary producer, even though the property is run by a salaried manager. The members of a partnership, or the beneficiaries entitled to the income of a trust, which carries on a primary production business would also qualify as primary producers.

A "primary production business" is defined (ITAA97 s 995-1(1)) as a business of:

- cultivating or propagating plants or fungi in any physical environment
- maintaining animals for the purpose of selling them or their bodily produce
- manufacturing dairy produce from raw material that a taxpayer has produced
- conducting operations relating directly to taking or catching fish, turtles, dugong, bêche-de-mer (sea cucumbers), crustaceans or aquatic molluscs
- conducting operations relating directly to taking or culturing pearls or pearl shell
- planting or tending trees in a plantation or forest that are intended to be felled
- felling trees in a plantation or forest, or
- transporting trees, or parts of trees, felled in a plantation or forest, directly to the place where they are first to be milled or processed, or transporting them to the place from which they are to be transported to be milled or processed.

The manufacture of dairy produce qualifies as primary production provided the manufacturer was also the producer of the raw material. On the other hand, timber milling is not primary production even though the miller may have planted, tended and felled the trees.

Primary production includes contract broiler growing (IT 233), prawn farming and the provision of artificial breeding services for the beef cattle industry by selling semen collected from bulls owned and maintained by the taxpayer (IT 219). However, the following activities are *not* regarded as primary production activities: kelp harvesting (IT 2006); beach worming (TD 93/39); and live sheep export (TD 93/94; TD 93/95). A cattle dealer would not usually be a primary producer.

[FITR ¶355-005]

¶18-020 Carrying on a primary production business

Whether or not a taxpayer's activities amount to carrying on a *business* of primary production is ''a question of fact and degree'' — this is judicial code for ''often it's very hard to tell''. A person can obtain a private ruling on ''ultimate conclusions of fact'' such as on the question of whether a business is being carried on (TR 2006/11). Relevant indicators of a primary production business include:

- whether the activities have a significant commercial purpose or character
- the size or scale of the activities
- whether the activities result in a profit and, in those cases where no profit is produced, whether the taxpayer has a genuine belief that eventually the activities will be profitable
- whether the activities are of the same kind or carried on in the same way as those which are characteristic of ordinary trade in the line of business in which the venture was made
- whether there is repetition and regularity of the activities
- whether the activities are conducted in a systematic and businesslike manner
- whether the taxpayer has had prior experience in related business activities
- whether the activities may more properly be described as the pursuit of a hobby or recreation rather than a business (¶10-105).

There is often a significant overlap between these indicators and no individual indicator should be regarded as decisive. In addition, the weighting to be given to each indicator will vary from case-to-case (TR 97/11).

For example, the scale of activities is important but not determinative. A person may carry on a business, if only in a small way (*Thomas*). In one case, a man was held to be carrying on a primary production business with just one goat: a female stud angora that cost $3,000 (*Walker*). This decision is all the more interesting because the taxpayer lived in Queensland but depastured the goat on a stud farm in Victoria. The Commissioner often argues that lack of personal involvement suggests something other than a business but, in this case, the distance between taxpayer and goat was not fatal to the claim. The fact that a taxpayer is experienced and competent in farming and has a genuine belief that the property will generate profits will indicate that a primary production business is being carried on (*Daff*). However, flower growing was not a business where the ''business'' premises (a hothouse) looked like a shambles, the taxpayer had never done a stocktake and there was no likelihood of breaking even for many years (*Crees*). Similarly, no business of growing palm trees was carried on where the taxpayer planted palms on a landscape, rather than a plantation, basis, and the small number of palms planted gave an insignificant potential return when compared with the cost of the land (*Reiger*).

If a business *has* started, expenses incurred in the early years of the business before any income commences to be derived may be deductible where this is a normal characteristic of the type of business (IT 2208: ¶16-154). The non-commercial loss provisions do not apply to an individual carrying on a primary production business if the assessable income from other sources is less than $40,000 (¶16-020).

A primary production business is no longer carried on when the primary production activities have ceased, even though there may be an intention of recommencing those activities in the future (*Inglis*).

Share-farming arrangements

Under share-farming or share-cropping arrangements, a farmer is allowed to farm and harvest a crop on someone else's land in return for payment of a percentage of the harvest proceeds to the owner of the land. The owner (or lessor) will be treated as being engaged in a primary production business only if the arrangement amounts to a partnership (¶5-010) or the landowner has a direct or immediate involvement in the activities that make up the business. The payment of expenses relating to the ownership of the land would not be sufficient and any receipts from the farmer for the use of the land would be income from property rather than from carrying on a primary production business (TD 95/62).

Preparatory activities

Sometimes a taxpayer's activities do not amount to carrying on a primary production business but are merely *preparatory* to engaging in such a business. For example, steps taken by a taxpayer to clear weeds and put the land into a state of readiness were no more than preparatory to establishing an orchard (*Dalton*). In *Nelson*, the taxpayer's activities over a number of years involved extensive research and planning but they had not reached the point where they constituted a primary production business.

On the other hand, in *Ferguson*, it was held that the taxpayer's preliminary activities in building up a herd of cattle through a leasing arrangement had sufficient commercial character to amount to a business. Substantial preparatory work, which may include the propagation of plant stock or the establishment of a sheep farm from which assessable income will ultimately be generated, may nevertheless amount to the carrying on of a business (*Case T12*; *Case 75/96*).

Although a taxpayer engaged in preparatory work may be regarded as carrying on a primary production business in appropriate cases, expenditure is not deductible under the general deduction provisions (¶16-010) if it is of a capital nature. Costs incurred in establishing a plantation of fruit or nut trees, at least up to the stage of getting seedlings established in the ground, would generally be non-deductible capital expenditure. On this basis, a taxpayer was denied a deduction for the cost of fertilising the soil prior to putting in chestnut trees (*Osborne*).

However, the establishment costs of new horticultural plants and grapevines (¶18-070) may be eligible for an accelerated write-off. It also seems that a person starting a business of raising *annual* crops may deduct the cost of fertiliser, even if no crop is ever harvested. Similarly, the cost of seedling trees to be used in an afforestation business is immediately deductible (TR 95/6).

Even where activities are held to be preparatory to engaging in a primary production business, depreciation may be deductible if the capital allowance provisions (¶17-000) are satisfied (*Dalton*).

Afforestation, cattle leasing and other managed investment schemes (MISs)

Participation in afforestation schemes generally takes one of 2 forms — an investment or a business pursuit. Where the participation is by way of investment in bonds, the expenditure so incurred is capital and not deductible (*Milne*); as is expenditure relating to the cost of research and development conducted before commencing the primary production business (*Howland-Rose*; *MacPherson (No 2)*; *Brody*; *Petersen*). Amounts outlaid in return for recurrent management services are on revenue account even if paid as a lump sum in advance (*Lau*), subject to the prepayment rules set out at ¶16-045 (¶18-125).

Investors were found to be carrying on a business in *Puzey* (sandalwood), *Iddles* (viticulture), *Sleight* (tea-trees), *Lenzo* (sandalwood), *Guest* (blueberries) and *Cooke* (horticulture). However, in the first 4 cases, deductions were disallowed on the basis of the general anti-avoidance provisions (¶30-170). In *Barham*, an investor in an aloe vera managed project was not carrying on a business and, in any case, due to the operation of the anti-avoidance provisions was not entitled to a deduction for management fees except to the extent that the amounts were actually paid.

Participation in a cattle or sheep leasing scheme may amount to a primary production business, even though it represents the initial stages of a long-term plan, provided the venture has a businesslike flavour, is conducted systematically and the taxpayer has the necessary funds to finance his/her participation in the scheme (TR 97/11; *Walker*; *Solling*; *Pepper*; *Hanlon*). Lease and management charges relating to cattle leasing schemes entered into for the purpose of upgrading the herd of an existing cattle raising business will be accepted as part of the outgoings of the existing business.

However, where the management agreement effectively guaranteed the provision by the manager of a set number of calves, as well as management services, and the taxpayer was not carrying on a business, the fees were on capital account (had the taxpayer carried on a business of breeding and selling cattle, the cattle would have been trading stock and on revenue account) (*Vincent*; ¶30-170). In another cattle breeding scheme, participants were neither considered to be carrying on a business nor undertaking a profit-making scheme (*Klein*).

Product rulings

There is a separate system of ''Product Rulings'' relating to promoted tax-effective investment arrangements of the kind typically associated with many afforestation and other investment schemes (¶24-540). The system gives investors access to binding public rulings on proposed schemes.

Registered agricultural managed investment schemes

Registered agricultural managed investment schemes (MIS) are registered with ASIC and they operate under the *Corporations Act 2001*. Depending on the circumstances, participants in such schemes may be carrying on a business and may be entitled to claim deductions for relevant expenses such as rent, management fees or responsible entity fees (*Hance*). Before the *Hance* decision, it was the Commissioner's view that contributions by investors to registered agricultural MIS were capital, or of a capital nature. The Commissioner accepts *Hance* as authoritative in relation to similar schemes (ATO *Decision Impact Statement* on *Hance*). The ATO has withdrawn rulings reflecting the earlier view (TR 2007/8; GSTR 2008/D1) and is issuing product rulings based on the current view.

There are specific tax concessions for forestry MISs (¶18-125).

If the responsible entity of a registered agricultural MIS changes, that does not affect the tax outcomes for participants in the scheme if it continues to be run according to the terms of a relevant product ruling (TD 2010/7). Investors in a non-forestry MIS may claim tax deductions in respect of contributions to the scheme. There is no clawback of deductions if an interest in a scheme is disposed of or terminated due to circumstances outside of the control of the investor (TD 2010/8). Payments received by an investor on the winding up of a non-forestry MIS may be assessable, depending on the circumstances (TD 2010/9).

[FITR ¶355-007 – ¶355-015]

¶18-030 What is income from primary production?

For a number of reasons it may be necessary to determine what constitutes income from primary production. This is relevant mainly for the purpose of the averaging provisions, which require a primary producer's "taxable primary production income" and "taxable non-primary production income" to be separately identified (¶18-210). Some common items of primary production income are:

- proceeds from the sale of produce
- proceeds from the sale of skins and hides
- profits on the sale of live stock
- insurance payments for loss of profits
- assessable balancing adjustments from the disposal of depreciating assets
- income from the short-term hiring of equipment to other primary producers or the granting of short-term agistment rights (but not where a substantial part of the property is used solely for agistment).

Guidelines on the tax treatment of income from particular activities

- **Cotton.** Cottongrowers derive income under a cotton contract when property in the cotton has passed from the grower to the merchant and a debt for an ascertainable sum has been created. Where cotton is placed in a pool, income is derived under the pool contract that provides for when a debt will become due and owing to the grower. A non-repayable advance distribution by the merchant to the grower is derived in the year in which the merchant declares or approves the distribution of a certain amount. In the case of fixed price and guaranteed minimum price pools, income is derived by the grower at the time of classing, which is completed within 14 days of ginning. Distributions in excess of the minimum guaranteed price are assessable to the growers when declared by the merchant (TR 94/13).
- **Dairy.** Dairy Regional Assistance Program grants are assessable (ID 2002/784). Dividends received by a dairy farmer on shares compulsorily held in a dairy cooperative are assessable primary production income (ID 2010/149).
- **Equine influenza hardship assistance.** Equine Influenza Hardship Wage Supplement Payments, Commercial Horse Assistance Payments (CR 2008/59) and Equine Influenza Business Assistance Grants are taxable. Equine Influenza Hardship Grants are not taxable. Grants for non-government not-for-profit equestrian organisations who have incurred expenses directly related to the outbreak are taxable unless the organisation is tax-exempt.
- **Fishing.** For the taxation treatment of payments made under the Securing our Fishing Future Package and similar entitlements, see CR 2007/47, CR 2007/49, CR 2007/64, CR 2007/65, CR 2007/72 and CR 2007/101.
- **Forest operations.** Receipts that may constitute assessable income from forest operations include proceeds from the sale of felled or standing timber, the royalties from granting rights to others to fell and remove timber, insurance recoveries and reafforestation incentive grants or payments (TR 95/6). For the market value of matured trees ventured into a new business of forest operations, see TD 96/8.
- **Government payments to industry.** A government payment made to assist a business to continue operating is included in the assessable income of the recipient under s 6-5 or s 15-10. A payment to industry to commence or cease a business or for agreeing to give up or sell part of the profit-yielding structure is not assessable (TR 2006/3). For example, an exceptional circumstances relief payment (ECRP) paid to a farmer under the *Farm Household Support Act 1992* is *not* primary

production income (TD 2008/16). Exit Assistance Program grants are not assessable income if the grant requires the taxpayer to transfer ownership of all their irrigated land and, as a result, the taxpayer's farming business ceases (¶10-160). A payment to a farmer under the Namoi River Groundwater Structural Adjustment Program, described as ''financial assistance to help licence holders adjust to changes in groundwater access'', was not liable to income tax (*Carberry*). The Commissioner considers that a GSAP payment may be income if the recipient completes all of the steps in the program (ATO *Decision Impact Statement* on *Carberry*).

- **Grazing/conservation payments.** Stewardship and on-ground works payments received under certain conservation programs are assessable, for example: on-ground establishment works payments and ongoing conservation management payments to landholders under the Western Catchment Management Authority's Enterprise Based Conservation Program (CR 2007/92); payments received under the Lower Murray Darling Catchment Management Authority Rangelands Incentive Strategy — Conservation Reserves and Sustainable Grazing Schemes (CR 2007/87); and conservation management payments under Murrumbidgee Catchment Management Authority EcoTender programs (CR 2010/1; CR 2010/76).

- **Hedging contracts on futures markets.** Income from hedging contracts on futures markets entered into by primary producers may be regarded as income from primary production. As a general rule, a sale of a futures contract by a primary producer for hedging purposes is an integral part of the primary production business where the quantity of goods specified in the contract corresponds to the estimated production and where there is a subsequent sale of goods of the kind covered by the contract. Where, as in a normal hedging operation, the futures contract is terminated by a subsequent buy-back contract, the resulting profit or loss will be accepted as arising from the primary production business (IT 2228).

- **Horses.** The taxation issues arising from horse breeding, racing and training are outlined in TR 2008/2. See also TR 93/26 (tax treatment of stallion syndicates). For the circumstances in which the activities qualify as a primary production business, see TR 97/11.

- **Interest and dividends.** Interest on a primary producer's term deposit account opened as a condition of obtaining finance to purchase a new farming property was held to be assessable income from primary production and, therefore, income subject to averaging (*Case X82*). Special dividends received by a primary production partnership from the purchaser of its produce are included in assessable primary production income (ID 2002/773).

- **Tobacco.** Grants under the Tobacco Growers Adjustment Assistance Programme 2006 to tobacco growers who undertake to exit all agricultural enterprises for at least 5 years are exempt (ss 53-10; 118-37). See also CR 2007/99.

- **Water entitlements.** Generally, receiving a lump sum for a permanent sale or disposal of water entitlements would not be an ordinary incident of a primary production business (the assessability of such amount depends on the surrounding facts). There may be income or CGT consequences from the receipt of government compensation for the reduction or cancellation of water entitlements. The ATO website contains information about the taxation of water entitlements in the *Landcare and water* chapter of its guide for primary producers *Primary producers essentials*. CGT roll-over relief is available for taxpayers who replace an entitlement to water with one or more different entitlements (¶12-445). For the taxation consequences of certain water entitlements, see CR 2008/28 (replacement of bore licence with aquifer access licence).

- **Sustainable Rural Water Use and Infrastructure Program.** The SRWUIP is a Commonwealth program to provide funding for projects to increase efficient water use in rural Australia. SRWUIP payments are generally taxable in the year they are received, either as ordinary income or as a subsidy, or as capital gains, to the extent that the payment is consideration for surrendered water rights (¶10-160). Expenditure under the program may be deductible over 3 years, as water facilities used in primary production. For SRWUIP payments made on or after 1 April 2010, taxpayers can choose either the existing tax treatment of payments and related expenditure or to make payments non-assessable non-exempt income and to disregard any capital gain or loss from transferring the water rights. If they do, expenditure related to the payments is not deductible and does not form part of the cost of any asset it is spent on. The ATO has administrative arrangements for assessing tax returns lodged for the period from 1 April 2010, including returns that anticipate the changes.

- **Wheat and barley.** For growers returning their income on an accruals basis, gross amounts from the sale of wheat or grain to the Australian Wheat Board for cash or at a previously agreed price are included in assessable income in the income year in which they sell the wheat or grain. For growers returning their income on a cash basis, gross amounts from the sale of wheat or grain are included in assessable income in the year in which they receive the payment (TR 2001/1). Similar rules apply where growers receive amounts from the sale of barley, grain or other commodities to the Australian Barley Board (TR 2001/5). See also CR 2004/122 to CR 2004/124. For the deductibility of certain underwriting fees payable to the Wheat Board and to the Barley Board under harvest payment agreements, see TD 2002/18.

- **Wind farming income.** Ordinary income earned by an individual from allowing wind farming infrastructure to be built and operated on farmland is not ''assessable primary production income'' for the purposes of ITAA97 Div 392 (TD 2013/2).

- **Wool.** The position of a woolgrower who returns income on an accruals basis is dealt with in TR 97/9. Woolgrowers returning income on the accruals basis derive income when all obligations necessary under a sale of wool contract have been performed to create an entitlement to the payment of an ascertainable sum. In an auction, income is derived when the property passes to the buyer at the fall of the hammer. At this time the wool ceases to be trading stock of the woolgrower. In sales by forward contracts, income is derived when the buyer, having taken delivery of the wool, receives the results of testing. In the case of sales of pooled wool, payments made in advance of the final payment are usually income when the pool operator declares them. For the final payment, income is derived when the grower becomes contractually entitled to it.

[FITR ¶27-380]

Special Deductions for Capital Expenditure

¶18-050 Special capital expenditure deductions for primary producers

Concessional tax treatment is given to capital expenditure relating to telephone lines (¶18-060), horticultural plants and new grapevines (¶18-070), water facilities (¶18-080), fodder storage assets (¶18-085), fencing assets (¶18-090), landcare operations (¶18-100) and timber depletion (¶18-120).

Generally, the amount of the deduction excludes the amount of any input tax credit to which the taxpayer may be entitled. Decreasing adjustments are included in assessable income and increasing adjustments are deductible (ITAA97 s 27-105).

Where a commercial debt is forgiven, the debtor's deduction under the capital allowance provisions in ITAA97 Div 40 may be reduced under the rules outlined at ¶16-910. Special provisions apply if property is acquired under limited recourse finance and the debt is terminated before full repayment (¶23-260).

If an entity joins or leaves a consolidated group under the consolidation regime (¶8-000), any deduction under the primary production provisions (other than for the decline in value of depreciating assets) is allocated between the 2 entities (ITAA97 ss 716-25; 716-70: ¶8-580). Special rules apply for depreciating assets.

The primary production deductions are subject to the rules for tax-preferred leasing provisions outlined at ¶23-210.

Special rules for partnerships

If the expenditure relating to some of the above items is incurred by a partnership, it is not deductible in arriving at the net income or loss of the partnership. Instead, each partner is treated as having personally incurred a part of the cost and is entitled to claim deductions based on that part. If the partners have not agreed on the share of the cost each will bear, the total cost is divided between them in the same ratio as their respective interests in the net partnership income or loss (¶5-130) of that year.

Non-arm's length dealings

Where the expenditure is incurred under a ''non-arm's length dealing'' and exceeds the ''market value'' (¶17-045, ¶17-050) of what the expenditure is for, only that market value is taken into account in calculating the deduction.

¶18-060 Telephone lines

The capital cost of a telephone line extending to, or situated on, land being used for a primary production business may, to the extent that it is not otherwise deductible, be written off in equal instalments over a 10-year period (ITAA97 ss 40-645; 40-650).

To qualify for this special deduction, the expenditure must have been incurred by: (a) the owner of the land or some other person (eg a tenant or lessee) having an interest in the land on which a primary production business was at that time being carried on (not necessarily by the claimant for the deduction); or (b) a sharefarmer carrying on a primary production business on that land.

Once the cost of a telephone line has qualified for deduction, it cannot be, or form part of, a deduction under any other provision of the income tax laws, whether in the hands of the taxpayer who incurred the expenditure or any other taxpayer. For example, there is no deduction for depreciation under the general capital allowance rules in Chapter 17.

The ordinary CGT rules (rather than CGT event K7) apply where the asset is subject to a CGT event such as a disposal (ITAA97 ss 104-235; 118-24).

Special rules apply if the expenditure is incurred by a partnership or in a non-arm's length dealing or if a commercial debt is forgiven (¶18-050). Recoupments of the telephone line expenditure are assessable (¶10-270).

[FITR ¶88-325, ¶88-330]

¶18-070 Horticultural plants

Capital expenditure incurred in establishing horticultural plants may be written off where the plants are used, or held ready for use, in a business of horticulture (ITAA97 ss 40-515 to 40-575). Total deductions cannot exceed the capital expenditure incurred on the plant.

A ''horticultural plant'' is a depreciating asset and is defined to mean any live plant or fungus that is cultivated or propagated for any of its products or parts.

The deduction is available where one of the following ownership conditions is satisfied:

- the taxpayer owns the plant and any holder of a lesser interest in the land (eg licensee or lessee) does not carry on a business of horticulture on the land
- the plant is attached to land held under a lease or under a quasi-ownership right granted by an exempt Australian or foreign government agency and the lease or right enables the taxpayer to carry on a business of horticulture on the land (and any holder of lesser interests does not carry on such business on the land), or
- the taxpayer holds a licence relating to the land to which the plant is attached and carries on a business of horticulture on the land.

In addition, the taxpayer must use the plant or hold it ready for use for commercial horticulture (ie for the purpose of producing assessable income in a business of horticulture).

Eligible expenditure

The cost of establishing horticultural plants may include the cost of: (a) acquiring and planting the plants or seeds; (b) preparing to plant (but not the initial clearing of land, although it may cover costs of top soil enhancement, soil analysis tests, forming up planting rows, planting site surveys, ploughing, contouring, top dressing, fertilising and stone removal that are attributable to the establishment of the plant); (c) pots and potting mixtures; (d) grafting trees; and (e) replacing existing plants and trees because of loss of fair economic return or declining popularity of a particular variety. Establishment expenditure also includes the cost of establishing plants used for associated purposes, such as for companion planting, if those plants are not horticultural plants in their own right (TD 2006/46). The cost of maintaining an established plantation (including replacing plants because of premature death or disease) may be a revenue expenditure.

Where a taxpayer purchases plants from a nursery and the plants are maintained by the nursery until an agreed delivery date, the total costs, including the maintenance costs, are of a capital nature (TD 2006/46).

Establishment expenditure does not include the cost of draining swamp or low-lying land or clearing land. Further, it excludes expenditure that is part of a pool of construction expenditure on capital works (¶20-470) as well as the cost of the land on which the plants are situated.

A taxpayer can get a deduction for the establishment expenditure even if it was incurred by a previous owner of the plant. If the ownership of a plant is transferred, the transferor may be required to give the transferee information that will help the transferee calculate the deduction. The ordinary CGT rules (rather than CGT event K7) apply if the plant is subject to a CGT event such as a disposal (ITAA97 ss 104-235; 118-24).

For the first taxpayer to satisfy the ownership conditions, the plant starts to decline in value in the income year in which its first commercial season starts. For later taxpayers, the plant starts to decline in value in the later of: (a) the income year in which the taxpayer first satisfied the ownership conditions; and (b) the income year in which the first commercial season starts.

If the effective life of a plant is less than 3 years, a taxpayer can get a deduction for 100% of the establishment expenditure in the year in which the plant starts to decline in value. If the effective life of a plant is 3 or more years, the taxpayer can get an annual deduction during the plant's "maximum write-off period", that is, the period beginning at the time when the plant first became capable of being used for commercial horticulture.

As a horticultural plant is a depreciating asset, its effective life is measured in accordance with the general rules for determining the effective life of depreciating assets (¶17-270). The taxpayer can self-assess the effective life or rely on the Commissioner's determination. The Commissioner's current determinations for specified plants are set out at ¶43-010. Where the plant is destroyed before the end of its maximum write-off period, a special deduction is available for the unrecouped expenditure relating to the plant as reduced by any amount received for the destruction, eg insurance proceeds (s 40-565).

Calculation of write-off

The deduction allowed for the decline in value of the plant is worked out using the following formula:

$$\text{establishment expenditure} \times \frac{\text{write-off days in income year}}{365} \times \text{write-off rate}$$

The ''write-off days in income year'' are essentially the days in a year: (a) on which the taxpayer used the plant or held it in readiness for use for commercial horticulture; (b) on which the taxpayer satisfied the ownership conditions (see above); and (c) within the maximum write-off period for the plant. The following table is used to work out the ''write-off rate'' and the maximum write-off period for a plant.

Years in effective life of plant	Annual write-off rate	Maximum write-off period
3 to fewer than 5	40%	2 years and 183 days
5 to fewer than 6 2/3	27%	3 years and 257 days
6 2/3 to fewer than 10	20%	5 years
10 to fewer than 13	17%	5 years and 323 days
13 to fewer than 30	13%	7 years and 253 days
30 or more	7%	14 years and 105 days

▶ Example

Thornbeauty Pty Ltd spent $200,000 to establish a commercial rose garden of 11,200 plants. When the plants entered their first commercial season at the start of September in Year 1, there were only 10,000 viable rose bushes remaining. At this time, the effective life of the rose bushes was estimated at 7 years.

Assuming none of the remaining 10,000 rose bushes are destroyed before the end of the maximum write-off period of 5 years, the annual deductions for Thornbeauty (or a subsequent owner) are calculated on the basis of the formula:

$$\text{establishment expenditure} \times \frac{\text{write-off days in income year}}{365} \times \text{write-off rate}$$

Thus, the deduction allowable in Year 1 is:

$$\$200{,}000 \times \frac{303}{365} \times 0.20 = \$33{,}206$$

The deductions available in the following years (ignoring leap years) are:

- In each of Years 2, 3, 4 and 5:

$$\$200{,}000 \times \frac{365}{365} \times 0.20 = \$40{,}000$$

- In Year 6:

$$\$200{,}000 \times \frac{62}{365} \times 0.20 = \$6{,}794$$

Other aspects

The rules about partnerships, non-arm's length dealings and commercial debt forgiveness referred to in ¶18-050 and the tax-preferred leasing rules outlined at ¶23-210 apply to expenditure on horticultural plants. Recoupments of establishment expenditure are assessable (¶10-270).

The rules for depreciating horticultural plants in Subdiv 40-F apply to expenditure incurred on or after 1 July 2001. Under transitional provisions, unrecouped expenditure on pre-1 July 2001 horticultural plants continues to be deductible under Subdiv 40-F, using the same establishment expenditure and the same effective life (ITTPA s 40-515).

The cost of establishing grapevines on or after 1 October 2004 is written off under the horticultural plants provisions. The Commissioner has determined the effective life of grapevines to be 15 years (dried and table) and 20 years (wine). For information on the former 4-year write-off for grapevines, see the 45th edition of the *Australian Master Tax Guide* and earlier editions.

[FITR ¶87-970 – ¶88-095]

¶18-080 Water facilities

Capital expenditure on water facilities for primary production land may qualify for an immediate deduction where it is incurred after 7.30 pm on 12 May 2015 (ITAA97 ss 40-515 to 40-575). Expenditure incurred before that (but after 1 July 2004) will qualify for deduction spread over 3 years.

For the deduction to apply, the following conditions must be satisfied:

(1) the taxpayer must incur capital expenditure on the construction, manufacture, installation or acquisition of a depreciating asset that is a water facility

(2) the expenditure must be incurred primarily and principally to conserve or convey water, and

(3) the water must be for use:

- in a primary production business conducted by the taxpayer on land in Australia, or
- if the expenditure is incurred by an irrigation water provider, the water must be for use in primary production businesses conducted by other entities on land in Australia, to whom water is supplied by the irrigation water provider.

"Water facility"

A water facility means:

- plant (¶17-040) or a structural improvement that is primarily and principally for the purpose of conserving or conveying water, eg a dam, tank, tank stand, bore, well, irrigation channel, pipe, pump, water tower, or windmill
- a structural improvement that is reasonably incidental to conserving or conveying water, eg a culvert, fence to prevent livestock entering an irrigation channel, or bridge over an irrigation channel, or
- alterations, additions, extensions or capital repairs to any of those assets.

The deduction would extend to the construction of power lines from an existing mains electricity connection to plant used for water conservation or conveyance (IT 252). It would not extend to the initial connection of mains electricity or upgrading an existing connection, but those costs may be deductible under other provisions (¶16-820).

A water facility would not include a water access entitlement. The cost of this also would not be deductible as a business deduction (ID 2004/392). However, it has been held that a levy paid by a canegrower to a weir construction co-operative was deductible in full as a business expense (*McLennan*).

Expenditure on long-lasting trickle irrigation systems would qualify for the water facilities deduction. The cost of lightweight systems that rest on the surface and are dug in each year would probably qualify for outright deductions as a business expense (IT 2339).

It is not necessary that the water facility be on the land on which the primary production business is carried on. For example, the deduction would apply to expenditure on the installation of a pump and piping on Crown land for the purpose of conveying water to land where the primary production business is being conducted.

Eligible purpose

The requirement that the expenditure be incurred ''primarily and principally'' for the purpose of conserving or conveying water means that this purpose must outweigh the total of all other ineligible purposes.

This is an objective test that requires an examination of the ''primary and principal function or purpose of the result'' produced by incurring the expenditure. Subjective factors are not taken into account (TD 94/9). For example, the installation of a new watering system would be covered irrespective of the subjective reason for the particular choice of system used.

This requirement is also designed to ensure that the 3-year water facilities deduction and the outright deduction available for landcare operations (¶18-100) are mutually exclusive.

▶ Example

The taxpayer incurs expenditure on constructing a dam primarily and principally for the purpose of holding water for irrigation. The dam also serves, to some degree, as a retention dam to prevent excessive water run-off that could lead to soil erosion. The expenditure is properly deductible over 3 years as a water facility expenditure rather than as a cost of landcare operation.

As long as the requisite purpose exists, it is irrelevant if, for example, a bore or well actually fails to produce the required quality or quantity of water (TD 96/41).

The installation costs of an in-ground swimming pool would not be eligible, even though the pool may occasionally be used to draw water for fire-fighting purposes. However, if the pool was equipped with an extra pump to be used solely for fire- fighting purposes, the cost of that pump would qualify (TD 92/190).

Other conditions and rules

If one taxpayer has already been eligible for a water facilities deduction for the acquisition, construction of manufacture of the facility, another taxpayer cannot claim the water facilities deduction for the cost of subsequently acquiring the facility (s 40-555).

▶ Example

A taxpayer buys second-hand commercial irrigation equipment that, presumably, has previously been used on primary production land. The water facilities deduction would not be available, as the ATO would assume that the previous owner would have been entitled to such a deduction. The ATO considers that the onus is on the purchaser to show on the balance of probabilities that such an entitlement did not in fact arise. (Based on ID 2004/15.)

In this example, however, the purchaser could claim the water facilities deduction for its own capital expenditure in installing the equipment, as distinct from acquiring it.

Similarly, the purchaser of primary production land cannot claim a deduction for that part of the purchase price attributable to water tanks, bores or other improvements for conserving or conveying water (*Case W9*; TD 96/40).

The ordinary CGT rules (rather than CGT event K7) apply if the water facility is subject to a CGT event such as a disposal (ITAA97 ss 104-235; 118-24).

The rules that apply to expenditure incurred by partnerships, to expenditure under non-arm's length dealings and to the forgiveness of commercial debts are referred to at ¶18-050. The deduction is also subject to the rules for tax-preferred leasing provisions outlined at ¶23-210. Recoupments of water conservation expenditure are assessable (¶10-270). See ID 2007/36 and ID 2007/37 for the interaction with Div 58 (assets previously owned by exempt entities) and with the consolidation provisions respectively.

[FITR ¶87-970 – ¶88-090]

¶18-085 Fodder storage assets

Primary producers may deduct capital expenditure on a fodder storage asset in the income year in which the expenditure is incurred for fodder storage assets first used or installed ready for use on or after 19 August 2018 (ITAA97 ss 40-515 to 40-575).

Expenditure incurred before that (but after 12 May 2015) qualifies for deduction spread over 3 years.

The deduction applies to capital expenditure incurred on the construction, manufacture, installation or acquisition of a fodder storage asset if that expenditure was incurred *primarily and principally* for use in a primary production business conducted on land in Australia.

A ''fodder storage asset'' is defined as an asset that is primarily and principally for the purpose of storing fodder. A fodder storage asset is also a structural improvement, a repair of a capital nature, or an alteration, addition or extension, to an asset or structural improvement, that is primarily and principally for the purpose of storing fodder. The term ''fodder'' takes its ordinary meaning and refers to food for livestock, usually dried, such as grain, hay or silage. Common examples of fodder storage assets include silos, liquid feed supplement storage tanks, bins for storing dried grain, hay sheds, grain storage sheds and above-ground bunkers for silage.

Although a fodder storage asset will primarily be used to store food for livestock, it may also store fodder which can be used for human consumption. Where a fodder storage asset is used to store fodder that can be used for animal consumption or human consumption, such as grain, it will still be an asset to which the deduction is available.

A repair of a capital nature or an alteration, addition or extension, to an asset or structural improvement, that is primarily and principally for the purpose of storing fodder will be a separate depreciating asset.

[FITR ¶87-970 – ¶88-070]

¶18-090 Fencing assets

Primary producers may claim an immediate deduction for capital expenditure on fencing assets in the year in which the expenditure is incurred, with effect from 12 May 2015 (ITAA97 ss 40-515 to 40-575). The deduction applies to capital expenditure incurred on the construction, manufacture, installation or acquisition of a fencing asset if that expenditure was incurred *primarily and principally* for use in a primary production business conducted on land in Australia. The total deduction cannot be more than the amount of the capital expenditure.

The words ''construction, manufacture, installation'' associated with ''acquisition'' were held to involve a fence coming into existence on the land and not just the acquiring of a pre-existing fence as part of a transfer of land, ie the meaning of the word ''acquisition'' was confined to an acquisition of a new fence or a fence that results in an improvement of the land (*AJ & PA McBride Ltd*).

The deduction is not available:

- if, in acquiring the fencing asset, any entity has deducted or can deduct an amount under ITAA97 Subdiv 40-F for any income year for earlier capital expenditure on the construction or manufacture of the fence or a previous acquisition of the fence
- to the extent that any person has deducted or can deduct the amount as expenditure on a landcare operation (¶18-100) under ITAA97 s 40-630(1), or
- if the fencing asset is (or is a repair, alteration, addition or extension to) a stockyard, pen or portable fence.

A ''fencing asset'' is an asset or structural improvement that is a fence, or a repair of a capital nature, or an alteration, addition or extension, to a fence. The term ''fence'' takes its ordinary meaning and includes an enclosure or barrier, usually of metal or wood, as around or along a field, or paddock. The term ''fence'' extends to parts or components of a fence including, but not limited to, posts, rails, wire, droppers, gates, fittings and anchor assemblies. A repair of a capital nature, or an alteration, addition or extension, to a fencing asset will be a separate depreciating asset.

Previously, a primary producer could deduct the capital expenditure on a fence in different ways depending on what the fence was used for. Generally, a primary producer could deduct the capital expenditure on a fence over the effective life of the asset. The Commissioner had determined that this could be up to 30 years, depending on the asset. Alternatively, in certain cases, primary producers could immediately deduct capital expenditure on fences as part of a landcare operation (¶18-100) (including fences built for certain purposes relating to landcare) or over 3 years on fences as part of a water facility (¶18-080).

[FITR ¶87-970 – ¶88-095]

¶18-100 Landcare operations

Capital expenditure incurred on landcare operations qualifies for outright deduction in the year the expenditure is incurred (ITAA97 ss 40-630 to 40-675).

The deduction applies to: (a) taxpayers carrying on a primary production business on land in Australia; (b) taxpayers carrying on a business (other than mining or quarrying) for a taxable purpose (¶17-010) from the use of rural land in Australia; and (c) rural land irrigation water providers whose main business is supplying water to primary producers and businesses using rural land. It does not apply to expenditure on ''plant'' (¶17-040) other than fences, dams or certain structural improvements. See generally ID 2004/714 (dealing with revegetation costs). A shed to store produce does not qualify (ID 2002/110).

Expenditure on the following operations qualifies for deduction:

(1) the eradication or extermination of animal or vegetable pests from the land

(2) the destruction of weed or plant growth detrimental to the land

(3) preventing or combating land degradation, otherwise than by the erection of fences on the land. The expression ''land degradation'' includes not only soil erosion but also other effects detrimental to the land, such as decline of soil fertility or structure, degradation of natural vegetation, deposits of eroded material or salinisation

(4) the erection of fences (including any alteration, extension or addition to fences) on the land to exclude live stock or vermin from areas affected by land degradation (see above) in order to prevent any aggravation of degradation in those areas and to assist in the reclamation of those areas

(5) the erection of fences (including any extension, alteration or addition to fences) to prevent land degradation where the fences separate different land classes and are erected in accordance with an approved land management plan in respect of the whole or part of the land

(6) the construction on the land of levee banks or similar improvements (including alterations, extensions and additions)

(7) the construction on the land of drainage works (including alterations, extensions and additions) for the purpose of controlling salinity or assisting in drainage control. This would include, for example, the sinking of drainage bores and the laying of surface or sub-surface piping in the course of constructing floodwater drainage work (IT 351). However, the draining of swamp or low-lying land is not included.

In each case (with the exception of (5) and (6)) the operation must be carried out *primarily and principally* for the purpose stated. The reason for this requirement is to ensure that the outright deduction for landcare measures and the 3-year write-off for water facilities (¶18-080) are mutually exclusive. See also TD 94/9.

▶ Example

A farmer constructs a dam primarily and principally for the purpose of holding water for irrigation. The dam also serves to a minor extent as a retention dam to prevent excessive water run-off that could lead to soil erosion. The expenditure is not incurred primarily and principally to combat erosion and is not deductible outright as landcare expenditure. Instead, it is deductible over 3 years as water conservation expenditure.

Expenditure on extending an operation, as well as the original operation itself, qualifies for deduction (eg expenditure on enlarging a levee bank or on extending an erosion-control fence for the purpose of excluding live stock or vermin from areas affected by soil erosion). Expenditure on the levelling of irrigated land by the use of laser-beam technology is generally acceptable where it is directed at combating or controlling salinity or drainage problems (IT 352).

The concession also applies to capital repairs as well as to structural improvements, alteration or additions that are reasonably incidental to assets deductible under the provisions (eg a bridge over a drain that was constructed to control salinity, or a fence constructed to prevent live stock entering a drain constructed to prevent salinity, but not a bulldozer used to dig such channel). If a deduction is available for the same expenditure under the water facilities provisions, no deduction is available under the landcare operations provisions.

Although the taxpayer must be carrying on a primary production business on the land, it is not necessary for the taxpayer to *own* the land. This means that a lessee who carries on a primary production business on the land may claim the deduction.

The amount of the deduction may be reduced where, after the expenditure is incurred, the land is used at any time during the balance of the income year for a purpose other than the carrying on of a primary production business or the carrying on of a business for the purpose of gaining assessable income from the use of rural land. For rural land irrigation water providers, there is a reduction if an entity's use of the land in the year after the provider incurred the expenditure was for a purpose other than a taxable purpose.

The ordinary CGT rules (rather than CGT event K7) apply when an asset is subject to a CGT event such as a disposal (ITAA97 ss 104-235; 118-24).

Special rules apply if the expenditure is incurred by partnerships or in a non-arm's length dealing or if a commercial debt is forgiven (¶18-050) or the tax-preferred leasing provisions outlined at ¶23-210 apply. A recoupment of deductible landcare expenditure is assessable (¶10-270).

[FITR ¶88-310 – ¶88-320]

¶18-120 Timber depletion

A deduction is available if a taxpayer acquires land carrying trees or a right to fell trees on another's land where the amount paid took the trees into account (ITAA97 s 70-120). The effect of the deduction is that the taxpayer is taxable only on the net proceeds from the disposal of the trees.

A proportion of the amount paid to acquire the land or rights is deductible if:

(1) some or all of the trees are felled during the income year for sale or use in manufacture by the taxpayer for income-producing purposes

(2) some or all of the trees are felled during the income year under a right granted by the taxpayer to another person in consideration of royalty payments, or

(3) the market value of some or all of the trees is included in the taxpayer's assessable income for the income year because of a disposal of the trees outside the ordinary course of business or a deemed disposal on the taxpayer's death.

In several cases it has been held that an amount paid by a taxpayer to purchase timber logging licences held by the vendor of a sawmilling business qualified for the deduction (*Marbut Gunnersen Industries*; *Monaro Sawmills*).

If the taxpayer and the seller of the land or of the felling rights did not deal with each other at arm's length and the taxpayer paid more than the market value of the land or rights, then the deduction is limited to the market value (¶17-045, ¶17-050).

No deduction is available under s 70-120 for an amount that has been deducted under the carbon sink forests deduction rules (¶19-120).

[FITR ¶115-110]

¶18-125 Timber plantation concessions

Certain prepaid expenditure that is invested in timber plantation managed investment schemes is excluded from the prepayment rules outlined at ¶16-045 (ITAA36 s 82KZMG). The exclusion allows investors to obtain an immediate deduction for funds contributed in one financial year for agronomic activities undertaken during the following year.

The concession applies if the following conditions are satisfied:

- the expenditure relates to an activity that is not wholly to be completed within the income year in which the expenditure was incurred
- the expenditure was incurred on or after 2 October 2001 and before 1 July 2008 under an agreement
- the agreement must be for planting and tending of trees for felling (not for their produce: ID 2003/487)
- the expenditure must be incurred on "seasonally-dependent agronomic activities" (as discussed in TD 2003/12). The operations must be carried out by the manager during the establishment period for the particular plantation, being the period *starting* when the first activity for that planting is done and *finishing* when either the planting is finished (excluding seedlings replacement) or, if later, when any fertilising, weed or pest control is done in conjunction with the planting. Failing to plant trees under a forestry scheme, for reasons outside the control of the parties, does not affect the timing of relevant deductions (TD 2010/14)

- the activities must be completed within 12 months of the prepayment being made or of the activity commencing (whichever is later), and by the end of the financial year following the year in which the expenditure was incurred
- the taxpayer must not have day-to-day control over the operations arising out of the agreement, and
- there must be more than one participant in the agreement as investor or the manager (or an associate) must manage, arrange or promote similar arrangements for other taxpayers.

The general prepayment provisions (¶16-045) continue to apply to the extent that any part of a prepayment does not satisfy the above conditions.

Managed investment companies must include the prepaid expenditure in assessable income in the year in which the deduction is first available to the investor and not when the work is done on the investor's behalf (ITAA97 s 15-45).

Plantation forestry investments

Initial investors in forestry managed investment schemes (MISs) receive a 100% tax deduction for their contributions to forestry schemes and secondary investors receive a 100% deduction for their ongoing contributions, provided that there is a reasonable expectation that at least 70% of the scheme manager's expenditure under the scheme, at arm's length prices, is direct forestry expenditure (ITAA97 Div 394). The arrangements apply: (a) to amounts paid by a participant under a scheme on or after 1 July 2007, provided that no other amounts were paid by the participant or any other participant under the scheme before 1 July 2007; and (b) to CGT events that happen on or after 1 July 2007.

Direct forestry expenditure (''DFE'') consists of amounts spent by the scheme manager (or an associate) under the scheme that are attributable to establishing, tending, felling and harvesting trees, as well as amounts of notional expenditure reflecting the market value of land, goods and services provided by the scheme manager that are used for establishing, tending, felling and harvesting trees (ITAA97 s 394-45). The 70% DFE rule must be satisfied on 30 June in the income year in which first payment is made or, if there is a contingency such as a minimum subscription requirement, in the year in which the contingency occurs.

The requirements for the deduction (ITAA97 s 394-10) are that:

- the entity claiming the deduction holds an interest in a forestry managed investment scheme
- the purpose of the scheme is establishing and tending trees for felling only in Australia. This precludes deductions for horticulture trees that are grown for their produce apart from timber, eg almond and avocadoes
- the investor ''pays'' an amount under the scheme. This excludes the acquisition of shares in forestry companies, or units in a forestry unit trust
- there must be more than one investor in the scheme or the scheme manager (or an associate) manages, arranges or promotes similar schemes for other entities
- the investor is an initial investor that holds the interest under the scheme for 4 years from the end of the income year in which they first paid an amount under the scheme. There are exceptions to this requirement: see below
- the investor does not have day-to-day control over the operation of the scheme, and
- under the scheme, all of the trees are established within 18 months of the end of the income year in which the first payment is made by an investor.

It is not necessary to demonstrate that a taxpayer is ''carrying on a business'' in order to access the deduction or that the amount paid is of a revenue nature. Failing to plant all of the trees under a forestry MIS means no Div 394 deduction is allowable for the investor's initial contribution. However, a deduction may be available under s 8-1. The initial investor's sale and harvest proceeds are treated as assessable income on revenue account.

Payments under the scheme exclude payments for financing (borrowing costs and interest and payments in the nature of interest), stamp duty, GST and processing forestry produce, for example in-field wood chipping or milling of logs, whether in-field or at a static facility.

Where an initial investor disposes of interests within 4 years, any deductions will be denied in the income years claimed. However, an investor does not fail the 4-year holding period rule if interests are disposed of within 4 years for reasons genuinely outside their control. Examples include: insolvency or accidental death; compulsory transfer of the scheme interest on marriage breakdown; compulsory government acquisition; the insolvency of the scheme manager causing the winding up of the scheme. The investor must not reasonably have been able to anticipate the circumstances when the investment was made.

Where a business is or was being carried on, the amount paid may be allowable under s 8-1. A market value pricing rule applies for disposals of forestry schemes interests by initial investors. Amounts received by initial and secondary investors for thinnings are assessable income on revenue account.

A secondary investor (ie an investor who acquires an interest in the scheme from another investor, eg by purchasing the interest from the initial investor on the secondary market) cannot claim a deduction under Div 394 for the cost of their interest but can claim a deduction for ongoing contributions under the scheme. The secondary investor's proceeds from sale and harvest are deemed to be held on revenue account to the extent that they ''recoup'' prior forestry deductions and the balance is deemed to be held on capital account (with the cost base increased to reflect the income deemed to be held on revenue account), provided that the secondary investor does not hold the forestry scheme interest as an item of trading stock. The measures allowing trading in forestry interests apply to interests in a pre-existing forestry MIS as well as future investment in newly established schemes. Therefore taxpayers who invested in a forestry MIS before 1 July 2003 may trade their interest from 1 July 2007.

If a scheme manager receives an amount from an investor and all of the requirements of s 394-10 are satisfied, the amount must be included in the scheme manager's assessable income in the year in which the investor is first able to claim the corresponding deduction (ITAA97 s 15-46).

If a taxpayer would be eligible for deductions under both s 8-1 and Div 394, the taxpayer may claim a deduction only under Div 394. If a forestry scheme does not qualify under Div 394, s 8-1 may continue to apply. If the new forestry provisions apply, the prepayment provisions (¶16-045) do not apply. The new arrangements do not apply for investments in non-forestry agribusiness MISs (¶18-020).

There are notification requirements for scheme managers (TAA 1953 s 394-5) and record keeping requirements for investors and scheme managers (ITAA36 s 262A). PS LA 2008/2 guides tax officers dealing with product ruling applications in relation to Div 394 and considering the 70% direct forestry expenditure rule, the arm's length pricing rule, net present value calculations and the 18-month establishment rule.

[FITR ¶363-000]

Abnormal Receipts

¶18-135 Primary production abnormal receipts

Special provisions apply to abnormal receipts relating to double wool clips (¶18-140), insurance recoveries for live stock and timber (¶18-150), and the forced disposal or death of live stock (¶18-160). Various elections apply in relation to the abnormal receipt provisions (see below).

Where an entity joins or leaves a consolidated group under the consolidation regime (¶8-000), amounts of assessable income spread over 2 or more years are split between the entity and the head of the group based on the period spent by the entity in the group (ITAA97 s 716-15: ¶8-580).

Elections

The elections available to a primary producer relating to abnormal receipts must be made on or before the date for lodging the first return where the effect of the election will be relevant or within any extended period allowed by the Commissioner (ITAA97 s 385-150). Where a partnership or trustee carries on a primary production business, only the partnership or trustee can make the election. Where a new partnership carries on the primary production business of a partnership that has ceased to exist, the new partnership can elect to be treated as a continuation of the old partnership and obtain the benefit of elections made by the old partnership, if the new partners together are entitled to 25% of the income and were partners in the old partnership (ITAA97 s 385-165; ID 2005/275). As to elections generally, see ¶24-040.

If a ‘‘disentitling event’’ happens, that is, if a taxpayer becomes bankrupt, leaves Australia permanently or ceases to carry on the primary production business, the assessable income in the year of bankruptcy, etc, includes the balance of the proceeds of disposal or death of livestock (¶18-160), of the insurance recovery for loss of live stock or trees (¶18-150), or of the proceeds of sale of 2 wool clips (¶18-140). If an election was made under ITAA97 s 385-110 (¶18-160), the unused tax profit on the disposal or death of the live stock is included in assessable income (ITAA97 s 385-160). The Commissioner has a discretion to ignore a disentitling event that happens to the beneficiary of a primary production trust (ITAA97 s 385-163).

[FITR ¶355-595]

¶18-140 Double wool clips

A measure of tax relief from the consequences of an advanced shearing caused by drought, fire or flood is available to primary producers carrying on a sheep grazing business in Australia (ITAA97 s 385-135).

A woolgrower may elect to have the assessment of the profit from the advanced shearing deferred to the succeeding income year where the effect of such an advanced shearing is that the grower’s assessable income in the year of income would otherwise include:

- the proceeds of sale of 2 wool clips from shearings in that year, or
- the proceeds of sale of the advanced shearing in that year, plus the proceeds of the previous year’s clip if its opening value taken in at the beginning of the year was at *cost price*.

The profit is the gross proceeds of the advanced shearing less the expenses directly attributable to the advanced shearing *and* sale that were incurred in the year in which the gross proceeds of the advanced shearing were receivable. These expenses include wages paid to shearers, classers and shed hands, payments to shearing contractors, and the costs of branding fluid, fuel for shearing-plant engines, food for shearers, etc, bales, freight to wool store, classing, storage, insurance and auctioneer's commission. Wages paid to persons normally employed in the taxpayer's business should not be taken into account.

▶ Example

Due to drought, Rex was forced to shear early, before the close of the 2021 income year. The advanced clip was sold in the 2021 year for $60,000. The expenses directly attributable to the advanced shearing and sale were $15,000. Earlier in the 2021 year, Rex had sold wool from the 2020 clip that had been brought to account as on hand on 1 July 2020 at cost price. He could elect to have the profit from the advanced shearing ($60,000 – $15,000), ie $45,000, excluded from his 2021 taxable income and taxed in the 2022 year.

Where an election has been made in one income year and its effect is that the profit from 2 clips will be taxed in the following year, a similar election can be made in the next year of income if there is an early shearing in that next year of income by reason of drought, fire or flood. As to the manner and time for making elections, see ¶18-135.

[FITR ¶355-590]

¶18-150 Insurance recoveries for live stock and timber losses

Insurance recoveries received for the loss of live stock (whether by reason of drought, fire, flood, disease or any other disaster) may be spread, for assessment purposes, in equal instalments over a 5-year period (ITAA97 s 385-130). This concession, which is not automatic, applies to cases where the live stock were assets of a primary production business carried on in Australia.

Unless an election is made to spread the insurance recovery, the whole of it would be taxable in the year of receipt (¶10-170). As to the manner and time for making elections, see ¶18-135.

The same concession is available in respect of assessable insurance recoveries for the loss of trees by fire. Such an amount may be assessable under the special rules applying to the loss of trading stock (¶10-170), ie where the amount has been received for the loss of trees on hand at the end of an income year that have been felled for the purpose of manufacture or sale in the course of carrying on a business of forest operations (TR 95/6). In addition, an amount will be assessable when received by way of insurance for the loss of income or profits that would have been assessable, ie where the income would have been derived from trees in a plantation or forest, planted or tended in the course of carrying on a business of forest operations.

[FITR ¶355-580]

¶18-160 Profit from forced disposal or death of live stock

Two forms of concessional tax treatment are available by election for assessable proceeds arising from the death or forced disposal of live stock that are assets of a primary production business carried on in Australia (ITAA97 ss 385-90 to 385-125).

An election is available where the live stock is disposed of or dies as a result of:

- the compulsory acquisition or resumption of land
- a state or territory leasing land for a cattle tick eradication campaign
- the destruction of pasture or fodder due to drought, fire or flood. In the case of destruction by drought, the election is available even where the disposal occurs after the relevant drought declaration is withdrawn (TD 95/6) or where the property has not been acknowledged as drought affected by the competent authority (ID 2002/780). The destruction of pasture by drought must be the compelling or decisive reason for the disposal of the livestock (ID 2011/6)
- compulsory destruction under an Australian law for the control of a disease or death through such disease, or
- receipt of a statutory notification regarding the contamination of property.

Spreading the tax profit

A taxpayer can elect to spread the tax profit from the forced disposal of live stock over 5 years (s 385-105). This is done by:

- including in assessable income for the disposal year the proceeds of the disposal or death as reduced by the tax profit
- including 20% of the tax profit in assessable income for the disposal year, and
- including 20% of the tax profit in assessable income for each of the 4 successive income years.

Depending on the circumstances, the ''proceeds of the disposal or death'' may include the proceeds of sale, or compensation received for the death or destruction of livestock (s 385-100(2)). The ''tax profit'' represents the difference between the proceeds and the sum of: (a) the purchase price of live stock acquired during the disposal year; and (b) the trading stock value of the live stock on hand at the start of the disposal year.

▶ Example

Beefco's cattle have to be destroyed because of a chemical contamination. The proceeds of the forced disposal are $66,000 and the tax profit is $18,000. Beefco elects to spread the tax profit over 5 years. Beefco's assessable income in the disposal year includes an amount of $51,600 in respect of the disposal. This amount is arrived at by reducing the proceeds of $66,000 by the tax profit of $18,000 and adding an amount of $3,600 (ie 20% of the tax profit of $18,000). For each of the 4 income years following the disposal year, Beefco must include an amount of $3,600 in its assessable income.

Deferring the tax profit

Alternatively, the taxpayer can elect to defer the tax profit by using it to reduce the cost of replacement live stock acquired in the disposal year and the subsequent 5 years (s 385-110). This is done by:

- including in assessable income for the disposal year the proceeds of the disposal or death as reduced by the tax profit
- reducing the cost of replacement live stock purchased in the disposal year or any of the following 5 years (s 385-120). The total of these reductions cannot exceed the tax profit, and
- including in assessable income on the last day of the fifth income year after the disposal year any unused tax profit on the disposal or death of the live stock. The ''unused tax profit'' is the tax profit reduced by the sum of: (a) any amounts that the taxpayer chooses to include in assessable income for replacement animals bred by the taxpayer (s 385-115); and (b) the extent to which the amount paid or payable for the purchase of replacement animals is reduced according to the rules in s 385-120.

▶ Example

Following a drought, a significant part of Mooco's pastoral land was rendered unfit for the grazing of cattle. As a result, the proceeds of the disposal of 100 cattle was $15,000. The tax profit on the disposal was $4,000. In the disposal year and in each of the 5 subsequent years, Mooco purchased 8 replacement cattle at $120 a head ($960). In each of the fourth and fifth years after the disposal year, Mooco also included an amount of $600 in its assessable income for 15 replacement cattle that it bred itself (under s 385-115).

In the disposal year, Mooco must include $11,000 in its assessable income, ie the proceeds of the disposal ($15,000) less the tax profit on the disposal ($4,000). In addition, the cost of the $960 in replacement cattle purchased during the disposal year is reduced by $320 (ie the reduction amount is calculated as 8 cattle × $40 (s 385-120)) to $640 for live stock trading account purposes.

For the 5 years following the disposal year, the cost of the $960 in replacement cattle purchased during the disposal year is also reduced by $320 to $640 for live stock trading account purposes.

In addition, for the fourth and fifth years after the disposal year, an amount of $600 is assessable for the 15 replacement cattle that Mooco bred itself.

Finally, in the fifth year after the disposal year, Mooco must also include the unused tax profit on the disposal of $880 in its assessable income. This figure is arrived at by reducing the tax profit on disposal ($4,000) by the reduction amounts affecting the cost of replacement cattle ($320 × 6 years) and by the amounts chosen to be assessable in respect of replacement cattle bred by Mooco ($600 × 2 years).

When a deferral election is made in relation to a disposal forced by bovine tuberculosis, the deferral period is extended to 10 years.

A deferral election is only available if the proceeds of the forced disposal are used mainly to purchase replacement live stock or to maintain breeding stock to produce replacement live stock. The Commissioner equates "mainly" with the application of at least two-thirds of the proceeds on purchasing or maintaining stock (IT 211). As to the manner and time for making elections, see ¶18-135.

[FITR ¶355-490]

Income Averaging

¶18-200 How the primary production averaging system works

The income averaging system (ITAA97 ss 392-1 to 392-95) is designed to ensure that primary producers with fluctuating incomes pay no more tax over a number of years than those on comparable but steady incomes. This is achieved by making an "averaging adjustment" in each year in which averaging applies. In high income years (when average income is less than taxable income) the adjustment takes the form of a tax offset that reduces tax. In low income years (when average income is greater than taxable income) the adjustment is made by increasing the tax that is payable.

For averaging purposes, a primary producer means an individual who carries on a primary production business in Australia (either alone or in partnership: ID 2003/359). As to when an individual is carrying on a primary production business, see ¶18-020.

A beneficiary will be treated as carrying on the primary production business carried on by a trust if they are presently entitled to income of the trust and, if the entitlement is less than $1,040, the Commissioner is satisfied that their interest in the trust was not acquired or granted wholly or primarily for the purpose of enabling the averaging provisions to apply.

If an individual is the beneficiary of a trust that has no trust income to which a beneficiary could be presently entitled (eg because the trust has a loss for trust law purposes in that income year), the beneficiary will be treated as carrying on the primary production business carried on by the trust if:

- for a non-discretionary trust — the beneficiary would have been entitled to trust income if the trust had income for that year that was available for distribution, or
- for a discretionary trust — the trustee makes a choice in writing that the beneficiary will receive the benefit of income averaging (ITAA97 s 392-20). The choice must be made before lodgment of the trust's income tax return for the year for which the choice applies.

The averaging provisions do not apply to the beneficiary of a corporate unit trust or a public trading trust.

A beneficiary of a discretionary trust will not generally be deemed to be carrying on a primary production business in any year in which the trustee does not exercise the discretion in favour of the beneficiary.

Where an individual dies and the trustee of the deceased's estate continues the primary production business, there is a new taxpayer and a new averaging calculation is made for the trustee.

Where averaging has applied to a taxpayer, it will continue to apply after the taxpayer ceases carrying on the primary production business provided, in each year after the year of the cessation of the business, the taxpayer either: (a) derives income from having carried on that business; or (b) carries on another primary production business.

The averaging provisions in ITAA97 Div 392 do *not* apply to a company carrying on a primary production business unless it does so in the capacity of trustee. Nor do they apply to a trustee on income that is assessed as net income of the trust to which no beneficiary is presently entitled, if the trustee is assessed under ITAA36 s 99A (¶6-230). The averaging provisions in ITAA36 s 156(5) to (8) continue to apply to trustees that are liable to be assessed under s 98 (¶6-120) and 99 (¶6-230). The averaging provisions apply to trust beneficiaries that are presently entitled to all or part of the trust income (¶6-110; ITAA97 s 392-20).

With effect from the 2016–17 income year, a primary producer can choose to withdraw from the averaging system and thereafter pay tax at ordinary rates. The primary producer can then access income tax averaging 10 income years after choosing to opt out, instead of that choice being permanent (¶18-270).

[FITR ¶362-000]

¶18-210 The averaging rules: a step-by-step process

The process set out in the steps below can be followed to determine: (a) whether the averaging adjustment applicable to a primary producer is a tax offset or extra income tax; and (b) how to calculate an averaging primary producer's overall tax liability taking into account whichever adjustment is applicable.

Step 1: Calculate basic taxable income for the current year

"Basic taxable income" is the primary producer's taxable income: (a) excluding certain superannuation benefits and employment termination payments (payments under ITAA97 s 82-65, 82-70 or 302-145) and any net capital gains; and (b) reduced by any amounts of above-average special professional income (¶2-140). Deductions excluded under the non-commercial loss provisions (¶16-020) are excluded from the calculation of basic taxable income.

Step 2: Calculate the comparison rate of tax

The comparison rate of tax is the rate of tax that a primary producer would pay in the current year at "basic rates of tax" (see below) on the producer's average income.

Average income

A primary producer's "average income" is the producer's basic taxable income averaged over the current year and a maximum of 4 previous years. This means that for a well-established primary producer, average income is calculated over a 5-year period.

▶ Example 1

Jack is a primary producer whose basic taxable income for the current year is $10,000. For the 4 previous years he had a basic taxable income of $12,000, $18,000, $15,000 and $20,000. His average income in the current year is:

($10,000 + $12,000 + $18,000 + $15,000 + $20,000) ÷ 5 = $15,000

For the first averaging calculation, a minimum period of 2 years is required in which the basic taxable income of the second year must be no less than the first year.

▶ Example 2

Fiona commenced business as a primary producer on 1 July of Year 1. Her basic taxable income was $18,000 in Year 1, $12,000 in Year 2 and $22,000 in Year 3. As her Year 2 income was less than her Year 1 income, Year 1 cannot be used as the first average year. Her first average year is Year 2 in which her income was less than in Year 3. Her average income for Year 3 is:

($12,000 + $22,000) ÷ 2 = $17,000

Provided a taxpayer carried on a primary production business in the current year, the fact that the producer had no taxable income for that year will not exclude the producer, even temporarily, from the averaging system and such a year can count as the first average year. An average year in which there is a tax loss is treated as a *nil* year.

▶ Example 3

Last year, Anton (a primary producer) incurred a tax loss of $2,500 due to non-primary production activities. This year, his taxable income, prior to the deduction of the previous year's loss, was $16,900. For calculating the average income for averaging purposes, his taxable income is nil for the previous year and $14,400 (ie $16,900 – $2,500) for the current year.

After the first year in which a primary producer uses the income averaging system, averaging will continue to be available in each year after the primary production business ceases, provided the producer either derives assessable income from having carried on that original business or carries on another primary production business within Australia.

Comparison rate of tax

The ''comparison rate of tax'' is worked out using the following formula:

$$\frac{\text{income tax at basic rates on average income}}{\text{average income}}$$

The basic rates of tax for a resident are the normal marginal rates of tax specified for residents (¶42-000). The Medicare levy is ignored for averaging purposes. Similarly, the basic rates of tax for a non-resident are the normal marginal rates of tax specified for non-residents (¶42-015).

▶ Example 4

Jessica is a primary producer with an average income of $36,000 in the 2020–21 income year. Her comparison rate would be calculated as follows:

$$\frac{\$36{,}000 \times \text{basic rates of tax}}{\$36{,}000} = \frac{\$3{,}382}{\$36{,}000} = 9.4\%$$

Step 3: Work out the averaging component

The averaging component is simply that part of a primary producer's basic taxable income that can be subject to an averaging adjustment.

The averaging component is made up of a primary producer's ''taxable primary production income'' (ITAA97 s 392-80) and ''taxable non-primary production income'' (ITAA97 s 392-85).

A primary producer has taxable primary production income when the producer's assessable primary production income exceeds the producer's primary production deductions (including a pro rata amount attributable to apportionable deductions). Deductions deferred under the non-commercial loss provisions (¶16-020) are not included in the calculation. ''Assessable primary production income'' is that part of the producer's basic assessable income derived from carrying on a primary production business (¶18-030).

When the income is less than the deductions, the producer's taxable primary production income is treated as being nil. Similar rules apply for calculating taxable non-primary production income.

Taxable primary production income always forms part of the averaging component. The extent to which taxable non-primary production income is included in the averaging component is determined according to the following rules:

- it is included in full where it is less than $5,000 (see Example 5)
- when it is between $5,000 and $10,000, a ''non-primary production shade-out amount'' is included. This amount is generally the amount remaining after deducting the taxable non-primary production income from $10,000 (see Example 6). Where a taxpayer makes a loss from primary production activities, the amount of that loss is also deducted, but the non-primary production shade-out amount cannot be less than nil (see Examples 8 and 9)
- it is not included at all when it is $10,000 or more (see Example 7).

▶ Example 5

Mary is a primary producer whose basic taxable income of $20,000 is made up of $16,000 in taxable primary production income and $4,000 in taxable non-primary production income. As the taxable non-primary production income does not exceed $5,000, her averaging component is the whole of her basic taxable income of $20,000.

▶ Example 6

Tom is a primary producer with a basic taxable income of $20,000 made up of $12,000 in taxable primary production income and $8,000 in taxable non-primary production income. His averaging component is:

$12,000 + non-primary production shade-out amount ($10,000 – $8,000) = $14,000

▶ Example 7

Cindy is a primary producer with a basic taxable income of $20,000 made up of $8,000 in taxable primary production income and $12,000 in taxable non-primary production income. As the taxable non-primary production income exceeds $10,000, Cindy's averaging component does not include any taxable non-primary production income, ie it is equivalent to the $8,000 in taxable primary production income.

▶ Example 8

Nubly is a primary producer whose primary production deductions exceed his assessable primary production income by $500. This means that his primary production income is nil. Nubly also has taxable non-primary production income of $4,000. After allowing for the primary production loss of $500, Nubly has a basic taxable income of $3,500. The averaging component is $3,500, ie the basic taxable income.

▶ Example 9

Adrian is a primary producer whose primary production deductions exceed his assessable primary production income by $2,000. He also has taxable non-primary production income of $7,000. This means that he has a basic taxable income of $5,000. Adrian is treated as having a taxable primary production income of nil and the averaging component is equal to the non-primary production shade-out amount, ie $10,000 – $7,000 (taxable non-primary production income) – $2,000 (primary production loss) = $1,000.

Step 4: Compare

(a) the tax payable on the basic taxable income for the current year at the comparison rate of tax with

(b) the tax payable on the basic taxable income for the current year at basic rates of tax. This amount of tax is calculated without taking into account the Medicare levy, the availability of any rebates, offsets or credits, and without applying the provisions governing uncontrolled partnership income (¶5-180) or the unearned income of minors (¶2-160).

Result:

- where (a) is less than (b) (because basic taxable income exceeds average income) the primary producer is entitled to an ''averaging adjustment'' in the form of a tax offset

- where (a) is greater than (b) (because average income exceeds basic taxable income) the primary producer must pay extra income tax on the producer's "averaging component" that is generally equal to the amount of the "averaging adjustment".

Step 5: Calculate the averaging adjustment

The averaging adjustment is calculated using the following formula:

$$\text{gross averaging amount} \times \frac{\text{averaging component}}{\text{basic taxable income}}$$

A primary producer's "gross averaging amount" is the difference between the tax payable at the comparison rate and the tax payable at basic rates calculated at Step 4.

Where tax payable at the comparison rate is less than tax payable at basic rates, the averaging adjustment will be a tax offset. In the reverse situation, the averaging adjustment will generally be extra income tax.

Step 6: Calculate the tax payable

The amount of tax payable is calculated after taking into account the averaging adjustment (tax offset or extra tax) calculated at Step 5.

Note: The formula for calculating the rate of tax payable where the averaging provisions apply is set out in *Income Tax Rates Act 1986* (ITRA), s 12A. The averaging provisions of ITRA can operate even though their application to a primary producer in a given case does not produce either a tax offset or extra tax (*Case 40/93*).

Trustees

Where a trustee is liable to be assessed and to pay tax in respect of the net income, or a share of the net income, of a trust estate to which the averaging provisions apply (¶18-200), the averaging system is calculated as for ordinary individuals with one exception. The exception is that the rates scale set out at ¶42-030 should be used where the trustee is assessed in respect of the net income of a trust estate other than the estate of a person who died less than 3 years before the end of the year of income.

[FITR ¶362-020 – ¶362-410]

¶18-250 Example: averaging adjustment — tax offset

The following example illustrates the operation of the averaging system where a primary producer is entitled to an averaging adjustment in the form of a tax offset. The steps in the example follow the sequence of those in the step-by-step process explained at ¶18-210. It is assumed that the taxpayer is a *resident*, so the appropriate rates of tax to be applied are those set out at ¶42-000, and eligibility for the rebate for low income earners (¶15-300) is ignored.

▶ Example

For the income year ended 30 June 2021, Barnaby, a primary producer, has a taxable income of $50,400 comprised of $40,800 in taxable primary production income and $9,600 in wages income. He has an average income of $33,600. He does not have any dependants.

Step 1: Basic taxable income = $50,400.

Step 2: Calculate the comparison rate of tax.

The comparison rate of tax is calculated as follows:

$$\frac{\text{income tax at basic rates on average income}}{\text{average income}} = \frac{\$2{,}926}{\$33{,}600} = 8.71\%$$

Step 3: Barnaby's averaging component is calculated as follows:

taxable primary production income ($40,800) + [$10,000 – taxable non-primary production income ($9,600)] = $41,200

Step 4: Compare the tax payable at the comparison rate of tax with the tax payable at basic rates of tax.

The tax payable on the basic taxable income at the comparison rate is:

$$\$50{,}400 \times 8.71\% = \$4{,}390$$

The tax payable on the basic taxable income at basic rates is $7,927.

As the tax payable at the comparison rate is less than the tax payable at basic rates, Barnaby is entitled to a tax offset equal to the averaging adjustment.

Step 5: Barnaby's averaging adjustment (tax offset) is calculated as follows:

$$\text{gross averaging amount} \times \frac{\text{averaging component}}{\text{basic taxable income}}$$

The gross averaging amount is the difference between the tax payable at the comparison rate ($4,390) and the tax payable at basic rates ($7,927), ie $3,537.

$$\text{averaging adjustment} = \$3{,}537 \times \frac{\$41{,}200}{\$50{,}400} = \$2{,}891$$

Step 6: Calculate tax payable after allowing for the tax offset derived at Step 5.

Tax payable (excluding the Medicare levy) on Barnaby's taxable income of $50,400 is $7,927. The tax offset of $2,891 will reduce Barnaby's tax liability to $5,036.

¶18-260 Example: averaging adjustment — extra income tax

The following example illustrates the operation of the averaging system where the primary producer is liable to pay extra tax on the averaging component of the producer's basic taxable income. The steps in the example follow the same sequence as those in the step-by-step process explained at ¶18-210. It is assumed that the taxpayer is a *resident*, so the appropriate rates of tax to be applied are those set out at ¶42-000, and eligibility for the rebate for low income earners (¶15-300) is ignored.

▶ Example

For the income year ended 30 June 2021, Clive, a primary producer, has a taxable income of $22,000 of which $16,000 is taxable primary production income. He has an average income of $23,000 and no dependants.

Step 1: Basic taxable income = $22,000.

Step 2: Calculate the comparison rate of tax.

The comparison rate of tax is calculated as follows:

$$\frac{\text{income tax at basic rates on average income}}{\text{average income}} = \frac{\$912}{\$23{,}000} = 3.96\%$$

Step 3: Calculate the averaging component.

Clive's averaging component is calculated as follows:

taxable primary production income ($16,000) + [$10,000 – taxable non-primary production income ($6,000)] = $20,000

Step 4: Compare the tax payable at the comparison rate of tax with tax payable at the basic rates of tax.

The tax payable on the basic taxable income at the comparison rate is: $22,000 × 3.96% = $871.

The tax payable on the basic taxable income at basic rates is $722.

As the tax payable at the comparison rate is more than the tax payable at basic rates, Clive is liable for extra tax equal to the averaging adjustment.

Step 5: The averaging adjustment (extra tax) is calculated as follows:

$$\text{gross averaging amount} \times \frac{\text{averaging component}}{\text{basic taxable income}}$$

The gross averaging amount is the difference between the tax payable at the comparison rate ($871) and the tax payable at basic rates ($722), ie $149.

$$\text{averaging adjustment} = \$149 \times \frac{\$20{,}000}{\$22{,}000} = \$135$$

Clive is liable to pay extra tax equivalent to the averaging adjustment, ie $135.

Step 6: Calculate tax payable including the extra tax derived at Step 5.

The tax payable on Clive's taxable income of $22,000 is $722.

The extra tax of $135 will increase Clive's total tax liability to $857. This does not take into account any rebates, offsets or credits to which he may be entitled. Clive may be liable for the Medicare levy (¶2-330).

¶18-270 Election to withdraw from averaging

A taxpayer can elect to withdraw from the averaging system (ITAA97 s 392-25). Where an election is made, tax will be payable at ordinary rates for the year of income specified in the election and all subsequent years. With effect from 2016–17 income year, primary producers are allowed to access income tax averaging 10 income years after choosing to opt out. Previously, an election to opt out, once made, was irrevocable.

After the 10 year opt-out period has ended, primary producers are treated as new primary producers in applying the basic conditions. The averaging adjustment applies again to a taxpayer's assessment if all of the following conditions are met:

- income tax averaging has not applied to the taxpayer because they permanently opted out 10 or more income years ago
- the taxpayer is carrying on a primary production business for 2 income years in a row, and
- their basic taxable income in the first year (after the 10-year opt-out period has passed) is less than or equal to their basic taxable income in the later year.

An election must be made in writing and should be lodged with the tax return for the income year in which the election is first to apply. The Commissioner has power to extend the time for making an election.

Taxpayers are given the right to elect out of the averaging system because the system can operate even where it does not result in a benefit to the taxpayer.

[FITR ¶362-140]

¶18-280 Permanent reduction of income

Primary producers may have calculations of average income started afresh, with high taxable incomes of previous years being dropped out. This will occur if they can establish that retirement from an occupation, or some other event, has resulted in taxable income (excluding income from unusual sources) being permanently reduced to an amount that is less than two-thirds of average taxable income. The taxpayer can then choose to recommence averaging based on the reduced level of income (ITAA97 s 392-95).

A reduction of income due to a change of investments from those producing assessable income to those producing exempt income is not a sufficient reason to bring this provision into operation. In one case, a grazier failed to show that his income was permanently reduced to the required level, despite his having newly brought his wife in as partner, when it became apparent that the partnership had considerable liquid resources not needed for working capital (*Case C79*).

There may be a permanent reduction of income, even though a primary producer has options available to increase income-earning potential, if it is unlikely that the taxpayer will take up any of these options (*Case V120*; IT 2526).

[FITR ¶362-410]

Farm Management Deposits

¶18-290 Farm management deposits scheme

The farm management deposits (FMD) scheme is designed to allow primary producers, in effect, to shift income from good to bad years in order to deal with adverse economic events and seasonal fluctuations (ITAA97 Div 393). The FMD scheme allows primary producers (with a limited amount of non-primary production income) to claim deductions for FMDs made in the year of deposit (and to reduce their PAYG instalment income accordingly). When an FMD is withdrawn, the amount of the deduction previously allowed is included in both their PAYG instalment income and their assessable income in the repayment year.

[FITR ¶362-500 – ¶362-700]

¶18-293 Farm management deposits eligibility rules

A deposit qualifies as an FMD only if it complies with the conditions affecting the agreement under which the relevant financial institution accepts money from a depositor. The conditions (ITAA97 ss 393-20 to 393-35) include the following:

- the owner of the FMD must be a primary producer when the deposit is made. The owner of an FMD can carry on a primary production business through a variety of structures including a sole trader, in partnership, with the owner being a partner, or through a trust, with the owner being either a beneficiary that is presently entitled to some or all of the net income of the trust or a unit holder in a fixed trust
- a deposit cannot be made by 2 or more persons jointly or be made on behalf of 2 or more persons
- a trustee acting as such can make a deposit only on behalf of a beneficiary who is presently entitled to a share of a trust estate and is under a legal disability
- the minimum deposit and withdrawal is $1,000 and the total of all deposits cannot exceed $800,000. The maximum amount that could be held as FMDs was $400,000 for income years commencing before 1 July 2016
- the depositor's rights in respect of the deposit cannot be transferred and the deposit cannot be charged or encumbered.

Failure to comply with the rules may result in the deposit not being treated as an FMD from the time the deposit was made.

[FITR ¶362-530, ¶362-600 – ¶362-660]

¶18-295 Making a farm management deposit

The owner of an FMD deposited during a particular income year can claim a deduction equal to the amount deposited, provided the owner did not, during that year:

- have more than $100,000 in non-primary production income (excluding net capital gains and certain superannuation amounts: ITAA97 s 995-1 definition of ''taxable non-primary production income''). The threshold was $65,000 for income years commencing before 1 July 2014
- die or become bankrupt, or
- cease to be a primary producer for at least 120 days.

No deduction is available where the deposit arises by way of transfer of an amount under the former income equalisation deposit scheme to an FMD account. The electronic transfer of an FMD from one institution to another is not treated as either a withdrawal or a deposit.

The sum of deductions in relation to FMDs for a particular year cannot exceed the owner's taxable primary production income for that year.

If a taxpayer makes a deposit during a period, the amount of the deposit reduces the taxpayer's PAYG instalment income for that period (¶27-260). The reduction is limited to the amount that the taxpayer reasonably expects to be able to claim as a deduction for the income year in which the deposit was made. The instalment income cannot be reduced below zero.

FMDs can be made only with ADIs or with financial institutions that have a Commonwealth, state or territory guarantee. Providers offering FMDs must make a declaration to depositors that they are either an ADI or have a relevant government guarantee. FMDs cannot become unclaimed moneys under the Banking Act. However, the status of amounts held as an FMD that had already become unclaimed moneys before that date does not change.

Amounts held in an FMD can be used to offset a loan or other debt offset a loan or other debt relating to the FMD owner's primary production business from 1 July 2016. Under such an arrangement, the amount of interest charged on the loan or other debt may be less than what it would otherwise be and there may be no entitlement or a reduced entitlement to earn interest on the FMD. To the extent that an FMD loan offset arrangement results in a lower amount of interest being charged on a loan or other debt used other than for the purposes of a primary production business of the FMD owner or a partnership in which they are a partner, an administrative penalty is payable.

[FITR ¶362-530]

¶18-310 Withdrawing a farm management deposit

Where an FMD is withdrawn in a year of income, the owner is required to include, as assessable income, an amount that equals the deductible amount previously allowed in respect of the deposit. A withdrawn FMD that is included in assessable income is treated as assessable primary production income for the purpose of working out the deductibility of any new FMD made in that income year.

The assessable amount is limited to the ''unrecouped FMD deduction'', which will generally be that part of a deposit for which a deduction has been claimed but which has yet to be included in assessable income on repayment. If the FMD contains both deductible and non-deductible deposits, withdrawals are considered to have been made from the non-deductible amounts first.

If, in an income year commencing on or after 1 July 2014, the taxpayer withdraws and immediately redeposits amounts for the purpose of consolidating FMDs, there are no income tax consequences. The deposits in those circumstances are not subject to the normal restrictions on making FMDs, provided all of the amounts are from FMDs more than 12 months old and gave rise to deductions when they were initially deposited.

Deposits repayable on death, bankruptcy or when primary production ceases, will be assessable in the income year in which the relevant event occurs (rather than in any later repayment year). Interest on an FMD is assessable in the year it is derived.

If a taxpayer withdraws funds from an FMD during a period, the amount repaid is included in the taxpayer's PAYG instalment income for that period (TAA s 45-120; ¶27-260). However, the instalment income only includes the amount repaid to the extent that it is assessable income for the income year in which the withdrawal is made. If neither the owner's TFN nor ABN have been quoted to the financial institution that holds the deposit, the amount withdrawn will also be subject to PAYG withholding (Income Tax Assessment Regulations 1997; ¶26-200).

Early withdrawal of FMDs

While deposits can be held in accounts of any term (including at call accounts), the general rule is that the deposit must not be repaid within 12 months. However, there are exceptions. Eligible primary producers may withdraw from their FMD earlier (ie within first 12 months of the deposit) if:

- the owner dies, becomes bankrupt, ceases to be a primary producer or the amount is transferred to another FMD provider
- part of the land used in carrying on the FMD owner's primary production business meets the prescribed rainfall conditions for the prescribed period (s 393-40(3)), or
- natural disaster relief and recovery arrangements in federal government regulations made under s 393-40(3A) apply to the primary production business. The conditions for early access are specified in the FMD regulations.

If part of a deposit is withdrawn within 12 months so that the remaining deposit is less than $1,000, the remaining deposit is not deductible as an FMD (s 393-40(2)).

Early withdrawal because of severe drought

From 1 July 2016, early access to amounts deposited by an individual as an FMD is only available for some classes of primary production businesses (ITAA97 s 995-1) that are likely to be directly affected by severe drought:

- cultivate or propagate plants, fungi or their products or parts (eg vegetable cropping, plant propagation, mushroom farming)
- maintain animals for sale or the sale of their bodily products or offspring (eg cattle farming, sheep farming including wool production, farming of aquatic animals such as fish, crustaceans and molluscs)
- produce dairy products from raw material produced by the primary producer (eg dairy farmers), or
- plant or tend trees in a plantation or forest for logging (eg tree cultivation for logging).

Early access to FMDs does not extend to an FMD owner that only carries on one or more of the following primary production businesses as drought conditions do not directly impact on these activities:

- commercial fishing, pearling and related activities (other than farming of aquatic animals)
- felling of trees, or
- transporting trees that the transporter logged for milling or processing or to a place for transport to a mill or processing plant.

The qualifying primary production business must demonstrate that any part of the land of the business has experienced a rainfall deficiency for at least 6 consecutive months. The deficiency must be equivalent to or worse (ie lower) than 5% of average rainfall (one in 20-year event) for that 6-month period based on the most recently available publicly released data from the Bureau of Meteorology at the time of the withdrawal. Further, the land must have been used in carrying on the primary production business and the deposit held for the prescribed period.

If an FMD owner carries on both qualifying and non-qualifying primary production businesses, they can access the early withdrawal concession for severe drought if they meet the rainfall deficiency test for land they use in carrying on their qualifying primary production business.

[FITR ¶362-540]

Chapter 19 Mining • Infrastructure • Environmental Protection

Mining, Infrastructure and Environmental Protection

¶19-000 Mining, infrastructure and environmental protection

Mining, quarrying and prospecting concessions

Special tax concessions are available to taxpayers engaged in mining, including petroleum mining, and quarrying operations for the following types of expenditure:

- exploration or prospecting expenditure (¶19-010)
- "pooled project expenditure" incurred in the working of mine sites, petroleum fields and quarries (¶19-050)
- expenditure incurred in rehabilitating former mine sites, petroleum fields and quarries (¶19-100)
- payments of PRRT (¶19-003).

These deductions are in addition to those allowable for general operating expenses (¶16-000) and specified business capital expenditure (''blackhole expenditure'': ¶16-156), assets used for taxable purposes (ie the purpose of producing assessable income, mining site rehabilitation, exploration or prospecting and environmental protection activities). For the uniform capital allowance (UCA) provisions dealing with assets see ¶17-005; see ¶43-000ff for the most recent ATO list of effective lives including assets used in the mineral processing and metallurgical laboratory industry. Depreciating assets include mining, quarrying or prospecting rights or information (¶19-010). If expenditure is deductible under both specific and general deduction provisions, the general rule against double deductions applies (¶16-100).

The CGT roll-over for prospecting and mining entitlements is automatic where relevant conditions are met (¶12-420).

If a commercial debt is forgiven, the debtor's deduction under the UCA provisions may be reduced under the rules discussed at ¶16-910. Special provisions apply if property is acquired under limited recourse finance and the debt is terminated without the debtor repaying the full amount of the debt (¶23-260).

Special rules apply to depreciating and exploration assets of consolidated entities (ITAA97 Subdiv 716-E). If an entity joins or leaves a consolidated group under the consolidation regime (¶8-000), any deduction is allocated between the entities under ss 716-25, 716-70 (¶8-580).

Foreign currency amounts are converted into Australian dollars at the rate applicable at the time of payment (¶23-070). The foreign exchange gains and losses provisions must also be considered (¶23-075).

Deductions covered in this chapter are subject to the application of the rules for tax-preferred leasing (¶23-210).

The treatment of natural resource incomes and payments derived by non-residents is discussed at ¶21-070, ¶22-070 and ¶26-270.

Other environmental initiatives

In addition to the measures noted above, there are other significant environmental protection initiatives:

- Carbon sink forests, ¶19-120
- Conservation covenants, ¶16-972
- Emissions reduction fund (ERF), ¶19-130
- Environmental impact studies (EIS), ¶19-040, ¶19-060
- Environmental protection activities, ¶19-110
- Environment protection earthworks, ¶20-480
- Gifts to environmental organisations, ¶16-960
- Green buildings withholding tax incentive, ¶19-135
- Landcare operations, ¶17-030, ¶18-100
- Water conservation or conveyance, ¶18-080.

Recoupments

A recoupment received by a taxpayer in respect of the various types of deductible expenditure referred to above is assessable (¶10-270).

Trading stock

The cost of trading stock for mining or quarrying operations is dealt with in TR 98/2. Absorption costing principles are recognised, however only tax-deductible expenditure incurred in the production process, the main components of which are direct material costs, direct labour costs and production costs (¶9-190), are absorbed as part of the cost of trading stock.

Non-arm's length dealings

Where capital expenditure is incurred in a ''non-arm's length dealing'' (ss 40-765, 40-855) and the expenditure is greater than the ''market value'' (¶17-045, ¶17-050) of what is received, the expenditure is taken to be that market value. This rule applies to exploration or prospecting expenditure, mining capital expenditure, transport capital expenditure, mining site rehabilitation expenditure, project infrastructure expenditure and environmental protection expenditure (Subdivs 40-H, 40-I).

ATO on infrastructure transactions

The ATO's web document *Infrastructure — Australian federal tax framework* provides guidance on infrastructure-related tax issues.

[FITR ¶88-410, ¶88-650]

¶19-003 Petroleum resource rent tax (PRRT)

The *Petroleum Resource Rent Tax Assessment Act 1987* (PRRTA87) applies to the PRRT to petroleum production, including coal seam gas and shale oil sourced from petroleum projects located onshore (up to 30 June 2019) and in territorial waters, as well as from the North West Shelf project area, and offshore petroleum projects in Australia's offshore areas beyond coastal waters. The joint petroleum development area (JPDA) in the Timor Sea (¶21-035), and resources that were subject to the former MRRT are not subject to the PRRT. For details of the application of the PRRT prior to 1 July 2012, see the 2012 *Australian Master Tax Guide* and earlier editions; MRRT 2015 *Australian Master Tax Guide*.

All payments or instalments of PRRT are tax deductible in the year in which they are paid (ITAA97 s 40-750), subject to the rules for tax-preferred leasing (¶23-210). Recoupments of such amounts are assessable income under the general recoupment provisions (¶10-270), or in the circumstances described in s 40-750(3).

General operation of PRRT

The PRRT is levied at the rate of 40% of the taxable profit of a person in a financial year in relation to a petroleum project.

A ''petroleum project'' exists when a production licence is in force. It also includes the operations, facilities and other things required, for the recovery, and the processing and treatment of petroleum; to produce and store ''marketable petroleum commodities'' (PRRTA87 s 2E). A petroleum project may comprise a single petroleum licence or, subject to Ministerial approval, a combination of sufficiently related licences.

Taxable profit is calculated by deducting eligible project expenses from the assessable revenues derived from the project (ID 2013/48). Assessable revenue includes receipts from the sale of petroleum or marketable petroleum commodities (including stabilised crude oil, sales gas, condensate, liquefied petroleum gas, ethane, and shale oil) from a project.

Deductible eligible project expenditure broadly includes capital or revenue expenditures that are directly incurred in relation to the petroleum project, including exploration expenditure, project development and operating expenditures, subject to specific exclusions. Expenditure in closing down a project (including offshore platform removal and environmental restoration) is deductible in the year incurred. ''Exploration'' takes its ordinary meaning (*ZZGN*); TR 2014/9 considers the meaning of petroleum exploration for PRRT purposes. State and federal resource taxes and native title payments under the *Native Title Act 1993* are deductible for PRRT purposes.

If a person's deductible expenditure exceeds their assessable revenue in a financial year, the excess is carried forward and uplifted to be deducted against assessable project receipts in later years. Payments in relation to a petroleum project may be apportioned from commencement of the project for the purposes of determining deductible expenditure under the PRRT law.

The ATO website has information on the PRRT, including PRRT entities, PRRT liabilities and instalments, PRRT concepts and record keeping. PCG 2016/12 and PCG 2016/13 explain the ATO's compliance approach to the deduction of general project expenditure under s 38 PRRTA87. TR 2018/1 allows that abandonment, decommissioning and rehabilitation expenditure (ADRE), incurred before a petroleum project is completely closed down, that falls under s 38 or 39 of that Act may be deductible. Guidance on the period within which a PRRT assessment can be amended to correct an error in a transfer of exploration expenditure is set out in PS LA 2017/1.

[FITR ¶88-500]

¶19-006 Withholding tax on Indigenous mining payments; native title benefits

Mining payments made to "Indigenous people" and distributing groups, relating to the use of "Indigenous land" for mining and exploration are subject to mining withholding tax (ITAA36 s 128V) at the rate of 4%. The amount withheld includes GST if the payment is for a taxable supply (ID 2010/115).

As a withholding tax, although formal liability for mining withholding tax rests with the Indigenous recipients, the actual responsibility for paying the tax rests on the mining company, government or other person who makes the payment. These bodies are required to withhold an amount from a mining payment in accordance with the PAYG withholding rules (¶26-270). Where an amount is withheld from a mining payment, the person liable to pay the mining withholding tax is generally entitled to a credit for the amount withheld (¶26-660).

The "mining payments" to which the withholding system applies are:

- amounts representing royalties received by the Commonwealth for the mining of Indigenous land
- certain payments made to Aboriginal Land Councils
- payments made in relation to Aboriginal land for the issue of a miner's right or mining interest, for permission to mine or explore, and payments of mining royalties in relation to Indigenous land.

Such payments (other than amounts of remuneration or consideration for goods or services) are treated as non-assessable non-exempt (NANE) income of the recipient (ITAA97 s 59-15; ¶10-895). For the deductibility of compensation payments made by a mining company to an Aboriginal community, see *Cape Flattery Silica Mines* (¶16-060).

Native title benefits

"Native title benefits" received from 1 July 2008 are NANE income and not subject to income tax (ITAA97 s 59-50; ¶10-187). In addition, certain CGT events involving native title rights do not have CGT implications (¶11-670).

A native title benefit is the amount or benefit that an "Indigenous person" or "Indigenous holding entity" (including a "distributing body" for Indigenous people) receives directly from entering into a relevant agreement or as compensation under the *Native Title Act 1993*.

The payee of a native title benefit is not required to withhold an amount from the payment as native title benefits are excluded from the definition of mining payment in ITAA36 s 128U.

[FITR ¶88-410, ¶88-650, ¶108-040; FTR ¶69-514, Archive ¶749-700]

Exploration or Prospecting Expenditure

¶19-010 Deduction for exploration or prospecting expenditure

Expenditure (net of GST and adjustments (ITAA97 s 27-105)) on ''exploration or prospecting'' (ITAA97 s 40-730(4); ¶19-040) for minerals (including petroleum) or quarry materials obtainable by ''mining or quarrying operations'' that satisfies at least one of the ''activity tests'' (s 40-730(1)) outlined below in the year of income, is fully deductible in the year in which it is incurred (s 40-730). The mining property may be located in or outside Australia, and the exploration or prospecting expenditure is deductible against income derived from any source.

The deduction under s 40-730 applies to both capital and revenue expenditure but is not available for the cost of depreciating assets (see below). Where *current* expenditure is potentially deductible under both the exploration provisions and another provision (eg the general deduction provision), the amount may only be deducted once under the most appropriate provision (¶16-100). TR 2017/1 contains detailed guidance on deductions for mining and petroleum exploration expenditure under both ss 40-730 and 8-1.

Satisfaction of at least one of the following activity tests during an income year is necessary for exploration or prospecting expenditure to be deductible:

- the taxpayer carried on general mining operations, petroleum mining operations or quarrying operations, eg *Case 4/2007* (¶19-050)
- it would be reasonable to conclude that the taxpayer proposed to carry on such operations, or
- the taxpayer carried on a business of, or including, exploration or prospecting for minerals (including petroleum) or quarry materials obtainable by such operations, and the expenditure was necessarily incurred in carrying on that business. A contractor in a business solely providing geophysical surveying services in the mining and mineral exploration industries is not carrying on a relevant business of exploration or prospecting (ID 2011/25).

A deduction is available under the exploration and prospecting provisions only if, when it is first used by the taxpayer, the asset is *not* used for development drilling for petroleum, or operations in the course of working a mining or quarrying property or petroleum field. There is *no* presumption that activities which answer the description of ''exploration or prospecting'' (¶19-040) and which occur in relation to a mining property, where there is an established mine, are operations in the course of working that mining property (TR 2017/1 para 49).

The deduction is subject to the rules for non-arm's length dealings (¶17-045; s 40-885) and tax-preferred leasing (¶23-210).

Depreciating assets

Where the expenditure is on a depreciating asset that is first used for exploration or prospecting (rather than on developing or working the mining or quarrying property, or petroleum field) and one of the 3 activity tests above is satisfied, an immediate deduction is available for the cost of the asset under the ordinary UCA provisions (ITAA97 s 40-80; ¶17-350) rather than under the exploration or prospecting provisions. Further, the balance of the general UCA provisions (from ¶17-005), including those about balancing adjustments (¶17-630), will apply. The deduction is available in the year in which the asset is first used or installed ready for use (rather than the year in which the expenditure is incurred). As a COVID-19 stimulus measure the threshold for instant asset write-offs has been significantly increased (¶17-330).

Special rules apply to consolidated groups (ITAA97 s 716-300).

Where a production licence gives the licence holder the right to carry out petroleum production activities as well as exploration, all of the expenditure is depreciable under s 40-95(10). Expenditure is not split in order to treat one part as relating to petroleum production and depreciable under s 40-95(10) and the other as relating to exploration and wholly deductible under s 40-80 (*Mitsui & Co (Australia) Ltd*).

Mining, quarrying or prospecting rights or information

An immediate deduction under s 40-80(1) for expenditure on mining, quarrying or prospecting rights or mining, quarrying or prospecting information first used in genuine exploration activities is only available in respect of the following types of expenditure:

- to create new mining information or to enhance mining information. The taxpayer may create the new information or may outsource the work to an agent. Expenditure to improve mining information is immediately deductible, regardless of whether an immediate deduction would have been available for the original information (s 40-80(1AB)(d)).
- to acquire a mining, quarrying or prospecting right or information from an Australian Government agency or entity, such as Geoscience Australia. This includes mining rights acquired through a cash bidding process.
- to acquire mining, quarrying or prospecting information in an "off the shelf" geological or geophysical data package, from someone whose main business is providing that information, such as an expert geologist or other specialist who analyses raw geological data. A geological or geophysical data package is a specific subset of mining information of a general and technical nature that does not relate to the more precise location of a particular resource in a particular tenement.

Mining, quarrying or prospecting rights and information not immediately deductible under s 40-80 are depreciable over the lesser of 15 years from the time the depreciating assets are first used, or their effective lives (¶17-015, ¶17-280). Where exploration is unsuccessful and ceases, the taxpayer may choose to immediately deduct any remaining undepreciated value. However, if the taxpayer recommences exploration or production activities on the tenement, a clawback amount may be included in assessable income. For what constitutes "use" of a mining, quarrying or prospecting right for depreciation purposes, see TD 2019/1.

For deductions for expenditure on mining, quarrying or prospecting rights and information before 14 May 2013, see the 2013 *Australian Master Tax Guide*.

A "mining, quarrying or prospecting right" is: (a) an authority, licence, permit or right (or interest therein) under Australian law to mine, quarry or prospect for minerals, petroleum or quarry materials (b) a lease of land (or interest in such lease) allowing the lessee to mine, quarry or prospect on the land, or (c) a right in respect of a building or other improvement on the land concerned or used in connection with operations on it, where such right is acquired with one of the rights referred to in (a) or (b). A right in respect of a housing and welfare facility relating to a quarrying site is excluded. Conversions of such rights are treated as a continuation of the existing right if the right ends and the new right relates to the same area.

"Mining, quarrying or prospecting information" is geological, geophysical or technical information relating to, or likely to help determine, the presence, absence or extent of deposits of minerals or quarry materials in an area (s 40-730(8)). This includes seismic information. Such information is also a depreciating asset and its decline in value is deductible over its effective life from when the taxpayer first uses it for income-producing purposes (¶17-010, ¶17-015; TR 2019/4). This definition is also relevant when considering what is ''mining information'' when determining whether shares in a mining exploration company can be principal assets (ITAA97 s 855-30; ¶12-725; *AP Energy Investments Ltd*).

The treatment of mining rights and mining information as depreciating assets has the consequence that the balancing adjustment provisions under UCA apply if a balancing adjustment event, eg sale or other disposal, occurs (¶17-630) and that certain costs can be claimed as second element costs (¶17-105).

Pre-1 July 2001 mining, quarrying and prospecting rights

Mining, quarrying or prospecting rights held before the introduction of the UCA provisions on 1 July 2001 are subject to the CGT provisions, rather than the UCA provisions (ITTPA s 40-77).

An amount received by a taxpayer for providing mining, quarrying or prospecting information to another entity is assessable income if it is not otherwise assessable as ordinary income and if the taxpayer continues to hold that information (ITAA97 s 15-40). If the taxpayer held the information before 1 July 2001, the assessable amount (or any assessable balancing adjustment) is reduced by the cost of the information incurred before that day that was not deductible under the former law (s 40-77).

The application of the above transitional provisions for pre-1 July 2001 mining rights and mining information is preserved for consolidated groups (ITTPA s 702-1: ¶8-000).

Relief for interest realignment arrangements

Roll-over relief is available to taxpayers who enter into an ''interest realignment arrangement'' (s 40-363(5)) after 14 May 2013. Under such an arrangement, each party holds mining, quarrying or prospecting rights relating to a common development project, and the parties jointly (or propose to) undertake the project to carry out mining and quarrying operations. An interest realignment arrangement occurs where additional payments are made because of changes in the perceived contributions of the parties to the common development project. The effect of the arrangement must be to align the interests that each party has in each right with their interest in the common development project. It must not involve any other transfer of a mining, quarrying or prospecting right (s 40-363(5)). If additional consideration is received as part of the adjustment, a similar outcome applies as if the consideration was made upfront; the tax outcome arises in the income year in which the adjustment payment is made (ITAA97 s 40-364). The adjustment provisions do not apply if an additional mining right is being contributed; such a transaction would be treated as a new interest alignment arrangement.

The form of relief depends on the type of rights disposed of. Broadly, where the original rights were acquired:

- after 1 July 2001 (ie UCA rights), the taxpayer may choose the balancing adjustment event roll-over under s 40-363. Any consideration other than mining, quarrying and prospecting rights forming part of the arrangement is included in the recipient's assessable income, and added to the payer's cost of the right received

- between 20 September 1985 and 1 July 2001 (ie post-CGT and pre-UCA rights), CGT roll-over relief applies such that capital gain or loss is disregarded, and the cost base of the original right disposed of is transferred to the right acquired (ITAA97 Subdiv 124-S). Further, rights received under the arrangement are deemed to have been acquired during that period (ITTPA s 40-77(1D)). Consideration other than mining, quarrying and prospecting rights forming part of the arrangement is not eligible for roll-over relief (s 124-1230), and

- before 20 September 1985 (ie pre-CGT rights), the rights received under the arrangement have pre-CGT status (s 124-1240).

Relief for farm-in farm-out (FIFO) arrangements

Tax relief is available to taxpayers entering into eligible "farm-in farm-out" (FIFO) arrangements after 14 May 2013. Under such an arrangement, the transferor/farmor transfers an interest in a mining, quarrying or prospecting right to the transferee/farmee, who provides *exploration benefits* to the transferor in return (ITAA97 s 40-1100). This includes both an *immediate* transfer, taking place at the time of agreement, and a *deferred* transfer, when the entities agree to a future transfer or grant an option relating to a future transfer.

"Exploration benefits" must be provided for an eligible FIFO arrangement to exist. This requires (s 40-1100):

(a) the transferee to either conduct (or undertake to) exploration activities, or fund (or undertake to) expenditure that the transferor incurs relating to exploration activities conducted by the transferor or another entity (other than the transferee)

(b) the benefits to relate to the part of the transferor's right not transferred under the FIFO arrangement, and

(c) the expenditure to be of a kind referred to in s 40-730 (including any amount ineligible for a deduction under s 40-730 merely because it was eligible under another provision: s 40-1100(3)(c)) or that would have been included in the transferor's cost of its mining information or in the cost of another depreciating asset that satisfied s 40-80.

The main tax consequences for the *transferor* of an eligible FIFO arrangement include:

- the value of any consideration received for disposing of a right is reduced to the extent the consideration is an exploration benefit (UCA rights: ITAA97 s 40-1105; pre-UCA rights: ITAA97 s 116-115(1)).

- the transferor ordinarily acquires a contractual right to receive exploration benefits as a CGT asset when entering into a FIFO arrangement. When this contractual right is satisfied, for example, upon receipt of the exploration benefits, CGT event C2 occurs. The cost base (and reduced cost base) of this contractual right is reduced by the market value of any entitlement to receive exploration benefits (ITAA97 s 40-1120); and the capital proceeds of the CGT event are deemed to be zero to the extent they are exploration benefits (s 116-115(2)).

- the transferor's mining right is taken to have been split into 2 depreciating assets immediately before the right is disposed of (ITAA97 s 40-115). The entire adjustable value is allocated to the retained part, though the transferor may attribute a reasonable proportion of the incidental costs of splitting the right to the part disposed (s 40-1110).

- to ensure tax neutral outcomes, deductions relating to the receipt of exploration benefits and benefits relating to the cost of mining information are reduced to the extent of the tax relief provided to the FIFO arrangement (ITAA97 ss 40-1115 and 40-1125).

The *transferee* is generally entitled to a deduction under s 40-730 for expenses incurred in conducting or funding exploration activities on the transferor's behalf. Any tax outcome arising is reduced to the extent the transferee agrees to provide exploration benefits. Accordingly, the first element of the cost base of the mining right received is reduced by the market value of the exploration benefits provided, and any income received for providing exploration benefits is treated as non-assessable non-exempt (NANE) income (ITAA97 s 40-1130). Further, CGT event D1 does not apply to bring about a capital gain for the transferee for creating a right in the transferor to receive exploration benefits (ITAA97 s 104-35(5)(g)).

A participant in a mining joint venture does not take undeducted exploration expenditure into account in calculating the balancing adjustment on disposal of interests in mining tenements to which former Div 330 applied (*Pratt Holdings Pty Ltd*; ¶19-050).

Mining exploration tax credit

The Junior Minerals Exploration Incentive (JMEI) (ITAA97 Div 418) replaces the exploration development incentive (EDI) from 2017–18 to 2020–21. The JMEI scheme facilitates the application by an explorer for tax credits distributable to resident investors in newly issued shares in exchange for tax losses in respect of greenfields exploration expenditure (s 418-80). Explorers must apply for and obtain an allocation of exploration credits from the Commissioner using the JMEI participation form. Applications are electronic and must be made in respect of each income year in which the JMEI is available, in June of the preceding income year. *Applications not lodged within the application period will not be considered.* Accordingly, applications in respect of the 2020–21 income year must have been lodged between 0:00 on 1 June 2020 and 23:59 on 30 June 2020, in respect of exploration credits up to the annual cap of $35 million (includes $5 million in unused exploration credits from a previous income year). Exploration credits are allocated on a first-come-first-serve basis subject to a cap of 5% of the annual exploration cap (or other prescribed limit) that can be allocated to any single applicant for an income year.

Once the exploration company has received a determination from the Commissioner (s 418-101) of the allocation of exploration credits for an income year, and the company has been assessed for tax for that year it may create and issue exploration credits to new investors in that year. Non-corporate investors receive a refundable tax offset, while corporate investors (other than in some cases a life insurance company) receive a franking credit. Investors receiving a JMEI tax offset can only claim it in the year to which it relates, accordingly where tax returns have already been lodged these will require amendment. Investors cannot claim credits in excess of their capital contribution. Exploration credits allocated to an explorer in respect of a particular year that are not issued to investors in that year, can be carried forward. However, explorers are required to exhaust an earlier allocation by issuing credits to earlier new investors before creating and issuing credits to new investors in the following year. Explorers creating exploration credits in excess of their maximum entitlement are subject to excess exploration credit tax and, potentially, shortfall penalties.

Exploration development incentive

The EDI was available for eligible expenditure in the income years from 2014–15 to 2016–17. It operated in a similar manner to the JMEI with some differences, the main ones in relation to the timing of the claim of EDIs, and that the distribution of the EDI was not restricted to investors in new shares. For further details see the 2017 *Australian Master Tax Guide.*

Compliance

Taxpayer compliance activity with laws on exploration expenditure deductions is outlined in PCG 2016/17.

[FITR ¶87-080, ¶87-726, ¶88-420, ¶88-960]

¶19-040 Scope of exploration or prospecting expenditure

"Exploration or prospecting" expenditure deductions are available for capital and current expenditure under ITAA97 s 40-730 where a taxpayer satisfies one or more of the "activity tests" outlined in ¶19-010. The expenditure need not be incurred in exploring or prospecting in an area for which a mining or exploration authority has been granted.

Whether a taxpayer is in the exploration or development stage is a question of fact and depends on the nature and purpose of the expenditure. The mere point in time at which expenditure is incurred does not determine its character or nature. The fact that an amount is incurred during the ''exploration phase'' (ie before a decision to mine has been made) does not determine its nature or character as ''exploratory''. Accordingly, any cost of long lead assets or early development activities (eg design work going beyond the level of detail required to evaluate a project's economic feasibility) incurred while the project is still being evaluated is not immediately deductible (TR 2017/1 para 9 to 11).

To be deductible under s 40-730, expenditure must be incurred *on* exploration or prospecting activities, ie there must be a direct or close link between the expenditure and the activities. Interest on moneys borrowed to finance exploration or prospecting do not have the required direct or close link (TR 2017/1 para 28 and 29) to be deductible as exploration or prospecting expenditure, although a deduction may be available under s 8-1; ¶16-740ff.

Exploration or prospecting is not exhaustively defined and includes its ordinary meaning, ie the discovery and identification of the existence, extent and nature of minerals; searching to discover the resource; the process of ascertaining the size of the discovery and appraising its physical characteristics; and activities that are incidental to (or closely connected with) actual exploration or prospecting, as to be reasonably considered part of it (TR 2017/1 para 35 and 36).

Exploration or prospecting includes, for general mining and quarrying: (a) geological mapping, geophysical surveys, systematic searches for areas containing minerals (other than petroleum) or quarry materials and searches by drilling or other means within those areas, and (b) searches for ore within, or near, an ore-body or searches for quarry materials by drives, shafts, cross-cuts, winzes, rises and drilling. In the case of petroleum mining, it includes: (a) geological, geophysical and geochemical surveys, and (b) exploration drilling and appraisal drilling.

Feasibility studies to evaluate the economic feasibility of mining minerals, petroleum or quarry materials once they have been discovered also qualify as exploration or prospecting. This includes studies undertaken for multiple purposes if, at least to a ''non-trivial extent'', they relate to assessing the economic viability of mining; there is no need for the studies to have a substantial, main or exclusive purpose of assessing the viability of mining (TR 2017/1 para 39). Matters relevant in interpreting the scope of feasibility studies and their deductibility are set out in TR 2017/1 para 38. The cost of other feasibility studies may be deductible as pooled project expenditure (ITAA97 Subdiv 40-I; ¶19-050). Certain feasibility study costs (eg into potential markets for certain minerals) may be deductible under the general deduction rules where the taxpayer has an existing mining or exploration business and is not, like the taxpayers in *Griffin* and *Esso* (¶16-154), extending its activities into a new area.

Exploration or prospecting also includes obtaining mining, quarrying or prospecting information (¶19-010) associated with the search for, and evaluation of, areas containing minerals, petroleum or quarry materials.

TR 2014/9 considers the meaning of petroleum exploration for PRRT purposes (¶19-003).

[FITR ¶88-430]

Mining or Infrastructure Project Pools

¶19-050 Deduction for pooled project expenditure

Certain mining project expenditure, and related transport expenditure or other infrastructure project expenditure (that is not the cost of a ''depreciating asset'': see below) may be deductible over the estimated life of the project (ITAA97 Subdiv 40-I: ss 40-830 to 40-885). The deduction is *not* limited to expenditure related to mining projects.

The deduction is calculated in accordance with the formula:

$$\frac{\text{pool value} \times 200\%^{1}}{\text{project pool life}}$$

[1] For project pools only containing project amounts incurred on or after 10 May 2006, for projects that start to operate on or after that day (s 40-832(1)). Prior to that date the applicable rate is 150%. The 200% rate does not apply to a taxpayer who abandons, sells or otherwise disposes of a project for the purpose of reviving the same project so as to qualify for the increased rate.

"Project pool life" (s 40-830(3)) is the number of years (including fractions of years) from when the taxpayer's project starts to operate until it stops operating (s 40-845; ID 2004/580). A project starts to operate when the taxpayer starts to do the things that produce assessable income (eg in the case of a mining operation, the project starts to operate when the extraction activities start). Project pool life is the *most recently recalculated* project life, as "project life" may be recalculated. It is the taxpayer's project and not other parties' projects that is the relevant project.

To make an estimate of project life, the taxpayer must take into account all relevant factors: factors personal to the taxpayer (eg how long the taxpayer intends to carry on the project) are not relevant, but factors outside the taxpayer's control (eg legislative or environmental restrictions or normal commercial practices) are relevant. The project must have a finite project life when the expenditure is incurred. If there is no finite project life, there is no relevant project (TR 2005/4; ID 2007/3). The project must have sufficient substance and be sufficiently identifiable (ie more than an idea or speculation) that it can be said that the expenditure is directly connected with it.

For the first income year that a "project amount" is allocated to a pool, "pool value" is the amount (net of GST and adjustments (ITAA97 s 27-100)) so allocated. In subsequent years, it is the previous year's closing pool balance plus any amounts allocated during the income year. The closing pool value is the closing pool value for the previous year, plus any amount allocated to the pool during the year, less any amount that would have been deductible from the pool during the year, had the project operated wholly for taxable purposes during the year.

In each year, the deduction is limited to the amount of the undeducted expenditure (ie the pool value). The deduction is reduced to reflect the extent to which the project operates for non-taxable purposes. The deduction becomes available for the first income year in which the project starts to operate. There is no apportionment to reflect the fact that a project amount was incurred during the year or that the project started or ended during the year.

If the project is abandoned, sold or otherwise disposed of, the whole undeducted amount becomes deductible in that year. A project can be abandoned at any time after it starts, even before it starts operating for a taxable purpose (eg if the taxpayer's tender for a property development is unsuccessful: ID 2003/728). The taxpayer's assessable income for the income year includes any amount received for the abandonment, sale or disposal. See also ID 2004/581.

In any income year, the taxpayer's assessable income includes other capital amounts derived in relation to a project amount, or something on which the project amount was expended.

Expenditure incurred in a foreign currency may be subject to the currency conversion rules (¶23-070) and foreign exchange gains and losses rules (¶23-075). If the gain or loss arises in relation to a project amount that became due for payment within 12 months of being incurred, the pool value for the year in which the amount was incurred is reduced by the gain (or increased by the loss) (ITAA97 ss 775-70, 775-75).

The deduction is subject to the rules for non-arm's length dealings (¶17-045) and for tax-preferred leasing (¶23-210).

For the deductibility of pre-1 January 2001 mining and quarrying expenditure, see below.

▶ Example: Pooled project expenditure

In Year 1, Rio Blanco Mining Co Ltd incurs mining capital expenditure of $3 million in respect of a mine at which time it has an estimated life of 10 years. In Year 2, it incurs expenditure of $1.2 million. Remaining project life is 9 years. The taxpayer is entitled to the following deductions in respect of that expenditure:

Year 1	
Pool value	$3,000,000
Less: Deduction[1]	600,000
Closing pool balance (and opening pool balance for Year 2)	$2,400,000
Year 2	
Pooled expenditure	$1,200,000
Less: Deduction[2]	800,000
Closing pool balance (and opening pool balance for Year 3)	$2,800,000

[1] In Year 1, the deduction is calculated as $\frac{\$3,000,000}{10} \times 200\%$.

[2] In Year 2, the deduction is calculated as $\frac{\$3,600,000}{9} \times 200\%$.

Project amount

A "project amount" consists of 2 types of expenditure provided that they: (a) are not otherwise deductible, and (b) do not form part of the cost of a depreciating asset held by the taxpayer. The first type of expenditure is "mining capital expenditure" that is directly connected with carrying on the mining operations in relation to which the expenditure is incurred (¶19-070), or "transport capital expenditure" that is directly connected with carrying on the business in relation to which the expenditure is incurred (¶19-090).

The second type of expenditure is infrastructure expenditure that is directly connected with a project carried on or proposed to be carried on for a "taxable purpose" (not necessarily a mining project) (s 40-840(2); ¶19-060). The words "carried on" require continuity of activity or active participation by the taxpayer (mere receipt of rental income is insufficient: TR 2005/4).

Something is done for a "taxable purpose" if it is done: (a) for the purpose of gaining or producing assessable income, or (b) in carrying on a business for the purpose of gaining or producing assessable income (eg ID 2007/3). Activities that are likely to produce a capital gain (eg the subdivision of land) do not satisfy the test, even though such gain is included in assessable income (ID 2005/157).

Depreciating assets

The cost of "depreciating assets" (¶17-015) does not form part of the project amount. A deduction for the decline in value of depreciating assets used for taxable purposes (including mining purposes) may be available under the UCA (depreciating asset) provisions (from ¶17-005) or the capital works provisions (from ¶20-470). Mudlakes, initial containment areas, dykes, tailings dams and other residue and waste storage or disposal facilities are plant and subject to the UCA provisions. See TR 1999/2 in relation to the cost of removal and disposal of overburden.

Mining operations

"Mining operations" comprise: (a) mining operations on a mining property for the extraction of minerals (other than petroleum) from their natural site, being operations carried on for assessable income-producing purposes (b) mining operations for the purpose of obtaining "petroleum" (s 40-730(6)) for assessable income-producing purposes ("petroleum" does not include coal and oil shale, even though they are sources of hydrocarbons (*Esso*)), and (c) quarrying operations on a quarrying property for extracting quarry materials from their natural site for assessable income-producing purposes.

Mining operations may include work done on or near the site that is preliminary or ancillary to the actual winning of the mineral (*Broken Hill*). The recovery of a mineral from the solution in which it occurs is a mining operation (*ICI Australia*).

Foreign exchange losses a mining company incurs in repaying foreign currency denominated loans (used to incur mining capital expenditure) are incurred in connection with the capital structure of the business itself not in carrying on prescribed mining operations (*Robe River Mining*). Payment made by the buyer of a mine to the seller for the removal of mine overburden is part of the purchase price of the mine not mining capital expenditure (*QCT Resources*).

Although the distinction between mining and quarrying expenditure for the purpose of deducting project expenditure is no longer relevant since 1 July 2001, it remains relevant because deductions are available for housing and welfare expenditure for mining but not quarrying operations (¶19-070) and the ordinary meaning of mining operations does not include quarrying operations. Mining operations refer to the extraction of useful minerals generally, whereas quarrying operations refer more specifically to the extraction of materials for building or civil engineering purposes. Mining operations include open cut extraction of gypsum (*Waratah Gypsum*); kaolin (IT 353), and open cut extraction of limestone for use in cement production (*North Australian Cement*).

Taxable purposes

A "taxable purpose" is the purpose of producing assessable income, the purpose of exploration or prospecting, the purpose of mining site rehabilitation or environmental protection activities (ITAA97 s 40-25).

Pre-1 July 2001 expenditure

Mining capital expenditure and mining transport expenditure (¶19-090) incurred before 1 July 2001 was deductible under ITAA97 former Div 330 over the shorter of the life of the mine or quarry, or 10 years (mining) or 20 years (quarrying). Under transitional provisions, unrecouped mining capital expenditure at 30 June 2001 is deducted as a depreciating asset using the prime cost method over the shorter of the remainder of the 10-year period (20 years for quarrying) and the life of the project. For details of the pre-1 July 2001 provisions, see the 2001 *Australian Master Tax Guide* and earlier editions.

[FITR ¶86-885, ¶88-440, ¶88-650]

¶19-060 Project infrastructure expenditure

As well as "mining capital expenditure" (¶19-070) and "transport capital expenditure" (¶19-090), a "project amount" (¶19-050) includes project infrastructure expenditure that is not otherwise deductible and that does not form part of the cost of a depreciating asset held by the taxpayer. The infrastructure expenditure must be directly connected with a project (not necessarily a mining project) carried on or proposed to be carried on for a "taxable purpose" (¶19-050; eg ID 2003/206 to ID 2003/208) and must be expenditure of an amount (s 40-840(2)):

- to create or upgrade community facilities associated with the project (eg a public road: ID 2003/1001)
- for site preparation costs for a depreciating asset (other than, for horticultural plants, expenditure in draining swamp or low-lying land, or expenditure in clearing land)
- for feasibility studies for the project (eg ID 2004/253, ID 2004/254)
- for environmental assessments for the project (eg ID 2004/582).
- incurred to obtain information associated with the project (eg ID 2004/253, ID 2004/583)
- incurred to obtain a right to intellectual property (¶17-015), or
- incurred for ornamental trees or shrubs.

[FITR ¶88-690]

¶19-070 What is mining capital expenditure?

Expenditure incurred in establishing, developing, extending or rejuvenating a mine is generally capital in nature (*Ampol Exploration Ltd*). A deduction may be available over the life of a project for a project amount consisting of mining capital expenditure that is directly connected with carrying on mining operations in relation to the expenditure (¶19-050). See TR 95/36 for what constitutes ''capital'' expenditure in the mining and quarrying industries. ''Mining capital expenditure'' of a mining or quarrying operator means capital expenditure incurred on the following:

- carrying on mining operations (¶19-050), including the cost of establishing access to an underground ore body; however, further costs maintaining access to the ore body as it is mined are on revenue account. In strip or open pit mining, mining capital expenditure includes the cost of constructing access roads or ramps to the ore body; however, removal of overburden to allow extraction is a revenue cost. The costs of diverting a highway to gain access to reserves under and beyond the road were considered mining capital expenditure in *Pine Creek Goldfields*. The treatment of haulage roads in open pit mining depends on their location and the size of the pit (TR 95/36)
- site preparation, buildings and improvements (such as workshops, storage facilities and offices), including expenditure on providing, or contributing to the cost of providing, services (on-site water, light or power) and access to, or communication with, the site of the mining operations
- buildings used in operating or maintaining treatment plant. ''Treatment'' broadly includes all processes applied to extracted ore up to and including the concentration stage, excluding sintering and calcining, and producing alumina or iron pellets or agglomerates (s 40-875(2))
- buildings or other facilities for the storage (before or after treatment) of minerals (including petroleum) and quarry materials, or to facilitate their treatment
- housing and welfare facilities, where the expenditure is incurred in carrying on mining (but not quarrying) operations. This refers to expenditure on health, education, recreation or similar facilities or facilities for meals, where the facilities are for the use of the taxpayer's or a contractor's employees and their dependants. It also includes expenditure on residential accommodation provided *by the taxpayer* at or adjacent to the mine site. Employees' housing located 50 km from a mine site was considered *adjacent to* the site in *BHP Minerals*. Also included is expenditure on infrastructure works such as water, light, power, and access to or communication with the facilities referred to above.

See also ID 2004/795, ID 2004/796 and ID 2004/797 in relation to hydraulic fracture stimulation.

Exclusions from mining capital expenditure

Mining capital expenditure does *not* include the following expenditure:

- railway lines, roads, pipelines or other facilities used to any extent in transporting minerals, quarry materials or their products *away from the site*. Expenditure on such facilities may be deductible as transport capital expenditure (¶19-090). This exclusion does not apply to expenditure on facilities used for transport *wholly within the mining or quarrying site*, such as on pipelines that form part of the mining or petroleum operations (eg flow lines from the wellhead to the separator)
- buildings, works, or other improvements constructed or acquired for use in the establishment, use or operation of port or shipping facilities (eg townships, wharves, roads, and harbour surveys and dredging)
- an office building not located at, or adjacent to, the site of the mining or quarrying operations
- housing and welfare facilities *relating to quarrying operations* (on the basis that quarries are usually located near existing urban areas). For the difference between mining and quarrying operations, see ¶19-050.

[FITR ¶88-725 – ¶88-740]

¶19-090 Mining and quarrying transport expenditure

Capital expenditure incurred on transport facilities and ancillary works used primarily and principally in transporting the products of mining and quarrying operations *away from the site* of those operations is deductible as transport capital expenditure over the effective life of the project (ITAA97 ss 40-865 to 40-875: ¶19-050).

The effective life of the project is from the first income year in which the project starts to operate until it stops operating (¶19-050). See ¶19-050 for the deductibility of pre-1 January 2001 mining or quarrying transport expenditure.

Deductions for the decline in value of depreciating assets used in mining or quarrying transport must be claimed under the general UCA (depreciating asset) provisions (¶17-010).

"Transport facility"

A ''transport facility'' is a railway, road, pipeline, port facility, shipping facility or other facility used primarily and principally for mining or quarrying transport. Expenditure on necessary earthworks, bridges, tunnels and cuttings, as well as payments to landholders as compensation or for construction rights; contributions to someone else's expenditure on the above facilities (ID 2012/17) or to the cost of publicly owned railway rolling stock qualify. Although the cost of ships, railway rolling stock and road vehicles does not qualify for the special deduction, a deduction for their decline in value may be available under the UCA provisions (¶17-000). Also excluded from deduction as transport capital expenditure is the cost of housing and welfare facilities (generally allowable as mining capital expenditure: ¶19-070) and infrastructure works (eg to provide water, light or power) at a port facility or other shipping facility. The cost of facilities for the transport of refined petroleum or petroleum reticulated to consumers does not qualify for the deduction.

Expenditure on port facilities or other facilities for ships that would be deductible as transport capital expenditure would include expenditure (other than on depreciating assets: ¶17-015) on navigational aids, the construction of breakwaters, site works and land reclamation, channel dredging, the provision of access roads and communications, and structural improvements at a port to provide storage facilities for products or materials awaiting shipment.

Connection with taxable purpose

To attract the special deduction for transport facilities, the expenditure must be: (a) directly connected with carrying on the business in relation to which the expenditure was incurred, and (b) incurred in carrying on a business for a "taxable purpose" (¶19-050) (eg the purpose of gaining assessable income). A deduction for a contribution to cost is not denied merely because the facility is owned or operated by a tax-exempt public authority or because the operator does not produce the products transported.

Off-site transport

A further condition of deductibility is that the transport facility must be used primarily and principally for mining or quarrying transport, ie for off-site transport of minerals or quarry materials obtained by persons in carrying on "mining or quarrying operations" (¶19-050), or transport of processed materials produced from quarry materials and minerals other than petroleum. The *principal and primary* use test should be applied with reference to all users of the facilities. The test would be satisfied where the use of a road for minerals transport in an income year exceeds 50% of total use by weight and 25% of total use by number of vehicles. The test can be applied independently for different road sections, and a recognised statistical sampling method may be used. Temporary cessation of use does not represent termination of use triggering automatic disallowance of deductions (TD 93/52, TD 93/53).

Other mining transport expenditure

Capital expenditure on facilities used for transport in connection with mining or quarrying operations wholly *within the site* of the operations is deductible as mining capital expenditure over the life of the project (¶19-050, ¶19-070). The deduction is only available if no other deduction for the expenditure is allowable.

Expenditure on transport as part of exploration or prospecting activities is immediately deductible as exploration or prospecting expenditure (¶19-010).

[FITR ¶88-750 – ¶88-780]

Site Rehabilitation Expenditure

¶19-100 Rehabilitating the site

Expenditure incurred in rehabilitating a mine, quarry or petroleum site (eg in removing redundant structures or restoring the terrain) is capital expenditure and not deductible as a revenue expense (although costs incurred by a mining company cleaning up residential land contaminated by landfill from a former mine site were deductible as a revenue expense in *Associated Minerals Consolidated*). However, an immediate deduction is available for current and capital expenditure (net of GST and adjustments (ITAA97 s 27-105)) on rehabilitation of sites (Australian and foreign) that have been used by the taxpayer for "mining or quarrying operations" (¶19-050), or ancillary activities (ITAA97 ss 40-735 to 40-745). Sites on which "exploration or prospecting" (¶19-040) was conducted also qualify, as do sites on which there are depreciating assets used in mining, quarrying or petroleum operations. "Ancillary mining activities" include preparing a site for mining, quarrying or petroleum operations, providing infrastructure for such a site, treating minerals or quarry materials, storing minerals and quarry materials (before or after treatment), and liquefying natural gas.

"Mining site rehabilitation" involves the full or partial restoration of the site to a reasonable approximation of its "pre-mining condition", ie its condition before general mining, quarrying or petroleum operations, exploration or prospecting or ancillary activities commenced. The removal or collapsing of an offshore oil platform would be a petroleum industry rehabilitation activity.

Expenditure incurred in respect of the acquisition of land, the construction of buildings, rehabilitation bonds or securities required under state laws, or housing and welfare or depreciating assets (¶17-015) is not deductible as rehabilitation expenditure (ITAA97 ss 40-45, 40-745). However, use of property for rehabilitation is taken to be a taxable purpose, and a deduction may be available for the decline in value of depreciating assets, (¶17-000) and buildings may be eligible for a capital works deduction (¶20-470).

Schemes under which a mining company seeks an immediate deduction for a payment to an offshore entity that agrees to carry out mine site rehabilitation in the future are the subject of TA 2009/3.

The seller of a mining tenement does not incur mining site rehabilitation expenditure where it makes payments to the buyer who incurs that expenditure after the sale (ID 2008/72). See TR 1999/2 for the deductibility of expenditure incurred on tailings dams or similar mining residue, waste storage or disposal facilities.

An immediate write-off of capital expenditure incurred on "environmental protection activities" is also available for a broader range of expenditure (eg preventive expenditure) than under the mine site rehabilitation measures (¶19-110).

Mining site rehabilitation expenditure that is deductible under this special provision or under another provision may only be deducted once, under the most appropriate provision (¶16-100). The rules about recoupments (¶10-270), non-arm's length dealings (¶17-045) and tax-preferred leasing (¶23-210) apply to rehabilitation expenditure.

Where the deductibility of expenditure under ITAA97 s 8-1 (¶16-000) is restricted by some other provision, (other than s 8-1 itself) that provision applies to the mining site rehabilitation provisions.

[FITR ¶88-460 – ¶88-550]

Environmental Protection

¶19-110 Deduction for environmental protection activities

Expenditure (net of GST and adjustments (ITAA97 s 27-105)), whether capital or revenue, that is incurred for the sole or dominant purpose of carrying on "environmental protection activities" is deductible in the income year in which it is incurred (ITAA97 ss 40-755 to 40-765). No deduction is available if protection of the environment is only a residual or subsidiary purpose of the taxpayer. If the expenditure is incurred for 2 or more purposes (eg environmental protection and improving the resale value of the land), it is necessary to establish the dominant purpose (TR 2020/2). The provisions do not accommodate apportionment on a fair and reasonable basis of a single outlay that serves multiple purposes indifferently. A deduction is also available for the decline in value of depreciating assets used for environmental protection activities (¶17-010), and construction costs may be deductible under the capital works provisions (¶20-470). TR 2020/2 outlines, with numerous examples, the operation of the provisions.

▶ Example: Environmental protection activities

A company buys a factory on polluted land. After testing the whole site, the contaminated portion is found to be 25%. All the contaminated soil is removed, clean soil is used to replace the contaminated soil and level the site. The cost of the fresh soil used for the purpose of replacing the removed soil, as well as testing for contaminants and removing the contaminated soil, is fully deductible.

The deduction does *not* apply to:

- expenditure that is deductible under another provision such as the general deduction provisions (¶16-010), the UCA provisions dealing with depreciating assets (¶17-000) or the project infrastructure expenditure provisions (¶19-060)
- the cost of acquiring land or the capital cost of constructing or altering buildings, structures or structural improvements, or
- environmental bonds or securities (eg a contribution to a fund for environmental disasters; a contingency fund) deposited, paid or subscribed by a taxpayer (such amounts may be deductible under the general deduction provisions: ¶16-010).

The rules about recoupments (¶10-270), non-arm's length dealings (¶17-045) and tax-preferred leasing (¶23-210) apply to environmental protection expenditure.

Where the deductibility of expenditure under ITAA97 s 8-1 (¶16-000) is limited by a provision (other than s 8-1 itself), that provision also applies to limit the environmental protection deduction.

Environmental protection activities

An "environmental protection activity" is an activity carried on in preventing, fighting or remedying pollution; or treating, cleaning up, removing or storing waste, where the pollution or waste:

- has resulted, or is likely to result, from an earning activity that was, is, or is proposed to be carried on by the taxpayer
- is on or from a site on which the taxpayer carried on, carries on, or proposes to carry on, an earning activity; or on which the taxpayer's predecessor (immediate or otherwise) carried on a business activity (eg if a lake is polluted by effluent discharged from a factory upstream, cleaning up the lake will be an environmental protection activity)

Pollution includes noise pollution and contamination by harmful or potentially dangerous substances, such as explosive chemicals, asbestos and chlorofluorocarbon gases. Merely improving the aesthetics of a site (eg vegetating the area beside a road) is not preventing, fighting or remedying pollution; nor will removing a redundant structure unless it is contaminated, or it is removed to enable pollution under it to be rectified.

Waste removal, treatment and storage may include any operation that leads to resource recovery, recycling, reclamation or reuse of waste at any stage of an industrial process and the disposal of waste by any means (eg by landfill, chemical conversion or incineration). This includes removing wood residue from a taxpayer's timber processing activities; geological sequestration of greenhouse gases such as carbon dioxide or other materials (TR 2008/6).

An earning activity is an activity, including an investment activity, carried on or proposed to be carried on for the purpose of producing assessable income, exploration or prospecting, or mining site rehabilitation. It also includes leasing a site or granting a right to use a site. The cost of demolishing an asbestos shed on a rental property is deductible. An investment made for the purpose of producing a net capital gain is not an earning activity.

Where more than one person is in a position to carry out an environmental protection activity on a particular site (eg a lessor who earns income from leasing a site and a lessee who carries on a business on the site), the deduction will be allowable to whomever incurs the expenditure. TR 2020/2 para 51 (Example 1) envisages a limitation on activities carried on "for" the taxpayer; the seller of a mining tenement does not carry on environmental protection activities where it makes payments to the buyer who carries on those activities after the sale.

Where the taxpayer's earning activity consists of a business acquired from a person who, or whose predecessor (immediate or otherwise), carried on that business on another site (the "old site"), expenditure on environmental protection activities in relation to pollution of, or waste on the old site, or pollution or waste from the old site, will be deductible provided the taxpayer acquired that business and carries it on substantially unchanged. Passive investment of renting a property does not satisfy this requirement.

[FITR ¶88-510ff]

¶19-120 Carbon sink forests

A deduction is available for the cost of establishing a qualifying carbon sink forest (ITAA97 Subdiv 40-J (ss 40-1000 to 40-1025)). An amount that is deductible under these provisions would not be deductible under ITAA97 Subdiv 40-G (landcare operations (¶18-100): s 40-630(2C)).

Qualifying conditions

The deduction is available under s 40-1010 if all of the following conditions are met:

(a) the trees are established in an income year

(b) the taxpayer or another entity as the "establishing entity" incurs the expenditure in the income year or an earlier income year for establishing the trees

(c) the establishing entity is carrying on a business in the income year

(d) the establishing entity's primary and principal purpose in establishing the trees is carbon sequestration by the trees, ie the process by which trees absorb carbon dioxide from the atmosphere (s 40-1015)

(e) the establishing entity did not establish the trees for the purpose of felling the trees or using the trees for commercial horticulture

(f) the expenditure was not incurred under a managed investment scheme or a forestry managed investment scheme (¶18-125).

The establishing entity must give the Commissioner a statement in an approved form (NAT 72196) that the following specific conditions relating to the trees are met:

(a) at the end of the income year, the trees occupy a continuous land area in Australia of 0.2 hectares or more

(b) at the time the trees are established, it is more likely than not that they will attain a crown cover of 20% or more and reach a height of at least 2 metres

(c) on 1 January 1990, the area occupied by the trees was clear of other trees that satisfied (b)

(d) the establishment of the trees meets the requirements of the *Environmental and Natural Resource Management in relation to the Establishment of Trees for the purposes of Carbon Sequestration Guidelines* (*Legislative Instrument* F2018L01578).

Expenditure is *not deductible* if the Climate Change Secretary gives the Commissioner a notice in relation to the trees. The decision to give a notice is reviewable by the AAT.

In addition, one of the following ownership conditions must be satisfied:

- the taxpayer owns the trees and any holder of a lesser interest in the land (eg licensee or lessee) does not use the land for the primary and principal purpose of carbon sequestration

- the trees occupy land held under a lease or under a quasi-ownership right granted by an exempt Australian or foreign government agency and the lease or right enables the taxpayer to use the land for the primary and principal purpose of carbon sequestration (and any holder of lesser interests does not use the land for that purpose), or
- the taxpayer holds a licence relating to the land occupied by the trees and uses the land for the primary and principal purpose of carbon sequestration, as a result of holding the licence.

Calculation of deduction

The deduction is calculated using the formula in s 40-1005(2) (which is the same as that used for horticultural plants (¶18-070)) using a write-off rate of 7%. The ‘‘write-off days in income year’’ is the number of days in the income year:

(a) that occur within the period starting on the first day of the income year in which the trees are established and ending 14 years and 105 days after that day

(b) on which the taxpayer used the land occupied by the trees for the primary and principal purpose of carbon sequestration, and

(c) on which the taxpayer satisfies the ownership conditions (see above).

The deduction is limited to the amount of capital expenditure incurred on establishing the trees up to the time when they are destroyed. Where a tree is destroyed during an income year, a deduction is available to the extent that any undeducted expenditure in relation to the tree exceeds any amounts received under an insurance policy or otherwise in respect of the destruction (s 40-1030).

If the expenditure incurred under a non-arm’s length arrangement exceeds the market value of what it was for, the amount of expenditure is limited to that market value (s 40-1025).

There is no deduction for the cost of purchasing land on which a carbon sink forest is established (ID 2009/60), nor is expenditure incurred in draining swamp or low-lying land, or in clearing land deductible (s 40-1020).

An eligible taxpayer who acquires trees from another entity may require the last taxpayer who deducted an amount for the trees to provide information about the amount of the expenditure deductible and the income year in which the trees were established (s 40-1035).

[FITR ¶88-850 – ¶88-880]

¶19-130 Emissions units

Division 420 ITAA97 governs the income tax treatment of acquiring, holding and surrendering emissions units. Emissions units include ACCUs (see below), Kyoto units and, before the carbon pricing regime was abolished, ‘‘carbon units’’ and prescribed international units (ITAA97 s 420-10). Together with other provisions, for holders of registered emissions units:

- the cost of acquiring units is generally deductible (s 420-15). However, where the purchase price for emission units that come into existence at a future time is an outgoing not necessarily incurred in carrying on the taxpayer’s business the deduction is not allowable *Academy Cleaning & Security Pty Ltd*. Part IVA and Sch 1 Div 290 TAA (promoter penalty rules (¶30-300; *Rowntree*)) may also apply to a scheme where a taxpayer pays a deposit on entering into a purchase agreement and immediately seeks to claim a deduction for the full purchase price
- the proceeds of disposing of units are assessable (s 420-25)

- emissions units are not trading stock (s 70-12). A rolling balance tax accounting system applies under which the value of units is compared at the start and the end of the income year; any increase in value included in assessable income, any decrease an allowable deduction (Subdiv 420-D)
- the holder of emissions units must make an irrevocable choice to value them using either the first-in first-out method, the actual cost method, or market value (¶9-200)
- capital gains and losses from emissions units, and rights to receive a free unit or an ACCU, are not subject to capital gains tax (s 118-15; ID 2011/26)
- the rules about taxation of financial arrangements in Div 230 do not apply to emissions units (ITAA97 s 230-481), although they may apply to derivatives of emissions units.

Supplies of eligible emissions units are GST-free (GST Act s 38-590; ¶34-165). The normal GST rules apply to registered emissions units that are *not* eligible emissions units and payments of grants of government assistance and other transactions under the former carbon pricing regime. Trading in financial derivatives of eligible emissions units is an input taxed financial supply.

ACCUs

An Australian carbon credit unit (ACCU) represents one tonne of carbon dioxide equivalent stored or avoided by a project. ACCUs are issued by the Clean Energy Regulator for greenhouse gas abatement activities undertaken as part of the government's Emissions Reduction Fund (¶19-135). The issuance of ACCUs is governed by the *Carbon Credits (Carbon Farming Initiative) Act 2011* and related rules and regulations. ACCUs can be sold to generate income, either to the government through a carbon abatement contract, or in the secondary market.

[FITR ¶390-015]

¶19-135 Other climate change initiatives

Withholding tax incentive for green buildings

A final withholding tax rate of 10% applies to payments from eligible clean building managed investment trusts made to foreign residents in countries with which Australia has effective exchange of information agreements. That rate applies to eligible trusts holding office buildings, retail centres and non-residential accommodation built after June 2012 that meet energy efficiency standards.

Emissions Reduction Fund

The Emissions Reduction Fund (ERF) enacted by the *Carbon Credits (Carbon Farming Initiative) Act 2011* is a voluntary scheme administered by the Clean Energy Regulator to encourage organisations and individuals to adopt practices and technologies to reduce their emissions.

A number of activities are eligible under the scheme and participants can earn ACCUs (¶19-130) for emissions reductions. The ERF also has a safeguard mechanism to encourage large businesses to keep their emissions within historical levels (see www.cleanenergyregulator.gov.au), to ensure the emission reductions are not displaced significantly by a rise in emissions elsewhere in the economy.

[FITR ¶355-700, ¶374-100]

Chapter 20 R&D • Films • Capital Works • NRAS • Innovation Incentives

Overview of Incentives

¶20-000 Available tax incentives

This chapter deals with the following special incentives for taxpayers:

- business expenditure on research and development (R&D) (¶20-150)
- the film concessions (¶20-330)
- the deduction for capital works expenditure (¶20-470)
- the national rental affordability scheme (¶20-600), and
- tax measures relating to the National Innovation and Science Agenda (¶20-700).

The availability of these concessions may be subject to the operation of special provisions dealing with limited recourse finance (¶23-260), certain leasing arrangements (¶23-210) and commercial debt forgiveness (¶16-910).

Foreign currency denominated amounts may be subject to the foreign currency conversion rules (¶23-070) and the foreign exchange gains and losses rules (¶23-075).

Research and Development

¶20-150 Outline of research and development (R&D) tax incentive

Companies that conduct R&D activities may be able to claim a tax incentive for their business expenditure on R&D (BERD). BERD is defined by the OECD's Frascati manual and its application to the tax incentive by ITAA97 Div 355. BERD can be to create new knowledge in ''basic or applied research'' or ''experimental development''. For the majority of companies, R&D is in the ''experimental development'' of new or improved products, processes, materials, services and devices. The incentives apply where the company needs to undertake experimental activities as part of the research or to develop the new or improved outcomes.

▶ Example

Crossing Pty Ltd designs and builds bridges. Where a bridge project is a simple adaptation of existing designs using standard construction methods and materials within known parameters, then these new bridges will not require R&D activities. However, a bridge may use an innovative design, new materials or improved construction methods or it may push existing understandings or parameters. If so then parts of the design, approval, construction and testing of the bridge will need to include R&D experiments.

The R&D tax incentive (¶20-160) provides a tax offset for the following expenditure:

(1) R&D expenditure (eg labour, contractors, consumables, services, hired equipment, software and feedstock inputs to experimental production trials) under s 355-205

(2) the decline in value of R&D assets (ie tax depreciation on tangible depreciating assets and non-building capital works assets used partly or exclusively to undertake R&D activities) — ss 355-305 and 355-520. Where the asset is used partly for R&D, the capital allowance will need to be apportioned

(3) balancing adjustments for these R&D assets — ss 355-315 and 355-580. Where a capital asset is used partly for R&D purposes, the adjustment on disposal is apportioned under ss 40-292 and 40-293

(4) R&D expenditure incurred by an associate in an earlier year — s 355-480, and

(5) R&D expenditure with an unassociated Research Service Provider (RSP) or as a contribution to a Cooperative Research Centre (CRC) — s 355-580.

The sum of expenditure on the first 4 items must exceed $20,000 pa to be eligible for the tax offset. However, there is no minimum expenditure requirement for RSP expenditure or CRC contributions. Certain entities with an aggregated turnover of less than $20 million may be eligible for a refundable tax offset at 43.5% on these expenditures. All other eligible entities may be entitled to a non-refundable carry-forward tax offset at 38.5% on these expenditures (¶20-170).

[FITR ¶335-001, ¶335-003, ¶335-005, ¶335-010]

¶20-160 The R&D tax incentive

The R&D tax incentive is a broadly based, activity-driven program that allows businesses to access tax offsets for expenditure on eligible activities. However, these R&D activities must be registered with Industry, Innovation and Science Australia, through AusIndustry, under Pt III of the *Industry Research and Development Act 1986* (IR&D Act).

ITAA97 Div 355, and s 355-100 in particular, provide for 2 R&D tax offsets depending on the size of the R&D business:

- the refundable tax offset at 43.5% for the first $100 million of eligible expenditure for eligible entities with an aggregated group turnover of less than $20 million (as determined under s 328-115), provided they are not controlled by income tax exempt entities, and
- the non-refundable tax offset at 38.5% for the first $100 million of eligible expenditure for all other eligible entities. Unused non-refundable offset amounts may be able to be carried forward to future income years under s 63-10(1).

The limit of $100 million applies on the amount of R&D expenditure that a company can claim as an offset at these uplifted rates under the incentive. If a company exceeds this amount, the offset claimable on the excess is reduced to the applicable corporate tax rate: ¶42-025 (¶20-170).

As the tax offset replaces tax deductions that may otherwise be available, the net after tax benefit of the offset is the difference between the tax offset rate and the applicable company tax rate. However, there is a timing benefit for companies eligible for the refundable offset if they are in tax loss.

The object of the rules is to encourage industry to conduct R&D activities that might otherwise not be conducted because of an uncertain return from the activities, where the knowledge gained is likely to benefit the wider Australian economy. This is achieved by providing a tax incentive for industry to conduct, in a scientific way, experimental activities for the purpose of generating new knowledge or information in either a general or applied form. As the incentive is meant to encourage development activities as well as research, it includes activities to develop new or improved materials, products, devices, processes or services. This can include production activities either as core experimental R&D activities or as activities that are directly related to these unless these latter supporting activities are done primarily for a dominant purpose other than R&D.

The incentive is jointly administered by Industry, Innovation and Science Australia (assisted by AusIndustry) and the ATO. Industry, Innovation and Science Australia is primarily responsible for administering the technical eligibility and registration of R&D activities under IR&D Act. Further information on the application process of applying for the incentive can be found at business.gov.au. The ATO works closely with AusIndustry in the guidance and review processes to encourage and ensure compliance in the self-assessment of eligibility for the tax credit and in documentary and administrative processes to support the taxpayer's R&D claim.

Changes to the R&D tax incentive for years commencing after 30 June 2021

The *Treasury Laws Amendment (A Tax Plan for the COVID-19 Economic Recovery) Act 2020* introduces a number of changes to the R&D tax incentive for years commencing on or after 1 July 2021. These include:

- Increasing the R&D expenditure threshold from $100 million to $150 million and making this threshold permanent. R&D expenditure over this threshold will continue to attract a tax offset equal to the R&D entity's company tax rate.
- Linking the R&D tax offset for refundable R&D tax offset claimants to the claimants' corporate tax rates plus an 18.5% premium on expenditure under the threshold. Effectively this will keep the refundable tax offset at 43.5% with a base rate entity company tax rate at 25% whilst providing an automatic adjustment if the company tax rate changes.
- The non-refundable offset rate for R&D expenditure will be the R&D entity's applicable company tax rate plus 8.5% for R&D expenditure up to 2% of total expenses. This will keep the net after tax benefit for large companies with an aggregated turnover of greater than $50 million at the current rate. However, it will reduce the net after tax benefit for R&D entities with an aggregated turnover of more than $20 million up to $50 million from 12.5% to 8.5%.
- The non-refundable offset rate for R&D expenditure over 2% of total expenses will be at the applicable company rate plus 16.5%.

  ▶ Example

  Large Group Ltd incurred R&D expenditure of $160 million and reports expenses of $2.9 billion in Item 6 of the company tax return. The tax offset of $56,110,000 is calculated as the sum of:

  (1) $160 million × the company tax rate of 30% = $48 million instead of a s 8-1 deduction plus

  (2) The R&D premium component of the tax offset:

  (a) $2.9 billion × 2% = $58 million × 8.5% = $4,930,000, plus

  (b) $150 million* – $58 million × 16.5% = $15,180,000

  = $20,110,000

  *There is no R&D premium amount for the $10 million over the $150 million cap.

- The rate at which the offset is recouped will be made accurate. The current provisions on the adjustments and clawbacks for grant recoupment (Subdiv 355-G), feedstock expenditure (Subdiv 355-H) and for balancing adjustments on the disposal of depreciating assets wholly (s 355-315 or 355-525) or partly (ss 40-292 and 40-293) used in R&D activities will be amended to correct the errors in the current legislation. These adjustments to the net after tax R&D benefit will no longer be different from the net after tax R&D benefit received (¶20-180).
- Extending the general anti-avoidance rules in ITAA36 Pt IVA to R&D tax offsets directly.
- Publicly reporting R&D expenditure and administration of the program by Industry, Innovation and Science Australia and AusIndustry after 2 years.

¶20-165 R&D activities and entities

R&D activities

The value of the tax offset available under the incentive is the expenditure (including decline in the value of R&D assets) on R&D activities (s 355-20). These activities include "core R&D activities" and "supporting R&D activities".

Core R&D activities

"Core R&D activities" (s 355-25) are experimental activities:

- whose outcome cannot be known (*Moreton Resources Ltd v Innovation and Science Australia (Taxation)*) or determined in advance on the basis of current knowledge but can only be determined by applying a systematic progression of work that is based on principles of established science and proceeds from hypothesis to experiment, observation and evaluation, and leads to logical conclusions (note, this requirement remains despite a successful Full Federal Court appeal in *Moreton Resources Ltd v Innovation and Science Australia*)
- that are conducted for the purpose of generating new knowledge including new knowledge in the form of new or improved materials, products, devices, processes or services. Clinical trials carried out to determine the safety and efficacy of a drug can be core R&D activities (*Case 1/2016*), and
- that are necessary to test a technical or scientific hypothesis and are conducted as a systematic progression of work based on principles of established science to generate new knowledge on the causal relationships between variables.

The following are "excluded activities" that may be R&D but cannot be considered "Core R&D activities":

(a) market research or sales promotion

(b) prospecting, exploring or drilling for minerals or petroleum for the purposes of discovering deposits, determining the location of deposits or determining the size or quality of deposits (*Coal of Queensland Pty Ltd v Innovation and Science Australia* and *Havilah Resources Ltd v Innovation and Science Australia*)

(c) management studies or efficiency surveys

(d) research in social sciences, arts or humanities

(e) commercial, legal and administrative aspects of patenting, licensing or other activities

(f) activities associated with complying with statutory requirements or standards, including routine testing (*Havilah Resources Ltd v Innovation and Science Australia*)

(g) any activity related to the reproduction of a commercial product or process by a physical examination of an existing system or from plans, blueprints, detailed specifications or publicly available information, and

(h) developing, modifying or customising computer software solely or primarily for use by the entity or an affiliate or connected entity for internal administration.

These "excluded activities" can be "supporting R&D activities". However, to be included as R&D activities they must be undertaken for the dominant purpose of supporting "core R&D activities".

Software exclusions

Activities to develop business administration software (eg office and staff management, payroll, accounting, ERP and CRM software, logistics, warehousing and payment processing) for the R&D entity and connected or affiliated entities are excluded from being a "core R&D activity". Software for production (eg PLC, SCADA and production controlling software) or for external purposes (for sales including cloud or software as a service or for customers) can be "core R&D activities". Internal business administration software may be included as "supporting R&D activities".

All experimental core or directly supporting R&D activities must be reasonably distinguishable from non-R&D activities. Where a task may be either R&D or non-R&D, the R&D purpose of performing that task must be evident, eg certain software development tasks, such as User Acceptance Trials may only form part of the R&D activities where their purpose is part of the systematic R&D process (TA 2017/5).

Relevant decisions

The following decisions were made in regards to the R&D tax incentive:

Coal of Queensland Pty Ltd v Innovation and Science Australia and *Havilah Resources Ltd v Innovation and Science Australia* both applied the exclusion of certain activities to discover and determine the location and size of mineral or petroleum deposits under s 355-25(2)(b). In the latter case it was found that discovering baseline hydrogeological conditions were excluded under s 355-25(2)(f) as associated with complying with statutory requirements or standards. The Deputy President considered this exclusion should be applied broadly. However, this exclusion would generally not be considered as applying where an eligible R&D activity must be conducted in compliance with statutory requirements or standards. For example, clinical trials, manufacturing process development experiments, or product trials are required to comply with safety, efficacy, environmental or occupational health and safety statutes and standards. An activity to prove compliance would be excluded but an activity to test a hypothesis in a compliant way would not be excluded.

In *Moreton Resources Ltd v Innovation and Science Australia*, the Full Federal Court set aside a previous AAT decision that supported Industry, Innovation and Science Australia's sharp narrowing of the meaning of a core R&D activity. The court confirmed the general understanding that the program is aimed at the creation of new knowledge including where this is in the form of new or improved materials, products, devices, processes and services. This means that the R&D activities are not restricted to high-level scientific experimentation and can include experiments to overcome more than insubstantial uncertainties in the application of existing technologies to a new site, product, process or circumstance. The court did not specifically decide on whether needing to meet environmental regulations meant the core activity would be excluded by s 355-25(2)(f) as a core R&D activity that is to meet a statutory requirement. However, the discussion in the decision on the uncertainty in whether the new process would be able to "operate in a safe and environmentally responsible manner" was not supportive of this view.

Ultimate Vision Inventions Pty Ltd v Innovation and Science Australia (Taxation) highlights the requirement that the R&D entity has identified the need for the R&D experiments and has conducted the experiments it registered. The AAT found that "none of this activity was carried out in accordance with the principles of established exercise science" and "the applicant did not have a purpose of generating new knowledge . . . it was indifferent to whether the knowledge generated through its field tests (if any) was new or not". The Applicant "was simply testing existing measures". For its claimed software development activity "the Applicant agreed that it never produced an application or source code, and therefore did not have anything to do alpha and beta testing on."

Activities in developing an online platform for the trading of water entitlements were neither core nor supporting R&D activities in *H2O Exchange Pty Ltd v Innovation and Science Australia (Taxation)*, as the AAT was not satisfied that the outcome of the activities was not known or able to be determined in advance. The outcome of some of the activities was partly known; other activities were not so difficult as would necessarily involve uncertainty of outcome.

JLSP v Innovation Australia was decided on the purpose for which the core R&D activities are conducted. This decision rejected the notion by Industry, Innovation and Science Australia that when conducting sets of experiments as part of a core R&D

activity, the R&D purpose must be the dominant purpose for the activities. Instead, it confirmed that core R&D activities are limited to those where the R&D purpose is a more than insubstantial purpose for conducting the activities.

RACV Sales and Marketing Pty Ltd v Innovation Australia was decided with regard to the previous R&D tax concession. However, it can be applied to the current law as it highlighted the need for core R&D activities to be experimental. The former concession required these activities to be ''systematic, investigative and experimental'' in nature whereas the incentive requires the core R&D activities to be sets of required experiments that are required to be conducted as a systematic progression of work based on principles of established science to determine outcomes. Both have as their outcomes the creation of new knowledge (including in the form of new or improved products, processes, material, services or devices). The core R&D activity must proceed from forming an hypothesis to conducting experiments to prove that hypothesis. This must be documented as observed, evaluated and responded to with a logical conclusion about the hypothesis. In RACV, the activities were undertaken but they did not answer an hypothesis; they merely produced safety star ratings for motor vehicles produced by others using a test developed by others for use by potential buyers.

Example of core R&D activity

Core R&D activity	**Not a core R&D activity**
Research by experimentation to develop new understandings to be used in creating new or improved products. Example: The use of a new material requires the company to do laboratory, pilot plant and full-scale testing to resolve uncertainty in using this material. The outcomes relied on the experiments to determine the causal links between the changed independent variables and the resulting measured dependent variables.	Upgrades to existing products that do not require the company to do more than apply a commonly understood solution. Example: The change to a different material is only new to this upgrade because this material is commonly used in known and similar ways. The upgrade's success was predictable and did not rely on experimental developments.

Engineering and software activities

The creation of new products or processes in engineering or software may involve core R&D activities. However, the development processes for engineering or software activities will be similar whether the task requires experiments or the simple application of what is already known or determinable in advance, eg software development often relies on Agile or Rapid processes and engineering developments may rely on a stage gate project management processes. The use of a process is not an indication of whether the activity is a core R&D activity, it always must meet the requirements in s 355-25. It must be the systematic resolution of a scientific or technical uncertainty in the creation of the knowledge including for new or improved materials, products, devices, processes or services.

The core R&D activities within an engineering or software project may be a large part of the project or limited to a specific and small part depending on the uncertainty requiring an experimental resolution. In a project, individual functions, modules or components may not require R&D experimentation but their aggregation or integration into a system or process may generate uncertainty requiring R&D experimentation.

The Frascati Manual 2015 definition gives guidance on where software developments may or may not be R&D. These concepts must be applied in line with requirements in s 355-25:

Activities that may be core R&D activities	Activities that may not be core R&D activities
Principle: The completion of the software development project must be dependent on a scientific or technical advance and the activity is to systematically resolve scientific or technical uncertainties. This can be for new software but generally it is incremental improvements, upgrades, additions or changes to existing software. The uncertainty can be at the functional level or at the integration or aggregation level or both. *Examples*: ● New or improved operating systems, environments or languages. ● The design and implementation of new functionality based on original technologies (eg new search engines). ● Experiments to resolve conflicts within hardware or software by systematically re-engineering a system or a network. ● The creation of new or improved algorithms based on new techniques with the algorithms (this does not require new development techniques). ● The creation of new and original techniques (eg new encryption or security techniques). ● Customising a product for a particular use where this requires new knowledge to significantly improve the product. ● Debugging processes that form part of the experimental development of new or improved software.	*Principle*: Routine activities to the extent they do not involve scientific and/or technological advances or the resolution of technological uncertainties. This includes work on system-specific or program-specific advances that were publicly available and understood prior to the commencement of the work, applying solutions to technical problems overcome in previous projects on the same operating systems and computer architecture, and routine computer and software maintenance. *Examples*: ● The development of business application software and information systems development using known functions or algorithms and existing software libraries or toolsets. ● Adding understood user functionality to existing application programs such as basic data entry functionalities. ● The creation of websites or software using existing libraries or toolsets. ● The use of standard methods of encryption, security verification and data integrity testing. ● Customising a product for a particular use within existing knowledge and without any significant improvement to the base program. ● Debugging of existing systems and programs where the debugging is not part of any experimental R&D development processes.

Supporting R&D activities

"Supporting R&D activities" (s 355-30) are activities that have a direct, close and relatively immediate relationship to the "core R&D activities". These are activities that will be usually required in order for the targeted "core R&D activities" to take place. This can include allocated direct overheads. Where the "supporting R&D activity" is an "excluded activity" or produces (or is related to producing) goods or services, the activity is only a "supporting R&D activity" if it is undertaken for the dominant purpose of supporting "core R&D activities".

Production and production-related activities

Where an R&D activity that produces goods or services is an experimental activity whose outcome cannot be known in advance and can only be determined by a systematic progression of work based on an applied scientific method, the activity is a "core R&D activity" and not subject to the dominant purpose test.

Production activities that can be "core R&D activities" include:

- Where the activities produce prototypes to be measured, tested or otherwise analysed and never sold or are broken up and reused or otherwise sold as scrap or downgraded product. For example: a company produces a batch of improved products to see if they can achieve a 5% performance gain in accordance with the hypothesis. This product is subjected to a range of tests to determine whether the gain is achieved.

- Where the activity has scientific or technical uncertainties in whether it can produce the desired result and it is not merely applying known things or solutions in understood ways. For example: It is understood that in a manufacturing process that changing from MX01 to MX02 will reduce power consumption per unit by 10%. However, changing to NY01 may reduce this by 20% but will have uncertain results. Initial R&D activities achieve an 8% reduction in an unstable way. Further R&D activities increased this to 18% and resulted in the development of new processes so this could be achieved safely and stably. As the 20% improvement was only achievable at higher risks, the company ceased the R&D activities at this point.

- Where the activity is no more than the minimum necessary activities to prove whether or not the hypothesis is statistically valid and repeatable across the necessary range of variables. For example: the core R&D activities in development of a new process often are not complete at the first point that the experiment successfully produces an answer to the hypothesis. In the example above, one of the uncertainties was whether the improvement could be achieved stably. This may require that the company use a valid statistical process to determine the minimum number of times the experiment needs to be repeated to determine if and when the results are stable and reliable. It could also require a range of variables to be tested. This could include testing in different seasons, weather conditions, with different colours, options or other variables before the core activities are complete.

- Where the knowledge generated by the experiment is in the form of new or improved materials, products, devices, processes or services and the knowledge sought by the experiment is dependent on uncertainty due to scale, volumetric or durational considerations. For example: A new product can be made in 2 grades and 6 sizes. The initial experiments are lab scale tests on the easiest grade and size. The core R&D activities may need to continue to successively larger scales but only while the scale increases have uncertainty. Core activities may still be required when moving from small volumes to larger volumes if the larger volumes create additional difficulties in producing the new products. If the 2 grades are significantly different from each other in a way that affects the R&D results, then the experimentation may continue to test both grades. Similarly, the changes in sizes may create uncertainty. This uncertainty may be able to be overcome by dividing the sizes into the 3 smallest and the 3 largest. If, in the small group, the results of testing one of the 3 sizes removes uncertainty about the other 2 then the core activities will cease with the testing of that size. For the larger group, it may be found that each size needs to be tested before the uncertainty is removed and the R&D is complete.

R&D activities that are production activities but are also directly related to the ''core R&D activities'' need to be assessed by the taxpayer for their dominant purpose on a case by case basis to determine if they are eligible R&D activities. ''Supporting R&D activities'' that have the dominant purpose of supporting ''core R&D activities'' could include the data collection phase that provides information upon which an hypothesis is developed or otherwise determines the type or direction of experimentation required to undertake the R&D. Indications that a production activity is an R&D activity, whether core or supporting can include:

- variations in the normal production process/line that may include changing/amending equipment, configurations or otherwise changing the standard production process

- smaller than usual production run size or time, eg the supporting R&D production run may be 1/4 the normal size of a standard production run as a direct result of the R&D objective

- higher level of monitoring or monitoring by additional staff including the R&D team, eg the production run may be controlled by the R&D team with twice the number of staff or with additional monitoring equipment
- additional testing over normal practices, eg standard quality assurance tests may test one out of every 1,000 using an indicative test but the R&D activities may require testing one out of every 100 or testing with a more intensive process
- procedures that require additional sign off prior to the activity being authorised to occur, eg the production activity includes aspects to support the core R&D activities but these are not able to be done without meeting formal requirements such as an authorised change control
- where the R&D entity has more than one production facility, site or units of plant and the trials are being performed on or at one of these locations prior to being implemented with the other ones, eg a new mill process is first implemented and tested at one site before this is applied to the other sites
- where the production run has significant product or process risks over and above normal risks due to the R&D activities, eg a mill normally has a yield loss of 2%, but following the development and introduction of a new product, the yield loss rose to 10%
- production scheduling that only allows the activity at certain times to limit the impact on normal operations, or, eg the supporting R&D activities are restricted to backshifts or after normal production targets have been reached, and
- costing of the activity to the R&D project or project team department instead of normal operations, eg a capital upgrade that included significant R&D activities to implement will not be handed over to the normal production team from the implementation team until it reaches certain performance capabilities in the project VURS (Valid User Requirements Specifications).

This classification of production activities between those that are:

- significantly for a core R&D activities purpose
- for the dominant purpose of directly supporting core R&D activities, or
- otherwise not able to be considered an R&D activity

applies to agricultural production activities. For example, large scale trials of broadacre farming including expenditure on fertilisers and other treatments need to exclude non R&D production activities (TA 2015/3).

R&D entities

Only eligible ''R&D entities'' can claim the offset. ''R&D entities'' (s 355-35) include bodies corporate incorporated under Australian or foreign law that are Australian residents, including companies and trustees of public trading trusts. A body corporate incorporated under a foreign law that is a resident of a foreign country with which Australia has a double tax agreement is an R&D entity to the extent that it carries on business through a permanent establishment in Australia. Exempt entities (¶10-604), individuals and trusts (other than public trading trusts) cannot be R&D entities.

There is no eligible R&D entity where the R&D activities are being conducted by a trustee company for a family trust (TA 2017/4).

The offset only applies to R&D partnerships where each of the partners is, or is able to be, an R&D entity, ie all the partners are companies. The benefits of the offset are directly available to the partners that are R&D entities, rather than being taken into account in determining a partner's individual interest in the net partnership income or loss (¶20-185). Eligibility for the offset and the determination of each partner's share is as modified by Subdiv 355-J. As some partners of corporate limited partnerships (¶3-475) cannot be R&D entities, R&D activities undertaken by a corporate limited partnership are not eligible for the offset.

The incentive applies to a consolidated group (¶8-000) or MEC group (¶8-610) as if it were a single entity. This means that expenditure incurred by the subsidiary member on R&D activities is taken to be incurred by the head company, R&D activities conducted for the subsidiary by a third party are taken to have been conducted for the head company and R&D activities conducted by one member of the group for another member of the same group are taken to have been conducted by the head company on its own behalf. This means that, in the case of a consolidated or MEC group, the head company must make the application for the R&D incentive, not the subsidiary members (*DZXP & Ors v Innovation and Science Australia*).

Entity eligible for R&D offset	**Entity not eligible for R&D offset**
A company incorporated under an Australian law — s 355-35(1)(a)	Entities that are not incorporated bodies
An Australian resident company incorporated under a foreign law — s 355-35(1)(b)	A company acting as a trustee
A permanent establishment operating in Australia of a foreign incorporated and foreign resident company. This is limited to where the residency is in a country with a double tax agreement with Australia that includes a definition of "permanent establishment" — s 355-35(2)	A tax exempt company — s 355-35(3)
A partnership made up exclusively of entities eligible to be R&D entities — s 355-505(1)	Corporate limited partnerships
Head companies of a tax consolidated group or MEC group whether the R&D is conducted by or for the head company, its subsidiary members or a combination of these.	
Where the R&D is "conducted for": ● the R&D entity where the activities are conducted in Australia or in accordance with an overseas finding — ss 355-210(1)(a), 355-210(1)(d), 355-210(1)(e) and 28C(1)(a) *Industry Research and Development Act 1986* ● the body corporate of an Australian permanent establishment not for the purposes of the permanent establishment solely in Australia with written evidence for whom the R&D is conducted — ss 355-210(1)(b) and 355-215 ● an associated and incorporated foreign resident by the R&D entity solely in Australia in accordance with a binding written agreement — ss 355-210(1)(c) and 355-220, or ● a combination of the above.	Where the R&D fails the "conducted for" test below — s 355-210(2)

[FITR ¶335-020]

¶20-170 Claiming the R&D incentive

The incentive consists of a 43.5% refundable tax offset for entities with an annual aggregated turnover of less than $20 million unless they are 50% or more controlled by exempt entities in a way described in s 328-125 (¶7-050). The concept of "aggregated turnover" is the same as in the small business concessions (¶7-050) and includes allocated turnover to an R&D entity in an R&D partnership.

Entities with a turnover of $20 million or more, or that are controlled by exempt entities, are entitled to a 38.5% non-refundable carry-forward offset. Entities undertaking R&D in Australia where the intellectual property is held offshore will also be able to access the non-refundable offset.

Entities that necessarily undertake R&D activities overseas are able to claim these costs so long as the total overseas expenditure over the life of the R&D activities is less than the expected total expenditure on the Australian R&D activities to which they are scientifically linked. This is subject to obtaining approval under s 28C of the IR&D Act for the foreign activities by Industry, Innovation and Science Australia. This registration is not required for minor incidental foreign expenditure (eg Australian researchers incurring foreign travel costs).

The 2 offset rates are limited to expenditure up to the $100 million cap. Where the R&D expenditure exceeds $100 million, the offset rate reduces to the applicable corporate tax rate (¶42-025). The cap will apply until 30 June 2024.

The minimum expenditure threshold of $20,000 pa applies, except in relation to expenditure on R&D activities performed for an R&D entity by an entity registered as a Research Service Provider and contributions to a Cooperative Research Centre.

The calculation relies on including the full cost in the offset with any required clawbacks being made by recognising additional deemed assessable income or tax payable (eg recoupments and recoveries of feedstock inputs, energy, and declines in value of assets to produce feedstock inputs by sale or application to own use). Prepayments are treated as per ITAA36 ss 82KZL to 82KZO.

To be eligible for the incentive in an income year:

- the R&D entity must be registered under s 27A of the IR&D Act for the R&D activities undertaken that year. Registration is normally required within 10 months after the end of the R&D entity's income year. This registration must be approved by Industry, Innovation and Science Australia (the Board) and is made through AusIndustry. The Board cannot register a company's activities after this period except in accordance with the decision-making principles (IR&D Act s 27D). A refusal to allow an extension of time is reviewable internally by the Board and subsequently by the AAT. Under the former concession, corporate restructuring and staff changes were not sufficient to warrant an extension of time in *Bloomfield Collieries Pty Ltd & Anor v Innovation Australia*, but an extension was granted for the year in which the Australian Coal Association Research Program (ACARP) had advised the taxpayer that an ongoing concession for ACARP levies was available without mentioning the need to apply for a registration. An extension was also not granted where the late preparation of the application was due to the failure of the company to have a system of checks in place to monitor its preparation and a lack of support for the relevant staff member who had become ill (*SFGV and Innovation Australia*)
- the R&D activities must have been conducted within Australia, an external territory or, if outside of these, covered by an overseas finding under s 28C of the IR&D Act. These activities can be conducted by a permanent establishment in Australia for other parts of that body corporate or for a foreign affiliate (ss 355-215; 355-220)

- the entity incurs notional deductions for the positive limbs linked to s 355-100, eg:
  - R&D expenditure under s 355-205 (eg labour, contractors, services, consumables, overheads, raw materials, energy, etc)
  - the decline in value of R&D assets under ss 355-305 and 355-520 (ie notional Div 40 tax depreciation of tangible assets including non-building related notional Div 43 deductions on owned and shared partnership R&D assets)
  - balancing adjustments on the disposal of these assets where they are only used for R&D activities under ss 355-315 and 355-525 or for amounts apportioned to R&D activities used under ss 40-292 and 40-293 over the asset's life (ie notional s 40-285 deductions including for non-building related notional Div 43 deductions on owned and shared partnership R&D only assets)
  - R&D expenditure constructively paid by the R&D entity in the current year where it was incurred by an associate in an earlier year under s 355-480, and
  - CRC contributions under s 355-580.
- the notional deductions are not for the negative limbs in s 355-225, eg:
  - R&D expenditure under s 355-205 that is to acquire or construct a building, part of a building or an extension, alteration or improvement to a building
  - R&D expenditure on tangible assets for which a decline in value notional deduction is able to be made under ss 355-305 and 355-520
  - R&D expenditure for interest payable to an entity
  - R&D expenditure on core technology. Core technology is technology acquired by the R&D entity so the R&D entity can further develop this. The subsequent R&D activities by the R&D entity are eligible but the core technology acquisition is not. This exclusion does not apply to activities conducted for the R&D entity by a contractor in the course of the R&D.

▶ Example

EnergyPlus manufactures alternative fuels and has an annual turnover of $3 million. It incurred the following costs in relation to R&D activities to do research into potential new fuels and to develop new products and processes to make these new fuels:

- $200,000 labour for the research team and for the product and process development teams. This includes those working directly on the R&D projects as well as those managing and directly supporting these teams. The value of the labour expenditure is claimed on the basis of the total cost (including on-costs, salary sacrifices and superannuation) of each person. The claim is limited to only the proportion of time these people spent on these R&D activities. This can be based on a reasonably apportionment methodology with timesheets or reasonable secondary documentary evidence
- $100,000 of business overheads that are needed to support the R&D activities. This can include a portion of rent, security, general consumables and services, etc each allocated using a reasonable allocation method determined on a case-by-case basis
- $300,000 on other costs including travel costs for the teams above or for experts brought into the project, contractor services, university or research laboratory studies, EnergyPlus' laboratory costs and consumables, etc. These costs should exclude recoverable GST amount and any intra-group mark-ups. They may need to be apportioned between R&D and normal activities. $50,000 of these costs relate to costs incurred with EnergyMinus, an associate of EnergyPlus. These costs were constructively paid by EnergyPlus in the current year for activities done in the prior year. By the associate payment rules (¶20-185) these are only claimable in the year they are constructively paid
- $225,000 of core R&D production trial costs. This includes the operating conversion costs (labour, services, consumables, energy, allocations of repairs and maintenance, depreciation, etc) as well as the feedstock inputs to the experimental trials. In this case, all the fuel produced is not sold so there is no feedstock adjustment required in feedstock inputs and energy. If the resulting

fuel was sold for a profit then the claim is reduced by a feedstock adjustment (¶20-180) to clawback only the feedstock inputs, energy and depreciation on processes prior to the R&D trial. All other conversion costs remain part of the R&D claim

- $175,000 of supporting R&D production trial costs. While these trials are to support the core R&D trials, the dominant purpose of conducting these trials was to produce fuel to be provided for free to a motor sport event to promote the fuel.

Under the incentive, for an income year that commenced on or after 1 July 2016, the tax offset would be $358,875 (ie $825,000 × 43.5%).

If EnergyPlus is part of R&D group with an annual turnover of $21 million, then EnergyPlus' tax offset would be $317,625 (ie $825,000 × 38.5%).

[FITR ¶335-100, ¶335-200, ¶335-300]

Evidence for activities and relevant expenditure

The Federal Court's decision in *Bogiatto & Ors 2020* on tax exploitation schemes involving R&D activities also addressed the requirement that the R&D entity must be able to substantiate that the R&D activities were carried out and the expenditure was incurred in line with the requirements of a statutory scheme. It established that the "entitlement to the tax offset is dependent on whether the taxable facts are such that the R&D claims were available" to the R&D entity and not just that the entitlement is dependent on keeping records. Adequate evidence should be kept to substantiate the tax offset claim. Primarily, this would be documentary evidence, but it may be supported by secondary evidence including accounting and business management processes, witness statements, statutory declarations, oral evidence and alike. For example, documentary evidence on total salary paid to particular employees together with other evidence, including oral testimony, on justifying the proportion of time they spent on R&D activities.

Bogiatto & Ors clarifies the application of AAT decisions on the former R&D tax concession to the R&D tax incentive, for example:

- *Ozone Manufacturing Pty Ltd* discussed the need for documentation. The decision affirmed that specific types of records such as time cards may not be required, and that apportionment of time and expenditure is acceptable. However, the company's ordinary business records used to substantiate this must be sufficient for a relevant independent third party to be able to readily verify the amount of the expenditure on R&D activities and the relationship of the expenditure to those activities. Records, documentation and other evidence to support the apportionment of expenditure between R&D activities and non-R&D activities should be maintained and be capable of reasonably straight-forward analysis.

- *Tier Toys Ltd* involved a case where contemporaneous records were claimed to have been lost in a fire 3 years after the R&D activities occurred. This highlighted the need to maintain sufficient records "directly in respect of" eligible R&D activities. Reasonable evidence should include the time a contractor spent on R&D activities and the specific nature of these R&D tasks, especially where the contractor did not exclusively engage in R&D tasks. Following *Bogiatto & Ors*, the records and secondary evidence must be adequate to reasonably satisfy a third party (eg the ATO or a court) that the expenditure claimed does relate to the R&D activities that were conducted for the R&D entity.

These decisions emphasise the importance of having adequate evidence that:

- the outcomes of the experiments could not be reliably or adequately predetermined by a competent professional without them conducting experiments. This is more than the competent professional considering that the outcome should be possible

- a substantial purpose in the activity is that these outcomes are required to answer the hypotheses on the causal links between variables and it is needed for the purpose of creating new knowledge including where this is in the form of new or improved materials, products, devices, processes or services
- the experiments were conducted by introducing or changing independent variables with their outcomes (the resulting dependent variables) measured, analysed and responded to in forming logical conclusions in meeting this purpose
- the R&D activities and expenditure on these R&D activities can be reasonably and verifiably split between the R&D activities and non-R&D activities.

¶20-175 R&D integrity rules

Expenditure not at arm's length

Section 355-400 adjusts R&D expenditure incurred with an associate back down to market value where that expenditure is charged at more than market value. Expenditure incurred within the R&D entity, including within the consolidated or MEC group, must be as incurred without any internal mark-up.

Reducing deductions for mark-ups within the R&D group

Section 355-415 requires the R&D expenditure to be reduced to remove any mark-ups on costs incurred with connected or affiliated entities so that the R&D expenditure reflects the cost to the R&D group for the inputs into the R&D activities.

▶ Example

BlueSky Research acquires 4 identical items for its latest R&D project. It pays GreenSky (a subsidiary member of the same consolidated group) and OrangeSky (a connected entity) $1,000 each for 2 of the items they produced for $800 each. It pays PurpleSky (an associate) $1,200 and BrownLand $1,100 for the other 2. The market value can be determined from the amount paid to Brownland as this is an arm's length transaction.

BlueSky can include $800 for the cost of producing each of the items acquired internally from subsidiary members and connected entities. It can include $1,100 for the cost of acquiring the item from BrownLand and $1,100 being the lower of the amount paid to PurpleSky and the market value.

Expenditure not at risk

Section 355-405 adjusts R&D expenditure where the R&D entity incurs the expenditure when, at the time it incurs this, the entity is deemed to be not at risk. It is to ensure that the R&D entity is bearing the risk of success or failure of the R&D activities without a guaranteed recovery of costs regardless of the outcome of the R&D. This guaranteed return includes indirect returns or returns received by an associate. It should not be applied against normal commercial returns from the successful completion of the R&D activities or recoveries such as those from normal plant insurance.

A normal example of this is where the entity seeking to claim the incentive is in fact only a contractor undertaking the R&D activities for another entity who may not be eligible to claim the R&D expenditure in their own right. This could be because the latter entity is an individual, trust, non-resident or is tax exempt and is funding the R&D.

Disposal of R&D results

Section 355-410 requires the recognition of income including CGT gains or profits on the disposal of depreciable assets when the results of the R&D are sold. This provision does not prevent the R&D entity from claiming the expenditure on R&D activities. It is to ensure that any revenue from the direct sale of R&D results, granting access to the results, payments receivable for undertaking the R&D (whether or not this is dependent on results) is captured as taxable revenue. Section 355-410 allows for apportioning an amount received by an R&D entity where the amount comprises payment for results from

R&D and non-R&D activities (ID 2015/4). It also includes amounts from the licensing of intellectual property payable in the future, subject to achieving future development and sales milestones (ID 2015/5).

No tax deduction for offset expenditure

Section 355-715 prevents a taxpayer from deducting under other Divisions expenditure or notional Division 40 deductions for which it, as an R&D entity, is entitled to receive a tax offset for under ss 355-100 through 355-205, 355-480, 355-580, 355-305, 355-315, 355-520 or 355-525.

[FITR ¶335-400]

¶20-180 Clawbacks of recoupments and feedstock recoveries

Where an R&D entity is entitled to an R&D tax offset that is greater than the company tax rate, there are 3 events that require adjustments to tax payable. These are:

- the calculation of a balancing adjustment on disposal of a depreciating asset to the extent was used in R&D activities during its life
- where the R&D activities are partly funded by a government grant or equivalent, and
- where the R&D activities also produce goods or materials from produced or acquired feedstock inputs.

For years ending 30 June 2021 or earlier these adjustments assume all businesses receive a 40% non-refundable tax offset instead of a 30% tax deduction thereby requiring a 10% adjustment. This was initially achieved for grants by a specific 10% additional tax and for feedstock and balancing adjustments by a one-third of 30% adjustment (with a one-fourth adjustment for pre-tax incentive R&D capital allowances). This allowed smaller R&D entities to retain a portion of these expenditures where they receive the refundable tax offset or pay less than 30% company tax. However, for R&D entities with $50 million or more aggregated turnover, these adjustments are higher than the net after tax benefit received. When this occurs, these activities should not be registered. See Specific Issue Guidance: ''Can companies avoid needing to report feedstock adjustments by not registering certain activities and not claiming associated feedstock input expenditure?'' from Industry, Innovation and Science Australia. This has been corrected for periods commencing after 30 June 2021.

The retained net after tax benefits after these adjustments for R&D entities paying current rates of tax (26% or 30%) are:

Retained benefit after adjustment	**Aggregated turnover**		
	<$20m	**$20m to <$50m**	**$50m or more**
Grant clawback	7.50%	2.50%	(1.5%)
Feedstock and balancing adjustment*	8.83%	3.83%	(1.5%)

* *Assets installed after 30 June 2010.*

Recoupment

Sections 355-430 to 355-450 require the payment of additional income tax when an R&D entity receives or becomes entitled to receive a government recoupment on costs (including notional Division 40 deductions) incurred on or in relation to R&D expenditure as part of a project.

The additional income tax is equal to 10% of the recoupment for the eligible R&D expenditure by reference to the qualifying R&D expenditure necessarily incurred to be eligible for that recoupment, subject to a cap (see below). This includes a recoupment from an Australian government agency or a State or Territory Body under ITAA36 Pt III Div 1AB, unless the recoupment is under a Cooperative Research Centre program.

Where the recoupment covers a project that is broader than the R&D expenditure, the additional income tax payable is capped by the proportion of the R&D expenditure to total project expenditure and reduced by any repayments of the recoupment. A further cap applies so that the additional income tax payable on recoupment cannot be more than the benefit of the offset.

▶ Example

New Furniture Ltd is developing and commercialising a range of new products. It is eligible for a government grant to cover aspects of its R&D efforts and commercialisation of resulting new products. To be eligible for the $100,000 grant New Furniture must spend $2 for every $1 of grant. $60,000 of the grant will partly fund the $250,000 expenditure on R&D activities and the remaining $40,000 is for commercialisation.

New Furniture is able to claim $250,000 expenditure for the offset. As its group aggregated turnover is less than $20 million, it is eligible for the 43.5% refundable offset. This will provide an offset of $108,750 (0.435 × $250,000). Assuming that New Furniture Ltd is not a small business entity, this is $33,750 more than the tax deduction foregone. 60% of the grant is for R&D related activities so a 10% tax is payable on 60% of the required expenditure. At $2 expenditure for every $1 of grant this is $120,000 ((2 × $60,000) × 10% = $12,000).

Feedstock adjustments

Sections 355-460 to 355-475 clawback any recovery made on the sale or own use of goods or materials produced by R&D activities by a feedstock adjustment. As feedstock inputs are included as R&D expenditure the clawback is by recognising an additional deemed assessable income amount. This amount is one-third of the lower of the:

- feedstock revenue, or
- attributable expenditure (s 355-465(2)) being the sum of:
  - feedstock inputs into an R&D activity
  - energy used in the R&D activity, and
  - decline in value of assets used to acquire or produce those feedstock inputs,

  where the feedstock inputs are goods or materials acquired or produced that are processed or transformed (ie not consumed) in R&D activities that produce tangible products.

The assessable income is recognised each time a good or material is sold out of the R&D group (or is applied to own use other than as a feedstock input by the R&D entity, any connected or affiliated entity) where that good or material is made from, or partly made from, tangible products made in R&D activities. Note, sales of like goods or materials in the same income year may be combined for convenience, but these sales may be in a different income year or income years from when the R&D activity occurred. They may be over many different sales of many different types of products with many different proportions of feedstock outputs produced by many different R&D activities. To calculate the feedstock revenue, the market value of the sold or used products must be apportioned to exclude value added after the last R&D activity that produced tangible products occurred and to exclude value added by activities that are not associated with any R&D activity. This is achieved by the following formula in s 355-470:

$$\text{Feedstock revenue} = \text{Market value of marketable product} \times \frac{\text{Cost of producing the feedstock output}}{\text{Cost of producing the marketable product}}$$

Where goods are acquired and transformed by a single set of R&D activities and then immediately sold in a single set of sales with little or no further processing, these calculations are straightforward.

▶ Example

EnergyPlus undertakes further core R&D production activities on its new fuel in the current income year. As this is to develop the production process, the resulting fuel is all sold in the year the experimental trials occurred. The cost of the trials is $100,000 conversion cost excluding energy, $200,000 feedstock inputs (including depreciation in prior processes) and $50,000 energy to process these inputs into the fuel. The trials occurred prior to the final stage of production. EnergyPlus includes in its R&D expenditure $100,000 as other R&D expenditure and $250,000 as feedstock input expenditure for a total of $350,000 to produce the fuel in the R&D trials. EnergyPlus incurred another $350,000 in later processes to complete the fuel for sale.

When the fuel is sold, EnergyPlus received revenue of $1,000,000 on the fuel partly completed in these R&D trials. The feedstock revenue is:

$$\$500{,}000 \quad = \quad \$1{,}000{,}000 \quad \times \quad \frac{\$350{,}000 \text{ Cost of producing the feedstock output}}{\$700{,}000 \text{ Cost of producing the marketable product}}$$

The additional assessable income is one-third the lower of the attributable expenditure ($250,000 feedstock inputs and energy) or feedstock revenue ($500,000). This is one-third of $250,000 or $83,333. This will result in EnergyPlus having to pay $21,666.58 tax (at 26%) as a feedstock adjustment.

EnergyPlus is eligible for the 43.5% tax offset, as it received a net benefit of $37,500 over the normal tax deduction so is $12,500 ahead. If EnergyPlus was only eligible for the 38.5% tax offset and pays 30% company tax, then its net benefit of $21,250 on attributable expenditure would be lower than the adjustment tax payable ($25,000) and it should exclude registering the acquisition of feedstock input expenditure as per *Specific Issue Guidance: Can companies avoid needing to report feedstock adjustments by not registering certain activities and not claiming associated feedstock input expenditure?* If the feedstock revenue was lower than the attributable expenditure (ie the R&D trials destroyed part of the value of the attributable expenditure), then this loss would compensate for this by reducing the tax payable on the feedstock adjustment.

However, in more complex circumstances, the calculations rely on ensuring that product tracking is able to determine how much of each affected sale is made from goods or materials made from potentially several sets of R&D activities on many component parts of the final sale. Where the clawback is made in a different income year after the R&D activity was undertaken, the R&D entity is able to claim the incentive on feedstock inputs, energy and depreciation in the year it performs the R&D and only repay this amount when it sells (or uses) the output. As the clawback is set at one-third of the entity's corporate tax rate, R&D entities that are eligible for the 43.5% tax offset are able to retain 8.8333% of this pre-R&D expenditure.

The concepts of ''applied to the entity's own use'', ''transformed'', ''costs of producing'' and others are considered in TR 2013/3.

A distinction was made in ID 2012/89 between the construction of a depreciating asset as a prototype that was subsequently used in R&D activities and expenditure on goods or materials that are processed or transformed in R&D activities that produce tangible feedstock outputs for sale or own use. Expenditure on capital assets does not form part of R&D expenditure under s 355-205. Instead, the notional decline in value of the asset is included by s 355-305. The R&D entity is not able to ''obtain under section 355-100'' (s 355-465(1)(b)) a tax offset for capital expenditure so there is no feedstock adjustment trigger when the capital asset is used by the R&D entity.

Balancing adjustments

Net income on the disposal of depreciating tangible assets must be increased where these assets are used solely (ss 355-315 and 355-525) or partly (ss 40-292 and 40-293) in R&D activities. This is adjusted for depreciation claimed in prior years as part of the R&D expenditure. It increases the balancing adjustment by one-third of the portion of depreciation claimed as R&D expenditure since the acquisition date or 1 July 2010, whichever is later. If the asset is older than this, any depreciation previously claimed under the R&D tax concession (former ITAA36 s 73BC) is increased by one-fourth under equivalent provisions in the *Income Tax (Transitional Provisions) Act 1997*.

▶ Example

At the end of the R&D activities, EnergyPlus sold the capitalised prototype pilot plant. Capital allowances of $600,000 were claimed prior to the sale of which $450,000 were claimed through R&D expenditure under s 355-305 over 3 years. The s 40-285 amount on the sale was $100,000. $75,000 of the s 40-285 amount is attributable to the R&D activities. This portion of this amount is increased by the formula in s 40-292:

$$\frac{\text{Sum of your R\&D deductions}}{\text{Total decline in value}} \times \text{Adjusted s 40-285 amount} \times 1\ 1/3$$

$450,000/$600,000 × $100,000 × 1 1/3 = $100,000.

As the adjusted s 40-285 amount of $100,000 plus the $25,000 s 40-285 amount unrelated to R&D is less than the total decline in value, the assessable balancing income is $125,000.

[FITR ¶335-430, ¶335-460]

¶20-185 Applying R&D to associates, R&D partnerships and CRCs

R&D expenditure paid to associates

Section 355-480 enables R&D expenditure for the R&D entity to include costs that it pays an associate for R&D activities the associate conducted for the R&D entity where the associate incurred these costs in a prior year.

▶ Example

A small business has 2 entities with at least 40% common ownership, Operating Co and Development Co. During the year all the costs of the group are paid through Operating Co. Under the concession after 30 June each year when the final accounts and income tax return are being prepared, the business would calculate the amount spent on R&D activities in the year and transfer these costs and any related revenue to Development Co. Development Co would then register its R&D activities with AusIndustry and claim the Concession with the ATO.

Under the incentive this method will result in Development Co not being able to claim these costs until the year it makes constructive payment to Operating Co. If it uses the procedure above it will need to register the activities with AusIndustry in the year the activities occurred and then again in the year Development Co paid Operating Co for doing these activities on its behalf. Constructive payment can be by bank payment or loan. The payment from the Development Co bank account to Operating Co must be made prior to the end of the financial year. If it is by loan, then this needs to be properly documented prior to the end of the financial year and Development Co should be able to demonstrate it has a clear intent to repay this loan. Any Div 7A implications need to be considered (¶4-200). If the 2 entities are in a tax consolidated group, then the head company is considered to be the R&D entity and the associate payment issue does not arise (¶8-000).

R&D partnerships

Sections 355-500 to 355-545 provide for the application of Div 355 to R&D partnerships including determining and allocating the incentive to each R&D partner. An R&D partnership is one where all partners at the time are R&D entities (¶20-165). Where the R&D is undertaken by the partnership, the incentive is claimed by each R&D entity. It does not apply to normal partnerships between individuals, nor to corporate limited partnerships as these can include entities that are not eligible R&D entities. R&D expenditures, including the decline in the value of depreciating assets, as well as any balancing adjustment assessable income on R&D only assets are allocated to the R&D entities that are R&D partners in the agreed proportions or on the basis of relative partnership interests. For the purposes of determining whether the R&D entity is eligible for the 43.5% refundable offset, the aggregated turnover includes the allocated proportion of the partnership turnover. The recoupments rules apply on the basis of allocated expenditure and allocated recoupments. Partnership net income and losses are amended to exclude R&D expenditures, deductions and recoupments under Subdiv 355-J.

Application to Cooperative Research Centres

Under s 355-580 an R&D entity can include, as expenditure on R&D activities, monetary contributions to Cooperative Research Centres (CRCs) so long as these contributions have or will be spent on R&D activities that are registered by the R&D entity under IR&D Act s 27A. This excludes expenditure to the extent that it is incurred out of Commonwealth funding. Where this expenditure is either eligible for the tax offset or is incurred out of Commonwealth funding, it is not deductible under any other provision.

[FITR ¶335-500, ¶335-580]

¶20-190 R&D registrations, reviews and objections

There is no separate provision for an R&D entity to object against an assessment of the amount of an R&D tax offset. Any objection is dealt with under the normal objection provisions if the offset is part of an assessment (¶28-010).

Section 355-705 has the effect of binding the Commissioner to the findings by Industry, Innovation and Science Australia on registrations (IR&D Act ss 27B and 27J) and core technology findings (IR&D Act s 28E). It also requires that these findings be made within 4 years after the end of the income year or last income year to which they relate.

Advance findings are binding on the Commissioner for the year the activities are conducted if they are completed in the year the application is made or, otherwise, the year of application and the next 2 years. For a finding on overseas expenditure this is for the life of the activity as described for the finding certificate.

The time in which the Commissioner can amend an assessment that is dependent on a finding by the Innovation Australia board is limited to 2 years if it will increase the taxpayer's liability or 4 years otherwise (s 355-710). However, if the amended assessment is as a result of a ''key decision'', the amendment can be made at any time. These key decisions can be made as a result of:

- internal review under IR&D Act s 30D(2)
- a decision in regards to an internal review under the *Administrative Appeals Tribunal Act 1975*, or
- a court decision relating to the above or any other decision under IR&D Act Pt III. These include registration, advance finding, core technology and foreign expenditure findings.

[FITR ¶335-700]

Investment in Australian Films

¶20-330 Film concessions

Three refundable tax offsets are available to companies involved in the Australian screen media industry under ITAA97 Div 376:

- the producer offset, for Australian expenditure in making Australian films (¶20-340)
- the location offset, for Australian production expenditure (¶20-350), and
- the PDV offset, for post, digital and visual effects production in Australia (¶20-360).

The basic concepts for each offset are ''production expenditure'' and ''qualifying Australian production expenditure'' (QAPE) (ITAA97 Subdiv 376-C).

"Production expenditure"

A company's production expenditure on a film is expenditure (of a capital or revenue nature) that the company incurs to the extent to which it:

(a) is incurred in, or in relation to, the making of the film, or

(b) is reasonably attributable to the use of equipment or other facilities for, or activities undertaken in, the making of the film.

The ''making of a film'' means the doing of the things necessary for the production of the first copy of the film and includes pre- and post-production activities and other activities undertaken to bring the film up to the state where it could be distributed or broadcast. It excludes developing the proposal for the making of the film, arranging finance, and distributing and promoting the film.

"Qualifying Australian production expenditure"

A company's QAPE on a film is the company's production expenditure on the film to the extent to which it is incurred for, or is reasonably attributable to goods and services provided in Australia, the use of land in Australia or the use of goods that are located in Australia at the time they are used in the making of the film.

It excludes expenditure incurred when the company is a foreign resident without both a permanent establishment in Australia and an ABN. It also excludes expenditure on remuneration and travel costs for an individual if the individual is not a member of the cast and enters Australia to work on the film for less than 2 consecutive calendar weeks.

Certain financing expenditure incurred in Australia prior to the end of the income year in which the film is complete can be claimed as QAPE, including:

- insurance related to making the film
- fees for audit and legal services provided in Australia in relation to raising and servicing the financing of the film, and/or
- fees for incorporation and liquidation of the company that makes or is responsible for making the film.

For the producer offset only, the following additional expenditure incurred in Australia can be claimed as QAPE:

- fees in obtaining an independent opinion of a film's QAPE
- expenditure in relation to offsetting carbon emissions created during the making of the film
- expenditure incurred in relation to distributing the film such as acquiring Australian classification certificates, sound mix mastering licences, re-versioning the film in Australia, freight services provided by a company in Australia for delivery of contracted deliverables in relation to the film and/or storing the film in a film vault in Australia
- certain publicity and promotion expenditure on publicist services provided in Australia, promotional stills, trailers and press kits (with Australian-owned copyright) that is incurred after the film's completion but prior to the end of the income year in which production is complete.

In determining an amount of expenditure for the purpose of applying the producer offset and the location offset, the expenditure is taken to exclude GST. In determining an amount of expenditure for the purpose of applying the PDV offset, the expenditure is taken to include GST.

Foreign currency translation rules (s 960-50(6))

When quantifying production expenditure, QAPE or total film expenditure for the purposes of issuing a certificate under the location and producer offset, foreign currency amounts are to be translated to Australian currency at the exchange rate applicable at the time when principal photography commences or production of the animated image commences. For the purposes of issuing a certificate under the PDV offset, foreign currency amounts are to be translated at the exchange rate applicable when post, digital and visual effects production for the film commences.

When quantifying production expenditure, QAPE or total film expenditure for the purposes of calculating the amount of the location, PDV or producer offset, foreign currency amounts are to be translated at the average of the exchange rates applicable from time to time during the period that QAPE is incurred on the film. However, when quantifying such expenditure for the producer offset and the company's QAPE is less than $15 million, foreign currency amounts are be translated at the exchange rate applicable at the time when expenditure is incurred on the film.

[FITR ¶351-655, ¶351-690]

¶20-340 Producer offset

The producer offset (ITAA97 ss 376-55 to 376-75) is available to a company for the making of an Australian film where:

- the film has a significant Australian content or is made under an arrangement between the Commonwealth and a foreign country
- the film was completed in the income year
- a certificate has been issued for the film by the film authority
- the offset is claimed in the income tax return for the year by the company, and
- the company is either an Australian resident or a foreign resident that has a permanent establishment in Australia and has an ABN.

The Producer Offset Rules 2018 (*Legislative Instrument* F2018L00112) provide for the way in which the Film Finance Corporation Australia Limited will issue provisional certificates and how applications for provisional certificates and final certificates are to be made.

An Australian residency requirement is imposed on individuals who perform services outside Australia through a company or a permanent establishment if a film reasonably requires a foreign location to be used for principal photography.

Eligible productions

The following productions qualify for the producer offset:

- a feature film (a film of at least one hour in length that is screened as the main attraction in commercial cinemas, or at least 45 minutes in length if designed for release in a large-format cinema, such as IMAX)
- a single episode program (such as a telemovie, ''movie-of-the-week'', films released direct to DVD or on the internet)
- the first 65 commercial hours of a series or a season of a series, and
- a short-form animation, short-form animated documentary or animated series or animated seasons of a series with episodes of at least 15 commercial minutes in duration.

The offset was denied in *Beyond Productions Pty Ltd v Screen Australia* for 2 new seasons of a television series because they had neither "significant Australian content" nor "a new creative concept" relative to the previous seasons.

The company must incur at least the following amounts of total QAPE to be eligible for the offset:

- $500,000 for a feature film and single episode program, other than a documentary. For a single episode program that is a documentary, there is an additional requirement that the company must incur at least $250,000 QAPE for each hour
- $250,000 for a short-form animated film, with the additional requirement that the company must incur at least $1 million QAPE for each hour
- $1 million for a series, or a season of a series, that is not a documentary, with the additional requirement that the company must incur at least $500,000 QAPE for each hour
- $500,000 for a series, or a season of a series, that is a documentary, with the additional requirement that the company must incur at least $250,000 QAPE for each hour. The offset was granted to a film series on household management as it was a "documentary" (*Screen Australia v EME Productions No 1 Pty Ltd*).

The normal rules about "incurring" expenditure apply (¶16-040). This means that, if a company is not under a presently existing liability nor definitively committed to the production expenditure, it will not qualify for the producer offset (*Creation Ministries International Ltd v Screen Australia*).

A company in receipt of financial assistance from the film authority's Producer Equity Program for the making of a documentary film is ineligible for the producer offset for that film.

A "film" does not include an advertising program or commercial, a discussion program, a quiz program, a panel program, a variety program or a program of a like nature, a film of a public event (other than a documentary), a training film, a computer game, a news or current affairs program or a reality program (other than a documentary).

As a result of the decision in EME Productions, a definition of "documentary" now applies (s 376-25). A "documentary" is a creative treatment of actuality excluding "infotainment or lifestyle programs" and "magazine programs". The TV series "Bride and Prejudice" was held not to be a documentary under the statutory definition as it was not a creative treatment of actuality (*Seven Network (Operations) Ltd v Screen Australia*).

Game shows are also specifically excluded from being eligible for the tax offsets as light entertainment programs (along with panel and quiz shows which are already excluded).

Amount of the offset

For a feature film, the amount of the offset is 40% of the total of the company's QAPE on the film; for all other films, the amount of the offset is 20%. There is no entitlement to the producer offset where the film has been granted a final certificate for either the location offset or the PDV offset.

Proposed changes

In a media release on 30 September, it was proposed to:

- make the offset rate for feature films and all other films 30%
- increase the minimum QAPE threshold for feature films to $1 million
- remove the "Gallipoli Clause" (which permits some costs incurred outside Australia to be claimed as QAPE)

- remove the 65 hours commercial hour cap for drama productions
- remove overheads as eligible expenditure
- cap the level of copyright expenditure that can be claimed at 30% of total production expenditure, and
- extend the ''above the line'' cap to non-feature documentaries (currently the producer tax offset caps ''above the line'' QAPE at 20% of total film expenditure for all content except non-feature documentaries).

These changes are proposed to apply to productions that commence principal photography or PDV activities on or after 1 July 2021.

[FITR ¶351-685]

¶20-350 Location offset

The location offset (ITAA97 ss 376-10 to 376-30) is available if the total of the company's QAPE on the film is at least $15 million and its QAPE ceased being incurred in the income year. In addition:

- the Arts Minister must have granted a certificate to the company
- the offset must be claimed by the company in its income tax return for the income year in which PDV effects production work ceased, and
- the company must be either an Australian resident company or a foreign resident company with a permanent establishment and an ABN. This must be the case both when the tax return is lodged and the offset is paid. While it is not strictly a requirement that the company be an eligible company when it makes its application to the minister for a certificate, it is expected that companies will meet this criterion when they make their application.

A film is eligible for the location offset if it is a feature film or a film of a like nature, a mini-series of television drama or a television series not otherwise covered. A production is ineligible for the location offset if it is a documentary (other than a television series), an advertisement or commercial, a discussion program, quiz program, panel program, variety or similar program, a film of a public event, a training film or a film forming part of a drama program series that is of a continuing nature. The location offset applies to online platforms, applicable for applications received from 11 April 2019.

There is no entitlement to the location offset where the film has been granted a final certificate for either the producer offset or the PDV offset.

The Location Offset Rules 2018 (*Legislative Instrument* F2018L00115) provide for the way in which the Board will issue provisional certificates and how applications for provisional and final certificates are to be made.

Amount of the offset

The amount of the offset is 16.5% of the total of the company's QAPE on the film.

Location incentive

The government also provides a location incentive worth $140 million for the Australian film industry over 4 years from 2019–20. The incentive is a grant of up to 13.5% of QAPE and productions must meet the eligibility criteria for the location offset to be eligible. The government has announced that an additional $400 million will be available under the location incentive, which will be extended so that it will be available until 2026–27 (Prime Minister's media release, 17 July 2020).

Proposed changes

In a media release on 30 September, it was proposed to:

- remove overheads as eligible expenditure, and
- cap the level of copyright expenditure that can be claimed at 30% of total production expenditure.

These changes are proposed to apply to productions that commence principal photography or PDV activities on or after 1 July 2021.

[FITR ¶351-675]

¶20-360 PDV offset

The PDV offset (ITAA97 ss 376-35 to 376-50) is available where:

- all eligible expenditure, PDV effects production-related expenditure, has ceased being incurred
- the Arts Minister has granted a certificate to the company
- the offset is claimed by the company in its income tax return for the income year in which PDV effects production work ceased, and
- the company is either an Australian resident company or a foreign resident company with a permanent establishment and an ABN (as in ¶20-350).

There is no entitlement to the PDV offset where the film has been granted a final certificate for either the producer offset or the location offset.

The PDV Offset Rules 2018 (*Legislative Instrument* F2018L00114) provide for the way in which the Board will issue provisional certificates and specify how applications for provisional and final certificates are to be made.

Eligible productions

The total of the company's QAPE on the film relating to PDV effect production must be at least $500,000.

Examples of PDV effects production include: 2D and 3D animation, green-screen photography (so long as the entire film is not shot against green-screen), pre-visualisation, music composition and recording, online and offline editing, still photography, matte painting and stills manipulation, credit design, models and miniatures, foley effects, additional dialogue recording and colour-correction. The hire of stages and facilities and other expenditures that are necessarily related to the undertaking of PDV effects production are also PDV effects production, as would salaries for actors recording additional dialogue or appearing in green-screen photography and expenditure on costumes for green-screen photography.

A production is ineligible for the PDV offset if it is a documentary (other than a television series), an advertisement or commercial, a discussion program, quiz program, panel program, variety or similar program, a film of a public event, a training film or a film forming part of a drama program series that is of a continuing nature. The PDV offset extends to online platforms, applicable for applications received from 11 April 2019.

Amount of the offset

The amount of the offset is 30% of the company's QAPE to the extent that the QAPE relates to the PDV effects production of a film.

Proposed changes

In a media release on 30 September, it was proposed to:

- increase the minimum PDV-QAPE threshold to $1 million
- remove overheads as eligible expenditure, and
- cap the level of copyright expenditure that can be claimed at 30% of total production expenditure.

These changes are proposed to apply to productions that commence principal photography or PDV activity on or after 1 July 2021.

[FITR ¶351-680]

Buildings and Structural Improvements

¶20-470 Deductions for capital works expenditure

A taxpayer can claim a deduction for capital expenditure incurred in constructing capital works, including buildings and structural improvements (ITAA97 Div 43: ss 43-1 to 43-260) (¶20-500). The deduction is either 2.5% or 4% of the construction expenditure, depending on when construction started and how the capital works are used (¶20-520). However, the deduction cannot exceed the undeducted construction expenditure (¶20-510) of the capital works.

A capital works deduction is generally available if the capital works (¶20-480) are used in a deductible way *during the income year* (¶20-490). In addition, for capital works started before 1 July 1997, the capital works must also have been intended for certain kinds of use *at the time of completion* (¶20-490).

Capital works deductions are not available until the construction of the capital works has been completed. Capital works deductions are calculated separately for each capital works project. For example, if a building is constructed at one time and is later extended, the construction expenditure for the later extension is treated as entirely separate from the construction expenditure for the original building.

A capital works deduction can be claimed if, at the time that the construction expenditure was incurred on the capital works, the taxpayer was to own or lease the capital works or hold the capital works under a quasi-ownership right over land granted by an exempt Australian or foreign government agency (eg a Crown lease).

Capital works deductible under these provisions are specifically excluded from the rules for calculating the decline in value of depreciating assets (¶17-030).

The capital works deduction is subject to the limited recourse finance provisions (¶23-260) and the debt forgiveness provisions (¶16-910).

Who can claim capital works deductions?

Generally, an entity is entitled to claim the deduction for capital works to the extent that the entity is the owner of the capital works (s 43-115). A subsequent owner can also claim capital works deductions based on the original construction expenditure of capital works. The actual purchase price of the capital works is not relevant in such a case. The construction expenditure for capital works purchased from a speculative builder is deductible to the first and subsequent buyers of the capital works even though the construction expenditure was not originally on capital account in the hands of the builder. If capital works are acquired under a deferred purchase agreement, deductions are available to the purchaser from the date of completion of construction when the purchaser takes possession, even though legal ownership may not pass for several years (IT 2254).

Certain anti-avoidance provisions dealing with leveraged (¶23-210) and non-leveraged leasing arrangements apply to taxpayers who are not owners of property as if they were the owners of that property for the purposes of the capital works deductions (s 43-45).

If the construction expenditure for capital works was incurred by a lessee or holder of quasi-ownership rights, the deduction is available to the lessee or rightholder, rather than the owner (s 43-120). A lessee or rightholder is also entitled to claim the deduction if the capital works have been continuously leased or held under a quasi-ownership right since construction was completed by another earlier lessee or rightholder that incurred the expenditure (or their assignee) (eg ID 2004/410; ID 2004/825). A taxpayer who enters into the novation of a lease is not ‘‘an assignee’’ of the earlier lessee's lease for the purposes of s 43-120 (ID 2012/4). If the lease or quasi-ownership right ends, the right to capital works deductions reverts to the owner of the capital works (s 43-125). However, capital works deductions are only available to the holder of quasi-ownership rights if: (a) in the case of hotel and apartment buildings (¶20-490), construction started after 30 June 1997; and (b) in the case of other capital works, construction started after 26 February 1992.

[FITR ¶98-000ff]

¶20-480 Capital works

‘‘Capital works’’ is an umbrella term covering a wide range of structures, and extensions, alterations and improvements to such structures. Capital works are divided into 3 broad categories: (a) buildings; (b) structural improvements; and (c) environment protection earthworks (ITAA97 s 43-20).

Buildings

Capital works deductions are available on the cost of constructing buildings, or extensions, alterations or improvements to buildings. Examples include factories, offices, shops, blocks of flats, rental home units, hotels, motels and R&D buildings. However, capital works deductions cannot be claimed if the building, extension, alteration or improvement was located in Australia and started being constructed before 22 August 1979 or was located outside Australia and started being constructed before 22 August 1990.

No deduction is available under ITAA97 Div 43 for the purchase price or original construction expenditure of a second-hand house constructed before 22 August 1979 that is relocated to the taxpayer's land and subsequently altered and improved (ID 2004/137).

Structural improvements

Capital works deductions are also available for the cost of constructing capital works started after 26 February 1992 that are structural improvements, or extensions, alterations or improvements to such structural improvements. It does not matter whether such structural improvements are made in or outside Australia.

Structural improvements include: (a) sealed roads, driveways, car parks and airport runways; (b) bridges, pipelines and lined road tunnels; (c) retaining walls (but not the improved area of land behind the wall or the reclaimed land behind a seawall: ID 2009/96), fences and concrete or rock dams (including breakwaters: ID 2004/270); and (d) artificial sports fields. Fences and gates installed by a child care provider generally qualify as structural improvements (TD 93/21). However, no deduction is allowable for structural improvements to a driveway of a private home which is partly used to produce assessable income (ID 2003/706). This is because, under ITAA97 s 43-170, if any part of the capital works are used mainly for, or in association with, the taxpayer's or an associate's residential accommodation, then they are not taken to be used for the purpose of producing assessable income. Structural improvements also include earthworks that are integral to the construction of a particular structural improvement that is itself eligible for capital works deductions. Examples include: (a) embankments, cuttings, culverts and tunnels associated with roads, railways or airport runways; and (b) the gravel underlay and bitumen surfacing for a car park.

Capital expenditure on certain kinds of structural improvements that are earthworks is specifically excluded from eligibility for capital works deductions, unless the improvements are environment protection earthworks (see below). These excluded earthworks are those that: (a) are not integral to the installation or construction of a structure; (b) are permanent (assuming they are maintained in reasonably good order and condition); and (c) can be economically maintained in reasonably good order and condition for an indefinite period. Examples of such earthworks include unlined channels, unlined basins, earth tanks, dirt tracks and dirt car parks. In addition, earthworks that simply create artificial landscapes (such as grass golf fairways and greens, gardens, and grass sports fields) are not structural improvements eligible for capital works deductions.

Environment protection earthworks

Capital works deductions are also available for the cost of constructing capital works that are environment protection earthworks, or extensions, alterations or improvements to such earthworks. ‘‘Environment protection earthworks’’ are capital works: (a) that are constructed as part of carrying out an environmental protection activity; (b) that can be economically maintained in reasonably good order and condition for an indefinite period; (c) that are not integral to the construction of capital works; and (d) for which the capital expenditure was incurred after 18 August 1992. An ‘‘environmental protection activity’’ refers to the act of: (a) preventing, fighting or remedying pollution; or (b) treating, cleaning up, removing or storing waste. In either case, the pollution or waste must be on the site of the taxpayer’s income-earning activity or have resulted, or be likely to result, from an income-producing activity of the taxpayer or from a business activity of the taxpayer’s predecessor on the polluted site.

[FITR ¶98-240]

¶20-490 Actual use and intended use of capital works

Both of the following ‘‘use’’ tests must be satisfied before a capital works deduction is available:

- the capital works must actually be used in a deductible way in the income year in which the deduction is claimed, and
- for pre-1 July 1997 works only, the capital works must have been intended for use for specified purposes at the time of completion.

Current year use of capital works

A capital works deduction is generally available if the capital works are used in a deductible way *during the income year*. To work out if capital works are used in a deductible way during the income year, reference must be made to when the capital works started being constructed (ITAA97 s 43-140).

Capital works are taken to start being constructed when the first step in the construction phase starts, eg the pouring of foundations or sinking of pilings for a building.

Capital works started *after* 30 June 1997 are used in a deductible way if used for the purpose of producing assessable income or carrying on R&D activities. Capital works started *before* 1 July 1997 are used in a deductible way if they are: (a) hotel or apartment buildings that provide short-term traveller accommodation (see below) used for the purpose of producing assessable income; or (b) other capital works used for the purpose of producing assessable income or carrying on R&D activities. The use of property for environmental protection activities or to carry out an activity for an environmental impact assessment of a project qualifies as a deductible purpose.

Capital works are used for a particular purpose if they are maintained ready for use for that purpose, provided that they are not used for any other purpose and the intended use has not been abandoned. Capital works are also taken to be used for a particular purpose if such use has temporarily stopped because of: (a) repairs or further construction work; or (b) seasonal or climatic factors. This means that deductions are available for commercial premises available for lease or a factory that has been temporarily closed down because of a lack of demand for certain products. An area may be used in a deductible way even if the rent received is below commercial levels (ID 2004/623). Where a rental property is destroyed, an amount can be deducted in the income year in which the capital works are destroyed for all of the construction expenditure that has not yet been deducted. However, this deduction is reduced by any insurance and salvage receipts (ATO's guide to Rental Properties 2019). If, however, a building is damaged and cannot be rented or made available for rent but it is expected to be made available for rent again, a deduction cannot be claimed for capital works for the number of days that the building is not available for rent. Similarly, a taxpayer cannot deduct an amount for structural improvements made to a rental property during the period when the property was advertised for sale and was not available to rent (ID 2004/593).

Capital works used for exhibition purposes, eg display homes, are not eligible for capital works deductions if they started being constructed before 1 July 1997.

Capital works deductions cannot be claimed for a home office. However, if part of the taxpayer's home represents a distinct and separate area used for income-producing purposes and is not used or suitable for residential accommodation by the taxpayer or an associate, eg if a business was conducted from home, capital works deductions are available (TR 97/25), but there may be CGT consequences on disposal of the building (¶11-760).

Temporary cessation of use

Capital works are taken to be used, or available for use, for a particular purpose or in a particular manner if the use of those capital works for that purpose or in that manner temporarily ceases because of:

- the construction or an extension, alteration or improvement
- the making of repairs, or
- seasonal or climatic factors (ITAA97 s 43-165).

Intended use of pre-1 July 1997 capital works

For capital works started before 1 July 1997, the capital works must also have been *intended* for use for a certain purpose *at the time of completion*. To work out if such capital works were intended for a purpose that would qualify for a capital works deduction, reference must be made to when the capital works started being constructed (ITAA97 s 43-90). The intended use test does not apply to post-30 June 1997 capital works.

The following table summarises what the intended use must have been at the time capital works were completed by reference to the various pre-1 July 1997 start dates:

Construction start date	Intended use at time of completion
22.8.79–19.7.82	Hotel or apartment buildings
20.7.82–17.7.85	Hotel or apartment buildings Non-residential buildings (eg factories, offices, shops) to be used for producing assessable or exempt income

Construction start date	Intended use at time of completion
18.7.85–20.11.87	Buildings to be used for producing assessable or exempt income, including hotel and apartment buildings Buildings to be used for providing residential accommodation (eg houses and flats), including hotel and apartment buildings
21.11.87–26.2.92	Buildings to be used for producing assessable or exempt income Buildings to be used for providing residential accommodation or for carrying on R&D activities
27.2.92–18.8.92	Certain hotel or apartment buildings to be used for short-term traveller accommodation Buildings or structural improvements to be used for producing assessable or exempt income Buildings or structural improvements to be used for, or in connection with, the provision of residential accommodation Buildings or structural improvements to be used for carrying on R&D activities
19.8.92–30.6.97	Certain hotel or apartment buildings to be used for short-term traveller accommodation Buildings, structural improvements or environment protection earthworks to be used for producing assessable or exempt income Buildings, structural improvements or environment protection earthworks to be used for, or in connection with, the provision of residential accommodation Buildings, structural improvements or environment protection earthworks to be used for carrying on R&D activities

''Residential accommodation'' is not limited to income-producing residential accommodation. For example, the intended use requirement will be satisfied even if the residential accommodation was intended to be used, after completion, for private purposes (provided the building is actually used for income-producing purposes in the year in which the deduction is claimed).

Hotel and apartment buildings

A hotel building is, broadly, a building used mainly to operate a hotel, motel or guesthouse where the building has at least 10 bedrooms that are for use mainly to provide short-term traveller accommodation. An apartment building is, broadly, a building consisting of at least 10 apartments, units or flats that are for use mainly to provide short-term traveller accommodation (ITAA97 s 43-95). A fully furnished, self-contained accommodation area within a building that consists of a fully-equipped kitchen, bathroom, laundry, fully-furnished bedroom, lounge and dining area, and full ironing facilities is generally an apartment and not a hotel (ID 2003/513). A building's status as an apartment building is not affected if it also has facilities (such as lounge rooms and games rooms) that are mainly for use in association with providing short-term traveller accommodation.

[FITR ¶98-000ff, ¶98-470, ¶98-480, ¶98-720]

¶20-500 Calculation of capital works deductions

Capital works deductions are calculated using the following formula (ITAA97 ss 43-210; 43-215):

$$\text{construction expenditure} \times \text{applicable rate} \times \frac{\text{days used}}{365}$$

The meaning of "construction expenditure" is discussed at ¶20-510. The "applicable rate" is 2.5% or 4% depending on: (a) when construction of the capital works started; and (b) the use to which the capital works are put (¶20-520). Separate calculations are made at both rates if capital works qualify partly for the 2.5% rate and partly for the 4% rate, so that an apportionment can be made. "Days used" is the number of days in the income year that the capital works were used either in a deductible way or so as to qualify for the 4% rate (¶20-520). The deduction cannot exceed the amount of the undeducted construction expenditure (¶20-510).

In the case of a leap year, the relevant number of days where the item has been used for the deductible purpose for the whole year is 366. This means that, if the capital works are so used for the whole of an income year that included 29 February, the "days used" component of the formula will be 366.

▶ Example 1

Construction of a block of flats started in March 2019 under a contract entered into in July 2018. The 2.5% rate therefore applies (¶20-520). The total construction expenditure is $2 million and the building is completed and first used for income-producing purposes on 24 February 2020. The taxpayer is entitled to a capital works deduction in 2019–20 of $17,534 (ie 128/365 × 2.5% × $2 million). In each of the following 39 years that is not a leap year, the taxpayer is entitled to an annual deduction of $50,000. For the leap years, the taxpayer is entitled to an annual deduction of $50,137. In 2059–60, the taxpayer is entitled to a deduction for the balance of $31,233, ie the remaining undeducted construction expenditure.

▶ Example 2

Construction of an R&D building started on 17 February 2019 under a contract entered into on 12 November 2018. The total construction expenditure is $1 million and the building is completed and first used for R&D purposes on 30 December 2019. The taxpayer is entitled to a capital works deduction in 2019–20 of $12,602 (ie 184/365 × 2.5% × $1 million). In each of the following 39 years that is not a leap year, the taxpayer is entitled to an annual deduction of $25,000. For those years that are leap years, the taxpayer is entitled to an annual deduction of $25,068. In 2059–60, the taxpayer is entitled to a deduction for the balance of $11,786, ie the remaining undeducted construction expenditure.

▶ Example 3

Construction of a fruit and vegetable canning factory started on 31 October 2018 and the building is completed and first used for income-producing purposes on 29 September 2019. As the factory is used for carrying on industrial activities (¶20-520), the 4% rate applies. The total construction expenditure is $5 million. The taxpayer is entitled to a capital works deduction in 2019–20 of $151,232 (ie 276/365 × 4% × $5 million). In each of the following 24 years that is not a leap year (assuming continual use as a fruit and vegetable canning factory or for any other eligible industrial activity), the taxpayer is entitled to an annual deduction of $200,000. For those years that are leap years, the taxpayer is entitled to an annual deduction of $200,548. In 2044–45, the taxpayer will be entitled to a deduction for the balance of $45,480, ie the remaining undeducted construction expenditure.

▶ Example 4

Construction of an R&D building is started on 17 February 2006 under a contract entered into on 12 November 2005. The total construction expenditure is $1 million and the building is completed and first used for R&D purposes on 30 December 2006. However, on 12 May 2013, the building's use changed and is, from that time onwards, used in carrying on an industrial activity. The taxpayer is entitled to a capital works deduction as follows:

Income year ended 30 June	Deduction using the 2.5% rate ($)	Deduction using the 4% rate ($)	Total deduction ($)
2007	12,534	0	12,534
2008	25,068	0	25,068
2009	25,000	0	25,000
2010	25,000	0	25,000
2011	25,000	0	25,000
2012	25,068	0	25,068

Income year ended 30 June	Deduction using the 2.5% rate ($)	Deduction using the 4% rate ($)	Total deduction ($)
2013	21,575	5,479	27,054
2014	0	40,000	40,000
2015	0	40,000	40,000
2016	0	40,110	40,110
2017	0	40,000	40,000
2018	0	40,000	40,000
2019	0	40,000	40,000
2020	0	40,110	40,110
2021	0	40,000	40,000
2022	0	40,000	40,000
2023	0	40,000	40,000
2024	0	40,110	40,110
2025	0	40,000	40,000
2026	0	40,000	40,000
2027	0	40,000	40,000
2028	0	40,110	40,110
2029	0	40,000	40,000
2030	0	40,000	40,000
2031	0	40,000	40,000
2032	0	40,110	40,110
2033	0	40,000	40,000
2034	0	34,726	34,726
Totals	159,245	840,755	1,000,000

Where only a part of capital works is used in a deductible way, an apportionment reducing the deduction should generally be made on a floor area basis. However, if another basis is more appropriate in a particular situation, that other basis should be adopted (TR 97/25).

[FITR ¶99-030, ¶99-040]

¶20-510 Construction expenditure

The deduction base for the purpose of working out capital works deductions is the construction expenditure incurred in building the relevant capital works. ''Construction expenditure'' is broadly defined as *capital* expenditure incurred on the construction of capital works (ITAA97 s 43-70(1)). Therefore, expenditure of a property developer on a building that was held as trading stock was revenue in nature and did not qualify as construction expenditure (ID 2003/377).

Construction expenditure is determined on the basis of the *actual cost* incurred in relation to the construction of a building, structural improvement, extension, etc. Construction expenditure includes preliminary expenses such as architect's fees, engineering fees, surveying fees, building fees, costs associated with obtaining the necessary building approvals and the cost of foundation excavations (TR 97/25). It also includes the cost of excavating existing roads where the excavation is integral to the construction of a building on land owned and leased by the taxpayer, and expenditure to build temporary roads and restore the area afterwards (ID 2014/37).

Certain types of capital expenditure are specifically *excluded* from being construction expenditure. These are: (a) the cost of acquiring land (but this does not include constructing a rock wall: ID 2007/142); (b) the cost of demolishing existing structures; (c) the cost of preparing a construction site (eg clearing, levelling, filling or draining) before carrying out excavation works; (d) the cost of landscaping (including landscaping design: ID 2006/235); (e) the cost of plant (¶17-040), eg mudlakes, tailings dams and similar industrial residue or waste disposal facilities (TR 1999/2), structural improvements on land used for agricultural or pastoral operations but not rock walls (ID 2007/160), air conditioning and lifts, plant or articles used in residential rental properties (TR 2004/16 which is discussed further at ¶17-040); (f) the cost of property for which a deduction is allowable under special provisions for mining and quarrying (¶19-010, ¶19-070 – ¶19-100), project infrastructure (¶19-060), scientific research, primary production (¶16-820, ¶18-060 – ¶18-100), forestry roads and timber mill buildings, and R&D buildings started before 21 November 1987; and (g) rebatable heritage conservation expenditure. A forestry road is a road constructed primarily and principally for providing access to enable trees to be planted, tended or removed. A timber mill building is a building for use primarily and principally in carrying on the taxpayer's timber milling business or for housing employees (or their dependants) engaged in that business (ITAA97 s 43-72). A deduction for the decline in value of depreciating assets (including plant, forestry roads and timber mill buildings) is available under the uniform capital allowance provisions (¶17-000).

Expenditure incurred by a taxpayer in relation to the relocation of a house to be used as residential rental premises, carried out before placing the moved house on the taxpayer's land, is not construction expenditure (ID 2004/138).

The value of an owner/builder's contribution to capital works (such as labour and expertise) and any notional profit element are not included in construction expenditure. This means that expenditure incurred in travelling between home and construction site, where the taxpayer manages and supervises the construction of a rental property, is not construction expenditure. Where a taxpayer buys capital works from a speculative builder, the construction expenditure of the capital works similarly excludes the builder's contribution and profit element (TR 97/25).

Indirect costs related to the construction of capital works *and* the construction or installation of plant can be allocated in accordance with the proportion that the direct cost of the plant bears to the direct cost of the buildings (*BP Refinery (Kwinana)*). If any other method is used, it must be justifiable on the basis of sound accounting principles and practical considerations (TR 97/25). Where items of furniture, fittings or plant are acquired and have no link to indirect costs, their cost should not be included in calculations apportioning their indirect costs.

Construction expenditure is reduced by the amount of any forgiven commercial debt (¶16-910).

Construction expenditure where original construction cost unknown

A person who disposes of the whole or a part of capital works to another person is required to provide a notice to the transferee containing information about the transferor's holding of the capital works, eg construction cost, when construction was completed (ITAA36 s 262A(4AJA)). The purpose of the notice is to provide enough information to enable the transferee to calculate its capital works deduction.

However, where a taxpayer is completely unable to obtain information about the actual cost of capital works, a building cost estimate by a quantity surveyor or other independent qualified person may be used. Examples of other qualified people may include clerks of works, builders experienced in estimating construction costs of similar building projects, supervising architects and project organisers. However, valuers, real estate agents, accountants and solicitors are not normally considered to be appropriately qualified.

The transferee's cost of obtaining such an estimate is deductible (¶16-850) even if the transferee did not request the information from the transferor.

Undeducted construction expenditure

"Undeducted construction expenditure" is the remaining balance of the construction expenditure that is still eligible for a capital works deduction (ITAA97 s 43-235). It is relevant for: (a) limiting the total amount of capital works deductions available in respect of capital works (¶20-500); and (b) working out the balancing deduction arising from the demolition or destruction of capital works (¶20-530).

In working out the undeducted construction expenditure, notional capital works deductions are calculated for any period that the capital works do not qualify for a deduction, eg if they are not used for producing assessable income during a particular income year (ID 2014/38).

Pre-27 February 1992 capital works

For capital works on which construction started before 27 February 1992, the undeducted construction expenditure is worked out depending on when construction started (ITAA97 s 43-240). If construction started after 21 August 1984 and before 16 September 1987, the undeducted construction expenditure is calculated by reducing the construction expenditure by 4% per year from the time the capital works were first used for any purpose. However, if construction started before 22 August 1984 or after 15 September 1987, the undeducted construction expenditure is calculated by reducing the construction expenditure by 2.5% per year from the time the capital works were first used for any purpose.

Post-26 February 1992 capital works

For capital works on which construction started after 26 February 1992, the undeducted construction expenditure is worked out by reducing the construction expenditure by 2.5% per year from the time the capital works were first used for any purpose (ITAA97 s 43-235). However, if a capital works deduction was actually claimed at the 4% rate during a period, the construction expenditure is instead reduced by the deductions actually claimed at the 4% rate for that period.

[FITR ¶98-430, ¶99-110, ¶99-120; FTR ¶785-080]

¶20-520 Rates of capital works deduction

A summary of applicable rates is at ¶43-115.

Pre-27 February 1992 capital works

The rate of deduction for capital works used in a deductible way during an income year (¶20-490) is (ITAA97 s 43-25):

- 4% of the construction expenditure if construction started after 21 August 1984 and before 16 September 1987 (or under a contract entered into before 16 September 1987, even if construction started after that time)
- 2.5% of the construction expenditure if construction started before 22 August 1984 or after 15 September 1987.

Post-26 February 1992 capital works

If capital works on which construction started after 26 February 1992 are used in a deductible way during an income year (¶20-490), there is a basic entitlement to a capital works deduction rate of 2.5% of the construction expenditure (s 43-25).

Use for which special 4% deduction rate is available

Expenditure on certain post-26 February 1992 capital works qualifies for a capital works deduction rate of 4% of the construction expenditure (ITAA97 s 43-145) if the capital works are assessable income-producing buildings:

- used mainly for: (a) industrial activities (see below); (b) the provision of employee amenities for workers (or their immediate supervisors) carrying out industrial activities; or (c) office accommodation for the immediate supervisors of those workers
- used mainly to operate a hotel, motel or guesthouse where the buildings have at least 10 bedrooms that are for use wholly to provide short-term traveller accommodation (ie hotel buildings), or
- consisting of at least 10 apartments, units or flats that are for use wholly to provide short-term traveller accommodation, ie apartment buildings. The 4% rate is still available if the buildings also have facilities that are mainly for use in association with providing short-term traveller accommodation.

Industrial activities

Industrial activities are (ITAA97 s 43-150):

- operations where manufactured items are made from other goods, even if those manufactured items are themselves then used as parts or materials in the manufacture of other items
- operations by which manufactured items are brought into or maintained in the form or condition in which they are sold or used (eg the painting of furniture or the provision of cold storage for perishables), even if they are for sale or use as parts or materials (but excluding packing, labelling or placing in containers)
- operations (including canning, bottling, freezing, milling, scouring, carbonising, curing or pasteurising) involved in processing primary products, as well as the separation of a metal or the treatment or processing of a metal after separation, the refining of petroleum and the production of various energy sources (other than from natural gas) for sale or use in other core activities
- printing, lithographing, engraving and other similar processes that take place in the course of carrying on a business as a publisher, printer, lithographer or engraver
- the preparation of foodstuffs in a factory or brewery (but not the preparation of food or drink in a hotel, motel, boarding house, restaurant, cafe, milk bar, coffee shop, retail shop, catering place or similar establishment, for consumption on the premises or elsewhere)
- activities associated with the above core activities, ie: (a) packing, labelling or placing in containers goods resulting from core activities; (b) disposing of waste from core activities; (c) cleansing or sterilising containers (including bottles and vats) used to store goods used in or resulting from core activities; (d) assembling, maintaining, cleansing, sterilising or repairing property (eg plant and equipment) used in core activities; and (e) storing on the premises where core activities are carried on (or on contiguous premises) goods to be used or in the process of being used in core activities, or completed core activity goods.

[FITR ¶98-250, ¶98-730, ¶98-740]

¶20-530 Consequences of demolition, destruction or disposal

If capital works are demolished or destroyed, whether voluntarily or involuntarily (TR 97/25), a balancing deduction is allowed (ITAA97 ss 43-40; 43-250). The amount of the balancing deduction is usually the undeducted construction expenditure (¶20-510) of the capital works at the time of the demolition or destruction. However, the balancing deduction is reduced by the excess of any insurance or salvage recoveries over demolition costs. If the insurance proceeds received in respect of the destruction exceed that building's undeducted construction expenditure, the amount of the deduction is nil. A right to receive an amount under an insurance policy for the destruction of works must also be taken into account (ID 2004/860). Insurance proceeds received in respect of the destruction of capital works that occurred in a previous year cannot be offset against the construction cost of replacement capital works (ID 2004/862). Demolition costs can increase the amount of deduction allowable to the extent that these costs reduce the amounts received for disposing of the destroyed capital works (ID 2003/833).

The balancing deduction is reduced to the extent that the taxpayer or another person did not use the capital works for the purpose of producing assessable income while it owned or held the capital works. If the amounts received or receivable on destruction or demolition of the capital works exceed the undeducted construction expenditure, no amount is assessable. It is reasonable to apportion the insurance proceeds receivable by taking into account the relative replacement costs of the deductible and non-deductible capital works (ID 2004/861).

While no balancing adjustment is required on disposal of capital works, there may be CGT consequences (¶11-240, ¶11-550, ¶11-560). In calculating the profit made on the disposal of a building held on revenue account, an insurance company was not required to exclude from cost the capital works deduction previously claimed for the building. In other words, there was no clawback of the capital works deduction under ITAA36 s 82 (*MLC*).

[FITR ¶99-220]

National Rental Affordability Scheme

¶20-600 Outline of NRAS

The National Rental Affordability Scheme (NRAS) is designed to encourage large-scale investment in housing by offering an incentive to participants so as to increase the supply of affordable rental dwellings and reduce rental costs for low and moderate income households. The principal legislation is the *National Rental Affordability Scheme Act 2008* and the National Rental Affordability Scheme Regulations 2008. It is administered by the Department of Social Services (the Housing Secretary). See also the *National Rental Affordability Scheme Guidelines*, available at www.dss.gov.au.

The NRAS offers incentives to providers of new dwellings on the condition that those dwellings are rented to low and moderate income households at 20% below market rates. The scheme operates on an ''NRAS year'' which runs from 1 May to 30 April. The incentive comprises a refundable tax offset, plus a state or territory contribution in the form of direct financial support or in-kind contribution, per dwelling per year.

The incentive is provided each year for 10 years to complying participants and is indexed in line with the rental component of the CPI. The amount of the incentive is reduced if the dwelling is not available for rent during the NRAS year or if it is vacant for a period of more than 13 weeks.

Not-for-profit entities do not ordinarily pay tax and so are not eligible to receive incentives in the form of refundable tax offsets. Instead, not-for-profit entities may receive incentives in the form of an amount payable for an NRAS year. To ensure that the charitable sector can participate fully in the scheme without jeopardising their charitable status, the definition of ''charitable purpose'' has been expanded to include the provision of rental dwellings under the NRAS, applicable to approved participants during the first 2 years of the scheme's operation (s 4A of the *Extension of Charitable Purpose Act 2004*).

Under the regulations, the Housing Secretary may make a call for applications. Round One of applications closed 4 September 2008. The last round was Round 4 which closed on 14 December 2010. The government announced on 13 May 2014 that it was not proceeding with Round 5 and no further rounds have been announced. The scheme will cease in 2026–27.

Eligible tenants

To be eligible, the dwelling must be rented to an "eligible tenant". To qualify as an eligible tenant, the household's gross income for the 12 months prior to commencement of tenancy of an NRAS dwelling must be equal to or less than the relevant income limit. All persons who ordinarily reside in an NRAS home must have their income included as a member of the household. A dwelling ceases to be eligible for an incentive if the tenants' household income exceeds the relevant income limit by 25% or more in 2 consecutive eligibility years. The annual gross income limits for the 2020–21 NRAS year (ie 1 May 2020 to 30 April 2021):

Household type	Initial income limit $*	Upper income limit $**
One adult	52,324	65,405
2 adults	72,341	90,427
3 adults	92,358	115,448
4 adults	112,375	140,469
Sole parent with 1 child	72,391	90,489
Sole parent with 2 children	89,748	112,185
Sole parent with 3 children	107,105	133,882
Couple with 1 child	89,698	112,123
Couple with 2 children	107,055	133,819
Couple with 3 children	124,412	155,515

* This limit must be met initially to qualify as an eligible tenant.

** A tenant ceases to be eligible when income exceeds this limit in 2 consecutive years.

The rent charged must be at least 20% less than the market value rent for the dwelling (as determined by an independent registered valuer).

For previous limits, see earlier editions of the *Australian Master Tax Guide*.

[FITR ¶352-255]

¶20-605 NRAS refundable tax offset

Entities participating in the NRAS can claim a refundable tax offset in their annual tax return (ITAA97 Div 380). The amount of tax offset available for the 2020–21 NRAS year is $8,452.94 ($8,436.07 for 2019–20) per dwelling. The offset claimable by each participant is notified in a certificate issued by the Housing Secretary.

Offsets claimable directly

An individual, corporate tax entity (ie a company, corporate limited partnership, corporate unit trust or a public trading trust) or superannuation fund is entitled to claim a refundable tax offset provided that:

- the Housing Secretary has issued the entity with a certificate in relation to an NRAS year, other than in the entity's capacity as the NRAS approved participant in an NRAS consortium, and
- the income year begins in the NRAS year (¶20-600) to which the certificate relates (s 380-5).

The amount of the refundable tax offset the entity is entitled to claim is the amount stated in the certificate.

If an individual, corporate tax entity or superannuation fund is a party to an NRAS consortium, those entities are entitled to claim the offset provided that:

- NRAS rent is derived by the party to an NRAS consortium in relation to the rental dwelling for an income year
- the NRAS approved participant of the NRAS consortium has been issued with a certificate by the Housing Secretary in relation to an NRAS year, and
- the income year begins in the NRAS year to which the certificate relates (s 380-10).

An NRAS consortium is a consortium, joint venture, or non-entity joint venture established by one or more contractual arrangements that facilitate the leasing of NRAS dwellings (s 995-1).

The amount of the offset per dwelling that such an entity may claim is the amount stated in the certificate for the rental dwelling apportioned by the NRAS rent derived by the entity from the dwelling for the income year and the total NRAS rent derived from the rental dwelling for the income year. The amounts per dwelling are summed to work out the total amount of the entity's (ie the individual's, corporate tax entity's, or superannuation fund's) offset.

A dwelling owner who leases their dwelling to an entity does not have an entitlement to the offset under s 380-10 if the entity subleases the dwelling as the dwelling owner does not derive NRAS rent (ID 2009/146).

Offset claimable indirectly

An entity may indirectly derive NRAS rent from a rental dwelling, as a partner of a partnership or a beneficiary of a trust. In this situation, the offset flows through the partnership or trust to the partners or beneficiaries. An entity is entitled to claim its share of the refundable tax offset consistent with its share of rental income from its participation in the NRAS through the trust or partnership (s 380-15).

A partner, trustee or beneficiary is entitled to claim the offset provided that:

- either the trust or partnership which directly receives the rental income has been issued with a certificate by the Housing Secretary under the NRAS applicable to the dwelling or the trust or partnership is a member of an NRAS consortium that has been issued with an NRAS certificate that covers one or more NRAS dwellings (in which case the partnership or trust will be deemed to be the NRAS approved participant to the extent of its interest in the consortium), and
- the income year of that trust or partnership begins in the NRAS year to which the certificate relates.

The entity indirectly receiving the NRAS rent may be:

- an individual
- a corporate entity (at the time the NRAS rent flows indirectly to it)
- the trustee of a trust that is liable to be assessed on a share of, or all or a part of, the trust's net income under ITAA36 s 98, 99 or 99A for that income year, or
- a superannuation fund, an approved deposit fund, or a pooled superannuation trust.

The amount of the offset that the partner or beneficiary is entitled to claim is equal to the amount stated in the certificate apportioned by the partner's or beneficiary's share of NRAS rent derived from a dwelling for the income year and the total NRAS rent derived from rental dwellings covered by the certificate for the relevant income year.

A beneficiary of a trust cannot receive NRAS rent indirectly in any year that the trust has no net income. In this situation, the trustee may be able to claim the offset under s 380-20. The amount of the offset that the trustee is entitled to claim is the trust's relevant share of the amount stated in the certificate.

Election to allow investors to claim NRAS tax offset

Some NRAS consortia may be structured in such a way that members receive rent which cannot be classified as NRAS rent. The NRAS approved participant (or a partnership or trust treated as the NRAS approved participant) may make an irrevocable election to transfer its entitlement to the tax offset to such members in proportion to the rent derived by the member (s 380-12). In this situation, it is the rent (net of any management fees and commission retained) that is used as the basis of apportionment. The entity making the election is not entitled to the tax offset. Any NRAS rent retained as a management fee or commission is treated as being passed to the other member(s).

The election must be made within 30 days of the issue of the certificate (or amended certificate). It must be in the approved form and the Commissioner may require that a copy of the election be given to the Commissioner and/or to each member of the NRAS consortium who may be entitled to a tax offset as a result of the election being made.

No CGT consequences

There are no CGT consequences arising from the provision to taxpayers of incentives or other benefits under the NRAS (ITAA97 s 118-37).

[FITR ¶352-265, ¶352-270, ¶352-285]

¶20-610 NRAS state and territory contribution

State and territory governments provide annual support for up to 10 years in the form of cash grants, stamp duty concessions or the provision of discounted land. For the 2020–21 NRAS year, the amount is $2,817.65 per property ($2,812.02 for 2019–20). ITAA97 s 380-35 ensures that state and territory contributions to entities participating in the NRAS, whether directly or indirectly (eg through an NRAS consortium) are non-assessable and non-exempt income.

[FITR ¶352-300]

National Innovation and Science Agenda Incentives

¶20-700 Outline of innovation incentives

The government's National Innovation and Science Agenda included a number of tax incentives designed to encourage innovation.

Early stage investors in start-ups

Concessional tax treatment in Subdiv 360-A applies to early stage investors in innovative start-ups, known as Early Stage Innovation Companies (ESICs), in relation to shares issued on or after 1 July 2016.

Investors may be entitled to a capital gains tax exemption (¶11-910).

In addition, entities (other than a trust or partnership) that acquire newly issued qualifying shares in an Australian ESIC may receive a non-refundable carry-forward tax offset of 20% of the value of the amount they paid for the shares, subject to a maximum offset cap amount of $200,000. A total annual investment limit of $50,000 applies to retail investors. There are no restrictions on the amount an entity may invest if it meets the requirements of the sophisticated investor test in s 708 of the *Corporations Act 2001* in relation to an offer of shares at any time in the income year.

"Qualifying shares" are newly issued equity interests (¶23-115) that are shares in a qualifying ESIC, where the issue of the shares does not constitute an acquisition of ESS interests under an employee share scheme (¶10-080). In order to qualify for the tax offset:

- the ESIC must not be an affiliate (¶7-050) of the investor nor can the investor be an affiliate of the ESIC at the time the relevant shares are issued, and
- the investor entity must not hold more than 30% of the equity interests of an ESIC, including any entities connected with (¶7-050) the ESIC, tested immediately after the time the equity interests are issued.

An equivalent tax offset is provided for members of trusts or partnerships who are, in substance, the ultimate investors. A beneficiary or unit holder of a trust, or a partner in a partnership, at the end of an income year is entitled to a carry-forward tax offset for that income year if the trust or partnership would have been entitled to a tax offset had it been an individual. A trustee is entitled to a tax offset if the trust would have been entitled to the tax offset had it been an individual and the trustee is liable to some extent for tax in respect of the activities of the trust (under ITAA36 s 98, 99 or 99A).

ESICs are required to report information annually about their investors to the ATO in order for the ATO to determine investor eligibility for the incentives.

Venture capital limited partnerships

The following tax treatment applies to Early Stage Venture Capital Limited Partnerships (ESVCLPs: ¶5-040):

- a 10% non-refundable carry-forward tax offset is available for partners on capital invested during the year (s 61-760). The amount of the tax offset is reduced to the extent that the amounts contributed by the partners are not, in effect, used by the ESVCLP to make eligible venture capital investments within that income year or the first 2 months after the end of that income year. If a limited partner is a partnership or trust, the offset will generally instead be available to the ultimate individual or corporate partners or beneficiaries
- the maximum fund size for new ESVCLPs is $200 million
- ESVCLPs are not required to divest a company when its value exceeds $250 million. However, if an ESVCLP does not dispose of an investment in an entity within 6 months after the end of an income year in which the investee's market value exceeds $250 million, then the ESVCLP will only be entitled to a partial CGT exemption (¶11-900), and
- entities in which a venture capital limited partnership (VCLP), ESVCLP or an Australian venture capital fund of funds (AFOF) has invested (the investee entity) are able to invest in other entities, provided that, after the investment: (i) the investee entity controls the other entity; and (ii) the other entity broadly satisfies the requirements to be an eligible venture capital investment under s 118-425.

FinTech businesses

Start-up FinTech businesses can access the early stage investor tax concession and the VCLP and ESVCLP regimes for investments made on or after 1 July 2018, following an amendment to the definition of "ineligible activities" with the result that activities are not "ineligible activities" if they are:

- developing technology in relation to finance, insurance or making investments
- ancillary or incidental to developing technology in relation to finance, insurance or making investments, or
- covered by a finding from Industry, Innovation and Science Australia that it is a substantially novel application of technology.

[FITR ¶110-350, ¶155-150, ¶336-003]

Chapter 21 Residence • Source • Foreign Tax Offsets • Accruals Taxation

¶21-000 Residence and source as criteria for liability

There are 2 main criteria for liability to Australian tax: *residence* and *source of income*. In general, it is necessary to determine whether or not the taxpayer concerned is a resident of Australia and then to determine the source of the income concerned.

A taxpayer, whether an individual or a company, who is a resident of Australia is generally assessable on ordinary and statutory income derived from all sources whether in or out of Australia (ITAA97 ss 6-5; 6-10). There are some exceptions to this rule, eg for limited types of overseas employment income (¶10-860), approved overseas projects (¶10-870) and certain temporary residents (¶22-125).

Income earned by some foreign companies and non-resident trusts is attributed to resident taxpayers and taxed on an accruals basis, eg it is taxed in the hands of resident taxpayers when it is derived, not when it is remitted to Australia. Income earned by resident taxpayers from certain other foreign investments may also be taxed on an accruals basis (¶21-105).

In contrast, a non-resident is generally liable to Australian tax only on ordinary and statutory income from Australian sources. This general rule is subject to a number of exceptions. For example, the liability of non-residents to withholding tax on dividends, interest and royalties is not dependent on the source of the amounts received. For the special CGT rules applying to non-residents, see ¶12-720 onwards.

Non-resident individuals are also subject to higher rates of tax than residents (¶42-015). A special rate of income tax applies to income earned by some working holiday makers (¶21-033).

Where the taxing powers of the source country and of the country of residence of the taxpayer are governed by a double taxation agreement, residence and source as determined according to Australian domestic law may be overridden by the provisions of the particular agreement (¶22-140).

Meaning of Australia

The geographical definition of ''Australia'' is a key factor for liability to Australian tax. It is important in working out whether an entity is a resident of Australia and whether an income or a gain has an Australian source. In summary, Australia, for income tax purposes, includes the states and internal territories (the Australian Capital Territory and the Northern Territory), Australia's territorial waters, all of Australia's external Territories (except the Australian Antarctic Territory) including the territorial waters surrounding them and much of the waters contained in Australia's exclusive economic zone. It also includes the airspace above and the seabed and subsoil beneath Australia's waters.

ITAA97 s 960-505(1) and (2) name the external territories and offshore areas that are part of Australia as:

- Norfolk Island
- the Coral Sea Islands Territory
- the Territory of Ashmore and Cartier Islands
- the Territory of Christmas Island
- the Territory of Cocos (Keeling) Islands
- the Territory of Heard Island and the McDonald Islands
- an offshore area for the purpose of the *Offshore Petroleum and Greenhouse Gas Storage Act 2006*, and
- the Joint Petroleum Development Area (within the meaning of the *Petroleum (Timor Sea Treaty) Act 2003*).

The GST and some other indirect taxes do not operate in Australia's external territories and in certain offshore areas. Those taxes operate in the ''indirect tax zone'', not Australia, to reflect their more limited geographic operation (¶34-000).

[FITR ¶28-500, ¶29-002]

Residence

¶21-010 Residence of individuals generally

An individual is an ''Australian resident'' if he/she either:

- resides in Australia (this is the primary or ''ordinary concepts'' test of residence), or
- satisfies one of 3 statutory residence tests (ITAA36 s 6(1)): ¶21-020.

Ordinary concept of residence

Residence according to ordinary concepts is quite different from domicile, nationality and citizenship.

Whether a person ''resides'' in Australia is essentially a question of fact and degree and there is no one rule which will determine the issue in every case. The dictionary definition of ''reside'' is ''have one's settled abode, dwell permanently or for a considerable time, live in or at a particular place''. It is not necessary for a person to reside in a particular structure such as a house. While physical presence alone may be insufficient evidence of residence, it does seem to be a prerequisite to a finding of residence in a particular place.

A person may be resident in more than one place (¶21-050). An individual may be held to be resident in Australia, even though living permanently abroad, if the individual visits Australia for part of the year as part of the regular order of his/her life. Conversely a sailor, for example, will be resident in Australia if he/she maintains a family home in Australia at which the sailor spends time while in Australia, even though absent from the country for most of the year.

Members of the Defence Forces serving abroad retain their residency, but may also be held to reside in the country in which they are serving. A person need not intend to remain permanently in a place to be found to reside there, but it seems that, where the duration of the stay is not decisive, the circumstances under which the person moved to that location should be considered.

The circumstances under which an individual entering Australia will be treated as "residing" here are considered in TR 98/17. The ruling is relevant to most persons entering Australia, including migrants (see below), academics teaching or studying in Australia, students, tourists and those on pre-arranged employment contracts.

Individuals are considered to be residing in Australia when their behaviour over a considerable time has the degree of continuity, routine or habit that is consistent with residing here. The Commissioner considers that 6 months is a "considerable time" for these purposes. When behaviour consistent with residing in Australia is demonstrated over a considerable time, an individual is regarded as a resident from when that behaviour commences. While each case must be considered on its facts, the following factors are useful in describing the quality and character of an individual's behaviour:

- the intention or purpose of the person's presence in Australia
- the extent of the person's family or business/employment ties with Australia
- the maintenance and location of the person's assets
- the person's social and living arrangements.

As examples, an engineer who took up a 2+ year appointment overseas, but maintained his Australian family home and ties in Australia to which he ultimately returned, was held to be a resident according to ordinary concepts (*Iyengar*). A similar result was reached where a doctor who worked in East Timor for many years returned to Australia each year for 6 to 8 weeks (*Pillay*); and where an Australian citizen was hired to work in Qatar for a total period of nearly two and a half years, but continued to maintain a residence in Australia, garaged a car there, maintained internet and telephone accounts, bank accounts and membership of an Australian superannuation fund (*Sneddon*; see also *Ellwood*, where the taxpayer was a New Zealand citizen). The fact that a taxpayer had acquired a residential property overseas was not considered sufficient to establish that he was no longer a resident of Australia in *Mulherin*. On the other hand, a person who had left Australia to live permanently in Bali, where he had personal and financial ties, was held to have ceased to be a resident, despite lengthy subsequent visits to Australia, his indication on the immigration cards that he was an Australian resident, and his receipt of Medicare benefits (*Murray*).

An unmarried French citizen who visited Australia on a working holiday for just over a year, doing casual jobs and living in various residential premises, was held to have established Australian residency (*Guissouma*). However, there is a trend of more recent cases holding that backpackers are less likely to be considered residents under ordinary principles. The cases include *Addy* (on appeal to the High Court), *MacKinnon*, *Coelho & Ors* and *Stockton*. Recent decisions also demonstrate the difficulties for a backpacker seeking to claim residency under the 183 day test and avoid the "usual place of abode outside Australia" exclusion (¶21-020).

Individuals who migrate to Australia are regarded as residents as soon as they arrive. The factors which the Commissioner regards as relevant to determining whether a business migrant is a resident according to ordinary concepts are set out in IT 2681.

The fact that a person comes to Australia under a business skills program is a strong indication that the person intends to reside in Australia. In addition, successful applicants under such programs are normally given permanent resident status on arrival in Australia under migration law and this fact should be given due weight. See *Murray* and *Guissouma*.

Residency test reform proposal

The Board of Taxation released an initial report in July 2018 on income tax residency rules for individuals, recommending the introduction of a simplified 2-step residency test.

[FITR ¶29-010; FTR ¶3-850]

¶21-020 Residence: 3 statutory tests

Even if a person does not reside in Australia within the ordinary meaning of ‘‘reside’’ (¶21-010), that person may nevertheless be a resident of Australia for tax purposes if any one of 3 additional statutory tests in the definition of ‘‘resident’’ in ITAA36 s 6(1) is satisfied.

(1) Domicile/permanent place of abode test

Under the first of these tests, a person whose *domicile* is in Australia is deemed to be a resident of Australia unless the Commissioner is satisfied that the person’s permanent place of abode is outside Australia (the ‘‘domicile/permanent place of abode’’ test).

The term ‘‘permanent’’ is not used in the sense of everlasting, but is used in contrast to temporary or transitory. It means something less than a place of abode in which the taxpayer subjectively intends to live for the rest of the taxpayer’s life. Thus, in *Applegate’s case*, an employed solicitor who was transferred to a Pacific island to open up a branch office, but returned 21 months later because of ill health, was held to have a permanent place of abode outside Australia during the period of his stay. This was so even though he always intended to return eventually to Australia after an indefinite, but lengthy, absence.

In *Applegate’s case*, the taxpayer’s overseas stay was intended to be indefinite. However, the absence of this element will not necessarily preclude a finding that the taxpayer has a permanent place of abode outside Australia. For example, in *Jenkins’ case*, a bank officer who, at the bank’s request, agreed to go abroad for 3 years and had not given any consideration to prolonging his stay there beyond that period, had a permanent place of abode outside Australia. In *Case W13*, Australian source rental income was taxed on the basis that the taxpayers were non-residents. They had returned to Greece in 1979 to care for their ageing relatives but maintained a family home in Australia for 9 years pending their return in 1988. It was held that, although they were domiciled in Australia, their permanent place of abode was in Greece.

IT 2650 examines the factors to be taken into account in determining whether a person who leaves Australia temporarily to live overseas acquires a permanent overseas place of abode there. These factors include the intended and actual length of the stay overseas (as a rule of thumb, a period of about 2 years would normally be considered to be a minimum), whether a fixed home has been established outside Australia and the durability of the person’s continuing association with a place inside Australia. However, none of these factors is conclusive by itself.

In *Case 2/98*, a physiotherapist who worked in Canada for more than 2 years, and who was present in Australia for only 4 weeks during 1995 and 1996, was nevertheless held to be a resident of Australia throughout her stay abroad because she had not established a permanent place of abode outside Australia. Similar results were reached in

Boer (oil field worker who worked on short-term contracts in Oman); *Sully* (marine engineer who worked on ocean-going vessels based in various parts of the world); *Bezuidenhout* (pilot who worked overseas but had house, family, private health insurance, bank account and an investment property in Australia); and *Case 5/2013* (Indian citizen with Australian permanent residence and a family home in Australia who spent most of 2 income years working either in Singapore or India). On the other hand, a New Zealand citizen with a long history of taking overseas postings, who left his home in Australia to take up a job in Abu Dhabi, was held to have established a permanent place of abode there (*Mayhew*). Although he retained some links with Australia, his actions were consistent with a person who had resolved to permanently leave. Similarly, a project manager domiciled in Australia who went to Saudi Arabia in 2007 to work under a contract of indefinite duration was held to have established a permanent place of abode there by the start of the 2009 income year. He was able to demonstrate that he had a genuine intention to live there for the duration of the project and beyond, even though he had maintained significant links with Australia (*Dempsey*; *Agius*). See also *Harding* (aircraft engineer who worked in Bahrain).

(2) The 183 day test

Under the second statutory test, *constructive residence* in Australia is attributed to a person who is actually present in Australia for a total period of more than half the year of income, unless it can be established that the person's usual place of abode is outside Australia and that there is no intention to take up residence here. This is called the "183 day" test. The test applies in relation to the relevant income year rather than a calendar year. The person's presence in Australia need not be continuous for these purposes, ie all the days the person is present in Australia during the income year will be counted (IT 2681).

However, the fact that the taxpayer spends more than 183 days *outside* Australia does not necessarily mean that they are not resident in Australia (*Gunawan*). The fact that a taxpayer does not have a usual place of abode in Australia does not necessarily mean that the taxpayer must have a usual place of abode somewhere else (*Subrahmanyam*).

(3) Commonwealth superannuation fund test

An individual is a resident under the third statutory test if he/she is a contributing member (or is the spouse or child under 16 of a person who is a contributing member) of the superannuation fund for Commonwealth government officers. The taxpayer in *Case 11/94* was held to be a resident under this test as he remained an "eligible employee" for the purposes of the *Superannuation Act 1976* throughout his period of service in the Solomon Islands. A taxpayer who had actually ceased to reside in Australia, but had retained membership of an Australian government superannuation scheme, was held to be resident within this test even though he had ceased contributing to the fund (*Baker*).

[FITR ¶29-085, ¶29-105, ¶29-120]

¶21-030 Part-year resident

Where a person resides in Australia within the ordinary meaning of that expression for less than one-half of the year of income, that person would be treated as a resident of Australia only during the actual time he/she is present in Australia. This means that the person would not be assessable to ordinary Australian tax on foreign source income derived during the period he/she was not actually in Australia.

Where, however, the individual has been present in Australia for more than half of any income year and is constructively a resident of Australia within the 183 day test, the position is not clear. In early cases, such an individual was treated as a resident of Australia *throughout* the year. However, a different view was expressed in *Case S19*. In that case, a bank officer departed from Australia in April 1978 for a posting in the Pacific. The Board of Review rejected the Commissioner's contention that the taxpayer could be deemed to be a resident for the whole of the 1977–78 income year because more than 6 months of that year had elapsed before his departure and he had no definite intention of not returning to Australia. The Board said that the 183 day test cannot deem a person who comes to Australia during an income year, and is here for more than 6 months of the year, to be a resident from the beginning of that year, nor can it deem a person who leaves Australia after being here for more than 6 months of an income year to be a resident from the time of departure until the end of that year.

Where a person is a resident of Australia for only part of the year, the tax-free threshold which applies to residents is only available on a pro-rated basis (¶2-130).

[FITR ¶29-130]

¶21-032 Temporary residents

Individuals with temporary visas who qualify as ''temporary residents'' are not assessable on most of their foreign source income, even if they qualify as residents under the normal tax rules. For details, see ¶22-125.

[FITR ¶587-100]

¶21-033 Working holiday makers

A special rate of income tax applies to income earned by some working holiday makers (also known as the ''backpacker tax''). A working holiday maker is an individual who holds a Subclass 417 (Working Holiday) visa, a Subclass 462 (Work and Holiday) visa or a bridging visa granted in relation to an application for one of the above visas. The rate applies regardless of the status of the individual as either a resident of Australia for income tax purposes or a non-resident.

A 15% income tax rate applies to working holiday maker taxable income on amounts up to $37,000, with ordinary tax rates applying to taxable income exceeding this amount. Working holiday maker taxable income is assessable income earned by a working holiday maker from Australian sources, less relevant deductions.

The special rate was enacted to ensure that all working holiday makers were taxed on a consistent basis. Before the introduction of the new rate, working holiday makers could be taxed at different rates, depending on whether they had established residency for income tax purposes or they were a non-resident.

The special rate is accompanied by the following measures:

- the rate of departing Australia superannuation payments tax for working holiday makers is 95% for those components of the payment that are subject to the tax (¶26-260)
- employers of working holiday makers must register with the Commissioner to be able to apply reduced rates of PAYG withholding on payments.

Any income earned by an individual from sources in Australia while a working holiday maker and which forms part of their taxable income is taxed as working holiday maker taxable income. That may include, for example, income other than employment income. The individual may claim tax deductions for expenses of earning the income, under the ordinary rules.

If a person is a working holiday maker for part of an income year, the working holiday maker tax rates only apply to income derived during that period. For the other part of the year, the person must assess their residency status, determined on a whole of year basis, and the relevant rates of tax will apply.

For a table with the working holiday maker income tax rates, see ¶42-018.

Court challenges to backpacker tax

The Full Federal Court rejected a legal challenge to the validity of the backpacker tax (*Addy*, on appeal to the High Court). The basis of the challenge was the effectiveness of the non-discrimination article (Art 25) contained in the Australia–UK Double Tax Agreement. Article 25 in effect prohibits the levying of Australian tax on UK nationals that is ''more burdensome'' than would apply to Australian nationals in the same circumstances. The Full Court held, by majority, that Art 25 did not invalidate the tax. However, the taxpayer has applied to the High Court for special leave to appeal from the decision of the Full Federal Court.

The ATO is administering the backpacker tax as if it is fully effective until the appeals process is exhausted. Employers should apply the PAYG withholding tax rate in accordance with their employee's tax file number declaration.

The ATO suggests working holiday makers potentially affected should wait until the court process ends before seeking a refund, amending their return or objecting. They will not be disadvantaged in such circumstances as they will have the opportunity to lodge an amendment request at a later time. The Commissioner will give favourable consideration to any requests to extend the time for lodging objections if a taxpayer's amendment period has expired.

[FITR ¶290-420]

¶21-035 Residents of Australia's territories

For income tax purposes, Australia's external territories are treated as if they were part of Australia (ITAA97 s 960-505: ¶21-000). Residents of these Islands are therefore generally treated as residents of Australia and are subject to tax on that basis. This means, for example, that income from sources within the Islands is treated as Australian-source income and withholding tax can apply to outgoing dividend, interest and royalty payments. In addition, the tax rules governing shipping freights and insurance contracts (¶22-110) apply as they do to Australia. After 1 July 2016, some special exemptions from paying personal and business taxes (but not the GST) for ''genuine'' residents of Norfolk Island ceased (¶10-640).

The Islands are included in Zone A (special area) for the purpose of the zone tax offsets (¶15-160).

The Joint Petroleum Development Area in the Timor Sea is treated by Australia as part of Australia and by East Timor as part of East Timor (ID 2009/95).

[FITR ¶762-732]

¶21-040 Residence of companies

Under the statutory definition, a company is resident in Australia if:

- it is incorporated in Australia, or
- although not incorporated in Australia, it carries on business in Australia and has either its central management and control in Australia, or its voting power controlled by shareholders who are residents of Australia (ITAA36 s 6(1)).

The leading case on the tax residency of overseas-incorporated companies is the High Court's decision in *Bywater Investments Ltd*. The case dealt with the question of the tax residency of 4 taxpayer companies who were incorporated overseas. They argued that they were not Australian tax residents under the central management and control test in s 6(1)(b) of ITAA36. The High Court found that they were all resident in Australia, having their central management and control in Australia.

The decision confirmed the principle that the place of a company's central management and control is determined by the reality of what happens, not by reference to legal formalities, or restrictions on who may exercise it or where it may be exercised. If a company's directors merely rubberstamp decisions made by others they do not exercise central management and control, rather it is those who actually make the decisions as a matter of fact. Further, the court affirmed the proposition of the High Court in the *Malayan Shipping case* that if a company carrying on business has its central management and control in Australia it will necessarily carry on business in Australia.

The *Esquire Nominees case* was distinguished by *Bywater*. It involved a company incorporated in Norfolk Island, with its voting shares and directorships in Norfolk Island hands. The High Court found that it was carrying on business as a trustee in Norfolk Island and, notwithstanding the influence and power of the Australian accountants who devised the scheme it was pursuing, doing so properly in the interests of its business. Its central management and control was therefore in Norfolk Island alone and it was not a resident of Australia.

Following the *Bywater* decision, the Commissioner issued TR 2018/5, about the central management and control test for foreign companies, applying from 15 March 2017. The Commissioner considers that: (a) if a company carries on business and has central management and control in Australia, it will carry on business in Australia. It does not also need for trading or investment operations to take place in Australia, because central management and control of a business is part of carrying on the business; (b) central management and control is the control and direction of a company's operations, that is, the making of high-level decisions that set the company's general policies and determine the direction of its operations and the type of transactions it will enter; (c) the conduct of the company's day-to-day activities and operations is not an act of central management and control; (d) mere legal power or authority to manage a company is not sufficient to establish the exercise of central management and control. A person who does not exercise their legal power or authority to control and direct a company does not exercise central management and control. Alternatively, a person who has no legal power or authority to control or direct a company may exercise central management and control of that company; (e) a company is controlled and directed where those making its decisions do so as a matter of fact and substance.

ATO guidance on determining the tax residency of foreign-incorporated companies in accordance with the principles in TR 2018/5 is found in PCG 2018/9. Determining whether a company is a tax resident of Australia or of another jurisdiction under domestic tax rules can be complicated by the potential application of a double tax agreement and the multilateral instrument (MLI: see ¶22-165). For an article discussing the potential application of the rules, see CCH *Tax Week*¶380 (2019).

Tax benefits denied to certain dual resident companies

''Prescribed dual residents'' are denied access to certain tax advantages available to ordinary resident companies. Prescribed dual residents are companies resident both in Australia and another country which:

- are treated as resident solely in another country for the purposes of one of Australia's double taxation agreements (¶22-140), or
- qualify as resident in Australia solely because their central management and control is in Australia, and which also have their central management or control in another country (s 6(1)). Effectively, this applies where there is a division of central management and control between the 2 countries.

Prescribed dual residents are denied CGT roll-over relief for certain assets (¶12-490) and the group transfer of income and capital losses (¶3-090, ¶11-110). Dual resident companies are also deemed to be non-residents for the purposes of the thin capitalisation (¶22-700) and other anti-avoidance provisions.

These deeming rules also apply to dual resident entities that are treated as companies under Australian income tax law (ie public trading trusts and corporate limited partnerships) even if they are not so treated under the relevant foreign law.

Government to amend corporate residency test

The government proposes to amend the law to clarify that foreign incorporated companies will be treated as Australian tax residents where there is a "significant economic connection to Australia". The test will be satisfied where the company's core commercial activities are undertaken in Australia, and its central management and control is in Australia (2020–21 Budget Paper No 2, p 13). The amendments will apply optionally from 15 March 2017 and will otherwise have effect from the first income year after the date of assent of the enabling legislation.

The government accepted the main recommendation of the Board of Taxation in its report on the corporate tax residency rules.

[FITR ¶29-205]

¶21-050 Residence for tax agreement purposes

In determining liability to Australian tax on the basis of residence or non-residence in Australia, it is necessary to consider not only the income tax laws, but also any applicable double taxation agreement (DTA).

Australia has concluded DTAs with over 40 countries to avoid the incidence of double taxation (see ¶22-140 and following for details of their operation). Most DTAs include a "tie-breaker" test under which a dual resident is deemed, for double taxation purposes, to be a resident solely of one of the 2 contracting countries.

For a discussion of the residence of trusts and trustees in the DTA context, see TR 2005/14; see also ¶6-060.

[FITR ¶29-005]

Source of Income

¶21-060 Source of income generally

The operation of the rules governing the taxation of foreign source income and the fact that non-residents are generally assessable only on income sourced in Australia make the identification of the source of a particular item of income fundamentally important.

Personal exertion — acts done by the taxpayer or the taxpayer's employees or agents — is one possible source of income. Property or rights over, or in relation to, property is another. The making of the contract or agreement, pursuant to which acts are done or moneys are paid and received, is also a possible source of income.

Often income may be the result of a combination of several factors occurring in different places. For example, the immediate source of income may be the sale of goods in Australia. The fact that the goods were purchased, produced or manufactured outside Australia would also be relevant in determining the source of the income. In cases where income has multiple sources, the dominant factor or factors must be determined. If necessary, the income must be apportioned among the various sources.

The source of income for tax purposes is determined according to the law of the country seeking to tax the recipient. Thus, while payments made by an Australian company for US "know-how" supplied in the US under a contract made in the US would probably have a US source according to generally accepted concepts of source, they are specifically deemed, for Australian tax purposes, to have an Australian source (ITAA36 s 6C; ¶22-030).

Under Australia's double taxation agreements, certain classes of income are deemed to be sourced in one or other country (¶22-150). In other cases, the source is undefined and falls to be determined under the laws of each country, which may or may not be the same.

[FITR ¶28-500]

¶21-070 Source of particular classes of income

Except where there is a specific statutory provision, determining the dominant source of an item of income is a practical, hard matter of fact to be determined separately in each case — the general comments below are intended merely as a guide.

Wages or salary, professional fees

The source of remuneration under a normal contract of employment or contract for services is generally the place where the duties or services are performed (*French*). If, however, creative powers or special knowledge is involved to such a high degree that the place where those powers or knowledge are utilised is relatively unimportant, the dominant source may be the place where the contract was made (*Mitchum*). In *Efstathakis' case*, salary paid by the Greek Government to a Greek national working in Sydney at the Greek Press and Information Service was taken to have an Australian source. Although the circumstances under which the taxpayer's employment was obtained, and the remuneration paid, included some factors occurring outside Australia, they were not significant enough to outweigh the importance of other factors relating to the employment which took place in Australia. In *Case X78*, a US resident was assessed on a payment made by his US employer of the tax payable on the salary he had received while working in Australia on secondment in the previous year of income. The AAT held that the payment was exempt income on the basis that the taxpayer derived the income at a time when he was a non-resident, and the source of the income was the US because the legal liability to make the payment arose from the taxpayer's employment contract which was entered into in the US.

An employment termination payment is more similar to a payment of compensation than a payment for services. Therefore, the most relevant factors in determining its source are where the liability to make the payment arose and where it was paid from, rather than where the services were performed.

Trading or business profits

The source of trading or business profits is generally determined by reference to the place where the trader (or its employees or agents) trades or renders services. Where the relevant acts consist largely of the making of contracts, and the place of their performance is unimportant, the place where the contracts are made may be the only significant determinant of source. Conversely, if the making of the contract is of little importance and the chief factor is its performance, then the place where the contract is performed may be the only relevant factor in determining source (*Thorpe Nominees*). The ATO considers that it is important to consider the substance of the transaction as a whole, particularly where it is plain that a transaction has been structured so as to avoid tax in Australia. In the case of a leveraged buyout arrangement, for example, the ATO does not consider the place of execution of the contracts to be determinative (TD 2011/24).

On this basis, income received by a Vanuatu-based insurance company was held *not* to have an Australian source where the insurance contracts were made and performed in Vanuatu, notwithstanding the taxpayer's close links to Australian companies (*Crown Insurance Services Ltd*). In contrast, income from trading in Australian-listed shares by a Vanuatu-based trader was held to have an Australian source, even where the transactions were conducted off-market, where the trading contracts were completed in Australia (*Picton Finance*).

Interest

The source is generally the place where the obligation to pay the interest arose, ie where the loan contract was made or the credit was given. The place where payment is to be made is also relevant. In *Spotless Services*, interest was paid to an Australian resident company by a Cook Islands bank on funds deposited against a certificate of deposit issued by the bank in the Cook Islands. However, the deposit was preceded by, and was dependent on, security being obtained for the deposit from a bank in Australia in the form of an irrevocable letter of credit. The Commissioner argued that the interest had its source in Australia from where all of the dealings between the parties originated and the contract for the letter of credit was made. However, the Full Federal Court identified the certificate of deposit as the crucial document and concluded that the interest had its source in the Cook Islands.

The source of tax indemnification payments made by a borrower to a non-resident lender will depend on where the contract is made and performed, the residence of the payer, the place and source of the payments and the reason the payment is made (TR 2002/4).

Dividends

The source of a dividend is not the location of the share register on which the shares giving rise to the dividend are effectively registered, but where the company paying the dividend made the profits out of which the dividend is paid (*Esquire Nominees*).

Royalties

If royalties are received in respect of property, such as a patent, trade mark, design, etc, or mine, owned by the recipient in the country from which the royalty flows, the source of those royalties will generally be that country. If received for technical know-how and services supplied outside that country under an agreement made outside that country, the source of those royalties would generally be outside that country. Note, however, that all "royalty" income derived by non-residents is deemed to have an Australian source to the extent that the payment is an outgoing of an Australian business (ITAA36 s 6C) and may therefore be subject to withholding tax when paid by a resident (¶22-030).

Pensions and annuities

The ATO treats the location of the fund from which a pension is paid as the source of the pension. On the other hand, it regards the source of an annuity payable under a contract to be the place where the contract was executed.

Income derived by residents of Norfolk Island

From 1 July 2016 the Australian taxation system applies to Norfolk Island resident individuals, companies and trustees in the same way it applies in mainland Australia with the exception of indirect taxes, including GST (¶10-640).

Natural resource payments to non-residents

Income derived by non-residents which is directly related to the development and exploitation of Australia's natural resources is treated as having a source in Australia where the payments of natural resource income are based on the level of production and recovery of natural resources (ITAA36 s 6CA).

The provisional views of the ATO on the application of s 6CA and the real property tax treaty articles to "override royalties" (payments made by the holder of a mining right based on the value of natural resources produced and/or sold) are given in *Draft* TR 2016/D3.

[FITR ¶28-520 – ¶28-620]

Offshore Banking Units

¶21-080 OBUs concessional income tax treatment

Income (other than capital gains) derived by an offshore banking unit (OBU) from offshore banking activities is taxed at an effective rate of 10%. The other income and capital gains of an OBU are taxed at normal company rates. Interest paid by an OBU on qualifying offshore borrowings and gold fees paid by an OBU on certain offshore gold borrowings are exempt from withholding tax.

OBUs are banks subject to the *Banking Act 1959*, state banks, fully-owned subsidiary companies of such banks, and other financial institutions authorised to deal in foreign exchange which have been given operational approval by the Treasurer. They can also include: (i) funds managers which are money market corporations or fully owned subsidiaries of such corporations; (ii) holders of a securities dealer's licence or investment adviser's licence; (iii) life insurance companies; and (iv) other companies, including providers of custodial services, determined by the Treasurer to be OBUs (ITAA36 s 128AE; ID 2008/8). Under the consolidation regime (¶8-000), the head company of a consolidated group may be treated as an OBU when a subsidiary member of the group is an OBU.

The government announced in October 2018 that it will amend the existing OBU regime to strengthen its integrity.

A special tax regime applies to Australian branches of foreign banks (ITAA36 Pt IIIB).

Offshore banking activity

To be an offshore banking activity (OB activity) the following conditions must be satisfied:

- the activity undertaken by the OBU must be one of the defined types of activity (see below)
- in relation to some kinds of activity, the other party to the transaction must be an "offshore person". Broadly, this is: (a) a non-resident entity excluding its Australian operations; (b) the overseas branches of a resident entity; or (c) another OBU (ITAA36 s 121E)
- the activity must be undertaken by a resident OBU (not being part of the offshore business of its overseas permanent establishment) or by a non-resident OBU (being part of the Australian business of its Australian permanent establishment) (ITAA36 s 121EA).

Eligible OB activities are listed in ITAA36 s 121D and include specified types of borrowing or lending, providing a guarantee or letter of credit, trading, investment, giving investment or other financial advice, hedging activities and leasing.

In income years starting on or after 1 July 2015, eligible trading activities do not include trading in subsidiaries or other entities where the OBU holds an interest of 10% or more. They also exclude trading in interests the OBU holds that are not held for trading according to the OBU's accounting records.

Record-keeping

An OBU is required to keep separate accounts for money used in its OB activities. Internal dealings of the OBU between units which carry on OB activities and those which do not carry on OB activities are treated as dealings by the OBU with separate entities. If the OB activities are not accounted for separately, the 10% effective tax rate does not apply. An OBU is not required to maintain a separate nostro account or vostro account for its OBU activities.

[FTR ¶59-250]

¶21-090 Calculation of OBU tax concession

A 10% effective tax rate on the income of an OBU is achieved by applying the general company tax rate to only a fraction (the ''eligible fraction'') of the OBU's ''assessable OB income'', less the eligible fraction of the OBU's ''allowable OB deductions''. The eligible fraction is 10 divided by the number of percent in the general company tax rate.

Assessable OB income

The assessable OB income of an OBU is so much of the OBU's assessable income as is derived from its OB activities except to the extent that the money used in carrying on those activities is ''non-OB money''. In this calculation the following are excluded from OBU assessable income: capital gains, income from managing the Australian asset component of its portfolio investment for a non-resident and income from managing a portfolio investment for an overseas charitable institution.

Allowable OB deductions

The deductions of an OBU may be classified into 5 mutually exclusive types, 3 of which are wholly or partly ''allowable OB deductions'' (ITAA36 s 121EF):

(1) *Exclusive OB deductions* are deductions (other than loss deductions) that relate exclusively to assessable OB income and are allowable OB deductions.

(2) *Exclusive non-OB deductions* are deductions (other than loss deductions) that relate exclusively to non-OB income and are not allowable OB deductions.

(3) *Apportionable deductions* are deductions (eg for gifts) which are apportioned by a formula as OB and non-OB deductions.

(4) *Loss deductions* are deductions allowable under ITAA97 Div 36 for carry-forward losses, and are not allowable OB deductions.

(5) *General deductions* are deductions which are not any of the other 4 types. An example would be rent and utilities for an office building which is used for both OB and non-OB activities. These are allocated as OB or non-OB deductions on an adjusted income basis.

For income years starting on or after 1 July 2015, a deduction that relates to both OB and non-OB income is allocated to the taxpayer's OBU to the extent that it relates to ''OB income''. As a result, the allocation rule applies to deductions that relate to expenses incurred in deriving non-assessable, non-exempt NANE income, as well as assessable income.

Foreign tax offsets

For the calculation of an OBU's foreign tax offsets, see ¶21-710.

Loss of concession where non-OB money used

Income derived from the use of ''non-OB money'' is taxed at normal company rates. Broadly defined, ''non-OB money'' consists of domestic funding and funding generated in non-OB dealings (ITAA36 s 121EE).

10% purity test

If more than 10% of the assessable income of an OBU which is attributable to OB activities is in turn attributable to the use of ''non-OB money'', then none of the income from OB activities qualifies for concessional treatment (ITAA36 s 121EH).

Exemptions for OBU offshore investment trusts

In general terms, an exemption applies where an OBU is a trustee or the central manager of a trust estate which carries on only investment-type OB activities, from which only non-residents may benefit. Where the specific requirements are met, the relevant trust income is exempt from income tax, and no capital gain or capital loss arises from a CGT event happening in relation to a CGT asset in connection with the relevant trust activities. However, this exemption does not apply to income, profits or capital gains derived from the Australian asset component of an investment portfolio managed for a non-resident by an OBU (¶21-080). A similar exemption applies to OBU trustees or managers carrying on investment activities solely for overseas charitable institutions (ITAA36 s 121EL).

[FTR ¶59-310 – ¶59-340]

Special Concessions

¶21-095 Exemption for non-portfolio dividends

A foreign equity distribution received by an Australian corporate tax entity from a foreign company is not assessable where the Australian entity holds a participation interest of at least 10% in the foreign company (s 768-5). Technically the distribution is treated as ''non-assessable, non-exempt'' (NANE) income (¶10-895). The exemption applies to distributions and non-share dividends made after 16 October 2014. It replaced the ''non-portfolio dividend'' exemption under ITAA36 former s 23AJ, operative before 17 October 2014.

For the purposes of the s 768-5 exemption:

- a ''corporate tax entity'' includes not only companies but also corporate limited partnerships and public trading trusts (¶4-440). In contrast, the former s 23AJ exemption was limited to companies
- a ''foreign equity distribution'' is a distribution or non-share dividend made by a company that is a foreign resident, in respect of an equity interest in that company (s 768-10). A ''non-share dividend'' is essentially a dividend on a non-share equity interest (¶23-125) and could include certain convertible notes. The reference to an ''equity interest'' (¶23-115) is wider than the ''voting interests'' to which the former s 23AJ exemption applied, but ensures that the exemption does not apply to returns on debt interests, such as redeemable interest shares
- the distribution may be received directly by the entity, or indirectly through interposed trusts or partnerships that are not themselves corporate tax entities. This application to indirect distributions, often called ''nominee'' or ''custodian'' arrangements, is an extension of the former s 23AJ exemption. However, the entity must not receive the distribution in the capacity of a trustee, unless it is in the capacity of a trustee of a public trading trust, and
- the 10% participation test requires that the direct and indirect participation interests held by the entity be calculated as if rights on winding up were disregarded (s 768-15). For the Commissioner's views on when an entity has a participation interest in a foreign company and when a distribution is made, see TR 2017/3; and when a company that is a partner or beneficiary can be taken to have a participation interest (TD 2017/21; TD 2017/22).

For more information about the ''non-portfolio dividend'' exemption under ITAA36 former s 23AJ, see the 2015 *Australian Master Tax Guide* (57th Edition) or earlier editions.

Deduction for outgoings

A specific deduction applies to losses or outgoings incurred in deriving dividends exempt under the above rules where the amount is a cost in relation to certain debt interests under the thin capitalisation rules (ITAA97 s 25-90). The ATO considers that to obtain the deduction it is not necessary for the taxpayer to actually derive the relevant dividend in the same income year as that in which the cost is incurred, provided that there is a sufficiently clear nexus between the incurring of the cost and the expected derivation of the dividend (TD 2009/21). The ATO has also warned that it is investigating certain artificial cross border arrangements that seek to exploit this deduction (TA 2009/9).

[FITR ¶585-100; FTR ¶9-990]

¶21-097 Exemption for previously attributed income

Certain ‘‘attribution account payments’’, ie income distributed by a CFC (¶21-150) which has previously been attributed to an Australian resident taxpayer, are exempt from tax (ITAA36 s 23AI).

Where an amount of attributable income is included in the assessable income of a taxpayer which maintains an attribution account for a CFC, an attribution account credit will arise in respect of that income (¶21-210). For this purpose, an attribution credit arises at the end of the CFC's statutory accounting period. When the CFC makes an ‘‘attribution account payment’’, ie actually distributes income to the taxpayer, and an attribution account debit is made to the account, the payment is treated either as non-attributable or exempt depending on the CFC's statutory accounting period and the taxpayer's year of income (TD 2003/27).

Where there is a payment of a non-portfolio dividend to a resident company that gives rise to an attribution debit, the s 23AI exemption applies to the extent of the attribution debit, and the foreign distribution exemption (¶21-095) applies to any part of the dividend that exceeds the attribution debit (TD 2006/51).

The fact that such income is exempt does not mean that expenses incurred in deriving that income cease to be deductible. An Australian entity can deduct a loss or outgoing if it is incurred in deriving income from a foreign source that is exempt under s 23AI provided the amount is a cost in relation to a debt interest issued by the entity that is covered by para (a) of the definition of ‘‘debt deduction’’ in the thin capitalisation regime (¶23-105, ¶22-700): ITAA97 s 25-90.

[FTR ¶9-980, ¶10-000, ¶51-120]

¶21-098 Exemption for foreign branch income

Most foreign income and gains derived by a resident company through a foreign permanent establishment (PE) are exempt (ITAA36 s 23AH). In more detail, this exemption applies to:

- ‘‘foreign income’’ derived by a resident company in carrying on business at or through a foreign PE of the company, or from the disposal of that business. In the case of PEs in listed countries, the exemption does not apply if the PE does not pass the active income test and the income is both adjusted tainted income and eligible designated concession income. In the case of PEs in unlisted countries, the exemption does not apply if the PE does not pass the active income test and the income is adjusted tainted income. Income from activities outside the exclusive economic zone of any country (eg on an oil rig) may not qualify as foreign income (ID 2010/46)
- capital gains made by a resident company on assets used wholly or mainly for the purpose of producing foreign income in carrying on a business at or through a foreign PE of the company, where the asset is not one that would expose a non-resident to CGT (¶12-720). In the case of PEs in listed countries, the exemption

does not apply if the gain is from a tainted asset and is eligible designated concession income in relation to a listed country. In the case of PEs in unlisted countries, the exemption does not apply where the gain is from a tainted asset. Corresponding provisions apply to capital losses.

A ‘‘PE’’ has its ordinary meaning, as modified by any applicable double tax agreement (¶22-150). The ‘‘active income’’ test and ‘‘adjusted tainted income’’ referred to above are based on the corresponding concepts that apply under the CFC rules (¶21-180). A ‘‘tainted asset’’ is, broadly, an asset that produces passive income. It does not include trading stock or other assets used solely in carrying on a business (ITAA36 s 317), such as business goodwill (ID 2006/17; ID 2006/181).

The exemption also applies correspondingly where a resident company has an indirect interest, through one or more partnerships or trusts, in:

- foreign income derived by the partnership or trustee through a foreign PE (eg ID 2011/35)
- capital gains or losses made on an asset of the partnership or trust in carrying on business through a foreign PE.

▶ Example

An Australian resident company (X) has a 50% interest in a partnership that carries on business through a PE in an unlisted country. In the income year, the income from the business is $1 million, and another $150,000 is net tainted rental income from equipment leases. This equipment is sold during the income year for a capital gain of $20,000.

The amount included in X’s assessable income is 50% of the net tainted income, and 50% of the capital gain, ie $75,000 + $10,000 = $85,000.

A debt interest cost is not deductible under s 25-90 or, alternatively, s 230-15(3) of ITAA97 where the amount is incurred in earning income that meets the requirements of both s 23AH of ITAA36 and s 768-5 of ITAA97 because such income is not non-assessable non-exempt income under s 768-5 for the purposes of s 25-90 (TD 2016/6).

The exemption does not apply to foreign branch income and capital gains from the operation of ships or aircraft in international traffic.

For the application of the exemption where the company has a PE on ‘‘substantial equipment’’ grounds (¶22-150), see TR 2014/3.

[FTR ¶9-970]

¶21-100 Conduit foreign income exemption

Any part of an unfranked distribution made by an Australian corporate tax entity that it declares to be ‘‘conduit foreign income’’ (CFI) is not assessable to a foreign resident, and is not subject to dividend withholding tax (ITAA97 s 802-15). The general aim of this measure is to reduce tax impediments for foreign investors who structure their foreign investments through Australian entities, instead of holding them directly. It replaces the more limited foreign dividend account rules (¶22-010).

An Australian corporate tax entity means a corporate tax entity (¶4-440) that is a resident or, in the case of a public trading trust, a resident unit trust (¶4-600) for the relevant income year. The entity must make its declaration in its distribution statement (¶4-690) on or before the day that the distribution is made.

Associated measures ensure that tax will not be attracted where the distribution declared to be CFI:

(1) flows through a trust to non-resident beneficiaries (ITAA97 s 802-17). In this situation, a presently entitled non-resident beneficiary is not assessed on its share of the net income of the trust to the extent that the share is reasonably attributable to all or part of the unfranked distribution. The trustee is also not liable to pay tax in relation to that beneficiary's share, or

(2) flows through interposed Australian entities to other Australian corporate tax entities (ITAA97 s 802-20). This concession applies where: (i) an Australian corporate tax entity receives an unfranked distribution from another Australian corporate tax entity that declares an amount of the unfranked distribution to be CFI; and (ii) the recipient entity itself makes an unfranked distribution and declares that part of it is CFI. This must be done after the start of the income year and before the due date for lodging its tax return for that year. The effect of this concession is that an amount calculated as follows will not be assessable to the recipient entity:

$$\text{total received CFI amounts*} \times \frac{\text{total declared CFI amounts**}}{\text{total received CFI amounts** – related expenses}}$$

* ie the total amounts of CFI received during the income year

** ie the total amounts declared to be CFI by the recipient entity before the due date for lodging its tax return for that year, excluding declared CFI amounts already taken into account for a previous income year.

The amount cannot exceed the total received CFI amounts. If the related expenses exceed that amount, none of the received CFI amounts is assessable.

▶ Example

Companies A, B and C are Australian corporate tax entities.

Company A pays an unfranked dividend of $1,000 to Company C and declares the whole amount to be conduit foreign income. Company C has $50 of expenses relating to the dividend.

Company B pays an unfranked dividend of $2,000 to Company C and declares $1,600 to be conduit foreign income. Company C has $150 of related expenses.

Company C itself pays an unfranked dividend of $1,800 and declares $1,200 to be conduit foreign income.

The amount that is not assessable to Company C is:

$$\$1,000 + \$1,600 \times \frac{\$1,200}{\$1,000 + \$1,600 - \$200}$$

$$= \$1,300$$

The balance ($2,600 – $1,300) = $1,300 is assessable to Company C. It can deduct $100 of its total $200 expenses.

If, instead, Company C had made a dividend that declared $2,400 as conduit foreign income, the whole of the $2,600 received CFI amounts would have been non-assessable.

The CFI in a distribution that flows through an interposed partnership or trust is worked out in the same way as would be the share of a franking credit on a franked distribution (¶4-860).

CFI is technically described as non-assessable non-exempt income (¶10-890), with the effect that it will not reduce Australian foreign tax losses of the foreign resident.

Calculation of CFI

In general terms, CFI is foreign income which is derived by a foreign resident through an Australian corporate tax entity (the conduit), and which would not normally be assessable to that Australian entity.

In more detail, the CFI of an Australian corporate tax entity is calculated as follows (ITAA97 s 802-30):

(1) calculate the amount of the entity's ordinary and statutory income (¶10-000) that has been or would be included in an Australian Accounting Standards income statement or similar financial statement, but that would not have been included if the entity had been a foreign resident. This is broadly the entity's foreign source income. Amounts applied for the benefit of the entity are also treated as if they were derived by it, eg withholding tax deducted by a foreign company from a payment to the entity

(2) reduce this by any amount that is or would be included in the entity's assessable income, ignoring the CFI rules. The balance, which can be described as the "basic CFI amount", is basically the foreign income on which no Australian company tax is payable. It would typically include non-assessable foreign non-portfolio dividends (¶21-095) and foreign branch income (¶21-098).

The basic CFI amount is then adjusted as follows:

- add the amount of any unfranked distribution paid to the entity that is declared to be CFI; and any non-portfolio dividends that would be non-assessable (¶21-095) but which would not have been included in an income statement, eg because they are treated as returns of capital under accounting principles
- reduce this by amounts that are non-assessable because they have previously been taxed under the accruals rules (¶21-097); non-assessable foreign income to the extent that it can be distributed fully franked; and certain "reasonably related" expenses (ID 2013/6).

The CFI also includes:

- certain capital gains that are not included in the calculation of the entity's net capital gain because of ITAA97 s 768-505 (¶12-745), ITAA36 s 23AH (¶21-098), or the Taxation Code for the Timor Sea Treaty (¶19-000). Conversely, reductions in capital losses under these provisions will reduce the CFI. These adjustments to CFI are made at the end of the income year in which the relevant CGT event occurred (ITAA97 s 802-35)
- any assessable foreign income to the extent that foreign tax credits effectively free that income of tax. This adjustment is made in the income year following the one for which the credit arose (ITAA97 s 802-40).

The CFI is reduced by any amount of an unfranked distribution made by the entity which the entity declares to be CFI (ITAA97 s 802-45); or by any part of a received CFI amount, net of expenses, that it does not on-distribute in accordance with the CFI rules (ITAA97 s 802-50).

There is also a rule to prevent double counting of benefits (ITAA97 s 802-55). This has the effect that where a non-portfolio dividend qualifies as CFI and also for deduction under ITAA36 s 46FA (¶3-540), the entity will have to choose which concession to adopt. Rules also apply to prevent exploitation of the CFI concession by "streaming" of distributions to particular shareholders — such as foreign shareholders — out of proportion to their interests in the company (ITAA97 s 802-60). Penalties may be imposed for over-declarations of CFI (TAA Sch 1 s 288-80).

An entity can, in general, calculate its CFI from the beginning of its first income year that started on or after 1 July 2005.

Investment Manager Regime

For measures designed to ensure that non-residents investing in foreign assets will not face further Australian tax on their investments when using Australian fund managers, see ¶22-122.

[FITR ¶610-200]

¶21-102 Other concessions for foreign income

- CGT relief applies on the disposal of certain interests in active foreign companies (ITAA97 Subdiv 768-G). This measure is intended to provide greater flexibility in corporate restructuring decisions by removing the Australian tax considerations (¶12-745).
- A limited exemption applies to certain foreign income derived by Australian residents from continuous employment in a foreign country (¶10-860) or from an approved overseas project (*Coventry*; ¶10-870).
- The *International Organisations (Privileges and Immunities) Act 1963* contains measures to exempt from income tax certain international organisations and the official salary of certain office holders (*Jayasinghe*; ¶10-605).

[FITR ¶25-020, ¶585-600]

Accruals Taxation System

¶21-105 Scope of accruals system

The broad objective of the accruals taxation system is to tax Australian residents on an accruals basis on their share of income derived by certain foreign entities which has not been comparably taxed offshore.

The main components of the accruals tax system are:

(1) the ''controlled foreign company'' (CFC) rules, which apply accruals taxation to ''tainted'' income derived by CFCs which has not been comparably taxed offshore (ITAA36 Pt X (ss 316 to 468; ¶21-110))

(2) the ''transferor trust measures'', which apply accruals taxation to the income of non-resident trusts to which resident Australian entities have transferred property or provided services (ITAA36 Pt III Div 6AAA (ss 102AAA to 102AAZG; ¶21-290)).

Foreign hybrids

Certain foreign ''hybrid'' business entities are treated as partnerships for Australian tax purposes (ITAA97 Div 830: ¶5-050). They include UK and US limited partnerships and US limited liability companies.

[FTR ¶51-370, ¶795-250, ¶797-350]

Controlled Foreign Companies

¶21-110 Scope of CFC rules

The broad purpose of the controlled foreign company (CFC) rules is to tax Australian shareholders on their share of a CFC's ''tainted income'' as it is earned, unless that income is comparably taxed offshore or the CFC derives its income almost exclusively from active business activities. This result is achieved by ''attributing'' tainted income to the Australian resident controllers of the CFC. ''Tainted income'' is generally income from investments or arrangements that are likely to be significantly affected by taxation considerations, eg interest, dividends, royalties or amounts arising from related party transactions (¶21-180).

The CFC rules generally apply accruals taxation to: (i) tainted income derived by CFCs resident in ''unlisted'' countries (¶21-130); and (ii) ''eligible designated concession income'' derived by CFCs resident in one of 7 ''listed'' countries (¶21-170). Accruals taxation will generally not apply, however, to income derived by CFCs which pass the ''active income test'', ie which derive more than 95% of their income from genuine business activities (¶21-180).

[FTR ¶795-250, ¶795-253]

¶21-130 "Listed" countries

''Listed'' countries comprise the 7 countries below (ITAA36 s 320; ITR15 reg 19). These are countries that are considered to have tax systems closely comparable to Australia's. All other countries are ''unlisted countries'' (s 320).

Canada	New Zealand
France	United Kingdom
Germany	United States of America
Japan	

[FTR ¶795-380]

¶21-140 Attributable taxpayer under CFC rules

The controlled foreign company (CFC) rules operate under the self-assessment regime. Therefore, the taxpayer bears the responsibility for determining whether, in a particular year of income, the taxpayer is required to include income derived by a CFC in the taxpayer's assessable income. For this purpose, the threshold question for each taxpayer is whether there is a CFC in relation to which the taxpayer is an ''attributable taxpayer'' (ITAA36 s 361).

A taxpayer will be an attributable taxpayer in relation to a CFC where the taxpayer:

- has a minimum 10% associate inclusive control interest in the CFC, or
- has a minimum 1% associate inclusive control interest in the CFC and is one of 5 or fewer Australian entities that controls the CFC.

''Associate inclusive control interest'' is the aggregate of the direct and indirect control interests held by the taxpayer and the taxpayer's associates. For the meaning of ''associate'', see ¶4-200. Two companies that were parties to a dual-listed company arrangement were associates for the purposes of the CFC rules (*BHP Billiton Ltd*). Direct control interests are determined using criteria based on interests, or entitlements to acquire interests, in issued capital (measured in terms of the paid-up value), voting rights and rights to distributions of capital (ITAA36 s 350). For these purposes, Australian entities that are members of a foreign company limited by guarantee may be treated as shareholders (TD 2007/20). Entitlements to acquire include absolute and contingent entitlements (ITAA36 s 322). This includes call options, but not put options, and does not include pre-emptive rights until such time as they are able to be exercised (TR 2002/3).

Indirect control interests are only traced through ''controlled foreign entities'' (CFCs, controlled foreign partnerships (ITAA36 s 341) and controlled foreign trusts (ITAA36 s 342)). Tracing of control interests stops where a foreign entity either has no interests in other entities or is not a controlled foreign entity. Indirect control interests are calculated by multiplying the control interest held by an Australian entity in the interposed entity by the control interest that the interposed entity has in the company being tested as a CFC. Where there is more than one interposed entity, the respective control interests are multiplied down the chain. For the purpose of determining whether a company is controlled, a resident or an interposed CFC with a majority interest in a non-resident company will be treated as having a 100% control interest.

Temporary residents

Individuals who qualify as ‘‘temporary residents’’ are not attributable taxpayers (¶22-125).

[FTR ¶795-710, ¶795-850]

¶21-150 What is a CFC?

A company is a CFC if it satisfies any one of the following 3 ‘‘control tests’’ in ITAA36 s 340:

(1) The company is a company in respect of which 5 or fewer Australian residents (each of which has at least a 1% control interest) have or are entitled to acquire at least a 50% associate inclusive control interest.

(2) A single Australian entity (and its associates) has at least a 40% control interest in the foreign company. There is a rebuttable presumption that such a shareholder controls the foreign company and the company is therefore a CFC. The presumption can be rebutted if the shareholder can demonstrate that the company is in fact controlled by another, unassociated, entity. For example, although an Australian entity may have a 45% control interest, the control test will not be satisfied where there is a single unassociated foreign entity holding a 55% control interest.

(3) Irrespective of the interests in a foreign company, a group of 5 or fewer Australian entities (either alone or together with associates) has *actual control* of the company.

For the purpose of applying the control tests, (1), (2) and (3) above are tested sequentially, ie it is first necessary to test whether situation (1) applies; if it does, no further testing is required.

For the treatment of foreign hybrid business structures, see ¶21-105. Individual cells in a Guernsey protected cell company are not CFCs (ID 2008/23).

Statutory accounting period

The control tests are to be applied at the *end* of the statutory accounting period of the relevant foreign company or another foreign company further up a chain of foreign companies. If a company ceases to exist before the end of its statutory accounting period, its statutory accounting period will be deemed to have ended immediately before it ceased to exist (¶21-200). In addition, the calculation of a CFC’s attributable income and the application of the active income test to a CFC (¶21-180) are both done in relation to the period covered by the company’s statutory accounting period.

The statutory accounting period of a company is generally each 12-month period ending on 30 June. However, the company can elect to adopt a statutory accounting period ending on a date other than 30 June or change a previously adopted statutory accounting period (ITAA36 s 319).

[FTR ¶795-370, ¶795-600]

¶21-160 CFC residency rules

It is important to determine whether a company is a resident of a listed country or an unlisted country for various reasons, including: (i) the income to be taken into account in the calculation of a CFC’s attributable income differs depending on whether the CFC is resident in a listed or unlisted country (¶21-200); (ii) the operation of the active income exemption differs depending on whether the CFC is resident in a listed or unlisted country (¶21-180); and (iii) only a listed country CFC qualifies for a *de minimis* exemption in relation to certain attributable income (¶21-200).

A company will be treated as a resident of a *listed* country where it satisfies both of the following conditions.

(1) The company must not be a ''Part X Australian resident'', which is defined as a resident in terms of ITAA36 s 6. However, a company that qualifies as a resident will not be regarded as a Part X Australian resident where it is treated for the purposes of the dual residency ''tie-breaker'' rules in a double taxation agreement as being solely a resident of another country.

For example, a company that is incorporated in Australia but has its central management and control in New Zealand will have dual residency. However, under the dual resident tie-breaker provisions in the New Zealand agreement the company will be deemed to be solely resident in New Zealand. Therefore, although the company would be a resident of Australia within s 6, it would not be a Part X Australian resident.

(2) The company must be treated as a resident of the relevant listed country for the purposes of that country's taxation laws.

Where a company is resident in both a listed country and an unlisted country, it will be treated as a resident of the listed country for the purposes of the CFC rules.

A company will be treated as a resident of an *unlisted* country where it is a resident of a particular unlisted country, or it is neither a Part X Australian resident nor a resident of a particular listed country (ITAA36 s 333).

TD 2004/31 considered the residency rules that apply to a non-resident ''corporate limited partnership'' which is a limited partnership (LP) or limited liability partnership (LLP) formed in the United Kingdom (UK) or United States (US). It says that the entity will be a resident of the UK or US (as the case may be) if it is subject to tax on its worldwide income in the UK or US. In all other cases, a UK or US LP or LLP will be a resident of no particular unlisted country. There are now specific statutory rules governing the tax treatment of such ''hybrid'' entities (¶5-050).

[FTR ¶795-500, ¶795-510]

¶21-170 Eligible designated concession income

There is an exception to the exemption from accruals taxation for CFCs which are residents of *listed countries*. This applies where the CFC derives ''eligible designated concession income''.

In general, designated concession income is income or profits that is either not taxed at all (eg capital gains), or is taxed at reduced rates to attract particular forms of business or financial activity. It also includes a capital gain arising because of CGT event J1 (¶11-340) (ITAA36 s 317). The specific types of designated concession income are set out in ITR15 reg 17.

Eligible designated concession income in relation to a listed country is simply designated concession income that is eligible to be attributed to an Australian resident taxpayer. It will be attributable where it is also not taxed on a current basis in any other listed country, or is subject to tax in another listed country but also on a concessional basis.

[FTR ¶795-284]

¶21-180 Active income test under CFC rules

Where a CFC passes the active income test in ITAA36 s 432, some or all of its income which would otherwise have been attributed will not be attributed to Australian resident shareholders. The test provides, in effect, an exemption from accruals taxation for small amounts of tainted income which are incidental to the overall operations of a CFC. The exemption is particularly important for Australian enterprises engaging in genuine business activities in unlisted countries.

The active income test requires a CFC to satisfy each of the following basic conditions:

- be in existence at the end of its statutory accounting period — this condition will always be satisfied (¶21-200) — and be a resident of a listed or unlisted country at all times during the accounting period when the company was in existence
- have at all times carried on business through a permanent establishment in its country of residence
- maintain accounts which are prepared in accordance with accounting standards and give a true and fair view of the financial position of the company
- have less than 5% of its gross turnover as stated in its recognised accounts in the form of tainted income. The calculation of gross turnover takes into account any capital gain or loss which arises when roll-over relief for an intra-group asset transfer is reversed, ie when the recipient CFC subsequently leaves the group (CGT event J1).

Tainted income

''Tainted income'' covers passive income, tainted sales income and tainted services income.

''Passive income'' includes dividends, tainted interest, rent and royalties, income derived from carrying on a business of trading in tainted assets and net gains from the disposal of tainted assets (ITAA36 s 446). In *Consolidated Press Holdings (No 2)*, it was held that a debt defeasance profit derived by a company in the course of its business was not passive income because it was not derived from ''trading'' in tainted assets or from the disposal of tainted assets. A UK company and an Australian resident company were parties to a dual-listed company arrangement carrying on a global commodities business. It was held that income sourced from sales by subsidiaries of the UK company was tainted sales income and attributable to the Australian resident company because the UK subsidiaries were associates of the Australian company (*BHP Billiton Ltd*). A lump sum received by a CFC in return for the assignment of an interest stream is passive income because it is ''tainted interest income'' (TD 98/20). An Australian financial institution (AFI) subsidiary carrying on a financial intermediary business may exclude certain tainted interest income from ''passive income'' (TD 2019/8).

''Tainted sales income'' is, broadly, income from the sale of goods to an associated person or income from the sale of goods originally purchased from an associate who had a connection with Australia (ITAA36 s 447).

''Tainted services income'' is broadly defined as income from the provision of services by a CFC to:

- a resident, but not where it is in connection with a business carried on by the resident at or through a foreign permanent establishment. In this context, ''resident'' means a Part X Australian resident (¶21-160), or
- a non-resident, in connection with a business carried on by the non-resident at or through a permanent establishment in Australia (ITAA36 s 448).

There are also anti-avoidance measures intended to ensure that services provided indirectly through interposed entities are treated as if they were provided directly.

The ATO has issued *Taxpayer Alert*TA 2015/5 concerning arrangements involving the use of offshore procurement hubs by Australian resident multinational enterprises. The ATO is concerned that the arrangements as described are being used to minimise ''tainted income'' under ss 447 and 448. Part IVA potentially applies and the ATO says the pricing of the arrangements raises transfer pricing issues.

Other aspects

The Commissioner can make adjustments to amounts included in a CFC's recognised accounts to reflect the application of arm's length transfer pricing principles to the CFC's transactions with related parties not covered by ITAA36 s 440. Under s 440, arm's length principles are used in applying the active income test to the calculation of gains and losses on the disposal of assets other than trading stock.

Where a CFC resident in an unlisted country passes the active income test, its attributable income will not include its ''adjusted tainted income''. This is its tainted income (ie passive income and tainted sales and services income) subject to certain modifications. These modifications essentially include gross amounts instead of net gains from the disposal of tainted assets and tainted commodity investments, and from currency exchange rate fluctuations.

Where a CFC resident in a listed country satisfies the test, there will be no attribution in respect of its designated concession income.

Special rules apply to the keeping of records needed to substantiate claims that the active income test has been passed (ITAA36 ss 451 to 453).

[FTR ¶795-298, ¶796-670, ¶796-890]

¶21-190 Attribution of CFC income to attributable taxpayers

The assessable income of a taxpayer who is an ''attributable taxpayer'' in relation to a CFC will include the taxpayer's share of the CFC's ''attributable income'' for the CFC's statutory accounting period that ended during the taxpayer's year of income.

Attribution percentage

The share of a CFC's attributable income that is attributable to a particular attributable taxpayer is called the ''attribution percentage''.

The attribution percentage is the sum of the taxpayer's direct and indirect ''attribution interests'' in the CFC. A direct attribution interest is calculated in the same manner as the taxpayer's direct control interest in the CFC (¶21-140). Indirect attribution interests can only be traced through controlled foreign entities. They are calculated by multiplying attribution tracing interests through interposed entities. Attribution does not apply where the taxpayer simply has de facto control, without either a direct or indirect attribution interest (ID 2008/5).

Attributable income provisions

The basic provision under which the attributable income of a CFC will be included in a resident taxpayer's assessable income is ITAA36 s 456. Special relief from double taxation is available under ITAA36 s 456A to ensure that there is no attribution under s 456 where an attributable taxpayer holds an interest in a CFC through an entity that is a resident of a listed country in which foreign tax is payable by the entity under an ''accruals taxation law'' of that country. The relevant accruals taxation laws are specified in ITR15 reg 18. The Commissioner will treat foreign tax as being payable in situations where no tax is paid due to the availability of a tax rebate, credit or deduction in the listed country (TD 96/37).

Attribution to resident attributable taxpayers will also occur where a CFC changes its country of residence from an unlisted country to a listed country or to Australia (ITAA36 s 457). The operation of this provision is modified where an unlisted country CFC is treated as having changed residence to a listed country as a result of the unlisted country becoming listed. In such a case, s 457 will not apply if the CFC was a resident of the newly listed country for 3 or more years prior to the country becoming listed. If the CFC has been a resident of a newly listed country for less than 3 years, s 457 will apply, but only to tax gains on the disposal of assets held at the residence-change time.

However, effective from 27 June 2005, this 3-year requirement will not apply, so there will be no attribution under s 457 simply because an unlisted country CFC becomes a listed country CFC due to its country of residence becoming listed.

Section 457 does not attribute adjusted distributable profits of past statutory accounting periods.

Attribution may also occur where ITAA36 s 459A is triggered to combat avoidance of attribution of income by the use of interposed Australian trusts or partnerships in conjunction with a CFC or a controlled foreign trust.

[FTR ¶796-980ff]

¶21-200 Attributable income of a CFC

The attributable income of a foreign company must be calculated where, at the end of the company's statutory accounting period:

- the company was a CFC (¶21-150). Where a CFC ceases to exist before the end of its statutory accounting period, its statutory accounting period will be deemed to have ended immediately before the CFC ceased to exist (ITAA36 s 319(6)), and
- there was at least one attributable taxpayer in relation to the CFC (¶21-140).

Where these conditions are satisfied, the attributable income of the CFC for that statutory period must be calculated separately for each attributable taxpayer.

A CFC's attributable income will be calculated on a *notional* basis using, in a modified form, the rules that apply for the calculation of the taxable income of a resident company (ITAA36 ss 381 to 431). The most important modifications relate to the application of the CGT provisions (see below), the treatment of depreciating assets and trading stock, currency translation and the deductibility of taxes paid. The commercial debt forgiveness provisions (¶16-910) do not apply for the purpose of attributing income derived by a CFC to resident taxpayers and neither do the thin capitalisation or debt creation rules.

The types of income that will be included in the attributable income of a CFC depend on whether it is resident in a listed or unlisted country and whether it passes the active income test (¶21-180).

The ATO considers that amounts deemed to be dividends under ITAA36 s 47A (¶21-250) are not included in the notional assessable income of either a listed or unlisted country CFC (TD 2007/16).

Unlisted country CFCs

Where a CFC that is a resident of an unlisted country does not pass the active income test, its attributable income is the amount that would have been its taxable income if the CFC was a resident of Australia and its only income (including income derived through a partnership) was: (i) adjusted tainted income (ie passive income and tainted sales and services income); and (ii) trust income (including trust income attributed under the transferor trust measures (¶21-300)). Where a CFC resident in an unlisted country passes the active income test, its attributable income will include the same forms of income as those listed above except for its adjusted tainted income (s 384).

Listed country CFCs

The attributable income of a CFC resident in a listed country which fails the active income test is calculated on the assumption that its income (including income derived through a partnership) consists of:

- adjusted tainted income that is eligible designated concession income (¶21-170)

- income that is not eligible designated concession income, is not derived from sources in the listed country and is adjusted tainted income not taxed in a listed country
- income derived as a beneficiary of a trust that is not taxed in a listed country or Australia or, being subject to tax in a listed country, is eligible designated concession income in relation to a listed country
- income attributed to the CFC under the transferor trust measures.

The attributable income of a listed country CFC that passes the active income test will include the same forms of income except for eligible designated concession income (s 385(2)).

Income excluded from attributable income

The attributable income of a CFC resident in an unlisted or a listed country does not include the following "notional exempt income" (ss 402 to 404):

- income of the CFC assessable for Australian tax purposes independently of the operation of the CFC measures
- dividends to the extent that they have been franked
- certain excluded insurance premiums.

For a CFC resident in an unlisted country, attributable income also does not include income derived in carrying on a business in a listed country, at or through a permanent establishment in that country, where the income is not eligible designated concession income (s 403).

Where a CFC is resident in a listed country at the end of the income year, a dividend paid to it by a company also resident in a listed country is also notional exempt income (s 404). For the purposes of this rule, the following countries are, in effect, treated as listed countries (ITAA36 s 320; ITR15 reg 19): Argentina, Austria, Bangladesh, Belgium, Brazil, Brunei, Bulgaria, China (except the Hong Kong Special Administrative Region), Czech Republic, Denmark, Fiji, Finland, French Polynesia, Greece, Hungary, Iceland, India, Indonesia, Iran, Ireland, Israel, Italy, Kenya, Kiribati, Republic of Korea, Luxembourg, Malaysia, Malta, Mexico, Myanmar, Netherlands, New Caledonia, Norway, Pakistan, Papua New Guinea, Philippines, Poland, Portugal, Romania, Russian Federation, Saudi Arabia, Singapore, Slovak Republic, Solomon Islands, South Africa, Spain, Sri Lanka, Sweden, Switzerland, Taiwan, Thailand, Tokelau, Tonga, Turkey, Tuvalu, Vietnam, Western Samoa and Zimbabwe. As a result of the changes to the rules on foreign dividend exemption (¶21-095), together with concerns about exploitation, s 404 was replaced with a new rule designed to ensure that CFCs would continue to have access to the foreign dividend exemption.

De minimis exemption for listed country CFCs

A *de minimis* exemption applies so that where the combined amount of: (i) eligible designated concession income; and (ii) income from sources outside the listed country that is *either* not taxed in a listed country or adjusted tainted income not taxed in a listed country, does not exceed certain levels (see below), such income is not included in the attributable income of a listed country CFC (s 385(4)). There is no similar exemption for CFCs that are residents of unlisted countries.

For a listed country CFC with a gross turnover of less than $1 million, the exemption applies where the sum of the 3 amounts does not exceed 5% of the gross turnover. Where a listed country CFC has a gross turnover of more than $1 million, it applies where the sum of the 3 amounts does not exceed $50,000.

Prior year losses

A CFC's attributable income may be reduced by prior year losses. A loss from a previous year can only be taken into account as a notional deduction if the CFC was a CFC during the year in which the loss was incurred and in all intervening years. In addition, a notional deduction is not generally available for prior year losses where a CFC changes its country of residence from a listed country to an unlisted country (or vice versa). A CFC's prior year losses will generally be reduced by the CFC's "sometimes-exempt income", ie broadly, an amount which was not included in the CFC's attributable income because the CFC passed the active income test or it fell within the *de minimis* exemption (see above) (ss 425 to 431).

Currency translation rules

For the rules governing the conversion of amounts expressed in a foreign currency into Australian or functional currency, see ¶23-070 and TD 2006/6.

Modified application of CGT provisions

A number of modifications to the operation of the CGT provisions apply for the purposes of calculating the attributable income of a CFC.

- When calculating the capital gain or loss in relation to a CGT event involving a CFC or the disposal of an asset by a CFC, all assets owned by the CFC immediately before it became a CFC which are not of a type that would expose a non-resident to CGT (¶12-720) (referred to as "commencing day assets") are treated as having been acquired by the CFC on its "commencing day". The cost base of the asset is deemed to be the greater of the asset's cost base or market value at the end of the commencing day; the first element of the reduced cost base of each such asset is the lesser of its market value or its cost base at the end of that day. For a CFC in existence as at 30 June 1990, its commencing day is 30 June 1990; for any other CFC, its commencing day is the first day after 30 June 1990 at the end of which it was a CFC. This means that, in relation to a post-30 June 1995 CGT event affecting an asset which is not of a type that would expose a non-resident to CGT (¶12-720), the attributable income of a CFC will include only the gain or loss accruing from the time the asset was acquired or its commencing day, whichever is later (ss 406; 411; 412). Where a company becomes a CFC after 30 June 1995, CGT events or asset disposals made before its commencing day will not be taken into account in the calculation of its attributable income. Note that, with general effect from 1 July 2005, the definition of "commencing day" is eased so that it will be the later of: (i) the last day of the most recent period during which there was not an attributable taxpayer with a positive attribution percentage in relation to the CFC; and (ii) 30 June 1990.

- Where the commencing day assets of a CFC include shares or units in a unit trust and, during the time from when they were acquired up to the CFC's commencing day, a payment representing a return of capital is made on those shares or units, their cost base as at the commencing day is reduced by the amount of the payment (s 413).

- Capital gains or losses on CGT events affecting assets which are of a type that would expose a non-resident to CGT (¶12-720) are not taken into account for attribution purposes. The usual CGT provisions applying to non-residents will, of course, apply to such assets in the calculation of the assessable income of the CFC in its own right.

- Capital losses incurred before 1 July 1990 are disregarded.

- Certain CGT provisions are disregarded, namely those which: (a) provide that no gain or loss is made from an asset used solely to produce exempt income; (b) reduce the capital proceeds from a CGT event as a result of the application of

ITAA36 s 47A (¶21-250); (c) allow group company transfers of a net capital loss; (d) apply to a CFC which becomes an Australian resident; (e) apply to a company changing its residence from an unlisted country; and (f) govern the acquisition date and cost base of certain assets of an individual or company that becomes a resident of Australia (s 410).

- Modifications are made to the roll-over relief provisions applicable to the transfer of an asset between wholly-owned group companies (s 419). A capital gain which arises when such roll-over relief is reversed (when the recipient CFC subsequently leaves the group (CGT event J1)), must be included in the CFC's attributable income if it fails the active income test.
- Adjustments are made to the consideration received on the happening of a CGT event in relation to a CGT asset that: (a) was owned by a CFC at the time when it changed its country of residence from an unlisted to a listed country (s 422); or (b) was transferred to the CFC by another CFC in circumstances which triggered s 47A (s 423).

For the CGT exemption applying to attributable income arising from the disposal of shares owned by a CFC in a foreign company, see ¶12-745.

[FTR ¶796-090, ¶796-170ff]

¶21-210 Attribution accounts for CFC distributions

In order to avoid double taxation of income which would otherwise arise where income attributed to an attributable taxpayer is subsequently distributed by the relevant CFC, an exemption is available under ITAA36 s 23AI for the distributed income, provided the recipient can establish a link between the distributed income and the previously attributed income.

Attribution accounts enable a taxpayer to do this by providing a mechanism for tracing dividends through interposed companies, partnerships and/or trusts in order to determine whether the distributable profits from which they have been paid have been previously attributed. Therefore, while there is no requirement that attributable taxpayers establish attribution accounts, there is a strong incentive to do so.

An attributable taxpayer can establish an attribution account in relation to a CFC when an amount of the CFC's attributable income is included in the taxpayer's assessable income. The taxpayer then makes an attribution *credit* entry representing the attributable income less the tax paid by the CFC on the income. When the CFC makes an attribution account payment (ie distributes the income), the taxpayer makes an attribution *debit* entry in the account.

The attribution debit cannot exceed the amount standing to the credit of the account at that time (the "attribution surplus"). This means that the attribution surplus is the maximum amount of previously attributed income against which the resident taxpayer can offset distributed CFC income for exemption purposes. Special rules apply for the operation of the successive levels of attribution accounts required in more complex situations where an Australian resident company has interests in a chain of CFCs (ITAA36 ss 363 to 373). Attribution account payments are exempt to the extent of the debit which arises when they are paid (¶21-097).

The various times at which an attribution credit can arise in the attribution account maintained in relation to a CFC are specified in ITAA36 s 371(5).

An attribution debit can arise only from an attribution payment made by a non-resident. This means that, where a CFC changes its country of residence to Australia, any profits that it distributes after coming onshore would not be exempt. To ensure that s 23AI does apply in such situations, a CFC that takes up residence in Australia will, for attribution debit purposes only, continue to be treated as a non-resident.

To prevent double taxation arising where a taxpayer disposes of an interest in a CFC, the capital or revenue proceeds are reduced by the amount of any attribution surplus for the CFC in relation to the taxpayer (ITAA36 ss 401; 461).

Consolidated groups

Only the head company of a consolidated group is able to operate attribution accounts during the period of consolidation (ITAA97 Div 717; ¶8-000 and following).

[FTR ¶795-880, ¶796-000]

¶21-220 Offshore information notices

To enforce the accruals taxation system, and for other purposes, the Commissioner may need to gain access to information and documents located in foreign countries. To this end, the Commissioner can issue a 90-day ''offshore information notice'' under TAA Sch 1 s 353-25 requesting a taxpayer to furnish information and/or documents which the Commissioner has reason to believe are relevant to the assessment of the taxpayer. The notice may be issued in respect of any tax administered by the Commissioner, including income tax, GST and Petroleum Resource Rent Tax. The relevant provisions, contained in TAA Sch 1 Subdiv 353-B, replaced former ITAA36 s 264A, with effect from 1 April 2019.

In the case of information, the Commissioner must reasonably believe that the information is: (i) within the knowledge of an entity outside Australia; (ii) recorded in a document outside Australia; or (iii) stored by any means whatsoever outside Australia. In the case of documents, the Commissioner must reasonably believe that the documents are outside Australia, whether or not copies of the documents are in Australia.

In *Pilnara*, the Full Federal Court said that: (i) the notice, issued under former s 264A, only had to identify the relevant taxpayer — it did not have to set out the objective facts which established the relevance of the documents sought to the assessment of the taxpayer; (ii) the scope of the information sought extended generally to the assessment of the taxpayer — it was not limited to the application of the CFC provisions; and (iii) there was no requirement that the Commissioner believe that each document sought actually existed.

The 90-day period can be extended on request by the taxpayer, and the Commissioner can issue subsequent notices varying the terms and compliance period stated in the original notice.

In *FH Faulding & Co*, the Federal Court ruled that certain requests made by the Commissioner in a former s 264A notice were invalid on the grounds that they were irrelevant or too uncertain. The court also held that the power to specify the manner in which information is to be provided does not extend to a power to specify that a third party make a statement or answer the questions asked of the taxpayer by the Commissioner.

Failing to comply with a s 353-25 notice is not an offence. The only sanction for failure to comply with a notice is that the information or documents which the taxpayer fails to produce will not be admissible in subsequent proceedings disputing the taxpayer's assessment. However, the Commissioner can consent to the admission into evidence of information or documents otherwise blocked under s 353-25. In circumstances where the refusal of the Commissioner to give consent would, constitutionally, have the effect of making a penalty or tax uncontestable, he cannot withhold consent.

[FTR ¶785-850]

¶21-230 Record-keeping by attributable taxpayers

A taxpayer whose assessable income includes an amount of attributable income from a CFC is required to maintain for 5 years records that show how the taxpayer came to be an attributable taxpayer, the basis on which the attributable income included in the taxpayer's assessable income was calculated, the aggregate of the taxpayer's indirect attribution interests in the CFC and the calculation of the taxpayer's attribution percentage in the CFC (ITAA36 ss 462 to 464A).

[FTR ¶797-080ff]

¶21-240 CFC elections and notices

For the purpose of calculating a CFC's attributable income, any elections, declarations, choices or notices that a CFC would be required to lodge are, instead, the separate responsibility of each taxpayer who is an attributable taxpayer in relation to the CFC (ITAA36 s 390). However, this rule does not always apply to elections in respect of CGT roll-over relief or variations of a CFC's statutory accounting period (see below).

The elections, etc, must be made in the attributable taxpayer's return for the relevant year or within such further period as the Commissioner allows.

Elections in respect of CGT roll-over relief and statutory accounting periods must generally be lodged by the CFC rather than the attributable taxpayers (TD 92/104). These elections, and requests for extensions of time to make them, must be lodged by the person authorised to act for the CFC whether under a foreign law or under the constituent document of the CFC. The requirement for a CFC to make an election will also be satisfied if an Australian agent (eg the Australian parent of a CFC or the CFC's tax agent) makes the election for or on behalf of the CFC, provided the person is authorised to do so. These elections must be lodged with the ATO branch where the largest attributable taxpayer's return is lodged.

An attributable taxpayer must make an election on behalf of a CFC in respect of CGT roll-over relief or a statutory accounting period variation if it is the only attributable taxpayer in relation to the CFC and has an attribution percentage of 100% (ITAA36 s 438).

[FTR ¶795-370, ¶796-760]

¶21-250 Payment of deemed dividends by CFCs

Certain ''distribution payments'' that represent the distribution of the profits of a CFC otherwise than by a dividend are treated as dividends under ITAA36 s 47A.

Where, at the time a CFC makes a distribution payment, the CFC has accumulated profits and is a resident of an *unlisted* country, the payment will be deemed to be a dividend paid by the CFC out of its profits to the extent that it does not exceed accumulated profits and would not otherwise be treated as a dividend.

Broadly, a distribution payment will be taken to have been made where the CFC transfers, or arranges for another entity to transfer, a ''distribution benefit'' to an associated entity. Given its anti-avoidance role against such ''disguised distributions'', and the many methods that could be employed to transfer profits in non-dividend form, s 47A is drafted to catch distribution benefits effectively transferred by the waiver of debts, the granting of a non-arm's length loan, transfers of property or services for no or inadequate consideration, the payment of a call on an allotment of shares and a variety of other arrangements involving the associated entity and the transfer of benefits involving third parties. TR 2002/2 explains the meaning of ''arm's length'' for the purposes of s 47A. Broadly, it looks at the nature of the dealing rather than the relationship between the parties.

The operation of s 47A may pose particular difficulties for a CFC resident in an unlisted country that seeks to limit its tainted income to 5% in order to satisfy the active income test (¶21-180), by transferring out of the company those assets that give rise to tainted income.

Special valuation rules govern the calculation of the amount of the deemed dividend.

Where a distribution payment is included in a taxpayer's return of assessable income, it will be treated as a dividend for tax purposes. If: (a) the payment is not treated as a dividend in the taxpayer's return; and (b) the taxpayer does not advise the Commissioner within 12 months after the year of income that it has been so treated and it is subsequently treated as a dividend (eg following an audit), no foreign tax credit will be available in respect of the amount taken to be a dividend, and the dividend will not be exempt from tax under ITAA36 s 23AI.

[FTR ¶21-700]

Transferor Trusts

¶21-290 Accruals taxation of non-resident trust income

In addition to its impact on the sheltered income of CFCs, the accruals taxation system also attacks tax avoidance/deferral arising from the accumulation of foreign source income in non-resident trust estates with Australian resident beneficiaries. The main elements in the accruals taxation and related measures affecting non-resident trusts contained in ITAA36 Div 6AAA (ss 102AAA to 102AAZG) are:

- the ''transferor trust'' measures which impose accruals taxation by attributing to an Australian resident income derived by a non-resident trust estate to which the Australian resident transferred property or provided services (¶21-300)
- an additional tax in the form of an interest charge payable by an Australian resident beneficiary on accumulated income distributed by a non-resident trust where that income has not been subject to the transferor trust measures or taxed on a current basis to the trustee or beneficiary (¶21-350).

[FTR ¶51-370]

¶21-300 Transferor trust measures

An entity that is an attributable taxpayer in relation to a non-resident trust estate and is resident in Australia during all or part of the taxpayer's year of income may have the attributable income of the trust estate included in its assessable income. An entity will be subject to attribution if it:

- has transferred property or services to a non-resident *discretionary* trust, or
- transfers property or services to a non-resident, *non-discretionary* trust for inadequate or no consideration.

Non-resident trust estate

A non-resident trust estate is defined as a trust estate that is not a ''resident trust estate''. A resident trust estate is a trust which had a trustee resident in Australia or its central management and control in Australia, a public trading trust taxed as a company, or an eligible superannuation fund, ADF or PST.

Discretionary trust

A trust is treated as a discretionary trust in any of the following circumstances:

(1) a person (including the trustee) has a power of appointment or other discretion, the exercise or non-exercise of which has an effect on the identity of the beneficiaries and/or how the beneficiaries are to benefit under the trust

(2) one or more of the beneficiaries has a contingent or defeasible interest in some or all of the corpus or income of the trust, or

(3) the trustee of another estate to which (1) applies benefits or is capable of benefiting under the trust.

Transfers

The scope of the expression ''transfer of property or services'' extends beyond transfers made to existing trusts to transfers which create the trust (eg a declaration of trust in respect of shares) and includes indirect transfers such as where property or services are applied to the benefit, or at the direction, of the trustee (ITAA36 s 102AAJ). The ATO considers that this would include a transfer of property or services to a non-resident company that is wholly or partly-owned by a non-resident trustee (TR 2007/13). There are special rules in ITAA36 s 102AAK which deem an entity to have made a transfer in situations such as in ''back to back'' arrangements in which one entity transfers property to another on condition that the second makes a transfer to the trust.

[FTR ¶51-372]

¶21-310 Attributable taxpayers of non-resident trusts

Where a company, partnership, trustee or any other entity, including a CFC, is an ''attributable taxpayer'' in relation to a non-resident trust estate, the attributable income of the trust is included in the entity's assessable income or, in the case of a CFC, in its attributable income.

The circumstances in which an entity will be an attributable taxpayer in relation to a non-resident trust estate differ according to whether the trust estate is a discretionary or non-discretionary trust (ITAA36 s 102AAT).

Transfers to discretionary trusts

The basic conditions that must be satisfied for an entity to be an attributable taxpayer in relation to a non-resident discretionary trust estate are that:

- at any time during the relevant year of income, the trust was a discretionary trust (and not a public unit trust for the whole year)
- the entity transferred property or services to the trust estate before or during the entity's relevant year of income.

There are exceptions for a transfer of property or services to a discretionary trust made in the ordinary course of business where there are similar arm's length transfers made to ordinary customers, or a transfer not made in the ordinary course of business but at arm's length, and neither the transferor entity nor any of its associates was in a position to control the trust.

There is a broad range of circumstances in which an entity will be taken to be in a position to control a trust estate (ITAA36 s 102AAG).

Transfers to non-discretionary trusts

The basic conditions that must be satisfied for an entity to be an attributable taxpayer in relation to a non-resident non-discretionary trust are that at all times during the transferor's year of income during which the trust was in existence, the trust estate was a non-discretionary trust or a public unit trust and the transfer was made for no consideration or less than the arm's length consideration.

There are 2 situations in which a natural person transferor to a non-resident trust estate (discretionary or non-discretionary) will *not* be an attributable taxpayer. These situations are outlined below.

Non-resident family trusts

Attribution to a resident taxpayer will not arise where the taxpayer is a natural person who transfers property or services to a trust which was a non-resident family trust at all times it was in existence from the beginning of the taxpayer's 1990–91 year of income until the end of the current year of income. In addition, a natural person who first becomes an Australian resident after 12 April 1989 and makes a transfer to a non-resident family trust before taking up residency will not be an attributable taxpayer, provided the trust remains a non-resident family trust. The natural person must not be a trustee of a trust.

There are 2 types of family trust (ITAA36 s 102AAH), those that come into existence by virtue of the breakdown of a marriage or a de facto marriage and family relief trusts, ie trusts established and operated for the relief of persons who are in necessitous circumstances.

Further, a natural person (not being a trustee of a trust), who first becomes a resident of Australia after 12 April 1989, will not be subject to attribution if the relevant transfer to a non-resident family trust was made before the person's change of residence and neither the person nor any associates could control the trust estate from the beginning of the year of income after that in which the person first became a resident.

Transfers by trustees of deceased estates

Generally, the transferor trust measures do not apply to transfers made by trustees of a deceased estate pursuant to directions contained in the deceased person's will or codicil, or to a court order which varies the terms of the will or codicil (ITAA36 s 102AAL). However, there are some specific exceptions.

Record-keeping by attributable taxpayers

Attributable taxpayers are required, under the sanction of a fine not exceeding 30 penalty units (¶29-700), to maintain records of the circumstances that resulted in the taxpayer being an attributable taxpayer and, except in the case of attributable income calculated on a "deemed rate of return" basis (¶21-340), how the attributable income of the trust is calculated.

Attributable taxpayers must also keep records which indicate the basis on which any amount of attributable income was included in their assessable income. One important concession to the record-keeping requirements applies where a taxpayer does not know, and had no reasonable grounds to suspect, that he/she was an attributable taxpayer (ITAA36 s 102AAZG).

[FTR ¶51-388 – ¶51-396, ¶51-410]

¶21-320 Attributable income of a non-resident trust estate

The attributable income of a non-resident trust estate depends on whether the trust estate is resident in a listed or unlisted country (¶21-130).

In general terms, a trust estate is a listed country trust estate in relation to a transferor's year of income where each item of income derived by the trust is either: (a) subject to tax in a listed country or in Australia in the hands of the trustee or a beneficiary in a period ending before the end of the year of income or commencing during that year of income; or (b) designated concession income (ITAA36 s 102AAE(1)).

The base amount of the attributable income of a trust estate that is *not* resident in a listed country is, subject to the modifications noted below, its net income under ITAA36 s 95(1). For a listed country trust estate it is its net income as calculated under s 95(1), having regard only to its eligible designated concession income (¶21-170).

The base amount of net income for both listed and unlisted country trust estates is then reduced by amounts that are otherwise subject to tax in Australia or a listed country (ITAA36 s 102AAU(1)).

Finally, any foreign or Australian income tax paid by the trustee or beneficiary that is attributable to the reduced amount is deducted from the trust estate's net income, or eligible designated concession income, as the case may be.

Modified application of certain provisions

For the purpose of calculating the net income of a non-resident trust estate under s 95(1), various provisions of ITAA36 and ITAA97 relating to trading stock, depreciating assets, transfer pricing, CGT and pre-1990–91 losses are applied in a modified form.

[FTR ¶51-384, ¶51-412 – ¶51-428]

¶21-330 Amounts included in assessable income of attributable taxpayers

The amount that will be included in the assessable income of each person who is an attributable taxpayer in relation to a non-resident trust estate depends on whether the taxpayer was resident in Australia during the whole of the year (ITAA36 s 102AAZD).

Where the attributable taxpayer was resident for the whole of the year, the amount included in the taxpayer's assessable income is the whole of the notional attributable income of the trust estate. For a part-year resident taxpayer, the notional attributable income is apportioned according to the number of days the taxpayer was resident during the year. Income can be attributed to a natural person who dies during the year of income, as distinct from the executor of the estate (ID 2008/9; ID 2008/10).

The fact that the *whole* of the trust's notional income can be attributed to *each* transferor in a multiple transferor situation is seen as a strong disincentive to such activities. However, the Commissioner has a discretion to reduce the amount included in the taxpayer's assessable income.

De minimis exemption

The attributable income of a trust estate that is resident in a listed country will not be included in the assessable income of a transferor if the total attributable income derived by all the non-resident trusts (including unlisted country trusts) to which the transferor has transferred property or services does not exceed the lesser of:

- $20,000, or
- 10% of the aggregate of the net incomes of the trust estates (ITAA36 s 102AAZE).

Attributable income not assessable when distributed

Attributable income of a trust estate that has been included in the assessable income of a transferor (other than a company) will be exempt from tax in the hands of a beneficiary to whom that income is subsequently distributed. Where the attributable income of a trust estate was included in the assessable income of a company transferor, subsequent distributions of that income to that company will be exempt from company tax.

Temporary residents

Individuals who qualify as ''temporary residents'' are not treated as residents for these purposes (¶22-125).

[FTR ¶51-432]

¶21-340 Deemed rate of return for some attributable taxpayers

One of the difficulties taxpayers will often face in complying with the accruals taxation system is gaining access to the information required to calculate their attributable income according to Australian law. However, if the Commissioner is satisfied that a transferor ''could not reasonably be expected to obtain'' the information, a deemed rate of return on the property or services transferred is calculated under ITAA36 s 102AAZD(4) to determine the amount of income to be included in the transferor's assessable income.

The deemed rate of return is 5 percentage points above the ''weighted statutory interest rate''. This is determined by reference to the ''basic statutory interest rate'' which is the same as the interest rate used to calculate additional tax on distributions of accumulated non-resident trust income (¶21-350).

[FTR ¶51-432/15]

¶21-350 Interest charge on distributions of accumulated trust income

In certain circumstances, an Australian resident beneficiary whose assessable income includes a distribution of accumulated income from a non-resident trust will be liable for an additional tax in the form of an interest charge imposed under the *Taxation (Interest on Non-resident Trust Distributions) Act 1990*.

The additional tax will apply to distributions of accumulated non-resident trust estate income which has not been caught by the transferor trust measures or been subject to tax on a current basis in the hands of the trustee or a beneficiary (ITAA36 s 102AAM). The interest charge is intended to compensate the revenue for the deferral of taxation that resulted from the income being accumulated in the trust rather than being distributed yearly. For listed country trust distributions, the interest charge applies only in relation to distributions made out of the trust's designated concession income (¶21-170).

To avoid the interest charge, a taxpayer has to provide evidence which overcomes the presumptions that, in relation to a listed country trust estate, the distribution was wholly attributable to the trust's designated concession income, or, in relation to an unlisted country trust estate, the distribution was wholly attributable to income and profits of the trust estate that have not been taxed in a listed country.

▶ Example

In the current income year A, an Australian resident individual, receives a distribution of $20,000 from an unlisted country trust estate. The distribution was made wholly out of foreign income derived by the trust in a prior year and is included in the taxpayer's assessable income by virtue of s 99B. No listed country tax has been paid on the income. In the prior year the trust derived foreign income of $40,000 and paid foreign tax of $10,000. This means that, on a pro rata basis, half ($5,000) of the foreign tax was attributable to the distribution included in A's assessable income as grossed up. Assuming that the applicable rate of tax is 45%, interest is payable on:

($20,000 + $5,000) × 45%	$11,250
Less	$5,000
Balance	$6,250

The rate of interest is the rate fixed under TAA s 8AAD, ie the GIC rate (¶29-510) less 7 percentage points.

[FTR ¶51-398]

Foreign Income Tax Offsets

¶21-670 Scope of FITO rules

The foreign income tax offset (FITO) rules in ITAA97 Div 770 are designed to protect a taxpayer from the double taxation that may arise where the taxpayer pays foreign tax on income that is also taxable in Australia. This is achieved by allowing a taxpayer to claim a tax offset where they have paid foreign tax on amounts included in their assessable income.

The operation of the general anti-avoidance provisions in ITAA36 Pt IVA (¶30-160) includes schemes designed to acquire or generate foreign tax offsets or credits (see, for example, *Citigroup*). The ATO also considers that certain arrangements in which Australian resident taxpayers seek to enhance their return on bond investments through access to foreign tax credits are not effective (TA 2007/3).

The position may also be affected by any double tax agreement that Australia may have with the foreign country (¶22-160).

The ATO has issued general guidelines in its *Guide to foreign income tax offset rules*.

[FITR ¶588-000]

¶21-680 Entitlement to foreign income tax offset

The general rule is that, to qualify for an offset for an income year, the taxpayer must have paid foreign income tax on an amount that is included in its assessable income for that year (s 770-10).

If only part of an amount on which foreign tax has been paid is assessable, only the same proportion of the foreign tax counts towards the offset. This could apply, for example, where foreign tax is paid on the foreign branch income of an Australian company (¶21-098).

Foreign capital gains and losses

If the taxpayer pays foreign tax on a foreign *capital gain*, the offset is available provided that the gain is taken into account in determining the taxpayer's net capital gain for the year. A taxpayer was entitled to an offset for only 50% of US tax paid on a US sourced capital gain because only half of the gain was included in his Australian assessable income. The other half of the gain was not included in income because of the operation of the CGT discount rule (*Burton*).

If the taxpayer has a net capital loss for a year, the foreign tax on the capital gain cannot be taken into account because it was not paid in respect of an amount included in assessable income. The offset also cannot be claimed in relation to a capital loss notwithstanding that it may be treated as a capital gain under foreign law due to differences in the method of calculating net gains and losses.

In some cases, taxpayers may be able to maximise their offset entitlements by taking advantage of the normal options available for applying capital losses against capital gains. The general idea is to maximise the proportion of foreign tax paid that qualifies for the offset. For example, it may be advantageous for a taxpayer to apply capital losses firstly against those capital gains on which no foreign tax is paid.

Tax on non-assessable income

Foreign income tax paid on *non*-assessable income generally does not qualify for the offset. As an exception to this rule, the offset extends to foreign tax paid by a resident in respect of amounts paid out of income previously attributed from a controlled foreign company which are non-assessable, non-exempt income under the rules explained at ¶21-097. However, this is limited to final or direct taxes such as dividend withholding tax. Underlying taxes are *not* covered by this provision, but some of these may be eligible under the rules at ¶21-770.

Foreign income tax must be "paid"

Under the general rule, to qualify for an offset for an income year, the taxpayer must have paid foreign income tax on an amount that is included in the taxpayer's assessable income for the claim year (ie the income year in relation to which the claim is made). Furthermore, the amount of the offset will be dependent on the amount of that foreign tax paid.

It is not necessary that the payment of foreign income tax actually occurs in the claim year. Payment in a different year may occur, for example, because of differences in tax accounting rules in the other country, or because foreign tax on a deferred interest security is not paid until maturity. In some cases where payment is made in a later year, this will mean that earlier year returns will need to be amended (¶21-775.)

The foreign tax must be *paid*, and it is not sufficient that the foreign tax has simply accrued, or that the liability for it has arisen. However, in relation to the corresponding requirement in the former FTC system, the ATO recognised that many foreign tax jurisdictions require progressive tax payments, and said that it would allow a credit for foreign taxes that the taxpayer could demonstrate had been paid as advance or instalment payments. Where there was a subsequent adjustment, an amended credit for that year would need to be calculated (former IT 2527).

Normally, the foreign tax must be paid by the entity claiming the offset. For special rules covering payment by other entities, see ¶21-765.

Foreign income tax is not considered to have been paid to the extent that it is refundable, either to the taxpayer or another entity. The same applies if the taxpayer or other entity is entitled to any other benefit worked out by reference to the amount of the foreign income tax. However, this does not apply if the only benefit is a reduction in tax liability, eg an imputation credit or rebate (s 770-140). Liability to pay foreign tax may also be affected by any applicable DTA. For the availability of offsets for tax paid on refunds from the New Zealand primary producer income equalisation scheme, see ID 2010/202.

As a result of the limitations placed on the exemption for foreign employment income (¶10-860), most taxpayers working overseas will be assessable in Australia on that income and be entitled to claim an offset for the foreign tax paid. The government has confirmed that these taxpayers will not be required to lodge a foreign tax return to demonstrate that the foreign tax has been paid — they should simply keep their normal pay slips identifying amounts withheld. These need only be provided to the ATO in the event of an audit (*Assistant Treasurer's media release No 57*, 1 April 2010).

Residence of taxpayer

Apart from the rule governing certain residence-based foreign taxes (¶21-700), there is no requirement that the entity claiming the offset must be an Australian resident. This extension enables Australia to give full effect to non-discrimination rules in its newer DTAs.

This also means that a foreign resident may theoretically be entitled to the offset for foreign income tax that it pays on a source basis (ie on the basis that the source of the income is in the foreign country), provided that they are also assessed in Australia on that income. However, situations in which Australia taxes non-residents on foreign source income are rare.

Offset is non-refundable

The offset is non-refundable, with the result that if it exceeds the amount of tax otherwise payable for the year, the excess is lost. The excess cannot be transferred to another taxpayer and the excess cannot be carried forward to a later income year. However, special transitional rules enable a limited form of carry forward for excess credits generated under the FTC system before 2008–09 (¶21-760).

[FITR ¶588-110]

¶21-700 What is foreign income tax?

"Foreign income tax" is intended to cover taxes that are substantially equivalent to Australian income tax. To qualify, the following requirements must be satisfied (s 770-15):

(1) the tax must be imposed by a law other than an Australian Commonwealth, state or territory law. The foreign law may be at the level of a national or supra-national government (such as the European Union), or at a state, provincial, local or municipal level. Unlike the situation that applied under the former FTC rules, it is not necessary that the foreign tax be imposed by a foreign country

(2) the tax must be:

- a tax on income, or on profits or gains (whether of an income or capital nature). This would extend to withholding taxes, or
- any other tax covered by a double tax agreement (eg a tax sparing amount, such as under the Philippines DTA).

Foreign income tax does not cover inheritance taxes, annual wealth taxes, net worth taxes, or taxes based on receipts, turnover or production.

Ineligible foreign income taxes

The following types of tax that may otherwise qualify as eligible foreign income tax are specifically excluded from the offset (ss 770-10; 770-15).

Certain residence-based taxes. The offset does not apply to foreign income tax paid to a foreign country by a taxpayer on the basis of their residence in that country on amounts sourced outside that country. This applies even though the taxpayer may also have residence in Australia.

▶ Example

A resident of a foreign country is obliged, by virtue of their residence, to pay tax on their Australian-source income. That residence-based tax would not qualify for the offset.

This forms a limited exception to the general rule that non-residents are not excluded from entitlement to the offset.

Ex-complying funds and ex-foreign funds. Superannuation funds that change their status from complying to non-complying, or from foreign to resident, are assessable on additional amounts based on the market value of the fund's assets just before the start of the income year, less undeducted contributions (¶13-200). Foreign tax paid by the superannuation provider on such amounts before the start of the income year does not qualify for the foreign income tax offset in that year.

Credit absorption or unitary taxes. Credit absorption taxes or unitary taxes are *not* excluded from ''foreign income tax'', but are specifically disqualified from counting towards the tax offset. A *credit absorption* tax is a tax that is imposed under a foreign law, to the extent that it is payable only because the taxpayer, or some other taxpayer, is entitled to a tax offset for that foreign tax against the Australian tax on the relevant foreign income. A *unitary* tax is a type of corporate tax imposed under a foreign law. Its distinguishing characteristic is that in determining the income, profits or gains of the company from that country, income, losses, outgoings or assets of the company (or an associated company) from *outside* that country are taken into account. Unitary taxes are relatively rare.

The ATO has ruled, under a similar but not identical definition that applied under the former FTC rules, that unitary taxes included ''worldwide'' unitary taxes, but not so-called ''water's edge'' unitary taxes, which limit a company group to associated companies conducting business in a particular country (TR 93/4). It also stated that where a company is able to elect, for a fee, to be taxed under the water's edge method instead of the worldwide method, the fee is not a ''tax'' and therefore did not qualify for credit.

Offshore banking units. In calculating the offset, only a proportion of the foreign income tax paid on offshore banking income of an offshore banking unit may be taken into account. This proportion is called the ''eligible fraction'' (¶21-090). Where the company tax rate is 30%, the eligible fraction is one-third. This restriction recognises that two-thirds of foreign income tax paid on offshore banking income relates to offshore banking income that is non-assessable, non-exempt income. The restriction was introduced because of the removal of quarantining of offshore banking tax credits.

Irish "pay related social insurance" (PRSI) deducted from salary was not foreign income tax (*Case 8/2014*). It appears that the "Free of Tax Reduction" made to certain New Zealand government superannuation pensions is not a tax, so no foreign tax offset can be claimed (ID 2009/75).

ATO list of eligible foreign taxes

The ATO has issued a list of foreign taxes imposed by Australia's major trading partners for which a foreign income tax offset may be available. The list is not exhaustive and generally does not include local or state taxes. If in doubt as to the status of a particular foreign tax, you should apply for a private binding ruling. The list is as follows:

Argentina: Income tax (Impuesto a las ganancias); *Canada*: Income taxes imposed by the Government of Canada under the Income Tax Act; *China*: Income tax; *France*: Income tax and corporation tax, including any related withholding tax, prepayment (precompte) or advance payment; *Germany*: Income tax (einkommensteuer), Corporation tax (korperschaftsteuer); *India*: Income tax, including any surcharge, Capital gains tax, Non-resident withholding tax, State government imposed taxes on various agriculture incomes; *Italy*: Individual income tax (l'imposta sul reddito delle persone fisiche), Corporate income tax (l'imposta sul reddito delle società, formerly l'imposta sul reddito delle persone giuridiche); *Japan*: Income tax, Corporation tax; *New Zealand*: Income tax, Non-resident withholding tax, Tax on profits from property sales; *Singapore*: Income tax; *South Africa*: Normal tax, Secondary tax on companies (due to be replaced with a withholding tax on dividends), Withholding tax on royalties; *South Korea*: Income tax, Corporations tax, Inhabitant tax; *United Kingdom*: Income tax, Capital gains tax, Corporations tax; *United States*: Federal income taxes imposed by the Internal Revenue Code (ATO *Guide to foreign income tax offset rules 2019*).

[FITR ¶588-120, ¶588-130]

¶21-710 Amount of foreign income tax offset

In general terms, the offset is based on the total foreign income tax paid (s 770-70), but is limited (or "capped") to the amount of Australian income tax that would have been payable on the relevant income (s 770-75).

To determine the amount of the tax offset in any particular year, you must first calculate the total foreign income tax paid on amounts included in the taxpayer's assessable income for the year.

If this amount is not more than $1,000, the taxpayer can simply claim the amount of the foreign income tax as the tax offset. In this situation, the amount of Australian tax on the relevant income is irrelevant, and therefore there is no need to work out the offset cap.

If, on the other hand, the amount *exceeds* $1,000, the taxpayer has 2 options:

- the first option is to claim only $1,000 as the offset. This would mean that the excess foreign income tax would effectively be wasted, but it would eliminate the need to calculate the offset cap. In marginal cases, this may possibly reduce compliance costs
- the second option applies where the taxpayer wishes to claim an offset greater than $1,000. In this case, the taxpayer must calculate the offset cap. This will enable them to claim an offset up to the amount of that cap. (If it turns out that the cap is less than $1,000, the taxpayer can simply claim the amount of foreign income tax paid, up to $1,000, as the offset.)

If a resident individual pays foreign income tax on the whole of a foreign capital gain, but is only assessable in Australia on half of the gain because of the 50% discount (¶11-036), only half of the foreign tax counts toward the tax offset (ID 2010/175).

Calculation of offset cap

The offset cap is generally calculated as the amount of Australian income tax that would be attributable to the income that has attracted the foreign income tax (the ''double-taxed amount'') (s 770-75).

The steps in calculating the cap are as follows:

Step 1: Calculate the amount of (Australian) income tax payable by the taxpayer for the income year. Of course, if this amount is nil (for example because there is a net loss), the offset limit calculated under this method must necessarily also be nil, and no further calculation is necessary.

The Medicare levy and levy surcharge, where relevant, can be included in the calculation of the offset limit. The offset that remains after being applied against a taxpayer's basic income tax liability can be applied first to reduce any liability for Medicare levy, and then against any Medicare levy surcharge liability. Medicare levy is also normally included in ''Australian tax'' under Australia's double tax treaties (ID 2011/75).

Step 2: Calculate the amount of tax that *would have been* payable if the following assumptions applied:

(a) the assessable income excluded:

  (i) the assessable amounts in respect of which eligible foreign income tax was paid, and

  (ii) any *other* ordinary or statutory income from a non-Australian source, irrespective of whether foreign tax has been paid on that income, and

(b) the taxpayer was not entitled to any deductions for:

  (i) debt deductions (¶22-700) attributable to the taxpayer's overseas permanent establishment, or

  (ii) any deductions that reasonably relate to the amounts of income excluded under (a) above.

Step 3: Calculate the offset limit by subtracting the amount calculated under Step 2 from the amount calculated under Step 1.

This method is designed to ensure that the tax attributable to the foreign income is calculated as if that income were the top slice of income, and therefore taxed at the taxpayer's highest marginal rate. In contrast, the method used under the former foreign tax credit rules required the cap to be calculated on the basis of an *average* tax rate.

For the ATO's guidelines on the application of the cap to an Australian resident company deriving gains and losses from foreign currency hedging transactions, see TR 2014/7.

Specific components of calculation

In calculating the offset limit, any other tax offsets are ignored.

In working out the income excluded under Step 2(a)(i), it is necessary to identify the extent to which the assessable income reflects the foreign taxed amount.

▶ Example

An Australian company derives a foreign capital gain of $5 million on which it pays foreign income tax. It also derives an Australian capital gain of $10 million (on which no foreign income tax is paid). Its net capital gain included in the company's assessable income is $15 million. Only the $5 million foreign capital gain is excluded from the offset cap calculations under Step 2(a)(i).

The reference to ''other'' foreign-source income in Step 2(a)(ii) means that the limit on the amount of the offset is based on the amount of Australian tax attributable to all non-foreign-source income, whether subject to foreign tax or not. This rule, which is inconsistent with a strict double-tax-relief approach, has the effect of increasing the offset limit. A capital gain in respect of which the taxpayer has not paid any foreign income tax is not included under Step 2(a)(i), with the result that it does not contribute to a higher offset limit (TD 2020/7).

Step 2(b)(ii) applies to deductions for expenses that "reasonably relate" to the excluded income amounts. This will be a question of fact depending on the circumstances of the taxpayer. The relationship may be direct or indirect, but where the expenses only relate *partly* to excluded amounts and partly to other amounts, they need to be apportioned on a reasonable basis. The types of expense that would fall under this head would include head office or general administration expenses incurred in carrying on a business in Australia and overseas, and interest expenses on funds borrowed to buy income-producing assets used in part to derive foreign income. Some guidance as to the ATO approach on "reasonable" apportionments may be obtained from former IT 2446, which concerned the similar test in the former FTC rules. That ruling says that:

- what constitutes a reasonable and appropriate basis of apportionment will depend on such factors as the nature and size of the businesses or other activities of the taxpayer in Australia and abroad, the types of income concerned and the methods used by the taxpayer to generally account for foreign income and expenses
- the same method of allocation of expenses may not be appropriate for all classes or categories of expenses or income
- a broad, practical approach is required. Provided that the method used is objective and results in a reasonable apportionment, it will generally be accepted.

Note however that, in contrast to the former test, what constitutes a reasonable apportionment is a matter of objective fact, and is not a matter of the Commissioner's opinion.

In a different context, the ATO has accepted an AAT conclusion that deductions for tax agents' fees and superannuation contributions are attributable exclusively to assessable income, and should not be apportioned between assessable income and exempt foreign income (TD 2000/12; *Case 67/96*).

Increase in offset limit

As noted at ¶21-680, amounts of foreign income tax paid by a resident in respect of amounts paid out of income previously attributed from a controlled foreign company may qualify for the offset. These amounts also operate to increase the offset limit calculated in accordance with the normal rules (s 770-80). Although these amounts do not include underlying taxes, their separate treatment means that there is effectively no limit on the foreign tax that qualifies, nor is there any requirement that they relate to the Australian tax paid on the relevant attributed income. However, as with other types of foreign tax, they cannot be taken into account in determining the offset limit in cases where the taxpayer is in a loss situation and the limit is consequently nil.

Example of FITO rules

The following example, adapted from the explanatory memorandum, illustrates the general operation of the offset limit rules.

An Australian resident company has assessable income of $3m, made up as follows:

Foreign portfolio dividend (foreign tax paid $100,000)	$1m	
Foreign interest (no foreign tax paid)	$1m	
Australian-sourced income	$1m	.... $3m

The company has deductions of $1m, made up as follows:

Interest expense (not attributable to overseas permanent establishment)	$500,000	

Other expenses related to Australian-sourced income	$500,000	.... $1m

The steps in calculating the company's offset limit, and offset entitlement, are as follows:

Assume the company is not a base rate entity (¶3-055) and the applicable tax rate is 30%.

Step 1: Australian tax

The company's taxable income is ($3m – $1m)	$2m	

Australian tax is therefore (30% × $2m) = $600,000

Step 2: Australian tax after foreign exclusions

Assume that the assessable income did not include:

the portfolio dividend (Step 2(a)(i))	$1m	
the interest income (Step 2(a)(ii))	$1m	.... $2m

Note: the $500,000 interest expense is not excluded from the company's deductions under Step 2(b)(i) because it is not attributable to an overseas permanent establishment.

On this basis, the taxable income would be nil (ie assessable income of $2 million less excluded income of $2 million). The Australian tax would therefore be nil.

Step 3: Subtract Step 2 amount from Step 1 amount

The offset limit is calculated as $600,000 – nil = $600,000.

As the foreign tax paid ($100,000) is less than the offset limit ($600,000), the offset is $100,000.

[FITR ¶588-210]

¶21-760 Treatment of excess foreign tax

To the extent that the foreign tax paid exceeds the amount claimable as an offset, the tax benefit of the payment is lost. It cannot be carried forward to be taken into account in determining the offset in subsequent income years, nor can it be transferred (s 63-10).

▶ Example

Assume that foreign tax of $20,000 is paid by a taxpayer on foreign income included in the taxpayer's assessable income, but the foreign income tax offset limit is $15,000. The taxpayer's offset is therefore $15,000. The $5,000 excess foreign tax cannot be carried forward in calculating the offset in any subsequent income year.

There is therefore an incentive for taxpayers to structure their affairs so as to ensure that as much as possible of their offset is utilised.

▶ Planning point

Where it appears that part of an offset may be ''wasted'', the taxpayer could possibly consider measures such as accelerating the derivation of some Australian income into the year in question, and therefore increasing the Australian tax, so as to enable the full benefit of the offset to be obtained.

[FITR ¶588-220, ¶588-230, ¶588-240]

¶21-765 Foreign tax paid on taxpayer's behalf

A taxpayer is deemed to have paid foreign income tax in respect of an amount of income where the tax has effectively been paid by someone else on their behalf under an arrangement, or under a foreign tax law (s 770-130). This deeming provision is intended to apply in cases such as where the tax has been paid by:

- deduction or withholding
- a trust in which the taxpayer is a beneficiary
- a partnership in which the taxpayer is a partner (ID 2010/94), or
- the taxpayer's spouse, eg where the foreign country taxes husband and wife as one unit.

Where foreign tax is withheld from an amount paid or credited to a taxpayer, the ATO considers that the assessable amount includes the amount of withheld tax.

▶ Example

A resident taxpayer receives dividends of $100 from a foreign company, from which $15 tax has been withheld, with the result that the taxpayer receives only a net $85. The consequences are as follows:

(1) the shareholder will be treated as having paid the $15 withholding tax

(2) even though the net dividend received by the shareholder was $85, the amount included in its assessable income will be $100, ie $85 ''grossed-up'' by the $15 of foreign tax paid

(3) the taxpayer is entitled to offset the $15 foreign tax against Australian tax liability on that $100.

The requirement that the foreign income tax paid must be ''in respect of'' the amount included in the taxpayer's income (the taxed amount) is intended to place some limit on the circumstances in which an entity can claim for tax paid by others. The ATO considers that this has the effect that there must be a material connection between the tax paid and the income in question. This requirement will evidently be met in cases where foreign entities elect for flow-through treatment of taxation.

However, a taxpayer who receives dividends from a foreign company evidently cannot claim for foreign company tax paid on the profits from which the dividend was distributed. Similarly, a taxpayer who receives a foreign pension from a foreign superannuation fund cannot claim for foreign income tax paid by the foreign fund on its income. This applies even though that tax effectively reduced the taxpayer's pension (ID 2008/135; *Jones*).

Where foreign tax on income is paid by a partnership, it should be apportioned among the partners according to their shares of partnership net income. A similar rule applies to other flow-through entities such as trusts (see further below).

A taxpayer who is assessable on a share of income in a foreign hybrid (¶5-050) can claim an offset for foreign tax on that income, whether the tax is paid by the taxpayer or someone else (TR 2009/6).

Special trust situations

In addition to situations where the tax is actually paid by the trust, a trust beneficiary may also be entitled to claim for foreign tax where the beneficiary receives a trust distribution that is attributable to another amount of income received by the trust on which foreign income tax has already been paid (s 770-130(3)). This special attribution rule could apply, for example, where the trust has received income on which foreign tax has already been withheld, or where the trust is a beneficiary in another trust that paid the tax. Under this rule, a beneficiary was able to claim an offset for foreign tax imposed on a dividend paid to the trust estate, where the beneficiary was assessable under the TOFA rules (¶23-020) in respect of their interest in the estate (ID 2010/216).

The amount of foreign tax that the taxpayer may claim is the amount by which the income included in the taxpayer's assessable income has been reduced because of the foreign income tax.

[FITR ¶588-255]

¶21-770 Tax paid by CFCs

A foreign income tax offset may apply to an entity that is an attributable taxpayer which is assessed under the controlled foreign company (CFC) rules. The circumstances in which this will apply are set out in s 770-135.

Where an Australian shareholder is assessed on amounts that are attributable to the profits of a CFC (¶21-190), an offset may be available where:

(1) the CFC has paid an amount of foreign tax, or Australian income tax or withholding tax, in relation to an amount included in its notional assessable income of the relevant statutory accounting period. This includes tax paid on reinsurance premiums, and

(2) the entity has an ''attribution percentage'' of 10% or more. This condition must be satisfied at the end of the statutory accounting period.

Where these conditions are satisfied, the entity is taken to have paid an amount of foreign tax equal to all the tax paid by the CFC for the statutory accounting period, multiplied by the entity's attribution percentage in relation to the CFC at the end of that period. The intention is that this represents the portion of income tax borne by the CFC that is relevant to the taxpayer.

Broadly corresponding rules apply where a company is assessed under ITAA36 s 457 (¶21-190), ie where a CFC changes residence from an unlisted to a listed country or to Australia. In this case, the requirement for a 10% attribution percentage must be met at the residence change time. The amount of foreign tax that is deemed to have been paid by the entity is the amount of tax paid by the CFC that is attributable to the amount assessable to the entity.

Grossing up of attributed amount

Although attributable income is net of foreign tax paid, a taxpayer claiming a foreign income tax offset under these rules will need to gross-up its assessable income by the amount of tax paid.

Indirect interests through foreign hybrids

A taxpayer who invests indirectly in a foreign company CFC through a foreign hybrid (¶5-050), cannot claim an offset for foreign tax paid by the CFC on its notional income. An offset may also be available where the taxpayer invests indirectly in a CFC through a foreign hybrid and foreign tax is paid on distributions that the CFC makes to the foreign hybrid (TR 2009/6).

Limitation to Australian entities

The offset is only available if the attributable taxpayer is an Australian entity, including a partnership with at least one partner that is an Australian entity.

[FITR ¶588-260, ¶588-280]

¶21-775 Extended period for amendment of FITO assessment

To qualify for a foreign income tax offset for an income year, the taxpayer must have paid foreign income tax on an amount that is included in the taxpayer's assessable income for the year of claim. However, as explained at ¶21-680, it is not necessary that the foreign income tax is paid in that year. To cover this eventuality, the normal amendment period is extended as follows (s 770-190):

(1) where the taxpayer pays foreign income tax after lodging the relevant return:

- the amendment period is 4 years, and
- this period starts at the time of payment.

▶ Example

The taxpayer lodges its return for Year 1 and receives its notice of assessment. It subsequently pays foreign income tax in relation to income included in the Year 1 return, giving rise to an entitlement to a foreign income tax offset in relation to Year 1. The period for amendment of the Year 1 return to give effect to the offset is 4 years from the time the foreign tax is paid, not the earlier time when notice of the Year 1 assessment was given.

(2) a corresponding rule applies if the foreign income tax is increased after the relevant return was lodged

(3) if the foreign tax is *decreased* after the relevant return was lodged, the 4-year amendment period starts from the time the amount of the tax paid was reduced, eg when the taxpayer receives a refund or credit.

These modified rules do not apply if there is merely an increase in the *offset limit*, as distinct from the amount of foreign tax paid. In such a case, the normal rules for determining amendment periods will apply.

[FITR ¶588-310]

Foreign Losses

¶21-800 Foreign losses

Effective for income years commencing on or after 1 July 2008, the rule that a foreign loss can only be offset against foreign income, and against income of its own class, has been repealed. However, special transitional rules applied to earlier-year foreign losses that were still unutilised at the time of the repeal (ITTPA Div 770).

Under these transitional rules, those foreign losses had to be ''de-quarantined'' by converting them to a single tax loss amount for each of the preceding 10 income years. These amounts can be carried forward to income years starting 1 July 2008 and beyond, subject to various restrictions including a phasing-in period for the first 4 years. Losses incurred beyond the 10-year period cannot be taken into account and are therefore effectively extinguished.

For further details of the transitional rules, see the 55th and previous editions of the *Australian Master Tax Guide*.

[FITR ¶85-007 – ¶85-009]

Chapter 22 Non-resident Withholding • DTAs • Transfer Pricing • Thin Capitalisation

Overview of Non-resident Tax Rules

¶22-000 Tax liability of non-residents

The primary rules governing the taxation of non-residents provide that non-residents are: (a) liable to Australian tax on all items of ordinary or statutory income which have their source in Australia; and (b) exempt from Australian tax on foreign source ordinary or statutory income (ITAA97 ss 6-5(3); 6-10(5)). However, there are some qualifications and exceptions to this rule.

With some notable exceptions, assessable income derived by non-residents is generally taxed on the same basis as income derived by residents. Unless specifically excluded or made applicable to residents only, the same exemptions (¶10-600) and exclusions (¶10-890) from assessable income apply, and the same business deductions (¶16-152) and special incentives are available against gross income. Non-residents may also be liable for FBT. From 8 May 2012 they are not entitled to the CGT discount (¶11-033). From 7.30 pm (AEST) on 9 May 2017, foreign resident individuals do not have access to the CGT main residence exemption (¶11-730).

While non-resident individuals are generally exempt from the Medicare levy (¶2-340), they cannot claim personal tax offsets (¶15-000). Moreover, non-resident individuals and non-resident trust estates are subject to higher tax and do not generally have the benefit of a zero-rated first step in the rates scale (¶2-120, ¶6-250).

Special tax regimes or concessions apply to particular industries or occupations (¶22-080 onwards). Taxpayers qualifying as "temporary residents" are also treated in a concessional way (¶22-125).

Non-resident companies are taxed at the same rates of tax as resident companies but are treated differently on important aspects such as dividend imputation and consolidation (¶3-010).

Dividends (¶22-010), interest (¶22-020) and royalties (¶22-030) paid to non-residents are generally subject to withholding tax at a flat rate (but there are many exemptions available under each category). This means that an amount representing the tax payable is withheld from the payment and is remitted by the payer direct to the ATO. Dividend, interest and royalty withholding taxes represent the final tax liability for those payments. Amounts which have been subject to withholding tax are excluded from the assessable income of non-residents. The collection of withholding taxes is dealt with at ¶22-040.

Additional withholding rules also apply on other income (¶22-050 onwards), including withholding on certain payments made in the course of carrying on an enterprise (¶26-265). For the special withholding rules that apply to distributions made by managed funds to foreign residents, see ¶22-045. A non-final withholding regime applies to the capital gains of non-residents (¶22-072).

A special tax regime applies to Australian branches of foreign banks (ITAA36 Pt IIIB). Special concessions apply to the transfer of assets and liabilities from Australian subsidiaries of foreign banks to their Australian branches (*Financial Corporations (Transfer of Assets and Liabilities) Act 1993*).

¶22-002 Foreign investment approval: tax conditions

The Foreign Investment Review Board (FIRB) is a non-statutory body that advises the government on foreign investment policy and its administration. The Board examines proposals by foreign interests to undertake direct investment in Australia and makes recommendations to the government on whether the proposals are suitable for approval.

Foreign investment proposals are reviewed on a case-by-case basis to ensure that they are not contrary to the national interest. In general, national interest considerations can include: national security, competition, other Australian government policies (including tax), impact on the economy and the community and the investor's character.

The applicant and its associates must:

- comply with Australian tax laws in relation to assets acquired
- provide documents or information to the ATO within the timeframe specified
- advise the ATO of any material transactions where the transfer pricing or anti-avoidance rules might apply and engage with the ATO in good faith to resolve tax issues
- pay any outstanding tax debt due at the time of the proposed investment
- where a significant tax risk is identified, periodically provide a forecast of tax payable and explain significant variations from the forecast, and
- report annually to the FIRB on compliance with the conditions.

Due to the significant impact of COVID-19 on the Australian economy, the monetary value thresholds for notifiable foreign investment proposals were reset to nil. The government announced that it will remove the temporary $0 foreign investment monetary screening thresholds from 1 January 2021.

[FTR ¶979-800]

¶22-005 Foreign-owned residential property vacancy fee

Foreign owners of residential real estate are liable to pay an annual vacancy fee where a residential property is not occupied or genuinely available on the rental market for at least 6 months in a 12-month period. The fee applies to foreign persons who submit a notice or an application to acquire a residential dwelling or residential land from 7:30 pm (AEST) on 9 May 2017.

The vacancy fee does not apply if the owner or a relative of theirs occupies their dwelling for 183 days or more in a 12-month period. Further, the fee does not apply if the dwelling is:

- subject to one or more leases or licences with a minimum duration of 30 days which total 183 days in a 12-month period, or
- made genuinely available on the rental market, with minimum durations of 30 days, for a total of 183 days in a 12-month period.

An owner will be liable to pay a vacancy fee if the dwelling is not residentially occupied, or genuinely available to be occupied, for at least 183 days in a 12-month period (referred to as a vacancy year). A vacancy year commences on the day of the owner's initial right to occupy the dwelling.

The foreign person is required to lodge a vacancy fee return with the ATO within 30 days after the end of each year during which the person may be liable for the fee for a dwelling. A civil penalty may apply where a foreign person fails to submit the vacancy fee return or keep the required records. The ATO will issue a notice to the foreign person if a vacancy fee is payable. The Treasurer has power to recover unpaid amounts and to waive or remit the vacancy fee.

Developers who sell dwellings under a new dwelling exemption certificate or a near-new dwelling exemption certificate to a foreign person are required to make reconciliation payments for sales to the ATO on a 6-monthly basis. Foreign persons who acquire an interest in residential land under a new dwelling exemption certificate or a near-new dwelling exemption certificate which was approved prior to 7.30 pm (AEST) on 9 May 2017 and who enter into the new contract after 7.30 pm (AEST) on 9 May 2017 are not liable for the vacancy fee.

The vacancy fee has been enacted as Pt 6A of the *Foreign Acquisitions and Takeovers Act 1975*. The amount of the fee is set by the *Foreign Acquisitions and Takeovers Fees Imposition Act 2015*. For an article discussing the vacancy fee, see CCH *Tax Week*¶38.

[FTR ¶979-825]

Non-resident Withholding

¶22-010 Dividend withholding tax

A final withholding tax is imposed on dividends paid by a resident company to non-residents regardless of whether the dividends are income according to ordinary concepts (ITAA36 s 128B(1)), unless an exception applies.

Dividend withholding tax is generally imposed at a flat rate of 30% (¶26-130) but, for dividends paid to residents of countries with which Australia has a double taxation agreement (DTA), the rate is generally 15%.

Withholding tax on dividends applies irrespective of:

- whether the dividends are received directly by a shareholder or indirectly through a nominee or trustee
- the source of the profits out of which the dividends are paid, and
- the location of the register on which the shares giving rise to the dividends are held.

Withholding tax is imposed on the gross amount of the dividends, ie no deductions may be made from the dividends, and the flat rate withholding tax applies whether or not the non-resident has other income subject to Australian tax under the ordinary assessment process.

The scope of the general anti-avoidance provisions of ITAA36 Pt IVA has been extended to include schemes which have the sole or dominant purpose of avoiding the payment of dividend withholding tax (¶30-160).

Where one or more tax-exempt bodies are interposed between an Australian resident payer and a non-resident recipient, withholding tax is payable as if the dividends had been paid directly to the non-resident recipient. Accordingly, withholding tax is payable unless the non-resident recipient is itself exempt.

Dividends paid in respect of non-equity shares (¶23-115) are treated as interest (¶22-020).

Dividends not subject to withholding tax

The following dividends are not subject to withholding tax under s 128B(1), (3):

- franked dividends, except where the Commissioner determines that the paying company has streamed the dividends or a franking credit scheme has occurred (¶4-900)
- unfranked dividends paid to non-residents by a resident company that are declared to be ''conduit foreign income'' (¶21-100)
- dividends paid to certain registered foreign charities, scientific institutions, public educational institutions and non-profit cultural, sporting and friendly societies whose income is exempt from Australian tax and from tax in the non-resident's home country (¶10-605). This exemption is generally restricted to those organisations which either: (a) have a presence in Australia and pursue their objectives principally in Australia; (b) are listed as institutions to which deductible gifts can be made; (c) are prescribed as exempt institutions; or (d) are prescribed charitable institutions which pursue their objectives principally outside Australia
- dividends paid to certain offshore testamentary charitable trusts established before 1 July 1997. Assets given to such testamentary charitable trusts (other than in return for valuable consideration) are deemed to be subject to a new trust which does not qualify for the exemption
- dividends paid to certain foreign non-profit aviation, tourism, agricultural and manufacturing associations
- dividends paid by PDFs
- certain dividends derived by a trust estate where the trustee is liable to be assessed
- dividends derived from assets included in the insurance funds of a non-resident life insurance company that carries on branch operations in Australia
- dividends in respect of which a taxpayer is assessed under special provisions dealing with tax avoidance schemes involving tax-exempt entities (¶10-620)
- dividends derived by a non-resident foreign superannuation fund from a resident company, where they are exempt in the country where the fund resides (ID 2009/77)
- dividends on which family trust distribution tax has been paid (¶6-268)
- certain dividends paid to an overseas charitable institution by an offshore banking unit (OBU) or the trustee of a trust managed or controlled by an OBU
- dividends paid by former exempting companies (exempt entities and companies owned by non-residents: ¶4-970) to the extent that they are franked as ''exempted dividends''
- certain non-frankable non-share dividends (¶23-125) paid by a resident authorised deposit-taking institution.
- dividends paid to the ICC Business Corporation for the International Cricket Council World Twenty20 to be held in Australia in 2022 (¶10-605)

Private company loans made to non-residents which are treated as deemed dividends under ITAA36 Pt III Div 7A (¶4-200) are not subject to withholding tax.

Dividends paid by non-resident companies to non-resident shareholders out of Australian sourced profits which are subject to the normal assessment process are not subject to withholding tax.

The declaration of a dividend was held to give rise to a liability for withholding tax, notwithstanding that the non-resident shareholder's right to receive the dividend was subsequently assigned (*ABB Australia*).

Dividends from non-resident companies received by a non-resident indirectly through a nominee or trustee are assessable to Australian tax only if the source of those dividends is in Australia.

Dividends attributable to foreign-owned branches

Where dividends paid by an Australian company to a non-resident company or individual are attributable to an Australian branch of the non-resident, they will be taxed on a net assessment basis instead of being subject to withholding tax. This will mean that the dividends will be included in the non-resident's assessable income, and that relevant expenses will be allowed as deductions against the non-resident's assessable income. In addition, where the dividend is franked, the non-resident recipient may be entitled to a franking tax offset.

[FTR ¶68-805, ¶68-825]

¶22-020 Interest withholding tax

Unless an exemption applies, withholding tax is payable on interest that is:

(1) derived by a non-resident, and

(2) paid by:

  (a) a resident, except where the interest is wholly incurred by the resident as an expense of carrying on a business overseas at or through a permanent establishment (such as a branch: ¶22-150), or

  (b) a non-resident and the interest is an expense wholly or partly incurred by the non-resident in carrying on a business in Australia at or through a permanent establishment in Australia (ITAA36 s 128B(2)).

Withholding is required not only where interest is actually "paid" to a non-resident, but also where interest is payable and has been dealt with on behalf of, or at the direction of, the non-resident by, for example, being reinvested (TD 93/146). If the interest is paid in foreign currency, it is converted to Australian currency for withholding purposes at the time of payment.

In addition, to avoid a possible loophole, interest derived by a *resident* in the course of carrying on a business through an overseas permanent establishment is subject to withholding tax if it is paid by:

- another resident and it is not wholly incurred by the payer in carrying on a business in a foreign country through a permanent establishment in that country, or
- a non-resident and it is wholly or partly incurred in carrying on business in Australia through a permanent establishment (s 128B(2A)).

Interest is not treated as incurred by a resident in carrying on business through an overseas permanent establishment unless it is paid in gaining income derived by that establishment. A similar rule applies to non-residents carrying on business in Australia through a permanent establishment.

Interest withholding tax is imposed at a flat rate of 10% on the *gross* amount of interest paid (ie without deducting expenses incurred in deriving that interest, etc). With some exceptions, this rate is unaffected by Australia's DTAs (¶26-130). A special rate of 45% may apply to interest not subject to the ordinary withholding tax provisions which is paid in respect of certain bearer debentures where the company has failed to disclose the names and addresses of the debenture holders to the Commissioner (ITAA36 s 126). For this purpose, the ''holder'' of the debenture is the person in possession of it (TD 2001/19). A concessional rate equal to half the normal rate may apply to interest notionally paid to a foreign bank by its Australian branch (ITAA36 s 160ZZZJ).

For guidelines on the application of the interest withholding tax provisions to interest paid to non-residents by resident authorised deposit-taking institutions, see TR 2006/9.

Where a United States limited liability company with Australian resident members was treated as if it were a partnership under the ''foreign hybrid'' rules (¶5-050), interest received by it from an Australian resident company was not subject to withholding tax and was assessable to those Australian resident members (ID 2012/70).

What is interest?

''Interest'' is generally regarded as an amount paid as compensation to a lender for not having the use of its capital (¶16-740). For withholding tax purposes, it includes amounts which:

- are in ''the nature of'' interest
- can reasonably be regarded as having been converted into a form that is ''in substitution for'' interest (eg a lump sum paid in lieu of interest). This may not cover a payment on a convertible security which does not constitute a loan (ID 2009/154)
- can reasonably be regarded as having been received for interest in connection with a ''washing arrangement''. This is an arrangement under which title to a security is transferred to a resident shortly before an interest payment is made and where the sole or dominant purpose of the arrangement is to reduce the amount of withholding tax payable by a person
- are dividends paid in respect of non-equity shares (¶23-115), or
- are paid on upper tier 2 capital instruments that are prescribed as debt interests and are issued on or after 21 March 2005 (ITAA36 s 128A(1AB)).

In *Century Yuasa Batteries*, amounts paid under a ''grossing-up'' tax indemnification clause in a loan agreement were held not to be amounts in the nature of interest (¶22-040). They would also not be interest under any of the statutory extensions noted above.

Forward exchange transactions, forward rate agreements, swaps and reciprocal purchase agreements do not generally fall within the interest withholding tax provisions as they do not involve the provision of finance. In most circumstances, income derived by non-residents on building society share accounts is treated as interest, not dividend, income and is subject to interest withholding tax (IT 2468).

The operation of the general anti-avoidance provisions of ITAA36 Pt IVA includes schemes which have the sole or dominant purpose of avoiding the payment of interest withholding tax (¶30-160). The ATO is reviewing arrangements which use offshore related entities to facilitate the avoidance of interest withholding tax (TA 2020/3).

Where one or more tax-exempt bodies are interposed between an Australian resident payer and a non-resident recipient of interest, withholding tax is payable as if the interest had been paid directly to the non-resident recipient. Accordingly, withholding tax is payable unless the non-resident recipient is itself exempt.

Discounted and deferred interest securities

Withholding tax may apply to certain discounted and deferred interest securities. Where a person transfers certain qualifying securities (¶23-320) and the transfer price exceeds the issue price, the excess is deemed to be interest. The same applies where the security has been partially redeemed and the transfer price exceeds the reduced issue price. In each case, the excess may therefore be subject to interest withholding tax (ITAA36 s 128AA). However, this does not apply in the case of debentures that satisfy the "public offer" test (¶22-022).

Hire purchase contracts

The withholding tax provisions also extend to hire purchase and similar arrangements involving Australian entities purchasing plant and equipment from non-residents. The withholding tax provisions apply to the "interest" component of such arrangements (ie the excess of the total payments made under the arrangements over the cost price of the goods). Further, where payments made under a cross-border equipment lease contain an implicit interest component, the interest is subject to interest withholding tax (ITAA36 s 128AC). The Commissioner will apply Pt IVA where lease transactions are structured to avoid withholding tax in such situations (TR 98/21).

Bills of exchange and promissory notes

Withholding tax is also payable on the discount element of a bill of exchange where a resident indemnifies or reimburses a non-resident acceptor for the face value of the bill at maturity. Any amount that constitutes the discount or interest factor under the bill is within the withholding tax provisions. A similar provision applies to promissory notes (ITAA36 s 128AD).

Interest payments not subject to withholding tax

The following interest payments are not subject to withholding tax:

- interest derived by a non-resident carrying on business in Australia at or through a permanent establishment. The rule that *deems* certain non-resident beneficiaries to be carrying on business in Australia through a branch (¶22-150) does not apply in this context (*GE Capital Finance*)
- interest on certain publicly offered debentures (¶22-022)
- interest paid to certain foreign charitable institutions, public hospitals and non-profit cultural, sporting and friendly societies whose income is exempt from Australian tax and from tax in the non-resident's home country (s 128B(3)). This exemption is generally subject to the same restrictions which apply when dividends are paid to such entities (¶22-010)
- interest paid to certain offshore testamentary charitable trusts established before 1 July 1997
- interest paid to certain foreign non-profit aviation, tourism, agricultural and manufacturing associations
- gold fees paid by an OBU in respect of an offshore gold borrowing (ITAA36 s 128GB). Gold fees are an additional amount of gold paid by a borrower under a gold loan contract. The Commissioner treats such fees as payments in the nature of interest (TR 92/5)
- certain interest derived by a trust estate where the trustee is liable to be assessed
- interest paid in relation to infrastructure borrowings
- interest derived by a non-resident foreign superannuation fund (¶13-250), where it is exempt in the country where the fund resides (ID 2009/78; ID 2009/79)
- interest on which family trust distribution tax has been paid (¶6-268)
- interest paid to non-residents from certain "nostro" accounts held by banks and other financial institutions that conduct banking business

- certain interest paid to an overseas charitable institution by an OBU or the trustee of a trust managed or controlled by an OBU
- a non-share dividend (¶23-125) to the extent to which an amount is a return on an equity interest
- interest paid by ‘‘temporary residents’’ (¶22-125) (ITAA97 s 768-980).
- interest paid to the ICC Business Corporation for the International Cricket Council World Twenty20 to be held in Australia in 2022 (¶10-605).

Withholding tax does not apply to interest paid to US and UK resident financial institutions that is not taxable by Australia under the relevant DTAs, eg because it is not effectively connected with an Australian branch of the institution (¶22-160). The scope of this exemption is discussed in TR 2005/5 and ID 2005/260: see also *Deutsche Asia Pacific Finance Inc*.

Exemption for government bonds

Interest paid on state and territory government bonds issued in Australia is eligible for exemption from interest withholding tax. Interest paid on debentures and debt interests issued in Australia by the Commonwealth Government or its authorities is also eligible for exemption. In each case, the public offer test (¶22-022) must be satisfied where applicable.

[FTR ¶68-510]

¶22-022 Interest on certain publicly offered debentures

Interest paid under a debenture is exempt from interest withholding tax if the issue of the debenture satisfies a ‘‘public offer’’ test (ITAA36 s 128F). If the issuing company is a resident, it must also be a resident at the time of payment. If the issuing company is a non-resident, the issue must be after 30 June 2001, the company must be a non-resident at the time of payment, and the issue and payment must be made through a permanent establishment of the company in Australia.

An exemption also applies where the sale of a debenture is deemed to give rise to deemed interest under ITAA36 s 128AA on or after 29 August 2001 (¶22-020), and the public offer test is satisfied. This is intended to ensure that there will be an exemption where the debenture is on-sold by a non-resident to an Australian resident before the debenture’s maturity date.

Public offer test

A company will satisfy the public offer test if the debentures were offered for issue in any of the following circumstances:

- to at least 10 persons operating in a capital market
- to at least 100 investors whom it was reasonable for the company to have regarded as either having previously acquired debentures or likely to be interested in acquiring debentures
- as a result of the debentures being accepted for listing by a stock exchange where the company had previously entered into an agreement with a dealer, manager or underwriter requiring the company to seek such a listing
- as a result of negotiations initiated publicly in electronic form (eg through Reuters or Bloomberg), or in another form, used by financial markets for dealing in debentures, or
- to a dealer, manager or underwriter for the purpose of placement of the debentures.

Debentures which are ‘‘global bonds’’ also satisfy the public offer test.

Associates

A debenture issue fails the public offer test if at the time of the issue the company knows, or has reasonable grounds to suspect, that the debentures would be acquired by an associate. There is an exception if that associate is a dealer, manager or underwriter involved in the placement of the debentures.

Interest paid on a debenture is not exempt in any event if the paying company knows, or has reasonable grounds to suspect, that interest is being paid to an associate of the company.

These general rules are subject to the following qualifications:

- in the case of debentures issued on or after 29 August 2001, there is no failure to satisfy the public offer test if the associate was either: (a) a non-resident that acquires the debenture in the course of carrying on business through a permanent establishment in Australia; or (b) a resident that does not acquire the debenture in the course of carrying on business through a permanent establishment overseas. Nor will be there be a failure to satisfy the test if the debenture is acquired by the associate as a clearing house, custodian, funds manager or responsible entity of a registered scheme, and
- in the case of payments on or after 29 August 2001, the exemption will not be denied if the associate fits any of the above descriptions or is a paying agent.

A wide range of issues relating to the operation of this exemption and the public offer test are examined in TD 1999/8 to TD 1999/26 and TD 2001/3.

Debentures issued through non-resident subsidiaries

A company is treated as having issued debentures itself if the debentures are issued through a wholly-owned non-resident subsidiary in a foreign country specified in the regulations (the United States has been listed). The subsidiary's sole business must be the raising of finance for its parent, and it must be resident in the country concerned.

Public unit trusts

In addition to the withholding tax exemption for interest paid by companies on publicly offered debentures, a corresponding exemption applies to similar debentures issued by eligible Australian unit trusts or eligible foreign unit trusts carrying on business at or through a permanent establishment in Australia (ITAA36 s 128FA). The debentures offered by the eligible unit trust must meet the public offer test that applies for companies, and must be issued on or after 23 June 2004.

For these purposes, eligible unit trusts are public unit trusts or widely-held unit trusts which have all their units held by 2 or more of the following: public unit trusts, complying superannuation funds with 50 or more members, PSTs, complying ADFs, life insurance companies, public companies or other unit trusts which are themselves widely held.

Interest on debt interests

Corresponding exemptions apply to interest paid on debt interests (¶23-105) that are issued on or after 21 March 2005.

To qualify for exemption, non-debenture debt interests issued on or after 7 December 2006 must either be: (1) non-equity shares; (2) syndicated loans; or (3) prescribed to be exempt by regulation. However, as a transitional concession, this requirement does not apply to debt interests that issued under, or result from, a written agreement entered into between 21 March 2005 and 7 December 2006. Subsequent extensions of such agreements will not be effective to extend the concession.

[FTR ¶68-600 – ¶68-800, ¶69-340]

¶22-030 Royalty withholding tax

Royalties derived by a non-resident are subject to withholding tax unless an exemption applies (ITAA36 s 128B(2B), (5A)).

Withholding tax applies where the royalties are paid by:

- a resident, except where they are outgoings wholly incurred by the payer in carrying on a business outside Australia at or through a permanent establishment, such as a branch, or
- a non-resident and are outgoings wholly or partly incurred by the payer in carrying on a business in Australia at or through a permanent establishment in Australia.

The broad definition of ''royalties'' in ITAA36 s 6(1) applies for these purposes (¶10-510). Where the sale element of a cross-border equipment lease is paramount (ie where the incidents of ownership and economic risk pass to the lessee), payments under the lease are not royalties. Conversely, where the main object of the lease is to hire the equipment, even if the hirer has an option to purchase the equipment, the lease payments are royalties and royalty withholding tax is payable (TR 98/21).

Where an agreement covers both distribution rights as well as intellectual property rights, there may be a question as to whether withholding tax can be limited to the component relating to intellectual property rights. In *International Business Machines Corporation*, the court considered that the agreement in question did not permit the components to be separated in this way, as the distribution rights were wholly subordinate to the intellectual property rights. Withholding tax was therefore payable on the whole amount payable under the agreement.

Any amounts paid as consideration for all forms of exploitation of a copyright short of an outright sale of the copyright should generally be treated as royalties. Amounts paid for outright sale are not royalties except where they are calculated by reference to the actual or intended use of the copyright (TR 2008/7). See also TD 2006/10. Payments for the right to broadcast digital TV signals of the Olympic Games were not royalties and were not subject to withholding tax. The signals were not a cinematograph film, a copyright or other like property or right (*Seven Network*).

''Permanent establishment'' is defined widely (¶22-150) and extends, for example, to a place where a person is using substantial equipment by sub-leasing it to another (TR 2007/11).

Withholding is required not only where royalties are actually ''paid'' to a non-resident, but also where royalties are payable and are dealt with on behalf of, or at the direction of, the non-resident by, for example, being reinvested. For the position where there is an indemnity, see ¶22-040.

In addition, to close loopholes, royalties derived by a resident in the course of carrying on a business through an overseas branch are subject to withholding tax if they are paid by:

- another resident and they are *not* wholly incurred by the payer in carrying on a business in a foreign country through a branch in that country, or
- a non-resident and they *are* wholly or partly incurred by the non-resident in carrying on business in Australia through a branch (s 128B(2C)).

A royalty will not be incurred by a resident in carrying on business through an overseas branch unless it is paid in gaining income derived by that branch. A similar provision applies to non-residents paying royalties when carrying on business in Australia through a branch.

The scope of the general anti-avoidance provisions of ITAA36 Pt IVA has been extended to include schemes which have the sole or dominant purpose of avoiding the payment of royalty withholding tax (¶30-160).

Where one or more tax-exempt bodies are interposed between an Australian resident payer and a non-resident recipient of royalties, withholding tax is payable as if the royalties had been paid directly to the non-resident recipient. Accordingly, withholding tax is payable unless the non-resident recipient is itself exempt.

Rate of withholding tax

The normal rate of royalty withholding tax is 30% (¶26-130). However, where royalties flow to a resident of a country with which Australia has a comprehensive DTA (¶22-140), the rate of royalty withholding tax is generally limited to 10% of the gross amount of the royalties, unless the royalties are effectively connected with a branch in Australia. If the country of residence of the recipient also taxes the income, that country gives credit against its tax for the Australian tax.

The withholding tax is based on the GST-inclusive amount of the payment (ID 2010/89).

Royalties exempt from withholding tax

The withholding tax provisions do not apply to royalties derived by a resident of a country with which Australia has a DTA where the royalties are effectively connected with a branch of the non-resident in Australia. Such royalties are treated as ‘‘business profits’’ and are taxed by assessment. Exemptions may also apply under specific DTAs (¶22-150; *McDermott Industries*); see also the guidelines on leasing arrangements in TR 2007/11.

Royalty payments received by a computer technology company resident in India from its Australian clients had an Australian source for income tax purposes by reason of the Australia-India DTA. The payments were therefore taxable in Australia (*Satyam* 2018 ATC ¶20-671).

The following royalties are also exempt from withholding tax under s 128B(3):

- royalties paid to certain foreign charitable institutions, public hospitals and non-profit cultural, sporting and friendly societies whose income is exempt from Australian tax and from tax in the non-resident's home country. This exemption is generally subject to the same restrictions which apply when dividends are paid to such entities (¶22-010)
- royalties paid to certain offshore testamentary charitable trusts established before 1 July 1997
- royalties paid to certain foreign non-profit aviation, tourism, agricultural and manufacturing associations
- certain royalties derived by a trust estate where the trustee is liable to be assessed
- royalties on which family trust distribution tax has been paid (¶6-268)
- certain royalties paid to an overseas charitable institution by an OBU or the trustee of a trust managed or controlled by an OBU
- royalties paid to foreign owners of qualifying vessels leased under a bareboat charter to an Australian resident company.
- royalties paid to the ICC Business Corporation for the International Cricket Council World Twenty20 to be held in Australia in 2022 (¶10-605).

Royalty withholding tax does not apply to a non-share dividend (¶22-010) to the extent to which an amount is a return on an equity interest.

Industrial, commercial or scientific equipment royalties

Withholding tax does not apply to equipment royalties paid to residents of tax treaty countries where the DTA does not treat the amount paid as a royalty, eg the United Kingdom and the United States (see, for example, ID 2008/140). An "equipment royalty" is a payment for the use of, or the right to use, any industrial, commercial or scientific (ICS) equipment.

For the Commissioner's views on payments to non-residents who charter ICS equipment such as ships or aircraft, or lease other ICS equipment to residents, see TR 2003/2.

[FTR ¶68-818, ¶68-825]

¶22-040 Collection of withholding tax on dividends, interest and royalties

The person liable for the tax is the non-resident person who derives the relevant dividends, interest or royalties (ITAA36 s 128B(4) to (6)). The tax is payable by the 21st day after the end of the month in which the income is derived (ITAA36 s 128C). However, an amount on account of the tax is required to be withheld, or deducted at source, by the payer of that income. As explained further below, this amount is credited against the payee's liability.

The rules governing how the tax is withheld and accounted for by the payer form part of the PAYG withholding system (¶26-250, ¶26-550). For the payer's reporting obligations, see ¶26-620.

Withholding tax is, in most cases, imposed as a final tax, ie income subject to withholding tax is excluded from assessable income (ITAA36 s 128D).

Where the correct amount of withholding tax is not withheld and paid, the payer of the dividend, interest or royalty is liable to pay the tax that should have been paid and the GIC on the unpaid amount (¶29-510). In addition, failure to deduct withholding tax is an offence punishable by a maximum fine of 10 penalty units (¶29-700).

Non-resident beneficiaries

A non-resident beneficiary who is presently entitled to a dividend, interest or a royalty included in a distribution of income from an Australian trust estate is deemed to have derived the income (and may therefore be liable for withholding tax) when the present entitlement arose (ITAA36 s 128A(3)). A beneficiary may be deemed to have derived the dividend, interest or royalty even if the trust estate has no net income, or has incurred a loss, for income tax purposes, in the year of income. Unitholders generally become entitled to the distributable income of a unit trust at the end of the quarterly or half-yearly distribution periods (IT 2680).

"Grossing-up" and tax indemnification clauses

In *Century Yuasa Batteries*, the Full Federal Court held that amounts paid under a "grossing-up" clause in a loan facility agreement were not subject to interest withholding tax. Under a grossing-up clause, the borrower undertakes to pay the interest withholding tax for which a foreign lender is liable. The court found that the amounts were not interest or in the nature of interest but were an indemnity against the lender's liability for withholding tax. However, the Commissioner considers that such payments will normally be income of the lender and will be assessable if their source is in Australia (¶10-112). The Commissioner also considers that the court's decision does not apply to certain royalty withholding tax indemnification clauses, such as may occur in equipment leases. In such cases, withholding tax would apply to the indemnity amount itself if it falls within the extended statutory definition of a royalty (TR 2004/17).

Where a borrowing was secured by a mortgage entered into on or before 27 June 1996, a grossing-up clause was void and unenforceable by virtue of ITAA36 former s 261 (*David Securities*).

Credit for withholding tax

A non-resident whose income includes a dividend, interest or a royalty from which withholding tax has been deducted is entitled to a credit against the withholding tax liability. Often the credit equals the withholding tax liability and, accordingly, the tax liability is extinguished.

A resident beneficiary of a non-resident trust estate is entitled to a credit for Australian withholding tax where the beneficiary receives a distribution of income which includes dividend, interest or royalty income from which withholding tax has been deducted. This is subject to the proviso that the tax was borne by the beneficiary and the tax is included in the beneficiary's assessable income in addition to the trust distribution received (ie the amount of the distribution is ''grossed up'' by the amount of withholding tax) (TR 93/10). This does not apply to: (a) distributions of income to resident unitholders of non-resident public unit trusts which are treated as companies; (b) trust income which is subject to the transferor trust measures (¶21-300); or (c) a resident beneficiary's foreign tax offset/credit entitlement (¶21-670).

Deduction rule

To ensure collection of the tax where the interest or royalty is paid to a person outside Australia, a payer of interest or a royalty is precluded from obtaining a deduction for the payment until the withholding tax is paid (TD 93/99).

[FTR ¶68-818]

¶22-045 Withholding on managed investment trust distributions

A concessional withholding tax regime applies to certain distributions made by Australian managed investment trusts (MITs) to foreign resident investors (TAA Sch 1 Subdiv 12-H; ss 12-375 to 12-420). The regime, which applies to certain MITs for income years starting from 1 July 2016, is intended to enhance the ability of managed investment trusts (particularly property trusts) to attract foreign investment. For more information, see ¶26-267.

[FTR ¶976-710]

¶22-050 TFN withholding tax on non-residents

Under the TFN system (¶33-000), an investment body is required to withhold tax from any income that it becomes liable to pay in connection with certain investments in respect of which the investor has not quoted a TFN (¶33-130). However, non-resident investors are exempt from the TFN quotation rules provided the investment body is required to withhold tax from the relevant interest or dividend payments (ITAA36 s 202EE(1)).

[FTR ¶690-140]

¶22-060 Withholding on other income

Every person in Australia holding moneys due to a non-resident who derives Australian source income or capital gains, or who is a shareholder, debenture holder or depositor in a company deriving such income or capital gains, is deemed to be the non-resident's agent (ITAA36 ss 254; 255). This ensures the collection of tax due by non-residents, particularly where they do not carry on business or furnish returns in Australia. Further, a banker may be treated as the agent of a non-resident in respect of moneys in the non-resident's account (ITAA36 s 257). For further details, see ¶24-050.

The Australian agent of an overseas shipper or charterer or the master of the ship is required to withhold and pay tax on the deemed taxable income (¶22-110) of the overseas principal. The same applies to an insured person in Australia, or the non-resident insurer's Australian agent (¶22-110).

Employers of non-resident employees must generally withhold tax from wages or salary paid to those employees in a similar way to that for resident employees. However, if the employee will be present in Australia for no more than 183 days in the tax year and the employee's Australian earnings are exempt under a DTA, an application should be made to the ATO for a certificate exempting the salary or wages from tax deductions.

A special withholding tax applies to superannuation payments made to persons who originally entered Australia temporarily, on particular classes of visa, and who subsequently left Australia permanently (¶14-390, ¶26-260).

PAYG withholding

PAYG withholding applies to certain payments made to, or received for, foreign residents where the payment is made in the course of carrying on an enterprise. This affects payments relating to casino junket tours, entertainment and sports activities, and building and construction contracts (¶26-265).

Non-resident individuals participating in the Seasonal Labour Mobility Program are subject to a 15% withholding tax, which represents their final liability to Australian tax on that income (¶26-275).

[FTR ¶782-060, ¶782-280]

¶22-070 Natural resource payments

A natural resource payment is a payment calculated by reference to the value or quantity of natural resources produced or recovered in Australia. However, natural resource payments do not include royalties, which have their own withholding tax rules (¶22-030).

The withholding rules for natural resource payments made to non-residents are part of the PAYG withholding system (¶26-270).

[FTR ¶976-700]

¶22-072 Withholding regime for non-resident CGT

A 12.5% non-final withholding tax on the disposal proceeds of certain taxable Australian property by foreign residents applies from 1 July 2017 (in 2016–17, the rate was 10%). The purchaser of taxable Australian property, indirect real property interests or options or rights to acquire such property or interest is required to pay 12.5% of the purchase price to the Commissioner and is entitled to withhold this amount from the payment to the foreign resident seller (¶26-269).

[FTR ¶976-776]

¶22-075 FATCA reporting and withholding requirements

The United States government imposes reporting and/or withholding obligations on financial institutions in Australia and other countries. The rules are contained in the US *Foreign Account Tax Compliance Act* (''FATCA''), supplemented by associated US regulations. Their stated purpose is to assist US efforts to combat evasion by US persons holding investments in offshore accounts.

Under an agreement between the Australian and US governments (the ''FATCA Agreement'', 28 April 2014), financial institutions provide information to the ATO, which then forwards it to the US Internal Revenue Service under the exchange of information provision (Art 25) in the Australia–US double tax agreement (¶22-140). This means Australian institutions do not deal directly with the IRS, thus avoiding problems that might otherwise arise under domestic privacy and anti-discrimination legislation.

A financial institution that does not comply with the FATCA Agreement becomes subject to a 30% US withholding tax on certain payments it receives from US sources, such as interest, dividends, rent, salaries, wages, premiums, annuities, compensation, remuneration, or the proceeds of sale of property that could produce US-sourced interest or dividends (TAA Sch 1 Div 396). To the extent that the Australia–US DTA limits maximum US rates on dividends (to 15%) and interest (to 10%), it appears that the institution will need to apply directly to the IRS for a refund. No interest is payable by the IRS on such refunds. Failure to provide the information to the ATO, or providing false or misleading information, may also expose the institution to penalties under domestic law (TAA Sch 1 Divs 284; 286).

Who is liable

The FATCA obligations are imposed on ''Reporting Australian Financial Institutions'' (defined in FATCA Agreement Art 1). These include banks, some building societies, some credit unions, specified life insurance companies, private equity funds, managed funds, exchange traded funds and brokers maintaining custodial accounts. However, it generally does *not* include Australian government entities; certain international bodies; or Australian retirement funds, including superannuation entities, public sector superannuation schemes, constitutionally protected funds or pooled superannuation trusts. It will not be necessary for all members of a multinational group to be FATCA-compliant in order for any one member to remain compliant (FATCA Agreement Art 4, Annex II).

The obligations apply where the financial institution has one or more ''US Reportable Accounts'' at any time during a calendar year (TAA Sch 1 s 396-5). In broad terms, these would include cheque and transaction accounts, savings accounts, term deposits, debt interests and equity interests (including derivatives) and certain annuities, where they are held by US taxpayers or foreign entities in which US taxpayers hold a controlling interest (see FATCA Agreement, Art 1).

Exempt products/accounts would include certain tax-favoured products (such as employee share schemes), accounts of deceased estates and escrow accounts (FATCA Agreement, Annex II).

Reporting and due diligence obligations

The institution must provide the following information about reportable accounts:

- account holder's name, address, account number
- US tax identification number
- account balance or value of the account at the end of the relevant year
- name and identifying number of the institution (FATCA Agreement Art 2).

The institution must normally provide the information to the ATO no later than the 31 July after the end of the year. Records of the due diligence procedures adopted in preparing the information must be kept for 5 years after providing the statement (TAA Sch 1 s 396-25). Procedures and deadlines apply for the provision of information by the ATO to the IRS (FATCA Agreement, Art 3). The ATO and IRS may notify each other of any significant non-compliance by a financial institution, in which case the usual domestic sanctions and penalties may apply.

The text of the FATCA Agreement is found on the Australian Treasury website. Information about FATCA is also found on the US IRS website.

The ATO has published administrative guidance on its website on FATCA reporting obligations (*Automatic exchange of information — guidance material*).

Australia has implemented the OECD Common Reporting Standard (CRS) for the automatic exchange of financial information between participating tax authorities (¶22-165).

[FTR ¶79-597]

Special Categories of Non-residents

¶22-080 Foreign government representatives

The official salary and foreign source income derived by foreign consular and diplomatic representatives and their official staff is exempt from tax in Australia where:

- they are not covered by the *Vienna Convention on Diplomatic Relations* or the *Vienna Convention on Consular Relations*
- they are not Australian citizens or ordinarily resident in Australia (*Efstathakis*), and
- the relevant country has enacted reciprocal tax exemption arrangements (ITAA97 s 768-100).

Where the Vienna Conventions apply, the following income of diplomatic or consular representatives, their staff and family is exempt from Australian tax by virtue of the *Diplomatic Privileges and Immunities Act 1967* and the *Consular Privileges and Immunities Act 1972*:

- the official salary and foreign source income of career consular heads and officers and of full-time technical and administrative staff
- the official salary of honorary consular heads and officers and of full-time domestic staff. However, there is no exemption in respect of the official income of honorary consuls who are nationals of, or permanent residents in, Australia (*Morris*)
- the foreign source income of non-working members of the families forming part of the household of career consular heads and officers and of the full-time non-domestic staff members (but, in the latter case, only when the head of the post is a career diplomat).

Exemption also applies to:

- official remuneration and foreign-source income of an officer of a Commonwealth of Nations country who is temporarily visiting Australia on behalf of that country, or of an Australian government agency, under an inter-governmental agreement (ITAA97 s 768-100)
- official remuneration of a foreign resident representative of a foreign country who is visiting Australia on behalf of that government, or a member of the entourage of that representative (ITAA97 s 842-105).

[FITR ¶585-205]

¶22-100 Australian earnings of other visitors

Australian earnings of certain other non-residents or visitors to Australia are also exempted from income tax. These exemptions cover:

- *expert advisers:* remuneration paid to a foreign resident by an Australian government agency for expert advice or as a member of a Royal Commission
- *conference delegates:* income of a foreign-resident representative of an educational, scientific, religious or philanthropic association who is visiting Australia for the purpose of attending an international conference or carrying on investigation or research
- *media representatives:* income of a foreign-resident representative of the foreign media who is visiting Australia to report proceedings relating to conferences or research in which exempt visitors to Australia are engaged, or reporting tours of exempt foreign government representatives

- *military representatives:* pay earned in Australia by members of the naval, military or air forces of a foreign government, excluding pay provided by the Commonwealth government
- *defence experts:* income of a foreign resident visiting Australia to assist in defence, provided that the income is not exempt in their home country, and
- *scholars:* Commonwealth government scholarships or education allowances paid to foreign residents pursuing a course of study or training in Australia (ITAA97 s 842-105).

A separate exemption applies to income of US-related persons in connection with specified projects of the US government in Australia, ie the North West Cape naval communication station, Joint Defence Space Research Facility, Sparta Project and the Joint Defence Space Communications Station (ITAA36 s 23AA).

[FITR ¶640-110]

¶22-110 Non-resident traders, insurers and shipowners

Insurers and reinsurers

Non-resident insurers with no principal or branch office in Australia are taxed on a deemed taxable income equal to 10% of gross premiums (excluding life policy premiums) receivable in respect of their Australian business. Where, however, the actual profit or loss on the Australian business is established to the Commissioner's satisfaction, the taxable income or loss is calculated by reference to actual receipts and expenditure (ITAA36 ss 141 to 144; 147).

No deduction for the premium paid is allowed to the insured person (eg in the case of deductible fire insurance on business premises) unless the Commissioner is satisfied the tax will be paid in respect of it (ITAA36 s 145). As to the insured person's liability as agent for payment of the tax, see ¶22-060.

The profit on reinsurances effected outside Australia with a non-resident by a person carrying on an insurance business in Australia is taxed in one of 2 ways: (a) the reinsurance premiums are non-deductible to the insurer and non-assessable to the reinsurer; or (b) the insurer may elect to claim the deduction and to furnish returns and pay tax, as agent for the reinsurer (ITAA36 s 148).

Australia's right to tax non-resident insurers on their Australian business is preserved in its DTAs.

Guidelines on the tax treatment of non-resident captive insurance arrangements are contained in PS LA 2007/8.

Shipping

A shipowner or charterer whose principal place of business is outside Australia is taxed on 5% of the gross fares or freight charges receivable in respect of the *outward* carriage (ie *from* Australia) of passengers, mail or freight (ITAA36 ss 129 to 135A). For guidelines, see TR 2014/2, and *Foreign ships visiting Australia* on the ATO website. For the treatment of ship charterparty arrangements, see ¶22-030.

If freight, etc, is transhipped to another vessel at a port outside Australia, only charges referable to the carriage from Australia to the point of transhipment are brought to account (*Ocean Steamship*).

Liability for this tax is limited in various ways by the relevant provisions in each of Australia's DTAs (TD 93/89).

[FTR ¶69-548, ¶71-005]

¶22-120 Venture capital concessions

Incentives apply to encourage foreign investment into the Australian venture capital market and to promote the development of the Australian venture capital industry by encouraging international venture capital managers to locate in Australia. The measures involve the taxation of certain venture capital institutions as ''flow-through'' vehicles (¶5-040) and a CGT exemption for certain gains made by foreign residents on venture capital investments (¶11-900).

[FITR ¶68-480, ¶68-490, ¶155-150]

¶22-122 Foreign managed funds and the Investment Manager Regime

The Investment Manager Regime (IMR) provides concessions designed to promote Australia as a leading regional financial services centre. One concession places individual foreign investors that invest into Australia through a foreign fund in the same income tax position in relation to disposal gains and disposal losses as they would typically have been had they made their share of the fund's investments directly (rather than through the fund). Further, a foreign investor that invests through an independent Australian fund manager is put in the same position, in relation to disposal gains and losses, as if they had invested directly.

An eligible managed investment trust (MIT) may elect into an attribution regime for the taxation of attribution managed investment trusts (AMITs), under ITAA97 Div 276 (¶6-405). For information about the tax rules applying to MITs, see ¶6-400.

[FITR ¶265-200, ¶265-220]

Temporary Residents

¶22-125 Concessions for temporary residents

Individuals who qualify as ''temporary residents'' are exempt from Australian tax on certain foreign source income or capital gains. In this respect, they are treated similarly to non-residents, even though in many cases they would normally have been classed as residents under the normal tax rules. They are also exempt from interest withholding tax, and special rules apply to employee shares and rights (¶12-630).

In general, these concessions apply for income years that begin on or after 1 July 2006. As an exception, the withholding tax concessions apply to payments made on or after 6 April 2006.

A special rate of income tax applies to income earned on or after 1 January 2017 by some working holiday makers, regardless of the residency status of the individual (¶21-033).

Who are temporary residents

A temporary resident is a person who holds a temporary visa under the *Migration Act 1958* (ITAA97 definition in s 995-1). A temporary visa is one that enables a person to remain in Australia during a specified period, or until a specified event occurs, or while the holder has a special status.

A person may be a temporary resident irrespective of whether they are a resident or a non-resident under the normal tax rules. However, a person will not be a temporary resident if they are residents under the separate test laid down in the *Social Security Act 1991*. In effect, this means that they cannot be an Australian-resident citizen, permanent resident, or person who holds a protected special category visa. The rationale for excluding protected special category visa holders is that they are entitled to government benefits on a similar basis to citizens. A person also cannot be a temporary resident if their *spouse* is a resident for social security purposes.

A New Zealand citizen who held a Special Category visa which lapsed when he left Australia for a short period was considered to remain a temporary resident during that period, as he continued to be entitled to re-enter Australia on presentation of his NZ passport (TD 2012/18).

There is no set time limit on how long a person can be a temporary resident. In addition, it is possible that a person can be a temporary resident even though they have been a temporary resident before. However, a person cannot be a temporary resident if, at any time after the legislation commences, they have been a resident that failed to satisfy the visa requirements.

Foreign-source income exemptions

In general, foreign-source income derived by a temporary resident will be exempt (ITAA97 s 768-910). This applies, for example, to foreign-source dividends, interest or rental income. It has also been applied to foreign-source pension income (ID 2006/161; ID 2006/162).

However, this exemption does *not* apply to:

- remuneration for employment undertaken or services provided while a person is a temporary resident. The reason for this exception is the government's view that permanent and temporary residents should compete on a level playing field for the supply of labour or services overseas
- alienated personal services income assessable under Div 86, and
- net capital gains (these are treated separately: see below).

The fact that the exemption does not apply to these types of income does not prevent them from being exempt under some other provision. For example, a temporary resident who is a resident for tax purposes and is employed overseas for at least 91 days on specified types of project may still be able to claim exemptions under ss 23AF and 23AG (¶10-860).

Australian-sourced income distributed from a non-resident trust to a temporary resident in Australia is considered to fall outside the exemption and to be assessable (ID 2007/108).

In technical terms, the income covered by the exemption is called ''non-assessable non-exempt income'' (¶10-890). This basically means that it is excluded from assessable income and is not taken into account when working out a taxpayer's losses.

The exemption also means that expenses incurred in deriving the income will not be deductible, and that foreign tax offsets/credits cannot be claimed for foreign tax paid on the income.

Special types of foreign income

It is specifically provided that a temporary resident will not be assessable on income attributed under the Controlled Foreign Companies (CFC) rules (¶21-140). This also means that they are relieved of the compliance burden associated with CFC calculations and the associated record-keeping requirements (ITAA97 s 768-960).

A temporary resident will not be treated as a resident for the purposes of the transferor trust measures (¶21-330). This means that they will not be attributed with any income of the trust under those measures during the period while they are a temporary resident (ITAA97 s 768-970). However the temporary resident will still be required to keep records under ITAA36 s 102AAZG that would be relevant to any period when they were not a temporary resident.

Capital gains and losses

Capital gains and losses made by a temporary resident will be treated as if they had been made by a non-resident (ITAA97 s 768-915). This means that only a limited range of capital gains or losses will be taken into account for Australian tax purposes (¶12-720). In addition, special rules apply where there is a change of residence status (¶12-760). Temporary residents are not entitled to the CGT discount (¶11-033).

From 7.30 pm (AEST) on 9 May 2017, foreign resident individuals do not have access to the CGT main residence exemption (¶11-730).

Interest withholding tax exemption

Residents who pay interest to foreign lenders are normally required to deduct and remit a 10% interest withholding tax, subject to some exceptions for US and UK lenders (¶22-020). Temporary residents are exempt from this obligation on payments made on or after 6 April 2006 (ITAA97 s 768-980(a)).

In addition, the interest will not be assessable if it is derived by a foreign resident lender that is not carrying on business in Australia at or through a permanent establishment here (ITAA97 s 768-980(b)).

In practice, foreign lenders commonly require a resident borrower to compensate them for the additional costs attributable to interest withholding tax. The exemption therefore not only removes a compliance burden from temporary resident borrowers, but also indirectly reduces their costs.

Superannuation

For details of the special rules applying to payment of superannuation for taxpayers who have entered Australia on certain classes of visa and are departing Australia permanently, see ¶14-390.

[FITR ¶587-100]

Double Taxation Agreements

¶22-140 Double taxation agreements

Australia has concluded double taxation agreements (DTAs) with the countries listed in the table at ¶22-160. These DTAs have twin aims:

- to relieve taxpayers from double taxation, and
- to counter fiscal evasion, eg in relation to transfer pricing (¶22-580).

The taxation agreements prevail in the event of conflicting provisions in ITAA36 and ITAA97 (except Pt IVA) or in the Rating Acts. It appears, however, that this principle does not prevent a unilateral amendment of the domestic law in contravention of the spirit of the agreements.

The primary legislation governing the DTAs is the *International Tax Agreements Act 1953* and the DTAs can be accessed through the Australian Treaty Series online database (www.austlii.edu.au/au/other/dfat/treaties).

"Residence" and "source" taxation

Two chief methods of relieving double taxation are adopted in the DTAs. Firstly, taxing rights over certain classes of income are reserved entirely to the country of residence of the person deriving the income. Secondly, all other income may be taxed (in some cases, only to a limited extent) by the country in which the income has its source; if the country of residence of the recipient also taxes that income, it is required to grant a credit against its tax for the tax levied by the source country.

Each agreement contains rules designed to classify each person (whether an individual, company or other entity) as either a resident of Australia or of the other country. These rules draw firstly on the domestic laws of each country and fall back on ''tie-breaker'' rules to attribute a sole country of residence to persons who would otherwise be regarded as dual residents. For example, they may provide that a dual resident is deemed to be a resident only of the country in which he/she has a permanent home available.

TR 2001/13 contains guidelines on the interpretation of Australia's DTAs as, in some situations, DTAs may be interpreted in a different way to the way in which domestic tax legislation is interpreted.

The Organisation for Economic Co-operation and Development (OECD) has a Model Tax Convention, plus associated commentary and guidelines, which may be used as a basis for the negotiation, application and interpretation of bilateral tax treaties.

The general anti-avoidance rules in Pt IVA (¶30-120) can apply to treaty shopping schemes, eg where there is an investment in the shares of an Australian company by an entity resident in the Cayman Islands though a complex series of interposed entities (TD 2010/20).

Reciprocal recovery of taxes

DTAs with specific provisions dealing with reciprocal recovery of tax include those with Germany, Finland, New Zealand, Norway, India and South Africa. There are also limited provisions in the *Foreign Judgments Act 1991* in relation to New Zealand and Papua New Guinea. For a case in which the ATO obtained freezing orders in the context of recovery of New Zealand tax under the reciprocal recovery provisions, see *Ma & Ors*.

Australia has also ratified the OECD *Convention of Mutual Administrative Assistance on Tax Matters*, effective 1 January 2013. This convention extends beyond the countries with which Australia has current bilateral agreements. It is intended to facilitate mutual recovery of tax by enabling the Commissioner to recover tax claims from foreign states, and to pursue tax claims in Australia on behalf of those states. More than 100 countries are covered by the Convention; for the current list, see the OECD website. For an article discussing the Convention, see CCH *Tax Week*¶964 (2012).

Domestic authority enabling the ATO to collect tax debts on behalf of a foreign tax authority, or to take measures to ensure the collection of that debt, are contained in TAA Sch 1 Div 263.

For information about tax information exchange agreements (TIEAs), Additional Benefits Agreements and the Common Reporting Standard (CRS) for the automatic exchange of financial account information, see ¶22-165.

[FTR ¶795-423]

¶22-150 Main scope of DTAs

The tax treatment of various forms of income under Australia's DTAs is summarised below.

Business profits and permanent establishments

The principal factor in the taxation of business profits is the presence of a branch, ie a ''permanent establishment'' (PE). Under the business profits articles of the agreements (generally Art 7), the profits of an enterprise of one country may be taxed in the other only if the enterprise carries on business in that other country through a permanent establishment, and only to the extent that the profits are attributable to the permanent establishment (and, in some agreements, to related sales or business activities). In addition, the limited rates of source country taxation applicable to dividend, interest and royalty income (see below) do not apply where such forms of income are "effectively connected" with a permanent establishment that the recipient maintains in the source country.

Where there is a permanent establishment in the source country, profits of that establishment may be taxed in the source country. In the case of an overseas business trust with such an establishment in Australia, overseas beneficiaries or unitholders entitled to a share of the trust are deemed to be carrying on business in Australia through a permanent establishment so that their share of distributions of the trust may be taxable here (either under the relevant DTA or under ITA Act, s 3(11); *Case X69*). It has been held that this deeming rule is simply an enabling provision which does not actually impose tax, and it therefore does not apply for the purpose of determining whether the withholding tax provisions apply (¶22-030), nor where the trust is actually resident in Australia (*GE Capital Finance*; see also the article at CCH *Tax Week*¶602 (2007)). In addition, where a business trust carries on funds management activities through a permanent establishment in Australia, income distributed to non-resident investors from those activities will be sourced in accordance with normal source rules. This means that, where the income arises from funds invested offshore, it will not be deemed to have an Australian source, and will therefore not be taxable in Australia (ITA Act s 3AA). For the application of the business profits rule where partners of a foreign limited liability partnership are resident in a tax treaty country, see TD 2011/25.

A Swiss resident successfully claimed that, under the business profits article in the Swiss agreement, he was taxable only in Switzerland on the profits arising from a speculative one-off share deal in Australia. This was because the profits were profits of an "enterprise carried on" by a resident of Switzerland who did not maintain a permanent establishment in Australia. The High Court held that the expression "enterprise carried on" does not require systematic activity or that the enterprise exist independently of the activity from which the profits are derived (*Thiel*).

"Permanent establishment" has a statutory meaning for general tax purposes (ITAA36 s 6), but the DTAs typically contain their own definition, which may share or extend the statutory meaning, and which should always be referred to in relevant cases. The primary meaning of permanent establishment under both s 6 and the DTAs is a fixed place of business through which the business of an enterprise is wholly or partly carried on. The most obvious example would be a branch. To qualify under this head, the place must have an element of permanence, both geographic and temporal. Permanence must be construed in the context of each particular business and is a question of fact and degree. However, "permanent" does not mean forever. As a rule of thumb, the Commissioner considers that there will be a permanent establishment where a business operates at or through a particular place continuously for 6 months or more, though shorter periods may suffice if the connection with Australia is very strong. This may apply, for example, where the business returns to a particular location in Australia on an ongoing and regular basis but only for short periods each time; or where the intention is to set up a permanent business in Australia but the owner unexpectedly dies or the business fails (TR 2002/5). The ATO considers that a non-resident does not have a permanent establishment in Australia solely as a result of selling trading stock through an internet website hosted by an Australian resident internet service provider (TD 2005/2). For the ATO's views on the activities of visiting foreign horse trainers, see ID 2012/23.

The statutory definition also includes places where: (1) the person is carrying on business through an agent; (2) the person has, uses or is installing substantial equipment or substantial machinery; (3) the person is engaged on a construction project; or (4) goods sold by the supplier are manufactured assembled, processed, packed or distributed by a related party. Variations on this are typically found in the DTAs. In determining whether equipment is "substantial", the ATO considers that the most important factor is size, though quantity, value and importance in the business are also relevant (TR 2007/10; ID 2006/337). On this basis a $200,000 computer used to carry on part of the business was considered not to be substantial. A provision in the Singapore DTA that a Singaporean enterprise would have a permanent establishment in Australia where substantial equipment was being used in Australia ''by, for or under contract with the enterprise'' was held to be satisfied even though the enterprise's role simply consisted of leasing the equipment to a business in Australia (*McDermott Industries*). Following that decision, the ATO accepts that a foreign resident may have a permanent establishment in Australia under such a provision even though it is not actively using equipment here. However, the ATO has also ruled that a Singaporean-resident enterprise that hires substantial equipment to an entity in Australia under a hire purchase agreement should not be treated as having a permanent establishment here (TD 2007/31). This view would extend to other similar DTAs. The ATO has also issued guidelines on the application of these rules to shipping and aircraft leasing under the UK and US DTAs (TR 2007/10) and non-resident sub-leases of substantial equipment (TR 2007/11).

Under the US DTA, a US enterprise has a permanent establishment here if it maintains substantial equipment for rental (Art 5(4)). However, for Australia to have the right to tax the rental income, the US enterprise would also have to carry on business here (Art 7), which would not be satisfied simply by the act of leasing alone (ID 2009/21).

For the application of the foreign branch income exemption (¶21-098) where the company has a PE on ''substantial equipment'' grounds, see TR 2014/3.

The statutory definition, like that in most of the DTAs, does not include a place where the business is carried on by an agent who does not have, or habitually exercise, a general authority to negotiate and conclude contracts. Merely executing a one-off licence arrangement may not be sufficient for this purpose (*Unisys Corporation*). However, in *Case 23/93*, it was held that an Australian share dealer who bought and sold shares on behalf of New Zealand principals habitually exercised authority to conclude contracts on their behalf and, accordingly, constituted a permanent establishment of the principals in Australia under the New Zealand agreement. An enterprise of one of the countries will not be deemed to be carrying on a business through a permanent establishment in the other country merely because of work performed for it by an agent acting in the ordinary course of the agent's business.

The DTA definitions commonly specifically include a factory, office, mine, market or ''long-term'' construction site (such as for 6 or 12 months). A Japanese company was considered to have a PE in Australia where it had a contract to undertake a long-term construction or installation project here and subcontracted some or all of that work to an Australian resident entity, under the supervision of the company's own personnel (ID 2014/29).

The ATO stated that it will not apply compliance resources to determine whether foreign companies have a permanent establishment in Australia because of the temporary presence of employees in Australia due to COVID-19 overseas travel restrictions. For an article discussing permanent establishment tax issues related to the ongoing disruption of construction projects from COVID-19, see CCH *Tax Week* ¶803 (2020).

Some DTA definitions also provide that the furnishing by an enterprise of one country of consultancy or other services will constitute a permanent establishment in the other country where those activities continue (for the same or a connected project) within the latter country for a period or periods aggregating more than 90 days in any year of income.

For the purpose of source country taxation, profits are attributed to a permanent establishment of an enterprise using arm's length principles, ie it will be treated as if it was a separate and distinct enterprise dealing wholly independently with both the enterprise of which it is a permanent establishment and other enterprises with which it deals. Usually, domestic laws regarding the taxation of profits from insurance with non-residents are not affected by the business profits article of the agreements.

The business profits article of the Australia/New Zealand DTA did not prevent the attribution of a NZ entity's income to an Australian entity under the personal services income rules (¶30-600), despite the fact that the NZ entity remained liable for NZ tax (*Russell*). The court acknowledged that hardship may result from such economic double taxation.

Income from real property

Income from real property may be taxed by the country in which the real property is located. This rule extends to income from real property of an enterprise and to income from real property used for the performance of independent personal services (see below).

Income from real property located in Australia is usually defined to include: (a) income from a lease or any other interest in land, including a right to explore for, or mine, minerals, oil, gas or other natural resources; and (b) royalties and other payments relating to the exploration for, and exploitation and extraction of, minerals, oil, gas or other natural resources. The country in which the real property is located can tax real property income whether or not the recipient maintains a permanent establishment in that country.

Income from the alienation of real property and capital gains

Income or gains derived by a resident of one country from the alienation of real property situated in the other country may be taxed in that other country. For these purposes, real property is often defined to include: (a) a lease of land or any other direct interest in or over land; (b) rights to exploit or explore natural resources; and (c) shares or rights in a company, the assets of which consist wholly or principally of direct interests in or over land.

Australia has extended its taxing right to situations in which Australian real property is owned by non-residents, either directly or indirectly or through a chain of interposed entities, and it is one of these entities which is alienated rather than the real property itself (ITA Act s 3A).

Income or gains from the alienation of property, other than real property which forms part of the business property of a permanent establishment or a fixed base used for the performance of independent personal services, may be taxed in the country in which the permanent establishment or fixed base is situated. This rule also applies to the disposal of the permanent establishment (alone or as part of the whole enterprise) or fixed base itself. Income or gains from the alienation of ships or aircraft operated in international traffic or property (other than real property) associated with such operations may be taxed only in the country of residence of the operator.

Australia's exclusive right to tax gains taxable in Australia under its capital gains tax regime is limited by its DTAs even though they may have been entered into before the 1987 introduction of CGT. For example, in *Virgin Holdings SA*, it was held that Australia's right to tax a non-resident company's capital gains in the circumstances of the case was denied by the business profits article in the Swiss DTA. A similar conclusion was reached in relation to the UK and Netherlands DTAs (*Undershaft No 1 and No 2*).

For the interaction of Australia's domestic CGT rules and the DTA with the United States in relation to limited partnerships, see *Resource Capital Fund IV LP*.

Some of Australia's post-CGT agreements contain a "sweep-up" provision which, from an Australian perspective, preserves the application of the domestic law in relation to the taxation of gains of a capital nature derived from the disposal of property that are not specifically dealt with elsewhere in the agreement. Where income or gains from the alienation of property result in an item of income or a gain being subjected to tax in both countries, the country of residence of the recipient is required to allow a credit against its own tax for the tax imposed by the source country.

Associated enterprises

There may be an arm's length reallocation of profits between "associated" Australian and foreign enterprises where the commercial or financial relations between them differ from those that might be expected to operate between enterprises dealing with each other on a wholly independent basis. Where this applies, either country may re-write the accounts of an enterprise to reflect arm's length principles. This "associated enterprises" article (typically Art 9) generally would not apply where it can be satisfactorily demonstrated that the transactions between the enterprises have taken place on normal, open market commercial terms.

Enterprises will be associated for these purposes where one enterprise participates in the management, control or capital of an enterprise of the other country, or the same persons participate in the management, control or capital of both enterprises. Parent and subsidiary companies and companies under common control are associated enterprises for these purposes.

Dividends

Dividends may be taxed in full in the country of residence of the beneficial owner of the relevant shares and in the source country subject to the tax limits shown in the table at ¶22-160. The source country tax limit on dividends does not apply where the recipient maintains a permanent establishment in the source country, or a fixed base for the performance of independent personal services, and the holding giving rise to the dividend is "effectively connected" with the permanent establishment or fixed base. In such circumstances, the dividends may be taxed as business profits or as income from independent personal services. In practice, where any Australian sourced dividends are franked they will generally remain exempt from tax in Australia, while Australian sourced unfranked dividends will generally be subject to withholding tax instead of being taxed by assessment.

Interest

Similar rules as apply to dividends also apply to interest. Interest is usually defined to include interest from government securities or from bonds or debentures, whether or not secured by mortgage and whether or not carrying rights to participate in the debtor's profits, interest from any other form of indebtedness as well as all other income assimilated to income from money lent under the tax law of the source country. The source country tax limit (see table at ¶22-160) does not apply where the person deriving the interest has a permanent establishment or fixed base in the source country for the performance of personal services and the indebtedness in respect of which the interest is incurred is effectively connected with the permanent establishment or fixed base.

Where the interest is "effectively connected" in the manner prescribed, it will be treated as forming part of the profits attributable to the permanent establishment or fixed base and will be subject to tax as business profits or income from independent personal services. Where, due to a special relationship that exists between the persons associated with a loan transaction, the amount of interest paid exceeds an arm's length amount, the source country tax limit applies only in respect of the arm's length amount of interest.

Withholding tax indemnification payments made by a borrower to a lender are not interest and would normally be treated as business profits for DTA purposes (TR 2002/4). Arm's length interest paid to US and UK resident financial institutions is normally not taxable by Australia under the relevant DTA unless it is effectively connected with a permanent establishment of the institution in Australia (TR 2005/5). However, this may not apply where the special provisions of Art 11(9) of the US DTA apply (*Deutsche Asia Pacific Finance Inc*).

Royalties

Royalties (¶22-030) may be taxed in full in the country of residence of the recipient of the royalties and in the source country, subject to the tax limits shown in the table at ¶22-160. The definition of royalties differs from agreement to agreement and must be checked in each case. In agreements concluded in recent years, it generally does not include natural resource payments which are treated as income from real property. The government will renegotiate Australia's DTAs to include spectrum licence payments in the definition of royalties for these purposes. Equipment royalties are not treated as royalties under the United Kingdom or United States DTAs. Under the Singapore DTA, there is a specific exclusion of royalties relating to literary, dramatic, musical or artistic copyright (eg see ID 2012/67).

The source country tax limit does not apply where the person beneficially entitled to the royalties carries on business in the source country through a permanent establishment or has a fixed base for the performance of personal services, and the property or right in respect of which the royalties are paid or credited is effectively connected with the permanent establishment or fixed base. Where the royalties are "effectively connected", they will be treated as forming part of the profits attributable to the permanent establishment or fixed base and will be subject to tax as business profits or income from independent personal services (*Tech Mahindra*, concerning the India DTA). The source country limit also does not apply where an arm's length rate of royalty is not applied because of a special relationship between the payer of a royalty and the payee, or between the payer, payee and some other person.

The decision in *McDermott Industries* (see above) means that in previous years some foreign residents who did not actively use equipment in Australia may have paid royalty withholding tax on the incorrect basis that they did not have a permanent establishment here. These foreign residents may apply to the ATO for refunds.

Payments made by an Australian software distributor to a Canadian resident software developer were held to be royalties subject to 10% withholding under the Australia–Canada DTA (*Task Technology Pty Ltd*). For the treatment of an agreement involving both distribution rights and intellectual property rights, see the *IBM case* at ¶22-030.

Independent professional or personal services income

Independent professional or personal services income (as derived by, for example, visiting doctors, lawyers and engineers, as well as persons engaged in scientific, educational or artistic activities) is generally taxable only in the country of residence of the recipient. However, it may be taxed in the source country where various combinations of the following conditions are satisfied: (a) the income is attributable to a fixed base in the source country; (b) the period during which the services are performed exceeds a specified period, usually 183 days; (c) the income is deductible in determining the profits of an enterprise or permanent establishment in the source country; and (d) the income derived exceeds a prescribed limit (eg A$8,000 in a 12-month period — Papua New Guinea, Fiji and Kiribati agreements).

Visiting employees, entertainers and athletes

Visiting employee remuneration is generally taxable in the country where the services are performed, but may be taxable solely in the country of residence of the employee where: (a) the duration of the visit does not exceed a specified limit (ranging from 90 to 183 days); (b) the remuneration is paid by a non-resident of the source country; and (c) the remuneration is not an expense of an enterprise or permanent establishment that the employer has in the source country. In determining whether an employment relationship genuinely exists, a "substance over form" approach should be adopted, and the actual behaviour of the parties may take precedence over the formal terms of the contract (TR 2013/1).

The remuneration of entertainers and athletes can be taxed in the country in which the entertainment or athletic activities are performed even where it accrues outside that country to a person other than the entertainer or athlete. The operation of DTAs and their interaction with domestic tax law in relation to income derived by foreign non-profit cultural bodies from performances in Australia are examined in TD 1999/7. For special PAYG rules, see ¶26-267.

International shipping and air transport profits

Profits from international shipping and air transport operations are generally taxable only in the country of residence of the operator. However, some agreements (eg Singapore and Thailand) allow both countries to tax such income with the source country reducing its tax by 50%. The Hungarian agreement is unusual in providing for the taxation of profits derived from international road transport operations. For ATO guidelines see TR 2008/8, TR 2014/2. Guidelines for calculating the taxable income of non-DTA airlines are in PS LA 2008/2 (GA).

Visiting teachers and students

Teaching and research remuneration of visiting professors and teachers is usually exempt from tax in the country being visited provided the visit does not exceed 2 years. In some agreements, the exemption does not apply to income from privately funded research work. Under other agreements (eg Singapore and the United States), teaching and research remuneration is treated as visiting employee remuneration. See further TD 2001/21 to TD 2001/24 (French, German, Italian and Japanese teachers). Payments received by visiting students from overseas for their maintenance, education or training are also exempt where they are visiting solely for educational or training purposes.

Government officials, pensions and annuities

The remuneration of government officials (other than income from services rendered in connection with a government business enterprise) is generally taxed only by the relevant government unless the official is a permanent resident (or, in some cases, a citizen or national) of the country in which the services are performed. These provisions normally apply only to employees, rather than contractors (TR 2005/8).

Pensions and purchased annuities are usually taxable only in the country of residence of the recipient. As there is no definition of pension in any of the agreements, it takes its ordinary meaning under domestic law (TD 93/151). The essential characteristic of a pension is that there be periodical payments (*Tubemakers of Aust Ltd*), so it would include periodic workers compensation, or ‘‘loss of earning’’ payments made under statutory transport accident schemes (ID 2008/145).

In some cases, pensions paid in respect of government service are taxable both in the state where they are paid and in the country of residence of the recipient (*Chong*).

Other income

Most of Australia’s agreements contain an article dealing with ‘‘other income’’, ie income not expressly covered by any other article of the agreement. This income is generally taxable only in the country of residence of the recipient unless it is sourced in, or connected with a permanent establishment in, the other country.

[FITR ¶29-005]

¶22-160 Checklist of Australia’s DTAs

Australia has entered into a number of comprehensive DTAs with other countries to avoid international double taxation and to prevent fiscal evasion. The following table summarises those DTAs and sets out the general source country tax limits applicable to most unfranked dividends, interest and royalties. In each case, reference must be made to the DTAs for details of precise requirements.

Country	Dividends (%)	Interest (%)	Royalties (%)
Argentina	10/15[1]	12	10/15[2]
Austria[3]	15	10	10
Belgium[4]	15	10	10
Canada[5]	5/15[5]	10	10
Chile[6]	5/15	5/10	5/10
China[7]	15	10	10
Czech Republic	5/15[8]	10	10
Denmark	15	10	10
Fiji	20	10	15
Finland[9]	0/5/15	10	5
France[10]	0/5/15	10	5
Germany[11]	5/15	10	5
Greece[12]	—	—	—
Hungary	15	10	10
India[13, 14]	15	15	10/15[13]
Indonesia	15	10	10/15[15]
Ireland	15	10	10
Israel[14A]	15	10	5
Italy[12]	15	10	10
Japan[16]	5/10	10	5
Kiribati	20	10	15
Korea	15	15	15
Malaysia[17]	15	15	15
Malta	15[18]	15	10
Mexico[19]	0/15[19]	10/15[19]	10[19]
Netherlands	15	10	10
New Zealand[20]	0/5/15	10	5
Norway	0/5/15[21]	10	5
Papua New Guinea	15/20[22]	10	10
Philippines	15/25[23]	15	15/25[24]
Poland	15	10	10
Romania	5/15[25]	10	10
Russia[26]	5/15[27]	10	10[28]
Singapore[29]	15	10	10
Slovakia	15	10	10
South Africa[30]	5/15	0/10	5
Spain	15[31]	10	10
Sri Lanka	15	10	10
Sweden	15	10	10
Switzerland[32]	5/15[32]	10	5
Taipei[33]	10/15[34]	10	12.5
Thailand[35]	15/20[36]	10/25[37]	15
Turkey[38]	5/15[38]	10	10

Country	Dividends (%)	Interest (%)	Royalties (%)
United Kingdom[39]	0/5/15[39]	0/10[39]	5[39]
United States[40]	0/5/15[40]	0/10[40]	5[40]
Vietnam	10/15[41]	10	10

Country notes:

(1) Australia limits its tax to 10% on franked dividends paid to a person who directly holds at least 10% of the voting power in the paying company. Argentina limits its tax to 10% on dividends paid to a person who directly holds at least 25% of the capital of the paying company. In all other cases the source country limit is 15%.

(2) The source country limit for royalties is: (a) 10% for copyright on literary works; the supply of industrial or scientific equipment or knowledge; ancillary assistance; other technical assistance (net of expenses); and (b) 15% for other copyright, patents and trademarks; commercial equipment; satellite reception of visual images or sounds; TV or radio broadcast of visual images or sounds; motion pictures and videos. A special rate of 3% applies in the case of Argentina to royalties in the form of payments to an Australian resident in respect of the transfer of news by an international news agency.

(3) Negotiations to update the DTA with Austria started in March 2010.

(4) A protocol amending the tax treaty between Australia and Belgium entered into force on 12 May 2014. The protocol allows for a full exchange of information in relation to several Australian federal taxes and Belgian federal taxes.

(5) Certain non-portfolio dividends are taxed at a maximum rate of 5% instead of 15%.

(6) The DTA took effect in Australia for withholding tax from 1 April 2013, for FBT from 1 April 2013 and in respect of other taxes from 1 July 2013. The 5% rate for dividends applies where the beneficial owner of the dividend is a company holding at least 10% of the paying company's voting power. For interest, the 5% rate applies to interest paid to financial institutions that are unrelated and independent of the payer, the 10% rate applies to other Australian-sourced interest and the 15% rate relates to other Chilean-sourced interest. The 5% royalty rate applies to equipment royalties.

(7) China does not include Hong Kong (TR 97/19) or Macau (TD 2000/9). Australia has also concluded a separate airline profits agreement with China.

(8) For Australia, a rate limit of 5% applies to franked dividends where, under Australian law, the rate of tax on franked dividends does not exceed 5%. The Czech Republic limit is 5% if the dividends are paid to a company which holds directly or indirectly at least 20% of the capital of the dividend paying company.

(9) An exemption in the source country applies to inter-corporate non-portfolio dividends where the recipient holds directly at least 80% of the voting power of the company paying the dividend, subject to certain conditions. A 5% rate limit applies on all other non-portfolio inter-corporate dividends where the recipient holds directly at least 10% of the voting power of the company paying the dividend. A general limit of 15% applies for all other dividends.

(10) Concessions apply to non-portfolio dividends, interest derived by government bodies and financial institutions, and a new 5% general rate limit for royalties. Amounts from equipment leasing are treated as business profits rather than royalties. The DTA does not apply to overseas French Territories (TD 93/220).

(11) On 12 November 2015, Australia and Germany signed a new DTA to replace the previous treaty signed in 1972. The treaty was ratified and entered into force on 7 December 2016. The general source country tax limits are those applicable under the 1972 treaty. Under the new treaty, the rate limit for interest will be 10% and for royalties, 5%. A lower limit of 5% for dividends will apply in certain circumstances.

(12) Australia has concluded separate airlines profits agreements with Italy and Greece, providing for each country to exempt from tax income derived by an enterprise of the other country from its international air transport operations. There is no comprehensive agreement with Greece.

(13) The source country limit under the Indian agreement is 10% for royalties paid in respect of the use of, or rights to use, industrial, commercial or scientific equipment or for the provision of consulting services related to such equipment. The limit for ''non-technical'' royalties is 15%.

(14) A 2011 protocol amending the DTA between Australia and India impacts the treatment of cross-border services, natural resource exploration and exploitation, substantial equipment, permanent establishments, tax discrimination, exchange of information and tax collection. Legislation to give effect to the protocol in Australia was passed on 27 March 2013 (*International Tax Agreements Amendment Act 2013*). The protocol will come into force when both countries have completed their domestic legislative requirements and exchanged diplomatic notes.

(14A) Australia and Israel signed a tax treaty on 28 March 2019. The treaty entered into force on 6 December 2019 with the effect that it applies, in the case of Australia, to (a) withholding taxes from 1 January 2020; (b) fringe benefits tax from 1 April 2020; and (c) other Australian taxes to which the convention applies from 1 July 2020.

(15) The 10% rate applies to rentals and other royalties including fees for related ancillary services concerning the use of industrial, commercial or scientific equipment, or the supply of scientific, technical, industrial or commercial knowledge or information. The 15% rate applies to all other royalties.

(16) An exemption applies for certain interest and inter-company dividends.

(17) A protocol allows the exchange of a range of tax-related information, including banking details and transaction.

(18) The 15% limit does not apply to Malta, which limits its tax to either: (a) the amount chargeable on the profits out of which the dividend is paid; or (b) if the profits out of which the dividends are paid are subject to tax at a reduced rate, that reduced rate.

(19) This agreement provides for withholding tax limits of 10% on royalties, and 10% for interest derived from bonds and securities traded on a recognised securities market and 15% for other interest. There is no withholding tax on dividends which have been fully taxed at the corporate level and where the recipient holds directly at least 10% of the voting power of the payer but, in other cases, the withholding rate on dividends is 15%.

(20) The source country limit is 5% for dividends paid to a company that owns directly at least 10% of the voting power in the company paying the dividends. An exemption from withholding tax applies for dividends paid to a company that owns directly or indirectly at least 80% of the voting rights in the paying company for 12 months prior to payment, and certain other conditions are fulfilled. An exemption also applies if the dividends are paid to a government organisation that owns no more than 10% of the voting rights in the paying company. In all other cases a limit of 15% applies.

(21) The source country limit is 5% for dividends paid to a company that owns directly at least 10% of the voting power in the company paying the dividends. An exemption from withholding tax applies for dividends paid to a company that owns directly or indirectly at least 80% of the voting rights in the paying company for 12 months prior to payment of the dividend, and certain other conditions are fulfilled. In all other cases a limit of 15% applies.

(22) For Australian source dividends the limit is 15%. Where they are sourced in Papua New Guinea, the limit is 20%.

(23) Source country tax is limited to 15% where relief by way of rebate or credit is given to the beneficial owner of the dividend. In any other case, source country tax is limited to 25%.

(24) Source country tax is generally limited to 15% of gross royalties if paid by an approved Philippines enterprise and, in all other cases, to 25% of the gross royalties.

(25) The source country limit is 5% for dividends paid to a company which holds directly at least 10% of the capital of the company paying the dividends and the dividends are paid out of profits that have been subject to Romanian profits tax (Romanian source dividends) or have been fully franked (Australian source dividends). In other cases the source country rate is 15%.

(26) The agreement contains a ''Lamesa'' provision (¶22-150).

(27) The general source country limit is 15%. However, the rate is reduced to 5% where the dividends have been fully taxed at the corporate level, the recipient company holds directly at least 10% of the capital of the paying company and has invested a minimum of A$700,000 or the Russian rouble equivalent in the paying company.

(28) The definition of royalties includes spectrum licences.

(29) A protocol to enable greater exchange of information between Australia and Singapore on a wide range of taxes came into force on 22 December 2010.

(30) A 5% withholding rate applies for non-portfolio inter-corporate dividends paid out of profits that have borne full company tax. A 15% rate applies to all other dividends. A withholding tax exemption applies to interest derived by overseas financial institutions.

(31) The 15% limit does not apply to income which, under Spanish tax law relating to transparent companies, is attributable to shareholders of such companies. Instead, Spain taxes such income under domestic law provided the income has not been subject to Spanish corporation tax.

(32) A revised DTA with Switzerland entered into force on 14 October 2014. The revised DTA reduces the withholding tax limit on royalties to 5%, and introduces lower limits for dividends in certain circumstances.

(33) For diplomatic reasons, the signatories to the agreement are the Australian Commerce and Industry Office and the Taipei Economic and Cultural Office. The agreement operates, however, in a very similar way to Australia's other agreements.

(34) In Australia, a limit of 10% applies to franked dividends. In Taiwan, a limit of 10% applies if the dividends are paid to a company which holds directly at least 25% of the capital of the dividend paying company.

(35) Negotiations to update the DTA with Thailand were foreshadowed in May 2012.

(36) Source country limit where the recipient has a minimum 25% direct holding in the paying company is 15% if the paying company engages in an ''industrial undertaking'', and 20% in other cases.

(37) Source country limit is 10% when interest is paid to a financial institution and 25% in all other cases.

(38) The 5% dividend rate applies where the beneficial owner of the dividend is a company holding at least 10% of the Australian paying company's voting power, or at least 25% of the Turkish paying company's capital.

(39) There is no tax on dividends where the recipient is a company directly holding 80% of the voting power of the payer, a 5% withholding tax rate applies where the beneficial owner of the dividend is a company which holds directly 10% of the voting power of the payer (TD 2014/13), and a 15% rate applies to other dividends. There is no withholding tax on interest derived by a financial institution (¶22-020) or government body.

(40) Royalty withholding tax does not apply on payments for industrial, commercial or scientific equipment. Dividend withholding tax is eliminated in certain cases where there are major shareholdings. Certain exemptions from interest withholding tax also apply, eg interest paid to certain financial institutions (¶22-020).

(41) For Australian source dividends, the limit is 15%. For Vietnamese source dividends, the limit is 10%.

[FTR ¶795-423]

¶22-165 Other agreements enabling international cooperation

Double taxation agreements typically include provisions enabling the exchange of information between the participating countries.

Tax information exchange agreements

Moreover, Australia has negotiated specific tax information exchange agreements (TIEAs) with Andorra, Anguilla, Antigua and Barbuda, Aruba, the Bahamas, Bahrain, Belize, Bermuda, British Virgin Islands, Brunei, Cayman Islands, Cook Islands, Costa Rica, Dominica, Gibraltar, Grenada, Guatemala (not yet in force), Guernsey, Isle of Man,

Jersey, Liberia, Liechtenstein, Macao, Marshall Islands, Mauritius, Monaco, Montserrat, Netherlands Antilles, Samoa, San Marino, St Kitts & Nevis, St Lucia, St Vincent and the Grenadines, Turks and Caicos Islands, Uruguay and Vanuatu.

For the current status and operative dates of TIEAs, see the Australian Tax Treaties Table on the Treasury website.

When in force, these agreements enable the countries concerned, where relevant, to be removed from the list of "tax havens" (¶22-640), and may entitle residents of those countries to concessional rates of withholding on managed investment trust distributions (¶26-267). The Australian and New Zealand governments have agreed to jointly negotiate tax information exchange agreements wherever possible.

An attempt to prevent the Commissioner from using information obtained under the TIEA with the Cayman Islands failed, despite the fact that a Cayman Islands court had ruled that the release of the information was invalid under their domestic law (*Hua Wang Bank Berhad (No 7)*).

The ATO has released internal guidelines on the exchange of information with foreign revenue authorities about indirect taxes under international tax agreements (PS LA 2016/6). There is specific ATO guidance on obtaining access to US Internal Revenue Service information relating to US territories (PS LA 2006/4). Protocols to the DTAs with countries such as Belgium and Singapore also contain expanded exchange of information provisions (¶22-160).

Domestic authority for collecting and dealing with information collected under current and future international tax agreements is contained in ITA Act s 23. The ATO's internal procedures for obtaining offshore tax-related information are set out in Chapter 3 of its online guidance *Our approach to information gathering*. Note that offshore information notices (¶21-220) may also be used in addition to the DTA exchange-of-information provisions and the TIEAs.

Australia has also entered into Additional Benefits Arrangements (ABAs) with Aruba, the British Virgin Islands, the Cook Islands, Guernsey, Isle of Man, Jersey, Marshall Islands, Mauritius and Samoa. ABAs are a limited version of a comprehensive Double Tax Agreement and are additional to the Tax Information Exchange Agreements which have also been signed with these countries (¶22-140). For current status and operative dates, see the Australian Tax Treaties Table on the Treasury website.

Exchanging financial information

Certain financial institutions (FI) are required to collect and report information to the ATO about financial accounts held by foreign tax residents (TAA 53 Sch 1 Subdiv 396-C). The ATO will exchange information about foreign residents with relevant national tax authorities in accordance with international agreements and in return it will receive information on Australian tax residents with financial accounts held overseas. FIs will report information for the period 1 July 2017 to 31 December 2017 in 2018 and the ATO will exchange information with other tax authorities by the end of 2018. Australia's commitment to participating in the scheme includes the adoption into domestic law of the Common Reporting Standard (CRS), an international reporting framework developed by the OECD.

The ATO has published administrative guidance on its website on CRS reporting obligations from 1 July 2017 (*Automatic exchange of information — guidance material*).

For information about the arrangement with the US for sharing financial information (FATCA), see ¶22-075.

Multilateral treaty to implement BEPS measures

Australia is a signatory to and has ratified the *Multilateral Convention to Implement Tax Treaty Related Measures to Prevent Base Erosion and Profit Shifting* (the MLI). The MLI entered into force for Australia on 1 January 2019. The purpose of the MLI is to implement a series of measures for updating Australia's international tax rules in its tax treaties and lessen the opportunity for tax avoidance by multinational enterprises. The measures have been developed under the OECD/G20 BEPS project.

A summary of the main features of the MLI and Australias final adoption provisions is available on the Australian Treasury website. The detailed list of reservations and notifications made by Australia upon ratification is available on the OECD website. It notes, for specific articles of the MLI, which of Australia's tax treaties will be covered, and any reservations where certain provisions will not apply to certain treaties.

For an article discussing the potential application of the MLI in the context of determining whether a company is a tax resident of Australia or of another jurisdiction, see CCH *Tax Week*¶380 (2019).

In 2019, the ATO began publishing ''synthesised texts'' on the ATO website for the majority of Australia's tax treaties being modified by the MLI. The purpose of a synthesised text is to facilitate understanding of the application of the MLI to a particular tax treaty. It is not an official source of law. The official legal texts of the tax treaty and the MLI take precedence. The synthesised texts are being made accessible on the *Wolters Kluwer Australian Tax Treaties Texts*.

Other international cooperation

In addition, Australia is represented on the Joint International Tax Shelter Information Centre (JITSIC) whose purpose is to increase collaboration and coordinate information about abusive tax transactions. Other members of JITSIC are Canada, the United Kingdom, the United States, Japan, Germany, South Korea, China and France.

In appropriate cases, the government may also have recourse to Australia's international treaties governing mutual assistance in criminal matters (see for example *Dunn & Anor v Australian Crime Commission & Ors*).

[FITR ¶620-220]

Transfer Pricing

¶22-580 Overview of transfer pricing

The transfer pricing provisions address arrangements under which profits are shifted out of Australia, primarily through the mechanism of inter-company and intra-company transfer pricing. The provisions seek to substitute arm's length conditions for the actual conditions operating between entities engaged in transfer pricing and for the tax payable to be based on the arm's length conditions.

A purpose of transfer pricing strategies may be to reduce Australian assessable income or increase allowable deductions in Australia. For example, an Australian resident might sell property at a low price to an affiliate in a low tax country which, in turn, sells the property at its market price. Another transfer pricing technique involves a foreign company borrowing funds at a low interest rate and lending them to a related Australian subsidiary at a higher rate (*Chevron*). Similarly, management or service fees may be inflated, or deductions more appropriately attributable to an overseas entity might be borne to an undue extent by a related resident entity. Moreover, there may be effective profit-shifting not only where separate entities are involved but also where there is only one entity with a number of branch operations.

Sources of transfer pricing rules

The ''traditional'' transfer pricing rules that applied for many years were contained in ITAA36 former Div 13. The government considered that cases such as *SNF* exposed some weaknesses in Div 13.

Reform of the transfer pricing rules was effected in 2 stages, the first being ITAA97 Subdiv 815-A which applied retrospectively to income years starting on or after 1 July 2004. It operated concurrently with former Div 13 but independently of it as a separate domestic transfer pricing measure. The second stage, effective from income years starting on or after 29 June 2013, is in Subdivs 815-B (entities), 815-C (permanent establishments) and 815-D, which replaced the previous provisions and aligned the application of the arm's length principle in Australian law with international transfer pricing standards. For full details, including other related changes, see ¶22-600.

Chevron case: Subdiv 815-A and former Div 13

Former Div 13 and Subdiv 815-A applied to a scheme in which a foreign company borrowed funds at a low interest rate and lent them to a related Australian subsidiary at a higher rate (*Chevron*). The Full Federal Court upheld amended assessments issued to Chevron in respect of income years from 2004 to 2008. In substance, each of the assessments in question was made on the basis that the interest paid by the taxpayer on a loan to a related company incorporated in the US was greater than it would have been under an arm's length dealing between independent parties.

The court found that the conditions for establishing that Chevron had received a ''transfer pricing benefit'' within the meaning of s 815-15(1) had been met. Former Div 13 and Subdiv 815-A both require a comparison between the taxpayer's situation and a hypothetical arm's length arrangement. However, Subdiv 815-A focuses on the ''conditions'' operating between associated entities and entertains the possibility that arm's length parties might have entered into different agreements.

The conditions for making a determination under former s 136AD(3) of former Div 13 had also been met, including the identification of the property acquired (the loan), the consideration for the property acquired and the comparison with the arm's length consideration, as defined, in respect of a hypothetical agreement.

The Commissioner had authority to issue the alternative Div 13 and Subdiv 815-A assessments, as long as only one amount of tax was recovered. However, the court rejected the Commissioner's argument that the assessments could be supported on the basis that Article 9 of the Australia–US double tax agreement was an independent taxing power. Rather, Subdiv 815-A was designed to provide the domestic law power required to give effect to the associated enterprises article in the double tax agreement. Chevron's challenge to the constitutional validity of Subdiv 815-A also failed.

In a more recent transfer pricing case, the Full Federal Court examined the application of the transfer pricing rules in Div 13 and Subdiv 815-A to sales of copper concentrate by an Australian subsidiary of the Glencore Group to its Swiss parent (*Glencore Investment Pty Ltd*). The decision provides guidance on the role of the OECD Transfer Pricing Guidelines, how to identify the hypothetical transaction and the role of experts and comparable transactions.

For further details of the measures in former Div 13 and Subdiv 815-A, see the 61st edition of the *Australian Master Tax Guide* and earlier editions.

ATO compliance and audit policy

Transfer pricing is a ''key compliance focus''. The ATO examines the comparative profitability and performance of multinationals across a wide range of industries and market sizes, including international companies with local headquarters. In recent years, the ATO's focus has included:

- restructures of Australian-based operations to shift functions, assets and risks offshore on a non-arm's length basis, such as the sale of intellectual property at a nominal price

- complex or novel financial arrangements that are not supported by a business need. See also TA 2016/3 (intra-group financing) and PCG 2017/4 (cross-border related party financing arrangements)
- international shipping operations; companies operating in the pharmaceutical industry; businesses with operations in emerging economies
- payment of excessive royalties, interest, guarantee and other fees. See also TA 2016/4 (cross-border leasing)
- provision of services by Australian-headquartered companies to overseas subsidiaries at no charge
- allocating income and expenses to Australian businesses which are inconsistent with the economic activities conducted here, and
- improper use of tax havens and bank secrecy provisions.

While the main focus is on large businesses, about a third of small-to-medium enterprises are involved in international activities, and that profit shifting remains an area of concern. The ATO says that it can assist these businesses with arm's length benchmarking analysis. Failure by an SME to lodge an appropriate International Dealings Schedule (¶22-630), where required, is also a common trigger for ATO review.

The ATO has issued guidance on its compliance approach to transfer pricing issues related to the structuring or relocation of certain business activities and operating risks into a centralised operating model, commonly referred to as a ''hub'' (PCG 2017/1).

International cooperation on transfer pricing enforcement

Revenue authorities around the world are developing their transfer pricing regulation and audit capacity to capture what they regard as their proper share of tax on profits from the rapidly increasing volume of international trade, especially in services and intangibles. OECD members, including Australia, have accepted the ''arm's length'' principle as the basis for their transfer pricing regulation, and a number of acceptable methodologies for determining those prices.

For other developments in relation to *bilateral* international cooperation, information sharing and profit shifting countermeasures, see ¶22-140. For developments in *multilateral* cooperation on transfer pricing, see ¶22-640.

Interactions with other rules

- Subdiv 815-B is not limited by other income tax rules. For example, the debt and equity rules cannot limit the operation of the transfer pricing rules (TD 2019/10).
- The transfer pricing rules have been supplemented by measures enabling the ATO to attack multinational profit shifting, including the multinational anti-avoidance law (s 177DA: ¶30-200) and the diverted profits tax (ss 177H to 177R: ¶30-205).
- Information gathered from multinational companies required to provide country-by-country (CbC) reports will be used to carry out transfer pricing risk assessments (¶22-630).
- For the purpose of applying the ''active income'' test to a CFC, the Commissioner can make adjustments to amounts included in the CFC's accounts to reflect arm's length transfer prices for certain transactions with related parties (¶21-180).
- For the relationship between the transfer pricing rules and the ''safe harbour'' provisions that apply under the thin capitalisation rules, see ¶22-610.

[FITR ¶620-010, ¶620-015]

¶22-600 Transfer pricing: 2013–14 and later

For income years starting on or after 29 June 2013, the transfer pricing rules are contained mainly in:

- Subdiv 815-B: applicable to entities in general (¶22-610)
- Subdiv 815-C: special rules for permanent establishments: (¶22-620), and
- Subdiv 815-D: special rules for trusts and partnerships (¶22-610, ¶22-630).

These replace the previous provisions, including the Div 13 rules and the interim rules in Subdiv 815-A. The main purpose of the current rules is to align the application of the arm's length principle in Australia's domestic law with international transfer pricing standards (currently set out in *OECD Transfer Pricing Guidelines for Multinational Enterprises and Tax Administrations*).

The new rules apply the arm's length principle:

- to relevant dealings between both associated and non-associated entities, and
- to attribute an entity's actual income and expenses between its parts.

The aim is that, regardless of whether the entities are related, the amount brought to tax in Australia from non-arm's length dealings should reflect the economic contribution made by the Australian operations. Thus independent parties engaging in, for example, collusive behaviour or other practices where they are not dealing exclusively in their own economic interests, will not circumvent the rules by reason of their non-association.

Unlike the former transfer pricing rules in Div 13 and in Subdiv 815-A, which both rely on the Commissioner making a determination, the new provisions are ''self-executing'' in their operation. Entities are required to determine their overall tax position that arises from their arrangements with offshore parties on the basis of independent commercial and financial relations or (in the case of the permanent establishment of an entity, on the basis of arm's length profits) occurring between the entities or parts of the entity.

''De minimis'' thresholds also apply to scheme shortfall amounts that arise as a result of a transfer pricing adjustment; below the threshold, scheme administrative penalties will not apply (¶22-630).

For further details of the measures in former Div 13 and Subdiv 815-A, see the 61st edition of the *Australian Master Tax Guide* and earlier editions.

[FITR ¶620-040]

¶22-610 "Transfer pricing benefit" in cross-border transactions

Subdivision 815-B, effective from 2013–14, applies where an entity would otherwise get a tax advantage in Australia from cross-border conditions that are inconsistent with internationally accepted arm's length principles. In this situation, the entity's Australian tax position should instead be determined as if the arm's length conditions in fact existed.

The tax advantage is called a ''transfer pricing benefit''. An entity gets a transfer pricing benefit where:

(1) the entity and another entity have ''commercial or financial relations''

(2) the benefit is from conditions that operate between the entities in connection with those relations (the ''actual conditions'')

(3) the actual conditions differ from the ''arm's length'' conditions

(4) the actual conditions satisfy the ''cross-border'' test, and

(5) if the arm's length conditions had operated:

- the entity's taxable income for an income year would have been greater, or
- its losses of a particular sort — whether a tax loss, film loss or net capital loss — for an income year would have been less, or
- its tax offsets for an income year would have been less, or
- the withholding tax payable by the entity in respect of interest or royalties would have been greater (s 815-120).

If this applies, the arm's length conditions are substituted for the actual conditions in working out the amount of the taxable income, loss, offset or withholding tax, as the case may be (s 815-115). This applies regardless of whether the entity had any purpose or motive of avoiding tax, and regardless of whether the entities are associated.

In the case of a trust or a partnership, references to the "taxable income" are treated as references to the net income. In the case of partnerships, references to tax losses are read as references to partnership losses (Subdiv 815-D: ss 815-305; 815-310). These are purely terminological changes, and do not affect the practical operation of the provisions.

Amendments to assessments to give effect to this provision may be made within 7 years of the date on which the Commissioner gives notice of the assessment to the entity concerned (s 815-150).

Commercial or financial relations

The term "commercial or financial relations" referred to in (1) is not defined in the legislation, but is intended to cover the totality of arrangements relating to the interaction of 2 entities. It could therefore include a single transaction, a series of transactions, a practice, understanding or arrangement, available options, unilateral actions, strategies, or overall profit outcomes achieved by the parties.

Actual conditions

The "actual conditions" referred to in (2) are those that in fact operate in connection with the commercial and financial relations between the parties, and that ultimately affect each of the entities' economic or financial positions. They are not limited to contractual terms. According to TR 2014/6, they may also include the price paid for the sale or purchase of goods or services, the terms of an agreement that have an economic impact on the margin of profits earned by one or both the entities, or a division of profits between the entities.

Arm's length conditions

The "arm's length" conditions referred to in (3) are those that might notionally be expected to operate between independent entities dealing wholly independently with one another in comparable circumstances (s 815-125).

In identifying the arm's length conditions, the method(s) used should be those that are the most appropriate and reliable in the circumstances. The internationally accepted arm's length methodologies are based on the concept of comparability — comparing the prices/margins achieved by associated enterprises in their dealings with each other to those achieved by independent enterprises for the same or similar dealings. The accepted methodologies are:

- the comparable uncontrolled price (CUP) method
- the resale price method
- the cost plus method
- the profit split method, and
- the transactional net margin method.

For the ATO's position on a number of issues relevant to using these pricing methodologies, see TR 97/20.

Relevant factors to take into account in choosing the method(s) include:

- the relative strengths and weaknesses of the methods available in the particular circumstances
- the functions performed, assets used and risks borne by the entities
- the availability of reliable information available to support the method, and
- the degree of comparability between the actual circumstances and the comparable circumstances, ie the notional circumstances postulated by the method used in determining arm's length conditions.

Circumstances are comparable if any differences between them do not materially affect any relevant condition, or if a reasonably accurate adjustment can be made to eliminate the difference. In identifying comparable circumstances, regard should be had to factors such as:

- the functions performed, assets used and risks borne by the entities. The types of functions that may be relevant include those relating to design, manufacture, assembly, research and development, servicing, purchasing, distribution, marketing, advertising, transportation, financing and management
- the characteristics of any property or services transferred, eg physical features, quality, reliability, availability and volume
- the contractual terms
- economic circumstances, eg location, market size, level of competition, availability of substitutes, level of supply and demand, consumer purchasing power, degree of governmental regulation, costs of production and transport, market level and the timing of transactions, and
- the entities' business strategies, eg a business pursuing a market penetration scheme may have temporarily depressed its price below that charged for comparable products.

Where reliable comparability adjustments cannot be made, this may indicate that another method based on different points of comparison should be used.

Identification of the arm's length conditions must normally be based on the commercial or financial relations in which the parties operate. It must also have regard to both the form and substance of these relations (s 815-130). However, there are some exceptions to the basic rule. If an exception applies, the Commissioner may disregard the actual conditions and compare "reconstructed" conditions to the arms' length conditions. The exceptions are:

- first, where there is an inconsistency between the form and the substance, the substance prevails (s 815-130). TR 2014/6 provides the Commissioner's views on determining if there is an inconsistency between the "form" of the relations between entities and their "substance"
- second, if independent entities in comparable circumstances would not have entered into those particular commercial or financial relations, and instead would have entered into relations that are different in substance, the identification should instead be based on those relations. It is not necessary that those relations be *entirely* different (TR 2014/6).

▶ Example

Parties enter into a sale, for a lump sum, of a long-term entitlement to intellectual property rights arising as a result of future research. This arrangement could be considered to be unlikely to have been entered into by independent parties, having regard to the inherent valuation difficulties and the lump sum nature of the payment. In this case, it may instead be appropriate to adjust the terms of the agreement in a commercially rational manner as a continuing research agreement, and identify the arm's length conditions on that basis. (Based on TR 2014/6.)

- third, if independent entities in comparable circumstances would not have entered into commercial or financial relations at all, the identification is based on that absence of relations.

Identifying the arm's length conditions must also be done so as best to achieve consistency with the OECD's *Transfer Pricing Guidelines for Multinational Enterprises and Tax Administrations* (2010) and, from 1 July 2016, the *Aligning Transfer Pricing Outcomes with Value Creation, Actions 8–10 — 2015 Final Reports*, of the OECD (October 2015).

PS LA 2015/3 sets out procedures for ATO officers dealing with the application of the reconstruction power in s 815-130, including tracking cases internally, engaging relevant technical experts and communicating with the taxpayer. For discussion of arm's length dealings in other contexts, see ¶17-045.

Cross-border test

The conditions satisfy the cross-border test in (4) above if they operate in connection with a business that the entity carries on in an area covered by an international tax sharing treaty that Australia has with another country.

Alternatively, the conditions satisfy the test if either or both of the entities concerned:

- is a resident of Australia and the conditions operate at or through an overseas permanent establishment of the entity (¶22-150), or
- is a non-resident and the conditions do not operate solely at or through an Australian permanent establishment of the entity (s 815-120(3)).

▶ Examples

(1) The cross-border test will *not* be satisfied, and a cross-border transfer pricing benefit therefore cannot arise, where:

- an Australian resident sells goods to another Australian resident and no overseas permanent establishment of either entity is involved, or
- the Australian resident sells the goods to a foreign resident, and the purchase is conducted solely through the Australian permanent establishment of that foreign resident.

(2) The cross-border test may be satisfied, and a cross-border transfer benefit therefore may arise, where:

- an Australian resident sells goods to a foreign resident, where the Australian resident is not acting through an overseas permanent establishment and the foreign resident is not acting through an Australian permanent establishment, or
- a foreign resident uses its Australian permanent establishment to sell goods to another foreign resident.

For these purposes, a resident will be treated as a non-resident if, under a tax treaty that Australia has, the entity is deemed to be a resident only of that country.

Consequential adjustments

The application of the cross-border rules to an entity may have consequential effects on other aspects of the entity's tax position, or the tax position of another entity. The Commissioner has the power to make consequential adjustments to that tax position where it would be "fair and reasonable" to do so (s 815-145). For example, if the application of the rules reduces the deduction for foreign interest that the entity has paid on the basis that it exceeds an arm's length amount, the Commissioner may determine that it is fair and reasonable that there be a corresponding reduction in the amount of withholding tax payable on that interest. This would normally be implemented by way of a refund to the foreign recipient. The ATO will provide information to assist taxpayers facing potential customs duty implications as the result of a transfer pricing adjustment made under Subdiv 815-C (PS LA 2016/1).

Amendments to assessments to give effect to a consequential adjustment may be made at any time (s 815-150).

Interaction of transfer pricing and thin capitalisation rules

The "thin capitalisation" rules apply to Australian entities that are foreign controlled or operate internationally, and to foreign entities that operate in Australia (Div 820). They enable deductions to be disallowed where there is an excessive amount of debt capital used to finance the entity's Australian operations (¶22-700). These rules have been used to effect profit shifting through exploitation of the "safe harbour" provisions.

A special rule governs the interaction between these rules and the transfer pricing rules in cases where they both potentially apply (s 815-140). Broadly, the arm's length rate determined under the transfer pricing rules is applied to the entity's actual amount of debt to determine the amount of the transfer pricing benefit, and the thin capitalisation rules are then applied to the amount of debt deductions remaining after the transfer pricing benefit has been negated. If this is still excessive under those rules, the relevant deductions will be reduced further under Div 820. Even if there is no excess debt under the thin capitalisation rules, the transfer pricing rules may still apply. For ATO guidelines, see TR 2014/6.

[FITR ¶620-360 – ¶620-415]

¶22-620 Transfer pricing benefit and permanent establishments

Subdivision 815-C, effective from 2013–14, sets out an additional way in which a transfer pricing benefit can arise. It applies where an entity that is operating a permanent establishment (PE) in Australia (¶22-150) obtains a tax advantage that it would not have obtained if the PE had been a separate entity dealing with the operating entity on an arm's length basis. The effect is that, in such a situation, the Australian tax position of the operating entity will be determined as if the parties were acting at arm's length.

An entity gets a transfer pricing benefit from the attribution of profits to a permanent establishment of the entity where:

(1) the actual amount of profits attributed to the PE differs from the arm's length profits for the PE, and

(2) if the arm's length profits had been attributed instead of the actual profits:

- the entity's taxable income for an income year would have been greater
- its losses of a particular sort — whether a tax loss, film loss or net capital loss — for an income year would have been less, or
- its tax offsets for an income year would have been less (s 815-220).

If this applies, the arm's length profits are notionally substituted for the actual profits in working out the amount of the taxable income, loss or offset, as the case may be (s 815-215). This applies regardless of whether the entity had any purpose or motive of avoiding tax.

In the case of a trust or a partnership, references to the "taxable income" are treated as references to the net income. In the case of partnerships, references to losses are read as including partnership losses (Subdiv 815-D: ss 815-305; 815-310).

Amendments to assessments to give effect to these provisions may be made within 7 years of the date on which the Commissioner gives notice of the assessment to the entity concerned (s 815-240).

The ATO has set out the circumstances in which internal derivatives that represent arm's length dealings can be used as an appropriate proxy for the purposes of allocating or attributing a bank's income, expenses or profit under Subdiv 815-C (PCG 2017/8).

Arm's length profits

The arm's length profits for the PE are worked out by allocating the actual expenditure and income of the operating entity between the PE and that entity on a notional arm's length basis (s 815-225). This means that the profits attributed to the PE are those which the PE might be expected to make if:

- the PE was a distinct and separate entity
- its activities and circumstances, including its functions, assets used and risks, were those of the separate entity, and
- the conditions that operated between that separate entity and the operating entity were the ''arm's length conditions'' that would apply (as explained at ¶22-600).

In this calculation, the operating entity's actual expenditure is taken to include losses and outgoings, and the actual income includes any amounts that would be assessable income of the entity.

This approach reflects the ''relevant business activity'' approach to the attribution of profits to PEs that is currently incorporated into Australia's tax treaties.

The arm's length profits, and the arm's length conditions, must be determined so as best to achieve consistency with:

- the OECD's *Model Tax Convention on Income and Capital*, and its Commentaries, relating to Art 7 (business profits) *before* its 2010 revision, as modified by regulations. The reason that the 2010 revision of Art 7 is not to be taken into account is that the revision adopts the ''functionally separate entity'' approach. The government has yet to determine whether it will change its current relevant business entity approach to reflect the revised OECD position
- the OECD's *Transfer Pricing Guidelines for Multinational Enterprises and Tax Administrations* (2010 revision), as modified by regulations
- the *Aligning Transfer Pricing Outcomes with Value Creation, Actions 8–10 — 2015 Final Reports* of the OECD published on 5 October 2015. Reference to this document only applies for income years starting on or after 1 July 2016, and
- any document prescribed by regulations (s 815-235).

The arm's length profits for the PE in Australia are taken to be attributable to sources in Australia, and the arm's length profits for the PE in a tax treaty country are taken to be attributable to sources in that country (s 815-230).

From 1 January 2016, ITAA36 s 177DA strikes down schemes by multinational entities to avoid the attribution of business profits to a taxable permanent establishment in Australia (¶30-200).

[FITR ¶620-440 – ¶620-480]

¶22-630 Transfer pricing records, penalties and thresholds

If an entity becomes liable for additional tax as a result of the Commissioner amending its assessment to give effect to the transfer pricing provisions, the entity also becomes liable for an administrative penalty. The same applies where the Commissioner serves the entity with a notice that additional withholding tax is payable (TAA Sch 1 s 284-145).

The penalty is based on the transfer pricing shortfall amount. This is the amount of additional tax and withholding tax payable as a result of the amendment or the serving of the notice (TAA Sch 1 s 284-150). The penalty is normally calculated as 25% of this amount, but is reduced to 10% where the entity treated the transfer pricing rules as applying in a way that was "reasonably arguable". These figures are increased to 50% and 25% respectively where it is reasonable to conclude that the entity entered into the scheme with the sole or dominant purpose (¶30-170) of obtaining a transfer pricing benefit for themselves or another entity (TAA Sch 1 s 284-160).

No penalty is imposed where the scheme shortfall amount is equal to, or less, than the "reasonably arguable threshold" (TAA Sch 1 s 284-165). This is $10,000 or 1% of income tax payable by the entity for the income year. For trusts and partnerships, the threshold is $20,000 or 2% of the entity's net income for the year (TAA Sch 1 s 284-90). For ATO guidelines on assessing penalties, see PS LA 2014/2.

Increased penalties

The administrative penalties that can be applied under TAA Sch 1 s 284-155 to large multinational companies that enter tax avoidance or profit shifting schemes have been doubled (¶29-180). The increased penalties apply to scheme benefits obtained by "significant global entities" (¶30-200) in relation to an income year commencing on or after 1 July 2015. The higher penalties do not apply where the taxpayer has a reasonably arguable position (¶29-160).

The amount of administrative penalty that applies for significant global entities that do not lodge a return, notice, statement, etc with the Commissioner on time increased with effect on or after 1 July 2017. The base penalty amount is multiplied by 500 if an entity is a significant global entity at the relevant time. A maximum penalty of $525,000 could apply if the lodgment is more than 16 weeks late. The penalties imposed on significant global entities under s 284-75, relating to statements and failing to give documents necessary to determine tax-related liabilities on time, have been doubled, with effect on or after 1 July 2017.

Documentation requirements

Transfer pricing arrangements must be properly documented in order to comply with the normal tax record-keeping requirements (¶9-045).

In addition, where the entity may be liable for an administrative penalty under the transfer pricing rules, it will not be able to obtain a reduction of that penalty on the grounds that it has a "reasonably arguable position" (¶29-160) unless it complies with specific documentation requirements (TAA Sch 1 s 284-250). These require that the entity keep records that:

- are prepared before the time by which the entity lodges its tax return for the relevant income year. According to TR 2014/8, this requires that the records be contemporaneous, ie they must actually exist and be in the entity's possession or ready and available to it at that time
- are in English, or readily accessible or convertible into English, and
- explain the particular way in which the transfer pricing provision applies (or does not apply), and why the application of the provisions in that way achieves consistency with the relevant OECD guidelines and regulations.

For example, the records must demonstrate matters such as the arm's length conditions, the actual conditions, the comparable circumstances, the particulars of the method used and its effect in the particular circumstances (TAA Sch 1 s 284-255). For detailed ATO guidelines, see TR 2014/8. The ATO has developed simplified transfer pricing record keeping options for eligible taxpayers (PCG 2017/2). The options reflect the types of transactions or activities considered to be low risk in the context of international related party dealings. For the ATO's policy when considering whether to undertake transfer pricing compliance action where entities have applied one or more of the simplification options in PCG 2017/2, see PS LA 2014/3.

If the entity has complied with these specific transfer pricing documentation requirements, that will be sufficient to ensure that it meets the normal tax record-keeping requirements, but the reverse does not necessarily apply.

Failure to have appropriate documentation may also attract ATO audit attention (*Daihatsu Australia Pty Ltd*).

Country-by-country reporting

For income years starting on or after 1 January 2016, large multinational companies are required to provide ''country-by-country'' (CbC) statements to the Commissioner annually (ITAA 1997 Subdiv 815-E). CbC reporting implements OECD guidelines and assists the Commissioner to carry out transfer pricing risk assessments. Entities that were ''significant global entities'' (entities with global annual income of $1 billion or more: ITAA97 Subdiv 960-U) in the previous income year must provide the following statements within 12 months of the end of the income year (or an allowed replacement reporting period) to which the statement relates:

- a master file providing an overview of the multinational enterprise group business, including the nature of its global business operations, its overall transfer pricing policies, and its global allocation of income and economic activity

- a local file focusing on specific transactions between the reporting entity and its associated enterprises in other countries, as well as the amounts involved in those transactions, and the entity's analysis of the transfer pricing determinations that it has made, and

- a CbC report containing certain information relating to the global allocation of the multinational enterprise's income and taxes paid together with certain indicators of the location of economic activity within the multinational enterprise group.

The ATO only accepts electronic lodgments of CbC reporting statements using one of the following channels:

- Business Portal or the Tax Agent Portal, using file transfer, or

- Standard Business Reporting (SBR) using SBR-enabled software.

Details of the content of these statements is set out in Chapter V of the Organisation for Economic Cooperation and Development's *Guidance on Transfer Pricing Documentation and Country-by-Country Reporting*. The ATO has developed guidelines for completing the local file (the *Local file — high level design*, on the ATO website). Among other things, the guidelines state that a company lodging a local file and meeting certain conditions does not need to complete some parts of the International Dealings Schedule (IDS).

A significant global entity must be an Australian resident, or a foreign entity with an Australian permanent establishment. The Commissioner may exempt specific entities or a class of entity from the reporting requirement. An entity may be exempted from providing one or more of the 3 reports. For example, a local entity may not need to provide the CbC report if its parent has provided it in another jurisdiction and the ATO can obtain it under an information sharing arrangement. The explanatory memorandum notes that an entity may be able to use content in documentation meeting TAA Sch 1 Subdiv 284-E requirements to produce the local file.

Entities may be liable for penalties where, for example, they fail to lodge statements on time or the statements contain false or misleading information.

A number of documents have been issued to assist taxpayers with implementing CbC, including: (a) the OECD's *Guidance on the Implementation of Country-by-Country (CbC) Reporting*; (b) the ATO's *Country by Country reporting* page, with links to other CbC guidance; (c) guidance on the ATO website about exercising the discretion to grant exemptions from CbC reporting obligations (*Country-by-Country reporting: Exemption Guidance*); (d) *Country-by-Country reporting guidance*; and (e) *Local file — Part B: Guidance on providing International Related Party agreements*, *Local file instructions* and *Local file — high level design*.

Australia is a signatory to the Multilateral Competent Authority Agreement on the Exchange of CbC reports (the CbC MCAA). The OECD website contains a useful table detailing the jurisdictions that have committed to CbC reporting, the status of domestic legislation to implement CbC, first reporting periods and whether local filing is required. Australia and the United States signed a bilateral Competent Authority Arrangement in August 2017 to exchange CbC reports.

A significant global entity that is a company must also give the Commissioner a general purpose financial statement if it does not lodge one with the Australian Securities and Investments Commission.

International Dealings Schedule

Taxpayers with international dealings that exceed certain thresholds must lodge additional documentation with their annual returns. This must be in the form of an *International Dealings Schedule* (''IDS''). The IDS is available on the ATO website (see ''International Dealings Schedule'' and instructions for the relevant year).

[FITR ¶620-070, ¶620-550, ¶762-733]

¶22-640 International cooperation on transfer pricing

The Australian Government is actively involved in dialogue and cooperation with governments and revenue authorities to target fraud, money laundering and tax evasion. For other developments in relation to international cooperation, information sharing and profit shifting countermeasures, see ¶22-165.

BEPS project

In October 2015, the OECD released a final package of tax reform measures under the Base Erosion and Profit Shifting (BEPS) Project. The OECD and G20 countries started the BEPS project in 2013 to address what is thought to be very significant losses in global corporate income tax revenues caused by aggressive tax planning by some multinational enterprises (MNEs), the interaction of domestic tax rules, lack of transparency and coordination between tax administrations, limited enforcement resources and harmful tax practices (eg special tax deals and concessions offered by countries). The final package of measures is the result of work on 15 Actions — problem areas identified by the OECD and G20 countries for action by participating states domestically and through treaty provisions.

The Australian Government has implemented a number of BEPS reform measures in domestic law.

Hybrid mismatch rules

ITAA 1997 Div 832 implements part of the OECD hybrid mismatch rules by preventing entities that are liable to income tax in Australia from being able to avoid income tax, or obtain a double non-taxation benefit, by exploiting differences between the tax treatment of entities and instruments across different countries. The hybrid mismatch rules apply to income years starting on or after 1 January 2019.

Broadly, a hybrid mismatch arises if an entity enters into a scheme that gives rise to a payment, and the payment gives rise to a ''deduction/non-inclusion mismatch'' or a ''deduction/deduction mismatch''.

Division 832 defines a set of factual scenarios to which the hybrid mismatch rules apply. If a relevant mismatch arises, it is neutralised by disallowing a deduction or including an amount in assessable income. An integrity rule targets the misuse of the rules by multinational groups using interposed country conduit type vehicles to invest into Australia, as an alternative to investing using hybrid instruments or entities.

The rules also limit the scope of the exemption for foreign branch income and prevent a deduction from arising for payments made by an Australian branch of a foreign bank to its head office in some circumstances.

Imputation benefits and foreign equity distributions

The rules deny imputation benefits on franked distributions made by an Australian corporate tax entity if all or part of the distribution gives rise to a foreign income tax deduction. In addition, certain foreign equity distributions received, directly or indirectly, by an Australian corporate tax entity are prevented from being non-assessable non-exempt income if all or part of the distribution gives rise to a foreign income tax deduction.

PCG 2018/7 sets out the ATOs compliance approach under Pt IVA of the ITAA 1936 in relation to restructures that preserve Australian tax benefits that would otherwise be disallowed under the hybrid mismatch rules. See also LCR 2019/3 (the meaning of a ''structured arrangement'' and related terms), PCG 2019/6 (guidance for taxpayers assessing the risk of the rules applying) and *Draft* LCR 2019/D1 (the targeted integrity rule).

Exchanging financial information

Australia has committed to participating in an OECD scheme for the automatic exchange of financial information between tax authorities (¶22-165). The international information exchange scheme is not formally part of the BEPS process but has been undertaken in parallel with it.

Tax havens

A tax haven is a country, region or state with a secretive tax or financial system that has minimal or low taxes for non-residents. Tax havens are used for tax evasion or tax avoidance, for example, by diverting income to an entity in a haven that is not taxable in Australia.

Tax havens may also be exploited for other reasons, including money laundering, the concealment of assets and breaches of Australian financial laws and regulations. The phrase ''secrecy haven'' has been coined to reflect the potential use of such places for a range of activities that is wider than tax avoidance or evasion.

Some tax provisions dealing with international transactions specifically recognise the existence of tax havens. For example, under the controlled foreign companies (CFC) rules, Australian shareholders are taxed on an accruals basis in respect of the income of some controlled foreign companies. The rules are tougher for companies located in tax havens (¶21-110). Other anti-avoidance provisions apply generally to international transactions but may reach dealings involving tax havens, such as the transfer pricing measures, thin capitalisation and value shifting that deal with arrangements to shift profits or value out of Australia. Part IVA may also apply to international arrangements.

The ATO uses a range of methods to detect and deal with tax haven arrangements and combat tax avoidance and evasion, including:

- tax return information-gathering tools like the *International Dealings Schedule* (IDS) and the *Reportable Tax Position Schedule* for company taxpayers (¶3-045)
- the Serious Financial Crime Taskforce, a multi-agency taskforce that conducts investigations and prosecutions addressing superannuation and investment fraud, identity crime and tax evasion
- the Financial account information obtained under the Common Reporting Standard (¶22-165) and the FATCA agreement with the US (¶22-075), and country-by-country (CbC) information about large multinational companies (¶22-630)
- the promoter penalty legislation targeted at promoters of tax avoidance and evasion schemes (¶30-300)
- working with international forums, such as the Organisation for Economic Co-operation and Development. Negotiating with cooperative tax havens to exchange relevant information under agreements such as Tax Information Exchange Agreements (TIEA) and Additional Benefits Agreements (listed at ¶22-165)
- taxpayer alerts (¶30-170) and other information that give early warning of significant new and emerging offshore tax schemes.

[FITR ¶620-220, ¶620-223; FTR ¶961-310]

¶22-650 Advance pricing arrangements

An Advance Pricing Arrangement (APA) is an agreement between the taxpayer, the ATO and, where appropriate, one or more foreign tax authorities regarding the income tax treatment of international transactions, agreements or arrangements between related parties or associates.

APAs give taxpayers the opportunity to reach agreement with the ATO on the method of applying the arm's length principle to their cross-border dealings on a prospective basis. Potential advantages include predictability about the tax treatment of relevant transactions, reduced compliance and record keeping burdens and, potentially, minimising the likelihood of double taxation. The term of an APA will usually be between 3 and 5 years.

A *unilateral* APA is concluded between the taxpayer and the ATO. A *bilateral* APA is made by the ATO and the relevant tax administration of a tax treaty partner, concerning the cross-border transactions of the taxpayer and third parties. A *multilateral* APA can be concluded between the ATO and more than one other tax treaty partner.

The APA process is set out in PS LA 2015/4, covering what happens from the commencement of discussions between the ATO and the applicant before lodgment of a formal application, to making the application and developing and concluding the APA, to monitoring compliance with the concluded agreement.

Collateral issues must be identified, addressed and resolved concurrently with the development of the APA and before it is concluded. Collateral issues are other tax or administrative issues relevant to and potentially affecting the outcome of the APA. Examples include the application of the CFC rules, carry-forward losses, Pt IVA or specific anti-avoidance provisions.

An APA will contain the agreement of the parties on at least the following matters:

- the names, addresses and countries of residence for taxation purposes of the parties
- terms of the APA
- the cross-border dealings covered
- the agreed transfer pricing methodology and how it is to be applied
- the arm's length amount, rate, range or other arm's length outcome
- critical assumptions which if breached must be disclosed to the ATO
- definitions of key terms
- the accounting standards on which the taxpayer's financial statements are based, and
- procedures for making a compensating adjustment, if necessary.

Other matters covered by PS LA 2015/4 include:

- renewing, revising or cancelling an APA
- roll-back (the ATO may use information gleaned from an APA application to resolve issues from prior years)
- the interaction between APAs and ATO audits and reviews, and
- the roles of ATO officers handling APA matters.

[FTR ¶70-180]

Thin Capitalisation

¶22-700 Thin capitalisation: overview

The thin capitalisation (''thin cap'') rules in Div 820 are intended to prevent multinational enterprises shifting profits out of Australia by funding their Australian operations with high levels of debt and relatively little equity in order to reduce their Australian taxable income.

The thin cap rules achieve their purpose by limiting deductions for interest expense and borrowing costs (''debt deductions'') where debt-to-equity gearing ratios exceed prescribed debt limits. If Australian operations have debt above the maximum allowed, debt deductions will be disallowed. The ATO is reviewing arrangements that artificially increase the maximum allowable debt limit (TA 2016/1) or under which a ''debt interest'' is used to reduce ''debt capital'' for thin capitalisation purposes (TA 2016/9). An entitys debt capital must be valued in its entirety in the manner required by the accounting standards, regardless of its classification (TD 2020/2).

A ''debt deduction'' is a cost incurred in connection with a ''debt interest'' that would otherwise be deductible, including interest, discount on a security and certain fees (eg ID 2003/973), but excluding foreign currency losses, salary or wages and rental expenses. Special rules apply for interest-free debt. Debt deductions disallowed under the thin cap rules cannot be added to the cost base of a CGT asset.

There are a number of different debt limits for calculating the maximum debt allowed including the ''safe harbour'' limit, ''arm's-length'' limit and the ''worldwide gearing'' limit. These debt limits vary depending on the kind of entity. Entities can choose the debt limit to use. Consideration of which debt limit to use will depend on which one gives the highest deduction and which one is easiest to apply.

Companies, partnerships and trusts subject to the thin cap rules must complete an International Dealings Schedule (IDS) as part of their self-assessment obligations (¶22-630).

An anti-avoidance measure targets, for income years starting on or after 1 July 2018, double gearing structures by lowering the associate entity threshold from 50% or more to 10% or more, to determine associate entity debt, associate entity equity and the associate entity excess amount for interests in trusts and partnerships. This prevents the use by foreign investors of multiple layers of flow-through entities to convert trading income into favourably taxed interest income.

With effect from 8 May 2018, an entity must comply with accounting standards in determining and calculating the value of its assets, liabilities (including debt capital) and equity capital. The entity must use the value of the assets, liabilities and equity capital in the entity's financial statements and may not revalue assets specifically for thin capitalisation purposes.

On or after 1 July 2019, non-ADI foreign controlled Australian tax consolidated groups and multiple entry consolidated groups that have foreign investments or operations are treated as both outward investing and inward investing entities.

[FITR ¶624-100 – ¶624-600]

¶22-710 Entities who may be subject to the thin cap rules

The thin cap rules may affect the following entities (companies, trusts, partnerships, unincorporated bodies):

- Australian entities that are foreign controlled
- foreign entities that either invest directly into Australia or operate a business through an Australian permanent establishment
- Australian entities that control foreign entities or operate a business through overseas permanent establishments and associate entities.

The definition of "Australian entity" ensures that the rules, for the most part, impact only upon companies, trusts and partnerships. This is because:

- a foreign-controlled Australian entity can only be a foreign-controlled Australian company, trust or partnership, and
- an Australian-controlled foreign entity can only be a controlled foreign company, trust or corporate limited partnership.

An Australian branch of a foreign bank or of a foreign non-bank financial entity can be part of a group's head company or part of a single resident company for the purpose of determining their thin cap position. This results in the branch being treated as a separate entity from the owner of the branch, ie similar to a subsidiary.

[FITR ¶624-100 – ¶624-325]

¶22-720 Entities not subject to the thin cap rules

The thin cap rules do not apply where the assets and liabilities concerned are wholly or principally private or domestic. The thin cap rules also do not apply to the following taxpayers:

(a) taxpayers and their associates who claim total annual debt deductions (eg interest expenses) that do not exceed a "de minimis" threshold (s 820-35). This threshold is $2 million for income years commencing on or after 1 July 2014 and $250,000 for previous years

(b) outward investing Australian entities where the sum of its average Australian assets and those of its associates represent 90% or more of the sum of its average total assets (including those of the associates) (s 820-37). This exempts Australian entities whose operations are substantially in Australia

(c) certain special purpose entities established for the purposes of managing some or all of the economic risk associated with assets, liabilities or investments where at least 50% of its assets are funded by debt interests and the entity is an insolvency remote special purpose entity (s 820-39). The ATO interprets this exclusion as potentially extending to a special purpose entity that seeks finance for the project established as part of the securitised licence structure used in some social infrastructure Public Private Partnerships (TD 2014/18).

[FITR ¶624-100 – ¶624-325]

¶22-730 Operation of thin cap rules

The thin cap rules apply in different ways depending on whether the entity is an inward investor (those controlled by non-residents) or outward investing entity (those with offshore investments) and whether it is an authorised deposit-taking entity (ADI), a financial entity or a general entity.

Financial entities who are not ADIs may elect to be treated as ADIs. A general entity is one that is not an ADI or a financial entity.

Where an entity is both an inward investing and outward investing entity, such as a foreign controlled Australian resident entity that controls a foreign entity, then the outward investing entity rules apply.

Application to ADIs

For authorised deposit-taking institutions (ADIs) such as banks, debt deductions will be reduced where the equity capital used to fund the Australian operations is less than the minimum equity requirement.

For *inward investing ADIs* (ie foreign ADIs with Australian permanent establishments), the minimum amount of equity capital is the lesser of:

- the safe harbour capital amount, ie 6% of Australian risk-weighted assets (4% for years previous to the income year commencing 1 July 2014), and
- the arm's length capital amount, determined in a similar manner to the arm's length debt amount for non-ADIs. The analysis results in a notional amount that represents what would reasonably be expected to have been the entity's minimum arm's length capital funding of its Australian business throughout the year.

Outward investing ADIs (ie Australian ADI entities with foreign investments) have the same requirement, but must also have capital to match certain other Australian assets. The minimum amount of equity capital for outward investing ADIs is the lesser of:

- the safe harbour capital amount ie 6% of the Australian risk-weighted assets (4% for years previous to the income year commencing 1 July 2014). For an example, see ID 2005/252
- the arm's length capital amount. This is a notional amount that represents what would reasonably be expected to have been the bank's minimum arm's length capital funding of its Australian business throughout the year, and
- the worldwide capital amount. This will allow an Australian ADI with foreign investments to fund its Australian investments with a minimum capital ratio equal to 100% of the Tier 1 capital ratio of its worldwide group (80% for years previous to the income year commencing 1 July 2014).

For the application of the above rules to the funding of a permanent establishment of a multinational bank, see TR 2005/11.

Application to non-ADIs

For non-ADIs, debt deductions will be reduced where the amount of debt used to fund an entity's Australian operations exceeds a specified maximum. This varies according to whether the entity is a financial institution and also whether it is an inward or outward investing entity.

For *inward investing non-ADI foreign entities with Australian investments*, the maximum amount of debt will be the greatest amount determined under:

- the safe harbour debt test
- the arm's length debt test, or
- the worldwide gearing debt test (s 820-190).

Under the *safe harbour debt test*, the amount of debt used to finance the Australian investments will be treated as being excessive when it is greater than that permitted by the safe harbour gearing limit of 1.5:1 (3:1 for years previous to the income year commencing 1 July 2014). For financial entities, this safe harbour gearing ratio only applies to their non-lending business. An on-lending rule will operate to remove from the calculations any debt that is on-lent to third parties or that is used for similar financing activities. The application of this on-lending rule will be limited by an additional safe harbour gearing ratio of 15:1 (20:1 for years previous to the income year commencing 1 July 2014) which will apply to the financial entity's total business. There are also special rules that result in higher allowable gearing ratios for financial entities that have assets which are allowed to be fully debt funded. For the purposes of the test, assets and liabilities are determined in accordance with accounting standards (TR 2002/20).

The *arm's length debt* amount is determined by conducting an analysis of the entity's activities and funding to determine a notional amount that represents what would reasonably be expected to have been the entity's maximum arm's length debt funding of its Australian business during the period. The ATO's provisional views on the arm's length debt test and its compliance approach are found in TR 2020/4 and PCG 2020/7 respectively.

The *worldwide gearing debt test* for inward investors (including those that are also outward investors) applies only from the income year commencing 1 July 2014 onwards. It does not apply if the entity's statement worldwide equity or assets (as defined) is nil or negative, or if audited consolidated financial statements do not exist. In addition, the entity must satisfy an asset threshold, ie its Australian assets must represent no more than 50% of the consolidated group's worldwide assets. Application of the test is optional — if, for example, the entity has applied the safe harbour test and determined that it has not exceeded its maximum allowable debt, it does not need to also apply the worldwide gearing debt test. The calculation of the worldwide gearing test amount depends on the type of entity (ss 820-216 to 820-219; Subdiv 820-JA).

For *outward non-ADI Australian entities with foreign investments*, the maximum debt amount will be the greatest amount determined under:

- the safe harbour debt test
- the arm's length debt test, or
- the worldwide gearing debt test.

The safe harbour limit and the arm's length test are fundamentally the same as those described for inward investing non-ADI foreign entities with Australian investments. They take account, however, of the amount and form of investment in the Australian non-ADI's controlled foreign investments.

The *worldwide gearing debt test* for outward investors allows an Australian entity with foreign investments to fund its Australian investments with gearing of up to 100% (120% for years previous to the income year commencing 1 July 2014) of the gearing of the worldwide group that it controls. However, this test is not available if the Australian entity is itself controlled by foreign entities.

For an example of the application of the rules, see ID 2002/942.

[FITR ¶624-155 – ¶624-325]

¶22-740 Interaction of thin cap rules with other taxing provisions

Debt/equity provisions

The thin cap rules require that a distinction is drawn between ''equity interests'' and ''debt interests'' under ITAA97 Div 974 (¶23-100). Where related schemes (¶23-105) that give rise to a debt interest in an entity include a hedging scheme (eg an interest rate swap used to hedge a loan), that scheme is disregarded in working out debt interest for thin capitalisation purposes (if the remaining scheme, without the hedging scheme, still gives rise to a debt interest). This means, for example, that any losses associated with the swap are not debt deductions under ITAA97 s 820-40.

Transfer pricing provisions

The thin cap rules are subject to the transfer pricing provisions. This means that even if the taxpayer falls within a safe harbour debt limit, their claim for deductions may still be adjusted or denied under the transfer pricing provisions: see ¶22-610.

Consolidated groups

The head company of a consolidated or MEC group containing one or more ADIs may apply the thin capitalisation rules as if the group did not contain an ADI, where all the ADIs in the group are specialist credit card institutions. Each ''specialist credit card institution'' will instead be treated as if it was a financial entity. The head company of a consolidated or MEC group or a single Australian resident company that cannot consolidate, that chooses to treat as part of itself the Australian permanent establishments of a foreign bank (the ''establishment entity''), can apply the thin capitalisation rules as if the head company or single company was an outward investing entity (non-ADI) or inward investing entity (non-ADI), where, if any of the head company, single company or establishment entity is an ADI, they are also a specialist credit card institution. The exemption from the thin capitalisation rules for the head company of a consolidated group does not apply where all of the ADIs in the group are specialist credit card institutions.

[FITR ¶624-100, ¶624-375]

Chapter 23 Financial Arrangements • TOFA

Introduction

¶23-000 Taxation of financial arrangements

This chapter discusses the taxation of financial arrangements and products. It also discusses the obligation of financial services entities, gambling service providers, bullion dealers and accountants/lawyers to report significant cash transactions and suspect transactions to AUSTRAC.

This chapter does not deal with all of the tax rules applicable to the taxation of financial arrangements and products. Other provisions of ITAA97 and ITAA36 which may apply include the following:

Topic	Source
Dividend imputation	¶4-400
Capital gains tax	¶11-000 and ¶12-000
Depreciating assets	¶17-000
Withholding tax	¶22-000
Tax-avoidance	¶30-000
Stamp duty	¶37-000
Taxation of interest	¶10-470 (assessability) and ¶16-740 (deductibility)
Derivation of income (such as interest and other income from financial products) and incurring of deductions for interest and other expenses	¶9-050, ¶9-100 and ¶16-748
Taxation treatment of returns from insurance products	¶10-210 – ¶10-240
Treatment of financing unit trust distributions	¶10-465
GST treatment of financial supplies	¶34-190

Taxation of Financial Arrangements (TOFA)

¶23-020 Overview of the TOFA regime

ITAA97 Div 230 contains comprehensive rules for the taxation of gains and losses arising on certain financial arrangements (also known as the ‘‘TOFA regime’’). The Division generally applies to large taxpayers although its scope is not limited to these taxpayers.

Division 230 applies in priority to other taxation rules unless specifically provided otherwise. Where Div 230 does not apply, taxpayers will need to consider whether other provisions of ITAA97 and ITAA36 apply, including the rules applicable to arrangements for financing the acquisition of income-producing assets, eg leasing (¶23-200 – ¶23-270), and the rules dealing with specific financial products such as discounted securities and traditional securities (¶23-300 – ¶23-430).

Division 230 applies to financial arrangements that taxpayers start to have in income years commencing on or after 1 July 2010. For transitional rules and elections, see the 2012 edition of the *Australian Master Tax Guide*.

When considering the application of Div 230 the following questions arise:

- *Is the taxpayer subject to Div 230?* (¶23-025) — Division 230 taxes net gains and losses arising from financial arrangements entered into by entities who meet certain asset and turnover threshold tests. Division 230 also applies to entities (including individuals) that may not meet the threshold tests, but who have entered into financial arrangements that are ''qualifying securities'' (¶23-320). Taxpayers (including individuals) not automatically subject to Div 230 can elect to apply the Division to gains and losses arising on their financial arrangements.

- *Is the arrangement a Div 230 financial arrangement?* (¶23-030) — An arrangement is a Div 230 financial arrangement if it is a cash settlable legal or equitable right to receive or provide a financial benefit (¶23-110) or a combination thereof. The following are also financial arrangements: foreign currency, non-equity shares, commodities or offsetting commodity contracts held by traders, certain equity interests, and rights or obligations in relation to equity interests.

- *How are gains and losses on Div 230 financial arrangements taxed?* (¶23-035) — In general, gains and losses are treated as arising on income account. However, certain gains and losses on financial arrangements are excluded from the taxation provisions in Div 230 and are instead taxed under other provisions of ITAA36 or ITAA97, eg gains and losses on leasing transactions.

- *What are the ways in which gains and losses on Div 230 financial arrangements are recognised?* (¶23-040) — Gains and losses on financial arrangements are recognised using one of 6 prescribed methods: compounding accruals method, realisation method, fair value method, foreign exchange retranslation method, hedging method, or financial reports method. When a financial arrangement is disposed of or ceases to be a financial arrangement a balancing adjustment may need to be made.

Proposed amendments to the TOFA regime

The 2016–17 Budget included an announcement that the TOFA regime would be redesigned and reformed to reduce its scope, decrease compliance costs and increase certainty. The proposed reform is intended to address concerns that the current rules, which are designed for the largest taxpayers, apply to a significant group of smaller taxpayers and have not delivered the envisaged compliance cost savings and simplification benefits. The reformed rules were scheduled to take effect for income years beginning on or after 1 January 2018, however, this start date has been deferred with the government announcing in December 2017, and again in the 2018–19 Budget, that additional time is required to design the new rules. The reformed rules will contain 4 key elements:

- a ''closer link to accounting'' that strengthens and simplifies the existing link between tax and accounting in the TOFA rules

- simplified accruals and realisation rules, which will significantly reduce the number of taxpayers subject to the TOFA rules, and will reduce the arrangements where spreading of gains and losses is required under TOFA and simplify required calculations

- a new tax hedging regime that is easier to access, encompasses more types of risk management arrangements (including risk management of a portfolio of assets) and removes the direct link to financial accounting
- simplified rules for the taxation of gains and losses on foreign currency to preserve current tax outcomes, but which streamlines the legislation.

[FITR ¶221-500, ¶221-510]

¶23-025 Taxpayers subject to the TOFA regime

The following entities must use the TOFA rules in Div 230 when self-assessing the net gains and losses arising on Div 230 financial arrangements to which they are a party:

- authorised deposit-taking institutions, securitisation vehicles and financial sector entities required to register under the *Financial Sector (Collection of Data) Act 2001*, with an aggregated turnover of $20 million or more
- superannuation entities, managed investment schemes, and foreign entities similar to managed investment schemes, if the value of their assets is $100 million or more
- other entities (not individuals) with aggregated turnover of $100 million or more, or assets of $300 million or more, or financial assets of $100 million or more.

Once an entity satisfies an applicable threshold, Div 230 will continue to apply even if that entity's turnover or value of assets subsequently falls below the relevant threshold.

In the case of tax consolidated groups, the entity being tested is the head company, which includes all its subsidiary members. In working out a tax consolidated group's turnover or value of assets, intra-tax consolidated group transactions and assets are not recognised.

Regardless of the above thresholds, Div 230 will apply to an arrangement held by any entity (including an individual) if it is a ''qualifying security'' within the meaning of ITAA36 Div 16E. A qualifying security is a security whose term at the time of issue will, or is reasonably likely to, exceed one year and is reasonably likely to result in the sum of the payments (excluding periodic interest) exceeding the issue price. For a fixed return security, this excess is greater than 1.5% of the sum of the payments multiplied by the number of years in the term of the security (¶23-320).

Electing into Div 230 regime

Taxpayers not automatically subject to Div 230 can elect to apply Div 230 to all their financial arrangements by completing a form *TOFA 3 & 4 election for Division 230 to apply*. It is not necessary to notify the ATO of the election but taxpayers should keep a copy of it with their tax records. Once an election is made it cannot be revoked and will apply to all financial arrangements that the taxpayer starts to have in the income year in which the election is made and all future income years. Reasons for making the election could include the ability to recognise losses on financial arrangements earlier, and to align gains/losses arising on hedging financial arrangements with those arising on the hedged item.

[FITR ¶221-510]

¶23-030 Meaning of financial arrangements

Division 230 applies to financial arrangements that are ''Div 230 financial arrangements''. A Div 230 financial arrangement is an arrangement where the legal or equitable rights to receive or obligations to provide a financial benefit (¶23-110) are cash settlable. An arrangement will not be a Div 230 financial arrangement, however, if the cash settlable rights and obligations are insignificant compared to other rights and obligations under the arrangement, or if the cash settlable rights and obligations no longer exist.

Division 230 also applies to certain equity interests (¶23-115), rights or obligations in relation to equity interests, and the following arrangements as if they were a right that constituted a financial arrangement:

- foreign currency
- non-equity shares in companies
- certain commodity contracts held by traders, and
- certain offsetting commodity contracts held by traders.

The broad definition of financial arrangement means that Div 230 extends to a wide range of arrangements including loans, bonds, derivatives (forwards, futures, options, swaps, etc), promissory notes, bills of exchange, shares and the like. ''Internal derivatives'' used by multinational banks may also be financial arrangements in certain instances (PCG 2017/8).

Arrangements not subject to Div 230

Division 230 does not apply to the following financial arrangements and the taxation rules in other parts of ITAA36 and ITAA97 will need to be considered:

- short-term cash settlable financial arrangements for the acquisition or provision of goods, property or services that are settlable within 12 months (excluding derivative financial arrangements) — eg short term trade credit arrangements
- most leasing and licensing arrangements (¶23-200) including:
  - luxury car leases to which Div 242 applies (¶17-220)
  - hire purchase agreements to which Div 240 applies (¶23-250)
  - assets put to tax-preferred use to which Div 250 applies (¶23-210)
- interests in partnerships (¶5-130) and trusts (¶6-060)
- certain rights or obligations under life insurance policies (¶10-240) and general insurance policies (¶10-230)
- certain worker's compensation arrangements (¶10-180)
- certain guarantees and indemnities unless a fair value or financial reports election is made (a term deposit provided as security for a performance bond is not a right or obligation under a guarantee or indemnity (ID 2014/25))
- personal arrangements (such as the right to receive maintenance payments) and arrangements in respect of personal injury (¶10-180, ¶10-210)
- superannuation and pension benefits (¶10-190)
- certain interests in a controlled foreign company (¶21-110)
- proceeds from certain business sales, including ''earn-outs'' (¶11-675)
- farm management deposits that are deductible under ITAA97 Div 394 (¶18-290)
- deemed interest payments to owners of offshore banking units (¶21-080)
- forestry managed investment schemes (¶18-125)
- exploration benefits provided under farm-in farm-out arrangements in the mining sector (¶11-520, ¶19-010), and
- any other arrangement specified by regulation.

Division 230 also does not apply:

- where losses arise on ceasing to hold an arrangement that is a ''marketable security'' (ITAA36 s 70B) where the taxpayer ceases to have the arrangement because of a belief that the other party to the arrangement would be unable to meet its obligations to discharge its liabilities under the arrangement
- where gains arise from the forgiveness of commercial debts. The commercial debt forgiveness provisions in ITAA97 Div 245 apply instead (¶16-910)
- to gains in the form of franked distributions or rights to receive franked distributions. These remain taxable under ITAA36 s 44
- where gains or losses are subject to the value shifting regime (ITAA97 Divs 723; 725; 727)
- where gains and losses arise on retirement village residence contracts, retirement village services contracts or arrangements for the provision of residential or flexible care. These arrangements are unlikely to be financial arrangements in any event as they are likely to include ''non-insignificant'' non-cash settlable rights and obligations (¶23-035), and
- to former registered emissions units (¶19-130).

Cash settlable arrangements

Division 230 financial arrangements include arrangements where the legal or equitable rights to receive or obligations to provide a financial benefit (¶23-110) are cash settlable. A right to receive or an obligation to provide a financial benefit is cash settlable where:

(a) the benefit is money or money equivalent

(b) the entity intends to satisfy or settle the right or obligation by money or a money equivalent, or by starting to have or ceasing to have another financial arrangement, other than an equity interest

(c) the entity has a practice of satisfying or settling similar rights or obligations mentioned in (b) above (whether or not there is the intention to satisfy or settle the right or obligation in that way)

(d) the entity deals with the right or obligation, or with similar rights or obligations, in order to generate a profit from short term fluctuations in price or from a dealers margin (or both)

(e) the entity is able to settle the right or obligation mentioned in (b) above, whether or not it intends to satisfy the right or obligation in that way, and does not have as its sole or dominant purpose for entering into the arrangement, the purpose of receiving or delivering the financial benefit as part of its expected purchase, sale or usage requirements, or

(f) the financial benefit is readily convertible into money or money equivalent, there is a highly liquid market for the benefit, and:

  - the financial benefit is not subject to a substantial risk of decrease in value for the recipient, or
  - a purpose of the entity entering into the arrangement is to raise or provide finance, or so that it may be converted or liquidated into money or a money equivalent (other than as part of expected purchase, sale or usage requirements).

Cash settlable financial arrangements include derivatives and debt instruments such as bonds, loans, bills of exchange and promissory notes (whether Australian or foreign currency denominated). Certain capital support payments made by a parent company to its subsidiary are not deductible under Div 230; such payments are not a loss from a financial arrangement because the subsidiary has a right which is not cash settlable and that right is significant (TD 2014/14).

Equity interests

Equity interests (¶23-115) which are shares in a company or interests in a trust or partnership are deemed to be financial arrangements. Rights to receive equity interests and obligations to provide equity interests (or combinations thereof) are also deemed to be financial arrangements provided that the right or obligation is not a cash settlable financial arrangement or does not form part of a cash settlable financial arrangement.

Where an arrangement is both cash settlable and an equity interest it will be treated as an equity interest for the purposes of applying Div 230 (TD 2011/12). This distinction is important as an equity interest is only subject to Div 230 where the taxpayer makes one of the following tax timing elections (¶23-040):

- a fair value election where the equity interest is held by the taxpayer (it does not apply where the equity interest is issued by the taxpayer)
- a financial reports election where the equity interest is held by the taxpayer, or
- a hedging financial arrangements election in respect of an equity interest which the taxpayer issues and it is a foreign currency hedge.

Identifying a financial arrangement

An arrangement may be made up of one or more financial arrangements. It is also possible that several arrangements may form one financial arrangement. TR 2012/4 provides guidance on when a contract consisting of a bundle of rights and obligations constitutes one or more financial arrangements for Div 230 purposes. For example, a convertible note which pays a coupon over its life and is convertible into shares of the issuing company on maturity is a single arrangement. Similarly, a loan facility which can be drawn down in stages is a single arrangement.

The time for determining whether an arrangement is a financial arrangement is the time the arrangement comes into existence or starts to be held. Division 230 also provides for testing throughout the life of the arrangement.

[FITR ¶221-515]

¶23-035 Calculating gains and losses on financial arrangements

Division 230 brings net gains and net losses on Div 230 financial arrangements to account in priority to other taxing provisions (including those in Div 775 which tax foreign exchange gains and losses (¶23-075)). Net gains and losses are recognised using one of the tax timing methods discussed below (¶23-040). Where a loss is deductible the thin capitalisation rules (¶22-700) may prevent it from being deductible in full. If a gain or loss is excluded from the application of Div 230 then other taxing provisions may apply.

Whether Div 230 applies to gains and losses is determined from the taxpayer's perspective. Holders and issuers of financial arrangements may, therefore, be treated in different ways by Div 230, eg one taxpayer may be subject to Div 230 and the other may be excluded, or a party to a financial arrangement may bring a financial benefit to account in a different way to the party providing the financial benefit. This could arise because different tax timing methods (¶23-040) are used.

Financial benefits

Under Div 230, a gain or loss from a financial arrangement is worked out by offsetting costs (financial benefits provided) against proceeds (financial benefits received). Cost attribution rules determine which costs should be subtracted from which proceeds.

To address arguments that the cost attribution rules only apply to financial benefits that taxpayers have received or provided, or are certain of receiving or providing, amendments have been made to clarify that taxpayers should also have regard to financial benefits that they might receive or provide when determining whether they have a gain or loss from a financial arrangement. This ensures that taxpayers may attribute a financial benefit that they are uncertain of providing or receiving as a cost or proceed when determining whether they have a gain or loss from a financial arrangement.

Gains and losses on revenue account

Division 230 treats most gains as assessable income and losses as deductible from assessable income. An exception to this is in the case of hedging financial arrangements where the gains and losses are characterised by reference to the tax characterisation of the underlying hedged item (ie capital, income, assessable, exempt or non-assessable non-exempt).

Gains and losses on financial arrangements relating to the gaining or producing of exempt income or non-assessable non-exempt income are disregarded as are gains or losses of a private or domestic nature. TR 2012/3 explains the principles that the ATO will apply in deciding whether a gain or loss from a financial arrangement is made in gaining or producing exempt income or non-assessable non-exempt income. A loss which is made by an Australian resident in deriving non-assessable non-exempt income under ITAA36 ss 23AI; 23AK or ITAA97 s 768-5 (ITAA36 former s 23AJ) may be deductible to the extent that it is a cost related to a debt interest issued by the taxpayer and is a debt deduction covered by s 820-40(1)(a).

TOFA and residence

Taxpayers who are not tax residents in Australia will only be taxable on gains arising from financial arrangements which have an Australian source. A person who becomes an Australian resident is taken to have acquired an existing financial arrangement at that time for its market value at that time. A person who ceases to be an Australian resident is taken to have disposed of an existing financial arrangement at that time for its market value at that time.

Division 230 and PAYG

Net gains, not net losses, made on financial arrangements subject to Div 230 are included in a taxpayer's instalment income (¶27-260).

Consolidation

When an entity holding a Div 230 financial arrangement joins or leaves a consolidated group (¶8-000) or MEC group (¶8-610), the existing consolidation rules generally prevail, however, specific rules have been made to enhance the interaction of the consolidation and TOFA regimes. These TOFA consolidation interaction provisions (Subdiv 715-F) are driven by 4 basic principles:

(1) where an entity joins a consolidated group or MEC group, the joining entity will apply Div 230 as if the joining time was the end of an income year

(2) the head company will apply the consolidation rules and Div 230 as if the head company had directly acquired assets that are or form part of financial arrangements from the joining entity

(3) where an entity leaves a consolidated group or MEC group, the head company will apply Div 230 as if the leaving time was the end of an income year

(4) a leaving entity whose financial arrangement gains and losses are subject to Div 230 will apply the Division as if the leaving entity took the financial arrangements with it at the leaving time.

Since the enactment of the TOFA consolidation interaction provisions, retrospective amendments taking effect from the commencement of the TOFA regime provide that:

- for liabilities subject to the fair value, reliance on financial reports or retranslation tax timing methods, the head company of a consolidated group is deemed to have received an amount for assuming the liability at the joining time. The deemed amount is the liability's accounting value at the joining time
- for liabilities subject to a tax timing method *other than* the fair value, financial reports or retranslation method, the head company of a consolidated group is deemed to have received an amount for assuming the liability at the joining time. The deemed amount is the liability's accounting value at the joining time applying the joining entity's accounting principles
- a tax value is set for an intra-group asset or liability that is, or is part of, a Div 230 financial arrangement when the asset or liability emerges from a consolidated group because a subsidiary member leaves the group. The broad objective of this amendment is to make the tax treatment of intra-group Div 230 financial arrangements consistent with the economic substance of transactions, and ensures that a lender is not assessed on a return of loan principal, and a borrower cannot claim a deduction for the repayment of that principal.

Amendments have also been made to the TOFA transitional provisions to ensure the TOFA consolidation interaction provisions apply when transitioning existing financial arrangements acquired or assumed by the head company of a consolidated group as part of a pre-TOFA joining, where the head company has made a TOFA transitional election. Note that the transitional election can no longer be made. For more information on the transitional election see the 2012 edition of the *Australian Master Tax Guide*.

Interaction of Div 230 with other tax provisions

The ITAA36 and ITAA97 contain rules for determining whether Div 230 or other tax provisions should take priority. The rules include:

- 12-month prepayment rule — where expenditure is prepaid and the prepayment period is more than 12 months Div 230 takes precedence over the prepayment rules in Subdiv H of Div 3 of ITAA36.
- Debt interests — Div 230 applies to debt interests (as defined in Div 974) which are financial arrangements.
- Trading stock — if an item of trading stock is a Div 230 financial arrangement it is dealt with under Div 230 and not Div 70.
- Superannuation funds — where a CGT event happens to a CGT asset that is a financial arrangement of a superannuation fund, the gain or loss is generally accounted for under the CGT provisions and not Div 230. Note the special provisions which apply in the context on instalment warrants and instalment receipts (¶23-390).
- Foreign income attribution — Div 230 is disregarded when calculating an entity's attributable income in relation to an interest in a CFC or a foreign trust under the transferor trust rules.
- Withholding tax — the withholding tax regime applies to financial arrangements held by a non-resident or a foreign permanent establishment of an Australian resident in priority to Div 230 (¶22-010).

- Forex rules — Div 230 applies in priority to the forex rules in Div 775 (¶23-075).
- Hybrid mismatches — where the hybrid mismatch (¶22-640) and Div 230 rules potentially apply to gains and losses on a Div 230 financial arrangement, adjustments may need to be made including splitting the gain or loss into 2 elements.

Integrity measures

Value shifting

The rules against value shifting target situations where, under a scheme, value is shifted away from equity or loan interests. Gains which are eliminated, or losses which are enlarged, in this manner are disregarded (to the extent of the excess) under Div 230 in determining tax outcomes for financial arrangements. Practically speaking, the value shifting rules apply to unrealised gains and losses from financial arrangements.

Arm's length rules

Division 230 incorporates arm's length rules that are similar to those applicable to arrangements not covered by the Division. Where a taxpayer starts to have a financial arrangement as consideration for something received or provided, the amount of the benefit obtained or provided is taken to be the market value of the arrangement at the time the taxpayer started to have the arrangement. The amount may be relevant for the purposes of applying tax provisions dealing with capital gains, capital allowances or trading stock to the thing received or acquired.

The arm's length rules in Div 230 are ''self-executing'' which means that the taxpayer must self-assess and the Commissioner does not need to exercise a discretion.

Tax exempt entities — privatisation

Integrity measures prevent tax exempt entities transferred to the private sector after 8 May 2018 from claiming tax deductions on the repayment of the principal of a concessional loan. The deductions arise due to unforeseen complex interaction between the TOFA rules and the rules dealing with deemed market values for tax exempt entities that become taxable. Concessional loans entered into by tax exempt entities that become taxable must be valued as if they were originally entered into on commercial terms.

[FITR ¶221-525]

¶23-040 TOFA tax timing methods

Division 230 provides that gains and losses on financial arrangements should be recognised by using one of 6 tax timing methods. There are 2 default methods: accruals method and realisation method; and 4 elective methods: fair value method, foreign exchange retranslation method, hedging financial arrangements method and financial reports method.

Once a method is chosen it must be applied in a consistent manner in future income years for the financial arrangement and all similar financial arrangements.

In addition to the 6 tax timing methods, there is a balancing adjustment method which applies where a taxpayer ceases to have a financial arrangement or the financial arrangement is disposed of or deemed to have been disposed of.

Accounting principles and auditing standards

To use an elective method a taxpayer must satisfy certain qualifying criteria including having its financial reports prepared and audited in accordance with relevant accounting principles and auditing standards. The ATO says financial reports must be prepared in accordance with those accounting standards and authoritative pronouncements of the Australian Accounting Standards Board which are relevant to financial arrangements and which are capable of being applied in respect of the affairs of the reporting taxpayer. This is the case regardless of whether those accounting principles mandatorily apply to the taxpayer or the financial report. The financial report does not need to be prepared in accordance with accounting principles which are not relevant to financial arrangements or which are not capable of being applied in respect of the affairs of the taxpayer whose financial position and performance is being reported (TD 2014/12).

Foreign authorised deposit-taking institutions (foreign ADIs) are able to satisfy the financial reports criterion by using the Statement of Financial Performance and the Statement of Financial Position that must be provided to the Australian Prudential Regulation Authority.

Priority of elections

It is possible that more than one tax timing method may apply to a financial arrangement. Where this is the case the tax timing rules should be applied in the following order:

- hedging financial arrangements method
- financial reports method
- fair value method
- foreign exchange retranslation method.

Making a tax timing election

A taxpayer can only use an elective tax timing method by completing a *TOFA 3 & 4 tax-timing method elections form*. In the case of a consolidated group or MEC group, the election is made by the head company of the group. The election applies to financial arrangements which the taxpayer starts to hold in the year the election is made. The election also applies to financial arrangements which the taxpayer starts to hold in earlier years where a transitional election (¶23-020) was made. Taxpayers do not need to notify the Commissioner of their election but must keep a copy of the election with their tax records. Once an election is made it is irrevocable. If a taxpayer ceases to satisfy the qualifying criteria for an elective method then the relevant financial arrangements are deemed to have been disposed of and reacquired and the election ceases to apply. Taxpayers may make new elections when the requirements are once more satisfied.

Accruals and realisation methods

Where no tax timing election is made the accruals and/or realisation methods apply to the financial arrangement (unless it is an equity interest, see ¶23-030). Both the accruals and realisation method can apply to a single financial arrangement where some of the financial benefits under the arrangement are sufficiently certain and some are not.

Accruals method

The accruals method applies where the overall gain or loss from an arrangement is "sufficiently certain" at the time the taxpayer starts to have the arrangement. The accruals method also applies where a particular gain is "sufficiently certain" at the time the taxpayer starts to have the arrangement or becomes sufficiently certain during the life of the arrangement. If there is neither a sufficiently certain overall gain or loss nor a sufficiently certain particular gain or loss then the gains and losses on a financial arrangement will be recognised using the realisation tax timing method (see below).

A gain or loss is sufficiently certain if it is reasonably expected that an entity will receive or provide a financial benefit and at least some of the amount or value of the benefit is fixed or determinable with reasonable accuracy, eg where a contingency under an interest rate swap is settled so that it is certain that a payment of a certain gain will be made. ATO guidance on the taxation of swaps under the accruals/realisation method is provided in TR 2016/2. The ATO has issued an alert raising concerns over cross-border arrangements that involve claiming interest deductions on the basis the loss is sufficiently certain (TA 2018/4).

Under the accruals method, the sufficiently certain gain or loss on the financial arrangement is spread over the term of the arrangement or the period to which the gain or loss relates.

The core method for spreading sufficiently certain gains of losses uses compounding accruals. This is conceptually identical to the effective interest rate method in Accounting Standard *AASB 9: Financial Instruments*. It is possible to use another type of accruals method but the outcome must approximate compounding accruals. There are specific rules in the accruals method concerning gains and losses from fees and costs (''portfolio fees'') and premiums/discounts (''portfolio premiums/discounts'') arising from a financial arrangement that is part of a portfolio of similar financial arrangements. If eligible, the taxpayer can elect to spread the portfolio fees and portfolio premiums/discounts over a period that equals the expected life of the portfolio of which the financial arrangement is a part. An election should be made using a *TOFA 3 & 4 election for portfolio treatment of fees, discounts and premiums* election form. This election does not need to be notified to the ATO but a copy should be kept with the taxpayer's records.

Running balancing adjustments must be made if the ultimate gain or loss on a financial arrangement is different from the estimated gain or loss. This recognises that the accruals method is an estimation of cash flows and that this may differ from actual cash flows.

Realisation method

If a gain or loss from the financial arrangement is not sufficiently certain, and no elective method applies, then the gain or loss is recognised using the realisation method. The realisation method allocates financial benefits in the form of gains and losses to income years in which they occur. A gain or loss will generally occur when the last financial benefit is provided or is to be provided.

Reassessment/re-estimate of gains or losses

A reassessment of gains or losses is required in cases involving material changes of circumstances, for the purposes of applying the accruals and realisation methods. A re-estimation of the gain or loss for the purposes of the accruals method (and corresponding balancing adjustments) is required if circumstances materially affect the amount or timing of the financial benefits under the arrangement. For example, a re-estimation may be necessary where financial benefits are no longer contingent and this changes the amount of the gain or loss which is sufficiently certain.

Fair value method

The fair value method is an elective tax timing method which calculates gains or losses on a financial arrangement by reference to the change in the arrangements' fair value between 2 points in time, generally the start and end of the income year. This gain or loss needs to be adjusted for amounts paid or received during the period. Division 230 does not define ''fair value'' but guidance on its meaning can be taken from AASB 9. AASB 9 generally recognises at fair value through profit or loss a financial asset or financial liability held for trading or a derivative.

A taxpayer that has issued its own equity interests is not permitted to apply the fair value method to those equity interests. This ensures a taxpayer does not obtain a deduction for dividends paid. The fair value method does not apply if an election is made to use the hedging financial arrangements method or the financial reports method.

Foreign exchange retranslation method

The foreign exchange retranslation method is an elective tax timing method which is relevant to taxpayers with arrangements denominated in foreign currency or where the gains and losses are determined by reference to a foreign currency. The foreign exchange retranslation method brings foreign exchange gains and losses to account in line with AASB 121 or its foreign equivalent. Where an entity has made a functional currency election (¶23-070) this method applies to a currency which is not the functional currency. Any gains and losses on a financial arrangement which do not arise by reference to currency movements will be brought to account using the accruals method. The foreign exchange retranslation method applies in priority to the forex rules in Div 775 (¶23-075).

There are 2 kinds of retranslation elections; the general retranslation election and the qualifying forex account election. A general retranslation election can be made in respect of all arrangements under Div 230 and those arrangements which are subject to Subdiv 775-F because Div 230 does not apply.

A qualifying forex account election can be made in respect of one or more arrangements that meet the definition of qualifying forex account provided that a general retranslation election has not already been made. A qualifying forex account is an account denominated in a foreign currency which is used for the primary purpose of facilitating transactions or is a credit card account.

The foreign exchange retranslation method does not apply if an election is made to use the fair value method, the hedging financial arrangements method, or the financial reports method.

Hedging financial arrangement method

The hedging financial arrangement method is an elective tax timing method which aligns the timing and character of gains and losses made on "hedging financial arrangements" with those arising on the item being hedged. For example, if the gain or loss on a hedged item is on capital account then the gain or loss on the hedging financial arrangement will also be on capital account.

The hedging financial arrangement method can only be made where the financial arrangement is a derivative financial arrangement or a foreign currency hedge; certain documentation requirements are met; and the hedge is "effective". Whether the arrangement is a derivative financial arrangement or a foreign currency hedge it must have been created, acquired or applied for the purpose of hedging risks in relation to a hedged item. The hedged item may be an existing liability or asset, a firm commitment or highly probable transaction. The hedged item does not need to be a financial arrangement. An anticipated dividend under ITAA 1997 Subdiv 768-A (formerly s 23AJ) can be a hedged item.

Derivative financial arrangement or a foreign currency hedge

A *derivative financial arrangement* is a financial arrangement whose value changes in response to changes in a specified variable(s) (interest rate, credit rating, commodity price, etc); and it requires no net investment or the net investment is smaller than would be required for other types of financial arrangement that would be expected to have similar response to changes in market values.

A *foreign currency hedge* is a financial arrangement which hedges risk in relation to movements in currency exchange rates and its value changes in response to changes in a specified variable(s) and it requires net investment that is not smaller than would be required for other types of financial arrangement that would be expected to have similar responses to changes in market values. For example, a taxpayer may enter into a foreign currency hedge to mitigate movements in foreign currency in respect of the purchase of machinery in a foreign currency at a future date. The timing and amount of gains and losses on this hedge would be recognised in accordance with the tax treatment of the hedged machinery.

Documentation requirements

To be eligible to use the hedging financial arrangement method certain recording requirements must be met, including: details of the hedge; details that are required under relevant accounting standards (eg AASB 9); and details of the basis for allocating gains and losses from the hedging financial arrangement for income tax purposes.

These records must be made, or in place, at or soon after the time the hedging financial arrangement is created, acquired or applied or at such other time as provided for by regulations.

The ATO has published sample hedging documentation on its website.

Effective

The hedge must be effective. The term ''effective'' is not defined but the Commissioner's view is that the effectiveness of a hedge is determined in accordance with Australian accounting principles (AASB 9) or equivalent foreign accounting standards (TD 2011/23). Whether a hedge is effective requires both retrospective and prospective testing of the hedge.

In TD 2012/13, the Commissioner gives the ATO's view on the proper allocation of gains and losses resulting from the expiration, sale, termination or exercise of a hedging financial arrangement to which a hedging financial arrangement election applies.

Proposed amendments to hedging financial arrangement method

The government announced in the 2016–17 Budget that it would amend the hedging financial arrangement method to make it easier to access, allow it to encompass more types of risk management arrangements (including risk management of a portfolio of assets) and remove the direct link to financial accounting. As part of this reform, the government said it would incorporate policy reflected in proposed amendments to the hedging rules first announced in the 2011–12 Budget, which have yet to be enacted. The changes to the hedging rules, which form part of the government's broader proposed reform of the TOFA regime, were originally intended to apply to income years beginning on or after 1 January 2018, however this has now been deferred to an unspecified future date.

Reliance on financial reports

The financial reports method is an elective tax timing method which allows a taxpayer to rely on their financial reports to bring gains and losses to account. A financial reports election takes precedence over other elective tax timing elections but only to the extent that the hedging financial arrangements method does not apply to the financial arrangement. The financial reports method does not apply if the arrangement is an equity interest issued by the taxpayer.

To make the financial reports election, the taxpayer must comply with the financial reporting and auditing requirements common to all elective tax timing methods (see above). In addition to these requirements the financial reports must not have been qualified by an auditor's report in the current or previous 4 years and there must have been no adverse assessment of the taxpayer's accounting systems in the current or previous 4 years.

Balancing adjustments and other special circumstances

If the rights and/or obligations under a financial arrangement are transferred wholly or in part to another entity or cease, or the arrangement ceases to be a financial arrangement, a balancing adjustment must be made. The general purpose of this rule is to bring to account any outstanding gains or losses from the arrangement. This is subject to a number of exceptions, eg certain equity interests, arrangements for which a hedging election was made, arrangements written off as a bad debt, the conversion or exchange of a traditional security, the settling or closing out of a derivative financial arrangement, or the subsidiary ceasing to be a member of a consolidated or MEC group.

The balancing adjustment is calculated by comparing the total of the financial benefits received under the arrangement and the deductions allowed or allowable for losses from the arrangement (Step 1); and the total of the financial benefits provided under the arrangement and the amounts assessed or assessable in relation to the gains from the arrangement (Step 2). The excess of the Step 1 amount over the Step 2 amount is an assessable balancing adjustment. The excess of the Step 2 amount over the Step 1 amount is a deductible balancing adjustment.

[FITR ¶221-530 – ¶221-560]

Conversion of Foreign Currency

¶23-070 General translation rules

Subdivisions 960-C and 960-D provide general translation rules for converting foreign currency amounts into Australian dollars for income tax purposes. Division 775 contains the ''forex rules'' which determine the tax treatment of foreign exchange gains and losses (¶23-075).

Cryptocurrencies

Cryptocurrencies such as Bitcoin are neither ''currency'' nor ''foreign currency'' for the purposes of Australian tax law, including Div 775 (TD 2014/25; *Seribu Pty Ltd*). Where cryptocurrency is held or used as part of a business any profits may be assessable as income. Disposals of cryptocurrency outside of a business are treated as the disposal of a CGT asset (TD 2014/26).

Core translation rule (Subdiv 960-C)

The core translation rule is that an amount of foreign currency is to be translated into Australian currency so that the Australian income tax liability is calculated by reference to a common unit of account (s 960-50). This rule applies to capital and revenue amounts generally and covers ordinary income, expenses, consideration, payments, receipts, obligations, values and liabilities denominated or expressed in a foreign currency.

The following special translation rules specify the exchange rate to be used for particular amounts (s 960-50(6)):

- forex realisation event 4 happens when the taxpayer ceases to have an obligation to pay foreign currency (¶23-075). The amount of the *obligation* is converted at the exchange rate prevailing at the ''tax recognition time'', as determined under ITAA97 s 775-55(7)
- the cost of *depreciating assets* is converted at the exchange rate which applied when the taxpayer began to hold the asset, or when satisfying the liability to pay for it, whichever occurs first
- the value of *trading stock* valued at market selling or replacement value is translated at the rate applicable at the end of the income year in which the trading stock is being valued. If trading stock is valued at cost, the value is to be translated at the rate applicable at the time the item became on hand
- amounts relevant to transactions or events to which the *CGT provisions* apply are to be converted at the exchange rate prevailing at the time of the transaction or event

- *ordinary income* is to be converted at the exchange rate prevailing at the earlier of the time it is derived or received (eg QC 17061; ID 2004/472; ID 2004/854)

- *non-CGT statutory income* is converted at the exchange rate prevailing at the time the amount must first be returned as income or at the time of receipt, whichever occurs first

- *deductible amounts* not falling within ITAA97 Div 40 must be converted at the exchange rate prevailing at the time the amount becomes deductible or the time of payment, whichever occurs first

- amounts relevant to a deduction for *film production expenditure* under ITAA97 Div 376 are translated at the average of the rate applicable during the period starting at the beginning of principal photography or production of animated images and ending on completion of the film

- *PAYG withholding amounts* must be translated at the rate applicable at the time when the amount is required to be withheld (¶27-100)

- *any other receipts or payments* must be converted at the exchange rate prevailing at the time of the receipt or payment.

Amounts that are elements in the calculation of other amounts are translated into Australian currency before the other amount is calculated (s 960-50(4), (5)). For example, this would apply to the calculation of a gain or loss on the disposal of a traditional security (TD 2006/30: ¶23-340). Similarly where a superannuation pension or annuity is payable in a foreign currency, the foreign pension or annuity payments and the deductible amount each have to be translated before working out the assessable amount (TD 2006/54). However, this does not apply to special accrual amounts as such amounts are calculated without translation and are then translated. ''Special accrual amounts'' are amounts subject to the luxury car leasing provisions (ITAA97 Div 242), the sale and loan provisions (ITAA97 Div 240), the tax-preferred leasing provisions (Subdiv 250-E), the provisions dealing with certain arrangements for the use of property (ITAA36 Pt III Div 16D), the deferred income securities provisions (ITAA36 Pt III Div 16E), the taxation of financial arrangements rules in Div 230 (unless Subdiv 230-B applies) and gains and losses that are subject to the accruals method under Subdiv 230-B where all financial benefits that are provided and received under the financial arrangement are denominated in a particular foreign currency (¶23-020).

The cost of obtaining an exchange rate for the above purposes is deductible (ID 2004/856).

The translation rules are modified by regulations which allow amounts in a foreign currency to be translated into Australian currency or an applicable functional currency using average rates, daily rates or rates that are consistent with the rates used in the preparation of an audited financial report, rather than using spot rates. Where the rates used in the preparation of an audited financial report are used by a tax consolidated group, there must be consistency in the translation methodology used across the group for the same kind of transaction (TD 2013/21).

Regulations also allow taxpayers to use the weighted average basis to calculate the cost of foreign currency, fungible rights to receive foreign currency, and the proceeds of assuming fungible obligations to pay foreign currency. The regulations provide that the settlement of certain foreign currency denominated spot contracts or the deduction of foreign currency denominated bad debts does not result in a forex realisation gain or loss.

Exceptions

The core translation rules contained in Subdiv 960-C do not affect the operation of the provisions dealing with notional loans under facility agreements (ITAA97 s 775-210), functional currency (Subdiv 960-D), valuation of financial benefits under the debt and equity rules (ITAA97 s 974-35(6)) and the former provisions dealing with foreign investment funds and life assurance (ITAA36 Pt XI).

ITAA36 former ss 20, 102AAX, 391 and ITAA97 former s 103-20 continue to apply to transactions or events which are not subject to the translation rules under Subdiv 960-C.

Functional currency rules (Subdiv 960-D)

Under the "functional currency" rules, the net income of an entity (or specified part of an entity) that functions predominantly in a particular foreign currency can be determined in that currency, with the net amount being translated into Australian currency. In other words, taxpayers can choose not to translate each transaction into Australian currency. In essence, each transaction may be translated from the other currency (say US$ or even A$) into a functional currency (eg Euro) (s 960-60), producing a net income amount in the functional currency, which is subsequently translated into the Australian currency (s 960-80).

The rules apply as follows (s 960-60):

- an Australian resident who is required to prepare financial reports under *Corporations Act 2001*, s 292 may choose to work out their taxable income or taxable loss in the functional currency, unless they make separate elections in respect of an overseas permanent establishment, an offshore banking unit (OBU), the attributable income from a controlled foreign company (CFC), or a transferor trust (these taxpayers may also be subject to the special rules in s 960-85)
- a resident carrying on a business through an overseas permanent establishment (PE) may choose to work out its taxable income or taxable loss from the PE in the functional currency
- a non-resident carrying on a business through an Australian PE may choose to work out its taxable income or taxable loss from the PE in the functional currency
- an OBU may choose to work out its total assessable OBU income or total allowable OBU deductions in the functional currency
- attributable taxpayers of a CFC may choose to work out the attributable income of the CFC in the functional currency
- a transferor trust may choose to work out its attributable income in the functional currency.

For a currency to be an applicable functional currency, it must be the sole or predominant foreign currency in which, at the time of the choice, the relevant entity or part of an entity kept its accounts (s 960-70). Such entities may choose to account for individual transactions using that currency (s 960-80). However, the net amount from those transactions (generally the taxable income) must be converted into Australian dollars.

The functional currency rules apply to amounts of a capital or revenue nature generally, including payments, receipts, obligations, values and liabilities, consideration, ordinary income, expenses and monetary limits (eg the car depreciation limit).

Special rules apply where an entity makes a choice to convert an amount to the applicable functional currency and the amount is attributable to an event that happened or a state of affairs that arose before the current choice took effect, for instance the sale of a car acquired prior to the choice and the cost of which was originally accounted for in A$ (s 960-85).

As a general rule, an amount to which s 960-80(1) applies will not be in the ''applicable functional currency'' where its source is a legal right or obligation denominated in any currency (including Australian currency), other than the non-Australian currency that is the entity's ''applicable functional currency'' (TR 2007/5). In rare cases the income tax law itself may be the source of a relevant amount, ie the amount may stem from a statutory concept which is separate and distinct from the underlying transactions and components which go to its makeup, or from a statutory Australian dollar amount.

Generally, a choice made in one year applies to the following income year but if the choice is made within 90 days of the start of the income year (or within 90 days of the taxpayer coming into existence), it can apply to the whole income year in which the choice is made (ss 960-60; 960-65). The choice can be withdrawn and substituted.

The applicable functional currency rules apply to the calculation of a capital gain or loss arising from a CGT event happening in relation to an indirect Australian real property interest of a foreign resident (s 960-61).

Where Australian currency is taken to be foreign currency under the functional currency rules, it is treated as a retained cost base asset under the consolidation rules (TD 2005/22).

An Australian resident entity, which is required to prepare financial statements in Australian dollars for statutory reporting purposes, can choose to use a foreign currency as its applicable functional currency, if that foreign currency is the sole or predominant foreign currency in which it kept its accounts at the time of making the choice (TD 2006/4).

The applicable functional currency is not relevant for the purpose of applying FBT, GST, SGC and PAYG withholding provisions (TD 2006/5). However, this does not mean that none of the amounts calculated under these provisions will be affected by a choice to use a particular foreign currency as the applicable functional currency (eg the amount of the deduction for FBT will need to be translated into the applicable functional currency).

If an ''attributable taxpayer'' makes a choice to use the applicable functional currency, the choice will not apply to its calculation of ''attribution surplus'' under the CFC provisions (TD 2006/6). The attribution surplus and all amounts included in the attribution account of the attributable taxpayer should be in Australian currency.

The head company of a consolidated group can make a choice to use the applicable functional currency. However, the fact that it is the head company of a consolidated group for certain income tax purposes does not affect its obligation to prepare financial reports under *Corporations Act 2001*, s 292 (TD 2006/7).

The applicable functional currency for the head company of a consolidated group is determined by looking at the accounts of all the group members, not just at the accounts of the head company. Whether there is such a currency depends on whether there is one particular foreign currency that is the currency predominantly used for the basic record keeping of the consolidated group (TD 2007/24).

A head company of a consolidated group that prepares a financial report for the group (a special purpose financial report) which accounts for the transactions of its subsidiaries must adopt the same translation methodologies for the same kinds of transactions. If it adopts different translation methodologies, it cannot be said to comply with the accounting standards and does not comply with the core foreign currency translation rule in s 960-50 (TD 2013/21).

A "small proprietary company", which is not required to prepare reports under s 292, can make a choice to use the applicable functional currency in limited circumstances (TD 2006/8).

Proposed amendments to functional currency rules

The government announced in the 2016–17 Budget that it would extend the range of entities that can use a functional currency. This measure was first announced in the 2011–12 Budget, but not enacted. The 2016–17 Budget announcement indicated that the proposed amendment would apply to income years beginning on or after 1 January 2018, however this has now been deferred to an unspecified future date.

[FITR ¶762-000 – ¶762-155]

¶23-075 Foreign currency gains and losses

The TOFA regime in Div 230 applies in priority to the "forex rules" in Div 775. Accordingly, Div 775 will only apply to determine the tax treatment of foreign exchange gains and losses where Div 230 does not apply, eg in the case of individuals and entities not automatically subject to Div 230 (¶23-025).

The forex rules in Div 775 have deferred application in respect of authorised deposit-taking institutions (ADI), non-ADI financial institutions, securitisation vehicles and certain special purpose vehicles (s 820-39). These entities became subject to Div 775 on the commencement of the TOFA regime in Div 230 (¶23-020) on 1 July 2010 (1 July 2009 where an early start election was made). As a result, until the commencement of the rules in Div 230 these entities remained subject to the ordinary income and general deduction provisions and the rules in former ITAA36 Pt III Div 3B.

If a forex gain or loss arises from a CGT event then the CGT provisions may be relevant. The relieving provision in s 118-20 is intended to prevent the double counting of gains.

Realisation of foreign gains or losses

Division 775 provides that a taxpayer must include in its assessable income forex realisation gains made as a result of a forex realisation event that happens during the income year. Forex realisation losses may be deducted as a result of a forex realisation event. The tax treatment of forex gains and losses is discussed below. Bitcoin is not a foreign currency for the purposes of the forex rules in Div 775 (TD 2014/25).

There are 5 main types of forex realisation events (FRE):

(1) "FRE 1" happens if a taxpayer disposes of foreign currency or a right to receive foreign currency to another entity. This is CGT event A1 (s 775-40).

(2) "FRE 2" happens if a taxpayer ceases to have a right to receive foreign currency (otherwise than because of having disposed of the right to another entity), eg where the right is discharged by receipt (s 775-45). Different rules apply depending on the type of the right. See ID 2005/318, ID 2005/321, ID 2005/323 and ID 2006/293.

(3) "FRE 3" happens if a taxpayer ceases to have an obligation to receive foreign currency, eg where an entity fulfils such an obligation (s 775-50).

(4) "FRE 4" happens if a taxpayer ceases to have an obligation to pay foreign currency (s 775-55). The ATO considers that where an entity elects to use a functional currency between the date on which a foreign currency loan is taken out and when it is repaid, that FRE 4 does not happen on repayment. This overturns the ATO's previous view expressed in TD 2014/D10 (withdrawn). The ATO says it will release a new draft determination in due course.

(5) "FRE 5" happens if a taxpayer ceases to have a right to pay foreign currency (s 775-60).

Where there is an option to buy or sell a particular foreign currency if the exercise price is payable in another currency, or there is a contract to buy a particular foreign currency in return for another currency, and more than one FRE is triggered, special rules apply to determine which one of those events is ignored (s 775-65).

Special rules have been included to address the treatment of currency derivatives. The "currency exchange rate effect" concept addresses synthetic currency exchange rate fluctuations. The definitions of "right to receive foreign currency" and "obligation to pay foreign currency" address synthetic rights to receive and obligations to pay foreign currency. Modifications to FREs address option costs and interactions between FREs 1 and 4 under derivative arrangements. Other provisions address expired currency options.

In applying the FREs to foreign currency or a fungible right or obligation to receive or pay foreign currency, the FRE is applied on a first-in first-out basis (s 775-145). For example, forex realisation gains and losses made as a result of the withdrawal of funds from a foreign currency denominated bank account opened before the commencement date are taken into account in determining taxable income but only to the extent that they are made as a result of the withdrawal of funds deposited on or after 1 July 2003. The first-in first-out ordering rule in s 775-145 is applied to determine which withdrawals relate to deposits made on or after 1 July 2003 (ID 2006/320).

Where there is a disposal of foreign currency or a right to receive foreign currency and FRE 1 happens, the amount attributable to a currency exchange rate effect is determined by subtracting the non-forex component of the capital gain (or loss) from the overall capital gain (or loss) (TD 2006/32). The non-forex component of the capital gain (or loss) is the foreign currency amount received on disposal less the foreign currency cost of acquisition, translated into Australian currency using the exchange rate applicable at the time of the disposal.

When, on novation, a foreign currency denominated debt is ended and a new party becomes the creditor or debtor in the substituted debt, FRE 2 occurs to the creditor and FRE 4 occurs to the debtor as the foreign currency denominated debt is ended and a new party has been substituted (TD 2006/11).

The effective assignment of a presently existing right to receive an amount under a foreign currency denominated debt from a creditor to a third party results in FRE 1 happening to that creditor if the assignment results in a change in beneficial ownership of the debt (as there is a disposal of a right to receive foreign currency). However, FRE 2 does not happen to the creditor as the cessation of the right occurred because of a disposal of a right to receive foreign currency. Regardless of whether the assignment conveys the beneficial ownership in the foreign currency denominated debt to a third party, no FRE 4 happens to the debtor as its obligation to pay foreign currency subsists (TD 2006/12).

The following 4 exceptions to the above rules are intended to reduce compliance costs.

Exception 1: Short-term forex realisation gains and losses

Exceptions to the general approach apply to certain short-term foreign currency realisation gains and losses where the gain or loss is closely linked to a capital asset (ss 775-70 to 775-80). In these cases, the foreign currency gain or loss is treated as having the same character as the gain or loss on the asset to which the foreign currency right or obligation relates. Thus, if a foreign currency gain or loss arises in respect of an FRE relating to a capital asset (eg relating to the acquisition, addition to cost, or disposal of a non-depreciating CGT asset), and the time between the date of the contract and the due date for payment is 12 months or less, then the gain or loss is taken into account in the cost base of the asset for CGT purposes (rather than being subject to Div 775).

If the asset is a depreciating asset, the forex gain or loss will affect the cost or opening adjustable value of the asset. For acquisitions of depreciating assets, the relevant time limit is a 24-month period beginning 12 months before the time when the asset begins to be held. In the case of a pooled asset (eg under ITAA97 Subdiv 328-D or 40-D), the opening pool balance is affected. Finally, if the foreign currency gain or loss relates to a project amount (under ITAA97 s 40-830), a forex gain or loss affects the pool value of the project pool. An entity can make a one-off irrevocable written election not to apply the short-term rules. For an example, see ID 2005/320.

Exception 2: Roll-over relief for facility agreements (Subdiv 775-C)

Optional roll-over relief will be available to the issuer of securities under certain finance facility agreements (ID 2004/158). The roll-over applies in respect of foreign currency gains and losses arising on roll-over of securities (ITAA97 Subdiv 775-C). A facility agreement is an agreement where: (a) a taxpayer has the right to issue eligible securities (such as discounted, non-interest bearing, fixed-term bills of exchange or promissory notes denominated in a foreign currency); (b) another entity or entities must acquire the securities; and (c) the economic effect of the agreement is to enable the issuer to obtain finance in a particular foreign currency. A roll-over happens if the issuer discharges an obligation under an existing security and at the same time issues a new security and other requirements are met (s 775-205).

If the taxpayer chooses roll-over relief for such an agreement (s 775-195), the consequences outlined in ss 775-200 to 775-220 (including FRE 6 and 7) apply.

The choice (which is irrevocable) must be made within 90 days after issuing an eligible security under the agreement for the first time.

Securitisation vehicles and special purpose vehicles under s 820-39(3) were unable to choose roll-over relief until the commencement of the Div 230 rules referred to at ¶23-020.

Exception 3: Qualifying forex accounts and the $250,000 test (Subdiv 775-D)

If the combined balance of all the accounts covered by the taxpayer's election does not exceed the foreign currency equivalent of $250,000, the account passes the "limited balance test". The taxpayer may then elect to disregard a forex realisation gain or loss made in relation to the account as a result of event 2 or 4 (but not as a result of event 1). The test also allows the combined balance to be more than $250,000, but not more than the foreign currency equivalent of $500,000 for not more than two 15-day periods in any income year. Any capital gain or loss made as a result of CGT event C1 or C2 happening in relation to a qualifying forex account as is attributable to a currency exchange rate effect is also disregarded (s 775-250). Such accounts do not need to be foreign currency denominated transaction accounts with an ADI or other financial institution (see the TOFA provisions in Div 230 and Exception 4 below).

The election, which is revocable, may be made at any time and applies from the time it is made.

A qualifying forex account is an account having the primary purpose of facilitating transactions or a credit card account (eg not a term deposit: ID 2014/32).

Exception 4: Retranslation for qualifying forex accounts (Subdiv 775-E)

These rules allow a taxpayer to bring to account any foreign currency gains or losses arising in respect of qualifying accounts by annually restating the balance by reference to deposits, withdrawals and the exchange rate prevailing at the beginning and end of each year. If a taxpayer chooses retranslation for a qualifying forex account, a forex realisation gain or loss made in relation to the account as a result of event 2 or 4 is disregarded. Similarly, any capital gain or loss made as a result of CGT event C1 or C2 in relation to withdrawals from the credit balance of the account is disregarded. In addition, FRE 8 enables any gains or losses to be worked out on a retranslation basis. FRE 8 happens if the taxpayer chooses retranslation for a qualifying forex account and there is either a positive or a negative retranslation amount for the retranslation period (such amount is essentially the closing balance for the period, less the opening balance, less total deposits, plus total withdrawals for the period). If the amount is positive, a gain arises and if the amount is negative, a loss arises.

A retranslation period may be in respect of part of a year and an entity can have more than one retranslation period in a year (eg by withdrawing the election and making a fresh election monthly) (ID 2004/157).

The election, which is revocable, may be made at any time and applies from the time it is made.

The election will not apply if an election is made under Subdiv 230-D (s 775-270(2A)).

Foreign exchange retranslation method (Subdiv 775-F)

Under Subdiv 230-D (¶23-020) a taxpayer may make an irrevocable foreign exchange retranslation election to bring foreign exchange gains and losses into account in line with the accounting treatment of such gains and losses. In this case, the gain or loss is the amount that the relevant accounting standard requires the taxpayer to recognise. Such election may be made if the taxpayer prepares a financial report in accordance with the Australian or equivalent foreign accounting standards. However the election does not apply if the financial arrangement is an equity interest, or right or obligation relating to an equity interest (under s 230-55).

Under Subdiv 775-F, if such an election is made, any forex realisation gain or loss arising from FRE 1 to 8 is disregarded and the gain (or loss) under FRE 9 is the amount that the relevant accounting standard requires the taxpayer to recognise in profit (or in loss) in relation to the arrangement. See ¶23-020 for application and transitional provisions.

Taxation treatment of forex gains and losses

A forex realisation gain which is not of a private or domestic nature is assessable where it arises from an FRE made during the year. While a forex realisation gain is specifically included in assessable income as statutory income, a gain arising under s 775-55 from the acquisition of foreign currency denominated trading stock (other than livestock that is only trading stock by reason of the statutory definition of trading stock) is ‘‘ordinary income’’ when calculating a taxpayer’s instalment income for PAYG purposes (TD 2006/29).

A forex realisation loss which is not of a private or domestic nature is deductible where it arises from an FRE made during the year.

A forex realisation gain which, if it had been a loss, would have been made in gaining or producing exempt income or non-assessable non-exempt (‘‘NANE’’) income, is treated as exempt or NANE income (eg ID 2004/571). A forex realisation loss is disregarded where it is made as a result of realising foreign currency or a right thereto (ie FRE 1, 2 or 5) and made in gaining or producing exempt or NANE income (s 775-35). Losses made as a result of ceasing to have an obligation to pay or receive foreign currency (ie FRE 3, 4 or 6) are disregarded to the extent that they are made in gaining or producing exempt or NANE income and the obligation does not give rise to a deduction (s 775-35; eg ID 2004/572).

Certain forex realisation gains of a private or domestic nature remain assessable if the gain would be taxable under the CGT provisions and the gain is: (a) a gain arising upon the disposal of foreign currency or a right; (b) a gain arising upon the discharge of a right acquired in return for the realisation of another kind of CGT asset; or (c) a gain arising upon the discharge of an obligation incurred to acquire a CGT asset.

Certain forex realisation losses of a private or domestic nature remain deductible if a gain or loss upon the realisation event would be recognised under the CGT provisions and it is: (a) a loss arising upon the discharge of a right acquired in return for the realisation of another kind of CGT asset; or (b) a loss arising upon the discharge of an obligation incurred to acquire a CGT asset.

Where an amount of exempt income is paid directly into a foreign currency denominated bank account, Div 775 does not operate to disregard any forex realisation loss made on withdrawal of that amount (TD 2006/16).

[FITR ¶590-400ff]

Debt and Equity

¶23-100 Debt and equity provisions overview

The debt and equity rules (ITAA97 Div 974) were introduced to classify certain financing arrangements as debt or equity for specified tax purposes including the thin capitalisation rules (¶22-700), the dividend and interest withholding rules (¶22-010, ¶22-020) and for determining whether a return paid by a company on a financing interest that it has issued is frankable. The debt and equity rules are intended to operate on the basis of the economic substance of the arrangement rather than merely its legal form.

ITAA97 Div 974 provides a test for determining whether an interest is to be treated as a debt interest or an equity interest for particular tax purposes. The tests must be applied every time there is a material change to the arrangement (ITAA97 s 974-110; ID 2004/611).

TD 2019/10 states that the debt and equity rules cannot limit the operation of the transfer pricing rules. Where the transfer pricing rules apply, a financing arrangement is classified as debt or as equity on the basis of the arm's length conditions that are taken to operate, rather than the actual conditions of the arrangement (¶22-580).

[FITR ¶762-748 – ¶762-925]

¶23-105 Debt interests

What is a debt interest?

The meaning of ''debt interest'' is relevant to companies and other entities. A scheme gives rise to a debt interest in an entity if, when it comes into existence, it satisfies the ''debt test'' in relation to the entity (ITAA97 s 974-15). The term ''scheme'' means any arrangement, scheme, plan, proposal, action, course of action or course of conduct.

Debt test

A scheme satisfies the debt test if:

(1) it is a financing arrangement for the entity, or the entity is a company and the scheme gives rise to an interest as a member or stockholder of the company, and

(2) the entity or a connected entity receives or will receive some financial benefit under the scheme, and

(3) the entity has, or both the entity and a connected entity have, an effectively non-contingent obligation under the scheme to provide financial benefit(s) to one or more entities after the time when the first of the financial benefits in (2) above is received, and

(4) it is substantially more likely than not that the value provided under (3) above will be at least equal to the value received under (2) above.

The value of financial benefit(s) to be provided is taken into account only if the entity or a connected entity has an effectively non-contingent obligation to provide them. Similarly, the value of financial benefit(s) to be received is taken into account only if another party has an effectively non-contingent obligation to provide them (ITAA97 s 974-20).

Where all but (4) above are satisfied, the debt test will still be satisfied if the Commissioner determines that it is substantially more likely than not that: (a) the non-contingent financial benefits provided under (3) above will offset the substantial part of the value received under (2) above; and (b) any shortfall will be offset by other financial benefits provided by the entity or its connected entity under the scheme (ITAA97 s 974-65).

A *''financing arrangement''* broadly is a scheme entered into or undertaken to raise finance for an entity or a connected entity, or to fund another financing arrangement (ITAA97 s 974-130). To be a debt interest or equity interest, a scheme must be a financing arrangement, shares in a company or units in a corporate trust estate.

The following will generally not be classified as financing arrangements: (a) ordinary *operating* leases; (b) securities lending arrangements under ITAA36 s 26BC; (c) general insurance and life insurance contracts undertaken as part of the issuer's ordinary course of business; and (d) royalty payment arrangements other than those specified in s 974-130. The obtaining of commitments from customers by cash or letters of credit does not qualify (ID 2003/664). A Certificate of Deposit is a debt interest in ID 2006/273.

A *''connected entity''* of an entity means an associate (¶4-200) of the entity or another member of the same ''wholly-owned group'' (¶3-090).

An *''effectively non-contingent obligation''* is an obligation that, in substance or effect, is not contingent on any event, condition or situation other than the ability or willingness of the relevant entity or connected entity to meet the obligation (ITAA97 s 974-135). See ID 2006/125 (term subordinated note), ID 2006/230 (revolving credit facility agreement) and ID 2007/52 (redeemable preference shares). Such an ''obligation'' need not be a legally enforceable obligation (TD 2009/1). Therefore, an effectively non-contingent obligation to provide a financial benefit can be found where a party has a right that it may exercise to provide a financial benefit but it does not have a legal obligation to take that action. This is primarily due to the interpretation of the expression ''in substance or effect'' to apply to both ''obligation'' and ''non-contingent''. This is also consistent both with the intention of the debt and equity provisions and with the other provisions that use the expression ''effectively non-contingent obligation''. An ''obligation'' does not have to be a legally enforceable obligation under s 974-135(1).

The issuer of a convertible note that can be converted at any time, at the issuer's discretion, into a share that is an equity interest in the issuer, does not have an effectively non-contingent obligation to provide financial benefits for the purposes of s 974-20(1)(c) (meaning the note will not be a debt interest), unless the option to convert should be disregarded on consideration of the pricing, terms and conditions under which the note was issued (TR 2008/3).

An issuer of an interest-bearing instrument that can change the rate of interest payable to any rate (including zero) that it chooses at its sole discretion does not have an ''effectively non-contingent obligation'' to provide ''financial benefits'' which means the instrument will not be a debt interest. If the holder of the instrument can compel the issuer to return the amount invested on any occasion that the issuer changes the interest rate, the instrument may be a debt interest (TD 2006/1).

▶ Example

An Australian company issues a redeemable security to its parent. Under the terms of the issue, the company must redeem it for 100% of its issue price in 5 years' time and, subject to profits being available, must pay returns of 8% pa. The interest is a debt interest. It passes the debt test criteria, even though the returns are contingent (eg ID 2003/527; ID 2003/665).

The Federal Court has held that redeemable shares issued to a partnership were debt interests as they were an effectively non-contingent obligation to provide a financial benefit. This was the case even though only 10 shares were issued and the redemption price was $1 per share (*D Marks Partnership*).

Regulations may be made to determine whether or not an obligation is contingent or whether or not it is effectively non-contingent. Currently, there are regulations in respect of the following arrangements: non-cumulative redeemable preference shares issued by credit unions and mutual building societies; redeemable preference shares (reg 974-135C); term cumulative subordinated notes with insolvency or capital adequacy conditions (reg 974-135D); perpetual cumulative subordinated notes with profitability, insolvency or negative earnings conditions (reg 974-135E); and term cumulative subordinated notes with non-viability conditions (reg 974-135F). The non-viability clause is disregarded in determining whether the entity's obligation to repay the principal amount on or after 1 January 2013 is effectively non-contingent.

Exception: short-term schemes

A scheme does not satisfy the debt test if:

- a substantial part of a financial benefit received or provided, as mentioned above, does not consist of money, or liquid or monetary asset(s)
- the scheme requires the financial benefit mentioned in (3) above to be provided within 100 days of receipt of the first financial benefit mentioned in (2) above, and: (a) it is provided within that period; or (b) the entity required to provide it is willing to do so but neglects or is unable to do so
- the scheme is not one of a number of related schemes (see below) that together are taken to give rise to a debt interest.

The Commissioner has no discretion to treat a scheme as having met the requirements for the exception (ID 2003/1040).

Related schemes

Two or more schemes that are in any way related (constituent schemes) may together give rise to a debt interest where the economic substance of the combined schemes is equivalent to a debt interest (s 974-15(2)). This will not be the case where each of the constituent schemes individually gives rise to a debt interest (ID 2006/230) or the Commissioner exercises the discretion to treat the schemes as not giving rise to a debt interest. Two schemes are not related to one another merely because one refers to the other or they have a common party. For examples of related schemes, see ID 2003/870 and ID 2004/430.

New scheme aggregation rule

The government has released draft legislation that proposes a new scheme aggregation rule, which replaces the existing related scheme rules in ss 974-15(2) and 974-70(2), and the equity override integrity provision in s 974-80. The new rule, discussed further at ¶23-115, ensures multiple schemes are only treated as a single scheme where this accurately reflects the economic substance of the schemes.

Debt interest where obligations owed by multiple entities

Where the same debt interest would otherwise be a debt interest of more than one entity, it is taken to be a debt interest only in the entity with the greatest "obligation value". The obligation value is the total value of the financial benefits that the entity is under an effectively non-contingent obligation to provide under the relevant scheme(s).

If it is not possible to determine which entity has the greatest obligation value, the debt interest is taken to be a debt interest in the entity agreed by all the entities or, failing such agreement, as determined by the Commissioner.

The Commissioner can determine that the debt interest is in a different entity from the one that was identified by either of the 2 methods (ITAA97 s 974-55).

Tie-breaker between debt and equity

An interest that could be characterised as both a debt interest and an equity interest will be treated as a debt interest. Accordingly, it is not necessary to apply the equity test (¶23-115) if the debt test has been satisfied.

Tax treatment of debt interest

A return paid on a debt interest will be deductible where it meets the general deduction criteria of ITAA97 s 8-1 (¶16-010).

Where the return would not otherwise meet the general deduction criteria of s 8-1, it may still be deductible up to a limit not exceeding the benchmark rate of return plus 150 basis points (1.5%). Subject to this limit and/or the regulations:

- it will not be prevented from being deductible merely because it is contingent upon economic performance or secures a permanent or enduring benefit, and
- if it is a dividend, it will be deductible to the extent that it would be deductible under s 8-1 if it were interest (ITAA97 s 25-85). A dividend payable in respect of a redeemable preference share (a debt interest) is deductible on or after the date of each payment, rather than on an accruals basis from the date of issue of the share (ID 2006/102).

The "benchmark rate of return" for an interest (the "test interest") in an entity is the annually compounded rate of return on an ordinary debt interest issued by the entity or a connected entity to a third party in the same market and currency, having a comparable maturity date, same credit status and same degree of debt subordination. Alternatively, if there is no such interest, it is the annually compounded internal rate of return on an interest that is closest to the test interest in the respects mentioned, adjusted appropriately to take account of the differences (ITAA97 s 995-1(1)). For an example, see ID 2006/319. An "ordinary debt interest" is one where the relevant obligations are not contingent on the economic performance of the issuer or a connected entity.

Certain interest expenses incurred in deriving certain non-assessable non-exempt income from a foreign source are deductible from assessable income if the amount is a cost in relation to certain debt interests (ITAA97 s 25-90). In TD 2009/21, the Commissioner expressed the view that a deduction under s 25-90 is not predicated on a taxpayer deriving a ITAA36 former s 23AJ dividend in the same income year that the cost is incurred. There must be a sufficiently clear nexus between the deduction and the production of the income to which s former 23AJ relates, and a reasonable expectation that there will be dividends paid in the future (note that from 17 October 2014, (former) s 23AJ has been replaced by Subdiv 768-A).

Where a debt interest is also a "financial arrangement" for the purposes of Div 230 (¶23-020), any gains or losses on that debt interest are brought to account under Div 230 (s 25-85(4A)).

[FITR ¶65-540, ¶762-767, ¶762-835, ¶762-895]

¶23-110 Financial benefits

A ''financial benefit'' means anything of economic value and includes property and services (ITAA97 s 974-160).

For the purposes of the debt and equity rules, a financial benefit is taken to be provided to an entity if it is provided: (a) to the entity; (b) on the entity's behalf; or (c) for the entity's benefit.

Neither the issue of an equity interest in itself by an entity or connected entity, nor an amount that is to be applied in respect of the issue, constitutes the provision of a financial benefit.

Valuation of financial benefits

Financial benefits in relation to debt interests having a term up to 10 years are valued in nominal terms. Where the term of the debt interest is, may or must exceed 10 years, they are valued in present value terms using the methodology provided in ITAA97 s 974-50 or in the regulations (ITAA97 s 974-35). Where a financing arrangement consists of a redeemable preference share having effectively non-contingent obligations and a term of 10 years, stapled to a perpetual ordinary share which has no effectively non-contingent obligations, the relevant performance period that is used to value the financial benefits provided and received under the related scheme is that of the instrument with effectively non-contingent obligations (ID 2006/103).

Where a future financial benefit is based on a variable factor such as a variable interest rate that cannot be accurately anticipated, the value of the financial benefit is calculated as if the factor's value retains its starting value over time.

Where all the financial benefits provided and received under a scheme are denominated in a particular foreign currency, commodity or other unit of account, they are not converted into Australian currency for the purpose of comparing their relative values.

Where a party to a scheme has a right or option to terminate the scheme early and has a non-contingent obligation to exercise that right or option, the life of the interest ends at the earliest time at which the party will have to exercise the right or option. Otherwise, the right or option is disregarded in working out the life of the interest (ITAA97 s 974-40).

Where a scheme gives rise to an interest that will or may convert into an equity interest in a company, the life of the interest ends no later than the time when it converts. If it is uncertain whether or when the interest will convert, the possibility of conversion is to be disregarded (ITAA97 s 974-45).

[FITR ¶762-785 – ¶762-805]

¶23-115 Equity interests

Equity interest

The meaning of ''equity interest'' is provided by ITAA97 Subdiv 974-C. A scheme gives rise to an equity interest in a company, when the scheme comes into existence, if it:

- is not a debt interest (¶23-105) in the company or a connected entity
- is not part of a larger interest that is a debt interest in the company or a connected entity
- satisfies the equity test in ITAA97 s 974-75(1) (see below).

The holder of an equity interest in a company is known as an ''equity holder''. A share that is not an equity interest (eg is or is part of a debt interest) is a ''non-equity share'' and a distribution relating to such share is unfrankable (¶4-620).

Regulations provide that certain non-cumulative redeemable preference shares issued by credit unions and mutual building societies are treated as equity interests.

Equity test

A scheme satisfies the equity test if:

(1) it gives rise to an interest in the company as a member or stockholder of the company

(2) it is a financing arrangement that gives rise to an interest carrying a right to a return from the company, and the right or return is contingent on the economic performance of the company, a connected entity or part of their activities

(3) it is a financing arrangement that gives rise to an interest carrying a right to a return from the company and the right or return is at the discretion of the company or a connected entity (eg ID 2003/752). Regulations may be made clarifying when a right or return is taken to be discretionary, or

(4) it is a financing arrangement that gives rise to an interest issued by the company that either: (a) gives its holder (or a connected entity of the holder) a right to be issued with an equity interest in the company or a connected entity of the company; or (b) is or may be convertible into such an interest.

The return referred to in (2) or (3) above may be a return of an amount invested in the interest. This is an exception to the general definition of "return", which states that "return on a debt interest or equity interest does not include a return of an amount invested in the interest".

The interest referred to in (2), (3) or (4) above may take the form of a proprietary right, a chose in action or any other form.

A share that falls within (1) will also be a convertible interest if it satisfies (4) above (TD 2007/26). For other examples of the application of the test, see ID 2003/325 to ID 2003/327 and ID 2003/873.

Related schemes — Two or more related schemes may also be categorised as together giving rise to an equity interest where the economic substance of the combined schemes is equivalent to an equity interest (ITAA97 s 974-70(2)). This will not be the case where each of the constituent schemes individually gives rise to an equity interest or the Commissioner exercises the discretion to treat the schemes as not giving rise to an equity interest.

Note that a new scheme aggregation rule has been proposed, which, if enacted, will replace the related schemes rule in s 974-70(2). The new rule is discussed below.

Equity override integrity provision — An equity override integrity provision in s 974-80 can apply to complex circumstances where a group raises capital by issuing an effective equity interest through the issue of debt to an interposed entity connected to the issuer. The central test is whether the return on a debt interest in one scheme is designed to be used to fund the return on an equity interest in a separate scheme. If these criteria are satisfied, the debt issued is treated as an equity interest. Clarification on this equity override provision is provided in TD 2015/3 and TD 2015/10. The equity override provision will not apply merely because a non-resident entity has chosen to invest indirectly in a debt interest issued by an Australian resident company and there are one or more equity interests interposed between the non-resident entity and the entity holding the debt interest (TD 2015/2).

Note that a new scheme aggregation rule has been proposed, which if enacted will replace the equity override integrity provision in s 974-80. The new rule is discussed directly below.

New scheme aggregation rule — The government has proposed a new scheme aggregation rule to replace the existing related scheme rules in ss 974-15(2) and 974-70(2), and the equity override integrity provision in s 974-80. The proposed new rule ensures multiple schemes are treated as a single scheme only where this accurately reflects the economic substance of the schemes. Under the proposed rule, it is necessary to consider whether the pricing, terms and conditions of the schemes are interdependent in a way that would change their debt or equity treatment under Div 974; and whether it would be concluded that the schemes were designed to operate to produce their combined economic effect — a link that is either accidental or present, without any element of design, is not sufficient to cause the schemes to be aggregated.

Exception for at call loans — From 1 July 2005, related party at call loans are deemed to be debt for a company if the company satisfies a less than $20 million annual turnover test in that year. This deeming rule applies whether the loan was made before or after 1 July 2005. As there may be fluctuations in turnover, the taxpayer may elect to alter the loan so that it is a debt interest (as if the change occurred at the beginning of the previous year). The election must be made before the earlier of the due date for the company's return or the actual lodgment date (ITAA97 s 974-110). See also ATO Guide ''Debt and equity tests: guide to 'at call' loans'', and CCH *Tax Week* ¶734 (2005).

''Non-share equity interest'' — A non-share equity interest in a company is an equity interest in the company that is not solely a share (ITAA97 s 995-1(1)), eg it may be an interest that is not a share or stapled security that includes a share (eg ID 2003/901; ID 2004/56). An investment in an unsecured note to be issued by a private investment company to a director is a non-share equity interest (ID 2002/794).

Tax treatment of equity interests

A company cannot deduct a dividend paid on an equity interest as a general deduction and cannot deduct a non-share distribution (¶23-125) or a return that has accrued on a non-share equity interest (ITAA97 s 26-26).

The dividend franking provisions (¶4-880) apply generally to a non-share equity interest and an equity holder in the same way that they apply to a share and a shareholder.

Most of the other relevant provisions of ITAA97 and ITAA36 apply in a similar manner, as noted in the commentary dealing with those provisions.

[FITR ¶762-823 – ¶762-850]

¶23-120 Non-share capital accounts

A company will have a notional account called a ''non-share capital account'' if it issues a non-share equity interest (¶23-115) in the company (ITAA97 s 164-10). Furthermore a company will have a non-share capital account if: (a) a debt interest changes to an equity interest as a result of a material change under s 974-110 (¶23-100); (b) a related party at call loan that was a debt interest becomes an equity interest on 1 July 2005 (¶23-115); or (c) the small company related party at call loan deeming rule ceases to apply to an interest (¶23-115). Special provisions applied to interests issued before 1 July 2001 that were still in existence on that date. The account records contributions to the company in relation to those non-share equity interests and returns of those contributions made by the company.

Once established, the non-share capital account continues indefinitely, even if the company ceases to have any non-share equity interests in existence. The balance cannot fall below nil.

Credits to non-share capital account

The only credits that may be made to the non-share capital account are those provided for in ITAA97 s 164-15. These are:

- where the company issues a non-share equity interest (¶23-115), the account is credited with the consideration the company receives *less* any credit made to its share capital account in respect of the issue (eg where the interest is a stapled security that includes a share). Where the consideration is other than money, it is valued at its market value at the time it is provided
- where a debt interest changes to an equity interest under (a) to (c) above, the account is credited with the consideration the company received for the issue of the interest, *less* any credit made to its share capital account in respect of the issue, *less* so much of the original consideration received that has been returned to the holder of the interest before the change occurs.

Debits to non-share capital account

The only debits that may be made to the non-share capital account are those that are provided for in ITAA97 s 164-20. These are as follows.

- All or part of a non-share distribution is debited to the account to the extent that: (a) the distribution is made as consideration for the surrender, cancellation or redemption of a non-share equity interest; or (b) the distribution is made in connection with a reduction in the market value of a non-share equity interest and equals that reduction.
- Where: (a) an equity interest changes at any time to a debt interest, as a result of a material change (¶23-100); or (b) the small company related party at call loan deeming rule applies to an interest that was an equity interest at the end of the previous year (¶23-115), the account is debited with the sum of all the credits that have been made to the account in relation to the interest *less* the sum of all the debits that have been made to the account in relation to the interest before the change occurs (ie the net balance in relation to that interest is offset to nil).

The total debits to the account in respect of a non-share equity interest cannot exceed the total credits in respect of the interest, ie there cannot be a negative balance in respect of any particular interest.

[FITR ¶178-000 – ¶178-030, ¶762-873]

¶23-125 Non-share distributions

A company makes a ''non-share distribution'' to a person if the person holds a non-share equity interest in the company and the company distributes money or other property, or credits an amount, to that person as the holder of the interest. A non-share distribution is characterised as: (a) a ''non-share dividend''; and/or (b) a ''non-share capital return''. Such distributions are not deductible (¶23-115).

Every non-share distribution is a non-share dividend, except to the extent that it is debited to the company's non-share capital account or share capital account. To the latter extent, it is a non-share capital return (ITAA97 Subdiv 974-E).

[FITR ¶762-873 – ¶762-880]

Asset and Project Financing

¶23-200 Financing projects or the acquisition of income-producing assets

The TOFA regime in Div 230 provides a comprehensive framework for the taxation of gains and losses arising in respect of financial arrangements (¶23-020), however it is not an exclusive code. Certain financial arrangements are specifically excluded from the application of Div 230 including certain leasing arrangements. Financial arrangements may also fall outside of the ambit of Div 230 because they pre-date the Div 230 commencement date of 1 July 2010 (1 July 2009 if an early start election was made) and no transitional election was made to bring them within the TOFA regime.

The commentary from ¶23-200 to ¶23-270 considers the taxation rules applicable to certain asset and project financing transactions to which Div 230 does not apply, namely:

- assets put to a tax-preferred use (¶23-210)
- sale and lease back arrangements (¶23-240)
- hire purchase arrangements (¶23-250)
- asset financing using non-recourse debt (¶23-260).

The rules applicable to these arrangements seek to charge tax on economic substance rather than legal form. Where these rules do not apply, the deductibility and assessability of lease payments will depend on the application of the ordinary principles outlined at ¶16-060 and ¶10-500 respectively. For the assessability of profits on the sale of lease equipment, see ¶10-380 to ¶10-422. The provisions dealing with luxury car leases are set out at ¶17-220. The taxation consequences of motor vehicle lease novation arrangements are at ¶16-310 and ¶35-150. For the implications of cross-border leases, see ¶22-020 and ¶22-030.

Depreciating assets and leases

Capital allowance deductions are available to the holder of a depreciating asset to the extent that the asset is used for taxable purposes (¶17-010). The depreciating assets that are subject to the capital allowance regime are tangible assets, but also include a limited number of specified intangible assets (¶17-015). Generally the holder of the asset is the owner, ie the lessor in the case of an ordinary lease. However, special provisions apply to deal with particular types of leases and other financing arrangements involving depreciating assets (¶17-020).

Proposed changes to taxation of asset backed financing arrangements

The government announced in its 2016–17 Budget that the tax treatment of asset backed financing arrangements will be clarified to ensure they are treated in the same way as financing arrangements based on interest bearing loans or investments. The proposed changes include the removal of key barriers to the use of asset backed financing arrangements, such as deferred payment and hire purchase arrangements. When enacted, the changes are intended to apply from 1 July 2018.

[FITR ¶19-200 – ¶19-230, ¶27-090]

¶23-210 Asset financing and tax-preferred entities

Assets put to tax-preferred use are subject to the rules in Div 250 of ITAA97 and are explicitly excluded from the TOFA regime in Div 230.

Where Div 250 applies, it has the effect of denying or reducing certain capital allowance deductions that would otherwise be available in relation to an asset if the asset is put to a tax-preferred use and the taxpayer has an insufficient economic interest in the asset. If such deductions are denied or reduced, certain financial benefits in relation to the tax-preferred use of the asset are assessed only to the extent of a notional gain component. This component is calculated by treating the arrangements as a loan that is taxed on a compounding accruals basis.

Prerequisites for the application of the rules

The rules apply if at a particular time (s 250-15):

- an asset is being put to a tax-preferred use
- the arrangement period for such use is greater than 12 months
- financial benefits in relation to the tax preferred use will be provided (ss 250-85 to 250-100) to the taxpayer by a tax-preferred end-user (or connected entity), or a tax-preferred entity (or connected entity), or a non-resident
- an entitlement would arise to a capital allowance deduction for the decline in value of the asset or for expenditure in relation to the asset, and
- the taxpayer lacks a predominant economic interest in the asset at the time. ''Predominant economic interest'' in an asset is determined under the rules in ss 250-110 to 250-140.

An entity (other than the taxpayer) is an ''end-user'' if the entity (or a connected entity) uses or will use, or is able to use or will be able to use the asset, or effectively controls, or will effectively control, or is able to or will be able to control, the use of the asset (s 250-50). Control may be direct or indirect. Temporary control for the purpose of ensuring public health and safety, protecting the environment or continuing the supply of an essential service is disregarded.

An end-user is a ''tax-preferred end user'' if the end-user (or connected entity) is a tax-preferred entity or the end-user is a non-resident. Tax-preferred entity is an exempt entity, an exempt Australian or foreign government agency, an associated government entity of an exempt Australian government agency, or a prescribed excluded state/territory body.

An asset is put to a tax-preferred use if an end-user is a lessee of the asset, and the asset is to be used by a tax-preferred end user or the asset is to be used wholly or principally outside Australia by a non-resident (s 250-60). An asset is also put to a tax-preferred use if the asset is to be used wholly or partly in connection with the production, supply, carriage, transmission or delivery of goods or the provision of services or facilities, to or for a tax-preferred end user (other than an exempt foreign government agency), or the asset is to be used wholly or principally outside Australia and the end-user is a non-resident.

The arrangement period for a tax-preferred use starts when such use starts, and ends on the date on which such use is reasonably expected to or is likely to end (s 250-65).

Improvements to and fixtures on land are taken to be assets that are separate from the land (s 250-75). Renewals or extensions of a right are taken to be a continuation of the original right. Whether a composite asset is one asset or whether the components are separate assets depends on the circumstances of each case. Non-lease arrangements for the use of real property or goods or personal chattels (other than money) giving the right to control the use of the asset are treated as leases (s 250-80).

Exclusions

However the rules in Div 250 do not apply in the following circumstances:

- the taxpayer is a small business entity (¶7-050) for the income year in which the arrangement period starts and applies Subdiv 328-D for the asset for that year (s 250-20)
- the total of the nominal value of the financial benefits to be provided by members of the tax-preferred sector under the arrangement is $5 million or less (this amount is indexed) (s 250-25)

- the arrangement period is 3 years or less, or in the case of a lease of real property, 5 years or less (s 250-30), except where s 250-35 applies
- the total of the nominal value of the financial benefits to be provided by members of the tax-preferred sector under the arrangement is $30 million, or in the case of a lease of real property, $50 million or less (this amount is indexed) (s 250-30), except where s 250-35 applies
- the total of the value of the assets that are put to a tax-preferred use under the arrangement is $20 million, or $40 million in the case of a lease of real property (s 250-30), except where s 250-35 applies
- the arrangement is a hire purchase arrangement subject to ITAA97 Div 240
- the present value of the amounts that would be assessable under Div 250 is less than the difference between the present value of the amounts that would be assessable if Div 250 did not apply and the deductions that would be available under Divs 40 and 43 if Div 250 did not apply (s 250-40), or
- the Commissioner determines (on the taxpayer's application) that it would be unreasonable for Div 250 to apply (s 250-45). The Commissioner's decision is reviewable under TAA Pt IVC.

Division 250 does not apply in respect of capital expenditure incurred by a taxpayer under Subdiv 40-I, where the taxpayer is not otherwise entitled to a capital allowance (ID 2010/31).

Denial of capital allowance deductions

If Div 250 applies to an asset and a taxpayer at a particular time, capital allowance deductions that would otherwise be available for the decline in value of an asset or and in respect of expenditure in relation to an asset are not available (s 250-145). Capital allowance deductions are deductions under Div 40 (capital allowances), Div 43 (capital works), Subdiv 328-D (capital allowances for small business entities) and ITAA97 former Div 10B and 10BA (Australian films). However, such deductions will be only partially disallowed if it is reasonable to expect that the financial benefits under the arrangement will be provided in respect of a use of the asset that is not tax-preferred nor private, or in respect of a tax-preferred use of the asset but not by members of the tax preferred sector (s 250-150). In such case, the taxpayer can make an irrevocable election to apportion the deduction, and the following percentage of the deductions is disallowed ("the disallowed capital percentage"):

$$\frac{\text{Sum of present values of financial benefits that are subject to deemed loan treatment}}{\text{Market value of asset}}$$

The Commissioner may determine an alternative apportionment method and such determination is reviewable under TAA Pt IVC.

Deemed loan treatment

Another consequence of ITAA97 Div 250 applying to an asset at a particular time is that a "financial arrangement" (ss 230-45; 230-50) in the form of a loan is taken to exist (s 250-155). The taxpayer receiving the benefits in relation to the tax-preferred use of the asset is taken to be the lender, over the arrangement period. The amount lent is taken to be the adjustable value of the asset (or other undeducted Div 40 capital expenditure, or undeducted capital expenditure under Div 43) less any financial benefits that have become due and payable before the start of the arrangement period and that are subject to the "deemed loan treatment" (s 250-160).

Gains and losses from such financial arrangements are recognised over the life of the arrangement using the compounding accruals method (or similar method) and ignoring distinctions between income and capital (ss 250-190 to 250-250). Changes in circumstances may cause a re-estimation of gains and losses that the accruals method is being applied to (ss 250-255; 250-260). A balancing adjustment is required if particular rights or obligations are transferred or cease (ss 250-265 to 250-275). In order to avoid double taxation, financial benefits provided by members of the tax-preferred segment to a taxpayer in relation to the tax-preferred use of an asset are not assessed as income if they are subject to the deemed loan treatment (s 250-185).

Other consequences

If Div 250 applies and the arrangement period for the tax-preferred use of an asset ceases at a particular time, the ''adjustable value'' of the asset under ITAA97 Div 40 is taken to be the end value of the asset under s 250-180 (s 250-285(1)). If the apportionment rules under s 250-150 have applied (see above), the adjustable value is the end value of the asset multiplied by the disallowed capital percentage plus the adjustable value multiplied by the allowed capital percentage.

If the arrangement period of the tax-preferred use of an asset ends because a particular event happens that would have qualified as a balancing adjustment event (if Div 250 had not applied), a balancing adjustment is made under Subdiv 40-D as if the event were a balancing adjustment event and the adjustable value of the asset were the amount worked out under s 250-285(1), and ss 40-290 and 40-292 (about reductions to the balancing adjustment amount to reflect non-taxable use of the asset) did not apply.

If the arrangement period for the tax-preferred use of an asset ceases at a particular time, the cost base or reduced cost base of the asset is reduced by the capital component of the deemed loan that has been excluded from assessable income. Similarly if the asset is on revenue account, the taxable profit is increased or loss is reduced by that amount on the sale of the asset.

For income years beginning on or after 1 July 2008, net gains under Subdiv 250-E are included in the taxpayer's instalment income under TAA s 45-120(2B).

[FITR ¶245-000 – ¶245-620]

¶23-230 Lease assignments

Division 45 provides specific rules to prevent the avoidance of tax in connection with assignments and disposals of leased plant. The TOFA regime in Div 230 does not apply to lease assignments and disposals.

Division 45 prevents avoidance of tax by taking into account all forms of consideration received from assigning leases (including the benefit of being relieved of debt) when calculating the assignor's assessable income.

Prior to the introduction of Div 45, tax could be avoided through assigning interests in leases to tax exempt or low tax entities by taking advantage of a balancing charge roll-over rule which applies where there is a partial change in ownership of the leased asset, or by effectively transferring debt along with interests in the leased asset or the lease. Lease assignments could also be undertaken by disposing of interests in a 100% subsidiary that owns the leased asset.

Division 45 applies when plant, or an interest in plant, is disposed of and:

- the plant was a leased asset on or after 22 February 1999
- the plant has been used by the lessor or an associate primarily for leasing to others
- the lessor or an associate has deducted amounts for depreciation.

If these circumstances exist, Div 45 applies as follows.

(1) Where the disposal constitutes a balancing adjustment event (¶17-630), the lessor's assessable income includes any excess of the money consideration and the value of other benefits obtained from disposing of the plant (or an interest in the plant) over the plant's written down value (or relevant proportion thereof). The ''written down value'' is the ''cost'' of the asset reduced by the sum of the amounts that the taxpayer has deducted, or can deduct, for the asset's decline in value (ie depreciation). However, if the taxpayer acquired the asset by way of a roll-over (¶17-710), the ''written down value'' of the asset is found by further reducing its cost by the amounts that the transferor, and any earlier successive transferor, deducted or can deduct for depreciation. For the meaning of ''plant'', see ¶17-040.

(2) If the lessor disposes of rights under the lease of the plant without disposing of the plant itself, the lessor's assessable income includes the money consideration for the disposal plus the value of other benefits obtained as a result of the disposal.

(3) Similar results as in (1) and (2) above follow if a partner in a partnership disposes of an interest in the partnership so as to reduce the partner's interest in plant which the partnership has used mainly to lease to other entities, or disposes of rights or an interest in the lease.

(4) If an interest in leased plant is effectively disposed of by selling more than 50% of the shares in a wholly-owned leasing subsidiary which owns the plant, the leasing subsidiary is treated as having disposed of the plant and reacquired it at market value. This means that the depreciation balancing adjustment rules would bring to tax any excess of the plant's market value over its written down value at the deemed disposal time. There is no such effect, however, if the main business of the new owners of the subsidiary is the same as the main business of the former group.

(5) If more than 50% of the shares in a wholly-owned subsidiary which is a partner in the leasing partnership changes hands, the subsidiary is treated as having disposed of its interest in plant that had been used by the partnership principally to lease to other entities. The consequence is that the de-grouped subsidiary becomes liable to tax on the difference between the market value of its interest in the leased plant and the proportion of its written down value attributable to that interest. This rule does not apply, however, if the main business of the new owners of the subsidiary is the same as the main business of the former group.

(6) In either of the cases outlined in (4) and (5) above, the companies that were in the same group as the de-grouped subsidiary become liable for the tax upon which the subsidiary was assessed, attributable to the transactions described above, if the former subsidiary does not pay the tax within 6 months of it becoming payable. This tax is imposed by the *New Business Tax System (Former Subsidiary Tax Imposition) Act 1999*.

(7) If the plant, or the interest in plant, is otherwise within Div 45, was acquired before 11.45 am EST on 21 September 1999 and was disposed of after that time, and the sum of the disposal benefits exceeds the cost of the plant or the part of the cost attributable to the disposed interest, the amount to be included in the lessor's assessable income under Div 45 is reduced by a factor that will allow for the indexation of assets subject to CGT. This is because CGT indexation of depreciable assets that were acquired before, but are disposed of after, that time is frozen as at 30 September 1999.

(8) An amount is not included in assessable income under Div 45 to the extent that it is already directly included in assessable income by another provision (eg as a balancing charge), or would be included except for specific relieving provisions, such as where it is subject to roll-over relief to a related entity (eg where a partnership disposes of a partnership asset: ID 2003/624).

▶ Example 1

Aldred Pty Ltd owns an item of plant which it leases to another business. There is no outstanding debt on the plant. Aldred has so far claimed depreciation on the plant totalling $4,500, and its current written down value is $5,000.

Aldred agrees to sell the plant to a superannuation fund for $7,500. This gives rise to the following possible consequences:

- a balancing charge of $2,500 would be included in Aldred's assessable income under ITAA97 s 40-285 (¶17-630), and
- an amount of $2,500 would be included in Aldred's assessable income under s 45-5(2).

In this case, the assessable amount under Div 45 is reduced to nil, because the same or a greater amount is assessable as a balancing adjustment.

▶ Example 2

Assume the same facts as in Example 1 except that, at the time of disposal, Aldred still owes a financier $3,000 which it had borrowed to acquire the asset in the first place. In addition to paying a cash consideration of $7,500 for the asset, the purchaser agrees to assume Aldred's remaining debt of $3,000. Thus, the sum of all the benefits received by Aldred in respect of the disposal is:

$7,500 + $3,000 = $10,500

The disposal gives rise to the following possible consequences:

- a balancing adjustment of $5,500 (ie $7,500 + $3,000 – $5,000) would be included in Aldred's assessable income under s 40-285, and
- an amount of $5,500 (ie $10,500 – $5,000) would be included in Aldred's assessable income under s 45-5(1).

In this case, the assessable amount under Div 45 is reduced to nil because the same amount is already assessable as a balancing adjustment.

Where an interest in a leased depreciating asset, or the lease itself, has been transferred in the circumstances regulated by Div 45 and roll-over relief has applied under the capital allowance provisions (¶17-710), the transferee is taken to have inherited the following characteristics from the transferor (ITAA97 s 40-350):

(1) if the transferor (or a partnership of which the transferor was a member) leased out the depreciating asset for most of the time that the transferor or partnership held the asset, the transferee is also taken to have done so

(2) if the transferor (or a partnership of which the transferor was a member) leased out the asset for a period on or after 22 February 1999, then the transferee is also taken to have done so, and

(3) if the main business of the transferor (or of the partnership of which the transferor was a member) was to lease assets to others then the transferee's main business is taken also to have been leasing assets.

However, this does not apply to elective roll-over relief if the sum of the amount of the benefits received by the lessor in respect of the disposal is at least equal to the market value of the plant or interest (s 40-350).

[FITR ¶99-490 – ¶99-610]

¶23-240 Sale and leaseback arrangements

A sale and leaseback transaction typically involves the sale by a taxpayer of a depreciable asset to a financier and the leasing of that asset directly back to the taxpayer as lessee. In such case, the lessor should return the lease income as assessable income and deduct from that income depreciation and any other deductions (the "asset method" of returning lease income). Payments to the lessor to make up the residual value of the asset will have an income character. Advantages of such arrangements include: (a) the lease payments are deductible in full (if the lessee borrowed funds to purchase the asset, the capital component of the loan repayment would not be deductible); (b) the financier can offer the lessee better terms if the financier can claim depreciation deductions or, in the case of buildings, deductions under ITAA97 Div 43; and (c) the lessee receives capital that would otherwise be consumed in the purchase of the asset.

The TOFA regime in Div 230 does not apply to sale and leaseback transactions. The taxation consequences of sale and leaseback financing arrangements which involve depreciating assets subject to Div 40 are as follows (TR 2006/13):

1. When a depreciating asset is sold, the balancing adjustment provisions apply. The Commissioner accepts a sale price representing the market value of the asset at the time of sale. Generally, the lessor's rights in respect of a leased asset would arise in circumstances where that asset would have to be separated from the business of the lessee, because the lease would have expired or because the lessee would be in default under the lease, and market value should reflect this fact. Where no ready market exists, the Commissioner will accept the adjustable value of the asset.

2. Deductions for decline in value of the asset are available to the lessor based on the cost of the asset to the lessor (ordinarily, the price paid under the sale to the lessor), not the cost to the lessee. If the lessee is the "holder" of the asset under Item 6 of the table in s 40-40 (¶17-020), the lessee, and not the lessor, claims decline in value deductions.

3. Periodic lease payments by the lessee to the lessor are deductible to the lessee and assessable to the lessor (the asset method of returning lease income: IT 2594; *Citibank Ltd*). Additional payments by the lessee to the lessor to make up the residual value of the asset to a required level (generally on expiry or termination of the lease) are also income of the lessor. See also IT 28 (¶16-060).

4. When the lease ends and the lessor sells the asset, the balancing adjustment provisions apply to the lessor. If, at the end of the lease, the lessor takes possession of the depreciating asset, the lessor continues to "hold" the asset and may continue to claim deductions for the decline in value of the asset if used for a taxable purpose. If the lessor continues to hold the asset but ceases to use it for a taxable purpose, then a balancing adjustment event may occur.

5. A different tax treatment results where a sale and leaseback arrangement includes a right of, or an obligation on, the lessee to repurchase the asset at the end of the lease. For example, if the arrangement is actually a hire purchase arrangement, ITAA97 Div 240 applies (¶23-250).

6. In some cases, a profit or gain derived by the lessee on disposal of the asset may constitute income apart from the balancing adjustment provisions (¶10-112).

7. Lease payments may have a capital component to the extent that the expected sale price of the asset is less than that actual market value at the end of the lease. The Commissioner accepts an up-front valuation of the expected market value of the asset at the end of the lease in the case of long term leases (for example, greater than 4 years), in the case of a bona fide valuation that is based on independent evidence or set no lower than in accordance with IT 28 and TD 93/142. The termination value, for the purposes of calculating any balancing adjustments arising at the end of the lease, is determined under the balancing adjustment provisions (¶17-640).

The ruling also deals with the consequences of sale and leaseback arrangements involving depreciating assets that are fixtures on land, as well as the potential application of the anti-avoidance provisions in ITAA36 Pt IVA (¶30-170) and s 51AD (TR 96/22). However, it does not apply to luxury car leases which are subject to the special rules outlined in ¶17-220.

The Full Federal Court has ruled that 2 large plant sale and leaseback arrangements were effective for tax purposes because, although one of the purposes of adopting a lease finance transaction instead of a loan was to obtain a tax benefit, the prevailing purpose was to obtain a large financial facility on the best terms reasonably available (*Eastern Nitrogen*; *Metal Manufactures*). The Commissioner's application for special leave to appeal to the High Court in both cases on the anti-avoidance issue was refused based on the view that the decisions turned on their own facts. The Commissioner considered arrangements featuring the use of inflated prices and artificially low residual values to be primarily designed as tax-avoidance measures (*ATO media release* NAT 02/16, 5 March 2002). Where a trading entity taxpayer enters into a sale and leaseback of a capital asset, expenditure incurred in establishing the transaction (eg valuation fees, establishment costs) is of a capital nature and not deductible (TD 2003/15).

[FTR ¶81-355; FITR ¶32-890]

¶23-250 Hire purchase arrangements

Hire purchase arrangements are subject to specific rules in ITAA97 Div 240. The TOFA regime in Div 230 does not apply to these arrangements.

Under Div 240, hire purchase and instalment sale transactions entered into after 27 February 1998 are treated as a sale of the property by the legal owner (the notional seller) to the entity having the right to use the asset, ie the hirer (the notional buyer), financed by a loan from the notional seller to the notional buyer. If Div 240 applies, the "Rule of 78" method does not apply (TR 93/16).

The rules have effect for all purposes of ITAA97 and ITAA36 including for the purpose of calculating balancing adjustment amounts (¶17-640). For the interaction of Div 240 and the capital allowance provisions, see TR 2005/20. However, the rules do not apply for CGT and withholding tax purposes (ID 2005/263). The CGT provisions apply in the usual manner to the actual transactions between the parties. Division 243 may apply if the notional loan is not fully repaid at the time the loan is terminated (¶23-260).

Where the leaseback component of a sale and leaseback arrangement is properly described as a hire purchase arrangement in respect of goods, Div 240 may treat the leaseback as a sale and loan and the lessee and lessor as a notional buyer and notional seller respectively (TR 2006/13; ¶23-240).

"Hire purchase agreement"

A contract for the hire of goods is a "hire purchase agreement" (as defined in ITAA97 s 995-1(1)) if the hirer has the right or obligation to purchase the goods and the charge that is made for the hire, together with any other amount payable under the contract (including an amount to buy the goods or to exercise an option to do so), exceeds the price of the goods. The excess represents the finance charge component of the contract.

If parties to a contract for the use or acquisition of goods add a nominal or trivial sum to the price of the goods to bring it within Div 240, the Commissioner considers that the addition of these *de minimis* amounts cannot reasonably represent a charge for the provision of finance. In fact, where the payment obligations of the hirer under the agreement are entirely prepaid or defeased by an up-front payment, there is no financing element in the arrangement. The question of what is *de minimis* in a particular case depends on all the facts and circumstances including the relative value of the goods concerned. As a guide, an amount added to the price of goods would be considered *de minimis* if it is so low that it could not reasonably be regarded as a finance charge (TD 2003/17). The Commissioner would also consider applying ITAA36 Pt IVA in these circumstances.

Taxation treatment of notional buyer (the hirer)

Where a hire purchase agreement is recharacterised as a sale of property by the notional seller to the notional buyer, combined with a loan (to finance the purchase), the consideration for the notional sale is taken to be the agreed cost or value, or the arm's length value. As a consequence of the notional sale, the notional buyer (rather than the notional seller) is considered to be the owner of the property for capital allowance purposes if it is reasonable to conclude that the notional buyer will acquire the asset, or that the asset will be disposed of at the direction and for the benefit of the notional buyer (¶17-020). If the property is acquired as trading stock, the normal consequences follow, ie the notional buyer is entitled to a deduction for the purchase price of the stock.

The notional interest on account of the finance charge on the loan, calculated for each payment period and subject to adjustment at the end of the arrangement, may be deductible to the notional buyer if the property is used for income-producing purposes. The actual payments are not deductible to the notional buyer.

If the arrangement is extended or renewed, the notional buyer continues to be treated as the owner and Div 240 applies to the extended or renewed arrangement as a new arrangement. If the arrangement ceases and the notional buyer acquires the property, the notional buyer continues to be treated as the owner and the transfer of the title to the property is not taken to be a disposal of the property (in addition, no amount is deductible to the notional buyer).

If the agreement ceases and the notional buyer ceases to have the right to use the property, the notional buyer is taken to have sold the property back to the notional seller at market value.

See also ID 2003/462 to ID 2003/464 and ID 2003/1196 to 2003/1199.

Taxation treatment of notional seller (the legal owner)

Where a hire purchase agreement is recharacterised as a sale of property by the notional seller to the notional buyer, combined with a loan (to finance the purchase), the consideration for the notional sale is taken to be the agreed cost or value, or the arm's length value. As a consequence of the notional sale, the notional seller loses the right to claim capital allowance deductions under ITAA97 Div 40 for the property (¶17-020).

Any profit made by the seller on the notional sale or on the sale of the property after a notional reacquisition is assessable income of the notional seller (if the property is trading stock, the usual consequences follow, ie the sale price is assessable).

The notional interest on account of the finance charge on the loan, calculated for each payment period and subject to adjustment at the end of the arrangement, is assessable to the notional seller. The actual payments are not assessable to the notional seller. Special provisions apply if the notional seller assigns the right to payments under the arrangement to a third party.

If the arrangement ceases and the notional buyer acquires the property, the notional buyer continues to be treated as the owner and the transfer of the title to the property is not taken to be a disposal of the property (in addition, no amount is assessable to the notional seller). If the agreement ceases and the notional buyer ceases to have the right to use the property, the notional seller is taken to have acquired the property from the notional buyer at market value.

The provisions do not apply to a hire purchase agreement where there is a notional buyer but no notional seller (a notional seller is a party to the agreement that either actually owns the goods or is taken to be the owner by a previous application of Div 240). This could arise where the supplier is a lessee of the goods under a head lease that is not a hire purchase agreement (eg because the charges under the agreement may not exceed the price of the goods) and is subleasing the goods to the hirer under a lease that is a hire purchase agreement. However, in such a case, the Commissioner would consider applying the general anti-avoidance provisions of Pt IVA (TD 2003/16).

Proposed changes to taxation of hire purchase arrangements

The government announced in its 2016–17 Budget that key barriers to the use of asset backed financing arrangements, which are supported by assets, such as deferred payment arrangements and hire purchase arrangements will be removed. The government will clarify the tax treatment of asset backed financing arrangements and ensure they are treated in the same way as financing arrangements based on interest bearing loans or investments. When enacted, the changes are intended to apply from 1 July 2018.

[FITR ¶225-000 – ¶225-810]

¶23-260 Limited recourse debt arrangements

Limited recourse debt arrangements are subject to specific rules in ITAA97 Div 243. The TOFA regime in Div 230 does not apply to these arrangements.

Division 243 limits the deductions that a taxpayer may claim in respect of property acquired using ''limited recourse debt''. The Division achieves this by recouping excess capital allowance deductions claimed with respect to capital expenditure where the taxpayer has not been fully at risk in relation to the expenditure because it is financed by a limited recourse debt and has not fully repaid the debt upon termination.

Limited recourse debt

Division 243 only applies where there is a limited recourse debt. A creditor's rights of recourse can be limited by contractual terms or by the overall effect of an arrangement, eg where a special purpose entity debtor predominantly holds and operates the financed assets. In both situations, the debtor is not fully at risk with respect to the debt and therefore the capital expenditure which is financed by the debt.

The definition of ''limited recourse debt'' was intended to apply to both contractually limited recourse debt arrangements as well as debt arrangements where recourse is effectively limited through arrangements. However, the High Court held that the definition only applied to contractually limited debt recourse arrangements (*BHP Billiton*).

To ensure that Div 243 applies to debt arrangements where recourse is effectively limited through arrangements, the definition of limited recourse debt has been amended to cover debt arrangements where it is reasonable to conclude that the debtor has not been fully at risk with respect to the debt because the creditor's recourse is effectively limited to the financed property or property provided to secure the debt. This amendment applies to debt arrangements terminated at or after 7.30 pm AEST in the ACT, on 8 May 2012.

Limit to capital allowance deductions

Where property is acquired under limited recourse debt (including hire purchase and instalment sales), the purchaser or hirer will only be able to obtain capital allowance deductions equal to the amount actually paid under the arrangement. The deduction limit applies where the debt is terminated and, on termination, the debtor does not fully pay out the capital amounts owing. Capital allowance deductions are those under ITAA97 Div 40 (depreciating assets and other expenditure: Chapters 17, 18 and 19), ITAA36 Pt III Divs 10B and 10BA (films: ¶20-340, ¶20-350), the capital works provisions (¶20-470) and the rules for small business entities (Chapter 7).

The amount to be included in the debtor's assessable income on termination of the debt arrangement is worked out by comparing:

(1) the deductions that would be allowable if the expenditure were reduced by the unpaid amount of debt (the ''deduction limit''), and

(2) "actual deductions".

If the actual deductions exceed the deduction limit, the excess is assessable.

"Actual deductions" comprise the deductions allowed or allowable in the years up to the end of the debt termination year in respect of the financed property (including any deductible balancing adjustment on disposal) *less* any amount assessable on disposal that effectively reverses such a deduction (eg an assessable balancing adjustment).

The "deduction limit" is calculated as if the deductions continued to be available after the debt was terminated. This means that generally a 100% write-off of the expenditure is assumed, reduced by the amount of the unpaid debt. No reduction to the deduction limit is made for any assessable balancing adjustments made as a result of the disposal.

Special rules apply if *after the debt arrangement is terminated*: (a) a capital allowance deduction entitlement arises (ITAA97 s 243-55); (b) an assessable balancing adjustment arises from a disposal (ITAA97 s 243-57); or (c) a payment is made for the debt or a replacement debt (ITAA97 ss 243-45; 243-50).

Such adjustments are not taken into account in calculating the cost base of the asset for CGT purposes.

For limited recourse finance arrangements which have triggered the operation of the general anti-avoidance provisions, see ¶30-160 and ¶30-170.

▶ Example

Property is bought under hire purchase for $100,000 on 1 July 2018. Its decline in value is calculated over 5 years using the prime cost method. A limited recourse loan of $100,000 finances the purchase. The arrangement is terminated on 30 June 2021 when the property is surrendered to the financier and the amount of $70,000 remains unpaid. The market value of the property on that date is $50,000.

The decline in value of the property for the 3 years is $60,000 and the adjustable value of the property on 30 June 2021 is $40,000. As the termination value of the property is $50,000, there is an assessable balancing adjustment of $10,000. "Actual deductions" are $50,000, ie the total capital allowance deductions ($60,000) less the assessable balancing adjustment ($10,000).

The amount of the deductions that would otherwise be allowable (ie the deduction limit) is $30,000, calculated on the assumption that the original expenditure ($100,000) was reduced by the unpaid loan amount ($70,000), and that deductions continued for the effective life of the property.

As the actual deductions ($50,000) exceed the deduction limit ($30,000), the excess ($20,000) is assessable.

[FITR ¶230-000 – ¶230-340]

¶23-270 Tax loss incentive for designated infrastructure projects

Nationally significant infrastructure projects designated by the Infrastructure CEO (a statutory officeholder under the *Infrastructure Australia Act 2008*) benefit from certain tax loss incentives. The window for receiving designation closed on 30 June 2017 and no new projects can benefit from the incentives unless prescribed by regulation. For details of this incentive see earlier editions of the *Australian Master Tax Guide*.

[*FITR* ¶389-000 – ¶389-050]

Financial Instruments

¶23-300 Financial instruments overview

The enactment of Div 230 changed the taxation rules applicable to gains and losses on financial arrangements (¶23-020). The rules in Div 230 do not apply, however, to all arrangements. The following paragraphs deal with the taxation consequences, under both general principles and specific provisions, of using certain financial instruments where the rules in Div 230 do not apply.

Financial instruments

For accounting purposes, a financial instrument is a contract that is a financial asset of one entity and the financial liability or equity instrument of another entity. A financial asset is an asset that is cash, or an equity instrument of another entity, or the contractual right to receive cash or another financial asset from another entity, or the contractual right to exchange other financial instruments on potentially favourable terms with another entity. Financial liability is a contractual obligation to deliver cash, or another financial asset to another entity, or to exchange other financial instruments on potentially unfavourable terms with another entity. Thus, financial instruments include a broad range of products, from simple debt instruments (eg loans) to derivative instruments (eg swaps, financial options, futures and forward contracts) and hybrids such as perpetual debt and certain preference shares.

¶23-320 Discounted and deferred interest securities

Discounted and deferred securities which are ‘‘qualifying securities’’ are now subject to taxation under the TOFA regime in Div 230 (¶23-020). A qualifying security is a security whose term at the time of issue will, or is reasonably likely to, exceed one year and is reasonably likely to result in the sum of the payments (excluding periodic interest) exceeding the issue price. For a fixed return security, this excess is greater than 1.5% of the sum of the payments multiplied by the number of years in the term of the security.

The commentary below relates to the taxation of qualifying securities to which Div 230 (¶23-020) does not apply.

Taxation of qualifying securities where TOFA regime does not apply

ITAA36 Div 16E imposes a statutory accruals regime on certain payments in relation to a ‘‘security’’ that is a ‘‘qualifying security’’. Division 16E only applies where the TOFA rules in Div 230 do not apply.

In the absence of Div 16E (and the rules in Div 230), holders of such securities would generally only be taxed at maturity or on earlier realisation. This, coupled with the fact that the borrower under such arrangements could be entitled to deductions on an accruals basis (*Australian Guarantee Corporation*), led to tax deferral and non-matching of income and deductions which Div 16E is designed to negate.

A security that falls within Div 16E is called a ‘‘qualifying security’’. To be a qualifying security, the security must be issued after 16 December 1984, its expected term must exceed or be likely to exceed 12 months (thus, 90 or 180 day bills of exchange do not qualify) and the sum of all payments under the security (other than payments of ‘‘periodic interest’’: TR 96/3; ID 2005/20) must exceed its issue price (s 159GP(1)). This excess is called the ‘‘eligible return’’ of the security (for an example, see ID 2003/261).

Where the amount of the eligible return can be established at the time a security is issued (eg a zero-coupon discounted security), Div 16E does not apply unless the excess is greater than 1.5% of the sum of the payments under the security, multiplied by the number of years and part years in the term of the security.

Division 16E applies to ‘‘stripped securities’’, but does not apply to non-residents who hold qualifying securities nor to qualifying securities held as trading stock. The declaration of a trust by which a named beneficiary obtains an equitable interest in the future coupon payments on a bond results in a transfer of payment rights for the purposes of s 159GZ (ID 2007/183).

The Full Federal Court rejected the Commissioner’s argument that certain agreements described as ‘‘annuity agreements’’ were qualifying securities and not agreements to purchase annuities (*ANZ Savings Bank*).

For a commercial bill facility that was not subject to the provisions, see ID 2003/849. For the meaning of ‘‘security’’, see TR 96/14.

TD 2004/84 (intra-group loans) and TD 2004/85 (intra-group income streams) deal with the application of the provisions to the head of a consolidated group where the principal of an intra-group loan or income stream are assigned by a member of the group to a non-member.

Where securities are issued in a series (ie they are all issued on the same terms and conditions) and the first security in the series is not a qualifying security, a subsequent security issued in that series will also not be a qualifying security even if its terms are such that it would otherwise be a qualifying security.

The income element of relevant deferred annuities issued after 19 September 1986 and of immediate annuities issued on or after 29 October 1987 is also taxed in accordance with Div 16E. Annuities issued by a life insurance company or registered organisation, including allocated annuities, which qualify for concessional tax treatment under ITAA36 s 27H (¶11-280) are *not* qualifying securities for Div 16E purposes.

Under PAYG, tax will be withheld at the top marginal rate where an investor does not quote a TFN or an ABN for certain deferred interest securities (¶33-030).

Tax treatment of eligible return

The eligible return from fixed return securities and variable return securities (which are qualifying securities) issued after 27 January 1994 is brought to account on a 6-month compounding accruals (yield to maturity) basis over the term of the security (ss 159GQ to 159GR; TD 94/95; ID 2003/848).

The eligible return from variable return securities (which are qualifying securities) issued before 28 January 1994 is separated into its fixed (non-varying) and varying elements. The fixed element is brought to account on a straight line basis, ie an equal amount of the fixed element of the return is brought to account in each income year during the term of the security. Where the security is held for only part of an income year, an apportioned amount is brought to account in that year. The varying element is brought to account on an attribution basis, ie so much of the varying element as is attributable to the relevant income year, or which the Commissioner considers may reasonably be attributed to the year, is included in the assessable income of the holder of the security.

The eligible return from any qualifying security is not assessable in accordance with Div 16E if it would not otherwise be assessable income (s 159GX).

Special provisions apply where a security is transferred or otherwise disposed of by a holder prior to maturity of the security (s 159GS).

[FTR ¶74-705 – ¶74-925]

¶23-325 Debt defeasance arrangements

The following commentary is relevant to the taxation of gains and losses on debt defeasance arrangements where the TOFA regime in Div 230 (¶23-020) does not apply. A debt defeasance arrangement arises when a borrower, liable to repay a loan at some future date, pays a third party an amount approximating the present value of the loan in consideration of the third party assuming the liability to pay the amount owed by the borrower when it becomes due. The assessability of the profit or gain arising from such an arrangement has been considered by the High Court in the *Orica case* and by the Full Federal Court in the *Unilever case* with contrasting results.

In the *Orica case* (known as *ICI* in earlier proceedings), the High Court held that the rights which the taxpayer acquired against the assumption party under the terms of the arrangement constituted an asset for CGT purposes. It also held that there was a disposal of part of the taxpayer's asset for CGT purposes each time the assumption party performed its obligations under the agreement by making a payment (¶11-270). The High

Court said that the difference between the amount paid by the taxpayer to the assumption party and the face value of the debentures was not assessable under ordinary concepts and was not a profit arising from a profit-making undertaking or scheme.

The High Court was not required to consider the finding of the Full Federal Court that ITAA36 Pt III Div 16E (¶23-320) did not apply because the Commissioner did not pursue his argument in support of Div 16E before it. The Full Federal Court had said that Div 16E could not apply because the taxpayer was not a ''holder'' of a qualifying security within the meaning of ITAA36 s 159GP(1).

In the *Unilever case*, the Full Federal Court held that the debt defeasance arrangement arose in the ordinary course of the taxpayer's business as a finance company and that the difference between the face value of the debentures and the amount paid by the taxpayer therefore constituted an assessable profit. The court also ruled that the profit was derived when the debentures matured and the taxpayer's obligations under each debenture trust deed were fully discharged. As in the subsequent *Orica case*, accruals taxation under ITAA36 Div 16E did not apply because the taxpayer was not the ''holder'' of a security in the required sense.

Despite the High Court decision in the *Orica case*, it has been argued that gains from debt defeasance arrangements will not necessarily be subject to tax under the CGT provisions. It is arguable that the decision in the *Orica case* may be distinguished on the basis that it involved a ''singular transaction, not part of the regular means whereby the taxpayer obtained returns''. The Commissioner has indicated that the *Unilever* decision will continue to apply to financial institutions and in-house finance entities (*Minutes of Capital Gains Tax Subcommittee meeting*, 10 June 1998). For the treatment of a debt defeasance arrangement involving a controlled foreign company, see ¶21-180.

[FITR ¶19-055]

¶23-330 Bills of exchange, promissory notes

The following commentary is relevant to the taxation of gains and losses on bills of exchange and promissory notes where the TOFA regime in Div 230 (¶23-020) does not apply. A deduction may be claimed for the discount factor associated with negotiating a bill of exchange or promissory note where the proceeds are used as working capital (*Energy Resources*). Where the bill or promissory note matures in a year of income later than the year of issue, and the term of the bill or note is 12 months or less, the deduction for the discount should be apportioned on an accounting straight line basis over the term of the bill or note (*Coles Myer Finance*; TR 93/21). However, where the proceeds of the notes were used by the taxpayer in the year of issue to discharge existing liabilities, the discount was allowed in the year of issue and no apportionment was required (*Energy Resources*). ''Annual financing costs'', paid in advance under a Fixed Rate Commercial Bill Facility, were incurred on the date that the facility was drawn down and on the subsequent anniversary date of the drawdown (ID 2003/849).

The Commissioner's practice is to regard the cost of the discount as deductible in the circumstances in which *Coles Myer Finance* would accrue the cost over the term of the discounted security, provided the funds raised are used in the taxpayer's assessable income-producing business. The *Energy Resources* decision would be limited to circumstances where the raising of funds through a discounted security occurred on a one-off basis and was not intended to be repeated in the near future.

In the case of bills or notes with a term longer than 12 months, the rules outlined in ¶23-320 apply. See also the rules outlined at ¶23-020.

[FITR ¶27-150]

¶23-340 Traditional securities

The following commentary is relevant to the taxation of gains and losses on traditional securities where the TOFA regime in Div 230 (¶23-020) does not apply.

Gains on realisation of "traditional securities" where the TOFA regime does not apply

Gains on the disposal or redemption of ''traditional securities'' are assessable under ITAA36 s 26BB in the year of disposal or redemption. A traditional security is, broadly, a security that is not issued at a discount of more than 1.5% multiplied by the number of years in the term of the security, does not bear deferred interest and is not capital indexed. Section 26BB does not apply to securities that are trading stock of the taxpayer or to discounted securities discussed at ¶23-320. For the purposes of s 26BB a ''security'' has the meaning given by ITAA36 s 159GP(1):

- stock, a bond, debenture, certificate of entitlement, bill of exchange, promissory note or other security
- a deposit with a bank, building society or financial institution
- a secured or unsecured loan, or
- any other contract under which a person is liable to pay an amount.

In TD 2008/21, Deferred Purchase Agreement warrants (DPA warrants) were not considered to be traditional securities. A DPA warrant is a listed or unlisted retail investment product offered by financial institutions to an investor who agrees to purchase ''assets'' (typically, listed shares or units). The number and value of the shares or units delivered to the investor under a DPA warrant is dependent on the performance of a nominated share market index from the date of the contract until a ''maturity date''. The determination concludes that the DPA warrants were not traditional securities under ITAA36 s 26BB(1) because they were not a security at all, essentially on the basis of not having enough debt-like obligations as required under ITAA36 s 159GP(1).

A number of interpretative issues affecting s 26BB are discussed in TR 96/14.

The application of the CGT provisions to traditional securities that are convertible notes/interests is considered at ¶12-620.

For an example of whether a security is a qualifying security under ITAA36 s 159GP(1) or a traditional security under ITAA36 s 26BB, see CR 2009/14.

Gains made by a taxpayer on receiving ordinary shares in return for the cancellation of capital notes were assessable under s 26BB. There was a redemption of the notes even though not for cash (*Proudfoot*).

UK Treasury bonds are traditional securities (ID 2003/982). In calculating the amount of any gain or loss on disposal or redemption of a traditional security denominated in a foreign currency, the foreign currency must be converted into Australian dollars at the time of payment or receipt (TD 2006/30; ¶23-070). In particular, the cost of acquiring the traditional security (translated into Australian dollars on the date the taxpayer pays for it) and the proceeds received on disposal or redemption (translated on the date the taxpayer receives payment for the traditional security) must be compared.

See ID 2005/281 for the treatment of a traditional security that is issued by a subsidiary member of a consolidated group to a non-group entity, reacquired by the head company of the group and later sold to a non-group entity.

For the treatment of securities transferred by a credit union under the *Financial Sector (Transfer and Restructure) Act 1999*, see ID 2004/885.

For the treatment of stapled securities comprising a note and preference shares, see TA 2008/1 and TD 2009/14 (*below*).

Loss on disposal of traditional securities where the TOFA regime does not apply

A loss on the disposal or redemption of a ''traditional security'' is deductible in the income year in which the disposal or redemption takes place (ITAA36 s 70B).

For the purpose of determining the amount of the loss, the Commissioner is entitled to substitute a commercial arm's length amount as the consideration for the transaction where the parties are not dealing at arm's length. Where an arm's length amount cannot be determined, the Commissioner can fix some other amount. In determining the arm's length consideration, a discounted cash flow analysis is used if there is no established market from which the arm's length value can be ascertained (TR 96/14).

Where a taxpayer disposed of a traditional security by exchanging his accounts with the Pyramid Building Society for 4-year bonds issued by the Victorian Government, the amount of any loss on the disposal was calculated by reference to the face value of the bonds, rather than to the (lower) market value (*Burrill*). In *Evenden*, the taxpayer's right of indemnity against a company (arising upon her making guarantee payments) that could not be satisfied was held to give rise to the loss of a traditional security.

Capital losses on the disposal or redemption of a traditional security are not deductible if the disposal or redemption is made in anticipation of the issuer not being able to meet all its obligations to pay out the security (eg ID 2006/214). In this case, the CGT provisions may be considered (¶11-250, ¶11-270). There will be no loss of the deduction, however, in cases where the traditional security is a marketable security and both the acquisition and the disposal occurred in the ordinary course of trading on a securities market. The acquisition of convertible notes by the exercise of the taxpayer's rights as a shareholder in the company and by the exercise of similar rights acquired on the stock exchange was not in the ordinary course of trading on a securities market (*Case 10/2006*).

A disposal occurred where a taxpayer divested itself of a traditional security or the right to receive payment under the security and exchanged personal property for a bundle of rights (*Rataplan*).

A loss incurred on the waiver or release of a debt under a traditional security does not give rise to a deduction. In any case, extinguishing a debt by deed of release or by the bankruptcy of the issuer is not a disposal, as the meaning of that term is consistent with "alienation" (*Case 23/95*). The mere writing off of a debt in the taxpayer's accounts (without formal documentation or release) does not constitute the discharge, disposal or redemption of the debt. Redemption and disposal both require that there is no outstanding legal liability on the part of the debtor to pay the amount of the security to the creditor (*Ashton Mining*). For the position where a life insurance company forgives an agency development loan made to an insurance agent, see TR 2001/9. For the Commissioner's views on the meaning of "disposal", see TR 96/14.

TA 2008/1, the ATO cautioned that it was considering arrangements where an Australian resident public company issues a stapled security (consisting of a note and a preference share) and the taxpayer disposes of the security at a loss on the occurrence of a so-called assignment event (specified circumstances which include the election of the company). Taxpayers were not to assume the losses were deductible under ITAA36 s 70B. In TD 2009/14, the Commissioner concluded that the above stapled security is a single instrument (a preference share with additional rights) and is not a traditional security for the purposes of ITAA36 s 26BB or 70B because it is not a security under ITAA36 s 159GP(1). Unless the stapled security was acquired in the ordinary course of business, the profit from the disposal was an assessable capital gain (¶23-350). A loss from a similar disposal is a capital loss (¶23-350).

A loss on disposal of convertible notes in a company after the company was put in receivership was held to be not deductible under s 70B(4). The AAT held that the purpose of s 70B(4) is to ensure that capital losses on the disposal of a traditional security arising from the issuer's perceived inability to discharge payment obligations are not deductible (*Case 3/2009*).

Conversion or exchange of post-14 May 2002 traditional securities

For a traditional security issued on or after 7.30 pm EST on 14 May 2002, no gain or loss arises under s 26BB or 70B respectively from the disposal or redemption of the security in 2 circumstances. Effectively, this defers recognition of the gain or loss until the shares acquired on conversion or exchange are disposed of. For the CGT consequences, see ¶12-625.

In the first case, no gain or loss arises if the traditional security is issued on the basis that it will or may convert into ordinary shares in the issuer of the security (or a connected entity) and the disposal or redemption occurs due to the security being *converted* into ordinary shares of the issuer of the security (or of a connected entity).

In the second case, no gain or loss arises if: (a) the traditional security is issued on the basis that it will or may be redeemed or disposed of to the issuer of the security (or a connected entity) in exchange for ordinary shares in a company that is not the issuer of the security (or a connected entity); (b) the disposal or redemption is in *exchange* for ordinary shares in that company; and (c) in the case of a disposal, the disposal is to the issuer of the security or a connected entity (this last requirement does not apply to redemption as, in any case, only the issuer can redeem the security).

If the security is exchanged for shares that are not ordinary shares (eg preference shares), or if the disposal is to an entity other than the issuer of the security, or if there is no conversion or exchange, s 26BB and 70B continue to apply to the gain or loss. In this case, the cost base of the share is increased by the amount of the assessed gain.

▶ Example

In Year 1, Josh acquires an exchangeable note with a face value of $100, for $100. Under the note, Josh is entitled to interest income of $5 per year. At the beginning of Year 3, Josh exchanges the note for an ordinary share with a market value of $110. As a result, no amount is included in assessable income under s 26BB and the capital gain is disregarded. The cost base of the share is $100 (ie the cost base of the note). Josh later sells the share for $130, thus making a capital gain of $30, ie $130 – $100. For the purposes of the CGT discount provisions, the share is taken to have been acquired at the beginning of Year 3 (ie not when the exchangeable note was acquired). The annual interest of $5 is not included in the cost base of the share.

See also ID 2003/1192.

[FTR ¶16-260, ¶35-695]

¶23-350 Other securities

The following commentary is relevant to the taxation of gains and losses in respect of shares and other securities where the TOFA regime in Div 230 (¶23-020) does not apply.

Gains from realisation of shares and other securities where the TOFA regime does not apply

The gains arising from the mere realisation of shares or other securities which are not traditional securities (ie where ITAA36 s 26BB (¶23-340) does not apply), and which were acquired as a long-term investment (eg *Case Z3*), will generally not be income according to ordinary concepts; nor will the gains arising from simply managing a share portfolio, even if conducted in a systematic and concerted way.

Gains may be caught by the CGT provisions in relation to shares or other securities acquired on or after 20 September 1985. Where an amount that is assessable as ordinary income is also assessable under the CGT provisions, the capital gain is reduced by the amount that is ordinary income (ITAA97 s 118-20; ¶11-690).

However, gains realised in the course of carrying on a business of investing for profit or trading in shares and other securities (¶9-150 – ¶9-300), or arising from individual transactions of a profit-making nature (¶10-112, ¶10-340), are assessable income. For example, the profit realised on the maturity of a discounted bill of exchange

(*Hurley Holdings*) and the profits realised on the sale of share options acquired as consideration for a loan (*Case W74*) have been held to be assessable. If the profit on the sale of bonus shares is assessable, the cost of those shares is determined in accordance with ITAA36 s 6BA (¶3-265).

Losses arising from share trading will be deductible if the taxpayer is in the business of trading shares (*Greig*; *Case* 10/2011), however many taxpayers have difficulty establishing they are carrying on a share trading business (*Hartley*; *Osborne*; *Devi*; *Hill*).

Where a company, in the course of its share trading business, issues warrants to its shareholders at non-refundable premiums which grant the warrant holders the right to purchase shares in another company at a fixed price within a certain period of time, the premiums are considered to be assessable to the share trader as ordinary income in the year in which the warrants are issued (TD 92/179).

Under short sale share transactions, the taxpayer ''borrows'' shares from a securities lender and sells them to a buyer. The taxpayer is then required to cover short sale transactions at a later date by buying, and returning to the securities lender, an equivalent number and type of shares.

Banks and insurance companies

In the case of banks and insurance companies (and seemingly also building societies: *Case F26*), the realisation or ''switching'' of investments will normally be regarded as acts done in the course of carrying on a banking or insurance business (and thus the profits will be assessable), even if the investments have stood for a number of years (*RAC Insurance*; *Employers' Mutual Indemnity Association*). This is particularly so in the case of life insurance companies as they need to obtain regular yields from investments.

In contrast, it has been held that a subsidiary of an insurance company was not assessable on profits made from the sale of shares, because they had been acquired as long-term investments and not to maintain the liquidity of the parent company (*AGC (Investments)*; ID 2005/334). However, merely shifting investment activity to a subsidiary may not make the profits tax-free to the subsidiary (*GRE Insurance*; *Unitraders Investments*).

In another case, the sale of all investments following the reorganisation of the group of which the taxpayer, a former insurance company, was a member represented the disposal of the business and thus the profits were capital (*Equitable Life and General Insurance*). In the same case, profits from the sale of investments in an earlier income year were also capital as the taxpayer did not carry on a share trading or investment business (¶16-665). The profits from the sale of an insurance company's head office will generally not be assessable as ordinary income (if the property is also used for rental purposes, the profits will be apportioned) and gains may also not be assessable where they result from the sale of investments from a special investment fund (IT 2276). Of course, where gains are not assessable as ordinary income, the CGT provisions may apply (¶11-000).

Where shares are held as revenue assets but are not trading stock (eg shares held by an insurance company), the profit arising on disposal of the shares for ordinary income purposes is calculated in accordance with TR 96/4.

Public investment companies, money lenders

Gains made by a public investment company on the realisation of securities have been held by the High Court to be assessable, even though the taxpayer's main object was to invest in securities for the purpose of producing dividend income and it generally did not buy shares for the purpose of profit-making by sale (*London Australia Investment*). In contrast, profits made by a public company were held to be capital where the company's business consisted mainly of borrowing or lending money, the relatively small share portfolio was used only as an investment asset, the number of share sales was modest and the investment policy was governed by long-term considerations unrelated to the business activities of the company (*Milton Corporation*).

Trustees

Where a trustee sells investments, it is more likely (depending on the nature of the trust) that it will be seen as the mere realisation of those investments rather than a sale in the course of carrying on a business of dealing in investments. This is because a trustee has a duty to invest trust funds and must not speculate. In the *Radnor case*, for example, the profits (and losses) realised by the investment arm of the trustee of trusts established and maintained primarily for the benefit of an intellectually and physically disabled person were held to be capital.

Investment commissions

Refunds of non-tax-deductible upfront service fees or commissions payable on investment products are capital in the hands of the investor, except where an ETP (¶14-000) has been rolled over and part of the payment was used to pay the service fee or commission. In such cases, any refund will be treated as assessable to the investor as an ETP (IT 2536). See also TR 93/36, which deals with the assessability of a commission (not being in the nature of an initial service fee or entry fee) paid by an investment fund to an intermediary (eg an investment adviser or accountant) where the latter is under an obligation to pay the commission to the investor (¶6-110).

[FITR ¶18-315, ¶18-350, ¶31-581, ¶31-589]

¶23-355 Conversion of semi-government securities

Where a security is issued by a state central borrowing authority (CBA) in substitution for an equivalent semi-government or local government security, the CBA security is deemed to be a continuation of the original security for tax purposes, including CGT purposes (ITAA36 s 23K). Without this provision, the substitution would be treated as involving a realisation of the original security and an acquisition of the new security. Dealers would therefore have been taxable on any gains and could have deducted any losses on the realisation.

[FTR ¶11-285]

¶23-370 Futures, hedging contracts

The following commentary is relevant to the taxation of gains and losses on futures and hedging contracts held by certain entities where the TOFA regime in Div 230 (¶23-020) does not apply.

Taxation of futures, hedging contracts where the TOFA regime does not apply

An investment in the futures market involves the purchase of a *contract*. The contract is for the purchase or sale of the underlying commodity or financial package at a specified date in the future. Where the rules in Div 230 do not apply, there are no special tax provisions dealing with futures contracts, and the taxation consequences of entering into such contracts depend on the application of the CGT rules and general assessability and deductibility principles. For the tax implications of various aspects of futures transactions, see IT 2228 (the part of the Ruling dealing with basis trading has been withdrawn).

Where a taxpayer is engaged in a business of trading in futures, profits from these activities will be assessable income and losses deductible. However, futures contracts are not regarded as trading stock and so the trading stock provisions (¶9-150) do not apply. Even if a business is not being carried on, profits from speculative dealings on the futures market will generally be of an income nature and accordingly assessable (TR 2005/15).

People who simply trade or speculate on the futures market are treated differently for tax purposes to commodity producers who use the market for bona fide hedging purposes, eg as a means of reducing the risk of falling prices for their commodities. A hedging transaction will be regarded as an integral part of a producer's business where: (a) the quantity of goods covered by the futures transaction is roughly equivalent to estimated production; and (b) there is a subsequent sale of goods of the kind covered by the trading. Thus, any profit or loss arising from the transaction will be taken into account in calculating the gross proceeds of the business (¶18-030). In the case of primary producers, the results of hedging transactions of this nature are taken into account for averaging purposes (¶18-200 and following).

If, however, a producer enters into a futures contract which covers goods in quantities significantly in excess of its own estimated production or goods which it does not produce, this would be regarded as outside the scope of the business activity. Whether the profit is assessable or the loss deductible will depend on whether the futures transaction represents an income-producing activity in its own right. The CGT provisions may also apply (¶11-380).

The tax implications of hedging in relation to currency fluctuations are discussed at ¶23-075. The Commissioner will disallow losses arising from ''straddle'' transactions.

Where losses arising from futures transactions are claimed as deductions, the taxpayer should retain copies of agreements with brokers, contract notes, settlement statements, details of sources and application of funds used to finance futures transactions and identification of any loan moneys used, so as to be able to verify the claim at a later date, eg if the taxpayer is audited. Only realised losses in any year plus associated expenses relating to those losses, eg commission, will be allowed.

Payments made on the novation of commodity hedging contracts are deductible and lump sums received on novation are assessable (ID 2003/796; ID 2003/797).

For the taxation of gold loan transactions and forward sales contracts, see TR 92/5.

Income from a financial contract for differences (CFD) is assessable (or a loss deductible) if the CFD is entered into as an ordinary incident of carrying on a business or in a business operation or commercial transaction for the purpose of profit-making. Such contracts are a cash-settled derivative, which allow investors to take risks on movements in the price of a subject matter without ownership of it (TR 2005/15).

TR 2005/15 does not apply to spread-betting arrangements. The ATO has cautioned that it is examining spread-betting arrangements that allow speculation on whether a share price, share index, commodity price or foreign exchange rate will rise or fall within a particular time period (ATO *media release* NAT 02/81, 6 September 2002). For further discussion, see CCH *Tax Week* ¶749 (2005).

The ATO intends to clarify the taxation of spread-betting arrangements through a suitable court case. Until the law is clarified, the ATO will determine the tax consequences for spread-betting arrangements having regard to the particular facts of the case and the principles outlined in TR 2005/15.

[FITR ¶19-515]

¶23-380 Options, rights, swaps

The following commentary is relevant to the taxation of gains and losses on options, rights and swaps held by certain entities where the TOFA regime in Div 230 (¶23-020) does not apply.

Taxation of options, rights and swaps where the TOFA regime does not apply

An *option* is the right (but not the obligation) of an asset holder to change the holding at or before a set date at a set price (the strike price). A call option is an option that gives the holder the right to buy. A put option is an option that gives the holder the right to sell. For example, a currency option involves the right (but not the obligation) to buy (call) or sell (put) a specific amount of one currency on or until a certain date (the exercise date) at the strike price. The option buyer may allow the option to lapse, exercise the option and take delivery of the bought currency or close out the option. For that right, the buyer pays a premium to the seller which the seller retains, whether or not the right is exercised.

If a put option is on revenue account, the premium may be an allowable deduction to the grantee and assessable income of the grantor. If the option is on capital account, the CGT provisions apply where the option is granted (¶11-280), exercised (¶11-250, ¶12-700) or expires (¶11-270). See also ID 2004/526. Margin payments made in respect of exchange-traded option and futures contracts are not deductible under s 8-1 being contributions of capital to a fund to provide for contingencies of the business rather than outgoings incurred in meeting such contingencies (TD 2006/25).

A trader in exchange-traded options (ETOs) is not entitled to a deduction for the market value of sold ETO positions that remain open at the end of their income year (ID 2006/313). The notional interest charged by an issuer on an outstanding amount for the purchase of an underlying share under an endowment warrant is not deductible to the holder of the warrant under s 8-1 (ID 2006/244).

With application from the 2001–02 income year, the treatment of rights issues that existed before the decision in *McNeil* is restored. The High Court there held that the market value of the sale of tradable put options was assessable as ordinary income. However, the government reversed the result by legislating that any amount that is assessable at the time the rights are issued will be included in the cost base of the rights or of the shares disposed of as a result of the exercise of the rights. Under s 59-40, the market value of rights issued by a company or unit trust to shareholders or unitholders to acquire further shares or units (ie call options) will be treated as non-assessable non-exempt income at the time the rights are issued, provided the original interests are held on capital account. A taxing point will not arise for the shareholders or unitholders in relation to the rights until a subsequent capital gains tax (CGT) event happens to the rights consequential to the exercise of the rights.

Expenditure associated with the conversion of options and rights to shares may be deductible (¶16-156).

A *swap* involves an exchange of one entitlement for another, such as holdings of currencies (currency swap) or borrowings with particular interest rates (interest rate swaps). In a currency swap, currencies are exchanged at one date with the agreement (a forward foreign currency contract) to re-exchange the amounts involved at a future date. Alternatively, a currency swap may involve the exchange of borrowings in one currency for liabilities in another. In an interest rate swap, parties may swap floating rate funds and fixed rate borrowings, or medium-term and long-term borrowings (IT 2050).

Floating and fixed rate payments made under interest rate swap contracts are incurred on a daily accruals basis over the term of each related calculation period (IT 2682).

Arrangements where a taxpayer enters into a scrip loan and takes out an option position over the same number of shares are discussed in TD 2003/32.

[FITR ¶27-100]

¶23-390 Instalment warrants

Special rules in ITAA97 Div 235 provide income tax look-through treatment for instalment warrants, instalment receipts, and other similar arrangements, and for certain limited recourse borrowing arrangements entered into by regulated superannuation funds. In particular, look-through treatment is provided:

- to investors, for instalment warrant and instalment receipt arrangements over certain assets (broadly, direct and indirect interests in listed securities as well as unlisted securities in widely held entities), and
- to regulated superannuation funds, for any limited recourse borrowing arrangement that satisfies the relevant requirements of the SIS Act.

This look-through treatment ensures that most income tax consequences associated with the underlying asset of the trust flows through to the investor, and not the trustee.

Instalment warrants and instalment receipts

Instalment warrants are financial products that entail borrowing to acquire an asset, such as a share. The asset is held on trust during the life of the loan to provide security for the lender. The investor is required to pay one or more instalments to repay any outstanding amounts before taking legal ownership of the asset. Nevertheless the investor is entitled to the benefit of any income flowing from the asset (eg dividends) while it is held on trust. It is common but not necessary (unless the investor is a trustee of a regulated superannuation fund) for the borrowing under these arrangements to be limited recourse in nature, meaning investors can ''walk away'' from the investment rather than pay any outstanding instalments.

Instalment receipts are similar to instalment warrants, with the key difference being that there is no ''borrowing''. Rather, there is a provision of credit to acquire an asset that is held on trust until the purchase price of the asset is fully paid by the investor.

[FITR ¶223-200]

¶23-400 Commonwealth Special Bonds

The amount representing accrued interest on Commonwealth Special Bonds is assessable on redemption of such Special Bonds (ITAA36 s 23E).

Premiums paid on redemption of such special bonds are generally exempt from tax and are not treated as income. This may be relevant, if the recipient is a company, in relation to liquidation distributions (¶4-300). The exemption does *not* apply to a dealer or trader in securities or a person who can be regarded as having a profit-making purpose in relation to the particular transaction.

[FTR ¶10-700]

¶23-410 Commonwealth Treasury Notes and other non-interest-bearing securities

The following commentary is relevant where the TOFA regime in Div 230 (¶23-020) does not apply. Certain Commonwealth securities and stock, such as treasury notes, inscribed stock and other seasonal securities, are non-interest-bearing but are redeemable at a price in excess of their issue price. The surplus on redemption over the cost of the security to the taxpayer is assessable (ITAA36 s 26C(1)(b)). Similarly, the excess of the value of the security at the date of its disposal by sale, gift, conversion or otherwise over its cost to the taxpayer is assessable (s 26C(1)(a)).

Where the security is *issued* to the taxpayer, the cost to the taxpayer will be the issue price. Where it is acquired by gift, purchase, inheritance or otherwise, its deemed cost to the taxpayer is its value on the date of acquisition (s 26C(2)(a)). If the owner (by whatever means) of the security dies, there is a deemed sale at the date of death and the person on whom it devolves by virtue of the owner's death is deemed to have purchased it for a cost equal to its value on that date (s 26C(2)(b)).

[FTR ¶16-350]

¶23-430 Sale of securities cum interest

If securities on which interest is accruing are sold cum interest, the purchaser is assessable on the whole of the interest subsequently received. The Commissioner's views on the basis of assessment of income derived from investments in fixed and variable securities cum interest are set out in TR 93/28 (¶9-050). Where securities acquired on or after 20 September 1985 are disposed of, the CGT provisions would usually be attracted.

For the position where there is a disposal of a discounted or deferred interest security issued after 16 December 1984, see ¶23-320. The tax implications of securities lending arrangements are considered at ¶12-430.

[FITR ¶27-100, ¶28-040]

Reporting Requirements

¶23-500 Financial transaction reporting

Businesses in the financial services industry, gambling service providers, bullion dealers, accountants and lawyers (to the extent they provide financial services) and others are required to report significant cash transactions of $10,000 or more and suspect transactions to the Australian Transactions Reports and Analysis Centre (AUSTRAC). These reporting obligations are imposed to combat money laundering, terrorism financing and tax evasion. The data collected is shared with the ATO and other government bodies.

The obligation to report significant cash transactions, and suspect transactions, is imposed by the *Anti-Money Laundering and Counter-Terrorism Financing Act 2006* (AML/CTF Act), the AML/CTF Regulations and the AML/CTF Rules issued by AUSTRAC. The AML/CTF Act largely replaces the *Financial Transaction Reports Act 1988* (FTRA). The FTRA continues to have limited application, including to "cash dealers" who are not subject to the AML/CTF Act (see below).

A Bill to introduce a $10,000 cash payment limit has failed to pass the Senate. If passed the Bill would have removed the requirement for most AUSTRAC reporting entities to report payments of $10,000 or more.

Persons subject to the AML/CTF Act

The AML/CTF Act applies to persons ("reporting entities") who provide "designated services". These reporting entities must enrol with AUSTRAC and fulfil certain reporting obligations described below.

Reporting entities include financial services entities (banks, insurance providers, superannuation funds, finance and leasing providers, stockbrokers, remittance dealers and digital currency exchange providers), bullion dealers and gambling service providers. Accountants and lawyers are also affected to the extent they provide financial services (they are not captured for providing advice and services relating to other aspects of their business).

Financial services, which are designated services, include opening an account, accepting money on deposit, making a loan, issuing a bill of exchange, a promissory note, or a letter of credit, issuing a debit or stored value card, issuing travellers' cheques, sending and receiving electronic funds transfer instructions, making money or property available under a designated remittance arrangement, acquiring or disposing of a bill of exchange, promissory note or letter of credit, issuing or selling a security or derivative, accepting a contribution, roll-over or transfer in respect of a member of a superannuation fund, exchanging currency and buying or selling emissions units.

AML/CTF obligations

The principal obligations for reporting entities under the AML/CTF Act are to:

- enrol with AUSTRAC
- register with AUSTRAC if the entity provides remittance services
- implement and maintain an AML/CTF program to identify, assess, mitigate, and manage the risk of money laundering and terrorism financing. Members of a designated business group may operate a joint AML/CTF program with other members of the group
- identify customers and undertake ongoing customer due diligence. This obligation includes a requirement to determine the ultimate beneficial owner of each customer and collect, and verify the beneficial owner's details, including full name, address and date of birth. Identification of a domestic company includes verifying their registered ASIC name, registered office and the company's ACN
- lodge transaction reports and compliance reports with AUSTRAC, including an annual AML/CTF compliance report, which can be submitted through AUSTRAC Online. The due date for the 2020 annual report is 31 March 2021, and
- comply with various AML/CTF related record-keeping obligations including reporting:
  - suspicious matters
  - the provision of a designated service, which is the transfer of an amount of $10,000 or more (physical currency or electronic transfer)
  - the provision of designated services in relation to international funds transfer instructions to or from Australia.

AUSTRAC may exempt certain persons from specified provisions of the AML/CTF Act — see further the AUSTRAC website.

Penalties for non-compliance

Penalties for non-compliance with the AML/CTF Act include civil penalties of up to $22.2 million for bodies corporate and $4.44 million for other persons. Criminal penalties may also be imposed. The AML/CTF Act establishes offences for producing false or misleading information or documents, forging a document for use in an applicable customer identification procedure, providing or receiving a designated service using a false customer name or customer anonymity, and structuring a transaction to avoid a reporting obligation.

In addition to the penalties imposed under the AML/CTF Act, producing false or misleading information or documents may also lead to penalties under other acts, eg under the *Corporations Act 2001* for failure to maintain proper records and under the *Criminal Code Act 1995* for false accounting.

Information exchange agreements

AUSTRAC has signed nearly 100 intelligence sharing agreements with foreign counterparts, including foreign law enforcement and national security agencies. Information exchange may also occur under tax information exchange agreements and some tax treaty articles (¶22-140), and the US Foreign Account Tax Compliance Act (¶22-075).

Australia has enacted legislation giving effect to a number of OECD/G20 initiatives allowing for the automatic exchange of information with partner countries. These initiatives include the Common Reporting Standard, the new single global standard for the collection, reporting and exchange of financial account information on foreign tax residents, and the OECD/G20 Inclusive Framework on Base Erosion and Profit Shifting (BEPS) (¶22-165). Australia is also member of the OECD's Global Forum on Transparency and Exchange of Information for Tax Purposes, which supports the fight against tax evasion by ensuring the effective implementation of international standards on tax transparency and exchange of ownership, accounting and financial account information (both "on request", and "automatically").

Financial Transaction Reports Act 1988

The FTRA has largely been replaced by the AML/CTF Act, but continues to have limited application to "cash dealers" who are not subject to the AML/CTF Act. In practice, the only entities with reporting obligations to AUSTRAC under the FTRA are:

- businesses selling traveller's cheques, such as Australia Post and travel agents
- insurers
- motor vehicle dealers who act as an insurer or insurance intermediary, and
- solicitors.

The reporting obligations imposed by the FTRA include:

- cash dealers must provide: a *significant cash transaction report* to AUSTRAC for any transaction that involves a cash component of $10,000 or more, or its equivalent in a foreign currency; an *international funds transfer instruction report* for any instruction for the transfer of funds, which is transmitted electronically into or out of Australia on behalf of a customer; a *suspect transaction report* where any transaction leads to reasonable grounds to suspect that information may be relevant to investigation of criminal offences, including terrorism financing, tax evasion and other criminal activity, or may assist in enforcing the proceeds of crime legislation, and
- solicitors must report significant cash transactions of $10,000 or more, or its equivalent in a foreign currency.

[FTR ¶979-360 – ¶979-630]

Chapter 24 Returns ● Activity Statements ● RBAs ● Rulings

¶24-000 Introduction: returns, BASs/IASs, RBAs, rulings

Under the system of self-assessment that applies in Australia, income tax return forms require taxpayers to provide only limited information (¶24-030). However, taxpayers are required to retain records in relation to transactions relevant to the calculation of their taxable income (¶9-045, ¶11-920, ¶16-320, ¶35-690). The substantiation rules also require taxpayers to retain records to verify claims for deductions (¶16-210 and following).

There are also requirements for making and lodging elections and notifications under self-assessment. Some elections and notifications do not have to be in writing, and many of those that are required to be in writing do not have to be lodged with the Commissioner, although they must be retained by taxpayers. Very few have to be lodged with the return (¶24-040).

In addition to lodging a separate income tax return, business taxpayers who are registered for GST must report their periodic tax obligations and entitlements by way of Business Activity Statements (BAS) (¶24-200). Other taxpayers (eg individuals with investment income) who are not registered for GST may need to complete Instalment Activity Statements (IAS) (¶24-220). A Running Balance Account (RBA) is used by the Commissioner to record a taxpayer's tax liabilities and payments on a single account (¶24-300). Upon receipt of a BAS or an IAS, the Commissioner will update the taxpayer's RBA to record any liability amounts or payments made.

To assist in the self-assessment process, the ATO provides various forms of advice, both to the public generally as well as in response to the specific circumstances of taxpayers. The different forms of advice provided by the ATO and the level of protection they afford the taxpayer are discussed at ¶24-500. Of these forms of advice, the ATO rulings system is perhaps the most important (¶24-520).

Returns

¶24-010 Lodgment of returns

In June of each year, the Commissioner issues a Legislative Instrument calling for the lodging of annual income tax returns. A person who fails to lodge a return by the due date stipulated may be liable to prosecution or to the payment of penalties (¶29-100).

Individuals required to lodge **2020–21 returns** *include*:

- residents whose taxable income was more than $18,200 (the minimum taxable income level for 2020–21)
- residents and non-residents who had amounts withheld from their pay or other income, incurred a loss or were claiming prior year losses exceeding $1,000, had a reportable fringe benefits amount or reportable employer superannuation contributions identified on their payment summary, or were liable to pay child support under the *Child Support (Assessment) Act 1989*, unless their ''adjusted taxable income'' (¶2-133) was less than $25,575 and they were in receipt of specified Australian government pensions, allowances or payments for the whole year
- unmarried individuals under 18 (at 30 June 2021) whose total 2020–21 income, other than for work personally performed, was more than $416 (¶2-160)
- individuals with prior year losses or a loss in the current year (¶16-880)
- individuals with a reportable fringe benefits amount included on their payment summary (¶35-055)
- individuals who wish to claim a refund of imputation credits (¶4-820)
- individuals with an individual interest in the net income or loss of a partnership (¶5-070)
- individuals (resident or otherwise) who carried on any business in Australia
- individuals entitled to claim the private health insurance tax offset (¶15-330)
- individuals entitled to a distribution from a trust which carried on a primary production business

- special professional covered by the income averaging provisions (¶2-140)
- individuals (resident or otherwise) entitled to income or loss as a beneficiary of a trust estate, or who had an individual interest in the net income or net loss of a partnership, that operated a business of primary production in Australia
- individuals who were Australian residents for only part of the year and whose taxable income exceeds $18,200 or $13,464 plus $395 for every month the individual was a resident of Australia (including the month in which he/she became, or ceased to be, a resident)
- individuals who, at any time during the 2020–21 year, were not residents of Australia and who derived assessable income from an Australian source other than dividends, interest or royalties that were subject to PAYG withholding.

A return must be lodged for every **partnership** (¶5-065) and **trust** (¶6-020, ¶6-030) showing the total income derived by the partnership or trust, as appropriate, during the income year. Special lodgment rules apply to **minor children** in receipt of unearned income (¶2-160) and to taxpayers entitled to only part of the tax-free threshold (¶2-130). A return must be lodged for a **deceased taxpayer** in respect of the period from the beginning of the income year to the date of death (¶2-080).

Companies are required to lodge an income tax return (¶3-045). If they are liable to pay franking deficit tax, they must lodge a franking account return. Companies are also required to lodge statements relating to interest and dividend payments made by the company. Superannuation funds, ADFs and PSTs are also required to lodge an income tax return (¶13-350).

The Commissioner may call on any person at any time to lodge a return, or a further or fuller return, for a year of income or a specified period, or to provide any information, statement or document about the person's financial affairs (irrespective of whether that person has derived income) (ITAA36 ss 162; 163).

Taxpayers must include in their returns all income and profits or gains of a capital nature derived in the 12 months up to and including the last day of the financial year or substituted accounting period. The most common types of exempt income (Chapter 10) do not have to be included. It is not permissible for taxpayers to defer income for inclusion in the return for the following year by closing their books of account before the end of the financial year or substituted accounting period (IT 2467).

Employers are required to lodge an FBT return by 21 May each year (¶35-030).

Electronic lodgment

The electronic lodgment system allows participating tax agents to lodge their clients' returns and other tax forms with the ATO electronically. Forms that can be lodged electronically include individual, partnership, trust, company, superannuation fund, FBT and GST returns. Estimates of company tax can also be lodged electronically, as well as applications for a private ruling. For lodgment programs applicable to tax agents, see ¶32-080. Individuals may lodge their returns electronically using "myTax", which is provided by the ATO (¶2-030).

The Commissioner will determine the software requirements for electronic forms where a return is to be lodged by electronic transmission (such as email) (ITAA36 s 161A). This applies to both returns lodged by registered tax agents on behalf of taxpayers and returns lodged electronically by those who do not use a tax agent.

Where a taxpayer uses a tax agent, the taxpayer is required to complete a declaration authorising the electronic transmission of the return (or request for an amendment) and state that he/she agrees with the information that is being transmitted. The tax agent is not entitled to transmit the taxpayer's document before receiving a copy of the declaration.

The original declaration must be kept by the taxpayer for a certain number of years, depending on the type of taxpayer concerned (TAA Sch 1 s 388-65; *Legislative Instrument* F2020L00564).

A notice, return or application for amendment that is given to the Commissioner by a taxpayer electronically has to contain the ‘‘electronic signature’’ of the taxpayer. Where this is given by a tax agent on a taxpayer's behalf, it has to contain the electronic signature of the registered tax agent (TAA Sch 1 s 388-75). An electronic signature is a unique identification in an electronic form that is approved by the Commissioner (PS LA 2005/20). Examples of electronic signatures are personal identification numbers, public and private key systems, and Auskey.

Any fees paid by the taxpayer for the electronic lodgment of tax-related information are deductible (¶16-850) (TD 93/63) and should be claimed in the return for the financial year in which paid (eg the fee for lodging a 2019–20 return would normally be claimed in the 2020–21 return).

Exemptions

Not all persons in receipt of income have to lodge a return. Resident individuals whose 2020–21 taxable income is less than $18,200 need not lodge a return if they have not had PAYG amounts withheld from their pay or other income and do not have current year or prior year losses. Resident and non-resident individuals who receive certain types of Australian government pension, benefit or allowance and whose taxable income is below the minimum threshold are also exempt from lodging a return. Taxpayers entitled to the maximum pensioner or beneficiary rebate generally do not have to lodge a return. The Commissioner may also exempt any particular taxpayer or classes of taxpayer from lodging an annual return, eg non-profit organisations, societies, clubs, etc, that are exempt from tax (¶10-605; *Australian Wool Testing Authority*).

Taxpayers who are not required to lodge returns should still do so if, for example, they wish to claim a refund of PAYG amounts withheld or excess imputation credits. Taxpayers who are not required to lodge returns may be required to send a non-lodgment advice form to the ATO.

[FTR ¶79-320]

¶24-030 Contents of returns

Income tax returns must be made on the applicable return form prescribed by the Commissioner, although a simpler form may be authorised and returns in a substantially similar form may be accepted. The ‘‘approved form’’ provisions in TAA Sch 1 Subdiv 388-B cover income tax return forms; see also PS LA 2005/19.

The returns must contain such information and particulars, and be accompanied by such documents, accounts and statements, as are indicated in the instruction booklets to the relevant return forms. The usual return forms are: (i) individuals — either the short tax return form or the ‘‘standard’’ tax return form (Form I if lodged by a tax agent) (¶2-030; ¶44-000); (ii) companies (including corporate limited partnerships, corporate unit trusts and public trading trusts) — Form C (¶3-045,¶44-020); (iii) superannuation funds, etc — Form F (¶13-350); (iv) partnerships (but not corporate limited partnerships) — Form P (¶5-065, ¶44-040); and (v) trusts — Form T (¶6-020, ¶44-060).

Under the self-assessment system (¶24-000), tax returns are not subject to technical or other scrutiny before assessment. In making an assessment, the Commissioner is authorised to accept, without examination, statements made by or on behalf of the taxpayer in the return or in any other relevant document (ITAA36 s 169A). As a consequence, many elections and notifications do not have to be in writing or lodged with the Commissioner. The information to be provided in a full self-assessment taxpayer's return includes the taxpayer's taxable income or net income, the amount (if any) of tax payable on that taxable income or net income, and any interest payable by the taxpayer under ITAA36 s 102AAM (¶21-350) for that year of income (ITAA36 s 161AA).

Records and statements showing how the taxpayer's taxable income is calculated are not lodged with returns (with certain exceptions such as an employee's payment summary), although they must be retained by a taxpayer for a certain period of time (¶9-045) and may have to be produced to the ATO, eg if the return is selected for audit. A business taxpayer's record-keeping requirements are discussed at ¶9-045.

It is likely that both the return form and any records, etc, retained by the taxpayer and made available to the ATO on request are to be read together in determining the extent to which tax shortfall penalties apply (¶29-160) (IT 2624; IT 2662).

It is important that returns contain all the required information and detail, and that they are correctly submitted for lodgment. The Commissioner warns that incomplete or substandard returns will be sent back to the taxpayer or tax agent concerned. Returns will not be regarded as lodged until they have been correctly completed and signed, and received by the ATO at the appropriate place. If the Commissioner has to send back the return, the taxpayer could be subject to late lodgment penalties (¶29-100).

Request for rulings

Where a taxpayer is uncertain about the proper tax treatment to be given to a particular matter, the taxpayer can apply for a private ruling (¶24-560). The fact that a taxpayer has applied for, or has objected against, a private ruling does *not* affect the taxpayer's obligation to lodge a return for the income year covered by the application or ruling; nor does it affect the Commissioner's power to make or amend an assessment in respect of the relevant year.

If the taxpayer is uncertain as to the proper tax treatment to be given to a particular matter but is not entitled to apply for a private ruling, the taxpayer may be able to apply to the ATO for an oral ruling (¶24-580), written advice (¶24-500) or include with the return a request for the Commissioner to consider the question (s 169A(2)). Statements made in relation to such requests are likely to be taken into account in determining the extent to which tax shortfall penalties apply (¶29-160). For the Commissioner's administrative guidelines in relation to these requests, see PS LA 2008/3.

Signature, address for service, etc

An individual return must be signed by the person making the return, verifying the information contained therein; this may be done electronically (¶24-010). A company return must be signed by the public officer. In the case of a trust or deceased estate, the return must be signed by any trustee resident in Australia or, if there is no such trustee, by the public officer or the agent in Australia for the trustee. A partnership return must be signed by any of the partners. If no partner is resident in Australia, then the return must be signed by the agent in Australia for the partnership. Documents, statements, etc, accompanying a return must also be signed by the person signing the return and must be endorsed so that they are identified as accompanying the return.

If a return or other document is prepared by a tax agent, the tax agent (or registered nominee if the tax agent is a partnership or company) must certify that the document was prepared in accordance with the information supplied by the taxpayer, the agent received a declaration from the taxpayer stating that the information provided to the agent was true and correct, and the agent was authorised by the taxpayer to give the document to the Commissioner (TAA Sch 1 s 388-70). If a tax agent gives a return to the Commissioner on a taxpayer's behalf in paper form, the document must contain a declaration made by the taxpayer with their signature and a declaration made by the tax agent with their signature, if the return so requires (TAA Sch 1 s 388-75).

A "preferred address for service" in Australia must be given in the return. Taxpayers may nominate an electronic address as their preferred address for service of notices and the Commissioner will use the preferred address where appropriate. Notice of a change of preferred address must be given (online using myGov, by phone or by post) within 28 days to the ATO. If a person provides no preferred address for service, eg where no return is lodged, or fails to notify the Commissioner of a change of preferred address, that person's preferred address for service will be the address in any record in the custody of the Commissioner. Failure to notify a change of address precludes a taxpayer from relying on the fact of the address having changed, eg in proceedings to recover outstanding tax (TAR reg 15 to 19).

Where a taxpayer has given the address of a registered tax agent as the address for service, that agent is required to give the taxpayer the original, or a copy, of any notice of assessment for that taxpayer delivered to that address. A penalty of 30 units (ie 30 × $210 = $6,300) applies for failing to comply (ITAA36 s 161G).

[FTR ¶79-305]

¶24-040 Elections, choices and notifications

As part of the process of determining the taxpayer's taxable income, the tax law allows a taxpayer to make various elections/choices and requests, and to give notice of certain matters (together, "elections"). Many elections are *not* required to be in writing and/or lodged with the Commissioner. For example, ITAA97 generally does not require choices made for CGT purposes to be lodged with the Commissioner.

Even though an election may not have to be in writing, it should be obvious from the return, and the taxpayer's records verifying the calculation of the relevant component of taxable income, whether the election was made.

Where an election has to be in writing, the taxpayer must retain it with his/her records (to be produced, for example, if the relevant return is selected for audit). In some cases an election, etc, must be lodged with the Commissioner by the time specified in the relevant provision, usually the due date for lodging the relevant return. In many cases, however, the Commissioner has a discretion to grant an extension of time. The Commissioner's current policy where he has such a discretion is that the election does *not* have to be lodged until specifically requested by him, except in the case of a specific election identified in IT 2624, the tax return instructions and other published ATO instructions (IT 2624; IT 2662). Before lodging a return, a taxpayer should check with the ATO whether an election is also required to be lodged.

Elections constituted by a written agreement between taxpayers do not have to be lodged with the Commissioner but must be retained by the taxpayers.

Elections required to be in writing and lodged include . . .

Consolidated groups

- Choice by a head company to form a consolidated group (ITAA97 s 703-50(2): ¶8-000).

Superannuation

- Election by PST in relation to exemption attributable to current pension liabilities (ITAA97 s 295-400: ¶13-440).
- Election by trustee of superannuation fund for fund to become a regulated superannuation fund (*Superannuation Industry (Supervision) Act 1993*, s 19: ¶8-100).

FBT

- Election to adopt operating cost method to determine the taxable value of car fringe benefits (FBTAA s 10(1): ¶35-170).

• Election to adopt current year as base year for the purpose of determining the taxable value of non-remote housing fringe benefits (FBTAA s 26(3)(aa): ¶35-420).

Trusts

• Request for Commissioner not to apply ITAA36 s 99A to income to which no beneficiary is presently entitled. Such a request may only be made by trustees of certain trusts (s 99A(2): ¶6-230).

Primary producers

• Election that income tax averaging not apply (ITAA97 s 392-25: ¶18-270).

CFCs

• Election by company of new statutory accounting period under the CFC rules (ITAA36 s 319(2): ¶21-140).

Gifts

• Election to spread deductions for certain cultural, environmental and heritage gifts and conservation covenants over a period of up to 5 income years (ITAA97 Subdiv 30-DB: ¶16-960, ¶16-965, ¶16-967, ¶16-972). Note that the election must be lodged with the Arts Secretary, the Environment Secretary or the Heritage Secretary (whichever is applicable).

Elections required to be in writing but not lodged include . . .

Trusts

• Election that a trust be treated as a family trust for tax purposes (ITAA36 Sch 2F s 272-80(2): ¶6-266). Although the election does not need to be lodged, the trustee is required to specify the year in which the election was made on the trust tax return each year.

Foreign currency

• Choice by certain entities to use the applicable functional currency to calculate their relevant annual net amounts and then to translate those annual net amounts into Australian currency for the purpose of determining the entity's income tax liability. (ITAA97 s 960-60: ¶23-070).

Trading stock

• Election where interests in trading stock have changed (ITAA97 s 70-100(4): ¶9-290).

Depreciation

• Joint election for roll-over relief where there is a disposal of a depreciating asset on change of ownership or interest (ITAA97 s 40-340(3): ¶17-710).

Substantiation

• Notice of nominated replacement car (ITAA97 s 28-130: ¶16-350).

CGT

• Choice that a residence continue to be the taxpayer's main residence even after it stopped being his/her main residence (ITAA97 s 118-145: ¶11-740).

• Election that specifies ''CGT exempt amount'' in relation to a small business retirement disposal (ITAA97 s 152-300: ¶7-185).

• Election for small business asset roll-over relief (ITAA97 s 152-410: ¶7-195).

Superannuation

• Notice by member of superannuation fund or holder of RSA of intention to claim a deduction for contributions to the fund or RSA (ITAA97 s 290-170: ¶13-730).

• Election to treat all or part of a transfer of overseas superannuation benefits to an Australian superannuation fund as assessable contributions (ITAA97 s 305-80: ¶14-420).

• Agreement by trustee of complying superannuation fund or complying ADF as to transfer of assessable contributions (ITAA97 s 295-260: ¶13-125).

• Election (given by an employee to his/her employer) that the employer not be liable for the superannuation guarantee charge because the employee's superannuation entitlements exceed the pension RBL (SGAA s 19: ¶39-030).

FBT

• Election to adopt either the statutory formula method or 12-week record-keeping method to determine the taxable value of car parking fringe benefits (FBTAA s 39FA(1) or 39GA(1): ¶35-256).

Dependants

• Family agreement allocating dependants for purposes of Medicare levy (ITAA36 s 251R(6D): ¶2-340).

[FTR ¶79-305, ¶785-090, ¶796-190, ¶796-540]

¶24-050 Duties and liabilities of agents

An agent is required to furnish an annual return of income, or profits or gains of a capital nature, derived by the agent in a representative capacity or by the principal through the agency (ITAA36 s 254). A separate return must be filed for each person for whom he/she is agent. If the agent is not the sole Australian agent for an overseas principal, an agent's return must still be furnished showing particulars of all transactions with that principal.

The definition of "agent" is very wide and includes not only agents in the generally accepted sense but also every entity who: (1) holds or has the control, receipt or disposal of money in Australia belonging to a person outside Australia; or (2) is declared by the Commissioner to be an agent. The last of these might include a bank at which a person outside of Australia has an account into which income is paid.

An agent's duties and liabilities are not limited to the furnishing of returns. The agent is authorised and required to retain funds received in their representative capacity to pay tax which is or will become due in respect of the income, profits or gains realised in that capacity (s 254(1)(d)). For this liability to arise, the Commissioner must have issued a notice of assessment of the taxpayer's taxable income and the tax payable (*Australian Building Systems*, High Ct).

Under the section, the agent is personally liable for the tax payable on income, profits or gains but only to the extent of any amount that the agent has retained or should have retained (s 254(1)(e)). However, s 254(1)(e) does not apply to limit a trustee's personal liability where the trustee is assessed on trust income under s 99 or 99A (*Barkworth Olives*).

Similarly, any other person in receipt or control of money from a non-resident may be required to retain, out of moneys coming to the person on behalf of the non-resident, sufficient funds to pay the tax due and payable by the non-resident (ITAA36 s 255). For a s 255 notice to be effective, a notice of assessment giving rise to the tax liability must have been issued (*Bluebottle*).

When a s 255 notice is given, the agent is required to retain tax out of the principal's money that is under, or will later come into, the agent's control, and then pay such tax to the Commissioner when required. This extends to money denominated in a foreign currency (*Resource Capital Fund*).

Where a s 255 notice is issued to a company in respect of dividends payable to a shareholder, the requirement to retain the money prevails even where the shareholder assigns the right to receive the dividend to a third party (*Bluebottle*).

Further, the Commissioner may issue an assessment to an agent. However, an assessment to an agent must clearly specify that the person is being assessed as an agent (*Case W56*).

Consolidating assessments

Where more than one person receives income, profits or capital gains on behalf of a non-resident or person absent from Australia who is liable to Australian tax, the Commissioner may consolidate the assessments. Further, he may declare any one of the non-resident's or absent person's ''agents'' to be his/her sole agent in respect of, and thus liable to pay the tax under, that consolidated assessment (ITAA36 s 169AA).

[FTR ¶79-886, ¶782-060, ¶782-280]

¶24-060 When to lodge returns

The final date for lodging income tax returns is specified by the Commissioner via Legislative Instrument (¶24-010). The due date for lodgment of returns for individuals, partnerships and trusts is generally 31 October. Where, however, the taxpayer is permitted to adopt a substituted accounting period, the return will not be due until 4 months after the close of the substituted accounting period. An income tax return is not treated as duly lodged until *received.*

Under the tax agent lodgment program, there are special extension of time arrangements for individual, partnership and trust returns lodged through tax agents. For the applicable lodgment dates and the various qualifications thereto, see the Lodgment Program on the ATO website at www.ato.gov.au.

Lodgment of returns by full self-assessment taxpayers (ie companies, superannuation funds, ADFs and PSTs) is currently as follows:

- companies and superannuation funds with returns 2 or more years outstanding — 31 October
- large/medium taxpayers (ie companies, superannuation funds, partnerships and trusts that have an annual income greater than $10 million or investment of more than $50 million, and all non-complying superannuation funds and PSTs) — 15 January, and
- all other companies and superannuation funds (including those which are new registrations) — 28 February.

Special, further or fuller returns must be lodged within the period prescribed by the Commissioner when he calls for them.

The Commissioner may grant a taxpayer an extension of time to lodge a return (¶24-070). A person who fails to lodge an annual or other return by the due date is liable to be prosecuted and/or to pay late lodgment penalties (¶29-100).

[FTR ¶79-310]

¶24-070 Additional time for lodgment

The Commissioner may defer the time for lodging a return (ITAA36 s 161; TAA Sch 1 s 388-55). A decision granting, or refusing to grant, an additional period of time is not reviewable by the AAT in proceedings under TAA Pt IVC (*AAT and AC Goode & Co*; *Fitzgibbon*), but may be reviewed under the *Administrative Decisions (Judicial Review) Act 1977* (¶28-180).

The ATO may grant either an arrangement to lodge or an extension to lodge. Where an *arrangement to lodge* is granted, the taxpayer is given additional time to lodge the return. If the return is not lodged within the additional time allowed, then late lodgment penalty (¶29-100) will be imposed from the original due date, not the later arranged due date. An *extension to lodge* is essentially the same as an arrangement to lodge except that, if the taxpayer fails to lodge, late lodgment penalty is calculated from the extended due date rather than the original due date. The ATO will grant extensions only in exceptional circumstances. Extensions were granted, for example, during the Gulf War to service personnel involved in the conflict. Normal practice within the ATO is to grant arrangements to lodge, and even these are only granted when the circumstances preventing lodgment are beyond the control of the person concerned.

An application for additional time to lodge should be made before the due date and should state the reason why the return cannot be lodged by the due date. If only a short period is required there will normally be no difficulty in obtaining the additional time.

The tax agent lodgment program provides for an extension of time for individual, partnership and trust returns lodged through a tax agent, provided certain conditions are fulfilled. However, returns lodged through tax agents after the final date for lodgment must be accompanied by payment of the estimated tax due. If tax agents have trouble obtaining information to complete clients' tax returns within the time allowed, they should apply to the Commissioner for an extension of time or, alternatively, advise their clients that they are at risk of incurring penalties if they do not provide the information. Failure to take either course of action may result in the client recovering damages for breach of contract.

In one case, not only did the taxpayers' accountants fail to lodge the relevant tax returns on time, some were not lodged at all. In addition, the accountants failed to lodge objections within the time allowed for some assessments that were issued to the taxpayers. The court awarded the taxpayers damages equal to the penalties imposed for late lodgment of the returns, damages for the "loss of the chance" to have the Commissioner's decisions not to allow their objections reviewed and damages equal to the amount of extra expense incurred in having their financial affairs sorted out by new accountants (*Markham v Lunt*).

[FTR ¶79-300, ¶978-835]

¶24-080 Where to lodge returns

The Commissioner normally directs the lodgment of a return to a particular address. If no such direction is given, the taxpayer may lodge the return at any office of a Deputy Commissioner. For individuals, the tax return instructions contain a pre-addressed envelope. As regards the electronic lodgment of returns, see ¶24-010.

Activity Statements

¶24-200 Business Activity Statement

Taxpayers who are registered for GST must report their periodic tax obligations and entitlements to the ATO on a single tax compliance form: the Business Activity Statement (BAS). The Instalment Activity Statement (IAS) is for taxpayers who are not registered for GST (¶24-220). Taxpayers still need to lodge separate income tax returns or FBT returns (where applicable) for their business.

The Commissioner will normally send a BAS to taxpayers who are registered for GST before they need to lodge it. Debts and any credit entitlements notified on the BAS will then be recorded on the taxpayer's running balance account (RBA) (¶24-300). Taxpayers will receive only one BAS for each reporting period even if they have both a monthly and a quarterly reporting obligation.

▶ Example

A business is required to lodge a quarterly BAS to report GST and PAYG instalments. However, as it is classified as a medium PAYG withholder (¶26-500), it is required to lodge a monthly BAS to report PAYG amounts withheld.

For the January–March quarter, the business is required to lodge:

- a BAS for its January PAYG withholding liability
- a BAS for its February PAYG withholding liability, and
- a BAS for both its March PAYG withholding liability and its quarterly GST and PAYG instalment liabilities.

Likewise for the remainder of the year.

Instructions for completing a BAS are available on the ATO's website (www.ato.gov.au).

Certain people other than registered tax agents may provide a ''BAS service'' on behalf of a taxpayer, eg preparing a BAS or giving advice in relation to a BAS provision (¶32-000).

Obligations to be reported

The following obligations and entitlements are reported on a BAS:

- GST (¶34-000)
- wine equalisation tax and luxury car tax (¶34-360)
- PAYG amounts withheld from payments (¶26-100)
- PAYG instalments (¶27-100)
- FBT instalments (¶35-000)
- deferred company instalments.

Amounts withheld by large PAYG withholders are not reported on a BAS but are notified separately as part of the process of making a mandatory electronic payment (¶26-550). Voluntary payments are also not reported on a BAS.

[FTR ¶978-830]

¶24-220 Instalment Activity Statement

Taxpayers who are not registered for GST are required to report their tax obligations on an Instalment Activity Statement (IAS) rather than a Business Activity Statement (BAS) (¶24-200). Taxpayers still need to lodge separate income tax returns. Some taxpayers may need to complete both a BAS and an IAS where, for example, a family business is run through a trust.

The IAS is mainly for individual taxpayers (including trustees) with investment income to report their obligations to the ATO. Investment income includes rental, dividend and interest income. The form can be used to report obligations for:

- PAYG instalments (¶27-100)
- PAYG amounts withheld from payments (¶26-100)
- FBT instalments (¶35-000)
- deferred company instalments.

Instructions for completing an IAS are available on the ATO's website (www.ato.gov.au).

¶24-240 Lodging activity statements

A penalty applies for failure to lodge an activity statement in the approved form (¶29-100). A document is in the ''approved form'' if it meets the requirements set out in TAA Sch 1 s 388-50. An activity statement that is incomplete will be in the approved form if it contains the information required by the Commissioner (s 388-50(1A)).

If the due date for lodgment falls on a Saturday or a Sunday, or on a public holiday for the whole of any state or territory, the activity statement may be lodged on the next business day without incurring a penalty (TAA Sch 1 s 388-52).

Both the BAS and IAS can be lodged via an automated phone service if taxpayers have zero amounts to report against all aspects of their monthly or quarterly activity statement.

Obligations reported on an activity statement originally had to be notified and paid to the ATO by the 21st day of the month after the end of the reporting period. However, extended due dates for meeting *quarterly* obligations apply to a taxpayer classified as a "deferred BAS payer" (ITAA97 s 995-1(1)). Taxpayers are *not eligible* for the extended due dates if they have monthly GST obligations or if their reporting obligation relates only to:

- PAYG amounts withheld by a medium withholder or a large withholder (¶26-500), or
- PAYG instalments of an annual payer (¶27-170).

The extended due dates are as follows:

Quarter ending	Due date
30 September	28 October
31 December	28 February
31 March	28 April
30 June	28 July

The due dates are generally extended by one week, except for the December quarter where a further one month is allowed due to the Christmas holiday period. A taxpayer can only be a deferred BAS payer where it has a quarterly obligation in a particular month. So, for example, a taxpayer that only has a monthly PAYG withholding obligation for a month will not be a deferred BAS payer for that month. In that case, the taxpayer is still required to lodge an activity statement by the 21st day of the month after the end of the reporting period. The ATO grants further lodgment concessions to tax agents and to those who lodge electronically (¶26-550).

The *general* reporting requirements are set out in the table below. For more details, and some qualifications, see the relevant paragraph indicated in the footnotes. For the reporting and payment of specific liabilities, the due dates for lodging activity statements are set out in the Tax Calendar at ¶45-100.

Liability	BAS/IAS due
GST[1]	
Annual turnover less than $20m (entities can choose to lodge monthly)	Quarterly
Annual turnover $20m or more	Monthly
PAYG withholding[2]	
Annual withholding obligations $25,000 or less (entities can choose to lodge monthly)	Quarterly
Annual withholding obligations more than $25,000 but do not exceed $1m	Monthly
PAYG instalments	
Taxpayers generally[3]	Quarterly
Large corporate entities[4]	Monthly
FBT instalments[5]	Quarterly

(1) If an entity's annual turnover is $20m or more, it must normally lodge electronically. Quarterly GST reporters whose annual turnovers do not exceed $2m may instead elect to lodge on an annual basis (¶34-120).

(2) Large withholders (amounts withheld of more than $1m a year) must lodge electronically approximately one week after the amount is withheld (¶26-550).

(3) Taxpayers can choose to make annual payments if they meet certain criteria (¶27-170).

(4) Corporate entities with a base assessment instalment income above the relevant threshold are required to lodge monthly, subject to transitional arrangements (¶27-170).

(5) Employers whose FBT liability in the previous year was less than $3,000 are only required to pay on an annual basis (¶35-050).

[FTR ¶978-830, ¶978-832]

¶24-260 Notification and payment of reported amounts

All the amounts reported in the activity statement will be aggregated to form a net amount owing to the Commissioner, or a net amount owing by the Commissioner. Upon receipt of the activity statement, the Commissioner will record the liability amounts on the entity's RBA (¶24-300). Any payments made in respect of those amounts for that period will also be recorded on the RBA. If there is a shortfall in the payment that results in a deficit balance on the RBA, GIC will be payable on that deficit (¶29-510).

A net amount on the activity statement that is a credit entitlement may result in a surplus on the RBA when recorded on the entity's account. The Commissioner may either apply the surplus against any other tax debt of the entity (¶24-360) or refund the amount (¶24-380). Where an amount that must be refunded is not refunded within 14 days, the entity may be entitled to deferred refund interest (¶24-380).

The Commissioner also has a discretion to refund an RBA surplus or credit rather than offsetting it against another tax debt (¶24-360).

The effect of these rules is that normally there will be a single payment or credit entitlement for each reporting period, rather than separate liabilities for each BAS amount.

A ''BAS amount'' refers to all credits and debts relating to GST (¶34-000), luxury car tax and wine equalisation tax (¶34-360), PAYG amounts withheld from payments (¶26-100), PAYG instalments (¶27-100), FBT instalments (¶35-000) and fuel tax credits (¶40-100) (''BAS amounts'' as defined in ITAA97 s 995-1(1)).

▶ Example

An entity reports the following obligations/entitlements on its BAS:

- GST credit of $12,500
- PAYG instalment liability of $2,500
- PAYG withholding liability of $5,000, and
- FBT liability of $1,000.

As there will be a credit entitlement of $4,000, ie $12,500 – ($2,500 + $5,000 + $1,000), the entity is not required to make any payments for the period.

Penalties apply where taxpayers fail to notify BAS amounts electronically where required (¶29-310).

Running Balance Accounts

¶24-300 What is a running balance account?

A running balance account (RBA) is used by the Commissioner to record a taxpayer's tax liabilities and payments on a single account. The Commissioner may set up an RBA to account for any primary tax debt, ie any liability due directly under a taxation law, including an amount that is not yet payable. Debts that arise indirectly through court or insolvency proceedings are not primary tax debts.

Rather than having a specific liability for various tax debts (eg PAYG instalments, FBT, GST obligations), a taxpayer has one consolidated balance, either debit or credit, reflected in the RBA. The RBA provisions are contained in TAA Pt IIB (ss 8AAZA to 8AAZN).

[FTR ¶963-050 – ¶963-090]

¶24-320 Operation of the RBA system

All debts notified on an activity statement (¶24-200) and any associated payments and credit entitlements for that business can be recorded on an RBA.

An RBA may be established for any entity. ''Entity'' means a company, a partnership, a person in the capacity of a trustee, a body politic, a corporation sole, and any other person. The Commissioner may establish RBAs on any basis that he determines, eg for different businesses conducted by the same entity, for different parts of the same business or for different periods (TAA s 8AAZC). For instance, a company with several operating divisions may have separate RBAs established for each division. In that case, the company's outstanding tax debt at a particular time would be determined by aggregating the ''RBA deficit debts'' (¶24-340) in the company's RBAs for each RBA class.

A person who is a trustee in more than one capacity is treated, for RBA purposes, as a separate entity in relation to each of those capacities.

The Commissioner may allocate a primary tax debt to an RBA that has been established for that type of tax debt. If 2 or more RBAs for an entity have been established for that kind of debt, the Commissioner may allocate the debt to any one of those RBAs, or between any 2 or more of those RBAs (TAA s 8AAZD).

[FTR ¶963-060, ¶963-065]

¶24-340 RBA deficit debt

An ''RBA deficit debt'' is a balance in favour of the Commissioner based on primary tax debts that remain unpaid after their due date and payments and credits that have been allocated to the RBA (TAA s 8AAZA). It is a debt due to the Commonwealth and may be recovered by the Commissioner under the collection and recovery regime (¶25-500). Outstanding liabilities may be recovered either as an RBA deficit debt or as individual debts. If there are several tax debtors (eg each partner in a partnership), each debtor is liable for the RBA deficit debt in the same way they are liable for the individual debts allocated to that RBA (TAA s 8AAZH).

An RBA statement, containing such particulars as the Commissioner determines, may be prepared at any time (TAA s 8AAZG). The production of an RBA statement is prima facie evidence that the RBA was duly kept and that the amount and particulars in the statement are correct (TAA s 8AAZI). However, the Commissioner is not required to issue an RBA statement before commencing recovery proceedings.

GIC is payable on any RBA deficit debt that exists at the end of each day (TAA s 8AAZF). Where an entity has several divisional RBAs for an RBA class of debts, the GIC is separately determined on the basis of each divisional RBA deficit debt. GIC also applies to the primary tax debts that are covered by an RBA.

[FTR ¶963-065, ¶963-070]

¶24-360 Allocation of credits to RBA

The Commissioner is generally required to deal with various credit amounts according to one of 2 methods. These rules apply to payments of current tax debts or anticipated tax debts, credits (including excess non-RBA credits) and RBA surpluses. In certain circumstances (outlined below), the Commissioner may refund a credit amount instead of applying it against a tax debt (TAA s 8AAZL). The 2 methods of applying credits are:

(1) the Commissioner may allocate the amount to an RBA of the entity or, if the entity is a member of an RBA group, to an RBA of another member of the group. The Commissioner must then also apply the amount against any tax debts allocated to that RBA or GIC on such tax debts. To the extent that the amount is not applied, it gives rise to an excess non-RBA credit in favour of the entity that relates to the RBA to which the amount was allocated (TAA s 8AAZLA), or

(2) the Commissioner may apply the credit amount against a non-RBA tax debt of the entity or, if the entity is a member of an RBA group, against a non-RBA tax debt of another member of the group. If the non-RBA tax debt is a tax debt allocated to an RBA, or GIC on such a tax debt, the Commissioner must then also allocate the amount to that RBA. To the extent that the amount is not applied, it gives rise to an excess non-RBA credit that relates to the RBA (if any) that the Commissioner determines (TAA s 8AAZLB).

A credit under the PAYG system must be applied against the tax debtor's HELP assessment debt, compulsory repayment amount (¶2-380) or FS assessment debt (¶2-385), in that order, before being applied against any other non-RBA tax debts (TAA s 8AAZLD).

A payment in respect of a tax debt is not considered to have been made until it is received by the Commissioner or a person acting on his behalf (TAA s 8AAZM).

In applying these rules, the Commissioner is not required to take account of any instructions from the entity (TAA s 8AAZLE).

The Commissioner is not required to apply a credit amount against a tax debt in accordance with one of the 2 methods set out above where the tax debt is:

- due but not yet payable
- one where the taxpayer has complied with an arrangement to pay by instalments (¶25-410), or
- one where the Commissioner has agreed to defer recovery (¶25-510).

[FTR ¶963-080 – ¶963-090]

¶24-380 Refunds of RBA surpluses

An RBA surplus is a balance in favour of the entity, based on primary tax debts that have been allocated to the RBA, payments made in respect of current or anticipated primary tax debts and credits to which the entity is entitled that have been allocated to the RBA.

The Commissioner must refund so much of the RBA surplus or excess non-RBA credit as the Commissioner does not allocate or apply according to the 2 methods set out in ¶24-360 (TAA s 8AAZLF(1); *Multiflex*); voluntary payments are only required to be refunded on request (TAA s 8AAZLF(2)). However, if the entity has not given the Commissioner a notification (eg a BAS) that may affect the amount of refund, the Commissioner may withhold the refund (TAA s 8AAZLG). Further, where the entity has given the Commissioner a notification but it is reasonable for the Commissioner to verify the information, he may withhold the refund. In deciding whether to withhold, the Commissioner must have regard to a number of factors, including the likely accuracy of the notified information, the impact on the entity's financial position, the impact on the revenue and the likelihood that there is fraud or evasion, intentional disregard of or recklessness as to a tax law. If the Commissioner wishes to retain the refund beyond 14 days for an RBA surplus and 30 days for an excess non-RBA credit, the Commissioner must inform the entity by the last day of the relevant period. The Commissioner can only retain the refund until it is no longer reasonable to require verification of the claims or there is a change to the refund (as a result of the issue of an amended assessment or a GST assessment), whichever happens first (TAA s 8AAZLGA; PS LA 2012/6). The entity has a right of objection against the decision to withhold — the right arises 60 days after when the Commissioner is required to inform of his decision to withhold but the period is extended by each day in which there is a request for information that remains outstanding. The objection must be lodged after the end of the 60-day period (or extended period) and before a change to the refund (as noted above) (TAA s 14ZW(1)(aac)).

Where an entity has an outstanding activity statement, a refund can be retained until a correct activity statement is lodged or the Commissioner makes an assessment of the amount, whichever happens first (TAA s 8AAZLG).

Any refund of an RBA surplus or credit must be paid into a financial institution account nominated by the entity in accordance with s 8AAZLH. The Commissioner will be able to withhold a refund until the entity nominates an account. However, the Commissioner may arrange to pay refunds to the entity in a different way, eg by cheque, or may direct that electronic refunds be paid into a nominated third party account when authorised to do so by the entity (PS LA 2011/22).

Delayed refund interest

A taxpayer is entitled to delayed refund interest where the Commissioner fails to refund an RBA surplus that he is required to refund within 14 days. The interest entitlement is governed by *Taxation (Interest on Overpayments and Early Payments) Act 1983* (TIOEPA) Pt IIIAA.

Specifically, delayed refund interest is payable by the Commissioner if a refund is not paid within 14 days where an RBA surplus arises from:

- the allocation of a BAS amount (¶24-260) to the RBA following lodgment of the activity statement (TIOEPA s 12AA)
- the remission of a penalty relating to a BAS amount (TIOEPA s 12AB)
- a voluntary payment that occurs because a payment is made in respect of an anticipated tax debt under a BAS provision (TIOEPA s 12AC).

The interest is payable from the *end* of the 14th day after the latest of either the day the RBA went into surplus, or the day the remission or refund request was made, until the *end* of the day the refund is paid. However, if there is an outstanding activity statement, or information that is necessary to process the activity statement has not been provided, the interest period does not commence until 15 days after the relevant statement or information is given to the Commissioner. Also, the interest period will not commence until the taxpayer provides details of the financial institution account to which the refund must be paid (TIOEPA ss 12AD; 12AF).

The applicable interest rate is equivalent to the base interest rate under TAA s 8AAD (¶28-170).

Delayed refund interest must be returned as income for the year of income in which it is either refunded or applied against a tax debt.

▶ Example

Mitzi lodged her first quarterly BAS for 2017–18, providing the ATO with all the information required for the BAS to be processed. The ATO processed the BAS on 3 November 2017 and this resulted in a $4,000 RBA surplus arising. The ATO calculated delayed refund interest from 18 November (the beginning of the date 15 days after the RBA surplus arose) to 26 November (the date the surplus was refunded), a period of 9 days:

$$\$4{,}000 \times 1.70\% \times \frac{9}{365} = \$1.67$$

Mitzi must include this amount as income in her income tax return for the year in which the interest was refunded to her, or the year in which the ATO set it off or applied it against a tax debt.

[FTR ¶963-086, ¶963-087, ¶963-087/10, ¶963-088, ¶972-830]

ATO Rulings and Advice

¶24-500 Provision of ATO advice

The forms of advice provided by the ATO can be split into advice provided to a particular entity (ie private rulings, administratively binding advice, written general advice and GST written advice) and advice to the public generally (ie public rulings and publications).

The various forms of ATO advice provide different levels of protection — as to penalties, interest or primary liability.

PS LA 2008/3 currently details the different forms of written technical advice which the ATO provides, the circumstances in which such advice is to be provided, and the extent to which such advice can be relied on. Essentially, the ATO will provide legally binding forms of written advice wherever possible. If a private ruling cannot be given because consent from all rulees has not been obtained and the request relates to many, a public ruling will be issued. A public ruling will also be issued if the matter on which a private ruling is sought is likely to be relevant to a wider range of persons.

Both public rulings and private rulings (as well as all written advice given or published on the GST) are legally binding on the Commissioner. Taxpayers are entitled to protection from additional primary tax, penalties and interest when they rely on a ruling. Taxpayers are entitled to protection from penalty and interest charges where they rely on other ATO written advice or administrative practice.

Interpretative Decisions (ATO ID series) indicate the Commissioner's view on the interpretation of the law on particular issues. They are produced to assist ATO officers to apply the law consistently and accurately to particular factual situations (PS LA 2001/8; PS LA 2003/3). However, IDs are not published as a form of ATO advice and, therefore, cannot be relied on; taxpayers who apply an ID in good faith but the ID is later found to be incorrect will be liable for underpaid tax, not penalty or interest.

Law Administration Practice Statements (PS LA series) provide direction to ATO staff on the approaches to be taken in performing their duties. They are not used to provide interpretative advice and do not convey extra statutory concessions to taxpayers (PS LA 1998/1).

Taxpayer Alerts (TA series) operate as an early warning to taxpayers of significant new and emerging tax planning issues or arrangements that the ATO has under risk assessment. Taxpayer Alerts give the title of the issue (which may be a scheme, arrangement or particular transaction), briefly describe it and highlight those features which the ATO considers as taxation problems (PS LA 2008/15).

All GST written advice given or published by the ATO is binding. In addition to formal rulings and determinations, this includes fact sheets, information booklets, advice manuals, bulletins and product rulings, but does not include GST Practice Statements and GST Case Decision Summaries (now being replaced by interpretative decisions: PS LA 2001/8) (GSTR 1999/1).

Publication of advice

Public rulings, determinations and bulletins, Interpretative Decisions, Law Administration Practice Statements and Taxpayer Alerts are all made publicly available on the legal database of the ATO website (law.ato.gov.au/atolaw/index.htm). Private rulings (with taxpayer identifiers deleted) are also published on the ATO legal database.

PS LA 2008/4 provides guidance on the requirement to publish written binding advice, editing such advice for publication, and the review mechanisms available for taxpayers on versions intended for publication.

[FTR ¶978-460]

¶24-520 Types of rulings

The Commissioner may make public rulings (¶24-540), private rulings (¶24-560) and oral rulings (¶24-580) under the TAA. These rulings are legally binding on the Commissioner where they apply to a taxpayer and the taxpayer relies on the ruling by acting (or omitting to act) in accordance with the ruling (TAA Sch 1 s 357-60). A ruling applies to a taxpayer if the taxpayer is a member of a class to whom the ruling applies (in the case of a public ruling), or it is given in response to an application (in the case of a private or oral ruling) and the facts, assumptions or conditions set out in the ruling are met.

Public rulings may apply to all entities or a class of entities, either generally or in relation to a particular ''scheme'' or class of schemes. Private rulings are statements about the way in which the Commissioner considers a relevant provision applies to a particular scheme, and may cover anything involved in the application of the provision, including valuations of any thing. Oral rulings are a form of binding advice provided by the Commissioner in response to an individual's oral application as to how a tax law applies to them.

''Scheme'' is defined to mean any ''arrangement'', or any scheme, plan, proposal, action, course of action or course of conduct, whether unilateral or otherwise. ''Arrangement'' is defined equally broadly to mean any arrangement, agreement, understanding, promise or undertaking, whether express or implied, and whether or not enforceable by legal proceedings (ITAA97 s 995-1(1)).

A public ruling will only be binding in relation to the schemes specified in it and not in relation to the underlying principle or reasoning behind the ruling (*Bellinz*). In *Bellinz*, the arrangements at issue could be distinguished from those in the binding rulings on which the taxpayers relied. If a contract requiring a scheme is entered into, the scheme began or begins to be carried out when the contract is entered into (TAA Sch 1 s 357-80).

A public, private or oral ruling can deal with any aspect of a person's liability for income tax, withholding tax, mining withholding tax, FBT, franking tax, Medicare levy and indirect tax (ie GST, luxury car tax or wine equalisation tax) or excise (including the administration or collection of such taxes), or their entitlement to a product grant or benefit (including the administration or payment of such a grant or benefit) (TAA Sch 1 s 357-55).

Neither a public ruling nor a private ruling is altered by a contrary court or AAT decision except, in the case of a private ruling, if the court or AAT decision is given on a review or appeal relating to the particular private ruling. However, if a court or AAT decision is more favourable than a public, private or oral ruling, the decision may be relied on by the taxpayer.

Status of old rulings

A legally binding ruling about a provision under ITAA36 (old law) will be a binding ruling about a corresponding provision under ITAA97 (new law) in so far as the old and new provisions express the same ideas (TAA Sch 1 s 357-85). In deciding whether the new law expresses the same ideas as the old law, taxpayers can assume that there has been no change in those ideas unless announced otherwise (TR 2006/10; TR 2006/11).

A public, private or oral ruling in force immediately before 1 January 2006 has effect on and after that day as if it were a public, private or oral ruling made under the new rulings framework (ie TAA Sch 1 Divs 358; 359; 360).

Conflicting rulings

Where more than one ruling applies to a taxpayer and the rulings are inconsistent, the following rules apply (TAA Sch 1 s 357-75):

(1) if the earlier ruling is a public ruling, the taxpayer may rely on either ruling regardless of the later type of ruling

(2) if both the earlier and the later rulings are private or oral rulings, the earlier ruling is taken not to have been made if the Commissioner was informed about the existence of the earlier ruling (otherwise the later ruling is taken not to have been made)

(3) if the earlier ruling is a private or an oral ruling and the later ruling is a public ruling, the earlier ruling is taken not to have been made if, when the later ruling is made, the period to which the rulings relate has not begun and the scheme to which the ruling relates has not begun to be carried out (otherwise either ruling can be relied on).

Disregard of rulings

There is no penalty for a shortfall resulting from failure to follow a ruling; however, such failure may go towards determining whether a position taken by a taxpayer is reasonably arguable or whether the shortfall was caused by a lack of reasonable care for the purposes of the tax shortfall penalty provisions (TAA Sch 1 s 357-65; ¶29-160).

[FTR ¶978-504, ¶978-520, ¶978-552]

¶24-540 Public rulings

The Commissioner may make public rulings (including determinations) on the way in which a tax law applies to: (i) entities generally or to a class of entities; (ii) entities in relation to a class of schemes; or (iii) entities in relation to a particular scheme (TAA Sch 1 s 358-5). The Commissioner can make public rulings on matters of administration, collection, ultimate conclusions of fact, risk management material, safe harbours, ABN matters and matters specific to a single entity.

TR 2006/10 explains the public rulings system. A public ruling must state that it is a public ruling and must contain a subject heading and a number for identification. The Commissioner must publish a brief description of the ruling in the *Commonwealth Gazette*. A public ruling is "made" at the later of the time when it is published and the time when the notice of it is published in the *Gazette*. However, if the latter does not occur, the ruling can still be relied on and will bind the Commissioner. A ruling does not apply to schemes that have already begun to be carried out if it changes the Commissioner's general administrative practice and is less favourable to a taxpayer than the practice (TAA Sch 1 ss 358-5; 358-10). Only part of a ruling may be a public ruling; the "explanations" part of a public ruling is not binding on the Commissioner (*Taneja*).

Rulings and determinations are usually first issued in draft form for public comment. Where a final ruling takes a position contrary to the draft ruling, and the draft ruling represents the Commissioner's general administrative practice, the final ruling cannot apply retrospectively to a taxpayer's detriment. A general administrative practice is a practice which is applied by the Commissioner generally as a matter of administration (TD 2011/19). Where the draft ruling represents the Commissioner's only public statement on an issue, it will usually represent the Commissioner's general administrative practice (Explanatory Memorandum to Tax Laws Amendment (Improvements to Self Assessment) Bill (No 2) 2005, para 3-53 and 3-130).

The expression of the Commissioner's opinion in a draft ruling is not, however, a decision of an administrative character made (or proposed to be made) under an enactment, and hence is not reviewable under the *Administrative Decisions (Judicial Review) Act 1977* (*Barkworth Olives Management Ltd*).

The Commissioner may withdraw a public ruling in whole or in part by publishing a notice of withdrawal in the *Commonwealth Gazette*. If a public ruling is withdrawn, it remains applicable to schemes begun to be carried out before the withdrawal (TAA Sch 1 s 358-20).

Product rulings

PR 2007/71 explains the operation of the product ruling system. The Commissioner issues product rulings to rule publicly on the availability of claimed tax benefits from "products". These are arrangements in which a number of taxpayers individually enter into substantially the same transactions with a common entity or a group of entities, eg primary production schemes or investment arrangements. Promoters, or the persons involved as principals in the carrying out of the arrangement (but not the participants), may make a written application for a product ruling using the format outlined in PR 2007/71.

A product ruling applies to all persons within a specified class who enter into the specified arrangement during the term of the ruling, ie the investors. These persons need not seek a private ruling on the tax consequences of their investment in the product. The product ruling is legally binding on the Commissioner and investors can rely on the statements it contains, provided that the arrangements are carried out in accordance with the details provided by the applicant and described in the ruling.

If the arrangement implemented is materially different from that described then the Commissioner may withdraw the ruling and the ruling will not apply to arrangements begun to be carried out after the date of withdrawal. In *Carey v Field* the Federal Court pointed out that the statutory provisions do not suggest that the Commissioner can only withdraw a public ruling if the differences between the arrangements ruled upon and the arrangements implemented *must* result in a different tax outcome. However, the court went on to say that the Commissioner is not expected to withdraw a ruling unless he is of the view that the differences are at least *likely* to result in a different tax outcome.

Product rulings only apply to arrangements entered into after the date the ruling is made. Persons investing in the product before the ruling is made cannot rely on the ruling.

Class rulings

CR 2001/1 outlines the class rulings system and the information that must be provided by an entity requesting such. Class rulings enable the Commissioner to provide advice in response to a request from an entity about the application of a tax law to a specific class of persons in relation to a particular arrangement. Their purpose is to provide certainty to participants and overcome the need for individual participants to seek private rulings. To this end, the Commissioner may also issue a class ruling where a member of a class of persons affected by a particular arrangement requests a private ruling on the arrangement.

A class ruling applies to all persons within a specified class who participate in the specified arrangement during the term of the ruling. Such rulings are legally binding on the Commissioner and participants can rely on the statements they contain, provided the arrangements are carried out as described in the ruling. Class rulings will *not* be issued in relation to investment schemes and similar products (for which a product ruling should be sought). Nor will a class ruling be issued where the Commissioner has announced a change to the law on which he has been asked to rule. Where the Commissioner is unable to rule favourably, a private ruling may be obtained to enable the issues to be tested through the relevant review processes.

No right of objection against public ruling

Public rulings relate to classes of entities or schemes. They are not given in relation to a specific entity and no right of objection exists against a public ruling. However, if a taxpayer is potentially affected by a public ruling they can apply for a private ruling on the same subject matter and, if the private ruling is adverse, object against it (¶24-560). In *Remuneration Planning*, the applicant sought a declaration that TR 1999/5 was invalid, or at least did not apply to the years of income before it was issued. The Federal Court summarily dismissed the application for relief on the basis that there were elaborate provisions for appeal against assessments pursuant to TAA Pt IVC.

[FTR ¶978-504 – ¶978-518]

¶24-560 Private rulings

The Commissioner may, on application, make a private ruling on the way in which he considers a tax law applies to a taxpayer in relation to a specified scheme (TAA Sch 1 s 359-5). A private ruling may deal with issues relating to liability, administration, procedure and collection, and ultimate conclusions of fact, including valuations that are necessary in dealing with the application of the law (see below).

The application must be made in the approved form (a standard form is available on the ATO website) by either the taxpayer, the taxpayer's agent or the taxpayer's legal personal representative (TAA Sch 1 s 359-10). Where a prospective transaction is time sensitive, of major commercial significance requiring corporate board consideration, involves complex matters of law or fact and the tax consequences are critical to the transaction, the ATO may accept it into the priority ruling process (PS LA 2009/2).

A private ruling may relate to a current, future or past income year or claim period (TAA Sch 1 s 359-25) but must specify the income year(s) or claim period to be valid (*Case 7/2006*). TR 2006/11 outlines the private rulings system.

The private ruling must be made in writing, must state that it is a private ruling, and must identify the taxpayer to whom it applies ("the rulee") as well as the relevant scheme and relevant provision to which it relates (TAA Sch 1 ss 359-15; 359-20). A private ruling that was sent to an applicant stating that it applied to the applicant for the relevant years of income, rather than the rulee on whose behalf the ruling was sought, was subsequently found to be invalid and unable to be objected against (*Corporate Business Centres*; ¶28-070).

An application for a private ruling can be lodged by: any taxpayer, their agent (or tax agent), or their legal personal representative; a partner as agent of the partnership (and its partners); or a trustee in regard to the affairs of the trust.

If further information is needed, the Commissioner must request the information. Private rulings were set aside in *Case 10/2006*, *CTC Resources* and *Payne* (1994) on the basis that the Commissioner did not have sufficient information to determine the issues raised by the taxpayers. The Commissioner cannot make his own enquiries as to the *accuracy* of the facts contained in the application (*Pierce*). He may, however, make assumptions and consider information other than that supplied by the taxpayer, provided such assumptions or information are made known to the taxpayer before being used (s 359-10).

The ATO has refused to consider applications that, in addition to specific tax provisions, seek clarification of the application of "any other provisions of the Act". An application can be withdrawn at any time before a private ruling is made.

Obligation to make ruling

The Commissioner *must* make a private ruling in response to an application unless: (1) he considers that making the ruling would prejudice or unduly restrict the administration of a taxation law; (2) the matter sought to be ruled on is already being or has been considered by the Commissioner; or (3) the matter is about how the Commissioner would exercise a power under a relevant provision and the Commissioner has decided whether or not to exercise that power. The Commissioner must give written reasons for declining to make a ruling (TAA Sch 1 s 359-35).

If the Commissioner considers that the correctness of a private ruling would depend on which assumptions were made about a future event or other matter, the Commissioner may make appropriate assumptions or decline to make the ruling (TAA Sch 1 s 357-110). In *Hacon*, the Full Federal Court held that the Commissioner was entitled to decline to make a private ruling about the application of ITAA36 Pt IV to particular facts because the correctness of the ruling would depend on which assumptions were made about a future event or other matter. Generally, however, where the Commissioner declines to make the ruling, the AAT may on review make the assumptions it considers appropriate and direct the Commissioner to grant the application for a private ruling (*Case 14/96*).

If, at the end of 60 days after an application for a private ruling is made, the Commissioner has neither made a ruling nor informed the applicant that the application will not be complied with, the applicant may give the Commissioner a written notice requiring him to make the ruling. (The 60-day period may be extended if further information is requested, assumptions are made, third party information is taken into account or a valuation is referred to a valuer.) If the ruling is not made within 30 days of notice being given, applicants may then assume a negative response to their application, triggering their objection and appeal rights (TAA Sch 1 s 359-50).

When considering an application for a private ruling, the Commissioner may make related private rulings, eg on the way in which another tax law would apply or on the way in which a tax law would apply to the person in respect of another year of income, or claim period, in relation to the scheme or in relation to a related scheme (TAA s 359-45). The Commissioner may also make a revised private ruling that negates an earlier ruling where the scheme or year to which the earlier ruling applies has not begun (TAA Sch 1 s 359-55).

Private rulings (with taxpayer identifiers deleted) are published on the ATO legal database.

Valuations

Where, in making a private ruling request, the Commissioner has to determine the value of any thing, he may refer the making of the valuation to a valuer or refer a valuation provided by the applicant to a valuer for review (only valuations by registered or approved valuers will be accepted). If so, the Commissioner can charge the applicant what he was charged for the valuer making or reviewing the valuation (TAA Sch 1 s 359-40). However, the Commissioner is required to provide an estimate of the charge to the applicant up front — the valuation will not commence until the estimated amount has been paid. If the final cost of the valuation differs from the estimate provided by the Commissioner, the applicant is either charged or refunded the difference.

Objection against private ruling

A rulee dissatisfied with a private ruling may object against the private ruling in accordance with the normal objection procedures (¶28-000) unless an assessment relating to the same period to which the ruling relates has issued or the ruling relates to withholding tax that is due and payable (TAA Sch 1 s 359-60). An objection must be lodged before the end of whichever of the following periods ends later (s 14ZW(1A)):

- the 60-day period after notice of the ruling is served on the person who applied for it
- for most individual or very small business taxpayers (¶25-310) — the 2-year period after the last day allowed to the rulee for lodging a return in relation to the income year to which the ruling relates, or
- for taxpayers with more complex affairs (¶25-310) — the 4-year period after the last day allowed to the rulee for lodging a return in relation to the income year to which the ruling relates.

A rulee may apply for an extension of time to lodge an objection. The AAT may review a decision of the Commissioner refusing such an extension (¶28-030).

If the rulee is dissatisfied with the Commissioner's decision on the objection, the rulee may apply to the AAT for review of, or appeal to the Federal Court against, the decision (¶28-080). In considering the correctness or otherwise of the objection decision, the AAT or court is limited to the facts as identified by the Commissioner in the ruling as constituting the arrangement or scheme (*McMahon*); the AAT or court cannot redefine the arrangement or engage in a fact finding exercise (*Rosgoe*). Where further facts subsequently come to light before the AAT or court, the Commissioner is permitted to request the rulee(s) to apply for another private ruling (*Case 2/2016*).

However, the AAT has no jurisdiction to review a private ruling where the Commisioner rules on a different question to the one asked by the taxpayer (*Investa Properties*), or where the scheme has not been implemented within the relevant period to which the ruling applies (*Hickey*).

There is effectively no right of appeal if the private ruling relates to an income year which has passed before the appeal has been instituted (or possibly before it has been heard) and the arrangement or scheme in question has not begun to be implemented (*CTC Resources*).

Other matters

No penalty applies for not following a private ruling. However, there is nothing preventing the Commissioner from issuing an assessment contrary to a private ruling; the question of whether the Commissioner is bound by the private ruling is then dealt with in the objection/appeal process (*Mt Pritchard*) (¶28-000).

[FTR ¶978-520 – ¶978-550]

¶24-580 Oral rulings

Individual taxpayers or their legal personal representative may also apply to the Commissioner for advice in the form of an oral ruling on the way in which the Commissioner considers a relevant provision applies in relation to a specified scheme.

In making the oral ruling, the Commissioner may request additional information from the taxpayer and make assumptions or take into account additional information provided by third parties, provided such assumptions or information are made known to the taxpayer before being used (TAA Sch 1 ss 357-105; 357-110; 357-115; 357-120).

The Commissioner must provide an oral ruling on application, unless the advice sought relates to a business or complex matter, or the relevant matter is already being or has been considered. The Commissioner may also decline to make an oral ruling if further information has been requested but not given or the correctness of the ruling depends on which assumptions were made about a future event or other matter.

The application for the ruling and the ruling itself must be made orally. A taxpayer is not entitled to a written record of the advice but a registration identifier must be provided for the ruling (TAA Sch 1 s 360-5).

Applicants cannot object to or appeal against the ruling. However, they can apply for a private ruling on the matter and that private ruling can be objected to (TAA Sch 1 s 359-60).

[FTR ¶978-580 – ¶978-670]

¶24-600 Law companion rulings

Law Companion Rulings (LCRs), as explained in LCR 2015/1, express the Commissioner's view on how recently enacted law applies to taxpayers. In particular, they seek to provide insight into the practical implications of new law in ways that may go beyond mere questions of interpretation. For example, an LCR may:

- set out the Commissioner's view on the meaning of an expression or concept in the new law
- set out practical examples of how the new law will or will not apply
- identify factors that the ATO may use to assess the risk of certain activities or transactions not being compliant with the new law, and examples of high and low risk scenarios
- contain general information about the new law and the ATO's approach to it, such as links to other useful material, and what the ATO is planning to do to implement the new law and foster compliance
- address practical considerations, such as documentation requirements and how they can be met
- explain how the new law interacts with existing tax law, and
- highlight issues that might emerge in the future.

LCRs will usually operate from the application date of the new law and will be a public ruling.

LCRs were originally released as Law Companion Guidelines (LCGs) but the naming was formally changed on 19 February 2018 to properly reflect their status as public rulings. The change did not effect any substantive changes to the way these rulings operate in practice.

[FTR ¶978-513]

¶24-620 Practical compliance guidelines

PCG 2016/1 explains that Practical Compliance Guidelines (PCGs) provide broad compliance guidance in respect of significant law administration issues. In particular, PCGs may set out administrative safe harbour approaches. Provided taxpayers follow them in good faith, the Commissioner will administer the law in accordance with them.

Although PCGs are generally not public rulings and are not legally binding, they represent guidance material on how the ATO will allocate its compliance resources according to assessments of risk.

PCGs will contain clear statements of how they can be relied upon by taxpayers and descriptions of the relevant classes of taxpayer to which they apply. They may also include statements concerning expectations of taxpayers in adopting relevant administrative approaches, as well as how and when the guidelines are to be reviewed to determine their effectiveness. If a PCG outlines an approach (eg an administrative safe harbour) that has clear consequences for determining tax liabilities of taxpayers who rely on that approach in good faith, and the ATO subsequently changes its view and/or the PCG is withdrawn or altered, the principles under PS LA 2011/27 will be relevant and the ATO will not take action to apply any changed view of the law to prior years. In these circumstances, any action in terms of applying the ATO view of the law will only occur on a prospective basis.

[FTR ¶978-565]

Chapter 25 Assessment • Audit • Collection

Assessments

¶25-100 Original assessments

The Commissioner is required to make an original assessment of a taxpayer's taxable income (or that there is no taxable income), the amount of tax payable thereon (or that there is no tax payable) and the total of the taxpayer's tax offset refunds (or that the taxpayer can get no such refunds) (ITAA36 s 166). The assessment is based on the annual return lodged by the taxpayer and/or any other information in the Commissioner's possession. In making an assessment, it has been held that the Commissioner could rely on information from a third party that was found to have been illegally obtained by that third party (*Awad*).

The assessment process is not completed until a notice of assessment is served on the taxpayer (*Batagol*). The existence of an assessment is central to whether the time limits on the Commissioner's power to amend an assessment apply (¶25-120, ¶25-300).

An assessment must be definitive; an interim or tentative assessment is not a valid assessment (*Bloemen*). The Commissioner is entitled to issue alternative assessments, ie to assess more than one taxpayer in respect of the same income, but may not be allowed to recover the tax owed until it is finally determined which taxpayer is liable (*Richard Walter*; *Futuris Corporation*, cf *Stokes*). According to PS LA 2006/7 on alternative assessments, a "primary" assessment will be made in accordance with the ATO's preferred view of how the tax law applies to the facts as understood at the time of issue; an "alternative" assessment will be made in accordance with an alternative view of how the tax law applies.

The validity of an assessment is not affected by non-compliance with any of the provisions of the income tax laws (ITAA36 s 175) but failure to exercise the assessment power in good faith is not protected. Deliberate double counting of assessable income subject to later compensating adjustments, however, does not constitute lack of good faith (*Futuris Corporation*). Further, stolen information obtained by the Commissioner from a third party may be used to support an assessment and use of the information in that way does not constitute conscious maladministration (*Denlay*). The same applies where information is obtained from a legal practitioner without the taxpayer's authorisation; also, legal professional privilege (¶25-220) did not apply to protect the information (*Donoghue*).

Production of a notice of assessment under the Commissioner's hand is conclusive evidence that the assessment was properly made and that, subject to the normal review and appeal procedures, the amount and particulars of the assessment are correct (TAA Sch 1 s 350-10).

Under the self-assessment system, returns are generally not subject to technical scrutiny before an assessment is made. The ATO relies on post-assessment checking and auditing to determine whether a taxpayer has disclosed all assessable income and whether deductions and rebates (or tax offsets) have been properly claimed. The Commissioner has fairly wide powers to amend assessments where, for example, any post-assessment checks reveal that the taxpayer's taxable income has been understated (¶25-300).

For the purposes of making an assessment, the Commissioner is specifically authorised to accept any statement made in a return, including a statement of the assessable income derived by the taxpayer and of any deductions or rebates claimed (ITAA36 s 169A). The Commissioner is also authorised to accept any other statement made by or on behalf of the taxpayer, eg a statement in a request for an assessment to be amended (¶25-300). Where a taxpayer is in doubt about how a particular matter is to be treated for tax purposes, the taxpayer should apply for a private ruling (¶24-560), an oral ruling (¶24-580) or include with the return a request for the Commissioner to consider the question (¶24-030).

Full self-assessment taxpayers

Companies (including corporate unit trusts and public trading trusts), superannuation funds, ADFs and PSTs are subject to a ''full'' self-assessment system under which they self-assess the amount of tax they have to pay. The Commissioner does not issue a formal notice of assessment after the company or fund has lodged its return. Instead, the Commissioner is taken to have made an assessment and the return itself is deemed to be a notice of the assessment of the entity's taxable or net income, as the case may be, and of the amount of tax payable thereon. The assessment is deemed to be made on the day the return is lodged (ITAA36 s 166A).

A company or fund has the same rights of objection, review and appeal in relation to a deemed assessment as an individual has in relation to an ordinary assessment.

Self-assessment for indirect taxes

Taxpayers are only liable to pay their GST, wine equalisation tax (WET), luxury car tax (LCT) and fuel tax credit (FTC) liabilities or receive the entitlements that have been established by an assessment. A deemed assessment of the amount returned in the GST return, fuel tax return or return given to Customs will arise on lodgment. However, where a return is lodged by a taxpayer who is not registered or required to be registered for GST, a non-business taxpayer is claiming fuel tax credits or no return is lodged, the Commissioner is required to issue an assessment. For GST, WET and LCT on importations, the Commissioner is deemed to have made an assessment when a taxpayer lodges an import declaration or a self-assessed clearance declaration with Customs and Customs issues an import declaration advice or a self-assessed clearance declaration advice, respectively; the 2 documents are together deemed to be a notice of assessment.

A 4-year period of review applies during which the Commissioner may amend an assessment either at the taxpayer's request or at the Commissioner's discretion. Where an assessment is amended, it is subject to a refreshed 4-year period of review in relation to the amended particular. Taxpayers will cease to be entitled to credits if they have not been taken into account in an assessment of the net amount or net fuel amount 4 years after the date the return to be lodged for the tax period to which the credit would be attributable.

Further, the Commissioner has the power to make a determination allowing a taxpayer to take into account, on his or her GST or fuel tax return for the current tax period or fuel tax return period, errors made in working out net amounts and net fuel amounts for preceding tax periods or fuel tax return periods, provided the error is corrected during the relevant period of review.

[FTR ¶79-500, ¶79-550]

¶25-110 Service of notice of assessment

The Commissioner is required to serve a written notice of an assessment, which need not be in any particular form, on the person liable to pay the assessed tax (ITAA36 s 174). A notice of assessment need not state the name of the person liable to pay the assessed tax, provided it brings to the attention of the person on whom it is served that it is an assessment of that person to tax on a particular taxable income (*Prestige Motors*).

''Assessment'' is defined as the ascertainment of the amount of taxable income (or that there is no taxable income), of the tax payable on that taxable income (or that no tax is payable) and of the total of a taxpayer's tax offset refunds (or that the taxpayer can get no such refunds). Where a notice of assessment is issued, generally rights of objection (¶28-010) will accrue; however, a taxpayer cannot lodge an objection against an assessment where there is no taxable income or where there is taxable income but there is no tax payable (ITAA36 s 175A(2)).

A notice of assessment may be served personally, by leaving it at the taxpayer's address for service (¶24-030); by sending it by prepaid post to that address; or by sending an electronic copy of the document to an electronic address or an electronic communication to that address that notifies the taxpayer is available for electronic retrieval (TAR reg 14). If sent by post, the notice of assessment is regarded as having been served at the time it would have arrived in the ordinary course of the post unless the contrary is proved (*Acts Interpretation Act 1901*, s 29). The date of service is vital for the purpose of calculating the period within which an objection against an assessment can be made (¶28-020) and the due date for payment of the tax (¶25-400).

Provided one of the prescribed procedures is followed, a notice of assessment will be treated as properly served, notwithstanding that it has not actually come to the personal notice of the taxpayer (*Taylor*). On the other hand, even if one of the set procedures is not followed, a notice of assessment may nevertheless be treated as served if it is clear that it was actually received, eg where it was posted to the taxpayer's residential address (not the address for service) and was admittedly received by the taxpayer there (*Briggs*).

For full self-assessment taxpayers (¶25-100), the return itself is deemed to be a notice of the assessment, deemed to be served on the taxpayer on the day on which the deemed assessment is made.

[FTR ¶80-800]

¶25-120 No time limit on original assessments

There is no time limit on making an original assessment. However, an individual taxpayer who has not received a notice of assessment within 12 months of filing a return may request in writing that the Commissioner make an assessment (ITAA36 s 171). If an assessment notice is not received within 3 months of the Commissioner's receipt of that request, the taxpayer is regarded as having been served, on the last day of the 3-month period, with a notional original assessment notice payable on that day. Theoretically, any subsequent assessment is deemed to be an amended assessment, the validity of which will depend on the usual time limits for amended assessments (¶25-300).

Section 171 is not relevant to returns lodged by full self-assessment taxpayers (¶25-100) because such returns are themselves deemed to be notices of assessment.

[FTR ¶80-500]

¶25-130 Special and miscellaneous assessments

The Commissioner may, at any time, make a special assessment of the taxable income derived by a taxpayer during the whole or part of any year (ITAA36 s 168). For example, the Commissioner may use this power to issue 2 assessments to a taxpayer who has become bankrupt; one for the part of the financial year ending with the bankruptcy, and a separate assessment from the end of the bankruptcy to the end of the financial year (*Jones*). This is complementary to the power to call for special returns in addition to, or instead of, the usual annual return (¶24-010).

The Commissioner may also make an assessment of the tax that any person is liable to pay under the tax law (ITAA36 s 169). Examples include assessments in respect of the deemed taxable income of an overseas shipowner from forward freight or the deemed taxable income of an overseas insurer (¶22-110). Assessments under one provision are separate and distinct from assessments under another provision. Consequently, assessments under different provisions in respect of the same income for a particular year are valid (*Case X36*), as are assessments against more than one taxpayer in respect of the same income (¶25-100).

[FTR ¶79-700, ¶79-800]

¶25-140 Default or arbitrary assessments

In certain circumstances, the Commissioner may make a default or arbitrary assessment of the amount on which, in the Commissioner's judgment, tax ought to be levied and that amount then becomes the taxpayer's taxable income (ITAA36 s 167). A default assessment may be made where a taxpayer has failed to furnish a return, or where the Commissioner is dissatisfied with the return filed, or has reason to believe that a person who has not made a return has derived taxable income. It may be issued as an original or amended assessment.

The Commissioner's policy on issuing a default assessment is set out in PS LA 2007/24. Reasonable grounds for determining a taxpayer's income may include information provided by third parties, any internal or external data matching information, indirect audit methodologies, relevant economic statistics or extrapolation from previous years' returns. The Commissioner will generally advise the taxpayer of the intention to issue a default assessment and the basis upon which it has been calculated.

A default assessment is commonly made where, following an investigation into a taxpayer's financial affairs, the increase in net assets over a fixed period is found to be inconsistent with the taxpayer's disclosed income. That increase, adjusted for private and other non-allowable expenditure and for non-assessable receipts, forms the basis of what is often called an assessment on an ''assets betterment'' basis.

If sufficient information is not available to enable the variation in net assets to be calculated separately for each year in the period under investigation, the practice is to apportion the increase from the beginning to the end of the period over the intervening years either equally or on some other basis considered appropriate.

The Commissioner is not required to correctly ascertain the taxpayer's assessable income and allowable deductions when making a default assessment (*Eldridge*; *Allard*). The Commissioner does not have to make inquiries of the taxpayer or the taxpayer's agent before issuing the assessment (*McCleary*). As long as the Commissioner makes a genuine estimate of the taxpayer's taxable income and does not simply pluck a figure out of the air, a default assessment may come close to guesswork and still be valid (*Briggs*). The onus is then on the taxpayer to object against the assessment (¶28-010) and, if necessary, prove in review or appeal proceedings that the assessment is excessive (¶28-130). To do this, the taxpayer must show what the assessment ought to have been, not merely that it was excessive (*Mulherin*).

An assessment is not rendered invalid because it effectively induces the taxpayer to discuss his/her affairs with the ATO so that a more accurate assessment of the taxable income can be made (this is likely to happen in any event as the taxpayer has to prove that the assessment is excessive: ¶28-130). The mere indication that an assessment will be reviewed later will not make that assessment invalid (*Simons*; *McCleary*). An assessment made for the purpose of opposing bail would not be a bona fide assessment, whereas one made for the purpose of issuing a notice to collect a tax liability from a third party (¶25-540) would be (*Madden v Madden*). The issue of a ''garnishee notice'' (¶25-540) before the issue of a notice of assessment did not affect the validity of the assessment in *Marijancevic* and there was no evidence of conscious maladministration of the assessment process, see *Futuris Corporation* (¶25-100).

[FTR ¶79-600]

Audits and Access Powers

¶25-200 Tax audits

A tax audit is the systematic examination of a taxpayer's affairs by the ATO to determine whether the taxpayer has fully complied with the tax laws. This includes whether the taxpayer has disclosed all assessable income and has correctly claimed deductions or tax offsets in the income years concerned (an audit may cover more than one year). The ATO's audit programs are also designed to promote voluntary compliance with the tax laws and to help the ATO identify areas of law that may need clarification.

Tax audits are not governed by any particular statutory provisions, except those that confer on the Commissioner responsibility for the general administration of relevant tax laws (ITAA36 s 8). In addition, the ATO relies on its access and information-gathering powers (¶25-220, ¶25-240) to carry out its audit programs effectively. It is lawful for the Commissioner (and duly authorised ATO officers) to randomly select for audit a taxpayer within a particular group (*Industrial Equity* (1990)).

Decisions made by the Commissioner in the course of an audit are only reviewable under the *Administrative Decisions (Judicial Review) Act 1977* where they are made under a specific provision (as distinguished from the general power of administration under ITAA36 s 8) (*Robinswood*).

Conduct of audits

Under the *Taxpayers' Charter*, the ATO undertakes to conduct audits in an impartial, fair, reasonable and professional manner and to treat taxpayers in accordance with the law, its policy and the principles outlined in the charter. It also undertakes to take into account the taxpayer's relevant circumstances when it makes decisions, try to minimise cost and inconvenience to the taxpayer, and complete audits as quickly as it can. This, however, will vary from case to case.

Broadly, the audit/review stages take the following cycle: (1) assessment or self-assessment; (2) ATO internal risk review; (3) selection for risk review; (4) contact with taxpayer; (5) information gathering; (6) decision on risk; (7) notification of audit; (8) intensive information gathering; (9) position paper; (10) taxpayer response; (11) statement of audit position; and (12) amended assessment. Taxpayer entities with a turnover or income of more than $250 million can apply for an independent review by the ATO within 10 working days of statement of audit position.

Although the ATO has a benchmark of 2 years for completing large business audits, there is no particular time period within which the Commissioner must complete an audit. It should be noted, however, that in the absence of fraud or evasion (¶25-330), there are specified time limits for amending assessments (¶25-310 – ¶25-320).

Further, it has been held that failure to comply with the Commissioner's Guidelines for the Conduct of Auditors and Taxpayers in Complex and Large Case Audits was not reviewable (*Robinswood*).

The ATO also undertakes during an audit to guide the taxpayer through the process, arrange mutually convenient interviews or meetings, explain the purpose of any interview or visit, ask clear and unambiguous questions and provide the taxpayer with all reasonable assistance and explanations to clarify their meaning, and allow the taxpayer to choose someone to act on their behalf or to attend interviews with them.

In turn, the ATO expects the taxpayer to: work cooperatively with them; be truthful and honest in their dealings with the ATO; provide complete, accurate and timely responses to requests for information; and provide tax officers with full and free access to buildings, premises, records and documents.

Completion of audit

When completing an audit or sometimes during the audit, the ATO will inform the taxpayer of the results and its decision. If an adjustment is made, it is required in accordance with the charter to clearly explain the basis for them as well as the reasons for any penalty imposed. The ATO must also give the taxpayer written notification of the outcome of the audit (generally within 7 days of the decision) and inform the taxpayer of their rights of review.

Managing audits

It has been suggested that the best way to manage tax audits is to: (1) understand the ATO's approach to assessing tax risks (see below); (2) conduct an objective risk assessment; (3) manage the ATO relationship throughout the review/audit cycle; and (4) understand the review/appeal process (¶28-000).

Compliance

The ATO uses a risk management approach to tax compliance. This approach recognises that different groups of taxpayers face different issues and, therefore, it is necessary to identify and target issues relevant to a particular group. Further, there is differentiation between the way the ATO engages with business taxpayers and tax practitioners. It uses certain risk-assessment processes to prioritise how it applies its resource. Tools it uses include data matching, industry benchmarking and the income tax refund integrity program. Its tax risk management and governance review guide provides more information to large businesses. For public and multinational businesses, it conducts justified trust and assurance programs, and also adopts an action differentiation framework.

The ATO compliance webpage "*Insight: building trust and confidence*" identifies various behaviours and activities the ATO focuses on, organised by reference to the types of taxpayers, such as individuals, small businesses and super funds and so on. The ATO's Tax Avoidance Taskforce targets multinationals, large public and private groups and wealthy individuals operating in Australia.

Annual compliance arrangements

The purpose of Annual Compliance Arrangements (ACAs) between the ATO and key/large taxpayers is to provide a compliance and risk management relationship framework between the parties. ACAs are available for income tax, GST, excise, petroleum resource rent tax, minerals resource rent tax and FBT or any combination of these taxes. Each tax covered by an ACA will have a separate schedule and is built around the taxpayer having sound tax risk management processes and a commitment to ongoing disclosure of tax risk.

Key benefits of entering into an ACA include: a speedier resolution of technical issues; administrative solutions to resolve compliance irritants; centralised points of contact and ongoing dialogue on technical matters, including access to ATO senior officers; a closure of returns to further ATO review; concessional treatments of penalties and interest; a plan outlining agreed processes and timelines; the possibility of extension of thresholds for correcting GST errors for a GST ACA; not being subject to post-lodgment risk reviews or audits for periods and income years covered by an ACA; not needing to complete the RTP schedule for income years covered by an ACA; and not being subject to a pre-lodgment compliance review.

[FTR ¶79-560]

¶25-210 Negotiated settlements

The ATO policy on the settlement of taxation and superannuation disputes are set out in PS LA 2015/1 (Code of settlement). Among other things, the code provides that settlements under the code must be finalised by the parties signing a deed of settlement. The ATO website has model deeds available to use as a basis for a deed of settlement and its *disputes policy*. "*Practical guide to the ATO code of settlement*" provides examples and illustrations of how the code operates.

PS LA 2007/6 provides practical guidance for the settlement of widely-based tax disputes, including disputes involving tax planning arrangements (whether subject to the general anti-avoidance rules or not). A panel has also been established to advise on widely-based settlements and this panel accepts submissions from taxpayers and/or their advisers through the ATO officer who is the decision-maker for the relevant case(s).

Settlement under the code involves an agreement between parties to resolve matters in dispute where one or more of the parties make concessions on what they consider is the legally correct position. The code focuses on resolving disputes as early as possible with settlement being part of good tax administration and all settlements being predicated on the following factors: (1) litigation risk; (2) cost vs benefit; and (3) the potential impact on future compliance.

The basic duty of the Commissioner is to administer tax law, but in exercising that duty the Commissioner must also provide for reasonable and sensible administration and good management of the tax system. The *Public Governance Performance and Accountability Act 2013*, which underpins the code, requires the Commissioner to manage ATO resources efficiently, effectively, ethically and economically.

A dispute that would be considered for settlement would ordinarily be one where the taxpayer has (or will have) a right to challenge the Commissioner's decision, however settlement is considered as potentially a way to resolve a wide range of disputes and disagreements.

The code states that settlement would generally not be considered where: (1) there is a contentious point of law that requires clarification; (2) it is in the public interest to litigate; (3) there is an impact on future compliance.

Generally speaking, the ATO prefers to settle cases on an issue-by-issue basis and "global" settlements will only be entered into in exceptional cases and as a last resort. Ability to pay is not relevant in determining a taxpayer's liability, but it may give rise to other administrative arrangements to assist the taxpayer. A taxpayer's ability to pay will affect the likely cost-effectiveness of any litigation action; inability to pay would normally result in the debt being written off as being uneconomical to pursue. However, where it is considered that inability to pay tax has been deliberately created, settlement will be considered inappropriate without first escalating the matter.

Where settlements are not appropriate

According to the "Practical guide to the ATO code of settlement", settlement should generally not be considered where: (1) there is a contentious point of the law which requires clarification — in such cases, it may be appropriate to fund the litigation under the test case litigation program; (2) it is in the public interest to litigate; (3) the behaviour is such that there is a need to send a strong message to the community — behaviour such as persistent, ongoing and/or expanding non-compliance, or blatant non-compliance which the community would expect the ATO to take action.

Alternative dispute resolution

A range of alternative dispute resolution (ADR) approaches, including mediation and conciliation, may be used to assist in reaching settlement of a tax dispute.

PS LA 2013/3 sets out what policies and guidelines must be followed by ATO officers when using ADR to resolve or limit disputes. It also suggests that ADR may be appropriate: (1) after the ATO issues a position paper (¶25-200); (2) during a review at the objection stage before a decision is made (¶28-070); or (3) during the litigation stage (¶28-080).

Individuals or small businesses can opt for the ATO's in-house facilitation service to resolve less complex disputes (see ATO webpage "*In-house facilitation*"). It is a mediation process where an impartial ATO facilitator meets with the taxpayers and the ATO case officers to identify the issues, develop options, consider alternatives, and attempt to reach a resolution.

Potential for prosecution

It is ATO policy that officers do not use the threat of either prosecution or the imposition of severe penalties as a lever in settlement negotiations.

ATO officers do not have authority to make it a condition of a settlement agreement that the taxpayer will not be prosecuted for a possible offence or that proceedings associated with a prosecution will not be taken. ATO officers must make it clear to taxpayers that settlements and prosecutions are separate and the decision whether to prosecute is the responsibility of the Director of Public Prosecutions. Where the ATO advises a taxpayer that there is no intention to prosecute, the taxpayer should also be advised that the matter may be reconsidered if further information comes to light that reveals that the misconduct is more serious than first thought. See also ¶29-700.

The settlement agreement

All settlements should be evidenced by a written agreement between the parties. The settlement agreement will normally include how each particular issue has been resolved, relevant undertakings by the parties, treatment in future years, withdrawal of objections, requests for reviews and appeals, and payment arrangements. *Grofam* exemplifies the need for clarity in drafting the agreement.

The settlement should represent the final agreed position between the parties. Consequently, the ATO expects the taxpayer to agree not to object to any subsequent assessment (*Jonshagen*), or to agree to withdraw any objection, application for review or appeal already lodged. The ATO will adhere to the terms of the settlement, unless it emerges that relevant facts were not disclosed to the ATO.

The ATO will adopt the settlement as the basis for treating similar issues in future year assessments of the taxpayer unless: (i) the agreement relates to a particular issue but the application of the law remains unclear; (ii) the taxpayer's circumstances are materially different; (iii) there are subsequent amendments to the law; (iv) a taxation ruling has been released on the particular issue; (v) the settlement agreement specifically indicates that it is not to apply for future years or it provides for a different basis for dealing with the relevant issue; or (vi) the ATO has reviewed the matter and at a suitably senior level determined that the ATO position should be different or that the settlement is not soundly based.

[FTR ¶79-595]

¶25-220 Commissioner's right of access

The Commissioner and an individual authorised by the Commissioner are entitled to full and free access at all reasonable times, to documents, books or other property (TAA Sch 1 s 353-15).

Full and free access to electronically-stored records extends to the provision of login codes, keys (including encryption keys), passwords, and system and software manuals, as well as access to printed copies of the records. It also includes access to electronic records that are stored in the cloud that are immediately accessible to the taxpayer (TR 2018/2). The Commissioner's requirements for keeping electronic records are set out in TR 2018/2 (¶9-045).

This access power enables the Commissioner to obtain tax-related information from, for example, the offices of solicitors and accountants whose clients are being investigated for tax avoidance. In one case, it was held that the access power could be used to obtain documents from a bank for use in proceedings to recover unpaid tax (*Simionato Holdings (No 2)*). In another case, the Commissioner could access affidavits filed by the taxpayer husband in the Family Court but had to get permission from the court to use them for audit purposes (*Darling*).

It is an offence for a person to hinder or obstruct ATO officers exercising their right of access (¶29-700). This access power is subject to legal professional privilege (see below) and the public interest immunity (*Middendorp Electric Co v Law Institute of Victoria*) but documents and records held by a law institute on the income or assessment of one of its members were not protected from disclosure by the public interest immunity (*Law Institute of Victoria*). Note, however, that the decision to utilise the access power is subject to judicial review (¶28-180).

Examples of cases where the Commissioner has used the access power include ones involving: significant risk of destruction of records; significant offshore funds not accounted for in Australia; offshore promotion of tax avoidance for Australian residents; phoenix operations; evasion of a range of taxes; lodgment of false BASs; and significant risk to the revenue (*National Tax Liaison Group minutes of 31 March 2010 meeting*).

Scope of access power

The access power can also be used to obtain documents that the Commissioner considers will assist in an audit of a taxpayer's affairs, including documents held at the premises of a person acting for or advising the taxpayer (*Industrial Equity* (1990)). The random selection of the taxpayer in the *Industrial Equity case* did not invalidate the access notices as the Commissioner was endeavouring to fulfil his statutory function of ascertaining the taxpayer's taxable income.

An occupier of a building or any other place is specifically required to provide a duly authorised ATO officer with all reasonable facilities and assistance for the effective exercise of the access power. Such an officer should therefore be able to make reasonable use of, for example, office space, lighting, telephones, photocopiers and facilities to extract information stored on computer. The officer is also entitled to reasonable assistance in the form of advice as to where relevant documents are located and the provision of access to areas where those documents are located. An occupier who fails to provide the necessary facilities or assistance is liable for a fine (¶29-700).

Authorised officers are entitled to take all reasonable and necessary steps to remove any physical obstruction to access but should not act in an excessive manner. For example, if the owner of a safe deposit box refuses to open it or supply a key, the officer would be entitled to attempt to open the box with the assistance of a locksmith and, if that fails, to break open the box by the reasonable use of force (*Kerrison*). Officers are not entitled to take possession of a taxpayer's records but they are entitled to make extracts or copies.

The access power does not permit ATO officers to take control of a taxpayer's offices or deny its staff access to their computer records. Nor does it permit the copying of all documents without any consideration of whether they are required for the purposes of the Act (*JMA Accounting*).

An officer is not entitled to enter or remain on premises if, after having been requested by the occupier to do so, the officer does not produce written proof of authority. An authorisation must be signed by the Commissioner or his delegate. It does not have to specify the premises to be searched or the documents that are to be the subject of the search. As written authorisation is only required to be produced on request, the existence of written authorisation is not a condition precedent to the exercise of the right of access (*Citibank*).

The ATO webpage "*Our approach to information gathering*" sets out the general principles it applies and the cooperative approach it adopts towards gathering information. It also has guidance relating to its formal notice powers; attending formal interviews; its formal access powers and their limits; gathering offshore information; and gathering electronic information.

PS LA 2004/14 sets out the ATO's policy regarding access to corporate board documents on tax compliance risk. These are documents created by advisers for the sole purpose of providing tax risk advice or opinion to the board of directors. Access to such documents will not be sought by the ATO during a compliance risk review or an audit of a corporate taxpayer except in exceptional circumstances. In that case, access would need to be approved by an appropriate ATO Senior Executive Service (SES) officer as described in the Accountants' Guidelines (¶25-230). These circumstances would include cases where the taxpayer has not cooperated with the ATO or has a history of serious non-compliance.

Treasury has issued a consultation paper to consider whether the ATO should be allowed to access third party information to investigate tax-related criminal offences and/or historical telecommunications data (including metadata).

Legal professional privilege

The access power is restricted by the doctrine of legal professional privilege (LPP) (*Citibank*). This doctrine protects communications made between a lawyer and client for the dominant purpose of giving or receiving legal advice. It does not currently apply to communications between an accountant and client but may be extended to tax advice documents prepared by accountants (¶25-230). The doctrine also applies to communications made between a client, the client's lawyer and third parties for the dominant purpose of use in existing or anticipated litigation (*Esso Australia Resources*). The Commissioner's power to obtain information under TAA Sch 1 s 353-10 is subject to legal privilege claims (¶25-240).

LPP is a shield and not a sword, ie it operates only as an immunity from disclosure, rather than a legal right that may found a cause of action. Thus, the High Court held that LPP could not compel the return of privileged documents already in the public domain (*Glencore*). The privilege belongs to the client, not the lawyer, and can only be waived by the client. If a lawyer is in any doubt as to whether a particular document is privileged, the lawyer should withhold the document and the Commissioner may then have to test the claim for privilege in the courts. In the *Citibank case*, a large-scale ''raid'' on the premises of a bank by ATO officers in search of documents was held to be beyond their power as lack of warning of the raid meant that the bank was not given sufficient opportunity to assert claims for LPP in relation to documents of its clients.

Privilege is not infringed merely by taking a copy of a privileged document. In some circumstances it may be appropriate for the ATO officer to look at a document for which privilege is claimed to determine whether it might be covered by the privilege. The document should not be looked at closely; just enough for the officer to decide whether it may be copied (*JMA Accounting*).

Examples of privileged documents or communications include a solicitor's advice, legal counsel's opinions, letters between a solicitor and a client, a solicitor's notes of a conference with a client or officers of a client company, and a detailed bill of costs if it discloses the nature of the advice sought or given. The following have also been held to be privileged: (i) communications between the Australian Government Solicitor and the ATO relating to tax recovery proceedings, including advice on the taxpayer's applications for an extension of time to pay and remission of late payment penalties (*Webb*); and (ii) documents held by the Australian Federal Police concerning the investigation of alleged tax offences (*Grofam v ANZ Banking Group*).

The following documents have been held *not* to be protected by LPP: (i) a solicitor's trust account records (*Allen, Allen & Hemsley*; *Clarke*); (ii) a bill of costs (*Packer*); and (iii) fax books recording faxes sent (*Sharp*), but only to the extent that they do not disclose the actual advice. It appears that legal advice prepared by a firm of solicitors but never offered to or used by clients is not protected by LPP (*May*: ¶25-240). The names of a lawyer's clients have also been held not to be protected by legal privilege (*Coombes (No 2)*: ¶25-240). Privilege does not extend to cases where documents were created in furtherance of a criminal, illegal or improper purpose. In *Clements, Dunne & Bell*, communications between a firm of accountants and a solicitor advising the accountants on the implementation of employee benefit schemes were held not to be privileged because there was evidence of fraudulent avoidance of income tax in relation to the schemes.

As noted above, legal privilege may attach to confidential communications between a client, the client's lawyer and third parties, for the dominant purpose of use in litigation. If litigation is not in prospect, legal privilege may extend to non-agent third party authored documentary communications, provided the dominant purpose test is met. However, where an accounting firm was employed to prepare a valuation and paper for use as part of taxation advice provided by the client's lawyer, most of the third party documents were not subject to the privilege as they were not brought into existence for the dominant purpose of obtaining legal advice (*Pratt Holdings*).

Where a witness for a taxpayer used a document, which would otherwise attract legal privilege, to refresh his memory in legal proceedings, there was a waiver of the privilege limited to that part of the document referred to in the evidence (*Case 29/97*). The Commissioner had impliedly waived his legal privilege by filing a statement of facts, issues and contentions in tax appeal proceedings and previously disclosing the substance of audit report documents in a freedom of information request (*Rio Tinto*). However, the Commissioner did not waive legal privilege by releasing documents in a freedom of information request that referred to legal advice in other documents over which he wished to claim privilege, as the reference did not disclose the substance of the advice (*Devereaux Holdings*).

The ATO webpage ''*Our approach to information gathering*'' contains its guidance on LPP, information on how to make an LPP claim, and links to forms for claiming LPP.

Confidentiality provisions

Taxpayers are entitled to the benefit of various confidentiality rules. The obligations apply not only to ATO officers but also to third parties to whom taxation information is disclosed in breach of a taxation law (¶1-220).

The collection, use and disclosure of personal information is prohibited in certain circumstances under the *Privacy Act 1988* (¶1-200). However, the collection of information by the ATO is permitted where it is ''necessary for one or more of its functions or activities''. The use or disclosure of information is also permitted where it is ''required or authorised by or under law'' or for the ''protection of the public revenue''. Because of the privacy rules, the Commissioner should normally use the formal access powers when seeking documents from third parties, rather than informally approaching them about a taxpayer's affairs.

[FTR ¶978-455 to ¶978-458/265]

¶25-230 Guidelines on access to accountants' papers

While the Commissioner considers that he has the power to request access to most documents (¶25-220), he also recognises that there are certain classes of documents that should generally remain within the confidence of taxpayers and their professional accounting advisers. This concession by the ATO is known as the accountants' concession, as set out in its webpage, ''*Guidelines to accessing professional accounting advisers' papers*''. The guidelines apply not only to documents sought under the access power (¶25-220), but also to requests to external accountants to furnish information and produce papers (¶25-240). The main features of the guidelines are as follows.

- The Commissioner will exercise his right of access without restriction to ''source'' documents, ie those documents that are prepared in connection with the conception, implementation and formal recording of a transaction or arrangement and which explain the setting, context and purpose of that transaction or arrangement. Examples of source documents include traditional accounting records such as ledgers, journals and balance sheets, documents comprising the permanent audit file held by a professional adviser performing a statutory audit and certain tax working papers. The Commissioner regards documents prepared before the completion of a tax return, and showing an analysis of shareholdings to establish continuity of ownership, as source documents (TD 93/222).

- The Commissioner will generally not seek access to ''non-source'' documents, except in exceptional cases such as cases of fraud, evasion or other illegality (*Stewart*) and, as a last resort, where other avenues through the taxpayer have been exhausted. Non-source documents include papers on the current audit file and papers prepared in the course of a prudential tax audit. They also include advisings provided after a transaction has been completed where the advisings do not affect the recording of the transaction or arrangement in the books of account or tax return.
- Access to certain source documents called ''restricted source'' documents will be sought only in the exceptional circumstances applicable to non-source documents. These documents are advice papers created prior to, or contemporaneously with, a relevant transaction or arrangement, which are likely to canvass the issues in circumstances in which a need for candour is a necessary element. In *White Industries*, a taxpayer sought to challenge a decision of a senior ATO officer granting access to such documents and the court ruled that the taxpayer was entitled to challenge that decision under s 39B of the Judiciary Act (¶28-180).
- Documents may maintain their confidential status when disclosed to nominated independent third parties only where both the taxpayer and their advisers agreed to such disclosure.
- Access to restricted source documents and non-source documents may only be sought with the written approval of a Deputy Commissioner (or another appropriate ATO Senior Executive Service (SES) officer).
- The ATO may request a taxpayer for further information if relevant source documents do not provide sufficient information. If the taxpayer fails to comply with this request on time, the ATO may seek access in accordance with the guidelines.
- ATO officers will not seek access to papers prepared by an accountant solely for the purpose of representing a taxpayer in legal proceedings under a tax law (eg objections, reviews, appeals). See also *Pratt Holdings* (¶25-220).
- Procedures are prescribed for resolving disputes as to whether access may be sought for particular documents.

Note that a decision to lift the concession may be set aside on the basis that the rules of procedural fairness were breached or that the decision is so unreasonable that a reasonable decision-maker would not have made it (*Stewart*).

The concession does *not* apply to documents obtained by other agencies such as the Australian Crime Commission and provided to the ATO (*Stewart*).

The doctrine of legal professional privilege (LPP, ¶25-220) does not apply to communications between accountants and their clients. The Australian Law Reform Commission has recommended extending LPP to tax advice documents prepared by accountants, and Treasury has issued a discussion paper on the subject.

[FTR ¶785-620]

¶25-240 Commissioner's power to obtain information

The Commissioner has wide powers to obtain information from a taxpayer or any other person (TAA Sch 1 s 353-10). This power also applies to PAYG and the related collection rules. The Commissioner also has powers to issue an ''offshore information notice'' where information or documents are located outside Australia (TAA Sch 1 s 353-25: ¶21-220).

The Commissioner may, by notice in writing under TAA Sch 1 s 353-10, require any person to:

- *provide such information* as he may require
- *attend and give evidence* before him or any authorised officer concerning that person's own or any other person's income or assessment, and
- *produce all documents* in that person's custody or control relating to that income or assessment.

A person who fails to comply with a notice may be guilty of an offence (¶29-700). Although it appears that the Commissioner ordinarily allows a period of at least 28 days to comply with the notice, this should not necessarily be regarded as the norm and lesser periods will not invalidate the notice, provided the time allowed is reasonable (*Holmes*).

A person served with a TAA Sch 1 s 353-10(b) notice cannot refuse to answer questions on the ground of self-incrimination (*Donovan*; *De Vonk*; *Binetter*). However, in certain circumstances, an examination under TAA Sch 1 s 353-10(b) may constitute a contempt of court (*De Vonk*; *Watson*). In *Watson's case*, the Federal Court granted the taxpayer an injunction restraining the Commissioner from acting on a TAA Sch 1 s 353-10 notice until criminal proceedings against the taxpayer were determined. While the issue of the notice did not interfere with or prejudice the proper conduct of AAT proceedings also on foot, an examination under TAA Sch 1 s 353-10 would have usurped the court's function in the criminal proceedings.

It has been held that a TAA Sch 1 s 353-10 notice may be issued to a liquidator of a company for the production of documents without consent of the court, as would otherwise be required under s 486 of the *Corporations Act 2001* (*Warner*).

A decision by the Commissioner to issue a TAA Sch 1 s 353-10 notice is subject to judicial review (¶28-180). Further, the Federal Court may grant an interim injunction, extending the time for compliance with a TAA Sch 1 s 353-10 notice (*Binetter*).

Provide such information . . .

The Commissioner may make wide-ranging inquiries that do not have to relate to a particular taxpayer or to a particular topic, provided they relate to the performance of the Commissioner's functions. This power enables a roving inquiry and a fishing expedition into the income or assessment of taxpayers. It can be used to gather information about the existence or prevalence of a particular arrangement or proposal that may have implications in relation to the tax laws. See, for example, *Daihatsu Australia*.

The power was validly used to require a large accounting firm to provide information on whether it had provided clients with advice or other services in connection with certain non-complying superannuation funds or trusts and to provide the names and addresses of such clients, funds or trusts (*Deloitte Touche Tohmatsu*). It was also validly used, as part of an ATO campaign against ''aggressive tax planning arrangements'', to require partners of another accounting firm to provide a list of clients for whom services had been provided over a particular period (*McCormack*). Inquiries can also extend to whether documents have ever been under the custody or control of the person being examined (*Griffin & Elliott v Marsh*).

The power has also been used to acquire the names of a lawyer's clients who had entered into certain arrangements (*Coombes (No 2)*; *Hart*). Further, the power was validly used to obtain information from a bank, stored on its Australian database, about customers who held accounts with any of its subsidiaries in Vanuatu; the court rejected arguments that the power infringed on foreign sovereignty or Vanuatu confidentiality laws (*ANZ v Konza*).

The Commissioner may exercise these powers for the purpose of conducting an audit of a taxpayer's affairs, including where the taxpayer is selected for audit at random, provided the audit is related to the ascertainment of the taxpayer's taxable income or tax liability (*Industrial Equity* (1990)). The powers can still be exercised after an assessment or amended assessment has been made (*Industrial Equity* (1990)). TAA Sch 1 s 353-10 notices can be issued seeking information about employee share plans and employee benefits trusts prepared by a firm of solicitors but never offered to or used by clients (*May*).

Attend and give evidence . . .

TAA Sch 1 s 353-10(1)(b), a person may be requested to attend before the Commissioner *or* before any officer authorised by him. A person may, however, be requested to attend before both the Commissioner *and* one or more officers (*Industrial Equity* (2000)).

Both the person being examined and the ATO officer conducting the examination are entitled to have legal counsel present at the examination to advise on legal issues such as legal professional privilege (*Dunkel*). To facilitate the investigatory process, counsel retained by the Commissioner are also permitted to ask questions during the examination (*Grant*).

A spouse cannot refuse to answer questions about their partner. The High Court has held that the common law does not recognise a privilege against spousal incrimination (*ACCC v Stoddart*).

Produce all documents . . .

A TAA Sch 1 s 353-10 notice served on a solicitors' firm will override the firm's clients' contractual right of confidentiality. Similarly, a person cannot be excused from complying with a notice by reason of the ''Harman obligation'', ie the obligation that when documents are generated or discovered in legal proceedings, they cannot be used by any person for any purpose unrelated to the proceedings being litigated without the leave of the court unless and until they are received into evidence (*Rennie Produce*). However, this power cannot be used to compel the production of documents covered by legal professional privilege (¶25-220) (*Baker v Campbell*). A TAA Sch 1 s 353-10 notice is not invalid simply because it requires production of a document that is prima facie privileged (*Perron Investments*). The spirit of the Commissioner's guidelines on access to documents held on lawyers' premises in circumstances where a claim of legal professional privilege is made (¶25-220) is intended to apply where a lawyer receives a TAA Sch 1 s 353-10 notice.

The Commissioner can require a person to produce documents only where these documents are in the custody of or under the control of that person. This covers persons who have the physical ability to produce the documents. So, for example, a bank has custody or control of the contents of a safe deposit box kept on its premises and can, therefore, be compelled to produce its contents (*ANZ Banking Group*; *Smorgon*).

The only documents that can be required to be produced are those that relate to the income or assessment of a particular person and that person must be named or otherwise indicated in the notice (*ANZ Banking Group*). On this basis, a notice requiring a solicitor to produce *all* his firm's trust account cash books, not just the cash books relating to the 2 clients named in the notice, was held to be too wide (*Clarke*). Note that the Commissioner's guidelines on access to accountants' papers (¶25-230) also apply in relation to requests to external accountants to furnish information and produce papers.

The Commissioner's powers to require production of documents do not extend to authorising him to require persons to make *copies* of documents (*Perron Investments*).

Give the information . . .

Where a TAA Sch 1 s 353-10 notice requires a person to both produce documents and attend and give evidence, the one requirement is severable from the other (*Elliott*).

[FTR ¶978-455, ¶978-455/10]

Amended Assessments

¶25-300 Amendment powers

The Commissioner's powers to amend an assessment, or further amend an amended assessment, are set out in ITAA36 s 170 and in s 170A.

The standard period in which the Commissioner can amend an assessment for most individuals, small business entities (¶7-050) and, from 1 July 2021, medium business entities (¶7-050), is 2 years from the day on which the Commissioner gives notice of the assessment (¶25-310). A 4-year period of review applies for taxpayers with more complex affairs (¶25-320).

A taxpayer wishing to challenge an amended assessment must lodge an objection within the prescribed time or such further time as allowed by the Commissioner (¶28-010 – ¶28-030). If the objection is disallowed, the taxpayer may seek a review by the AAT or appeal to the Federal Court (¶28-080 and following).

The Commissioner is required to amend an assessment where this is necessary to give effect to an AAT or court decision, but only when any appeals from the decision have been finalised (¶28-160). Such an amendment must be made within 60 days of the decision becoming final. The normal specified time limits do not apply for this purpose. The Commissioner may amend an assessment to give effect to a private ruling even though the normal specified time limit for making amendments has expired.

Although the Commissioner cannot be compelled to amend an assessment if he does not think it necessary, it is arguable that he must make all alterations and additions to make the assessment correct (including allowing deductions previously unclaimed).

A taxpayer may apply to the Commissioner for an amendment to an assessment. Any information necessary to decide the application must be supplied to the Commissioner within that time. If these conditions are satisfied, the Commissioner may amend the assessment at any time and for any reason. For example, a taxpayer may want to apply for an amendment of an assessment to reflect a changed interpretation of the law in his/her favour. Where an application is made electronically it must contain the taxpayer's electronic signature (¶24-010) or, if given to the Commissioner by a tax agent on behalf of the taxpayer, the tax agent's electronic signature (TAA Sch 1 s 388-75).

In considering an application to amend an assessment, the Commissioner is authorised to accept a statement made by or on behalf of the taxpayer. Accordingly, the Commissioner can amend an assessment without, at that time, checking any claims made by or on behalf of the taxpayer in connection with the application for an amendment. This effectively allows a taxpayer to "self-amend" an assessment.

The Commissioner's power to amend an assessment to reduce liability, and particularly his power to amend on the taxpayer's application, is discretionary, not mandatory. It is, therefore, imperative that taxpayers preserve their rights to dispute an incorrect or invalid assessment by lodging an objection (¶28-010). This power extends to any error in the return, whether it is an error of law, an error in calculation or a mistake of fact.

Further amendment rectifying excessive reduction

The Commissioner may amend an assessment (including a deemed assessment in the case of companies and funds) so as to *reduce* the taxpayer's liability on the basis of an amendment request by the taxpayer. In such a case, the Commissioner can, within the relevant timeframe for amending assessments, further amend the assessment in respect of the particular that was earlier amended, to *increase* the taxpayer's liability (ITAA36 s 170(3)). This could happen where an audit of the taxpayer's affairs reveals that the reduction in liability was excessive. In these circumstances, the taxpayer will not be entitled to a further amendment (to reduce liability) of an assessment that has already been amended twice.

Extensions of the amendment period

The Commissioner may amend an assessment even if the limited period of amendment has ended where:

- the taxpayer applies for an amendment in the approved form before the end of the amendment period (s 170(5))
- the taxpayer applies for a private ruling before the end of the amendment period and the Commissioner makes a ruling in response to the application (s 170(6)), and
- the Commissioner has started to examine a taxpayer's affairs but has not completed that examination by the end of the amendment period. In that case, the period can be extended by:
  - a Federal Court order where it is satisfied that the failure to complete the examination was due to the taxpayer's behaviour (eg instigating court proceedings) or the taxpayer's failure to take action (eg failing to comply with a TAA Sch 1 s 353-10 notice to provide information), or
  - written consent of the taxpayer (s 170(7)).

Where a taxpayer has applied for an amendment or a private ruling within the limited amendment period allowed under particular legislation (ie outside of s 170), the Commissioner is allowed to amend an assessment to give effect to his decision or ruling after that period has expired. Further, where the Commissioner has started to examine the affairs of a taxpayer in relation to that particular legislation but has not completed the examination by the limited amendment period, he may apply to the Federal Court or seek the taxpayer's consent to extending the limited amendment period for a specified period (s 170A).

Profit or loss from extended operations

The Commissioner also has the power to amend an assessment to ensure its completeness and accuracy where the assessment contains an estimated amount of income or capital gain from a series of incomplete operations extending over more than one year. The amended assessment may be made within 4 years after the Commissioner ascertains the actual profit or loss (s 170(9)).

Protection for anticipating certain announcements

The Commissioner cannot amend an assessment in a less favourable manner to the taxpayer where the taxpayer has reasonably and in good faith anticipated in a statement in a tax return or otherwise a government-announced legislative amendment but which the government subsequently decided on 14 December 2013 not to proceed with (ITAA36 s 170B). To obtain the benefit of the "protection provision", the government announcement must be one of those specifically listed in s 170B(8), the taxpayer's anticipation of the amendment must be reasonably within the terms of the announcement and timing requirements in s 170B(3) must be met.

However, the protection provision does not prevent the Commissioner from amending an assessment, in the relevant circumstances, where the taxpayer applies for the amendment or where the amendment is to give effect to an objection decision or a decision on review or appeal (s 170B(6)). Further, the protection provision does not apply where the taxpayer makes a statement for a later income year, in a tax return or otherwise, that is inconsistent with the taxpayer's previous position (ss 170(10), item 27A; 170B(7)).

[FTR ¶79-900, ¶80-200]

¶25-310 Standard 2-year amendment period

The period during which the Commissioner may amend an assessment for most individuals or some small to medium business taxpayers is 2 years. The amendment period applies from the day on which the Commissioner gives notice of the assessment to the taxpayer (s 170(1)).

Taxpayers with more complex tax affairs are subject to a 4-year amendment period. These include businesses that are not small business entities or, from 1 July 2021, medium business entities (¶7-050). The period for review and amendment of assessments involving arrangements with a dominant tax avoidance purpose is also 4 years. For details of the exclusions from the standard 2-year period, see ¶25-320.

Eligibility for the standard 2-year amendment period depends on the actual tax affairs of the taxpayer for that year, and not the taxpayer's or the Commissioner's understanding of the status of the affairs at the time of the assessment.

▶ Example 1

George includes in his 2016–17 tax return his salary and a share of his interest in the net income of a partnership that he wrongly believes to be a small business entity for that year. In December 2017, the Commissioner issues a notice of assessment to George based on his return as lodged. Subsequently, in August 2020, the Commissioner adjusts the net partnership income and issues an amended assessment to George reflecting that adjustment. The amended assessment was issued more than 2 years after George received his original assessment. He is not eligible for the standard amendment period for the 2016–17 year because he is a partner in a partnership that was not a small business entity.

▶ Example 2

In her 2016–17, Rachel declares as part of her assessable income her salary and a distribution from a trust. It appears that the trust is not a small business entity so she is not eligible for the standard amendment period. Three years after she receives her notice of assessment for 2016–17, she discovers that the trust was a small business entity and, therefore, Rachel was subject to the standard amendment period for the 2016–17 year.

[FTR ¶79-905]

¶25-320 4-year amendment period

Certain taxpayers are not eligible for the standard 2-year amendment period, but are subject to a 4-year amendment period (s 170(1)). Exclusions from the standard 2-year amendment period apply to:

- a taxpayer that carries on a business (or is a partner in a business) unless the taxpayer is a ''small business entity'' or, for assessments for income years starting on or after 1 July 2021, a ''medium business entity'' (¶7-050)
- a taxpayer in the capacity of a trustee of a trust
- a taxpayer who is a beneficiary of a trust unless the trust is a small business entity (or, from 1 July 2021, a medium business entity) or the trustee of the trust (in that capacity) is a full self-assessment taxpayer. For these purposes, a taxpayer who is an object of a discretionary trust is considered to be a beneficiary (*Yazbek*)
- a taxpayer who (either alone or with others) entered into or carried out a scheme for the sole or dominant purpose of obtaining a scheme benefit, and
- a taxpayer in a high risk category or special case to be prescribed by regulation (see below).

Avoidance schemes

The avoidance exclusion is not limited to cases where ITAA36 Pt IVA applies. The exclusion can also apply where the benefit sought is unavailable because of any provision of the law, if the relevant purpose is present. In that case, the 4-year amendment period will apply regardless of whether the taxpayer is actually entitled to the benefit.

High risk categories

The following "high risk" categories are excluded from the standard 2-year amendment period (ITR15 reg 14).

- **Non-arm's length transactions between associates where there is a mismatch in the review periods of the parties involved.** This exclusion applies, for example, where a private company has a 4-year amendment period and a shareholder in the company with a majority voting interest has a 2-year amendment period. The exclusion would not apply to transactions that do not have income tax consequences, eg gifts between parties in a personal relationship.

- **Distributions to entities connected with a private company.** This excludes taxpayers involved in transactions to which Div 7A applies, where there is a mismatch between the company's amendment period of at least 4 years and the related entity's amendment period. The exclusion applies to related entities that are shareholders, former shareholders and their associates.

- **Unpaid present entitlements.** This excludes taxpayers involved in transactions where, as a result of Subdiv EA of Div 7A applying, certain amounts are included in assessable income as if they were dividends.

- **Employee share scheme anti-avoidance rule.** An anti-avoidance rule operates in respect of employee shares and rights offered by a company whose predominant business is the acquisition, sale or holding of shares, securities or other investments. Employee shareholders who are subject to this rule are excluded from the 2-year amendment period unless the company is a small or medium business entity that itself has a 2-year amendment period.

- **Omitted income from foreign transactions.** This exclusion applies to individual taxpayers who omit income from foreign transactions from their tax returns. However, this does not mean that taxpayers have to correctly identify income from foreign transactions at a correct label on the tax return (*Elliott*).

- **Transfer of property and services and tainted services income.** Exclusions apply where information is required from overseas in relation to 2 specific anti-avoidance provisions, namely deemed transfers of property and services and tainted services income.

- **Other specific anti-avoidance provisions.** This excludes taxpayers whose affairs fall under various specific anti-avoidance provisions not covered by the general avoidance exclusion (see above). The provisions relate to distributions of preferentially taxed capital, excluded income of minors, stripping of company profits, franking debit creation and franking credit cancellation schemes, schemes to take advantage of deductions, expenses for a leisure facility or boat, the use of a company's losses and the cancellation of gross up or tax offset where the imputation system has been manipulated.

[FTR ¶79-905]

¶25-330 No time limits for certain amendments

If an under-assessment of tax was due to fraud or evasion, the Commissioner can amend the assessment at any time. There are also other specific provisions that give rise to unlimited review periods.

Fraud or evasion

The essence of "fraud" is the absence of a genuine belief in the truth of a statement or representation, or a reckless carelessness as to its truth or falsity. "Evasion" is something less than fraud but something more than avoidance or mere withholding of information. There must be some blameworthy act or omission on the taxpayer's part, eg deliberately withholding information so that the Commissioner does not consider that the taxpayer has a larger taxable income than the taxpayer is prepared to concede.

Failure to keep proper records of a business due to carelessness and indifference has been held to amount to evasion. There was also evasion where a taxpayer, who had doubts about the tax treatment of share transactions, failed to seek advice from the Commissioner and also failed to give full particulars to a broker, accountant and solicitor he consulted (10 TBRD *Case* K88). Wilful overstatement of expenditure or understatement of receipts is, of course, evasion at the very least.

The Commissioner was not precluded from issuing amended assessments on the basis of fraud or evasion even though the AAT had made orders to set aside an objection decision by consent (*Case 18/2006*).

As to the respective powers of the AAT and courts to review the Commissioner's opinion that the avoidance of tax is due to fraud or evasion, see ¶28-080. The question of whether there has been an avoidance of tax is a matter of fact (to be disproved by the taxpayer) and is not a matter that depends on the Commissioner's opinion. Guidelines for ATO officers on how to deal with suspected cases of fraud or evasion are set out in PS LA 2008/6.

Other unlimited amendment periods

There are no time limits restricting the Commissioner's power to amend an assessment to reflect the fact that a contract that is found to be void *ab initio* has no CGT consequences (ITAA36 s 170(9D)).

The Commissioner may also amend an assessment at any time to give effect to specified provisions (ITAA36 s 170(10), (10AA)) although some of these unlimited review periods are being pared back.

The Commissioner had thought that he could amend an assessment at any time to include the amount of a capital gain taken to have been made in an income year because of the timing rule in ITAA97 s 104-10(3)(a) (¶11-250). Under that rule, the disposal of an asset is deemed to occur at the time when the contract is made rather than when the change of ownership occurs, ie at settlement. However, the Full Federal Court held in *Metlife Insurance* that where settlement has already occurred at the time of lodgment/deemed assessment of the taxpayer company's return, s 170(10AA) could not operate.

[FTR ¶79-905ff]

Payment

¶25-400 Time for payment

In the case of individuals or trustees, income tax is due for payment 21 days after the due date for lodgment of the taxpayer's return or 21 days after a notice of assessment is given to the taxpayer, whichever is the later (ITAA97 s 5-5(5), (6)) (see ¶25-110 as to when a notice of assessment is served). This rule also applies to the payment of administrative penalties imposed under TAA Sch 1 Pt 4-25 (¶29-000) and to GIC (¶29-510). It does *not* apply to late lodgment penalties payable by a company or fund.

The 21-day period is a minimum period and the Commissioner may, and often does, specify a date for payment which is more than 21 days after the service of the notice of assessment. The period of 21 days is calculated by excluding the date of service or deemed service and including the 21st day. Thus, for example, the earliest due date for payment of tax where the notice of assessment is posted on 29 September to an address in the same town or city as the branch office of the ATO issuing the notice would be 21 October (the notice of assessment would be deemed to be served on 30 September). If an amended assessment *increases* liability (¶25-300), a new 21-day due date period calculated from the date of service applies to the excess amount. If an amended assessment *decreases* liability, no new period may be calculated for the reduced amount.

The tax liability of a full self-assessment taxpayer (with a 30 June balance date) is due and payable on 1 December of the following year of income or such later date as notified by the Commissioner. For full self-assessment taxpayers with substituted accounting periods, tax is due and payable on the first day of the sixth month of the following year of income or such later date as notified by the Commissioner (ITAA36 former s 204(1A); ITAA97 s 5-5(4)).

Liability to pay the assessed tax is not suspended pending the Commissioner's consideration of the taxpayer's objections against the assessment, nor while a review or an appeal is pending (¶25-510). The Commissioner has the power to defer the time for payment of tax (¶25-410). In certain circumstances, interest is payable by the Commissioner on early payments and overpayments of tax (¶25-440, ¶28-170).

If the Commissioner has reason to believe that a person is about to leave the country before the due date for payment of tax assessed to that person, the tax is due and payable on such (earlier) date (if any) as the Commissioner notifies to the taxpayer (TAA Sch 1 s 255-20). This notice can operate as a notice of assessment in its own right and its validity is not dependent upon the Commissioner having previously issued a notice of assessment specifying a later date for payment as otherwise required (*Thai*). The Commissioner also has the power to prevent a person with undischarged tax liabilities from leaving Australia (¶25-550).

[FITR ¶16-110]

¶25-410 Deferring of time for payment

The Commissioner may defer the time for payment of tax for particular taxpayers and may permit the tax to be paid by instalments (TAA Sch 1 ss 255-10(1); 255-15(1)). The Commissioner may also defer the time for payment for a class of taxpayers by publishing a notice on the ATO website (TAA Sch 1 s 255-10(2A) to (2C)).

Taxpayers seeking an individual deferment of time to pay should apply to the ATO. The application should ideally be made before the due date for payment and include details of the assessment number, TFN, due date for payment and a brief statement of the taxpayer's financial position and the reasons for seeking an extension. It should also contain a definite offer to pay by a specific date, or by instalments beginning and ending on specified dates, otherwise the application may be refused (*Lawrence*). If the deferment sought is for more than 6 months, a statement of assets and liabilities and other information should be supplied.

If the Commissioner defers the time at which tax is due and payable, then GIC (¶29-510) only becomes payable, in the event of non-payment, from the extended date.

If the taxpayer intends to lodge an objection, the proposed grounds of objection should be indicated in the application (*Lawrence*). However, an application for a deferment of time for payment should not be incorporated in the same letter as an objection against the assessment, as the objection and the application are dealt with in separate sections of the ATO. The inclusion of both in the one letter could result in delay.

A taxpayer does not have any right under the income tax legislation to challenge a decision of the Commissioner refusing a deferment of time for payment. However, the taxpayer may apply for judicial review of such a decision (¶28-180). A company director seeking judicial review of the Commissioner's refusal to accept payment by instalments was unsuccessful in *Stojic*.

Commissioner's guidelines on deferment

Guidelines on the circumstances in which the Commissioner will exercise the power to defer the time for payment of a tax-related liability are set out in PS LA 2011/14. The time for payment will not normally be deferred unless the taxpayer can demonstrate that:

- payment cannot be, or has not been, made by the original time for payment because of circumstances beyond their control, and the taxpayer has taken reasonable steps to mitigate the effects of those circumstances
- payment in full can be made at a later time (when the circumstances that led to non-payment have been alleviated)
- once the circumstances are under control, continuing tax-related liabilities will be paid as and when they fall due.

Each request will be considered on its merits and the deferred payment time will be determined having regard to the particular circumstances of the taxpayer and the circumstances that led to the inability to pay on time. Examples where deferment will normally be granted include natural disasters, serious illness or a legal impediment.

Disputed assessment cases

In considering an application for an extension of time to pay the whole of the tax in dispute, the Commissioner should take into account the fact that an objection has been lodged against the assessment in question or that an appeal is pending (*Ahern*; *ARM Constructions*). Where there is a genuine dispute, the Commissioner is bound to take into account a claim that immediate payment of the tax would cause total or partial liquidation of the taxpayer's business (*ARM Constructions*). In one case, a relevant factor in the court's decision to set aside the Commissioner's refusal to grant an extension of time was that assessments covering an 11-year period were issued suddenly after a long investigation into the taxpayer's affairs and the taxpayer was required to pay $20 million in tax within one month (*Nestle Australia*).

Where the Commissioner lodges an appeal against an AAT or court decision in favour of a taxpayer on a matter which directly affects other taxpayers, the ATO does not apply that decision in making assessments pending the determination of the appeal. In such a case, any extension of time to pay the disputed tax will be on terms requiring GIC to be paid on any amount ultimately found to be payable. However, GIC will not be imposed for the period during which a decision in the taxpayer's favour still subsists (IT 2250).

[FTR ¶977-615]

¶25-420 Security for payment

The Commissioner may require a taxpayer to give security for the payment of an existing or future tax-related liability where the Commissioner: (1) has reason to believe that a taxpayer establishing or carrying on a business in Australia intends to carry it on only for a limited period (including "phoenix activities" where a company with significant unpaid debts is wound up but the same business is conducted through a new company with the same directors/management); or (2) reasonably believes that the requirement is otherwise appropriate having regard to all the circumstances (TAA Sch 1 s 255-100(1)). In *Keris*, the Full Federal Court held that the Commissioner could require a taxpayer to provide security for estimated GST liability even before the proposed transaction had taken place. Similarly, the taxpayers in *Fastbet Investments* were required to give security for future liabilities expected to arise from their property development activities.

The Commissioner may require security to be given by way of a bond, deposit or by any other means that the Commissioner believes is appropriate, eg a mortgage over property (real or personal), floating charges, liens and guarantees (TAA Sch 1 s 255-100(2)).

The Commissioner is required to give written notice to a taxpayer required to give security (TAA Sch 1 s 255-105(1)). The notice must explain why the Commissioner has asked for security, describe the means by which security can be provided; set out by when security must be provided and advise of the procedures available to have the Commissioner's decision reviewed (TAA Sch 1 s 255-105(2)).

In making the decision to require security and how much security, the Commissioner must consider all relevant matters and act reasonably (TAA Sch 1 s 255-100(3)) — since the decisions are administrative in nature, they are subject to judicial review by the Federal Court. However, to avoid taxpayers challenging or defeating the notice on purely technical grounds, a failure to comply with specific technicalities of the notice requirements does not invalidate the notice (TAA Sch 1 s 255-105(5)).

Failing to provide a security as required by the Commissioner is a criminal offence which carries with it a maximum penalty of 100 penalty units (¶29-000) for individuals and 500 penalty units for bodies corporate (TAA Sch 1 s 255-110; *Crimes Act 1914*, s 4B). It follows that the Criminal Code defences apply to the criminal offence of refusing to provide security, eg the defence of involuntariness may apply to a taxpayer who is incapable of providing the security required.

Further, the Commissioner may apply for a Federal Court order to compel a taxpayer to provide security (TAA Sch 1 s 255-115).

The collection of security deposits is not subject to the general collection and recovery rules that apply to tax-related liabilities (¶25-500). Accordingly, security deposits cannot be allocated to a running balance account, and the general interest charge is not applicable for failing to provide a security within the required timeframe.

[FTR ¶977-670, ¶977-674]

¶25-430 Means of payment

Payment of a tax-related liability (¶25-500) must be in Australian currency. The tax-related liability must be paid using a method approved by the Commissioner and in accordance with any instructions provided by the Commissioner (TAR reg 21).

The methods of payment approved by the Commissioner include payment: by using the BPAY system; by credit/debit card online; by using the Government EasyPay service or via an individual's myGov account; by direct credit or direct debit; by posting a cheque together with payment details to the Australian Taxation Office, Locked Bag 1936, Albury NSW 1936; in person at an Australia Post office by cash (up to $3,000), EFTPOS, or cheque or money order; and by transfer from an overseas bank account through the SWIFT system.

Tax refunds can also be directly credited to the taxpayer's bank, building society or credit union account. EFT refunds can also be made to any one specified account that need not be the taxpayer's account, eg it could be the account of the tax agent or another third party (TAA s 8AAZLH). The refund is credited on the day the notice of assessment is issued.

A tax-related liability must be paid in full, unless the Commissioner gives written permission for part payment (TAR reg 21(3)). The Commissioner is not required to give a receipt unless one is requested (TAR reg 22).

The ATO as the Australian Peppol Authority uses Peppol, the common e-invoicing international standard for electronic invoicing (or e-invoicing) (TAA s 3G).

[FTR ¶976-150]

¶25-440 Interest on early payments

The Commissioner is required to pay interest where income tax or certain other amounts are paid by the taxpayer more than 14 days before the day on which the relevant amount becomes due and payable (the "appropriate due day") (*Taxation (Interest on Overpayments and Early Payments) Act 1983*, ss 8A to 8D).

The amounts in respect of which early payment interest may be payable include payments of, or on account of, income tax, a HELP or FS assessment debt (¶2-380, ¶2-385), administrative penalties under TAA Sch 1 Pt 4-25 (¶29-000), interest on accumulated non-resident trust income (¶21-350), shortfall interest charge and GIC for liabilities arising from amended assessments (¶29-550) and GIC for late lodgment of returns by non-instalment taxpayers (¶29-510).

Interest is *not* payable on:

- any part of a payment that exceeds the amount of income tax that is due
- amounts deducted from payments under arrangements for the advance collection of tax (eg amounts withheld from an employee's salary under the PAYG system), and
- amounts credited in payment of a tax liability but which are not directly paid by the taxpayer (eg overpayments of income tax liabilities for an earlier year), or other tax liabilities such as FBT or GST.

The period for which early payment interest is calculated is:

- for companies, superannuation funds, ADFs and PSTs — from the day the early payment is made until the appropriate due day, and
- for other taxpayers — from the later of the day of payment or the day the relevant notice (eg of assessment) is issued until the appropriate due day.

If an amount that is paid early is refunded before the day it becomes due and payable, early payment interest is not payable in respect of any period after the day it is refunded.

See ¶28-170 for the rates at which early payment interest is payable, and payment of interest on overpayment of tax.

A taxpayer can ask the ATO for payment of the interest or can claim the interest as a credit in the return for the income year in which the entitlement to the interest arises. The Commissioner can offset interest on early payments against income tax and other tax liabilities (TAA Pt IIB Div 3).

Early payment interest is assessable in the year in which it is received or applied against another tax liability (¶10-470). If the interest is claimed as a credit in one year, it should be included as income in the return for the following year.

The Commissioner is also required to pay interest on overpayments of tax in certain circumstances (¶28-170). Note that early payment interest is not payable for any period where interest is also payable as a result of a credit, refund or remission.

[FTR ¶910-200]

¶25-450 Release from payment

Taxpayers may apply to the Department of Finance and Deregulation for a waiver of their tax debts, ie the right to pursue and recover the debt is irrevocably abandoned. Under the *Public Governance Performance and Accountability Act 2013*, the Finance Minister has the general power to waive a debt due to the Commonwealth, and the decision-maker has a very broad discretion to consider each request on a case-by-case basis. Debts may be waived where the decision-maker considers recovery of the debt would be inequitable or cause ongoing financial hardship, and that other debt treatment options (such as an agency writing off the debt or deferring payment) are not appropriate (see below).

While not delegated with the general power to waive tax debts, the Commissioner may approve release from the payment of some tax debts, in whole or part, on the grounds of serious hardship. TAA Sch 1 Div 340 provides for an individual or the trustee of the estate of a deceased person to be released from paying certain liabilities if payment of the liability will cause serious hardship. An application for release should be made before the due date for payment. The taxpayer's application should be made on the approved form and should contain sufficient detail to satisfy the ATO that payment of the tax debts would cause serious hardship and that release would be appropriate (PS LA 2011/17).

Liabilities from which release may be granted are income tax (including Medicare levy, Medicare levy surcharge and withholding tax), together with administrative penalties (¶29-000), shortfall interest charge (¶29-550), GIC and other penalties associated with those liabilities. Applications may also include instalments of PAYG and FBT. However, where release is granted from a PAYG or an FBT instalment, a taxpayer is not entitled to a credit for the instalment to the extent of that release. If the taxpayer's circumstances have not improved by the time of the final assessment, the taxpayer could apply for release from the overall liability at that time. The Commissioner does not have the power to grant release from a debt arising from an administrative overpayment (*Anderson*).

A taxpayer who is dissatisfied with the Commissioner's decision has a right of objection under TAA Pt IVC (¶28-010). A taxpayer who is dissatisfied with the objection decision may request that the AAT review the merits of that decision. The ATO will pay the AAT fee for a review of a decision refusing release from taxation liability based on serious hardship (PS LA 2011/17).

If the Commissioner refuses an application or only grants partial release, a taxpayer may make a further application in relation to the same liability, even if the taxpayer has unsuccessfully objected against the decision. However, a taxpayer cannot apply for the return of taxes previously paid.

The estates of deceased Australian Defence Force personnel and deceased civilians who have served in a prescribed UN peacekeeping force are also eligible for release under ITAA36 s 265A (¶10-750, ¶10-780).

What is serious hardship?

The decision to grant relief is based on whether payment of the liability would cause the taxpayer (or the dependants of a deceased taxpayer) to suffer serious hardship.

Guidelines on determining whether there is serious hardship can also be found in PS LA 2011/17. According to that policy, serious hardship would exist where a taxpayer is left without the means to achieve reasonable acquisitions of food, medical supplies, accommodation, education for children and other basic requirements.

Serious hardship has been defined as something less severe than extreme financial hardship or destitution but nevertheless hardship of a significant kind in terms of normal community standards (*Ferguson*; *ZDCW*). In *Van Grieken v Veilands*, the taxpayer's financial affairs, including financial relations with other members of his household or with any family company, were held to be relevant matters to consider. Further, there needs to be a causal relationship between the requirement to satisfy the tax liability and the serious hardship; the existence of the liability itself does not impose serious hardship especially in circumstances where it was not yet due (*XLPZ*). Other relevant factors in determining whether relief should be granted include the taxpayer's level of discretionary spending, payment of rent, the priority given to investments or debts, and tax compliance history resulting in a spike in liability (*Moriarty*).

Release will not normally be granted if it would *not* relieve hardship, eg where the existence of other creditors make bankruptcy inevitable. In *Rollo v Morrow*, an application by a tax consultant was refused because of his knowledge of the tax laws and his obligations under them, his ability to earn large sums of money and the fact that money was owing to him.

A solicitor in receipt of a very substantial income was granted release from his tax debt on the basis of serious hardship. The Federal Court found that, while the AAT's decision to grant relief was initially surprising, it was based on a consideration of the taxpayer's particular circumstances. These included whether he could achieve acquisitions of food, clothing, accommodation, medical supplies, education and other basic requirements that were not excessive or unreasonable in the circumstances. The court accepted that the taxpayer's income was highly vulnerable should he be made bankrupt (*Taxpayer*). Similarly, in *Milne*, because of the taxpayer's age and serious health problems, the few remaining years of his working life, the dependency of his 2 children and the likely loss of his practicing certificate in the event of bankruptcy, his circumstances constituted serious hardship.

In *Rollason*, however, a solicitor failed to obtain relief. Although the taxpayer established that serious hardship arose from misfortune for which he was not responsible his compliance record was very bad and the hardship was attributable to his own conduct. The AAT considered that the relief provisions were not designed to allow a taxpayer to escape an obligation that he did not discharge through his own fault. Similarly, in *Rasmussen*, the AAT found that the taxpayer would suffer serious hardship but that did not arise merely because of his tax liability but rather his other liabilities. Accordingly, he did not satisfy the condition that he would suffer serious hardship if required to satisfy the tax liability (s 340-5(3), item 1).

[FTR ¶978-415]

Collection and Recovery

¶25-500 Collection and recovery regime

The collection and recovery of unpaid tax-related liabilities (including penalties) is covered by a common set of rules in TAA Sch 1 Pt 4-15. This regime applies to all tax-related liabilities, including PAYG instalment and PAYG withholding amounts. A tax-related liability is defined as a pecuniary liability to the Commonwealth arising under a taxation law (TAA Sch 1 s 255-1). A ''taxation law'' is defined in TAA s 2.

A full list of the different types of tax-related liabilities that arise throughout the various taxation laws is contained in 2 tables in TAA Sch 1 s 250-10. The tables also set out the various provisions that specify when those liabilities become due and payable.

Guidelines on the Commissioner's policy in relation to the collection and recovery of tax-related liabilities are set out in PS LA 2011/14. Guidelines on the recovery of tax liabilities from trustees is set out in PS LA 2012/2.

The IGTO has commenced a review into the underlying causes for the rise in uncollected and undisputed tax debts (ie the ATO's collectable debts).

[FTR ¶977-550 – ¶977-890]

¶25-510 Recovery of tax

Income tax (and other tax-related liabilities), when it becomes due and payable (¶25-400), is a debt due to the Commonwealth of Australia (TAA Sch 1 s 255-5(1)). Liability to pay tax is a civil one and failure to pay exposes the taxpayer to civil but not criminal remedies. However, a criminal offence may be committed where arrangements are entered into with the purpose of rendering a company or trustee unable, or likely not to be able, to pay tax (¶30-000).

Unpaid tax may be sued for and recovered as a civil debt by the Commissioner or Deputy Commissioner in any court of competent jurisdiction, ie in every court which by enactment is made competent to entertain a claim for recovery of unpaid tax (TAA Sch 1 s 255-5(2)). For these purposes, tax includes penalty tax under ITAA36 former Pt VII (¶29-000) and GIC (¶29-510). In this regard, both the Australian National Audit Office (ANAO) and the Australian Small Business and Family Enterprise Ombudsman have called on the ATO to improve its management of small business tax debts.

Recovery proceedings

If a taxpayer cannot be found after reasonable inquiry, or has left Australia and has no agent or attorney in Australia, service of any process in proceedings for the recovery of tax (eg a Supreme Court writ) may be effected by posting it to the taxpayer's last known place of business or abode in Australia or, in certain circumstances, an overseas address (TAA Sch 1 s 255-40). This does not apply to service of a bankruptcy notice and creditors' petition by the Commissioner (they must be served personally in accordance with the *Bankruptcy Rules*) (*Re Kassab*), however, the Commissioner may obtain an order for substituted service from the court. For example the court may order that the document be sent to the debtor or given to another person who will bring the document to the attention of the debtor.

An application may also be made to the Federal Court for service outside Australia. Rule 10.43 of the Federal Court Rules 2011 allows this if it is permitted under Australia's double tax agreements (¶22-160), the Hague Convention or the law of the foreign country. Some of Australia's double tax agreements provide for mutual assistance on the collection of taxes such that the Commissioner could collect foreign tax debts (and serve documents) on behalf of the foreign revenue authorities (TAA Sch 1 Div 263).

The taxpayer is prevented from challenging the assessment(s) creating the tax liability (ITAA36 s 175; TAA Sch 1 s 350-10) although the taxpayer is not prevented from arguing that the assessment(s) are invalid for lack of bona fides (*Broadbeach Properties*; *Futuris Corporation*). TAA Sch 1 Div 350 (ss 350-1 to 350-25) deals with procedural and evidentiary matters, as well as the evidentiary effect of official tax documents for the purposes of taxation laws.

Income tax is recoverable only from a person who is given a legal right to contest the correctness of an assessment. For example, tax under an assessment issued to the trustee of a deceased estate who, having had no reason to believe there was any unpaid liability for tax, had distributed the assets to the beneficiaries, was not recoverable from the beneficiaries (*Brown*). However, see ¶25-540 for the Commissioner's right to recover tax from any person owing money to the taxpayer.

The Commissioner does not have to comply with time limitations in state legislation when seeking to recover a tax debt (*Moorebank*). The federal regime excludes the operation of state limitations and extends to the collection of tax-related liabilities that arose before 1 July 2000 and remained payable after that date (*Muc (No 2)*; High Court special leave application refused). Tax debts can be recovered at any time. State legislation allowing for judgment debts to be paid by instalments does not apply to tax debts (*Zarzycki*; *Re Mazuran*; *Homewood*).

Where a husband and wife resided in and spent substantial amounts rebuilding a property that was orally gifted to them by the husband's parents (who remained the registered owners), a constructive trust existed in favour of the taxpayers. Consequently, in the event of proceedings to recover a tax debt, the taxpayers could not contend that they did not have an interest in the property (*Sarkis*; *Karas*).

Liability not suspended pending review

Liability to pay assessed tax, additional tax or any other amount is *not* suspended pending the outcome of an application for review or appeal (TAA ss 14ZZM; 14ZZR). Thus, once assessed tax or any other amount (eg penalties and GIC) becomes due and payable, the Commissioner is entitled to take whatever steps necessary and appropriate to recover the tax or other amount. This rule applies even if any objection, review or appeal under TAA Pt IVC, or any further appeal, is still outstanding (*Broadbeach Properties*). Further, the AAT is specifically prevented from granting a stay of execution of the judgment debt pending determination of the review proceedings before it (TAA s 14ZZB; *Coshott*).

If the taxpayer is a company, the Commissioner can serve a statutory demand under s 459E of the *Corporations Act 2001* which may ultimately lead to the company being wound up: *Kalis Nominees*. There are a number of bases on which a court may set aside a statutory demand, eg on the ground that there is a ''genuine dispute'' about the existence or amount of the debt (*Corporations Act 2001*, s 459H). In *Hoare Bros*, the Full Federal Court held that challenging an assessment under the provisions of Pt IVC was not a genuine dispute to justify setting aside a demand as, in the meantime, the tax had to be paid. In *Broadbeach Properties*, the High Court upheld the correctness of *Hoare Bros*.

Where there is a risk of asset dissipation, the Commissioner may apply for a Mareva injunction or freezing order preventing the taxpayer and his/her associates from dealing with certain assets (*Ousley*; *Gashi*; *Hua Wang Bank Berhard*). The granting of a freezing order is discretionary; the relevant factors for and against are weighed up to see what the balance of convenience requires. In *Uysal*, the taxpayer breached a Mareva injunction by deliberately mortgaging his family home; he was found guilty of contempt of court and imprisoned (*Uysal*).

Where an extension of time for payment of tax has been granted (¶25-410), recovery action will normally be held in abeyance but will recommence if the taxpayer defaults on the terms of the extension.

Stay of proceedings or execution

If the Commissioner commences proceedings to recover unpaid tax, or petitions the court for a sequestration or winding-up order on the basis of the taxpayer's failure to pay a tax debt, the taxpayer can apply to the court for a stay of proceedings or dismissal of the petition (the AAT has no power to stay recovery proceedings: TD 93/226). A taxpayer may also apply for a stay of execution where judgment is entered against the taxpayer. Whatever the nature of the proceedings, the taxpayer will have to show good cause before the court will grant a stay. Hardship to the taxpayer, the merits of any objection or appeal against the assessment(s) in question and abuse of office are relevant factors, although the fact that an objection or appeal is pending or that it has substance will not of itself justify a stay (eg *Palumbo*). However, where the taxpayers had an arguable case that an agreement with the Commissioner for settlement of the amount of tax owing had been entered into under economic duress, a summary judgment for money owing under the agreement was set aside (*Caratti*).

In *Pollock*, although the taxpayer was not represented at his bankruptcy hearing, through no fault of his own, the sequestration order made at the hearing was not set aside as he could not show that his grounds of objection to the assessment in question had any substance. Similarly, a taxpayer who argued that the Commissioner had delayed instituting recovery proceedings in order that penalty taxes would accrue was unsuccessful in having the judgment entered against him set aside on grounds of unconscionability (*Pickering*). It seems that the taxpayer could obtain an injunction in recovery proceedings where the assessment imposing the unpaid tax was made contrary to representations made to the taxpayer, eg in a private ruling (*Atkinson*).

Except in quite exceptional circumstances, a stay of proceedings will not be granted where the taxpayer has been a party to a scheme to avoid liability for tax (*Mackey*). The Federal Court refused to stay recovery proceedings pending the outcome of criminal proceedings in which the taxpayers were charged with conspiracy to defraud the Commissioner (*Alvaro*). However, a stay of execution was granted to a mother of 4 dependent children whose only means of financial support was social security benefits; significant factors in the decision were that she and her estranged husband, who was being held in custody on armed robbery charges, had been assessed on an assets betterment basis (¶25-140) and she was ignorant of her husband's alleged criminal activities (*Gergis*).

[FTR ¶977-595]

¶25-520 Liability of liquidators, receivers and agents

A liquidator of a company or a receiver for a debenture holder is required to notify the Commissioner *within 14 days* of the fact of: (i) being appointed as liquidator; or (ii) taking possession of the assets of the company (TAA Sch 1 Subdivs 260-B; 260-C).

As soon as practicable after notice has been given, the Commissioner is required to notify the liquidator or receiver of the amount which would be sufficient to cover income tax (including penalties and GIC: ¶29-000, ¶29-510) which the Commissioner considers is payable or will become payable. Until this notification is received, the liquidator or receiver must not, without the leave of the Commissioner, part with any of the assets of the company except to pay secured or preferred debts (eg debts owed to employees of an insolvent company for unpaid wages, accrued leave or a similar entitlement). If there are any assets available for payment of ordinary debts, the liquidator or receiver must set aside a pro rata share of them for payment of the amount of income tax notified by the Commissioner (and also for payment of any other amounts, such as FBT and GST, which the Commissioner considers are or may become payable and are notified by him under the relevant Acts).

A liquidator's general duty to act honestly and impartially may require the liquidator to notify the Commissioner where he/she subsequently becomes aware that the Commissioner's claim for tax is clearly understated (*Re Autolook*). On the other hand, once the liquidator has finally distributed the assets of the company and paid the tax notified by the Commissioner, it appears that the Commissioner cannot subsequently vary the notice so as to increase the amount of tax for which the liquidator should have made provision (*Bettina House of Fashion*).

Similar duties are imposed on agents for non-resident principals (TAA Sch 1 Subdiv 260-D). The agent must notify the Commissioner within 14 days after being required by the principal to wind up the business or realise the assets. However, unlike a liquidator or receiver, the agent cannot part with any of the assets to pay out secured or preferred debts until after receiving notification from the Commissioner of the tax likely to be payable. The agent is required to set aside out of the assets enough to pay the full amount of the tax.

A refusal or failure to comply with these requirements renders the liquidator, receiver or agent personally liable for the tax to the extent of the value of the assets that were in his/her possession and required to be set aside for payment of the tax. The liquidator, etc, is also guilty of an offence carrying a fine of up to 10 penalty units (¶29-000). In *Tideturn's case*, the liquidator continued the trading operations of the company and was subsequently held personally liable for group tax which the company had failed to remit to the Commissioner during his administration. However, as the liquidator's decision to continue trading was based on promised finance (which never materialised) and he had not been remunerated, the court reduced his liability to some extent.

[FTR ¶977-785 – ¶977-820]

¶25-530 Liability of trustees of deceased taxpayer

Special rules apply where the whole of a deceased's tax liability up to the time of death has not been satisfied (TAA Sch 1 s 260-140). The Commissioner has the same powers and remedies for the assessment and recovery of tax against the trustees of the deceased's estate (including the executors and administrators) after death as he would have had against the taxpayer had he/she not died.

The trustees must furnish any returns required from them for that purpose. The trustees are also specifically required to furnish a return of any income or profits or gains of a capital nature of the deceased not covered by previous returns. This would generally include: (i) a return for such income or profits derived by the deceased for the period from the end of the last income year for which the deceased filed a return to the date of death; (ii) a return for any earlier year not filed by the deceased; and (iii) a return disclosing amounts omitted from a previous return (¶2-080).

The Commissioner may issue original or amended assessments to the trustees and the trustees can become liable to penalties for late payment or default in furnishing returns in the same way as the deceased would have been. Notification from the Commissioner in the form of a notice of assessment or nil tax advice may be relied on by a trustee to distribute the assets of the estate.

The trustees may be personally liable for the tax if they do not set aside sufficient assets to pay it (¶6-040).

Where the trustees are unable, refuse or fail to furnish a return, or where probate or letters of administration are not taken out within 6 months of death, the Commissioner can make an arbitrary assessment of the taxable income and the tax (including relevant penalties) payable thereon (TAA Sch 1 ss 260-145; 260-150). In cases where probate or administration is not granted within 6 months, a person who claims an interest in the estate may object against such an assessment in accordance with TAA Pt IVC (the objection is called a ''delayed administration (beneficiary) objection''). Where probate or letters of administration are eventually granted, the executor or administrator may also object against the assessment in accordance with Pt IVC (the objection is called a ''delayed administration (trustee) objection''). See ¶28-020 for the time limits for lodging a delayed administration (beneficiary) objection or a delayed administration (trustee) objection. (Note that the Commissioner may grant an extension of time: ¶28-030.)

For a checklist of the tax consequences of death, see ¶44-170.

[FTR ¶977-845]

¶25-540 Recovery from third party

Where a tax-related liability (¶25-500) is payable, the Commissioner may issue a notice under TAA Sch 1 s 260-5 requiring any person who owes money to the taxpayer to pay that money to the Commissioner instead. This power enables the Commissioner to collect the tax-related liability without proceeding to judgment or execution against the taxpayer.

The s 260-5 procedure is akin to garnishee proceedings and, accordingly, a s 260-5 notice is sometimes referred to as a garnishee notice or third party notice. The service of a notice on a third party creates a statutory charge in favour of the Commissioner over any moneys payable, or which become payable, by the recipient of the notice to the taxpayer (*Donnelly*; *Lanstel*). However, it does not create a proprietary interest in the moneys (*Hansen Yuncken v Ericson*) and may be subject to a pre-existing charge (*Market Nominees*).

Notices were ineffective where the recipients did not owe money to the taxpayer (*Ultra Thoroughbred Racing*) or would not owe money until they had received its share of a retained sum (*Elsinora Global*). A notice attempting to recover tax owing by a company in liquidation was void because it was an attachment to the property of the company in contravention of the *Corporations Act 2001* (*Bell Group*). However, in *Park*, a notice to the purchasers of real property in respect of the vendor's tax liabilities was effective even though the property was subject to 2 registered mortgages which exceeded the value of the property.

A s 260-5 notice may be issued to the third party where there is a debt or tax-related liability due by the taxpayer to the Commissioner whether or not the debt has become due and payable. However, a breach of s 260-5 does not in itself give rise to a "tax-related liability" within the meaning of s 255-1 that can found the issuing of further notices (*Fyna Projects*). Further, a decision to issue a notice in respect of tax liabilities for which judgment was stayed by the Queensland Supreme Court was held to be unreasonable (*Denlay*).

Unless there are special circumstances, the Commissioner is not required to give advance notice before issuing a notice to a third party (*Woodroffe*; *Saitta*). In *Shail*, notices were invalid because a notice of assessment left at the taxpayer's post office box on the same day was not validly served, so there was no debt due and payable on that date.

Failure by a third party to comply with a notice is an offence (TAA Sch 1 s 260-20) — the penalty is a 20 penalty units (¶29-000) and the offender may also be required to pay the amount sought by the Commissioner. Alternatively, the Commissioner may sue in debt for the recovery of the amount due under the notice when the time for payment has arrived (*Barnes*). Any person making a payment under the notice is indemnified for the amount paid. The validity of a notice can be challenged, eg on grounds of bad faith or improper purpose, by any person with an interest in the matter, including the person on whom the notice is served (*Sunrise Auto*). However, any such person cannot challenge the correctness of the underlying assessment giving rise to the tax debt unless the taxpayer challenges the assessment under TAA Pt IVC (*Sunrise Auto*) (¶28-000).

The Commissioner's power to issue a notice to a third party is not confined to the collection of debts due to the taxpayer, but may also apply where the third party owes or may later owe money to the taxpayer (*Saitta*). The Commissioner used the comparable power under ITAA36 former s 218 to require a solicitor to hand over money held in the solicitor's trust account on behalf of a client as security for future costs (*Gilshenan & Luton*).

Minor errors in a notice issued under TAA Sch 1 s 260-5 will not necessarily invalidate it (*Goodin*). However, a notice which was ambiguous as to whether payments were to be made to the Commissioner every 2 or 4 weeks was invalid (*De Martin and Gasparini*).

A Mareva injunction obtained by the Commissioner preventing a taxpayer from dealing with his/her assets does not nullify a notice served on a third party (*Zumtar*).

In *Brown v Brown & Ors*, a notice issued to a third party in respect of a debt owed by a company that was subsequently wound up was effective. The court also rejected an argument that, by lodging a proof of debt, the Commissioner had surrendered the security interest created by the notice.

The ATO has agreed to the IGTO's 2019 recommendations in its review into the ATO's use of garnishee notices. Separately, a 2017 consultation paper proposed to allow the ATO to use the garnishee power to garnishee an amount to cover a security deposit (¶25-420) to address phoenix behaviour.

Where notice will be ineffective

A notice to a third party is ineffective against money held in a joint account, even though tax is owing by each of the joint account holders (*Westpac Savings Bank*). A notice directed to the Official Trustee is also ineffective (*Kunz*). Where taxpayers assign money due to them before the issuing of a notice, that notice will not defeat the right of the assignee, even if the person holding the money received the notice before receiving notice of the assignment (*Zuks*).

A notice requiring the payment by a bank of moneys held on account of a taxpayer will be invalid where the moneys held in the account are denominated in foreign currency (*Conley*).

The Commissioner cannot use the power to collect from a third party as an instrument of oppression to deprive a taxpayer of virtually all his/her income flow. Nor can it be used to collect tax owed not by the taxpayer but by companies associated with the taxpayer (*Edelsten v Wilcox*).

Where a taxpayer who owes tax sells mortgaged land, the purchaser will generally not be required to pay the whole, or part, of the purchase price to the Commissioner to the detriment of the mortgage provider's secured interest. In these cases, the Commissioner says that he will generally only seek to apply a notice to so much of the purchase moneys to be paid to the vendor, or as the vendor directs, as remains after the mortgage has been discharged (PS LA 2011/18). However, the result in *Park*, where the Commissioner enforced a notice ahead of 2 secured creditors, seems to sit uneasily with his stated policy in PS LA 2011/18.

A notice does not override an equitable lien held by the taxpayer's solicitor over the moneys charged by a notice for costs reasonably incurred in recovering those moneys (*Government Insurance Office of NSW*; *Heath*).

A notice issued to a third party after the commencement of the winding up of the taxpayer company, ie where a liquidator has been appointed, is invalid (*Bruton Holdings*); TAA Sch 1 s 260-45 provides a specific regime for the collection and recovery of tax liabilities of such companies, ie by requiring liquidators to set aside from the available assets of the company an amount sufficient to pay the Commissioner the amount recoverable as an unsecured creditor in the liquidation.

Further, once the taxpayer's debt is discharged, whether by payment or otherwise (eg where the taxpayer successfully challenges the relevant assessment), the notice ceases to have effect (*Government Insurance Office of NSW* — in that case, the tax debt was discharged upon the taxpayer being discharged from bankruptcy).

Review of s 260-5 notices

A decision to issue a notice under TAA Sch 1 s 260-5 is subject to judicial review (*Edelsten v Wilcox*); however, it is not reviewable by the AAT under TAA Pt IVC because it is not a reviewable objection decision (*Rossi*).

[FTR ¶977-690]

¶25-550 Departure prohibition orders

The Commissioner can issue a departure prohibition order (DPO) to stop a person with a tax debt leaving Australia (TAA ss 14Q to 14ZA). The issue of a DPO ensures that the debtor does not leave Australia without discharging an outstanding tax liability or without making satisfactory arrangements for it to be discharged. The penalty for defying a DPO is severe: a fine of up to 50 penalty units (¶29-000); and/or one year's imprisonment.

Where a DPO is in force, the debtor may still leave Australia temporarily if he/she obtains a departure authorisation certificate from the Commissioner. These will generally only be issued if the Commissioner is satisfied that the debtor will return to Australia and the tax liability will be discharged or that a temporary departure should be allowed on humanitarian or general policy grounds.

The Commissioner is required to revoke a DPO if: (1) the debtor's tax liabilities have been wholly discharged and the Commissioner is satisfied that any future tax liabilities in respect of matters that have occurred will be wholly discharged or completely irrecoverable; or (2) the Commissioner is satisfied that the debtor's tax liabilities are completely irrecoverable.

An appeal lies to the Federal Court or the Supreme Court against the making of a DPO. An appeal is not simply a rehearing of the matter and the onus is on the debtor to prove the DPO is invalid (*Poletti*). A decision to make a DPO is also reviewable under the *Administrative Decisions (Judicial Review) Act 1977* (ADJR Act) (¶28-180), but is not reviewable by the AAT (*Case 7/95*). The Commissioner's refusal to revoke a DPO or to issue a departure authorisation certificate is reviewable by the AAT or, in appropriate circumstances (eg where the matter involves the interpretation of the legislation), by the Federal Court under the ADJR Act (¶28-180). A taxpayer who wanted to go overseas to visit sick relatives, spend time with his wife and children and participate in certain volunteer works was granted a departure authorisation certificate by the AAT on humanitarian grounds (*Crockett*). However, the Commissioner's refusal to issue a departure authorisation certificate has been upheld in cases where taxpayers had previously breached DPOs and failed to provide any security for their return (*Eid*; *Koueider*). Further, a taxpayer who owed $23 million in tax debts and offered some security but not enough to satisfy the Commissioner could not obtain a departure authorisation certificate even though his wife was dying overseas (*Lui*).

Penalties will be attracted if a person fails to answer questions from police or Customs officers directed at determining whether the person is affected by a DPO (maximum penalty is a fine of 10 penalty units: ¶29-000) and for knowingly making a false reply to such a question (maximum penalty is a fine of 10 penalty units (¶29-000) or 6 months' imprisonment, or both).

Appeals against DPOs were unsuccessful in the *Briggs*, *Winter* and *Poletti cases*.

However, an appeal was successful in *Pattenden* because the DPO had been altered by an ATO officer after it had been authorised by the decision-maker and reasonable grounds did not exist for the belief that the taxpayer was a flight risk. Further, in *Skase's case*, the Federal Court said that because the taxpayer had very few assets in Australia, the recovery of tax could not be affected by his departure. In *Edelsten's case*, the Federal Court held that the taxpayer's bankruptcy released him from his tax liabilities at the time the sequestration order was made. Similarly, the AAT in *Walsh* revoked a DPO the ATO granted almost 3 years previously, after balancing its severe intrusion on the taxpayer's freedom of movement (his principal place of residence was in the USA with his wife and young daughter) against the protection of the revenue.

[FTR ¶970-700]

¶25-560 Directors penalties

Special regimes enable the Commissioner to recover from the directors of companies unpaid amounts under the PAYG withholding system (¶26-500), unpaid superannuation guarantee charge (SGC: ¶39-000) and from 1 April 2020, liabilities under the GST Act relating to GST (¶34-000), luxury car tax (LCT: ¶34-220) and wine equalisation tax (WET: ¶34-360).

Estimates of liabilities

Under Div 268, the Commissioner may make a reasonable estimate of a person's liability for unpaid and overdue amount of PAYG under TAA Sch 1 s 16-70, SGC for a quarter (to the extent that the charge has not already been assessed), and/or a net amount for a tax period under the GST Act relating to GST, LCT and WET (to the extent that the net amount has not been assessed), having regard to anything that the Commissioner considers is relevant (s 268-10).

When the Commissioner makes such an estimate, the person must be notified in writing of the estimate, and that the estimate may be reduced if the person makes a statutory declaration or affidavit specifying the actual amount of liability or declaring that no amounts had to be withheld or paid (TAA Sch 1 ss 268-40(1), item 1; 268-90). Where an estimate remains unpaid after 7 days, GIC is payable (TAA Sch 1 s 268-75).

Once an estimate has been made, the Commissioner may commence recovery proceedings based on that estimated liability (TAA Sch 1 s 268-20(2)). The person liable may defend the recovery proceedings by proving, by means of an affidavit, that the actual liability never existed, has been discharged or is less than the Commissioner's estimate (TAA Sch 1 ss 268-40(1), items 2 and 3; 268-90).

Company directors personally liable

In conjunction with the regime for the recovery of unremitted amounts, the director of a non-remitting company may be personally liable to pay an amount equal to the company's tax liabilities (TAA Sch 1 Div 269). The regime applies where a company is required to remit an amount in respect of PAYG withheld; an alienated personal services payment received; a non-cash benefit provided; SGC for the relevant quarter; an assessed net amount under the GST Act for the relevant tax period from 1 April 2020; or a GST instalment for the relevant GST instalment quarter from 1 April 2020 (TAA Sch 1 s 269-10).

Under Div 269, there is a duty on a director to ensure that the company:

- meets its obligations to remit amounts deducted or pay estimated liabilities (see above)
- goes into voluntary administration, or
- begins to be wound up (TAA Sch 1 s 269-15).

If the company has not undertaken one of these options on or before the due date for the remittance of the deductions or amounts withheld, the directors of the company are each personally liable to pay to the Commissioner, by way of penalty, an amount equal to the unpaid amount of the company's liability or the estimate. This liability applies to persons who were directors at any time during the period from the date the deductions were made to the due date for payment (TAA Sch 1 s 269-20(1), (2)). Importantly, new directors may be liable where, 30 days after they become directors, the company has still not complied with the above requirements (TAA Sch 1 s 269-20(3)). However, the Commissioner cannot take action to enforce an obligation or to recover a penalty if there was an instalment arrangement in force under s TAA Sch 1 s 255-15.

A director will also remain liable for penalty in certain cases, even if there is an appointment of an administrator or the commencement of winding up, if the underlying liability remains unpaid and unreported before the relevant "lockdown date" (TAA Sch 1 s 269-30(2); *Lee; Silverbrook*). The lockdown date is:

- for a withheld amount or an assessed net amount under the GST Act — the last day of the 3 months after the due day for its payment
- for an estimated amount of PAYG withholding liabilities — the last day of the 3 months after the due day for payment of the underlying liability
- for an estimated amount of a net amount under the GST Act — the last day of the 3 months after the due day for the relevant GST return
- for an SGC — the due day for its payment
- for an estimated amount of SGC which has not been paid — the due day for payment of the underlying liability.

In these cases, the subsequent appointment of an administrator, or the beginning of the winding up of the company, will not have the effect of remitting the directors penalty. That penalty will therefore continue to be payable. However, remission may continue to be applicable to the extent that the company has:

- for withheld amounts, notified the Commissioner within the 3-month period of the amount of its liability
- for SGC, lodged an accurate SG statement by the due day, or
- for net amounts, lodged the relevant GST return within the 3-month period.

Notice of penalty

The Commissioner must give 21 days' notice before instituting proceedings to recover, by way of penalty, the unpaid amount of the company's liability or the unpaid amount of the estimate of that liability (TAA Sch 1 s 269-25(1)).

The notice must set out what the Commissioner thinks is the unpaid amount (s 269-25(2); *Snell*). The person to whom a notice is sent does not have to be a current director. It is sufficient if the person is in office for at least some of the period before the due date when the company became liable to make the payment (*Canty*).

Penalties imposed on directors are not subject to GIC (¶29-510), but may be subject to pre-judgment interest (*Canty*).

A 2017 consultation paper proposed to remove the 21-day notice period for high risk phoenix operators.

Service of penalty notice

If it appears from information held by the Registrar that a person is or has been a director of the company within the last 7 days, the penalty notice can be served by delivering it or posting it to the person's place of residence or business as it appears on those documents (TAA Sch 1 s 269-50). The Commissioner may also send a copy of the notice to the director's tax agent's address (TAA Sch 1 s 269-52). The notice is taken to be given at the time that the notice is left or posted by the Commissioner (TAA Sch 1 s 269-25(4)), not at the time the letter would ordinarily have been delivered under s 29 of the *Acts Interpretation Act 1901* (*Roche*); the Commissioner does not need to satisfy the court that a notice was actually received by the director (*Tannous*).

Defences to personal liability

A director has 3 defences against proceedings to recover the penalty:

(1) because of illness or for some other good reason, it would have been unreasonable to expect the person to take part, and the person did not take part, in the management of the company at any time when the person was a director and the directors were under a duty to comply

(2) the person took all reasonable steps to ensure that the directors complied or there were no reasonable steps that could have been taken

(3) in relation to the SGC or assessed net amounts under the GST Act, the company treated the SGC legislation or GST Act as applying to a matter in a way that was "reasonably arguable" and the company took reasonable care in applying the legislation (TAA Sch 1 s 269-35).

A defence will be established if the Commissioner is satisfied of the relevant matters on the basis of the information provided by the director. If the Commissioner fails to pay due regard to such information, the Commissioner's decision could be declared invalid (*Brown*).

In practice, it can be difficult to meet the requirements of these defences. In *Saunig*, a director who had concerns about the management of a company was unable to rely on the second defence that he had taken all reasonable steps to ensure compliance. The court noted that, although he had tried unsuccessfully to convince the other directors to comply, as a single director he could have caused the company to begin to be wound up and should have obtained professional advice at an earlier stage. The need to seek legal advice as soon as a director becomes aware of the true state of a company's financial obligations was also underscored in *Solomon*.

A person who, 2 months after the unremitted amounts were due, became a director of a company for 17 days and who received a notice nearly 3 months after ceasing to be a director was also unable to rely on the defences (*Fitzgerald*). Although the director had not been aware of the company's financial position or the amounts due while he was a director, this was not sufficient to provide a defence. The court warned that it was the responsibility of new directors at the time of, or before taking up, their appointments to make inquiries of the relevant officers of the company as to whether there were any moneys owing. If incorrect information was given to such an inquiry, a defence may be available.

A director who fails to make out the defence that he has taken reasonable steps to ensure compliance is also unable to obtain relief under the s 1318 of the *Corporations Act 2001* (TAA Sch 1 s 269-35(5)).

A director is entitled to be indemnified by the company, and any other persons from whom the Commissioner is entitled to recover, for any payment made by way of penalty under these provisions (TAA Sch 1 s 269-45).

PAYG withholding non-compliance tax

Directors and their associates who are entitled to a credit attributable to a payment made by a company that has failed to pay amounts withheld under PAYG withholding to the Commissioner, can be liable to pay a new PAYG withholding non-compliance tax. This tax effectively reverses any PAYG credit to which the director was entitled (¶26-710).

[FTR ¶977-900, ¶977-930]

¶25-570 Reinstatement of deregistered companies

The Commissioner may apply for a company that has been deregistered (whether by the company voluntarily, ASIC's initiative or court order) to be reinstated (*Corporations Act 2001*, s 601AH). On application, the court may make an order that ASIC reinstate the registration of the company if the court is satisfied that it is just that the company's registration be reinstated.

In *DFC of T v ASIC; in the matter of Anttila Enterprises*, the Commissioner was successful in having the company's registration reinstated to enable him to recover unpaid tax. Further, in *DFC of T; in the matter of James Hardie Australia Finance*, the company's registration was reinstated so that the Commissioner could issue a Pt IVA determination and an amended assessment.

Chapter 26 PAYG Withholding

Para

Para

ADMINISTRATION

Introduction

¶26-100 Introduction to PAYG withholding

The Pay As You Go (PAYG) withholding system is found in TAA Sch 1 Pt 2-5 (ss 10-1 to 20-80). Under PAYG withholding, a person who makes certain kinds of payments must withhold an amount from the payment, and then pay that amount to the Commissioner. PAYG also applies to non-cash benefits, and may also apply to certain payments of personal services income.

The obligation to withhold and pay an amount to the Commissioner is imposed on the entity making the withholding payment. An ''entity'' is an individual, a body corporate, a body politic, a partnership, any other unincorporated association or body of persons, a trust, a superannuation fund or an approved deposit fund.

An obligation otherwise imposed on a partnership is imposed on each partner and may be discharged by any of the partners. Partners are jointly and severally liable to pay an amount that would otherwise be payable by the partnership. Similarly, an obligation otherwise imposed on an unincorporated association is imposed on each member of the committee of management and may be discharged by any of those members.

Apart from determining status (¶26-500), PAYG withholding obligations are not affected by the consolidation regime (¶8-000) — withholding obligations of a subsidiary continue while the subsidiary entity is a member of the consolidated group.

[FTR ¶976-502]

Withholding Payments

¶26-120 Payments from which amounts must be withheld

Payments and other transactions subject to PAYG withholding are called ''withholding payments''; these are listed in TAA Sch 1 s 10-5(1). An amount is taken to have been ''paid'' when it is applied or dealt with in any way on behalf of the payee or as the payee directs (TAA Sch 1 s 11-5).

Payments excluded from PAYG

There is no requirement to withhold an amount from a payment (or part of a payment) if (TAA Sch 1 s 12-1):

- the whole of the payment is exempt income of the payee
- the whole of the payment is not assessable income and is not exempt income of the payee
- that part of the payment that is a living-away-from-home allowance benefit (¶35-460), or
- that part of the payment that is an expense payment benefit (¶35-330). However, if the expense payment benefit is a reimbursement of car expenses calculated by reference to the distance travelled, the benefit is not disregarded when working out how much to withhold. Those payments are exempt from FBT but are assessable income (¶10-060).

Payments to volunteers are generally not subject to PAYG withholding. However, an organisation may be required to withhold from a payment to a volunteer where the payment is for a supply of goods or services made in the course of an enterprise carried on by the volunteer, and the volunteer has not quoted an ABN (*Volunteers and tax* NAT 4612).

▶ Example 1

Tom volunteers at a charity and operates a bakery business. He volunteers to paint a community centre for the charity. Tom needs to purchase some additional material not supplied by the charity (which costs $80). The charity reimburses Tom $80 for the cost of the additional material. As Tom has not made the supply in the course of his enterprise as a baker, he does not need to quote his ABN to the charity and the charity will not be required to withhold from the payment to Tom.

Tom also agrees to make pies at his bakery for the charity's pie drive for the cost of the ingredients. The charity reimburses Tom $150 for the cost of the ingredients. As Tom has made a supply in the course of his enterprise, he will need to quote his ABN to the charity to avoid an amount being withheld from the payment. The rate of withholding in this situation is 47% of the total payment.

Most specific provision applies

If more than one provision in the PAYG withholding legislation requires a payer to withhold an amount from a single payment, only one amount is to be withheld. The general rule, subject to the exceptions in TAA Sch 1 s 12-5(2), is that the payer must apply the provision that is most specific to the circumstances of the payment (s 12-5).

Currency requirements

If a payment is made in a foreign currency, the amount withheld must be expressed in Australian dollars, using the exchange rate at the time the amount is required to be withheld (ITAA97 s 960-50(6), item 10). The functional currency rules (¶23-070) are not relevant to PAYG withholding (TD 2006/5).

[FTR ¶976-518 – ¶976-532]

¶26-130 How much to withhold

The amount required to be withheld from a withholding payment is worked out either under the withholding schedules or under the regulations (TAA Sch 1 s 15-10). There is an exception in relation to a natural resource payment where the amount to be withheld is calculated under the Commissioner's notice or certificate (¶26-270).

Regulations

Regulations may specify the amounts, formulae and procedures to be used for working out the amount required to be withheld by an entity from a withholding payment (TAA Sch 1 s 15-35). Regulations apply to withholding payments where a TFN or an ABN is not quoted or where dividends, interest, royalty or mining payments are made.

Withholding schedules

The Commissioner may make withholding schedules specifying the amounts, formulae and procedures to be used for working out the amount required to be withheld from a withholding payment (TAA Sch 1 ss 15-25; 15-30). Withholding schedules cover payments for work and services (including payments under voluntary agreements and labour hire arrangements), retirement and superannuation payments, annuities, benefits and compensation payments, certain payments made to or for foreign residents, non-cash benefits, alienated personal services payments and additional withholding amounts under an upwards variation declaration.

In working out how much to withhold under the withholding schedules, a payer may disregard any part of a payment that is paid, or is to be paid, as a donation to a deductible gift recipient at the direction of the payee under a regular planned giving arrangement, unless the payee advises the payer of a variation to the amount withheld (*Legislative*

Instrument F2016L01641). Similar arrangements apply for payees who make donations to a deductible gift recipient under an occasional workplace giving arrangement (*Legislative Instrument* F2011L02733).

The PAYG withholding schedules for 2020–21 are in *Legislative Instrument* F2020L01297; for 2019–20, see *Legislative Instrument* F2019L00894.

The Commissioner has also issued a tax table for back payments, commissions, bonuses and similar payments (*Legislative Instrument* F2012L01068). A further legislative instrument helps employers and other payers who have to withhold PAYG amounts in addition to the required amounts (*Legislative Instrument* F2014L01665). For the withholding schedules applicable to working holiday makers, see *Legislative Instrument* F2016L01964.

Withholding rates

Withholding payment	How much to withhold
Salary, wages, etc, of an employee Remuneration of a director or office holder Payment to a religious practitioner Return to work payment Payment under a labour hire arrangement Payment specified by regulations Superannuation income stream or annuity Superannuation lump sum or employment termination payment Unused leave payment Social security and other benefit payment Commonwealth education or training payment Compensation, sickness or accident payment Alienated personal services payment	The amount worked out under the withholding schedules, based on progressive rates. Where the payee has not provided a TFN declaration, 47% of the payment to be withheld. Note that a voluntary agreement may affect how much is required to be withheld.
Payment from an investment where the investor does not quote a TFN or, in some cases, an ABN (including becoming presently entitled to income of a unit trust)	47% of the payment, unless it is a partly franked dividend (in which case the 47% rate applies only to the unfranked portion). These rules, in TAR reg 35, are subject to special rules in TAR reg 28 where the investor is a minor.
Accrued gain in relation to a Pt VA investment	47% of the accrued gain.
Payment for a supply where no ABN is quoted	47% of the payment (TAR reg 38).
A distribution to a beneficiary of a closely held trust or a beneficiary of a closely held trust is beneficially entitled to a share of the trust income and no TFN is quoted	47% of the distribution or beneficiary's share (TAR regs 36; 37).
Dividend paid to an overseas person; dividend received for a foreign resident	30% of the dividend or as provided in a double tax agreement (TAR reg 40).

Withholding payment	How much to withhold
Interest paid to an overseas person; interest received for a foreign resident; interest derived through an overseas permanent establishment	10% of the interest (TAR reg 41).
Royalty paid to an overseas person; royalty received for a foreign resident	30% of the royalty or as provided in a double tax agreement (TAR reg 42).
Departing Australia superannuation payment	For tax free component — nil. For untaxed element of the taxable component — 45%. For a person who was a temporary working holiday maker — 65%. Remainder — 35%.
Departing Australia superannuation payment that is a roll-over superannuation benefit paid to a former temporary resident	For amount that is not an excess untaxed roll-over amount — 45%. For amount that is an excess untaxed roll-over amount — nil.
Payment to foreign residents	Amount specified in the regulations.
Payment under the Seasonal Labour Mobility Program	15%
Payment to working holiday makers	Up to a taxable income of $45,000 — 15%. Taxable income $45,001 and above — normal marginal rates.
Mining payment	4% of the payment (TAR reg 53).
Natural resource payment	The rate set by the Commissioner.
Excess untaxed roll-over amount	47% of the amount.
Distributions of withholding MIT income	Where the income is non-concessional MIT income (NCMI) and the transitional exclusions do not apply, or the recipient is not in an exchange of information jurisdiction — 30%. Where the recipient is in an exchange of information jurisdiction and the payment relates to payments from a clean building MIT — 10%. Where the recipient is in an exchange of information jurisdiction, the transitional exclusions from NCMI apply and the payment does not relate to a payment from a clean building MIT — 15%.
Voluntary agreement	Either the payee's instalment rate (¶27-450) as notified by the ATO or a flat rate of 20% (ATO Fact Sheet NAT 2772). If the instalment rate is greater than 20%, the payer must withhold at that higher rate. If the instalment rate is less than 20%, the payer must withhold at the rate of 20%, unless the payer and payee agree to use the instalment rate.
Employee share schemes where TFN not quoted	47% of the assessable discount.
Disposal of CGT assets by foreign residents	12.5% of the purchase price.

Withholding payment	How much to withhold
Withholding of GST from certain real estate supplies	1/11th of the contract price. If the margin scheme applies, 7% of the contract price (or such percentage as has been determined by legislative instrument).
FHSS released amounts	The amount of tax that the Commissioner estimates will be payable by the individual in relation to the assessable FHSS released amount for an income year or If the Commissioner is unable to make an estimate — 17% of the individual's assessable FHSS released amount for an income year.

Commissioner's power to vary amounts to be withheld

The Commissioner may vary the amount to be withheld (including to nil) for the purposes of meeting the special circumstances of a particular case (TAA Sch 1 s 15-15). ''Special circumstances'' usually only arise where the payee's final liability for all income types for that year does not justify the standard withholding rate. Taxpayers who wish to request a variation can do so using the form available from the ATO website (PAYG withholding variation application). For foreign entities, the Commissioner may use this discretion to reduce the rate of withholding to nil if the relevant income is not assessable in Australia, or to reduce the rate of withholding to a more appropriate level, where the prescribed withholding rates are excessive in comparison to the amount of tax which will ultimately be payable by the foreign entity (PS LA 2006/10).

However, the Commissioner cannot vary a withholding amount in relation to an investment where the investor does not quote a TFN (or an ABN), employee share schemes where an employee does not quote a TFN or an investor becomes presently entitled to income of a unit trust. This is because the rate of withholding for those events is designed as a sanction. Further, the Commissioner's power to vary the withholding rate will generally not be relevant to a natural resource payment because, in that case, the Commissioner sets the rate of withholding on a case-by-case basis and is able to take into account any special circumstances affecting the recipient as part of that process.

A variation must be made by a written notice given to each entity affected. In the case of a class of entities, a copy of the notice may be published in the *Commonwealth Gazette*. Details of current variations are discussed in the relevant withholding payment.

▶ Planning point

A salaried individual who is entitled to significant deductions during an income year (eg if he/she enters into a negatively geared investment) may ask the ATO to vary the PAYG withholding rate, thus increasing take-home pay. It would, of course, be an offence to knowingly or recklessly make a false or misleading statement in a variation request (¶29-700).

[FTR ¶976-785, ¶976-795]

¶26-150 PAYG: payments for work or services

Employees

An entity that pays salary, wages, commission, bonuses or allowances to an individual as an employee must withhold an amount from the payment (TAA Sch 1 s 12-35). The individual may be an employee of the payer or of another entity. ''Employee'' in the PAYG system has its ordinary meaning (TR 2005/16). Whether a person is an employee of another is a question of fact to be determined by examining the terms and circumstances of the contract between them, having regard to the key indicators expressed in the relevant case law. Withholding may be required, not only from payments of salary or wages made to an employee as such, but also where there is a constructive payment of salary or wages to an employee.

An employer will be required to withhold an amount from a contribution to the trustee of an employee remuneration trust (ERT) when the contribution constitutes a payment of salary, etc, that is not exempt income or non-assessable non-exempt income (TR 2018/7). A trustee of an ERT that makes a payment to an employee (or deals with an amount on the employee's behalf or as the employee directs) of salary, etc, that is not exempt income or non-assessable non-exempt income must also withhold an amount. Where an employee has entered into an employee benefits trust arrangement in which bonus units are issued to the employee that are considered to be salary or wages, the trustee must withhold an amount from the payment (TR 2010/6).

Resident employers that have employees working in a foreign country may have withholding obligations. Foreign earnings that do not meet any of the exemption conditions (¶10-860) are assessable income and subject to PAYG withholding.

A non-resident employer can be subject to PAYG withholding in respect of Australian resident employees working overseas (TD 2011/1). A non-resident employer who pays an Australian resident for work performed overseas is subject to withholding obligations if the non-resident employer has a sufficient connection with Australia, ie if the non-resident carries on an enterprise or income-producing activities in Australia and has a physical presence in Australia.

Employees at common law

For a payment to be made to an employee, there must be a contract *of service* (formerly referred to as a ''master/servant'' relationship) between the payer and the payee. This exists where one person contracts to perform work for another and is substantially subject to the control and direction of that person in the manner in which the work is done. This is the basis of the employer/employee relationship at common law, as distinct from a principal/independent contractor relationship involving a contract *for services*.

The following persons have been found to be employees:

- certain land salespersons paid by way of commission only and over whom no detailed control was exercised (*Barrett*)
- workmen, and a supervisor, paid by the proprietor of a painting and decorating business (*Glambed*)
- lecturers in the Weight Watchers organisation who were under contractual obligations as to the manner in which the lectures were to be conducted and the information that was to be imparted (*Narich*)
- interviewers engaged by a survey research company and given very detailed instructions on how to proceed (*Roy Morgan Research Centre*)
- delivery drivers working for the taxpayer that had contracted with another company to make its bakery deliveries (*Trustee for the Farant Family Trust*).

However, consultants who sold a company's cosmetic products at private houses under a party plan system were not employees (*Mary Kay Cosmetics*).

The distribution of profits of a business to employees on the basis of their worth to the company were ''wages'' for payroll tax purposes even though they were paid pursuant to directions in the will of the founder of the business (*George Adams Estate Trustees*).

An employer may seek to change the status of an employee to that of an independent contractor by including a clause to that effect in the contract of engagement. However, that clause will have no effect if it does not reflect the true nature of the relationship under the contract as a whole. If the terms of the relationship (such as leave entitlements and other employee benefits) are not changed, it is likely that the worker's status would remain that of an employee (TR 2005/16).

The requirement to withhold an amount under s 12-35 extends to the payment of a creditor dividend to a former employee of an employer company that is being wound up (*Applied Design*). This is because the dividend represents wages owing to the former employee. See also TR 2003/15.

Distinguishing between employee and independent contractor

As withholding under s 12-35 is not required from an amount paid to an independent contractor, it becomes crucial to distinguish between an employee and an independent contractor. An independent contractor undertakes to perform certain work for another person but is not, in the execution of the work, subject to the order and control of that person.

A contract undertaken to produce a given result will usually result in the contractor not being held to be an employee. On this basis, commission paid by a bookseller to an agent under a contract to sell books was held not to be subject to tax instalment deductions (*World Book (Australia)*).

Clothing industry outworkers, who used their own sewing machines at home to sew pre-cut garments from given materials in accordance with a sample, were held not to be employees as such (*Filsell v Top Notch Fashions*).

Taxi drivers were held not to be employees of taxi operators as the relationship between the operators and the drivers was one of bailment and not one of employment (*De Luxe Red and Yellow Cabs*).

Couriers engaged by a courier company were held not to be employees for superannuation guarantee purposes (where similar tests apply) (*Vabu*). However, in a subsequent negligence case, the High Court ruled that Vabu (the courier company) was vicariously liable for the negligence of one of its bicycle couriers because the relationship between the company and the courier was that of employer and employee (*Hollis v Vabu*). As a result, the Commissioner requires employers of bicycle couriers to withhold amounts from payments of salary or wages.

No withholding required from employees in certain circumstances

Withholding is not required from a payment to an employee where the payment is exempt income of the payee, or to the extent that the payment is a living-away-from-home allowance or expense payment benefit (¶26-120). Unless the Commissioner has given written approval not to withhold amounts, all other allowances should be added to normal earnings when calculating the amount to be withheld.

Company directors

An incorporated company that pays remuneration to an individual as a director or as a person who performs the duties of a director must withhold an amount from the payment (TAA Sch 1 s 12-40).

An unincorporated company that pays remuneration to a member of its committee of management must withhold an amount from the payment. This extends to a person who, although not on the committee, performs the duties of such a member.

Officeholders

An entity that pays salary, wages, commission, bonuses or allowances to an individual who is in the service of the Commonwealth, a state or a territory must withhold an amount (TAA Sch 1 s 12-45). This includes payments to Members of Parliament, the Defence Force, the police force and certain local governing bodies. TR 2002/21 provides guidance in determining whether a person holds an appointment, office or position under the Constitution or an Australian law and whether a person is otherwise in the service of the Commonwealth, a state or a territory. PAYG amounts do not have to be withheld from payments to members of a local governing body unless it has unanimously resolved that the remuneration of members be subject to withholding.

Religious practitioners

A withholding event (TAA Sch 1 s 12-47) covers payments received by religious practitioners for activities done in the pursuit of a vocation as a religious practitioner and as a member of a religious institution. All entities who make payments to religious practitioners in the course or furtherance of an enterprise are required to withhold. This includes an entity carrying on an enterprise as a wedding planner, which is required to withhold tax from payments made to religious practitioners for conducting marriage services (see further the ATO's document "Religious Practitioners").

Return to work payment

An entity that makes a payment to induce a person to resume working or to provide services must withhold an amount if the payment is included in the payee's assessable income (¶10-074) (TAA Sch 1 s 12-50).

Voluntary agreement to withhold

A voluntary agreement to withhold is a written agreement between a business (the payer) and a worker (the payee) to bring work payments into the PAYG withholding system (TAA Sch 1 s 12-55). The worker must be an individual who has an ABN and the payments must not be subject to any other PAYG withholding (eg they must not be payments arising from an employment relationship or under a labour hire arrangement).

A voluntary agreement must be a written agreement between the payer and payee that includes the following:

- the commencement date of the agreement
- the purpose of the payments (eg painting services)
- a statement that the payments made under the arrangement are subject to a voluntary agreement
- both the payer's and the payee's ABN, name and address
- the rate of withholding
- the signatures of both the payer and payee.

A voluntary agreement can cover a specific task or apply to successive arrangements between the payer and payee. Either party can end a voluntary agreement at any time by notifying the other in writing.

Labour hire arrangements

An entity that carries on a business that is wholly or partially concerned with arranging for persons to perform work or services directly for clients is liable to withhold an amount from payments it makes to an individual in the course of the enterprise (TAA Sch 1 s 12-60(1); *T T Lam and HT Ngo*). This also applies if the entity's activities include a business of that kind that is not merely incidental to its main activities. The client of the labour hire firm has no PAYG obligations in respect of payments made to the individual.

For withholding to apply, the payment must be made under an arrangement, the performance of which (in whole or in part) involves the performance of work or services by the individual directly for a client of the entity, or directly for a client of another entity.

▶ Example 1

Staffprovider Ltd keeps a database of skilled persons who are willing to provide their services to third parties. Staffprovider arranges with Corporate Pty Ltd to provide to it the services of a computer programmer in return for payment. Staffprovider arranges with Jane for her to undertake computer programming for Corporate. Staffprovider must withhold amounts from payments it makes to Jane under the arrangement with her.

Effectively, this means that an entity is only required to withhold if it is carrying on a labour hire business. It is not necessary that the labour hire activities be the sole business, or even the main business, of the payer. However, a merely incidental business is not sufficient to require withholding.

▶ Example 2

Ian is a solicitor who regularly briefs barristers to represent his clients. Briefing barristers is merely incidental to Ian's main activities as a solicitor, so he does not have to withhold amounts from payments he makes to barristers.

PAYG withholding is required where a chain of labour hire firms is involved, but not where payments are made by a contractor to a sub-contractor (because work is not being done "directly" for the client of the payer).

PAYG withholding only applies if the payment is made to an individual. This individual must not be an employee of either the client or the labour hire firm. However, there is no scope for quoting an ABN to avoid withholding and the priority rules state that the labour hire provisions are to be applied in priority to the ABN provisions. As a result, an individual carrying on business could consider incorporating so as to fall outside labour hire withholding (although operating through an entity raises the possibility that PAYG withholding will still apply because of the alienated personal services income provisions: ¶26-280).

Work of a prescribed kind

An entity that carries on an enterprise and which makes a payment to an individual in the course of the enterprise must withhold an amount if the payment is for work or services of a kind prescribed by the regulations (s 12-60(2)). This provides flexibility to extend the categories of payments for work or services that can be subject to withholding.

The following payments have been prescribed (TAR reg 27):

- payments for tutorial services provided to improve the education of indigenous people and that are financially supported by the Commonwealth
- payments for translation and interpretation services provided for the Translating and Interpreting Service conducted by the Department of Immigration and Multicultural and Indigenous Affairs
- payments made under a contract to an individual performing artist for performing in a promotional activity, unless the individual is engaged primarily because he/she is a sportsperson, and
- payments of green army allowance.

Withholding variations

The Commissioner has varied the amount required to be withheld to 20% of a payment made under a contract to an individual engaged as a performing artist to perform in a promotional activity where the individual has provided the payer with a TFN Declaration (¶26-350) quoting his/her TFN (*Legislative Instrument* F2016L01639).

The Commissioner has varied the amount of withholding from amounts paid: (i) as a wage to a participant in the Community Development Employment Projects (CDEP) program from the wages component of a grant made under the program; (ii) by way of a CDEP Scheme Participant Supplement; and (iii) as top up payments associated with these payments. The amount to be withheld is calculated using the rules set down in *PAYG withholding guide — a guide for payers participating in Community Development Employment Projects (CDEP)* (*Commonwealth Gazette* No GN 37, 15 September 2004).

The amount to be withheld from payments made by trustees of bankrupt estates and external administrators (as a result of the *Applied Designs case*) covered by TAA Sch 1 s 12-35 has been varied to an amount equal to 34.5% of the total payment (*Legislative Instrument* F2015L01528). The payments subject to the variation include amounts paid as:

- a back payment of wages, including unpaid amounts of leave already taken that were accrued prior to the date on which the administrator was appointed
- unused annual leave
- payment in lieu of notice
- redundancy pay
- long service leave.

A variation applies to payments made to individuals engaged in foreign service whose foreign earnings from that service are not exempt under s 23AG (¶10-860). The amount to be withheld is the amount which would normally be withheld in Australia from the Australian dollar equivalent of those earnings, under the relevant withholding tax table as if the earnings were not foreign earnings *less* the Australian dollar equivalent of the amount of tax to be withheld and paid to the foreign country in relation to the individual's foreign income tax liability for the provision of the service for the relevant period in that country. If the resulting withholding amount is nil or negative, there is no amount to withhold (*Legislative Instrument* F2019L01282.).

Variations to nil

The Commissioner has varied the withholding rate to nil for the following payments:

- amounts paid by an entity to an individual who is under 18 years of age and who has not provided the entity with a TFN declaration, where the amount paid by the paying entity does not exceed $350 weekly, $700 fortnightly or $1,517 monthly (*Legislative Instrument* F2012L00884)
- certain allowances (*Legislative Instrument* F2013L00521):
  - car expense payments up to amounts calculated using the approved cents per kilometre rate, to a maximum of 5,000 business kilometres (*Legislative Instrument* F2015L01047)
  - award transport payments for deductible transport expenses
  - laundry (not dry cleaning) allowance for deductible clothing up to the threshold amount (currently $150: ¶16-210)
  - award overtime meal allowances up to the reasonable allowances amount (published in an annual ATO ruling: ¶16-210), and
  - domestic or overseas travel allowance (excluding overseas accommodation allowance) involving an overnight absence from the payee's ordinary place of residence up to reasonable allowances amount (published in the annual ATO ruling: ¶16-210)

  where the payee is expected to incur expenses that may be able to be claimed as tax deduction at least equal to the amount of the allowance, and the allowance is shown separately in the accounting records of the payer
- payments made to an individual partner as a director of a company because of its connection with the partnership where the partner agrees to remit the director's fees to the partnership

- payments made by an entity that is not a religious institution to a religious practitioner (*Legislative Instrument* F2016L00107):
  - for work or services except for the performance of chaplaincy and/or counselling services, and
  - for chaplaincy and/or counselling services, where the payment does not exceed $100 (if paid weekly), $200 (if paid fortnightly), or $433 (if paid monthly)
- payments made by a religious institution to a religious practitioner for locum services performed for a period of not greater than 2 days in a quarter (*Legislative Instrument* F2016L00107)
- a payment for reimbursement of actual expenses incurred by a payee for work performed under a labour hire arrangement where the expenses may be deductible and can be substantiated (*Legislative Instrument* F2016L01580)
- remuneration to a company director, committee member or office holder where the recipient is required to remit those payments to another entity (*Legislative Instrument* F2016L00222), and
- allowance payments to Green Army Programme participants made by Green Army service providers.

[FTR ¶976-550 – ¶976-570]

¶26-180 PAYG: retirement payments

An entity that makes a payment to an individual must withhold an amount if the payment is:

- a superannuation income stream or annuity (TAA Sch 1 s 12-80) (¶14-120)
- a superannuation lump sum or employment termination payment (TAA Sch 1 s 12-85) (¶14-120, ¶14-600), or
- an unused leave payment (TAA Sch 1 s 12-90) (¶14-720, ¶14-730).

In *Bennett v Higgins*, an amount was held to be required to be withheld from an award of compensation for unfair dismissal made to a former employee as the award constituted an ETP.

In *Flack*, the AAT did not have jurisdiction to review the imposition of PAYG withholding on an ETP because the taxpayer could not validly object against the imposition of PAYG.

Withholding variations

Reduced rates of withholding apply for payments made from a taxed element of a superannuation income stream benefit to a payee who is 59 years of age and will turn 60 in the financial year in which the payment is made (*Legislative Instrument* F2018L00775). This is to ensure that superannuation beneficiaries are not subject to excessive withholding in the financial year in which they turn 60.

The Commissioner has also varied the amount to be withheld from payments made by trustees of bankrupt estates and external administrators covered by TAA Sch 1 ss 12-85 and 12-90 to an amount equal to 34.5% of the total payment (*Legislative Instrument* F2015L01528). The payments subject to the variation include amounts paid as:

- a back payment of wages, including unpaid amounts of leave already taken, that were accrued prior to the date on which the administrator was appointed
- unused annual leave

- payment in lieu of notice
- redundancy pay
- long service leave.

The withholding obligations arise as a consequence of the *Applied Designs case* (¶26-150).

Variations to nil

The Commissioner has varied the withholding rate to nil for payments made to recipients with a terminal medical condition of lump sum superannuation member benefits in circumstances where the payment will not be subject to income tax (*Legislative Instrument* F2008L01854).

No withholding is required for payments of non-assessable non-exempt income to superannuation beneficiaries that have not provided a tax file number (*Legislative Instrument* F2017L01280).

[FTR ¶976-580, ¶976-585]

¶26-190 PAYG: benefit and compensation payments

Social security

An entity that makes certain payments to an individual under the *Social Security Act 1991*, the *Veterans' Entitlements Act 1986*, the *Disability Services Act 1986* and the *Farm Household Support Act 1992* must withhold an amount (TAA Sch 1 s 12-110). PAYG amounts must also be withheld from CDEP Scheme Participant Supplement payments and parental leave pay (within the meaning given of the *Paid Parental Leave Act 2010*: ¶2-133). PAYG does not apply to so much of a payment as is exempt income of the individual (eg certain payments on the death of the taxpayer's partner).

Commonwealth education or training payments

An entity that makes a Commonwealth education or training payment (¶10-700) to an individual must withhold an amount (TAA Sch 1 s 12-115). PAYG withholding does not, however, apply to so much of the payment as is exempt income of the individual (eg isolated children payments).

Compensation payments

An entity that makes a payment of compensation, or sickness or accident pay, to an individual must withhold an amount if the payment is:

- made because of incapacity for work
- calculated at a periodical rate, and
- not a payment made under an insurance policy to the policy owner (TAA Sch 1 s 12-120).

Variations to nil

The Commissioner has varied the withholding rate to nil for the following payments:

- a payment by an insurer to an entity in settlement of a claim under an insurance policy
- a payment by an entity operating a statutory compensation scheme to another entity in settlement of a claim for compensation under the scheme, and
- a payment by an entity operating a compulsory third party scheme to another entity in settlement of a claim for compensation under that scheme (*Legislative Instrument* F2016L00433).

[FTR ¶976-590 – ¶976-594]

¶26-200 PAYG: investments where TFN or ABN not quoted

If an investor fails to quote a TFN (¶33-030), or an ABN (¶33-130) in the case of a business, to the investment body in relation to an investment, the investment body is required to withhold an amount, at the top marginal rate plus Medicare, from income on the investment, meaning that the withholding rate is 47%.

Part VA investments where a payment is made

An investment body that makes a payment to another entity in respect of an ITAA36 Pt VA investment must withhold an amount if:

- all or some of the payment is ordinary or statutory income of the entity, and
- the entity did not quote its TFN by the required time (TAA Sch 1 s 12-140(1)). For transferable investments (eg shares or units in a unit trust), this is the time the entity had to be registered with the investment body as the investor to be entitled to the payment. For non-transferable investments, it is the time the payment became payable.

For the meaning of ‘‘Pt VA investment’’, see ¶33-030.

If an investment body makes a payment in respect of an eligible deferred interest investment (¶23-320) and no TFN has been quoted, withholding is required only: (a) to the extent that the payment consists of a periodic interest payment; or (b) if the payment became payable at the end of the term of the investment, to the extent of the accrual amount included in the investor's assessable income for the income year (TAA Sch 1 s 12-150). TFN withholding tax may be payable on the amount not subject to PAYG withholding (see below).

Part VA investments — TFN withholding tax on accrued gains

Subdivision 14-B of TAA Sch 1 contains the TFN withholding arrangements that apply where there has been an accrued gain in relation to a Pt VA investment. TFN withholding tax is payable if:

- an amount (the accrued gain) is included in the investor's assessable income for an income year under ITAA36 s 159GQ (¶23-320)
- the investment is an interest-bearing account or interest-bearing deposit with a financial institution, or a non-transferable loan to a government body or to a body corporate
- the term of the investment does not end during the income year, and
- s 12-140 would have required the investment body to withhold an amount if the investment body had made a payment equal to the accrued gain to the investor at the end of the income year. This is the amount of TFN withholding tax payable in relation to the accrued gain.

The adoption of a substituted accounting period (¶9-010) is disregarded for the purposes of TFN withholding tax.

Unit trusts

If the investment is units in a unit trust, the paying entity must withhold an amount from a payment it makes in respect of the investment if the payment is income to the payee and no TFN has been quoted (s 12-140(2)).

In addition, an entity must withhold an amount when an investor becomes presently entitled to a share of income of the trust before any of that share is paid (TAA Sch 1 s 12-145). The amount to be withheld is the amount that would be withheld if the share were paid to the investor. If an amount is withheld on present entitlement, no amount is to be withheld from a subsequent payment of that share to the investor.

Withholding from closely held trusts

The TFN withholding arrangements extend to closely held trusts, including family trusts (ss 12-175 to 12-185).

The withholding rules apply if the trustee of a resident trust estate that is a closely held trust (within the meaning of ITAA36 s 102UC: ¶6-275) makes a distribution to a beneficiary during the income year and some or all of the distribution is from the ordinary or statutory income of the trust. The beneficiary must be an Australian resident, not an exempt entity and not under a legal disability (eg minors).

The trustee must withhold an amount from the distribution if the following conditions are met:

- the beneficiary did not quote a tax file number to the trustee before the distribution time
- the trustee is not liable to pay tax under ITAA36 s 98 in connection with the distribution
- the trustee is not required to make a correct TB statement (¶6-275) in connection with the distribution, and
- family trust distribution tax (¶6-268) is not payable in connection with the distribution.

Similar rules apply if the beneficiary becomes presently entitled to a share of the net income of the trust.

The ATO has provided a guide to the withholding rules at *TFN withholding for closely held trusts*.

The TFN withholding rate to be used for working out how much of a distribution or present entitlement amount is to be withheld is 47% (TAR regs 36; 37). Only amounts above $120 are subject to withholding, apportioned for payments for part of an income year (TAR reg 30).

Certain classes of trusts are excluded from the operation of TFN withholding:

- discretionary mutual funds (ie within the meaning of the *Financial Sector (Collection of Data) Act 2001* or a fund that provides professional indemnity insurance to a legal practitioner)
- employee share trusts for employee share schemes (¶12-630), and
- law practice trusts (ie a trust created and maintained in connection with the provision of legal services by a duly qualified legal practitioner or the deposit of money to a solicitor and regulated by a state or territory law (TAR reg 29)).

PAYG withholding exceptions

An investment body is not required to withhold an amount from a payment to another entity in respect of a Pt VA investment in 4 cases.

(1) *Quotation of ABN.* Instead of quoting a TFN, certain investors can quote an ABN (TAA Sch 1 s 12-155). This option is only available to an entity that made the investment in the course of an enterprise.

▶ Example

Simone, a sole trader, may quote her ABN in relation to her business bank accounts (ie where the income from the investment will be properly returned as part of business receipts) but not in relation to her personal accounts.

(2) *Exemption from quoting TFN.* Withholding is not required if an exemption from quoting a TFN has applied to the investor entity but no longer applies when the payment is made, and the investment body has not been informed that the exemption no longer applies (TAA Sch 1 s 12-160).

(3) *Fully franked dividends.* No amount need be withheld on the payment of fully franked dividends from a public company (¶3-015) (TAA Sch 1 s 12-165).

(4) *Payment below threshold.* No amount need be withheld if the payment is below the amount worked out under the regulations (TAA Sch 1 s 12-170). TAR reg 28 sets out the threshold amounts (generally, $420 for a person aged under 16 and $120 in other cases) below which PAYG withholding does not apply.

Where an adult opens an interest bearing account ''in trust'' for a child and no TFN is quoted, the $120 threshold will apply because the account is deemed to belong to the trustee. If it is a formal trust account (ie a trust relationship that is legally acknowledged), the trust's TFN should be quoted to avoid amounts being withheld. If it is an informal trust account, the informal trustee's personal TFN should be quoted to avoid amounts being withheld.

[FTR ¶976-600 – ¶976-630, ¶976-760 – ¶976-765]

¶26-220 PAYG: payments for a supply

A payer who makes a payment to an entity for a supply that the entity has made, or proposes to make, to the payer in the course of an enterprise carried on in Australia must withhold an amount if none of the following exceptions applies (TAA Sch 1 s 12-190(1)). ''Supply'' has the same meaning as for GST purposes (¶34-100). The meaning of an entity carrying on an enterprise is discussed in MT 2006/1.

First exception: ABN correctly quoted

The payer does not have to withhold an amount if, when the payment is made, the entity has given the payer an invoice that relates to the supply and that quotes the entity's ABN. Further, no withholding is required if, when the payment is made, the payer has some other document relating to the supply on which the entity's ABN is quoted (s 12-190(2)). ''Some other document'' includes a letterhead, order form, business card provided in relation to a supply, a record of an over-the-telephone quotation, email or internet record (TR 2002/9). However, it is not sufficient to receive another document *after* the payment has been made that quotes, or purports to quote, the supplier's ABN (*Queensland Harvesters Pty Ltd*).

An ABN may be quoted in writing, in an electronic document, over the telephone or on an internet site (TR 2002/9). An oral quotation needs to be recorded on a document (paper or electronic) held by the payer. In all cases, the ABN must be quoted before or at the time payment is made. A list of ''approved suppliers'' that contains the suppliers' ABNs is sufficiently connected with a later supply where it is reasonably calculated to cover future supplies of that nature. For periodic supplies, the payer should check the list with suppliers at least once a year.

Where a supply is made through an agent, the payer need not withhold from the payment if the agent has given the payer an invoice that relates to the supply and gives the agent's ABN, or the payer has some other document relating to the supply on which the agent's ABN is quoted (s 12-190(2A)).

Second exception: payer has no reason to believe the ABN is incorrectly quoted

The payer may have an invoice or document that purports to quote an entity's ABN but the entity does not have an ABN or the invoice or document does not, in fact, quote the entity's ABN. In this case, the payer need not withhold an amount if there are no reasonable grounds to believe that the entity does not have an ABN, or that the invoice or document does not quote the entity's ABN (s 12-190(3)). A payer is not required to check the validity of an ABN on the Australian Business Register (TR 2002/9). An example of ''reasonable grounds'' would be where a supplier uses different names on different occasions.

Similarly, a payer is not required to withhold where an ABN is quoted by an agent that does not in fact have an ABN but the payer has no grounds to believe that the ABN quoted is invalid (s 12-190(3A)).

Third exception: no need to quote ABN

A payer does not have to withhold an amount if any of the following apply (s 12-190(4)).

- The payer makes the payment for a supply that is not ''in the course or furtherance of an enterprise'' carried on in Australia by the payer — this means withholding is not required from payments that are wholly of a private or domestic nature for the payer, and payments by an employer or labour hire worker relating to their work in that capacity.

  This exception applies where residential premises are used by the tenant for private or domestic purposes. If the tenant uses the premises partly for business purposes (eg as a beauty salon), PAYG applies if the *main* use is for business, rather than private, purposes (GSTD 2000/9).

- The payment (disregarding the GST component) does not exceed $75 (A New Tax System (Goods and Services Tax) Regulations 2019, s 29-80.01) or the sum of all the payments made to the entity for the supply does not exceed $75.

- The supply is made in the course of an activity done as a member of a local governing body.

- The supply is wholly input taxed (¶34-100).

Fourth exception: investments

A payer need not withhold an amount under s 12-190 if the payment is subject to PAYG withholding for investments where no TFN has been quoted, or would have been subject to withholding had the investor not quoted a TFN or ABN or had an exemption not applied (¶26-200) (s 12-190(5)). No amount needs to be withheld from an employment termination payment or a superannuation lump sum where no TFN declaration is made if the payment is non-assessable non-exempt income under s 12-1(1A) (¶26-120).

Fifth exception: private or domestic transactions

A payer need not withhold an amount from a payment for a supply if the payee is an individual and the supply is made in the course of a private recreational pursuit or hobby, or is wholly of a private or domestic nature for the *payee*. The payee must give the payer a written statement to that effect and the payer must have no reasonable grounds to believe that the statement is false or misleading in a material way (s 12-190(6)).

Variations to nil

The Commissioner has varied the withholding rate to nil for the following payments:

- a payment made to an individual under the age of 18 that does not exceed $120 per week where the supplier does not quote an ABN to the payer (TD 2000/48)

- a payment to an indigenous artist for artistic works where the artist qualifies for a special Zone A rebate and does not quote an ABN (*Legislative Instrument* F2016L00358)

- a payment to a body corporate of a residential or commercial property made by a member of the body corporate in respect of levies, access fees to inspect accounts and fees for the collection of rents from the common property (TD 2000/49; *Legislative Instrument* F2016L01640)
- a payment for financial supplies where no ABN is quoted, and
- payments covered by s 12-190 that relate to entertainment activities carried on in Australia, and are made to support staff (TAR reg 32) who are residents of a country with which Australia has an international tax agreement and present in Australia for a period not exceeding 183 days in the financial year (*Legislative Instrument* F2019L00407).

[FTR ¶976-635]

¶26-250 PAYG: dividend, interest and royalty payments

A payer who makes a dividend, interest or royalty payment to an "overseas person" or an entity that receives such a payment on behalf of a non-resident must withhold an amount.

In the relation to dividends, the PAYG withholding requirements apply to:

- part of a dividend in the same way they apply to a whole dividend
- a distribution by a liquidator to the extent that it is treated as a dividend (¶4-300). The liquidator is treated as if it were the company.

"Interest" refers to an amount:

- in the nature of interest (eg a discount on a security), and
- to the extent that it could reasonably be regarded as being in substitution for interest (eg a lump sum instead of interest payments).

The meaning of "royalty" is discussed at ¶10-640.

No deduction will be allowed for an amount of interest or royalty unless the withholding obligations have been fulfilled (ITAA97 s 26-25).

Payment to an overseas person

A resident company that pays a dividend to a shareholder who has an address outside Australia must withhold an amount (TAA Sch 1 s 12-210). The address of the shareholder is determined according to the register of the company's members. If shares are held by more than one entity and one of the entities has an address outside Australia, the paying company must also withhold an amount.

An entity that pays interest or a royalty to an entity must withhold an amount if the recipient has an address outside Australia (TAA Sch 1 ss 12-245; 12-280). The recipient's address is to be determined according to any record in the payer's possession, or that which is kept or maintained on the payer's behalf, about the transaction to which the interest or royalty relates. Where s 12-280 requires an entity to withhold an amount from a payment that it makes to a non-resident in relation to royalties, the withholding is based on the GST inclusive amount of the payment (ID 2010/89).

The payer must also withhold an amount from a dividend, interest or royalty if it is authorised to pay it at a place outside Australia.

Receiving a payment for a non-resident

An entity in Australia (or an Australian government agency) that receives a dividend, interest or royalty from a resident must withhold an amount if a foreign resident is entitled to:

- receive the dividend, interest or royalty (or part of it) from the entity
- receive the amount of the dividend, interest or royalty (or part of it) from the entity, or
- have the entity credit it with the dividend, interest or royalty (or the amount of it or part of it) or otherwise deal with it on its behalf or as it directs (TAA Sch 1 ss 12-215; 12-250; 12-285).

The entity must withhold the amount immediately after receiving the payment if the foreign resident is entitled at that time to receive the payment, or, if the foreign resident becomes entitled to receive the payment at a later time, immediately after that time. An Australian entity acting as agent for a non-resident licensor is required, under s 12-285, to withhold tax from royalty payments it receives in Australia on behalf of the non-resident licensor (ID 2006/305).

Overseas permanent establishment

An Australian resident entity (or an Australian government agency) that derives interest, payable in Australia, in carrying on business in a foreign country through a permanent establishment in that country must notify the payer of those facts (TAA Sch 1 s 12-260). This also applies if interest is payable to entities, at least one of whom is an Australian resident, that derive the interest through an overseas permanent establishment.

The notice must be in writing and given before the payer and payee enter into the transaction in relation to which the interest is payable, or within one month afterwards. Immediately after giving the notice, the entities must also notify the Commissioner of the particulars of the transaction, including the dates on which interest is payable and the day when the notice was given to the payer. A payer who receives such a notice must withhold an amount from the interest payment (TAA Sch 1 s 12-255).

Interaction with withholding tax

A payer does not have to withhold an amount from a dividend, interest or royalty if no withholding tax is payable in respect of it under ITAA36 s 128B (¶22-010, ¶22-020, ¶22-030). Further, a payer does not have to withhold more than the withholding tax payable (reduced by each amount already withheld under the PAYG system) (TAA Sch 1 s 12-300).

[FTR ¶976-650, ¶976-680]

¶26-260 PAYG: departing Australia superannuation payments

An entity (usually a superannuation fund) must withhold an amount from a departing Australia superannuation payment it pays to an entity (TAA Sch 1 s 12-305). A "departing Australia superannuation payment" is defined in ITAA97 s 301-170 (¶14-390). However, an entity does not have to withhold an amount if no withholding tax is payable in respect of the departing Australia superannuation payment; further, an entity is not required to withhold more than the withholding tax payable in respect of such a payment (TAA Sch 1 s 12-310). ITAA97 s 301-175 deals with the withholding tax liability (¶14-390).

[FTR ¶976-690]

¶26-262 PAYG: excess untaxed roll-over amount

An entity must withhold an amount from an excess untaxed roll-over amount it pays to an entity (TAA Sch 1 s 12-312). An "excess untaxed roll-over amount" is an amount that may form part of a roll-over superannuation benefit that includes an element untaxed in the fund (ITAA97 s 306-15). However, no amount is required to be withheld if no withholding tax is payable on the amount. Further, only the amount of withholding tax payable on the amount is required to be withheld, (reduced by each amount already withheld from the excess untaxed roll-over amount under PAYG withholding). Section 306-15 deals with liability to this form of withholding tax (¶14-450).

[FTR ¶976-693]

¶26-265 PAYG: payments to foreign residents

TAA Sch 1 ss 12-315 to 12-319 requires that an entity making a payment to a foreign resident, or receiving a payment for a foreign resident, must withhold an amount in certain situations.

In order for a payment *made* to a foreign resident to be subject to PAYG withholding, the following conditions must be satisfied:

- the payment must have been made by the entity in the course of carrying on an enterprise
- the recipient must be a foreign resident or, where the payer does not have reasonable grounds to believe that the recipient is an Australian resident, the recipient has a foreign address or has authorised payment to a place outside Australia
- the payment must be of a type prescribed by regulations (see below). Such regulations can only apply to payments of a type that could reasonably be related to assessable income of foreign residents. This means that, if a payment is exempt income for all foreign residents, it will not be prescribed by regulation. However, withholding could be required from a payment that is exempt for a particular foreign resident where it would not necessarily be exempt for other foreign residents.

In order for an entity that *receives* a payment on behalf of a foreign resident to be required to withhold an amount from that payment, the following conditions must be satisfied:

- the recipient (the intermediary) is a person in Australia or an Australian government agency
- a foreign resident is entitled to receive the payment (or a part of it) from the intermediary or have the intermediary deal with the payment on behalf of the foreign resident
- the person for whom the intermediary received the payment (the likely foreign resident) must be a foreign resident or, where the intermediary does not have reasonable grounds to believe that the likely foreign resident is an Australian resident, the likely foreign resident has a foreign address or has authorised payment to a place outside Australia
- the payment must be of a type prescribed by regulations (see below). In this regard, the payment must be of a type that could reasonably be related to assessable income of foreign residents (ie withholding could be required from a payment that is exempt for a particular foreign resident where it would not necessarily be exempt for other foreign residents).

In *both* cases:

- the payment must not be:
  - a dividend, interest or royalty
  - a departing Australia superannuation payment
  - a natural resource payment

  - a mining payment, or
  - a fund payment from a managed investment trust

  (as these payments are covered by other PAYG withholding requirements)

- the recipient must not have been granted an exemption by the Commissioner (see below).

The Commissioner may grant an exemption from withholding by notice where the Commissioner is satisfied that the foreign resident has an established compliance history and that he/she/it is likely to continue to comply with his/her/its taxation obligations. This exemption applies for the specific period stated in the exemption notice. The Commissioner's power to vary the amount withheld under TAA Sch 1 s 15-15 may be exercised in favour of a foreign resident where the relevant income is not assessable in Australia, or to reduce the rate of withholding to a more appropriate level, where the prescribed withholding rates are excessive in comparison to the amount of tax which will ultimately be payable by the foreign entity (PS LA 2006/10).

This withholding obligation applies to a payment *made* to a partnership or joint venture if one or more of the partners or venturers is a foreign resident. However, where a payment is *received* on behalf of such a partnership or joint venture, the obligation to withhold only extends to those partners or venturers who are foreign residents. Distributions from trusts to foreign residents are subject to ITAA36 s 98(3) and (4) (¶6-220).

All other withholding obligations have priority over this withholding obligation, except for voluntary agreement withholding (which only applies if no other withholding obligation applies).

The foreign resident withholding rules extend to alienated personal services payments (¶26-280) (TAA Sch 1 s 12-7). Amounts must be withheld from payments that are included in an individual's assessable income under ITAA97 Div 86 (¶30-600) and payments which are specified under the regulations.

Prescribed foreign resident withholding

The following foreign resident withholding obligations are prescribed in TAR regs 31, 32 and 33. Withholding is required from:

- payments for operating or promoting a casino junket tour. Withholding is required at a rate of 3%
- payments for entertainment and sports activities, including payments to support staff. Withholding is required at individual non-resident marginal tax rates or the company tax rate, as appropriate
- payments for the construction, installation and upgrading of buildings, plant and fixtures, and related activities. Withholding is required at a rate of 5%. See further TR 2006/12.

Any amount to be withheld is to be reduced by any amount already withheld (TAR reg 48).

Variation to nil

The Commissioner has varied the withholding rate to nil for the following payments:

- payments that relate to entertainment activities carried on in Australia made to support staff who are residents of a country with which Australia has an international tax agreement and who are present in Australia for a period not exceeding 183 days in the financial year (*Legislative Instrument* F2007L03532), and

- payments to entertainers and sportspersons who are USA residents for entertainment and sports activities carried on in Australia where the combined payments from such activities do not exceed US $10,000 (or its Australian dollar equivalent) for the relevant income year (*Legislative Instrument* F2014L00379).

[FTR ¶976-695 – ¶976-697]

¶26-267 PAYG: distributions of withholding MIT income

Withholding also applies to certain distributions (''fund payments'') from ''withholding MITs'' (Subdiv 12-H). Liability to this withholding tax is imposed under ITAA97 Div 840 (¶22-045). If there is no underlying liability to managed investment trust withholding tax, then there is no obligation to withhold.

Withholding MIT

A trust is a ''withholding MIT'' (s 12-383) if it is a managed investment trust (within the meaning in ITAA97 s 275-10(1)(a) or (2): see ¶12-660) and a substantial proportion of the investment management activities carried out by the trust in relation to certain assets are carried out in Australia throughout the income year. The relevant assets are all of the trust's assets that are, at any time in the income year:

- situated in Australia
- taxable Australian property (¶12-725), or
- shares, units or other interests listed on an approved Australian stock exchange.

Further, an AMIT (¶26-268) which only makes deemed payments and not cash distributions can be a withholding MIT if the other requirements are satisfied.

Fund payment

A fund payment is defined in TAA Sch 1 s 12-405 and is basically a component of a payment made by the trustee of a withholding MIT that, in effect, represents a distribution of the net income of the withholding MIT, disregarding:

- dividend, interest or royalty income subject to PAYG withholding
- capital gains and losses from a capital gains tax asset that is not taxable Australian property
- amounts that are not from an Australian source, and
- deductions relating to any of those amounts.

A fund payment must be made during the income year, within 3 months after the income year or within a longer period if agreed to by the Commissioner (but not exceeding 6 months from the end of the income year).

Section 12-405 generally applies to a trust that is not an AMIT; the meaning of ''fund payment'' for AMITs is contained in TAA Sch 1 s 12A-110 (¶26-268).

When withholding is required

For withholding to apply, the recipient of the fund payment must have a relevant connection outside Australia. This will occur if either: (i) according to any record in the payer's possession, the recipient has an address outside Australia; or (ii) the payer is authorised to make payment at a place outside Australia. This connection does not exist in relation to payments made to a recipient that carried on business in Australia at or through an Australian permanent establishment and the payment is associated with that establishment.

If the payer does not have an obligation to withhold at that time, it may have an obligation to give a notice to the recipient or make certain information available on a website in respect of the payment. The obligation to give a notice or make information available on a website will continue through a chain of entities until the obligation to withhold is triggered.

Where a foreign resident invests in a withholding MIT through an interposed entity (a custodian), the custodian is required to withhold from a payment it makes where:

- the payment is reasonably attributable to a payment received by the custodian that was covered by a notice or information that was made available on a website, and
- the recipient of the payment has a relevant connection outside Australia.

Withholding is not required in respect of a payment made by a corporate custodian unless the custodian is acting in the capacity of a trustee or as an agent for a principal. For this purpose, both a public trading trust and a corporate unit trust is a company.

A non-custodian is required to withhold an amount where:

- the non-custodian receives a payment, all or part of which is covered by a notice or information made available on a website, and
- a foreign resident is, or becomes entitled to, an amount attributable to the payment received by the non-custodian.

Amount to be withheld

If the place, address or country of residence of the recipient is in a jurisdiction with which Australia has effective exchange of information on tax matters (¶22-165), withholding is required at the rate of:

1. 30% for fund payments to the extent that they are attributable to non-concessional MIT income (see below), or
2. If 1 does not apply, 10% for fund payments to the extent that they are, or are attributable to, fund payments from a clean building MIT (see below), or
3. If 1 and 2 do not apply, 15%.

If the place, address or country of residence of the recipient is ***not*** in a jurisdiction with which Australia has effective exchange of information on tax matters, withholding is required at the rate of 30%.

Information exchange countries are specified in TAR reg 34.

Where a non-custodian is a trust that is required to withhold an amount and that trust has a different year end to the withholding MIT to which the payment relates, then the amount that is required to be withheld is calculated by reference to the withholding rate that corresponds to the income year of the withholding MIT to which the fund payment relates, not the resident trust's income year in which the beneficiary's entitlement arises (ID 2013/63).

Withholding from clean building MITs

A final withholding tax at the rate of 10% applies to fund payments from eligible clean building MITs that are made to foreign residents in information exchange countries. An eligible clean building MIT is a withholding MIT that holds one or more clean buildings (TAA Sch 1 ss 12-425; 12-430). These are new energy efficient buildings for which construction began on or after 1 July 2012 and must be office buildings, hotels or shopping centres, or a building consisting of a combination of these. The building must meet and maintain at least a 5-star Green Star rating as certified by the Green Building Council of Australia or a 5.5-star energy rating as accredited by the National Australian Built Environment Rating System. Land on which the clean building is a fixture is also included as a clean building. A clean building MIT cannot derive assessable income from any taxable Australian property other than its clean buildings and assets ‘‘reasonably incidental to’’ those clean buildings.

Foreign pension funds and MIT withholding tax

A foreign pension fund that receives a fund payment as a trustee will be taken to be a beneficiary in its own right and therefore is liable to tax at the MIT withholding tax rate as determined by the residency of the fund (ITAA97 s 840-805(4A), (4B), (4C)).

Non-concessional MIT income

An amount of a fund payment is non-concessional MIT income if it is attributable to income that is:

- MIT cross staple arrangement income
- MIT trading trust income
- MIT agricultural income, or
- MIT residential housing income (TAA Sch 1 ss 12-435, 12-436).

For members who are residents of an exchange of information country, to the extent that the fund payment is attributable to non-concessional MIT income, the rate of MIT withholding tax will be 30%. Transitional rules apply to fund payments that are attributable to existing investments with the effect that the current MIT withholding tax rate of 15% will continue to apply. Non-concessional MIT income is further discussed in *Law Companion Ruling* LCR 2020/2.

MITs can invest in affordable housing for income years commencing on or after 1 July 2017. MIT distributions that are attributable to investments in residential housing that are *not* used to provide affordable housing are non-concessional MIT income.

Proposed non-resident withholding taxes for collective investment vehicles

The government has released a draft Bill to implement the withholding arrangements that will apply to the Corporate Collective Investment Vehicle (CCIV) regime (Treasury Laws Amendment (Corporate Collective Investment Vehicle) Bill 2018: Tax Treatment). See further ¶6-410.

[FTR ¶976-710ff]

¶26-268 PAYG: distributions to foreign residents from attribution MITs

Certain managed investment trusts (MITs) are governed by a special tax system (¶6-405). As it applies to PAYG withholding, the system basically draws a distinction between those MITs that are covered by the system (attribution MITs or AMITs) and those that are not.

For those MITs that are not AMITs, the existing rules continue to apply. In addition, the current dividend, interest and royalty withholding provisions (¶27-250), and the MIT withholding provisions (¶26-267), continue to apply to relevant cash payments made by an AMIT to a foreign resident prior to the time that a deemed payment is made.

Members of AMITs are taxed on amounts attributed to them. Under the attribution model, the amount included in the assessable income of a member is based on the amount of the ‘‘determined trust component’’ that has been attributed to the member by an AMIT. This amount is the ‘‘taxable member component’’ and is disclosed in the AMMA statement that is given to the member by the AMIT. The AMMA statement categorises each type of income into separate ‘‘AMIT characters’’. These concepts are discussed further at ¶6-400.

To impose PAYG withholding on these deemed payments, Div 12A modifies the operation of Subdiv 12-F (in relation to dividends, interest and royalty payments to overseas persons) and Subdiv 12-H (in relation to fund payments to overseas persons).

For AMITs, the operation of the dividend, interest and royalty withholding provisions is modified so that they apply to a taxable member component of a dividend, interest or royalty income AMIT character that is attributed to a member by an AMIT as shown on an AMMA statement. The operation of the MIT withholding provisions is also modified so that a fund payment includes a relevant taxable member component that is attributed to a member by an AMIT as shown on an AMMA statement.

The AMIT must pay to the Commissioner an amount that is equal to the amount that the trustee would have had to withhold if the deemed payment was an actual payment. In addition, if an AMIT attributes a taxable member component to a member that is a custodian and does not pay the custodian an amount of cash that is sufficient to cover the custodian's PAYG withholding obligation in relation to the deemed payment, the custodian can transfer the remaining part of the obligation back to the AMIT.

A member of an AMIT is liable to withholding tax on a relevant taxable member component that is attributed to the member by an AMIT. However, the member can reduce his/her/its liability to withholding tax by the amount that is withheld or paid by an AMIT under the PAYG withholding regime in respect of the attributed amount.

LCR 2015/12 explains how the withholding rules for dividends, interest and royalties apply to an AMIT and its members. LCR 2015/13 explains changes that have been made to the MIT withholding rules applying to fund payments.

¶26-269 PAYG: foreign resident CGT withholding

A 12.5% non-final withholding tax obligation applies to the purchaser of certain Australian real property and related interests where the property is acquired from a foreign resident vendor.

TAA Sch 1 Subdiv 14-D applies to the acquisition of an asset that is:

- taxable Australian real property, ie TARP (¶12-725)
- an indirect Australian real property interest (¶12-725), or
- an option or right to acquire such property or interest. LCR 2016/7 contains further guidance where options are involved.

Financial benefits obtained under CGT look-through earnout rights (¶11-675) are also subject to withholding.

The obligation arises where any vendor of the relevant property is a foreign resident. It consists of a requirement to withhold 12.5% of the first element of the cost base of the asset (¶11-550), ignoring any financial benefits under earnout rights, and paying that amount to the Commissioner at the time of acquisition, ie at settlement. LCR 2016/6 explains how to work out the amount to be paid to the Commissioner under Subdiv 14-D.

The administrative penalties in TAA Sch 1 ss 16-30 and 16-35 (¶29-300) apply where there is a failure to withhold.

There is no obligation to withhold in these situations:

- transactions involving taxable Australian real property and certain indirect Australian real property interests valued at less than $750,000
- a transaction that is conducted through an approved stock exchange (ITAR Sch 5) or a crossing system
- an arrangement that is already subject to an existing withholding obligation
- a securities lending arrangement, and
- transactions involving vendors who are subject to formal insolvency or bankruptcy proceedings.

Where the asset is TARP or a company title interest, the vendor is *assumed* to be a foreign resident, unless the vendor obtains a clearance certificate from the Commissioner that he/she/it is a resident. Clearance certificates should be provided by the vendor to the purchaser before settlement to ensure that no withholding is made.

For an indirect Australian real property interest (other than a company title interest) and for an option or right to acquire TARP or an indirect Australian real property interest (other than a company title interest), the obligation to withhold arises if the purchaser knows or reasonably believes the vendor to be a foreign resident. For these interests, the vendor may make a declaration to the effect that he/she/it is a resident and this should be provided to the purchaser before settlement. There are, however, penalties for making false or misleading declarations.

For all relevant Australian property interests and related interests, the vendor or the purchaser may apply for a variation of the amount of the withholding obligation. Where the vendor applies for a variation, the Commissioner's notice of variation should be provided to the purchaser before settlement to ensure the reduced withholding rate applies. Reasons for seeking a variation include: the asset is a pre-CGT asset; a CGT roll-over or exemption is claimed; and the liability is less than 12.5% of the proceeds and any non-monetary consideration. The Commissioner's variation power is further explained in LCR 2016/5.

Where there is a sale of Australian property by multiple vendors and one of them is an Australian resident and at least one is a foreign resident, *Legislative Instrument* F2016L01123 ensures that the PAYG amount is based on the proportion of the acquisition cost and the market value of the financial benefit attributable to foreign resident entities.

ATO administrative arrangements

Three online forms are available on the ATO website:

- a clearance certificate application for Australian residents
- a variation application for foreign residents and other parties, and
- purchaser payment notification. This needs to be completed when withholding is required.

In straightforward cases where the ATO has all the required information, it is expected that clearance certificates will be provided within days of being submitted. Where there are data irregularities or exceptions, the clearance certificates will be provided within 14–28 days. Higher risk and unusual cases may take longer. Further information can be found on the ATO website at Instructions for withholding rate variation.

Withholding variations to nil

The amount that would otherwise have had to be withheld and paid under s 14-200 is reduced to nil where:

- a deceased's legal personal representative
- beneficiaries of a deceased estate, or
- surviving joint tenants that acquire a deceased joint tenant's interest in a relevant asset

would otherwise have to pay the amount (*Legislative Instrument* F2016L01396).

There is also a nil withholding amount where an entity proves to the purchaser that it was an income tax exempt entity, either by a private ruling or documentation showing it was endorsed as a registered charity (*Legislative Instrument* F2017L00390).

There is also no requirement for any withholding when ownership of a relevant asset is transferred following a relationship breakdown between spouses resulting in a roll-over under ITAA97 Subdiv 126-A (*Legislative Instrument* F2016L01642).

The amount to be withheld under s 14-200 is varied to nil when land is acquired under the following circumstances:

- there is a transaction where a mortgagee that is an authorised deposit-taking institution exercises a power of sale over the land
- the mortgagee has determined that the residue from the sale proceeds will be zero or less than zero, and
- the mortgagee has provided the transferee with a written declaration, stating that the amount to withhold is varied to nil (*Legislative Instrument* F2020L01291).

[FTR ¶976-776, ¶976-779/3]

¶26-270 PAYG: mining payments

Mining payments in respect of Aboriginal land

An entity that makes a mining payment to another entity, or that applies a mining payment for the benefit of another entity, must withhold an amount (TAA Sch 1 s 12-320). A ‘‘mining payment’’ is a payment made in consideration for the issuing or renewing of mining rights on Aboriginal land or by way of mineral royalties in respect of mining on Aboriginal land. The payer is not required to withhold more than the mining withholding tax payable in respect of the payment (¶19-000) and therefore no amount is to be withheld if no mining withholding tax is payable. The amount to be withheld from the mining payment should be calculated on a GST inclusive basis (ID 2010/115).

Natural resource payments

An entity that makes a payment to a foreign resident that is worked out wholly or partly by reference to the value or quantity of natural resources produced or recovered in Australia must withhold an amount (TAA Sch 1 s 12-325). The payer must notify the Commissioner in writing of the amount of the proposed payment. The Commissioner then notifies the payer in writing of the amount (if any) to be withheld. A payer that makes the payment without the proper notice is liable for a penalty (unless the payment is covered by a certificate).

The Commissioner may issue a certificate exempting the payer from the requirement to notify. However, a payer must still withhold, from a payment covered by the certificate, the amount in respect of tax that is payable by a foreign resident to whom the payment is made. The Commissioner may, by written notice to the payer, revoke or vary a certificate. The decision not to give, revoke or vary a certificate is a reviewable decision (¶28-180).

[FTR ¶976-700, ¶976-705]

¶26-275 PAYG: seasonal labour mobility program

An amount must be withheld from salary, wages, commission, bonuses or allowances paid to an individual as an employee of an approved employer under the Seasonal Labour Mobility Program when the employee is a foreign resident who holds a Special Program Visa (subclass 416).

The rate of tax payable under the *Income Tax (Seasonal Labour Mobility Program Withholding Tax) Act 2012* is 15% and so the amount to be withheld is 15% of the payment (TAR reg 52). The employee is entitled to a credit for the amount withheld (TAA Sch 1 s 18-33).

[FTR ¶976-698]

¶26-277 PAYG: working holiday makers

Special arrangements apply to ''working holiday makers'', known as the ''backpacker tax'' (¶21-033). A working holiday maker is an individual who holds a working holiday visa (subclass 417), a work and holiday visa (subclass 462), or one of certain related bridging visas (ss 3(1) and 3A(1) of the *Income Tax Rates Act 1986*).

In the absence of these special arrangements, working holiday makers would either be taxed as residents or non-residents, depending on their circumstances. The Commissioner issued a statement to the effect that he believed most working holiday makers are transient and that they would, absent these special arrangements, be taxable as non-residents. Where these special arrangements apply, a rate of 15% is applied up to a taxable income of $45,000 (instead of 32.5%) — normal rates apply after $45,000 (for the withholding schedules, see ¶26-130).

The validity of the ''backpacker tax'' was challenged in *Addy*, where it was held that it did not contravene a non-discrimination clause in the tax treaty between Australia and the United Kingdom. The taxpayer has applied to the High Court for special leave to appeal from the decision. For details of Australia's tax treaties, see ¶22-140.

The ATO continues to administer the working holiday maker income tax rates in line with the law as enacted until the appeals process is exhausted and notes that the impact of the *Addy* decision is limited to working holiday makers from Chile, Finland, Germany, Japan, Norway, Turkey and the United Kingdom, who also qualify as residents of Australia for tax purposes.

Employer registration

In order for the special arrangements for working holiday makers to apply, the employer must be registered with the ATO. This application must be made in the approved form and by the day on which the employer is first required to withhold an amount from a working holiday maker (or such further time as the Commissioner allows) (s 16-146). The approved form requires the employer to make a declaration to the Commissioner, stating that (s 16-147):

- if the entity is carrying on a business, the employer has a genuine business requirement to employ one or more working holiday makers
- the employer agrees to comply with the requirements of the *Fair Work Act 2009* in relation to his/her/its employment of any working holiday maker, and
- the employer agrees to check that any working holiday maker holds a visa that qualifies that person to be a working holiday maker.

Employers can check a person's visa details by registering for the Department of Immigration and Border Protection's free, online system (Visa Entitlement Verification Online). Alternatively, employers can ask the prospective employee to send visa details directly using the Visa Entitlement Verification Online email function.

Administrative penalties exist for false and misleading statements made in an application, which range from 20 to 60 penalty units. The Commissioner must decide on an application within 30 days and notify the employer of his decision (including its effective date if successful). If the employer has an ABN, a successful registration will be noted on the Australian Business Register. This allows prospective employees to search the ABR for registered employers (s 16-147). The Commissioner can cancel an employer's registration if notified in the approved form that working holiday makers will no longer be employed. Registration can also be cancelled if the Commissioner believes that the employer is not a fit and proper person (s 16-148).

Employers can object to the Commissioner's decision to fail to register the employer or to cancel registration if dissatisfied.

Reporting by the Commissioner

The Commissioner must present an annual report to parliament on the taxation of working holiday makers and the registration of their employers (s 352-25). The Commissioner will also be permitted to disclose information to ensure an entity's compliance with the Fair Work Act, without breaching secrecy provision in the *Taxation Administration Act 1953*.

¶26-280 PAYG: alienated personal services payments

A personal services entity (¶30-630) must pay an amount to the Commissioner if it: (a) receives an alienated personal services payment; and (b) receives that payment during a PAYG payment period for which it is a personal services payment remitter (TAA Sch 1 s 13-5(1)).

An ‘‘alienated personal services payment’’ is a payment of personal services income that is received by a personal services entity and assessed to an individual under the rules in ITAA97 Div 86 (¶30-600). ‘‘Personal services income’’ is income that is gained mainly as a reward for the personal efforts or skills of an individual. A ‘‘personal services entity’’ is a company, partnership or trust whose income includes the personal services income of one or more individuals.

Is the entity a personal services payment remitter?

To determine whether a personal services entity is a personal services payment remitter for a PAYG payment period (quarterly for small withholders and monthly for medium and large withholders), the entity must look to the income year preceding the relevant year. For example, for an entity with a 30 June year end, if the PAYG payment period is the quarter ending 31 March 2021, the entity must consider the 2019–20 income year.

The personal services entity will be a personal services payment remitter for the period if, during that preceding income year:

- the entity's income included an individual's personal services income, and
- the entity was not conducting a personal services business when it received that income (TAA Sch 1 s 13-15).

In the case of a personal services entity that commences during a PAYG payment period or that begins to receive personal services income for the first time during a PAYG payment period, the decision as to whether it is a personal services payment remitter is based on a reasonable expectation of the entity's circumstances for the income year in which that period occurs. If it is reasonable to expect that the entity will receive personal services income during that year but not in the course of conducting a personal services business, it will be a personal services payment remitter.

An entity is not a personal services payment remitter for a PAYG payment period if a personal services business determination (¶30-680) applies during that period or an earlier period in the same income year.

Working out how much to withhold

A method statement for calculating the amount to be paid is set out in TAA Sch 1 s 13-5(2). As a general rule, the personal services entity is required to pay to the Commissioner the amount that would have been required to be withheld from the relevant personal services income if it had been paid as salary, minus what was, in fact, withheld from any personal services income that was paid as salary to the individual.

A personal services entity is not required to pay any amounts to the Commissioner if it pays the personal services income to the relevant individual as salary or wages within 14 days of the end of the PAYG payment period. There is, in such a case, no alienated personal services payment. Nor does the obligation apply to entities who were conducting a personal services business in the previous income year or who have a personal services business determination in force.

A personal services entity can satisfy its obligations by withholding or paying amounts that are calculated by applying the applicable withholding rate to a ''minimum personal services income payout measure'' (PS LA 2003/6). The applicable withholding rate is the rate listed in the relevant PAYG withholding tax tables, unless the Commissioner has granted the individual service provider a withholding variation.

The minimum personal services income payout measure will be an amount that is either equal to or greater than:

- 70% of the gross personal services income (exclusive of GST) received by the personal services entity during the current PAYG payment period, or
- a ''net personal services income percentage'' applied to the gross personal services income (exclusive of GST) received by the personal services entity during the current PAYG payment period.

The net personal services income percentage is worked out as follows:

$$\frac{\text{individual's gross personal services income (excl GST) for the previous income year} - \text{amount worked out under the method statement in ITAA97 s 86-20 for the previous income year}}{\text{personal services entity's gross personal services income (excl GST) for the previous income year}} \times \frac{100}{1} = \text{net personal services income percentage}$$

Where a personal services entity withholds or pays amounts in accordance with this measure but does not withhold or pay amounts that are exactly equal to that required by the method statement in s 13-5(2) resulting in a shortfall, the Commissioner will remit any failure to withhold penalty to nil (¶26-750).

After the end of the income year, the personal services entity must attribute the remaining personal services income (after allowing for certain deductions) to the individual service provider.

Variations to nil

The Commissioner has varied to nil the amount required to be withheld from any alienated personal services payment that is:

- received by a personal services entity that relates to one or more individuals' personal services income
- salary or wages paid to the individual, or individuals, within 14 days after the end of the relevant PAYG payment period, and
- the payment is equal to, or greater than either:
  - 70% of the gross personal services income (exclusive of GST) received by the personal services entity during the current PAYG payment period, or
  - a net personal services income percentage applied to the gross personal services income (exclusive of GST) received by the personal services entity during the current PAYG payment period (calculated by dividing the personal services entity's gross personal services income (exclusive of GST) less allowable deductions (excluding salary or wages) for the previous income year by the personal services entity's gross personal services income (exclusive of GST) for the previous income year and multiplying this amount by 100).

(*Legislative Instrument* F2013L00522.)

[FTR ¶976-720 – ¶976-740]

¶26-300 PAYG: non-cash benefits

An entity that provides a non-cash benefit, and an entity that receives such a benefit, is in the same position as an entity that pays or receives money. This prevents entities from avoiding their PAYG withholding obligations by providing non-cash benefits.

A "non-cash benefit" is property or services in any form except money, eg a barter transaction. A benefit is taken to have been provided to an entity if it is dealt with on the entity's behalf or is provided, or dealt with, as the entity directs.

Provider of benefit must pay an amount

The provider of a non-cash benefit must pay an amount to the Commissioner in respect of the benefit if it would have been required to withhold an amount had the benefit been paid in money equal to the market value of the benefit (TAA Sch 1 s 14-5). The market value of a benefit is determined at the time it is provided but anything that would prevent or restrict the conversion of the benefit to money is disregarded. The amount withheld must be paid before providing the benefit. The amount to be paid is equal to the amount that would have been withheld from a cash payment.

▶ Example

Nick is a building contractor who has entered into a voluntary agreement with Mike. Nick proposes to give Mike his old utility van (the market value of which is $1,000) as payment for work Mike has done for him over a fortnight. If, instead, Nick paid Mike $1,000, Nick would have had to withhold $200. Nick is therefore required to pay $200 to the Commissioner before giving the van to Mike.

No amount is to be paid if the benefit is:

- a fringe benefit or an exempt benefit for FBT purposes (¶35-060), or
- the acquisition of an ESS interest under an employee share scheme (¶10-080). Instead, specific withholding rules apply (¶26-320).

The provision of Bitcoin by an employer to an employee in respect of his/her employment is a property fringe benefit and excluded from PAYG withholding (TD 2014/28).

Recovery of an amount paid

The provider of the benefit may recover from the payee the amount it paid to the Commissioner. The amount to be recovered can also be set off against debts due by the provider to the payee (TAA Sch 1 s 14-15).

[FTR ¶976-750, ¶976-755]

¶26-320 PAYG: employee share schemes

Withholding tax is payable if an employer provides discounted shares and/or rights to an employee under an employee share scheme (ESS) and that employee has not quoted his/her TFN or ABN to the employer by the end of the income year (Subdiv 14-C). This withholding applies to shares, rights, and stapled securities and is imposed in the income year that the employee would be liable to pay tax in relation to the ESS under Div 83A (¶10-085).

The withholding tax is payable on the amount of employee share scheme discount included in an employee's assessable income for an income year under Div 83A at the top marginal rate plus Medicare levy. Any upfront concession that may be available to the employee (reducing the amount of discount that is included in his/her assessable income) is disregarded.

Withholding tax is payable 21 days after the end of the income year in which the ESS interest is included in the employee's assessable income. This will be the year that the shares or rights were provided in the case of upfront taxation schemes, or the year of the ESS deferred taxing point for deferred tax schemes. Employers can recover the amount of withholding tax that they have paid from the employee to whom the amount of tax relates by offsetting the amount they can recover from the employee against an amount they otherwise owed the employee, such as the employee's salary. The employee is given a credit for any withholding tax that has been paid (¶26-660).

[FTR ¶976-770]

¶26-330 PAYG: GST on certain real estate supplies

Purchasers of new residential premises or new subdivisions of potential residential land must withhold an amount of the purchase price, representing the GST payable on the transaction (TAA Sch 1 ss 14-250, 14-255). These rules apply to supplies for which any of the consideration (other than a deposit) is first provided on or after 1 July 2018, whether a contract for the supply was entered into before, on or after that date. However, the obligation to withhold does not apply if the contract was entered into before 1 July 2018 and consideration for the supply, other than a deposit, is first provided before 1 July 2020.

The obligation applies to a purchaser who is the recipient of a taxable supply (¶34-105) of:

- new residential premises, other than those created through a substantial renovation and commercial residential premises or
- subdivisions of potential residential land

by way of sale or long-term lease. There is no requirement to withhold if the purchaser is registered for GST and acquires the potential residential land for a creditable purpose.

The amount withheld must be remitted to the ATO on or before the day on which any of the consideration for the supply is first provided (other than consideration provided as a deposit). To facilitate this, suppliers of residential premises or potential residential land will be required to issue a notification to the purchaser 14 days before making the supply of the requirement to withhold an amount. However, purchasers will not be required to register with the ATO under PAYG withholding.

The administrative penalty under s 16-30 (¶29-300) will not apply where the purchaser reasonably believes that the premises are not new residential premises.

Entities that make a taxable supply of new residential premises or new subdivisions of potential residential land will be entitled to a credit on their BAS for the amount of the payment made to the ATO. Where a supply of new residential premises is made under the margin scheme (¶34-230), the supplier may apply to the ATO for a refund of a portion of the amount withheld by the purchaser.

The rules are further explained in LCR 2018/4.

¶26-335 PAYG: First Home Super Saver released amounts

The Commissioner must withhold an amount from the First Home Super Saver (FHSS) released amounts paid in respect of a person (s 12-460). For details of the FHSS Scheme, see ¶13-790.

The amount to be withheld is: (a) the amount of tax that the Commissioner estimates will be payable by the individual in relation to the individual's assessable FHSS released amount for an income year; or (b) if the Commissioner is unable to make such an estimate — 17% of the individual's assessable FHSS released amount for an income year (TAR reg 53A).

Declarations

¶26-350 TFN and withholding declarations

TFN declarations

A person who receives a payment for work or services (including non-cash benefits), a retirement payment, annuity, benefit or compensation payment, or is likely to receive such a payment, may give the payer a TFN declaration (ITAA36 s 202C). A TFN declaration cannot be given in relation to a voluntary agreement to withhold (¶26-150) — instead, the voluntary agreement discloses the payee's ABN, which is sufficient. A person can choose whether to provide a TFN declaration but, if one is not provided, the payment is subject to withholding at the top marginal rate plus Medicare levy. A payer making a payment for which a payee may make a TFN declaration must notify the Commissioner if the payee does not provide a declaration.

To avoid amounts being withheld at the top marginal rate, an individual should complete a TFN declaration each time a new relationship is commenced with a payer (eg starting a job or converting a superannuation entitlement into a pension). An individual is exempt from quoting a TFN if he/she is:

- under 16 years of age and not earning enough to pay tax, or
- receiving certain Centrelink pensions, benefits or allowances or a service pension from the Department of Veterans Affairs.

The payer must forward the declaration to the Commissioner within 14 days after the payee has given it, and must take information contained in the declaration into account when working out how much to withhold.

Optional arrangements

An employer may inform an employee that he/she is able to make a TFN declaration using the Commissioner's online service, rather than the employee providing the form directly to the employer (ITAA36 s 202C(2)). The Commissioner will then make available to the employer the information in the employee's TFN declaration where the employee has made a TFN declaration in relation to that employer to the Commissioner (ITAA36 s 202CG).

An employer that receives information from the Commissioner, rather than a TFN declaration from an employee, does not need to sign and send an original TFN declaration to the Commissioner. However, employers will need to continue to keep a record of the TFN declaration information made available by the Commissioner. An employer will not be required to notify the Commissioner that an employee has not provided a TFN declaration if the Commissioner has made the employee's TFN declaration available to the employer. However, if the Commissioner has not made the employee's TFN declaration available to the employer within 14 days after the commencement of the employment relationship, then the employer must give notice to the Commissioner in the approved form (ITAA36 s 202CF(1A)).

Employers are still required to on-disclose an employee's TFN to a superannuation entity, where the employee quotes his/her TFN to the Commissioner and the Commissioner makes the TFN available to the employer (SISA s 299C(4)).

Optional TFN validation

The Commissioner can provide employers with both positive and negative validation of an employee's personal details, including his/her TFN, where the Commissioner is satisfied that the person is an employee of the employer and the employee has given a TFN declaration to the employer (ITAA36 s 202CEA).

Employers are not required to validate their employees' TFN information.

A negative validation notice is not a notice that the TFN quoted by the recipient is invalid. This is because a validation notice is not a notice under ITAA36 s 202CE(3) as that section relates exclusively to TFNs stated in a TFN declaration. If the Commissioner is unable to validate the information, then the employer can seek further information from the employee to resolve any discrepancies. The Commissioner may provide an electronic interface to receive information and give a notice.

Withholding declarations

A person who expects to receive a payment for work or services, a retirement payment, annuity, benefit or compensation payment, or an alienated personal services payment, and who wishes a matter relating to the person's income tax or certain other liabilities to be taken into account in working out the amount to be withheld from the payment, may give the payer a withholding declaration about the matter (TAA Sch 1 s 15-50). The declaration must be in the approved form (see further the ATO website Withholding declaration (NAT 3093)).

An individual may only make a withholding declaration if he/she has given the payer a TFN declaration or has entered into a voluntary agreement. A withholding declaration may also be used to change any information given in a TFN declaration. A withholding declaration can only be given about a particular matter to one payer at any given time.

Section 15-50(1)(b) lists the matters that may be taken into account in working out the amount to be withheld are any matters relating to the individual's liability to:

- income tax
- the Medicare levy, and
- repayments of accumulated higher education and trade support loans.

A payer must take the information in the declaration into account when working out how much to withhold. Where the payee's circumstances change in relation to a prescribed matter, the payee must provide a new withholding declaration (TAR reg 56).

[FTR ¶976-805]

Payer's Obligations

¶26-450 Obligation to withhold

If an entity is required to withhold an amount from a cash payment, it must do so when making the payment (TAA Sch 1 s 16-5). The provider of a non-cash benefit must pay the required amount to the Commissioner before providing the benefit.

If the obligation to withhold arises as a result of an investor becoming presently entitled to the income of a unit trust, the amount must be withheld at the time the investor becomes presently entitled.

If an entity is required to withhold an amount from a payment received by it, the entity must do so immediately after receiving the payment. Where a dividend, interest or a royalty is received for a foreign resident, an amount must be withheld either immediately or when the foreign resident becomes entitled to the payment (¶26-250).

Discharge of liability

An entity that withholds an amount (or pays to the Commissioner an amount associated with alienated personal services income or a non-cash payment) is discharged from all liability to pay or account for that amount to any entity except the Commissioner (TAA Sch 1 s 16-20). However, the entity may be required to refund the amount in some circumstances (¶26-680).

No deduction if amount not withheld

For certain payments and non-cash benefits, no deduction is allowed for the payer where the payer has not complied with the PAYG withholding requirements (s 26-105). This applies to a payment:

- of salary, wages, commissions, bonuses or allowances to an employee (¶26-150)
- of directors' fees (¶26-150)
- to a religious practitioner (¶26-150)
- under a labour hire arrangement (¶26-150), or
- for a supply of services where the payee has not quoted its ABN (excluding supplies of goods and supplies of real property) (¶26-220).

Withholding an incorrect amount will not affect the entitlement to a deduction. The payer will be entitled to a deduction if, in the original income year, the payer voluntarily notifies the Commissioner, in the approved form, of the mistake before the Commissioner commences an audit or other compliance activity. An employer will also not be denied a deduction if it honestly, but mistakenly, believes an employee is a contractor and has complied with the no ABN withholding rule.

[FTR ¶976-820, ¶976-825]

¶26-500 Obligation to pay: determining PAYG withholder status

The rules for when a withheld amount must be paid to the Commissioner depend on whether the "withholder" is a large, medium or small withholder. To determine an entity's status for a particular month, apply the following tests.

Withholder status	Test to be satisfied
Large (TAA Sch 1 s 16-95)	• it was a large withholder for June 2001 • the amounts withheld during a financial year ending at least 2 months before the current month exceeded $1m • at the end of a financial year ending at least 2 months before the current month, the entity was a member of a wholly-owned group of companies and the amounts withheld by those companies during that year exceeded $1m, or • the Commissioner determines that the entity is a large withholder.
Medium (TAA Sch 1 s 16-100)	It is not a large withholder and: • it was a medium withholder for June 2001 • the amounts withheld during a financial year ending before the current month exceeded $25,000, or • the Commissioner determines that the entity is a medium withholder.
Small (TAA Sch 1 s 16-105)	It has withheld at least one amount during the month and it is neither a large nor a medium withholder for that month.

Commissioner may vary an entity's status

The Commissioner may make a determination varying an entity's status either upwards or downwards (TAA Sch 1 ss 16-110; 16-115). The determination must be in writing and must state that the determination applies for specified months. The Commissioner may revoke or vary any such determination.

In making a determination varying an entity's status upwards, the Commissioner may have regard to:

- the sum of the amounts likely to be withheld by the entity in the following 12 months
- the extent to which the entity makes or receives withholding payments that were previously made or received by another entity
- any failure by the entity to comply with its obligations
- any arrangement that was entered into or carried out for the purpose of lengthening the intervals at which the entity is required to pay amounts withheld
- such other matters as the Commissioner considers relevant.

An entity may apply in writing to the Commissioner for a determination varying its status downwards.

An entity that is dissatisfied with a decision in relation to status may object to it in the usual manner (¶28-010).

[FTR ¶976-840 – ¶976-850]

¶26-550 Obligation to pay: timing of payments

Amounts withheld are to be paid in accordance with the following table (TAA Sch 1 ss 16-75; 16-85).

Withholder status	Due date of payments		Method of payment
Large	*If withholder withholds on:*	*Withholder must pay by:*	Electronic
	Saturday or Sunday	The second Monday after that day	
	Monday or Tuesday	The first Monday after that day	
	Wednesday	The second Thursday after that day	
	Thursday or Friday	The first Thursday after that day	
Medium	Payment due by the 21st or 28th day after the end of the month in which the amount was withheld (see below)		Electronic or other means approved by the Commissioner
Small	Payment due by the 21st or 28th day after the end of the quarter in which the amount was withheld (see below)		Electronic or other means approved by the Commissioner

The extended dates (ie to the 28th day) apply to any entity that has a Business Activity Statement (BAS) (¶24-200) or Instalment Activity Statement (IAS) (¶24-220) quarterly obligation, apart from an entity that has chosen or is required to pay GST monthly. These taxpayers are referred to as "deferred BAS payers" (¶24-240). Therefore, small withholders may be eligible as they pay quarterly but large withholders are not.

Medium withholders who do not qualify for the deferral (eg because they pay GST monthly) are required to pay by the 21st day of the next month. Medium withholders who qualify for the deferral will be entitled to pay on the 28th day of the month (or 28 February in relation to amounts withheld in December) only if they are a deferred BAS payer for that month (ie only if they have another quarterly BAS obligation due on that day). If they do not have another quarterly BAS obligation due on that day, they are required to pay by the 21st day of the next month. This means that, during a year, a medium withholder's due dates may vary between the 21st and the 28th day of a particular month.

▶ Example 1: Large withholder

Abbott Manufacturing makes a payment of salary to its employees on the first Tuesday of every month. It is required to pay the amount withheld on that Tuesday on or before the following Monday.

▶ Example 2: Medium withholder

Surfboards'n'More pays its directors fortnightly on a Thursday. It pays its GST monthly. If it withholds an amount on Thursday, 3 June 2021, it must pay that amount to the Commissioner on or by Wednesday, 21 July 2021.

If Surfboards'n'More had quarterly GST obligations, it must pay the amount withheld on 3 June by Wednesday, 28 July 2021. However, amounts withheld on 1 July 2021 are due by Monday, 23 August 2021 as the company did not have another quarterly BAS obligation due in that month.

▶ Example 3: Small withholder

The Tipperary Cake Shop pays its employees on a monthly basis. The amount withheld from salaries in June 2021 must be paid to the Commissioner on or before 28 July 2021.

The Commissioner may, with a withholder's agreement and written notice, vary the means by which it pays amounts.

Where a due date for payment of a tax debt falls on a Saturday, a Sunday or a public holiday, taxpayers may pay on the next business day without incurring a penalty or GIC (TAA s 8AAZMB).

Lodgment concessions

The ATO lodgment concession for tax agents *generally* offers a 4-week extension for lodgment of the first, third and fourth quarterly activity statements if lodged electronically. Full details of the tax agent lodgment program 2020–21 are available on the ATO website (www.ato.gov.au).

There is also a lodgment concession for entities that do not use tax agents for the lodgment of activity statements. This concession *generally* offers a 2 week extension for lodgment of the first, third and fourth quarterly activity statements if lodged electronically. However, this concession does *not* apply to:

- monthly activity statements
- monthly GST payers with quarterly PAYG instalments (or other quarterly obligations)
- monthly PAYG withholding payers
- head companies of consolidated groups
- large businesses with substituted accounting periods (a large business is one with annual total income over $10 million, annual GST turnover over $20 million, annual withholding payments over $1 million, or a member of a company group where at least one member of the group has annual total income over $10 million)
- statements that did not have an original due date of the 28th of the month
- quarterly instalment notices (PAYG instalment only, GST instalment only, or PAYG and GST instalment only).

TFN withholding tax

TFN withholding tax (¶26-200) is due and payable at the end of 21 days after the end of the income year in which the accrued gain is included in the investor's assessable income (s 14-55).

It is payable jointly and severally by the investor and the investment body except if the investment body is the Commonwealth or an untaxed Commonwealth entity, in which case it is payable by the investor who is taken to have authorised the investment body to pay it on his/her/its behalf.

The investment body may recover from the investor any TFN withholding tax it pays. It is also entitled to set off an amount that it can recover from the investor against a debt due by it to the investor or an amount accruing to the investor or that stands to the investor's credit.

Recovery of amounts by Commissioner

The Commissioner can take recovery action under TAA Div 268 by estimating a debt for *all* PAYG withholding amounts that have been withheld but not paid to the Commissioner (¶25-560). The taxpayer can have the estimate reduced or revoked by giving the Commissioner a statutory declaration. The Commissioner may then recover the amount under the collection and recovery rules in TAA Sch 1 Pt 4-15 (¶25-500). The Commissioner's power to issue, and revoke, a PAYG liability estimate notice is discussed in *DFC of T v Armstrong Scalisi Holdings Pty Ltd*.

[FTR ¶976-840 – ¶976-850]

¶26-600 Obligation to register under PAYG

Registration of withholders

An entity required to pay an amount to the Commissioner under PAYG withholding must apply to be registered with the Commissioner (TAA Sch 1 s 16-140). The entity must apply in the approved form by the first day on which it is required to withhold an amount (or pay an amount in respect of a non-cash benefit). However, the Commissioner may grant an extension (eg where an unregistered entity must withhold an amount from a payment for a cash-on-delivery supply because the payee did not quote an ABN). Purchasers of certain real property who are required to withhold GST (¶26-330) are not required to be registered.

The Commissioner may register an entity, or cancel registration, at any time.

Registration of branches

The Commissioner may register a branch of a registered entity if:

- the entity applies for registration of the branch in the approved form
- the entity has an ABN or has applied for one — the ABN allows the Commissioner to link each branch's running balance account (¶24-300) to the entity
- the Commissioner is satisfied that the branch maintains an independent system of accounting and can be separately identified by reference to its activities or location, and
- the Commissioner is satisfied that the entity is carrying on an enterprise through the branch (or intends to carry on an enterprise through the branch) (TAA Sch 1 s 16-142).

The Commissioner must cancel a branch's registration if it no longer satisfies these last 2 requirements (TAA Sch 1 s 16-144).

A branch that is registered is a ''PAYG withholding branch''. Note, however, that the entity remains legally responsible for all amounts that relate to its branches. PAYG withholding applies to an entity with a PAYG withholding branch as if the amounts it must pay to the Commissioner were separated into:

- a class of amounts that relate to each such branch, and
- a class of amounts that do not relate to any of the entity's branches.

These amounts are worked out as if the branch were a separate entity and all payments made through the branch were made by that entity (TAA Sch 1 s 16-143).

If an entity's registration is cancelled, the registration of any PAYG withholding branches is also cancelled (TAA Sch 1 s 16-145).

Impact of COVID-19 for foreign employers

If a foreign employer has employees working in Australia temporarily because of the COVID-19 effect on travel, the foreign employer does not need to register for PAYG withholding if its employees left Australia before 30 June 2020 and the only reason the employees were working in Australia was because of the effects of COVID-19 on travel (ATO website).

Foreign employers may need to register for PAYG withholding if their employees continue to work in Australia after 30 June 2020 and the employees are either Australian residents or foreign residents who are not exempt from income tax under a double taxation agreement (¶22-140).

An employee may not be taxed in Australia if they are not residents of Australia and a relevant double taxation agreement applies. If the employee's income is not taxable in Australia, the employer does not need to withhold tax from their wages.

[FTR ¶976-860, ¶976-862]

¶26-620 Obligation to provide information to the Commissioner

An entity that must pay an amount (even if it is a nil amount) to the Commissioner (as an amount withheld, an alienated personal services payment or as a payment in respect of a non-cash benefit), must notify the Commissioner of the amount (TAA Sch 1 s 16-150). The notification must be in the approved form and lodged with the Commissioner on or before the day on which the amount is due to be paid (regardless of when it is paid). However, most employers notify the Commissioner of certain withholding payments using Single Touch Payroll (STP) reporting (¶26-630).

The Commissioner must also be given a copy of some payment summaries (¶26-640).

Annual reports

An entity that makes a payment subject to PAYG withholding must give an annual report to the Commissioner (TAA Sch 1 s 16-153). The report must either: (a) be in the approved form; or (b) consist of: (i) copies of all payment summaries (¶26-640) that the entity gave in respect of the financial year for payments, non-cash benefits, alienated personal services payments and reportable fringe benefits amounts; and (ii) an accompanying statement in the approved form.

The due date for the annual report is:

- 31 October, if the report relates to:
  - payments for a supply where the recipient does not quote an ABN
  - dividend, interest and royalty payments
  - payments to foreign residents
  - departing Australia superannuation payments
  - the seasonal labour mobility program
  - mining payments, or
  - non-cash benefits in relation to any of those items

- 14 August, if the report relates to:
  - work or services payments
  - superannuation payments, employment termination payments and unused leave payments
  - benefit and compensation payments
  - non-cash benefits relating to any of those items
  - alienated personal services payments
  - reportable fringe benefits, or
  - reportable employer superannuation contributions.

If a payer withholds under both categories, it must still make the report by the appropriate due date but may choose to provide both reports by 14 August.

Reports relating to managed investment trust withholding must be given to the Commissioner not later than 14 days after the end of 6 months after the end of the income year of the managed investment trust or within a longer period allowed by the Commissioner.

The Commissioner may vary the obligation to make an annual report but such a variation must be: (a) published in the *Commonwealth Gazette* if it relates to a class of payers; or (b) made by written notice to the payer if it affects a single payer.

Under the *Lodgment program 2020–21*, most taxpayers that engage a tax agent or BAS agent generally have to lodge their annual reports by 30 September 2020. A further extension applies for tax agents only if the taxpayer has only closely held employees (eg family members of a family business, directors of a company, shareholders or beneficiaries) and they meet the compliance test. In this case, the taxpayer has to lodge its report by the due date of the income tax return. This concession does not apply to large withholders who have to lodge by 14 August 2020.

Investment bodies are not required to give an annual report but continue to give TFN reports and annual investment income reports under TAA Sch 1 Div 393. An entity's ABN must be reported if this has been quoted in place of a TFN. Managed investment trusts, custodians and other investment bodies must also include in their annual investment income report information about amounts withheld under Subdiv 12-H from payments to foreign residents.

Single Touch Payroll (STP) reporting

Employers utilising STP reporting (¶26-630) are not required to provide an annual report. This exclusion covers reportable employer superannuation contributions and reportable fringe benefit amounts voluntarily notified to the Commissioner using STP reporting by 14 July after the end of the financial year.

However, an employer must give a declaration to the Commissioner that he/she/it has given all the information that he/she/it would otherwise be required to give under ss 16-153 (annual reports), 16-155 (annual payment summaries) and 16-165 (payment summaries for superannuation lump sums and employment termination payments) for payments made in the financial year by 14 July to be exempt from the annual reporting obligations (TAA s 389-20(2)). The Commissioner has specified the last ''finalised'' STP report for the financial year as the approved form for this purpose.

Information about payment recipient

A payer that commences a relationship with another person under which that person is entitled to receive a payment for work or services, a retirement payment, an annuity or pension, or a benefit or compensation payment must give notice to the Commissioner about the payment recipient (ITAA36 s 202CF). This notice must be given within 14 days of entering into the relationship, unless a TFN declaration is in force at the end of that period (¶26-350).

No deduction if Commissioner not notified

Similar to the denied deduction where a payer fails to withhold (¶26-450), a deduction is denied for payments made from 1 July 2019 where the payer did not notify the Commissioner when required under s 16-150 (s 26-105). This applies to a payment: of salary, wages, commissions, bonuses or allowances to an employee; of directors' fees; to a religious practitioner; under a labour hire arrangement; or for a supply of services where the payee has not quoted its ABN (excluding supplies of goods and supplies of real property). A deduction will also be denied in relation to a non-cash benefit provided in lieu of a cash payment where an amount must be paid and reported to the Commissioner but no notification is made.

[FTR ¶976-880]

¶26-630 Single Touch Payroll reporting

Single Touch Payroll (STP) is a reporting framework for employers to provide payroll information to the Commissioner in line with their payroll cycle, which is usually at a time earlier than that which applies under other reporting provisions. It applied from 1 July 2018 to ''substantial employers'' (ie, an entity with 20 or more employees) but it applies to most employers from 1 July 2019. Entities that report to the Commissioner using STP do not have to comply with some other reporting obligations. The main STP reporting provisions are contained in TAA Sch 1 Div 389.

Exemptions

The Commissioner can exempt entities of a particular class or individual entities from STP reporting by written notice, as a result of an application by the entity or on the Commissioner's own volition (TAA Sch 1 s 389-10). Where the entity has applied for an exemption, the Commissioner must notify the entity if the application is refused and there is a deemed refusal if the Commissioner does not notify the entity within 60 days of the application being made. The entity can object in the usual way against a refused application or the Commissioner's decision to limit the exemption. The following exemptions currently apply:

- *Legislative Instrument* F2019L00121 exempts an entity from reporting contribution amounts paid to a superannuation fund from 1 July 2018
- *Legislative Instrument* F2020L00800 exempts entities that administer a Portable Long Service Leave scheme or a Portable Redundancy scheme from reporting in respect of payments made to members of the scheme from 1 July 2020, and
- *Legislative Instrument* F2020L00801 exempts employers for 2020–21 who do not have an Australian Business Number (ABN) but instead have a Withholding Payer Number (WPN).

Small employers (19 or less employees) were exempt from reporting through STP for their closely held payees for the 2019–20 financial year. A closely held payee is one who is directly related to the entity from which they receive payments (eg family members of a family business, directors or shareholders of a company or beneficiaries of a trust). The ATO website reports that this exemption has been extended until 1 July 2021 (STP 2020/D3).

Withholding payments covered

The withholding payments (including nil amounts) covered by STP are (s 389-5):

- A payment that constitutes an employee's ordinary time earnings or salary or wages (within the meaning of the *Superannuation Guarantee (Administration) Act 1992* (SGAA)) — this excludes contractors, and

- The following payments:
  - under the Seasonal Labour Mobility Program (¶26-275)
  - for work and services (¶26-150), with the exception of payments under voluntary agreements, labour hire arrangements, and those prescribed by regulations
  - for termination of employment (¶26-180)
  - for unused leave (¶26-180)
  - for parental leave pay (¶26-190), and
  - for dad and partner pay (¶26-190).

Reportable employer superannuation contribution (RESC) and reportable fringe benefit (RFB) amounts are not required to be reported using STP reporting. However, an entity may nonetheless choose to report these amounts to the Commissioner using STP reporting by 14 July (s 389-15(3)).

From 1 July 2020, voluntary reporting has been extended to include the employer withholding the child support deductions and child support garnishee amounts from salary or wages that are paid to the Child Support Registrar.

Proposed extension of information to be reported

Draft Taxation Administration - Single Touch Payroll - Amounts to be Notified Determination 2020 (STP 2020/D4) provides that the following kinds of amounts must be in the approved form for STP reporting purposes:

- an amount that is not an SGAA sacrificed ordinary time earnings amount (having the same meaning as the term "sacrificed ordinary time earnings amount" defined in the SGAA) but which, as the result of an effective salary sacrifice arrangement, reduces the ordinary time earnings of an employee
- an amount that is not an SGAA sacrificed salary or wages amount but which, as the result of an effective salary sacrifice arrangement, reduces the salary and wages payable to an employee
- a superannuation liability amount
- a tax offset amount
- a foreign tax paid amount
- an exempt foreign income amount
- a foreign employment income amount
- a lump sum D amount (the amount of a genuine redundancy payment or an early retirement payment)
- a payment made under the Community Development Employment Project scheme
- a voluntary agreement to withhold amount, and
- a labour hire arrangement amount.

When finalised, the draft legislative instrument will replace the current determination (*Legislative Instrument* F2019L00122), which prescribes additional information the approved form may require using Standard Business Reporting (SBR) enabled software.

Amounts included in this instrument, which are not currently required, will not become amounts that are required by the approved form until the earlier of either: (a) the date after 1 January 2021 that an entity chooses to commence reporting those amounts, or (b) 1 July 2021.

[FTR ¶978-870]

Timing and method of reporting

Although STP reporting applies to all employers from 1 July 2019, small employers (ie, those with less than 20 employees) could start reporting any time from 1 July to 30 September 2019 and the ATO will grant deferrals to any small employer who requests additional time to start. The ATO has also provided a concession for micro employers to have their tax or BAS agent report on their behalf.

Payments that constitute an employee's ordinary time earnings or salary or wages must be notified to the Commissioner on or before the day on which the amount is paid. All other amounts must be notified to the Commissioner on or before the day by which the PAYG withholding amount is required to be withheld from the payment (regardless of whether the withholding has been made by that time).

Under STP reporting, employers must report information to the Commissioner in the approved form (s 389-5(2)). The approved form can only cover the withholding payments covered by STP reporting. The Commissioner has prescribed STP as the approved form and failure to use the approved form would render the employer liable to a failure to lodge penalty under TAA Div 286.

¶26-640 Obligation to provide information to a payment recipient

Standard annual payment summary rules

Under PAYG withholding (s 16-155), a payer must give a payment summary to an entity (the recipient) if:

(1) during the year, the payer made a withholding payment to the payee (other than a withholding payment in relation to a superannuation lump sum or an ETP, a payment for a supply where the recipient does not quote an ABN, a dividend, interest or royalty or other specified payment received for a foreign resident (see ¶26-265 for the types of payments that are specified), a closely held trust payment or a managed investment trust fund payment)

(2) during the year, the payer received a withholding payment in relation to a dividend, interest or royalty payment received for a foreign resident and the payee is the foreign resident

(3) during the year, the payer received a withholding payment of a specified type (see ¶26-265 for the types of payments that are specified) for a likely foreign resident and the payee is the likely foreign resident

(4) during the year, the payer received a withholding payment which is alienated personal services income, or is taken to have paid alienated personal services income as salary on the last day of the year

(5) the payee is an individual and has a reportable fringe benefits amount for the income year ending at the end of that financial year, in respect of his/her employment by the payer, or

(6) the recipient is an individual and reportable employer superannuation contributions have been made by the payer, in respect of the individual's employment, during the year.

A "payment summary" is a written statement that:

- names the payer and recipient
- states the recipient's TFN or ABN (if these have been given to the payer)

- states the total of the withholding payments (if any) that it covers and the total of the amounts withheld by the payer from those withholding payments
- specifies the financial year in which the withholding payments were made
- specifies the reportable fringe benefits amount and/or reportable employer superannuation contributions (if any) that it covers and the income year to which that amount relates
- includes other information that the Commissioner requires to be included (TAA Sch 1 s 16-170).

The Commissioner may vary any requirements by written notice and may do so in such instances and to such extent as he thinks fit.

Generally, the payment summary must be given within 14 days after the end of a financial year (ie generally, by 14 July) and it must cover each withholding payment and the reportable fringe benefits amount/employer superannuation contributions, where relevant, except where it is covered by a previous payment summary. However, Single Touch Payroll (STP) (¶26-630) automatically reports payroll information to the ATO and employers using that system no longer have to report employee-related PAYG withholding in their payment summaries.

Where a payer makes a withholding payment for a supply to a recipient who does not quote an ABN, the payer must give the recipient a payment summary when making the payment, or as soon as practicable afterwards (TAA Sch 1 s 16-167). The payment summary must cover only that payment.

Other payment summary rules

Standard payment summary rules do not apply to the managed investment trust withholding. Entities required to withhold must provide a statement each year to the payees that details the amounts of the payments from which withholding has occurred and the amounts withheld from those payments. The statement must be provided within 14 days after the end of 6 months after the end of the managed investment trust's income year. The statement may be provided in electronic form and a copy is not required to be given to the payee.

Generally, where a payer pays a superannuation lump sum, ETP or a departing Australia superannuation payment, the payer must give a payment summary covering the payment to the recipient within 14 days of the payment being made (TAA Sch 1 ss 16-165; 16-166). A copy must also be given to the Commissioner. However, this has been deferred in respect of ETPs or departing Australia superannuation payments until 14 August following the end of the financial year in which the payments are made (F2012L00584).

An entity that makes a withholding payment in relation to a payment to recipients who do not quote an ABN must give the recipient a payment summary and a copy of it that covers that payment, unless the amount required to be withheld is nil. This must be done when making the payment, or as soon as practicable afterwards.

The ATO requires that an information statement be prepared in relation to TFN amounts withheld from ESS interests, which discloses the amount withheld.

A payment summary must not cover a withholding payment that is a payment of an amount purported to have been parental leave pay which was not lawfully payable. In this case, within 28 days of becoming so aware, the payer must give the recipient an amended payment summary, a notice in the approved form or inform the Secretary of the Department of Families, Housing, Community Services and Indigenous Affairs (FaHCSIA) that the payer does not intend to give the recipient an amended payment summary or notice.

Part-year payment summary

The payer must give a part-year payment summary to the payee if the payee asks in writing for a payment summary covering one or more withholding payments (TAA Sch 1 s 16-160):

- made during the year, other than one in relation to an ETP, a supply where the payee hasn't quoted an ABN, or a dividend, interest, royalty or other specified amounts received for a foreign resident (see ¶26-265 for the types of payments that are specified). Further the payment summary must not cover a withholding payment that is a payment of an amount purported to have been parental leave pay if, at the time the recipient asks for the payment summary, the payer is aware that the amount was not lawfully payable
- that are dividend, interest or royalty withholding payments received for a foreign resident if the payee is the foreign resident
- that are of a type specified in the regulations received for a foreign resident, if the payee is the likely foreign resident (see ¶26-265 for the types of payments that are specified), or
- that are taken to be alienated personal services income and included in the payee's assessable income for the income year.

The application does not necessarily depend on the cessation of employment.

The recipient must ask for the payment summary not later than 21 days before the end of a financial year. The payer must comply with the request within 14 days after receiving it, unless the recipient is an individual and has a reportable fringe benefits amount for the income year ending at the end of that financial year. This is because there are reportable amounts that can only be calculated at the end of the FBT year on 31 March.

Where an employee ceases employment between 1 April and 30 June in a particular financial year, the reportable fringe benefits amount for the period from 1 April to when the employee ceased employment will be included on a payment summary issued by 14 July after the end of the *following* financial year. The withholding payments for this period are included on the payment summary issued by 14 July after the end of the *current* financial year together with any reportable fringe benefits amount calculated to 31 March of the current financial year.

▶ Example

David ceased employment on 12 April 2020 and there was a reportable fringe benefits amount in respect of his employment. David's employer, George, is required to issue a separate payment summary for the reportable fringe benefits amount paid from 1 April 2020 to 12 April 2020 no later than 14 July 2021.

Amounts withheld from payments made to David up to 12 April 2020 and the reportable fringe benefits amounts calculated to 31 March 2020 must be included on a payment summary provided by George to David by 14 July 2020.

Payers are not required to provide a part-year payment summary where the payer has made a reportable employer superannuation contribution in respect of the recipient's employment during the financial year (TAA Sch 1 s 16-160(2)).

Exemption from giving payment summaries

The Commissioner may exempt an entity from the payment summary obligations (TAA Sch 1 s 16-180). The following exemptions apply:

- where payments are made to a company director, committee member or office holder and the recipient is required to remit those payments to another entity (*Gazette* No S 676, 28 December 2000)

- where payments are made to a religious practitioner by an entity that is not a religious institution for work or services performed. In the case of chaplaincy and/or counselling services, the weekly payment must not exceed $100 or $433 monthly (*Legislative Instrument* F2006B00322)
- where a payment is made under a contract to an individual engaged as a performing artist to perform in a promotional activity that is: (a) conducted in the presence of an audience; (b) intended to be communicated to an audience by print or electronic media; (c) for a film or tape; or (d) for a television or radio broadcast and the payer has issued a payment summary to the performing artist at the time each individual payment is made (*Gazette* No GN 8, 27 February 2002)
- in relation to terminally ill recipients of lump sum superannuation member benefits (*Legislative Instrument* F2008L01999)
- for withholding amounts made on a passbook savings account where a TFN or ABN is not quoted and for dividends, interest and royalty payments (*Legislative Instrument* F2012L02333). However, entities are required to provide payment summaries if passbook savings account holders specifically request them
- an entity is exempted from its obligations to provide payment summaries and annual reports to the extent that the relevant information has been reported under Single Touch Payroll (¶26-630) (*Legislative Instrument* F2018L00494).

Exemption from giving copies of payment summaries

Entities are not required to provide employees and other payees with a duplicate copy of a PAYG withholding payment (*Legislative Instrument* F2008L01659). This exemption applies to entities making payments covered under Subdivs 12-B, 12-C, 12-D, 12-E, 12-F, 12-FA, 12-FAA, 12-FB, 12-G, Div 13 and ITAA97 s 86-40.

Implications of STP reporting

Employers that notify the Commissioner using STP reporting (¶26-630) no longer need to comply with their obligations under ss 16-155 and 16-165 to provide payment summaries to their employees in relation to amounts reported through STP (TAA s 389-20), although they will continue to be required to provide payment summaries in relation to amounts that are not reported through STP.

Employers may still choose to provide an annual payment summary if requested to do so by an employee. While it is not mandatory for employers to notify the Commissioner of reportable employer superannuation contribution and reportable fringe benefit amounts through STP, an employer may nonetheless choose to report these amounts to the Commissioner through STP by 14 July and, if so, that employer no longer needs to provide an annual payment summary covering these amounts (TAA ss 389-20(1)(c); 389-15(3)) as the Commissioner has prescribed STP as the approved form.

Employers are not be required to comply with their obligation under s 16-160 to provide a part-year payment summary to the extent that it would relate to an amount that the employer has notified under STP.

[FTR ¶976-883]

Recipient's Rights and Obligations

¶26-660 Right to a credit for amounts withheld

In general, an entity that receives a withholding payment is entitled to a credit for the amount withheld. Also, the foreign resident for whom a dividend, interest or royalty withholding payment, or other payment, is received is entitled to a credit for the amount withheld. Special rules exist for determining entitlement to the credit in the case of a partnership or trust.

As a general rule, a person is not entitled to a credit for an amount withheld to the extent that it must be refunded (TAA Sch 1 s 18-5).

A decision by the Commissioner to refuse a taxpayer's claim for PAYG credits is not subject to judicial review (*Perdikaris*; *James*).

Credits for withholding payment

Direct credit to recipient

A recipient of a withholding payment is entitled to a credit equal to the amounts withheld during an income year if, for the income year, an assessment has been made of the income tax payable by the recipient or an assessment has been made that no income tax is payable by the recipient (TAA Sch 1 s 18-15). Entitlement to the credit arises at the time of the issue of the assessment (*Cumins*). If a taxpayer can show that the total of the amount withheld is greater than the amount of the credit for PAYG withholding shown on the notice of assessment, then the taxpayer is entitled to a credit for the greater amount and nothing in the notice of assessment prevents this (*Cassaniti*). However, if there is no evidence to show that salary or wages were ever paid then there was no withholding payment from which an amount could have been withheld and no entitlement to a credit (*Cassaniti (No 2)*; *Cameron*). See also *Cassaniti* where the Commissioner accepted that, as a matter of law, remission to the Commissioner was not a pre-condition to the obtaining of credits; rather, what was critical was whether the act of withholding had taken place contemporaneously with the payment of salary or wages. A payment summary is only prima facie evidence that amounts have been withheld; if there is other evidence that establishes that no amounts were withheld, then the taxpayer is not entitled to a credit (*Price*).

Recipient is a partnership

If the recipient of a withholding payment is a partnership, a person with an individual interest in the partnership net income or loss that is wholly or partly attributable to withholding payments is entitled to a credit in respect of amounts withheld (TAA Sch 1 s 18-20). In addition, the partnership must have lodged its income tax return for the income year and either an assessment has been made of the tax payable by the partner or the Commissioner is satisfied that no tax is payable.

The amount of the credit is worked out using the formula:

$$\text{amounts withheld} \times \frac{\text{partner's individual interest attributable to the withholding payments}}{\text{net income/partnership loss attributable to the withholding payments}}$$

Recipient is a trustee

If the recipient of a withholding payment is a trustee, the entitlement to a credit is worked out according to the following rules (TAA Sch 1 s 18-25).

A *beneficiary* of the trust is entitled to a credit if:

- an amount is included in the beneficiary's assessable income under ITAA36 s 97 in respect of a share of the net income of the trust (¶6-110)
- the share is wholly or partly attributable to the withholding payments, and
- an assessment has been made of the tax payable by the beneficiary for the income year or the Commissioner is satisfied that no tax is payable.

The *trustee* of the trust is entitled to a credit if:

- the trustee is liable to be assessed, and to pay tax, under ITAA36 s 98 on an amount in respect of a share of the net income of the trust to which a beneficiary is presently entitled (¶6-210, ¶6-220)
- the share is wholly or partly attributable to the withholding payments, and
- either an assessment has been made of that tax or the Commissioner is satisfied that no tax is payable.

In both cases, the amount of the credit is worked out using the formula:

$$\text{amounts withheld} \times \frac{\text{share of net income attributable to the withholding payments}}{\text{so much of the net income as is attributable to the withholding payments}}$$

The *trustee* may also be entitled to a credit, calculated in the same manner, if liable to be assessed, and to pay tax, under ITAA36 s 99 or 99A on the net income of the trust, or on part of it, to which no beneficiary is presently entitled (¶6-230).

If there is no net income of the trust for the income year, the trustee is entitled to a credit equal to the sum of the amounts withheld.

Credits for foreign resident capital gains withholding tax

The normal credit rules are modified to ensure an entity's entitlement to a credit for amounts paid under the foreign resident capital gains tax withholding provisions (¶26-269) is available in the income year in which the transaction that caused the withholding is recognised (*Legislative Instrument* F2017L00992).

Credits for dividend, interest and royalty withholding

A person is entitled to a credit if:

- a dividend, interest or royalty has been included in the person's ordinary or statutory income, and
- the person has borne all or part of an amount withheld from the dividend, interest or royalty.

The amount of the credit is that amount or part (TAA Sch 1 s 18-30).

If an entity has paid a penalty for failing to withhold in relation to a dividend, interest or royalty payment, or GIC in relation to the penalty, the person liable to pay the withholding tax for the withholding payment is entitled to a credit equal to the amount of the penalty or GIC.

If the Commissioner remits the whole or a part of the penalty or GIC, then the credit is reduced by the amount that is remitted and the Commissioner refunds that amount (TAA Sch 1 s 18-35). A credit is similarly available where a penalty or GIC has been imposed in relation to a scheme to avoid withholding tax (TAA Sch 1 s 18-40).

Credit for withholding under the Seasonal Labour Mobility Program

An employee who has had an amount withheld under Subdiv 12-FC (¶26-275) is entitled to a credit (TAA Sch 1 s 18-33).

Credits for departing Australia superannuation payment withholding

A person liable to withholding tax under ITAA97 s 301-175 is entitled to a credit equal to the amount withheld from a departing Australia superannuation payment (TAA Sch 1 s 18-42).

If an entity has paid a penalty for failing to withhold in relation to departing Australia superannuation payment, or GIC in relation to the penalty, the person liable to pay the withholding tax under s 301-175 is entitled to a credit equal to the amount of penalty or GIC. (See ¶25-410 for a discussion of how GIC is calculated.)

If the Commissioner remits the whole or a part of the penalty or GIC, then the credit is reduced by the amount that is remitted and the Commissioner refunds that amount.

Credits for mining payments

If an amount is withheld from a mining payment in relation to Aboriginal land, the general rule is that the person liable to pay mining withholding tax (¶19-000) is entitled to a credit of an amount equal to the amount withheld (TAA Sch 1 s 18-45).

If separate mining payments are taken to have been made to, or applied for the benefit of, 2 or more persons because of that payment, the credit entitlement is divided between them. For example, if the payments have been made to 3 persons, each is entitled to one-third of the available credit.

If an entity has paid a penalty amount for failing to withhold in relation to a mining payment, the person liable to the mining withholding tax is entitled to a credit equal to the penalty amount. If separate mining payments are taken to have been made, the credit is divided between them.

If the Commissioner remits the whole or a part of the amount of penalty, any credit is reduced by the amount that is remitted and the Commissioner must pay to the entity an amount equal to the amount that is remitted.

[FTR ¶976-910 – ¶976-940]

¶26-680 Right to a refund from the payer

The payer must refund an amount to the recipient of a withholding payment if the payer:

- withheld the amount from a payment to the recipient (whether the amount has been paid to the Commissioner or not), or
- paid the amount to the Commissioner in relation to an alienated personal services payment or a non-cash benefit,

and the amount was withheld or paid in error or, in the case of an amount withheld from a purported parental leave payment, the amount was not lawfully payable (TAA Sch 1 s 18-65). For example, an investor may quote his/her TFN to an investment body but the body fails to record the number and later withholds from a payment of investment income.

The payer must refund a withheld amount if it becomes aware of the error or the recipient applies to the payer for the refund. In both cases, this must occur before the end of the financial year in which the amount was withheld or paid. The amount that must be refunded is a debt recoverable by the recipient from the payer.

If the payer refunds an amount, it may either:

- offset that amount against another payment it is required to make to the Commissioner, or
- recover from the Commissioner so much of the amount that is withheld and paid to the Commissioner, and which the payer has not recorded as being offset.

Request for information

In order to be eligible for a refund, the recipient must have provided any information requested by the payer (or the time for making such a request must have passed). The payer may request the recipient's:

- TFN or evidence of the basis on which the recipient is taken to have quoted the TFN to the payer, or
- ABN if the payment or non-cash benefit was in respect of an investment made in the course or furtherance of an enterprise,

if the payment or non-cash benefit was in respect of payments for work or services, retirement payments and ETPs, benefits and compensation payments or an investment where the recipient did not quote a TFN or an ABN.

Such a request must be made within 7 working days (of the payer) after the payer receives the application for the refund or after the payer otherwise becomes aware of the error. This request enables payers to correct their records before refunding an amount withheld in error, thereby reducing the risk of future errors. If the recipient does not provide a TFN or an ABN to the payer, the payer is not required to refund the amount.

[FTR ¶976-950]

¶26-700 Right to a refund from the Commissioner

A payment recipient may apply in writing to the Commissioner for the refund of an amount if the payer:

- withheld an amount from a payment made to, or received for, the recipient, or
- paid to the Commissioner an amount for an alienated personal services payment in relation to which an amount is included in the recipient's assessable income or for a non-cash benefit provided to, or received for, the recipient,

and the amount was so withheld or paid in error or, in the case of an amount withheld from a purported parental leave payment, the amount was not lawfully payable (TAA Sch 1 s 18-70).

However, the recipient may only apply for a refund from the Commissioner if it cannot apply for a refund from the payer (¶26-680) and the payer has already paid the withheld amount to the Commissioner.

The Commissioner must refund the amount if the application sets out:

- the recipient's TFN or, if the recipient does not have a TFN but was taken to have quoted one before the amount was withheld or paid, the basis on which the recipient was taken to have quoted the TFN, or
- if the payment or non-cash benefit was in respect of an ITAA36 Pt VA investment (¶26-200) made by the recipient in the course or furtherance of an enterprise — the recipient's ABN,

and the Commissioner is satisfied that it would be fair and reasonable to refund the amount, having regard to the circumstances that gave rise to the withholding obligation, the nature of the error and any other matter the Commissioner considers relevant (eg whether the recipient would suffer hardship if a refund is not given).

A person who is dissatisfied with the Commissioner's decision in relation to a refund may object against the decision in the usual manner (¶28-010).

Refunds in relation to investments

The Commissioner must refund all or part of an amount withheld from a withholding payment in relation to an investment for which no TFN is quoted, or where the investor became presently entitled to income from a unit trust, if the investor applies for a refund and the Commissioner is satisfied that the investor was effectively exempt from the TFN reporting requirements and that it is fair and reasonable to make the refund.

[FTR ¶976-953 – ¶976-960]

¶26-710 Directors of PAYG non-complying companies

TAA Sch 1 Subdiv 18-D reverses the economic benefit of a credit of a director received under TAA Sch 1 s 18-15 if the company does not comply with its withholding obligations.

The *Pay As You Go Withholding Non-Compliance Tax Act 2012* imposes the PAYG withholding non-compliance tax on company directors and their associates. This tax is payable where the company has withheld more amounts that it has paid to the Commissioner for the income year and the director has an entitlement to a withholding credit attributable to an amount withheld from a payment made by the company to the director (TAA Sch 1 s 18-125). Liability extends to an individual that became a director after the amount withheld was due to be paid to the Commissioner where the individual is still a director 30 days after the amount became due. The amount of tax payable is the lesser of:

- the total amounts withheld from payments to the individual by the company in the income year, and
- the company's PAYG withholding liability for payments made during the income year.

Where the Commissioner is satisfied that the director had grounds for allowing the company to fail to meet its withholding obligations, the amount of the tax may be reduced (TAA Sch 1 s 18-130). These grounds are:

(a) the director was not involved in the management of the company and it was reasonable for the director not to be involved because of illness or some other good reason

(b) the director took all reasonable steps to ensure that the directors caused: (i) the company to pay the withholding liability; (ii) an administrator to be appointed; or (iii) the company to begin to be wound up, or

(c) there were no reasonable steps that could have been taken to ensure one of those 3 things occurred.

The amount of the reduction is determined by the Commissioner.

An individual who is an associate of the director (within the meaning of ITAA36 s 318: ¶4-200) can be liable for the non-compliance tax where the associate is entitled to a credit which can be attributed to some extent to amounts withheld from payments made to the associate by the company (TAA Sch 1 s 18-135). The individual must be an associate of a director, either when the company was due to pay the amounts withheld to the Commissioner or after the amount became due and 30 days later the director was still a director. In addition, the Commissioner must be satisfied that:

- due to the associate's relationship with the director or the company, the associate knew or could reasonably be expected to have known, that the company had failed to pay amounts withheld to the Commissioner and the associate did not take reasonable steps to influence the directors to cause the company to notify the Commissioner about the amounts withheld, pay the amounts withheld to the Commissioner, appoint an administrator, have the company wound up, report to the Commissioner or other authority that the company has not paid the amounts withheld, or
- where the associate is an employee of the company, the associate was treated more favourably than other employees.

The Commissioner may commence proceedings to recover the tax after a notice has been issued to the individual (TAA Sch 1 s 18-140). GIC is payable on any unpaid non-compliance tax. For examples where company directors were liable to penalties for a company's failure to make payment of PAYG withholding amounts, despite the company entering liquidation, see *Lee; Silverbrook* and *Snell.*

[FTR ¶976-975]

¶26-720 Obligation to keep records under PAYG

Where certain conditions are satisfied, a payment summary given to an individual must be retained for a period of 2 years after the Commissioner issues a notice of assessment for the relevant year. The conditions that must be satisfied are, broadly:

- the individual's assessable income for the income year consists only of salary or wages, interest or a dividend from an Australian resident company, and
- the only amounts deducted from the individual's assessable income for the income year are expenditure incurred in managing tax affairs (¶16-850), bank account fees and charges or certain specified deductible gifts.

In addition, none of the following circumstances must exist in relation to the individual for the income year: the individual is not an Australian resident for the whole of the year; the individual is entitled to a foreign tax offset; an amount of expenditure incurred by an associate was deducted from the individual's assessable income; the individual derived income from an associate; the individual has a capital gain or capital loss for the income year; or the individual derived exempt foreign income (¶10-870) (Shortened Document Periods (Individuals with Simple Tax Affairs) Determination 2006 (*Legislative Instrument* F2006L00216)).

A payment summary given to an individual where the above conditions are not satisfied, must be retained for 5 years after the end of that year.

If the payer gives an entity other than an individual a payment summary, the entity must retain that copy for 5 years after the end of that year (TAA Sch 1 s 18-100).

Each party must keep a copy of a voluntary agreement to withhold from when it is made until 5 years after the making of the last payment covered by the agreement (TAA Sch 1 s 12-55).

A record-keeping checklist can be found at ¶44-100.

[FTR ¶976-970]

Administration

¶26-730 Commissioner's powers relating to PAYG withholding

The Commissioner may, by written notice, require any person to:

- give information
- attend and give evidence before the Commissioner or an authorised officer
- produce any documents in the person's custody or control,

covering any matters relevant to the administration or operation of PAYG withholding (TAA Sch 1 s 353-10).

[FTR ¶978-455]

¶26-750 PAYG withholding offences and penalties

The main offences connected with PAYG withholding are discussed at ¶29-300.

As an alternative to an administrative penalty for failing to withhold and in cases of serious non-compliance, the Commissioner can seek to have an offence prosecuted (s 16-25).

Offences by partnerships and unincorporated associations

An offence that would otherwise be committed by a partnership or unincorporated association is taken to have been committed by each partner or member of the committee of managements (as appropriate) who aided, abetted, counselled or procured the relevant act or omission or was in any way knowingly concerned in it.

[FTR ¶976-825]

Chapter 27 PAYG Instalments

Introduction

¶27-100 Introduction to PAYG instalments

The Pay As You Go (PAYG) instalments system (in TAA Sch 1 Pt 2-10 Div 45) is designed to ensure the efficient collection of income tax, Medicare levy, and tertiary education loan repayments. The due date for lodgment of a taxpayer's income tax return is not affected by the payment of PAYG instalments. The system requires most taxpayers to pay a quarterly instalment after the end of the quarter to which it relates based on the income derived during that quarter. Other taxpayers pay annually or monthly, depending on eligibility.

Business Activity Statements and Instalment Activity Statements

Notification of instalment income and payment of instalments is closely connected with the lodgment of a Business Activity Statement or an Instalment Activity Statement (¶24-200 and following).

[FTR ¶977-100]

Liability for Instalments

¶27-120 Liability to pay PAYG instalments

A taxpayer is only liable to pay PAYG instalments if the Commissioner has, by written notice, given the taxpayer an instalment rate (TAA s 45-15). An instalment rate will not be given to a taxpayer whose assessable income has always consisted wholly of withholding payments (¶26-120), other than non-quotation withholding payments (eg payments of investment income where a TFN or an ABN is not quoted). A taxpayer first starting in business will not be given an instalment rate until after the first income tax return for the business is assessed. To avoid the bunching of payments in the second year of business, a new business can make voluntary payments of PAYG instalments before an instalment rate is issued.

The fact that the Commissioner is under no obligation to give an instalment rate to a taxpayer effectively authorises the Commissioner to exempt certain taxpayers from the PAYG instalments system.

A taxpayer who has been given an instalment rate by the Commissioner is liable to pay the first instalment:

- *for the instalment month* in which the Commissioner first gives the instalment rate if, at the end of that month, the taxpayer is a monthly payer
- *for the instalment quarter* in which the Commissioner first gives the taxpayer an instalment rate (even if it is not the first instalment quarter for the year), or
- *for the income year* in which the Commissioner first gives the instalment rate if, at the end of the instalment quarter in which the Commissioner first gives the instalment rate, the taxpayer becomes an annual payer (TAA s 45-50).

An instalment does not have to be paid if the Commissioner withdraws the instalment rate.

Unpaid amounts of PAYG instalments are collected under TAA Sch 1 Pt 4-15 (¶25-500).

While partnerships are not liable to pay PAYG instalments, they are required to notify their partners of the amount of instalment income derived during an instalment period to enable the partners to correctly determine any amount payable. There are special rules for trustees (¶27-500) and consolidated groups (¶27-550).

Exemptions from the PAYG instalment system

Individuals in receipt of the seniors and pensioners tax offset (SAPTO: ¶15-310) are exempted from paying PAYG instalments if they qualified for a full or partial SAPTO in the latest income year for which an assessment has been issued.

Individuals and trusts with a balance on their last assessment of less than $1,000 are exempt from the PAYG instalment system. Further, individuals and trusts are exempt from the PAYG instalment system if the business and investment income shown in the most recent income tax return is less than $4,000 for residents ($1 for non-residents), or the notional tax is less than $500. These taxpayers will only need to pay tax on annual assessment.

Companies and superannuation funds are generally only required to pay PAYG instalments where:

- their ATO calculated instalment rate is greater than 0% and their notional tax is more than $500
- business and/or investment income (excluding capital gains) in the most recent income tax assessment is $2 million or more, or
- the taxpayer is the head company of a consolidated group.

[FTR ¶977-105]

¶27-130 PAYG instalment information to be given to the Commissioner

A taxpayer liable to pay a PAYG instalment for a period (even if that amount is nil) must notify the Commissioner of the amount of instalment income for that period (TAA s 45-20). This must be done on or before the date the instalment is due (¶27-200) (even if the taxpayer does not make the payment at that time) and it must be in the approved form (ie on a Business Activity Statement (BAS) or an Instalment Activity Statement (IAS): ¶24-240 and following).

Notification is not required in relation to:

- a quarterly instalment calculated on the basis of GDP-adjusted notional tax or estimated benchmark tax (¶27-220), or
- an annual instalment, unless it is worked out using the instalment rate given to the taxpayer by the Commissioner, multiplied by the taxpayer's instalment income for the year.

A taxpayer that fails to notify the Commissioner of the instalment income by the due date is liable to an administrative penalty (TAA s 286-75) (¶29-300). Monthly payers are required to notify the Commissioner electronically.

[FTR ¶977-105]

¶27-150 Credit for instalments

A taxpayer is entitled to a credit at the time the Commissioner makes an assessment of income tax payable by the taxpayer or determines that the taxpayer does not have a taxable income for the income year (TAA s 45-30). The credit is equal to the total of each instalment payable for the income year (even if it has not yet been paid), reduced by any variation credits claimed in respect of such instalments (¶27-280, ¶27-300).

The fact that the Commissioner has made such an assessment or determination does not affect the taxpayer's liability to pay an instalment.

The application of the credit, ie whether it is allocated to the taxpayer's running balance account (RBA) or applied by the Commissioner against a non-RBA tax debt of the taxpayer, is discussed at ¶24-360 and ¶24-380.

[FTR ¶977-105]

¶27-170 How many PAYG instalments are payable?

PAYG instalments may be payable annually, quarterly or monthly. The rules for determining the frequency of PAYG instalments are summarised below:

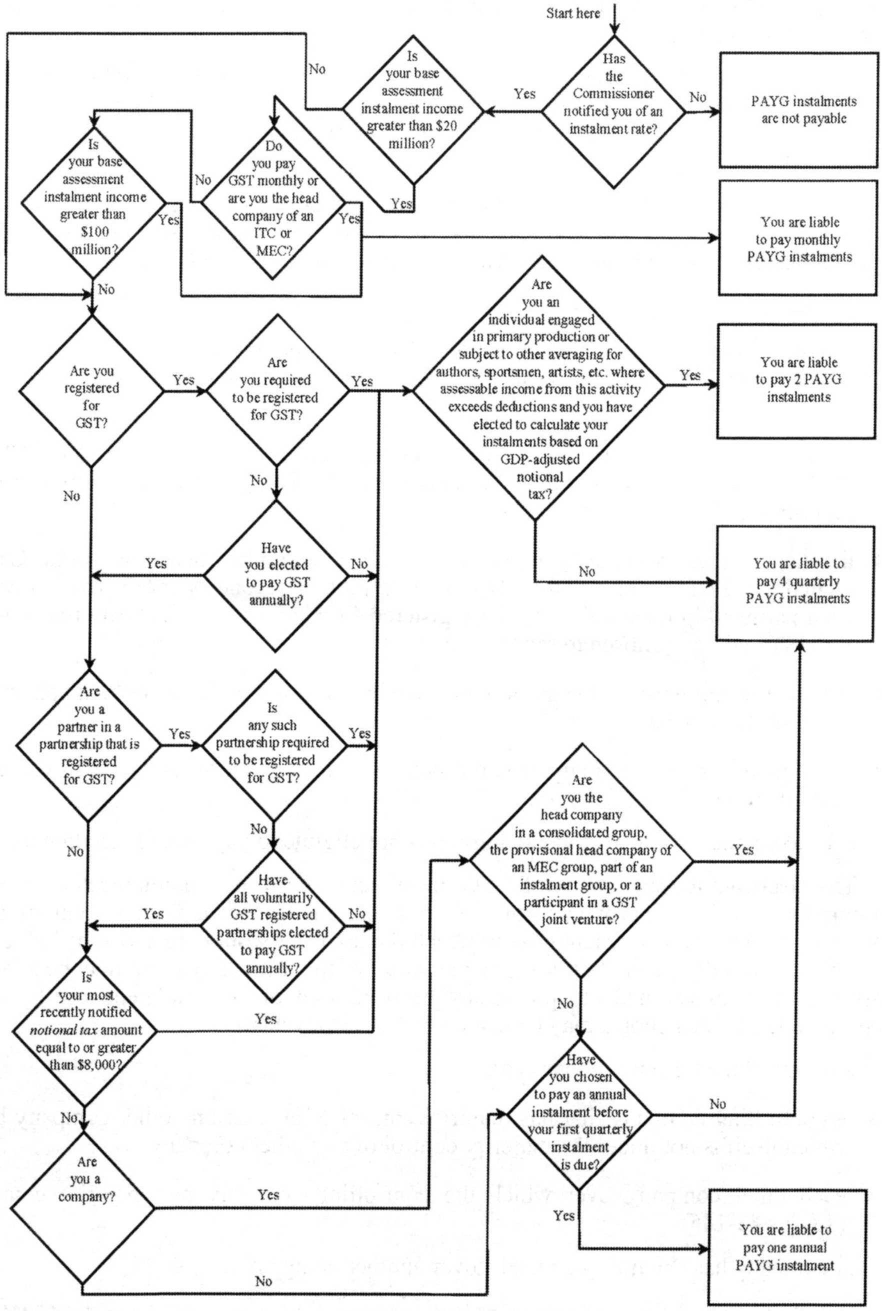

Quarterly instalments

A taxpayer who has been given an instalment rate by the Commissioner is liable to pay quarterly PAYG instalments, one for each quarter of the income year, unless the taxpayer is eligible to pay an annual instalment and chooses to do so or is required to pay monthly (TAA s 45-50).

Certain quarterly taxpayers are eligible to pay only 2 quarterly instalments each year, payable at the end of the third and fourth quarters (¶27-200). The eligible taxpayers are individuals who either carry on primary production businesses or who are authors, artists or other special professionals.

A taxpayer who is required to pay a quarterly instalment is required to continue to pay quarterly instalments unless the taxpayer becomes an annual or monthly PAYG instalment payer or the Commissioner withdraws the taxpayer's instalment rate.

Annual instalments

A taxpayer can choose to pay one annual PAYG instalment if, at the end of the first instalment quarter in the income year that the taxpayer would otherwise be required to pay:

- the taxpayer is not registered for GST and not required to be registered for GST (¶34-110) and is not a partner in a partnership that is registered or required to be registered for GST, or
- the taxpayer is voluntarily registered for GST and has chosen to remit GST annually (¶34-150) and, if the taxpayer is a partner in one or more partnerships, each partnership must either not be registered for GST or be voluntarily registered for GST and have chosen to remit annually, and
- the most recent notional tax amount notified by the Commissioner to the taxpayer is less than $8,000, and
- if the taxpayer is a company, it is not part of an instalment group (see below) or a participant in a GST joint venture (TAA s 45-140).

A head company of a consolidated group is not eligible to pay annual instalments.

The decision to pay annual PAYG instalments must be communicated to the Commissioner, in the approved form, on or before the due date for payment of the instalment for the first instalment quarter which the taxpayer would otherwise be liable to pay. This will usually be the first instalment quarter of the income year but may be a later quarter if the taxpayer had not previously been advised of an instalment rate by the Commissioner. Such a choice may be made via the ATO website.

An "instalment group" consists of:

- a controlling company that has majority control of at least one other company but which itself is not under the majority control of any other company
- each other company over which the controlling company has majority control (TAA s 45-145).

A company has "majority control" over another company if:

- the first company is in a position to cast, or control the casting of, more than 50% of the maximum number of votes that might be cast at a general meeting of the other company
- the first company has the power to appoint or remove the majority of the directors of the other company, or

- the other company is, or a majority of its directors are, accustomed or under an obligation, whether formal or informal, to act according to the directions, instructions or wishes of the first company.

A taxpayer required to pay an annual instalment continues to pay annual instalments unless the taxpayer ceases to be eligible to be an annual instalment payer, the taxpayer chooses to pay quarterly or the Commissioner withdraws the taxpayer's instalment rate.

Monthly instalments

Large entities are liable to pay monthly PAYG instalments if, on the "MPR test day", their income exceeds the following threshold:

- if the taxpayer is the head company of an income tax consolidated ("ITC") group or the provisional head company of a multiple entry consolidated ("MEC") group — $20 million
- if the taxpayer is not the head company of an ITC or MEC group:
  - if required to report and pay GST monthly — $20 million
  - otherwise — $100 million.

Determining the threshold

The threshold amount is the amount of "base assessment instalment income" that the entity has for a particular income year as provided by the Commissioner. Broadly, this is so much of the entity's assessable income for a year (the base year) as the Commissioner determines is instalment income (s 45-320(2): ¶27-260).

Those entities that have financial arrangements to which ITAA97 Div 230 applies ("TOFA entities") are required to use an "adjusted" base assessment instalment income calculation if the base assessment instalment income provided by the Commissioner does not exceed the threshold amount. This is because the base assessment instalment income calculated by the Commissioner uses net calculations for TOFA arrangements rather than gross figures; the adjusted base assessment instalment income includes the gross income of the entity's financial arrangements. This adjusted amount will need to be determined by the entity and notified to the Commissioner.

"MPR test day"

The threshold amount is tested at a particular point in time, namely, the start of the entity's monthly payer requirement test day (the "MPR test day").

If an entity is already paying PAYG instalments, the MPR test day is the first day at the start of the third last month of the previous income year (s 45-138(4)(b)). This means that, for an income year ending 30 June, the MPR test day for the 2020–21 income year is 1 April 2020. An entity currently paying PAYG instalments that satisfies the monthly payer requirement on a MPR test day becomes a monthly payer from the commencement of its next income year (the last day of the starting instalment month).

For entities first entering the PAYG instalment system, the MPR test day is the last day of the month in which the Commissioner has given them the instalment rate. Such entities that satisfy the monthly payer requirement at the relevant time will become monthly payers from the last day of the month (the starting instalment month) after the month in which the Commissioner gives the entity their first instalment rate. This is the first month commencing immediately after the MPR test day.

An entity continues to be liable for monthly PAYG instalments until it no longer meets the monthly payer requirement and gives notice to the Commissioner that it will no longer pay monthly instalments. Where such notice has been given, the entity remains a monthly payer until the next income year.

[FTR ¶977-125]

¶27-200 When PAYG instalments are payable

When quarterly PAYG instalments are payable

A taxpayer's first instalment will be payable for the PAYG instalment quarter in which the Commissioner first gives the taxpayer an instalment rate (TAA s 45-50). This need not be the first quarter of that income year.

If a taxpayer's income year ends on 30 June, the following table sets out the taxpayer's instalment quarters and the days on which the instalments for those quarters are due (TAA s 45-60). These dates generally apply to any entity that has a Business Activity Statement (BAS) (¶24-200) or Instalment Activity Statement (IAS) (¶24-220) quarterly obligation, apart from an entity that has chosen or is required to pay GST monthly. These entities are referred to as ''deferred BAS payers''.

For the quarter ending on:	The instalment is due on or before:
30 September	28 October
31 December	28 February
31 March	28 April
30 June	28 July

A quarterly instalment payable by a head company of a consolidated group will be due on or before 21 days after the end of the instalment quarter. This will be so even if the head company is a deferred BAS payer that is not due to pay its other BAS amounts until 28 days after the end of the quarter. The due date for paying those other BAS amounts is not affected.

The due dates for entities which are not eligible for the extended dates above (eg entities which pay GST monthly) are as follows:

For the quarter ending on:	The instalment is due on or before:
30 September	21 October
31 December	21 January
31 March	21 April
30 June	21 July

A taxpayer that uses 13 4-weekly accounting periods or 12 accounting periods, some of 4 weeks and others of 5 weeks, may calculate the PAYG instalment amount (and remit the instalment) for an instalment quarter having regard to the taxpayer's normal accounting periods, as long as the taxpayer has approval under the GST legislation (¶34-130) to have different tax periods (TD 2000/53). If a taxpayer has changed the day on which a tax period ends to reflect its commercial accounting practice, the taxpayer can also calculate its instalment income for the instalment quarter over the equivalent tax period. This does not, however, change the due dates for lodging a BAS or making payments (TD 2000/54).

If a taxpayer's income year ends on a day other than 30 June:

- the first PAYG instalment quarter is for the first 3 months of the taxpayer's income year
- the second PAYG instalment quarter is for the fourth, fifth and sixth months of the taxpayer's income year
- the third PAYG instalment quarter is for the seventh, eighth and ninth months of the taxpayer's income year, and

- the fourth PAYG instalment quarter is for the last 3 months of the taxpayer's income year.

The due dates for payment of PAYG instalments do not affect the due date for lodgment of the taxpayer's income tax return — the existing rules continue to apply (¶24-060).

A PAYG instalment is not payable if the Commissioner withdraws a taxpayer's instalment rate during the instalment quarter (TAA s 45-90).

Quarterly taxpayers with 2 instalments

Certain individual taxpayers who pay quarterly instalments are eligible to pay only 2 instalments in an income year rather than 4 (''the two instalments payer''). This applies to individuals who either:

- carry on primary production businesses (¶18-020), or
- are an author, artist or other special professional (¶2-142).

However, the concession is only available if the individual's assessable income from the business or professional activities in the most recent income year exceeded the deductions for that year that reasonably relate to that income. The instalments will be worked out using the GDP-adjusted notional tax method (¶27-220). They will be due 21 days after the end of the third and fourth quarters in the case of a two instalments payer who is not a deferred BAS payer, and 28 days after the end of the third and fourth quarters for deferred BAS payers. This allows those individuals to pay PAYG instalments more in accordance with the fluctuating nature of their income flows. The two instalments payer will be able to vary the amount of an instalment by estimating their expected tax liability for the year, but GIC will be imposed if the varied amount is too low (¶27-320).

Lodgment concessions

The ATO grants lodgment concessions which *generally* offer a 4-week extension for the first, third and fourth quarterly activity statements if lodged electronically by agents. Full details of the *Lodgment program 2020–21* are available on the ATO website.

There is also a lodgment concession for entities that do not use tax agents for the lodgment of activity statements. This concession *generally* offers a 2-week extension for lodgment of the first, third and fourth quarterly activity statements if lodged electronically. However, this concession does *not* apply to:

- monthly activity statements
- monthly GST payers with quarterly PAYG instalments (or other quarterly obligations)
- monthly PAYG withholding payers
- head companies of consolidated groups
- large businesses with substituted accounting periods (a large business is one with annual total income over $10 million, annual GST turnover over $20 million, annual withholding payments over $1 million, or a member of a company group where at least one member of the group has annual total income over $10 million)
- statements that did not have an original due date of the 28th of the month
- quarterly instalment notices (PAYG instalment only, GST instalment only, or PAYG and GST instalment only).

When annual PAYG instalments are payable

The first instalment for annual instalment payers is the instalment for the year in which the Commissioner first gives the taxpayer an instalment rate.

A PAYG instalment is not payable if the Commissioner withdraws a taxpayer's instalment rate during the income year.

All annual PAYG instalment payers must pay the annual PAYG instalment on or before the 21st day of the fourth month following the end of the income year (TAA s 45-70). For a taxpayer whose income year ends on 30 June, this means that the annual PAYG instalment is due on or before *21 October*.

Taxpayers should finalise their annual PAYG instalment before lodging their income tax return for the year, especially if they will have tax to pay. This will ensure that taxpayers receive credit in their income tax assessments for their annual PAYG instalments. Where taxpayers wish to vary their annual PAYG instalment, they should lodge the variation **before** lodging their annual income tax return (allowing enough time for postage and processing where the variation is lodged by mail). If taxpayers lodge their annual income tax return before finalising their annual PAYG instalment, they will receive a credit with their assessment for the amount notified on their instalment notice. Taxpayers are required to pay their annual PAYG instalment amount by 21 October even if their income tax return has been assessed. To alleviate this timing issue, for June balancing taxpayers the ATO generally issues the instalment notice in early July. However, if the taxpayer's income tax return has already been assessed, the ATO should be contacted to confirm whether the amount payable has changed.

When monthly instalments are payable

Notification and payment of monthly instalments must be undertaken on or before the 21st day of the next month, unless specified by other means by the Commissioner.

If a monthly payer is a deferred BAS payer, the payment must be made by the 28th day of the next month. The payment of a December monthly PAYG instalment by a deferred BAS payer must be made on or before the 28th of February.

Method of payment

Monthly PAYG instalments must be paid electronically. Other PAYG instalments must be paid electronically if the taxpayer is required to pay a net amount of GST electronically for that period (¶34-150) or is a large PAYG withholder (¶26-500) with a net amount payable for that month (TAA s 8AAZMA). Otherwise, the taxpayer is free to pay the instalment by any other method acceptable to the Commissioner.

Extensions of time to pay PAYG instalments

The Commissioner may extend the due date for the payment of a PAYG instalment for a period that is warranted by the circumstances (TAA s 255-10).

An amount due and payable on a non-business day (ie Saturday, Sunday or public holiday) is due and payable on the next business day (TAA s 8AAZMB).

Consequences of not paying a PAYG instalment on time

PAYG instalments are a debt due to the Commonwealth and may be sued for and recovered in any court of competent jurisdiction. Further, GIC is payable if a taxpayer fails to pay some or all of a PAYG instalment by the due date (TAA s 45-80). The GIC is payable on the amount that remains unpaid for the period that commences on the due date of the PAYG instalment and ends when the instalment, and the associated GIC, has been fully paid (¶29-510).

[FTR ¶977-125]

Calculation of Instalments

¶27-220 Amount of quarterly PAYG instalments

Instalment income as a basis for calculating quarterly instalments

Where a quarterly payer is not eligible to pay quarterly instalments on the basis of GDP-adjusted notional tax (¶27-470) or, if eligible, has elected to become a quarterly payer who pays on the basis of instalment income, the amount of a PAYG instalment for a particular quarter is calculated as follows (TAA s 45-110):

applicable instalment rate × instalment income for the quarter

The ''applicable instalment rate'' means whichever of the following is applicable:

- the latest instalment rate notified to the taxpayer by the Commissioner before the end of the quarter (¶27-450)
- where the taxpayer has chosen to use a different instalment rate for the current quarter — the rate chosen by the taxpayer, or
- if the taxpayer has chosen in a previous quarter in the current income year to use a rate other than the one notified by the Commissioner — the rate previously chosen by the taxpayer. In subsequent years, the taxpayer must use the most recent rate given by the Commissioner or may choose another instalment rate (TAA s 45-205).

The procedure for varying the instalment rate is discussed at ¶27-280.

The ''instalment income for the quarter'' is the taxpayer's instalment income for the particular PAYG instalment quarter worked out under the rules in ¶27-260.

▶ Example 1

Mighty Big Tractors Pty Ltd is required to pay quarterly PAYG instalments based on its instalment rate and instalment income for each quarter. The Commissioner has advised Mighty Big Tractors Pty Ltd of an instalment rate of 22.57% prior to the end of the current instalment quarter. The company has decided not to vary its instalment rate. During this instalment quarter, Mighty Big Tractors Pty Ltd derived instalment income of $1,025,891. Therefore, the PAYG instalment for Mighty Big Tractors Pty Ltd for the current quarter is:

22.57% × $1,025,891 = $231,543.60

GDP-adjusted notional tax as a basis for calculating quarterly instalments

Individual taxpayers and multi-rate trustees

All individual taxpayers and multi-rate trustees (¶27-500) that are quarterly payers are eligible to pay quarterly instalments using the GDP-adjusted notional tax method (whether they pay 2 or 4 instalments annually). This is the default basis and applies unless the taxpayer has chosen to pay on the basis of instalment income. The choice is made by notifying the Commissioner in the approved form on or before the due date for payment of the instalment for the starting instalment quarter (generally, the first instalment quarter of the year).

Other taxpayers eligible

Other quarterly payers are eligible to have their quarterly PAYG instalments calculated for them by the Commissioner using the GDP-adjusted notional tax method. This is the default method for calculating quarterly PAYG instalments for all companies, superannuation funds and other entities taxed as companies that have:

- $2 million or less in base assessment instalment income (¶27-450) for the previous income year, or
- more than $2 million in instalment income for the previous income year and are eligible to pay annual PAYG instalments but have chosen not to do so (s 45-130).

"Small business entities" (¶7-050) are also able to have their liability for PAYG instalments calculated under the GDP-adjusted notional tax method. The turnover threshold for determining whether an entity is a small business will increase from $10 million to $50 million from 1 July 2021.

Ceasing to be eligible to use GDP-adjusted notional tax to calculate quarterly instalments

A quarterly payer ceases to be eligible to calculate PAYG instalments on the basis of GDP-adjusted notional tax at the start of the first quarter of the next income year if the payer:

- chooses to become an annual payer at the end of the first instalment quarter of a later income year
- chooses to be a quarterly payer who pays on the basis of instalment income at the end of the first instalment quarter of a later income year
- in the case of a company or superannuation fund, it fails to meet the eligibility criteria mentioned above, or
- the taxpayer becomes a monthly payer.

Amount of instalment using GDP-adjusted notional tax

The amount of a PAYG instalment for a taxpayer for a particular quarter where the taxpayer has chosen to pay quarterly PAYG instalments based on GDP-adjusted notional tax is whichever of the following is applicable (TAA s 45-112):

- the amount notified to the taxpayer by the Commissioner as being the amount of the instalment
- where the taxpayer has chosen to work out the amount of the instalment on the basis of the taxpayer's estimate of benchmark tax for that income year and the taxpayer has notified the Commissioner of that benchmark tax amount (¶27-300) — the applicable amount, or
- if the taxpayer has chosen in a previous quarter in the current income year to base instalments on an estimate of benchmark tax (¶27-490) — the amount notified to the taxpayer by the Commissioner as being the amount of the instalment.

For the GDP adjustment factor, see ¶27-470.

Amount notified by the Commissioner

The following table sets out the amount that the Commissioner will notify the taxpayer as being payable for a particular PAYG instalment where the taxpayer is eligible to pay instalments based on GDP-adjusted notional tax and has not decided to calculate instalments on the basis of an estimate of benchmark tax for that income year (¶27-300).

If the instalment quarter is:	The amount of the instalment is:
the first in that income year for which the taxpayer is liable to pay a PAYG instalment	25% of the GDP-adjusted notional tax
the second in that income year for which the taxpayer is liable to pay a PAYG instalment	50% of the GDP-adjusted notional tax, less the amount of any previous instalment in that income year
the third in that income year for which the taxpayer is liable to pay a PAYG instalment	75% of the GDP-adjusted notional tax, less the amount of any previous instalments in that income year
the fourth in that income year for which the taxpayer is liable to pay a PAYG instalment	100% of the GDP-adjusted notional tax, less the amount of any previous instalments in that income year

▶ Example 2

Marlene is eligible to pay her quarterly PAYG instalments on the basis of GDP-adjusted notional tax and has chosen to do so. Marlene has not chosen to work out her instalments based on her estimate of her benchmark tax.

At the time Marlene's first instalment was payable, her GDP-adjusted notional tax was $76,000. Accordingly, the Commissioner notified Marlene of an instalment of $19,000.

During the second quarter of the income year, Marlene's assessment for the prior income year issued. Her GDP-adjusted notional tax was now $102,000. Accordingly, the second quarterly PAYG instalment notified to Marlene by the Commissioner was:

$$(50\% \times \$102{,}000) - \$19{,}000 = \$32{,}000$$

Assuming no other changes to her GDP-adjusted tax, Marlene's third and fourth instalments will be $25,500 each.

Two instalments payers

Individuals who are quarterly payers who pay 2 instalments annually pay on the basis of GDP-adjusted notional tax (¶27-200). The amount of the quarterly instalment will be worked out in the same way as for those who are already entitled to pay on the basis of GDP-adjusted notional tax.

Generally, the instalment payable for the third quarter is 75% of the taxpayer's GDP-adjusted notional tax. The instalment payable for the fourth quarter is 100% of the taxpayer's GDP-adjusted notional tax less the previous instalment unless the amount is negative, in which case the amount of instalment is nil. This method is used if the individual becomes a 2 instalment payer before the end of the first instalment quarter in an income year. The amount is reduced if the individual becomes a 2 instalment payer at the end of the second, third or fourth instalment quarter of the income year. The reduction ensures that the individual does not pay more than would have been required had he/she been a quarterly payer who pays 4 instalments annually on the basis of GDP-adjusted notional tax, or if he/she had chosen to pay quarterly instalments on the basis of instalment income.

Instalment quarter in which instalment rate is first notified	**Instalment quarter for which the instalment is payable**	**Amount of instalment**
Before the end of the first	Third	75% of the taxpayer's GDP-adjusted notional tax
	Fourth	100% of the taxpayer's GDP-adjusted notional tax, less the third instalment
During the second	Third	50% of the taxpayer's GDP-adjusted notional tax
	Fourth	75% of the taxpayer's GDP-adjusted notional tax, less the third instalment
During the third	Third	25% of the taxpayer's GDP-adjusted notional tax
	Fourth	50% of the taxpayer's GDP-adjusted notional tax, less the third instalment
During the fourth	Third	Not applicable
	Fourth	25% of the taxpayer's GDP-adjusted notional tax

Impact of IFRS

Guidelines have been issued by the ATO for Australian entities reporting PAYG instalment income where International Financial Reporting Standards (IFRS) issues are not resolved (¶23-000, ¶22-700). Companies affected by the implementation of IFRS should lodge and pay using the following methods:

- PAYG instalment amount payers can pay the pre-notified PAYG instalment amount by the due date and vary their instalment amount on a subsequent activity statement (or instalment notice) if required
- PAYG instalment rate payers who have an unresolved IFRS issue beyond their control will be allowed to calculate their instalment income under the previous reporting standards or use a best estimate of the impact of IFRS on the relevant transactions when reporting their PAYG instalments,

provided a revised activity statement is lodged as soon as practical after the issue is resolved.

Taxpayers who make a genuine attempt to comply with IFRS and revise their obligation as soon as practical or lodge under previous reporting standards, or use a best estimate approach, will have GIC attributable to the revision remitted to the base rate. Penalties on shortfall or variation amounts would also be remitted, provided a genuine attempt to comply with IFRS has been made.

Where a PAYG instalment issue has not been resolved by the time the annual income tax return is lodged, any adjustments need only be made to the income tax return when the issue is resolved. Revisions that reduce a taxpayer's tax liability may give rise to an entitlement to interest.

[FTR ¶977-145, ¶977-155]

¶27-240 Amount of annual PAYG instalments

The amount of an annual PAYG instalment is whichever of the following the taxpayer chooses:

- the amount worked out using the formula:

  instalment rate × taxpayer's instalment income for the year

- the notional tax amount most recently notified to the taxpayer by the Commissioner prior to the end of the income year, or
- the amount the taxpayer estimates will be the benchmark tax amount for the income year (TAA s 45-115).

Annual PAYG payers cannot substitute their own estimate of the instalment rate for that which the Commissioner advises (¶27-450). If an annual payer wishes to pay a different amount (eg the instalment rate is considered to be too high), the taxpayer must choose to pay either: (a) the notional tax amount most recently notified by the Commissioner prior to the end of the income year; or (b) the amount the taxpayer estimates will be the benchmark tax amount for the income year.

▶ Example

For the current income year, Albert is eligible to pay an annual PAYG instalment. The notional tax amount most recently notified to Albert before the end of the current income year is $6,845. Further, the Commissioner has advised Albert of an instalment rate of 42.90%. Albert's instalment income for the current income year is $14,096. Albert has not chosen to pay his annual PAYG instalment based on his estimate of benchmark tax.

If Albert chooses to pay his annual instalment based on the instalment rate notified to him by the Commissioner, the amount of his annual instalment is:

42.90% × $14,096 = $6,047.18

Alternatively, Albert could choose to pay an annual instalment of $6,845, being the amount of his most recently notified notional tax.

[FTR ¶977-165]

¶27-250 Amount of monthly PAYG instalments

The amount of a monthly instalment is calculated as follows (TAA s 45-114):

the applicable instalment rate × the instalment income for that instalment month

The ''applicable instalment rate'' means whichever of the following is applicable:

- the latest instalment rate notified to the taxpayer by the Commissioner before the end of the month (¶27-450)
- where the taxpayer has chosen to use a different instalment rate for the current month — the rate chosen by the taxpayer, or
- if the taxpayer has chosen in a previous month in the current income year to use a rate other than the one notified by the Commissioner — the rate previously chosen by the taxpayer. In subsequent years, the taxpayer must use the most recent rate given by the Commissioner or may choose another instalment rate (TAA s 45-205).

The procedure for varying the instalment rate is discussed at ¶27-280.

The ''instalment income for the month'' is the taxpayer's instalment income for the particular PAYG instalment month worked out under the rules in ¶27-260.

''Instalment month'' means a month that starts on the first day of an income year and each subsequent month, which equates to each calendar month of the year.

The Commissioner may determine additional methods for calculating the amount of a monthly instalment by legislative instrument. In this case, a monthly payer may choose to use an additional method (if eligible) or calculate instalment income under the general provisions.

*Legislative Instrument*F2013L01933 prescribes an additional method. Basically, this method allows the taxpayer to calculate the first 2 instalments of a quarter as the applicable instalment rate multiplied by ''a reasonable estimate'' of his/her/its instalment income for the month. If the Commissioner considers that the estimate is not reasonable, then the application of this determination is taken to be invalid and the Commissioner can require the taxpayer to calculate the instalment in accordance with s 45-114. Where this method has been used for the first and second months in an instalment quarter, the third instalment in the quarter is calculated as:

$$\text{applicable instalment rate} \times \left(\begin{array}{c}\text{taxpayer's actual}\\ \text{instalment income for}\\ \text{the instalment quarter}\end{array} - \begin{array}{c}\text{the instalment income}\\ \text{used for the first and second}\\ \text{instalment months}\end{array} \right)$$

If the amount worked out using the formula is negative, the instalment for the third month of the instalment quarter is $0 and the taxpayer is able to revise the instalment income in the second instalment month and, if that is insufficient, the first instalment month.

The rules that apply to the operation and administration of quarterly PAYG instalment payers apply to monthly payers, including penalties where the varied instalment rate is too low.

[FTR ¶977-160]

Calculation of Instalment Income

¶27-260 General rule for calculation of instalment income

A taxpayer's instalment income for a period includes the taxpayer's ordinary income derived during that period, but only to the extent that it is assessable during the income year that is, or includes, the period (TAA s 45-120(1)).

▶ Example

A primary producer derives a tax profit of $500,000 from the forced disposal of live stock. The $500,000 would be considered to be ordinary income in the month/quarter/year derived. However, the primary producer can elect to spread this profit over a 5-year period such that only $100,000 is assessable income in the year of derivation. In this case, only $100,000 is considered to be instalment income. In Years 2, 3, 4 and 5, the $100,000 returned as assessable income from the forced disposal does not constitute ordinary income and, therefore, is not part of the primary producer's instalment income for those years. Of course, the taxpayer's instalment rate could be expected to increase in this situation.

Ordinary income includes amounts such as sales (excluding GST and gross of expenses), fees, interest, dividends (excluding franking credits) and royalties (¶10-010). Ordinary income from shipping activities that relate to a vessel in respect of which the taxpayer expects to be issued with a shipping exempt income certificate can be excluded from instalment income (ID 2013/45).

An entity can include a net forex realisation gain in instalment income if the entity accounts for forex realisation gains and losses on a net basis in its books of account, and the net basis of accounting is reflected in the manner in which the entity reported information about forex realisation gains and losses in the income tax return (before reconciliation to taxable income) on which the instalment rate for that instalment period is based (PS LA 2005/17). However, the net forex realisation gain cannot include a forex realisation loss that is known to be material, at the time of determining instalment income. (Note that PS LA 2005/17 does not apply to individuals who do not derive income from a business or entities that pay PAYG instalments on the basis of GDP-adjusted notional tax.) A forex realisation gain made under ITAA97 s 775-55 upon payment for the acquisition of foreign currency denominated trading stock (other than livestock) is ordinary income (TD 2006/29).

Statutory income (eg capital gains) is not, as a general rule, included as part of a taxpayer's instalment income. Further, exempt income is not included as part of instalment income.

Special rules apply for calculating the instalment income of a partner in a partnership (¶27-265) and a beneficiary of a trust estate (¶27-270).

If there is no instalment income for a period, the taxpayer must advise the Commissioner of that fact.

Statutory income included for some taxpayers

Financial arrangements

The definition of "instalment income" includes net gains (to the extent the gains equal or exceed the losses) from Div 230 financial arrangements, applicable to the first quarter of an income year following a TOFA entity's first base assessment that applied the TOFA provisions to their Div 230 financial arrangements. It does not apply to individuals, and entities whose only gains and losses are from financial arrangements that are qualifying securities. To ensure that there is no double counting of an ordinary or statutory income amount in instalment income calculations for any instalment period, where an amount of ordinary or statutory income is taken into account in working out a net TOFA gain for an instalment period (including nil), it is not taken into account again in the instalment income calculations for any instalment period.

Other statutory income

The instalment income of PSTs and of complying/non-complying superannuation funds and ADFs for a period also includes statutory income that is reasonably attributable to the period and is assessable income of the income year that is, or includes, that period (s 45-120(2)).

Certain statutory income is also included in the instalment income of a life insurance company, including a consolidated group that includes a life insurance company (s 45-120(2A)).

PAYG withholding payments

Generally, a taxpayer's instalment income does not include: (a) amounts that have been, or should have been, subject to PAYG withholding (¶26-120); or (b) personal services amounts required to be included in a taxpayer's assessable income and for which amounts are required to be paid under TAA Sch 1 Div 13 (¶26-280) (s 45-120(3)).

However, amounts that have been subject to PAYG withholding because the taxpayer failed to quote a TFN or an ABN (¶26-200) will be included in instalment income.

Farm management deposits

If a taxpayer makes a farm management deposit (FMD) (¶18-290) during a period, the taxpayer's instalment income for that period is reduced (but not below nil) by the amount of that deposit to the extent that the taxpayer reasonably expects to be able to claim a deduction for it for the income year that is, or includes, the period (s 45-120(4)). Conversely, where a taxpayer makes an FMD withdrawal during a period, the taxpayer's instalment income for that period includes that withdrawal to the extent that it is assessable income for the income year that is, or includes, that period (s 45-120(5)).

Clean energy initiatives

Instalment income for a period also includes an amount that is included in a taxpayer's assessable income under ITAA97 s 420-25 for the income year that is or includes that period because the taxpayer ceases to hold a registered emissions unit during that period (s 45-120(5A)).

[FTR ¶977-145]

¶27-265 Instalment income for partners in a partnership

The instalment income of a taxpayer who is a partner in a partnership at any time during a period includes an amount calculated in accordance with the following formula for each such partnership (TAA s 45-260):

$$\frac{\text{taxpayer's assessable income from the partnership for the last income year}}{\text{partnership's instalment income for that income year}} \times \text{partnership's instalment income for the current period}$$

The "taxpayer's assessable income from the partnership for the last income year" is so much of the taxpayer's individual interest in the partnership's net profit as was included in the taxpayer's assessable income for the most recent income year that ended before the start of the current period and for which the taxpayer has been assessed or has been advised by the Commissioner that no tax is payable. This will usually be the amount of the partnership distribution included in the taxpayer's assessable income for the income year that has most recently been assessed.

The ''partnership's instalment income for that income year'' is the instalment income for the partnership (calculated using all of the rules involving calculation of instalment income, including this one) for the most recent income year that ended before the start of the current period and for which the taxpayer has been assessed or has been advised by the Commissioner that no tax is payable.

The ''partnership's instalment income for the current period'' is the instalment income for the partnership for the current period. Therefore, the partnership will be required to calculate its instalment income on a monthly, quarterly and annual basis. Further, the partnership will need to notify each partner of the amount calculated in accordance with the above formula (or each of the components so that the partners can calculate the amount) on a monthly, quarterly and annual basis.

The amount included in a taxpayer's instalment income from a partnership is in addition to any other amounts already included in instalment income (eg other business income, interest and dividends). However, no deduction is made if the partnership is expected to make a loss.

The general rule in s 45-260 does not apply to a partner in a corporate limited partnership. Instead, the general rule in TAA s 45-120 (¶27-260) applies, and the partner includes in instalment income any distribution from the corporate limited partnership for the instalment period in which the distribution is made.

Instalment income may include a "fair and reasonable" amount

If the taxpayer's share from the partnership for the last income year or the partnership's instalment income for that year is nil or did not exist, the taxpayer's instalment income for the current period includes an amount that is fair and reasonable having regard to the following factors:

- the extent of the taxpayer's interest in the partnership during the current period
- the partnership's instalment income for the current period
- any other relevant circumstances (s 45-260(3)).

This could occur where the partnership is new or incurred a loss in the last year, or the taxpayer has only recently become a partner in the partnership. There is no guidance as to what may constitute ''other relevant circumstances''. This qualification has no application where the partnership's instalment income for the current period is nil.

See ¶27-270 for an example showing the calculation of instalment income for a taxpayer who is a partner in a partnership and also a beneficiary of a trust.

[FTR ¶977-195]

¶27-270 Instalment income for beneficiaries of a trust estate

If a taxpayer is a beneficiary of a trust estate at any time during the period, the general rule is that the taxpayer's instalment income, in relation to each trust of which the taxpayer is a beneficiary during the period, includes an amount calculated in accordance with the following formula (TAA s 45-280):

$$\frac{\text{taxpayer's assessable income from the trust for the last income year}}{\text{trust's instalment income for that income year}} \times \text{trust's instalment income for the current period}$$

The ''taxpayer's assessable income from the trust for the last income year'' is so much of the taxpayer's share of the net income of the trust as was included in the taxpayer's assessable income for the most recent income year that ended before the start of the current period and for which the taxpayer has been assessed or advised by the

Commissioner that no tax is payable. This will usually be the amount of the trust distribution included in the taxpayer's assessable income for the income year that has most recently been assessed.

In general, a taxpayer's assessable income does not include a share of the trust net income that is attributable to a capital gain made by the trust. There are, however, 2 circumstances in which a capital gain is included: (a) if the beneficiary is an eligible ADF, an eligible superannuation fund or a PST; or (b) to the extent that the share of the trust's net income is included in the complying superannuation class of a life insurance company's taxable income (TAA s 45-290).

In determining the taxpayer's assessable income from the trust, only amounts assessed under ITAA36 Pt III Div 6 (¶6-080) are taken into account. Amounts assessed under other provisions (eg a distribution from a superannuation fund) are not included. Effectively, this means that only the flow-through distributions are included for this purpose. The PAYG instalment system applies separately to certain trustees where such trustees are taxable on some or all of the net income of the trust estate (¶27-500).

The "trust's instalment income for that income year" is the instalment income for the trust for the most recent income year that ended before the start of the current period and for which the taxpayer has been assessed or has been advised by the Commissioner that no tax is payable.

The "trust's instalment income for the current period" is the instalment income for the trust for the current period. Therefore, a trust will be required to calculate the trust's instalment income on a monthly, quarterly and annual basis. Also, on a monthly, quarterly and annual basis, the trustee will need to notify each beneficiary of the amount calculated in accordance with the above formula (or each of the components so that the beneficiaries can calculate the amount).

The amount included in a taxpayer's instalment income as a beneficiary is in addition to any other amounts already included in the instalment income.

Instalment income may include a "fair and reasonable" amount

If the taxpayer's share of the net income of the trust estate for the last income year or the trust's instalment income for that year is nil or did not exist, the taxpayer's instalment income for the current period includes an amount that is fair and reasonable having regard to the following factors:

- the extent of the taxpayer's interest in the trust, or in the income of the trust, during the current period
- the trust's instalment income for the current period
- any other relevant circumstances.

This could occur where the trust is new or incurred a loss in the last year, or the taxpayer has only recently become a beneficiary of the trust. There is no guidance as to what may constitute "other relevant circumstances". This qualification has no application where the trust's instalment income for the current period is nil.

▶ Example

Calculation of instalment income for partner/beneficiary

During a particular instalment quarter (the current period), Marcia derived the following assessable income:

Gross sales	$45,000
Interest	$10,000

Unfranked dividends	$2,000
Net capital gain	$4,500

During the previous income year, Marcia was a beneficiary of the Jan Fan Trust. For that year, Marcia derived assessable income from the trust of $2,300 and the trust had total instalment income of $67,094. The Jan Fan Trust has informed Marcia that it has derived $23,000 instalment income for the current period.

Marcia has also gone into partnership with Greg and Peter during the current period. This partnership did not exist during the last income year. Under the partnership agreement with Greg and Peter, profits are to be divided equally. During the current period, the partnership derived instalment income of $3,300.

Marcia's instalment income for the current period is calculated as follows:

Instalment income = $45,000 + $10,000 + $2,000 + $788.45 (from the trust) + $1,100 (from the partnership)
= $58,888.45

The trust amount of $788.45 was calculated as follows:

$$\text{Trust amount} = \frac{\$2{,}300}{\$67{,}094} \times \$23{,}000$$
$$= \$788.45$$

The partnership amount of $1,100 is a fair and reasonable amount given that the partnership did not exist last year and given Marcia's interest in the partnership and the instalment income derived by the partnership during the period.

The net capital gain of $4,500 is not included as it is not ordinary income and Marcia is not a superannuation fund, ADF, PST or life insurance company.

Exceptions to general rule in s 45-280

There are 4 exceptions to the general rule for calculating the instalment income of the beneficiary of a trust.

(1) The instalment income of a *beneficiary of a corporate unit trust or public trading trust* is calculated under the general rule in TAA s 45-120 (¶27-260). Such a beneficiary includes any distribution from the trust in its instalment income for the period in which the distribution is made (s 45-280(4)).

(2) *Beneficiaries who are absolutely entitled* to the assets of a trust include in their instalment income for an instalment period their proportionate share of the instalment income earned by the trust in that period (s 45-280(6)). This applies to a beneficiary where:

(a) the trustee's only active duties in managing the trust are to deal with trust income and trust capital according to the requests or directions of the beneficiaries

(b) the beneficiary is absolutely entitled to the trust assets, and

(c) the beneficiary has a vested and indefeasible interest in all of the trust income or, if there is more than one beneficiary, each beneficiary has a vested and indefeasible interest in a proportion of the trust income that corresponds with the beneficiary's proportional interest in the trust capital.

The beneficiary is treated as having received its share of the trust income as soon as that income is earned in the trust.

(3) Certain *beneficiaries of broadly held resident investment unit trusts* calculate their instalment income by applying the rules in TAA s 45-285(1). The beneficiary's instalment income for an instalment period includes any trust income or trust capital that the trust distributes to them, or applies for their benefit. In working out the instalment income on this ''receipts basis'', it does not matter whether the trust income or trust capital is included in the beneficiary's assessable income for the income year in which the distribution or application occurs.

A *unit trust* is required to satisfy 4 conditions before the beneficiaries are entitled to determine their instalment income on this basis:

(a) the unit trust is resident

(b) the unit trust is broadly held, ie throughout the relevant instalment period the units in the unit trust are listed on a stock exchange in Australia or elsewhere, are offered to the public, or are held by at least 50 persons

(c) ownership of the trust is not concentrated in 20 or fewer individuals (tests about ''ownership'' of the trust are contained in TAA s 45-287)

(d) the trust's activities are limited to investment activities listed in the ITAA36 s 102M definition of ''eligible investment business'' throughout the relevant instalment period (these activities include investing in land to earn rent and investing or trading in various securities) (¶6-320).

(4) *Beneficiaries of certain other resident investment unit trusts* (ie certain ''narrowly held'' trusts) can determine their instalment income from the trust on a receipts basis if the unit trust and the beneficiary satisfy certain conditions (s 45-285(2)). The tests that the *unit trust* must satisfy are that:

(a) the unit trust is a resident trust

(b) the trust's activities consist only of activities listed in the s 102M definition of ''eligible investment business''.

The *beneficiary* must satisfy 2 conditions:

(a) the beneficiary is not required to include in instalment income the trust income or trust capital distributed to, or applied for, it under s 45-285(1) (ie under the exception in (3) above)

(b) the beneficiary must, throughout the instalment period, be one of the following: (i) the trustee of a broadly held resident investment unit trust that satisfies the 4 conditions in (3) above; (ii) exempt from tax; (iii) a complying superannuation fund, complying ADF or PST; (iv) a statutory fund of a life insurance company; or (v) the trustee of one or more trusts that meets specified requirements (TAA s 45-288), including that the beneficiaries are absolutely entitled to the assets of the trust.

A taxpayer's instalment income for a period also includes trust income or trust capital that a trust distributes to the taxpayer, or applies for the taxpayer's benefit, during that period in certain situations (s 45-286). This applies where:

(a) the income or capital is not included in the taxpayer's instalment income under s 45-280 or 45-285

(b) the trust satisfies the condition in s 12-400(1)(a) (¶26-267) in relation to the income year that is or includes that period

(c) the trust is a managed investment trust or is treated as a managed investment trust for that income year, and

(d) the trust meets the requirement in ITAA97 s 275-110 throughout the income year (ie it is not a corporate unit trust or trading trust).

The liability to PAYG instalments of *trustees* in respect of a beneficiary's share of the trust's net income, or the income to which no beneficiary is entitled, is discussed at ¶27-500.

[FTR ¶977-200]

Variation of Instalments

¶27-280 Variation of instalments based on instalment income

All monthly PAYG instalment payers and some quarterly PAYG instalment payers are ineligible to pay quarterly PAYG instalments based on GDP-adjusted notional tax. Further some quarterly payers, being eligible, have declined to use this method. Such taxpayers may wish to use an instalment rate other than that which has been advised by the Commissioner. Note that annual payers can use the instalment rate method but are not eligible to use a varied rate. (Variation of instalments by taxpayers who use the GDP-adjusted notional tax basis is discussed at ¶27-300.)

Some situations in which it may be appropriate to vary an instalment include:

- reducing or expanding investment activity (or receiving significantly lower or higher dividends from a share portfolio)
- changes in the level of business activity and, therefore, business income
- having much higher or lower than expected tax deductions for about the same level of investment and business income
- having repaid all amounts owed under HELP or Student Financial Supplement Scheme (SFSS)
- changes in business structure, eg mergers, takeovers or internal restructuring.

Once a taxpayer has decided to use a different instalment rate to that notified by the Commissioner, the varied instalment rate must be notified to the Commissioner in order to be effective (TAA s 45-210). This notification forms part of the Business Activity Statement or the Instalment Activity Statement (¶24-200, ¶24-220) and must be notified on or before the due date for payment of the instalment.

Once the Commissioner has been notified, the taxpayer must use that instalment rate for that instalment month or quarter, even if the Commissioner notifies the taxpayer of a different instalment rate after that time (TAA s 45-205). In fact, this rate must continue to be used by the taxpayer for the remaining months or quarters in the income year, unless the taxpayer chooses to use a different instalment rate and notifies the Commissioner accordingly. Therefore, a taxpayer can effectively vary the instalment rate up to 4 times (for quarterly payers) or 12 times (for monthly payers) in any given income year, once for each instalment period.

However, the varied instalment rate is only applicable for the income year for which it was notified to the Commissioner. For the subsequent income year, the taxpayer must either revert to using the rate most recently notified by the Commissioner, or again vary the instalment rate and notify the Commissioner accordingly.

Penalties may apply if the varied instalment rate is too low (¶27-320).

Claiming a variation credit for previous overpaid instalments

If a taxpayer has already paid a monthly or quarterly PAYG instalment before choosing to use a varied instalment rate, the taxpayer may be entitled to claim a variation credit (TAA s 45-215). To claim such a credit, the instalment rate chosen for the calculation of the current monthly or quarterly instalment must be less than the instalment rate used to calculate the instalment for the previous instalment month or quarter (if any) in the same income year.

Further, the amount calculated in accordance with the following method statement must be positive.

Step 1: Add up all the instalments the taxpayer has paid, or is liable to pay, for the instalment periods in the current income year prior to the current instalment period (even if they have not yet been paid).

Step 2: Subtract from the step 1 amount each earlier variation credit that the taxpayer has claimed in respect of the current income year.

Step 3: Multiply the total of the taxpayer's instalment income for the earlier periods by the instalment rate to be used for the current period.

Step 4: Subtract the step 3 amount from the step 2 amount.

Step 5: If the result at step 4 is positive, this is the amount of the variation credit.

The variation credit claim must be made in the approved form on or before the day on which the instalment for the current quarter is due. Further, an entitlement to a variation credit does not affect the taxpayer's liability to pay an instalment. The variation credit claimed by the taxpayer will be credited to the taxpayer's running balance account (¶24-300).

▶ Example

The Merry Widow Axe Co Pty Ltd (''the taxpayer'') is a quarterly payer and has been notified by the Commissioner of an instalment rate of 15%. The taxpayer uses that rate to calculate its first quarterly instalment for the income year. Its instalment income for that quarter is $80,000 and, therefore, its first instalment is $12,000.

The taxpayer's instalment income for the second quarter is $100,000. For the second instalment, the taxpayer notified the Commissioner that it wished to vary its instalment rate to 10%. The taxpayer's variation credit is determined as follows.

Step 1: The taxpayer's earlier instalments add up to $12,000.

Step 2: There were no previous variation credits, therefore no reduction is required.

Step 3: Multiply $80,000 by the varied rate of 10% = $8,000.

Step 4: $12,000 – $8,000 = $4,000.

Step 5: The amount at step 4 is positive, therefore, the variation credit is $4,000.

Thus, the taxpayer's second instalment is $10,000 ($100,000 × 10%) and the taxpayer may claim a variation credit of $4,000.

In the third instalment quarter, the taxpayer's instalment income was $70,000 and again the taxpayer chose to vary its instalment rate, this time to 8%. The taxpayer's variation credit for the third instalment quarter is determined as follows.

Step 1: The taxpayer's earlier instalments add up to $22,000.

Step 2: The taxpayer has previously claimed a variation credit of $4,000, therefore $22,000 – $4,000 = $18,000.

Step 3: Multiply $180,000 ($80,000 + $100,000) by the varied rate of 8% (ie $14,400).

Step 4: $18,000 – $14,400 = $3,600.

Step 5: The amount at step 4 is positive, therefore the variation credit is $3,600.

Thus, the taxpayer's third instalment is $5,600 ($70,000 × 8%) and the taxpayer may claim a variation credit of $3,600.

Where a taxpayer varies the instalment rate upwards, there is no need to make additional payments. However, the taxpayer may make voluntary payments if desired.

When a taxpayer makes a claim for a variation credit, the instalment income for all previous quarters is required. This information will also need to be advised to the Commissioner in order for the Commissioner to determine if the taxpayer is liable to a penalty where the varied instalment rate is too low.

[FTR ¶977-175]

¶27-300 Variation of instalments based on GDP-adjusted notional tax

A quarterly PAYG instalment payer who uses the GDP-adjusted notional tax basis can vary the amount of a quarterly instalment by making an estimate of benchmark tax (¶27-490) (TAA s 45-112). For situations in which such a variation may be appropriate, see ¶27-280.

The taxpayer must notify the Commissioner, in the approved form, of the estimated benchmark tax amount on or before the due date of the instalment (see ¶27-200 for when the instalment is due). In subsequent quarters, unless the taxpayer chooses to vary the estimated benchmark tax amount, the Commissioner will advise the taxpayer of the amount of the instalment and the taxpayer will have at least 21 days from the date of the notice in which to pay the instalment.

Once the Commissioner has been notified, the taxpayer must use that amount as the basis for calculating the instalment for that instalment quarter. This amount must be used by the taxpayer for the remaining quarters in the income year unless the taxpayer chooses to estimate a different benchmark tax amount for later instalment quarters and notifies the Commissioner accordingly. Therefore, a taxpayer can effectively vary the benchmark tax amount up to 4 times in any given income year, once for each instalment quarter.

However, the estimated benchmark tax amount calculated by the taxpayer is only applicable for the income year for which it was notified to the Commissioner. It does not carry over to subsequent income years.

Amount of instalments once a taxpayer has chosen to use benchmark tax

Taxpayers who pay 4 quarterly instalments

The amount of the instalment for an instalment quarter depends upon the number of the quarter (TAA s 45-410). That is, the first instalment quarter refers to the first instalment quarter for the current income year for which the taxpayer is liable to pay an instalment. This will usually be the first instalment quarter of the income year, but may be a later quarter if the taxpayer was not required to pay instalments for those previous quarters (eg because the Commissioner had not previously advised the taxpayer of an instalment rate).

The following table sets out the amount payable for a particular instalment where the taxpayer has chosen to pay instalments based on GDP-adjusted notional tax and has subsequently decided to work out instalments on the basis of an estimate of benchmark tax for that income year.

If the instalment quarter is:	The amount of the instalment is:
The first in that income year for which the taxpayer is liable to pay a PAYG instalment	25% of the estimated benchmark tax amount
The second in that income year for which the taxpayer is liable to pay a PAYG instalment	50% of the estimated benchmark tax amount, less the amount of any previous instalment in that income year

If the instalment quarter is:	The amount of the instalment is:
The third in that income year for which the taxpayer is liable to pay a PAYG instalment	75% of the estimated benchmark tax amount, less the amount of any previous instalments in that income year, plus any variation credit claimed in respect of the second instalment
The fourth in that income year for which the taxpayer is liable to pay a PAYG instalment	100% of the estimated benchmark tax amount, less the amount of any previous instalments in that income year, plus any variation credit claimed in respect of the second and third instalments

An instalment calculated in accordance with this table is only payable where the amount is positive. If the amount is negative, no amount is payable and the taxpayer may be entitled to a variation credit.

▶ Example

Rupert is eligible to pay his quarterly PAYG instalments on the basis of GDP-adjusted notional tax and has chosen to do so. Rupert did not choose to work out his first instalment on his estimate of benchmark tax. At the time Rupert's first instalment was payable, his GDP-adjusted notional tax was $26,000. Accordingly, the Commissioner notified Rupert of an instalment of $6,500.

During the second quarter of the income year, Rupert decided to estimate his benchmark tax amount at $14,000 and notified the Commissioner accordingly. Therefore, Rupert's second quarterly PAYG instalment is:

$$(50\% \times \$14,000) - \$6,500 = \$500$$

For the third and fourth quarterly PAYG instalments, the Commissioner will notify Rupert of the amount payable. On the basis that Rupert does not wish to vary his estimate of benchmark tax, these instalments will each be $3,500.

Taxpayers who pay 2 quarterly instalments

The amount of the varied instalment depends on when the taxpayer is first provided with an instalment rate, as follows:

Instalment quarter in which instalment rate is first notified	Instalment quarter for which the instalment is payable	Amount of instalment
Before the end of the first	Third	75% of the taxpayer's estimate of benchmark tax
	Fourth	100% of the taxpayer's estimate of benchmark tax, less the third instalment
During the second	Third	50% of the taxpayer's estimate of benchmark tax
	Fourth	75% of the taxpayer's estimate of benchmark tax, less the third instalment
During the third	Third	25% of the taxpayer's estimate of benchmark tax
	Fourth	50% of the taxpayer's estimate of benchmark tax, less the third instalment
During the fourth	Third	Not applicable
	Fourth	25% of the taxpayer's estimate of benchmark tax

Claiming a variation credit for prior overpaid instalments

Where an instalment calculated in accordance with either of the above tables is a negative amount, the taxpayer is entitled to a variation credit (TAA s 45-420). The amount of the variation credit is the negative amount expressed as a positive.

The variation credit claim must be made in the approved form on or before the day on which the instalment for the current quarter is due. Further, an entitlement to a variation credit does not affect the taxpayer's liability to pay an instalment. The variation credit claimed by the taxpayer will be credited to the taxpayer's running balance account (¶24-300).

[FTR ¶977-145, ¶977-240]

¶27-320 Penalties where the varied instalment rate is too low

A taxpayer is liable to GIC for each instalment month or quarter in which the taxpayer chooses to use an instalment rate that is less than 85% of the benchmark instalment rate (¶27-490) for that income year (¶27-280). GIC is payable on the following amount (TAA s 45-225; 45-230):

$$\text{rate discrepancy} \times \text{taxpayer's instalment income for the variation month or quarter} + \text{credit adjustment}$$

The "rate discrepancy" is the difference between the varied instalment rate chosen by the taxpayer and the lesser of the following:

- the benchmark instalment rate
- the most recent instalment rate notified to the taxpayer by the Commissioner prior to the end of the instalment month or quarter.

The "credit adjustment" is only relevant where the taxpayer has claimed a variation credit in relation to the instalment month or quarter (¶27-280, ¶27-300). Where this has occurred, the credit adjustment is the lesser of:

- the amount of the credit actually claimed
- the amount calculated by multiplying the instalment income of the previous instalment months or quarters by the rate discrepancy.

▶ Example

Continuing the example of The Merry Widow Axe Co Pty Ltd from ¶27-280, the taxpayer's instalment income for the fourth instalment quarter was $50,000 and therefore the fourth PAYG instalment was $4,000. There was no variation credit for this quarter. After lodgment of the taxpayer's income tax return, the Commissioner determines that the taxpayer's benchmark instalment rate is 10%.

There will be no amount on which to impose GIC for the first instalment quarter as the taxpayer did not use a varied instalment rate for that quarter. Further, there will be no amount on which to impose GIC for the second instalment quarter as the taxpayer had chosen to use 10% for that quarter which is not less than 85% of the benchmark instalment rate.

The amount on which GIC will be imposed for the third instalment quarter is calculated as follows:

$$\text{rate discrepancy} \times \text{taxpayer's instalment income for the variation quarter} + \text{credit adjustment}$$

= [(10% – 8%) × $70,000] + [lesser of $3,600 or (10% – 8%) × $180,000]
= $1,400 + $3,600
= $5,000

The amount on which GIC will be imposed for the fourth instalment quarter is calculated as follows:

[(10% – 8%) × $50,000] + [lesser of $0 or (10% – 8%) × $250,000]
= $1,000 + $0
= $1,000

Impact of COVID-19

The ATO has advised that, to assist businesses affected by COVID-19, penalties and interest will not be applied for excessive PAYG instalment variations for the 2020–21 income year if a ''best attempt'' is made to estimate the end of year tax. However, GIC (¶29-510) may apply to any outstanding PAYG instalment balances.

[FTR ¶977-185]

¶27-330 Penalties where the estimated benchmark tax is too low

A taxpayer is liable to GIC for each instalment quarter in which the taxpayer chooses to use an estimate of benchmark tax (¶27-490) that is less than 85% of the benchmark tax amount for that income year as calculated by the Commissioner (¶27-300) (TAA s 45-232).

For a particular instalment quarter, GIC is imposed on the amount worked out as follows (if it is a positive amount):

acceptable amount of the instalment – actual amount

The ''actual amount'' is the amount of the instalment for the particular quarter as worked out in accordance with the applicable table at ¶27-300. However, where the taxpayer claimed a variation credit, the actual amount is the amount of that credit expressed as a negative.

The ''acceptable amount of the instalment'' is whichever of the following is applicable:

- if the taxpayer has not varied the particular instalment, or any earlier instalments in that income year — the amount notified by the Commissioner (which will be based on the GDP-adjusted notional tax of the taxpayer), or
- if the taxpayer has varied an instalment — the amount calculated using the applicable table below.

If the amount on which GIC is payable is negative, there is no GIC penalty for that instalment quarter.

Taxpayers who pay 4 quarterly instalments

If the instalment quarter is:	The acceptable amount of the instalment is:
the first in that income year for which the taxpayer is liable to pay a PAYG instalment	the lower of: (a) the amount the Commissioner notified the taxpayer as the amount of the instalment for that instalment quarter (this will be based on GDP-adjusted notional tax), and (b) 25% of the benchmark tax amount for that income year

If the instalment quarter is:	The acceptable amount of the instalment is:
the second in that income year for which the taxpayer is liable to pay a PAYG instalment	the lower of: (a) the amount the Commissioner would have notified the taxpayer as the amount of the instalment for that instalment quarter if the taxpayer had not chosen to vary the instalments (this will be based on GDP-adjusted notional tax), and (b) 50% of the benchmark tax amount for that income year, less the acceptable amount for the earlier instalment quarter in that income year
the third in that income year for which the taxpayer is liable to pay a PAYG instalment	the lower of: (a) the amount the Commissioner would have notified the taxpayer as the amount of the instalment for that instalment quarter if the taxpayer had not chosen to vary the instalments (this will be based on GDP-adjusted notional tax), and (b) 75% of the benchmark tax amount for that income year, less the sum of the acceptable amounts for the earlier instalment quarters in that income year
the fourth in that income year for which the taxpayer is liable to pay a PAYG instalment	the lower of: (a) the amount the Commissioner would have notified the taxpayer as the amount of the instalment for that instalment quarter if the taxpayer had not chosen to vary the instalments (this will be based on GDP-adjusted notional tax), and (b) 100% of the benchmark tax amount for that income year, less the sum of the acceptable amounts for the earlier instalment quarters in that income year

▶ Example 1

Tony is a quarterly PAYG instalment payer (and deferred BAS payer) who has chosen to pay his instalments based on his GDP-adjusted notional tax. The Commissioner has notified Tony that his GDP-adjusted notional tax is $42,000 and therefore his instalments will be $10,500 per quarter. Tony paid his first quarterly instalment of $10,500 as per the Commissioner's notice.

At the end of the second quarter, Tony estimated his benchmark tax to be $28,000 and notified the Commissioner accordingly. Tony's instalments for the remainder of the year were therefore $3,500, $7,000 and $7,000.

Subsequently, the Commissioner determined that Tony's benchmark tax was $40,000. As Tony's estimate of his benchmark tax of $28,000 is less than 85% of the amount of the benchmark tax calculated by the Commissioner, Tony is liable to GIC.

There is no penalty for the first quarter as Tony had not estimated his benchmark tax at that time.

The amount on which GIC is imposed for the second quarter is calculated as follows:

acceptable amount of the instalment – actual amount
= [$10,500 or (50% × $40,000 – $10,500), whichever is lower] – $3,500
= [$10,500 or $9,500] – $3,500
= $9,500 – $3,500
= $6,000

The amount on which GIC is imposed for the third quarter is calculated as follows:

[$10,500 or (75% × $40,000 – ($10,500 + $9,500)), whichever is lower] – $7,000
= [$10,500 or ($30,000 – $20,000)] – $7,000
= $10,000 – $7,000
= $3,000

The amount on which GIC is imposed for the fourth quarter is calculated as follows:

[$10,500 or (100% × $40,000 – ($10,500 + $9,500 + $10,000)), whichever is lower] – $7,000
= [$10,500 or ($40,000 – $30,000)] – $7,000
= $10,000 – $7,000
= $3,000

Taxpayers who pay 2 quarterly instalments

Special rules in s 45-232 apply for the calculation of GIC where there is a shortfall in instalments following a variation by a taxpayer who pays 2 PAYG quarterly instalments annually using the GDP-adjusted notional tax method (¶27-200).

The acceptable amount of the instalment depends on when the taxpayer is first provided with an instalment rate, as follows:

Instalment quarter in which instalment rate is first notified	Instalment quarter for which the instalment is payable	Acceptable amount of instalment
Before the end of the first	Third	the lower of: (a) the amount the Commissioner notified the taxpayer as the amount of the instalment for that instalment quarter (this will be based on GDP-adjusted notional tax), and (b) 75% of the benchmark tax amount for that income year
	Fourth	the lower of: (a) the amount the Commissioner would have notified the taxpayer as the amount of the instalment for that instalment quarter if the taxpayer had not chosen to vary the instalments (this will be based on GDP-adjusted notional tax), and (b) 100% of the benchmark tax amount for that income year less the sum of the acceptable amount for the earlier instalment quarter in that income year
During the second	Third	the lower of: (a) the amount the Commissioner notified the taxpayer as the amount of the instalment for that instalment quarter (this will be based on GDP-adjusted notional tax), and (b) 50% of the benchmark tax amount for that income year

Instalment quarter in which instalment rate is first notified	Instalment quarter for which the instalment is payable	Acceptable amount of instalment
	Fourth	the lower of: (a) the amount the Commissioner would have notified the taxpayer as the amount of the instalment for that instalment quarter if the taxpayer had not chosen to vary the instalments (this will be based on GDP-adjusted notional tax), and (b) 75% of the benchmark tax amount for that income year less the sum of the acceptable amount for the earlier instalment quarter in that income year
During the third	Third	the lower of: (a) the amount the Commissioner notified the taxpayer as the amount of the instalment for that instalment quarter (this will be based on GDP-adjusted notional tax), and (b) 25% of the benchmark tax amount for that income year
	Fourth	the lower of: (a) the amount the Commissioner would have notified the taxpayer as the amount of the instalment for that instalment quarter if the taxpayer had not chosen to vary the instalments (this will be based on GDP-adjusted notional tax), and (b) 50% of the benchmark tax amount for that income year less the sum of the acceptable amount for the earlier instalment quarter in that income year
During the fourth	Third	Not applicable
	Fourth	the lower of: (a) the amount the Commissioner notified the taxpayer as the amount of the instalment for that instalment quarter (this will be based on GDP-adjusted notional tax), and (b) 25% of the benchmark tax amount for that income year

Reduction of amount on which GIC is imposed

The amount on which GIC is imposed can, in certain circumstances, be too high. This will occur where a taxpayer has estimated the benchmark tax for a quarter and that estimate was too low and, in a later instalment quarter in that income year, the taxpayer estimates the benchmark tax at a higher level. This upwards estimation has the effect of ''catching-up'' some of the previous underpayment.

The amount on which GIC is imposed for a particular instalment quarter is reduced if, in a later instalment quarter in the same income year, the amount worked out using the following formula is a negative amount (TAA s 45-233):

$$\begin{array}{c}\text{acceptable amount of the instalment}\\ \text{for the later instalment quarter}\end{array} - \begin{array}{c}\text{actual amount of}\\ \text{that instalment}\end{array}$$

The above amount, expressed as a positive, is called the ''top up''.

The "actual amount of that instalment" is the amount of the instalment for the particular quarter as worked out in accordance with the applicable table in ¶27-300. However, where the taxpayer claims a variation credit, the actual amount is the amount of that credit expressed as a negative.

The "acceptable amount of the instalment for the later instalment quarter" is the amount calculated using the applicable table above.

A top up has the effect of reducing the amount on which GIC is imposed by that amount (but not below nil). Where the top up exceeds the amount on which GIC is imposed, any amount not applied can be carried forward to offset the amount on which GIC is imposed for a later instalment quarter in the same income year.

▶ Example 2

Continuing the example of Tony — assume that Tony made another estimate of his benchmark tax in the fourth quarter. This time he estimated that his benchmark tax would be $32,000. Accordingly, his instalment for the fourth quarter will be $11,000 (100% × $32,000 – $21,000).

Tony is still liable to the GIC penalty in respect of the second, third and fourth quarters as both of his estimates of benchmark tax are less than 85% of the amount of benchmark tax calculated by the Commissioner. However, the amount on which GIC is imposed for the fourth quarter is calculated as follows:

acceptable amount of the instalment – actual amount

= [$10,500 or (100% × $40,000 – ($10,500 + $9,500 + $10,000)), whichever is lower] – $11,000

= [$10,500 or ($40,000 – $30,000)] – $11,000

= $10,000 – $11,000

= ($1,000)

As this amount is negative, no GIC penalty will be imposed for the fourth quarter. Further, this means that there is a top up of $1,000. This amount will reduce the amount on which GIC will be imposed for the second quarter from $6,000 to $5,000.

Therefore, for the second quarter, GIC will be imposed on $6,000 for the period from 28 February to 28 July and on $5,000 for the period from 28 July to the due date for payment of Tony's assessed tax (or the date the assessed tax is paid if this is earlier).

Imposition of GIC

GIC is payable for each day in the period that:

- starts on the due date by which the instalment for the variation quarter is due to be paid, and
- finishes at the end of the day on which the taxpayer's assessed tax for the income year is due to be paid.

The Commissioner must give written notice of the liability to GIC, and the charge must be paid within 14 days of the notice being given. If GIC is unpaid at the end of those 14 days, additional GIC is payable on the unpaid GIC.

Payment of GIC is considered at ¶29-510; remission of GIC is considered at ¶29-530.

Impact of COVID-19

The ATO has advised that, to assist businesses affected by COVID-19, penalties and interest will not be applied for excessive PAYG instalment variations for the 2020–21 income year if a "best attempt" is made to estimate the end of year tax. However, GIC (¶29-510) may apply to any outstanding PAYG instalment balances.

[FTR ¶977-185]

¶27-340 How an annual instalment payer varies an instalment

An annual instalment payer normally has 3 choices as to the amount of the annual instalment (TAA ss 45-115; 45-175):

(1) the amount worked out by multiplying the Commissioner's instalment rate by the taxpayer's instalment income for the income year

(2) the most recently notified notional tax, or

(3) the taxpayer's estimate of benchmark tax.

Annual PAYG instalment payers cannot estimate an instalment rate as quarterly PAYG instalment payers can (¶27-280). If an annual taxpayer believes that the instalment rate is too high and the notional tax amount is also not appropriate, the taxpayer can pay a different amount by estimating benchmark tax. For situations in which such a variation may be appropriate, see ¶27-280. In this case, the taxpayer must notify the Commissioner in the approved form of the estimated benchmark tax amount on or before the due date of the instalment. The amount of the annual instalment is then the benchmark tax amount as estimated by the taxpayer.

Penalty where the estimated benchmark tax is too low

A taxpayer is liable to GIC if the taxpayer chooses to use an estimate of benchmark tax that is less than 85% of the benchmark tax amount for that income year as calculated by the Commissioner (TAA s 45-235).

The amount on which GIC is imposed is calculated as follows:

acceptable amount of the instalment – actual amount

The ''actual amount'' is the amount of the estimated benchmark tax advised by the taxpayer to the Commissioner (ie it is the amount of the instalment as estimated by the taxpayer).

The ''acceptable amount of the instalment'' is the lowest of the following:

- the most recent instalment rate given to the taxpayer by the Commissioner before the end of the income year multiplied by the taxpayer's instalment income for the income year
- the most recent notional tax amount notified to the taxpayer by the Commissioner before the end of the income year
- the taxpayer's benchmark tax amount for the income year as calculated by the Commissioner (¶27-490).

Calculation of GIC

GIC is payable for each day in the period that:

- starts on the due date of the instalment that is subject to the penalty, and
- finishes at the end of the date on which the taxpayer's assessed tax for the income year is due to be paid.

Payment and remission of GIC are considered at ¶29-510 and ¶29-530.

[FTR ¶977-165, ¶977-185]

Changing Instalment Frequency

¶27-380 Change from an annual instalment payer

Ceasing to be annual instalment payer immediately

A taxpayer ceases to be an annual instalment payer at the start of an instalment quarter if the taxpayer becomes the head company of a consolidated group or the provisional head company of a MEC group during that quarter. In this case, the taxpayer must pay an instalment for that instalment quarter and later instalment quarters. Such a taxpayer may again become an annual instalment payer if it ceases to be the head company of a consolidated group or provisional head company of a MEC group, satisfies the other conditions to be an annual instalment payer (¶27-170) and elects to do so (TAA s 45-160).

Ceasing to be an annual instalment payer at the end of the income year

A taxpayer ceases to be an annual PAYG instalment payer *at the end of an income year* if, during that year:

- the Commissioner notifies the taxpayer of a notional tax amount of $8,000 or more
- on the taxpayer's MPR test day, the taxpayer's base assessment instalment income is greater than the threshold (¶27-170), or
- the taxpayer chooses to pay PAYG instalments quarterly instead of annually (TAA s 45-155).

A taxpayer also ceases to be an annual PAYG instalment payer if, *during an instalment quarter*:

- the taxpayer becomes required to be registered for GST
- the taxpayer becomes a partner in a partnership that is required to be registered for GST
- a partnership in which the taxpayer is a partner becomes required to be registered for GST
- a taxpayer company becomes part of an instalment group or a participant in a GST joint venture, or
- an annual GST election for the taxpayer, or a partnership in which the taxpayer is a partner, ceases to have effect (TAA s 45-150).

Where these rules are satisfied, the taxpayer will commence paying monthly or quarterly instalments from the first instalment period of the following income year for which the taxpayer is required to pay an instalment. A taxpayer required to pay 4 instalments annually will commence paying quarterly PAYG instalments from the first instalment quarter of the following income year. A taxpayer eligible to pay 2 quarterly instalments annually will commence paying quarterly PAYG instalments from the third instalment quarter of the following income year. A taxpayer required to pay monthly instalments will commence from the first month of the following income year (although the legislation has ''current year'' which cannot be the intention — s 45-136(2)(b)). In all cases, taxpayers are still required to pay an annual instalment for the year in which they become ineligible to be annual PAYG instalment payers. Monthly or quarterly instalments continue to be payable after that time, unless and until the taxpayer again satisfies the requirements for being an annual PAYG instalment payer (¶27-170) and chooses to pay on that basis or the Commissioner withdraws the taxpayer's instalment rate.

[FTR ¶977-165]

¶27-420 Change from a quarterly instalment payer

Becoming an annual instalment payer

An eligible taxpayer can only choose to be an annual PAYG instalment payer before the due date of the first quarterly PAYG instalment that the taxpayer would otherwise be required to pay for the income year (TAA s 45-140(2)).

Becoming a monthly instalment payer

A taxpayer becomes a monthly payer if, on the taxpayer's MPR test day, its base assessment instalment income is greater than the threshold (¶27-170). Where this occurs, the taxpayer will commence paying monthly instalments from the first instalment month of the following income year. Such a taxpayer is still required to pay any remaining quarterly instalments for the year in which the taxpayer became a monthly payer. Monthly instalments continue to be payable after that time unless and until the taxpayer ceases to be a monthly instalment payer (¶27-430) or the Commissioner withdraws the taxpayer's instalment rate.

¶27-430 Change from a monthly instalment payer

A monthly instalment payer ceases to be a monthly payer for a later tax year where (TAA s 45-136(4)):

- on the taxpayer's MPR test day for that year (ie the first day of the third last month of the previous income year), the taxpayer's base assessment instalment income is less than the threshold (¶27-170), and
- the taxpayer gives the Commissioner a notice (an MP stop notice) in the approved form for that year before the start of that later income year.

Such a taxpayer is still required to pay any remaining monthly instalments for the year in which the taxpayer ceased to be a monthly payer.

The taxpayer will become a quarterly payer for the first instalment quarter of the later income year unless the taxpayer is eligible to pay an annual instalment and chooses to be an annual PAYG instalment payer before the due date of the first quarterly PAYG instalment that the taxpayer would otherwise be required to pay for the income year (TAA s 45-140(2)).

Calculations by the Commissioner

¶27-450 PAYG instalment rate

The Commissioner calculates a taxpayer's instalment rate (to 2 decimal places) using the following formula (TAA s 45-320):

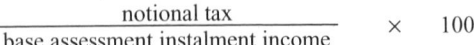

$$\frac{\text{notional tax}}{\text{base assessment instalment income}} \times 100$$

If either the notional tax (¶27-460) or the base assessment instalment income is nil, the instalment rate is also nil.

Base assessment instalment income

The taxpayer's "base year" is the latest income year for which an assessment has been made. However, if the Commissioner is satisfied that there is a later income year for which the taxpayer does not have a taxable income and therefore no assessment has been made, the base year will be that income year. This could occur where the taxpayer is in a loss position in that year.

▶ Example 1

At the time the Commissioner is determining the instalment rate for Enterprises Ltd, the company has lodged its 2018–19 return and has been assessed. The company has also lodged its 2019–20 return which disclosed an overall loss for that year. The Commissioner will determine that Enterprises Ltd's base year is the 2019–20 income year.

The "base assessment" is the assessment for the base year. If the base year is one in which an assessment has not been made (eg because the taxpayer was in a loss position), then the base assessment is the return or other information from which an assessment for that year would have been made.

The "base assessment instalment income" is so much of the taxpayer's assessable income taken into account for the base assessment as the Commissioner determines is instalment income. For the definition of "instalment income", see ¶27-260.

▶ Example 2

In the assessment for her base year, Joan Smith derived $25,000 salary, $30,000 business income, $2,000 interest and incurred $10,000 in business expenses. Joan's base assessment instalment income is $32,000 (ie $30,000 + $2,000).

High instalment rates

There are situations where the instalment rate calculated using TAA Sch 1 s 45-320 can produce a very high rate. This is usually caused by amounts that are included in the calculation of notional tax but are not included in base assessment instalment income. Examples include employee share scheme income from deferral schemes, excess superannuation contributions, and the second to fifth years after a primary producer has received an amount on the forced disposal of livestock. In these situations, it is not uncommon for the instalment rate to be greater than 100%.

The Commissioner limits the instalment rate calculated using TAA Sch 1 s 45-320 to a "more reasonable rate" (see the ATO website). The reasonable rates are set out below:

Entity type	Reasonable rate
Individuals	55%
Trusts	55%
Superannuation funds and self managed superannuation funds	45%
Companies (including entities taxed as companies)	30%

[FTR ¶977-210]

¶27-460 PAYG notional tax

A taxpayer's "notional tax" for the base year is calculated as follows (TAA s 45-325):

$$\text{adjusted tax on adjusted taxable income} - \text{adjusted tax on adjusted withholding income}$$

Where a taxpayer's adjusted tax on adjusted withholding income is greater than the adjusted tax on adjusted taxable income for the base year, the notional tax is nil.

In working out a taxpayer's notional tax, the Commissioner may take account of:

- changes in the law that may reasonably be expected to apply to the year for which the Commissioner is calculating the instalment rate and which did not apply in the base year

- proposed changes in the law that, in the Commissioner's opinion, are likely to be enacted and have the effect of lowering the taxpayer's instalment rate.

The calculation of a superannuation or RSA provider's notional tax is modified to ensure that no-TFN contributions income and the tax offset for no-TFN contributions income are not taken into account. However the contributions are still assessable contributions that are taken into account when working out the provider's notional tax and base assessment instalment income.

Adjusted taxable income

A taxpayer's ''adjusted taxable income'' for the base year is the taxpayer's total assessable income for the base year, reduced by (TAA s 45-330):

- any net capital gains included in assessable income (except if the taxpayer is a superannuation fund, an ADF or a PST)
- all deductions allowed for the base year, except tax losses
- if the taxpayer is a company or it is a head company that had tax losses transferred to it under ITAA97 Subdiv 707-A, the lesser of:
  - any tax loss to the extent that it can be carried forward to the next income year, and
  - the deduction for tax losses claimed in the base year, and
- if the taxpayer is neither a company nor a head company that had tax losses transferred to it under Subdiv 707-A, any tax loss to the extent that it can be carried forward to the next income year.

The adjusted taxable income of a life insurance company is calculated using the formula in s 45-330(3).

Adjusted withholding income

A taxpayer's ''adjusted withholding income'' for the base year is the amount of assessable income from which PAYG withholding has been, or should have been, made for the base year (¶26-120) (except for amounts that have been subject to PAYG withholding because the taxpayer did not quote a TFN or an ABN), reduced by the deductions allowed for the base year to the extent that they reasonably relate to those amounts (TAA s 45-335).

There is no legislative guidance as to what deductions reasonably relate to the amounts from which PAYG withholding has been, or should have been, made. There is also no mention of how such deductions are to be allocated where they do not fully relate to PAYG withholding income.

Adjusted tax

Calculation of the adjusted tax on either the adjusted taxable income or the adjusted withholding income is a 4-step process (TAA s 45-340).

Step 1: Calculate the income tax payable on the adjusted taxable income or the adjusted withholding income (as relevant). The following tax offsets are disregarded:

- private health insurance offset (¶15-330)
- tax offset arising from franking deficit tax liabilities (¶4-780)
- low income rebate/tax offset (¶15-300)
- offset for superannuation contributions made on behalf of the taxpayer's spouse (¶13-770)
- offset for Medicare levy surcharge (lump sum payments in arrears) (¶15-350)

- offset for early stage investors in innovation companies (¶20-700), and
- the junior minerals exploration incentive tax offset (¶19-010).

Step 2: Calculate the Medicare levy payable on the adjusted taxable income or the adjusted withholding income (as the case may be), disregarding the Medicare levy surcharge.

Step 3: Calculate the amount of any tertiary education loan assessment debt that would have been repayable for the base year on the assumption that the taxpayer's taxable income was equal to the adjusted taxable income or the adjusted withholding income (as the case may be).

Step 4: Add up the amounts determined for steps 1, 2 and 3.

▶ Example 1: Corporate taxpayer

Happy Toys Ltd derived the following assessable income during the base year:

Gross sales	$120,000
Interest	$10,000
Royalties	$25,000

It incurred the following deductions during the base year:

Cost of sales	$50,000
Tax agent's fees	$2,000

Happy Toys Ltd did not quote its TFN in relation to the interest income and, consequently, tax was withheld. On the assumption that Happy Toys is a base rate entity and the tax rate of 26% applies for the year for which the instalment rate is calculated, Happy Toys Ltd's instalment rate is calculated as follows:

Happy Toys Ltd's adjusted taxable income	=	assessable income of base year	–	net capital gains of base year	–	allowable deductions (except tax losses) of base year	–	tax losses carried forward from base year
	=	$155,000 – $0 – $52,000 – $0						
	=	$103,000						

Happy Toys Ltd's adjusted withholding income	=	nil, since amounts subject to PAYG withholding due to the non-quotation of either the taxpayer's TFN or ABN do not count

Adjusted tax on adjusted taxable income

Step 1:	=	Income tax payable on $103,000
	=	26% × $103,000
	=	$26,780
Step 2:		Not applicable
Step 3:		Not applicable
Step 4:		Add Steps 1 to 3
	=	$26,780 + $0 + $0
	=	$26,780

Happy Toys Ltd's notional tax is therefore $26,780.

Happy Toys Ltd's base assessment instalment income equals so much of its assessable income for the base year that is instalment income. This would be $155,000 (ie $120,000 + $10,000 + $25,000).

$$\text{Happy Toys Ltd's instalment rate} = \frac{\text{Happy Toys Ltd's notional tax}}{\text{Happy Toys Ltd's base assessment instalment income}} \times 100$$

$$= \frac{\$26{,}780}{\$155{,}000} \times 100$$

$$= 17.28\% \text{ (rounded to 2 decimal places)}$$

▶ Example 2: Individual taxpayer

Hilary derived the following assessable income during the year ended 30 June 2020 (the base year):

Salary	$30,000
Net capital gain	$12,000
Interest	$8,000
Dividends (fully franked from a large public company)	$2,000
Dividend gross-up amount ($2,000 × 30/70)	$857

She incurred the following deductions during the base year:

Work-related expenses	$800
Interest and dividend deductions	$200

Hilary did not quote her TFN in relation to the interest income and, consequently, tax was withheld. Further, on her assessment for the year ended 30 June 2020, Hilary was allowed an offset for a superannuation contribution she made on behalf of her spouse, Herbert. Hilary does not have a tertiary education assessment debt. Using the personal tax rates for the year ending 30 June 2021, Hilary's instalment rate is calculated as follows:

Hilary's adjusted taxable income	=	assessable income of base year	–	net capital gains of base year	–	allowable deductions (except tax losses) of base year	–	tax losses carried forward from base year
	=	$52,857 – $12,000 – $1,000 – $0						
	=	$39,857						

Hilary's adjusted withholding income = $30,000 – $800
= $29,200

The interest subject to PAYG withholding due to the fact that Hilary did not quote her TFN does not count as adjusted withholding income.

Adjusted tax on adjusted taxable income

Step 1:	=	Income tax payable on $39,857
	=	Tax on $39,857 using 2020–21 rates (¶42-000) – franking credit of $857
	=	$4,114.83 – $857
	=	$3,257.83
Step 2:	=	Medicare levy on $39,857
	=	$39,857 × 2%
	=	$797.14
Step 3:		Not applicable
Step 4:		Add steps 1 to 3
	=	$3,257.83 + $797.14 + $0
	=	$4,054.97

Adjusted tax on adjusted withholding income

Step 1:	=	Income tax payable on $29,200
	=	Tax on $29,200 using 2020–21 rates (¶42-000)
	=	$2,090
Step 2:	=	Medicare levy on $29,200
	=	$29,200 × 2%
	=	$584
Step 3:		Not applicable
Step 4:		Add steps 1 to 3
	=	$2,090 + $584 + $0
	=	$2,674

Hilary's notional tax is therefore $1,380.97 (ie $4,054.97 – $2,674).

Hilary's base assessment instalment income equals so much of her assessable income for the base year that is instalment income. This would be $10,000 (ie $8,000 + $2,000). The dividend gross-up amount is not instalment income as it is statutory income.

$$\text{Hilary's instalment rate} = \frac{\text{Hilary's notional tax}}{\text{Hilary's base assessment instalment income}} \times 100$$

$$= \frac{\$1,380.97}{\$10,000} \times 100$$

$$= 13.81\% \text{ (rounded to 2 decimal places)}$$

Special rules provide a methodology for the Commissioner to work out one or more instalment rates for a trustee who has more than one PAYG instalment liability in respect of:

- a beneficiary under a legal disability
- a beneficiary that has a vested and indefeasible interest in the trust income but cannot require the trustee to pay that amount to them, and
- income to which no beneficiary is entitled (¶27-500).

[FTR ¶977-210]

¶27-470 GDP-adjusted notional tax

The Commissioner calculates GDP-adjusted notional tax in much the same way as notional tax is calculated (¶27-460). However, the adjusted taxable income for the base year is increased by the GDP adjustment and the adjusted tax is calculated based on this increased adjusted taxable income. Further, the adjusted withholding income for the base year is also increased by the GDP adjustment and the adjusted tax is calculated based on this increased adjusted withholding income.

The GDP adjustment factor is 5% for 2019–20 and 0% for 2020–21. The 0% rate applies for instalment quarters that commence on or after 1 July 2020.

[FTR ¶977-235]

¶27-490 Benchmark tax and benchmark instalment rate

The calculations of benchmark tax and the benchmark instalment rate are used to determine a taxpayer's liability to penalties where the taxpayer has varied the PAYG instalment rate (¶27-280 – ¶27-380).

Benchmark tax

Benchmark tax is calculated as follows (TAA s 45-365):

$$\text{adjusted assessed tax on adjusted assessed taxable income} - \text{PAYG withholding credits}$$

If the amount of PAYG withholding credits is greater than the adjusted gross tax on adjusted assessed taxable income, then the benchmark tax is nil (ie the above formula cannot produce a negative amount). PAYG withholding credits cover: (a) credits for amounts withheld from withholding payments to the taxpayer during the variation year (¶26-660); and (b) credits for amounts of personal services income included in the taxpayer's assessable income for amounts paid under TAA Sch 1 Div 13 (¶26-280).

A taxpayer's "adjusted assessed taxable income" for a particular income year is the taxpayer's taxable income for that year, reduced by any net capital gains (except if the taxpayer is a superannuation fund, an ADF or a PST) (TAA s 45-370). Special rules apply if the taxpayer is a life insurance company.

Calculation of the "adjusted assessed tax" on adjusted assessed taxable income for a particular year is a 4-step process (TAA s 45-375).

Step 1: Calculate the income tax payable on the adjusted assessed taxable income. The following tax offsets are disregarded:

- private health insurance offset (¶15-330)
- tax offset arising from franking deficit tax liabilities (¶4-780)
- low income rebate/tax offset (¶15-300)
- an offset for superannuation contributions made on behalf of the taxpayer's spouse (¶13-770)
- offset for Medicare levy surcharge (lump sum payments in arrears) (¶15-350)
- offset for early stage investors in innovation companies (¶20-700), and
- the junior minerals exploration incentive tax offset (¶19-010).

Step 2: Calculate the Medicare levy payable on the adjusted assessed taxable income, disregarding the Medicare levy surcharge.

Step 3: Calculate the amount of any tertiary education assessment debt that would have been repayable for the particular income year on the assumption that the taxpayer's taxable income was equal to the adjusted assessed taxable income.

Step 4: Add up the amounts determined for steps 1, 2 and 3.

The application of s 45-365 is modified when working out a superannuation or RSA provider's benchmark tax to ensure that no-TFN contributions income and the tax offset for no-TFN contributions income are not taken into account.

Benchmark instalment rate

A taxpayer's benchmark instalment rate for an income year is calculated using the following formula (calculated to 2 decimal places, rounded up if the third decimal place is 5 or more) (TAA s 45-360):

$$\frac{\text{taxpayer's benchmark tax for the income year}}{\text{instalment income for that income year}} \times 100$$

The "instalment income for that income year" is so much of the taxpayer's assessable income for that income year that the Commissioner determines is instalment income for that year (¶27-260).

▶ Example

Grail Tours Pty Ltd was assessed on the following income during the 2019–20 income year:

Gross sales	$120,000
Interest	$7,500
Net capital gain	$3,500

It also incurred $48,000 in expenses.

Grail Tours Pty Ltd's adjusted assessed taxable income is $79,500 (ie $120,000 + $7,500 – $48,000). The $3,500 capital gain is not taken into account.

Grail Tours Pty Ltd's adjusted assessed tax on adjusted assessed taxable income, calculated on an assumed 26% company tax rate (as Grail Tours Pty Ltd is a base rate entity and the tax rate for base rate entities for the year ending 30 June 2021 is 26%), is $20,670.00 (ie $79,500 × 26%). Steps 2, 3 and 4 above are not relevant for a non-individual taxpayer.

Accordingly, Grail Tours Pty Ltd's benchmark tax is $20,670.00.

Grail Tours Pty Ltd's instalment income for the 2019–20 income year is $127,500 (ie $120,000 + $7,500). The capital gain of $3,500 is not included.

Accordingly, Grail Tours Pty Ltd's benchmark instalment rate is:

$$\frac{\$20,670.00}{\$127,500} = 16.21\% \text{ (rounded to 2 decimal places)}$$

[FTR ¶977-220]

Trustees and Consolidated Groups

¶27-500 PAYG calculations for trustees of trust estates

A trustee that is liable to pay tax in respect of a beneficiary's share of the trust's net income, or the income to which no beneficiary is entitled, is liable to pay PAYG instalments in respect of such a liability. Special rules in TAA Sch 1 Subdiv 45-N (ss 45-450 to 45-535) explain how the PAYG instalments regime applies to a trustee.

Single-rate trustees

A single-rate trustee is a trustee covered by any of items 4 to 8, 12 and 13 of the table in ITAA97 s 9-1, ie a trustee of a corporate unit trust, a public trading trust, a complying or non-complying superannuation fund, a complying or non-complying ADF, and a PST (s 45-450). Each of these trustees will be given a single instalment rate by the Commissioner.

If the single-rate trustee is a trustee of a corporate unit trust or a public trading trust, the PAYG instalments system applies as if the trustee had a taxable income for the income year that is equal to the net income of the trust (s 45-450(3)). This allows the Commissioner to treat the trust's net income as taxable income of the trustee for the purposes of calculating an instalment rate, benchmark instalment rate or benchmark tax for the trustee.

Multi-rate trustees

Some trustees have several separate liabilities to pay tax as the trustee of a particular trust and may, therefore, have more than one liability to pay PAYG instalments. A trustee may be liable to pay tax for a previous income year in respect of: (a) a beneficiary who is under a legal disability or a beneficiary who has a vested and indefeasible interest in trust income but cannot require the trustee to pay the amount (ITAA36 s 98(1), (2)); or (b) income to which no beneficiary is entitled (ITAA36 ss 99; 99A). Such trustees are multi-rate trustees (s 45-455). A trustee that is liable to pay tax under s 98(1) for a particular beneficiary for a particular year does not, however, have to pay PAYG instalments if that beneficiary will no longer be under a legal disability at the end of the subsequent year.

Instalments of a multi-rate trustee

The trustee works out the amount of its instalments by multiplying the total instalment income (calculated in the same way as for other entities: ¶27-260) of the trust by the instalment rate (s 45-465). The Commissioner works out the separate instalment rates for a trustee. The matching of the instalment income to the rate calculation enables the correct amount of an instalment to be worked out by the trustee in respect of each of the trustee's different instalment liabilities.

A multi-rate trustee may choose to pay quarterly instalments on a GDP-adjusted notional basis (¶27-300) if the trustee has a liability to pay instalments in respect of a beneficiary or income to which no beneficiary is entitled (s 45-468).

The Commissioner works out instalment rates for a multi-rate trustee on the basis of a formula in s 45-470. This formula is essentially the same as for other PAYG instalment payers. The "notional tax" in the formula is the notional tax in respect of a particular liability for a beneficiary or income to which no beneficiary is entitled (s 45-475). In effect, the notional tax is worked out on a share of the trust's net income. The "base assessment instalment income" in the formula is, however, the total base assessment instalment income of the trust, not a share of it (s 45-470(2)).

The instalment rate is worked out in this way to allow the trustee, in calculating the amount of an instalment, to apply the instalment rate to the total instalment income of the trust for an instalment period. The trustee does not need to work out each beneficiary's share of the trust's instalment income in order to calculate the amount of the trustee's various instalment liabilities.

The Commissioner's methods of working out a benchmark instalment rate and benchmark tax where the trustee has varied an instalment or an instalment rate are set out in ss 45-525 to 45-535.

[FTR ¶977-250]

¶27-550 Liability for PAYG instalments in a consolidated group

The consolidation regime allows wholly-owned groups of entities to make a choice to consolidate and therefore be treated as a single entity for the purposes of determining income tax liability (¶8-000). This has consequences for the operation of the PAYG instalment system. The rules are contained in TAA Sch 1 Subdivs 45-Q and 45-R.

Transitional rules

Where entities opt to be treated as a consolidated group, the head company of the group is responsible for the PAYG instalments obligations of the group once the Commissioner gives it an instalment rate worked out from its first assessment as the head company of that group.

For the transitional period from formation of the consolidated group until the head company is given an instalment rate, each member of the consolidated group continues to pay PAYG instalments as it did previously, ie as if it were not a member of a consolidated group. Instalments payable by the subsidiary members of a consolidated group in the transitional period will be credited against the assessment of tax payable by the head company of the group (¶27-150).

Rules once an instalment rate is given

Once the head company of a consolidated group has been given an instalment rate, the PAYG instalments provisions apply to the head company in much the same way as they do to any other company. Head companies will be liable to pay monthly or quarterly instalments and will pay using either the GDP-adjusted notional tax method (if eligible) or the instalment income method if ineligible to use the GDP method or chooses not to do so (¶27-220).

The head company will have to work out its instalment income for an instalment month or quarter on the basis that each subsidiary member of the group is a part of the head company, ie as if it derives the income or gains arising from transactions carried out by the members of the group. It also has to take account of the attributes of its subsidiary members. For example, if a subsidiary member is a partner in a partnership, or a beneficiary of a trust, the head company will be treated as being the partner or beneficiary where that partnership or trust is not itself a member of the group. However, the head company will not be required to include in its instalment income ordinary income arising from intra-group transactions under the mutuality principle.

A monthly instalment payable by a head company will be due on or before 21 days after the end of the instalment month (¶27-200). A quarterly instalment payable by a head company will be due on or before 21 days after the end of the instalment quarter (¶27-200). Head companies are not eligible to pay annual instalments.

Joining or leaving a consolidated group

An entity that becomes a subsidiary member of a consolidated group will be liable to pay a PAYG instalment for the instalment month or quarter (or income year if it is an annual payer) in which it joins the group. However, it will not be liable to pay an instalment for any subsequent month or quarter (or year) unless it later leaves the group.

If, at the time the subsidiary member joins the group, it pays its instalments using the instalment income method, its instalment income for the joining month or quarter will be the ordinary income it derives before joining the group. Any income derived after joining will be treated as if it is derived by, and assessable to, the head company and therefore will not be instalment income of the subsidiary.

If, at the time it joins the group, the subsidiary member pays its instalments using the GDP-adjusted notional tax method (and therefore cannot be a monthly payer), the entity will, for the joining quarter, pay the amount notified by the Commissioner but may choose to vary the amount on the basis of its estimate of its expected tax liability for the income year.

An entity will become liable to pay PAYG instalments immediately on leaving a consolidated group. The entity will be required to pay quarterly instalments using the instalment income method and must use the most recent instalment rate given to the head company before the end of the instalment quarter in which the entity leaves the group.

The entity will continue to pay on the instalment income basis until the first instalment quarter of the first income year that starts after it has been assessed in its own right. It can then determine whether it is eligible to pay instalments annually, quarterly or monthly and if it is a GDP-adjusted notional tax payer or instalment income payer.

However, no PAYG instalments are payable by a company that leaves one consolidated group to join another consolidated group.

The Commissioner has the power to give a head company a new instalment rate or instalment amount in certain circumstances when there is a change in the membership of a mature consolidated group.

Rules for head companies

The rules refine the circumstances in which the head company of a consolidated group will be liable to pay PAYG instalments and when it will cease to be liable to pay PAYG instalments.

A head company of a consolidated group will *start* to be treated as a ''mature'' head company (and therefore be liable to pay PAYG instalments on behalf of the consolidated group) at the start of the instalment quarter (or at the beginning of the next instalment month if it is a monthly payer) during which one or more of the following occurs:

- the Commissioner gives the head company an instalment rate
- the consolidated group is created from a mature MEC group, or
- a company is interposed between a mature head company and its shareholders and the interposed company elects to continue the consolidated group.

A head company will *cease* to be a mature head company at the earliest of the following times:

- at the end of the instalment quarter in which the consolidated group ceases to exist (but a MEC group is not thereby created)
- at the end of the instalment quarter in which a MEC group is created from the consolidated group (if the Commissioner is notified of the creation of the MEC group in that quarter)
- just before the instalment quarter during which the Commissioner is notified of the creation of a MEC group from the consolidated group (if the MEC group was created in an earlier quarter), or
- just before the instalment quarter in which a company is interposed between the head company and its shareholders and the interposed company elects to continue the consolidated group and becomes the head company of that group.

When an interposed company elects to continue a consolidated group, it will be endowed (at the time of the interposition) with the PAYG attributes of the head company it has replaced.

Special rules for members of consolidated groups

When a mature head company becomes a wholly-owned subsidiary of another entity that is a member of a group that is not yet mature, the old head company continues to pay PAYG instalments as if it were still the head company of the mature group until the new group matures or the old head company ceases to be a member of the new group.

When a subsidiary (which also has one or more subsidiaries) ceases to be a member of a mature group but, at that time, also becomes the head company of a consolidatable group and that company elects to form a consolidated group, that company may be treated as if it immediately becomes a mature head company from the date of consolidation.

Multiple entry consolidated groups

There are additional PAYG instalment rules for MEC groups (¶8-610). These rules are in TAA Sch 1 Subdiv 45-S.

Generally, the PAYG instalments regime applies to the members of a MEC group in much the same way as it applies to the members of a consolidated group — a rule that applies to a head company of a consolidated group will generally apply to the provisional head company of a MEC group; a rule that applies to a subsidiary member of a consolidated group will generally apply to a member (other than the provisional head company) of a MEC group.

A provisional head company of a MEC group *becomes* a ''mature'' provisional head company for PAYG instalment purposes at the start of an instalment quarter (or the start of the next instalment month if the company is a monthly payer) in which:

- the Commissioner gives the provisional head company an instalment rate

- the Commissioner is notified that a MEC group has been created from a mature consolidated group, or
- a new provisional head company is appointed after a cessation event happens to a former provisional head company that is a mature provisional head company.

A provisional head company of a MEC group *ceases* to be a mature provisional head company at the earlier of the following:

- at the end of the instalment quarter in which the group ceases to exist (but a consolidated group is not thereby created)
- at the end of the instalment quarter in which a consolidated group is created from the MEC group, or
- just before the instalment quarter in which another company is appointed as provisional head company of the MEC group.

When a provisional head company of a MEC group ceases to be eligible to be a provisional head company and a replacement provisional head company is appointed, the replacement provisional head company is endowed (at the time the replacement takes effect) with the PAYG attributes of the company it replaces.

Credits for instalments

A head company of a consolidated group will be entitled to a credit for instalments payable by an entity that is a subsidiary member of that group at any time during the head company's consolidation transitional year. This credit will be in addition to the credit to which the head company is entitled for its own instalments under s 45-30.

The head company will be entitled to credits after the Commissioner makes an assessment of the income tax the head company is liable to pay for a consolidation transitional year for the head company or determines that the head company is not liable to pay tax on its taxable income or that it has no taxable income for that year. The amount of the credit to which a head company is entitled in respect of a particular subsidiary member is worked out by:

- totalling each instalment payable by that subsidiary member, and
- subtracting any variation credits claimed by it,

to the extent to which those instalments and variation credits are reasonably attributable to that head company's assessment for a consolidation transitional year.

Penalties for variation of instalments where varied amount is too low

A head company of a consolidated group that is a quarterly payer (whether or not some of the other members of the group are monthly payers) will be liable to pay the GIC for an instalment quarter of a consolidation transitional year if:

- any member of the consolidated group has varied its instalment for that quarter or, if the member's instalment quarters differ from the head company's, the last instalment quarter of the member that finishes before the end of that particular quarter of the head company (called the equivalent quarter), and
- the sum of the instalments payable by the members of the group for the quarter (and any equivalent quarters of the members) reduced by any variation credits claimed by those members is less than 85% of one-quarter of the head company's benchmark tax for that consolidation transitional year.

The amount on which a head company will be liable to pay the GIC will be determined by reference to the lesser of:

- the sum of all the instalments that would have been payable by the members of the group had no member varied

- the amount that would have been payable by the head company if it had been required to pay one quarter of its benchmark tax as its instalment for that quarter.

The lesser of those 2 amounts will be reduced by the sum of the instalments actually payable by all the members of the group reduced by any variation credits claimed by them. If the result is positive, the GIC is imposed on that amount.

For a head company which is a monthly payer and all members of the group are also monthly payers, the above rules for quarterly payers apply as if all references to quarters were references to months.

For a head company which is a monthly payer and any of the other members of the group are quarterly payers (''subsidiary quarterly payers''), the above rules apply as if all references to quarters were references to months. In addition, the quarters of the subsidiary quarterly payers are divided into 3 notional instalment months and the amounts for that quarter are allocated to those notional instalment months.

[FTR ¶977-300, ¶977-355]

PAYG Anti-avoidance Rules

¶27-600 PAYG anti-avoidance rules

Penalties may be applied to an entity whose tax position, so far as it relates to PAYG instalments, is altered by a scheme that is inconsistent with the purposes and objects of the PAYG instalments regime (TAA Sch 1 Subdiv 45-P: ss 45-595 to 45-640). These anti-avoidance rules are not, however, intended to apply to ''a straightforward use of structural features'' of the PAYG instalments system (eg a choice to use a varied instalment rate or to pay instalments on the basis of notional tax) if that use is consistent with the legislative purposes and policy (s 45-595(2)).

Liability to GIC

An entity is liable to GIC if there is a scheme (¶30-140) that, judged objectively, was entered into or carried out for the *sole* or *dominant purpose* of obtaining one or more tax benefits (s 45-600). An entity that obtains a tax benefit is liable to pay GIC even if:

- the entity did not enter into the scheme from which it gets the tax benefit
- the entity that carries out the scheme did so alone or with others
- the scheme is carried out outside Australia, or
- that tax benefit is different from the tax benefit sought to be obtained.

Whether an entity gets a tax benefit is worked out using the following steps (s 45-605):

Step 1: Work out the entity's *actual tax position* for the income year (ie the tax position as a result of the scheme).

Step 2: Work out the entity's *hypothetical tax position* (ie what would have been, or could reasonably be expected to have been, the entity's tax position for the same income year if the scheme had not been entered into or carried out).

Step 3: Each component of the entity's actual tax position is *compared* with the corresponding component of the hypothetical tax position. If the amount of a component of the actual tax position is less than the amount of that component of the hypothetical tax position, the difference between the 2 amounts is a tax benefit from the scheme. If there is also a difference in relation to another component, that is a separate tax benefit.

There are 4 different types of components of an entity's tax position: (i) the quarterly instalment component (ie the instalment for each instalment quarter, regardless of whether the entity pays its instalments quarterly or annually); (ii) the annual instalment component (ie the annual instalment regardless of whether the entity pays its instalments quarterly or annually); (iii) the variation credit component (ie the credit claimed by the entity for an instalment quarter because it has chosen a lower instalment rate: ¶27-280); and (iv) the variation GIC component (ie the GIC payable in respect of a varied instalment rate or an entity's estimated benchmark tax: ¶27-320). For monthly payers, these provisions have the same effect for an instalment month in the same way in which they apply to an instalment quarter (s 45-597).

Calculation of GIC

An entity is liable to pay GIC on twice the tax benefit obtained from a scheme for each day in the period that:

- starts on the day by which the instalment to which the component relates was due, or would have been due, to be paid, and
- finishes on the due date for payment of the assessed tax (s 45-620).

The Commissioner must give the entity written notice of the GIC, and the penalty must be paid within 14 days of receipt of the notice. Late payment GIC is payable for each day the GIC remains unpaid after the due date. The Commissioner may remit the whole or a part of the GIC if satisfied that there are special circumstances that would make it fair and reasonable to do so (s 45-640).

An entity is entitled to a credit if it is liable to GIC because it gets a tax benefit from a scheme and the Commissioner is also satisfied that the entity gets a tax detriment from that scheme and the tax detriment relates to a component of that entity's tax position for an income year (s 45-625). The credit allowed to the entity cannot exceed the total GIC that the entity is liable to pay because it gets a tax benefit from the scheme.

Payment and remission of GIC are considered at ¶29-510 and ¶29-530.

Rights of review

A taxpayer does not have a right of review under TAA Pt IVC in relation to GIC imposed under the PAYG instalments anti-avoidance rules. However, an entity that is dissatisfied with the imposition of the penalty or with a decision not to remit the penalty may seek a review of the decision under the *Administrative Decisions (Judicial Review) Act 1977* (¶28-180).

[FTR ¶977-280]

Chapter 28 Objections • Appeals

Para

Challenging Taxation Decisions

¶28-000 Introduction to challenging taxation decisions

A taxpayer dissatisfied with an assessment (¶25-100, ¶25-110) or other taxation decision may challenge that decision in accordance with the objection, review and appeal procedures in TAA Pt IVC (ss 14ZL to 14ZZS). The Pt IVC procedures apply where various federal tax and superannuation Acts or Regulations provide that a taxpayer may object against a taxation decision, ie an assessment, determination, notice or decision. For example, Pt IVC applies where:

- a taxpayer is dissatisfied with an assessment of tax where there is a taxable income and there is tax payable, including the total of tax offsets (¶25-100), or administrative penalties (¶29-000 and following)

- a company is dissatisfied with a franking deficit tax assessment (¶4-780)
- a company is dissatisfied with the Commissioner's determination as to whether the company is entitled to offset franking deficit tax against company tax (¶4-780)
- a taxpayer is dissatisfied with the Commissioner's decision on a request for a compensating adjustment where the Commissioner has made a determination to cancel a tax benefit pursuant to the general anti-avoidance provisions (¶30-180)
- a person claiming an interest in the estate of a deceased taxpayer is dissatisfied with an assessment in respect of the deceased's tax liability, where probate has not been granted or letters of administration have not been taken out within 6 months after death, or a person subsequently appointed executor or administrator is dissatisfied with such an assessment (¶25-530)
- a person is dissatisfied with decisions under the PAYG system, eg a decision to vary a withholder's status (¶26-500), the Commissioner's refund decision (¶26-700) or the Commissioner's decision on remission of penalties (¶26-750)
- an employer is dissatisfied with an assessment of FBT liability (¶35-730)
- an entity is dissatisfied with an ABN decision, eg setting the date of effect of registration, refusing ABN registration, cancelling or refusing to cancel registration, setting the date of effect of a cancellation and refusing an application not to disclose details (ABN Act s 21) (¶33-115)
- an entity is dissatisfied with the Commissioner's decision to withhold refund of an RBA surplus or excess non-RBA credit pending verification of the entity's claims (¶24-360).

If the Act under which a taxation decision is made does *not* give a person dissatisfied with the decision the right to challenge it under Pt IVC, the taxpayer will have to seek an alternative remedy. For example, certain decisions of the Commissioner which do not actually relate to the assessment or calculation of tax, such as the exercise of one of the Commissioner's many discretions, may be reviewed under the *Administrative Decisions (Judicial Review) Act 1977* (¶28-180). In some cases, a taxpayer has the option of using the review/appeal procedures in Pt IVC or applying to the Federal Court for judicial review. A person dissatisfied with the administrative actions of the ATO may also have the matter examined by lodging a written complaint with the Inspector-General of Taxation (¶1-200). The ATO also has its own Complaints Unit (¶28-190).

Liability to pay tax is not suspended pending the outcome of an objection, review or appeal (¶25-510) and the lodgment of an objection, etc, cannot be regarded as an effective delaying tactic. However, as a matter of practice, where there is a genuine dispute about the taxpayer's liability, the Commissioner usually allows payment of some or all of the tax in dispute to be deferred (¶25-410).

Companies, superannuation funds, ADFs and PSTs which fully self-assess their liability to tax (¶25-100) still retain rights of objection, review and appeal. For example, such an entity may object against its own calculation of tax payable where it wishes to challenge a view of the Commissioner (eg as expressed in a ruling: ¶24-500) which it had nevertheless adopted for prudence in self-assessing its tax liability.

Expenses in disputing a taxation decision, including AAT and court fees (¶28-085), may be deductible (¶16-850, ¶16-854).

Amendment requests

If a mistake has been made on an income tax return or assessment, a credit amendment may be requested in writing, rather than lodging an objection. In addition to the taxpayer's name, preferred address for service, telephone number and TFN, this request should include: (1) the year shown on the tax return to be amended; (2) the tax return item number and the change to be made; (3) an explanation of why this information was not included (or incorrectly included) in the original return; and (4) a signed and dated declaration by the taxpayer as follows: "I declare that all the information I have given in this letter, including any attachments, is true and correct". For individuals, a standard amendment request form is available on the ATO website at www.ato.gov.au. See further ¶25-300 and following.

[FTR ¶972-500, ¶972-540]

Objections

¶28-010 Lodging an objection

Where a taxpayer has taxable income, there is tax payable (¶25-100) and a notice of assessment has been served (¶25-110), a right of objection will accrue against the assessment. There is no right of objection where the taxpayer has no taxable income or there is taxable income but no tax is payable, unless the taxpayer is seeking an increase in the taxpayer's liability or the total of the taxpayer's tax offset refunds (ITAA36 s 175A). It is not sufficient for a taxpayer to foreshadow the mere *possibility* of an increase in liability (*Case 1/2018*).

Where a taxpayer is dissatisfied with an assessment (or any other taxation decision) or a deemed assessment (¶25-100), the taxpayer may, and should, object against it. To be valid and effective, an objection must:

- be in the form approved by the Commissioner (standard forms for professionals and non-professionals are available on the ATO website). However, it is not necessary to use a standard form provided the objection is in writing and contains a signed and dated declaration that all the information provided is true and correct
- be lodged with the Commissioner within the appropriate time limits, although a taxpayer may be able to obtain an extension of time (¶28-020, ¶28-030), and
- state fully and in detail the grounds on which the taxpayer relies in disputing the assessment or deemed assessment (¶28-040).

If the prescribed course of action is not followed explicitly, the taxpayer's rights may be irrevocably lost. An objection may be withdrawn at any time, as may a pending review or appeal against a disallowed objection, so there is everything to be gained and nothing to be lost by lodging an objection to an assessment or deemed assessment.

Where an assessment of penalty is included in the notice of assessment of ordinary tax, both are treated as one assessment (TAA s 14ZR). This means that the taxpayer does not have to object independently against each assessment and the one notice of objection can cover both the ordinary tax and the penalty.

A taxpayer may lodge more than one objection against an assessment within the allowable time limit. After an objection has been made to an element of an assessment, further objections to that element can be made until the Commissioner makes an objection decision. Further, the taxpayer can continue to object against other elements of the assessment within the allowable time limit (TR 2011/5).

A taxpayer may also lodge a single notice of objection against multiple assessments where common questions of law and fact are involved (*McDermott*). However, a taxpayer's right to object against an *amended* assessment or determination is limited to matters connected with the particular item(s) that has been amended and with which the taxpayer is dissatisfied (TAA s 14ZV; *Case 21/94*).

Another restriction on a taxpayer's right to object against an assessment is where the assessment reflects the application of a private ruling against which the taxpayer had previously objected. In such a case, the objection against the assessment cannot include grounds that were, or could have been, grounds for objection against the private ruling (TAA s 14ZVA) (¶24-560).

Where a taxpayer enters into a deed of settlement with the Commissioner (¶25-210) concerning tax in dispute, the deed will usually provide for the waiver of objection rights and these clauses are binding (*Jonshagen*; *EE&C Pty Ltd as Trustee for the Tarcisio Cremasco Family Trust*).

Allowance of credits

There is no right to object against the amount of a credit allowed by the Commissioner for PAYG amounts that have been withheld (¶26-660). This is because the allowance of the credit does not form part of the assessment as such; the credit is only taken into account once the assessment or deemed assessment has actually been made (TR 2011/5; *Cassiniti*). In these cases, an amendment request should be lodged rather than an objection as amendments are processed faster.

Where the Commissioner fails to allow a credit, it would be open to the taxpayer to pursue some administrative remedy (eg an approach to the Inspector-General of Taxation: see ¶1-200) or to sue the Commissioner for the amount involved.

However, it has been held that the Commissioner's decision not to allow PAYG credits to a taxpayer, in circumstances where the employer had never remitted the PAYG credits, was not reviewable under the *Administrative Decisions (Judicial Review) Act 1977* (*Perdikaris*).

[FTR ¶972-690]

¶28-020 Time limit for lodging objections

The time limit for lodging objections against assessments (and certain other taxation decisions) is generally 2 years after service of the notice of assessment for most individuals and small business taxpayers, and 4 years for taxpayers with more complex affairs (or, in the case of companies, superannuation funds, ADFs and PSTs, 4 years after the deemed service of the deemed notice of assessment) (¶25-310; TAA s 14ZW). This 2 or 4-year limit applies to objections against assessments of income tax, administrative penalties (¶29-000), franking deficit tax (¶4-780), FBT (¶35-730), or income tax and FBT due to delayed administration of deceased estates (¶25-530, ¶35-730).

A 4-year limit also applies to objections against determinations (the 4 years running from after service of the notice of the determination) regarding a claim for credits under the former foreign tax credit system or a double taxation agreement (¶28-010), and as to whether a company is entitled to offset franking deficit tax against company tax (¶4-780).

For the time limits for lodging an objection against a private ruling, see ¶24-560.

Amended assessments

Where an assessment or determination is amended by the Commissioner and a 2-year or 4-year time limit would otherwise apply, an objection against the amended assessment or determination must be lodged within the *later* of:

- *2 years* (for most individuals and small business taxpayers) or *4 years* (for taxpayers with more complex affairs) after service (or deemed service) of the notice (or deemed notice) of the assessment or determination that has been amended (if an assessment or determination has been amended more than once, the relevant notice is the notice of the first assessment or determination), and
- *60 days* after service of the notice of amended assessment or amended determination.

Other cases

For all other determinations, notices or decisions, a *60-day* objection limit applies.

Calculating the objection period

An objection must actually be physically *received* by the Commissioner within the relevant objection period and is not considered as lodged until that occurs. The *first* day of the objection period is the day *after* the date of service of the notice of assessment (or taxation decision) or, in the case of companies, superannuation funds, ADFs and PSTs, the date of deemed service of the deemed notice of assessment (¶25-110). In practice, there should be some evidence of the date of service (or deemed service) of the assessment (such as a contemporaneous diary note or stamping the date of receipt on the assessment notice) and of the date when the objection notice was lodged.

Days that are not business days (ie Saturdays, Sundays, public and bank holidays) are counted in calculating when the objection period begins and ends. However, if the *last* day of the objection period is not a business day, the objection may be lodged on the next business day.

▶ Example 1

An individual taxpayer, Tom, is notified via a message on myGov that a notice of assessment for the 2017–18 income year, dated 8 December 2018, is available on myTax. The first day of the 2-year objection period is 9 December 2018 and that period would expire at midnight on 10 December 2020. An objection would have to be received by the Commissioner by that time and, therefore, an objection posted on or before midnight on 10 December 2020, but not received by the Commissioner until after that date, would be out of time (although an extension of time may be granted: ¶28-030).

▶ Example 2

A notice of assessment for the 2014–15 income year is served on a business taxpayer that is not a small business entity on 6 September 2016. Following an audit of the taxpayer's affairs, an amended assessment for that year is served on the taxpayer on 9 November 2017. The taxpayer is required to lodge an objection to the amended assessment by midnight on 6 September 2020, ie 4 years after the notice of the original assessment was served on the taxpayer (although an extension of time may be granted: ¶28-030).

If the notice of the amended assessment is served on the taxpayer on 9 August 2020, the taxpayer would be required to lodge the objection by midnight on 8 October 2020, ie 60 days after service of the notice of the amended assessment. If the assessment is further amended and notice of the further amended assessment is served on the taxpayer on 16 December 2020, the objection to the further amended assessment would have to be lodged by midnight on 14 February 2021, ie 60 days after service of the notice of the further amended assessment (although an extension of time may be granted: ¶28-030).

[FTR ¶972-830]

¶28-030 Extensions of time to object

An objection lodged outside the relevant period (¶28-020) cannot be considered unless an extension of time is granted. A taxpayer who is out of time should lodge the objection with the Commissioner *together with* a written application requesting him to deal with the objection as if it had been lodged in time. The application must provide full details of the reasons why the objection was not lodged in time (TAA s 14ZW(2), (3)). The Commissioner has the discretion to refuse or grant the application and must give the taxpayer written notice of the decision. Where an application for an extension of time is granted, the objection is taken to have been duly lodged within the relevant period (TAA s 14ZX). If the Commissioner refuses to grant an extension of time, the taxpayer must be notified of the right to have the decision reviewed by the AAT (*Administrative Appeals Tribunal Act 1975* (AAT Act), s 27A: ¶28-070).

Factors taken into account

The taxpayer bears the onus of establishing why an extension of time should be granted. The taxpayer should establish that the objection and the application for an extension were lodged as soon as circumstances reasonably permitted and must have an acceptable explanation for the delay (eg *Windshuttle*; *Case 36/94*). According to PS LA 2003/7, relevant factors to be taken into account by the Commissioner include:

- the reasons for the delay (eg the taxpayer's illness or absence overseas, postal delays, legislative amendments, new case law or rulings, and incorrect tax advice or misleading conduct by the ATO are all examples of where an extension of time may be appropriate)
- the circumstances of the delay, including whether the taxpayer took steps to inform the Commissioner that the decision in question was to be contested
- whether the taxpayer has an arguable case
- any prejudice to the Commissioner in granting an extension (eg the lapse of time may give rise to evidentiary difficulties if documents have been destroyed)
- evidence of negligence on the part of the taxpayer's tax agent.

Where an individual or STS taxpayer has a 2-year time limit for lodging an objection against an income tax assessment under s 14ZW(1), the Commissioner will generally accept a request for an extension of time to lodge an objection if it is received within 4 years after the original notice of assessment was given to the taxpayer and the objection discloses an arguable case for allowing the objection (PS LA 2003/7).

Appeal to AAT

A taxpayer who is dissatisfied with the Commissioner's decision to refuse an extension of time may have the decision reviewed by the AAT (s 14ZX(4)). An application for review must be made to the AAT and lodged within 60 days of the decision being furnished to the taxpayer (or such further time as may be allowed). An application fee is payable, subject to certain exceptions (¶28-085). The application is not taken to be lodged unless the prescribed fee (if any) is paid. A taxpayer seeking a review is entitled to request the Commissioner supply a statement of reasons for the decision refusing the extension (AAT Act s 28).

Given the wide discretion conferred by s 14ZX(1), a degree of inconsistency in the case law has evolved. However, the AAT will generally assess the evidence against the 4 considerations outlined in *Brown*, ie the taxpayer's explanation for the delay, the circumstances attendant upon that delay, whether the taxpayer has an arguable case, and such other matters as the circumstances of the case make relevant.

The merits of the substantive application may be properly taken into account in considering whether an extension of time should be granted. An insurance company was allowed an extension of time to lodge an objection nearly 4 years after the expiry of the objection period because it had an arguable case (based on rulings issued after the lodgment of its return) and the complexity of the objection meant that a lengthy delay was not unreasonable (*Case 15/96*). Similarly, a medical centre operator was allowed an extension of time to lodge an objection to claim deductions for earlier income years after a successful ''test case'' objection for a later income year (*Primary Health*).

Taxpayers who fail to provide an acceptable explanation for the delay in seeking a review of the objection decision are likely to be refused an extension of time (eg *Zizza*). However, this is not always the case (eg *Case 4/2000*). The weight to be given to various factors is a matter of fact for the AAT to determine. An inappropriate decision about the weight to be given to a finding about a particular factor is not an error of law (*Zizza*).

It may not be considered to be in the public interest to reopen a matter which had been settled after protracted negotiations (*Case Y58*). Public interest was also an important factor in refusing an extension of time where the taxpayer did not seek to challenge his assessment until after the High Court handed down a decision which, if applied to his assessment, would have resulted in a reduction in his tax liability (*Case 33/93*). However, this decision can be contrasted with *Case 9/98* where a court decision overturning the Commissioner's established view was the trigger for a successful extension of time application.

A gold mining company was refused an extension of time to lodge objections against FBT assessments over 5 years after the expiry of the objection period partly because, notwithstanding that the objections would have been allowed if the extension of time were to be granted, it was a commercial case in which the taxpayer had the benefit of professional advice and assistance in the preparation and lodgment of the relevant tax returns (*Mt Gibson Manager*). Conversely, a taxpayer was allowed an extension of time for FBT objections lodged up to 6 years out of time where the taxpayer relied on a suspect public ruling in self-assessing its FBT liability (*Minproc Engineers*), but not where the taxpayer did not rely on a ruling (*Boral Resources*). In *Ciaglia* the taxpayer was successful in obtaining an extension to object nearly 13 years late on the basis that extreme domestic and family circumstances caused the delay.

The fact that the delay is the fault of the taxpayer's accountant or tax agent is only one of the factors to be taken into account and will not automatically entitle the taxpayer to an extension of time. *Fardon*, *Case 8/93*, *Case 18/94* and *Case 26/95* are examples of where a taxpayer was represented by a tax agent or other professional adviser but was refused an extension of time. However, in *Case 27/97*, a taxpayer who was content to be guided by his accountant and solicitor but who was confused regarding his tax affairs was allowed an extension of nearly 3 years as the Commissioner would suffer no prejudice and it was likely that the assessment was incorrect owing to an error on the part of the tax agent.

If the AAT decides that an extension of time should be granted, the Commissioner must, within 60 days of that decision becoming final, take such action as is necessary to give effect to the decision (¶28-160).

[FTR ¶972-855, ¶972-865]

¶28-040 Contents of objection

An objection against an assessment must comply with the general guidelines stipulated in TAA Sch 1 s 388-50, ie it must be in the form approved by the Commissioner (standard forms for professionals and non-professionals are available on the ATO website), and contain the required information and declaration (¶28-010). See ¶28-050 for more sample notices of objection.

The objection should convey why the taxpayer considers the assessment to be incorrect and the reasons for that view (*Lancey Shipping*). The Commissioner will treat a request for amendment as an objection where there is: (1) any dispute over facts, issues or his interpretation of the law; (2) a challenge to an entitlement (other than against PAYG credits); or (3) a suggestion or request to preserve rights of review (PS LA 2008/19).

A statement merely to the effect that the assessment is excessive or wrong, without providing any further information, is unlikely to constitute a valid objection (*Lancey Shipping*). Nevertheless, a letter which simply stated that: (a) tax returns had been lodged indicating that there was no tax payable for the relevant years; and (b) the assets betterment statement on which the assessments were based was wrong, was held to be a valid objection (*Szajntop*). However, in that case, the Full Federal Court acknowledged that the taxpayer would have little chance of success unless she was allowed to amend the grounds of objection to directly challenge the assets betterment statement. It should not be assumed that the AAT or court will exercise its discretion to allow a taxpayer to amend the grounds of objection; if it is not exercised, the taxpayer will be restricted to the grounds stated in the objection (¶28-130).

There are restrictions on a taxpayer's right to object against an amended assessment or determination (¶28-010) and against an assessment which reflects the application of a private ruling to which the taxpayer previously objected (¶24-560).

[FTR ¶972-715]

¶28-050 Sample notices of objection

The sample objections that follow are intended as a guide only. It is generally desirable to have an objection drawn up by a tax agent, accountant or tax lawyer unless only a small amount is involved. The objection should be signed by the taxpayer personally or, in the case of a company, by its public officer. Here are some practical points to keep in mind when preparing an objection.

• All possible **grounds of objection**, with sufficient detail, should be included so as to avoid the uncertainties and costs involved in applying to the AAT or court for an amendment (¶28-130). For example, in the case of an assets betterment assessment, the objection should refer to each aspect of the assets betterment statement that is considered to be wrong. Reference should be made to any relevant private ruling (¶24-560).

• Under the **penalty and offence provisions**, a statement made in a notice of objection which is false or misleading, or an omission from a statement which makes the statement misleading, may expose the taxpayer and the person who drafted the notice of objection (eg a tax agent) to prosecution (¶29-700). An incorrect statement in an objection may also result in the imposition of a penalty under the administrative penalty regime (¶29-140). It is therefore of utmost importance that what is alleged in an objection is correct and not misleading. It is suggested that the grounds of objection should be stated as *claims* rather than as positive assertions.

• A ground relating to **quantum** should be included. For example, if the Commissioner has wholly disallowed a deduction claimed by the taxpayer, the objection should contain a ground claiming that the deduction is wholly allowable and also a ground that, if the deduction is not wholly allowable, then it is allowable in part.

• Grounds relating to the general **anti-avoidance provisions** (¶30-120) and, in appropriate cases, to specific anti-avoidance provisions (eg prepayment schemes and expenditure recoupment schemes: ¶16-110), should be included where it is known or likely that the Commissioner has applied those provisions.

• If an **administrative penalty** has been imposed, eg for late lodgment of the return or for a shortfall amount, it may be necessary to object on the ground that the conditions for the imposition of the penalty do not exist. A request that the Commissioner exercise the discretion under the relevant provision to remit the penalty to nil, or to a greater extent than already allowed, should also be included.

• Where the taxpayer is an individual liable for the **Medicare levy** and it is claimed in the objection that the taxable income as assessed is excessive, an appropriate ground of objection should be included claiming that the levy should be calculated by reference to the taxable income as reduced in accordance with the objection or, alternatively, a taxable income less than that assessed by the Commissioner.

• **Companies, superannuation funds, etc**, that self-assess (¶25-100) should refer in the objection to the relevant deemed assessment and to any request for a private ruling (¶24-560) or other ruling (¶24-030), as appropriate. In such a case, there will be no assessment number.

- An objection may incorporate an **election** that the taxpayer is required to make and, if necessary, a request for an extension of time to make the election (¶24-040).

[FTR ¶972-730 – ¶972-800]

¶28-052 Precedent: Objection — profit not assessable and capital loss reduced capital gain

An objection against an assessment must comply with the general guidelines stipulated in TAA Sch 1 s 388-50, ie it must be in the form approved by the Commissioner, and contain the required information and declaration (¶28-010). This precedent for an objection is intended as a guide only — please see the disclaimer below.

It is generally desirable to have an objection drawn up by a tax agent, accountant or tax lawyer unless only a small amount is involved. The objection should ideally be signed by the taxpayer personally or, in the case of a company, by its public officer.

It is assumed that the capital gain is a discount capital gain and that the taxpayer does not have a net capital loss carried forward from a previous income year.

COMMONWEALTH OF AUSTRALIA
INCOME TAX ASSESSMENT ACT 1997 (ITAA97)

ASSESSMENT No ____________ FILE No ____________

NOTICE OF OBJECTION AGAINST ASSESSMENT

I, Jerry Smyth, object against the assessment of income tax based on income derived by me during the year of income ended 30 June 2017, and issued to me by notice of assessment dated 14 February 2018. I contend that the taxable income of $98,345 shown on the notice of assessment should be reduced by the amount of $45,444, being the difference between the amount of $64,560 included in the assessment as profit from the sale of 16 Hart Street, Baulkham Hills (''the property''), and the amount of $19,116 being the amount of the net capital gain which is properly included in my assessable income for the year of income.

In support of my contention I claim that:

1. The proceeds of sale of the property are of a capital nature and are not to any extent assessable as income pursuant to ITAA97 Div 6.

2. Neither the proceeds of sale of the property nor any part thereof is assessable under ITAA97 Div 6 or any other provision other than ITAA97 Pt 3-1.

3. The sale of the property gave rise to a capital gain within the meaning of ITAA97 Pt 3-1 equal to $50,670 calculated as follows:

Capital proceeds	$220,000
Cost base	$169,330
Capital gain	$50,670

4. A capital loss of $12,438 accrued to me during the year of income on the disposal on 7 May 2017 of 3,000 shares in Owls and Magpies Forest Holdings Ltd which were acquired by me on 15 April 2003. The loss is calculated as follows:

Capital proceeds	$15,630
Reduced cost base	$28,068
Capital loss	$12,438

5. The capital gain of $50,670 is a discount capital gain as defined in ITAA97 Div 115 and accordingly after applying Step 3 of the method statement in ITAA97 s 102-5 the amount of the net capital gain which is included in my assessable income for the year of income under ITAA97 s 102-5 is $19,116.

6. If, contrary to the above, the amount of the net capital gain to be included in my assessable income for the year of income under ITAA97 s 102-5 is not $19,116 it is some other amount and the assessment should be amended and reduced accordingly.

7. I did not omit from my tax return for the year of income any assessable income derived by me during that year, nor include in the return as a deduction for, or as a rebate in respect of, expenditure incurred by me an amount in excess of the expenditure actually incurred by me during the year of income. Accordingly, there is no shortfall amount for the year of income and I am not liable to an administrative penalty under any of the provisions of TAA Sch 1 Div 284.

8. If there is a shortfall amount for the year of income, which is not admitted, then none of the conditions prescribed in TAA Sch 1 Subdiv 284-B for the imposition of penalty have been satisfied and, accordingly, I am not liable to pay a penalty under TAA Sch 1 Div 284 in respect of the year of income.

9. If I am liable to pay an amount of penalty under TAA Sch 1 Div 284 in respect of the year of income, which is not admitted, such penalty should be remitted, pursuant to TAA Sch 1 s 298-20, to nil or, alternatively, to an amount less than $ which has been included in the assessment.

10. The Medicare levy payable by me pursuant to ITAA36 Pt VIIB should be calculated by reference to a taxable income of $72,017 or, alternatively, a taxable income less than that shown on the notice of assessment.

[Signed declaration, date and address for service of notices]

[FTR ¶972-801/2]

Disclaimer: *This document must at all times be used cautiously and will need to be modified to reflect the particular circumstances in which it is proposed to be used. This document does not comprise legal, accounting or other professional advice. No person should rely on this document without first obtaining legal advice from a qualified lawyer and reviewing the document to ascertain if it is appropriate for the indended use. CCH does not warrant that this document is fit for any specific purpose, including without limitation compliance with any legal requirements that may be applicable to your organisation.*

¶28-054 Precedent: Objection — deductibility of overseas travelling expenses

An objection against an assessment must comply with the general guidelines stipulated in TAA Sch 1 s 388-50, ie it must be in the form approved by the Commissioner and contain the required information and declaration (¶28-010). This precedent for an objection is intended as a guide only — please see the disclaimer below.

It is generally desirable to have an objection drawn up by a tax agent, accountant or tax lawyer unless only a small amount is involved. The objection should ideally be signed by the taxpayer personally or, in the case of a company, by its public officer.

COMMONWEALTH OF AUSTRALIA
INCOME TAX ASSESSMENT ACT 1997 (ITAA97)

ASSESSMENT No FILE No

NOTICE OF OBJECTION AGAINST ASSESSMENT

I, Regi Blinker, object against the assessment of income tax based on income derived by me during the year of income ended 30 June 2017, and issued to me by notice of assessment dated 18 January 2018. I contend that the assessment should be amended by the allowance, as a deduction from my assessable income of $47,650, of the sum of $5,420 or some part thereof, representing certain expenses incurred by me in respect of an overseas trip undertaken during the year of income.

In support of my contention I claim that:

1. The sum of $5,420 is an allowable deduction under the provisions of ITAA97 s 8-1.

2. The sum of $5,420 was a loss or outgoing incurred by me in gaining or producing my assessable income, or necessarily incurred by me in carrying on a business for the purpose of gaining or producing assessable income and was not a loss or outgoing of capital or of a capital, private or domestic nature or incurred in relation to the gaining or production of exempt income and is an allowable deduction under ITAA97 s 8-1.

3. Even if some part of the sum of $5,420 was not incurred by me in gaining or producing my assessable income, or was not necessarily incurred by me in carrying on a business for the purpose of gaining or producing assessable income, or was a loss or outgoing of capital or of a capital, private or domestic nature or was incurred in relation to the gaining or production of exempt income, none of which is conceded, then the remainder of the sum of $5,420 which was incurred by me in gaining or producing my assessable income, or was necessarily incurred by me in carrying on a business for the purpose of gaining or producing assessable income, and was not a loss or outgoing of capital or of a capital, private or domestic nature or incurred in relation to the gaining or production of exempt income, is an allowable deduction under ITAA97 s 8-1 and a deduction should have been allowed for that portion of the sum of $5,420.

4. The Medicare levy payable by me pursuant to ITAA36 Pt VIIB should be calculated by reference to a taxable income of $42,230 or, alternatively, a taxable income less than that shown on the notice of assessment.

[Signed declaration, date and address for service of notices]

[Note: see sample objection (1), cl 6 to 8, for precedent clauses objecting to the imposition of penalties.]

[FTR ¶972-801/3]

Disclaimer: *This document must at all times be used cautiously and will need to be modified to reflect the particular circumstances in which it is proposed to be used. This document does not comprise legal, accounting or other professional advice. No person should rely on this document without first obtaining legal advice from a qualified lawyer and reviewing the document to ascertain if it is appropriate for the indended use. CCH does not warrant that this document is fit for any specific purpose, including without limitation compliance with any legal requirements that may be applicable to your organisation.*

¶28-056 Precedent: Objection — deductibility by company of retiring allowance

An objection against an assessment must comply with the general guidelines stipulated in TAA Sch 1 s 388-50, ie it must be in the form approved by the Commissioner, and contain the required information and declaration (¶28-010). This precedent for an objection is intended as a guide only — please see the disclaimer below.

It is generally desirable to have an objection drawn up by a tax agent, accountant or tax lawyer unless only a small amount is involved. The objection should ideally be signed by the taxpayer personally or, in the case of a company, by its public officer.

It is assumed the taxpayer has self-assessed its taxable income on the basis of an unfavourable private ruling made by the Commissioner in relation to the deductibility of the retiring allowance.

COMMONWEALTH OF AUSTRALIA
INCOME TAX ASSESSMENT ACT 1997 (ITAA97)

FILE No __________

NOTICE OF OBJECTION AGAINST ASSESSMENT

Princes and Paupers Pty Ltd (''the Company'') by its Public Officer, Luis Batty, objects against the assessment of income tax based on income derived by it during the year of income ended 30 June 2017, deemed to have been made under ITAA36 s 166A on 1 March 2018, notice of which was deemed by that section to have been served on the Company on 1 March 2017. The Company contends that the amount of taxable income as deemed to have been assessed should be reduced by the sum of $34,500, being that part of the retiring allowance paid to Jonathan Seagull during the year of income which, in accordance with the private ruling [No] made by the Commissioner on 11 August 2017, was not claimed as a deduction in the return for the year of income.

In support of this contention the Company claims that:

1. The sum of $60,000 paid by the Company to Jonathan Seagull was paid as a gratuity or retiring allowance to a former employee of the Company in good faith in consideration of his past services in business operations carried on by the Company for the purpose of gaining or producing assessable income and is an allowable deduction under ITAA97 s 25-50.

2. The relationship of employer and employee formerly existed between Jonathan Seagull and the Company and the sum of $60,000 was paid to Jonathan Seagull on his retirement from the employment of the Company, so that the sum was paid as a gratuity or retiring allowance to a person who was an employee of the Company within the meaning of ITAA97 s 25-50.

3. The sum of $60,000 was paid, as required by ITAA97 s 25-50, in good faith in consideration of the past services of Jonathan Seagull in business operations carried on by the Company for the purpose of gaining or producing assessable income, and there are no relevant facts or circumstances, then or now, from which an alternative objective conclusion could be reached by the Commissioner and the conclusion reached by the Commissioner was decided on improper principles and should be reconsidered and corrected by him.

4. Having regard to the services rendered to the Company by Jonathan Seagull and the length of time during which those services were performed, the sum of $60,000 is not in excess of a reasonable amount within the meaning of ITAA36 s 109 and, if the Commissioner has formed an opinion that the sum is in excess of a reasonable amount within the meaning of s 109, then there were no relevant facts or circumstances or, alternatively, there are now no relevant facts or circumstances which would justify the formation of such an opinion and the opinion formed by the Commissioner was formed on improper principles and should be reviewed, reconsidered and corrected by him.

5. Even if the sum of $60,000 paid to Jonathan Seagull is in excess of a reasonable amount within the meaning of ITAA36 s 109, which is not admitted, then that part of the sum of $60,000 which is in excess of a reasonable amount is less than the sum of $34,500 which was not claimed as a deduction.

6. The sum of $60,000 paid to Jonathan Seagull was a loss or outgoing incurred in gaining or producing the assessable income of the Company or was necessarily incurred in carrying on a business for the purpose of gaining or producing such income and was not a loss or outgoing of capital, or of a capital, private or domestic nature, or incurred in relation to the gaining or producing of exempt income and is an allowable deduction under ITAA97 s 8-1.

7. If the whole of the sum of $60,000 is not deductible under either ITAA97 s 25-50 or s 8-1, which is not admitted, then the part of the sum which is deductible exceeds the sum of $25,500 which was claimed as a deduction on the basis of private ruling [number].

[Signed declaration, date and address for service of notices]

[FTR ¶972-801/6]

Disclaimer: *This document must at all times be used cautiously and will need to be modified to reflect the particular circumstances in which it is proposed to be used. This document does not comprise legal, accounting or other professional advice. No person should rely on this document without first obtaining legal advice from a qualified lawyer and reviewing the document to ascertain if it is appropriate for the indended use. CCH does not warrant that this document is fit for any specific purpose, including without limitation compliance with any legal requirements that may be applicable to your organisation.*

¶28-060 Taxpayer's right to further information

The income tax legislation does not specifically require the Commissioner to provide information to a taxpayer. In preparing an objection, however, it would obviously be helpful if the taxpayer had all relevant information, as an adjustment sheet, if issued, usually contains only brief details. Of course, if an assessment is amended after an audit of the taxpayer's affairs, it is likely that the issues will have been fully canvassed during the audit. It is also likely that, in determining whether the grounds of objection have been stated "fully and in detail" (¶28-040), the court or AAT would take into account the information available to the taxpayer when drafting the objection.

If further information is needed, a taxpayer may have to use the *Freedom of Information Act 1982* (Cth) (FOI Act). A taxpayer will not be charged for accessing their personal information. Requests must be in writing using, if possible, a "Request under the *Freedom of Information Act 1982*" form available on the ATO website. The FOI Act can prove quite fruitful. For example, a taxpayer successfully applied for access to ATO internal working documents, including reports by advising officers, inter-office memoranda and an objection report, which related to a purely routine assessment (*Murtagh*). Another applicant was granted access to a final report by a consultant to the ATO on proposals to simplify the personal income tax system as the document was of overwhelming public interest (*McKinnon*). In another case, taxpayers were granted access to file notes disclosing the views of ATO officers on the application of the anti-avoidance provisions (*Walker*).

However, access to documents may be denied on various grounds of exemption, including:

- where disclosure of documents could reasonably be expected to prejudice the conduct of an investigation into tax evasion or prejudice the proper administration of the law (s 37) (*Re Kingston Thoroughbred Horse Stud*)
- where disclosure of documents or the information contained in them is prohibited under the secrecy provisions (¶1-220) (s 38) (*Re Harts*; *Collie*)
- where the documents are protected by legal professional privilege (s 42) (*Collie*)
- where documents contain material obtained in confidence (s 45), or
- where documents disclose trade secrets or commercially valuable information (s 47).

If the ATO refuses to provide relevant information, the applicant can seek review either by the ATO or the Australian Information Commissioner, with a further right of review by the AAT.

If the taxpayer applies to the AAT for review of an objection decision, the Commissioner is required to lodge a statement of reasons for his decision and relevant documents in his possession (¶28-090). The AAT may also order the Commissioner to disclose documents. If the taxpayer appeals to the Federal Court, the Commissioner is required to lodge a statement outlining his contentions (¶28-110). The court also has jurisdiction to require the parties to give particulars if it appears just, although there may be restrictions on the power to order particulars where a default assessment has been issued (*George*). In an appropriate case, a taxpayer may obtain a court order requiring the Commissioner to produce documents on which an assessment is based (*Tomlinson*; *Bailey*).

There is some authority for the view that where the exercise of a discretionary power by the Commissioner is in issue, a taxpayer is entitled to be informed of the matters taken into account by the Commissioner in exercising the discretionary power (*Giris*; *Kolotex Hosiery*; *Brian Hatch Timber*). Where the AAT itself exercises the discretion, on appeal the Federal Court is concerned with the AAT's exercise of the discretion and the Commissioner's state of mind when making the assessment may be irrelevant (*BOA*).

[FTR ¶930-000]

¶28-070 Consideration of objection

The Commissioner is bound to consider the taxpayer's objection and to serve the taxpayer with written notice of the decision to disallow it, or to allow it wholly or in part (an ''objection decision'') (TAA s 14ZY). Objections are considered by ATO officers who are independent of the original ATO officer issuing the assessment. This is designed to enable the ATO to reach a final, considered position at the objection stage.

The issue of a further assessment amending the assessment objected against does not qualify as a notice of the objection decision. The Commissioner is required to notify the taxpayer of the right to have the objection decision reviewed by the AAT but not of the right to appeal to the Federal Court. In fulfilling this obligation, the Commissioner must have regard to ''The Code of Practice for Notification of Reviewable Decisions and Rights of Review'' (AAT Act ss 27A; 27B).

If the Commissioner has not dealt with an objection (other than one under s 359-50 in relation to a private ruling) within the later of:

- 60 days of the objection being lodged
- 60 days of a decision to allow an extension of time for lodging the objection, or
- where the Commissioner has requested additional information, 60 days of the Commissioner receiving that information,

a taxpayer can serve a written notice requiring the Commissioner to make a decision on the objection (TAA s 14ZYA). Such a request may only be made if the objection was lodged (or is taken to have been lodged: ¶28-030) within the required period (¶28-020) (*Case 32/97*). If no decision is made within 60 days of the Commissioner receiving the notice, the Commissioner is deemed to have disallowed the objection and the taxpayer can apply for review or appeal.

A taxpayer who lodges a notice under TAA s 14ZYA is able to subsequently withdraw it (*McGrouther*).

[FTR ¶972-880, ¶972-890]

Reviews and Appeals

¶28-080 Application for review or appeal

A taxpayer dissatisfied with the Commissioner's objection decision, eg decision to disallow or only to allow in part an objection against an assessment (¶28-070), has the option of either:

- applying to the AAT for a review of the decision (¶28-090), or
- appealing to the Federal Court against the decision (¶28-110) (TAA s 14ZZ).

It is the Commissioner's objection decision as a whole that is referred to the AAT or court, ie even the part that the Commissioner has allowed in full and not just that part of the decision with which the taxpayer is dissatisfied (*ANZ Savings Bank*). However, it appears that a taxpayer may seek review of one part of the objection decision before the AAT and another part before the Federal Court (*Ferguson*).

On review or appeal, the Commissioner is not restricted to responding to the particular grounds of objection and may vary the grounds for defending the assessment (*Wade*). One consequence of this is that, once the AAT or court determines that the taxpayer is assessable on a basis different from that originally relied on by the Commissioner, the Commissioner is entitled to argue, for example, that deductions previously allowed by him are not in fact allowable (*ANZ Savings Bank*). The taxpayer should be given time to respond to any new arguments, even if the hearing has to be adjourned. See also ¶28-130 for limitations on review or appeal.

The ATO will generally attempt to resolve disputes but litigation is more likely where clarification of the law is required, it is in the public interest to litigate or the behaviour is such that there is a need to send a strong message to the community (¶25-210).

ATO test case litigation program

The ATO conducts a test case litigation program, under which it provides funding to taxpayers for litigation that it regards as being important. The purpose of the program is to develop legal precedent where: (1) there is uncertainty or contention in the tax law; (2) the issue is of significant interest to a substantial segment of the public or has significant commercial implications for an industry segment; and (3) it is in the public interest for the issue to be litigated. Generally, cases involving tax avoidance schemes or attempts to obtain benefits clearly not intended by the tax law will not be funded.

Taxpayers wishing to obtain funding under the program must complete an application for test case litigation funding (a form is available on the ATO website). Generally, applications will be considered by a test case litigation panel. Where test case funding is refused, taxpayers are able to apply to the ATO for review.

ATO's litigation conduct

According to PS LA 2009/9, the ATO conducts litigation in accordance with its obligations under the law, the Attorney-General's *Legal Services Directions 2017* (in particular, the obligation to act as a model litigant), court and tribunal rules and directions, and relevant internal and external policies and guidelines. However, there have been rare instances where the ATO has maintained a position that is contrary to a court or AAT decision which was not appealed against (*Indooroopilly Children Services*).

Appeals by entities other than the taxpayer

An entity other than the taxpayer may only appeal against the Commissioner's decision if it has standing. In *Pearson*, a trustee objected to an assessment issued to it but went into liquidation by the time the objection decision had been determined. A new trustee was appointed and the new trustee, a beneficiary of the trust and the public officer of the new trustee all sought to appeal against the objection decision. However, the

Federal Court ruled that none of the 3 had standing to appeal. They were neither the person who had objected (ie s 14ZZ was not satisfied) nor were they the dissatisfied taxpayer for ITAA36 s 175A purposes (¶28-010). On appeal by the beneficiary alone, the Full Federal Court upheld the decision.

If a taxpayer is bankrupt, generally it is the trustee in bankruptcy who is entitled to appeal against, or apply for review of, the Commissioner's decision (*McCallum*). The bankrupt taxpayer will have standing only in very limited circumstances, eg where the outcome of the appeal or review will have consequences for the taxpayer in years following discharge from bankruptcy. However, this is likely to be rare (*Robertson*; *Spirakos*). If the taxpayer lacks standing and the trustee in bankruptcy decides not to seek further review of the Commissioner's decision, the court may nevertheless order the trustee to do so where appropriate, eg to prevent injustice or oppression, at least if this can be done without cost to the estate. These rules apply even where the appeal, etc, was instituted before the bankruptcy (*McCallum*).

For similar reasons, a taxpayer who is subject to a guardianship order has no right to appeal in his own name (*Abuothman*).

[FTR ¶972-900]

¶28-085 Choosing between Tribunal and court

Some of the factors to bear in mind when deciding whether to apply to the AAT for review of, or to appeal to the Federal Court against, the Commissioner's decision on an objection are given below.

Type of case. If the question in dispute simply concerns an item of expenditure such as travelling or self-education expenses, an appeal to the court would not generally be warranted. If, however, a question of law is involved, it may be desirable that a test case be brought before the court so that a decisive determination of the question of law can be obtained. In the more usual case, where the issue is a question of fact, it would generally be better to have the matter reviewed by the AAT.

If the dispute concerns the way in which the Commissioner has exercised a *discretion*, it would normally be advisable to apply for review by the AAT as the AAT can exercise all the powers and discretions of the Commissioner. It can, therefore, consider the matter afresh and its opinion will be substituted for the Commissioner's. On the other hand, the court cannot interfere with a discretion exercised by the Commissioner unless it finds that the discretion was not exercised in accordance with legal principles. The court cannot interfere simply because it would have come to a different conclusion on the facts. Note that public, private and oral rulings on the way the Commissioner would exercise a discretion may be legally binding on the Commissioner (¶24-500).

Nature of proceedings. The AAT is not bound by the rules of evidence and a hearing before the AAT is less formal than the proceedings before the court. A taxpayer may appear in person before the AAT or may be represented by, for example, a tax agent without having to engage a solicitor or barrister. On the other hand, a tax agent cannot represent the taxpayer before the court and, if an appeal to the court is justified, legal representation is virtually a necessity (see *Tanner*). The court, but not the AAT, has the power to stay recovery proceedings (¶25-510).

Publicity. AAT hearings on tax matters may be held in private if the taxpayer so requests (TAA s 14ZZE) despite the general AAT rule that proceedings are to be held in public except in special circumstances (AAT Act s 35). If a matter is heard in private, the reasons for the decision must not disclose the identity of the taxpayer (unless a notice of appeal has been lodged). On the other hand, in an appeal to the court, generally the name of the taxpayer is disclosed and appears in the reported case (*Herald & Weekly Times v Williams*).

Costs. In a case before the AAT, the taxpayer and the Commissioner generally bear their own costs. In contrast, the Federal Court may award costs against the unsuccessful party. Note, however, that if the taxpayer succeeds and is awarded costs, the taxpayer would not recover all costs either under a typical costs order or a higher indemnity costs order. Court proceedings are generally more expensive because the proceedings are more formal and the fees are higher (see below).

The Commonwealth will generally agree to pay a taxpayer's reasonable costs where the Commissioner appeals from a decision of the AAT to the Federal Court and where there are any consequent appeals (eg to the High Court). However, no undertaking to meet costs will be given to taxpayers ''who are seeking to avoid tax or obtain some benefit that the legislature had clearly not intended to grant'' (*Treasurer's Statement*, 1 August 1986).

Small businesses. A Small Business Taxation Division (SBTD) exists in the AAT where unrepresented small businesses receive one hour of legal advice for $100 (with a possibility for an extra hour); a reduced application fee (see Tribunal fees below); and a dedicated case manager with decisions to be made within 28 days of hearing. In addition, if the ATO has legal representation and the small business does not, the ATO will pay for their equivalent representation. Further, the ATO will generally not enforce recovery of tax debts before the SBTD.

Rights of appeal. The question of further rights of appeal in the event of an unfavourable AAT or court decision may also be a relevant factor (¶28-120).

Court and Tribunal fees

The following AAT, Federal Court and High Court fees are payable, except for applicants who are eligible for a reduction or an exemption. Fees are different for publicly listed companies (PLC), corporations (a public authority is treated as a corporation) and others (these *include* small businesses, ie those with no more than 19 employees and an annual turnover of less than $2 million, and unincorporated not-for-profit associations).

An appeal to the High Court against a decision of the Full Federal Court is dependent on a special leave application (SLA) being lodged and granted.

<table>
<tr><td></td><td colspan="18">Application fee ($)</td></tr>
<tr><td>AAT[1]</td><td colspan="9">AAT</td><td colspan="9">952 (94[2] or 511[3])</td></tr>
<tr><td rowspan="2">FED CT[4]</td><td colspan="6">Filing fee ($)</b></td><td colspan="6"><b>Setting down fee ($)</td><td colspan="6">Daily hearing fee ($)</td></tr>
<tr><td colspan="3">corp</td><td colspan="3">other</td><td colspan="3">corp</td><td colspan="3">other</td><td colspan="3">corp</td><td colspan="3">other</td></tr>
<tr><td>First instance</td><td colspan="3">4,190</td><td colspan="3">1,440</td><td colspan="3">7,000</td><td colspan="3">2,875</td><td colspan="3">2,795</td><td colspan="3">1,140</td></tr>
<tr><td>On appeal from AAT</td><td colspan="3">10,455</td><td colspan="3">4,840</td><td colspan="3">7,000</td><td colspan="3">2,875</td><td colspan="3">2,795</td><td colspan="3">1,140</td></tr>
<tr><td>On appeal from Fed Ct</td><td colspan="3">10,460</td><td colspan="3">4,835</td><td colspan="3">7,000</td><td colspan="3">2,875</td><td colspan="3">2,795</td><td colspan="3">1,140</td></tr>
<tr><td rowspan="3">HIGH CT[5]</td><td colspan="6">Filing fee ($)
(for SLA)</b></td><td colspan="6"><b>Hearing fee ($)
(other than SLA)</td><td colspan="6">Daily hearing fee ($)
(other than SLA)</td></tr>
<tr><td colspan="2">PLC</td><td colspan="2">corp</td><td colspan="2">other</td><td colspan="2">PLC</td><td colspan="2">corp</td><td colspan="2">other</td><td colspan="2">PLC</td><td colspan="2">corp</td><td colspan="2">other</td></tr>
<tr><td colspan="2">15,570</td><td colspan="2">10,370</td><td colspan="2">3,440</td><td colspan="2">21,125</td><td colspan="2">14,075</td><td colspan="2">5,780</td><td colspan="2">7,030</td><td colspan="2">4,690</td><td colspan="2">1,920</td></tr>
</table>

Notes:

1. Amounts are applicable from 1 July 2020 and increase on 1 July each year in line with inflation: Administrative Appeals Tribunal Regulations 2015 reg 27.

Where a taxpayer lodges 2 or more applications for review in the same Tribunal, only one fee is payable if the applications may be conveniently heard together (that will usually be the case where a number of assessments concerning the same taxpayer are in dispute). A refusal to order that only one fee is payable is reviewable by the AAT.

2. The lower fee of $94 applies to small business taxation disputes where the amount of tax in dispute is less than $5,000.

3. The lower fee of $511 applies to the review of Small Business Taxation Decisions.

4. Amounts are applicable from 1 July 2020 and increase every 2 years in line with inflation: Federal Court and Federal Circuit Court Regulation 2012 reg 2.20.

   Where a taxpayer appeals to the Federal Court against more than one decision (either of the AAT or of a single judge but not both), only one fee is payable if a registrar is satisfied that the appeals concern substantially the same issue (other than a procedural issue).

   The Federal Court daily hearing fees listed are payable for the second, third and fourth days. The fees increase for the fifth to ninth days, and further increase for the 10th and subsequent days.

5. Amounts are applicable from 1 July 2020 and increase every year in line with inflation: High Court of Australia (Fees) Regulation 2012 reg 16.

   The High Court daily hearing fees listed are payable for the second and subsequent days.

Reduced fees and exemptions

For the AAT, the categories of persons eligible for a reduced, flat fee of $100 are:

- legal aid recipients
- health care card, pensioner concession card and Commonwealth health concession card holders
- persons serving a term of imprisonment or otherwise lawfully detained in a public institution
- persons under 18 years of age, and
- those receiving youth allowance, Austudy payments or benefits under the ABSTUDY scheme.

For the Federal Court and High Court, the same categories of persons are eligible for a complete fee exemption.

Financial hardship

AAT and court fees can be waived or partly waived on the basis of financial hardship. Where, a registrar of the AAT or court (as applicable) determines that a person is in financial hardship, the AAT fee is reduced to $100 ($94 if the tax in dispute is less than $5,000), the Federal Court fees are waived completely and the High Court fees are reduced by approximately two-thirds. A refusal to waive fees either by a registrar of the AAT or court is reviewable by the AAT.

Refunds and costs

AAT fees will generally be refunded where an application is determined in a manner favourable to the taxpayer. Court costs awarded in favour of a successful taxpayer are likely to include court fees. Court setting down and hearing fees will be refunded if the hearing does not proceed and the court is given at least 10 working days' notice that it will not proceed.

Costs associated with an application for review or an appeal, including the relevant fees, may be deductible (¶16-850). Where a deduction is allowable, any refund or reimbursement of those costs, including any refund of fees, must be included in assessable income (¶10-270).

[FTR ¶972-905]

¶28-090 Review by Tribunal

An application for review by the AAT of the Commissioner's decision on an objection is heard by the Taxation and Commercial Decisions Division. Proceedings before the AAT are governed by the AAT Act, subject to various modifications which apply specifically to taxation reviews (TAA ss 14ZZA to 14ZZJ). It seems that the AAT will *not* have jurisdiction to review an objection decision if the objection is itself invalid, eg because the original decision against which the objection was lodged was not adverse to the taxpayer (*Case 21/94*), or if the application for review predates the objection decision (*Andres*; cf *Walters*).

An application for review of an objection decision must be lodged within 60 days of the applicant being served with notice of the decision, although the AAT may grant an extension of time (¶28-100). An application for review must be in writing (a form is available from the AAT) and set out a statement of the reasons for the application. Documents may be lodged with the AAT electronically.

The AAT may convene a preliminary conference of the parties or their representatives to clarify the issues. The AAT may also refer suitable matters to conciliation/mediation with the consent of the parties. If the matter proceeds to a hearing, no evidence is to be given of what occurred at the preliminary conference, conciliation/mediation unless both parties agree. If an agreement is reached at a preliminary conference or conciliation/mediation, the AAT may make a decision giving effect to that agreement (if within its powers) without holding a hearing. Once the matter has been referred to the AAT, the applicant may, if desired, request an early hearing date.

The Commissioner is obliged to lodge with the AAT copies of: (a) a statement of the reasons for his decision on an objection; (b) the notice of the taxation decision concerned (eg the assessment), the objection and the notice of the objection decision; (c) any other document which is in the Commissioner's possession or under his control and which he considers is necessary to the review of the objection decision; and (d) a list of the documents being lodged (in the case of an AAT extension application (¶28-100), the Commissioner is required to lodge copies of all relevant documents). The AAT may also issue oral orders at a preliminary conference, or serve a notice, requiring the Commissioner or applicant to lodge additional documents in their possession or under their control. If the statement of reasons lodged by the Commissioner is inadequate, the AAT may order the Commissioner to lodge an additional statement setting out further and more adequate reasons for the decision, findings of fact and/or details of evidence. The AAT has extensive powers to summon a person to give evidence and/or produce documents at the hearing (eg *Case 25/95*).

The AAT may dismiss an application if the applicant fails to proceed with the application within a reasonable time or if it is satisfied that the application is frivolous or vexatious. However, in the absence of bad faith, the AAT will be reluctant to dismiss an application merely because the taxpayer's case appears to be weak (eg *The Christ Circle Oriona Community*). The AAT may also dismiss an application if the applicant fails to appear or be represented at a preliminary conference, a conciliation or directions hearing, or the hearing itself. In such a case, the AAT can order that the applicant pay the Commissioner's costs (¶28-085).

Taxation review proceedings are generally heard by a single member, although a 3-member AAT may sit in certain cases. If a presidential member is presiding, any question of law is decided by that member (eg *Case 30/95*; AAT Act s 42). Unlike most other proceedings before the AAT, taxation hearings are held in private if the applicant so requests. Where a matter is heard in private, the AAT must ensure, as far as practicable, that the reasons for its decision do not disclose the applicant's identity (this does not apply if a notice of appeal to the Federal Court has been lodged). The AAT *may* allow a person to participate in a hearing by means of electronic communication, eg by telephone, closed-circuit television or video conference (*Grbich & Shen*; *Dunn*). The AAT is not required to apply the laws of evidence, but may take evidence on oath or affirmation.

Powers of the AAT

The AAT may exercise all the powers and discretions of the Commissioner, but only for the purposes of reviewing the Commissioner's objection decision (*Liedig*). There are, however, minor restrictions on the AAT's power to review decisions relating to the remission of penalties (¶29-410).

In its proceedings, the AAT must comply with the rules of natural justice or procedural fairness. This would normally require that the parties be given the opportunity to make submissions on any issues decided by the AAT. For example, the AAT was not entitled to decide a case against a taxpayer on the ground that the anti-avoidance provisions applied where the question of the application of those provisions had not been raised at any time during the hearing (*Fletcher*). Procedural fairness also means that only in exceptional circumstances will the Commissioner be allowed to withhold relevant documents (eg *Case 25/95*; but see also *VAI v Forgie* where the AAT determined that the particulars supplied by the Commissioner were sufficient to give the taxpayer a fair picture of the fraud or evasion case made against him). However this does not include internal legal advice (*ACN 154 520 199 Pty Ltd (in liq)*).

The process contemplated by the AAT Act is not to be fragmented by applications seeking to challenge intermediate directions or determinations made along the way to reaching an ultimate determination of the issue before the Tribunal. Hence a direction by the AAT requiring a party to proceedings to provide further information (or the dismissal of an application for such a direction) is not a judicially reviewable decision (¶28-180) (*Beddoe*; *VAI v Forgie*).

The AAT may confirm, vary or set aside the Commissioner's decision on an objection. The AAT does not have the power to actually make, amend or set aside an assessment (*Stevenson*). Thus, if the AAT concludes that the taxpayer's taxable income, and the tax payable thereon, is less than as assessed, it must remit the matter to the Commissioner with a direction that he amend the assessment accordingly. In *Case Z36*, where the AAT concluded that a taxpayer's assessed income had been understated, it could only affirm the objection decisions under review and leave it to the Commissioner to decide whether he had the power to amend the relevant assessments (¶25-300). Once a decision of the AAT becomes final, the Commissioner must give effect to that decision within 60 days (¶28-160). The AAT must give either oral or written reasons for its decision. If the AAT gives oral reasons and it later issues written reasons, it cannot change the oral reasons or add different ones (*MA*).

The AAT is ordinarily bound to follow previous court decisions although, where there are conflicting decisions of similar authority, it may have to decide which one to follow (*Salenger*).

The AAT may refer a question of law arising before it to the Federal Court, but only with the consent of the President (AAT Act s 45(1)(a)). Where that happens, neither the applicant nor the Commissioner will be liable for filing, setting down or hearing fees.

An appeal against an AAT decision may be made to the Federal Court on a question of law (¶28-120).

[FTR ¶972-950, ¶973-055]

¶28-100 Extension of time for review application

A taxpayer may apply to the AAT for an extension of the prescribed 60-day period (¶28-090) for lodging an application for review of an objection decision (TAA s 14ZZA; AAT Act s 29(7) to (11)). Such an application (known as an "AAT extension application") may be made even though the original 60-day period has expired (in contrast, there is no provision for applying for an extension of time for lodging an appeal to the Federal Court: ¶28-110). No additional fee is payable upon lodging an AAT extension application.

The following were found to be relevant factors in allowing an extension of time for lodging an application for review: (a) the failure to lodge in time was the fault of the taxpayer's representative; (b) the Commissioner would not be prejudiced by an extension of time; (c) the taxpayer's objection had merit; and (d) the taxpayer had always intended to apply to the AAT for review (*Case 27/94*; *Case 28/94*; *Case 34/94*; *Case 17/95*). By way of contrast, in *Case X75* the taxpayers failed to obtain an extension of time where the delay was due to their agent's neglect; and in *Case 12/93* an extension was refused where a 4-year delay could not be justified (see also *Case 31/94*; *Case 22/97*; *Bird*).

An extension of time is likely to be granted where the delay is solely due to an excusable oversight (which an ordinary person may occasionally experience). In *Case 58/96*, the AAT accepted the taxpayer's excuse that he was under the impression that he had 60 days from the cessation of negotiations with the ATO.

The AAT has recommended (in *Case U175*) that taxpayers should attach copies of the following documents to an AAT extension application: (a) the assessment in question (presumably in the case of a deemed assessment (¶25-100) a copy of the return should be attached); (b) the adjustment sheet (if any); (c) the objection; and (d) the notice of the objection decision, accompanied by any explanatory memoranda and/or any amended assessment issued by the Commissioner with the notice.

[FTR ¶973-057]

¶28-110 Appeal to Federal Court

An appeal to the Federal Court against the Commissioner's decision on an objection (¶28-080) is heard by a single judge. An appeal is conducted in accordance with the Federal Court Rules.

An appeal must be lodged within 60 days after service of the notice of the objection decision (TAA s 14ZZN). There is no provision which allows for an extension of the prescribed 60-day period for lodging an appeal to the Federal Court against an appealable objection decision (*Bayeh*).

An appeal is commenced by the applicant filing an application (a form is available on the Federal Court website). As to the fees payable, see ¶28-085. An application for an appeal must: (a) set out brief details of the objection decision appealed against and the address of the relevant ATO; and (b) be filed in the registry of the court in the state or territory in which that ATO is located. The applicant must also serve a sealed copy of the application on the Commissioner. The notion of ''lodging'' an appeal connotes the filing of a document with the court (*Carter*). In that case, a taxpayer who had commenced proceedings applied to have 4 other taxpayers joined to the proceedings. The court refused on the ground that, without applications by the other taxpayers, the court lacked jurisdiction in relation to them. However, a number of taxpayers are allowed to appeal in the one Federal Court appeal application where they have joined in filing or lodging the appeal (*Krampel*). Similarly, a single proceeding can be commenced by a taxpayer in respect of multiple objection decisions where common questions of law or fact are involved (*McDermott*).

Within 28 days (or 14 days if the appeal relates to a private ruling) after being served with the sealed copy of the application, the Commissioner must file a number of documents including: (i) a copy of the notice of the objection decision; (ii) a copy of the decision against which the objection was lodged; (iii) if the appeal relates to a matter other than a private ruling, any return or other document in his possession or under his control which is relevant to the hearing; (iv) if the appeal relates to a private ruling, a copy of that ruling; and (v) either a statement outlining the Commissioner's contentions and the facts and issues in the appeal as he perceives them or, if the appeal relates to a private ruling, a statement of any assumption made by the Commissioner which is not stated in the notice of the ruling. The Commissioner must serve on the applicant a copy of the statement and a list of the other documents mentioned above.

Genuine steps statement

An applicant must also file a "genuine steps statement" (Form 16) with the application. The statement must set out the steps that have been taken to try and resolve the issues in dispute or the reasons why no such steps were taken. Genuine steps that can be taken to resolve a dispute include considering whether the dispute could be resolved by an alternative dispute resolution process. In response, the respondent must also file a genuine steps statement (Form 11) stating either that they agree with the applicant's statement or that they disagree and specifying the reasons why they disagree. A party that fails to file a genuine steps statement as required may have an adverse costs order made against them.

Powers of the court

The court reviews the Commissioner's decision on the objection and may make such order as it thinks fit, including an order confirming or varying the decision, although it cannot actually amend an assessment (TAA s 14ZZP). Once the decision of the court has become final, the Commissioner must give effect to it within 60 days (¶28-160). Appeal proceedings were adjourned in one case pending the determination of the trial of 2 taxpayers on charges which involved facts crucial to their assessments (*Hurley*). An appeal may be dismissed where an applicant has not done any act required to be done by or under the Federal Court Rules, or otherwise has not prosecuted the appeal with due diligence.

The Federal Court can transfer proceedings on an appeal against an objection decision pending before it to the Family Court for hearing and determination (TAA s 14ZZS). There is no right of appeal against a decision to transfer proceedings.

A single judge of the Federal Court hearing a taxation appeal may state a case or reserve a question for the consideration of the Full Federal Court.

[FTR ¶973-210]

¶28-120 Further appeal

Appeal to the Federal Court

The Commissioner or the taxpayer may appeal to the Federal Court from a decision of the AAT on a question of law (AAT Act s 44). For example, the AAT's findings on the evidence is a question of fact, not law. The appeal is restricted to a question of law (including a mixed question of fact and law: *Great Western Railway Co v Bater*; *Haritos*) and does not amount to a fresh hearing of the matter (*Brixius*; *Rawson Finances*).

However, the court may, under AAT Act s 44(7), make findings of fact consistent with the AAT's findings of fact (other than findings made by the AAT as a result of an error of law) (*Holzberger v Secretary, Department of Health and Ageing*); the court may also receive further evidence for the purpose of making findings of fact (AAT Act s 44(8)).

An issue may seemingly be raised for the first time on appeal, but only if it is one of construction or of law and it is in the interests of justice for the court to consider it (*Water Board v Moustakas*). An appeal must be initiated within 28 days of the AAT's decision being furnished. If the AAT initially gives short reasons for its decision and later gives full reasons, the decision is not given until the later date (*Fletcher*).

The court may grant an extension of time for lodging an appeal. In *Osborne*, an extension was granted where there was only a 6-week delay and the disputed tax had been paid. In *Logounov*, the taxpayer's mental illness and failure of the AAT to inform the taxpayer of its decision to dismiss his application were taken into account in granting the extension after a 2-year delay. Where there is a real issue to be decided on appeal, a court will rarely order an individual taxpayer to provide security for costs (*Fletcher*). A single judge may state a case or reserve a question for the consideration of the Full Federal Court.

On appeal from an AAT decision, the Federal Court may make such order as it thinks fit including, but not limited to, an order affirming or setting aside the AAT decision or an order remitting the case to the AAT to be heard and determined again. An AAT decision can be set aside where it is so unreasonable that no reasonable decision-maker would have made it (eg *McCabe*). An AAT decision can also be set aside where its reasons were mostly an unattributed reproduction of the Commissioner's submissions; this meant that the AAT failed to exercise its jurisdiction and committed an error of law (*Thorpe*). In limited circumstances, the court may make new findings of fact in order to completely dispose of the matter rather than remit it to the AAT (s 44(7)).

If a matter is remitted to the AAT to be heard again, the AAT is not bound by the earlier AAT's findings of fact (*Blackman*). It may, however, reach a decision on the basis of the transcript of the earlier hearing (*Fletcher*) unless the court orders that further evidence be heard. The AAT need not be constituted by the same person(s) who made the earlier decision, and a person who was a member of the earlier AAT is not automatically disqualified from being a member of the later AAT (*Fletcher*). However, the court may order that it be heard by a differently constituted AAT (*Jagelman*).

Appeal to the Full Federal Court

An appeal may be made against a decision of a single judge of the Federal Court. An appeal must be lodged within 28 days of the relevant judgment being handed down or within such further time as may be allowed. An extension of time will not be granted merely because this would be administratively convenient for the applicant (*Martin*). An extension may also be refused where the taxpayer has no prospects of succeeding in the appeal (*Atkinson*). The Full Court may affirm, reverse or vary the judgment appealed, set aside (in whole or in part) the judgment appealed and remit it to the lower court or AAT for further hearing and determination, or make such order as it thinks fit. For fees payable on appeal, see ¶28-085.

If a party wants to argue a new case before the Full Court, it must seek the leave of the court to do so. The Commissioner was refused such leave in *Dismin Investments*. In that case, the Commissioner resiled from the position he had argued at first instance and sought to attach the disputed tax liability to another step in the transaction. The taxpayer argued that it would have led other evidence had it known this was the Commissioner's position.

Appeal to the High Court

An appeal against a decision of the Full Federal Court lies to the High Court, but only with special leave of the High Court. The application should be lodged within 28 days of judgment or within such further time as may be allowed. Special leave to appeal will generally only be granted where the appeal involves a question of fundamental principle and it has been considered by an intermediate appeal court (*Australian National Hotels*). The High Court may affirm, reverse or modify the judgment appealed.

[FTR ¶973-020, ¶973-210]

¶28-130 Limitations on review or appeal

On a review by the AAT of, or an appeal to the Federal Court against, an objection decision, the taxpayer is generally limited to the grounds stated in the objection (TAA ss 14ZZK(a); 14ZZO(a)). Having said that, the Federal Court has held that the AAT's decision to remit a penalty, even though not raised on objection, was within the AAT's power as it was relevant to the substantive issue before it (*Hornibrook*). Even though the Federal Court decision was subsequently overturned on appeal (as the relevant objection decision was an ineligible income tax remission decision), the Full Federal Court affirmed that the AAT had jurisdiction to review the Commissioner's objection decision in relation to additional tax where the additional tax was not directly raised in the objection decision (*Hornibrook*).

The AAT and the court have a discretion to allow the taxpayer to amend the grounds of objection, although the AAT or court is not obliged to exercise the discretion of its own volition. Note that the court does *not* have a discretion to allow the grounds of objection to be amended when the substantive matter comes before it by way of an appeal from an AAT decision (*Liedig*), although the taxpayer may, of course, appeal to the court against an AAT decision rejecting an application to amend the grounds of objection (*McLean*). There are also restrictions on the Commissioner relying on the general anti-avoidance provisions to support an assessment originally made without reference to those provisions (¶30-120).

Exercising the discretion to amend grounds

The discretion to allow the grounds of objection to be amended is very wide. For example, the AAT or court may allow a taxpayer to amend an objection to rely on entirely new grounds, even if they require consideration of matters not considered by the Commissioner in the original assessment process (*Lighthouse Philatelics*). The discretion may also be exercised to allow a taxpayer to rely on a fresh ground to dispute a matter already put in issue by the objection, or to include additional claims not already in dispute (*Scott*). A taxpayer should also be allowed to amend the grounds of objection to increase the amount of deductions already claimed. However, a taxpayer would not be allowed to amend the grounds of objection to challenge the validity of the assessment itself (¶28-000; *Case 19/93*).

The Full Federal Court has commented that the decision to allow the grounds of objection to be amended ought to be made on the merits of the particular case and on the same considerations of justice upon which such decisions are regularly made in litigation (*Lighthouse Philatelics*). In a subsequent case, the court refused to allow a taxpayer to amend the grounds of objection to raise new issues, partly on the basis that the court had already given directions to ensure that the parties were aware of the relevant legal and evidentiary issues (*Gilder*). However, in a case in which the taxpayer's counsel raised a new argument during the closing address (that retention payments paid to the taxpayers were fringe benefits and therefore exempt income), the court said that the AAT was wrong to refuse to allow the grounds of objection to be amended as the Commissioner knew of the relevant exempt income provisions and it should have been apparent that the retention payments could constitute exempt income (*McLean*). If the AAT or court allows the taxpayer to amend the grounds of objection to raise an entirely new matter, the hearing should be adjourned to allow the Commissioner to prepare his response.

It is the objection decision as a whole, and not just that part of the decision with which the taxpayer is dissatisfied, which is referred to the AAT or court (¶28-080). Thus, in defending an assessment, the Commissioner is not restricted by a statement on an adjustment sheet accompanying the assessment; and he may generally support an assessment on a ground not taken into account at the time the assessment was made, if that does not result in injustice to the taxpayer (*Reynolds*). Where such a course of action would result in unfairness to the taxpayer, it seems that the AAT or court would allow the taxpayer to amend the grounds of objection. In one case the Commissioner was refused leave to amend his grounds of appeal, to rely on an anti-avoidance provision which he had not raised before, as it would have been unfair to the taxpayer (*Raymor*).

Burden of proof

In proceedings before the AAT or court, including on any further appeal such as against an AAT decision, the taxpayer bears the burden or onus of proving:

- in the case of an income tax assessment made under s 166 — that the assessment is excessive (*Trautwein*; *McCormack*; *Macmine*)
- in the case of an income tax assessment made under s 167 — that the assessment is excessive; what the actual taxable income should be (*Dalco*; *Mulherin*; *Rigoli*); the burden of proof remains with the taxpayer even where the Commissioner issues the default assessment on the basis of fraud (*Binetter; Bai*)
- in the case of a franking account assessment (¶4-780) — that the assessment is wrong, and
- in the case of any other taxation decision — that the decision should not have been made or should have been made differently (ss 14ZZK(b); 14ZZO(b)).

The standard of proof is on the balance of probabilities. In fraud or evasion cases, the taxpayer bears the onus of proving on the balance of probabilities that there was no fraud or evasion — this can be done by proving that the assessment was excessive (*Bai*).

If the taxpayer is unable to establish that the assessment in question is excessive, then the assessment will stand irrespective of whether or not there are any facts or circumstances which would prima facie support the Commissioner's assessment (*McCormack*; *Macmine*). In a taxation appeal, a taxpayer may lead evidence which contradicts facts decided against the taxpayer in previous criminal proceedings (*Saffron* — the taxpayer in that case had been convicted of criminal conspiracy to defraud the Commonwealth of income tax). However, where the issues in the criminal proceedings and in the taxation appeal are closely related, the fact of the taxpayer's conviction may be given great weight where the taxpayer leads evidence that was the same as that rejected by the jury in the criminal trial (*Rogerson*).

The manner in which the taxpayer discharges the burden of proof varies with the circumstances. However, the taxpayer will not necessarily prove that an assessment is excessive by showing the Commissioner made an error in forming a judgment as to the amount of the assessment, although in some cases the taxpayer may be able to prove an assessment is excessive by showing an error in computation (*Dalco*; *Ma*). In *Trustee of Balmain Trust*, the taxpayer failed even though the ATO issued 2 sets of assessments (¶25-100). In the case of an assets betterment assessment (¶25-140), the taxpayer should show that the increase in net assets is due to non-assessable receipts and/or is less than claimed by the Commissioner (eg *Scallan*; *Favaro*; *Luu*). It is not sufficient for the taxpayer to show that the discrepancy disclosed in the betterment statement is probably not correct. Each assessment, for each year, must be considered separately and acceptable evidence must be produced that provides material for determining the amount by which each assessment is alleged to be wrong (*Krew*).

Where a taxpayer asserts that the tax in an assessment is too low, the burden of proof is on the taxpayer to show that the relevant tax decision should not have been made or should have been made differently under TAA s 14ZZK(b)(iii) (*Waverley Council*).

[FTR ¶973-130, ¶973-140, ¶973-310]

¶28-160 Implementation of decisions

Once a decision of the AAT or court has become final, the Commissioner must give effect to that decision within 60 days (TAA ss 14ZZL; 14ZZQ). Where the taxpayer has been partly or wholly successful, the Commissioner is required to amend the relevant assessment (¶25-300; ITAA36 s 170(1), item 6). The AAT or court cannot itself amend an assessment, whether to reduce or increase the amount of taxable income, as part of the process of reviewing an objection decision (¶28-090, ¶28-110).

A decision is not "final" until all subsequent appeals have been finalised. Where no appeal is lodged against a decision, it will be regarded as final as soon as the time for lodging the appeal has expired (however, the Commissioner has indicated that there may be instances where he will not follow a Federal Court decision in relation to taxpayers other than those in the particular case because the decision is, on the basis of legal advice, incorrect. In those instances, he will either appeal or take prompt action to test the issue before the Full Federal Court). A decision of the Full Federal Court becomes final 30 days after the decision is given, unless an application for special leave to appeal to the High Court has been lodged within that time.

Where an assessment has been amended to reduce a taxpayer's liability as a result of a review or an appeal, any overpaid tax is refunded to the taxpayer or applied in accordance with TAA Pt IIB Divs 3 and 3A, which deals with payments, credits and running balance account surpluses (ITAA36 s 172). The taxpayer is entitled to be paid interest on the refunded amount (¶28-170).

[FTR ¶973-165, ¶973-330]

¶28-170 Interest on overpayments

Interest is payable by the Commissioner on overpayments of tax in the circumstances outlined below at (1) to (5). Interest may also be payable on certain early payments of tax (¶25-440). The interest payable by the Commissioner is governed by the *Taxation (Interest on Overpayments and Early Payments) Act 1983* (Interest Act) and the Taxation (Interest on Overpayments and Early Payments) Regulations.

Where an overpayment results from a downward correlative adjustment made to relieve international double taxation that has arisen as a result of a foreign tax administration making a transfer pricing or profit/expense allocation debit adjustment, interest is not payable if the foreign country does not impose interest on the corresponding underpayment of tax.

The applicable interest rate is the "base interest rate" (ie 90-day bank accepted bill rate — see TAA s 8AAD(2)). The rates applicable for recent years are as follows:

Period	**Rate % pa**
1 January 2016–31 March 2016	2.22
1 April 2016–30 June 2016	2.28
1 July 2016–30 September 2016	2.01
1 October 2016–31 December 2016	1.76
1 January 2017–31 March 2017	1.76
1 April 2017–30 June 2017	1.78
1 July 2017–30 September 2017	1.73
1 October 2017–31 December 2017	1.70
1 January 2018–31 March 2018	1.72
1 April 2018–30 June 2018	1.77
1 July 2018–30 September 2018	1.96
1 October 2018–31 December 2018	1.96
1 January 2019–31 March 2019	1.94
1 April 2019–30 June 2019	1.96
1 July 2019–30 September 2019	1.54
1 October 2019–31 December 2019	0.98
1 January 2020–31 March 2020	0.91
1 April 2020–30 June 2020	0.89
1 July 2020–30 September 2020	0.10
1 October 2020–31 December 2020	0.10
1 January 2021–31 March 2021	0.02

Interest is calculated as simple and not compound interest (*Consolidated Fertilizers*). The amount of interest payable by the Commissioner is rounded down to the nearest 5 cents and the minimum amount of interest payable is 50 cents.

Interest payable by the Commissioner can be offset against any tax liability of the taxpayer including, in the Commissioner's opinion, assessed tax not yet due and payable (TD 92/150). For the operation of running balance accounts (RBAs) and the treatment of payments, credits and RBA surpluses, see ¶24-360. A tax liability will be discharged in full if, after applying an amount of interest in discharge of the liability, it is reduced to less than 50 cents.

Taxpayers entitled to receive interest on an overpayment do not need to approach the ATO for payment. If interest is not credited against another liability, it will be paid when the overpayment is refunded. Interest received by a taxpayer is assessable (¶10-470).

(1) Refund where successful objection or amended assessment. A taxpayer who receives a refund of tax as a result of a successful objection against an assessment, or as a result of a successful review of or appeal against the Commissioner's decision disallowing an objection, is entitled to interest on the amount of the refund (Interest Act s 9). Interest is also payable on a refund of tax where the Commissioner decides of his own motion to amend an assessment to reduce a taxpayer's liability (eg as a result of an audit of the taxpayer's affairs). In addition, where the amendment results from a request to amend an assessment (including another person's assessment) or from a successful objection or appeal by another taxpayer, interest is payable on a refund of tax.

Interest is not only payable on overpaid income tax but also on other overpaid amounts such as PAYG instalments (¶27-100), franking deficit tax (¶4-780) or penalties under TAA Sch 1 Pt 4-25, GIC resulting from an amended assessment (¶29-510) and HELP and FS assessment debts (¶2-380, ¶2-385).

Where a taxpayer entitled to averaging (eg a primary producer or artist, writer or sportsperson) successfully objects to an income tax assessment for a particular year, subsequent assessments may need to be amended to reduce the tax payable because of the lower taxable income in the earlier year. In such a case, interest will be payable on the reductions of tax in those later years even though no objection was lodged against them.

The period for which interest is payable on an overpayment of tax resulting from a successful objection or an amended assessment is essentially *from* the later of the day on which the notice of the relevant assessment, determination or decision is issued and the day the tax is paid *to* the day the tax is refunded (Interest Act s 10).

Where an amount paid by one person is applied against the tax liability of another person, the latter is deemed to have paid that amount to the Commissioner on the day on which it is applied against that person's liability. For example, where PAYE instalments were credited against the taxpayer's income tax liability, he/she was deemed to have paid the tax, to the extent of the amount so credited, on the day the instalments were credited (usually the day on which the relevant assessment was made) (TD 93/50).

Where tax is paid by instalments (whether by agreement or otherwise), interest is calculated from the date of payment of each instalment. If part only of the tax paid by instalments is overpaid, the "last-in first-out rule" applies and thus interest accrues only in respect of the most recently paid instalments that actually result in the overpayment of tax.

(2) Refund in ordinary assessment process. Interest is also payable on a refund made in the ordinary assessment process (Interest Act ss 8E; 8G; 8H). Interest is payable where the sum of amounts credited or applied against the taxpayer's tax liabilities for an income year (eg tax amounts withheld from salary and wages, PAYG instalments and amounts withheld for failure to supply an ABN) exceeds the sum of the taxpayer's income tax liabilities for the year (including Medicare levy, any HELP or FS assessment debt, administrative penalties under Pt 4-25 and ITAA36 s 102AAM interest). However, interest is only payable:

- if the taxpayer is *not* a full self-assessment taxpayer — where the notice of assessment (showing that amounts have been credited or applied against the taxpayer's tax liabilities) is issued more than 30 days after the relevant return is lodged (the 30-day requirement does not apply where the overpayment results from the crediting, etc, of an amount after the assessment is made) (a "post-notice crediting"), or
- if the taxpayer is a full self-assessment taxpayer — where the first crediting or applying of an amount occurs either: (a) 30 days or more after the return is lodged (if lodged 30 days or more before the entity's due date for payment); or (b) after the due date for payment of the assessed tax (if the return is lodged after 30 days or more before the due date for payment).

A notice that no tax is payable is deemed to be a nil assessment for these purposes.

The period for which interest is payable in these circumstances is:

- if the taxpayer is *not* a full self-assessment taxpayer — *from* the 30th day after the return is lodged *to* the day on which the notice of assessment is issued. However, where the overpayment results from a post-notice crediting, the interest period runs *from* the later of: (a) the day the original assessment is made; and (b) the day a subsequent payment of tax is made *to* the day the post-notice crediting occurs (the excess is attributable to payments of tax in reverse order to the order in which they were made), or
- if the taxpayer is a full self-assessment taxpayer — *from* the earliest of: (a) the beginning of the 30th day after the day of lodgment of the return; or (b) the due date for payment of the assessed tax, *to* the end of the day the first crediting occurs.

(3) Refund of advance payments or instalments, remission of penalties. Interest is also payable where the Commissioner, as a result of a request by a person, refunds a payment on account of income tax (including a HELP or FS assessment debt, and s 102AAM interest), GIC or shortfall interest charge (Interest Act s 12A) and the refund, crediting or remission occurs *more than* 30 days after the request is made. In these circumstances, interest is payable from the 30th day after the request is made until the day the refund, crediting or remission takes place.

(4) Refunds of RBA surpluses. A taxpayer is entitled to interest where a refund of an RBA surplus is not made within 14 days of the surplus arising (¶24-380) (*Travelex Ltd*, on appeal to High Court). Interest is payable *from* the end of the RBA interest day until the end of the day on which the refund takes place. The "RBA interest day" is the 14th day after the latest of: the day on which the surplus arises or the request is made; notification is given to the Commissioner; or the taxpayer nominates a financial institution account.

[FTR ¶910-000]

¶28-180 Administrative review of Commissioner's decisions

Certain decisions of the Commissioner may be reviewed by the Federal Court under the *Administrative Decisions (Judicial Review) Act 1977* (ADJR Act), the *Judiciary Act 1903*, s 39B or, it appears, under general administrative law principles. For example, generally, the exercise of Commissioner's discretion is not subject to review under Pt IVC (*AAT*). Nevertheless, the Commissioner has a legal duty to act fairly when exercising an administrative discretion (*Pickering*). It may therefore be arguable that, where the Commissioner exercises his discretion favourably in respect of one taxpayer, the Commissioner must exercise his discretion in the same way in respect of another taxpayer who is in a like situation. In practice, a taxpayer's ability to rely on this principle will, outside of family situations, depend largely on the extent to which the taxpayer can obtain information from the Commissioner (eg under the *Freedom of Information Act 1982*: ¶28-060) regarding the manner in which he has exercised his discretion in relation to other taxpayers. However, the Commissioner is not required to exercise different discretions to bring about the same result for taxpayers in similar positions (*Pickering*).

Some decisions may be either challenged under TAA Pt IVC or reviewed under the ADJR Act (eg the refusal to issue a certificate that a film is a qualifying Australian film for tax purposes). If a decision is reviewable by another tribunal, the court may refuse to exercise its review powers under the ADJR Act (eg *Szajntop*).

Reviewable decisions

Decisions of the Commissioner which have been subject to judicial review include:

- refusal to grant an extension of time to pay tax (*Ahern*; *Lawrence*; *Rawson Finances*)
- refusal to vary an amount of PAYE instalment deductions (*Coco*)
- refusal to issue a certificate that a film is a qualifying Australian film for the purposes of the special concessions for film investors (*Willarra v Minister for Home Affairs and Environment*)
- refusal to grant an extension of the 3-year period allowed for the dissolution of a company after distributions are made in an informal liquidation (*Constable Holdings*)
- decisions relating to the exercise of the Commissioner's investigatory powers to gain access (¶25-220) (*Southern Farmers Group*; *Robinswood*) or information (¶25-240) (*Clarke & Kann*)
- issue of a notice to collect tax from a third party (*Edelsten v Wilcox*; *Heath*)
- refusal to grant a tax agent further extensions of time for lodging clients' returns under the tax agent lodgment program (*Balnaves*)
- withdrawal of earlier advice that a taxpayer is exempt from income tax (*Australian Wool Testing Authority*)
- issue of a departure prohibition order (*Briggs*) and refusal to revoke such an order (*Edelsten*) (¶25-550), and
- decisions approving access to accounting documents in tax appeal proceedings (*White Industries*: ¶25-230).

The following decisions of the Commissioner should also be reviewable under the ADJR Act:

- a refusal to allow a taxpayer to adopt a substituted accounting period
- a decision relating to the remission of GIC (¶29-530), and
- a decision to impose GIC under the PAYG anti-avoidance rules (¶27-600).

The grounds on which judicial review may be sought include: (i) breach of natural justice; (ii) failure to follow proper procedures for making a decision; (iii) lack of jurisdiction to make a decision; (iv) improper exercise of power; (v) decision not justified on the evidence; (vi) decision involving an error of law or fraud; and (vii) unreasonable delay in making a decision.

In relation to certain types of tax decisions which may be subject to judicial review, the taxpayer is entitled to obtain a written statement of the reasons for the decision.

The Federal Court has power to transfer judicial review proceedings pending before it to the Family Court for hearing and determination. This power is similar to the power it has in relation to income tax proceedings (¶28-110).

Decisions which are not reviewable

The following are specifically *not* reviewable under the ADJR Act:

- decisions forming part of the process of making, or leading up to the making of, assessments or calculations of tax (eg a threatened assessment: *Independent Holdings* or refusal to remit penalty tax: *Qld Trading*)
- decisions disallowing objections to assessments or calculations of tax (¶28-070)
- decisions making, reducing and revoking estimates of unremitted deductions (¶25-560) (ADJR Act s 3; Sch 1).

Other decisions found by the courts to be *not* reviewable include:

- a refusal by the Commissioner to waive liability under an assessment (*Pickering*)
- decisions to commence proceedings to recover unpaid income tax (*Ruddy*; *Golden City Car & Truck Centre*; but compare the earlier decision in *Terrule*)
- a decision by the Commissioner to vote against a motion put (under the Bankruptcy Act) at a meeting of a taxpayer's creditors (*Hutchins*)
- the decision by the Commissioner to establish the Work Related Expenses Audit Program, and a decision to include a tax agent in that Program; however, these decisions could be challenged under *Judiciary Act 1903*, s 39B, although they were held not to be invalid on that basis (*Knuckey*)
- decisions leading up to the making of ITAA36 Pt IVA determinations (*Meredith*)
- alleged failure by the ATO to comply with the ATO's Guidelines for the Conduct of Auditors and Taxpayers in Complex and Large Case Audits (*Robinswood*)
- a refusal by the AAT to grant an adjournment (*Szajntop*).

Non-binding oral advice, eg as to the deductibility of certain payments or the assessability of certain receipts, is unlikely to be a ''decision'' for the purposes of the ADJR Act and thus will not be reviewable (*Pegasus Leasing*). A demand for withholding tax alleged to be payable is also not a ''decision'' (*Century Yuasa Batteries*).

Decisions that are not reviewable can only be challenged (if at all) under the objection, review and appeal provisions of Pt IVC or, in exceptional circumstances, under s 39B (¶28-000).

Unless there are exceptional circumstances, the Federal Court will decline to review an alleged abuse of process in instituting a prosecution in a Local Court, because the Local Court has its own power to grant a permanent stay if an abuse of process is established (*Smiles*; *Bryant's case (No 2)*).

[FTR ¶934-100]

¶28-190 ATO complaints

Taxpayers who are dissatisfied with a decision, service or action of the ATO have the right to complain. The ATO recommends that dissatisfied taxpayers should first try to resolve the issue with the tax officer they have been dealing with and then, if necessary, talk to the tax officer's manager. If still not satisfied, the matter can be escalated by contacting the ATO complaints line on 1800 199 010. Complaints can also be made online using the complaints form provided, or by writing to: Complaints, Australian Taxation Office, PO Box 1271, Albury NSW 2640. Once a complaint is lodged in the

ATO complaints system, a tax officer (the resolver) will contact the dissatisfied taxpayer within 3 working days and then work with the taxpayer to resolve the issue, keeping them informed of the progress of the case.

If dissatisfied with the ATO's administrative action, taxpayers may complain to the Inspector-General of Taxation (¶1-200).

[FTR ¶935-600]

Chapter 29 Penalties • Offences

Introduction

¶29-000 Overview of penalties

Administrative penalty regime

A uniform administrative penalty regime applies to all ''taxation laws'' (other than, for certain provisions, excise laws) as defined in ITAA97 s 995-1(1) (TAA s 3AA). Uniform penalties apply irrespective of the type of tax involved, provided the tax is imposed under a relevant taxation law.

The main regime is located in TAA Sch 1 Pt 4-25. Specifically, it imposes penalties for:

- failure to lodge activity statements, returns and other documents on time (¶29-100)
- making false or misleading statements or, in respect of income tax laws or PRRT (¶19-003) laws, taking positions in statements that are not reasonably arguable (¶29-140)
- scheme benefits relating to schemes (¶29-180)

- failure to make a statement required for determining a tax-related liability (¶29-140), and
- failure to meet various other tax obligations (¶29-300, ¶29-310).

Penalty unit

A penalty unit is $222 for an offence committed on or after 1 July 2020 and $210 for an offence committed between 1 July 2017 and 30 June 2020 (*Crimes Act 1914*, s 4AA and Notice of Indexation of the Penalty Unit Amount (F2020N00061)).

Penalties for failure to lodge by due date or in approved form (¶29-100)

Type of entity	Penalty
Small entity	Base penalty: 1 penalty unit for each 28-day period or part thereof not lodged, up to a maximum of 5 penalty units
Medium entity	Double the base penalty
Large entity	5 times the base penalty
Significant global entity	5 hundred times the base penalty

Penalties relating to statements and schemes (¶29-140, ¶29-180)

Culpable behaviour	Base penalty amount (%)[(1)]	Adjusted penalty (%)		
		if hindrance (or in some repeat cases)	*if voluntary disclosure*	
			during examination	*before examination*[(2)]
No shortfall amounts:[(3)(4)]				
Intentional disregard	60 p.u.	72 p.u.	48 p.u.	0
Recklessness	40 p.u.	48 p.u.	32 p.u.	0
No reasonable care	20 p.u.	24 p.u.	16 p.u.	0
Shortfall amounts:[(4)]				
Intentional disregard	75	90	60	15
Recklessness	50	60	40	10
No reasonable care	25	30	20	5
No reasonably arguable position	25	30	20	5
Failure to make statement	75	90	N/A	N/A
Scheme shortfall amounts:[(5)(6)]				
Tax avoidance provision applied	50 (25)	60 (30)	40 (20)	10 (5)
Profit shifting (tax avoidance purpose)	50 (25)	60 (30)	40 (20)	10 (5)
Profit shifting (no dominant tax avoidance purpose)	25 (10)	30 (12)	20 (8)	5 (2)

(1) Unless otherwise specified, this is the percentage of the shortfall amount or, in the case of failure to make a statement, the percentage of the tax-related liability. The base penalty amount can be reduced to the extent that a taxation law was applied in an accepted way under TAA Sch 1 s 284-224.

(2) The penalty is reduced to nil if voluntary disclosure is made before examination and the shortfall, if any, is less than $1,000. The $1,000 threshold does not apply in scheme cases (¶29-190).

(3) For statements that do not result in shortfall amounts, the penalty is expressed in penalty units (p.u.).

(4) Penalties are doubled for significant global entities from 1 July 2017 (TAA Sch 1 s 284-90(1A)).

(5) Penalties are doubled for significant global entities entering into tax avoidance and profit shifting schemes without a reasonably arguable position (TAA Sch 1 s 284-155(3): ¶29-180, ¶22-630).

(6) Bracketed rates of penalty apply if the taxpayer's position is reasonably arguable.

Other administrative penalties (¶29-310)

Culpable behaviour	Penalty
Failure to keep or retain records	20 penalty units
Failure to retain or produce declarations	20 penalty units
Preventing access	20 penalty units

The Commissioner is required to provide written notice of a penalty and the reasons why the taxpayer is liable to pay the penalty (TAA Sch 1 s 298-10).

The rules relating to the recovery of income tax (¶25-510) also generally apply in relation to administrative penalties. Assessments of penalties and, with certain exceptions, decisions relating to the remission of penalties are reviewable in accordance with TAA Pt IVC (¶28-000, ¶29-410).

Former penalty provisions applying to 1999–2000 and earlier income years are dealt with in the *Australian Master Tax Guide 2000* (31st Edition) or earlier editions.

GIC for late payment

A taxpayer who fails to pay the correct amount of tax on time is liable to pay GIC on the tax unpaid after the due date (¶29-500ff).

Offences

In some cases, the circumstances that give rise to a liability for penalties also constitute an offence. Failing to lodge a return or making a false or misleading statement are 2 examples. If a prosecution is instituted, the person ceases to be liable to pay the administrative penalty (¶29-700).

Reform recommendations

The government has indicated that it would consider a recommendation of an 2019 independent review to introduce an administrative penalty regime against tax practitioners who make (or are involved in making) false statements to the ATO with intentional disregard of the taxation laws. The review also recommended that the safe harbour protection to taxpayers (for penalties relating to failure to lodge (¶29-100) and false or misleading statements (¶29-140)), be extended to cover instances where the tax agent or BAS agent has demonstrated recklessness or intentional disregard with respect to a taxation law.

Separately, the IGTO recommended in 2014 that the government should conduct a broad review of the penalties regime. The government should also consider specific issues including the lack of sufficient differentiation between a range of taxpayer behaviours (¶29-160), the application of false or misleading statement penalties where tax no shortfall arises (¶29-140) and the inability to receive interest on money paid for unsustained penalties.

Proposed measures

Treasury issued a consultation paper in 2018 on proposed measures to combat the black economy including:

- introducing penalties for repeat offenders to equal to double the amount of a tax shortfall
- introducing non-financial penalties, such as travel bans on individuals who engage in black economy and tax avoidance behaviour, and
- ensuring that penalties are only remitted if criminal proceedings result in a conviction (currently, the penalty is withdrawn under TAA s 8ZE where criminal prosecution is commenced: ¶29-700).

The government proposed to provide the Commissioner a discretion to direct taxpayers to undertake an approved record keeping course instead of applying financial penalties if he reasonably believes there has been a failure by the taxpayer to comply with their reporting obligations (2019–20 MYEFO). The discretion, however, could not be applied to those who disengage with the tax system or who deliberately avoid their record keeping obligations.

[FTR ¶977-950]

Lodgment Penalties

¶29-100 Failure to lodge on time

Taxpayers who fail to lodge tax returns and other documents by the due date or, if required, in the "approved form" (see below) are liable to a penalty (TAA Sch 1 Div 286). However, the penalty provisions do not apply to tax documents required to be given to the Commissioner under the *Superannuation Contributions Tax (Assessment and Collection) Act 1997*, the *Superannuation Guarantee (Administration) Act 1992* and the *Superannuation (Self Managed Superannuation Funds) Supervisory Levy Imposition Act 1991* because of the particular reporting obligations in those laws.

Refusal or failure to lodge a return also constitutes an offence that renders the taxpayer liable to prosecution (¶29-700). If a prosecution is instituted, however, a penalty is not payable.

Working out the base penalty amount

All entities, including individuals, are liable for the "base penalty amount" where they fail to lodge relevant documents as required. The base penalty amount is one penalty unit (¶29-000) for each 28-day period (or part period) that the tax document remains outstanding, up to a maximum of 500 penalty units. The amount of the penalty payable increases according to the size of the entity as follows:

- small entity — the base penalty amount for every 28 days overdue
- medium entity — double the base penalty amount for every 28 days overdue
- large entity — 5 times the base penalty amount for every 28 days overdue, and
- significant global entity — from 1 July 2017, 500 times the base penalty amount for every 28 days overdue.

A small entity is one that is not a medium or a large entity.

A medium entity is one that, at the time it is required to give the relevant document to the Commissioner:

- is a medium withholder under the PAYG withholding system (¶26-500)
- has assessable income of more than $1 million but less than $20 million for the income year in which the return or other document is required, or
- has a current annual turnover for GST purposes, worked out in the month in which the return or other document is required, of more than $1 million but less than $20 million.

A large entity is one that, at the time it is required to give the relevant document to the Commissioner:

- is a large withholder under the PAYG withholding system (¶26-500)
- has an assessable income of $20 million or more for the income year in which the return or other document is required, or
- has a current annual turnover for GST purposes, worked out in the month in which the return or other document is required, of $20 million or more.

A significant global entity is broadly one that, at the time it is required to give the relevant document to the Commissioner:

- a global parent entity with an annual global income of $1 billion or more, or
- any member of such a global parent entity's group (s 960-550).

▶ Example

A medium PAYG withholder was due to submit a BAS (¶24-200) by 21 October 2020 but lodged it on 5 December 2020. The taxpayer was therefore 45 days late in lodging the BAS. The base penalty amount (2 penalty units) is then multiplied by 2 because the taxpayer is a medium entity, ie 4 penalty units.

Approved forms

The requirements for a return, notice, statement, application or other document under a taxation law to be an approved form are set out in TAA Sch 1 s 388-50.

The BAS is the approved form for lodging a GST return and notifying PAYG withholding amounts, PAYG instalments, FBT instalments and deferred company instalments (¶24-200). Failure to lodge a BAS on time or in the approved form could result in multiple applications of the administrative penalty, depending on the number of tax obligations that were reportable. Each kind of payment imposes a separate notification obligation for penalty purposes.

Engaging a registered tax agent or BAS agent — safe harbour exemption

A taxpayer who engages a registered tax agent or BAS agent is exempt from the penalty if a document is lodged late, and the late lodgment did not result from the agent's intentional disregard, or recklessness as to the operation of, a taxation law (other than excise laws), provided the taxpayer has given the agent all relevant taxation information to lodge the document in the approved form on time (TAA Sch 1 s 286-75(1A)).

[FTR ¶978-180]

Penalties Relating to Statements and Schemes

¶29-140 Penalties relating to statements

Penalties may be imposed where a taxpayer makes a statement (or fails to make a statement) about tax under TAA Sch 1 Div 284. A penalty may apply if a taxpayer (or agent) makes a statement to the Commissioner and:

- the statement is on a taxation law (other than excise laws), and the statement is *false or misleading* in a material particular (TAA Sch 1 s 284-75(1))
- the taxpayer treated an income tax law or the PRRT (¶19-003) law applying to a matter in a way that was *not reasonably arguable* (s 284-75(2))
- the taxpayer has *failed to give a statement* to the Commissioner to determine a tax-related liability (other than one arising under excise laws) on time, eg has not lodged a return (s 284-75(3)), or
- the taxpayer has entered into a scheme involving tax avoidance or transfer pricing (¶29-180).

The base penalty amount may then be increased or reduced (¶29-190), or remitted (¶29-400).

False or misleading statement

Penalties apply if a statement that is false or misleading in a material particular is made:

- to the Commissioner or an entity exercising powers or performing functions under a taxation law (other than excise laws) (TAA Sch 1 s 284-75(1)). Statements made to the Commissioner include statements made to an ATO employee in the course of that person's duties or to a person other than a taxation officer about a tax-related matter, for example a tax agent preparing an income tax return (TAA Sch 1 s 284-25)
- to an entity that is neither the Commissioner nor an entity exercising powers or performing functions under a taxation law (other than excise laws), where the statement is (or purports to be) one required or permitted by a taxation law (other than excise laws) or might reasonably be expected to be used for certain GST purposes (TAA Sch 1 s 284-75(4)). It includes, for example, statements the trustee of a super fund provides to members, and statements employees provide to employers relating to the amount of tax withheld from their wages.

A "statement" can be made orally, in a document or in any other way (including electronically) for a purpose connected with a taxation law other than excise laws (TAA Sch 1 s 284-20). If something in a statement is false or misleading, or information is omitted from a statement, the statement is false or misleading in a material particular. For example if assessable income is omitted from an income tax return, that omission is taken to be a statement that the taxpayer did not derive the assessable income during the return period. Where a taxpayer's tax return includes a claim for a deduction to which the taxpayer is not entitled, the return contains a false or misleading statement.

PS LA 2012/4 and PS LA 2012/5 deal with the ATO's administration of the penalty imposed under TAA Sch 1 s 284-75(1) (¶29-400).

Statement that is not reasonably arguable

A penalty applies if a statement is made that treats an income tax law or the PRRT law as applying to a matter in a way that is not reasonably arguable (TAA Sch 1 s 284-75(2)). A matter is *reasonably arguable* if it would be concluded in the circumstances and having regard to the relevant authorities that what is argued for is "*about* as likely to be correct as incorrect, or is more likely to be correct than incorrect" (TAA Sch 1 s 284-15). A relevant authority includes a taxation law, material for the purposes of the *Acts Interpretation Act 1901*, s 15AB(1), a decision of a court (Australian or otherwise) or the AAT, or a public ruling (¶24-540). The reasonably arguable test applies only to income tax laws or the PRRT law, and not to other tax laws such as FBT or GST.

For more discussion on this test, see ¶29-160.

Failure to make a statement

A penalty is payable if a taxpayer fails to provide a return, notice or other document from which a tax liability (other than one arising under excise laws) can be established (s 284-75(3)). The penalty is 75% of the tax-related liability concerned (rather than the shortfall amount; s 284-90(1), item 7; *Kakavas* and *Case 7/2016*). PS LA 2014/4 contains ATO guidelines on the administration of the penalty. The taxpayer may also be liable to an additional penalty for failing to give the document on time (¶29-100).

Exemptions

Relevant exemptions from the administrative penalty for making false or misleading statements include:

- *reasonable care.* No penalty under s 284-75(1) or (4) applies if the taxpayer or its agent took reasonable care (s 284-75(5)).

- *safe harbour*. No penalty under s 284-75(1) or (4) applies against a taxpayer who engages a registered tax agent or BAS agent if the taxpayer has given the agent all relevant tax information and the statement did not result from the agent's intentional disregard of, or recklessness as to the operation of, a taxation law (other than excise laws) (TAA Sch 1 s 284-75(6); *The Executors of the Estate of the late Peter Fowler*), and
- *Single Touch Payroll (STP) reporting*. No s 284-75(1) penalty applies for making a false or misleading statement under the STP reporting system if a further statement correcting the original statement is lodged within 14 days after the end of the income year in which the original statement was made (s 284-75(8): ¶26-630). The Commissioner may provide an ongoing grace period for correcting errors in relation to STP reports without penalty (TAA Sch 1 s 389-25).

Relief for inadvertent errors

The ATO may provide penalty relief during their audits to inadvertent errors in tax returns and activity statements that are due to failure to take reasonable care or taking a position on income tax that is not reasonably arguable (¶29-160).

Relief would be provided once every 3 years to eligible individuals, and eligible entities with a turnover of less than $10 million. Eligible entities include small businesses, SMSFs, strata title bodies, not-for-profit organisations and co-operatives. Ineligible entities include wealthy individuals and their businesses; associates of wealthy individuals that may be classed as a small business entity (SBE: ¶7-050) in their own right; entities that do not meet the SBE eligibility criteria; and public groups, significant global entities and associates. Relief is also not available if in the past 3 years the taxpayer has: had penalty relief applied; been penalised for reckless or intentional disregard of the law; evaded tax or committed fraud; been involved in the control or management of another entity, which has evaded tax; or incurred debts without the intention of being able to pay, such as phoenix activity.

[FTR ¶978-005]

¶29-160 Penalties relating to statements — base penalty amounts

A scale of penalties applies for false or misleading statements or statements whose positions as to income tax law or the PRRT law are not reasonably arguable (TAA Sch 1 s 284-90):

- where a statement does not result in a shortfall amount, a fixed penalty applies, and
- where there is a shortfall amount above any applicable threshold, the penalty is worked out as a fixed percentage of the shortfall amount.

Where a taxpayer fails to make a statement under s 284-75(3), the penalty is 75% of the tax-related liability.

This ''base penalty amount'' differs depending on the conduct of the taxpayer with respect to the statement. For example, the penalty is highest (75%) where there was a shortfall that was caused by intentional disregard of the tax law. The base penalty amount may then be adjusted up or down, depending on a range of factors such as whether the taxpayer made a voluntary disclosure, or hindered or obstructed the Commissioner in finding out about the statement (¶29-190). No penalty applies if reasonable care has been taken (TAA Sch 1 s 284-75(5)). For relevant base penalty amounts, see ¶29-000 and scheme shortfall amounts (TAA Sch 1 s 284-160), ¶29-180. Penalties are doubled for significant global entities from 1 July 2017 (TAA Sch 1 s 284-90(1A)).

Certain conduct that gives rise to an administrative penalty, eg deliberate evasion, also constitutes an offence that renders the taxpayer liable to prosecution (¶29-700). If a prosecution is instituted, however, the penalty is not payable.

Shortfall amount

A "shortfall amount" is the difference between the amount of tax, credit, payment entitlement or excess exploration credit tax (¶19-010), calculated on the basis of the taxpayer's statement, and the amount of tax, credit, payment entitlement or excess exploration credit tax according to law (TAA Sch 1 s 284-80). The shortfall is worked out by reference to a tax liability, credit or payment entitlement in the accounting period for the particular liability or credit. A taxpayer may be liable to a fixed penalty even if no shortfall amount arises.

A shortfall amount arises where the tax liability is less, or the credit or payment entitlement is more, than it would have been if the statement had not been false or misleading, or treated an income tax law or the PRRT law as applying in a way that was not reasonably arguable.

▶ Example

Caroll's tax liability (ignoring Medicare levy) for the income year is $20,000. However, the tax payable on the basis of an incorrect deduction claim for $5,000 in her return is $17,750. Caroll's shortfall amount is $2,250 (ie $20,000 – $17,750).

Intentional disregard of tax law

Where there is a shortfall amount and part or all of it is caused by the intentional disregard of a taxation law (other than excise laws) by the taxpayer or its agent, the taxpayer is liable to a penalty of 75% of the amount of the shortfall, or part of the shortfall, as appropriate (s 284-90(1), item 1). Where there is no shortfall amount, 60 penalty units applies (s 284-90(1), item 3A).

Culpable behaviour falling within this category would include the exclusion of an amount from assessable income, knowing it to be assessable, or the claiming of a deduction, rebate, credit or offset, knowing that it is not allowable. The Commissioner's view is that intentional disregard requires actual knowledge that a statement is false. Evidence of intention may be found through direct evidence or by inference from all the surrounding circumstances, including the taxpayer's conduct — see MT 2008/1. Penalties were correctly imposed for intentional disregard where a director of a company (who was also a tax agent) lodged 14 BASs falsely claiming GST credits (*Case 10/2005*). Penalties were also correctly imposed where a taxpayer intentionally failed to return income that he had received, and took steps to disguise such receipts as loans or advances (*Case 11/2009*). Similarly, a penalty was imposed where a tax agent had lodged returns with falsified information, regardless of whether the taxpayer was aware of the falsity (*Weyers & Anor*; *Case 5/2006*).

Recklessness

Where there is a shortfall amount and part or all of it is caused by the recklessness of the taxpayer or its agent with regard to the correct operation of a taxation law (other than excise laws), the taxpayer is liable to a penalty of 50% of the amount of the shortfall, or part of the shortfall, as appropriate (s 284-90(1), item 2). Where there is no shortfall amount, 40 penalty unit applies (s 284-90(1), item 3B).

The Commissioner considers that recklessness involves conduct that goes beyond mere carelessness or inadvertence by displaying a high degree of carelessness. It includes conduct that shows disregard of, or indifference to, risks that are foreseeable by a reasonable person (MT 2008/1). For case law examples, see *Hart*, *BRK (Bris)*.

Lack of reasonable care

Where there is a shortfall amount and part or all of it is caused by the failure of the taxpayer or its agent to take reasonable care to comply with a taxation law (other than excise laws), the taxpayer is liable to a penalty of 25% of the amount of the shortfall, or part of the shortfall, as appropriate (s 284-90(1), item 3). Where there is no shortfall amount, 20 penalty unit applies (s 284-90(1), item 3C). No penalty arises if the taxpayer or agent has taken reasonable care (TAA Sch 1 s 284-75(5)). Note the safe harbour exemption for taxpayers in respect of conduct of tax agents or BAS agents under s 284-75(6) (¶29-140).

The reasonable care test requires a taxpayer to take the same care in fulfilling their tax obligations as could be expected of a reasonable ordinary person in their shoes. The statements below, based on MT 2008/1, provide some guidance.

- The standard of care required of a taxpayer takes account of the taxpayer's personal circumstances (age, health and background), their knowledge, education, experience and skill, and their understanding of the relevant tax laws. For example, a salary and wage earner who diligently follows the *Individual tax return instructions* is likely to have taken reasonable care. A professional person with specialist tax knowledge will be subject to a higher standard of care.
- For business taxpayers, reasonable care requires the putting into place of an appropriate record-keeping system and other procedures to ensure that the income and expenditure of the business are properly recorded and classified for tax purposes. What is reasonable will depend on factors such as the nature and size of the business, regular internal audits, sample checking, adequate staff training and preparation of instruction manuals.
- If a taxpayer is uncertain about the correct tax treatment of an item, the taxpayer should make reasonable inquiries (eg contacting the ATO or referring to an ATO publication or other authoritative statement).
- In determining the standard of care that is reasonable, factors such as the complexity of the law and whether the relevant law involves new measures are relevant. Failure to understand fully the effects of the law does not necessarily amount to failure to take reasonable care (*Taneja*).
- Engaging a tax agent does not of itself excuse the taxpayer from the obligation to take reasonable care (*Sparks*; *Necovski*; *Sinclair*; *Aurora Developments (No 2)*). However, engaging a tax agent in some circumstances would suffice (see, eg *Taneja*). Note also the safe harbour exemption under s 284-75(6) (¶29-140). Even when advice has been obtained from a range of sources, a taxpayer has an additional obligation to exercise professional judgment and common sense when interpreting the advice (*Outbound Logistics*).
- Failure to obtain a private ruling does not invariably amount to failure to take reasonable care (*North Ryde RSL*; *MLC Limited*).

Penalty relief may apply to inadvertent errors in tax returns and activity statements that are due to failing to take reasonable care (¶29-140).

No reasonably arguable position

Where in a statement the taxpayer or its agent treats an income tax law or the PRRT law as applying in a particular way, but the position taken is not "reasonably arguable", the penalty is 25% of the shortfall amount (TAA Sch 1 s 284-90, item 4).

However, the penalty only applies if there is a shortfall amount which exceeds the "reasonably arguable threshold" (TAA Sch 1 s 284-90(3)). For an entity other than a trust or partnership, the threshold is the greater of $10,000 or 1% of the income tax or PRRT payable for the relevant tax year, worked out on the basis of the taxpayer's relevant tax return. For a trust or a partnership, the threshold is the greater of $20,000 or 2% of the entity's net income for the income year, worked out on the basis of the taxpayer's income tax return.

The threshold is applied separately to each non-identical situation in which the taxpayer did not take a reasonably arguable position. Thus, if the taxpayer lacks a reasonably arguable position in respect of 2 non-identical matters, each of which involves a shortfall amount of, for example, $9,000, no penalty will be attracted under TAA Sch 1 s 284-75(2) even though the shortfall totals $18,000. If, on the other hand, the matters were identical, the penalty would apply because identical matters are treated as a single matter and there is a shortfall of $18,000. Similar but distinct matters will not be treated as a single matter (MT 2008/2).

The Commissioner's views based on MT 2008/2 are outlined below.

- The position taken must involve a contentious area of the law.
- The test does not require the taxpayer's position to be the "better view"; the standard is "about as likely as not". However, the taxpayer's position must be defensible and sufficient to support a reasonable expectation that the taxpayer could win in court.
- An opinion expressed by an accountant, lawyer or other adviser is not in itself an authority, although the authorities used to support that an opinion may support the position taken by the taxpayer.
- The absence of authority for a position will not be fatal provided the taxpayer has a well-reasoned construction of the particular provision that is about as likely as not to be the correct interpretation (*Cameron Brae*).
- Other authorities could include statements in texts recognised by professionals as being authoritative about how the law operates, particularly where there are few relevant authorities, although the weight of the authority would depend on the circumstances.
- The mere existence of a contrary public ruling does not mean that alternative treatments cannot be reasonably arguable.
- As a broad rule, liability will not arise under this category where the false or misleading nature of a statement is caused by an error of primary fact or calculation.

The test is a purely objective test (*Orica Ltd*; *Thomas & Ors* and *Traviati*). On the other hand, the reasonable care standard is an objective standard that considers the subjective circumstances of the individual in question. Hence, these 2 independent standards are to be determined separately (*Sanctuary Lakes* and ATO *Decision Impact Statements* on *Sanctuary Lakes* and *Shin*).

A taxpayer who is uncertain whether a position is reasonably arguable may be able to seek a private ruling on the matter.

No penalty applies where a taxpayer, with circumstances similar to those of an ID, relies on the ID, if the ID is subsequently found to be incorrect. However, GIC (¶29-510) may be payable (PS LA 2001/8).

Penalty relief may apply to inadvertent errors in tax returns and activity statements that are due to taking a position on income tax that is not reasonably arguable (¶29-140).

Where 2 or more penalties apply

Where 2 or more penalties may apply, the taxpayer is liable to pay only one of the penalties. In such cases, the highest applicable rate of penalty applies. For example, if a particular part of a shortfall is attributable to both recklessness and failure to take reasonable care, only the 50% penalty for recklessness applies (s 284-90(2)).

Where there is a shortfall and various parts of it are attributable to different categories of behaviour, the shortfall amount must be broken into its component parts for calculation of penalties. Factors such as overstatements and progressive tax rates are considered and illustrated by worked examples in TR 94/3.

Partners and trustees

All of the partners in a partnership can be made liable to penalties under TAA Sch 1 Div 284 where one of the partners, or the partnership's agent, makes a statement about the partnership net income or partnership loss or the partnership participates in a scheme (TAA Sch 1 s 284-35).

Where the false or misleading nature of a statement is caused by intentional disregard, recklessness or lack of reasonable care, the normal penalties for such behaviour apply (s 284-90(1), item 6). Where a shortfall is caused by lack of a reasonably arguable position, the relevant threshold is the greater of $20,000 or 2% of the net income of the partnership.

For penalties other than those relating to partnership net income or loss, for example a PAYG withholding amount, TAA Sch 1 s 444-30 makes each partner jointly and severally liable. If one partner is not at fault, then that partner may take action against the culpable partner. However, this does not affect that partner's liability to pay the penalty.

The trustee of a trust is liable to pay any penalty arising from statements made about the trust's net income or obligations, or any penalty arising from the trust's participation in a scheme. Where relevant, any shortfall amount or scheme shortfall amount of a beneficiary that relates to the trust's net income or obligations is treated as if it were the shortfall amount of the trustee (TAA Sch 1 s 284-30). Where there are multiple trustees to a trust, the penalty applies to all trustees and they are jointly liable for the whole amount owing by the trust (*Hutson*). As with partnerships, where there is a shortfall which is caused by lack of a reasonably arguable position, the relevant threshold is the greater of $20,000 or 2% of the net income of the trust (s 284-90(1), item 5).

If SMSF corporate trustees are liable to a penalty under s 284-75(1) or (4), the directors (at the time the liability arises) are jointly and severally liable to the tax-related liability in respect of the penalty (s 284-95).

[FTR ¶978-055]

¶29-180 Penalties relating to schemes

Different base penalty amounts apply to benefits (scheme benefits) that would arise where the taxpayer has entered into a tax avoidance scheme under a taxation law. Broadly, the amounts of the scheme benefits are ''scheme shortfall amounts'' (TAA Sch 1 ss 284-145 to 284-160). Scheme shortfall amounts can arise under the anti-avoidance provisions of the income tax law and of other taxation laws, eg *A New Tax System (Goods and Services Tax) Act 1999* Div 165 and FBTAA s 67.

For most taxpayers, the penalty applies if the *sole or dominant purpose* of participating in the scheme was for the taxpayer (or another entity) to obtain a scheme benefit. For a scheme that limits a non-resident entity's taxable presence in Australia under ITAA36 s 177DA (¶30-200), the penalty applies if a *principal purpose* was for the taxpayer (or another entity) to obtain a scheme benefit. For Div 165 schemes, the penalty may be triggered where the *principal effect* of the scheme is that the entity itself obtained a scheme benefit from the scheme, either directly or indirectly (s 284-145(1)).

The base penalty amount in respect of schemes is expressed as a percentage of the scheme shortfall amount, and reduced where the taxpayer has a ''reasonably arguable'' case that the relevant anti-avoidance provisions do not apply (s 284-160). Penalties are doubled for significant global entities entering into tax avoidance and profit shifting schemes without a reasonably arguable position (TAA Sch 1 s 284-155(3): ¶22-630).

Different base penalty amounts apply to schemes involving transfer pricing under ITAA97 Div 815 (¶22-630) or non-arm's length income of managed investment trusts (MITs: ¶6-405) under ITAA97 Subdiv 275-L (TAA Sch 1 s 284-145(2A) to (2C)). The scheme shortfall amount would be the amount of additional income tax or withholding tax one is liable to pay (TAA Sch 1 s 284-150(4) and (6)). A smaller penalty may apply to a transfer pricing scheme, even if the entity did not participate in the scheme with the sole or dominant purpose of obtaining a scheme benefit (s 284-160(3)).

The above penalties are subject to adjustments (¶29-190) and possible remission (¶29-400).

If an entity has a scheme shortfall amount, 2 or more penalties may apply under the provisions relating to shortfall amounts and to scheme shortfall amounts. Generally, penalties will not be assessed cumulatively. However, where an entity has entered into a scheme and has made a false or misleading statement relating to the scheme, penalties may be imposed cumulatively. The Commissioner has a discretion to remit the cumulative penalty amount (PS LA 2008/18).

Different tests apply for determining the purpose of the scheme under s 284-145 and ITAA36 former s 226L. For former s 226L, reference is made to a taxpayer's actual purpose or subjective state of mind (*Starr*; *Faigenbaum*; *Star City (No 2)*). The position for s 284-145 is less certain. While Jessup J applied a subjective test in *Lawrence*, the ATO followed the approach of Dowsett J in *Star City (No 2)* and used an objective test (ATO *Decision Impact Statement* on *Lawrence*). Subsequently, Robertson J said that although not a solely subjective test, the entity's subjective purpose is relevant (*Chevron Australia Holdings Pty Ltd*). In *Orica Ltd*, Pagone J said that the words "it is reasonable to conclude" in s 284-145(1)(b) did not impose an objective test in place of the actual subjective purpose; rather, the words sought to qualify the factual finding of an actual purpose, namely, that an actual purpose will be found if it can reasonably be concluded from the evidence.

In *Star City (No 2)*, the Full Federal Court stated that s 284-145 and former ITAA36 s 226L did not operate in the same way. Section 284-145 contemplated an underlying tax-related liability, a scheme which reduced that liability, and the existence of a taxation law, or the taking of action under a taxation law, the effect of which was to restore the underlying liability. In the present case, there was no effective scheme to reduce liability or scheme benefits. On the other hand, former s 226L operated if a scheme was entered into or carried out for the sole or dominant purpose of enabling the taxpayer to pay no tax or less tax. Unlike s 284-145, former s 226L applied even if a tax avoidance scheme was ineffective and there was no tax benefit for the taxpayer. The ATO has acknowledged that a legislative amendment would be necessary to ensure that s 284-145 is consistent with former s 226L (ATO *Decision Impact Statement* on *Star City (No 2)*).

Penalty regime for scheme promoters

A civil penalty regime applies to deter the promotion and implementation of tax avoidance and tax evasion schemes (TAA Sch 1 Subdiv 290-B) (¶30-300).

[FTR ¶978-100]

¶29-190 Increase or decrease in penalty rates

Penalties payable for statements (¶29-160) and those relating to schemes (¶29-180) may be reduced or eliminated where certain mitigating factors apply or voluntary disclosure is made. Further, the base penalty rates may be increased if the taxpayer hinders the Commissioner or where a second or subsequent occurrence is involved.

A penalty does not arise in respect of a false or misleading statement if the taxpayer or its agent took reasonable care in making it (TAA Sch 1 s 284-75(5)), eg if the taxpayer made a genuine attempt to flag the issue by seeking a private ruling before lodging the return.

Increase in base penalty amount

The base penalty amount is increased by 20% (eg from 50% to 60% of the amount of a shortfall) where (TAA Sch 1 s 284-220):

- the taxpayer takes steps to prevent or hinder the Commissioner from finding out about the false or misleading nature of a statement, a shortfall amount or scheme shortfall amount. Examples of hindering might be failing to respond to inquiries (*Leighton*), unreasonable delay in responding to inquiries, failing to keep an appointment for interview without reasonable excuse, destruction of relevant records or collusion with others to conceal a shortfall. A tax agent's failure to respond to a notice to produce documents, however, did not justify an increase in penalty (*Bosanac*)
- the taxpayer was liable to pay a penalty for a scheme shortfall amount (¶29-180) in an earlier accounting period
- the taxpayer became aware of the false or misleading nature of a statement or the shortfall after the statement had been made and the taxpayer failed to tell the Commissioner or a relevant entity about it within a reasonable time. An example is where the taxpayer relies upon factual information from a third party in preparing the taxpayer's return and subsequently finds out that the information supplied is incorrect
- the base penalty amount is payable for lack of reasonable care, recklessness or intentional disregard of the law and the taxpayer was liable to the penalty for any of those reasons previously, or
- the base penalty amount is payable because the taxpayer does not have a reasonably arguable case, or failed to provide a document to establish a tax liability on time, and was penalised for the same failure previously.

Reduction of base penalty amount

A base penalty amount is reduced to the extent that the false or misleading nature of a statement, a shortfall or a scheme shortfall is attributable to advice received from the Commissioner, a statement in an ATO publication or the general administrative practice of the Commissioner (TAA Sch 1 s 284-224(1)). A general administrative practice is a practice which the Commissioner applies generally as a matter of administration, and consists of the habitual, customary or repeated adoption of a view in multiple cases (TD 2011/19).

The base penalty amount may also be reduced for voluntary disclosure by taxpayers. Broadly (TAA Sch 1 s 284-225):

- the penalty is reduced where a taxpayer voluntarily tells the Commissioner about a false or misleading statement, a shortfall amount or scheme shortfall amount *before* being informed that an examination of the taxpayer's affairs relating to taxation laws ("examination") is to be conducted. The penalty is also reduced where the taxpayer responds to a public request by the Commissioner for voluntary disclosures about participation in tax avoidance schemes or other arrangements by a particular date. Where the false or misleading statement does not result in the taxpayer having a shortfall amount, the base penalty amount is reduced to nil. Where there is a shortfall amount, the base penalty amount is reduced by 80% where the shortfall amount is $1,000 or more, or to nil where the shortfall amount is less than $1,000. For a scheme shortfall amount, the penalty is reduced by 80% and the $1,000 threshold does not apply, and
- the base penalty amount is reduced by 20% in respect of a false or misleading statement, a shortfall or a scheme shortfall where, after being informed of an examination, the taxpayer voluntarily tells the Commissioner in the approved form about the relevant matter. The Commissioner may, if appropriate, deem the notification to have taken place before the taxpayer was informed of an examination (s 284-225(5)). The notification to the Commissioner must also arguably save the ATO significant time or resources in the examination.

The Commissioner's views on voluntary disclosure are set out in MT 2012/3. If the Commissioner makes a public statement requesting voluntary disclosures by a particular day, the disclosure must be made before the earlier of:

- the day the taxpayer is told by the Commissioner that an examination is to be conducted, or
- the day by which the Commissioner, in his public statement, requests the disclosure to be made.

As a general rule, a taxpayer will be treated as having disclosed voluntarily before being informed that an audit is to be conducted under TAA Sch 1 s 284-225(5) where, during the initial notification, the ATO invites the taxpayer to make a voluntary disclosure within a specified period or by a specified date, and the taxpayer fully discloses within the time period (*Mold*).

To qualify for a reduction in penalty, the taxpayer must disclose information not otherwise known to the Commissioner — merely agreeing with what the Commissioner has already identified is not enough.

[FTR ¶978-140]

Other Administrative Penalties

¶29-300 PAYG penalties and offences

The uniform penalty regime applies generally to many obligations imposed on entities under the PAYG system. In addition, a number of specific penalties and offences are imposed under PAYG withholding (¶26-100) and PAYG instalments (¶27-100). These are outlined below.

Failure to withhold or pay an amount

The failure to withhold an amount as required by TAA Sch 1 Div 12 (¶26-120) or pay an amount to the Commissioner as required by TAA Sch 1 Div 13 (¶26-280) or 14 (¶26-300) is a strict liability offence subject to a penalty of 10 penalty units. In addition to a penalty, the person convicted may be ordered to pay to the Commissioner an amount up to or equivalent to what was required to be withheld (TAA Sch 1 s 16-25).

As an *alternative* to the penalties that may be imposed under TAA Sch 1 s 16-25, an administrative penalty equal to the amount not withheld may be imposed under TAA Sch 1 s 16-30.

The Commissioner has a discretion to remit penalties imposed under s 16-30 for failure to withhold (TAA Sch 1 s 298-20). Guidelines on the remission of penalties are set out in PS LA 2007/22.

Under the current guidelines, the level of remission is based on the entity's conduct, ranging from a voluntary disclosure to a deliberate decision not to comply (ie intentional disregard). Stricter guidelines apply to penalties for failure to withhold from dividend, interest and royalty payments. In general, remission of these penalties would only be granted in exceptional circumstances, at a rate of no more than 10% (PS LA 2007/22).

An entity that has paid an administrative penalty for failure to withhold in relation to a dividend, interest, royalty or mining payment may recover an amount equal to the amount of penalty from the person liable to pay the withholding tax in relation to the withholding payment (TAA Sch 1 s 16-195).

Failure to pay an amount withheld

If an amount required to be paid (either as an amount withheld, an alienated personal services payment or a payment in relation to a non-cash benefit) remains unpaid after its due date, the entity is liable to pay GIC on the unpaid amount (¶29-510). GIC is also payable on any unpaid penalty amounts.

Withholder's failure to register

A withholder that fails to register with the Commissioner is liable to a civil penalty of 5 penalty units (TAA Sch 1 s 16-140).

Withholding amounts payment information

A withholder must notify the Commissioner of withholding amounts that it must pay, on or before the due date (TAA Sch 1 s 16-150). Failure to do so incurs the administrative penalty under TAA Sch 1 s 284-75(3).

Failure to give annual reports

An entity that fails to give an annual report to the Commissioner about withholding payments and reportable fringe benefits (TAA Sch 1 s 16-153) incurs an administrative penalty under TAA Sch 1 Div 286.

Payee information

A payer that fails to provide the Commissioner with a report about a payee who has not given a TFN declaration commits an offence that may result in a civil penalty of 10 penalty units (ITAA36 s 202CF).

Payment summaries

An entity that fails to comply with the requirements for providing payment summaries incurs the administrative penalty under Div 286. Should there be a failure to keep a payment summary for the required period of 5 years, the administrative penalty for failing to keep and retain records applies (TAA Sch 1 ss 18-100; 288-25).

A person must not, with the intention of obtaining a credit, payment or any other benefit, present a copy of a payment summary or a document purporting to be a copy of a payment summary that is not a copy duly given to the person (TAA Sch 1 s 20-35). The penalty is 60 penalty units, imprisonment for 12 months or both.

Record-keeping

Entities required to withhold amounts under the PAYG withholding system must keep appropriate records for the statutory 5-year period (except where a withholding event has its own record-keeping requirements). If relevant records are not kept or retained, the administrative penalty under s 288-25 applies (¶29-310).

Refunds and credits

A person who presents a document issued by the Commissioner and who falsely pretends to be the person specified in the document with the intention of obtaining payment of an amount withheld or a credit, commits an offence (s 20-35). Similarly, a person commits an offence by presenting a copy of a payment summary that is not duly theirs with the intention of obtaining a credit, a payment or any other benefit. It is also an offence to try to obtain a credit where there is no entitlement to one. The penalty in each case is 60 penalty units, imprisonment for 12 months or both.

Voluntary agreements

A party to a voluntary agreement to withhold (¶26-150) that fails to keep a copy of the agreement from when it is made until 5 years after the making of the last payment covered by it is liable for a penalty of 30 penalty units (TAA Sch 1 s 12-55).

Natural resource payments

A payer that makes a natural resource payment (¶26-270) without the proper notice from the Commissioner is liable for a penalty of 20 penalty units, unless the payment is covered by a certificate (TAA Sch 1 s 12-330). However, failure to notify the Commissioner of a proposed payment is not an offence.

Failure to pay PAYG instalment

Failure to pay a PAYG instalment by the due date incurs GIC calculated for the period on and from the due date to the date on which the instalment is paid (TAA Sch 1 s 45-80).

Instalment payment information

An entity required to pay an instalment (even a nil amount) must notify the Commissioner of the amount of the instalment income for the period (TAA Sch 1 s 45-20). Failure to do so incurs the administrative penalty under Div 286.

Variation of instalment amounts

A range of penalties apply where a taxpayer chooses an instalment rate that is too low. The penalties are explained in detail at ¶27-320 and ¶27-340. Where a variation results in an underestimation by more than 15%, the taxpayer is liable to pay GIC on the underestimated instalment.

PAYG instalment anti-avoidance provisions

The specific anti-avoidance measures targeted at schemes to alter an entity's PAYG instalments position are explained at ¶27-600.

[FTR ¶976-530, ¶976-860, ¶977-125]

¶29-310 Miscellaneous penalties

Electronic sales suppression tools

In order to deter the use or distribution of sales suppression technology to keep incorrect electronic point of sale records, penalties apply for:

- producing or supplying electronic sales suppression tools (TAA Sch 1 s 288-125: 60 penalty units)
- possessing such tools (s 288-130: 30 penalty units), and
- incorrectly keeping tax records using such tools (or aiding, abetting etc) (s 288-135: 60 penalty units).
  An ''electronic sales suppression tool'' is essentially a device, software program or other thing, or any part or combination of such things capable of falsifying, manipulating, hiding, obfuscating, destroying, or preventing the creation of certain records from electronic point of sale systems (s 8WAB). Offences relating to such tools also apply (¶29-700).

Non-electronic reporting

An entity whose annual turnover is $20 million or more is required to lodge a GST return (incorporated in a Business Activity Statement (BAS)) and notify other BAS amounts electronically. There is also a similar requirement for electronic payment where an entity (with a turnover of $20 million or more) is liable to pay an assessed net amount of GST, or a large PAYG withholder (¶26-500) is required to pay an amount withheld.

If the entity fails to make an electronic notification or payment as required (but notifies or pays in another way), it will be liable to a civil penalty of 5 penalty units (TAA Sch 1 ss 288-10; 288-20).

Failure to keep records

An administrative penalty of 20 penalty units applies for failure to keep or retain records that are required to be kept under a taxation law (TAA Sch 1 s 288-25). The penalty does not apply to documents that must be kept under the income tax substantiation provisions (¶16-210) or statutory evidentiary documents for FBT purposes (¶35-690). PS LA 2005/2 provides guidelines on remission of the penalties imposed by s 288-25.

SMSFs

SISA Pt 20 contains administrative penalties for contraventions relating to SMSFs (¶13-060). PS LA 2020/3 provides guidance on the administrative penalties in SISA s 166(1).

[FTR ¶978-235]

Remission of Penalties

¶29-400 Commissioner's discretion to remit penalties

The Commissioner has discretion to remit an administrative penalty in whole or in part (TAA Sch 1 s 298-20). This discretion is unconfined, provided it is exercised within the boundaries of the subject matter, scope and purpose of the legislation (*Burness & Anor*).

The question is whether one is satisfied, having regard to the taxpayer's particular circumstances, that it is appropriate to remit the penalty (*Sanctuary Lakes* and ATO *Decision Impact Statement*). Rather than seeing it as a reconsideration of the appropriate level of penalty, the question actually involves making a ''separate call'' on whether a taxpayer's personal circumstances warranted the exercise of the discretion (*Bosanac*). A penalty should be remitted if an outcome would otherwise be harsh (*Dixon*), though ''harshness'' is not necessarily an essential element to the exercise of the discretion (*Sanctuary Lakes* and ATO *Decision Impact Statement*). Further, special circumstances need not be established, and the mere fact that no harm has been done is not of itself a matter that can be taken into account (*Dixon*).

It is unclear whether the fact that a taxpayer had a reasonably arguable position is relevant to the issue of remission. In *Traviati*, the taxpayer's individual circumstances were held to be relevant and not, for example, the fact that his approach accorded with an overturned court decision. However, the majority of the Full Federal Court in *Sanctuary Lakes* considered that any reasonably arguable position the taxpayer had was relevant in determining whether a penalty imposed for failing to take reasonable care should be remitted.

If the Commissioner refuses to remit some or all of the penalty, written notice of the decision and its reasons must be provided to the taxpayer. The Full Federal Court has held (by majority) that an ATO letter accepting a taxpayer's lump sum payment to discharge their tax liabilities did not evidence the Commissioner's decision to remit all applicable GIC in *Pintarich*. The ATO did acknowledge that the template upon which the letter in *Pintarich* was based could have been more clearly expressed, and had subsequently amended that template (*Decision Impact Statement on Pintarich*).

If the amount of unremitted penalty is more than 2 penalty units (for the current value of a penalty unit, see ¶29-000), the taxpayer may object against the decision in accordance with TAA Pt IVC (¶28-000); otherwise it is not reviewable.

Statement penalties

The ATO has guidelines on the remission of statement penalties:

- PS LA 2012/4 for a false and misleading statement that *does not* result in a shortfall amount
- PS LA 2012/5 for a false and misleading statement that *does* result in a shortfall amount, and
- PS LA 2011/30 for scheme shortfall amounts.

Full remission has been granted, for example, in *Johnston*, where the taxpayer had failed to prepare his paperwork to obtain a deduction that would have reduced his taxable income by almost 75%. The AAT found that it was harsh that he should pay a $10,000 penalty when it was merely a shortcoming in the paperwork that led to the denial of the deduction.

Partial remission has been granted where:

- the taxpayer, had he been properly advised, would not have suffered a financial penalty (*Egan*)
- the taxpayer faced some difficulties because of the death of her husband (who had structured the original partnership investment) (*Ryvitch*)
- the taxpayer's mistake was an isolated one and there was no evidence that the taxpayer had acted dishonestly (*Tavco Group*)
- the taxpayer was advised to lodge a BAS reducing GST payable to nil on the incorrect assumption that the ATO would request further information and adjust the return later (*Nitram Consulting*). The Commissioner has warned taxpayers against speculative lodgments (*Decision Impact Statement on Nitram Consulting*), and
- the taxpayer had suffered depression, had unwisely relied on staff and agents, and 11 of his companies were under administration or in liquidation (*Sonntag*).

Lodgment penalties

According to PS LA 2011/19, full remission of the penalty for failure to lodge on time will be granted where the taxpayer or their tax agent can establish that delay occurred due to circumstances beyond their control. Remission may nevertheless be granted where the circumstances are not beyond the taxpayer's control, provided it would be fair and reasonable to do so. For example, it would generally be fair to remit a penalty where the taxpayer has a good compliance history. In *Kizquart*, remission of lodgment penalties was justified where the delay was caused by the taxpayer's failure to understand the new tax system, pressure of work and personal difficulties.

Remission guidelines applying to the penalty for non-electronic reporting (¶29-310) are contained in PS LA 2011/2. Guidelines applying to the penalty for failure to lodge a document (¶29-140), including remission of penalties, are contained in PS LA 2014/4.

[FTR ¶978-295]

¶29-410 Review of penalty remission decisions

Generally, the AAT may review decisions of the Commissioner relating to the remission of penalties. However, certain "ineligible income remission decisions" relating to the former penalty provisions under ITAA36 cannot be reviewed (TAA s 14ZS). These restrictions only apply where the decision under review relates wholly to the remission of penalties. They do not apply where the decision under review also relates to an assessment of income tax and only partly relates to the remission of penalties

(*Grollo Nominees*). Where the primary tax is not reduced in a decision, a decision relating to remission of related penalties does not cease to be an ''ineligible income tax remission decision'' (*Hornibrook*).

In all cases, an appeal may be made to the Federal Court against a remission decision, but the court is restricted to examining whether the Commissioner has acted in accordance with correct legal principles. Accordingly, where possible, it may be advisable to first go to the AAT rather than the court (¶28-080).

An objection against an assessment should include a ground to the effect that the conditions for imposing a penalty do not exist and that any penalty imposed is excessive (¶28-050).

[FTR ¶972-635]

Late Payment Penalties

¶29-500 Failure to pay by due date

A taxpayer who fails to pay an amount of tax on time is liable to pay GIC. GIC applies not only to primary tax debts, but also to running balance account deficit debts (TAA ss 8AAA to 8AAH: ¶29-510).

The rules allowing the Commissioner to collect and recover GIC (and other tax-related liabilities) are contained in TAA Sch 1 Pt 4-15 (¶25-500).

[FTR ¶962-921]

¶29-510 General interest charge

Liability to GIC usually arises where an amount of tax is not paid by the payment due date. GIC is calculated daily on a compounding basis (TAA s 8AAC). It applies on each day in the period starting on the day on which the tax was due for payment to the day on which any of the tax remained unpaid. The provisions of ITAA36 and other taxation laws that impose a liability for GIC are set out in TAA s 8AAB. GIC may also apply where an individual or trustee fails to lodge an income tax return on time; the GIC is payable from the date tax is taken to be due and payable, which could be a day before an assessment is made (ITAA97 s 5-5(3)). For further information on when tax becomes due, see ¶25-400.

The GIC rate for a day is worked out by dividing the base interest rate plus 7% by the number of days in the calendar year (TAA s 8AAD). The base interest rate is determined by reference to the monthly average yield of 90-day Bank Accepted Bills.

Recent GIC rates are as follows:

Quarter	GIC annual rate (simple interest) (%)	GIC daily rate (compounding) (%)
Apr–Jun 2019	8.96	0.02454794
Jul–Sep 2019	8.54	0.02339726
Oct–Dec 2019	7.98	0.02186301
Jan–Mar 2020	7.91	0.02161202
Apr–Jun 2020	7.89	0.02155738
Jul–Sep 2020	7.10	0.01939891
Oct–Dec 2020	7.10	0.01939891
Jan–Mar 2021	7.02	0.01923288

▶ **Example**

Marjorie's outstanding tax is $10,000. It became due and payable on 21 October 2020 but was not paid until 21 November 2020 (ie 30 days overdue). GIC is payable on the $10,000 for each day in the period from the beginning of 21 October 2020 (ie the day the tax was due to be paid) to the end of 20 November 2020 (ie the last day on which any tax or GIC remains unpaid). Marjorie is liable to pay GIC for 30 days. The applicable daily GIC rate is 0.01939891%. Marjorie's total debt, made up of the outstanding tax and GIC, is:

$$\$10,000 \times (1.0001939891)^{30} = \$10,058.36.$$

The GIC daily compounding rate now applies to most taxes, including income tax, FBT, GST and PAYG, although the Commissioner has a discretion to apply the simple interest rate.

GIC is deductible (ITAA97 s 25-5(1); ¶16-850). It is to be deducted in the year in which the notice of assessment for the relevant tax debt is issued (*Nash*). This does not apply to GIC accruing after the assessment has been issued, from which point GIC is deductible on a daily basis (ATO *Decision Impact Statement* on *Nash*). It is a debt due to the Commonwealth that may be sued for and recovered in the usual way. GIC is also a "present legal obligation" (¶4-200) on each day an amount of tax remains unpaid (*H* and *Decision Impact Statement*).

Running balance accounts

Running balance accounts (RBAs) record a taxpayer's tax liabilities and credits that are notified on an activity statement (¶24-300). GIC is payable on any RBA deficit that exists at the end of each day (TAA s 8AAZF).

GIC has been held to have been payable for an RBA deficit debt, notwithstanding that the debt was the consequence of an administrative overpayment from the ATO, in respect of which the ATO had not given a notice specifying a payment due date (*Price*).

[FTR ¶962-921]

¶29-530 Remission of GIC

The Commissioner has discretion to remit GIC in whole or in part. However, if GIC is payable because an amount remains unpaid after the time by which it is due to be paid, GIC may only be remitted if:

- the circumstances that contributed to the delay in payment were not due to, or caused directly or indirectly by, an act or omission of the person liable to pay the GIC and that person has taken reasonable action to mitigate those circumstances
- where the circumstances contributing to the delay in payment were caused, directly or indirectly, by an act or omission of the person liable to pay the GIC, that person has taken reasonable action to mitigate those circumstances or their effect and it would be fair and reasonable to remit the GIC or any part of it, or
- there are special circumstances that make it fair and reasonable to remit all or part of the GIC or it is otherwise appropriate to do so (TAA s 8AAG).

A taxpayer's intentional disregard of the consequences of non-compliance with tax laws has been held to have been a legitimate basis to exclude the circumstances listed in TAA s 8AAG, so that it was not fair or reasonable or otherwise appropriate to remit GIC (*Melbourne Car Shop Pty Ltd*).

Where a taxpayer pays late payment penalty and the penalty tax or the GIC is later remitted, the Commissioner is required to pay interest (¶28-170).

ATO guidelines

PS LA 2011/12 contains guidelines on remission of GIC imposed for late payment or underestimation of liability. Generally the taxpayer bears the onus of proving remission is warranted. Relevant considerations include factors beyond the debtor's control; acts or omissions of the debtor; actions to relieve the circumstances affecting the liability to pay; and whether it is fair and reasonable to remit.

PS LA 2006/8 contains guidelines on remission of interest charges on shortfall amounts that arise where a tax liability is amended or revised. It deals with the remission of interest charges that accrue before the tax liability is amended or revised. The amount remitted depends on the circumstances and the extent to which factors beyond the taxpayer's control were responsible for the size and duration of the shortfall.

Activity statements

Where the due date for an activity statement falls on a Saturday, a Sunday or a public holiday, payment may be made on the next business day without incurring a penalty or GIC (TAA Sch 1 s 388-52). The GIC is automatically imposed on amounts remaining unpaid after that date.

However, GIC may be remitted where a taxpayer can demonstrate that reasonable steps were taken to mitigate the reasons for the delay in payment or there are special circumstances, because of which it would be fair and reasonable to remit the GIC. Where there are no other unpaid debts on the taxpayer's account and the amount of GIC is small, the Commissioner may remit the GIC.

Review of remission decisions

The Commissioner's decision on the remission of GIC cannot be objected under TAA Pt IVC (¶28-000), but may be judicially reviewed under the *Administrative Decisions (Judicial Review) Act 1977* (*Sharp*) (¶28-180).

[FTR ¶962-945]

¶29-550 Shortfall interest charge

Where an assessment is amended to increase the amount of tax payable (¶25-300), the taxpayer is liable to pay a shortfall interest charge (SIC) on the amount of the increase (TAA Sch 1 Div 280).

Liability for the SIC applies for each day in the period from the due date for payment of the understated assessment to the end of the day before the assessment is amended. The annual rate of the SIC is 4 percentage points lower than the GIC rate (¶29-510).

The SIC is payable even if the amendment results in liability to any penalty. The Commissioner must give a notice to the taxpayer specifying the amount of the SIC liability. The amount can be included in any other notice, such as the notice of amended assessment.

The due date for payment of the tax shortfall and any SIC is 21 days from when the taxpayer is given notice (ITAA36 former s 204(2), (2A); ITAA97 ss 5-5(7); 5-10). Once this due date has passed, the GIC will apply to any unpaid tax and SIC (ITAA36 former s 204(3); ITAA97 s 5-15).

The Commissioner has the discretion to remit the SIC. In deciding whether to grant remission, the Commissioner must have regard to 2 principles:

(1) remission should not occur just because the benefit the taxpayer received from the temporary use of the shortfall amount is less than the SIC, and

(2) remission should occur where the circumstances justify the Commonwealth bearing part of the cost of delayed payment, eg where the ATO took longer to complete an audit than could reasonably have been expected.

The Commissioner must provide a written statement of reasons for not remitting the SIC where the taxpayer has requested remission in the approved form. Where the unremitted amount of the SIC exceeds 20% of the shortfall, the taxpayer may contest a decision not to remit the SIC under the objection and appeal provisions (¶28-000).

SIC is tax-deductible (¶16-850).

[FITR ¶16-110, ¶16-120, ¶16-130]

Tax Offences

¶29-700 Prosecution for tax offences

Various taxation offences are created by TAA Pt III (ss 8A to 8ZN). The offences carry fairly substantial fines and, in some cases, a term of imprisonment. The penalties are higher for second or subsequent offences.

Certain offences, if committed by a natural person, are punishable by a fine and/or imprisonment. Where such an offence is committed by a company, the maximum penalty is 5 times the maximum fine that could be imposed on a natural person (s 8ZF).

Where an offence is not punishable by a term of imprisonment, the proceedings take the form of proceedings for the recovery of a pecuniary penalty. This means that the proceedings are civil, rather than criminal, in nature. Such proceedings may be instituted in a court of summary jurisdiction or, where the maximum penalty for the offence exceeds 50 penalty units (¶29-000) for a natural person or 250 penalty units for companies, in the relevant Supreme Court. If the prosecution has been commenced in a court of summary jurisdiction and the penalty for the offence exceeds those amounts, the person or company being prosecuted may elect to have the matter tried in the relevant Supreme Court. Where a person is charged with several offences for keeping incorrect records or falsifying or concealing the identity or location of a person, which individually would be summary offences, each conviction in a single sitting of the court is a summary offence (ie the first conviction does not make the remaining offences before the court indictable offences).

Company officers and managers may be liable for taxation offences committed by their companies (¶29-710).

In certain circumstances (eg where a person fails to lodge a return), the Commissioner may prosecute the offender as an alternative to imposing a penalty. However, the ATO will generally consider whether an administrative penalty is an appropriate sanction and will not use the threat of prosecution as a lever in settlement negotiations (¶25-210). When deciding whether to prosecute, the ATO would consider *Prosecution policy of the Commonwealth* and its policy on *Fraud Control and the Prosecution Process* (see ATO website on its disputes policy). If a person is liable to a penalty and a prosecution is instituted (based on the same offence), the person ceases to be liable to pay that penalty, even if the prosecution is later withdrawn. In such a case, any amount paid, or applied by the Commissioner, to discharge that liability for the penalty must be refunded or applied towards any other tax liability of the person.

There is also a variety of other offences for which a person may be prosecuted and penalties imposed, for example for breaches of the PAYG system obligations (¶29-300) or the TFN withholding tax (¶33-080) provisions, or for the misuse of TFNs (¶33-085).

The chart below sets out the specific taxation offences and the maximum penalties. The offences are not restricted to cases where the *taxpayer* commits the offence — they can apply where any person commits the offence. Costs may also be awarded by the court against any party under s 8ZN (*MacPherson*).

CHART OF OFFENCES AND PENALTIES*

<table>
<tr><th rowspan="2">Offence</th><th colspan="2">Maximum penalty if committed by (see Note 1 below)</th></tr>
<tr><th>Natural person</th><th>Corporation (s 8ZF; see Note 8 below)</th></tr>
<tr><td rowspan="2">Refusal or failure to comply with a requirement of a tax law to furnish a return or information, produce (or permit access to) documents, answer questions, attend before the Commissioner or give evidence on oath or affirmation (see Note 2 below) (ss 8C; 8D; 8E).</td><td>First offence: 20 penalty units.

Second offence: 40 penalty units.

Third and each subsequent offence: 50 penalty units and/or 12 months' imprisonment.</td><td>First offence: 20 penalty units.

Second offence: 40 penalty units.

Third and each subsequent offence: 250 penalty units.</td></tr>
<tr><td colspan="2">A convicted person may also be ordered to pay up to double or, for subsequent offences, treble the amount of tax avoided (see Notes 3 and 4 below) (s 8HA).</td></tr>
<tr><td rowspan="2">Refusal or failure to comply with a court order to give evidence or furnish a return or information (ss 8G; 8H).</td><td>50 penalty units and/or 12 months' imprisonment.</td><td>250 penalty units.</td></tr>
<tr><td colspan="2">A convicted person may also be ordered to pay up to double or, for subsequent offences, treble the amount of tax avoided (see Notes 3 and 4 below) (s 8HA).</td></tr>
<tr><td rowspan="2">Making a false or misleading statement or an omission that makes the statement misleading, subject to a statutory defence (see Note 5 below) (ss 8K; 8M).

Incorrectly keeping records, subject to a statutory defence (see Note 6 below) (ss 8L; 8M).</td><td>First offence: 20 penalty units.

Second and each subsequent offence: 40 penalty units.</td><td>First offence: 20 penalty units.

Second and each subsequent offence: 40 penalty units.</td></tr>
<tr><td colspan="2">A convicted person may also be ordered to pay the Commissioner up to double the amount of tax avoided (s 8W).</td></tr>
<tr><td rowspan="2">Recklessly making a false or misleading statement or recklessly omitting something from a statement which makes it misleading (ss 8N; 8R).

Recklessly incorrectly keeping records (ss 8Q; 8R).</td><td>First offence: 30 penalty units.

Second and each subsequent offence: 50 penalty units and/or 12 months' imprisonment.</td><td>First offence: 30 penalty units.

Second and each subsequent offence: 250 penalty units.</td></tr>
<tr><td colspan="2">A convicted person may also be ordered to pay the Commissioner up to double or, for second and subsequent offences, treble the amount of tax avoided (see Notes 3 and 4 below) (s 8W).</td></tr>
<tr><td rowspan="2">Falsifying, concealing, destroying or altering records with intent to deceive or obstruct (ss 8T; 8V).

Falsifying or concealing identity or address with intent to deceive or obstruct (ss 8U; 8V).</td><td>First offence: 50 penalty units and/or 12 months' imprisonment.

Second and each subsequent offence: 100 penalty units and/or 2 years' imprisonment.</td><td>First offence: 250 penalty units.

Second and each subsequent offence: 500 penalty units.</td></tr>
<tr><td colspan="2">A convicted person may also be ordered to pay the Commissioner up to double or, for second and subsequent offences, treble the amount of tax avoided (see Notes 3 and 4 below) (s 8W).</td></tr>
<tr><td>Obstructing ATO officers (see Note 7 below) (Criminal Code, s 149.1; former s 8X).</td><td>2 years' imprisonment.</td><td></td></tr>
<tr><td>Unauthorised access to tax records (s 8XA).</td><td>100 penalty units and/or 2 years' imprisonment.</td><td>500 penalty units.</td></tr>
<tr><td>Unauthorised disclosure of protected tax information by an entity other than a taxation officer (Sch 1 s 355-155; former s 8XB).</td><td>2 years' imprisonment.</td><td></td></tr>
</table>

CHART OF OFFENCES AND PENALTIES*

Offence	Maximum penalty if committed by (see Note 1 below)	
	Natural person	*Corporation* **(s 8ZF; see Note 8 below)**
TFN offences		
Unauthorised obtaining of a TFN (s 8WA).	100 penalty units and/or 2 years' imprisonment.	500 penalty units.
Unauthorised use or disclosure of a TFN (s 8WB).		
Conducting affairs to avoid the use of TFN requirements (s 8WC).		
Electronic sales suppression tools (¶29-310)		
Producing or supplying such tools (s 8WAC).	5,000 penalty units.	25,000 penalty units.
Possessing such tools (s 8WAD).	500 penalty units.	2,500 penalty units.
Incorrectly keeping records using such tools (s 8WAE).	1,000 penalty units.	5,000 penalty units.

* All sections referred to are of the TAA (unless otherwise specified).

Note 1: For the current value of a penalty unit, see ¶29-000.

Note 2: The following range of penalties has been recommended as appropriate in ordinary cases of failing to lodge returns (*Hagidimitriou*).

- For a first offence in a run-of-the-mill case, the fine should be between $250 and $500.
- For offenders who have a previous conviction under ITAA36 former s 223 for failing to lodge a return (a pre-14 December 1984 offence), the fine should be in the order of $500 to $1,000.
- For offenders who have a previous conviction for a post-13 December 1984 offence, the penalty should be in the order of $1,000 to $2,000.

These amounts should be regarded as starting points, which may be increased or reduced according to the particular circumstances of the case. In *Dahia*, a tax agent who failed to lodge 2 returns was fined $400 for each offence; in *Petherbridge*, a taxpayer was fined $1,200 for a second conviction for failing to lodge returns. In *Harrex v Fraser*, a taxpayer who failed to lodge 11 returns was fined $200 for the first offence, $450 for the second, and $550 each for the remaining 9 offences, together with court costs of $111. The court did not consider his circumstances, including his mental condition, justify non-conviction orders.

The fact that the taxpayer still has not lodged the return at the time of the hearing may be an aggravating factor justifying a higher penalty than would otherwise have applied (*Simmons*).

Note 3: For the purposes of ss 8HA and 8W, a reference to a conviction of a person for an offence includes a reference to the making of an order under *Crimes Act 1914*, s 19B, eg where the court is satisfied that a charge is proved but places a person on a good behaviour bond without proceeding to a conviction.

Note 4: Unless there are exceptional circumstances, a court should exercise the discretion under s 8HA (*Bulyee Nominees*). In determining the amount that ought to be paid under s 8HA or 8W on conviction, there is authority for the view that the administrative penalties that would have been imposed if the offender had not been prosecuted should be used as the starting point (*Taplin v Pickford*). However, there is conflicting authority that considers that the discretion under ss 8HA and 8W is to be exercised without reference to those penalties (*Bulyee Nominees*). There is also authority for the view that, usually, an additional penalty under s 8W should be imposed to reinforce the element of general deterrence (*Thomas v Schwager*).

Note 5: It is a defence to a charge under s 8K if the person proves on the balance of probabilities that he/she did not know and could not reasonably be expected to have known that the statement was false or misleading.

Note 6: It is a defence to a charge under s 8L if the person proves on the balance of probabilities that he/she did not know and could not reasonably be expected to have known that the records did not correctly record the facts.

Note 7: A person was held not to be guilty of obstruction by refusing ATO officers access to documents before obtaining legal advice (*Scanlan v Swan*).

Note 8: A person who is concerned in, or takes part in, the management of a corporation is deemed to have committed the offence in certain circumstances: s 8Y.

General criminal offences

In addition to the specific taxation offences set out in Pt III, prosecutions for a number of general offences may be instituted under various provisions of the *Criminal Code* (eg ss 134.2 and 135.2) or the *Crimes Act 1914*. Some examples are set out below.

- Several company directors who understated a company's assessable income by almost $242,000 were convicted of fraud. The court commented that deliberate and systematic tax fraud should result in imprisonment unless there are substantial mitigating factors. The directors, however, were placed on good behaviour bonds and not imprisoned because: (i) their culpability was largely due to carelessness and incompetence; (ii) they pleaded guilty; (iii) they had cooperated with the ATO; and (iv) they had paid all the avoided tax plus penalties (*Elvin*).
- Two persons were convicted of conspiring to defraud the Commonwealth for creating artificial deductions and accessing money through ATMs using foreign credit cards. Their sentences were reduced because of the fact that over $1 million in penalty taxes had been paid; the relatively short duration of the offending conduct; the absence of prior criminal histories; the jury's inferential finding that the accused did not intentionally set up an unlawful scheme; and the fact that the accused did not abuse a position of trust (*R v Hargraves & Stoten*).
- A taxpayer was convicted of fraud and imposition for making false representations in his notices of objection and was sentenced to 2 years' imprisonment (together with a recognisance release order) (*Saxby v R*).
- A taxpayer was convicted for intentionally omitting his CGT position (and thus avoiding tax of between $1.9 million and $2.4 million) and for omitting income of approximately $1 million in 3 years' tax returns. He was given an aggregate sentence of 4.5 years' imprisonment (together with a recognisance release order) (*Milne v R*; *Milne v R*; *R v Milne*; *Milne v R*; *R v Milne (No 6)*). The NSW Court of Criminal Appeal noted that firm custodial sentences for serious white collar crime were required; and that there was a high community expectation that serious tax fraud would be properly punished and offenders, no matter their business acumen and high status in the commercial world, dealt with sternly and appropriately.
- Two company co-directors were sentenced to imprisonment (with non-parole periods of 9 years and 3 months for one and 7 years and 6 months for the other) for making false depreciation claims in company tax returns. The risk of loss that was intended to be caused in the sophisticated scheme approximated $135 million (*Dickson v R* and *R v Issakidis*).

As for the period of imprisonment an offender should serve before being released on a recognizance release order, the High Court has indicated that there is no judicially determined norm or starting point (*Hili & Jones*). In *Hili & Jones*, 2 accused were convicted for tax-related offences covering over $750,000 of income tax and each had been sentenced to 18 months' total imprisonment, with a recognisance release order to take effect after 7 months. The Court of Criminal Appeal increased the sentences to 3 years each, with a recognisance release order to take effect after 18 months. The High Court upheld the revised sentences, though it considered that the Court of Criminal Appeal was incorrect in saying that the norm for a period of mandatory imprisonment was between 60% and 66%.

A person who aids or abets the commission of a taxation offence is also guilty of that offence (*Criminal Code* s 11.2; *Crimes Act 1914*, former s 5). The aiding and abetting provisions are particularly relevant to tax agents and other professional advisers. Where tax agents omit income or invent (or inflate) claims on their own initiative in a return prepared for a client, it seems that the client will nevertheless be treated as the person who makes the misstatement (*Grapsas v Unger*). However, the agent is likely to be guilty as an accomplice (in addition, the agent's registration may be suspended or cancelled). A taxpayer's recourse in these circumstances is to sue the agent for recovery of any penalty. There are also provisions in the *Crimes (Taxation Offences) Act 1980* that make it an offence to participate in, or aid or abet participation in, arrangements that render a company or trustee unable, or likely to be unable, to meet an income tax liability (¶30-110).

[FTR ¶963-700 – ¶967-900]

¶29-710 Prosecution of company officers and managers for tax offences

Any person who is concerned in or takes part in the management of a company is liable to be prosecuted for a tax offence committed by the company as if that person had committed the offence personally (TAA s 8Y).

An ''officer'' of a company is automatically presumed to be concerned in and to take part in the company's management unless the contrary is proved. An officer is defined to mean a director, secretary, receiver and manager, official manager, liquidator appointed in a voluntary winding up or a trustee or other person administering a compromise or arrangement made between the company and any other person. It also includes a de facto director and any person in accordance with whose directions or instructions the directors of the company are accustomed to act (TAA s 8A(1)). A person will not be included merely because the directors act on advice given by that person in a proper professional or business capacity, for example an advising solicitor or accountant (s 8A(2)).

It is a defence to a prosecution under s 8Y if the person proves that he/she did not aid, abet, counsel or procure the act or omission of the company and was not in any way knowingly concerned in, or a party to, that act or omission. A director of several companies failed to establish this defence in *Buist's case*. The director had simply accepted a statement by an employee of the companies' firm of accountants that steps were being taken to comply with notices requiring the companies to lodge returns for several years.

As a matter of policy, the ATO will usually prosecute the company, rather than the individuals who manage it. However, prosecution of company officers may be appropriate where the company does not have sufficient assets to meet any penalty imposed. Prosecution referrals may also occur in relation to a company officer where that person is the controlling mind of the company.

In addition to being convicted under s 8Y, the company officer or manager may be personally liable to make reparation to the Commissioner for the amount of tax owed by the company (*Crimes Act 1914*, s 21B). A company director, who was fined $500 for each of 13 sales tax offences under s 8Y, was also required to pay the company's sales tax debt of $250,000 (*Bonham*). A reparation order can be made even if the director has not been morally culpable (*Gould*). However, in the exercise of its discretion whether to make a reparation order, the court may have regard to the personal circumstances and means of the offender (*Vlahov*; *Hookham*; *Gould*). Further, directors in breach of their duties for entering into tax evasion schemes on behalf of a company may be liable to compensate liquidators for tax debts incurred (*BCI Finances Pty Ltd (in liq) v Binetter (No 4)*).

[FTR ¶963-700, ¶966-250]

Chapter 30 Tax Avoidance • Alienation of Income • PSI

Tax Avoidance

¶30-000 Countering tax avoidance

What tax avoidance means is not completely clear and the boundaries of what is acceptable or unacceptable tax behaviour shift over time. There is a long history of legislative action against artificial, contrived or deceptive schemes employed by taxpayers to avoid paying tax.

Australia and many other nations are grappling with the challenges of globalisation and digital disruption which present new opportunities for tax avoidance, fraud and money laundering (¶30-005). This was illustrated by the publication in 2017 of a massive leak of documents — the ''Paradise Papers'' — revealing the extensive use of tax havens, offshore deals, schemes and trusts to hide wealth around the world.

A number of measures have been enacted to tackle cross-border tax avoidance, including the multinational anti-avoidance law (the MAAL: ¶30-200) and the diverted profits tax (¶30-205). Australia is implementing tax reform measures under the Base Erosion and Profit Shifting (BEPS) Project (¶22-640). The government has enacted a law to protect, from 1 July 2018, whistleblowers — individuals who disclose information to the ATO relating to tax avoidance behaviour and other tax issues (¶1-220).

This chapter examines the following measures dealing with tax avoidance:

- Pt IVA, the general anti-avoidance provisions (¶30-110)
- the promoter penalty laws targeting the promoters of tax avoidance or tax evasion schemes (¶30-300)
- the personal services income regime which targets the alienation of personal services income (¶30-600)
- the tax laws relating to the transfer of rights to receive income (¶30-900).

[FTR ¶81-150, ¶978-282/1]

¶30-005 Emerging challenges to the tax base

Globalisation and rapid technological change are major causes of social, legal and economic disruption. The digital revolution is fuelling radical changes in business and personal life and the pace of change is accelerating. Rapid change challenges the capacity of governments to raise revenue and tax authorities globally are responding to a range of threats.

Some of the emerging challenges to the tax base are described below.

Base erosion and profit shifting

The OECD and G20 countries started the base erosion and profit shifting (BEPS) project in 2013 to address the problem of significant losses in national corporate income tax revenues, facilitated by globalisation. Losses were attributed to aggressive tax planning by some multinational enterprises, mismatches between national tax rules, lack of transparency and coordination between tax administrations, limited enforcement resources and harmful tax practices (eg special tax deals and concessions).

Under the BEPS project, over 130 countries and jurisdictions are collaborating to implement a range of BEPS measures. For more information, see ¶22-640.

Sharing economy

Defining the sharing economy is difficult because the term encompasses a large number of modes of operation. The sharing economy can be defined very broadly as new kinds of economic and social interactions facilitated by the internet. Alternative terms for describing the same or similar concepts include: the collaborative economy or collaborative consumption, the access economy and the on-demand economy. Examples of businesses participating in the sharing economy are: eBay, Uber, Airbnb, Etsy, and Airtasker.

The ATO describes the sharing economy as buyers (users) and sellers (providers) connected through a facilitator who usually operates an app or a website. The sale of goods and services via the sharing or collaborative economy is growing at a phenomenal rate, raising challenges for collection of tax revenues. Tax issues for participants in the sharing economy include:

- if a business is being carried on, whether an ABN is needed (¶33-105) and whether the person should register for GST (¶34-100) and lodge activity statements (¶24-240)
- whether the price of the goods or services provided includes GST (¶34-110)
- if tax invoices are needed for sales (¶34-140)
- if assessable income has been earned (¶2-135)
- whether GST credits and income tax deductions can be claimed for expenses (¶34-110)
- how sharing economy activities added together impact GST and income tax (¶10-105) obligations.

The government intends to implement a new reporting regime for information on taxpayers who earn income from sharing economy websites or platforms.

Black economy

The black economy (or cash economy) is the part of a country's economic activity which is unrecorded and untaxed by its government. It is not a new problem but accelerating technological change presents governments and revenue authorities with new challenges and opportunities for dealing with it.

The government announced the formation of the Black Economy Taskforce in 2016 and described the problem as:

> "... people who operate entirely outside the tax system or who are known to the tax system but deliberately understate their income or overstate their expenses. Black economy participants evade taxes and may also be over-claiming welfare and other government benefits."

Measures that have been implemented include:

- measures to prevent "phoenix" companies from making creditor-defeating dispositions of property; prevent improper director resignations leaving a company with no directors; make company directors personally liable for their company's GST and greater ATO data gathering power; and authorise the retention of tax refunds where a taxpayer has not lodged a tax return or provided relevant information
- measures to establish the legal framework for director identification numbers (DIN) (¶33-090)
- increased funding for ATO audit activity including mobile strike teams, and a Black Economy Hotline (Tel 1800 807 875)
- new offences to deter the production, use and distribution of electronic sales suppression tools to manipulate or falsify electronic point of sale records (¶29-700)
- the taxable payment reporting system (TPRS) has been extended to include the road freight, security and information technology sectors from 1 July 2019 (¶33-200), and

- after 1 July 2019, businesses are not able to claim deductions for payments to employees or certain payments to contractors where they have not met PAYG obligations.

Proposed measures include:

- a new, strengthened regulatory framework for the Australian Business Number (ABN) system (¶33-100) in 2018–19 (consultation paper, July 2018). The government announced measures in the 2019–20 Federal Budget to require ABN holders to lodge tax returns and update their ABN details to be able to retain their ABN registration, and
- an announcement by government in 2018 of a review of existing criminal offences, and civil and administrative penalties for black economy activity. The government held a public consultation on how to implement the Black Economy Taskforce recommendation to introduce a modern offences regime.

The OECD has released a non-binding international framework to enable collection of information from digital platforms used by the sharing and gig economy. Nations may participate by enacting the rules in domestic law and thereby obtain data on the sellers of accommodation, transport, food delivery and other gig economy services.

Cryptocurrencies

Revenue authorities are concerned that cryptocurrencies like Bitcoin present opportunities for tax evasion, money laundering and other undesirable activities.

Bitcoin allows users to transfer money on the internet without using a bank, credit card issuer or other third party. The network is controlled by those using it, on a platform of encrypted software, ensuring security and anonymity. Bitcoin transactions are recorded publicly and permanently on a register called the Blockchain, which means anyone can see the balance and transactions of any bitcoin address. However, the identity of the user behind a transaction is not easily revealed.

The ATO and other agencies like AUSTRAC and ASIC are concerned by the ability of participants to conduct transactions anonymously. It is possible to use Bitcoin and other cryptocurrencies in a similar way to using foreign bank accounts to facilitate tax evasion. Transactions using cryptocurrencies present difficult tax compliance and record-keeping challenges.

In February 2019, the government sought public comment on Initial Coin Offerings (ICOs) in Australia and the application of Australia's regulatory framework, including the tax rules, to ICOs.

For information about current tax rules for recognising cryptocurrency transactions, see ¶10-030 and ¶23-070.

[FTR ¶79-560, ¶958-010; FITR ¶19-545, ¶620-220, ¶620-223]

General Anti-avoidance Provisions

¶30-110 Introduction to Pt IVA

The general income tax anti-avoidance provisions appear in ITAA36 Pt IVA. They supplement the numerous anti-avoidance rules directed at particular types of arrangements which appear elsewhere in the Act. Part IVA is also referred to by the acronyms GAAP (general anti-avoidance provision) and GAAR (general anti-avoidance rule).

Part IVA is a provision of "last resort", so it does not apply unless the taxpayer's claim is otherwise allowable. For example, it will not apply if a claimed deduction is not allowable in any event under the general deduction provisions, or if the transaction is set aside by some other specific anti-avoidance measure. Nor need it apply where a commercially unrealistic transaction is entered into solely to generate tax deductions, and is not effective for tax purposes in any event (*Fletcher*: ¶16-010).

The Commissioner also will not need to rely on Pt IVA if the transaction is a sham, and not intended to have legal effect, as that transaction will be inherently ineffective (*Jaques*; *Hancock*; *Richard Walter*). However, when a transaction is evidenced by apparently valid documents it would be necessary to establish, to the satisfaction of the court, that those documents were not in fact acted upon or were a mere facade or cloak for some other transaction before the court could conclude that the transaction evidenced by the documents was a sham (*Normandy Finance*).

Part IVA strengthened

The government amended Pt IVA in 2013 to remedy deficiencies in ss 177C (tax benefits) and 177D, as revealed by a number of Full Federal Court decisions, including *RCI* in 2011 (¶30-160) and *Futuris* in 2012 (¶30-160). Part IVA was amended to make it more effective against tax avoidance schemes carried out as part of broader commercial transactions. The amendments apply in relation to schemes that were entered into, or that started to be carried out, on or after 16 November 2012.

Multinational tax avoidance measures

The government has enacted a number of measures to address multinational tax avoidance, including:

- the doubling of administrative penalties that can be applied to large multinational companies entering tax avoidance or profit shifting schemes (¶29-180)
- the multinational anti-avoidance law (MAAL) which targets multinational entities using artificial or contrived arrangements to avoid the attribution of business profits to a taxable permanent establishment in Australia (¶30-200), and
- the diverted profits tax (DPT: ¶30-205).

These measures apply to ‘‘significant global entities’’ (¶30-200).

Fiscal nullity doctrine

The High Court has held that the doctrine of fiscal nullity, developed by the UK courts to strike down artificial tax avoidance arrangements, does not apply in Australia because of the general anti-avoidance provisions contained in Pt IVA (*John*).

Criminal sanctions for tax fraud or evasion

The *Crimes (Taxation Offences) Act 1980* (Taxation Offences Act) creates a number of criminal offences relating to the fraudulent evasion of various federal taxes — specifically income tax, GST-related taxes, FBT, petroleum resource rent tax and the superannuation guarantee charge. The Act is directed against stripping arrangements which are designed to render a company or trust incapable of paying tax.

In relation to income tax, the Act makes it an offence to enter into an arrangement with a purpose of securing that a company or trust will be, or will be likely to be, unable to pay income tax that is then payable (Taxation Offences Act s 5), or that will or may reasonably be expected to become payable in the future. It is also an offence to aid, abet, counsel or procure another person to enter such an arrangement (Taxation Offences Act ss 6; 7). The maximum penalty is 10 years’ gaol, a fine of $210,000 (1,000 penalty units: ¶29-000) or both. The person convicted may also be ordered to pay some or all of the tax involved (Taxation Offences Act ss 9; 12). The Act operates in a similar way in relation to the other taxes within its scope.

Note that the directors of a company may be personally liable to pay compensation for tax liabilities arising from participation in tax avoidance schemes or tax evasion. In *BCI Finances Pty Ltd (in liq) v Binetter (No 4)*, the Federal Court found that directors of companies involved in tax evasion schemes had sufficient knowledge of and involvement in the schemes to support a finding that they had breached their statutory and common law duties as directors of the companies. The liquidators of the companies succeeded in claims against directors, based on rights to equitable compensation.

[FTR ¶81-150, ¶942-005]

¶30-120 Scope of Pt IVA

ITAA36 Pt IVA (ss 177A to 177F) applies to schemes entered into with the sole or dominant purpose of obtaining a tax benefit. The operation of Pt IVA is not limited by any other provision of ITAA36, ITAA97 or by any provision of the *International Tax Agreements Act 1953*.

When Pt IVA was enacted, the then Treasurer said that:

- ''arrangements of a normal business or family kind, including those of a tax planning nature'', would be beyond its scope
- Pt IVA is designed to operate against ''blatant, artificial, or contrived arrangements, but not cast unnecessary inhibitions on normal commercial transactions by which taxpayers legitimately take advantage of opportunities available for the arrangement of their affairs''.

Despite these statements, the language used in the provisions is extremely wide. However, since the practical application of Pt IVA depends on the Commissioner making a determination in accordance with the powers conferred under s 177F, it is reasonable to expect that the ATO will only exercise these powers where it considers that a scheme is blatant, artificial or contrived, although it is somewhat uncertain which schemes would be treated as falling within that description. It is also worth noting that in recent years the original function of Pt IVA as a general anti-avoidance regime has been significantly expanded by the enactment of provisions designed to combat more specific arrangements, such as those involving withholding tax (¶30-160) and franking credit trading (¶30-195).

Part IVA specifically does *not* affect tax benefits under the income equalisation deposit or farm management deposit schemes.

Part IVA is intended to apply to trusts and trustees even though in certain circumstances they may not technically be ''taxpayers'' (*Grollo Nominees*). It may also apply to some schemes involving the group consolidation provisions (¶8-950).

Part IVA may also apply to treaty shopping schemes (TD 2010/20). Treaty shopping refers to the structuring of an arrangement in a manner that attracts the operation of a tax treaty between Australia and another country to obtain a particular benefit or advantage.

Guidelines for ATO staff in dealing with the application of Pt IVA are contained in PS LA 2005/24. In addition, PS LA 2008/6 provides guidelines for dealing with taxpayers who have committed fraud or evasion. See also ¶30-170.

The ATO has published a practical guide outlining the basic principles of how and when Pt IVA applies to tax schemes. The guide, *Part IVA: the general anti-avoidance rule for income tax — basic principles about how and when it applies* (2005), is available on the ATO website. A fact sheet entitled *Recognising, rejecting and reporting tax avoidance schemes* (2013) is also available on the ATO website.

Effect of applying Pt IVA

Where Pt IVA applies, the Commissioner may cancel the relevant tax benefit (¶30-180) and, in addition, impose penalty tax (¶29-180).

[FTR ¶81-190]

¶30-130 Does Pt IVA apply?

Section 177D determines when Pt IVA applies to a scheme. Separate rules apply to some other specific schemes or benefits (eg franking credit schemes: ¶30-195). The conditions for the application of s 177D are as follows:

- there is a scheme (¶30-140)
- there is a tax benefit (¶30-160)
- it must be possible to conclude that a participant in the scheme did so for the purpose (determined objectively) of enabling one or more taxpayers to obtain a tax benefit in connection with the scheme (¶30-170).

Part IVA applies if the conditions of s 177D are met. However, consequences flow from the application of Pt IVA only if and when the Commissioner makes a determination under s 177F to cancel tax benefits (¶30-180).

[FTR ¶81-195]

¶30-140 Is there a scheme?

To work out if Pt IVA applies, it is necessary to identify a ''scheme'' as defined in ITAA36 s 177A. A ''scheme'' means any agreement, arrangement, understanding, promise or undertaking — whether express or implied and whether legally enforceable or not — and any scheme, plan, proposal, course of action or course of conduct (ITAA36 s 177A). Anything done either alone or in association with another or others may constitute a scheme.

Schemes involving franking credit trading and dividend streaming, or franking credits and consolidation, are separately defined in ss 177EA (¶30-195) and 177EB, respectively. The Pt IVA consequences of those kinds of schemes are set out in those sections.

The role of artificial entities and their controllers may call for particular consideration. Where a company is concerned, the company itself will probably be a party, its purpose being determined by the collective purpose of its directors (or sometimes the shareholders). However, the directors individually may also be parties, if not otherwise than as a result of their involvement as directors. The role played by directors in discussions of the arrangement should be carefully considered.

A similar question may arise in relation to advisers, particularly when the client of the adviser is relatively unsophisticated and relies heavily on the skill and comprehension of the adviser. In such circumstances, the adviser may well be a party to the scheme.

The simple disposition of an income-producing asset by a natural person to a wholly-owned private company is not an arrangement to which ITAA36 Pt IVA will be applied. However, where there are other associated transactions, transfers or arrangements (whether antecedent or subsequent), the application of Pt IVA may need to be considered in that broader context (TD 95/4).

In any particular situation, it is likely that there will be a number of schemes that can be identified. For example, there may be a scheme involving a large number of the steps that were actually taken, and another scheme involving a fewer number of those steps. In *Peabody*, the High Court said that a set of circumstances will not constitute a scheme if they are incapable of standing on their own without being robbed of all practical meaning, although whether this is still the case as a result of the subsequent High Court decision in *Hart* (¶30-170) is uncertain. Unfortunately, there was no clear precedent arising from the 3 separate judgments in *Hart* as to the definition of ''scheme'', as noted by Hill J at first instance in *Macquarie Finance*.

On appeal to a court against a Pt IVA determination, the Commissioner is entitled to put his case in alternative ways. If, within a wider scheme which has been identified, the Commissioner also seeks to rely on a sub-scheme as meeting the requirements of Pt IVA, the Commissioner may rely on it as well as the wider scheme. The ability to isolate sub-schemes to which Pt IVA can apply may make it easier to assert that a scheme was entered into for the sole or dominant purpose of obtaining a tax benefit.

In *British American Tobacco Australia Services Limited*, the Full Federal Court held the relevant scheme included the transfer of assets between related companies, the making of a CGT roll-over election by the first company and sale of the assets outside of the group by the second company which used significant capital losses to offset the capital gain. The effect of the scheme was to reduce tax by shifting a profit into a related company that could offset tax losses against it on ultimate sale. The court rejected an argument that the scheme was limited to the making of the CGT roll-over election as it would have opened the possibility that Pt IVA did not apply by virtue of s 177C(2A).

[FTR ¶81-200, ¶81-303]

¶30-160 Was a tax benefit obtained?

There must be a "tax benefit" in connection with a scheme for Pt IVA to apply (s 177D). Establishing a tax benefit is a 2-step enquiry (s 177C). First, a taxpayer must have achieved at least one of the following beneficial outcomes from the scheme:

- an amount is not included in assessable income (s 177C(1)(a))
- a deduction is allowable (s 177C(1)(b))
- a capital loss is incurred by the taxpayer (s 177C(1)(ba))
- a foreign income tax offset is allowable (s 177C(1)(bb)), or
- withholding tax is not payable on an amount (s 177C(1)(bc)).

Second, it must be established that the beneficial tax outcome would not have happened, or it is reasonable to expect that it would not have happened, if the scheme had not been entered into or carried out. So, for example, a tax benefit may be obtained by a taxpayer if an amount is not included in the taxpayer's assessable income which would have been or might reasonably be expected to have been included if the scheme had not been entered into or carried out (ITAA36 s 177C(1)(a)).

The prediction about events which would have taken place if the relevant scheme had not been entered into or carried out is known as the alternative postulate or the counterfactual. The prediction must be sufficiently reliable for it to be regarded as reasonable (*Peabody*).

Before the amendments to Pt IVA that apply on and from 16 November 2012 (¶30-110), the courts had interpreted the requirements in s 177C(1) that a tax effect "would have" or "might reasonably be expected" to have happened, as a composite phrase representing a range of certainty or likelihood of the alternative postulate. However, the amendments applying on and from 16 November 2012 are intended to have the effect that the "would have" and "might reasonably be expected to have" limbs in the paragraphs of s 177C(1) are *alternative bases* upon which the existence of a tax benefit can be established. Further, there are rules for working out when and how a tax benefit is established under the 2 limbs (s 177CB).

The "would have" limb

A decision, for example, that an amount "would have" been included in assessable income if the scheme had not been entered into or carried out, must be made solely on the basis of a postulate comprising all of the events or circumstances that actually happened or existed, other than those that form part of the scheme (s 177CB(2)). This is described in the relevant explanatory memorandum (EM) as the "annihilation approach". When postulating what would have occurred in the absence of the scheme, the scheme must be assumed not to have happened, ie it must be ''annihilated'' or extinguished. Cases that appear to have been decided on the basis of this approach to the first limb include the Full Federal Court decisions *Puzey* (2003) and *Sleight* (2004).

The "might reasonably be expected to have" limb

A decision, for example, that a deduction ''might reasonably be expected not to have been allowable'' if the scheme had not been entered into or carried out, must be made on the basis of a postulate that is a reasonable alternative to the scheme (s 177CB(3)). Whether a postulate is a reasonable alternative to a scheme must be worked out having particular regard to the substance of the scheme and its results and consequences for the taxpayer, and disregarding any potential tax results and consequences.

This is referred to in the relevant EM as the ''reconstruction approach''. The EM states that a reconstruction approach is a way to identify a tax benefit in relation to a scheme that also achieves substantive non-tax results and consequences. In these cases, simply annihilating the scheme would be inconsistent with the non-tax results and consequences sought by the participants in the scheme.

▶ **Example 1** (based on the EM to the amending Bill)

Mr and Mrs H want to borrow money to acquire both a family home and a holiday house that they plan to rent to holidaymakers. They borrow the money under an arrangement in which the repayments are applied exclusively to the borrowing in relation to the family home. The result is that the deductible interest payments are increased for the holiday home borrowing and the non-deductible interest payments for the family home borrowing are minimised.

Merely annihilating the scheme would not leave a sensible result because there would be no borrowing at all, so some reconstruction is necessary. It is therefore necessary to consider what might reasonably be expected to have happened if the scheme had not been entered into. A reasonable alternative in this case might be that Mr and Mrs H took out 2 loans, one for each of the homes they wished to acquire, each of which was entered into on normal commercial terms.

Examining the substance of a scheme requires a consideration of its commercial and economic substance as distinct from its legal form or shape. Where a scheme forms part of a broader commercial transaction, a postulate would be a reasonable alternative to the scheme if it performed the same role in relation to the broader transaction as the scheme itself performs, disregarding its tax effects. If a scheme is integral to a broader transaction in the sense that it is intertwined with it and facilitates it in some way, then it would be reasonable for an alternative postulate to involve a reconstruction of the broader transaction, so long as that produces the same non-tax results and consequences as were in fact achieved by the broader transaction.

▶ **Example 2** (based on the EM to the amending Bill)

Assume that in order for Kerry to secure a tax deduction for borrowing money to invest in an offshore company (Offshore Co) it is necessary for her to interpose a resident Australian company. She does this by using the borrowed funds to buy shares in an Australian shelf company (Oz Co). In turn, Oz Co buys ordinary shares in Offshore Co. Oz Co performs no other role.

The Commissioner makes a Pt IVA determination on the basis that the interposition of Oz Co is a scheme to which Pt IVA applies. Objectively viewed, the interposition of Oz Co achieves 2 effects. One is securing a deduction for interest on the borrowing, and the other is the acquisition of shares in Offshore Co.

A correct alternative postulate should be another way in which Kerry could reasonably be expected to have acquired ordinary shares in Offshore Co. An alternative postulate that involved Kerry lending the borrowed monies to Offshore Co would achieve a different effect. So too would be a postulate that involved Kerry investing the borrowed monies in a completely different company.

Potential tax liabilities are not to be taken into account in assessing the likelihood or reasonableness of any alternative postulate. As a result, an alternative course of action cannot be rejected on the basis that the tax costs involved in undertaking it would have caused the parties to do nothing, including deferring or abandoning a wider transaction of which the scheme was a part (see, eg *RCI*).

A tax benefit may arise if the effect of a scheme is that an amount is assessable under a different provision, or is differently characterised, thus altering its tax treatment (IT 2456).

Exclusion for tax benefits arising from making agreements, choices, etc

Tax benefits obtained as a result of the making of an agreement, choice, declaration, election, selection, notification or option which is expressly provided for in ITAA36 or ITAA97 are not caught by Pt IVA, provided the relevant scheme was not entered into for the purpose of creating the preconditions necessary for making the relevant agreement, choice, etc (s 177C(2)). Thus, the mere fact that a taxpayer takes advantage of the option in ITAA97 s 70-45 for valuing trading stock on hand at the end of a year at cost price, market selling price or replacement price will not attract Pt IVA.

There is an exception to this where the tax benefit consists of the incurring of a capital loss. In this case, the exemption does not apply if the loss is attributable to an agreement etc, to roll over an asset under the group company provisions, or to transfer a group company loss, and this forms part of a wider scheme.

In one case, a taxpayer argued that ITAA36 offered him a choice of conducting his affairs either as an employee or as a consultant to a family company/family trust. The AAT held that the fact that ITAA36 recognises entities such as trusts does not mean that the choice of the trust mechanism for income-splitting was ‘‘expressly provided for’’ (*Case W58*).

Cases about tax benefits

The cases about tax benefits in the following commentary were decided based on Pt IVA before it was amended with effect from 16 November 2012 (¶30-110).

In *Peabody* (1994), the High Court set out what is required, when considering what might ‘‘reasonably be expected’’ to have happened in the absence of a Pt IVA scheme. A reasonable expectation requires more than a possibility and the prediction must be ‘‘sufficiently reliable for it to be regarded as reasonable’’. In *Peabody*, Pt IVA did not apply. The Commissioner could not establish an alternative postulate under which the taxpayer would have received the amount on which she was assessed if the scheme in question had not been implemented.

In *Spotless* (1996), the High Court held that Pt IVA applied to a scheme to invest surplus funds in the Cook Islands to derive interest income that would have been exempt from Australian income tax. It found that if the scheme had not been entered into, the ‘‘reasonable expectation’’ was that an amount would have been included in the taxpayer’s assessable income as a result of investing the funds in Australia. The Commissioner identified the tax benefit as the actual amount of overseas interest, less withholding tax, rather than the higher amount of ‘‘notional’’ Australian interest. It appears that the court considered the notional amount more accurately reflected the tax benefit but it ruled that the Commissioner’s quantification was not adverse to the taxpayer and there was no alteration of the amount.

In a number of recent cases, the taxpayer has successfully challenged the application of Pt IVA on the basis that the Commissioner could not establish the existence (and/or the amount) of a tax benefit by reference to a reasonable alternative postulate. The cases, including *AXA Asia Pacific Holdings* (2010), *RCI* (2011) and *Futuris* (2012), prompted the amendments to Pt IVA that apply on and from 16 November 2012 (¶30-110). The Commissioner believes that the introduction of s 177CB into Pt IVA has significantly altered the framework of the tax benefit test in s 177C(1), to the extent that cases such as *AXA* should be treated with extreme caution when applied to the current version of Pt IVA (ATO *Decision Impact Statement on FCT v AXA*).

RCI was a company involved in a complicated restructure of the international James Hardie group. The Commissioner identified a scheme for Pt IVA purposes under which the market value of shares held by RCI were reduced by the payment of a dividend. As a result, on a later transfer of the shares, the capital gain was less than it would otherwise have been in the absence of the scheme. The Full Federal Court found that there was no tax benefit because RCI would not have transferred the shares and participated in the restructure if the costs of doing so, including the tax costs, were unacceptably high. It was a reasonable alternative postulate that RCI would have done nothing, meaning that no amount would have been included in its assessable income.

In *Futuris* (2012), the Commissioner unsuccessfully tried to apply Pt IVA to a series of steps that occurred in anticipation of the sale of the Futuris group's building products division. The scheme had the effect of reducing the amount of net capital gain assessable. The Full Federal Court accepted that Futuris could not have been expected to carry out the float in the way postulated by the Commissioner because it would have generated significant tax costs and was not commercially feasible. Futuris produced expert evidence of what its commercial options were if it had not entered the scheme. It discharged its onus of proving the amended assessment excessive by putting forward a credible alternative postulate to the Commissioner's counterfactual.

In the course of litigation that led to *Futuris* (2012), the Federal Court refused Futuris' application for the Commissioner to provide particulars as to what the taxpayer might have done had it not entered the scheme, as that was not consistent with the taxpayer's burden of proving the Pt IVA assessment excessive (*Futuris* (2009)).

AXA Asia Pacific Holdings (2010) concerned the sale by the taxpayer of a wholly owned subsidiary to a third party and the effectiveness of CGT rollover relief. The Full Federal Court held that no tax benefit arose because the Commissioner's alternatives to the scheme were not reasonable.

By contrast, Pt IVA applied to the taxpayer in a case involving the disposal of assets to a third party in a way that minimised CGT (*British American Tobacco Australia*). The scheme involved an internal sale of assets within the group and a CGT rollover before sale to the third party. The Full Federal Court accepted the reasonableness of the Commissioner's alternative hypothesis which was a direct sale of assets by the taxpayer to the third party, generating an assessable capital gain.

In *Lenzo* (2008), a case involving an investment by an individual in a forestry managed investment scheme, the Full Federal Court held that a taxpayer can satisfy the onus of showing that he/she has not obtained a tax benefit in connection with a scheme if: (a) he/she would have undertaken or might reasonably be expected to have undertaken a particular activity in lieu of the scheme; and (b) the activity would or might reasonably be expected to have resulted in an allowable deduction of the same kind as the deduction claimed by the taxpayer in consequence of the scheme.

Part IVA applied to deny deductions for payments made to an ''employee welfare fund'' established by an employer for the benefit of employees (*Trail Bros Steel & Plastics Pty Ltd*). An employer stopped making contributions to a self managed superannuation fund on behalf of the employees and instead made payments to the fund, after a change in the law limiting the amount of deductible contributions that could be made to a superannuation fund. The Full Federal Court affirmed the Commissioner's Pt IVA determination, disallowing deductions for the substituted payments. The court did not accept the taxpayer's contention that if the scheme had not been entered into and the payments had not been made to the fund, the taxpayer would have made deductible payments to its employees in some other way.

However, the court considered that, if the scheme had not been carried out, it was reasonable to conclude the employer would have made deductible payments up to the amount of deductible contributions that could have been made to a superannuation fund. In that case, the *amount* of the tax benefit was not the full amount of the deduction claimed but the difference between it and the deductible superannuation contributions.

In *Grollo Nominees*, the Full Federal Court ruled that Pt IVA can apply to a trustee although the relevant tax benefit accrued to beneficiaries of the trust.

[FTR ¶81-210, ¶81-330]

¶30-170 What was the dominant purpose?

In order for the general anti-avoidance provisions to apply, it must be able to be concluded that at least one person who entered into or carried out the scheme did so for the sole or dominant purpose of obtaining a tax benefit (ITAA36 ss 177A(5); 177D). In determining this, the Commissioner must take into account the following 8 matters listed in s 177D(2):

(a) the manner in which the scheme was entered into or carried out

(b) the form and substance of the scheme

(c) the time at which the scheme was entered into and the length of the period during which it was carried out

(d) the income tax result that, but for Pt IVA, would be achieved by the scheme

(e) any change in the financial position of the relevant taxpayer that has resulted, will result, or may reasonably be expected to result, from the scheme

(f) any change in the financial position of any person who has, or has had, any connection (whether of a business, family or other nature) with the relevant taxpayer, being a change that has resulted, will result, or may reasonably be expected to result, from the scheme

(g) any other consequence for the relevant taxpayer, or for any person referred to in (f), of the scheme having been entered into or carried out

(h) the nature of any connection (whether of a business, family or other nature) between the relevant taxpayer and any person referred to in (f).

Relevant cases

Each of the 8 matters involves an objective finding of fact (*Spotless*). The parties' subjective intentions are certainly not decisive. In fact, it may well be that they are irrelevant (*CC (NSW) Pty Ltd (in liq)*; *Eastern Nitrogen*; *Vincent*).

Although each of the 8 matters must be considered, it is not necessary that they be unbundled from a global consideration of purpose and "slavishly ticked off" (*Consolidated Press Holdings*).

The time for testing the dominant purpose is ordinarily when the scheme was entered into or carried out, and by reference to the law as it then stood (*Consolidated Press Holdings*). It is no defence that the taxpayer is either innocent or ignorant.

It is not necessary that all, a majority, or even any 2, of the parties to the scheme in question should have the relevant dominant purpose. It is enough that just one of them has the purpose, even if that party conceals it from the others. Where parties enter into a scheme on the advice of professional advisers, the objective purpose of those advisers may be attributed to the parties (*Consolidated Press Holdings*). The purpose of a scheme promoter and the entities that it controls may also be taken into account (*Vincent*; ¶18-020).

It is not necessary that the person with the relevant purpose be the taxpayer who obtains the benefit. Indeed, the taxpayer obtaining the benefit need not be a party to the scheme at all.

The fact that a transaction represents a rational commercial decision does not mean that there cannot also be a dominant purpose to obtain a tax benefit within Pt IVA. In *Spotless*, the High Court denied that there was a dichotomy between commercial and tax decisions, pointing out that: "A particular course of action may be . . . both 'tax driven' and bear the character of a rational commercial decision. The presence of the latter characteristic does not determine the answer to the question whether . . . [there was a] 'dominant purpose' of enabling the taxpayer to obtain a 'tax benefit' ". In concluding that the companies' dominant purpose was to obtain a tax benefit, the court equated dominant purpose with the "most influential, and prevailing or ruling purpose". Thus, for example, if there are 3 purposes of a scheme, one of which is to obtain a tax benefit, the dominant purpose requirement will arguably be satisfied if the most influential purpose is to obtain a tax benefit even if, by itself, it is less than 50% of the overall purpose.

In *Hart*, the High Court held that Pt IVA applied to split loan arrangements and denied the taxpayers a deduction for the extra interest on the investment loan. Under the taxpayers' split loan arrangements, their home and investment loans were combined. They could direct loan repayments to their home loan while allowing interest to capitalise on the investment loan. This increased the interest on the investment loan, while allowing the interest payable on the home loan to be reduced. Although all 5 judges took the view that the dominant purpose of the split loan arrangements was to obtain tax benefits, there was no clear majority among the judges in the reasoning adopted to arrive at that conclusion. For a detailed analysis of the *Hart* decision, see CCH *Tax Week*¶488 (2004).

Examples of other cases in which a dominant purpose of obtaining a tax benefit was found to exist include *CC (NSW) Pty Ltd (in liq)* and *Clough Engineering*, both of which involved schemes implemented to make use of otherwise inaccessible losses; and *Hart*, a scheme which purported to convert a solicitor's practice income into a loan. Part IVA was also held to apply to deny claims for interest deductions under a mass-marketed tax scheme involving limited recourse loans, where there was a low likelihood of any commercial returns (*Howland-Rose* (the *"Budplan" case*)); to deny deductions in 3 Budplan projects (*Brody*); to deny deductions for the grossly inflated cost of seedlings under a sandalwood plantation scheme (*Puzey*); to deny deductions for a taxpayer's investment in a tea-tree project (*Sleight*; *Calder*; *Princi*; *Carter*); to deny deductions for management fees (*Tolich*); to deny a deduction for a prepayment of $15 million into an employee benefit trust (*Pridecraft*); to a marine pilot's arrangements to use a company to provide his personal services (*Case 2/2004*); to deny a capital loss generated by a share transfer (*Cumins*); to include a capital gain generated by a share transfer (*Walters*), and to deny deductions from investing in a eucalyptus oil project (*Clampett*), a wine grape project (*Macpherson*; *Iddles*), a managed investment project (*Burrows*), a managed agricultural project (*Forward*), an aloe vera project (*Barham*), an olive growing project (*O'Brien*) and a sandalwood plantation project (*Lenzo*). However, in *Cooke*, a horticultural scheme case, it was held that Pt IVA did not apply as the dominant purpose was to generate income for the taxpayer's retirement.

Business restructures and reorganisations

In *News Australia Holdings*, Pt IVA did not apply to a tax benefit which arose from a global corporate restructure because the dominant purpose of the arrangement was a commercial one. In particular, the dominant purpose of the share buy-back aspect of the scheme in question was to avoid a sandwiching of 2 Australian companies between 2 US companies). It did not follow that merely because a taxpayer took taxation considerations into account in selecting one form of transaction over another, any tax benefit which resulted from the choice was within Pt IVA. The *News Australia* decision is analysed in

CCH *Tax Week*¶1057 (2009). The Commissioner could not establish a dominant purpose of obtaining a tax benefit in a case involving a complex restructuring of a multinational group that included Australian subsidiaries (*Noza Holdings*, Federal Court).

The profitable resale by an investment bank of a minority interest in a mining company in a way that reduced the taxable profit was not motivated by tax avoidance (*Macquarie Bank Limited*). After an offer by Macquarie Bank Limited (MBL) to acquire the minority interest from a US private equity firm was rejected, the parties agreed on a scheme under which MBL acquired the mining company indirectly through a corporate structure that became part of the MBL consolidated group. The Commissioner challenged the scheme under Pt IVA on the basis that MBL had used the consolidation provisions of Pt 3-90 to engineer a smaller tax profit on the ensuing sale of the mining company. This could happen because of the way the consolidation rules allocated the cost of the acquisition of the subsidiary to the tax cost setting amount of the asset (the mining company) disposed of by the subsidiary. By majority, the Full Federal Court found that no tax benefit arose in connection with the relevant scheme and, even if a tax benefit had existed, there was no dominant purpose of enabling it to be obtained.

The dominant purpose of a series of transactions within a large company group that involved intra-group loans, interest payments and bad debt write-offs was refinancing for asset protection, not tax minimisation (*Ashwick*, Full Federal Court). However, the Federal Court found that Pt IVA applied to an inter-company loan arrangement that generated tax deductions for interest in Australia and used up significant tax losses in the US (*Orica*; TA 2016/10).

A scheme had 2 principal commercial purposes: (i) it permitted the taxpayer to obtain an indemnity against health risks that otherwise was not available to it; and (ii) it provided a number of commercial advantages, including more efficient risk management (*WD & HO Wills (Australia)*). Although there were possible tax advantages, these were not at the forefront of the parties' minds, and the proposal still made commercial sense even if they were disregarded. The tax advantages were incidental to the principal objectives of the scheme and Pt IVA was not attracted.

Part IVA did not apply to an investment consultant acting as an agent for stockbroking firms who conducted his business through a family trust (*Mochkin*). Although the structure used by the taxpayer had tax advantages, these were subsidiary to the dominant purpose of obtaining protection from the very real risk of personal liability.

For obiter comments on the application of Pt IVA after the *Spotless* and *Hart* decisions, see the Full Federal Court decision in *Macquarie Finance*. An analysis of the *Macquarie Finance* decision is given at CCH *Tax Week*¶828 (2005). In the New Zealand High Court case of *Westpac Banking Corporation v C of IR, High Court Auckland, CIV 2005-404-2843*, the question was whether a bank could claim a deduction for a guarantee procurement fee paid to another subsidiary of the group of companies. The court held that each relevant transaction had a genuine commercial purpose but also a separate purpose of tax avoidance that was not merely incidental or subsidiary to the commercial purpose. There was no "objectively ascertainable business purpose" served by the payment of the fee. The court was in no doubt that the function of the fee was to generate a statutory deduction for an expense that appeared genuine but was actually a contrivance.

Part IVA applied to a complex set of cross-border financing transactions, resulting in the cancellation of foreign tax credits claimed by the taxpayer (*Citigroup*, Full Federal Court). Citigroup, in partnership with a subsidiary company, subscribed for bonds issued in Hong Kong and immediately sold the interest and principal entitlements under the bonds. Hong Kong tax was paid on the gross proceeds on the sale of the coupons. In Australia, Citigroup returned the Hong Kong profit in the year the bonds were purchased as assessable income and claimed foreign tax credits for the Hong Kong tax paid. The court held Citigroup's dominant purpose was to obtain the foreign tax credits in Australia.

Splitting personal exertion income

Part IVA has been applied to various arrangements involving the splitting of personal exertion income. Although specific statutory limitations have applied since 1 July 2000 (¶30-600), Pt IVA continues to have potential application (¶30-690).

Application of Pt IVA: Commissioner's view

The Commissioner has issued extensive guidance and opinion on the application of Pt IVA to specific transactions. The following information is organised under the broad categories of schemes benefiting individuals, loans, leasing and other financial transactions and companies, shares and other securities.

Schemes benefiting individuals

Part IVA may be applied to schemes involving the creation of tax benefits for employees, including: fringe benefits such as cars provided by service or service/administration companies for the private use of employees (IT 2494); an employee benefit trust arrangement, where bonus units are issued to employees and neither ITAA97 s 6-5 nor 15-2 apply (TR 2010/6); an employee savings plan, where an employer contributes what would otherwise be salary or wages to a benefits trust and the employee receives bonus units (TD 2010/10); and a salary deferral arrangement as described in TD 2010/11.

Schemes involving professionals and their legal structures include: service arrangements with unusual features (eg the service fees are excessive (TR 2006/2)); a professional person's practice company makes no attempt to distribute income or it holds unacceptable investments (IT 2503); schemes involving professional services providers earning personal services income who enter into a partnership with unrelated taxpayers. Income is re-characterised as partnership income to enable the taxpayer to split the income with a spouse or related party (TD 2002/24); schemes to claim deductions for purported partnership losses claimed to have been incurred as a result of entering into prepaid service warrant arrangements (TD 2003/9). The ATO has published a guide on its website *Your service entity arrangements* to assist professional firms in determining whether fees paid under their service arrangements are tax deductible.

Schemes involving individuals in business include: incentives given to enter into a lease of business premises (IT 2631: ¶10-116, ¶16-650); large deductions claimed for internet marketing expenses paid to tax-haven based marketers (TD 2002/23; ¶16-725); and deductions claimed by a retailer for volume allowances contributed to a mutual association (TR 2004/5).

Trusts may be used as a vehicle for delivering tax benefits of the following kinds: a deduction for interest claimed as part of an uncommercial trust arrangement (TD 2009/17); capital gains streamed to a beneficiary where there is a deliberate mismatch between trust income entitlements and amounts actually taxable (TA 2013/1); and deductions claimed under certain home loan unit trust arrangements (TR 2002/18). The arrangement in TR 2002/18 involves borrowing to acquire units in a unit trust that acquires a private residence and leases it to the taxpayer. The unit trust claims deductions for property outgoings and the taxpayer claims deductions for interest on borrowings.

Professional firms and Pt IVA

Until 14 December 2017, the ATO website contained materials and guidelines, titled *Assessing the risk: allocation of profits within professional firms*, to help taxpayers assess the risk of Pt IVA applying to the allocation of profits from a professional firm carried on through a partnership, trust or company. As a result of a review of the guidelines, the ATO advised that they did not apply after 13 December 2017 and they would be revised and replaced after consultation with stakeholders.

The withdrawn guidelines set out how the ATO would assess the risk of Pt IVA applying to allocation of profits within a professional firm, from 30 June 2015. In particular, the ATO had formed the view that Pt IVA could apply to an Everett assignment (¶5-160), unless certain benchmarks were met for it to be rated low risk.

The ATO believes that the guidance material was being misinterpreted in relation to arrangements that went beyond its scope. It also identified arrangements exhibiting high risk factors not specifically addressed within the materials, including the use of related party financing and SMSFs.

Taxpayers who entered into arrangements before 14 December 2017 which comply with the guidelines and do not exhibit any of the high risk factors can continue to rely on the suspended guidelines for the year ending 30 June 2020. Such arrangements which do not exhibit high risk factors will not be reviewed but those exhibiting any of the high risk factors may be subject to review. Individual professional practitioners contemplating entering into new arrangements from 14 December 2017 are invited to contact the ATO.

Loans, leasing and other financial transactions

Part IVA may be applied to loan and financing schemes including: margin lending arrangements (IT 2513) or certain financing unit trust arrangements (IT 2512: ¶10-465); arrangements designed to provide a non-resident beneficiary with an entitlement to interest income earned by a resident trust estate from associates (IT 2344; IT 2466); an "investment loan interest payment arrangement" where the subjective purpose is "to pay off a home loan sooner" (TD 2012/1); and schemes under which an Australian lender seeks to convert otherwise assessable interest income from a non-resident borrower into non-assessable non-exempt dividends (TD 2011/22).

Leasing schemes that may be attacked by Pt IVA include: certain forms of leveraged leasing (IT 2051) or equity leasing (IT 2169); cross border equipment leasing arrangements structured to avoid withholding tax on royalty or interest payments (TR 98/21); and sale and leaseback arrangements where appropriate values are not used, eg in respect of the sale price of the asset, the lease payments, the residual value of the asset or any balancing adjustments (TR 2006/13: ¶23-240).

Part IVA may apply to arrangements where life policy premiums are paid by an employer on behalf of an employee with the expectation that the employee will obtain the amounts paid as premiums shortly after they are paid (TD 92/164); and where premiums are paid under arrangements known as "financial insurance" and "financial reinsurance" (TR 96/2).

Financial transactions that have tax-driven features to which Pt IVA may apply include: an asymmetric swap scheme — typically 2 swap transactions entered into between an Australian resident company and an unrelated non-resident counterparty (TD 2010/12); a non-arm's length disposal of a traditional security (eg an assignment to a related party) (TR 96/14); and wash sale arrangements used to minimise CGT (TR 2008/1: ¶11-250).

Other targeted transactions in this category include: tax benefit transfer arrangements involving the licensing of intellectual property (TR 2002/19); the use of interposed entities to transform plant expenditure into R&D expenditure for the purpose of the R&D concession in ITAA36 former s 73B (TR 2002/1); film schemes involving claims by taxpayers with no or limited commercial exposure to the success or failure of the film (TR 2002/13; *Case 2/2002*); and R&D arranged on a syndicated basis that is not bona fide (IT 2635).

Companies, shares and other securities

The kinds of schemes and arrangements that may be targeted by Pt IVA in this category include: distribution of the accumulated profits of a private company in a substantially tax-free form under a dividend access share arrangement (TD 2014/1); deductions claimed for payments made under certain stapled security arrangements (TR

2002/16); CGT reduction arrangements involving the disposal of a CGT asset by a corporate group to an unrelated third party (TD 2003/3); a profit-washing arrangement involving a chain of trusts and a loss company (TD 2005/34); a New Zealand based foreign discretionary trust provides services at a mark-up to an Australian resident business (TR 2005/14); a deduction claimed under s 70B of ITAA36 on the sale of certain stapled securities involving notes and preference shares (TD 2009/14); the restructuring of a multinational conglomerate including Australian subsidiaries that involved generating interest deductions under ITAA97 ss 25-85 and 25-90 — the main purpose was to utilise the capacity of the Australian group to decrease the overall tax liability of the international group (ATO ID 2012/50); and deductions generated from the purchase of offshore "emission units" that are not legitimately generated through offshore carbon reduction activities (TA 2012/6).

The ATO expects that businesses may have undertaken restructuring in anticipation of the hybrid mismatch rules that apply from 1 January 2019 (¶22-640). The ATO has released views on how Pt IVA could apply to restructures to preserve Australian tax benefits that would otherwise be disallowed (PCG 2018/7).

Part IVA may apply to certain schemes involving an election to consolidate (¶8-950) and also to certain thin capitalisation situations (¶22-700). For the application of Pt IVA to an assignment of an interest in a partnership, see ¶5-160.

Taxpayer alerts

The ATO issues "taxpayer alerts" to give early warning of significant new and emerging tax planning arrangements that it has under risk assessment (PS LA 2008/15). The subjects of some of the alerts are later examined in taxation determinations or rulings. Taxpayer alerts are available on the ATO website.

[FTR ¶81-235, ¶81-345]

¶30-180 Cancellation of tax benefits

If a taxpayer obtains a tax benefit in connection with a scheme to which ITAA36 Pt IVA applies, the Commissioner is authorised to take the following actions:

- if the tax benefit relates to an amount not being included in assessable income — determine that the whole or part of that amount is assessable
- if the tax benefit relates to a deduction or foreign tax credit not being allowable — determine that the whole or part of that deduction or credit be disallowed
- if the tax benefit relates to the incurring of a capital loss — determine that the whole or part of the loss was not incurred
- if the tax benefit relates to withholding tax on an amount — determine that the taxpayer is subject to withholding tax on the whole of that amount (ITAA36 s 177F).

For specific provisions for counteracting benefits under franking credit schemes, see ¶30-195.

Where the Commissioner makes such a determination, he is required to take such action as is considered necessary to give effect to it.

Section 177F gives no clear guidance as to *when* a determination may be made. In *Jackson*, the Full Federal Court held that the Commissioner cannot raise Pt IVA for the first time after the lodging of an appeal, as this would substantially change the nature of the matters at issue. The appropriate action is to issue an amended assessment to give effect to a Pt IVA determination.

The Full Federal Court held (in *BHP Billiton Finance*) that the Commissioner's Pt IVA determination to cancel a tax benefit was valid in circumstances where the Commissioner issued an assessment to disallow the taxpayer's bad debt deductions but did not make a Pt IVA determination at that time. Later, in the course of considering the taxpayer's objection to the assessment, the Commissioner made a Pt IVA determination but did not give effect to it by issuing an amended assessment. The court said the determination was valid and the Commissioner was entitled to rely on ITAA36 s 169A(3) (relevantly, a Pt IVA determination made when considering an objection to an assessment is deemed to be made when the assessment was made).

Where the tax benefit relates to a deduction being allowable, it is not necessary for the Commissioner to actually allow the deduction before cancelling it by the issue of a determination (*Dan & Ors*).

If the Commissioner does not make a determination but, on the facts, such a determination is appropriate, it is open to the AAT to make the determination (*Fletcher*). The AAT must give the taxpayer a fair opportunity of presenting a case against the application of Pt IVA (*Fletcher*). In *Fabry*, the taxpayer was unsuccessful in claiming that the Commissioner's powers under Pt IVA were spent once the matter was referred to the AAT. The Federal Court does not have a similar discretionary power to make such a determination (¶28-080).

Consolidated groups

The Commissioner may give effect to a s 177F determination made in respect of a subsidiary member of a consolidated group by issuing an assessment or an amended assessment to it. Doing so is not inconsistent with the single entity rule in ITAA97 Div 701 (*Channel Pastoral*).

Compensating adjustments

Where the Commissioner cancels a tax benefit, he/she may make a "fair and reasonable" compensating adjustment in respect of *any* taxpayer to prevent injustice, eg double taxation, which might otherwise result from cancelling a tax benefit. However, in determining what is fair and reasonable, it is not permissible to make assumptions about what alternative transactions might have been entered into if there had been no scheme (*Egan*).

A taxpayer who considers that the Commissioner ought to make a compensating adjustment may request the Commissioner to make it. There is no time limit for the making of such a request. The Commissioner is required to consider the request and give the taxpayer a written decision. If dissatisfied with the Commissioner's decision, the taxpayer may object to it (¶28-000).

The Commissioner is authorised to amend an assessment *at any time* to give effect to a compensating adjustment. Decisions forming part of the process of making an amended assessment to give effect to Pt IVA are not subject to judicial review (¶28-180) (*Meredith*).

[FTR ¶81-252, ¶81-380]

¶30-190 Dividend stripping

ITAA36 Pt IVA contains a provision which is specifically directed at "dividend stripping" schemes. This provision applies where:

(1) as a result of a dividend stripping scheme, any property of the company is disposed of

(2) the Commissioner is of the opinion that the disposal of the property represents, wholly or in part, a distribution of profits (whether of the current, a past or a future accounting period) of the company, and

(3) if the profits represented by the disposal of the property had been paid as a dividend immediately before the scheme was entered into, it would be reasonable to expect that this would result in an amount being included in a taxpayer's assessable income (ITAA36 s 177E).

Where these conditions are satisfied, the scheme is taken to be a scheme to which Pt IVA applies. The taxpayer who would have been assessable on the payment of the notional dividend referred to in (3) above is taken to have obtained a tax benefit in connection with the scheme that is referable to the notional amount not being included in assessable income. The amount of the tax benefit is the notional amount.

The Commissioner may then make a determination to cancel the tax benefit in whole or in part and also, if the circumstances are appropriate, a determination to effect any compensating adjustment or adjustments that may be necessary (¶30-180).

Section 177E applies only to schemes that have the dominant purpose of tax avoidance. Ordinarily, this purpose is to enable the vendor shareholders to receive profits of the company in a substantially (if not entirely) tax-free form, thus avoiding tax that could be payable if the company's profits were paid as dividends to shareholders. Therefore, it did not apply where the dominant purpose was to carry out a complex corporate reorganisation, the sale of the shares was only incidental, and significant *assessable* capital gains were received (*Consolidated Press Holdings*).

The section applies not only to schemes ''by way of or in the nature of'' dividend stripping, but also to schemes that have ''substantially the effect'' of dividend stripping (see *Lawrence* and the article in CCH *Tax Week*¶35 (2009)). This is intended to catch schemes where the distribution by the company is not in the form of dividends, eg where an irrecoverable loan is made to associates of the purchaser.

An example of a dividend stripping scheme for the purposes of s 177E is given in TD 2014/1. Broadly, the arrangement involves accessing the tax-paid profits of a private company using dividend access shares, in a way that transfers the economic benefit of the company's profits to the original shareholder and his/her associates in a tax-free or substantially tax-free form.

[FTR ¶81-360]

¶30-195 Franking credit schemes

ITAA36 Pt IVA is also attracted where a scheme involving a disposition of shares is entered into with a purpose of enabling the taxpayer to obtain a franking credit benefit (ITAA36 s 177EA). Unlike the general provisions of Pt IVA, this provision does not depend on the formal identification of a ''tax benefit in connection with'' a scheme. It applies where:

- there is a disposal of shares or an interest in shares
- a franked dividend is paid
- the shareholder would or could reasonably be expected to receive franking credit benefits from the dividend, and
- having regard to specified circumstances, it would be concluded that a purpose of at least one of the participants was to obtain a franking credit benefit. It is not necessary that this purpose is the dominant purpose, but it is not sufficient that it is merely incidental.

In these circumstances, the Commissioner has a choice as to whether to debit the company's franking account or deny the franking credit benefit to the recipient of the dividend. This provision applies to dividends and distributions paid after 7.30 pm on 13 May 1997. It operates in association with other rules that are designed for companies preferentially streaming dividends to advantage certain shareholders (¶4-920). It also potentially applies to any scheme involving the issue of certain types of convertible notes (TR 2009/3).

The issue in *Mills* was whether there was a non-incidental purpose of enabling investors in stapled securities issued by a bank to obtain imputation benefits in the form of franked dividends. The High Court held that while there was a purpose of enabling taxpayers who became holders of the securities to obtain franking credits, that purpose was incidental to the Bank's purpose of raising capital. Therefore, s 177EA did not apply. The High Court reached a different conclusion to the Federal Court judge at first instance and the majority decision of the Full Federal Court.

The fact that the parties to a scheme made investment management decisions on a proper commercial basis and to achieve long-term commercial objectives did not mean that s 177EA could not apply (*Electricity Supply Industry Superannuation (Qld)*).

The Commissioner believes that s 177EA will generally apply to a dividend washing scheme of the kind described in TD 2014/10. Dividend washing occurs when a shareholder who places a relatively high value on franking credits (such as a superannuation fund or an income tax exempt not-for-profit entity) enters a series of transactions with a shareholder who places a lower value on franking credits (such as a non-resident), resulting in a transfer of the value of franking credits from the latter to the former.

An integrity rule in the imputation provisions limits, from 1 July 2013, an entity's ability to obtain the benefits of any additional franking credits received as a result of dividend washing (ITAA97 s 207-157: ¶4-975). In March 2016, the ATO stated that the application of s 207-157 to distributions on or after 1 July 2013 is expected to relieve the Commissioner from making determinations under s 177EA to target dividend washing (ATO statement on *Norman Superannuation Fund*). The AAT confirmed that a dividend washing scheme that took place after 1 July 2013 was caught both by ss 207-157 and 177EA (*Lynton*).

The ATO has warned that s 177EA may apply to a scheme in which a private company with accumulated profits channels franked dividends to a self managed superannuation fund (TA 2015/1). Section 177EA may also apply to arrangements where a company raises new capital to fund the payment of franked dividends (TA 2015/2). Artificial arrangements involving derivatives to access franking credits may infringe s 177EA and are under investigation by the ATO (TA 2020/5).

Franking credit schemes and consolidated groups

On the introduction of the consolidation regime (¶8-000), a specific anti-avoidance rule was targeted at schemes entered into with a purpose of enabling franking credits to be transferred from a subsidiary to a head company on consolidation (s 177EB).

Section 177EB applies to schemes entered into on or after 1 July 2002. It supplements the general franking credit trading rules in s 177EA by applying to the specific circumstances of the consolidation of a company within a corporate group. Section 177EB does not limit s 177EA, nor does s 177EA limit s 177EB (s 177EB(2)).

Section 177EB applies where:

(a) there is a scheme for the disposition of membership interests in an entity (called "the joining entity")

(b) as a result of this disposition the joining entity becomes a subsidiary member of a consolidated group

(c) a credit arises in the franking account of the head company of the group, and

(d) having regard to specified relevant circumstances, it would be concluded that any person involved in entering into or carrying out the scheme or any part of the scheme did so for a purpose (not necessarily the dominant purpose, but not an incidental purpose) of enabling the franking credit to arise in the head company's account.

If s 177EB applies, the Commissioner is authorised to make a determination to the effect that no franking credit arises in the franking account of the relevant head company.

[FTR ¶81-275, ¶81-370, ¶81-379/10]

¶30-200 Multinational tax avoidance

Section 177DA applies to artificial or contrived arrangements to avoid the attribution of business profits to a taxable permanent establishment in Australia. Known as the multinational anti-avoidance law (MAAL), the measure applies to tax benefits obtained on or after 1 January 2016 under both new and existing schemes if, in connection with a scheme, a non-resident entity:

- derives income from the making of a supply of goods or services to Australian customers, with an entity in Australia supporting that supply, and
- avoids the attribution of the income from the supply to a permanent establishment in Australia.

It must be reasonable to conclude that the division of activities between the non-resident entity, the Australian entity, and any other related parties has been designed to ensure that the relevant taxpayer is not deriving income from making supplies that would be attributable to an Australian permanent establishment. *Taxation Determination* TD 2018/12 discusses when activities undertaken in Australia are ''directly in connection with'' a supply by a foreign entity to an Australian customer.

The relevant taxpayer who entered into or carried out the scheme must have done so for a principal purpose of enabling a taxpayer to obtain a tax benefit with or without the reduction of other non-income tax liabilities under Australian law or under a foreign law. Special rules apply to determine if a foreign entity satisfies the conditions for the multinational anti-avoidance law to apply where supplies are made by a trust or partnership.

Where s 177DA applies, the Commissioner has the power to look through the scheme and apply the tax rules as if the non-resident had been making a supply through an Australian permanent establishment. This includes the business profits from the supply that would have been attributable to an Australian permanent establishment and obligations arising under royalty and interest withholding tax (for the relevant taxpayer or another taxpayer).

The measure only applies to a non-resident entity that is a ''significant global entity'' in the income year in which it sought to obtain a tax benefit under the scheme.

In addition, it only applies to non-residents that are or have a related entity or entities in their corporate structure that are subject to no corporate tax or a low corporate tax rate, either under the law of a foreign country or through preferential regimes.

Significant global entity

An entity is a significant global entity (SGE) for a period if it is a global parent entity with annual global income of AU$1 billion or more (ITAA97 Subdiv 960-U). It may also be a significant global entity if it is a member of a group of entities that are consolidated for accounting purposes, with the global parent entity of the group having annual global income of AU$1 billion or more.

From 1 July 2019, the definition of significant global entity was broadened so that it applies to groups of entities headed by an entity other than a listed company in the same way as it applies to groups headed by a listed company.

ATO rulings on s 177DA

The ATO has identified strategies being developed to avoid the MAAL that may not be legally effective and may trigger other anti-avoidance rules. It has issued taxpayer alerts focusing on a number of arrangements, including *Taxpayer Alert* TA 2016/11 (interposed partnership structures) and TA 2016/8 (artificial structures to avoid GST).

Law Companion Ruling LCR 2015/2 explains the conditions that must be satisfied for s 177DA to apply, including the principal purpose test (where there is a combined purpose of obtaining a tax benefit and reducing or deferring a liability to foreign tax). The ruling also provides examples of high risk and low risk scenarios and a checklist for assessing the potential application of the law.

[FTR ¶81-357; FITR ¶762-733]

¶30-205 Diverted profits tax

The diverted profits tax (DPT) gives the Commissioner power to deal with multinationals who transfer profits to offshore associates using arrangements carried out with a principal purpose of avoiding Australian tax. Under the DPT, a 40% tax rate will apply to tax benefits under a relevant scheme, derived in income years commencing on or after 1 July 2017.

The DPT is not self-activating; the Commissioner must make an assessment of liability. A taxpayer has a DPT liability (ITAA36 Pt IVA ss 177H to 177R) if:

- it is reasonable to conclude that a scheme (or a part of a scheme) was carried out for a principal purpose of, or for more than one principal purpose that includes a purpose of, enabling one or more taxpayers to obtain a DPT tax benefit, or both to obtain a tax benefit and reduce a foreign tax liability
- the relevant taxpayer is a significant global entity — ¶30-200
- the relevant taxpayer obtains a tax benefit in connection with a scheme involving a foreign associated entity, and
- the taxpayer is not on a list of excluded entities that includes managed investment trusts, foreign widely-held collective investment vehicles, foreign entities owned by a foreign government, complying superannuation funds and foreign pension funds.

However, the DPT will not apply if one of the following tests applies:

- the $25 million turnover test (a de minimis test applying to the Australian turnover of the relevant taxpayer and any associated entities that are part of the same significant global group)
- the sufficient foreign tax test (the increase in the foreign tax liability from the scheme is 80% or more of the reduction in the Australian tax liability), or
- the sufficient economic substance test (the income of each entity connected with the scheme reasonably reflects the economic substance of the entity's activities in connection with the scheme).

If the DPT applies to a scheme, the Commissioner may issue a DPT assessment to the relevant taxpayer within 7 years of issuing an original assessment. Tax is payable within 21 days of the assessment on the amount of the diverted profits at a penalty rate of 40%, plus an interest charge.

The DPT liability is not reduced by any foreign tax paid on the diverted profits. A franking credit will arise for DPT paid but it will be at the ordinary company tax rate, not the 40% DPT rate.

After receiving the DPT assessment, there will be a 12-month period of review to permit the taxpayer to convince the Commissioner to reduce the assessment by providing further information. The Commissioner may amend the DPT assessment to either increase or decrease the liability and it is also possible for the Commissioner to agree to an outcome that involves both a reduction in the DPT liability and an increase in an income tax assessment.

At the end of the 12-month period of review, the taxpayer will have 60 days to challenge the assessment by appealing to the Federal Court (not the AAT). However, generally, only evidence provided to the Commissioner during the period of review will be admissible in the court proceedings.

The ATO has issued administrative guidance on some of the DPT concepts, including exceptions to the DPT (LCR 2018/6). *Practical Compliance Guideline* PCG 2018/5, sets out the ATO's client engagement framework for the DPT. It outlines the ATO's approach to risk assessment and compliance activity when the DPT is identified as a potential area of concern. *Practice Statement*PS LA 2017/2 explains to ATO staff the administrative process for making a DPT assessment. Find more information on developments on the ATO website.

The ATO is reviewing cross-border transactions involving intangible assets (TA 2020/1); and cross-border arrangements that misrepresent the nature of direct foreign investment in Australian businesses as debt or equity interests (TA 2020/2). The arrangements under review may warrant the application of the transfer pricing provisions, the general anti-avoidance rules or the DPT.

For more information about the DPT, see CCH *Tax Week*¶191 (2017) and ¶918 (2016).

[FTR ¶81-357; FITR ¶762-733]

Tax Scheme Promoters

¶30-300 Measures to deter promotion of tax schemes

The consequences of non-compliance with tax laws, including the anti-avoidance provisions, fall on taxpayers. Generally, where non-compliance occurs, the tax laws operate to change the tax outcome for participants in transactions (eg by disallowing a deduction or deeming income to be earned, etc).

The promoter penalty laws in (TAA Sch 1 Div 290) target *promoters* of tax avoidance and tax evasion schemes, rather than the participants. A promoter may be subject to a civil penalty (fine), injunction or enforceable undertaking if:

- it or another entity is a promoter of a tax exploitation scheme, or
- it implements a scheme that has been promoted on the basis of conformity with a product ruling in a way that is materially different from the way it is described in the ruling.

Who is a promoter?

An entity (which includes an individual, a company, a partnership, an unincorporated association, a trust or a superannuation fund) is a promoter of a tax exploitation scheme if:

- it markets a scheme or otherwise encourages the growth of a scheme or interest in it
- the entity or an "associate" (ITAA36 s 318) receives (directly or indirectly) consideration in respect of marketing or encouraging the scheme, and
- it is reasonable to conclude that the promoter has had a substantial role in respect of marketing or encouraging the scheme (TAA Sch 1 s 290-60(1)).

A scheme is a tax exploitation scheme if, at the time the scheme is promoted, it is reasonable to conclude that an entity that entered into or carried out the scheme has a sole or dominant purpose of getting a ''scheme benefit'', and it is not reasonably arguable that the benefit is available under the tax laws (TAA Sch 1 s 290-65). The provisions cover schemes involving taxes such as income tax, GST and FBT and any impugned conduct occurring either in or outside Australia.

The Commissioner successfully applied to the Federal Court in 2013 to have penalties imposed on 2 promoters of a tax exploitation scheme under s 290-50(1) (*Ludekens*, Full Federal Court). Dr Ludekens and another person had marketed and implemented a tax exploitation scheme involving a number of elements that included them and others investing in ''woodlots'' in a forestry managed investment scheme and financing their arrangements by on-selling some of the woodlots to other groups of investors. All of the elements of s 290-50(1) were established. The promoters' efforts in convincing others to invest and in on-selling some investments constituted marketing of the scheme and were substantial. They received consideration in respect of the marketing that included commission for acquiring the woodlots and GST refunds from the ATO. They carried out the scheme with the dominant purpose of the participants getting tax benefits that were not reasonably arguable.

The Commissioner has successfully obtained civil penalty orders in the Federal Court against tax scheme promoters in other cases: *Barossa Vines* (managed investment schemes where the scheme actually carried out was materially different from the scheme described in a product ruling); *Arnold* (''highly artificial'' scheme to inflate tax deductions for charitable donations of medicines); *Bogiatto* (bogus R&D expenditure claims); and *Rowntree & Ors* (emissions reduction scheme).

An employee is not taken to have had a substantial role in respect of marketing or encouraging a scheme merely because he/she distributes information or material prepared by another entity (TAA Sch 1 s 290-60(3)).

A promoter may still be penalised if it uses another entity as a ''front'' for the promotion of a scheme with the aim of avoiding the promoter laws.

However, financial planners, tax agents, accountants, legal practitioners and others are not promoters if they merely provide independent and objective advice about a tax exploitation scheme, even if that advice provides alternative ways to structure a transaction, or sets out the tax risks of the alternatives (TAA Sch 1 s 290-60(2)).

Penalties and other sanctions

The Commissioner has the following options regarding penalties and sanctions:

(1) request the Federal Court of Australia to impose a civil penalty (a fine)

(2) seek an injunction to stop the promotion or implementation of a scheme in a way not conforming with a product ruling

(3) accept a voluntary undertaking from a promoter about the way in which schemes are promoted or implemented

(4) obtain a Federal Court order to restrain a breach of an undertaking, or any other order considered appropriate.

The maximum penalty the Federal Court can impose is the greater of: (a) 5,000 penalty units (¶29-000) for an individual or 25,000 penalty units for a body corporate; and (b) twice the consideration received or receivable, directly or indirectly, by the promoter or its associates in respect of the scheme (TAA Sch 1 s 290-50(4)). For a case in which the Federal Court considered the imposition of promoter penalties, see *Ludekens*.

Penalties do not apply to entities or their employees who are only peripherally involved in a contravention of the promoter penalties through giving advice or minor involvement in implementing the scheme. In addition, an entity is not liable for a penalty if:

- the conduct in respect of which the proceedings are instituted is due to a reasonable mistake of fact, or the act or default of another, or due to an accident or some other cause beyond the entity's control, if they took reasonable precautions and exercised due diligence to avoid the conduct, or
- a scheme treats the taxation law as applying in a way that agrees with a statement or advice given to the promoter or their agent by, or on behalf of, the Commissioner, or
- more than 4 years have passed since the entity last engaged in the relevant conduct. This mirrors the period for which *taxpayers* are at risk of scheme penalties (TAA Sch 1 s 290-55).

The ATO may refer registered tax agents to the Tax Practitioners Board where there is evidence that they are in breach of obligations under the *Tax Agent Services Act 2009*. The Board can deregister a practitioner who is penalised for promoting a tax exploitation scheme (¶32-050).

ATO guidelines

The ATO has issued PS LA 2008/7 (about promotion of tax exploitation schemes) and PS LA 2008/8 (about schemes involving product rulings) to explain how ATO officers administer the promoter penalty laws. The ATO has also published on its website the *Promoter penalty laws* guide to help tax advisers and any other intermediaries in the tax system to manage compliance risks, with a focus on promoter penalties.

[FTR ¶978-282/1]

Personal Services Income Regime

¶30-600 Summary of PSI regime

A special tax regime for personal services income (PSI) applies to prevent individuals from reducing their tax by alienating their PSI to an associated company, partnership, trust or individual, or by claiming inappropriate ''business'' deductions.

Where it applies, the PSI regime has the following main effects:

- PSI is included in the assessable income of the individual whose personal efforts or skills generated the income, notwithstanding that it may have been alienated to another interposed entity (¶30-610)
- there are restrictions on the deductions that may be claimed by the individual or interposed entity, so that they broadly correspond to the deductions available to employees, eg expenses relating to the individual's private residence, certain travel expenses and payments made to spouses or other associates (¶30-620, ¶30-630)
- interposed entities may have additional PAYG withholding obligations (¶26-280).

The PSI regime does not apply if:

- the income is not PSI
- the income is derived as an employee or office holder, or
- the income is derived as part of a personal services business (¶30-660).

Although the PSI regime is intended to level the playing field between an employee and a contractor who has PSI, it does not deem contractors to be employees and does not alter the legal relationship between the parties (ITAA97 s 84-10).

Relationship to general anti-avoidance rules

The PSI regime does not overrule the operation of the general anti-avoidance rules of ITAA36 Pt IVA (¶30-690).

[FITR ¶133-000]

¶30-610 Assessment of personal services income

Income which is **mainly** a reward for an individual's personal efforts or skills is the individual's *personal services income* (PSI), regardless of whether it is income of another entity (eg a company, trust, partnership or other individual), whether it is for doing work or producing a result or whether it is payable under a contract (ITAA97 s 84-5). Only individuals can have PSI.

Examples of PSI include salary or wages, income payable under a contract which is wholly or principally for the labour or services of a person, and income derived by consultants (eg computer consultants) from the exercise of personal expertise (*Fowler*). Payments made to an individual's personal service entity when he/she is not actually providing services can still be PSI (TD 2015/1). That could include annual or personal leave payments or gardening leave and retainer payments.

Personal services income does not include income that is mainly generated by the use of assets, the sale of goods, or a business structure.

The characterisation of income as PSI is a question of fact depending on the circumstances of each case, including the substance of the agreement under which services are provided. ''Mainly'' means more than half of the relevant amount of ordinary or statutory income. This requires the exercise of practical judgment as to whether the value contributed by the efforts or skills of the individual exceeds the value of all other inputs, such as the efforts of other workers, and the use of plant and equipment or machinery, or intellectual or other property (TR 2001/7).

A company, partnership or trust whose ordinary income or statutory income includes the PSI of one or more individuals is referred to as a *personal services entity* (PSE).

Subject to the following exceptions, an individual's PSI that is income of a PSE is included in the assessable income of the individual (ITAA97 s 86-15). This is called ''attribution'' (see further TR 2003/6). The exceptions are:

- the part of the PSE's income that is income from conducting a personal services business (¶30-660)
- amounts that are paid to the individual as employee salary or wages before the end of the 14th day after the PAYG payment period during which the amount became income of the entity
- exempt income of the PSE
- deductions of the PSE that are permitted to be offset against PSI.

If a personal services entity that is an Australian resident earns income that is the PSI of an individual who is a resident of a foreign country, the income is not assessable to the individual under ITAA97 s 6-10(5) (ID 2010/214). However, the Australian personal services entity is assessable on the foreign-sourced PSI.

The income of a *non-resident company* may be attributed to an Australian resident taxpayer under the PSI rules (*Russell*, Full Federal Court). The Australia–New Zealand DTA did not prevent the income being taxed both to the New Zealand company in New Zealand and to the taxpayer as PSI in Australia.

Offsetting the personal services entity's deductions against PSI

The amount of PSI included in the individual's assessable income may be reduced (but not below nil) by the amount of certain deductions to which the PSE is entitled (ITAA97 s 86-20). The reduction consists of 2 elements:

(1) deductions to which the PSE is entitled that are deductions relating to the PSI (this excludes entity maintenance deductions (¶30-630) and deductions for wages paid to the individual)

(2) the part (if any) of the PSE's entity maintenance deductions that exceeds the entity's *assessable* income from sources other than PSI. If the PSI is identified with more than one individual, any reduction for this element is apportioned to the individuals on a pro rata basis.

▶ Example

Interco has $200,000 of income that is the PSI of Louisa ($80,000) and Bruce ($120,000), as well as $10,000 of assessable income that is not PSI. Interco is entitled to deductions of $11,000 that relate directly to Louisa's PSI and $15,000 that relate to Bruce's PSI. Interco is entitled to entity maintenance deductions of $16,000.

$10,000 of the entity maintenance deductions must be allocated to Interco's other assessable income, leaving only $6,000 to be offset against the PSI which is assessable to Louisa and Bruce.

The entity maintenance offset apportionable to Bruce's PSI is:

$$\frac{\$120{,}000}{\$200{,}000} \times \$6{,}000 = \$3{,}600$$

The net PSI which is to be included in Bruce's assessable income is therefore:

Bruce's gross PSI		$120,000
Less:	Interco's deductions relating to Bruce's PSI	15,000
Less:	pro rata entity maintenance deductions	3,600
Amount to be included in Bruce's assessable income		$101,400

Similar calculations would be made for Louisa.

An individual is entitled to deduct a net PSI loss from other income. An individual can deduct an amount equal to the excess of the individual's "personal services deduction amount" over the individual's "unreduced personal services income". This excess (ie the net PSI loss) can be deducted from the individual's other income or, in the case where the individual's current income cannot absorb the loss, it can be carried forward and deducted against future income (ITAA97 s 86-27).

The individual's personal services deduction amount is the sum of:

- the amount of allowable PSE deductions relating to the individual's PSI
- the entity maintenance deductions less any non-PSI income of the PSE, if this amount is greater than zero (s 86-27(a)).

The individual's unreduced personal services income is the amount of personal services income that would have been included in the individual's assessable income if there had been no reduction under s 86-20 (s 86-27(b)).

The total amount of the deductions to which a PSE is entitled is reduced by the amount of any deduction that an individual, whose personal services income is income of the PSE for that income year, is entitled to under s 86-27 (ITAA97 s 86-87). This ensures that the PSE and individual cannot both deduct the net PSI loss.

Exclusion of PSI from a PSE's assessable income

To the extent that an individual's PSI is included in the individual's assessable income, the PSE is not taxed on that income, but is still entitled to the deductions that were offset against the individual's PSI in calculating the individual's assessable amount (ITAA97 s 86-30).

Later payments of or entitlements to the PSI are disregarded

Once PSI has been included in an individual's assessable income, the income will not be taxed again if the individual or an associate subsequently receives or becomes entitled to a share of that income (ITAA97 s 86-35).

Payments shortly after an income year

Where an individual performs services in the last PAYG period of an income year, and receives the relevant PSI as salary or wages before 15 July of the next income year, the PSI is treated as income received on 30 June of the year in which the services were performed. However, this will not change the time at which the PSE is treated as having paid the salary or wages for deduction purposes (ITAA97 s 86-40).

[FITR ¶133-200]

¶30-620 Deductions relating to personal services income

Where an individual generates personal services income (PSI) as a non-employee (and not as part of a personal services business: ¶30-660), the individual's deductions relating to that income are generally restricted to the amount that they would be entitled to deduct if the income had been received as an employee (ITAA97 s 85-10). This means, for example, that the individual cannot deduct rent, mortgage interest, rates or land tax relating to their residence or associate's residence (ITAA97 s 85-15), although home office heating and lighting expenses remain deductible. Various aspects of these restrictions are discussed in TR 2003/10.

Permitted deductions

The PSI regime specifically does not prohibit deductions to the extent that they relate to:

- gaining work (eg advertising, tendering, quoting)
- insuring against loss of income or earning capacity
- insuring against liability arising from income-earning activities (eg public liability and professional indemnity insurance)
- engaging an entity that is not an associate to perform work
- personal superannuation contributions
- meeting obligations under workers compensation law
- meeting obligations or exercising rights under GST law (s 85-10), or
- deductions by small business entities (¶7-250) in respect of depreciating assets, including up to one benefit car, as discussed below (ITAA97 s 328-235).

Payments to or on behalf of associates

An individual cannot deduct payments to an associate or payments arising from obligations to an associate to the extent that they relate to gaining or producing the individual's PSI. However, this does not apply to the extent that an amount relates to engaging the associate to perform part of the principal work for which the individual's PSI is received (ITAA97 s 85-20). The term ''principal work'' has its ordinary meaning. It does not include support services such as maintaining records and preparing billings to the client.

To the extent that a payment is not deductible because of this rule, it is not income of the individual's associate.

An individual also cannot deduct superannuation contributions made on behalf of an associate, to the extent that the associate's work relates to gaining the individual's PSI but does not form part of the principal work for which that income is received. Deductions for contributions related to the principal work category cannot exceed the amount which the individual would be required to contribute under the superannuation guarantee legislation (¶39-000 and following), taking into account only deductible salary or wages (ITAA97 s 85-25).

For the meaning of ‘‘associate’’, see ¶4-200. However, in the context of the PSI regime, a federal, state or territory government agency is not taken to be an associate of another such agency (ITAA97 s 85-35).

[FITR ¶133-100]

¶30-630 Deduction entitlements of personal services entities

A ‘‘personal services entity’’ (PSE) is a company, partnership or trust whose ordinary income or statutory income includes the personal services income (PSI) of one or more individuals. The rules for deduction entitlements of PSEs are set out in ITAA97 Subdiv 86-B. Various aspects of these deductions are discussed in TR 2003/10.

General rule

As a general rule, a PSE is not entitled to a deduction to the extent that it relates to gaining or producing an individual's PSI unless either:

- the individual could have deducted the amount if the entity's circumstances had applied to the individual, or
- the entity receives the individual's PSI in the course of conducting a personal services business (¶30-660).

This general rule is modified by specific provisions covering deductions for entity maintenance costs, car expenses, superannuation, salary or wages promptly paid, and income of the entity which has been included in an individual's assessable income. The general rule is ignored for the purposes of depreciation by small business entities (ITAA97 s 328-235; ¶7-250). The existence of ITAA97 Div 86 does not cause the car expense (¶16-310) and substantiation rules (¶16-210) to apply to a PSE.

Entity maintenance deductions

The general rule does not preclude ‘‘entity maintenance deductions’’ such as:

- bank account fees
- tax-related expenses (¶16-850)
- costs of preparing and lodging documents required under the corporations law (other than payments to associates), or
- licence, registration, approval, etc, fees payable to an Australian government agency under an Australian law (ITAA97 s 86-65).

Car expenses

The general rule does not stop the entity deducting a car expense for a car which has no private use, or deducting a car expense and related FBT for a car fringe benefit. However, there can be only one benefit car at a time in relation to one individual's PSI. If there is more than one benefit car in relation to one individual, the entity must choose which car will generate deductions. The choice remains in effect until the entity ceases to hold that car (ITAA97 s 86-70).

Superannuation deductions

The general rule does not prevent the entity deducting a contribution it makes to a fund or RSA to provide superannuation benefits for an individual whose PSI is included in the entity's income. However, where 2 or more such individuals are associated, the deduction for an individual who performs less than 20% (by market value) of the entity's principal work is limited to the amount which the entity is required to contribute under the superannuation guarantee scheme (ITAA97 s 86-75).

Salary and wages

If an individual's PSI is included in a PSE's ordinary income or statutory income and the entity promptly pays the PSI to the individual, the entity may be able to deduct the amount paid. To qualify for the deduction, the PSI must be paid to the individual as salary or wages before the end of the 14th day after the PAYG payment period (month or quarter, as the case may be: ¶26-550) during which the amount became income of the entity.

If the PSI is not paid to the individual within the specified time, then a similar result is achieved by the operation of ITAA97 ss 86-15 and 86-30 (¶30-610).

Costs related to individual's assessable income

The Act generally does not permit deductions for costs incurred in gaining or producing a different taxpayer's assessable income. This technical difficulty is overcome by ITAA97 s 86-85, so that a PSE is not denied deductions on this basis alone where its income becomes assessable income of an individual.

[FITR ¶133-300]

¶30-660 Exemption for personal services business

Income from the conduct of a genuine personal services business (PSB) is exempt from the personal services income (PSI) regime.

There are various tests for determining whether a PSB is being conducted (ITAA97 s 87-15). There will be a PSB if:

- the ''results'' test is satisfied (¶30-665)
- less than 80% of the PSI is from one source and any of 3 additional tests are satisfied (¶30-670), or
- a PSB determination is obtained from the Commissioner (¶30-680).

Detailed guidelines on each of these tests are in TR 2001/8.

Personal services business flow chart

This ATO flow chart shows how to ascertain whether PSI is income from conducting a PSB.

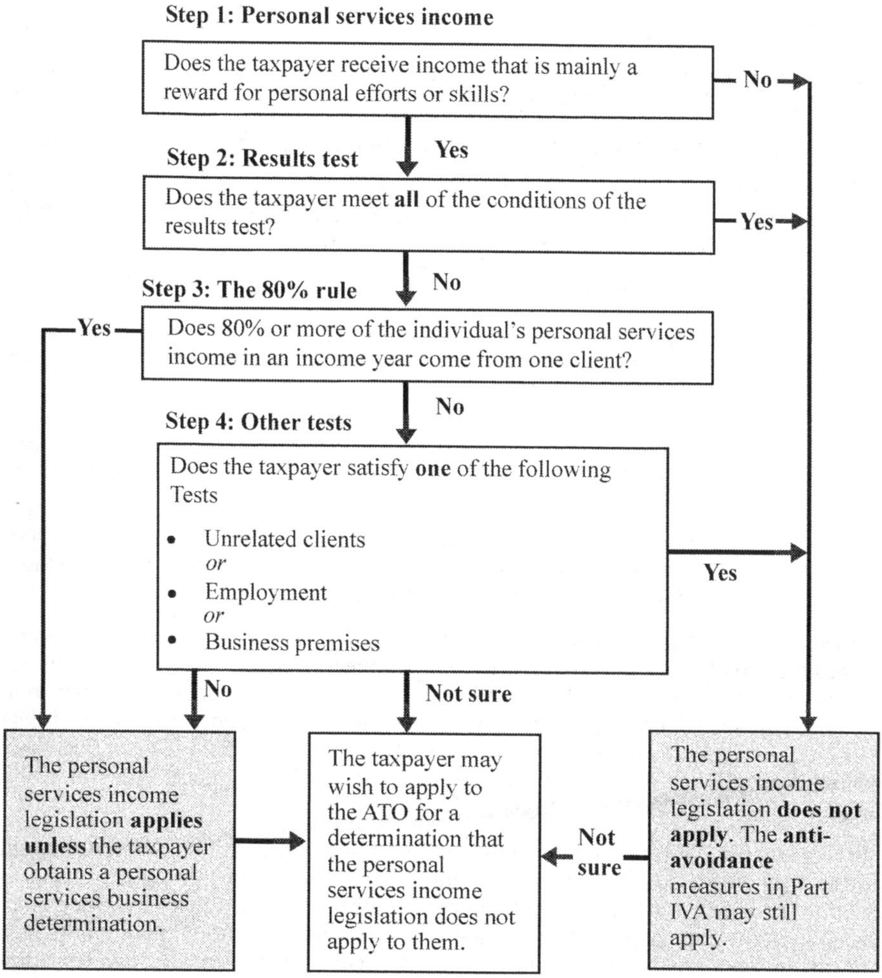
Step 1: Personal services income
Does the taxpayer receive income that is mainly a reward for personal efforts or skills?
No
Yes
Step 2: Results test
Does the taxpayer meet all of the conditions of the results test?
Yes
No
Step 3: The 80% rule
Yes
Does 80% or more of the individual's personal services income in an income year come from one client?
No
Step 4: Other tests
Does the taxpayer satisfy one of the following Tests
• Unrelated clients
or
• Employment
or
• Business premises
Yes
No
Not sure
The personal services income legislation applies unless the taxpayer obtains a personal services business determination.
The taxpayer may wish to apply to the ATO for a determination that the personal services income legislation does not apply to them.
Not sure
The personal services income legislation does not apply. The anti-avoidance measures in Part IVA may still apply.

[FITR ¶133-400]

¶30-665 PSI results test

An individual or personal services entity (PSE) that satisfies the results test will be taken to be conducting a personal services business (ITAA97 s 87-15). The income from that business is therefore exempt from the personal services income (PSI) regime.

The results test is based on the traditional criteria for distinguishing independent contractors from employees (TR 2005/16: ¶26-150). For an individual to satisfy the results test in a particular income year, the individual must satisfy the following 3 conditions in relation to at least 75% of his or her PSI during the year (excluding employee or office-holder income):

(1) the income is for producing a result (eg delivering a completed software component, by contrast with performing a week of programming work)

(2) the individual is required to supply the plant and equipment or tools of trade (if any) needed to perform the work, and

(3) the individual is, or would be, liable for the cost of rectifying any defect in the work performed (ITAA97 s 87-18). Where physical rectification is not possible, condition (3) will be satisfied if the individual or PSE is liable for damages in relation to the defect (TR 2001/8).

For each of these conditions, industry custom and practice will be taken into account.

Corresponding conditions apply to a PSE, except that in condition (1) it is the PSE's income from the individual's PSI that must be for producing a result.

▶ Example: Courier drivers

A courier company engages individuals to perform courier services. The company receives orders then arranges for one of the couriers to do the delivery. Each courier provides its own van with corporate fit-out and is paid a fee for each delivery. The courier is liable for any damage and any incorrect deliveries.

The couriers satisfy the results test because: (a) they are paid for producing a result, ie successful delivery; (b) they are required to supply any necessary plant and equipment, ie the van; and (c) they are liable for the costs of rectifying any mistakes. The couriers would therefore not be subject to the PSI regime. (Based on TR 2001/8.)

In determining whether the results test has been satisfied, the Commissioner considers that contractual statements will not be conclusive if they are mere "window dressing" and do not reflect the real contractual position (TR 2001/8).

In *IRG Technical Services*, the Federal Court held that 2 taxpayer entities, each of which was effectively controlled by a (different) engineer, failed to satisfy the results test. According to Allsop J, who said the central relationship for examination was between the individual whose exertions produce the personal service income and the acquirer of those exertions or services, it would be a "misuse of language" and not a "reflection of substantial reality" to say that the income received by the engineers was for results produced.

In *Nguyen*, the AAT held that a computer consultancy firm did not satisfy the results test as the terms of its contracts were not consistent with those that could reasonably be expected in the case of an independent contractor. Further, there was no evidence that it was customary for entities providing the services of IT personnel to be paid on the basis of a result. In *Cooper*, the AAT held that the provision of the "professional business services" by the company in question did not satisfy the results test in s 87-18(3) because: (1) the agreements did not specify any result; (2) remuneration was not based on the result but was time-based; (3) the company was not permitted to sub-contract the work; and (4) the remuneration was payable only up to the termination of the work relationship and was not calculated on the production of any result.

For similar decisions by the AAT on this point, see: *Skiba* (engineering services); *Taneja* (computer analyst); *Prasad* (project management); and *Douglass* (engineering consultant).

The PSI rules applied to attribute income derived by a New Zealand resident company to an Australian resident taxpayer who was the primary controller of the company (*Russell*). The taxpayer could not satisfy the results test in s 87-18(3)(a). In addition, the New Zealand company could be a PSE despite being a non-resident and the tax treaty with New Zealand did not prevent the attribution of the amounts earned by the New Zealand company to the taxpayer as part of his assessable income.

[FITR ¶133-422]

¶30-670 The 80% rule and additional tests

If the results test is *not* satisfied, it is necessary to consider the 80% rule (ITAA97 s 87-15). This rule operates in the following way:

- if 80% or more of an individual's personal services income (PSI) in the income year is from one entity (eg one client), the income will be subject to the PSI regime unless the individual obtains a personal services business determination from the Commissioner (¶30-680)
- if 80% or more of the PSI is not from one entity, the income will be exempt from the PSI regime if the individual satisfies any of the following tests:
  - the unrelated clients test
  - the employment test, or
  - the business premises test.

The 80% rule does not apply to income earned by an employee or, after the 2001–02 year, payments to an individual as an officeholder or as a religious practitioner. Special rules apply to commission-based agents that make it easier for them to show that their income is from more than one source (¶30-675).

The source of the PSI is determined by reference to the contract under which the services are rendered. The source is not necessarily the entity that physically pays the income. For example, a doctor receives income from his/her multiple patients, even though he/she may actually be paid by a single medical fund (TR 2001/8).

Unrelated clients test

An individual or personal services entity (PSE) (service provider) meets the unrelated clients test in an income year if:

- the service provider gains income from providing services to 2 or more entities that are not associates of each other and are not associates of the service provider, and
- the services are provided as a direct result of the service provider making offers or invitations (eg by advertising) to the public at large or to a section of the public (ITAA97 s 87-20). Offers or invitations may also be made by public tenders or word of mouth referrals. They are less likely to be made to a ''section of the public'' if they are made to a limited number of entities or to related entities (TR 2001/8).

The second limb of the test is not satisfied by the service provider merely being available to provide the services through an entity that conducts a business of arranging for persons to provide services directly for its clients (eg an agent or labour hire firm).

▶ Example

At the instigation of her employer (Appliances), an engineer has her employment contract terminated and replaced by a contract for the provision of engineering services. The engineer provides services to Appliances and to Products, an associate of Appliances. She also, as a result of placing advertisements in industry journals, provides services to another company (Metals) that is not related to any other relevant parties.

The engineer will not satisfy the unrelated clients test as she only has one unrelated client (Metals). Appliances does not qualify because the services are provided to it as a result of its own actions, rather than the engineer making an offer or invitation to the public. Products does not qualify because it is an associate of Appliances.

If the engineer had a second eligible unrelated client, she would have satisfied the unrelated clients test. In that event, and assuming that 80% or more of her income was not from one source, she would not be subject to the PSI regime. (Based on TR 2001/8.)

In *Yalos Engineering*, the taxpayer's sole income in the 2003–04 and 2004–05 income years was from the one labour hire firm under a contract for services as an offshore installation engineer for BHP Billiton. The taxpayer's expertise was relevant only to a very small number of companies engaged in offshore petroleum exploration and mining. It had regular personal contact with the companies to assess their needs and learned of work opportunities by word of mouth and personal recommendations. It did not advertise in newspapers, brochures or other media which would have been inappropriate in the circumstances. The court found the taxpayer satisfied the unrelated clients test. The taxpayer's clients constituted "a section of the public". The services were provided either as a direct result of the taxpayer having made offers or invitations to the public or to a section of the public.

A taxpayer who provided drafting services to a small number of personal contacts and relationships, but did not advertise the services, failed the unrelated clients test (*Cameron*). The one-off approaches to or from the taxpayer's clients were not offers or invitations to the public at large or a section of the public. A taxpayer did not satisfy the unrelated clients test just by having a LinkedIn profile which, it was argued, was an advertisement of his services to the public. None of the taxpayer's clients made their decision to engage the taxpayer's services as a direct result of an offer or invitation constituted by the taxpayer's LinkedIn profile (*Fortunatow*, on appeal to the High Court).

Special rules apply to commission-based agents that make it easier to comply with the unrelated clients test (¶30-675).

Employment test

An *individual* service provider meets the employment test in an income year if at least 20% (by market value) of the individual's principal work for the year is performed by an entity or entities engaged by the individual. The entities cannot be non-individuals that are associates of the individual.

A *PSE* meets the employment test where the 20% criterion above is met and the entity or entities engaged are neither individuals whose PSI is included in the PSE's income, nor non-individuals that are associates of the PSE. If the PSE entity is a partnership, work done by a partner is taken to be work done by an entity engaged by the partnership. An individual or a PSE can also meet the employment test by having one or more apprentices for at least half the income year (ITAA97 s 87-25).

The Commissioner considers that "principal work" does not include incidental clerical or administrative work (TR 2001/8).

Business premises test

An individual or a PSE (service provider) meets the business premises test in an income year if, at all relevant times during the year, the service provider maintains and uses business premises:

- at which they mainly conduct activities from which PSI is gained
- of which they have exclusive use (this would typically require ownership or a lease)
- that are physically separate from any premises that the service provider or service provider's associate uses for private purposes, and
- that are physically separate from the premises of the service provider's client or client's associate (ITAA97 s 87-30).

It is not necessary to use the *same* premises for the entire year.

In *Dixon Consulting*, the AAT held that a building consisting of an office and a garage adjacent to residential premises occupied by a director of the taxpayer and his family did not satisfy the business premises test because the taxpayer did not have exclusive use of the garage.

The car of a travelling salesperson does not qualify as business premises (TR 2001/8).

[FITR ¶133-420]

¶30-675 Special rules for commission-based agents

Special rules apply to certain commission-based agents (ITAA97 s 87-40). These rules are intended to make it easier for agents who bear entrepreneurial risk to show that they are carrying on a personal services business (PSB).

Agents eligible for these special rules must satisfy all of the following conditions:

(1) they are an individual or a personal services entity

(2) they are agents, not employees, of another entity (the principal)

(3) they receive income from the principal that is for services that the agent provides to customers on the principal's behalf

(4) at least 75% of that income is performance-based commissions or fees

(5) they actively seek other customers for the principal (eg by advertising rather than merely accepting referrals)

(6) they do not provide services to the customers from the premises of the principal or an associate of the principal, unless the agent has an arm's length arrangement for the use of those premises.

▶ Example 1

Christopher is a financial planner who acts as an agent for Colossus (*conditions (1) and (2)*). He receives 85% of his income as performance-based commission from Colossus for services provided to customers (*conditions (3) and (4)*). He advertises regularly in financial papers and professional journals (*condition (5)*). He operates from an office, which he leases from Colossus on commercial terms, and does not have access to any other facilities of Colossus (*condition (6)*). As he satisfies all the conditions, he is eligible for the special rules explained below.

Where the agent satisfies these conditions, the following special rules apply:

- in determining whether at least 80% of the agent's personal services income (PSI) is from one source, PSI income that the agent receives from the principal for services provided to customers on the principal's behalf is treated as though it were received directly from the customers
- in determining whether the agent satisfies the unrelated clients test, those services are treated as if they were provided by the agent, not the principal.

▶ Example 2

Assume that Christopher (from Example 1 above) provides services to 20 of Colossus' customers. In the absence of the special rule, all of Christopher's PSI would be from one source (Colossus), so he would not satisfy the 80% test. However, under the special rule, the income he receives from Colossus that is attributable to those customers can be treated as being from 20 sources. On this basis, 80% or more of his PSI is not from one source.

Christopher also satisfies the first limb of the unrelated clients test as he is treated as providing services to 2 or more unrelated customers. If those services were provided as a direct result of his advertising, he would also satisfy the second limb of the unrelated clients test and, as such, would be treated as carrying on a PSB. He would therefore be outside the scope of the PSI regime.

[FITR ¶133-450]

¶30-680 Personal services business determinations

Any individual can apply for a personal services business (PSB) determination from the Commissioner (ITAA97 s 87-60). A personal services entity (PSE) may also apply for a determination relating to an individual's personal services income (PSI) that is included in the entity's income (ITAA97 s 87-65).

If granted, the determination means that the individual or PSE is taken to be conducting a PSB, so that the income is exempt from the PSI regime (ITAA97 s 87-15).

A determination may be appropriate, for example, where the applicant does not formally satisfy any of the other tests, or where it wants its status to be more conclusively determined.

To make a determination in relation to an individual, the Commissioner must be satisfied that one or more of these conditions are met:

- the individual met, or could reasonably be expected to meet, one or more of the results test (¶30-665), the employment test or the business premises test (¶30-670) *and* the individual's PSI was, or could reasonably be expected to be, from the individual conducting activities that met one or more of those tests (s 87-60(3A))
- but for unusual circumstances applying to the individual in that year, the individual would have met, or could reasonably have been expected to meet, one or more of the results test, the employment test or the business premises test (¶30-670) *and* the PSI of the individual was, or could reasonably be expected to be, from the individual conducting activities that met one or more of those tests (s 87-60(3B))
- the individual met, or could reasonably be expected to meet, the unrelated clients test but because of unusual circumstances 80% or more of the PSI of the individual would have been, or could reasonably have been expected to be, from the same source *and* the PSI of the individual was, or could reasonably be expected to be, from the individual conducting activities that met the unrelated clients test (s 87-60(5)), or
- but for unusual circumstances applying to the individual in that year, the individual would have met, or could reasonably have been expected to meet, the unrelated clients test *and* if 80% or more of the individual's PSI would have been, or could reasonably have been expected to be, from the same entity, this was only because of unusual circumstances applying to the individual in the income year *and* the individual's PSI was, or could reasonably be expected to be, from the individual conducting activities that met the unrelated clients test (s 87-60(6)).

The provisions ensure that the Commissioner may not provide a PSB determination to those individuals who, but for unusual circumstances, would satisfy the unrelated clients test but did not satisfy, and would not normally have satisfied, the 80% rule.

In determining what can ''reasonably be expected'', the Commissioner will take into account the experience of previous years, and current and projected contractual arrangements (TR 2001/8).

The Commissioner can also make a determination where satisfied that unusual circumstances have prevented the individual from satisfying the results test, the unrelated clients test, the employment test or the business premises test. This may be appropriate, for example, where an individual who normally enters into monthly contracts with numerous clients enters into a 12-month contract with just one client, or where a barrister is engaged for an unusually long trial or Royal Commission. The Commissioner considers that circumstances are not unusual unless they are exceptional and temporary (TR 2001/8). A state of affairs that existed for 7 years probably could not be described as unusual (*Creaton*).

In connection with the unrelated clients test, unusual circumstances specifically cover a situation where:

- the individual starts a business during the income year and can reasonably be expected to meet the test in subsequent income years, or
- the individual provides services to only one entity during the income year, but met the test in one or more preceding years and can reasonably be expected to meet the test in subsequent income years (s 87-60(4)). The preceding years referred to do not have to be the immediately preceding years (*Creaton*).

Corresponding requirements apply to applications by PSEs (s 87-65).

In *Scimitar Systems*, the AAT held that the phrase ''unusual circumstances'' referred to circumstances other than those affecting the information technology industry generally and which were not regular or recurring incidents of the PSE's activities that produced the PSI.

In *Dibarr*, a case involving a company which was paid monthly in arrears for labour supplied by it to its only client, the AAT was not satisfied that unusual circumstances existed to justify the making of a personal services business determination.

In *BRMJCQ Pty Ltd*, the AAT upheld the Commissioner's refusal to make personal services business determination in respect of an IT company which provided the services of its sole director and shareholder. In coming to its decision, the AAT held that the remuneration the taxpayer received was not for producing a result within the meaning of s 87-18(3)(a), 100% of its income in the relevant year came from one contract and the ''unrelated'' client's test was not satisfied because the taxpayer had not made public offers of its services.

Procedural aspects

Application for determination or variation

An application for a PSB determination or a variation of an existing determination must be made in the approved form. If the Commissioner has not decided the application within 60 days, the applicant may give the Commissioner written notice that the applicant wishes to treat the application as having been refused. The 60-day period excludes any time period(s) starting when the Commissioner requests an applicant for specified information or documentation and ending when the applicant provides the specified information or document (ITAA97 s 87-70). A person who is dissatisfied with the Commissioner's decision may object to the decision under TAA Pt IVC (¶28-010).

Effective dates

A determination or variation is effective from the day specified in the notice or (if a day is not specified) the day on which the notice is given. A determination can therefore have retrospective effect. The determination ceases to have effect at the end of the earliest day on which one or more of the following occurs:

- one or more conditions to which the determination is subject are not met
- the Commissioner revokes the determination, or
- the period for which the determination has effect comes to an end (ITAA97 s 87-75).

The Commissioner says that it would be prudent to consider making an application for a determination at the start of any income year in which there is a reasonable expectation that the 80% rule will not be satisfied (TR 2001/8).

Revocation

The Commissioner is required to revoke the determination by written notice if the Commissioner is no longer satisfied that there are grounds on which the determination could be made (ITAA97 s 87-80).

[FITR ¶133-505, ¶133-510]

¶30-690 Application of general anti-avoidance rules

The personal services income (PSI) regime was enacted partly because of the perceived inadequacies of the general anti-avoidance provisions (ITAA36 Pt IVA) in dealing with diverted income on a case-by-case basis. However, it does not take the place of Pt IVA. For example, even if a taxpayer is exempted from the PSI regime because it is carrying on a personal services business, Pt IVA is still potentially applicable.

The Commissioner may seek to apply Pt IVA where the income is generated predominantly from the personal activities of the independent contractor — as distinct from the use or sale of property or from a business structure — and the dominant purpose of the arrangement is income splitting (TR 2001/8).

▶ Example

A taxpayer who earned wages of $1,200 a week for driving a truck enters into an arrangement through his personal company with his former employer under which his personal company is paid $2,000 a week, but has to provide its own truck. The personal company pays the taxpayer wages of $200 and either retains the balance or distributes it as dividends to the taxpayer's wife and children who are all on low marginal rates. The Commissioner considers that this arrangement could be subject to challenge under Pt IVA. (Based on TR 2001/8.)

The Commissioner regards Pt IVA as applicable to arrangements under which individuals try to split their personal exertion income among family members by diverting it to a family company or trust (IT 2121). Other relevant rulings include IT 2330, IT 2501 and IT 2503.

Splitting business income

Although IT 2121 is primarily concerned with cases involving personal exertion income of an employee kind, it is clear that arrangements that involve interposing entities in relation to the personal exertion income of a business or professional practice may be struck down where income from the practice is split between family members. This was the effect of the decisions of the High Court in *Gulland*, *Watson* and *Pincus* where unit trusts were established to carry on medical practices. Attempts by professional consultants to split income through the use of trustees or companies have been struck down under Pt IVA (*Case 3/99*; *Case W58*; *Case X90*; *Case Y13*; *Egan*) and under its predecessor, ITAA36 former s 260 (*Bunting*). See also ¶31-180.

Contract for services

A person cannot avoid being taxed on salary or wage income which the person earns by agreeing to bring it to account as income of a partnership formed with another, or by assigning it for value or otherwise to some other person.

Different considerations may result where the remuneration arises under a contract for services (eg a contract made with an independent contractor, retained accountant, lawyer or doctor) rather than a contract of service (ie between an employee and an employer). If the right to remuneration is not inextricably integrated with the personal obligation to perform the service, the right may be assignable in such a fashion that the remuneration is derived, not by the assignor, but by the assignee.

[FTR ¶81-355]

Transfer of Rights to Receive Income

¶30-900 Rights to future income

Alienation of income versus application of income

Instead of transferring the property which gives rise to the receipt of assessable income, a taxpayer may prefer simply to transfer the right to that income, while retaining the property. However, a transfer of this type faces a number of difficulties.

There is an important distinction between the *alienation* of income and the *application* of income. If a person directs his/her bank to pay all interest accruing on his/her account to another person, that would simply be an application of the income. The interest, as it arises, belongs to the transferor, but it is applied for the benefit of another. For tax purposes, it is still derived by the transferor and is assessable to him/her (ITAA97 ss 6-5(4); 6-10(3)). The same applies, for example, where an employee's wages are garnished against payment of a debt, or PAYG amounts are withheld from wages. Thus, a retired coal miner who received an additional pension payment "in respect of his wife" was held assessable on the whole amount (*Case L53*).

An obligation to pay a percentage of gross receipts or profits as royalties does not have the effect that the party under the obligation does not derive that percentage of receipts or profits: he/she derives the income representing that percentage but may, in some cases, be entitled to claim a deduction for the royalty payment.

While transactions of this type simply result in an *application* of or payment out of income, other transactions may be formulated under which the taxpayer has *assigned* or *alienated* income. Income which has been properly alienated is no longer the person's income so that the person neither receives nor derives it, and thus escapes tax on it (although the CGT provisions may be attracted in some cases). Where the arrangement is effective, the income that arises becomes the property of, and is taxable to, the assignee — even where the assignor receives it as trustee for the assignee.

In *Howard* (2014), the High Court found the taxpayer to be assessable in respect of damages awarded as compensation for joint venture losses. The taxpayer argued unsuccessfully that he had assigned the right to receive the damages to an associated company under a litigation agreement. French CJ and Keane J found that the assignment of mere future income apart from the associated proprietary interest was not effective to prevent the income from being derived. Hayne and Crennan JJ, Gageler J agreeing, found that the better construction of the litigation agreement was that it provided for the assignment of the proceeds of the action and not for the underlying rights to receive those sums.

Transfer of rights to, and expectancies of, future income

Where income is to be alienated, so that it is derived by another, the nature of the rights to be assigned must be ascertained. The law draws a distinction between the rights to income existing at law and those existing in equity, and between presently subsisting rights to income and the mere expectation that income will be received. A presently existing right to income is a chose in action (ie an intangible right enforceable by legal or equitable action) which is capable of assignment as such. The entirety of a legal chose in action may be assigned either at law or in equity and, in either case, with or without consideration. A part of, or a partial interest in, a legal chose in action, and an equitable chose in action, may be assigned only in equity, again either with or without consideration.

However, the mere expectancy or possibility of a future receipt of income is not an existing chose in action and can be assigned, if at all, only in equity and for consideration. Examples of an expectancy are: (i) any interest which might be paid on a loan repayable at the option of the borrower; and (ii) undeclared future dividends (*Norman*). Purported voluntary assignments of such income are not effective to achieve its derivation by the assignee.

In contrast, where the owner of a patent, who had granted a licence in consideration of royalty payments, unconditionally assigned to third parties 90% of the benefit of the right to receive royalties under the licence agreement, it was held that there had been an effective equitable assignment of a present right and the assigned income was derived by the assignee (*Shepherd*).

Derivation of expectancy income

Where an expectancy and not a present right is assigned, the effect in equity of a purported present assignment for value is that the assignment is treated as a contract to assign and the contract transfers the beneficial interest to the assignee immediately on acquisition of the property. The question then arises whether the accrual of the income to its assignor precedes or succeeds (or is contemporaneous with) the affixing of the trust arising under the assignment, ie whether the assignor derives the income and then holds it on trust for the assignee, or whether the assignor holds the income on trust for the assignee who derives it. The issue is unsettled, although 15 TBRD *Case* Q17 supported the latter alternative and consequently an assignor was not assessable on dividends, the right to which had been previously assigned for value.

Special tax considerations

Even though an assignment may be effective under the general law, this does not necessarily mean that it is effective for tax purposes. Statutory restrictions on the tax benefits of various types of assignment of income from property are imposed by ITAA36 Pt III Div 6A (¶30-940) and certain purported assignments of income, for example from personal exertion, may be ineffective under the general anti-avoidance provisions of ITAA36 Pt IVA (¶30-690). Where consideration is paid for the assignment, the question also arises whether the consideration is assessable in the hands of the assignor (¶30-960).

Assignment of share in partnership

For the assignment of a share in a partnership, see ¶5-160.

[FITR ¶28-030]

¶30-940 Transfer of rights to income from property

Special statutory provisions restrict the tax benefits of a transfer of a right to receive income from property where there is no accompanying transfer of the income-producing property itself (ITAA36 Pt III Div 6A: ss 102A to 102CA). The effect is that:

- in some cases where the income is alienated for less than 7 years, the alienation may be treated as void for tax purposes
- in certain other cases, where the right to income is alienated in return for payment, the alienation may be effective for tax purposes but the payment will be treated as assessable income of the person receiving it.

Where a transfer of the right to receive income from property without the transfer of the property itself occurs, the transfer is ineffective for tax purposes if: (i) the transfer will or may terminate before the expiration of 7 years; (ii) the parties to the transfer are associated persons; *and* (iii) any consideration for the transfer was less than would have been expected under an arm's length transfer (s 102B). However, this rule does not apply to transfers effected by will or transfers that may terminate within the 7-year period solely because of death or disability.

In all other cases where there is a transfer of the right to receive income from property without the transfer of the property itself, the transfer is effective for tax purposes. However, any consideration for the transfer is included in the transferor's assessable income in the year in which the right is transferred, regardless of the duration of the transfer (s 102CA). These rules do not apply to maintenance payments which are not exempt because they are received as a result of a transfer of a right to income, or to transfers effected by will (¶10-855).

Division 6A does *not* apply to an assignment of the right to receive royalties arising on the sale of iron ore because it is not a right to receive income from property (*SP Investments*). There may also be CGT implications.

Termination within 7 years

In order to satisfy the 7-year requirement, the right to income must be one which by its nature subsists for more than 7 years (*Booth*). For example, where there is a periodic tenancy from year to year, the right to rent subsists for only one year. It cannot be assigned for 7 years and Div 6A may therefore apply. It has also been suggested that assignments of rental are *always* likely to be caught by this rule, because leases typically contain a provision enabling the lease to be terminated if the rent is in arrears (*Davis*).

CGT implications

For CGT purposes, the transfer of a right to receive income from property is the disposal of a CGT asset (¶11-250). Accordingly, if the right was acquired by the transferor on or after 20 September 1985, a capital gain or loss may arise when it is subsequently transferred. If an amount is assessable under Div 6A and a capital gain arises as a result of the transfer, ITAA97 s 118-20 (¶11-690) reduces the capital gain to avoid double taxation.

From 8 May 2018, the CGT small business concessions are not available to partners who alienate their income by creating, assigning or otherwise dealing in rights to the future income of a partnership (Everett assignments) (¶7-120).

[FTR ¶52-201]

¶30-960 Character of consideration for assignment

Where what is assigned is a present right to future income, the right itself may be of a capital nature but the consideration may nevertheless be an income receipt. This is illustrated in *Myer Emporium*, where the High Court ruled that the consideration paid for the transfer of a right to future interest income was itself assessable income (¶10-020).

In *Henry Jones (IXL),* the Full Federal Court held that a lump sum received by a taxpayer in return for assigning its rights to royalties over a 10-year period was assessable. The court considered that *Myer Emporium* had established that, except in the case of an assignment of an annuity where the income arises from the very contract assigned, an assignment of income from property without assignment of the underlying property right will, no matter what its form, result in the consideration for that assignment being on revenue account — the consideration being a substitution for the future income that is to be derived. This is so even if the income is produced by a contractual right rather than by the relevant property. However, *Myer Emporium* does not apply where the right is related to underlying property which the transferor has not previously owned (eg where the transferor owns a right to income under a licence contract granting a right to use a trade mark) or where the right to income is not related to any underlying property (eg a right to an annuity) (TR 92/3).

Where what is assigned is an expectancy or a right of a revenue nature which is not a right to income from property (eg the right to payment under a contract for services or the supply of goods), the consideration for the assignment is itself income of the assignor.

[FTR ¶52-310]

¶30-970 Other ways of transferring income

There are other ways to transfer income from one taxpayer to another:

- transfer of income-producing assets (¶31-290)
- deductible payments by high-rate taxpayer to low-rate taxpayer (¶31-370)
- discretionary distributions (¶31-420).

Chapter 31 Tax Planning • Year End Tax Strategies

Tax Planning in General

¶31-000 What is tax planning?

This chapter aims to provide an overview of tax planning issues and concepts. It is a general guide only and does not purport to discuss all relevant issues. Some planning pointers on specific issues are contained within the commentary in other chapters:

- ATO compliance policy (¶25-200), including its particular emphasis on international business restructures: ¶22-580
- the implications of the tax avoidance legislation: ¶30-110
- checklist of tax changes coming into effect during 2019–20: ¶2
- checklists relevant to particular transactions, situations or occupations, see Chapter 44.

What is tax planning?

Broadly, tax planning is the process of organising the affairs of a taxpayer or a group of taxpayers so that, as far as legally or commercially possible, the liability of the taxpayer or group of taxpayers to income and other taxes is minimised.

Tax planning is not limited to complex, high risk or sophisticated arrangements. Taxpayers contemplating even the most ordinary transactions should give proper consideration to tax planning (and, in particular, to CGT issues) to ensure that they do not suffer adverse tax consequences.

Tax planning advice is usually given in the following general situations:

- when considering the overall structure of a business or business group
- where the overall structure of a business or business group is being reconsidered due to a change in circumstances, eg a change in the tax laws that has reduced the viability or suitability of the present structure
- where there is a change in ownership of a business or business group or a merger or amalgamation of 2 businesses or groups
- where a business or individual needs advice as to how a proposed transaction, project or asset acquisition may best be structured from a tax point of view
- where a business or individual is likely to achieve a large taxable income for a particular income year, in which case consideration may be given to ways of reducing the taxable income before the end of the year
- where there is a change in personal circumstances, eg on retirement or marriage breakdown, and
- where an individual prepares for the devolution or disposal of assets on death (succession planning).

Specific situations where tax advice is particularly important include: the acquisition or disposal of an asset otherwise than in the ordinary course of business; the sale of a business (¶31-610); making a will and dealing with a deceased estate (¶44-170); long-term contracts; restructuring companies, trusts and partnerships; changes to the issued capital of a company; changes to the issued units of a unit trust; variations of rights attaching to shares or units; the liquidation of a company and the winding up of a trust; constructing premises and the rezoning or subdivision of real estate; contracts with overseas concerns, raising issues of transfer pricing (¶22-580); the borrowing of money overseas; and the extension by Australian companies of their operations to other countries or to new areas of operation within Australia.

Tax planning often involves consideration of the *interaction* of a number of separate tax provisions. For example:

- one method of effecting profit shifting involves the interaction of the thin capitalisation rules (¶22-700), the exemption for foreign non-portfolio dividends, and the deduction for interest expense incurred in deriving certain exempt foreign income (¶21-095)
- foreign investment in the Australian agricultural sector may involve consideration not only of the existing specific concessions for primary producers (¶18-000) but also the managed investment trust rules (¶6-400) and the investment manager regime (¶22-122). For an article discussing the interaction, see the CCH *Tax Week* at ¶615 (2013).

Other taxes such as GST (¶34-000) and stamp duties (¶37-000) or considerations such as social security entitlements will often also need to be taken into account.

¶31-005 Different needs of different taxpayers

Different considerations apply to different types of taxpayer. For example, where companies are concerned, although directors' duties will include ensuring that the company does not incur unnecessary tax, consideration should be given to the practicality of any proposal, its economic impact (if any) and its effect on personnel and the company's reputation. In the case of individuals or small private companies, other considerations will arise as there are often great differences in the capabilities and attitudes of individual persons towards tax minimisation arrangements. Financial position and the importance of reducing the incidence of tax should be taken into account. For example, in the case of a growing business, a portion of the profits will usually be represented by increases in stock or debtors and will not be available in cash, while the growth of the business will require additional capital expenditure that frequently has to be met, at least partly, out of profits. Thus, tax planning may become an economic necessity as well as a matter of business prudence.

All businesses should consider the long-term ramifications of any arrangement and, in particular, the likely costs, taxation and otherwise, of being audited by the ATO (¶25-200). Having appropriate systems for identifying and managing both the short-term and long-term tax risks facing an organisation may reduce the risk of an audit, and may reduce the cost of an audit once it is instituted.

Taxpayers should also be aware that the authorities are increasingly willing to prosecute people (¶29-700). In the corporate context, directors and other persons concerned in the management of a company should not overlook the fact that they may be charged and convicted for aiding and abetting or otherwise, being knowingly concerned in taxation offences committed by the company (¶29-710). Further, the system governing the recovery of unremitted PAYG withholdings (and other deductions) is potentially very onerous for directors (¶25-560).

¶31-015 Duties and liabilities of tax advisers

A tax adviser is clearly under a duty to advise the client on the ramifications of any tax planning arrangements, including the penalties that may be payable where there is a shortfall amount (¶29-160). Failure to do so may expose the tax adviser to an action for damages for professional negligence (*Sacca v Adam*; *Jindi (Nominees) v Dutney*; *Jones v WHK Sherwin Chan & Walshe*). Default may also in certain circumstances amount to a breach of the contract of retainer with the client and, if incorrect statements are made, constitute false or misleading conduct under trade practices legislation (*Symond v Gadens Lawyers Sydney Pty Ltd*).

The standard of care is higher where the adviser professes to have a special skill in taxation law. However, general professional advisers such as solicitors and accountants are also arguably under a duty to advise their clients on the tax implications of any proposed transactions or, if they lack tax expertise, to refer the client to a tax specialist (*Hurlingham Estates v Wilde*; *Balkin v Peck*). In highly technical cases or those involving large amounts, even a specialist may be well advised to recommend the client seek a second opinion.

A tax adviser will discharge their duty of care if the advice is soundly based and the client is made fully aware of the consequences before acting on the advice or entering into the transaction (*Zelino & Ors v Budai*). However, if an adviser is guilty of negligence, the client also needs to prove that the negligence caused it some loss (*Tip Top Dry Cleaners v Mackintosh*).

In recommending one particular course of action, it appears that a tax adviser is also under an obligation to advise the client of: (1) alternatives that may achieve the objective in a more tax-efficient way; (2) the existence of any anti-avoidance provisions which may be applicable; and (3) the possibility that the arrangement will attract ATO scrutiny (*Symond v Gadens Lawyers Sydney Pty Ltd*). The advisability of obtaining a private ruling should also be considered in appropriate cases. In view of the complexity of taxation law, advisers should be wary of giving advice that is expressed in unqualified terms.

Financial advisers were held liable for losses suffered by investors in tax schemes as a result of their negligent and misleading investment advice (*Newman v Financial Wisdom*). The court found that the advisers had failed to ensure that there were reasonable grounds for recommending the investments and that the investors were prepared to accept the risks involved.

The amount of damages for negligence may be based on matters such as the amount of additional tax and penalties associated with adopting the advice, audit costs, compensation for any net losses associated with adoption of the advice, and interest (*Symond v Gadens Lawyers Sydney Pty Ltd No 2*).

Advisers to a mass marketed tax evasion scheme involving the sale of franchises to investors were convicted of conspiring to defraud the Commonwealth in *Pearce v R*.

Registration requirements apply to persons charging a fee for tax advice or for other ''tax agent services'' (¶32-010, ¶32-055). To be registered, the person must be a ''fit and proper person'' (¶32-025).

Advisers and scheme promoters

Promoters of tax schemes may be liable for penalties or other sanctions if they contravene the ''scheme promoter'' rules (TAA Sch 1 Div 290). However, advisers are not liable under these rules if they merely provide independent and objective advice about a scheme, even if that advice provides alternative ways to structure a transaction, or sets out the tax risks of the alternatives. For details, see ¶30-300.

[FTR ¶978-282/1]

¶31-020 Tax avoidance and tax evasion

The distinction between tax avoidance and tax evasion is often misunderstood by taxpayers. A simplistic, and therefore not strictly accurate, distinction is to say that avoidance involves arrangements within the law that take the taxpayer outside the scope of particular tax legislation, while evasion involves arrangements outside the law where liability to tax, having been incurred, is wilfully concealed or ignored.

The distinction between avoidance and evasion is important, not least because of the *Crimes (Taxation Offences) Act 1980* (¶30-110), which makes it an offence to participate in, or aid or abet participation in, arrangements that render a taxpayer unable, or likely to be unable, to pay income tax for which it is or will be liable.

The taxation offences listed in TAA Pt III should also be noted (¶29-700).

Taxpayers and their advisers must realise that tax evasion may result in imprisonment. Indeed, it seems that the courts in all states are now more willing to imprison people for serious breaches of the tax laws.

Apart from considering the legal effectiveness of any proposed tax planning arrangement, the planner should consider the ATO's likely approach or attitude to the arrangement. In particular, he/she should be aware of any pronouncements by the government or the ATO, and any relevant public rulings (¶24-540).

The ATO also issues ''taxpayer alerts'' as early warning that certain tax planning activities are under risk assessment (PS LA 2008/15). Taxpayers should exercise caution in relation to arrangements described in a taxpayer alert and should consider obtaining a private ruling or professional advice before acting.

[FTR ¶81-155 – ¶81-165, ¶81-290]

¶31-030 Part IVA provision of last resort

In addition to considering any specific anti-avoidance provisions that may be relevant to a particular transaction, the tax planner must pay constant regard to the general anti-avoidance provisions of ITAA36 Pt IVA (¶30-120). If a transaction is a sham, it will be inherently ineffective and the Commissioner would not need to rely on Pt IVA to strike it down (¶30-110).

[FTR ¶81-150]

¶31-040 Commercial considerations

As previously indicated (¶31-015), tax planning should not be confined to taxation considerations, as commercial considerations and other legislative requirements may make an otherwise attractive tax plan impossible or at least inadvisable (eg the direct and indirect costs may outweigh the tax savings). Some of the possible pitfalls are mentioned below.

- *Existing contractual relationships* — regard must be had to the effect of the tax plan on the taxpayer's continuing contractual relationships with, for example, suppliers, customers, tenants etc. Where a change in the operating vehicle is involved, as on the sale of a business, the other parties to these continuing relationships must be advised; if they are not, there are not only the difficulties that may arise under contract law, but also the possibility that the transfer may be treated as a sham or that any resulting tax benefits may be nullified by the general anti-avoidance provisions of ITAA36 Pt IVA. Difficulties may also arise in obtaining GST input tax credits (¶34-100) where the wrong party is invoiced.

The approval of creditors, including suppliers, to the substitution of one entity for another in the course of a tax plan must be obtained. In this regard, it should be remembered that it is not possible to assign a liability; all that can be done is to obtain a release of an existing liability in consideration of the assumption of a similar liability by the substituted party, or to have the substituted entity covenant to reimburse the other entity for any amount paid pursuant to an obligation for which the other entity remains primarily liable. For further discussion, see ¶23-325.

In certain instances, the costs associated with such practical problems may justify the implementation of a court approved scheme of arrangement. This would streamline asset transfers and avoid the need for the specific approval of contracting parties (although such parties may seek to approve such a scheme).

• *Effect on employees* — where a business is transferred from one associated taxpayer to another, it will usually be desirable for the new proprietor to assume liability for employee benefits such as annual leave, sick leave and long service leave payments, as the vendor will not, after ceasing to carry on business, be entitled to a deduction for those liabilities. In certain circumstances, a payment made in respect of accrued leave entitlements of an employee transferred from one employer to another is deductible to the employer making the payment, eg where the payment is made under an industrial award or agreement (ITAA97 s 26-10: ¶16-040). The payment is assessable in the hands of the purchaser (ITAA97 s 15-5: ¶10-110). Consideration should also be given to the rights of employees under superannuation fund deeds and to any necessary amendments of those deeds.

• *Insurance* — upon a transfer, all relevant insurances should be rearranged to ensure that the transferee is fully insured.

• *Licences, etc* — it may be necessary to re-negotiate licences of patents and other forms of intellectual property, although this may have CGT consequences.

• *Liquidity of parties* — where the liquidity or viability of one of the parties is in doubt (eg where a loss company is involved) account should be taken of the provisions of the *Bankruptcy Act 1966* and the fact that the *Corporations Act 2001* may allow the transactions involved in the tax planning exercise to be set aside.

¶31-045 Tax "shelters"

Taxpayers may be tempted to invest in tax shelters towards the end of each income year. Essentially, these tax shelters have a common element: the investment of borrowed funds by the taxpayer in circumstances where deductions are generated in the early years of the transaction and offset by assessable income in later years (provided representations as to the assessable income flows are met), with the net result that the taxpayer obtains the benefit of a deferral of tax. In the case of a high income earner, such tax savings can generate significant cash flow advantages in the early years of the arrangement.

Taxpayers should seek independent professional advice before entering into a tax shelter as the Commissioner may challenge the arrangement on a number of grounds, eg under Pt IVA (¶30-120), or on the basis that it is a sham (¶30-110).

Tax shelters should also be closely scrutinised from a commercial point of view. Tax shelters will often expose participants to commercial risks (such as personal exposure to liabilities) and should therefore only be considered after expert advice has been taken.

The ATO issues "product rulings" (¶24-540) that publicly rule on the availability of claimed tax benefits from tax-effective investments. Taxpayer alerts warn taxpayers of schemes that are under scrutiny, and the ATO provides information on its website to investors in relation to aggressive tax planning. The ATO has issued practice instructions to ATO staff on the treatment of aggressive tax planning (PS LA 2008/15).

One "tax shelter" that usually carries low commercial risks is the family home. Investment in the main residence is particularly attractive, as capital gains arising from such an investment will generally be tax-free (¶11-730). If the main residence has also been used for income-producing purposes, part of any capital gain may be assessable (¶11-760). For a checklist of tax rules affecting family homes, see ¶44-108.

¶31-050 Tax compliance requirements of other statutes

Apart from commercial considerations (¶31-040) and the possible application of multiple tax rules to particular situations (¶31-000), the requirements of other statutes and the difficulties that may be encountered in satisfying them should also be assessed in formulating a tax plan. Some of the relevant provisions are:

- the requirements for registration of transfers of interests in real property, leases, patents, etc
- the requirement that dispositions of interests in real estate or of equitable interests be effected in writing
- the liabilities that various steps or documents in the tax plan may attract under other revenue legislation, principally stamp duty, and liabilities of the new structure to other taxes (eg GST) and payroll tax
- the requirements imposed by various statutes to obtain licences to carry on particular types of business
- the corporations law (¶4-682)
- the *Anti-Money Laundering and Counter-Terrorism Financing Act 2006* (www.austrac.gov.au)
- the requirements and constraints imposed by the *Competition and Consumer Act 2010*, and
- the likely application of testators family maintenance provisions in situations involving deceased estates (see article in CCH *Tax Week* at ¶41 (2014)).

¶31-080 Checklist: methods of reducing tax liability

The objective of any tax planning arrangement is to reduce the tax payable in respect of a given quantity of profits or earnings, including profits on the realisation of assets within the CGT regime. In broad terms, there are several ways of reducing liability to tax. These are summarised below.

Aim	Possible methods
Reduce assessable income	Derive capital, not income (¶31-100) Avoid deriving assessable amounts (¶31-120) Select best CGT option for calculating gain (¶31-125) Maximise CGT cost base (¶31-130) Take advantage of tax exemptions (¶31-140)
Increase deductions and offsets	Maximise present deductions and concessions (¶31-160) Deductions for individuals (¶31-170) Deductions for businesses (¶31-180)
Reduce rate of tax/defer payment of tax	Maximise offsets (¶31-220) Averaging for primary producers, authors, inventors, etc (¶31-240) Delay derivation of income (¶31-270)
Divert income	Alienate income to another (¶30-900, ¶31-500) Transfer income-producing assets (¶31-290) Contract with associated taxpayers (¶31-370) Use discretionary distributions (¶31-420)

Aim	Possible methods
Select tax planning "vehicle"	Family members (¶31-510) Family partnerships (¶31-520) Family companies (¶31-530) Family trusts (¶31-540) Loss companies (¶31-550) Unit trusts (¶31-560) Loss trusts (¶31-540)
Common situations	Sale of business (¶31-610) CGT issues (¶31-620)

These strategies may conflict in a particular case. For example, a high income earner may be desirable as a holder of a negatively geared property from an income tax perspective, but would be undesirable from a CGT perspective if that property was expected to increase significantly in value. Thus, it is necessary to balance different tax considerations. *Non-tax* issues must also be considered, eg the high income earner may be an undesirable owner of an asset if that person is a professional who may be subject to a negligence action.

Reducing Assessable Income

¶31-095 Overview: reducing assessable income

There are a number of ways in which the assessable income of a taxpayer may be reduced. The CGT provisions must also be considered to ensure that assets are acquired by the most appropriate taxpayer in the most appropriate circumstances. Further, the provisions that tax certain non-cash business benefits even though they are not convertible into money must be considered (¶10-030).

¶31-100 Derive capital, not income

In some cases the benefit of an asset or right may be realised in the form of either a capital receipt or a revenue receipt. For example, see ¶10-020.

Where an asset being disposed of is a pre-CGT asset it is clearly advantageous to derive a capital receipt, as it will generally not be assessable. The same applies to CGT-exempt assets such as family homes or sales of small business assets. However, even with non-exempt, post-CGT assets, realisation of capital gains is generally preferable to realisation of income gains because of the benefits of the discounted capital gains rules applying to individuals, complying superannuation entities and trusts (¶11-033, ¶12-005). Taxpayers should also consider whether they are eligible for the small business CGT concessions (¶7-110).

Realisation of a capital gain, rather than income, may also be desirable to enable the taxpayer to take advantage of current year capital losses or unused capital losses from previous years.

The proceeds of extraordinary business or commercial transactions are likely to be income rather than capital if a significant intention was to make a profit (¶10-112).

¶31-120 Avoid deriving assessable amounts

Taxpayers will not usually be assessed on amounts that are not derived (the time of derivation will depend on whether the taxpayer adopts a cash or accruals basis of tax accounting). However, where the taxpayer does not receive an amount under a proposed arrangement, care must be taken if the economic benefit of the right or asset concerned is to be derived by the taxpayer or their family. Some provisions are designed to ensure that even if the taxpayer does not receive and is not entitled to receive an amount, he/she is taxed as if an amount had been received (eg the "constructive receipt" rules (¶9-080), certain provisions governing the disposal of trading stock (¶9-290) and the CGT rules (¶11-500)).

Two obvious ways of avoiding a receipt are to give the asset concerned to someone who is able to realise it without suffering tax in consequence (but see ¶31-300) or to divert income to another taxpayer (¶31-280).

Change of accounting basis

In certain circumstances, a change of accounting basis may lead to amounts received by a taxpayer being treated as not having been derived for income tax purposes, although the appropriate basis of accounting depends on an objective assessment of the taxpayer's business (it is recommended that the Commissioner's approval be obtained).

There are 2 alternative methods of accounting for the derivation of income — the cash or receipts basis and the accruals or earnings basis (¶9-030). The Commissioner's views on the appropriate accounting method are set out in TR 98/1.

Use of roll-overs

Certain transactions that would otherwise give rise to an income tax liability may be sheltered by the use of roll-overs. One example is where there is a deemed disposal of trading stock on the dissolution or reorganisation of a partnership, provided the partners in the old partnership retain at least a 25% interest in the trading stock (¶9-290). Roll-over relief may also be available in respect of balancing adjustments arising from changes in ownership interests in depreciated property (¶17-710).

Deferral of receipts

For commercial reasons, avoiding the receipt of assessable income may not be possible or advisable. Nevertheless, it may be possible to defer derivation of assessable income (which includes the realisation of a capital gain) until a future year of income. Because tax rates are invariably higher than interest rates, this will result in savings to taxpayers and will be of particular benefit where tax rates fall from one year to the next. Readers should accordingly consider when the relevant item of assessable income will be "derived" for income tax purposes (¶31-270).

Salary packaging and salary sacrifice arrangements

Salary packaging can produce tax advantages where it enables concessionally taxed benefits to replace higher taxed income: see generally ¶35-057.

The tax consequences of salary sacrifice arrangements (SSAs) vary according to whether or not the arrangement is "effective". The ATO accepts that an employee may enter into an effective SSA with his/her employer under which the employee sacrifices a *future* entitlement to salary or wages in return for the employer making superannuation contributions (or providing other fringe benefits) of an equivalent value for the employee. If, on the other hand, the salary or wages that are forgone are those to which the employee is *already* entitled, the arrangement is not treated as effective (TR 2001/10; *Wood*).

Under effective SSAs:

- benefits are not assessable to the employee (s 23L: ¶10-030)
- benefits are not subject to PAYG withholding (¶26-150)
- benefits are subject to FBT (¶35-070)
- the employer's contributions may qualify as contributions under the superannuation guarantee (SG) scheme (¶39-240)
- the employer's contributions to complying funds may be deductible as superannuation contributions (¶13-710).

Under *in*effective SSAs, benefits are derived as salary or wages and are assessable to the employee (ss 6-5; 6-10) and are subject to PAYG withholding (¶26-150). Benefits are not subject to FBT (¶35-070). The employer's contributions do not qualify as contributions under the SG scheme (¶39-240) and they are not deductible as superannuation contributions (¶13-710).

An effective SSA may include an arrangement entered into with an ''employee'' within the extended meaning of that term in the superannuation guarantee legislation, eg a person who works under a contract that is wholly or principally for the labour of the person, or artists, musicians, sportspersons, etc (SGD 2006/2).

¶31-125 Selecting best CGT option for calculating gain

Individuals, complying superannuation entities and trusts may have a choice as to how to calculate the capital gain on disposal of assets — the frozen indexation option or the discounted basis. For factors relevant to this decision, see ¶11-038.

¶31-130 Maximising the cost base of an asset

Maximising the cost base of an asset acquired (or deemed to have been acquired) after 19 September 1985 will reduce any capital gain (or increase any capital loss) on a subsequent disposal of the asset, thereby reducing assessable income.

The cost base of an asset may often be increased by a simple variation to the proposed structure of a transaction, subject as always to other commercial considerations. For example, a taxpayer proposing to fund a company would maximise the cost base of that company by subscribing all of the money by way of share capital, instead of providing the money by way of loans (¶31-530). This may result in favourable CGT consequences on a sale or winding up of the company (although the freezing of indexation and reflection of the funding in the selling price may minimise any advantage). Of course, other tax considerations may suggest a different approach (eg depending on the tax consequences in its country of residence, a non-resident proposing to fund an Australian company may prefer to maximise debt funding within the constraints of the thin capitalisation rules (¶22-700) due to favourable treatment of interest paid to non-residents and ease of access to the funds once cash flows are positive).

¶31-140 Take advantage of tax exemptions

For details of *tax exemptions*, see ¶10-600 and the checklist at ¶10-005.

Note particularly the exemption for superannuation benefits paid to taxpayers aged 60 or over (¶14-220) and the rules affecting commencement and cessation of superannuation income streams (¶14-120).

Increasing Deductions

¶31-160 Overview: increasing deductions

Increasing the tax deductions allowable in an income year is another way to reduce the tax liability for that year.

In practice, taxpayers often lose deductions they could have validly claimed because they are either unaware of their entitlement or because they have not kept the records required to substantiate the deductions. This is particularly important in relation to claims attracting specific substantiation requirements, such as claims for the work-related use of motor vehicles (¶16-320). The Commissioner has a discretion to overlook any failure to comply with the substantiation requirements when the ATO is satisfied that the taxpayer is entitled to the deduction claimed (¶16-210). Where there are no specific substantiation provisions, record-keeping is still important as taxpayers who are audited will be required to prove their entitlement to any deductions claimed.

Taxpayers will often benefit by ‘‘accelerating’’ deductions so as to ‘‘incur’’ them in the current year, rather than in subsequent years. This may be particularly beneficial if the tax rates in the current year are higher than in subsequent years. Whether a deduction is ‘‘incurred’’ in a particular income year will depend on the requirements of the particular deductibility provision. The principles that determine when losses or outgoings are ‘‘incurred’’ are discussed at ¶16-040.

Capital expenditure, even though it is not deductible under ITAA97 s 8-1, may be of benefit as the legislation contains various provisions that specifically allow deductions for certain kinds of expenditure and amortisation of the cost of acquiring or creating depreciating assets used for income-producing purposes (¶17-000).

¶31-170 Increasing deductions for individuals

The consequences of deductions for individuals will depend on the type of assessable income earned:

- deductions against salary income will generate a tax reduction, the size of which depends on the taxpayer’s marginal tax rate, and
- deductions against non-salary income will reduce current year tax and possibly also the PAYG instalment rate (¶27-220 and following) for the following income year.

A salaried individual who is entitled to significant deductions during an income year may ask the ATO to vary the PAYG withholding rate (¶26-130).

Expenditure must be apportioned (between deductible and non-deductible expenditure) where it is incurred for both income-producing and non-income-producing purposes. See, for example, *Madigan* (outgoings on a rental property apportioned because the property was let partly for private purposes: ¶16-650).

Broadly, employed taxpayers are entitled to fewer deductions than their self-employed or employer counterparts. Nevertheless, employees who incur expenditure that clearly relates to their employment may be able to claim deductions in some circumstances (¶16-160 and following).

Superannuation: member contributions

An individual is entitled to a deduction for personal superannuation contributions (¶13-730). However, excess contributions tax may be payable if the contributions exceed specified levels.

Certain contributions may be eligible for a government co-contribution (¶13-760). A tax offset is available for superannuation contributions on behalf of a taxpayer’s low income spouse (¶13-770).

Borrowing expenses

Where a taxpayer borrows money and invests that money for the purpose of earning assessable income or as part of a business carried on for that purpose, interest on those borrowings will generally be deductible on general principles (¶16-740). Thus, interest on borrowings to acquire a rent-producing property will generally be deductible, whereas interest on borrowings to acquire vacant land (which did not produce any income) would generally not be deductible. Interest of the second kind is allowed as part of the CGT cost base of an asset (¶11-550).

Negative gearing

As noted above, an outgoing may be deductible in a year of income although the assessable income motivating the outgoing is not generated until a subsequent year of income. Where deductions associated with an investment exceed the assessable income derived from the investment in any particular income year (‘‘negative gearing’’), the excess can be used to reduce the tax payable on other assessable income of the investing taxpayer (¶16-740).

¶31-180 Increasing deductions for businesses

Tax planning for business taxpayers often raises different considerations, not least because business taxpayers are more likely to be subject to non-tax regulations and considerations (eg industrial awards and enterprise agreements) that may constrain available options. The fact that non-compliance with regulatory requirements may give rise to a non-deductible penalty, eg the superannuation guarantee charge (see below), is a tax planning consideration.

Tax advisers should be aware that the commercial debt forgiveness measures provide that the net amount of certain commercial debts that are forgiven is applied to reduce the debtor's accumulated revenue losses, net capital losses, certain undeducted expenditures and cost bases of assets (¶16-910).

Borrowing expenses

Interest on borrowings used for working capital of a business should generally be deductible (¶16-740). However, particular attention should be paid to the requirement that there be a connection between the expense and the taxpayer's business or other income-producing activities. The courts appear to be adopting a more lenient line in situations, for example, where borrowed funds are used to acquire and hold a capital asset to be developed for income-producing purposes in the future (¶16-740).

As to whether interest can be included in the cost base of an asset for CGT purposes, see ¶11-550.

Superannuation

Contributions paid to a complying superannuation fund in respect of eligible employees are tax-deductible (subject to limits) and FBT-exempt (¶13-710).

Contributions knowingly made to non-complying superannuation funds are not deductible (¶13-710). The tax treatment of such contributions is highly punitive, as they are also subject to FBT (¶35-070). If a non-complying fund was a complying fund in the immediately preceding income year, it is also assessed on its net previous income (ie asset values less undeducted contributions) (¶13-200).

Bad debts

Bad debts that have previously been brought to account by the taxpayer as assessable income are deductible under ITAA97 s 25-35 (bad debts in respect of money lent in the ordinary course of a moneylending business are also deductible). A deduction is only allowable in the year in which the debt is physically written off, so timing is crucial (¶16-582). Under the commercial debt forgiveness measures (¶16-910), the amount of the deduction may be reduced in certain circumstances. In addition, the forgiveness of a debt by a shareholder to a private company may be deemed to be a dividend (¶4-220).

Where the requirements of s 25-35 are not strictly met, a write-off for bad debts of business taxpayers may be allowed under ITAA97 s 8-1.

There are restrictions on trusts (other than family trusts) deducting bad debts and debt-for-equity swaps (¶6-262 and following).

Capital allowances (depreciation)

Capital allowances are not available if income-producing operations have not commenced (¶17-480).

Capital allowances are available to the "holder" of a depreciating asset. The "holder" of an asset is identified by reference to the particular circumstances. For example, a lessor is the holder of a leased depreciating asset that becomes a fixture attached to another person's land, where the lessor has the right to recover the asset (¶17-020).

A number of other provisions, such as the primary production provisions (¶18-000), mining provisions (¶19-000), R&D provisions (¶20-150) and capital works provisions (¶20-470), allow similar deductions in special circumstances.

Blackhole expenditure

A business may be able to claim a deduction for capital expenditure if the expenditure relates to the carrying on of a current, former or a proposed business and if the expenditure is not otherwise deductible under another section. These amounts are specifically made deductible over 5 years (¶16-156).

Trading stock

Those businesses that involve buying and selling may often fall within the specific provisions dealing with trading stock (¶9-150). The trading stock provisions may give rise to a deduction where stock on hand can be devalued as at year-end below its book value. Expenditure incurred in acquiring trading stock is generally not deductible until the stock is on hand (¶16-040); a taxpayer cannot therefore claim a deduction in an income year before the year in which the trading stock is delivered. The Commissioner's views on the assessability and deductibility of discounts offered by traders for prompt settlement of accounts should also be noted (¶9-050). A simplified trading stock regime applies for small business taxpayers (¶9-170).

Incentive deductions

Various tax incentives apply to encourage investment in activities regarded as economically or environmentally desirable. More recent incentives have been hedged about with many qualifications and anti-avoidance provisions, so that benefits are now evaluated more as a reduction in effective cost than as a simple tax saving. The principal incentive deductions relate to income-producing buildings (¶20-470), gifts (¶16-942), Australian films (¶20-330), R&D (¶20-150), environmental protection and primary production (¶18-000).

Reducing Rate and Deferring Liability to Tax

¶31-210 Overview: reducing rate and tax deferral

Another tax planning device is to arrange a taxpayer's affairs so that the rate of tax payable on the same aggregate amount of taxable income is reduced (principally by diverting income to a lower rate taxpayer: ¶31-280), or so that the liability to pay tax is deferred with consequent cash flow savings. Deferring the liability to tax may also lead to a reduction in the rate of tax (by spreading income over a number of years rather than over a number of taxpayers). This is especially beneficial when tax rates reduce in later years of income.

Arrangements to reduce the tax payable on a particular level of taxable income should not give rise to a "tax benefit" for the purposes of ITAA36 Pt IVA (¶30-160).

¶31-220 Taking advantage of tax offsets and other benefits

Tax offsets, unlike deductions, do not enter the calculation of taxable income. Rather, once taxable income has been determined, a tax offset is subtracted from the tax payable in respect of that taxable income. If the sum of any tax offsets exceeds the tax payable, the excess is "wasted" as it cannot be carried forward to a subsequent income year. For some exceptions, see ¶15-010.

Franking credits

Receipt of franked dividends by a company will generate franking credits regardless of whether the company has any taxable income and, subject to various anti-avoidance provisions, will not affect that company's tax liability in respect of those dividends (¶4-110).

However, franking credits affect the tax liability of individuals, whether franked dividends are received directly or flow through trusts or partnerships. The following points should be noted by taxpayers wishing to maximise the benefits of franking credits:

- rebatable recipients may offset the balance of those credits against tax payable on their other income and are entitled to refunds of any remaining excess (¶4-800, ¶4-820)
- franking credits are effectively of less benefit to non-residents than to residents (¶4-840), and
- benefits to associates of private companies that are deemed to be dividends may not be franked (¶4-200, ¶4-220).

For details of the various anti-avoidance measures associated with franked dividends, including dividend washing, see ¶4-900.

Foreign income tax offsets

A taxpayer should structure their affairs to ensure that all of their foreign income tax offsets are utilised in the same income year. This is because taxpayers can no longer carry forward excess offsets except where transitional rules apply (¶21-760).

Concessions for personal superannuation contributions

Certain lower-income employees may be entitled to concessions for their personal superannuation contributions (¶13-760). A rebate may also be available for contributions made on behalf of a low income or non-working spouse (¶13-770).

Personal tax offsets

For year end strategies to maximise personal tax offset entitlements (¶15-000), see the checklist at ¶31-700.

¶31-240 Benefits of averaging

Primary producers

The benefits of the averaging provisions for primary producers in ITAA97 Div 392 (¶18-200) are substantial only in the case of taxpayers whose income is high in relation to their average income and whose income includes a high proportion of primary production income. On the other hand, the averaging system will disadvantage a primary producer in any year in which their taxable income is less than their average income (the averaging system can apply even where it would increase the tax payable). Primary producers have the option of permanently withdrawing from the averaging system.

Authors, performers, inventors, sportspersons, etc

The averaging system applicable to ‘‘authors’’ (ie artists, composers and writers), inventors, performers, production associates and sportspersons (¶2-140) can confer significant benefits.

In tax planning for certain categories of eligible persons, eg authors and inventors, the benefits of capital/income conversions (¶31-100) can also be very significant. In some circumstances, a lump sum received by an author or inventor for the assignment of a copyright or patent may be a capital receipt, provided it is not received as part of the proceeds of the assignor’s business or profession.

As far as the assignor is concerned, the CGT provisions may only apply if the copyright or patent was acquired (or deemed to be acquired) after 19 September 1985. In determining the time of acquisition for CGT purposes, the Commissioner considers that the crucial time is when some positive work commenced on the manuscript, invention, etc (¶11-450).

[FITR ¶361-900; ¶385-000]

¶31-270 Delaying the derivation of income

Cash versus accruals basis

In determining when income is derived, different rules apply to different kinds of income and different kinds of taxpayers. For example, it seems that a sole practitioner is assessable on a receipts (or cash) basis, whereas a large professional firm (eg of accountants or solicitors) is assessable on an earnings (or accruals) basis (¶9-030).

In most instances, the tax planner will wish to ensure that professional clients and others in a similar position commence to return their income on a receipts basis and continue to do so for as long as possible, since this will provide an effective deferral of tax payable (¶31-120).

The Commissioner's guidelines on whether the receipts or earnings method applies are set out in TR 98/1. Note also the views (in TR 96/20 and TD 96/45) on the assessability and deductibility of prompt payment discounts (¶9-050). For example, there may be cases where the full invoice price, which is considered to be assessable at the time of sale, is returned in one income year while the discount, which is considered to be deductible when the account is settled, is not claimed as a deduction until the following year.

Services provided over period

The decision in the *Arthur Murray case* (¶9-090) has been the basis of arrangements designed to confer immediate deductions on one taxpayer (eg by the payment of a management charge) while the recipient returns the income over the period during which the income is said to be earned (ie as the services are provided). From a commercial point of view, the viability of such arrangements may depend on the accounting treatment of the payments and on what will happen if the services are not in fact performed.

In considering such arrangements, it is necessary to take into account not only the general anti-avoidance provisions of ITAA36 Pt IVA, but also the various prepayment rules (¶16-045, ¶16-110). ITAA36 Div 16E (ss 159GP to 159GZ) is also designed to match the assessability and deductibility of payments (other than periodic interest) on qualifying securities, thus overcoming potential mismatch opportunities arising from the *Australian Guarantee Corporation case* (¶23-320).

The TOFA regime provides rules for taxing gains and losses arising on certain financial arrangements (ITAA97 Div 230). The rules generally apply to large taxpayers but their scope is not limited to these taxpayers (¶23-020).

Instalments of profit

In *Thorogood's case*, it was held that the profit on the sale of certain land, where the purchase price was payable by instalments over a period, was derived only over the term of those instalment payments. The principle recognised in this case may be utilised by a taxpayer who anticipates that the profit on a sale of property would be assessable income under ITAA97 s 6-5 (¶10-112). Note *Gasparin's case* (¶9-170), where blocks of land ceased to be trading stock of a developer on settlement of the contracts of sale and not when the contracts became unconditional (which was before settlement). Where the arrangement is commercially justifiable, a taxpayer may arrange to sell the relevant property on terms to an appropriate recipient, eg a trust or company, with the recipient subsequently making the sale to the ultimate purchaser on terms that result in little or no profit to the recipient. The taxpayer then returns in each year only that proportion of the total profit that is appropriate to the instalments received in that year from the interposed recipient. However, the Commissioner does not agree to the spreading of profit in this manner where the disposal occurs in the course of carrying on a business. Further, the CGT provisions may apply even if the profit is not assessable under s 6-5.

Where there is a disposal of property under an instalment contract and the CGT provisions apply, it is important to remember that the whole of the capital gain accrues to the vendor in the income year in which the disposal occurs, ie usually the income year in which the contract is entered into.

Trading stock valuation options

By taking advantage of the option conferred by ITAA97 s 70-45 in relation to the valuation of trading stock on hand at the end of an income year, a taxpayer may adjust the respective taxable incomes of that year and the succeeding year (¶9-180). It is normal practice to value stock on hand at the end of the year at the lower of cost or market selling value, effectively postponing the taxation of any increase in the value of stock on hand.

Where there is a change in ownership of, or interests in, trading stock (eg on the formation or dissolution of a partnership), there is a notional disposal of the trading stock at market value (ITAA97 s 70-100). However, where there is at least a 25% continuing interest, the capacity of the old and new owners to elect to value the trading stock at its tax value (¶9-295) may enable there to be a derivation of profits on a notional sale of the entirety of trading stock.

Small business taxpayers are subject to modified trading stock provisions (¶9-170).

Disposal of depreciating assets

Roll-over relief may be available where a change occurs in the ownership of, or in the interests of persons in, depreciating assets, eg where a partnership is created, varied or dissolved (¶17-780). The disposal of depreciated plant for a consideration in excess of its cost may, in appropriate circumstances, give rise to income, eg where the taxpayer trades in that kind of property and the disposal in fact occurs as part of the conduct of the business (¶17-630).

Capital gains

A capital gain (or loss) accrues in the income year in which the disposal of an asset occurs, ie regardless of whether any of the consideration for the disposal has been received. Where an asset is disposed of under a contract, the time of the disposal is the time of the making of the contract. For example, land is generally disposed of at the time the contract of sale is made, although the gain (or loss) is not returned until the change of ownership actually occurs (eg on settlement). Thus it is not possible to spread the derivation of a capital gain.

This should be taken into account when considering the disposal of an asset in circumstances involving the provision of vendor finance to the purchaser (¶11-250).

Methods of Diverting Income

¶31-280 Overview: diverting income

A common method of tax planning has been to ''divert'' income from a taxpayer who bears tax at high rates (the high rate taxpayer) to one who is taxed at low rates or not at all (the low rate taxpayer). Some methods by which income might be diverted are:

- the alienation of income or the transfer of the right to receive it (¶30-900)
- channelling of an individual's income from personal services into a ''business'' structure such as a company, partnership, trust or contractual arrangement, to facilitate income splitting and access to business deductions (for counter measures, see ¶30-600)
- the transfer of income-producing assets (¶31-290)

- deductible payments by the high rate taxpayer to the low rate taxpayer (¶31-370), and
- discretionary distributions (¶31-420).

The various possible *recipients* of the diverted income are discussed at ¶31-500 and following.

¶31-290 Transfer of income-producing assets

If a taxpayer sells, settles on trust or gives away assets of which the taxpayer is the legal and beneficial owner or in which the taxpayer has a beneficial interest and all legal and equitable requirements or formalities are complied with, the taxpayer is not assessable on any income arising from that asset or beneficial interest after the assignment. This is so even though some of that income (eg rent, interest, dividends) may have accrued, but was not payable, before the assignment. This applies, for example, to outright sales of shares or securities cum dividend (¶4-100) or cum interest (¶23-430).

Tax benefits may arise if income is received by a low rate taxpayer instead of an associated high rate taxpayer, particularly where the asset can be made available to the high rate taxpayer in a non-taxable form. The general anti-avoidance provisions of ITAA36 Pt IVA (¶30-120) generally will not apply to the simple disposition of an income-producing asset by a natural person to a wholly-owned private company (TD 95/4). Some of the possibilities are as follows.

- A business carried on by the high rate taxpayer may be sold, or in appropriate circumstances leased or licensed, to the low rate taxpayer who carries on the business and derives the resultant income.
- Investments, such as shares, real property, interests in trust estates, etc, may be sold or given to an associated low rate taxpayer.
- Moneys that would otherwise be invested by the high rate taxpayer may be given or advanced, interest-free and repayable on demand, to a low rate taxpayer who in turn deposits them at interest. If moneys are deposited in joint names, the high rate taxpayer will be assessable on half the interest (subject to any specific apportionment).
- Where both members of a couple are high rate taxpayers, spouse superannuation contributions (¶13-770) might be considered. This can facilitate accumulation of retirement wealth at concessional tax rates and splitting of retirement incomes.
- An investment property may be leased to a low rate taxpayer at a rent sufficient to cover expenses only and then sub-leased by the low rate taxpayer at the market rent (¶16-650). If a premium is paid for the head lease, it would be non-deductible to the sub-lessee but would give rise to a CGT liability for the lessor (¶11-300).
- The interest of the high rate taxpayer in a partnership may be assigned to a low rate taxpayer, the former remaining a member of the partnership to the exclusion of the latter (*Everett*; *Galland*). However, such "Everett assignments" will generally result in the assignor deriving a large capital gain (¶11-200). Further, CGT is imposed where a prospective partnership interest is assigned and the subsequently created interest is held by its creator as trustee of a discretionary trust (a "pre-admission Everett assignment") (¶11-290).

Sale and leaseback transactions may also provide tax benefits (¶23-240). However, the Commissioner will challenge sale and leaseback arrangements that are primarily designed as tax avoidance measures, eg they contain inflated prices or artificially low residual values.

What transfers are to be made, and on what terms, can only be decided by a careful examination of the circumstances of each particular case and the application of the legislation. The difficulties in effecting the transfer of the relevant asset, as well as the tax and commercial consequences of the transfer, will need to be taken into account.

Where the transfer of an asset is contemplated, one of the most important considerations is the impact of the CGT provisions. If the asset was acquired by the transferor before 20 September 1985, it will lose the status of a pre-CGT asset in the hands of the transferee, unless roll-over relief is available (¶12-035).

¶31-300 Problems arising from the transfer of assets

The transfer of assets may give rise to unfavourable taxation and other consequences. Some of the more common problems are mentioned below.

Work in progress

To overcome the potential double taxation of work in progress (most commonly with the transfer of professional partnerships), a deduction is allowed for amounts paid for the transfer of work in progress (ITAA97 s 25-95) (¶16-158).

Nevertheless, work in progress should be treated with care. If a payment to a retiring partner cannot be dissected into distinct components, the whole amount will be treated as a capital sum subject to the CGT provisions (*Crommelin*) — a partner's right to receive work in progress payments on the dissolution of a partnership is clearly an ''asset'' (¶11-200). It may be possible to adjust retirement payments between capital and income to suit the parties (eg *Nandan's case* where a retiring partner's partnership income was determined in accordance with the dissolution agreement: ¶5-160).

Repairs

Where a property requiring repairs is to be transferred, it is preferable for the repairs to be effected before the transfer (¶16-700). Of course, expenditure in relation to a newly acquired asset that is capital in nature may, depending on the facts, be part of the depreciable cost and/or cost base of the asset. In this regard, the circumstances in which capital expenditure to enhance the value of an asset may form part of the cost base of the asset should be noted (¶11-550).

Depreciating assets

Where a deduction has been claimed on a depreciating asset that is being transferred, attention must be paid to the rules governing balancing adjustments and possible CGT liabilities (¶17-670), and to any balancing adjustment relief that may be available (¶17-710, ¶17-720).

Improvements to land

In certain situations, a building or other capital improvement to land is treated as a separate asset for CGT purposes (¶11-410). On disposal of the property, there may be a separate capital gain or loss for each asset. If the land and improvement(s) are sold under an arm's length transaction and there is an allocation of the sale price in the contract, the Commissioner will accept that allocation for CGT purposes; if there is no agreed allocation, the parties will need to make their own reasonable apportionment based on market values (TD 98/24; *Collis*).

Trading stock

Where the assets of the business sold include trading stock, ITAA97 s 70-90 requires an amount equal to the market value of the stock on hand to be included in the seller's assessable income (¶9-290). Where the transferee is a partnership of which the seller and buyer are members, or where the asset transferred is an interest in a partnership, it may be possible to take advantage of the right to elect that s 70-90 not apply, although the circumstances in which an election may be made are restricted.

Goodwill

Small businesses may be eligible for a 50% CGT exemption in a capital gain arising on the sale of the business under the 50% "active asset" reduction (¶7-175). This concession may apply in addition to the general 50% discount (¶11-036) so that only 25% of the original capital gain is taxable. This exemption may be claimed in addition to the other CGT small business concessions.

Unsolicited gifts

Property acquired by a taxpayer as a passive recipient (eg by way of an unsolicited gift or inheritance) cannot be said to have been acquired by the taxpayer with a profit-making purpose.

For CGT purposes, an *inter vivos* gift of property, or a disposal and acquisition between parties not dealing with each other at arm's length, constitutes the disposal of the property by the transferor and the acquisition of the property by the transferee for a consideration equal to the market value of the property (¶11-510, ¶11-570). As to the position where property passes on death, see ¶12-570.

The fixing of a transfer price in relation to an *inter vivos* transfer may itself cause difficulties: a price at the higher end of the acceptable market range for the asset concerned may increase the amount on which the vendor is possibly exposed to a tax liability, while a price towards the lower end of that range may increase the possible tax liability on a resale by the purchaser. Further, the Commissioner may fix a transfer price irrespective of that selected by the parties.

Practical problems

There are other difficulties that may stand in the way of a convenient transfer of an income-producing asset from a high rate to a low rate taxpayer. Some assets, by their nature, are incapable of transfer: they may be rights that by the instrument creating them are expressed to be personal to the high rate taxpayer; or they may be assets that a company or trustee is prohibited from owning (eg certain Crown land leases) or the transfer of which requires third party consent (eg ministerial consent required for the transfer of certain mining tenements).

Some business activities (particularly those of a professional nature) are capable of being carried on only by registered persons, who are usually high rate taxpayers. These problems are not always insurmountable, as exemplified by *Everett* (solicitor assigned part of his share in a partnership), *Peacock* (surveyor in partnership with his non-practising wife) and *Liedig* (registered landbroker carried on landbroking business in trust for himself and his wife). However, even if they are overcome, there is still a risk that the general anti-avoidance provisions of Pt IVA will apply (¶5-160). The personal services income regime (¶30-600) should also be considered, with particular attention to the exclusion of income from the conduct of a genuine personal services business (¶30-660).

The transfer of assets may also involve unacceptably high costs in stamp duties.

In many cases it is possible to devise arrangements that circumvent these practical problems, but the structure that is required for these purposes may in turn affect the incidence of income tax and, in particular, may indicate that the dominant purpose of the arrangement is obtaining a tax benefit within the scope of Pt IVA.

¶31-370 Contracting with associated taxpayers

The methods of diverting income already discussed concern the redirection of income at its source, so that it is not in fact derived by the high rate taxpayer at all. An alternative method of diverting income is to contract with an associated low rate taxpayer for the payment of amounts that, although income to the recipient, are deductible (¶6-010) to the high rate taxpayer. It will be crucial to ensure that the outgoing is deductible and, of course, that the perceived low rate taxpayer is in fact a low rate taxpayer, eg provisions such as the CFC rules (¶21-110) strictly limit access to low rate taxpayers in the foreign context.

Different considerations arise depending on whether a transaction involves a non-resident taxpayer or is purely a domestic transaction. Great caution is urged in respect of transactions that are not purely domestic, because of:

- the broad powers of the ATO under the transfer pricing provisions (¶22-580)
- increasing moves against multinational profit shifting (¶22-640), and
- the increased willingness of the ATO to counter international arrangements through the general anti-avoidance rules (¶30-110).

Taxpayers should create and keep contemporaneous documentation to show that they were dealing with associated enterprises at arm's length. It may be advisable to obtain an Advance Pricing Arrangement regarding the tax treatment of international transactions, agreements or arrangements between related parties (¶22-650).

Where the arrangement involves an element of prepayment, the high rate taxpayer will not be permitted a deduction until, in effect, the associated low rate taxpayer is assessable on the receipt (ITAA36 s 82KK: ¶16-110). Further, losses or outgoings of an excessive amount incurred in respect of payments to a third party are not deductible if associated with an acquisition of property by the taxpayer or an associate at an undervalue. If the parties are not associated, the prepayment may only be deductible to the extent that the prepayment rules permit (¶16-045).

¶31-380 Employing the family

In many cases the simplest way of diverting income is to employ family members, eg the spouse or older children may act as receptionists, gardeners, secretaries, etc. However, the Commissioner has the power (under ITAA97 s 26-35) to reduce the amount of the deduction claimed by the employer for salary or wages paid to a relative to an amount that, in the Commissioner's opinion, is reasonable (¶16-530). In practice, it is advisable to keep records of the duties performed by the family employee and to have regard to the award rates for work of a similar type.

In some cases employing the family is not a good idea because family members may lose access to other forms of government assistance such as the family tax benefit which is exempt from income tax (¶10-197). For the application of these rules to partnerships, see ¶5-100.

In determining the salary payable to a low rate taxpayer by a family company, ITAA36 s 109 (concerning excessive payments) should be considered (¶4-220).

Where the taxpayer is a child under the age of 18, the provisions of ITAA36 Div 6AA (including the arm's length provisions), under which the child's unearned income is taxable at a punitive rate of personal tax, may apply (¶2-160).

¶31-420 Using discretionary distributions

Some income sources are by their nature subject to direction or diversion (directly or indirectly) by a taxpayer who can control the allocation of income among members or beneficiaries of the entities earning it. These entities, the ''vehicles'' of tax planning, are principally the family partnership (¶31-520), the family trust estate (¶31-540) and the family company (¶31-530).

The general anti-avoidance provisions of ITAA36 Pt IVA must be taken into account when establishing arrangements for the allocation of income. Part IVA can apply to arrangements involving a trust, irrespective of whether the tax benefit is obtained by the trustee or the beneficiaries (*Grollo Nominees*).

One question that needs to be considered is whether any particular person (eg a partner or beneficiary) might reasonably be expected to have received income that is diverted to someone else. If so, the former will obtain a tax benefit (within the meaning of Pt IVA) and may therefore be assessed on the diverted income (¶30-160). Taxpayers should also be careful in the case of ‘‘vehicles’’ with significant pre-CGT assets, as the Commissioner may argue that changes to a previous pattern of income distributions are relevant to whether those assets are deemed to be subject to CGT (¶12-870).

Partnerships and trusts

A partnership may be constituted so that one or more of the partners has the power to direct the distribution of the net partnership profit among the partners. However, partnerships formed on such terms are uncommon because the joint and several unlimited liability of partners for the liabilities of the partnership tends to lead partners to require a degree of certainty as to their respective rights. Income derived by a partner as a result of such a distribution is not thereby subject to additional tax under ITAA36 s 94 (¶5-180) since that provision applies only to an uncontrolled share in partnership income; ie the question is not whether the determination of the amount of the share is controlled, but whether the share of partnership income, once ascertained, is effectively controlled by the partner. A net partnership loss may be subject to allocation in a similar fashion. Care must be exercised in drafting the partnership agreement to ensure that the income is not in fact derived by the partner having the power of direction but is merely dealt with as he/she directs (*Jones*).

Further, the profits of the partnership cannot, for tax purposes, be so allocated that one partner receives a share of partnership income and another incurs a share of partnership loss — there is only one amount, either net income of the partnership or a partnership loss, available for distribution pursuant to ITAA36 s 92.

In *McDonald's case*, where the taxpayer and his wife acquired investments as joint tenants and agreed between themselves that any net profit would be apportioned 75% to the wife and 25% to the husband and any loss would be wholly absorbed by the husband, it was held that there was no partnership at general law and therefore the husband was entitled to claim only half of the losses (¶5-000). The position may well have been otherwise had there been a partnership at general law, although it is unlikely that the joint ownership of a rental property will of itself be sufficient to establish a partnership at general law (eg *Case 12/95*).

Most states have legislation allowing for the establishment of limited partnerships. Limited liability partnerships are generally taxed as if they are companies (¶3-475) and thus have no partnership tax advantages (eg individual partners do not have access to partnership losses).

The income of a trust estate may, if the trust deed so permits, be allocated among the beneficiaries with a view to incurring the minimum liability to tax (although in some circumstances it is questionable whether the trustee properly exercises a discretion if it is exercised on the basis of overall tax liabilities). Where the trust fund is a ‘‘discretionary trust’’ (¶31-540), ITAA36 s 101 deems the income allocated by the trustee to the beneficiary in exercise of the trustee's discretion to be income to which the beneficiary is presently entitled (¶6-105). In considering the use of a trust estate in tax planning, care should be taken to avoid the application of ITAA36 s 100A (¶6-270). For the position on income ‘‘streaming’’, see ¶6-077.

Recipients of Diverted Income

¶31-500 Choosing recipients of diverted income

The choice of an appropriate recipient (or recipients) for income diverted from a high rate taxpayer by one of the means already discussed will depend on the circumstances of each case, and opportunities available to some taxpayers will be denied to others. That choice may well call for as much skill and judgment on the part of the tax planner as the method of achieving the income diversion itself. Matters to be considered include comparative costs, the possibility of legislative changes, estate planning implications, the degree of sophistication of the taxpayer and their appreciation of legal principles and general understanding of the nature of the vehicle(s) that might be used.

The possible recipients are as follows:

- members of the taxpayer's family (¶31-510)
- a partnership of members of the taxpayer's family (¶31-520)
- a family company (¶31-530)
- a discretionary family trust (¶31-540)
- a "loss" company (¶31-550)
- a unit trust (¶31-560), and/or
- administration companies/service entities (¶31-570).

The purpose of this chapter is not to undertake a detailed consideration of each of the possible recipients, but simply to provide a brief summary of the more important issues. Whatever vehicle is chosen, an important issue will be the degree of control the taxpayer is able to maintain over the diverted income and any assets transferred to assist in the diversion of income.

¶31-510 Diversion to family members

Ordinarily, the most obvious recipients of diverted income would be the members of a taxpayer's family. However, as a result of the provisions of ITAA36 Div 6AA (¶2-160), and restrictions on the use of the low income tax rebate, the diversion of unearned income to minors (ie children under 18), even if married, may in many instances be disadvantageous.

The special penal rates under Div 6AA apply to the unearned income of minors, irrespective of whether such income is derived by them directly from investments owned absolutely by them, or is paid to them or applied for their benefit, etc, through a family trust. Income may still, of course, be diverted to children who are 18 or older. However, such a person would be entitled to demand actual payment of the diverted income and this might not be desirable.

Frequently, the most convenient means of diverting income is by the payment of salaries but, in view of ITAA97 s 26-35, those salaries must be reasonable (¶31-380). Attempts to arrange loans among family members, so that interest is deductible to a high income borrower and assessable in the hands of a selected low income recipient, must be treated with great caution for a number of reasons.

(1) The general anti-avoidance provisions of ITAA36 Pt IVA (¶30-120).

(2) Loans by family companies and family trusts to family members are likely to be reviewed by the ATO to see whether any FBT liabilities exist or whether the loans should be deemed to be dividends (¶4-200).

(3) A loan (or other payment or crediting) by a private company to shareholders or their associates will generally be treated as unfranked assessable dividends unless it is an excluded transaction — such as the payment of a genuine debt owed by the company or a loan that meets minimum interest rate and maximum term criteria (¶4-230).

If there is an absolute diversion of income from a parent to a family member, this will usually result in the parent losing control over the income diverted. The loss of control over income might not be a serious problem where the amounts are relatively small, but it might create a problem if large amounts are involved and the parent does not desire the relevant family member to have control of the diverted income. The problem may be mitigated by encouraging the recipient to incur expenditure that the parent might otherwise have incurred. The disadvantage of the loss of control of income where children are minors can be overcome by using a family trust. However, the high rates of tax on unearned income derived by minors apply irrespective of whether the unearned income is derived by the children directly or through a trust distribution.

For a useful discussion of the relative merits of various methods of drawing funds from a company, see *Symond v Gadens Lawyers Sydney Pty Ltd*.

¶31-520 Diversion through family partnerships

The use of a family partnership, as a device for splitting income between the various members of a family, has declined somewhat because of the greatly increased use of discretionary family trusts (¶31-540) which are more flexible vehicles than partnerships. Another disadvantage is that partners have unlimited liability, unlike the shareholders in a company (including a corporate trustee). The requirements to establish the existence of a partnership are discussed at ¶5-010.

A problem with family partnerships is that, because of the high tax rates on the ‘‘unearned income’’ of minors (¶2-160), the diversion of income to children may be ineffective in achieving a reduction in tax. Another difficulty is that provisions in a partnership agreement of a kind that may be desirable to protect the position of the client might result in the payment of tax on ‘‘uncontrolled partnership income’’ at a penal rate (¶5-180). Accordingly, family partnerships are often only of benefit where the potential partners are all over 18 or, in the case of a non-business, property-owning partnership, the client is not concerned by the fact that the partnership agreement gives family members substantial rights in relation to property.

One advantage of a partnership is that a partner may benefit directly from the CGT small business roll-over and retirement exemptions (¶7-110). Individuals may also be entitled to discount capital gains (¶11-038).

¶31-530 Diversion through family companies

The relatively low rate of tax paid by companies obviously makes the use of a company attractive. Companies have long been used as vehicles for the derivation of income by families. Family companies are also frequently used as vehicles to obtain superannuation benefits. A company can provide greater flexibility than a partnership in the manner of dealing with profits, eg by providing for shares with different classes of rights. In addition, companies may have only one shareholder and director (making it easier for sole traders to incorporate) and various accounting and other requirements have been removed or relaxed in order to reduce the administrative burden on small business.

Other advantages of a company are: (i) unlike a natural person, it does not die and thus most difficulties in relation to devolution of property on death are avoided; (ii) it provides shareholders with the benefits of limited liability; and (iii) it is a well-recognised commercial vehicle with an established body of law concerning its operations. On the other hand, a director has substantial and stringent legal duties and, in certain circumstances, may be liable for certain debts of the company.

Tax advisers should be aware that the Commissioner regards the use of a family company to split an individual’s personal exertion income among family members as a potential tax avoidance arrangement, unless the family company has significant income-producing activities or assets, or engages a number of employees (IT 2121). Further, such arrangements may be thwarted by the personal services income regime (¶30-600). However, the simple disposition of an income-producing asset by an individual to a company wholly-owned by that individual will not generally attract the operation of ITAA36 Pt IVA, eg where an individual incorporates a company to which he/she transfers a rental property or share portfolio (TD 95/4).

The imputation system

The fact that excess imputation credits are refundable to resident individuals, superannuation funds and other eligible taxpayers (¶4-820) has increased the flexibility of family companies.

Other points to note include the following.

- A tax refund received by a company may reduce the available franking credits below the level necessary to frank the distribution.
- A distribution should not be paid unless the franking account(s) have been reconciled (¶4-700).
- The resolution declaring a distribution must be dated at least one day before the payment date, even where payment is by crediting a loan account.
- An entity other than a private company must provide a distribution statement in an approved format to the recipient no later than the time the distribution is made.

The state of the company's franking account should always be kept in mind. For example, if the account has a nil balance and it is expected that a franking credit will soon arise, such as by the payment of a PAYG tax instalment (¶4-700) or the receipt of franked dividends, there may be a window of opportunity to declare an unfranked dividend. Alternatively, if franked dividends are declared in anticipation of franking credits arising but those credits do not arise, over-franking may occur (this can be rectified later in the year by generating franking credits, otherwise franking deficit tax will be payable: ¶4-780). Under-franking may create more problems than over-franking because a full franking debit arises but the shareholders get only a partial credit.

The rules for distinguishing debt from equity (¶23-100) may also need to be considered to determine whether a distribution is to be treated as a frankable distribution or an interest payment.

Other factors

It would seem that some tax ''incentives'' may be effectively lost where a business is conducted by, or property is held in, a company. For example, where a company is entitled to some incentive deduction that reduces its taxable income below the amount of its accounting profit, distributions out of the excess of the accounting profit over the taxable income will ultimately be fully taxable in the hands of the shareholder as no franking credits will be generated to cover the excess.

If a person is both a shareholder in and an employee of a private company, an employment-related benefit provided to that person will generally be deductible and subject to FBT (¶35-120).

A private company loan to a shareholder and/or director may be a loan fringe benefit (¶35-270) and thus give rise to an FBT liability, or may be deemed to be a dividend (¶4-210). The deemed dividend rule is likely to apply if there is no intention to repay the ''loan''. However, it should not apply if the loan is properly documented and complies with the rules concerning minimum interest rate and maximum term. Minimum annual repayments must be made while the loan is outstanding. Reference should also be made to the anti-avoidance rules applying where capital is returned to shareholders (¶4-682) and the rules governing the tax consequences of off-market share buy-backs (¶3-170).

CGT issues

In some cases it may be desirable to inject additional funds into the company as capital. However, if the shares in the company are pre-CGT shares great care must be taken to ensure that the CGT provisions are not triggered — a substantial change in the underlying interests may deem a pre-CGT asset to have been acquired after 19 September

1985 (¶12-870). Additionally, attention should be given to the value shifting provisions (¶12-800). Alternatively, it may be desirable that the assets of the business be sold rather than the shares in the company.

If the business of the company commenced before 20 September 1985 but substantial share capital was issued on or after that date, it may be advantageous to sell the assets rather than the shares, as the assets may include a substantial amount of goodwill that could attract concessional CGT treatment. Roll-over relief may be available where active assets of a small business are sold and the proceeds are reinvested in other active assets within 2 years (¶7-195).

Companies should generally not be used to hold capital appreciating assets. Companies are not eligible for capital gains discounts, whereas a gain realised directly by an eligible investor (eg individual or superannuation fund) may be eligible to be discounted before tax is calculated (¶11-033).

¶31-540 Diversion through family trusts

The most significant features of a typical family trust are as follows.

- The trustee — which is usually a shelf company controlled by the client (eg the parent who contributed the bulk of the trust estate), but may be a trusted friend or family member of the client — is given wide discretionary powers in relation to the distribution of income and the appointment of capital among members of the client's family (ie a discretionary trust). In particular, the trustee should have the discretion to distribute different categories of income to different beneficiaries and to treat, as trust income, capital gains or receipts deemed to be income for tax purposes — otherwise the tax advantages of a family trust are greatly reduced.
- A clause in the trust deed gives the client the power to remove any trustee and to appoint a new trustee or trustees, thereby giving the client indirect control.
- The trustee is given wide power to acquire or dispose of property, to carry on business and to borrow money.

Discretionary family trusts

Discretionary family trusts provide flexibility in relation to distributions of income and assets among members of the client's family, while at the same time permitting the client to maintain either direct or indirect control over funds or other assets that have become the property of the family members. ''Streaming'' a category of trust income to a particular beneficiary provides tax planning opportunities. For example, foreign tax offsets can be best utilised by resident individual beneficiaries with high marginal tax rates and net capital gains can be best utilised by beneficiaries with carry-forward capital losses, low income beneficiaries with carry-forward revenue losses and minors able to receive excepted trust income (¶2-210). The streaming of net capital gains and franked distributions are governed by specific statutory rules (¶4-860, ¶11-060).

Note also the provisions directed at disclosure of ultimate beneficiaries in closely held trusts (¶6-275).

For an article analysing the use of a family discretionary trust to hold a negatively-geared investment property, see CCH *Tax Week* at ¶1059 (2013).

Loss trusts

The trust loss measures, which limit the circumstances in which trusts can deduct prior year and current year losses and certain debt deductions (¶6-262), generally do not apply to family trusts (¶6-266).

Other potential pitfalls are:

- whether transactions have been entered into that are void or voidable pursuant to the *Bankruptcy Act 1966* or *Corporations Act 2001*

- the risks of undisclosed liabilities, etc — in this regard, any warranties given by vendors may be of more doubtful value than would be the case where, for example, a profitable company is acquired, and
- the problems of diverting income to the loss trust to absorb available losses — in particular, ITAA36 s 100A may apply where the diversion is effected by means of a distribution from another trust (¶6-270).

Loans

As noted at ¶31-530, the ATO may review loans by family trusts to beneficiaries and by trustee companies to shareholders and/or directors, to determine whether they may be loan fringe benefits (¶35-270) giving rise to an FBT liability, or whether, in the case of loans by private companies, the loans should be deemed to be dividends (¶4-210).

Diversion to children

The diversion of income to children who are too young to have independent incomes is affected by ITAA36 Div 6AA, as a result of which most of this income is taxed at higher than normal rates (¶2-160). Minors covered by Div 6AA also cannot claim the benefit of the low income earner's rebate (¶15-330).

Distributions to superannuation funds

Discretionary trust distributions to superannuation funds are generally taxed at 45% (¶6-170). Distributions to superannuation funds by a unit trust are taxed at 15%, except to the extent that the distribution exceeds an arm's length amount (the excess is taxed at 45%).

Distributions to tax-exempt beneficiaries

For rules that may expose tax-exempt beneficiaries to tax on trust distributions, see ¶6-274.

Corporate trustees

If the trustee of a trust is a company, then the trust can be provided with most of the advantages of company status including perpetual succession and limited liability as far as the trustee is concerned. The use of a company trustee also facilitates control over the trust by the client, ie by giving the client some means of controlling the company that acts as trustee. Generally speaking, it is unnecessary for customers to know that they are dealing with a trustee, although the accounts of a trustee company (which would disclose that the company did not own the trust assets beneficially) would make this plain to anyone who had access to them. This latter circumstance sometimes causes difficulties with lending institutions but they are not insuperable. Where a company acts as trustee, the requirements of the *Corporations Act 2001* must, of course, be complied with.

Drafting trust deeds

An inadequately drafted trust deed can give rise to serious problems, sometimes long after the establishment of the trust. Forward planning is particularly important, eg by identifying a class of beneficiaries that is appropriate not only for the settlor(s) but also for their successors, and by including in the trust deed mechanisms to minimise or resolve any disputes that may occur. Resettling the trust or amending the trust deed may have undesirable stamp duty consequences (although rectification of the trust deed is possible to give effect to the true intention of the parties, eg *Carlenka*).

One issue to be considered is that, in some circumstances, there may be a difference between the amount of net income for trust law purposes and the amount of net income for income tax purposes (¶6-200), particularly where there is a net capital gain. This situation should be covered in the trust deed.

Another issue is that a beneficiary, on turning 18, will be entitled to demand payment or delivery of the balance of their allocated fund, or at least so much as remains after payment of tax and deduction of amounts applied for their benefit (eg living and education expenses). The amounts to which minor beneficiaries remain entitled may be substantial and thus considerable skill in drafting (as well as understanding legal principles) is necessary to avert the difficulties that might flow from demands for payment made by beneficiaries on turning 18.

Other potential pitfalls include:

- losing (in whole or in part) an entitlement to a deduction where trust property is let at less than market rent (eg *Madigan*: ¶16-650)
- the application of the thin capitalisation rules (¶22-700)
- the application of the continuity of ownership test to determine whether a company can carry forward losses where the company is owned by a family discretionary trust (¶3-110)
- the difficulty for a discretionary trust to take advantage of the CGT roll-over relief or exemption where the proceeds of sale of active assets of a small business are either reinvested in active assets of another business or used for retirement purposes (see above), and
- the "prudent person principle" in most states' legislation regulating trusts — in the absence of a provision in the trust deed specifying otherwise, this principle requires trustees to make investments in light of the beneficiaries' tax requirements (including whether they can use imputation credits, the effect of selling pre-CGT assets and the CGT consequences of changing investments).

It is important for beneficiaries, particularly non-residents, to keep written evidence that they received (actually or constructively) trust distributions. In the absence of such evidence, it may be more difficult to establish that the trust distributions were not shams (*Hasmid Investments*).

¶31-545 Comparison of family trusts and family companies

Whether a family company or a discretionary family trust is the appropriate vehicle will depend on the circumstances of each case. Considerations other than tax (eg the costs of establishing and maintaining a particular structure) must also be taken into account. Of course, as much flexibility as possible should be maintained in any set-up. In some cases, this may be obtained by having a discretionary family trust with both individual and company beneficiaries — the shareholders of the company being the persons whom it is intended should eventually benefit.

¶31-550 Diversion through loss companies

There are 2 kinds of loss companies that may be considered as possible income recipients — "current year loss companies" and "past year loss companies".

Broadly speaking, losses incurred by a company in previous years will not be deductible unless the company meets either a continuity of ownership test (¶3-105), a "same business" test (¶3-123) or a "similar business" test (¶3-125). Great care must be taken when seeking to utilise losses of past years where the losses are to be recouped from the profits of a different business from that in which the losses were incurred. Where a family trust directly or indirectly holds the relevant interests in a company, the trustee will be taken to beneficially own the interests as an individual for the purposes of the continuity of ownership test (¶3-110).

Note the potential application of the inter-entity loss multiplication rules ¶3-135.

"Current year loss companies" are companies that have incurred losses in the current income year. The tests used to determine the deductibility of carry-forward losses are applicable in determining the availability of deductions in one income year against profits for the same year. There is very little opportunity to take advantage of current year losses except in similar situations to those where it may still be possible to obtain a deduction for carry-forward losses. Even where other entities in the same ''stable'' seek to take advantage of losses incurred by a current year loss company, great care must be taken to ensure that the various requirements of the legislation are satisfied (¶3-065).

¶31-560 Diversion through unit trusts

A unit trust is a trust in which the beneficial ownership of the trust property is divided into a number of units. Although discretionary unit trusts do exist (see below), the property of a unit trust is normally held on trust absolutely for the persons who for the time being are the holders of units in the unit trust (although the unitholders may themselves be the trustees of discretionary trusts). There is normally no discretion to redistribute the beneficial interests in capital or income among the unitholders. Thus, like a company, a unit trust permits the association of a number of unrelated parties in a venture. A unit trust is governed by the same principles as other trusts and there must be property vested in the trustee for the benefit of beneficiaries. Like any other trust, a unit trust imposes obligations with respect to the trust property; and the trustee of a unit trust has, and in general is subject to, the same duties, obligations and liabilities as the trustee of any other trust. Public trading trusts (¶6-310) are taxed as companies.

In recent years, unit trusts have been used less for tax planning purposes as various disadvantages associated with companies have been removed, eg the reduction in the company tax rate. The trust loss measures also affect unit trusts (¶6-262) as well as CGT event E4 (¶11-290). However, the recipients of income who may benefit from a unit trust structure include low income individuals, individuals with carry-forward losses (subject to the trust loss measures), tax-exempt organisations and trustees of child support or maintenance trusts.

A CGT roll-over is available where a fixed trust transfers all its assets to a shelf company having the same ownership (¶12-395).

Character of unit trusts

The character of each unit trust will be determined by the provisions of the relevant unit trust deed. There are a number of different kinds of unit trusts and unit trust deeds. Generally speaking, units in a unit trust are negotiable, ie capable of being transferred, although often the most convenient method of effecting transfers of units is to have the units of a retiring unitholder redeemed and fresh units issued to an incoming unitholder. Normally a unit trust deed will confer on the trustee a wide discretion in relation to the management of the trust and the day-to-day running of the business. On the other hand, the trustee would normally have no discretion in relation to distributions of income or capital among the unitholders. It is thought to be desirable in almost all cases that the trustee of a unit trust should be a company. It is necessary to exercise great care in determining the shareholding composition and in drafting the constitution of the company.

Relevant matters in setting up a unit trust

Some of the issues to be considered when setting up a unit trust are:

- the composition and control of the trustee company, the method of arriving at decisions (eg whether unanimity should be required in certain cases) and the method of removing the trustee and appointing a new trustee (the fact that 2 or more unrelated parties may be associated in the operation of a unit trust and the fact that the unit trust will normally be under the control of more than one person, increases the risk of disputes as to the management of the trust assets and the construction of the relevant documents)
- the powers of the trustee to determine whether receipts, receivables, outgoings and other charges are on income or capital account with particular regard to the effect of special tax concessions

- the extent of control that should be exercised by unitholders over the activities of the trustee
- the means of transferring units or permitting unitholders to have their units transferred or redeemed
- whether units should, in any circumstances, be subject to compulsory redemption and how this should be achieved
- the means of introducing new unitholders
- the extent of the indemnity that should be provided to the trustee for breaches of trust and the effect of these provisions on potential lenders to the trustee
- the means of excluding a unitholder (eg the trustee of a deceased individual's family trust) from a continued interest in a closely held unit trust, in a manner that is fair to the deceased person's family and yet not onerous for continuing unitholders that are involved in the ongoing business activities of the trust, and
- the protection of unitholders from personal liability to the extent that this is possible.

The assessability of distributions to unitholders in a unit trust is discussed at ¶10-460. The CGT implications for unit trusts are discussed at ¶11-290 and following.

¶31-570 Diversion through administration companies/service entities

Self-employed professional persons, whether sole practitioners or in partnership, can set up administration companies to provide themselves with access to employer-sponsored superannuation.

This is generally achieved by the administration company employing the practitioner to carry out the administrative duties of the practice for a proportion of that practitioner's total working time. However, the Commissioner requires that the company be established only for the purpose, so far as income tax is concerned, of providing employer-sponsored superannuation benefits for professional practitioners (IT 2494; IT 2503). The Commissioner accepts that the benefits will arise to the professional person in their capacity as a partner, and not as an employee, and therefore there are no FBT consequences (TD 95/57). An administration company can also provide fringe benefits as part of an employee's remuneration package, provided no material taxation advantage is gained, other than access to greater superannuation benefits: see below (TD 95/34). It is accepted that there is no material taxation advantage simply because the amount of FBT payable is less than the amount of income tax that would have been payable if the benefit had been provided in the form of salary or wages. An administration company should not provide exempt benefits unless required to do so by legislation (eg workers compensation).

In the case of professional partnerships, it is also common to establish a service entity to provide various services to the business, including premises, plant, equipment and the services of support staff. The partnership will pay the service entity for those services, effectively splitting income to the extent that the service entity makes a profit on the services and is owned by family members of the partnership on lower marginal tax rates than the partners. The Commissioner may apply the general anti-avoidance provisions (¶30-120) if it is considered that obtaining a tax benefit is the dominant purpose for establishing the service entity. To avoid problems, partnerships using a service entity should: (i) enter into a written agreement setting out the nature of the services and the fees to be charged; (ii) ensure that those fees are at commercial rates; (iii) ensure that the service entity invoices the business regularly for the services performed; (iv) separate the administration of the service entity from the rest of the business; (v) ensure that employees know who their employer is (ie the service entity or the partnership); and (vi) review the operation of the service entity from time to time, including the fees charged.

An arrangement involving a service trust was upheld in *Phillips' case* (¶16-070), where the court emphasised that the charges in question were reasonable. However, the Commissioner's view is that the decision in *Phillips' case* does not mean that service fees calculated using the particular mark-ups adopted in that case will always be deductible. Where the benefits passing to the taxpayer under the service trust arrangement are not obviously connected to the conduct of the taxpayer's income-earning activities or business, or where the service fees are not commercially realistic, a broader examination of the circumstances surrounding the expenditure may be necessary. If it is determined that the expenditure was in fact incurred in pursuit of an independent advantage then, to that extent, based on a fair and reasonable apportionment, it will not be deductible (TR 2006/2; ATO guide entitled *Your service entity arrangements*).

Some Common Planning Situations

¶31-610 Tax planning in business sales

Parties to a business sale should consider the income tax and CGT consequences for each asset (tangible or intangible) being sold, and also any associated matters such as the provision of services or the grant of a restrictive covenant. As taxpayers will be required to prove that an adverse assessment is excessive, it would not generally be desirable to leave any of the sale consideration unallocated. If the consideration is not allocated, the Commissioner may so allocate (generally using market values). Allocations of consideration by taxpayers should, of course, be commercially justifiable. From the vendor's point of view, as much of the consideration as possible should be allocated to pre-CGT assets. Where assets are subject to CGT, the vendor may wish to consider other alternatives. In the case of small businesses, an important factor will be the various CGT concessions that apply (¶7-110). The GST implications of buying or selling a business are discussed at ¶34-240.

The purchaser should seek to maximise any tax benefits of the assets being acquired. For example, where the cost of purchased assets may be subject to depreciation or amortisation for tax purposes (eg a unit of industrial property or fixtures in a building), consideration should be specifically allocated to those assets. The purchaser should also request the original construction cost details where a building is eligible for amortisation under ITAA97 Div 43. Where a business may later be sold by the purchaser, it may be desirable to maximise the payment for goodwill (particularly for a pre-CGT business of the vendor) so as to maximise the purchaser's cost base of the goodwill. See also ¶31-300.

Where it is intended to sell a business conducted by a company or unit trust, it may in some cases be advantageous to sell the shares in the company or units in the trust, rather than the business itself, so as to avoid balancing adjustments in respect of depreciating assets that have a higher value than their written down value or to avoid the application of the rules on the sale of trading stock, etc (¶9-290). However, the usefulness of this will also depend on the implications of the CGT provisions: see ¶31-530. In considering a sale of shares, it should also be kept in mind that there may be other factors in addition to taxation. For example, an acquisition of shares may be commercially undesirable where the purchaser is not being protected against the potential liabilities of the company.

The sale of business assets for variable consideration is a particularly difficult area, for example where there is an "earnout" arrangement. The government changed the law to simplify the CGT treatment of business sales involving earnout rights (ie rights to future payments linked to the performance of an asset or assets after sale). Capital gains and losses arising in respect of look-through earnout rights are disregarded. Instead, payments received or paid under the earnout arrangements affect the capital proceeds and cost base of the underlying asset or assets to which the earnout arrangement relates. The changes apply generally to earnout arrangements on or after 24 April 2015 (¶11-675).

If a taxpayer sells business assets and goodwill in return for a percentage of future profits for life, those receipts will generally be income in the taxpayer's hands; but they are not the proceeds of the business which, when carried on by the purchaser, will constitute the *purchaser's* income.

Where the business sale involves land, timing of settlement may be important for land tax purposes. Depending upon the state jurisdiction, the owner at 30 June, 1 July or 31 December will generally be responsible for a full year's land tax (¶38-010 – ¶38-070).

Business sales are also an area where unintended stamp duty consequences may arise. For example, if documents need to be stamped in more than one jurisdiction, there is a potential for double stamp duty if the consideration is not properly allocated between jurisdictions and the authorities in those jurisdictions disagree on the value of tangible assets within their control. The availability of stamp duty exemptions for transfers, consequent on the sale of a business, that do not themselves transfer the beneficial ownership of property also needs to be considered.

Treatment of debtors

Consideration must also be given to the manner in which the debtors of the former proprietor are dealt with. If a proprietor on a cash basis assigns debtors for value, the amount received from the assignee will be assessable income to the proprietor and the payment will not be deductible to the assignee. If the business is conducted on an accruals basis (as most are), care must be taken in the treatment of prospective or actual bad debts. A debt assigned and subsequently found to be bad may not be claimed as a deduction by the assignor, who has realised it, nor by the assignee, who has not returned it as income (¶16-580). However, a capital loss for the purposes of the CGT provisions may be incurred in some cases. A ''traditional security'' deduction is not available under ITAA36 s 70B in this situation (¶23-340). For a deduction to be obtained for a debt written off before the transfer of the business, the debt must be bad at the time it is written off. Writing off a debt may have adverse consequences for the debtor under the commercial debt forgiveness measures: ¶16-910.

The above difficulties may often be avoided if the vendor of the business retains the debtors, but the purchaser collects the debts in return for a commission. This may also be advantageous from a stamp duty perspective. A mechanism for consequential adjustments to the sale price of the business may be required depending on how the arrangements were structured. If such arrangements can be justified as part of an ordinary business transaction, it is most unlikely that the general anti-avoidance provisions of ITAA36 Pt IVA would apply.

For an article on CGT planning for business sales, see CCH *Tax Week* at ¶996 (2014).

For work in progress, see ¶31-300. For other commercial considerations, see ¶31-040.

¶31-620 Tax planning for CGT

In considering the application of CGT, particular attention should be paid to:

- ascertaining which, if any, CGT event has occurred (as this affects the calculation and timing of any assessable gain)
- the potential for maintaining the status of pre-CGT assets
- the possible loss of an asset's pre-CGT status where the underlying beneficial interests change

- the diminution of the value of pre-CGT assets
- non-assessable amounts which give rise to CGT consequences (such as CGT event E4 (¶11-290))
- value shifts that give rise to a deemed capital gain or reduce the cost base of the relevant asset (¶12-800)
- the immediate assessability of the consideration, even where paid by instalments (¶11-500)
- the taxpayer incurring non-deductible expenditure in relation to an asset where the expenditure does not form part of the cost base of the asset
- disposals involving multiple taxpayers (eg there may be ordinary income to one taxpayer and a capital gain to another)
- a taxable CGT event (¶11-240) arising in relation to a pre-CGT asset
- the requirements (including residence) for obtaining the CGT discount (¶11-036), and
- the availability and appropriateness of using a CGT rollover, for example, the rollover for business restructures (¶12-370) or the rollover for small business restructures (¶12-380).

Care should be taken to ensure that an asset-rich individual preparing a will is aware of the likely CGT consequences of creating interests such as life estates where final distribution of the assets is effectively postponed (¶11-000).

For other CGT planning aspects, see ¶31-125 and ¶31-130.

Year End Tax Strategies

¶31-700 Year end tax strategies checklist

The following is a checklist of some of the income tax planning strategies outlined in this chapter or elsewhere in the *Master Tax Guide* that may be particularly relevant as the tax year draws to a close. Note that, as in all tax planning situations, other considerations must also be taken into account — for example, personal factors, commercial considerations, common sense, the general economic climate and the potential impact of other taxes. For simplicity, a tax year ending on 30 June is assumed.

As a general planning consideration, you should also be aware of upcoming tax changes. These are summarised in the Checklist of tax changes at ¶2.

For a recent article discussing tax planning ideas and strategies, see CCH *Tax Week* at ¶273 (2020).

Personal tax

- The government has brought forward personal income tax cuts by 2 years, starting with the 2020–21 income year (¶42-000), and has increased the low income tax offset (LITO) (¶15-300), effective from the 2020–21 income year.
- Be aware of the annual income levels at which certain dependant tax offsets cut out (¶15-025).
- Be aware of the income cut-off for LITO. A low and middle income tax offset (LMITO) is also available for the 2020–21 income year (¶15-300).
- Consider making deductible gifts before year's end, particularly if you expect that your average tax rate (and therefore the value of your deduction) will fall in the next year. However, the effects on liquidity, and the possible loss of interest income

on the accelerated payment, must be kept in mind. Note, too, that the gifts deduction is limited to the taxable income for the year, and cannot create a carry forward loss, so deferment of "excess" gifts may be appropriate in some cases (¶16-942).

- Where spouses are on different marginal rates, consider ensuring that all deductible gifts are made by the spouse in the higher tax bracket so as to maximise the benefit of the deduction (¶16-942).
- Consider if the working holiday maker tax rates and related obligations apply to wages paid (¶21-033).
- A minor can avoid being taxed at the penal rates applicable to minors' income if they are in a full-time occupation at 30 June. A minor who is intending to take up a post in July may therefore be better off if they are able to take it up in June (¶2-170).
- A taxpayer who is considering retiring near year end may find it worthwhile to defer discretionary income until after 30 June. In that subsequent year, their income will normally be smaller and the marginal rate may therefore be less (¶31-210).
- When considering the timing of retirement, keep in mind the restrictions on the concessional treatment of employment termination payments that apply (¶14-610).

Superannuation

- For taxpayers wishing to claim deductions for concessional superannuation contributions, or to qualify for the government's co-contribution, ensure that the payment is made (and received by the fund) by year's end. Bear in mind the annual caps that apply and consider whether any excess contribution over the cap should be deferred (¶13-760, ¶13-775).
- Consider making a tax deductible personal superannuation contribution to supplement concessional contributions but be careful not to exceed the concessional contributions cap for the year (¶13-730).
- Take care not to exceed annual caps for concessional and non-concessional superannuation contributions (¶13-730, ¶13-785).
- Individuals with superannuation account balances of $500,000 or less can make "catch-up" superannuation contributions using their unused concessional contributions caps, for up to 5 years (¶13-775).
- Individuals may withdraw voluntary contributions made under the First Home Super Saver Scheme (up to certain limits) together with associated earnings for the purposes of purchasing their first home (¶13-790).
- Individuals aged 65 years or older can make downsizer contributions of up to $300,000 into their superannuation using the proceeds from the sale of their main residence where sale contracts are exchanged on or after 1 July 2018 (¶13-795, ¶13-825).
- To qualify for the government superannuation co-contribution, a contribution must have been made by 30 June and meet various other tests (¶13-760).

Income

- Subject to cash flow considerations and anti-avoidance rules, consider deferring income to the following year, particularly if: (1) income for that year is likely to be lower; or (2) tax rates for that year are expected to be lower (¶31-210).

- Consider the availability of statutory roll-overs to defer liability arising in the current year, eg partnerships' trading stock (¶9-290), depreciation (¶17-710) and capital gains (¶12-035).
- In general, under the *Arthur Murray* rule, income is not derived until it has been earned by the provision of the relevant services. Service contracts should be reviewed accordingly (¶9-090).
- Interest income credited on the maturity of a fixed term deposit in June may be fully assessable in the current year, but may not be assessable until the following year if the term deposit matures in July (¶9-080, ¶10-470).
- An accruals based professional person is normally not assessable on work in progress unless there is a recoverable debt, eg when the client is invoiced (¶9-050).
- Where feasible, and subject to anti-avoidance rules, consider acquiring income-producing assets in the hands of a low income taxpayer rather than a high income taxpayer (¶31-500).
- If seeking to avoid having a private company loan treated as a dividend, the loan must comply with the requirements relating to minimum interest and maximum term of the loan (¶4-230).
- The special averaging rules for authors, inventors, performing artists, production associates and sportspersons can provide relief in years in which their professional income fluctuates above their average income (¶2-140).
- Primary producers may consider permanently withdrawing from the special averaging system where their income is consistently lower than their average income (¶31-240).
- Long-term visitors to Australia should consider their resident status — in particular, the rule that a person may be classed as a resident if they have been in Australia continuously or intermittently for more than one half of the year of income (¶21-020).

Capital gains and losses

- Consider realising a capital gain in a low income year rather than a high income year. However, as a capital gain accrues on disposal, simply deferring the derivation of the sale proceeds to a later year may not be effective (¶31-270).
- Where appropriate, consider realising capital losses by year's end so that they may be offset against realised capital gains of that year (¶11-030).
- Where appropriate, consider realising capital gains by year's end so that they may be reduced by current year capital losses (or unused capital losses from previous years) (¶11-030).
- Where it is intended to stream a capital gain to a particular beneficiary, take care to ensure that "specific entitlement" requirements are satisfied (¶11-060).
- The government proposes a targeted CGT exemption for granny flat arrangements (2020–21 Budget Paper No 2, p 23). If enacted, there will be conditions, including the need for a formal written agreement to be in place (¶11-915).

Deductions

- Businesses with an aggregated turnover of less than $5 billion may deduct the full cost of eligible depreciating assets that are first held, and first used or installed ready for use for a taxable purpose, between 7.30 pm (ACT legal time) on 6 October 2020 and 30 June 2022 ("full expensing"; ¶17-430).

- Be aware of the availability of the immediate deduction for small business assets (the ''instant asset write-off'') (¶7-250).
- The instant asset write-off is also available for medium-sized businesses (¶17-330). Businesses with eligible turnover of between $50 million and $500 million can deduct the full cost of an asset costing less than $150,000 if purchased by 30 June 2021 (¶17-330).
- In general, deductions are not allowed where there is merely an accounting provision or reserve set up for estimated costs — the actual expense must be incurred (¶9-120).
- If using the logbook method for substantiating car expense deductions, be aware of the need to keep a logbook and take odometer readings (¶16-320); or if claiming travel expenses, the need to keep a travel diary or similar record (¶16-240).
- Be aware of the need to keep a diary over a representative period to support the apportionment of computer or home office expenses (¶16-480).
- Consider claiming working from home expenses using the short-cut method (the ''COVID-hourly rate'') that applies in the period from 1 March 2020 to 30 June 2020 and the 2020–21 income year (¶16-480).
- Ensure that deductible wages to spouses are actually incurred by year's end and that this is documented. Be aware that deductions are limited where the payment is considered unreasonable (¶31-380).
- Small business entities may be able to take advantage of special prepayment rules (¶16-045).
- Subject to cash flow considerations and prepayment rules, consider making deductible purchases by year's end in order to accelerate deductions. This applies particularly if tax rates for the following year — and therefore the tax benefit of the deduction — are expected to be lower than in the current year (¶16-040).
- Consider year-end tax shelter investments with caution (¶31-045).
- For PAYG individuals, significant deductions in the current year may justify lower PAYG withholding rates in the following year (¶26-500).
- For taxpayers on higher incomes, consider the use of negatively-geared investments to generate excess deductions that can be offset against current year income (¶16-740).
- To be deductible, a bad debt may need to be actually written off by year's end (¶16-582).
- To claim a current year deduction for directors' fees, the company should have definitively committed itself to the payment, eg by passing a properly authorised resolution (¶16-040).
- To claim a current year deduction for annual or long service leave, it is not sufficient for the employer merely to have made a provision in its accounts to cover the employees' entitlements (¶16-040).
- If claiming a deduction for a retiring allowance under s 25-50 (as distinct from the business deduction provisions), be aware that these deductions cannot produce a tax loss. If this would be the effect of paying the full amount of the allowance during the current year, consideration may need to be given to deferring the payment (or the appropriate part of it) to the next year (¶16-540).
- Tax agent fees are not deductible until they have been incurred, irrespective of the year of the tax return to which they may relate (¶16-850).

- Consider whether the rules denying deductions for travel expenses related to inspecting, maintaining or collecting rent for a residential rental property could apply (¶16-650).

Offsets and losses

- In response to the COVID-19 pandemic, businesses with an aggregated turnover below $500 million can write off half of the cost of eligible assets on installation. The concession applies to eligible assets first used or installed between 12 March 2020 and 30 June 2021 (¶17-430).
- Be aware that capital allowances (ie depreciation) are not available for a year unless the asset has been used or installed ready for use, and the taxpayer's income-producing operations have commenced (¶17-480).
- If claiming a concession for R&D expenditure, be aware of the various thresholds and time limits that may apply (¶20-150).
- Subject to transitional rules, if the foreign tax paid exceeds the amount claimable as a foreign tax offset, the tax benefit of the excess is lost. It cannot be taken into account in determining the offset in subsequent income years, nor can it be transferred (¶21-760).
- Consider whether a family trust election needs to be made where the trust has made losses (¶6-266).
- Consider whether a loss claim may be affected by the non-commercial loss rules (¶16-020).
- Where a company is seeking to carry forward a prior year loss, pay attention to the requirements for the continuity of ownership test to be satisfied up to the end of the claim year (¶3-105).
- By accelerating income and deferring deductible expenditure, it may be possible to increase the taxable income of a loss company in the period before consolidation, thus utilising or reducing some if its pre-consolidation losses (¶8-110).
- A company may carry back a tax loss incurred in the 2019–20, 2020–21 or 2021–22 income years and apply it against profits made in or after the 2018–19 income year, to receive a tax refund (¶3-080).

Depreciation and trading stock

- Consider opting for roll-over relief where there is a partial change of interests in a depreciable partnership asset (¶17-780).
- If seeking to vary the effective life of a depreciating asset, the choice should be made for the year in which the asset is first used or installed ready for use (¶17-270).
- Consider whether a change of stock valuation method is appropriate (¶9-180).
- The normal practice of valuing stock at the end of year at the lower of cost or market selling value may not be appropriate if the taxpayer is a company that has incurred a loss (¶31-270).
- Trading stock in transit at year's end may have to be taken into account in calculating the value of stock on hand at the end of the year (¶9-170).
- For obsolete stock, or in other special circumstances, consider whether to adopt a special lower valuation (¶9-240).
- Where there is a change of interests in trading stock, consider the special valuation options available where the continuity test is satisfied (¶31-270).
- Business deductions for trading stock will generally not be available until the stock is actually on hand (¶9-170, ¶31-180).

Other

- If expecting a refund, lodge early and expedite assessment by lodging electronically (¶24-010).
- In determining liability for franking deficit tax, an income tax refund received within 3 months after the end of the income year is treated as having been received immediately before the end of that year (¶4-780).
- Where land is involved in the sale of a business, the timing of the settlement before or after year's end may affect land tax liabilities (¶31-610).
- Consolidating on the first day of the tax year is not essential, but each member of the consolidating group will need to file a return if it consolidates part-way through the year (¶8-000).
- Check compliance with the thin capitalisation measures (¶22-700).
- Check compliance with the commercial debt forgiveness rules (¶16-910).
- Trustee resolutions will not be accepted as giving rise to present entitlements for an income year unless they are made by the end of that year. The 2-month period of grace formerly allowed no longer applies (¶6-105).
- Consider the application of the trust streaming measures (¶6-077).
- Exercise caution in examining the tax and commercial bona fides of year-end investments in promoted schemes.
- Be aware of upcoming tax changes (¶2).

Chapter 32 Tax Agents and BAS Agents

Para

¶32-000 Introduction to tax agent services regime

The registration of tax agents is governed by the *Tax Agent Services Act 2009* (TASA) which is administered by the Tax Practitioners Board. The registration regime also provides for the registration of BAS agents and financial planners (called tax (financial) advisers) who provide a tax (financial) advice service.

Unless otherwise indicated, legislative references in this chapter are to sections of the *Tax Agents Services Act 2009* (TASA) and references to the Board are to the Tax Practitioners Board.

The final report of an independent review into the effectiveness of the Tax Practitioners Board and the TASA to ensure that tax agent services are provided to the public in accordance with appropriate professional and ethical standards was released by the government on 27 November 2020. The final report made 28 recommendations of which the government supports 20 in full, in part or in principle. Additional consultation is to be carried out before some of recommendations are implemented.

¶32-005 The key features of the tax agent registration regime

The following sets out the key features of the present tax agent registration regime. There is further discussions of some matters later in the chapter.

Tax Practitioners Board

The Tax Practitioners Board ("the Board") is a national Board which has the responsibility for registering tax agents, BAS agents and, most recently, tax (financial) advisers, ensuring that registered entities maintain appropriate skills and knowledge, investigating complaints against registered entities and ensuring that unregistered entities do not hold themselves out to be registered. See further www.tpb.gov.au.

BAS agents

The registration regime as originally enacted extended to the registration of BAS agents who can only provide a limited range of services relating to the taxation laws that are relevant to a "BAS provision" in the law (¶32-065).

Tax (financial) advisers

The registration regime has now been extended to require the registration of financial advisers who provide tax agent services that constitute tax (financial) advice services. For an information sheet issued by the Board that deals with what constitutes a tax (financial) advice service, see (TPB(I) 20/2014). The registration of financial advisers is not further considered in this chapter.

Registration rules

Meeting the fit and proper person test (¶32-025), as well as minimum educational qualifications and relevant experience requirements (¶32-030), are required in order to obtain registration to provide tax agent services for a fee or other reward. The minimum educational qualifications and relevant experience requirements are set at a less demanding level for registration as a BAS agent than for registration as a tax agent, in recognition of the narrower scope of services provided by BAS agents.

A significant feature of the registration regime is that the registration of "specialist" tax agents (and BAS agents) is possible. For this purpose, the Board may impose one or more conditions on registration. A condition limits the scope of the services that an agent may provide to a particular area of the taxation laws or a particular type of tax agent service (¶32-035).

Also, appropriate professional indemnity insurance must be maintained by a registered entity (¶32-035), and registered individuals must undertake continuing professional education that meets the Board's requirements.

While registration is restricted to individuals, partnerships and companies, there is flexibility for a registered entity to conduct its business through a trust structure. See ¶32-020.

Code of Professional Conduct

A key element of the registration regime is a statutory Code of Professional Conduct which prescribes the ethical and professional standards that must be adhered to by tax agents (and BAS agents and tax (financial) advisers). The Code is set out as a statement of principles and the Board has issued guidelines relating to the interpretation and application of the Code (¶32-045).

Safe harbour from penalties

A taxpayer who uses a registered tax agent (or BAS agent) can benefit from safe harbours from statement and late lodgment administrative penalties in certain circumstances. Administrative penalties do not apply:

- where a false or misleading statement is made by a taxpayer's agent carelessly, provided the taxpayer gave the tax agent all relevant taxation information necessary to make the statement, and
- where a document (such as a return, notice or statement) is not lodged on time in the approved form due to the agent's carelessness, provided the taxpayer gave the agent all relevant taxation information in sufficient time to enable the agent to lodge the document on time and in the approved form.

Legal practitioners

The general position is that a barrister or solicitor may provide a taxation service as a legal service without being a registered tax agent (¶32-015).

COVID-19

In response to COVID-19 the Board has made several changes to assist practitioners, including in relation to the annual declaration and continuing professional education requirements.

¶32-010 What is a tax agent service?

The fundamental concept that underlies the registration regime for tax agents is that of a tax agent service. An unregistered entity that provides a tax agent service for a fee or other reward, that advertises they will provide tax agent services or that represents that they are registered will contravene civil penalty provisions (TASA Subdiv 50-B).

The definition of tax agent service has 2 elements (TASA s 90-5). The first element is that the service must relate to:

(1) ascertaining liabilities, obligations or entitlements of an entity that arise, or could arise, under a taxation law

(2) advising an entity about liabilities, obligations or entitlements of the entity or another entity that arise, or could arise, under a taxation law, or

(3) representing an entity in their dealings with the Commissioner.

The second element of the definition is that the service must be provided in circumstances where the entity can reasonably be expected to rely on the service for either or both of the following purposes:

- to satisfy liabilities or obligations that arise, or could arise, under a taxation law
- to claim entitlements that arise, or could arise, under a taxation law.

A taxation law is (broadly) any Act of which the Commissioner has the general administration. This means, for example, that each of the ITAA36, ITAA97, GST Act, FBTAA and TAA is a taxation law. Although the Commissioner does not have the general administration of the *Tax Agents Services Act 2009*, it is expressly provided that this Act is a taxation law. This is of particular relevance in relation to the references to a taxation law in the Code of Professional Conduct.

The following are examples of tax agent services:

- preparing or lodging a return, notice, statement, application or other document about a taxpayer's liabilities, obligations or entitlements under a taxation law
- preparing or lodging on behalf of a taxpayer an objection against an assessment, determination, notice or decision under a taxation law
- applying to the Commissioner or the AAT for a review of, or instituting an appeal against, a decision on an objection
- giving a taxpayer advice about a taxation law that the taxpayer can reasonably be expected to rely upon to satisfy their taxation obligations, or
- dealing with the Commissioner on behalf of a taxpayer.

The regulations specify a range of services that are not a tax agent service (Tax Agent Services Regulations 2009, reg 13). These *include*: a service that is provided by an auditor of a self managed superannuation fund under the *Superannuation Industry (Supervision) Act 1993*; a service provided between related entities (related entities include associated entities within the meaning of the *Corporations Act 2001* (Cth) and entities under common ownership (as defined)); a service provided by the trustee of a trust to the trust or an entity wholly controlled or owned by the trust; a service provided between partners in a partnership in relation to the partnership; and a service provided between the members of a joint venture in relation to the joint venture.

For the Board's views on how the registration regime operates in relation to: insolvency practitioners, see TPB(I) 12/2012; valuers, see TPB(I) 16/2012; labour hire/on-hire firms, see TPB(I) 26/2016; and payroll service providers, see TPB(I) 31/2016.

For a recent decision in which the Federal Court held that both an unregistered individual and an unregistered corporation for which the individual provided services breached the prohibition on unregistered entities providing tax agent services, see *Tax Practitioners Board v Hacker & Ors*. For the penalties imposed in this case (including for contempt of court), see *Tax Practitioners Board v Hacker & Ors (No 3)*.

¶32-015 Legal practitioners and tax agent services

The provision of a tax agent service as a legal service which is not prohibited under the relevant legal profession legislation does not give rise to the contravention of the civil penalty provision that applies to the provision of tax agent services by an unregistered entity (TASA s 50-5(1)(e)). However, subject to a minor exception, the service must not consist of preparing, or lodging, a return or a statement in the nature of a return.

¶32-020 Tax agent registration rules

An individual who is at least 18 years of age is eligible for registration as tax agent if the Board is satisfied that the individual:

- is a fit and proper person (¶32-025)
- meets the requirements prescribed by the regulations, including requirements relating to qualifications and experience (¶32-030)
- maintains (or will be able to maintain) professional indemnity insurance that meets the Board's requirements (TPB(EP) 03/2010), and
- in the case of a renewal of registration, has completed continuing professional education that meets the Board's requirements (TASA s 20-5(1)).

Note that there is a grandfathering provision that applies if an individual was registered as a tax agent (or as a nominee) under the former registration regime immediately before both 1 March 2010 and 1 November 1988 (TASA s 20-5(4)).

A company is eligible for registration as a tax agent if the Board is satisfied that:

- each director of the company is a fit and proper person (¶32-025)
- the company is not under external administration and has not been convicted of a serious taxation offence or of an offence involving fraud or dishonesty during the previous 5 years
- the company has a sufficient number of individual registered tax agents to provide tax agent services to a competent standard and to carry out supervisory arrangements, and
- the company maintains (or will be able to maintain) professional indemnity insurance that meets the Board's requirements (TASA s 20-5(3)).

A partnership is eligible for registration as a tax agent if the Board is satisfied that:

- each partner who is an individual is at least 18 years of age and is a fit and proper person (¶32-025)
- if a company is a partner, the requirements of the first 2 dot points above for a company to be registered are met

- the partnership has a sufficient number of individual registered tax agents to provide tax agent services to a competent standard, and to carry out supervisory arrangements, and
- the partnership maintains (or will be able to maintain) professional indemnity insurance that meets the Board's requirements (TASA s 20-5(2)).

Under the TASA, there is flexibility for a registered entity to conduct its tax agent or BAS agent business through a trust structure. The registered entity needs to be a trustee of the trust. The TASA applies to a trustee who is an individual in the same way as it applies to an individual. Similarly, the TASA applies to a trustee that is a company in the same way as it applies to a company. The Board has issued an information paper dealing with the registration of a trust (TPB(I) 03/2011).

For the Board's views on the need for an applicant for registration to demonstrate his/her knowledge of the TASA (including the Code of Professional Conduct, see TPB(I) 10/2011).

The registration application

An application for registration as a tax agent must be made in an approved form and be accompanied by any required supporting document and the prescribed fee (TASA s 20-20).

The Board must decide an application for registration within 6 months of receiving it and (unless the application is for re-registration) is taken to have rejected it if it has not been decided within that time. Registration is for the period determined by the Board, but must be for at least 3 years.

Renewal of registration

An application for renewal of registration is determined by the Board on the same basis as an original application for registration. However, the application for renewal must be made at least 30 days before the day on which the existing registration expires or within such shorter period as the Board allows (TASA s 20-50). The existing registration is taken to continue until the application for renewal has been decided.

Annual declaration

The Board requires all registered tax and BAS agents to complete an annual declaration to demonstrate that they are meeting their obligations as a registered tax practitioner, including having professional indemnity insurance cover (the annual declaration will replace the professional indemnity insurance notification form) and (for individuals) undertaking continuing professional education.

The annual declaration is due on the anniversary of the agent's renewal date (but will not be required for the year in which the renewal of registration falls due). The Board gives 45 days' notice by email of the due date for lodgment of the declaration.

Review of decision

A decision by the Board to refuse registration or re-registration is reviewable on its merits by the AAT.

¶32-025 Fit and proper person

In deciding whether it is satisfied that an individual is a fit and proper person for the purposes of applying the eligibility requirements for registration, the Board must have regard to:

(1) whether the individual is of good fame, integrity and character, and

(2) without limiting (1):

- (a) whether an event described below has occurred during the previous 5 years
- (b) whether the individual had the status of an undischarged bankrupt at any time during the previous 5 years, and

(c) whether the individual served a term of imprisonment, in whole or in part, at any time during the previous 5 years (TASA s 20-15).

The events relevant for the purposes of (2)(a) above are:

- being convicted of a serious taxation offence
- being convicted of an offence involving fraud or dishonesty
- having a penalty imposed for contravention of the scheme promoter penalty provisions
- becoming an undischarged bankrupt or going into external administration, or
- being sentenced to a term of imprisonment (TASA s 20-45).

The application of the fit and proper person test must obviously be applied on a case-by-case basis and involves the exercise of a discretionary judgment. The pre-1 March 2010 registration regime also imposed a fit and proper person test and decisions in relation to the operation of the former registration regime are of continuing relevance.

A fit and proper person is one who is ''a person of good reputation, has a proper knowledge of taxation laws, is able to prepare income tax returns competently and is able to deal competently with any queries which may be raised by [ATO] officers . . . He should be a person of such competence and integrity that others may entrust their taxation affairs to his care. He should be a person of such reputation and ability that [ATO] officers . . . may proceed upon the footing that the taxation returns lodged by the agent have been prepared by him honestly and competently'' (*Su*). In *Ray*, the AAT set aside a decision to cancel the registration of an agent who had acrimonious dealings with the ATO and imposed a 90-day suspension instead, stating that the power to deregister a tax agent was designed to protect the public and ought to be reserved for the most serious of cases.

The fit and proper person test encompasses matters beyond financial and technical capabilities and requires fitness and propriety in the widest sense. Thus, an applicant who demonstrated a serious lack of honesty in not disclosing his status as an undischarged bankrupt in his application for re-registration as a tax agent was not a fit and proper person to be registered (*Fitzgibbon*). Nor was a tax agent nominee who resorted to bullying tactics in the hope of intimidating a client into withdrawing a complaint made against him (*Bond Patterson*).

The expression ''good fame, integrity and character'' (see (1) above) is one of wide import; the meaning of each constituent part is obvious enough as a matter of ordinary English and that, in turn, leads to a conclusion that those constituent parts are not necessarily mutually exclusive (*Ham v Tax Practitioners Board*). In that case the Federal Court, affirming a decision of the AAT, held that the fact that the appellant (a formerly registered tax agent) was knowingly concerned over a lengthy period in equitable fraud when acting otherwise than as tax agent was a relevant matter to be taken into account when concluding that he was not a fit and proper person for the purposes of the TASA.

Another tax agent who had failed to note in his application for re-registration a conviction for failing to lodge his own tax returns was refused re-registration as the failure amounted to a gross dereliction of a fundamental duty of a tax agent and, therefore, he was not a fit and proper person (*Carbery*; *Adamec*). A former tax agent who had been convicted of misappropriating clients' funds over 5 years previously was also deemed not to be a fit and proper person to be re-registered; notwithstanding the lapse of 5 years since his convictions, the nature of the convictions meant that the applicant was not of good fame, integrity and character (*Jones*).

The AAT upheld the Board's decision that a tax agent who acted with wilful blindness in preparing and lodging erroneous returns for some 346 taxpayers whom he had never contacted nor sought their proof of identity, was not a fit and proper person and should be deregistered and debarred from seeking registration for 3 years (*Tung v Tax Practitioners Board*). An application for registration was refused because the applicant was knowingly concerned in defrauding the ATO and some clients of a former accounting firm and was, therefore, not a fit and proper person to be registered (*Hourani v Tax Practitioners Board*).

On the other hand, in *Case 6/2004* (upheld by the Federal Court in *Bray*) the AAT found the applicant tax agent to be a fit and proper person despite the disrespect shown to the Tax Agents' Board, a significant tax debt owed to the ATO, a serious complaint by one of the tax agent's clients, and the fact that the tax agent had permitted an independent contractor to prepare returns contrary to ITAA36 former s 251N. The AAT accepted that the tax agent's past derelictions were caused by marital difficulties, ill health and the introduction of the GST and PAYG withholding regimes, and granted his application for re-registration. A similar result occurred in *Marzol* where a tax agent was found to be a fit and proper person despite failing to lodge his own income returns because he was suffering from psychiatric problems and dealing with family illnesses. However the AAT found that no special circumstances existed in the case of *Toohey* even though the tax agent claimed ill health and family illness as the reason for not discharging his tax agent duties.

The Board has issued an explanatory paper on the fit and proper person test (TPB(EP) 02/2010).

¶32-030 Prescribed requirements for registration

To satisfy the prescribed requirements for registration as an individual tax agent, the Tax Agent Services Regulations 2009 provide that the individual must satisfy one of a number of academic and relevant experience combinations (reg 8 and Pt 2 Sch 2). The relevant information is set out out on the Tax Practitioners Board website.

Board's mix and match practice

The Board has issued an information sheet which sets out the views of the Board in relation to the practice adopted by the Board of identifying a number of subjects or units which have been successfully completed by an applicant for registration which, taken together, will satisfy the requirements of a Board-approved course (TPB(I) 06/2011). This practice is called the "mix and match" approach and enables applicants for registration to satisfy the requirements of courses which are referred to in Sch 2 of the Tax Agent Services Regulations 2009.

¶32-035 Conditions on registration and professional indemnity insurance

If the Board considers it appropriate to do so, the Board may impose one or more conditions to which an entity's registration is subject (TASA s 20-25(5) to (7)). If a condition is imposed, it must relate to the subject area in respect of which tax agent services may be provided. In deciding whether to impose a condition, the Board must have regard to the educational and experience requirements prescribed by the regulations in relation to:

- in the case of an individual — the individual's registration as a tax agent, and
- in the case of a partnership or company — the registration of individuals who will provide tax agent services for the partnership or company.

On an application being duly made, the Board may vary a condition of registration (TASA s 20-40).

If the Board grants an application for registration, the Board may give a written notice requiring the maintenance of professional indemnity insurance as specified in the notice (TASA s 20-30(3)). Such a notice may be given at the same time as the giving of the notification of registration, or subsequently. The Board has released an explanatory paper on what is required to satisfy its requirements in relation to professional indemnity insurance (TPB(EP) 03/2010).

¶32-040 Tax agent notification obligations

If:

- a registered tax agent ceases to meet one of the ''tax practitioner registration requirements'' (ie one of the matters as to which the Board must be satisfied in order to grant registration)
- an event listed at ¶32-025 occurs in relation to an individual registered tax agent, an individual partner in a registered partnership or a director of a registered company, or
- there is a change in business or email address or of any other circumstance relevant to registration,

then notice must be given to the Board within 30 days of the day on which the agent became, or ought to have become, aware that the event occurred (TASA s 30-35).

In addition (within the same 30-day period):

- a partnership must notify the Board when the composition of the partnership changes, and
- a company must notify the Board when an individual becomes, or ceases to be, a director of the company (TASA s 30-35).

¶32-045 The Code of Professional Conduct

An important feature of the tax agent registration regime is a statutory Code of Professional Conduct which must be adhered to by a registered tax agent, a registered BAS agent and a registered tax (financial) adviser.

The Board has released an explanatory paper that deals with the Code of Professional Conduct generally (TPB(EP) 01/2010) and also information sheets and an explanatory paper which consider specific principles of the Code.

Code principles

The principles of the Code are that a registered tax entity must:

(1) act honestly and with integrity

(2) comply with the taxation laws in the conduct of their personal affairs

(3) account to a client for any money or other property received from or on behalf of a client and which is held on trust. The Board has issued an information sheet on this principle

(4) act lawfully in the best interests of a client

(5) have in place adequate arrangements for the management of conflicts of interest that may arise in relation to the activities that are undertaken in the capacity of a registered tax agent. The Board has issued an information sheet on this principle

(6) subject to any legal duty, not disclose any information relating to a client's affairs to a third party without the client's permission. The Board has issued an information sheet on this principle

(7) ensure that a tax agent service that they provide, or that is provided on their behalf, is provided competently

(8) maintain knowledge and skills relevant to the tax agent services that are provided

(9) take reasonable care in ascertaining a client's state of affairs, to the extent that ascertaining the state of those affairs is relevant to a statement to be made or a thing being done on behalf of the client. The Board has issued an information sheet on this principle

(10) take reasonable care to ensure that taxation laws are applied correctly to the circumstances in relation to which advice is provided to a client. The Board has issued an information sheet on this principle

(11) not knowingly obstruct the proper administration of the taxation laws

(12) advise a client of the client's rights and obligations under the taxation laws that are materially related to the tax agent services provided

(13) maintain professional indemnity insurance that meets the Board's requirements, and

(14) respond to requests and directions from the Board in a timely, responsible and reasonable manner (TASA s 30-10).

The operation of principles (1), (3) and (7) of the Code was considered by the AAT in *SRBP & Tax Practitioners Board*. The operation of principle (7) was considered in *DTMP* in the context of the drafting of a notice of objection.

Principle (1) is not confined in its operation to the provision of tax agent services; in other words, the principle may be infringed by conduct that is not itself the provision of a tax agent service (*Kishore v Tax Practitioners Board*).

The Board has released information products on various principles of the Code.

A practice note issued by the Board provides practical guidance and assistance in relation to the use of letters of engagement (TPB(PN) 3/2019). While letters of engagement are not a specific requirement of the Code, the Board considers that the provision of such letters is an important and effective mechanism to assist tax practitioners in ensuring that they comply with the requirements of the Code.

The Board has released an exposure draft practice note that considers the use and disclosure of a client's TFN and TFN information in email communications (TPB(PN) D42/2020).

Sanctions for failure to comply with Code

If the Board is satisfied, after conducting an investigation, that a registered agent has failed to comply with the Code of Professional Conduct, the Board may decide to take no action or to do one or more of the following:

- give the agent a written caution
- give the agent an order that requires the agent to take one or more actions (for example, to complete a specified course of education or training specified in the order, to provide tax agent services for which they are registered only under the supervision of a registered agent specified in the order or to provide only those tax agent services that are specified in the order)
- suspend the agent's registration
- terminate the agent's registration (¶32-050) (TASA ss 30-15 to 30-30).

With the exception of a decision to give a written caution, a decision of the Board to impose a sanction for a failure to comply with the Code is reviewable by the AAT.

Continuing professional education

The Board has developed a continuing professional education (CPE) policy to assist agents to meet their obligations in this regard under the Code. The annual declaration requires CPE details to be supplied (¶32-020). The Board has issued explanatory papers on its CPE policy for tax agents and registered BAS agents (TPB(EP) 04/2012) and for registered tax (financial) advisers (TPB(EP) 06/2014).

¶32-050 Termination of tax agent registration

In addition to the power to terminate registration of a tax agent, BAS agent or tax (financial) adviser for a failure to comply with the Code of Professional Conduct (¶32-045), the Board has power to terminate registration where an event listed at ¶32-025 occurs in relation to a registered individual, in relation to an individual partner of a registered partnership or in relation to a director of a registered company or of a company that is a partner in a registered partnership. Where such an event occurs in relation to a partner or a director, the Board has the power to direct that the partner or director be removed.

The Board may also terminate registration if the registered agent ceases to meet one of the ''tax practitioner registration requirements'' or breaches a condition of registration (TASA s 40-5). The ''tax practitioner registration requirements'' are the requirements as to which the Board must be satisfied in order to grant registration.

Where the Board terminates an agent's registration it may also determine a period (of not more than 5 years) during which registration may not be reapplied for (TASA s 40-25).

Where a registered agent surrenders his registration in writing the Board does not have to cancel the registration if the Board considers that, due to a current investigation or the outcome of an investigation, it would be inappropriate to terminate the registration (TASA s 40-15(2)).

A decision of the Board to terminate registration or to determine a period during which registration may not be reapplied for is reviewable by the AAT.

There is an increasing number of cases where a tax agent seeking to challenge a termination of registration decision of the Board has sought to have the Board's termination decision stayed by the AAT until the hearing of the substantive application for the review of the Board's termination decision (eg see *Gao v Tax Practitioners Board*; *Le'Sam Accounting Pty Ltd and Tax Practitioners Board* and *Norman and Tax Practitioners Board*).

¶32-055 TASA civil penalties and injunctions

The integrity of the registration regime is protected by:

- the sanctions that may be imposed by the Board for a failure to comply with the Code (¶32-045)
- the termination of registration provisions (¶32-050)
- a range of civil penalty provisions, and
- injunctive powers conferred on the Federal Court.

An important civil penalty provision is contravened where an unregistered entity provides a service that the entity knows (or ought reasonably to know) is, as the case may be, a tax agent service, a BAS service or a tax (financial advice) service and the entity charges or receives a fee or other reward for providing the service (TASA s 50-5). An unregistered entity will also breach civil penalty provisions if they advertise the provision of tax agent services, BAS services or tax (financial) advice services (TASA s 50-10) or represent that they are registered (TASA s 50-15). Where the prohibition on the provision of tax agent services by an unregistered entity was breached on 86 occasions giving rise to a financial benefit of $17,370, a penalty of $43,000 ($500 per breach) was imposed (*Tax Practitioners Board v Dedic*).

In addition to the civil penalty provisions which apply to unregistered entities, there are civil penalty provisions that will be contravened by a registered agent where (broadly):

- the registered agent makes a statement to the Commissioner, or prepares a statement that the agent knows is likely to be made to the Commissioner, and the agent knows, or is reckless as to whether, the statement is false, incorrect or misleading in a material particular or omits any matter or thing without which the statement is misleading in a material respect (TASA s 50-20)
- the registered agent employs or uses the services of an entity whose registration was terminated within the preceding 12 months (TASA s 50-25), or
- in the course of providing a tax agent or BAS service, the registered agent signs a declaration or other statement in relation to a taxpayer that is required or permitted by a taxation law and the document in relation to which the declaration or statement is being made was prepared otherwise than by an individual registered tax agent or by an individual who is working under the supervision and control of an individual registered tax agent (TASA s 50-30).

Where a civil penalty provision is contravened, the Board may apply to the Federal Court for an order for the payment of a civil penalty. The maximum penalties that may be ordered to be paid are provided for in relation to each particular civil penalty provision. The maximum penalty payable by a company is 5 times the maximum penalty that may be payable by an individual. For cases where civil penalties were ordered to be paid in respect of the provision of tax agent services when not registered, see *Tax Practitioners Board v Munro* and *Tax Practitioners Board v Caolboy*. An application for an order for the payment of civil penalty must be made by the Board within 4 years after the particular contravention. Where a partnership contravenes a civil penalty provision each partner at the time of the particular conduct is taken to have contravened the civil penalty provision unless the partner proves (on the balance of probabilities) that they did not engage in the conduct, did not aid, abet, counsel or procure the conduct and were not in any way knowingly concerned in, or party to, the conduct (TASA s 50-40).

The Federal Court also has the power, on application by the Board, to grant injunctions (interim or final) to prevent a civil penalty provision being contravened (TASA s 70-5). For a case where an injunction was granted by the Federal Court on the application of the Board, see *Tax Practitioners Board v Zada Dedic*.

¶32-060 Investigations by Tax Practitioners Board

A significant function of the Board is to investigate applications for registration or any conduct that may breach the *Tax Agent Services Act 2009* (TASA s 60-95).

In conducting an investigation, the Board has the power to request information or documents to be produced and to require a witness to attend to give evidence (TASA ss 60-100; 60-105).

An investigation is taken to have commenced on the date of the notification that is given to the investigated entity that an investigation is to be carried out and the Board must make a decision as a result of an investigation within 6 months after that date or a longer period determined by the Board. The Board may only determine a longer period if it is satisfied that, for reasons beyond the control of the Board, a decision in relation to the investigation cannot be made within the prescribed 6-month period (s 60-125). If a decision is not made within the 6-month period (or longer period determined) the Board is taken to have decided to take no further action in relation to the matter that was the subject of investigation. A decision of the Board to determine a longer period for the carrying out of an investigation is reviewable by the AAT.

¶32-065 BAS agents

The present registration regime also provides for the registration of BAS agents.

A BAS service is a limited form of tax agent service. It is a service that relates to ascertaining (or advising about) liabilities, obligations or entitlements of an entity that arise, or could arise, under a BAS provision, or representing an entity in their dealings with the Commissioner in relation to a BAS provision (s 90-10). A BAS provision means the collection and recovery of tax provisions in the FBTAA, the indirect tax law (including the GST Act) and the PAYG provisions in the TAA. BAS agents are now also able to provide certain other specified services, including: (1) determining and reporting the superannuation guarantee shortfall amount and any associated administrative fees; (2) dealing with superannuation payments made through a clearing house; (3) completing and lodging the Taxable payments annual report to the ATO, on behalf of a client; (4) sending a TFN declaration to the Commissioner on behalf of a client; and (5) applying for an ABN on behalf of a client. The BAS service concept has been extended by legislative instrument to advising about entitlements under the JobKeeper payment and cash flow COVID-19 support for business initiatives.

The educational and work experience requirements for registration as a BAS agent, which are set out in Pt 1 of Sch 2 of the Regulations, can be found on the Tax Practitioners Board website.

The Code of Professional Conduct (¶32-045) applies to BAS agents and there are civil penalty provisions that correspond to those that apply to tax agents.

¶32-075 Liabilities of tax agents

Tax agents may be sued at common law for breach of contract or negligence. Examples of cases where taxpayers have been successful against their tax agents include:

- an accountant (also a de-registered tax agent) who breached his fiduciary duty when he used his client's tax money for his own purposes (*Stambulich v Ekamper*)
- a firm of accountants who failed to carry out clients' instructions relating to the distribution of shares on the winding up of a company (*Jindi (Nominees) v Dutney*)
- a chartered accountant/tax agent who failed to advise his client on the introduction and effect of the thin capitalisation provisions that impacted on the advice he had given (*Bell v Vahexi Pty Ltd*).

Accountants responsible for the preparation of a taxpayer's return cannot necessarily rely on the accuracy of the information provided by the taxpayer (*Walker v Hungerfords*).

In general, liability for negligent advice is limited to the area in which the tax agent holds himself/herself out as being competent (*Mohr v Cleaver*). The mere fact that an accountant advised a taxpayer to enter into a tax scheme, which the Commissioner much later rejected as a sham, did not prove that the accountant had been negligent (*Doug Sim Enterprises v Patrick Wan*). Even where it was found that the accountant failed to meet the standard of a prudent and reasonable tax adviser, he was not liable for the damages suffered by his client as it did not necessarily follow that, but for the accountant's advice, the relevant transaction would not have gone ahead (*Leda v Weerden*).

Specific measures are now in place to deter the promotion of tax avoidance and tax evasion schemes, under which a civil penalty, injunction or enforceable undertaking may apply to an entity that engages in conduct that results in that entity or another entity being a promoter of such a scheme, or that implements a scheme that has been promoted on the basis of conformity with a product ruling in a way that is materially different from that described in the product ruling (TAA Div 290; ¶30-300).

Financial planners, tax agents, accountants, legal practitioners and others are not promoters merely because they provide advice about a tax exploitation scheme, even if that advice provides alternative ways to structure a transaction, or sets out the tax risks of the alternatives (TAA s 290-60(2)). However, tax advisers will fail in their duty if they do not take reasonable steps to ensure that a client understands the risks involved in a particular tax plan (*EVBJ v Greenwood*).

To successfully sue for damages, a taxpayer must prove that the agent's negligence caused it loss. For example, the disallowance of a claim for the pre-purchase of trading stock did not cause the taxpayer any loss in *Tip Top Dry Cleaners*. In addition: (i) the transaction that the taxpayer entered into was not the transaction that the agent had advised on; (ii) the taxpayer decided to enter into that transaction after receiving advice that, if it proceeded with the purchase and claimed a deduction, it would not be able to sustain the deduction if it were disallowed; and (iii) the agent explained the alternatives to the taxpayer and the consequences of each alternative. This meant that the agent had discharged the duty of care and, accordingly, the claim of negligence was unsuccessful.

It should be noted that the Board requires registered entities to maintain professional indemnity insurance (¶32-035).

¶32-080 Tax agent lodgment programs

Although taxpayers must normally lodge their income tax returns by a fixed date each year, special extension arrangements are made for clients of tax agents to enable agents to spread their work over a substantial part of the year. They apply to individual, partnership and trust returns, but not company or superannuation fund returns (¶24-070). The tax agent *Lodgment program 2020–21* is available on the ATO website (www.ato.gov.au). This details the concessional lodgment due dates that a tax agent receives as a registered agent during the 12 months ending 30 June 2021. There is also a lodgment program for FBT returns (¶35-030).

Chapter 33 Tax File Numbers • Australian Business Numbers • Third Party Reporting

Para

Tax File Numbers

¶33-000 What are tax file numbers?

A tax file number (TFN) is a unique number issued by the ATO for each taxpayer (ITAA36 s 202A). The TFN system is designed to detect non-disclosure of income and to enable the ATO to "match" the details of income disclosed in a taxpayer's return with details which it receives from other sources, primarily in the areas of employment and investment income, and also in relation to the paid parental leave scheme. Quotation of TFNs is also relevant in other tax areas, such as superannuation (¶33-025).

Quotation of TFNs also applies to other areas not directly related to tax. For example, quotation of a TFN may be a precondition to receiving a Commonwealth income support payment and may be necessary for enrolment at a higher education institution or in an Open Learning course.

Application for TFN

A taxpayer without a TFN may apply for one through any ATO office (ITAA36 s 202B). All online registrations for a business TFN must be lodged via the Australian Business Register (ABR) at abr.gov.au. TFNs can also be applied for online at Apply for a TFN on the web and verified at Australia Post retail outlets. It is necessary to provide several proofs of identity (POI).

For individuals, this will usually be satisfied by a passport, certificate of citizenship, university degree and so on. Secondary school students are able to apply through the ATO's Secondary Schools TFN program using a simpler application form available through the school and with either a birth certificate, Australian citizenship papers or overseas passport.

For non-individuals, proofs of identity include certificates of incorporation or registration, extracts from trust deeds, partnership agreements, etc. Details of individual directors, partners and trustees may be required. Further details are provided on the application forms.

More stringent POI requirements apply to non-resident individuals and entities.

[FTR ¶689-000]

¶33-020 TFNs and salary and wages

Where an employee has *not* quoted a TFN on a TFN declaration lodged with his/her employer, the employer must deduct tax from the salary and wages of the employee and any discount on shares and/or rights provided to the employee under an employee share scheme at the top marginal tax rate (¶42-000), plus Medicare levy (¶42-010) (¶26-150, ¶26-350). Amounts withheld are allowed as a credit in the employee's assessment.

An employee will be treated as having quoted a TFN in a TFN declaration if the declaration includes a statement that an application or enquiry about a TFN has been made (ITAA36 s 202CB). The employer must then allow the employee 28 days (or any further period notified by the ATO) to quote the number. If the TFN has not been quoted by the end of the relevant period, tax must be deducted at the top marginal rate, plus Medicare levy.

Where a TFN has been quoted, the employer must include the number on the employee's payment summary, including payment summaries issued in respect of ETPs (¶26-640).

Where a TFN is not quoted on a TFN declaration but, before the declaration is sent to the Commissioner, the employee informs the employer of the TFN, the employer must write the number on the declaration and the copy (¶26-350). There is a fine of 10 penalty units for failing to do so (ITAA36 s 202CD(4)).

Where an employee has a TFN but quotes it incorrectly to the employer, the Commissioner may notify the correct TFN directly to the employer and the employee is treated as having quoted the correct TFN in the first place (ITAA36 s 202CE). If the employee does not have a TFN but quotes a fictitious one to the employer, the Commissioner may notify the employer and the employee will be treated as not having quoted a TFN.

TFN declarations can be made using the Commissioner's online service. The Commissioner will then make the information contained in the online TFN declaration available to the employer in respect of whom the declaration was made (¶26-350).

Where the Commissioner is satisfied that a person is an employee of an employer and the employee has given a TFN declaration to the employer, the Commissioner will provide employers with both positive and negative validation of the employee's personal details, including his/her TFN (ITAA36 s 202CEA).

[FTR ¶689-760ff]

¶33-022 TFNs and trusts

The TFN withholding arrangements apply to closely held trusts, including family trusts (s 202DN to 202DR; ¶26-200). The beneficiary is required to quote a TFN to the trustee who must then report the TFN to the Commissioner. Such trusts will need to withhold amounts from trust distributions at the top marginal rate (¶42-000) plus Medicare (¶42-010) if the TFN has not been provided to the trustee. Taxpayers who have tax withheld by trustees can claim a credit for that tax in their tax returns.

The measure does not apply to income on which tax is directly payable by the trustee of the trust (eg income assessable to minors).

[FTR ¶690-035]

¶33-025 TFNs and superannuation

Individuals making a TFN declaration to their employer are taken to also provide authority for their employer to quote their TFN to the relevant superannuation provider (ITAA36 s 202DHA). Superannuation entities can also request that a beneficiary, or an applicant to become a beneficiary, of the entity or superannuation scheme quote his/her TFN: *Legislative Instruments* F2017L01262 and F2017L01270.

In relation to superannuation contributions, where a TFN is not attached to an individual's account, deductible contributions are included in the superannuation fund or RSA provider's ''no-TFN contributions income'' under ITAA97 Subdiv 295-I and taxed at the rate of 32% for complying funds and 2% for non-complying funds (which is in addition to the ordinary income tax payable on contributions: ¶42-035). Where a TFN is subsequently provided within a 4-year period, a superannuation fund or RSA provider is entitled to claim a tax offset for the amount of tax paid on the no-TFN contributions income (¶13-180).

Superannuation fund trustees and RSA providers can use TFNs to locate member accounts and to facilitate the consolidation of multiple member accounts.

Certain superannuation fund members can electronically request the consolidation of their superannuation benefits through the ATO. Under the scheme, the Commissioner is permitted to request a member's TFN and disclose it to a superannuation fund trustee for the purposes of the scheme, and to include the TFN on the transfer request.

[FTR ¶690-026]

¶33-030 TFNs and investments

The failure by an investor to quote a TFN in connection with an investment means that the investment body must withhold an amount under PAYG withholding from any income that it becomes liable to pay in connection with that investment (TAA Sch 1 s 12-140: ¶26-200). The amount of tax is calculated using the maximum personal marginal tax rate (¶42-000), plus Medicare (¶42-010). An entity that made an investment in the course of an enterprise may quote its ABN, rather than its TFN, to the investment body to avoid withholding (¶33-130). Amounts withheld will be allowed as a credit in the taxpayer's assessment. Income is treated as being paid to an investor even though it is merely reinvested, accumulated, capitalised or dealt with on the investor's behalf. See ¶33-045 for the various exemptions available.

The TFN quotation rules apply to the following types of investment (ITAA36 s 202D; also known as ''Pt VA investments''):

(1) interest-bearing accounts with financial institutions such as banks, credit unions and building societies, eg savings accounts, interest-bearing cheque and card accounts

(2) interest-bearing deposits with financial institutions, eg term deposits, fixed deposits

(3) loans to government bodies or companies, eg Treasury bonds, debentures and money market securities (see chart below). This does not include deposits to interest-bearing accounts or deposits covered by (1) or (2), or loans made in the ordinary course of the business of providing business or consumer finance. In determining whether a person is in the business of providing finance, the person's scale of lending operations, the continuity and repetition of providing loans and the commercial character of the operations are relevant (IT 2634). A company that is set up within a company group to raise and provide finance for the group would normally be considered to be in the business of providing finance

(4) moneys deposited into the trust account of a legal practitioner for reinvestment or on-lending

(5) units in a unit trust

(6) shares in a company that is a ''public company'' according to company law

(7) certain investment-related lottery prizes (¶10-440). In this case, the amount of cash paid or credited to the taxpayer is classified as income for the purposes of the TFN provisions.

The TFN rules also apply to certain money market securities (TD 92/185). Uninscribed securities (ie those where a register of investors is not maintained) and derivatives (eg interest rate futures contracts, forward rate agreements and repurchase agreements) are *not* subject to the TFN rules. Inscribed securities (ie those where a register of investors is maintained) are generally subject to the TFN rules. The situation is illustrated in the following chart.

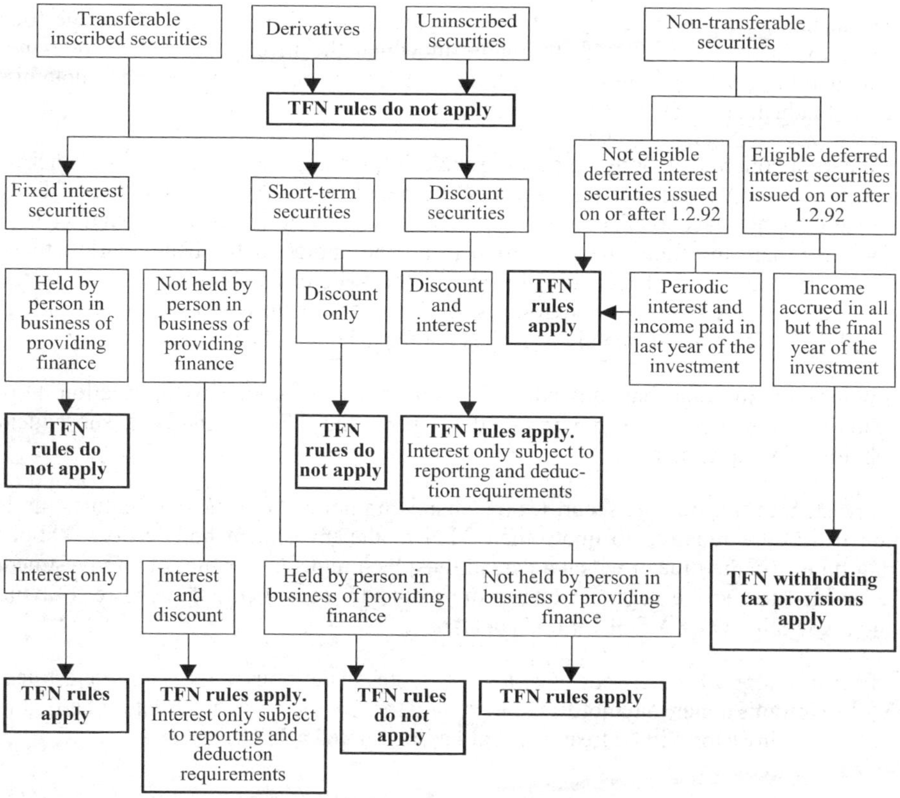

Entrepot nominee companies (ie nominee companies operated and controlled *solely* by securities dealers and *only* used to facilitate the settlement of securities transactions) are not investment bodies for the purposes of the TFN arrangements.

For the provisions dealing with collecting the tax payable for not quoting a TFN for investments such as deferred interest securities (‘‘TFN withholding tax’’), see ¶26-200.

Information requirements

The investment body’s obligations to provide information to the Commissioner and to the taxpayer are discussed at ¶26-620.

[FTR ¶689-880, ¶976-600, ¶976-765]

¶33-040 How an investor quotes a TFN

The rules for quoting a TFN in relation to an investment are in ITAA36 ss 202D to 202DM. An investor quotes a TFN to an investment body by informing it, either directly or via an agent, of the number in the approved manner. For investments made through a securities dealer, it is sufficient to inform the dealer of the number. The dealer must, in turn, notify the investment body.

If an investment is made jointly by 2 persons, both must quote their TFNs (unless exempt). If the investment is made jointly by more than 2 persons, at least 2 must quote their TFNs or be deemed to have quoted their TFNs. For investments by partnerships, the partnership’s TFN must be quoted.

If an investment is made by a trustee, the trustee may quote the TFN of the trust estate (if available), even though the name in which the investment is held does not indicate that the person is investing as a trustee. Alternatively, the trustee may quote his/her/its individual TFN (TD 93/61).

Where a solicitor or body corporate reinvests funds as trustee (either in his/her/its own name or in only some of the names of the beneficiaries) and the solicitor or body corporate does not have a TFN for the trust estate, an Australian Business Number may be quoted. Where the funds are reinvested in all the names of the beneficiaries, those persons may quote their TFNs directly, or via the solicitor or body corporate, to the investment body. In this case, the solicitor or body corporate has no TFN obligations provided that at least one of the investors has quoted a TFN to the investment body.

Where an investor has quoted a TFN to a public company in relation to a shareholding, the investor is not required to quote the TFN again for a subsequent shareholding in that company.

Investors in transferable securities (eg shares in public companies, debentures, units in unit trusts) are required to quote their TFN to the investment body *before* ‘‘books closing time’’ (ie the time at which a person must be a registered owner of an investment to be entitled to receive payment of income from the investment) if they are to avoid having tax withheld (TAA Sch 1 s 12-140(1)).

If an investor who does not have a TFN quotes a fictitious TFN to the investment body, the Commissioner may notify the body and the investor. From the date specified in the notice, the investor will be treated as not having quoted a TFN.

[FTR ¶689-940]

¶33-045 TFN exemptions for investors

There are various exemptions from the TFN quotation rules governing investments (ITAA36 ss 202EB to 202EH; TAA Sch 1 ss 12-165 and 12-170).

• People receiving specified social security pensions or benefits are exempt from the TFN quotation rules in relation to their investments, provided they notify the investment body of their full name and pension entitlement. These include: age, disability support, carer's, parenting payment and special needs pensions; special benefit; and pensions under the *Veterans' Entitlements Act 1986*.

• Companies or unincorporated associations that are exempt from lodging returns and that do not have TFNs (eg charitable, social and other non-profit organisations and non-profit companies with taxable incomes below the relevant threshold) are not subject to the TFN quotation rules in relation to their investments, provided they notify the investment bodies of their full name, address and the reason for their exempt status.

• Non-residents: (i) who are liable for non-resident withholding tax on dividends, interest or royalties from the investment; or (ii) whose income is exempt from Australian tax, are deemed to have provided their TFN. However, in respect of distributions from the trustee of a managed investment trust, this deeming only applies at a particular point in time and does not deem the TFN to have been quoted in relation to future distributions (ID 2012/8).

Where an investment body receives an exemption declaration from an investor, the body must retain it for the period specified by the Commissioner and forward it to the Commissioner when required to do so.

There are other situations where the PAYG withholding requirements in relation to investments have been varied (¶26-200).

[FTR ¶690-080ff]

¶33-080 TFN avoidance safeguards

Investors are prohibited from structuring their investments to exploit the interest thresholds for accounts with banks, building societies or credit unions and certain investments of children under 16 through the use of multiple accounts (¶33-045). Investors are also prohibited from structuring their investments to ensure that TFN withholding tax (¶26-200) is not payable.

Where it is reasonable to conclude that a person has structured investments for the sole or dominant purpose of ensuring or attempting to ensure that: (i) amounts are not deducted and the person has not quoted a TFN; (ii) the investment is not referred to in a report under ITR36; or (iii) TFN withholding tax is not payable, the person is liable to a fine of up to 100 penalty units (¶29-700) and/or 2 years' imprisonment (TAA s 8WC).

[FTR ¶965-960]

¶33-085 TFN privacy guidelines

Various penalties apply where TFN information is misused. For example, the maximum penalty for the unauthorised collecting, recording, use or disclosure of TFN information is 100 penalty units (¶29-700) and/or 2 years' imprisonment (TAA ss 8WA; 8WB).

Employers and other TFN recipients must also comply with the Privacy (Tax File Number) Rule 2015 (F2015L00249), made under the *Privacy Act 1988* to ensure the security of TFN information relating to individuals. The guidelines require recipients of TFNs to protect TFN information from misuse and loss, and from unauthorised access, use, modification or disclosure. Recipients must ensure that access to records containing TFN information is restricted to individuals who need to handle that information for taxation law, personal assistance law or superannuation law purposes.

[FTR ¶689-520]

Director Identification Numbers

¶33-090 Director identification number (DIN)

The new ''director identification number'' (DIN) is designed to tackle illegal phoenixing activities. It will commence 2 years after assent (which was 22 June 2020) or on such earlier date as is proclaimed.

A director of a registered body corporate must apply for a DIN before becoming a director unless an exemption applies (note that transitional arrangements provide additional time to apply for a DIN when the new requirements first start to apply). Initially, the DIN will operate only in relation to appointed directors and acting alternate directors and not to de facto or shadow directors. The requirements apply to both Australian companies and registered foreign companies that are body corporates.

Civil and criminal penalties will apply to directors who fail to apply for a DIN within the relevant timeframe. It is a defence if the director applied to the registrar for a DIN prior to being first appointed as a director and the application has not yet been dealt with. It is also a defence if the director was appointed without his/her knowledge.

Once the applicant's identity has been established, the registrar will give him/her a unique DIN. The registrar can request a person's tax file number to facilitate the administration of the DIN, particularly in establishing the person's identity. Penalties will also apply to conduct designed to undermine the DIN system, eg deliberately providing false identity information, intentionally providing a false DIN to a government body or body corporate, or intentionally applying for multiple DINs.

The ATO started consultation in November 2019 to understand the user experience for affected directors, company office holders and intermediaries. This process is due to be completed by March 2021.

The ATO expects that the required changes will be implemented in early 2021 (ATO Corporate Plan 2020–21).

Australian Business Numbers

¶33-100 What are Australian Business Numbers?

The Australian Business Number (ABN) is a single business identifier that allows businesses to deal with the whole of government at one place and with one identifier (*A New Tax System (Australian Business Number) Act 1999* (ABNA), s 3). It operates in conjunction with the Australian Business Register, of which the Commissioner is the Registrar.

An entity required to register for GST purposes (¶34-110) must have an ABN; other eligible entities may also register (¶33-105). The ABN is also relevant for a range of other dealings with the ATO, including the Business Activity Statement (BAS) (¶24-200) and the PAYG withholding system (¶26-200). A charity seeking exemption from tax must obtain an ABN (¶10-610) and an entity seeking deductible gift recipient status must also obtain an ABN and be registered (¶16-942). People who manage their own superannuation funds should obtain an ABN for the fund.

The Registrar of the ABR also acts as the Multi-agency Registration Authority and can register and maintain details about representatives of businesses to enable electronic communication with government agencies.

Online security when dealing with government agencies

"myGovID" is a single online security credential to access government online services. Most Australians can apply for a myGovID and be authorised to act on behalf of enterprises. For more information, see www.mygovid.gov.au. "myGovID" replaced AUSkeys from 31 March 2020.

[FTR ¶958-000]

¶33-105 Registering for an ABN

An ABN is available to: all companies registered under the Corporations Act; government entities; other entities carrying on an enterprise in Australia; an entity that, in the course or furtherance of an enterprise, makes supplies that are connected with Australia and other entities required to be registered for the GST (¶34-110) (ABNA s 8).

An "enterprise" has the same meaning as for GST purposes (¶34-100) (ABNA s 41; *A New Tax System (Goods and Services Tax) Act 1999*, s 9-20). MT 2006/1 further explains an entity's entitlement to an ABN.

An entity that lets out a rental property on a regular and continuous basis is carrying on an enterprise and is therefore entitled to an ABN (MT 2000/2). If the whole of the premises is to be used for residential accommodation, the entity may obtain an ABN but does not need one for PAYG withholding purposes (¶26-220). Where, however, the entity lets out commercial premises and the supply is a taxable supply, an ABN must be quoted to avoid amounts being withheld.

An entity must apply to be registered on the Australian Business Register to get an ABN. The application must be in the approved form and may be mailed to the Registrar or lodged via the Business Entry Point (www.business.gov.au) (ABNA s 9). An entity may also apply for the Registrar to register details about a nominated representative (who is an individual) for the purpose of facilitating electronic dealings with government entities (ABNA s 9A). Various application forms relevant for ABNs can be found at www.ato.gov.au. All online registrations for an ABN must be lodged via the Australian Business Register (ABR) at abr.gov.au.

The Registrar must register an entity or representative if satisfied that the entity is entitled to have an ABN and that its identity has been established (ABNA ss 10; 10A). The Registrar then sends a written notice informing the entity of its registration, its ABN, the date from which registration is effective and the entity's details on the register. The date of registration may be any date, including a date before the application was made (ABNA s 11).

The Registrar must give written notice to an entity of a refusal to register, including reasons for the refusal. If an application has not been decided within 28 days of it being made, the entity may give written notice to the Registrar that it wishes the application to be treated as having been refused and the Registrar is taken to have refused registration on the day on which the notice is given (ABNA s 13).

ABN not required

Certain taxpayers are not required to obtain or quote an ABN for the purposes of the withholding tax regime (¶26-220). In certain situations, the amount to be withheld for PAYG purposes has been varied.

[FTR ¶958-010ff]

¶33-110 The Australian Business Register

The Registrar of the Australian Business Register (ABR) must maintain the register (ABNA s 24). Entered into the register in relation to each entity is (where appropriate):

- the entity's name, registered business name and ABN/ACN/ARBN
- the entity's principal place of business, an address for service of notices and email address
- the date of effect of registration
- details about the entity's associates that were requested in the approved form
- the kind of entity that is being registered
- whether the entity is endorsed as a charitable or public benevolent institution
- the Australian New Zealand Standard Industrial Classification (ANZSIC) code for the business conducted by the entity
- the name of the entity's public officer or trustee
- the date of effect of any change to the entity's ABN, and
- the date of effect of the cancellation of the entity's registration (ABNA s 25; A New Tax System (Australian Business Number) Regulations 1999 (ABNR), reg 5; 6).

Where a representative is registered in the Register, the representative's name, email address and date of effect of registration are kept. The register also expressly identifies private ancillary funds (¶16-962) and the provision under which they are entitled to be endorsed as a deductible gift recipient. It also contains information relevant to the administration of the employment of working holiday makers (¶21-033). PS LA 2016/4 outlines the Registrar's policy on how the ABR is maintained.

Access and privacy guidelines

PS LA 2016/5 outlines the Registrar's policy on when information and documents collected by the Registrar can be disclosed and to whom.

The register is available for inspection by any person and copies of entries may be made (on payment of a fee: ABNR reg 7). No fee is payable for a single copy of an entity's own entry in the register and, in any case, the Registrar may reduce or waive the fee in cases of financial hardship.

However, public access to the details contained in the register is broadly limited to: the entity's name and ABN; date of registration; the entity's business name; the entity type; its ACN or ARBN; GST and deductible gift recipient details; the state or territory in which its business is located and its postcode; and any date of change in the entity's ABN or date of cancellation of registration (ABNA s 26; ABNR reg 8).

There are also restrictions on the use of information obtained by a person in the course of official employment, eg employment with the Commonwealth (ABNA s 30). The restrictions apply to:

- any document made or given for the purposes of the ABN legislation, or
- any information relating to the affairs of an entity which was obtained by a person in the course of employment and that was disclosed or obtained under the ABN legislation.

The information about employers of working holiday makers cannot be made publicly available and can only be disclosed to the Fair Work Ombudsman where an entity is actually or reasonably suspected of non-compliance with a taxation law.

A person who obtains such a document or information must not make a record of it and must not disclose it to anyone else. This does not prevent the recording or disclosure of information for the purposes of the ABN legislation, in the course of official employment or where it is otherwise authorised.

Modernisation of the ABR

Legislation has been enacted to modernise the ABR and the various Australian Securities and Investments Commission (ASIC) business registers into a single platform — a new Commonwealth business registry regime. The regime initially applies to the business registers administered by ASIC and the Australian Business Register but additional government registers may be included.

[FTR ¶958-085ff]

¶33-115 Obligations and rights once registered on the ABR

A registered entity must inform the Registrar of any change in circumstances that makes information contained in the Australian Business Register incorrect. This must be done within 28 days after becoming aware of the change (ABNA s 14). To this end, entities can now access and change their details via the Internet. Tax agents are also able to access the ABN register online in order to update their clients' information.

A registered entity must also comply with any request from the Registrar for information relevant to: its entitlement to be registered; confirming its identity; or the details entered in the register (ABNA s 15). Failure to comply with these requirements is an offence under TAA s 8C (¶29-700).

An entity may object against a reviewable ABN decision with which it is dissatisfied (ABNA s 21). The usual objection procedure is to be followed (¶28-010). Each of the following is a reviewable ABN decision: setting the date of effect of registration; a refusal of registration; cancelling or refusing to cancel registration; setting the date of effect of a cancellation; and refusing an application not to disclose details.

[FTR ¶958-040, ¶958-075]

¶33-120 Variation and cancellation of ABN registration

The Registrar may vary an entity's ABN by making an appropriate change to the Australian Business Register (ABR) and notifying the entity in writing (ABNA s 17).

The Registrar may cancel an entity's registration if satisfied that the entity is registered under a false identity, the entity was not entitled to have an ABN at the time of registration, or the entity is no longer entitled to have an ABN (ABNA s 18). For example, an individual's ABN was correctly cancelled when he was in prison as, during that time, he would be unable to carry on an enterprise (*Maksimovic v Registrar of Australian Business Register*). Written notice must be given of the cancellation with reasons. The Registrar may also cancel registration if the entity applies for cancellation in the approved form. See further PS LA 2016/3 which outlines the Registrar's policy on cancellation of registrations of entities in the ABR.

Once registration is cancelled, the entity ceases to have an ABN. In *Case 2/2007*, the AAT held that an applicant, which had commenced a business in 2000 and obtained an ABN, should have the registration cancelled from the end of 2004 when the business failed.

Currently, ABN holders are able to retain their ABN regardless of whether they are meeting their income tax return lodgment obligation or the obligation to update their ABN details. However, it was announced in the 2019 Federal Budget that ABN holders:

- with an income tax return obligation will be required to lodge their income tax return, from 1 July 2021, and
- will be required to confirm the accuracy of their details on the ABR annually, from 1 July 2022

to retain their ABN.

The ATO has announced that, from October 2019, it will focus on cancelling the ABNs for businesses that are no longer carrying on an enterprise. To determine if ABNs are inactive, the ATO will check: information in the ABN holder's tax return and other lodgments; if the ABN holder's lodgments are outstanding; and third party information.

Reinstatement of registration

If the Registrar is satisfied that registration should not have been cancelled, the Registrar must reinstate the entity's registration (ABNA s 19). The entity must be notified in writing of the reinstatement and the reinstatement has effect from the day on which the registration was cancelled.

If the ATO mistakenly cancels an ABN, or a business with a cancelled ABN wants to start a business again, the business can reapply for the same ABN, if their business structure remains the same. The business will be issued with a new ABN if the business structure is different, for example a change from sole trader to company.

[FTR ¶958-055ff, ¶958-075]

¶33-130 Quoting an ABN

Quoting an ABN on investments

Under PAYG withholding, the general rule is that an investment body must withhold tax from investment income if a TFN is not quoted (¶26-200). However, a business may quote either an ABN or a TFN to avoid such withholding. The option to quote an ABN is only available to an entity that made the investment in the course of an enterprise (¶26-200).

Quoting an ABN in relation to a supply

A payer who makes a payment to an entity for a supply that the entity has made in the course of an enterprise carried on in Australia must withhold an amount under PAYG withholding (¶26-220). However, the payer does not have to withhold if:

- the entity (or the entity's agent) has given the payer an invoice that relates to the supply and that quotes his/her/its ABN
- the payer has some other document relating to the supply on which the entity's (or the entity's agent's) ABN is quoted, or
- the payment is $75 or less, or the supplier is under 18 years of age and the payment is less than $120 (TAA Sch 1 s 12-190; TR 2002/9).

Quoting an ABN in relation to a voluntary agreement

An entity that makes a payment to an individual under an arrangement for the performance of work or services must withhold an amount under PAYG withholding if the entity and the individual agree to the withholding and the individual has an ABN (¶26-150).

ABN offences

In addition to offences relating to privacy (¶33-110), an entity must not purport to identify itself, or an associate, by using a number that is not an ABN or an ABN that is not the entity's own (ABNA s 23). The penalty for such an offence is imprisonment for 2 years.

[FTR ¶958-080, ¶976-635]

Third Party Reporting

¶33-200 Taxable payments reporting system

A transaction, ABN and identification verification system, contained in TAA Sch 1 Pt 5-30 (Div 400 to 425), applies to payments for supplies that are specified in regulations, known as the taxable payments reporting system (TPRS).

Transaction reporting for building and construction services

Certain businesses in the building and construction industry are required to report to the ATO on payments made to contractors in the industry.

A purchaser that makes, or is liable to make, a payment for a specified supply during a year must give a report (the ‘‘taxable payments annual report’’) to the Commissioner within 21 days after the end of the year (ie by 21 July). However, the ATO has granted a permanent extension for lodging this report to 28 August (ATO website: taxable payments annual report — businesses in building and construction). The report must identify the purchaser, supplier and the supplier's ABN (if known) and specify the total payments made, or liable to be made, to the supplier during the quarter. Failing to give a report as required results in a penalty of 20 penalty units.

The regulations (F2012L00666) specify the following supplies by a supplier to a purchaser:

(a) the purchaser is a business that is primarily in the building and construction industry (ie broadly more than 50% of the purchaser's business income is derived from providing building and construction services)

(b) the purchaser has an ABN

(c) the supplier supplies to the purchaser building and construction services or a combination of goods and building and construction services, if the supply of the services is not incidental to the supply of the goods.

‘‘Building and construction services’’ include any of the following activities, if performed on, or in relation to, any part of a building, structure, works, surface or sub-surface: alteration; assembly; construction; demolition; design; destruction; dismantling; erection; excavation; finishing; improvement; installation; maintenance; management of building and construction services; modification; organisation of building and construction services; removal; repair; and site preparation.

Note that the legislation upon which the transaction reporting is based requires quarterly reporting (TAA s 405-10). However, the Commissioner has the power to vary this requirement by written notice (TAA s 405-10(4)). The fact sheet on the ATO website states that the Commissioner has varied the reporting requirements from quarterly to annual reporting to ‘‘minimise compliance costs for businesses’’. In addition, the transaction reporting legislation also provides for transaction reporting by suppliers (TAA Div 410); however, this is not part of the transaction reporting regime for the building and construction industry.

Transaction reporting for courier and cleaning industries

The TPRS also applies to the courier and cleaning industries. ‘‘Courier’’ and ‘‘cleaning’’ are not defined and take their ordinary meaning. A courier service includes any service where an entity collects goods from one place and delivers them to another place. A cleaning service refers to any service where a structure, vehicle, place, surface, machinery or equipment has been subject to a process in which dirt or similar material has been removed from it. Entities are not required to report where the total amount of payments received for courier or cleaning services is less than 10% of the entity's GST turnover (¶34-115) (*Legislative Instrument* F2019L00864).

An entity providing a courier or cleaning service and that has an ABN is required to report information to the ATO about transactions where the entity has provided consideration to a contractor wholly or partly to undertake courier or cleaning services for them. LCR 2019/4 provides further guidance.

Transaction reporting for road freight, IT and security industries

In addition, the TPRS applies to these industries:

- security and surveillance providers and investigation services
- road freight transport, and
- IT, computer system design and related services.

Entities that have an ABN and make supplies of road freight, IT or security, investigation or surveillance services will be required to report information to the Commissioner about transactions with contractors providing such services on behalf of these entities. Further details are provided in LCR 2019/4. Entities are not required to report where the total amount of payments received for these services is less than 10% of the entity's GST turnover (¶34-115) (*Legislative Instrument* F2019L00864).

The terms ''road freight'', ''IT'' and ''security, investigation or surveillance'' are not defined and are intended to take their ordinary meaning. ''Road freight'' refers to the transport of goods by freight over road, which is not included in the meaning of a courier service. It includes services such as road freight transport, log haulage, road freight forwarding, taxi trucks, furniture removal and road vehicle towing. An ''IT'' service involves the provision of expertise in relation to computer hardware or software to meet the needs of a client. These services may be performed on site, or may be provided remotely through the internet, and include services that support or modify the operation of hardware or software. It does not include the mere sale or lease of hardware or off-the-shelf software. However, if the seller or lessor of the hardware or software modifies it for the purchaser or lessee, or develops specific software for them, then those services will be an IT service. ''Security'' refers to protection from, or measures taken against, injury, damage, espionage, theft, infiltration, sabotage or the like and includes services such as locksmithing, burglary protection, body guards, security guards and armoured cars. A ''surveillance service'' refers to a general watch or observation maintained over an area or location, by one or more persons or by using devices such as motion detector alarms, cameras or recorders. This includes watchmen services, alarm monitoring and services that involve the use of closed circuit television cameras for the purpose of maintaining security. An ''investigation'' refers to a searching inquiry in order to ascertain facts, typically conducted by a detective or an enquiry agency but not including any service which may be used to compile or gather information, such as online search engines or databases.

[FTR ¶978-970ff]

¶33-210 Sharing economy online platforms

The government announced in the 2019–20 MYEFO that it will introduce a third party reporting regime which will require sharing economy online platforms to report identification and income information regarding participating sellers to the ATO. A consultation paper was released by Treasury in January 2019. Under this proposal, the reporting regime will apply to:

- ride-sourcing and short-term accommodation platforms from 1 July 2022, and
- asset sharing, food delivery, tasking-based platforms and other platforms (except for marketplaces) from 1 July 2023.

At this stage it is unclear whether this will form part of the taxable payments reporting system (¶33-200) or be a separate regime. The ATO currently uses its data matching programs to obtain information about the sharing economy.

¶33-220 Third party reporting of tax-related information

A third party reporting regime requires certain entities to report information to the ATO about transactions that could have tax consequences for other entities.

Subdivision 396-B of TAA Sch 1 applies to:

(i) government-related entities, other than local governing bodies, who are required to report on government grants

(ii) government-related entities, who are required to report on financial benefits for services

(iii) states and territories who are required to report on real property transfers

(iv) ASIC, market participants, listed companies and trustees with an absolutely entitled beneficiary, who are required to report on security transactions

(v) trustees of unit trusts, who are required to report on transactions relating to units in unit trusts, and

(vi) administrators of payment systems — on electronic business transactions.

The entity must prepare a report in the approved form setting out information it has about any relevant transactions that happened during the financial year (or other specified period) and give the report to the Commissioner within 31 days after the end of the financial year (or other reporting period). For government-related entities ((i) and (ii) above), the report is the "taxable payments annual report" and the ATO has extended the date of lodgment to 28 August (ATO website: taxable payments annual report — government entities). The reporting period for states and territories ((iii) above) has been varied to 3-month periods ending 30 September, 31 December, 31 March and 30 June (*Legislative Instrument* F2016L00541).

The information about the transaction must relate to the identification, collection or recovery of a possible tax-related liability of the other entities involved in the transaction and may relate to the identification of those other entities. Any possible tax exemption is disregarded as reporting entities may not know whether the entity they are reporting on is exempt from a taxation law.

An administrative penalty may apply under TAA Sch 1 s 284-75 to any false or misleading statements made in reporting.

Exemptions from tax-related third party reporting

Certain classes of electronic payment system transactions and other transactions have been exempted from the third party reporting regime:

- companies listed on an Australian financial market, trustees of a unit trust and trustees of other trusts holding shares or units are not required to report in relation to transactions that relate to shares listed on Australian financial markets or transactions on that Australian financial market where data is not required to be delivered to the Australian Securities and Investments Commission under the market integrity rules (*Legislative Instrument* F2018L00473; TPRE 2020/D2)

- administrators of a payment system are not required to report payments processed by Bulk Electronic Clearing System Framework Participants and payments processed by New Payment Platform Participants (*Legislative Instrument* 2020/SDP/0023)

- administrators of a payment system are not required to report: payments made to a carriage service provider; payments made to a utility for the provision of electricity, water, sewerage or gas; payments made to a government-related entity; payments made to a general insurer, life insurer or private health insurer which are received in the course of the insurer's insurance business; payments made to a superannuation fund, approved deposit fund, pooled superannuation trust or retirement savings account provider; and payments processed by High Value Clearing System Framework Participants (*Legislative Instrument* F2017L00629), and
- government related entities are not required to report: electronic payments made to a BPAY biller, by recurring direct debit, by debit or credit card payment through a merchant acquiring system or via third party payment processors facilitating any of the above payments; provision of consideration to a carriage service provider for a carriage service; provision of consideration to a utility for the provision of electricity, water, sewerage or gas; provision of consideration for transportation of employees; provision of consideration to a general insurer for services provided in the course of the insurer's insurance business; provision of consideration for accommodation in commercial premises, a hotel, motel, inn, hostel, boarding house, caravan park or camping ground; provision of consideration for the lease of goods; provision of consideration for the creation, grant, transfer, assignment or use under licence of a right; provision of consideration for a financial supply; provision of consideration for membership of a professional association or body; provision of consideration for services relating to the exercise of court or tribunal functions; provision of consideration for a supply to another government related entity; or provision of a grant to another government related entity (*Legislative Instrument* F2016L00526).

For details of prior year exemptions, see previous editions of the *Australian Master Tax Guide*.

Other third party reporting requirements for financial institutions

Subdivision 396-A gives effect to the FATCA Agreement between Australia and the US under which Australian financial institutions must give the Commissioner certain information about US reportable accounts (¶22-075).

Subdivision 396-C imposes obligations on Australian financial institutions to report certain information about accounts of foreign residents under the OECD Common Reporting Standard (CRS: ¶23-500).

Chapter 34 Goods and Services Tax

Introduction to GST

¶34-000 What is GST?

A 10% goods and services tax (GST) started full operation in Australia on 1 July 2000. GST is an indirect, broad-based consumption tax.

- *Indirect* means that it is levied on the supply of goods, services or activities, rather than directly on income. Other indirect taxes include stamp duty.

- A *broad-based* tax applies generally to all transactions by all types of taxpayers, with only limited exceptions. It can be contrasted with taxes such as sales tax, which was generally limited to transactions involving sales, and transactions involving certain types of goods.

- *Consumption tax* means that instead of being applied to income (as measured by the amounts that are received), GST is applied to consumption (as measured by the amounts that are spent). The tax is ultimately borne by consumers, not by producers or suppliers.

Despite its name, GST is not limited to ''goods and services'' in the normally understood sense. For example, it also applies to real property and the creation of rights. GST is therefore a convenient but not an entirely accurate shorthand term.

GST is governed principally by the *A New Tax System (Goods and Services Tax) Act 1999* (GST Act). All section or Division references in this chapter are to this Act unless otherwise stated. For details of other GST-related legislation, see ¶34-360.

GST applies where an entity makes a ''taxable supply'' (Div 7). For there to be a taxable supply, the entity — called the ''supplier'' — must be registered or required to be registered (¶34-100). In addition, the supply must be connected with Australia and made for consideration in the course or furtherance of an enterprise that the supplier carries on. The requirements of a taxable supply are discussed at ¶34-105. GST also applies to ''taxable importations''. However, in such cases, it is the importer, rather than the supplier, which is required to account for the GST (¶34-250).

From 1 July 2015, the term ''indirect tax zone'' (s 195-1) replaced the term ''Australia'' in nearly all instances in the GST Act, without significant alteration in meaning. However, for simplicity, this commentary continues to use the term ''Australia''.

The amount of GST that an entity is liable to pay is 10% of the value of the taxable supply (s 9-70). In effect, this means that 1/11th of the consideration received by a supplier will be regarded as being the GST on the supply. Legal liability for the GST rests with the supplier (s 9-40).

If an entity *acquires* goods or services for a ''creditable purpose'' (ie in carrying on its enterprise), it can claim a credit for the GST component of the price (¶34-110). This is called an input tax credit because it is a credit on business inputs. For this to apply, the entity — called the ''recipient'' — must be registered, or required to be registered (¶34-100) and provide, or be liable to provide, consideration for the acquisition. Also, the supply to the recipient must be a taxable supply (Div 11; ¶34-110).

The combined effect of these rules is that the ultimate burden of the GST will normally fall on the end-user or private consumer. The businesses that form part of the chain of supply act as progressive collectors of the tax, but do not ultimately bear the burden of it.

The following example gives an idea of how GST is accounted for at the various stages of production.

▶ Example

A customer buys a leather briefcase from a retailer. The retailer had acquired the briefcase from a leathergoods manufacturer that had acquired the leather to make the briefcase from a tannery. The tannery had bought cow hide from an abattoir to make the leather. Assume that all parties are registered except for the customer. The GST rules apply as follows:

(1) The abattoir sells the cow hide to the tannery for $22 (including $2 GST). When the abattoir fills in its GST return, it takes the GST it collected on its sale to the tannery ($2), subtracts any GST it paid for input (its input tax credit, in this case assume nil) and sends the net amount ($2) to the ATO.

(2) The tannery processes the cow hide into leather and sells it to the leathergoods manufacturer for $44 (including $4 GST). When the tannery fills in its GST return, it takes the GST it collected on its sale to the manufacturer ($4), subtracts the GST it paid on its inputs ($2 paid to the abattoir on purchase of the cow hide) and sends the net amount ($2) to the ATO. The ATO has therefore collected $4 in total so far.

(3) The leathergoods manufacturer makes the leather into a briefcase that it sells to a retailer for $88 (including $8 GST). When the manufacturer fills in its GST return, it takes the GST it collected from the retailer ($8), subtracts the GST it paid on its inputs ($4 paid to the tannery) and sends the net amount ($4) to the ATO. The ATO has therefore collected $8 in total so far.

(4) The retailer sells the briefcase to the final consumer for $110 (including $10 GST). When the retailer fills in its GST return, it takes the GST it collected on the sale to the consumer ($10), subtracts the GST it paid on its inputs ($8 paid to the manufacturer) and sends the difference ($2) to the ATO. The ATO has therefore collected $10 in total.

This means that the total GST payable on the briefcase was $10, which was the total amount sent to the ATO. It is also clear that the businesses did not ultimately bear the GST — this was totally borne by the final customer as part of the price paid.

¶34-010 A 10-point guide to GST

Below is a 10-point *simplified* snapshot of how GST works. Each of these steps is explained later in this chapter.

(1) GST liability. Liability for GST arises where a registered business makes taxable supplies to its customers. The GST is imposed at the rate of 10%. Typically, it is included in the price paid by the recipient of the goods and services. The supplier must account for the amount of GST to the ATO (¶34-105).

(2) Getting credits for GST. If the recipient of goods or services is a registered business entity, it will normally be able to claim a credit for the amount of GST it has paid, provided it holds a tax invoice. This credit — called an input tax credit — is offset against any GST on goods or services that the recipient supplies to its own customers (¶34-110, ¶34-140).

(3) Burden on end-consumer. The net effect is that registered business entities receive an amount representing GST but do not keep it, and pay GST but get a credit for it. This means that they act essentially as collecting agents for the tax. The ultimate burden of the tax falls on the private consumer of the goods and services, as this person gets no credit for the GST they pay (¶34-110).

(4) Registration. Most business entities have to register for GST, although there are some exceptions. If an entity is not registered, it normally is not liable for GST and cannot claim credits for the GST it pays (¶34-100).

(5) Returns and tax periods. Businesses account to the ATO for the GST on the supplies they make and the credits they claim by making a GST return in their Business Activity Statement (BAS) (¶34-150). A separate GST return is made for each tax period, which may, according to the circumstances, be monthly, quarterly or — for some smaller businesses — annual. Monthly returns are compulsory in some situations, such as where GST turnover is $20 million or more (¶34-120).

(6) Accounting basis. GST and input tax credits are allocated to particular tax periods either on a cash basis (based on when amounts are received or paid out) or on an accruals basis (based on when invoices are sent or received). There are restrictions on who can use the cash basis (¶34-130).

(7) Tax or refund? If the GST allocated to a tax period is more than the credits for that period, the business is liable for the balance to the ATO. If the credits exceed the GST, the business is entitled to a credit or refund (¶34-150). Adjustments may need to be made later if there is a change of circumstances (¶34-145).

(8) GST exemptions. Some transactions are outside the scope of GST altogether because, for example, they are gifts, are made by unregistrable people or have no connection with Australia (¶34-160). Others are ‘‘GST-free’’ which means that there is no liability for GST on the supply, but the supplier can claim credits for the GST on its own related acquisitions. The main GST-free items are specified exports, health, food, education, international travel and certain charitable activities (¶34-165).

(9) Input taxed supplies. A small range of supplies is ''input taxed''. This means that there is no liability for GST on supplies made and that the supplier cannot claim credits for the GST on its own acquisitions. The main input taxed items are financial services and the supply of residential rental premises (¶34-170).

(10) Special rules apply to a wide range of items including charities and non-profit bodies (¶34-175), GST groups and joint ventures (¶34-180), financial supplies (¶34-190), superannuation funds (¶34-200), insurance (¶34-210), vehicles (¶34-220), real property (¶34-230), buying and selling a business (¶34-240), importations (¶34-250), and second-hand goods (¶34-260). Other special rules are noted at ¶34-270.

How GST Operates

¶34-100 Registration for GST

Registration is fundamental to the operation of the GST system. An entity must normally be registered, or required to be registered, to be liable for GST or to claim input tax credits (Div 23). As far as registration is concerned there are:

(1) entities that cannot be registered

(2) entities that can be registered, but are not required to be, and

(3) entities that are required to be registered.

An entity *cannot* be registered unless it is carrying on an enterprise (see below), or is intending to do so from a particular date (s 23-10).

An entity *can* be registered if it is carrying on an enterprise, or is intending to do so from a particular date (s 23-10). Non-residents as well as residents are eligible.

An entity is *required* to be registered if it is carrying on an enterprise, and its GST turnover is $75,000 or more (s 23-5). This is called the registration turnover threshold (s 23-15). For non-profit bodies (including body corporate entities: ID 2016/1), the corresponding threshold is generally $150,000. For the calculation of GST turnover, see ¶34-115. An entity that is required to register, but fails to do so, becomes liable for penalties and even prosecution.

Meaning of ''entity''

An entity means:

- an individual
- a ''body corporate''. This includes a company, building society, credit union, trade union, statutory body, strata title body corporate, municipal council, incorporated association, and certain governing bodies of various religious institutions (MT 2006/1)
- a ''corporation sole''. This is a corporation consisting of one person and that person's successors to a particular position, eg a bishopric
- a ''body politic'', ie a government. Government departments are technically not entities but can be separately registered
- a partnership (see below)
- any other unincorporated association or body of persons, eg charities, clubs or certain syndicates. To qualify, something more than a common aim or purpose is necessary. Typical characteristics would include: members of the association; a

contract binding the members among themselves; a constitutional arrangement for meetings of members and for appointing officers; freedom to join or leave the association; continuity of existence; and a moment in time when a number of persons combined to form the association. However, not all these characteristics are essential (*Conservative and Unionist Central Office v Burrell (Inspector of Taxes)*; MT 2006/1)

- a trust, or the trustee of the trust at any given time (see below)
- a superannuation fund, or the trustee of the fund at any given time (s 184-1).

Non-charitable public ancillary and prescribed private funds may also register and operate as enterprises for GST purposes. For the Commissioner's guidelines on the meaning of entity, see MT 2006/1.

Types of partnership

Both a "general law" partnership and a "tax law" partnership (¶5-000) are registrable "entities" for GST purposes (GSTR 2003/13; GSTR 2004/6). A tax law partnership commences when the persons associate and carry on the activity from which the income will be received — this means, for example, that it can claim input tax credits on the acquisition of the property from which income may be derived jointly (GSTR 2004/6).

Trusts

Although a trust is specified as an entity, a trustee of a trust or superannuation fund is also taken to be an entity consisting of the person or persons who are the trustees at any given time (s 184-1(2)). This is because a right or obligation cannot be conferred or imposed on an entity (eg a trust) that is not a legal person (MT 2006/1).

This does not mean that the GST Act creates 2 separate entities — the trust and the trustee. Rather, the relevant entity is the trust with the trustee standing as that entity if legal personality is required. A consequence of this is that there will only ever be one ABN registration for the trust and only one ABN issued irrespective of the number of trustees for the trust (MT 2006/1). A public company acting as the responsible entity of a managed investment scheme is entitled to register as a trust entity (ID 2007/7).

Persons acting in different capacities

A legal person may act in more than one capacity. For example, an individual may act in his or her personal capacity, as well as in the capacity of a trustee. In such cases the person will be treated for GST purposes as a different entity in each of those capacities (s 184-1(3)).

▶ Example 1

Individual X and Company Y are the trustees of Z Trust. X is an entity in his or her personal capacity. Y is an entity in its capacity as a body corporate. X and Y together are an entity in their capacity as trustees of the trust.

▶ Example 2

An insolvency practitioner may also act as the representative of an incapacitated entity. In such a case, the same legal person is acting in 2 different capacities and is registered twice for GST — once as an entity pursuant to Div 58 of the GST Act and once as an entity under Div 23 of the GST Act (ID 2012/6).

Carrying on an enterprise

An entity cannot be registered unless it is carrying on an "enterprise" (ss 23-5; 23-10). An enterprise is defined to mean an activity or series of activities done (s 9-20(1)):

- in the form of a business (including any profession, trade, employment, vocation or calling). The Commissioner interprets this as including business-like activities that are not carried out for profit, or non-profit clubs or associations (MT 2006/1; GSTD 2006/6)
- in the form of an adventure or concern in the nature of trade. This is intended to catch a commercial activity that does not amount to a business
- on a regular or continuous basis, in the form of a lease, licence or other grant of an interest in property. An activity is ''regular'' if it is repeated at reasonably proximate intervals, and ''continuous'' if there is no significant cessation or interruption to the activity (MT 2006/1; GSTD 2006/6)
- by the trustee of a fund, authority or institution covered by ITAA97 Subdiv 30-B and to which deductible gifts can be made
- by the trustee of a complying superannuation fund or, if there is no trustee of the fund, by a person who manages the fund
- by a charity
- by the Commonwealth, a state or a territory (including government departments and certain local governments: GSTR 2006/5) or by a body corporate or corporation solely established for a public purpose by one of those entities
- by a non-charitable public ancillary fund or a prescribed private fund where the fund is covered by item 2 of the table in ITAA97 s 30-15 or would be covered by that item if it had an Australian Business Number (ABN).

It is not necessary that there be a series of activities. A single activity can be an enterprise.

It may also happen that a single entity carries on more than one enterprise, or carries on some activities that are an enterprise and some that are not.

The sale of subdivided vacant land by a company which owned several rental properties and operated a sheep grazing business was held to be liable to GST even though the sales were not connected with those enterprises (*San Remo Heights Pty Ltd*). The AAT said there was no evidence that the company acquired the land other than for commercial purposes and it was not satisfied that the series of activities undertaken by the company in relation to the land did not constitute an enterprise.

▶ Example 3

A self-employed doctor also runs a profitable farm. The doctor is carrying on 2 enterprises. If the doctor registers, that will cover both enterprises.

Commencing or terminating an enterprise

An entity is treated as carrying on an enterprise if it is doing anything in the course of commencing or terminating the enterprise (s 195-1). The ATO considers that this would include conducting a feasibility study involving genuine business activities where there has been serious contemplation of developing an enterprise. However, activities undertaken to establish an entity, for example drawing up of a trust deed and the settlement of trust property (MT 2006/1), or preparatory activities (*Clayton*; *Guru 4U*), would not be included.

Similarly, acts done in the course of selling the business will be treated as carrying on the enterprise, for example finalising accounts, paying creditors, repaying loans, cancelling licences and business registrations (MT 2006/1); or the realisation of business assets as part of winding up a partnership (GSTR 2003/13). The ATO's view is that an enterprise would normally be taken to have terminated when all assets are disposed of or converted to another purpose, and all obligations have been satisfied (MT 2006/1).

*What is **not** an enterprise*

An enterprise does *not* include the following activities:

- activities carried out as an employee, or other person subject to specified PAYG withholding rules (company directors, officeholders, labour hire). This means that — subject to the special rule noted below — these people are not treated as carrying on an enterprise themselves. However, their activities are still treated as part of the enterprise of their employer or work provider
- private recreational pursuits or hobbies. These are normally characterised by their small scale, irregularity and lack of profit motive (TR 97/11; MT 2006/1)
- activities by an individual, or partnership consisting wholly or mostly of individuals, where there is no "reasonable expectation" of profit or gain. A reasonable expectation requires more than just a possibility (MT 2006/1; GSTD 2006/6). However, the fact that no profit was in fact made over a significant period does not necessarily mean that there was no reasonable expectation that a profit would eventually be made (*Case 2/2007*)
- activities by certain members of local governing bodies, for example, councillors (s 9-20(2), (4)).

A special rule applies where a person accepts a position as an officeholder in connection with other business activities. An example of this is where a partner of a legal or accounting firm becomes a director of one of the firm's client companies. Directors are generally treated as employees, so the services they provide are not normally subject to GST. However, in this particular case, the partner/director will be treated as an enterprise, not an employee, and the supply of the partner/director's services to the company is therefore potentially subject to GST (s 9-20(2)(a)).

Meaning of "business"

The most common form of enterprise is a business. Normally there is little dispute about whether a business is being carried on (¶10-105). However, borderline situations arise in areas such as primary production (¶18-020), writing, sport or gambling (¶10-430). Activities may constitute a business even though they are only carried on in a small way. However, it would normally need to be shown that there was a real expectation of profit emerging. Where activities are of a very small size and scale, they would normally not be treated as a business if they are carried on in an ad hoc manner and there is little repetition or regularity (MT 2006/1).

Procedure for registration

An entity has to apply for registration within 21 days of becoming required to do so (s 25-1). Normally, this means that the entity has to apply within 21 days after the time when the enterprise it is carrying on first meets the relevant turnover threshold test (¶34-115).

If an entity is entitled to be registered, but not required to do so, it may apply for registration at any time.

Applications may be made online at the Australian Business Register (www.abr.gov.au) or by using the appropriate ABN registration form. Separate forms apply to sole traders, superannuation funds, companies and other organisations, and government bodies.

The ATO must grant an entity's application if satisfied that it is carrying on an enterprise, or intending to do so from a specified date. If the ATO is satisfied that it is required to be registered, it must register the entity even if the entity has not applied.

On registration, the ATO will notify the entity of the date of effect, the entity's GST registration number and the tax periods that apply to it (s 25-5).

Generally, the registration takes effect from the day specified in the application. This cannot be earlier than the date on which the entity commenced to carry on an enterprise. Registration may be backdated beyond the date specified in the application if the ATO is satisfied that it was required to be registered earlier. If so, the entity will be treated as being subject to the GST system from that date (ss 25-10; 25-15). However, the Commissioner cannot backdate the registration beyond 4 years, unless there has been fraud or evasion (ss 23-20; 25-10).

Simplified registration for certain non-residents

Simplified GST registration arrangements are available for non-residents who make or intend to make:

- supplies of inbound intangible consumer supplies, or
- for tax periods starting on or after 1 July 2018, offshore supplies of low value goods (this also applies to redeliverers of these supplies) (¶34-250).

For this to apply, the non-resident must elect to become a ‘‘limited registration’’ entity (Div 146). This means that the non-resident will only need to provide minimal information when they register and provide GST returns. Limited registration entities will not be entitled to input tax credits, are not entitled to an ABN, are not recorded in the Australian Business Register, must have quarterly tax periods, do not issue tax invoices, and cannot elect to pay GST by instalments (ss 146-5 to 146-25).

These rules were formerly contained in former Subdiv 84-D. Elections made under those provisions continue in effect.

[AMGST ¶3-000; GSTG ¶5-000]

¶34-105 Taxable supplies

GST is charged or levied on the making of every ‘‘taxable supply’’ and ‘‘taxable importation’’ (s 7-1). The amount of GST that a supplier is liable to pay is 10% of the value of the taxable supply (s 9-70). In effect, this means that 1/11th of the consideration received by a supplier will be regarded as being the GST on the supply.

For an entity to make a ‘‘taxable supply’’ 5 cumulative conditions must usually be satisfied. An entity makes a ‘‘taxable supply’’ and therefore must charge GST if (s 9-5):

(1) it makes a supply for consideration

(2) the supply is made in the course or furtherance of an enterprise that it carries on

(3) the supply is connected with Australia (the indirect tax zone)

(4) the entity is either registered or required to be registered, and

(5) the supply is not GST-free or input taxed.

There are some provisions, however, that ignore these requirements and simply deem the elements needed to create taxable supplies — for example, supplies between associates (¶34-270) and sales in satisfaction of debts (Div 105).

"Supply for consideration"

The first requirement for a taxable supply is that an entity makes a ‘‘supply for consideration’’.

A supply is ‘‘any form of supply whatsoever’’ (s 9-10(1)) and is clearly intended to be all-encompassing, extending well beyond supplies of goods and services to include many transactions that result in an entity receiving money or property (Byron [2019] AATA 2042). In order to clarify the breadth of the definition, s 9-10(2) provides, without limiting the general definition in s 9-10(1), that ‘‘supply’’ includes any of the following:

(a) a supply of goods

(b) a supply of services

(c) a provision of advice or information

(d) a grant, assignment or surrender of real property

(e) a creation, grant, transfer, assignment or surrender of any right

(f) a financial supply

(g) an entry into, or release from, an obligation:

  (i) to do anything

  (ii) to refrain from an act, or

  (iii) to tolerate an act or situation

(h) any combination of any 2 or more of the matters referred to in items (a) to (g).

Despite the breadth of this definition, it should not be automatically assumed that a supply exists and that GST consequences follow where there is a transaction and consideration is payable. Rather, it is necessary in any case where a payment is made to determine whether anything is supplied and, if so, whether the payment has a sufficient nexus to be consideration for what is supplied. The meaning of "supply for consideration" was considered by the Full Federal Court in *AP Group*. Although its comments were only obiter the court said:

> "The consideration must be 'in connection with' the supply but the supply must also be 'for' the consideration . . . It ensures that not every connection between the giving of consideration and the provision satisfy the first condition of making a taxable supply. If it were otherwise, any form of connection of any character between the making of a supply and the payment of consideration would suffice."

The meaning of "supply for consideration" is also discussed in GSTR 2014/1 in the context of motor vehicle incentive payments.

In some cases, the one consideration may be received for more than one supply (*Qantas*). In that case, the High Court held that GST was payable by an airline where a passenger books and pays for airline travel, but subsequently cancels the booking or does not turn up for the flight and does not receive a refund. The High Court said that the airline's contractual conditions did not provide an unconditional promise to carry the passenger and baggage on a particular flight. It said the taxpayer supplied something less than that, namely (at the least) a promise to use its best endeavours to carry the passenger and baggage, having regard to the circumstances of the business operations of the airline. This was a "taxable supply" for which the consideration, being the fare, was received.

A supply is normally something that passes from one entity to another (GSTR 2001/4; GSTR 2006/9). There may be a supply even though there is no element of consumption. On this view, agreeing to refrain from producing goods would still be a supply (GSTR 2001/4).

Prior to the High Court decision in *MBI Properties*, there was a widely accepted view that a supply cannot be "made" unless the supplier does something or takes some action. For example, it has been suggested that there cannot be a supply constituted by a release of an obligation that occurs independently of the act of the releasor (*Shaw v Director of Housing and State of Tasmania (No 2)*). In *MBI Properties*, however, the High Court stated (at para 33) that it was incorrect to consider that the making of a supply must always involve the taking of some action on the part of the supplier (GSTR 2006/9).

Compulsory acquisitions

On a similar basis, the compulsory resumption of land from an entity does not involve a "surrender" or other supply unless the entity has taken some action to cause its interest to be transferred or surrendered to the relevant authority. Accordingly, there is no supply by the entity where its legal interest is divested by operation of the resumption statute, for example, upon gazettal of the acquisition notice, and the authority initiated the resumption process pursuant to a statutory right (GSTR 2006/9; *CSR Ltd v Hornsby Shire Council*).

Supplies of money

A payment of money for the supply of something else is not a ''supply'' — otherwise there would be a doubling up of GST (s 9-10(4)).

However, if money is provided as consideration for the supply of other money, that will be treated as a supply. This may apply, for example, where there is a foreign exchange transaction or a cheque is cashed for a fee. This is treated as a financial supply (¶34-190).

For supplies or payments made on or after 1 July 2017, the GST treatment of digital currency such as bitcoin is aligned with that of money. The effect is that a supply of digital currency is not treated as a supply unless it is provided as consideration for another supply of money or digital currency, eg in debt trading or foreign currency speculation. If there is such a supply, it will be treated as a financial supply.

Commissioner's summary of ''supply'' rules

The Commissioner considers that the following propositions generally apply in identifying and characterising typical 2-party supplies:

(1) for every supply there is a supplier

(2) generally, for every supply there is a recipient and an acquisition

(3) a supply may be mixed, composite or neither

(4) a transaction may involve 2 or more supplies

(5) to ''make a supply'', an entity must do something

(6) ''supply'' usually, but not necessarily, requires something to be passed from one entity to another

(7) an entity cannot make a supply to itself

(8) a supply cannot be made by more than one entity

(9) creation of expectations alone does not establish a supply

(10) it is necessary to analyse the transaction that occurs, not a transaction that might have occurred (GSTR 2006/9).

Consideration

Consideration is defined broadly and means, in effect, just about anything of value (s 9-15). In the straightforward example of a sale of goods for money, the consideration is simply the payment.

As well as payment, consideration also covers situations where someone does something or refrains from doing something. Any of these things are treated as consideration for a supply if they are:

- ''in connection with'' the supply (this is interpreted widely)
- made in response to the supply, or
- made to induce the supply.

It is not necessary that the consideration is provided by the recipient of the goods or services — it may be provided by a third party. Nor is it necessary that there was any legal obligation to make the payment, or that it was made to the supplier (*TT-Line Company*; GSTR 2006/9). However, in such cases, it would be necessary to establish that there is a sufficient connection between the supply and the third party payment.

"In the course or furtherance of an enterprise"

The second requirement for a taxable supply is that the supply is made ''in the course or furtherance of an enterprise'' that the supplier is carrying on (s 9-5). For the meaning of ''enterprise'', see ¶34-100.

This covers any supplies that are made in connection with the enterprise. The necessary relationship is established if the asset is applied, or intended to be applied, in the enterprise, even if the application or intended application is minor or secondary. It is irrelevant what the recipient intends to use the asset for. It is also irrelevant, for example, whether the asset is sold or whether it is distributed ''in specie'' (eg where a discretionary trust makes a distribution to a beneficiary by directly transferring an asset to them). However, it would not cover the supply of private commodities, such as when a car dealer privately sells his/her own car that is not used to any extent in the business (GSTD 2009/1).

"Connected with Australia"

The third requirement for a taxable supply is that the supply is connected with Australia (the indirect tax zone) (s 9-25). This test varies according to whether the supply is of goods, real property or other things such as services. Special rules also apply to telecommunications, and there are important exemptions for certain supplies by non-residents (see below).

(1) Goods

A supply of *goods* has the relevant connection with Australia in the following circumstances (GSTR 2018/2):

- in the case of goods supplied wholly *within* Australia, the goods have the relevant connection if they are delivered or made available in Australia. The ATO considers that this means *physically* delivered or made available

- in the case of goods supplied *from* Australia, the goods have the relevant connection if they are removed from Australia (but for the exemption for exports, see ¶34-165), or

- in the case of goods supplied *to* Australia, the supply has the relevant connection if either:

  - the supplier imports the goods into Australia. The Commissioner considers that, in this context, ''import'' includes completing the customs formalities, for example by entering the goods for home consumption, warehousing or transhipment (GSTR 2003/15). Special rules apply to imports (¶34-250), or

  - the supply is an offshore supply of low value goods to a consumer (¶34-250). This particular measure applies for tax periods starting on or after 1 July 2018.

''Goods'' include any form of tangible personal property (s 195-1). Goods therefore include trading stock, plant, equipment, food, vehicles and raw materials. Goods do *not* include real property, interests in real property, or intangible property such as contractual rights, goodwill, copyright or trademarks.

Supply of goods involving installation or assembly services

Where a supply of goods (other than a luxury car) involves the goods being brought to Australia and the goods into Australia, the supply is treated as if it were 2 separate supplies (s 9-25(6)). The prices of each of the separate supplies is so much of the price of the actual supply that reasonably represents the price of each of the deemed supplies (s 9-75(4)).

Prior to 1 October 2016, the installation or assembly component of a supply that was connected with Australia could be treated as part of a single supply of the goods (former s 9-25(3)).

(2) Real property

A supply of *real property* has the relevant connection if the real property is situated in Australia, or if the land to which the real property relates is in Australia (GSTR 2018/1). "Real property" includes rights, interests, options and licences over land (s 195-1). So, for example, if an entity has a licence to occupy land situated in Australia, that licence is treated as real property which is connected with Australia.

(3) Other things such as services and intangibles

A supply of anything else (eg services, digital products, rights, advice or obligations) has the relevant connection if (GSTR 2019/1):

(a) it is done in Australia

(b) the supplier makes the supply through an enterprise that the supplier carries on in Australia (see below)

(c) there is a supply of a right or option to acquire some other thing, and the supply of that thing would be connected with Australia. An offshore supply of a right or option to acquire something is also connected with Australia if the supply of that thing would be connected with Australia (s 9-25(5)(c)). This provision is primarily designed to catch non-resident tour operators who acquire Australian package holidays from resident tour wholesalers and then on-supply them to tourists. However, it is not specifically restricted to that situation, or

(d) for tax periods starting on or after 1 July 2017, where the recipient of the supply is an "Australian consumer". An Australian consumer means a resident of Australia that either: (1) is not registered; or (2) is registered, but does not acquire the supply solely or partly for the purpose of an enterprise that it is carrying on (s 9-25(5)(d); GSTR 2017/1; ¶34-250).

Enterprise carried on in Australia

With effect from 1 October 2016, an enterprise of an entity is carried on in Australia if the enterprise of the entity is carried on by one or more specified individuals who are in Australia and any of the following apply:

(i) the enterprise is carried on through a "fixed place" in Australia

(ii) the enterprise has been carried on through one or more places in Australia — not necessarily fixed places — for more than 183 days in a 12-month period, or

(iii) the entity *intends* to carry on the enterprise through one or more places in Australia for more than 183 days in a 12-month period (ss 9-25; 9-26; 9-27).

For the Commissioner's rulings on how he will apply the test, see LCR 2016/1. Prior to 1 October 2016, an enterprise was carried on in Australia if it was carried on through a permanent establishment (former s 9-25(6); ¶22-150).

Creation, grant, transfer, assignment or surrender of a right

In general, the rule in (c) may be satisfied irrespective of whether the supply of that other thing is actually made. However, in the case of a *surrender* of a right or option to acquire something, the rule in (c) will not apply. This would mean that the surrender would only be connected with Australia if (a) or (b) is satisfied (GSTR 2003/8).

Non-resident's supplies that are not connected with Australia

For tax periods starting on or after 1 October 2016, the following types of supply are not connected with Australia if they are made by a non-resident and the supply is not made through an enterprise carried on in Australia:

(1) supply of an intangible (anything other than goods or real property) made to an ''Australian-based business recipient'', where the thing is done in Australia. An entity is an Australian-based business recipient of a supply if it is registered and carries on an enterprise in Australia, and its acquisition of the supply is not solely private or domestic.

(2) supply of an intangible to another non-resident that acquires it solely for the purpose of carrying on its enterprise outside Australia, and the thing is done in Australia

(3) transfer of ownership of leased goods to another non-resident that does not acquire them solely or partly for an enterprise that it carries on in Australia (GSTR 2018/2). The lessee must have made a taxable importation of the goods before the supply was made and must continue to lease them on substantially similar terms and conditions, or

(4) supply of the lease if the recipient in (3) is the lessee (s 9-26; GSTR 2018/2).

These exclusions override the special rules applying to telecommunication supplies. Although these supplies are not connected with Australia, the supply may be ''reverse charged'', so that GST is instead paid by the recipient (¶34-250), if the acquisition would not have been fully creditable to the recipient.

Telecommunication supplies

Telecommunication supplies are connected with Australia if the recipient will ''effectively use or enjoy them'' in Australia (s 85-5). For tax periods starting on or after 1 October 2016, this rule is subject to the exclusions relating to non-resident's supplies above.

Registration

The fourth requirement for a taxable supply is that the supplier is either registered or required to be registered (s 9-5; ¶34-100).

Supplies not GST-free or input taxed

The fifth requirement is that taxable supplies do not include supplies that are GST-free or input taxed (ss 9-5; 9-30). If a supply is GST-free, this means that no GST is payable on it and that the supplier is entitled to claim credits for the GST payable on its related business inputs. If a supply is input taxed, no GST is payable on the supply, but the supplier generally *cannot* claim input tax credits on its related business inputs. For details of GST-free and input taxed supplies, see ¶34-165 and ¶34-170, respectively.

A supply of a right to receive a supply that would be input taxed is itself input taxed, and the supply of a right to receive a supply that would be GST-free is itself GST-free (s 9-30).

[AMGST ¶4-000; GSTG ¶10-000]

¶34-110 Input tax credits

GST can be claimed back for any "creditable acquisition" made by an entity (s 11-20). The GST which attaches to a creditable acquisition is called an "input tax credit".

Creditable acquisition

There are 4 cumulative tests that must be satisfied for an acquisition to qualify as a "creditable acquisition" and thus give rise to an input tax credit entitlement. Similar tests apply to "creditable importations" (¶34-250).

An entity makes a creditable acquisition if (s 11-5):

(1) it acquires anything solely or partly for a creditable purpose

(2) the supply of the thing to the entity is a taxable supply

(3) it provides, or is liable to provide, consideration for the supply (¶34-105; *McKinnon Holdings (NSW)*), and

(4) it is registered, or required to be registered (¶34-100).

Meaning of "acquisition"

"Acquisition" is defined to mean "any form of acquisition whatsoever" (s 11-10(1)) and is clearly intended to be very broad.

In order to clarify the breadth of the definition, s 11-10(2) provides, without limiting the general definition in s 11-10(1), that "acquisition" includes any of the following:

(a) acquiring goods or services

(b) receiving advice or information

(c) accepting a grant, assignment or surrender of real property

(d) accepting a grant, transfer, assignment or surrender of any right

(e) acquiring something the supply of which is a financial supply

(f) acquiring a right to require another person:

  (i) to do anything, or

  (ii) to refrain from an act, or

  (iii) to tolerate an act or situation

(g) any combination of any of the acquisitions listed above.

However, it does not include an acquisition of money unless the money is provided as consideration for a supply that is a supply of money (s 11-10(3)).

An employer cannot claim an input tax credit for an expense paid on behalf of a superannuation fund that makes an acquisition. This is because, although the employer is providing consideration for the supply, the employer has not acquired anything (GSTD 2016/1).

Meaning of "creditable purpose"

In order to be entitled to input tax credits on an acquisition that was a taxable supply, the acquisition must have been made for a "creditable purpose" (s 11-15). This means that:

(a) the entity must have acquired it in carrying on its "enterprise" (¶34-100). This requires that the particular enterprise be identified. This is determined on the basis of matters such as the business's income-earning activities, its formation documents, contracts, business records, business plans and minutes. On the basis of analogous income tax cases, whether a thing is acquired in carrying on an entity's enterprise depends on the purpose for which it acquired the thing (GSTR 2008/1; *304 Wanda Street Pty Ltd*).

Some of the factors that would suggest that an acquisition is made in carrying on an enterprise are that:

- it is incidental or relevant to the commencement, continuance or termination of the enterprise
- the thing acquired is used by the enterprise in making supplies
- the acquisition secures a real benefit or advantage
- it is one which an ordinary business person would be likely to make
- it does not meet the *personal* needs of individuals such as partners or directors
- it helps to protect or preserve the enterprise entity, structure or organisation, and
- it is made by the entity in accordance with statutory requirements (GSTR 2008/1)

In *Skourmallas*, a small-scale luxury car dealer who had already purchased and resold 7 luxury cars was held to have acquired an eighth car in the course of an enterprise, even though there was a degree of private use and the car was resold at a loss. The taxpayer's pattern of purchases and sales, his going to the trouble and expense of undertaking 9 subjects in a course of study relating to motor vehicle trading and obtaining a motor dealer's licence was held to be consistent with his professed intention of operating a motor dealership.

(b) the acquisition must not be of a private or domestic nature. The ATO considers, on the basis of analogous income tax cases, that this would normally cover matters such as living expenses, childminding expenses and most home/work travel (GSTR 2008/1), and

(c) the acquisition must not relate to making supplies that would be input taxed, unless specified exceptions apply (eg the supply is made through an enterprise (or part of an enterprise) carried on outside Australia, or the business provides financial supplies as only an incidental part of their operations or the acquisition relates to making financial supplies consisting of a borrowing other than through a deposit account: s 11-15(3), (4), (5)). Typical input taxed supplies include financial supplies (¶34-170) and residential accommodation (¶34-230). The relationship must be real and substantial, not just trivial. However, it is not necessary that there be a direct link between the acquisition and an actual supply that is input taxed (*HP Mercantile Pty Limited*; GSTR 2008/1). Nor is the relationship subject to some overriding "purpose" test. For example, where a mining company acquired residential accommodation to lease to its employees in remote areas, it was denied input tax credits on associated acquisitions, as they related to the (input taxed) supply of the premises. In the Full Federal Court's view, the acquisitions related wholly to the making of supplies that would be input taxed albeit that they did so for the wider purpose of the enterprise (*Rio Tinto Services Ltd*).

Acquisition must have been a taxable supply

In order for an acquisition to be creditable, the supply of the thing to the recipient must be a taxable supply (s 11-5(b); ¶34-105).

The determination of whether there has been a taxable supply to the recipient should be looked at from the perspective of the entity making the supply (*Secretary to the Department of Transport (Vic)*).

No input tax credits for non-deductible expenses

Acquisitions will not qualify as creditable acquisitions to the extent that they involve certain expenses that are *specifically* made non-deductible under the income tax law (s 69-5). These include expenses that are not deductible under the following provisions:

- recreational club expenses (ITAA97 s 26-45)
- leisure facility expenses (ITAA97 s 26-50)
- non-compulsory uniforms (ITAA97 Div 34)
- family maintenance (ITAA97 s 26-40)
- relatives' travel (ITAA97 s 26-30)
- entertainment (ITAA97 Div 32; ITAA36 ss 51AEA; 51AEB; 51AEC)
- penalties (ITAA97 s 26-5)
- agreements for the provision of non-deductible non-cash business benefits (ITAA36 s 51AK).

Calculation of input tax credit

Normally, the amount of the input tax credit for a creditable acquisition is simply the amount of GST payable on the supply acquired (s 11-25).

▶ Example

An entity buys equipment that it uses wholly in carrying on its business. The GST-inclusive cost is $22,000. It can claim an input tax credit of $2,000.

However, some transactions involve acquisitions that are only *partly* eligible for credit (s 11-30). Typically, these involve acquisitions that relate partly to making private or input taxed supplies. In these cases, it is necessary to work out the creditable amount by a process of apportionment. The general rule is that the method for doing this must be fair and reasonable, must reflect the intended use of the acquisition, and must be appropriately documented. For the Commissioner's apportionment guidelines, see GSTR 2006/4.

Time limit for claiming input tax credits

Generally, an entity's entitlement to input tax credits for creditable acquisitions ceases unless they are included in its assessed net amounts within a period of 4 years, although this time limit does not apply in certain limited cases (ss 93-1; 93-10; ATO *Decision Impact Statement* on *Coles Supermarkets Australia*).

[AMGST ¶5-000; GSTG ¶15-000]

¶34-115 GST turnover

An entity's GST turnover is relevant in determining whether the entity is required to register (¶34-100). It is also relevant in determining whether it is required to lodge monthly or electronic returns (¶34-120).

For entities that are carrying on an enterprise that does *not* constitute a business (eg some charities, trustees of superannuation funds and government bodies), GST turnover is also relevant for determining entitlement to:

- use the cash basis of accounting (¶34-130)
- pay GST by instalments (¶34-150), and
- make an annual apportionment of input tax credits.

In determining an entity's GST turnover, both the current year and the projected year are taken into account (Div 188). For example, an entity's GST turnover will be $75,000 or more — and it will therefore be required to register — if *either*:

- its current GST turnover is $75,000 or more, and the ATO is not satisfied that the projected GST turnover is below $75,000, or
- its projected GST turnover is $75,000 or more (s 188-10).

At any particular time, the current GST turnover is measured over the 12-month period ending at the end of the current month. The projected GST turnover is measured over the 12-month period starting at the beginning of the current month.

The turnover does not include the GST component of taxable supplies and also does not include:

- input taxed supplies
- supplies where there is no consideration provided
- supplies that are not made in connection with an enterprise
- supplies that are not connected with Australia. You also disregard: (1) an offshore supply of rights or options that is deemed to be connected with Australia, unless (from 1 July 2017) it is made to an ''Australian consumer'' (¶34-105), the underlying supply is not a supply of goods or real property and the supply is not GST-free; and (2) offshore supplies of rights or options to use commercial accommodation in Australia
- GST-free supplies made by a non-resident that are not made through an enterprise carried on by the non-resident in Australia. The exclusion applies in working out net amounts for tax periods starting on or after 1 October 2016, or
- insurance payouts (ss 188-15; 188-20; 188-22).

If the supply is a loan of money, the value for turnover purposes is generally the amount of the loan (s 188-35). If the entity is a member of a GST group (¶34-180), supplies made between members are excluded.

In addition, projected turnover does not include transfers of capital assets, or any transfers associated with closing down the business or substantially and permanently reducing its size or scale (s 188-25). For guidelines on the meaning of GST turnover, see GSTR 2001/7.

Offshore suppliers of hotel accommodation

From 1 July 2019, offshore suppliers of the right to use commercial accommodation (eg hotels) in Australia are required to include these supplies in working out their GST turnover in the same way as local sellers. This affects supplies:

- for which any of the consideration is first provided on or after 1 July 2019, or
- where the invoice is issued on or after 1 July 2019.

If the supplier's GST turnover equals or exceeds the registration turnover threshold then GST must be remitted for supplies that are taxable supplies.

[AMGST ¶3-030; GSTG ¶5-070]

¶34-120 GST tax periods

Tax periods are either monthly or quarterly, depending on the circumstances. In certain situations, annual tax periods may also apply.

Quarterly tax periods

The general rule is that tax periods are quarterly, ie for 3 months. These periods end on 31 March, 30 June, 30 September and 31 December (s 27-5).

However, as explained below, monthly tax periods will be compulsory in certain situations. In other cases, optional monthly tax periods may be adopted.

Compulsory monthly tax periods

An entity *must* use monthly tax periods if any of the following apply:

- its GST turnover is $20 million or more
- it will be carrying on its enterprise in Australia for less than 3 months
- it has a history of failing to comply with its tax obligations (s 27-15).

If these circumstances change (eg the entity's GST turnover falls below $20 million) it can elect to change to quarterly tax periods, provided that it has been using one-month periods for at least 12 months (s 27-25). Unlike the position with optional monthly tax periods (see below) the ATO does not have a discretion to reduce this 12-month period.

If an entity is a resident agent for a non-resident, monthly tax periods will apply if the non-resident's GST turnover is $20 million or more (s 57-35).

Optional monthly tax periods

Even if monthly tax periods are not compulsory, an entity may elect to use them (s 27-10). This election can take effect from 1 January, 1 April, 1 July or 1 October.

Once an entity has been using optional monthly tax periods for at least 12 months, it can change to quarterly tax periods, provided that its GST turnover is less than $20 million (s 27-20). This simply requires the relevant notification to the ATO.

The ATO has a discretion to reduce this 12-month period if an entity makes a request in the approved form (s 27-22). In exercising this discretion, the ATO may take all relevant matters into account, including how long it has been using monthly tax periods and whether monthly tax periods applied to it under an earlier registration.

Annual tax periods

Entities that are *voluntarily* registered have the option of reporting and paying GST on an annual basis (Div 151). This applies to ordinary enterprises with a GST turnover of less than $75,000 and non-profit organisations with a GST turnover of less than $150,000 (¶34-100). However, this option is not available to entities if the only reason that they are not required to be registered is because offshore supplies of rights or options have been disregarded in calculating their turnover (s 151-5(2)). Nor is it available to entities that have made an election under s 162-15 to pay GST by instalments (s 151-5(1)).

The tax period for "small business entities" (¶7-050) and entities not carrying on a business with GST turnovers of $2 million or less that elect to pay by instalments will normally be the same as the financial year (Div 162).

Liquidators, receivers and trustees

Liquidators, receivers, interim managers, controllers and trustees in bankruptcy have the same tax period as the entity they represent (s 58-35). The entity's tax period at the time that it becomes incapacitated is taken to have ended on the day prior to that time. The next tax period starts on the day after the tax period ends, and ends when the first tax period would have ended (s 27-39).

Non-standard tax periods

There may be modifications to normal tax periods to fit individual circumstances.

(1) "Non-calendar" monthly tax periods

The compulsory monthly tax periods may be modified for businesses that do not use calendar months as the basis of their commercial accounting. Entities that are in this position, and that have GST turnovers of $20 million or more, can apply to the ATO to have tax periods that reflect their normal accounting practice (s 27-37). For example, this may be appropriate if the entity uses 13 four-weekly accounting periods, or 12 accounting periods, with some of 4 weeks and others of 5 weeks. Approval will be withdrawn if the entity subsequently fails to satisfy any of these preconditions (s 27-38).

(2) 7-day leeway for aligning tax periods

An entity can also change the day in each year on which a tax period would normally end, so as to be consistent with its normal accounting practice. However, the changed period must end no more than 7 days before or after the end of the original period. It does not need to get the ATO's consent for this (s 27-35).

If the day is changed in this way, the next period commences on the day after the changed period ends.

(3) Transitional tax periods

If an entity has changed tax periods, the ATO can nominate a particular period as a tax period to ensure a continuous transition. The nominated period cannot be less than 3 months, and cannot overlap with any other tax period for which a GST return has already been lodged (s 27-30). This also applies at the time the entity registers.

Concluding tax periods

An entity's final (or ''concluding'') tax period ends at the following time:

- at the end of the day before the individual dies or the entity ceases to exist
- at the end of the day on which the entity ceases to carry on any enterprise
- at the end of the day on which the entity's cancellation of registration takes effect (s 27-40).

If an entity is on a cash basis and its registration is cancelled, any GST, input tax credits or adjustments that have not been attributed to any previous tax period will be attributed to the entity's concluding tax period (s 138-15). Increasing adjustments may apply where registration is cancelled (s 138-5).

[AMGST ¶7-100; GSTG ¶20-500]

¶34-130 Basis of GST accounting

The GST and the input tax credits that belong to each period are worked out according to attribution rules, which vary according to whether the entity is on a cash basis or an accruals basis of accounting (Div 29).

If it is on the cash basis, the GST and input tax credits for each tax period are worked out on the basis of amounts actually received and paid out. An entity can use the cash basis if:

- it is a ''small business entity'' (¶7-050) or, if it does not carry on a business, its GST turnover does not exceed $2 million
- it accounts on a cash basis for income tax purposes
- it is a charity or related body, or
- it can convince the ATO that it is appropriate.

If the entity uses the accruals basis, it works out the GST and input tax credits for each tax period on the basis of its *entitlement* to be paid and its obligation to pay. This will normally be when it gives or receives an invoice.

In either case, the entity normally cannot claim an input tax credit unless it also has a complying tax invoice for the purchase at the time of lodging the return (¶34-140).

▶ Example 1

Assume that a seller and buyer both operate on a cash basis and both have the same tax periods. The seller sells goods and issues a tax invoice in the first tax period of the year. The buyer pays for the goods in the second tax period of the year.

The seller should attribute the GST on the sale to the second tax period because that is when payment is received. The buyer should attribute the input tax credit to the second period because it paid for the goods in that period and had a tax invoice.

▶ Example 2

Assume that a seller and buyer both operate on a cash basis and both have the same tax periods. The buyer makes a part payment for goods in the first tax period, receives the goods in the second period, together with a tax invoice, and pays the balance owing in the third period.

The seller should attribute the GST on the part payment to the first tax period, and the GST on the balance to the third tax period.

As the buyer does not receive a tax invoice until the second tax period, the input tax credit for the part payment should be attributed to that period. The input tax credit for the balance should be attributed to the third period.

▶ Example 3

Assume that the seller and the buyer operate on an accruals basis and that both have the same tax periods. The seller sells goods and issues an invoice in the first tax period of the year. The invoice does not comply with the requirements for a tax invoice. The buyer pays for the goods in the second tax period of the year.

The seller becomes entitled to be paid when it issues the invoice and should therefore attribute all of the GST on the sale to the first tax period.

The buyer becomes liable to pay when it receives the invoice in the second tax period, but cannot attribute the input tax credit to that period because it does not have a tax invoice. Until it receives this, it cannot claim the credit.

▶ Example 4

Assume that the seller and the buyer operate on an accruals basis and that both have the same tax periods. The buyer makes a deposit on goods in the first tax period, receives the goods in the second period, together with a tax invoice, and pays the balance owing in the third period.

As the seller receives some of the consideration (ie the deposit) in the first tax period, all of the GST on the sale should be attributed to that period.

As the buyer does not receive a tax invoice until the second tax period, all of the input tax credit for the purchase should be attributed to that period.

▶ Example 5

Assume that the seller and the buyer operate on an accruals basis and that both have the same tax periods. The seller requires payment in advance in the first tax period, and delivers the goods in the second tax period, together with a tax invoice.

The seller should attribute all the GST on the sale to the first period.

As the buyer does not receive a tax invoice until the second tax period, all of the input tax credit for the purchase should be attributed to that period.

[AMGST ¶7-200; GSTG ¶21-000]

¶34-140 GST tax invoices

In general, an input tax credit for a creditable acquisition cannot be claimed unless the recipient holds a ‘‘tax invoice’’ at the time it lodges its GST return for the tax period to which the credit is attributable (s 29-10(3); *Chalmers*). If this requirement is not satisfied, the credit claim will be deferred until the tax period for which the requirement is satisfied. However, the mere existence of a tax invoice is not, by itself, sufficient to establish that a creditable acquisition has in fact occurred (*GH1 Pty Ltd (In Liq)*). There is no obligation to hold a tax invoice if the value of the supply (excluding GST) is $75 or less (s 29-80(1)).

The tax invoice must be issued by the supplier (s 29-70(1)), except in the case of "recipient created" tax invoices (see below). However, in certain circumstances another entity can issue a tax invoice on behalf of a supplier where there is an agreement between them (ID 2010/146). If the recipient requests a tax invoice from the supplier, the supplier must issue it within 28 days after the request (s 29-70(2)).

An invoice is issued for the purposes of s 29-5(1)(b) when some act has been done to convey it to the intended recipient (*Tavco*). An invoice is also issued when it is posted on a website, provided certain conditions are met (GSTD 2005/2).

The required contents for a tax invoice are as follows:

(1) it must be issued by the supplier (for *recipient* created tax invoices, see below)

(2) it must be in the approved form

(3) it must contain enough information to enable the following to be "clearly ascertained":

- the supplier's identity (eg its legal name, business name or trading name) and ABN
- if the total price of the supply/ies is $1,000 or higher, the recipient's identity or ABN
- what is supplied, including quantity and price
- the extent to which each supply to which the document relates is taxable. This requirement is satisfied if the document includes the amount of GST payable for each taxable supply, or a statement of the extent to which the supply is taxable, or each taxable supply is asterisked with a corresponding statement of the extent to which the supply is taxable (GSTR 2013/1)
- date of issue
- the amount of GST payable in relation to each supply to which the document relates
- such other matters as may be specified in the regulations, and

(4) it must be clearly ascertainable from the document itself that it was *intended* to be a tax invoice. The most obvious way would be to include the words "Tax Invoice", though alternatives such as "GST Invoice" may suffice in appropriate circumstances (s 29-70).

The tax invoice may cover more than one supply, provided that it meets the requirements for each of those supplies. If it meets the requirements for some but not all of the supplies, it qualifies as a tax invoice in relation to the former supplies, but not the latter. So far as price is concerned, GSTR 2013/1 says that it is not necessary to specify the actual price of each item, provided that the price can be determined from the invoice.

The $1,000 threshold for requiring the recipient's identity or ABN is designed to accommodate smaller business transactions, such as from a cash register, where that information may not be readily available. Of course, a supplier retains the option of including this information if it wishes, even if the transaction is for less than $1,000.

Modifications to tax invoice requirements

The Commissioner can waive or modify the requirement that a tax invoice must be held before an input tax credit can be claimed (s 29-10(3)). For example, this has been done, subject to various conditions, in relation to:

- acquisitions under an agency relationship (WTI 2013/1)
- acquisitions from or by a beneficiary of a bare trust (WTI 2013/2)

- acquisitions through electronic purchasing systems (WTI 2013/3)
- acquisitions where total consideration not known (WTI 2013/4)
- offer documents and renewal notices (WTI 2013/5)
- acquisitions from or by a partnership (WTI 2013/6)
- acquisitions from property managers (WTI 2013/7)
- taxi travel (WTI 2013/8)
- creditable acquisitions by a lessee or sub-lessee following a sale of a reversion in commercial premises (WTI 2013/9)
- acquisition of a motor vehicle under a novated lease (WTI 2013/10)
- acquisition of a motor vehicle from a dealer who is entitled to a motor vehicle incentive payment (WTI 2014/1)
- direct entry services (WTI 2015/30)
- customer of Choice Hotels Asia-Pac Pty Ltd (WTI 2016/33)
- government law enforcement agencies who reimburse work expenses incurred by their employees or agents working as undercover officers (WTI 2016/40)
- intangible supplies from offshore (WTI 2017/3)
- corporate credit or charge card statements.

For a full list and further details, see Appendix 2 to GSTR 2013/1.

Documents that do not strictly comply

The Commissioner also has a discretion to treat a document as a tax invoice even though it does not strictly comply (s 29-70(1B)). The ATO says that this discretion is exercised in a practical way. According to PS LA 2004/11, the preconditions are:

- if the taxpayer has not yet claimed the credit, it must have made a genuine and reasonable attempt — preferably in writing — to obtain a valid tax invoice from the supplier, although it is not necessary that they go to extraordinary lengths or great expense
- if the claim for a credit has already been made in a BAS, the taxpayer must show that it has made a genuine attempt to meet the invoice requirements, bearing in mind the practical and commercial realities of record-keeping. The ATO will take into account factors such as: (1) whether the error is minor in legal or money terms; (2) whether any missing information is provided in other documentation; (3) the taxpayer's compliance record; (4) the adequacy of their record-keeping systems; and (5) their GST ''experience'' level.

Further details are given in PS LA 2004/11 and in GSTR 2013/1.

Recipient created tax invoices

A tax invoice is normally issued by the supplier. However, sometimes this will not be practicable, for example where the recipient determines the value of the goods or services, rather than the supplier. In these cases it may be more appropriate for the tax invoice to be issued by the recipient. The situations in which these ''recipient created tax invoices'' (RCTIs) can be issued are determined by the Commissioner (s 29-70(3)).

The Commissioner has authorised the use of recipient created tax invoices for some general situations and for a variety of more specific industry transactions. The general situations are specified in GSTR 2000/10. They are as follows:

(1) Supplies of agricultural products made to registered recipients who determine the value of the products after a qualitative or quantitative analysis. This applies to products derived from viticulture, horticulture, pasturage, apiculture (bees), poultry farming and dairy farming, and other operations connected with cultivation, crop gathering or livestock rearing.

▶ **Example 1**

A tax invoice could be issued by a sugar mill that tests crushed sugar cane it receives to establish the sugar content or by an abattoir that weighs, slaughters, grades and prices the animals that are supplied to it.

(2) Supplies made to registered government entities such as a department, branch or other approved body.

(3) Supplies made to registered recipients that have a turnover of at least $20 million. If the recipient is a member of a group that meets the requirements for a GST group — even though the group is not actually registered as such — it will be sufficient that one of the members of the group has GST turnover of at least $20 million. If the recipient is the operator of a GST joint venture, it will be sufficient that one of the participants has turnover of at least $20 million, or is a member of a qualifying group as described above. The turnover is measured in the same way as explained at ¶34-115, including the value of input taxed supplies.

▶ **Example 2**

Company X has turnover of $25 million. It satisfies the turnover test even if $10 million of that turnover is for financial supplies that are input taxed.

▶ **Example 3**

Company Y has turnover of $5 million. It is 100% owned by Company Z that has a turnover of $21 million. As Company Z's turnover exceeds $20 million, and Companies Y and Z can be treated as a group, Company Y satisfies the turnover test. Company Z satisfies the turnover test in any event by virtue of its own turnover.

For a recipient created tax invoice to be effective in any of these situations, various additional conditions must be satisfied, for example there must be a written agreement (which may alternatively be embedded in the invoice) and both parties must be registered.

RCTIs for specific industry transactions

The Commissioner has also determined that recipient created tax invoices may be used in specific industry situations.

These determinations, which are subject to various qualifications, are contained in a series of *Recipient Created Tax Invoice (RCTI) Determinations*. They may be accessed under ''Legislative Determinations'' at www.ato.gov.au.

[AMGST ¶5-100; GSTG ¶16-000]

¶34-145 GST adjustments

Adjustments to previously declared GST or input tax credits are required where, because of subsequent events or circumstances, the GST paid or payable or input tax credit claimed or claimable is incorrect. Adjustments arise from:

- changes in price or GST status. These are called adjustment events (Div 19, see below)
- debts becoming bad or overdue (Div 21)
- changes in intended use (Divs 129; 130)
- changes associated with starting, transferring or ceasing business, or altering registration status (Divs 137; 138; 139)

- other miscellaneous adjustments (eg arrangements involving agents, groups, joint ventures, amalgamation of property, annual apportionment of input tax credits and gross-up clauses).

Adjustment events

An adjustment event is an event which has the effect of:

- cancelling a supply or acquisition
- changing the consideration for a supply or an acquisition, or
- causing a supply or an acquisition to become (or stop being) a taxable supply or a creditable acquisition (s 19-10).

For the Commissioner's views on which events are, and are not, adjustment events, see GSTR 2000/19. The Commissioner considers that rental guarantee payments made by a vendor to a purchaser of real property give rise to an adjustment event in certain circumstances (GSTD 2014/3).

Increasing and decreasing adjustments

Adjustments can be either increasing adjustments or decreasing adjustments. An increasing adjustment increases the net amount of GST for a tax period, ie by increasing the GST on supplies or reducing the input tax credit on acquisitions (ss 19-50; 19-75; 19-80). A decreasing adjustment reduces the net amount of GST for a tax period, ie by reducing the GST on supplies or increasing the input tax credit on acquisitions (ss 19-55; 19-75; 19-85).

An increasing adjustment made under s 19-50 can give rise to an amount of excess GST within the meaning of Div 142 of the GST Act (¶34-150) (GSTD 2016/2).

Attribution to tax periods

Adjustments are generally attributed to the tax period in which the entity becomes aware of them (s 29-20). However, special attribution rules apply for adjustment events and on cessation of registration.

In the case of adjustment events, the adjustments are attributed to the tax period(s) in which the entity becomes aware of them. However, if an entity accounts on a cash basis and the adjustment event results in it paying consideration, the adjustment is attributable to the period(s) in which the consideration is paid (s 29-20). In the case of decreasing adjustments, the entity must also hold an adjustment note (see below). In cases where a business's registration is cancelled, the adjustment is made in the business's concluding tax period (s 138-10).

Adjustment notes

If an adjustment event results in a decreasing adjustment — ie a reduction of GST or an increase in input tax credits — the entity will need to hold an adjustment note at the time it lodges its return for the tax period in which the adjustment is claimed (s 29-20). However, an adjustment note is not necessary if the amount of the decreasing adjustment is $75 or less, excluding GST (s 29-80(2)).

An adjustment note must be issued by the supplier within 28 days after the recipient requests. Even if a request is not made, the supplier must issue an adjustment note within 28 days of becoming aware of the adjustment, provided that a tax invoice was issued (or requested) in relation to the original supply (s 29-75).

Content of adjustment notes

The required contents for an adjustment note which is issued by a supplier are as follows:

(1) it must be in the approved form. No particular format has been prescribed, as long as it complies with (2) and (3)

(2) it must set out the ABN of the supplier

(3) it must contain enough information to enable the following to be "clearly ascertained":

- that it is intended as an adjustment note, and the effect of the adjustment, eg whether it is for an increasing or decreasing adjustment
- the identity and ABN of the supplier or supplier's agent
- the identity or ABN of the recipient or the recipient's agent. This, however, is only essential where the note relates to a tax invoice showing the total price for the supply was at least $1,000; or relates to a supply that was not taxable but becomes taxable and its price is at least $1,000
- the issue date
- a brief explanation of the reason for the adjustment
- the amount of the adjustment to the GST payable. Where the amount of GST is 1/11th of the price (as is usual), it will be sufficient to make it clear that the difference in the price of the supply includes GST
- the difference between the price of the supply before the adjustment event and the price after the adjustment event. If the supply is not wholly taxable, the price is apportioned accordingly (s 29-75; A New Tax System (Goods and Services Tax) Adjustment Note Information Requirements Determination 2012 and A New Tax System (Goods and Services Tax) Adjustment Note Information Requirements Amendment Determination 2013: GSTR 2013/2).

Recipient created adjustment notes — ie those issued by the recipient of the supply — must contain the same information as those issued by suppliers, except that they must make it clear that they are intended to be recipient created adjustment notes, and must in *all* cases show the recipient's identity *and* ABN.

Modifications to adjustment note requirements

The Commissioner has the discretion to modify the adjustment note requirements in various ways.

(1) Where adjustment note not required

An entity does not need to have an adjustment note to claim an adjustment if the Commissioner has given a written determination that it is not required (s 29-20). This will apply, for example, where a non-resident makes supplies connected with Australia that are "reverse charged" to the recipient (Div 83) or an entity imports services and is liable for GST under the "reverse charge" rules (Div 84) (GSTR 2013/2). It is also expected that it may apply in special circumstances, such as:

- a natural disaster
- where the supplier is not contactable or repeatedly refuses to issue the adjustment note.

The Commissioner considers that the discretion to waive or modify the requirements will be exercised on a case-by-case basis. The automatic waiver that applied in certain cases where a court or tribunal had conclusively found that there was an entitlement to a decreasing adjustment no longer applies (Notice of Withdrawal of former GSTD 2004/1). Other specific exemptions have been granted by Legislative Determination, and may be accessed via the Legal Database on the ATO website.

(2) Documents that do not strictly comply

The Commissioner may also treat a document as an adjustment note even though it does not strictly comply (s 29-75). The Commissioner has stated that this discretion will be exercised on a case-by-case basis (GSTR 2013/2). For further details, see PS LA 2004/11.

[AMGST ¶6-000; GSTG ¶17-000]

¶34-150 GST returns, payments and refunds

A registered entity must lodge a GST return for each tax period (Div 31). Where the entity has monthly tax periods, the return must normally be lodged by the 21st day of the month following the end of the tax period (s 31-10). For example, the monthly return for June is due by 21 July. For quarterly taxpayers, returns must normally be lodged by 28 April (for the March quarter), 28 July (for the June quarter), 28 October (for the September quarter) and 28 February (for the December quarter). Extensions typically apply where returns are lodged through tax agents.

Quarterly taxpayers also have the option of lodging simplified quarterly remittance forms and an annual information statement. If the quarterly taxpayer is a ''small business entity'' (¶7-050) or an entity that carries on an enterprise that does *not* constitute a business and its GST turnover does not exceed $2 million, it may instead elect to lodge on the basis of an annual tax period, with GST instalments being paid quarterly and an annual reconciliation statement being made in the annual return. This return is due by the date for lodging the income tax return, or by the following 28 February if no tax return is required to be lodged.

From 1 July 2017, small businesses with a turnover of less than $10 million have reduced reporting requirements for their annual BAS (*Simpler BAS*).

Small businesses and non-profit bodies that are voluntarily registered for GST have the option of reporting and paying their GST on an annual basis (Div 151).

If the entity's GST turnover is $20 million or more, it must normally lodge electronically. The GST return is incorporated into a Business Activity Statement (BAS) (¶24-200).

The amount that the entity is liable to pay for each tax period is the GST for that period less the input tax credits for that period. If the credits exceed the GST, the entity is eligible for a refund or a credit against any other tax due (Div 17).

The GST is normally paid at the same time as the return is lodged (Div 33). If the entity's GST turnover is $20 million or more, it must pay electronically.

Assessments and objections

An entity's GST liabilities and entitlements are determined by an assessment. The Commissioner is taken to have made an assessment of an amount determined in a GST return on lodgment by the entity. The return is treated as a notice of assessment and is conclusive evidence that the assessment is correct (TAA Sch 1 Div 155).

Once an assessment has been made, a 4-year period of review applies during which time the Commissioner may amend an entity's assessment, either at the request of the entity or at the Commissioner's discretion.

In certain situations, the Commissioner can make an *estimate* of unpaid amounts of GST, luxury car tax (LCT) and wine equalisation tax (WET), with the aim of recovering those amounts from taxpayers even if they have not been assessed. This brings GST into line with the rules that apply to income tax liabilities (TAA Sch 1 Div 268). It applies to tax periods starting on or after 1 April 2020.

Liability of directors for unpaid GST liability

Directors may be personally liable for their company's outstanding GST, LCT and WET liabilities in certain circumstances of non-payment by the company. These changes, applicable from 1 April 2020, essentially extend the Commissioner's powers which previously used to only apply to the superannuation guarantee and PAYG withholding (TAA Sch 1 Div 269).

Circumstances where directors can be made personally liable include, eg if there is an indication of phoenix behaviour, assets being dissipated or actions being taken to defeat creditors (PCG 2020/2).

Refunds of overpaid GST

A supplier may overpay an amount of GST by incorrectly:

- treating a GST-free or input taxed supply as a taxable supply (this would include incorrectly apportioning the taxable and non-taxable components of a mixed supply)
- treating a transaction or arrangement which is not a supply as a taxable supply
- calculating the amount of GST payable on a supply, or
- reporting an amount of GST on a GST return.

Where GST has been overpaid, Div 142 of the GST Act provides that the overpaid GST is only refundable in certain circumstances. Generally, a refund of overpaid GST can only be claimed where the GST has not been passed on or the GST has been reimbursed. However, the Commissioner retains a discretion to refund an amount of overpaid GST if refunding the amount would not give an entity a windfall gain (s 142-15(1)). The Commissioner's views on the meaning of the terms ''passed on'' and ''reimburse'' are set out in GSTR 2015/1.

Division 142 replaced TAA Sch 1 s 105-65 which applied to tax periods starting before 31 May 2014.

Under TAA Sch 1 s 105-65, the ATO was not obliged to give a refund to the supplier if either:

- the recipient was registered, or required to be registered, or
- the supplier failed to reimburse the recipient for the incorrectly imposed GST.

Guidelines on the operation of TAA Sch 1 s 105-65 are contained in MT 2010/1.

[AMGST ¶8-000, ¶8-110; GSTG ¶25-000]

¶34-160 Non-taxable supplies

The GST rules generally do not apply to gifts, supplies made by unregistrable entities, supplies made by business entities that are not registered and are not required to be registered, transactions that have no connection with Australia, or supplies made before 1 July 2000.

The Commonwealth Government itself is not liable to pay GST (s 177-1). Appropriations made between government agencies are also not subject to GST (s 9-17(3)).

Services provided as an employee are not subject to GST.

[AMGST ¶1-160; GSTG ¶1-160]

¶34-165 GST-free supplies

If a supply is GST-free, this means that no GST is payable on it, but that the supplier is entitled to claim credits for the GST payable on its business inputs that relate to that supply (ss 9-5; 11-15). For this reason, it is quite different from a supply which is outside the GST system altogether (¶34-160).

▶ Example

A registered greengrocer's business consists wholly of selling fresh food. The sale of that food is GST-free. The greengrocer therefore will not charge GST on the food it sells but will claim input tax credits for the GST it pays on goods and services it acquires in carrying on its business.

Note that if the greengrocer used some of those goods for private, non-business purposes, only a proportion of the input tax credit for GST on those goods would be allowed.

The greatest impact of GST-free status will normally be felt where the customer is a private consumer. It will not matter so much where the customer is a business that can get an input tax credit for any GST in any event, though there may be some cash flow implications.

The main types of GST-free supply, as set out in Div 38, are as follows.

Exports

Exports of goods or services are GST-free (Subdiv 38-E). This also applies to leases of goods for use outside Australia (the indirect tax zone).

Health and medical care

Most health and medical services are GST-free (Subdiv 38-B). These include:

- services of a medical practitioner or pathologist (s 38-7)
- services of allied health practitioners such as physiotherapists, naturopaths, nurses and optometrists (s 38-10)
- hospital treatment (s 38-20)
- residential, community care and specialist disability services, including National Disability Insurance Scheme funded supports (ss 38-25 to 38-40)
- medical aids and appliances (s 38-45; Sch 3)
- drugs, medicines and health goods (ss 38-47; 38-50), and
- health insurance (s 38-55).

Education and child care

Most educational services are GST-free (Subdiv 38-C). This applies to:

- education courses (s 38-85)
- certain course materials, hired goods and excursions (ss 38-90 to 38-97)
- certain student accommodation (s 38-105)
- professional and trade courses (s 38-85).

Approved child care is GST-free (s 38-140).

Food

Most food for human consumption is GST-free (Subdiv 38-A). However, GST applies to:

- food which is not for human consumption
- restaurant, catered or eat-in food

- hot takeaways
- prepared meals and other prepared food
- bakery products (except bread)
- confectionery, snacks, ice-cream and biscuits, and
- alcohol, most soft drinks and certain other drinks (ss 38-3; 38-4; Sch 1; 2).

Simplified accounting methods apply to food retailers (including cafes and restaurants) with annual turnovers under specified levels (Div 123). They apply to:

- a small business entity (¶7-001), or
- an entity that does not carry on a business but has a GST turnover (¶34-115) that does not exceed $2 million

that makes mixed supplies or has mixed inputs.

From 1 July 2021, this concession available for small business entities has been extended to medium business entities (¶7-050).

Charities, religions and gift-deductible bodies

Certain activities of charities and related bodies are GST-free (Subdivs 38-G; 38-H). This will apply to sales for nominal consideration, sales of second-hand goods, raffles, bingo and religious services. For other special rules that apply, see ¶34-175.

International transport and travel

International travel is GST-free, but domestic travel is generally subject to GST except where it forms part of an overseas trip (Subdiv 38-K). The cost of transporting goods overseas is also GST-free.

Tourists may be entitled to refunds of GST on items purchased in Australia and taken overseas (Div 168). This Tourist Refund Scheme (TRS) applies to goods costing $300 or more that were bought from the same store within 60 days before leaving Australia. Refunds are claimed at TRS booths at airports and terminals. Residents of Australia's External Territories (eg Norfolk, Cocos (Keeling) and Christmas Islands) may also claim refunds under the TRS on goods that are exported otherwise than as accompanied baggage to their External Territory.

GST-free status also applies to certain international mail costs and supplies through inwards duty-free shops (Subdivs 38-M; 38-Q).

Other GST-free supplies

Other GST-free supplies include:

- the sale of a ''going concern'' (¶34-240)
- a grant of Crown land (¶34-230)
- certain sales of farm land (¶34-230)
- certain post-1 July 2000 supplies under pre-8 July 1999 contracts (¶34-300)
- certain transactions involving precious metals (s 38-385)
- water, sewerage and drainage (Subdiv 38-I)
- cars for disabled people (¶34-220)
- global roaming services provided to visitors to Australia (Subdiv 38-R), and
- eligible emissions units (Subdiv 38-S).

[AMGST ¶25-010; GSTG ¶41-000, ¶50-000, ¶50-500, ¶55-000, ¶58-000, ¶65-200]

¶34-170 Input taxed supplies

If a supply is "input taxed", no GST is payable on it, but the supplier cannot claim input tax credits for the GST payable on its business inputs that relate to that supply (ss 9-5; 11-15).

▶ Example

A registered landlord's business consists wholly of letting private residential premises. These are input taxed supplies. The landlord therefore will not charge GST on the rent, and cannot claim input tax credits for the GST it pays on the goods and services it acquires to run the business.

Note that if the landlord also used some of the goods and services in other business activities that were taxable (or GST-free), it could claim a proportion of the GST as an input tax credit.

Input taxed supplies, as set out in Div 40, include:

- financial supplies such as loans, dealings in money and issuing securities (¶34-190)
- supply of private residential premises for rent (¶34-230)
- sales of residential premises (but not new homes or commercial premises) (¶34-230)
- food at school tuckshops (optional) (s 40-130)
- fundraising activities of charities (optional) (s 40-160), and
- certain transactions involving precious metals (s 40-100).

It is possible that a supply can be categorised as both a GST-free supply and an input taxed supply. In these cases, the GST-free status prevails (s 9-30).

[AMGST ¶25-020; GSTG ¶30-000, ¶35-000, ¶65-300]

GST Special Rules

¶34-175 GST and charities and non-profit bodies

Apart from their GST-free concessions (¶34-160), charities and non-profit bodies will not have to register unless their GST turnover is $150,000 or more, and have the option of splitting their operations into separate independent branches for GST purposes.

Charities are also entitled to use the cash basis of accounting irrespective of GST turnover, and can take advantage of simplified accounting methods in relation to supplies of food (¶34-165), second-hand goods and other sales for nominal value. They may also opt to have specified fundraising events treated as input taxed (s 40-160). Non-profit bodies that are voluntarily registered for GST have the option of reporting and paying their GST on an annual basis (Div 151).

[AMGST ¶15-000; GSTG ¶58-000]

¶34-180 GST groups and joint ventures

Certain groups of related companies, trusts, individuals, partnerships, non-profit bodies and government bodies can be treated as a single taxpayer for GST purposes (Div 48). Entities can self-assess their eligibility to form, change and dissolve a GST group. They can also nominate or change the representative member responsible for lodging returns on behalf of the group.

Each member of the GST group must be registered and have the same tax periods and accounting basis as the other members. Each member must also satisfy an ownership test. For example, in the case of a group consisting entirely of companies, each company must be a member of the same "90% owned group" as any other companies in the group. Companies are members of the same 90% owned group if one has at least a 90% stake in the other or if a third company has at least a 90% stake in the other 2 (s 190-1).

The main effects of having a GST group are:

- the group is treated as a single body, with the result that supplies and acquisitions made wholly within the group are ignored for GST purposes
- the representative member is responsible for paying the GST on all supplies outside the group and for claiming all input tax credits for acquisitions made from outside the group, and
- the income tax liabilities of group members are calculated as if they had individually paid the GST or claimed the input tax credit, even though this in fact was done by the representative member (ITAA97 ss 17-20; 27-25).

GST does not apply where tax losses are transferred between members of wholly-owned company groups even if they are not members of a GST group (Div 110). Exemptions also apply to transactions carried out as part of the operation of the consolidation regime (Div 110).

Special rules also apply where companies amalgamate, ie where companies merge and become a new company (Div 90). These rules are intended to ensure that GST generally does not apply to transactions made as part of the amalgamation process.

Joint ventures

Similarly, entities engaged in specified types of joint venture can self-assess their eligibility to form, change and dissolve a GST joint venture. Where a GST joint venture is formed the operator of the venture is responsible for the GST liabilities and entitlements arising from the operator's dealings on behalf of the venture participants (Div 51). Guidelines on what constitutes a joint venture are set out in GSTR 2004/2. In certain circumstances, joint venture operators in the petroleum and mining industries can account for ‘‘non-product’’ sales made on behalf of the participants in the joint venture (PS LA 2007/2 (GA)).

Practical Compliance Guideline PCG 2016/7 sets out the compliance approach to the GST treatment of supplies made between 2 GST joint ventures in the energy and resource industry with common participants, as well as supplies made involving a GST joint venture where the supplier is a participant in that GST joint venture.

[AMGST ¶17-010; GSTG ¶43-000]

¶34-190 Financial supplies

Supplies that are classed as ‘‘financial supplies’’ — including loans, share trades and life insurance — are input taxed (s 40-5). In general, this means that the financial supplier cannot claim input tax credits on the things it acquires for the purpose of making that supply.

As an exception to this general rule, certain acquisitions will entitle a financial supplier to claim input tax credits, but only at a reduced rate of 75% (see below). Further exceptions apply where an entity does not exceed the financial acquisitions threshold (sometimes called the ‘‘de minimis’’ test), where credits are being claimed for borrowing expenses or where supplies are made through overseas branches (s 11-15). The first limb of the financial acquisitions threshold is $150,000 (ss 189-5; 189-10).

What constitutes a financial supply is specified in the A New Tax System (Goods and Services Tax) Regulations 2019 (GST Regulations) Div 40. Comprehensive guidelines are also contained in GSTR 2002/2. For there to be a financial supply, the following must apply:

(1) there must be a provision, acquisition or disposal of an interest in specified items in return for consideration. Those items include:
   - bank, building society and credit union accounts
   - lending and borrowing, or providing credit

- mortgages or charges over real or personal property
- superannuation
- annuities and allocated pensions
- life insurance
- guarantees and indemnities
- credit under hire purchase agreements entered into before 1 July 2012
- currency
- securities such as shares, debentures, units in unit trusts and promissory notes
- derivatives including futures contracts, swaps, options and forward contracts
- supplies of bank accounts and superannuation interests by foreign financial institutions (tax periods starting on or after 1 July 2017), and
- services incidental to any of these

(2) the transaction must be in the course of an enterprise and must be connected with Australia (¶34-105)

(3) the entity that provides, acquires or disposes of the interests must be a ''financial supply provider''. This covers the owner of the interest immediately before its supply, the creator of the interest or the acquirer of the interest. For example, if an entity sells shares through an agent, the entity will be a financial supply provider, but the agent is only a financial supply *facilitator*. This means that if all the other relevant conditions are fulfilled, the entity's sale of the shares will be input taxed, but the provision of the agent's services to the entity would be taxable, and

(4) the financial supply provider must be registered or required to be registered.

What are not financial supplies

The supply of any of the following items, or interests in them, is not a financial supply:

- providing legal or accounting advice, taxation advice, actuarial advice or rating services in relation to a financial supply
- payment facilities for transaction cards
- stored value facility cards and prepayments, other than those linked to a bank, building society or credit union account
- providing cheque and deposit forms to banks
- finance leases
- deliverable commodity options (but the provision of margin on exchange traded futures is input taxed)
- supplies made as a result of the exercise of an option or right to make or receive a taxable supply
- facilities for trading securities or derivatives and the clearance and settlement of those trades
- insurance and reinsurance (but life insurance is input taxed)
- broking services
- investment portfolio investment, administration services for trusts and funds

- sales accounting services under factoring arrangements
- debt collection
- trustee and custodian services
- currency whose market value exceeds the face value
- providing goods for display or demonstration pending disposal to a third party
- goods or credit supplied under hire purchase agreements entered into on or after 1 July 2012, and
- warranties for goods.

Reduced credit for certain services

As mentioned above, the acquisition of certain services may entitle a financial supplier to the reduced 75% input tax credit (s 70-5). These services are specified in GST Regulations Div 70. They include:

- transaction banking and cash management services such as operating accounts, processing account information and credit reference services
- certain payment and funds transfer services
- arranging the provision, acquisition or disposal of interests in securities
- securities and unit registry services
- specified loan services
- services supplied to a credit union by jointly-owned subsidiaries
- debt collection
- arranging hire purchase
- trade finance processing, recording and remittance
- services in connection with the supply of derivatives, sale or purchase of currency, or sale of a forward contract
- certain investment portfolio management services and administration services (but not taxation and auditing services)
- certain services remunerated by commission and franchise fees, and
- trustee and custodial services (but not safe custody of money, documents or other things).

Comprehensive guidelines on what acquisitions are ‘‘reduced credit acquisitions’’ are contained in GSTR 2004/1.

Certain acquisitions made by ‘‘recognised trust schemes’’, including managed investment schemes and regulated superannuation funds, are subject to 55% input tax credits (GST Regulations s 70-5.03).

[AMGST ¶10-000; GSTG ¶30-000]

¶34-200 GST and superannuation funds

Although a superannuation fund and its trustees are both ‘‘entities’’, only the trustees can be registered, as funds do not have the legal capacity to carry out GST obligations. In accordance with the normal rules, registration is compulsory where the GST turnover of the enterprise is $75,000 or more. However, most of the supplies — including the provision of superannuation benefits — will typically be input taxed, and will therefore not be included in GST turnover (¶34-115). It follows that for some smaller funds the turnover will be less than $75,000, so registration will be optional. In deciding whether to register, the trustee will need to compare the costs of compliance with the limited amount of input tax credits it could claim.

[AMGST ¶10-080; GSTG ¶31-200]

¶34-210 GST and insurance

The supply of life insurance is treated as a financial supply (¶34-190) and is input taxed. Health insurance is GST-free. General insurance is taxable.

On an insurance settlement, the insured is technically making a supply to the insurance company by giving up its rights under the policy. However, the settlement it receives from the insurance company — whether in the form of money or goods and services — is generally not treated as consideration received or provided. GST will therefore not be payable (s 78-45) and the insurance company will not claim an input tax credit (s 78-20).

There is an exception to this where the insured — or other entity paying the premium — was entitled to an input tax credit for the premium, but failed to notify the insurance company of its credit entitlement, or understated it (s 78-50). To this extent a pro rata amount of GST will be payable on the settlement. The notification may be made when, or at any time before, a claim is first made under the policy. However, there is no requirement to make the notification if the insured was not registered or required to be registered (s 78-80).

In limited circumstances, the insurance company making a settlement will be eligible for a ‘‘decreasing adjustment’’ reducing its net GST. This will apply if the insured was not entitled to a full input tax credit on the premiums it paid under the policy (s 78-10). The adjustment only applies if the issue of the policy was taxable — it will not apply to wholly GST-free insurance (eg health insurance) or input taxed insurance (eg life insurance). The decreasing adjustment is calculated as 1/11th of the settlement amount.

Special rules also apply to subrogation, insurance excesses and the treatment of goods and services used in settlement of a claim (Div 78). Separate rules apply to CTP insurance settlements (Divs 79; 80).

For the GST consequences of insurance settlements, see GSTR 2006/10.

Transitional measures

- The GST rules do not apply if the loss or injury occurred before 1 July 2000, even though the settlement is on or after that date (*A New Tax System (Goods and Services Tax Transition) Act 1999* (GST Transition Act), s 22).
- Input tax credits cannot be claimed for motor vehicle compulsory third party (CTP) insurance premiums paid for cover commencing before 1 July 2003 (GST Transition Act s 23).
- If a *non-refundable* commission or fee was paid to an insurance broker or agent for arranging insurance cover before 1 July 2000, GST does not apply to that payment even though the cover extends beyond 1 July 2000 (GSTR 2000/5).

[AMGST ¶10-100; GSTG ¶32-000, ¶76-600]

¶34-220 Vehicles

In accordance with the normal rules, the supply of a car as part of an enterprise may be subject to GST. The GST would apply to the retail selling price, the cost of accessories, dealer delivery charges and insurance, but not to registration or stamp duty.

An additional luxury car tax applies where the market value exceeds a certain limit (see below). Input tax credits may also be limited in that situation.

Luxury cars

In addition to GST, a special tax known as the ''luxury car tax'' applies where the GST inclusive price of a car exceeds the luxury car tax threshold. For 2020–21, the luxury car tax threshold is normally $68,740, though a higher limit of $75,565 applies to certain ''fuel-efficient cars''. The amounts for 2019–20 were $67,525 and $75,526, respectively.

The tax is imposed at the rate of 33%, although the former rate of 25% continues to apply where the contract was entered into before 7.30 pm AEST on 13 May 2008. Primary producers and tourist operators are also entitled to refunds that may reduce their effective rates to 25% for certain cars.

The rate is applied to the amount of the excess, excluding GST (*A New Tax System (Luxury Car Tax) Act 1999*).

▶ Example

In 2020–21, Tuan buys a car (not a fuel-efficient car) for the GST inclusive price of $90,000. The luxury car tax is calculated as 33% × 10/11 × ($90,000 − $68,740) = $6,378. The total payable is therefore ($90,000 + $6,378) = $96,378.

Where the GST inclusive price of a vehicle exceeds the car limit ($59,136 in 2020–21, up from $57,581 in 2019–20), and an input tax credit is available, the credit is limited to 1/11th of that limit (s 69-10). Guidelines on how to claim input tax credits for car expenses are set out in *GST Bulletin* GSTB 2006/1.

Reimportation of luxury cars

From 1 January 2019, the liability for luxury car tax on cars that are reimported into Australia following service, repair or refurbishment overseas has been removed.

Other rules affecting vehicles

- Taxi operators are required to be registered for GST, irrespective of GST turnover (s 144-5). In *Uber*, the Federal Court ruled that services supplied by an Uber driver constituted the supply of ''taxi travel'' within the meaning of s 144-5. The decision confirms a view previously expressed by the ATO that providers of ''ride-sourcing services'' are essentially providing taxi travel services and are required to be registered for GST (*Ride-sourcing and tax*).
- Supplies of cars to disabled veterans (s 38-505) and other disabled people (s 38-510; Taxation Administration (Remedial Power — Certificate for GST-free supplies of Cars for Disabled People) Determination 2020) may be GST-free in certain circumstances. Concessions also apply to motor cycles (ss 38-505; 38-510).

[AMGST ¶12-080, ¶23-200; GSTG ¶68-300, ¶76-760]

¶34-230 Real property

In general, the sale of pre-existing residential premises is input taxed if the premises are real property to be used predominantly for residential purposes (s 40-65; *Sunchen*). In most cases, the sale of an existing home will not be subject to GST in any event, as the owner will normally not be selling in the course of business and will not be required to be registered.

The sale of *new* residential premises is generally taxable, but will be input taxed in certain exceptional situations. ''New'' residential premises fall into the following 3 categories (s 40-75):

(1) those that have not previously been sold as residential premises, or have not previously been subject to a long-term lease

(2) those that have been created by ''substantial'' renovations, or

(3) those that have been built to replace demolished premises.

''New'' residential premises do not include residential premises that have been used solely for rental purposes for the period of at least 5 years since they were built, substantially renovated or replaced (s 40-75(2)). The Commissioner considers that this 5-year period may include short periods between tenancies, but not periods when the premises are used for a private purpose or left vacant with no attempt to rent (GSTR 2003/3). In *Case 6/2016*, the AAT held that 4 properties constructed on vacant land were new residential premises despite the land having being held by the taxpayer for more than 5 years at the time of sale and the properties being rented for several years. According to the AAT, each of the properties was rented for less than 5 years and therefore did not satisfy the 5-year rule.

The sale of non-residential premises and commercial residential premises is taxable. Vacant land does not come within the definition of ''residential premises'' (*Vidler*).

The Commissioner's views on the application of the GST provisions to supplies of residential premises and commercial residential premises are set out in GSTR 2012/5 (residential premises), GSTR 2012/6 (commercial residential premises) and GSTR 2012/7 (long-term accommodation in commercial residential premises).

A summary of the GST consequences of selling leased residential premises and leased commercial premises are set out in GSTD 2012/1 and GSTD 2012/2, respectively.

From 1 July 2018, purchasers of new residential premises or new residential subdivisions need to remit the GST on the purchase price directly to the ATO as part of the settlement process. Where an entity (the supplier) makes a taxable supply of new residential premises or a subdivision of potential residential land by way of sale or long-term lease, the recipient of the supply (the purchaser) is required to make a payment of part of the consideration to the ATO directly, prior to or at the time consideration is first provided for the supply (other than as a deposit). For the Commissioner's rulings on the operation of these rules, see LCR 2018/4.

The "margin" scheme

Where a sale of real property is taxable, the purchaser and seller may, in certain circumstances, agree to calculate the GST by using what is called the ''margin scheme'' (Div 75). Under the margin scheme, the GST payable is calculated on the ''margin'' for the supply (rather than on the consideration). Broadly, the margin is the excess of the consideration for the supply over the acquisition consideration or, if the real property was acquired by the seller before 1 July 2000, its value at that date. Guidelines on how the margin scheme applies are set out in GSTR 2000/21, GSTR 2006/7 and GSTR 2006/8. For an example of a developer's use of the transitional margin scheme provisions, see *Brady King*. For specific guidelines on how the margin scheme applies to general law partnerships, see GSTR 2009/1.

Special rules may apply where the seller acquired the real property from a deceased estate, an associate, a fellow member of a GST group or a joint venture operator of a GST joint venture. In addition, there are integrity measures to ensure that the interaction between the margin scheme provisions and the going concern, farmland and associates provisions does not allow property sales to be structured in a way that results in GST not applying to the value added to real property on or after 1 July 2000.

If the margin scheme is used, the purchaser cannot claim an input tax credit on the acquisition. It follows that the margin scheme may be particularly relevant where the purchaser may not have been entitled to an input tax credit in any event, eg where a developer sells new residential units to private individuals.

Subdivided land

Taxpayers may use the consideration method, the valuation method or the GST-inclusive market value method, whichever is appropriate, when calculating the margin on a taxable supply of subdivided land (s 75-15).

Rented or leased premises

The lease of private residential premises is input taxed if the premises are to be used predominantly for residential purposes (s 40-35). However, the provision of accommodation in commercial residential premises (eg a hotel) is generally taxable. In the case of commercial residential premises that are used for long-term accommodation (such as some caravan parks), there is a choice of treatment — the transaction may either be treated as input taxed or be treated as taxable on a concessional basis (Div 87). Leases of ordinary commercial premises such as shops are taxable in accordance with the normal rules.

The treatment of various supplies made in relation to a hotel was considered in *South Steyne*. In *ECC Southbank*, certain supplies of student residential accommodation were held to be supplies of ''commercial residential accommodation''.

Other relevant rules

- In general, long-term leases of 50 years or more are treated in the same way as a sale.
- The initial grant of unimproved Crown land is GST-free (s 38-445).
- Where a taxable lease spans 1 July 2000, only the post-30 June 2000 component of the lease is subject to GST. However, if a lease was entered into before 8 July 1999, it may be entitled to GST-free status until 1 July 2005 unless there is an earlier opportunity to review the rent to take account of GST.

[AMGST ¶11-000, ¶11-300; GSTG ¶35-000]

¶34-240 Buying and selling a business

The supply of a going concern — such as a continuing business — is GST-free in certain circumstances (s 38-325). For this to apply, the buyer must be registered or be required to be registered. The buyer and the seller must have agreed in writing that the sale is of a going concern (*Midford*; *Case 12/2009*; *SDI Group*; *Brookdale Investments*), and the seller must be obliged to carry on the business until the date of sale. The seller must also supply the buyer with all the things necessary for the business' continued operation. In *Debonne Holdings*, it was held that the going concern provisions applied to the sale of a hotel business, notwithstanding that there were separate contracts for the sale of the land and the sale of the business. However, the sale of a development site by a developer was not a supply of a going concern because the developer was not carrying on an enterprise in relation to the development of the site at the date of the contract (*Aurora Developments*).

If the exemption does not apply, any GST payable could normally be claimed back by a registered buyer as an input tax credit when the next GST return is lodged. To this extent, the only disadvantage to the buyer is one of cash flow. The exemption basically only relieves the purchaser of having to fund the tax on settlement.

A business operated by a company may also be sold by disposing of the shares in the company. In this situation, the going concern exemption is not relevant. Instead, the sale of the shares is treated as a financial supply and is input taxed (¶34-190).

The ATO's guidelines on the operation of the going concern exemption are set out in GSTR 2002/5.

Where the recipient of a supply of a going concern intends to make supplies through the enterprise that are neither taxable supplies nor GST-free supplies, an increasing adjustment will arise under s 135-5. The operation of s 135-5 was considered by the High Court in *MBI Properties* and also by the AAT in 2 related cases (with different results) in *Case 6/2013* and *MSAUS*. In *MBI*, the High Court held that the recipient of a supply of a going concern was liable to an increasing adjustment following its purchase of premises, subject to an existing lease, because its assumption of the lessor's rights and obligations resulted in the making of supplies which were neither taxable supplies nor GST-free supplies. Following the decision in *MBI*, the AAT ruled in *MSAUS* that the sale of a residential apartment subject to a lease did not result in the purchaser becoming liable to an increasing adjustment under Div 135 because a special condition in the contract of sale operated to apply the margin scheme (rather than the supply of going concern provisions) to the sale of the property. The decision in *MAUS* is in contrast to the earlier decision in *Case 6/2013* which upheld a decision of the Commissioner making the purchaser of leased residential apartments liable for an increasing adjustment.

Farm businesses

Apart from the going concern exemption, the sale of farm land will be GST-free if:

- there has been a farming business carried out on the land for at least 5 years before the sale, and
- the buyer intends that a farming business will be carried out on the land (s 38-480).

A limited exemption also applies where farm land is subdivided and sold to associates for residential purposes (s 38-475).

[AMGST ¶11-410, ¶11-500; GSTG ¶48-000, ¶49-000]

¶34-250 Importations

Where goods are imported into Australia, the GST is payable by the importer, not by the overseas supplier (s 13-15). This applies whether or not the importer is registered, and whether or not it was carrying on an enterprise. However, if the importer is registered, it may be able to claim an input tax credit for the GST paid.

From 1 July 2015, the term "indirect tax zone" (s 195-1) replaced the term "Australia" in nearly all instances in the GST Act, without significant alteration in meaning. However, for simplicity this commentary continues to use the term "Australia".

The GST is calculated as 10% of the value of the importation. The value is the CIF (customs, insurance, freight) value. Technically, the GST is paid to Customs, in the same way as customs duty. In practice, however, a special Deferred GST Scheme enables approved importers to defer the GST until the first Business Activity Statement is submitted after the goods are entered for home consumption. In most cases, this deferral will mean that the GST is cancelled out, as a corresponding input tax credit will be claimed in the same return. This will overcome the cash flow disadvantage for importers of having to pay GST "up front". The value of the importation does not include the value of any assembly or installation services (see below).

In the case of temporary importations, the importer may be required to give a security or undertaking to pay any relevant customs duty or GST. If the goods are subsequently exported within the required time and other relevant conditions are complied with, GST will not be payable.

GST does not apply where the importation is of goods that would have been GST-free or input taxed if supplied in Australia (s 13-10). An importation will also not be taxable if the goods qualify for specified exemptions under customs law, eg goods of insubstantial value, or goods imported under the Tradex scheme. A further exemption applies if goods that were exported are returned to Australia in an unaltered condition, eg where a manufacturer sends its goods for sale overseas and they are returned unsold (Div 42).

Currently, a GST and customs duty exemption generally applies to imported goods with a customs value of no more than $1,000. The exemption — referred to as the "low value threshold" (LVT) — was abolished, effective for tax periods commencing on or after 1 July 2018, and replaced by a new system imposing GST at the point of sale (see below). The exemption does not apply to alcoholic beverages, tobacco products or goods that are the accompanied or unaccompanied effects of passengers or crew of a ship or aircraft.

Installation or assembly of goods brought to Australia

For tax periods starting on or after 1 October 2016, special rules apply where the supply of goods involves them being brought into Australia, and being installed or assembled here (s 9-25(6)). In this situation:

- the part of the supply that involves the installation or assembly in Australia is treated as if it were a separate supply. This will potentially be connected with Australia because it is a supply of services that is ''done'' here (¶34-105), but there are important exceptions to this, for example, if the recipient is an ''Australian–based business recipient''
- the rest of the supply is treated as another separate supply, ie a supply of goods. This will be connected with Australia if the supplier was the importer (¶34-105). If the supplier was not the importer, the supplier does not have to pay GST, though the actual importer will be liable to GST on the taxable importation.

The price of each supply is apportioned according to what reasonably represents the price for that component (s 9-75(4)).

Previously, the installation or assembly of goods brought into Australia was connected with Australia as part of the supply of the goods (former s 9-25(3)).

Option to "reverse charge" on non-resident supplies

If a service or right — as distinct from goods — is supplied from overseas, but is not provided through an Australian enterprise of the supplier, GST normally would not apply because the supply is not ''connected with Australia'' (¶34-105). However, in certain situations, this result is overcome by providing that GST will be payable by the recipient. For this to apply, the *recipient* must be registered or be required to be registered, and must use the supply partly for non-creditable purposes. This ''reverse charge'' rule is intended to overcome the fact that the supplier will often not be subject to the Australian GST system (Div 84). In certain situations, a non-resident supplier may also agree with a resident recipient for the recipient to pay the GST (Div 83).

Effective for supplies made on or after 1 July 2017, a separate procedure for shifting GST liability will apply where electronic supplies are made from offshore to Australian consumers through electronic distribution services (Subdiv 84-B). This will have the effect that the operator of the distribution service is treated as the supplier, and therefore assumes any GST liability, unless it has no control over any of the key elements of the supply (such as delivery, charging or terms and conditions). For further details of these measures, see ¶34-105.

Offshore supplies of digital products and other intangible supplies to consumers

For tax periods starting on or after 1 July 2017, supplies of things other than goods or real property, ie services or rights, are treated as having a connection with Australia if they are made to an ''Australian consumer'' (s 9-25(5); GSTR 2017/1). An Australian consumer means a resident of Australia that either: (1) is not registered; or (2) is registered, but does not acquire the supply solely or partly for the purpose of an enterprise that it is carrying on. Those supplies therefore may become subject to GST even though the supplier is overseas. This rule is largely directed at supplies of digital products, such as streaming or downloading of movies, music, apps, games and e-books, as well as consultancy and professional services. However, it is not restricted to those things.

Special rules apply in allocating GST liability for such ''inbound intangible consumer supplies'' (s 84-65). For these supplies:

- no tax invoice or adjustment note is required (s 84-50)
- non-resident suppliers may elect to be limited registration entities (s 84-140). Limited registration entities will not be entitled to input tax credits, are not entitled to an ABN, are not recorded in the Australian Business Register, must have quarterly tax periods, and cannot elect to pay GST by instalments

- where they are made through an electronic distribution platform, such as an e-store, the operator of the platform, not the actual supplier, is liable for the GST (s 84-55).

These rules do *not* apply where the thing is done wholly in Australia or is supplied through an enterprise that the supplier carries on in Australia.

For the Commissioner's rulings on the operation of these rules, see LCR 2018/2. These rules as to electronic distribution platforms will also apply under the provisions governing supplies of low value goods (see below).

Offshore supplies of "low-value" goods to consumers

Until 1 July 2018, a GST and customs duty exemption generally applies to imported goods with a customs value of no more than $1,000. This exemption is to be abolished and is to be replaced by a new system imposing GST at the point of sale (Subdiv 84-C; LCR 2018/1) effective for tax periods commencing on or after 1 July 2018.

The effect is that an offshore supplier will normally be required to register, collect and remit GST where the following conditions are satisfied:

- there is an offshore supply of goods, ie goods are brought to Australia with the assistance of the supplier, eg where the supplier delivers the goods to Australia, or procures, arranges or facilitates their delivery to Australia (s 84-77)

- the goods are "low value". This requires that their customs value would have been $1,000 or less if they had been exported at the time when the consideration for the supply was first agreed. Tobacco or alcoholic beverages are excluded and continue to be treated as taxable importations, as under the former rules (s 84-79). Where multiple low value goods are purchased in one order, GST applies even if the total order amount is over $1,000

- the supplier has a (Australian) GST turnover of $75,000 or more ($150,000 for non-profit bodies), including the GST turnover from the relevant supply, and

- the supply is connected with Australia (¶34-105). This requirement is satisfied if the recipient is a "consumer" of the supply — eg is not GST-registered, or is GST-registered but does not acquire the thing for use in an enterprise that it carries on in Australia (s 84-75). There is a "safe harbour" for suppliers where the customer provides its ABN and a declaration that it is GST-registered (s 84-105). A reverse charge mechanism also applies where the recipient misrepresents that the supply is being made to a consumer. Where a purchaser arranges for the goods to be delivered to someone else, the purchaser is still the recipient.

An entity may also be treated as the supplier if the entity is the operator of an "electronic distribution platform" through which the supply is made, or the entity is a "redeliverer" of the goods (ss 84-77; 84-81; LCR 2018/3). In these cases, the operator or redeliverer is liable to pay the GST. An entity is liable as operator or as redeliverer if it delivers the goods into Australia, or "procures, arranges or facilitates" the delivery of the goods into Australia, eg by providing offshore mailbox or shopping services. If there are multiple redeliverers, generally, the first redeliverer to deal with the customer is liable for the GST.

Non-residents who make offshore supplies of low value goods — including operators of electronic distribution platforms — can elect to take advantage of simplified registration requirements (¶34-100).

[AMGST ¶9-000, ¶9-095, ¶9-100, ¶9-120; GSTG ¶40-000, ¶40-700]

¶34-260 Second-hand goods

In certain cases, dealers are able to claim input tax credits on second-hand goods even though the person that supplied them was not registered (Div 66). The amount of the credit is 1/11th of the cost of the goods. However, if the goods cost more than $300, the credit cannot be more than the amount of GST on their later resale.

The rationale for this concession is that the unregistered supplier would normally have paid GST when buying the goods but would not have been able to claim input tax credits. The price the recipient dealer pays for the goods therefore includes some embedded GST for which a credit should be able to be claimed.

If the payment for the goods is $300 or less, the normal rules apply for attributing the credit to a tax period (¶34-130). If the payment is more than $300, the rules are:

- if the dealer is on the accruals basis, the credit normally cannot be claimed until the dealer subsequently sells the goods as part of its business. The credit will be attributed to the tax period in which the dealer receives any payment for the sale, or the period when it issues an invoice, whichever is the earlier, or
- if the dealer is on a cash basis, the credit can be claimed only to the extent that payment is received for the dealer's subsequent sale of the goods (s 66-15).

One of the requirements for claiming an input tax credit is that the dealer keeps accurate identity records of the supplier (s 66-17; *Case 5/2008*). Another is that the second-hand goods are acquired for the purposes of sale or exchange in the ordinary course of business (s 66-5; *LeasePlan*). For guidelines on when second-hand goods are acquired for the purposes of sale or exchange, see GSTD 2013/2.

Global accounting methods

Dealers in second-hand goods may be entitled to use a special ''global'' method of accounting. This method, which is intended to reduce the need to track individual goods for GST purposes, applies in 2 situations:

- where second-hand goods are acquired from an unregistered supplier and are divided up for re-supply to the dealer's customers (s 66-40), or
- where specified categories of second-hand goods are acquired from a registered or unregistered supplier, and the dealer exercises the option to apply the global method (s 66-70).

Using the global basis, the dealer works out the input tax credits on all of its acquisitions of the relevant description and offsets that amount against the total GST on everything it sells from that pool of purchases (s 66-65). This, however, does not affect the GST position of the person to whom the dealer supplies the goods.

Goods held at 1 July 2000

Both the special input tax credit and the global accounting method extend to second-hand goods that the dealer acquired as stock before 1 July 2000, provided that it still held them as stock at that date (*A New Tax System (Goods and Services Tax Transition) Act 1999*, s 18).

[AMGST ¶16-100; GSTG ¶15-660, ¶22-200, ¶76-780]

¶34-270 Other GST special rules and situations

Some special rules and situations that have not already been covered are set out below in alphabetical order.

Agents. A principal and an agent can agree that the agent should be treated as a principal for GST purposes (s 153-50). This is also the case where principals enter into agreements with other intermediaries, such as billing agents and paying agents. If a non-resident acts through an agent resident in Australia, the agent is responsible for the GST consequences

(Div 57). A property management company was held to be carrying out its services as agent for the owners, not as a principal, and was therefore not entitled to claim input tax credits in relation to those services (*Crown Estates*). In *Paul J Castan & Son Pty Ltd Atf Castan Investments Unit Trust*, it was held that under the terms of a management agreement the operator of a hotel was acting as the agent of the hotel owner. As a consequence, the owner was found to be the entity making supplies of accommodation in commercial residential premises. For tax periods starting on or after 1 October 2016, the normal agency rules do not apply if the supplier would not be liable for GST on the supply, or makes it through an enterprise that it carries on in Australia (s 57-5). This is designed to prevent overlap with the reverse charge rules (¶34-250). The question of whether a tour operator is acting as an agent or a principal will depend on the contractual arrangements (PCG 2018/6).

Associates. Special rules apply if something is supplied to an associate at a price below market value or as a gift. The supply will be treated as if it had been for market value, unless the associate would have been entitled to a full input tax credit. Since 24 March 2010 the fact that a supply to an associate is without consideration will not result in an otherwise input taxed (or GST-free) supply being treated as a taxable supply. An associate includes a relative, business partner, entities in trustee/beneficiary relationships, and companies and their controllers (Div 72).

Avoidance. The Commissioner has wide powers to cancel GST benefits that arise from contrived schemes and may also impose substantial penalties (Div 165; *Unit Trend Services*; *Case 14/2006*). Guidelines on the application of Div 165 are set out in PS LA 2005/24.

Barter transactions. The Commissioner's guidelines on the GST implications of transactions between members of a barter scheme conducted by a trade exchange are set out in GSTR 2003/14. Simplified compliance rules for certain countertrade transactions are outlined in PCG 2016/18.

Branches. Special rules allow business branches to be registered separately. This procedure is intended to avoid the administrative and accounting costs of having to amalgamate branch accounts every tax period (Div 54).

Court orders. The ATO considers that GST normally will not apply to awards of damages for negligence or personal injury, but may apply if the settlement of a dispute amounts to an adjustment of consideration for an earlier supply (GSTR 2001/4). GST has been held not to apply in various damages cases, eg *Shaw v Director of Housing and State of Tasmania (No 2)*. Where the award is compensation for outgoings for which the plaintiff would be eligible to claim input tax credits, the amount of the compensation should be reduced accordingly (*Millington v Waste Wise Environmental Pty Ltd*).

Deposits. Special rules apply to deposits made as security for the performance of an obligation (Div 99). Typical transactions to which these rules will apply are: (1) a contract for the hire of goods, where the supplier holds a security deposit to secure the return of the goods; or (2) a contract for the purchase of real property, goods or services, where the purchaser pays a deposit to secure the obligation to complete the purchase. The Commissioner's guidelines on security deposits are set out in GSTR 2006/2. In *Reliance Carpet*, the High Court held that a deposit forfeited by a purchaser when a contract for the sale of commercial property was rescinded was subject to GST.

Gambling. Special simplified rules for calculating GST apply if gambling services are provided. This includes selling tickets in lotteries or raffles, or accepting bets on races, games, sporting events or any other events (Div 126). The Commissioner's guidelines are in GSTR 2002/3. In *TSC 2000*, it was held that the operator of a lotto syndicate was making gambling supplies to the syndicate members. As a result of the introduction of the offshore intangible consumer supply rules from 1 July 2017 (¶34-105), it is specifically provided that offshore gambling supplies are connected to Australia if the recipient is an Australian resident (s 126-27). This ensures that consistent GST treatment will continue to apply to all gambling supplies made to Australian residents.

Incapacitated entities. As a consequence of the decision in *PM Developments*, measures have been enacted to ensure that representatives of incapacitated entities are liable for GST on post-appointment transactions (Div 58). Representatives are only liable for GST on taxable supplies, and entitled to input tax credits on creditable acquisitions, which they actually make, and not on supplies and acquisitions made before their appointment by an entity over which they had no control (*Albarran & Ors as administrators of Cooper & Oxley Builders Pty Ltd*).

Pre-establishment costs. A company may be entitled to input tax credits for acquisitions and importations made before it was incorporated (Div 60).

Precious metals. Supplies of precious metals are input taxed (s 40-100), except for the first supply after refinement to a dealer, which is GST-free (s 38-385). Precious metal does not include scrap gold, which is treated as a taxable supply on which input tax credits may be available provided relevant tax invoices are held (*Cash World Gold Buyers Pty Ltd*). From 1 April 2017, a taxable supply of goods consisting of valuable metal (ie gold, silver, platinum or any other substance specified in regulations for the purposes of definition of a precious metal) is subject to a mandatory reverse charge if the recipient is registered or required to be registered and, at the time of the supply, the market value of the goods does not exceed the valuable metal threshold (Div 86). Goods to the extent that they consist of valuable metal are not subject to the special rules in Div 66 applying to second-hand goods (¶34-260). The introduction of the reverse charge requirement follows extensive ATO investigations into fraud and GST evasion in the gold bullion and precious metals industries (*ACN 154 520 199 Pty Ltd (in liq)* 2019 ATC ¶10-518; 2020 ATC ¶20-772 (on appeal to the High Court)).

Redeemable vouchers. are subject to GST on redemption rather than on the original acquisition (Div 100). The liability to GST will therefore depend on the GST status of the goods or services supplied on redemption. The Commissioner's guidelines are set out in GSTR 2003/5. Prepaid phone cards or facilities are treated as vouchers for the purposes of Div 100.

Reimbursements. In certain circumstances, input tax credits can be claimed where employees, agents, company officers or partners are reimbursed for expenses they incur in the course of their duties (Div 111). These rules also apply to charitable volunteers. Direct payments by employers of employees' work-related expenses also qualify for input tax credits.

Small business entities. Taxpayers that qualify as small business entities can claim various concessions (¶7-001).

GST Transitional and Related Matters

¶34-300 GST transitional rules

Transitional rules are contained in the *A New Tax System (Goods and Services Tax Transition) Act 1999* (GST Transition Act).

The general rule is that GST is payable only on supplies and importations made on or after 1 July 2000 (GST Transition Act s 7). Similarly, input tax credits can only be claimed on acquisitions and importations made on or after 1 July 2000.

The time at which a supply or acquisition takes place is determined according to the nature of the supply (GST Transition Act s 6). *Goods* are supplied or acquired when they are removed. If they are not to be removed, the relevant time is when they are made available to the recipient. *Real property* is supplied or acquired when it is made available. This will typically occur on settlement, even though there may be an earlier contract for sale. *Services* are supplied or acquired when they are performed. *Other things* are supplied or acquired when they are performed or done. This would include transactions such as a transfer of copyright or the release of a right. If the contract provides for a mixture of any of the above (eg goods and services), each type of supply is considered separately.

The general rule is modified in various ways:

- special transitional rules apply to particular types of transaction, and
- special concessions apply to contracts made before 8 July 1999.

For more details on these special rules, see earlier editions of the *Australian Master Tax Guide*.

Various other transitional rules apply. These include:

- stocks of second-hand goods on hand at 1 July 2000 (¶34-260)
- insurance claims for events occurring before 1 July 2000 (¶34-210)
- prepaid funerals (s 15)
- pre-1 July 2000 payments or invoicing for post-30 June 2000 supplies (GST Transition Act, s 10)
- GST-free status of pre-8 July 1999 contracts (GST Transition Act, s 13)
- redeemable vouchers (GST Transition Act, ss 11; 24A)
- offshore supplies of intangibles to Australian consumers (¶34-250).

Separate credit rules applied to pre-GST stocks of alcoholic beverages (GST Transition Act, ss 16A; 16AB; 16B) and petroleum products (GST Transition Act, s 16C).

[AMGST ¶19-000; GSTG ¶75-500]

¶34-360 Other GST-related measures

"Locking in" the GST rate

Measures intended to lock in the GST rate at 10% are contained in the *A New Tax System (Commonwealth-State Financial Arrangements) Act 1999*. This Act provides that no alteration can be made to the rate unless each state and territory agrees, as well as both Houses of Federal Parliament.

Relationship with other taxes

In general, the GST component of the price of goods or services is not assessable to the supplier (ITAA97 s 17-5: ¶10-000). Similarly, the GST component is not deductible to the purchaser/recipient except to the extent that an input tax credit cannot be claimed (ITAA97 s 27-5: ¶16-860). The cost of assets that you can depreciate is reduced by the amount of any input tax credit entitlement (¶17-080). Periodical payments of net GST made to the ATO by suppliers are not deductible (ITAA97 s 27-15).

Supplies of goods and services to employees as fringe benefits will not be subject to GST if the supply is subject to FBT or is an exempt fringe benefit. However, GST may apply where the employee makes a contribution or payment to the employer towards the cost of the fringe benefit (s 9-75; GSTR 2001/3).

Wine equalisation tax and luxury car tax

The wine equalisation tax and luxury car tax are both designed to cushion the effect that the abolition of sales tax would otherwise have had. The operative provisions for these taxes are contained in the *A New Tax System (Wine Equalisation Tax) Act 1999* and the *A New Tax System (Luxury Car Tax) Act 1999*.

Administration

General machinery provisions for the administration of the taxation laws (including GST) are contained in the TAA.

GST-related offences

Penalties for failing to comply with various GST obligations are contained in the TAA. Guidelines for remission of some of these penalties are set out in several ATO Practice Statements, including PS LA 2012/4 and PS LA 2012/5 (false or misleading statements), PS LA 2007/3 (tax invoices) and PS LA 2007/4 (registration obligations).

GST Regulations

Some important GST rules are contained in the A New Tax System (Goods and Services Tax) Regulations 2019 — eg the detailed requirements for tax invoices (¶34-140) and the definition of input taxed financial supplies (¶34-190). The GST Regulations originally issued in 1999 were reissued with minor procedural and numbering changes (A New Tax System (Goods and Services Tax) Regulations 2019).

Australian Business Numbers

In general, an entity's GST registration number is its Australian Business Number (ABN). Rules governing the use of ABNs are contained in the *A New Tax System (Australian Business Number) Act 1999.*

Chapter 35 Fringe Benefits Tax

Introduction

¶35-000 Outline of fringe benefits tax

Fringe benefits tax (FBT) is a tax payable by employers on the value of certain benefits that have been provided to their employees or to associates of those employees in respect of their employment, known as ''fringe benefits''.

The principal legislation dealing with FBT is the *Fringe Benefits Tax Assessment Act 1986* (FBTAA) and the Fringe Benefits Tax Assessment Regulations 2018 (FBTAR). Section references in this chapter are to the FBTAA unless otherwise indicated. Other legislation affecting fringe benefits comprises the *Fringe Benefits Tax Act 1986* (FBTA) and the *Fringe Benefits Tax (Application to the Commonwealth) Act 1986*. The ATO publishes *Fringe benefits tax: a guide for employers* (NAT 1054).

Employers are generally required to pay FBT in 4 instalments but FBT is assessed on an annual basis. The FBT year runs from 1 April to 31 March and so references to a ''year'' in relation to FBT mean a year ending on 31 March. The system of FBT is based on self-assessment by employers. The statutory due date for lodgment of FBT returns and payment of any FBT liability is 21 May following the end of the FBT year. However, for taxpayers who are on a tax agent's lodgment programme, concessions apply (¶35-030).

FBT is imposed on the fringe benefits taxable amount which is the employer's aggregate fringe benefits amount for the year grossed-up (¶35-025). If certain conditions are satisfied, employers exempted from the record-keeping requirements are able to calculate the FBT payable based on the aggregate fringe benefits amount of an earlier year and not the aggregate fringe benefits amount of the current year (¶35-692).

FBT rate

For the 2020 and 2021 FBT years, the FBT rate is 47%.

Interaction with other taxes

Income tax

A benefit that is taxable under the FBTAA (or specifically exempted under that Act, except for certain car expense payment benefits) is free from income tax. The scheme of ITAA36, ITAA97 and the FBTAA is that monetary remuneration, including most allowances, is subject to income tax in the employee's hands, and that non-cash benefits (and certain living-away-from-home allowances) are subject to FBT, which is payable by the employer, and are not subject to income tax.

However, an employer is required to record on an employee's payment summary the taxable value of certain fringe benefits provided during the year (¶35-055).

Employers can claim an income tax deduction for the cost of providing fringe benefits (¶16-520) and for any FBT incurred (¶16-858). Where an FBT assessment is issued or amended for an earlier FBT year, FBT is incurred at the end of the earlier FBT year rather than in the year in which the assessment is raised (TD 2004/20).

The taxable value of fringe benefits is reduced by the amount of a payment that is non-deductible because of the personal services income rules (¶30-620, ¶30-630; s 61G).

GST

Although the provision of services by an employee would normally be treated as the consideration for the supply of a fringe benefit, no GST arises unless the employee makes a contribution for the benefit (*A New Tax System (Goods and Services Tax) Act 1999* (GST Act), s 9-75(3); GSTR 2001/3). If no contribution is made, no GST is charged. If the employee makes a ''recipient's payment'' towards a car fringe benefit or a ''recipients contribution'' towards another benefit, the employer must remit 1/11th of the contribution as GST in respect of the supply of the fringe benefit. No GST is charged if the provision of the fringe benefit is a GST-free (¶34-165) or input-taxed (¶34-170) supply.

Where the taxable value of a benefit includes the "cost" of providing the benefit, this means the GST-inclusive cost (TR 2001/2).

Interaction with foreign employment income rules

Where resident taxpayers derive foreign earnings (¶10-860), there is the potential for double taxation as FBT is levied on employers whereas most foreign jurisdictions tax such benefits to the employee. A non-resident employer can be subject to PAYG withholding (¶26-100) and FBT in respect of Australian resident employees working overseas (TD 2011/1). A non-resident employer who pays an Australian resident for work performed overseas is subject to withholding obligations if the non-resident employer has a sufficient connection with Australia, ie if the non-resident carries on an enterprise or income-producing activities in Australia and has a physical presence in Australia. If there is a withholding obligation, FBT obligations will arise in relation to benefits provided to that employee. However, if there is no withholding obligation, amounts paid to the employee by the non-resident employer will not be "salary and wages" and no FBT obligations can arise for the non-resident employer in relation to benefits provided to that employee.

[AFB ¶5-000]

¶35-025 Fringe benefits taxable amount — gross-up rules

An employer's fringe benefits taxable amount is calculated by "grossing-up" the taxable values of fringe benefits provided during the FBT year. The gross-up has the effect that FBT is calculated as if the employer provided fringe benefits with a taxable value that included the FBT paid by the employer.

An employer's fringe benefits taxable amount is calculated using 2 gross-up methods: one for benefits for which the employer is entitled to GST input tax credits on the acquisition price, and the other for benefits for which there is no entitlement to GST input tax credits. The reason for the 2 gross-up calculations is to distinguish between persons and benefits receiving different treatment under the GST legislation (TR 2001/2). The employer is then allowed a deduction for the FBT.

The effect of the gross-up rules in s 5B(1A) to (1D) is that the fringe benefits taxable amount is calculated as follows:

$$\text{s 5B(1B) amounts} + \text{s 5B(1C) amount} + \text{aggregate non-exempt amount}$$

The s 5B(1B) and (1C) amounts are calculated by applying the relevant gross-up formula to the "type 1" or "type 2" aggregate fringe benefits amounts of the employer, calculated using method statements in s 5C(3) and (4). Type 1 and type 2 aggregate fringe benefits amounts are determined according to whether or not GST input tax credits are available on acquisitions of goods or services acquired to provide the benefits.

- *Type 1 aggregate fringe benefits amounts* broadly represent the sum of the individual fringe benefits amounts and the excluded fringe benefits (¶35-055) that are provided to the employer's employees and that are "GST-creditable benefits", ie the provider of the benefit is entitled to GST input tax credits at the time the benefit was acquired.
- *Type 2 aggregate fringe benefits amounts* are all other fringe benefits.

The gross-up of type 1 aggregate fringe benefits amounts under s 5B(1B) essentially applies where the provider of the benefit is entitled to GST input tax credits on the acquisition of the thing it provides as a fringe benefit. The gross-up of type 2 aggregate fringe benefits amounts under s 5B(1C) applies where the provider is not entitled to GST input tax credits (eg because the provider is not registered for GST or because the thing supplied is GST-free or input taxed).

GST-creditable benefit

The first category of GST-creditable benefit is one that relates to the acquisition or importation of a thing, which is essentially anything that can be supplied or imported (s 149A).

The second type of GST-creditable benefit is one where the person who provided the benefit was entitled to an input tax credit (¶34-010) for that benefit by the operation of GST Act Div 111 (¶34-270). It also applies to GST group arrangements and ensures that a benefit may also be a GST-creditable benefit where another member of the GST group, rather than the person who is providing the benefit, is entitled to input tax credits.

GSTR 2001/3 explains the circumstances under which supplies of fringe benefits are subject to GST, and the entitlement to input tax credits for acquisitions and importations related to the provision of fringe benefits.

Gross-up formulae

Type 1 benefits

If an employer is entitled to input tax credits in respect of the value of fringe benefits at the time the benefits were provided (type 1 benefits), then the total value of the fringe benefits is grossed up to a tax-inclusive value using the formula:

$$\frac{\text{FBT rate} + \text{GST rate}}{(1 - \text{FBT rate}) \times (1 + \text{GST rate}) \times \text{FBT rate}}$$

This formula is aimed at recouping any input tax credits arising from the provision of fringe benefits by an employer or associate, or under an arrangement between the employer and a third party. For the 2020 and 2021 FBT years, the rates are 47% and 10%, resulting in a gross-up rate of 2.0802.

Type 2 benefits

These benefits comprise:

- those that are wholly GST-free
- those that represented goods or services not acquired by the employer (such as goods manufactured by the employer)
- those provided by an employer that is a small business employer who has opted not to register for GST
- those benefits provided by an employer whose activities are input taxed.

In the above cases, the gross-up formula is:

$$\frac{1}{(1 - \text{FBT rate})}$$

This formula results in a gross-up rate of 1.8868 for the 2020 and 2021 FBT years.

An "employer's fringe benefits taxable amount" (s 5B) represents the total of the type 1 and type 2 aggregate fringe benefits amounts calculated using the above formulae, plus any aggregate non-exempt amount.

Aggregate non-exempt amount

An employer's aggregate non-exempt amount is calculated according to s 5B(1E) to (1L). Only employers that are qualifying public or non-profit hospitals, public ambulance services, health promotion charities or public benevolent bodies and that provide benefits exempted by s 57A (¶35-100) have aggregate non-exempt amounts. Such an employer's aggregate non-exempt amount is the sum of the grossed-up value of an employee's individual fringe benefits amounts and most excluded fringe benefits (¶35-055) provided to the employee that exceeds the relevant threshold. This sum is basically all fringe benefits other than entertainment facility leasing expenses and meal entertainment (except if provided as part of a salary packaging arrangement) and car parking. For the 2020 and 2021 FBT years, the relevant thresholds are:

- $17,000, if the employee is engaged in duties connected with qualifying public or non-profit hospitals or public ambulance services, or
- $30,000, if the employee is engaged in duties connected with a public benevolent institution or a health promotion charity that is not covered by the $17,000 threshold, eg an institution that is not a public hospital (¶35-100).

Salary packaged meal entertainment and entertainment facility leasing expenses are not excluded fringe benefits. In order to provide a $5,000 threshold before such benefits become taxable, the aggregate non-exempt amount is reduced by the lesser of $5,000 and the total grossed-up taxable value of salary packaged meal entertainment and entertainment facility leasing expense benefits.

For an illustration of the application of the rules, see CR 2005/82. Where the employer's status changes during the FBT year from being an endorsed public benevolent institution to a hospital that is not endorsed, the employer remains entitled to the $30,000 capped exemption for each employee who was employed both before and after this change while being provided with benefits throughout the FBT year (ID 2009/159).

▶ Example

During the FBT year ending 31 March 2021, an employer provides its employees with these fringe benefits:

- employee A received a television with a taxable value of $2,000 and an overseas holiday with a taxable value of $7,000
- employee B received a $3,000 reimbursement of his children's school fees.

The employer is registered for GST and input tax credits are available on the acquisition of the television. None of the benefits are exempted by s 57A, so there is no aggregate non-exempt amount. The employer's fringe benefits taxable amount is calculated as follows.

Step 1: calculate the type 1 aggregate fringe benefits amount

Add each employee's individual fringe benefits amount for benefits where the employer was entitled to input tax credits for GST paid.

employee A	=	$2,000 for the television
employee B	=	$0 (tuition fees are GST-free)
	=	$2,000

Step 2: calculate the type 2 aggregate fringe benefits amount

Add each employee's individual fringe benefits amount for benefits where the employer did not pay GST or input tax credits were not allowed.

employee A	=	$7,000 (no GST on overseas holiday)
employee B	=	$3,000 (tuition fees are GST-free)
	=	$10,000

Step 3: calculate the s 5B(1B) amount

Multiply the type 1 aggregate fringe benefits amount by the relevant gross-up formula (ie by the rate of 2.0802), ie $2,000 × 2.0802 = $4,160.40

Step 4: calculate the s 5B(1C) amount

Multiply the type 2 aggregate fringe benefits amount by the relevant gross-up formula (ie by the rate of 1.8868), ie $10,000 × 1.8868 = $18,868

Step 5: calculate the fringe benefits taxable amount

Add together the s 5B(1B) and (1C) amounts:

$4,160.40 + $18,868 = $23,028.40

The employer's FBT liability for the year is:

$23,028 × 47% = $10,823.16

The amount of $10,823 is deductible to the employer (ITAA97 s 8-1).

[AFB ¶56-520]

¶35-030 FBT annual returns and assessments

FBT is collected via a self-assessment system. Each year an employer who has provided fringe benefits to its employees is required to:

(1) obtain declarations and make elections

For type 1 benefits

(2) identify the employee's individual fringe benefits amounts that are GST-creditable benefits for the year of tax in respect of the employment of the employee (¶35-025)

(3) add up the taxable value of every ''excluded fringe benefit'' (¶35-055) for the year (other than an amortised fringe benefit under s 65CA: ¶35-650) that is a GST-creditable benefit (¶34-010) relating to an employee and the employer

(4) total items (2) and (3). This represents the employer's type 1 aggregate fringe benefits amount

(5) calculate that part of the ''employer's fringe benefits taxable amount'' that comprises type 1 benefits (ie multiply item (4) by 2.0802 for the 2020 and 2021 FBT years)

For type 2 benefits

(6) identify all other employee's individual fringe benefits amounts for the year of tax in respect of the employment of the employee

(7) add up the taxable value of every other excluded fringe benefit for the year (other than an amortised fringe benefit) relating to an employee and the employer

(8) total items (6) and (7). This represents the employer's type 2 aggregate fringe benefits amount if there are no amortised or reducible (s 65CC: ¶35-650) fringe benefits

(9) calculate the amortised amount for the year of each amortised fringe benefit relating to an employee and the employer

(10) total items (8) and (9)

(11) calculate the reduction amount for the year of tax of each reducible fringe benefit relating to an employee and the employer

(12) deduct item (11) from item (10). This represents the employer's type 2 aggregate fringe benefits amount (s 5C(4))

(13) calculate that part of the "employer's fringe benefits taxable amount" that comprises type 2 benefits (ie multiply item (12) by 1.8868 for the 2020 and 2021 FBT years)

FBT payable

(14) total items (5) and (13)

(15) calculate the FBT payable on the "employer's fringe benefits taxable amount" (ie multiply item (14) by 47% for the 2020 and 2021 FBT years: ¶42-380)

(16) deduct the FBT rebate if applicable (¶35-642), and

(17) prepare and lodge an annual FBT return (unless the taxable amount of fringe benefits is nil: s 68) and pay any tax due or obtain a refund after allowing for instalments of FBT paid during the year.

The 2020 FBT return form is available from the ATO website at 2020 FBT return. A single return must be lodged for each employer. An employer with decentralised operations cannot divide its FBT responsibilities among different branches. The consolidation regime (¶8-000) does not apply to an employer's FBT obligations and each entity within a consolidated group must comply with its own FBT obligations.

The ATO recommends that employers register once they have established that they have to pay FBT. To register for FBT, employers complete an *Application for registration — fringe benefits tax* (NAT 1055) and send it to the ATO. There is no legal requirement to register.

Although there is no requirement to lodge an FBT return if the fringe benefits taxable amount for the year is nil, employers that are registered for FBT but do not need to lodge an FBT return are asked by the ATO to lodge with the ATO a *Notice of non-lodgment of FBT return* (NAT 3094).

Deemed assessment

The lodging of a return gives rise to a deemed assessment of the employer's liability for FBT (s 72). That assessment is deemed to have been made by the Commissioner and served on the employer at the time when the return is lodged. If a return is not lodged, the Commissioner can make an assessment of the fringe benefits taxable amount and the amount of tax for which, in the Commissioner's opinion, the employer would have been liable (s 73). Alternatively, the Commissioner can require any person to lodge a return for a particular year (s 69).

Amendment of assessment

An assessment may be amended where the employer requests an adjustment, or where an audit or subsequent check by the Commissioner reveals undisclosed or undervalued benefits. An application for amendment must be made in the approved form (s 74(6A)). A refund or reduction of the FBT liability as a result of an amended assessment is an assessable recoupment (TD 2004/21).

An assessment may be amended within 3 years of the lodgment of a return. Where there has not been full and true disclosure and there has been an avoidance of tax, the assessment may be amended within 6 years of the lodgment of the return. Where, in the Commissioner's opinion, there has been tax fraud or evasion, an amendment may be made at any time (s 74(3); *Case 17/2006*).

Lodgment dates

For employers *not* on a tax agent lodgment programme, the annual return form must be lodged by 21 May (or such later date as the Commissioner allows). Taxpayers can lodge a ''Request for additional time to lodge'' where there are exceptional or unforeseen circumstances that prevent lodgment by the due date.

For employers on a tax agent lodgment programme the ATO provides a lodgment-only deferral to 25 June for electronic lodgments. Paper returns are still required by 21 May.

To continue to be eligible for the lodgment programme due date, the tax agent must lodge 85% or more of the FBT returns from his/her client list by the due date.

Due to COVID-19, the lodgment and payment due date for all 2019–20 FBT annual returns was automatically deferred to 25 June 2020.

Tax agents

Generally, only a registered tax agent can charge a fee for preparing FBT returns or objections on behalf of another person (*Tax Agent Services Act 2009*, Div 50). The prohibition on charging fees for tax services does not extend to solicitors or barristers acting in a professional capacity in preparing an objection, in tax litigation or proceedings, and in advising on tax matters. Only a registered tax agent or registered BAS agent can provide a BAS service (¶32-000), which would include preparing FBT information on a BAS.

[AFB ¶7-500]

¶35-050 Payment of FBT

An employer's FBT liability is due and payable on 21 May following the FBT year ended on 31 March if the employer is not on a tax agent's lodgment programme (s 90). If the employer is on a tax agent's lodgment programme, the due date is 28 May.

If the previous year's FBT liability was $3,000 or more, the employer is required to pay the tax in quarterly instalments (ss 101 to 113). The instalments are notified in each quarter's BAS or IAS with a final payment being due, if necessary, with the lodgment of the annual FBT return.

Instalments are based on either: (a) the employer's ''notional tax amount'' — generally, the amount of the employer's tax for the most recent year of tax for which the Commissioner has made an assessment (s 110) (this amount is modified where the FBT rate has changed); or (b) if the employer chooses, the employer's estimate of its current year's FBT liability (s 112).

GIC is payable if the estimate and consequent instalments are too low (¶29-510).

For deferred BAS payers (¶24-240), the instalments of tax are due on 28 July, 28 October, 28 February and 28 April (s 103(2)). The balance is paid on lodgment of the annual FBT return (s 90).

For employers other than deferred BAS payers, the instalments of tax are due on 21 July, 21 October, 21 January and 21 April (s 103(1)). The balance is paid on lodgment of the annual FBT return (s 90).

Due dates on weekends

Where a due date for payment of a tax debt or lodgment of an approved form falls on a Saturday, a Sunday or a public holiday, the payment or lodgment may be made on the next business day without incurring a penalty or GIC.

No instalments if FBT less than $3,000

Instalments do not have to be paid by employers whose FBT liability in the previous year was less than $3,000 (s 111). Such employers need only pay on an annual basis.

[AFB ¶7-650]

¶35-055 Reporting of benefits on payment summaries

Employers are required to record on payment summaries the grossed-up taxable value of certain fringe benefits (other than excluded fringe benefits) provided to employees during the FBT year, where the taxable value of the benefits provided to an employee exceeds $2,000 (a grossed-up value of $3,773 for the 2020 and 2021 FBT years) (ss 135M to 135Q). Special rules apply where the employer is exempt from FBT (¶35-100).

The ‘‘reportable fringe benefits amount’’ (ie the individual’s grossed-up fringe benefits amount) is used to determine a taxpayer’s entitlement to certain income-tested tax concessions and liability to income-tested surcharges for the year.

Employers can elect to notify the Commissioner of reportable fringe benefits amounts using single touch payroll reporting (¶26-630). Where this is done, the employer is not required to issue a payment summary covering the reportable fringe benefits amount.

Excluded fringe benefits

These ‘‘excluded fringe benefits’’ are not included in the reporting requirements (s 5E(3)):

- car parking fringe benefits (¶35-252). Certain motor vehicle parking expense payment benefits are exempt under s 58G and therefore are not fringe benefits and not subject to the reporting requirements
- fringe benefits attributable to entertainment facility leasing expenses, entertainment by way of food or drink, and accommodation, travel or reimbursement of expenses in relation to that entertainment (¶35-617). However, salary packaged meal entertainment benefits and entertainment facility leasing expense benefits are included in the reporting requirements
- an expense payment, property or residual fringe benefit arising in relation to the provision of remote area residential fuel where the taxable value of the fringe benefit is reduced under s 59 (¶35-650)
- a remote area housing loan whose taxable value is reduced under s 60 (¶35-650)
- fringe benefits that relate to occasional travel to a major population centre in Australia provided to employees and family members not resident in or adjacent to an ‘‘eligible urban area’’ (as defined in s 140). For a list of such centres, see the Australian Bureau of Statistics, *Year Book Australia* for 2009–10 (*NTLG FBT minutes*, 12 May 2011). Regular trips will not qualify (ID 2009/24)
- fringe benefits that relate to freight costs for food provided to employees not resident in or adjacent to an eligible urban area
- amortised and reducible fringe benefits (ss 65CA; 65CC: ¶35-650)
- benefits provided to address security concerns relating to the personal safety of an employee, or an associate, arising from the employee’s employment, where a threat assessment was made by a relevant industry body or government body or other competent person
- the following fringe benefits prescribed by regulation:

(a) the provision of parking facilities to an employee who is entitled to the use of a disabled persons' car parking space and who is the driver of, or a passenger in, the car and who displays a valid disabled persons' car parking permit on the car (FBTAR s 12)

(b) emergency and essential health care costs incurred by Australian resident employees, or their associates who are also Australian residents, while the employee is serving overseas (provided the costs are not covered by Medicare) (FBTAR s 6)

(c) benefits provided to Australian Defence Force members relating to the removal and storage of household effects resulting from a Department of Defence direction to change residence (FBTAR s 7)

(d) use by a police officer of a car that is garaged at the employee's place of residence to enable the employee's quick response to crime-related incidents where the car is fitted with a police radio, warning lights and sirens (FBTAR s 8)

(e) benefits associated with the removal or storage of household effects of police officers who move at the direction of the police force (FBTAR s 8)

(f) benefits provided to police officers in relation to housing attached to a police station, remote area housing rent, and costs incidental to the purchase of a new dwelling where the officer was required to move in order to perform the duties of the employment (FBTAR s 8)

(g) pooled or shared private use by employees of their employer's car, ie a vehicle provided for the private use of 2 or more employees resulting in a car benefit for more than one employee (FBTAR s 10). The exclusion does not apply to the use of a motor vehicle that is not a car, such as a utility designed to carry a load of one tonne. However, the private use of a car is an excluded fringe benefit for an employee where a second employee's private use of the same car is an exempt benefit (ID 2008/21). It is sufficient for record-keeping purposes if the employee preparing the odometer records also confirms that, during the FBT year, the car was used by more than one employee for either private purposes or was parked overnight at the employee's home in accordance with the employer's written policy; the records should also provide the names of the 2 employees concerned (*NTLG meeting*, 12 November 2009), and

(h) living-away-from-home (LAFH) allowances and benefits, including certain expense payment benefits and residual benefits, for Commonwealth employees required to live away from their normal residence to undertake their official duties of employment (FBTAR s 11).

Determining employee's share

Where one fringe benefit is provided for 2 or more employees, the employer must allocate the taxable value in a way that reasonably reflects the amount of benefit received by each employee (s 5F).

Reportable fringe benefits amount

Where the individual fringe benefits amount for an employee exceeds $2,000 for the FBT year ending 31 March, that amount, after being grossed-up (¶35-025), is the reportable fringe benefits amount to be included by the employer on the employee's payment summary for that income year ending 30 June. The factor used for gross-up purposes is the FBT gross-up factor used for type 2 benefits (¶35-025), irrespective of whether GST has been included in the benefits (s 135P(2)).

If, as a result of an FBT assessment being amended, there is an understatement of up to $195 in a payment summary, the employer is nonetheless considered to have satisfied the reporting requirements, provided the understatement was not deliberate (Chapter 5.9 of the ATO's fringe benefits tax guide for employers).

[AFB ¶7-800]

¶35-057 Salary packaging and salary sacrifice arrangements

"Salary packaging" is the structuring of an employee's total remuneration so that it provides the most value to the employee in relation to its cost to the employer. Two common ways of structuring a salary package are:

(1) on a gross salary plus benefits basis, eg the package might be expressed as $80,000 salary, plus compulsory superannuation and a fully-maintained car of a certain class, and

(2) on a total remuneration cost basis, eg the package may be expressed in terms of the total cost to the employer, being $130,000. The employee can select a mix of salary and permitted benefits so that the total cost to the employer, including FBT on the benefits, is $130,000.

The latter method allows employees to give up part of their salary entitlement in return for desired benefits that are not assessable to the employee, but are taxable or exempt fringe benefits. Where such "salary sacrifice" arrangements (SSAs) are effective (¶31-120), a taxpayer (in particular a taxpayer paying tax at the highest marginal rate) may be able to reduce his/her tax bill. The tax benefit arises where the fringe benefit provided by the employer is taxed concessionally under the FBT regime. As a result, although the amount of salary that has been sacrificed equals the cost to the employer of providing the benefit (and therefore is a neutral transaction from the employer's point of view, subject to any additional administration costs that, in any event, the employee could be required to pay), the cost of the benefit to the employee is less than if the employee used after-tax salary to obtain the same benefit.

Generally, the principal benefits are cars (providing greatest advantages for employees on a high marginal tax rate), FBT-exempt portable computers (¶35-645) and FBT-exempt superannuation contributions (¶13-710, ¶35-070). Where the employer is FBT-exempt, a wide range of salary sacrifice benefits are tax-effective within specified limits (¶35-100). This is also generally the case for high marginal rate employees where the employer is eligible for an FBT rebate (¶35-100, ¶35-642).

The provision of child care facilities on the employer's business premises is an exempt fringe benefit and therefore also provides salary sacrifice opportunities (¶35-580). The provision of a low interest loan by an employer to an employee may be beneficial if the loan is used for investment purposes (to the extent that the loan is used for investment purposes, the "otherwise deductible" rule reduces the amount of FBT payable: ¶35-680). Alternatively, a loan provided for private purposes at the benchmark interest rate may be beneficial where it provides better terms or greater access to funds than the employee could have otherwise obtained (¶35-290).

Not-for-profit salary packaging and COVID-19

Not-for-profit employers can provide salary-packaged meal entertainment to employees up to the applicable exempt or rebatable cap (¶35-025, ¶35-642). The ATO has stated that compliance resources will not be applied to scrutinise expenditure under these arrangements for the period:

- FBT year ended 31 March 2020 — when restaurants and public venues were closed, and

- FBT year ending 31 March 2021 — where meals are provided by a supplier that was authorised as a meal entertainment provider as at 1 March 2020.

[AFB ¶80-000]

General Criteria for Fringe Benefits

¶35-060 Outline of fringe benefits

A taxable fringe benefit will arise where:

- a benefit is provided to an employee, an associate of an employee, or some other person at the direction of an employee or an associate of an employee
- the benefit is provided by the employee's employer, by an associate of the employer, or by a third party under an arrangement with the employer or with an associate of the employer, and
- the benefit is provided in respect of the employment of the employee (s 136(1)).

The tax extends to benefits that are provided to prospective or former employees in connection with their prospective or past employment.

Connection with Australia

FBT applies to benefits provided in relation to an employee who is a resident of Australia, except where the relevant salary or wage of the employee is exempt from income tax, and to a non-resident employee whose salary or wage from the employment has an Australian source (definition of ''employee'' in s 136(1); ID 2007/25). Where an employee is a non-resident for part of the year, benefits provided during the year will be taxable in proportion to the period of residence. Whether FBT is included as a tax to which a particular DTA applies depends on how ''Australian tax'' is defined in the agreement. For example, the New Zealand DTA and the United Kingdom DTA include references to FBT. For the application of FBT to benefits provided to a non-resident employee from New Zealand or the United Kingdom, see ID 2005/166.

FBT applies irrespective of whether the acts, omissions, and so on giving rise to a liability under the Act occurred inside or outside Australia (s 163(1)).

[AFB ¶6-000, ¶5-700]

¶35-070 Benefit must be provided

A ''benefit'' includes any right, privilege, service or facility. Some benefits are expressly *excluded* as fringe benefits and do not give rise to any FBT liability. The main exclusions are:

- exempt benefits (¶35-645)
- salary or wages
- most superannuation fund contributions (see below)
- payments from certain superannuation funds
- benefits under employee share schemes or employee share trusts, including in respect of individuals engaged in foreign service, and including certain stapled securities acquired under such schemes and indeterminate rights (¶10-085; ID 2010/142)
- payments on termination of employment
- capital payments for enforceable contracts in restraint of trade
- capital payments for personal injury

- payments deemed to be dividends for income tax purposes and loans that comply with the deemed dividend provisions in ITAA36 Div 7A (¶4-200, eg ID 2011/33)
- payments to an associated person to the extent that they are not considered by the Commissioner to be deductible
- amounts that have been subject to family trust distribution tax (¶6-268)
- certain distribution entitlements of individual venture capital managers (s 136(1)).

The following are salary and wages (rather than fringe benefits):

- an allowance paid to employees in place of medical benefits insurance (*Tubemakers of Australia*)
- payments made to employees for the cost of fares to and from work, regardless of whether public transport was used (*Roads and Traffic Authority of NSW*: ¶35-330)
- retention payments made to a person in consideration of the person providing services for 12 months and paid in addition to normal periodic salary (*Dean*).

Benefits provided under an ''effective'' salary sacrifice arrangement are not salary and wages and, conversely, benefits provided under ''ineffective'' arrangements are salary and wages and not subject to FBT (TR 2001/10: ¶31-120). Costs incurred by an employer in administering such arrangements do not give rise to a fringe benefit (ID 2001/333). Where a person is being paid parental leave pay by an employer in accordance with the *Paid Parental Leave Act 2010*, the employee can salary sacrifice his/her parental leave pay for non-cash remuneration as parental leave pay is salary and wages as defined for FBT purposes when paid by the person's employer.

A benefit is not ''provided'' if it is obtained through the employee's fraudulent activity that is not condoned by the employer (ID 2003/458).

Superannuation contributions

Employer superannuation contributions are not fringe benefits if they are contributions for an *employee* to:

- a complying superannuation fund or a fund that the contributor reasonably believed was complying (¶13-100)
- a non-resident superannuation fund where the employee for whom the benefit is provided is a temporary resident of Australia (generally an employee with a temporary visa), or
- an RSA under the *Retirement Savings Accounts Act 1997* (¶13-470).

Employer superannuation contributions not falling under any of those exclusions may constitute a fringe benefit. In particular, superannuation contributions on behalf of *associates* of employees (eg a spouse) are subject to FBT (s 136(1), definition of ''fringe benefit'').

Payments by an employer of a superannuation fund's expenses (that are treated as a superannuation contribution) are not a fringe benefit (MT 2005/1).

[AFB ¶6-020, ¶6-360]

¶35-080 Benefit provided to employee

To be a fringe benefit, a benefit must be provided to an employee of the employer concerned (s 136(1)). Additionally, a fringe benefit arises where a benefit is provided to an associate of the employee, or to a third party under an arrangement between the employer or an associate of the employer, and an employee or an associate of the employee (s 148(2): ¶35-110).

The test of whether there is an employment relationship is — if the benefit had been provided in cash form, would it have been salary or wages for PAYG purposes? In addition, past and prospective employees are treated as employees, so that benefits provided to such people or to their associates are subject to FBT if those benefits meet the other criteria. However, benefits provided to relatives of deceased employees (eg travel benefits provided to a widow or widower of a Member of Parliament) are not subject to FBT (TR 1999/10) nor is the payment of funeral expenses of a deceased employee (ID 2006/159). An ''employee'' is a person who is entitled to receive ''salary or wages'', ie payments to employees, company directors and office holders, as well as other specified payments that are subject to PAYG (TR 2005/16).

Where an employee directs the employer to pay part of the agreed salary to a third party (such as a bank by way of loan repayment) the amount remains part of the employee's salary (*Wood*; *Case 1/97*).

A person who is provided only with non-cash benefits instead of salary or wages is treated as an employee if, had any benefit been in the form of cash, that cash would have been salary or wages and that person would have been an employee (s 137).

Contributions made by an employer to an industry welfare trust (CR 2004/76) and contributions of apprentice levies to a redundancy fund (CR 2004/97) do not give rise to a fringe benefit. See also CR 2004/113 (payments for worker income protection and portable sick leave insurance policies) and ID 2002/848 (employee share plan).

A low-interest loan by an insurance agency to its agents does not give rise to a fringe benefit because insurance agents are not employees (TR 93/38). Local government councillors are not treated as employees unless the council resolves that its members are subject to PAYG withholding (definition of ''salary or wages''; TAA Sch 1 ss 12-45 and 446-1).

Requirement for a particular employee to be identified: employee benefits trusts

A particular employee (rather than a number of employees) must be identified in connection with the benefit. Therefore a payment made into an Employee Incentive Trust in relation to 3 employees was not a fringe benefit and was not deductible (*Essenbourne*; see also *Spotlight Stores*; *Cameron Brae*; *Benstead Services*; ¶16-010, ¶35-110). The Full Federal Court declined to consider the issue in *Pridecraft* (on appeal from *Spotlight Stores*). The required connection with a particular employee was present in *Walstern* where the trustee of a foreign superannuation fund allocated the contribution to a particular employee.

This approach is confirmed in TR 2018/7 which states that a contribution to an employee remuneration trust (ERT) will be a fringe benefit where the trustee is an associate of an employee and the contribution is a benefit provided in respect of the employment of a particular employee, or 2 or more employees, provided the identity of each of the employees who will take a share of the benefit is known with sufficient particularity. Accordingly, both the employee, and the share of the benefit the employee will take, must be known at the time of the contribution. ''In respect of employment'' requires a sufficient or material, rather than a causal, connection or relationship between the benefit and the employment. A contribution is *not* a fringe benefit to the extent that it is remuneration of an employee, assessable as salary or wages or if it is a deemed dividend under ITAA36 Div 7A.

In *Caelli Constructions*, an employer's contributions to a redundancy fund on behalf of employees were subject to FBT as property fringe benefits. The fund's trust deed fixed the weekly amount of the contributions to be made by employers for each worker, and provided for how the contributions were to be applied. Further, the trust deed provided that the amount standing to the credit of a particular worker's account was available for distribution to the worker if the employment ceased.

In *Indooroopilly Children Services*, the proposed issue of shares by a franchisor to the trustee of an employee share plan for the benefit of its franchisees' employees was not considered to give rise to a fringe benefit. The Commissioner had taken the view in former TR 1999/5 (now withdrawn) that a payment by an employer to the trustee of a trust or a non-complying superannuation fund set up to provide benefits to employees gave rise to a property fringe benefit. However, as a result of the decision in *Indooroopilly*, the Commissioner accepted that: (a) it is necessary to identify a particular employee in respect of whose employment a benefit is provided before a fringe benefit can exist; and (b) a benefit provided to a common associate of a number of employees, eg the trustee of an employee benefit trust, can be a fringe benefit if the identity of employees is known when the benefit is provided (ATO *Decision Impact Statement*; ID 2007/194). Thus employer contributions to a social club do not constitute a fringe benefit as they do not relate to a particular employee (ID 2007/208).

The issue of bonus units to employees as part of an employee benefit trust arrangement is a fringe benefit at the time of issue or transfer, provided the issue of the bonus unit does not create a right to receive salary or wages (TR 2010/6). A right to receive salary or wages or bonus income is not a fringe benefit.

[AFB ¶6-040, ¶6-060]

¶35-090 Employer liable for FBT

It is the employer whose employee (or the associate of the employee) receives the benefit who is liable for FBT (s 66). This is so whether the employer is a sole trader, partnership, trustee, corporation, unincorporated body, government or government body (ss 165; 166).

Where an employer disposes of a business and the new owner continues to provide fringe benefits to persons who were employed by the former owner, the new owner is liable for FBT in respect of those benefits.

A payment made by an employee in reimbursement of an FBT liability does not constitute an employee contribution capable of reducing the taxable value of a benefit (s 136A). However, the employer is assessable on such reimbursements.

The application of the FBT regime to certain Commonwealth agencies is discussed in ID 2007/200.

[AFB ¶5-500]

¶35-100 FBT exempt employers

There are specific exemptions for these employers:

- *religious institutions* for benefits provided to a minister or full-time member of a religious order in respect of that person's religious work (s 57; TR 2019/3; ID 2001/332). Benefits provided to a religious practitioner for the performance of pastoral or related duties are exempt benefits, regardless of whether the religious practitioner is a common law employee of the religious institution
- *international bodies* that are exempt generally from taxation (s 55)
- *foreign government representatives* that are exempt under the *Consular Privileges and Immunities Act 1972* or the *Diplomatic Privileges and Immunities Act 1967* (s 56)
- *public benevolent institutions* (¶16-950) (and certain hospitals) (s 57A). The exemption does not extend to benefits provided by a state department of health to an employee whose duties are not exclusively performed in connection with a public hospital (ID 2003/40). In *SIM Australia (as trustee for SIMAID Trust)*, a

trust failed to qualify as a PBI because, despite being public and benevolent, it was not an institution. Benefits provided for certain live-in carers may also be exempt (s 58) (¶35-380).

There are a number of exemptions for particular classes of benefit . There are also specific exemptions for certain miscellaneous benefits (¶35-645) and there is an FBT rebate available to certain non-profit employers (¶35-642).

Public benevolent institutions, hospitals and health promotion charities

The s 57A exemption applies where the employer is:

- a public benevolent institution (PBI). For the meaning of ''public benevolent institution'', see ACNC Commissioner's Interpretation Statement: Public Benevolent Institutions (*CIS 2016/03*; ¶16-950)
- a government body, and the employee performs his or her duties in a public hospital or a hospital carried on by a rebatable non-profit society or association
- a public hospital or a hospital carried on by a rebatable non-profit society or association (see further TD 2015/12)
- a public ambulance service, or
- a health promotion charity (as discussed in TR 2004/8), ie a charitable institution whose principal activity is promoting the prevention or control of disease in humans. See TR 2011/4 for a discussion of the meaning of ''charitable institution''. A cycling association was not entitled to be endorsed as a health promotion charity because the prevention and control of disease in human beings was not its principal activity (*Bicycle Victoria Inc*).

Benefits that are exempt under s 57A are limited in the amount of concessional treatment they attract.

In particular, for health promotion charities and public benevolent institutions that are not public hospitals, the exemption is limited to certain excluded fringe benefits (meal entertainment, car parking and entertainment facility leasing expenses) and $30,000 of each employee's individual grossed-up non-exempt amount. Where the s 57A employer is a public hospital or a hospital carried on by a non-profit society or association, or the employer is a government body and the employee works exclusively for a public hospital or a non-profit hospital, or a public ambulance service, the cap is $17,000 (¶35-025). The cap applies even if the employee was employed for part of the year only. For example, see CR 2007/15 to CR 2007/17.

Benefits provided by public benevolent institutions and health promotion charities only attract concessional treatment if they are endorsed by the Commissioner under ss 123C to 123E. The endorsement process is discussed at ¶10-610.

There is a cap on the total amount of salary packaged entertainment benefits that certain employees can be provided by exempt employers (covered by s 57A) and rebatable employers (covered by s 65J) that are subject to a reduced amount of FBT. Salary packaged entertainment benefits are now included in the standard threshold. Further, if the total value of fringe benefits exceeds the standard threshold in a particular year, the threshold is raised by the lesser of:

- $5,000, and
- the total grossed up taxable value of salary packaged entertainment benefits.

[AFB ¶5-520]

¶35-110 Benefit provided to associates of employers and employees

Generally, a benefit provided by an associate of an employer or to an associate of an employee is subject to FBT in the same manner as if the employer had provided it or the employee had received it. In addition, a benefit provided by a third party under an arrangement with the employer *or with an associate of the employer* will be caught, as will a benefit provided to a third party at the request of the employee *or of an associate of the employee* (s 148).

A fringe benefit may arise where a benefit is provided by a *third party*, if the employer or associate knew or ought reasonably to have known that it was doing so:

- because there was an arrangement between the employer or an associate of the employer and the arranger, or
- because the employer participated in or facilitated the provision of the benefit.

For example, a fringe benefit arises where a franchisor issues shares to a trust for the benefit of franchisee employees, whether the franchisees provide specific information to the trustee in relation to each of the beneficiaries (eg position held and length of service) or whether the information is available to the franchisor as a result of the pay-roll function that it performs under licence agreements between the franchisor and franchisees (ID 2005/195).

A benefit that is effectively only one benefit, although provided to more than one person (such as an employee and an associate of an employee), will only give rise to one liability (s 138).

''Associate'' has the meaning provided in ITAA36 s 318 (¶4-200). The term includes spouses, relatives, partners, trustees and beneficiaries, and related companies (s 136(1); 159; eg ID 2006/196). The trustees of employee benefit trusts or non-complying superannuation funds (whether resident or non-resident) established to provide benefits to employees are associates of the employees notwithstanding that no employee is a beneficiary or member when the benefit is provided (*Caelli Constructions*; *Decision Impact Statement* on *Indooroopilly Children Services*). If a partnership is reconstituted, the old partnership is an associate of the new.

The deeming rule in s 148(2) applies where a benefit is provided to a person other than an employee or an associate of the employee under an arrangement between the provider, the employer or an associate of the employer and the employee or an associate of the employee. In this situation, the recipient of the benefit is deemed to be an associate of the employee.

The deeming rule does not apply if the employee would be entitled to a deduction under ITAA97 Div 30 (¶16-942) had the employee, rather than the provider, provided the benefit to the recipient (s 148(2A)).

[AFB ¶6-040]

¶35-120 Benefit must have nexus with employment

For a benefit to be a fringe benefit, it must be provided ''in respect of'' the employment of an employee — even if provided to an associate of the employee or to a third party at the request of the employee or an associate (ss 136(1); 148).

A benefit is provided ''in respect of'' employment if it is provided by reason of the employment, or in relation to the employment — whether directly or indirectly. This includes a benefit provided for more than one reason, eg because of employment or a family relationship (*Curtain World*).

MT 2016 sets out these examples of where there would *not* be a fringe benefit: (a) where accommodation and meals are provided in the family home to children of a primary producer who work on the family farm; (b) where board is provided in the family home to a son who is apprenticed to his father as a motor mechanic; (c) where birthday presents are given by parents to their children who work in a family small business; (d) where a wedding gift is given to a child by the parents where earlier the child had worked in the family business; and (e) where parents give a child an interest-free or low-interest loan to purchase a matrimonial home.

Flight rewards received under a consumer loyalty programme are generally not subject to FBT as they result from a personal contractual relationship. An FBT liability may arise, however, where:

- the person with the personal contract is also an employer and provides the flight reward to an employee (who is a family member) in respect of the employment, or
- in respect of the employment, a flight reward is provided to an employee or the employee's associate under an arrangement that results from business expenditure (TR 1999/6).

Rewards received under a consumer loyalty programme that result from points accrued from business expenditure may be subject to FBT if there is a sufficient and material connection with employment (eg the employee uses his/her own credit card to pay reimbursed employer's expenses so that reward points arise for the employee) (PS LA 2004/4 (GA); ¶10-030).

In the case of a benefit provided to a shareholder who is also an employee, there is potential for the benefit to either be a fringe benefit or a dividend. In the case of a private company, ITAA36 s 109ZB provides that ITAA36 Div 7A applies to a loan and the forgiveness of debt, even if the loan or debt forgiveness was provided to the individual in his/her capacity as an employee or in respect of the employment of the person (¶4-200). For other benefits, ITAA Div 7A does not apply to benefits provided to shareholders in their capacity as an employee. For other such benefits, and for companies to which ITAA36 Div 7A does not apply, the benefit will generally be a fringe benefit if the company claims an income tax deduction for it (MT 2019). Otherwise, it will generally be regarded as being provided to a shareholder as such and not as being a fringe benefit. To be a fringe benefit, there must be a *sufficient* or *material*, rather than merely a *causal*, connection between the benefit and the employment (*J&G Knowles*; see also *Starrim*; *Case 28/97*).

▶ Planning point

As the tax consequences for the company and recipient are different, the manner in which a benefit is paid requires consideration. For the company, the tax consequences are more beneficial if the amount is non-deductible and not subject to FBT. For the recipient, however, the tax consequences will depend on whether the benefit received is a dividend (assessable) or non-assessable amount.

Benefits provided by a company to its director/shareholder in repayment of a loan were not provided "in respect of" the employment as they related to the shareholders' entitlement as creditors of the taxpayer (*Slade Bloodstock*). See also ID 2001/253, ID 2003/316, ID 2003/688, ID 2003/690, ID 2003/692 and ID 2003/836. In CR 2007/112, the required connection with employment was absent where the payer had no PAYG withholding obligation in relation to any payments to the recipients for services provided. The provision of a share to satisfy the exercise of a right granted under an employee share scheme comes as a consequence of the employee exercising the rights previously obtained under the scheme, and not in respect of employment (ID 2010/219).

Benefits provided to an employee/partner through an administration/service entity are not considered to have been provided in respect of employment (TD 95/57) (¶31-180).

Benefits provided to genuine volunteer workers will not, in most cases, give rise to a fringe benefit (ATO: *Volunteers and tax* NAT 4612).

[AFB ¶6-060]

Employee Contributions

¶35-135 Employee contributions to benefits

Generally, any employee contribution towards the cost of providing a fringe benefit will reduce the taxable value of the fringe benefit. For example, rent paid by an employee in receipt of a housing fringe benefit will be deducted from the market or statutory value of the benefit used to calculate the taxable value. Journal entries in an employer's accounts reflecting a set-off between the employer and employee can be such a payment, subject to certain conditions (MT 2050). See also ID 2012/88 where interest was not paid ''in respect of the provision of'' an expense payment fringe benefit and therefore was not a recipients contribution.

▶ Example

An employee is provided with a motor vehicle and makes payments to an employer of $30 per week for the cost of fuel charged to the employer's fleet card. These payments would reduce the employer's FBT liability for running costs of that employee's car.

Any consideration received by an employer in reimbursement of an FBT liability does not, however, constitute an employee contribution capable of reducing the taxable value of the fringe benefit (s 136A).

A contribution by an employee towards the cost of a car fringe benefit is known as a ''recipient's payment'' (¶35-190). An employee contribution towards a housing fringe benefit is known as ''recipients rent''. A contribution by an employee towards the cost of most other fringe benefits is known as a ''recipients contribution''.

Employee contributions will generally be assessable income to the employer.

The taxable value of a fringe benefit is reduced by the full amount of the contribution, irrespective of whether the contribution includes an amount to compensate the employer for any GST liability that may arise from the employee contribution. GST is usually payable by the employer on a ''recipient's payment'' made by the employee towards the cost of a car fringe benefit, and a ''recipients contribution'' made by the employee towards the cost of other benefits, but not on recipient's rent paid in relation to a housing fringe benefit (¶35-000). See GSTR 2001/3.

[AFB ¶57-060]

Car Benefits

¶35-150 Conditions giving rise to a car benefit

A car benefit arises on any day where an employer's car is used by an employee for private purposes or is available for such use. Even if the car is not actually owned or leased by the employer or an associate, there will still be a car benefit if it is used or is available for use for private purposes by an employee under an arrangement between the employer or an associate of the employer and a third party who actually owns or leases the car. The existence of a car benefit is determined on a daily basis.

There must be a "car"

A car benefit only arises from the provision of a ''car'', defined as any motor-powered road vehicle (including a 4-wheel drive vehicle) (except a motor cycle or similar vehicle) designed to carry a load of less than one tonne and fewer than 9 passengers.

The designed load of a vehicle is determined on the same basis as that applied for determining the vehicles that are subject to CGT (¶11-640; MT 2024). A car that has been destroyed as a result of a natural disaster ceases to be a ''car'' from the date of the natural disaster (ID 2011/28).

A car does not include a motor cycle or a 4-wheeled motor cycle of the sort used on farms. Provision of a motor vehicle that is not a car will not give rise to a car benefit, but may give rise to a residual benefit if it is used by an employee.

Private use of an unregistered car (one that cannot be driven legally on a public road) will be an exempt benefit where the car is unregistered at all times during the year when it is held by the provider of the benefit and where it is held principally for use in business operations (s 8(3); 162N).

Car owned or leased by employer

To give rise to a car benefit, a car must be ''held'' by the employer, or by an associate of the employer, or by the third party with whom the employer or associate makes an arrangement for the car to be provided.

A car is held by a person if that person owns or leases it or it is otherwise made available to that person (s 162). A car under a hire purchase agreement is deemed to be owned by the hirer (s 7(6)). More than one person can hold a car at the same time (eg an owner and a lessee of the same car).

The provision of a motor car by an employer to an employee under a lease novation arrangement gives rise to a car fringe benefit. In a full novation and a split full novation, the lease payment obligations are transferred to the employer. There are no income tax implications for the employee while the employer makes the lease payment. The employer is entitled to a deduction for the lease expenses where the motor car is used in the business or is provided to an employee or associate of an employee as part of a salary packaging arrangement (IT 2509; TR 1999/15).

A car used for taxi travel or a short-term hire car (eg a rental car) is not ''held'' by the hirer (s 7(7)). If an employer pays for such a car for an employee, the benefit will either be an expense payment benefit or a residual benefit unless it is an exempt benefit (¶35-645). The provision of a chauffeur to drive a car at the employee's direction for business or private purposes gives rise to a residual benefit, rather than a car benefit (ID 2003/498).

Private use by employee, etc

For there to be a car benefit on any particular day, the car must either:

- be used on that day for private purposes by an employee or an associate of an employee, or
- be *taken to be available* for private use on that day by such a person.

(1) Private use

''Private use'' by an employee or an associate of an employee means use other than in the course of producing assessable income of the employee.

Home/work travel is generally regarded as private use, even if taking the car home is a condition of employment. The Commissioner's views on private use are set out in MT 2027. Even where home/work travel is not private use, the car will normally be taken to be available for private use by virtue of being garaged at an employee's home.

(2) Taken to be available for private use

In 2 situations, a car will be taken to be available for private use by an employee or an associate of an employee regardless of whether it is actually so used.

(a) Car garaged by employee. Where a car held by an employer (or an associate of an employer) is, on any day, garaged or kept at or near the place of residence of an employee of the employer, or of an associate of such an employee, it is taken to be available for the private use of the employee or associate on that day (s 7(2)). A car will, therefore, give rise to a car benefit for 2 days when garaged at an employee's home overnight, regardless of actual private use. The employee's place of residence is the home

or any other place where the employee resides or has sleeping accommodation (s 136(1)), including a motel (ID 2004/852). In *Case 58/94*, a car was taken to be available for private use where it was garaged at the employer's place of business because that place was also the employee's residence. See also *Jetto Industrial Pty Ltd*.

(b) Car in employee's custody or control. A car will generally be deemed to be available for the private use of an employee or associate on any day that person has custody or control of the car while it is away from any business premises of the employer and the employee is not performing employment duties (s 7(3); TR 2000/4). Where an employee leaves a car in an airport car park while away from the employee's home city and the car park is not in the vicinity of the employee's residence, the car will not be taken to be available for private use if the employer removes the custody and control of the car from the employee (eg takes the car keys) (TD 94/16).

When a car is parked by an employee or an associate in a Sydney Airport Corporation Ltd parking facility under an agreement between the Corporation and the employer, neither s 7(2) nor s 7(3) is satisfied because the employee and the associate are not entitled to use the car for any purpose and do not have custody or control of the car (CR 2009/3).

Where the person with the car is an employee (not an associate) who is performing duties of employment at the time and who is not entitled to use the car for private purposes, then the car is not deemed to be available for private use subject to the prohibition being consistently enforced (s 7(4)).

(3) Emergency vehicles

Cars that are used by an ambulance, a police or firefighting service and that are visibly marked for that purpose and are fitted with a flashing warning light and horn, bell or alarm are not considered to be available for private use (s 7(2A)).

Impact of COVID-19

The ATO has advised that, where a car has been garaged at an employee's home due to the impact of COVID-19 and is not being driven at all, or is only being driven for maintenance purposes, the car will not be taken to be held for the purposes of providing fringe benefits. Therefore, where the operating cost method is used, there may not be an FBT liability for that car. However, if an exemption does not apply and a work car is garaged at an employee's home, it will still be deemed to be available for private use (and give rise to an FBT liability).

[AFB ¶20-000, ¶20-010]

¶35-160 Work-related travel in commercial vehicles

Employee use of certain commercial vehicles will be an exempt benefit where the only private use, apart from minor, infrequent and irregular use by an employee or an associate of an employee, is for "work-related" travel by the employee (not by an associate of the employee) (s 8(2)). Transporting a family member by the employee on their journey from home to a work location in the employer's car is a "private use" of the car (ID 2012/97). A one-off transportation of a family member may be an excepted "private use" (ID 2012/98). Travel between the employee's place of residence and the place of employment in relation to a second employer is not "work-related travel" (ID 2013/34).

Work-related travel is home/work travel by an employee, or travel by an employee that is incidental to travel in the course of performing employment duties (s 136(1)).

Commercial vehicles

The exemption applies to:

- cars used for taxi travel, panel vans or utilities designed to carry a load of less than one tonne

- other vehicles that are designed to carry a load of less than one tonne and that are not designed mainly to carry passengers.

These factors should be considered in determining whether any ''other road vehicle'' is ''designed for the principal purpose of carrying passengers'': (a) the appearance and presentation of the vehicle; (b) relevant promotional literature; (c) the vehicle's specifications, load and passenger carrying capacity; and (d) the marketing of the vehicle (TD 94/19).

A similar exemption applies to commercial vehicles that would otherwise give rise to a residual benefit where used for private purposes (s 47(6)). This exemption applies essentially to vehicles that are designed to carry a load of one tonne or more, or 9 or more passengers.

See MT 2024 for a discussion of the exemption; a list of eligible vehicles can be found on the ATO website under Fringe Benefits Tax — exempt motor vehicles. See MT 2033 for the application of the exemption to certain modified cars.

Employers may purchase a motor vehicle cab/chassis designed to carry a load of one tonne or more and then have a work specific tray or other items (eg metal bars, toolboxes, etc) fitted which reduce the carrying capacity of the vehicle to less than one tonne. The ATO has advised that if, after the fitting, the load capacity is found to be less than one tonne in accordance with the methodology set out in MT 2024, the vehicle would be classed as a ''car'' (*NTLG FBT Sub-committee minutes* — 13 August 2009). Accordingly, an employer could use the statutory formula method.

Minor, infrequent and irregular use

PCG 2018/3 provides guidance on the ATO's compliance approach to the exemption in s 8(2) for private use of a commercial vehicle that is minor, infrequent and irregular. Employers who meet the requirements and who rely on the Guideline do not need to keep records about employee's minor private use of the vehicle and the Commissioner will not devote compliance resources to review the exemption for that employee. An employer may rely on the Guideline if:

(a) it provides an eligible vehicle to a current employee

(b) the vehicle is provided to the employee for business use to perform their work duties

(c) the vehicle had a GST-inclusive value less than the luxury car tax threshold (¶34-220) at the time the vehicle was acquired

(d) the vehicle is not provided as part of a salary packaging arrangement and the employee cannot elect to receive additional remuneration in lieu of the use of the vehicle

(e) it has a policy in place that limits private use of the vehicle and obtain assurance from its employee that their use is limited to use as outlined in subparagraphs (f) and (g)

(f) the employee uses the vehicle to travel between their home and their place of work and any diversion adds no more than 2 kilometres to the ordinary length of that trip, and

(g) for journeys undertaken for a wholly private purpose, the employee does not use the vehicle to travel more than 1,000 km in total and a return journey that exceeds 200 km.

[AFB ¶20-160]

Value of Car Fringe Benefits

¶35-170 Car benefits

The taxable value of a car fringe benefit can be determined in one of 2 ways — by the *statutory formula* method or by the *operating cost* method (ss 9; 10). An employer can choose either method each year for each car giving rise to a car fringe benefit. If an employer makes no express choice, then the statutory formula method automatically applies. If the employer elects to use the operating cost method for a particular car for any year, but the statutory formula would in fact result in a lower value for that year, then the lower statutory formula value applies for the year (s 10(5)). The taxpayer may request an amendment of an FBT return after the return has been lodged, to change the method used from the statutory formula to the operating cost method (ID 2002/102). Regardless of the method used, FBT is payable on the grossed-up taxable value of the benefit (¶35-025).

See CR 2014/73 for the treatment of employer clients of Toyota Finance Australia Limited who provide car fringe benefits under novated lease arrangements incorporating the payment of insurance premiums.

[AFB ¶20-200]

¶35-180 Statutory formula method

The effect of the statutory formula is to value a car fringe benefit by applying a statutory fraction to a specially determined value of the car. The formula reduces the benefit value to take account of any days during the year when the car was not applied to private use or taken to be available for private use. The value is also reduced by the amount of any payments for the benefit by a recipient.

The formula (s 9) for calculating the benefit value is:

$$\left(0.2 \times \text{Base value of the car} \times \frac{\text{Number of days during that year of tax on which the car fringe benefits were provided by the provider}}{\text{Number of days in that year of tax}}\right) - \text{Amount (if any) of the recipient's payment}$$

The meaning of each of the formula's components is discussed at ¶35-190.

[AFB ¶20-310]

¶35-190 Statutory formula components

Base value of car

The calculation of the base value of a car depends on whether the provider (the employer or associate) originally owned or leased the car (s 9(2)). It is the manner of originally holding the car that counts, not the manner in which it is currently held. In addition, if an associate of the current provider first held the car, the position is determined according to whether that associate originally owned or leased the car. This counters arrangements designed to reduce the value. Non-arm's length transactions are adjusted to arm's length terms (s 13).

Whether the car was originally owned or leased, the base value of a car also includes the cost price of any subsequently fitted non-business accessory that remains on the car. No reduction is made to this component after 4 years.

The ATO considers that the cost of repairs to a car, including the replacement of damaged or stolen non-business accessories, does not affect the base value of the car.

Car originally owned

Where the provider originally owned the car, the base value is the *cost price* of the car to the provider when the provider first held it (s 9(2)(a)). The base value is reduced to two-thirds of the cost price if the provider has held the car for more than 4 years at the beginning of the FBT year concerned (TD 94/28; ID 2004/527).

The "cost price" of a car is the expenditure directly attributable to the acquisition or delivery of the car, exclusive of registration costs and of any tax on registration or transfer (s 136(1)). Customs duty privileges and exemptions are disregarded. Where the provider actually manufactured the car, the cost price is the amount that would have been paid at arm's length for the car. Any costs associated with the delivery of the car are included in the cost price, including dealer delivery charges not otherwise included in the purchase price but excluding insurance costs and extended car warranties (TR 2011/3). Where an employee provides a trade-in vehicle to a car dealer who sells a car to either the employer or the lessor, the expenditure incurred by the purchaser is the purchase price, reflecting the value of the trade-in amount. Similarly, a cash payment made by an employee, either to the car dealer or to the employer, reduces the amount of the purchase price. Fleet discounts, manufacturer rebates or any other incentives or discounts that reduce the purchase price, reduce the expenditure incurred by the purchaser in acquiring the car.

A car let under a hire purchase agreement is deemed to have been purchased. The "cost price" is the original leased car value (see below) even after the eventual purchase in fact occurs (s 136(1)).

The cost price of a car also includes the cost of any non-business accessories fitted to the car at or about the time of purchase (or deemed purchase). A "non-business accessory" means any accessory (factory fitted or otherwise) fitted to the car, other than an accessory required to meet the special needs of any business operations for which the car is used (s 136(1)). A mobile phone or 2-way radio fitted to a car used by a sales representative would not be a non-business accessory and its cost would not be added to the cost price of the car. "Signage" for the purposes of advertising that is placed on a car is also not a non-business accessory (*NTLG minutes*, 12 May 2011). Non-business accessories include an air-conditioning system, CD player or radio, paint, fabric or rust protection, and window tinting (ID 2011/47). A portable electronic device that is exempt from FBT under s 58X (¶35-645), eg a GPS, is not an "accessory" (*NTLG FBT Sub-committee meeting*, 26 February 2009).

"Cost price" of a car includes the normal new car warranty provided by the manufacturer, but not an extended car warranty which is acquired under a separate contract (ID 2006/253). Cost price may be reduced by the amount of any trade-in. For further examples of the application of the cost price rules, see ID 2003/584 to ID 2003/587.

Car originally leased

Where the provider did not originally own the car when first holding it, the base value is the original *leased car value* of the car at the earliest time when it was so held (s 9(2)(a)). The base value is reduced to two-thirds of the original leased car value if the provider has held the car for more than 4 years at the beginning of the FBT year concerned. For examples of the application of the rules, see ID 2004/527 and ID 2004/528.

Where the lessor purchased the car at or about the time the provider commenced to lease the car from the lessor, the leased car value of the car is the cost price of the car to the lessor.

Where the lessor did not purchase the car at or about the time the provider commenced to lease it from the lessor, the leased car value is simply the arm's length purchase price of the car at the time when the provider or associate first held the car.

Impact of GST

The cost of cars purchased from 1 July 2000 is GST inclusive, as is the cost of non-business accessories fitted to cars. The base values of leased cars and operating costs are also GST inclusive. Cost also includes any luxury car tax.

Most employers were not entitled to GST input tax credits for cars purchased before 23 May 2001, in which case the gross-up rate is the rate for type 2 benefits (¶35-025). If the employer is entitled to an input tax credit for a car bought on or after 23 May 2001, the gross-up rate for type 1 benefits should be used (TR 2001/2).

Statutory fraction (0.2)

For new vehicle contracts entered into *after* 7.30 pm (AEST) on 10 May 2011, the statutory fractions were phased out and replaced by a flat rate of 20% over the next 4 years (s 9; see previous editions of the *Australian Master Tax Guide* for the rates that applied to earlier contracts). The 20% rate applies regardless of the distance travelled during the year.

Number of days benefit provided

The number of days during the year concerned on which the car gave rise to a car fringe benefit is the number of days during the year on which the conditions for a car benefit were present (¶35-150). Each day on which a car does not give rise to a car benefit reduces this value in the formula, and thereby reduces the taxable value of the benefit arising from the car. This would be the case where the employer retains custody of a car while an employee is away overseas.

Number of days during year of tax

This is the number of days during the relevant FBT year.

Recipient's payment

The "recipient's payment" may be a payment by a recipient to the employer (or the provider if not provided by the employer) in consideration for provision of the car benefit (s 9(2)(e)). The recipient must actually make a payment before it can be taken into account. However, journal entries in an employer's accounts reflecting a set-off may be accepted (¶35-135). A non-reimbursed payment of car expenses (registration, insurance, repairs and maintenance or fuel: ¶35-230) by the recipient during the year may also be a recipient's payment. The recipient must obtain documentary evidence of the payment (except in the case of oil or fuel, where a declaration in respect of the expense is also acceptable) and give it to the employer before the relevant return date. The documentary evidence requirements are similar to the income tax substantiation requirements affecting car expenses (¶16-320). See also ID 2005/210.

Pool cars and cars in trading stock

Where an employer allows employees to use any of a number of cars that are on hand, it is difficult to apply the statutory formula on an individual car basis. The Commissioner will accept a figure based on an average value of such cars, if the numbers and total costs are ascertained quarterly (MT 2023). The average for the year will be the total of the quarterly vehicle costs divided by the total of the number of vehicles on hand at the end of each quarter.

▶ Example

At the end of a quarter to 30 June, a dealer has 8 pool cars costing a total of $136,000. At the end of the quarter to 30 September there are 12 cars costing $240,000. At 31 December there are 8 cars costing $128,000. At 31 March there are 12 cars costing $216,000. The average cost for the pool vehicles for the year ending 31 March will be:

$$\frac{\$720{,}000}{40} = \$18{,}000$$

The benefit value can be calculated by reference to the average number of employees (calculated quarterly) having use of pool cars during the year. The value will be the average number of employees, multiplied by the average vehicle cost, multiplied by the statutory fraction.

▶ Example

A car dealer's pool of cars has an average value of $18,000, as shown in the example above. There are on average 10 employees having access to the car pool for the year. The total base value is:

$$\$18,000 \times 10 = \$180,000$$

Assuming that there are no recipient's payments for use of the cars, the taxable value for the year would be:

$$\$180,000 \times 0.20 = \$36,000$$

FBT is payable on the grossed-up taxable value of the benefit (¶35-025).

[AFB ¶20-350ff, ¶20-750]

¶35-200 Examples applying statutory formula

▶ Example 1: Car held for whole year

This example shows the application of the formula to a car that was originally owned by the employer before the commencement of the year, is held by the employer for the whole year and is available for private use on every day during the year.

FBT year ending 31 March 2021

Date car purchased	1 October 2017
Time car held at commencement of year	3 years 6 months
Cost price of car	$30,000
Number of days in year	365
Number of days when car benefit arises	365
Recipient's payments	$0

Taxable value of benefit:

$$\left(0.2 \times \begin{array}{c}\text{Base value}\\ \text{of the car}\end{array} \times \frac{\begin{array}{c}\text{Number of days}\\ \text{during that year of tax}\\ \text{on which the car fringe benefits}\\ \text{were provided by the provider}\end{array}}{\begin{array}{c}\text{Number of days}\\ \text{in that year of tax}\end{array}} \right) - \begin{array}{c}\text{Amount}\\ \text{(if any)}\\ \text{of the}\\ \text{recipient's}\\ \text{payment}\end{array}$$

Taxable value of benefit:

$$\frac{0.2 \times \$30,000 \times 365}{365} - 0 = \$6,000$$

FBT is payable on the grossed-up taxable value (being a type 1 benefit: ¶35-025), assuming GST input tax credits are available, ie

$6,000 × 2.0802	=	$12,481
Tax at 47%	=	$5,866.07

▶ Example 2: Car held for part of year

This example shows the application of the formula to a car that is held by the employer for part of the year and is available for private use on every day during that part of the year.

FBT year ending 31 March 2021

Date car purchased	1 October 2020
Time car held at commencement of year	0 years
Cost price of car	$30,000
Number of days in year	365
Number of days when car benefit arises	182
Recipient's payments	$0

Taxable value of benefit:

$$\left(0.2 \times \text{Base value of the car} \times \frac{\text{Number of days during that year of tax on which the car fringe benefits were provided by the provider}}{\text{Number of days in that year of tax}}\right) - \text{Amount (if any) of the recipient's payment}$$

Taxable value of benefit:

$$\frac{0.2 \times \$30{,}000 \times 182}{365} - 0 = \$2{,}991.78$$

FBT is payable on the grossed-up taxable value (being a type 1 benefit: ¶35-025), assuming GST input tax credits are available, ie:

$2,991.78 × 2.0802	=	$6,223.50
Tax at 47%	=	$2,925.04

[AFB ¶20-420]

¶35-210 Operating cost method

If the operating cost method is used, the taxable value of a car fringe benefit is based on the operating cost of the car during the period over which the benefit arises (s 10). That cost is apportioned between the business use of the car during that period and the non-business use. The portion related to non-business use is the taxable value.

Employers using the operating cost method of valuing a car fringe benefit must ensure that various records are kept to show the total car expenses incurred during the relevant period and the proportions of business and non-business use of the car.

The value of a car fringe benefit under the operating cost method is determined by the formula (s 10(2)):

$$[C \times (100\% - BP)] - R$$

where:

C is the *operating cost* of the car during the *holding period*

BP is the *business use percentage* applicable to the car for the *holding period*

R is the amount of any *recipient's payment* attributable to *the holding period.*

The relevant "holding period" is the period during the FBT year of tax during which the provider "held" (¶35-150) the car for the purpose of providing the car fringe benefit (ss 162(2); 162C). If the provider holds the car for only part of the year, or holds the car to provide the benefit during only part of the year, then the relevant holding period is that part of the year.

The ''recipient's payment'' is the amount, if any, contributed by the recipient (the employee) of the benefit concerned. It is determined in the same way as the recipient's payment under the statutory formula method (¶35-190) (s 10(3)(c)). Where the payment is in the form of a payment of car expenses, it is subject to the same evidentiary or declaration requirements as apply in the case of the statutory formula method. See also ID 2005/210.

[AFB ¶20-450, ¶20-850]

¶35-230 Meaning of operating cost

In general terms, the operating cost of a car consists of ''car expenses'', registration and insurance costs (see below), and:

- where the car is owned (or deemed to be owned), depreciation and an imputed interest cost on the value of the car and of any non-business accessories fitted to the car, or
- where the car is leased, lease costs (s 10(3)).

Where a recipient of a car fringe benefit incurs a car expense, registration or insurance cost on the car, that amount is included as part of the operating cost. However, if the recipient is not reimbursed for the expense, it will also qualify as a recipient's payment.

In determining operating costs, any non-arm's length transactions are converted to an arm's length basis and any property acquired without expenditure is deemed to have been acquired at market value (s 13(2), (4)).

Operating costs such as lease payments, repairs, fuel, registration and insurance are to be included at their GST-inclusive value, whether the car is owned, manufactured or leased, and whether non-business accessories are fitted (TR 2001/2).

Most employers were not entitled to GST input tax credits for cars purchased before 23 May 2001, in which case the gross-up rate is the rate for type 2 benefits (¶35-025). If the employer is entitled to an input tax credit for a car bought on or after 23 May 2001, the gross-up rate for type 1 benefits should be used (TR 2001/2).

Car expenses

A ''car expense'' is an expense incurred on repairs, maintenance or fuel for the car, eg a car wash (s 136(1)). The car expenses to be included in the operating cost are those incurred during the holding period (¶35-210). Repairs include the cost of replacing damaged or stolen non-business accessories. It also includes the cost of a map update of an in-built satellite navigation system (ID 2014/18).

An insured repair expense is not included as a car expense. This covers accident repair expenses where the expenses are paid by an insurer or by the party responsible for the damage.

If the provider leases the car, expenses incurred by the lessor under the lease are not included as a car expense.

Membership fees that give rise to a road service entitlement are car expenses (*NTLG FBT Sub-committee minutes*, 1 December 1994), but road tolls are not (*NTLG FBT Sub-committee minutes*, 18 March 1999).

Insurance and registration expenses

The insurance and registration expenses to be included in the operating cost are those relating to the holding period. See also ID 2006/253.

Even if the provider holds the car for the whole year and uses it to provide car fringe benefits for the whole year, an apportionment will be necessary if the period of registration or insurance does not correspond with the FBT year.

Depreciation

Depreciation on the car is included in the operating cost of the car where the provider owns the car. If the provider holds the car on hire purchase, the provider is deemed to own it and to have purchased it at the time when first held (s 7(6)). Deemed depreciation is also included where the provider neither owns nor leases the car and it is calculated on the assumption that the car was purchased at its leased car value (¶35-190) at the time the car was first held by the provider.

Where a car is owned by a provider and a non-business accessory has been fitted to the car after the provider purchased, or is deemed to have purchased, the car, depreciation on that accessory has to be calculated separately but in the same manner as though the non-business accessory (¶35-190) were a car.

Depreciation is calculated using the formula (s 11):

$$\frac{ABC}{D}$$

where:

A is the ''depreciated value'' of the car if the provider already owned (or was deemed to own) the car at the beginning of the year, or the GST-inclusive ''cost price'' (¶35-190) of the car in other cases. The deemed depreciation is not limited by reference to the depreciation cost limits that apply for income tax purposes (¶17-200). ''Depreciated value'' is the cost price of the car to the provider, less depreciation calculated using the above depreciation formula from the time when the provider first held the car to the beginning of the year (s 12)

B is:

- 0.225 for cars acquired before 1 July 2002
- 0.1875 for cars acquired on or after 1 July 2002 and before 10 May 2006, and
- 0.25 for cars acquired on or after 10 May 2006.

C is the number of days during the year on which the provider held the car

D is the number of days in the FBT year (s 11(1)).

▶ Example 1

An employer owns a car with a depreciated value of $14,051.64 at 1 April 2020 (the car was bought on 2 February 2006). There are 365 days in the year to 31 March 2021. The deemed depreciation on that car for that year is calculated as follows:

$$\frac{\$14{,}051.64 \times 0.1875 \times 365}{365} = \$2{,}634.68$$

If, instead, the car was acquired in 2001 and sold for $15,000 on 31 October 2020 (there being 214 days in the year from 1 April to 31 October), the deemed depreciation on that car for the year to 31 March 2021 would be calculated as follows:

$$\frac{\$14{,}051.64 \times 0.225 \times 214}{365} = \$1{,}853.66$$

Assume instead that an employer bought a car on 2 November 2020 for $24,000 and retained it for the rest of the year to 31 March 2021. There are 150 days from 2 November to 31 March. The deemed depreciation on the car for the year to 31 March 2021 is calculated as follows:

$$\frac{\$24{,}000 \times 0.25 \times 150}{365} = \$2{,}465.75$$

Where, for some part of the year, the provider held the car but did not hold it for the purpose of providing car fringe benefits, deemed depreciation is apportioned using the formula:

$$\text{DEP} \times \frac{\text{DHP}}{\text{DCO}}$$

where:

DEP is the deemed depreciation calculated under the depreciation formula

DHP is the number of days in the year when the car was held by the provider for the purpose of providing car fringe benefits

DCO is the total number of days in the year for which the provider held the car (s 11(1A)).

Imputed interest

An imputed interest cost on the value of the car is included in the operating cost of the car where the provider owns the car. If the provider holds the car on hire purchase, the provider is deemed to own it and to have purchased it at the time when it was first held (s 7(6)). A deemed imputed interest cost is also included where the provider neither owns nor leases the car. This cost is calculated on the basis that the provider purchased the car at its leased car value at the time it was first held.

If any non-business accessory (¶35-190) has been fitted to the car after the provider purchased (or is deemed to have purchased) the car, an imputed interest cost on the value of that accessory must be calculated separately. Imputed interest is calculated in the same manner as though the non-business accessory were a car.

The formula for calculating imputed interest is similar to the depreciation formula, except that component B is a statutory interest rate, rather than the rate of depreciation (s 11(2)). Imputed interest is calculated on the same cost price or depreciated value as is used for calculating depreciation.

The statutory interest rate (also referred to as the FBT benchmark interest rate) is the standard variable rate for owner-occupied housing loans of the major banks, last published by the Reserve Bank of Australia before the commencement of the year of tax. For the year ended 31 March 2020, it was 5.37% (TD 2019/6); for the year ending 31 March 2021, it is 4.80% (ATO website).

▶ Example 2

An employer owns a car with a depreciated value of $9,069 at 1 April 2020. The imputed interest cost on the car for the year to 31 March 2021 is calculated as follows:

$$\frac{\$9,069 \times 0.048 \times 365}{365} = \$435.31$$

If instead the car was sold for $11,000 on 31 October 2020, the imputed interest cost for the year to 31 March 2021 is calculated as follows:

$$\frac{\$9,069 \times 0.048 \times 214}{365} = \$255.22$$

If, on the other hand, the employer purchased a car on 1 November 2020 for $30,000 and retained it for the rest of the year to 31 March 2021, the imputed interest cost for the year to 31 March 2021 is calculated as follows:

$$\frac{\$30,000 \times 0.048 \times 151}{365} = \$595.72$$

An apportionment formula similar to that for deemed depreciation (see above) applies to apportion the imputed interest cost for the year concerned if, for some part of the year, the provider held the car but did not hold it for the purpose of providing car fringe benefits (s 11(1B)).

Lease charges

Where the provider leases the car, the operating cost of the car includes so much of the charges paid or payable under the lease as relate to the time during the year for which the provider held the car for the purpose of providing the benefit. If the lessor of the car obtained the car without paying customs duties, the lease charges are adjusted to reflect the level of charges that would have applied had the lessor incurred the costs.

[AFB ¶20-460ff]

¶35-240 Meaning of business use percentage

The business use percentage component of the operating cost formula (¶35-210) is the percentage of the total distance travelled by the car during the relevant period that relates to business use. The percentage is based on the number of business kilometres travelled during the year and is calculated using the formula:

$$\frac{\text{number of business kilometres travelled by the car during the holding period}}{\text{total number of kilometres travelled by the car during the holding period}} \times 100\%$$

The employer must establish the business use percentage in accordance with the rules discussed below. Unless the employer complies with these rules, the business use percentage will be treated as nil and the taxable value of the benefit will be the whole operating cost of the car for the period concerned, reduced by any recipient's payment (¶25-230; ID 2004/385). The resultant taxable value is likely to exceed the taxable value of the benefit as determined under the statutory formula, in which case the lower statutory formula value will apply for the year (s 10(5)).

To establish the business use percentage of a car, an employer must ensure that the logbook and odometer records showing the business use of the car are maintained (s 10A). If the employer is not the provider, the provider must give the employer any relevant logbook and odometer records for the car. Furthermore, the employer must specify in writing an estimate of the number of business kilometres travelled by the car during the holding period as well as an estimate of the business use percentage for the car during the holding period. Generally, each of these requirements must be completed on or before the date on which the employer's FBT return for the year is due to be lodged. An employer must retain odometer and logbook records for 5 years from the assessment date of the last year to which they relate (ss 123; 136(1)).

Employers with a fleet of 20 or more cars

Guidelines in PCG 2016/10 apply to employers with a fleet of 20 or more cars for working out the taxable value of car fringe benefits where:

- the cars are ''tool of trade'' cars
- employees are required to maintain logbooks in a logbook year and the employer holds valid logbooks for at least 75% of the cars in the logbook year
- the cars are of a make and model chosen by the employer
- each car had a GST-inclusive value less than the luxury car limit applicable at the time the car was acquired, and

- the cars are not provided as part of an employee's remuneration package (for example, under a salary packaging arrangement), and employees cannot elect to receive additional remuneration in lieu of the use of the cars.

In this situation, an "average business use percentage" can be applied to all tool of trade cars held in the fleet in the logbook year and the following 4 years. The average business use percentage is calculated by determining which fleet logbooks are valid, confirming there are valid logbooks for at least 75% of the cars in the fleet and calculating the average of the business use percentages determined in accordance with each of the valid logbooks. This simplified approach can be applied for a period of 5 years in respect of the fleet (including replacement and new cars) provided the fleet remains at 20 cars or more, and subject to there being no material and substantial changes in circumstances (eg a change in location of the employer's depot that would substantially alter the business use percentage of the fleet).

Logbook records

An employer is generally required to keep a logbook for the first year the operating cost method is used and then every 5 years. The logbook must be kept for a minimum of 12 weeks. This period may overlap 2 tax years (eg from 1 March to 24 May). For examples of the application of the requirements, see ID 2002/925, ID 2003/1099 and CR 2006/104. Commercial applications provided by TomTom, Fleet Partners, GPSI, Telogis, mTrax, Smartrak, IntelliTrac, Ctrack, Fleetsu and Two10degrees can also satisfy the definition of "logbook records" (CR 2014/69; CR 2015/1; CR 2015/60; CR 2015/105; CR 2016/31; CR 2016/44; CR 2016/47; CR 2016/56; CR 2016/91; CR 2019/8). In *Jetto Industrial Pty Ltd*, a logbook covering a period of only 2 months was an insufficient basis for an inference that the same practice prevailed uniformly over the previous 4 years.

During the period in which a logbook is being maintained, an entry must be made to record each business journey in the car concerned, detailing the date each journey began and ended, the various odometer readings and the purpose of each journey. Private journeys do not have to be recorded.

Consecutive business journeys in the same car on the same day are deemed to constitute a single journey (s 161).

Odometer records

Odometer records must be maintained for the holding period and, in a logbook year, for the logbook period (ss 10A; 10B). The record must show the odometer reading of the car at the beginning and at the end of the period (s 136(1)). The TomTom Telematics system taken together with the TomTom Logbook Report satisfies the definition of "odometer records" (CR 2014/69).

Employer's estimate of business kilometres

Employers are required to estimate the number of "business kilometres" travelled by the car during the holding period (s 10A; 10B). A business kilometre is one travelled by a car in the course of a business journey, ie a non-private journey (eg ID 2007/140; ID 2012/96). Employers are required to take all relevant matters into account when making this estimate, including any logbook, odometer or other records and any variations in the pattern of use of the car (s 162F).

Employer to specify business use percentage

Employers are also required to specify a business use percentage of a car during the holding period (ss 10A; 10B), defined in accordance with the formula set out above.

Replacement car

Where a car is replaced, the original business use percentage for the old car can be used for the new car, subject to any changes in the business use of the replacement car (s 162K). The employer must specifically nominate the replacement car, giving the make, model and registration number of both cars.

Impact of COVID-19

The ATO has advised that, where the operating cost method is used, employers can take into account the impact of COVID-19 on the business use of a car if it is being driven during the period it is garaged at home. Further, business use estimates may be adjusted to reflect changes in employees' driving patterns due to COVID-19.

[AFB ¶20-600]

Car Parking Benefits

¶35-252 Car parking benefits

Car parking facilities provided by an employer to an employee (or an associate of the employee) may give rise to a car parking benefit (s 39A). A car parking benefit arises where, on a particular day, these conditions are satisfied:

- a ''car'' (¶35-150) is parked on ''business premises'' or ''associated premises'' of the provider (premises owned, leased or otherwise controlled) that are within one kilometre of a ''commercial parking station'' (s 136(1)). ''Business premises'' are premises which are used for the business operations of the employer. The employer does not need to have exclusive proprietary rights in respect of the business premises (*Esso Australia*). For further guidance on the meaning of business premises, see TR 2000/4. See also ID 2001/255
- the commercial car parking station ordinarily charges members of the public more than the car parking threshold for all-day parking at the start of the FBT year. Where a parking station charges a fee for all-day parking which becomes progressively lower after a number of days parking, the lowest fee the parking station is taken to charge for all-day parking on a particular day is calculated by dividing the total fee payable for the period (eg for the year) by the ''business days in the period'' (s 39E; ID 2006/93). For the year ended 31 March 2020, the threshold was $8.95 (TD 2019/9); for the year ending 31 March 2021, the threshold is $9.15 (ATO website).
- the car is parked on those premises for a total period of more than 4 hours between 7 am and 7 pm on the particular day
- a car benefit relating to the car is provided on that day to an employee or an associate in respect of the employment of the employee, or the car is owned or leased by the employee or an associate, or the car is made available to the employee
- the provision of parking facilities for the car on that day is ''in respect of'' the employee's employment (¶35-120). No car parking facilities are considered to have been provided where a car dealer provides a car from the car yard to employees for travel to or from work (TD 94/54)
- the employee has a ''primary place of employment'' on that day
- the car is parked at, or in the vicinity of, that primary place of employment. The word ''vicinity'' is a reference to places which are near, meaning in close spatial proximity to each other. Therefore, a car park which was approximately 2 km away from the employee's primary place of employment was not near, proximate or close to that place (*Virgin Blue Airlines*)
- the car is used on that day by the employee to travel between the employee's place of residence and primary place of employment, and
- the provision of car parking facilities is not exempted by regulation (¶35-254).

The Commissioner's views on the car parking benefit provisions are contained in *Draft*TR 2019/D5 which, when finalised, will apply to benefits provided from 1 April 2021 (deferred for one year as a result of significant feedback). In TR 2019/D5, the ATO takes the view that a car park that allows all-day parking but charges high fees to discourage such parking can still be considered a commercial parking station, which differs from its previous view contained in (now withdrawn) TR 96/26. For benefits provided before this date, TR 96/26 applies.

Commercial parking station

A ''commercial parking station'' is defined to mean a permanent commercial car parking facility where car parking spaces are available in the ordinary course of business to members of the public for all-day parking on payment of a fee (s 136(1)). A kerbside parking meter does not qualify. ''All-day parking'' is defined to mean the parking of a single car for a continuous period of 6 hours or more in a daylight period (s 136(1)). A fee charged for vehicles entering the parking station from 1.00 pm is not a fee for ''all-day parking'' as it is impossible to park for a continuous period of 6 hours or more during a daylight period on that day as a ''daylight period'' ends before 7.00 pm on that same day (ID 2014/12).

The former view was that a car parking facility that did not have the primary purpose of providing all-day parking (eg parking for short-term shoppers or hotel guests) was not treated as a commercial parking station, nor was a car park that was not operated to make a profit (withdrawn TR 96/26). However, there is no requirement that the parking station be provided principally, or primarily, for use by commuters driving their cars to and from work (*Qantas Airways Limited*). TR 96/26 also stated that car parking facilities that have a primary purpose other than providing all-day parking, that is, one that usually charges penalty rates significantly higher than the rates chargeable for all-day parking at commercial all-day parking facilities, were not commercial parking stations. This view will no longer apply in recognition of the *Qantas* decision.

The current view, in *Draft*TR 2019/D5, is that if a car park allows all-day parking but its fee structure discourages it with higher fees, the car park can still be considered a commercial parking station if it satisfies other requirements. This is because the parking facility makes car parking spaces available to the public for all-day parking, on payment of a fee.

Car parking fee must be representative

If the fee charged for all-day parking on the first day of the FBT year is not representative, it is to be disregarded for the purposes of deciding whether it exceeds the threshold figure. A fee will not be representative if it is substantially less or more than the average fee charged during the 4-week period either beginning or ending on the first day of the FBT year (whichever period is chosen by the employer).

[AFB ¶53-000, ¶53-030]

¶35-254 Exemptions for certain car parking benefits

Small business employers

An exemption applies to car parking benefits provided in respect of the employment of an employee if all of these conditions are satisfied (s 58GA):

- the car is not parked at a commercial parking station
- the employer is neither a public company nor a subsidiary of a public company on the day on which the benefit is provided
- the employer is not a government body of a state or of a territory

- the employer is either a ''small business entity'' (¶7-050) for the year of income ending before the FBT year or the employer's ordinary and statutory income for the income year ending most recently before the start of the FBT year is less than $10 million (increasing to $50 million from 1 April 2021). The employer's income is calculated on a single entity basis rather than a group basis (ID 2003/25) and on a GST-inclusive basis (ID 2004/935). If the employer did not start to carry out business operations until after the start of the relevant income year, the condition is deemed to be satisfied if the employer makes a reasonable estimate that its ordinary and statutory income for the income year would be less than the threshold amount. Similar rules apply if all of an employer's income is wholly exempt from income tax and the employer did not start to carry out operations or activities until after the start of the income year. If an employer unreasonably estimates that the amount of income would have been less than the threshold, a reasonable estimate may be substituted by the Commissioner. If the Commissioner's estimate is over the threshold, penalty tax may become payable (TAA Sch 1 Pt 4-25).

Residual benefits and certain expense payment benefits

The provision of car parking facilities is exempt from FBT where the benefit is an expense payment fringe benefit (¶35-330) that is not also an ''eligible car parking expense payment benefit'' or where the benefit is a residual fringe benefit (s 58G(1)).

An ''eligible car parking expense payment benefit'' is an expense payment benefit where the recipient is an employee or an associate of an employee, the recipient's expenditure is for the provision of car parking facilities for a car on one or more days and these conditions are satisfied for any of those days:

- the employee had a primary place of employment on that day
- the car was parked at, or in the vicinity of, that primary place of employment for a total period of more than 4 hours between 7 am and 7 pm on that day
- the whole or part of the recipient's expenditure was for the provision of parking facilities to which that parking relates
- the car was used on that day by the employee to travel between the employee's place of residence and that primary place of employment, and
- the provision of car parking facilities was not exempted by regulation (s 136(1)).

Where an employer reimburses an employee for fees incurred to park the employee's car at the local airport while the employee is working interstate at a remote location, the reimbursement constitutes an exempt benefit (ID 2012/18).

Other exempt car parking benefits

Other car parking benefits that are exempt from FBT are:

- benefits provided by certain non-profit bodies (certain scientific institutions, religious institutions, charitable institutions and public educational institutions) (s 58G(2), (3))
- ''minor benefits'' (s 58P; ¶35-645) and
- car parking benefits for disabled persons (FBTAR s 12) or car parking expense payment benefits for disabled persons (FBTAR s 14).

[AFB ¶53-210]

¶35-256 Valuing car parking benefits

The taxable value of a car parking benefit may be ascertained by using one of these methods:

- the commercial parking station method (s 39C)
- the market value method (s 39D)

- the average cost method (s 39DA)
- the statutory formula method (s 39FA), or
- the 12-week register method (s 39GA).

An employer may choose any of the methods for a year in which a car parking fringe benefit arises and, in the case of the commercial parking station, market value or average cost methods, for each such benefit. If the employer elects to use either the statutory formula method or the 12-week register method, the selected method must be used for all benefits covered by the election.

Where a commercial parking station charges a periodic fee for all-day parking, the daily rate necessary for the valuation is ascertained by dividing the total fee by the "business days in period" (s 39E(1)). Business days exclude weekends and public holidays (s 136(1)).

Generally, the taxable value of the benefit is reduced by the employee's contribution. No reduction is made for any amount that would have been deductible, had the expenditure been incurred by the employee.

Anti-avoidance provisions apply where: (a) a transaction between the operator of a commercial parking station and a customer is not at arm's length; and/or (b) the operator sets a level of fee for the sole or dominant purpose of enabling an employer to obtain a reduced taxable value for car parking fringe benefits. In case (a), the fee is assumed to be that which would have been payable if the parties had been dealing at arm's length, and in case (b), the fee is assumed to be the fee that would have been payable if it had been set without that purpose in mind (s 39E(2)).

FBT is payable on the grossed-up taxable value of the benefit (¶35-025).

Commercial parking station valuation method

Under the commercial parking station method of valuation, the taxable value of a car parking fringe benefit on a particular day is the lowest public parking fee charged for any continuous period of 6 daylight hours in the ordinary course of business by any commercial parking station within a one kilometre radius of the relevant business premises or associated premises on which the car is parked (s 39C; ¶35-252). A nil fee cannot be taken into account in determining the lowest fee charged (TR 96/26).

Market value method

The taxable value of a car parking fringe benefit on a particular day, under the market value method of valuation, is the amount that the recipient could reasonably be expected to have been required to pay for the benefit if the provider and the recipient were dealing with each other at arm's length (s 39D).

Under this method, the relevant market value is to be determined by a suitably qualified arm's length valuer and reported to the employer in a form approved by the Commissioner. The employer's FBT return must be based on that report. An employer can elect to use the market value method where the car parking space is located in a commercial car park (*NTLG FBT Sub-committee minutes*, 14 August 2008).

The Commissioner's views on issues concerning the market value method, including: who is a suitably qualified valuer; the relevance of the cost of nearby car parking; and approved forms of valuation, are set out in TR 96/26.

Average cost method

Under the average cost method, the taxable value of the car parking benefit is determined by reference to an average of the lowest fees charged by any operator of a commercial parking station within a one kilometre radius of the employer's premises on particular days, ie the first and last days on which the benefit is provided in the FBT year (s 39DA).

The lowest fee must be representative, ie it must not be substantially greater or lower than the average daily fee charged by an operator 4 weeks before or after the particular day.

Statutory formula method

Under this method, the taxable value of each space for which there is at least one car parking benefit for an employee is calculated by using the formula:

$$\frac{\text{daily rate amount} \times \text{number of days in availability period} \times 228}{366}$$

The ''daily rate amount'' is the value of the benefit provided (ie the space) as determined under the ''average cost method'', ''commercial parking station method'' or ''market value method'', assuming no recipient's contribution (s 39FA).

The total taxable value of the car parking benefits under this method will be the sum of each of the taxable values, reduced by any recipient's contribution. The employer must record the number of car parking spaces available over the FBT year.

Where the average number of employees covered by the election is less than the average number of spaces provided, the taxable value of the benefits is reduced proportionately by a formula set out in s 39FB. In this case, the employer must keep a record of the number of employees and spaces at the beginning and end of the FBT year (TR 96/26). The average number of employees is the number of employees at the beginning plus the number of employees at the end of the relevant period, divided by 2.

▶ Example 1

An employer elects to use the statutory formula method to determine the taxable value of car parking benefits provided to its employees. There are 44 employees at the beginning and 56 at the end of the FBT year, ie an average of 50 ((44 + 56) ÷ 2). The employer provides 60 parking spaces. The benefits are provided for only half the FBT year and the taxable value of each benefit calculated under the ''average cost'' method is $10. The taxable value of one benefit is $1,140, calculated as follows:

$$\$10 \quad \times \quad 228 \quad \times \quad \frac{183}{366}$$

For the 50 employees the total taxable value is $57,000 (ie $1,140 × 60 × 50/60).

The employer may elect to use the statutory formula method, and can choose whether it applies to all or merely some employees.

12-week record-keeping method

Under this method, the total taxable value of car parking benefits provided during the full FBT year is based on the total value of the car parking benefits provided during a 12-week period (s 39GA).

The taxable value of the benefits provided during the 12-week period is determined in accordance with a register which the employer must keep to record the details of the benefits provided in that period. The total taxable value of the benefits for the year is then calculated using the formula:

$$\text{total value of car parking benefits (register)} \times \frac{52}{12} \times \frac{\text{number of days of car parking benefits}}{366}$$

The taxable value of each benefit provided during the 12-week period must be determined in accordance with the commercial parking station method, the market value method or the average cost method (s 39GB).

▶ Example 2

After keeping a register for a 12-week period, an employer determines that 250 car parking benefits, each with a taxable value of $10, have been provided to employees during the 12-week period. Car parking benefits are provided by the employer from 1 October to the end of the FBT year. The total taxable value of the benefits is $5,387.06, calculated as follows:

$$250 \times \$10 \times \frac{52}{12} \times \frac{182}{366}$$

Where this method is used, the 12-week period chosen must be representative of the car parking usage over the year of tax. A new register must be kept after 4 years or in the FBT year following any year in which the number of car spaces (or the number of employees if this is less) increases by more than 10% on any day (eg ID 2007/45).

The register must set out the date on which each car is parked, whether the car is parked for more than 4 hours on that day, whether the car travelled between the place of residence of the relevant employee and the employee's primary place of employment on that day, and the place where the car is parked. Entries in the register must be made as soon as practicable after a vehicle has entered or left the car parking facilities.

Record-keeping requirements

If no election is made to use either the statutory formula or the 12-week record-keeping method, the employer must keep records of the actual usage of car parking spaces and complete a declaration. The declaration must state: (a) the number of car parking spaces available to be used by employees (and their associates); (b) the daily value of those spaces; (c) the number of business days in the year; and (d) the method of valuation chosen by the employer. In addition, the employer may record: (e) the actual number of employees parking on the premises (if always fewer than the number of car parking spaces); (f) the number of parking spaces not occupied for more than 4 hours; and (g) the number of business days when parking spaces were not occupied (eg because members of staff were absent) (TR 96/26). There are commercial solutions available which enable the employer to establish the actual number of car parking benefits provided during the year (CR 2015/2).

[AFB ¶53-310, ¶53-500]

Loan and Debt Waiver Benefits

¶35-270 Loan fringe benefits

A loan benefit arises where a provider (generally the employer) makes a loan to another person called the recipient (generally the employee) (ss 16; 17; 147; 148). Loans include those made by an associate of an employer, or by a third party under an arrangement with an employer, and loans to an associate of an employee, or to some other person at the request of an employee or of an associate of an employee. For examples, see ID 2003/315 and ID 2003/347.

A loan fringe benefit exists in any year in which the recipient is under an obligation to repay the whole or any part of the loan (ie there is a benefit for as long as any part of the loan remains unpaid). A private company loan to a shareholder (who is also an employee) will be deemed to be a dividend and no fringe benefit arises (¶35-120). See also the anti-avoidance rules applying where capital is returned to shareholders (¶4-682) and the rules governing the tax consequences of off-market share buy-backs (¶3-170).

▶ Planning point

The deemed dividend rule is likely to apply if there is no intention to repay the ''loan''. However, it should not apply if the loan is properly documented and complies with the rules concerning minimum interest rate and maximum term. Minimum annual repayments must be made while the loan is outstanding.

A loan includes an advance of money, the provision of credit, the payment of an amount on account of another person where there is some sort of obligation on the person to repay the amount, or any other transaction that in substance effects a loan (s 136(1)). A loan of property is generally valued as a residual benefit. A loan fringe benefit also arises where an employer allows a debt owed by an employee to run past the due date for payment and exists for as long as the debt remains unpaid (s 16(2)).

A loan on which interest accrues, but where the interest is not payable at least every 6 months, gives rise to a new loan of that ''deferred'' interest (s 16(3), (4)). Once interest has accrued for 6 months on such a loan, there is deemed to be a separate and additional interest-free loan of the accrued unpaid interest. Such a new loan arises at the end of each 6-month period and continues until the interest accruing in that 6 months is paid. For example, if interest on a loan is payable every 24 months, there will be 3 deemed loans between one payment of interest and the next payment 24 months later (one lasting 18 months, one 12 months and one 6 months). These provisions do not apply where the original loan is interest-free, or where interest is payable at least every 6 months.

A loan fringe benefit will also arise where a financial institution offers an interest offset arrangement to its employees only, or offers an arrangement that is materially different from that offered to other customers (TR 93/6). Failure to charge a loan establishment fee on a loan provided by a financial institution to an employee does not give rise to a loan fringe benefit, but rather may give rise to a residual benefit (*Westpac*) (¶35-570). An employer's allowing of time for an employee to repay a mistakenly paid amount to which the employee is not legally entitled, but which the employee is obliged to repay, gives rise to a loan benefit (TD 2008/10).

A company that allows its directors to make cash drawings for personal expenses is not necessarily providing loan fringe benefits. What must be established is a sufficient or material (and not merely a causal) connection or relationship between the benefit and employment as a director. An authorisation of a payment by a director is not sufficient to characterise a benefit as one of employment (*J&G Knowles*; *Starrim*).

A loan provided by the trustee of an employee remuneration trust (ERT) to an employee is a fringe benefit if it is made under an arrangement between the trustee and the employee's employer and in respect of the employment of the employee (TR 2018/7). However, if ITAA36 Div 7A (¶4-200) deems the loan to be a dividend (or would so deem a dividend to be paid if the loan did not comply with s 109N) it is not a fringe benefit.

Exempt loan benefits

These loans are exempt from FBT (s 17):

- a loan made by an employer that is a money lender (eg a bank or credit union) to its employees at a commercial rate of interest that is no less than the rate available to the public for the same sort of loan from the employer (TD 95/18)
- a loan to a current employee to meet employment-related expenses that will be incurred within 6 months of the loan (such as a business travel advance) (eg ID 2006/294), and
- a temporary advance by an employer to an employee, to enable the employee to pay security deposits (such as a rental bond or electricity deposit) in connection with temporary accommodation paid for by the employer, is an exempt loan benefit where the need for the accommodation arises from the employment.

[AFB ¶25-000, ¶25-100]

¶35-290 Taxable value of loan fringe benefits

The taxable value of a loan fringe benefit is the difference between a notional amount of interest, calculated on the daily balance of the loan during the year at a statutory interest rate, and any interest actually accruing on the loan (s 18). If the interest actually accruing is at least as great as the notional amount of interest, then the loan benefit has no taxable value. The taxable value is determined by reference to the whole period in the year during which the loan existed (not just the period during which the actual rate was below the statutory rate) (TD 95/17). Subject to the special rules referred to in ¶35-300 about car loans used for income-producing purposes, the general rules dealing with the calculation of the taxable value of loan fringe benefits apply to loans used to purchase any item, including cars. FBT is payable on the grossed-up taxable value of the benefit (¶35-025).

Except for pre-1 July 1986 fixed interest loans and pre-3 April 1986 variable interest housing loans, the statutory interest rate is a benchmark interest rate based on the standard variable rate for owner-occupied housing loans of the major banks, last published by the Reserve Bank of Australia before the commencement of the year of tax (ie 1 April). For the year ended 31 March 2020, it was 5.37% (TD 2019/6); for the year ending 31 March 2021, it is 4.80% (ATO website).

▶ Example

At 1 April 2020, an employee had a loan of $50,000 at 3%. The employee did not repay any principal during the year to 31 March 2021. The actual interest accruing for the year was $1,500 (ie $50,000 × 3%). The notional interest, at the benchmark rate of 4.80%, is $2,400 (ie $50,000 × 4.80%). The difference between the notional amount of interest and the actual amount of interest ($2,400 – $1,500) is $900. This is the taxable value of the loan fringe benefit for the employee for the year. FBT is payable on the grossed-up taxable value, ie $900 × 1.8868 = $1,698.12.

Pre-1 July 1986 fixed interest loans. The statutory interest rate for fixed interest loans made before 1 July 1986 is the lesser of the benchmark rate for the year and the rate specified in the Schedule to the FBTAA for the time when the loan was made. The specified rate for fixed interest loans made before 1 January 1946 is 3.875%. For fixed interest loans made from 1 January 1946 to 30 June 1986, the specified rates are obtained from the Schedule plus the definition of ‘‘benchmark interest rate’’ in s 136(1).

Pre-3 April 1986 variable interest housing loans. For variable interest housing loans made before 3 April 1986, the statutory rate of interest is the lesser of the benchmark rate for the year and 13.5%.

Remote area housing loans. Where a loan is a remote area housing loan (s 142(1)), the taxable value of any loan benefit arising from the loan is reduced by 50% (s 60(1)). As to what is a ‘‘remote area’’, see ¶35-430.

Employee remuneration trust loans. The taxable value of a loan fringe benefit may be reduced by the otherwise deductible rule in s 19 only where (and to the extent) that had the employee incurred interest, it would have been deductible (TR 2018/7). This generally requires the loan to be used for a purpose attended with a reasonable expectation of sufficient income.

[AFB ¶25-200, ¶25-235]

¶35-300 Loan used for income-producing purposes

The taxable value of a loan fringe benefit may be reduced where an employee (but not an associate of an employee) uses all or part of the loan concerned for income-producing purposes (s 19; ¶35-680). The test for whether a reduction of the taxable value is allowable is based on the assumption that the employee was liable for interest on the loan during the year at the statutory rate (¶35-290). On this basis, the amount of the reduction is the amount the employee would have been allowed as a once-only income tax deduction for all or part of the (notional) interest liability. Deductibility is determined on the last day of the FBT year while the loan exists, and on the date of final repayment.

The taxable value of a loan fringe benefit will not be reduced by the premiums on a life assurance policy held by an insurance agent where that policy is required to be held as a condition of the granting of the loan (TD 95/38).

Jointly held assets

Where a benefit is provided jointly to an employee and an associate, the benefit is deemed to have been received solely by the employee (s 138(3); *National Australia Bank*). In that case, an employer provided low interest loans jointly to the employee husband and his wife which were invested in a jointly held investment property. The court held that the employee was the sole recipient of the loan fringe benefit. As sole recipient and sole investor of the proceeds, if the employee husband had incurred and paid unreimbursed interest on the loan, he would have been entitled to a deduction for the expense. Thus, under the otherwise deductible rule, the taxable value of the loan fringe benefit is reduced to nil so that the employer had no FBT liability arising from the loan fringe benefit provided to both the employee and his spouse.

However, the otherwise deductible rule was amended to ensure that the full value of a benefit that has been provided to both an employee and an associate in relation to a jointly held asset or thing (eg a low interest loan related to a rental property) is subject to FBT. This is designed to overcome the decision in the *National Australia Bank case* and reinstate the principle that deductions arising from jointly held assets should be allocated between owners according to their legal interests. The amount of the notional deduction is reduced to reflect the employee's percentage of interest in the income producing asset or thing purchased or paid for using all or part of the loan to which the loan fringe benefit relates.

Loans other than car loans

For a loan other than one used to purchase a car, the starting point for determining the amount of the reduction is to determine the amount of the notional income tax deduction that the employee would have been allowed for the notional interest at the statutory rate during the year. This depends on the deduction provisions of the income tax legislation (¶16-740).

▶ Example 1

Before 1 April 2020, an employee received an interest-free loan of $10,000 from the employer. The loan is available during the whole year to 31 March 2021. The relevant statutory interest rate for the loan is 4.80%. The employee used the loan for 2 purposes: $2,000 for a holiday and $8,000 to buy an income-producing investment. If the employee had paid interest at the statutory rate, 80% of that interest would have been deductible. The amount of the deduction would be:

$$80\% \times (\$10{,}000 \times 4.80\%) = \$384.00.$$

If the employee was, in fact, not liable for any interest on the loan, then the taxable value of the loan fringe benefit would be reduced by the amount of the notional income tax deduction.

▶ Example 2

The taxable value of the loan fringe benefit on the facts set out in the example above would be calculated as follows:

(1) Original taxable value: $\$10{,}000 \times 4.80\% = \$480$.

(2) Reduced taxable value: $\$480 - \$384 = \$96$.

The taxable value of the loan fringe benefit for the year (no input tax credits are applicable) is $96. FBT is payable on the grossed-up taxable value, ie $\$96 \times 1.8868 = \$181.13$.

If the employee was in fact liable for some interest on the loan during the year, then whether the employee is entitled to an income tax deduction for the actual interest depends on whether the employer set the interest rate to reflect the level of income-producing use to which the loan is put (ITAA36 s 51AJ). If the interest rate was not set by reference to the income-producing use, then the amount by which the taxable value of the loan fringe benefit is reduced is the amount of the notional income tax deduction *minus* the amount of the income tax deduction in fact allowable to the employee for the actual interest.

▶ Example 3

If, on the facts set out above, the employee is liable to pay interest at 3%, such rate being set without reference to the level of income-producing use to which the loan is put, the taxable value of the loan fringe benefit would be calculated as follows:

(1)	Original taxable value:	($10,000 × 4.80%) – ($10,000 × 3%) = $180
(2)	Reduced taxable value:	$180 – [($480 × 0.8) – ($300 × 0.8)] = $36

The taxable value of the loan fringe benefit for the year is $36. FBT is payable on the grossed-up taxable value, ie $36 × 1.8868 = $67.92. The employee is entitled to a deduction for 80% × $300 = $240.

If the employer has set an interest rate that reflects the income-producing use to which the loan is put, ie the employer charges an interest rate to reflect the balance of the loan that is used for private purposes, the employee is not allowed an income tax deduction for interest payments which are really for the private portion of the loan (ITAA36 s 51AJ). Instead, the fact that the loan is used partly for income-producing purposes is reflected in a reduction of the taxable value of the loan benefit.

▶ Example 4

Before 1 April 2020, an employer lends an employee $10,000. The loan subsists during the whole year to 31 March 2021. Of the $10,000, $2,000 was used for private purposes and $8,000 was used to purchase equipment used by the employee for employment purposes. The relevant statutory interest rate for the loan is 4.80%. To reflect the level of income-producing use, the employer charges interest at the rate of only 0.96% during the year (ie 20% × 4.80%). If the employee had been liable for interest at the statutory rate, the employee would have been entitled to a deduction of 80% of that interest. The amount of the deduction would be:

80% × ($10,000 × 4.80%) = $384

Because the level of interest reflects the income-producing use to which $8,000 of the loan was put, the employee is not entitled to any deduction for any of the actual interest of 0.96%. The amount by which the taxable value of the loan fringe benefit is reduced is therefore the whole of the notional income tax deduction of $384. The taxable value of the loan fringe benefit would be calculated as follows:

(1) Original taxable value:

Interest at statutory rate, ie $10,000 × 4.80%	$480
Less: interest actually accruing, ie $10,000 × 0.96%	$96
Taxable value	$384

(2) Reduced taxable value: $384 – $384 = nil.

The taxable value of the loan fringe benefit for the year is nil.

Car loans

Where a loan to an employee is used to purchase a car, the deductible percentage of interest depends on the percentage of business use of the car during the year.

The business use percentage of a car needs to be established under the general substantiation rules relating to car benefits (¶35-240), including the keeping of odometer and logbook records (ss 65D to 65F). The employee's loan benefit declaration substantiating the reduction must show that the relevant records have been kept and those records must be given to the employer. Where these rules have been complied with for the relevant year, the value of the loan fringe benefit will be reduced by the appropriate business use percentage.

Alternatively, where odometer records and any necessary logbook records have not been kept, but the employee is able to declare in the loan benefit declaration:

- the total number of kilometres travelled during the relevant period, and
- the percentage of those kilometres that related to business use,

then a reduction of the business proportion will be allowable up to a maximum of one-third.

If the employer charges a lower than normal interest rate on the car loan because of the income-producing use to which the car is put, then any deduction to which the employee would otherwise be entitled in respect of actual interest payments is reduced or eliminated under ITAA36 s 51AJ. That adjustment, combined with the amount allowed as a reduction of the taxable value of the loan benefit, is such that the 2 together account for the appropriate business use percentage.

▶ Example 5

An employer lends an employee $20,000 for the whole year to 31 March 2021 to purchase a car. Business use of the car is 80%. The statutory interest rate is 4.80% and the employer charges 0.96% interest (representing the private component only, ie 20% × 4.80%). The taxable value of the fringe benefit before any reduction would be $768, ie ($20,000 × 4.80%) – ($20,000 × 0.96%).

The notional amount of interest is $960, ie ($20,000 × 4.80%). Therefore the reduction of the taxable value is $768, ie 80% × $960. The taxable value of the loan fringe benefit therefore is nil, ie $768 – $768. No deduction is allowable to the employee for the interest actually paid.

Substantiation of deductibility

To establish that interest would be deductible, the employee must generally complete a loan benefit declaration, showing the uses made of the loan and the percentage of interest for which the employee would have been entitled to an income tax deduction if interest had been paid at the relevant statutory rate.

Where a car loan is involved, the declaration must include additional information relating to odometer records and logbook records for the car and the business use of the car.

A loan benefit declaration is *not* required where:

- the employee used the loan solely to purchase shares in the employer company and held those shares throughout the year concerned while the loan subsisted, or
- the loan consists of a provision of credit to the employee for the purchase of goods or services used exclusively in the employee's employment.

[AFB ¶25-410, ¶25-420, ¶25-510]

¶35-310 Debt waiver fringe benefits

A taxable benefit arises where an employer (or an associate or arranger) releases an employee (or an associate of an employee) from a debt, ie ''waives'' the debt (s 14). The actual waiver must be connected with the employment. A debt waived, for example, for commercial reasons, such as where the employee has no assets and is unable to repay it, would not give rise to a benefit. Where under a commercial loan agreement a lender accepts a transfer of shares in full satisfaction of the loan, there is no waiver (ID 2003/316; ID 2003/317). A debt can be waived before the actual time for payment arises. The taxable value is the amount waived (s 15). FBT is payable on the grossed-up taxable value of the benefit (¶35-025). If the waiver constitutes a fringe benefit, the commercial debt forgiveness provisions (¶16-910) do not apply. A remuneration advance received by an insurance agent and offset against commissions actually earned was assessable income and did not give rise to a debt waiver fringe benefit (*Cohen*).

Where an employer mistakenly pays to their employee an amount that the employee is not legally entitled to but is obliged to repay, the employer's subsequent waiver of that obligation constitutes a ''debt waiver benefit'' provided at the time of the waiver.

However if the employer gives the employee a bonus equal to the amount of the debt outstanding and agrees to set-off this bonus against that debt these actions will not be a debt waiver (TD 2008/11).

A debt that is not waived but remains unpaid gives rise to a loan benefit (¶35-270). The loan benefit remains until the loan is repaid or repayment is waived. Waiver creates a debt waiver benefit.

[AFB ¶28-020, ¶28-210, ¶28-500]

Expense Payment Benefits

¶35-330 Expense payment fringe benefits

An expense payment benefit arises where an employer pays or reimburses expenses incurred by an employee (s 20). A reimbursement giving rise to an expense payment benefit is excluded from the amount subject to PAYG withholding and, as a consequence, does not fall within the definition of "salary or wages" in s 136(1). Where an employee directs the employer to pay part of the agreed salary to a third party (such as a bank by way of loan repayment) the amount remains part of the employee's salary (*Case 1/97*; ID 2002/614). Where an employee sacrifices amounts into a home mortgage account (with or without a redraw facility) under a salary sacrifice arrangement that satisfies TR 2001/10, an expense fringe benefit arises (ID 2001/532). Where an employer reimburses an employee for costs the employee incurs in preparing or administering an employment agreement, the employer is providing a fringe benefit (TR 2000/5).

As with other benefits, an expense payment benefit is a taxable fringe benefit where it has the necessary nexus with the employment relationship (¶35-120; eg ID 2003/836) and is not exempt (¶35-340). The benefit may be provided by an associate of the employer, or by a third party under an arrangement with the employer, as well as by the employer personally. It may also be provided to an associate of an employee, or to some other person at the request of an employee or an associate of an employee, as well as to an employee personally.

A "reimbursement" by an employer of expenses incurred by an employee needs to be distinguished from an "allowance" paid by the employer to the employee (allowances are generally assessable: ¶10-060). A reimbursement seems to require that an employee be compensated exactly for an expense already incurred although not necessarily disbursed (IT 2614; TR 92/15). A payment by an employer in discharge of an employee's income tax liability does not give rise to an expense payment benefit because income tax is not "expenditure incurred", although it may give rise to a residual benefit (*Kumagai Gumi*). For the GST implications, see ATO Fact Sheet *Employee reimbursements and GST* (NAT 7755 at www.ato.gov.au). See also CR 2003/36, CR 2003/111 and CR 2004/44 (payments into an employee's salary packaging payment card account) and ATO Fact Sheet "*Fringe benefits tax and road tolls*".

[AFB ¶30-000]

¶35-340 Specific exemptions for expense payment fringe benefits

Benefits covered by a no-private-use declaration

An expense payment fringe benefit is exempt if it is covered by a no-private-use declaration (s 20A). A no-private-use declaration may be made in respect of expense payment fringe benefits where the employer reimburses only employment-related expenses or where the employer enforces a policy that benefits be used only for employment-related expenses. The declaration must be in the form approved by the Commissioner. The exemption can be relied upon in circumstances where employees travel overseas on business that extends for more than 5 nights and in circumstances where an employer has strict policies in place that the employer will only ever pay for work-related expenses (*NTLG FBT Sub-committee meeting*, 12 August 2010).

Accommodation expenses

An expense payment benefit may be exempt if it relates to expenses that an employee incurs on accommodation. This includes accommodation for any spouse and children normally living with the employee, where the accommodation is required solely because the employee is required to live away from the employee's usual place of residence to carry out employment duties (s 21). See also ID 2001/803.

To qualify for the exemption, the employer must obtain a declaration from the employee on an approved living-away-from-home declaration form stating that the employee had to live away from home for employment reasons, the period involved, the usual place of residence and the actual place of residence during that period.

Car expenses

An expense payment benefit is exempt if it is a reimbursement of the employee for car expenses where the car is owned or leased by the employee, and if the reimbursement is calculated according to the distance travelled (ie on a cents per kilometre basis) (s 22). Relevant car expenses include registration, insurance, repair, maintenance and fuel costs (¶35-230) incurred by the employee (but not by any associate).

The exemption does not apply if the benefit relates to a holiday taken by the employee or if the employment had ceased at the time when the travel occurred. Nor does it apply to benefits to which certain other specific exemptions or concessions apply, ie where the travel relates to relocation, a job interview or work-related medical, counselling or migrant language training purposes (¶35-645). In these situations, the taxable value of the expense payment fringe benefit can be reduced, but the reduction is limited to the amount the employee would have been able to claim based on the applicable cents per kilometre rate (¶16-370) if income tax deductions were claimed for that amount of travel. For the FBT return for the year to 31 March 2021, employers should use the per kilometre rate determined by the Commissioner for the income year ending 30 June 2021.

Where the exemption applies, the relevant payment will be income of the employee (¶10-060), who will have to claim any offsetting deductions and meet the income tax substantiation requirements in so doing (¶16-320).

Car expenses paid by an employer where the employer owns or leases the car are not an expense payment benefit (s 53). They are effectively represented in the value of any resultant car benefit (¶35-150).

[AFB ¶30-100]

¶35-350 Taxable value of expense payment fringe benefits

The taxable value of an expense payment benefit is generally the amount of the expenditure incurred by the employee that is paid or reimbursed by the employer (s 23). FBT is payable on the grossed-up taxable value of the benefit (¶35-025).

The valuation is different where the expenditure to which the benefit relates is incurred:

- in purchasing goods which the employer normally produces for sale to the public, or which the employer purchased for resale to the public (¶35-510), or
- in purchasing a benefit which is similar to benefits which the employer normally supplies to the public (s 22A; ID 2006/197; ¶35-590).

Where the benefit arises from the payment by the employer of a liability incurred by the employee, the taxable value is reduced by any amount that the employee pays to the employer by way of a contribution.

The taxable value of an expense payment benefit may be reduced in a number of situations, eg where the expenditure concerned would have been an income tax deduction for the employee (¶35-360) or where it relates to a living-away-from-home food benefit, residential fuel for remote area housing, remote area residential property, interest on a remote area housing loan, rent for housing in a remote area or remote area holiday transport (¶35-650).

Where an expense payment benefit is provided in connection with remote area residential property (eg the reimbursement of the cost of building a home), the value of the benefit may be spread over the period (generally up to 7 years) of the reimbursement.

[AFB ¶30-200]

¶35-360 Expenditure for tax-deductible purpose

If the employee would have been allowed a once-only income tax deduction for the expenditure had the employer not paid or reimbursed it (eg for the cost of deductible work clothing: TR 97/12), the taxable value of the benefit is reduced accordingly (s 24). The general conditions for this type of reduction are discussed at ¶35-680. For a "once only deduction" to arise, there must be a tax deduction in a year of income in respect of a percentage of that expenditure. Expenditure that is hypothetically affected by the loss deferral rule in ITAA97 s 35-10(2) (¶16-020), ie it would have been disallowed in the year incurred, can never satisfy the above condition and can never give rise to a once only deduction, for the purposes of s 24 (TR 2013/6).

Substantiation of deductibility

In most cases, evidence of the recipient's expenditure is required before any reduction in the taxable value of an expense payment benefit is available. Two types of evidence are normally required— documentary evidence and a declaration.

Neither documentary evidence nor a declaration is necessary for expenditure on food and drink in connection with overtime worked by the employee, or on food, drink or other incidentals in connection with work travel by the employee away from home within or outside Australia (or on accommodation relating to such travel within Australia).

Documentary evidence

The type of documentary evidence required to substantiate a reduction in the taxable value varies. However, to substantiate the amount and nature of expenditure for which an employee would have been entitled to an income tax deduction, the employer must normally obtain documentary evidence of the expenditure from the employee by the time the relevant FBT return is to be furnished. This will usually be the original or a copy of the receipt or invoice. For expense items of less than $10 each, which do not total more than $200 a year for the employee, entries in a petty cash book that set out the particulars that would be set out in documentary evidence of the recipient's expenditure are sufficient. Such petty cash book entries are also sufficient for cases where the nature of the expenditure (such as train fares) would make it unreasonable to expect the employee to obtain documentary evidence.

Declarations

In many cases, an employer must obtain a declaration from the recipient employee in an approved form substantiating the income-producing nature of the recipient's expenditure. The need for, and the contents of, a declaration and the supporting records for it depend on the type of expenditure. Where the general declaration requirement applies, it must describe the expenditure and show the percentage of it that would have been deductible by the employee. An employee receiving a number of similar benefits may make a single declaration (a "recurring fringe benefit declaration").

A general declaration is *not* required where:

- the recipient's expenses (other than interest) are incurred exclusively in gaining salary or wages from the employment to which the expense payment relates
- the recipient's expenditure is on travel within or outside Australia involving more than 5 nights away from home. In this case, the employer must obtain a travel diary from the employee, recording business activities on the trip to substantiate the deductible nature of the expenditure, unless the recipient is a member of a crew on an international airline flight.

  Where a travel diary is required to be kept, the record must be made before, at the time of, or as soon as reasonably practicable after, the conclusion of the activity. The diary entry must contain sufficient detail to give a reasonable guide as to the extent to which the trip was undertaken for deductible purposes (MT 2038)
- the recipient's expenditure is reasonable and is on food or drink relating to overtime work
- the recipient's expenditure is reasonable and is for accommodation, food or drink while travelling away from home within Australia, or for food or drink while travelling outside Australia, in the course of performing employment duties, or
- the recipient's expenditure relates to car expenses (¶35-230).

Car expenses

Special substantiation requirements apply where an employer provides car expense payment benefits in respect of a car owned or leased by the employee. One of the following methods can be used, depending on what records have been maintained.

If odometer records and (where necessary) logbook records have been kept properly (¶35-240), then the benefit value will be reduced by the appropriate business use percentage established by those records. The employee must also make a declaration substantiating the reduction on an approved form.

Alternatively, where odometer records and any necessary logbook records have not been kept, but the employee is able to declare:

- the total number of kilometres travelled during the relevant period, and
- the percentage of those kilometres that related to business use,

the taxable value of the benefit is reduced on the basis of a car business percentage (up to 33¹/3%) estimated by the employer.

[AFB ¶30-400, ¶30-440, ¶30-500]

Housing Benefits

¶35-380 Housing fringe benefits

A housing fringe benefit arises where an employer grants an employee a ''housing right'' — a right to occupy or use a unit of accommodation as a usual place of residence — which must be for more than one day (s 25; 149). The right to occupy may be under a lease or licence, either formal or informal. It may cover any type of accommodation, as long as it is the employee's usual place of residence — house, flat, unit, hotel, motel, guesthouse, bunkhouse, ship, oil rig, caravan or mobile home. If the accommodation is not the employee's usual place of residence, the benefit will not be a housing benefit but will be a residual benefit subject to the rules discussed at ¶35-570. The right can include the provision of water under the tenancy agreement (ID 2005/158).

As with other benefits, a housing benefit is a taxable fringe benefit where it has the necessary nexus with the employment relationship (¶35-120). The benefit may be provided by an associate of the employer or by a third party under an arrangement with the employer, as well as by the employer personally. It may also be provided to an associate of an employee or to some other person at the request of an employee or an associate of an employee, as well as to an employee personally. Where an employee has been previously granted a housing right, but is unable to continue to occupy the house as it has been destroyed in a natural disaster, a housing fringe benefit no longer exists from the date the house was destroyed (ID 2011/57).

Exemption for live-in carers

Where an employee of a government, religious institution or non-profit body lives, together with persons who are elderly (ie aged over 60), or who are mentally or physically handicapped or in necessitous circumstances, in residential premises of the employer, any benefit which arises is exempt (s 58). The exemption extends to the spouse and children of the employee, and covers the supply of electricity and gas, as well as accommodation.

The benefit may also be exempt if the employer of the employee providing the live-in help is a natural person (s 58U), or if the employer of a live-in domestic worker is a religious institution or religious practitioner (s 58T).

[AFB ¶35-000, ¶35-100]

¶35-400 Taxable value of housing fringe benefits

The valuation rules applying to a housing fringe benefit depend on whether the accommodation is outside Australia, in a non-remote part of Australia (¶35-420) or in a remote area of Australia (¶35-430).

The starting point for most calculations is the market value of the accommodation in the first year. In determining the market value of the right to occupy accommodation, any associated expenses of the occupant that might be paid by another person are disregarded, as are any onerous conditions attached to the occupation and relating to the employee's employment (s 27(1), (2)). Acceptable standard values and discounts for various types of accommodation and situations are set out in MT 2025.

Accommodation outside Australia

If the accommodation is outside Australia, or in an external territory, the taxable value of the housing benefit will be the market value of the accommodation for the time it is occupied during the year, less any rent or other consideration paid (s 26(1)(a)).

[AFB ¶35-200]

¶35-420 Non-remote area accommodation

If the accommodation is in Australia and is not in a remote area, the taxable value of the housing fringe benefit depends on the type of accommodation.

If the accommodation is in a hotel, motel, hostel, guesthouse, caravan or mobile home and the provider is in the business of providing similar benefits to the public, the taxable value of the housing fringe benefit is either:

- if the provider is not the employer, the market value of the accommodation *less* any rent paid (s 26(1)(b)), or
- if the provider is the employer, 75% of the amount that the public would pay *less* any rent paid.

For any other type of accommodation in a non-remote area, the taxable value is the "statutory annual value" of the right to occupy the accommodation (s 26(1)(c)). This is reduced proportionately where the housing right does not exist for the whole year. Any rent paid by the employee is subtracted. Rent would include an amount paid to make a property habitable (*Case 28/97*).

In the first year in which the accommodation is used to provide a housing fringe benefit, the statutory annual value is the market value of the right to occupy the accommodation for a year (s 26(2)(a)).

In subsequent years, the market value may be used again, and it must be used where there is a break of at least a year in which the accommodation does not give rise to a housing benefit for any employee or where a material alteration to the accommodation results in an increase or decrease in the market value of at least 10% (s 26(3) to (6)). Alternatively, the most recently determined market value for a preceding year is simply indexed according to movements since that year in the Consumer Price Index (CPI) rent sub-group for the capital city of the state or territory in which the accommodation is situated (s 26(2)(b)).

For accommodation being valued by the CPI method for the year ending 31 March 2021, the indexation factors are (ATO website):

NSW	Vic	Qld	SA	WA	Tas	ACT	NT
1.000	1.017	1.002	1.010	0.969	1.056	1.029	0.948

For the year ended 31 March 2020, the indexation factors were (TD 2019/5):

NSW	Vic	Qld	SA	WA	Tas	ACT	NT
1.020	1.019	0.997	1.008	0.937	1.043	1.028	0.948

If the indexation method is used, then the actual market value must be redetermined at least each tenth year (s 26(3)(c)).

[AFB ¶35-230, ¶35-240, ¶35-277]

¶35-430 Remote area accommodation

A remote area housing benefit is an exempt benefit (s 58ZC). A "housing benefit" arises where an employee is granted a right to occupy, as a usual place of residence, a unit of accommodation provided by an employer (s 25).

Four conditions must be satisfied for the remote area housing exemption to apply.

- The accommodation must be located in a remote area, ie not in, or adjacent to, an "eligible urban area". An eligible urban area is generally defined (s 140(1)) as a town or city with a 1981 census population of at least 14,000 (or 28,000 if in Zone A or Zone B for income tax purposes). A location is "adjacent to" an eligible urban area if it is less than 40 km by the shortest practicable surface route from the centre point of an eligible urban area with a 1981 census population of less than 130,000, or is less than 100 km from an eligible urban area with a census population of 130,000 or more. A list of relevant towns is available on the ATO website at *Remote areas*.

  Accommodation located at least 100 km from a town with a census population of 130,000 or more is treated as being in a remote area if the employer is the police service, a charitable institution, a hospital carried on by a non-profit society or association, a public hospital, or a public ambulance service.

Where the shortest practicable route involves travel solely over water, the total kilometres of the surface route that are by water are doubled for the purposes of determining whether the location is remote. Where the shortest practicable route involves travel over both land and water, the total number of kilometres by water are doubled and added to the total number of kilometres by land.

- The recipient of the benefit must be employed by the employer for the whole tenancy period and the employee's usual place of employment must not have been at a location in or adjacent to an eligible urban area during that period.
- It must be necessary for the employer to provide free or subsidised accommodation to employees for any of these reasons:
  - the employees are likely to move frequently from one residential location to another because of the nature of the employer's business
  - there is not sufficient suitable accommodation otherwise available in the employment area, or
  - it is customary in the employer's industry to provide free or subsidised housing to employees.
- The arrangement must be an arm's length arrangement and not entered into for the purpose of gaining the s 58ZC exemption concessions. See ID 2010/183, ID 2005/156, ID 2002/412, ID 2001/761.

The Commissioner has a discretion to treat a person who resides in an area adjacent to an eligible urban area as residing outside that area if persons who live nearby are outside that area.

For other remote area concessions, see ¶35-650.

[AFB ¶35-220]

Living-away-from-home Allowance Benefits

¶35-460 Living-away-from-home allowance benefits

A living-away-from-home allowance (LAFHA) benefit arises where an employer pays an employee an allowance to compensate for additional expenses or disadvantages suffered because the employee (with or without family) has to live away from home for employment purposes (s 30(1)). A LAFHA benefit cannot be paid by an associate of an employer or by a third party, or paid to an associate of an employee. Where a LAFHA falls within s 30(1), it cannot be assessable income of the taxpayer and expenses incurred by the taxpayer for accommodation and food are not deductible (*Hancox*).

"Additional expenses" do not include expenses for which the employee would be entitled to an income tax deduction (*Roads and Traffic Authority of NSW*; *Draft* TR 2017/D6). An allowance to compensate only for "other additional disadvantages" without some clear connection with likely additional expenses will not be a taxable fringe benefit (*Atwood Oceanics Australia*; TD 94/14). For example, a location allowance will generally not be a LAFHA but is assessable income of the employee (TD 94/14). A "hardlying" allowance paid to a seaman in relation to the standard of and requirement to share accommodation on board ship was an assessable allowance and not a LAFHA (*Best*; *Crane*). See also ID 2002/232 (sleepover allowance paid to a disabilities support worker). For the distinction between a LAFHA and a travelling allowance, see *Hancox*.

A LAFHA benefit may also arise where an employee works on an oil or gas rig at sea with accommodation provided at or near the worksite (including on a drill ship), and an allowance is paid to compensate the employee for the additional disadvantages of having to live away from the employee's usual place of residence (s 30(2); for an example, see ID 2005/314; *Case* 3/2007).

One of the conditions for a LAFHA is that employees must live away from their usual place of residence. These employees are normally required to live away from home:

- construction workers living in camps, barracks or huts
- oil industry employees living on offshore oil rigs
- marine industry employees living on board vessels
- trainee employees (eg trainee teachers) living away from home in order to undergo extended training courses.

Transitory workers, such as those who follow construction work around, and employees regularly required to transfer (eg police officers, school teachers and bank employees), are not regarded as living away from home. However, an employee may be regarded as living away from home when transferred overseas or interstate for a limited period and expected to return home. As a general rule, an allowance paid for up to 21 days will be treated as a travelling allowance and not as a LAFHA (ATO's Fringe benefits tax — a guide for employers at 11.12).

In addition to living away from their usual place of residence, in order to qualify for a LAFHA, employees must be required to do so. In *Compass Group*, an employee who lived about 60 km from his place of employment was not required to reside in accommodation closer to his work in order to carry out his employment duties. In that case, the allowance he was paid by his employer to compensate him for so doing did not constitute a LAFHA, despite the fact that he was living away from his usual place of residence.

[AFB ¶40-000]

¶35-470 Taxable value of living-away-from-home allowance fringe benefit

The taxable value of a LAFHA fringe benefit in a year of tax is the amount of the fringe benefit reduced by any exempt accommodation component and any exempt food component, provided the employee satisfies all of the following for the fringe benefit and the period to which it relates (s 31):

(a) the requirement to maintain an Australian home (s 31C — see below)

(b) the requirement that the fringe benefit relates only to all or part of the first 12 months that the duties of that employment require the employee to live away from home (s 31D — see below), and

(c) the declaration requirements (s 31F — see below).

This also applies to LAFHA benefits provided to fly-in fly-out (FIFO) and drive-in drive-out (DIDO) employees, provided they satisfy (s 31A):

(a) the requirement that the employee has residential accommodation at or near his/her usual place of employment

(b) the fly-in fly-out and drive-in drive-out requirements (s 31E — see below), and

(c) the declaration requirements (s 31F — see below).

In any other case, taxable value of the fringe benefit in relation to the year of tax is the amount of the fringe benefit (s 31B).

Substantiation

The exempt accommodation and food components must be substantiated (s 31G). However, where the total does not exceed the amount the Commissioner considers reasonable, those expenses do *not* have to be substantiated. TD 2020/4 sets out the amounts that the Commissioner considers reasonable for the FBT year that commenced on 1 April 2020; the amounts for the FBT year that commenced on 1 April 2019 are in TD 2019/7.

Reasonable amounts for food and drink — within Australia

The reasonable food and drink amounts for locations within Australia per week are:

	2020–21 per week	2019–20 per week
One adult	$276	$269
2 adults	$414	$404
3 adults	$552	$539
One adult and one child	$345	$337
2 adults and one child	$483	$472
2 adults and 2 children	$552	$540
2 adults and 3 children	$621	$608
3 adults and one child	$621	$607
3 adults and 2 children	$690	$675
4 adults	$690	$674

An ''adult'' is a person who was aged 12 before the beginning of the FBT year. For larger family groups for the 2020–21 FBT year, the Commissioner accepts the reasonable food and drink amount based on the above figures plus $138 for each additional adult and $69 for each additional child ($135 and $68 for the 2019–20 FBT year).

Reasonable amounts for food and drink — overseas

These determinations also set out the amounts the Commissioner considers to be reasonable food and drink amounts for a LAFHA paid to employees living away from home outside Australia for the relevant FBT years, covering approximately 150 countries and assigning each to one of 6 ''cost groups'' to determine the reasonable amount. For further details, see the text of the determinations.

Maintaining a home in Australia

An employee is considered to be maintaining a home in Australia if the place where the employee usually resides in Australia is a unit of accommodation in which the employee or his/her spouse has an ownership interest and it continues to be available for the employee's immediate use during the period that the employee is required to live away from it (s 31C). In addition, it must be reasonable to expect that the employee will resume living at that place when the period ends.

12-month period

Section 31D is satisfied if the fringe benefit relates only to all or part of the first 12 months that the duties of that employment require the employee to live away from the employee's usual place of residence. However, the 12-month period may be paused by the employer. Further, a separate 12-month period may be started if the employer later requires the employee to live at a different location and it would be unreasonable to expect the employee to commute to the new location from an earlier location. Other changes in the nature of the employee's employment are irrelevant and employers and their associates are treated as if they are one employer.

Fly-in fly-out and drive-in drive-out employees

The s 31E requirements for fly-in fly-out and drive-in drive-out employees are that:

- the employee, on a regular and rotational basis, works for a number of days and has a number of days off and, on completion of the working days, the employee travels from the usual place of employment to his/her normal residence and, on completion of the days off, returns to that usual place of employment
- it is customary for such arrangements to exist for employees performing similar duties in the industry
- it would be unreasonable to expect the employee to travel on a daily basis on work days between the place of employment and residence, and
- it is reasonable to expect the employee will resume living at his/her normal residence when his/her duties no longer require him/her to live away from it.

These requirements are not satisfied where an employee works for 5 and half days and remains on call on the seventh day (ID 2013/43).

Declarations

Where the employee maintains an Australian home, the employee is required to give the employer a declaration that sets out the address of that home, the fact that s 31C is satisfied in relation to that home, and the places where the employee actually resided during the period he/she was required to live away from that home.

A fly-in fly-out or drive-in drive-out employee is required to give the employer a declaration that sets out the address of the employee's usual place of residence, that it is reasonable to expect the employee will resume living at his/her normal residence when his/her duties no longer require him/her to live away from it, and the places where the employee actually resided during the period he/she was required to live away from home.

The declaration must be given to the employer before the lodgment date of the return, or such later date as the Commissioner allows, in the approved form.

[AFB ¶40-310, ¶40-362, ¶40-502]

Property Benefits

¶35-490 Property fringe benefits

A property benefit arises where one person provides property to another person (s 40). This applies to all types of property, both tangible and intangible, such as goods, real property, shares, other securities or rights and bitcoin (TD 2014/28). It also covers gas and electricity which is not reticulated (provision of reticulated gas and electricity is a residual benefit: ¶35-570). Property benefit also covers the payment of money, other than salary or wages, by an employer to the trustee of a trust in respect of the employment of an employee (*Walstern*; *Caelli Constructions*; ID 2007/204). The issue of bonus units to employees who enter into certain employee benefits trust arrangement may be treated as the provision of a property fringe benefit (TR 2010/6). The transfer from the employer capital/unallocated trust capital account to the employee's bonus unit account may be treated as a property fringe benefit or a residual fringe benefit (¶35-570). The payment of a marginally higher than market rate of interest by the employer to an employee/investor does not have the required connection with employment and is not a fringe benefit (ID 2003/688).

Property is generally "provided" when ownership passes. However, where a person has the use of property before title passes, the property is deemed to be provided at the time of obtaining use of the property (s 155(1)). If title never passes, then there is deemed never to have been a property benefit and any assessment made in the meantime can be amended at any time (s 155(2)). There would instead be a residual benefit from the use of the property. Where a person does anything that results in the creation of property in another person, such as the issue of shares by a company, the property is provided when it comes into existence (s 154).

[AFB ¶45-000, ¶45-500]

¶35-500 Property provided on work premises

Goods supplied to, and consumed by, an employee on a working day and on the employer's premises, or on premises of a related company, are an exempt property benefit (s 41). Examples are a daily ration of beer consumed by brewery workers at work and morning and afternoon teas provided to employees (IT 2675), as well as hand-food and non-elaborate meals provided on the employer's premises through a dining card facility (CR 2005/89; CR 2006/81) but not a massage voucher (ID 2005/109).

Food or drink provided as part of a salary sacrifice arrangement (eg a meal card) is excluded from the exemption. The exemption also does not apply to food or drink provided to an employee where:

- an employee has agreed to receive the food or drink in return for a reduction in the employee's entitlement to receive salary or wages and this would not have happened apart from the agreement, or
- it is reasonable to conclude that the employee's salary or wages would be greater if the food or drink were not provided as part of the employee's remuneration package.

This type of agreement or arrangement includes arrangements whereby an employee forgoes salary and wages to have food and drink supplied to them on their employer's premises. The exclusion does not apply to a subsidised canteen which is available to all employees and which does not form part of a salary sacrifice arrangement. Under such arrangements, an employer pays for an employee's meals which have been provided by an independent caterer located on, or the independent caterer delivers to, the employer's premises.

[AFB ¶45-110]

Taxable Value of Property Fringe Benefits

¶35-510 Valuation rules for property fringe benefits

There are different rules for valuing property fringe benefits, depending on whether the concession for ''in-house'' benefits applies.

Non-concessional rules

Except where the concessional rules for in-house benefits apply, the taxable value of a property fringe benefit is generally the amount by which the arm's length cost of the goods to the employer exceeds the price charged to the employee (¶35-530). FBT is payable on the grossed-up taxable value of the benefit (¶35-025).

In-house benefits

Concessional valuation rules apply where the benefit is an in-house benefit (¶35-520). An ''in-house property fringe benefit'' is one provided in respect of tangible property where:

- the employer or an associate (not a third party) provides the benefit, and the property is of a sort normally sold as part of the provider's business, or

- a third party provides the property, after acquiring it from the employer or an associate of the employer, and the property is of a sort normally sold by both the provider and the person from whom it is acquired as part of their businesses (s 136(1)).

"Tangible property" means goods and includes animals, gas and electricity. It does not include real property (ID 2004/211), gift cards (ID 2010/135) or a payment of money (ID 2010/151). When a retail store employer provides an employee with a voucher/coupon, entitling the employee to merchandise from the store, the employer provides the employee with an in-house property fringe benefit only when the employee redeems the voucher/coupon for merchandise (ID 2014/17).

The concessional valuation rules extend to cases where, rather than being directly provided with in-house property, the employee purchased the property and the employer either paid the bill or reimbursed the employee for the cost. It does not matter whether the employee purchased the property from the employer, an associate or a third party supplier. Although the benefit in these cases is an expense payment benefit, it is valued under the concessional rules applying to in-house property (¶35-350). The only special rules to be taken into account are:

- the employee must obtain a receipt or invoice from the supplier and give it to the employer, and

- any amount paid to the supplier by the employee and not reimbursed is treated as a contribution for the benefit by the employee and deducted from the taxable value of the property.

Where employee could have obtained deduction

Where there is a property fringe benefit and the employee could have obtained a once-only income tax deduction for all or part of the expenditure on the property (such as the cost of deductible work clothing: TR 97/12), the taxable value of the benefit is reduced accordingly (s 44). For details of the reduction, see ¶35-680. For example, light lunches provided by a computer training company to its trainers as part of the conduct of the training courses were property benefits subject to the "otherwise deductible rule" which reduced the taxable value of the benefit (*Pollak Partners*). Generally, the value of the benefit is reduced by the same amount as the amount that would have been allowed as an income tax deduction to the employee. Where the employee would have received only a partial deduction, the value of the benefit is reduced only by that partial amount.

[AFB ¶45-200]

¶35-520 Valuing in-house property benefits

There are 2 sets of rules for valuing in-house benefits, depending on who provided the property and the activities of that person.

Property produced for sale

Where the property is provided by an employer or associate, and that person manufactures, produces, processes or treats the type of property concerned, the valuation rules are as follows:

- If the goods are identical to goods normally sold by the employer to manufacturers, wholesalers or retailers, the taxable value of the benefit is the amount by which the employer's lowest arm's length selling price exceeds the amount, if any, paid by the employee.

- If the goods are identical to goods normally sold by the employer to the public by retail, the taxable value of the benefit is the amount by which 75% of the lowest price charged to the public exceeds the amount, if any, paid by the employee.

- Where the goods are similar, but not identical, to those sold by the employer (eg "seconds"), the taxable value of the benefit is 75% of the amount which the employee could be expected to pay for the goods at arm's length, less the amount, if any, paid by the employee (s 42(1)(a)).

Property purchased for resale

Where the property was acquired by the provider, and is of a sort that the person would normally sell in the course of business, the taxable value of the benefit is the arm's length price paid by that person less the amount, if any, paid by the employee (s 42(1)(b)).

If the goods have lost value (eg through obsolescence or deterioration), the taxable value is the amount the employee would have paid for them at arm's length if that is less than the employer's purchase price.

Arm's length price

Where the property is acquired by the provider of the benefit in the ordinary course of business under an arm's length transaction (s 42(2)(a)), the arm's length price is the "cost price" of the property, ie the expenditure that is directly attributable to purchasing or obtaining delivery of the property (s 136(1)). Where the property is either not acquired in the ordinary course of business or is not acquired in an arm's length transaction, the arm's length price is the amount the provider could reasonably be expected to pay for the property if the acquisition had been in the ordinary course of business under an arm's length transaction (s 42(2)(b)). An arm's length transaction is a transaction in relation to which the parties are dealing with each other at arm's length (s 136(1)).

Airline transport benefits

The taxable value of airline transport benefits is calculated as 75% of the stand-by airline travel value of the benefit, less the employee contribution. Where the transport is on a domestic route, the stand-by airline travel value is 50% of *the* carrier's lowest standard single economy airfare for that route as publicly advertised during the year of tax. Where the transport is on an international route, the stand-by airline travel value is 50% of the lowest of *any* carrier's standard single economy airfare for that route as publicly advertised during the year of tax.

An airline transport benefit is taxed as an in-house property fringe benefit to the extent that the benefit includes the provision of transport in a passenger aircraft operated by a carrier (including any related incidental services on board the aircraft) and is subject to the stand-by restrictions that customarily apply in the airline industry.

Additional concession

For in-house benefits, including in-house property benefits valued under any of the above rules, there is a general exemption for the first $1,000 of the taxable value for each recipient employee each year (¶35-660).

Removal of concessional treatment if accessed through a salary packaging arrangement

The concessional treatment for in-house fringe benefits is removed if they are accessed by way of a salary packaging arrangement; instead, the taxable value of the benefit is based on the "notional value" of the benefit. A "salary packaging arrangement" is an arrangement under which a benefit is provided to an employee if:

(a) the benefit is provided in return for the employee agreeing to a reduction in salary or wages that would not have happened apart from the arrangement, or

(b) the arrangement is part of the employee's remuneration package, and the benefit is provided in circumstances where it is reasonable to conclude that the employee's salary or wages would be greater if the benefit were not provided.

Additionally, the exemption that applies for residual benefits that are provided for transport from home to work for employers in the transport business is removed where it is accessed through a salary packaging arrangement. The annual $1,000 reduction of aggregate taxable value in respect of in-house fringe benefits is also removed where they are provided under a salary packaging arrangement.

▶ Example (from the EM to Tax Laws Amendment (2012 Measures No 6) Bill 2012)

Cecilia works for an appliance rental franchise and, as part of her remuneration, she agreed to salary package the rental of a flat screen television and video gaming console for a six-month period. Ordinarily her employer would value the rental for the purposes of FBT at 75% of the lowest price paid by other customers. However, under this measure, the employer would instead determine the taxable value on the basis of its notional value which is its market value and is therefore determined to be the retail price of the rental contract.

[AFB ¶45-230]

¶35-530 Valuing general property benefits

For property fringe benefits to which the in-house concessions (¶35-520) do not apply, the taxable value of the benefit is generally the arm's length cost of the property to the employer, less the amount, if any, paid by the employee (s 43). Where this is not appropriate, the Commissioner will accept the lowest value obtained using these valuation methods (TD 93/231):

- the price of comparable goods advertised in local newspapers or relevant magazines or similar publications
- the price paid for comparable goods at a public auction
- the price of comparable goods at a secondhand store
- the market value of the goods determined by a qualified valuer.

The Commissioner will *not* accept a value determined using the tax written down value or the "best offer" made by an employee (TD 93/231). Following the decision in *Granby*, the Commissioner has accepted that a residual value nominated in a lease may be used where the parties are actually at arm's length (TD 95/63). Accordingly, where an employer has an arm's length finance lease of a car which is later acquired at its residual value and on-sold to an employee at the residual value specified in the lease, no FBT will be payable. For the minimum residual values required by the Commissioner for income tax purposes, see ¶16-310.

Where the employee obtains property from a third party at arm's length under an arrangement by which the employer pays for the property (eg where the employee uses a credit card provided by the employer), the taxable value of the benefit is the expenditure incurred by the employer less the amount, if any, paid by the employee (s 150).

If the employer paid less than market price for the property (such as where a manufacturer provides a "free" item with a large order), the taxable value is the notional market price less the amount, if any, paid by the employee.

In the case of a remote area housing scheme, where the employer sells a house at a discount to an employee or pays an option fee to the employee for the right to purchase the house, the value of the benefit is spread over the period it is enjoyed, rather than being taxed "up-front" as a lump sum. In most cases, the value of the benefit is spread over a 7-year period, but in limited cases a 15-year amortisation period may apply (s 65CA).

Where an employer made contributions to a redundancy fund (*Caelli Constructions*) and to a superannuation fund (*Walstern*), the taxable value of the benefit was the amount of the employer's contributions. The value of the property benefit (shares) provided by a company to 2 key employees was the amount of the premium allocated to each employee (*Experienced Tours*).

[AFB ¶45-310]

Residual Benefits

¶35-570 Residual fringe benefits

Any fringe benefit not covered by any other valuation rules is treated as a residual fringe benefit.

The only criteria are that there must be something that can be identified as a benefit, and the necessary employment relationship must exist to make the benefit a fringe benefit (¶35-060). The benefit may be provided by the employer, an associate of the employer, or by a third party under an arrangement with the employer or an associate of the employer. The benefit may be provided to an employee, an associate of an employee, or to some other person at the request of an employee or an associate of an employee.

Examples of residual benefits are free or discounted services, such as travel or the performance of work, the use of property, the provision of insurance coverage (eg CR 2004/113 and CR 2005/103), the provision of vehicles that are not cars (eg vehicles designed to carry more than one tonne or 9 or more passengers, hire cars, and e-bikes: CR 2015/80) and use of a travel smartcard provided by the employer (CR 2016/58). Specifically, the provision of reticulated gas or electricity is a residual benefit (s 156), as is the provision of a car used for taxi travel, rental car or motor cycle (¶35-150). Where the provision of a taxi by an employer gives rise to a taxable benefit, the value of the benefit is the amount paid to the taxi operator and does not include any additional service charges (eg Cabcharge) referable to the taxi fare (*National Australia Bank*). A free loan establishment service provided by a bank to an employee, being a service for which the bank charges customers, gives rise to a residual benefit (*Westpac Banking Corporation*), as does the provision of investment services, chauffeur services (ID 2003/498) and the use of the employer's electronic road toll tag. In *Kumagai Gumi Co*, the payment by a foreign company of the Australian income tax liabilities of Japanese executives transferred to Australia gave rise to a residual fringe benefit.

In cases where property is provided at the same time as a residual benefit (eg spare parts are provided when a television set is repaired), the 2 benefits are treated as one residual benefit if the provider is in the business of supplying such goods and services (s 153). If the goods are supplied by one provider and the services by another, the 2 types of benefit are valued separately.

A residual benefit generally arises at the time when the benefit is provided. If the benefit is provided over a period, such as where an employee has the use of property for a period of time, the benefit arises during that period (s 149(1)). If the period straddles more than one FBT year, the benefit is taxable on a proportional basis in each year (s 46(1)).

In some cases, the benefit arises when the time for payment for the benefit is due (s 46(2)). This is where:

- the benefit is a continuing one which would normally be billed on a regular basis, and
- the same services are provided to members of the public in the ordinary course of the employer's business.

For example, where electricity or gas is supplied at a discounted rate with quarterly billing periods, a benefit will arise at each quarterly payment due date rather than over the period of the quarter. This can affect the year into which the benefit will fall — where the period of supply spans the end of one tax year and the beginning of the next, the benefit falls into the year in which the payment due date occurs, rather than being spread over the 2. This does not apply where the benefit arises from a lease or licence of property. In that case the benefit is provided over the whole of the relevant period (s 149(2)).

[AFB ¶50-000]

¶35-580 Exempt residual benefits

A number of residual benefits are specifically exempted from tax (s 47). These can be summarised as:

- free or discounted transport (not air transport) provided to current employees in the course of the employer's business of providing such transport to the public (s 47(1))
- certain recreational or child care facilities for the benefit of employees (such facilities being located on the "business premises of the employer") (s 47(2)) and certain contributions to secure priority of access to child care facilities (eg ID 2012/58) (s 47(8)). "Recreational facility" includes general attendance or reserved seating at a sporting event organised by the employer on its business premises. The exemption may apply to the provision of gym facilities (CR 2015/9) but not fitness classes (ID 2015/25)
- the use by an employee of an employer's equipment that is ordinarily located on the business premises (other than a motor vehicle) (s 47(3))
- "work-related" use, and other minor, infrequent and irregular private use, of vehicles not being "cars" (the same as the exemption applying to work-related and other minor private use of commercial vehicles: ¶35-160, particularly PCG 2018/3) (s 47(6), eg use of a bus is exempt (ID 2001/313; CR 2017/35) but not a tram (ID 2010/163))
- private use of an unregistered motor vehicle (one which cannot be legally driven on a public road) which is used principally for business purposes (s 47(6A))
- transport provided under certain "fly-in fly-out" travel arrangements for employees in designated remote areas or working on oil rigs and other off-shore installations (TD 95/49) (s 47(7))
- living-away-from-home accommodation provided to employees who are required for work purposes to live away from their usual place of residence and who satisfy the requirements in ¶35-470 (*Draft* TR 2017/D6) (s 47(5)). For the meaning of "usual place of residence", see CR 2003/19 and Ch 11 of the ATO's "Fringe benefits tax — a guide for employers".

The exemption of contributions to secure priority of access to child care facilities must relate to:

- a child care facility run by an eligible organisation under the *Child Care Act 1972*, or
- an approved centre-based long day care service, family day care service, outside school hours care service or in-home care service, within the meaning of *A New Tax System (Family Assistance) (Administration) Act 1999*, Pt 8 Div 1.

A residual fringe benefit covered by a "no-private-use declaration" is exempt. This declaration can be made where a benefit is covered by a consistently enforced policy that it is provided only for employment-related purposes (s 47A).

The term ‘‘business premises of the employer’’ was considered by the Federal Court in *Esso Australia*. The court held that the employer does not have to have exclusive proprietary or occupancy rights in respect of the premises and may hold the premises jointly with other employers. Reference should also be made to TR 2000/4 on the meaning of ‘‘business premises’’.

[AFB ¶50-100]

¶35-590 Taxable value of residual benefits

In-house residual benefits

Concessional valuation rules apply where the benefit is an ‘‘in-house residual fringe benefit’’. This is one where:

- the employer or an associate (not a third party) provided the benefit, and the benefit was of a kind normally provided to the public as part of the provider’s business, or
- a third party provided the benefit, after acquiring it from the employer or an associate of the employer, and the benefit was of a kind normally provided by both the provider and the employer, or the associate, as part of their businesses (s 136(1)).

A benefit provided under a contract of investment insurance is expressly excluded from the definition of in-house residual fringe benefit.

The concessional valuation rules extend to cases where, rather than being directly provided with an in-house residual benefit, the employee acquired it and the employer either paid the bill or reimbursed the employee for the cost. It does not matter whether the employee acquired the benefit from the employer, an associate or a third party supplier. Although the benefit in these cases is an expense payment benefit, it is valued under the concessional rules applying to in-house residual benefits (¶35-350). The only special rules to be taken into account are:

- the employee must obtain a receipt or invoice from the supplier and give it to the employer, and
- any amount paid to the supplier by the employee and not reimbursed is treated as a contribution for the benefit by the employee and deducted from the taxable value.

The taxable value of an in-house residual fringe benefit is generally 75% of the lowest price charged to the public for the same type of benefit, less any amount actually paid for the benefit (s 48; 49). If the benefit is similar, but not identical, to benefits provided to the public, the taxable value is 75% of the amount that would reasonably be paid at arm’s length for the benefit, *less* any amount actually paid by the employee. For examples, see ID 2004/487, ID 2008/30, ID 2012/85 and ID 2012/86.

Airline transport benefits

The taxable value of airline transport benefits is calculated as 75% of the stand-by airline travel value of the benefit, less the employee contribution. Where the transport is on a domestic route, the stand-by airline travel value is 50% of *the* carrier’s lowest standard single economy airfare for that route as publicly advertised during the year of tax. Where the transport is on an international route, the stand-by airline travel value is 50% of the lowest of *any* carrier’s standard single economy airfare for that route as publicly advertised during the year of tax.

An airline transport benefit is taxed as an in-house residual fringe benefit to the extent that the benefit includes the provision of transport in a passenger aircraft operated by a carrier (including any related incidental services on board the aircraft) and is subject to the stand-by restrictions that customarily apply in the airline industry.

$1,000 exemption

For in-house benefits, including in-house residual benefits valued under the above rules, there is a general exemption for the first $1,000 of the taxable value for each recipient employee each year (¶35-660).

General residual benefits

For residual fringe benefits to which the in-house concessions do *not* apply, the taxable value of the benefit is generally the arm's length cost of the benefit to the employer, *less* any amount paid by the employee (ss 50; 51).

Where the benefit is obtained from a third party at arm's length under an arrangement by which the employer pays for it (eg where the employee uses a credit card provided by the employer), the taxable value of the benefit is the expenditure incurred by the employer, *less* any amount paid by the employee (s 150).

Where the benefit was not purchased at arm's length by the employer, the value of the benefit is the amount that the employee could reasonably be expected to have paid at arm's length *less* any amount paid by the employee.

Where the employer paid the expatriate employee's income tax obligations and the income tax refund was returned to the employer (and the employee received the net salary only), the employee's income tax refund was not a "recipient's contribution". However, the refund reduced the taxable value of the benefit (ID 2001/758).

Private use of a non-car motor vehicle

The taxable value of a fringe benefit arising from the private use of a motor vehicle other than a car may be calculated using one of the methods outlined in MT 2034. If the cents per kilometre basis is used, the rates per kilometre for the year ended 31 March 2020 (TD 2019/3) and ending 31 March 2021 (TD 2020/3) are:

Engine capacity	Rate per km (2019–20)	Rate per km (2020–21)
0–2500cc	55 cents	56 cents
Over 2500cc	66 cents	67 cents
Motorcycles	16 cents	17 cents

[AFB ¶50-200, ¶50-372, ¶50-400]

Entertainment Benefits

¶35-617 Entertainment benefits

"Entertainment", for the purposes of the FBTAA, is defined by reference to ITAA97 s 32-10 (¶16-390). The Commissioner's views on what constitutes entertainment by way of the provision of food and drink and when FBT is payable on entertainment are set out in TR 97/17.

A fringe benefit which consists of entertainment is taxed under the ordinary rules that apply to that benefit. Depending on the type of entertainment and the circumstances in which the benefit is provided, entertainment can be one of a number of types of fringe benefit (eg expense payment fringe benefit or property fringe benefit). However, an employer may elect that "meal entertainment" fringe benefits be taxed in accordance with special rules designed to reduce compliance costs. Once an election is made, it applies to all meal entertainment fringe benefits provided by the employer in respect of all employees, their associates and others, throughout the whole year.

Generally the cost of providing a fringe benefit is deductible as an ordinary business expense under s 8-1 (¶16-520). Subject to certain exceptions, where entertainment expenses are incurred in providing a fringe benefit (eg not an exempt benefit), the general prohibition on deductibility does not apply (s 32-20; ¶16-390; CR 2007/71).

Meal entertainment fringe benefits

A meal entertainment fringe benefit arises where an employer provides a fringe benefit (¶35-060) that is a meal entertainment benefit which generally consists of: (a) entertainment by way of food or drink; (b) travel or accommodation connected with (a); or (c) the reimbursement or payment of expenses incurred in providing (a) or (b).

An employer is able to elect to calculate the taxable value of meal entertainment fringe benefits provided to employees (and associates) under either a "50/50 split method" (s 37B) or a "12-week register method" (s 37C). If no election is made, the taxable value is determined on the basis of the actual expenditure. The election is not available in respect of meal entertainment which is not provided by the employer (eg if it is provided by an associate of the employer or by another person).

Under the 50/50 split method, the taxable value of the meal entertainment fringe benefits is one-half of the expenses incurred in providing the meal entertainment benefits to all persons (whether employees, clients or others, and whether or not the expenditure would otherwise be exempt). If this method is chosen, half the cost of the meal entertainment is deductible for income tax purposes (¶16-390) and subject to FBT, and the remaining half is non-deductible for income tax purposes but not subject to FBT. The 50/50 split method can also be used to calculate the taxable value of "entertainment facility leasing expenses" incurred by the employer, ie the leasing and hiring costs of corporate boxes and other hospitality arrangements, including where the employer reimburses expenses incurred by the employee on leasing or hiring a private function room or hotel room (ID 2009/45) (s 152B).

Under the 12-week register method, the taxable value of the benefits is determined by reference to a 12-week register. The taxable value is the total meal entertainment expenditure incurred by the employer on all persons in the year multiplied by the register percentage (such an amount is deductible for income tax purposes: ¶16-390). The register percentage is calculated on the basis of the formula:

$$\frac{\text{total value of meal entertainment fringe benefits provided in the 12-week period}}{\text{total value of meal entertainment provided in the 12-week period}}$$

▶ Example

An employer's total meal entertainment expenditure in an FBT year is $100,000. The employer maintains a 12-week register which allows the employer to determine that 30% of meal entertainment expenditure was provided as a fringe benefit. The taxable value of meal entertainment fringe benefits provided is 30% × $100,000, ie $30,000.

The employer must keep a register for a continuous 12-week period which is representative of the expenditure in the relevant year. Generally, the register can be used for the year in which it is kept and the subsequent 4 years. However a new register must be kept if the meal entertainment expenses are more than 20% higher than the corresponding expenses for the first year for which the register was valid.

The 50/50 split method and the register method do not apply to calculate the taxable value of meal entertainment benefits that are either:

- not provided by an employer (ie they are provided by an associate of the employer or by a third party under an arrangement with the employer or an associate of the employer), or
- where the benefit is provided under a salary packaging arrangement.

Where either of the above apply, the taxable value is determined on the basis of the actual expenditure.

Expenses incurred by the employer are reduced by any amount contributed by the employee or an associate of the employee that is not reimbursed by the employer (s 37AB), but not by an amount contributed by a third party (ID 2005/146).

Taxi fares incurred in connection with the provision of entertainment by way of food or drink fall within the definition of "meal entertainment" where the employer uses the 50/50 method or 12-week register method (*NTLG FBT Sub-committee meeting*, 13 August 2009). However, under the 12-week register method, taxi fares incurred during the register period that satisfy the requirements of s 58Z are not included and therefore do not increase the register percentage.

The use of a Meal Entertainment Purchasing Card to acquire entertainment by way of food or drink constitutes the "provision of meal entertainment". If the employer chooses the 50/50 split method, and the requirements of Div 111 of the GST Act are met, 50% of the employer's total meal entertainment expenditure is GST-creditable (¶35-025; CR 2006/47; CR 2006/48). If the benefit is not provided under a salary packaging arrangement and it is provided by a public benevolent institution, health promotion charity or other employer exempt under s 57A it is exempt (¶35-100), as well as being disregarded for the purposes of the capping thresholds (¶35-100) and excluded from the reportable fringe benefits provisions (¶35-055; CR 2007/15; CR 2007/16; CR 2007/35; CR 2007/88). Other situations are considered in CR 2016/18 ("Salary Packaging Card"), CR 2008/25 ("Corporate Advantage Card"), CR 2016/85 (Meal Entertainment Card), CR 2017/33, CR 2017/34 and CR 2019/16. See also ¶35-500.

Other entertainment

If the provisions relating to meal entertainment fringe benefits do *not* apply, then, depending on the circumstances, the entertainment may be:

- an expense payment benefit, eg reimbursement of entertainment expenditure incurred on a personal credit card of an employee to the extent that the entertainment was provided to employees or their associates
- a property benefit, eg an entertainment meal provided in a restaurant to an employee
- a residual benefit, eg use by an employee of sporting facilities owned by an employer
- a board fringe benefit (¶35-630), eg an entertainment meal provided to an employee who is entitled under an industrial award to accommodation and at least 2 meals per day, or
- a tax-exempt body entertainment benefit (see below), eg the provision of an entertainment meal to an employee by an employer which is a tax-exempt body.

The taxable value of entertainment which is a fringe benefit is determined according to the rules applicable to the specific type of fringe benefit. Subject to those valuation rules, the taxable value of the benefit may qualify for some limited exemptions (eg an exempt property benefit (¶35-500) or a minor benefit (¶35-645)) or a reduction in taxable value (eg because the employee could have obtained a deduction had the employee provided the benefit: ¶35-680). If the entertainment provided is an expense payment fringe benefit provided to an employee, the taxable value of the benefit will be reduced to the extent that the expenditure relates to persons who are not employees or associates of employees (s 63A).

A "per head" basis of apportionment will be accepted, unless the special rules for meal entertainment fringe benefits have applied (TD 94/25). Other determinations have been released in relation to in-house dining meals (TD 94/24), the provision of property as entertainment (TD 94/55), the provision of morning and afternoon teas and light meals (IT 2675; CR 2005/89) and Christmas parties (ATO Fact Sheet *Fringe benefits tax and Christmas parties*).

Entertainment benefits provided by income tax-exempt employers

Entertainment provided to an employee or to an associate of an employee by an income tax-exempt employer, which is provided in respect of employment, is a tax-exempt body entertainment benefit if the expenditure would be non-deductible were the body a taxable entity (s 38; see also the ATO Fact Sheet *FBT and Christmas parties for tax-exempt bodies*). Such a benefit will generally be a fringe benefit subject to FBT (¶35-060). A tax exempt local government council that provided an employee with the use of the local recreation centre which it owned was providing a residual benefit and not a tax-exempt body entertainment benefit (ID 2008/60).

The taxable value of the benefit is the expenditure incurred in providing the entertainment to the employee or the employee's associate. Where the expenditure is used to provide entertainment for more than one person, the taxable value is the appropriate proportion of the total expenditure. Tax-exempt employers may also use either the 50/50 split method or the 12-week register method of valuing meal entertainment fringe benefits.

FBT is payable on the grossed-up taxable value of the benefit (¶35-025). However, a rebate is available to certain non-profit employers (¶35-642).

If the provision of food or drink constitutes a property benefit, rather than tax-exempt body entertainment, the exemption in s 41 may apply (¶35-500). The ATO has published ''Fringe benefits tax (FBT) and entertainment for non-profit organisations'', ''Fringe benefits tax (FBT) and entertainment for government'', and ''Fringe benefits tax (FBT) and entertainment for small business'' to provide guidance on FBT and entertainment. See also CR 2007/86 (tax-exempt body entertainment benefits and exempt benefits under s 57A).

[AFB ¶60-000, ¶60-100, ¶60-300, ¶60-650, ¶60-800]

Board Benefits

¶35-630 Board benefits

A board benefit arises where an employee is entitled under an industrial award or employment arrangement to accommodation and to at least 2 meals a day. The board benefit consists of any meal provided to such an employee, or to a family member who has similar entitlements, under an award or arrangement, by the employer (or by a related company in a whollyowned group) where the meal is prepared and supplied on the employer's or related company's premises or at or adjacent to a worksite (s 35).

Except for employees of restaurants, hotels, motels, etc, the meal must not be provided in a public dining facility. Meals at a party, reception, etc, are excluded, as are meals prepared in a facility exclusive to the employee concerned.

Where an employee is providing live-in care to elderly (ie aged over 60), handicapped or necessitous persons, so that accommodation provided to the employee would be an exempt benefit (¶35-380), then meals provided to the employee and members of the employee's family are exempt to the same extent (ss 58; 58T; 58U).

Meals provided on a working day by a primary producer carrying on business in a remote area (s 58ZD; ¶35-645) and remote area housing benefits (s 58ZC; ¶35-430) are exempt.

Taxable value of board fringe benefits

The taxable value of a board benefit is $2 per meal where the recipient was 12 years old or more at the beginning of the year concerned, and $1 per meal if less than 12 years old (s 36). Any amount paid for the meal is deducted.

Where the employee would have been entitled to an income tax deduction for expenditure on the meal, the taxable value is reduced proportionately (s 37; ¶35-680; *Draft*TR 2017/D6). The income tax substantiation requirements are disregarded for this purpose.

[AFB ¶37-000, ¶37-300]

Rebates of Fringe Benefits Tax

¶35-642 Rebate of FBT for certain non-profit employers

FBT is payable on the grossed-up taxable value of benefits for the year, and an offsetting income tax deduction is allowed (¶35-025). To ensure that certain non-profit employers that are unable to claim an income tax deduction for FBT are not disadvantaged, a rebate of FBT at the rate of 47% is available under s 65J.

An employer will qualify for the rebate if it is not a public benevolent institution or a health promotion charity (¶35-100) and is:

- a religious institution
- a scientific or public educational institution (other than an institution of the Commonwealth, a state or territory)
- a charitable ''institution'' (¶35-100) other than a Commonwealth, state or territory institution. TR 2011/4 discusses the meaning of charitable institution (¶10-605). The mere incorporation of a charitable institution does not mean that the institution is ''established by a law of the Commonwealth, a State or a Territory'' (TD 2008/2). Charitable institutions must be endorsed by the Commissioner (¶10-610). In *Navy Health Ltd*, a company providing private health insurance to defence force members as well as to others did not qualify as charitable institution. Charitable ''funds'' are not taken to be rebatable employers
- a non-profit scientific institution engaged solely in researching human disease which is established under a state, Commonwealth or territory law but which is not conducted on behalf of the state, Commonwealth or territory
- a trade union
- an association of employers or employees registered or recognised under the *Fair Work (Registered Organisations) Act 2009* or under a law of the Commonwealth, a state or territory relating to the settlement of industrial disputes
- a non-profit, non-government school (including a pre-school, but not a tertiary institution) established under Commonwealth, state or territory law, or
- a non-profit society, non-profit association or non-profit club established for:
  - the encouragement of music, art, science or literature
  - the encouragement or promotion of a game or sport
  - the encouragement or promotion of animal races

- community service purposes (not being political or lobbying purposes), eg an industry ombudsman (ID 2003/721) but not a company providing private health insurance for defence force members as well as to others (*Navy Health Ltd*) or a health care association whose members were public hospitals and community health centres (*Victorian Healthcare Association*)
- the purpose of promoting the development of aviation or tourism
- the purpose of promoting the development of the agricultural, pastoral, horticultural, viticultural, aquacultural, fishing, manufacturing or industrial resources of Australia, or
- the purpose of promoting the development of Australian information and communication technology.

A non-profit society, non-profit association or non-profit club qualifies for the rebate if it is not carried on for profit or gain to the individual members, is not a company where all the shares are beneficially owned by, or by an authority of, the Commonwealth, a state or territory, and is not a company limited by guarantee where members' interests and rights are beneficially owned by, or by an authority of, the Commonwealth, a state or territory. An association that is an incorporated company limited by guarantee and that includes in its membership both government bodies and non-government bodies can be a non-profit association (ID 2009/127).

Bodies formed and controlled by government and performing functions on behalf of government are not ''associations'' (TD 95/56).

Calculation of rebate

The amount of the rebate is worked out using the formula:

$$0.47 \times (\text{gross tax} - \text{aggregate non-rebatable amount}) \times \frac{\text{rebatable days in year}}{\text{total days in year}}$$

where:

- *gross tax* is the amount of FBT that would be payable if the rebate did not exist
- *rebatable days in year* is the number of whole days in the year of tax on which the employer qualified for the rebate
- *total days in year* is the number of days in the year of tax excluding the days on which the employer did not engage in activities as an employer
- *aggregate non-rebatable amount* is an amount calculated by complex formulae in s 65J(2B) to (2H) similar to the formulae required to calculate the ''aggregate non-exempt amount'' for a s 57A employer (¶35-025). The application of these formulae has the effect that the rebate does not apply to the individual grossed-up amounts of benefits that exceed $30,000: s 65J(2A). The aggregate non-rebatable amount is further reduced by the lesser of $5,000 and so much of the individual grossed-up amounts of benefits that represents salary packaged meal entertainment and entertainment facilities leasing expense benefits.

See the ATO publications *Fringe benefits tax: a guide for employers* (NAT 1054) Chapter 6 ''Non-profit organisations and FBT'' and *Fringe Benefits Tax for non-profit organisations* (NAT 14947).

[AFB ¶58-000, ¶58-100]

Miscellaneous Exemptions

¶35-645 Exemptions from fringe benefits tax

In addition to the exemptions applying to particular classes of benefit, there are specific exemptions for a number of benefits. FBT is not payable on an exempt benefit and the benefit does not form part of an employee's reportable fringe benefits amount.

Reimbursement of car expenses

Where the benefit is in the form of a reimbursement of car expenses (¶35-230) calculated on a cents per kilometre basis, it is effectively exempt if the amount is within the prescribed rates (s 60A; 61; 61A; 61B; 61E; 61F) — the "basic car rate" (being the rate prescribed under the income tax substantiation provisions for the year ending on 30 June following the 31 March of the FBT year: ¶16-370) and the "supplementary car rate" (0.63 cents per kilometre: FBTAR s 15).

Work-related items

A portable electronic device, computer software, protective clothing, a briefcase and a tool of trade is exempt where it is primarily for use in the employee's employment (s 58X). Wireless broadband access to the internet provided as part of the use of a laptop could be exempt where it is subject to security requirements and policies as to private use (*NTLG FBT Sub-committee meeting*, 12 August 2010), but not home internet access. The use of a mobile phone, including internet access, will be exempt provided it is provided primarily for use in the employee's employment (*NTLG FBT minutes*, 12 August 2011).

The exemption is restricted to one item per year for items that have a substantially identical function (s 58X(3)) but the exemption is available for an item that replaces another item acquired earlier in the FBT year (s 58X(4)). A replacement item is one that is required because the earlier item was lost, destroyed or needed to be replaced due to developments in technology. A second item provided as a back-up — eg because the earlier item is being washed — is not exempt (*NTLG FBT Sub-committee meeting*, 14 May 2009). A combination of a tablet PC and a laptop computer or a phablet and a tablet PC would be eligible for the exemption but not a combination of a smartphone and a phablet or a tablet PC hybrid and a laptop computer because they are considered to have "substantially identical functions" and an exemption would not be available for the second item provided to an employee in the same FBT year unless s 58X(3) or (4) applied (*NTLG FBT Sub-committee meeting*, 16 May 2013). Employees are also denied decline in value deductions for eligible work-related items exempt under s 58X.

Small business entities (¶7-050) or employers whose ordinary and statutory income for the income year ending most recently before the start of the FBT year is less than $10 million (increasing to $50 million from 1 April 2021) that provide their employees with more than one qualifying work-related portable electronic device can access the FBT exemption even if the additional items have substantially similar functions as the first device (s 58X(4)(b)).

Working from home due to COVID-19

The ATO has reminded employers who have provided employees with items to allow them to work from home (or from another location) due to COVID-19 that items primarily used by employees for work, including laptops, portable printers, and other electronic devices will usually be exempt from FBT. In addition, the minor benefits exemption or the otherwise deductible rule may apply if employees are allowed to use a monitor, mouse or keyboard they otherwise use in the workplace, are provided with stationery or computer consumables, or their phone and internet access is paid or reimbursed.

Fly-in fly-out (FIFO) arrangements

The provision of transport to and from an employee's home base and a remote area worksite (including a ship, vessel or floating structure: TD 95/49) is an exempt benefit (s 47(7)). The exemption applies even where the employee takes a rest day during the period at the worksite (TD 94/96). A full list is provided on the ATO website at Fringe benefits tax — remote areas.

The exemption covers Australian residents working in remote overseas areas who are employed under FIFO arrangements. Whether an overseas location is "remote" is determined on a case-by-case basis, using a number of factors such as distance to, and population of, the nearest urban area, amenities and facilities, safety and health risks. A list of remote overseas areas is also available on the ATO website at FBT exemption for fly-in/fly-out arrangements remote and non-remote overseas locations.

Temporary accommodation due to COVID-19

The ATO has advised that temporary accommodation and meals provided to fly-in fly-out and drive-in drive-out employees will be considered emergency assistance and therefore exempt from FBT where the employees are unable to return to their normal residences due to COVID-19 domestic and/or international travel restrictions.

Relocation expenses

Benefits relating to the movement of an employee from one locality to another for employment purposes are exempt, including:

- relocation travel costs (including meals and accommodation en route) of the employee and family members (ss 58F; 61B; 143A; ID 2004/293). This can include "look-see trips", ie trips for employees and their families to familiarise themselves with a new location after a transfer has been accepted but before the actual relocation (*NTLG FBT Sub-committee meeting*, 13 November 2008) but not the costs of a visa application for a non-resident employee to remain in Australia (ID 2013/35)
- the cost of removal of furniture and personal effects (including insurance and storage) (s 58B)
- costs of temporary accommodation, both at the old locality and the new (subject to time limits) (s 61C)
- the cost of leasing furniture for temporary accommodation (s 58E)
- the cost of connecting telephone, electricity or gas services to temporary accommodation (s 58D)
- necessary meal costs at a hotel, motel, etc (in excess of $2 per meal per adult or $1 per meal per child under 12) (s 61D)
- advances to cover such items as rental bond or electricity or gas deposits, provided the advance is repayable within one year (s 17)
- home sale and purchase costs (stamp duty, legal fees, estate agent's commission) (s 58C), provided the employee sells the old dwelling within 2 years of the relocation
- the engagement of relocation consultants (s 58AA).

Cancelled events

Non-refundable costs for cancelled events (including events cancelled due to COVID-19) which employees were due to attend do not give rise to an FBT liability where the arrangement was between the employer and event organisers. However, where the employee was required to pay for his/her attendance at the event and the non-refundable costs were reimbursed to the employee, then this will constitute an expense payment fringe benefit — although the otherwise deductible rule may apply for work-related events (ATO website).

Items that protect employees from COVID-19

Items provided to employees to protect them from COVID-19 while at work (such as gloves, masks, sanitisers and anti-septic sprays) will be exempt from FBT under s 58N if they are provided to employees who:

- have physical contact with (or are in close proximity to) customers or clients as part of their duties, or
- are involved in cleaning premises.

If the employees are not involved in these functions, the minor benefits exemption under s 58P may apply if the benefits have a value of less than $300 and are minor, infrequent and/or irregular (ATO website).

Other FBT exemptions

Other benefits covered by exemptions are:

- **Australian traineeship scheme** — food and accommodation provided to trainees under the scheme (s 58S)
- **compassionate travel** — travel (including necessary accommodation and meals) by an employee or close relative at times of serious illness or death in the family (s 58LA)
- **emergency assistance** — benefits such as food, clothing and shelter, provided to employees and family members at a time of emergency (s 58N). It can also include emergency relief cash payments (ID 2011/60). The ATO has stated that this exemption extends to emergency assistance to provide immediate relief where the employee is, or is at risk of being, adversely affected by COVID-19. It also extends to emergency treatment on the employer's premises (or those of a related company) provided to an employee affected by COVID-19 by an employee (or an employee of a related company) at or adjacent to the employee's work-site. However, payment for ongoing medical treatment is not exempt (ATO website)
- **employment interviews** — benefits relating to travel (including meals and accommodation en route) by a current or future employee for the purpose of attending a job interview or selection test (ss 58A; 61E; 143D)
- **live-in and non-live-in help** — food and accommodation provided to a live-in domestic employee of a religious institution, priest or minister (s 58T) or to live-in help employed to care for the elderly (ie aged over 60) or disadvantaged (s 58U), and food and drink provided to such employees who do not live in (s 58V) (¶35-380)
- **long service awards** — awards for long service of at least 15 years, provided the benefit is no more than $1000 for 15 years service and $100 for each additional year (s 58Q). Prior year long service award benefits for which an exemption was not available must be taken into account in determining the availability of current year exemptions (*NTLG meeting*, 12 November 2009). For example, an employee was provided with an artwork valued at $1,200 in respect of 15 years of service. The employer was not able to claim an exemption for the artwork as its value exceeded $1,000. After a further 5 years, the employee is provided with a watch valued at $600 in recognition of 20 years service. The watch is also not eligible for an exemption as its value exceeds $500 ((20 – 15) × $100), notwithstanding that the total exemption otherwise available for 20 years service is $1,500, the current award is less than that and no previous exemption has been claimed

- **meals on working days** — meals provided for consumption on working days to employees of primary production employers where the business is not located in or adjacent to an eligible urban area (eg ID 2006/333). It is also necessary that the benefit not be meal entertainment, as defined in s 37AD. The reimbursement by the employer of an employee's car parking fees incurred when attending an entertainment venue is an expense incurred in providing the employee with travel under s 37AD (ID 2014/15). The meal benefit must be either a board benefit, property benefit, expense benefit or residual benefit (s 58ZD)

- **membership fees and subscriptions** — an employee's subscription to a trade or professional journal, membership fees for a corporate credit card and membership fees for an airport lounge membership (s 58Y)

- **military compensation and other benefits** — benefits provided to Commonwealth employees who receive payments under the *Military Rehabilitation and Compensation Act 2004* and health care and other benefits provided to members of the Defence Force (*Fringe Benefits Tax (Application to the Commonwealth) Act 1986*)

- **minor benefits** — benefits with a value of less than $300 if, having regard to various matters such as infrequency and irregularity, it would be unreasonable to treat the benefit as a fringe benefit (s 58P). "Infrequent and irregular benefits" is not to be equated with "isolated or rare" (*Case 2/96*). See TR 2007/12 and ID 2005/366 (gift jointly purchased by employer and employee)

- **newspapers and periodicals** — newspapers and periodicals provided to employees for use for business purposes (s 58H)

- **occupational health and counselling** — work-related medical tests (including pre-employment tests: ID 2007/141 and COVD-19 testing carried out by a legally qualified medical practitioner or nurse and it is available to all employees: ATO website), preventive health care including certain vaccinations (including flu vaccinations for employees working from home provided they are offered to all employees) (ID 2002/963; ID 2004/301; ATO website), work-related counselling (including services to former employees who were made redundant: TD 93/153 but not training courses or activities for employees being made redundant: ID 2015/1), optical aids for screen-based equipment (ID 2004/557) and lifestyle and weight loss counselling (CR 2011/41) and migrant language training, but not massages (ID 2003/689) or the payment of employee health insurance premiums (*Lake Fox Ltd*) (ss 58M; 143E). See generally CR 2007/81

- **remote area housing** — essentially accommodation not located in or adjacent to an eligible urban area (¶35-430)

- **retraining and reskilling** — employer-provided retraining or reskilling expenses where the employee will be redeployed to a different role in the business (proposed to apply from 2 October 2020). The exemption will not apply to retraining provided through a salary packaging arrangement or Commonwealth supported places at universities

- **safety awards** — awards genuinely related to occupational safety achievements (provided the value is $200 or less per recipient) (s 58R)

- **student exchange programs** — places provided in an approved student exchange program for an employee or an associate of the employee (s 58ZB)

- **superannuation deposits** — certain deposits made under the *Small Superannuation Accounts Act 1995* (s 58W; ¶39-650)

- **taxi travel** — taxi travel (other than by limousine) provided by employers to employees for travel beginning or ending at the employee's place of work or for sick employees for travel home or to any other place to which it is necessary or appropriate for the employee to go as a result of illness or injury, including COVID-19 (eg to a doctor or a relative) (s 58Z). "Taxi travel" has the same meaning as for GST purposes, namely "travel that involves transporting passengers by taxi or limousine, for fares" and includes taxis and ride-sourcing or ride-sharing services provided in a vehicle that is not licensed as a taxi, such as Uber

- **transport for police force** — certain free public transport provided to police officers (s 47)

- **travel for medical treatment** — travel (including necessary accommodation and meals) by an employee or family member from a foreign country in order to obtain medical treatment (including in relation to COVID-19) at the least cost necessary (s 58L)

- **vehicle parking** — motor vehicle parking facilities in a limited number of circumstances (¶35-254)

- **worker entitlement funds** — contributions to funds set up to protect employee entitlements in the event of insolvency or to provide for entitlements such as redundancy and long service leave (ss 58PA; 58PB). The payments into the fund must be made under an industrial instrument for the purpose of making leave payments or payments when an employee ceases employment. Funds must be either prescribed by regulation or be a long service leave fund established under a Commonwealth, state or territory law. Approved worker entitlement funds are listed on the Australian Business Register (www.abr.business.gov.au). Contributions made by an employer to an approved worker entitlement fund to provide income protection insurance to employees do not constitute exempt benefits (ID 2012/95)

- **workers compensation** — provision of workers compensation insurance coverage and provision of actual compensation for work-related injuries (s 58J; TD 93/64; CR 2005/103)

- **worksite medical facilities** — work-related and incidental medical services and health care benefits provided at a worksite, first aid post or medical clinic (s 58K).

[AFB ¶55-000, ¶55-580]

Miscellaneous Reductions and Concessions

¶35-650 FBT concessions for employees in remote areas

There are several concessions for benefits provided to employees working in remote areas. The areas that are "remote" for these purposes are discussed at ¶35-430.

Housing assistance. The taxable value of certain benefits arising from housing assistance provided to an employee in a remote area is generally reduced by 50% (s 60). This applies where the employer pays or reimburses interest on a housing loan, sells a house with interest-free or low-interest instalments, sells a house below value, pays a fee for an option to purchase a house from an employee, reimburses an employee for expenses connected with a home, or pays or reimburses rent. These factors must be present:

- the employee must work and live in a remote area

- it must be customary in the employer's industry for employers to provide housing assistance to employees

- one of a set of prescribed circumstances must make it necessary for the employer to provide the assistance.

In some cases, the value of remote area housing assistance is spread over the period the benefit is enjoyed (up to 7 years generally but, in exceptional cases, up to 15 years), rather than being taxed ''up-front'' as a lump sum (s 65CA). For examples, see ID 2003/157 to ID 2003/160.

Residential fuel. Where an employer supplies, or pays for, or reimburses the cost of electricity, gas or other residential fuel (not water: ID 2005/158) for an employee in a remote area, the value of the benefit is reduced by 50% (s 59; ID 2004/276).

Remote area holiday travel. Where an employee working in a remote area is given transport (including appropriate meals and accommodation en route) for taking leave of more than 3 days under an award or industry custom, or is reimbursed for the costs of such transport, the value of the benefit, up to a certain limit, is reduced by 50% (ss 60A; 61; 143). The 50% of the value of the fringe benefit is calculated after deducting any recipients contribution (ID 2014/9). The reduction also applies to such benefits given to members of an employee's family living with the employee in a remote area including *cash allowances* paid to employees' spouses and children to cover the cost of remote area holiday travel. For details of the conditions of the concession, see MT 2048.

Loss incurred by employee on sale of home to employer. Where a loss occurs on the forced disposal of an employee's home under the terms of a buy-back arrangement with an employer, the employer's fringe benefits taxable amount in that year may be reduced (s 65CC). Such a situation could occur, for example, where house prices rise sharply but the employee is locked into a below-market figure. The aim of the reduction (limited to 50% of the employee's loss) is to offset tax paid by the employer on the fringe benefit given to the employee to facilitate the original purchase of the house. A reduction cannot give rise to a negative fringe benefits amount capable of being carried forward.

[AFB ¶57-400]

¶35-655 Employees posted overseas

There are concessions applying to a number of benefits provided to employees who are posted overseas — whether from Australia to a foreign country or from a foreign country to Australia. The effect of the definition of ''employee'' in s 136 is that the FBT provisions (including any concessions) only apply to benefits provided to a person who receives or is entitled to receive payments that are subject to PAYG withholding, ie not exempt income (¶35-060; ID 2007/25).

Where the employee is provided with travel for a holiday, the taxable value of the benefit is reduced by 50% (s 61A; 143B; 143C). The amount to which this reduction applies is limited to the equivalent of a return economy class air fare to the employee's home each year. Where travel is to the employee's home country for a holiday, the amount to which the reduction applies is the actual cost of travel if this exceeds the cost of a return economy class air fare to the employee's home. The same concession and limit applies to holiday travel provided for family members, regardless of whether they live overseas with the employee.

Fringe benefits in respect of the education costs of the employee's children are exempt to the extent that the costs relate to a school term while the employee is overseas (ss 65A; 143B; ID 2006/52). The child must be aged under 25.

[AFB ¶57-560, ¶57-570]

¶35-660 First $1,000 of in-house benefits

The first $1,000 of the aggregate of the taxable values of certain ''in-house'' benefits given to an employee in a year is exempt from FBT (s 62). The exemption includes benefits provided to an associate of the employee (MT 2044).

The benefits to which this applies are: in-house property fringe benefits (¶35-520); in-house residual fringe benefits (¶35-590); and in-house expense payment benefits (¶35-350). However, the $1,000 reduction is removed where the benefits are provided under a salary packaging arrangement (¶35-520).

[AFB ¶57-090]

¶35-680 Employee entitled to deduction: the "otherwise deductible rule"

Where an employee receives a benefit, and would have been entitled to an income tax deduction for expenditure on the benefit if the employee had provided the benefit, then the taxable value of the benefit is reduced by the amount of that notional deduction (eg work-related clothing expenditure: TR 97/12; work-related telephone expenses: TD 93/96; but not HELP fees: *Draft*TR 2017/D6). The reduction is available in respect of loan fringe benefits (s 19; ¶35-300), expense payment fringe benefits (s 24; ¶35-360), board fringe benefits (s 37; ¶35-630), property fringe benefits (s 44; ¶35-510), and residual fringe benefits (s 52; ¶35-570); eg where accommodation is provided to an employee travelling in the course of employment: *Draft*TR 2017/D6; and where an employee provided with air travel is travelling from his/her home city to a remote work location and employment commences and ends at the home city airport (*John Holland Group*). The reduction is available regardless of whether the employer would have been entitled to a deduction for the expenditure (TD 93/20). The reduction is *not* available to reduce the taxable value of benefits provided to associates of employees (TD 93/90).

Generally, the value of the benefit is reduced by the same amount as the amount that would have been allowed as an income tax deduction to the employee. Where the employee would have received only a partial deduction, the value of the benefit is reduced only by that partial amount.

This concession does *not* apply where the employee's notional deduction would have been for decline in value of a depreciating asset or some other deduction (eg borrowing expenses on a loan or a prepayment: TD 93/46) spread over more than one year.

In determining the amount of the employee's notional deduction, the threshold for self-education expenses (¶16-450) and the income tax substantiation requirements (¶16-210) are disregarded. The application of the non-commercial loss provisions (ITAA97 Div 35) to the employee's expenses is also disregarded. However, this is contradicted by TR 2013/6 in the situation where the deduction would not have been allowed in the year incurred if it was incurred by the taxpayer. In most cases, specific substantiation requirements (such as an employee declaration, provision of receipts, petty cash book entries, a travel diary or car odometer and logbook records) are imposed.

The employer must normally obtain any relevant declaration and documentary evidence from the employee before the date by which the annual FBT return is due. However, where an employee receives a series of benefits that are essentially the same but for differences in their value or the proportion of their business use (ie "recurring fringe benefits"), a declaration will need to be provided by the employee only for the first benefit (s 152A). If the employee has died before making the declaration, the employer may obtain the declaration from the executor of the employee's estate (*NTLG FBT Sub-committee minutes*, 14 February 2008).

Another recurring fringe benefit declaration will need to be obtained 5 years after the last such declaration or if there has been a decrease in the business use of the benefit of more than 10%.

Declarations must be in a form approved by the Commissioner. They must generally show the nature of the expenditure to establish its relationship to the production of assessable income, and state the extent to which it would have been deductible to the employee.

An employee who incurs unreimbursed expenditure on a benefit may be entitled to a whole or partial income tax deduction for the amount incurred. In such a case, the amount of the deduction allowable to the employee is excluded from the amount by which the taxable value of the benefit is reduced — in other words, the benefit of deductibility is apportioned between the employee and the employer. Where the employee's contribution to the benefit is for any private component, then the notional deduction goes towards reducing the taxable value of the benefit and the employee is not allowed a deduction for the contribution.

Jointly held assets

Where a benefit is provided jointly to an employee and an associate, the benefit is deemed to have been received solely by the employee (s 138(3); *National Australia Bank*: ¶35-300).

However, changes to the otherwise deductible rule ensure that the full value of a loan benefit, expense payment benefit, property benefit or residual benefit that has been provided to both an employee and an associate in relation to a jointly held asset or thing is subject to FBT. This is designed to overcome the decision in the *National Australia Bank case* and reinstate the principle that deductions arising from jointly held assets should be allocated between owners according to their legal interests.

The rule provides a different method of calculating the notional deduction where, because of s 138(3), a fringe benefit is provided jointly to an employee and their associate and is deemed to be provided solely to the employee. In this situation, the amount of the notional deduction is reduced to reflect the employee's percentage of interest in the income producing asset or thing to which the benefit relates, but not the associate's.

[AFB ¶57-070]

Records and Administration

¶35-690 Retention of FBT records

Records of transactions

An employer must keep records to identify and explain all transactions and acts relevant to ascertaining its FBT liability (s 132). The records must be in English or readily accessible and convertible into English. Records must be kept for 5 years after completion of the relevant transaction or act. For the Commissioner's approach to record-keeping, including the use of electronic records, see TR 2005/9. PS LA 2005/2 provides guidelines on record-keeping obligations and the remission of administrative penalty for a failure to keep records.

An associate who provides benefits to an employer's employee must keep similar records for relevant transactions and must give the employer a copy within 21 days after the end of the relevant year.

Where a benefit is provided by a third party under an arrangement, the employer must take all reasonable steps to obtain details of the transaction.

Failure to comply with these requirements is an offence (¶35-750).

Employers who adopt the record-keeping exemption arrangements (¶35-692) must maintain records for the base year.

Statutory evidentiary documents

Where the taxable value of a fringe benefit has been reduced on the basis that the employee would have been entitled to an income tax deduction for expenditure on the benefit, the employer must generally obtain relevant declarations, receipts and other evidence from the employee (¶35-680). In the case of small or undocumentable expenses which may reduce the taxable value of an expense payment fringe benefit, the employer may maintain a petty cash book or similar document that sets out the particulars of the expenses incurred by employees if there are no actual receipts (¶35-360). In other cases, the employer must obtain from the employee documents or declarations substantiating the number of business and total kilometres travelled by a car and expenditure on car expenses (¶35-210 and following). All these are called "statutory evidentiary documents" (s 136(1)).

Generally, the employer must keep these documents for 5 years, starting from the date of the FBT assessment for the last year to which they relate, and longer if there is an outstanding dispute (ss 123; 136(1)). Except for employee declarations, it is sufficient if the employer obtains a copy of the relevant documents from the employee.

The employer can rely on a copy of a lost or destroyed document if it was in existence when the original document was lost or destroyed. If there is no copy and reasonable precautions were taken to prevent the loss or destruction of the document, the Commissioner may effectively exempt the employer from the retention requirement.

Commissioner's substantiation discretion

The Commissioner has a discretion to disregard non-compliance with the record-keeping requirements (but not the requirements to provide declarations) where the nature and quality of the evidence satisfies the Commissioner that the taxable value of a benefit is not greater than that specified by the employer (s 123B; eg ID 2003/1099). The Commissioner can only exercise this discretion while reviewing the affairs of the taxpayer (eg during an audit or when considering an objection).

Proposed reduction to FBT record-keeping requirements

It was announced in the 2020–21 Budget that employers will be allowed to use existing corporate records, rather than prescribed records, to comply with their FBT obligations. Under the proposal, instead of requiring employers to create additional records and employee declarations, the Commissioner will have the power to determine adequate alternative records, allowing employers to rely on existing corporate records and reduce compliance costs. The proposed measure will have effect from the start of the first FBT year after the date of assent of the enabling legislation.

[AFB ¶62-000, ¶66-520]

¶35-692 FBT record-keeping exemption

Generally, the FBT payable by an employer is calculated on the grossed-up aggregate fringe benefits amount for the year (¶35-025). Also, an employer is generally required to maintain certain records (¶35-690). However, certain employers are exempted from the record-keeping requirements and are able to calculate FBT on the aggregate fringe benefits amount of an earlier year (the "base year") when such records were maintained (ss 135A to 135L).

Conditions

To qualify for this exemption, the employer must:

- have established a base year, and
- not have been given a notice by the Commissioner during the FBT year immediately before the current year requiring the employer to resume record-keeping (s 135B).

An employer who satisfies these conditions for an FBT year will not be required to maintain FBT records for that year (subject to certain exceptions). An employer will be required to keep and retain records for a base year for a period of 5 years after the end of the last FBT year for which the base year is relevant in determining the employer's liability.

Base year

A base year is established in relation to the current FBT year where either:

- the FBT year immediately before the current year was a base year, or

- an earlier FBT year was a base year and the employer's FBT liability for every FBT year after that base year (and before the current year) was determined by using the employer's aggregate fringe benefits amount for that earlier FBT year (s 135C).

An FBT year is a base year in relation to an employer if:

- the employer has carried on business operations throughout the FBT year
- the employer has lodged an FBT return for the FBT year (even if the employer is not generally required to lodge a return)
- all the records for the FBT year have been kept and retained as required (s 132; ¶35-690). An employer who is relying on s 132A to obtain the necessary documentary evidence within a reasonable time may still treat a year as the base year where that evidence is obtained
- the employer's FBT liability for the FBT year is worked out from the aggregate fringe benefits amount for that year and not an earlier base year, and
- the aggregate fringe benefits amount for the FBT year does not exceed the "exemption threshold". The exemption threshold for the FBT year ended 31 March 2020 was $8,714 (TD 2019/4); for the year ending 31 March 2021, it is $8,853 (ATO website). For earlier years, see ¶42-410.

▶ **Example 1**

An employer establishes a base year and is exempt from keeping records in the following year (Year 1). In Year 2 the employer no longer qualifies for the record-keeping exemption. The employer must retain the base year records until the end of Year 6.

▶ **Example 2**

An employer establishes a base year and uses that base year for the record-keeping exemption in the following year (Year 1). In Year 2 the employer decides to establish a second base year which is used for the record-keeping exemption in Year 3. The records for the first base year must be retained for 5 years after the end of Year 1, while the records for the second base year must be retained for 5 years after the end of Year 3. Thus, the employer is retaining records for 2 base years during Years 4 to 6.

Exceptions

An employer who qualifies for the record-keeping exemption is still required to maintain records where:

- the employer is a government body or an income tax-exempt body at any time during the year. If an employer becomes a government body or an income tax-exempt body, FBT records must be kept from the day the employer's status changes
- an associate of the employer provides to the employer copies of records relating to benefits provided by the associate to the employer's employees, or
- the employer receives from the Commissioner a notice requiring it to recommence keeping and retaining records (this will apply from the date the notice is given) (s 135E).

FBT liability

Where an employer qualifies for the record-keeping exemption, the FBT liability for the current year is worked out using the aggregate fringe benefits amount for the most recent base year, instead of the aggregate fringe benefits amount for the current year (s 135G).

An employer may also choose to use the current year aggregate fringe benefits amount (rather than the base year amount) to determine the FBT liability for the current year (s 135H). For example, an employer may choose to use the current year aggregate fringe benefits amount where it is less than the base year amount.

The base year aggregate fringe benefits amount cannot be used where:

- the employer is a government body or an income tax-exempt body at any time during the current year (s 135J), or

- the current year aggregate fringe benefits amount is more than 20% greater than the most recent base year amount. However, this 20% rule does not apply where the difference between the current year and most recent base year amount is $100 or less (s 135K).

Special rules dealing with the retention of statutory evidentiary documents and the valuation of car fringe benefits apply to assist employers in determining their aggregate fringe benefits amount for the current year (given that, under the record-keeping exemption provisions, they may not have retained records for the current year) (s 135K(4), (5)).

An employer who ceases business during the current year is able to pro rate its base year aggregate fringe benefits amount in accordance with the proportion of the current year during which it was in business (s 135L).

[AFB ¶65-800, ¶65-840]

¶35-710 FBT collection and recovery

The mechanical provisions for the collection and recovery of FBT generally correspond to those applying to income tax (TAA Sch 1 Pt 4-15: ¶25-510).

GIC (s 93; ¶29-510) applies to any late payment of tax and/or instalment of tax. If an underpayment occurs because of an amendment to an assessment, other than an amendment to correct a false or misleading statement or an amendment due to a tax avoidance arrangement, the per annum rate is the lower rate which applies to overpayments of tax (¶28-170). For the Commissioner's power to remit late payment penalties, see ¶29-530.

[AFB ¶65-340]

¶35-720 FBT administrative provisions

The following summary outlines a number of administrative provisions:

- In the absence of sufficient information to make a proper assessment, the Commissioner can make a reasonable assessment (s 124).
- Where it is reasonable to assume that an employee's eligible foreign remuneration or foreign earnings during a year of tax will be exempt but the anticipated circumstances do not eventuate and the income is not exempt, the assessment can be amended at any time (s 124A).
- Authorised officers have wide powers to enter buildings, inspect documents and make copies, and are entitled to all reasonable assistance from the occupier (TAA Sch 1 s 353-15).
- The Commissioner can require any person to attend before the Commissioner or an authorised officer, to answer questions and to produce documents in the person's custody or control (TAA Sch 1 s 353-10).
- Agents acting for employers, employers in the capacity of trustees, and trustees in respect of the affairs of employers, who provide or arrange fringe benefits are required, as agent or trustee, to lodge returns and pay FBT (s 129).
- There is provision for relief from FBT in cases of serious hardship (TAA Div 340: ¶25-450).

[AFB ¶7-500, ¶63-040, ¶75-500, ¶75-600]

¶35-730 FBT objections, reviews and appeals

An employer's rights to object against an FBT assessment are similar to a taxpayer's rights in regard to an income tax assessment (TAA Pt IVC: ¶28-000). This applies to deemed assessments made by the lodgment of an FBT return as well as to assessments made by the Commissioner.

An objection must be in writing and made within 4 years from the date of service of the notice of assessment. Deemed assessments are made on the date on which the return is lodged. If an employer is dissatisfied with the Commissioner's decision on an objection, a request for a review of the decision by the AAT or an appeal to the Federal Court can be made within 60 days.

Rights of review and appeal, and provisions for extension of time limits, etc, effectively correspond to those applying to income tax (¶28-000). For the employer's right to request an amended assessment, see ¶35-030. There is no right to a refund of FBT under the general law of restitution, eg where the objection time limits have expired and the extension of time provisions are not satisfied (*Mt Gibson Manager*). In *Minproc Engineers*, an employer which followed a ruling in self-assessing its FBT liability was allowed to lodge an objection which was 5 and a half years out of time, but not an objection which was more than 6 years out of time. However, in *Boral Resources (WA)*, where the facts were similar to *Minproc Engineers*, the AAT refused to allow objections against FBT assessments lodged out of time because the employer had not relied on a ruling when self-assessing its FBT liability.

[AFB ¶8-000, ¶70-020, ¶70-200]

¶35-750 FBT penalties and offences

The uniform penalty regime contained in TAA Sch 1 Pt 4-25 applies for all FBT related matters (¶29-000). Penalties may also be imposed under the FBTAA for:

- a tax agent's failure to provide a taxpayer with the original of, or a copy of, any notice of assessment (s 70D; ¶35-030) (30 penalty units), and
- failing to record or retain records (s 132) (30 penalty units).

The Commissioner can remit all or part of a penalty (¶29-400).

In addition to the specific offences under the FBTAA, the general offences under the TAA (such as failing to furnish returns or supply information, making false or misleading statements, obstruction and so on) apply to FBT (¶29-700; see, for example, *Case 7/2016*). Government bodies are excluded from the offence provisions of the FBT legislation (s 167). Persons stripping companies or trusts to make them incapable of paying FBT may be convicted under the *Crimes (Taxation Offences) Act 1980*.

A partner is deemed to have committed any offence committed by another in the partnership, but has a defence if it can be shown that the partner was in no way connected with the offence (s 165). The same applies to members of the committee of management of an unincorporated company (s 166).

FBT avoidance arrangements

Where, on an objective view of an arrangement and the surrounding circumstances, the arrangement was entered into for the sole or dominant purpose of reducing liability for FBT, the Commissioner can effectively cancel any tax benefit from the arrangement (s 67). Section 67 operates in a similar way to ITAA36 Pt IVA (¶30-000). Ceasing or reducing a benefit, or replacing it with cash remuneration, or requiring the employee to make a contribution does not constitute a tax avoidance arrangement.

[AFB ¶8-080, ¶71-400]

Chapter 36 Payroll Tax

¶36-000 Payroll tax: introduction

Payroll tax is a state and territory (state) impost controlled by 8 separate legislatures. Accordingly, the requirements, liabilities and rates of tax vary from state to state so that, for example, a particular allowance or benefit that is subject to payroll tax in Victoria may well be exempt in Queensland (and vice versa).

The states have enacted legislation to have common provisions and definitions of a range of payroll tax arrangements while retaining individual control over rates and thresholds. The legislation in each state broadly provides for payroll tax to be levied on "wages", in cash or in kind, provided by employers to their employees. However, factors determining an employer's liability, which may differ from state to state, include: the tax-exempt wage level threshold; any allowable deduction applying to the payroll tax threshold; and the applicable rate of tax.

¶36-010 Liability for payroll tax

Payroll tax is a tax on wages paid or payable by an employer to an employee. Most employer/employee relationships are readily identifiable. However, there are occasions where the issue is not clear cut and the various legislatures operate to deem certain relationships to be that of an employer/employee so that payments are subject to payroll tax.

Generally speaking, allowances or other benefits that are provided to employees (other than as a reimbursement for work-related expenses incurred by the employee) are deemed to be wages for the purposes of the payroll tax law in each of the states, whether they are paid in cash or in kind. The most common types of benefits and allowances that may be provided by employers to employees are listed in the table at ¶36-140, together with their status (assessable or exempt) for payroll tax purposes.

Payroll tax is generally required to be paid within the time in which an employer must lodge the return of wages in respect of which the tax is payable. In most states, monthly returns must be lodged within 7 days after the end of each month (except June). An annual adjustment return incorporating the June return must then be lodged within 21 days after the end of the financial year, ie by 21 July. In the Northern Territory, monthly returns are required to be lodged within 21 days after the end of each month with the annual adjustment return to be lodged by 21 July. In New South Wales, the return relating to the month of June 2019 and any subsequent year, and the annual adjustment return for the 2018–19 and subsequent financial years, must be lodged within 28 days after the end of June (ie by 28 July).

¶36-020 Payroll tax registration requirements

In Queensland and Western Australia, an employer who is a member of a group must register for payroll tax within 7 days after the month in which that employer pays or is liable to pay taxable wages. In the other states, an employer who is a member of a group must register within 7 days (21 days in the Northern Territory) after the month in which it pays or is liable to pay wages where the group's weekly wages for that month exceeds the prescribed threshold.

Employers who are *not* members of a group must register within 7 days (21 days in the Northern Territory) after the end of a month in which they commence to pay wages in that state, where wages exceed the threshold indicated below.

State	Threshold ($)
New South Wales[1]	23,013 weekly
Victoria	12,500 weekly
Queensland	25,000 weekly
South Australia[2]	28,846 weekly
Western Australia	83,333 monthly
Tasmania	24,038 weekly
ACT	166,666.66 monthly
Northern Territory[3]	28,767 weekly

(1) Revenue NSW advises that employers must register if during any one month their total Australian wages are above the relevant monthly threshold.

(2) Revenue SA recommends that employers register when taxable wages consistently exceed the relevant monthly threshold.

(3) The NT Territory Revenue Office advises that employers must register if total Australian wages exceed the monthly exemption level.

¶36-030 Rates and thresholds of payroll tax

The following payroll tax rates and thresholds are applicable in the various states for the financial year commencing 1 July 2020:

State	Rate (%)	Annual wages threshold ($)	Monthly wages threshold ($)
New South Wales	4.85[1]	1,200,000	92,055; 98,630; 101,918[2]
Victoria	4.85; 2.02; 1.2125[3]	650,000[4]	54,166[5]
Queensland	4.75; 4.95[6]	1,300,000 (¶36-040)	108,333
South Australia	4.95[7]	1,500,000	125,000
Western Australia	5.5; 6; 6.5[8]	1,000,000[9] (¶36-040)	83,333[10]
Tasmania	4; 6.1[11]	1,250,000	95,890; 102,740; 106,164[12]
ACT	6.85	2,000,000	166,666.66
Northern Territory	5.5	1,500,000 (¶36-040)	125,000

(1) NSW rate applies from 1 July 2020 to 30 June 2022. From 1 July 2022 the rate will be 5.45%.

(2) NSW monthly threshold is based on 28, 30 or 31 days in the month.

(3) Victoria payroll tax rate is 4.85% for employers other than regional employers, 2.02% for regional employers and 1.2125% for bushfire relief regional employers. In 2019–20, the payroll tax rate for regional employers (other than bushfire relief regional employers) was 2.425%.

(4) Victoria annual threshold will increase to $675,000 in 2021–22 and $700,000 in 2022–23 and subsequent years.

(5) Victoria monthly threshold will increase to $56,250 in 2021–22 and $58,333 in 2022–23 and subsequent years.

(6) Queensland payroll tax rate is 4.95% for employers paying more than $6,500,000 in Australian taxable wages and 4.75% for other employers. For the 2019–20 to 2022–23 financial years a 1% rate discount applies to regional employers paying at least 85% of taxable wages to regional employees.

(7) In South Australia, a payroll tax variable rate of 0% to 4.95% applies for annual taxable wages between $1,500,000 and $1,700,000 and 4.95% for annual wages above $1,700,000.

(8) From 1 July 2020 to 30 June 2021 a tiered payroll tax rate scale applies in Western Australia as follows:

- employers or group of employers with annual taxable wages of not more than $1 million will pay no tax
- employers or group of employers with annual taxable wages of $1 million to $7.5 million will pay tax at the rate of 5.5% with an entitlement to a diminishing exemption threshold (¶36-040)
- employers or group of employers with annual taxable wages of $7.5 million to $100 million will pay tax at the rate of 5.5% with no entitlement to a diminishing exemption threshold
- employers or group of employers with annual taxable wages of $100 million to $1.5 billion will pay tax at the effective marginal rate of 6%
- employers or group of employers with annual taxable wages of more than $1.5 billion will pay tax at the effective marginal rate of 6.5%.

(9) Western Australia annual threshold was $850,000 from 1 July 2019 to 31 December 2019 and $950,000 from 1 January 2020 to 30 June 2020.

(10) Western Australia monthly threshold was $70,833 from 1 July 2019 to 31 December 2019 and $79,167 from 1 January 2020 to 30 June 2020.

(11) Tasmania payroll tax rate is 4% for taxable wages between $1,250,000 and $2,000,000 and 6.1% for taxable wages over $2,000,000.

(12) Tasmania monthly threshold is based on 28, 30 or 31 days in the month.

¶36-040 Payroll tax deduction amounts

Employers are entitled to a deduction, so that where taxable wages exceed a specified threshold, only the excess is subject to payroll tax. In most states, a flat deduction is allowed for all employers.

In South Australia, the maximum annual deduction entitlement is $600,000 ($50,000 monthly). However, a nil payroll tax rate applies where the annual Australian wages do not exceed $1.5 million.

In Queensland and the Northern Territory the deduction is reduced by $1 for every $4 by which the wages exceed the tax free threshold until the deduction tapers to zero.

In Western Australia, the tax-free threshold gradually phases out for employers or group of employers with annual taxable wages in Australia between the annual threshold amount (¶36-030) and the upper threshold amount of $7,500,000. The deduction amount is calculated using the ‘‘tapering value’’ (2/13 in 2020–21) as follows:

Annual threshold amount – [(Total annual wages – Annual threshold amount) × 2/13]

Where employers are grouped, one member claims the exemption threshold and the remaining members must pay a flat amount of tax. Generally, the deduction available is first calculated based on total Australian wages. The result is then reduced on a pro rata basis by comparing the wages paid in a particular state with the total Australian wages.

¶36-050 Wages subject to payroll tax

The definition of ''wages'' in each state is prescribed in either the *Payroll Tax Act* or *Pay-roll Tax Assessment Act*, as applicable. The term ''wages'' is generally defined to mean any wages, salary, remuneration, commission, bonuses or allowances paid or payable (whether at piece work rates or otherwise and whether paid or payable in cash or in kind) to an employee as such. This may include:

- any amount paid or payable by way of remuneration to a person holding office under, or in the service of, the Crown in right of the state
- any amount paid or payable under any prescribed classes of contracts to the extent to which that payment is attributable to labour (¶36-100)
- any amount paid or payable by a company by way of remuneration to a director or member of the governing body of that company, and
- any amount paid or payable by way of commission to an insurance or time-payment canvasser or collector.

Additionally, the definition of wages expressly includes benefits (¶36-080) and extends to include employer contributions to superannuation funds and employee share schemes (¶36-140).

For other payments considered as ''wages'' for payroll tax purposes, see the table at ¶36-140.

¶36-060 Payroll tax exemptions and concessions

Not all wages are subject to payroll tax. The legislation in each state prescribes specific wages that are not subject to the tax and these generally include wages paid or payable:

- by religious institutions
- by public benevolent institutions
- by public or non-profit hospitals
- by schools or colleges providing education at or below the secondary level of education
- by municipal councils
- by charitable organisations, or
- to a person who is a member of the armed forces, being wages paid or payable by the employer from whose employment the person is on leave by reason of his/her being such a member.

Clarification should be sought in each state as the exemption provisions are not necessarily the same in each state.

Further, each state may have additional employers who pay wages that may qualify for exemption. The legislation may also provide for certain elements of wages to be exempt from payroll tax.

In Tasmania, a 3-year payroll tax exemption from 1 July 2018 to 30 June 2021 is provided for wages paid by an employer to its employees in regional Tasmania, where the business relocates to Tasmania and establishes its operations in the state permanently and the employees conduct 80% of their work in regional Tasmania.

In the Northern Territory, a payroll tax exemption is provided from 1 May 2018 to employers when they hire a new employee who is a resident in the Territory or relocate an existing employee to the Territory, or replace a non-resident employee with a resident employee, provided the new hiring or residency occurs by 30 June 2021.

States also provide payroll tax concessions including the following:

- In New South Wales, wages paid or payable on or after 1 June 2020 but before 1 January 2021 are exempt from payroll tax to the extent that they are funded by an Aged Care Workforce payment under the Commonwealth Aged Care Workforce Retention Grant Opportunity program.
- In Queensland, a payroll tax rebate is provided for wages of apprentices and trainees payable for 2009–10 to 2011–12 and the 2015–16 to 2020–21 financial years. This is in addition to the payroll tax exemption for wages paid to apprentices and trainees. For the 2016–17 to 2020–21 financial years, the rebate is 50% of the amount calculated by applying the payroll tax rate to the exempt apprentices and trainee wages.
- In Queensland, for the 2019–20 and 2020–21 financial years, a payroll tax rebate (the employment growth rebate) of up to $20,000 is available to eligible employers that, over a relevant full financial year, have employed more than their level of full-time employees (*Public Ruling* PTAQ000.4.1).

The states have determined that no payroll tax is payable on wages subsidised by the Commonwealth JobKeeper Payment scheme (¶36-140).

The states have also provided payroll tax relief to businesses affected by COVID-19 including the following measures that apply in 2020–21:

- In New South Wales, eligible employers have the option to establish a Stimulus Payment Arrangement for up to 24 months to include the tax payable for the 2019–20 annual reconciliation and any monthly liability for the July, August and September 2020 return periods.
- In Victoria, eligible employers with payrolls up to $10 million can defer their payroll tax liabilities for 2020–21 until the 2021–22 financial year.
- In Queensland, businesses affected by COVID-19 may be eligible for a deferral of payroll tax for the 2020 calendar year. Although payroll tax has been deferred, payroll tax returns must continue to be lodged on their due dates.
- In South Australia, employers (and employer groups) with Australian (annualised group) wages up to $4 million will be granted a payroll tax waiver for the months of April 2020 to June 2021 (for the return periods of March 2020 to May 2021). Employers whose employees qualify for the JobKeeper payments between 4 January 2021 and 28 March 2021 will also receive a payroll tax waiver on other wages paid for the months of January to June 2021 (for the return periods of December 2020 to May 2021). Employers with Australian (annualised group) wages above $4 million who have been adversely impacted by COVID-19 can defer their payroll tax payments for the March to November 2020 return periods until 14 January 2021.
- In Western Australia, wages subsidised by the Boosting Apprenticeship Commencements scheme from 5 October 2020 to 30 September 2021 are exempt from payroll tax.

- In Tasmania, a payroll tax waiver is available for eligible employers providing hotel quarantine services in respect of a wage supplement amount paid to their employees.
- In the NT, employers with estimated total Australian taxable wages under $7.5 million for 2019–20 and with a reduction in turnover of at least 30% due to COVID-19 when compared to the same month or quarter in 2019 can apply for a waiver of payroll tax for the March 2020 to April 2021 return periods. Employers with estimated total Australian taxable wages over $7.5 million for 2019–20 can apply for a deferral until 21 May 2021 of the payment of their monthly payroll tax for the March 2020 to April 2021 return periods if they have a reduction in turnover of at least 50% due to COVID-19 when compared to the corresponding month or quarter in 2019.
- In the ACT, an employer or group with Australia-wide wages up to $10 million can defer their 2020–21 payroll tax interest-free until 1 July 2022. A payroll tax exemption is also provided for wages paid to new apprentices or trainees employed for the period 1 August 2020 to 30 June 2021. Payroll tax exemptions or waivers will continue to be provided until 30 June 2021 to businesses that are unable to operate or can only operate on a very limited basis.

A table showing the assessable and exempt status of common types of payments and benefits is set out in ¶36-140.

¶36-070 Payroll tax treatment of allowances

The definition of ‘‘wages’’ in the payroll tax legislation in each state includes ‘‘allowances’’ so that all payments to employees as ‘‘allowances’’ are subject to tax. However, allowances such as accommodation and motor vehicle/travelling allowances are not subject to payroll tax to the extent that the allowance is within specified statutory amounts (¶36-140).

Reimbursements of expenses incurred by employees on behalf of an employer are only taxable where they are subject to the provisions of the *Fringe Benefits Tax Assessment Act 1986* (FBTAA) (¶36-080).

¶36-080 Payroll tax on non-cash benefits

The legislation of all of the states expressly provides for payroll tax to be levied on non-cash ‘‘benefits’’ provided to employees by employers. However, certain benefits have been prescribed to be not a fringe benefit for payroll tax purposes.

The value of benefits are to be calculated in accordance with the FBTAA.

Generally, the value of fringe benefits for payroll tax purposes is determined by using the ‘‘fringe benefits taxable amount’’ under FBTAA s 5B, ie the ‘‘grossed-up’’ component of taxable fringe benefits is included in the payroll tax base.

¶36-100 Payroll tax on payments to contractors

Generally, payroll tax is a tax on ‘‘wages’’ paid or payable to an employee by an employer. While a contractor is not ordinarily considered to be an ‘‘employee’’, persons/contractors may be deemed to be employees where a ‘‘relevant’’ contract exists between the person supplying the services (the contractor) and the end-user (the employer).

Broadly, the contractor provisions deem payments to certain contractors to be ‘‘wages’’ for payroll tax purposes.

The basic situations that will give rise to a ‘‘relevant’’ contract are:

(1) where a person, in the course of carrying on a business, supplies to another person services for or in relation to the performance of work

(2) where a person, in the course of carrying on a business, is supplied with the services of another person for or in relation to the performance of work, and

(3) where a person, in the course of carrying on a business, provides goods to persons who perform work and resupply the goods. This is intended to deal with the practice of a person in business providing goods to ''outworkers'' or ''home workers'' who perform specified work and return the goods.

Under the contractor provisions, the term ''contract'' includes an agreement, arrangement or undertaking, whether formal or informal and whether express or implied. Although the provisions relate to the supply of services, the term ''services'' is defined to include ''results (whether goods or services) of work performed''. However, only the amount of the payment that relates to labour is liable to tax and not the cost of materials and equipment incurred by the contractor. Some states have issued guidelines on the deductions available for materials and equipment for particular types of contractors.

Although the situations covered are very broad, at least one party to the contract must enter into the agreement while in the course of carrying on a business.

The legislation also provides for specific exclusions from the contractor provisions, supplemented by rulings from the various state revenue offices. Where any exclusions apply, the contract payments by the person engaging the contractor will be exempt from payroll tax. Contracts may be exempted if any of the following apply.

- The labour component of the contract is ancillary to the supply of materials or equipment.
- The services provided are not normally required by the business receiving the services and the person supplying those services provides them to the general public.
- The services provided are not required by the business for more than 180 days per financial year regardless of how many different contractors provide the same service.
- Any one contractor is not engaged for more than 90 days in total per financial year or provides one person or the same people for no more than 90 days in total to carry out the contract.
- Services provided under contract are ordinarily rendered to the general public.
- The services under the contract are provided by 2 or more persons supplied by the contractor.
- The services are those of an owner/driver, an insurance agent or a direct selling agent. Note that the exemptions that apply in relation to insurance agents and direct selling agents are not available in New South Wales, Tasmania, the Northern Territory and the ACT.

Where the contractor provisions do not apply the liability for payroll tax will generally depend on whether an employer/employee relationship exists. Accordingly, payroll tax does not fall on payments made to independent contractors provided the intention of the contract is not to reduce or avoid the liability to payroll tax.

In all states, provisions apply to make employment agents liable for payroll tax on payments made to persons engaged to provide services to the agents' clients (see (12) at ¶36-140).

¶36-110 Payroll tax grouping provisions

The legislation in all states provides for the ''grouping'' of related or associated businesses so that, where 2 or more businesses are grouped, their wages are aggregated in order to determine whether a liability exists. However, each employer in the group remains primarily responsible for the payment of payroll tax on its own wages. The principal circumstances in which businesses will be grouped by the various state tax authorities are as follows:

- where companies are "related" under *Corporations Act 2001* (ie in a holding/subsidiary relationship)
- where employees of one business perform duties solely or mainly for the benefit of another business
- where there is an agreement between 2 businesses relating to the performance of duties by employees of one, for the benefit of the other
- where the same person (or persons) has a controlling interest in 2 or more businesses. Different rules apply to companies, trusts, partnerships or businesses owned by one person, and
- where an employer has controlling interest in another employer (being a corporation) under tracing provisions.

Determining whether a group exists largely hinges on the opinion of the Commissioner in each state, having regard to the circumstances of each particular case. Generally, the legislation provides that, other than in respect of companies related under the corporations law, the Commissioner has a discretion to exclude an employer from the operation of the grouping provisions. The discretion may be exercised where it can be demonstrated that the grouped businesses are substantially independent and unconnected, and that the relationship is not designed to reduce or avoid payroll tax. Each state has separate guidelines as to the circumstances in which a person may seek to gain exclusion from the respective grouping provisions.

Generally, where employers are grouped, one group member claims the exemption threshold and the remaining members must pay a flat rate of tax (¶36-040).

¶36-120 Payroll tax jurisdiction issues

The legislation in each state prescribes the circumstances in which wages are liable to payroll tax to ensure that tax in respect of services rendered by a particular employee is payable in only one state for any given month.

Under the nexus provisions common to all states, wages are taxable in a state if they relate to services performed wholly in that jurisdiction. For wages relating to services performed in 2 or more Australian jurisdictions, or partly in one or more Australian jurisdictions and partly outside all Australian jurisdictions, they are taxable in a particular state if:

- the employee is based in that state
- where the employee is not based in an Australian jurisdiction, the employer is based in that state
- where both the employee and employer are not based in an Australian jurisdiction, the wages are paid or payable in that state, or
- where both the employee and employer are not based in an Australian jurisdiction and the wages are not paid or payable in an Australian jurisdiction, the services are performed mainly in that state.

Wages will also be taxable in a state if they relate to services performed wholly outside all Australian jurisdiction and are paid in that state.

An employee is based in a particular state if his or her principal place of residence is in that jurisdiction. In cases where the employee is a company, the test for where the employee is based is the same as it is for an employer. An employer is based in a state if the employer's registered business address (for ABN purposes) is in that jurisdiction. If the employer does not have a registered business address, or has a registered business address in more than one Australian jurisdiction, the employer is based in a particular state if the employer's principal place of business is in that jurisdiction.

The question of where services were provided is determined by reference to services provided by the employee in the month in which the wages are paid or payable or, if no services were provided in that month, in the most recent prior month in which services were provided.

An exemption may be available where an employee has been working overseas for a continuous period of more than 6 months.

Accordingly, it is important for employers to be aware that both the place where services are provided and the place where wages are paid need to be taken into consideration when determining a potential payroll tax liability.

¶36-140 Table of payroll tax assessable and exempt items

The following table shows the assessable or exempt status of common types of payments and benefits provided by employers to employees for payroll tax purposes. The table is current as at 1 January 2021.

The letter A denotes assessable status and the letter E denotes exempt status. Numbered items are explained in the notes that follow the table.

Description	NSW	Vic	Qld	SA	WA	Tas	ACT	NT
Wages	A	A	A	A	A	A	A	A
Salaries	A	A	A	A	A	A	A	A
Remuneration	A	A	A	A	A	A	A	A
Commissions	A	A	A	A	A	A	A	A
Bonuses	A	A	A	A	A	A	A	A
Allowances (1)	A	A	A	A	A	A	A	A
Benefits	(2)	(2)	(2)	(2)	(2)	(2)	(2)	(2)
Accident pay	A	A	A	A	A	A	A	A
Adoption leave	(3)	(3)	(3)	(3)	(3)	(3)	(3)	(3)
Apprentices' wages	(4)	(4)	(4)	(4)	(4)	(4)	(4)	(4)
Back pay	A	A	A	A	A	A	A	A
Compensation other than workers compensation	A	A	A	A	A	A	A	A
Directors allowances								
– working	A	A	A	A	A	A	A	A
– non-working	(5)	(5)	(5)	(5)	(5)	A	(5)	A
Directors fees	A	A	A	A	A	A	A	A
Dividends	E	E	E	E	E	E	E	E
Fees to employees	A	A	A	A	A	A	A	A
Free holidays	A	A	A	A	A	A	A	A
Gifts (6)	A	A	A	A	A	A	A	A
GST on wages	(7)	(7)	(7)	(7)	(7)	(7)	(7)	(7)
Holiday pay (8)	A	A	A	A	A	A	A	A
Indirect payments	A	A	A	A	A	A	A	A
JobKeeper payments	(9)	(9)	(9)	(9)	(9)	(9)	(9)	(9)

Description	NSW	Vic	Qld	SA	WA	Tas	ACT	NT
Loans	A	A	A	A	A	A	A	A
Long service leave (10)	A	A	A	A	A	A	A	A
Maternity leave	(11)	(11)	(11)	(11)	(11)	(11)	(11)	(11)
Meal money	A	A	A	A	A	A	A	A
Meals	A	A	A	A	A	A	A	A
Motor vehicles	A	A	A	A	A	A	A	A
Overtime	A	A	A	A	A	A	A	A
Parental leave	*	(12)	*	*	*	*	*	*
Paternity leave	(13)	A	(13)	A	(13)	A	(13)	(13)
Payments through/by employment agents	(14)	(14)	(14)	(14)	(14)	(14)	(14)	(14)
Payment by third party to an employee/third party	(15)	(15)	(15)	(15)	(15)	(15)	(15)	(15)
Piece work payments	A	A	A	A	A	A	A	A
Prizes (16)	A	A	A	A	A	A	A	A
Quarters	A	A	A	A	A	A	A	A
Reimbursements	E	E	E	E	E	E	E	E
Relevant contracts	(17)	(17)	(17)	(17)	(17)	(17)	(17)	(17)
Retirement allowances	(18)	(18)	(18)	(18)	(18)	(18)	(18)	(18)
Share scheme contributions	(19)	(19)	(19)	(19)	(19)	(19)	(19)	(19)
Shift allowances	A	A	A	A	A	A	A	A
Sick pay	A	A	A	A	A	A	A	A
Staff discounts	A	A	A	A	A	A	A	A
Study expenses	A	A	A	A	A	A	A	A
Superannuation contributions	(20)	(20)	(20)	(20)	(20)	(20)	(20)	(20)
Surrogacy leave	*	*	(21)	*	*	*	*	*
Termination payments	(22)	(22)	(22)	(22)	(22)	(22)	(22)	(22)
Trust distributions	(23)	*	*	*	*	(23)	*	*
Volunteer firefighters/ emergency services volunteers	(24)	(24)	(24)	(24)	(24)	(24)	(24)	(24)
Vouchers	A	A	A	A	A	A	A	A
Workers compensation (25)	E	E	E	E	E	E	E	E

* Not expressly included in wages definition.

(1) Allowances

Allowances cover cash amounts paid to employees (eg dirt money, tool allowances, meal allowances, currency translation allowances, tax equalisation payments) and are generally taxable in full. However, genuine reimbursements of work-related expenses are not allowances and not subject to payroll tax.

Travelling allowance

Travelling allowances are exempt to the extent that they do not exceed the exempt rate. The exempt rate of travelling allowance is the rate determined under the income tax legislation for calculating a deduction for car expenses (68 cents per kilometre for 2020–21) or, if no such rate is determined, the rate prescribed under the payroll tax regulations.

Accommodation allowance

The exempt rate of accommodation allowance is the reasonable daily travel allowance expenses using the lowest capital city for the lowest salary band determined by the ATO ($283.45 per night for 2020–21) or, if no such determination is in force, the rate prescribed by the payroll tax regulations.

(2) Benefits

These are assessable on the value assessed for Commonwealth FBT purposes and include:

- waiver of a debt
- payment or reimbursement of expenditure that is not actually incurred in the course of employment
- free or cheap housing or board
- certain living-away-from-home allowances, and
- entertainment provided to employees by employers who are exempt from income tax.

(3) Adoption leave

New South Wales, Queensland, South Australia, Western Australia, Tasmania and Northern Territory

Wages payable in respect of adoption leave given to an employee in connection with the adoption of a child by that employee are exempt from payroll tax. The exemption does not apply to any fringe benefits component of the wages.

Victoria

An exemption for wages payable in respect of adoption leave given to an employee applied from 1 January 2003 to 30 June 2019. From 1 July 2019, the exemption was replaced by an exemption for wages payable in respect of parental leave for the employee's role as primary caregiver or secondary caregiver for a child (see "Parental leave").

ACT

Wages payable to an employee on adoption leave or primary carer leave in relation to a newly adopted child are exempt from payroll tax.

(4) Apprentices' wages

New South Wales

From 1 July 2008, the exemption in relation to apprentices, trainees and group apprenticeship or traineeship schemes ceased to apply and was replaced with a rebate scheme. However, the exemption in relation to apprentices and trainees employed by non-profit organisations continues to apply.

Victoria

Wages paid to eligible apprentices or trainees ("new entrants") employed by an organisation declared by the Treasurer to be an approved training organisation are exempt from payroll tax. Prior to 1 July 2018, the declaration as an approved training organisation was restricted to non-profit organisations. From 1 July 2016, the exemption applies to wages paid to an apprentice or trainee who resumes an apprenticeship or traineeship with a different employer.

Queensland

Wages payable to an apprentice or trainee for the period of the apprenticeship or traineeship are exempt. The exemption does not apply to wages paid to a trainee who, immediately before the current traineeship started, has been employed by the employer for a continuous period of at least 3 months as a full-time employee or 12 months as a casual employee. However, the exemption applies if the employee commenced a Certificate II traineeship and, having successfully completed the traineeship, commences a Certificate III traineeship with the same employer. For the 2009–10 to 2011–12 and 2015–16 to 2020–21 financial years, employers may be entitled to claim a payroll tax rebate on the exempt wages paid to apprentices and trainees. The effect of the rebate is to reduce the payroll tax payable on the wages of other employees of the employer.

South Australia

The payroll tax exemption that applied from 1 July 2010 to 30 June 2012 for wages of eligible trainees and apprentices was abolished from 1 July 2012.

Tasmania

From 1 July 2008, wages paid or payable to an employee who is employed by a non-profit training organisation under a group apprenticeship or group training scheme are exempt. A payroll tax rebate is also provided for employers who pay payroll tax and employ eligible apprentices, trainees and youth employees between 1 July 2017 and 30 June 2022. In response to the impact of COVID-19, a one-year rebate is also available for employers who commence employment of youth employees between 1 April 2020 and 30 June 2022.

Western Australia

Wages paid or payable by an employer to or in relation to person who is an apprentice under a registered training contract or a trainee employed under a training agreement are exempt. With effect from 1 December 2017 the exemption for trainees is restricted to new employees with annual wages of $100,000 or less at the time the training contract is lodged for registration. The new employee must have been continuously employed for more than 3 months full time or not more than 12 months casual or part-time, or a combination of both, immediately prior to the commencement date of the training contract.

ACT

Wages payable to a ''new starter'' who is employed for the first time in an industry or occupation and is receiving eligible training in the industry or occupation are exempt. Wages payable to trainees by approved group training organisations are also exempt. As a relief measure to help businesses impacted by COVID-19, a payroll tax exemption is also provided for wages paid to apprentices or trainees employed for the period 1 August 2020 to 31 January 2021.

Northern Territory

Before 1 July 2015, wages payable to certain classes of probationers and apprentices, and to graduates of tertiary educational institutions employed under approved trainee agreements, were exempt.

(5) Directors' allowances

New South Wales, Victoria, Queensland, South Australia, Western Australia, ACT

To qualify for exemption from payroll tax, these allowances must be bona fide allowances paid to non-working directors for expenses incurred in carrying out the duties of their office.

(6) Gifts

A gift provided by an employer to a person in his/her capacity as an employee may be a benefit liable for payroll tax in all states. The value of the benefit is assessed on the same basis as property benefits for Commonwealth FBT purposes. Examples of such benefits are gifts of goods produced by the employer or the reduction in price of such goods.

(7) GST on wages

The GST component of wages is excluded from the payroll tax base.

(8) Holiday pay

In all states holiday pay is assessable if paid to an employee who will be continuing in employment. Payments made in a lump sum in lieu of holidays in consequence of the termination of employment of an employee are also subject to payroll tax.

(9) JobKeeper payments

New South Wales

Any additional wages paid to employees to meet the requirements of the Commonwealth JobKeeper scheme are exempt from payroll tax.

Victoria

Additional payments made to bridge the gap between an employee's normal wages and the $1,500 per fortnight required to qualify for JobKeeper payments are exempt from payroll tax.

Queensland

The Australian Government's JobKeeper payment is not liable for payroll tax.

South Australia

Wages paid or payable by an employer to an employee that are subsidised by the JobKeeper payment are exempt from payroll tax.

Western Australia

Wage subsidies paid by employers to employees under the Australian Government's JobKeeper Payment scheme are exempt from payroll tax.

Tasmania

An employer is not required to pay payroll tax in respect of the amount of taxable wages paid or payable to the employee that is equal to the amount of the Commonwealth JobKeeper payment that the employer is entitled to receive for that employee for those wages.

Northern Territory

Employers receiving payments under the Commonwealth JobKeeper scheme for employees working in the Northern Territory do not have to pay payroll tax on those payments.

ACT

Wages paid or payable to an eligible employee that are subsidised under the Commonwealth Government JobKeeper subsidy program are exempt from payroll tax.

(10) Long service leave

In all states, if paid to a continuing employee, long service leave is assessable. Payments of accrued long service leave made on termination of employment also form part of taxable wages.

(11) Maternity leave

New South Wales, Queensland, South Australia, Western Australia, Tasmania and Northern Territory

Wages payable in respect of maternity leave given to a female employee in connection with her pregnancy or birth of her child are exempt from payroll tax. Wages in respect of paternity leave are also exempt in New South Wales. The exemption is limited to wages paid or payable for a maximum 14 weeks' leave. The exemption does not apply to any fringe benefits component of the wages.

Victoria

Wages payable in respect of maternity leave were exempt from payroll tax from 1 January 2003 to 30 June 2019. From 1 July 2019 the exemption was replaced by an exemption for wages payable in respect of parental leave for the employee's role as primary caregiver or secondary caregiver for a child (see ''Parental leave'').

ACT

Wages payable to an employee on maternity leave or primary carer leave in relation to the birth of a child are exempt from payroll tax.

(12) Parental leave

From 1 July 2019, wages are exempt from Victorian payroll tax if they are paid to an employee in respect of parental leave for the employee's role as primary caregiver or secondary caregiver for a child. The exemption is limited to wages paid or payable for a maximum 14 weeks' leave. The exemption does not apply to any fringe benefit component of the wage (see also ''Adoption leave'' and ''Maternity leave'').

Paid parental leave scheme payments

Payments made under the Commonwealth government's Paid Parental Leave (PPL) scheme do not constitute wages and are not liable to payroll tax (*Revenue Ruling* PTA 037).

(13) Paternity leave

New South Wales, Queensland and Northern Territory

Wages in respect of paternity leave are exempt. The exemption is limited to wages paid or payable for a maximum 14 weeks' leave. The exemption does not apply to any fringe benefit component of the wages.

Western Australia

A similar exemption applies for wages in respect of ''parental leave'' given to an employee in connection with the pregnancy of a female carrying the employee's unborn child or the birth of the employee's child.

ACT

Wages payable to an employee on primary carer leave in relation to the birth or adoption of a child are exempt from payroll tax.

Paid parental leave scheme payments

See ''Adoption leave''.

(14) Payments through/by employment agents

New South Wales, Victoria, Queensland and Tasmania

Employment agents are liable to payroll tax on amounts paid to service providers who are provided to a client under an employment agency contract. However, the employment agent will not be liable if the payments to the service provider would be exempt if they had been paid to the service provider by the client and a declaration to this effect is given by the client to the employment agent.

South Australia, Western Australia and ACT

The employment agent is the employer. Broadly, an employment agent is defined as a person who by arrangement procures the services of another person for a client as a result of which the agent receives directly or indirectly payment, by way of lump sum or ongoing fee. Certain exemptions may apply.

In the ACT, from 1 January 2015 no exemption applies in respect of wages paid or payable by employment agents to subcontractors where the subcontractor was a genuine employer of the individuals who performed the work for which wages were paid.

Northern Territory

Employment agents are liable to payroll tax on amounts paid to service providers who are provided to a client under an employment agency contract. However, the employment agent will not be liable if the payments to the service provider would be exempt if they had been paid to the service provider by the client and a declaration to this effect is given by the client to the employment agent.

(15) Payments by third party to an employee or another third party

New South Wales, Victoria, Queensland, South Australia, Tasmania, ACT and Northern Territory

Money or other valuable consideration paid or given by: (a) a third party to the employee; (b) the employer to a third party; or (c) a third party to another third party, for an employee's services will be treated as wages.

Western Australia

Wages include payments to or in relation to an employee by someone acting on behalf of the employer.

(16) Prizes

Prizes that have a functional utility in the form of valuable and useful goods such as cars, TVs, stereos and holidays, provided to a person as an employee, are taxable in all states. Taxable value is that assessed for Commonwealth FBT purposes. Prizes and awards such as medals, plaques and cups that in essence recognise achievements are not taxable.

(17) Relevant contracts

New South Wales, Victoria, Queensland, South Australia, Tasmania and ACT

Payments under relevant contracts are deemed to be wages, subject to certain exemptions (¶36-100).

Western Australia

Relevant or service contracts (¶36-100) are not expressly provided for in the legislation. The liability to payroll tax *generally* depends on the existence of an employer/employee relationship. The tax does not fall on payments to independent contractors provided the contract is not made to reduce or avoid the liability to payroll tax. However, regard should be had to (12) above concerning employment agents.

Northern Territory

Payments under relevant contracts are taken to be wages from 1 July 2009. Prior to that date, there were no relevant/service contract provisions in the legislation and the liability to payroll tax generally depended on the existence of an employer/employee relationship.

(18) Retirement allowances

See (22) Termination payments.

(19) Share scheme contributions

New South Wales, Victoria, Queensland, South Australia and Tasmania

Employer contributions to an employee share acquisition scheme constitute wages subject to payroll tax in New South Wales from 1 July 2003, in Victoria from 1 July 2007 and in Queensland, South Australia and Tasmania from 1 July 2008. Contributions to a share scheme provided to directors or members of the governing body of a company by way of remuneration also constitute wages subject to tax.

Western Australia and Northern Territory

Employer contributions to an employee share acquisition scheme are subject to payroll tax in Western Australia (from 1 July 1997) and in the Northern Territory (from 1 July 1999).

ACT

In the ACT, employer contributions to employee share schemes are subject to payroll tax from 1 July 2005.

(20) Superannuation contributions

Employer contributions to, or the setting apart of money for, any form of superannuation, provident or retirement fund or scheme are taxable in all states. This includes payments under the superannuation guarantee scheme, and may include non-monetary contributions and top-up contributions to a defined benefit fund (*CSR Ltd v Chief Commr of State Revenue (NSW)*). All states tax employee contributions to superannuation funds on the basis that such contributions form part of gross salaries.

In South Australia, the *Payroll Tax Act 2009* specifically provides that amounts credited to members' accounts so as to increase the employee's superannuation entitlements are taxable.

(21) Surrogacy leave

Wages for surrogacy leave (other than annual leave, recreation leave, sick leave or similar leave) given to an employee in connection with a child residing with the employee under a surrogacy arrangement (as defined under the *Surrogacy Act 2010* (Qld)) are exempt in Queensland from 14 October 2010. The exemption is limited to wages paid or payable for not more than 14 weeks' surrogacy leave for any one surrogacy arrangement. Wages comprising a fringe benefit are excluded from the exemption.

(22) Termination payments

New South Wales, Victoria, Queensland, South Australia, Tasmania and Northern Territory

Termination payments made in consequence of the retirement from, or termination of, any office or employment of an employee are wages for payroll tax purposes. These include:

- unused annual leave and long service leave payments
- employment termination payments within the meaning of ITAA97 s 82-130 that would be included in the assessable income of an employee, including transitional termination payments within the meaning of ITTPA s 82-10, and any payment that would be an employment termination payment but for the fact that it was received more than 12 months after termination
- amounts paid or payable by a company as a consequence of terminating the services or office of a director

- amounts paid or payable by a person taken to be an employer under the contractor provisions (¶36-100), as a consequence of terminating the supply of services by the deemed employee under those provisions.

Western Australia

Payroll tax is payable on:

- unused annual leave and long service leave payments
- employment termination payments within the meaning of ITAA97 s 82-130 that would be included in the assessable income of an employee, including transitional termination payments within the meaning of ITTPA s 82-10, and any payment that would be an employment termination payment but for the fact that it was received more than 12 months after termination
- amounts paid or payable by a company as a consequence of terminating the service or office of a director (from 1 July 2009).

ACT

The legislation specifically provides for the following termination payments to be taxable in the ACT:

- payments for unused annual leave, including loading or additional payment relating to that leave
- payments for unused long service leave
- employment termination payments paid or payable by an employer that would be included in the assessable income of the employee if the whole of the payment had been paid to the employee
- payments by a company in consequence of the termination of the services of a director, and
- payments by an employer under a service contract in consequence of the termination of the services of an employee under the contract.

(23) Trust distributions

New South Wales

Under the repealed *Pay-roll Tax Act 1971* (NSW), from 1 July 2003 a distribution to a beneficiary under a trust constituted wages to the extent that the distribution is in lieu of wages for work done for the trust by the beneficiary. This provision has been deleted from the new *Payroll Tax Act 2007* (NSW) so that from 1 July 2007 these trust distributions are no longer liable to payroll tax.

Tasmania

Under the repealed *Pay-roll Tax Act 1971* (Tas), trust distributions made in lieu of wages were included in the definition of wages from 1 July 2005. This provision has been omitted from the new *Payroll Tax Act 2008* (Tas) which came into effect from 1 July 2008.

(24) Volunteer firefighters/emergency services volunteers

Wages paid or payable to an employee in respect of any period during which the employee was taking part as a volunteer in emergency or bushfire fighting activities exempt. The exemption does not include payments as recreation leave, annual leave, long service or sick leave.

(25) Workers compensation

All compensation payments made in accordance with any workers compensation legislation are exempt whether paid by an employer or an insurer.

''Make-up pay'' is taxable.

Chapter 37 Stamp Duty

Para

¶37-000 Introduction to stamp duty

Stamp duty, or ''duty'' as it is now called in most jurisdictions, is a tax imposed by the states and territories on various transactions either at a fixed rate or at an ''ad valorem'' rate on the value of the transaction.

This chapter provides a general outline of the more important transactions on which stamp duty is imposed by the various states and territories. References are to the *Duties Act 1997* (NSW) unless otherwise stated.

The general administration of tax collection in NSW is governed by the *Taxation Administration Act 1996* (NSW) and comparable administration legislation exists in other states. However, primary liability for payment of tax arises under the following legislation:

- New South Wales — *Duties Act 1997*
- Victoria — *Duties Act 2000*
- Queensland — *Duties Act 2001*
- Western Australia — *Duties Act 2008*
- South Australia — *Stamp Duties Act 1923*
- Tasmania — *Duties Act 2001*
- Australian Capital Territory — *Duties Act 1999*
- Northern Territory — *Stamp Duties Act 1978.*

The rates and information in this chapter are based on the law as at 1 July 2020.

Stamp duty and GST

Stamp duty will, in most cases, apply to the GST inclusive amount of the consideration. For example, stamp duty will be payable on the GST inclusive amount paid by a purchaser for the conveyance or transfer of real property. If the agreed purchase price is $1 million and, in addition to this amount, the vendor collects from the purchaser $100,000 on account of GST, duty will be payable on $1.1 million.

As a general rule, the converse will not apply. That is, GST will not have to be paid on stamp duty payable on a dutiable matter by a purchaser to a state or territory.

¶37-005 Rewrite of stamp duty law

Rewritten legislation was adopted in NSW, Victoria, Queensland, Tasmania, Western Australia and the ACT between 1999 and 2008 (¶37-000). These states are referred to in this chapter as the ''Rewrite States''.

The duties legislation in the Rewrite States imposes duty on certain transactions and documents. In particular, duty is charged on a transfer of, and certain other dealings in, ''dutiable property'' (¶37-020). Broadly, transfer duty replaced conveyance duty and duty on undocumented transactions of the ''old'' legislation.

Other states

Stamp duty in South Australia and the Northern Territory (the ''non-Rewrite States'') is imposed largely in the ''traditional'' manner, ie on documents (''instruments'') necessary to evidence such things as transfers of land, although the legislation has been widened over time to impose duty where no written document is brought into existence.

¶37-020 Duty on transfers of property

In the Rewrite States (¶37-005), duty is payable on transfers of dutiable property. In the non-Rewrite States (ie South Australia and the Northern Territory), duty is imposed on conveyances of property (unless an exempt category of property).

Rewrite states

In NSW duty is imposed on transfers of specified items of dutiable property. Dutiable property includes the following (s 11):

- land (there are provisions for landholder corporations and unit trusts: ¶37-030)
- transferable floor space
- land use entitlements
- a partnership interest, if it is an interest in a partnership that has partnership property which is dutiable property
- goods, if they are the subject of an arrangement that includes a dutiable transaction over certain other dutiable property (other than certain exempt categories of goods such as stock-in-trade)
- options to purchase land, and
- interests in any dutiable property (with some exceptions).

The following transactions in relation to dutiable property are also potentially dutiable: (a) agreements for sale or transfer; (b) declarations of trust; (c) surrenders of interests in land; (d) foreclosures of mortgages; (e) vesting of dutiable property by, or as a consequence of, a court order and (f) certain leases (s 9).

Generally, duty is payable by the transferee (s 13). It is levied on the higher of the consideration for the dutiable transaction and the unencumbered value of the dutiable property (s 21). Duty has to be paid within 3 months after an agreement for sale or transfer. This period begins for a written instrument when the instrument is first executed, ie when any party signs or seals an instrument regardless of whether the other parties have done so.

Duty is payable on an upward sliding scale (s 32), set out in the tables below. Concessions may be available for certain transfers, eg first home buyers may pay duty at a discounted rate (s 69).

The legislation contains provisions aggregating dutiable transactions for the purpose of assessing duty (s 25). The dutiable transactions must occur within 12 months and the transferees must be associated persons. The dutiable transactions must together form, evidence, give effect to or arise from what is substantially one *arrangement* relating to the relevant dutiable property. The term ''arrangement'' is likely to cover a wider range of situations than the word ''transaction'', used in the former legislation (¶37-000).

There are additional anti-avoidance provisions going to dutiable value that enable the Chief Commissioner to disregard certain arrangements affecting the dutiable value of dutiable property that has the effect of reducing the dutiable value (s 24). There are also wider anti-avoidance provisions dealing with schemes generally (Ch 11A).

The relevant provisions of the Victorian, Queensland, Tasmanian, Western Australian and ACT legislation are broadly similar. However, in Queensland and Western Australia the duty base also includes non-real business assets. The Northern Territory also levies duty in respect of certain categories of non-real business assets.

Duty on the transfer of non-real core business assets (eg goodwill, intellectual property and statutory licences) was abolished in the ACT from 1 July 2006, in Tasmania from 1 July 2008, in South Australia from 18 June 2015 and in NSW from 1 July 2016. Similar duties are proposed to be abolished in Queensland, Western Australia and the Northern Territory but with no certain date for abolition (¶37-060). In South Australia a phased abolition of duty on transfers of non-residential, non-primary production real property commenced on 7 December 2015 (RevenueSA Information Circular No 86). That abolition was completed on 1 July 2018.

NEW SOUTH WALES	
Value of consideration ($)	**Duty payable ($)**
0 – 14,000	1.25 for every 100 (or part thereof)
14,001 – 31,000	175 + 1.50 for every 100 (or part thereof) in excess of 14,000
31,001 – 83,000	430 + 1.75 for every 100 (or part thereof) in excess of 31,000
83,001 – 310,000	1,340 + 3.50 for every 100 (or part thereof) in excess of 83,000
310,001 – 1,033,000	9,285 + 4.50 for every 100 (or part thereof) in excess of 310,000
1,033,001 or more	41,820 + 5.50 for every 100 (or part thereof) in excess of 1,033,000

Note: Premium property duty of 7% is payable on excess over $3,101,000 of dutiable value of residential property. This duty has been levied since 1 June 2004 and the current threshold of $3,101,000 came into effect on 1 July 2020. An 8% duty surcharge generally applies to foreign purchasers of residential property from 1 July 2017 (the surcharge was previously 4%). Certain exemptions may apply. Commercial residential property is exempt from the surcharge. From 1 July 2017, no duty is payable by first home buyers purchasing new and existing homes up to $650,000, with duty reduced for amounts between $650,000 and $800,000.

On 27 July 2020, stamp duty was eliminated for newly built homes below $800,000 benefiting first home buyers. The concession reduces on higher values before phasing out at $1 million. The change will last for a 12-month period, commencing on 1 August 2020. Lower thresholds apply for existing homes and vacant land.

The NSW Treasurer announced on 5 November 2018 that NSW will index stamp duty brackets to CPI. This stamp duty brackets change will affect transactions made on or after 1 July 2019. The above table shows the indexed rates applicable from 1 July 2020.

The NSW government has also announced a significant tax reform package which will, if implemented, see the ultimate replacement of stamp duty with a property tax levied annually. The package is still a proposal with a period for public consultation ending on 15 March 2021.

VICTORIA	
Value of consideration ($)	**Duty payable ($)**
0 – 25,000	1.40 for every 100 (or part thereof)
25,001 – 130,000	350 + 2.40 for every 100 (or part thereof) in excess of 25,000
130,001 – 960,000	2,870 + 6 for every 100 (or part thereof) in excess of 130,000
960,001 or more	5.50 for every 100 (or part thereof)
Note: Concessional rates apply for a principal place of residence. From 1 July 2017, duty is abolished for first home buyers purchasing a property up to $600,000, with a duty concession for properties valued between $600,001 and $750,000. An 8% duty surcharge applies to foreign purchasers of residential property from 1 July 2019. The previous rate was 7%. Duty concessions also apply for bushfire affected and regional areas.	

TASMANIA	
Value of consideration ($)	**Duty payable ($)**
0 – 3,000	50
3,001 – 25,000	50 + 1.75 for every 100 (or part thereof) in excess of 3,000
25,001 – 75,000	435 + 2.25 for every 100 (or part thereof) in excess of 25,000
75,001 – 200,000	1,560 + 3.50 for every 100 (or part thereof) in excess of 75,000
200,001 – 375,000	5,935 + 4 for every 100 (or part thereof) in excess of 200,000
375,001 – 725,000	12,935 + 4.25 for every 100 (or part thereof) in excess of 375,000
725,001 or more	27,810 + 4.50 for every 100 (or part thereof) in excess of 725,000
Note: A surcharge of 3% applies to foreign persons purchasing residential property from 1 July 2018. The rate increased to 7% from 1 January 2020.	

QUEENSLAND	
Value of consideration ($)	**Duty payable ($)**
0 – 5,000	Nil
5,001 – 75,000	1.50 for every 100 (or part thereof) in excess of 5,000
75,001 – 540,000	1,050 + 3.50 for every 100 (or part thereof) in excess of 75,000
540,001 – 1,000,000	17,325 + 4.50 for every 100 (or part thereof) in excess of 540,000
1,000,001 or more	38,025 + 5.75 for every 100 (or part thereof) in excess of 1,000,000
Note: Concessions may apply for home buyers. A 3% duty surcharge applied to foreign purchasers of residential property from 1 October 2016. From 1 July 2018, the surcharge rate increased to 7%.	

AUSTRALIAN CAPITAL TERRITORY	
Value of consideration ($)	**Duty payable ($)**
0 – 200,000	20 or 1.20 for every 100 or part thereof, whichever is greater
200,001 – 300,000	2,400 + 2.20 for every 100 (or part thereof) in excess of 200,000
300,001 – 500,000	4,600 + 3.40 for every 100 (or part thereof) in excess of 300,000
500,001 – 750,000	11,400 + 4.32 for every 100 (or part thereof) in excess of 500,000
750,001 – 1,000,000	22,200 + 5.90 for every 100 (or part thereof) in excess of 750,000
1,000,001 – 1,455,000	36,950 + 6.40 for every 100 (or part thereof) in excess of 1,000,000

AUSTRALIAN CAPITAL TERRITORY	
Value of consideration ($)	**Duty payable ($)**
1,455,000 or more	A flat rate of 4.54 for every 100 applied to the total transaction value
Note: The above rates only apply for non-commercial transactions (ie where the property is used for residential or rural purposes) from 1 July 2019. For commercial transactions (ie where the property is used wholly or partly for commercial purposes) and the value of the property is below $1.5 million, the duty rate is nil. Where the value of the property is $1.5 million and above, a flat rate of 5% applies.	

WESTERN AUSTRALIA	
Value of consideration ($)	**Duty payable ($)**
0 – 80,000	1.90 for every 100 (or part thereof)
80,001 – 100,000	1,520 + 2.85 for every 100 (or part thereof) in excess of 80,000
100,001 – 250,000	2,090 + 3.80 for every 100 (or part thereof) in excess of 100,000
250,001 – 500,000	7,790 + 4.75 for every 100 (or part thereof) in excess of 250,000
500,001 or more	19,665 + 5.15 for every 100 (or part thereof) in excess of 500,000
Note: Concessional rates apply to principal places of residence, residential rental properties and vacant land on which a residence is built within 5 years. From 1 January 2019, a 7% duty surcharge applies to foreign purchasers of residential property.	

SOUTH AUSTRALIA	
Value of consideration ($)	**Duty payable ($)**
0 – 12,000	1 for every 100 (or part thereof)
12,001 – 30,000	120 + 2 for every 100 (or part thereof) in excess of 12,000
30,001 – 50,000	480 + 3 for every 100 (or part thereof) in excess of 30,000
50,001 – 100,000	1,080 + 3.50 for every 100 (or part thereof) in excess of 50,000
100,001 – 200,000	2,830 + 4 for every 100 (or part thereof) in excess of 100,000
200,001 – 250,000	6,830 + 4.25 for every 100 (or part thereof) in excess of 200,000
250,001 – 300,000	8,955 + 4.75 for every 100 (or part thereof) in excess of 250,000
300,001 – 500,000	11,330 + 5 for every 100 (or part thereof) in excess of 300,000
500,001 or more	21,330 + 5.50 for every 100 (or part thereof) in excess of 500,000
Note: A 7% duty surcharge applies to foreign purchasers of residential property from 1 January 2018. Duty on property that is not residential or primary production land was abolished from 1 July 2018.	

NORTHERN TERRITORY	
Value of consideration ($)	**Duty payable ($)**
0 – 525,000	see formula below
525,001 – 2,999,999	4.95%
3,000,000 – 4,999,999	5.75%
5,000,000 or more	5.95%
Note: A discount of up to $18,601 may be available for the purchase of a principal place of residence. Previously (before 6 May 2019), a full stamp duty concession may have been available for first home buyers who purchased an established home up to the value of $650,000 on the initial $500,000 value of the home.	

The duty payable on amounts of consideration up to $525,000 is calculated according to the following formula:

$$D = (0.06571441 \times V^2) + 15V$$

where:

D = the duty payable in $, and

$V = \dfrac{\text{the value}}{1{,}000}$

Thus, where the consideration is $400,000:

$$\begin{aligned} D &= \$(0.06571441 \times 400^2) + 15 \times 400 \\ &= \$(0.06571441 \times 160{,}000) + 6{,}000 \\ &= \$16{,}514.30 \end{aligned}$$

¶37-030 Landholder duty

The stamp duty legislation in each state and territory contains provisions which are designed to levy duty at land conveyance rates on transfers of shares or units in certain landholder corporations and unit trusts. These provisions seek to ensure that the duty payable on transfers of land is not avoided by transferring the shares or units in land-holding entities, rather than the land itself.

Accordingly, duty is imposed on the acquisition of certain interests in landholder companies or unit trusts at the same rates applying to transfers of dutiable property (¶37-020).

Details of the landholder provisions in each state and territory are as follows:

- *New South Wales*: landholder duty is payable where there is an acquisition of a significant interest, or an acquisition which results in a significant interest, in a landholder which has land holdings in NSW with a value of $2 million or more. A landholder includes a unit trust scheme, a listed company and a private company. A significant interest is a 50% or greater interest in a private landholder, or a 90% interest in a public landholder.

- *Victoria*: landholder duty is payable where there is an acquisition of a significant interest, or an interest which results in a significant interest, in a landholder. A landholder is a company or unit trust scheme (whether private or public) that has land holdings in Victoria with an unencumbered value of $1 million or more. The thresholds for a ''significant interest'' are: 20% for a private unit trust scheme; 50% for a private company or wholesale unit trust scheme; and 90% for a listed company or public unit trust scheme.

- *Queensland*: landholder duty is payable where there is an acquisition of a significant interest, or an acquisition which results in a significant interest, in a landholder. A landholder is a listed unit trust, a listed corporation or an unlisted corporation that has landholdings in Queensland with an unencumbered value of $2 million or more. A significant interest is a 50% or greater interest in a private landholder, or a 90% or greater interest in a public landholder.

- *South Australia*: landholder duty applies when a person or group of associates acquires 50% or more of the shares or units in a private company or unit trust and the private company or unit trust owns land. Landholder duty also applies where there is an acquisition of 90% or more of the shares or units of a listed ''landholder'' company or trust. Landholder duty replaced land rich duty in South Australia from 1 July 2011.

- *Western Australia*: landholder duty is payable where there is an acquisition of a significant interest, or an acquisition which results in a significant interest, in a landholder. A landholder is any corporation or unit trust scheme that has an entitlement to land in Western Australia, either directly or through a linked entity, with an unencumbered value of $2 million or more. A significant interest is a 50% or greater interest in a landholder that is not on the official list of a prescribed financial market, or a 90% or greater interest in a landholder that is on the official list of a prescribed financial market and whose shares are quoted.

- *Tasmania*: landholder duty is payable where there is an acquisition of a significant interest, or an interest which results in a significant interest, in a landholder. A landholder is a company or unit trust scheme (whether private or public) that has land holdings in Tasmania with an unencumbered value of $500,000 or more. The thresholds for a ''significant interest'' are: 50% for a private company or unit trust scheme and 90% for a listed company or public unit trust scheme. Landholder duty replaced land-rich duty in Tasmania from 6 December 2016.

- *Australian Capital Territory*: landholder duty is payable where there is an acquisition of a significant interest, or an acquisition which results in a significant interest, in an entity that has a landholding in the ACT. A person holds a significant interest in a landholder where, in the event of a distribution of all of the property of the landholder, they are entitled to at least 50% of the property distributed.

- *Northern Territory*: landholder duty is payable where there is an acquisition of a significant or a further interest in a land-holding corporation or a unit trust scheme that is entitled to an interest in land in the Northern Territory with an unencumbered value of $500,000 or more.

¶37-035 Duty on dealings in shares and units

In certain circumstances, conveyance rates may apply to sales of shares in land-owning corporations or units in land-owning trusts (¶37-030). In Queensland, transfer duty is payable in certain cases on acquisitions of units in non-public unit trusts.

The allotment or issue of a share or unit is generally exempt from duty (unless the landholder provisions apply (¶37-030)).

¶37-060 Timetable for abolishing various stamp duties

As part of the arrangements for the introduction of the GST, all states and territories agreed to review the need for retention of a number of stamp duties by 2005 (¶1-110). The terms of this agreement are set out in the Intergovernmental Agreement on the Reform of Commonwealth-State Financial Relations (IGA) made in 1999.

On 20 April 2005, the governments of Victoria, Queensland, South Australia, Tasmania, the ACT and the Northern Territory advised the federal government that they were prepared to abolish certain stamp duties progressively between 2005–06 and 2010–11.

Details of the timetable agreed to by these states and territories are set out below. In some cases the abolition of certain duties was subsequently deferred to a later date.

	VIC	QLD	SA	TAS	ACT	NT
2005–06		• 100% of Lease Duty • Credit Business Duty — 1 Jan 2006	(Part) Mortgage Duty — 1 Jan 2006			100% of Electronic Tax (included in IGA Cheque Duty Totals)
2006–07	100% of Rental Duty — 1 Jan 2007	• 100% of Hire Duty • Marketable Securities Duty — 1 Jan 2007	100% of other minor duties (a)	50% of Mortgage Duty	100% of Non-realty Conveyances	• 100% of Marketable Securities Duty • Lease Duties
2007–08		50% of Mortgage Duty — 1 Jan 2008	• 33% of Rental Duty • (remaining) Mortgage Duty	100% of Mortgage Duty	100% of Rental Duty	100% of Rental Duty
2008–09		100% of Mortgage Duty — 1 July 2008	• 67% of Rental Duty • (remaining) Mortgage Duty	100% of Non-realty Conveyances		
2009–10		50% of Non-realty Conveyances — 1 Jan 2010 (now deferred indefinitely*)	• 100% of Rental Duty and (remaining) Mortgage Duty • 50% of Non-realty Conveyances & Marketable Securities Duty**		100% of Lease Duty	100% of Non-realty Conveyances (now deferred indefinitely***)
2010–11		100% of Non-realty Conveyances — 1 Jan 2011 (now deferred indefinitely*)	100% of Non-realty Conveyances & Marketable Securities Duty**		100% of Marketable Securities Duty	
Taxes abolished/ never had	• Mortgage Duty • Lease Duty and other minor duties • Marketable Securities Duty • Non-realty Conveyances (never had)	Rental Duty (partial)	• Lease Duty • Mortgage Duty (partial) • Cheque Duty	• Lease Duty and other minor duties**** • Rental Duty • Marketable Securities Duty	Mortgage Duty (never had)	Mortgage Duty (abolished before 2000)

** Duty on non-realty conveyances in Queensland was originally proposed to be abolished by 1 Jan 2011. It has now been deferred indefinitely as part of Qld's Mid Year Fiscal and Economic Review released on 13 January 2012.*

*** Duty on non-realty conveyances and non-quoted marketable securities in South Australia was originally proposed to be abolished between 2009–10 and 2010–11 but this was deferred on several occasions. It was finally abolished from 18 June 2015 as part of SA's 2015–16 Budget.*

**** Duty on non-realty conveyances in the Northern Territory was originally proposed to be abolished in 2009–10 but has been deferred "until the budget situation permits" as part of the NT's 2012–13 Budget handed down on 1 May 2012.*

***** Minor duties includes all stamp duties specified for review in the IGA but not explicitly identified in the table.*

Western Australia and New South Wales

Western Australia and New South Wales were not signatories to the above timetable. However, both states subsequently agreed to abolish a number of stamp duties.

Western Australia

Western Australia agreed to:

- reduce mortgage duty by 50% from 1 July 2006 and abolish it completely by 1 July 2008
- abolish hiring transactions duty from 1 January 2007, and
- abolish duty on "non-real" business assets such as goodwill, intellectual property and statutory licences, from 1 July 2010 (since deferred indefinitely).

The proposed abolition of duty on non-real business assets was deferred indefinitely by measures in the *Duties Legislation Amendment Act 2013* (WA).

New South Wales

New South Wales agreed to:

- abolish hire of goods duty from 1 July 2007
- abolish lease duty from 1 January 2008
- abolish duty on unlisted marketable securities from 1 January 2009 (since deferred to 1 July 2016)
- abolish mortgage duty on owner-occupied residences from 1 September 2007, on residential investment properties from 1 July 2008 and on commercial properties from 1 July 2009 (since deferred to 1 July 2016), and
- abolish conveyance duty on business assets other than land from 1 January 2011 (since deferred to 1 July 2016).

The dates initially proposed in NSW for the abolition of duty on unlisted marketable securities, mortgages on commercial properties and transfers of business assets other than land were deferred on several occasions and were eventually abolished from 1 July 2016 as announced in the 2014–15 NSW Budget.

¶37-070 Abolished duties

Hire of goods duty

Duty on rental or hiring of goods has been abolished in every Australian state and territory. Hire of goods duty was abolished in Tasmania from 1 July 2002, in Victoria, Queensland and Western Australia from 1 January 2007, and in NSW, the Northern Territory and the ACT from 1 July 2007. Rental business duty was abolished in South Australia from 1 July 2009.

Mortgage duty

Mortgage duty is not payable in any Australian state or territory. It was abolished in Victoria with effect from 1 July 2004, in Tasmania from 1 July 2007, in Queensland and Western Australia from 1 July 2008, in South Australia from 1 July 2009 and in NSW from 1 July 2016 (¶37-060). The Northern Territory and the ACT have never imposed mortgage duty.

Lease duty

Lease duty is not payable in any Australian state or territory. However, transfer or conveyance duty may apply to certain leases for consideration other than market rent.

Duty on dealings in shares and units

Duty on transfers of shares or units quoted on the Australian Stock Exchange, or other recognised stock exchanges, was abolished in every state and territory with effect from 1 July 2001.

Duty on unlisted marketable securities was abolished in Victoria and Tasmania with effect from 1 July 2002, in Western Australia from 1 January 2004, in the Northern Territory from 1 July 2006, in Queensland from 1 January 2007, in the ACT from 1 July 2010, in South Australia from 18 June 2015 and in NSW from 1 July 2016.

Chapter 38 Land Tax

¶38-000 Land tax: introduction

Land tax is an annual tax on the ownership of land. It is imposed by all states and by the Australian Capital Territory, but not by the Northern Territory.

In all jurisdictions liability to land tax falls to the owner or owners of non-exempt land in that jurisdiction. An owner may be an individual, a company, a trustee or beneficiary of a landholding trust, a life tenant, or a purchaser or mortgagee in possession. Ownership generally arises out of a freehold estate in land, although in some circumstances a lessee or a person having a legal right to occupy land or receive rents and profits may also be an owner.

Factors that affect a taxpayer's land tax liability include:

- whether the land is owned by a natural person or a company, directly or through a trust, and whether there are joint owners or other ownership interests
- whether an owner is a foreign person
- land values, tax-free thresholds, and the marginal rates of tax imposed, and
- the exemptions specifically provided in each state.

In all jurisdictions except the ACT, a taxpayer's liability to land tax is assessed by reference to land owned on a taxing date in the year prior to the year for which land tax is assessed. In the ACT land tax is assessed quarterly. The values of all assessable land interests held on the taxing date are aggregated to determine the quantum to which tax rates are applied. Land values are determined by a statutory valuing authority in each jurisdiction and are generally based on the unimproved value of the land at the time of the valuation. In some cases (eg NSW, Qld, ACT), land values may be averaged over up to 3 years to smooth out spikes in property values over time.

Because assessment to land tax depends on ownership on a prior year taxing date, an owner who owns that land on the taxing date bears the land tax liability for the entire year. Owners who sell land are usually required to provide a certificate showing the amount, if any, of the land tax liability in respect of land, and the parties apportion that amount accordingly.

Foreign owners

New South Wales, Vic, Qld and the ACT all impose surcharges where interests in land are held, directly or indirectly, by foreign owners. In Vic and Qld the surcharge applies with respect to "taxable land", whereas in NSW and the ACT it is limited to foreign ownership of "residential land". Tax-free thresholds apply with respect to the surcharge in all jurisdictions except for NSW; accordingly a foreign owner of land in NSW may be liable for surcharge where no land tax liability arises. Foreign owners may eligible for the exemptions applying to land tax assessment, although the principal place of residence exemption cannot be claimed by absentees or foreign owners in Qld.

Duty surcharges may also apply where ownership of land is transferred to a foreign person.

Objections and appeals

Taxpayers have rights to object to assessments and other decisions and to seek judicial review of the Commissioner's determination of those objections from tribunals and courts. Objections must be lodged in writing stating the grounds of the objection. Lodgment of an objection or an application for review does not of itself freeze or stay the obligation to pay the outstanding tax, although in some cases payment arrangements may be made pending the outcome.

Time limits apply to lodging objections and to applications for review. In most jurisdictions the Commissioner has a discretion to accept late lodgment of objections. In some jurisdictions (eg NSW) tribunals and courts have power to accept applications for review made out of time. Challenges to land valuations should generally be made to the rating or valuing authority in the state or territory, and may be subject to different time limits and other requirements.

¶38-010 New South Wales land tax

Land tax is charged on the aggregate value of taxable land located in NSW and owned by a person on the taxing date. For the 2021 land tax year the taxing date is 31 December 2020. For most taxpayers, a general rate is applied to the taxable value of land held by an owner in excess of a tax-free threshold, and a premium rate applies to any component above a premium tax threshold. In certain circumstances the tax-free threshold may not apply where land is owned by a company or through a trust.

Tax reform

The NSW Budget 2020–21 includes a policy proposal to replace existing stamp duty and land tax imposts with a broad-based annual property tax. The proposed tax would apply to the unimproved land value of each individual property. Purchasers could elect to pay stamp duty or (much lower) property tax at the time of purchase, but this election would bind subsequent owners. Owner-occupiers and primary producers would pay lower rates than those apply to residential investment and commercial properties. NSW Treasury has issued a consultation paper and an invitation for public feedback.

Bushfire and COVID-19 measures

Taxpayers affected by the 2019–20 bushfires can apply for extensions to lodgment and payment deadlines, and interest may be waived on outstanding land tax debts.

Landlords who lease land to a residential or business tenant suffering financial distress as a result of the COVID-19 outbreak may be entitled to land tax reductions totalling up to 50% of the land tax attributable to the parcel of leased land in the 2020 land tax year. A further reduction is available in the 2021 land tax year for a more limited range of retail leases. The reductions are conditional on the benefit being passed on to tenants in the form of a reduction in rent.

A reduction of up to 25% of land tax attributable to the land is available in respect of the amount by which rent payable by an affected tenant is reduced during the periods from 1 April 2020 to 30 September 2020 and from 1 October 2020 to 31 December 2020. Separate applications should be made in respect of each of these periods. The landlord must be able to verify that a business tenant has annual turnover of less than $50 million and has suffered a 30% drop in revenue because of COVID-19. Residential tenants must have suffered a drop in household income due to COVID-19 of at least 25%. Eligible landlords can also have payments of outstanding land tax deferred for 3 months. Where 2020 land tax has already been paid, any reduction can be refunded.

In 2021, landlords can receive up to a further 25% reduction in land tax chargeable on land leased to retail tenants where rents are reduced during the period from 1 January 2021 to 28 March 2021. This reduction is limited to rent reductions provided to retail tenants with annual turnover of up to $5 million.

Details on applications and required documentation are available from Service NSW.

Build-to-rent construction projects

Property developers may be able to claim a 50% reduction in land tax in respect of build-to-rent developments. The concession applies to land in metropolitan areas on which construction commences on or after 1 July 2020 and applies until the 2040 land tax year. The development must produce at least 50 longer-term rental units which comply with guidelines to be issued by the Treasurer. The measure was introduced to promote affordable housing and to boost the construction sector in the wake of the COVID-19 economic downturn.

For 2021 and later land tax years, foreign developers may also be eligible for an exemption from foreign owner surcharge (see below).

Companies and trusts

Related companies are assessed using a grouping mechanism to ensure that the overall taxable value of group land holdings benefits from no more than one tax-free threshold and one premium rate threshold. Companies are ''related'' where one company holds a controlling interest in another, or where a person or persons hold a controlling interest in both. A ''controlling interest'' in a company means control of the composition of the board of directors or more than 50% of voting power at a general meeting, or holding more than 50% of share capital.

One or more companies in the group may be designated ''concessional'', and be assessed, jointly if more than one company, on the taxable value of land above the tax-free threshold at the general rate, and on the premium rate above the premium rate threshold. Other group companies holding land are ''non-concessional'' and assessed at 1.6% on the full taxable value, unless the aggregate taxable value of group land holdings exceeds the premium tax threshold, in which case a rate of 2% applies on the full taxable value of land held by each non-concessional company.

Fixed trusts, including family unit trusts, are assessed with the benefit of tax-free and premium rate thresholds. Most discretionary trusts are taxed as ''special trusts'', at 1.6% of the full taxable value up to the premium rate threshold and at the premium rate thereafter. Testamentary discretionary trusts can be treated as fixed trusts for the 2 years following the testator's death, or longer if approved by the Chief Commissioner.

A trust in which a foreign person is, *or could be*, a beneficiary may incur the surcharge on foreign ownership (see below). Trust deeds should be carefully drafted to avoid inadvertent ownership interests arising in favour of foreign persons. Trustees of existing trusts had until 31 December 2020 to irrevocably alter the terms of the trust to exclude actual and prospective foreign person owners. Unless the necessary amendments were put in place trustees face potential surcharge liability for each year of foreign ownership since 2017.

Surcharge on foreign ownership

From 2018 a land tax surcharge of 2% of taxable value (0.75% in 2017) is charged on residential land in NSW owned by foreign persons. An individual is a foreign person if they are not an Australian citizen, or a foreign national entitled to permanently reside in Australia who has been in Australia for 200 or more days in the 12 months preceding the taxing date. Companies, trustees and general partners in a limited partnership will themselves be foreign persons where another foreign person holds a substantial interest (20%), or, where there is more than one foreign person, an aggregate substantial interest (40%), in the company, trust or partnership. A foreign government or government entity is a foreign owner.

The surcharge is levied on the foreign owner's proportionate interest in each parcel of land owned on the taxing date. No tax-free threshold applies and there are no joint assessments. A trust which has no beneficiaries who are foreign persons but is, on its terms, open to a foreign person having or coming into an interest in trust property in the future may incur the surcharge (see above).

Hotels, motels and inns, hostels and boarding houses, student accommodation, aged care and other care facilities, certain B&B accommodation, and other forms of short or medium-term accommodation provided on a commercial basis are not subject to the surcharge (*Revenue Ruling* G 011).

Australian-based foreign-owned developers who subdivide land for residential construction, or who sell land on which newly constructed dwellings have been built, can claim exemption from the surcharge, or a refund of surcharge already paid. Time limits apply (*Revenue Ruling* G 013).

Exemptions

The following categories of land are exempt from land tax.

- Residential land (including strata lots) in NSW used and occupied as the owner's principal place of residence. The property must be the owner's principal place of residence out of all residences owned anywhere in the world. The land must be used for no other purpose. The exemption is available for only one property per family, and cannot be claimed if the land is owned by, or jointly with, a company or a special trust. Concessions on these restrictions allow the exemption where:

  - there is one other residential tenancy on the land. This applies to boarding and lodging arrangements, bedsits, bed and breakfast arrangements, and granny flats
  - the owner is moving house and holds both the former home and the new home on the taxing date. Both can be treated as exempt where the purchase of the new home and the sale of the old both occur within 6 months of the taxing date
  - the owner has acquired unoccupied land and intends to build or renovate and has no other principal place of residence. The vacant land can be treated as exempt for up to 4 years
  - the owner moves away for a period of up to 6 years and owns no other principal place of residence during that time
  - the owner dies. The property will be exempt for 2 years after the date of the person's death or until the land is transferred to any person other than the deceased's personal representative or a beneficiary of the deceased's estate. Land will also be exempt where a person occupies the land as a residence under rights conferred by the will
  - a partial exemption can be claimed in the form of a reduction in the land value used for assessment when land is used partly as a principal place of residence and partly for other purposes, such as a development containing both residential flats and commercial or professional offices.

- Rural zoned land predominantly used for primary production is exempt. Stricter commercial requirements apply if the land is not zoned as rural land.

- Land used and occupied primarily for low-cost accommodation or as a boarding house (subject to certain pricing and vacancy thresholds), as an aged-care establishment or a retirement village; and land owned by religious societies, non-profit associations, charitable institutions, Aboriginal land councils, licensed child care centres and registered non-government schools.

Concessions can be revoked and land tax reassessed if the relevant conditions are not met. In some situations the Chief Commissioner has discretion to extend time periods.

Objections and appeals

A taxpayer may lodge a written objection to an assessment within 60 days from date of service of the notice of assessment or later if allowed by Commissioner. Appeals against adverse objection decisions may be lodged up to 60 days from the date of the objection decision, or if no objection decision has been made after 90 days from lodgment of the objection.

Rates and thresholds for the 2021 land tax year

Taxable value of land ($)	Land tax payable ($)
Not more than 755,000	Nil
More than 755,000 but not more than 4,616,000	100 + 1.6% of the excess over 755,000
More than 4,616,000	61,876 + 2% of the excess over 4,616,000

¶38-020 Victoria land tax

Land tax is charged on the taxable value of land located in Victoria and owned by a person on the taxing date. For the 2021 land tax year, the taxing date is 31 December 2020.

Land tax is assessed to the owner of land, such as a holder of freehold title, a life tenant, a lessee of Crown land, a person having legal right to occupy land and receive rents and profits, a trustee, and the manager of a timeshare scheme.

Related companies may be grouped together and land tax will be assessed on the aggregate taxable value of all lands owned by group members. The Commissioner's approach to land tax grouping provisions affecting related corporations is outlined in *Revenue Ruling* LTA-008.

Bushfire and COVID-19 measures

Land tax payable for 2020 in respect of properties destroyed or substantially damaged in the 2019–20 summer bushfire emergency may be waived, and a reduction is available where property is affected but not destroyed. Similar concessions apply where land is used to provide free accommodation to those affected by the bushfires.

Landlords who lease land to a residential or business tenant suffering financial distress as a result of the COVID-19 outbreak, and landlords unable to secure a tenant because of the pandemic, may be entitled to land tax reductions totalling up to 50% of the land tax attributable to the parcel of leased land in the 2020 land tax year. A further reduction is available in the 2021 land tax year for landlords of residential properties. The reductions are conditional on the benefit being passed on to tenants in the form of a reduction in rent.

Reductions of up to 25% of 2020 land tax attributable to the land are available in respect of the amount by which rent payable by an affected tenant is reduced from 29 March to 29 September and from 30 September to 31 December 2020. Separate applications must be made in respect of each of these periods. Landlords of properties with multiple tenancies can make a single application for a 25% reduction in land tax attributable to the whole property. This increases to a 50% reduction where the rent of at least half of those tenants is reduced by 50% or more.

Commercial landlords are eligible where tenants have had annual turnover of less than $50 million in either of the last 2 financial years and are receiving the Commonwealth Government's JobKeeper payment. Where a tenant operates a licensed pub, club or restaurant in premises on the land turnover must have reduced by at least 30% since March 2020.

Commercial owner-occupiers may also be eligible for a 25% reduction in 2020 land tax charged on land used for their businesses. Owners of at least one non-residential property who have total taxable landholdings below $1 million can defer payment of their entire 2020 land tax liability until 31 March 2021, and obtain refunds of amounts of 2020 land tax already paid.

Landlords of residential properties may also be eligible for a 25% reduction on 2021 land tax on the leased land, and can defer the balance of their 2021 land tax liability, and any outstanding 2020 land tax, until 30 November 2021.

Vacancy tax liabilities arising in 2021 have been waived (see below). From 1 January 2022, eligible new build-to-rent developments will receive a 50% land tax discount.

Details on applications for bushfire and COVID-19 relief are available from the Victoria SRO.

Trusts

A surcharge rate applies generally to trusts which hold non-exempt land. Trustees are assessed on the aggregate value of land held in each trust. Trusts excluded from the surcharge include charitable trusts, public unit trust schemes, certain testamentary trusts, complying superannuation trusts and trusts for disabled persons.

Trustees of fixed and unit trusts who advise the Commissioner of certain beneficial interests or unit holdings in land held in trust may be taxed at the general rate. Trustees of discretionary trusts may be taxed at the general rate if the land was acquired on or before 31 December 2005 and a nominated beneficiary has been named. Trustees are under an obligation to notify the SRO of any land acquisition or change in trust land within one month of the change.

Exemptions

An owner's principal place of residence is exempt from land tax, including where:

- the owner is absent from the residence for up to 6 years and has not claimed a principal place of residence exemption elsewhere. This period can be extended where the owner dies, or the land becomes unfit for occupation
- the owner is moving house and holds both the former home and the new home on the taxing date
- land held in trust is used as a principal place of residence by a beneficiary
- land is used partly as a principal place of residence and partly for other purposes, such as a mixed residential/commercial development. A partial exemption can be claimed for the residential use in the form of a reduction in the land value used for assessment.

Land outside greater Melbourne which is used primarily for primary production is exempt. For 2020 and later land tax years the owner of urban-zoned land located within greater Melbourne must demonstrate a connection to the entity carrying on a business of primary production on the land.

Land owned by charitable, religious or educational bodies, local municipalities, and public statutory authorities is exempt. So is land used for residential and disability care and services, rooming houses, caravan parks, mines, and land used for sporting, recreational or cultural purposes. Starting in 2021, land owned and used by non-profit clubs for members' social, cultural, recreational, literary or educational interests will be exempt.

Abolition of special tax on land which ceases to be exempt

''Special land tax'' has been abolished with effect from 16 December 2020. The tax was charged at a rate of 5% of taxable value, or 7% where the owner was an absentee. It applied on a one-off basis where land with a taxable value of $250,000 or more ceased to be exempt (eg was sold to be applied to a different use) and was payable by the person who owned the land immediately after the exemption ceased to apply. Land which ceases to be exempt on or after 16 December 2020 will no longer attract the tax.

Absentee owners

From 2016 a surcharge has applied to taxable land in Victoria owned by absentee owners. The rate for 2020 and later years is 2% of the site value of the land. Broadly, an ''absentee owner'' is:

- a natural person who is not an Australian citizen or permanent resident, does not ordinarily reside in Australia and is either absent from Australia on the taxing date or absent from Australia for more than 6 months in the year prior to the relevant land tax year
- an Australian company in which an absentee person has a controlling interest, or
- a trustee of a trust in which an absentee person is a beneficiary or unit holder.

Australian-based companies or trusts that conduct commercial operations engaging local labour and using local materials and services may be exempt from the surcharge under guidelines issued by the Treasurer. Starting in 2022 absentee owners engaged in eligible build-to-rent developments will be exempt from the surcharge.

The surcharge is applied to the joint assessment of joint owners only if all joint owners are absentees. Otherwise, the surcharge is applied only with respect to the separate assessment of each absentee owner. The absentee owner surcharge applies to trusts in addition to the trusts surcharge rate.

Absentee owners are required to advise the Victorian SRO of their absentee status by 15 January in the year after they first owned the land as an absentee.

Vacancy tax

A vacant residential land tax (''vacancy tax'') applies to residential properties in the inner or middle ring of Melbourne which are left vacant for 6 months in the preceding calendar year. Vacancy tax is charged at a rate of 1% of the property's ratable value. Holiday homes and city properties maintained for work are exempt. Broadly, if a home is exempt from land tax it is also exempt from vacancy tax. For properties under construction or renovation, or which have been left derelict or uninhabitable, vacancy tax begins to apply after 2 years.

Vacancy tax liabilities arising in 2021 in respect of properties vacant in 2020 have been waived.

Objections and appeals

A taxpayer may lodge a written objection to an assessment within 60 days from date of service of the notice of assessment or later if allowed by the Commissioner. Appeals may be lodged up to 60 days from the date of the objection decision or anytime after 90 days from lodgment of the objection if no objection decision has been made.

General rates and thresholds

General land tax rates from 2009 and general rates with absentee owner surcharge from 2020

Taxable value of land ($)	Land tax payable ($)	Land tax payable with absentee owner surcharge ($)
0 – <250,000	Nil	Nil
250,000 – <600,000	275 + 0.2% of the excess over 250,000	5,275 + 2.2% of the excess over 250,000
600,000 – <1,000,000	975 + 0.5% of the excess over 600,000	12,975 + 2.5% of the excess over 600,000
1,000,000 – <1,800,000	2,975 + 0.8% of the excess over 1,000,000	22,975 + 2.8% of the excess over 1,000,000
1,800,000 – <3,000,000	9,375 + 1.3% of the excess over 1,800,000	43,375 + 3.3% of the excess over 1,800,000
3,000,000 or more	24,975 + 2.25% of the excess over 3,000,000	84,975 + 4.25% of the excess over 3,000,000

Trust rates and thresholds

Trust surcharge rates from 2009 and trust surcharge with absentee owner surcharge from 2020

Taxable value of land ($)	Land tax payable ($)	Land tax payable with absentee owner surcharge ($)
0 – <25,000	Nil	Nil
25,000 – <250,000	82 + 0.375% of the excess over 25,000	582 + 2.375% of the excess over 25,000
250,000 – <600,000	926 + 0.575% of the excess over 250,000	5,926 + 2.575% of the excess over 250,000
600,000 – <1,000,000	2,938 + 0.875% of the excess over 600,000	14,938 + 2.875% of the excess over 600,000
1,000,000 – <1,800,000	6,438 + 1.175% of the excess over 1,000,000	26,438 + 3.175% of the excess over 1,000,000
1,800,000 – <3,00,000	15,838 + 0.7614% of the excess over 1,800,000	51,838 + 2.7614% of the excess over 1,800,000
3,000,000 or more	24,975 + 2.25% of the excess over 3,000,000	84,975 + 4.25% of the excess over 3,000,000

¶38-030 Queensland land tax

Land tax for 2020–21 is levied on the taxable value of all freehold land owned in Queensland as at midnight on 30 June 2020. The taxable value is the lesser of the statutory land value under the *Land Valuation Act 2010* and the averaged value of the land. The averaged value is based on the statutory value for the current year and the previous 2 years. If previous year values are unavailable, the current statutory value is multiplied by a factor based on overall land values across the state in the current year.

Companies and trustees, including superannuation funds, have a lower tax-free threshold and pay higher rates than those applying to resident individuals. Surcharges also apply to foreign owners in some circumstances. Joint owners are assessed separately as owners of their respective ownership interests in the jointly owned land, along with any other taxable land they own.

COVID-19 measures

The due date for payment of land tax in the 2020–21 land tax year is deferred by 3 months. Accordingly, notices of assessment for 2020–21 will issue 3 months later than in the corresponding period in 2019–20.

A land tax rebate is available to residential and commercial landlords in the 2019–20 and 2020–21 land tax years in respect of land leased to a tenant whose ability to pay rent is affected by COVID-19. The amount of the rebate is equal to 25% of the land tax payable in respect of each qualifying parcel of leased land in each land tax year. To qualify for the rebate the landlord must provide rent reductions to a tenant of at least that amount, and comply with leasing principles designed to regulate relations between landlords and affected tenants. Where there are multiple tenants for a single property, the requirements and conditions need only be met for at least one tenancy. The reduction is also available to those landlords unable to secure a tenant because of COVID-19.

The application deadline for the 2019–20 land tax year was 31 October 2020. The deadline for the 2020–21 land tax year is 26 February 2021. Further information is available from Queensland OSR and applications should be made via the OSR Online web portal.

The absentee surcharge for foreign entities was waived in respect of land tax assessments for the 2019–20 land tax year.

Exemptions

Land used exclusively as the home of an owner who is a natural person is exempt from land tax. While generally only one property can be eligible for the exemption, a concession applies where a person who is moving homes is the owner of both the new home and the old home on the taxing date. In this situation both homes may be exempt provided the owner sells the old home prior to the next taxing date. The exemption can apply to land owned by a trustee where all the beneficiaries of the relevant trust so use the land.

Other exemptions include:

- land used for the business of agriculture, pasturage or dairy farming. Natural persons, relevant proprietary companies, exempt charitable institutions or trustees can apply for this deduction. A trustee must be either a natural person who is not an absentee or a relevant proprietary company
- land owned by non-profit clubs, associations, societies and charitable institutions, provided qualifying criteria are satisfied
- land used predominantly as a caravan or residential park. More than 50% of the total number of sites must be occupied or available for residential occupation minimum periods of 6 weeks at a time
- land on which an aged care facility is located
- land on which a supported accommodation service is conducted.

Foreign ownership and absentee rates

Land tax liability of absentee individuals, foreign companies and foreign trusts which own or hold land in Queensland is charged at surcharge rates. From 2019–20 the surcharge rate is 2% of the taxable value of taxable land in excess of an absentee threshold. As the absentee threshold is lower that the land tax threshold, an absentee surcharge may arise where there is no land tax liability. As part of the state's COVID-19 response, absentee surcharge was waived for assessments in the 2019–20 financial year.

Generally, individuals who are not Australian citizens or permanent residents and who were absent on the taxing date will be ''absentees'' if they were out of the country for more than 6 months in total during the land tax year.

A company is subject to absentee rates if it is incorporated outside Australia or if a foreign person or persons have a controlling interest in the company. A "controlling interest" in a company means control of more than 50% of voting power or potential voting power at a general meeting, or holding more than 50% of share capital.

A trust is subject to surcharge rates if at least 50% of the trust interests in the trust are foreign interests. "Foreign interests" are interests held by individuals who are not Australian citizens or permanent residents, or by foreign companies, trustees of foreign trusts, or persons who are related to foreign interest holders. Special rules apply to discretionary trusts and superannuation funds.

Foreign individuals may have to provide information on time spent outside the country, places of residence, and other matters relevant to absentee status (see FORM OSR – LT16).

Objections and appeals

A taxpayer may lodge a written objection to an assessment within 60 days from date of service of the notice of assessment. Later lodgments may be allowed. Appeals may be lodged up to 60 days from the date of the objection decision.

Rates and thresholds

Resident individual rates in 2018–19 and later land tax years

Taxable value of land ($)	Land tax payable ($)
0 – 599,999	Nil
600,000 – 999,999	500 + 1.0% of the excess over 600,000
1,000,000 – 2,999,999	4,500 + 1.65% of the excess over 1,000,000
3,000,000 – 4,999,999	37,500 + 1.25% of the excess over 3,000,000
5,000,000 – 9,999,999	62,500 + 1.75% of the excess over 5,000,000
10,000,000 or more	150,000 plus 2.25 cents for each $1 more than 10,000,000

Companies and trustee rates for 2018–19 and later land tax years

Taxable value of land ($)	Land tax payable ($)
0 – 349,999	Nil
350,000 – 2,249,999	1,450 + 1.7% of the excess over 350,000
2,250,000 – 4,999,999	33,750 + 1.5% of the excess over 2,250,000
5,000,000 – 9,999,999	75,000 + 2.25% of the excess over 5,000,000
10,000,000 or more	187,500 + 2.75 cents for each $1 more than 10,000,000

Absentee rates for 2019–20 and later land tax years

Taxable value of land ($)	Land tax payable ($)
0 – 349,999	Nil
350,000 – 2,249,999	1,450 + 1.7% of the excess over 350,000
2,250,000 – 4,999,999	33,750 + 1.5% of the excess over 2,250,000
5,000,000 – 9,999,999	75,000 + 2.0% of the excess over 5,000,000
10,000,000 or more	175,000 + 2.5 cents for each $1 more than 10,000,000

¶38-040 South Australia land tax

Land tax in South Australia for 2020–21 is levied on the aggregated site value of all land owned in South Australia as at midnight on 30 June 2020. The site value of land is, broadly, the market value of unimproved land.

COVID-19 measures

Landlords who lease land to a residential or business tenant suffering financial distress resulting from the COVID-19 outbreak may be entitled to land tax reductions totalling up to 50% of the land tax attributable to the parcel of leased land in the 2019–20 land tax year. The land tax reductions are conditional on the benefit being passed on to tenants in the form of a reduction in rent and are also available to landlords who are unable to secure a tenant because of COVID-19 provided that the land was leased as at 30 March 2020.

A reduction of up to 25% of land tax attributable to the leased land is available in respect of the amount by which rent payable by an affected tenant is reduced during the period from 30 March 2020 to 30 October 2020 and the period from 31 October 2020 to 30 April 2021. Separate applications must be made in respect of each of these periods.

In the case of residential tenancies, at least one of the residential tenants must be able to declare that they are experiencing financial hardship due to COVID-19. Where the tenancy is non-residential, a tenant must have annual turnover of no more than $50 million, and at least one tenant must be eligible for the Federal government's JobKeeper payment.

Businesses who operate from their own land as at 31 October 2020 may also be eligible for a 25% reduction on the property's 2019–20 land tax where they have annual turnover of $50 million or less and are eligible for the JobKeeper payment.

Taxpayers paying quarterly in 2019–20 could defer payment of their third instalment by up to 6 months from the due date, and defer their fourth instalment payment by up to 3 months. Taxpayers who have already paid 2019-20 land tax can claim a refund or a credit against a future land tax debt. Details on application for relief are available from Revenue SA.

Ownership

Land tax liability is assessed on the land interest held by an owner of the land. An "owner" includes the registered owner of freehold land, any person entitled to legal or equitable ownership, persons with a right to purchase the land and a shareholder in a home unit company. Lessees of land under a crown lease, tenants in common who lease a portion of the land and certain long-term lessees or occupiers of "shack sites" on privately owned land near the Murray river may also be owners for land tax purposes.

Where there is more than one owner of land, all owners may be treated as a single owner for assessment purposes, and the Commissioner may assess owners in one capacity (eg trustees, equitable owners, a lessee under a perpetual lease) as the sole owner or owners of the land. Minor interests in land of 5% or less are disregarded in the assessment. Any interest in land less than 50% may be disregarded in the assessment if it appears the interest was created to reduce a land tax liability.

Assessment

For 2020–21 and later land tax years, land tax assessments include all land owned by a person on the taxing date, irrespective of whether the land is held directly, or through a trust or company. This is similar to assessment of land tax in NSW, whereby the value of ownership interests held through trust or company arrangements are aggregated for the purpose of assessment (see ¶38-010). The new regime replaces the taxation of land on the basis of separate legal holdings.

Taxpayers who have an increase in their land tax liability which is solely the result of the aggregation changes can seek transitional relief in the form of a reduction in land tax liability. The land tax reduction is assessed for each relevant parcel of land owned as at 16 October 2019 and assessed by reference to the increase in land tax payable under the new regime over that which would have been payable on that parcel in a 2019-20 assessment. This transitional relief is available in each of the 2020-21, 2021-22 and 2022-23 land tax years for a minimum increase of $2,500 and capped at $50,000, $30,000 and $15,000 in each of those years respectively. Applications for transitional relief should be made by 31 March in each land tax year to RevenueSA.

Property developers who subdivide land for affordable housing may seek an ex gratia concession for the difference between the assessed land tax liability and the amount which would have been payable on each parcel of land absent any aggregation of land holdings. From 1 March 2020 ex gratia relief is also available to lessors who provide affordable housing through a participating community housing provider.

Related companies

For 2020–21 and later land tax years, related corporations that own land are assessed as if they were a single corporation. Related companies are grouped together and land tax is assessed on the aggregate taxable value of all lands owned by group members as if the land were owned by a single entity.

Exemptions

Land that is exempt from the tax includes:

- land used as a principal place of residence, including retirement villages, is fully exempt. If a home business activity is carried on at the property a partial exemption may be available. Exemption may be available for up to 3 years after a home is destroyed or rendered uninhabitable if an owner intends to rebuild or repair the building within that time
- certain land used for primary production
- land that is owned by prescribed associations and is used for relevant purposes (eg sporting, recreational, historical and agricultural shows, literature, science, languages, the arts or the preservation of historical, traditional or cultural heritage or for similar purposes)
- land used for religious, hospital or library purposes
- land owned (or in certain situations occupied) by certain charitable, educational, benevolent or philanthropic organisations
- land owned by a prescribed body and used for the benefit of indigenous people
- land used for caravan parks, residential parks for retired persons and licensed supported residential facilities
- land used for the provision of residential care by an approved provider under the *Aged Care Act 1997* (Cth).

A 5-year land tax exemption is available for investors who entered into off-the-plan apartment contracts between 22 June 2017 and 30 June 2018. The exemption does not apply to foreign purchasers.

Deceased estates

In certain circumstances, land used by a deceased person as a principal place of residence immediately before their death may qualify for *ex gratia* relief from land tax for the first financial year following the death of the owner (*Revenue Ruling* LT 001). Similar relief is provided where an owner moves into residential care (*Revenue Ruling* LT 003).

Trusts surcharge

From 2020–21 owners of land held in trust with a taxable value greater than $25,000 may be assessed at trust rates of land tax. Trust rates are only payable on a separate assessment, not on a joint assessment.

Trustees must have notified RevenueSA that they own South Australian land on trust by 31 July 2020, and of any subsequent change in ownership within one month of those changes. Notifications can be made via the RevenueSA Online portal.

Fixed, discretionary and unit trusts which would otherwise be taxed at trust rates may be taxed at general rates where appropriate notification of beneficial interests in the trust is made to RevenueSA. A trustee of a fixed trust or a unit trust must notify RevenueSA of all the beneficial interests in the trust. Land which was subject to a discretionary trust as at 16 October 2019 may be taxed at general rates where the trustee lodges a written notice specifying a single beneficiary as the designated beneficiary of the trust by 30 June 2021. Land acquired by a trustee of a discretionary trust from 17 October 2019 onwards is taxed at trust rates.

Charitable trusts, superannuation trusts, estate administration trusts and various public and concessional trusts are excluded from surcharge. Land tax exemptions, including the principal place of residence exemption, can apply to the trust surcharge where the land is used and/or occupied in the requisite manner by a beneficiary or beneficiaries.

Objections and appeals

Taxpayers can lodge written objections to assessments within 60 days from date of service of a notice of assessment or up to 12 months later if allowed by the Minister. Appeals can be lodged up to 60 days from the date of the objection decision or anytime after 90 days from lodgment of the objection if no objection decision has been made and the taxpayer has given 14 days notice of the intention to appeal.

Rates and thresholds

Land tax thresholds are indexed annually based on the average percentage change in site values.

General land tax rates for 2020–21

Taxable value of land ($)	Land tax payable ($)
0 – 450,000	Nil
450,000 – 723,000	0.50 for every 100 (or fractional part) over 450,000
723,000 – 1,052,000	1,365 + 1.25 for every 100 (or fractional part) over 723,000
1,052,000 – 1,350,000	5,477.50 + 2.00 for every 100 (or fractional part) over 1,052,000
above 1,350,000	11,437.50 + 2.40 for every 100 (or fractional part) over 1,350,000

Trust land tax rates for 2020–21

Taxable value of land ($)	Land tax payable ($)
0 – 25,000	Nil
25,000 – 450,000	125 + 0.50 for every 100 (or fractional part) over 25,000
450,000 – 723,000	2,250 + 1.00 for every 100 (or fractional part) over 450,000

Taxable value of land ($)			Land tax payable ($)
723,000	–	1,052,000	5,477.50 + 2.00 for every 100 (or fractional part) over 723,000
1,052,000	–	1,350,000	10,737.50 + 2.40 for every 100 (or fractional part) over 1,052,000
above 1,350,000			17,899.50 + 2.40 for every 100 (or fractional part) over 1,350,000

¶38-050 Western Australia land tax

Land tax for 2020–21 is levied on the taxable value of land held by the same owners on 30 June 2020. The taxable value of land is the lesser of the unimproved value of the land and the capped value of the land, which is 150% of the value on which land tax was charged in the previous year.

COVID-19 measures

Landlords who provide rent relief to small business tenants may be eligible for a grant payment equivalent to 25% of the land tax payable in respect of the land in the 2019–20 land tax year. The small business tenant must have suffered at least a 30% drop in turnover due to the impact of COVID-19 and the landlord must reduce the overall rent paid over the period from 1 March 2020 to 31 August 2020 by half. Grants are paid through a capped grant program of $100 million and awarded on a first come, first served basis. Information on applications is available at the Small Business Development Corporation website.

Exemptions

There are a number of categories of land that may qualify for exemption depending on dimensions, usage and/or ownership, including:

- the land is the sole or principal place of residence of an owner. Concessions apply in certain circumstances, such as where owners are moving house or constructing or refurbishing a new residence
- land owned by an individual that a disabled family member uses as their primary residence
- land used for primary production
- land owned and used by sports associations to provide facilities for members to engage in sports
- land owned by other non-profit associations where it is used solely for association purposes
- land owned by a non-profit, charitable or religious body, provided it is used for those purposes
- land used for caravan parks, park homes and camping grounds, and
- land used as an aged care facility or retirement village.

The state government has indicated that it will introduce amendments to ensure that residential parks with owner-occupied relocatable homes can continue to be licensed as caravan parks and eligible for land tax exemption. The changes, proposed to have effect for the 2020-21 land tax year, come as the result of a tribunal decision which held that a caravan park home must be a ‘‘vehicle’’.

If a land tax liability exists in respect of land in the metropolitan area, Metropolitan Region Improvement Tax (MRIT) is payable in addition to land tax at a rate of 0.14 cents per dollar of the aggregated taxable value of the land in excess of $300,000. A useful summary of affected suburbs is provided on the Western Australian Department of Finance website at www.finance.wa.gov.au.

Objections and appeals

A taxpayer may lodge a written objection to an assessment within 60 days from date of service of the notice of assessment or later if allowed by Commissioner. An appeal to the State Administrative Tribunal should be made within 60 days of an objection decision or 90 days after lodgment of the objection if no decision has been made and no further evidence requested. An appeal to the Supreme Court is available within 28 days of a tribunal decision.

Rates and thresholds for 2018–19 and later land tax years

Taxable value of land ($)	Land tax payable ($)
0 – 300,000	Nil
300,001 – 420,000	Flat rate of 300
420,001 – 1,000,000	300 + 0.0025 for each $1 over 420,000
1,000,001 – 1,800,000	1,750 + 0.009 for each $1 over 1,000,000
1,800,001 – 5,000,000	8,950 + 0.018 for each $1 over 1,800,000
5,000,001 – 11,000,000	66,550 + 0.02 for each $1 over 5,000,000
11,000,001 or more	186,550 + 0.0267 for each $1 over 11,000,000

¶38-060 Tasmania land tax

Land tax for 2020–21 is levied on the aggregate assessed value of land owned on 1 July 2020.

COVID-19 measures

On 17 March 2020 the state government declared a public emergency in Tasmania as a result of the COVID-19 pandemic. Commercial land which has been adversely affected as a result of the effects of COVID-19 during the period of the emergency is exempt from land tax for the 2020–21 land tax year. The Commissioner may also defer outstanding land tax due for 2019–20 until 30 June 2020, as well as offering payment arrangements in cases of financial hardship.

To qualify, the business must have suffered an adverse financial impact that is unexpected and not insignificant during the pandemic period. That may include a reduction in the amount of income derived in respect of the land, or the impact on business conducted on the land, or the land being available for rent but failing to attract a tenant because of the pandemic. Landlords and business owners have until 1 July 2021 to apply for the exemption. Information on making an application for exemption is available from Tasmania SRO.

Exemptions and rebates

There are 3 categories of land in Tasmania: principal residence land, primary production land and general land. Land used as an owner's main place of residence as at 1 July of each financial year and land used for primary production are exempt. General land, including rental properties, holiday homes, vacant land and commercial land, is usually taxable. It may, however, be exempt where it is owned by a charitable institution, or used by owners for religious purposes, as a specialist medical establishment, to operate a retirement village, in furtherance of a conservation covenant, or for Aboriginal cultural activities. Sporting clubs are entitled to a special rate of tax. Where land is used partly for an exempt purpose and partly for a non-exempt purpose, land tax is assessed on the proportion of the land used for the non-exempt purpose.

A land owner may be eligible for a rebate of land tax paid where they are building on vacant land on the taxing date or where they have purchased a new principal place of residence on or after 1 April and have entered into a contract for sale of the other property on or before 30 September. In this circumstance, the owner will own 2 residences on 1 July and be entitled to receive a rebate of tax paid on the property which is not their principal place of residence.

From 1 July 2017, where an owner dies, a property which was used as a principal residence by that owner may continue to be exempt as a principal residence in the financial year following death (*Land Tax Act 2000*, s 6(9)).

A land tax exemption applies for newly built housing built on general land where a dwelling is made available for a residential tenancy of at least 12 months. The exemption applies for the 3 financial years immediately following the issue of an occupancy certificate where the certificate is issued between 8 February 2018 and 30 June 2023.

A one-year land tax exemption is available for general land made available for a residential tenancy of at least 12 months after being used or advertised for use as short-stay accommodation during the majority of the 3-month period prior to the commencement of the residential tenancy. The lease must commence between 15 March 2018 and 30 June 2023.

Objections and appeals

A taxpayer may lodge a written objection to an assessment within 60 days from date of service of the notice of assessment or later if allowed by Commissioner. Appeals may be lodged up to 60 days from the date of the objection decision or anytime after 90 days from lodgment of the objection if no objection decision has been made.

Rates and thresholds (applicable since 1 July 2010)

Aggregated assessed value ($)	Rate of tax ($)
Less than 25,000	Nil
25,000 – 349,999	50 + 0.55% of value above 25,000
350,000 and over	1,837.50 + 1.5% of value above 350,000

¶38-070 Australian Capital Territory land tax

Land tax in the ACT is assessed quarterly to the owner of the land as at 1 July, 1 October, 1 January and 1 April in each year. It applies to all residential property that is not an owner's principal place of residence whether owned by an individual, company or trust, and whether rented or not. Land tax does not apply to commercial properties.

Rented residential properties can include dual occupancies, granny flats, multiple dwellings and boarding houses.

COVID-19 measures

Land tax relief is available to residential landlords, commercial landlords and owner-operators of land used for business.

Residential landlords who reduce rent payable by tenants because of the impact of COVID-19 are eligible for a land tax rebate of 50% of that rental reduction. The rebate is available in respect of rent reductions of at least 25% of the rent payable as at 1 March 2020 and is capped at $1,300 per quarter. Originally available in respect of rent reductions provided over 6 months from 1 April 2020, the scheme has been extended to cover rent reductions up until 30 June 2021.

Land tax relief is available to commercial landlords of properties with an average unimproved value (AUV) of up to $2 million who provide rent reductions to tenants. Where tenants have suffered at least 30% reduction in business income, commercial landlords can receive a rebate equal to 25% of that rent reduction, capped at the lower of $5,000 per quarter, or total quarterly rates. Where tenants have effectively shut down (at least 80% reduction in business income) landlords can receive a rebate equal to 50% of that rent reduction, capped at the lower of $8,000 per quarter, or total quarterly rates.

Owner-operators of properties with an AUV of up to $2 million who have suffered at least 30% reduction in business income can receive a rebate equal to 50% of their rates, capped at $5,000 per quarter. For an 80% or more reduction in business income the rebate is equal to 80% of their rates, capped at $8,000 per quarter.

Applications for the rebate should be made to ACT Revenue. Owners of commercial property with an AUV of more than $2 million can still apply for assistance, but support will be provided on a case-by-case basis.

Exemptions

Land tax exemptions apply to the principal place of residence of an owner, including;

- where the owner is moving from one home to another, the former home is exempt for the first full quarter after the owner vacates the property and the new home is exempt for the first full quarter after settlement of the purchase
- where the owner dies the former principal place of residence is exempt from land tax for up to 2 years after the date of death, or until the land is transferred to a beneficiary or is rented. The 2-year period can be extended provided these conditions prevail. Homes occupied by a person with a life or term interest under a will are also exempt
- where the owner can no longer live independently and resides at a hospital or hospice, nursing home, an approved mental health or approved community care facility, or with a carer eligible for a carer payment under the *Social Security Act 1991* (Cth). The property must remain unoccupied for the full period of exemption
- where the home is unfit for occupation as a place of residence because the home is under construction, being significantly renovated, or has been damaged
- where the home is occupied rent free or where the rent only covers the cost of rates, repairs, maintenance or insurance.

Other exemptions apply to rural land, land owned by the Housing Commissioner, retirement villages, nursing homes, religious accommodation, land owned by a not-for-profit housing corporation, land transferred for community housing to entities declared under the *Duties Act 1999*, s 73A and land used for prescribed purposes.

From 28 March 2019, exemption is available for up to 100 properties rented through a registered affordable community housing provider under a pilot program that expires on 30 June 2021. On 10 September 2020 the maximum number of properties which could be exempted was increased to 125.

Exemption may also be granted for up to one year on compassionate grounds.

Calculation and rates

Land tax is assessed quarterly and calculated using a fixed charge (FC) plus progressive marginal rates applied to the AUV of the land.

FC + (AUV × rate) × number of days in the quarter divided by number of days in the year

The AUV of land is the average of the unimproved values of the land over up to 3 years.

From 1 July 2017, land tax on residential units is based on that proportion of the AUV of the whole residential complex represented by the owner's residential unit entitlement in the total aggregate of residential properties in the complex, and not on the AUVs of the individual units.

Foreign owners

From 1 July 2018 an additional annual land tax surcharge of 0.75% of average unimproved value is payable by foreign owners of land in the ACT.

Objections and appeals

A taxpayer may lodge a written objection to an assessment within 60 days from date of service of the notice of assessment or later if allowed by Commissioner. Appeals must be lodged within 28 days of the date of the objection decision.

Rates and thresholds

For 2020–21, the fixed charge component is $1,326.

Average unimproved value (AUV) ($)	Land tax rates and thresholds ($)
0 – 150,000	0.52% of the AUV
150,001 – 275,000	$780 + 0.62% AUV above 150,000
275,001 – 2,000,000	$1,555 + 1.10% AUV above 275,000
2,000,001 or more	$20,530 + 1.12% AUV above 2,000,000

Chapter 39 Superannuation Guarantee Charge

The SG Scheme

¶39-000 Outline of SG scheme

The superannuation guarantee (SG) scheme, administered by the ATO, requires employers to provide a minimum level of superannuation support for each of their employees, subject to limited exemptions. The SG regime applies on a quarterly basis, with the SG year divided into 4 quarters ending 30 September, 31 December, 31 March and 30 June.

The legislation governing the scheme is the *Superannuation Guarantee Charge Act 1992*, the *Superannuation Guarantee (Administration) Act 1992* (SGAA) and the Superannuation Guarantee (Administration) Regulations 2018 (SGAR). The High Court has held that the SG charge is a tax under the Commonwealth Constitution (see below).

The required rate of SG contributions is 9.5% of an employee's ordinary time earnings in the 2015–16 to 2020–21 financial years. The SG rate is legislated to increase by 0.5% in each later year from 1 July 2021 until it reaches 12% for the year beginning 1 July 2025 (¶39-100). The level of superannuation support provided for each employee is measured quarterly (¶39-230). To avoid incurring an SG charge liability in a quarter, the SG contributions must be made within 28 days after the end of the quarter (¶39-240).

Employers who have an SG shortfall in a quarter are liable to pay an SG charge (¶39-400) to the ATO, made up of the amount of the shortfall plus an interest component and an administrative charge. The shortfall and interest component of the charge is redistributed by the ATO to a complying superannuation fund, complying ADF, RSA or the Superannuation Holding Accounts Special Account (SHASA) for the benefit of the employees for whom the charge was paid (¶39-600).

SG contributions must be made to a complying superannuation fund (¶13-100) or RSA (¶13-470) for the benefit of the employee, either directly or through a clearing house (¶39-240).

Employers must offer eligible employees a choice of funds for receiving the SG contributions made for them (¶39-260).

SG contributions for employees are generally tax deductible (where the relevant conditions for deductibility are met: ¶13-710). Payment of the SG charge is not deductible (¶39-500).

Employer superannuation contributions for employees which are made in accordance with a Commonwealth, state or territory law, an industrial award or an occupational superannuation arrangement may be counted towards the employer's SG obligations (¶39-230).

The SG scheme is administered on a self-assessment basis. An employer with an SG shortfall in a quarter is required to lodge an SG statement with the ATO by the 28th day of the second month following the end of the quarter. The statement is the employer's notice of assessment for that quarter and payment of the SG charge is due on lodgment of the statement (¶39-500).

Wolters Kluwer provides additional commentary on the superannuation guarantee scheme in the *Australian Master Superannuation Guide 2020/21*.

Constitutional validity of the SG charge

The High Court has dismissed a constitutional challenge that the charge under the SG Charge Act and SGAA was not a "tax" as it was not imposed for "public purposes" and it conferred "a private and direct benefit" on the relevant employees. The Court held that the receipt of the proceeds of the charge into Consolidated Revenue Fund (CRF) established that the charge was imposed for "public purposes", and where other necessary constitutional criteria of a tax are met as they were in the case, the receipt of funds into the CRF conclusively established the character of the SG charge as a law with respect to taxation within the meaning of s 51(ii) of the Constitution (*Roy Morgan Research*; *Decision Impact Statement, 2011 (M177 of 2010)*).

[AMSG ¶12-000ff; FTR ¶794-600; SLP ¶50-100]

Application to Employers

¶39-020 Employers and employees under the SGA Act

The SG scheme applies to employers in respect of their full-time, part-time and casual employees, with only limited exemptions (¶39-030).

The terms ''employer'' and ''employee'' in the SGAA have their ordinary common law meanings (¶26-150, ¶39-022), but have an expanded meaning to expressly cover various other persons as provided in SGAA s 12(2) to (11).

Certain workers who are otherwise employees may be regarded not to be employees under the SGAA (see ''Persons who are not employees'' below). If 2 contracts of employment exist simultaneously between an employer and an employee, the employer will have an obligation under each contract to make SG contributions for the employee (ID 2006/321).

Guidelines on the common law and statutory meaning of ''employee'' are found in SGR 2005/1 and SGR 2005/2 (¶39-022).

Employers and employees — statutory meanings

In general terms, an ''employee'' is a person who receives payment in the form of salary or wages (¶39-026) in return for work or services rendered, or payment for work under a contract that is wholly or principally for the person's labour, and the person liable to make the payment is the employer.

Under its expanded meaning in the SGAA, a person is an ''employee'' or ''employer'' in the following circumstances.

- A person who is entitled to payment for the performance of duties as a member of the executive body (whether described as the board of directors or otherwise) of a body corporate is an employee of the body corporate (*Kelly (No 2)* — concept of ''entitled to be paid''; SGD 97/1 — director who is a partner in a professional partnership: ¶39-024). The *Kelly* decision affirms the ATO view on the circumstances in which a director is deemed to be an employee under s 12(2) (TR 2010/1 para 238 to 243).

- A person who works under a contract that is wholly or principally for the labour of the person is an employee of the other party to the contract (see below) (*On Call Interpreters and Translators Agency Pty Ltd*, *Dental Corporation Pty Ltd v Moffet*: ¶39-022, ¶39-024).

- A member of the Commonwealth Parliament, state parliament or territory Legislative Assembly is an employee of the Commonwealth, state or territory.

- A person who receives payment to perform or present, or to participate in the performance or presentation of, any music, play, dance, entertainment, sport, display or promotional activity, or any similar activity involving the exercise of intellectual, artistic, musical, physical or other personal skill, or who receives payment to provide services in connection with any of these activities, is an employee of the person liable to make the payment (see below) (*General Aviation Maintenance*: ¶39-022; *Racing Queensland Board*, *Scone Race Club Ltd*: ¶39-024).

- A person who is paid to perform services in, or in connection with, the making of any film, tape, disc, or of any television or radio broadcast is an employee of the person liable to make the payment.
- A person who holds, or performs the duties of, an appointment, office or position under the Constitution or under a law of the Commonwealth or of a state or territory (including service as a member of the Defence or Police Force) is an employee of the Commonwealth, a state or a territory (SGAA s 12(2) to (9)).

Persons who are not employees

A person is *not* an employee for SG purposes in the following circumstances:

- a person who holds office as a member of a local government council (other than members of an eligible local governing body, see below) (s 12(9A))
- a person who receives payment to do work wholly or principally of a *domestic or private nature* (see below) for not more than 30 hours per week (eg as a nanny) (s 12(11)).

A person covered by TAA Sch 1 s 12-45(1)(e) (about members of local governing bodies subject to PAYG withholding) is an employee of the body (s 12(10)). This means that a person who is a member of an eligible local governing body and whose remuneration is covered by the PAYG system is an employee of the body for SG purposes.

SGAA s 12 — expanded meaning to both the terms "employee" and "employer"

The Full Federal Court has stated that it was apparent that s 12(2)-(11) expand both terms ''employee'' and ''employer'' for 2 reasons. First, s 12(1)(a) identifies that subsections (2)-(11) expand ''those terms'', referring to both ''employee'' and ''employer''. Given the word ''employer'' does not appear in any of subsections (2) to (11), the plural terms require that ''employer'' is coordinately expanded in meaning to ''employee''. Second, subsections (2)-(11) would be otiose if they did not expand the term ''employer''. The necessary implication of the terms of the subsections is that the term ''employee'' is expanded, and the person with whom they have a relationship as identified in each subsection is their ''employer'' (*Racing Queensland Board*).

Section 12(11) — work of a domestic or private nature

The expression *domestic or private nature* in s 12(11) was examined by the Federal Court in *Newton*, an appeal from *Care Provider*. The Commissioner had submitted that s 12(11) was not intended to relieve a labour hire business, or other businesses that provide domestic services for clients, from an SG obligation, and the words of s 12(11) suggest that it was concerned with work of a domestic or private nature only from the payer's perspective. Essentially, the phrase ''work of a domestic or private nature'' is a composite one. While some work done in a boarding school, hotel or hospital or in a retirement village might be characterised as domestic in some sense, it could not fairly be characterised as being of a domestic or private nature in the context of the SGAA.

The Court agreed that the language of s 12(11) is by no means clear. In summary, whether the exemption in s 12(11) applies requires an examination of the nature of the work carried out by the worker, the identity or attributes of the payer, the relationship between the payer and the worker, or the nature of the work or services that the worker provides to the payer. The AAT, on remittal of the case, found strong indications that the workers were employees pursuant to s 12(3) (ie persons engaged for their labour), and probably were also employees under its common law meaning in s 12(1) (*Newton, T/A as Combined Care for the Elderly*) (¶39-022).

Section 12(3) — contract wholly or principally for the labour of the person

The diversity of arrangements where people work under a contractual relationship is discussed in ¶39-022.

In *On Call*, the Federal Court (Bromberg J) was of the view that s 12(3) would apply where an independent contractor provided personal services in an employment-like setting which was not of a domestic or private nature. In determining what an employment-like setting was, his Honour thought it was appropriate to ask "whether in all the circumstances, the labour component of the contract in question could have been provided by the recipient of the labour employing an employee". In *Dental Corporation Pty Ltd v Moffet*, the Full Federal Court held that such an approach "is erroneous because it has no textual anchor in the provision and constitutes a gloss on the provision". The Full Court opined that s 12(3) requires: (a) there should be a "contract"; (b) which is wholly or principally "for" the labour of a person; and (c) that the person must "work" under that contract. So far as (b) is concerned, the word "for" is purposive but even the simplest employment relationship has 2 purposes depending on the perspective from which it is viewed. Since s 12(3) poses the question of whether the contract is "for" the labour of a person, this shows that parliament was mandating an inquiry into the purpose of the contract from the perspective of the person obtaining the benefit of the labour (ie the quasi-employer) ([80]–[84]).

Scope of SGAA application

The SGAA extends to every external territory referred to in the definition of Australia (SGAA s 4). When used in a geographical sense, Australia is defined as having the same meaning as in ITAA97 (SGAA s 6(1); ITAA97 ss 960-505; 995-1(1)). Under its income tax definition, Australia includes Norfolk Island, the Coral Sea Islands Territory, the Territory of Ashmore and Cartier Islands, the Territory of Christmas Island, the Territory of Cocos (Keeling) Islands, and the Territory of Heard Island and the McDonald Islands. It extends to offshore areas and expressly includes an offshore area for the purpose of the *Offshore Petroleum and Greenhouse Gas Storage Act 2006* and to the Joint Petroleum Development Area (within the meaning of the *Petroleum (Timor Sea Treaty) Act 2003*). The income tax definition clarifies the SG entitlements and obligations of employers and employees in Australia, subject to specific persons being expressly excluded by the general exemptions in SGAA s 27 (¶39-030).

SGAA application to Commonwealth and untaxable Commonwealth authorities

The Commonwealth, Commonwealth Departments and untaxable Commonwealth authorities are not liable to pay SG charge. For SGAA purposes, they are treated as employers in respect of the employment of a Commonwealth employee and the Act is taken to apply to them in all operational aspects (like any other employer), other than the provisions imposing liability to pay the charge and penalties and the provisions allowing appeal and review rights. However, a Commonwealth authority whose enabling legislation otherwise exempts it from Commonwealth taxation is liable to pay the SG charge unless it is expressly exempted by the legislation (SGAA ss 5; 5A).

Partnerships, unincorporated associations and trusts

Specific provisions clarify the status of partnerships and unincorporated associations as employers for SG purposes (SGAA ss 72; 73).

A partnership is treated as if it were a separate legal person so that a person can be an employee of the partnership, rather than an employee of the individual partners themselves. A partner in a partnership cannot be an employee of the partnership, and an agreement that enables a partner to draw a salary does not create an employer/employee relationship but operates simply to vary the sharing of partnership profits between the parties (SGR 2005/1 para 15, 99–102). Whether an individual (other than a partner) who is engaged by a partnership to perform work for the partnership is an employee of the partnership depends on the circumstances of the contractual arrangement (¶39-022).

An unincorporated association is treated as a legal person so that it may be an employer even though it is not otherwise a legal entity with the capacity to enter into contracts.

A trust is not a legal entity (¶6-010). At common law, a trustee cannot be an employee of the trust as that would require the trustee to enter into a contract of service with himself/herself. However, in a particular case, there may be an employment relationship between individual trustees (in their capacity as workers who are receiving remuneration for their services) and the trust (ie the trustees) and, in those circumstances, the trustees of the trust (as the employer) have an obligation to make SG contributions for themselves as employees (*Christie*).

[AMSG ¶12-060ff; FTR ¶794-628, ¶794-628/10; SLP ¶50-200]

¶39-022 Employer–employee relationship

The relationship between an employer and employee is a contractual one, often referred to as a ''contract of service''. This may be contrasted with an independent contractor relationship that is referred to as a ''contract for service''. An independent contractor typically contracts to achieve a result whereas an employee contracts to provide his/her labour typically to enable the employer to achieve a result. Where the substance of a contract is to achieve a specified result, it is likely (but not conclusive) that it is a contract for service (*World Book (Australia) Pty Ltd*: ¶26-150).

An employee at common law is an employee under SGAA s 12(1) (unless expressly excluded, for example, by s 12(9A) or (11): ¶39-020). The leading cases on the common law meaning of employee and the key indicators of whether an individual is an employee or independent contractor at common law (such as the ''control test'', the ''integration or organisation test'': see below) are discussed in ¶26-150 and SGR 2005/1.

SGR 2005/1 states that determining if a person is a common law employee is a question of fact, based on all the circumstances in each case and having regard to the key indicators expressed in case law. The classic test for determining the nature of the relationship between a person who engages another to perform work and the person so engaged is the degree of control which the former can exercise over the latter. Basically, a common law employee is told not only what work is to be done, but how and where it is to be done. With the increasing usage of skilled labour and consequential reduction in supervisory functions, the importance of control lies not so much in its actual exercise as in the right of the employer to exercise it. While control is important, it is not the sole indicator of whether or not there is an employment relationship but rather one of a number of indicia which must be considered in determination of that question (SGR 2005/1, para 33, 36).

Key points from SGR 2005/1 on when an individual is an employee under the SGAA are noted below.

- The question of whether a person is an employee for SG purposes is not determined by reference to whether the person is a full-time, part-time or casual worker.
- Defining the contractual relationship is often a process of examining a number of factors and evaluating them within the context of the relationship between the parties (SGR 2005/1, para 32 to 60). The totality of the relationship between the parties must be considered as no one indicator of itself is determinative (see further ''Employer–employee and other contractual relationships'' below).
- Where an individual performs work for another party through an entity (such as a company or trust), there is no employer-employee relationship between the individual and other party either at common law or under the SGAA extended definition of employee as the entity has entered into an agreement with the party,

rather than the individual. However, the individual may be the employee of the intermediary entity, depending on the terms of the agreement (see ''Work arranged by intermediary'' below).

- A partner in a partnership is not an employee of the partnership. If a partnership has contracted to provide services, the person who actually does the work is not the employee of the other party to the contract. This is so even if the worker is a partner and the contract requires the partner to do the work. However, if partners contract outside the partnership in their personal capacity to provide their labour to fulfil a contractual obligation, they can be an employee of the other party to the contract.
- A person who holds an ABN may still be an employee for SGAA purposes, as a person who carries on a business or trade may also at certain times perform work for another as an employee (SGR 2005/1, para 108).
- The application or otherwise of the personal services income (PSI) measures (¶30-600) to an individual is not determinative, nor does it imply, that an individual is an employee under the SGAA (ITAA97 s 84-10) (ID 2015/9: ¶39-200).
- An arrangement structured between parties in a way that does not give rise to a payment for services rendered but rather a payment for something entirely different (eg a lease or a bailment) does not give rise to an employer-employee relationship (see *De Luxe Red and Yellow Cabs* below: taxi owner and driver arrangement).

Employer–employee and other contractual relationships

A person who works under a contract that is wholly or principally for the labour of the person is an employee of the other party to the contract under the expanded definition of employee and employer in SGAA s 12(3) (¶39-020).

Most contractual conditions are equivocal as indicators of the true character of a contract, ie whether the contract establishes an employer-employee or an independent contractor relationship. For example, worker discretion in matters such as time and place of work, and a performance-based mode of payment, may be consistent with an independent contractor relationship; on the other hand, payer prescription as to time and place of work, and a time-based mode of payment, may be consistent with an employment relationship (TR 2005/16).

A contract for a person's labour is one where the work must be done by that particular person. If the contract leaves the person completely free to have the work performed by another person, it is not a contract for labour of a particular person and a person working under such a contract is not an employee under SGAA s 12(3), ie a person who works under a contract wholly or principally for the labour of the person (¶39-020).

In particular circumstances, an independent contractor at common law may still be an ''employee'' under the SGAA. SGR 2005/1 states that a contract is considered to be wholly or principally for the labour of the individual engaged (and the individual will be an employee under s 12(3)) where the terms of the contract in light of the parties' subsequent conduct indicate:

- the individual is remunerated (either wholly or principally) for his/her personal labour and skills
- the individual must perform the contractual work personally (ie there is no right of delegation), and
- the individual is not paid to achieve a result (para 11).

A pizza delivery driver who operates under an ''Independent Contract Driver Agreement'' for a fixed rate per delivery is an employee of the person operating the pizza delivery franchise business within the ordinary meaning of employee in s 12(1)

(¶39-020). The fact that the drivers are required to provide and maintain their own vehicles is not an overriding factor when considering the arrangement as a whole (ID 2014/28).

In *Vabu*, the court held that some courier drivers who supplied and maintained their own motor vehicles could not be classified, on balance, as employees at common law (¶26-150). The ATO noted in ID 2014/28 that the Vabu courier arrangement was different from that involving pizza delivery drivers. Vabu's business was essentially an organising role, ie organising couriers to collect various items from clients for delivery of those items to the requested destination. In this regard, Vabu had more of an agency-type or intermediary role between the client and the courier as the service of the courier (delivery of parcels, etc) was being provided to a third party. This is different from the arrangement in ID 2014/28, where the service of the driver (delivery of pizzas) was being provided to the entity engaging the driver (the pizza delivery franchisee). The couriers engaged by Vabu to collect and make deliveries were not integrated into Vabu's business, whereas with the pizza delivery drivers, the item (pizza) being delivered represented the core business of the employer. The ATO also noted that due to the decision and associated reasoning in Vabu, pizza delivery drivers who provide their own vehicles do not fall within the extended definition of ''employee'' in s 12(3). That is, they are employees by virtue of s 12(1) only.

On the ''integration or organisation test'' for determining the existence of a common law employee relationship, the majority of the High Court in *Hollis and Vabu* (a subsequent negligence action in *Vabu's case*) held that: ''. . . the distinction between an employee and independent contractor is rooted fundamentally in the difference between a person who serves his employer in his, the employer's business, and a person who carries on a trade or business of his own''. The majority found that, viewed as a practical matter, the bicycle couriers in the *Hollis case* were not running their own business or enterprise, nor did they have independence in the conduct of their operations. The Commissioner accepted that, in addition to consideration of the control test and other relevant aspects of the relationship between the parties, the High Court was at the same time concerned with the fundamental question of whether the workers were operating their own business or operating within Vabu's business. That is, when applying the indicators of employment, it is also necessary to keep in mind the distinction between a worker operating on his/her own account and a worker operating in the business of the payer (SGR 2005/1, para 41; ¶26-150) (*Probin*; *Toowong Pastures Pty Ltd as trustee for the DB Family Trust*: control test and delegation of duties test).

In *De Luxe Red and Yellow Cabs*, the Full Federal Court held that the relationship between taxi operators and taxi drivers is not one of employer and employee, but one of bailment. Accordingly, taxi operators have no SG obligations in respect of their drivers.

Casual market research interviewers in the field and those who conducted computer-assisted interviews were found by the AAT to be employees at common law and employees within the meaning of s 12(3) as they were engaged under contracts that were wholly or principally for their labour. On appeal, the Full Federal Court agreed that the interviewers were employees as they were not employed to produce a result (*Roy Morgan Research Pty Ltd*). In the *Morgan case*, the court also held that the SG legislation was constitutionally valid; this decision was upheld by the High Court (¶39-000).

In *On Call Interpreters and Translators Agency* (*On Call*), the Federal Court (Bromberg J) reviewed the legal principles governing the distinction between a common law employee or independent contractor relationship, in particular the question of whether a person is an independent contractor in relation to the performance of particular work. The court concluded that the interpreters and translators in that case were common law employees under s 12(1) and, if not, they would be employees within the extended meaning of employee in s 12(3).

The ATO agreed that the *On Call* conclusions were consistent with its submissions in the case, even though the reasoning differed from its view in SGR 2005/1. The ATO states that his Honour's observations in this regard were *obiter dicta*, and although they are to be given great weight, the principles established in *Vabu* (based on the High Court decision in *Neale v Atlas Products (Vic) Pty Ltd* and the NSW Court of Appeal in *World Book*) represent the current authority on the application of s 12(3). Hence, the ATO will continue to administer s 12(3) in accordance with the *Vabu* line of authority and will maintain the views set out in SGR 2005/1 (ATO *Decision Impact Statement* on *On Call*) (*SR & K Hall Family Trust*: workers in plumbing business were employees under s 12(3), not independent contractors; *OEM Supplies Pty*: principles in *On Call* applied). Note also that the Full Federal Court has stated that the *On Call* approach to interpreting s 12(3) was erroneous and has provided guidelines on the interpretation of s 12(3) (see ¶39-020 and *Dental Corporation Pty Ltd v Moffet* below).

The Federal Court has held that a dental corporation was liable to pay superannuation contributions on behalf of a dentist (Dr Moffet) it engaged. The court found that Dr Moffet was engaged as an independent contractor, and not as an employee or worker as defined in the *Fair Work Act 2009* and the *Long Service Leave Act 1955* (NSW), respectively. Notwithstanding that, the court concluded that the Services Agreement entered into between Dental Corporation and Dr Moffet was a contract that was *wholly or principally* for the labour of Dr Moffet within the meaning of SGAA s 12(3) (¶39-020) and, therefore, he was an employee for SG purposes (*Moffet v Dental Corporation Pty Ltd*; Dental Corporation's appeal dismissed by the Full Federal Court:). It should be noted that this case dealt with a Services Agreement/Independent Contractor Agreement under which Dr Moffet, in the capacity as a dentist, was engaged to provide services to the patients of Dental Corporation. Such arrangements are different from those under a genuine Services and Facilities Agreement where the dental practice is engaged to provide services to the practitioner in exchange for a fee.

An "expert tradesman" engaged by a partnership as an independent contractor was held to be an employee. The fact that there was an agreement with the worker not to make superannuation contributions on his behalf is irrelevant. Once an employment relationship is established, the employer cannot "contract out" of its SG obligations (*Griffiths*). Licensed contractors and tradespersons engaged as workers by a taxpayer who carried on a business of a plumbing services subcontractor were held to be independent contractors, not employees of the taxpayer (*Case 3/2014*). A technician contracting his services to a repair and maintenance services company was held to be in an independent contractor relationship, and not an employee of the company (*MWWD*).

Workers engaged by a taxpayer company engaged in the business of providing facilities for its clients to make video-recorded or unrecorded tandem parachute jumps were held to be common law employees, or employees under the extended meaning in s 12(3) (person working under a contract wholly or principally for the person's labour) and s 12(8) (person performing certain activities or services in connection with making a disc) (¶39-020) (*General Aviation Maintenance*).

In *Brinkley*, the captain and deckhand of a commercial fishing boat, who were remunerated based on set percentages of the catch in-line with the common practice in the industry, were held to be employees of the boat owner. The AAT found that the captain and deckhand were not conducting their own business, but were an integral part of the owner's business and subject to his direction (see also *Floorplay*: crew members of commercial fishing vessel licensee held to be employees). By contrast, in *Re Dominic B Fishing*, the AAT held that the crew members (fishermen) on a commercial fishing vessel operated by the taxpayer were neither "employees" at common law nor employees under s 12(3) as the parties' contract terms contemplated a joint venture intended to produce fish for sale and the fishermen were remunerated on the basis of an outcome. The ATO considered that the AAT's finding was limited to its own facts and did not provide authoritative guidance on cases concerning whether a worker was an employee for the

SG purposes. The ATO also stated it did not have an opportunity to make submissions on the AAT's finding of a "joint venture" in the case, but would do so on this point in similar cases that arise in the future so as to further clarify when a fisherman is or is not in a joint venture with a boat owner (*Decision Impact Statement, 2014 VRN M177 of 2010*).

Work arranged by intermediaries

Working arrangements involving 3 (or more) parties, which may take different forms and are often labelled in different ways, involve various relationships (whether contractual or otherwise) between the entity requiring the services or work of an individual (end-user), an intermediary firm, and the individual performing the work or services.

In these tripartite working arrangements, more than one contract is often formed in contrast to the conventional working relationship between an entity and worker under a single contract. Accordingly, it can sometimes be difficult to tell whether the worker engaged through an intermediary is an employee of the intermediary or end-user, or neither. SGR 2005/2 sets out the principles to apply in determining whether there is an employment relationship for the purposes of s 12(1) and (3) where work is arranged by intermediaries.

TA 2011/2 describes an arrangement where a labour hire firm makes a discretionary trust structure available for the use of individual taxpayers for the purpose of alienating income from personal services and splitting it between the individual taxpayers who perform the services and their associates. The Alert states such an arrangement, which attempts to circumvent the personal services income (PSI) regime (¶30-600) and other tax and superannuation obligations, may be ineffective. For example, it may constitute an arrangement under s 30 of the SGAA to avoid payment of the SG charge (¶39-550).

Practice tools

The ATO's *Employee/contractor decision tool* enables businesses which engage and make payments to workers to determine if the worker is an employee or contractor for tax and superannuation purposes (www.ato.gov.au/Calculators-and-tools/Employee-or-contractor). The tool is not designed for use by labour hire firms, individual workers, or operators or drivers deriving income in connection with ride-sourcing arrangements.

For a practitioner article which examines whether an incorporated contractor is automatically outside the scope of the SG regime, see *Reconsidering incorporated contractors in an SG context* in the CCH *Tax Week*¶53 (2016).

¶39-024 Particular categories of employers and employees

SGR 2005/1 and SGR 2005/2 provide guidelines to determine whether a person is an employee for SG purposes, whether at common law or under the extended definition of "employee" in SGAA s 12 (¶39-020, ¶39-022).

Other ATO views on particular categories of persons and payments for SG purposes include the following:

- A partner in a professional partnership who is a director of a company is not an employee of the company if he/she must pass on any directors' fees received to the partnership; however, where the partner's appointment as a director is unrelated to membership of the partnership, the partner is an employee of the company notwithstanding any agreement to pay the fees over to another entity or person (SGD 97/1).
- If a medical practitioner provides medical services within a practice (clinic) under an arrangement (eg fee-splitting, management services etc) with the clinic, the totality of the relationship between the parties must be considered to determine

whether, on balance, he/she is an employee or independent contractor (ID 2011/87: medical practitioner neither a common law employee nor employee under any expanded meanings in s 12).

- A person who provides home-based child care is generally not an employee, unless the carer provides the child care in the parents' own home (former SGD 94/4 covered arrangements which are less common in the current child care environment; most family day care services and in-home care programs are now being established as commercial ventures, see SGR 2005/1). Basically, the s 12(11) exemption applies to persons who are paid for work principally or wholly of a domestic or private nature for not more than 30 hours per week and the exemption would not apply to carers engaged by labour hire entities to provide child care services in the parent's home (*Decision Impact Statement* on *Newton's case*: ¶39-020).

- A sportsperson may be an employee under s 12(1) if his/her relationship to the payer conforms to the indicators and factors that typify a common law employment relationship (as discussed in SGR 2005/1). If a common law employment relationship does not exist, the SGAA provisions below must be considered:

  - s 12(3) dealing with payments to work under a contract that is wholly or principally for the labour of the person (SGR 2009/1) (see *Dental Corporation Pty Ltd v Moffet* in ¶39-020), and

  - s 12(8) dealing with payments to a persons who is paid to perform, present or participate in the performance or presentation of any sport, or where services are provided ''in connection with'' a sporting activity, or for payments for provision of services in, or in connection with, any television or radio broadcast (¶39-020) (see *Racing Queensland Board* and *Scone Race Club Ltd* below).

  A sportsperson paid ''appearance fees'' and similar payments to participate in sporting activity is an employee of the payer under the SGAA. However, a sportsperson paid ''prize money'' would not be an employee of the payer (unless the sportsperson is an employee at common law) because the prize money is not paid for the sportsperson's participation in a sporting activity. Prize money is only payable if a specific result has been achieved. A sportsperson who is paid to appear on a television or radio broadcast will be an employee of the payer under s 12(8)(c).

  The SGAA will apply to non-resident sportspersons paid to participate in sports in Australia, unless the payer is exempted under a certificate of coverage (SGAA s 27(1)(e): ¶39-030). Team officials and non-resident event organisers may also be excluded from the scope of the SGAA if they are a prescribed employee under SGAR s 11 (SGAA s 27(1)(d): ¶39-030).

Miscellaneous payments

The ATO has successfully appealed against 2 Federal Court decisions with similar issues concerning the SG liability for payments to jockeys. In the first case, the court at first instance held that jockeys were not employees of the Racing Queensland Board (RQB) and that the RQB was not liable for unpaid SG charges on various payments made to the jockeys under a Centralised Prizemoney System (CPS), which makes prize money percentage payments and riding fee payments to jockeys on behalf of race clubs for all Queensland race meetings. In the second case, the court held that the Scone Race Club (SRC) was not liable to make SG contributions in relation to riding fees paid by it to jockeys. In upholding the ATO's appeal, the Full Federal Court held that the RQB and SRC were the entities liable to pay riding fees to jockeys for riding in a horse race and therefore were deemed to be their employers for the purposes of the SG legislation (*Racing Queensland Board*; *Scone Race Club Ltd*; the High Court has denied special leave to appeal the Full Court decisions). The ATO has stated that both decisions were consistent with its interpretation of s 12(8) that the RQB and SRC were the "employer" of jockeys to whom they had paid riding fees; it did not form the view that they were the "employer" of jockeys under the ordinary meaning of that term, or for any effect other than under the SG legislation.

The Fair Entitlements Guarantee (FEG) scheme provides assistance to employees who have lost their employment due to their employer's liquidation or bankruptcy and are owed certain employee entitlements. Where the Department of Employment (DE) makes a FEG advance to a former employee in relation to unpaid employee entitlements, the DE pays as a representative of, or in the interest of, the company in liquidation, ie a payment made "on behalf of the employer" within the scope of SGAA s 6(3) even though there is no agency relationship between the DE and the company. This is the case even if the advance is ultimately paid to the employee by a third party (eg an accounting firm) or the DE makes the payment directly to the employee (SGD 2017/1). The advance to the former employee is "salary or wages" paid by the employer to an employee for the purposes of working out an SG liability (¶39-026) and the employer is the entity with the liability for the SG charge.

A person can accrue long service leave credits with different employers under a worker entitlement fund (WEF) arrangement where the employers make contributions to the WEF to provide for the person's long service leave. Once the required credits have been accrued, the person is entitled to receive a payment from the WEF. Neither the WEF nor the employer have an SG obligation on WEF long service leave payments to the individual. There is no employer-employee relationship between the WEF and the individual receiving the long service leave payments, and the employer is not making, or is not liable to make, the payments to the individual (ID 2005/33).

Scholarship payments by an Australian university to a student undertaking a relevant course of study (where the scholarships are funded by industry-based organisations) are not subject to the SG scheme. The university has no obligation to make SG contributions on the scholarship payment as there is no employer-employee relationship (ID 2005/53).

Gig economy activities

The sharing economy is activity through a digital platform (such as a website or an app) where people share assets or services for a fee (sometimes referred to as the "gig economy"). People sharing services include those who provide ride-sourcing services for a fare (eg Uber, GoCatch) or provide personal services, including creative or professional services like graphic design, creating websites or odd jobs (eg OneFlare).

Whether an individual providing services in the gig economy will receive SG contributions depends on the individual's working arrangements with the platform, that is, whether as an employee or a contractor (ATO Fact Sheet *The sharing economy and tax*).

[AMSG ¶12-070ff; FTR ¶794-630, ¶794-631; SLP ¶50-250]

¶39-026 Salary or wages for superannuation guarantee

The meaning of "salary or wages" is important because their recipients are generally employees (¶39-020) under the SGAA so that their employers are required to make SG contributions for them.

In addition, an employer's individual SG shortfall in respect of employees in each quarter is worked out using an employee's "quarterly salary or wages base", which comprises the total salary and wages paid to the employee for the quarter and any salary sacrificed amounts for the quarter that would have been salary or wages but for a salary sacrificed arrangement (¶39-300).

Inclusive definition of "salary or wages"

The term ''salary or wages'' is defined inclusively in the SGAA (s 11(1)). Salary or wages therefore has its ordinary meaning to mean all amounts paid as reward for an employee's services. The term ''salary'' ordinarily means a fixed periodical payment paid to a person for regular work or service. A ''wage'' or ''wages'' is an amount paid for work or services whether by the day or the week or on any other basis (Macquarie Dictionary, 4th edition). The court has held that ''wages'' are ''. . . payments made to an employee in connection with and by reason of his service as an employee or in respect of some incident of his service . . . a bonus paid to employees because they were employees would be so included'' (*Mutual Acceptance* at 396).

In the SGAA, ''salary or wages'' *includes* the following: commissions; directors' fees; payments under a contract made in respect of the labour of the person working under the contract; payments for activities involving the exercise of creative talents; payments for services in connection with the making of any film, tape, disc or television or radio broadcast; remuneration for members of the Commonwealth and state parliaments, members of the Legislative Assembly of a territory, and members of a local government council that is an eligible local governing body; and remuneration for members of the Defence or Police Force (SGAA s 11(1)). These forms of salary or wages reflect the payments made to persons who come within the extended definition of employee in the SGAA s 12(2) to (10) (¶39-020).

Certain remuneration and benefits are not salary or wages

The following payments and benefits are *not* salary or wages for the SGAA purposes:

- remuneration under a contract for work of not more than 30 hours per week of a domestic or private nature (SGAA s 11(2)) (these workers are excluded as employees for SG purposes: ¶39-020), and
- fringe benefits under the FBTAA (s 11(3)).

The Commissioner considers that other ''benefits'' (within the meaning of the FBTAA) given by employers to employees that are neither fringe benefits nor salary or wages within the meaning of that Act are not salary or wages for SGAA purposes. Examples are employer contributions to a complying superannuation fund for the benefit of an employee and the acquisition of a share, or of a right to acquire a share, under an employee share scheme within the meaning of ITAA36 Pt III Div 13A (SGR 2009/2, para 58).

In a case which involved payments to employees from a profit sharing bonus scheme based on specified revenue targets achieved, the AAT held that the bonuses were clearly paid in an employment context and by reference to the specific performance of the employees as a group; they were ordinary time earnings as well as salary or wages for SG purposes (*Prushka*).

In *Falcote*, employees were paid under awards that provided for employer superannuation contributions to be based on each employee's ''ordinary time earnings'', exclusive of overtime, allowances, bonuses and other extraneous payments of a like nature. The AAT upheld the Commissioner's decision that the employer should have made SG contributions on the basis of the employees' ordinary time earnings, which included the over-award amounts. For SG purposes, the ''attendance bonuses'' were, in fact, wages. In *Penrowse*, the employer had an agreement with the delivery drivers it employed that their remuneration payments would be allocated as to 80% for allowances for motor vehicle expenses (''MVRE'', an acronym used in the company's accounts for amounts paid to drivers for motor vehicle ''allowances'' or ''reimbursements'' of motor vehicle expenses) and the remaining 20% would be regarded as wages. The AAT held that the MVRE amounts were salary or wages, and not reimbursement of motor vehicle expenses, and are relevant to the calculation of SG charge (¶39-400).

Where a person is an employee under SGAA s 12(3) (ie persons contracted wholly or principally for their labour: ¶39-020), the salary or wages of the employee are the payments for the labour component of the contract or a reasonable market value if this component cannot be worked out. Employers must keep records for this purpose (SGD 96/2; *Floorplay*: wages of commercial fishing crew net of operating expenses).

An advance that is paid to a former employee of a company in liquidation is ''salary or wages'' under its ordinary meaning because the advance is paid in consideration of the services rendered by the former employee prior to the company entering into liquidation. An advance paid under s 28 of the *Fair Entitlements Guarantee Act 2012* to a former employee is ''salary or wages'' for the purposes of working out an SG charge liability (SGD 2017/1).

Certain salaries or wages and income are excluded for SGAA purposes

The employee earnings below are not taken into account as salaries or wages for particular SG purposes:

- earnings of employees as specified in SGAA s 27 (¶39-030), and salaries or wages paid to part-time employees under the age of 18 (see below) (SGAA s 28) — the salaries or wages paid to these employees are not taken into account when calculating the employee's SG shortfall under SGAA s 19 (¶39-300)
- tax-exempt earnings of reserve force members under SGAA s 29 — the salaries or wages paid to these employees are not taken into account for all SGAA purposes.

The effect of the above is that the employers will not have an SG shortfall even if they do not make SG contributions for these employees, ie they are ''exempt'' employees (¶39-030).

A ''part-time employee'' means a person who is employed to work not more than 30 hours per week (SGAA s 6(1)). The term ''employed to work'' means actual hours worked. A person who actually works for more than 30 hours per week is not a part-time employee, even where a contract stipulates the person is to work fewer hours (SGD 93/1).

▶ Example

Diana is employed under a contract which states she is to work 25 hours per week. During the school holidays she works an additional 10 hours per week. For those weeks, Diana is ''employed to work'' 35 hours per week and is not a part-time employee.

Checklist of salary or wages and ordinary time earnings

ATO guidelines on the meaning of ''salary or wages'' and ''ordinary time earnings'' (¶39-200), including a checklist of whether certain payments and amounts are included in ''ordinary time earnings'' and/or ''salary or wages'' for SG purposes, are set out in SGR 2009/2.

[AMSG ¶12-080; FTR ¶794-626, ¶794-648; SLP ¶50-350]

¶39-030 Employees "exempt" from SG

The following are ''exempt'' employees for SG purposes and an employer is not required to make SG contributions for them in respect of certain salary or wages amounts paid to them:

(1) non-resident employees paid for ''work done outside Australia'' (see below), except to the extent covered by a certificate under SGAA s 15C (s 27(1)(b)) (see ''Scheduled international social security agreement'' below)

(2) resident employees employed by non-resident employers for work done outside Australia (see below), or non-resident employees for work done in the Joint Petroleum Development Area within the meaning of the *Petroleum (Timor Sea Treaty) Act 2003* (s 27(1)(c), (ca))

(3) employees who hold visas or entry permits prescribed by the SGAR (s 27(1)(d); SGAR s 11) (*Sushi Yachiyo Pty Ltd*: cook not an exempt employee)

(4) employees receiving salary or wages prescribed by the SGAR (s 27(1)(e); SGAR ss 12, 12A), namely:

   (i) salary or wages paid to an employee for a period of parental leave

   (ii) salary or wages paid to an employee who is engaging in an eligible community service activity

   (iii) salary or wages paid to an employee who is undertaking service with the Australian Defence Force

   (iv) salary or wages paid to an employee consisting of a payment of green army allowance (within the meaning of the Social Security Act 1991)

   (v) salary or wages paid to an employee as a result of a bonus payment under the Aged Care Workforce Retention Grant Opportunity (see ''Employees receiving parental leave and other prescribed payments'' below)

   (vi) salary or wages paid to an employee where a scheduled international social security agreement provides that the employer is not subject to the SG scheme in respect of the work for which the payment was made (see ''Scheduled international social security agreement'' below)

   (vii) salary or wages paid to an employee that enables the employer to satisfy the JobKeeper wage condition (see ''Salary or wages paid in respect of a JobKeeper fortnight'' below)

(5) employees receiving salary or wages of less than $450 in a month (based on the salary or wages actually paid by the employer in the month) (s 27(2)) (see example in ¶39-300).

How does the "exempt" employee status arise?

The SG exemption for employees in the categories covered by s 27 is achieved by not taking the salary or wages paid to the employee into account when calculating the individual SG shortfall of the employee under SGAA s 19 (¶39-300).

The ''exempt'' employee status therefore arises as there is no SG shortfall in respect of those employees, even though they receive salaries or wages and the employer does not make SG contribution for them.

However, any excluded salary or wages are still taken into account when determining whether the employee is paid less than $450 a month under the low income earners' exemption in category (5) (SGD 2003/5: ¶39-300).

New Zealand citizens do not require a visa to work in Australia. The exemption in s 27(1)(d) (category (3) above) is not relevant and employers must provide SG for employees who are NZ citizens.

Apart from the s 27 categories, certain other employees are also ''exempt'' employees or may opt out of the SG scheme (see ''Other employees exempted from the SG scheme'' below).

Work done outside Australia

The expression ''work done outside Australia'' is used in s 27(1)(b) and (c) (see categories (1) and (2) above). The term ''Australia'', when used in a geographical sense, includes certain territories and their offshore areas (¶39-020). ''Australia'' in the expression ''work done outside Australia'' includes the coastal sea of Australia and the coastal sea of each of its territories, and work done at sea at a location which satisfies all of the following is ''work done outside Australia'' for the purposes of s 27(1):

- it is outside the outer limits of the "coastal sea" of Australia
- it is outside the outer limits of the "coastal seas" of the Territories, including the Coral Sea Islands Territory, the Territory of Ashmore and Cartier Islands, the Territory of Christmas Island, the Territory of Cocos (Keeling) Islands and the Territory of Heard Island and the McDonald Islands, and
- it is outside the offshore areas, including an offshore area for the purpose of the *Offshore Petroleum* and *Greenhouse Gas Storage Act 2006* and the Joint Petroleum Development Area (within the meaning of the *Petroleum (Timor Sea Treaty) Act 2003*) (ITAA97 s 960-505, Note 1; ID 2015/24).

Norfolk Island employers and employees

The SG scheme covers salary and wages paid to Norfolk Island resident employees for work done in Norfolk Island and salary and wages paid by Norfolk Island resident employers for work done in Norfolk Island from 1 July 2016. These employees and employers previously did not come within the SG regime (former s 27(1)(b) and (c): categories (1) and (2) above).

A transitional SG rate applies for Norfolk Island employers and employees over a 12-year period (¶39-100).

Employees receiving parental leave and other prescribed payments

The exemption under category (4)(i)–(v) covers salary or wages paid to employees:

- for a period of parental leave or ancillary leave. This applies regardless of whether the payments are made under current awards or agreements, or a statutory paid parental leave scheme "Parental leave" includes maternity leave, early paid leave relating to an inability to be transferred to a safe job, paternity leave and other leave taken by partners at the time of birth or adoption, pre-adoption leave and adoption leave (SGAR s 12(1)(a))
- who are engaging in an "eligible community service" activity (as defined in s 109(1) of the *Fair Work Act 2009*) and paid by the employee's usual employer while absent from their usual employment. Eligible community service includes jury service or another activity (SGAR s 12(1)(b)). This does not apply to the salary or wages of an employee who engages in the eligible community service activity as an employee of the employer that carries on the activity, or to a payment relating to annual leave, sick leave or long service leave that is paid in relation to the period during which the employee is engaged in the relevant activity or performing the relevant work (SGAR s 12(2), (4))
- who are undertaking service with the Australian Defence Force and paid by the employee's usual employer while absent from their usual employment (SGAR s 12(1)(c)). This does not apply to salary or wages paid by the Australian Defence Force (other than salary or wages to which SGAA s 29 applies) (see "Other employees exempted from the SG scheme" below), or to a payment relating to annual leave, sick leave or long service leave that is paid in relation to the period during which the employee is engaged in the relevant activity or performing the relevant work (SGAR s 12(2), (4))
- consisting of payments of "green army allowance" (within the meaning of the *Social Security Act 1991*), ie payments to Green Army Programme participants by Green Army service providers (SGAR s 12(1)(d))
- that is funded by a payment made to the employer under the Commonwealth program known as the Aged Care Workforce Retention Grant Opportunity (the Grant) on or after 1 June 2020. The Grant funds 2 bonus payments for eligible aged care workers as part of the government's response to COVID-19 to ensure the continuity of the aged care workforce in residential and home care. The Grant is

paid to employers on the condition that the funds are used to make bonus payments to their eligible employees (including at a pro-rata rate for part-time employees). This exception ensures that an employer does not incur SG-related liabilities as a result of their employees receiving a bonus payment under the Grant (SGAR s 12(1)(f)).

Scheduled international social security agreement

The exemption for employees under category (4)(vi) deals with potential ''double superannuation coverage'' that can arise where an employee is sent to work temporarily in another country and the employer is required to make superannuation contributions for the employee under the legislation of both Australia and the foreign country (SGAA ss 15C, 27(1)(e); SGAR s 12(1)(e)).

To address that problem, the government has entered into ''scheduled international social security agreements'' (defined by reference to *Social Security (International Agreements) Act 1999*, s 5) with a number of countries. These agreements which form a part of the broader agreement on social security have the effect that only the home country's superannuation scheme will apply. Current agreements exist with: the United States of America, Portugal, the Netherlands, Croatia, Chile, Belgium, Ireland, Norway, Switzerland, Korea, Greece, Germany, Japan, Finland, Poland, the former Yugoslav Republic of Macedonia, Czech Republic, Austria, the Slovak Republic, Latvia, Hungary and India.

Where an Australian employee is sent to work in a foreign country, an exemption from that country's compulsory superannuation arrangements is only available if the employee remains covered by Australia's SG legislation while working overseas. To qualify for the exemption, the employer must apply to the ATO for a ''Certificate of Coverage'' before the employee leaves Australia. On approval, the ATO will give a Certificate of Coverage to the employer (who will be required to give a copy to the employee) and a copy of the certificate to the authorities in the relevant foreign country (ID 2006/336: USA agreement and non-Australian resident coverage). The double superannuation coverage issue does not arise for self-employed persons as they are not covered by the SGAA.

Salary or wages paid in respect of a JobKeeper fortnight

The exemption under category (4)(vii) deals with payments to employees under the JobKeeper scheme, established by the Coronavirus Economic Response Package (Payments and Benefits) Rules 2020 (the JobKeeper Rules) (¶10-040).

As a condition of entitlement under the JobKeeper scheme, an employer must have satisfied the *wage condition* (set out in the JobKeeper Rules) by paying salary or wages (in combination with any superannuation contributions made under a salary sacrifice arrangement (SSA) or other amounts dealt with as agreed with the employee) of at least the JobKeeper payment amount to each eligible employee in the fortnight. In some cases, an eligible employee will receive an amount greater than their usual salary or wages, for example, where the employee has been stood down or the amount required to be paid to the employee for the performance of work is less than the JobKeeper payment amount per fortnight.

To ensure that employers are only required to make SG contributions in respect of the amount paid to an employee for the *performance of work*, the salary or wages paid to an employee in respect of a ''jobkeeper fortnight'' (see below) is prescribed for the purposes of s 27(1)(e) to the extent (if any) that:

- the salary or wages for the fortnight exceeds the amount that the employer is required to pay to the employee in respect of the fortnight for the performance of work (including in relation to any leave entitlements), and

- the excess amount is reasonably attributable to amounts paid by the employer to the employee for the purpose of satisfying the wage condition for getting a JobKeeper payment in respect of the employee for the fortnight (SGAR s 12A(2)).

In addition, if an amount of less than $450 remains (the remaining amount) after reducing the salary or wages the employer pays to the employee in a calendar month by so much of those salary or wages as prescribed under s 12A(2) (see above), the remaining amount is also excluded salary or wages under s 27(2) (see example below).

▶ Example: Employee earns less than $450 a month

Betty, an employee, earns $400 in April 2020 for the performance of work. To satisfy the wage condition for JobKeeper payment for Brendon, her employer pays her $400 for the month, plus an additional $2,600, totalling $3,000 before tax for that month. Her employer is entitled to JobKeeper payment for Betty.

The additional payment of $2,600 is excluded from being salary or wages because it is not an amount that is required to be paid to Betty for the performance of work.

The remaining $400 is also excluded salary or wages (under s 27(2)) because Betty's earnings for the performance of work during the calendar month is less than $450.

Therefore, Betty's salary or wages and ordinary time earnings (OTE) for the month of April are nil for SGAA purposes and her employer is not required to make SG contributions for her.

A "jobkeeper fortnight" means a fortnightly period in which an employer may be entitled to a JobKeeper payment for an employee, ie the fortnight beginning on 30 March 2020, and each subsequent fortnight (s 12A(4)).

The s 12A exceptions achieve the intended policy outcome as employer payments to employees to satisfy the wage condition for getting JobKeeper payment would otherwise be considered salary or wages and OTE under the SGAA. That is, the amounts for the purposes of s 27(1)(e) are excluded from the calculation of the minimum SG contribution the employer is required to make for the employees to avoid an SG charge liability, and the calculation of the individual SG shortfall in respect of the employees.

Section 12A(1) does not require an employer to be entitled to a JobKeeper payment. This allows the provision to apply where an employer has a reasonable belief that it is entitled to a JobKeeper payment and has satisfied the wage condition but is ultimately found not to be entitled.

Other employees exempted from the SG scheme

In addition to the categories of "exempt" employee by operation of s 27 (as discussed above), employers do not have to make SG contributions for part-time employees who are under 18 years of age and for employees who receive tax-exempt salaries or wages as a member of the reserve forces, as any salary or wages paid to these employees are not taken into account for the purpose of making employee SG shortfall calculations (¶39-300) or for SGAA purposes (SGAA ss 28; 29: ¶39-026).

Certain employees can opt out of the SG scheme

Employee with multiple employers can apply to opt out of the SG scheme from 1 July 2018 (¶39-050).

Also, a transitional arrangement provides an exemption for employees who had elected not to receive SG support because their accumulated superannuation benefits had exceeded the pension reasonable benefit limit (RBL) by deeming the employer's quarterly shortfall (¶39-300) for the employee to be nil (SGAA former s 19(4)–(7)). The RBL system has been abolished from 1 July 2007 and there are no new "exempt" employees under this category from that date. However, the exemption continues for employees who were exempt before that date as the employee's election is irrevocable.

An employer has a right to protection from the SG charge for employees who had made the election despite the repeal of the law as this right is preserved for the duration of the employment contract (ID 2007/199).

[AMSG ¶12-100; FTR ¶794-648, ¶794-668; SLP ¶50-300, ¶50-800]

¶39-050 Employees with multiple employers can opt out of SG scheme

Individuals who receive superannuation from multiple employers may apply to opt out of the SG scheme in respect of an employer so as to avoid unintentionally breaching their concessional contributions cap (SGAA ss 19AA–19AC). In these cases, the employee may instead negotiate with the employer to receive additional cash or non-cash remuneration.

A person may apply to the Commissioner to issue an ''employer shortfall exemption certificate'' in relation to a specified employer (which must be the person's employer at the time the application is made) and a specified quarter in a specified financial year. The application must be in the approved form, specify the employer, the quarter and the financial year, and must be made at least 60 days before the first day of the quarter (s 19AB(1), (2)).

The Commissioner may issue the employee an employer shortfall exemption certificate only if satisfied that, if the certificate is not issued, the employee is likely to have excess concessional contributions for the financial year (whether or not issuing the certificate would prevent that result), and having regard to any other matter in accordance with s 19AB(3)–(6). This process is to ensure that the employer shortfall exemption certificates target those employees who are likely to inadvertently breach their concessional contributions cap through employer contributions.

The Commissioner may issue multiple certificates in relation to a single employee, with each certificate covering a different employer. However, at least one employer must still be required to make contributions for the benefit of the employee in order to avoid liability for SG charge. This ensures that an employee will still receive a minimum level of contributions for the financial year.

The Commissioner may not vary or revoke an employer shortfall exemption certificate that is issued. There is no legislative mechanism for an employer to be forced back into the SG scheme in respect of the employee for the quarter covered by a certificate (s 19AB(8),(9)).

A person who is dissatisfied with a decision of the Commissioner may object against the decision in the manner set out in TAA Pt IVC.

SG exemption under a shortfall exemption certificate

An employer covered by a shortfall exemption certificate will have a maximum contribution base of nil (¶39-220) in relation to the employee for the quarter to which the certificate relates (s 19AA). This means the total salary or wages paid by the employer to the employee for the quarter is taken to be nil when calculating the employer's individual SG shortfall for the employee for the quarter (¶39-300). The effect of this is that the employee is exempt from the SG scheme as the employer does not have an SG charge liability (or face other SG consequences) for not making SG contributions for the employee for the quarter.

A shortfall exemption certificate does not prevent an employer from making contributions into superannuation on behalf of the employee. The certificate only removes the consequences of the employer not making contributions for the employee for the quarter covered by the certificate. This means an employer may choose to disregard a certificate and continue to make contributions. For example, this may arise where an employee and employer do not agree on the terms of an alternative remuneration package for the relevant quarter, or there is insufficient time to make payroll or other business software adjustments to discontinue contributions for the employee.

[AMSG ¶12-070, ¶12-220; FTR ¶794-648/10; SLP ¶50-810]

Measuring SG Support

¶39-100 Employer's charge percentage

The minimum level of superannuation support that an employer must provide for each employee so as to avoid incurring liability for the SG charge is calculated by reference to a ''charge percentage'' (commonly called the SG rate) of the employee's ordinary time earnings (or, in pre-2008–09 years, the employee's notional earnings base). All employers are subject to the same charge percentage, regardless of the size of their annual national payroll.

The meaning of ''ordinary time earnings'' is discussed at ¶39-200. For the calculation of an employer's superannuation support for an employee, see ¶39-230.

The process for reducing the employer's charge percentage in respect of each employee based on the employer support provided is discussed at ¶39-300 and the calculation of the SG charge payable by an employer is discussed at ¶39-400.

General SG rate

The general SG rate is noted in the table below. The rate is legislated to remain at 9.5% for years up to and including 2020–21, and will increase by 0.5% on 1 July of each later year until it reaches 12% for years starting on or after 1 July 2025 (SGAA s 19(2)).

Financial year	SG rate
2014–15 to 2020–21	9.5%
2021–22	10%
2022–23	10.5%
2023–24	11%
2024–25	11.5%
2025–26 and later years	12%

Transitional SG rate for Norfolk Island employers and employees

Norfolk Island residents are covered by the SG scheme from 1 July 2016 (SGAA former s 27(1)(b), (c): ¶39-030).

A transitional SG rate starting at 1% for 2016–17, and increasing by 1% in each later year over a 12-year period, applies to Norfolk Island employers and employees in respect of salary and wages that were previously exempt from the SG scheme (to the extent that they were exempt) (*Tax and Superannuation Laws Amendment (Norfolk Island Reforms) Act 2015*, Act No 53 of 2015 Sch 2 item 2).

Employers will apply the general SG rate to all salary and wages that were not previously exempt from SG under the former Norfolk Island exemption (¶39-030), while salary and wages that were exempt are subject to the transitional SG rate. Employers will need to apportion the salary and wages they pay between the 2 categories (amounts subject to SG and amounts previously exempt from SG) and apply the correct SG rate to each category.

[AMSG ¶12-150; FTR ¶794-648; SLP ¶50-485]

¶39-200 Employee's ordinary time earnings

The level of employer SG support for an employee in each quarter is calculated as a percentage of the employee's ordinary time earnings (¶39-230).

In a quarter, an employee's ''ordinary time earnings'' (OTE) is the *lesser* of:

(a) the total of the employee's:

  (i) earnings in respect of ordinary hours of work, *other than* earnings consisting of a lump sum payment on termination of employment, ie (A) a payment in lieu of unused sick leave, and (B) an unused annual leave or unused long service leave payment, and

  (ii) earnings consisting of ''over-award payments, shift loading or commission'' (see below), and

(b) the maximum contribution base (¶39-220) for the quarter (SGAA s 6(1)).

In practical terms, the expression ''earnings'' means ''salary or wages'' (¶39-026). An amount can only be part of an employee's OTE if it is ''salary or wages'' of the employee, but the employee's salary or wages may include amounts that are not OTE (eg the lump sum payments for accrued leave which are expressly excluded from OTE, see above).

SGR 2009/2 sets out guidelines on the OTE definition and the meaning of ''ordinary hours of work'', ''ordinary time earnings'' and ''salary or wages'' (including a checklist). ''Earnings'' for the purpose of the OTE definition is the remuneration paid to the employee as a reward for the employee's services. Generally, the ordinary hours specified in an award or other documents are the ordinary hours of work for an employee, provided a distinction is made between ordinary hours and other hours. If not specified, the ordinary hours of work will be the normal or regular hours worked by the employee. Where it is not possible to determine the normal or regular hours of work (eg with casual workers), the actual hours of work are to be taken as the ordinary hours of work. If the actual hours worked exceed what is considered to be standard full-time hours, the total actual hours worked is used to calculate OTE, and not a capped number of hours.

The Full Federal Court in its appeal decision in *BlueScope Steel (AIS) Pty Ltd v Australian Workers' Union* (see below) stated as below, when agreeing with the Commissioner's interpretation of the terms ''ordinary time earnings'' and ''ordinary hours of work'' within the meaning of SGAA s 6:

> ''. . . The meaning that best reflects these considerations and the text, context, purpose and history of the provision is earnings in respects of ordinary or standard hours of work at ordinary rates of pay as provided for in a relevant industrial instrument, or contract of employment, but if such does not exist (and there is no distinction between ordinary or standard hours and other hours by reference to rates of pay) earnings in respect of the hours that the employee has agreed to work or, if different, the hours usually or ordinarily worked ...''

Over-award payments, shift-loading, commission, paid leave and leave loading

- An over-award payment is the component of a payment in excess of an award entitlement. The specific inclusion of these payments does not apply to over-award payments that are specifically referable to hours worked that are not ordinary time hours. For example, an employer may offer a higher rate of overtime pay for some overtime hours worked than the penalty rate required by an award. Even though these are technically over-award payments, such additional payments are not covered by the OTE definition.

- A shift-loading is an amount paid in addition to a worker's basic hourly rate for having to work outside the usual span of time for ''day workers''. Shift-loadings payable on ordinary hours of work must be distinguished from overtime payments under awards and agreements. Often these are mutually exclusive under awards and agreements, but if an employee is entitled to a shift-loading in respect of hours other than ordinary hours of work, the specific inclusion of shift-loadings in the OTE definition does not apply in that circumstance.

- A commission is a payment made to an employee (eg a salesperson) on the basis of the volume of sales achieved or other similar criteria. These are always OTE except in the unusual case where they can be shown to be wholly referable to overtime hours worked (SGR 2009/2, para 21 to 23).

Salary or wages that employees receive, at or below their normal rate of pay for ordinary hours of work, in respect of periods of paid leave (except parental or ancillary leave: see below) is simply a continuation of their ordinary time pay and is OTE. This is also the case with salary or wages received at the ordinary time rate in respect of public holidays and rostered days off.

Annual ''leave loading'' payments, and like payments, are OTE unless they are demonstrably referable to a notional loss of opportunity to work overtime (eg an annual leave loading that is payable under some awards and industrial agreements). However, loading is always salary or wages (SGR 2009/2, para 32 to 35). Most awards do not specifically state the reason the annual leave loading entitlement is provided and that relying on historical opinions of the initial purpose of annual leave loading is not enough to demonstrate that annual leave loading is a lost opportunity to work overtime. The ATO's guidelines on identifying the purpose for annual leave loading entitlements and its compliance approach are set out in fact sheet *Ordinary time earnings – annual leave loading*.

A payment to an employee in lieu of notice of termination of employment is OTE and salary or wages for SG purposes (SGR 2009/2, para 38).

▶ Example

Darren was dismissed from employment and, was paid the equivalent of 2 weeks' salary in lieu of notice of termination. The employer also made a payment to Darren for unused annual leave.

- Both payments are ''salary or wages'' — the payment in lieu of notice is effectively a payment of salary or wages that Darren was entitled to receive during the notice period. The payment for unused leave is a salary or wage payment to which Darren was entitled but had not previously received.
- Although Darren did not perform work to receive the payment in lieu of notice, the payment is nonetheless made ''in respect of ordinary hours of work'' rather than overtime hours. To this extent, the amount is OTE.
- The unused annual leave payment is not OTE, being specifically excluded from the definition of ''ordinary time earnings'' (see above), but is salary or wages.

With respect to the meaning of ''ordinary hours of work'' in SGAA ss 6 and 23, the court has stated that ''there may be cases in which the working of hours beyond fixed standard hours becomes so regular, normal, customary or usual that the additional hours are to be regarded as ordinary hours for a particular employee. This may be so notwithstanding that the additional hours are remunerated at overtime rates or penalty rates'' (*Quest Personnel Temping Pty Ltd*). That approach focusses upon giving the term ''ordinary'' no technical meaning but rather a meaning directed to determining as a matter of fact what is ''regular, normal, customary or usual''.

In *Australian Workers' Union v BlueScope Steel (AIS) Pty Ltd*, employees were required under their employment agreements to work shifts and to be available 24 hours per day, 365 days of the year under an ''annualised salary'' system. Under the agreements, employees also regularly worked on public holidays. At first instance, the court held that the ''ordinary hours of work'' for SGAA purposes included the ''additional hours'' and ''public holidays''. As a consequence, the relevant payments were OTE and the employer was liable to make SG contributions on the ''additional hours'' and ''public holidays'' component amounts.

In overturning that decision, the Full Federal Court held that the definition of ''OTE'', including the phrase ''earnings in respect of ordinary hours of work'' in s 6(1), had (and has) within it the well-known conception of ordinary hours at ordinary rates. The relevant agreements are clear in the present case. The annualised salary contains a clear component of ordinary or standard (38) hours at an ordinary rate, and that conception is what the term ''ordinary time earnings'' defined in s 6(1) is directed to. The court further stated that the superannuation legislation is structured upon standard hours at ordinary rates, where present in an industrial instrument. That that operation gives a less favourable financial consequence to some employees than calculating superannuation on the whole annualised salary is a consequence of the proper construction of the superannuation legislation. That legislation is not intended to give superannuation benefits for the total salary. It was and is a system to encourage national savings for retirement based on standard hours at ordinary rates (*BlueScope Steel (AIS) Pty Ltd v Australian Workers' Union*; *Decision Impact Statement*).

A payment in lieu of a flex credit to an employee under the terms of a certified agreement is not OTE as the amount is not in respect of the employee's ordinary hours of work (ID 2010/113).

Guidelines on how to calculate SG contributions for drivers in the transport industry can be found in ATO fact sheet *Super for long-distance drivers.*

Salary sacrifice amounts and OTE base

Salary sacrifice arrangements are discussed in ¶39-250.

For the purposes of determining the reduction in an employer's charge percentage from contributions made by an employer for an employee under SGAA s 23, the OTE base is the sum of the employee's OTE and any salary sacrificed amounts that would have been OTE, but for a salary sacrifice arrangement (¶39-230).

This means that any amount that an employee salary sacrifices to superannuation cannot reduce an employer's SG charge, and that the mandatory employer contributions to reduce the SG charge are calculated on a pre-salary sacrifice base (¶39-250).

Personal services income

The personal services income (PSI) regime is discussed in ¶30-600. In certain circumstances, income derived by a personal services entity (PSE) from the personal services (principal work) provided by an individual may be included in the individual's assessable income (ie attribution under ITAA97 s 86-15). Some exceptions apply, for example, attributed amounts do not include payments made promptly by the PSE to the individual, as an employee, as salary or wages (ie payments made before the end of the 14th day after the relevant PAYG payment period).

Attributed PSI will not generally give rise to an SG obligation. This is because the attributed PSI amount is generally *not paid* to the individual personal services provider and an employer's SG obligation hinges upon the notion of receipt of payment for work. However, where the individual receives salary or wages and the payment is made after the end of the 14th day after the PAYG payment period, this amount is treated as attributed PSI (s 86-15(4)). Such a case will give rise to an SG obligation as the payment is considered to be ''earnings in respect of ordinary hours of work'' in relation to an individual under the definition of ordinary time earnings (ID 2015/9: attributed PSI).

As the SGAA imposes obligations only in respect of amounts paid in the relevant quarter, any amount of late salary or wages paid in the first quarter of a financial year (ie July to September), but reported as attributable PSI for the prior year under ITAA97 s

86-40 does not give rise to an SG obligation in the quarter or financial year in which it is declared. The SG obligation will arise in the quarter of the subsequent year when it is paid.

¶39-220 Maximum contribution base

The maximum contribution base for each quarter is $57,090 in 2020–21.

The base acts as a ceiling on the maximum amount of the SG contribution payable by the employer for an employee in each quarter which are calculated based on the employee's "ordinary time earnings" (¶39-200) in the quarter. For 2020–21, the effect of the $57,090 ceiling means that an employer is only required to make maximum SG contributions of $5,424 (ie $57,090 × 9.5% charge percentage) for a quarter in the 2020–21 financial year, or $21,696 for the year, even if the employee's annual salary in 2020–21 is more than $228,360 (ie $57,090 × 4 quarters).

Where an employer fails to make the prescribed amount of SG contributions for an employee in a quarter (¶39-200), the employee's salary or wages for that quarter is used to calculate the individual employee's SG shortfall (¶39-300). For this purpose, the amount of the employee's salary or wages for the quarter is also limited to the maximum contribution base (SGAA s 19(3)).

Contribution base limited by concessional contributions cap

The maximum contribution base for a quarter in a year is indexed using the indexation factor for the year (ss 9, 15(3)).

To ensure that the SG contributions for an employee in a year will not exceed the concessional contributions cap for the year (which is indexed under different rules: ¶13-775), the maximum contribution base for a quarter from 2017–18 onwards is the amount calculated using the formula in s 15(5) if this amount is *less* than the indexed maximum contribution base under s 15(3). This means that an employer who makes SG contributions for an employee based on the maximum contribution base for a quarter will not result in the employee exceeding the concessional contributions cap for the year. Based on the 2020–21 concessional contributions cap ($25,000) and SG charge percentage (9.5%), such a situation will not arise until the maximum contribution base is greater than $65,789 in a quarter.

Employees with multiple employers

Employees who receive superannuation from multiple employers may apply to opt out of the SG regime in respect of an employer so as to avoid unintentionally breaching their concessional contributions cap (¶39-050).

[AMSG ¶12-220; FTR ¶794-635/10, ¶794-637; SLP ¶50-560]

¶39-230 Measuring actual level of superannuation support

An employer is required to measure the actual level of superannuation support that is provided for each employee in each quarter, based on the employee's ordinary time earnings base (¶39-200). This level of employer superannuation support (expressed as a percentage) is then used to reduce the charge percentage to determine whether there is an SG shortfall in respect of the employee in the quarter (¶39-300).

Any period of time during which excluded salary or wages (¶39-030) are paid to an employee is not counted as a period of employment (SGAA s 26(1)).

An employer's superannuation contributions for employees which are made in accordance with a Commonwealth, state or territory law, an industrial award or an occupational superannuation arrangement will generally be counted towards the employer's SG obligations (¶39-200). A contribution to a fund, other than the superannuation fund nominated in an industrial award, is deemed to be made "in accordance with the award'' if the award does not require contributions to be made to the nominated fund, or a court decision has held that the award cannot specify the fund into which non-members' contributions should be made (SGD 94/6).

The method of measuring the level of employer superannuation support is set out in SGAA ss 22 and 23, based on whether the contribution is made to a defined benefit superannuation scheme or another type of fund. In all cases, the scheme or fund must be a complying superannuation fund or an RSA. An employer who pays a contribution to the ''approved clearing house'' under SGAA s 79A (¶39-240) is taken to have made the contribution to a complying superannuation fund or an RSA for the purposes of s 23 (and SGAA s 23A dealing with late contribution payments to offset an SG charge: ¶39-500).

A non-defined benefit superannuation scheme may elect to be treated as one for SG purposes by giving the ATO a conversion notice (SGAA ss 6A; 6B). Sub-plans within master trusts can provide the ATO with a conversion notice allowing them to be treated as defined benefit funds without causing other sub-plans within the master trust to be treated in a similar manner.

Employer contributions may be deemed to have been made to a complying superannuation fund (or a benefit certificate may be deemed to be in relation to a complying scheme) where there were reasonable grounds for believing that the fund was a complying fund at the time the contributions were paid (SGAA ss 24; 25).

Contributing to a defined benefit superannuation scheme

If an employer contributes to a defined benefit superannuation scheme (or a fund which has elected to be treated as one), the employer must obtain a benefit certificate from an actuary stating the ''notional employer contribution rate'' (NECR) for each class of employees in the scheme (SGAA s 10; SGAR s 8; SGD 2003/3; SGD 2003/4). The NECR is then used to reduce the charge percentage in respect of each employee within that class (SGAA s 22). If an employee is not included in a class of employees specified in the benefit certificate, the employer cannot use the defined benefit scheme to which the certificate relates to satisfy its SG obligations for that employee (ID 2015/18).

The NECR must be adjusted to reflect any period when the employee was employed (excluding any period when the employee was on leave without pay) but was not a member of the scheme or not covered by the benefit certificate (s 22(2)).

▶ Example 1

(1) Albert was employed for the whole of the first quarterly period in the year (ie 1 July to 30 September = 92 days).

(2) Albert was enrolled in a defined benefit fund from 1 September, so that his fund membership period in the quarter is 30 days (ie 1 September to 30 September). The proportion of the fund membership period to the employment period in the quarter is:

$$\frac{\text{fund membership period}}{\text{employment period in quarter}} = \frac{30}{92}$$

(3) A benefit certificate was in effect from 1 August in relation to the defined benefit fund, so that the benefit certificate effective period in the quarter is 61 days (ie 1 August to 30 September). The proportion of the benefit certificate effective period to the employment period in the quarter is:

$$\frac{\text{benefit certificate effective period}}{\text{employment period in quarter}} = \frac{61}{92}$$

(4) The benefit certificate specified a NECR of 7%.

(5) Apportionment of NECR:

$$\text{NECR in benefit certificate} \times \text{lower fraction of (2) and (3)}$$

$$= 7\% \times \frac{30}{92} = 2.282\%$$

The employer's NECR for Albert in the quarter is 2.282%.

Contributing to an RSA or a non-defined benefit superannuation scheme

If an employer contributes to an RSA or a superannuation fund other than a defined benefit superannuation scheme, the contribution amount made for the benefit of each employee in each quarter is expressed as a percentage of the employee's "ordinary time earnings base" (OTE base) for the quarter using the formula in s 23(2) (see example 2 below). The percentage is then used to reduce the charge percentage in respect of that employee.

The OTE base is the sum of the OTE of the employee for the quarter and any "sacrificed OTE amounts" of the employee for the quarter in respect of the employer. A "sacrificed OTE amount" (¶39-200) is the amount by which an employee agrees for their OTE to be reduced for a quarter under a salary sacrifice arrangement (SSA).

If an employee's salary or wages is not taken into account because of s 27 or 28 (ie excluded salary or wages for the purpose of determining if there is an individual employee SG shortfall under s 19: ¶39-030), the employee's OTE is taken to be reduced by that amount for the purpose of calculating the employer's superannuation support level for the employee (s 23(12)).

▶ Example 2

Carol was employed for the whole of the first quarter in the year (ie 1 July to 30 September) and has ordinary time earnings of $8,000 for the whole period. Her employer contributed $300 in the quarter to a complying superannuation fund.

The employer's percentage level of superannuation support for the quarter is:

$$\frac{\text{Contributions during quarter}}{\text{OTE base for the quarter}} \times \frac{100}{1}$$

$$= \frac{\$300}{\$8{,}000} \times \frac{100}{1}$$

$$= 3.75\%$$

Sacrificed OTE amounts do not include amounts that would have been excluded salary and wages (¶39-030) if they had been paid to the employee. That is, the employee's OTE earnings base reduced by an amount of excluded salary or wages only if that amount has been included as part of OTE (ss 15A(3), (4); 23(12)).

Where sacrificed OTE amounts under an SSA are taken into account for one quarter, but not actually contributed to the fund in that quarter, the amount will be counted in the quarter to which the SSA relates. Where sacrificed OTE amounts are never contributed (eg they are paid as OTE instead), they are disregarded to avoid double counting (s 23(7A)). SG contributions by employers and under SSAs are discussed further in ¶39-240 and ¶39-250.

[AMSG ¶12-230; FTR ¶794-654, ¶794-656; SLP ¶50-610, ¶50-650]

¶39-240 Payment of SG contributions for employees

Employer superannuation provided under the SG scheme for each employee is calculated in each quarter in the year (¶39-230).

To avoid incurring an SG charge liability in a quarter, the required employer SG contributions must be made to a complying superannuation fund or an RSA by the 28th day in the month following the end of the quarter (SGAA s 23(6): ¶39-230). If an employer fails to make the required SG contributions, the employer has an SG shortfall for the quarter and is required to lodge an SG statement with the ATO by the 28th day of the second month following the end of the quarter (¶39-500). An employer contribution includes a contribution made on behalf of the employer (SGAA s 6(2); SGD 2017/1: ''on behalf of'' has its ordinary and natural meaning taking into account its context in the SGAA (¶39-024)).

An employer contribution may be taken into account as having been made in any quarter if it is made not more than 12 months before the beginning of the quarter. Contributions which are taken into account in one quarter cannot be taken into account for any other quarter (s 23(7), (8)).

The SGAA does not provide for any extension of time for employers to make SG contributions beyond their due date (¶39-500), and the Commissioner has no discretion to overlook a failure to make the contributions by the due date. Employers are liable to pay the SG charge for non-compliance with the contributions deadline (*Jarra Hills*; *Kancroft*; *Benross*; *Williams*; *IWEC*; *Pyke*).

An employer may elect for SG contributions that are made for an employee after the due date to be used to offset the SG shortfall and interest portion of the SG charge payable for the quarter in respect of the employee (¶39-500).

Contribution to a complying fund or RSA and other rules

The SGAA requires an employer's SG contributions to be made to a complying superannuation fund or an RSA (*Coreta*). An amount that is simply paid to an employee allegedly for ''superannuation'' would not suffice; nor would payments of the SG shortfall amounts directly to employees (*Payne*).

An employer's SG obligations in respect of a deceased employee may be satisfied by paying to the deceased employee's legal personal representative an amount equal to the employer SG contributions that would otherwise have been made for the employee directly (s 23(9A)). Such a payment is treated as a contribution to a complying superannuation fund for the benefit of the employee (ID 2014/31).

TR 2010/1 discusses the ordinary meaning of contribution, how a contribution can be made and when a contribution is made for ITAA97 purposes (¶13-700). Generally, a contribution by a personal cheque is made when received by the superannuation fund trustee so long as the cheque is promptly presented and is honoured. If the cheque is subsequently dishonoured, the contribution is taken not to have been made at all. For a post-dated personal cheque, the contribution will be made on day when payment can be demanded as shown on the cheque. Prompt payment of a personal cheque or related party promissory note is taken to have taken place if payment is demanded within a few business days. Where it is clear that payment has not been promptly sought, the contribution will, in the absence of extenuating circumstances, be taken to be made if, and when, a payment of cash (or its electronic equivalent) actually occurs (TR 2010/1, para 13 to 15, 189).

Where the last day for making superannuation contributions in a quarter falls on a weekend, public holiday or bank holiday, contributions may be made in respect of the quarter on the next working day (SGD 2003/2; TAA s 388-52).

An employer contribution made through a payroll provider or a clearing house other than the Small Business Superannuation Clearing House (SBSCH) (which is the SGAA ''approved clearing house'', see below) is made when the contribution is received by the trustee of the complying superannuation fund or RSA provider. This is the case even if the clearing house is operated by the superannuation fund (SGD 2005/2, para 1, 3). By contrast, employer contributions made to the SBSCH are taken to be contributions made to a complying fund or RSA at the time of payment of the contributions when accepted by the clearing house (SGAA s 23B).

An employer who mistakenly made SG contributions for subcontractors who were, in effect, not ''employees'' was held to be entitled to a refund of the contributions (*Personalised Transport Services Pty Ltd v AMP Superannuation Ltd*). An employer who paid increased salaries to casual employees in lieu of making SG contributions for them was held to be liable to the SG charge (*Weston*).

For SGAA purposes, the Commissioner will only accept a contribution made into a fund, other than those nominated in an award, as being in accordance with the award if the award does not require contributions into a nominated fund, or a court decision has held that the particular award cannot specify the fund into which the relevant employees' contributions should be made. A decision by a court will apply only to the particular award before the court (SGD 94/6).

Small Business Superannuation Clearing House

The SBSCH is the ''approved clearing house'' for SGAA purposes (s 79A; SGAR s 24). This is a free online clearing house service administered by the ATO for:

- employers with 19 or fewer employees (whether employed on a full-time, part time or casual basis), and
- businesses with an annual turnover below the small business entity turnover threshold (currently $10 million: see ¶7-050).

The SBSCH service aims to reduce employers' compliance costs by simplifying and streamlining the process of making employee superannuation contributions. Employers can make a single lump contribution payment to the SBSCH each quarter and that payment can be divided into individual payments to be contributed to each employee's respective superannuation fund or RSA. For details of the SBSCH registration and usage process, see www.ato.gov.au/Business/Super-for-employers/In-detail/Small-Business-Superannuation-Clearing-House/Clearing-house-terms-and-conditions-of-use-and-access-(employers).

An employer payment to the SBSCH for the benefit of an employee is taken to be a contribution to a complying superannuation fund or an RSA at the time of payment if the SBSCH accepts the contribution (SGAA s 23B). This applies for the purpose of determining whether an employer is liable for the SG charge and does not extend to determining when an employer is entitled to claim an income tax deduction for the contribution (¶13-710). That is, the contribution counts at that time to measure the employer's superannuation support for the employee under SGAA s 23 (reduction of employer's SG charge percentage: ¶39-230) and s 23A (late contribution used to offset a charge: ¶39-500). The employer's contribution will also meet the choice of fund rules if other relevant conditions are met (¶39-260).

There may be a time gap between an employer's payment to the SBSCH and its actual receipt by a superannuation fund or an RSA provider (eg the SBSCH may be unavailable close to the end of the financial year for scheduled system maintenance). The ATO has stated that it would not apply compliance resources to consider whether an employer contribution was received by the superannuation fund or RSA provider in the same income year as the payment to the SBSCH provided the payment was made before the close of business on the last business day on or before 30 June. Employers therefore do not need to check with the employees' superannuation funds or RSA providers to determine in which income year the contributions were received from the SBSCH prior to claiming an income tax deduction in the income year the payment was made to the SBSCH. This approach does not apply for contributions made through a clearing house other than the SBSCH (a commercial clearing house) (PCG 2020/6: ¶13-710).

[AMSG ¶12-010, ¶12-230; FTR ¶794-656; SLP ¶50-700ff]

¶39-250 Salary sacrifice arrangements

A ''salary sacrifice arrangement'' (SSA) between an employer and employee is one under which:

- a contribution is made, or will be made to a complying superannuation fund or an RSA by the employer for the benefit of the employee, and
- the contribution was made because the employee agreed for it to be made in return for the employee's salary or wages for the quarter being reduced (s 15A).

A ''sacrificed contribution'' means a contribution to a complying superannuation fund or an RSA under an SSA.

Salary sacrifice does not affect an employer's SG obligations

From 1 January 2020, the rules below apply to prevent employers from using an employee's salary sacrificed contributions to reduce their SG obligations and ensure that an employee's pre-salary sacrifice base is used to calculate the employer's SG shortfall:

- when working out the reduction of an employer's charge percentage for contributions made for an employee, the employee's ordinary time earnings (OTE) base will comprise their OTE and any salary sacrificed amount that would have been OTE but for the SSA, ie the employer contributions are calculated on a pre-OTE sacrifice base (¶39-200)
- a salary sacrificed amount cannot form part of any late employer contributions to offset against the SG charge (¶39-500), and
- when working out an employer's SG shortfall amount for an employee, the employee's salary or wages base will comprise their salary and wages and any salary sacrificed amount that would have been salary or wages but for the SSA (ie the employee's pre-salary sacrifice base: ¶39-300).

Sacrificed salary or wages amounts and sacrificed OTE amounts do not include amounts that, had they been paid to an employee, would have been excluded salary and wages or excluded OTE (eg salary and wages paid to a part-time employee under 18 years of age or an employee to whom an international social security agreement applies, or an employee who earns less than $450 a month) (¶39-030).

Where sacrificed salary or wages amounts or sacrificed OTE amounts are taken into account for one quarter, but are not actually contributed to the fund in that quarter, the amounts will be counted in the quarter to which the SSA relates. Where these amounts are never contributed and instead are paid to the employee in a later quarter (eg at the employee's request), they are disregarded to avoid double counting (s 23(7A)).

ATO Guidance Note GN 2020/1 provides guidelines for employers applying the SSA rules for quarters commencing on or after 1 January 2020.

Other SSA rules and guidelines

TR 2001/10, which provides guidelines on the tax consequences of SSAs, states that only an effective SSA involving the employee giving up a future entitlement to salary or wages (ie using pre-tax salary or wages) can be tax-effective for SG and other purposes (*Wood*; *Turner*: SSA ends on resignation; *Kander*: no effective SSA due to mistaken salary-deduction instructions to employer).

Where permitted by the *Fair Work Act 2009*, an employer and employee can agree to an SSA which reduces the cash portion of the employee's wages to an amount below the minimum award wage (*Casey Grammar School v Independent Education Union of Australia*).

An employer and employee must refer to any written SSA to determine whether salary sacrifice can continue while the employee is receiving workers compensation payments in lieu of wages. In the absence of any restriction, they can agree for the SSA to continue in relation to the workers compensation payments.

An ''employee'' covered by SGAA s 12(3) or 12(8) (ie a person who works under a contract that is wholly or principally for the labour of the person, or artists, musicians, sportspersons, etc: ¶39-020) can enter into an effective SSA (SGD 2006/2).

[AMSG ¶12-250; FTR ¶794-656; SLP ¶50-750]

Choice of Funds

¶39-260 Choice of fund rules

The choice of fund rules in SGAA Pt 3A (ss 32A to 32ZA) requires employers to provide eligible employees with a choice of superannuation funds to which SG contributions made for them would be paid.

The choice rules apply separately to each employer of an employee. For example, an employee's chosen fund as a result of a standard choice form being given by an employer is only a chosen fund in relation to the operation of the choice rules to that employer (s 32X).

An employer that makes contributions which do not comply with the choice of fund requirements will have an increased SG shortfall for the quarter (see below).

How an employer complies

The choice rules apply to employer SG contributions made for employees so that potentially all employees must be offered a choice of funds. However, contributions made for employees to certain funds or in certain circumstances, or under certain superannuation arrangements, comply or are taken to comply with the choice rules so that choice need not be given to the affected employees.

Employers comply or are deemed to comply with the choice of fund rules in one of the ways below by making SG contributions:

- to an employee's chosen fund, including a former employee's fund (s 32C(1), (10))
- to a ''default fund'' chosen by the employer (ie the employee does not make a choice of fund) and the requirements of s 32C(2) and SGAR s 14 are met
- to prescribed Commonwealth or public sector superannuation schemes, except where otherwise provided by regulations (ie deemed compliance) (s 32C(3) to (5))
- to a fund under or in accordance with certain industrial agreements or awards, or workplace determinations or enterprise agreements made before 1 January 2021 (ie deemed compliance) (s 32C(6) to (8)), or
- to a fund under a Commonwealth, state or territory law prescribed by the SGAR (ie deemed compliance) (s 32C(9); SGAR s 15).

Industrial agreements, awards, workplace determinations or enterprise agreements may specify a given superannuation fund or funds to which the employer's contributions are to be made for the benefit of the employee.

Employer contributions made to a successor fund or to the SBSCH (ie the SGAA approved clearing house: ¶39-240) for the benefit of an employee also comply with the choice requirements where certain conditions are met (s 32C(2AB), (2B)).

An employer's contribution to a fund does not comply with s 32C if the employer imposes a direct cost or charge on the employee for making the contribution to that fund (s 32CA).

Chosen fund and default fund

The meaning of ''chosen fund'' is set out in ss 32F to 32J.

A ''default fund'' must be an eligible choice fund (ie a complying superannuation fund or scheme or an RSA: s 32D) which offers MySuper products and complies with prescribed requirements in relation to the provision of death insurance cover or benefits for members (s 32C(2)(c), (d); SGAR s 14).

The rules for the approval of registrable superannuation entity licensees (generally trustees of superannuation funds open to the public) that are authorised to offer MySuper products, and the operation of MySuper products, are set out in SISA Pt 2C. The *Fair Work Act 2009* sets out the criteria for the selection and ongoing assessment of superannuation funds that are eligible for nomination as default funds in modern awards.

Employees covered by industrial agreements and workplace determinations

Employers that make contributions under or in accordance with an enterprise agreement or workplace determination made before 1 January 2021 comply with the choice of fund requirements and their employees do not have the right to choose their own superannuation fund (see above: s 32C(6)(g) and (h)).

The terms ''workplace determination'' and ''enterprise agreement'' have the same meaning they have in the Fair Work Act 2009. Whether a determination or agreement is ''made'' and ''applies'' is determined in accordance with that Act.

For workplace determinations or enterprise agreements made on or after 1 January 2021, the rules below apply:

- Employers must allow their employees to choose their own superannuation fund (unless other circumstances exempt the employer from doing so) (s 32C(6)(g) and (h)). In these cases, the employees must be given a standard choice form as required under s 32N (see ''Choice procedures'' below).
- Existing employees on 1 January 2021 do not need to be given a standard choice of fund form, but can request a choice form from their employer.

If an existing employee does not make a choice of fund, the employer can continue to make compulsory superannuation contributions to the same fund to which the employer previously contributed for the employee under the pre-1 January 2021 workplace determination or enterprise agreement (s 32C(6AA)). An employer can specify such a fund as a default fund in the standard choice form given by the employer to the existing employee.

Where a workplace determination or enterprise agreement made on or after 1 January 2021 includes a term that restricts choice of funds, such a term is not enforceable under s 32Z to the extent that the employer instead makes contributions to an employee's chosen fund. Terms restricting choice include those which specify the name of the fund to which the employer must contribute, or those which list several funds the employer must choose between to make contributions to.

Choice procedures

The choice procedures require employers to give eligible employees a standard choice form as set out in s 32N (eg on commencement of employment or if requested by the employee in writing), except in certain circumstances (see below).

The standard choice form must be given by the time specified in s 32N and must contain certain information (s 32P; SGAR s 17; ATO *Choice of superannuation fund — Standard choice form* (NAT 13080) or *Choice of superannuation fund — Standard choice form — defined benefit member* (NAT 13842)).

An employee is not obliged to choose a superannuation fund or RSA, but if no choice is made, the employer's SG contributions for the employee are paid to the default fund specified in the standard choice form (s 32P(1); SGAR ss 14; 16).

Choice form need not be given to employees in certain circumstances

An employer does not have to give a standard choice form to employees where:

- the employee has chosen a fund (s 32NA(1)), or the employer is making contributions for the employee as mentioned in s 32C(3) to (9) (see above) (s 32NA(2))
- the employee is a member of an unfunded public sector scheme (except certain Commonwealth employees) or is a defined benefit member of a defined benefit superannuation scheme and certain conditions are met (ss 32F(3); 32NA(4), (7) to (9)) (see "Defined benefit schemes" below) (ID 2005/141: defined benefit fund cannot be chosen fund)
- the employee holds a "temporary visa" (as defined in s 30(2) of the *Migration Act 1958*) (ss 32C(2AA); 32NA(11)), and
- the employees' superannuation benefits are transferred from a chosen fund or default fund to a successor fund as a result of a superannuation fund merger (ss 32C(2AB); 32NA(1A)).

Defined benefit schemes

Employees who are existing members of certain defined benefit schemes cannot choose another fund (SGAA Pt 3A Div 4). These are schemes where a member's retirement, resignation or retrenchment benefit in the fund would remain unchanged if the employer made contributions to another fund under the choice of fund arrangements (s 32F(3)).

An employer is not required to give an employee who is an existing member of a defined benefit scheme a standard choice form where:

- the scheme is in surplus and s 20(2) is satisfied (ie employee has been a member of the defined benefit fund before 1 July 2005)
- the employee has accrued their maximum benefit in the scheme and s 20(3) is satisfied (ie the employee's accrued benefit will not increase other than in prescribed circumstances, such as a salary increase or by indexation), or
- the employee is a defined benefit member of a defined benefit scheme and the employee's benefits in the scheme will remain the same if the employer contributes to another fund for the employee (s 32NA(7) to (9)).

These provisions deny choice of fund to employees who are members of defined benefit schemes because their employers do not incur an increase in their SG shortfall in the circumstances above (see "Consequences of non-compliance with choice rules" below).

Existing employees who are not defined benefit members and who become newly eligible to join a defined benefit scheme do not need to be given a standard choice form unless requested by the employee or another subsection of s 32N applies. New employees who are not existing defined benefit members but are eligible to join a defined benefit scheme must be given a standard choice form within 28 days of commencing employment.

Consequences of non-compliance with choice rules

Where an employer's SG contributions for an employee do not comply with the choice rules, the employer's individual SG shortfall for the employee for the quarter is increased by the amount worked out under SGAA s 19(2A) (for contributions to non-defined benefit funds) or s 19(2B) (for contributions to defined benefit funds). The total shortfall amount that is increased under s 19(2A) or 19(2B) is limited to a maximum of $500 in a particular quarter or notice period.

Employer contributions to a defined benefit scheme do not attract an increase in SG shortfall where, for a given quarter, the scheme is in surplus, the employee concerned has accrued their maximum benefit in the scheme, or the employee's benefit from the defined benefit scheme on retirement, resignation or retrenchment is not affected by the employer making contributions for the employee's benefit to another fund (ss 20(1)–(3A), 32F(3), 32NA(7)–(9)). These provisions mirror the circumstances in which employers do not have to provide a choice of fund form to employees who are members of defined benefit schemes (see above).

[AMSG ¶12-040ff; FTR ¶794-675; SLP ¶50-400]

SG Shortfall and SG Charge

¶39-300 Calculating an individual employee's shortfall

To determine if there is an SG shortfall for an employee, an employer needs to calculate the level of superannuation support provided for the employee in a quarter and compare this with the prescribed level of support to be provided (ie the charge percentage).

The SG shortfall calculation process involves the following steps:

Step 1: Determine the charge percentage that applies for the year (¶39-100).

Step 2: Determine the actual percentage level of superannuation support that is provided for each employee (or the total of the percentage levels if support is provided in more than one fund) (¶39-230).

Step 3: Compare the percentage levels in steps 1 and 2:

(a) if the actual percentage level of support provided (step 2) equals or exceeds the charge percentage (step 1), the employer has no SG shortfall in respect of that employee, or

(b) if the actual percentage level of support provided is less than the charge percentage, the employer has an **SG shortfall** in respect of the employee as calculated in step 4.

Step 4: The individual SG shortfall of the employee for the quarter is calculated as the difference between the percentage levels in steps 1 and 2 (as reflected in step 3(b)) multiplied by the "**quarterly salary or wages base**" (or total *salary or wages* before 1 January 2020) of the employee in the relevant quarter (SGAA s 19).

The SG shortfall amount in Step 4 forms part of the SG charge payable in respect of the employee (¶39-400).

The meaning of salary or wages is discussed in ¶39-026 and salary sacrifice arrangements are discussed in ¶39-250.

An employee's "quarterly salary or wages base" in Step 4 is the sum of the total salary or wages paid by the employer to the employee for the quarter and any salary or wages amounts of the employee for the quarter that have been sacrificed into superannuation. The inclusion of sacrificed salary or wages amounts ensures that the SG shortfall and charge is calculated on the pre-salary sacrifice base and that employers cannot calculate their SG obligations on reduced salary and wages. An employee's quarterly salary or wages base for a quarter is also limited to the maximum contribution base (s 19(4)) (¶39-220).

Excluded salary or wages

For the purposes of Step 4, salary or wages paid do not include payments while the employee was ''exempt'' (¶39-030). These payments are referred to as ''excluded salary or wages'', ie payments of salary or wages that, under SGAA s 27 or 28, are not to taken into account for the purpose of calculating an SG shortfall under s 19 (s 15A(3), (4)).

The above rule applies to any amounts that remain after excluding any salary or wages under s 27(1) (¶39-030). This means, for example, that any remaining amount that is less than $450 in a calendar month is also considered excluded salary or wages for the purpose of calculating individual SG shortfalls (s 27(2)).

The interaction of s 19 and the exempt employee provisions in ss 27 and 28 is discussed in SGD 2003/5 and the example below.

▶ Example

Brenda is 17 and works part-time. In September she was paid $810 over 4 weeks, as follows:

Week	Hours	Wage
1	25	$200
2	15	$110
3	35	$340
4	20	$160

As Brenda was paid over $450 in the month, her employer must make SG contributions for her or incur an SG shortfall. The contributions or shortfall will be based only on the earnings paid in week 3, where Brenda worked more than 30 hours (ie $340) as the amounts paid in the other weeks are excluded under s 28 (¶39-030).

If Brenda was paid the total amount of $810 in week 4 instead of receiving weekly payments, the answer would still be the same. In this situation Brenda is still a part-time employee in the weeks in which she is employed to work. As she is under 18, any payments for work in respect of the weeks when she works less than 30 hours are excluded by s 28 regardless of when they are paid.

An employer that has an SG shortfall in a quarter is required to lodge an SG statement with the ATO by the 28th day of the second month following the end of the quarter (¶39-500).

The Commissioner may also require an employer to lodge a statement stating whether the employer has an SG shortfall (SGAA s 34).

PS LA 2006/14 provides guidelines when assessing an employer's SG compliance where the ATO identifies one or more individuals engaged under a contract that is wholly or principally for their labour.

Former employees

Employers have an SG obligation in respect of a former employee in a quarter following the termination of employment as salary or wages paid to, and contributions made for, the former employee are treated as if the former employee was still an employee (SGAA s 15B). This ensures that employer SG contributions are payable on wages or salary paid in a quarter following the termination of an employment relationship.

A deceased employee falls within the meaning of former employee in s 15B. An employer will have an individual SG shortfall under s 19(1) where an amount of salary and wages owing to a deceased employee at the time of the employee's death is paid to the employee's estate, and the employer does not make sufficient SG contributions in respect of the payment by the relevant quarterly due date (ID 2014/31).

▶ Example

Barry, an employee, dies on 10 April and the accrued salary or wages for the fortnightly pay period of 1 April to 14 April is unpaid at time of Barry's death.

The employer pays salary or wages accrued for the period 1 April to 10 April to the executor of Barry's estate on 18 April, but does not make SG contributions to a complying superannuation fund for Barry for the 1 April to 30 June quarter.

The employer will have an individual superannuation guarantee shortfall in respect of Barry for the quarter in which the salary or wages were paid to the Barry's estate.

Penalty for failure to comply with choice of fund rules

An increased SG shortfall amount arises as an additional penalty if an employer fails to comply with the choice of fund requirements (¶39-260).

[AMSG ¶12-300; FTR ¶794-640, ¶794-648; SLP ¶50-800]

¶39-400 Calculating the SG charge

The SG charge payable by an employer is calculated as the sum of: (a) the total of the employer's individual SG shortfalls for the quarter (¶39-300); (b) the employer's nominal interest component for the quarter; and (c) the employer's administration component for the quarter (SGAA s 17).

The Commissioner has no discretion to remit any components of the SG charge (*Jarra Hills*; *Benross*; *IWEC*; *Roy Morgan Research Pty Ltd*; *Australian Medical Services*; *Payne*; ID 2002/309).

Allowances paid to employees for motor vehicle expenses were held by the AAT to be salary or wages and relevant to the calculation of SG charge (*Penrowse*: ¶10-060).

Nominal interest component

The employer's nominal interest component is a substitute for fund earnings that would have accrued if the employer had provided the prescribed minimum SG support. For a quarter, this component is calculated by multiplying the total of the employer's individual SG shortfalls for the quarter by 10% pa from the beginning of the quarter in which the SG liability arose until the date the SG charge is payable (SGAA s 31; SGAR s 13). The SG charge is payable when an SG statement is lodged with the ATO, or when a default assessment is made if no SG statement was lodged (SGAA s 46, Note 1; ¶39-500; *Australian Medical Services*: interest calculation where contributions were made before SG statement lodgment).

▶ Example

Walter (an employer) had total individual SG shortfalls of $500 for the last quarter (April to June) in 2020–21. Walter lodged an SG statement with the ATO on 28 August 2021 as required. The number of days from 1 April to 28 August 2021 is 150 days. The rate for calculation of the interest component is 10% pa.

The interest component is calculated as follows:

$$\$500 \quad \times \quad \frac{150}{365} \quad \times \quad 10\% \quad = \quad \$20.54$$

The AAT has held that the Commissioner was not authorised to remove or reduce the nominal interest component that has been calculated in accordance with s 31, following the issue of amended SG assessments (¶39-500) to a taxpayer under SGAA s 37 (*Trustee for Rane Haulage Trust*). The nominal interest component was held to be correctly calculated in that case, based on the entire period from the beginning of the relevant quarter to the delayed date of lodgment of the SG statements by the taxpayer following the amended assessments.

Administration component

The employer's administration component for a quarter is a flat amount of $20 for each employee in respect of whom the employer has an individual SG shortfall for the quarter (SGAA s 32).

▶ Example

An employer has individual SG shortfalls in respect of 5 employees in a quarter. The administration component for the quarter is $20 × 5 = $100.

[AMSG ¶12-300, ¶12-360; FTR ¶794-640, ¶794-672, ¶794-674; SLP ¶50-910]

Assessment and Payment of SG Charge

¶39-500 SG statements and payment of SG charge

The calculation of an employer's SG shortfall and SG charge is discussed in ¶39-300 and ¶39-400.

Employers are required to self-assess their liability to the SG charge and make payment of the charge, if any, to the ATO by the due date in each quarter. The charge is *not* tax-deductible, except where it is covered by the SG amnesty discussed in ¶39-505 (ITAA97 s 26-95).

An employer with an SG shortfall must lodge an SG statement in the approved form with the ATO by the 28th day of the second month following the end of the quarter, or by any later date allowed by the Commissioner. The statement is deemed to be the employer's notice of assessment for the quarter. Payment of the SG charge is due when the statement is lodged (SGAA ss 33; 46).

The Commissioner may also require an employer to lodge a statement stating whether the employer has an SG shortfall (SGAA s 34), and may direct a person to pay an amount of SG charge that is payable (¶39-505, ¶39-550).

Assessments and default assessments

Where an employer lodges an SG statement for a quarter, and no previous statement has been lodged and no previous assessment has been raised, the lodged statement has effect as an assessment of the employer's SG shortfall and the SG charge payable for the quarter, based on the shortfall specified in the statement. The deemed assessment is taken to be made on the later of: (a) the 28th day of the second month following the end of the quarter to which it relates (eg 28 May for the quarter ended 31 March); or (b) the day on which the statement is lodged (SGAA s 35).

The Commissioner may issue default assessments and amend assessments where necessary (SGAA ss 36; 37; *Pye*). PS LA 2007/10 outlines when a default assessment can be made and the factors the Commissioner will consider when making default assessments.

An employer who is dissatisfied with an SG charge assessment may object in the manner set out in TAA Pt IVC (¶28-010) (SGAA s 42; *Ripamz*). PS LA 2007/1 (GA) outlines the circumstances in which the ATO may decide, for administrative reasons, not to raise an SG assessment or allow an employer's objection to an assessment.

An employer who has entered into a court-ordered settlement with an employee on termination of employment is not relieved of its SG charge obligation as the charge is a debt owed by the employer to the Commonwealth, not to the employee. This is the case even if the settlement terms include a waiver of the employee's rights in respect of or in connection with the employee's employment (ID 2006/6: settlement payment).

Due date for paying SG charge

Payment of the SG charge for a quarter is due on:

- if the employer lodges an SG statement *before* the lodgment day for the quarter — on the lodgment day
- if the employer lodges an SG statement *after* the lodgment day for the quarter — on the day the statement is lodged
- if a default assessment under s 36 is made for a quarter — on the day the assessment is made (SGAA s 46).

The "lodgment day" in a quarter is the 28th day of the second month in the next quarter (see "Summary — SG contribution and SG statement lodgment" below).

Where the last day for lodging an SG statement or paying the SG charge falls on a weekend, public holiday or bank holiday, the statement may be lodged or the charge may be paid on the next working day (SGD 2003/2).

An employer who fails to pay the SG charge by its due date is liable to pay the GIC (see below).

Extension of time to lodge SG statement or pay SG charge

The Commissioner may extend the lodgment date for the SG statement (TAA Sch 1 s 388-55; SGAA s 33(1A)), and defer the time by which the SG charge is payable (TAA Sch 1 s 255-10).

The Commissioner may also permit an employer to pay the SG charge in instalments, but this does not alter the time that the full SG charge is due and payable (TAA Sch 1 s 255-15). Despite an arrangement between an employer and the Commissioner for payment by instalments, GIC for any unpaid amount begins to accrue when the SG charge is due and payable or at that time as varied under s 255-10.

Summary — SG contribution and SG statement lodgment

The table below sets out the due dates for:

- making SG contributions for employees in an SG quarter to avoid incurring an SG shortfall (¶39-240)
- lodging an SG statement with the ATO and paying the SG charge ("lodgment day", see above).

SG quarter	Due date for payment of SG contributions	Due date for lodgment of SG statement and payment of SG charge
1 Jul–30 Sept	28 October	28 November
1 Oct–31 Dec	28 January	28 February
1 Jan–31 Mar	28 April	28 May
1 Apr–30 Jun	28 July	28 August

The ATO may consider it not necessary to assess an employer for the SG charge if there is evidence that the employer has done what could reasonably be expected to have done to comply with the law by the due date (PS LA 2007/1 (GA)).

Offsetting late contribution payments against an SG charge

An employer may make an election for late contributions to offset an SG charge in respect of an employee if the contribution is made *after* the end of 28 day period after the end of the relevant quarter (see the due dates table above) and *before* the employer's original assessment for that quarter is made (s 23A).

An election is irrevocable and must be made:

- in a statement having effect under SGAA s 35 as the employer's assessment for the quarter, or
- within 4 years after the employer's original assessment of SG charge for the quarter is made (SGAA s 23A(1), (2)) (*Payne*: no election made).

▶ Example

Cory is required to make an SG contribution of $1,000 for the September 2020 quarter for Jay (an employee).

She failed to make the contribution by the due date of 28 October 2020, but makes a late contribution into Jay's superannuation fund on 1 December 2020.

Cory was assessed on 31 January 2021 with an SG charge liability in respect of Jay for the September 2020 quarter.

Cory may elect to use the late contribution made for Jay to offset the unpaid SG charge liability for Jay for the September 2020 quarter if she makes the election in the approved form to the Commissioner by 31 January 2025.

If an election happens after the employer's assessment for the quarter is made, the assessment must be amended accordingly under SGAA s 37 for the offset to take effect (s 23A(4A)). The reference in s 23A(4A) to the possibility of amending assessments only relates to late elections, not late contributions. Section 23(4A) does not open the door to amended assessments to take account of late contributions (*Jordyn Properties Pty Ltd*).

The contribution is offset against the employer's liability to pay SG charge to the extent that the liability relates to that part of the employer's nominal interest component or the employer's individual superannuation guarantee shortfall for the employee for the quarter (s 23A(3)).

Any amount used as an offset cannot be taken into account as a contribution for any other quarter or be used to reduce the employer's charge percentage under SGAA ss 22 and 23 (¶39-230).

An offsetting contribution under s 23A is not deductible (except where it is covered by the SG amnesty: ¶39-505) (ITAA97 s 290-95; ¶13-710).

An employee's salary sacrifice amount does not form part of any offsetting contributions under s 23A from 1 January 2020. Salary sacrifice arrangements are discussed in ¶39-250.

GIC on late payment of SG charge

An employer who fails to pay the SG charge by its due date is liable to pay the GIC (¶29-510) as calculated under SGAA s 49(3).

When a contribution offset election is made for the first time under s 23A (see above), GIC accrues on the original SG shortfall amount from the day the relevant SG charge became payable to the day when the election is lodged with the ATO.

Where an employer elects to offset late contribution payments against SG charge, GIC accrues on the remaining shortfall component of the unpaid SG charge amount (after the offset is applied) from the original SG assessment date for the quarter, not from the date of the election (s 49(3A)).

If a Part 7 penalty (¶39-550) is imposed, the penalty will apply to the full amount of the original SG charge before the s 23A late contribution offset is taken into account (SGAA s 62A).

[AMSG ¶12-350, ¶12-370ff; FTR ¶794-678; SLP ¶51-000]

¶39-505 SG amnesty for employers

A one-off amnesty applies to encourage employers to voluntarily disclose and pay previously unpaid SG charge (SGC), including nominal interest, that they owe their employees, for quarters starting from 1 July 1992 to 31 March 2018, without incurring the administration component of the SGC or a SGAA Part 7 penalty. In addition, SG shortfall payments covered by the amnesty made after 24 May 2018 and before the end of 7 September 2020 are tax deductible (see ''Benefits under the SG amnesty'' below).

The SG amnesty period ended on 7 September 2020. The ATO's guidelines for employers in respect of applications received before 7 September 2020 (including the amnesty disqualification consequences), and applications received after 7 September 2020, may be found in the Fact Sheet *Superannuation guarantee amnesty*.

The SG amnesty

Employers who disclose their previously unpaid SGC to the ATO in accordance with SGAA s 74 (see below) during the **amnesty period** from 24 May 2018 to 7 September 2020 are eligible for the SG amnesty. The amnesty (which was first proposed on 24 May 2018 by the lapsed Treasury Laws Amendment (2018 Superannuation Measures No 1) Bill 2018 was passed as law by the *Treasury Laws Amendment (Recovering Unpaid Superannuation) Act 2020* on 6 March 2020.

Employers who have already disclosed unpaid SGC to the ATO between 24 May 2018 and 6 March 2020 are not required to apply for the amnesty. The ATO will review the disclosures and apply the amnesty to employers who are eligible (see ''Eligibility conditions for SG amnesty'' below). Other employers must apply to the ATO in the approved form from 6 March 2020 up to the end of 7 September 2020.

An employer who is notified by the ATO of eligibility for the amnesty is required to pay the SG shortfall amount owing (see ''Employer must pay SG charge or make offset contributions'' below) or set up a payment plan so as to avoid being disqualified and losing the benefits of the amnesty.

Benefits under the SG amnesty

The benefits under the SG amnesty are as follows:

- ***Deductibility of SGC and offset contributions***. Payments to the ATO for the SGC imposed on the SG shortfall disclosed under the amnesty are deductible for employer payments made during the amnesty period (ITAA97 s 26-95(1), (2)). Employers who already have an outstanding SGC debt before making a disclosure under the amnesty are able to claim a deduction for the payments made but the Commissioner will first apply the payments to clear the employer's existing debt (if any).

  Employer contributions that are made to offset the SGC imposed on the SG shortfall disclosed under the amnesty are similarly deductible. This ensures commensurate benefits for employers that contribute directly to their employees' superannuation funds and employers who make payments to the ATO.

- ***No administration component***. An employer does not have an administration component (¶39-400) in the SGC payable on the employees' SG shortfalls that qualify under the amnesty (SGAA s 32(1), (2) and (3)). However, if an employer already had an administration component in respect of an employee because of an earlier assessment, the previous administration component imposed is unaffected (see Example below).

  ▶ Example — Previous administration component (adapted from the EM)

  An employer with 25 employees for a quarter covered by the amnesty previously had individual SG shortfalls in respect of 12 of those employees for the quarter. The employer's SGC (then calculated in respect of the 12 employees) before the amnesty included an administration component for each of those employees.

During the amnesty period, the employer discloses that it became aware of a further individual SG shortfall in respect of all 25 employees. For the 12 employees for whom SGC was paid previously, this shortfall is in addition to the previous individual SG shortfalls.

As the disclosure occurred under the amnesty, the employer does not have an administration component included in their (increased) SG shortfall for the quarter. However, the earlier administration component in respect of the original 12 employees remains unaffected.

- ***No liability to pay Part 7 penalty***. An employer is not liable to a Part 7 penalty (¶39-550) for a failure to provide an SG statement in respect of SG shortfalls covered by the amnesty (SGAA s 60). Like the administration component, the Part 7 penalty exemption does not affect any historical penalties, ie the protection applies only to any further Part 7 penalty amount to which the employer would have been liable as a result of a disclosure under the amnesty.

Restriction on Commissioner's discretion to remit Part 7 penalties

A Part 7 penalty where it applies to an employer is an amount of additional SGC equal to 200% of the SGC amount payable by the employer for the quarter. The Commissioner may remit all or a part of the Part 7 penalty (SGAA ss 59(1), 62(3)) (¶39-550).

From 8 September 2020 (ie the day after the amnesty period ends), the Commissioner cannot remit the Part 7 penalty below 100% of the amount of SGC payable by the employer for a historical quarter that was covered by the amnesty (s 62(4) and (5)). This restriction on the Commissioner's general discretion to remit Part 7 penalties strengthens the operation of the amnesty by providing employers with higher minimum penalties for failing to come forward during the amnesty in relation to historical SG shortfalls, subject to certain exceptions (¶39-550).

Eligibility conditions for SG amnesty

An employer must meet all of the following criteria to be eligible for the SG amnesty:

- The employer has not been informed that the ATO is examining or intends to examine the employer's SG obligation for the quarter(s) to which the employer's disclosure relates to (as disclosed in the application for amnesty form, see below).
- The employer must disclose an SG shortfall for an employee that the employer has not already disclosed to the ATO (or disclose additional amounts of SG shortfall for a quarter previously disclosed).
- The disclosure is for the quarters starting from 1 July 1992 to 31 March 2018.
- The employer has lodged the approved SG amnesty form with the ATO by no later than 7 September 2020 (SGAA s 74(1)–(3)).

The Commissioner may, by written notice, disqualify an employer from the beneficial treatment provided by the amnesty if the employer:

- fails to pay the amounts equivalent to any SGC (imposed on the disclosed SG shortfall) on or before the day the SGC becomes payable, or
- does not enter into a payment arrangement with the ATO in relation to that amount or comply with such a payment arrangement (s 74(5)).

In such cases, the Commissioner can unwind any benefits that have accrued to the employer under the amnesty by amending the employer's assessments.

Employer must pay SG charge or make offset contributions

The SGC (imposed on SG shortfalls disclosed under the amnesty) is due and payable on the day an SG statement is lodged by the employer (¶39-500). The SGC under the amnesty will comprise the total of individual shortfalls and the nominal interest for the quarter.

Where an employer does not have an existing SGC assessment for the quarter, the employer may choose to make contributions (of the employee's individual shortfall and nominal interest) directly into an employee's superannuation account and elect to offset these amounts against the employer's liability for SGC in accordance with SGAA s 23A (¶39-500).

Employers who have an existing SGC assessment for the quarter, or are otherwise unable to contribute directly into their employee's superannuation accounts, will need to pay the SGC to the Commissioner.

Employers must pay the components of the SGC imposed on the disclosed amounts that reflect their employees' SG entitlements (individual SG shortfall for relevant employees and nominal interest), as well as any general interest charge imposed on the overdue SGC. This allows the Commissioner to deal with these amounts for the benefit of employees to ensure employees would still be paid their full SG entitlement.

Employers who have difficulty in paying SGC by the due date may pay the amount under a payment arrangement agreed with the Commissioner.

Employers who are adversely affected by COVID-19 can make special payment arrangements with the ATO, including flexible payment terms and amounts and extending a payment plan beyond 7 September 2020 (*Superannuation guarantee amnesty* fact sheet).

Related tax rules arising from SG amnesty contributions

Two tax-related rules apply so that employees are not disadvantaged from an employer benefiting from the SG amnesty in relation to the 2017–18 and later income years.

The first rule is to ensure that the employees do not exceed their concessional contributions cap. Under the SG amnesty, employers may pay SG charge which represents late SG payments covering a number of years to the ATO and the Commissioner must pay these amounts to an employee's superannuation account for the employee's benefit in accordance with the SGAA. These contributions would be considered concessional contributions and may cause employees to exceed their annual concessional contributions cap (¶13-775).

This rule provides an exception to the requirement in ITAA s 295-465(2)(i) that an individual must apply to the Commissioner to make a determination to disregard or reallocate a contribution (¶13-785). It is relevant where the Commissioner has made contributions on behalf of the individual and the contributions represent amounts recovered under the SG amnesty from the individual's employer. The exception therefore means that such a determination may be made on the Commissioner's own initiative. The exception does not apply where employers make the contributions directly to an employee's superannuation fund as late SG offset contributions (¶39-500). In this case, the employee can still request the Commissioner to exercise to the discretion under s 295-465(2).

The second rule ensures that the contributions made by the Commissioner and employer SG offset contributions for the purposes of the SG amnesty are not included in the calculation of an employee's "low tax contributed amounts". This means that such contributions do not attract additional Division 293 tax or cause other low tax contributed amounts to attract additional Division 293 tax (s 293-30(4)(d): ¶13-750).

[AMSG ¶12-415; SLP ¶50-760]

SG Administration and Penalties

¶39-510 SG record-keeping and information disclosure

An employer must retain records of all transactions and acts in relation to its SG obligations, regardless of whether the employer is liable to the SG charge. Records must be kept in writing, in English and be retained for 5 years (SGAA s 79).

An employer who, without reasonable excuse, fails to comply with the record-keeping requirements may be subject to a fine. An administrative penalty may also be imposed (TAA Sch 1 s 288-25).

An employer who is liable to pay the SG charge is further required to keep records of the calculation of amounts shown in the SG statement that is lodged with the ATO (¶39-550).

Secrecy and disclosure of information under the TAA

Employees or former employees may make a complaint to the ATO where they think that their employer has not complied with their SG obligations.

Specific rules in TAA Div 355 in Sch 1 govern the recording and disclosure of protected information by taxation officers (ss 355-25; 355-50). ''Protected information'' includes written documents, any other form in which information can be recorded, information obtained directly from a taxpayer or information generated by the ATO, and information about the ATO's compliance activity against a particular taxpayer (s 355-30).

Except as permitted by Div 355, the Commissioner cannot disclose information or provide details about the progress of any action in relation to or against another person in response to an employee's SG inquiries or complaints. In this regard, where the disclosure is to an employee or former employee, the ATO may record or disclose information relating to its response to a complaint about the employer's failure or suspected failure to comply with the SGAA in relation to the employee, but not information about the employer's general financial affairs (TAA Sch 1 s 355-65, table 2 item 7 and 7A) (see further ¶39-530).

Employee's recourse against employers for non-compliance with SG obligations

The ATO has no enforceable legal duty to recover alleged unpaid superannuation contributions by an employer on a person's behalf. In *Kronen*, the taxpayer had a disputed claim with his employer about unpaid superannuation. The Federal Court held that there was no prospect of the taxpayer successfully arguing that he had, in the circumstances, an enforceable legal right to require the ATO to take action under either s 36 or 37 (ATO default assessments or amended assessments: ¶39-500), or any other SGAA provision, to compel the employer to make the additional contributions claimed to be payable, or that the ATO had in the circumstances a corresponding legal duty to do so.

The interaction between the SGAA and industrial instruments with clauses about the making of superannuation contributions may give employees a right of action against their employer under the terms of their employment contract or industrial agreement, for instance, by seeking relief under civil remedy provisions such as ss 539(2); 540; 545(1), (2)(a) and (b) of the *Fair Work Act 2009*. This will arise if the employer does not comply with obligations to pay superannuation where the prescribed contribution amounts in the contract or agreement are over and above the minimum contributions required under the SGAA (*BlueScope Steel (AIS) Pty Ltd v Australian Workers' Union*; ATO *Decision Impact Statement*: www.ato.gov.au/law/view/document?DocID=LIT/ICD/NSD542of2018/00001).

[AMSG ¶12-420, ¶12-510; FTR ¶794-742, ¶794-786; SLP ¶51-500]

¶39-530 Reporting contributions and member information to the ATO

Superannuation entities are required to give the ATO a statement in the approved form in relation to individuals who hold an interest in a superannuation plan (fund members) at any time during the period specified in a determination by the Commissioner. The statement may contain information about contributions made to the superannuation plan (including if no contributions are made), the value of an individual's superannuation interest or account, and information relating to the *Superannuation (Unclaimed Money and Lost Members) Act 1999* (TAA Sch 1 ss 390-5, 390-20: life insurance companies) (see ''Events-based reporting'' below).

The ATO uses the information for various purposes, including administration of the SG, co-contribution and contributions cap regimes, and total superannuation balance and transfer balance account regimes (¶13-760, ¶13-775, ¶14-050, ¶14-320).

A person who is dissatisfied with a statement given to the ATO by a superannuation entity may make a complaint under the Australian Financial Complaints Authority (AFCA) scheme (see *Corporations Act 2001* Pt 7.10A).

Penalties are imposed for failure to comply with the TAA information and reporting requirements (eg no or late lodgment or not using the approved form). An administrative penalty may also apply for non-compliance or providing information that is false or misleading in a particular matter (TAA Sch 1 s 286-75; Subdiv 284-B).

The Commissioner may give superannuation entities an ongoing grace period for correcting false or misleading statements in relation to member information statements without giving rise to penalties (TAA Sch 1 s 390-7).

Events-based reporting

Superannuation providers are required to comply with events-based reporting using the member account transactions service (MATS) and member account attribute service (MAAS).

The MATS is used to report contributions received and annual member balances (ie reporting account phases at a transactional level) and the MAAS is used to report attribute changes to a member's account (ie reporting account phases and changes in real time). Superannuation account phases and attributes include, but are not limited to, opening and closing of accounts, defined benefit interests and acceptance of contributions and roll-overs.

The MATS and MAAS complement other superannuation information reporting to the ATO, for example, via the transfer balance account report (TBAR) (¶14-340) or the Single Touch Payroll regime (see below).

The MAAS includes an optional Provision of Details service to assist in reuniting members who are at risk of becoming lost with their account (ATO protocol document).

MATS reporting and dates

The MATS form is the approved form for giving a statement to the Commissioner under TAA Sch 1 ss 390-5 and 390-20 in relation to a superannuation account transaction for an individual.

Superannuation providers (other than SMSFs) and life insurance companies are required to lodge a MATS form relating to the following superannuation account transactions by the dates below (or such later date as the Commissioner may allow under TAA Sch 1 s 388-55):

(i) Employer contributions and non-employer transactions — no later than 10 business days after the day the contribution amount or transaction amount is allocated to the individual's superannuation account

(ii) Retirement phase events — no later than 10 business days after the day the relevant reporting event occurs

(iii) Acknowledgements by the provider of valid notices of intent to claim a personal superannuation contribution deduction — no later than 10 business days after the day the notice is acknowledged

(iv) Member contribution balance amounts — no later than 31 October following the end of the financial year to which the amount relates (*Taxation Administration Member Account Transaction Service — the Reporting of Information Relating to Superannuation Account Transactions 2018:* F2018L00906).

''Non-employer transactions'' include all contributions made by an entity other than an employer and amounts allocated from a reserve.

''Retirement phase events'' are transactions that result in a credit or debit in an individual's transfer balance account, including new income streams commencing or beginning to be in the retirement phase, limited recourse borrowing arrangement repayments, member commutations and income streams that stop being in the retirement phase.

''Member contribution balance amounts'' include account balances, retirement phase values and accumulation phase values as at 30 June of a financial year, and ''notional taxed contributions'' (uncapped) and ''defined benefit contributions''.

MAAS reporting and dates

The MAAS form is the approved form for giving a statement to the Commissioner under ss 390-5 and 390-20 in relation to an individual's superannuation account phases and attributes.

Superannuation providers (excluding SMSFs) and life insurance companies must lodge a MAAS form in relation to an individual's superannuation account phases and attributes no later than 5 business days after the day on which:

(i) an account is opened or a life insurance policy is first held, and

(ii) any changes to the account phases and/or attributes relating to the account or policy occur (Taxation Administration Member Account Attribute Service – the Reporting of Information Relating to Superannuation Account Phases and Attributes 2018: F2018L00467).

Other employer contributions reporting obligations

Employers are required to report (on payslips) to an employee either the person's entitlements to superannuation accrued during the pay-period or the actual contributions made (*Fair Work Act 2009*, s 536; Fair Work Regulations 2009, reg 3.46).

Employers, when making superannuation contributions for their employees, are required to provide the payments and associated data to superannuation funds in a specific electronic format, in accordance with the ''Superannuation data and payment standards - SuperStream'' (see ¶13-800).

Single Touch Payroll

Single Touch Payroll (STP) reporting by employers under TAA Sch 1 Div 389 and its interaction with other ATO reporting and withholding payments obligations are discussed in ¶26-620 (see also *STP reporting guidelines*).

Employers are required to include ''sacrificed ordinary time earnings amounts'' and ''sacrificed salary or wages amounts'' within the meaning of the SGAA (salary sacrificed amount) that are paid to their employees' superannuation funds when reporting under the STP (TAA Sch 1 s 389-5(1)) (¶39-200, ¶39-250).

ATO may disclose superannuation information

As an exception to the TAA secrecy provisions (¶39-510), the ATO may disclose information held by it about a member's superannuation interests to superannuation entities and their administrators for the purpose of assisting members to find and manage their superannuation interests (eg consolidate, transfer, cash or deal with their interests in any other way). The disclosure may cover amounts held by the ATO (TAA Sch 1 s 355-65(3), item 10). Information can also be disclosed where it relates to an individual who has applied to become a member of a superannuation entity.

[AMSG ¶12-530; SLP ¶51-370]

¶39-550 Penalties for SG breaches

Penalties may be imposed on employers for a breach of their SG obligations. These include:

- an SG charge for entering into arrangements to avoid payment of the charge (SGAA s 30)
- a Part 7 penalty for failing to provide an SG statement, or statements or information for the purposes of assessing the employer's SG liability (SGAA s 59) (see below)
- a TAA administrative penalty, for example, for failing to provide statements to the ATO or to keep records or produce documents, or for providing false or misleading statements (TAA Sch 1 ss 286-75; 286-80; Subdiv 284-B) (see below).

GIC is imposed under the TAA for late payment of the SG charge (see below).

No deduction is allowed for any charge under the SGAA, but employer payments in relation to an SG charge imposed on SG shortfalls disclosed under the SG amnesty discussed in ¶39-505 are deductible up to the charge amount (ITAA97 s 26-95(2)).

For the purposes of the TAA, an SG charge or additional SG charge under s 59 is a "tax related liability" (TAA Sch 1 s 250-10(2), table item 60).

Employers may object to an assessment of a Part 7 penalty or TAA administrative penalty in accordance with TAA Pt IVC (SGAA s 42; TAA Sch 1 s 298-30(2)) (¶28-010).

Chapter 2 of the *Criminal Code* (which sets out the general principles of criminal responsibility) applies to all offences against the SGAA.

Part 7 penalty — failure to provide SG statements or information

A Part 7 penalty is payable by an employer who fails to provide, when and as required, an SG statement or information relevant to assessing the employer's liability to pay an SG charge for a quarter, for example:

- where an employer lodges an SG statement for a quarter after the due date (¶39-500), or
- where the ATO makes a default assessment of an employer's liability for the SG charge because the employer has not lodged an SG statement for a quarter (¶39-500), and the ATO is of the opinion the employer is liable to pay SG charge for the quarter.

An employer who is liable to pay an SG charge for a quarter must also keep records of the calculation of the amounts shown in the SG statement lodged with the ATO (SGAA s 59(2)).

The Part 7 penalty, which is automatically imposed on an employer by law, is equal to 200% of the amount of the SG charge payable for the quarter (minimum penalty is $20) (SGAA s 59).

A Part 7 penalty is based on the full amount of the SG charge. In working out the amount of the SG charge payable for a quarter, employer contributions under s 23A which are made to offset the SG charge (¶39-500) are disregarded (SGAA s 62A).

The AAT has jurisdiction to review the assessment of the SG charge and the penalty for failing to provide SG statements but not the late payment penalty or the GIC imposed under s 49 (see below) (*Pye*).

TAA administrative penalty

An administrative penalty may be imposed under the TAA where the Commissioner determines a tax-related liability without the assistance of a return, notice or other document that is both required by a specified time and is necessary to determine the tax-related liability ("TAA default assessment administrative penalty") (TAA Sch 1 s 284-75(3)).

The base penalty amount of the TAA default assessment administrative penalty is 75% of the tax-related liability concerned (TAA Sch 1 s 284-90(1), table item 7).

Remission of Part 7 penalty and review

The Commissioner may remit all or a part of a Part 7 penalty and TAA default assessment administrative penalty, and may do so as part of the assessment of the penalty (an audit decision) or after the penalty is assessed (an objection decision) (TAA Sch 1 s 298-20; SGAA s 62(3); *Weston*; *DB Mahaffy & Associates*).

PS LA 2020/4 sets out guidelines on what the ATO will consider in making a decision to remit a Part 7 penalty, when relief is appropriate, and how a Part 7 penalty interacts with other administrative penalties (see Appendix 1 for the 4-step penalty remission process).

Restriction on Commissioner's discretion to remit Part 7 penalty

From 8 September 2020 (the date the SG amnesty for employers ends: see ¶39-505), the Commissioner cannot remit a Part 7 penalty below 100% of the amount of SG charge payable by an employer for a historical quarter that was covered by the amnesty (ie quarters from 1 July 1992 to 31 March 2018) (s 62(4) and (5)). The amnesty period is the period from 24 May 2018 to the end of 7 September 2020. This restriction serves to strengthen the operation of the amnesty by ensuring that employers will have higher minimum penalties for failing to come forward during the amnesty in relation to historical SG shortfalls.

The circumstances in which the Commissioner's ability to remit the Part 7 penalty is restricted or may be unaffected are set out in s 62(4) and (5).

Generally, the power of remission is restricted where an employer fails to disclose to the Commissioner during the amnesty period information that is relevant to the employer's SG shortfall amount for a historical quarter (s 62(4)(a)). Where a disclosure has been made, the remission power is not necessary because employers who qualify for the amnesty would already have their liability to pay additional SG charge for the quarter reduced to nil (SGAA s 60) (¶39-505).

There may be cases, however, where disclosures are made but the employer does not qualify for the amnesty or is disqualified under the amnesty. For example:

- the employer is disqualified from the beneficial treatment under the amnesty for failing to pay the SG charge imposed on the disclosed SG shortfall by the due date, or
- the employer does not qualify for the amnesty because the information was previously disclosed to the Commissioner before the amnesty period.

In these circumstances, the discretion to remit a penalty is unaffected so as to allow the Commissioner to flexibly manage outcomes for employers that come forward during the amnesty but fail to qualify for the amnesty or are later disqualified.

The discretion to remit the Part 7 penalty is also unaffected where the Commissioner is satisfied that "exceptional circumstances" prevented an employer from either disclosing information relevant to the employer's historical SG shortfall after the start of the amnesty period, or disclosing such information before the ATO notified the employer of an examination into their SG compliance (s 62(5)).

GIC for late payment of SG charge

If an amount of SG charge is not paid or not paid in full by its due date (¶39-500), the employer is liable to pay GIC (¶29-510) on the unpaid amount (SGAA s 49). This is so even if the Commissioner has extended the date for payment of the charge.

The GIC is deductible under ITAA97 s 25-5(1).

Director penalty regime extended to SG amounts

The director penalty regime in TAA Sch 1 Div 269 (¶25-560) applies to cover SG amounts as follows:

- directors may be made personally liable for their company's unpaid SG amounts
- directors cannot discharge their director penalties by placing their company into administration or liquidation when PAYG withholding or superannuation guarantee remains unpaid and unreported 3 months after the due date, and
- directors and their associates may be liable to PAYG withholding non-compliance tax (effectively reducing credit entitlements) where the company has failed to pay amounts withheld to the Commissioner (*DFC of T v Lawson*: directors penalty notices issued to a director of a company which had failed to pay SG charge validly served).

The director penalty represents the amount of the company's SG charge as assessed, either by the employer through the lodgment of an SG statement or by the Commissioner through a default assessment (¶39-500) or a notice of an estimate issued by the Commissioner (TAA Sch 1 ss 268-10(1), (3); 269-10(1), table items 4 and 5).

Any amount collected under the director penalty regime that represents the SG charge is dealt with in the same way as SG charge amounts collected under the SGAA (¶39-600) (SGAA s 63A(3)).

ATO may give a direction to pay SG charge

The Commissioner may, by written notice, direct a person to pay an amount of SG charge that is payable or an amount under an estimate in force under TAA Sch 1 Div 268 of an amount of the person's liability to pay SG charge for a quarter (as referred to in s 268-10) (TAA Sch 1 s 265-90). A penalty applies if the amount set out in the Commissioner's direction is not paid by the end of the period specified in the direction.

[AMSG ¶12-395, ¶12-550; FTR ¶794-718, ¶794-740; SLP ¶51-100]

Distribution of SG Shortfall

¶39-600 Distribution of shortfall component

When an employer pays the SG charge to the ATO under the SGAA (¶39-500), the Commissioner must apply the "shortfall component" of the charge for the benefit of each employee in respect of whom the charge was paid (a "benefiting employee"), as worked out under SGAA s 64A (or s 64B if there is more than one benefiting employee). For this purpose, a former employee is treated as if he/she was an employee of the former employer (SGAA s 63A(1A)).

Any amount collected under the director penalty regime (¶39-550) that represents an SG charge is dealt with in the same way as SG charge amounts collected under the SGAA (s 63A(3), (4)).

The process for payment of the shortfall component to the benefiting employees is set out in SGAA s 65(1) and regulations. An employee may request a complying fund or ADF, or an RSA provider, to collect his/her entitlement to the shortfall component from the ATO, or lodge a written nomination of a fund with the ATO. This allows funds to approach the Commissioner, with the employee's consent, to seek payment of any outstanding shortfall amounts directly to the employee's account (SGAR ss 18 to 22).

If an employee does not nominate a fund or an RSA to receive the shortfall component amount, the Commissioner must credit the amount to an account in the SHASA (¶39-650) for the benefit of the employee (SGAA s 65(1)(c)).

Direct payments of shortfall component by ATO

If an employee has died or has retired from the workforce because of permanent incapacity or invalidity, the ATO can, on proper notification of the employee's death or retirement, pay the shortfall component amount directly to the deceased employee's legal personal representative or the retired employee (SGAA ss 66; 67; SGAR s 19).

Except in a case covered by s 65AA (see below), the ATO must make direct payment of the shortfall component amount to an individual (whether or not still an employee) upon request in the ATO approved form if:

- the individual is 65 years of age or over, or
- the individual has a terminal medical condition (within the meaning of the ITAA97: ¶14-310) (SGAA ss 65A; 66A).

A direct payment of the shortfall component need not be made if the individual was a former temporary resident within the meaning of the *Superannuation (Unclaimed Money and Lost Members) Act 1999*. No ATO payment is required as the shortfall component amount is treated as if it had been paid to the Commissioner by a superannuation fund under s 20F of that Act (SGAA s 65AA).

[AMSG ¶12-500; FTR ¶794-754ff; SLP ¶51-200]

Superannuation Holding Accounts Special Account

¶39-650 Operation of the SHASA

The SHASA is constituted under the *Small Superannuation Accounts Act 1995* and is administered by the ATO. It is not a superannuation fund or scheme, but is a repository for an employee's superannuation entitlements or government co-contributions. The SHASA was used voluntarily by employers before 1 July 2006 to make SG contributions as employer deposits to the SHASA were treated as contributions to a complying superannuation fund or an RSA for employees (SGAA s 23(13)).

The SHASA ceased to accept employer contributions after 30 June 2006, but is still used as a repository for the ATO's distributions of the shortfall component of an SG charge where an employee does not nominate a superannuation fund to receive the shortfall component (¶39-600), or for payments of government co-contributions for the benefit of a person (¶13-760).

Operation of SHASA

The SHASA maintains separate notional accounts (the ''individual's account'') for each employee. The ATO must notify an individual of his/her account balance as soon as practicable: (a) on the first occasion that an amount is credited to the account; (b) at the individual's request; (c) after the end of each financial year (only if the balance exceeds nil); and (d) when the account balance first exceeds $1,200 (*Small Superannuation Accounts Act 1995* (SSA Act), ss 20 to 23).

Interest accrues daily on an individual's account, and is credited quarterly on the "allocation day". An individual's account for interest calculation purposes is deemed never to exceed $1,200 so that interest is not paid on balances over $1,200 (SSA Act s 49).

An individual's account in the SHASA may be debited for the following:

- transfer of the individual's account to a regulated superannuation fund, an exempt public sector superannuation scheme or an RSA
- direct withdrawal by the individual or the legal personal representative of a deceased individual
- transfer of the individual's account to the Consolidated Revenue Fund (eg "inactive" accounts, where no employer deposit or SG shortfall component is credited at any time during a period of 10 consecutive financial years)
- refund to employers or former employers (eg deposits made due to a clerical error, or a defect or irregularity in a deposit form) or overpayments of government co-contributions.

Withdrawals from SHASA

Applications may be made to the Commissioner for withdrawals from an individual's account in the SHASA if:

- the balance of the account is less than $200 and the individual has ceased employment (not applicable to deposits from government co-contributions)
- the individual is in receipt of "Commonwealth income support payments" for a prescribed period
- the individual has retired due to permanent disability
- a terminal medical condition (within the meaning of the ITAA97: ¶14-310) exists in relation to the individual
- the individual turns 65
- the individual is at least 55 years old, is not an Australian resident and is not employed, or is employed but the duties of the employment are performed wholly or principally outside Australia
- the individual was the holder of an eligible temporary visa that has ceased to be in effect, has left Australia, is not holding a permanent visa, and is neither an Australian citizen nor New Zealand citizen
- the individual dies, and his/her legal personal representative applies for withdrawal of the account balance (SSA Act ss 61; 63 to 68; 76).

Relationship with other tax laws

The operation of the SHASA and its relationship with other income tax laws are outlined below.

- Credits of the shortfall component of an SG charge to an employee's account in the SHASA are treated as employer contributions to a complying superannuation fund for the employee for SG purposes (¶39-600).
- If a deduction had been allowed for deposits made to the SHASA, any refund of those deposits is assessable income (ITAA36 former s 82AAQA).

- Interest earned on an individual's account in the SHASA is free from tax (ie it is not taxed in the employee's hands), but will be treated as employer contributions when the individual's account balance is transferred to a superannuation fund or an RSA. The amounts transferred are assessable in the fund or RSA provider except to the extent that they represent government co-contributions (ITAA97 s 295-160: ¶13-125, ¶13-480).
- An amount paid from an individual's account to the individual or to the trustee of the estate of a deceased individual (including payments made from the Consolidated Revenue Fund) (a ''small superannuation account payment'' under ITAA97 s 307-5(1), item 4) is assessable as a superannuation benefit or superannuation death benefit (¶14-100).

[AMSG ¶12-620; SLP ¶55-100]

Chapter 40 Fuel Tax Credits

¶40-000 Overview of fuel tax credits

Most businesses are entitled to fuel tax credits in accordance with the *Fuel Tax Act 2006* (FTA) for fuel used in a range of business activities, *excluding* the use of light vehicles on public roads. The rate of credit varies according to the use to which the fuel is put.

Fuel tax credits are administered by the ATO, and aspects such as registration and accounting periods are similar to those applying for GST (¶34-000). The credits are claimed on the Business Activity Statement (BAS) in a similar way to input tax credits.

Fuel tax credits are assessable income, and should be disclosed in the tax return as "Assessable government industry payments". They are also treated as instalment income for the purpose of calculating PAYG instalments. Fuel tax credits are not subject to GST.

Basic Entitlement Rules

¶40-100 Entitlement to fuel tax credit

Fuel tax credits may be claimed where:

- you acquire, manufacture or import "taxable fuel". This is fuel that is liable for duty under excise or customs legislation, with certain minor exceptions. The main examples are diesel and petrol (FTR 2007/1)
- you do so "for use in carrying on your enterprise" (¶34-110; FTD 2006/3). Fuel is not "used" if it is sold or otherwise disposed of (FTD 2009/1; *PXTY*). Subsequent evaporation and leakage of the fuel acquired for resale to customers was held to be wholly incidental to making a taxable supply of fuel (ie not "used" in carrying on the enterprise) (*Coles Supermarkets Australia*), and
- at that time, you are registered for GST, or are required to be (¶34-110). This requirement does not apply if you are a non-profit body and the fuel is for use in a vehicle or vessel that provides emergency services and is clearly identifiable as such.

Fuel tax credits may also be claimed if you manufacture or acquire:

- kerosene, heating oil or other prescribed fuel in order to sell it to someone who will use it for domestic heating, or
- kerosene, mineral turpentine, white spirit or other prescribed fuel in order to repackage it in containers of 20 litres or less for sale for a use other than in an internal combustion engine.

For the ATO's views on fuel tax credit entitlements where a vehicle is hired, see FTR 2009/1.

Non-eligible fuels and uses

Fuel tax credits *do not* apply to:

- fuel used in light vehicles, ie vehicles with a gross vehicle mass (GVM) of 4.5 tonnes or less travelling on a public road (eg a car or small van)
- fuel used in pre-1996 heavy vehicles, ie vehicles with a GVM of more than 4.5 tonnes, travelling on public roads, that do not meet specified environmental criteria (FTA s 41-25)
- fuel for which another entity has claimed a credit which is not likely to be increased
- aviation fuel.

Biodiesel and ethanol

Blended fuels are blends of 2 or more liquid fuels, eg diesel with biodiesel, or petrol with ethanol. Petrol/ethanol blends are treated as entirely petrol (ie taxable fuel) if the ethanol component does not exceed 10% (eg E10). Diesel/biodiesel blends are treated as entirely diesel (ie taxable fuel) if the biodiesel component does not exceed 20% (eg B20).

Gaseous fuels

Liquefied petroleum gas (LPG), compressed natural gas (CNG) and liquefied natural gas (LNG) were previously not subject to fuel tax. However, where used for transport (and certain other limited purposes), they were phased into the fuel taxation regime at discounted rates over the period up to 1 July 2015, and fuel tax credits may be available to end-users.

Claiming credits

To claim fuel tax credits, you should be registered. The credits are normally claimed on the BAS in a similar way to GST input tax credits. See the ATO's *Fuel Tax Credits: How to Complete Your BAS*. Entitlement to a credit ceases to the extent that the credit has not been taken into account in an assessment within the 4-year entitlement period (FTA s 47-5(1); ATO *Decision Impact Statement* on *Coles Supermarkets Australia*).

Fuel tax credits are attributed to the same tax period as the GST input tax credit for the fuel (¶34-130). Where adjustments to fuel tax credits are made, they are attributed to the tax period in which the taxpayer became aware of the adjustment.

A claimant for fuel tax credits must keep records that record and explain all transactions and acts that are relevant to the claim (TAA Sch 1 s 382-5). In *O'Brien,* a penalty at the rate of 25% of the shortfall was imposed for failing to take reasonable care in complying with this requirement.

Non-business taxpayers

Fuel tax credits may also be claimed by householders using fuel to generate domestic electricity. For details, see the ATO's *Fuel tax credits — domestic electricity generation and non-profit emergency vehicles or vessels*.

¶40-110 Rates of fuel tax credit: summary

The credit is generally based on the amount of fuel tax payable, and varies according to the type of fuel and its usage.

For heavy on-road vehicles (¶40-200), the full rate is reduced by the road user charge (FTA s 43-10; ¶40-210). The relevant rate of road user charge is that in force at the start of the tax period to which the fuel tax credit is attributable.

The fuel excise rate is indexed, effective from 10 November 2014 (*Excise Tariff Amendment (Fuel Indexation) Act 2015* and *Customs Tariff Amendment (Fuel Indexation) Act 2015*; Excise Tariff Proposal (No 1) 2014 and Customs Tariff Proposal (No 1) 2014; FTA s 43-6).

Heavy On-road Vehicles

¶40-200 Heavy on-road vehicles

Fuel tax credits apply to fuel used in vehicles with a gross vehicle mass (GVM) greater than 4.5 tonnes travelling on a public road.

The ATO considers that the GVM of a vehicle is the GVM accepted by the authority that registered the vehicle. Trailers are not included in the GVM of a rigid vehicle. In the case of prime movers, the GVM is the gross combination mass.

''Vehicle travelling on a public road'' is not defined in the FTA. The ATO considers that it is not restricted to registered vehicles and should be construed broadly to include any vehicle that can be authorised to travel on a public road by the relevant road traffic authority. This may include plant, equipment or machinery that is capable of locomotion. It is not necessary that the vehicle be self-propelled, or that it be for the carriage of people or passengers (FTR 2008/1). A public road is a road generally accessible as of right to the public and includes privately operated toll roads (*Linfox Australia* [2019] FCAFC 131; *ATO Decision Impact Statement* on *Linfox*). A public road does not include a road maintained by a public authority that is not responsible for the provision of road transport infrastructure where the public access to the road is subordinate to the authority's objects (FTR 2008/1).

Travelling on a public road includes those parts of a journey where the vehicle is stationary, or is a safety vehicle moving along a public road providing safety services (ID 2013/16), but it would not cover a situation where the vehicle is simply engaged in constructing, maintaining or repairing a public road (former ID 2013/22).

The requirement that the GVM *exceed* 4.5 tonnes was modified for vehicles acquired before 1 July 2006. For those vehicles, it was sufficient that the GVM was 4.5 tonnes or more.

¶40-210 Rate of credit: heavy on-road vehicles

Vehicles with a GVM greater than 4.5 tonnes travelling on a public road are normally only entitled to a reduced rate of credit. This is calculated as:

Full credit rate *less* road user charge

For diesel and petrol, the effect is that the full credit rate (currently 40.9) is reduced as set out below. Note that the road user charge was reduced from 25.90 to 25.80 from 1 July 2017 (*Fuel Tax (Road User Charge) Determination 2017*):

1/7/10 to 30/6/11: (38.143 less 22.600)	15.543 cents per litre
1/7/11 to 30/6/12: (38.143 less 23.100)	15.043 cents per litre
1/7/12 to 30/6/13: (38.143 less 25.50)	12.643 cents per litre

1/7/13 to 9/11/14: (38.143 less 26.140)	12.003 cents per litre
10/11/14 to 1/2/15: (38.6 less 26.140)	12.460 cents per litre
2/2/15 to 31/7/15: (38.9 less 26.140)	12.760 cents per litre
1/8/15 to 31/1/16: (39.2 less 26.140)	13.060 cents per litre
1/2/16 to 30/6/16: (39.5 less 26.140)	13.360 cents per litre
1/7/16 to 31/7/16: (39.5 less 25.90)	13.60 cents per litre
1/8/16 to 31/1/17: (39.6 less 25.90)	13.70 cents per litre
1/2/17 to 30/6/17: (40.1 less 25.90)	14.20 cents per litre
1/7/17 to 31/7/17: (40.1 less 25.80)	14.30 cents per litre
1/8/17 to 4/2/18: (40.3 less 25.80)	14.50 cents per litre
5/2/18 to 31/7/18: (40.9 less 25.80)	15.10 cents per litre
1/8/18 to 3/2/19: (41.2 less 25.80)	15.40 cents per litre
4/2/19 to 4/8/19: (41.6 less 25.80)	15.80 cents per litre
5/8/19 to 2/2/20: (41.8 less 25.80)	16.00 cents per litre
3/2/20 to 30/6/20: (42.3 less 25.80)	16.50 cents per litre
1/7/20 to 31/1/21: (42.3 less 25.80)	16.50 cents per litre

The above rate is indexed twice a year generally on 1 February and 1 August.

From 1 November 2019, this rate includes fuel used to power passenger air-conditioning of buses and coaches.

For gaseous fuels (¶40-100), the road user charge effectively reduces the credit rate to zero.

For blended fuels, except where the blend is treated as entirely petrol or diesel (¶40-100), fuel tax credits apply to the extent that the blend is taxable, ie petrol or diesel. The road user charge applies to the entire quantity of fuel, irrespective of the amount of the renewable component.

Where public road use is incidental to main use

The rate of credit for these vehicles is *not* reduced by the road user charge if the vehicle's travel on a public road is only incidental to the vehicle's main use (FTA s 43-10).

A vehicle's "main use" is a question of fact, to be decided on the facts and circumstances of each case. Relevant factors include:

- the purpose for which the vehicle is designed
- any specific alterations or modifications which make the vehicle's use different from the use for which it was originally designed
- the ordinary pattern of use of the vehicle
- time spent or distance travelled (as appropriate) by the vehicle in carrying out a particular operation, compared to the time or distance spent in carrying out other operations, and
- the nature of the entity's enterprise (FTR 2008/1).

▶ Example 1: concrete truck

A company uses a concrete truck to transport concrete from its premises to construction sites of its customers. During the journey, the plastic state of the concrete is maintained by agitation. The ATO would consider that the "main use" of the concrete truck includes using public roads to transport concrete in its plastic state. The travel on the public roads is therefore integral, not incidental, to the main use of the vehicle. The fuel tax credit rate for this travel would therefore be reduced by road user charge.

▶ Example 2: harvester

A farmer carries on business on an agricultural property. A public road separates parts of the property. The farmer uses a harvester it owns to harvest crops on its farm. In the course of harvesting, the harvester travels 2 kilometres on the public road to get from one part of the property to another. The ATO would consider that the harvester's main use is to harvest crops, and that it only travels on the public road to go from one part of the farm to another during the course of harvesting. The travel on the public roads is insubstantial in extent, and occurs in the course of the harvester's off-road use. The travel on the public road is therefore incidental to the harvester's main use and would not affect the amount of the fuel tax credit. As the activity is an eligible agricultural activity (¶40-300), the credit would be allowed at the full rate. For the ATO's views on what a motor vehicle is and when a motor vehicle is used ''primarily'' on an agricultural property, see FTD 2019/1.

The amount of fuel tax credit for taxable fuel used in a vehicle on a public road (*Linfox Australia* [2019] FCAFC 131; *ATO Decision Impact Statement* on *Linfox*) for idling and cabin air-conditioning is reduced by the amount of the road user charge (FTD 2016/1; *Linfox Australia* [2019] AATA 222). However, the credit for fuel used for the refrigeration unit attached to a truck was not reducible by the road user charge, as the fuel was used for refrigeration and not for propelling the vehicle (*Linfox Australia* [2012] AATA 517; FTR 2008/1). The ATO has released ''safe harbour'' rates that it considers to be fair and reasonable for determining credits for fuel used in powering such auxiliary equipment (PCG 2016/11).

Other Business Activities

¶40-300 Eligible business uses other than heavy vehicles on public roads

For eligible business uses other than heavy vehicles on public roads, the credit rate for taxable liquid fuels since 1 July 2014 is:

- 1/7/14 to 9/11/14: 38.143 cents per litre
- 10/11/14 to 1/2/15: 38.6 cents per litre
- 2/2/15 to 31/7/15: 38.9 cents per litre
- 1/8/15 to 31/1/16: 39.2 cents per litre
- 1/2/16 to 31/7/16: 39.5 cents per litre
- 1/8/16 to 31/1/17: 39.6 cents per litre
- 1/2/17 to 31/7/17: 40.1 cents per litre
- 1/8/17 to 4/2/18: 40.3 cents per litre
- 5/2/18 to 31/7/18: 40.9 cents per litre
- 1/8/18 to 3/2/19: 41.2 cents per litre
- 4/2/19 to 4/8/19: 41.6 cents per litre
- 5/8/19 to 2/2/20: 41.8 cents per litre
- 3/2/20 to 30/6/20: 42.3 cents per litre
- 1/7/20 to 31/1/21: 42.3 cents per litre.

The above rate is indexed twice a year generally on 1 February and 1 August.

Gaseous fuels

The credit rates for transport gaseous fuels are set out in the following table:

Acquisition date of fuel	LNG or CNG	LPG
1/7/14 – 9/11/14	20.9	10.0
10/11/14 – 1/2/15	21.2	10.1
2/2/15 – 30/6/15	21.3	10.2
1/7/15 – 31/7/15	26.6	12.7
1/8/15 – 31/1/16	26.8	12.8
1/2/16 – 31/7/16	27.0	12.9
1/8/16 – 31/1/17	27.1	12.9
1/2/17 – 30/6/17	27.4	13.1
1/7/17 – 31/7/17	27.4	13.1
1/8/17 – 4/2/18	27.6	13.2
5/2/18 – 31/7/18	28.0	13.3
1/8/18 – 3/2/19	28.2	13.4
4/2/19 – 4/8/19	28.5	13.6
5/8/19 – 2/2/20	28.7	13.7
3/2/20 – 30/6/20	29.0	13.8
1/7/20 – 31/1/21	29.0	13.8

The above rates are indexed twice a year generally on 1 February and 1 August.

Separate rates apply to ''non-transport'' gaseous fuels. For further details, see the ATO's *Fuel tax rates and eligible fuels*.

Blended fuels

Except where blends are treated as entirely petrol or diesel (¶40-100), fuel tax credits apply to the extent that the blend is taxable, ie petrol or diesel. For further details, see ''Fuel tax credits rates and eligible fuels'' at www.ato.gov.au.

Calculation of Credit

¶40-400 Basic formula for calculating fuel tax credit

The fuel tax credit is calculated as:

Number of eligible litres of fuel × Applicable rate

However, as different credit rates apply to different types of business activity, it will often be necessary to identify how many litres of fuel have been used in each of those activities. The claim will be the total of these separate calculations.

The applicable rate of credit is generally determined as at the date the fuel is acquired. However, for heavy vehicles travelling on public roads, taxpayers should continue to use the rate in effect when completing the relevant BAS.

For the BAS period ending 31 March 2016 and later periods, taxpayers that claim less than $10,000 in fuel tax credits each year can use the rate that applies at the end of a BAS period if there has been a change of rate during that period. They can also work out their litres based on the cost of the fuel purchased.

For guidelines on correcting earlier credit claims, see *ATO Simplified fuel tax credits*.

¶40-410 ATO methods of calculating eligible quantities

The Commissioner says that an apportionment method that is fair and reasonable may be used to determine the credit that is available for the taxable fuel that is acquired. Where there is more than one fair and reasonable way of apportioning, the taxpayer may choose any of those methods. In the following situations, a taxpayer will generally have to perform separate calculations:

- where there is one type of taxable fuel in multiple activities that attract differential rates or the credit is subject to reduction, eg by road user charge
- where there is more than one type of taxable fuel in the same activity
- where there is more than one type of taxable fuel for multiple activities that attract differential rates or the credit is reducible.

However, in certain circumstances, a taxpayer may find it fair and reasonable to perform a single calculation, eg if the same type of equipment uses 2 types of taxable fuel and has the same average hourly consumption for both types (FTD 2010/1; PCG 2016/8). For substantiation methods, see FTD 2006/2. For further ATO guidelines, see *Keeping records* and *Calculating eligible quantities*.

The ATO has also issued the following *Practical Compliance Guidelines* to assist claimants in complying with their fuel tax credit obligations:

- PCG 2016/2: Fuel tax credits — practical compliance methods for small claimants
- PCG 2016/3: Fuel tax credits — fuel tax credit rate for non-business claimants
- PCG 2016/4: Fuel tax credits — incidental travel on public roads by certain vehicles
- PCG 2016/11: Fuel tax credits — apportioning taxable fuel used in a heavy vehicle with auxiliary equipment
- PCG 2019/2: Fuel tax credits — practical compliance methods for farmers in disaster affected areas.

Chapter 41 Pending Tax and Superannuation Legislation

Bills

¶41-000 Introduction to pending tax and superannuation legislation

Details of pending tax and superannuation legislation are usually integrated into the commentary in the relevant substantive chapters. However, the coverage in this chapter provides an additional point of reference for readers who wish to see an overview of proposed measures in the form of a Bill before parliament or exposure draft legislation released by Treasury.

The information provided below is up to date as at 31 December 2020.

¶41-100 Reuniting more superannuation Bill

The Treasury Laws Amendment (Reuniting More Superannuation) Bill 2020 was introduced into the House of Representatives on 6 February 2020 and is currently before the Senate.

The Bill contains measures amending the SISA, RSAA and SUMLMA, to facilitate the closure of eligible rollover funds (ERFs) by 30 June 2021 and allow amounts transferred to the ATO from ERFs to be included in the amounts that the Commissioner can proactively reunite with a member's active superannuation account.

Specifically, the Bill amends the SUMLMA to require the balance of all accounts less than $6,000 held by ERFs on 1 June 2020 to be transferred to the ATO by 30 June 2020 (to be extended to 30 June 2021, see below) and the balance of all remaining accounts held by ERFs to be transferred to the ATO by 30 June 2021 (to be extended to 31 January 2022, see below).

The Bill also amends the SISA and RSAA to prevent superannuation funds and retirement savings account providers from transferring new amounts to ERFs from the later of 7 days after assent, or 1 May 2020.

The amendments commence the day after assent.

Note: In the July 2020 *Economic and Fiscal Update* the government announced that it proposes to defer:

- by 12 months the start date of the measure that prevents superannuation funds transferring new amounts to ERFs
- the date by which ERFs are required to transfer accounts below $6,000 to the ATO to 30 June 2021, and
- the date by which ERFs are required to transfer remaining accounts to the ATO to 31 January 2022.

See ¶13-850.

¶41-150 More flexible superannuation Bill

The Treasury Laws Amendment (More Flexible Superannuation) Bill 2020 was introduced into the House of Representatives on 13 May 2020 and is currently before the Senate.

The Bill partially implements the *Improving flexibility for older Australians* measure from the 2019–20 Budget and amends ITAA97 s 292-85(3)(c) so that the cut-off age for accessing the bring forward non-concessional contributions cap is increased from 65 to 67 years.

The amendments are proposed to apply to non-concessional contributions made on or after 1 July 2020.

See ¶13-780.

¶41-200 Self managed superannuation funds Bill

The Treasury Laws Amendment (Self Managed Superannuation Funds) Bill 2020 was introduced into the Senate on 2 September 2020.

This Bill amends the SISA, ITAA97, SUMLMA and *Corporations Act 2001* to increase the maximum number of allowable members in SMSFs and small APRA funds from 4 to 6.

The amendments will apply from the first day of the first quarter following assent.

See ¶13-060.

Draft Legislation

¶41-900 Exposure draft legislation

Exposure draft legislation released by Treasury at the time of writing includes the following:

- *Corporate collective investment vehicle (CCIV) — tax framework* — These measures propose a new tax framework that will give effect to the CCIV. The policy intent of the CCIV is to establish a new form of passive investment vehicle with a tax treatment that is broadly aligned with the attribution tax regime for managed investment trusts (¶6-410).
- *Your Future, Your Super* — These measures propose to implement the *Your Future, Your Super* package of reforms announced in the 2020–21 Budget. The exposure draft legislation includes amendments to:
  - limit the creation of multiple superannuation accounts for new employees
  - require trustees and directors of corporate trustees of superannuation funds to perform their duties and exercise their powers in the best financial interests of the beneficiaries, and
  - require APRA to conduct an annual performance test for MySuper products and other products to be specified in regulations (¶13-800).

Chapter 42 Tax Rates and Tables

Income Tax Rates

¶42-000 Resident individual rates for 2020–21

2020–21 taxable income (column 1) ($)	Tax on column 1 ($)	% on excess (marginal rate)
18,200	Nil	19
45,000	5,092	32.5
120,000	29,467	37
180,000	51,667	45

A ready reckoner enabling quick calculation of gross tax payable on taxable incomes of up to $180,000 is provided at ¶42-023.

▶ Example 1

Ben, a resident with no dependants, has a taxable income of $60,000. His gross tax is $9,967, ie $5,092 (tax at 19% on $45,000, with first $18,200 tax-free) + $4,875 (tax at 32.5% on [$60,000 – $45,000]). This is before the low income rebate (¶15-300) and low and middle income tax offset (¶15-300) are taken into account.

▶ Example 2

Jessica, also a resident with no dependants, has a taxable income of $121,000. Her gross tax is $29,837, ie $29,467 (tax on $120,000) + $370 (37% × [$121,000 – $120,000]). This is before the low and middle income tax offset (¶15-300) is taken into account.

Notes

1. The above scales enable the calculation of *gross* tax payable by most resident individual taxpayers. However, special rules apply in calculating tax payable where:

(a) the taxpayer is a primary producer (¶18-200)

(b) the taxpayer is an author, inventor, performing artist, production associate or sportsperson (¶2-140)

(c) the taxpayer is a minor with unearned income (¶2-160).

2. Tax offsets (eg rebates for dependants) and credits (eg for franked dividends) must be subtracted from gross tax to give net tax payable (¶15-000).

3. A low income rebate is available to taxpayers whose taxable income is less than $66,667. For 2020–21, the maximum rebate is $700 (¶15-300). An additional rebate is available to certain low income aged persons (¶15-310).

4. A low and middle income tax offset is available to taxpayers whose taxable income does not exceed $126,000. The maximum offset amount is $1,080 (¶15-300).

5. For 2020–21, the standard tax-free threshold for resident individuals is $18,200. The tax-free threshold may effectively be higher where the taxpayer is entitled to rebates such as the low income rebate and low and middle income tax offset. The tax-free threshold is pro-rated in a year of income in which a taxpayer becomes or ceases to be a resident (¶2-130).

6. Medicare levy is payable at the rate of 2% of taxable income, subject to relief for low income earners (¶2-330). An additional levy, the Medicare levy surcharge, of 1%, 1.25% or 1.5% (depending on income for surcharge purposes) is imposed on higher income earners who do not have private patient hospital insurance cover (¶2-335).

7. The rates scale for prescribed non-resident individuals is set out at ¶42-015.

8. Special rules apply to superannuation fund payments (¶14-200) and employment termination payments (¶14-600).

9. Rates for individuals who are working holiday makers (¶21-033) are set out at ¶42-018.

10. Further changes to reduce the income tax rates and thresholds will take effect from the 2024–25 year (¶2-120).

¶42-010 Medicare levy and Medicare levy surcharge rate and thresholds

Resident individuals are liable to pay a Medicare levy based on the amount of their taxable income for the income year. The Medicare levy rate is 2% of taxable income.

Relief from the Medicare levy is provided for low income earners, including those who qualify for the Senior Australians and Pensioners Tax Offset (¶2-330).

Medicare levy surcharge

An additional levy surcharge of 1%, 1.25% or 1.5% depending on level of income is payable by an unmarried person whose ''income for surcharge purposes'' for the 2020–21 year is more than $90,000 if the person is not covered by private patient hospital insurance (¶2-335).

¶42-015 Non-resident individual rates for 2020–21

2020–21 taxable income (column 1) ($)	Tax on column 1 ($)	% on excess (marginal rate)
Nil	Nil	32.5
120,000	39,000	37
180,000	61,200	45

▶ **Example**

Nick, a prescribed non-resident, has a taxable income of $122,000. His gross tax is $39,740, ie $39,000 (tax on $120,000) + $740 (37% × [$122,000 – $120,000]).

Notes

1. The above scale enables the calculation of *gross* tax payable by prescribed non-resident individuals. A ''prescribed non-resident'' is a person who at all times during the income year was a non-resident, other than a person in receipt of a taxable Australian social security or veterans' entitlement pension (¶2-120).

2. A non-resident who does not qualify as a prescribed non-resident is taxable at the same rates as a resident, although the standard tax-free threshold may be pro-rated to account for the period of non-residency (¶42-000).

3. Prescribed non-residents pay tax on the very first dollar of taxable income.

4. A non-resident is generally only taxable on Australian source income (¶22-000).

5. A non-resident is exempt from liability for the Medicare levy (¶2-340).

6. Income derived by non-resident individuals participating in the Seasonal Labour Mobility Program is taxed at 15%, administered as a final withholding tax.

7. Rates for individuals who are working holiday makers (¶21-033) are set out at ¶42-018.

8. Further changes to reduce the income tax rates and thresholds will take effect from the 2024–25 year (¶2-120).

¶42-018 Working holiday maker rates

The rates of tax applicable to individual taxpayers who are working holiday makers (¶21-033) for the 2020–21 year are as follows.

2020–21 taxable income (column 1) ($)	Tax on column 1 ($)	% on excess (marginal rate)
Nil	Nil	15
45,000	6,750	32.5
120,000	31,125	37
180,000	53,325	45

Note

1. Further changes to reduce the income tax rates and thresholds will take effect from the 2024–25 year (¶2-120).

¶42-020 Rates for minors

The following are the special rates of tax applicable under ITAA36 Pt III Div 6AA to the eligible taxable income of a minor (¶2-220) for 2020–21.

Resident minors

- Where the eligible taxable income is $416 or less, the special rates do not apply. The general rates applicable to resident individuals simply apply to the whole of the taxable income.
- Where the eligible taxable income exceeds $416 but does not exceed $1,307, the tax on the eligible taxable income is the greater of: (i) 66% of the excess over $416; and (ii) the difference between tax on the whole of the taxable income and tax on the taxable income other than the eligible taxable income.
- Where the eligible taxable income exceeds $1,307, tax is payable on the whole of the eligible taxable income at the rate of 45%.
- Resident minors are not entitled to the low income rebate in respect of their eligible income (¶15-300).

Prescribed non-resident minors

- Where the eligible taxable income does not exceed $416, the tax payable on that income is the greater of: (i) 32.5% of the eligible taxable income; and (ii) the difference between tax on the total taxable income and tax on the taxable income other than the eligible taxable income, using in both cases the rates applicable to prescribed non-residents (¶42-015).
- Where the eligible taxable income exceeds $416 but does not exceed $663, the tax payable on that income is the greater of: (i) $135.20 plus 66% of the excess over $416; and (ii) the difference between tax on the total taxable income and tax on the taxable income other than the eligible taxable income, using in both cases the rates applicable to prescribed non-residents (¶42-015).
- Where the eligible taxable income exceeds $663, tax is payable on the whole of the eligible taxable income at the rate of 45%.

¶42-023 Tax calculator for resident individuals

The individual tax calculator below enables quick calculation of gross tax payable by resident individuals.

2020–21 TAX CALCULATOR FOR RESIDENT INDIVIDUALS

Taxable income	Resident Individuals: Gross Tax Payable at 2020–21 Rates*									
	$0	$10	$20	$30	$40	$50	$60	$70	$80	$90
18200	0.00	1.90	3.80	5.70	7.60	9.50	11.40	13.30	15.20	17.10
18300	19.00	20.90	22.80	24.70	26.60	28.50	30.40	32.30	34.20	36.10
18400	38.00	39.90	41.80	43.70	45.60	47.50	49.40	51.30	53.20	55.10
18500	57.00	58.90	60.80	62.70	64.60	66.50	68.40	70.30	72.20	74.10
18600	76.00	77.90	79.80	81.70	83.60	85.50	87.40	89.30	91.20	93.10
18700	95.00	96.90	98.80	100.70	102.60	104.50	106.40	108.30	110.20	112.10
18800	114.00	115.90	117.80	119.70	121.60	123.50	125.40	127.30	129.20	131.10
18900	133.00	134.90	136.80	138.70	140.60	142.50	144.40	146.30	148.20	150.10
19000	152.00	153.90	155.80	157.70	159.60	161.50	163.40	165.30	167.20	169.10
19100	171.00	172.90	174.80	176.70	178.60	180.50	182.40	184.30	186.20	188.10
19200	190.00	191.90	193.80	195.70	197.60	199.50	201.40	203.30	205.20	207.10
19300	209.00	210.90	212.80	214.70	216.60	218.50	220.40	222.30	224.20	226.10
19400	228.00	229.90	231.80	233.70	235.60	237.50	239.40	241.30	243.20	245.10
19500	247.00	248.90	250.80	252.70	254.60	256.50	258.40	260.30	262.20	264.10
19600	266.00	267.90	269.80	271.70	273.60	275.50	277.40	279.30	281.20	283.10
19700	285.00	286.90	288.80	290.70	292.60	294.50	296.40	298.30	300.20	302.10
19800	304.00	305.90	307.80	309.70	311.60	313.50	315.40	317.30	319.20	321.10
19900	323.00	324.90	326.80	328.70	330.60	332.50	334.40	336.30	338.20	340.10
20000	342.00	343.90	345.80	347.70	349.60	351.50	353.40	355.30	357.20	359.10
20100	361.00	362.90	364.80	366.70	368.60	370.50	372.40	374.30	376.20	378.10
20200	380.00	381.90	383.80	385.70	387.60	389.50	391.40	393.30	395.20	397.10
20300	399.00	400.90	402.80	404.70	406.60	408.50	410.40	412.30	414.20	416.10
20400	418.00	419.90	421.80	423.70	425.60	427.50	429.40	431.30	433.20	435.10
20500	437.00	438.90	440.80	442.70	444.60	446.50	448.40	450.30	452.20	454.10
20600	456.00	457.90	459.80	461.70	463.60	465.50	467.40	469.30	471.20	473.10
20700	475.00	476.90	478.80	480.70	482.60	484.50	486.40	488.30	490.20	492.10
20800	494.00	495.90	497.80	499.70	501.60	503.50	505.40	507.30	509.20	511.10
20900	513.00	514.90	516.80	518.70	520.60	522.50	524.40	526.30	528.20	530.10
21000	532.00	533.90	535.80	537.70	539.60	541.50	543.40	545.30	547.20	549.10
21100	551.00	552.90	554.80	556.70	558.60	560.50	562.40	564.30	566.20	568.10
21200	570.00	571.90	573.80	575.70	577.60	579.50	581.40	583.30	585.20	587.10
21300	589.00	590.90	592.80	594.70	596.60	598.50	600.40	602.30	604.20	606.10
21400	608.00	609.90	611.80	613.70	615.60	617.50	619.40	621.30	623.20	625.10
21500	627.00	628.90	630.80	632.70	634.60	636.50	638.40	640.30	642.20	644.10
21600	646.00	647.90	649.80	651.70	653.60	655.50	657.40	659.30	661.20	663.10
21700	665.00	666.90	668.80	670.70	672.60	674.50	676.40	678.30	680.20	682.10
21800	684.00	685.90	687.80	689.70	691.60	693.50	695.40	697.30	699.20	701.10
21900	703.00	704.90	706.80	708.70	710.60	712.50	714.40	716.30	718.20	720.10
22000	722.00	723.90	725.80	727.70	729.60	731.50	733.40	735.30	737.20	739.10
22100	741.00	742.90	744.80	746.70	748.60	750.50	752.40	754.30	756.20	758.10
22200	760.00	761.90	763.80	765.70	767.60	769.50	771.40	773.30	775.20	777.10
22300	779.00	780.90	782.80	784.70	786.60	788.50	790.40	792.30	794.20	796.10
22400	798.00	799.90	801.80	803.70	805.60	807.50	809.40	811.30	813.20	815.10
22500	817.00	818.90	820.80	822.70	824.60	826.50	828.40	830.30	832.20	834.10
22600	836.00	837.90	839.80	841.70	843.60	845.50	847.40	849.30	851.20	853.10

To the above amounts, add the appropriate figure for the odd dollar amount								
$1	$2	$3	$4	$5	$6	$7	$8	$9
0.19	0.38	0.57	0.76	0.95	1.14	1.33	1.52	1.71

***Tax offsets must be deducted, and Medicare levy added, to give net tax payable (see notes at ¶42-000)**

Taxable income	Resident Individuals: Gross Tax Payable at 2020–21 Rates*									
	$0	**$10**	**$20**	**$30**	**$40**	**$50**	**$60**	**$70**	**$80**	**$90**
22700	855.00	856.90	858.80	860.70	862.60	864.50	866.40	868.30	870.20	872.10
22800	874.00	875.90	877.80	879.70	881.60	883.50	885.40	887.30	889.20	891.10
22900	893.00	894.90	896.80	898.70	900.60	902.50	904.40	906.30	908.20	910.10
23000	912.00	913.90	915.80	917.70	919.60	921.50	923.40	925.30	927.20	929.10
23100	931.00	932.90	934.80	936.70	938.60	940.50	942.40	944.30	946.20	948.10
23200	950.00	951.90	953.80	955.70	957.60	959.50	961.40	963.30	965.20	967.10
23300	969.00	970.90	972.80	974.70	976.60	978.50	980.40	982.30	984.20	986.10
23400	988.00	989.90	991.80	993.70	995.60	997.50	999.40	1001.30	1003.20	1005.10
23500	1007.00	1008.90	1010.80	1012.70	1014.60	1016.50	1018.40	1020.30	1022.20	1024.10
23600	1026.00	1027.90	1029.80	1031.70	1033.60	1035.50	1037.40	1039.30	1041.20	1043.10
23700	1045.00	1046.90	1048.80	1050.70	1052.60	1054.50	1056.40	1058.30	1060.20	1062.10
23800	1064.00	1065.90	1067.80	1069.70	1071.60	1073.50	1075.40	1077.30	1079.20	1081.10
23900	1083.00	1084.90	1086.80	1088.70	1090.60	1092.50	1094.40	1096.30	1098.20	1100.10
24000	1102.00	1103.90	1105.80	1107.70	1109.60	1111.50	1113.40	1115.30	1117.20	1119.10
24100	1121.00	1122.90	1124.80	1126.70	1128.60	1130.50	1132.40	1134.30	1136.20	1138.10
24200	1140.00	1141.90	1143.80	1145.70	1147.60	1149.50	1151.40	1153.30	1155.20	1157.10
24300	1159.00	1160.90	1162.80	1164.70	1166.60	1168.50	1170.40	1172.30	1174.20	1176.10
24400	1178.00	1179.90	1181.80	1183.70	1185.60	1187.50	1189.40	1191.30	1193.20	1195.10
24500	1197.00	1198.90	1200.80	1202.70	1204.60	1206.50	1208.40	1210.30	1212.20	1214.10
24600	1216.00	1217.90	1219.80	1221.70	1223.60	1225.50	1227.40	1229.30	1231.20	1233.10
24700	1235.00	1236.90	1238.80	1240.70	1242.60	1244.50	1246.40	1248.30	1250.20	1252.10
24800	1254.00	1255.90	1257.80	1259.70	1261.60	1263.50	1265.40	1267.30	1269.20	1271.10
24900	1273.00	1274.90	1276.80	1278.70	1280.60	1282.50	1284.40	1286.30	1288.20	1290.10
25000	1292.00	1293.90	1295.80	1297.70	1299.60	1301.50	1303.40	1305.30	1307.20	1309.10
25100	1311.00	1312.90	1314.80	1316.70	1318.60	1320.50	1322.40	1324.30	1326.20	1328.10
25200	1330.00	1331.90	1333.80	1335.70	1337.60	1339.50	1341.40	1343.30	1345.20	1347.10
25300	1349.00	1350.90	1352.80	1354.70	1356.60	1358.50	1360.40	1362.30	1364.20	1366.10
25400	1368.00	1369.90	1371.80	1373.70	1375.60	1377.50	1379.40	1381.30	1383.20	1385.10
25500	1387.00	1388.90	1390.80	1392.70	1394.60	1396.50	1398.40	1400.30	1402.20	1404.10
25600	1406.00	1407.90	1409.80	1411.70	1413.60	1415.50	1417.40	1419.30	1421.20	1423.10
25700	1425.00	1426.90	1428.80	1430.70	1432.60	1434.50	1436.40	1438.30	1440.20	1442.10
25800	1444.00	1445.90	1447.80	1449.70	1451.60	1453.50	1455.40	1457.30	1459.20	1461.10
25900	1463.00	1464.90	1466.80	1468.70	1470.60	1472.50	1474.40	1476.30	1478.20	1480.10
26000	1482.00	1483.90	1485.80	1487.70	1489.60	1491.50	1493.40	1495.30	1497.20	1499.10
26100	1501.00	1502.90	1504.80	1506.70	1508.60	1510.50	1512.40	1514.30	1516.20	1518.10
26200	1520.00	1521.90	1523.80	1525.70	1527.60	1529.50	1531.40	1533.30	1535.20	1537.10
26300	1539.00	1540.90	1542.80	1544.70	1546.60	1548.50	1550.40	1552.30	1554.20	1556.10
26400	1558.00	1559.90	1561.80	1563.70	1565.60	1567.50	1569.40	1571.30	1573.20	1575.10
26500	1577.00	1578.90	1580.80	1582.70	1584.60	1586.50	1588.40	1590.30	1592.20	1594.10
26600	1596.00	1597.90	1599.80	1601.70	1603.60	1605.50	1607.40	1609.30	1611.20	1613.10
26700	1615.00	1616.90	1618.80	1620.70	1622.60	1624.50	1626.40	1628.30	1630.20	1632.10
26800	1634.00	1635.90	1637.80	1639.70	1641.60	1643.50	1645.40	1647.30	1649.20	1651.10
26900	1653.00	1654.90	1656.80	1658.70	1660.60	1662.50	1664.40	1666.30	1668.20	1670.10
27000	1672.00	1673.90	1675.80	1677.70	1679.60	1681.50	1683.40	1685.30	1687.20	1689.10
27100	1691.00	1692.90	1694.80	1696.70	1698.60	1700.50	1702.40	1704.30	1706.20	1708.10
27200	1710.00	1711.90	1713.80	1715.70	1717.60	1719.50	1721.40	1723.30	1725.20	1727.10
27300	1729.00	1730.90	1732.80	1734.70	1736.60	1738.50	1740.40	1742.30	1744.20	1746.10
27400	1748.00	1749.90	1751.80	1753.70	1755.60	1757.50	1759.40	1761.30	1763.20	1765.10
27500	1767.00	1768.90	1770.80	1772.70	1774.60	1776.50	1778.40	1780.30	1782.20	1784.10
27600	1786.00	1787.90	1789.80	1791.70	1793.60	1795.50	1797.40	1799.30	1801.20	1803.10

To the above amounts, add the appropriate figure for the odd dollar amount								
$1	$2	$3	$4	$5	$6	$7	$8	$9
0.19	0.38	0.57	0.76	0.95	1.14	1.33	1.52	1.71

***Tax offsets must be deducted, and Medicare levy added, to give net tax payable (see notes at ¶42-000)**

Resident Individuals: Gross Tax Payable at 2020–21 Rates*

Taxable income	$0	$10	$20	$30	$40	$50	$60	$70	$80	$90
27700	1805.00	1806.90	1808.80	1810.70	1812.60	1814.50	1816.40	1818.30	1820.20	1822.10
27800	1824.00	1825.90	1827.80	1829.70	1831.60	1833.50	1835.40	1837.30	1839.20	1841.10
27900	1843.00	1844.90	1846.80	1848.70	1850.60	1852.50	1854.40	1856.30	1858.20	1860.10
28000	1862.00	1863.90	1865.80	1867.70	1869.60	1871.50	1873.40	1875.30	1877.20	1879.10
28100	1881.00	1882.90	1884.80	1886.70	1888.60	1890.50	1892.40	1894.30	1896.20	1898.10
28200	1900.00	1901.90	1903.80	1905.70	1907.60	1909.50	1911.40	1913.30	1915.20	1917.10
28300	1919.00	1920.90	1922.80	1924.70	1926.60	1928.50	1930.40	1932.30	1934.20	1936.10
28400	1938.00	1939.90	1941.80	1943.70	1945.60	1947.50	1949.40	1951.30	1953.20	1955.10
28500	1957.00	1958.90	1960.80	1962.70	1964.60	1966.50	1968.40	1970.30	1972.20	1974.10
28600	1976.00	1977.90	1979.80	1981.70	1983.60	1985.50	1987.40	1989.30	1991.20	1993.10
28700	1995.00	1996.90	1998.80	2000.70	2002.60	2004.50	2006.40	2008.30	2010.20	2012.10
28800	2014.00	2015.90	2017.80	2019.70	2021.60	2023.50	2025.40	2027.30	2029.20	2031.10
28900	2033.00	2034.90	2036.80	2038.70	2040.60	2042.50	2044.40	2046.30	2048.20	2050.10
29000	2052.00	2053.90	2055.80	2057.70	2059.60	2061.50	2063.40	2065.30	2067.20	2069.10
29100	2071.00	2072.90	2074.80	2076.70	2078.60	2080.50	2082.40	2084.30	2086.20	2088.10
29200	2090.00	2091.90	2093.80	2095.70	2097.60	2099.50	2101.40	2103.30	2105.20	2107.10
29300	2109.00	2110.90	2112.80	2114.70	2116.60	2118.50	2120.40	2122.30	2124.20	2126.10
29400	2128.00	2129.90	2131.80	2133.70	2135.60	2137.50	2139.40	2141.30	2143.20	2145.10
29500	2147.00	2148.90	2150.80	2152.70	2154.60	2156.50	2158.40	2160.30	2162.20	2164.10
29600	2166.00	2167.90	2169.80	2171.70	2173.60	2175.50	2177.40	2179.30	2181.20	2183.10
29700	2185.00	2186.90	2188.80	2190.70	2192.60	2194.50	2196.40	2198.30	2200.20	2202.10
29800	2204.00	2205.90	2207.80	2209.70	2211.60	2213.50	2215.40	2217.30	2219.20	2221.10
29900	2223.00	2224.90	2226.80	2228.70	2230.60	2232.50	2234.40	2236.30	2238.20	2240.10
30000	2242.00	2243.90	2245.80	2247.70	2249.60	2251.50	2253.40	2255.30	2257.20	2259.10
30100	2261.00	2262.90	2264.80	2266.70	2268.60	2270.50	2272.40	2274.30	2276.20	2278.10
30200	2280.00	2281.90	2283.80	2285.70	2287.60	2289.50	2291.40	2293.30	2295.20	2297.10
30300	2299.00	2300.90	2302.80	2304.70	2306.60	2308.50	2310.40	2312.30	2314.20	2316.10
30400	2318.00	2319.90	2321.80	2323.70	2325.60	2327.50	2329.40	2331.30	2333.20	2335.10
30500	2337.00	2338.90	2340.80	2342.70	2344.60	2346.50	2348.40	2350.30	2352.20	2354.10
30600	2356.00	2357.90	2359.80	2361.70	2363.60	2365.50	2367.40	2369.30	2371.20	2373.10
30700	2375.00	2376.90	2378.80	2380.70	2382.60	2384.50	2386.40	2388.30	2390.20	2392.10
30800	2394.00	2395.90	2397.80	2399.70	2401.60	2403.50	2405.40	2407.30	2409.20	2411.10
30900	2413.00	2414.90	2416.80	2418.70	2420.60	2422.50	2424.40	2426.30	2428.20	2430.10
31000	2432.00	2433.90	2435.80	2437.70	2439.60	2441.50	2443.40	2445.30	2447.20	2449.10
31100	2451.00	2452.90	2454.80	2456.70	2458.60	2460.50	2462.40	2464.30	2466.20	2468.10
31200	2470.00	2471.90	2473.80	2475.70	2477.60	2479.50	2481.40	2483.30	2485.20	2487.10
31300	2489.00	2490.90	2492.80	2494.70	2496.60	2498.50	2500.40	2502.30	2504.20	2506.10
31400	2508.00	2509.90	2511.80	2513.70	2515.60	2517.50	2519.40	2521.30	2523.20	2525.10
31500	2527.00	2528.90	2530.80	2532.70	2534.60	2536.50	2538.40	2540.30	2542.20	2544.10
31600	2546.00	2547.90	2549.80	2551.70	2553.60	2555.50	2557.40	2559.30	2561.20	2563.10
31700	2565.00	2566.90	2568.80	2570.70	2572.60	2574.50	2576.40	2578.30	2580.20	2582.10
31800	2584.00	2585.90	2587.80	2589.70	2591.60	2593.50	2595.40	2597.30	2599.20	2601.10
31900	2603.00	2604.90	2606.80	2608.70	2610.60	2612.50	2614.40	2616.30	2618.20	2620.10
32000	2622.00	2623.90	2625.80	2627.70	2629.60	2631.50	2633.40	2635.30	2637.20	2639.10
32100	2641.00	2642.90	2644.80	2646.70	2648.60	2650.50	2652.40	2654.30	2656.20	2658.10
32200	2660.00	2661.90	2663.80	2665.70	2667.60	2669.50	2671.40	2673.30	2675.20	2677.10
32300	2679.00	2680.90	2682.80	2684.70	2686.60	2688.50	2690.40	2692.30	2694.20	2696.10
32400	2698.00	2699.90	2701.80	2703.70	2705.60	2707.50	2709.40	2711.30	2713.20	2715.10
32500	2717.00	2718.90	2720.80	2722.70	2724.60	2726.50	2728.40	2730.30	2732.20	2734.10
32600	2736.00	2737.90	2739.80	2741.70	2743.60	2745.50	2747.40	2749.30	2751.20	2753.10

To the above amounts, add the appropriate figure for the odd dollar amount

$1	$2	$3	$4	$5	$6	$7	$8	$9
0.19	0.38	0.57	0.76	0.95	1.14	1.33	1.52	1.71

***Tax offsets must be deducted, and Medicare levy added, to give net tax payable (see notes at ¶42-000)**

Resident Individuals: Gross Tax Payable at 2020–21 Rates*

Taxable income	$0	$10	$20	$30	$40	$50	$60	$70	$80	$90
32700	2755.00	2756.90	2758.80	2760.70	2762.60	2764.50	2766.40	2768.30	2770.20	2772.10
32800	2774.00	2775.90	2777.80	2779.70	2781.60	2783.50	2785.40	2787.30	2789.20	2791.10
32900	2793.00	2794.90	2796.80	2798.70	2800.60	2802.50	2804.40	2806.30	2808.20	2810.10
33000	2812.00	2813.90	2815.80	2817.70	2819.60	2821.50	2823.40	2825.30	2827.20	2829.10
33100	2831.00	2832.90	2834.80	2836.70	2838.60	2840.50	2842.40	2844.30	2846.20	2848.10
33200	2850.00	2851.90	2853.80	2855.70	2857.60	2859.50	2861.40	2863.30	2865.20	2867.10
33300	2869.00	2870.90	2872.80	2874.70	2876.60	2878.50	2880.40	2882.30	2884.20	2886.10
33400	2888.00	2889.90	2891.80	2893.70	2895.60	2897.50	2899.40	2901.30	2903.20	2905.10
33500	2907.00	2908.90	2910.80	2912.70	2914.60	2916.50	2918.40	2920.30	2922.20	2924.10
33600	2926.00	2927.90	2929.80	2931.70	2933.60	2935.50	2937.40	2939.30	2941.20	2943.10
33700	2945.00	2946.90	2948.80	2950.70	2952.60	2954.50	2956.40	2958.30	2960.20	2962.10
33800	2964.00	2965.90	2967.80	2969.70	2971.60	2973.50	2975.40	2977.30	2979.20	2981.10
33900	2983.00	2984.90	2986.80	2988.70	2990.60	2992.50	2994.40	2996.30	2998.20	3000.10
34000	3002.00	3003.90	3005.80	3007.70	3009.60	3011.50	3013.40	3015.30	3017.20	3019.10
34100	3021.00	3022.90	3024.80	3026.70	3028.60	3030.50	3032.40	3034.30	3036.20	3038.10
34200	3040.00	3041.90	3043.80	3045.70	3047.60	3049.50	3051.40	3053.30	3055.20	3057.10
34300	3059.00	3060.90	3062.80	3064.70	3066.60	3068.50	3070.40	3072.30	3074.20	3076.10
34400	3078.00	3079.90	3081.80	3083.70	3085.60	3087.50	3089.40	3091.30	3093.20	3095.10
34500	3097.00	3098.90	3100.80	3102.70	3104.60	3106.50	3108.40	3110.30	3112.20	3114.10
34600	3116.00	3117.90	3119.80	3121.70	3123.60	3125.50	3127.40	3129.30	3131.20	3133.10
34700	3135.00	3136.90	3138.80	3140.70	3142.60	3144.50	3146.40	3148.30	3150.20	3152.10
34800	3154.00	3155.90	3157.80	3159.70	3161.60	3163.50	3165.40	3167.30	3169.20	3171.10
34900	3173.00	3174.90	3176.80	3178.70	3180.60	3182.50	3184.40	3186.30	3188.20	3190.10
35000	3192.00	3193.90	3195.80	3197.70	3199.60	3201.50	3203.40	3205.30	3207.20	3209.10
35100	3211.00	3212.90	3214.80	3216.70	3218.60	3220.50	3222.40	3224.30	3226.20	3228.10
35200	3230.00	3231.90	3233.80	3235.70	3237.60	3239.50	3241.40	3243.30	3245.20	3247.10
35300	3249.00	3250.90	3252.80	3254.70	3256.60	3258.50	3260.40	3262.30	3264.20	3266.10
35400	3268.00	3269.90	3271.80	3273.70	3275.60	3277.50	3279.40	3281.30	3283.20	3285.10
35500	3287.00	3288.90	3290.80	3292.70	3294.60	3296.50	3298.40	3300.30	3302.20	3304.10
35600	3306.00	3307.90	3309.80	3311.70	3313.60	3315.50	3317.40	3319.30	3321.20	3323.10
35700	3325.00	3326.90	3328.80	3330.70	3332.60	3334.50	3336.40	3338.30	3340.20	3342.10
35800	3344.00	3345.90	3347.80	3349.70	3351.60	3353.50	3355.40	3357.30	3359.20	3361.10
35900	3363.00	3364.90	3366.80	3368.70	3370.60	3372.50	3374.40	3376.30	3378.20	3380.10
36000	3382.00	3383.90	3385.80	3387.70	3389.60	3391.50	3393.40	3395.30	3397.20	3399.10
36100	3401.00	3402.90	3404.80	3406.70	3408.60	3410.50	3412.40	3414.30	3416.20	3418.10
36200	3420.00	3421.90	3423.80	3425.70	3427.60	3429.50	3431.40	3433.30	3435.20	3437.10
36300	3439.00	3440.90	3442.80	3444.70	3446.60	3448.50	3450.40	3452.30	3454.20	3456.10
36400	3458.00	3459.90	3461.80	3463.70	3465.60	3467.50	3469.40	3471.30	3473.20	3475.10
36500	3477.00	3478.90	3480.80	3482.70	3484.60	3486.50	3488.40	3490.30	3492.20	3494.10
36600	3496.00	3497.90	3499.80	3501.70	3503.60	3505.50	3507.40	3509.30	3511.20	3513.10
36700	3515.00	3516.90	3518.80	3520.70	3522.60	3524.50	3526.40	3528.30	3530.20	3532.10
36800	3534.00	3535.90	3537.80	3539.70	3541.60	3543.50	3545.40	3547.30	3549.20	3551.10
36900	3553.00	3554.90	3556.80	3558.70	3560.60	3562.50	3564.40	3566.30	3568.20	3570.10

To the above amounts, add the appropriate figure for the odd dollar amount

$1	$2	$3	$4	$5	$6	$7	$8	$9
0.19	0.38	0.57	0.76	0.95	1.14	1.33	1.52	1.71

***Tax offsets must be deducted, and Medicare levy added, to give net tax payable (see notes at ¶42-000)**

Resident Individuals: Gross Tax Payable at 2020–21 Rates*

Taxable income	$0	$10	$20	$30	$40	$50	$60	$70	$80	$90
37000	3572.00	3573.90	3575.80	3577.70	3579.60	3581.50	3583.40	3585.30	3587.20	3589.10
37100	3591.00	3592.90	3594.80	3596.70	3598.60	3600.50	3602.40	3604.30	3606.20	3608.10
37200	3610.00	3611.90	3613.80	3615.70	3617.60	3619.50	3621.40	3623.30	3625.20	3627.10
37300	3629.00	3630.90	3632.80	3634.70	3636.60	3638.50	3640.40	3642.30	3644.20	3646.10
37400	3648.00	3649.90	3651.80	3653.70	3655.60	3657.50	3659.40	3661.30	3663.20	3665.10
37500	3667.00	3668.90	3670.80	3672.70	3674.60	3676.50	3678.40	3680.30	3682.20	3684.10
37600	3686.00	3687.90	3689.80	3691.70	3693.60	3695.50	3697.40	3699.30	3701.20	3703.10
37700	3705.00	3706.90	3708.80	3710.70	3712.60	3714.50	3716.40	3718.30	3720.20	3722.10
37800	3724.00	3725.90	3727.80	3729.70	3731.60	3733.50	3735.40	3737.30	3739.20	3741.10
37900	3743.00	3744.90	3746.80	3748.70	3750.60	3752.50	3754.40	3756.30	3758.20	3760.10
38000	3762.00	3763.90	3765.80	3767.70	3769.60	3771.50	3773.40	3775.30	3777.20	3779.10
38100	3781.00	3782.90	3784.80	3786.70	3788.60	3790.50	3792.40	3794.30	3796.20	3798.10
38200	3800.00	3801.90	3803.80	3805.70	3807.60	3809.50	3811.40	3813.30	3815.20	3817.10
38300	3819.00	3820.90	3822.80	3824.70	3826.60	3828.50	3830.40	3832.30	3834.20	3836.10
38400	3838.00	3839.90	3841.80	3843.70	3845.60	3847.50	3849.40	3851.30	3853.20	3855.10
38500	3857.00	3858.90	3860.80	3862.70	3864.60	3866.50	3868.40	3870.30	3872.20	3874.10
38600	3876.00	3877.90	3879.80	3881.70	3883.60	3885.50	3887.40	3889.30	3891.20	3893.10
38700	3895.00	3896.90	3898.80	3900.70	3902.60	3904.50	3906.40	3908.30	3910.20	3912.10
38800	3914.00	3915.90	3917.80	3919.70	3921.60	3923.50	3925.40	3927.30	3929.20	3931.10
38900	3933.00	3934.90	3936.80	3938.70	3940.60	3942.50	3944.40	3946.30	3948.20	3950.10
39000	3952.00	3953.90	3955.80	3957.70	3959.60	3961.50	3963.40	3965.30	3967.20	3969.10
39100	3971.00	3972.90	3974.80	3976.70	3978.60	3980.50	3982.40	3984.30	3986.20	3988.10
39200	3990.00	3991.90	3993.80	3995.70	3997.60	3999.50	4001.40	4003.30	4005.20	4007.10
39300	4009.00	4010.90	4012.80	4014.70	4016.60	4018.50	4020.40	4022.30	4024.20	4026.10
39400	4028.00	4029.90	4031.80	4033.70	4035.60	4037.50	4039.40	4041.30	4043.20	4045.10
39500	4047.00	4048.90	4050.80	4052.70	4054.60	4056.50	4058.40	4060.30	4062.20	4064.10
39600	4066.00	4067.90	4069.80	4071.70	4073.60	4075.50	4077.40	4079.30	4081.20	4083.10
39700	4085.00	4086.90	4088.80	4090.70	4092.60	4094.50	4096.40	4098.30	4100.20	4102.10
39800	4104.00	4105.90	4107.80	4109.70	4111.60	4113.50	4115.40	4117.30	4119.20	4121.10
39900	4123.00	4124.90	4126.80	4128.70	4130.60	4132.50	4134.40	4136.30	4138.20	4140.10
40000	4142.00	4143.90	4145.80	4147.70	4149.60	4151.50	4153.40	4155.30	4157.20	4159.10
40100	4161.00	4162.90	4164.80	4166.70	4168.60	4170.50	4172.40	4174.30	4176.20	4178.10
40200	4180.00	4181.90	4183.80	4185.70	4187.60	4189.50	4191.40	4193.30	4195.20	4197.10
40300	4199.00	4200.90	4202.80	4204.70	4206.60	4208.50	4210.40	4212.30	4214.20	4216.10
40400	4218.00	4219.90	4221.80	4223.70	4225.60	4227.50	4229.40	4231.30	4233.20	4235.10
40500	4237.00	4238.90	4240.80	4242.70	4244.60	4246.50	4248.40	4250.30	4252.20	4254.10
40600	4256.00	4257.90	4259.80	4261.70	4263.60	4265.50	4267.40	4269.30	4271.20	4273.10
40700	4275.00	4276.90	4278.80	4280.70	4282.60	4284.50	4286.40	4288.30	4290.20	4292.10
40800	4294.00	4295.90	4297.80	4299.70	4301.60	4303.50	4305.40	4307.30	4309.20	4311.10
40900	4313.00	4314.90	4316.80	4318.70	4320.60	4322.50	4324.40	4326.30	4328.20	4330.10
41000	4332.00	4333.90	4335.80	4337.70	4339.60	4341.50	4343.40	4345.30	4347.20	4349.10
41100	4351.00	4352.90	4354.80	4356.70	4358.60	4360.50	4362.40	4364.30	4366.20	4368.10
41200	4370.00	4371.90	4373.80	4375.70	4377.60	4379.50	4381.40	4383.30	4385.20	4387.10
41300	4389.00	4390.90	4392.80	4394.70	4396.60	4398.50	4400.40	4402.30	4404.20	4406.10
41400	4408.00	4409.90	4411.80	4413.70	4415.60	4417.50	4419.40	4421.30	4423.20	4425.10
41500	4427.00	4428.90	4430.80	4432.70	4434.60	4436.50	4438.40	4440.30	4442.20	4444.10
41600	4446.00	4447.90	4449.80	4451.70	4453.60	4455.50	4457.40	4459.30	4461.20	4463.10

To the above amounts, add the appropriate figure for the odd dollar amount

$1	$2	$3	$4	$5	$6	$7	$8	$9
0.19	0.38	0.57	0.76	0.95	1.14	1.33	1.52	1.71

***Tax offsets must be deducted, and Medicare levy added, to give net tax payable (see notes at ¶42-000)**

Resident Individuals: Gross Tax Payable at 2020–21 Rates*

Taxable income	$0	$10	$20	$30	$40	$50	$60	$70	$80	$90
41700	4465.00	4466.90	4468.80	4470.70	4472.60	4474.50	4476.40	4478.30	4480.20	4482.10
41800	4484.00	4485.90	4487.80	4489.70	4491.60	4493.50	4495.40	4497.30	4499.20	4501.10
41900	4503.00	4504.90	4506.80	4508.70	4510.60	4512.50	4514.40	4516.30	4518.20	4520.10
42000	4522.00	4523.90	4525.80	4527.70	4529.60	4531.50	4533.40	4535.30	4537.20	4539.10
42100	4541.00	4542.90	4544.80	4546.70	4548.60	4550.50	4552.40	4554.30	4556.20	4558.10
42200	4560.00	4561.90	4563.80	4565.70	4567.60	4569.50	4571.40	4573.30	4575.20	4577.10
42300	4579.00	4580.90	4582.80	4584.70	4586.60	4588.50	4590.40	4592.30	4594.20	4596.10
42400	4598.00	4599.90	4601.80	4603.70	4605.60	4607.50	4609.40	4611.30	4613.20	4615.10
42500	4617.00	4618.90	4620.80	4622.70	4624.60	4626.50	4628.40	4630.30	4632.20	4634.10
42600	4636.00	4637.90	4639.80	4641.70	4643.60	4645.50	4647.40	4649.30	4651.20	4653.10

To the above amounts, add the appropriate figure for the odd dollar amount

$1	$2	$3	$4	$5	$6	$7	$8	$9
0.19	0.38	0.57	0.76	0.95	1.14	1.33	1.52	1.71

***Tax offsets must be deducted, and Medicare levy added, to give net tax payable (see notes at ¶42-000)**

Resident Individuals: Gross Tax Payable at 2020–21 Rates*

Taxable income	$0	$10	$20	$30	$40	$50	$60	$70	$80	$90
42700	4655.00	4656.90	4658.80	4660.70	4662.60	4664.50	4666.40	4668.30	4670.20	4672.10
42800	4674.00	4675.90	4677.80	4679.70	4681.60	4683.50	4685.40	4687.30	4689.20	4691.10
42900	4693.00	4694.90	4696.80	4698.70	4700.60	4702.50	4704.40	4706.30	4708.20	4710.10
43000	4712.00	4713.90	4715.80	4717.70	4719.60	4721.50	4723.40	4725.30	4727.20	4729.10
43100	4731.00	4732.90	4734.80	4736.70	4738.60	4740.50	4742.40	4744.30	4746.20	4748.10
43200	4750.00	4751.90	4753.80	4755.70	4757.60	4759.50	4761.40	4763.30	4765.20	4767.10
43300	4769.00	4770.90	4772.80	4774.70	4776.60	4778.50	4780.40	4782.30	4784.20	4786.10
43400	4788.00	4789.90	4791.80	4793.70	4795.60	4797.50	4799.40	4801.30	4803.20	4805.10
43500	4807.00	4808.90	4810.80	4812.70	4814.60	4816.50	4818.40	4820.30	4822.20	4824.10
43600	4826.00	4827.90	4829.80	4831.70	4833.60	4835.50	4837.40	4839.30	4841.20	4843.10
43700	4845.00	4846.90	4848.80	4850.70	4852.60	4854.50	4856.40	4858.30	4860.20	4862.10
43800	4864.00	4865.90	4867.80	4869.70	4871.60	4873.50	4875.40	4877.30	4879.20	4881.10
43900	4883.00	4884.90	4886.80	4888.70	4890.60	4892.50	4894.40	4896.30	4898.20	4900.10
44000	4902.00	4903.90	4905.80	4907.70	4909.60	4911.50	4913.40	4915.30	4917.20	4919.10
44100	4921.00	4922.90	4924.80	4926.70	4928.60	4930.50	4932.40	4934.30	4936.20	4938.10
44200	4940.00	4941.90	4943.80	4945.70	4947.60	4949.50	4951.40	4953.30	4955.20	4957.10
44300	4959.00	4960.90	4962.80	4964.70	4966.60	4968.50	4970.40	4972.30	4974.20	4976.10
44400	4978.00	4979.90	4981.80	4983.70	4985.60	4987.50	4989.40	4991.30	4993.20	4995.10
44500	4997.00	4998.90	5000.80	5002.70	5004.60	5006.50	5008.40	5010.30	5012.20	5014.10
44600	5016.00	5017.90	5019.80	5021.70	5023.60	5025.50	5027.40	5029.30	5031.20	5033.10
44700	5035.00	5036.90	5038.80	5040.70	5042.60	5044.50	5046.40	5048.30	5050.20	5052.10
44800	5054.00	5055.90	5057.80	5059.70	5061.60	5063.50	5065.40	5067.30	5069.20	5071.10
44900	5073.00	5074.90	5076.80	5078.70	5080.60	5082.50	5084.40	5086.30	5088.20	5090.10

To the above amounts, add the appropriate figure for the odd dollar amount

$1	$2	$3	$4	$5	$6	$7	$8	$9
0.32	0.65	0.98	1.30	1.63	1.95	2.27	2.60	2.93

***Tax offsets must be deducted, and Medicare levy added, to give net tax payable**
(see notes at ¶42-000)

Resident Individuals: Gross Tax Payable at 2020–21 Rates*

Taxable income	$0	$10	$20	$30	$40	$50	$60	$70	$80	$90
45000	5092.00	5095.25	5098.50	5101.75	5105.00	5108.25	5111.50	5114.75	5118.00	5121.25
45100	5124.50	5127.75	5131.00	5134.25	5137.50	5140.75	5144.00	5147.25	5150.50	5153.75
45200	5157.00	5160.25	5163.50	5166.75	5170.00	5173.25	5176.50	5179.75	5183.00	5186.25
45300	5189.50	5192.75	5196.00	5199.25	5202.50	5205.75	5209.00	5212.25	5215.50	5218.75
45400	5222.00	5225.25	5228.50	5231.75	5235.00	5238.25	5241.50	5244.75	5248.00	5251.25
45500	5254.50	5257.75	5261.00	5264.25	5267.50	5270.75	5274.00	5277.25	5280.50	5283.75
45600	5287.00	5290.25	5293.50	5296.75	5300.00	5303.25	5306.50	5309.75	5313.00	5316.25
45700	5319.50	5322.75	5326.00	5329.25	5332.50	5335.75	5339.00	5342.25	5345.50	5348.75
45800	5352.00	5355.25	5358.50	5361.75	5365.00	5368.25	5371.50	5374.75	5378.00	5381.25
45900	5384.50	5387.75	5391.00	5394.25	5397.50	5400.75	5404.00	5407.25	5410.50	5413.75
46000	5417.00	5420.25	5423.50	5426.75	5430.00	5433.25	5436.50	5439.75	5443.00	5446.25
46100	5449.50	5452.75	5456.00	5459.25	5462.50	5465.75	5469.00	5472.25	5475.50	5478.75
46200	5482.00	5485.25	5488.50	5491.75	5495.00	5498.25	5501.50	5504.75	5508.00	5511.25
46300	5514.50	5517.75	5521.00	5524.25	5527.50	5530.75	5534.00	5537.25	5540.50	5543.75
46400	5547.00	5550.25	5553.50	5556.75	5560.00	5563.25	5566.50	5569.75	5573.00	5576.25
46500	5579.50	5582.75	5586.00	5589.25	5592.50	5595.75	5599.00	5602.25	5605.50	5608.75
46600	5612.00	5615.25	5618.50	5621.75	5625.00	5628.25	5631.50	5634.75	5638.00	5641.25
46700	5644.50	5647.75	5651.00	5654.25	5657.50	5660.75	5664.00	5667.25	5670.50	5673.75
46800	5677.00	5680.25	5683.50	5686.75	5690.00	5693.25	5696.50	5699.75	5703.00	5706.25
46900	5709.50	5712.75	5716.00	5719.25	5722.50	5725.75	5729.00	5732.25	5735.50	5738.75
47000	5742.00	5745.25	5748.50	5751.75	5755.00	5758.25	5761.50	5764.75	5768.00	5771.25
47100	5774.50	5777.75	5781.00	5784.25	5787.50	5790.75	5794.00	5797.25	5800.50	5803.75
47200	5807.00	5810.25	5813.50	5816.75	5820.00	5823.25	5826.50	5829.75	5833.00	5836.25
47300	5839.50	5842.75	5846.00	5849.25	5852.50	5855.75	5859.00	5862.25	5865.50	5868.75
47400	5872.00	5875.25	5878.50	5881.75	5885.00	5888.25	5891.50	5894.75	5898.00	5901.25
47500	5904.50	5907.75	5911.00	5914.25	5917.50	5920.75	5924.00	5927.25	5930.50	5933.75
47600	5937.00	5940.25	5943.50	5946.75	5950.00	5953.25	5956.50	5959.75	5963.00	5966.25
47700	5969.50	5972.75	5976.00	5979.25	5982.50	5985.75	5989.00	5992.25	5995.50	5998.75
47800	6002.00	6005.25	6008.50	6011.75	6015.00	6018.25	6021.50	6024.75	6028.00	6031.25
47900	6034.50	6037.75	6041.00	6044.25	6047.50	6050.75	6054.00	6057.25	6060.50	6063.75
48000	6067.00	6070.25	6073.50	6076.75	6080.00	6083.25	6086.50	6089.75	6093.00	6096.25
48100	6099.50	6102.75	6106.00	6109.25	6112.50	6115.75	6119.00	6122.25	6125.50	6128.75
48200	6132.00	6135.25	6138.50	6141.75	6145.00	6148.25	6151.50	6154.75	6158.00	6161.25
48300	6164.50	6167.75	6171.00	6174.25	6177.50	6180.75	6184.00	6187.25	6190.50	6193.75
48400	6197.00	6200.25	6203.50	6206.75	6210.00	6213.25	6216.50	6219.75	6223.00	6226.25
48500	6229.50	6232.75	6236.00	6239.25	6242.50	6245.75	6249.00	6252.25	6255.50	6258.75
48600	6262.00	6265.25	6268.50	6271.75	6275.00	6278.25	6281.50	6284.75	6288.00	6291.25
48700	6294.50	6297.75	6301.00	6304.25	6307.50	6310.75	6314.00	6317.25	6320.50	6323.75
48800	6327.00	6330.25	6333.50	6336.75	6340.00	6343.25	6346.50	6349.75	6353.00	6356.25
48900	6359.50	6362.75	6366.00	6369.25	6372.50	6375.75	6379.00	6382.25	6385.50	6388.75
49000	6392.00	6395.25	6398.50	6401.75	6405.00	6408.25	6411.50	6414.75	6418.00	6421.25
49100	6424.50	6427.75	6431.00	6434.25	6437.50	6440.75	6444.00	6447.25	6450.50	6453.75
49200	6457.00	6460.25	6463.50	6466.75	6470.00	6473.25	6476.50	6479.75	6483.00	6486.25
49300	6489.50	6492.75	6496.00	6499.25	6502.50	6505.75	6509.00	6512.25	6515.50	6518.75
49400	6522.00	6525.25	6528.50	6531.75	6535.00	6538.25	6541.50	6544.75	6548.00	6551.25
49500	6554.50	6557.75	6561.00	6564.25	6567.50	6570.75	6574.00	6577.25	6580.50	6583.75
49600	6587.00	6590.25	6593.50	6596.75	6600.00	6603.25	6606.50	6609.75	6613.00	6616.25
49700	6619.50	6622.75	6626.00	6629.25	6632.50	6635.75	6639.00	6642.25	6645.50	6648.75
49800	6652.00	6655.25	6658.50	6661.75	6665.00	6668.25	6671.50	6674.75	6678.00	6681.25
49900	6684.50	6687.75	6691.00	6694.25	6697.50	6700.75	6704.00	6707.25	6710.50	6713.75

To the above amounts, add the appropriate figure for the odd dollar amount

$1	$2	$3	$4	$5	$6	$7	$8	$9
0.325	0.65	0.975	1.30	1.625	1.95	2.275	2.60	2.925

***Tax offsets must be deducted, and Medicare levy added, to give net tax payable (see notes at ¶42-000)**

Resident Individuals: Gross Tax Payable at 2020–21 Rates*

Taxable income	$0	$10	$20	$30	$40	$50	$60	$70	$80	$90
50000	6717.00	6720.25	6723.50	6726.75	6730.00	6733.25	6736.50	6739.75	6743.00	6746.25
50100	6749.50	6752.75	6756.00	6759.25	6762.50	6765.75	6769.00	6772.25	6775.50	6778.75
50200	6782.00	6785.25	6788.50	6791.75	6795.00	6798.25	6801.50	6804.75	6808.00	6811.25
50300	6814.50	6817.75	6821.00	6824.25	6827.50	6830.75	6834.00	6837.25	6840.50	6843.75
50400	6847.00	6850.25	6853.50	6856.75	6860.00	6863.25	6866.50	6869.75	6873.00	6876.25
50500	6879.50	6882.75	6886.00	6889.25	6892.50	6895.75	6899.00	6902.25	6905.50	6908.75
50600	6912.00	6915.25	6918.50	6921.75	6925.00	6928.25	6931.50	6934.75	6938.00	6941.25
50700	6944.50	6947.75	6951.00	6954.25	6957.50	6960.75	6964.00	6967.25	6970.50	6973.75
50800	6977.00	6980.25	6983.50	6986.75	6990.00	6993.25	6996.50	6999.75	7003.00	7006.25
50900	7009.50	7012.75	7016.00	7019.25	7022.50	7025.75	7029.00	7032.25	7035.50	7038.75
51000	7042.00	7045.25	7048.50	7051.75	7055.00	7058.25	7061.50	7064.75	7068.00	7071.25
51100	7074.50	7077.75	7081.00	7084.25	7087.50	7090.75	7094.00	7097.25	7100.50	7103.75
51200	7107.00	7110.25	7113.50	7116.75	7120.00	7123.25	7126.50	7129.75	7133.00	7136.25
51300	7139.50	7142.75	7146.00	7149.25	7152.50	7155.75	7159.00	7162.25	7165.50	7168.75
51400	7172.00	7175.25	7178.50	7181.75	7185.00	7188.25	7191.50	7194.75	7198.00	7201.25
51500	7204.50	7207.75	7211.00	7214.25	7217.50	7220.75	7224.00	7227.25	7230.50	7233.75
51600	7237.00	7240.25	7243.50	7246.75	7250.00	7253.25	7256.50	7259.75	7263.00	7266.25
51700	7269.50	7272.75	7276.00	7279.25	7282.50	7285.75	7289.00	7292.25	7295.50	7298.75
51800	7302.00	7305.25	7308.50	7311.75	7315.00	7318.25	7321.50	7324.75	7328.00	7331.25
51900	7334.50	7337.75	7341.00	7344.25	7347.50	7350.75	7354.00	7357.25	7360.50	7363.75
52000	7367.00	7370.25	7373.50	7376.75	7380.00	7383.25	7386.50	7389.75	7393.00	7396.25
52100	7399.50	7402.75	7406.00	7409.25	7412.50	7415.75	7419.00	7422.25	7425.50	7428.75
52200	7432.00	7435.25	7438.50	7441.75	7445.00	7448.25	7451.50	7454.75	7458.00	7461.25
52300	7464.50	7467.75	7471.00	7474.25	7477.50	7480.75	7484.00	7487.25	7490.50	7493.75
52400	7497.00	7500.25	7503.50	7506.75	7510.00	7513.25	7516.50	7519.75	7523.00	7526.25
52500	7529.50	7532.75	7536.00	7539.25	7542.50	7545.75	7549.00	7552.25	7555.50	7558.75
52600	7562.00	7565.25	7568.50	7571.75	7575.00	7578.25	7581.50	7584.75	7588.00	7591.25
52700	7594.50	7597.75	7601.00	7604.25	7607.50	7610.75	7614.00	7617.25	7620.50	7623.75
52800	7627.00	7630.25	7633.50	7636.75	7640.00	7643.25	7646.50	7649.75	7653.00	7656.25
52900	7659.50	7662.75	7666.00	7669.25	7672.50	7675.75	7679.00	7682.25	7685.50	7688.75
53000	7692.00	7695.25	7698.50	7701.75	7705.00	7708.25	7711.50	7714.75	7718.00	7721.25
53100	7724.50	7727.75	7731.00	7734.25	7737.50	7740.75	7744.00	7747.25	7750.50	7753.75
53200	7757.00	7760.25	7763.50	7766.75	7770.00	7773.25	7776.50	7779.75	7783.00	7786.25
53300	7789.50	7792.75	7796.00	7799.25	7802.50	7805.75	7809.00	7812.25	7815.50	7818.75
53400	7822.00	7825.25	7828.50	7831.75	7835.00	7838.25	7841.50	7844.75	7848.00	7851.25
53500	7854.50	7857.75	7861.00	7864.25	7867.50	7870.75	7874.00	7877.25	7880.50	7883.75
53600	7887.00	7890.25	7893.50	7896.75	7900.00	7903.25	7906.50	7909.75	7913.00	7916.25
53700	7919.50	7922.75	7926.00	7929.25	7932.50	7935.75	7939.00	7942.25	7945.50	7948.75
53800	7952.00	7955.25	7958.50	7961.75	7965.00	7968.25	7971.50	7974.75	7978.00	7981.25
53900	7984.50	7987.75	7991.00	7994.25	7997.50	8000.75	8004.00	8007.25	8010.50	8013.75
54000	8017.00	8020.25	8023.50	8026.75	8030.00	8033.25	8036.50	8039.75	8043.00	8046.25
54100	8049.50	8052.75	8056.00	8059.25	8062.50	8065.75	8069.00	8072.25	8075.50	8078.75
54200	8082.00	8085.25	8088.50	8091.75	8095.00	8098.25	8101.50	8104.75	8108.00	8111.25
54300	8114.50	8117.75	8121.00	8124.25	8127.50	8130.75	8134.00	8137.25	8140.50	8143.75
54400	8147.00	8150.25	8153.50	8156.75	8160.00	8163.25	8166.50	8169.75	8173.00	8176.25
54500	8179.50	8182.75	8186.00	8189.25	8192.50	8195.75	8199.00	8202.25	8205.50	8208.75
54600	8212.00	8215.25	8218.50	8221.75	8225.00	8228.25	8231.50	8234.75	8238.00	8241.25
54700	8244.50	8247.75	8251.00	8254.25	8257.50	8260.75	8264.00	8267.25	8270.50	8273.75
54800	8277.00	8280.25	8283.50	8286.75	8290.00	8293.25	8296.50	8299.75	8303.00	8306.25
54900	8309.50	8312.75	8316.00	8319.25	8322.50	8325.75	8329.00	8332.25	8335.50	8338.75

To the above amounts, add the appropriate figure for the odd dollar amount

$1	$2	$3	$4	$5	$6	$7	$8	$9
0.325	0.65	0.975	1.30	1.625	1.95	2.275	2.60	2.925

***Tax offsets must be deducted, and Medicare levy added, to give net tax payable (see notes at ¶42-000)**

Resident Individuals: Gross Tax Payable at 2020–21 Rates*

Taxable income	$0	$10	$20	$30	$40	$50	$60	$70	$80	$90
55000	8342.00	8345.25	8348.50	8351.75	8355.00	8358.25	8361.50	8364.75	8368.00	8371.25
55100	8374.50	8377.75	8381.00	8384.25	8387.50	8390.75	8394.00	8397.25	8400.50	8403.75
55200	8407.00	8410.25	8413.50	8416.75	8420.00	8423.25	8426.50	8429.75	8433.00	8436.25
55300	8439.50	8442.75	8446.00	8449.25	8452.50	8455.75	8459.00	8462.25	8465.50	8468.75
55400	8472.00	8475.25	8478.50	8481.75	8485.00	8488.25	8491.50	8494.75	8498.00	8501.25
55500	8504.50	8507.75	8511.00	8514.25	8517.50	8520.75	8524.00	8527.25	8530.50	8533.75
55600	8537.00	8540.25	8543.50	8546.75	8550.00	8553.25	8556.50	8559.75	8563.00	8566.25
55700	8569.50	8572.75	8576.00	8579.25	8582.50	8585.75	8589.00	8592.25	8595.50	8598.75
55800	8602.00	8605.25	8608.50	8611.75	8615.00	8618.25	8621.50	8624.75	8628.00	8631.25
55900	8634.50	8637.75	8641.00	8644.25	8647.50	8650.75	8654.00	8657.25	8660.50	8663.75
56000	8667.00	8670.25	8673.50	8676.75	8680.00	8683.25	8686.50	8689.75	8693.00	8696.25
56100	8699.50	8702.75	8706.00	8709.25	8712.50	8715.75	8719.00	8722.25	8725.50	8728.75
56200	8732.00	8735.25	8738.50	8741.75	8745.00	8748.25	8751.50	8754.75	8758.00	8761.25
56300	8764.50	8767.75	8771.00	8774.25	8777.50	8780.75	8784.00	8787.25	8790.50	8793.75
56400	8797.00	8800.25	8803.50	8806.75	8810.00	8813.25	8816.50	8819.75	8823.00	8826.25
56500	8829.50	8832.75	8836.00	8839.25	8842.50	8845.75	8849.00	8852.25	8855.50	8858.75
56600	8862.00	8865.25	8868.50	8871.75	8875.00	8878.25	8881.50	8884.75	8888.00	8891.25
56700	8894.50	8897.75	8901.00	8904.25	8907.50	8910.75	8914.00	8917.25	8920.50	8923.75
56800	8927.00	8930.25	8933.50	8936.75	8940.00	8943.25	8946.50	8949.75	8953.00	8956.25
56900	8959.50	8962.75	8966.00	8969.25	8972.50	8975.75	8979.00	8982.25	8985.50	8988.75
57000	8992.00	8995.25	8998.50	9001.75	9005.00	9008.25	9011.50	9014.75	9018.00	9021.25
57100	9024.50	9027.75	9031.00	9034.25	9037.50	9040.75	9044.00	9047.25	9050.50	9053.75
57200	9057.00	9060.25	9063.50	9066.75	9070.00	9073.25	9076.50	9079.75	9083.00	9086.25
57300	9089.50	9092.75	9096.00	9099.25	9102.50	9105.75	9109.00	9112.25	9115.50	9118.75
57400	9122.00	9125.25	9128.50	9131.75	9135.00	9138.25	9141.50	9144.75	9148.00	9151.25
57500	9154.50	9157.75	9161.00	9164.25	9167.50	9170.75	9174.00	9177.25	9180.50	9183.75
57600	9187.00	9190.25	9193.50	9196.75	9200.00	9203.25	9206.50	9209.75	9213.00	9216.25
57700	9219.50	9222.75	9226.00	9229.25	9232.50	9235.75	9239.00	9242.25	9245.50	9248.75
57800	9252.00	9255.25	9258.50	9261.75	9265.00	9268.25	9271.50	9274.75	9278.00	9281.25
57900	9284.50	9287.75	9291.00	9294.25	9297.50	9300.75	9304.00	9307.25	9310.50	9313.75
58000	9317.00	9320.25	9323.50	9326.75	9330.00	9333.25	9336.50	9339.75	9343.00	9346.25
58100	9349.50	9352.75	9356.00	9359.25	9362.50	9365.75	9369.00	9372.25	9375.50	9378.75
58200	9382.00	9385.25	9388.50	9391.75	9395.00	9398.25	9401.50	9404.75	9408.00	9411.25
58300	9414.50	9417.75	9421.00	9424.25	9427.50	9430.75	9434.00	9437.25	9440.50	9443.75
58400	9447.00	9450.25	9453.50	9456.75	9460.00	9463.25	9466.50	9469.75	9473.00	9476.25
58500	9479.50	9482.75	9486.00	9489.25	9492.50	9495.75	9499.00	9502.25	9505.50	9508.75
58600	9512.00	9515.25	9518.50	9521.75	9525.00	9528.25	9531.50	9534.75	9538.00	9541.25
58700	9544.50	9547.75	9551.00	9554.25	9557.50	9560.75	9564.00	9567.25	9570.50	9573.75
58800	9577.00	9580.25	9583.50	9586.75	9590.00	9593.25	9596.50	9599.75	9603.00	9606.25
58900	9609.50	9612.75	9616.00	9619.25	9622.50	9625.75	9629.00	9632.25	9635.50	9638.75
59000	9642.00	9645.25	9648.50	9651.75	9655.00	9658.25	9661.50	9664.75	9668.00	9671.25
59100	9674.50	9677.75	9681.00	9684.25	9687.50	9690.75	9694.00	9697.25	9700.50	9703.75
59200	9707.00	9710.25	9713.50	9716.75	9720.00	9723.25	9726.50	9729.75	9733.00	9736.25
59300	9739.50	9742.75	9746.00	9749.25	9752.50	9755.75	9759.00	9762.25	9765.50	9768.75
59400	9772.00	9775.25	9778.50	9781.75	9785.00	9788.25	9791.50	9794.75	9798.00	9801.25
59500	9804.50	9807.75	9811.00	9814.25	9817.50	9820.75	9824.00	9827.25	9830.50	9833.75
59600	9837.00	9840.25	9843.50	9846.75	9850.00	9853.25	9856.50	9859.75	9863.00	9866.25
59700	9869.50	9872.75	9876.00	9879.25	9882.50	9885.75	9889.00	9892.25	9895.50	9898.75
59800	9902.00	9905.25	9908.50	9911.75	9915.00	9918.25	9921.50	9924.75	9928.00	9931.25
59900	9934.50	9937.75	9941.00	9944.25	9947.50	9950.75	9954.00	9957.25	9960.50	9963.75

To the above amounts, add the appropriate figure for the odd dollar amount

$1	$2	$3	$4	$5	$6	$7	$8	$9
0.325	0.65	0.975	1.30	1.625	1.95	2.275	2.60	2.925

***Tax offsets must be deducted, and Medicare levy added, to give net tax payable (see notes at ¶42-000)**

Resident Individuals: Gross Tax Payable at 2020–21 Rates*

Taxable income	$0	$10	$20	$30	$40	$50	$60	$70	$80	$90
60000	9967.00	9970.25	9973.50	9976.75	9980.00	9983.25	9986.50	9989.75	9993.00	9996.25
60100	9999.50	10002.75	10006.00	10009.25	10012.50	10015.75	10019.00	10022.25	10025.50	10028.75
60200	10032.00	10035.25	10038.50	10041.75	10045.00	10048.25	10051.50	10054.75	10058.00	10061.25
60300	10064.50	10067.75	10071.00	10074.25	10077.50	10080.75	10084.00	10087.25	10090.50	10093.75
60400	10097.00	10100.25	10103.50	10106.75	10110.00	10113.25	10116.50	10119.75	10123.00	10126.25
60500	10129.50	10132.75	10136.00	10139.25	10142.50	10145.75	10149.00	10152.25	10155.50	10158.75
60600	10162.00	10165.25	10168.50	10171.75	10175.00	10178.25	10181.50	10184.75	10188.00	10191.25
60700	10194.50	10197.75	10201.00	10204.25	10207.50	10210.75	10214.00	10217.25	10220.50	10223.75
60800	10227.00	10230.25	10233.50	10236.75	10240.00	10243.25	10246.50	10249.75	10253.00	10256.25
60900	10259.50	10262.75	10266.00	10269.25	10272.50	10275.75	10279.00	10282.25	10285.50	10288.75
61000	10292.00	10295.25	10298.50	10301.75	10305.00	10308.25	10311.50	10314.75	10318.00	10321.25
61100	10324.50	10327.75	10331.00	10334.25	10337.50	10340.75	10344.00	10347.25	10350.50	10353.75
61200	10357.00	10360.25	10363.50	10366.75	10370.00	10373.25	10376.50	10379.75	10383.00	10386.25
61300	10389.50	10392.75	10396.00	10399.25	10402.50	10405.75	10409.00	10412.25	10415.50	10418.75
61400	10422.00	10425.25	10428.50	10431.75	10435.00	10438.25	10441.50	10444.75	10448.00	10451.25
61500	10454.50	10457.75	10461.00	10464.25	10467.50	10470.75	10474.00	10477.25	10480.50	10483.75
61600	10487.00	10490.25	10493.50	10496.75	10500.00	10503.25	10506.50	10509.75	10513.00	10516.25
61700	10519.50	10522.75	10526.00	10529.25	10532.50	10535.75	10539.00	10542.25	10545.50	10548.75
61800	10552.00	10555.25	10558.50	10561.75	10565.00	10568.25	10571.50	10574.75	10578.00	10581.25
61900	10584.50	10587.75	10591.00	10594.25	10597.50	10600.75	10604.00	10607.25	10610.50	10613.75
62000	10617.00	10620.25	10623.50	10626.75	10630.00	10633.25	10636.50	10639.75	10643.00	10646.25
62100	10649.50	10652.75	10656.00	10659.25	10662.50	10665.75	10669.00	10672.25	10675.50	10678.75
62200	10682.00	10685.25	10688.50	10691.75	10695.00	10698.25	10701.50	10704.75	10708.00	10711.25
62300	10714.50	10717.75	10721.00	10724.25	10727.50	10730.75	10734.00	10737.25	10740.50	10743.75
62400	10747.00	10750.25	10753.50	10756.75	10760.00	10763.25	10766.50	10769.75	10773.00	10776.25
62500	10779.50	10782.75	10786.00	10789.25	10792.50	10795.75	10799.00	10802.25	10805.50	10808.75
62600	10812.00	10815.25	10818.50	10821.75	10825.00	10828.25	10831.50	10834.75	10838.00	10841.25
62700	10844.50	10847.75	10851.00	10854.25	10857.50	10860.75	10864.00	10867.25	10870.50	10873.75
62800	10877.00	10880.25	10883.50	10886.75	10890.00	10893.25	10896.50	10899.75	10903.00	10906.25
62900	10909.50	10912.75	10916.00	10919.25	10922.50	10925.75	10929.00	10932.25	10935.50	10938.75
63000	10942.00	10945.25	10948.50	10951.75	10955.00	10958.25	10961.50	10964.75	10968.00	10971.25
63100	10974.50	10977.75	10981.00	10984.25	10987.50	10990.75	10994.00	10997.25	11000.50	11003.75
63200	11007.00	11010.25	11013.50	11016.75	11020.00	11023.25	11026.50	11029.75	11033.00	11036.25
63300	11039.50	11042.75	11046.00	11049.25	11052.50	11055.75	11059.00	11062.25	11065.50	11068.75
63400	11072.00	11075.25	11078.50	11081.75	11085.00	11088.25	11091.50	11094.75	11098.00	11101.25
63500	11104.50	11107.75	11111.00	11114.25	11117.50	11120.75	11124.00	11127.25	11130.50	11133.75
63600	11137.00	11140.25	11143.50	11146.75	11150.00	11153.25	11156.50	11159.75	11163.00	11166.25
63700	11169.50	11172.75	11176.00	11179.25	11182.50	11185.75	11189.00	11192.25	11195.50	11198.75
63800	11202.00	11205.25	11208.50	11211.75	11215.00	11218.25	11221.50	11224.75	11228.00	11231.25
63900	11234.50	11237.75	11241.00	11244.25	11247.50	11250.75	11254.00	11257.25	11260.50	11263.75
64000	11267.00	11270.25	11273.50	11276.75	11280.00	11283.25	11286.50	11289.75	11293.00	11296.25
64100	11299.50	11302.75	11306.00	11309.25	11312.50	11315.75	11319.00	11322.25	11325.50	11328.75
64200	11332.00	11335.25	11338.50	11341.75	11345.00	11348.25	11351.50	11354.75	11358.00	11361.25
64300	11364.50	11367.75	11371.00	11374.25	11377.50	11380.75	11384.00	11387.25	11390.50	11393.75
64400	11397.00	11400.25	11403.50	11406.75	11410.00	11413.25	11416.50	11419.75	11423.00	11426.25
64500	11429.50	11432.75	11436.00	11439.25	11442.50	11445.75	11449.00	11452.25	11455.50	11458.75
64600	11462.00	11465.25	11468.50	11471.75	11475.00	11478.25	11481.50	11484.75	11488.00	11491.25
64700	11494.50	11497.75	11501.00	11504.25	11507.50	11510.75	11514.00	11517.25	11520.50	11523.75
64800	11527.00	11530.25	11533.50	11536.75	11540.00	11543.25	11546.50	11549.75	11553.00	11556.25
64900	11559.50	11562.75	11566.00	11569.25	11572.50	11575.75	11579.00	11582.25	11585.50	11588.75

To the above amounts, add the appropriate figure for the odd dollar amount

$1	$2	$3	$4	$5	$6	$7	$8	$9
0.325	0.65	0.975	1.30	1.625	1.95	2.275	2.60	2.925

***Tax offsets must be deducted, and Medicare levy added, to give net tax payable (see notes at ¶42-000)**

Resident Individuals: Gross Tax Payable at 2020–21 Rates*

Taxable income	$0	$10	$20	$30	$40	$50	$60	$70	$80	$90
65000	11592.00	11595.25	11598.50	11601.75	11605.00	11608.25	11611.50	11614.75	11618.00	11621.25
65100	11624.50	11627.75	11631.00	11634.25	11637.50	11640.75	11644.00	11647.25	11650.50	11653.75
65200	11657.00	11660.25	11663.50	11666.75	11670.00	11673.25	11676.50	11679.75	11683.00	11686.25
65300	11689.50	11692.75	11696.00	11699.25	11702.50	11705.75	11709.00	11712.25	11715.50	11718.75
65400	11722.00	11725.25	11728.50	11731.75	11735.00	11738.25	11741.50	11744.75	11748.00	11751.25
65500	11754.50	11757.75	11761.00	11764.25	11767.50	11770.75	11774.00	11777.25	11780.50	11783.75
65600	11787.00	11790.25	11793.50	11796.75	11800.00	11803.25	11806.50	11809.75	11813.00	11816.25
65700	11819.50	11822.75	11826.00	11829.25	11832.50	11835.75	11839.00	11842.25	11845.50	11848.75
65800	11852.00	11855.25	11858.50	11861.75	11865.00	11868.25	11871.50	11874.75	11878.00	11881.25
65900	11884.50	11887.75	11891.00	11894.25	11897.50	11900.75	11904.00	11907.25	11910.50	11913.75
66000	11917.00	11920.25	11923.50	11926.75	11930.00	11933.25	11936.50	11939.75	11943.00	11946.25
66100	11949.50	11952.75	11956.00	11959.25	11962.50	11965.75	11969.00	11972.25	11975.50	11978.75
66200	11982.00	11985.25	11988.50	11991.75	11995.00	11998.25	12001.50	12004.75	12008.00	12011.25
66300	12014.50	12017.75	12021.00	12024.25	12027.50	12030.75	12034.00	12037.25	12040.50	12043.75
66400	12047.00	12050.25	12053.50	12056.75	12060.00	12063.25	12066.50	12069.75	12073.00	12076.25
66500	12079.50	12082.75	12086.00	12089.25	12092.50	12095.75	12099.00	12102.25	12105.50	12108.75
66600	12112.00	12115.25	12118.50	12121.75	12125.00	12128.25	12131.50	12134.75	12138.00	12141.25
66700	12144.50	12147.75	12151.00	12154.25	12157.50	12160.75	12164.00	12167.25	12170.50	12173.75
66800	12177.00	12180.25	12183.50	12186.75	12190.00	12193.25	12196.50	12199.75	12203.00	12206.25
66900	12209.50	12212.75	12216.00	12219.25	12222.50	12225.75	12229.00	12232.25	12235.50	12238.75
67000	12242.00	12245.25	12248.50	12251.75	12255.00	12258.25	12261.50	12264.75	12268.00	12271.25
67100	12274.50	12277.75	12281.00	12284.25	12287.50	12290.75	12294.00	12297.25	12300.50	12303.75
67200	12307.00	12310.25	12313.50	12316.75	12320.00	12323.25	12326.50	12329.75	12333.00	12336.25
67300	12339.50	12342.75	12346.00	12349.25	12352.50	12355.75	12359.00	12362.25	12365.50	12368.75
67400	12372.00	12375.25	12378.50	12381.75	12385.00	12388.25	12391.50	12394.75	12398.00	12401.25
67500	12404.50	12407.75	12411.00	12414.25	12417.50	12420.75	12424.00	12427.25	12430.50	12433.75
67600	12437.00	12440.25	12443.50	12446.75	12450.00	12453.25	12456.50	12459.75	12463.00	12466.25
67700	12469.50	12472.75	12476.00	12479.25	12482.50	12485.75	12489.00	12492.25	12495.50	12498.75
67800	12502.00	12505.25	12508.50	12511.75	12515.00	12518.25	12521.50	12524.75	12528.00	12531.25
67900	12534.50	12537.75	12541.00	12544.25	12547.50	12550.75	12554.00	12557.25	12560.50	12563.75
68000	12567.00	12570.25	12573.50	12576.75	12580.00	12583.25	12586.50	12589.75	12593.00	12596.25
68100	12599.50	12602.75	12606.00	12609.25	12612.50	12615.75	12619.00	12622.25	12625.50	12628.75
68200	12632.00	12635.25	12638.50	12641.75	12645.00	12648.25	12651.50	12654.75	12658.00	12661.25
68300	12664.50	12667.75	12671.00	12674.25	12677.50	12680.75	12684.00	12687.25	12690.50	12693.75
68400	12697.00	12700.25	12703.50	12706.75	12710.00	12713.25	12716.50	12719.75	12723.00	12726.25
68500	12729.50	12732.75	12736.00	12739.25	12742.50	12745.75	12749.00	12752.25	12755.50	12758.75
68600	12762.00	12765.25	12768.50	12771.75	12775.00	12778.25	12781.50	12784.75	12788.00	12791.25
68700	12794.50	12797.75	12801.00	12804.25	12807.50	12810.75	12814.00	12817.25	12820.50	12823.75
68800	12827.00	12830.25	12833.50	12836.75	12840.00	12843.25	12846.50	12849.75	12853.00	12856.25
68900	12859.50	12862.75	12866.00	12869.25	12872.50	12875.75	12879.00	12882.25	12885.50	12888.75
69000	12892.00	12895.25	12898.50	12901.75	12905.00	12908.25	12911.50	12914.75	12918.00	12921.25
69100	12924.50	12927.75	12931.00	12934.25	12937.50	12940.75	12944.00	12947.25	12950.50	12953.75
69200	12957.00	12960.25	12963.50	12966.75	12970.00	12973.25	12976.50	12979.75	12983.00	12986.25
69300	12989.50	12992.75	12996.00	12999.25	13002.50	13005.75	13009.00	13012.25	13015.50	13018.75
69400	13022.00	13025.25	13028.50	13031.75	13035.00	13038.25	13041.50	13044.75	13048.00	13051.25
69500	13054.50	13057.75	13061.00	13064.25	13067.50	13070.75	13074.00	13077.25	13080.50	13083.75
69600	13087.00	13090.25	13093.50	13096.75	13100.00	13103.25	13106.50	13109.75	13113.00	13116.25
69700	13119.50	13122.75	13126.00	13129.25	13132.50	13135.75	13139.00	13142.25	13145.50	13148.75
69800	13152.00	13155.25	13158.50	13161.75	13165.00	13168.25	13171.50	13174.75	13178.00	13181.25
69900	13184.50	13187.75	13191.00	13194.25	13197.50	13200.75	13204.00	13207.25	13210.50	13213.75

To the above amounts, add the appropriate figure for the odd dollar amount

$1	$2	$3	$4	$5	$6	$7	$8	$9
0.325	0.65	0.975	1.30	1.625	1.95	2.275	2.60	2.925

***Tax offsets must be deducted, and Medicare levy added, to give net tax payable (see notes at ¶42-000)**

Resident Individuals: Gross Tax Payable at 2020–21 Rates*

Taxable income	$0	$10	$20	$30	$40	$50	$60	$70	$80	$90
70000	13217.00	13220.25	13223.50	13226.75	13230.00	13233.25	13236.50	13239.75	13243.00	13246.25
70100	13249.50	13252.75	13256.00	13259.25	13262.50	13265.75	13269.00	13272.25	13275.50	13278.75
70200	13282.00	13285.25	13288.50	13291.75	13295.00	13298.25	13301.50	13304.75	13308.00	13311.25
70300	13314.50	13317.75	13321.00	13324.25	13327.50	13330.75	13334.00	13337.25	13340.50	13343.75
70400	13347.00	13350.25	13353.50	13356.75	13360.00	13363.25	13366.50	13369.75	13373.00	13376.25
70500	13379.50	13382.75	13386.00	13389.25	13392.50	13395.75	13399.00	13402.25	13405.50	13408.75
70600	13412.00	13415.25	13418.50	13421.75	13425.00	13428.25	13431.50	13434.75	13438.00	13441.25
70700	13444.50	13447.75	13451.00	13454.25	13457.50	13460.75	13464.00	13467.25	13470.50	13473.75
70800	13477.00	13480.25	13483.50	13486.75	13490.00	13493.25	13496.50	13499.75	13503.00	13506.25
70900	13509.50	13512.75	13516.00	13519.25	13522.50	13525.75	13529.00	13532.25	13535.50	13538.75
71000	13542.00	13545.25	13548.50	13551.75	13555.00	13558.25	13561.50	13564.75	13568.00	13571.25
71100	13574.50	13577.75	13581.00	13584.25	13587.50	13590.75	13594.00	13597.25	13600.50	13603.75
71200	13607.00	13610.25	13613.50	13616.75	13620.00	13623.25	13626.50	13629.75	13633.00	13636.25
71300	13639.50	13642.75	13646.00	13649.25	13652.50	13655.75	13659.00	13662.25	13665.50	13668.75
71400	13672.00	13675.25	13678.50	13681.75	13685.00	13688.25	13691.50	13694.75	13698.00	13701.25
71500	13704.50	13707.75	13711.00	13714.25	13717.50	13720.75	13724.00	13727.25	13730.50	13733.75
71600	13737.00	13740.25	13743.50	13746.75	13750.00	13753.25	13756.50	13759.75	13763.00	13766.25
71700	13769.50	13772.75	13776.00	13779.25	13782.50	13785.75	13789.00	13792.25	13795.50	13798.75
71800	13802.00	13805.25	13808.50	13811.75	13815.00	13818.25	13821.50	13824.75	13828.00	13831.25
71900	13834.50	13837.75	13841.00	13844.25	13847.50	13850.75	13854.00	13857.25	13860.50	13863.75
72000	13867.00	13870.25	13873.50	13876.75	13880.00	13883.25	13886.50	13889.75	13893.00	13896.25
72100	13899.50	13902.75	13906.00	13909.25	13912.50	13915.75	13919.00	13922.25	13925.50	13928.75
72200	13932.00	13935.25	13938.50	13941.75	13945.00	13948.25	13951.50	13954.75	13958.00	13961.25
72300	13964.50	13967.75	13971.00	13974.25	13977.50	13980.75	13984.00	13987.25	13990.50	13993.75
72400	13997.00	14000.25	14003.50	14006.75	14010.00	14013.25	14016.50	14019.75	14023.00	14026.25
72500	14029.50	14032.75	14036.00	14039.25	14042.50	14045.75	14049.00	14052.25	14055.50	14058.75
72600	14062.00	14065.25	14068.50	14071.75	14075.00	14078.25	14081.50	14084.75	14088.00	14091.25
72700	14094.50	14097.75	14101.00	14104.25	14107.50	14110.75	14114.00	14117.25	14120.50	14123.75
72800	14127.00	14130.25	14133.50	14136.75	14140.00	14143.25	14146.50	14149.75	14153.00	14156.25
72900	14159.50	14162.75	14166.00	14169.25	14172.50	14175.75	14179.00	14182.25	14185.50	14188.75
73000	14192.00	14195.25	14198.50	14201.75	14205.00	14208.25	14211.50	14214.75	14218.00	14221.25
73100	14224.50	14227.75	14231.00	14234.25	14237.50	14240.75	14244.00	14247.25	14250.50	14253.75
73200	14257.00	14260.25	14263.50	14266.75	14270.00	14273.25	14276.50	14279.75	14283.00	14286.25
73300	14289.50	14292.75	14296.00	14299.25	14302.50	14305.75	14309.00	14312.25	14315.50	14318.75
73400	14322.00	14325.25	14328.50	14331.75	14335.00	14338.25	14341.50	14344.75	14348.00	14351.25
73500	14354.50	14357.75	14361.00	14364.25	14367.50	14370.75	14374.00	14377.25	14380.50	14383.75
73600	14387.00	14390.25	14393.50	14396.75	14400.00	14403.25	14406.50	14409.75	14413.00	14416.25
73700	14419.50	14422.75	14426.00	14429.25	14432.50	14435.75	14439.00	14442.25	14445.50	14448.75
73800	14452.00	14455.25	14458.50	14461.75	14465.00	14468.25	14471.50	14474.75	14478.00	14481.25
73900	14484.50	14487.75	14491.00	14494.25	14497.50	14500.75	14504.00	14507.25	14510.50	14513.75
74000	14517.00	14520.25	14523.50	14526.75	14530.00	14533.25	14536.50	14539.75	14543.00	14546.25
74100	14549.50	14552.75	14556.00	14559.25	14562.50	14565.75	14569.00	14572.25	14575.50	14578.75
74200	14582.00	14585.25	14588.50	14591.75	14595.00	14598.25	14601.50	14604.75	14608.00	14611.25
74300	14614.50	14617.75	14621.00	14624.25	14627.50	14630.75	14634.00	14637.25	14640.50	14643.75
74400	14647.00	14650.25	14653.50	14656.75	14660.00	14663.25	14666.50	14669.75	14673.00	14676.25
74500	14679.50	14682.75	14686.00	14689.25	14692.50	14695.75	14699.00	14702.25	14705.50	14708.75
74600	14712.00	14715.25	14718.50	14721.75	14725.00	14728.25	14731.50	14734.75	14738.00	14741.25
74700	14744.50	14747.75	14751.00	14754.25	14757.50	14760.75	14764.00	14767.25	14770.50	14773.75
74800	14777.00	14780.25	14783.50	14786.75	14790.00	14793.25	14796.50	14799.75	14803.00	14806.25
74900	14809.50	14812.75	14816.00	14819.25	14822.50	14825.75	14829.00	14832.25	14835.50	14838.75

To the above amounts, add the appropriate figure for the odd dollar amount

$1	$2	$3	$4	$5	$6	$7	$8	$9
0.325	0.65	0.975	1.30	1.625	1.95	2.275	2.60	2.925

***Tax offsets must be deducted, and Medicare levy added, to give net tax payable (see notes at ¶42-000)**

Resident Individuals: Gross Tax Payable at 2020–21 Rates*

Taxable income	$0	$10	$20	$30	$40	$50	$60	$70	$80	$90
75000	14842.00	14845.25	14848.50	14851.75	14855.00	14858.25	14861.50	14864.75	14868.00	14871.25
75100	14874.50	14877.75	14881.00	14884.25	14887.50	14890.75	14894.00	14897.25	14900.50	14903.75
75200	14907.00	14910.25	14913.50	14916.75	14920.00	14923.25	14926.50	14929.75	14933.00	14936.25
75300	14939.50	14942.75	14946.00	14949.25	14952.50	14955.75	14959.00	14962.25	14965.50	14968.75
75400	14972.00	14975.25	14978.50	14981.75	14985.00	14988.25	14991.50	14994.75	14998.00	15001.25
75500	15004.50	15007.75	15011.00	15014.25	15017.50	15020.75	15024.00	15027.25	15030.50	15033.75
75600	15037.00	15040.25	15043.50	15046.75	15050.00	15053.25	15056.50	15059.75	15063.00	15066.25
75700	15069.50	15072.75	15076.00	15079.25	15082.50	15085.75	15089.00	15092.25	15095.50	15098.75
75800	15102.00	15105.25	15108.50	15111.75	15115.00	15118.25	15121.50	15124.75	15128.00	15131.25
75900	15134.50	15137.75	15141.00	15144.25	15147.50	15150.75	15154.00	15157.25	15160.50	15163.75
76000	15167.00	15170.25	15173.50	15176.75	15180.00	15183.25	15186.50	15189.75	15193.00	15196.25
76100	15199.50	15202.75	15206.00	15209.25	15212.50	15215.75	15219.00	15222.25	15225.50	15228.75
76200	15232.00	15235.25	15238.50	15241.75	15245.00	15248.25	15251.50	15254.75	15258.00	15261.25
76300	15264.50	15267.75	15271.00	15274.25	15277.50	15280.75	15284.00	15287.25	15290.50	15293.75
76400	15297.00	15300.25	15303.50	15306.75	15310.00	15313.25	15316.50	15319.75	15323.00	15326.25
76500	15329.50	15332.75	15336.00	15339.25	15342.50	15345.75	15349.00	15352.25	15355.50	15358.75
76600	15362.00	15365.25	15368.50	15371.75	15375.00	15378.25	15381.50	15384.75	15388.00	15391.25
76700	15394.50	15397.75	15401.00	15404.25	15407.50	15410.75	15414.00	15417.25	15420.50	15423.75
76800	15427.00	15430.25	15433.50	15436.75	15440.00	15443.25	15446.50	15449.75	15453.00	15456.25
76900	15459.50	15462.75	15466.00	15469.25	15472.50	15475.75	15479.00	15482.25	15485.50	15488.75
77000	15492.00	15495.25	15498.50	15501.75	15505.00	15508.25	15511.50	15514.75	15518.00	15521.25
77100	15524.50	15527.75	15531.00	15534.25	15537.50	15540.75	15544.00	15547.25	15550.50	15553.75
77200	15557.00	15560.25	15563.50	15566.75	15570.00	15573.25	15576.50	15579.75	15583.00	15586.25
77300	15589.50	15592.75	15596.00	15599.25	15602.50	15605.75	15609.00	15612.25	15615.50	15618.75
77400	15622.00	15625.25	15628.50	15631.75	15635.00	15638.25	15641.50	15644.75	15648.00	15651.25
77500	15654.50	15657.75	15661.00	15664.25	15667.50	15670.75	15674.00	15677.25	15680.50	15683.75
77600	15687.00	15690.25	15693.50	15696.75	15700.00	15703.25	15706.50	15709.75	15713.00	15716.25
77700	15719.50	15722.75	15726.00	15729.25	15732.50	15735.75	15739.00	15742.25	15745.50	15748.75
77800	15752.00	15755.25	15758.50	15761.75	15765.00	15768.25	15771.50	15774.75	15778.00	15781.25
77900	15784.50	15787.75	15791.00	15794.25	15797.50	15800.75	15804.00	15807.25	15810.50	15813.75
78000	15817.00	15820.25	15823.50	15826.75	15830.00	15833.25	15836.50	15839.75	15843.00	15846.25
78100	15849.50	15852.75	15856.00	15859.25	15862.50	15865.75	15869.00	15872.25	15875.50	15878.75
78200	15882.00	15885.25	15888.50	15891.75	15895.00	15898.25	15901.50	15904.75	15908.00	15911.25
78300	15914.50	15917.75	15921.00	15924.25	15927.50	15930.75	15934.00	15937.25	15940.50	15943.75
78400	15947.00	15950.25	15953.50	15956.75	15960.00	15963.25	15966.50	15969.75	15973.00	15976.25
78500	15979.50	15982.75	15986.00	15989.25	15992.50	15995.75	15999.00	16002.25	16005.50	16008.75
78600	16012.00	16015.25	16018.50	16021.75	16025.00	16028.25	16031.50	16034.75	16038.00	16041.25
78700	16044.50	16047.75	16051.00	16054.25	16057.50	16060.75	16064.00	16067.25	16070.50	16073.75
78800	16077.00	16080.25	16083.50	16086.75	16090.00	16093.25	16096.50	16099.75	16103.00	16106.25
78900	16109.50	16112.75	16116.00	16119.25	16122.50	16125.75	16129.00	16132.25	16135.50	16138.75
79000	16142.00	16145.25	16148.50	16151.75	16155.00	16158.25	16161.50	16164.75	16168.00	16171.25
79100	16174.50	16177.75	16181.00	16184.25	16187.50	16190.75	16194.00	16197.25	16200.50	16203.75
79200	16207.00	16210.25	16213.50	16216.75	16220.00	16223.25	16226.50	16229.75	16233.00	16236.25
79300	16239.50	16242.75	16246.00	16249.25	16252.50	16255.75	16259.00	16262.25	16265.50	16268.75
79400	16272.00	16275.25	16278.50	16281.75	16285.00	16288.25	16291.50	16294.75	16298.00	16301.25
79500	16304.50	16307.75	16311.00	16314.25	16317.50	16320.75	16324.00	16327.25	16330.50	16333.75
79600	16337.00	16340.25	16343.50	16346.75	16350.00	16353.25	16356.50	16359.75	16363.00	16366.25
79700	16369.50	16372.75	16376.00	16379.25	16382.50	16385.75	16389.00	16392.25	16395.50	16398.75
79800	16402.00	16405.25	16408.50	16411.75	16415.00	16418.25	16421.50	16424.75	16428.00	16431.25
79900	16434.50	16437.75	16441.00	16444.25	16447.50	16450.75	16454.00	16457.25	16460.50	16463.75

To the above amounts, add the appropriate figure for the odd dollar amount

$1	$2	$3	$4	$5	$6	$7	$8	$9
0.325	0.65	0.975	1.30	1.625	1.95	2.275	2.60	2.925

***Tax offsets must be deducted, and Medicare levy added, to give net tax payable (see notes at ¶42-000)**

Resident Individuals: Gross Tax Payable at 2020–21 Rates*

Taxable income	$0	$10	$20	$30	$40	$50	$60	$70	$80	$90
80000	16467.00	16470.25	16473.50	16476.75	16480.00	16483.25	16486.50	16489.75	16493.00	16496.25
80100	16499.50	16502.75	16506.00	16509.25	16512.50	16515.75	16519.00	16522.25	16525.50	16528.75
80200	16532.00	16535.25	16538.50	16541.75	16545.00	16548.25	16551.50	16554.75	16558.00	16561.25
80300	16564.50	16567.75	16571.00	16574.25	16577.50	16580.75	16584.00	16587.25	16590.50	16593.75
80400	16597.00	16600.25	16603.50	16606.75	16610.00	16613.25	16616.50	16619.75	16623.00	16626.25
80500	16629.50	16632.75	16636.00	16639.25	16642.50	16645.75	16649.00	16652.25	16655.50	16658.75
80600	16662.00	16665.25	16668.50	16671.75	16675.00	16678.25	16681.50	16684.75	16688.00	16691.25
80700	16694.50	16697.75	16701.00	16704.25	16707.50	16710.75	16714.00	16717.25	16720.50	16723.75
80800	16727.00	16730.25	16733.50	16736.75	16740.00	16743.25	16746.50	16749.75	16753.00	16756.25
80900	16759.50	16762.75	16766.00	16769.25	16772.50	16775.75	16779.00	16782.25	16785.50	16788.75
81000	16792.00	16795.25	16798.50	16801.75	16805.00	16808.25	16811.50	16814.75	16818.00	16821.25
81100	16824.50	16827.75	16831.00	16834.25	16837.50	16840.75	16844.00	16847.25	16850.50	16853.75
81200	16857.00	16860.25	16863.50	16866.75	16870.00	16873.25	16876.50	16879.75	16883.00	16886.25
81300	16889.50	16892.75	16896.00	16899.25	16902.50	16905.75	16909.00	16912.25	16915.50	16918.75
81400	16922.00	16925.25	16928.50	16931.75	16935.00	16938.25	16941.50	16944.75	16948.00	16951.25
81500	16954.50	16957.75	16961.00	16964.25	16967.50	16970.75	16974.00	16977.25	16980.50	16983.75
81600	16987.00	16990.25	16993.50	16996.75	17000.00	17003.25	17006.50	17009.75	17013.00	17016.25
81700	17019.50	17022.75	17026.00	17029.25	17032.50	17035.75	17039.00	17042.25	17045.50	17048.75
81800	17052.00	17055.25	17058.50	17061.75	17065.00	17068.25	17071.50	17074.75	17078.00	17081.25
81900	17084.50	17087.75	17091.00	17094.25	17097.50	17100.75	17104.00	17107.25	17110.50	17113.75
82000	17117.00	17120.25	17123.50	17126.75	17130.00	17133.25	17136.50	17139.75	17143.00	17146.25
82100	17149.50	17152.75	17156.00	17159.25	17162.50	17165.75	17169.00	17172.25	17175.50	17178.75
82200	17182.00	17185.25	17188.50	17191.75	17195.00	17198.25	17201.50	17204.75	17208.00	17211.25
82300	17214.50	17217.75	17221.00	17224.25	17227.50	17230.75	17234.00	17237.25	17240.50	17243.75
82400	17247.00	17250.25	17253.50	17256.75	17260.00	17263.25	17266.50	17269.75	17273.00	17276.25
82500	17279.50	17282.75	17286.00	17289.25	17292.50	17295.75	17299.00	17302.25	17305.50	17308.75
82600	17312.00	17315.25	17318.50	17321.75	17325.00	17328.25	17331.50	17334.75	17338.00	17341.25
82700	17344.50	17347.75	17351.00	17354.25	17357.50	17360.75	17364.00	17367.25	17370.50	17373.75
82800	17377.00	17380.25	17383.50	17386.75	17390.00	17393.25	17396.50	17399.75	17403.00	17406.25
82900	17409.50	17412.75	17416.00	17419.25	17422.50	17425.75	17429.00	17432.25	17435.50	17438.75
83000	17442.00	17445.25	17448.50	17451.75	17455.00	17458.25	17461.50	17464.75	17468.00	17471.25
83100	17474.50	17477.75	17481.00	17484.25	17487.50	17490.75	17494.00	17497.25	17500.50	17503.75
83200	17507.00	17510.25	17513.50	17516.75	17520.00	17523.25	17526.50	17529.75	17533.00	17536.25
83300	17539.50	17542.75	17546.00	17549.25	17552.50	17555.75	17559.00	17562.25	17565.50	17568.75
83400	17572.00	17575.25	17578.50	17581.75	17585.00	17588.25	17591.50	17594.75	17598.00	17601.25
83500	17604.50	17607.75	17611.00	17614.25	17617.50	17620.75	17624.00	17627.25	17630.50	17633.75
83600	17637.00	17640.25	17643.50	17646.75	17650.00	17653.25	17656.50	17659.75	17663.00	17666.25
83700	17669.50	17672.75	17676.00	17679.25	17682.50	17685.75	17689.00	17692.25	17695.50	17698.75
83800	17702.00	17705.25	17708.50	17711.75	17715.00	17718.25	17721.50	17724.75	17728.00	17731.25
83900	17734.50	17737.75	17741.00	17744.25	17747.50	17750.75	17754.00	17757.25	17760.50	17763.75
84000	17767.00	17770.25	17773.50	17776.75	17780.00	17783.25	17786.50	17789.75	17793.00	17796.25
84100	17799.50	17802.75	17806.00	17809.25	17812.50	17815.75	17819.00	17822.25	17825.50	17828.75
84200	17832.00	17835.25	17838.50	17841.75	17845.00	17848.25	17851.50	17854.75	17858.00	17861.25
84300	17864.50	17867.75	17871.00	17874.25	17877.50	17880.75	17884.00	17887.25	17890.50	17893.75
84400	17897.00	17900.25	17903.50	17906.75	17910.00	17913.25	17916.50	17919.75	17923.00	17926.25
84500	17929.50	17932.75	17936.00	17939.25	17942.50	17945.75	17949.00	17952.25	17955.50	17958.75
84600	17962.00	17965.25	17968.50	17971.75	17975.00	17978.25	17981.50	17984.75	17988.00	17991.25
84700	17994.50	17997.75	18001.00	18004.25	18007.50	18010.75	18014.00	18017.25	18020.50	18023.75
84800	18027.00	18030.25	18033.50	18036.75	18040.00	18043.25	18046.50	18049.75	18053.00	18056.25
84900	18059.50	18062.75	18066.00	18069.25	18072.50	18075.75	18079.00	18082.25	18085.50	18088.75

To the above amounts, add the appropriate figure for the odd dollar amount

$1	$2	$3	$4	$5	$6	$7	$8	$9
0.325	0.65	0.975	1.30	1.625	1.95	2.275	2.60	2.925

***Tax offsets must be deducted, and Medicare levy added, to give net tax payable (see notes at ¶42-000)**

Taxable income	Resident Individuals: Gross Tax Payable at 2020–21 Rates*									
	$0	$10	$20	$30	$40	$50	$60	$70	$80	$90
85000	18092.00	18095.25	18098.50	18101.75	18105.00	18108.25	18111.50	18114.75	18118.00	18121.25
85100	18124.50	18127.75	18131.00	18134.25	18137.50	18140.75	18144.00	18147.25	18150.50	18153.75
85200	18157.00	18160.25	18163.50	18166.75	18170.00	18173.25	18176.50	18179.75	18183.00	18186.25
85300	18189.50	18192.75	18196.00	18199.25	18202.50	18205.75	18209.00	18212.25	18215.50	18218.75
85400	18222.00	18225.25	18228.50	18231.75	18235.00	18238.25	18241.50	18244.75	18248.00	18251.25
85500	18254.50	18257.75	18261.00	18264.25	18267.50	18270.75	18274.00	18277.25	18280.50	18283.75
85600	18287.00	18290.25	18293.50	18296.75	18300.00	18303.25	18306.50	18309.75	18313.00	18316.25
85700	18319.50	18322.75	18326.00	18329.25	18332.50	18335.75	18339.00	18342.25	18345.50	18348.75
85800	18352.00	18355.25	18358.50	18361.75	18365.00	18368.25	18371.50	18374.75	18378.00	18381.25
85900	18384.50	18387.75	18391.00	18394.25	18397.50	18400.75	18404.00	18407.25	18410.50	18413.75
86000	18417.00	18420.25	18423.50	18426.75	18430.00	18433.25	18436.50	18439.75	18443.00	18446.25
86100	18449.50	18452.75	18456.00	18459.25	18462.50	18465.75	18469.00	18472.25	18475.50	18478.75
86200	18482.00	18485.25	18488.50	18491.75	18495.00	18498.25	18501.50	18504.75	18508.00	18511.25
86300	18514.50	18517.75	18521.00	18524.25	18527.50	18530.75	18534.00	18537.25	18540.50	18543.75
86400	18547.00	18550.25	18553.50	18556.75	18560.00	18563.25	18566.50	18569.75	18573.00	18576.25
86500	18579.50	18582.75	18586.00	18589.25	18592.50	18595.75	18599.00	18602.25	18605.50	18608.75
86600	18612.00	18615.25	18618.50	18621.75	18625.00	18628.25	18631.50	18634.75	18638.00	18641.25
86700	18644.50	18647.75	18651.00	18654.25	18657.50	18660.75	18664.00	18667.25	18670.50	18673.75
86800	18677.00	18680.25	18683.50	18686.75	18690.00	18693.25	18696.50	18699.75	18703.00	18706.25
86900	18709.50	18712.75	18716.00	18719.25	18722.50	18725.75	18729.00	18732.25	18735.50	18738.75
87000	18742.00	18745.25	18748.50	18751.75	18755.00	18758.25	18761.50	18764.75	18768.00	18771.25
87100	18774.50	18777.75	18781.00	18784.25	18787.50	18790.75	18794.00	18797.25	18800.50	18803.75
87200	18807.00	18810.25	18813.50	18816.75	18820.00	18823.25	18826.50	18829.75	18833.00	18836.25
87300	18839.50	18842.75	18846.00	18849.25	18852.50	18855.75	18859.00	18862.25	18865.50	18868.75
87400	18872.00	18875.25	18878.50	18881.75	18885.00	18888.25	18891.50	18894.75	18898.00	18901.25
87500	18904.50	18907.75	18911.00	18914.25	18917.50	18920.75	18924.00	18927.25	18930.50	18933.75
87600	18937.00	18940.25	18943.50	18946.75	18950.00	18953.25	18956.50	18959.75	18963.00	18966.25
87700	18969.50	18972.75	18976.00	18979.25	18982.50	18985.75	18989.00	18992.25	18995.50	18998.75
87800	19002.00	19005.25	19008.50	19011.75	19015.00	19018.25	19021.50	19024.75	19028.00	19031.25
87900	19034.50	19037.75	19041.00	19044.25	19047.50	19050.75	19054.00	19057.25	19060.50	19063.75
88000	19067.00	19070.25	19073.50	19076.75	19080.00	19083.25	19086.50	19089.75	19093.00	19096.25
88100	19099.50	19102.75	19106.00	19109.25	19112.50	19115.75	19119.00	19122.25	19125.50	19128.75
88200	19132.00	19135.25	19138.50	19141.75	19145.00	19148.25	19151.50	19154.75	19158.00	19161.25
88300	19164.50	19167.75	19171.00	19174.25	19177.50	19180.75	19184.00	19187.25	19190.50	19193.75
88400	19197.00	19200.25	19203.50	19206.75	19210.00	19213.25	19216.50	19219.75	19223.00	19226.25
88500	19229.50	19232.75	19236.00	19239.25	19242.50	19245.75	19249.00	19252.25	19255.50	19258.75
88600	19262.00	19265.25	19268.50	19271.75	19275.00	19278.25	19281.50	19284.75	19288.00	19291.25
88700	19294.50	19297.75	19301.00	19304.25	19307.50	19310.75	19314.00	19317.25	19320.50	19323.75
88800	19327.00	19330.25	19333.50	19336.75	19340.00	19343.25	19346.50	19349.75	19353.00	19356.25
88900	19359.50	19362.75	19366.00	19369.25	19372.50	19375.75	19379.00	19382.25	19385.50	19388.75
89000	19392.00	19395.25	19398.50	19401.75	19405.00	19408.25	19411.50	19414.75	19418.00	19421.25
89100	19424.50	19427.75	19431.00	19434.25	19437.50	19440.75	19444.00	19447.25	19450.50	19453.75
89200	19457.00	19460.25	19463.50	19466.75	19470.00	19473.25	19476.50	19479.75	19483.00	19486.25
89300	19489.50	19492.75	19496.00	19499.25	19502.50	19505.75	19509.00	19512.25	19515.50	19518.75
89400	19522.00	19525.25	19528.50	19531.75	19535.00	19538.25	19541.50	19544.75	19548.00	19551.25
89500	19554.50	19557.75	19561.00	19564.25	19567.50	19570.75	19574.00	19577.25	19580.50	19583.75
89600	19587.00	19590.25	19593.50	19596.75	19600.00	19603.25	19606.50	19609.75	19613.00	19616.25
89700	19619.50	19622.75	19626.00	19629.25	19632.50	19635.75	19639.00	19642.25	19645.50	19648.75
89800	19652.00	19655.25	19658.50	19661.75	19665.00	19668.25	19671.50	19674.75	19678.00	19681.25
89900	19684.50	19687.75	19691.00	19694.25	19697.50	19700.75	19704.00	19707.25	19710.50	19713.75

To the above amounts, add the appropriate figure for the odd dollar amount								
$1	$2	$3	$4	$5	$6	$7	$8	$9
0.325	0.65	0.975	1.30	1.625	1.95	2.275	2.60	2.925

***Tax offsets must be deducted, and Medicare levy added, to give net tax payable (see notes at ¶42-000)**

Resident Individuals: Gross Tax Payable at 2020–21 Rates*

Taxable income	$0	$10	$20	$30	$40	$50	$60	$70	$80	$90
90000	19717.00	19720.25	19723.50	19726.75	19730.00	19733.25	19736.50	19739.75	19743.00	19746.25
90100	19749.50	19752.75	19756.00	19759.25	19762.50	19765.75	19769.00	19772.25	19775.50	19778.75
90200	19782.00	19785.25	19788.50	19791.75	19795.00	19798.25	19801.50	19804.75	19808.00	19811.25
90300	19814.50	19817.75	19821.00	19824.25	19827.50	19830.75	19834.00	19837.25	19840.50	19843.75
90400	19847.00	19850.25	19853.50	19856.75	19860.00	19863.25	19866.50	19869.75	19873.00	19876.25
90500	19879.50	19882.75	19886.00	19889.25	19892.50	19895.75	19899.00	19902.25	19905.50	19908.75
90600	19912.00	19915.25	19918.50	19921.75	19925.00	19928.25	19931.50	19934.75	19938.00	19941.25
90700	19944.50	19947.75	19951.00	19954.25	19957.50	19960.75	19964.00	19967.25	19970.50	19973.75
90800	19977.00	19980.25	19983.50	19986.75	19990.00	19993.25	19996.50	19999.75	20003.00	20006.25
90900	20009.50	20012.75	20016.00	20019.25	20022.50	20025.75	20029.00	20032.25	20035.50	20038.75
91000	20042.00	20045.25	20048.50	20051.75	20055.00	20058.25	20061.50	20064.75	20068.00	20071.25
91100	20074.50	20077.75	20081.00	20084.25	20087.50	20090.75	20094.00	20097.25	20100.50	20103.75
91200	20107.00	20110.25	20113.50	20116.75	20120.00	20123.25	20126.50	20129.75	20133.00	20136.25
91300	20139.50	20142.75	20146.00	20149.25	20152.50	20155.75	20159.00	20162.25	20165.50	20168.75
91400	20172.00	20175.25	20178.50	20181.75	20185.00	20188.25	20191.50	20194.75	20198.00	20201.25
91500	20204.50	20207.75	20211.00	20214.25	20217.50	20220.75	20224.00	20227.25	20230.50	20233.75
91600	20237.00	20240.25	20243.50	20246.75	20250.00	20253.25	20256.50	20259.75	20263.00	20266.25
91700	20269.50	20272.75	20276.00	20279.25	20282.50	20285.75	20289.00	20292.25	20295.50	20298.75
91800	20302.00	20305.25	20308.50	20311.75	20315.00	20318.25	20321.50	20324.75	20328.00	20331.25
91900	20334.50	20337.75	20341.00	20344.25	20347.50	20350.75	20354.00	20357.25	20360.50	20363.75
92000	20367.00	20370.25	20373.50	20376.75	20380.00	20383.25	20386.50	20389.75	20393.00	20396.25
92100	20399.50	20402.75	20406.00	20409.25	20412.50	20415.75	20419.00	20422.25	20425.50	20428.75
92200	20432.00	20435.25	20438.50	20441.75	20445.00	20448.25	20451.50	20454.75	20458.00	20461.25
92300	20464.50	20467.75	20471.00	20474.25	20477.50	20480.75	20484.00	20487.25	20490.50	20493.75
92400	20497.00	20500.25	20503.50	20506.75	20510.00	20513.25	20516.50	20519.75	20523.00	20526.25
92500	20529.50	20532.75	20536.00	20539.25	20542.50	20545.75	20549.00	20552.25	20555.50	20558.75
92600	20562.00	20565.25	20568.50	20571.75	20575.00	20578.25	20581.50	20584.75	20588.00	20591.25
92700	20594.50	20597.75	20601.00	20604.25	20607.50	20610.75	20614.00	20617.25	20620.50	20623.75
92800	20627.00	20630.25	20633.50	20636.75	20640.00	20643.25	20646.50	20649.75	20653.00	20656.25
92900	20659.50	20662.75	20666.00	20669.25	20672.50	20675.75	20679.00	20682.25	20685.50	20688.75
93000	20692.00	20695.25	20698.50	20701.75	20705.00	20708.25	20711.50	20714.75	20718.00	20721.25
93100	20724.50	20727.75	20731.00	20734.25	20737.50	20740.75	20744.00	20747.25	20750.50	20753.75
93200	20757.00	20760.25	20763.50	20766.75	20770.00	20773.25	20776.50	20779.75	20783.00	20786.25
93300	20789.50	20792.75	20796.00	20799.25	20802.50	20805.75	20809.00	20812.25	20815.50	20818.75
93400	20822.00	20825.25	20828.50	20831.75	20835.00	20838.25	20841.50	20844.75	20848.00	20851.25
93500	20854.50	20857.75	20861.00	20864.25	20867.50	20870.75	20874.00	20877.25	20880.50	20883.75
93600	20887.00	20890.25	20893.50	20896.75	20900.00	20903.25	20906.50	20909.75	20913.00	20916.25
93700	20919.50	20922.75	20926.00	20929.25	20932.50	20935.75	20939.00	20942.25	20945.50	20948.75
93800	20952.00	20955.25	20958.50	20961.75	20965.00	20968.25	20971.50	20974.75	20978.00	20981.25
93900	20984.50	20987.75	20991.00	20994.25	20997.50	21000.75	21004.00	21007.25	21010.50	21013.75
94000	21017.00	21020.25	21023.50	21026.75	21030.00	21033.25	21036.50	21039.75	21043.00	21046.25
94100	21049.50	21052.75	21056.00	21059.25	21062.50	21065.75	21069.00	21072.25	21075.50	21078.75
94200	21082.00	21085.25	21088.50	21091.75	21095.00	21098.25	21101.50	21104.75	21108.00	21111.25
94300	21114.50	21117.75	21121.00	21124.25	21127.50	21130.75	21134.00	21137.25	21140.50	21143.75
94400	21147.00	21150.25	21153.50	21156.75	21160.00	21163.25	21166.50	21169.75	21173.00	21176.25
94500	21179.50	21182.75	21186.00	21189.25	21192.50	21195.75	21199.00	21202.25	21205.50	21208.75
94600	21212.00	21215.25	21218.50	21221.75	21225.00	21228.25	21231.50	21234.75	21238.00	21241.25
94700	21244.50	21247.75	21251.00	21254.25	21257.50	21260.75	21264.00	21267.25	21270.50	21273.75
94800	21277.00	21280.25	21283.50	21286.75	21290.00	21293.25	21296.50	21299.75	21303.00	21306.25
94900	21309.50	21312.75	21316.00	21319.25	21322.50	21325.75	21329.00	21332.25	21335.50	21338.75

To the above amounts, add the appropriate figure for the odd dollar amount

$1	$2	$3	$4	$5	$6	$7	$8	$9
0.325	0.65	0.975	1.30	1.625	1.95	2.275	2.60	2.925

***Tax offsets must be deducted, and Medicare levy added, to give net tax payable (see notes at ¶42-000)**

Resident Individuals: Gross Tax Payable at 2020–21 Rates*

Taxable income	$0	$10	$20	$30	$40	$50	$60	$70	$80	$90
95000	21342.00	21345.25	21348.50	21351.75	21355.00	21358.25	21361.50	21364.75	21368.00	21371.25
95100	21374.50	21377.75	21381.00	21384.25	21387.50	21390.75	21394.00	21397.25	21400.50	21403.75
95200	21407.00	21410.25	21413.50	21416.75	21420.00	21423.25	21426.50	21429.75	21433.00	21436.25
95300	21439.50	21442.75	21446.00	21449.25	21452.50	21455.75	21459.00	21462.25	21465.50	21468.75
95400	21472.00	21475.25	21478.50	21481.75	21485.00	21488.25	21491.50	21494.75	21498.00	21501.25
95500	21504.50	21507.75	21511.00	21514.25	21517.50	21520.75	21524.00	21527.25	21530.50	21533.75
95600	21537.00	21540.25	21543.50	21546.75	21550.00	21553.25	21556.50	21559.75	21563.00	21566.25
95700	21569.50	21572.75	21576.00	21579.25	21582.50	21585.75	21589.00	21592.25	21595.50	21598.75
95800	21602.00	21605.25	21608.50	21611.75	21615.00	21618.25	21621.50	21624.75	21628.00	21631.25
95900	21634.50	21637.75	21641.00	21644.25	21647.50	21650.75	21654.00	21657.25	21660.50	21663.75
96000	21667.00	21670.25	21673.50	21676.75	21680.00	21683.25	21686.50	21689.75	21693.00	21696.25
96100	21699.50	21702.75	21706.00	21709.25	21712.50	21715.75	21719.00	21722.25	21725.50	21728.75
96200	21732.00	21735.25	21738.50	21741.75	21745.00	21748.25	21751.50	21754.75	21758.00	21761.25
96300	21764.50	21767.75	21771.00	21774.25	21777.50	21780.75	21784.00	21787.25	21790.50	21793.75
96400	21797.00	21800.25	21803.50	21806.75	21810.00	21813.25	21816.50	21819.75	21823.00	21826.25
96500	21829.50	21832.75	21836.00	21839.25	21842.50	21845.75	21849.00	21852.25	21855.50	21858.75
96600	21862.00	21865.25	21868.50	21871.75	21875.00	21878.25	21881.50	21884.75	21888.00	21891.25
96700	21894.50	21897.75	21901.00	21904.25	21907.50	21910.75	21914.00	21917.25	21920.50	21923.75
96800	21927.00	21930.25	21933.50	21936.75	21940.00	21943.25	21946.50	21949.75	21953.00	21956.25
96900	21959.50	21962.75	21966.00	21969.25	21972.50	21975.75	21979.00	21982.25	21985.50	21988.75
97000	21992.00	21995.25	21998.50	22001.75	22005.00	22008.25	22011.50	22014.75	22018.00	22021.25
97100	22024.50	22027.75	22031.00	22034.25	22037.50	22040.75	22044.00	22047.25	22050.50	22053.75
97200	22057.00	22060.25	22063.50	22066.75	22070.00	22073.25	22076.50	22079.75	22083.00	22086.25
97300	22089.50	22092.75	22096.00	22099.25	22102.50	22105.75	22109.00	22112.25	22115.50	22118.75
97400	22122.00	22125.25	22128.50	22131.75	22135.00	22138.25	22141.50	22144.75	22148.00	22151.25
97500	22154.50	22157.75	22161.00	22164.25	22167.50	22170.75	22174.00	22177.25	22180.50	22183.75
97600	22187.00	22190.25	22193.50	22196.75	22200.00	22203.25	22206.50	22209.75	22213.00	22216.25
97700	22219.50	22222.75	22226.00	22229.25	22232.50	22235.75	22239.00	22242.25	22245.50	22248.75
97800	22252.00	22255.25	22258.50	22261.75	22265.00	22268.25	22271.50	22274.75	22278.00	22281.25
97900	22284.50	22287.75	22291.00	22294.25	22297.50	22300.75	22304.00	22307.25	22310.50	22313.75
98000	22317.00	22320.25	22323.50	22326.75	22330.00	22333.25	22336.50	22339.75	22343.00	22346.25
98100	22349.50	22352.75	22356.00	22359.25	22362.50	22365.75	22369.00	22372.25	22375.50	22378.75
98200	22382.00	22385.25	22388.50	22391.75	22395.00	22398.25	22401.50	22404.75	22408.00	22411.25
98300	22414.50	22417.75	22421.00	22424.25	22427.50	22430.75	22434.00	22437.25	22440.50	22443.75
98400	22447.00	22450.25	22453.50	22456.75	22460.00	22463.25	22466.50	22469.75	22473.00	22476.25
98500	22479.50	22482.75	22486.00	22489.25	22492.50	22495.75	22499.00	22502.25	22505.50	22508.75
98600	22512.00	22515.25	22518.50	22521.75	22525.00	22528.25	22531.50	22534.75	22538.00	22541.25
98700	22544.50	22547.75	22551.00	22554.25	22557.50	22560.75	22564.00	22567.25	22570.50	22573.75
98800	22577.00	22580.25	22583.50	22586.75	22590.00	22593.25	22596.50	22599.75	22603.00	22606.25
98900	22609.50	22612.75	22616.00	22619.25	22622.50	22625.75	22629.00	22632.25	22635.50	22638.75
99000	22642.00	22645.25	22648.50	22651.75	22655.00	22658.25	22661.50	22664.75	22668.00	22671.25
99100	22674.50	22677.75	22681.00	22684.25	22687.50	22690.75	22694.00	22697.25	22700.50	22703.75
99200	22707.00	22710.25	22713.50	22716.75	22720.00	22723.25	22726.50	22729.75	22733.00	22736.25
99300	22739.50	22742.75	22746.00	22749.25	22752.50	22755.75	22759.00	22762.25	22765.50	22768.75
99400	22772.00	22775.25	22778.50	22781.75	22785.00	22788.25	22791.50	22794.75	22798.00	22801.25
99500	22804.50	22807.75	22811.00	22814.25	22817.50	22820.75	22824.00	22827.25	22830.50	22833.75
99600	22837.00	22840.25	22843.50	22846.75	22850.00	22853.25	22856.50	22859.75	22863.00	22866.25
99700	22869.50	22872.75	22876.00	22879.25	22882.50	22885.75	22889.00	22892.25	22895.50	22898.75
99800	22902.00	22905.25	22908.50	22911.75	22915.00	22918.25	22921.50	22924.75	22928.00	22931.25
99900	22934.50	22937.75	22941.00	22944.25	22947.50	22950.75	22954.00	22957.25	22960.50	22963.75

To the above amounts, add the appropriate figure for the odd dollar amount

$1	$2	$3	$4	$5	$6	$7	$8	$9
0.325	0.65	0.975	1.30	1.625	1.95	2.275	2.60	2.925

***Tax offsets must be deducted, and Medicare levy added, to give net tax payable (see notes at ¶42-000)**

Taxable income	Resident Individuals: Gross Tax Payable at 2020–21 Rates*									
	$0	**$10**	**$20**	**$30**	**$40**	**$50**	**$60**	**$70**	**$80**	**$90**
100000	22967.00	22970.25	22973.50	22976.75	22980.00	22983.25	22986.50	22989.75	22993.00	22996.25
100100	22999.50	23002.75	23006.00	23009.25	23012.50	23015.75	23019.00	23022.25	23025.50	23028.75
100200	23032.00	23035.25	23038.50	23041.75	23045.00	23048.25	23051.50	23054.75	23058.00	23061.25
100300	23064.50	23067.75	23071.00	23074.25	23077.50	23080.75	23084.00	23087.25	23090.50	23093.75
100400	23097.00	23100.25	23103.50	23106.75	23110.00	23113.25	23116.50	23119.75	23123.00	23126.25
100500	23129.50	23132.75	23136.00	23139.25	23142.50	23145.75	23149.00	23152.25	23155.50	23158.75
100600	23162.00	23165.25	23168.50	23171.75	23175.00	23178.25	23181.50	23184.75	23188.00	23191.25
100700	23194.50	23197.75	23201.00	23204.25	23207.50	23210.75	23214.00	23217.25	23220.50	23223.75
100800	23227.00	23230.25	23233.50	23236.75	23240.00	23243.25	23246.50	23249.75	23253.00	23256.25
100900	23259.50	23262.75	23266.00	23269.25	23272.50	23275.75	23279.00	23282.25	23285.50	23288.75
101000	23292.00	23295.25	23298.50	23301.75	23305.00	23308.25	23311.50	23314.75	23318.00	23321.25
101100	23324.50	23327.75	23331.00	23334.25	23337.50	23340.75	23344.00	23347.25	23350.50	23353.75
101200	23357.00	23360.25	23363.50	23366.75	23370.00	23373.25	23376.50	23379.75	23383.00	23386.25
101300	23389.50	23392.75	23396.00	23399.25	23402.50	23405.75	23409.00	23412.25	23415.50	23418.75
101400	23422.00	23425.25	23428.50	23431.75	23435.00	23438.25	23441.50	23444.75	23448.00	23451.25
101500	23454.50	23457.75	23461.00	23464.25	23467.50	23470.75	23474.00	23477.25	23480.50	23483.75
101600	23487.00	23490.25	23493.50	23496.75	23500.00	23503.25	23506.50	23509.75	23513.00	23516.25
101700	23519.50	23522.75	23526.00	23529.25	23532.50	23535.75	23539.00	23542.25	23545.50	23548.75
101800	23552.00	23555.25	23558.50	23561.75	23565.00	23568.25	23571.50	23574.75	23578.00	23581.25
101900	23584.50	23587.75	23591.00	23594.25	23597.50	23600.75	23604.00	23607.25	23610.50	23613.75
102000	23617.00	23620.25	23623.50	23626.75	23630.00	23633.25	23636.50	23639.75	23643.00	23646.25
102100	23649.50	23652.75	23656.00	23659.25	23662.50	23665.75	23669.00	23672.25	23675.50	23678.75
102200	23682.00	23685.25	23688.50	23691.75	23695.00	23698.25	23701.50	23704.75	23708.00	23711.25
102300	23714.50	23717.75	23721.00	23724.25	23727.50	23730.75	23734.00	23737.25	23740.50	23743.75
102400	23747.00	23750.25	23753.50	23756.75	23760.00	23763.25	23766.50	23769.75	23773.00	23776.25
102500	23779.50	23782.75	23786.00	23789.25	23792.50	23795.75	23799.00	23802.25	23805.50	23808.75
102600	23812.00	23815.25	23818.50	23821.75	23825.00	23828.25	23831.50	23834.75	23838.00	23841.25
102700	23844.50	23847.75	23851.00	23854.25	23857.50	23860.75	23864.00	23867.25	23870.50	23873.75
102800	23877.00	23880.25	23883.50	23886.75	23890.00	23893.25	23896.50	23899.75	23903.00	23906.25
102900	23909.50	23912.75	23916.00	23919.25	23922.50	23925.75	23929.00	23932.25	23935.50	23938.75
103000	23942.00	23945.25	23948.50	23951.75	23955.00	23958.25	23961.50	23964.75	23968.00	23971.25
103100	23974.50	23977.75	23981.00	23984.25	23987.50	23990.75	23994.00	23997.25	24000.50	24003.75
103200	24007.00	24010.25	24013.50	24016.75	24020.00	24023.25	24026.50	24029.75	24033.00	24036.25
103300	24039.50	24042.75	24046.00	24049.25	24052.50	24055.75	24059.00	24062.25	24065.50	24068.75
103400	24072.00	24075.25	24078.50	24081.75	24085.00	24088.25	24091.50	24094.75	24098.00	24101.25
103500	24104.50	24107.75	24111.00	24114.25	24117.50	24120.75	24124.00	24127.25	24130.50	24133.75
103600	24137.00	24140.25	24143.50	24146.75	24150.00	24153.25	24156.50	24159.75	24163.00	24166.25
103700	24169.50	24172.75	24176.00	24179.25	24182.50	24185.75	24189.00	24192.25	24195.50	24198.75
103800	24202.00	24205.25	24208.50	24211.75	24215.00	24218.25	24221.50	24224.75	24228.00	24231.25
103900	24234.50	24237.75	24241.00	24244.25	24247.50	24250.75	24254.00	24257.25	24260.50	24263.75
104000	24267.00	24270.25	24273.50	24276.75	24280.00	24283.25	24286.50	24289.75	24293.00	24296.25
104100	24299.50	24302.75	24306.00	24309.25	24312.50	24315.75	24319.00	24322.25	24325.50	24328.75
104200	24332.00	24335.25	24338.50	24341.75	24345.00	24348.25	24351.50	24354.75	24358.00	24361.25
104300	24364.50	24367.75	24371.00	24374.25	24377.50	24380.75	24384.00	24387.25	24390.50	24393.75
104400	24397.00	24400.25	24403.50	24406.75	24410.00	24413.25	24416.50	24419.75	24423.00	24426.25
104500	24429.50	24432.75	24436.00	24439.25	24442.50	24445.75	24449.00	24452.25	24455.50	24458.75
104600	24462.00	24465.25	24468.50	24471.75	24475.00	24478.25	24481.50	24484.75	24488.00	24491.25
104700	24494.50	24497.75	24501.00	24504.25	24507.50	24510.75	24514.00	24517.25	24520.50	24523.75
104800	24527.00	24530.25	24533.50	24536.75	24540.00	24543.25	24546.50	24549.75	24553.00	24556.25
104900	24559.50	24562.75	24566.00	24569.25	24572.50	24575.75	24579.00	24582.25	24585.50	24588.75

To the above amounts, add the appropriate figure for the odd dollar amount								
$1	$2	$3	$4	$5	$6	$7	$8	$9
0.325	0.65	0.975	1.30	1.625	1.95	2.275	2.60	2.925

***Tax offsets must be deducted, and Medicare levy added, to give net tax payable (see notes at ¶42-000)**

Taxable income	Resident Individuals: Gross Tax Payable at 2020–21 Rates*									
	$0	**$10**	**$20**	**$30**	**$40**	**$50**	**$60**	**$70**	**$80**	**$90**
105000	24592.00	24595.25	24598.50	24601.75	24605.00	24608.25	24611.50	24614.75	24618.00	24621.25
105100	24624.50	24627.75	24631.00	24634.25	24637.50	24640.75	24644.00	24647.25	24650.50	24653.75
105200	24657.00	24660.25	24663.50	24666.75	24670.00	24673.25	24676.50	24679.75	24683.00	24686.25
105300	24689.50	24692.75	24696.00	24699.25	24702.50	24705.75	24709.00	24712.25	24715.50	24718.75
105400	24722.00	24725.25	24728.50	24731.75	24735.00	24738.25	24741.50	24744.75	24748.00	24751.25
105500	24754.50	24757.75	24761.00	24764.25	24767.50	24770.75	24774.00	24777.25	24780.50	24783.75
105600	24787.00	24790.25	24793.50	24796.75	24800.00	24803.25	24806.50	24809.75	24813.00	24816.25
105700	24819.50	24822.75	24826.00	24829.25	24832.50	24835.75	24839.00	24842.25	24845.50	24848.75
105800	24852.00	24855.25	24858.50	24861.75	24865.00	24868.25	24871.50	24874.75	24878.00	24881.25
105900	24884.50	24887.75	24891.00	24894.25	24897.50	24900.75	24904.00	24907.25	24910.50	24913.75
106000	24917.00	24920.25	24923.50	24926.75	24930.00	24933.25	24936.50	24939.75	24943.00	24946.25
106100	24949.50	24952.75	24956.00	24959.25	24962.50	24965.75	24969.00	24972.25	24975.50	24978.75
106200	24982.00	24985.25	24988.50	24991.75	24995.00	24998.25	25001.50	25004.75	25008.00	25011.25
106300	25014.50	25017.75	25021.00	25024.25	25027.50	25030.75	25034.00	25037.25	25040.50	25043.75
106400	25047.00	25050.25	25053.50	25056.75	25060.00	25063.25	25066.50	25069.75	25073.00	25076.25
106500	25079.50	25082.75	25086.00	25089.25	25092.50	25095.75	25099.00	25102.25	25105.50	25108.75
106600	25112.00	25115.25	25118.50	25121.75	25125.00	25128.25	25131.50	25134.75	25138.00	25141.25
106700	25144.50	25147.75	25151.00	25154.25	25157.50	25160.75	25164.00	25167.25	25170.50	25173.75
106800	25177.00	25180.25	25183.50	25186.75	25190.00	25193.25	25196.50	25199.75	25203.00	25206.25
106900	25209.50	25212.75	25216.00	25219.25	25222.50	25225.75	25229.00	25232.25	25235.50	25238.75
107000	25242.00	25245.25	25248.50	25251.75	25255.00	25258.25	25261.50	25264.75	25268.00	25271.25
107100	25274.50	25277.75	25281.00	25284.25	25287.50	25290.75	25294.00	25297.25	25300.50	25303.75
107200	25307.00	25310.25	25313.50	25316.75	25320.00	25323.25	25326.50	25329.75	25333.00	25336.25
107300	25339.50	25342.75	25346.00	25349.25	25352.50	25355.75	25359.00	25362.25	25365.50	25368.75
107400	25372.00	25375.25	25378.50	25381.75	25385.00	25388.25	25391.50	25394.75	25398.00	25401.25
107500	25404.50	25407.75	25411.00	25414.25	25417.50	25420.75	25424.00	25427.25	25430.50	25433.75
107600	25437.00	25440.25	25443.50	25446.75	25450.00	25453.25	25456.50	25459.75	25463.00	25466.25
107700	25469.50	25472.75	25476.00	25479.25	25482.50	25485.75	25489.00	25492.25	25495.50	25498.75
107800	25502.00	25505.25	25508.50	25511.75	25515.00	25518.25	25521.50	25524.75	25528.00	25531.25
107900	25534.50	25537.75	25541.00	25544.25	25547.50	25550.75	25554.00	25557.25	25560.50	25563.75
108000	25567.00	25570.25	25573.50	25576.75	25580.00	25583.25	25586.50	25589.75	25593.00	25596.25
108100	25599.50	25602.75	25606.00	25609.25	25612.50	25615.75	25619.00	25622.25	25625.50	25628.75
108200	25632.00	25635.25	25638.50	25641.75	25645.00	25648.25	25651.50	25654.75	25658.00	25661.25
108300	25664.50	25667.75	25671.00	25674.25	25677.50	25680.75	25684.00	25687.25	25690.50	25693.75
108400	25697.00	25700.25	25703.50	25706.75	25710.00	25713.25	25716.50	25719.75	25723.00	25726.25
108500	25729.50	25732.75	25736.00	25739.25	25742.50	25745.75	25749.00	25752.25	25755.50	25758.75
108600	25762.00	25765.25	25768.50	25771.75	25775.00	25778.25	25781.50	25784.75	25788.00	25791.25
108700	25794.50	25797.75	25801.00	25804.25	25807.50	25810.75	25814.00	25817.25	25820.50	25823.75
108800	25827.00	25830.25	25833.50	25836.75	25840.00	25843.25	25846.50	25849.75	25853.00	25856.25
108900	25859.50	25862.75	25866.00	25869.25	25872.50	25875.75	25879.00	25882.25	25885.50	25888.75
109000	25892.00	25895.25	25898.50	25901.75	25905.00	25908.25	25911.50	25914.75	25918.00	25921.25
109100	25924.50	25927.75	25931.00	25934.25	25937.50	25940.75	25944.00	25947.25	25950.50	25953.75
109200	25957.00	25960.25	25963.50	25966.75	25970.00	25973.25	25976.50	25979.75	25983.00	25986.25
109300	25989.50	25992.75	25996.00	25999.25	26002.50	26005.75	26009.00	26012.25	26015.50	26018.75
109400	26022.00	26025.25	26028.50	26031.75	26035.00	26038.25	26041.50	26044.75	26048.00	26051.25
109500	26054.50	26057.75	26061.00	26064.25	26067.50	26070.75	26074.00	26077.25	26080.50	26083.75
109600	26087.00	26090.25	26093.50	26096.75	26100.00	26103.25	26106.50	26109.75	26113.00	26116.25
109700	26119.50	26122.75	26126.00	26129.25	26132.50	26135.75	26139.00	26142.25	26145.50	26148.75
109800	26152.00	26155.25	26158.50	26161.75	26165.00	26168.25	26171.50	26174.75	26178.00	26181.25
109900	26184.50	26187.75	26191.00	26194.25	26197.50	26200.75	26204.00	26207.25	26210.50	26213.75

To the above amounts, add the appropriate figure for the odd dollar amount								
$1	$2	$3	$4	$5	$6	$7	$8	$9
0.325	0.65	0.975	1.30	1.625	1.95	2.275	2.60	2.925

***Tax offsets must be deducted, and Medicare levy added, to give net tax payable (see notes at ¶42-000)**

Resident Individuals: Gross Tax Payable at 2020–21 Rates*

Taxable income	$0	$10	$20	$30	$40	$50	$60	$70	$80	$90
110000	26217.00	26220.25	26223.50	26226.75	26230.00	26233.25	26236.50	26239.75	26243.00	26246.25
110100	26249.50	26252.75	26256.00	26259.25	26262.50	26265.75	26269.00	26272.25	26275.50	26278.75
110200	26282.00	26285.25	26288.50	26291.75	26295.00	26298.25	26301.50	26304.75	26308.00	26311.25
110300	26314.50	26317.75	26321.00	26324.25	26327.50	26330.75	26334.00	26337.25	26340.50	26343.75
110400	26347.00	26350.25	26353.50	26356.75	26360.00	26363.25	26366.50	26369.75	26373.00	26376.25
110500	26379.50	26382.75	26386.00	26389.25	26392.50	26395.75	26399.00	26402.25	26405.50	26408.75
110600	26412.00	26415.25	26418.50	26421.75	26425.00	26428.25	26431.50	26434.75	26438.00	26441.25
110700	26444.50	26447.75	26451.00	26454.25	26457.50	26460.75	26464.00	26467.25	26470.50	26473.75
110800	26477.00	26480.25	26483.50	26486.75	26490.00	26493.25	26496.50	26499.75	26503.00	26506.25
110900	26509.50	26512.75	26516.00	26519.25	26522.50	26525.75	26529.00	26532.25	26535.50	26538.75
111000	26542.00	26545.25	26548.50	26551.75	26555.00	26558.25	26561.50	26564.75	26568.00	26571.25
111100	26574.50	26577.75	26581.00	26584.25	26587.50	26590.75	26594.00	26597.25	26600.50	26603.75
111200	26607.00	26610.25	26613.50	26616.75	26620.00	26623.25	26626.50	26629.75	26633.00	26636.25
111300	26639.50	26642.75	26646.00	26649.25	26652.50	26655.75	26659.00	26662.25	26665.50	26668.75
111400	26672.00	26675.25	26678.50	26681.75	26685.00	26688.25	26691.50	26694.75	26698.00	26701.25
111500	26704.50	26707.75	26711.00	26714.25	26717.50	26720.75	26724.00	26727.25	26730.50	26733.75
111600	26737.00	26740.25	26743.50	26746.75	26750.00	26753.25	26756.50	26759.75	26763.00	26766.25
111700	26769.50	26772.75	26776.00	26779.25	26782.50	26785.75	26789.00	26792.25	26795.50	26798.75
111800	26802.00	26805.25	26808.50	26811.75	26815.00	26818.25	26821.50	26824.75	26828.00	26831.25
111900	26834.50	26837.75	26841.00	26844.25	26847.50	26850.75	26854.00	26857.25	26860.50	26863.75
112000	26867.00	26870.25	26873.50	26876.75	26880.00	26883.25	26886.50	26889.75	26893.00	26896.25
112100	26899.50	26902.75	26906.00	26909.25	26912.50	26915.75	26919.00	26922.25	26925.50	26928.75
112200	26932.00	26935.25	26938.50	26941.75	26945.00	26948.25	26951.50	26954.75	26958.00	26961.25
112300	26964.50	26967.75	26971.00	26974.25	26977.50	26980.75	26984.00	26987.25	26990.50	26993.75
112400	26997.00	27000.25	27003.50	27006.75	27010.00	27013.25	27016.50	27019.75	27023.00	27026.25
112500	27029.50	27032.75	27036.00	27039.25	27042.50	27045.75	27049.00	27052.25	27055.50	27058.75
112600	27062.00	27065.25	27068.50	27071.75	27075.00	27078.25	27081.50	27084.75	27088.00	27091.25
112700	27094.50	27097.75	27101.00	27104.25	27107.50	27110.75	27114.00	27117.25	27120.50	27123.75
112800	27127.00	27130.25	27133.50	27136.75	27140.00	27143.25	27146.50	27149.75	27153.00	27156.25
112900	27159.50	27162.75	27166.00	27169.25	27172.50	27175.75	27179.00	27182.25	27185.50	27188.75
113000	27192.00	27195.25	27198.50	27201.75	27205.00	27208.25	27211.50	27214.75	27218.00	27221.25
113100	27224.50	27227.75	27231.00	27234.25	27237.50	27240.75	27244.00	27247.25	27250.50	27253.75
113200	27257.00	27260.25	27263.50	27266.75	27270.00	27273.25	27276.50	27279.75	27283.00	27286.25
113300	27289.50	27292.75	27296.00	27299.25	27302.50	27305.75	27309.00	27312.25	27315.50	27318.75
113400	27322.00	27325.25	27328.50	27331.75	27335.00	27338.25	27341.50	27344.75	27348.00	27351.25
113500	27354.50	27357.75	27361.00	27364.25	27367.50	27370.75	27374.00	27377.25	27380.50	27383.75
113600	27387.00	27390.25	27393.50	27396.75	27400.00	27403.25	27406.50	27409.75	27413.00	27416.25
113700	27419.50	27422.75	27426.00	27429.25	27432.50	27435.75	27439.00	27442.25	27445.50	27448.75
113800	27452.00	27455.25	27458.50	27461.75	27465.00	27468.25	27471.50	27474.75	27478.00	27481.25
113900	27484.50	27487.75	27491.00	27494.25	27497.50	27500.75	27504.00	27507.25	27510.50	27513.75
114000	27517.00	27520.25	27523.50	27526.75	27530.00	27533.25	27536.50	27539.75	27543.00	27546.25
114100	27549.50	27552.75	27556.00	27559.25	27562.50	27565.75	27569.00	27572.25	27575.50	27578.75
114200	27582.00	27585.25	27588.50	27591.75	27595.00	27598.25	27601.50	27604.75	27608.00	27611.25
114300	27614.50	27617.75	27621.00	27624.25	27627.50	27630.75	27634.00	27637.25	27640.50	27643.75
114400	27647.00	27650.25	27653.50	27656.75	27660.00	27663.25	27666.50	27669.75	27673.00	27676.25
114500	27679.50	27682.75	27686.00	27689.25	27692.50	27695.75	27699.00	27702.25	27705.50	27708.75
114600	27712.00	27715.25	27718.50	27721.75	27725.00	27728.25	27731.50	27734.75	27738.00	27741.25
114700	27744.50	27747.75	27751.00	27754.25	27757.50	27760.75	27764.00	27767.25	27770.50	27773.75
114800	27777.00	27780.25	27783.50	27786.75	27790.00	27793.25	27796.50	27799.75	27803.00	27806.25
114900	27809.50	27812.75	27816.00	27819.25	27822.50	27825.75	27829.00	27832.25	27835.50	27838.75

To the above amounts, add the appropriate figure for the odd dollar amount

$1	$2	$3	$4	$5	$6	$7	$8	$9
0.325	0.65	0.975	1.30	1.625	1.95	2.275	2.60	2.925

***Tax offsets must be deducted, and Medicare levy added, to give net tax payable (see notes at ¶42-000)**

Taxable income	Resident Individuals: Gross Tax Payable at 2020–21 Rates*									
	$0	**$10**	**$20**	**$30**	**$40**	**$50**	**$60**	**$70**	**$80**	**$90**
115000	27842.00	27845.25	27848.50	27851.75	27855.00	27858.25	27861.50	27864.75	27868.00	27871.25
115100	27874.50	27877.75	27881.00	27884.25	27887.50	27890.75	27894.00	27897.25	27900.50	27903.75
115200	27907.00	27910.25	27913.50	27916.75	27920.00	27923.25	27926.50	27929.75	27933.00	27936.25
115300	27939.50	27942.75	27946.00	27949.25	27952.50	27955.75	27959.00	27962.25	27965.50	27968.75
115400	27972.00	27975.25	27978.50	27981.75	27985.00	27988.25	27991.50	27994.75	27998.00	28001.25
115500	28004.50	28007.75	28011.00	28014.25	28017.50	28020.75	28024.00	28027.25	28030.50	28033.75
115600	28037.00	28040.25	28043.50	28046.75	28050.00	28053.25	28056.50	28059.75	28063.00	28066.25
115700	28069.50	28072.75	28076.00	28079.25	28082.50	28085.75	28089.00	28092.25	28095.50	28098.75
115800	28102.00	28105.25	28108.50	28111.75	28115.00	28118.25	28121.50	28124.75	28128.00	28131.25
115900	28134.50	28137.75	28141.00	28144.25	28147.50	28150.75	28154.00	28157.25	28160.50	28163.75
116000	28167.00	28170.25	28173.50	28176.75	28180.00	28183.25	28186.50	28189.75	28193.00	28196.25
116100	28199.50	28202.75	28206.00	28209.25	28212.50	28215.75	28219.00	28222.25	28225.50	28228.75
116200	28232.00	28235.25	28238.50	28241.75	28245.00	28248.25	28251.50	28254.75	28258.00	28261.25
116300	28264.50	28267.75	28271.00	28274.25	28277.50	28280.75	28284.00	28287.25	28290.50	28293.75
116400	28297.00	28300.25	28303.50	28306.75	28310.00	28313.25	28316.50	28319.75	28323.00	28326.25
116500	28329.50	28332.75	28336.00	28339.25	28342.50	28345.75	28349.00	28352.25	28355.50	28358.75
116600	28362.00	28365.25	28368.50	28371.75	28375.00	28378.25	28381.50	28384.75	28388.00	28391.25
116700	28394.50	28397.75	28401.00	28404.25	28407.50	28410.75	28414.00	28417.25	28420.50	28423.75
116800	28427.00	28430.25	28433.50	28436.75	28440.00	28443.25	28446.50	28449.75	28453.00	28456.25
116900	28459.50	28462.75	28466.00	28469.25	28472.50	28475.75	28479.00	28482.25	28485.50	28488.75
117000	28492.00	28495.25	28498.50	28501.75	28505.00	28508.25	28511.50	28514.75	28518.00	28521.25
117100	28524.50	28527.75	28531.00	28534.25	28537.50	28540.75	28544.00	28547.25	28550.50	28553.75
117200	28557.00	28560.25	28563.50	28566.75	28570.00	28573.25	28576.50	28579.75	28583.00	28586.25
117300	28589.50	28592.75	28596.00	28599.25	28602.50	28605.75	28609.00	28612.25	28615.50	28618.75
117400	28622.00	28625.25	28628.50	28631.75	28635.00	28638.25	28641.50	28644.75	28648.00	28651.25
117500	28654.50	28657.75	28661.00	28664.25	28667.50	28670.75	28674.00	28677.25	28680.50	28683.75
117600	28687.00	28690.25	28693.50	28696.75	28700.00	28703.25	28706.50	28709.75	28713.00	28716.25
117700	28719.50	28722.75	28726.00	28729.25	28732.50	28735.75	28739.00	28742.25	28745.50	28748.75
117800	28752.00	28755.25	28758.50	28761.75	28765.00	28768.25	28771.50	28774.75	28778.00	28781.25
117900	28784.50	28787.75	28791.00	28794.25	28797.50	28800.75	28804.00	28807.25	28810.50	28813.75
118000	28817.00	28820.25	28823.50	28826.75	28830.00	28833.25	28836.50	28839.75	28843.00	28846.25
118100	28849.50	28852.75	28856.00	28859.25	28862.50	28865.75	28869.00	28872.25	28875.50	28878.75
118200	28882.00	28885.25	28888.50	28891.75	28895.00	28898.25	28901.50	28904.75	28908.00	28911.25
118300	28914.50	28917.75	28921.00	28924.25	28927.50	28930.75	28934.00	28937.25	28940.50	28943.75
118400	28947.00	28950.25	28953.50	28956.75	28960.00	28963.25	28966.50	28969.75	28973.00	28976.25
118500	28979.50	28982.75	28986.00	28989.25	28992.50	28995.75	28999.00	29002.25	29005.50	29008.75
118600	29012.00	29015.25	29018.50	29021.75	29025.00	29028.25	29031.50	29034.75	29038.00	29041.25
118700	29044.50	29047.75	29051.00	29054.25	29057.50	29060.75	29064.00	29067.25	29070.50	29073.75
118800	29077.00	29080.25	29083.50	29086.75	29090.00	29093.25	29096.50	29099.75	29103.00	29106.25
118900	29109.50	29112.75	29116.00	29119.25	29122.50	29125.75	29129.00	29132.25	29135.50	29138.75
119000	29142.00	29145.25	29148.50	29151.75	29155.00	29158.25	29161.50	29164.75	29168.00	29171.25
119100	29174.50	29177.75	29181.00	29184.25	29187.50	29190.75	29194.00	29197.25	29200.50	29203.75
119200	29207.00	29210.25	29213.50	29216.75	29220.00	29223.25	29226.50	29229.75	29233.00	29236.25
119300	29239.50	29242.75	29246.00	29249.25	29252.50	29255.75	29259.00	29262.25	29265.50	29268.75
119400	29272.00	29275.25	29278.50	29281.75	29285.00	29288.25	29291.50	29294.75	29298.00	29301.25
119500	29304.50	29307.75	29311.00	29314.25	29317.50	29320.75	29324.00	29327.25	29330.50	29333.75
119600	29337.00	29340.25	29343.50	29346.75	29350.00	29353.25	29356.50	29359.75	29363.00	29366.25
119700	29369.50	29372.75	29376.00	29379.25	29382.50	29385.75	29389.00	29392.25	29395.50	29398.75
119800	29402.00	29405.25	29408.50	29411.75	29415.00	29418.25	29421.50	29424.75	29428.00	29431.25
119900	29434.50	29437.75	29441.00	29444.25	29447.50	29450.75	29454.00	29457.25	29460.50	29463.75

To the above amounts, add the appropriate figure for the odd dollar amount								
$1	$2	$3	$4	$5	$6	$7	$8	$9
0.325	0.65	0.975	1.30	1.625	1.95	2.275	2.60	2.925

***Tax offsets must be deducted, and Medicare levy added, to give net tax payable (see notes at ¶42-000)**

Taxable income	Resident Individuals: Gross Tax Payable at 2020–21 Rates*								
	$0	$10	$20	$30	$40	$50	$60	$70	$80	$90
120000	29467.00	29470.70	29474.40	29478.10	29481.80	29485.50	29489.20	29492.90	29496.60	29500.30
120100	29504.00	29507.70	29511.40	29515.10	29518.80	29522.50	29526.20	29529.90	29533.60	29537.30
120200	29541.00	29544.70	29548.40	29552.10	29555.80	29559.50	29563.20	29566.90	29570.60	29574.30
120300	29578.00	29581.70	29585.40	29589.10	29592.80	29596.50	29600.20	29603.90	29607.60	29611.30
120400	29615.00	29618.70	29622.40	29626.10	29629.80	29633.50	29637.20	29640.90	29644.60	29648.30
120500	29652.00	29655.70	29659.40	29663.10	29666.80	29670.50	29674.20	29677.90	29681.60	29685.30
120600	29689.00	29692.70	29696.40	29700.10	29703.80	29707.50	29711.20	29714.90	29718.60	29722.30
120700	29726.00	29729.70	29733.40	29737.10	29740.80	29744.50	29748.20	29751.90	29755.60	29759.30
120800	29763.00	29766.70	29770.40	29774.10	29777.80	29781.50	29785.20	29788.90	29792.60	29796.30
120900	29800.00	29803.70	29807.40	29811.10	29814.80	29818.50	29822.20	29825.90	29829.60	29833.30
121000	29837.00	29840.70	29844.40	29848.10	29851.80	29855.50	29859.20	29862.90	29866.60	29870.30
121100	29874.00	29877.70	29881.40	29885.10	29888.80	29892.50	29896.20	29899.90	29903.60	29907.30
121200	29911.00	29914.70	29918.40	29922.10	29925.80	29929.50	29933.20	29936.90	29940.60	29944.30
121300	29948.00	29951.70	29955.40	29959.10	29962.80	29966.50	29970.20	29973.90	29977.60	29981.30
121400	29985.00	29988.70	29992.40	29996.10	29999.80	30003.50	30007.20	30010.90	30014.60	30018.30
121500	30022.00	30025.70	30029.40	30033.10	30036.80	30040.50	30044.20	30047.90	30051.60	30055.30
121600	30059.00	30062.70	30066.40	30070.10	30073.80	30077.50	30081.20	30084.90	30088.60	30092.30
121700	30096.00	30099.70	30103.40	30107.10	30110.80	30114.50	30118.20	30121.90	30125.60	30129.30
121800	30133.00	30136.70	30140.40	30144.10	30147.80	30151.50	30155.20	30158.90	30162.60	30166.30
121900	30170.00	30173.70	30177.40	30181.10	30184.80	30188.50	30192.20	30195.90	30199.60	30203.30
122000	30207.00	30210.70	30214.40	30218.10	30221.80	30225.50	30229.20	30232.90	30236.60	30240.30
122100	30244.00	30247.70	30251.40	30255.10	30258.80	30262.50	30266.20	30269.90	30273.60	30277.30
122200	30281.00	30284.70	30288.40	30292.10	30295.80	30299.50	30303.20	30306.90	30310.60	30314.30
122300	30318.00	30321.70	30325.40	30329.10	30332.80	30336.50	30340.20	30343.90	30347.60	30351.30
122400	30355.00	30358.70	30362.40	30366.10	30369.80	30373.50	30377.20	30380.90	30384.60	30388.30
122500	30392.00	30395.70	30399.40	30403.10	30406.80	30410.50	30414.20	30417.90	30421.60	30425.30
122600	30429.00	30432.70	30436.40	30440.10	30443.80	30447.50	30451.20	30454.90	30458.60	30462.30
122700	30466.00	30469.70	30473.40	30477.10	30480.80	30484.50	30488.20	30491.90	30495.60	30499.30
122800	30503.00	30506.70	30510.40	30514.10	30517.80	30521.50	30525.20	30528.90	30532.60	30536.30
122900	30540.00	30543.70	30547.40	30551.10	30554.80	30558.50	30562.20	30565.90	30569.60	30573.30
123000	30577.00	30580.70	30584.40	30588.10	30591.80	30595.50	30599.20	30602.90	30606.60	30610.30
123100	30614.00	30617.70	30621.40	30625.10	30628.80	30632.50	30636.20	30639.90	30643.60	30647.30
123200	30651.00	30654.70	30658.40	30662.10	30665.80	30669.50	30673.20	30676.90	30680.60	30684.30
123300	30688.00	30691.70	30695.40	30699.10	30702.80	30706.50	30710.20	30713.90	30717.60	30721.30
123400	30725.00	30728.70	30732.40	30736.10	30739.80	30743.50	30747.20	30750.90	30754.60	30758.30
123500	30762.00	30765.70	30769.40	30773.10	30776.80	30780.50	30784.20	30787.90	30791.60	30795.30
123600	30799.00	30802.70	30806.40	30810.10	30813.80	30817.50	30821.20	30824.90	30828.60	30832.30
123700	30836.00	30839.70	30843.40	30847.10	30850.80	30854.50	30858.20	30861.90	30865.60	30869.30
123800	30873.00	30876.70	30880.40	30884.10	30887.80	30891.50	30895.20	30898.90	30902.60	30906.30
123900	30910.00	30913.70	30917.40	30921.10	30924.80	30928.50	30932.20	30935.90	30939.60	30943.30
124000	30947.00	30950.70	30954.40	30958.10	30961.80	30965.50	30969.20	30972.90	30976.60	30980.30
124100	30984.00	30987.70	30991.40	30995.10	30998.80	31002.50	31006.20	31009.90	31013.60	31017.30
124200	31021.00	31024.70	31028.40	31032.10	31035.80	31039.50	31043.20	31046.90	31050.60	31054.30
124300	31058.00	31061.70	31065.40	31069.10	31072.80	31076.50	31080.20	31083.90	31087.60	31091.30
124400	31095.00	31098.70	31102.40	31106.10	31109.80	31113.50	31117.20	31120.90	31124.60	31128.30
124500	31132.00	31135.70	31139.40	31143.10	31146.80	31150.50	31154.20	31157.90	31161.60	31165.30
124600	31169.00	31172.70	31176.40	31180.10	31183.80	31187.50	31191.20	31194.90	31198.60	31202.30
124700	31206.00	31209.70	31213.40	31217.10	31220.80	31224.50	31228.20	31231.90	31235.60	31239.30
124800	31243.00	31246.70	31250.40	31254.10	31257.80	31261.50	31265.20	31268.90	31272.60	31276.30
124900	31280.00	31283.70	31287.40	31291.10	31294.80	31298.50	31302.20	31305.90	31309.60	31313.30

To the above amounts, add the appropriate figure for the odd dollar amount								
$1	$2	$3	$4	$5	$6	$7	$8	$9
0.37	0.74	1.11	1.48	1.85	2.22	2.59	2.96	3.33

***Tax offsets must be deducted, and Medicare levy added, to give net tax payable (see notes at ¶42-000)**

Taxable income	Resident Individuals: Gross Tax Payable at 2020–21 Rates*									
	$0	$10	$20	$30	$40	$50	$60	$70	$80	$90
125000	31317.00	31320.70	31324.40	31328.10	31331.80	31335.50	31339.20	31342.90	31346.60	31350.30
125100	31354.00	31357.70	31361.40	31365.10	31368.80	31372.50	31376.20	31379.90	31383.60	31387.30
125200	31391.00	31394.70	31398.40	31402.10	31405.80	31409.50	31413.20	31416.90	31420.60	31424.30
125300	31428.00	31431.70	31435.40	31439.10	31442.80	31446.50	31450.20	31453.90	31457.60	31461.30
125400	31465.00	31468.70	31472.40	31476.10	31479.80	31483.50	31487.20	31490.90	31494.60	31498.30
125500	31502.00	31505.70	31509.40	31513.10	31516.80	31520.50	31524.20	31527.90	31531.60	31535.30
125600	31539.00	31542.70	31546.40	31550.10	31553.80	31557.50	31561.20	31564.90	31568.60	31572.30
125700	31576.00	31579.70	31583.40	31587.10	31590.80	31594.50	31598.20	31601.90	31605.60	31609.30
125800	31613.00	31616.70	31620.40	31624.10	31627.80	31631.50	31635.20	31638.90	31642.60	31646.30
125900	31650.00	31653.70	31657.40	31661.10	31664.80	31668.50	31672.20	31675.90	31679.60	31683.30
126000	31687.00	31690.70	31694.40	31698.10	31701.80	31705.50	31709.20	31712.90	31716.60	31720.30
126100	31724.00	31727.70	31731.40	31735.10	31738.80	31742.50	31746.20	31749.90	31753.60	31757.30
126200	31761.00	31764.70	31768.40	31772.10	31775.80	31779.50	31783.20	31786.90	31790.60	31794.30
126300	31798.00	31801.70	31805.40	31809.10	31812.80	31816.50	31820.20	31823.90	31827.60	31831.30
126400	31835.00	31838.70	31842.40	31846.10	31849.80	31853.50	31857.20	31860.90	31864.60	31868.30
126500	31872.00	31875.70	31879.40	31883.10	31886.80	31890.50	31894.20	31897.90	31901.60	31905.30
126600	31909.00	31912.70	31916.40	31920.10	31923.80	31927.50	31931.20	31934.90	31938.60	31942.30
126700	31946.00	31949.70	31953.40	31957.10	31960.80	31964.50	31968.20	31971.90	31975.60	31979.30
126800	31983.00	31986.70	31990.40	31994.10	31997.80	32001.50	32005.20	32008.90	32012.60	32016.30
126900	32020.00	32023.70	32027.40	32031.10	32034.80	32038.50	32042.20	32045.90	32049.60	32053.30
127000	32057.00	32060.70	32064.40	32068.10	32071.80	32075.50	32079.20	32082.90	32086.60	32090.30
127100	32094.00	32097.70	32101.40	32105.10	32108.80	32112.50	32116.20	32119.90	32123.60	32127.30
127200	32131.00	32134.70	32138.40	32142.10	32145.80	32149.50	32153.20	32156.90	32160.60	32164.30
127300	32168.00	32171.70	32175.40	32179.10	32182.80	32186.50	32190.20	32193.90	32197.60	32201.30
127400	32205.00	32208.70	32212.40	32216.10	32219.80	32223.50	32227.20	32230.90	32234.60	32238.30
127500	32242.00	32245.70	32249.40	32253.10	32256.80	32260.50	32264.20	32267.90	32271.60	32275.30
127600	32279.00	32282.70	32286.40	32290.10	32293.80	32297.50	32301.20	32304.90	32308.60	32312.30
127700	32316.00	32319.70	32323.40	32327.10	32330.80	32334.50	32338.20	32341.90	32345.60	32349.30
127800	32353.00	32356.70	32360.40	32364.10	32367.80	32371.50	32375.20	32378.90	32382.60	32386.30
127900	32390.00	32393.70	32397.40	32401.10	32404.80	32408.50	32412.20	32415.90	32419.60	32423.30
128000	32427.00	32430.70	32434.40	32438.10	32441.80	32445.50	32449.20	32452.90	32456.60	32460.30
128100	32464.00	32467.70	32471.40	32475.10	32478.80	32482.50	32486.20	32489.90	32493.60	32497.30
128200	32501.00	32504.70	32508.40	32512.10	32515.80	32519.50	32523.20	32526.90	32530.60	32534.30
128300	32538.00	32541.70	32545.40	32549.10	32552.80	32556.50	32560.20	32563.90	32567.60	32571.30
128400	32575.00	32578.70	32582.40	32586.10	32589.80	32593.50	32597.20	32600.90	32604.60	32608.30
128500	32612.00	32615.70	32619.40	32623.10	32626.80	32630.50	32634.20	32637.90	32641.60	32645.30
128600	32649.00	32652.70	32656.40	32660.10	32663.80	32667.50	32671.20	32674.90	32678.60	32682.30
128700	32686.00	32689.70	32693.40	32697.10	32700.80	32704.50	32708.20	32711.90	32715.60	32719.30
128800	32723.00	32726.70	32730.40	32734.10	32737.80	32741.50	32745.20	32748.90	32752.60	32756.30
128900	32760.00	32763.70	32767.40	32771.10	32774.80	32778.50	32782.20	32785.90	32789.60	32793.30
129000	32797.00	32800.70	32804.40	32808.10	32811.80	32815.50	32819.20	32822.90	32826.60	32830.30
129100	32834.00	32837.70	32841.40	32845.10	32848.80	32852.50	32856.20	32859.90	32863.60	32867.30
129200	32871.00	32874.70	32878.40	32882.10	32885.80	32889.50	32893.20	32896.90	32900.60	32904.30
129300	32908.00	32911.70	32915.40	32919.10	32922.80	32926.50	32930.20	32933.90	32937.60	32941.30
129400	32945.00	32948.70	32952.40	32956.10	32959.80	32963.50	32967.20	32970.90	32974.60	32978.30
129500	32982.00	32985.70	32989.40	32993.10	32996.80	33000.50	33004.20	33007.90	33011.60	33015.30
129600	33019.00	33022.70	33026.40	33030.10	33033.80	33037.50	33041.20	33044.90	33048.60	33052.30
129700	33056.00	33059.70	33063.40	33067.10	33070.80	33074.50	33078.20	33081.90	33085.60	33089.30
129800	33093.00	33096.70	33100.40	33104.10	33107.80	33111.50	33115.20	33118.90	33122.60	33126.30
129900	33130.00	33133.70	33137.40	33141.10	33144.80	33148.50	33152.20	33155.90	33159.60	33163.30

To the above amounts, add the appropriate figure for the odd dollar amount								
$1	$2	$3	$4	$5	$6	$7	$8	$9
0.37	0.74	1.11	1.48	1.85	2.22	2.59	2.96	3.33

***Tax offsets must be deducted, and Medicare levy added, to give net tax payable (see notes at ¶42-000)**

Taxable income	Resident Individuals: Gross Tax Payable at 2020–21 Rates*									
	$0	**$10**	**$20**	**$30**	**$40**	**$50**	**$60**	**$70**	**$80**	**$90**
130000	33167.00	33170.70	33174.40	33178.10	33181.80	33185.50	33189.20	33192.90	33196.60	33200.30
130100	33204.00	33207.70	33211.40	33215.10	33218.80	33222.50	33226.20	33229.90	33233.60	33237.30
130200	33241.00	33244.70	33248.40	33252.10	33255.80	33259.50	33263.20	33266.90	33270.60	33274.30
130300	33278.00	33281.70	33285.40	33289.10	33292.80	33296.50	33300.20	33303.90	33307.60	33311.30
130400	33315.00	33318.70	33322.40	33326.10	33329.80	33333.50	33337.20	33340.90	33344.60	33348.30
130500	33352.00	33355.70	33359.40	33363.10	33366.80	33370.50	33374.20	33377.90	33381.60	33385.30
130600	33389.00	33392.70	33396.40	33400.10	33403.80	33407.50	33411.20	33414.90	33418.60	33422.30
130700	33426.00	33429.70	33433.40	33437.10	33440.80	33444.50	33448.20	33451.90	33455.60	33459.30
130800	33463.00	33466.70	33470.40	33474.10	33477.80	33481.50	33485.20	33488.90	33492.60	33496.30
130900	33500.00	33503.70	33507.40	33511.10	33514.80	33518.50	33522.20	33525.90	33529.60	33533.30
131000	33537.00	33540.70	33544.40	33548.10	33551.80	33555.50	33559.20	33562.90	33566.60	33570.30
131100	33574.00	33577.70	33581.40	33585.10	33588.80	33592.50	33596.20	33599.90	33603.60	33607.30
131200	33611.00	33614.70	33618.40	33622.10	33625.80	33629.50	33633.20	33636.90	33640.60	33644.30
131300	33648.00	33651.70	33655.40	33659.10	33662.80	33666.50	33670.20	33673.90	33677.60	33681.30
131400	33685.00	33688.70	33692.40	33696.10	33699.80	33703.50	33707.20	33710.90	33714.60	33718.30
131500	33722.00	33725.70	33729.40	33733.10	33736.80	33740.50	33744.20	33747.90	33751.60	33755.30
131600	33759.00	33762.70	33766.40	33770.10	33773.80	33777.50	33781.20	33784.90	33788.60	33792.30
131700	33796.00	33799.70	33803.40	33807.10	33810.80	33814.50	33818.20	33821.90	33825.60	33829.30
131800	33833.00	33836.70	33840.40	33844.10	33847.80	33851.50	33855.20	33858.90	33862.60	33866.30
131900	33870.00	33873.70	33877.40	33881.10	33884.80	33888.50	33892.20	33895.90	33899.60	33903.30
132000	33907.00	33910.70	33914.40	33918.10	33921.80	33925.50	33929.20	33932.90	33936.60	33940.30
132100	33944.00	33947.70	33951.40	33955.10	33958.80	33962.50	33966.20	33969.90	33973.60	33977.30
132200	33981.00	33984.70	33988.40	33992.10	33995.80	33999.50	34003.20	34006.90	34010.60	34014.30
132300	34018.00	34021.70	34025.40	34029.10	34032.80	34036.50	34040.20	34043.90	34047.60	34051.30
132400	34055.00	34058.70	34062.40	34066.10	34069.80	34073.50	34077.20	34080.90	34084.60	34088.30
132500	34092.00	34095.70	34099.40	34103.10	34106.80	34110.50	34114.20	34117.90	34121.60	34125.30
132600	34129.00	34132.70	34136.40	34140.10	34143.80	34147.50	34151.20	34154.90	34158.60	34162.30
132700	34166.00	34169.70	34173.40	34177.10	34180.80	34184.50	34188.20	34191.90	34195.60	34199.30
132800	34203.00	34206.70	34210.40	34214.10	34217.80	34221.50	34225.20	34228.90	34232.60	34236.30
132900	34240.00	34243.70	34247.40	34251.10	34254.80	34258.50	34262.20	34265.90	34269.60	34273.30
133000	34277.00	34280.70	34284.40	34288.10	34291.80	34295.50	34299.20	34302.90	34306.60	34310.30
133100	34314.00	34317.70	34321.40	34325.10	34328.80	34332.50	34336.20	34339.90	34343.60	34347.30
133200	34351.00	34354.70	34358.40	34362.10	34365.80	34369.50	34373.20	34376.90	34380.60	34384.30
133300	34388.00	34391.70	34395.40	34399.10	34402.80	34406.50	34410.20	34413.90	34417.60	34421.30
133400	34425.00	34428.70	34432.40	34436.10	34439.80	34443.50	34447.20	34450.90	34454.60	34458.30
133500	34462.00	34465.70	34469.40	34473.10	34476.80	34480.50	34484.20	34487.90	34491.60	34495.30
133600	34499.00	34502.70	34506.40	34510.10	34513.80	34517.50	34521.20	34524.90	34528.60	34532.30
133700	34536.00	34539.70	34543.40	34547.10	34550.80	34554.50	34558.20	34561.90	34565.60	34569.30
133800	34573.00	34576.70	34580.40	34584.10	34587.80	34591.50	34595.20	34598.90	34602.60	34606.30
133900	34610.00	34613.70	34617.40	34621.10	34624.80	34628.50	34632.20	34635.90	34639.60	34643.30
134000	34647.00	34650.70	34654.40	34658.10	34661.80	34665.50	34669.20	34672.90	34676.60	34680.30
134100	34684.00	34687.70	34691.40	34695.10	34698.80	34702.50	34706.20	34709.90	34713.60	34717.30
134200	34721.00	34724.70	34728.40	34732.10	34735.80	34739.50	34743.20	34746.90	34750.60	34754.30
134300	34758.00	34761.70	34765.40	34769.10	34772.80	34776.50	34780.20	34783.90	34787.60	34791.30
134400	34795.00	34798.70	34802.40	34806.10	34809.80	34813.50	34817.20	34820.90	34824.60	34828.30
134500	34832.00	34835.70	34839.40	34843.10	34846.80	34850.50	34854.20	34857.90	34861.60	34865.30
134600	34869.00	34872.70	34876.40	34880.10	34883.80	34887.50	34891.20	34894.90	34898.60	34902.30
134700	34906.00	34909.70	34913.40	34917.10	34920.80	34924.50	34928.20	34931.90	34935.60	34939.30
134800	34943.00	34946.70	34950.40	34954.10	34957.80	34961.50	34965.20	34968.90	34972.60	34976.30
134900	34980.00	34983.70	34987.40	34991.10	34994.80	34998.50	35002.20	35005.90	35009.60	35013.30

To the above amounts, add the appropriate figure for the odd dollar amount								
$1	$2	$3	$4	$5	$6	$7	$8	$9
0.37	0.74	1.11	1.48	1.85	2.22	2.59	2.96	3.33

***Tax offsets must be deducted, and Medicare levy added, to give net tax payable (see notes at ¶42-000)**

Resident Individuals: Gross Tax Payable at 2020–21 Rates*

Taxable income	$0	$10	$20	$30	$40	$50	$60	$70	$80	$90
135000	35017.00	35020.70	35024.40	35028.10	35031.80	35035.50	35039.20	35042.90	35046.60	35050.30
135100	35054.00	35057.70	35061.40	35065.10	35068.80	35072.50	35076.20	35079.90	35083.60	35087.30
135200	35091.00	35094.70	35098.40	35102.10	35105.80	35109.50	35113.20	35116.90	35120.60	35124.30
135300	35128.00	35131.70	35135.40	35139.10	35142.80	35146.50	35150.20	35153.90	35157.60	35161.30
135400	35165.00	35168.70	35172.40	35176.10	35179.80	35183.50	35187.20	35190.90	35194.60	35198.30
135500	35202.00	35205.70	35209.40	35213.10	35216.80	35220.50	35224.20	35227.90	35231.60	35235.30
135600	35239.00	35242.70	35246.40	35250.10	35253.80	35257.50	35261.20	35264.90	35268.60	35272.30
135700	35276.00	35279.70	35283.40	35287.10	35290.80	35294.50	35298.20	35301.90	35305.60	35309.30
135800	35313.00	35316.70	35320.40	35324.10	35327.80	35331.50	35335.20	35338.90	35342.60	35346.30
135900	35350.00	35353.70	35357.40	35361.10	35364.80	35368.50	35372.20	35375.90	35379.60	35383.30
136000	35387.00	35390.70	35394.40	35398.10	35401.80	35405.50	35409.20	35412.90	35416.60	35420.30
136100	35424.00	35427.70	35431.40	35435.10	35438.80	35442.50	35446.20	35449.90	35453.60	35457.30
136200	35461.00	35464.70	35468.40	35472.10	35475.80	35479.50	35483.20	35486.90	35490.60	35494.30
136300	35498.00	35501.70	35505.40	35509.10	35512.80	35516.50	35520.20	35523.90	35527.60	35531.30
136400	35535.00	35538.70	35542.40	35546.10	35549.80	35553.50	35557.20	35560.90	35564.60	35568.30
136500	35572.00	35575.70	35579.40	35583.10	35586.80	35590.50	35594.20	35597.90	35601.60	35605.30
136600	35609.00	35612.70	35616.40	35620.10	35623.80	35627.50	35631.20	35634.90	35638.60	35642.30
136700	35646.00	35649.70	35653.40	35657.10	35660.80	35664.50	35668.20	35671.90	35675.60	35679.30
136800	35683.00	35686.70	35690.40	35694.10	35697.80	35701.50	35705.20	35708.90	35712.60	35716.30
136900	35720.00	35723.70	35727.40	35731.10	35734.80	35738.50	35742.20	35745.90	35749.60	35753.30
137000	35757.00	35760.70	35764.40	35768.10	35771.80	35775.50	35779.20	35782.90	35786.60	35790.30
137100	35794.00	35797.70	35801.40	35805.10	35808.80	35812.50	35816.20	35819.90	35823.60	35827.30
137200	35831.00	35834.70	35838.40	35842.10	35845.80	35849.50	35853.20	35856.90	35860.60	35864.30
137300	35868.00	35871.70	35875.40	35879.10	35882.80	35886.50	35890.20	35893.90	35897.60	35901.30
137400	35905.00	35908.70	35912.40	35916.10	35919.80	35923.50	35927.20	35930.90	35934.60	35938.30
137500	35942.00	35945.70	35949.40	35953.10	35956.80	35960.50	35964.20	35967.90	35971.60	35975.30
137600	35979.00	35982.70	35986.40	35990.10	35993.80	35997.50	36001.20	36004.90	36008.60	36012.30
137700	36016.00	36019.70	36023.40	36027.10	36030.80	36034.50	36038.20	36041.90	36045.60	36049.30
137800	36053.00	36056.70	36060.40	36064.10	36067.80	36071.50	36075.20	36078.90	36082.60	36086.30
137900	36090.00	36093.70	36097.40	36101.10	36104.80	36108.50	36112.20	36115.90	36119.60	36123.30
138000	36127.00	36130.70	36134.40	36138.10	36141.80	36145.50	36149.20	36152.90	36156.60	36160.30
138100	36164.00	36167.70	36171.40	36175.10	36178.80	36182.50	36186.20	36189.90	36193.60	36197.30
138200	36201.00	36204.70	36208.40	36212.10	36215.80	36219.50	36223.20	36226.90	36230.60	36234.30
138300	36238.00	36241.70	36245.40	36249.10	36252.80	36256.50	36260.20	36263.90	36267.60	36271.30
138400	36275.00	36278.70	36282.40	36286.10	36289.80	36293.50	36297.20	36300.90	36304.60	36308.30
138500	36312.00	36315.70	36319.40	36323.10	36326.80	36330.50	36334.20	36337.90	36341.60	36345.30
138600	36349.00	36352.70	36356.40	36360.10	36363.80	36367.50	36371.20	36374.90	36378.60	36382.30
138700	36386.00	36389.70	36393.40	36397.10	36400.80	36404.50	36408.20	36411.90	36415.60	36419.30
138800	36423.00	36426.70	36430.40	36434.10	36437.80	36441.50	36445.20	36448.90	36452.60	36456.30
138900	36460.00	36463.70	36467.40	36471.10	36474.80	36478.50	36482.20	36485.90	36489.60	36493.30
139000	36497.00	36500.70	36504.40	36508.10	36511.80	36515.50	36519.20	36522.90	36526.60	36530.30
139100	36534.00	36537.70	36541.40	36545.10	36548.80	36552.50	36556.20	36559.90	36563.60	36567.30
139200	36571.00	36574.70	36578.40	36582.10	36585.80	36589.50	36593.20	36596.90	36600.60	36604.30
139300	36608.00	36611.70	36615.40	36619.10	36622.80	36626.50	36630.20	36633.90	36637.60	36641.30
139400	36645.00	36648.70	36652.40	36656.10	36659.80	36663.50	36667.20	36670.90	36674.60	36678.30
139500	36682.00	36685.70	36689.40	36693.10	36696.80	36700.50	36704.20	36707.90	36711.60	36715.30
139600	36719.00	36722.70	36726.40	36730.10	36733.80	36737.50	36741.20	36744.90	36748.60	36752.30
139700	36756.00	36759.70	36763.40	36767.10	36770.80	36774.50	36778.20	36781.90	36785.60	36789.30
139800	36793.00	36796.70	36800.40	36804.10	36807.80	36811.50	36815.20	36818.90	36822.60	36826.30
139900	36830.00	36833.70	36837.40	36841.10	36844.80	36848.50	36852.20	36855.90	36859.60	36863.30

To the above amounts, add the appropriate figure for the odd dollar amount

$1	$2	$3	$4	$5	$6	$7	$8	$9
0.37	0.74	1.11	1.48	1.85	2.22	2.59	2.96	3.33

***Tax offsets must be deducted, and Medicare levy added, to give net tax payable (see notes at ¶42-000)**

Resident Individuals: Gross Tax Payable at 2020–21 Rates*

Taxable income	$0	$10	$20	$30	$40	$50	$60	$70	$80	$90
140000	36867.00	36870.70	36874.40	36878.10	36881.80	36885.50	36889.20	36892.90	36896.60	36900.30
140100	36904.00	36907.70	36911.40	36915.10	36918.80	36922.50	36926.20	36929.90	36933.60	36937.30
140200	36941.00	36944.70	36948.40	36952.10	36955.80	36959.50	36963.20	36966.90	36970.60	36974.30
140300	36978.00	36981.70	36985.40	36989.10	36992.80	36996.50	37000.20	37003.90	37007.60	37011.30
140400	37015.00	37018.70	37022.40	37026.10	37029.80	37033.50	37037.20	37040.90	37044.60	37048.30
140500	37052.00	37055.70	37059.40	37063.10	37066.80	37070.50	37074.20	37077.90	37081.60	37085.30
140600	37089.00	37092.70	37096.40	37100.10	37103.80	37107.50	37111.20	37114.90	37118.60	37122.30
140700	37126.00	37129.70	37133.40	37137.10	37140.80	37144.50	37148.20	37151.90	37155.60	37159.30
140800	37163.00	37166.70	37170.40	37174.10	37177.80	37181.50	37185.20	37188.90	37192.60	37196.30
140900	37200.00	37203.70	37207.40	37211.10	37214.80	37218.50	37222.20	37225.90	37229.60	37233.30
141000	37237.00	37240.70	37244.40	37248.10	37251.80	37255.50	37259.20	37262.90	37266.60	37270.30
141100	37274.00	37277.70	37281.40	37285.10	37288.80	37292.50	37296.20	37299.90	37303.60	37307.30
141200	37311.00	37314.70	37318.40	37322.10	37325.80	37329.50	37333.20	37336.90	37340.60	37344.30
141300	37348.00	37351.70	37355.40	37359.10	37362.80	37366.50	37370.20	37373.90	37377.60	37381.30
141400	37385.00	37388.70	37392.40	37396.10	37399.80	37403.50	37407.20	37410.90	37414.60	37418.30
141500	37422.00	37425.70	37429.40	37433.10	37436.80	37440.50	37444.20	37447.90	37451.60	37455.30
141600	37459.00	37462.70	37466.40	37470.10	37473.80	37477.50	37481.20	37484.90	37488.60	37492.30
141700	37496.00	37499.70	37503.40	37507.10	37510.80	37514.50	37518.20	37521.90	37525.60	37529.30
141800	37533.00	37536.70	37540.40	37544.10	37547.80	37551.50	37555.20	37558.90	37562.60	37566.30
141900	37570.00	37573.70	37577.40	37581.10	37584.80	37588.50	37592.20	37595.90	37599.60	37603.30
142000	37607.00	37610.70	37614.40	37618.10	37621.80	37625.50	37629.20	37632.90	37636.60	37640.30
142100	37644.00	37647.70	37651.40	37655.10	37658.80	37662.50	37666.20	37669.90	37673.60	37677.30
142200	37681.00	37684.70	37688.40	37692.10	37695.80	37699.50	37703.20	37706.90	37710.60	37714.30
142300	37718.00	37721.70	37725.40	37729.10	37732.80	37736.50	37740.20	37743.90	37747.60	37751.30
142400	37755.00	37758.70	37762.40	37766.10	37769.80	37773.50	37777.20	37780.90	37784.60	37788.30
142500	37792.00	37795.70	37799.40	37803.10	37806.80	37810.50	37814.20	37817.90	37821.60	37825.30
142600	37829.00	37832.70	37836.40	37840.10	37843.80	37847.50	37851.20	37854.90	37858.60	37862.30
142700	37866.00	37869.70	37873.40	37877.10	37880.80	37884.50	37888.20	37891.90	37895.60	37899.30
142800	37903.00	37906.70	37910.40	37914.10	37917.80	37921.50	37925.20	37928.90	37932.60	37936.30
142900	37940.00	37943.70	37947.40	37951.10	37954.80	37958.50	37962.20	37965.90	37969.60	37973.30
143000	37977.00	37980.70	37984.40	37988.10	37991.80	37995.50	37999.20	38002.90	38006.60	38010.30
143100	38014.00	38017.70	38021.40	38025.10	38028.80	38032.50	38036.20	38039.90	38043.60	38047.30
143200	38051.00	38054.70	38058.40	38062.10	38065.80	38069.50	38073.20	38076.90	38080.60	38084.30
143300	38088.00	38091.70	38095.40	38099.10	38102.80	38106.50	38110.20	38113.90	38117.60	38121.30
143400	38125.00	38128.70	38132.40	38136.10	38139.80	38143.50	38147.20	38150.90	38154.60	38158.30
143500	38162.00	38165.70	38169.40	38173.10	38176.80	38180.50	38184.20	38187.90	38191.60	38195.30
143600	38199.00	38202.70	38206.40	38210.10	38213.80	38217.50	38221.20	38224.90	38228.60	38232.30
143700	38236.00	38239.70	38243.40	38247.10	38250.80	38254.50	38258.20	38261.90	38265.60	38269.30
143800	38273.00	38276.70	38280.40	38284.10	38287.80	38291.50	38295.20	38298.90	38302.60	38306.30
143900	38310.00	38313.70	38317.40	38321.10	38324.80	38328.50	38332.20	38335.90	38339.60	38343.30
144000	38347.00	38350.70	38354.40	38358.10	38361.80	38365.50	38369.20	38372.90	38376.60	38380.30
144100	38384.00	38387.70	38391.40	38395.10	38398.80	38402.50	38406.20	38409.90	38413.60	38417.30
144200	38421.00	38424.70	38428.40	38432.10	38435.80	38439.50	38443.20	38446.90	38450.60	38454.30
144300	38458.00	38461.70	38465.40	38469.10	38472.80	38476.50	38480.20	38483.90	38487.60	38491.30
144400	38495.00	38498.70	38502.40	38506.10	38509.80	38513.50	38517.20	38520.90	38524.60	38528.30
144500	38532.00	38535.70	38539.40	38543.10	38546.80	38550.50	38554.20	38557.90	38561.60	38565.30
144600	38569.00	38572.70	38576.40	38580.10	38583.80	38587.50	38591.20	38594.90	38598.60	38602.30
144700	38606.00	38609.70	38613.40	38617.10	38620.80	38624.50	38628.20	38631.90	38635.60	38639.30
144800	38643.00	38646.70	38650.40	38654.10	38657.80	38661.50	38665.20	38668.90	38672.60	38676.30
144900	38680.00	38683.70	38687.40	38691.10	38694.80	38698.50	38702.20	38705.90	38709.60	38713.30

To the above amounts, add the appropriate figure for the odd dollar amount

$1	$2	$3	$4	$5	$6	$7	$8	$9
0.37	0.74	1.11	1.48	1.85	2.22	2.59	2.96	3.33

***Tax offsets must be deducted, and Medicare levy added, to give net tax payable (see notes at ¶42-000)**

Resident Individuals: Gross Tax Payable at 2020–21 Rates*

Taxable income	$0	$10	$20	$30	$40	$50	$60	$70	$80	$90
145000	38717.00	38720.70	38724.40	38728.10	38731.80	38735.50	38739.20	38742.90	38746.60	38750.30
145100	38754.00	38757.70	38761.40	38765.10	38768.80	38772.50	38776.20	38779.90	38783.60	38787.30
145200	38791.00	38794.70	38798.40	38802.10	38805.80	38809.50	38813.20	38816.90	38820.60	38824.30
145300	38828.00	38831.70	38835.40	38839.10	38842.80	38846.50	38850.20	38853.90	38857.60	38861.30
145400	38865.00	38868.70	38872.40	38876.10	38879.80	38883.50	38887.20	38890.90	38894.60	38898.30
145500	38902.00	38905.70	38909.40	38913.10	38916.80	38920.50	38924.20	38927.90	38931.60	38935.30
145600	38939.00	38942.70	38946.40	38950.10	38953.80	38957.50	38961.20	38964.90	38968.60	38972.30
145700	38976.00	38979.70	38983.40	38987.10	38990.80	38994.50	38998.20	39001.90	39005.60	39009.30
145800	39013.00	39016.70	39020.40	39024.10	39027.80	39031.50	39035.20	39038.90	39042.60	39046.30
145900	39050.00	39053.70	39057.40	39061.10	39064.80	39068.50	39072.20	39075.90	39079.60	39083.30
146000	39087.00	39090.70	39094.40	39098.10	39101.80	39105.50	39109.20	39112.90	39116.60	39120.30
146100	39124.00	39127.70	39131.40	39135.10	39138.80	39142.50	39146.20	39149.90	39153.60	39157.30
146200	39161.00	39164.70	39168.40	39172.10	39175.80	39179.50	39183.20	39186.90	39190.60	39194.30
146300	39198.00	39201.70	39205.40	39209.10	39212.80	39216.50	39220.20	39223.90	39227.60	39231.30
146400	39235.00	39238.70	39242.40	39246.10	39249.80	39253.50	39257.20	39260.90	39264.60	39268.30
146500	39272.00	39275.70	39279.40	39283.10	39286.80	39290.50	39294.20	39297.90	39301.60	39305.30
146600	39309.00	39312.70	39316.40	39320.10	39323.80	39327.50	39331.20	39334.90	39338.60	39342.30
146700	39346.00	39349.70	39353.40	39357.10	39360.80	39364.50	39368.20	39371.90	39375.60	39379.30
146800	39383.00	39386.70	39390.40	39394.10	39397.80	39401.50	39405.20	39408.90	39412.60	39416.30
146900	39420.00	39423.70	39427.40	39431.10	39434.80	39438.50	39442.20	39445.90	39449.60	39453.30
147000	39457.00	39460.70	39464.40	39468.10	39471.80	39475.50	39479.20	39482.90	39486.60	39490.30
147100	39494.00	39497.70	39501.40	39505.10	39508.80	39512.50	39516.20	39519.90	39523.60	39527.30
147200	39531.00	39534.70	39538.40	39542.10	39545.80	39549.50	39553.20	39556.90	39560.60	39564.30
147300	39568.00	39571.70	39575.40	39579.10	39582.80	39586.50	39590.20	39593.90	39597.60	39601.30
147400	39605.00	39608.70	39612.40	39616.10	39619.80	39623.50	39627.20	39630.90	39634.60	39638.30
147500	39642.00	39645.70	39649.40	39653.10	39656.80	39660.50	39664.20	39667.90	39671.60	39675.30
147600	39679.00	39682.70	39686.40	39690.10	39693.80	39697.50	39701.20	39704.90	39708.60	39712.30
147700	39716.00	39719.70	39723.40	39727.10	39730.80	39734.50	39738.20	39741.90	39745.60	39749.30
147800	39753.00	39756.70	39760.40	39764.10	39767.80	39771.50	39775.20	39778.90	39782.60	39786.30
147900	39790.00	39793.70	39797.40	39801.10	39804.80	39808.50	39812.20	39815.90	39819.60	39823.30
148000	39827.00	39830.70	39834.40	39838.10	39841.80	39845.50	39849.20	39852.90	39856.60	39860.30
148100	39864.00	39867.70	39871.40	39875.10	39878.80	39882.50	39886.20	39889.90	39893.60	39897.30
148200	39901.00	39904.70	39908.40	39912.10	39915.80	39919.50	39923.20	39926.90	39930.60	39934.30
148300	39938.00	39941.70	39945.40	39949.10	39952.80	39956.50	39960.20	39963.90	39967.60	39971.30
148400	39975.00	39978.70	39982.40	39986.10	39989.80	39993.50	39997.20	40000.90	40004.60	40008.30
148500	40012.00	40015.70	40019.40	40023.10	40026.80	40030.50	40034.20	40037.90	40041.60	40045.30
148600	40049.00	40052.70	40056.40	40060.10	40063.80	40067.50	40071.20	40074.90	40078.60	40082.30
148700	40086.00	40089.70	40093.40	40097.10	40100.80	40104.50	40108.20	40111.90	40115.60	40119.30
148800	40123.00	40126.70	40130.40	40134.10	40137.80	40141.50	40145.20	40148.90	40152.60	40156.30
148900	40160.00	40163.70	40167.40	40171.10	40174.80	40178.50	40182.20	40185.90	40189.60	40193.30
149000	40197.00	40200.70	40204.40	40208.10	40211.80	40215.50	40219.20	40222.90	40226.60	40230.30
149100	40234.00	40237.70	40241.40	40245.10	40248.80	40252.50	40256.20	40259.90	40263.60	40267.30
149200	40271.00	40274.70	40278.40	40282.10	40285.80	40289.50	40293.20	40296.90	40300.60	40304.30
149300	40308.00	40311.70	40315.40	40319.10	40322.80	40326.50	40330.20	40333.90	40337.60	40341.30
149400	40345.00	40348.70	40352.40	40356.10	40359.80	40363.50	40367.20	40370.90	40374.60	40378.30
149500	40382.00	40385.70	40389.40	40393.10	40396.80	40400.50	40404.20	40407.90	40411.60	40415.30
149600	40419.00	40422.70	40426.40	40430.10	40433.80	40437.50	40441.20	40444.90	40448.60	40452.30
149700	40456.00	40459.70	40463.40	40467.10	40470.80	40474.50	40478.20	40481.90	40485.60	40489.30
149800	40493.00	40496.70	40500.40	40504.10	40507.80	40511.50	40515.20	40518.90	40522.60	40526.30
149900	40530.00	40533.70	40537.40	40541.10	40544.80	40548.50	40552.20	40555.90	40559.60	40563.30

To the above amounts, add the appropriate figure for the odd dollar amount

$1	$2	$3	$4	$5	$6	$7	$8	$9
0.37	0.74	1.11	1.48	1.85	2.22	2.59	2.96	3.33

***Tax offsets must be deducted, and Medicare levy added, to give net tax payable (see notes at ¶42-000)**

Resident Individuals: Gross Tax Payable at 2020–21 Rates*

Taxable income	$0	$10	$20	$30	$40	$50	$60	$70	$80	$90
150000	40567.00	40570.70	40574.40	40578.10	40581.80	40585.50	40589.20	40592.90	40596.60	40600.30
150100	40604.00	40607.70	40611.40	40615.10	40618.80	40622.50	40626.20	40629.90	40633.60	40637.30
150200	40641.00	40644.70	40648.40	40652.10	40655.80	40659.50	40663.20	40666.90	40670.60	40674.30
150300	40678.00	40681.70	40685.40	40689.10	40692.80	40696.50	40700.20	40703.90	40707.60	40711.30
150400	40715.00	40718.70	40722.40	40726.10	40729.80	40733.50	40737.20	40740.90	40744.60	40748.30
150500	40752.00	40755.70	40759.40	40763.10	40766.80	40770.50	40774.20	40777.90	40781.60	40785.30
150600	40789.00	40792.70	40796.40	40800.10	40803.80	40807.50	40811.20	40814.90	40818.60	40822.30
150700	40826.00	40829.70	40833.40	40837.10	40840.80	40844.50	40848.20	40851.90	40855.60	40859.30
150800	40863.00	40866.70	40870.40	40874.10	40877.80	40881.50	40885.20	40888.90	40892.60	40896.30
150900	40900.00	40903.70	40907.40	40911.10	40914.80	40918.50	40922.20	40925.90	40929.60	40933.30
151000	40937.00	40940.70	40944.40	40948.10	40951.80	40955.50	40959.20	40962.90	40966.60	40970.30
151100	40974.00	40977.70	40981.40	40985.10	40988.80	40992.50	40996.20	40999.90	41003.60	41007.30
151200	41011.00	41014.70	41018.40	41022.10	41025.80	41029.50	41033.20	41036.90	41040.60	41044.30
151300	41048.00	41051.70	41055.40	41059.10	41062.80	41066.50	41070.20	41073.90	41077.60	41081.30
151400	41085.00	41088.70	41092.40	41096.10	41099.80	41103.50	41107.20	41110.90	41114.60	41118.30
151500	41122.00	41125.70	41129.40	41133.10	41136.80	41140.50	41144.20	41147.90	41151.60	41155.30
151600	41159.00	41162.70	41166.40	41170.10	41173.80	41177.50	41181.20	41184.90	41188.60	41192.30
151700	41196.00	41199.70	41203.40	41207.10	41210.80	41214.50	41218.20	41221.90	41225.60	41229.30
151800	41233.00	41236.70	41240.40	41244.10	41247.80	41251.50	41255.20	41258.90	41262.60	41266.30
151900	41270.00	41273.70	41277.40	41281.10	41284.80	41288.50	41292.20	41295.90	41299.60	41303.30
152000	41307.00	41310.70	41314.40	41318.10	41321.80	41325.50	41329.20	41332.90	41336.60	41340.30
152100	41344.00	41347.70	41351.40	41355.10	41358.80	41362.50	41366.20	41369.90	41373.60	41377.30
152200	41381.00	41384.70	41388.40	41392.10	41395.80	41399.50	41403.20	41406.90	41410.60	41414.30
152300	41418.00	41421.70	41425.40	41429.10	41432.80	41436.50	41440.20	41443.90	41447.60	41451.30
152400	41455.00	41458.70	41462.40	41466.10	41469.80	41473.50	41477.20	41480.90	41484.60	41488.30
152500	41492.00	41495.70	41499.40	41503.10	41506.80	41510.50	41514.20	41517.90	41521.60	41525.30
152600	41529.00	41532.70	41536.40	41540.10	41543.80	41547.50	41551.20	41554.90	41558.60	41562.30
152700	41566.00	41569.70	41573.40	41577.10	41580.80	41584.50	41588.20	41591.90	41595.60	41599.30
152800	41603.00	41606.70	41610.40	41614.10	41617.80	41621.50	41625.20	41628.90	41632.60	41636.30
152900	41640.00	41643.70	41647.40	41651.10	41654.80	41658.50	41662.20	41665.90	41669.60	41673.30
153000	41677.00	41680.70	41684.40	41688.10	41691.80	41695.50	41699.20	41702.90	41706.60	41710.30
153100	41714.00	41717.70	41721.40	41725.10	41728.80	41732.50	41736.20	41739.90	41743.60	41747.30
153200	41751.00	41754.70	41758.40	41762.10	41765.80	41769.50	41773.20	41776.90	41780.60	41784.30
153300	41788.00	41791.70	41795.40	41799.10	41802.80	41806.50	41810.20	41813.90	41817.60	41821.30
153400	41825.00	41828.70	41832.40	41836.10	41839.80	41843.50	41847.20	41850.90	41854.60	41858.30
153500	41862.00	41865.70	41869.40	41873.10	41876.80	41880.50	41884.20	41887.90	41891.60	41895.30
153600	41899.00	41902.70	41906.40	41910.10	41913.80	41917.50	41921.20	41924.90	41928.60	41932.30
153700	41936.00	41939.70	41943.40	41947.10	41950.80	41954.50	41958.20	41961.90	41965.60	41969.30
153800	41973.00	41976.70	41980.40	41984.10	41987.80	41991.50	41995.20	41998.90	42002.60	42006.30
153900	42010.00	42013.70	42017.40	42021.10	42024.80	42028.50	42032.20	42035.90	42039.60	42043.30
154000	42047.00	42050.70	42054.40	42058.10	42061.80	42065.50	42069.20	42072.90	42076.60	42080.30
154100	42084.00	42087.70	42091.40	42095.10	42098.80	42102.50	42106.20	42109.90	42113.60	42117.30
154200	42121.00	42124.70	42128.40	42132.10	42135.80	42139.50	42143.20	42146.90	42150.60	42154.30
154300	42158.00	42161.70	42165.40	42169.10	42172.80	42176.50	42180.20	42183.90	42187.60	42191.30
154400	42195.00	42198.70	42202.40	42206.10	42209.80	42213.50	42217.20	42220.90	42224.60	42228.30
154500	42232.00	42235.70	42239.40	42243.10	42246.80	42250.50	42254.20	42257.90	42261.60	42265.30
154600	42269.00	42272.70	42276.40	42280.10	42283.80	42287.50	42291.20	42294.90	42298.60	42302.30
154700	42306.00	42309.70	42313.40	42317.10	42320.80	42324.50	42328.20	42331.90	42335.60	42339.30
154800	42343.00	42346.70	42350.40	42354.10	42357.80	42361.50	42365.20	42368.90	42372.60	42376.30
154900	42380.00	42383.70	42387.40	42391.10	42394.80	42398.50	42402.20	42405.90	42409.60	42413.30

To the above amounts, add the appropriate figure for the odd dollar amount

$1	$2	$3	$4	$5	$6	$7	$8	$9
0.37	0.74	1.11	1.48	1.85	2.22	2.59	2.96	3.33

***Tax offsets must be deducted, and Medicare levy added, to give net tax payable (see notes at ¶42-000)**

Resident Individuals: Gross Tax Payable at 2020–21 Rates*

Taxable income	$0	$10	$20	$30	$40	$50	$60	$70	$80	$90
155000	42417.00	42420.70	42424.40	42428.10	42431.80	42435.50	42439.20	42442.90	42446.60	42450.30
155100	42454.00	42457.70	42461.40	42465.10	42468.80	42472.50	42476.20	42479.90	42483.60	42487.30
155200	42491.00	42494.70	42498.40	42502.10	42505.80	42509.50	42513.20	42516.90	42520.60	42524.30
155300	42528.00	42531.70	42535.40	42539.10	42542.80	42546.50	42550.20	42553.90	42557.60	42561.30
155400	42565.00	42568.70	42572.40	42576.10	42579.80	42583.50	42587.20	42590.90	42594.60	42598.30
155500	42602.00	42605.70	42609.40	42613.10	42616.80	42620.50	42624.20	42627.90	42631.60	42635.30
155600	42639.00	42642.70	42646.40	42650.10	42653.80	42657.50	42661.20	42664.90	42668.60	42672.30
155700	42676.00	42679.70	42683.40	42687.10	42690.80	42694.50	42698.20	42701.90	42705.60	42709.30
155800	42713.00	42716.70	42720.40	42724.10	42727.80	42731.50	42735.20	42738.90	42742.60	42746.30
155900	42750.00	42753.70	42757.40	42761.10	42764.80	42768.50	42772.20	42775.90	42779.60	42783.30
156000	42787.00	42790.70	42794.40	42798.10	42801.80	42805.50	42809.20	42812.90	42816.60	42820.30
156100	42824.00	42827.70	42831.40	42835.10	42838.80	42842.50	42846.20	42849.90	42853.60	42857.30
156200	42861.00	42864.70	42868.40	42872.10	42875.80	42879.50	42883.20	42886.90	42890.60	42894.30
156300	42898.00	42901.70	42905.40	42909.10	42912.80	42916.50	42920.20	42923.90	42927.60	42931.30
156400	42935.00	42938.70	42942.40	42946.10	42949.80	42953.50	42957.20	42960.90	42964.60	42968.30
156500	42972.00	42975.70	42979.40	42983.10	42986.80	42990.50	42994.20	42997.90	43001.60	43005.30
156600	43009.00	43012.70	43016.40	43020.10	43023.80	43027.50	43031.20	43034.90	43038.60	43042.30
156700	43046.00	43049.70	43053.40	43057.10	43060.80	43064.50	43068.20	43071.90	43075.60	43079.30
156800	43083.00	43086.70	43090.40	43094.10	43097.80	43101.50	43105.20	43108.90	43112.60	43116.30
156900	43120.00	43123.70	43127.40	43131.10	43134.80	43138.50	43142.20	43145.90	43149.60	43153.30
157000	43157.00	43160.70	43164.40	43168.10	43171.80	43175.50	43179.20	43182.90	43186.60	43190.30
157100	43194.00	43197.70	43201.40	43205.10	43208.80	43212.50	43216.20	43219.90	43223.60	43227.30
157200	43231.00	43234.70	43238.40	43242.10	43245.80	43249.50	43253.20	43256.90	43260.60	43264.30
157300	43268.00	43271.70	43275.40	43279.10	43282.80	43286.50	43290.20	43293.90	43297.60	43301.30
157400	43305.00	43308.70	43312.40	43316.10	43319.80	43323.50	43327.20	43330.90	43334.60	43338.30
157500	43342.00	43345.70	43349.40	43353.10	43356.80	43360.50	43364.20	43367.90	43371.60	43375.30
157600	43379.00	43382.70	43386.40	43390.10	43393.80	43397.50	43401.20	43404.90	43408.60	43412.30
157700	43416.00	43419.70	43423.40	43427.10	43430.80	43434.50	43438.20	43441.90	43445.60	43449.30
157800	43453.00	43456.70	43460.40	43464.10	43467.80	43471.50	43475.20	43478.90	43482.60	43486.30
157900	43490.00	43493.70	43497.40	43501.10	43504.80	43508.50	43512.20	43515.90	43519.60	43523.30
158000	43527.00	43530.70	43534.40	43538.10	43541.80	43545.50	43549.20	43552.90	43556.60	43560.30
158100	43564.00	43567.70	43571.40	43575.10	43578.80	43582.50	43586.20	43589.90	43593.60	43597.30
158200	43601.00	43604.70	43608.40	43612.10	43615.80	43619.50	43623.20	43626.90	43630.60	43634.30
158300	43638.00	43641.70	43645.40	43649.10	43652.80	43656.50	43660.20	43663.90	43667.60	43671.30
158400	43675.00	43678.70	43682.40	43686.10	43689.80	43693.50	43697.20	43700.90	43704.60	43708.30
158500	43712.00	43715.70	43719.40	43723.10	43726.80	43730.50	43734.20	43737.90	43741.60	43745.30
158600	43749.00	43752.70	43756.40	43760.10	43763.80	43767.50	43771.20	43774.90	43778.60	43782.30
158700	43786.00	43789.70	43793.40	43797.10	43800.80	43804.50	43808.20	43811.90	43815.60	43819.30
158800	43823.00	43826.70	43830.40	43834.10	43837.80	43841.50	43845.20	43848.90	43852.60	43856.30
158900	43860.00	43863.70	43867.40	43871.10	43874.80	43878.50	43882.20	43885.90	43889.60	43893.30
159000	43897.00	43900.70	43904.40	43908.10	43911.80	43915.50	43919.20	43922.90	43926.60	43930.30
159100	43934.00	43937.70	43941.40	43945.10	43948.80	43952.50	43956.20	43959.90	43963.60	43967.30
159200	43971.00	43974.70	43978.40	43982.10	43985.80	43989.50	43993.20	43996.90	44000.60	44004.30
159300	44008.00	44011.70	44015.40	44019.10	44022.80	44026.50	44030.20	44033.90	44037.60	44041.30
159400	44045.00	44048.70	44052.40	44056.10	44059.80	44063.50	44067.20	44070.90	44074.60	44078.30
159500	44082.00	44085.70	44089.40	44093.10	44096.80	44100.50	44104.20	44107.90	44111.60	44115.30
159600	44119.00	44122.70	44126.40	44130.10	44133.80	44137.50	44141.20	44144.90	44148.60	44152.30
159700	44156.00	44159.70	44163.40	44167.10	44170.80	44174.50	44178.20	44181.90	44185.60	44189.30
159800	44193.00	44196.70	44200.40	44204.10	44207.80	44211.50	44215.20	44218.90	44222.60	44226.30
159900	44230.00	44233.70	44237.40	44241.10	44244.80	44248.50	44252.20	44255.90	44259.60	44263.30

To the above amounts, add the appropriate figure for the odd dollar amount

$1	$2	$3	$4	$5	$6	$7	$8	$9
0.37	0.74	1.11	1.48	1.85	2.22	2.59	2.96	3.33

***Tax offsets must be deducted, and Medicare levy added, to give net tax payable**
(see notes at ¶42-000)

Taxable income	Resident Individuals: Gross Tax Payable at 2020–21 Rates*									
	$0	**$10**	**$20**	**$30**	**$40**	**$50**	**$60**	**$70**	**$80**	**$90**
160000	44267.00	44270.70	44274.40	44278.10	44281.80	44285.50	44289.20	44292.90	44296.60	44300.30
160100	44304.00	44307.70	44311.40	44315.10	44318.80	44322.50	44326.20	44329.90	44333.60	44337.30
160200	44341.00	44344.70	44348.40	44352.10	44355.80	44359.50	44363.20	44366.90	44370.60	44374.30
160300	44378.00	44381.70	44385.40	44389.10	44392.80	44396.50	44400.20	44403.90	44407.60	44411.30
160400	44415.00	44418.70	44422.40	44426.10	44429.80	44433.50	44437.20	44440.90	44444.60	44448.30
160500	44452.00	44455.70	44459.40	44463.10	44466.80	44470.50	44474.20	44477.90	44481.60	44485.30
160600	44489.00	44492.70	44496.40	44500.10	44503.80	44507.50	44511.20	44514.90	44518.60	44522.30
160700	44526.00	44529.70	44533.40	44537.10	44540.80	44544.50	44548.20	44551.90	44555.60	44559.30
160800	44563.00	44566.70	44570.40	44574.10	44577.80	44581.50	44585.20	44588.90	44592.60	44596.30
160900	44600.00	44603.70	44607.40	44611.10	44614.80	44618.50	44622.20	44625.90	44629.60	44633.30
161000	44637.00	44640.70	44644.40	44648.10	44651.80	44655.50	44659.20	44662.90	44666.60	44670.30
161100	44674.00	44677.70	44681.40	44685.10	44688.80	44692.50	44696.20	44699.90	44703.60	44707.30
161200	44711.00	44714.70	44718.40	44722.10	44725.80	44729.50	44733.20	44736.90	44740.60	44744.30
161300	44748.00	44751.70	44755.40	44759.10	44762.80	44766.50	44770.20	44773.90	44777.60	44781.30
161400	44785.00	44788.70	44792.40	44796.10	44799.80	44803.50	44807.20	44810.90	44814.60	44818.30
161500	44822.00	44825.70	44829.40	44833.10	44836.80	44840.50	44844.20	44847.90	44851.60	44855.30
161600	44859.00	44862.70	44866.40	44870.10	44873.80	44877.50	44881.20	44884.90	44888.60	44892.30
161700	44896.00	44899.70	44903.40	44907.10	44910.80	44914.50	44918.20	44921.90	44925.60	44929.30
161800	44933.00	44936.70	44940.40	44944.10	44947.80	44951.50	44955.20	44958.90	44962.60	44966.30
161900	44970.00	44973.70	44977.40	44981.10	44984.80	44988.50	44992.20	44995.90	44999.60	45003.30
162000	45007.00	45010.70	45014.40	45018.10	45021.80	45025.50	45029.20	45032.90	45036.60	45040.30
162100	45044.00	45047.70	45051.40	45055.10	45058.80	45062.50	45066.20	45069.90	45073.60	45077.30
162200	45081.00	45084.70	45088.40	45092.10	45095.80	45099.50	45103.20	45106.90	45110.60	45114.30
162300	45118.00	45121.70	45125.40	45129.10	45132.80	45136.50	45140.20	45143.90	45147.60	45151.30
162400	45155.00	45158.70	45162.40	45166.10	45169.80	45173.50	45177.20	45180.90	45184.60	45188.30
162500	45192.00	45195.70	45199.40	45203.10	45206.80	45210.50	45214.20	45217.90	45221.60	45225.30
162600	45229.00	45232.70	45236.40	45240.10	45243.80	45247.50	45251.20	45254.90	45258.60	45262.30
162700	45266.00	45269.70	45273.40	45277.10	45280.80	45284.50	45288.20	45291.90	45295.60	45299.30
162800	45303.00	45306.70	45310.40	45314.10	45317.80	45321.50	45325.20	45328.90	45332.60	45336.30
162900	45340.00	45343.70	45347.40	45351.10	45354.80	45358.50	45362.20	45365.90	45369.60	45373.30
163000	45377.00	45380.70	45384.40	45388.10	45391.80	45395.50	45399.20	45402.90	45406.60	45410.30
163100	45414.00	45417.70	45421.40	45425.10	45428.80	45432.50	45436.20	45439.90	45443.60	45447.30
163200	45451.00	45454.70	45458.40	45462.10	45465.80	45469.50	45473.20	45476.90	45480.60	45484.30
163300	45488.00	45491.70	45495.40	45499.10	45502.80	45506.50	45510.20	45513.90	45517.60	45521.30
163400	45525.00	45528.70	45532.40	45536.10	45539.80	45543.50	45547.20	45550.90	45554.60	45558.30
163500	45562.00	45565.70	45569.40	45573.10	45576.80	45580.50	45584.20	45587.90	45591.60	45595.30
163600	45599.00	45602.70	45606.40	45610.10	45613.80	45617.50	45621.20	45624.90	45628.60	45632.30
163700	45636.00	45639.70	45643.40	45647.10	45650.80	45654.50	45658.20	45661.90	45665.60	45669.30
163800	45673.00	45676.70	45680.40	45684.10	45687.80	45691.50	45695.20	45698.90	45702.60	45706.30
163900	45710.00	45713.70	45717.40	45721.10	45724.80	45728.50	45732.20	45735.90	45739.60	45743.30
164000	45747.00	45750.70	45754.40	45758.10	45761.80	45765.50	45769.20	45772.90	45776.60	45780.30
164100	45784.00	45787.70	45791.40	45795.10	45798.80	45802.50	45806.20	45809.90	45813.60	45817.30
164200	45821.00	45824.70	45828.40	45832.10	45835.80	45839.50	45843.20	45846.90	45850.60	45854.30
164300	45858.00	45861.70	45865.40	45869.10	45872.80	45876.50	45880.20	45883.90	45887.60	45891.30
164400	45895.00	45898.70	45902.40	45906.10	45909.80	45913.50	45917.20	45920.90	45924.60	45928.30
164500	45932.00	45935.70	45939.40	45943.10	45946.80	45950.50	45954.20	45957.90	45961.60	45965.30
164600	45969.00	45972.70	45976.40	45980.10	45983.80	45987.50	45991.20	45994.90	45998.60	46002.30
164700	46006.00	46009.70	46013.40	46017.10	46020.80	46024.50	46028.20	46031.90	46035.60	46039.30
164800	46043.00	46046.70	46050.40	46054.10	46057.80	46061.50	46065.20	46068.90	46072.60	46076.30
164900	46080.00	46083.70	46087.40	46091.10	46094.80	46098.50	46102.20	46105.90	46109.60	46113.30

To the above amounts, add the appropriate figure for the odd dollar amount								
$1	$2	$3	$4	$5	$6	$7	$8	$9
0.37	0.74	1.11	1.48	1.85	2.22	2.59	2.96	3.33

***Tax offsets must be deducted, and Medicare levy added, to give net tax payable (see notes at ¶42-000)**

Resident Individuals: Gross Tax Payable at 2020–21 Rates*

Taxable income	$0	$10	$20	$30	$40	$50	$60	$70	$80	$90
165000	46117.00	46120.70	46124.40	46128.10	46131.80	46135.50	46139.20	46142.90	46146.60	46150.30
165100	46154.00	46157.70	46161.40	46165.10	46168.80	46172.50	46176.20	46179.90	46183.60	46187.30
165200	46191.00	46194.70	46198.40	46202.10	46205.80	46209.50	46213.20	46216.90	46220.60	46224.30
165300	46228.00	46231.70	46235.40	46239.10	46242.80	46246.50	46250.20	46253.90	46257.60	46261.30
165400	46265.00	46268.70	46272.40	46276.10	46279.80	46283.50	46287.20	46290.90	46294.60	46298.30
165500	46302.00	46305.70	46309.40	46313.10	46316.80	46320.50	46324.20	46327.90	46331.60	46335.30
165600	46339.00	46342.70	46346.40	46350.10	46353.80	46357.50	46361.20	46364.90	46368.60	46372.30
165700	46376.00	46379.70	46383.40	46387.10	46390.80	46394.50	46398.20	46401.90	46405.60	46409.30
165800	46413.00	46416.70	46420.40	46424.10	46427.80	46431.50	46435.20	46438.90	46442.60	46446.30
165900	46450.00	46453.70	46457.40	46461.10	46464.80	46468.50	46472.20	46475.90	46479.60	46483.30
166000	46487.00	46490.70	46494.40	46498.10	46501.80	46505.50	46509.20	46512.90	46516.60	46520.30
166100	46524.00	46527.70	46531.40	46535.10	46538.80	46542.50	46546.20	46549.90	46553.60	46557.30
166200	46561.00	46564.70	46568.40	46572.10	46575.80	46579.50	46583.20	46586.90	46590.60	46594.30
166300	46598.00	46601.70	46605.40	46609.10	46612.80	46616.50	46620.20	46623.90	46627.60	46631.30
166400	46635.00	46638.70	46642.40	46646.10	46649.80	46653.50	46657.20	46660.90	46664.60	46668.30
166500	46672.00	46675.70	46679.40	46683.10	46686.80	46690.50	46694.20	46697.90	46701.60	46705.30
166600	46709.00	46712.70	46716.40	46720.10	46723.80	46727.50	46731.20	46734.90	46738.60	46742.30
166700	46746.00	46749.70	46753.40	46757.10	46760.80	46764.50	46768.20	46771.90	46775.60	46779.30
166800	46783.00	46786.70	46790.40	46794.10	46797.80	46801.50	46805.20	46808.90	46812.60	46816.30
166900	46820.00	46823.70	46827.40	46831.10	46834.80	46838.50	46842.20	46845.90	46849.60	46853.30
167000	46857.00	46860.70	46864.40	46868.10	46871.80	46875.50	46879.20	46882.90	46886.60	46890.30
167100	46894.00	46897.70	46901.40	46905.10	46908.80	46912.50	46916.20	46919.90	46923.60	46927.30
167200	46931.00	46934.70	46938.40	46942.10	46945.80	46949.50	46953.20	46956.90	46960.60	46964.30
167300	46968.00	46971.70	46975.40	46979.10	46982.80	46986.50	46990.20	46993.90	46997.60	47001.30
167400	47005.00	47008.70	47012.40	47016.10	47019.80	47023.50	47027.20	47030.90	47034.60	47038.30
167500	47042.00	47045.70	47049.40	47053.10	47056.80	47060.50	47064.20	47067.90	47071.60	47075.30
167600	47079.00	47082.70	47086.40	47090.10	47093.80	47097.50	47101.20	47104.90	47108.60	47112.30
167700	47116.00	47119.70	47123.40	47127.10	47130.80	47134.50	47138.20	47141.90	47145.60	47149.30
167800	47153.00	47156.70	47160.40	47164.10	47167.80	47171.50	47175.20	47178.90	47182.60	47186.30
167900	47190.00	47193.70	47197.40	47201.10	47204.80	47208.50	47212.20	47215.90	47219.60	47223.30
168000	47227.00	47230.70	47234.40	47238.10	47241.80	47245.50	47249.20	47252.90	47256.60	47260.30
168100	47264.00	47267.70	47271.40	47275.10	47278.80	47282.50	47286.20	47289.90	47293.60	47297.30
168200	47301.00	47304.70	47308.40	47312.10	47315.80	47319.50	47323.20	47326.90	47330.60	47334.30
168300	47338.00	47341.70	47345.40	47349.10	47352.80	47356.50	47360.20	47363.90	47367.60	47371.30
168400	47375.00	47378.70	47382.40	47386.10	47389.80	47393.50	47397.20	47400.90	47404.60	47408.30
168500	47412.00	47415.70	47419.40	47423.10	47426.80	47430.50	47434.20	47437.90	47441.60	47445.30
168600	47449.00	47452.70	47456.40	47460.10	47463.80	47467.50	47471.20	47474.90	47478.60	47482.30
168700	47486.00	47489.70	47493.40	47497.10	47500.80	47504.50	47508.20	47511.90	47515.60	47519.30
168800	47523.00	47526.70	47530.40	47534.10	47537.80	47541.50	47545.20	47548.90	47552.60	47556.30
168900	47560.00	47563.70	47567.40	47571.10	47574.80	47578.50	47582.20	47585.90	47589.60	47593.30
169000	47597.00	47600.70	47604.40	47608.10	47611.80	47615.50	47619.20	47622.90	47626.60	47630.30
169100	47634.00	47637.70	47641.40	47645.10	47648.80	47652.50	47656.20	47659.90	47663.60	47667.30
169200	47671.00	47674.70	47678.40	47682.10	47685.80	47689.50	47693.20	47696.90	47700.60	47704.30
169300	47708.00	47711.70	47715.40	47719.10	47722.80	47726.50	47730.20	47733.90	47737.60	47741.30
169400	47745.00	47748.70	47752.40	47756.10	47759.80	47763.50	47767.20	47770.90	47774.60	47778.30
169500	47782.00	47785.70	47789.40	47793.10	47796.80	47800.50	47804.20	47807.90	47811.60	47815.30
169600	47819.00	47822.70	47826.40	47830.10	47833.80	47837.50	47841.20	47844.90	47848.60	47852.30
169700	47856.00	47859.70	47863.40	47867.10	47870.80	47874.50	47878.20	47881.90	47885.60	47889.30
169800	47893.00	47896.70	47900.40	47904.10	47907.80	47911.50	47915.20	47918.90	47922.60	47926.30
169900	47930.00	47933.70	47937.40	47941.10	47944.80	47948.50	47952.20	47955.90	47959.60	47963.30

To the above amounts, add the appropriate figure for the odd dollar amount

$1	$2	$3	$4	$5	$6	$7	$8	$9
0.37	0.74	1.11	1.48	1.85	2.22	2.59	2.96	3.33

***Tax offsets must be deducted, and Medicare levy added, to give net tax payable (see notes at ¶42-000)**

Resident Individuals: Gross Tax Payable at 2020–21 Rates*

Taxable income	$0	$10	$20	$30	$40	$50	$60	$70	$80	$90
170000	47967.00	47970.70	47974.40	47978.10	47981.80	47985.50	47989.20	47992.90	47996.60	48000.30
170100	48004.00	48007.70	48011.40	48015.10	48018.80	48022.50	48026.20	48029.90	48033.60	48037.30
170200	48041.00	48044.70	48048.40	48052.10	48055.80	48059.50	48063.20	48066.90	48070.60	48074.30
170300	48078.00	48081.70	48085.40	48089.10	48092.80	48096.50	48100.20	48103.90	48107.60	48111.30
170400	48115.00	48118.70	48122.40	48126.10	48129.80	48133.50	48137.20	48140.90	48144.60	48148.30
170500	48152.00	48155.70	48159.40	48163.10	48166.80	48170.50	48174.20	48177.90	48181.60	48185.30
170600	48189.00	48192.70	48196.40	48200.10	48203.80	48207.50	48211.20	48214.90	48218.60	48222.30
170700	48226.00	48229.70	48233.40	48237.10	48240.80	48244.50	48248.20	48251.90	48255.60	48259.30
170800	48263.00	48266.70	48270.40	48274.10	48277.80	48281.50	48285.20	48288.90	48292.60	48296.30
170900	48300.00	48303.70	48307.40	48311.10	48314.80	48318.50	48322.20	48325.90	48329.60	48333.30
171000	48337.00	48340.70	48344.40	48348.10	48351.80	48355.50	48359.20	48362.90	48366.60	48370.30
171100	48374.00	48377.70	48381.40	48385.10	48388.80	48392.50	48396.20	48399.90	48403.60	48407.30
171200	48411.00	48414.70	48418.40	48422.10	48425.80	48429.50	48433.20	48436.90	48440.60	48444.30
171300	48448.00	48451.70	48455.40	48459.10	48462.80	48466.50	48470.20	48473.90	48477.60	48481.30
171400	48485.00	48488.70	48492.40	48496.10	48499.80	48503.50	48507.20	48510.90	48514.60	48518.30
171500	48522.00	48525.70	48529.40	48533.10	48536.80	48540.50	48544.20	48547.90	48551.60	48555.30
171600	48559.00	48562.70	48566.40	48570.10	48573.80	48577.50	48581.20	48584.90	48588.60	48592.30
171700	48596.00	48599.70	48603.40	48607.10	48610.80	48614.50	48618.20	48621.90	48625.60	48629.30
171800	48633.00	48636.70	48640.40	48644.10	48647.80	48651.50	48655.20	48658.90	48662.60	48666.30
171900	48670.00	48673.70	48677.40	48681.10	48684.80	48688.50	48692.20	48695.90	48699.60	48703.30
172000	48707.00	48710.70	48714.40	48718.10	48721.80	48725.50	48729.20	48732.90	48736.60	48740.30
172100	48744.00	48747.70	48751.40	48755.10	48758.80	48762.50	48766.20	48769.90	48773.60	48777.30
172200	48781.00	48784.70	48788.40	48792.10	48795.80	48799.50	48803.20	48806.90	48810.60	48814.30
172300	48818.00	48821.70	48825.40	48829.10	48832.80	48836.50	48840.20	48843.90	48847.60	48851.30
172400	48855.00	48858.70	48862.40	48866.10	48869.80	48873.50	48877.20	48880.90	48884.60	48888.30
172500	48892.00	48895.70	48899.40	48903.10	48906.80	48910.50	48914.20	48917.90	48921.60	48925.30
172600	48929.00	48932.70	48936.40	48940.10	48943.80	48947.50	48951.20	48954.90	48958.60	48962.30
172700	48966.00	48969.70	48973.40	48977.10	48980.80	48984.50	48988.20	48991.90	48995.60	48999.30
172800	49003.00	49006.70	49010.40	49014.10	49017.80	49021.50	49025.20	49028.90	49032.60	49036.30
172900	49040.00	49043.70	49047.40	49051.10	49054.80	49058.50	49062.20	49065.90	49069.60	49073.30
173000	49077.00	49080.70	49084.40	49088.10	49091.80	49095.50	49099.20	49102.90	49106.60	49110.30
173100	49114.00	49117.70	49121.40	49125.10	49128.80	49132.50	49136.20	49139.90	49143.60	49147.30
173200	49151.00	49154.70	49158.40	49162.10	49165.80	49169.50	49173.20	49176.90	49180.60	49184.30
173300	49188.00	49191.70	49195.40	49199.10	49202.80	49206.50	49210.20	49213.90	49217.60	49221.30
173400	49225.00	49228.70	49232.40	49236.10	49239.80	49243.50	49247.20	49250.90	49254.60	49258.30
173500	49262.00	49265.70	49269.40	49273.10	49276.80	49280.50	49284.20	49287.90	49291.60	49295.30
173600	49299.00	49302.70	49306.40	49310.10	49313.80	49317.50	49321.20	49324.90	49328.60	49332.30
173700	49336.00	49339.70	49343.40	49347.10	49350.80	49354.50	49358.20	49361.90	49365.60	49369.30
173800	49373.00	49376.70	49380.40	49384.10	49387.80	49391.50	49395.20	49398.90	49402.60	49406.30
173900	49410.00	49413.70	49417.40	49421.10	49424.80	49428.50	49432.20	49435.90	49439.60	49443.30
174000	49447.00	49450.70	49454.40	49458.10	49461.80	49465.50	49469.20	49472.90	49476.60	49480.30
174100	49484.00	49487.70	49491.40	49495.10	49498.80	49502.50	49506.20	49509.90	49513.60	49517.30
174200	49521.00	49524.70	49528.40	49532.10	49535.80	49539.50	49543.20	49546.90	49550.60	49554.30
174300	49558.00	49561.70	49565.40	49569.10	49572.80	49576.50	49580.20	49583.90	49587.60	49591.30
174400	49595.00	49598.70	49602.40	49606.10	49609.80	49613.50	49617.20	49620.90	49624.60	49628.30
174500	49632.00	49635.70	49639.40	49643.10	49646.80	49650.50	49654.20	49657.90	49661.60	49665.30
174600	49669.00	49672.70	49676.40	49680.10	49683.80	49687.50	49691.20	49694.90	49698.60	49702.30
174700	49706.00	49709.70	49713.40	49717.10	49720.80	49724.50	49728.20	49731.90	49735.60	49739.30
174800	49743.00	49746.70	49750.40	49754.10	49757.80	49761.50	49765.20	49768.90	49772.60	49776.30
174900	49780.00	49783.70	49787.40	49791.10	49794.80	49798.50	49802.20	49805.90	49809.60	49813.30

To the above amounts, add the appropriate figure for the odd dollar amount

$1	$2	$3	$4	$5	$6	$7	$8	$9
0.37	0.74	1.11	1.48	1.85	2.22	2.59	2.96	3.33

***Tax offsets must be deducted, and Medicare levy added, to give net tax payable (see notes at ¶42-000)**

Taxable income	Resident Individuals: Gross Tax Payable at 2020–21 Rates*									
	$0	**$10**	**$20**	**$30**	**$40**	**$50**	**$60**	**$70**	**$80**	**$90**
175000	49817.00	49820.70	49824.40	49828.10	49831.80	49835.50	49839.20	49842.90	49846.60	49850.30
175100	49854.00	49857.70	49861.40	49865.10	49868.80	49872.50	49876.20	49879.90	49883.60	49887.30
175200	49891.00	49894.70	49898.40	49902.10	49905.80	49909.50	49913.20	49916.90	49920.60	49924.30
175300	49928.00	49931.70	49935.40	49939.10	49942.80	49946.50	49950.20	49953.90	49957.60	49961.30
175400	49965.00	49968.70	49972.40	49976.10	49979.80	49983.50	49987.20	49990.90	49994.60	49998.30
175500	50002.00	50005.70	50009.40	50013.10	50016.80	50020.50	50024.20	50027.90	50031.60	50035.30
175600	50039.00	50042.70	50046.40	50050.10	50053.80	50057.50	50061.20	50064.90	50068.60	50072.30
175700	50076.00	50079.70	50083.40	50087.10	50090.80	50094.50	50098.20	50101.90	50105.60	50109.30
175800	50113.00	50116.70	50120.40	50124.10	50127.80	50131.50	50135.20	50138.90	50142.60	50146.30
175900	50150.00	50153.70	50157.40	50161.10	50164.80	50168.50	50172.20	50175.90	50179.60	50183.30
176000	50187.00	50190.70	50194.40	50198.10	50201.80	50205.50	50209.20	50212.90	50216.60	50220.30
176100	50224.00	50227.70	50231.40	50235.10	50238.80	50242.50	50246.20	50249.90	50253.60	50257.30
176200	50261.00	50264.70	50268.40	50272.10	50275.80	50279.50	50283.20	50286.90	50290.60	50294.30
176300	50298.00	50301.70	50305.40	50309.10	50312.80	50316.50	50320.20	50323.90	50327.60	50331.30
176400	50335.00	50338.70	50342.40	50346.10	50349.80	50353.50	50357.20	50360.90	50364.60	50368.30
176500	50372.00	50375.70	50379.40	50383.10	50386.80	50390.50	50394.20	50397.90	50401.60	50405.30
176600	50409.00	50412.70	50416.40	50420.10	50423.80	50427.50	50431.20	50434.90	50438.60	50442.30
176700	50446.00	50449.70	50453.40	50457.10	50460.80	50464.50	50468.20	50471.90	50475.60	50479.30
176800	50483.00	50486.70	50490.40	50494.10	50497.80	50501.50	50505.20	50508.90	50512.60	50516.30
176900	50520.00	50523.70	50527.40	50531.10	50534.80	50538.50	50542.20	50545.90	50549.60	50553.30
177000	50557.00	50560.70	50564.40	50568.10	50571.80	50575.50	50579.20	50582.90	50586.60	50590.30
177100	50594.00	50597.70	50601.40	50605.10	50608.80	50612.50	50616.20	50619.90	50623.60	50627.30
177200	50631.00	50634.70	50638.40	50642.10	50645.80	50649.50	50653.20	50656.90	50660.60	50664.30
177300	50668.00	50671.70	50675.40	50679.10	50682.80	50686.50	50690.20	50693.90	50697.60	50701.30
177400	50705.00	50708.70	50712.40	50716.10	50719.80	50723.50	50727.20	50730.90	50734.60	50738.30
177500	50742.00	50745.70	50749.40	50753.10	50756.80	50760.50	50764.20	50767.90	50771.60	50775.30
177600	50779.00	50782.70	50786.40	50790.10	50793.80	50797.50	50801.20	50804.90	50808.60	50812.30
177700	50816.00	50819.70	50823.40	50827.10	50830.80	50834.50	50838.20	50841.90	50845.60	50849.30
177800	50853.00	50856.70	50860.40	50864.10	50867.80	50871.50	50875.20	50878.90	50882.60	50886.30
177900	50890.00	50893.70	50897.40	50901.10	50904.80	50908.50	50912.20	50915.90	50919.60	50923.30
178000	50927.00	50930.70	50934.40	50938.10	50941.80	50945.50	50949.20	50952.90	50956.60	50960.30
178100	50964.00	50967.70	50971.40	50975.10	50978.80	50982.50	50986.20	50989.90	50993.60	50997.30
178200	51001.00	51004.70	51008.40	51012.10	51015.80	51019.50	51023.20	51026.90	51030.60	51034.30
178300	51038.00	51041.70	51045.40	51049.10	51052.80	51056.50	51060.20	51063.90	51067.60	51071.30
178400	51075.00	51078.70	51082.40	51086.10	51089.80	51093.50	51097.20	51100.90	51104.60	51108.30
178500	51112.00	51115.70	51119.40	51123.10	51126.80	51130.50	51134.20	51137.90	51141.60	51145.30
178600	51149.00	51152.70	51156.40	51160.10	51163.80	51167.50	51171.20	51174.90	51178.60	51182.30
178700	51186.00	51189.70	51193.40	51197.10	51200.80	51204.50	51208.20	51211.90	51215.60	51219.30
178800	51223.00	51226.70	51230.40	51234.10	51237.80	51241.50	51245.20	51248.90	51252.60	51256.30
178900	51260.00	51263.70	51267.40	51271.10	51274.80	51278.50	51282.20	51285.90	51289.60	51293.30
179000	51297.00	51300.70	51304.40	51308.10	51311.80	51315.50	51319.20	51322.90	51326.60	51330.30
179100	51334.00	51337.70	51341.40	51345.10	51348.80	51352.50	51356.20	51359.90	51363.60	51367.30
179200	51371.00	51374.70	51378.40	51382.10	51385.80	51389.50	51393.20	51396.90	51400.60	51404.30
179300	51408.00	51411.70	51415.40	51419.10	51422.80	51426.50	51430.20	51433.90	51437.60	51441.30
179400	51445.00	51448.70	51452.40	51456.10	51459.80	51463.50	51467.20	51470.90	51474.60	51478.30
179500	51482.00	51485.70	51489.40	51493.10	51496.80	51500.50	51504.20	51507.90	51511.60	51515.30
179600	51519.00	51522.70	51526.40	51530.10	51533.80	51537.50	51541.20	51544.90	51548.60	51552.30
179700	51556.00	51559.70	51563.40	51567.10	51570.80	51574.50	51578.20	51581.90	51585.60	51589.30
179800	51593.00	51596.70	51600.40	51604.10	51607.80	51611.50	51615.20	51618.90	51622.60	51626.30
179900	51630.00	51633.70	51637.40	51641.10	51644.80	51648.50	51652.20	51655.90	51659.60	51663.30

To the above amounts, add the appropriate figure for the odd dollar amount								
$1	$2	$3	$4	$5	$6	$7	$8	$9
0.37	0.74	1.11	1.48	1.85	2.22	2.59	2.96	3.33

***Tax offsets must be deducted, and Medicare levy added, to give net tax payable (see notes at ¶42-000)**

Taxable income	Resident Individuals: Gross Tax Payable at 2020–21 Rates*									
	$0	$10	$20	$30	$40	$50	$60	$70	$80	$90
180000	51667.00	51671.50	51676.00	51680.50	51685.00	51689.50	51694.00	51698.50	51703.00	51707.50

To the above amounts, add the appropriate figure for the odd dollar amount								
$1	$2	$3	$4	$5	$6	$7	$8	$9
0.45	0.90	1.35	1.80	2.25	2.70	3.15	3.60	4.05

***Tax offsets must be deducted, and Medicare levy added, to give net tax payable (see notes at ¶42-000)**

¶42-025 Company rates for 2020–21

TYPE OF COMPANY	TAX RATE
PRIVATE COMPANIES	
• Private companies (other than life insurance companies) that are not base rate entities (BREs)	30%
• Private companies (other than life insurance companies) that are BREs	26%[1]
PUBLIC COMPANIES	
• Public companies (other than life insurance companies) that are not BREs	30%
• Public companies (other than life insurance companies) that are BREs	26%[1]
LIFE INSURANCE COMPANIES	
• Ordinary class of taxable income	30%
• Complying superannuation class of taxable income	15%
RSA PROVIDERS	
• Companies (other than life insurance companies) that are RSA providers	
– Standard component of taxable income	
(i) if a BRE	26%[1]
(ii) if not a BRE	30%
– RSA component of taxable income	15%
NON-PROFIT COMPANIES	
• First $416 of taxable income	Nil
• Shade-in above $416 to $832 for BREs; otherwise $416 to $915	55%
• Taxable income above shade-in range of $832 for BREs	26%[1]
• Taxable income above shade-in range of $915 for other non-profit companies	30%
POOLED DEVELOPMENT FUNDS (PDFs)	
• Companies that are PDFs throughout the year of income:	
– on SME income component	15%
– on unregulated investment component	25%
• Companies that become PDFs during the year of income and are still PDFs at the end of the year:	
– on SME income component	15%
– on unregulated investment component	25%

TYPE OF COMPANY		TAX RATE
–	on so much of the taxable income as exceeds the PDF component	
	(i) if a BRE	26%[1]
	(ii) if not a BRE	30%
CREDIT UNIONS		
–	Small credit unions (taxable income less than $50,000) that are BREs	26%[1]
–	Small credit unions (taxable income less than $50,000) that are not BREs	30%
–	Medium credit unions (taxable income of $50,000 to $149,999) that are BREs	41.25%
–	Medium credit unions (taxable income of $50,000 to $149,999) that are not BREs	45%
–	Large credit unions (taxable income of $150,000 and above) that are BREs	26%[1]
–	Large credit unions (taxable income of $150,000 and above) that are not BREs	30%

Notes

1. This rate applies to base rate entities. An entity is a base rate entity if no more than 80% of its assessable income is ''base rate entity passive income'' (¶3-055) and it has an aggregated turnover (¶7-050) of less than $50 million. This rate is 25% for 2021–22.

2. For the operation of the PAYG instalments system for 30 June balancing companies see ¶27-200. The time for lodging income tax returns is discussed at ¶24-060.

3. Friendly societies that conduct life insurance business are taxed under the same regime as life insurance companies (¶3-480). Other friendly societies are generally taxed as non-profit companies (¶3-470).

4. For the definitions of public company, private company and non-profit company, see ¶3-015.

5. Companies that are taxable in the capacity of trustee pay tax at the appropriate trustee rate (¶42-030).

6. Partnerships that qualify as ''corporate limited partnerships'' (¶3-475) are taxed at the rate of tax applicable to public companies.

¶42-027 Small business income tax offset

For 2020–21, individuals who receive business income from a small business entity (¶7-050), other than via a company, are entitled to a discount of 13% of the income tax payable on that business income up to a maximum of $1,000 a year. This applies for entities with an annual aggregated turnover of less than $5 million (¶7-210). The discount increases to 16% in 2021–22.

¶42-030 Trustee rates

The rates of tax payable by trustees for 2020–21 are set out below. A trustee assessed under ITAA36 s 98, 99 or 99A may also be liable for the Medicare levy (MLA s 251S: ¶42-033, ¶6-250). A trustee assessed under s 98 may also be liable for the Medicare levy surcharge where the relevant beneficiary does not have adequate private patient hospital cover (¶42-033, ¶2-335).

For the rates of tax payable by trustees of superannuation funds, ADFs and PSTs, see ¶42-035; for rates payable by trustees who derive primary production income subject to averaging, see ¶18-200.

(1) Presently entitled beneficiary under legal disability — ITAA36 s 98(1)

Where a beneficiary is presently entitled to a share of the net income of a trust estate but is under a legal disability (eg is a minor: ¶6-210), the trustee is taxed at general individual rates (¶42-000 — except where the minors' income rules apply: ¶2-250).

In the case of a *resident beneficiary*, the 2020–21 rates are:

Share of net income (column 1) ($)	Tax on column 1 ($)	% on excess (marginal rate)
18,200	Nil	19
45,000	5,092	32.5
120,000	29,467	37
180,000	51,667	45

In the case of a *prescribed non-resident beneficiary* (¶2-210), the 2020–21 rates are:

Share of net income (column 1) ($)	Tax on column 1 ($)	% on excess (marginal rate)
Nil	Nil	32.5
120,000	39,000	37
180,000	61,200	45

Where a presently entitled beneficiary under 18 years of age is subject to the minors' income rules, the trustee will be assessed at the special rates which apply under that Division (¶2-250).

(2) Beneficiary with vested and indefeasible interest — ITAA36 s 98(2)

Where a beneficiary has a vested and indefeasible interest in the income of a trust estate but is not presently entitled, the trustee is deemed by s 95A(2) to be presently entitled and is assessed under s 98(2) on the beneficiary's share of the trust net income at the general individual rates (set out at (1) above).

(3) Non-resident beneficiary presently entitled — ITAA36 s 98(2A), (3) and (4)

A trustee assessed under s 98(2A), (3) or (4) (¶6-220) in respect of: (i) a presently entitled beneficiary who is a non-resident at the *end* of the income year; or (ii) a presently entitled beneficiary where that beneficiary is a trustee of another trust which has a non-resident trustee; is taxed at the following rates for 2020–21:

- where the beneficiary is a company — the trustee is taxed on the beneficiary's share of the net income at 26% if the company is a base rate entity, or otherwise at 30%.
- where the beneficiary is a natural person and is a prescribed non-resident — the trustee is taxed at the rates set out at (1) above for prescribed non-resident beneficiaries, and
- where the beneficiary is presently entitled to trust income as trustee of another trust with a non-resident trustee — the trustee of the first trust is taxed on the relevant share of the trust net income at 45%.

(4) No beneficiary presently entitled — ITAA36 s 99A

The net income of a trust estate to which no beneficiary is presently entitled and in respect of which the trustee is assessed under s 99A (¶6-230) is taxed at a flat rate of 45% for 2020–21. In a limited number of cases the Commissioner has a discretion to assess the trustee under ITAA36 s 99 (see (5) below) if the ATO is of the opinion that it would be unreasonable that s 99A should apply.

(5) No beneficiary presently entitled — ITAA36 s 99

A trustee assessed under s 99 in respect of the net income of a deceased estate is taxed at the general individual rates for the first 3 income years after the death of the taxpayer. Thus, in the case of a resident trust estate, the rates set out at (1) above for resident beneficiaries apply. In the case of a non-resident trust estate, the rates set out at (1) above for non-resident beneficiaries apply.

Otherwise, a trustee assessed under s 99 in respect of the net income of a resident trust estate is taxed at the following rates for 2020–21:

Share of net income (column 1) ($)	Tax on column 1 ($)	% on excess (marginal rate)
416	Nil	50
670	127	19*
45,000	8,549	32.5
120,000	32,924	37
180,000	55,124	45

* If the share of net income is between $670 and $45,000, it is taxed at a flat rate of 19%.

A trust estate is a ‘‘resident trust estate’’ if at any time during the year either a trustee was a resident or the central management and control of the estate was in Australia. A trustee assessed under s 99 in respect of the net income of a non-resident trust estate is taxed at the rates set out at (1) above for prescribed non-resident beneficiaries.

(6) Public trading trusts

The trustee of a public trading trust is liable to pay tax at the relevant corporate rate on the net income of the trust estate for the 2020–21 income year (¶42-025).

¶42-033 Medicare levy and Medicare levy surcharge for trustees

Section 98 assessments

A trustee of a trust assessable under s 98 in respect of a share of the net income of the trust to which a resident beneficiary under a legal disability is presently entitled is liable for the Medicare levy (MLA s 251S(1)). The levy liability is determined in the same way as if the income were assessed to the beneficiary (MLA s 10). Thus, the normal reliefs and exemptions apply (¶2-330 and following).

Further, Medicare levy will not be payable by the trustee under a s 98 assessment to the extent the beneficiary was a ‘‘prescribed person’’ for Medicare levy purposes during the income year (MLA ss 251T; 251U).

The trustee may also be liable for the Medicare levy surcharge if the beneficiary is a high income earner without adequate private patient hospital insurance (¶2-335).

Section 99 assessments

Where a trustee of a trust (other than a deceased estate) is assessable under s 99 in respect of the whole or part of the net income of the trust, the trustee is liable for the Medicare levy as follows.

Net income	Medicare levy payable
$0 – $416	Nil
$417 – $520	10% of the excess over $416
$521 and above	2% on the entire amount

A trustee of a deceased estate assessable under s 99 in respect of the whole or part of the net income of the trust is not liable for the Medicare levy (MLA s 251S(1)(c)).

Section 99A assessments

Where a trustee is assessable under s 99A on the net income of the trust, the Medicare levy payable by the trustee is 2% of the entire amount assessed.

¶42-035 Superannuation fund rates for 2020–21

Entity	2020–21
Complying superannuation funds	
(i) Assessed on income, including realised capital gains and assessable contributions	15%
(ii) Assessed on non-arm's length income, private company dividends and certain trust distributions	45%
Non-complying superannuation funds	
Assessed on income, including realised capital gains and assessable contributions	45%
Complying ADFs	
(i) Assessed on income, including realised capital gains and assessable contributions	15%
(ii) Assessed on non-arm's length income, private company dividends and certain trust distributions	45%
Non-complying ADFs	
Assessed on income, including realised capital gains and assessable contributions	45%
PSTs	
(i) Assessed on income, including realised capital gains and assessable contributions transferred to the PST	15%
(ii) Assessed on non-arm's length income, private company dividends and certain trust distributions	45%

Note

Superannuation funds that receive no-TFN contributions income are required to pay additional tax on such income, subject to a tax rebate if a TFN is subsequently provided (¶13-180).

Withholding Rates

¶42-100 Withholding schedules

The ATO issues various Schedules setting out the weekly, fortnightly or monthly amounts required to be withheld from withholding payments covered by the PAYG withholding system (¶26-130). PAYG withholding rates on other types of withholding payments are also explained at ¶26-130.

¶42-115 Withholding for dividends, interest and royalties

DIVIDENDS — Withholding tax: 30% on gross amount of dividends or, where there is a double taxation agreement, the lower rate specified in the agreement (generally, 15%; ¶22-160). Franked dividends paid to non-residents are exempt from dividend withholding tax unless the dividends have been streamed or a franking credit scheme has occurred (¶22-010). Unfranked dividends are also exempt to the extent that they consist of a ''foreign dividend account declaration amount'' (¶22-010).

INTEREST — Withholding tax: 10% on gross amount of interest, unaffected by double taxation agreements. (Certain foreign loan interest not liable: ¶22-020.)

ROYALTIES — Withholding tax: 30% of gross amount of royalties (¶22-030) or, where there is a double taxation agreement, the lower rate specified in the agreement (¶22-160).

¶42-125 Withholding for departing Australia superannuation payments

A departing Australia superannuation payment (DASP: ¶14-390) is not taxed as a superannuation lump sum benefit (¶14-200) but is subject to withholding tax at the rates below.

Component of DASP	2020–21	Rate for working holiday makers*
The tax free component	0%	0%
The element taxed in the fund	35%	65%
The element untaxed in the fund	45%	65%

DASP is a roll-over superannuation benefit

Component of DASP	2020–21	Rate for working holiday makers*
The amount of the element untaxed in the fund that is an excess untaxed roll-over amount	0%	0%
The amount of the element untaxed in the fund that is not an excess untaxed roll-over amount	45%	65%

* For DASPs paid on or after 1 July 2017 where the DASP includes amounts attributable to superannuation contributions made while the person was a working holiday maker.

Individuals

¶42-165 Personal tax offsets and rebates for 2020–21

Offset/Rebate	Maximum amount for 2020–21
Dependant (Invalid and Carer) (¶15-100)	$2,816
Low income tax offset (¶15-300)	$700 (amounts vary according to taxable income levels)
Low and middle income tax offset (¶15-300)	$1,080 (amounts vary according to taxable income levels)
Senior Australians and pensioners (¶15-310) Recipients of social security payments and allowances and of certain educational allowances (¶15-315)	Rebate levels vary according to taxpayer's circumstances
Private health insurance (¶15-330, ¶2-335)	Dependent on age of person(s) covered by policy and income level(s)
Zone rebates (¶15-160) • Ordinary Zone A • Ordinary Zone B • Special Zone A or B Overseas defence force (¶15-180) UN peacekeeping force (¶15-190)	 $338 + 50% of relevant rebate amount $57 + 20% of relevant rebate amount $1,173 + 50% of relevant rebate amount Same as for Ordinary Zone A
Income arrears (¶15-340) Medicare levy surcharge lump sum arrears (¶15-350)	Applicable to lump sum payments of income paid in arrears

¶42-170 Cents per kilometre for motor vehicle expense claims

The prescribed rates per kilometre for motor vehicle expense claims (¶16-370) is 72 cents per kilometre for 2020–21 and 68 cents per kilometre for 2019–20.

Capital Gains Tax

¶42-225 CGT index numbers

The rules regarding CGT indexation are explained at ¶11-610.

Year	Quarterly CPI number			
	March	**June**	**September**	**December**
1985	—	—	39.7	40.5
1986	41.4	42.1	43.2	44.4
1987	45.3	46.0	46.8	47.6
1988	48.4	49.3	50.2	51.2
1989	51.7	53.0	54.2	55.2
1990	56.2	57.1	57.5	59.0
1991	58.9	59.0	59.3	59.9
1992	59.9	59.7	59.8	60.1
1993	60.6	60.8	61.1	61.2
1994	61.5	61.9	62.3	62.8

Year	Quarterly CPI number			
1995	63.8	64.7	65.5	66.0
1996	66.2	66.7	66.9	67.0
1997	67.1	66.9	66.6	66.8
1998	67.0	67.4	67.5	67.8
1999	67.8	68.1	68.7	69.1
2000	69.7	70.2	—	—

¶42-230 Improvements to pre-CGT assets

The CGT improvement threshold is discussed at ¶11-410.

Year of income ended 30 June	Threshold	Year of income ended 30 June	Threshold
1986	$50,000	2004	$104,377
1987	$53,950	2005	$106,882
1988	$58,859	2006	$109,447
1989	$63,450	2007	$112,512
1990	$68,018	2008	$116,337
1991	$73,459	2009	$119,594
1992	$78,160	2010	$124,258
1993	$80,036	2011	$126,619
1994	$80,756	2012	$130,418
1995	$82,290	2013	$134,200
1996	$84,347	2014	$136,884
1997	$88,227	2015	$140,443
1998	$89,992	2016	$143,392
1999	$89,992	2017	$145,401
2000	$91,072	2018	$147,582
2001	$92,802	2019	$150,386
2002	$97,721	2020	$153,093
2003	$101,239	2021	$155,849

Superannuation and Termination of Employment

¶42-250 Superannuation benefits — lump sums and income streams

The tax treatment of a superannuation benefit (other than a death benefit: ¶42-260) is explained at ¶14-200 and following.

Preservation age

For a person born . . .	Preservation age
Before 1 July 1960	55
1 July 1960–30 June 1961	56
1 July 1961–30 June 1962	57
1 July 1962–30 June 1963	58

Preservation age

For a person born . . .	Preservation age
1 July 1963–30 June 1964	59
After 30 June 1964	60

The tables below set out the tax treatment of a superannuation member benefit paid from an element taxed and an element untaxed in the fund The tax free component of the benefit is not included in the tables. Medicare levy (¶42-010) is added to whichever rate of tax (other than 0%) applies.

Special rules apply to certain superannuation benefit payments (¶14-300, ¶14-310).

Taxable component — element taxed in the fund

Age of taxpayer	Lump sum	Income stream
Age 60 and over	● Not assessable, not exempt income	● Not assessable not exempt income
Preservation age to age 59	● 0% for amount of component up to **low rate cap amount** (see below) ● Amount of component exceeding the low rate cap amount is taxed at a maximum rate of 15%	● Taxed at marginal tax rates ● Tax offset of 15% of the taxable component is available
Below preservation age	● Amount of component is taxed at a maximum rate of 20%	● Taxed at marginal tax rates, with no tax offset ● Tax offset of 15% of the taxable component is available if a disability superannuation benefit

Taxable component — element untaxed in the fund

Age of taxpayer	Lump sum	Income stream
Age 60 and over	● Amount of component up to the **untaxed plan cap amount** (see below) is taxed at a maximum rate of 15% ● Amount of component exceeding the untaxed plan cap amount is taxed at the top marginal rate (45%)	● Taxed at marginal rates, with a 10% tax offset

Taxable component — element untaxed in the fund

Age of taxpayer	Lump sum	Income stream
Preservation age to age 59	● Amount of component up to the **low rate cap amount** (see below) is taxed at a maximum rate of 15% ● Amount of component exceeding the low rate cap amount up to the untaxed plan cap amount is taxed at a maximum rate of 30% ● Amount of component exceeding the untaxed plan cap amount is taxed at the top marginal rate	● Taxed at marginal rates, with no tax offset
Below preservation age	● Amount of component up to untaxed plan cap amount is taxed at a maximum rate of 30% ● Amount of component exceeding the untaxed plan cap amount is taxed at the top marginal rate	● Taxed at marginal rates, with no tax offset

Low rate cap amount and untaxed plan cap amount

Income year	Low rate cap amount	Untaxed plan cap amount
2018–19	$205,000	$1.480m
2019–20	$210,000	$1.515m
2020–21	$215,000	$1.565m

The low rate cap amount and the untaxed plan cap amount are indexed in line with AWOTE, in increments of $5,000 rounded down (ITAA97 s 960-285). For the cap amount in pre-2018–19 years, see earlier editions of the *Australian Master Tax Guide*.

¶42-260 Superannuation death benefits

The taxation of a superannuation lump sum or income stream death benefit is discussed at ¶14-270.

The tables below summarise the tax treatment of superannuation death benefits. The tax free component is not included in the tables. Medicare levy (¶42-010) is added to whichever rate of tax applies, except where the recipient is the trustee of the deceased estate. In that case, the tax payable, if any, is imposed on the trustee depending on how beneficiaries will benefit from the death benefit payment.

There are additional tax consequences if the defined benefit income stream payments to a taxpayer exceed $100,000 in a year (¶14-370).

Payments to dependants

Age of deceased	Superannuation death benefit	Age of recipient	Taxation treatment
Any age	Lump sum	Any age	Not assessable income, not exempt income
Aged 60 and above	Income stream	Any age	Taxable component: ● element taxed in the fund is not assessable income, not exempt income ● element untaxed in the fund is taxed at marginal tax rates. Recipient entitled to a 10% tax offset on this amount
Below age 60	Income stream	Age 60 and above	Taxable component: ● element taxed in the fund is not assessable income, not exempt income ● element untaxed in the fund is taxed at marginal tax rates. Recipient entitled to a 10% tax offset on this amount
Below age 60	Income stream	Below age 60	Taxable component: ● element taxed in the fund is taxed at marginal tax rates. Recipient entitled to a 15% tax offset on this amount ● element untaxed in the fund is taxed at marginal tax rates

Payment to non-dependants

Age of deceased	Superannuation death benefit	Age of recipient	Tax treatment
Any age	Lump sum	Any age	Taxable component: ● element taxed in the fund is taxed at a maximum rate of 15% ● element untaxed in the fund is taxed at a maximum rate of 30%
Any age	Income stream	Any age	● Benefit cannot be paid as an income stream to non-dependants ● Income streams that had commenced before 1 July 2007 are taxed as if received by a dependant (see table above)

¶42-265 Transfer balance cap and defined benefit income cap

Transfer balance cap

An individual is liable to pay excess transfer balance tax if the transfer balance cap is exceeded (¶14-320). The cap is $1.6 million for the 2017–18 to 2020–21 financial years. A child who receives a death benefit income stream is subject to a modified transfer balance cap (¶14-330). An individual who has an excess transfer balance is liable to pay excess transfer balance tax at 15% on the excess transfer balance earnings

(¶14-360). From 1 July 2018 onwards, the tax rate is 15% for the first time that the taxpayer has an excess transfer balance, but the rate increases to 30% if the individual has an excess transfer balance for a second or subsequent time.

Defined benefit income cap

The defined benefit income cap is $100,000 for the 2017–18 to 2020–21 financial years. From 2017–18, additional tax consequences apply where the defined benefit income received by an individual exceeds the cap in a financial year (¶14-370).

¶42-270 Employment termination payments

The taxable component of an employment termination payment (ETP) is assessable income (¶14-620); however, a tax offset may be available.

The tables below set out the tax treatment of ETPs. Medicare levy (¶42-010) is added to whichever rate of tax applies. For the tax treatment of death benefit termination payments, see ¶42-290.

Depending on the type of ETP, access to the tax offset for ETPs is limited to the ETP cap or the smaller of the ETP cap and a whole-of-income cap (¶14-620). Amounts in excess of the applicable cap are taxed at the top marginal rate (plus Medicare levy).

The table below sets out the types of ETPs and the applicable cap for each type of payment.

Column 1	Column 2
ETP cap only applies to:	**Smaller of the ETP cap and whole-of-income cap applies to:**
An early retirement scheme payment that exceeds the tax-free limit* (only the amount in excess of the limit is an ETP)	A "golden handshake" whether paid: ● under a contract or an industrial award obligation ● in recognition of prior service
A genuine redundancy payment that exceeds the tax-free limit* (only the amount in excess of the limit is an ETP)	A gratuity
A payment made because of the employee's permanent disability	A payment in lieu of notice
Compensation payment for personal injury	A payment for unused sick leave
Compensation for unfair dismissal	A payment for unused rostered days off
Compensation for harassment	A payment not covered in column 1
Compensation for discrimination	
Lump sum payments paid on the death of an employee	

* For the tax-free limit, see "Redundancy and early retirement scheme payments" below.

Taxation of employment termination payments

Employment termination payments

Component	Tax treatment
Tax free component	Not assessable income and not exempt income
Taxable component	Preservation age (¶42-250) and over ● amount up to applicable cap amount (see the table below) — taxed at a maximum rate of 15% ● amount over the applicable cap amount — taxed at top marginal rate (45%) Below preservation age ● amount up to the applicable cap amount — taxed at a maximum rate of 30% ● amount over the applicable cap amount — taxed at top marginal rate

Applicable cap amount — life benefit termination payment

Income year	ETP cap amount (indexed yearly)	Whole-of-income cap (not indexed)
2018–19	$205,000	$180,000
2019–20	$210,000	$180,000
2020–21	$215,000	$180,000

The ETP cap amount is indexed in line with AWOTE, in increments of $5,000 rounded down (ITAA97 s 960-285). The whole-of-income cap amount is not indexed. For the cap amount in pre-2018–19 years, see earlier editions of the *Australian Master Tax Guide*.

Redundancy and early retirement scheme payments

Conditions must be met for a termination payment to be treated as a genuine redundancy payment (¶14-700) or an early retirement scheme payment (¶14-710). These payments comprise an amount which is non-assessable non-exempt income and an assessable amount which is taxed as an ETP. The non-assessable non-exempt amount is worked out by the formula:

Base amount + (Service amount × Years of service)

Base amount and service amount

Income year	Base amount	Service amount
2018–19	$10,399	$5,200
2019–20	$10,638	$5,320
2020–21	$10,989	$5,496

The base amount and service amount are increased by indexation in line with AWOTE each year (ITAA97 s 960-275). For the base and service amounts in pre-2018–19 years, see earlier editions of the *Australian Master Tax Guide*.

¶42-290 Death benefit termination payments

A death benefit termination payment (¶14-680) may have 2 components — a tax free component and a taxable component.

The table below summarises the tax treatment of death benefit termination payments. Medicare levy is added to whichever rate of tax applies, except where the recipient is the trustee of the deceased estate. In this case, the tax payable, if any, depends on how beneficiaries will benefit from the death benefit payment. Any tax payable is imposed on the trustee.

Component	Tax treatment
Tax free component	Not assessable income and not exempt income
Taxable component	Payment to a dependant: ● amount up to the **ETP cap amount** (see below) is not assessable income and not exempt income ● amount over the ETP cap amount is taxed at the top marginal rate (45%) Payment to a non-dependant: ● amount up to the ETP cap amount is taxed at a maximum rate of 30% ● amount over the ETP cap amount is taxed at the top marginal rate Payment to trustee of deceased estate: ● taxed in the estate, based on whether the beneficiary is a dependant or non-dependant as above

ETP cap amount — death benefit termination payment

Income year	ETP cap amount
2018–19	$205,000
2019–20	$210,000
2020–21	$215,000

The ETP cap amount is increased by indexation in line with AWOTE each year, in increments of $5,000 rounded down (ITAA97 s 960-285). For the cap amount in pre-2018–19 years, see earlier editions of the *Australian Master Tax Guide*.

The cap amount is reduced for any death benefit termination payment previously received in consequence of the same termination, whether in an earlier income year or the year of receipt. The cap amount is not reduced because of the receipt of a life benefit termination payment in the same year.

¶42-305 Unused leave payments

A lump sum payment to a taxpayer in lieu of unused annual leave (¶14-720) or unused long service leave (¶14-730) in consequence of termination of employment may receive concessional tax treatment:

Unused annual leave payments

Unused annual leave — period of accrual	Assessable portion	Maximum tax rate
General termination of employment:		
– accrual before 18.8.93	100%	30%

Unused annual leave payments

Unused annual leave — period of accrual	**Assessable portion**	**Maximum tax rate**
– accrual on or after 18.8.93	100%	Marginal
Genuine redundancy amount, early retirement scheme amount or invalidity amount paid on or after 18.8.93	100%	30%

Unused long service leave payments

Unused long service leave — period of accrual	**Assessable portion**	**Maximum tax rate**
General termination of employment:		
– accrual before 16.8.78	5%	Marginal
– accrual 16.8.78 to 17.8.93	100%	30%
– accrual on or after 18.8.93	100%	Marginal
Genuine redundancy amount, early retirement scheme amount or invalidity amount:		
– accrual before 16.8.78	5%	Marginal
– accrual on or after 16.8.78	100%	30%

The assessable portions are aggregated with other assessable income of the taxpayer, and the maximum rates are effected by way of a tax offset if the tax (as calculated in the usual manner) attributable to those portions exceeds the relevant maximum rates. Medicare levy is added to whichever rate is applicable.

¶42-320 Concessional contributions cap

An individual is liable to pay excess contributions charge if the concessional contributions made by or for the individual exceed the concessional contributions cap for the year (¶13-775). The excess contributions are included in the individual's assessable income and taxed at marginal tax rates.

Concessional contributions cap

Income year	**Age on 30 June**	**Cap amount**	**Age on 30 June**	**Cap amount**
2016–17	49 +	$35,000	< 49	$30,000
2017–18	Any age	$25,000	NA	NA
2018–19	Any age	$25,000	NA	NA
2019–20	Any age	$25,000	NA	NA
2020–21	Any age	$25,000	NA	NA

The general concessional contributions cap is indexed in line with AWOTE, in increments of $5,000 rounded down (except in certain years) (ITAA97 s 960-285). For the cap amount in pre-2016–17 years, see earlier editions of the *Australian Master Tax Guide*.

Where an individual's concessional contributions exceed a prescribed income threshold of $250,000, they are liable to a 15% Division 293 tax on the excess (¶13-750).

Unused concessional cap carry forward

From 1 July 2018, an individual who has a total superannuation balance (¶14-050) of less than $500,000 on 30 June of the previous financial year is entitled to contribute more than the general concessional contributions cap amount under a ''carry forward'' arrangement by making additional concessional contributions using any unused concessional cap amounts from an earlier year.

The first year of entitlement to the carry forward unused amounts is the 2019–20 financial year. Unused amounts are available for a maximum of 5 years, and will expire after this period. The table below illustrates how the unused cap carry forward operates.

Unused concessional cap carry forward *

	2017–18	2018–19	2019–20	2020–21	2021–22
General contributions cap*	$25,000	$25,000	$25,000	$25,000	$25,000
Total unused available cap accrued	NA	$0	$22,000	$44,000	$69,000
Maximum cap available	$25,000	$25,000	$47,000	$25,000	$94,000
Superannuation balance 30 June prior year	NA	$480,000	$490,000	$505,000	$490,000
Concessional contributions made (assumed)	$0	$3,000	$3,000	$0	$0
Unused concessional cap amount accrued in the relevant financial year	$0	$22,000	$22,000	$25,000	$25,000

* This table assumes there is no indexation increase to the general concessional contributions cap in the tax periods covered.

¶42-325 Non-concessional contributions cap

An individual is liable to pay excess contributions tax if the individual's non-concessional contributions exceed the non-concessional contributions cap for the year (¶13-780). For 2017–18 through to 2020–21, an individual's non-concessional contributions cap is:

- $100,000 (general non-concessional contributions cap), or
- nil — if, immediately before the start of the year, the individual's total superannuation balance (¶14-050) equals or exceeds the general transfer balance cap (¶14-320) for the year.

An individual's cap for a year may be affected by the bring forward rule (see ¶13-780). For the non-concessional contributions cap amount in pre-2017–18 years, see earlier editions of the *Australian Master Tax Guide.*

CGT cap amount

A CGT cap (a lifetime limit for each taxpayer) operates in conjunction with the non-concessional contributions tax regime under which certain contributions are counted towards the CGT cap, rather than the general non-concessional contributions cap (¶13-780).

CGT cap amount

Income year	Cap amount
2018–19	$1.480m
2019–20	$1.515m
2020–21	$1.565m

The CGT cap amount is indexed in line with AWOTE, in increments of $5,000 rounded down (ITAA97 s 960-285). For the CGT cap amount in pre-2018–19 years, see earlier editions of the *Australian Master Tax Guide*.

¶42-330 Government co-contributions and low income tax offset

Individual taxpayers may qualify for government co-contribution and low income superannuation tax offset for their personal superannuation contribution if they satisfy certain conditions (¶13-760).

Government co-contributions

The matching co-contribution rate and maximum co-contribution amount payable in a year are as follows.

Year	Matching rate (%)	Maximum co-contribution payable ($)	Co-contribution shading-out
2012–13 and later years	50%	$500	Contributions are matched at $0.50 for each $1 contributed up to a maximum co-contribution of $500 if the person's income is at or below the lower income threshold. The maximum co-contribution is reduced by 3.333 cents for each $1 by which the person's income exceeds the lower income threshold. No co-contribution is payable when the person's income is at or more than the higher income threshold.

Lower and higher income thresholds

Year	Lower income threshold	Higher income threshold
2018–19	$37,697	$52,697
2019–20	$38,564	$53,564
2020–21	$39,837	$54,837

For the lower and higher income threshold amounts in pre-2018–19 years, see earlier editions of the *Australian Master Tax Guide*.

Calculation of government co-contribution amount

Contributor's income (TI)	Maximum government co-contribution (MGC) payable is . . .
$0 to lower income threshold (**LIT**)	**MGC**
LIT + $1 to higher income threshold (**HIT**)	MGC – [(TI – LIT) × reduction percentage (**RP**)]
HIT + $1	$0

TI is the sum of the taxpayer's assessable income, reportable fringe benefits total and reportable employer superannuation contributions.

LIT and **HIT** are the income thresholds, see ''Lower and higher income thresholds'' above.

MGC is $500.

RP is 3.333%.

Low income superannuation tax offset

For 2017–18 and later years, an individual taxpayer whose adjusted taxable income is below $37,000 may be entitled to a low income superannuation tax offset (LISTO) where certain conditions are met (¶13-760). The LISTO replaced the low income superannuation contribution which was payable in pre-2017–18 years.

The LISTO in a year is based on 15% of the taxpayer's eligible concessional contributions for the year, subject to a maximum amount of $500 and a minimum amount of $10.

¶42-335 Tax offset — spouse contributions

An individual may be entitled to a tax offset for superannuation contributions made for the benefit of the individual's non-working or low income spouse (receiving spouse) whose total assessable income, reportable fringe benefits total and reportable employer superannuation contributions (**TI**) for an income year is less than $40,000 (¶13-770).

The maximum tax offset in a year of income is $540, based on 18% of the *lesser* of: (i) the actual contributions made to a complying superannuation fund or RSA; and (ii) the maximum contributions (**MC**) entitled to the tax offset ($3,000). The MC is reduced by $1 for each $1 that the receiving spouse's TI exceeds $37,000 so that the tax offset ceases to be available when the TI is $40,000 or more.

Receiving spouse's TI	Maximum contributions entitled to tax offset (MC)	Maximum tax offset (18% of lesser of)
$0 to $37,000	$3,000	MC or actual contributions
$37,001 to $39,999	$3,000 – (TI – $37,000)	MC or actual contributions
$40,000+	$0	$0

¶42-340 Superannuation guarantee charge

Employers who provide less than a prescribed level of superannuation support (the ''charge percentage'') for their employees in each quarter in a financial year are liable to pay a superannuation guarantee (SG) charge based on the shortfall plus an interest component and an administration charge (¶39-000).

Financial year	SG charge percentage*
2014–15 to 2020–21	9.5%
2021–22	10%

Financial year	SG charge percentage*
2022–23	10.5%
2023–24	11%
2024–25	11.5%
2025–26 and later years	12%

* A transitional SG charge percentage starting at 1% in 2016–17, and increasing by 1% in each later year over a 12-year period, applies to Norfolk Island employers and employees (¶39-100).

Maximum contribution base

The maximum contribution base (¶39-220) for a quarter is $57,090 in 2020–21 ($55,270 in 2019–20, $54,030 in 2018–19).

Fringe Benefits Tax

¶42-380 Fringe benefits tax rate

For the FBT year from 1 April 2020 to 31 March 2021, the rate of FBT is 47%, and is applied to the tax-inclusive value of the fringe benefits provided in the year. The tax-inclusive value of a benefit depends on whether the employer who provides the benefit is entitled to a GST input tax credit for the acquisition.

For Type 1 benefits, the gross-up rate is 2.0802 and for Type 2 benefits, the gross-up rate is 1.8868.

¶42-400 Statutory fractions for car benefit valuation

Fringe Benefits Tax Assessment Act 1986 s 9(1) sets out the formula that applies to determine the taxable value of a car fringe benefit where the employer has not elected to use the operating cost valuation method (¶35-180). The statutory fraction is a flat rate of 0.2, regardless of distance travelled during the year. For details of the phased out statutory rates for previous years, see earlier editions of the *Australian Master Tax Guide*.

¶42-405 Interest rates for car and loan fringe benefits

The taxable value of most loan fringe benefits is determined by reference to a notional amount of interest called the statutory interest rate for the year for which the benefit is being valued (¶35-290).

In calculating the taxable value of a car fringe benefit, an imputed interest cost equal to the statutory benchmark interest rate is included in the operating cost of the car where the provider owns the car (¶35-230).

The statutory benchmark interest rates for recent years are as follows.

Year ended 31 March	Rate of interest (%)
2015	5.95
2016	5.65
2017	5.65
2018	5.25
2019	5.20
2020	5.37
2021	4.80

¶42-410 FBT record-keeping exemption thresholds

In some cases, employers are exempted from FBT record-keeping requirements and are able to calculate FBT on the aggregate fringe benefits amount of an earlier year when such records were maintained (¶35-692). The exemption thresholds for recent years are:

FBT year	$
2014–15	7,965
2015–16	8,164
2016–17	8,286
2017–18	8,393
2018–19	8,552
2019–20	8,714
2020–21	8,853

Chapter 43 Capital Allowances (Depreciation) • Effective Life

¶43-000 Effective life of depreciating assets (depreciation)

The decline in value of a depreciating asset (ie capital allowance or depreciation) acquired *on or after* 1 July 2001 (¶17-480) is generally calculated on the basis of the effective life of the asset. Taxpayers may either make their own estimates of effective life or use the Commissioner's effective life determinations as a safe harbour (¶17-270). The effective life of a depreciating asset is determined at the time that it is first used (or installed ready for use) by the taxpayer for any purpose. The estimate may be changed at a later date (where the asset was acquired after 11.45 am EST on 21 September 1999 and accelerated depreciation rates are not being used). Effective lives generally do not need to be worked out if the temporary full expensing rules apply, unless an asset's opening adjustable value needs to be determined (¶17-430).

The Commissioner's effective life determinations for a broad range of assets are shown in tables which are regularly updated by the Commissioner. The latest tables (below) are reproduced from TR 2020/3 (applicable from 1 July 2020). If an asset does not appear in either table, taxpayers must make their own determination of the effective life of the asset.

Table A (¶43-005) is an industry table which contains assets under industry headings generally derived from the Australian and New Zealand Standard Industry Classification (ANZSIC) subject categories. *This table may only be used by members of the specified industry.*

Table B (¶43-100) is an asset table which contains generic assets which may be used by more than one industry. If an asset is only listed in Table B, that rate is to be used both by industry and non-industry members. If an item is listed in both tables, industry members must use the Table A rate and non-industry members must use the Table B rate. Note that the assets in Table B are common assets (eg rental property assets, cars, computers) used by a broader range of taxpayers (including salary and wage earners, landlords, small businesses) than the ones who can rely on Table A.

Taxpayers that are small business entities (¶7-050) are eligible for the small business depreciation regime (¶7-250) and need only distinguish between effective lives of less than 25 years and those of 25 years or more.

Since 1 July 2001, the legislation does not refer to "depreciation rates": the decline in value is simply calculated by spreading the cost of the asset over its effective life. For convenience, however, the table below sets out the rates of decline in value corresponding to the effective lives in Tables A and B. The table uses the diminishing value rate of 200% applicable to assets that start to be held on or after 10 May 2006 (¶17-500).

Effective life (years)	Prime cost method (%)	Diminishing value method (%)
1 1/2	66.67	100
2	50	100
3	33.33	66.67
3 1/3	30	60
4	25	50
4 1/2	22.22	44.44
5	20	40
5 1/2	18.18	36.36
6 2/3	15	30
7	14.29	28.57
8	12.5	25
8 1/3	12	24
9	11.11	22.22
10	10	20
12	8.33	16.67
13	7.69	15.38
13 1/3	7.5	15
15	6.67	13.33
16 2/3	6	12
20	5	10
25	4	8

Effective life (years)	Prime cost method (%)	Diminishing value method (%)
33 1/3	3	6
40	2.5	5
50	2	4
66 2/3	1.5	3
100	1	2

¶43-005 1 July 2020 effective life Table A (industry items)

Table A is an industry table which contains assets under industry headings generally derived from the Australian and New Zealand Standard Industry Classification (ANZSIC) subject categories. This table may only be used by members of the specified industry. If an item is listed in both Table A and Table B, industry members must use the Table A rate and non-industry members must use the Table B rate (¶43-100). If an asset does not appear in either table, taxpayers must make their own determination of the effective life of the asset (¶17-270).

New and reviewed items have been marked with an asterisk (*) in the third column of the table. Where the Commissioner has determined effective lives for assets in excess of the statutory caps for those assets (¶43-105), they have been marked with a hash (#). Assets marked with a plus (+) are fodder storage assets used in a primary production business (see also ¶18-085). Table A incorporates the 1 July 2020 Schedule of effective life determinations.

¶43-010 Effective life — agriculture, forestry and fishing

AGRICULTURE, FORESTRY AND FISHING
(01110 to 05290)

Asset	Life (Years)	Reviewed	Date Of Application
All terrain vehicles (ATVs) used in primary production activities	5	*	1 Jul 2007
Environmental control structures (including glasshouses, hothouses, germination rooms, plastic clad tunnels and igloos)	20	*	1 Jul 2006
Fences (excluding stockyard, pen and portable fences): Being fencing constructed at a time for a particular function (eg a line of fencing forming a side of a boundary or paddock) not being in the nature of a repair:			
General (incorporating anchor assemblies, intermediate posts, rails, wires, wire mesh and droppers)	30	*	1 Jul 2008
Electric	20	*	1 Jul 2008
Fence energisers for electric fences:			
Mains power	10	*	1 Jul 2008
Portable	5	*	1 Jul 2008
Fertigation systems:			
Pumps	3	*	1 Jul 2008
Tanks	10	*	1 Jul 2008
Grading and packing line assets used on farm:			
Banana assets:			
Air rams	3	*	1 Jul 2008
Bunch lines	10	*	1 Jul 2008
Choppers/mulchers	8	*	1 Jul 2008
Rails (including points)	15	*	1 Jul 2008
Scrap conveyors	5	*	1 Jul 2008
Tops	8	*	1 Jul 2008
Water troughs	10	*	1 Jul 2008

AGRICULTURE, FORESTRY AND FISHING
(01110 to 05290)

Asset	Life (Years)	Reviewed	Date Of Application
Coffee assets:			
Dryers	15	*	1 Jul 2008
Processors (including pulpers)	10	*	1 Jul 2008
Fermentation tanks	10	*	1 Jul 2008
Hullers	12	*	1 Jul 2008
Washers/separators	10	*	1 Jul 2008
General assets:			
Bin tippers	15	*	1 Jul 2008
Conveyors (including elevators)	10	*	1 Jul 2008
Drying tunnels	15	*	1 Jul 2008
Fungicide units	12	*	1 Jul 2008
Receival hoppers (including water dumps)	15	*	1 Jul 2008
Tables (including packing and sorting tables)	15	*	1 Jul 2008
Washing assets (including brush and barrel washers)	10	*	1 Jul 2008
Waxing assets	12	*	1 Jul 2008
Graders:			
Electronic	10	*	1 Jul 2008
Mechanical	15	*	1 Jul 2008
Optical	8	*	1 Jul 2008
Labelling assets:			
Labelling applicators (including in line labellers)	8	*	1 Jul 2008
Labelling guns	3	*	1 Jul 2008
Olive oil processing assets – see Table A Oil and fat manufacturing (11500)			
Packing assets (including bagging and wrapping machines)	10	*	1 Jul 2008
Scales (excluding platform scales)	5	*	1 Jul 2008
Tree nut assets:			
De-husking units	8	*	1 Jul 2008
Drying silos	20	*	1 Jul 2008
Trommels	15	*	1 Jul 2008
Livestock grids	40	*	1 Jul 2008
Motorcycles used in primary production activities	5	*	1 Jul 2007
Post drivers/hole diggers	10	*	1 Jul 2008
Protective structures (including shade houses and netting constructions)	20	*	1 Jul 2006
Sheds on land that is used for agricultural or pastoral operations (including machinery sheds, workshop sheds and farm production sheds)	40	*	1 Jan 2007
Tractors[6]	12	*#	1 Jul 2007
Water assets:			
Bores	30	*	1 Jul 2008
Dams (including earth or rock fill and turkey nests)	40	*	1 Jul 2008
Dam liners and covers	20	*	1 Jul 2008
Effluent channels	40	*	1 Jul 2008
Effluent recycle tanks	12	*	1 Jul 2008
Effluent sedimentation ponds	40	*	1 Jul 2008
Irrigation assets:			
Drip, micro spray or mini sprinkler systems:			
Above ground polyethylene (PE) pipes	10	*	1 Jul 2008
Drippers, micro sprays and mini sprinklers	5	*	1 Jul 2008

AGRICULTURE, FORESTRY AND FISHING
(01110 to 05290)

Asset	Life (Years)	Reviewed	Date Of Application
Control systems	10	*	1 Jul 2008
Filtration systems	15	*	1 Jul 2008
Pumps	12	*	1 Jul 2008
Variable speed drives (VSDs)	15	*	1 Jul 2008
Irrigation earth channels	40	*	1 Jul 2008
Irrigators (including centre pivot, lateral and travelling guns):			
Fresh water	20	*	1 Jul 2008
Effluent	10	*	1 Jul 2008
Pumps:			
Bore pumps, effluent and manure pumps	7	*	1 Jul 2008
Other	12	*	1 Jul 2008
Water mains:			
Aluminium	20	*	1 Jul 2008
Galvanised steel	25	*	1 Jul 2008
Polyethylene (PE)	20	*	1 Jul 2008
Polyvinylchloride (PVC)	30	*	1 Jul 2008
Water tanks:			
Concrete	30	*	1 Jul 2008
Galvanised steel	25	*	1 Jul 2008
Polyethylene (PE)	15	*	1 Jul 2008
Water troughs:			
Concrete	25	*	1 Jul 2008
Galvanised steel	15	*	1 Jul 2008
Polyethylene (PE)	10	*	1 Jul 2008
Windmills	30	*	1 Jul 2008
Water pressure cleaners	5	*	1 Jul 2008
Agriculture (01110 to 01990)			
Bee farming assets:			
Beehives	13	*	1 Jul 2016
Processing assets	20	*	1 Jul 2016
Bridges (wooden)	20		1 Jan 2001
Grain, cotton, peanut and rice assets:			
Chemical spraying assets:			
Generally (including broad acre trailed or linkage boom and utility)	10	*	1 Jan 2007
Self-propelled	8	*	1 Jan 2007
General assets:			
Aeration assets:			
Controllers	10	*	1 Jan 2007
Kits	15	*	1 Jan 2007
Augers (including conveyors)	15	*	1 Jan 2007
Dryers	20	*	1 Jan 2007
Moisture meters	5	*	1 Jan 2007
Mulchers	10	*	1 Jan 2007
Peanut pre-cleaners	10	*	1 Jan 2007
Slashers	7	*	1 Jan 2007
Harvesting assets:			
Boll buggies	15	*	1 Jan 2007

AGRICULTURE, FORESTRY AND FISHING
(01110 to 05290)

Asset	Life (Years)	Reviewed	Date Of Application
Chaser bins	15	*	1 Jan 2007
Combine harvesters[7]	12	*#	1 Jul 2007
Cotton picker/strippers	10	*#	1 Jul 2007
Field bins	20	*	1 Jan 2007
Fuel trailers	15	*	1 Jan 2007
Module builders	15	*	1 Jan 2007
Module tarpaulins	5	*	1 Jan 2007
Peanut diggers (including peanut pullers)	10	*#	1 Jan 2007
Peanut threshers	12	*#	1 Jul 2007
Precision farming assets (including GPS, controllers, lightbars, variable rate technology assets, but excluding hydraulic automated steering)	5	*	1 Jan 2007
Seeding and fertilizing assets:			
Fertilizer spreaders (including linkage and trailed)	10	*	1 Jan 2007
Planters (including bar, box, combined seeders, precision planters and row crop planters)	15	*	1 Jan 2007
Seed and fertilizer bins[8]	15	*+	1 Jan 2007
Tillage assets:			
Generally	15	*	1 Jan 2007
Harrows	5	*	1 Jan 2007
Laser controlled scraping assets:			
Buckets	10	*	1 Jan 2007
Transmitters	7	*	1 Jan 2007
Rippers	10	*	1 Jan 2007
Harvesters/sweepers	6 2/3	#	1 Jan 2001
Hay and foraging assets:			
Bale handling attachments (including accumulator grabs, bale stackers, hay forks/spikes/spears (incorporating metal frame), round bale grabs)	12	*	1 Jan 2007
Balers	10	*	1 Jan 2007
Bale wrappers	10	*	1 Jan 2007
Baler and wrappers	10	*	1 Jan 2007
Forage harvesters	10	*#	1 Jul 2007
Hay rakes (including finger wheel, rotary and parallel)	10	*	1 Jan 2007
Moisture probes	5	*	1 Jan 2007
Mower conditioners:			
Self-propelled:			
Attachments	8	*	1 Jan 2007
Prime movers	12	*	1 Jan 2007
Trailed	8	*	1 Jan 2007
Super conditioners (hay re-conditioners)	8	*	1 Jan 2007
Tedders	10	*	1 Jan 2007
Trailed bale handling assets:			
Big square bale stackers	10	*	1 Jan 2007
Generally (including accumulators and bale carriers)	15	*	1 Jan 2007
Windrowers:			
Self-propelled:			
Attachments	8	*	1 Jan 2007
Prime movers	12	*	1 Jan 2007
Trailed	8	*	1 Jan 2007

AGRICULTURE, FORESTRY AND FISHING
(01110 to 05290)

Asset	Life (Years)	Reviewed	Date Of Application
Hop growers' plant:			
Hop picking machines	13 1/3		1 Jan 2001
Kilns	20		1 Jan 2001
Horse stalls (Breeze way, Shed row)	33 1/3		1 Jan 2001
Horticultural plants:			
Citrus:			
Grapefruits	30	*	1 Jan 2001
Lemons	20	*	1 Jan 2001
Limes	20	*	1 Jan 2001
Mandarins	25	*	1 Jan 2001
Oranges	30	*	1 Jan 2001
Grapevines, dried	15	*	1 Oct 2004
Grapevines, table	15	*	1 Oct 2004
Grapevines, wine	20	*	1 Oct 2004
Nuts:			
Almonds	25	*	1 Jul 2001
Cashews	25	*	1 Jul 2001
Chestnuts	25	*	1 Jul 2001
Hazelnuts	25	*	1 Jul 2001
Jojoba	30	*	1 Jul 2001
Macadamia	25	*	1 Jul 2001
Pecans	25	*	1 Jul 2001
Pistachios	25	*	1 Jul 2001
Walnuts	25	*	1 Jul 2001
Pome:			
Apples	20	*	1 Jan 2001
Pears	25	*	1 Jan 2001
Stone Fruit:			
Apricots	10	*	1 Jan 2001
Cherries	18	*	1 Jan 2001
Nectarines	10	*	1 Jan 2001
Olives	30	*	1 Jan 2001
Peaches	10	*	1 Jan 2001
Plums	15	*	1 Jan 2001
Prunes	20	*	1 Jan 2001
Tropical:			
Avocados	20	*	1 Jan 2001
Mangoes	30	*	1 Jan 2001
Levee banks and revetments	40		1 Jan 2001
Pea-viners, pea cleaners, vine and straw conveyors	10	*	1 Jul 2016
Silos:			
Ancillary equipment	20		1 Jan 2001
Grain (metal)[9]	30	*+	1 Jul 2001
Stud stock and thoroughbred horses	10		1 Jan 2001
Trellis	20		1 Jan 2001

AGRICULTURE, FORESTRY AND FISHING
(01110 to 05290)

Asset	Life (Years)	Reviewed	Date Of Application
Nursery and floriculture production (01110 to 01150)			
Chemical spraying assets:			
Generally (including broad acre trailed or linkage boom and utility)	10	*	1 Jul 2006
Environmental control assets:			
Boilers (including piping)	20	*	1 Jul 2006
Control systems	10	*	1 Jul 2006
Evaporative coolers	10	*	1 Jul 2006
Heating assets	10	*	1 Jul 2006
Instruments (including sensors)	10	*	1 Jul 2006
Retractable screens	8	*	1 Jul 2006
Ventilation fans	5	*	1 Jul 2006
Fertigation system assets (incorporating control systems, pumps and tanks)	10	*	1 Jul 2006
General assets:			
Bins and pallets	5	*	1 Jul 2006
Fertiliser spreaders	10	*	1 Jul 2006
Fumigation assets	5	*	1 Jul 2006
Pasteurisation assets:			
Pasteurisation rooms	20	*	1 Jul 2006
Steam boilers	15	*	1 Jul 2006
Racks	15	*	1 Jul 2006
Ride on mowers	5	*	1 Jul 2006
Refrigeration assets:			
Insulation panels used in cool rooms	40	*	1 Jul 2006
Refrigeration generally	10	*	1 Jul 2006
Trailers	15	*	1 Jul 2006
Trolleys	15	*	1 Jul 2006
Weed mats	5	*	1 Jul 2006
Harvesting assets:			
Bed lifters and diggers	10	*	1 Jul 2006
Tree spades[10]	15	*#	1 Jul 2006
Packaging assets:			
Bunching and bundling machines	15	*	1 Jul 2006
Deleafers	15	*	1 Jul 2006
Grading machines	15	*	1 Jul 2006
Planting assets:			
Benches and tables	10	*	1 Jul 2006
Conveyors	15	*	1 Jul 2006
Dibblers and seeders	15	*	1 Jul 2006
Hoppers	15	*	1 Jul 2006
Pot, punnet and tray dispensers	12	*	1 Jul 2006
Potting machines (including pot and bag fillers)	10	*	1 Jul 2006
Soil elevators	10	*	1 Jul 2006
Soil mixers	10	*	1 Jul 2006
Transplanters (plugs and seedlings)	8	*	1 Jul 2006
Tray and punnet fillers	10	*	1 Jul 2006
Tray washers	15	*	1 Jul 2006

AGRICULTURE, FORESTRY AND FISHING
(01110 to 05290)

Asset	Life (Years)	Reviewed	Date Of Application
Vermiculite dispensers and coverers	15	*	1 Jul 2006
Propagation assets:			
Heated propagators	10	*	1 Jul 2006
Seedling and punnet trays, reusable	3	*	1 Jul 2006
Turf growing assets:			
Chemical spraying assets:			
Generally (including broad acre trailed or linkage boom and utility)	10	*	1 Jul 2006
Fertiliser spreaders	10	*	1 Jul 2006
Field top makers	10	*	1 Jul 2006
Land planes	25	*	1 Jul 2006
Line planters	10	*	1 Jul 2006
Mowers (including reel and rotary mowers)	10	*	1 Jul 2006
Net layers	10	*	1 Jul 2006
Power harrows	10	*	1 Jul 2006
Roll layers	10	*	1 Jul 2006
Soil aerators	10	*	1 Jul 2006
Trailers	15	*	1 Jul 2006
Turf harvesters (including pedestrian and tractor mounted harvesters)[11]	10	*#	1 Jul 2006
Turf rollers	15	*	1 Jul 2006
Turf seeders	15	*	1 Jul 2006
Turf vacuums	10	*	1 Jul 2006
Mushroom growing (01210)			
Air handling systems (incorporating cooling coils, filter blowers, mixing boxes, environment sensors and air ducting)	10	*	1 Jul 2008
Boilers (used for humidification and pasteurisation)	10	*	1 Jul 2008
Casing machines (includes casing mixers)	10	*	1 Jul 2008
Compost phase 1 assets:			
Bunkers	10	*	1 Jul 2008
Machinery (including forklifts, front end loaders, bunker fillers and pre-wet turners)	4	*	1 Jul 2008
Protective structures	10	*	1 Jul 2008
Pumps	3	*	1 Jul 2008
Control systems (excluding personal computers)	10	*	1 Jul 2008
Filling and emptying machines (including bag fillers, bed winches, cassette fillers and tunnel fillers)	10	*	1 Jul 2008
Growing systems:			
Shelves:			
Aluminium	15	*	1 Jul 2008
Other materials	10	*	1 Jul 2008
Trays:			
Wood	5	*	1 Jul 2008
Mushroom graders	5	*	1 Jul 2008
Sheds	40	*	1 Jul 2008
Slicing machines	5	*	1 Jul 2008
Spawning machines (including supplement machines)	12	*	1 Jul 2008
Trolleys	10	*	1 Jul 2008

AGRICULTURE, FORESTRY AND FISHING
(01110 to 05290)

Asset	Life (Years)	Reviewed	Date Of Application
Tunnels/rooms (incorporating doors, floors, drains, frames, insulation, lighting, roofs and walls):			
Growing	15	*	1 Jul 2008
Peak heat and spawn running	10	*	1 Jul 2008
Vacuum coolers	10	*	1 Jul 2008
Weighing machines	10	*	1 Jul 2008
Vegetable growing (under cover) (01220)			
Hydroponic growing assets (including cut flower growing):			
Hanging gutters	10	*	1 Jul 2007
Troughs	10	*	1 Jul 2007
Hydroponics growers may also use the effective life for relevant assets shown in Nursery and floriculture production (01110 to 01150)			
Vegetable growing (outdoors) and sugar cane growing (01230 and 01510)			
Chemical spraying assets:			
Generally	10	*	1 Jul 2007
Self-propelled	8	*	1 Jul 2007
Fertilizer spreaders:			
Generally	10	*	1 Jul 2007
Spinner	5	*	1 Jul 2007
General assets:			
Bins:			
Plastic	10	*	1 Jul 2007
Timber	5	*	1 Jul 2007
Mulch layers	12	*	1 Jul 2007
Mulch lifters	12	*	1 Jul 2007
Mulchers	8	*	1 Jul 2007
Rakes (eg cane trash rakes)	10	*	1 Jul 2007
Slashers	8	*	1 Jul 2007
Harvesting assets:			
Cane haul out bins	12	*	1 Jul 2007
Harvesters (including cane, carrot, onion, potato and tomato)[12]	10	*#	1 Jul 2007
Harvesting aids (incorporating trailers and conveyor belts)	15	*	1 Jul 2007
Onion lifters[13]	10	*#	1 Jul 2007
Trailers	15	*	1 Jul 2007
Windrowers (including potato diggers, onion and potato windrowers)[14]	10	*#	1 Jul 2007
Planting assets:			
Billet planters	12	*	1 Jul 2007
Potato cutters	15	*	1 Jul 2007
Potato planters	10	*	1 Jul 2007
Precision seeders	10	*	1 Jul 2007
Transplanters:			
Automated	7	*	1 Jul 2007
Manual	10	*	1 Jul 2007
Tillage assets:			
Generally	15	*	1 Jul 2007
Power take-off (PTO) operated (including rotary hoes and power harrows)	8	*	1 Jul 2007

AGRICULTURE, FORESTRY AND FISHING
(01110 to 05290)

Asset	Life (Years)	Reviewed	Date Of Application
Trellising assets:			
Stake drivers	12	*	1 Jul 2007
Stake pullers	12	*	1 Jul 2007
Trellising (incorporating stakes and wire)	5	*	1 Jul 2007
Wire winders	15	*	1 Jul 2007
Fruit growing (01310 to 01360 and 01390)			
Cleaning and mulching assets:			
Mowers (including zero turn and ride on)	8	*	1 Jul 2008
Mulchers	6	*	1 Jul 2008
Slashers	8	*	1 Jul 2008
Sweeper attachments	10	*	1 Jul 2008
Crop protection assets:			
Applicators (including temporary bird netting applicators and vine cover rollers)	15	*	1 Jul 2008
Banana bagging machines	10	*	1 Jul 2008
Banana ripening bags	3	*	1 Jul 2008
Sprayers	10	*	1 Jul 2008
Temporary bird netting	5	*	1 Jul 2008
Under vine weeder	10	*	1 Jul 2008
Vine covers	3	*	1 Jul 2008
Dried fruit assets:			
Generally (including bin dryers, boxing machines, dehydration tunnels, dippers, rack dehydrators, scrapers, trolleys and wetting machines)	15	*	1 Jul 2008
Drying sheets (including ground sheets)	10	*	1 Jul 2008
Trays	10	*	1 Jul 2008
Fertilising assets:			
Fertigation systems:			
Pumps	3	*	1 Jul 2008
Tanks	10	*	1 Jul 2008
Spreaders:			
Generally	10	*	1 Jul 2008
Spinners	5	*	1 Jul 2008
General assets:			
Bins:			
Plastic	10	*	1 Jul 2008
Timber	5	*	1 Jul 2008
Crates (including picking lugs)	5	*	1 Jul 2008
Elevating work platforms	10	*	1 Jul 2008
Frost fans	15	*	1 Jul 2008
Mulch layers	12	*	1 Jul 2008
Mulch lifters	12	*	1 Jul 2008
Orchard ladders	10	*	1 Jul 2008
Post driver/hole diggers	10	*	1 Jul 2008
Refractometers	10	*	1 Jul 2008
Water pressure cleaners	5	*	1 Jul 2008
Harvesting assets:			
Grape harvesters [15]	10	*#	1 Jul 2008

AGRICULTURE, FORESTRY AND FISHING
(01110 to 05290)

Asset	Life (Years)	Reviewed	Date Of Application
Harvest aids	15	*	1 Jul 2008
Picking bags	3	*	1 Jul 2008
Picking platforms	10	*	1 Jul 2008
Picking trolleys	5	*	1 Jul 2008
Trailers (including grape chaser bins)	15	*	1 Jul 2008
Tree shakers [16]	10	*#	1 Jul 2008
Planting assets:			
Hole burners	10	*	1 Jul 2008
Planters	12	*	1 Jul 2008
Tree guards	2	*	1 Jul 2008
Trellising	20	*	1 Jul 2008
Weed matting	5	*	1 Jul 2008
Pruning assets:			
Chain saws	3	*	1 Jul 2008
Electric hand pruners	3	*	1 Jul 2008
Manual hand pruners	2	*	1 Jul 2008
Mechanical pruning assets (including cutter bars and cane strippers, but excluding vine leaf removers)	10	*	1 Jul 2008
Pneumatic pruners:			
Compressors	10	*	1 Jul 2008
Hand tools	5	*	1 Jul 2008
Vine leaf removers	15	*	1 Jul 2008
Tillage assets:			
Generally	15	*	1 Jul 2008
Power take-off (PTO) operated (including rotary hoes and power harrows)	8	*	1 Jul 2008
Coffee, olive and tree nut growing (01370, 01390 and 01590)			
Chemical spraying assets (including air blast sprayers and linkage sprayers)	10	*	1 Jul 2007
Cleaning and mulching assets:			
Blowers	10	*	1 Jul 2007
Mowers (including zero turn and ride on)	8	*	1 Jul 2007
Mulchers	8	*	1 Jul 2007
Slashers	10	*	1 Jul 2007
Sweeper attachments	10	*	1 Jul 2007
Fertilizer spreaders	10	*	1 Jul 2007
General assets:			
Bins:			
Plastic	10	*	1 Jul 2007
Timber	5	*	1 Jul 2007
Stakes (including trellising)	3	*	1 Jul 2007
Harvesting assets:			
Bankouts (almonds)	15	*	1 Jul 2007
Catcher nets	10	*	1 Jul 2007
Elevators (almonds)	12	*	1 Jul 2007
Harvesters [17]:			
Coffee	10	*#	1 Jul 2007
Harvesting pole rakes	5	*	1 Jul 2007

AGRICULTURE, FORESTRY AND FISHING
(01110 to 05290)

Asset	Life (Years)	Reviewed	Date Of Application
Olive	10	*#	1 Jul 2007
Nuts:			
Generally	10	*#	1 Jul 2007
Macadamia mower mounted	8	*	1 Jul 2007
Pick ups (eg almonds)	12	*#	1 Jul 2007
Sweepers	12	*#	1 Jul 2007
Tree shakers	10	*#	1 Jul 2007
Reservoir carts (almonds)	15	*	1 Jul 2007
Trailers	15	*	1 Jul 2007
Pruning assets:			
Chain saws	5	*	1 Jul 2007
Electric hand pruners	3	*	1 Jul 2007
Manual hand pruners	2	*	1 Jul 2007
Pneumatic pruners:			
Compressor	10	*	1 Jul 2007
Hand tools	5	*	1 Jul 2007
Sheep farming (01410)			
Crutching machines, portable type	10	*	1 Jan 2007
Dipping and spraying assets for parasite control:			
Jet spray system assets (including the race or handler dedicated to the jet spray system)	10	*	1 Jan 2007
Mobile plunge dips	5	*	1 Jan 2007
Feeders (including grain feeders, oat feeders, hay feeders)	15	*	1 Jan 2007
Footbaths	10	*	1 Jan 2007
Instruments for measuring wool fibre fineness, laser type	10	*	1 Jan 2007
Instruments for measuring backfat or eye muscle or detecting pregnancy, ultrasound type (incorporating probe and monitor)	5	*	1 Jan 2007
Sheep handling assets (including autodrafter, conveyor, cradle, crate, crutching trailer, elevator, ewe lifter, handler, hydraulic lift, rollover unit, shearing table, weigh crate, winch used to lift sheep)	15	*	1 Jan 2007
Weigh bars, weigh indicators and weigh platforms	10	*	1 Jan 2007
Yards, races, leadup systems and loading ramps:			
Permanent types	40	*	1 Jan 2007
Portable types	25	*	1 Jan 2007
Woolshed assets:			
Grinding machines for sharpening cutters	30	*	1 Jan 2007
Shearing machines	30	*	1 Jan 2007
Shearing or crutching handpieces	10	*	1 Jan 2007
Wool bale movers	10	*	1 Jan 2007
Wool presses	20	*	1 Jan 2007
Wool tables, steel types	20	*	1 Jan 2007
Woolsheds and shearing sheds	50	*	1 Jan 2007
Beef cattle farming (01420)			
Cattle handling assets:			
Calf cradles	10	*	1 Jan 2007
Cattle crushes (hydraulic and manual)	10	*	1 Jan 2007
NLIS and other readers	5	*	1 Jan 2007
Scales, weigh indicators and loading bars	5	*	1 Jan 2007

AGRICULTURE, FORESTRY AND FISHING
(01110 to 05290)

Asset	Life (Years)	Reviewed	Date Of Application
Cattle yards (including races and coolers (steel and timber)):			
Permanent types	30	*	1 Jan 2007
Portable types	20	*	1 Jan 2007
Feed bins (including hay racks)18	15	*+	1 Jan 2007
Feed handling assets:			
Bale feeders	10	*	1 Jan 2007
Feed mixers	10	*	1 Jan 2007
Silage and feedout wagons	10	*	1 Jan 2007
Loading ramps	20	*	1 Jan 2007
Manure and fertilizer spreaders	10	*	1 Jan 2007
Saddlery and harness	10	*	1 Jan 2007
Beef cattle feedlots (01430)			
Cattle handling assets:			
Cattle crushes (hydraulic and manual)	6	*	1 Jan 2007
Cattle induction and transfer yards (steel and timber)	20	*	1 Jan 2007
Cattle treatment yards (steel and timber)	20	*	1 Jan 2007
Cattle wash yards (steel and timber)	20	*	1 Jan 2007
NLIS and other readers	5	*	1 Jan 2007
Scales, weigh indicators and loading bars	5	*	1 Jan 2007
Cattle pen assets:			
Bunk sweepers	8	*	1 Jan 2007
Cattle pen infrastructure assets:			
Feed bunks or troughs and aprons	20	*	1 Jan 2007
Feed roads	20	*	1 Jan 2007
Pen earthworks	20	*	1 Jan 2007
Pen fences and gates (steel and timber)	20	*	1 Jan 2007
Shade structures	20	*	1 Jan 2007
Pen scrapers	10	*	1 Jan 2007
Feed milling and handling assets:			
Ancillary grain handling equipment:			
Augers	10	*	1 Jan 2007
Conveyors and elevators	15	*	1 Jan 2007
Bulk and segregated commodity storage facilities (incorporating bunkers)	30	*	1 Jan 2007
Feed mixers	7	*	1 Jan 2007
Feed mixer trucks	7	*	1 Jan 2007
Grain cleaners	10	*	1 Jan 2007
Grain processing assets:			
Roller mills	15	*	1 Jan 2007
Steam flaking chests	15	*	1 Jan 2007
Steam flaking surge bins	15	*	1 Jan 2007
Tempering silos:			
Glass fused to steel	50	*	1 Jan 2007
Stainless steel	15	*	1 Jan 2007
Galvanised steel	12	*	1 Jan 2007
Receival pits and hoppers	25	*	1 Jan 2007
Roughage processing assets (including tub rinders)	7	*	1 Jan 2007
Sampling and testing assets	5	*	1 Jan 2007

AGRICULTURE, FORESTRY AND FISHING
(01110 to 05290)

Asset	Life (Years)	Reviewed	Date Of Application
Silos and bins used for storing dry grain:[19]			
Concrete	50	*+	1 Jan 2007
Steel	20	*+	1 Jan 2007
Tank storages for liquid feed supplements	15	*	1 Jan 2007
Loading ramps	20	*	1 Jan 2007
Manure composting and screening machines	15	*	1 Jan 2007
Dairy cattle farming (01600)			
Automatic calf feeders	10	*	1 Jul 2016
Barn fed dairy farms:			
Bulk and segregated commodity storage facilities (incorporating bunkers)	30	*	1 Jul 2007
Exercise yards	20	*	1 Jul 2007
Feeding barns and maternity barns (incorporating cow beds, fans, and feed alleys)	20	*	1 Jul 2007
Cattle handling assets:			
Air operated gates	10	*	1 Jul 2007
All terrain vehicles (ATVs)	3	*	1 Jul 2007
Automatic drafting systems	7	*	1 Jul 2007
Automatic ID systems	7	*	1 Jul 2007
Automatic weighing systems and cattle scales	5	*	1 Jul 2007
Backing gates	15	*	1 Jul 2007
Calf cradles	10	*	1 Jul 2007
Cattle crushes (including automatic)	10	*	1 Jul 2016
Cattle laneways	30	*	1 Jul 2007
Cattle yards (including loading ramps)	30	*	1 Jul 2007
Dairy milking sheds	30	*	1 Jul 2007
Dairy yards and races	20	*	1 Jul 2007
Teat spraying systems:			
Automatic	7	*	1 Jul 2007
Manual	10	*	1 Jul 2007
Clean up assets:			
High pressure pumps and hoses	10	*	1 Jul 2007
Hot water services	10	*	1 Jul 2016
Milk line washing systems:			
Automatic	10	*	1 Jul 2007
Manual	10	*	1 Jul 2007
Feed milling and handling assets:			
Augers	10	*	1 Jul 2007
Conveyors and elevators	15	*	1 Jul 2007
Feed mixers	7	*	1 Jul 2007
Feed pads and bunkers	30	*	1 Jul 2007
Feeding systems:			
Automatic	12	*	1 Jul 2007
Manual	15	*	1 Jul 2007
Grain mills (including roller mills, disc mills and hammer mills)	15	*	1 Jul 2007
Manure spreaders	10	*	1 Jul 2007
Silage pits	40	*	1 Jul 2007
Silage wagons	10	*	1 Jul 2007

AGRICULTURE, FORESTRY AND FISHING
(01110 to 05290)

Asset	Life (Years)	Reviewed	Date Of Application
Silos (steel)[20]	20	*+	1 Jul 2007
Telescopic handlers	10	*	1 Jul 2007
Tub grinders	7	*	1 Jul 2007
Milking and milk handling assets:			
Automatic cluster removers	10	*	1 Jul 2007
Bailing systems:			
Herringbone (including swing over, double up and rapid exit)	15	*	1 Jul 2007
Rotary	15	*	1 Jul 2007
Walk through	15	*	1 Jul 2007
Filters	15	*	1 Jul 2016
Milking systems (incorporating clusters, swing over arms, hoses, pipes, pulsators, vacuum pumps, variable speed control)	15	*	1 Jul 2007
Milk meters and recording jars (including conductivity sensors)	10	*	1 Jul 2007
Milk vats	25	*	1 Jul 2016
Plate coolers	15	*	1 Jul 2007
Receivers	15	*	1 Jul 2007
Refrigeration compressors	10	*	1 Jul 2007
Robotic milking system assets:			
Air compressors	5	*	1 Jul 2016
Automated milking systems:			
Rotary	10	*	1 Jul 2016
Single box and multi box	10	*	1 Jul 2016
Automatic feeding systems	10	*	1 Jul 2016
Automatic footbaths	8	*	1 Jul 2016
Control systems (excluding personal computers) – see Table B Control systems and control system assets			
Cow comfort systems:			
Cow brushes	3	*	1 Jul 2016
Rubber matting	7	*	1 Jul 2016
Cow identification systems (including weights, bands, numbers and transponders)	7	*	1 Jul 2016
Cow traffic systems	7	*	1 Jul 2016
Milk chillers/plate coolers/energy recovery systems	10	*	1 Jul 2016
Vacuum pumps	7	*	1 Jul 2016
Poultry farming for breeding, eggs and meat (01710 to 01720)			
Animal housing environmental control assets:			
Control systems (excluding personal computers)	10	*	1 Jan 2007
Curtains:			
Baffles, brooders	10	*	1 Jan 2007
Sidewalls	5	*	1 Jan 2007
Tunnel inlets	10	*	1 Jan 2007
Evaporative cooling systems (including frames, pipes, pumps, tanks and coolpads)	10	*	1 Jan 2007
Foggers	10	*	1 Jan 2007
Heaters	15	*	1 Jan 2007
Minimum vents (including cabling)	12	*	1 Jan 2007
Sensors	4	*	1 Jan 2007
Tunnel inlet panels	15	*	1 Jan 2007
Ventilation fans:			

AGRICULTURE, FORESTRY AND FISHING
(01110 to 05290)

Asset	Life (Years)	Reviewed	Date Of Application
Exhaust fans (tunnel, minivent)	12	*	1 Jan 2007
Stirrer fans	15	*	1 Jan 2007
Animal housing structures (incorporating frames, walls, rooves, insulation, doors, floors and lighting)	20	*	1 Jan 2007
Cages (for egg layers)	20	*	1 Jan 2007
Egg belt systems (under cage/nest housing) (including belts, rollers, tensioners and drive units)	15	*	1 Jan 2007
Egg conveyors (including drive units)	15	*	1 Jan 2007
Egg counters	15	*	1 Jan 2007
Egg elevators (including drive units)	15	*	1 Jan 2007
Egg grading and packing assets:			
Egg grader and packing systems (including box erectors, box sealers, candling machines, conveyors, crack, dirt, leak and blood detectors, denesters (egg inners and trays), egg loaders, egg oilers, egg tray stackers, egg washers, egg weigher and transfer systems, imprinters (egg and box), packers (inners, trays and boxes) and wrappers)	10	*	1 Jan 2007
Pallet levellers (coil spring)	25	*	1 Jan 2007
Palletisers	10	*	1 Jan 2007
Trolley lifters	15	*	1 Jan 2007
Farm trolleys:			
Chicken transport	10	*	1 Jan 2007
Egg transport	10	*	1 Jan 2007
Feeding systems (including troughs, trolleys, chains, hoppers, pans, tubes with auger and drive units)	10	*	1 Jan 2007
Generators (emergency)	20	*	1 Jan 2007
Hanging cable systems (for feeders, drinkers and nest housing)	15	*	1 Jan 2007
Manure belt systems (under cage/nest housing) (including polypropylene belts, scrapers, rollers, tensioners and drive units)	15	*	1 Jan 2007
Manure conveyors (including drive units)	10	*	1 Jan 2007
Nest housing (including slatted walkways)	15	*	1 Jan 2007
Silos for feed:[21]			
Metal	20	*+	1 Jan 2007
Ancillary equipment:			
Augers	10	*	1 Jan 2007
Conveyors and elevators	15	*	1 Jan 2007
Water assets:			
Drinking systems (including tubing, nipple drinkers, drinking cups, pressure regulators and filter units)	10	*	1 Jan 2007
Winches	10	*	1 Jan 2007
Poultry hatcheries (01710 to 01720)			
Air handlers	20	*	1 Jan 2007
Boilers	20	*	1 Jan 2007
Candling equipment	20	*	1 Jan 2007
Chick counters	20	*	1 Jan 2007
Chilled water plants	20	*	1 Jan 2007
Control systems (excluding personal computers)	10	*	1 Jan 2007
Condensers/heat exchangers	10	*	1 Jan 2007
Conveyors	20	*	1 Jan 2007
Generators (emergency)	20	*	1 Jan 2007

AGRICULTURE, FORESTRY AND FISHING
(01110 to 05290)

Asset	Life (Years)	Reviewed	Date Of Application
Hatcher baskets	10	*	1 Jan 2007
Hatcher trolleys/dollies	10	*	1 Jan 2007
Hatchers (including integrated controller units)	20	*	1 Jan 2007
Hatchery buildings (incorporating frames, walls, rooves, insulation, doors, floors and lighting)	40	*	1 Jan 2007
Macerators	20	*	1 Jan 2007
Separators – chick and egg	20	*	1 Jan 2007
Setter trays	10	*	1 Jan 2007
Setter trolley unloaders	20	*	1 Jan 2007
Setter trolleys	10	*	1 Jan 2007
Setters/incubators (including integrated controller unit)	20	*	1 Jan 2007
Stacker/destacker systems	20	*	1 Jan 2007
Transfer machines – farm trolley to setter trolley	20	*	1 Jan 2007
Transfer machines – setter tray to hatcher basket	20	*	1 Jan 2007
Vaccinators	15	*	1 Jan 2007
Vacuum/auger systems (waste)	20	*	1 Jan 2007
Washing assets	20	*	1 Jan 2007
Pig farming (01920)			
Animal housing assets:			
Animal housing structures (incorporating frames, covers, walls, roof, insulation, shutters and doors)	20	*	1 Jul 2008
Curtains – sidewalls	10	*	1 Jul 2008
Floors (suspended types):			
Concrete	10	*	1 Jul 2008
Plastic	10	*	1 Jul 2008
Steel	5	*	1 Jul 2008
Control systems (excluding personal computers)	10	*	1 Jul 2008
Dry feed systems (incorporating troughs, trolleys, chains, hoppers, pans, tubers with auger and drive units)	10	*	1 Jul 2008
Effluent separators/effluent fan extractors	10	*	1 Jul 2008
Evaporative cooling systems (incorporating frames, pipes, pumps, tanks and coolpads)	10	*	1 Jul 2008
Fans:			
Exhaust (tunnel, minivent)	10	*	1 Jul 2008
Stirrer	10	*	1 Jul 2008
Farrowing crates	10	*	1 Jul 2008
Generators (emergency)	20	*	1 Jul 2008
Heaters and heat lamps	5	*	1 Jul 2008
High pressure cleaners	3	*	1 Jul 2008
Instruments for measuring backfat or detecting pregnancy, ultrasound types (incorporating probes and monitors)	5	*	1 Jul 2008
Liquid feed systems (incorporating feed valves, tanks, pumps, pipelines, mixers and troughs)	10	*	1 Jul 2008
Milling assets	10	*	1 Jul 2008
Mixing assets	10	*	1 Jul 2008
Pens (including fences, gates, stalls, farrowing crates, ramps)	10	*	1 Jul 2008
Silos:22			
Grain storage	20	*+	1 Jul 2008
Readyfeed	10	*+	1 Jul 2008

AGRICULTURE, FORESTRY AND FISHING
(01110 to 05290)

Asset	Life (Years)	Reviewed	Date Of Application
Tank storage for liquid feed supplements	20	*	1 Jul 2008
Water assets:			
Drinking systems (incorporating tubing, nipple drinkers, drinking cups, pressure regulators and filter units)	10	*	1 Jul 2008
Effluent tanks (concrete)	20	*	1 Jul 2008
Weigh bars, weigh indicators and weigh platforms	5	*	1 Jul 2008
Aquaculture (02011 to 02039)			
Aeration assets:			
Direct supply systems (including paddlewheels and aspirators):			
Fresh water	6	*	1 Jul 2007
Salt water[23]	3	*	1 Jul 2007
Remote or indirect supply systems (incorporating blowers, diaphragm pumps, diffusers, upwellers and pipelines)	10	*	1 Jul 2007
Aquaculture tanks:			
Concrete	20	*	1 Jul 2007
Fibreglass	15	*	1 Jul 2007
Polyethylene (PE)	20	*	1 Jul 2007
Raceways	20	*	1 Jul 2007
Transport of live products	10	*	1 Jul 2007
Bins and crates	5	*	1 Jul 2007
Commercial vessels and support assets – see Table A Water transport and support services (48100 to 48200 and 52110 to 52190)			
Control systems	10	*	1 Jul 2007
Cooling assets (including water chillers)	10	*	1 Jul 2007
Environmental control structures and protective structures used in salt water environment	15	*	1 Jul 2007
Feeders (including belt, pendulum, scatter and blower)	5	*	1 Jul 2007
Graders	10	*	1 Jul 2007
Harvesting nets	4	*	1 Jul 2007
Hatching assets (including hatching containers)	10	*	1 Jul 2007
Heating assets:			
Direct heating system (including immersion heaters):			
Fresh water	10	*	1 Jul 2007
Salt water	5	*	1 Jul 2007
Indirect heating system (including heat exchangers and passive heating)	10	*	1 Jul 2007
Instruments (including sensors and water quality meters)	5	*	1 Jul 2007
Oyster farming assets:			
Baskets	8	*	1 Jul 2007
Oyster growing structures (incorporating posts and racks or lines)	10	*	1 Jul 2007
Rumblers	10	*	1 Jul 2007
Sticks	5	*	1 Jul 2007
Trays:			
Plastic	8	*	1 Jul 2007
Timber	5	*	1 Jul 2007
Vats, treatment	15	*	1 Jul 2007
Power supply assets, emergency or standby:			
Generators (incorporating attached engine management and generator monitoring instruments)	15	*	1 Jul 2007

AGRICULTURE, FORESTRY AND FISHING
(01110 to 05290)

Asset	Life (Years)	Reviewed	Date Of Application
Processing assets:			
Conveyors, elevators and hoppers	10	*	1 Jul 2007
Cookers	10	*	1 Jul 2007
Packaging assets (including vacuum and modified atmospheric packing)	10	*	1 Jul 2007
Refrigeration assets:			
Insulation panels in cool or freezer rooms used in salt water environment	20	*	1 Jul 2007
Sea cages (incorporating rings, nets, ropes, anchors, weights and stanchions)	10	*	1 Jul 2007
Water assets:			
Aquaculture channels and ponds	20	*	1 Jul 2007
Liners and erosion matting for ponds and channels	15	*	1 Jul 2007
Pipes and pipelines:			
Above ground (polyethylene (PE) and polyvinylchloride (PVC) including lay flat hoses)	10	*	1 Jul 2007
In ground (polyethylene (PE) and polyvinylchloride (PVC))	30	*	1 Jul 2007
Pumps:			
Generally:			
Fresh water	10	*	1 Jul 2007
Salt water	5	*	1 Jul 2007
Single phase transfer pumps:			
Fresh water	5	*	1 Jul 2007
Salt water	3	*	1 Jul 2007
Water treatment assets (including filtration assets, foam fractionators, oxygen and ozone generators and UV sterilizers)	10	*	1 Jul 2007
Weighing machines	5	*	1 Jul 2007
Forestry and logging (03010 to 03020)			
Logging plant:			
Cable systems (including winches and high leads)	8	*	1 Jan 2001
Forwarders	8	*	1 Jan 2001
Harvesters and feller bunchers (includes heads)	7	*	1 Jan 2001
Log trailers	10	*	1 Jan 2001
Saws:			
Mobile	8	*	1 Jan 2001
Portable chain	2	*	1 Jan 2001
Snigging plant (including cable and grapple skidders, wheel loaders with log grabs, bulldozers, excavators, arches and winches)	7	*	1 Jan 2001
Fishing (04111 to 04199)			
Fishing plant:			
Commercial vessels and support assets – see Table A Water transport and support services (48100 to 48200 and 52110 to 52190)			
Fish holding baskets	10		1 Jan 2001
Purse seine fishing net	5		1 Jan 2001

AGRICULTURE, FORESTRY AND FISHING
(01110 to 05290)

Asset	Life (Years)	Reviewed	Date Of Application
Other agriculture and fishing support services (05290)			
Pulse and seed processing assets:			
Harvesting assets:			
Headers – flex drapers/pea pluckers	5	*	1 Jul 2017
Land rollers – steel	8	*	1 Jul 2017
Packaging assets:			
Bagging machines	10	*	1 Jul 2017
Bag sewers – see Table B Packaging machines			
Labellers	5	*	1 Jul 2017
Palletisers and depalletisers – see Table B Packaging machines			
Platform scales	10	*	1 Jul 2017
Wrapping machines (including shrink wrappers, stretch wrappers, pallet wrappers and strapping machines) – see Table B Packaging machines			
Processing assets:			
Cleaning and pre-cleaning assets:			
Air screen	15	*	1 Jul 2017
Flat bed	8	*	1 Jul 2017
Screens	10	*	1 Jul 2017
Conditioning assets:			
Clippers/debearders	9	*	1 Jul 2017
Conditioning units/drying units/heaters	7	*	1 Jul 2017
Hullers	15	*	1 Jul 2017
Mixers	12	*	1 Jul 2017
Seed treaters	10	*	1 Jul 2017
Separating assets:			
Gravity tables	15	*	1 Jul 2017
Rotary sieves	10	*	1 Jul 2017
Indented cylinders	15	*	1 Jul 2017
Spirals	15	*	1 Jul 2017
Splitters	12	*	1 Jul 2017
Product and raw material handling and receiving assets:			
Augers	12	*	1 Jul 2017
Chaser bins	15	*	1 Jul 2017
Crates:			
Wooden	5	*	1 Jul 2017
Wooden (mesh reinforced)	20	*	1 Jul 2017
Elevators (including bucket elevators)	15	*	1 Jul 2017
Field bins	10	*	1 Jul 2017
Silos – conditioning	20	*	1 Jul 2017
Tubulators/Mobile belt conveyors/Belt shifters	10	*	1 Jul 2017
Weighbridges – See Table B Weighbridges			
Quality control assets:			
Magnets	7	*	1 Jul 2017
Metal detectors	8	*	1 Jul 2017
Sorting and sizing assets:			
Colour sorters	8	*	1 Jul 2017

AGRICULTURE, FORESTRY AND FISHING
(01110 to 05290)

Asset	Life (Years)	Reviewed	Date Of Application
Support assets:			
Air Compressors	7	*	1 Jul 2017
Extraction assets (including dust collectors and fans)	9	*	1 Jul 2017

Footnotes:

6 A capped effective life of 6 2/3 years is available – see subsection 40-102(5)

7 A capped effective life of 6 2/3 years is available for harvesters listed in this sub-category (assets marked with #) – see subsection 40-102(5)

8 Primary producers may be entitled to an immediate deduction for capital expenditure incurred on a fodder storage asset if the asset was first used or installed ready for use on or after 19 August 2018 – see sections 40-515 and 40-548, and subsections 40-525(3) and 40-555(4).

9 Primary producers may be entitled to an immediate deduction for capital expenditure incurred on a fodder storage asset if the asset was first used or installed ready for use on or after 19 August 2018 – see sections 40-515 and 40-548, and subsections 40-525(3) and 40-555(4)

10 A capped effective life of 6 2/3 years is available – see subsection 40-102(5)

11 A capped effective life of 6 2/3 years is available – see subsection 40-102(5)

12 A capped effective life of 6 2/3 years is available – see subsection 40-102(5)

13 A capped effective life of 6 2/3 years is available – see subsection 40-102(5)

14 A capped effective life of 6 2/3 years is available – see subsection 40-102(5)

15 A capped effective life of 6 2/3 years is available – see subsection 40-102(5)

16 A capped effective life of 6 2/3 years is available – see subsection 40-102(5)

17 A capped effective life of 6 2/3 years is available where applicable (assets marked with #) – see subsection 40-102(5)

18 Primary producers may be entitled to an immediate deduction for capital expenditure incurred on a fodder storage asset if the asset was first used or installed ready for use on or after 19 August 2018 – see sections 40-515 and 40-548, and subsections 40-525(3) and 40-555(4)

19 Primary producers may be entitled to an immediate deduction for capital expenditure incurred on a fodder storage asset if the asset was first used or installed ready for use on or after 19 August 2018 – see sections 40-515 and 40-548, and subsections 40-525(3) and 40-555(4).

20 Primary producers may be entitled to an immediate deduction for capital expenditure incurred on a fodder storage asset if the asset was first used or installed ready for use on or after 19 August 2018 – see sections 40-515 and 40-548, and subsections 40-525(3) and 40-555(4).

21 Primary producers may be entitled to an immediate deduction for capital expenditure incurred on a fodder storage asset if the asset was first used or installed ready for use on or after 19 August 2018 – see sections 40-515 and 40-548, and subsections 40-525(3) and 40-555(4).

22 Primary producers may be entitled to an immediate deduction for capital expenditure incurred on a fodder storage asset if the asset was first used or installed ready for use on or after 19 August 2018 – see sections 40-515 and 40-548, and subsection 40-525(3) and 40-555(4).

23 Defined as water containing in excess of 10 parts of salt per 1,000 parts of water.

¶43-015 Effective life — mining

MINING
(06000 to 10900)

Asset	Life (Years)	Reviewed	Date Of Application
Crushing and milling assets:			
Crushers:			
Cone and gyratory	25	*	1 Jul 2003
Feeder breaker	20	*	1 Jul 2003
Generally	25	*	1 Jul 2003
Impact and rotary	20	*	1 Jul 2003
Jaw	25	*	1 Jul 2003
Roller (including roll sizers)	20	*	1 Jul 2003
Grinding mills:			
Ball and rod	25	*	1 Jul 2003
Generally	25	*	1 Jul 2003
Hammer	15	*	1 Jul 2003
SAG (autogenous)	25	*	1 Jul 2003
Hydrometallurgy and Pyrometallurgy assets:			
Adsorption process assets	20	*	1 Jul 2003
Agglomeration (pelletizing) assets	25	*	1 Jul 2003
Calcination process assets (including kilns)	25	*	1 Jul 2003
Casting process assets for casting billets or ingots	30	*	1 Jul 2003
Converting process assets (including rotatable cylindrical furnaces)	30	*	1 Jul 2003
Cooling process assets (including cooling towers)	25	*	1 Jul 2003
Counter current decantation (CCD) process assets	20	*	1 Jul 2003
Drying process assets (including rotary dryers, spray dryers and indirect heat exchanger dryers)	25	*	1 Jul 2003
Electrolysis process assets (including electrowinning process and electro refining process assets including tanks)	20	*	1 Jul 2003
Filtration process assets	15	*	1 Jul 2003
Gas cleaning process assets (including electrostatic precipitators and baghouses)	20	*	1 Jul 2003
Gas recovery process assets (including stripping and absorption assets)	25	*	1 Jul 2003
Ion exchange process assets	15	*	1 Jul 2003
Leaching process assets:			
Atmospheric	15	*	1 Jul 2003
Generally	25	*	1 Jul 2003
Pressure	25	*	1 Jul 2003
Neutralisation process assets	20	*	1 Jul 2003
Pots and ladles used for molten materials	30	*	1 Jul 2003
Precipitation process assets (including tanks and agitators)	20	*	1 Jul 2003
Pressure vessels	30	*	1 Jul 2003
Roasting process assets (including kilns and furnaces)	30	*	1 Jul 2003
Sintering process assets (including continuous sintering machines)	30	*	1 Jul 2003
Smelting process assets (including furnaces)	25	*	1 Jul 2003
Solution treatment and metal recovery assets	20	*	1 Jul 2003
Solvent extraction process assets (including mixer-settler units)	20	*	1 Jul 2003
Tailings stills	20	*	1 Jul 2003
Infrastructure support assets:			
Compressors	15	*	1 Jul 2003

MINING
(06000 to 10900)

Asset	Life (Years)	Reviewed	Date Of Application
Control systems and communication systems assets:			
Generally	10	*	1 Jul 2003
Instruments	10	*	1 Jul 2003
Towers or other supporting structures	30	*	1 Jul 2003
Electrical infrastructure assets (including power reticulation, substations, switchgear and transformers)	25	*	1 Jul 2003
Mineral treatment structure	40	*	1 Jul 2003
Pipes and pipelines (including valves and fittings):			
Generally	25	*	1 Jul 2003
Slurry pipework within processing facility (including slurry pipe to thickener)	10	*	1 Jan 2006
Pumps:			
Generally	20	*	1 Jul 2003
Positive displacement pumps	15	*	1 Jul 2003
Materials handling assets:			
Belt magnets, samplers, metal detectors and analysers	15	*	1 Jul 2003
Bins, chutes, hoppers, bunkers and silos	30	*	1 Jul 2003
Bucket elevators	25	*	1 Jul 2003
Conveyors	25	*	1 Jul 2003
Feeders:			
Generally (including apron and belt)	20	*	1 Jul 2003
Vibrating	15	*	1 Jul 2003
Fuel storage tanks	30	*	1 Jul 2003
Gas storage tanks and spheres	25	*	1 Jul 2003
Grizzly bars and scalpers	25	*	1 Jul 2003
Overhead cranes/gantries	30	*	1 Jul 2003
Stacks (chimney)	30	*	1 Jul 2003
Stockpile assets:			
Reclaim tunnel flow valves and activators	25	*	1 Jul 2003
Stackers, reclaimers and stacker/reclaimers	25	*	1 Jul 2003
Train loaders	30	*	1 Jul 2003
Trippers/stackers and stacking conveyor systems	25	*	1 Jul 2003
Tunnel vent and exhaust fans	15	*	1 Jul 2003
Water recycling facilities	20	*	1 Jul 2003
Water storage tanks	30	*	1 Jul 2003
Weighing machines (including weighers for feeders and conveyors)	20	*	1 Jul 2004
Mineral dressing assets:			
Classification, gravity separation and dewatering assets:			
Centrifuges	15	*	1 Jul 2003
Cyclones:			
Dense medium and heavy medium	8	*	1 Jul 2003
Generally (including classifying, desliming, and hydrocyclones)	15	*	1 Jul 2003
Generally	18	*	1 Jul 2003
Hydraulic classifiers and teetered bed separators	20	*	1 Jul 2003
Jigs	25	*	1 Jul 2003
Pneumatic tables and air separators	25	*	1 Jul 2003
Settling cones	25	*	1 Jul 2003

MINING
(06000 to 10900)

Asset	Life (Years)	Reviewed	Date Of Application
Shaking tables	25	*	1 Jul 2003
Sluices and cone concentrators	25	*	1 Jul 2003
Spirals	12	*	1 Jul 2003
Electrostatic separation assets	20	*	1 Jul 2003
Filtration assets (including pressure filtration and vacuum filtration equipment)	15	*	1 Jul 2003
Flotation assets (including tanks, launders, agitators, air supply and reagent dosing equipment)	20	*	1 Jul 2003
Magnetic separation assets (including cross belt, drum and disc types)	20	*	1 Jul 2003
Screening assets	15	*	1 Jul 2003
Thickening assets	25	*	1 Jul 2003
Port assets – see Table A Water transport and support services (48100 to 48200 and 52110 to 52190)			
Railway infrastructure assets and rolling-stock – see Table A Rail freight and passenger transport services (47100 to 47200)			
Surface mobile mining machines:			
Bucket wheel excavators	30	*	1 Jul 2002
Compressors	20	*	1 Jul 2002
Cranes	20	*	1 Jul 2002
Dozers	9	*	1 Jul 2002
Draglines	30	*	1 Jul 2002
Drill rigs (Production)	10	*	1 Jul 2002
Electric rope shovels	25	*	1 Jul 2002
Generators	10	*	1 Jul 2002
Graders	10	*	1 Jul 2002
Hydraulic excavators (including hydraulic front shovels)	10	*	1 Jul 2002
Lighting systems	10	*	1 Jul 2002
Off highway trucks (including articulated, rigid dump, service, fuel and water trucks)	10	*	1 Jul 2002
Rollers	15	*	1 Jul 2002
Scrapers	7	*	1 Jul 2002
Skid steer loader	7	*	1 Jul 2002
Tool carriers	10	*	1 Jul 2002
Wheel loaders	8	*	1 Jul 2002
Tailings dams	20		1 Jan 2001
Underground mobile mining machines:			
Compressors	10	*	1 Jul 2002
Continuous haulage systems	10	*	1 Jul 2002
Continuous miners	10	*	1 Jul 2002
Drill rigs:			
Diamond	20	*	1 Jul 2002
Production	7	*	1 Jul 2002
Feeder breakers	15	*	1 Jul 2002
Graders	10	*	1 Jul 2002
Jumbos	10	*	1 Jul 2002
Load-haul-dump machines	6	*	1 Jul 2002
Long-wall equipment:			
Armoured face conveyors	6	*	1 Jul 2002
Beam stage loaders	7	*	1 Jul 2002

MINING
(06000 to 10900)

Asset	Life (Years)	Reviewed	Date Of Application
Hydraulic pump modules	15	*	1 Jul 2002
Hydraulic roof supports	10	*	1 Jul 2002
Impact crushers	10	*	1 Jul 2002
Mobile conveyors tail end	5	*	1 Jul 2002
Roof support relocation vehicles	10	*	1 Jul 2002
Shearers	7	*	1 Jul 2002
Shearer carriers	10	*	1 Jul 2002
Maintenance vehicles	8	*	1 Jul 2002
Personnel transporters	8	*	1 Jul 2002
Raise borers and down reamers	20	*	1 Jul 2002
Roof bolters	8	*	1 Jul 2002
Scissor lifts	6	*	1 Jul 2002
Shuttle cars	12	*	1 Jul 2002
Skid steer loaders	12	*	1 Jul 2002
Underground haulage trucks	6	*	1 Jul 2002
Wheel loaders	6	*	1 Jul 2002
Workshop plant	20		1 Jan 2001
Coal mining (06000)			
Coal preparation assets:			
Centrifuges	15	*	1 Jul 2003
Crushing assets (including feeder breakers, impact, roller and rotary crushers)	20	*	1 Jul 2003
Cyclones:			
Dense medium, heavy medium	6	*	1 Jul 2003
Generally (including classifying, desliming and hydrocyclones)	10	*	1 Jul 2003
Filtration assets (including belt, drum and vacuum filters)	15	*	1 Jul 2003
Flotation assets (including agitation air supply systems, launders, reagent dosing systems and tanks)	20	*	1 Jul 2003
Grizzly bars and scalpers	25	*	1 Jul 2003
Jigs and heavy medium baths	25	*	1 Jul 2003
Magnetic separators	20	*	1 Jul 2003
Spirals	12	*	1 Jul 2003
Thickening assets	25	*	1 Jul 2003
Infrastructure support assets:			
Analysers, belt magnets, grinding mills, metal detectors and samplers	15	*	1 Jul 2003
Coal preparation facility framework/structure	40	*	1 Jul 2003
Compressors	15	*	1 Jul 2003
Control systems and communication systems assets:			
Generally	10	*	1 Jul 2003
Instruments	10	*	1 Jul 2003
Towers or other supporting structures	30	*	1 Jul 2003
Electrical infrastructure assets (including reticulation assets, substations, switch gear and transformers)	25	*	1 Jul 2003
Fuel storage tanks	30	*	1 Jul 2003
Gas storage tanks	25	*	1 Jul 2003
Overhead cranes/gantries	30	*	1 Jul 2003
Pipes and pipelines (including valves and fittings):			

MINING
(06000 to 10900)

Asset	Life (Years)	Reviewed	Date Of Application
Generally	25	*	1 Jul 2003
Slurry pipework within processing facility (including slurry pipe to thickener)	10	*	1 Jan 2006
Pumps:			
Generally (including centrifugal pumps)	20	*	1 Jul 2003
Positive displacement pumps	15	*	1 Jul 2003
Train loaders	30	*	1 Jul 2003
Tunnel vent or exhaust fans	15	*	1 Jul 2003
Valves and other non pipe fittings	10	*	1 Jul 2003
Water recycling facility	20	*	1 Jul 2003
Water storage dams (including fire services dams and water storage dams generally)	30	*	1 Jul 2003
Water storage tanks	30	*	1 Jul 2003
Materials handling assets:			
Bins, chutes, hoppers, silos and storage bunkers	30	*	1 Jul 2003
Bucket elevators	25	*	1 Jul 2003
Conveyors	25	*	1 Jul 2003
Feeders:			
Generally (including apron and belt feeders)	20	*	1 Jul 2003
Vibrating feeders	15	*	1 Jul 2003
Stockpile spraying system	20	*	1 Jul 2003
Stockpile stackers, reclaimers and stacker reclaimers:			
Generally (including all machinery)	25	*	1 Jul 2003
Reclaim tunnels	25	*	1 Jul 2003
Trippers/stackers	25	*	1 Jul 2003
Oil and gas extraction (07000)			
Assets used to manufacture condensate, crude oil, domestic gas, liquid natural gas (LNG) or liquid petroleum gas (LPG) but not if the manufacture occurs in an oil refinery[24]:			
Control systems	10	*	1 Jul 2002
Domestic gas processing assets (including centrifugal compressor, column, gas turbine, heat exchanger, piping and turbo expander)	30	*#	1 Jul 2002
Electricity generation assets – see Table A Electricity supply (26110 to 26400)			
Flare towers for gas flares	25	*#	1 Jul 2002
Fractionation train assets (including air coolers, columns, compressors, heat exchangers, piping and pumps)	30	*#	1 Jul 2002
Hot water system assets	17½	*#	1 Jul 2002
Instruments	12½	*	1 Jul 2002
LNG holding facility assets (including boil off gas compressors, cryogenic storage tanks, loading arms, pumps and tanks)	30	*#	1 Jul 2002
LNG train assets (including centrifugal compressors, columns, cryogenic heat exchangers, gas turbine drivers and other heat exchangers)	30	*#	1 Jul 2002
Stabiliser process assets (including columns, heat exchangers, pumps and reciprocating compressors)	30	*#	1 Jul 2002
Storage and loading assets (including cryogenic storage tanks, jetties, loading arms, LPG chillers and pumps)	30	*#	1 Jul 2002
Trunkline onshore terminal (TOT) assets:			
Flash tanks	20	*#	1 Jul 2002
Slugcatcher and associated piping	30	*#	1 Jul 2002

MINING
(06000 to 10900)

Asset	Life (Years)	Reviewed	Date Of Application
Valves including control valves	12 1/2	*	1 Jul 2002
Gas production assets[25]:			
Central production facility assets:			
Boilers	10	*	1 Jul 2002
Cabling for power and control systems	30	*#	1 Jul 2002
Diesel systems	15	*	1 Jul 2002
Drains systems	20	*#	1 Jul 2002
Drill rigs	10	*	1 Jul 2002
Flare system assets:			
Carbon steel piping	15	*	1 Jul 2002
Flare tips	5	*	1 Jul 2002
Stainless steel piping	30	*#	1 Jul 2002
Fuel gas systems	30	*#	1 Jul 2002
Gas compression and reinjection assets:			
Gas compressors used offshore	10	*	1 Jul 2002
Gas turbine drivers used offshore	12 1/2	*	1 Jul 2002
Generally (including piping, skid, vessels and assets used onshore)	30	*#	1 Jul 2002
Power turbines used offshore	12 1/2	*	1 Jul 2002
Heat exchangers	30	*#	1 Jul 2002
Major carbon steel vessels	12 1/2	*	1 Jul 2002
Major stainless steel (or lined) vessels	30	*#	1 Jul 2002
Offshore platforms:			
Generally (including accommodation modules, flare structures, helidecks, jackets, primary steel work and topsides secondary steel work)[26]	30	*#	1 Jul 2002
Topsides tertiary steelwork (including handrails, ladders and stairs)	15	*	1 Jul 2002
Piping	30	*#	1 Jul 2002
Pumps:			
Circulation pump	12 1/2	*	1 Jul 2002
Generally	20	*#	1 Jul 2002
Seawater lift pumps	15	*	1 Jul 2002
Shutdown and fire/gas systems	15	*	1 Jul 2002
Tempered water system assets:			
Chemical treatment assets	12 1/2	*	1 Jul 2002
Piping and vessels	30	*#	1 Jul 2002
Utility air compressors	15	*	1 Jul 2002
Coal seam gas extraction assets:			
Infield gathering systems used for gas and associated water (including polyethylene (PE) pipes and pumps)	20	*#	1 Jul 2016
Water assets:			
Storage ponds and tanks for water and brine	30	*#	1 Jul 2016
Treated water distribution assets	30	*#	1 Jul 2016
Treated water irrigation assets – see Table A Agriculture, Forestry and Fishing (01110 to 05290), water assets			
Water treatment facility assets (including desalination plants, reverse osmosis, brine concentration and crystallisation assets)	20	*#	1 Jul 2016

MINING
(06000 to 10900)

Asset	Life (Years)	Reviewed	Date Of Application
Well assets:			
Downhole equipment (including pumps, but excluding well casing)	5	*	1 Jul 2016
Wellpad surface assets (including christmas trees, separators and telemetry equipment)	20	*#	1 Jul 2016
Wells	20	*#	1 Jul 2016
Control systems	10	*	1 Jul 2002
Electricity generation assets – see Table A Electricity supply (26110 to 26400)			
Floating production storage and offloading (FPSO) vessels (incorporating mooring systems)	20	*#	1 Jul 2002
Floating storage and offloading (FSO) vessels (incorporating mooring systems)	20	*#	1 Jul 2002
Infield pipeline	30	*#	1 Jul 2002
Instruments (including level, pressure and temperature indicators)	12½	*	1 Jul 2002
Offshore bulk loading transfer systems	10	*	1 Jul 2002
Subsea production assets (including control umbilical, flowline and manifold)	20	*#	1 Jul 2002
Trunklines	30	*#	1 Jul 2002
Valves	12½	*	1 Jul 2002
Wells and downhole equipment	15	*	1 Jul 2002
Wellheads and christmas trees	30	*#	1 Jul 2002
Oil production assets[27]:			
Central production facility assets (excluding FPSOs):			
Boilers	10	*	1 Jul 2002
Circulation pumps	12½	*	1 Jul 2002
Drill rigs	10	*	1 Jul 2002
Flare tips	5	*	1 Jul 2002
Gas compression and reinjection assets:			
Gas compressors used offshore	10	*	1 Jul 2002
Gas turbine drivers used offshore	12½	*	1 Jul 2002
Generally (including piping, skids, vessels and assets used onshore)	15	*	1 Jul 2002
Power turbines used offshore	12½	*	1 Jul 2002
Generally (including offshore platforms)	15	*	1 Jul 2002
Major carbon steel vessels	12½	*	1 Jul 2002
Pumps:			
Circulation pumps	12½	*	1 Jul 2002
Other	15	*	1 Jul 2002
Tempered water system assets:			
Chemical treatment assets	12½	*	1 Jul 2002
Piping and vessels	15	*	1 Jul 2002
Control systems	10	*	1 Jul 2002
Electricity generation assets – see Table A Electricity supply (26110 to 26400)			
Floating production storage and offloading (FPSO) vessels (incorporating mooring systems)	20	*#	1 Jul 2002
Floating storage and offloading (FSO) vessels (incorporating mooring systems)	20	*#	1 Jul 2002
Infield pipelines	15	*	1 Jul 2002
Instruments (including level, pressure and temperature indicators)	12½	*	1 Jul 2002

MINING
(06000 to 10900)

Asset	Life (Years)	Reviewed	Date Of Application
Offshore bulk loading transfer systems	10	*	1 Jul 2002
Subsea production assets (including control umbilical, flowline and manifold)	15	*	1 Jul 2002
Trunklines	30	*#	1 Jul 2002
Valves	12 1/2	*	1 Jul 2002
Wells and downhole equipment	10	*	1 Jul 2002
Wellheads and christmas trees	15	*	1 Jul 2002
Port assets – see Table A Water transport and support services (48100 to 48200 and 52110 to 52190)			
Iron ore mining (08010)			
Infrastructure support assets:			
Blowers, high pressure	15	*	1 Jan 2006
Dust suppression/control equipment	15	*	1 Jan 2006
Materials handling assets:			
Feeders:			
Vibrating	10	*	1 Jan 2006
Mineral dressing assets:			
Cyclones, dense/heavy medium (unlined nihard)	1	*	1 Jan 2006
Dense medium separation assets (including baths and drums)	20	*	1 Jan 2006
Magnetic separation assets:			
LIMS (low intensity magnetic separators)	20	*	1 Jan 2006
WHIMS (wet high intensity magnetic separators)	15	*	1 Jan 2006
Screening assets	10	*	1 Jan 2006
Gold ore mining (08040)			
Gold ore processing assets:			
Adsorption process assets	15	*	1 Jul 2004
Carbon regeneration kilns	12	*	1 Jul 2004
Concentrators (including inline pressure jigs and mechanical concentrators)	10	*	1 Jul 2004
Crushing assets:			
Cone/gyratory crushers	20	*	1 Jul 2004
Hydraulic rock breakers	12	*	1 Jul 2004
Jaw crushers	20	*	1 Jul 2004
Electrowinning/electrorefining assets	17	*	1 Jul 2004
Elution columns	12	*	1 Jul 2004
Elution storage tanks	17	*	1 Jul 2004
Laboratory assets:			
Atmospheric adsorption spectrometers	10	*	1 Jul 2004
Generally (including drying ovens, pulverisers, crushers, gas fired ovens, fume cupboards)	15	*	1 Jul 2004
Leaching process assets (including carbon in pulp and carbon in leach processes)	15	*	1 Jul 2004
Shaking tables	12	*	1 Jul 2004
Smelting furnaces	15	*	1 Jul 2004
Thickening assets	20	*	1 Jul 2004

MINING
(06000 to 10900)

Asset	Life (Years)	Reviewed	Date Of Application
Mineral sand mining (08050)			
Aeration assets (including aerators, attritioners, blowers and turbine impeller agitated vessels)	20	*	1 Jan 2003
Classification and gravity separation assets (including centrifuges, cones, cyclones, screw classifiers, spirals and tables)	15	*	1 Jan 2003
Crushing assets (including drum scrubbers)	30	*	1 Jan 2003
Dredges	20	*	1 Jul 2009
Drying assets:			
Generally (including flash and fluid bed dryers and fluid bed heaters)	20	*	1 Jan 2003
Rotary dryer kilns	30	*	1 Jan 2003
Dust management assets:			
Baghouse filters and extractors	30	*	1 Jan 2003
Cyclones	15	*	1 Jan 2003
Multiclones	20	*	1 Jan 2003
Electrostatic separation assets (including curve plates, electrostatic roll separators, high tension roll separators and screen plates)	20	*	1 Jan 2003
Filtration/dewatering assets (including candle filter presses, dewatering towers, horizontal belt filters and hydrocyclones)	15	*	1 Jan 2003
Magnetic separation assets (including belt and drum separators, electromagnetic separators, induced roll and rare earth magnetic separators and wet high intensity magnets)	20	*	1 Jan 2003
Materials handling assets (including bins, bucket and conveying elevators, conveyors, feeders, hoppers, loading systems, paddle mixers and tailings stackers)	30	*	1 Jan 2003
Screening assets (including screens and trommels)	15	*	1 Jan 2003
Support assets:			
Control systems	10	*	1 Jan 2003
Pipes and pipelines (including valves and fittings):			
Generally	20	*	1 Jan 2003
Slurry pipework within processing facility (including slurry pipe to thickener)	10	*	1 Jan 2006
Pumps	20	*	1 Jan 2003
Tanks:			
Constant density and thickening	20	*	1 Jan 2003
Generally (including acid leaching and water)	15	*	1 Jan 2003
Thermal reduction assets (including cooler kilns, cooling towers, heat exchangers and reduction kilns)	30	*	1 Jan 2003
Waste gas handling assets:			
Afterburners	20	*	1 Jan 2003
Cyclones	15	*	1 Jan 2003
Electrostatic precipitators	30	*	1 Jan 2003
Scrubbers and stacks	20	*	1 Jan 2003
Nickel ore mining (08060)			
Nickel ore processing assets:			
Mineral treatment structures (including structure holding walkways, supporting assets and thoroughfares)	20	*	1 Jul 2004
Reagent pumps (including high pressure acid leach pumps)	5	*	1 Jul 2004

MINING
(06000 to 10900)

Asset	Life (Years)	Reviewed	Date Of Application
Construction material mining (09110 to 09190)			
Control systems (for conveying, crushing and screening assets)	10	*	1 Jul 2003
Conveyors:			
Gravity take-up	25	*	1 Jul 2003
Screw take-up	15	*	1 Jul 2003
Crushers:			
Generally	20	*	1 Jul 2003
Mobile (track or wheel mounted machinery including screening and conveying components)	15	*	1 Jul 2003
Cyclones	15	*	1 Jul 2003
Dredges	20	*	1 Jul 2009
Drill rigs	8	*	1 Jul 2003
Electrical switching assets	20	*	1 Jul 2003
Graders	15	*	1 Jul 2003
Heavy mobile quarry assets not specifically listed – see Table A Mining (06000 to 10900)			
Hydraulic oversize rock breakers (mounted above primary crusher)	8	*	1 Jul 2003
Material handling assets (including chutes, feeders, hoppers, product bins and surge bins)	20	*	1 Jul 2003
Pug mills	15	*	1 Jul 2003
Screening assets	12	*	1 Jul 2003
Wheel loaders	10	*	1 Jul 2003
Wire saws	10	*	1 Jul 2003
Petroleum exploration services (10112)			
Exploration assets used offshore:			
Down hole geophysics units – skid mounted	10	*	1 Jan 2007
Drill strings	3	*	1 Jan 2007
Offshore drilling rigs (including blow out preventers, drilling fluid circulation systems, hoisting and rotary systems, platforms, rig powering and transmissions)	20	*	1 Jan 2007
Exploration assets used onshore:			
Down hole geophysics units – truck mounted	12	*	1 Jan 2007
Drill strings	4	*	1 Jan 2007
Onshore surface drilling rigs (including blow out preventers, derricks, drilling fluid circulation systems, hoisting and rotary systems, rig powering and transmissions)	15	*	1 Jan 2007
Portable messing and sleeping huts	7	*	1 Jan 2007
Seismic survey assets:			
Airguns	5	*	1 Jan 2007
Hydrophones	5	*	1 Jan 2007
Mineral exploration services (10122)			
Exploration assets:			
Drill rigs:			
Surface (including blow out preventers, drilling fluid circulation systems, hoisting and rotary systems, rig powering and transmission and trucks)	10	*	1 Jan 2007
Underground	5	*	1 Jan 2007
Geophysical survey assets:			

MINING
(06000 to 10900)

Asset	Life (Years)	Reviewed	Date Of Application
Airborne geophysical assets (including magnetometers, receivers and transmitters):			
Aircraft integrated	10	*	1 Jan 2007
Aircraft demountable	8	*	1 Jan 2007
Down hole geophysical assets (including acoustic televiewers, callipers, density tools, dipmeters, draw works, neutron probes, sonic probes, receiver/transmitter modules and sondes):			
Portable assets	5	*	1 Jan 2007
Vehicle integrated assets	8	*	1 Jan 2007
Ground geophysical assets (including gravity instruments, resistivity receivers and transmitters, scintillometers and spectrometers)	5	*	1 Jan 2007
Portable ground geophysical assets (including electromagnetics, ground magnetics, ground penetrating radars and radiometrics)	5	*	1 Jan 2007
Seismic survey assets:			
Cabling	3	*	1 Jan 2007
Geophones	5	*	1 Jan 2007
Global positioning systems	5	*	1 Jan 2007
Processing systems	3	*	1 Jan 2007
Recording systems	10	*	1 Jan 2007
Total stations (including mechanical, manual, motorised, auto lock, robotic, universal and multi-stations)	5	*	1 Jul 2015
Vibration source assets:			
Buggy mounted shear wave vibrators	10	*	1 Jan 2007
Drilling rigs – shot hole	10	*	1 Jan 2007
Ground impactors	4	*	1 Jan 2007
Portable messing and sleeping huts	7	*	1 Jan 2007
Other mining support services (10900)			
Gas and oil mining support services (excluding offshore services):			
Cementing assets:			
Batch mixing assets:			
Batch mixing units (excluding batch mixing units incorporated with trailers)	8	*	1 Jul 2018
Trailers (incorporating batch mixing unit and trailer)	10	*	1 Jul 2018
Cement silos:			
Fixed steel	30	*	1 Jul 2018
Mobile	10	*	1 Jul 2018
Cement tankers (incorporating tank and trailer) – see Table B Motor vehicles and trailers, trailers having a gross vehicle mass greater than 4.5 tonnes			
Pumping units	10	*	1 Jul 2018
Drilling assets:			
Bottom hole assemblies (including logging while drilling tools, measuring while drilling tools, motors and stabilisers)	5	*	1 Jul 2018
Coil tubing assets:			
Pumping units	7	*	1 Jul 2018
Reel and power units	10	*	1 Jul 2018
Downhole fishing and remedial tools (including casing swages, junk magnets and milling tools)	5	*	1 Jul 2018

MINING
(06000 to 10900)

Asset	Life (Years)	Reviewed	Date Of Application
Drill rigs	10	*	1 Jul 2018
Drill strings	5	*	1 Jul 2018
Fluid assets (including centrifuges, pumps and shear units)	10	*	1 Jul 2018
Mobile fluid tanks	10	*	1 Jul 2018
Well control equipment (including blow out preventers and choke manifolds)	5	*	1 Jul 2018
Hydraulic fracturing assets:			
Blenders	8	*	1 Jul 2018
Frac tanks	10	*	1 Jul 2018
Pumps	8	*	1 Jul 2018
Mineral mining support services:			
Blasting assets:			
Augers	10	*	1 Jul 2017
Blast hole pumps	7	*	1 Jul 2017
Explosive boxes	5	*	1 Jul 2017
Magazines	10	*	1 Jul 2017
Mobile processing units (MPUs):			
Surface			1 Jul 2017
Motor vehicles – see Table B Motor vehicles and trailers			
MPUs	9	*	1 Jul 2017
Underground MPUs (incorporating motor vehicle and MPU)	6	*	1 Jul 2017
Remote control blasting units	5	*	1 Jul 2017
Stemming buckets	7	*	1 Jul 2017
Dewatering pumps	12	*	1 Jul 2017
Surface drill rigs (production)	10	*	1 Jul 2017

Footnotes:

24 A capped effective life of 15 years is available where applicable (assets marked with #) – see subsection 40-102(5)

25 A capped effective life of 15 years is available for assets marked with #, except offshore platforms – see subsection 40-102(5)

26 A capped effective life of 20 years is available – see subsection 40-102(5)

27 A capped effective life of 15 years is available where applicable (assets marked with #) – see subsection 40-102(5)

¶43-020 Effective life — manufacturing

MANUFACTURING
(11110 to 25990)

Asset	Life (Years)	Reviewed	Date Of Application
Meat processing (11110)			
Boning room assets:			
Boneless meat packing stations	20	*	1 Jul 2013
Boning and slicing stations	20	*	1 Jul 2013
Boning hoists	5	*	1 Jul 2013

MANUFACTURING
(11110 to 25990)

Asset	Life (Years)	Reviewed	Date Of Application
Chine bone removal machines	10	*	1 Jul 2013
De-sinewed mince meat machines	10	*	1 Jul 2013
Dicing and mincing machines	10	*	1 Jul 2013
Dump and product bins	15	*	1 Jul 2013
Frenching machines	8	*	1 Jul 2013
Knuckle and aitch bone pullers	5	*	1 Jul 2013
Loin/saddle deboning machines	10	*	1 Jul 2013
Overhead in-feed carcass conveyors (incorporating housings, handles, chains and motors)	20	*	1 Jul 2013
Pneumatic knives (including meat trimmers/round knives and de-fatting knives)	2	*	1 Jul 2013
Pork brine and marinade mixers	10	*	1 Jul 2013
Pork de-rinders	10	*	1 Jul 2013
Pork marinade injectors	10	*	1 Jul 2013
Rise and fall platforms	15	*	1 Jul 2013
Sausage filling machines	10	*	1 Jul 2013
Saws:			
Band saws	10	*	1 Jul 2013
Bone saws	5	*	1 Jul 2013
Breaking saws:			
Circular electric	3	*	1 Jul 2013
Circular hydraulic	2	*	1 Jul 2013
Reciprocating electric	5	*	1 Jul 2013
Reciprocating pneumatic	3	*	1 Jul 2013
Skinning or denuding machines	10	*	1 Jul 2013
Transfer belt and screw conveyors (incorporating belt, drive motors and supporting structure)	10	*	1 Jul 2013
Weight graders	5	*	1 Jul 2013
X-ray and chemical lean analysis machines	10	*	1 Jul 2013
Cold storage assets:			
Air curtains	5	*	1 Jul 2013
Ammonia condensers	10	*	1 Jul 2013
Blast freezer tunnels	20	*	1 Jul 2013
Blast freezers	20	*	1 Jul 2013
Carbon dioxide (CO_2) snow making machines	10	*	1 Jul 2013
Carton conveyors (incorporating belt, drive motors and supporting structure)	10	*	1 Jul 2013
Chiller tunnels	20	*	1 Jul 2013
Chillers (incorporating pneumatic gates)	15	*	1 Jul 2013
Desiccant	10	*	1 Jul 2013
Refrigerant	15	*	1 Jul 2013
Door controls and motor drive systems for automatic opening doors (incorporating controls, motors and sensors, but excluding doors)	5	*	1 Jul 2013
Evaporators	15	*	1 Jul 2013
Freezers	20	*	1 Jul 2013
Load out bays (incorporating air tight truck pads and hydraulic platforms)	15	*	1 Jul 2013
Overhead carcass conveyors (incorporating housings, handles, chains and motors)	20	*	1 Jul 2013
Plate freezers	20	*	1 Jul 2013

MANUFACTURING
(11110 to 25990)

Asset	Life (Years)	Reviewed	Date Of Application
Pressure vessels	20	*	1 Jul 2013
Refrigeration compressors	15	*	1 Jul 2013
Storage racking and stillages	10	*	1 Jul 2013
Transfer roller conveyors	10	*	1 Jul 2013
Livestock handling assets:			
Cattle soaker pens	15	*	1 Jul 2013
Cattle wash/soaker control systems	10	*	1 Jul 2013
Cattle washes	15	*	1 Jul 2013
Cattle yards (incorporating concrete base and galvanised steel posts and rails)	20	*	1 Jul 2013
Feed auger systems	10	*	1 Jul 2013
Hydraulic forcing pen gates	10	*	1 Jul 2013
Lead-up races	20	*	1 Jul 2013
Loading ramps stationary and height adjustable (hydraulic, pneumatic and electronic)	15	*	1 Jul 2013
Pig lairages (incorporating concrete slat floor and concrete panel walls or concrete floor and galvanised steel posts and rails)	20	*	1 Jul 2013
Sheep lairages (incorporating galvanised web mesh base and galvanised steel posts and rails)	10	*	1 Jul 2013
Water troughs	12	*	1 Jul 2013
Packaging assets:			
Automatic carton erecting and lidding machines	10	*	1 Jul 2013
Bagging machines	5	*	1 Jul 2013
Bar code label printers	3	*	1 Jul 2013
Bar code readers	4	*	1 Jul 2013
Carton weigh label stations	7	*	1 Jul 2013
Flow wrappers	10	*	1 Jul 2013
Labelling machines	5	*	1 Jul 2013
Meat compactors	10	*	1 Jul 2013
Metal detectors	10	*	1 Jul 2013
Netting machines	5	*	1 Jul 2013
Palletisers and de-palletisers	10	*	1 Jul 2013
Shrink wrappers	10	*	1 Jul 2013
Strapping machines	5	*	1 Jul 2013
Transfer belt conveyors (incorporating belts, drive motors and supporting structures)	10	*	1 Jul 2013
Vacuum packaging systems (incorporating vacuum pumps and booster pumps):			
Rotary systems	12	*	1 Jul 2013
Tunnel systems	12	*	1 Jul 2013
Weighing scales	4	*	1 Jul 2013
Rendering plant:			
Bagging/weigh batching machines	10	*	1 Jan 2001
Bins (includes raw material bins, charging hopper/feedbins, cake bins and holding bins)	15	*	1 Jan 2001
Blood drying equipment (includes blood holding tanks, agitated holding tanks, coagulators, driers, decanters and dried blood hoppers)	10	*	1 Jan 2001
Cookers and driers (includes batch cookers, continuous cookers, continuous driers and pre-heater)	15	*	1 Jan 2001
Decanters/centrifuges	12	*	1 Jan 2001

MANUFACTURING
(11110 to 25990)

Asset	Life (Years)	Reviewed	Date Of Application
Environmental control equipment (including condensers and associated equipment, bio-filters, air-scrubbers, after-burners and dissolved air flotation systems)	10	*	1 Jan 2001
Feathrolysers/feather hydrolysers	10	*	1 Jan 2001
Magnets	15	*	1 Jan 2001
Mills	10	*	1 Jan 2001
Mincers/grinders	5	*	1 Jan 2001
Pans and screens (includes percolator pans/screen and shaker screens)	15	*	1 Jan 2001
Pre-breakers/pre-hoggers	10	*	1 Jan 2001
Screw and bucket elevators	10	*	1 Jan 2001
Screw presses/expeller presses	13	*	1 Jan 2001
Separators/polishers	15	*	1 Jan 2001
Tallow storage tanks	15	*	1 Jan 2001
Waste heat evaporators	15	*	1 Jan 2001
Slaughter floor assets:			
Beef hide pullers (fixed and traversing)	15	*	1 Jul 2013
Bung ring expanders:			
Pneumatic	3	*	1 Jul 2013
Manual hand held	5	*	1 Jul 2013
Cattle restrainers (incorporating centre track belly conveyors)	12	*	1 Jul 2013
Carcass cleaning systems:			
Cutting line sanitising systems (incorporating vacuum pumps and collection tanks)	8	*	1 Jul 2013
Decontamination chambers	20	*	1 Jul 2013
Dehomers	5	*	1 Jul 2013
Electrical immobilisers	12	*	1 Jul 2013
Electrical stimulators	12	*	1 Jul 2013
Evisceration tables (incorporating organ pans)	15	*	1 Jul 2013
Head cutters and droppers:			
Automatic	10	*	1 Jul 2013
Hand held hydraulic	5	*	1 Jul 2013
Hock cutters	5	*	1 Jul 2013
Knife blade sharpening machines	5	*	1 Jul 2013
Knocking boxes (incorporating head restrainers)	12	*	1 Jul 2013
Landing tables and bleed slat conveyors	15	*	1 Jul 2013
NLIS readers:			
Hand held wands	2	*	1 Jul 2013
Fixed gate readers	10	*	1 Jul 2013
Swinging gate readers	5	*	1 Jul 2013
Offal processing assets:			
Chilled water systems	10	*	1 Jul 2013
Fat vacuum transfer systems	10	*	1 Jul 2013
Head splitters	7	*	1 Jul 2013
Intestine processing machines	10	*	1 Jul 2013
Jaw breakers	5	*	1 Jul 2013
Offal bins	15	*	1 Jul 2013
Offal chutes	15	*	1 Jul 2013
Offal cutting tables	15	*	1 Jul 2013

MANUFACTURING
(11110 to 25990)

Asset	Life (Years)	Reviewed	Date Of Application
Offal packing stations	15	*	1 Jul 2013
Offal transfer conveyors (incorporating belts, drives, motors and supporting structure)	10	*	1 Jul 2013
Offal tumblers	10	*	1 Jul 2013
Offal washers	10	*	1 Jul 2013
Tongue cleaners	10	*	1 Jul 2013
Tripe cookers/centrifuges	10	*	1 Jul 2013
Overhead bleed, dressing and trim conveyors ((incorporating housings, handles, chains and motors) including elevators and lowerators)	20	*	1 Jul 2013
Pneumatic knives:			
De-hiding knives	2	*	1 Jul 2013
Meat trimmers/round knives and de-fatting knives	2	*	1 Jul 2013
Preparation and trimming stations	15	*	1 Jul 2013
Rise and fall platforms	15	*	1 Jul 2013
Saws:			
Brisket saws	5	*	1 Jul 2013
Splitting saws	5	*	1 Jul 2013
Scribing saws	3	*	1 Jul 2013
Sheep brisket scissors	5	*	1 Jul 2013
Sheep restrainers (incorporating belts, pulleys, drives and motors)	10	*	1 Jul 2013
Sheep skin pullers	10	*	1 Jul 2013
Specialised pork slaughter floor assets:			
Carbon dioxide (CO_2) stunning chambers (incorporating carousels)	10	*	1 Jul 2013
Carcass grading probes	4	*	1 Jul 2013
De-hairing machines	10	*	1 Jul 2013
Gambrel tables	15	*	1 Jul 2013
Polishers	10	*	1 Jul 2013
Scalding tanks	15	*	1 Jul 2013
Singers	10	*	1 Jul 2013
Spinal cord removal systems (incorporating hand pieces, vacuum pumps and tanks)	8	*	1 Jul 2013
Stunners:			
Electric stunners	5	*	1 Jul 2013
Manual bolt stunners with cartridges	5	*	1 Jul 2013
Pneumatic bolt stunners	7	*	1 Jul 2013
Waste belt conveyors (incorporating drives, motors and supporting structure)	10	*	1 Jul 2013
Waste screw conveyors (incorporating drives, motors and supporting structure)	10	*	1 Jul 2013
Support assets:			
Air and spring balancers and counter weights	5	*	1 Jul 2013
Compressed air assets:			
Air compressors	10	*	1 Jul 2013
Air dryers	10	*	1 Jul 2013
Air receivers	20	*	1 Jul 2013
Control systems	10	*	1 Jul 2013
Control systems assets:			
Flow meters	10	*	1 Jul 2013

MANUFACTURING
(11110 to 25990)

Asset	Life (Years)	Reviewed	Date Of Application
Instruments and sensors	10	*	1 Jul 2013
Turbidity meters	7	*	1 Jul 2013
Variable speed drives (VSDs)	10	*	1 Jul 2013
Fire protection systems	15	*	1 Jul 2013
Hand air driers	3	*	1 Jul 2013
Hand wash basins	15	*	1 Jul 2013
Hide preparation assets:			
Bale presses	10	*	1 Jul 2013
Sheep skin and hide mixers, salt tumblers and agitators	6	*	1 Jul 2013
Hydraulic power packs	10	*	1 Jul 2013
Laboratory assets	10	*	1 Jul 2013
Sterilisers	15	*	1 Jul 2013
Truck and livestock crate washes	20	*	1 Jul 2013
Waste water assets:			
Aerators and agitators	10	*	1 Jul 2013
Aerobic ponds	30	*	1 Jul 2013
Anaerobic ponds	30	*	1 Jul 2013
Belt filter presses	15	*	1 Jul 2013
Chlorine dosing systems	10	*	1 Jul 2013
Dissolved air flotation systems	15	*	1 Jul 2013
Effluent distribution pipes	15	*	1 Jul 2013
Effluent drum filters	10	*	1 Jul 2013
Effluent irrigators (including centre pivot, lateral and travelling gun)	10	*	1 Jul 2013
Effluent pumps	7	*	1 Jul 2013
Effluent screens	10	*	1 Jul 2013
Effluent storage tanks	15	*	1 Jul 2013
Methane gas cogeneration assets – see Table A Electricity supply (26110 to 26400) and Gas supply (27000)			
Pond covers	10	*	1 Jul 2013
Pond liners	10	*	1 Jul 2013
Sequential batch reactors	10	*	1 Jul 2013
Settling ponds	30	*	1 Jul 2013
Solids dewatering presses	10	*	1 Jul 2013
Water assets:			
Boilers	20	*	1 Jul 2013
Bore pumps	7	*	1 Jul 2013
Bores	30	*	1 Jul 2013
Chlorine dosing systems	10	*	1 Jul 2013
Clarifiers	20	*	1 Jul 2013
High stage pump sets	7	*	1 Jul 2013
Hot water systems	10	*	1 Jul 2013
Heat exchangers	10	*	1 Jul 2013
Raw water filters	15	*	1 Jul 2013
Raw water in-feed pump sets	10	*	1 Jul 2013
Reverse osmosis systems (incorporating pumps, pipe work, membranes and controls)	10	*	1 Jul 2013

MANUFACTURING
(11110 to 25990)

Asset	Life (Years)	Reviewed	Date Of Application
Water distribution pipes	20	*	1 Jul 2013
Water softeners	10	*	1 Jul 2013
Water storage tanks	20	*	1 Jul 2013
Water tank liners	15	*	1 Jul 2013
Poultry processing (11120)			
Chilling assets:			
Freezers (including blast tunnels, in-line air chillers, and spiral freezers)	15	*	1 Jul 2017
Spin chillers and immersion chillers	15	*	1 Jul 2017
Conveyors: overhead chains (carrying birds)	1	*	1 Jul 2017
Cut up & portion cutting assets:			
Cut-up machines (for body, breast, legs, necks, wings, etc)	12	*	1 Jul 2017
Dicers, flatteners and portion cutters (including air, bowl, vacuum, vertical, water jet, etc)	6	*	1 Jul 2017
Deboning area assets:			
Automatic deboners	10	*	1 Jul 2017
Bone scanners (x-ray or photo)	7	*	1 Jul 2017
Cone lines	10	*	1 Jul 2017
Extruders, grinders and mechanical deboned meat (MDM) machines	10	*	1 Jul 2017
Saws and pneumatic guns	5	*	1 Jul 2017
Skinners	6	*	1 Jul 2017
Defeathering equipment:			
Pluckers or pickers	13	*	1 Jul 2017
Pluckers (waterfowl necks or tails)	7	*	1 Jul 2017
Pluckers (drums and wax peelers)	6	*	1 Jul 2017
Scalders (air or water)	11	*	1 Jul 2017
Waxing tanks	8	*	1 Jul 2017
Evisceration equipment:			
Croppers, feet removers, giblet processors, head removers, heart lung harvesters, heart lung separators, openers, vent cutters, etc)	11	*	1 Jul 2017
Inside/outside bird washers	15	*	1 Jul 2017
Further processing assets:			
Coating machines, breaders, dusters, etc	10	*	1 Jul 2017
Filling machines (including Kiev, sausage, stuffing, etc)	10	*	1 Jul 2017
Injectors (including brine, saline, seasoning etc)	15	*	1 Jul 2017
Marinating machines (including marinade sprayers, mixers, vacuum tumbler massagers, etc)	10	*	1 Jul 2017
Ovens and cookers (including gyro, spiral, steam, thermal fluid fryers, vertical airflow, etc)	15	*	1 Jul 2017
Grading equipment:			
Camera vision scanners	6	*	1 Jul 2017
Overhead chain weighing, sorting, and transfer systems	7	*	1 Jul 2017
Killing equipment:			
Controlled atmosphere stunning (CAS) machines	10	*	1 Jul 2017
Electric water stunners	12	*	1 Jul 2017
Killers	12	*	1 Jul 2017
Live bird handling systems (including live bird containers)	12	*	1 Jul 2017

MANUFACTURING
(11110 to 25990)

Asset	Life (Years)	Reviewed	Date Of Application
Packaging machines generally (bagging machines, batchers, carton and case erecting and closing machines, inspection equipment (checkweighers, metal detectors etc), multihead and singlehead weighers, palletisers and depalletisers, product identification labellers, robotic pick and place machines and wrapping machines) – see Table B Packaging machines			
Shrink dip tanks and shrink wrap tunnels	10	*	1 Jul 2017
Cured meat and smallgoods manufacturing (11130)			
Ancillary assets:			
Analysers (including meat analysers)	10	*	1 Jul 2016
Barcode readers, RF guns, scanner guns etc	5	*	1 Jul 2016
Benches and tables	15	*	1 Jul 2016
Bin and tray washers	12	*	1 Jul 2016
Bin lifters and tippers	15	*	1 Jul 2016
Bins:			
Plastic	5	*	1 Jul 2016
Stainless steel	15	*	1 Jul 2016
Boot washers	10	*	1 Jul 2016
Cages, stillages and trolleys (stainless steel)	15	*	1 Jul 2016
Chillers	15	*	1 Jul 2016
Conveyors (including belt loaders, bucket elevators, vibratory feeders etc)	10	*	1 Jul 2016
Die sets	15	*	1 Jul 2016
Flake ice machines	10	*	1 Jul 2016
Freezers (including blast freezers, crust freezers etc)	15	*	1 Jul 2016
Hoppers	12	*	1 Jul 2016
Piping, pipelines and pipework (stainless steel)	20	*	1 Jul 2016
Platforms and gantries	15	*	1 Jul 2016
Racking and shelving	10	*	1 Jul 2016
Tray stackers/destackers	10	*	1 Jul 2016
Waste water management and treatment systems	20	*	1 Jul 2016
Post-production and packaging assets:			
Carton tapers	5	*	1 Jul 2016
Clipping/tying/stringing machines (including tie clipping machines)	10	*	1 Jul 2016
Dicing and shredding assets	15	*	1 Jul 2016
Packaging machines generally (bagging machines, carton and case erecting and closing machines, inspection equipment (checkweighers, metal detectors etc), multihead and singlehead weighers, palletisers and depalletisers, product identification labellers, robotic pick and place machines and wrapping machines) – see Table B Packaging machines			
Pasteurisers	15	*	1 Jul 2016
Rods and smoke sticks	12	*	1 Jul 2016
Shrink dip tanks and shrink tunnels	10	*	1 Jul 2016
Slicers and slicing line assets	17	*	1 Jul 2016
Smokehouses	20	*	1 Jul 2016
Thermoformers	15	*	1 Jul 2016

MANUFACTURING
(11110 to 25990)

Asset	Life (Years)	Reviewed	Date Of Application
Production assets generally for bacon, ham, meat emulsion products, smallgoods etc (including band saws, cookers, cutters, deboning machines, dicing machines, emulsifiers, filling machines, grinding machines, guillotines, injecting machines, massaging machines, meat pumps, microwave cooking tunnels, mixing machines, netting machines, pump grinders, sausage linkers, shredders, tumbling machines etc)	12	*	1 Jul 2016
Raw material preparation and receiving assets:			
Brine/pickle preparation system assets	15	*	1 Jul 2016
Carton lifters and pallet lifters	10	*	1 Jul 2016
Carton shredding/stripping machines	10	*	1 Jul 2016
Curing machines	17	*	1 Jul 2016
Decartoning machines	10	*	1 Jul 2016
Floor scales (platform scales)	10	*	1 Jul 2016
Thawing assets (including defrosters, tempering systems and thawers)	15	*	1 Jul 2016
Support assets generally (including boilers, control systems, cranes (gantry and overhead), fire control and alarm assets, laboratory assets, loading bay assets (dock levellers, pallet jacks and pallet trucks, scissor lifts), refrigeration assets etc) – see Table B			
Dairy product manufacturing (11310 to 11330)			
Ancillary and support assets:			
Air compression assets – see Table B Air compression assets			
Ammonia gas detectors	12	*	1 Jul 2018
Automated guided vehicles (AGVs)	12	*	1 Jul 2017
Bag and cardboard compactors	15	*	1 Jul 2017
Benches and tables	15	*	1 Jul 2016
Bin and drum tippers	15	*	1 Jul 2018
Bins generally:			
Plastic	8	*	1 Jul 2017
Stainless steel	15	*	1 Jul 2017
Boilers – see Table B Boilers			
Boot washers	10	*	1 Jul 2016
Cages (including cardboard cages and pallet cages)	10	*	1 Jul 2016
Chemical and flammable storage cabinets	10	*	1 Jul 2016
Clean-in-place (CIP) system assets (including pipes, pumps and tanks)	15	*	1 Jul 2016
Contaminant detectors (including magnets, metal detectors and x-ray units)	10	*	1 Jul 2017
Control systems – see Table B Control systems and control system assets			
Conveyors	15	*	1 Jul 2016
Cooling assets:			
Chillers	15	*	1 Jul 2016
Cooling towers	15	*	1 Jul 2016
Crate handling assets (including lifters, stackers and de-stackers, turners etc)	12	*	1 Jul 2016
Dehumidifiers	15	*	1 Jul 2017
Dock levellers	15	*	1 Jul 2016
Dosing systems	15	*	1 Jul 2016
Dust extractors and collectors	20	*	1 Jul 2017

MANUFACTURING
(11110 to 25990)

Asset	Life (Years)	Reviewed	Date Of Application
Fire control and alarm assets – see Table B Fire control and alarm assets			
Floor scrubbers and polishers	10	*	1 Jul 2016
Foamers	10	*	1 Jul 2016
Infeed water treatment assets (excluding water storage tanks)	15	*	1 Jul 2017
Instrumentation (including flow meters, level transmitters, pressure transmitters etc)	10	*	1 Jul 2016
Laboratory equipment:			
Generally (excluding penetrometers) – see Table B Laboratory assets used in quality control, sample checking etc			
Penetrometers	13	*	1 Jul 2018
Lifting and handling assets:			
Forklifts – see Table B Forklifts			
Hoists	10	*	1 Jul 2016
Lifters (including small bin, box, drum, roll and vacuum lifters)	10	*	1 Jul 2017
Pallet jacks and pallet trucks	10	*	1 Jul 2016
Scissor lifts	15	*	1 Jul 2016
Milk tankers (incorporating tank and trailer)[28]	15	*#	1 Jul 2017
Piping, pipelines and pipework	20	*	1 Jul 2016
Power transformers	40	*	1 Jul 2017
Pumps:			
Chemical pumps	10	*	1 Jul 2017
Product pumps	12	*	1 Jul 2017
Vacuum pumps	12	*	1 Jul 2017
Water pumps	15	*	1 Jul 2017
Racking	15	*	1 Jul 2016
Refrigeration assets – see Table B Refrigeration assets			
Resin beads for milk and protein processing and water filtration	5	*	1 Jul 2016
Scales	10	*	1 Jul 2016
Shelving	12	*	1 Jul 2016
Silos	20	*	1 Jul 2016
Steelwork structures (including ladders, platforms and walkways)	20	*	1 Jul 2016
Tanks:			
Chemical storage tanks	15	*	1 Jul 2016
Water storage tanks	20	*	1 Jul 2016
Trolleys	10	*	1 Jul 2016
Valves	15	*	1 Jul 2016
Washers (including bottle and crate washers)	15	*	1 Jul 2016
Waste water treatment assets	20	*	1 Jul 2016
Water filtration system assets (excluding resin beads)	15	*	1 Jul 2016
Weighbridges	20	*	1 Jul 2016
Assets commonly used for product manufacturing and processing:			
Feeders (including loss-in-weight feeders and volumetric feeders)	10	*	1 Jul 2017
Heat exchangers	15	*	1 Jul 2016
Heaters (including air heaters and concentrate heaters)	20	*	1 Jul 2017
Homogenisers	15	*	1 Jul 2016
Hoppers	15	*	1 Jul 2017
In-line moisture meters and moisture controllers	10	*	1 Jul 2017

MANUFACTURING
(11110 to 25990)

Asset	Life (Years)	Reviewed	Date Of Application
Membrane filtration system assets	15	*	1 Jul 2016
Mixers and blenders	15	*	1 Jul 2016
Pasteurisers and thermalisers	15	*	1 Jul 2017
Separators, decanters, clarifiers and bactofuges	15	*	1 Jul 2017
Standardisers	15	*	1 Jul 2016
Tanks (including storage, mixing, process and balance tanks)	20	*	1 Jul 2016
UHT aseptic processing system assets	15	*	1 Jul 2016
Valve matrixes	15	*	1 Jul 2016
Assets for butter manufacturing:			
Butter churns (including continuous buttermakers and butter reworkers)	20	*	1 Jul 2018
Butter melters	25	*	1 Jul 2018
Crystallisers	20	*	1 Jul 2018
In-line titrators	10	*	1 Jul 2018
Salt crushers	20	*	1 Jul 2018
Assets for cheese manufacturing:			
Blockformers	15	*	1 Jul 2017
Cheese cutting machines (including cutters, grinders, shredders and slicers)	15	*	1 Jul 2017
Cheese washers	15	*	1 Jul 2017
Continuous cheese making machines	15	*	1 Jul 2017
Cooker stretchers	15	*	1 Jul 2017
Extruders	15	*	1 Jul 2017
Moulding machines	15	*	1 Jul 2017
Moulds:			
Plastic	10	*	1 Jul 2017
Stainless steel	15	*	1 Jul 2017
Presses	20	*	1 Jul 2017
Vats:			
Cheese making vats	20	*	1 Jul 2017
Culture vats	15	*	1 Jul 2017
Assets for dairy powder manufacturing:			1 Jul 2017
Blowers	15	*	1 Jul 2017
Crystallisers	20	*	1 Jul 2017
Dryers (including fluid bed and spray)	20	*	1 Jul 2017
Evaporators (including circulation/vacuum chamber and falling film)	20	*	1 Jul 2017
Powder bins	20	*	1 Jul 2017
Sifters	15	*	1 Jul 2017
Assets for ice cream manufacturing:			
Blenders and mixers:			
Bench mounted planetary mixers	15	*	1 Jul 2018
Hand-held stick blenders	5	*	1 Jul 2018
Enrobers (including dippers)	15	*	1 Jul 2018
Extruders and extrusion line stick inserters	15	*	1 Jul 2018
Freezing assets:			
Blast freezers and freezer tunnels/hardening tunnels (excluding cabinet style self-contained blast freezers)	15	*	1 Jul 2018
Cabinet style self-contained blast freezers	10	*	1 Jul 2018

MANUFACTURING
(11110 to 25990)

Asset	Life (Years)	Reviewed	Date Of Application
Ice cream churners/freezers	15	*	1 Jul 2018
Moulding machines, moulds and moulding line stick inserters	15	*	1 Jul 2018
Ovens	15	*	1 Jul 2018
Portable batch pasteurisers	12	*	1 Jul 2018
Slush machines	10	*	1 Jul 2018
Assets for yoghurt manufacturing:			1 Jul 2017
Aerators	15	*	1 Jul 2017
Fruit dosing system assets	15	*	1 Jul 2017
Fermentation tanks	20	*	1 Jul 2017
Incubation room assets:			
Fans	4	*	1 Jul 2017
Heaters	8	*	1 Jul 2017
Insulated sandwich panels	20	*	1 Jul 2017
Packaging assets:			
Bottle and lid unscramblers	15	*	1 Jul 2018
Butter patting machines	20	*	1 Jul 2018
Cartoning assets (including carton and case erecting, packing and closing machines, and carton and box sealers/tapers)	15	*	1 Jul 2016
Checkweighers	10	*	1 Jul 2016
Cheese wrapping machines (including overwrappers and thermoforming machines)	12	*	1 Jul 2017
Debaggers (debagging tables)	20	*	1 Jul 2016
Filling and sealing/capping machines (including various types used in the industry such as bag, bin, bottle, bulk, can, carton, pouch and tub filling and sealing/capping machines; form fill and seal machines; preformed cup filling and sealing machines; seamers and clinchers)	15	*	1 Jul 2018
Flow wrappers (including continuous heat seal wrappers)	15	*	1 Jul 2018
Inkjet and laser label printers	7	*	1 Jul 2016
Palletisers and depalletisers	15	*	1 Jul 2016
Palletising robots	10	*	1 Jul 2016
Product identification labellers (including coding machines and label applicators)	10	*	1 Jul 2016
Shrink tunnels	10	*	1 Jul 2017
Wrapping machines (including shrink wrappers, stretch wrappers and strapping machines)	12	*	1 Jul 2016
Fruit and vegetable processing (11400)			
Dried fruit (other than sun-dried) manufacturing assets:			
Packaging assets:			
Box sealers (including taping machines)	10	*	1 Jul 2018
Carton erecting, packing and closing machines (including cartoners)	15	*	1 Jul 2018
Form fill and seal machines – see Table B Packaging machines			
Labellers – see Table B Packaging machines			
Multihead weighers – see Table B Packaging machines			
Palletisers – see Table B Packaging machines			
Wrapping machines (including pallet wrappers, shrink wrappers and stretch wrappers) – see Table B Packaging machines			
Processing assets:			

MANUFACTURING
(11110 to 25990)

Asset	Life (Years)	Reviewed	Date Of Application
Aspirators	20	*	1 Jul 2018
Cappers and destemmers	15	*	1 Jul 2018
Cookers	15	*	1 Jul 2018
Cooling tunnels	15	*	1 Jul 2018
Drying assets (including dehydrators and dryers)	20	*	1 Jul 2018
Mixers	15	*	1 Jul 2018
Pitters	15	*	1 Jul 2018
Riddles (including pre-riddles and rotary sieves)	15	*	1 Jul 2018
Shaker tables	15	*	1 Jul 2018
Sulphur tanks	15	*	1 Jul 2018
Washing assets (including barrel washers, brush washers and ripple washers)	15	*	1 Jul 2018
Product and raw material handling assets:			
Bins	10	*	1 Jul 2018
Bin tippers	15	*	1 Jul 2018
Conveyors and elevators	15	*	1 Jul 2018
Quality control and inspection assets:			
Colour sorters and laser scanners	10	*	1 Jul 2018
Inspection equipment (including checkweighers and metal detectors) – see Table B Packaging machines	10	*	1 Jul 2018
Testing equipment	15	*	1 Jul 2018
Support assets:			
Cool rooms – see Table B Refrigeration assets			
Weighers	20	*	1 Jul 2018
Fruit juice and fruit juice drink manufacturing assets:			
Evaporators (used in concentrate manufacture)	20	*	1 Jul 2010
Extraction assets:			
Break tanks	20	*	1 Jul 2010
Centrifugal decanters	15	*	1 Jul 2010
Crushing and milling assets (including hammer mills)	15	*	1 Jul 2010
Extractors (including presses and reamers)	20	*	1 Jul 2010
Filters (including membrane, pressure and vacuum filters)	20	*	1 Jul 2010
Finishers	20	*	1 Jul 2010
Fruit sizing assets (including sizing belts/heads and sorting tables)	10	*	1 Jul 2010
Pulp and rind mincers	20	*	1 Jul 2010
Pulper-finishers	15	*	1 Jul 2010
Roller/spreaders	20	*	1 Jul 2010
Tomato choppers	15	*	1 Jul 2010
Washers (including brush washers, flume tanks and pre-clean water hoppers)	15	*	1 Jul 2010
Filling and sealing assets:			
Bottle inverters	20	*	1 Jul 2010
Capping machines	15	*	1 Jul 2010
Cap sorters	10	*	1 Jul 2010
Container dryers (incorporating air knives and blowers)	10	*	1 Jul 2010
Cooling and warming tunnels (including bottle warmers and water spray cooling tunnels)	15	*	1 Jul 2010
Filling machines (including aseptic fillers, bag in box fillers, cup fillers, gable top carton fillers and plastic bottle fillers)	20	*	1 Jul 2010

MANUFACTURING
(11110 to 25990)

Asset	Life (Years)	Reviewed	Date Of Application
Handling assets:			
Bottle rinsing machines	20	*	1 Jul 2010
Bottle unscramblers	15	*	1 Jul 2010
Depalletisers	20	*	1 Jul 2010
Palletisers	20	*	1 Jul 2010
Stretch wrappers (pallet wrappers)	15	*	1 Jul 2010
Inspection assets:			
Checkweighers	10	*	1 Jul 2010
Vacuum seal testers	10	*	1 Jul 2010
Vision inspection assets (including cap inspection/rejection systems and label inspection machines)	6	*	1 Jul 2010
Packing assets:			
Cartoning assets (including carton and case erectors, carton sealers, case packers and overpackers)	15	*	1 Jul 2010
Coding machines (including container coders and outer date coders)	7	*	1 Jul 2010
Hot melt adhesive (spot glue) applicators	10	*	1 Jul 2010
Label applicators	7	*	1 Jul 2010
Labellers	10	*	1 Jul 2010
Multipack machines	10	*	1 Jul 2010
Shrink sleeve applicators	15	*	1 Jul 2010
Shrinkwrappers	15	*	1 Jul 2010
Straw applicators	20	*	1 Jul 2010
Support assets:			
Air compressors and receivers	20	*	1 Jul 2010
Bins, cages and hoppers	20	*	1 Jul 2010
Boilers	20	*	1 Jul 2010
Clean-in-place (CIP) system assets (including pipes, pumps and tanks)	15	*	1 Jul 2010
Control system assets (excluding personal computers but including program logic controllers (PLCs) and switchgear)	10	*	1 Jul 2010
Conveyors (including augers, belt conveyors and bucket elevators)	15	*	1 Jul 2010
Fruit concentrate drum tippers	15	*	1 Jul 2010
Laboratory equipment:			
Electronic (including high performance liquid chromatography or HPLC machines, refractometers, spectrometry machines and titrimetric analysers)	7	*	1 Jul 2010
Non-electronic	10	*	1 Jul 2010
Pasteurisation assets:			
Pasteurisers (including heat exchangers)	15	*	1 Jul 2010
Tunnel pasteurisers	10	*	1 Jul 2010
Pipes	25	*	1 Jul 2010
Pumps:			
Cavity pumps	10	*	1 Jul 2010
Others (including centrifugal pumps)	15	*	1 Jul 2010
Refrigeration assets (including compressors, cooling towers, condensers and pumps)	15	*	1 Jul 2010
Valves	10	*	1 Jul 2010
Water treatment filters:			
Carbon filters	15	*	1 Jul 2010

MANUFACTURING
(11110 to 25990)

Asset	Life (Years)	Reviewed	Date Of Application
Membrane filters generally (including microfiltration (MF), nanofiltration (NF) and reverse osmosis (RO) membrane filters)	7	*	1 Jul 2010
UF membrane filters	5	*	1 Jul 2010
Weighbridges	20	*	1 Jul 2010
Tanks:			
Blending and mixing tanks	25	*	1 Jul 2010
Debittering tanks	30	*	1 Jul 2010
Storage tanks:			
Generally	30	*	1 Jul 2010
Jacketed	20	*	1 Jul 2010
Refrigerated	20	*	1 Jul 2010
Waste water storage/treatment tanks	20	*	1 Jul 2010
Jam, pickles and sauces manufacturing assets:			
Filling and sealing assets:			
Bottle rinsing machines	10	*	1 Jul 2018
Capping machines	15	*	1 Jul 2018
Denesters	10	*	1 Jul 2018
Filling machines (including aseptic, bucket and portion control)	15	*	1 Jul 2018
Jar de-palletisers	15	*	1 Jul 2018
Lid descramblers, cap sorters and hoppers	15	*	1 Jul 2018
Packaging assets:			
Carton erecting, packing and closing machines (including cartoners)	12	*	1 Jul 2018
Labellers – see Table B Packaging machines			
Palletisers	10	*	1 Jul 2018
Wrapping machines (including pallet wrappers, shrink wrappers and stretch wrappers) – see Table B Packaging machines			
Processing assets:			
Brush finishers and pulper finishers	15	*	1 Jul 2018
Cookers	10	*	1 Jul 2018
Cooling tunnels (including water cooling tunnels)	15	*	1 Jul 2018
Micro filters	20	*	1 Jul 2018
Pasteurisers	15	*	1 Jul 2018
Pectin mixers	10	*	1 Jul 2018
Pipes and pipelines (including pigging)	15	*	1 Jul 2018
Tanks and vats (including blending, holding and mixing tanks)	15	*	1 Jul 2018
Quality control and inspection assets:			
Metal detectors and camera vision scanners	10	*	1 Jul 2018
Support assets:			
Accumulation tables and turntables	15	*	1 Jul 2018
Air compression assets (including air compressors, air dryers and air receivers)	10	*	1 Jul 2018
Boilers – see Table B Boilers			
Conveyors	15	*	1 Jul 2018
Exhaust systems	10	*	1 Jul 2018
Heat exchangers	10	*	1 Jul 2018

MANUFACTURING
(11110 to 25990)

Asset	Life (Years)	Reviewed	Date Of Application
Pumps (including cavity, diaphragm and lobe)	15	*	1 Jul 2018
Preserved fruit and vegetable manufacturing assets:			
Filling and sealing assets:			
Canning assets (including can loaders, closers and seamers)	10	*	1 Jul 2018
Capping machines:			
Cappers	10	*	1 Jul 2018
Induction sealers	5	*	1 Jul 2018
Filling machines (including aseptic, bag in box, cup, direct and piston)	10	*	1 Jul 2018
Packaging assets:			
Carton erecting, packing and closing machines (including cartoners)	15	*	1 Jul 2018
Labellers	10	*	1 Jul 2018
Palletisers and depalletisers – see Table B Packaging machines			
Wrapping machines (including pallet wrappers, shrink wrappers and stretch wrappers) – see Table B Packaging machines			
Processing assets:			
Blanchers and paste finishers (including bean and spaghetti)	12	*	1 Jul 2018
Concentrates and syrup assets (including centrifuges, decanters and syrupers)	15	*	1 Jul 2018
Cookers:			
Rotary atmospheric sterilisers	20	*	1 Jul 2018
Rotary pressure sterilisers	10	*	1 Jul 2018
Static retorts	15	*	1 Jul 2018
Crushing mills	30	*	1 Jul 2018
Graders	15	*	1 Jul 2018
Peelers:			
Chemical (including caustic)	10	*	1 Jul 2018
Mechanical (including ginacas and magnesium scrubbers)	5	*	1 Jul 2018
Pitters and repitters	20	*	1 Jul 2018
Slicers and resizers	15	*	1 Jul 2018
Tanks and vats (including blending, holding and mixing tanks)	15	*	1 Jul 2018
Quality control and inspection assets:			
Colour sorters	10	*	1 Jul 2018
Inspection equipment (including checkweighers and metal detectors) – see Table B Packaging machines			
Support assets:			
Bin tippers	20	*	1 Jul 2018
Control systems – see Table B Control systems and control system assets			
Conveyors and elevators	15	*	1 Jul 2018
Filtration systems	15	*	1 Jul 2018
Pasteurisers (including heat exchangers)	10	*	1 Jul 2018
Pumps	10	*	1 Jul 2018

MANUFACTURING
(11110 to 25990)

Asset	Life (Years)	Reviewed	Date Of Application
Oil and fat manufacturing (11500)			
Edible oil or fat, blended, modified, refined or solvent extracted manufacturing assets (including canola, safflower, soybean):			
Preparatory and extraction assets:			
Preparatory and mechanical extraction assets:			
Breaking assets (including dehullers and crackers)	20	*	1 Jul 2012
Cookers (including conditioners and preheaters)	25	*	1 Jul 2012
Extruders (including screw presses)	20	*	1 Jul 2012
Milling and grinding assets (including flakers, hammer mills and roller mills)	20	*	1 Jul 2012
Pumps	8	*	1 Jul 2012
Vibratory screens	15	*	1 Jul 2012
Solvent extraction system assets:			
Distillation system assets (incorporating distillation columns, steam economisers, condensers, evaporators and oil strippers)	30	*	1 Jul 2012
Meal and cake processing assets (incorporating desolventisers, toasters, drying and cooling assets)	30	*	1 Jul 2012
Mineral oil recovery system assets (incorporating heat exchangers, mineral oil scrubbers and oil strippers)	30	*	1 Jul 2012
Solvent extractors (including hoppers and conveyors)	30	*	1 Jul 2012
Solvent water separation system assets (incorporating condensers, solvent water separators, steam ejectors and solvent receivers)	30	*	1 Jul 2012
Margarine and shortening processing assets:			
Pasteurisers	15	*	1 Jul 2012
Pin rotor machines (including plasticators and complectors)	25	*	1 Jul 2012
Refrigeration assets (including compressors, condensers, evaporators and pumps)	15	*	1 Jul 2012
Scraped surface heat exchangers (including perfectors and crystallisers)	25	*	1 Jul 2012
Measuring and monitoring assets:			
Belt weighers	15	*	1 Jul 2012
Flow meters	10	*	1 Jul 2012
Laboratory assets:			
Colorimeters	10	*	1 Jul 2012
Furnace ovens	15	*	1 Jul 2012
Gas chromatograph analysers	10	*	1 Jul 2012
Moisture and protein analysers, electronic (including near infrared analysers)	10	*	1 Jul 2012
Spectrophotometers	15	*	1 Jul 2012
Vacuum separators	10	*	1 Jul 2012
Seed samplers, hydraulic driven	10	*	1 Jul 2012
Support assets:			
Centrifuges, decanters and separators	20	*	1 Jul 2012
Cooling towers (including packaged type)	20	*	1 Jul 2012
Deodorisers	30	*	1 Jul 2012
Drying assets (including vacuum dryers)	20	*	1 Jul 2012
Emission control assets:			
Dust collection assets (including ductwork, dust collectors, scrubbers and fans)	20	*	1 Jul 2012

MANUFACTURING
(11110 to 25990)

Asset	Life (Years)	Reviewed	Date Of Application
Environmental control assets (including scrubbers, ductwork, fans, biofilters and concrete containers)	20	*	1 Jul 2012
Filtration assets:			
Plate and frame presses and polished filters	30	*	1 Jul 2012
Pressure leaf filters	20	*	1 Jul 2012
Heat exchangers	15	*	1 Jul 2012
Pipes and pipelines	25	*	1 Jul 2012
Pumps	15	*	1 Jul 2012
Stacks (steel flues)	20	*	1 Jul 2012
Tanks and vessels:			
Bulk oil storage tanks	30	*	1 Jul 2012
Other:			
Steel	20	*	1 Jul 2012
Stainless steel	30	*	1 Jul 2012
Linseed or flaxseed and other edible, non-modified, refined or solvent extracted oil processing assets (including chai, hemp, acacia and excluding olive oil):			
Preparatory and extraction assets:			
Cleaning and pre-cleaning assets (including seed cleaners and vibratory screens)	15	*	1 Jul 2017
Cookers	15	*	1 Jul 2017
Crushing and breaking assets (including grinders, flaking machines and seed crackers)	20	*	1 Jul 2017
Extruders (including expellers and screw presses)	15	*	1 Jul 2017
Filtration assets (including plate and frame presses and pressure leaf filters)	15	*	1 Jul 2017
Pipes and pipelines	20	*	1 Jul 2017
Tanks and vats	15	*	1 Jul 2017
Olive oil processing assets	15	*	1 Jul 2008
Packaging assets:			
Bag sewers – see Table B Packaging machines			
Capping machines	15	*	1 Jul 2012
Cartoning assets (including carton and case erecting, packing and closing machines)	15	*	1 Jul 2017
Coding machines	10	*	1 Jul 2012
Filling machines	20	*	1 Jul 2017
Labellers	10	*	1 Jul 2017
Palletisers and depalletisers	20	*	1 Jul 2012
Platform scales – see Table B Platform scales			
Robots (pick and place packaging machines)	10	*	1 Jul 2012
Wrapping machines (including shrink and stretch wrappers)	15	*	1 Jul 2012
Quality control assets (including metal detectors and magnets)	10	*	1 Jul 2012
Receiving and storage assets:			
Bins and containers	20	*	1 Jul 2017
Silos:			
Conditioning/sealed	20	*	1 Jul 2017
Meal	20	*	1 Jul 2012
Seed	30	*	1 Jul 2012
Underground seed storage assets (including concrete dump pits)	40	*	1 Jul 2012
Seed and product handling assets:			

MANUFACTURING
(11110 to 25990)

Asset	Life (Years)	Reviewed	Date Of Application
Augers, conveyors, elevators and hoppers	15	*	1 Jul 2017
Support assets:			
Control systems (excluding personal computers) - see Table B Control systems and control system assets			
Cool rooms – see Table B Refrigeration assets			
Forklifts – see Table B Forklifts			
Generators – see Table B Power supply assets			
Weighbridges – see Table B Weighbridges			
Grain mill product manufacturing (11610)			
Flour milling assets:			
Grain cleaning, milling and refining assets:			
Extraction and evaporation assets:			
Blowers, fans and evaporative coolers	15	*	1 Jul 2017
Control systems (dust collectors) – see Table B Control systems and control system assets			
Cyclones and dust collectors	20	*	1 Jul 2017
Grain screen cleaners	12	*	1 Jul 2017
Gravity tables or separators	20	*	1 Jul 2017
Hammer mills	15	*	1 Jul 2017
Horizontal scourers	13	*	1 Jul 2017
Intake separators	20	*	1 Jul 2017
Intensive dampeners	20	*	1 Jul 2017
Plan sifters	20	*	1 Jul 2017
Purifiers	20	*	1 Jul 2017
Roller mills	20	*	1 Jul 2017
Rotary sieves	12	*	1 Jul 2017
Packaging assets:			
Bag sewers – see Table B packaging machines			
Carton erecting, packing and closing machines (including cartoners)	15	*	1 Jul 2017
Hoists	15	*	1 Jul 2017
Inspection equipment (including check weighers, metal detectors, counting machines etc) — see Table B Packaging machines			
Label applicators	10	*	1 Jul 2017
Multihead and singlehead weighers – see Table B Packaging machines			
Palletisers and depalletisers	15	*	1 Jul 2017
Vertical form fill and seal/volumetric fillers (including valve bag fillers)	15	*	1 Jul 2017
Weighers	25	*	1 Jul 2017
Wrapping machines (including pallet wrappers, shrink wrappers, stretch wrappers) – see Table B Packaging machines			
Product and raw material handling and receiving assets:	15	*	1 Jul 2017
Conveyors (including belt, chain, drag, screw)	20	*	1 Jul 2017
Elevators			
Silos:			
Concrete	50	*	1 Jan 2004
Conditioning/sealed	20	*	1 Jul 2017

MANUFACTURING
(11110 to 25990)

Asset	Life (Years)	Reviewed	Date Of Application
Flexible	10	*	1 Jul 2017
Galvanised	30	*	1 Jan 2004
Steel	40	*	1 Jan 2004
Weighbridges – see Table B Weighbridges			
Quality control assets:			
Laboratory testing equipment (including near infrared analysers)	10	*	1 Jul 2017
Test kitchen assets (including dough makers, breadmakers, ovens, provers)	10	*	1 Jul 2017
Test mills	25	*	1 Jul 2017
Malt manufacturing assets:			
Barley and malt cleaning assets (including deculmers, dust extractors, indented cylinders, magnetic cleaners, malt shakers, screeners)	15	*	1 Jul 2008
Barley and malt handling assets:			
Augers, conveyors and elevators	15	*	1 Jul 2008
Silos:			
Galvanised construction	30	*	1 Jul 2008
Steel construction	40	*	1 Jul 2008
Weighbridges/weighers	20	*	1 Jul 2008
Clean-in-place (CIP) system assets (including pipes, pumps and tanks)	15	*	1 Jul 2008
Control systems (excluding personal computers)	10	*	1 Jul 2008
Germination assets:			
Above/below floor cleaning systems	15	*	1 Jul 2008
Aeration blowers	15	*	1 Jul 2008
Carbon dioxide (CO_2) extraction units	15	*	1 Jul 2008
Loaders/unloaders/turners	15	*	1 Jul 2008
Vessels:			
Concrete	40	*	1 Jul 2008
Rotating drums	20	*	1 Jul 2008
Stainless steel	25	*	1 Jul 2008
Kiln assets:			
Fans	15	*	1 Jul 2008
Gas burners	15	*	1 Jul 2008
Heat exchanger systems	20	*	1 Jul 2008
Heat recovery systems	20	*	1 Jul 2008
Kilns:			
Concrete	40	*	1 Jul 2008
Stainless steel	25	*	1 Jul 2008
Loaders/unloaders/turners	15	*	1 Jul 2008
Refrigeration assets (including chillers, compressors, condensers, evaporative coolers and pumps)	15	*	1 Jul 2008
Steeping assets:			
Above floor/below floor cleaning systems	15	*	1 Jul 2008
Slurry tanks	25	*	1 Jul 2008
Steeping vessels:			
Concrete	40	*	1 Jul 2008
Rotating drums	20	*	1 Jul 2008
Stainless steel	25	*	1 Jul 2008

MANUFACTURING
(11110 to 25990)

Asset	Life (Years)	Reviewed	Date Of Application
Waste water treatment assets:			
Aerators	20	*	1 Jul 2008
Blowers	20	*	1 Jul 2008
Clarifiers	20	*	1 Jul 2008
Digester/aeration tanks	25	*	1 Jul 2008
Reverse osmosis system assets	20	*	1 Jul 2008
Rice milling assets:			
Grain cleaning, milling and refining assets:			
Colour sorters	10	*	1 Jul 2017
De-stoners (including aspirators)	15	*	1 Jul 2017
Extraction and evaporation assets (including blowers, dust collectors, dryers, fans)	15	*	1 Jul 2017
Flow weighers	20	*	1 Jul 2017
Hullers	15	*	1 Jul 2017
Intake separators	20	*	1 Jul 2017
Length graders	20	*	1 Jul 2017
Paddy cleaners and pre-cleaners	20	*	1 Jul 2017
Paddy separators	15	*	1 Jul 2017
Plan sifters	20	*	1 Jul 2017
Thickness grading assets (including scalpers and rotary screens)	20	*	1 Jul 2017
Whiteners (including abrasive and friction whiteners)	15	*	1 Jul 2017
Packaging assets:			
Cartoning assets (including bagging machines, bag sealers, carton and case erecting, packing and closing machines) – see Table B Packaging machines			
Palletisers and depalletisers	15	*	1 Jul 2017
Weighers	20	*	1 Jul 2017
Wrapping machines (including pallet wrappers, shrink wrappers, stretch wrappers and strapping machines) – see Table B Packaging machines			
Product and raw material handling and receiving assets:			
Augers, conveyors and elevators	15	*	1 Jul 2017
Quality control assets:			
Inspection equipment (including check weighers and metal detectors)	10	*	1 Jul 2017
Laboratory equipment (including moisture testing machines)	10	*	1 Jul 2017
Magnets	10	*	1 Jul 2017
Support assets:			
Air compressors – see Table B Air compression assets generally (including air compressors, air dryers and air receivers)			
Fumigation systems	15	*	1 Jul 2017
Cereal and pasta product manufacturing (11620)			
Ancillary assets:			
Bin washers	15	*	1 Jul 2008
Blowers and fans:			
Generally	25	*	1 Jul 2008
Used in materials handling	15	*	1 Jul 2008
Clean-in-place (CIP) systems	15	*	1 Jul 2008

MANUFACTURING
(11110 to 25990)

Asset	Life (Years)	Reviewed	Date Of Application
Control systems (excluding personal computers)	10	*	1 Jul 2008
Dust collection assets (including cyclones)	20	*	1 Jul 2008
Extrusion die washers	5	*	1 Jul 2008
Racks and shelving	20	*	1 Jul 2008
Scales (electronic scales and load cells)	10	*	1 Jul 2008
Water chillers	20	*	1 Jul 2008
Water filtration and softening assets (including reverse osmosis assets)	15	*	1 Jul 2008
Cereal food manufacturing assets:			
Baked cereal bar product manufacturing assets – see Table A Bakery product manufacturing (11710 to 11740)			
Cold formed and nut based cereal bar manufacturing assets:			
Cooling tunnels	20	*	1 Jul 2008
Enrobers	12½	*	1 Jul 2008
Guillotines	15	*	1 Jul 2008
Slab formers (sheeters)	15	*	1 Jul 2008
Slitters	15	*	1 Jul 2008
Spreaders	15	*	1 Jul 2008
Syrup cookers and kettles (including fire cookers)	15	*	1 Jul 2008
Tempering machines	15	*	1 Jul 2008
General cereal food processing assets:			
Blenders and mixers (including drum mixers, paddle blenders/mixers and ribbon blenders/mixers)	15	*	1 Jul 2008
Ovens (electric and gas-fired)	20	*	1 Jul 2008
Ready-to-eat cereal manufacturing assets (including extruded, co-extruded, flaked and puffed cereal manufacturing assets):			
Coating assets (including coating applicators and drum coaters)	15	*	1 Jul 2008
Cookers	15	*	1 Jul 2008
Delumpers (lump breakers)	10	*	1 Jul 2008
Dryers:			
Flite dryers	30	*	1 Jul 2008
Fluid bed dryers	20	*	1 Jul 2008
Others (including belt and coating dryers)	15	*	1 Jul 2008
Extruders	20	*	1 Jul 2008
Feeders (including loss-in-weight and screwtype feeders)	10	*	1 Jul 2008
Milling machines (including flaking mills, pellet mills and shredding mills)	20	*	1 Jul 2008
Steam preconditioners	10	*	1 Jul 2008
Packaging assets (including cartoners, casepackers, case palletisers, checkweighers, fillers, label applicators, robotic pick and place packaging machines, shrink wrappers and stretch wrappers etc)	12	*	1 Jul 2008
Pasta manufacturing assets:			
Blenders and mixers	15	*	1 Jul 2008
Cooling assets (including chillers and coolers)	10	*	1 Jul 2008
Dryers	15	*	1 Jul 2008
Extrusion dies	2	*	1 Jul 2008
Fill preparation assets:			
Cookers/kettles	15	*	1 Jul 2008
Mincers	15	*	1 Jul 2008

MANUFACTURING
(11110 to 25990)

Asset	Life (Years)	Reviewed	Date Of Application
Long goods/short goods pasta making assets (including blanchers/ cookers, formers, gnocchi making machines, laminators, presses, ravioli making machines, sheeters etc)	$12^1/_2$	*	1 Jul 2008
Pasteurisers	15	*	1 Jul 2008
Product and raw material receiving and handling assets:			
Aspirators	20	*	1 Jul 2008
Bins and hoppers (including tote bins, intermediate bulk containers, scaling bins etc):			
Mild and stainless steel	15	*	1 Jul 2008
Others (including plastic and fibreglass)	10	*	1 Jul 2008
Bulker bag unloaders (including electric hoist, forklift and trolley based unloaders)	15	*	1 Jul 2008
Conveyors (including belt, bucket, roller and screw conveyors)	15	*	1 Jul 2008
Silos:			
Steel	30	*	1 Jul 2008
Used for flour (semolina)	25	*	1 Jul 2008
Storage tanks (including jacketed tanks)	20	*	1 Jul 2008
Tipping stations (tote bin dumpers)	15	*	1 Jul 2008
Quality control assets:			
Metal detectors	10	*	1 Jul 2008
X-ray detectors	5	*	1 Jul 2008
Bakery product manufacturing (11710 to 11740)			
Baking assets used by large-scale manufacturers of biscuits, bread, cakes, pastries and pies:			
Ancillary assets (including basket/crate washers, basket stack movers, crate/pan stackers and unstackers, depanners/detinners, foil handling denesters, oil spray units, pan cleaners, and topping applicators)	15	*	1 Jan 2002
Automatic pan storage units	20	*	1 Jan 2002
Automatic product handling assets (including basket loaders and basket stackers)	15	*	1 Jan 2002
Bread crumb assets (including baggers, debaggers, hammer mills, ovens, screw conveyors and sifters)	20	*	1 Jan 2002
Conveyors:			
Generally	15	*	1 Jan 2002
Infloor	12	*	1 Jan 2002
Cooling and refrigeration assets:			
Cooling tunnels, tray and vacuum coolers	20	*	1 Jan 2002
Freezers (including blast freezer, plate freezer)	15	*	1 Jan 2002
Spiral coolers, spiral freezers	10	*	1 Jan 2002
Final provers (mechanical type)	15	*	1 Jan 2002
Final provers (rack type)	8	*	1 Jan 2002
Make-up assets (including croissant making machines, crumpet making machines, crumbers, cutters, depositors, dividers, dough pumps, dough piece check weighers, extruders, final moulder/ panners, first/intermediate provers, gauge rolls, laminators, meat cookers, meat extruders, moulders, muffin making machines, pie making machines, roll making machines, rounder/airflow handers, sheeters and stampers)	$12^1/_2$	*	1 Jan 2002
Mixing assets (including bowl/dough hoists/tippers, meat mincers, meat mincer/blenders, mixers generally and mixer water assets)	15	*	1 Jan 2002
Ovens:			

MANUFACTURING
(11110 to 25990)

Asset	Life (Years)	Reviewed	Date Of Application
Rack ovens	8	*	1 Jan 2002
Tray type ovens (including swing tray)	20	*	1 Jan 2002
Tunnel ovens:			
Generally	20	*	1 Jan 2002
Lidding systems	10	*	1 Jan 2002
Packaging assets (including accumulators, bag closers, bread baggers, box and carton making machines, finished product check weighers, flow wrappers, metal detectors, robotic pick and place assets and shrink wrappers)	10	*	1 Jan 2002
Proof and bake systems:			
Spiral oven	15	*	1 Jan 2002
Spiral prover	10	*	1 Jan 2002
Secondary process assets (including cake folders, creamers, depositors, enrobers, icing machines, sandwiching machines and sprinklers)	12½	*	1 Jan 2002
Slicers (including bread band slicers, cake slicers and reciprocating blade slicers)	10	*	1 Jan 2002
Storage, feeding and ingredient handling assets:			
Flour silos	25	*	1 Jan 2002
Blowers, flour sifters and grain soak systems	15	*	1 Jan 2002
Weighers	10	*	1 Jan 2002
Bakery product manufacturing (non-factory based) (11740)			
Retail bread, biscuit, cake and pastry baking assets:			
Bread slicers	7	*	1 Jan 2002
Bun dividers/rounders	8	*	1 Jan 2002
Fixed bowl spiral mixers	7	*	1 Jan 2002
Hydraulic dough dividers	7	*	1 Jan 2002
Moulders	8	*	1 Jan 2002
Ovens (convection)	8	*	1 Jan 2002
Ovens (multi-decked, rotating rack or static rack, rotating deck)	10	*	1 Jan 2002
Planetary mixers	7	*	1 Jan 2002
Provers/prover retarders	6	*	1 Jan 2002
Semi-automated baguette, bread and bread roll making assets	12	*	1 Jan 2002
Semi-automated doughnut making assets	8	*	1 Jan 2002
Sugar manufacturing (11810)			
Sugar milling assets:			
Cane delivery assets:			
Cane bin assets:			
Rail bins	20	*	1 Jul 2011
Rail bin automatic coupling/de-coupling devices	12	*	1 Jul 2011
Road bins	12	*	1 Jul 2011
Rail assets (excluding cane bin assets) – see Table A Rail freight and passenger transport services (47100 to 47200)			
Receival station assets:			
Cane levellers	20	*	1 Jul 2011
Cane receival hoppers	25	*	1 Jul 2011
Tipplers	25	*	1 Jul 2011
Weighbridges	20	*	1 Jul 2011
Cane juice extraction assets:			

MANUFACTURING
(11110 to 25990)

Asset	Life (Years)	Reviewed	Date Of Application
Cane shredding machines (incorporating drives)	30	*	1 Jul 2011
Crushing mills (incorporating drives)	30	*	1 Jul 2011
Rotary juice screens	15	*	1 Jul 2011
Cane juice filtration and clarification assets:			
Clarifiers	25	*	1 Jul 2011
Flash tanks	20	*	1 Jul 2011
Juice heaters	20	*	1 Jul 2011
Lime and mud storage bins	25	*	1 Jul 2011
Lime slakers	20	*	1 Jul 2011
Mud mixers/minglers	20	*	1 Jul 2011
Rotary vacuum mud filters	20	*	1 Jul 2011
Evaporation and crystallisation assets:			
Centrifugals	25	*	1 Jul 2011
Crystallisers	20	*	1 Jul 2011
Evaporators	30	*	1 Jul 2011
Magma mixers	20	*	1 Jul 2011
Magma/massecuite distributors and receivers	20	*	1 Jul 2011
Massecuite re-heaters	20	*	1 Jul 2011
Seed vessels	20	*	1 Jul 2011
Sugar melters	20	*	1 Jul 2011
Vacuum pans	30	*	1 Jul 2011
Vapour condensers:			
Mild steel	20	*	1 Jul 2011
Stainless steel	30	*	1 Jul 2011
Molasses storage assets:			
Coolers	15	*	1 Jul 2011
Dams (earthworks only)	40	*	1 Jul 2011
Dam bladders and covers	12	*	1 Jul 2011
Tanks	30	*	1 Jul 2011
Power generation assets:			
Ash filters (including rotary and horizontal belt vacuum filters)	15	*	1 Jul 2011
Bagasse handling assets:			
Bagacillo collection systems	15	*	1 Jul 2011
Bagasse bins (incorporating stacking and reclaim systems)	30	*	1 Jul 2011
Other power generation assets – see Table A Electricity supply (26110 to 26400)			
Sugar drying and storage assets:			
Hoppers (weigh and feed)	25	*	1 Jul 2011
Lump breakers	15	*	1 Jul 2011
Rotary sugar dryers	25	*	1 Jul 2011
Sugar storage bins and silos	30	*	1 Jul 2011
Vibratory screens	15	*	1 Jul 2011
Support assets:			
Air compression assets:			
Air dryers	12	*	1 Jul 2011
Air receivers	20	*	1 Jul 2011
Compressors	12	*	1 Jul 2011

MANUFACTURING
(11110 to 25990)

Asset	Life (Years)	Reviewed	Date Of Application
Packaged air compression systems	12	*	1 Jul 2011
Blowers and fans	15	*	1 Jul 2011
Control system assets:			
Control cabinets and switchgear	10	*	1 Jul 2011
Instrumentation	10	*	1 Jul 2011
Programmable logic controllers (PLCs)	10	*	1 Jul 2011
Switchboards	20	*	1 Jul 2011
Variable speed drives (VSDs)	10	*	1 Jul 2011
Conveyors (including framework and enclosures)	20	*	1 Jul 2011
Conveyor belt weighers	15	*	1 Jul 2011
Dust collectors (including ducting, but excluding bagacillo collection systems)	20	*	1 Jul 2011
Heat exchangers	15	*	1 Jul 2011
Laboratory assets:			
Cutter grinders	15	*	1 Jul 2011
Moisture determination ovens	10	*	1 Jul 2011
Polarimeters	10	*	1 Jul 2011
Rotary juice samplers	15	*	1 Jul 2011
Spectrometers	10	*	1 Jul 2011
Wet disintegrators	15	*	1 Jul 2011
Overhead cranes – see Table B Cranes			
Piping and valves:			
Piping:			
Mild steel	15	*	1 Jul 2011
Non ferrous	20	*	1 Jul 2011
Stainless steel	25	*	1 Jul 2011
Valves	10	*	1 Jul 2011
Pumps	15	*	1 Jul 2011
Tanks (excluding molasses storage tanks):			
Water storage tanks	25	*	1 Jul 2011
Other tanks:			
Mild steel	20	*	1 Jul 2011
Plastic	15	*	1 Jul 2011
Stainless steel	30	*	1 Jul 2011
Water treatment and cooling assets:			
Clarifiers	25	*	1 Jul 2011
Cooling and effluent ponds	40	*	1 Jul 2011
Cooling towers:			
Field erected	25	*	1 Jul 2011
Packaged	15	*	1 Jul 2011
Ion exchange systems	15	*	1 Jul 2011
Sugar refining assets:			
Affination assets:			
Centrifugals	25	*	1 Jul 2011
Magma mixers	20	*	1 Jul 2011
Melter liquor screens	15	*	1 Jul 2011
Sugar melters	20	*	1 Jul 2011
Clarification and de-colourising assets:			

MANUFACTURING
(11110 to 25990)

Asset	Life (Years)	Reviewed	Date Of Application
Carbon regeneration kilns	15	*	1 Jul 2011
Clarifiers	25	*	1 Jul 2011
Deep bed filters	30	*	1 Jul 2011
De-colourising columns:			
Carbon based	30	*	1 Jul 2011
Resin based	20	*	1 Jul 2011
Evaporation and crystallisation assets:			
Centrifugals	25	*	1 Jul 2011
Evaporators	30	*	1 Jul 2011
Magma/massecuite distributors and receivers	20	*	1 Jul 2011
Vacuum pans	30	*	1 Jul 2011
Vapour condensers:			
Mild steel	20	*	1 Jul 2011
Stainless steel	30	*	1 Jul 2011
Packaging assets:			
Bagging machines (including flow wrappers, form fill and seal machines, and roll wrapping machines)	15	*	1 Jul 2011
Bottling assets:			
Bottle capping, filling and unscrambling machines	15	*	1 Jul 2011
Syrup and treacle filter presses	15	*	1 Jul 2011
UV disinfectors	15	*	1 Jul 2011
Carton erecting, packing and closing machines (including cartoners)	15	*	1 Jul 2011
Case erecting, packing and closing machines (including casepackers)	15	*	1 Jul 2011
Inspection equipment (including check weighers, metal detectors, counting machines)	10	*	1 Jul 2011
Multihead and singlehead weighers	15	*	1 Jul 2011
Palletisers and de-palletisers	15	*	1 Jul 2011
Product identification labellers (including decorating, applicator and coding machines)	10	*	1 Jul 2011
Wrapping machines (including shrink wrappers, stretch wrappers and strapping machines)	15	*	1 Jul 2011
Sugar receival, drying, screening, and storage assets:			
Bins, hoppers and silos	30	*	1 Jul 2011
Lump breakers	15	*	1 Jul 2011
Rotary sugar dryers	25	*	1 Jul 2011
Sugar throwers	15	*	1 Jul 2011
Vibratory screens (including graders and scalpers)	15	*	1 Jul 2011
Support assets:			
Air compression assets:			
Air dryers	12	*	1 Jul 2011
Air receivers	20	*	1 Jul 2011
Compressors	12	*	1 Jul 2011
Packaged air compression systems	12	*	1 Jul 2011
Blowers and fans	15	*	1 Jul 2011
Boilers (packaged type only)	20	*	1 Jul 2011
Control system assets:			
Control cabinets and switchgear	10	*	1 Jul 2011
Instrumentation	10	*	1 Jul 2011

MANUFACTURING
(11110 to 25990)

Asset	Life (Years)	Reviewed	Date Of Application
Program logic controllers (PLCs)	10	*	1 Jul 2011
Switchboards	20	*	1 Jul 2011
Variable speed drives (VSDs)	10	*	1 Jul 2011
Conveyors (including framework and enclosures):			
Packaging conveyors	15	*	1 Jul 2011
Other conveyors	20	*	1 Jul 2011
Cooling towers:			
Field erected	25	*	1 Jul 2011
Packaged	15	*	1 Jul 2011
Dust collectors (including ducting)	20	*	1 Jul 2011
Heat exchangers	15	*	1 Jul 2011
Pipes and valves:			
Pipes:			
Mild steel	15	*	1 Jul 2011
Non ferrous	20	*	1 Jul 2011
Stainless steel	25	*	1 Jul 2011
Valves	10	*	1 Jul 2011
Pumps	15	*	1 Jul 2011
Refractometers	10	*	1 Jul 2011
Spectrometers	10	*	1 Jul 2011
Tanks:			
Water storage tanks	25	*	1 Jul 2011
Other tanks:			
Mild steel	20	*	1 Jul 2011
Plastic	15	*	1 Jul 2011
Stainless steel	30	*	1 Jul 2011
Weighbridges	20	*	1 Jul 2011
Confectionery manufacturing (11820)			
Chocolate making assets:			
Conches	20	*	1 Jul 2016
Pre-refiners	12	*	1 Jul 2016
Refiners	10	*	1 Jul 2016
Tempering machines	15	*	1 Jul 2016
Enrobers (chocolate, coconut etc)	15	*	1 Jul 2016
Extruders and depositors (including egg spinners, fingers, formers, frozen cone, sheeting slab and slit, truffle rollers etc)	15	*	1 Jul 2016
Jelly and sugar lolly making assets:			
Cleaners (brush and laser)	10	*	1 Jul 2016
Coating and dusting machines	15	*	1 Jul 2016
Depositors (including nozzle plates, pistons and pumps)	12	*	1 Jul 2016
Mouldboards and trays	7	*	1 Jul 2016
Oiling machines	15	*	1 Jul 2016
Starch conditioners	10	*	1 Jul 2016
Starch moguls	10	*	1 Jul 2016
Packaging assets:			
Bagging machines (including flow wrappers, form fill seal machines, shaped foil wrappers, stick/bunch/sleeve wrappers etc)	15	*	1 Jul 2016

MANUFACTURING
(11110 to 25990)

Asset	Life (Years)	Reviewed	Date Of Application
Cartoning and boxing machines (including erectors, robots, case packers, palletisers, strappers etc)	12	*	1 Jul 2016
Inspection equipment (including check weighers, metal detectors, scales, vision scanners etc)	8	*	1 Jul 2016
Multihead and singlehead weighers	10	*	1 Jul 2016
Panning assets:			
Belt panners	15	*	1 Jul 2016
Coating and polishing panners	20	*	1 Jul 2016
Sugar panners	12	*	1 Jul 2016
Support assets:			
Cookers, drying rooms, ovens, roasters, mixers and melting stations (caramel, fruit, nougat, wafer etc)	15	*	1 Jul 2016
Cooling tunnels	17	*	1 Jul 2016
Cutters and guillotines	12	*	1 Jul 2016
Moulds	4	*	1 Jul 2016
Tanks and vats (chocolate, egg, syrup etc)	14	*	1 Jul 2016
Prepared animal and bird feed manufacturing (11920)			
Pet food manufacturing assets:			
Dry process assets:			
Batching systems	15	*	1 Jul 2013
Blowing systems	15	*	1 Jul 2013
Coating assets (including oil, tumble and vacuum coaters)	10	*	1 Jul 2013
Coolers (including counterflow, horizontal and vertical)	15	*	1 Jul 2013
Cooling systems (including fans and cyclones)	10	*	1 Jul 2013
Dehumidifying systems (including silo munters)	10	*	1 Jul 2013
Dosing systems (including liquid)	10	*	1 Jul 2013
Dryers	15	*	1 Jul 2013
Extruders	15	*	1 Jul 2013
Hammer mills	15	*	1 Jul 2013
Hoppers (including batch and surge)	15	*	1 Jul 2013
Mixers (including batch and paddle)	15	*	1 Jul 2013
Ovens (including horizontal, tunnel and vertical)	15	*	1 Jul 2013
Pre-conditioners	10	*	1 Jul 2013
Packaging assets:			
Bagging machines (including flow wrappers, form fill and seal machines and roll wrapping machines)	10	*	1 Jul 2013
Can and tray labelling assets	10	*	1 Jul 2013
Case erecting, packing and closing machines (including cartoners)	10	*	1 Jul 2013
Inspection equipment (including checkweighers, metal detectors, counting machines etc)	10	*	1 Jul 2013
Multihead and singlehead weighers	10	*	1 Jul 2013
Palletisers and depalletisers	15	*	1 Jul 2013
Robotic lid, tray and sealing assets	10	*	1 Jul 2013
Robotic pick and place assets	10	*	1 Jul 2013
Wrapping machines (including shrink wrappers, stretch wrappers and strapping machines)	10	*	1 Jul 2013
Raw material receiving, storage and handling assets:			
Chutes	15	*	1 Jul 2013

MANUFACTURING
(11110 to 25990)

Asset	Life (Years)	Reviewed	Date Of Application
Conveyors (including belt, chain, drag, screw and walking beam conveyors)	15	*	1 Jul 2013
Elevators and distributors (including bucket and transfer elevators)	15	*	1 Jul 2013
Hoppers (including batch and weigh hoppers)	15	*	1 Jul 2013
Receival assets	15	*	1 Jul 2013
Screw and weigh belt feeders	10	*	1 Jul 2013
Silos	20	*	1 Jul 2013
Storage bins	20	*	1 Jul 2013
Tanks (including holding, liquid storage and water)	20	*	1 Jul 2013
Support assets:			
Access platforms	20	*	1 Jul 2013
Air compressors and receivers	10	*	1 Jul 2013
Bins (including tippers and raw material bins)	15	*	1 Jul 2013
Boilers	20	*	1 Jul 2013
Cleaning systems (including vacuum)	15	*	1 Jul 2013
Contra shears and drum filters	10	*	1 Jul 2013
Control systems	10	*	1 Jul 2013
Dust management assets (including bag and dust filters, dust collectors, dust extraction hood and ducting and exhaust fans and socks)	15	*	1 Jul 2013
Effluent pumps	10	*	1 Jul 2013
Effluent screens and filters	10	*	1 Jul 2013
Emissions and odour control systems (incorporating exhaust fans, ducting and biofilters)	15	*	1 Jul 2013
Fire prevention systems (incorporating fire protection system and water tanks)	20	*	1 Jul 2013
Laboratory and analysing assets (including probes and samplers)	10	*	1 Jul 2013
Pumps (including liquid feed)	10	*	1 Jul 2013
Racking	20	*	1 Jul 2013
Safety systems	20	*	1 Jul 2013
Waste water ponds	25	*	1 Jul 2013
Waste water treatment assets	20	*	1 Jul 2013
Weighing assets (including weigh cells, heads and hoppers)	10	*	1 Jul 2013
Wet process assets:			
Air purification and recycling systems	10	*	1 Jul 2013
Basket tippers	10	*	1 Jul 2013
Blending, dicing and mincing assets	10	*	1 Jul 2013
Blowers	15	*	1 Jul 2013
Canning and tray assets (including closers and fillers)	10	*	1 Jul 2013
Chillers	15	*	1 Jul 2013
Cooling towers	15	*	1 Jul 2013
Cool rooms	15	*	1 Jul 2013
Cutting assets (including knife and blade assemblies)	10	*	1 Jul 2013
Dewatering assets	10	*	1 Jul 2013
Drying assets	15	*	1 Jul 2013
Extruders	15	*	1 Jul 2013
Freezers	15	*	1 Jul 2013
Frozen block warmers	10	*	1 Jul 2013

MANUFACTURING
(11110 to 25990)

Asset	Life (Years)	Reviewed	Date Of Application
Gravy make-up stations	15	*	1 Jul 2013
Grinders	10	*	1 Jul 2013
Hoppers (including batch and surge)	15	*	1 Jul 2013
Mix slides and chutes	15	*	1 Jul 2013
Mixers (including batch and paddle)	15	*	1 Jul 2013
Pallet lifters and hoists	10	*	1 Jul 2013
Refrigeration compressors	15	*	1 Jul 2013
Retort cooking vessels	15	*	1 Jul 2013
Retort trays	15	*	1 Jul 2013
Seal thickness testing assets	10	*	1 Jul 2013
Slicing and shredding assets	10	*	1 Jul 2013
Stacking assets	15	*	1 Jul 2013
Prepared animal and bird feed manufacturing assets generally:			
Batching, grinding and mixing assets:			
Bins (including mash, outloading, surge, supply and raw material bins)	30	*	1 Jul 2012
Control systems (including batching systems)	10	*	1 Jul 2012
Dressers	10	*	1 Jul 2012
Drum magnets	10	*	1 Jul 2012
Evaporative coolers	10	*	1 Jul 2012
Grinders	10	*	1 Jul 2012
Hammer and roller mills	15	*	1 Jul 2012
Heating chambers (including coils and heat exchangers)	12	*	1 Jul 2012
Hoppers (including expansion, grinder, weigh and surge hoppers)	25	*	1 Jul 2012
Liquid tanks (including molasses and tallow)	20	*	1 Jul 2012
Load cells	10	*	1 Jul 2012
Mixers (including paddle, premix and ribbon screw)	20	*	1 Jul 2012
Pumps (including heat, molasses and water pumps)	7	*	1 Jul 2012
Rotary valves	15	*	1 Jul 2012
Shears	15	*	1 Jul 2012
Turn heads	20	*	1 Jul 2012
Drying, coating, cooling and addition assets:			
Coating assets (including oil, tumble and vacuum coaters)	12	*	1 Jul 2012
Coolers (including counterflow, horizontal and vertical)	15	*	1 Jul 2012
Cooling fans and cyclones	10	*	1 Jul 2012
Dryers	15	*	1 Jul 2012
Injection systems (including tallow)	15	*	1 Jul 2012
Meters (including counterflow meters)	10	*	1 Jul 2012
Post pellet addition systems (incorporating mixers)	10	*	1 Jul 2012
Screening and sieving assets	10	*	1 Jul 2012
Vacuum pump and piping	15	*	1 Jul 2012
Liquid feed assets:			
Augers, conveyors and elevators	7	*	1 Jul 2012
Bladders for molasses ponds	10	*	1 Jul 2012
Bulk bag hangers	10	*	1 Jul 2012
Covers for molasses ponds	10	*	1 Jul 2012
Hoppers	10	*	1 Jul 2012
Liners for tanks	5	*	1 Jul 2012

MANUFACTURING
(11110 to 25990)

Asset	Life (Years)	Reviewed	Date Of Application
Micro scales	7	*	1 Jul 2012
Mixers	10	*	1 Jul 2012
Mixing tanks for clay and other products	15	*	1 Jul 2012
Pumps:			
Acid and urea pumps	3	*	1 Jul 2012
Heat, molasses and water pumps	10	*	1 Jul 2012
Silos (including polyvinylchloride (PVC) and steel construction)	15	*	1 Jul 2012
Storage tanks (including polyvinylchloride (PVC) and steel construction)	15	*	1 Jul 2012
Packaging assets:			
Bagging machines (including flow wrappers, form fill and seal machines and roll wrapping machines)	10	*	1 Jul 2012
Case erecting, packing and closing machines (including cartoners)	10	*	1 Jul 2012
Inspection equipment (including checkweighers, metal detectors, counting machines)	10	*	1 Jul 2012
Multihead and singlehead weighers	10	*	1 Jul 2012
Palletisers and depalletisers	15	*	1 Jul 2012
Robotic pick and place, lid, tray and sealing assets	10	*	1 Jul 2012
Wrapping machines (including shrink wrappers, stretch wrappers and strapping machines)	10	*	1 Jul 2012
Pre-conditioning and extrusion assets:			
Boilers	20	*	1 Jul 2012
Conditioners	10	*	1 Jul 2012
Crumble rollers	20	*	1 Jul 2012
Extruders	15	*	1 Jul 2012
Pellet presses (including air flow and die feeder presses)	15	*	1 Jul 2012
Pellet testers	10	*	1 Jul 2012
Raw material receiving, storage and handling assets:			
Augers	10	*	1 Jul 2012
Bulkheads	20	*	1 Jul 2012
Chutes, deadboxes and diverters	10	*	1 Jul 2012
Conveyors (including belt, drag, grain and screw conveyors)	15	*	1 Jul 2012
Elevators and distributors (including bucket and transfer elevators)	15	*	1 Jul 2012
Grain cleaning and shifting assets (including grain blowers and grain shifters)	15	*	1 Jul 2012
Grain transfer drag chains	15	*	1 Jul 2012
Portable conveying assets (including augers and belt conveyors)	5	*	1 Jul 2012
Receival pits	30	*	1 Jul 2012
Rotary and slide gates	10	*	1 Jul 2012
Silos	30	*	1 Jul 2012
Storage bins	20	*	1 Jul 2012
Support assets:			
Air compressors	10	*	1 Jul 2012
Dust management assets (including bag and dust filters, dust collectors, dust extraction hood and ducting and exhaust fans and socks)	15	*	1 Jul 2012

MANUFACTURING
(11110 to 25990)

Asset	Life (Years)	Reviewed	Date Of Application
Emissions and odour control systems (incorporating exhaust fans, ducting and biofilters)	15	*	1 Jul 2012
Feed delivery bins	15	*	1 Jul 2012
Fire prevention systems (incorporating fire protection system and water tanks)	20	*	1 Jul 2012
Grain vacuum and silo sampling probes	5	*	1 Jul 2012
Laboratory assets (including grain testing assets)	10	*	1 Jul 2012
Near infrared transmission systems and analysers	7	*	1 Jul 2012
Racking	20	*	1 Jul 2012
Waste water treatment assets	20	*	1 Jul 2012
Weighbridges	25	*	1 Jul 2012
Other food product manufacturing n.e.c. (11990)			
Coffee processing assets:			
Bins and hoppers (including gravity bins and holding bins)	20	*	1 Jul 2012
De-stoners, gravity separators and magnetic separators	20	*	1 Jul 2012
Extraction and evaporation assets (including decanters, evaporators/finishers, flash vessels/stripping columns, pressure vessels/cells, separators/clarifiers, spray driers, strainers and wet scrubbers)	20	*	1 Jul 2012
Grinders	20	*	1 Jul 2012
Material handling assets (including augers, belt conveyors, bucket elevators, elevators and vibratory conveyors)	15	*	1 Jul 2012
Packaging assets:			
Form fill and seal packaging machines (including flat bottom, flat top and bottom, pillow shape, stand up and vacuum brick pack packaging machines)	12	*	1 Jul 2012
Inspection equipment (including checkweighers, metal detectors, counting machines etc)	12	*	1 Jul 2012
Multihead weighers	12	*	1 Jul 2012
Process control valves	10	*	1 Jul 2012
Roasters (including cooling trays)	20	*	1 Jul 2012
Sample roasters	15	*	1 Jul 2012
Silos	25	*	1 Jul 2012
Smoke/odour elimination systems (incorporating afterburners, housing and piping)	15	*	1 Jul 2012
Support assets:			
Air compressors	12	*	1 Jul 2012
Boiler house assets	20	*	1 Jul 2012
Clean-in-place (CIP) systems	15	*	1 Jul 2012
Control system assets (including programmable logic controllers (PLCs) and variable speed drives (VSDs))	10	*	1 Jul 2012
Laboratory assets:			
Electronic (including analysers and spectrometers)	7	*	1 Jul 2012
Generally	10	*	1 Jul 2012
Pipes	20	*	1 Jul 2012
Pumps	20	*	1 Jul 2012
Racks	20	*	1 Jul 2012
Scales	10	*	1 Jul 2012
Tanks	30	*	1 Jul 2012
Waste water treatment assets	20	*	1 Jul 2012

MANUFACTURING
(11110 to 25990)

Asset	Life (Years)	Reviewed	Date Of Application
Weighbridges	25	*	1 Jul 2012
Frozen pre-prepared food manufacturing assets (including frozen appetisers and finger foods such as dim sims and spring rolls, frozen french fries/potato chips, frozen pizzas and frozen pre-prepared meals):			
Ancillary and support assets:			
Air compression assets:			
Air dryers	10	*	1 Jul 2012
Air receivers	20	*	1 Jul 2012
Compressors and packaged air compression systems	15	*	1 Jul 2012
Blowers and fans	15	*	1 Jul 2012
Boilers	20	*	1 Jul 2012
Clean-in-place (CIP) assets	10	*	1 Jul 2012
Control systems generally	10	*	1 Jul 2012
Conveyors (including auger conveyors, belt conveyors, bucket elevators, flume conveyors roller conveyors, web conveyors etc)	15	*	1 Jul 2012
Dust collection systems	20	*	1 Jul 2012
Fire control assets – use any relevant determination in Table B			
Frying oil reclaiming and cleansing systems (incorporating filtration equipment, storage tanks and ventilation hoods)	20	*	1 Jul 2012
Heat exchangers	15	*	1 Jul 2012
Holding and storage tanks generally (including water storage tanks)	20	*	1 Jul 2012
Piping and reticulation lines (excluding fire water pipes)	25	*	1 Jul 2012
Pumps (including cavity pumps, centrifugal pumps, lobe pumps etc)	10	*	1 Jul 2012
Refrigeration and freezing assets:			
Chilled water systems generally (including chillers, condensers and cooling towers)	15	*	1 Jul 2012
Cooling tunnels	20	*	1 Jul 2012
Freezers:			
Generally (including blast freezers and plate freezers)	15	*	1 Jul 2012
Spiral freezers	10	*	1 Jul 2012
Insulation panels used in cold stores, cool rooms, freezer rooms etc – see Table B Refrigeration assets			
Uninterruptible power supply (UPS) assets – see Table B Power supply assets			
Valves	10	*	1 Jul 2012
Waste water treatment assets:			
Aerators	20	*	1 Jul 2012
Biogas system assets (excluding lagoon and pond covers)	25	*	1 Jul 2012
Blowers	20	*	1 Jul 2012
Clarifiers (including dissolved air floatation equipment and screens)	20	*	1 Jul 2012
Digester/aeration tanks	25	*	1 Jul 2012
Lagoons and ponds	40	*	1 Jul 2012
Lagoon and pond covers	12	*	1 Jul 2012
Lagoon and pond liners	20	*	1 Jul 2012
Reverse osmosis system assets	20	*	1 Jul 2012

MANUFACTURING
(11110 to 25990)

Asset	Life (Years)	Reviewed	Date Of Application
Sludge dewatering assets (including filters, separators etc)	15	*	1 Jul 2012
Water treatment filters (including carbon filters and membrane filters)	10	*	1 Jul 2012
Frozen appetiser and finger food manufacturing assets:			
Appetiser forming machines	15	*	1 Jul 2012
Cookers	12	*	1 Jul 2012
Fryers	12	*	1 Jul 2012
Mixing assets (including meat mincers, meat mincer/blenders, mixer/grinding machines and mixers generally)	15	*	1 Jul 2012
Frozen lasagne manufacturing assets generally (including cookers, cutters, depositors, extruders, lasagne making machines, mixers and sheeters)	15	*	1 Jul 2012
Frozen pasta product manufacturing assets generally – use any relevant determination made for pasta manufacturing assets in Table A Cereal and pasta product manufacturing (11620)			
Frozen pizza manufacturing assets:			
Pizza base making assets:			
Dough mixers	15	*	1 Jul 2012
Ovens	20	*	1 Jul 2012
Pizza base forming and sheeting assets (including chunking units, cutters, extruders, laminators, spiker rollers etc)	15	*	1 Jul 2012
Proofers	15	*	1 Jul 2012
Pizza sauce and topping application assets (including can opening machines, cheese shredding assets, depositors, enrobers, topping applicators and water coating sprayers)	15	*	1 Jul 2012
Pocket pizza making machines	15	*	1 Jul 2012
Frozen potato product manufacturing assets (including french fries/ potato chips, potato flake, potato shred and shred product manufacturing assets):			
Pre-processing assets:			
Deskinners and peelers:			
Abrasive/brush peelers	12	*	1 Jul 2012
Steam peelers	10	*	1 Jul 2012
Destoners	20	*	1 Jul 2012
Sizing and sorting assets:			
Electronic sorters	10	*	1 Jul 2012
Mechanical sizers (including roller sizers and screen shaker sizers)	15	*	1 Jul 2012
Trim tables (roller inspection tables)	20	*	1 Jul 2012
Washers and brushers (including barrel washers, flat bed brushers, polishers and pre-cleaner wet hopper washers)	12	*	1 Jul 2012
Processing assets generally:			
Batter enrobers	10	*	1 Jul 2012
Blanchers	15	*	1 Jul 2012
Cookers	12	*	1 Jul 2012
Cutters:			
Mechanical cutters	10	*	1 Jul 2012
Water based (hydro) cutters	15	*	1 Jul 2012
Dicers	10	*	1 Jul 2012
Dosing systems for dextrose and SAPP application etc	15	*	1 Jul 2012

MANUFACTURING
(11110 to 25990)

Asset	Life (Years)	Reviewed	Date Of Application
Dryers:			
Flake drum dryers	20	*	1 Jul 2012
Generally (including dewatering dryers)	15	*	1 Jul 2012
Flake breakers	10	*	1 Jul 2012
Forming drums/machines	10	*	1 Jul 2012
Fryers	12	*	1 Jul 2012
Mixers	15	*	1 Jul 2012
Pre-heaters	15	*	1 Jul 2012
Shredders	10	*	1 Jul 2012
Trimming and grading assets (including shaker screen tables used in grading finished products and nubbin removal, sliver removers etc)	10	*	1 Jul 2012
Frozen pre-prepared meal manufacturing assets (including cookers and kettles, depositors, fillers, meat injectors and tenderisers, mixers, multihead weighers, ovens, particle and sauce applicators and rice/pasta cookers)	15	*	1 Jul 2012
Ingredient receiving and handling assets:			
Bins and hoppers (including holding bins, intermediate bulk containers, tote bins etc):			
Mild and stainless steel	15	*	1 Jul 2012
Others (including plastic and fibreglass)	8	*	1 Jul 2012
Potato storage assets:			
Air handling system assets used in potato storage structures:			
Aeration pipes	25	*	1 Jul 2012
Control systems	15	*	1 Jul 2012
Fans	15	*	1 Jul 2012
Humidification assets (humidifiers etc)	10	*	1 Jul 2012
Refrigeration assets (refrigeration units etc)	12	*	1 Jul 2012
Potato pilers (bin pilers)	20	*	1 Jul 2012
Silos (flour)	25	*	1 Jul 2012
Tippers and unloaders (including bin tippers and unloaders, bulker bag unloaders and tote tippers and unloaders)	12	*	1 Jul 2012
Trolleys (for cooked rice etc)	5	*	1 Jul 2012
Packaging and quality control assets:			
Accumulators	12	*	1 Jul 2012
Adhesive applicators	7	*	1 Jul 2012
Cartoners (including inner and outer cartoning machines)	15	*	1 Jul 2012
Case erecting, packing and closing machines (including casepackers)	15	*	1 Jul 2012
Case sealing machines	10	*	1 Jul 2012
Checkweighers	10	*	1 Jul 2012
Coding machines (including laser coding machines)	8	*	1 Jul 2012
Flow wrappers	10	*	1 Jul 2012
Form fill and seal assets (including bagging units and multihead weighers)	15	*	1 Jul 2012
Heat shrink tunnels	10	*	1 Jul 2012
Metal detectors	10	*	1 Jul 2012
Palletisers	12	*	1 Jul 2012
Palletising robots	10	*	1 Jul 2012
Pallet wrappers	12	*	1 Jul 2012

MANUFACTURING
(11110 to 25990)

Asset	Life (Years)	Reviewed	Date Of Application
Product loaders and stackers	15	*	1 Jul 2012
Tray denesters	15	*	1 Jul 2012
Tray sealers	15	*	1 Jul 2012
Weighbridges	20	*	1 Jul 2012
X-ray detectors	10	*	1 Jul 2012
Peanut processing assets:			
Aeration units	15	*	1 Jul 2009
Aspirators	10	*	1 Jul 2009
Bins and hoppers (including gravity bins, holding bins, shell bins, surge bins etc)	15	*	1 Jul 2009
Blanchers	10	*	1 Jul 2009
Cleaning assets:			
De-stoners and gravity separators	20	*	1 Jul 2009
Pre-cleaners (intake cleaners)	15	*	1 Jul 2009
Control systems	10	*	1 Jul 2009
Door controls and motor drive systems for rapid roller doors (incorporating chains, controls, motors and sensors, but excluding doors)	10	*	1 Jul 2009
Dust collection assets (including ductwork, dust collectors, extraction fans etc)	20	*	1 Jul 2009
Fryers	10	*	1 Jul 2009
Granulators	12	*	1 Jul 2009
Laboratory assets:			
Generally	10	*	1 Jul 2009
Laboratory analysers	5	*	1 Jul 2009
Materials handling assets (including augers, belt conveyors, bucket elevators, elevators and vibratory conveyors)	15	*	1 Jul 2009
Ovens (including roasters and dryers)	10	*	1 Jul 2009
Packaging assets (including packers, palletisers, shrink wrappers and strapping machines)	10	*	1 Jul 2009
Peanut oil crushing assets:			
Cookers	15	*	1 Jul 2009
Screw presses/expeller presses	13	*	1 Jul 2009
Quality control assets:			
Magnets and magnetic separators	7	*	1 Jul 2009
Metal detectors	10	*	1 Jul 2009
X-ray units	5	*	1 Jul 2009
Refrigeration units	20	*	1 Jul 2009
Sampling assets:			
Sample grinders and shellers	10	*	1 Jul 2009
Sieve tables and picking belt decks	20	*	1 Jul 2009
Moisture meters	5	*	1 Jul 2009
Scales	5	*	1 Jul 2009
Shellers	20	*	1 Jul 2009
Silos (metal)	30	*	1 Jul 2009
Sorting and sizing assets:			
Electronic/laser sorters (including colour sorters)	10	*	1 Jul 2009
Generally (including vibrating sieves, shaker decks and sizing shakers)	20	*	1 Jul 2009
Tipping units	20	*	1 Jul 2009

MANUFACTURING
(11110 to 25990)

Asset	Life (Years)	Reviewed	Date Of Application
Transformers	40	*	1 Jul 2009
Tea processing assets:			
Bins (including receiving and refrigerated)	15	*	1 Jul 2012
Bin tippers	20	*	1 Jul 2012
Classifiers and shredders	20	*	1 Jul 2012
Dryers (including primary, secondary and final)	20	*	1 Jul 2012
Fermenters (oxidizers)	20	*	1 Jul 2012
Fibre extractors	20	*	1 Jul 2012
Laboratory assets:			
Generally	15	*	1 Jul 2012
Laboratory analysers	10	*	1 Jul 2012
Materials handling assets (including augers, belt conveyors, bucket elevators, vibratory conveyors, structures, gearboxes and motors)	15	*	1 Jul 2012
Packaging assets:			
Bagging machines (including flow wrappers and roll wrapping machines)	15	*	1 Jul 2012
Packaging machines:			
Form fill and seal packaging machines	15	*	1 Jul 2012
Generally (including flat bottom, flat top and bottom, pillow shape and stand up packaging machines)	15	*	1 Jul 2012
Vacuum brick pack packaging machines	15	*	1 Jul 2012
Tea packaging assets generally (including cartoners, casepackers, case palletisers, checkweighers, fillers, label applicators, shrink wrappers and stretch wrappers etc)	15	*	1 Jul 2012
Pre dryers	20	*	1 Jul 2012
Rollers (including crush tear and curl (CTC), electrostatic, secondary and final)	20	*	1 Jul 2012
Rotovanes	20	*	1 Jul 2012
Support assets:			
Air compression assets (including air dryers, air receivers and compressors)	12	*	1 Jul 2012
Blowers and fans	15	*	1 Jul 2012
Boilers	20	*	1 Jul 2012
Bulka bags	5	*	1 Jul 2012
Control system assets (including control cabinets and switchgear, instrumentation, programmable logic controllers (PLCs) and variable speed drives (VSDs))	10	*	1 Jul 2012
Switchboards	20	*	1 Jul 2012
Vibratory screens	20	*	1 Jul 2012
Withering troughs (incorporating controls and sensors)	25	*	1 Jul 2012
Soft drink, cordial and syrup manufacturing (12110)			
De-aerated water system assets (including pipes, pumps and tanks)	20	*	1 Jul 2009
Filter assets (including bag filters, carbon filters, cartridge filters, ozone filters and UV filters)	15	*	1 Jul 2009
Fruit juice drink manufacturing assets – see Table A Fruit and vegetable processing (11400)			
Ice manufacturing assets (excluding dry ice manufacturing assets):			
Ammonia tank liquid receivers	20	*	1 Jul 2016
Compressors	12	*	1 Jul 2016
Condensers and cooling towers	10	*	1 Jul 2016

MANUFACTURING
(11110 to 25990)

Asset	Life (Years)	Reviewed	Date Of Application
Ice cabinets:			
Display merchandisers	5	*	1 Jul 2016
Hydraulic lift trailers	10	*	1 Jul 2016
Mobile ice boxes	7	*	1 Jul 2016
Ice makers	25	*	1 Jul 2016
Support assets:			
Augers	20	*	1 Jul 2016
Bagging assets (including air compressors, baggers, sealers etc)	8	*	1 Jul 2016
Block pressers	10	*	1 Jul 2016
Conveyors (including elevators, conveyors and belts)	10	*	1 Jul 2016
Ice rake assemblies	8	*	1 Jul 2016
Ice storage bins, feed bins and rake bins	20	*	1 Jul 2016
Packaging assets:			
Filling and sealing assets:			
Capping machines	15	*	1 Jul 2009
Container dryers (incorporating air knives and blowers)	10	*	1 Jul 2009
Cooling and warming tunnels	10	*	1 Jul 2009
Filling machines (including bag in box fillers, cup fillers and aseptic fillers)	20	*	1 Jul 2009
Induction sealers	10	*	1 Jul 2009
Inspection machines	10	*	1 Jul 2009
Handling assets:			
Bottle and can rinsing machines	20	*	1 Jul 2009
Depalletisers	20	*	1 Jul 2009
Pallet binders	10	*	1 Jul 2009
Palletisers	20	*	1 Jul 2009
Strap cutting machines	10	*	1 Jul 2009
Stretch wrappers	15	*	1 Jul 2009
Packing assets:			
Carton packers	15	*	1 Jul 2009
Coding machines (including container coders and outer date coders)	7	*	1 Jul 2009
Label applicators	7	*	1 Jul 2009
Labellers	15	*	1 Jul 2009
Multipack machines	10	*	1 Jul 2009
Shrink wrappers	15	*	1 Jul 2009
Tunnel pasteurisers	10	*	1 Jul 2009
Support assets:			
Additive dosing systems assets (including pipes, pumps and tanks)	20	*	1 Jul 2009
Air compressors and receivers	20	*	1 Jul 2009
Boilers	20	*	1 Jul 2009
Carbonators (including controls, pumps and valves)	20	*	1 Jul 2009
Centrifuges	15	*	1 Jul 2009
Clean-in-place system (CIP) assets (including pipes, pumps and tanks)	15	*	1 Jul 2009
Control system assets (excluding personal computers, but including program logic controllers (PLCs) and switchgear)	10	*	1 Jul 2009
Conveyers	15	*	1 Jul 2009
Heat exchangers	15	*	1 Jul 2009

MANUFACTURING
(11110 to 25990)

Asset	Life (Years)	Reviewed	Date Of Application
Laboratory equipment	10	*	1 Jul 2009
Refrigeration assets (including compressors, cooling towers, condensers, evaporators and pumps)	15	*	1 Jul 2009
Pipes	25	*	1 Jul 2009
Pumps	15	*	1 Jul 2009
Syrup preparation assets (including tanks)	15	*	1 Jul 2009
Valves	10	*	1 Jul 2009
Waste water treatment assets:			
Aerators	20	*	1 Jul 2009
Anaerobic bio gas system assets	25	*	1 Jul 2009
Blowers	20	*	1 Jul 2009
Clarifiers	20	*	1 Jul 2009
Digester/aeration tanks	25	*	1 Jul 2009
Reverse osmosis system assets	20	*	1 Jul 2009
Weighers	20	*	1 Jul 2009
Tanks:			
Hot water	25	*	1 Jul 2009
Liquid carbon dioxide (CO_2) storage	20	*	1 Jul 2009
Storage:			
Chemical storage	20	*	1 Jul 2009
Generally	30	*	1 Jul 2009
Beer manufacturing (except non-alcoholic beer) (12120)			
Beer filtration assets:			
Beer filters	20	*	1 Jul 2008
Filter media make up assets	20	*	1 Jul 2008
Mash filters	20	*	1 Jul 2008
Brewing assets:			
Grist hoppers	25	*	1 Jul 2008
Mash tuns	25	*	1 Jul 2008
Lauter tuns	25	*	1 Jul 2008
Spent grains transfer system assets	20	*	1 Jul 2008
Wort kettles	25	*	1 Jul 2008
Whirlpool vessels	25	*	1 Jul 2008
Cellaring assets:			
Carbonators (including controls, pumps and valves)	20	*	1 Jul 2008
Centrifuges	15	*	1 Jul 2008
De-aerated water system assets (including pipes, pumps and tanks)	20	*	1 Jul 2008
Yeast filters/dryers	15	*	1 Jul 2008
Yeast propagators	20	*	1 Jul 2008
Malt handling and cleaning assets:			
Augers/conveyers and elevators	15	*	1 Jul 2008
Dust extractors	20	*	1 Jul 2008
Grain cleaning assets (including screeners, destoners and magnetic separators)	20	*	1 Jul 2008
Malt milling machines (including hammer and roller mills)	20	*	1 Jul 2008
Silos:			
Galvanised construction	30	*	1 Jul 2008
Steel construction	40	*	1 Jul 2008

MANUFACTURING
(11110 to 25990)

Asset	Life (Years)	Reviewed	Date Of Application
Weighers	20	*	1 Jul 2008
Packaging assets:			
Bottle and can filling and sealing assets:			
Filling machines	20	*	1 Jul 2008
Inspection machines	10	*	1 Jul 2008
Bottle and can handling assets:			
Bottle and can rinsing machines	20	*	1 Jul 2008
Depalletisers	20	*	1 Jul 2008
Palletisers	20	*	1 Jul 2008
Bottle and can packing assets:			
Carton packers	15	*	1 Jul 2008
Date coders	7	*	1 Jul 2008
Labellers	15	*	1 Jul 2008
Multipack machines	10	*	1 Jul 2008
Outer date coders	7	*	1 Jul 2008
Shrink wrappers	15	*	1 Jul 2008
Tunnel pasteurisers	10	*	1 Jul 2008
Conveyers	15	*	1 Jul 2008
Keg line assets:			
Capping machines	15	*	1 Jul 2008
Coding machines	7	*	1 Jul 2008
External washing machines	20	*	1 Jul 2008
Internal washer and filler machines	20	*	1 Jul 2008
Kegs (stainless steel)	15	*	1 Jul 2013
Pasteurisers	20	*	1 Jul 2008
Support assets:			
Additive and hops dosing systems assets (including pipes, pumps and tanks)	20	*	1 Jul 2008
Air compressors and receivers	20	*	1 Jul 2008
Boilers	20	*	1 Jul 2008
Carbon dioxide (CO_2) recovery system assets:			
Gas collection and storage assets (including pipes bladders and tanks)	25	*	1 Jul 2008
Gas processing assets	20	*	1 Jul 2008
Vaporisation system assets	20	*	1 Jul 2008
Clean-in-place system (CIP) assets (including pipes, pumps and tanks)	15	*	1 Jul 2008
Control system assets (excluding personal computers)	10	*	1 Jul 2008
Heat exchangers	15	*	1 Jul 2008
Refrigeration assets (including compressors, condensers, evaporators and pumps)	15	*	1 Jul 2008
Pipes	25	*	1 Jul 2008
Pumps	15	*	1 Jul 2008
Valves	10	*	1 Jul 2008
Vapour condensers	15	*	1 Jul 2008
Waste water treatment assets:			
Aerators	20	*	1 Jul 2008
Anaerobic bio gas system assets	25	*	1 Jul 2008
Blowers	20	*	1 Jul 2008

MANUFACTURING
(11110 to 25990)

Asset	Life (Years)	Reviewed	Date Of Application
Clarifiers	20	*	1 Jul 2008
Digester/aeration tanks	25	*	1 Jul 2008
Reverse osmosis system assets	20	*	1 Jul 2008
Tanks:			
Beer fermentation and storage	30	*	1 Jul 2008
Chemical storage	20	*	1 Jul 2008
Cold service storage	25	*	1 Jul 2008
Condensate collection	25	*	1 Jul 2008
Hot service storage	25	*	1 Jul 2008
Liquid carbon dioxide (CO_2) storage	20	*	1 Jul 2008
Trub	25	*	1 Jul 2008
Yeast storage	25	*	1 Jul 2008
Spirit manufacturing (12130)			
Barrels, tanks and tuns:			
Barrels or casks (wooden):			
Capacity greater than 150 litres	10	*	1 Jul 2018
Capacity of 150 litres or less	4	*	1 Jul 2018
Fermenters, washbacks, vats and holding tanks	25	*	1 Jul 2018
Intermediate bulk containers (IBC)	8	*	1 Jul 2018
Mash tuns and lauter tuns	20	*	1 Jul 2018
Bottling assets:			
Bottle fillers:			
Automated (including bottle r insers/washers, cappers, capsule applicators and foilers)	15	*	1 Jul 2018
Manual	7	*	1 Jul 2018
Labellers	10	*	1 Jul 2018
Printers and ink coders	8	*	1 Jul 2018
Distillation assets			
Laboratory and testing assets (including alcoholmeters, alcolyzers, density meters, gas chromatographs, Graham condensers, homogenisers, hydrometers, Inland Revenue condensers and sugar testers)	7	*	1 Jul 2018
Stainless steel stills (continuous/vacuum stills, marc stills producing grape spirit, neutral spirit or potable ethanol [incorporating analyser/stripping columns, purifier columns, rectifying columns, condensers and dephlegmators/reflux condensers and methanol/fusel oil isolators])	25	*	1 Jul 2018
Stills generally (copper stills, pot stills, spirit stills and wash stills [incorporating botanical baskets, condensers, head tubes/necks, rectifiers, rectifying columns and still columns])	15	*	1 Jul 2018
Support assets:			
Barrel racks:			
Steel	20	*	1 Jul 2018
Wooden	15	*	1 Jul 2018
CCTV, security and monitoring systems assets – see Table B Security and monitoring assets			
Chillers	15	*	1 Jul 2018
Floor scales (platform scales)	10	*	1 Jul 2018
Flow meters	10	*	1 Jul 2018
Furnaces, barley smokers, crispers and malt kilns	15	*	1 Jul 2018

MANUFACTURING
(11110 to 25990)

Asset	Life (Years)	Reviewed	Date Of Application
Gristmills	15	*	1 Jul 2018
Heat exchangers (plate or tube)	15	*	1 Jul 2018
Programmable logic control (PLC) system assets – see Table B Control systems and control system assets			
Pumps (including macerating pumps)	7	*	1 Jul 2018
Water filters, reverse osmosis (RO) filters and water softeners	10	*	1 Jul 2018
Water heating assets:			
Boilers – see Table B Boilers			
Water heaters (including small steam boilers [up to 500KW])	10	*	1 Jul 2018
Wine and other alcoholic beverage manufacturing (12140)			
Barrel assets:			
Barrel racks	20	*	1 Jul 2008
Barrel washers	7	*	1 Jul 2008
Oak barrels	4	*	1 Jul 2008
Grape handling assets:			
Conveyors and elevators	15	*	1 Jul 2008
Crushers/destemmers	15	*	1 Jul 2008
Electronic scales (mobile)	10	*	1 Jul 2008
Grape bins (plastic)	5	*	1 Jul 2008
Grape receival hoppers	20	*	1 Jul 2008
Grape waste pits (concrete)	20	*	1 Jul 2008
Presses:			
Basket	20	*	1 Jul 2008
Continuous (screw)	15	*	1 Jul 2008
Pneumatic (airbag)	15	*	1 Jul 2008
Weighbridges/weighers	20	*	1 Jul 2008
Packaging assets:			
Bottle and cask filling, sealing and coding assets:			
Cap feed systems	15	*	1 Jul 2008
Cappers	15	*	1 Jul 2008
Carton packing machines	15	*	1 Jul 2008
Corkers	15	*	1 Jul 2008
Crown sealers (sparkling wine)	15	*	1 Jul 2008
Date coders	7	*	1 Jul 2008
Fillers	15	*	1 Jul 2008
Foilers	15	*	1 Jul 2008
Inspection machines	10	*	1 Jul 2008
Labellers	10	*	1 Jul 2008
Rinsers	15	*	1 Jul 2008
Handling and packing assets:			
Carton erectors/sealers/tapers	15	*	1 Jul 2008
Conveyors (loose bottle, carton and pallet)	15	*	1 Jul 2008
Depalletisers	15	*	1 Jul 2008
Outer date coders	5	*	1 Jul 2008
Palletisers	15	*	1 Jul 2008
Shrink wrappers	15	*	1 Jul 2008
Separation/filtration assets:			
Centrifuges	10	*	1 Jul 2008

MANUFACTURING
(11110 to 25990)

Asset	Life (Years)	Reviewed	Date Of Application
Filtration units (incorporating housing and filters):			
Cross flow filter units	10	*	1 Jul 2008
Diatomaceous earth filter units (including earth make-up system)	10	*	1 Jul 2008
Lees filter units	10	*	1 Jul 2008
Membrane cartridge filter units (including lenticular)	10	*	1 Jul 2008
Plate and frame filter units	15	*	1 Jul 2008
Rotary drum vacuum filter units	15	*	1 Jul 2008
Sparkling wine equipment:			
Carbonation equipment	10	*	1 Jul 2008
Corking/wiring equipment	15	*	1 Jul 2008
Disgorging and dosing equipment	10	*	1 Jul 2008
Riddling equipment	15	*	1 Jul 2008
Support assets:			
Additive liquid dosing systems	10	*	1 Jul 2008
Air compressors	15	*	1 Jul 2008
Air receivers	20	*	1 Jul 2008
Boilers	15	*	1 Jul 2008
Cooling towers	15	*	1 Jul 2008
Electrical and Process control systems:			
Control cabinets, switchgear	10	*	1 Jul 2008
Programmed logic controllers (PLCs)	10	*	1 Jul 2008
Transformers	40	*	1 Jul 2008
Flow meters	10	*	1 Jul 2008
Grape/wine testing equipment:			
Grape must analyzers	10	*	1 Jul 2008
Laboratory – glassware	2	*	1 Jul 2008
Laboratory – other equipment	10	*	1 Jul 2008
Heat exchangers	15	*	1 Jul 2008
Hoses	5	*	1 Jul 2008
Hot water systems	10	*	1 Jul 2008
Inert gas systems:			
Dry ice machines	10	*	1 Jul 2008
Gas storage pressure tanks	20	*	1 Jul 2008
Nitrogen generators	10	*	1 Jul 2008
Pipes and fittings:			
Mild steel	10	*	1 Jul 2008
Non-ferrous	20	*	1 Jul 2008
Stainless steel	25	*	1 Jul 2008
Valves	10	*	1 Jul 2008
Pumps	15	*	1 Jul 2008
Refrigeration assets (including compressors, condensors, evaporators and storage tanks)	15	*	1 Jul 2008
Reverse osmosis plant	10	*	1 Jul 2008
Waste water treatment assets:			
Aerators	10	*	1 Jul 2008
Blowers	10	*	1 Jul 2008
Clarifiers	10	*	1 Jul 2008
Digesters	10	*	1 Jul 2008

MANUFACTURING
(11110 to 25990)

Asset	Life (Years)	Reviewed	Date Of Application
Tanks (including insulation, agitators, pump over systems and monitoring instrumentation):			
Pressure tanks (for sparkling wine)	20	*	1 Jul 2008
Waste water storage/treatment tanks	15	*	1 Jul 2008
Water storage tanks	30	*	1 Jul 2008
Wine fermenters:			
Open	30	*	1 Jul 2008
Rotary	30	*	1 Jul 2008
Static	30	*	1 Jul 2008
Sweeping arm	30	*	1 Jul 2008
Wine storage tanks	30	*	1 Jul 2008
Tank accessories:			
Micro oxygenation systems	5	*	1 Jul 2008
Tank plungers	10	*	1 Jul 2008
Textile, leather, clothing and footwear manufacturing (13110 to 13520)			
Boot and shoe-making machinery:			
Machinery and general plant	13 1/3		1 Jan 2001
Moulds for plastic heels	3		1 Jan 2001
Vulcanising moulds	5		1 Jan 2001
Carpet manufacturing assets:			
Accumulators	20	*	1 Jul 2017
Beamers (including warpers)	15	*	1 Jul 2017
Creels	20	*	1 Jul 2017
Cutting tables	15	*	1 Jul 2017
J Bins	20	*	1 Jul 2017
Lapping and mending frames	15	*	1 Jul 2017
Lapping trolleys	15	*	1 Jul 2017
Latex application assets	17	*	1 Jul 2017
Offline mending tables	15	*	1 Jul 2017
Ovens	20	*	1 Jul 2017
Pre-coat assets (including direct coat applicators and steamers)	15	*	1 Jul 2017
Re-wind machines	13	*	1 Jul 2017
Roll-up machines	15	*	1 Jul 2017
Sample binding assets (including binders and sewing machines)	15	*	1 Jul 2017
Sample cutting assets (including stamping presses)	15	*	1 Jul 2017
Shearers	20	*	1 Jul 2017
Stretchers (including pre-tenters)	15	*	1 Jul 2017
Tufters	15	*	1 Jul 2017
Clothing and millinery manufacturing plant:			
General plant	20		1 Jan 2001
Hat manufacturing plant and machinery	13 1/3		1 Jan 2001
Sewing machines	10	*	1 Jul 2014
Cotton manufacturers' machinery:			
Conveyors	10		1 Jan 2001
Engines, gas	20		1 Jan 2001
Gas producer plant	13 1/3		1 Jan 2001
Gins	10		1 Jan 2001

MANUFACTURING
(11110 to 25990)

Asset	Life (Years)	Reviewed	Date Of Application
Flock manufacturing plant:			
Carding machines	13 1/3		1 Jan 2001
General plant	20		1 Jan 2001
Knitting machines	13 1/3		1 Jan 2001
Rope and twine manufacturers' plant	20		1 Jan 2001
Tanners' plant:			
General plant	20		1 Jan 2001
Modern plant used in 'wet' process	13 1/3		1 Jan 2001
Weaving machinery (silk and cotton)	13 1/3		1 Jan 2001
Wool dumping machinery	13 1/3		1 Jan 2001
Wool and fleece scouring and carbonising assets:			
Baker	16	*	1 Jul 2017
Bale breaker (including wool feeder and wool opener)	15	*	1 Jul 2017
Crusher (including duster)	13	*	1 Jul 2017
Dryers:			
Used in carbonising	13	*	1 Jul 2017
Used in scouring	18	*	1 Jul 2017
Dust extraction plant	15	*	1 Jul 2017
Grease separators	15	*	1 Jul 2017
High density press	15	*	1 Jul 2017
Scour machine	15	*	1 Jul 2017
Waste treatment system	10	*	1 Jul 2017
Woollen manufacturers' machinery	16 2/3		1 Jan 2001
Log sawmilling and timber dressing (14110 to 14130)			
Saw milling equipment:			
Dry or planner mill plant:			
Generally (includes multi saw/trimmer, pack docker, planner/molder, resaw or optimiser docker, stress grader and tilt hoist)	10	*	1 Jan 2001
Stackers	15	*	1 Jan 2001
Tray sorters	15	*	1 Jan 2001
Green mill plant:			
Edger line plant (includes board edger and resaw)	10	*	1 Jan 2001
Heating plant (includes storage bins/silos)	15	*	1 Jan 2001
Kiln drying plant:			
Generally (includes kiln trolleys/carriages, traverser and weights)	10	*	1 Jan 2001
Timber drying kilns and reconditioners	15	*	1 Jan 2001
Main saw line plant (includes saws, chipper canter, board separator and cant turner)	10	*	1 Jan 2001
Sorter and trimming line plant:			
Generally (includes grade mark reader and multi trimmer)	10	*	1 Jan 2001
Stackers	15	*	1 Jan 2001
Vertical bin sorters	15	*	1 Jan 2001
Log debarking plant (includes decks, carriages, hydraulic grabs and fixed cranes, butt reducer, debarker, kicker sorter and bins/pockets)	10	*	1 Jan 2001
Log, lumber and waste transfer equipment	15	*	1 Jan 2001

MANUFACTURING
(11110 to 25990)

Asset	Life (Years)	Reviewed	Date Of Application
Log yard equipment:			
Fixed and mobile cranes	12	*	1 Jan 2001
Mobile equipment (including log loaders with log grabs)	7	*	1 Jan 2001
Watering systems	15	*	1 Jan 2001
Miscellaneous plant:			
Generally (includes air compressors, extraction systems and pollution and air monitoring equipment)	10	*	1 Jan 2001
Moisture meters	3	*	1 Jan 2001
Saw and knife sharpening equipment	10	*	1 Jan 2001
Walkways	15	*	1 Jan 2001
Waste processing equipment:			
Bins – waste, chip and fuel	15	*	1 Jan 2001
Chippers, shakers/screens and hoggers	10	*	1 Jan 2001
Other wood product manufacturing (14910 to 14990)			
Clothes peg manufacturing plant (wood)	13 1/3		1 Jan 2001
Case-making plant	13 1/3		1 Jan 2001
Cork manufacturers' plant	10		1 Jan 2001
Frame (picture) manufacturing plant	13 1/3		1 Jan 2001
Joinery plant	13 1/3		1 Jan 2001
Moulding machinery (wood)	13 1/3		1 Jan 2001
Wood working plant	13 1/3		1 Jan 2001
Plywood and veneer manufacturing (14930)			
Debarking assets	15	*	1 Jan 2005
Dry clipping assets	25	*	1 Jan 2005
Glue mixing assets	25	*	1 Jan 2005
Heating unit assets	20	*	1 Jan 2005
Lay-up and glue spreading assets (including roller, curtains, and spray coaters, liquid and foam extruders)	25	*	1 Jan 2005
Log conditioning, heating and steaming assets	25	*	1 Jan 2005
Log sizing assets	20	*	1 Jan 2005
Log yard assets (see Table A Log sawmilling and timber dressing (14110 to 14130), saw milling equipment)			
Materials handling assets (including belt, chain and screw conveyors)	20	*	1 Jan 2005
Packaging assets	20	*	1 Jan 2005
Presses	25	*	1 Jan 2005
Sanding and finishing assets	25	*	1 Jan 2005
Sharpening assets	30	*	1 Jan 2005
Trimming and sawing assets	25	*	1 Jan 2005
Veneer composing, jointing and splicing assets	20	*	1 Jan 2005
Veneer dryers	25	*	1 Jan 2005
Veneer patching and grading assets	20	*	1 Jan 2005
Veneer peeling and slicing assets (including rotary peelers, longitudinal, crosscut, and staylog lathe slicers, log chargers and reelers)	20	*	1 Jan 2005
Veneer reconditioning assets	25	*	1 Jan 2005
Veneer sorting assets	20	*	1 Jan 2005
Wet clipping assets	25	*	1 Jan 2005

MANUFACTURING
(11110 to 25990)

Asset	Life (Years)	Reviewed	Date Of Application
Reconstituted wood product manufacturing (14940)			
Board coolers	25	*	1 Jan 2005
Board curing assets	20	*	1 Jan 2005
Board storage assets	25	*	1 Jan 2005
Chipping, milling and flaking assets	15	*	1 Jan 2005
Debarking assets	15	*	1 Jan 2005
Driers	15	*	1 Jan 2005
Fibre sifters	15	*	1 Jan 2005
Flake and fibre storage assets	25	*	1 Jan 2005
Glue, resin and wax mixing and blending assets	15	*	1 Jan 2005
Heat plant and boiler assets	25	*	1 Jan 2005
Lamination assets	15	*	1 Jan 2005
Log conditioning, heating and steaming assets	25	*	1 Jan 2005
Log sizing assets	20	*	1 Jan 2005
Log yard assets (see Table A Log sawmilling and timber dressing (14110 to 14130), saw milling equipment)			
Magnetic separators	25	*	1 Jan 2005
Mat forming and weighing assets (including pendistor)	20	*	1 Jan 2005
Materials handling assets (including belt, chain and screw conveyors)	20	*	1 Jan 2005
Packaging assets	20	*	1 Jan 2005
Presses (including pre-press, hot and cold presses)	25	*	1 Jan 2005
Quality measuring assets (including blow detectors, thickness detectors and weighing bridges)	15	*	1 Jan 2005
Refiner assets	20	*	1 Jan 2005
Sanding and finishing assets	25	*	1 Jan 2005
Trimming and sawing assets	25	*	1 Jan 2005
Ventilation and dust extraction assets	15	*	1 Jan 2005
Woodchip screening and washing assets	15	*	1 Jan 2005
Pulp, paper and converted paper product manufacturing (15100, 15210, 15220 and 15290)			
Pulp and paper mill assets:			
Auxiliary assets (including agitators, blowers/fans conveyors, heat exchangers and condensers, pipes and pumps)	15	*	1 Jan 2002
Box and carton making assets (including box converting assets and corrugators)	10	*	1 Jan 2002
Chemical preparation assets (including tanks and pipes used for chemical preparation)	10	*	1 Jan 2002
Electrical and instrumentation assets:			
Control systems	10	*	1 Jan 2002
Control valves	15	*	1 Jan 2002
Local indicators (pressure, level and temperature)	15	*	1 Jan 2002
Power plant assets (including switchgear, transformers and turbo generators) – see Table A Electricity supply (26110 to 26400)			
Sensors:			
Specialised	8	*	1 Jan 2002
Standard	15	*	1 Jan 2002
Paper machine assets:			
Dry end assets (including calenders, coaters and reelers)	15	*	1 Jan 2002
Dryers (including MG cylinder and yankee cylinder)	25	*	1 Jan 2002

MANUFACTURING
(11110 to 25990)

Asset	Life (Years)	Reviewed	Date Of Application
Size press	15	*	1 Jan 2002
Wet end assets (including forming section, head box and press section)	10	*	1 Jan 2002
Pulp process assets:			
Major assets (including bleaching towers, digesters, electrostatic precipitators, evaporators, lime kilns, pulp baling lines, recovery boilers, and strippers)	20	*	1 Jan 2002
Other assets (including cleaners, flotation cells, pulpers and repulpers, refiners, screens and washers/thickeners)	15	*	1 Jan 2002
Stock preparation assets (including cleaners, flotation cells, pulpers and repulpers, refiners, screens and washers/thickeners)	15	*	1 Jan 2002
Tanks	20	*	1 Jan 2002
Wood yard assets (including chip screens, chippers, reclaimers/live bottom scrappers and rotating drum debarkers)	10	*	1 Jan 2002
Paper stationery manufacturing (15230)			
Stationers' manufacturing plant	13$^1/_3$		1 Jan 2001
Sanitary paper product manufacturing (15240)			
Finishing and converted paper product manufacturing assets:			
Generally (including machines for manufacturing disposable facial and toilet tissues, paper tablecloths, paper table napkins, interleaved and rolled paper towels)	15	*	1 Jul 2013
Rolled paper core manufacturing assets (including feeder racks, glue applicators and cutting carriages)	10	*	1 Jul 2013
Hygienic paper product manufacturing assets:			
Fluff preparation assets (including hammer mills, cutting machines, fluff forming drums, compacting rollers and carding machines)	13	*	1 Jul 2013
Generally (including machines for manufacturing disposable nappies, sanitary napkins, sanitary liners and tampons)	13	*	1 Jul 2013
Packaging assets:			
Cartoning assets (including bundlers, carton and case erectors, packing and closing machines)	10	*	1 Jul 2013
Coding and labelling machines	10	*	1 Jul 2013
Robots (including automatic guided vehicles (AGVs) and pick and place packaging machines)	10	*	1 Jul 2013
Stackers and baggers	10	*	1 Jul 2013
Wrapping machines (including shrink and stretch wrappers)	10	*	1 Jul 2013
Support assets:			
Air compressors and air dryers	15	*	1 Jul 2013
Control system and monitoring assets (including programmable logic controllers (PLCs), variable speed drives (VSDs), instruments and sensors)	10	*	1 Jul 2013
Dust control assets (including ductwork, dust collectors, scrubbers and fans)	15	*	1 Jul 2013
Laboratory assets (including quality control and material testing assets)	10	*	1 Jul 2013
Material handling assets (including conveyors, elevators, hoists, feeders and hoppers)	15	*	1 Jul 2013
Metal detectors	10	*	1 Jul 2013
Storage assets (including bins and trolleys)	10	*	1 Jul 2013

MANUFACTURING
(11110 to 25990)

Asset	Life (Years)	Reviewed	Date Of Application
Printing (16110)			
Digital printing assets (including flatbed digital printers, ink based thermal imaging printers, ink jet printers, spray jet digital printers and toner based printers)	5	*	1 Jan 2006
Flexographic printing assets:			
Ancillary assets:			
Anilox roll cleaning machines	15	*	1 Jul 2006
Anilox trolley tugs	10	*	1 Jul 2006
Ink dispensing systems	10	*	1 Jul 2006
Sleeve mounting machines	10	*	1 Jul 2006
Sleeves	2	*	1 Jul 2006
Printing assets:			
Die cutters, flexo/folder/gluers (see Table A Pulp, paper and converted paper product manufacturing (15100, 15210, 15220 and 15290), box and carton making assets)			
Presses (including mid web, narrow web, very wide web and wide web flexographic presses)	12 1/2	*	1 Jul 2006
Newspaper printing assets:			
Ancillary assets:			
Automated guided vehicles (AGVs) (including laser guided vehicles and track mounted automated vehicles)	10	*	1 Jan 2007
Gripper conveyor systems (incorporating drive chains, grippers and tracks)	15	*	1 Jan 2007
Ink pumps (mechanical)	6	*	1 Jan 2007
Buffering/print line storage assets:			
Storage devices (including discs, rolls, spools and associated mountings)	15	*	1 Jan 2007
Unwinders and winders (including single, double and triple stations and buffer docking stations)	15	*	1 Jan 2007
Newspaper wrapping machines – see Table A Other store-based retailing (42110 to 42799)			
Offset lithography printing presses:			
Hybrid heatset and non-heatset webfed offset presses (incorporating integrated control systems, dryers and other peripheral equipment)	15	*	1 Jan 2007
Non-heatset (coldset) webfed offset presses (incorporating integrated control systems, folders, pasters, reelstands and other peripheral equipment)	15	*	1 Jan 2007
Reel processing, storage and transport assets:			
Conveyors	12 1/2	*	1 Jan 2007
Racks	20	*	1 Jan 2007
Reel trolleys (incorporating controls and drive chains)	15	*	1 Jan 2007
Shredders	15	*	1 Jan 2007
Stripping machines	15	*	1 Jan 2007
Offset lithography printing presses used in commercial printing generally:			
Heatset webfed offset presses (incorporating integrated control systems, coaters and other peripheral equipment)	15	*	1 Jan 2006
Sheetfed presses (incorporating integrated control systems, coaters and other peripheral equipment)	12 1/2	*	1 Jan 2006
Post-press (finishing) trade services assets – see Table A Printing support services (16120)			

MANUFACTURING
(11110 to 25990)

Asset	Life (Years)	Reviewed	Date Of Application
Pre-press trade services assets – see Table A Printing support services (16120)			
Quality control assets:			
Automatic web inspection systems	6	*	1 Jul 2006
Gas Chromatograph (GC) testers	8	*	1 Jul 2006
Others (including densitometers, plate readers and spectrophotometers)	5	*	1 Jul 2006
Screen printing assets:			
Ancillary assets:			
Dryers (including conventional air dryers, flash curers and UV dryers)	12½	*	1 Jan 2006
Drying racks	20	*	1 Jan 2006
Emulsion coaters	10	*	1 Jan 2006
Exposure lights	5	*	1 Jul 2006
Screen frames	10	*	1 Jan 2006
Sign cutting machines	5	*	1 Jan 2006
Squeegee cutters	10	*	1 Jan 2006
Vacuum frames	20	*	1 Jan 2006
Press assets:			
Heat presses used in sublimation finishing	25	*	1 Jan 2006
Pen and pad print machines	20	*	1 Jan 2006
Screen printing presses:			1 Jan 2006
Automatic presses (including in-line multicolour presses)	15	*	1 Jan 2006
Cylinder presses	15	*	1 Jan 2006
Others (including manual, semi-automatic and three quarter automatic carousel, flatbed and rotary screen printing presses)	20	*	1 Jan 2006
Screen reclamation assets:			
Screen cleaning bays	10	*	1 Jan 2006
Screen washers (automatic)	6	*	1 Jan 2006
Water blasters	4	*	1 Jan 2006
Support assets:			
Afterburners	10	*	1 Jan 2006
Dust/waste extraction systems:			
Compactors	12½	*	1 Jan 2007
Ducting	15	*	1 Jan 2007
Vacuum pumps	6	*	1 Jan 2007
Printing support services (16120)			
Post-press (finishing) trade services assets:			
Addressing and mailing assets:			
Combination addressing, folding and gluing mailing units	10	*	1 Jan 2006
Inkjet addressing printers	5	*	1 Jan 2006
Bagging and wrapping machines (including palletisers)	10	*	1 Jan 2006
Banding and tying machines	12½	*	1 Jan 2006
Benchtop finishing assets used in small printing establishments (including benchtop guillotines, coil, plastic comb and spiral binders, portable banding and tying machines, small roll laminators and tabletop folders)	5	*	1 Jan 2006

MANUFACTURING
(11110 to 25990)

Asset	Life (Years)	Reviewed	Date Of Application
Binding assets:			
Binding lines (including case binding lines and perfect binding lines)	15	*	1 Jan 2006
Perfect binders – standalone	10	*	1 Jan 2006
Stitchers:			
Generally (including drum stitchers, saddle stitching lines and side stitchers)	12½	*	1 Jan 2006
Saddle stitchers – standalone (bookletmakers)	7½	*	1 Jan 2006
Casemakers	10	*	1 Jan 2006
Collators	15	*	1 Jan 2006
Die cutters	15	*	1 Jan 2006
Drilling units	10	*	1 Jan 2006
Foil stamping machines	10	*	1 Jan 2006
Folders	12½	*	1 Jan 2006
Guillotines and ancillary assets (including joggers, stackers and transomats)	15	*	1 Jan 2006
Laminators	10	*	1 Jan 2006
Mail inserters	5	*	1 Jan 2006
Newspaper mailroom assets:			
Bundle conveying and sorting systems (including bundle sorting and barcode reading stations and bundle conveyors)	12½	*	1 Jan 2007
Inserters and inserting systems (incorporating feeders and feeder chains)	10	*	1 Jan 2007
Stackers	15	*	1 Jan 2007
Trimmers (including rotary and scissor action trimmers)	15	*	1 Jan 2007
Perforators	10	*	1 Jan 2006
Sewing machines	15	*	1 Jan 2006
Three knife trimmers	15	*	1 Jan 2006
Pre-press trade services assets:			
Conventional flexographic plate making assets (including combination units, dryers, post exposure units, UV light exposure units and washout units)	7	*	1 Jan 2006
Film and plate processors	6	*	1 Jan 2006
Film projection camera systems (including backing board and processing assets)	10	*	1 Jan 2006
Platesetters:			
Computer-to-plate (CtP) platesetters (including thermal and visible-light platesetters) and Direct-to-plate flexographic platesetters (Computer digital imagers)	5	*	1 Jan 2006
Film image platesetters (imagesetters)	7	*	1 Jan 2006
Plate punch benders:			
Automatic (optical)	5	*	1 Jan 2007
Manual	10	*	1 Jan 2007
Plotters	5	*	1 Jan 2006
Proofers:			
Analogue film or photographic proofers	7	*	1 Jan 2006
Digital and ink-jet proofers	5	*	1 Jan 2006
Scanners:			
Drum	10	*	1 Jan 2006
Flatbed	5	*	1 Jan 2006

MANUFACTURING
(11110 to 25990)

Asset	Life (Years)	Reviewed	Date Of Application
Petroleum refining (17010)			
Assets used to manufacture condensate, crude oil, domestic gas, liquid natural gas (LNG) or liquid petroleum gas (LPG) but not if the manufacture occurs in an oil refinery - see Table A Oil and gas extraction (07000)			
Oil refinery assets:			
Assets used in acid, caustic or clay treating, alkylation, polymerisation or sour water stripping	15	*	1 Jul 2002
Assets used in sulphur recovery:			
Generally	15	*	1 Jul 2002
Sulphur pits	10	*	1 Jul 2002
Assets used in other processes:			
Air compressors	30	*	1 Jul 2002
Catalyst regenerators	20	*	1 Jul 2002
Chemical injection systems	5	*	1 Jul 2002
Coke drums	20	*	1 Jul 2002
Distillation columns	30	*	1 Jul 2002
Drums:			
Generally	20	*	1 Jul 2002
Used in amine treating, bitumen blowing, potassium carbonate treating or vacuum distillation	15	*	1 Jul 2002
Electric desalters	25	*	1 Jul 2002
Expansion turbines	25	*	1 Jul 2002
Fans/blowers	30	*	1 Jul 2002
Filters/coalescers:			
Generally	25	*	1 Jul 2002
Used in amine treating, continuous coking, delayed coking, potassium carbonate treating, visbreaking or vacuum distillation	20	*	1 Jul 2002
Flare stacks	25	*	1 Jul 2002
Flare tips	5	*	1 Jul 2002
Fractionating columns	30	*	1 Jul 2002
Furnaces:			
Generally	25	*	1 Jul 2002
Used in continuous coking, delayed coking or visbreaking	20	*	1 Jul 2002
Gas absorbers:			
Generally	25	*	1 Jul 2002
Used in amine treating or potassium carbonate treating	20	*	1 Jul 2002
Gas adsorbers	25	*	1 Jul 2002
Heat exchangers:			
Generally	25	*	1 Jul 2002
Used in amine treating, bitumen blowing, catalytic de-waxing, continuous coking, delayed coking, hydrodesulphurisation, hydrotreating, potassium carbonate treating, vacuum distillation or visbreaking	20	*	1 Jul 2002
Jet ejectors	20	*	1 Jul 2002
Liquid extraction columns:			
Generally	25	*	1 Jul 2002
Used in amine treating	20	*	1 Jul 2002

MANUFACTURING
(11110 to 25990)

Asset	Life (Years)	Reviewed	Date Of Application
Piping	30	*	1 Jul 2002
Process gas compressors	30	*	1 Jul 2002
Pumps:			
Generally	25	*	1 Jul 2002
Used in amine treating, bitumen blowing, catalytic de-waxing, continuous coking, delayed coking, potassium carbonate treating, vacuum distillation or visbreaking	20	*	1 Jul 2002
Reactors	25	*	1 Jul 2002
Rotary filters	20	*	1 Jul 2002
Scrubbers	25	*	1 Jul 2002
Side stream strippers	25	*	1 Jul 2002
Storage tanks:			
Generally	25	*	1 Jul 2002
Used in amine treating, merox extraction, merox sweetening or potassium carbonate treating	20	*	1 Jul 2002
Strippers:			
Generally	25	*	1 Jul 2002
Used in amine treating or potassium carbonate treating	20	*	1 Jul 2002
Bunds (other than formed with earth)	100		1 Jan 2001
Control systems assets (excluding computers)	10	*	1 Jul 2002
Effluent separators (concrete)	40		1 Jan 2001
Laboratory equipment	20		1 Jan 2001
Industrial gas manufacturing (18110)			
Industrial gas – general manufacturing assets:			
Air and gas cooling and heating assets:			
Heat exchangers	15	*	1 Jul 2011
Moisture condensers	20	*	1 Jul 2011
Quench drums	20	*	1 Jul 2011
Refrigeration units	20	*	1 Jul 2011
Air and gas purification assets:			
Adsorption systems	25	*	1 Jul 2011
Gas scrubbers	20	*	1 Jul 2011
Reactors	25	*	1 Jul 2011
Compressors	25	*	1 Jul 2011
Gas buffer and surge tanks	25	*	1 Jul 2011
Silencers/mufflers	20	*	1 Jul 2011
Industrial gas – manufacturing assets for specific gases:			
Acetylene manufacturing assets (carbide process):			
Acetylene compressors	25	*	1 Jul 2011
Acetylene generators (incorporating hoppers)	30	*	1 Jul 2011
Acetylene purification assets (including cooling condensers, driers, purifier vessels and scrubbers)	20	*	1 Jul 2011
Calcium hydroxide settling ponds and tanks	20	*	1 Jul 2011
Carbide handling assets (including carry skips, drum conveyor system and drum opening, lifting and tipping apparatus)	12	*	1 Jul 2011
Dust collection systems	20	*	1 Jul 2011
Flashback arrestors	10	*	1 Jul 2011

MANUFACTURING
(11110 to 25990)

Asset	Life (Years)	Reviewed	Date Of Application
Ammonia manufacturing assets – see Table A Basic chemical and chemical product manufacturing (18120, 18130 and 18310)			
Argon, nitrogen and oxygen manufacturing assets (cryogenic process):			
Air filtering units for process air (incorporating housing and filters)	20	*	1 Jul 2011
Cold boxes (incorporating distillation columns, expansion valves, heat exchangers, piping, separators and vacuum insulated enclosures)	30	*	1 Jul 2011
Evaporative coolers (nitrogen cooled) and spray coolers	20	*	1 Jul 2011
Nitrogen liquefiers (incorporating, expansion valves, heat exchangers, piping, separators and vacuum insulated enclosures)	30	*	1 Jul 2011
Turbine expansion engines	25	*	1 Jul 2011
Carbon dioxide (CO_2) manufacturing assets:			
Amine based absorption/desorption systems	20	*	1 Jul 2011
Liquefaction assets (including condensers, condensate receivers and separators)	25	*	1 Jul 2011
Dry ice manufacturing assets:			
Dry ice cutting machines	10	*	1 Jul 2011
Dry ice packaging systems (incorporating conveyors, shrink tunnels and wrapping and sealing machines)	10	*	1 Jul 2011
Dry ice presses	20	*	1 Jul 2011
Dry ice shipping boxes	10	*	1 Jul 2011
Extraction fans for waste carbon dioxide (CO_2)	10	*	1 Jul 2011
Pelletisers	15	*	1 Jul 2011
Helium manufacturing assets:			
Helium liquefiers (incorporating cryogenic adsorbers, expansion valves, heat exchangers, piping, separators and vacuum insulated enclosures)	30	*	1 Jul 2011
Turbine expansion engines	25	*	1 Jul 2011
Hydrogen manufacturing assets:			
Gasifiers and steam reformer furnaces	25	*	1 Jul 2011
Industrial gas distribution assets:			
Compressor assets:			
Air receivers	20	*	1 Jul 2011
Compressors (including those for helium gas, industrial air and medical air)	15	*	1 Jul 2011
Cylinder filling assets:			
Cylinder filling station assets:			
High pressure hoses	10	*	1 Jul 2011
Manifolds and piping (incorporating flashback arrestors):			
Acetylene gas	10	*	1 Jul 2011
Other gases	20	*	1 Jul 2011
Water cooling system for acetylene cylinders (incorporating piping and spray nozzles)	20	*	1 Jul 2011
Cylinder frames (incorporating manifolds and piping)	15	*	1 Jul 2011
Cylinders:			
Gas cylinders	30	*	1 Jul 2011
Liquid gas cylinders:			

MANUFACTURING
(11110 to 25990)

Asset	Life (Years)	Reviewed	Date Of Application
Flasks	7	*	1 Jul 2011
Other liquid gas cylinders	15	*	1 Jul 2011
Cylinder valves	10	*	1 Jul 2011
Cylinder handling assets:			
Baskets, crates, and pallets	12	*	1 Jul 2011
Tippers and trolleys	10	*	1 Jul 2011
Cylinder preparation assets:			
Boilers	10	*	1 Jul 2011
Cylinder brushing machines	10	*	1 Jul 2011
Cylinder drying cabinets (incorporating heaters and fans)	15	*	1 Jul 2011
Cylinder inspection lights	10	*	1 Jul 2011
Cylinder spray booths	15	*	1 Jul 2011
Cylinder stamping machines	10	*	1 Jul 2011
Cylinder testing machines	10	*	1 Jul 2011
Cylinder valving machines (incorporating safety enclosures)	15	*	1 Jul 2011
Tank truck assets:			
Gas storage tanks	20	*	1 Jul 2011
Hoses	5	*	1 Jul 2011
Metering systems	7	*	1 Jul 2011
Pipes and valves	10	*	1 Jul 2011
Pumps	10	*	1 Jul 2011
Tanker filling station assets:			
Breakaway couplings	12	*	1 Jul 2011
Framework, manifolds and piping	20	*	1 Jul 2011
Tanker filling hoses	10	*	1 Jul 2011
Weighbridges	20	*	1 Jul 2011
Vapourisers	20	*	1 Jul 2011
Support and other assets:			
Air drying systems for industrial and instrument air	15	*	1 Jul 2011
Control system assets:			
Control cabinets and panels, programmable logic controllers (PLCs) and variable speed drives (VSDs)	10	*	1 Jul 2011
System monitoring assets (including instrumentation and sensors and transmitters for level, pressure, speed and temperature measurement)	10	*	1 Jul 2011
Cooling towers:			
Field erected	20	*	1 Jul 2011
Packaged	15	*	1 Jul 2011
Customer installations assets:			
Adsorption based nitrogen and oxygen generation systems (skid type) assets:			
Membrane systems	10	*	1 Jul 2011
Pressure swing adsorption (PSA) systems	12	*	1 Jul 2011
Vacuum swing adsorption (VSA) systems	15	*	1 Jul 2011
Blowers and compressors	15	*	1 Jul 2011
Freezers (including batch freezers, freeze tunnels, and tumble freezers)	15	*	1 Jul 2011
Gas supply metering, monitoring and control systems (incorporating meters, telemetry assets, sensors, transmitters and supply switching devices)	4	*	1 Jul 2011

MANUFACTURING
(11110 to 25990)

Asset	Life (Years)	Reviewed	Date Of Application
Gas analysis assets:			
Chromatographs	15	*	1 Jul 2011
Other analysers	10	*	1 Jul 2011
Gas storage assets:			
Liquid carbon dioxide (CO_2) storage assets:			
Tanks	30	*	1 Jul 2011
Tank refrigeration units	10	*	1 Jul 2011
Vacuum insulated tanks	30	*	1 Jul 2011
Piping assets:			
Flow meters	10	*	1 Jul 2011
Pipes:			
Carbon steel	20	*	1 Jul 2011
Stainless steel	30	*	1 Jul 2011
Pipelines	30	*	1 Jul 2011
Valves	10	*	1 Jul 2011
Platform scales	20	*	1 Jul 2011
Pumps:			
Cryogenic pumps	15	*	1 Jul 2011
Liquid carbon dioxide (CO_2) pumps	15	*	1 Jul 2011
Other pumps	15	*	1 Jul 2011
Safety assets:			
Fire control and alarm assets (see Table B)			
Gas leakage monitors:			
Fixed	10	*	1 Jul 2011
Portable	4	*	1 Jul 2011
Basic chemical and chemical product manufacturing (18120, 18130 and 18310)			
Ammonia manufacturing assets:			
Air and gas reforming and separation assets:			
Adsorption systems (including pressure and thermal swing)	25	*	1 Jul 2013
Carbon dioxide (CO_2) absorption systems (incorporating absorber and stripping columns, flash drums, heat exchangers, piping, pumps and tanks)	20	*	1 Jul 2013
Cryogenic separation process assets:			
Air cooling and drying assets (excluding adsorption systems shown above)	20	*	1 Jul 2013
Cold boxes (incorporating cryogenic distillation columns, expansion valves, heat exchangers, piping, separators and vacuum insulated enclosures)	30	*	1 Jul 2013
Desulphurisers	25	*	1 Jul 2013
Methanators	25	*	1 Jul 2013
Pre-heaters (for air and gas feedstock)	25	*	1 Jul 2013
Pre-reformers	25	*	1 Jul 2013
Primary reformers	20	*	1 Jul 2013
Secondary reformers	25	*	1 Jul 2013
Shift converters (high and low temperature)	25	*	1 Jul 2013
Compressor assets:			
Air filtering units (incorporating filters and housing filters)	25	*	1 Jul 2013
Blowers and compressors (incorporating drives)	25	*	1 Jul 2013

MANUFACTURING
(11110 to 25990)

Asset	Life (Years)	Reviewed	Date Of Application
Conversion and liquefaction assets:			
Ammonia converters	25	*	1 Jul 2013
Chillers, condensers, flash drums, receivers and separators	25	*	1 Jul 2013
Purge gas recovery systems (incorporating heat exchangers, membranes, packing, piping pumps and vessels)	25	*	1 Jul 2013
Distribution, handling and storage assets:			
Ammonia bullet tanks (including storage and surge tanks)	30	*	1 Jul 2013
Ammonia deluge and vapour suppression systems	30	*	1 Jul 2013
Ammonia pipelines (incorporating fittings and valves)	30	*	1 Jul 2013
Ammonia pumps	15	*	1 Jul 2013
Ammonia storage tank refrigeration systems (incorporating compressors, condensers, flash drums and receivers)	20	*	1 Jul 2013
Ammonia storage tanks	30	*	1 Jul 2013
Ammonia vapour scrubber systems	25	*	1 Jul 2013
ISOtainers and portable tanks	15	*	1 Jul 2013
Loading arm systems – marine	25	*	1 Jul 2013
Rail and road tank filling assets:			
Breakaway couplings	10	*	1 Jul 2013
Filling hoses	10	*	1 Jul 2013
Loading arm systems	10	*	1 Jul 2013
Gas pipelines (incorporating fittings and valves)	30	*	1 Jul 2013
Heat exchangers:			
Process gas	20	*	1 Jul 2013
Waste heat boilers	20	*	1 Jul 2013
Support assets:			
Air compression assets (for industrial air and instrument air):			
Air compressors (incorporating air drying and filtering assets)	15	*	1 Jul 2013
Air receivers	20	*	1 Jul 2013
Blowers and fans (generally)	20	*	1 Jul 2013
Boiler assets:			
Boilers	25	*	1 Jul 2013
De-aerators	25	*	1 Jul 2013
Economisers	25	*	1 Jul 2013
Steam drums	25	*	1 Jul 2013
Chemical storage tanks:			
Polyethylene (PE)	12	*	1 Jul 2013
Other	20	*	1 Jul 2013
Control system assets:			
Control cabinets and panels, program logic controllers (PLCs), switchgear and variable speed drives (VSDs)	10	*	1 Jul 2013
System monitoring assets (including instrumentation and sensors and transmitters for level, pressure, speed and temperature measurement)	10	*	1 Jul 2013
Cooling towers	20	*	1 Jul 2013
Electricity supply assets:			
Emergency supply assets – see Table B Power supply assets, emergency or standby			
Steam turbine generators	25	*	1 Jul 2013

MANUFACTURING
(11110 to 25990)

Asset	Life (Years)	Reviewed	Date Of Application
Other electricity supply assets – see Table A Electricity supply (26110 to 26400)			
Emission control assets:			
Flare tips	10	*	1 Jul 2013
Silencers	20	*	1 Jul 2013
Stacks (exhaust, vent and flare)	20	*	1 Jul 2013
Fire control and alarm systems:			
Fire fighting systems (incorporating hose boxes, hydrants and ring mains)	30	*	1 Jul 2013
Other fire control and alarm assets – see Table B Fire control and alarm assets			
Gas detectors:			
Fixed	10	*	1 Jul 2013
Portable	4	*	1 Jul 2013
Heat exchangers (not specified elsewhere)	20	*	1 Jul 2013
Laboratory assets:			
Analysers	10	*	1 Jul 2013
Other laboratory equipment (including centrifuges, drying ovens, fume cupboards etc)	10	*	1 Jul 2013
Overhead cranes	25	*	1 Jul 2013
Piping assets:			
Flow meters	10	*	1 Jul 2013
Pipes and fittings	25	*	1 Jul 2013
Valves	10	*	1 Jul 2013
Pumps:			
Boiler feedwater and cooling water pumps	20	*	1 Jul 2013
Dosing pumps	5	*	1 Jul 2013
Other pumps (not specified elsewhere)	15	*	1 Jul 2013
Safety showers and eye wash stations	20	*	1 Jul 2013
Water storage and treatment assets:			
Clarifiers and settling tanks	20	*	1 Jul 2013
Dam and pond liners	20	*	1 Jul 2013
Dams and effluent ponds	40	*	1 Jul 2013
Ion exchange systems	20	*	1 Jul 2013
Reverse osmosis systems	15	*	1 Jul 2013
Water storage tanks:			
Polyethylene (PE)	15	*	1 Jul 2013
Other	25	*	1 Jul 2013
Weighbridges	20	*	1 Jul 2013
Ammonium nitrate manufacturing assets:			
Ammonia handling and storage assets – see above in Ammonia manufacturing assets, distribution, handling and storage assets			
Ammonium nitrate prill manufacturing assets:			
Coating, cooling, drying and screening assets:			
Bulk flow coolers	20	*	1 Jul 2013
Chilling systems (incorporating chillers, ducting and piping)	20	*	1 Jul 2013
Coating product tanks	25	*	1 Jul 2013
Fluid bed coolers	20	*	1 Jul 2013

MANUFACTURING
(11110 to 25990)

Asset	Life (Years)	Reviewed	Date Of Application
Rotary drum machines (including coaters, coolers, driers and granulators)	20	*	1 Jul 2013
Screeners	20	*	1 Jul 2013
Distribution, handling and storage assets:			
Bagging machines	15	*	1 Jul 2013
Conveyor belt weighers	15	*	1 Jul 2013
Conveyors and elevators	15	*	1 Jul 2013
Load out bins/silos	25	*	1 Jul 2013
Reclaim hoppers	20	*	1 Jul 2013
Scales	15	*	1 Jul 2013
Prill tower blowers and fans	20	*	1 Jul 2013
Prill towers (incorporating head tanks and lifts)	25	*	1 Jul 2013
Scrubber systems (incorporating ducting, fans, scrubbers and tanks)	20	*	1 Jul 2013
Ammonia nitrate solution manufacturing assets:			
Evaporation assets:			
Condensate tanks, flash drums and separators	20	*	1 Jul 2013
Evaporators	20	*	1 Jul 2013
Neutralisers	25	*	1 Jul 2013
Pipe reactors (titanium)	3	*	1 Jul 2013
Remelt and solution storage tanks (incorporating heating coils and stirrers)	25	*	1 Jul 2013
Solution filters	20	*	1 Jul 2013
Solution pumps	15	*	1 Jul 2013
Nitric acid manufacturing assets:			
Ammonia liquid filtering vessels (incorporating filters)	25	*	1 Jul 2013
Ammonia vapour filtering vessels (incorporating filters)	20	*	1 Jul 2013
Ammonia/air mixers	20	*	1 Jul 2013
Compressor assets:			
Air filtering units (incorporating housing and filters)	25	*	1 Jul 2013
Compressors (incorporating drives)	25	*	1 Jul 2013
Tail gas expanders	25	*	1 Jul 2013
Conversion and absorption assets:			
Absorber columns (including bleachers)	25	*	1 Jul 2013
Catalyst filters	25	*	1 Jul 2013
Converters	25	*	1 Jul 2013
Cooler condensers:			
Zirconium	25	*	1 Jul 2013
Other	10	*	1 Jul 2013
Nitric acid heaters:			
Zirconium	20	*	1 Jul 2013
Other	10	*	1 Jul 2013
Nitric acid pumps	15	*	1 Jul 2013
Nitrous oxide (NOx) abaters	25	*	1 Jul 2013
Weak acid tanks	30	*	1 Jul 2013
Heat exchangers:			
Air coolers and heaters	25	*	1 Jul 2013
Ammonia vapourisers	20	*	1 Jul 2013
Gas coolers and heaters	20	*	1 Jul 2013

MANUFACTURING
(11110 to 25990)

Asset	Life (Years)	Reviewed	Date Of Application
Superheaters	15	*	1 Jul 2013
Waste heat boilers	20	*	1 Jul 2013
Nitric acid storage assets:			
Scrubbers	20	*	1 Jul 2013
Tanks	25	*	1 Jul 2013
Support assets – see above in Ammonia manufacturing assets, support assets			
Chemical manufacturing plant (not listed elsewhere):			
General plant	13 1/3		1 Jan 2001
Organic peroxides explosion (cell block)	20		1 Jan 2001
Ethanol manufacturing assets:			
Cooking assets:			
Filters and strainers	15	*	1 Jul 2012
Flash tanks	20	*	1 Jul 2012
Jet cookers	10	*	1 Jul 2012
Liquefaction tanks (including cook tubes and slurry tanks)	20	*	1 Jul 2012
Meal mixers	15	*	1 Jul 2012
Distillation and purification assets:			
Distillation columns	25	*	1 Jul 2012
Molecular sieve adsorption systems (incorporating condensers, control systems, coolers, heaters, molecular sieves, pumps, tanks and vacuum equipment)	25	*	1 Jul 2012
Reboilers	20	*	1 Jul 2012
Side stream strippers	20	*	1 Jul 2012
Feedstock handling and storage assets:			
Grain assets:			
Cleaning assets (including magnetic separators, screeners and sieves)	20	*	1 Jul 2012
Conveyor belt weighers	15	*	1 Jul 2012
Conveyors (including belt, drag and screw conveyors, bucket and rake elevators and chutes)	15	*	1 Jul 2012
Hoppers (including weigh hoppers)	25	*	1 Jul 2012
Milling machines (including hammer and roller mills)	20	*	1 Jul 2012
Silo aerators	15	*	1 Jul 2012
Silos	30	*	1 Jul 2012
Starch tanks	25	*	1 Jul 2012
Molasses assets:			
Dam covers	12	*	1 Jul 2012
Dam liners	20	*	1 Jul 2012
Dams	40	*	1 Jul 2012
Pipelines (incorporating fittings and valves)	25	*	1 Jul 2012
Receival station control systems	10	*	1 Jul 2012
Receival troughs (incorporating protective cladding, rails and roofing)	40	*	1 Jul 2012
Tanks	30	*	1 Jul 2012
Fermentation assets:			
Chillers	20	*	1 Jul 2012
Fermentation tanks	30	*	1 Jul 2012
Scrubbers	20	*	1 Jul 2012
Yeast propagation vessels	20	*	1 Jul 2012

MANUFACTURING
(11110 to 25990)

Asset	Life (Years)	Reviewed	Date Of Application
Yeast recovery assets (molasses feedstock):			
Centrifugal separators	20	*	1 Jul 2012
Filtering assets (including feed tanks, filtering vessels and hydrocyclone systems)	20	*	1 Jul 2012
Hoppers, mixing tanks and storage tanks	25	*	1 Jul 2012
Stillage assets:			
Distillers grain assets:			
Centrifugal decanters	15	*	1 Jul 2012
Conveyors	15	*	1 Jul 2012
Cooling assets for dried distillers grain (including blowers and fans, chillers, ducting and other cooling assets)	20	*	1 Jul 2012
Evaporators	25	*	1 Jul 2012
Mixers	15	*	1 Jul 2012
Rotary drum dryers	20	*	1 Jul 2012
Stillage and syrup tanks	25	*	1 Jul 2012
Dunder and stillage assets (molasses feedstock):			
Conveyors and hoppers for fertiliser additives	15	*	1 Jul 2012
Dam covers	12	*	1 Jul 2012
Dams	40	*	1 Jul 2012
Pipelines (incorporating fittings and valves)	25	*	1 Jul 2012
Tanks (including fertiliser additive mixing and buffer tanks)	20	*	1 Jul 2012
Support and other assets:			
Additive dosing systems (including pipes, pumps and tanks):			
Plastic	5	*	1 Jul 2012
Other	20	*	1 Jul 2012
Air compression assets:			
Air compressors	15	*	1 Jul 2012
Air drying and filtering systems	12	*	1 Jul 2012
Air receivers	20	*	1 Jul 2012
Blowers and fans	20	*	1 Jul 2012
Boilers	20	*	1 Jul 2012
Control system assets:			
Control cabinets and panels, programmable logic controllers (PLCs), switchgear and variable speed drives (VSDs)	10	*	1 Jul 2012
System monitoring assets (including instrumentation and sensors and transmitters for level, pressure, speed and temperature measurement)	10	*	1 Jul 2012
Cooling towers	20	*	1 Jul 2012
Dust collection systems (including baghouses, cyclones and other dust collection assets)	20	*	1 Jul 2012
Heat exchangers (excluding column reboilers)	15	*	1 Jul 2012
Laboratory assets:			
Analysers	10	*	1 Jul 2012
Other laboratory equipment (including autoclaves, centrifuges, drying ovens, fume cupboards and UV sterilisers)	10	*	1 Jul 2012
Piping assets:			
Flow meters	10	*	1 Jul 2012

MANUFACTURING
(11110 to 25990)

Asset	Life (Years)	Reviewed	Date Of Application
Pipes	25	*	1 Jul 2012
Valves	10	*	1 Jul 2012
Pumps	15	*	1 Jul 2012
Safety assets:			
Fire control and alarm assets – see Table B			
Gas detectors:			
Fixed	10	*	1 Jul 2012
Portable	4	*	1 Jul 2012
Tanker filling assets:			
Automated dispensing systems	10	*	1 Jul 2012
Automatic tank gauges	10	*	1 Jul 2012
Fire protection systems (incorporating auxiliary monitors, fire and UV detectors, fire indicator panels, fire retardant lines and foam storage tanks)	15	*	1 Jul 2012
Hoses	2	*	1 Jul 2012
Loading and unloading arms (incorporating balance mechanisms, couplers, drop hoses and swivels)	10	*	1 Jul 2012
Meters and metering systems	7	*	1 Jul 2012
Overfill protection systems	10	*	1 Jul 2012
Tanks:			
Chemical tanks (including clean–in-place (CIP) tanks):			
Plastic	15	*	1 Jul 2012
Other	20	*	1 Jul 2012
Ethanol and petroleum tanks:			
Stainless steel	30	*	1 Jul 2012
Other	25	*	1 Jul 2012
Water tanks (including condensate collection tanks)	25	*	1 Jul 2012
Vapour condensers	20	*	1 Jul 2012
Waste water treatment assets:			
Aerators	20	*	1 Jul 2012
Biogas system assets (excluding effluent pond covers)	25	*	1 Jul 2012
Digester/aeration tanks	25	*	1 Jul 2012
Effluent channels and ponds	40	*	1 Jul 2012
Pond covers	12	*	1 Jul 2012
Pond liners	20	*	1 Jul 2012
Water filtration assets (including ion exchange assets and reverse osmosis assets)	15	*	1 Jul 2012
Weighbridges	20	*	1 Jul 2012
Fertiliser manufacturing plant (excluding ammonia manufacturing assets and ammonium nitrate manufacturing assets listed in Table A Basic chemical and chemical product manufacturing (18120, 18130 and 18310))	20		1 Jan 2001
Salt manufacturing and refining plant	10		1 Jan 2001
Sulphuric acid plant:			
Acid chambers (irrespective of raw material used)	20		1 Jan 2001
Plant:			
Where pyrites used in manufacture of the acid	10		1 Jan 2001
Where natural sulphur (brimstone) so used	13 1/3		1 Jan 2001

MANUFACTURING
(11110 to 25990)

Asset	Life (Years)	Reviewed	Date Of Application
Human pharmaceutical and medicinal product manufacturing (18410)			
Laboratory assets:			
Bench top autoclaves	5	*	1 Jan 2004
Incubators	6	*	1 Jan 2004
Laboratory analysers (including coagulators, carbon analysers, colour readers, gas chromatographs, high performance liquid chromatographs (HPLCs), and spectrophotometers)	5	*	1 Jan 2004
Particle sizers	5	*	1 Jan 2004
Packaging assets:			
Accumulators	10	*	1 Jan 2004
Batch, barcode, label, and volume readers	10	*	1 Jan 2004
Blister pack packaging machines	10	*	1 Jan 2004
Blow-fill-seal (BFS) machines	12	*	1 Jan 2004
Bottle and vial inverters and blowers	10	*	1 Jan 2004
Bottle and vial unscramblers	10	*	1 Jan 2004
Bundlers and bundle packing machines	10	*	1 Jan 2004
Cappers and sealers (including tamper proof sealers)	10	*	1 Jan 2004
Cartoners	10	*	1 Jan 2004
Check weighers	10	*	1 Jan 2004
Cream, liquid and powder filling and sealing machines (including bag, bottle, syringe and tube fillers and sealers)	12	*	1 Jan 2004
Desiccant and cotton wool depositors/inserters	10	*	1 Jan 2004
Dropper and leaflet inserters	10	*	1 Jan 2004
Flaming stations	10	*	1 Jan 2004
Flow wrappers and shrink wrappers	10	*	1 Jan 2004
Ink jet batch label printers	7	*	1 Jan 2004
Labelling machines	10	*	1 Jan 2004
Palletisers	10	*	1 Jan 2004
Pinhole inspectors	10	*	1 Jan 2004
Robotic pick and place packaging machines	10	*	1 Jan 2004
Sleevers	10	*	1 Jan 2004
Tablet/capsule fillers, feeders and counters	10	*	1 Jan 2004
Production assets:			
Autoclaves (for terminal sterilisation)	10	*	1 Jan 2004
Drying ovens	10	*	1 Jan 2004
Encapsulators	10	*	1 Jan 2004
Fluid bed dryers	12	*	1 Jan 2004
Granulators and mixer/granulators	12	*	1 Jan 2004
Homogenisers	7	*	1 Jan 2004
Intermediate bulk containers, bins and vessels (including instruments, pipes, pumps and valves) used to hold and transfer formulations during various stages of production	10	*	1 Jan 2004
Metal detectors	10	*	1 Jan 2004
Mixers and blenders (including cream, liquid, powder, and syrup mixers and blenders)	10	*	1 Jan 2004
Sizing mills	10	*	1 Jan 2004
Tablet and capsule coating machines, coating drums and coating pans	12	*	1 Jan 2004
Tablet dedusters	10	*	1 Jan 2004

MANUFACTURING
(11110 to 25990)

Asset	Life (Years)	Reviewed	Date Of Application
Tablet presses	10	*	1 Jan 2004
Vibrating sieves	10	*	1 Jan 2004
Raw material storage and dispensing assets:			
Demountable strong rooms	20	*	1 Jan 2004
Dispensing booths and associated air filtration systems	10	*	1 Jan 2004
Laminar flow benches and biohazard cabinets	8	*	1 Jan 2004
Safes	20	*	1 Jan 2004
Weighing scales	10	*	1 Jan 2004
Scientific medical and pharmaceutical research assets – see Table A Scientific research services (69100)			
Services:			
Air filtration systems	10	*	1 Jan 2004
Water purification plant	10	*	1 Jan 2004
Cleaning compound and toiletry preparation manufacturing (18510 to 18520)			
Boot and shoe polish manufacturing plant	13 1/3		1 Jan 2001
Other basic chemical product manufacturing (18910 to 18990)			
Eucalyptus oil plant:			
Stills (coolers)	40		1 Jan 2001
Tanks	40		1 Jan 2001
Explosives manufacturing and chemical plant (excluding ammonia manufacturing assets and ammonium nitrate manufacturing assets listed in Table A Basic chemical and chemical product manufacturing (18120, 18130 and 18310))	13 1/3		1 Jan 2001
Polymer film and sheet packaging material manufacturing (19110)			
Extrusion assets:			
Extruder dies	15	*	1 Jul 2014
Extruders and co-extruders (incorporating barrels, screws, towers and treatment units, but excluding dies)	20	*	1 Jul 2014
Heat exchangers	15	*	1 Jul 2014
Laminating machines	20	*	1 Jul 2014
Packaging assets:			
Labelling machines	7	*	1 Jul 2014
Palletisers	12	*	1 Jul 2014
Wrapping machines (including shrink and stretch wrappers)	10	*	1 Jul 2014
Pouch and bag making machines	10	*	1 Jul 2014
Printing assets – see Table A Printing (16110)			
Racking machines	25	*	1 Jul 2014
Recycling machines	10	*	1 Jul 2014
Resin preparation assets (including hoppers mixers/blenders and weigh batchers)	15	*	1 Jul 2014
Slitting machines and perforation units	15	*	1 Jul 2014
Support assets:			
Air compressors and receivers	15	*	1 Jul 2014
Boilers	20	*	1 Jul 2014
Control system assets (including control cabinets and panels, programmable logic controllers (PLCs), switchgear and variable speed drives (VSDs))	10	*	1 Jul 2014
Jib cranes	15	*	1 Jul 2014

MANUFACTURING
(11110 to 25990)

Asset	Life (Years)	Reviewed	Date Of Application
Laboratory assets:			
Generally	15	*	1 Jul 2014
Laboratory analysers	10	*	1 Jul 2014
Silos	25	*	1 Jul 2014
Vacuum transfer system assets (incorporating blowers, ductwork, fans and pumps)	10	*	1 Jul 2014
Rigid and semi-rigid polymer product manufacturing (19120)			
Agglomerators, shredders, granulators and grinders	10	*	1 Jul 2016
Air compressor systems (incorporating compressor, drier and receiver) – see Table B Air compression assets generally (including air compressors, air dryers and air receivers)			
Annealing ovens	25	*	1 Jul 2016
Bagging and de-bagging machines	15	*	1 Jul 2016
Bandsaws	10	*	1 Jul 2016
Bending machines	10	*	1 Jul 2016
Bins	10	*	1 Jul 2016
Blow moulding machines	13	*	1 Jul 2016
Boilers – see Table B Boilers			
Chilled water plant (incorporating chiller, pipes, pumps etc)	12	*	1 Jul 2016
Control system assets – see Table B Control systems and control system assets (including control cabinets and panels, instruments, programmable logic controllers (PLCs), sensors, switchgear telemetry and variable speed drives (VSDs))			
Conveyor systems (including framework)	15	*	1 Jul 2016
Cooling towers	15	*	1 Jul 2016
Die carts	15	*	1 Jul 2016
Driers (pellet or resin)	10	*	1 Jul 2016
Drop testers and strength testers	16	*	1 Jul 2016
Extruder dies:			
Foamed polyethylene (PE) or extruded polystyrene extruder dies	10	*	1 Jul 2016
Generally	12	*	1 Jul 2016
Extruders:			
Foamed polyethylene (PE) or extruded polystyrene extruders	10	*	1 Jul 2016
Generally	13	*	1 Jul 2016
Flange makers (pipes) and belling machines	10	*	1 Jul 2016
Forklifts – see Table B Forklifts			
Granule transfer assets (including feeders, loaders, and vacuum transfer systems)	10	*	1 Jul 2016
Heat exchangers	15	*	1 Jul 2016
Hydraulic power packs	12	*	1 Jul 2016
Hydraulic presses	10	*	1 Jul 2016
Injection moulding machines (incorporating hydraulic power packs but excluding moulds):			
Expanded polystyrene and expanded polypropylene moulding machines	10	*	1 Jul 2016
Generally	13	*	1 Jul 2016
Laboratory assets:			
Generally	15	*	1 Jul 2016
Laboratory analysers	10	*	1 Jul 2016
Lifting platforms (including scissor lifts)	15	*	1 Jul 2016

MANUFACTURING
(11110 to 25990)

Asset	Life (Years)	Reviewed	Date Of Application
Moulds:			
Expanded polystyrene and expanded polypropylene moulds	4	*	1 Jul 2016
Generally	8	*	1 Jul 2016
Mould heaters, die heaters and coolers	10	*	1 Jul 2016
Offset rollers, hot stamping machines, ink jet coders and printers and indent printers	5	*	1 Jul 2016
Overhead gantry cranes – see Table B Cranes (gantry and overhead)			
Palletisers – see Table B Packaging assets, palletisers and depalletisers			
Pipe cutters	10	*	1 Jul 2016
Pipe winders	12	*	1 Jul 2016
Pits	15	*	1 Jul 2016
Plastic welders	9	*	1 Jul 2016
Polystyrene pre-expanders	10	*	1 Jul 2016
Pullers/haul-offs/haul-throughs/Caterpillar pullers	10	*	1 Jul 2016
Pumps (including hydraulic, water and vacuum)	8	*	1 Jul 2016
Punch machines	5	*	1 Jul 2016
Racking	20	*	1 Jul 2016
Rainwater collection systems (incorporating pipes, tanks, and pumps)	15	*	1 Jul 2016
Resin preparation assets (including hoppers, mixers/blenders, and batch weighing)	15	*	1 Jul 2016
Robot control pendants	5	*	1 Jul 2016
Robots – see Table B Robots (industrial)			
Safety fencing	15	*	1 Jul 2016
Screen changers	12	*	1 Jul 2016
Silos:			
Bag silos for expanded polystyrene beads	10	*	1 Jul 2016
Generally – see Table B Silos			
Splitting/skiving machines	9	*	1 Jul 2016
Transformers	20	*	1 Jul 2016
Trimming machines	12	*	1 Jul 2016
Water baths/tanks, spray tanks, vacuum cooling	15	*	1 Jul 2016
Water tanks	15	*	1 Jul 2016
Polymer product and rubber product manufacturing (19130 to 19200)			
Gelatine and glue manufacturing plant	13 1/3		1 Jan 2001
Rubber manufacturers' plant:			
Moulds	5		1 Jan 2001
Process plant	13 1/3		1 Jan 2001
Paint and coatings manufacturing (19160)			
Ink factory plant	20		1 Jan 2001
Paint and coatings manufacturing assets:			
Air compressors	10	*	1 Jul 2013
Bead mills	20	*	1 Jul 2013
Bulk storage tanks	25	*	1 Jul 2013
Control system assets	10	*	1 Jul 2013
Disperser and mixer motors	15	*	1 Jul 2013
Dispersers	20	*	1 Jul 2013
Dust collectors and fume extracting assets (including bag dust collectors, blowers, cyclones and fans)	20	*	1 Jul 2013

MANUFACTURING
(11110 to 25990)

Asset	Life (Years)	Reviewed	Date Of Application
Filling and packing assets:			
Conveyors	15	*	1 Jul 2013
Denesters	10	*	1 Jul 2013
Filling machines	15	*	1 Jul 2013
Filtration assets	15	*	1 Jul 2013
Labellers (including laser coders and label applicators)	7	*	1 Jul 2013
Printers	7	*	1 Jul 2013
Robotic palletisers	10	*	1 Jul 2013
Wrappers	10	*	1 Jul 2013
Gantry cranes	25	*	1 Jul 2013
Hoists	10	*	1 Jul 2013
Mixers	20	*	1 Jul 2013
Paint tinting and colour blending machines (manual and automatic)	7	*	1 Jul 2014
Piping assets:			
Manifolds	20	*	1 Jul 2013
Meters	10	*	1 Jul 2013
Piping	25	*	1 Jul 2013
Pumps	10	*	1 Jul 2013
Racking:			
External	15	*	1 Jul 2013
Internal	20	*	1 Jul 2013
Scales	10	*	1 Jul 2013
Spray booths	15	*	1 Jul 2013
Testing assets:			
Air conditioning assets (including room units and split systems)	8	*	1 Jul 2013
Gloss meters	10	*	1 Jul 2013
Ovens	15	*	1 Jul 2013
Spectrometers	10	*	1 Jul 2013
Viscometers	10	*	1 Jul 2013
Vacuum lifters	10	*	1 Jul 2013
Non-metallic mineral product manufacturing (20100 to 20900)			
Monumental masons' plant	13 1/3		1 Jan 2001
Slate works plant	20		1 Jan 2001
Glass and glass product manufacturing (20100)			
Container glass and flat (float) glass manufacturing assets:			
Ancillary assets:			
Blowers and fans	25	*	1 Jul 2008
Conveyors generally (including bottle conveyors, bucket elevators, pallet transport conveyors and pneumatic conveyors)	25	*	1 Jul 2008
Ducting, pipes and piping	40	*	1 Jul 2008
Steelwork structures (including gantries, platforms and walkways)	40	*	1 Jul 2008
Vacuum pumps:			
Liquid ring pumps	10	*	1 Jul 2008
Oil sealed pumps	20	*	1 Jul 2008
Annealing lehrs	25	*	1 Jul 2008

MANUFACTURING
(11110 to 25990)

Asset	Life (Years)	Reviewed	Date Of Application
Batch house assets:			
Cullet handling and return assets:			
Cullet crushers	25	*	1 Jul 2008
Scraping conveyor systems:			
Container glass	12	*	1 Jul 2008
Flat glass	25	*	1 Jul 2008
Other assets (including batch conveyors, batch mixers, bins, hoppers and weigh hoppers)	25	*	1 Jul 2008
Silos	40	*	1 Jul 2008
Coating assets (cold and hot end)	12	*	1 Jul 2008
Control systems (excluding personal computers)	10	*	1 Jul 2008
Flat glass ribbon cutting assets (including cross cutters, longitudinal cutters and snap rolls)	25	*	1 Jul 2008
Float baths	25	*	1 Jul 2008
Forehearths	12	*	1 Jul 2008
Forming machines (incorporating shearing and distribution systems)	12	*	1 Jul 2008
Glass furnace assets:			
Batch chargers	12	*	1 Jul 2008
Exhaust stacks:			
Brick lined	40	*	1 Jul 2008
Steel	12	*	1 Jul 2008
Furnace support assets (including bubbler systems and electro boost systems)	12	*	1 Jul 2008
Furnace tanks	12	*	1 Jul 2008
Regenerators and recuperators	12	*	1 Jul 2008
Glass product handling and packaging assets (including case packers, flat glass lifters and stackers, palletisers, strapping machines, shrink wrappers, stretch wrappers and trolley shuttle cars)	12	*	1 Jul 2008
Inspection assets	10	*	1 Jul 2008
Lehr stackers	12	*	1 Jul 2008
Moulds	2	*	1 Jul 2008
Glass product manufacturing assets:			
Automotive glass product manufacturing assets:			
CNC controlled edgers and grinders	15	*	1 Jul 2009
CNC controlled scorers and cutters	15	*	1 Jul 2009
Inspection assets:			
Automotive laminated glass product inspection assets (including automated distortion checking assets and conveyors)	15	*	1 Jul 2009
Automotive toughened glass product inspection assets (including thermal imaging testing assets)	10	*	1 Jul 2009
Post-processing assets used in automotive laminated glass production and toughened glass production processes:			
Automated back window soldering units	10	*	1 Jul 2009
Others (including conveyor handling assets, encapsulation presses, hot melt adhesive applicators, robots and tooling)	15	*	1 Jul 2009
CNC machines	7	*	1 Jul 2009
Control systems (excluding personal computers)	10	*	1 Jul 2009

MANUFACTURING
(11110 to 25990)

Asset	Life (Years)	Reviewed	Date Of Application
Cutting tables:			
Automated cutting and break-out tables	10	*	1 Jul 2009
Laminated glass cutting tables	10	*	1 Jul 2009
Manual cutting tables (including air float tables)	15	*	1 Jul 2009
Digital printing assets:			
Digital printers	5	*	1 Jul 2009
Dryers	$12^{1}/_{2}$	*	1 Jul 2009
Double glazing assets (including butyl coating machines, conveyors, presses, sealing machines and spacer robots)	15	*	1 Jul 2009
Drilling and/or milling machines (including horizontal and vertical drilling machines)	10	*	1 Jul 2009
Edgers:			
Arrissing machines	8	*	1 Jul 2009
Horizontal double edgers	10	*	1 Jul 2009
Straight line edgers and bevellers	7	*	1 Jul 2009
Glass handling and storage assets:			
Automated loaders and unloaders (used with automated cutting tables, laminating lines, toughening lines etc)	10	*	1 Jul 2009
Bulk glass handling assets:			
Straddle carriers	10	*	1 Jul 2009
Vertical glass handlers (sideloaders, tuning forks)	17	*	1 Jul 2009
Cranes (gantry and overhead)	25	*	1 Jul 2014
Racks (including A-frame racks, hydraulic concertina racks and freefall racks)	20	*	1 Jul 2009
Steel grabs	12	*	1 Jul 2009
Trolleys	7	*	1 Jul 2009
Vacuum lifters and scissor grabs	8	*	1 Jul 2009
Vertical masts and other elevating work platforms – see Table A Rental and hiring services (except real estate) (66110 to 66400), Elevating work platforms (EWPs)			
Glass laminating assets (including assembly clean room assets, autoclaves, heaters, laminating lehr furnaces, ovens, pre-presses, presses and vacuum bag furnaces)	15	*	1 Jul 2009
Glass toughening (tempering) assets:			
Furnaces and quenches used in toughening, bending/toughening and bending/slumping	20	*	1 Jul 2009
Heat soaking ovens	20	*	1 Jul 2009
Glass washing machines	10	*	1 Jul 2009
Plastic film applicators (spotstick machines)	8	*	1 Jul 2009
Screen printing assets – see Table A Printing (16110)			
Support assets:			
Air compressors	20	*	1 Jul 2014
Boilers	20	*	1 Jul 2014
Waterjet cutting machines	10	*	1 Jul 2009
Note: Determinations for assets used in mining clay are shown under the Construction material mining (09110 to 09190) sub-category			

MANUFACTURING
(11110 to 25990)

Asset	Life (Years)	Reviewed	Date Of Application
Ceramic product manufacturing (20210 to 20290)			
Clay brick and paver manufacturing assets:			
Box feeders	20	*	1 Jul 2011
Control systems	10	*	1 Jul 2011
Conveyors	20	*	1 Jul 2011
Cutters	15	*	1 Jul 2011
De-hackers (excluding robots)	20	*	1 Jul 2011
Dryers	25	*	1 Jul 2011
Extruders	15	*	1 Jul 2011
Kiln/dryer car cable hauler system assets (incorporating cable, gearbox, pulling wheels and motors)	10	*	1 Jul 2011
Kiln/dryer/transfer car track work	12	*	1 Jul 2011
Kiln/dryer cars	10	*	1 Jul 2011
Kilns	20	*	1 Jul 2011
Robots	10	*	1 Jul 2011
Setting assets (excluding robots)	20	*	1 Jul 2011
Transfer cars	15	*	1 Jul 2011
Wrapping and strapping machines	10	*	1 Jul 2011
Pottery plant	20		1 Jan 2001
Rapid fire shuttle kilns (used in the manufacture of ceramic tiles)	$13^1/_3$		1 Jan 2001
Cement manufacturing (20310)			
Cooling assets:			
Air to air coolers	20	*	1 Jul 2011
Evaporation coolers:			
Cement coolers	20	*	1 Jul 2011
Conditioning towers (incorporating spray systems)	20	*	1 Jul 2011
Grate coolers (incorporating grate conveyor and quenching fans)	25	*	1 Jul 2011
Drying assets:			
Fluid bed dryers	20	*	1 Jul 2011
Hot gas generators	15	*	1 Jul 2011
Rotary dryers	20	*	1 Jul 2011
Electrical installation assets (including cabling):			
Power generators	15	*	1 Jul 2011
Switchboards	20	*	1 Jul 2011
Transformers	20	*	1 Jul 2011
Emissions control assets:			
Dedusting fans	20	*	1 Jul 2011
Particulate filtering assets (excluding filter units incorporated in kiln bypass systems):			
Bagfilter systems (incorporating housing and filters)	20	*	1 Jul 2011
Electrostatic precipitators	20	*	1 Jul 2011
Stacks (excluding stacks incorporated in kiln bypass systems)	25	*	1 Jul 2011
Milling assets (used for raw material and cement milling including gearbox and drives):			
Ball mills (including dryer systems and separators/classifiers where incorporated in the mill)	25	*	1 Jul 2011
Hammer mills (including dryer systems and separators/classifiers where incorporated in the mill)	20	*	1 Jul 2011

MANUFACTURING
(11110 to 25990)

Asset	Life (Years)	Reviewed	Date Of Application
Roller mills (vertical) (including dryer systems and separators/classifiers where incorporated in the mill)	25	*	1 Jul 2011
Roller presses	20	*	1 Jul 2011
Separators/classifiers (including single and multi cyclones)	15	*	1 Jul 2011
Preheat and clinker production assets:			
Cyclone preheaters (incorporating tower structure, lifts, cyclones, precalciners, ducts, inlet chambers and meal pipes)	20	*	1 Jul 2011
Kilns (incorporating kiln shell, inlet chamber, roller stations, thrust unit, kiln hood, burner and drive)	25	*	1 Jul 2011
Kiln bypass systems (incorporating bypass ducts, heat exchangers, spray towers, filter units, ID fans and stacks)	10	*	1 Jul 2011
Kiln guns	5	*	1 Jul 2011
Kiln shell scanners	10	*	1 Jul 2011
Quarrying assets:			
Construction material mining assets – see Table A Construction material mining (09110 to 09190)			
Scrapers	7	*	1 Jul 2011
Storage, handling and packing assets:			
Conveyor systems (mechanical and pneumatic types incorporating structures, moving media, gearboxes, motors, fans, feeders, flowgates, feed valves and weighers):			
Mechanical:			
Belt, screw, drag chain, apron/pan conveyors	15	*	1 Jul 2011
Bucket elevators	20	*	1 Jul 2011
Pneumatic:			
Air lift elevators	15	*	1 Jul 2011
Air slides	15	*	1 Jul 2011
Hoppers, bins and tanks	20	*	1 Jul 2011
Packaging assets:			
Packing/bagging machines	15	*	1 Jul 2011
Palletisers	15	*	1 Jul 2011
Wrappers	10	*	1 Jul 2011
Pressure vessels (other than air/shock blast units)	25	*	1 Jul 2011
Silos:			
Concrete, generally	50	*	1 Jan 2004
Concrete (used for gypsum or wetslag, or at port facilities)	40	*	1 Jan 2004
Steel, generally	30	*	1 Jan 2004
Steel (used for gypsum or wet slag, or at port facilities)	20	*	1 Jan 2004
Stockpile assets:			
Reclaim tunnels	25	*	1 Jul 2011
Reclaimers	25	*	1 Jul 2011
Stackers	25	*	1 Jul 2011
Unloading/loading assets:			
Bulk loading devices (including loading spouts and telescopic chutes)	10	*	1 Jul 2011
Railcar and truck unloaders (including pump unloading and vacuum pressure unloading systems)	20	*	1 Jul 2011
Ship unloading/loading assets – see Table A Water transport and support services (48100 to 48200 and 52110 to 52190)			
Weighbridges	20	*	1 Jul 2011

MANUFACTURING
(11110 to 25990)

Asset	Life (Years)	Reviewed	Date Of Application
Support assets:			
Air compression assets:			
Packaged air compressors (compressor, drier and receiver in one integrated unit)	10	*	1 Jul 2011
Other air compressor systems	15	*	1 Jul 2011
Air/shock blast units	8	*	1 Jul 2011
Control systems (process and safety control systems incorporating PLCs, cabling, monitors, sensors and switchgear, but excluding software)	10	*	1 Jul 2011
Cranes	20	*	1 Jul 2011
Hoists	20	*	1 Jul 2011
ID (induced draught) fans	15	*	1 Jul 2011
Pumps	15	*	1 Jul 2011
Testing equipment:			
Generally (including spectrometers, gas chromatographs, titrators, calorimeters, laser granulometers, photometers, moisture analysers, drying ovens)	8	*	1 Jul 2011
Raw material analysers	5	*	1 Jul 2011
XRF/XRD analysers	5	*	1 Jul 2011
Plaster product manufacturing (20320)			
Plasterboard and cornice manufacturing assets:			
General:			
Bins	20	*	1 Jul 2011
Control systems	10	*	1 Jul 2011
Conveyors (including belt conveyors, belt stacker conveyors, bucket elevators and screw conveyors)	20	*	1 Jul 2011
Dust collection assets (including bag dust collectors, blowers, cyclones and fans)	20	*	1 Jul 2011
Dust detectors	5	*	1 Jul 2011
Fans/blowers (excluding blowers used with hot pits)	20	*	1 Jul 2011
Feeders	15	*	1 Jul 2011
Flow meters	10	*	1 Jul 2011
Hoppers	20	*	1 Jul 2011
Lump breakers	20	*	1 Jul 2011
Pumps	10	*	1 Jul 2011
Rotary valves	15	*	1 Jul 2011
Silos (steel)	20	*	1 Jul 2011
Tanks	20	*	1 Jul 2011
Plaster milling assets:			
Bulk bag handling assets	20	*	1 Jul 2011
Calciners	20	*	1 Jul 2011
Grinding/hammer mills	20	*	1 Jul 2011
Heat generators	15	*	1 Jul 2011
Hot pits:			
Blowers	12	*	1 Jul 2011
Vessels	20	*	1 Jul 2011
Stucco coolers	20	*	1 Jul 2011
Plasterboard/cornice plant assets:			
Chillers (volumetric air-cooled)	15	*	1 Jul 2011

MANUFACTURING
(11110 to 25990)

Asset	Life (Years)	Reviewed	Date Of Application
Dry end handling assets (including bookers, cascades, conveyors and stackers)	20	*	1 Jul 2011
Dryers	25	*	1 Jul 2011
Dunnage assets used to make dunnage	25	*	1 Jul 2011
Forming line assets (including belt conveyors and roller conveyors)	20	*	1 Jul 2011
Forming plates	10	*	1 Jul 2011
Forming station assets (excluding forming plates and pin mixers)	20	*	1 Jul 2011
Hydropulpers	25	*	1 Jul 2011
Knives (used for plasterboard or cornice)	25	*	1 Jul 2011
Paper and tape assets (including creasers, magazines, splicing assets, tape rollers, tension stations and unwinders)	20	*	1 Jul 2011
Pin mixers	13	*	1 Jul 2011
Printers	5	*	1 Jul 2011
Start-up pullers (used for cornice)	20	*	1 Jul 2011
Wet-end-transfer assets (including conveyors, dryer in-feeds, turners)	20	*	1 Jul 2011
Ready-mixed concrete manufacturing (20330)			
Air compressors	10	*	1 Jul 2014
Air dryers	10	*	1 Jul 2014
Bins (including weigh bins, but excluding concrete bins)	15	*	1 Jul 2014
CCTV systems	5	*	1 Jul 2014
Cement tankers (incorporating tank and trailer) – see Table B Motor vehicles and trailers, trailers having a gross vehicle mass greater than 4.5 tonnes			
Chillers	15	*	1 Jul 2014
Control systems	10	*	1 Jul 2014
Conveyors	20	*	1 Jul 2014
Dust extraction systems	15	*	1 Jul 2014
Fuel storage assets:			
Card reading systems	6	*	1 Jul 2014
Dispensers (incorporating electronic circuitry, hoses, LCD displays, meters and nozzles)	10	*	1 Jul 2014
Pumps	10	*	1 Jul 2014
Tanks	25	*	1 Jul 2014
Hoppers (including weigh hoppers)	15	*	1 Jul 2014
Mixers used in wet ready-mixed plants	15	*	1 Jul 2014
Mobile concrete batching plants (incorporating bins, conveyors, tanks, hoppers and trailers, but excluding demountable plant)	10	*	1 Jul 2014
Silos	30	*	1 Jul 2014
Slump stands	10	*	1 Jul 2014
Testing assets:			
Concrete testers	10	*	1 Jul 2014
Ovens	8	*	1 Jul 2014
Truck transit mixers:			
Mixers (incorporating barrel, chutes, frame and hydraulic pumps)	5	*	1 Jul 2014
Trucks – see Table B Motor vehicles and trailers			
Volumetric concrete batching trucks:			
Trucks – see Table B Motor vehicles and trailers			

MANUFACTURING
(11110 to 25990)

Asset	Life (Years)	Reviewed	Date Of Application
Volumetric concrete batching units (incorporating bins, hoppers, mixing augurs and water tanks)	10	*	1 Jul 2014
Waste water treatment assets:			
Catchment and settlement ponds	20	*	1 Jul 2014
Concrete slurry pumps	3	*	1 Jul 2014
Polyethylene (PE) water tanks	8	*	1 Jul 2014
Water pumps	5	*	1 Jul 2014
Concrete product manufacturing (20340)			
Concrete block, brick and paver manufacturing assets:			
Batching and mixing assets:			
Bins (excluding concrete bins)	15	*	1 Jul 2011
Colour dosing assets	12	*	1 Jul 2011
Colour tanks (incorporating stirrers)	15	*	1 Jul 2011
Hoppers	15	*	1 Jul 2011
Mixers	15	*	1 Jul 2011
Block/brick/paver making assets:			
Block/brick/paver making machines	15	*	1 Jul 2011
Moulds	5	*	1 Jul 2011
Splitters	10	*	1 Jul 2011
Curing assets:			
Boilers (including steam generators)	20	*	1 Jul 2011
Drying chambers	25	*	1 Jul 2011
Elevators/lowerators (including loaders/unloaders)	15	*	1 Jul 2011
Racks (excluding racks fixed to drying chambers)	5	*	1 Jul 2011
Transfer car (incorporating finger cars) track works	15	*	1 Jul 2011
Transfer cars (incorporating finger cars)	15	*	1 Jul 2011
General assets:			
Control systems	10	*	1 Jul 2011
Conveyors	15	*	1 Jul 2011
Plates	10	*	1 Jul 2011
Palletising and packaging assets:			
Cubing assets (including cubers, doublers and squeezers)	15	*	1 Jul 2011
Robots	10	*	1 Jul 2011
Wrapping and strapping machines	10	*	1 Jul 2011
Concrete roof tile manufacturing assets:			
Air compressors (rotary screw)	10	*	1 Jul 2012
Applicator batching assets (including hoppers, mixers and tanks, but excluding batching assets for anti-scuff hot glue/max applicators and oil applicators)	15	*	1 Jul 2012
Applicators:			
Anti-scuff hot glue/wax	10	*	1 Jul 2012
General (including colour, sealer and sheen)	20	*	1 Jul 2012
Oil (excluding oil tanks)	10	*	1 Jul 2012
Bins	15	*	1 Jul 2012
Control systems	10	*	1 Jul 2012
Conveyors	20	*	1 Jul 2012
Curing assets:			
Boilers	20	*	1 Jul 2012

MANUFACTURING
(11110 to 25990)

Asset	Life (Years)	Reviewed	Date Of Application
Curing bays:			
Concrete	25	*	1 Jul 2012
Foam sandwich (incorporating insulated panel walls, roof and doors)	10	*	1 Jul 2012
Rackers/deracker (including loaders/unloaders)	20	*	1 Jul 2012
Racks (used in curing bays)	10	*	1 Jul 2012
Depalleters	20	*	1 Jul 2012
Extruders	15	*	1 Jul 2012
Hoppers	15	*	1 Jul 2012
Mixers	15	*	1 Jul 2012
Oil tanks	30	*	1 Jul 2012
Packaging assets:			
General (including collectors, compilers and cranes)	20	*	1 Jul 2012
Robots	10	*	1 Jul 2012
Shrink wrappers	10	*	1 Jul 2012
Strapping assets	10	*	1 Jul 2012
Wrapping assets	10	*	1 Jul 2012
Plates:			
General	7	*	1 Jul 2012
Trim (including plates used for barge and ridge tiles)	5	*	1 Jul 2012
Fibre cement building boards manufacturing assets:			
Curing assets:			
Autoclaves (incorporating rails)	30	*	1 Jul 2012
Boilers	20	*	1 Jul 2012
Chargers (including traversers)	15	*	1 Jul 2012
Trackwork	20	*	1 Jul 2012
Trolley chain hauling systems (incorporating chains, gearboxes, motors and tappets)	15	*	1 Jul 2012
Trolley transfer platforms (including transversals)	20	*	1 Jul 2012
Trolleys (including trucks) used inside and outside autoclaves	10	*	1 Jul 2012
Trolleys (including trucks) used only outside autoclaves	20	*	1 Jul 2012
Tunnels (including steamers)	25	*	1 Jul 2012
Finishing line and packaging assets:			
Applicators (including coating and sealing applicators)	7	*	1 Jul 2012
Drying tunnels (including heating ovens)	10	*	1 Jul 2012
Machining assets (including sanding and trimming assets)	15	*	1 Jul 2012
Printers	5	*	1 Jul 2012
Robots	10	*	1 Jul 2012
General assets:			
Air compressors (rotary screw)	10	*	1 Jul 2012
Control systems	10	*	1 Jul 2012
Conveyors	20	*	1 Jul 2012
Dust collection assets	20	*	1 Jul 2012
Oil tanks	30	*	1 Jul 2012
Stackers/unstackers (including pilers/unpilers)	15	*	1 Jul 2012
Steel templates	7	*	1 Jul 2012
Manufacturing, trimming and pressing assets:			
Cranes (used to load boards into presses and unload boards from presses)	15	*	1 Jul 2012

MANUFACTURING
(11110 to 25990)

Asset	Life (Years)	Reviewed	Date Of Application
Guillotines	20	*	1 Jul 2012
Hatschek machines (including tub machines)	25	*	1 Jul 2012
Presses	20	*	1 Jul 2012
Scrap return assets (including pulpers and shredders)	15	*	1 Jul 2012
Trimmers	20	*	1 Jul 2012
Storage, preparation and mixing assets:			
Ball mills	25	*	1 Jul 2012
Batching vessels (including feeding vessels) (excluding silica thickener vessels)	20	*	1 Jul 2012
Classifiers (including cyclones)	15	*	1 Jul 2012
Hoppers	20	*	1 Jul 2012
Hydropulpers	20	*	1 Jul 2012
Mixers	15	*	1 Jul 2012
Refiners	20	*	1 Jul 2012
Storage tanks (including silica thickener vessels)	25	*	1 Jul 2012
Prefabricated concrete product manufacturing assets:			
Air compressors	10	*	1 Jul 2013
Automated panel manufacturing assets:			
Automated trowel machines (incorporating crane and trowel)	15	*	1 Jul 2013
Concrete distribution stations:			
Distributors	10	*	1 Jul 2013
Flying buckets	10	*	1 Jul 2013
Hoppers	15	*	1 Jul 2013
Curing chambers	25	*	1 Jul 2013
Laser beam alignment systems	10	*	1 Jul 2013
Pallet cleaning machines	15	*	1 Jul 2013
Pallet receivable stands (excluding pallet vibrating stands)	20	*	1 Jul 2013
Pallet transport systems:			
Pallet drive mechanisms (incorporating drive units, motors, sensors and wheels)	10	*	1 Jul 2013
Track work	20	*	1 Jul 2013
Transversals (including continuous transfer wagons)	10	*	1 Jul 2013
Pallet vibrating stands	10	*	1 Jul 2013
Pallets	15	*	1 Jul 2013
Rack feeders	15	*	1 Jul 2013
Shutter cleaning machines	15	*	1 Jul 2013
Shutter transporting assets (including automated roller conveyors)	15	*	1 Jul 2013
Shutters	8	*	1 Jul 2013
Turning machines (including flippers and tilting assets)	20	*	1 Jul 2013
Buckets (including kibbles, skips and tippers)	6	*	1 Jul 2013
Casting tables	10	*	1 Jul 2013
Concrete manufacturing assets:			
Bins (excluding concrete bins)	15	*	1 Jul 2013
Conveyors	20	*	1 Jul 2013
Hoppers	15	*	1 Jul 2013
Mixers	15	*	1 Jul 2013
Concrete testers	10	*	1 Jul 2013
Control system assets	10	*	1 Jul 2013

MANUFACTURING
(11110 to 25990)

Asset	Life (Years)	Reviewed	Date Of Application
Gantry cranes	25	*	1 Jul 2013
Lifting gear (including chains, lugs and swivels)	7	*	1 Jul 2013
Moulds	10	*	1 Jul 2013
Pipe manufacturing assets:			
Cage machines	20	*	1 Jul 2013
Load testers	25	*	1 Jul 2013
Moulds	7	*	1 Jul 2013
Pallets	15	*	1 Jul 2013
Pipe making machines	20	*	1 Jul 2013
Prestressing assets	10	*	1 Jul 2013
Shutter saws	7	*	1 Jul 2013
Steel cutters and benders	7	*	1 Jul 2013
Trowel machines	4	*	1 Jul 2013
Work tables	10	*	1 Jul 2013
Silos	30	*	1 Jul 2012
Tile manufacturing plant (cement and concrete, but excluding concrete roof tiles):			
General plant	10		1 Jan 2001
Pallets (aluminium used in extrusion process)	5		1 Jan 2001
Iron smelting and steel manufacturing (21100)			
Assets used in common in iron smelting and steel manufacturing processes:			
Automated guided vehicles (AGVs)	20	*	1 Jul 2010
CCTV systems	3	*	1 Jul 2010
Coil cars (including hydraulic sliding floor plates)	13	*	1 Jul 2010
Coil car tracks and rails	7	*	1 Jul 2010
Control systems assets:			
Instruments (including temperature probes, control panels, gas analysers, location sensors, carbon monoxide monitors, pressure controls, temperature controls, pyrometers, strip position sensors, gamma ray detectors, hot metal detectors, x-ray gauges, width gauges, thickness gauges)	7	*	1 Jul 2010
Programmable logic controllers (PLCs) and distributed control systems (DCS)	10	*	1 Jul 2010
Uninterruptible power supplies (UPS)	5	*	1 Jul 2010
Cranes and gantries	20	*	1 Jul 2010
Electricity distribution, generation or transmission assets:			
Aerials or underground cables	30	*	1 Jul 2010
Electronic protection relays	10	*	1 Jul 2010
High voltage switchgear	25	*	1 Jul 2010
Transformers	20	*	1 Jul 2010
Use any relevant determinations made in Electricity supply (26110 to 26400) for any other electricity distribution, generation or transmission assets			
Gasometers	30	*	1 Jul 2010
Rail infrastructure and rolling stock except torpedo cars – use any relevant determinations made for Rail freight and passenger transport services (47100 to 47200)			
Rolls for mill roll stands (including roughing mill rolls, finishing mill rolls and skin conditioning mill rolls)	2	*	1 Jul 2010

MANUFACTURING
(11110 to 25990)

Asset	Life (Years)	Reviewed	Date Of Application
Roller tables (incorporating gearboxes, motors, drives, rolls, table frames, aprons, side guards and foundations)	15	*	1 Jul 2010
Scale or transfer car rail tracks and turntables	20	*	1 Jul 2010
Scale or transfer cars (incorporating cable reel and drive units)	20	*	1 Jul 2010
Ship ore unloaders	20	*	1 Jul 2010
Slag processing assets:			
Crushers	20	*	1 Jul 2010
Granulators	15	*	1 Jul 2010
Slag pots	20	*	1 Jul 2010
Slag pot carriers	10	*	1 Jul 2010
Stacks (including flare off stacks (incorporating burners and derricks))	20	*	1 Jul 2010
Stackers, reclaimers, stacker/reclaimers and sequencers	25	*	1 Jul 2010
Basic oxygen steelmaking (BOS) and electric arc furnace (EAF) steel making assets:			
BOS vessels (incorporating motors, gearboxes, bull gear, vessel, torsion bar, lube pumps, pulse generators, tacho generators, brakes, limit switches, pressure switches and support structures)	10	*	1 Jul 2010
Desulphurising lances (incorporating masts, winch control boxes, hydraulic cylinders carriage system, motors, gearboxes, brake lance carriages, lance guides, lances and switches)	10	*	1 Jul 2010
Electric arc furnaces (EAFs)	10	*	1 Jul 2010
Electrode control arms	10	*	1 Jul 2010
Emissions control assets:			
Baghouses	20	*	1 Jul 2010
De-dusting ducts and mains	15	*	1 Jul 2010
Electrostatic precipitators	15	*	1 Jul 2010
Primary and secondary scrubbers (incorporating support structure and spray systems)	20	*	1 Jul 2010
Waste gas radiation cooling systems (incorporating water sprays and ducts)	20	*	1 Jul 2010
Waste gas extractor fans and silencers	20	*	1 Jul 2010
Flux making assets:			
Kiln contact coolers (including agitator, agitator hydraulic system and rotary valves)	15	*	1 Jul 2010
Kiln burner units (incorporating gas and firing systems)	15	*	1 Jul 2010
Lime kiln discharge conveyors (incorporating structures, belts, pulleys, motors and gearboxes)	15	*	1 Jul 2010
Lime kilns (incorporating rollers, tyres, support structures, drives, motors and gearboxes)	25	*	1 Jul 2010
Raw material crushers and ball mills	15	*	1 Jul 2010
Grinders (incorporating motors, drive pullies and belts, drive shafts, roller crusher units and whizzer separators)	15	*	1 Jul 2010
Heat shielding for vessels incorporating supports	30	*	1 Jul 2010
Hot metal pots	20	*	1 Jul 2010
Lance pumps and motor assemblies	15	*	1 Jul 2010
Liquid oxygen lances (incorporating carriage system, motors, gearboxes, brake lance carriages, lance guides, lances and switches)	10	*	1 Jul 2010
Liquid oxygen supply pipes	10	*	1 Jul 2010
Materials handling assets:			
Air blowers	15	*	1 Jul 2010

MANUFACTURING
(11110 to 25990)

Asset	Life (Years)	Reviewed	Date Of Application
Bins	20	*	1 Jul 2010
Bucket elevators	20	*	1 Jul 2010
Conveyor systems (incorporating structures, belts, gearboxes and motors)	20	*	1 Jul 2010
Cyclones	10	*	1 Jul 2010
Hoppers, weigh hoppers, chutes, silos	20	*	1 Jul 2010
Scrap metal buckets, skips and stands	20	*	1 Jul 2010
Screens and weighing systems	15	*	1 Jul 2010
Vibro feeders	15	*	1 Jul 2010
Vibrators	15	*	1 Jul 2010
Weighbridges (incorporating load cells)	20	*	1 Jul 2010
Pneumatic air tube systems (incorporating blower units)	20	*	1 Jul 2010
Scull breakers	10	*	1 Jul 2010
Secondary treatment assets:			
Composition adjustment stations (including Injection Reheating Up Temperature (IRUT) stations incorporating snorkels, support structures and motors)	20	*	1 Jul 2010
Ladle metallurgical furnaces (LMFs)	20	*	1 Jul 2010
Vacuum degassers (incorporating steam pumps and vacuum pumps)	10	*	1 Jul 2010
Slag rakes	10	*	1 Jul 2010
Steel ladles (incorporating tilting bales, thrusters, cassettes, shells, lids and linings)	20	*	1 Jul 2010
Sub or sampling lances (incorporating motors, drives, gearboxes, limit switches, over speed switches, drums, cables and slow motors)	10	*	1 Jul 2010
Water treatment assets:			
Cooling towers (incorporating fans, motors, access platforms and stairs)	20	*	1 Jul 2010
Heat exchangers	10	*	1 Jul 2010
Launder distribution and collection systems	15	*	1 Jul 2010
Pipes and pipelines:			
Slurry disposal pipelines	15	*	1 Jul 2010
Water pipes	20	*	1 Jul 2010
Valves and other non-pipe fittings	10	*	1 Jul 2010
Pumps (including slurry disposal pumps)	15	*	1 Jul 2010
Settling ponds	30	*	1 Jul 2010
Tanks:			
Conditioner, slurry, polymer, liquid flocculants and mixer tanks	20	*	1 Jul 2010
Water tanks	25	*	1 Jul 2010
Thickeners and clarifiers (incorporating tanks, rakes and access platforms)	30	*	1 Jul 2010
Blast furnace assets:			
Cast house assets:			
Cast house floor iron and slag runner systems, covers, and tilting spouts	5	*	1 Jul 2010
Cast house structure	40	*	1 Jul 2010
Common hydraulic systems	15	*	1 Jul 2010
Manipulators	15	*	1 Jul 2010
Mud guns	15	*	1 Jul 2010

MANUFACTURING
(11110 to 25990)

Asset	Life (Years)	Reviewed	Date Of Application
Taphole drills	15	*	1 Jul 2010
Emissions control assets:			
Baghouses	20	*	1 Jul 2010
Chimney mains	30	*	1 Jul 2010
De-dusting ducts and mains	15	*	1 Jul 2010
Dust catchers (incorporating supporting structures)	15	*	1 Jul 2010
Excess gas bleeder systems	20	*	1 Jul 2010
Furnace top recovery turbine systems (incorporating hydraulic system, inlet and outlet mains and valves)	20	*	1 Jul 2010
Scrubbers (incorporating support structure and spray systems)	15	*	1 Jul 2010
Uptakes, bleeders and platforms, downcomers, dust dumping, valves and hydraulics	15	*	1 Jul 2010
Waste gas collector mains and ducts	15	*	1 Jul 2010
Furnace proper assets:			
Furnace charging tops (incorporating charging valves and hydraulics)	15	*	1 Jul 2010
Furnace elevators	15	*	1 Jul 2010
Furnace shells (incorporating hearths, refractory linings, staves, probes, profile meters and sondes)	15	*	1 Jul 2010
Furnace support assets (including maintenance platforms and control and switch rooms)	15	*	1 Jul 2010
Furnace support structure (incorporating foundations)	40	*	1 Jul 2010
Hot blast system assets:			
Cold blast mains (incorporating snorts and mixer valves)	15	*	1 Jul 2010
Hot blast mains (incorporating bustle mains, back draught mains and tuyere stock)	15	*	1 Jul 2010
Stoves (incorporating refractory, shell, foundations, fan and valves)	30	*	1 Jul 2010
Stoves mixed gas main systems	15	*	1 Jul 2010
Materials handling assets:			
Furnace charging bins	15	*	1 Jul 2010
Furnace charging conveyor systems (incorporating structures, belts, gearboxes and motors)	20	*	1 Jul 2010
Furnace charging skip hoist	20	*	1 Jul 2010
Furnace charging skip tracks	30	*	1 Jul 2010
Furnace charging skips	15	*	1 Jul 2010
Screens and weighing systems	15	*	1 Jul 2010
Torpedo cars	17	*	1 Jul 2010
Water treatment assets:			
Basins	30	*	1 Jul 2010
Cooling towers (incorporating fans, motors, access platforms and stairs)	20	*	1 Jul 2010
Heat exchangers	10	*	1 Jul 2010
Thickeners and clarifiers (incorporating tanks, rakes and access platforms)	30	*	1 Jul 2010
Valves and other non-pipe fittings	8	*	1 Jul 2010
Water distribution systems	10	*	1 Jul 2010
Water pumps	10	*	1 Jul 2010
Coke making assets:			
Coal screening assets:			
Crushers	20	*	1 Jul 2009

MANUFACTURING
(11110 to 25990)

Asset	Life (Years)	Reviewed	Date Of Application
Hammer mills	15	*	1 Jul 2009
Hydrowashers	20	*	1 Jul 2009
Primary, secondary and tertiary screens and chutes	10	*	1 Jul 2009
Coke ovens batteries assets:			
Breeze basins	30	*	1 Jul 2009
Charging car rails	20	*	1 Jul 2009
Charging cars	20	*	1 Jul 2009
Coke ovens batteries (including ovens, doors, individual oven gas off takes from supply and extraction mains)	30	*	1 Jul 2009
Coke ploughs	15	*	1 Jul 2009
Coke transfer cars	25	*	1 Jul 2009
Coke wharves (including concrete end barriers and skids)	30	*	1 Jul 2009
Hot car spur lines	30	*	1 Jul 2009
Hot cars (incorporating locomotive, wagon, tray and bogies)	15	*	1 Jul 2009
Quenchers (incorporating stack structures, water tanks, pipes, pumps, sprays, pneumatic systems and water pump pits)	15	*	1 Jul 2009
Ram tracks and live rails	30	*	1 Jul 2009
Rams	30	*	1 Jul 2009
Coke ovens gas by-products assets:			
Acid compound assets:			
Acid compound structures, pumps, overflow and storage tanks	15	*	1 Jul 2009
Ammonia absorbers (including pumps, ammonia storage tanks, and distribution pipes including valves)	15	*	1 Jul 2009
Ammonia plant assets:			
Ammonia incinerators, ammonia stills, tanks, decanters, pumps, condensers (including support structures, stacks)	15	*	1 Jul 2009
Benzine, toluene and xylene plant assets:			
Distillation columns, dephlegorators, pumps, tanks, coolers, condensers and pre heaters	30	*	1 Jul 2009
Benzol scrubbers (including pumps and distribution pipe work including valves)	35	*	1 Jul 2009
Exhausters (including support structures and hydraulic systems)	5	*	1 Jul 2009
Final coolers	35	*	1 Jul 2009
Napthalene plant assets:			
Sludge tanks, pre heaters, distillation columns, tanks, decanters, condensers, and pumps	35	*	1 Jul 2009
Primary cooler assets:			
Electric and steam pumps, tar tanks, strainers, salt water coolers (including supporting structures and distribution pipes to cooler off takes including valves)	40	*	1 Jul 2009
Sulphate plant assets:			
Feed tanks, evaporators, centrifuge units, conveyors (including belts, structures, drives and chutes, jet condensers, hot water tanks, driers including chutes, drives, and support structures, pumps, vibrating screens, cyclones, and scraper conveyors)	10	*	1 Jul 2009
Tar plant assets:			
Decanters, make tanks (incorporating scrapers and drives, storage tanks, steam and electric pumps, liquor tank and strainers)	15	*	1 Jul 2009

MANUFACTURING
(11110 to 25990)

Asset	Life (Years)	Reviewed	Date Of Application
Tar precipitators	20	*	1 Jul 2009
Emissions control assets:			
Waste gas cleaning and dedusting assets:			
Baghouses	20	*	1 Jul 2009
Dedusting fans (including extraction dusting incorporating gearboxes and drives)	20	*	1 Jul 2009
Dust collection systems, dust drop out boxes and dust disposal rotary valves (incorporating motors and gearboxes)	20	*	1 Jul 2009
Fume extraction hoods	20	*	1 Jul 2009
Waste gas collector mains and ducts	25	*	1 Jul 2009
Materials handling assets:			
Bins (including furnace coke, dust disposal bins)	20	*	1 Jul 2009
Conveyor systems (incorporating structures, belts, gearboxes and motors)	15	*	1 Jul 2009
Conveyor systems transfer houses	15	*	1 Jul 2009
Feed bunkers	15	*	1 Jul 2009
Motorised feeders	15	*	1 Jul 2009
Water treatment assets:			
Cooling towers (incorporating fans, motors, access platforms and stairs)	25	*	1 Jul 2009
Hot strip mill assets:			
Coil and slab weighers	15	*	1 Jul 2010
Coil box and crop shear assets:			
Coil boxes (incorporating side guard drives and transfer mechanism assemblies)	8	*	1 Jul 2010
Coil box shear and scale breakers	17	*	1 Jul 2010
Crop shears (incorporating assemblies and main drive motors)	17	*	1 Jul 2010
Crop shear maintenance jigs and pinch rolls	15	*	1 Jul 2010
Transfer bed oxy cutting stations	15	*	1 Jul 2010
Coil handling assets:			
Cooling tunnel ventilation fans	10	*	1 Jul 2010
Cooling tunnel conveyors	13	*	1 Jul 2010
Marking machines	15	*	1 Jul 2010
De-scaling systems (incorporating scale breakers, nozzles, pipe works, valves and high pressure pumps)	10	*	1 Jul 2010
Down coiler assets (including coilers (incorporating side guards, mandrel, mandrel drives, wrappers and unit roll drives))	15	*	1 Jul 2010
Finishing mill assets:			
Finishing mill flumes	20	*	1 Jul 2010
Finishing mills (incorporating mill stands, side guides, strippers, screw downs, drive shafts, pinion boxes, main drive motors, transformers, loopers, grease systems, oil circulation systems, and hydraulic systems)	20	*	1 Jul 2010
Laminar flow cooling systems	15	*	1 Jul 2010
Mill roll shop assets:			
Bearing washing machines	10	*	1 Jul 2010
Chuck changers	15	*	1 Jul 2010
Floor plate or checker plate machines	15	*	1 Jul 2010
Roll grinders	15	*	1 Jul 2010
Roll lathes	20	*	1 Jul 2010

MANUFACTURING
(11110 to 25990)

Asset	Life (Years)	Reviewed	Date Of Application
Roll racks and sleds	20	*	1 Jul 2010
Reversing roughing mill assets:			
Reversing roughing mills (incorporating mill stands, entry side guards, delivery side guards, main drive motors and hydraulic systems)	20	*	1 Jul 2010
Vertical edgers (incorporating drive motors, gearboxes and edger adjustments)	20	*	1 Jul 2010
Roll changing assets	20	*	1 Jul 2010
Scale scrapers	15	*	1 Jul 2010
Skin pass mill assets:			
Skin pass mills (incorporating mill entry assets, gap control and auxiliary hydraulics, main drive motors, payoff reel, un-coiler mandrels and re-coiler mandrels)	20	*	1 Jul 2010
Tension reels and belt wrappers	15	*	1 Jul 2010
Laser systems mill entry	5	*	1 Jul 2010
Slab tracking systems	5	*	1 Jul 2010
Strapping machines (including radial and circumferential)	13	*	1 Jul 2010
Walking beam furnace assets:			
Air dilution manifolds	20	*	1 Jul 2010
Air ducts	10	*	1 Jul 2010
Coke ovens gas systems	15	*	1 Jul 2010
Cold combustion air systems	20	*	1 Jul 2010
Dilution blowers	10	*	1 Jul 2010
Extractors	10	*	1 Jul 2010
Furnaces (incorporating structure, charging machines with synchronising drive trains, refractories, walking beam floors, furnace hydraulic systems, and charge and discharge doors)	20	*	1 Jul 2010
Nitrogen purge systems	15	*	1 Jul 2010
Tracking lasers (incorporating cables and adapters)	5	*	1 Jul 2010
Pellet making assets:			
Balling assets:			
Balling drums	20	*	1 Jul 2010
Bentonite tanks	20	*	1 Jul 2010
Mixers	20	*	1 Jul 2010
Seed screens	10	*	1 Jul 2010
Cooler assets:			
Cooler fans	10	*	1 Jul 2010
Annular coolers (incorporating pans, pan conveyors and drives)	25	*	1 Jul 2010
Roller screens	10	*	1 Jul 2010
Dewatering assets:			
Launders	20	*	1 Jul 2010
Pressure filter pumps	5	*	1 Jul 2010
Process water tanks	20	*	1 Jul 2010
Return water pipes	20	*	1 Jul 2010
Slurry feed pipes	10	*	1 Jul 2010
Slurry pumps	10	*	1 Jul 2010
Slurry tanks (incorporating agitators)	15	*	1 Jul 2010
Sumps	20	*	1 Jul 2010
Thickeners (incorporating tanks, rakes and access platforms)	20	*	1 Jul 2010

MANUFACTURING
(11110 to 25990)

Asset	Life (Years)	Reviewed	Date Of Application
Vertical plate pressure filters (incorporating filters, plates, membranes, water sprays, ladders, bomb bay doors)	20	*	1 Jul 2010
Emissions control assets:			
Compressors	20	*	1 Jul 2010
Dust collection system	20	*	1 Jul 2010
Multi-cone	20	*	1 Jul 2010
Scrubbers	20	*	1 Jul 2010
Waste gas collector mains and ducts	20	*	1 Jul 2010
Waste gas extractor fans	20	*	1 Jul 2010
Fluxing tanks	20	*	1 Jul 2010
Grinding mills	15	*	1 Jul 2010
Induration assets:			
Kiln burner units (incorporating gas and firing systems)	15	*	1 Jul 2010
Rotary kilns (incorporating bearings, drive gear and drive system)	30	*	1 Jul 2010
Travelling grates (incorporating motors, gearboxes or drives and rollers)	30	*	1 Jul 2010
Waste heat recovery ducts	15	*	1 Jul 2010
Waste heat recovery fans	10	*	1 Jul 2010
Materials handling assets:			
Conveyor systems (incorporating structures, belts, gearboxes and motors):			
Conveyors to and from balling drums	20	*	1 Jul 2010
Filter cake conveyors	20	*	1 Jul 2010
Finished pellet conveyor	20	*	1 Jul 2010
Flux bins	20	*	1 Jul 2010
Roller feeders	10	*	1 Jul 2010
Table feeders	10	*	1 Jul 2010
Vibrating feeders	10	*	1 Jul 2010
Weigh feeders	10	*	1 Jul 2010
Plate mill assets:			
Cold levellers (incorporating motor, gearbox spindles, hydraulic traverse cylinders, fill-in table rolls, motor, gearbox, rolls and catenaries)	30	*	1 Jul 2010
De-scaling boxes (incorporating sprays, mechanicals, control valves pipe work after isolation valves, de-scaling box table rolls, tables, chains, covers, side guides and covers)	10	*	1 Jul 2010
Edgers (incorporating motors, hydraulic controls, mechanical controls, anvil (carryover table), hand rails and walkways)	20	*	1 Jul 2010
Furnace entry skids	20	*	1 Jul 2010
Furnaces (incorporating slab pushers, bumpers, pyrometers, off takes from king valve to outlets and all structures and equipment from after entry skids up to and including circular apron skids)	20	*	1 Jul 2010
Hot levellers (incorporating motors, gearboxes, spindles, rolls, leveller AGC capsules, screws, crowning device, de-scaling header and valves)	20	*	1 Jul 2010
Inter-roll stand cooling sprays	15	*	1 Jul 2010
Reversing finishing mill (incorporating housing, side guides and covers, guards, motors, drives, spindles, water sprays, gearboxes, screw down, spindles, AGC capsules, hydraulics, mill de-scaling, filler plates, and oil systems within the mill)	20	*	1 Jul 2010

MANUFACTURING
(11110 to 25990)

Asset	Life (Years)	Reviewed	Date Of Application
Reversing roughing mill (incorporating housing, side guides and covers, guards, motors, drives, spindles, water sprays, gearboxes, screw down, spindles, AGC capsules, hydraulics, mill de-scaling, filler plates, and oil systems within the mill)	20	*	1 Jul 2010
Rope driven cooling transfer bed	20	*	1 Jul 2010
Shears (including crop, divide, scrap, rotary trim, guillotine and end shears)	20	*	1 Jul 2010
Slab sizing systems (incorporating side guard measuring devices and stands, slab sizing unit supports, cameras and light banks)	5	*	1 Jul 2010
Turnover inspection table (incorporating barriers and hydraulics)	20	*	1 Jul 2010
Walking beam cooling beds (incorporating carry on section, carry off section, moving (walking) section, chain drives and hydraulics)	20	*	1 Jul 2010
Primary metal product casting assets:			
Continuous casting machines (incorporating turrets, tundishes (incorporating lids and cassettes), tundish cars, moulds, dummy bars, segments, oscillators, rolls, water sprays, hydraulics, motors and gearboxes):			
Billet casters	17	*	1 Jul 2010
Combination casters	17	*	1 Jul 2010
Slab casters	17	*	1 Jul 2010
Cooler transfer arms (incorporating motors, gearboxes and drive shafts)	17	*	1 Jul 2010
Crop removal machines	20	*	1 Jul 2010
Cut to length machines and torch cutters	15	*	1 Jul 2010
De-burring machines (incorporating fixed drives)	15	*	1 Jul 2010
Emissions control assets:			
Baghouses	20	*	1 Jul 2010
Dedusting fans (including extraction dusting incorporating gearboxes and drives)	15	*	1 Jul 2010
Dedusting ducts and mains	15	*	1 Jul 2010
Steam exhaust fans	10	*	1 Jul 2010
Hydraulic shears	17	*	1 Jul 2010
Materials handling assets:			
Conveyor systems (including structures, belts, gearboxes and motors)	20	*	1 Jul 2010
Mould powder bins	23	*	1 Jul 2010
Screw feeders	15	*	1 Jul 2010
Scarfing machines (incorporating catenary system of hoses, power supply cables and support structures)	20	*	1 Jul 2010
Slab or billet cooler tanks (incorporating grid stands)	30	*	1 Jul 2010
Slab or billet marking machines	17	*	1 Jul 2010
Transfer beds	17	*	1 Jul 2010
Up-enders (including hydraulics)	17	*	1 Jul 2010
Walking beam cooling beds and run out tables	17	*	1 Jul 2010
Water treatment assets:			
Basins and ponds	30	*	1 Jul 2010
Cooling towers (incorporating fans, motors, access platforms and stairs)	20	*	1 Jul 2010
Gravel and sand filters	25	*	1 Jul 2010
Heat exchangers	10	*	1 Jul 2010
Pipelines:			
Water pipelines	20	*	1 Jul 2010

MANUFACTURING
(11110 to 25990)

Asset	Life (Years)	Reviewed	Date Of Application
Valves and other non-pipe fittings	10	*	1 Jul 2010
Pumps:			
Water pumps	10	*	1 Jul 2010
Chemical dosing pumps	5	*	1 Jul 2010
Skimmers and scrapers	15	*	1 Jul 2010
Tanks:			
Sludge, chemical storage and dosing tanks	20	*	1 Jul 2010
Water tanks	25	*	1 Jul 2010
Thickeners and clarifiers (incorporating tanks, rakes and access platforms)	30	*	1 Jul 2010
Rod, bar, structural and rail mill assets:			
Controlled tempering quenching cars	10	*	1 Jul 2010
Cut to length machines	17	*	1 Jul 2010
De-scaling systems (incorporating scale breaker, nozzles, pipe work, valves and high pressure pump)	10	*	1 Jul 2010
Finishing mills (incorporating motors, gearboxes, drives, guides and cassettes)	20	*	1 Jul 2010
Furnace charging skids	20	*	1 Jul 2010
Intermediate mills (incorporating motors, gearboxes, drives, guides and cassettes)	20	*	1 Jul 2010
Reversing roughing mills (incorporating motors, gearboxes, drives, guides and cassettes)	20	*	1 Jul 2010
Roughing mills (incorporating motors, gearboxes, drives, guides and cassettes)	20	*	1 Jul 2010
Shears (incorporating motors and drives)	17	*	1 Jul 2010
Stacker/bundlers	12	*	1 Jul 2010
Straighteners	20	*	1 Jul 2010
Walking beam cooling beds	20	*	1 Jul 2010
Walking beam, natural gas furnaces (incorporating structure, refractories, walking beam floors, furnace hydraulic systems, and charge and discharge doors)	20	*	1 Jul 2010
Sinter making assets:			
Cooler assets:			
Cooler fans	10	*	1 Jul 2009
Coolers (incorporating pan conveyors and drives)	25	*	1 Jul 2009
Emissions control assets:			
Waste gas cleaning and dedusting assets:			
Activated carbon packed bed filters	15	*	1 Jul 2009
Dedusting fans	10	*	1 Jul 2009
Electrostatic precipitators and scraper chains	20	*	1 Jul 2009
Waste gas collector mains and ducts	20	*	1 Jul 2009
Feed sequence assets:			
Feed rolls	7	*	1 Jul 2009
Mixing and rolling drums	30	*	1 Jul 2009
Materials handling assets:			
Belt weighers	5	*	1 Jul 2009
Bins:			
Coke bins	15	*	1 Jul 2009
Ore bins	23	*	1 Jul 2009
Sinter bins	17	*	1 Jul 2009

MANUFACTURING
(11110 to 25990)

Asset	Life (Years)	Reviewed	Date Of Application
Chutes	15	*	1 Jul 2009
Conveyor systems (incorporating structures, belts, gearboxes and motors)	17	*	1 Jul 2009
Feeders:			
Coke	15	*	1 Jul 2009
Ore	23	*	1 Jul 2009
Sinter	17	*	1 Jul 2009
Weigh feeders:			
Coke	15	*	1 Jul 2009
Ore	23	*	1 Jul 2009
Strand assets:			
Ignition furnaces (incorporating associated air and gas mains)	15	*	1 Jul 2009
Preheat hoods (incorporating waste heat recovery fans and mains)	7	*	1 Jul 2009
Spike roll crushers (incorporating bogey flex, electric motors, primary gearboxes, fluid couplings, grillage bars and crash decks)	10	*	1 Jul 2009
Strand structures and drives (including conveyors, wind legs and dust troughs)	20	*	1 Jul 2009
Water treatment assets:			
Thickeners and clarifiers (incorporating tanks, rakes and access platforms)	30	*	1 Jul 2009
Steel railway track product manufacturing assets:			
Steel railway clip manufacturing assets:			
Anti-corrosion dip tanks	20	*	1 Jul 2011
Coil transfer arms (incorporating motors, gearboxes and drive shafts)	15	*	1 Jul 2011
End spades	20	*	1 Jul 2011
Gas temper furnaces	20	*	1 Jul 2011
Induction heaters	20	*	1 Jul 2011
Noise reduction enclosures	30	*	1 Jul 2011
Presses	20	*	1 Jul 2011
Quench systems (incorporating heat exchangers, transfer arms, tanks, pipes and pumps)	20	*	1 Jul 2011
Shears	20	*	1 Jul 2011
Tooling	15	*	1 Jul 2011
Transfer systems (incorporating flat bed transfer table)	30	*	1 Jul 2011
Quality control test rigs	30	*	1 Jul 2011
Materials handling assets:			
Conveyor systems	20	*	1 Jul 2011
Hoppers	20	*	1 Jul 2011
Racks for storage	20	*	1 Jul 2011
Weigh scales	15	*	1 Jul 2011
Water treatment assets:			
Cooling towers	20	*	1 Jul 2011
Pumps	10	*	1 Jul 2011
Tanks	20	*	1 Jul 2011
Steel railway sleeper manufacturing assets:			
Crop shear and presses	20	*	1 Jul 2011
Form presses	20	*	1 Jul 2011

MANUFACTURING
(11110 to 25990)

Asset	Life (Years)	Reviewed	Date Of Application
Punch presses	20	*	1 Jul 2011
Steel strip metallic coating assets:			
Accumulators (incorporating rolls, drive gear, winches and rope)	17	*	1 Jul 2010
Air knife assemblies	13	*	1 Jul 2010
Crop shears	17	*	1 Jul 2010
Curing ovens	15	*	1 Jul 2010
Horizontal air coolers (incorporating ducting fans and nozzles)	15	*	1 Jul 2010
Horizontal furnaces	20	*	1 Jul 2010
Levellers (incorporating gearboxes and drives)	15	*	1 Jul 2010
Metal coating pots	15	*	1 Jul 2010
Passivators (incorporating tanks and pumps)	17	*	1 Jul 2010
Payoff reels	15	*	1 Jul 2010
Pot hardware (incorporating zinc roll frames and roll assemblies)	13	*	1 Jul 2010
Pre melt pots	5	*	1 Jul 2010
Quench systems (incorporating rolls, spray bars and tanks)	10	*	1 Jul 2010
Re-coilers	15	*	1 Jul 2010
Resin coaters	15	*	1 Jul 2010
Scrapers	13	*	1 Jul 2010
Skin conditioning mills (incorporating entry and exit tension rolls)	20	*	1 Jul 2010
Steering rolls and bridles (incorporating motors, gearboxes and rolls)	15	*	1 Jul 2010
Vertical air coolers (incorporating ducting, fans and motors)	15	*	1 Jul 2010
Vertical preheat furnaces	15	*	1 Jul 2010
Welders	17	*	1 Jul 2010
Steel strip organic coating assets:			
Accumulators (incorporating rolls, drive gear, winches and rope)	17	*	1 Jul 2010
Banders	15	*	1 Jul 2010
Branders	10	*	1 Jul 2010
Chemical rinsing, cleaning and pre-treatment assets	15	*	1 Jul 2010
Cooler and cooling assets	15	*	1 Jul 2010
Curing ovens	15	*	1 Jul 2010
Finishing assets	15	*	1 Jul 2010
Inspection assets	17	*	1 Jul 2010
Payoff reels	15	*	1 Jul 2010
Primer and main coaters	13	*	1 Jul 2010
Quench systems	10	*	1 Jul 2010
Re-coilers	15	*	1 Jul 2010
Shears	15	*	1 Jul 2010
Stitchers	17	*	1 Jul 2010
Tin-plating mill assets:			
Accumulators and loopers	17	*	1 Jul 2011
Acid and alkaline cleaning baths (including scrubbing units, rolls and electrical grids)	13	*	1 Jul 2011
Batch annealing assets:			
Annealing furnaces	6	*	1 Jul 2011
Bases	4	*	1 Jul 2011
Convector plates	4	*	1 Jul 2011
Inner covers	4	*	1 Jul 2011
Cold reduction mills	20	*	1 Jul 2011

MANUFACTURING
(11110 to 25990)

Asset	Life (Years)	Reviewed	Date Of Application
Continuous annealing furnaces	15	*	1 Jul 2011
Crop shears	15	*	1 Jul 2011
Dryers	15	*	1 Jul 2011
Electro plating baths (including scrubbing units, rolls and electrical grids)	13	*	1 Jul 2011
Pickling tanks (including scrubbing units and rolls and electrical grids)	13	*	1 Jul 2011
Preheat furnaces	20	*	1 Jul 2011
Recoilers, bridles and uncoilers	15	*	1 Jul 2011
Rinse tanks	15	*	1 Jul 2011
Side trimmers	15	*	1 Jul 2011
Temper mills	20	*	1 Jul 2011
Tension control system (including steering)	10	*	1 Jul 2011
Welders	17	*	1 Jul 2011
Alumina production (21310)			
Alumina manufacturing (including bauxite refining and calcined alumina manufacturing):			
Bauxite crushing and handling assets:			
Conveyors	30	*	1 Jan 2003
Crushing assets	30	*	1 Jan 2003
Screening assets	15	*	1 Jan 2003
Stockpile reclaimers, stackers and stacker/reclaimers	30	*	1 Jan 2003
Train loading assets (including conveyors, product bins and towers)	30	*	1 Jan 2003
Bauxite residue disposal assets:			
Initial containment areas	20		1 Jan 2001
Mudlakes	10		1 Jan 2001
Calcination assets:			
Calciners and kilns	25	*	1 Jan 2003
Generally (including alumina cooling assets, hydrate storage tanks and hydrate washing assets)	30	*	1 Jan 2003
Clarification of liquor stream assets (including counter current washing tanks, flash tanks, lime burning assets, lime handling assets, lime slaking assets, settling tanks and other tanks and vessels)	30	*	1 Jan 2003
Control systems assets	10	*	1 Jan 2003
Digestion assets (including desilication tanks, digester vessels, flash tanks, heat exchangers, heaters, mills and trihydrate bauxite treatment assets)	30	*	1 Jan 2003
Emissions control assets (including baghouse filters and electrostatic precipitators)	20	*	1 Jan 2003
Filtration assets for hydrate and slurry (including filters used for clarification of liquor and filters used for coarse hydrate)	15	*	1 Jan 2003
Pipework (including slurry pipes)	30	*	1 Jan 2003
Precipitation assets (including classification assets, cooling towers, crystallisation assets, heat exchangers, tanks and vessels)	30	*	1 Jan 2003
Pumps	20	*	1 Jan 2003
Steam raising and electrical infrastructure assets (including switchgear and transformers)	30	*	1 Jan 2003

MANUFACTURING
(11110 to 25990)

Asset	Life (Years)	Reviewed	Date Of Application
Aluminium smelting (21320)			
Anode baking assets (including crucibles and furnaces)	20	*	1 Jan 2003
Anode (green) pasting assets:			
Crushing assets	30	*	1 Jan 2003
Mixing and forming assets	15	*	1 Jan 2003
Screening assets	15	*	1 Jan 2003
Anode rodding assets (including aluminium spray station assets, furnaces and metal casting assets)	20	*	1 Jan 2003
Compressors	20	*	1 Jan 2003
Control systems assets	10	*	1 Jan 2003
Cranes and gantries (including cell tending machines)	20	*	1 Jan 2003
Emissions control assets (including baghouse filters and electrostatic precipitators)	20	*	1 Jan 2003
Materials handling assets:			
Anode transport vehicles and hot metal carriers	10	*	1 Jan 2003
Generally (including conveyors, silos and stockpile reclaiming assets)	30	*	1 Jan 2003
Metal casting assets (including casting machines, casting wheels, crucibles, foam filters, furnaces, in-line metal treatment assets, stacking machines and weighing machines)	20	*	1 Jan 2003
Pot line/reduction line assets (excluding cell tending machines, cranes and gantries)	25	*	1 Jan 2003
Pumps	20	*	1 Jan 2003
Steam raising and electrical infrastructure assets:			
Generally (including switchgear and transformers)	30	*	1 Jan 2003
Rectiformers	20	*	1 Jan 2003
Non-ferrous metal casting (21410)			
Metal casting assets (non-ferrous eg aluminium, brass and magnesium):			
Cooling assets (including tables, conveyors, towers)	15	*	1 Jan 2004
Deodorising machines/fume extraction systems	15	*	1 Jul 2013
Die casting machines (including high pressure, low pressure and gravity type machines)	15	*	1 Jan 2004
Die tools (moulds used for casting)	4	*	1 Jan 2004
Heating assets:			
Degassing assets	5	*	1 Jan 2004
Furnaces (including dosing, holding and melting)	15	*	1 Jan 2004
Heat treatment baskets	5	*	1 Jan 2004
Heat treatment ovens	20	*	1 Jan 2004
Ingot pre-heaters	20	*	1 Jan 2004
Quenching tanks	20	*	1 Jan 2004
Impregnation machines	10	*	1 Jul 2013
Machining/finishing assets:			
Blast machines (including shot, sand, bead)	20	*	1 Jan 2004
CNC lathes	10	*	1 Jan 2004
CNC machining centres	10	*	1 Jan 2004
CNC milling machines	10	*	1 Jan 2004
Drilling machines	15	*	1 Jan 2004
Linishing belt machines	10	*	1 Jan 2004
Trim presses (hydraulic type and crank type)	15	*	1 Jan 2004

MANUFACTURING
(11110 to 25990)

Asset	Life (Years)	Reviewed	Date Of Application
Trim tools used in trim press machines	4	*	1 Jan 2004
Vibrating machines (including rumbling and knock out machines	10	*	1 Jan 2004
Materials handling conveyors	10	*	1 Jan 2004
Molten metal transfer ladles	3	*	1 Jan 2004
Paint line conveyors	15	*	1 Jan 2004
Robots	10	*	1 Jan 2004
Sand casting assets:			
Core boxes	4	*	1 Jan 2004
Core making machines (core blowers)	15	*	1 Jan 2004
Gas generators for sand curing	15	*	1 Jan 2004
Sand core dies	7	*	1 Jul 2013
Sand core making machines	15	*	1 Jul 2013
Testing assets:			
Co-ordinate measurement machines	10	*	1 Jan 2004
Leak and pressure testing machines	4	*	1 Jan 2004
Spectrometers	10	*	1 Jan 2004
X-ray machines	15	*	1 Jan 2004
Tinsmiths' plant	20		1 Jan 2001
Fabricated metal product manufacturing (22100 to 22990)			
Galvanising plant	10		1 Jan 2001
Metal crushing plant (core fragmentised)	13 1/3		1 Jan 2001
Nail manufacturing plant	20		1 Jan 2001
Saw-making plant	20		1 Jan 2001
Spring manufacturers' plant:			
Cooling furnaces	10		1 Jan 2001
Power presses, rotary cambering, scale testing and scragging machines	20		1 Jan 2001
Steel coil roll forming, slitting and blanking and sheet metal forming (22210 to 22290)			
Steel coil blanking or shear line assets:			
Coil cars (including stationary coil cars)	15	*	1 Jul 2012
Cut to length shears and guillotines	15	*	1 Jul 2012
De-coilers/un-coilers (incorporating drives, motors, mandrels, gearboxes, snubbers and brakes)	15	*	1 Jul 2012
Flying shears	10	*	1 Jul 2012
Grip feeders	10	*	1 Jul 2012
Levellers	15	*	1 Jul 2012
Meter wheels	7	*	1 Jul 2012
Peeler tables	15	*	1 Jul 2012
Run out tables	15	*	1 Jul 2012
Scissor lifts	15	*	1 Jul 2012
Stackers	15	*	1 Jul 2012
Steel coil roll forming assets:			
Auto banders	10	*	1 Jul 2012
Closed section induction welders	15	*	1 Jul 2012
Closed section laser welders	10	*	1 Jul 2012
CNC laser cutting units	10	*	1 Jul 2012
Coil cars	15	*	1 Jul 2012

MANUFACTURING
(11110 to 25990)

Asset	Life (Years)	Reviewed	Date Of Application
Coil joining welding units	15	*	1 Jul 2012
Coil levellers and straighteners	15	*	1 Jul 2012
Coil magazines	15	*	1 Jul 2012
Coil tilters	15	*	1 Jul 2012
Coil tilting coil cars	15	*	1 Jul 2012
Control systems assets:			
Motion controllers	10	*	1 Jul 2012
Programmable logic controllers (PLCs)	10	*	1 Jul 2012
Potentiometers	5	*	1 Jul 2012
Variable speed drives (VSDs)	10	*	1 Jul 2012
Control systems (including roll former control systems (incorporating end coders), de-coiler/un-coiler control systems and snubber control systems)	10	*	1 Jul 2012
De-coilers/un-coilers (incorporating drives, motors, mandrels, gearboxes, snubbers and brakes)	15	*	1 Jul 2012
Embossing units	5	*	1 Jul 2012
Flying shears	10	*	1 Jul 2012
In-line presses and punches	15	*	1 Jul 2012
In-line printers and labellers	7	*	1 Jul 2012
Metal saws:			
Band saws	10	*	1 Jul 2012
Rotary cut off saws	10	*	1 Jul 2012
Roll former tooling	8	*	1 Jul 2012
Roll formers (incorporating entry guides, fixed and height adjustable pinch rollers, drive motor and gearboxes, base and power supply unit):			
Fixed	15	*	1 Jul 2012
Mobile	10	*	1 Jul 2012
Run out tables	15	*	1 Jul 2012
Shears and guillotines	15	*	1 Jul 2012
Snubbers (incorporating drives, motors and gearboxes)	15	*	1 Jul 2012
Strip lubricators	10	*	1 Jul 2012
Support assets:			
Controlled access gates	10	*	1 Jul 2012
Conveyors:			
Gravity feed conveyors (incorporating belts, rollers and frames)	15	*	1 Jul 2012
Motorised conveyors (incorporating gearboxes, belts, rollers, bearings, motors, frames and controls)	15	*	1 Jul 2012
Engineering workshop assets:			
CNC and NC lathes	10	*	1 Jul 2012
Drilling machines	10	*	1 Jul 2012
Keyway broaching presses	15	*	1 Jul 2012
Guard lights (incorporating red eye guard lights and stands)	7	*	1 Jul 2012
Lifting assets:			
C-hooks	15	*	1 Jul 2012
Overhead cranes and gantries	25	*	1 Jul 2012
Spreader bars	10	*	1 Jul 2012
Manual strapping machines	7	*	1 Jul 2012

MANUFACTURING
(11110 to 25990)

Asset	Life (Years)	Reviewed	Date Of Application
Measuring assets (including micrometers, protractors, tapes, and vernier callipers)	7	*	1 Jul 2012
Perimeter fencing	15	*	1 Jul 2012
Pneumatic systems assets:			
Air compressors	7	*	1 Jul 2012
Air driers	7	*	1 Jul 2012
Air receivers	15	*	1 Jul 2012
Racking	20	*	1 Jul 2012
Stackers (drop and suction)	15	*	1 Jul 2012
Stretch wrappers	10	*	1 Jul 2012
Tunnel guarding (including safety cages)	15	*	1 Jul 2012
Steel coil slitting assets:			
Anti-flutter rolls	10	*	1 Jul 2012
Auto banders (incorporating conveyors, strapping heads, coil lift systems, strapping dispensers, accumulators and controls)	10	*	1 Jul 2012
Carryover tables	15	*	1 Jul 2012
Coil cars	15	*	1 Jul 2012
Coil stacking systems	20	*	1 Jul 2012
Control systems	10	*	1 Jul 2012
Controlled access gates	10	*	1 Jul 2012
Conveyors:			
Gravity feed conveyors (incorporating belts, rollers and frames)	15	*	1 Jul 2012
Motorised conveyors (incorporating gearboxes, belts, rollers, bearings, motors, frames and controls)	15	*	1 Jul 2012
De-coiler/un-coiler edge guides	10	*	1 Jul 2012
De-coilers/un-coilers (incorporating drives, motors, mandrels, gearboxes, snubbers and brakes)	15	*	1 Jul 2012
Downenders (incorporating conveyors, hydraulics and controls)	20	*	1 Jul 2012
Entry and exit coil carousels/capstans	20	*	1 Jul 2012
Entry shears	15	*	1 Jul 2012
Exit edge guides	10	*	1 Jul 2012
Exit feed up units (incorporating deflector and lift rolls, shears, separators, tables and traverse drives)	20	*	1 Jul 2012
Exit turnstile/coil stackers	20	*	1 Jul 2012
Lifting assets:			
C-hooks	15	*	1 Jul 2012
Magnet cranes	20	*	1 Jul 2012
Overhead cranes and gantries	25	*	1 Jul 2012
Main hydraulic power pack (incorporating interconnecting pipe work to valve stands)	15	*	1 Jul 2012
Pallet conveyor monorails	10	*	1 Jul 2012
Peeler tables	15	*	1 Jul 2012
Perimeter guarding	15	*	1 Jul 2012
Pinch rollers/breakers	20	*	1 Jul 2012
Pneumatic systems assets:			
Air compressors	7	*	1 Jul 2012
Air driers	7	*	1 Jul 2012
Air receivers	15	*	1 Jul 2012

MANUFACTURING
(11110 to 25990)

Asset	Life (Years)	Reviewed	Date Of Application
Re-coilers (incorporating drives, motors, mandrels, gearboxes, snubbers, and brakes)	15	*	1 Jul 2012
Scrap baller	15	*	1 Jul 2012
Scrap chopper bins and carriages	20	*	1 Jul 2012
Scrap chopper conveyors (incorporating gearboxes, belts, rollers, bearings, motors, frames and controls)	15	*	1 Jul 2012
Scrap choppers	20	*	1 Jul 2012
Separator blades	10	*	1 Jul 2012
Slitter tooling (incorporating blades, rubbers and spacers)	5	*	1 Jul 2012
Slitting head building stations (incorporating rotating rigs)	20	*	1 Jul 2012
Slitting head entry side guides	10	*	1 Jul 2012
Slitting heads (incorporating electric motors, gearboxes and drive shafts)	15	*	1 Jul 2012
Tension units (incorporating entry and exit quadrants, rolls, separators, drag pads, motors, gearboxes and drives)	15	*	1 Jul 2012
Weighing scales (incorporating load cells and controls)	20	*	1 Jul 2012
Steel sheet metal forming assets:			
Blankers	15	*	1 Jul 2012
Brake presses	20	*	1 Jul 2012
CNC multi head combined slitter/blankers	15	*	1 Jul 2012
Control systems	10	*	1 Jul 2012
Folders	10	*	1 Jul 2012
Guillotines	15	*	1 Jul 2012
Mini slitters	15	*	1 Jul 2012
Boiler, tank and other heavy gauge metal container manufacturing (22310)			
Sheet metal tanks manufacturing assets:			
Band saws	5	*	1 Jul 2012
Coil holders	10	*	1 Jul 2012
Curving rollers	10	*	1 Jul 2012
Drilling machines (including bench and radial drills)	5	*	1 Jul 2012
Gang and turret punching machines	15	*	1 Jul 2012
Hand tools	5	*	1 Jul 2012
Hoists:			
Electric	5	*	1 Jul 2012
Hydraulic	15	*	1 Jul 2012
Hooks (including c-hooks and slinger hooks)	5	*	1 Jul 2012
Jib cranes	15	*	1 Jul 2012
Laser cutters	7	*	1 Jul 2012
Overhead cranes and gantries	25	*	1 Jul 2012
Pallet jacks	10	*	1 Jul 2012
Plate grabs	5	*	1 Jul 2012
Racking	20	*	1 Jul 2012
Riveting machines	15	*	1 Jul 2012
Shears:			
Hand-held type	3	*	1 Jul 2012
Guillotine type	15	*	1 Jul 2012
Spreader bars	15	*	1 Jul 2012
Trolleys	5	*	1 Jul 2012
Welders	5	*	1 Jul 2012

MANUFACTURING
(11110 to 25990)

Asset	Life (Years)	Reviewed	Date Of Application
Motor vehicle manufacturing (23110)			
Bus and truck manufacturing assets (including bus vehicle body assembling assets and truck body manufacturing assets):			
Ancillary and support assets:			
Air compressors	15	*	1 Jul 2011
Battery assets for warehouse vehicles (including pallet trucks and forklifts) – see Table B Warehouse and distribution centre equipment and machines			
Brake hose cleaning machines	10	*	1 Jul 2011
Calibration assets	10	*	1 Jul 2011
Control systems	10	*	1 Jul 2011
Door controls and motor drive systems for rapid roller doors (incorporating chains, controls, motors and sensors, but excluding doors)	10	*	1 Jul 2011
Dust and fume extraction assets:			
Fixed extraction systems (incorporating ducting, extraction arms etc)	15	*	1 Jul 2011
Mobile	7	*	1 Jul 2011
Floor sweepers/scrubbers	10	*	1 Jul 2011
Glycol and water mixing plant assets	15	*	1 Jul 2011
Hose reels	7	*	1 Jul 2011
Power supply assets (including generators) – use any relevant determinations made for Power supply assets in Table B			
Racks and shelving	20	*	1 Jul 2011
Stillages, storage bins tote boxes and trolleys	15	*	1 Jul 2011
Storage tanks:			
Fuel storage tanks	20	*	1 Jul 2011
Gas storage tanks (including argon, compressed natural gas (CNG) and nitrogen gas storage tanks)	30	*	1 Jul 2011
Lubricant storage tanks	20	*	1 Jul 2011
Tooling:			
Dies (for press brakes)	12	*	1 Jul 2011
Jigs and fixtures	7	*	1 Jul 2011
Moulds (including fibreglass moulds)	7	*	1 Jul 2011
Vehicle platforms and runways (used in wheel alignment etc)	20	*	1 Jul 2011
Ventilation fans	20	*	1 Jul 2011
Waste oil collection and storage assets	10	*	1 Jul 2011
Waste water treatment assets:			
Meters	5	*	1 Jul 2011
Pipework	15	*	1 Jul 2011
Pumps	12	*	1 Jul 2011
Separators	15	*	1 Jul 2011
Tanks	30	*	1 Jul 2011
Water demineralising plant assets (including containers, pipework, pumps and reverse osmosis assets)	15	*	1 Jul 2011
Weighers:			
Fixed (weighbridges)	20	*	1 Jul 2011
Mobile	10	*	1 Jul 2011
Assembly and body shop assets:			
Adhesive mixing and dispensing assets	15	*	1 Jul 2011

MANUFACTURING
(11110 to 25990)

Asset	Life (Years)	Reviewed	Date Of Application
Alignment, positioning and verification assets:			
Axle and frame alignment assets (including frame presses)	15	*	1 Jul 2011
Computer and laser based contact and non-contact devices (including 'Faro arms')	10	*	1 Jul 2011
Dumpy levels	7	*	1 Jul 2011
Coupling machines	15	*	1 Jul 2011
Power tool and rivet gun power packs and rigs	15	*	1 Jul 2011
Power tools:			
Nut runners (including cables and controllers)	7	*	1 Jul 2011
Others (including angle grinders, fastening tools, hand operated saws, rivet guns etc) – see Table B Power tools, hand tools			
Sawing machines (including aluminium cutting saws, bandsaws and cold saws)	12	*	1 Jul 2011
Welding assets:			
Automatic stud well bowl feeder units	10	*	1 Jul 2011
Hand held and portable spot welders (including transformers)	10	*	1 Jul 2011
MIG welders	15	*	1 Jul 2011
Stud welding machines	15	*	1 Jul 2011
TIG welders	15	*	1 Jul 2011
Vertical electric welders (pedestal welders)	15	*	1 Jul 2011
Welding reels	7	*	1 Jul 2011
Handling assets:			
Conveyors:			
Floor and in-floor conveyors (including belt conveyors, skid conveyors, skillet conveyors, slat conveyors, turntables etc)	15	*	1 Jul 2011
Monorails and overhead conveyors	20	*	1 Jul 2011
Cranes (including gantry cranes, overhead cranes and turnover cranes)	25	*	1 Jul 2011
Elevating work platforms – see Table A Rental and hiring services (except real estate) (66110 to 66400), Elevating work platforms (EWPs)			
Forklift trucks (including pallet jacks, pallet stackers and reach trucks) – see Table B Forklifts			
Mobile hoists/floor cranes (including engine and radiator hoists)	15	*	1 Jul 2011
Pushers, rollers and tug units	10	*	1 Jul 2011
Vehicle hoists/lifters (including column lifters and post hoists)	25	*	1 Jul 2011
Paint shop assets:			
Booths and ovens:			
Generally (including baking/curing ovens, paint mixing booths/rooms, pre-treatment/sanding booths and wash down booths including cab degreasers)	20	*	1 Jul 2011
Spray booths and combination spray booth baking ovens	15	*	1 Jul 2011
Dip tank electro coating assets (including alkaline cleaner tanks, electro application tanks, surface conditioner tanks and water rinse tanks)	15	*	1 Jul 2011
Infrared paint dryers	7	*	1 Jul 2011
Paint proportioning assets:			

MANUFACTURING
(11110 to 25990)

Asset	Life (Years)	Reviewed	Date Of Application
Electronic component proportioning systems	10	*	1 Jul 2011
Paint tinting and colour blending machines	5	*	1 Jul 2011
Press shop assets:			
Bending machines:			
Chassis rail/frame bending machines	20	*	1 Jul 2011
Folders (including pan brakes)	20	*	1 Jul 2011
Press brakes (brake presses)	25	*	1 Jul 2011
Tube benders	12	*	1 Jul 2011
Chassis rail drilling/punching machines:			
Chassis rail processing machines (incorporating drilling and profiling)	20	*	1 Jul 2011
Punching machines	20	*	1 Jul 2011
CNC milling machines	10	*	1 Jul 2011
CNC routing machines	10	*	1 Jul 2011
Drilling machines (bench drills, pedestal drills and pillar drills)	12	*	1 Jul 2011
Guillotine shears	20	*	1 Jul 2011
Lathes:			
CNC lathes	10	*	1 Jul 2011
Conventional or non-CNC lathes	15	*	1 Jul 2011
Plasma cutters	15	*	1 Jul 2011
Scribing and number stamping machines (including chassis number scribing/stamping machines and vehicle identification number stamping machines)	10	*	1 Jul 2011
Trim and final shop assets:			
Air conditioning charging units	10	*	1 Jul 2011
Brake testing units	20	*	1 Jul 2011
Bus and truck wash assets – see Table A Automotive body, paint and interior repair n.e.c. (94129), large vehicle wash assets			
Electrical systems testing assets	15	*	1 Jul 2011
Fluid filling assets:			
Fluid filling machines (including coolant, fuel, lubrication and power steering fluid filling machines)	10	*	1 Jul 2011
Urea dispensing systems (incorporating intermediate bulk containers, hose reels, meters and pumps)	10	*	1 Jul 2011
Headlight aiming equipment	10	*	1 Jul 2011
Torque testing machines (including chassis dynamometers and engine dynamometers)	12	*	1 Jul 2011
Wheel alignment assets:			
Wheel alignment lasers	4	*	1 Jul 2011
Wheel alignment systems (incorporating alignment machines housing computer hardware and software, probes and sensors)	15	*	1 Jul 2011
Metal stamping and blanking assets:			
Ancillary assets (including building and services assets):			
Air compressors	15	*	1 Jul 2012
Air dryers	10	*	1 Jul 2012
Generally (including air conditioning assets, air cooling assets, fencing (removable), fire control and alarm assets, power supply assets) – use any applicable determination in Table B			

MANUFACTURING
(11110 to 25990)

Asset	Life (Years)	Reviewed	Date Of Application
Steelwork structures (including access and storage platforms, bollards, ladders etc)	15	*	1 Jul 2012
Blanking and stamping press assets:			
Presses (including production presses and production supporting presses such as die spotting presses, tryout presses etc)	15	*	1 Jul 2012
Support assets (including decoilers, loaders, unloaders, pallet transfer, sheet feeders, crane savers etc)	15	*	1 Jul 2012
Die change over assets (die trailers, die trucks, die trolleys etc)	15	*	1 Jul 2012
Die racks	15	*	1 Jul 2012
Dies (stamping dies)	7	*	1 Jul 2012
Inspection and measuring assets (including accelerometers, accuracy measurement tools, desktop friction and wear testers, dualscopes and measuring and evaluation machines generally)	10	*	1 Jul 2012
Maintenance workshop and tool room assets:			
Benches and cutting tables (including magnetic field benches, marking out tables, welding benches etc)	15	*	1 Jul 2012
Cutting machines (including gas cutters and plasma cutting machines)	10	*	1 Jul 2012
Exhaust fans	10	*	1 Jul 2012
Fixtures (including rotary work fixtures and set up fixtures)	10	*	1 Jul 2012
Hand tools (including portable power tools, sealer guns and spray guns)	3	*	1 Jul 2012
Heat treatment assets (including furnaces and quench tanks etc)	15	*	1 Jul 2012
Lifting equipment (including vertical elevators and hoists)	15	*	1 Jul 2012
Maintenance machines and tool room assets generally (including boring machines, folding machines, grinding machines, guillotines, hydraulic benders and presses, lapping machines, lathes, milling machines, NC machines and pipe threaders)	15	*	1 Jul 2012
Measuring assets (including height gauges, micrometers, surface measuring machines and vernier calipers)	10	*	1 Jul 2012
Washing machines and tanks (including ultrasonic cleaners/washers and other hot solvent small parts washing assets)	15	*	1 Jul 2012
Welders (including ARC welders, MIG welders and TIG welders)	10	*	1 Jul 2012
Pallets	10	*	1 Jul 2012
Production control systems	10	*	1 Jul 2012
Robots (including press tending robots, press transfer robots and pressed parts rack loading robots)	10	*	1 Jul 2012
Scrap metal baling assets (including balers and conveying systems)	15	*	1 Jul 2012
Steel coil and steel sheet handling assets:			
Automated guided vehicles (AGVs) (used in blank/stamped parts handling)	10	*	1 Jul 2012
Coil loaders (including hydraulic carts, lift tables and platforms)	15	*	1 Jul 2012
Conveyors	15	*	1 Jul 2012
Forklifts – see Table B			
Overhead cranes and hoists	20	*	1 Jul 2012
Steel coil and steel sheet processing assets:			
Blank/sheet turnover machines	15	*	1 Jul 2012
Destacking/stacking machines	10	*	1 Jul 2012
Washing machines	10	*	1 Jul 2012

MANUFACTURING
(11110 to 25990)

Asset	Life (Years)	Reviewed	Date Of Application
Motor car engine assembly and manufacturing assets:			
Ancillary and support assets:			
Air compressors	15	*	1 Jul 2012
Air curtains	10	*	1 Jul 2012
Control systems (including mimic panels)	10	*	1 Jul 2012
Cooling water supply assets (including cooling towers, storage tanks and water conditioning/dosing assets)	15	*	1 Jul 2012
Dust and fume extraction assets (including ducting, extraction fans, hoppers etc)	15	*	1 Jul 2012
Engine lubrication storage, filtration and feed plant assets	15	*	1 Jul 2012
Engine pallets	10	*	1 Jul 2012
Lighting (production)	15	*	1 Jul 2012
Racks, shelving, stands and tables generally	15	*	1 Jul 2012
Robots generally (including assembly robots, gantry robots and pick and place robots etc)	10	*	1 Jul 2012
Safety assets generally (including guarding, matting, railing etc, where separately identifiable and not incorporated into an existing asset)	10	*	1 Jul 2012
Stillages, storage bins, tote boxes and trolleys	10	*	1 Jul 2012
Swarf and machining line coolant separation and refrigeration systems (incorporating coolant circulation pumps and tanks, outfeed extractors, refrigeration chiller packs, separators and swarf tote excavators)	15	*	1 Jul 2012
Tooling assets:			
Electronic and laser tool pre-setting and setting machines (including coordinate measurement machines)	10	*	1 Jul 2012
Tooling (for drills, lathes, mills etc)	3	*	1 Jul 2012
Engine assembly and engine component sub-assembly assets:			
Adhesive application assets used in form-in-place gasket systems etc (including adhesive unloading equipment and robots)	10	*	1 Jul 2012
Assembly and sub-assembly assets generally (including assembly machines, balancing machines, bearing shell detection assets, crank and piston spin test machines, oil filling machines etc)	10	*	1 Jul 2012
Coding assets (including automated ink or spray jet coders and automated pin coding stamping machines)	10	*	1 Jul 2012
Nut runner assets:			
Automated nut runner and fastening systems (incorporating cables and controllers, and including bolt torquing robots)	10	*	1 Jul 2012
Manually operated nut runners (pre-torque applications etc)	5	*	1 Jul 2012
Power tools generally	3	*	1 Jul 2012
Engine component machining line assets (including broaching machines, deburring machines, gauging machines, honing machines, leak testing machines, machining centres, pallet loading systems, surface grinding machines, transfer machines, washing machines etc)	15	*	1 Jul 2012
Engine function testing assets (including cold test machines, engine dynamometers, engine ignition testing machines and hot test machines)	10	*	1 Jul 2012
Handling assets:			
Conveyors:			

MANUFACTURING
(11110 to 25990)

Asset	Life (Years)	Reviewed	Date Of Application
Elevating conveyors (including engine block elevating conveying assets etc)	15	*	1 Jul 2012
Floor and in-floor standalone conveyors (including belt conveyors, infeed and outfeed conveyors)	15	*	1 Jul 2012
Monorails and overhead conveyors	15	*	1 Jul 2012
Cranes and hoists (including bridge cranes, gantry cranes, overhead cranes and turnover cranes)	20	*	1 Jul 2012
Lifting fixtures, magnets, slings etc	10	*	1 Jul 2012
Quality control assets generally (including cylinder head thickness testers, digital torque wrenches, gauges, inspection equipment generally, measuring equipment generally, microscopes, scales, scanners, testing equipment generally, thermometers, vibration meters etc)	10	*	1 Jul 2012
Toolroom assets:			
Benches and cutting tables (including magnetic field benches, marking out tables, welding benches etc)	15	*	1 Jul 2012
Degreasing plant systems (incorporating float valves, hoists, monorails, pumps etc)	15	*	1 Jul 2012
Fixtures (including rotary work fixtures and set up fixtures)	10	*	1 Jul 2012
Heat treatment assets (including furnaces and quench tanks)	15	*	1 Jul 2012
Tool grinding and maintenance machines (including boring machines, broach sharpening machines, grinding machines, guillotines, lapping machines, milling machines, toolroom lathes etc)	15	*	1 Jul 2012
Washing machines and tanks (including ultrasonic cleaners/ washers and other hot solvent small parts washing assets)	15	*	1 Jul 2012
Welders (ARC welders, MIG welders etc)	10	*	1 Jul 2012
Waste treatment assets:			
Laboratory equipment (including balancers, chart recorders, dryers, pH sampling devices, rotameters and simulators etc)	10	*	1 Jul 2012
Meters and sensors (including chart recorders, dosing meters, level meters, level sensors and pH method meters and sensors etc)	10	*	1 Jul 2012
Pumps (including dosing pumps, recirculation pumps etc)	10	*	1 Jul 2012
Tanks and pools (including recycling tanks, sludge tanks and pools, storage tanks etc)	20	*	1 Jul 2012
Waste treatment assets generally (including dosing systems, flotation waste treatment systems, heaters, oil removing systems, skimmers and sludge presses etc)	15	*	1 Jul 2012
Motor vehicle manufacturing plant (not listed elsewhere):			
Basic machinery	10		1 Jan 2001
Tooling (ie jigs, dies, press tools and specialty attachments such as working heads and work-holding tools)	3		1 Jan 2001
Non-ferrous metal casting assets – see Table A Non-ferrous metal casting (21410)			
Motor vehicle body and trailer manufacturing (23120)			
Bus vehicle body assembly assets (on supplied motor and chassis) – see Table A Motor vehicle manufacturing (23110), bus and truck manufacturing assets (including bus vehicle body assembling assets and truck body manufacturing assets)			
Truck body manufacturing assets – see Table A Motor vehicle manufacturing (23110), bus and truck manufacturing assets (including bus vehicle body assembling assets and truck body manufacturing assets)			

MANUFACTURING
(11110 to 25990)

Asset	Life (Years)	Reviewed	Date Of Application
Other motor vehicle parts manufacturing (23190)			
Metal stamping and blanking assets – see Table A Motor vehicle manufacturing (23110), metal stamping and blanking assets			
Piston ring manufacturing plant:			
Engineering works plant	20		1 Jan 2001
Motors	20		1 Jan 2001
Overhead gear, equipment, belting etc	20		1 Jan 2001
Precision machines	13 1/3		1 Jan 2001
Railway rolling stock manufacturing and repair services (23930)			
Assembly assets:			
Access and assembly platforms	15	*	1 Jul 2014
Alignment assets (including gearbox alignment assets)	10	*	1 Jul 2014
Bearing puller assets	10	*	1 Jul 2014
Blast chamber assets (incorporating shot recovery systems)	10	*	1 Jul 2014
Cutting assets (including plate profilers, profile cutters and saws)	10	*	1 Jul 2014
De-coiling assets	15	*	1 Jul 2014
Drilling assets (including radial drills)	10	*	1 Jul 2014
Foam filling station assets	10	*	1 Jul 2014
Furnaces and ovens (including ladles and stress relief ovens)	20	*	1 Jul 2014
Jigs (including rollover jigs and lifting jigs)	15	*	1 Jul 2014
Lathes (including above floor and under floor wheel lathes)	20	*	1 Jul 2014
Milling machines (including gantry)	20	*	1 Jul 2014
Pipe and tube bending assets	10	*	1 Jul 2014
Presses (including bearing mounting, bench, brake, hydraulic power and wheel presses)	20	*	1 Jul 2014
Riveting assets	5	*	1 Jul 2014
Specialised hydraulic tool assets	10	*	1 Jul 2014
Stretch formers	10	*	1 Jul 2014
Sweeping assets	10	*	1 Jul 2014
Turning assets	10	*	1 Jul 2014
Wash bay assets	10	*	1 Jul 2014
Welding assets (including robot welders and spot welding towers)	10	*	1 Jul 2014
Wire cutting and stripping assets	10	*	1 Jul 2014
Handling assets:			
Cranes (including overhead gantry cranes)	25	*	1 Jul 2014
Lifting assets generally (including hydraulic double lift jacks, locomotive jacks and stands)	20	*	1 Jul 2014
Pallet lifters	10	*	1 Jul 2014
Scissor lifts	10	*	1 Jul 2014
Maintenance and refurbishment assets:			
Boring assets	10	*	1 Jul 2014
Cutting assets (including guillotines, plasma cutters and profilers)	15	*	1 Jul 2014
Detecting assets (including flaw detectors)	10	*	1 Jul 2014
Drilling assets (including radial drills)	10	*	1 Jul 2014
Grinding and milling assets	20	*	1 Jul 2014
Hydraulic drop and work tables	10	*	1 Jul 2014
Lathes (including above floor and under floor wheel lathes)	20	*	1 Jul 2014

MANUFACTURING
(11110 to 25990)

Asset	Life (Years)	Reviewed	Date Of Application
Paint spraying booths (incorporating baking ovens, extractor fans and gas heaters)	15	*	1 Jul 2014
Portable presses (including hydraulic power presses)	10	*	1 Jul 2014
Presses (including bearing mounting, bench, brake, hydraulic power and wheel presses)	20	*	1 Jul 2014
Tanks (including washing and water tanks)	20	*	1 Jul 2014
Vacuum assets	10	*	1 Jul 2014
Washing assets (including bearing and bogie washers)	10	*	1 Jul 2014
Welding assets (including robot welders and spot welding towers)	10	*	1 Jul 2014
Wheel condition monitoring systems	7	*	1 Jul 2014
Support assets:			
Cleaning assets (including high pressure cleaners)	5	*	1 Jul 2014
Compressed air system assets (including compressors, dryers and filters and receivers)	10	*	1 Jul 2014
Computer measuring and monitoring assets (including load and pressure indicators)	7	*	1 Jul 2014
Control system assets (including supervisory control and data acquisition (SCADA) systems and vehicle preparation systems)	10	*	1 Jul 2014
Cooling towers	15	*	1 Jul 2014
Dust and fume extraction system assets	15	*	1 Jul 2014
Electricity supply assets – see Table A Electricity supply (26100 to 26400)			
Fastening and riveting assets	5	*	1 Jul 2014
Fire prevention systems (incorporating fire protection systems and water tanks)	15	*	1 Jul 2014
Induction heaters	10	*	1 Jul 2014
Portable train weighing assets	10	*	1 Jul 2014
Pumps (including hydraulic pumps)	10	*	1 Jul 2014
Racking and storage assets	20	*	1 Jul 2014
Rail vehicle moving and placing assets (including crabs, shunting locomotives and trackmobiles)	10	*	1 Jul 2014
Railway tracks – see Table A Rail freight and passenger transport services (47100 to 47200)			
Refrigerant recovery assets	10	*	1 Jul 2014
Traversers and turntables	20	*	1 Jul 2014
Vehicle progression systems assets (including rabbits)	10	*	1 Jul 2014
Waste water and effluent treatment assets	10	*	1 Jul 2014
Weighing assets for carriages and locomotives	20	*	1 Jul 2014
Testing assets:			
Bogie, brake and spring testing assets	10	*	1 Jul 2014
Cab test benches and CRC cable testing assets	5	*	1 Jul 2014
Earth testing assets	10	*	1 Jul 2014
Electrical testing assets (including multimeters)	10	*	1 Jul 2014
Post production testing assets (excluding weighing assets – see above in support assets):			
Water test facility assets (incorporating control systems, gantries, pipes, pumps etc)	10	*	1 Jul 2014
Other post production testing assets	5	*	1 Jul 2014
Test sheds for testing locomotives and other rolling stock	30	*	1 Jul 2014

MANUFACTURING
(11110 to 25990)

Asset	Life (Years)	Reviewed	Date Of Application
Aircraft manufacturing and repair services (23940)			
Air compression assets:			
Generally (including air compressors, air dryers and air receivers) (excluding portable air compressors)	13	*	1 Jul 2020
Portable:			
Reciprocating	7	*	1 Jul 2020
Rotary screw	10	*	1 Jul 2020
Aircraft testing and measurement equipment:			
Instrumentation, dynamometers and calibrating equipment (including testing equipment for engines, radios)	10	*	1 Jul 2020
Maintenance stands (including rigs and engine stands)	20	*	1 Jul 2020
Test cell tunnels	40	*	1 Jul 2020
Air start units	15	*	1 Jul 2020
Benches and tables	10	*	1 Jul 2020
Borescope equipment:			
Fixed probes	3	*	1 Jul 2020
Flexible probes	3	*	1 Jul 2020
Light source	5	*	1 Jul 2020
Video scopes	5	*	1 Jul 2020
Cabin pressurisation test units	15	*	1 Jul 2020
Carbon fibre cutters used in manufacturing	10	*	1 Jul 2020
Computer numerical control (CNC) machines	10	*	1 Jul 2020
Cranes (gantry and overhead)	25	*	1 Jul 2020
Degreasing machines (including washing machines)	7	*	1 Jul 2020
Elevating work platforms:			
Boom lifts	15	*	1 Jul 2020
Personnel lifts	10	*	1 Jul 2020
Scissor lifts	10	*	1 Jul 2020
Hand tools, manual (including screw drivers, spanners, wrenches)	10	*	1 Jul 2020
Hand tools, powered:			1 Jul 2020
Air	5	*	1 Jul 2020
Battery	3	*	1 Jul 2020
Electric	5	*	1 Jul 2020
Hydraulic power units (including hydraulic mules)	15	*	1 Jul 2020
Industrial autoclaves	30	*	1 Jul 2020
Industrial ovens	15	*	1 Jul 2020
Jacks	10	*	1 Jul 2020
Maintenance work platforms	20	*	1 Jul 2020
Measuring tools, manually operated (including vernier calipers, micrometers, depth gauges, tyre pressure gauges)	5	*	1 Jul 2020
Metal working precision machines (including automatic lathes, milling machines, jig borers)	10	*	1 Jul 2020
Mobile cranes	10	*	1 Jul 2020
Nitrogen carts	15	*	1 Jul 2020
Oxygen carts	15	*	1 Jul 2020
Racks	20	*	1 Jul 2020
Robots	10	*	1 Jul 2020
Sandblasters	7	*	1 Jul 2020

MANUFACTURING
(11110 to 25990)

Asset	Life (Years)	Reviewed	Date Of Application
Sheet metal machines (including benders and folders, guillotines and roll formers)	15	*	1 Jul 2020
Tow bars	10	*	1 Jul 2020
Tow tractors:			
Generally (excluding remote controlled tugs)	20	*	1 Jul 2020
Remote controlled tugs	10	*	1 Jul 2020
Tyre bead breakers	15	*	1 Jul 2020
Welders – see Table B Welders			
Other transport equipment manufacturing n.e.c. (23990)			
Motor cycle building plant	10		1 Jan 2001
Photographic, optical and ophthalmic equipment manufacturing (24110)			
Optical lens grinding and contact lens manufacturing:			
CNC milling machines	7	*	1 Jul 2004
Combined surface generators and grinders and finers	10	*	1 Jul 2004
Deblocking and lens cleaning machines (including ultrasonic washers)	9	*	1 Jul 2004
Finers	10	*	1 Jul 2004
Finishing blockers	8	*	1 Jul 2004
Frame tracers	5	*	1 Jul 2004
Lap tools	10	*	1 Jul 2004
Layout blockers	8	*	1 Jul 2004
Lens coating machines	10	*	1 Jul 2004
Lens curing and drying ovens	10	*	1 Jul 2004
Lens edgers	7	*	1 Jul 2004
Lens tinting machines	8	*	1 Jul 2004
Lensmeters:			
Automated	5	*	1 Jul 2004
Manual	10	*	1 Jul 2004
Polishers	10	*	1 Jul 2004
Protective lacquering or surface saver taping machines	9	*	1 Jul 2004
Surface generators and grinders	10	*	1 Jul 2004
Surface lathes	8	*	1 Jul 2004
Other professional and scientific equipment manufacturing n.e.c. (24190)			
Watchmakers' plant	10		1 Jan 2001
Furniture and other manufacturing (25110 to 25990)			
Broom and brush manufacturing plant	13 1/3		1 Jan 2001
Furniture-making plant	13 1/3		1 Jan 2001
Jewellers' plant	10		1 Jan 2001
Umbrella manufacturers' plant:			
Cutting boards	10		1 Jan 2001
Lathes	13 1/3		1 Jan 2001
Motors	20		1 Jan 2001

Footnotes:

28 A capped effective life of 10 years is available – see subsection 40-102(4)

¶43-025 Effective life — electricity, gas, water and waste services

**ELECTRICITY, GAS, WATER AND WASTE SERVICES
(26110 to 29220)**

Asset	Life (Years)	Reviewed	Date Of Application
Electricity supply (26110 to 26400)			
Electricity distribution:			
Control, monitoring, communications and protection systems	10	*	1 Jan 2002
Customer meters (incorporating load and time switches if fitted)	25	*	1 Jan 2002
Customer service mains or cable, above ground	40	*	1 Jan 2002
Customer service mains or cable, underground	50	*	1 Jan 2002
Distribution lines:			
Above ground (incorporating conductors; cross arms, insulators and fittings; poles – concrete, wood, steel or stobie; and transformers – pole or ground pad mounted)	45	*	1 Jan 2002
Combination of above ground and underground	47 1/2	*	1 Jan 2002
Underground (incorporating cables, fittings and ground pad mounted transformers)	50	*	1 Jan 2002
Distribution substations/transformers, pole or ground pad mounted	40	*	1 Jan 2002
Distribution zone substations (excluding control, monitoring, communications and protection systems)	40	*	1 Jan 2002
Nightwatchman's lights	15	*	1 Jan 2002
Street lights	15	*	1 Jan 2002
Electricity generation:			
Ash and dust handling and disposal:			
Ash dams	20	*	1 Jan 2002
Ash slurry systems	15	*	1 Jan 2002
Conveyors	30	*	1 Jan 2002
Crushers	15	*	1 Jan 2002
On-site storage silos, concrete or steel	30	*	1 Jan 2002
Fuel supply and handling:			
On-site gaseous fuel supply systems (incorporating downstream delivery pipelines)	30	*	1 Jan 2002
On-site liquid fuel supply systems (incorporating downstream delivery pipelines)	30	*	1 Jan 2002
Solid fuels:			
Coal handling assets (including conveyors, slot bunker, transfer towers, and weighers)	30	*	1 Jan 2002
Day bunkers and silos, concrete or steel (incorporating top side conveyor system)	30	*	1 Jan 2002
On-site coal storage assets (including stacking and reclaiming assets)	30	*	1 Jan 2002
On-site storage silos, concrete or steel	30	*	1 Jan 2002
Quality control assets (including coal sampling assets and secondary crushers)	30	*	1 Jan 2002
Power generators:			
Co-generation:			
Condensing and feed heating assets	30	*	1 Jan 2002
Control and monitoring system	15	*	1 Jan 2002
Emergency power supply assets (including batteries and uninterruptible power supply (UPS) assets)	15	*	1 Jan 2002
Gas turbine generators	30	*	1 Jan 2002
Generator transformers and unit transformers in sub-tropical areas	30	*	1 Jan 2002

ELECTRICITY, GAS, WATER AND WASTE SERVICES
(26110 to 29220)

Asset	Life (Years)	Reviewed	Date Of Application
Generator transformers and unit transformers in tropical areas	25	*	1 Jan 2002
Heat recovery steam generators	30	*	1 Jan 2002
Miscellaneous assets	30	*	1 Jan 2002
On-site switchyards with conventional outdoor switchgear	30	*	1 Jan 2002
On-site switchyards with gas insulated switchgear	30	*	1 Jan 2002
Reciprocating engines, diesel fired	20	*	1 Jan 2002
Reciprocating engines, gas spark ignition	20	*	1 Jan 2002
Station and auxiliary electrical systems within the power station	30	*	1 Jan 2002
Steam turbine generators	30	*	1 Jan 2002
Combined cycle:			
Condensing and feed heating assets	30	*	1 Jan 2002
Control and monitoring systems	15	*	1 Jan 2002
Emergency power supply assets (including batteries and uninterruptible power supply (UPS) assets)	15	*	1 Jan 2002
Gas turbine generators	30	*	1 Jan 2002
Generator transformers and unit transformers in sub-tropical areas	30	*	1 Jan 2002
Generator transformers and unit transformers in tropical areas	25	*	1 Jan 2002
Heat recovery steam generators	30	*	1 Jan 2002
Miscellaneous assets	30	*	1 Jan 2002
On-site switchyards with conventional outdoor switchgear	30	*	1 Jan 2002
On-site switchyards with gas insulated switchgear	30	*	1 Jan 2002
Station and auxiliary electrical systems within the power station	30	*	1 Jan 2002
Steam turbine generators	30	*	1 Jan 2002
Diesel or gas engine:			
Control and monitoring systems	15	*	1 Jan 2002
Diesel reciprocating engines	20	*	1 Jan 2002
Emergency power supply assets (including batteries and uninterruptible power supply (UPS) assets)	15	*	1 Jan 2002
Gas spark ignition reciprocating engines	20	*	1 Jan 2002
Generator transformers and unit transformers in sub-tropical areas	30	*	1 Jan 2002
Generator transformers and unit transformers in tropical areas	25	*	1 Jan 2002
Miscellaneous assets	30	*	1 Jan 2002
On-site switchyards with conventional outdoor switchgear	30	*	1 Jan 2002
On-site switchyards with gas insulated switchgear	30	*	1 Jan 2002
Station and auxiliary electrical systems within the power station	30	*	1 Jan 2002
Gas turbine:			
Control and monitoring systems	15	*	1 Jan 2002
Emergency power supply assets (including batteries and uninterruptible power supply (UPS) assets)	15	*	1 Jan 2002
Gas turbine generators	30	*	1 Jan 2002

ELECTRICITY, GAS, WATER AND WASTE SERVICES (26110 to 29220)

Asset	Life (Years)	Reviewed	Date Of Application
Generator transformers and unit transformers in sub-tropical areas	30	*	1 Jan 2002
Generator transformers and unit transformers in tropical areas	25	*	1 Jan 2002
Miscellaneous assets	30	*	1 Jan 2002
On-site switchyards with conventional outdoor switchgear	30	*	1 Jan 2002
On-site switchyards with gas insulated switchgear	30	*	1 Jan 2002
Station and auxiliary electrical systems within the power station	30	*	1 Jan 2002
Hydro-electric:			
Control and monitoring system	15	*	1 Jan 2002
Emergency power supply assets (including batteries and uninterruptible power supply (UPS) assets)	15	*	1 Jan 2002
Generator transformers and unit transformers in sub-tropical area	30	*	1 Jan 2002
Generator transformers and unit transformers in tropical areas	25	*	1 Jan 2002
Hydro turbines and generators	40	*	1 Jan 2002
Miscellaneous assets	40	*	1 Jan 2002
On-site switchyards with conventional outdoor switchgear	40	*	1 Jan 2002
On-site switchyards with gas insulated switchgear	35	*	1 Jan 2002
Station and auxiliary electrical systems within the power station	40	*	1 Jan 2002
Solar:			
Photovoltaic electricity generating system assets (incorporating photovoltaic panels, mounting frames and inverters)	20	*	1 Jul 2011
Thermal:			
Condensing and feed heating assets	30	*	1 Jan 2002
Control and monitoring systems	15	*	1 Jan 2002
Emergency power supply assets (including batteries and uninterruptible power supply (UPS) assets)	15	*	1 Jan 2002
Generator transformers and unit transformers in sub-tropical areas	30	*	1 Jan 2002
Generator transformers and unit transformers in tropical areas	25	*	1 Jan 2002
Miscellaneous assets	30	*	1 Jan 2002
On-site switchyards with conventional outdoor switchgear	30	*	1 Jan 2002
On-site switchyards with gas insulated switchgear	30	*	1 Jan 2002
Primary dust collection systems (incorporating electrostatic precipitators or baghouse filters)	30	*	1 Jan 2002
Solid fuel preparation assets (including fuel feeders and milling assets)	30	*	1 Jan 2002
Station and auxiliary electrical systems within the power station	30	*	1 Jan 2002
Steam generators	30	*	1 Jan 2002
Steam turbine generators	30	*	1 Jan 2002
Wind:			
Generator transformers and unit transformers in sub-tropical areas	30	*	1 Jan 2002

ELECTRICITY, GAS, WATER AND WASTE SERVICES
(26110 to 29220)

Asset	Life (Years)	Reviewed	Date Of Application
Generator transformers and unit transformers in tropical areas	25	*	1 Jan 2002
Wind turbines	20	*	1 Jan 2002
Power station civil and structural works:			
Chimney stacks:			
Concrete surrounds	30	*	1 Jan 2002
Steel flues	20	*	1 Jan 2002
Cooling towers (concrete or timber)	30	*	1 Jan 2002
Cooling water systems (excluding cooling towers and condensing assets)	30	*	1 Jan 2002
Power station buildings, to the extent that they form an integral part of plant	30	*	1 Jan 2002
Workshop machinery and tools	20	*	1 Jan 2002
Electricity transmission:			
Control, monitoring, communications and protection systems	12½	*	1 Jan 2002
Power transformers	40	*	1 Jan 2002
Transmission lines (incorporating conductors, insulators and towers)	47½	*	1 Jan 2002
Transmission substations (excluding power transformers and control, monitoring, communications and protection systems)	40	*	1 Jan 2002
Gas supply (27000)			
Gas distribution[29]:			
Control systems (excluding computers)	10	*	1 Jul 2002
Gas meters	15	*	1 Jul 2002
Low pressure (LP) gas storage holders	40	*#	1 Jul 2002
Pigging devices	5	*	1 Jul 2002
Pipelines (including high, medium or low pressure trunk, primary or secondary mains or services):			
Generally	50	*#	1 Jul 2002
Polyvinylchloride (PVC) pipelines	30	*#	1 Jul 2002
Regulators (including gate stations, subgate stations, block valve stations, pressure regulating stations and district regulating stations)	40	*#	1 Jul 2002
Gas transmission[30]:			
Compressor gas turbine (GT) drivers	20	*	1 Jul 2002
Compressor station assets	30	*#	1 Jul 2002
Control systems (excluding computers)	10	*	1 Jul 2002
Gas meters	15	*	1 Jul 2002
Gas pipeline LNG station assets	30	*#	1 Jul 2002
Pigging devices	5	*	1 Jul 2002
Pipelines – transmission, spur or lateral	50	*#	1 Jul 2002
Regulators (including gate stations, subgate stations, block valve stations, pressure regulating stations and district regulating stations)	40	*#	1 Jul 2002
Underground gas storage asset	40	*#	1 Jul 2002

ELECTRICITY, GAS, WATER AND WASTE SERVICES
(26110 to 29220)

Asset	Life (Years)	Reviewed	Date Of Application
Water supply (28110)			
Assets used by irrigation water providers:			
Channel regulators	80	*	1 Jan 2005
Cranes (including gantries)	40	*	1 Jan 2005
Dams and weirs ((incorporating gates and actuators) consisting of a barrier to obstruct the flow of water constructed from any or all of the following: concrete, earth and rockfill)	100	*	1 Jan 2005
Drain inlet	50	*	1 Jan 2005
Drainage channels (measured from the point of intersection with another drainage channel to the following intersection)	100	*	1 Jan 2005
Escapes	50	*	1 Jan 2005
Flow meters	20	*	1 Jan 2005
Irrigation channels (incorporating siphons and subways) measured from offtake or regulator to regulator:			
Concrete	50	*	1 Jan 2005
Earth	80	*	1 Jan 2005
Measurement flumes	50	*	1 Jan 2005
Metered outlets:			
Electronic	40	*	1 Jan 2005
Mechanical	50	*	1 Jan 2005
Piped	40	*	1 Jan 2005
Offtakes	80	*	1 Jan 2005
Pipes: measured from valve to valve, that are of the same age and same material (not being in the nature of a repair)	80	*	1 Jan 2005
Pump inlets	50	*	1 Jan 2005
Pump sets (incorporating switchboards, starters, motors and pumps)	40	*	1 Jan 2005
Reservoirs and tanks	80	*	1 Jan 2005
Valves	40	*	1 Jan 2005
Assets used in water supply:			
Aerators and blowers	20	*	1 Jan 2005
Cathodic protection systems	20	*	1 Jan 2005
Chemical dosing pumps	25	*	1 Jan 2005
Pump sets (incorporating switch boards, starters, motors and pumps)	25	*	1 Jan 2005
Raw water storage and supply assets:			
Bores	30	*	1 Jan 2005
Dam or weir intake structures	100	*	1 Jan 2005
Dams and weirs	100	*	1 Jan 2005
Reservoirs, elevated tanks and standpipes: whether made from steel or concrete	80	*	1 Jan 2005
Service connections:			
Water meters	20	*	1 Jan 2005
Valves:			
Generally	30	*	1 Jan 2005
Pressure reducing valves	25	*	1 Jan 2005
Water mains: Being lengths of trunk, distribution and reticulation mains within a section, measured from valve to valve that are of the same age and same material (not being in the nature of a repair)	80	*	1 Jan 2005

ELECTRICITY, GAS, WATER AND WASTE SERVICES
(26110 to 29220)

Asset	Life (Years)	Reviewed	Date Of Application
Water supply control systems assets:			
Air scour flow meters, level sensors, transmitters and meters	10	*	1 Jan 2005
Chlorine analysers, mini labs, pH meters, turbidity analysers and meters	7	*	1 Jan 2005
Flow meters	20	*	1 Jan 2005
Pressure sensors, transmitters and meters	10	*	1 Jan 2005
Telemetry (including modems and remote transfer units)	10	*	1 Jan 2005
Variable speed drives (VSDs)	15	*	1 Jan 2005
Water supply pumping station detention tanks	80	*	1 Jan 2005
Water treatment assets:			
Balance tanks	80	*	1 Jan 2005
Bore water treatment assets:			
Aerators and blowers	20	*	1 Jan 2005
Backwash pumps	25	*	1 Jan 2005
Batching tanks	80	*	1 Jan 2005
Clear water tanks	80	*	1 Jan 2005
Drying beds	50	*	1 Jan 2005
Filtration tanks	80	*	1 Jan 2005
Lime pump sets (incorporating switch boards, starters, motors and pumps)	25	*	1 Jan 2005
Lime silos	50	*	1 Jan 2005
Reactors	25	*	1 Jan 2005
Sludge thickeners	50	*	1 Jan 2005
Chemical blowers	15	*	1 Jan 2005
Chemical dosing systems	15	*	1 Jan 2005
Chemical feeders and hoppers	25	*	1 Jan 2005
Chemical mixers and blenders	25	*	1 Jan 2005
Chemical storage tanks	30	*	1 Jan 2005
Clarifiers (incorporating scrapers)	80	*	1 Jan 2005
Clear water tanks	80	*	1 Jan 2005
Dissolved air flotation systems	25	*	1 Jan 2005
Filtration tanks (incorporating scrapers)	80	*	1 Jan 2005
Flocculation tanks (incorporating scrapers)	80	*	1 Jan 2005
Inline mixers	15	*	1 Jan 2005
Penstocks	25	*	1 Jan 2005
Raw water inlet screening systems	25	*	1 Jan 2005
Sludge treatment lagoons	50	*	1 Jan 2005
Wash water holding tanks	80	*	1 Jan 2005
Sewerage and drainage services (28120)			
Chemical dosing pumps	25	*	1 Jan 2005
Dams:			
Lined earth dams	100	*	1 Jan 2005
Dam covers	20	*	1 Jan 2005
Effluent outfalls:			
Shoreline ocean	100	*	1 Jan 2005
Extended ocean	100	*	1 Jan 2005
River or estuary	100	*	1 Jan 2005

ELECTRICITY, GAS, WATER AND WASTE SERVICES
(26110 to 29220)

Asset	Life (Years)	Reviewed	Date Of Application
Methane gas and cogeneration assets – see Table A Electricity supply (26110 to 26400) and Gas supply (27000)			
Pump sets (incorporating switch boards, starters, motors and pumps)	25	*	1 Jan 2005
Sewage pump station assets:			
Detention tanks	80	*	1 Jan 2005
Overflow screens	25	*	1 Jan 2005
Sewage service connection assets:			
Low pressure pumps	25	*	1 Jan 2005
Vacuum pumps	25	*	1 Jan 2005
Sewage treatment assets:			
Air filtration systems	20	*	1 Jan 2005
Air scrubbers	10	*	1 Jan 2005
Chemical blowers	15	*	1 Jan 2005
Chemical feeders and hoppers	25	*	1 Jan 2005
Chemical mixers and blenders	25	*	1 Jan 2005
Chemical storage tanks	30	*	1 Jan 2005
Grit removal assets	25	*	1 Jan 2005
Penstocks	25	*	1 Jan 2005
Screenings removal assets	25	*	1 Jan 2005
Sludge processing assets:			
Anaerobic digesters	80	*	1 Jan 2005
Anaerobic digester gas handling and blowing systems	25	*	1 Jan 2005
Anaerobic digester heating systems	25	*	1 Jan 2005
Bio-filters	80	*	1 Jan 2005
Dissolved air flotation systems	25	*	1 Jan 2005
Lime disinfection dosing units	25	*	1 Jan 2005
Sludge dewatering assets:			
Belt presses	15	*	1 Jan 2005
Centrifuges	20	*	1 Jan 2005
Screw conveyors	25	*	1 Jan 2005
Screw presses	20	*	1 Jan 2005
Sludge driers	20	*	1 Jan 2005
Sludge heating units	20	*	1 Jan 2005
Sludge thickening tanks (incorporating scrapers)	80	*	1 Jan 2005
Treatment assets:			
Primary treatment assets:			
Primary clarifiers (incorporating scrapers)	80	*	1 Jan 2005
Primary sedimentation lagoons	50	*	1 Jan 2005
Primary sedimentation tanks (incorporating scrapers and weirs)	80	*	1 Jan 2005
Scum collection and transfer systems	25	*	1 Jan 2005
Secondary treatment assets:			
Biological nutrient removal (BNR) assets:			
Aerators and blowers	20	*	1 Jan 2005
BNR tanks (incorporating mixed liquor stream, anoxic, anaerobic and swing zones and diffusers)	80	*	1 Jan 2005
Mixers	25	*	1 Jan 2005
Secondary clarifiers (incorporating scrapers)	80	*	1 Jan 2005

ELECTRICITY, GAS, WATER AND WASTE SERVICES
(26110 to 29220)

Asset	Life (Years)	Reviewed	Date Of Application
Secondary treatment lagoons	50	*	1 Jan 2005
Secondary treatment tanks (incorporating scrapers and weirs)	80	*	1 Jan 2005
Sequenced batch reactors	80	*	1 Jan 2005
Sludge aerators and blowers	80	*	1 Jan 2005
Tertiary treatment assets:			
Backwash air blowers	20	*	1 Jan 2005
Chlorine contact tanks	80	*	1 Jan 2005
Filtration tanks	80	*	1 Jan 2005
Reverse osmosis assets:			
Fine screening systems	15	*	1 Jan 2005
Micro filtration units	15	*	1 Jan 2005
Reverse osmosis membrane filtration units	10	*	1 Jan 2005
UV disinfectors	25	*	1 Jan 2005
Water storage tanks	80	*	1 Jan 2005
Sewerage control systems assets:			
Chlorine residual analysers and pH meters	7	*	1 Jan 2005
Dissolved oxygen probes, level sensors, transmitters and meters	10	*	1 Jan 2005
Flow meters	20	*	1 Jan 2005
Telemetry (including modems and remote transfer units)	10	*	1 Jan 2005
Variable speed drives (VSDs)	15	*	1 Jan 2005
Sewer mains: Being lengths of collection sewers measured from manhole to manhole (including branch, main, pressure, reticulation, sub-main and trunk sewers) (not being in the nature of a repair)	80	*	1 Jan 2005
Valves:			
Generally	25	*	1 Jan 2005
Pressure reducing valves	30	*	1 Jan 2005
Solid waste collection services (29110)			
Air compressors and receivers	7	*	1 Jul 2015
Balers	7	*	1 Jul 2015
Bins:			
Domestic mobile bins (plastic)	10	*	1 Jul 2015
Industrial mobile rubbish bins (metal)	8	*	1 Jul 2015
Industrial mobile rubbish bins (plastic)	5	*	1 Jul 2015
Metal skips for hire	8	*	1 Jul 2015
Roll-on roll-off containers	10	*	1 Jul 2015
Stationary and portable compactor bins	8	*	1 Jul 2015
Bin delivery vehicle cranes/bin and skip lifters	10	*	1 Jul 2015
Compactors and collection bodies on trucks (including lifting arms)	8	*	1 Jul 2015
Fans	10	*	1 Jul 2015
Forklifts	11	*	1 Jul 2015
Garbage compactor trucks (excluding the compactor)[31]	10	*#	1 Jul 2015
Hook lifts on truck body	10	*	1 Jul 2015
Truck hoists	20	*	1 Jul 2015
Washing assets (including pressure washers)	4	*	1 Jul 2015
Waste water treatment systems	10	*	1 Jul 2015

ELECTRICITY, GAS, WATER AND WASTE SERVICES
(26110 to 29220)

Asset	Life (Years)	Reviewed	Date Of Application
Waste treatment and disposal services (29210)			
Transfer stations and landfill operation assets:			
Air compressors and receivers	7	*	1 Jul 2015
Balers	7	*	1 Jul 2015
Bins:			
Bins generally (including metal bins)	7	*	1 Jul 2015
Compactor bins	6	*	1 Jul 2015
Mobile bins (including rubbish bins)	5	*	1 Jul 2015
Bulk fuel above ground tanks	20	*	1 Jul 2015
Bulldozers and drotts (including landfill compaction assets)	5	*	1 Jul 2015
CCTV and security systems	4	*	1 Jul 2015
Concrete crushing assets	15		1 Jul 2015
Dust and odour control assets	12	*	1 Jul 2015
Excavators and front end loaders	5	*	1 Jul 2015
Fans	10	*	1 Jul 2015
Forklifts used in waste handling	5	*	1 Jul 2015
Forklifts not used in waste handling	11	*	1 Jul 2015
Gas capture assets:			
Extraction assets (including wells, laterals and headers, and condensate systems)	8	*	1 Jul 2015
Flare skid assets generally (including blowers, monitoring systems and flame arresters, but excluding flare stacks)	7 1/2	*	1 Jul 2015
Flare stacks – continuous use	15	*	1 Jul 2015
Flare stacks – standby stacks	7 1/2	*	1 Jul 2015
Monitoring systems (excluding wells)	5	*	1 Jul 2015
Off-site monitoring wells	15	*	1 Jul 2015
Green waste mulchers and shredders	7	*	1 Jul 2015
Hoppers	7	*	1 Jul 2015
Push pits	15	*	1 Jul 2015
Sweepers – road sweepers	10	*	1 Jul 2015
Transfer trailers	10	*	1 Jul 2015
Water treatment systems	10	*	1 Jul 2015
Weighbridges	15	*	1 Jul 2015
Waste remediation and materials recovery services (29220)			
Materials recovery facility (MRF) assets:			
Air compressors and receivers	7	*	1 Jul 2014
Balers	7	*	1 Jul 2014
Ballistic separators	10	*	1 Jul 2014
Bins:			
Bins generally (including metal bins)	7	*	1 Jul 2014
Compactor bins	6	*	1 Jul 2014
Mobile bins (including rubbish bins)	5	*	1 Jul 2014
Bunkers	10	*	1 Jul 2014
CCTV and security systems	4	*	1 Jul 2014
Chippers and shredders	7	*	1 Jul 2014
Control systems	10	*	1 Jul 2014
Conveyors and conveyor systems:			

ELECTRICITY, GAS, WATER AND WASTE SERVICES
(26110 to 29220)

Asset	Life (Years)	Reviewed	Date Of Application
Bounce conveyors and feeders	10	*	1 Jul 2014
Conveyors generally ((incorporating belt, drive, motors and supporting structure) including walking floor conveyors)	9	*	1 Jul 2014
Hand sort conveyors	10	*	1 Jul 2014
Door controls and motor drive systems for automatic opening doors (incorporating controls, motors and sensors, but excluding doors)	10	*	1 Jul 2014
Ducted air transfer system assets	10	*	1 Jul 2014
Dust collectors	12	*	1 Jul 2014
Eddy current separators	7	*	1 Jul 2014
Excavators and front end loaders	5	*	1 Jul 2014
Fans	10	*	1 Jul 2014
Feed hoppers (incorporating steel drag chain, conveyor belt, metering feed roller, motor and gearbox)	5	*	1 Jul 2014
Ferrous and magnetic separators	10	*	1 Jul 2014
Food separation and screening assets	10	*	1 Jul 2014
Forklifts	5	*	1 Jul 2014
Glass breakers and crushers	6	*	1 Jul 2014
Hoppers	7	*	1 Jul 2014
Leachate pumps and filters	10	*	1 Jul 2014
Lifting assets (including pallet jacks)	10	*	1 Jul 2014
Optical sorters	5	*	1 Jul 2014
Screen separators	10	*	1 Jul 2014
Sweepers and scrubbers	10	*	1 Jul 2014
Trommels (incorporating wheels, motors and gearboxes):			
Fixed	7	*	1 Jul 2014
Portable	7	*	1 Jul 2014
Vacuum extraction and cleaning assets	10	*	1 Jul 2014
Vibrating screen separators	10	*	1 Jul 2014
Waste compactors	9	*	1 Jul 2014
Weighbridges	15	*	1 Jul 2014

Footnotes:

29 A capped effective life of 20 years is available where applicable (assets marked with #) – see subsection 40-102(5)

30 A capped effective life of 20 years is available where applicable (assets marked with #) – see subsection 40-102(5)

31 A capped effective life of 7 1/2 years may be available – see subsection 40-102(4)

¶43-030 Effective life — construction

CONSTRUCTION
(30110 to 32990)

Asset	Life (Years)	Reviewed	Date Of Application
Air compressors:			
Compressors – reciprocating	7	*	1 Jul 2008
Compressors – rotary screw	10	*	1 Jul 2008
Backhoe loaders	9	*	1 Jul 2002

CONSTRUCTION
(30110 to 32990)

Asset	Life (Years)	Reviewed	Date Of Application
Bending machines (bar, angle or rod)	10	*	1 Jul 2008
Block and brick elevators (portable)	10	*	1 Jul 2008
Chain blocks, rod shears, jacks etc	13 1/3		1 Jan 2001
Compaction:			
Compactors – flat plate	8	*	1 Jul 2008
Compactors – vertical rammer	6	*	1 Jul 2008
Concreting assets:			
Brick and paving saws	5	*	1 Jul 2008
Buggies or dumpers (motorised)	5	*	1 Jul 2001
Concrete demolition saws	3	*	1 Jul 2008
Concrete kibble buckets	15	*	1 Jul 2008
Concrete mixers	4	*	1 Jul 2008
Concrete surface preparation assets (including floor grinders, planers and scarifiers)	5	*	1 Jul 2008
Concrete trowels:			
Ride on	7	*	1 Jul 2008
Walk behind	5	*	1 Jul 2008
Concrete vibrating screeders	5	*	1 Jul 2008
Concrete vibrators:			
Brushcutter style	5	*	1 Jul 2008
Drive units	6	*	1 Jul 2008
Flexible shaft pumps	6	*	1 Jul 2008
Vibrating shaft	3	*	1 Jul 2008
Concrete wheeled saws	6	*	1 Jul 2008
Hoppers, skips and hoist buckets	10		1 Jan 2001
Mobile concrete pumping units	6 2/3		1 Jan 2001
Cranes (mobile):			
Light and medium	15	*	1 Jul 2002
Heavy (over 15.24 tonnes lift)	20	*	1 Jul 2002
Tower and hoists	10		1 Jan 2001
Dozers/front end loaders	9	*	1 Jul 2002
Forklifts	11	*	1 Jul 2002
Formwork, beams and props, steel	10	*	1 Jul 2008
Hydraulic excavators	10	*	1 Jul 2002
Lift slab assets (incorporating spreader bars, clutches, pulleys and cables)	5	*	1 Jul 2008
Mini excavators	8	*	1 Jul 2002
Motor graders	10	*	1 Jul 2002
Pavers	12	*	1 Jul 2002
Power supply assets:			
Generators, portable (incorporating attached engine management and generator monitoring instruments):			
Diesel	10	*	1 Jul 2008
Petrol	5	*	1 Jul 2008
Power tools:			
Chain saws	3	*	1 Jul 2008
Hand tools:			
Air	5	*	1 Jul 2008
Battery	3	*	1 Jul 2008

CONSTRUCTION
(30110 to 32990)

Asset	Life (Years)	Reviewed	Date Of Application
Electric	5	*	1 Jul 2008
Jack hammers:			
Air	7	*	1 Jul 2008
Electric	3	*	1 Jul 2008
Nail guns – air	3	*	1 Jul 2008
Profilers	10	*	1 Jul 2002
Pumps	10		1 Jan 2001
Road rollers	15	*	1 Jul 2002
Saws, bench and mitre, portable	7	*	1 Jul 2008
Scrapers	8	*	1 Jul 2002
Skid steer loaders	7	*	1 Jul 2002
Stabiliser recyclers	12	*	1 Jul 2002
Surveying assets (including levels) – see Table A Surveying and mapping services (69220)			
Telescopic handlers	10	*	1 Jul 2002
Tool carriers	10	*	1 Jul 2002
Track loaders	9	*	1 Jul 2002
Traffic management assets (use the relevant lives given under Table A Rental and hiring services (except real estate) (66110 to 66400), whether or not the assets are in fact hired or leased)			
Welders:			
Diesel	10	*	1 Jul 2008
Electric	5	*	1 Jul 2008
Wheel loaders	8	*	1 Jul 2002
Winches	$13^1/_3$		1 Jan 2001
Other heavy and civil engineering construction n.e.c. (31099)			
Automatic welding machines (used at sea in construction of submarine pipelines)	10		1 Jan 2001

¶43-035 Effective life — wholesale trade

WHOLESALE TRADE
(33110 to 38000)

Asset	Life (Years)	Reviewed	Date Of Application
Barcode readers/scanners - see Table B Warehouse and distribution centre equipment and machines			
Benches	15	*	1 Jul 2019
Dimensioning machines	15	*	1 Jul 2019
Ice making machines	8	*	1 Jul 2019
Intermediate bulk containers:			
Mild and stainless steel	15	*	1 Jul 2019
Others	8	*	1 Jul 2019
Lifting and handling assets:			
Elevating work platforms	10	*	1 Jul 2019
Forklifts - see Table B Warehouse and distribution centre equipment and machines			
Pallet conveyers – see Table B Warehouse and distribution centre equipment and machines			

WHOLESALE TRADE
(33110 to 38000)

Asset	Life (Years)	Reviewed	Date Of Application
Pallet jacks - see Table B Loading bay assets			
Picking and collating machines - see Table B Warehouse and distribution centre equipment and machines			
Ladders	4	*	1 Jul 2019
Livestock scales, weigh indicators and loading bars	5	*	1 Jul 2019
Racks - see Table B Warehouse and distribution centre equipment and machines			
Packaging assets:			
Carton sealers and box taping machines	12	*	1 Jul 2019
Pallet wrappers - see Table B Packaging machines			
Pumps:			
Chemical pumps	10	*	1 Jul 2019
Product pumps	12	*	1 Jul 2019
Vacuum pumps	12	*	1 Jul 2019
Water pumps	15	*	1 Jul 2019
Refrigeration assets - see Table B Refrigeration assets			
Scales (excluding livestock scales)	10	*	1 Jul 2019
Signs - see Table B Advertising signs			
Tanks:			
Chemical storage tanks	15		1 Jul 2019
Water storage tanks	20		1 Jul 2019
Trailers - see Table B Motor vehicles and trailers			
Trolleys - see Table B Warehouse and distribution centre equipment and machines			
Unmanned aerial vehicles (drones/remotely piloted aircraft) - see Table B Unmanned aerial vehicles			
Wool wholesaling (33110)			
Wool presses	20	*	1 Jul 2006
Petroleum product wholesaling (33210)			
Bulk fuel regional depot assets (excluding LPG assets):			
Cathodic protection systems:			
Sacrificial anode	10	*	1 Jul 2010
Impressed current	20	*	1 Jul 2010
Effluent treatment system (incorporating pumps, motors and electronic circuitry)	15	*	1 Jul 2010
Electric pumps	10	*	1 Jul 2010
Hoses	2	*	1 Jul 2010
Loading gantries and racks (incorporating meters and metering systems)	15	*	1 Jul 2010
Petroleum product storage tanks – fibreglass and steel	20	*	1 Jul 2010
Rigid fuel tank truck assets:			
Aluminium tanks or barrels	10	*	1 Jul 2010
Filters	5	*	1 Jul 2010
Metering systems	5	*	1 Jul 2010
Overfill protection systems	10	*	1 Jul 2010
Pumping systems:			
Guns and nozzles	3	*	1 Jul 2010
Hose reels	7	*	1 Jul 2010

WHOLESALE TRADE
(33110 to 38000)

Asset	Life (Years)	Reviewed	Date Of Application
Hoses	2	*	1 Jul 2010
Hydraulically driven pumps	8	*	1 Jul 2010
Pipes and fittings	10	*	1 Jul 2010
Tailgate loaders	15	*	1 Jul 2010
Single or multi product gasoline and diesoline dispensers (incorporating meters, electronic circuitry, LCD displays, cash presets, hoses, automatic nozzles and steel cabinets and, where applicable, vapour recovery monitoring and collection systems)	10	*	1 Jul 2010
Single or multi product gasoline and diesoline pumps (incorporating pump units, meter, electronic circuitry, LCD displays, cash presets, hoses, automatic nozzles, steel cabinets and, where applicable, vapour recovery monitoring and collection systems)	10	*	1 Jul 2010
Submersible turbine pumps	8	*	1 Jul 2010
Underground distribution piping systems (incorporating pipes, fittings and manholes) fibreglass and steel	20	*	1 Jul 2010
Bulk fuel terminal assets (excluding LPG assets):			
Automatic tank gauges	10	*	1 Jul 2010
Effluent treatment systems (incorporating air pump, pipes, separator and tank)	10	*	1 Jul 2010
Fire protection systems (incorporating auxiliary monitors, fire and UV detectors, fire indicator anels, fire retardant lines and foam storage tank)	15	*	1 Jul 2010
Hoses	2	*	1 Jul 2010
Loading and unloading arms (incorporating balance mechanisms, couplers, drop hoses and swivels)	10	*	1 Jul 2010
Marketing pumps	7	*	1 Jul 2010
Meters and metering systems	7	*	1 Jul 2010
Overfill protection systems	10	*	1 Jul 2010
Product piping (steel)	20	*	1 Jul 2010
Terminal automation equipment	10	*	1 Jul 2010
Vapour recovery units	15	*	1 Jul 2010
LPG depot and terminal assets:			
Automatic tank gauges	10	*	1 Jul 2010
Cathodic protection systems:			
Sacrificial anode	10	*	1 Jul 2010
Impressed current	20	*	1 Jul 2010
Depot and terminal storage vessels – aboveground and underground	30	*	1 Jul 2010
Electronic scales	10	*	1 Jul 2010
Forklift fuel tanks:			
Galvanised steel or steel tanks coated with zinc rich enamel	15	*	1 Jul 2010
Aluminium tanks	12	*	1 Jul 2010
Hoses	5	*	1 Jul 2010
In-situ permanently installed cylinders	30	*	1 Jul 2010
Leak detection systems	8	*	1 Jul 2010
Leisure market cylinders (4.5 and 9 kgs capacity)	15	*	1 Jul 2010
Loading arms:			
Terminal	10	*	1 Jul 2010
Marine	25	*	1 Jul 2010
LPG fleet refuelling facility:			
Dispenser	10	*	1 Jul 2010

WHOLESALE TRADE
(33110 to 38000)

Asset	Life (Years)	Reviewed	Date Of Application
Guns and nozzles	3	*	1 Jul 2010
Hoses	5	*	1 Jul 2010
Meters	7	*	1 Jul 2010
Piping	20	*	1 Jul 2010
Pump sets	10	*	1 Jul 2010
Storage tanks	30	*	1 Jul 2010
Valves	10	*	1 Jul 2010
LPG tank truck assets:			
LPG storage tanks	20	*	1 Jul 2010
Metering systems	7	*	1 Jul 2010
Pumping systems:			
Guns and nozzles	3	*	1 Jul 2010
Hoses	5	*	1 Jul 2010
Hose reels	7	*	1 Jul 2010
Pipes and fittings	7	*	1 Jul 2010
Pumps	7	*	1 Jul 2010
Valves	7	*	1 Jul 2010
Product piping systems:			
Pipes	20	*	1 Jul 2010
Valves	10	*	1 Jul 2010
Pumps	7	*	1 Jul 2010
Stillages	5	*	1 Jul 2010
Vapour recovery units and vapour compressors	7	*	1 Jul 2010
Weighbridges	25	*	1 Jul 2010
Commission-based wholesaling (38000)			
Sale yards (used by stock and station agents)	30	*	1 Jul 2014

¶43-040 Effective life — retail trade

RETAIL TRADE
(39110 to 43209)

Asset	Life (Years)	Reviewed	Date Of Application
Counters, freestanding (including check-out and service counters)	10	*	1 Jul 2005
Door controls and motor drive systems for automatic sliding doors (incorporating chains, controls, motors and sensors, but excluding doors)	15	*	1 Jul 2005
Electronic article surveillance (EAS) system assets (including barcodes or tag deactivators and detachers, door pedestals, electronic tag release assets, receivers and transmitters)	5	*	1 Jul 2005
Floor coverings (removable without damage):			
Carpet	8	*	1 Jul 2005
Floating timber	10	*	1 Jul 2005
Linoleum	10	*	1 Jul 2005
Vinyl	10	*	1 Jul 2005
Furniture, freestanding (including chairs, cupboards, racks, showcases and tables)	10	*	1 Jul 2005
Hot food display assets (including bain marie)	10	*	1 Jul 2005
Loading bay assets – see Table B Loading bay assets			

RETAIL TRADE
(39110 to 43209)

Asset	Life (Years)	Reviewed	Date Of Application
Overhead track scales (including meat rail scales)	10	*	1 Jul 2005
Power supply assets, emergency or standby:			
Generator assets – see Table B Power supply assets			
Uninterruptible power supply (UPS) system:			
Line interactive type	5	*	1 Jul 2013
On line double conversion type	10	*	1 Jul 2013
Public address and paging system assets (including amplifiers, audio speakers and microphones) – see Table B Public address and paging system assets			
Refrigeration assets:			
Generally (including blast chillers, condensers, evaporators, refrigeration cabinets, standalone freezers and standalone refrigerators)	10	*	1 Jul 2014
Ice making machines	8	*	1 Jul 2014
Insulation panels used in cool or freezer rooms	40	*	1 Jul 2014
Roller shutter electric motors	20	*	1 Jul 2005
Shelving	10	*	1 Jul 2005
Signage used for business identification (including lighting for signs) – see Table B Advertising signs			
Trolleys, customer shopping type	7	*	1 Jul 2005
Trolleys, stock type	10	*	1 Jul 2005
Visual display assets (including body forms, head displayers, mannequins and seasonal decorations)	7	*	1 Jul 2005
Motor vehicle tyre or tube retailing (39220)			
Air tools (including ratchet guns)	2	*	1 Jul 2011
Compressed air assets:			
Air compressors:			
Reciprocating	10	*	1 Jul 2011
Rotary screw	10	*	1 Jul 2011
Rotary vane	10	*	1 Jul 2011
Air receivers	10	*	1 Jul 2011
Air driers and dehumidifiers	10	*	1 Jul 2011
Hose reels	3	*	1 Jul 2011
Reticulation lines:			
Aluminium	15	*	1 Jul 2011
Copper	20	*	1 Jul 2011
Polyethylene (PE)	15	*	1 Jul 2011
Steel	10	*	1 Jul 2011
Floor jacks:			
Used for car and light truck repairs	3	*	1 Jul 2011
Used for heavy vehicle repairs	5	*	1 Jul 2011
Hand tools	10	*	1 Jul 2011
Stillages	15	*	1 Jul 2011
Storage shelving	10	*	1 Jul 2011
Tyre conveyors:			
Horizontal	10	*	1 Jul 2011
Vertical	8	*	1 Jul 2011
Tyre fitting machines	5	*	1 Jul 2011
Tyre inflation cages	10	*	1 Jul 2011

RETAIL TRADE
(39110 to 43209)

Asset	Life (Years)	Reviewed	Date Of Application
Tyre inflators (automatic and manual)	3	*	1 Jul 2011
Tyre spreaders	8	*	1 Jul 2011
Vehicle hoists:			
Used for car and light truck repairs	10	*	1 Jul 2011
Used for heavy vehicle repairs	20	*	1 Jul 2011
Wheel alignment machines	7	*	1 Jul 2011
Wheel balancing machines	5	*	1 Jul 2011
Wheel balancing plates, flanges and finger adaptors	5	*	1 Jul 2011
Wheel lifters	5	*	1 Jul 2011
Wheel lifters (incorporating tyre spreaders)	8	*	1 Jul 2011
Fuel retailing (40000)			
Air compressors and air lines	7	*	1 Jul 2010
Automatic tank gauges	10	*	1 Jul 2010
Canopy lighting:			
Liquid emitting diode	10	*	1 Jul 2010
Radiant gas positive	5	*	1 Jul 2010
Convenience store assets:			
Air conditioning systems	7	*	1 Jul 2010
Back-loading refrigerated cabinets (incorporating fans, boosters and compressors)	10	*	1 Jul 2010
CCTV video surveillance systems	4	*	1 Jul 2010
Coffee making machines (including espresso and drip filter type machines)	5	*	1 Jul 2010
Counters – freestanding	10	*	1 Jul 2010
Display shelving and racking	10	*	1 Jul 2010
Door controls and motor drive systems for automatic opening doors (incorporating controls, motors and sensors, but excluding doors)	7	*	1 Jul 2010
Hot food display assets (including bain maries)	10	*	1 Jul 2010
Microwave ovens	5	*	1 Jul 2010
Pie warmers and heating units	10	*	1 Jul 2010
Refrigerated cabinets and freezers	10	*	1 Jul 2010
PA systems	12	*	1 Jul 2010
Point of sale assets:			
Barcode scanners	6	*	1 Jul 2010
Electronic funds transfer point of sale machines (EFTPOS)	6	*	1 Jul 2010
Forecourt controllers	6	*	1 Jul 2010
Safes:			
Cash storage	10	*	1 Jul 2010
Cash vending	7	*	1 Jul 2010
Cigarette safes	7	*	1 Jul 2010
Emergency shut off systems	10	*	1 Jul 2010
Facility signs	7	*	1 Jul 2010
Gasoline and diesoline assets:			
Effluent treatment systems (incorporating motors, electronic circuitry, pumps, and separators)	8	*	1 Jul 2010
Leak protection pressure systems	8	*	1 Jul 2010

RETAIL TRADE
(39110 to 43209)

Asset	Life (Years)	Reviewed	Date Of Application
Single or multi product gasoline and diesoline dispensers (incorporating meters, electronic circuitry, LCD displays, cash presets, hoses, automatic nozzles, steel cabinets and, where applicable, vapour recovery monitoring and collection systems)	10	*	1 Jul 2010
Single or multi product gasoline and diesoline pumps (incorporating pump units, meters, electronic circuitry, LCD displays, cash presets, hoses, automatic nozzles, steel cabinets and, where applicable, vapour recovery monitoring and collection systems	7	*	1 Jul 2010
Pay at pump card reading systems	6	*	1 Jul 2010
Submersible turbine pumps	8	*	1 Jul 2010
Underground fuel distribution and containment piping systems (incorporating pipes, fittings and manholes)	20	*	1 Jul 2010
Underground fuel storage tanks – steel and fibreglass	20	*	1 Jul 2010
Hot water systems	10	*	1 Jul 2010
LPG assets:			
LPG pumps	7	*	1 Jul 2010
LPG dispensers (incorporating meters, electronic circuitry, LCD displays, cash presets, hoses, automatic nozzles and steel cabinets)	10	*	1 Jul 2010
LPG storage tanks – aboveground and underground	30	*	1 Jul 2010
Underground steel piping systems (incorporating pipes, fittings and manholes)	20	*	1 Jul 2010
Food retailing (41100 to 41290)			
Butchers' plant	20		1 Jan 2001
Supermarket and grocery stores (41100)			
Bakery assets:			
Bakery display assets, non-refrigerated (including freestanding display cabinets, cases, racks, shelves and stands)	10	*	1 Jul 2020
Bakery trolleys	12	*	1 Jul 2020
Bread slicers	10	*	1 Jul 2020
Bun divider rounders	10	*	1 Jul 2020
Doughnut making machines	8	*	1 Jul 2020
Hydraulic dough dividers	10	*	1 Jul 2020
Mixers (including planetary and spiral mixers)	10	*	1 Jul 2020
Moulders	12	*	1 Jul 2020
Ovens	10	*	1 Jul 2020
Provers and retarder provers	8	*	1 Jul 2020
Butcher assets:			
Bandsaws	10	*	1 Jul 2020
Meat:			
Mincers	10	*	1 Jul 2020
Tenderisers	10	*	1 Jul 2020
Meat trolleys	12	*	1 Jul 2020
Sausage filling machines	10	*	1 Jul 2020
Deli Assets:			
Cheese cutters	10	*	1 Jul 2020
Cheese graters	10	*	1 Jul 2020
Coffee making machines (including espresso and drip filter type machines)	5	*	1 Jul 2020
Contact grills	10	*	1 Jul 2020

RETAIL TRADE
(39110 to 43209)

Asset	Life (Years)	Reviewed	Date Of Application
Deep fryers	10	*	1 Jul 2020
Deli slicers	10	*	1 Jul 2020
Hot food display assets (including bain marie, hot boxes and pie warmers)	10	*	1 Jul 2020
Juicing machines, commercial type	8	*	1 Jul 2020
Ovens (including chicken ovens and smoker ovens)	10	*	1 Jul 2020
Popcorn machines	8	*	1 Jul 2020
Sushi making assets (including rice cookers, rice mixers and sushi robots)	7	*	1 Jul 2020
Produce assets:			
Display barrels	10	*	1 Jul 2020
Produce bins	12	*	1 Jul 2020
Scales (including bench scales and hanging scales)	8	*	1 Jul 2020
Refrigeration and freezing assets:			
Compressors, condensers and evaporators	10	*	1 Jul 2020
Freezers and refrigerators generally (including refrigeration cabinets and cases, standalone chillers, standalone freezers and standalone refrigerators)	10	*	1 Jul 2020
Insulation panels used in cool or freezer rooms	30	*	1 Jul 2020
Night blinds/covers	10	*	1 Jul 2020
Support and other assets:			
Automatic entrance swing gates	10	*	1 Jul 2020
Balers (for cardboard and plastic) – see Table B Warehouse and distribution centre equipment and machines			
Benches (stainless steel), free standing	20	*	1 Jul 2020
Bin lifters	15	*	1 Jul 2020
Cash handling assets:			
Coin counters and sorters	10	*	1 Jul 2020
Note counters and sorters	10	*	1 Jul 2020
Safes	15	*	1 Jul 2020
Cigarette cabinets, free standing	15	*	1 Jul 2020
Counters, free standing (including checkout and service counters)	10	*	1 Jul 2020
Dishwashers	10	*	1 Jul 2020
Display racks and stands (including magazine racks/stands)	10	*	1 Jul 2020
Hot water systems (excluding piping)	12	*	1 Jul 2020
Label printers	5	*	1 Jul 2020
Label printing scales	8	*	1 Jul 2020
Labelling guns	5	*	1 Jul 2020
Microwave ovens	5	*	1 Jul 2020
Nut grinders/peanut butter makers	5	*	1 Jul 2020
Packaging assets:			
Automatic labelling wrappers, modified atmosphere packaging (MAP) and vacuum chamber packaging machines	10	*	1 Jul 2020
Benchtop heat wrappers	10	*	1 Jul 2020
Point of sale assets:			
Generally (excluding self-checkout registers) – see Table B Point of sale assets			
Self-checkout registers	6	*	1 Jul 2020
Power generators (emergency or standby)	20	*	1 Jul 2020
Racking	20	*	1 Jul 2020

RETAIL TRADE
(39110 to 43209)

Asset	Life (Years)	Reviewed	Date Of Application
Range hood exhaust fans	12	*	1 Jul 2020
Safety steps	10	*	1 Jul 2020
Shelving	15	*	1 Jul 2020
Signage:			
Aisle signs	7	*	1 Jul 2020
Others (such as advertising signs and signage for business identification) – see Table B Advertising signs			
Stock ladders	12	*	1 Jul 2020
Trolleys, customer shopping type	7	*	1 Jul 2020
Trolleys, stock type (including roll cages, platform trolleys, etc)	10	*	1 Jul 2020
UV insect exterminators	7	*	1 Jul 2020
Other store-based retailing (42110 to 42799)			
Newspaper wrapping machines	10		1 Jan 2001
Paint tinting and colour blending machines (manual and automatic)	7	*	1 Jul 2014

¶43-045 Effective life — accommodation and food services

ACCOMMODATION AND FOOD SERVICES
(44000 to 45302)

Asset	Life (Years)	Reviewed	Date Of Application
Accommodation (44000)			
Accommodation providers using assets not listed here may rely on determinations shown for Residential property operators (67110)			
Accommodation providers who operate a pub, tavern, bar, cafe, restaurant or club within their premises should use the effective life determinations shown for cafes, restaurants, takeaway food services, pubs, taverns, bars and clubs (hospitality) (45110 to 45302) for assets used in that business			
Audio visual entertainment assets (including those used in conference and function rooms (including amplifier, audio speaker, digital disc player, microphone, television sets, turntable, video projection equipment))	5	*	1 Jul 2005
Carpets	7	*	1 Jul 2005
Door controls and motor drive systems for automatic sliding doors and revolving doors (incorporating chains, controls, motors and sensors, but excluding doors)	10	*	1 Jul 2005
Furniture, freestanding:			
Generally (including guestrooms)	7	*	1 Jul 2005
Outdoor	5	*	1 Jul 2005
Garage doors, electric (excluding doors):			
Controls and motors	5	*	1 Jul 2005
Gates, electric (excluding gates):			
Controls and motors	5	*	1 Jul 2005
Guestroom assets:			
Bathroom assets:			
Accessories, freestanding (including sanitary assets, shower caddies, soap holders and toilet brushes)	1	*	1 Jul 2005
Hair dryers	3	*	1 Jul 2005
Heated towel rails, electric	5	*	1 Jul 2005

ACCOMMODATION AND FOOD SERVICES
(44000 to 45302)

Asset	Life (Years)	Reviewed	Date Of Application
Scales	5	*	1 Jul 2005
Spa bath pumps	7	*	1 Jul 2005
Towels	1	*	1 Jul 2005
Bedding (including mattress protectors, pillows and sheets)	2	*	1 Jul 2005
Bed mattresses	7	*	1 Jul 2005
Beds:			
Generally (including ensembles)	7	*	1 Jul 2005
Foldout and rollaway beds (excluding sofas)	3	*	1 Jul 2005
Bed spreads, blankets and quilts	5	*	1 Jul 2005
Clocks and clock radios	5	*	1 Jul 2005
Kitchen assets:			
Bar refrigerators	10	*	1 Jul 2005
Cooking utensils (including electric jugs, kettles, pans, pots and toasters, but excluding portable cook tops and ovens)	2	*	1 Jul 2005
Crockery and cutlery	4	*	1 Jul 2005
Glassware	2	*	1 Jul 2005
Microwave ovens	5	*	1 Jul 2005
Laundry assets in guestrooms:			
Clothes dryers	7	*	1 Jul 2005
Irons and ironing boards	3	*	1 Jul 2005
Washing machines	7	*	1 Jul 2005
Window blinds and curtains	6	*	1 Jul 2005
Hot water systems (excluding commercial boilers and piping)	10	*	1 Jul 2005
Housekeeping assets (including bins, buckets, floor signs and toilet brushes)	1	*	1 Jul 2005
Laundry assets used by hotel/motel operators:			
Dryers	10	*	1 Jul 2005
Linen bins	15	*	1 Jul 2005
Pressers	15	*	1 Jul 2005
Roller irons	20	*	1 Jul 2005
Washing machines	10	*	1 Jul 2005
Public address and paging system assets (including amplifiers, audio speakers and microphones)	10	*	1 Jul 2005
Sauna heating assets	10	*	1 Jul 2005
Swimming pools and spas:			
Chlorinators	8	*	1 Jul 2005
Filtration assets (including pumps)	8	*	1 Jul 2005
Heaters	10	*	1 Jul 2005
Trolleys	10	*	1 Jul 2005
Vacuum cleaners	3	*	1 Jul 2005
Water pumps used to deliver water to residences above ground level	10	*	1 Jul 2005
Cafes, restaurants, takeaway food services, pubs, taverns, bars and clubs (hospitality) (45110 to 45302)			
Audio visual entertainment assets (including amplifiers, audio speakers, digital disc players, microphones, television sets, turntables and video projection equipment)	5	*	1 Jul 2005
Bars, freestanding (including drink service counters and wet bars)	15	*	1 Jul 2005
Beer dispensing system assets (including, tanks, taps tubes and valves)	15	*	1 Jul 2005
Coffee making machines (including espresso and drip filter type machines)	5	*	1 Jul 2005

ACCOMMODATION AND FOOD SERVICES
(44000 to 45302)

Asset	Life (Years)	Reviewed	Date Of Application
Counters for customer service, freestanding	15	*	1 Jul 2005
Dance floor assets, freestanding (including wooden surface, fog and smoke machines, strobe lights and disco balls)	5	*	1 Jul 2005
Dishwasher machines	8	*	1 Jul 2005
Drink blenders	3	*	1 Jul 2005
Drink dispensing machines (including hot water urns, post mix dispensers, refrigerated and frozen drink dispensers and dairy dispensers, but excluding beer dispensing systems)	10	*	1 Jul 2005
Electronic spirits dispensers	5	*	1 Jul 2005
Floor coverings, removable without damage:			
Carpet	5	*	1 Jul 2005
Rubber safety mats	5	*	1 Jul 2005
Food preparation and service assets:			
Bench top appliances – small portable type (including blenders, food processors, grills, rice cookers and toasters)	3	*	1 Jul 2005
Cooking appliances, large commercial type (including cook tops, deep fryers, grills, kebab machines, ovens and salamanders)	10	*	1 Jul 2005
Cookware, handheld (including frypans, pans, pots, trays and woks)	2	*	1 Jul 2005
Crockery, cutlery and glassware	1	*	1 Jul 2005
Hot food display assets (including bain marie)	10	*	1 Jul 2005
Microwave ovens	5	*	1 Jul 2005
Preparation benches, freestanding	20	*	1 Jul 2005
Wok burners, large commercial type	8	*	1 Jul 2005
Furniture, freestanding, for customer use:			
In drinking areas of pubs, bars, clubs	5	*	1 Jul 2005
In dining areas	8	*	1 Jul 2005
Furniture, not freestanding:			
Chairs and tables fixed to ground or building	20	*	1 Jul 2005
Glassware	1	*	1 Jul 2005
Glass washer machines	5	*	1 Jul 2005
Kitchen exhaust fans	5	*	1 Jul 2005
Menu boards	5	*	1 Jul 2005
Poker/gaming machines	7	*	1 Jul 2009
Refrigeration assets:			
Generally (including blast chillers, condensers, evaporators, refrigeration cabinets, standalone freezers and standalone refrigerators)	10	*	1 Jul 2014
Ice making machines	8	*	1 Jul 2014
Insulation panels used in cool or freezer rooms	40	*	1 Jul 2014

¶43-050 Effective life — transport and storage

TRANSPORT, POSTAL AND WAREHOUSING
(46100 to 53090)

Asset	Life (Years)	Reviewed	Date Of Application
Road transport (46100 to 46239)			
Containers, transportable (used to transport goods by road, rail and sea)	10	*	1 Jan 2001
Motor vehicles and trailers:			

TRANSPORT, POSTAL AND WAREHOUSING
(46100 to 53090)

Asset	Life (Years)	Reviewed	Date Of Application
Buses having a gross vehicle mass of more than 3.5 tonnes[32]	15	*#	1 Jan 2005
Cars (motor vehicles designed to carry a load of less than one tonne and fewer than 9 passengers):			
Generally	8	*	1 Jan 2006
Hire cars:[33]			
Cars used to provide basic service ride-sourcing, ride-hailing or ride-sharing services (eg uberX)	8	*	1 Jul 2016
Generally (including cars used to provide premium service ride-sourcing, ride-hailing or ride-sharing services eg UberBLACK)	6	*	1 Jul 2016
Rental cars:[34]	5	*	1 Jul 2016
Taxis	4	*	1 Jul 2015
Light commercial vehicles designed to carry a load of one tonne or greater and having a gross vehicle mass of 3.5 tonnes or less[35]	12	*#	1 Jan 2005
Limousines:			
Sedan limousines	6	*	1 Jul 2016
Stretch limousines	12	*	1 Jul 2016
Minibuses having a gross vehicle mass of 3.5 tonnes or less and designed to carry 9 or more passengers[36]	12	*#	1 Jan 2005
Trailers having a gross vehicle mass greater than 4.5 tonnes[37]	15	*#	1 Jan 2005
Trailers having a gross vehicle mass of 4.5 tonnes or less:			
Aluminium, galvanised steel, galvanised hot dipped steel and powder coated trailers	10	*	1 Jul 2015
Mild steel trailers (painted and unpainted)	5	*	1 Jul 2015
Trucks having a gross vehicle mass greater than 3.5 tonnes (excluding off highway trucks used in mining operations)[38]	15	*#	1 Jan 2005
Tramway and light rail passenger transport services (46220)			
Infrastructure assets:			
Communication, computer and passenger support assets:			
Automatic vehicle monitoring computer systems	10	*	1 Jul 2010
Automatic vehicle monitoring tram borne equipment (including transponders)	10	*	1 Jul 2010
CCTV systems	4	*	1 Jul 2010
Control systems	10	*	1 Jul 2010
Hand-held passenger ticketing machines	5	*	1 Jul 2010
Passenger information displays	10	*	1 Jul 2010
Passenger ticketing machines	15	*	1 Jul 2010
Radio base stations, intercoms	7	*	1 Jul 2010
Electrification assets:			
Lighting	15	*	1 Jul 2010
Overhead distribution lines (incorporating conductors, cross arms, feeders, insulators, inverters, fittings and poles)	30	*	1 Jul 2010
Power transformers	40	*	1 Jul 2010
Substations (incorporating switchgear and circuit breakers)	40	*	1 Jul 2010
Signalling assets (including automatic points)	15	*	1 Jul 2010
Track maintenance assets:			
Truck mounted maintenance assets (including points cleaning, sweeping and welding machines)	15	*	1 Jul 2010
Trackwork (incorporating track drainage):			
Ballasted track	25	*	1 Jul 2010

TRANSPORT, POSTAL AND WAREHOUSING
(46100 to 53090)

Asset	Life (Years)	Reviewed	Date Of Application
Curved track	20	*	1 Jul 2010
Embedded track	30	*	1 Jul 2010
Points (excluding automatic points) and crossings	20	*	1 Jul 2010
Track within depots	40	*	1 Jul 2010
Tramway and light rail rolling stock:			
Bogies	30	*	1 Jul 2010
Carriages, modules, saloons	30	*	1 Jul 2010
Pantographs	15	*	1 Jul 2010
Rail freight and passenger transport services (47100 to 47200)			
Containers, transportable (used to transport goods by road, rail and sea)	10	*	1 Jan 2001
Infrastructure assets:			
Electrification assets:			
Overhead distribution lines (incorporating conductors, contact catenary, cross arms, insulators and fittings, and poles)	33 1/3	*	1 Jan 2002
Power transformers	30	*	1 Jan 2002
Substations (incorporating switchgear and circuit breakers)	40	*	1 Jan 2002
Passenger information and ticketing system	15	*	1 Jan 2002
Signalling assets (including axle detectors, block signals, dragging equipment detector, hot boxes, interlockings, level crossings, and train control and train describer)	15	*	1 Jan 2002
Trackwork (incorporating rails, sleepers, ballast, permanent way/ top 600, and integral bridges, culverts and tunnels):			
Freight (trackwork used by vehicles with gross axle loads of 30 tonnes and below per vehicle):			
Heavy haul (trackwork carrying >20 GMT per annum)	30	*	1 Jan 2002
Light haul (trackwork carrying <1 GMT per annum)	50	*	1 Jan 2002
Medium haul (trackwork carrying between 1 GMT and 20 GMT per annum)	40	*	1 Jan 2002
Freight (trackwork used by vehicles with gross axle loads above 30 tonnes per vehicle)	20	*	1 Jan 2002
Passenger	40	*	1 Jan 2002
Turnouts and crossings	20	*	1 Jan 2002
Monorail operation assets:			
Infrastructure assets:			
Communication, computer and passenger assets:			
CCTV systems	4	*	1 Jul 2010
Control systems (including commutators)	10	*	1 Jul 2010
Hand held passenger ticketing machines	5	*	1 Jul 2010
Passenger information displays	10	*	1 Jul 2010
Passenger ticketing machines	15	*	1 Jul 2010
Phones, radio base stations, intercoms	7	*	1 Jul 2010
Rescue and recovery vehicles	30	*	1 Jul 2010
Electrification assets:			
Collector rails	30	*	1 Jul 2010
Lighting	15	*	1 Jul 2010
Power transformers	40	*	1 Jul 2010
Standby generators	25	*	1 Jul 2010
Substations (incorporating switchgear and circuit breakers)	40	*	1 Jul 2010

TRANSPORT, POSTAL AND WAREHOUSING
(46100 to 53090)

Asset	Life (Years)	Reviewed	Date Of Application
Uninterruptible power supply (UPS) systems	5	*	1 Jul 2010
Track and maintenance assets:			
Beams and columns	30	*	1 Jul 2010
Maintenance vehicles	15	*	1 Jul 2010
Track	30	*	1 Jul 2010
Track switches	30	*	1 Jul 2010
Traversers	30	*	1 Jul 2010
Monorail rolling stock:			
Bogies	30	*	1 Jul 2010
Carriages, modules, saloons	30	*	1 Jul 2010
Railway rolling stock:			
Locomotives:			
Generally (including diesel-electric and electric)	25	*	1 Jan 2002
Heavy haul (bulk minerals/coal)	20	*	1 Jan 2002
Underground (diesel-battery)	15	*	1 Jan 2002
Passenger:			
Electric/diesel power cars and trailers	30	*	1 Jan 2002
Locomotive hauled carriages (including baggage vans, diners, mail vans, sit-up cars, and sleepers)	30	*	1 Jan 2002
Power vans	15	*	1 Jan 2002
Rail mounted track infrastructure assets:			
Generally (including ballast wagons/cleaners/regulators, rail grinders, sleeper laying machines and track recorders)	20	*	1 Jan 2002
Mainline and switch tampers	15	*	1 Jan 2002
Wagons – bulk freight:			
Mineral ores and coal:			
Carbon steel	20	*	1 Jan 2002
Ferritic steel	30	*	1 Jan 2002
Other:			
Coke quenchers	15	*	1 Jan 2002
Grain hoppers	20	*	1 Jan 2002
Limestone	20	*	1 Jan 2002
Pneumatic discharge – cement	20	*	1 Jan 2002
Used on tram lines	40		1 Jan 2001
Tank cars	20	*	1 Jan 2002
Wagons – non bulk freight (including all wagons used for general and inter-modal freight)	30	*	1 Jan 2002
Note: From the 2012-13 income year, a capped life of 10 years is available for the decline in value of eligible shipping vessels but only if certain conditions are met (see subsection 40-102(4) item 10 and subsection 40-102(4A))			
Water transport and support services (48100 to 48200 and 52110 to 52190)			
Commercial vessels:			
Canoes	10	*	1 Jul 2009
Dinghies and punts (not longer than 6 metres)	12	*	1 Jul 2009
Fishing vessels (including trawlers, long liners, seiners, fin fish boats, pearling boats, lobster boats, aquaculture and other fishing boats):			
Longer than 10 metres	20	*	1 Jul 2009
Not longer than 10 metres	15	*	1 Jul 2009
Houseboats	20	*	1 Jul 2009

TRANSPORT, POSTAL AND WAREHOUSING (46100 to 53090)

Asset	Life (Years)	Reviewed	Date Of Application
Inflatable boats (excluding rigid hull inflatable boats)	7	*	1 Jul 2009
Jet skis	4	*	1 Jul 2009
Kayaks	5	*	1 Jul 2009
Offshore supply and support vessels	20	*	1 Jul 2009
Passenger vessels (including cruise vessels, skippered charter vessels, vehicle and passenger ferries, semi submersible vessels and water taxis):			
Longer than 10 metres	20	*	1 Jul 2009
Not longer than 10 metres	15	*	1 Jul 2009
Pedal boats	10	*	1 Jul 2009
Pontoon boats (excluding pontoons or floating jetties used for storage or walkway only)	15	*	1 Jul 2009
Sail boats (not longer than 6 metres and including 'off the beach' boats)	10	*	1 Jul 2009
Ski boats	10	*	1 Jul 2009
Thrill boats (including jet boats)	10	*	1 Jul 2009
Trading ships:			
Bulk carriers	20	*	1 Jul 2009
Cargo ships	20	*	1 Jul 2009
Container ships	20	*	1 Jul 2009
Roll on/roll off ships	20	*	1 Jul 2009
Tankers:			
Oil and chemical	20	*	1 Jul 2009
LNG and LPG	30	*	1 Jul 2009
Work vessels (including barges, coastal supply boats, dredges, general work boats, landing craft, launches, lighters, line boats, pilot boats, runabouts and tug boats):			
Longer than 10 metres	20	*	1 Jul 2009
Not longer than 10 metres	15	*	1 Jul 2009
Yachts and motor cruisers – bare boat charter (including monohulls, catamarans and trimarans)	15	*	1 Jul 2009
Support assets (acquired separately from the vessel):			
Desalinators	10	*	1 Jul 2009
Hot water units:			
Domestic	5	*	1 Jul 2009
Marine	10	*	1 Jul 2009
Lifting assets:			
Hoists and winches:			
Electric	5	*	1 Jul 2009
Hydraulic and mechanical	10	*	1 Jul 2009
Navigational and communication assets acquired separately from the vessel (including autopilots, chart plotters, depth sounders, GPS, radar systems and marine radios)	5	*	1 Jul 2009
Outboard motors	5	*	1 Jul 2009
Power supply assets:			
Batteries (deep cycle)	3	*	1 Jul 2009
Generators (stand alone)	10	*	1 Jul 2009
Inverters	6	*	1 Jul 2009
Safety assets:			
Emergency signalling assets (including EPIRBS)	5	*	1 Jul 2009
Life rafts	10	*	1 Jul 2009

TRANSPORT, POSTAL AND WAREHOUSING
(46100 to 53090)

Asset	Life (Years)	Reviewed	Date Of Application
Trailers	8	*	1 Jul 2009
Port assets:			
Cargo handling equipment:			
Containers, transportable (used to transport goods by road, rail and sea)	10	*	1 Jan 2001
Cranes:			
Container/portainer	20	*	1 Jul 2002
Fixed	25	*	1 Jul 2002
Mobile (over 15.24 tonnes lift)	20	*	1 Jul 2002
Dozers	9	*	1 Jul 2002
Forklifts:			
Container handling	7 1/2	*	1 Jul 2002
General handling	11	*	1 Jul 2002
Rail mounted gantries	15	*	1 Jul 2002
Reach stackers	10	*	1 Jul 2002
Ship loaders	30	*	1 Jul 2002
Ship unloaders	20	*	1 Jul 2002
Spreaders	5	*	1 Jul 2002
Stackers, reclaimers and stackers/reclaimers	25	*	1 Jul 2002
Straddle carriers	12 1/2	*	1 Jul 2002
Wheel loaders	8	*	1 Jul 2002
Control systems:			
Control system assets – programmable logic controllers (PLCs) and hardware	10	*	1 Jul 2002
Motor control centre and motor control field devices	20	*	1 Jul 2002
Environmental equipment:			
Current, tidal, wave and wind monitoring systems	5	*	1 Jul 2002
Oil spill containment boom	10	*	1 Jul 2002
Intermodal facilities:			
Receival station assets (including belt feeder, hopper and tippler)	30	*	1 Jul 2002
Truck and rail receival dump pit	50	*	1 Jul 2002
Land based facilities:			
Concrete rail beams and rails	30	*	1 Jul 2002
Conveyor systems (incorporating chutes, gravity take-up assemblies, headframes, structures, surge bins, transfer towers and weigh towers)	30	*	1 Jul 2002
Dust suppression systems	30	*	1 Jul 2002
Electricity supply assets – see Table A Electricity supply (26110 to 26400)			
Storage sheds, to the extent they form an integral part of bulk handling equipment	40	*	1 Jul 2002
Navigational aids:			
Land based navigational aids	20	*	1 Jul 2002
Offshore beacons, channel markers and lead lights:			
Floating buoys	10	*	1 Jul 2002
Piled structures	20	*	1 Jul 2002
Other facilities:			
Cathodic protection:			
Impressed current system	30	*	1 Jul 2002

TRANSPORT, POSTAL AND WAREHOUSING
(46100 to 53090)

Asset	Life (Years)	Reviewed	Date Of Application
Sacrificial system	15	*	1 Jul 2002
Dry docks (including floating dry docks)	40	*	1 Jul 2013
Fender systems:			
Elastomeric	20	*	1 Jul 2002
Timber	10	*	1 Jul 2002
Gangways – removable	10	*	1 Jul 2002
Mooring facilities (including bollards)	40	*	1 Jul 2002
Mooring quick release hooks	20	*	1 Jul 2002
Pontoons – floating	20	*	1 Jul 2002
Slipways (incorporating rails, ramps, runners and winching systems)	30	*	1 Jul 2002
Wharves, dolphins and jetties	40	*	1 Jul 2002
Salvage machinery:			
Boilers, vertical	40		1 Jan 2001
Engine hoisting	40		1 Jan 2001
Pumps:			
Centrifugal, direct acting, and connections	40		1 Jan 2001
Duplex boiler feed	40		1 Jan 2001
Other air and space transport (49009)			
Aircraft:			
Aeroplanes:			
General use[39]	20	*#	1 Jul 2002
Used predominantly for agricultural spraying or agricultural dusting[40]	10	*#	1 Jul 2002
Helicopters:			
General use[41]	20	*#	1 Jul 2002
Used predominantly for mustering, agricultural spraying or agricultural dusting[42]	10	*#	1 Jul 2002
Scenic and sightseeing transport (50100)			
Gliders (including motor gliders)	20	*	1 Jul 2013
Hot air balloon ride operation assets:			
Flight instruments	10	*	1 Jul 2013
Hot air balloon assets:			
Baskets	6	*	1 Jul 2013
Burners	10	*	1 Jul 2013
Envelopes	5	*	1 Jul 2013
Fuel cylinders and tanks (incorporating shut off valves)	20	*	1 Jul 2013
Inflator fans	15	*	1 Jul 2013
Monocable circulating detachable, reversible and fixed ropeway assets operated in non-snowfield areas:			
Cabins (including carriers)	25	*	1 Jul 2009
Communications assets:			
Communications cables	10	*	1 Jul 2009
Radios	5	*	1 Jul 2009
Drive and return station assets (including braking systems, drive systems, gear boxes, motors, variable speed drives (VSDs) and tensioning systems)	15	*	1 Jul 2009
Rescue vehicles	30	*	1 Jul 2009

TRANSPORT, POSTAL AND WAREHOUSING
(46100 to 53090)

Asset	Life (Years)	Reviewed	Date Of Application
Ropes:			
Haul ropes	10	*	1 Jul 2009
Track ropes	20	*	1 Jul 2009
Standby power drives	25	*	1 Jul 2009
Towers:			
Tower heads	15	*	1 Jul 2009
Tower structures	30	*	1 Jul 2009
Transportation systems (incorporating drives and belts)	3	*	1 Jul 2009
Pipeline transport (50210)			
Pipes and pipelines (including valves and fittings):			
Generally	25	*	1 Jul 2003
Slurry pipework within processing facility (including slurry pipe to thickener)	10	*	1 Jan 2006
Pumps:			
Generally	20	*	1 Jul 2003
Positive displacement pumps	15	*	1 Jul 2003
Other transport n.e.c. (50290)			
Monocable circulating fixed grip and detachable ropeway assets operated in snowfield areas (including double, triple and quad chair lifts, T-bar, poma and surface lifts):			
Chair head grips	15	*	1 Jul 2009
Chairs, T-bars and pomas	25	*	1 Jul 2009
Communication assets:			
Communications cables – above ground	10	*	1 Jul 2009
Communications cables – under ground	25	*	1 Jul 2009
Radios and telephone systems	5	*	1 Jul 2009
Covered moving walkways (including covered walkways and carpets)	10	*	1 Jul 2009
Drive and return station assets (including braking systems, drive systems, gear boxes, motors, variable speed drives (VSDs) and tensioning systems)	20	*	1 Jul 2009
Oversnow transport assets:			
Oversnow transporters	8	*	1 Jul 2009
Skidoos	5	*	1 Jul 2009
Ropes:			
Main hauling rope for detachable lifts etc	15	*	1 Jul 2009
Main hauling rope for fixed grip, t-bars lifts etc	20	*	1 Jul 2009
Snow grooming assets (including free groomers, snow blowers and winches)	8	*	1 Jul 2009
Snowmaking assets including:			
Air water guns and fan guns	10	*	1 Jul 2009
Compressors, pumps, water mains and pipes	20	*	1 Jul 2009
Cooling towers	15	*	1 Jul 2009
Electrical cables – above ground	10	*	1 Jul 2009
Electrical cables – under ground	25	*	1 Jul 2009
Weather stations	5	*	1 Jul 2009
Standby power drives	25	*	1 Jul 2009
Tower heads and structures	30	*	1 Jul 2009

TRANSPORT, POSTAL AND WAREHOUSING
(46100 to 53090)

Asset	Life (Years)	Reviewed	Date Of Application
Postal services (51010)			
Mail house assets:			
Envelope inserters	7	*	1 Jul 2015
Folders	12½	*	1 Jul 2015
Guillotines	15	*	1 Jul 2015
Heat sealers	10	*	1 Jul 2015
Printers	5	*	1 Jul 2015
Racks	20	*	1 Jul 2015
Scales	5	*	1 Jul 2015
Scanners	5	*	1 Jul 2015
Trolleys	8	*	1 Jul 2015
Postal delivery services:			
Control systems and control system assets	10	*	1 Jul 2016
Flat mail optical character reading and sorting machines	12	*	1 Jul 2016
Letter boxes (bulk private)	30	*	1 Jul 2016
Letter sorting assets (including bar code sorters, culler facer cancellers and multiline optical character readers)	12	*	1 Jul 2016
Motorcycles	5	*	1 Jul 2016
Parcel lockers	10	*	1 Jul 2016
Parcel sorting system assets (excluding control systems and control system assets)	15	*	1 Jul 2016
Post boxes (street type)	20	*	1 Jul 2016
Courier pick-up and delivery services (51020)			
Inspection assets:			
Scales:			
Bench	10	*	1 Jul 2011
Floor (platform)	20	*	1 Jul 2011
Weight dimension capture system assets (including checkweighers, in motion scales and readers)	10	*	1 Jul 2011
Materials handling equipment:			
Ball transfer mats and castor decks	20	*	1 Jul 2011
Control systems and control system assets	10	*	1 Jul 2016
Conveyors (including shoe sorters)	15	*	1 Jul 2011
Forklifts – see Table B			
Parcel sorting system assets (including sortation system assets) (excluding control systems and control system assets)	15	*	1 Jul 2016
Scissor lifts	10	*	1 Jul 2015
Storage racks	20	*	1 Jul 2011
Trolleys, freight barrows, cages and bins	10	*	1 Jul 2011
Pick up and delivery equipment:			
Barcode label printers	5	*	1 Jul 2011
Portable hand held barcode readers (including point of delivery capture devices and delivery information acquisition devices)	4	*	1 Jul 2011

TRANSPORT, POSTAL AND WAREHOUSING
(46100 to 53090)

Asset	Life (Years)	Reviewed	Date Of Application
Airport operations and other air transport support services (52200)			
Aircraft maintenance assets – see Table A Aircraft manufacturing and repair services (23940)			
Aircraft training assets:			
Flight simulators	8		1 Jan 2001
Link trainers	8		1 Jan 2001
Airport assets:			
Aerobridges	20	*	1 Jan 2003
Baggage handling assets:			
Baggage check-in stations (incorporating scales and check-in conveyors)	10	*	1 Jan 2003
Baggage outbound conveyor systems (incorporating belts, diverters, gearboxes, motors, ploughs, rollers, structures and tag readers)	15	*	1 Jan 2003
Baggage reclaim conveyor systems (incorporating belts, gearboxes, motors, rollers and structures)	15	*	1 Jan 2003
Control systems (excluding computers)	10	*	1 Jan 2003
Fire safety and rescue assets:			
Breathing units	10	*	1 Jan 2003
Drills, air powered	10	*	1 Jan 2003
Fire fighting vehicles	20	*	1 Jan 2003
Rescue boats:			
Aluminium	20	*	1 Jan 2003
Inflatable	8	*	1 Jan 2003
Rescue units (jaws of life)	15	*	1 Jan 2003
Fuel supply assets:			
Aircraft fueller vehicles	15	*	1 Jan 2003
Aircraft hydrant dispenser vehicles	15	*	1 Jan 2003
Filters, fuel	25	*	1 Jan 2003
Fire fighting systems	25	*	1 Jan 2003
Piping	25	*	1 Jan 2003
Pumps, fuel	25	*	1 Jan 2003
Tanks	25	*	1 Jan 2003
Ground support assets:			
Aircraft loader/unloader vehicles	15	*	1 Jan 2003
Aircraft stairs:			
Manual	20	*	1 Jan 2003
Vehicle mounted	15	*	1 Jan 2003
Airstart units	15	*	1 Jan 2003
Containers, air cargo (used to transport goods by air)	5	*	1 Jan 2001
Ground power units	15	*	1 Jan 2003
High lift service vehicles (including catering, lavatory, maintenance and water vehicles)	15	*	1 Jan 2003
Tow tractors	20	*	1 Jan 2003
Tractors, baggage	15	*	1 Jan 2003
Tractor trolleys (including baggage and container trolleys, and dollies)	10	*	1 Jan 2003
Navigation aids:			
Distance measuring assets	15	*	1 Jan 2003

TRANSPORT, POSTAL AND WAREHOUSING (46100 to 53090)

Asset	Life (Years)	Reviewed	Date Of Application
Instrument landing systems	10	*	1 Jan 2003
Non-directional beacons (excluding towers)	15	*	1 Jan 2003
Radar sensors	15	*	1 Jan 2003
Towers	30	*	1 Jan 2003
VHF omni range assets (excluding towers)	15	*	1 Jan 2003
Runway sweepers	15	*	1 Jan 2003
Terminal building assets:			
Flight information display signs (including monitors and LED screens)	7	*	1 Jan 2003
Security scanning assets (including explosive detection systems, hand-held and walk through detectors, and x-ray screening systems)	5	*	1 Jan 2003
Visual aids assets:			
Docking guidance systems	10	*	1 Jan 2003
Lighting systems (including apron floodlighting, runway lighting and taxiway lighting)	15	*	1 Jan 2003
Movement area guidance signs	10	*	1 Jan 2003
Visual approach slope indicator systems (PAPI)	15	*	1 Jan 2003
Wind direction indicators, illuminated	10	*	1 Jan 2003
Other transport support services n.e.c. (52999)			
Electronic toll collection assets:			
Digital measuring instruments (including vehicle classifiers (laser or infrared) and electronic toll collection readers (radio frequency))	4	*	1 Jul 2005
Electronic toll collection transponders	4	*	1 Jul 2005
Optical character recognition cameras	4	*	1 Jul 2005
Other warehousing and storage services (53090)			
Warehouse and distribution centre equipment and machines:			
Automated storage and retrieval machines	20	*	1 Jul 2011
Balers	15	*	1 Jul 2011
Battery assets for warehouse vehicles (including pallet trucks and forklifts):			
Batteries (detachable for recharging)	5	*	1 Jul 2011
Battery chargers:			
Forklifts	11	*	1 Jul 2011
Other	10	*	1 Jul 2011
Handling assets:			
Battery tuggers	10	*	1 Jul 2011
Racking roller beds	15	*	1 Jul 2011
Transfer carts	10	*	1 Jul 2011
Washers	10	*	1 Jul 2011
Carts/buggies	15	*	1 Jul 2011
Conveyors	15	*	1 Jul 2011
Dock levellers, pallet jacks, pallet trucks and scissor lifts – see Table B Loading bay assets			
Door controls and motor drive systems (incorporating chains, controls, motors and sensors, but excluding doors):			
External	20	*	1 Jul 2011
Internal	10	*	1 Jul 2011
Floor sweepers/scrubbers	10	*	1 Jul 2011

TRANSPORT, POSTAL AND WAREHOUSING
(46100 to 53090)

Asset	Life (Years)	Reviewed	Date Of Application
Forklift attachments:			
Cages	10	*	1 Jul 2011
Push pull units	11	*	1 Jul 2011
Inflatable dock bags/seals/shelters	10	*	1 Jul 2011
Packaging machines and wrapping machines – see Table B Packaging machines			
Pallet assets:			
Dispensers	15	*	1 Jul 2011
Lift tables	10	*	1 Jul 2011
Racks	20	*	1 Jul 2011
Radio frequency terminal assets:			
Barcode readers/scanners	5	*	1 Jul 2011
Portable/handheld and vehicle mounted terminal devices	4	*	1 Jul 2011
Refrigeration assets – see Table B			
Roll cages	10	*	1 Jul 2011
Trolleys	10	*	1 Jul 2011
Voice picking assets:			
Battery chargers	4	*	1 Jul 2011
Headsets	4	*	1 Jul 2011
Terminals (on person)	4	*	1 Jul 2011
Waste compactors (used for cardboard and plastic):			
Electric	15	*	1 Jul 2011
Hydraulic	20	*	1 Jul 2011

Footnotes:

32 A capped effective life of $7^1/2$ years is available – see subsection 40-102(4).

33 A hire car is a passenger car hired with a driver, not being a taxi

34 A hire car is a passenger car hired with a driver, not being a taxi

35 A capped effective life of $7^1/2$ years is available – see subsection 40-102(4).

36 A capped effective life of $7^1/2$ years is available – see subsection 40-102(4).

37 A capped effective life of 10 years is available – see subsection 40-102(4).

38 A capped effective life of $7^1/2$ years is available – see subsection 40-102(4).

39 A capped effective life of 10 years is available – see subsection 40-102(4).

40 A capped effective life of 8 years is available – see subsection 40-102(4).

41 A capped effective life of 10 years is available – see subsection 40-102(4).

42 A capped effective life of 8 years is available – see subsection 40-102(4).

¶43-055 Effective life — information media and telecommunications

INFORMATION MEDIA AND TELECOMMUNICATIONS
(54110 to 60200)

Asset	Life (Years)	Reviewed	Date Of Application
Motion picture and video activities (55110 to 55140)			
Camera accessories:			
Aspect ratio converters	12	*	1 Jan 2006

INFORMATION MEDIA AND TELECOMMUNICATIONS
(54110 to 60200)

Asset	Life (Years)	Reviewed	Date Of Application
Digital or electronic time code slates	5	*	1 Jan 2006
Speed control, time lapse and phase adjustment controls	10	*	1 Jan 2006
Time code generators and master clocks	10	*	1 Jan 2006
Underwater and marine housings and rain deflectors	12	*	1 Jan 2006
Video assist systems (incorporating monitors, video recorder with playback, transmitters and receivers)	3	*	1 Jan 2006
Cameras:			
16mm and 35mm film cameras	10	*	1 Jan 2006
Digital cameras	5	*	1 Jan 2006
Camera lens accessories:			
Coloured and graduated filters and filter stages	3	*	1 Jan 2006
Fish eye and wide angle lens adapters	10	*	1 Jan 2006
Follow focus, remote focus, shutter and zoom controls	10	*	1 Jan 2006
Image stabilisers, matte boxes, and teleprompters	10	*	1 Jan 2006
Camera lenses	10	*	1 Jan 2006
Camera supports (including heads, legs mounts and tripods)	10	*	1 Jan 2006
Copyright in a feature film (not including a licence relating to a copyright in a feature film)	5	*	1 Jul 2004
Grips' assets:			
Camera cranes	10	*	1 Jan 2006
Camera heads	10	*	1 Jan 2006
Car rigs, sea rigs and other specialised rigs	2	*	1 Jan 2006
Communications systems	5	*	1 Jan 2006
Dollies	12	*	1 Jan 2006
Dolly and camera attachments	10	*	1 Jan 2006
Dolly track	5	*	1 Jan 2006
Remote camera control systems	10	*	1 Jan 2006
Towers, rigging, and dance floors	10	*	1 Jan 2006
Tracking vehicles and insert trailers – see Table B Motor vehicles and trailers			
Lighting assets:			
Accessories (including gaffer grips, clamps, mounts, and stands)	10	*	1 Jan 2006
Portable lights	10	*	1 Jan 2006
Studio lights – fixed	15	*	1 Jan 2006
Lighting control systems	10	*	1 Jan 2006
Lighting grids – fixed	20	*	1 Jan 2006
Lighting hoists	15	*	1 Jan 2006
Motion picture film processing assets:			
Chemical agitators and mixers	10	*	1 Jan 2006
Chemical storage tanks	15	*	1 Jan 2006
Film cleaning machines	10	*	1 Jan 2006
Film colour analysers and colour grading machines	8	*	1 Jan 2006
Film densitometers	10	*	1 Jan 2006
Film printing machines	10	*	1 Jan 2006
Film processing machines	10	*	1 Jan 2006
Film re-winders	15	*	1 Jan 2006
Flat bed and rear projection film viewers	15	*	1 Jan 2006
Mixed chemical pumps	10	*	1 Jan 2006

INFORMATION MEDIA AND TELECOMMUNICATIONS
(54110 to 60200)

Asset	Life (Years)	Reviewed	Date Of Application
Optical sound camera systems (incorporating soundtrack and time code generators)	10	*	1 Jan 2006
Silver recovery units	8	*	1 Jan 2006
Sound quality control processors	5	*	1 Jan 2006
Waste water treatment assets	10	*	1 Jan 2006
Post production sound assets:			
Amplifiers and pre-amplifiers	5	*	1 Jan 2006
Audio effects units (incorporating aural exciters, compressors, delay and effects control processors graphic equalisers, harmonisers, limiters, noise reduction processors, reverberation processors, telephone simulators and time controllers)	5	*	1 Jan 2006
Digital audio players and recorders (including CD, DVD, digital audio tape (DAT), mini disc and hard disc players and recorders)	3	*	1 Jan 2006
Digital film projectors	5	*	1 Jan 2006
Digital sound conversion processors (including encoders and decoders)	5	*	1 Jan 2006
Hard disc video players and recorders	3	*	1 Jan 2006
Microphones and microphone accessories	10	*	1 Jan 2006
Motion picture film projectors	10	*	1 Jan 2006
Screens	5	*	1 Jan 2006
Sound mixing desks and consoles	5	*	1 Jan 2006
Speakers	7	*	1 Jan 2006
Time code synchronisation units	5	*	1 Jan 2006
Video routers and servers	5	*	1 Jan 2006
Post production video assets:			
DVD players	3	*	1 Jan 2006
Edit controllers (used in linear editing)	4	*	1 Jan 2006
High definition digital film scanners	4	*	1 Jan 2006
High definition laser film recorders	5	*	1 Jan 2006
Monitors	5	*	1 Jan 2006
Motion capture and analysis systems	5	*	1 Jan 2006
Non-linear editing systems (incorporating computer control, interface and hard disc system)	5	*	1 Jan 2006
Telecine chains (incorporating colour correctors, film time code readers, grain and noise reduction systems and telecine machines)	7	*	1 Jan 2006
VHS video cassette players and recorders	2	*	1 Jan 2006
Video routers and servers	5	*	1 Jan 2006
Videotape players and recorders	5	*	1 Jan 2006
Screening theatre assets:			
Audio amplification and processing equipment (includes component racks systems)	5	*	1 Jan 2006
Digital audio players, digital film projectors and digital sound conversion processors	5	*	1 Jan 2006
Motion picture film projectors	10	*	1 Jan 2006
Screens	8	*	1 Jan 2006
Speakers	10	*	1 Jan 2006
Sound recording assets:			
Amplifiers and pre-amplifiers	5	*	1 Jan 2006
Sound mixing consoles	5	*	1 Jan 2006
Boom poles	2	*	1 Jan 2006
Compressors, expanders and limiters	5	*	1 Jan 2006

INFORMATION MEDIA AND TELECOMMUNICATIONS
(54110 to 60200)

Asset	Life (Years)	Reviewed	Date Of Application
Digital audio players and recorders (including CD, DVD, digital audio tape (DAT), mini disc and hard disc players and recorders)	2	*	1 Jan 2006
Digital or electronic time code slates	5	*	1 Jan 2006
Headphones:			
Generally	2	*	1 Jan 2006
Miniature in-ear headphones	1	*	1 Jan 2006
Microphones:			
Field or boom microphones	7	*	1 Jan 2006
Lapel microphones	1	*	1 Jan 2006
Microphone accessories (including adapters, connectors, stands, suspension mounts, pistol grips, windscreens and windjammers)	5	*	1 Jan 2006
Microphone cables	2	*	1 Jan 2006
Radio microphone systems (incorporating antennas, miniature microphones, receivers and transmitters)	5	*	1 Jan 2006
Studio microphones	10	*	1 Jan 2006
Monitors	2	*	1 Jan 2006
Speakers	5	*	1 Jan 2006
Vision switchers	5	*	1 Jan 2006
Video monitors	5	*	1 Jan 2006
Motion picture exhibition (55130)			
Audio amplification and processing equipment (including component rack systems)	10	*	1 Jan 2001
Carpets	5	*	1 Jan 2001
Cinema automation systems	10	*	1 Jan 2001
Cinema and sound processors	8	*	1 Jan 2001
Cinema seating (including frames, seat bodies and covers)	7	*	1 Jan 2001
Curtains, wall and acoustic treatments	7	*	1 Jan 2001
Drive-in plant:			
Sound transmission equipment	10	*	1 Jan 2001
Listening units (including posts, wiring and speaker equipment)	10	*	1 Jan 2001
Screens and screen framing	15	*	1 Jan 2001
Film handling and maintenance equipment (including splicers, footage counters, spools and reels, stripper plates, rewinders, spinners, trolleys and cleaners)	10	*	1 Jan 2001
Film transport systems (including platter systems, tower, make-up tables and interlock systems)	15	*	1 Jan 2001
Lighting (including dimmers, aisle and seat)	10	*	1 Jan 2001
Loud speakers and sound reproduction equipment	10	*	1 Jan 2001
Motion picture and slide projection equipment:			
Motion picture projectors	10	*	1 Jan 2001
Projector heat extraction systems	10	*	1 Jan 2001
Projection ports	20	*	1 Jan 2001
Slide projectors	10	*	1 Jan 2001
Screen installations (including screens, framing and masking equipment)	8	*	1 Jan 2001
Radio broadcasting (56100)			
Amplifiers and pre-amplifiers	10	*	1 Jul 2012
Audio monitors	10	*	1 Jul 2012

INFORMATION MEDIA AND TELECOMMUNICATIONS
(54110 to 60200)

Asset	Life (Years)	Reviewed	Date Of Application
Audio processing assets (including rack mounted effects units etc)	10	*	1 Jul 2012
Audio routers	10	*	1 Jul 2012
Automation systems (including broadcast playout automation systems, content creation systems, music scheduling systems and traffic and billing automation systems)	6	*	1 Jul 2012
Consoles:			
Broadcast consoles (incorporating audio logging and routing, intercommunication etc)	7	*	1 Jul 2012
Production consoles	10	*	1 Jul 2012
Control room assets generally:			
Electronically based assets (including audio processors, audio switchers, aural studio to transmitter linkage assets, distribution amplifiers, monitor receivers etc)	10	*	1 Jul 2012
Personal computer based assets (including delay units, logging units, program fail detectors, RDS generators etc)	6	*	1 Jul 2012
Digital audio players and recorders (including CD, DVD, mini disc, hard disc and solid state players and recorders)	5	*	1 Jul 2012
Headphones and headsets	2	*	1 Jul 2012
Intercommunication systems (standalone)	10	*	1 Jul 2012
Microphones:			
Field and portable microphones	5	*	1 Jul 2012
Studio based microphones (including recording microphones)	10	*	1 Jul 2012
Microwave and satellite telecommunications assets – see Table A Telecommunications services (58010 to 58090)			
Mobile production vehicles (excluding the assets contained within) – see Table B Motor vehicles and trailers			
On air lights	15	*	1 Jul 2012
Racks	20	*	1 Jul 2012
Servers, domain controllers, switches, transcoders etc	6	*	1 Jul 2012
Studio based digital audio broadcasting infrastructure (encoding assets etc)	10	*	1 Jul 2012
Telephone systems:			
Telephone interface assets generally (used for sending and receiving audio to and from connected telephone lines)	10	*	1 Jul 2012
Telephone screening systems and other personal computer based telephone systems (excluding software)	6	*	1 Jul 2012
Voice over internet protocol (VoIP) based systems	7	*	1 Jul 2012
Time code generators	10	*	1 Jul 2012
Transmission assets:			
Antennas	20	*	1 Jul 2012
Codecs	10	*	1 Jul 2012
Fibre optic terminal equipment generally	10	*	1 Jul 2012
Generators (backup)	15	*	1 Jul 2012
Obstruction lighting	15	*	1 Jul 2012
Power conditioners	15	*	1 Jul 2012
RF switching units	15	*	1 Jul 2012
Signal receiving and monitoring assets (including audio processors, decoders, modulation monitors, spectrum analysers etc)	10	*	1 Jul 2012
Silence detection and switching units	10	*	1 Jul 2012
Surge arresters	10	*	1 Jul 2012
Translators	15	*	1 Jul 2012

INFORMATION MEDIA AND TELECOMMUNICATIONS (54110 to 60200)

Asset	Life (Years)	Reviewed	Date Of Application
Transmission towers	40	*	1 Jul 2012
Transmitters	15	*	1 Jul 2012
Uninterruptible power supply (UPS) assets – see Table B Power supply assets			
Television broadcasting (56210 to 56220)			
Audio boards, consoles and mixers	12	*	1 Jul 2005
Audio delay units	10	*	1 Jul 2005
Audio effects units (including compression units, delay units, graphic equalisers and reverberation units)	12	*	1 Jul 2005
Automated tape library systems (incorporating robotic controls and tape drives)	10	*	1 Jul 2005
Broadcast antennas	20	*	1 Jul 2005
Broadcast interfacing assets (including aspect ratio converters, distribution amplifiers, sync pulse generators, timecode generators and readers and other 'glue' assets)	12	*	1 Jul 2005
Cameras:			
Portable cameras (including camcorders, electronic field production (EFP) and electronic news gathering (ENG) cameras)	8	*	1 Jul 2005
Studio cameras	10	*	1 Jul 2005
Camera control units	10	*	1 Jul 2005
Camera lens accessories (including adapters, filters, matte boxes and stabilisers)	12	*	1 Jul 2005
Camera lenses	12	*	1 Jul 2005
Camera mounting heads	15	*	1 Jul 2005
Camera mounts (including cranes, jibs, pedestals and tripods)	25	*	1 Jul 2005
Camera pan tilt and pedestal robotic systems (incorporating integrated hardware and control unit)	12	*	1 Jul 2005
Character and graphics generating assets – standalone (including character generators, paintboxes and stillstores)	10	*	1 Jul 2005
Digital audio players and recorders (including CD players and recorders, digital audio tape (DAT) players, DVD players and recorders, and mini disc players and recorders)	5	*	1 Jul 2005
Digital video effects (DVE) units – standalone	10	*	1 Jul 2005
Edit controllers (used in linear editing and audio post-production)	8	*	1 Jul 2005
Hard disk recorders	5	*	1 Jul 2005
Intercommunication systems	15	*	1 Jul 2005
Lighting:			
Portable lighting	12	*	1 Jul 2005
Studio lighting	15	*	1 Jul 2005
Lighting control systems	10	*	1 Jul 2005
Lighting grids – fixed	40	*	1 Jul 2005
Lighting hoists	15	*	1 Jul 2005
Microphones:			
Field or boom microphones	5	*	1 Jul 2005
Miniature or 'lapel' microphones	5	*	1 Jul 2005
Radio microphone systems (incorporating antennas, miniature microphones, receivers and transmitters)	5	*	1 Jul 2005
Studio or fixed microphones	10	*	1 Jul 2005
Microphone booms	10	*	1 Jul 2005
Microwave telecommunications assets – see Table A Telecommunications services (58010 to 58090)			

INFORMATION MEDIA AND TELECOMMUNICATIONS
(54110 to 60200)

Asset	Life (Years)	Reviewed	Date Of Application
Mobile production vehicles (excluding the assets contained within) – see Table B Motor vehicles and trailers			
Monitors:			
Audio monitors	10	*	1 Jul 2005
Video monitors:			
Cathode ray tube (CRT) monitors	8	*	1 Jul 2005
LCD and Plasma monitors	5	*	1 Jul 2005
Virtual monitor wall systems (including rear projection monitor walls)	5	*	1 Jul 2005
Non-linear editing systems (incorporating computer control, interface and hard disk system)	4	*	1 Jul 2005
Presentation automation systems	10	*	1 Jul 2005
Racks	20	*	1 Jul 2005
RF Modulation units	12	*	1 Jul 2005
Routing systems (incorporating control panels, hardware and switchers)	11	*	1 Jul 2005
Satellite telecommunications assets – see Table A Telecommunications services (58010 to 58090)			
Servers (excluding data servers)	8	*	1 Jul 2005
Signal measurement, monitoring and testing assets (including modulation monitors, RF analysers, test signal generators, vectorscopes and waveform monitors)	12	*	1 Jul 2005
Slow motion controllers	10	*	1 Jul 2005
Switchers (including master control, presentation and production switchers)	10	*	1 Jul 2005
Teleprompters	10	*	1 Jul 2005
Translators	15	*	1 Jul 2005
Transmission towers	40	*	1 Jul 2005
Transmitters	15	*	1 Jul 2005
Transmitting masts (for mobile production vehicles)	10	*	1 Jul 2005
Under monitor and tally display systems	10	*	1 Jul 2005
Videocassette recorders	5	*	1 Jul 2005
Videotape players and recorders	8	*	1 Jul 2005
Internet publishing and broadcasting (57000)			
Internet only audio broadcasting assets – use any relevant determination in Table A Radio broadcasting (56100)			
Telecommunications services (58010 to 58090)			
Backbone network assets:			
Conduits	40	*	1 Jul 2003
Cross connects (including digital and optical)	15	*	1 Jul 2003
Multiplexers (including wave division, terminal, and add-drop)	15	*	1 Jul 2003
Optical amplifiers	15	*	1 Jul 2003
Optical fibre cables	25	*	1 Jul 2003
Optical patch panels	25	*	1 Jul 2003
Regenerators	15	*	1 Jul 2003
International telecommunications submarine cables	15	*	1 Jul 2002
Microwave radio telecommunications assets:			
Antennas (incorporating wave guide, pressurisation unit, dehydrator and data cable):			

INFORMATION MEDIA AND TELECOMMUNICATIONS (54110 to 60200)

Asset	Life (Years)	Reviewed	Date Of Application
High capacity licensed microwave radio	10	*	1 Jul 2004
Medium capacity licensed microwave radio	8	*	1 Jul 2004
Low capacity licensed microwave radio	5	*	1 Jul 2004
Microwave radio system (including modulator, demodulator, receiver, transmitter, monitoring/supervisory system, RF filter):			
High capacity licensed microwave radio system ≥ 68Mb	10	*	1 Jul 2004
Medium capacity licensed microwave radio system ≥ 16Mb to <68Mb	8	*	1 Jul 2004
Low capacity licensed microwave radio system < 16Mb	5	*	1 Jul 2004
Class licence microwave radio system (including antenna)	3	*	1 Jul 2004
Multiplexers	10	*	1 Jul 2004
Towers (including guyed, lattice and steel or concrete poles)	25	*	1 Jul 2004
Mobile telecommunications assets:			
Base station assets:			
Antennas, battery backup, radio transmitters/receivers and rectifiers	6	*	1 Jul 2002
Towers	25	*	1 Jul 2002
Base station controller hardware	10	*	1 Jul 2002
Microwave assets (including antennas, electronic multiplexers and transmitters/receivers)	10	*	1 Jul 2002
Mobile switching centre hardware	10	*	1 Jul 2002
Payphones (public telephones)	10		1 Jan 2001
Satellite communication assets:			
Communications satellites (geosynchronous orbit)	15	*	1 Jan 2005
High power amplifiers	12	*	1 Jan 2005
Multiplexers	10	*	1 Jan 2005
Satellite antennas:			
Electronic components, external (including low noise amplifiers)	8	*	1 Jan 2005
Non-tracking antenna systems (incorporating data cables, dehydrators, pressurisation units, and wave guides)	8	*	1 Jan 2005
Tracking antenna systems (incorporating antenna tracking motors, controllers, data cables, dehydrators, gearboxes, pressurisation units and wave guides)	20	*	1 Jan 2005
Satellite earth station electronic assets (including bandwidth managers, decoders, demodulators downconverters, encoders, filters, modulators, receivers, transmitters and upconverters)	10	*	1 Jan 2005
Satellite telemetry and control systems	15	*	1 Jan 2005
Telecommunications assets:			
Air-conditioning units	5	*	1 Jul 2002
Batteries, rectifiers	6	*	1 Jul 2002
Racks	20	*	1 Jul 2003
Equipment shelters (transportable)	25	*	1 Jul 2003
Electronic information storage services (59220)			
Aisle containments (including hot aisle containments (HAC), cold aisle containments (CAC))	15	*	1 Jul 2017
Data centre control systems – see Table B control systems and control system assets			
Data centre cooling assets:			
Chillers	15	*	1 Jul 2017

INFORMATION MEDIA AND TELECOMMUNICATIONS
(54110 to 60200)

Asset	Life (Years)	Reviewed	Date Of Application
Computer room air conditioning (CRAC) units (including direct expansion (DX) systems)	10	*	1 Jul 2017
Computer room air handling (CRAH) units (including chilled water systems)	15	*	1 Jul 2017
Cooling towers	10	*	1 Jul 2017
Humidifier assets:			
Others (including ultrasonic humidifiers)	10	*	1 Jul 2017
Steam humidifiers (including steam generators)	5	*	1 Jul 2017
Rear door heat exchangers (RDHx)	15	*	1 Jul 2017
Row-based cooling units assets:			
Others (including direct expansion (DX) cooling system units)	10	*	1 Jul 2017
Water-chilled	15	*	1 Jul 2017
Water buffer tanks	20	*	1 Jul 2017
Diesel rotary uninterruptible power supply (DRUPS)	22	*	1 Jul 2017
Fire protection and suppression systems assets – see Table B Fire control and alarm assets			
Generators – see Table B Power supply assets: Emergency or standby			
Leak detection systems	10	*	1 Jul 2017
Load banks	15	*	1 Jul 2017
Modular data centre (including portable containerised data centre modules, prefabricated data centre modules – able to be transported)	10	*	1 Jul 2017
Rack based power rails (including rack based power distribution unit (PDU))	10	*	1 Jul 2017
Racks	10	*	1 Jul 2017
Raised floors	25	*	1 Jul 2017
Rectifiers	12	*	1 Jul 2017
Static transfer switches (STS)	12	*	1 Jul 2017
Switchboards – see Table B Switchboards			
Security and monitoring systems assets – see Table B Security and monitoring assets			
Uninterruptible power supply (UPS) systems (excluding batteries)	12	*	1 Jul 2017
Uninterruptible power supply (UPS) systems batteries	5	*	1 Jul 2017
Library and other information services (60100 to 60200)			
Libraries:			
Circulating (all classes of books)	10		1 Jan 2001
Music lending	6 2/3		1 Jan 2001

¶43-060 Effective life — financial and insurance services

FINANCIAL AND INSURANCE SERVICES
(62100 to 64200)

Banking, building society and credit union operations (62210 to 62230)			
Asset	**Life (Years)**	**Reviewed**	**Date Of Application**
Automatic teller machines (ATMs) - see Table B Automatic teller machines (ATMs)			
Cheque processing machines (including proof machines, endorsers, MICR encoders, printers, readers, sorters and scanners)	5	*	1 Jul 2019

FINANCIAL AND INSURANCE SERVICES
(62100 to 64200)

Banking, building society and credit union operations (62210 to 62230)			
Asset	**Life (Years)**	**Reviewed**	**Date Of Application**
Cash handling assets:			
Coin cabinets, secure coin storage units and coin trolleys	15	*	1 Jul 2019
Coin counters and sorters, and coin deposit machines (CDMs)	10	*	1 Jul 2019
Note counters and sorters	8	*	1 Jul 2019
Teller cash recyclers (TCRs), teller cash dispensers (TCDs), teller assist units (TAUs) and automated teller safes (ATSs)	7	*	1 Jul 2019
Weighing machines (such as coin scales, digital weighing machines, and note scales)	7	*	1 Jul 2019
EFTPOS machines and EFTPOS terminals (such as PIN pads) - see Table B Point of sale assets			
Safes:			
Safes (portable)	40	*	1 Jul 2019
Strongroom door and frame	100		1 Jan 2001
Teller safes, counter safes and teller time-delay safes	25	*	1 Jul 2019
Vaults (demountable or portable) and demountable strongrooms	100	*	1 Jul 2019
Security assets:			
Anti-jump barriers (cables or partitions)	15	*	1 Jul 2019
Ballistic and blast resistant screens and barriers (including fixed and rising types) not forming part of the building - see Table B Security and monitoring assets			
Variable message signs, such as electronic FX boards and digital LED screens - see Table B Advertising signs			

¶43-065 Effective life — rental, hiring and real estate services

RENTAL, HIRING AND REAL ESTATE SERVICES
(66110 to 67200)

Note: If the asset is hired or leased to and used predominantly by a particular industry and not listed below, see the entry under Table A for that industry			
Asset	**Life (Years)**	**Reviewed**	**Date Of Application**
Rental and hiring services (except real estate) (66110 to 66400)			
Air Compressors:			
Compressors – reciprocating	7	*	1 Jul 2005
Compressors – rotary screw	10	*	1 Jul 2005
Compaction:			
Compactors – flat plate	8	*	1 Jul 2005
Compactors – vertical rammer	6	*	1 Jul 2005
Concreting assets:			
Brick/paving saws	5	*	1 Jul 2005
Concrete demolition saws	3	*	1 Jul 2005
Concrete kibble buckets	15	*	1 Jul 2005
Concrete mixers	4	*	1 Jul 2008
Concrete trowels:			
Ride on	7	*	1 Jul 2008
Walk behind	5	*	1 Jul 2008
Concrete surface preparation assets (including floor grinders, planers and scarifers)	5	*	1 Jul 2008

RENTAL, HIRING AND REAL ESTATE SERVICES
(66110 to 67200)

Asset	Life (Years)	Reviewed	Date Of Application
Concrete vibrators:			
Brushcutter style	5	*	1 Jul 2008
Drive units	6	*	1 Jul 2008
Flexible shaft pumps	6	*	1 Jul 2008
Vibrating shafts	3	*	1 Jul 2008
Concrete wheeled saws	6	*	1 Jul 2005
Elevating work platforms (EWPs):			
Boom lifts (including knuckle and telescopic boom lifts)	15	*	1 Jul 2015
Personnel lifts	10	*	1 Jul 2015
Scissor lifts	10	*	1 Jul 2015
Generators:			
Cables	5	*	1 Jul 2005
Distribution boards	10	*	1 Jul 2005
Diesel	10	*	1 Jul 2005
Petrol	5	*	1 Jul 2005
Generator with attached lighting plant	10	*	1 Jul 2005
Household assets:			
Clothes dryers	5	*	1 Jan 2006
DVD players	5	*	1 Jan 2006
Dishwashers	8	*	1 Jan 2006
Evaporative coolers, portable	5	*	1 Jan 2006
Freezers	6	*	1 Jan 2006
Microwave ovens	6	*	1 Jan 2006
Refrigerators	6	*	1 Jan 2006
Stereo systems (incorporating amplifiers, cassette players, CD players, radios and speakers)	5	*	1 Jan 2006
Surround sound systems (incorporating audio-video receivers and speakers)	5	*	1 Jan 2006
Television sets	8	*	1 Jan 2006
Vacuum cleaners, portable	5	*	1 Jan 2006
Video cassette recorder systems (VCR)	5	*	1 Jan 2006
Washing machines	6	*	1 Jan 2006
Ladders (including stepladders, work platforms extension ladders, trestles and planks):			
Aluminium	4	*	1 Jul 2015
Fibreglass	4	*	1 Jul 2015
Portable structures (sheds, site office trailers, portable toilets and washrooms etc) used for a temporary period in offsite locations (eg construction sites)	10	*	1 Jul 2014
Power tools:			
Chainsaws	3	*	1 Jul 2005
Hand tools – air	5	*	1 Jul 2005
Hand tools – battery	3	*	1 Jul 2008
Hand tools – electric	5	*	1 Jul 2005
Jackhammers – air	7	*	1 Jul 2005
Jackhammers – electric	3	*	1 Jul 2005
Nail guns – air	3	*	1 Jul 2005
Recreational vehicles:			
Campervans and motorhomes:			

RENTAL, HIRING AND REAL ESTATE SERVICES
(66110 to 67200)

Asset	Life (Years)	Reviewed	Date Of Application
Vehicles having a gross vehicle mass greater than 3 tonnes and 4WD vehicles	5	*	1 Jul 2015
Vehicles having a gross vehicle mass of 3 tonnes or less	8	*	1 Jul 2015
Caravans and camper trailers	12	*	1 Jul 2015
Rental cars[43]	5	*	1 Jul 2016
Scaffolding:			
Aluminium	5	*	1 Jul 2015
Fibreglass	5	*	1 Jul 2015
Steel	15	*	1 Jul 2015
Traffic management assets:			
Crash prevention assets:			
Barriers:			
Concrete	30	*	1 Jan 2006
Plastic	5	*	1 Jan 2006
Crash attenuators (truck mounted)	10	*	1 Jan 2006
Road marking assets:			
< 100 litre capacity	5	*	1 Jan 2006
100 to 500 litre capacity	9	*	1 Jan 2006
> 500 litre capacity	11	*	1 Jan 2006
Line grinders (walk behind)	5	*	1 Jan 2006
Traffic management signs:			
Arrow boards	10	*	1 Jan 2006
Speed observation signs	10	*	1 Jan 2006
Traffic lights – mobile	10	*	1 Jan 2006
Variable message signs	10	*	1 Jan 2006
Static signage (including safety cones, barricades, warning signs and bollards)	3	*	1 Jan 2006
Video recorder or equipment hiring	$6^{2}/_{3}$		1 Jan 2001
Video tapes and games hiring	$^{1}/_{2}$	*	1 Jan 2001
Welders:			
Diesel	10	*	1 Jul 2005
Electric	5	*	1 Jul 2005
Note where the terms 'freestanding' and 'fixed' are used in entries for residential property operators, they have the following meaning. ***Freestanding*** – items designed to be portable or movable. Any attachment to the premises is only for the item's temporary stability. ***Fixed*** – annexed or attached by any means, for example screws, nails, bolts, glue, adhesive, grout or cement, but not merely for temporary stability.			
Residential property operators[44] ***(67110)***			
Assets generally:			
Air conditioning assets (excluding ducting, pipes and vents):			
Air handling units	20	*	1 Jul 2003
Chillers:			
Absorption	25	*	1 Jul 2003
Centrifugal	20	*	1 Jul 2003
Volumetrics (including reciprocating, rotary, screw, scroll):			
Air-cooled	15	*	1 Jul 2003
Water-cooled	20	*	1 Jul 2003
Condensing sets	15	*	1 Jul 2003
Cooling towers	15	*	1 Jul 2003

RENTAL, HIRING AND REAL ESTATE SERVICES
(66110 to 67200)

Asset	Life (Years)	Reviewed	Date Of Application
Damper motors (including variable air volume box controller)	10	*	1 Jul 2003
Fan coil units (connected to condensing set)	15	*	1 Jul 2003
Mini split systems up to 20KW (including ceiling, floor and high wall split system)	10	*	1 Jul 2003
Packaged air conditioning units	15	*	1 Jul 2003
Pumps	20	*	1 Jul 2003
Room units	10	*	1 Jul 2003
Ceiling fans	5	*	1 Jul 2004
Clocks, electric	10	*	1 Jul 2004
Digital peep holes	10	*	1 Jul 2019
DVD players	5	*	1 Jul 2004
Door closers	10	*	1 Jul 2004
Door stops, freestanding	10	*	1 Jul 2004
Escalators (machinery and moving parts)	20	*	1 Jan 2003
Evaporative coolers:			
Fixed (excluding ducting and vents)	15	*	1 Jul 2019
Portable	10	*	1 Jul 2005
Floor coverings (removable without damage):			
Carpet	8	*	1 Jul 2019
Floating timber	15	*	1 Jul 2004
Linoleum	10		1 Jan 2001
Vinyl	10		1 Jan 2001
Furniture, freestanding	13 1/3		1 Jan 2001
Garbage bins	10	*	1 Jul 2004
Garbage compacting systems (excluding chutes)	6 2/3		1 Jan 2001
Generators	20		1 Jan 2001
Gym assets:			
Cardiovascular	5	*	1 Jul 2004
Resistance	10	*	1 Jul 2004
Hand dryers, electrical	10		1 Jan 2001
Heaters:			
Fixed:			
Electric	15	*	1 Jul 2004
Gas:			
Ducted central heating unit	20	*	1 Jul 2004
Other	15	*	1 Jul 2004
Freestanding	15	*	1 Jul 2004
Home automation control assets	10	*	1 Jul 2019
Hot water systems (excluding piping):			
Electric	12	*	1 Jul 2004
Gas	12	*	1 Jul 2004
Solar	15	*	1 Jul 2004
Hydronic assets:			
Controls	10	*	1 Jul 2019
Water heaters	15	*	1 Jul 2019
Intercom system assets	10	*	1 Jul 2004
Lifts (including hydraulic and traction lifts)	30	*	1 Jan 2003
Lights:			

RENTAL, HIRING AND REAL ESTATE SERVICES (66110 to 67200)

Asset	Life (Years)	Reviewed	Date Of Application
Fittings (excluding hardwired)	5	*	1 Jul 2004
Freestanding	5	*	1 Jul 2004
Shades, removable	5	*	1 Jul 2004
Linen	5	*	1 Jul 2004
Master antenna television (MATV) assets:			
Amplifiers	10	*	1 Jul 2004
Modulators	10	*	1 Jul 2004
Power sources	10	*	1 Jul 2004
Mirrors, freestanding	15	*	1 Jul 2004
Radios	10		1 Jan 2001
Rugs	7	*	1 Jul 2004
Skylights:			
Controls	10	*	1 Jul 2019
Motors	10	*	1 Jul 2019
Solar power generating system (incorporating batteries, inverters, solar panels, regulators)	20	*	1 Jul 2004
Stereo systems (incorporating amplifiers, cassette players, CD players, radios and speakers)	7	*	1 Jul 2004
Surround sound systems (incorporating audio-video receivers and speakers)	10	*	1 Jul 2004
Telecommunications assets:			
Cordless phones	4	*	1 Jul 2004
Telephone hand sets	6	*	1 Jul 2019
Telephone systems - see Table B Telephony			
Television antennas, freestanding	5	*	1 Jul 2004
Television sets	8	*	1 Jul 2019
Vacuum cleaners:			
Ducted:			
Hoses	10	*	1 Jul 2004
Motors	10	*	1 Jul 2004
Wands	10	*	1 Jul 2004
Portable	10		1 Jan 2001
Ventilation fans	20	*	1 Jul 2004
Video cassette recorder systems (VCRs)	5	*	1 Jul 2004
Water pumps:			
Multi-storey	20	*	1 Jul 2019
Rainwater tanks	5	*	1 Jul 2019
Single residence pressure pumps	8	*	1 Jul 2019
Window blinds, internal	10	*	1 Jul 2004
Window curtains	6	*	1 Jul 2004
Window shutters, automatic:			
Controls	10	*	1 Jul 2004
Motors	10	*	1 Jul 2004
Bathroom assets:			
Accessories, freestanding (including shower caddies, soap holders, toilet brushes)	3	*	1 Jul 2019
Exhaust fans (including light/heating)	10	*	1 Jul 2004
Heated towel rails, electric	10	*	1 Jul 2004
Shower curtains (excluding curtain rods and screens)	2	*	1 Jul 2004

RENTAL, HIRING AND REAL ESTATE SERVICES
(66110 to 67200)

Asset	Life (Years)	Reviewed	Date Of Application
Spa bath pumps	10	*	1 Jul 2019
Fire control assets:			
Alarms:			
Heat	6	*	1 Jul 2004
Smoke	6	*	1 Jul 2004
Detection and alarm systems:			
Alarm bells	12	*	1 Jul 2004
Detectors (including addressable manual call points, heat, multi type and smoke)	20	*	1 Jul 2004
Fire indicator panels	12	*	1 Jul 2004
Emergency warning and intercommunication systems (EWIS):			
Master emergency control panels	12	*	1 Jul 2004
Speakers	12	*	1 Jul 2004
Strobe lights	12	*	1 Jul 2004
Warden intercom phones (WIPs)	12	*	1 Jul 2004
Extinguishers	15	*	1 Jul 2004
Hoses and nozzles	10	*	1 Jul 2004
Pumps (including diesel and electric)	25	*	1 Jul 2004
Stair pressurisation assets:			
AC variable speed drives (VSDs)	10	*	1 Jul 2004
Pressurisation and extraction fans	25	*	1 Jul 2004
Sensors	10	*	1 Jul 2004
Kitchen assets:			
Cook tops	12	*	1 Jul 2004
Crockery	5	*	1 Jul 2004
Cutlery	5	*	1 Jul 2004
Dishwashers	8	*	1 Jul 2019
Freezers	12	*	1 Jul 2004
Garbage disposal units	10	*	1 Jul 2004
Microwave ovens	8	*	1 Jul 2019
Ovens	12	*	1 Jul 2004
Range hoods	12	*	1 Jul 2004
Refrigerators	12	*	1 Jul 2004
Stoves	12	*	1 Jul 2004
Water filters, electrical	15	*	1 Jul 2004
Laundry assets:			
Clothes dryers	7	*	1 Jul 2019
Ironing boards, freestanding	5	*	1 Jul 2019
Irons	5	*	1 Jul 2004
Washing machines	8	*	1 Jul 2019
Outdoor assets:			
Automatic garage doors:			
Controls	5	*	1 Jul 2004
Motors	10	*	1 Jul 2004
Barbecue assets:			
Fixed barbecue assets:			
Sliding trays and cookers	10	*	1 Jul 2004
Freestanding barbecues	5	*	1 Jul 2004

RENTAL, HIRING AND REAL ESTATE SERVICES (66110 to 67200)

Asset	Life (Years)	Reviewed	Date Of Application
Floor carpet (including artificial grass and matting)	5	*	1 Jul 2004
Folding arm awnings:			
Controls	10	*	1 Jul 2019
Motors	10	*	1 Jul 2019
Furniture, freestanding	5	*	1 Jul 2004
Gardening watering installations:			
Control panels	5	*	1 Jul 2004
Pumps	5	*	1 Jul 2004
Timing devices	5	*	1 Jul 2004
Garden lights, solar	5	*	1 Jul 2019
Garden sheds, freestanding	15	*	1 Jul 2004
Gates, electrical:			
Controls	5	*	1 Jul 2004
Motors	10	*	1 Jul 2004
Operable pergola louvres:			
Controls	15	*	1 Jul 2004
Motors	15	*	1 Jul 2004
Rainwater tanks:			
Galvanised steel	25	*	1 Jul 2019
Polyethylene	15	*	1 Jul 2019
Roller blinds			
Controls	10	*	1 Jul 2019
Motors	10	*	1 Jul 2019
Sauna heating assets	15	*	1 Jul 2004
Sewage treatment assets:			
Controls	8	*	1 Jul 2004
Motors	8	*	1 Jul 2004
Spas:			
Fixed spa assets:			
Chlorinators	10	*	1 Jul 2019
Filtration assets (including pumps)	10	*	1 Jul 2019
Heaters (electric or gas)	15	*	1 Jul 2004
Freestanding spas (incorporating blowers, controls, filters, heaters and pumps)	17	*	1 Jul 2004
Swimming pool assets:			
Chlorinators	10	*	1 Jul 2019
Cleaning assets	7	*	1 Jul 2004
Covers (including blankets)	8	*	1 Jul 2019
Filtration assets (including pumps)	10	*	1 Jul 2019
Heaters:			
Electric	15	*	1 Jul 2004
Gas	15	*	1 Jul 2004
Solar	20	*	1 Jul 2004
Tennis court assets:			
Cleaners	3	*	1 Jul 2004
Drag brooms	3	*	1 Jul 2004
Nets	5	*	1 Jul 2004
Rollers	3	*	1 Jul 2004

RENTAL, HIRING AND REAL ESTATE SERVICES
(66110 to 67200)

Asset	Life (Years)	Reviewed	Date Of Application
Umpire chairs	15	*	1 Jul 2004
Security and monitoring assets:			
Access control systems:			
Code pads	5	*	1 Jul 2004
Door controllers	5	*	1 Jul 2004
Readers:			
Proximity	7	*	1 Jul 2004
Swipe card	3	*	1 Jul 2004
CCTV systems:			
Cameras	4	*	1 Jul 2004
Monitors	4	*	1 Jul 2004
Recorders:			
Digital	4	*	1 Jul 2004
Time lapse	2	*	1 Jul 2004
Switching units (including multiplexes)	5	*	1 Jul 2004
Security systems:			
Code pads	5	*	1 Jul 2004
Control panels	5	*	1 Jul 2004
Detectors (including passive infrared, photo sensors and vibration)	5	*	1 Jul 2004
Global System for Mobiles (GSM) Units	5	*	1 Jul 2004
Noise makers (including bells and sirens)	5	*	1 Jul 2004
Non-residential property operators (67120)			
Commercial office building assets:			
Boilers	20	*	1 Jul 2005
Boiler pumps	5	*	1 Jul 2005
Building maintenance units	35	*	1 Jul 2005
Carpets	8	*	1 Jul 2005
Door controls and motor drive systems for automatic sliding doors (incorporating chains, controls, motors and sensors, but excluding doors)	15	*	1 Jul 2005
Hot water installations (excluding commercial boilers and piping)	15	*	1 Jul 2005
Power supply assets:			
Emergency or standby:			
Generator assets:			
Acoustic hoods and canopies	20	*	1 Jul 2005
Generators (incorporating attached engine management and generator monitoring instruments)	25	*	1 Jul 2005
Power management units	15	*	1 Jul 2005
Lighting control systems (microprocessor based)	5	*	1 Jul 2014
Uninterruptible power supply (UPS) systems:			
Line interactive types	5	*	1 Jul 2013
On line double conversion types	10	*	1 Jul 2013
Window blinds	20	*	1 Jul 2005

Footnotes:

43 A rental car is a passenger car hired, leased or rented for short-term use without a driver.

44 From 1 July 2017, certain investors in residential properties will not be able to deduct the decline in value of plant and equipment that has been used previously by an entity (other than as trading stock), subject to limited exceptions. This measure applies to plant and equipment acquired at or after 7:30pm (AEST), 9 May 2017.

¶43-070 Effective life — professional, scientific and technical services

PROFESSIONAL, SCIENTIFIC AND TECHNICAL SERVICES
(69100 to 70000)

Asset	Life (Years)	Reviewed	Date Of Application
Scientific research services (69100)			
Scientific, medical and pharmaceutical research assets:			
Autoclaves:			
Bench top autoclaves	5	*	1 Jul 2014
Others	10	*	1 Jul 2014
Automated cell counters	5	*	1 Jul 2014
Automated colony pickers	5	*	1 Jul 2014
Balances	10	*	1 Jul 2014
Biological safety cabinets	10	*	1 Jul 2014
Cell harvesters	10	*	1 Jul 2014
Centrifuges:			
Bench top centrifuges	5	*	1 Jul 2014
Others	10	*	1 Jul 2014
Computed tomography (CT) scanners	10	*	1 Jul 2014
Digital cameras	3	*	1 Jul 2014
DNA sequencers	5	*	1 Jul 2014
Electrophoresis systems (incorporating power supplies and tanks)	7	*	1 Jul 2014
Electroporators	8	*	1 Jul 2014
Fermenters	10	*	1 Jul 2014
Flow cytometers	8	*	1 Jul 2014
Freeze dryers	10	*	1 Jul 2014
Freezers	10	*	1 Jul 2014
Gel documentation systems	5	*	1 Jul 2014
Glassware washers	8	*	1 Jul 2014
Heating blocks	10	*	1 Jul 2014
Homogenisers	7	*	1 Jul 2014
Incubators	6	*	1 Jul 2014
Liquid chromatography systems	5	*	1 Jul 2014
Liquid nitrogen assets (including dewars and tanks)	10	*	1 Jul 2014
Microscopes	10	*	1 Jul 2014
Microtomes	10	*	1 Jul 2014
Mixers	7	*	1 Jul 2014
Nano spectrophotometers	8	*	1 Jul 2014
Ovens	6	*	1 Jul 2014
Peristaltic pumps	7	*	1 Jul 2014
pH meters	7	*	1 Jul 2014
Plate readers	5	*	1 Jul 2014
Polymerase chain reaction (PCR) thermal cyclers	8	*	1 Jul 2014
Real-time PCR detection machines	5	*	1 Jul 2014
Refrigerators	8	*	1 Jul 2014

PROFESSIONAL, SCIENTIFIC AND TECHNICAL SERVICES
(69100 to 70000)

Asset	Life (Years)	Reviewed	Date Of Application
Robotic systems (including robotic liquid handling systems and robotic sampler systems)	5	*	1 Jul 2014
Shakers	7	*	1 Jul 2014
Sonicators (including water bath sonicators and sonicators with probes)	7	*	1 Jul 2014
Spectrophotometers (excluding nano spectrophotometers)	10	*	1 Jul 2014
Surface plasmon resonance (SPR) machines	5	*	1 Jul 2014
Vacuum concentrators	7	*	1 Jul 2014
Water baths (including refrigerated and shaking water baths)	7	*	1 Jul 2014
Water purification systems	8	*	1 Jul 2014
Surveying and mapping services (69220)			
Airborne imaging (cameras)	7	*	1 Jul 2015
Automatic optical levels (dumpy levels)	7	*	1 Jul 2015
Controllers	4	*	1 Jul 2015
Digital (electronic) levels	5	*	1 Jul 2015
Echo sounders	5	*	1 Jul 2015
GNSS/GIS handhelds (asset receivers)	3	*	1 Jul 2015
GNSS/GPS survey equipment (including receivers, reference/base stations, rover receivers, data radios, antennas and integrated GNSS)	5	*	1 Jul 2015
Ground imaging (pole cameras)	5	*	1 Jul 2015
Laser detectors/receivers (rod-eye receivers)	4	*	1 Jul 2015
Laser distance measurers/meters (DISTOs)	4	*	1 Jul 2015
Laser levels:			
Grade laying (dial-in grade)	6	*	1 Jul 2015
Laser plummets	5	*	1 Jul 2015
Line and plumb/point and cross line	4	*	1 Jul 2015
Pipe laying	6	*	1 Jul 2015
Rotating	6	*	1 Jul 2015
Tunnelling and plumbing	6	*	1 Jul 2015
Laser scanners – 3D (high definition surveying) – ground LIDAR	5	*	1 Jul 2015
Laser scanners – vehicle mounted – ground LIDAR	5	*	1 Jul 2015
LIDAR (airborne)	7	*	1 Jul 2015
Rail surveying assets:			
Mobile rail surveying equipment	5	*	1 Jul 2015
Platform clearance gauges	6	*	1 Jul 2015
Rail profile gauges	6	*	1 Jul 2015
Stereoplotters – digital/softcopy (hardware only)	10	*	1 Jul 2015
Tablets	4	*	1 Jul 2015
Theodolites (digital)	7	*	1 Jul 2015
Total stations (including mechanical, manual, motorised, auto lock, robotic, universal and multi-stations)	5	*	1 Jul 2015
Traverse kits (incorporating tripods, tribrachs, prisms, poles and optical plummets)	5	*	1 Jul 2015
Unmanned aerial vehicles (drones/remotely piloted aircraft):			
Fixed wing	3	*	1 Jul 2015
Rotary wing	2	*	1 Jul 2015
Unmanned surface vehicles	4	*	1 Jul 2015
Utility locator (underground service locator) assets:			
Ground penetrating radars (GPRs)	5	*	1 Jul 2015

PROFESSIONAL, SCIENTIFIC AND TECHNICAL SERVICES (69100 to 70000)

Asset	Life (Years)	Reviewed	Date Of Application
Magnetic locators	5	*	1 Jul 2015
Service locators	5	*	1 Jul 2015
Signal generators	5	*	1 Jul 2015
Signal tracer for locators	4	*	1 Jul 2015
Scientific testing and analysis services (69250)			
Coal laboratory assets:			
Sample preparation assets:			
Drop shatters	20	*	1 Jul 2018
Drum tumblers	15	*	1 Jul 2018
Drying ovens:			
Benchtop	7	*	1 Jul 2018
Others (including floor size with trolleys)	15	*	1 Jul 2018
Dust extraction system	15	*	1 Jul 2018
Float-sink buckets	8	*	1 Jul 2018
Float-sink testing units (incorporating ventilation ducting, fans, density separation apparatus etc, but excluding float-sink buckets)	15	*	1 Jul 2018
Flotation machines (including froth rotation machines)	20	*	1 Jul 2018
Jaw crushers	10	*	1 Jul 2018
Pulverisers	10	*	1 Jul 2018
Riffle splitters	10	*	1 Jul 2018
Rotary Sample Dividers (RSDs)	15	*	1 Jul 2018
Sample storage assets:			
Cool room assets - see Table B Refrigeration assets			
Portable refrigerators/freezers	10	*	1 Jul 2018
Sample trays	5	*	1 Jul 2018
Sample trolleys	10	*	1 Jul 2018
Sieve shakers (excluding sieves)	10	*	1 Jul 2018
Sieves (including various meshes and sizes)	7	*	1 Jul 2018
Weighing scales	10	*	1 Jul 2018
Laboratory analytical equipment and instruments:		*	1 Jul 2018
Analytical balances	7	*	1 Jul 2018
Calorimeters	10	*	1 Jul 2018
Carbon and sulphur analysers	7	*	1 Jul 2018
CHN analysers (including carbon, hydrogen and nitrogen)	7	*	1 Jul 2018
Coal ash fusibility furnaces	10	*	1 Jul 2018
Crucible Swell Number (CSN) burners	10	*	
Dilatometers	9	*	1 Jul 2018
Fume cabinets	15	*	1 Jul 2018
Moisture testing ovens (including nitrogen setup apparatus)	10	*	1 Jul 2018
Muffle furnaces	15	*	
Particle size analysers	10	*	1 Jul 2018
Petrographic microscopes	10	*	1 Jul 2018
Plastometers	9	*	1 Jul 2018
Water baths (including ultrasonic water baths)	7	*	1 Jul 2018

PROFESSIONAL, SCIENTIFIC AND TECHNICAL SERVICES
(69100 to 70000)

Asset	Life (Years)	Reviewed	Date Of Application
X-Ray Fluorescence (XRF) and X-Ray Diffraction (XRD)	7	*	1 Jul 2018
Mineral processing and metallurgical laboratory assets:			
Sample preparation assets:			
Benchtop (including work benches and tables)	10	*	1 Jul 2019
Centrifugal concentrators	15	*	1 Jul 2019
Cone crushers	20	*	1 Jul 2019
Drying ovens:			
Benchtop	7	*	1 Jul 2019
Others (including floor size with trolleys)	10	*	1 Jul 2019
Dust cabinet (including extracted workstations)	20	*	1 Jul 2019
Dust extraction systems	15	*	1 Jul 2019
Flotation machines (including froth rotation machines)	20	*	1 Jul 2019
Gravity separation assets (including centrifuges and cyclones)	10	*	1 Jul 2019
Grinding mills	12	*	1 Jul 2019
Jaw crushers	10	*	1 Jul 2019
Laboratory tumblers (including cyanide leach test tumblers)	10	*	1 Jul 2019
Micro dosing peristaltic pumps	7	*	1 Jul 2019
Overhead tank mixers	5	*	1 Jul 2019
pH control systems	15	*	1 Jul 2019
Pressure filters	8	*	1 Jul 2019
Pulverisers	10	*	1 Jul 2019
Riffle splitters	10	*	1 Jul 2019
Rotary Sample Dividers (RSDs)	10	*	1 Jul 2019
Sample storage assets:			
Cool room assets - See Table B under 'Refrigeration'			
Portable refrigerators/freezers	8	*	1 Jul 2019
Sample trays	3	*	1 Jul 2019
Sample trolleys	7	*	1 Jul 2019
Scrubbers	15	*	1 Jul 2019
Shaking tables (including wet tables)	20	*	1 Jul 2019
Sieve shakers (excluding sieves)	10	*	1 Jul 2019
Sieves (including various meshes and sizes)	3	*	1 Jul 2019
Solvent extraction & electrowinning equipment	15	*	1 Jul 2019
Vacuum filters	7	*	1 Jul 2019
Water purification systems	15	*	1 Jul 2019
Weighing scales	7	*	1 Jul 2019
Laboratory analytical equipment and instruments:			
Analytical balances	7	*	1 Jul 2019
Atomic Absorption Spectroscopy (AAS) instruments	10	*	1 Jul 2019
Auto dilutors	7	*	1 Jul 2019
Auto titration instruments	7	*	1 Jul 2019
Carbon and sulphur analysers	7	*	1 Jul 2019
Cupellation furnaces	10	*	1 Jul 2019
Fume cabinets	15	*	1 Jul 2019
Fusion furnaces	10	*	1 Jul 2019
Fourier Transform Infrared (FTIR) spectroscopy	7	*	1 Jul 2019

PROFESSIONAL, SCIENTIFIC AND TECHNICAL SERVICES
(69100 to 70000)

Asset	Life (Years)	Reviewed	Date Of Application
Hot blocks	7	*	1 Jul 2019
Hotplate magnetic stirrers	10	*	1 Jul 2019
Incubators	7	*	1 Jul 2019
Inductively coupled plasma mass spectrometry (ICP-MS), and Inductively coupled plasmas optical emission spectroscopy (ICP-OES)	10	*	1 Jul 2019
Ion Chromatography (IC) equipment	15	*	1 Jul 2019
Muffle furnaces	12	*	1 Jul 2019
Overhead stirrers	8	*	1 Jul 2019
Particle size analysers	10	*	1 Jul 2019
Petrographic microscopes	10	*	1 Jul 2019
Robotic cells (including robotic fusion cells, robotic preparations cells)	10	*	1 Jul 2019
Robotic TGA cells	7	*	1 Jul 2019
Thermogravimetric Analysers (TGAs)	7	*	1 Jul 2019
Water baths	5	*	1 Jul 2019
X-Ray Fluorescence (XRF) and X-Ray Diffraction (XRD)	7	*	1 Jul 2019
Advertising services (69400)			
Advertising signs – see Table B Advertising signs			
Veterinary services (69700)			
Veterinarians' assets:			
Anaesthesia machines	10	*	1 Jan 2004
Animal blow dryers	5	*	1 Jan 2004
Animal cages:			
Fibreglass, plastic and polyethylene (PE) cages	10	*	1 Jan 2004
Stainless steel cages	20	*	1 Jan 2004
Animal patient monitoring assets (including blood pressure monitors, carbon dioxide (CO_2) end-tidal monitors, ECGs and pulse oximeters)	7	*	1 Jan 2004
Animal scales	7	*	1 Jan 2004
Dental assets:			
Dental units	10	*	1 Jan 2004
Ultrasonic scalers (standalone)	10	*	1 Jan 2004
Diagnostic assets (including ophthalmoscope, otoscope, handles and power supply)	10	*	1 Jan 2004
Electrocautery units	10	*	1 Jan 2004
Electroejaculators	6	*	1 Jan 2004
Hydrobaths	8	*	1 Jan 2004
Pathology assets:			
Centrifuges	5	*	1 Jan 2004
Laboratory analysers:			
Electrolyte analysers	4	*	1 Jan 2004
Generally	5	*	1 Jan 2004
Microscopes	10	*	1 Jan 2004
Surgery lights	10	*	1 Jan 2004
Tables and tubs	20	*	1 Jan 2004
Ultrasound systems (incorporating scanner, transducers, integrated computer and integrated software)	5	*	1 Jan 2004

PROFESSIONAL, SCIENTIFIC AND TECHNICAL SERVICES
(69100 to 70000)

Asset	Life (Years)	Reviewed	Date Of Application
X-ray assets (excluding direct radiography assets):			
Mobile or portable x-ray units	10	*	1 Jan 2004
X-ray processors – automatic	10	*	1 Jan 2004
Professional photographic services (69910)			
Audio assets (including microphones, preamplifiers, sound recording devices, transmitters and receivers)	3	*	1 Jul 2015
Camera lenses	5	*	1 Jul 2015
Digital cameras:			
Compact cameras (including point and shoot cameras)	3	*	1 Jul 2015
Compact system cameras (including bridge cameras, micro four-thirds cameras, mirrorless cameras)	3	*	1 Jul 2015
Medium format single lens reflex (SLR) camera systems (including camera bodies and digital backs)	4	*	1 Jul 2015
SLR cameras (including full-frame SLR cameras)	3	*	1 Jul 2015
Lighting assets:			
Electronic flash units (including compact flash heads, monolights):			
Portable	3	*	1 Jul 2015
Studio lightings	5	*	1 Jul 2015
Light meters	5	*	1 Jul 2015
Light shaping tools (including modelling glass protectors, reflectors and scrims, softboxes and umbrellas)	3	*	1 Jul 2015
Portable flash units (including flashguns)	2	*	1 Jul 2015
Power packs (including battery packs and compact flash generators)	4	*	1 Jul 2015
Support assets:			
Backdrop support systems (including background elevation systems)	10	*	1 Jul 2015
Bags and cases	5	*	1 Jul 2015
Camera track sliders	2	*	1 Jul 2015
Light stands (including boom arms)	5	*	1 Jul 2015
Photographic printers/plotters	4	*	1 Jul 2015
Tent and shooting tables	2	*	1 Jul 2015
Tripods	5	*	1 Jul 2015
Unmanned aerial vehicles (drones/remotely piloted aircraft) – rotary	2	*	1 Jul 2015
Wind machines	5	*	1 Jul 2015

¶43-075 Effective life — administrative and support services

ADMINISTRATIVE AND SUPPORT SERVICES
(72110 to 73200)

Asset	Life (Years)	Reviewed	Date Of Application
Building and other industrial cleaning services (73110)			
Air purifiers, deodorising and mould remediation assets (including air filtering machines, air scrubbers and ozone generators)	5	*	1 Jul 2010
Batteries, deep cycle (including those used in ride-on polishers, scrubbers, sweepers and vacuum cleaners)	2	*	1 Jul 2010
Drying and restoration assets (including air movers and dehumidifiers)	5	*	1 Jul 2010

ADMINISTRATIVE AND SUPPORT SERVICES
(72110 to 73200)

Asset	Life (Years)	Reviewed	Date Of Application
Extractors for carpet and upholstery cleaning:			
Spot extractors (including portable handheld and brief case size extractors for stain removal)	3	*	1 Jul 2010
Other (including walk behind and self-contained carpet extractors)	5	*	1 Jul 2010
Truck or van mounted	10	*	1 Jul 2010
Polishing, carpet cleaning and floor stripping assets (including floor polishers, burnishers, rotary scrubbers, encapsulation machines and floor strippers):			
Portable	5	*	1 Jul 2010
Ride-on	5	*	1 Jul 2010
Pressure washers:			
Portable	4	*	1 Jul 2010
Trailer or truck mounted	7	*	1 Jul 2010
Scrubbers, hard floor:			
Portable	5	*	1 Jul 2010
Ride-on	7	*	1 Jul 2010
Steam cleaners for sanitising floor and surfaces	5	*	1 Jul 2010
Sweepers, hard floor:			
Portable	5	*	1 Jul 2010
Ride-on	7	*	1 Jul 2010
Road sweeper trucks (including sweepers)[45]	10	*#	1 Jul 2010
Vacuum cleaners:			
Backpack and pull along machines	3	*	1 Jul 2010
Other portable (including upright machines)	5	*	1 Jul 2010
Ride-on or stand on	7	*	1 Jul 2010
Gardening services (73130)			
Arboriculture and gardening services:			
Blowers	3	*	1 Jan 2004
Brushcutters (including whipper snippers)	2	*	1 Jan 2004
Chainsaws (including pole pruners)	2	*	1 Jan 2004
Elevating work platforms	15	*	1 Jan 2004
Hand tools (including pruner, rake, hedge shears, loppers and tree saws)	3	*	1 Jan 2004
Hedge trimmers	4	*	1 Jan 2004
Lawn edgers (excluding brushcutters)	4	*	1 Jan 2004
Lawn mowers:			
Cylinder	7	*	1 Jan 2004
Push (rotary)	2	*	1 Jan 2004
Ride-ons	5	*	1 Jan 2004
Self propelled (rotary)	2	*	1 Jan 2004
Stump grinders	5	*	1 Jan 2004
Tractors	8	*	1 Jan 2004
Tractor attachments:			
Roller mowers	4	*	1 Jan 2004
Slashers	4	*	1 Jan 2004
Trailers used to carry tree and grass clippings	5	*	1 Jan 2004
Tree climbing assets:			
Climbing hardware (including carabineers, figure of 8 and lowering pullies)	1	*	1 Jan 2004

ADMINISTRATIVE AND SUPPORT SERVICES (72110 to 73200)

Asset	Life (Years)	Reviewed	Date Of Application
Climbing spurs	10	*	1 Jan 2004
Friction lowering devices	10	*	1 Jan 2004
Harness	3	*	1 Jan 2004
Ropes	1	*	1 Jan 2004
Wood chippers	8	*	1 Jan 2004
Packaging services (73200)			
Fruit and vegetables pack houses assets used off farm:			
Banana assets:			
Air rams	3	*	1 Jul 2008
Bunch lines	10	*	1 Jul 2008
Choppers/mulchers	4	*	1 Jul 2008
Rails (including points)	15	*	1 Jul 2008
Scrap conveyors	5	*	1 Jul 2008
Tops	8	*	1 Jul 2008
Water troughs	10	*	1 Jul 2008
General assets:			
Bins	5	*	1 Jul 2008
Bin tippers	15	*	1 Jul 2008
Conveyors (including elevators)	10	*	1 Jul 2008
Drying tunnels	15	*	1 Jul 2008
Fungicide units	10	*	1 Jul 2008
Receival hoppers (including water dumps)	10	*	1 Jul 2008
Tables (including packing and sorting tables)	15	*	1 Jul 2008
Washing assets (including brush and barrel washers)	10	*	1 Jul 2008
Waxing assets	10	*	1 Jul 2008
Graders:			
Electronic	10	*	1 Jul 2008
Mechanical	15	*	1 Jul 2008
Optical	8	*	1 Jul 2008
Labelling assets:			
Labelling applicators (including in line labellers)	8	*	1 Jul 2008
Labelling guns	3	*	1 Jul 2008
Packing assets (including bagging and wrapping machines)	10	*	1 Jul 2008
Scales (excluding platform scales)	5	*	1 Jul 2008
Tree nuts assets:			
Crackers	7	*	1 Jul 2008
Drying silos	15	*	1 Jul 2008
Separating assets (including air separators, trommels and vibrating screens)	10	*	1 Jul 2008

Footnotes:

45 A capped effective life of 7 1/2 years may be available – see subsection 40-102(4)

¶43-080 Effective life — education and training

EDUCATION AND TRAINING
(80100 to 82200)

Asset	Life (Years)	Reviewed	Date Of Application
Kindergarten furniture an play equipment – see Table A Child care services (87100)			

¶43-085 Effective life — health care and social assistance

HEALTH CARE AND SOCIAL ASSISTANCE
(84010 to 87900)

Asset	Life (Years)	Reviewed	Date Of Application
Medical assets (used in common across all health care industry segments):			
Benchtop sterilisers	5	*	1 Jul 2003
Benchtop ultrasonic cleaners	7	*	1 Jul 2003
Clinical furniture	10	*	1 Jul 2003
X-ray viewers	10	*	1 Jul 2003
Hospitals (84010 to 84020)			
Hospital assets:			
Anaesthesia machines	10	*	1 Jan 2003
Angiography assets:			
Image acquisition systems (incorporating computers with digital subtraction capability, digital cameras, monitors and integrated software)	4	*	1 Jul 2002
Image intensifiers	7	*	1 Jul 2002
Patient gantries or tables, patient monitoring assets, positioning assets and pressure injectors	10	*	1 Jul 2002
Cell savers and cell separators	7	*	1 Jan 2003
Colposcopes	10	*	1 Jan 2003
Defibrillators	10	*	1 Jan 2003
Diathermy and cautery machines/electrosurgical generators	10	*	1 Jan 2003
Endoscopic surgery assets (excluding disposable accessories):			
Arthroscopic fluid management systems	7	*	1 Jan 2003
Endoscopes (flexible and rigid) and endoscopic surgical instruments	4	*	1 Jan 2003
Endoscopic camera systems:			
Beam splitters and light sources	10	*	1 Jan 2003
Printers, video cameras, video camera adaptors, couplers and heads, video image capture systems and video processors	5	*	1 Jan 2003
Still cameras	7	*	1 Jan 2003
Video monitors and video recorders	7	*	1 Jan 2003
Endoscopic electrosurgical generators	10	*	1 Jan 2003
Endoscopic lasers	10	*	1 Jan 2003
Endoscopic ultrasound systems (incorporating scanner, transducers/probes, integrated computer and integrated software)	5	*	1 Jan 2003
Haemodialysis machines	7	*	1 Jan 2003
Head lights	7	*	1 Jan 2003
Hospital furniture:			

HEALTH CARE AND SOCIAL ASSISTANCE
(84010 to 87900)

Asset	Life (Years)	Reviewed	Date Of Application
Beds:			
Electronic	7	*	1 Jan 2003
Mechanical	10	*	1 Jan 2003
Bedside cabinets/lockers, carts and poles, blanket warming cabinets, blood warming cabinets, medical refrigerators and overbed tables	10	*	1 Jan 2003
Infusion pumps:			
General, pain management and rapid	8	*	1 Jan 2003
Syringe driven	6	*	1 Jan 2003
Insufflators	10	*	1 Jan 2003
Lithotriptors used for extra-corporeal shock wave lithotripsy	7	*	1 Jan 2003
Mechanical assist assets:			
Calf and cuff compression devices	8	*	1 Jan 2003
Cardiac bypass and heart lung machines	8	*	1 Jan 2003
Intra-aortic balloon pumps	8	*	1 Jan 2003
Ventricular assist heart pumps	8	*	1 Jan 2003
Natal care assets (including incubators, infant warmers and mobile infant warmers)	7	*	1 Jan 2003
Operating tables and attachments:			
Electronic	10	*	1 Jan 2003
Mechanical	13	*	1 Jan 2003
Operating theatre lights	8	*	1 Jan 2003
Pan flushers	10	*	1 Jan 2003
Patient hoists and lifters	10	*	1 Jan 2003
Patient monitoring assets:			
Bedside monitoring systems	7	*	1 Jan 2003
Cardiac monitors	7	*	1 Jan 2003
ECGs	7	*	1 Jan 2003
Foetal monitors	7	*	1 Jan 2003
Pulse oximeters	7	*	1 Jan 2003
Vital signs monitors	7	*	1 Jan 2003
Patient warming assets (excluding disposable accessories):			
Fluid warmers	10	*	1 Jan 2003
Forced air patient warmers	10	*	1 Jan 2003
Smoke evacuators	8	*	1 Jan 2003
Sterilisation and autoclave processing assets:			
Drying cabinets	10	*	1 Jan 2003
Endoscope sterilisers and disinfectors	5	*	1 Jan 2003
Flash sterilisers	10	*	1 Jan 2003
Instrument washers	10	*	1 Jan 2003
Pre-vacuum sterilisers	10	*	1 Jan 2003
Ultrasonic cleaners and baths	7	*	1 Jan 2003
Surgical instruments:			
Hand held manually operated instruments	8	*	1 Jan 2003
Powered instruments (including drills, saws, shavers, non-disposable instrument accessories and power sources)	7	*	1 Jan 2003
Ultrasonic aspirators	10	*	1 Jan 2003
Ultrasonic scalpels	10	*	1 Jan 2003
Surgical lasers (excluding ophthalmic surgical lasers)	10	*	1 Jan 2003

HEALTH CARE AND SOCIAL ASSISTANCE
(84010 to 87900)

Asset	Life (Years)	Reviewed	Date Of Application
Surgical microscopes	10	*	1 Jan 2003
Ultrasonic bladder scanners	10	*	1 Jan 2003
Ultrasonic needle guides	10	*	1 Jan 2003
Ultrasound systems (incorporating scanner, transducers, integrated computer and integrated software) used by cardiologists, obstetricians and vascular surgeons	5	*	1 Jul 2002
Ventilators:			
Fixed	7	*	1 Jan 2003
Portable	5	*	1 Jan 2003
Wheelchairs	10	*	1 Jan 2003
General practice medical services (85110)			
Anatomical medical models, plastic	10	*	1 Jul 2020
Autoclaves and sterilisers	8	*	1 Jul 2020
Automated ankle brachial pressure index (ABPI) measurement devices	6	*	1 Jul 2020
Automated external defibrillators (AEDs) – see Table B			
Blood coagulation (INR) meters	5	*	1 Jul 2020
Cryosurgical assets:			
Cryosurgical flasks and guns	5	*	1 Jul 2020
Liquid nitrogen storage dewers and tanks	10	*	1 Jul 2020
Dermatoscopes	5	*	1 Jul 2020
Ear irrigators	5	*	1 Jul 2020
Electrocardiograph (ECG) machines	7	*	1 Jul 2020
Examination lights:			
Desktop/trolley	3	*	1 Jul 2020
Procedure	7	*	1 Jul 2020
Foetal heart monitors, external	7	*	1 Jul 2020
Hyfrecators – electrosurgical units	6	*	1 Jul 2020
Magnifying loupes	10	*	1 Jul 2020
Medical examination beds (adjustable/electric)	8	*	1 Jul 2020
Medical plaster saws	7	*	1 Jul 2020
Medical refrigerators	8	*	1 Jul 2020
Nebulisers	5	*	1 Jul 2020
Ophthalmoscopes, direct and otoscopes	6	*	1 Jul 2020
Oxygen tank regulators	10	*	1 Jul 2020
Portable observation machines (including vital signs monitors)	7	*	1 Jul 2020
Privacy curtains and rails	8	*	1 Jul 2020
Pulse oximeters	4	*	1 Jul 2020
Resuscitation kits	15	*	1 Jul 2020
Saddle chairs	7	*	1 Jul 2020
Scales:			
Baby scales	3	*	1 Jul 2020
General, heavy duty, mother/baby scales	5	*	1 Jul 2020
Sphygmomanometers (including aneroid and digital)	5	*	1 Jul 2020
Spirometers	7	*	1 Jul 2020
Stethoscopes	10	*	1 Jul 2020
Suction machines, portable	8	*	1 Jul 2020
Surgical instruments (including forceps, needle holders, scissors, skin graft knives)	8	*	1 Jul 2020

HEALTH CARE AND SOCIAL ASSISTANCE (84010 to 87900)

Asset	Life (Years)	Reviewed	Date Of Application
Thermometers, digital	4	*	1 Jul 2020
Trolleys (including instrument and treatment trolleys)	10	*	1 Jul 2020
Wheelchairs	8	*	1 Jul 2020
X-ray viewers	10	*	1 Jul 2020
Specialist medical services n.e.c (85129)			
Neurologists' assets:			
Electroencephalography (EEG) systems (incorporating electrodes, amplifiers, integrated software and integrated computers)	5	*	1 Jul 2003
Electromyography (EMG) systems (incorporating electrodes, amplifiers, integrated software and integrated computers)	5	*	1 Jul 2003
Thoracic physicians' assets:			
Body plethysmographs (incorporating flow sensors, gas analysers, integrated software and integrated computers)	7	*	1 Jul 2003
Continuous positive airway pressure (CPAP) and variable positive airway pressure (VPAP) systems	7	*	1 Jul 2003
Lung function analysis exercise systems (incorporating flow sensors, treadmills or ergometers, ECGs, pulse oximeters, integrated software and integrated computers)	7	*	1 Jul 2003
Lung function analysis systems (incorporating flow sensors, gas analysers, integrated software and integrated computers)	7	*	1 Jul 2003
Spirometers	7	*	1 Jul 2003
Sleep laboratory systems (incorporating amplifiers, sensors, integrated CPAP monitors, integrated carbon dioxide (CO_2) monitors, integrated pulse oximeters, integrated computers and integrated software)	7	*	1 Jul 2003
Pathology and diagnostic imaging services (85201, 85202, 85203 and 85209)			
Pathologists' assets:			
Batch slide stainer	6	*	1 Jan 2002
Bio hazard chambers	10	*	1 Jan 2002
Centrifuges	5	*	1 Jan 2002
Incubators	6	*	1 Jan 2002
Laboratory analysers	5	*	1 Jan 2002
Microscopes	10	*	1 Jan 2002
Rotary microtomes	6	*	1 Jan 2002
Tissue embedding systems	6	*	1 Jan 2002
Tissue processors	6	*	1 Jan 2002
Radiologists' diagnostic imaging assets:			
Bone densitometry (BMD) systems (incorporating either whole body scanners, integrated computer and integrated software, or spine and hip scanners, holding devices, integrated computers and integrated software)	10	*	1 Jul 2002
Computed radiography (CR) digitisers	4	*	1 Jul 2002
Computed tomography (CT) systems (incorporating scanners, integrated computers and integrated software)	10	*	1 Jul 2002
Film digitisers	4	*	1 Jul 2002
Fluoroscopy assets (excluding direct radiography assets):			
Fixed systems (incorporating buckies, generators, screening tables and suspensions)	15	*	1 Jul 2002
Image acquisition systems (incorporating computers, digital cameras, integrated software and monitors)	4	*	1 Jul 2002
Image intensifiers	7	*	1 Jul 2002

HEALTH CARE AND SOCIAL ASSISTANCE
(84010 to 87900)

Asset	Life (Years)	Reviewed	Date Of Application
Mobile systems (incorporating buckies, generators, screening tables and suspensions)	10	*	1 Jul 2002
Magnetic resonance imaging (MRI) systems (incorporating scanners, cooling systems, radio frequency coil accessories, integrated computer and integrated software)	7	*	1 Jul 2002
Mammography systems (incorporating either prone core biopsy scanners, quality assurance equipment, stereotaxis, integrated computers and integrated software, or conventional upright scanners, quality assurance equipment, stereotaxis, integrated computer and integrated software)	7	*	1 Jul 2002
Nuclear medicine systems (incorporating cameras, gantries, collimators, integrated computers, integrated software and hot lab equipment, but excluding Positron Emission Tomography (PET) systems)	10	*	1 Jul 2002
Orthopantomography (OPG) systems (incorporating scanners, integrated computers and integrated software)	15	*	1 Jul 2002
Patient archival and communication systems (PACS)	4	*	1 Jul 2002
Processing assets:			
Daylight imaging processors	9	*	1 Jul 2002
Dry laser imaging processors	8	*	1 Jul 2002
Wet laser imaging processors	10	*	1 Jul 2002
Teleradiology assets (excluding the imaging device)	4	*	1 Jul 2002
Ultrasound systems (incorporating scanner, transducers, integrated computer and integrated software)	5	*	1 Jul 2002
X-ray assets (excluding direct radiography assets):			
Fixed systems (incorporating buckies, control panels, generators, screening table, suspensions, tube column and x-ray tube)	15	*	1 Jul 2002
Image intensifier	7	*	1 Jul 2002
Mobile systems (incorporating buckies, control panels, generators, screening table, suspensions, tube column and x-ray tube)	15	*	1 Jul 2002
Mobile systems (incorporating buckies, control panels, generators, screening table, suspensions, tube column and x-ray tube)	10	*	1 Jul 2002
Dental services (85310)			
Dentists' assets:			
Air abrasion units	10	*	1 Jul 2003
Air compressors	10	*	1 Jul 2003
Amalgamators	7	*	1 Jul 2003
Amalgam separators	7	*	1 Jul 2003
Computerised (CAD/CAM) ceramic restoration systems:			
Imaging units	7	*	1 Jul 2003
Milling units	5	*	1 Jul 2003
Curing lights (halogen)	5	*	1 Jul 2003
Dental chairs	10	*	1 Jul 2003
Dental instruments:			
Hand-held manually operated instruments	3	*	1 Jul 2003
Handpieces (driven by compressed air, compressed gas or electricity)	3	*	1 Jul 2003
Dental lasers:			
Hard tissue and soft tissue lasers	7	*	1 Jul 2003
Soft tissue and whitening lasers	7	*	1 Jul 2003

HEALTH CARE AND SOCIAL ASSISTANCE
(84010 to 87900)

Asset	Life (Years)	Reviewed	Date Of Application
Soft tissue lasers	10	*	1 Jul 2003
Dental loupes	10	*	1 Jul 2003
Dental operating lights	10	*	1 Jul 2003
Dental units	10	*	1 Jul 2003
Dental x-ray assets:			
Conventional x-ray film systems (incorporating control boxes, swing arms and x-ray heads, but excluding orthopantomogram (OPG) systems)	15	*	1 Jul 2003
Digital x-ray systems (including intra-oral storage phosphor plate systems and intra-oral digital sensor systems)	7	*	1 Jul 2003
Intra-oral x-ray film processors	10	*	1 Jul 2003
Handpiece cleaners	5	*	1 Jul 2003
Intra-oral camera systems (incorporating camera and integrated processor/docking station)	7	*	1 Jul 2003
Nitrous oxide sedation units	20	*	1 Jul 2003
Oral surgical motors	5	*	1 Jul 2003
Suction units	10	*	1 Jul 2003
Ultrasonic scalers (standalone)	10	*	1 Jul 2003
Optometry and optical dispensing (85320)			
Optical assets:			
Automatic refractometers/keratometers	5	*	1 Jan 2004
Cameras (including anterior segment cameras, retinal cameras, fundus cameras):			
Analogue	8	*	1 Jan 2004
Digital	4	*	1 Jan 2004
Colour vision testers (automated)	8	*	1 Jan 2004
Corneal topography systems	5	*	1 Jan 2004
Examination chairs	10	*	1 Jan 2004
Glaucoma diagnostic assets (including ocular coherence tomographs (OCTs), scanning laser ophthalmoscopes and scanning laser polarimeters)	5	*	1 Jan 2004
Keratometers (Ophthalmometers):			
Automated	5	*	1 Jan 2004
Manual	12	*	1 Jan 2004
Ophthalmic surgery assets:			
Microkeratome	3	*	1 Jan 2004
Ophthalmic cryo surgery systems	5	*	1 Jan 2004
Ophthalmic diathermy surgery systems	5	*	1 Jan 2004
Ophthalmic lasers:			
Non-refractive	10	*	1 Jan 2004
Refractive (including eye tracking systems)	4	*	1 Jan 2004
Phacoemulsification systems	4	*	1 Jan 2004
Pupillometers (used for refractive surgery)	5	*	1 Jan 2004
Vitrectomy systems	4	*	1 Jan 2004
Wave front analysers	4	*	1 Jan 2004
Ophthalmic viewers	5	*	1 Jan 2004
Ophthalmoscopes:			
Direct (including power supply)	8	*	1 Jan 2004
Indirect	9	*	1 Jan 2004

HEALTH CARE AND SOCIAL ASSISTANCE
(84010 to 87900)

Asset	Life (Years)	Reviewed	Date Of Application
Optical dispensing assets – see Table A Photographic, optical and ophthalmic equipment manufacturing (24110)			
Refraction units (including examination chair, instrument arms, table and light source)	10	*	1 Jan 2004
Refractometers (automated)	5	*	1 Jan 2004
Slit lamp biomicroscopes:			
Hand-held	9	*	1 Jan 2004
Mounted	12	*	1 Jan 2004
Telemedicine digital imaging systems (excluding the imaging devices)	4	*	1 Jan 2004
Tonometers:			
Contact tonometers:			
Applanation:			
Hand-held	6	*	1 Jan 2004
Mounted	8	*	1 Jan 2004
Electronic	6	*	1 Jan 2004
Non-contact tonometers:			
Hand-held	5	*	1 Jan 2004
Table mounted	8	*	1 Jan 2004
Trial lens sets	20	*	1 Jan 2004
Ultrasound diagnostic assets (including A-scan biometers, A/B scan biometers, B-scan biometers, laser interference biometers, pachymeters and ultrasound biomicroscopes (UBMs))	5	*	1 Jan 2004
Visual acuity testing assets:			
Automated vision testers	6	*	1 Jan 2004
Manual vision testers (phoropters)	12	*	1 Jan 2004
Visual acuity charts (illuminated)	10	*	1 Jan 2004
Visual acuity chart projectors (automated)	8	*	1 Jan 2004
Visual field testing assets (perimeters) – automated	5	*	1 Jan 2004
Podiatry services (85399)			
Podiatrists' assets:			
Computerised orthoses manufacturing assets:			
Carving mills	7	*	1 Jul 2003
Contact pin digitisers	7	*	1 Jul 2003
Doppler vascularscopes	5	*	1 Jul 2003
Electric nail drills:			
Dust extraction drills	7	*	1 Jul 2003
Portable dust extraction drills	5	*	1 Jul 2003
Water and alcohol based spray drills	4	*	1 Jul 2003
Examination/magnifying lamps	10	*	1 Jul 2003
Footrests	10	*	1 Jul 2003
Gait analysis assets:			
Computerised systems (incorporating in-shoe pressure analysis or platform based pressure mats, integrated hardware and integrated software)	4	*	1 Jul 2003
Non-computerised:			
Treadmills	10	*	1 Jul 2003
Video cameras	5	*	1 Jul 2003
Video monitors and video recorders	7	*	1 Jul 2003

HEALTH CARE AND SOCIAL ASSISTANCE
(84010 to 87900)

Asset	Life (Years)	Reviewed	Date Of Application
Orthotic benchtop grinders	6	*	1 Jul 2003
Patient chairs	12	*	1 Jul 2003
Podiatric instruments	3	*	1 Jul 2003
Vacuum presses	3	*	1 Jul 2003
Vascular neurological assessment assets:			
Monofilaments	2	*	1 Jul 2003
Tuning forks	10	*	1 Jul 2003
Retirement village and accommodation for the aged operation (86011 to 86012)			
Assistance and medical assets:			
Beds:			
Electronic (including hi-lo and lo-lo beds)	7	*	1 Jul 2019
Mechanical	10	*	1 Jul 2004
Bedside cabinets, lockers and overbed tables	10	*	1 Jul 2019
Blood pressure machines	3	*	1 Jul 2019
Call systems	7	*	1 Jul 2019
Chairs			
Commode	7	*	1 Jul 2019
Electronic recliner (including electric lift)	10	*	1 Jul 2019
Fallout/floating/princess	7	*	1 Jul 2019
Shower	5	*	1 Jul 2019
Wheelchair - electric, manual, tilt in space	5	*	1 Jul 2019
Defibrillators	8	*	1 Jul 2019
Drug safes	15	*	1 Jul 2019
Electronic arms for toilets	10	*	1 Jul 2019
Hoists			
Ceiling (incorporating tracks)	12	*	1 Jul 2019
Mobile (floor, full, standing)	10	*	1 Jul 2019
Lifting slings	2	*	1 Jul 2019
Mattresses			
Air	3	*	1 Jul 2019
Foam	7	*	1 Jul 2019
Medication trolleys	10	*	1 Jul 2019
Mobile suction machines	3	*	1 Jul 2019
Pan flushers/pan sanitisers	10	*	1 Jul 2019
Sensor beams and sensor mats	3	*	1 Jul 2019
Shower trolleys/mobile baths	8	*	1 Jul 2019
Syringe driven infusion pumps	5	*	1 Jul 2019
Treatment trolleys	15	*	1 Jul 2019
Walking belts	3	*	1 Jul 2019
Walking frames (including forearm walkers)	12	*	1 Jul 2019
Weighing machines and scales (including chair scales and wheelchair scales)	10	*	1 Jul 2019
Common area assets:			
Artificial grass/synthetic lawn (removable without damage)	15	*	1 Jul 2019
Audio visual assets	8	*	1 Jul 2019
Carpets - see Table B Floor coverings (removable without damage)			
Curtains and drapes - see Table B Curtains and drapes			

HEALTH CARE AND SOCIAL ASSISTANCE
(84010 to 87900)

Asset	Life (Years)	Reviewed	Date Of Application
Furniture:			
General/indoor	10	*	1 Jul 2019
Outdoor	7	*	1 Jul 2019
Hair salon assets (including chairs and dryers)	15	*	1 Jul 2019
Hot water dispensers	8	*	1 Jul 2019
Television sets	5	*	1 Jul 2019
Window blinds - see Table B Window blinds			
Fitness and recreation assets:			
Billiard/pool tables	20	*	1 Jul 2019
Bowling greens - artificial grass or carpet (removable without damage)	15	*	1 Jul 2019
Gymnasium and exercise equipment	10	*	1 Jul 2019
Support assets:			
Annunciator panels	15	*	1 Jul 2019
Boilers - see Table B Boilers			
Buggies to transport people	8	*	1 Jul 2019
Cleaning carts and trolleys - see Table B Cleaning carts and trolleys			
Cool rooms - see Table B Refrigeration assets			
Electronic mops and floor scrubbers	5	*	1 Jul 2019
Hot water systems (excluding commercial boilers and piping)	10	*	1 Jul 2019
Kitchen assets:			
Blast chillers	8	*	1 Jul 2019
Bowl mixers	10	*	1 Jul 2019
Dishwashers	8	*	1 Jul 2019
Food preparation assets - large commercial type (including cooktops, fryers, multi-function centres, self-cooking centres, single tray meal service, soup kettles, stoves)	10	*	1 Jul 2019
Hot food display and warming assets (including bain marie, banquet units, buffet units, hot boxes, plate warmers)	10	*	1 Jul 2019
Ice making machines	10	*	1 Jul 2019
Kitchen trolleys	5	*	1 Jul 2019
Small appliances (including blenders, food processors, meat slicers, stick mixers)	4	*	1 Jul 2019
Toasters	6	*	1 Jul 2019
Laundry assets:			
Dryers	12	*	1 Jul 2019
Spring loaded trolleys	10	*	1 Jul 2019
Washing machines	12	*	1 Jul 2019
Lockers, freestanding - see Table B Lockers, freestanding			
Master antenna television (MATV) assets - see Table A Residential property operators (67110)			
Refrigerators (including controlled temperature medication refrigerators)	10	*	1 Jul 2019
Swimming pool assets:			
Dehumidifiers	15	*	1 Jul 2019
Filtration equipment (including chlorinators and pumps) - see Table B Swimming pool assets			
Pool covers (including blankets) - see Table B Swimming pool assets			
Vacuum cleaners, ride on	7	*	1 Jul 2019

HEALTH CARE AND SOCIAL ASSISTANCE
(84010 to 87900)

Asset	Life (Years)	Reviewed	Date Of Application
Child care services (87100)			
Audio visual assets	5	*	1 Jul 2020
Augmented reality (AR) interactive sandboxes (incorporating projectors)	5	*	1 Jul 2020
Electronic whiteboards (including touch screen interactive digital boards)	6	*	1 Jul 2020
Furniture used by children, freestanding:			
Age specific (including cots, changing tables, floor sleeping mattresses, high and low feeding chairs, and stackable beds)	5	*	1 Jul 2020
Carpet mats (including rugs and floor mats/cushions)	5	*	1 Jul 2020
Others (including bookcases, chairs and sofas, coat/dress-up racks, easels, room dividers, tables and storage shelving units)	10	*	1 Jul 2020
Play area assets:			
Furniture, freestanding (including tables, seating and toy storage boxes)	5	*	1 Jul 2020
Pet enclosures and structures, freestanding (including bird aviaries, chicken coops, fish tanks, guinea pig cages and rabbit hutches)	10	*	1 Jul 2020
Playground flooring:			
Artificial grass/synthetic lawn	7	*	1 Jul 2020
Soft fall flooring (including wet pour rubber and rubber mats)	5	*	1 Jul 2020
Playsets (including cubby houses, forts, slides, swing sets and trestle frames)	8	*	1 Jul 2020
Pole and post padding/protectors	5	*	1 Jul 2020
Sandpits, freestanding (including portable sandpits and sandpit covers)	7	*	1 Jul 2020
Tents, portable (including gazebos, marquees and tepee play tents)	5	*	1 Jul 2020
Toys (not specified elsewhere)	3	*	1 Jul 2020
Tricycles and bicycles (including balance bicycles and tricycle scooters)	5	*	1 Jul 2020
Water play area filtration assets and water pumps	7	*	1 Jul 2020
Support assets:			
Automated external defibrillators (AEDs) – see Table B Automated external defibrillators (AEDs)			
Fascia signs (including freestanding signs) – see Table B Advertising signs			
Fire control and alarm assets – see Table B Fire control and alarm assets			
Floor coverings – see Table B Floor coverings (removable without damage)			
Garden sheds, freestanding	15	*	1 Jul 2020
Hand dryers – see Table B Hand dryers (electrical)			
Kiosk stands, freestanding	10	*	1 Jul 2020
Kitchen assets:			
Dishwashers	5	*	1 Jul 2020
Food cooking assets (including combination ovens, cooktops, fryers, soup kettles and stoves)	10	*	1 Jul 2020
Grease traps	10	*	1 Jul 2020
Kitchen trolleys	5	*	1 Jul 2020
Microwave ovens	5	*	1 Jul 2020
Refrigerators/freezers	10	*	1 Jul 2020

HEALTH CARE AND SOCIAL ASSISTANCE
(84010 to 87900)

Asset	Life (Years)	Reviewed	Date Of Application
Small appliances (including blenders, food processors, mixers and toasters)	4	*	1 Jul 2020
Laundry assets:			
Dryers	5	*	1 Jul 2020
Washing machines	5	*	1 Jul 2020
Reception furniture, freestanding (including lobby chairs, desks, lounges, sofas and tables) – see Table B Office furniture, freestanding			
Security and monitoring assets - see Table B Security and monitoring assets			
Steam cleaners	3	*	1 Jul 2020
Strollers:			
Commercial multi seat (including buggies)	10	*	1 Jul 2020
Others	5	*	1 Jul 2020
Time attendance devices (including fingerprint and vein scanners)	7	*	1 Jul 2020
Vacuum cleaners	3	*	1 Jul 2020
Table games	5	*	1 Jul 2020
Television sets	8	*	1 Jul 2020

¶43-090 Effective life — arts and recreation services

ARTS AND RECREATION SERVICES
(89100 to 92099)

Asset	Life (Years)	Reviewed	Date Of Application
Heritage activities (89100 to 89220)			
Museum displays in aircraft/war museums	100		1 Jan 2001
Parks and gardens:			
Lion parks:			
Animal cages and sheds	20		1 Jan 2001
Animal huts	10		1 Jan 2001
Planetarium domes	33 1/3		1 Jan 2001
Sea life centres:			
Fibreglass aquarium tanks	20		1 Jan 2001
Ketches	13 1/3		1 Jan 2001
TV audio systems	10		1 Jan 2001
Creative and performing arts activities (90010 to 90030)			
Theatre equipment:			
Accessories (theatrical – wigs, costumes etc)	5		1 Jan 2001
Performing dogs – see Table B Working dogs			
Health and fitness centres and gymnasia operation (91110)			
Health and fitness centre operation assets:			
Cardiovascular training machines:			
Cross trainers, steppers and treadmills	4	*	1 Jul 2012
Exercise bicycles (including spin bicycles, upright and recumbent bicycles)	4	*	1 Jul 2012
Rowing machines	5	*	1 Jul 2012

ARTS AND RECREATION SERVICES
(89100 to 92099)

Asset	Life (Years)	Reviewed	Date Of Application
Free weight training assets:			
Barbells, dumbbells, kettle bells, weight plates and storage racks	6	*	1 Jul 2012
Benches (including abdominal crunch, adjustable, declined, inclined and flat benches)	8	*	1 Jul 2012
Resistance training machines (including abdomen, arm, back, chest, hip, leg, shoulder and multiple training machines)	8	*	1 Jul 2012
Support assets:			
Audio visual entertainment assets (including amplifiers, audio speakers, digital disc players and television sets)	4	*	1 Jul 2012
Fans (including wall mounted)	5	*	1 Jul 2012
Lockers	8	*	1 Jul 2012
Platform scales	5	*	1 Jul 2012
Sport and recreation services (91121 to 91390)			
Amusement machines and equipment:			
Coin-operated amusement machines:			
Children's rides	5	*	1 Jul 2001
Convertible video games/simulators (cabinet)	5 1/2	*	1 Jul 2001
Dedicated video games/simulators	3 1/2	*	1 Jul 2001
Interchangeable video game kits	1	*	1 Jul 2001
Juke boxes (CD)	10	*	1 Jul 2001
Photo-image machines	3 1/2	*	1 Jul 2001
Pinball machines	3 1/2	*	1 Jul 2001
Pool/billiard tables	10	*	1 Jul 2001
Redemption games (prizes/tickets)	5 1/2	*	1 Jul 2001
Table games (including air hockey, soccer etc)	5 1/2	*	1 Jul 2001
Billiard tables	40		1 Jan 2001
Rides and devices (fixed or mobile):			
Chair-o-planes	15	*	1 Jan 2002
Children's indoor soft playgrounds	5	*	1 Jan 2002
Children's rides (designed for the carriage of children less than 8 years old)	15	*	1 Jan 2002
Ferris wheels	25	*	1 Jan 2002
Free falls (including giant drop and tower of terror)	25	*	1 Jan 2002
Inflatables (including jumping castles)	5	*	1 Jan 2002
Overhead transit devices (including chair lifts and cabin lifts)	25	*	1 Jan 2002
Roller coasters:			
Non-powered (including corkscrew loop, looping coasters and mini roller coasters – wild cat, madmouse)	25	*	1 Jan 2002
Powered (including tornado)	15	*	1 Jan 2002
Round rides with or without additional motions (including merry-go-rounds)	15	*	1 Jan 2002
Self-drive non-powered gravity rides (including toboggans and bob-sleds):			
Track	20	*	1 Jan 2002
Vehicle	5	*	1 Jan 2002
Self-drive powered rides (including dodgems and go-karts):			
Track	15	*	1 Jan 2002
Vehicle	5	*	1 Jan 2002
Simulators	10	*	1 Jan 2002

ARTS AND RECREATION SERVICES
(89100 to 92099)

Asset	Life (Years)	Reviewed	Date Of Application
Swinging rides (including pirate ship, spaceloop, and rainbow)	15	*	1 Jan 2002
Trains, tracked or trackless (including tractor trains and miniature railways)	10	*	1 Jan 2002
Water rides	20	*	1 Jan 2002
Water slides (gravity powered)	20	*	1 Jan 2002
Bowling centres (plant and equipment):			
Bowling alleys (timber – including ball return tracks, gutters, pit signals and terminals)	13 1/3		1 Jan 2001
Bowling balls	5		1 Jan 2001
Carpets	4		1 Jan 2001
Masking units	10		1 Jan 2001
Pin setters and pin spotters	10		1 Jan 2001
Other equipment	13 1/3		1 Jan 2001
Golf courses (miniature):			
Carpets on stairways	3		1 Jan 2001
Lighting plant, electric motors, moving parts	20		1 Jan 2001
Lighting standards	40		1 Jan 2001
Marina operation:			
Boat cradles	10	*	1 Jul 2002
Boat storage racks	10	*	1 Jul 2002
Forklifts	11	*	1 Jul 2002
Marina – wet berths (incorporating piling, decking and floating pontoons)	20	*	1 Jul 2002
Mooring buoys	10	*	1 Jul 2002
Travel lifts	15	*	1 Jul 2002
Racehorses	10		1 Jan 2001
Racing cars	2		1 Jan 2001
Shuffle boards	10		1 Jan 2001
Skating rink plant:			
Fittings (open air)	20		1 Jan 2001
General freezing plant and equipment	13 1/3		1 Jan 2001
Hired ice skating boots	5		1 Jan 2001
Roller skates	5		1 Jan 2001
Surface (synthetic panels)	10		1 Jan 2001
Ski equipment (skis, boots and stocks for hiring to public)	3		1 Jan 2001
Ski maintenance machines	13 1/3		1 Jan 2001
Space theatre domes	33 1/3		1 Jan 2001
Tennis court surfaces:			
Bitumen	20		1 Jan 2001
Plexipave	20		1 Jan 2001
Synthetic lawn	10		1 Jan 2001
Trampolines	10		1 Jan 2001
Gambling activities (92010 to 92099)			
Poker/gaming machines	7	*	1 Jul 2009
Totalisators:			
Computer equipment	10		1 Jan 2001
Ancillary equipment (eg ticket issuing machines)	13 1/3		1 Jan 2001

¶43-095 Effective life — other services

OTHER SERVICES
(94110 to 96030)

Asset	Life (Years)	Reviewed	Date Of Application
Automotive repair and maintenance (94110 to 94199)			
Automotive and heavy vehicle repair and maintenance assets:			
Air conditioning assets:			
Refrigerant leak detectors	3	*	1 Jul 2011
Refrigerant management systems	5	*	1 Jul 2011
Refrigerant recovery machine	5	*	1 Jul 2011
Refrigerant recovery and recycling machines	5	*	1 Jul 2011
Vacuum pumps	5	*	1 Jul 2011
Air tools (including ratchet guns)	2	*	1 Jul 2011
Automatic transmission flush and fill machines	5	*	1 Jul 2011
Axle and ball joint play testers or shakers	10	*	1 Jul 2011
Battery chargers	5	*	1 Jul 2011
Battery testers	5	*	1 Jul 2011
Brake disc and drum grinding lathes:			
Fixed	10	*	1 Jul 2011
Portable on-car	5	*	1 Jul 2011
Brake fluid testers	5	*	1 Jul 2011
Brake shoe riveters	5	*	1 Jul 2011
Brake system flushers	5	*	1 Jul 2011
Compressed air assets:			
Air compressors:			
Reciprocating	10	*	1 Jul 2011
Rotary screw	10	*	1 Jul 2011
Rotary vane	10	*	1 Jul 2011
Air driers and dehumidifiers	10	*	1 Jul 2011
Air receivers	10	*	1 Jul 2011
Hose reels	3	*	1 Jul 2011
Reticulation lines:			
Aluminium	15	*	1 Jul 2011
Copper	20	*	1 Jul 2011
Polyethylene (PE)	15	*	1 Jul 2011
Steel	10	*	1 Jul 2011
Continuous diesel engine particulate testers	5	*	1 Jul 2011
Cooling system flushers	5	*	1 Jul 2011
Decelerometer brake testers	7	*	1 Jul 2011
Diagnostic assets:			
Diagnostic and roller dynamometers, performance and emissions testers	10	*	1 Jul 2011
Engine analysers	5	*	1 Jul 2011
Electrical test benches	10	*	1 Jul 2011
Fuel injection pump test benches	5	*	1 Jul 2011
Oscilloscopes	10	*	1 Jul 2011
Scan tools	5	*	1 Jul 2011
Diesel engine emission testers	5	*	1 Jul 2011
Drill presses	15	*	1 Jul 2011
Drive-on plate brake, steering and suspension testing machines	10	*	1 Jul 2011

OTHER SERVICES
(94110 to 96030)

Asset	Life (Years)	Reviewed	Date Of Application
Drive-on shock absorber testers	10	*	1 Jul 2011
Dual wheel removers	8	*	1 Jul 2011
Effluent treatment systems incorporating motors, electronic circuitry, pumps, and separators	8	*	1 Jul 2011
Engine cranes	10	*	1 Jul 2011
Exhaust gas analysers for petrol engines:			
Computer operated	5	*	1 Jul 2011
Standalone	10	*	1 Jul 2011
Exhaust stands	11	*	1 Jul 2011
Flywheel grinders	13	*	1 Jul 2011
Hand tools	10	*	1 Jul 2011
Headlight testers	7	*	1 Jul 2011
Hydraulic brake hose machines	5	*	1 Jul 2011
Hydraulic presses	10	*	1 Jul 2011
Jacks:			
Floor jacks:			
Used for car and light truck repairs	3	*	1 Jul 2011
Used for heavy vehicle repairs	5	*	1 Jul 2011
Transmission jacks:			
Used for car and light truck repairs	8	*	1 Jul 2011
Used for heavy vehicle repairs	5	*	1 Jul 2011
Vehicle positioning jacks	3	*	1 Jul 2011
Lathes	20	*	1 Jul 2011
Measuring assets:			
Micrometers	10	*	1 Jul 2011
Tension wrenches	5	*	1 Jul 2011
Tyre pressure gauges	5	*	1 Jul 2011
Noise level meters	5	*	1 Jul 2011
Oil and grease delivery systems:			
Bunding:			
Polyethylene (PE) pallets	5	*	1 Jul 2011
Rubber	3	*	1 Jul 2011
Distribution lines:			
Polyethylene (PE)	5	*	1 Jul 2011
Rubber	3	*	1 Jul 2011
Steel	10	*	1 Jul 2011
Guns and pumps	3	*	1 Jul 2011
Reels:			
Plastic	3	*	1 Jul 2011
Steel	7	*	1 Jul 2011
Tanks (including waste oil tanks)	20	*	1 Jul 2011
Oil filter crushers	10	*	1 Jul 2011
Parts cleaners and washers	7	*	1 Jul 2011
Pipe and tube benders	10	*	1 Jul 2011
Pipe and tube saws and cutters	10	*	1 Jul 2011
Power steering flushing systems	5	*	1 Jul 2011
Pressure washers	4	*	1 Jul 2011
Sand blasters	7	*	1 Jul 2011

OTHER SERVICES
(94110 to 96030)

Asset	Life (Years)	Reviewed	Date Of Application
Spring compressors	5	*	1 Jul 2011
Stillages	15	*	1 Jul 2011
Storage shelving	10	*	1 Jul 2011
Toolbox roller cabinets	7	*	1 Jul 2011
Trolleys	10	*	1 Jul 2011
Truck brake imbalance testers	5	*	1 Jul 2011
Tyre conveyors:			
Horizontal	10	*	1 Jul 2011
Vertical	8	*	1 Jul 2011
Tyre fitting machines	5	*	1 Jul 2011
Tyre inflation cages	10	*	1 Jul 2011
Tyre inflators (automatic and manual)	3	*	1 Jul 2011
Tyre spreaders	8	*	1 Jul 2011
Vehicle hoists:			
Used for car and light truck repairs	10	*	1 Jul 2011
Used for heavy vehicle repairs	20	*	1 Jul 2011
Vehicle service and inspection lane assets:			
Control consoles	10	*	1 Jul 2011
Data collection devices (including bar code readers, mobile recorders and transponders)	5	*	1 Jul 2011
Floor unit assets:			
Axle and ball joint play testers or shakers	10	*	1 Jul 2011
Roller brake testers	10	*	1 Jul 2011
Shock absorber testers	10	*	1 Jul 2011
Side slip testers	10	*	1 Jul 2011
Speedometer tester	10	*	1 Jul 2011
Suspension play detectors	10	*	1 Jul 2011
Vehicle special tools	5	*	1 Jul 2011
Waste oil evacuators	5	*	1 Jul 2011
Welders:			
Electric	10	*	1 Jul 2011
Oxy-acetylene	10	*	1 Jul 2011
Wheel alignment machines	7	*	1 Jul 2011
Wheel balancing machines	5	*	1 Jul 2011
Wheel balancing plates, flanges and finger adaptors	5	*	1 Jul 2011
Wheel lifters	5	*	1 Jul 2011
Wheel lifter incorporating tyre spreaders	8	*	1 Jul 2011
Work platform ladders	10	*	1 Jul 2011
Automotive body, paint and interior repair n.e.c. (94129)			
Car wash and detailing assets:			
Activation and entry station assets (including bay controllers, pay station assets and bank note change machines)	10	*	1 Jul 2009
Automatic car wash assets (including rollover and tunnel washes):			
Friction washer system assets (including gantry, rails and arches and driers)	10	*	1 Jul 2009
Touch free pressure washer system assets (including gantry, rails and arches and driers)	10	*	1 Jul 2009
Car conveyor system assets (incorporating correlators, sensors, tracks and rails)	15	*	1 Jul 2009

OTHER SERVICES
(94110 to 96030)

Asset	Life (Years)	Reviewed	Date Of Application
Detailing assets:			
Steam cleaners	10	*	1 Jul 2009
Vacuum cleaners	10	*	1 Jul 2009
Hand and self serve car wash assets:			
Ceiling and wall booms	10	*	1 Jul 2009
Large vehicle wash assets:			
Hoists	20	*	1 Jul 2009
Side brush cleaning system assets	10	*	1 Jul 2009
Support assets:			
Door controls and motor drive systems for rapid roller doors (incorporating chains, controls, motors and sensors, but excluding doors)	10	*	1 Jul 2009
Plant room assets:			
Air compressors			
Compressors – reciprocating	7	*	1 Jul 2009
Compressors – screw	10	*	1 Jul 2009
Boilers	20	*	1 Jul 2009
Control systems	10	*	1 Jul 2009
Pumps	12	*	1 Jul 2009
Water treatment assets:			
Filter system assets (including reverse osmosis)	10	*	1 Jul 2009
Tanks	20	*	1 Jul 2009
Vending machines	5	*	1 Jul 2009
Smash repair assets:			
Air compressors	10	*	1 Jul 2009
Dust extraction systems:			
Metal arms	15	*	1 Jul 2009
Stationary vacuum dust collection units	5	*	1 Jul 2009
Frame straightening assets:			
Aligning benches	15	*	1 Jul 2009
Chassis measuring assets:			
Computerised	10	*	1 Jul 2009
Manual	10	*	1 Jul 2009
Hoists	20	*	1 Jul 2009
Painting assets:			
Buffing machines	3	*	1 Jul 2009
Infrared paint dryers:			
Heating arches	20	*	1 Jul 2009
Mobile	7	*	1 Jul 2009
Sanders	3	*	1 Jul 2009
Spectrophotometers	4	*	1 Jul 2009
Spray bake ovens	12	*	1 Jul 2009
Spray guns	3	*	1 Jul 2009
Spray gun washing machines	5	*	1 Jul 2009
Vacuum dust collection mobile units	3	*	1 Jul 2009
Waste water filtering system assets:			
Oil and water separators	15	*	1 Jul 2009
Pumps	5	*	1 Jul 2009
Tanks	15	*	1 Jul 2009

OTHER SERVICES
(94110 to 96030)

Asset	Life (Years)	Reviewed	Date Of Application
Water pressure cleaners	3	*	1 Jul 2009
Welders	5	*	1 Jul 2009
Other machinery and equipment repair and maintenance (94290)			
Agriculture, construction and mining heavy machinery and equipment repair and maintenance assets:			
Field service assets:			
Assets used in field service that are not listed under this sub-heading – use any relevant determination listed under Workshop assets below			
Air compressors	8	*	1 Jul 2015
Cranes	10	*	1 Jul 2015
Cutting machines	8	*	1 Jul 2015
Diagnostic assets	5	*	1 Jul 2015
Lathes	5	*	1 Jul 2015
Line boring machines	10	*	1 Jul 2015
Milling machines	8	*	1 Jul 2015
Turning machines	8	*	1 Jul 2015
Trailers:			
Generally (including comb trailers and tilt trailers) – see Table B Motor vehicles and trailers			
Service trailers (incorporating built-in hoses, built-in pumps, built-in tanks etc)	10	*	1 Jul 2015
Workshop assets:			
Air conditioning service assets (including refrigerant management/charging stations, refrigerant recovery machines, refrigerant recovery and recycling machines and vacuum pumps)	5	*	1 Jul 2015
Air compression assets (including air dryers, air receivers, compressors and packaged air compression systems)	10	*	1 Jul 2015
Battery chargers	5	*	1 Jul 2015
Battery load testers	5	*	1 Jul 2015
Bending machines:			
Folders	15	*	1 Jul 2015
Pipe and tube benders	10	*	1 Jul 2015
Press brakes	20	*	1 Jul 2015
Brake shoe riveting machines	5	*	1 Jul 2015
Brake testers (including in-ground and mobile roller brake testers)	10	*	1 Jul 2015
Boring machines (including floor borers, jib borers, horizontal and vertical boring machines)	15	*	1 Jul 2015
Diagnostic, measuring and testing assets:			
Generally (including co-ordinate measuring machines, dynamometers, electrical testers, flow meters, hardness testers, hydraulic testers and multimeters)	10	*	1 Jul 2015
Laptop diagnostic systems:			
Laptops – see Table B Computers, Laptops			
Machine interface units	3	*	1 Jul 2015
Tyre pressure gauges	5	*	1 Jul 2015
Vehicle specific diagnostic assets	5	*	1 Jul 2015
Drilling machines (including drill presses, magnetic drills, pedestal drills and radial arm drills)	10	*	1 Jul 2015

OTHER SERVICES
(94110 to 96030)

Asset	Life (Years)	Reviewed	Date Of Application
Flange facers	5	*	1 Jul 2015
Forklift attachments	10	*	1 Jul 2015
Forklifts	11	*	1 Jul 2015
Grinding machines (including gear grinding machines)	10	*	1 Jul 2015
Guillotine shears	15	*	1 Jul 2015
Heat treatment assets (including furnaces and quenches)	15	*	1 Jul 2015
Hydraulic hose crimpers	10	*	1 Jul 2015
Lathes:			
CNC lathes	10	*	1 Jul 2015
Manual lathes	20	*	1 Jul 2015
Lifting assets:			
Cranes:			
Jib cranes (including column/wall mounted, floor mounted/freestanding and portable jib cranes)	15	*	1 Jul 2015
Overhead cranes	25	*	1 Jul 2015
Pick & carry cranes/yard cranes	10	*	1 Jul 2015
Portable cranes generally (including engine cranes, engine hoists, floor cranes, mobile gantries, shop cranes etc)	15	*	1 Jul 2015
Hoists	10	*	1 Jul 2015
Jacks (including air hydraulic jacks, hydro pneumatic jacks, floor jacks, transmission jacks, trolley jacks and truck jacks)	5	*	1 Jul 2015
Scissor lifts	15	*	1 Jul 2015
Vehicle lifters (including mobile column lifts and post hoists)	20	*	1 Jul 2015
Machining centres	10	*	1 Jul 2015
Milling machines (including bed mills and universal mills)	10	*	1 Jul 2015
Oil recovery, service and treatment assets:			
Collection vessels/tanks	20	*	1 Jul 2015
Dangerous goods containers	15	*	1 Jul 2015
Pumps	5	*	1 Jul 2015
Painting assets:			
Buffing machines	3	*	1 Jul 2015
Paint agitators	3	*	1 Jul 2015
Space heaters	10	*	1 Jul 2015
Spray booths	15	*	1 Jul 2015
Spray gun washing machines	5	*	1 Jul 2015
Parts washing machines	7	*	1 Jul 2015
Pipe cutting machines	10	*	1 Jul 2015
Plasma cutters	10	*	1 Jul 2015
Presses:			
Hydraulic presses	10	*	1 Jul 2015
Punch and shear machines	15	*	1 Jul 2015
Saws (including band saws and cold cut saws)	10	*	1 Jul 2015
Stands (including axle stands, engine stands and transmission stands)	10	*	1 Jul 2015
Storage assets (including racking, shelving, safety cabinets and storage cabinets)	10	*	1 Jul 2015
Surface preparation assets:			

OTHER SERVICES
(94110 to 96030)

Asset	Life (Years)	Reviewed	Date Of Application
Abrasive blasting assets:			
Abrasive blasting machines (incorporating blasting pots, hoses, nozzles, valves etc)	10	*	1 Jul 2015
Abrasive recovery/recycling machines and associated equipment (including storage hoppers)	12	*	1 Jul 2015
Blast booths/chambers	12	*	1 Jul 2015
Dust collection and ventilation systems	12	*	1 Jul 2015
Pressure cleaners/washers	4	*	1 Jul 2015
Toolboxes and toolbox roller cabinets	7	*	1 Jul 2015
Tooling:			
Moulds	7	*	1 Jul 2015
Press brake dies	10	*	1 Jul 2015
Tooling for lathes, machining centres, milling machines and other machine tools	7	*	1 Jul 2015
Vehicle specific specialised tooling	5	*	1 Jul 2015
Workholding devices (including jigs and fixtures)	7	*	1 Jul 2015
Tools:			
Hand tools (manually operated)	10	*	1 Jul 2015
Hand held power tools (air, battery and electric)	3	*	1 Jul 2015
Power packs	5	*	1 Jul 2015
Torque/tension wrenches	5	*	1 Jul 2015
Torque wrench pumps (pneumatic and electric driven)	5	*	1 Jul 2015
Trolleys (including powered and electrodrive trolleys)	10	*	1 Jul 2015
Turning machines	10	*	1 Jul 2015
Waste water recovery and treatment assets:			
Grease traps	10	*	1 Jul 2015
Pumps	5	*	1 Jul 2015
Tanks and separators	15	*	1 Jul 2015
Waterjet cutting machines	10	*	1 Jul 2015
Weight scales (corner weight)	10	*	1 Jul 2015
Welding assets:			
Welders (including ARC, MIG, TIG, multi process and oxy-acetylene welders/cutters)	10	*	1 Jul 2015
Weld tables and positioners (including rotary tables)	10	*	1 Jul 2015
Welding helmets incorporating respirators	3	*	1 Jul 2015
Wire feeders	5	*	1 Jul 2015
Wheel service assets:			
Bead breaker kits	5	*	1 Jul 2015
Tyre changers	5	*	1 Jul 2015
Wheel aligners	7	*	1 Jul 2015
Wheel balancers	5	*	1 Jul 2015
Wheel handlers and lifters	5	*	1 Jul 2015
Wheel play detectors	10	*	1 Jul 2015
Work benches and tables	15	*	1 Jul 2015
Hairdressing and beauty services (95110)			
Beauty industry assets:			
Electrical treatment assets:			
Faradic, galvanic, high frequency and multi function units	10	*	1 Jul 2010

OTHER SERVICES
(94110 to 96030)

Asset	Life (Years)	Reviewed	Date Of Application
Light therapy units (including intense pulse light (IPL) systems)	10	*	1 Jul 2010
Micro dermabrasion units	5	*	1 Jul 2010
Hydrotherapy assets:			
Spa capsules	10	*	1 Jul 2010
Vichy shower units	10	*	1 Jul 2010
Wet tables	10	*	1 Jul 2010
Massage and treatments beds:			
Dry hydrotherapy (including flotation)	7	*	1 Jul 2010
Electronic	7	*	1 Jul 2010
Non electronic (including folding)	10	*	1 Jul 2010
Reception furniture, freestanding (including lobby chairs, desks, lounges, sofas and tables)	10	*	1 Jul 2010
Sterilisation processing assets (including autoclaves and hot towel cabinets)	5	*	1 Jul 2010
Hairdressing industry assets:			
Barber chairs	15	*	1 Jul 2010
Coffee making machines (including espresso and drip filter type)	5	*	1 Jul 2010
Cutting chairs (including styling chairs and cutting stools)	10	*	1 Jul 2010
Cutting and styling workstations, freestanding	10	*	1 Jul 2010
Display shelving, freestanding	10	*	1 Jul 2010
Hairdryers and heat accelerator machines (excluding hand held)	15	*	1 Jul 2010
Reception furniture (including lobby chairs, desks, lounges, sofas and tables)	10	*	1 Jul 2010
Shampoo units and wash lounges, freestanding	10	*	1 Jul 2010
Funeral, crematorium and cemetery services (95200)			
Cemetery assets:			
Casket lowering devices	10	*	1 Jul 2020
Mini excavators and skid steer loaders	10	*	1 Jul 2020
Crematorium assets:			
Ash processors/granulators	7	*	1 Jul 2020
Cremators	20	*	1 Jul 2020
Dust collection assets	10	*	1 Jul 2020
Funeral assets:			
Bench seating	10	*	1 Jul 2020
Broadcasting equipment (including audio visual devices and streaming equipment)	5	*	1 Jul 2020
Church trolleys/trucks	15	*	1 Jul 2020
Coffin racks	13	*	1 Jul 2020
Engravers:			
Electronic/laser cutters	7	*	1 Jul 2020
Manual	20	*	1 Jul 2020
Lecterns	15	*	1 Jul 2020
Scissor lift tables – see Table B Loading bay assets			
General assets:			
Funeral coaches/hearses	15	*	1 Jul 2020
Mortuary cots/stretchers	15	*	1 Jul 2020
Refrigeration assets:			
Cool rooms – see Table B Refrigeration assets			

OTHER SERVICES
(94110 to 96030)

Asset	Life (Years)	Reviewed	Date Of Application
Refrigeration racks	20	*	1 Jul 2020
Scales:			
Animal scales	5	*	1 Jul 2020
Platform scales – see Table B			
Transfer vehicles (including fitouts) – see Table B Motor vehicles and trailers – Generally			
Mortuary assets:			
Embalming machines	10	*	1 Jul 2020
Embalming/morgue tables	15	*	1 Jul 2020
Floor coverings – linoleum and vinyl (removable without damage)	15	*	1 Jul 2020
Hoists and lifting machines	10	*	1 Jul 2020
Hydro-aspirators	10	*	1 Jul 2020
Laundry and dry cleaning services (95310)			
Carpet, upholstery and rug cleaning services assets:			
Air purifiers, deodorising and mould remediation assets (including air filtering machines, air scrubbers and ozone generators)	5	*	1 Jul 2010
Carpet cleaning assets, portable (including rotary scrubbers and encapsulation machines)	5	*	1 Jul 2010
Drying and restoration assets (including air movers and dehumidifiers)	5	*	1 Jul 2010
Extractors for carpet and upholstery cleaning:			
Spot extractors (including portable handheld and brief case size extractors for stain removal)	3	*	1 Jul 2010
Others (including walk behind and self-contained carpet extractors)	5	*	1 Jul 2010
Truck or van mounted	10	*	1 Jul 2010
Vacuum cleaners:			
Backpack and pull along machines	3	*	1 Jul 2010
Other portable cleaners (including upright machines)	5	*	1 Jul 2010
Dry cleaning and laundry assets:			
Dry cleaning machines	12	*	1 Jul 2011
Washers:			
Continuous batch washer systems (including washers, moisture extraction units and dryers)	17	*	1 Jul 2011
Extractors, standalone	12	*	1 Jul 2011
Drying assets:			
Tumble dryers, standalone	12	*	1 Jul 2011
Tunnel dryers and garment finishers (including steam cabinets)	15	*	1 Jul 2011
Finishing assets:			
Flatwork processing assets (including automatic pickers, feeders, folders and stackers)	13	*	1 Jul 2011
Garment finishers (including collar and cuff presses, form finishers, pant toppers and puff irons)	10	*	1 Jul 2011
Presses (including flat, utility and scissor legger presses):			
Air operated, semi automatic	15	*	1 Jul 2011
Manual	20	*	1 Jul 2011
Roller ironers	17	*	1 Jul 2011
Support assets:			
Air vacuum units, standalone	10	*	1 Jul 2011
Control systems	10	*	1 Jul 2011

OTHER SERVICES
(94110 to 96030)

Asset	Life (Years)	Reviewed	Date Of Application
Heat seal machines for labelling laundry items	10	*	1 Jul 2011
Hot water systems	12	*	1 Jul 2011
Ironing and spotting boards and tables:			
Vacuum operated	10	*	1 Jul 2011
Non vacuum operated	15	*	1 Jul 2011
Laundry handling assets:			
Conveyors and garment sorting and storage systems	15	*	1 Jul 2011
Hoppers	20	*	1 Jul 2011
Monorail and bag loading systems	20	*	1 Jul 2011
Tipplers	10	*	1 Jul 2011
Pipes	20	*	1 Jul 2011
Soap dispenser machines	20	*	1 Jul 2011
Trolleys and bins:			
Generally	10	*	1 Jul 2011
Stainless steel	15	*	1 Jul 2011
Waste water treatment and recycling system assets:			
Filters (including carbon and sand)	10	*	1 Jul 2011
Lint shakers (including circular vibratory screens)	20	*	1 Jul 2011
Ozone generators and UV sterilisers	7	*	1 Jul 2011
Pumps	5	*	1 Jul 2011
Tanks	20	*	1 Jul 2011
Photographic film processing (95320)			
Binding assets:			
Binders	7	*	1 Jul 2017
Building-in machines	15	*	1 Jul 2017
Casemakers	8	*	1 Jul 2017
Casing-in machines	7	*	1 Jul 2017
Comb binders (including ring wire binders and spiral binders)	5	*	1 Jul 2017
Cutting machines (guillotines)	10	*	1 Jul 2017
Die cutting machines	15	*	1 Jul 2017
Folding machines	10	*	1 Jul 2017
Glue binders	6	*	1 Jul 2017
Hole punching machines	7	*	1 Jul 2017
Sewing machines	5	*	1 Jul 2017
Stich liners	5	*	1 Jul 2017
Finishing assets:			
Laminators:			
Cold	10	*	1 Jul 2017
Heat assisted	7	*	1 Jul 2017
Vacuum press	23	*	1 Jul 2017
UV coaters	7	*	1 Jul 2017
Framing assets:			
Automatic measuring stops	10	*	1 Jul 2017
Board and glass wall cutters	12	*	1 Jul 2017
Dust extractors	10	*	1 Jul 2017
Mat cutters	10	*	1 Jul 2017
Mitre guillotines	25	*	1 Jul 2017

OTHER SERVICES
(94110 to 96030)

Asset	Life (Years)	Reviewed	Date Of Application
Mitre saws	10	*	1 Jul 2017
Trimmers	15	*	1 Jul 2017
Underpinners	15	*	1 Jul 2017
Vinyl cutters	5	*	1 Jul 2017
Printing assets:			
Colour matching booths	10	*	1 Jul 2017
Digital minilabs:			
Dry:			
Commercial	5	*	1 Jul 2017
Compact	3	*	1 Jul 2017
Wet	10	*	1 Jul 2017
Digital presses	5	*	1 Jul 2017
Film processers	10	*	1 Jul 2017
Heat presses:			
Automatic, manual, mug and multipurpose	4	*	1 Jul 2017
Large format flatbed	6	*	1 Jul 2017
ID card printers	10	*	1 Jul 2017
Kiosks	5	*	1 Jul 2017
Large format flatbed digital printers	5	*	1 Jul 2017
Laser cutters (incorporating laser printing):			
Desktop	3	*	1 Jul 2017
Floor mounted	7	*	1 Jul 2017
Photo calibration monitors	8	*	1 Jul 2017
Photo scanners (including photo and film scanners)	9	*	1 Jul 2017
Roll to roll printers	15	*	1 Jul 2017
Textile printers (including direct to fabric printers and direct to garment printers)	5	*	1 Jul 2017
Wide format printers:			
Dye sublimation (including desktop)	5	*	1 Jul 2017
Solvent	4	*	1 Jul 2017
Specialist photo	6	*	1 Jul 2017
Parking services (95330)			
Car park operation assets – see Table B Car park assets			

¶43-100 1 July 2020 effective life Table B (asset categories)

Table B is an asset table which contains generic assets which may be used by more than one industry. If an asset is only listed in Table B, that rate is to be used both by industry and non-industry members. If an item is listed in both tables, industry members must use the Table A rate (¶43-005) and non-industry members must use the Table B rate. If an asset does not appear in either table, taxpayers must determine the effective life of the asset (¶17-270). The assets in Table B are common assets (eg rental property assets, cars, computers etc) used by a broader range of taxpayers (including salary and wage earners, landlords, small businesses) than the ones who can rely on Table A.

New and reviewed items have been marked with an asterisk (*) in the third column of the table. Where the Commissioner has determined effective lives for assets in excess of the statutory caps for those assets, they have been marked with a hash (#) in the third column of the table.

Table B incorporates the 1 July 2020 Schedule of effective life determinations.

Asset	Life (years)	Reviewed	Date of application
A			
Accommodation units in caravan/tourist parks being articles, not fixtures, and used for a specified purpose[46]:			
Relocatable homes and tourist park cabins constructed with chassis	20	*	1 Jul 2015
Other accommodation units (eg manufactured homes)	30	*	1 Jul 2015
Additive manufacturing printers (including 3D printers)	3	*	1 Jul 2016
Advertising signs:			
Billboard assets:			
Billboard lighting:			
HID/Metal halide lighting systems	5	*	1 Jul 2015
LED lighting systems (including solar powered LED lighting systems)	10	*	1 Jul 2015
Solar power generating assets – see Table B Solar photovoltaic electricity generation system assets			
Billboard steel structures (incorporating electrical systems, footings, scaffolding and walking platforms and steel frame sign panels)	20	*	1 Jul 2015
Computer hardware – see Table B Computers			
Digital LED screens	6	*	1 Jul 2015
Electronic message centre (EMC) units	3	*	1 Jul 2015
Mobile billboard assets:			
Digital LED screens	4	*	1 Jul 2015
Mobile billboard trucks and trailers – see Table B Motor vehicles and trailers			
Floor mounted internal advertising panels (used in airports and shopping centres etc)	7	*	1 Jul 2015
Kiosks and other external standalone advertising panel structures	15	*	1 Jul 2015
LED advertising screens (used in office tower foyers etc)	5	*	1 Jul 2015
Wall mounted advertising panels (used in airports, rail concourses and platforms, shopping centres etc):			
Digital LED advertising panels	5	*	1 Jul 2015
Static advertising panels	10	*	1 Jul 2015
Air compression assets:			
Air compression assets generally (including air compressors, air dryers and air receivers)	15	*	1 Jul 2014
Air compressors (portable):			
Compressors – reciprocating	7	*	1 Jul 2014
Compressors – rotary screw	10	*	1 Jul 2014
Air-conditioning assets (excluding pipes, duct work and vents):			
Air handling units	20	*	1 Jul 2003
Cooling towers	15	*	1 Jul 2003
Condensing sets	15	*	1 Jul 2003
Chillers:			
Absorption	25	*	1 Jul 2003
Centrifugal	20	*	1 Jul 2003
Volumetrics (including reciprocating, rotary, screw, scroll):			
Air-cooled	15	*	1 Jul 2003
Water-cooled	20	*	1 Jul 2003
Damper motors (including variable air volume box controllers)	10	*	1 Jul 2003
Fan coil units (connected to a condensing set)	15	*	1 Jul 2003
Humidifiers (steam generator)	10	*	1 Jul 2003
Mini split systems up to 20KW (including ceiling, floor and high wall split systems)	10	*	1 Jul 2003

Asset	Life (years)	Reviewed	Date of application
Packaged air conditioning units	15	*	1 Jul 2003
Pumps	20	*	1 Jul 2003
Room units	10	*	1 Jul 2003
Aircraft:			
Aeroplanes:			
General use[47]	20	*#	1 Jul 2002
Used predominantly for agricultural spraying or agricultural dusting[48]	10	*#	1 Jul 2002
Helicopters:			
General use[49]	20	*#	1 Jul 2002
Used predominantly for mustering, agricultural spraying or agricultural dusting[50]	10	*#	1 Jul 2002
Airless sprayers (used in painting, epoxy and polyurethane coating, priming etc):			
Electrically and petrol-driven units	7	*	1 Jul 2013
Pneumatically-driven units	15	*	1 Jul 2013
Artworks qualifying as depreciating assets (restricted to works of art and reproductions of artwork that are tangible in nature, such as paintings, sculptures, drawings, engravings and photographs, that are displayed in open viewing areas in premises used for taxable purposes including reception areas, waiting rooms and foyers)	100	*	1 Jul 2013
Automated external defibrillators (AEDs)	8	*	1 Jul 2020
Automatic teller machines (ATMs)	7	*	1 Jul 2019
B			
Bending machines (bar, angle and rod)	10	*	1 Jul 2008
Block and brick elevators, portable	10	*	1 Jul 2008
Boilers	20	*	1 Jul 2005
Boom gates:			
Electromechanically operated boom gates	7	*	1 Jul 2013
Hydraulically operated boom gates	10	*	1 Jul 2013
C			
Car park assets:			
Automatic and semi-automatic parking systems (including platforms, stackers, turntables etc)	20	*	1 Jul 2016
Automatic payment machines/stations	10	*	1 Jul 2016
Barrier gates/boom gates – see Table B Boom gates			
Car park floodlighting	20	*	1 Jul 2016
Car park signage	7	*	1 Jul 2016
Entry and exit stations/columns (including RFID card readers, ticket dispensing machines, ticket readers etc)	10	*	1 Jul 2016
Licence plate recognition cameras and systems	5	*	1 Jul 2016
Parking guidance assets:			
Automatic vehicle counter systems (incorporating counter modules and signage)	7	*	1 Jul 2016
Parking guidance systems (incorporating controllers, detectors, dynamic signage, lighting etc)	7	*	1 Jul 2016
Pay and display machines/Pay and go machines	8	*	1 Jul 2016
Security and monitoring assets:			
Generally (including CCTV systems) – see Table B Security and monitoring assets			
Intercommunication (intercom) system assets	7	*	1 Jul 2016
Two-way radios – see Table B Two-way radios			
Ceiling fans	10	*	1 Jul 2016

Asset	Life (years)	Reviewed	Date of application
Cleaning carts and trolleys	5	*	1 Jul 2019
Compaction assets:			
Compactors – flat plate	8	*	1 Jul 2008
Compactors – vertical rammer	6	*	1 Jul 2008
Computers and computer equipment:			
Computers and computer equipment (not specified elsewhere below)	4	*	1 Jul 2016
Computer monitors	4	*	1 Jul 2016
Desktop computers (including personal computers)	4	*	1 Jul 2016
Mainframe computers	5	*	1 Jul 2016
Mobile/portable computers (including laptops, tablets)	2	*	1 Jul 2016
Network equipment (including hubs, modems routers, switches, etc)	5	*	1 Jul 2016
Raised floors	25	*	1 Jul 2017
Servers	4	*	1 Jul 2016
Concrete truck mixers (incorporating barrel, chutes, frame and hydraulic pumps)	5	*	1 Jul 2014
Concreting assets:			
Brick and paving saws	5	*	1 Jul 2008
Concrete demolition saws	3	*	1 Jul 2008
Concrete kibble buckets	15	*	1 Jul 2008
Concrete mixers	4	*	1 Jul 2008
Concrete surface preparation assets (including floor grinders, planers and scarifers)	5	*	1 Jul 2008
Concrete trowels:			
Walk behind	5	*	1 Jul 2008
Ride on	7	*	1 Jul 2008
Concrete vibrating screeders	5	*	1 Jul 2008
Concrete vibrators:			
Brushcutter style	5	*	1 Jul 2008
Drive units	6	*	1 Jul 2008
Flexible shaft pumps	6	*	1 Jul 2008
Vibrating shafts	3	*	1 Jul 2008
Concrete wheeled saws	6	*	1 Jul 2008
Control systems and control system assets (including control cabinets and panels, instruments, programmable logic controllers (PLCs), sensors, switchgear telemetry and variable speed drives (VSDs))	10	*	1 Jul 2015
Cranes (gantry and overhead)	25	*	1 Jul 2014
Curtains and drapes	6	*	1 Jul 2004
D			
Digital cameras:			
Camera lenses	5	*	1 Jul 2015
Medium format single lens reflex (SLR) system (including camera bodies and digital backs)	4	*	1 Jul 2015
Others	3	*	1 Jul 2015
Door controls and motor drive systems for automatic sliding doors (incorporating chains, controls, motors and sensors, but excluding doors)	15	*	1 Jul 2005
Dozers/front end loaders	9	*	1 Jul 2002
Drink dispensing machines	10	*	1 Jul 2005
Drones/remotely piloted aircraft – see Table B Unmanned aerial vehicles			

Asset	Life (years)	Reviewed	Date of application
E			
Employee time and attendance recorders (including bundy clocks, time clocks etc):			
Computerised time and attendance recorders (including fingerprint and face recognition systems and swipe card digital time clock systems)	10	*	1 Jul 2013
Standalone electronic time and attendance recorders (card based etc)	10	*	1 Jul 2013
Escalators (machinery and their moving parts)	20	*	1 Jan 2003
F			
Fences:			
Portable electric fences	20	*	1 Jul 2014
Wire mesh (demountable used for partitioning purposes, including portable electric fences)	20	*	1 Jul 2014
Fire control and alarm assets:			
Alarms:			
Heat	6	*	1 Jul 2004
Smoke	6	*	1 Jul 2004
Detection and alarm systems:			
Alarm bells	12	*	1 Jul 2004
Detectors:			
Aspirated smoke	12	*	1 Jul 2004
Heat	20	*	1 Jul 2004
Manual call point (addressable type only)	20	*	1 Jul 2004
Multi type	20	*	1 Jul 2004
Smoke	20	*	1 Jul 2004
Fire indicator panels	12	*	1 Jul 2004
Gas suppression cylinders	25	*	1 Jul 2004
Emergency warning and intercommunication systems:			
Master emergency control panels	12	*	1 Jul 2004
Speakers	12	*	1 Jul 2004
Strobe lights	12	*	1 Jul 2004
Warden intercom phones	12	*	1 Jul 2004
Extinguishers	15	*	1 Jul 2004
Hoses and nozzles	10	*	1 Jul 2004
Pumps (including diesel and electric)	25	*	1 Jul 2004
Stair pressurisation assets:			
AC variable speed drives (VSDs)	10	*	1 Jul 2004
Pressurisation and extraction fans	25	*	1 Jul 2004
Sensors	10	*	1 Jul 2004
Floor coverings (removable without damage):			
Carpets (excluding fixed carpet tiles)	8	*	1 Jul 2016
Floating timber	15	*	1 Jul 2016
Linoleum and vinyl	10	*	1 Jul 2016
Fogging machines (insecticide, including cold foggers and thermal foggers):			
Portable	6	*	1 Jul 2013
Vehicle mounted	10	*	1 Jul 2013
Forklifts	11	*	1 Jul 2002
Forklift battery chargers	11	*	1 Jul 2013
Formwork, beams and props, steel	10	*	1 Jul 2008

Asset	Life (years)	Reviewed	Date of application
Foundations for plant and machinery (integral to the operation of such plant and machinery, but not incorporated into the plant and machinery itself)	40	*	1 Jul 2014
G			
Generators – see Table B Power supply assets			
H			
Hand dryers (electrical)	10	*	1 Jul 2013
Hand tools (manually operated)	10	*	1 Jul 2014
J			
Judges' robes:			
Ceremonial robes	15	*	1 Jul 2013
Working robes	10	*	1 Jul 2013
L			
Laboratory assets used in quality control, sample checking etc:			
Automated and electronically based laboratory assets (including analysers, refractometers, spectrometry machines etc)	7	*	1 Jul 2014
Other laboratory assets (including autoclaves, centrifuges, microscopes, ovens etc)	10	*	1 Jul 2014
Laser cutting machines	10	*	1 Jul 2014
Levels:			
Automatic optical levels (dumpy levels)	7	*	1 Jul 2015
Laser levels:			
Grade laying (dial-in grade)	6	*	1 Jul 2015
Laser plummets	5	*	1 Jul 2015
Line and plumb/point and cross line	4	*	1 Jul 2015
Pipe laying	6	*	1 Jul 2015
Rotating	6	*	1 Jul 2015
Tunnelling and plumbing	6	*	1 Jul 2015
Libraries (professional)	10	*	1 Jul 2014
Lift slab assets (incorporating spreader bars, clutches, pulleys and cables)	5	*	1 Jul 2008
Lifts (including dumbwaiters, hydraulic lifts and traction lifts)	30	*	1 Jan 2003
Light fittings and freestanding lights (excluding hardwired light fittings)	10	*	1 Jul 2016
Light shades (removable)	5	*	1 Jul 2016
Lighting control systems (microprocessor based)	5	*	1 Jul 2014
Loading bay assets:			
Dock levellers	20	*	1 Jul 2005
Pallet jacks and pallet trucks	10	*	1 Jul 2005
Scissor lifts	15	*	1 Jul 2005
Lockers, freestanding	20	*	1 Jul 2019
M			
Machine tools (grinding machines, lathes, milling machines etc):			
CNC and NC based machines	10	*	1 Jul 2014
Conventional or manual machines	20	*	1 Jul 2014
Mini-skid steer loaders (with a carrying capacity less than or equal to 1100 kg)	5	*	1 Jul 2005
Mini-skid steer loader attachments:			
Others (including auger and bucket)	5	*	1 Jan 2004
Stump grinders	2	*	1 Jan 2004
Motor graders	10	*	1 Jul 2002
Motor vehicles and trailers:			

Asset	Life (years)	Reviewed	Date of application
Buses having a gross vehicle mass of more than 3.5 tonnes[51]	15	*#	1 Jan 2005
Cars (motor vehicles designed to carry a load of less than one tonne and fewer than 9 passengers):			
Generally	8	*	1 Jan 2006
Hire cars:[52]			
Cars used to provide basic service ride-sourcing, ride-hailing or ride-sharing services (eg uberX)	8	*	1 Jul 2016
Generally (including cars used to provide premium service ride-sourcing, ride-hailing or ride-sharing services eg UberBLACK)	6	*	1 Jul 2016
Rental cars[53]	5	*	1 Jul 2016
Taxis	4	*	1 Jul 2015
Garbage compactor trucks – see Table A Solid waste collection services (29110)			
Light commercial vehicles designed to carry a load of one tonne or greater and having a gross vehicle mass of 3.5 tonnes or less[54]	12	*#	1 Jan 2005
Limousines:			
Sedan limousines	6	*	1 Jul 2016
Stretch limousines	12	*	1 Jul 2016
Minibuses having a gross vehicle mass of 3.5 tonnes or less and designed to carry 9 or more passengers[55]	12	*#	1 Jan 2005
Motorcycles (including courier motorcycles and mailbox delivery motorcycles)	7	*	1 Jul 2015
Scooters	3	*	1 Jul 2015
Trailers having a gross vehicle mass greater than 4.5 tonnes[56]	15	*#	1 Jan 2005
Trailers having a gross vehicle mass of 4.5 tonnes or less:			
Aluminium, galvanised steel, galvanised hot dipped steel and powder coated trailers	10	*	1 Jul 2015
Mild steel trailers (painted and unpainted)	5	*	1 Jul 2015
Trucks having a gross vehicle mass greater than 3.5 tonnes (excluding off highway trucks used in mining operations)[57]	15	*#	1 Jan 2005
Moving walks	20	*	1 Jan 2003
Musical instruments and associated equipment:			
Associated portable equipment (including amplifiers, microphones, speakers, mixers and music stands)	6 2/3	*	1 Jan 2001
Brass instruments	10	*	1 Jan 2001
Keyboard instruments (acoustic)	10	*	1 Jan 2001
Keyboard instruments (electric)	5	*	1 Jan 2001
Percussion instruments	5	*	1 Jan 2001
Stringed instruments	10	*	1 Jan 2001
Woodwind instruments	10	*	1 Jan 2001
O			
Office furniture, freestanding:			
Bookcases:			
Metal	20	*	1 Jul 2005
Timber	15	*	1 Jul 2005
Cabinets (including credenzas, cupboards, filing, mapping, mobile, stationery and storage type):			
Metal	20	*	1 Jul 2005
Timber/laminated	15	*	1 Jul 2005
Chairs	10	*	1 Jul 2005
Desks	20	*	1 Jul 2005
Mobile storage units (compactus type)	25	*	1 Jul 2005

Asset	Life (years)	Reviewed	Date of application
Reception assets (including lobby chairs, desks, lounges, sofas and tables)	10	*	1 Jul 2005
Screens	20	*	1 Jul 2005
Tables:			
Boardroom	20	*	1 Jul 2005
General	10	*	1 Jul 2005
Workstations (including desks and partitions)	20	*	1 Jul 2005
Office machines and equipment:			
Electronic whiteboards	6	*	1 Jan 2001
Enveloping machines	6	*	1 Jan 2001
Facsimile machines	5	*	1 Jan 2001
Letter folding and inserting machines (including envelope inserters and letter inserters – desktop/low volume units)	5	*	1 Jul 2013
Mailing machines	5	*	1 Jan 2001
Multi function machines (includes fax, copy, print and scan functions)	5	*	1 Jan 2001
Photo copying machines	5	*	1 Jan 2001
Projectors (including lenses)	5	*	1 Jul 2014
Shredders	15	*	1 Jul 2005
Trolleys	15	*	1 Jul 2005
Whiteboards	10	*	1 Jul 2005
P			
Packaging machines:			
Bagging machines (including flow wrappers, form fill and seal machines, and roll wrapping machines)	10	*	1 Jul 2009
Bag sewers	7	*	1 Jul 2017
Carton erecting, packing and closing machines (including cartoners)	10	*	1 Jul 2009
Case erecting, packing and closing machines (including casepackers)	10	*	1 Jul 2009
Inspection equipment (including checkweighers, metal detectors, counting machines etc)	10	*	1 Jul 2009
Multihead and singlehead weighers	10	*	1 Jul 2009
Palletisers and depalletisers	12	*	1 Jul 2009
Product identification labellers (including decorating, applicators and coding machines)	8	*	1 Jul 2009
Robotic pick and place packaging machines	10	*	1 Jul 2009
Wrapping machines (including pallet wrappers, shrink wrappers, stretch wrappers and strapping machines)	10	*	1 Jul 2017
Partitions (demountable)	20	*	1 Jul 2005
Platform scales	15	*	1 Jul 2014
Plumbing fixtures and fittings (including wall and floor tiles) provided mainly for employees and/or children of employees of an entity carrying on a business for the purpose of producing assessable income:			
Floor and wall tiles	20	*	1 Jul 2015
Generally (including basins, bidets, sinks, toilets, urinals etc)	20	*	1 Jul 2015
Tapware (including taps, mixers and shower heads and assemblies)	15	*	1 Jul 2015
Pneumatic air tube systems	10	*	1 Jul 2013
Point of sale assets:			
Cash registers, standalone type	10	*	1 Jul 2005
Cash transfer system assets, pneumatic type (including printer circuit board, transfer pipes and turbines)	10	*	1 Jul 2005

Asset	Life (years)	Reviewed	Date of application
Generally (including barcode scanners, cash drawers, dedicated computers, electronic funds transfer point of sale (EFTPOS) machines, keyboards, monitors, printers and terminals)	6	*	1 Jul 2005
Weighing machines and scales (including weigh labelling machines)	10	*	1 Jul 2005
Portable structures (sheds, site office trailers, portable toilets and washrooms etc) used for a temporary period in offsite locations (eg construction sites)	15	*	1 Jul 2014
Powder coating machines and systems (automatic and manual)	10	*	1 Jul 2014
Power regulation systems (PRS)	5	*	1 Jul 2016
Power supply assets:			
Emergency or standby:			
Generator assets:			
Acoustic hoods and canopies	20	*	1 Jul 2005
Generators (incorporating attached engine management and generator monitoring instruments)	25	*	1 Jul 2005
Power management units	15	*	1 Jul 2005
Uninterruptible power supply (UPS) systems	15	*	1 Jul 2013
Generators, portable (incorporating attached engine management and generator monitoring nstruments):			
Diesel	10	*	1 Jul 2008
Petrol	5	*	1 Jul 2008
Private electricity line assets (where used for a specified purpose[58]):			
Distribution lines:			
Combination of overhead and underground	47 1/2	*	1 Jul 2014
Overhead (incorporating poles – concrete, wood, steel or stobie – and electrical equipment the responsibility of the private landholder such as conductors, cross arms etc)	45	*	1 Jul 2014
Underground (incorporating cables, fittings and ground pad mounted transformers)	50	*	1 Jul 2014
Service cables, overhead	40	*	1 Jul 2014
Service cables, underground	50	*	1 Jul 2014
Storage batteries	15	*	1 Jul 2013
Power tools:			
Chain saws	3	*	1 Jul 2008
Hand tools:			
Air	5	*	1 Jul 2008
Battery	3	*	1 Jul 2008
Electric	5	*	1 Jul 2008
Jack hammers:			
Air	7	*	1 Jul 2008
Electric	3	*	1 Jul 2008
Nail guns – air	3	*	1 Jul 2008
Power transformers	45	*	1 Jan 2002
Public address and paging system assets (including amplifiers, audio speakers and microphones)	12	*	1 Jul 2005
R			
Rainwater tanks:			
Galvanised steel	25	*	1 Jul 2019
Polyethylene	15	*	1 Jul 2019
Refrigeration assets:			

Asset	Life (years)	Reviewed	Date of application
Compressors, condensers, evaporators etc	15	*	1 Jul 2014
Insulation panels used in cool or freezer rooms	40	*	1 Jul 2014
Robots (industrial)	10	*	1 Jul 2014
S			
Saws, bench and mitre, portable	7	*	1 Jul 2008
Security and monitoring assets:			
Access control systems:			
Code pads	5	*	1 Jul 2004
Door controllers	5	*	1 Jul 2004
Readers:			
Proximity	7	*	1 Jul 2004
Swipe card	3	*	1 Jul 2004
Ballistic and blast resistant screens and barriers (including fixed and rising types) not forming part of the building	20	*	1 Jul 2014
CCTV systems:			
Cameras	4	*	1 Jul 2004
Monitors	4	*	1 Jul 2004
Recorders:			
Digital	4	*	1 Jul 2004
Time lapse	2	*	1 Jul 2004
Switching units (including multiplexers)	5	*	1 Jul 2004
Security systems:			
Code pads	5	*	1 Jul 2004
Control panels	5	*	1 Jul 2004
Detectors (including glass, passive infrared and vibration)	5	*	1 Jul 2004
Global system for mobiles (GSM) units	5	*	1 Jul 2004
Noise maker (including alarms and bells)	5	*	1 Jul 2004
Sewing machines	10	*	1 Jan 2014
Signage for business identification (including lighting for signs) – see Table B Advertising signs			
Silos:			
Bulk handling:			
Ancillary mechanical assets (including augers, bucket elevators, conveyors etc)	15	*	1 Jul 2014
Concrete construction	50	*	1 Jan 2004
Galvanised construction	30	*	1 Jan 2004
Steel construction	40	*	1 Jan 2004
Solar photovoltaic electricity generation system assets	20	*	1 Jul 2011
Spas used as plant in a business (incorporating blowers, controls, filters, heaters and pumps)	17	*	1 Jul 2014
Spray booths	15	*	1 Jul 2014
Stacks (chimney stacks, exhaust stacks, flues etc):			
Concrete stacks (including concrete reinforced stacks)	30	*	1 Jul 2014
Flare stacks	25	*	1 Jul 2014
Reinforced plastic stacks	25	*	1 Jul 2014
Steel stacks (steel flues)	20	*	1 Jul 2014
Suitcases	10	*	1 Jul 2013
Swimming pool assets:			
Chlorinators	12	*	1 Jul 2004
Cleaning assets	7	*	1 Jul 2004
Covers (including blankets)	8	*	1 Jul 2019

Asset	Life (years)	Reviewed	Date of application
Filtration assets (including pumps)	12	*	1 Jul 2004
Heaters:			
Electric	15	*	1 Jul 2004
Gas	15	*	1 Jul 2004
Solar	20	*	1 Jul 2004
Swimming pools (used as plant in a business):			
Above-ground	10	*	1 Jul 2005
Concrete	50	*	1 Jul 2005
Fibreglass	20	*	1 Jul 2005
Switchboards	20	*	1 Jul 2014
Synthetic lawn surfaces	5	*	1 Jul 2014
T			
Tarpaulins	5	*	1 Jul 2014
Telephony:			
Mobile phones	3	*	1 Jul 2014
Telephone systems (including analogue and digital telephone systems, PABX/PBX systems, key/commander systems, VoIP systems and hybrid telephone systems such as IP-PBX systems etc)	7	*	1 Jul 2015
Television sets	10	*	1 Jul 2014
Tractors	12	*	1 Jul 2007
Trailers – see Table B Motor vehicles and trailers			
Two-way radios:			
Base stations	6	*	1 Jul 2014
Mobile units	6	*	1 Jul 2014
Portable units	3	*	1 Jul 2014
Repeaters	7	*	1 Jul 2014
U			
Unmanned aerial vehicles (drones/remotely piloted aircraft):			
Fixed wing	3	*	1 Jul 2015
Rotary wing	2	*	1 Jul 2015
V			
Vending machines	5	*	1 Jul 2001
Ventilation fans (excluding ducting, piping and vents)	20	*	1 Jan 2005
W			
Warehouse and distribution centre equipment and machines:			
Automated storage and retrieval machines	20	*	1 Jul 2011
Balers	15	*	1 Jul 2011
Battery assets for warehouse vehicles (including pallet trucks and forklifts):			
Batteries (detachable for recharging)	5	*	1 Jul 2011
Battery chargers:			
Forklifts	11	*	1 Jul 2011
Other	10	*	1 Jul 2011
Handling assets:			
Battery tuggers	10	*	1 Jul 2011
Racking roller beds	15	*	1 Jul 2011
Transfer carts	10	*	1 Jul 2011
Washers	10	*	1 Jul 2011
Carts/buggies	15	*	1 Jul 2011
Conveyors	15	*	1 Jul 2011

Asset	Life (years)	Reviewed	Date of application
Dock levellers, pallet jacks, pallet trucks and scissor lifts – see Table B Loading bay assets			
Door controls and motor drive systems (incorporating chains, controls, motors and sensors, but excluding doors):			
External	20	*	1 Jul 2011
Internal	10	*	1 Jul 2011
Floor sweepers/scrubbers	10	*	1 Jul 2011
Forklift attachments:			
Cages	10	*	1 Jul 2011
Push pull units	11	*	1 Jul 2011
Inflatable dock bags/seals/shelters	10	*	1 Jul 2011
Packaging machines and wrapping machines – see Table B Packaging machines			
Pallet assets:			
Dispensers	15	*	1 Jul 2011
Lift tables	10	*	1 Jul 2011
Racks	20	*	1 Jul 2011
Radio frequency terminal assets:			
Barcode readers/scanners	5	*	1 Jul 2011
Portable/handheld and vehicle mounted terminal devices	4	*	1 Jul 2011
Refrigeration assets – see Table B Refrigeration assets			
Roll cages	10	*	1 Jul 2011
Trolleys	10	*	1 Jul 2011
Voice picking assets:			
Battery chargers	4	*	1 Jul 2011
Headsets	4	*	1 Jul 2011
Terminals (on person)	4	*	1 Jul 2011
Waste compactors (used for cardboard and plastic):			
Electric	15	*	1 Jul 2011
Hydraulic	20	*	1 Jul 2011
Waste storage and disposal bins (including crane bins, hooklift bins, skip bins and other industrial use bins)	10	*	1 Jul 2016
Weighbridges	20	*	1 Jul 2014
Welders:			
Diesel	10	*	1 Jul 2008
Electric	5	*	1 Jul 2008
Oxygen welders and cutters	10	*	1 Jul 2014
Window blinds	15	*	1 Jul 2016
Working beasts and beasts of burden (including camels and horses but excluding working dogs) used in a business other than primary production	15	*	1 Jul 2014
Working dogs (including certified therapy dogs used by qualified therapists, detection dogs, guard dogs, performing dogs, police dogs and security dogs; but excluding assistance dogs (such as guide dogs, hearing dogs and service dogs), pet dogs, racing dogs, support dogs, and working dogs used in primary production)	8	*	1 Jul 2019

Footnotes:

46 A specified purpose is a taxable purpose, the purpose of producing exempt income or non-assessable non-exempt income, or the purpose of conducting R&D activities (assuming that this is reasonably likely)

47 A capped effective life of 10 years is available – see subsection 40-102(4)

48 A capped effective life of 8 years is available – see subsection 40-102(4)

49 A capped effective life of 10 years is available – see subsection 40-102(4)

50 A capped effective life of 8 years is available – see subsection 40-102(4)

51 A capped effective life of 7 1/2 years is available – see subsection 40-102(4)

52 A hire car is a passenger car hired with a driver, not being a taxi.

53 A rental car is a passenger car hired, leased or rented for short-term use without a driver.

54 A capped effective life of 7 1/2 years is available – see subsection 40-102(4).

55 A capped effective life of 7 1/2 years is available – see subsection 40-102(4).

56 A capped effective life of 10 years is available – see subsection 40-102(4).

57 A capped effective life of 7 1/2 years is available – see subsection 40-102(4).

58 A specified purpose is a taxable purpose, the purpose of producing exempt income or non-assessable non-exempt income, or the purpose of conducting R&D activities (assuming that this is reasonably likely).

¶43-105 Statutory caps on effective life

Capped effective lives apply to assets that correspond exactly to those specified in the table below. For items 1 to 4, the capped lives apply where the assets start being used or installed ready for use from 1 July 2002. For items 5 to 9, the capped lives apply where the start time occurs on or after 1 January 2005. For item 10, the capped life applies to an eligible vessel that a taxpayer holds on or after 1 July 2012 (¶17-280).

Effective lives do not need to be worked out if the temporary full expensing rules apply, unless an asset's opening adjustable value needs to be determined (¶17-430).

Capped life of certain depreciating assets

Item	Kind of depreciating asset	Period
1	Aeroplane used predominantly for agricultural spraying or agricultural dusting	8 years
2	Aeroplane to which item 1 does not apply	10 years
3	Helicopter used predominantly for mustering, agricultural spraying or agricultural dusting	8 years
4	Helicopter to which item 3 does not apply	10 years
5	Bus with a gross vehicle mass of more than 3.5 tonnes	7.5 years
6	Light commercial vehicle with a gross vehicle mass of 3.5 tonnes or less and designed to carry a load of 1 tonne or more	7.5 years
7	Minibus with a gross vehicle mass of 3.5 tonnes or less and designed to carry 9 or more passengers	7.5 years
8	Trailer with a gross vehicle mass of more than 4.5 tonnes	10 years
9	Truck with a gross vehicle mass of more than 3.5 tonnes (other than a truck that is used in mining operations and that is not of a kind that can be registered to be driven on a public road in the place in which the truck is operated)	7.5 years
10	Vessel for which the taxpayer has a certificate under Pt 2 of the *Shipping Reform (Tax Incentives) Act 2012*	10 years

Capped effective lives apply to assets that are used in the industries and which are of a kind specified in the table below. For items 1 to 6, the capped lives apply where the assets start being used or installed ready for use from 1 July 2002. For items 7 and 8, the capped lives apply where the start time occurs on or after 1 July 2007 (¶17-280).

Capped life of certain depreciating assets used in specified industries			
Item	**Kind of depreciating asset**	**Industry in which the asset is used**	**Period**
1	Gas transmission asset	Gas supply	20 years
2	Gas distribution asset	Gas supply	20 years
3	Oil production asset (other than an electricity generation asset or an offshore platform)	Oil and gas extraction	15 years
4	Gas production asset (other than an electricity generation asset or an offshore platform)	Oil and gas extraction	15 years
5	Offshore platform	Oil and gas extraction	20 years
6	Asset (other than an electricity generation asset) used to manufacture condensate, crude oil, domestic gas, liquid natural gas or liquid petroleum gas but not if the manufacture occurs in an oil refinery	Petroleum refining	15 years
7	Harvester	Primary production sector	6 2/3 years
8	Tractor	Primary production sector	6 2/3 years

¶43-110 Car depreciation limit

The car depreciation limit (known as the ‘‘car limit’’) for various income years is set out in the following table (¶17-200).

Income year	Car limit
2001–02	$55,134
2002–03	$57,009
2003–04	$57,009
2004–05	$57,009
2005–06	$57,009
2006–07	$57,009
2007–08	$57,123
2008–09	$57,180
2009–10	$57,180
2010–11	$57,466
2011–12	$57,466
2012–13	$57,466
2013–14	$57,466
2014–15	$57,466
2015–16	$57,466
2016–17	$57,581
2017–18	$57,581
2018–19	$57,581
2019–20	$57,581
2020–21	$59,136

¶43-115 Capital works deductions for buildings and structural improvements

A special system of tax deductions applies to capital expenditure incurred on the construction of buildings and structural improvements (¶20-470).

The table below shows the rates of deduction for capital works expenditure on residential and non-residential buildings, and structural improvements.

Construction start date	Capital works deduction rate (%)
Non-residential buildings	
Industrial	
27.2.92 onwards[1]	4
Non-industrial	
16.9.87 onwards	2.5[2, 3]
22.8.84 – 15.9.87	4
20.7.82 – 21.8.84	2.5
Residential buildings	
Short-term traveller accommodation	
27.2.92 onwards	4
16.9.87 – 26.2.92	2.5[2]
22.8.84 – 15.9.87	4
22.8.79 – 21.8.84	2.5
Other residential accommodation	
16.9.87 onwards	2.5[2]
18.7.85 – 15.9.87	4
Structural improvements	
27.2.92 onwards	2.5[4]

(1) An industrial building constructed before 27 February 1992 qualifies for a capital works deduction under the rates given for non-industrial non-residential buildings.

(2) Where the construction relates to certain pre-16.9.87 contracts, the rate is 4%.

(3) This includes expenditure on R&D buildings where construction started on or after 21 November 1987.

(4) This includes environment protection earthworks expenditure incurred after 18 August 1992.

Chapter 44 Tax Checklists

¶44-000 Instructions: Individual tax return 2020

These instructions enable you to find explanations of each item in the 2020 Individual Tax Return. It also directs you to the relevant explanations in the ATO *Individual tax return instructions 2020*, *Individual tax return instructions supplement 2020* and *Business and professional items instructions 2020.*

The ATO website has details of the ATO occupation codes for 2020 and the ATO codes for CGT exemptions and roll-overs.

For lodgment requirements, see ¶24-010.

Return form item		Return form label	Explanation	Individual tax return instructions 2020 page
Taxpayer details				
	Tax file number		¶33-000	
	Residence		¶21-010	
Income				
1	Salary or wages	C–G	¶10-050	9
2	Allowances, earnings, tips, director's fees, etc	K	¶10-060 – ¶10-076	10
3	Employer lump sum payments	R, H	¶14-720, ¶14-730	11

Return form item		Return form label	Explanation	Individual tax return instructions 2020 page
4	Employment termination payments	I	¶14-610	12
5	Australian Government allowances and payments (incl JobSeeker)	A	¶10-195, ¶10-040	13
6	Australian Government pensions and allowances	B	¶10-195, ¶10-190, ¶10-200	14
7	Australian annuities and superannuation income streams	J, M, N, Y, Z	¶14-200	15
8	Australian superannuation lump sum payments	Q, P	¶14-120	17
9	Attributed personal services income	O	¶30-610	18
10	Gross interest	L M	¶10-470 ¶33-030	19
11	Dividends	S–U V	¶4-100, ¶4-800 ¶33-030	20
12	Employee share schemes (assessable amounts)	D–F, B	¶10-085 – ¶10-089	21
	TFN amounts withheld from ESS discounts	C	¶26-640	
	Foreign source ESS discounts	A	¶10-089	
	Deductions			
D1	Work-related car expenses	A	¶16-310	24
D2	Work-related travel expenses	B	¶16-220	26
D3	Work-related clothing, laundry and dry cleaning expenses	C	¶16-180	27
D4	Work-related self-education expenses	D	¶16-450	28
D5	Other work-related expenses			30
	generally	E	¶16-170	
	subscriptions	E	¶16-430	
	meals	E	¶16-175	
	seminars and conferences	E	¶16-450, ¶16-390	
	home office	E	¶16-480	
	telephone expenses	E	¶16-400	
	books and trade magazines	E	¶16-440, ¶16-170	
	safety items	E	¶16-180	
	computers	E	¶16-725	
	tools and equipment	E	¶16-170	
D6	Low-value pool deduction	K	¶17-810	31
D7	Interest deductions	I	¶16-660	32
D8	Dividend deductions	H	¶16-660, ¶4-180	33

Return form item		Return form label	Explanation	Individual tax return instructions 2020 page
D9	Gifts or donations	J	¶16-942	34
D10	Cost of managing tax affairs	L, M, N	¶16-850	34
Losses				
L1	Tax losses of earlier income years	Q, F R, Z	¶16-880 ¶16-895 ¶18-020	36
Tax offsets				
T1	Senior Australians and pensioners	N, Y	¶15-310	37
T2	Australian superannuation income stream	S	¶14-220, ¶14-240	40
Medicare levy related items				
M1	Medicare levy reduction or exemption	Y, V, W	¶2-330, ¶2-340	42
M2	Medicare levy surcharge	E, A	¶2-335	46
Private health insurance policy details				
	Private health insurance	B, C, J, K, L	¶15-330	49
Adjustments				
A1	Under 18	J	¶2-160	52
A2	Part-year tax-free threshold	N	¶2-130	53
A3	Government super contributions	F, G, H	¶13-760, ¶13-765	54
A4	Working holiday maker net income	D	¶21-033, ¶26-277	59
Income tests				
IT1	Total reportable fringe benefits	N, W	¶35-055	60
IT2	Reportable employer superannuation contributions	T	¶26-640	61
IT3	Tax-free government pensions or benefits	U	¶10-195	61
IT4	Target foreign income	V	¶2-133	62
IT5	Net financial investment loss	X	¶2-133	62
IT6	Net rental property loss	Y	¶2-133	64
IT7	Child support paid	Z	¶2-133	65
IT8	Number of dependent children	D	¶15-120	65
Spouse details				
	Spouse details — married or de facto	L–F	Generally, see ‘‘Income tests’’ (above)	66

The *Individual tax return instructions supplement 2020* is only available online; it is not available in print.

SUPPLEMENTARY SECTION

Return form item		Return form label	Explanation	Link to online instructions
Income				
13	Partnerships and trusts			13
	partnerships generally	N, O	¶5-130	
	trusts generally	L, U	¶6-110	
	primary production generally	N	¶18-010	
	landcare operations	I, J	¶18-100	
	water facilities	I, J	¶18-080	
	fencing assets	I, J	¶18-090	
	fodder storage assets	I, J	¶18-085	
	franked distributions from trusts	C	¶4-860	
	ABN credits	P	¶26-200	
	franking credits	Q	¶4-640	
	TFN credits	R, M	¶26-200	
	credit for tax paid by trustee	S	¶6-210, ¶6-220	
	foreign resident withholding credit	A	¶26-265	
	NRAS tax offset	B	¶20-605	
14	Personal services income	See Business and professional items section		14
15	Net income or loss from business	See Business and professional items section		15
16	Deferred non-commercial business losses	See Business and professional items section		16
17	Net farm management deposits or withdrawals	D N R	¶18-293 ¶18-295 ¶18-310	17
18	Capital gains			18
	Did you have a capital gains tax event during the year?	G	¶11-240	

SUPPLEMENTARY SECTION

Return form item		Return form label	Explanation	Link to online instructions
	Have you applied an exemption or rollover?	M	¶12-150, ¶12-450	
	Total current year capital gains	H	¶11-180	
	Net capital gain	A	¶11-030	
	Net capital losses carried forward to later income years	V	¶11-040	
	Credit for foreign resident capital gains withholding amounts	X	¶26-269	
19	Foreign entities	I K W B	¶21-190 ¶21-200 ¶21-300 ¶21-330	19
20	Foreign source income and foreign assets or property			20
	source	E	¶21-070	
	employment income	T, N	¶10-860	
	pensions, annuities	L, D	¶14-510	
	franking credits from a NZ franking company	F	¶4-490	
	foreign income tax offsets	O	¶21-680	
21	Rent	P Q, U F	¶10-500 ¶16-650 ¶20-470	21
22	Bonuses from life insurance companies and friendly societies	W	¶10-240	22
23	Forestry managed investment scheme income	A	¶18-125	23
24	Other income			24
	Category 1			
	lump sum payments in arrears (except for those relating to superannuation income streams)	Y	¶15-340	
	Business Services Wage Assessment Tool (BSWAT) lump sum payment in arrears	Y	¶15-340	
	foreign exchange gains	Y	¶23-075	
	benefits or prizes from investment-related lotteries and some game-show winnings	Y	¶10-440	

SUPPLEMENTARY SECTION

Return form item		Return form label	Explanation	Link to online instructions
	assessable balancing adjustment when the taxpayer stops holding a depreciating asset	Y	¶17-630	
	a gain on the disposal or the redemption of traditional securities	Y	¶23-340	
	work-in-progress amounts not included at item 15	Y	¶16-158	
	Category 2			
	reimbursement or recoupment of tax-related expenses or election expenses that the taxpayer is claiming as a deduction (ie ATO interest)	X	¶10-270	
	Category 3			
	Assessable FHSS released amount	R	¶13-790	
	Category 4			
	jury attendance fees	V	¶10-050	
	royalties	V	¶10-510	
	bonus amounts distributed from friendly society income bonds	V	¶3-470	
	scholarships and educational awards	V	¶10-740	
	special professional income	V	¶2-142	
	payments under an income protection, sickness or accident insurance policy where the premiums were deductible and payments not already shown at item 1 or 2	V	¶10-210	
	interest from infrastructure borrowings where the taxpayer intends to claim a tax offset at item T10	V	¶23-030	
	allowances or payments received as a member of a local government council not shown at item 1 or 2	V		

SUPPLEMENTARY SECTION

Return form item		Return form label	Explanation	Link to online instructions
	other taxable allowances or payments from the Department of Human Services not shown at item 5 or 6	V	¶10-190	
	an amount released by a superannuation fund greater than the excess contributions tax liability stated on the release authority	V	¶13-777	
	any other amount of income not already shown on the taxpayer's tax return	V	¶10-005	
	tax withheld — lump sum payments in arrears	E	¶15-340	
	tax withheld — assessable FHSS released amount	S	¶13-790	
	special professional income	Z	¶2-142	
Deductions				
D11	Deductible amount of UPP of foreign pension or annuity	Y	¶14-510	D11
D12	Personal superannuation contributions	H	¶13-730	D12
D13	Deduction for project pool	D	¶19-050	D13
D14	Forestry managed investment scheme deduction	F	¶18-125	D14
D15	Other deductions			D15
	election expenses	E	¶16-500	
	losses on traditional securities	J	¶23-340	
	debt deductions	J	¶16-800	
	blackhole expenditure	J	¶16-156	
	sickness/accident/income protection insurance premiums	J	¶16-560	
	net personal services income loss of a personal services entity	J	¶30-610	
	foreign exchange losses	J	¶23-075	
	capital expenditure not claimed before ceasing a primary production business	J	¶18-050	

SUPPLEMENTARY SECTION

Return form item		Return form label	Explanation	Link to online instructions
	infrastructure borrowings interest	J	¶23-030	
	small business pool deductions for depreciating assets that the taxpayer cannot claim at item P8	J	¶7-250	
	self-education expenses incurred in satisfying the study requirements of a bonded scholarship	J	¶16-450	
Tax offsets				
T3	Superannuation contributions on behalf of spouse	A	¶13-770	T3
T4	Zone or overseas forces	R	¶15-160 ¶15-180	T4
T5	Invalid and invalid carer	B	¶15-100	T5
T6	(Former) landcare and water facility — unused from previous years	T		T6
T7	Early stage venture capital limited partnership	K, M	¶5-040, ¶20-700	T7
T8	Early stage investor	L, O	¶20-700	T8
T9	Other non-refundable tax offsets			T9
	(former) interest from infrastructure borrowings scheme	C		
	income from Joint Petroleum Development area	C	¶19-003	
T10	Other refundable tax offsets			T10
	conservation tillage	P	¶18-000	
	special disability trust income	P	¶6-230	
Adjustments				
A5	Amount on which family trust distribution tax has been paid	X	¶6-268	A5
Credit for interest on tax paid				
C1	Credit for interest on early payments	L	¶25-440	C1

The *Business and professional items 2020* (ie the instructions) is available online only; it is not available in print.

BUSINESS AND PROFESSIONAL ITEMS

Return form item		Return form label	Explanation	Link to online instructions
	General			
P1	Personal services income (PSI) generally		¶30-600	P1
	results test	P	¶30-665	
	personal services business determination	C	¶30-680	
	80% test	Q	¶30-670	
	unrelated clients test	D1	¶30-670	
	employment test	E1	¶30-670	
	business premises test	F1	¶30-670	
	withholding from PSI	M–J	¶26-280	
	deductions	K, L	¶30-620	
	[P2–P7 are taxpayer-specific items]			
P8	Business income			P8 P8 income
	ABN not quoted	C, D	¶26-200	
	payments subject to foreign resident withholding	B	¶26-265	
	voluntary agreement	E, F	¶26-150	
	labour hire	N, O	¶26-150	
	government industry payments	G, H	¶10-160	
	gross sales of trading stock	I, J	¶9-160	
	stock for private use	I, J	¶9-245	
	livestock	I, J	¶9-250	
	services	I, J	¶10-050	
	sharing economy income	I, J	¶2-135	
	rental income from rental business	I, J	¶10-105, ¶10-500	
	recoupment of expenses	I, J	¶10-270	
	bad debts recovered	I, J	¶10-270	
	profit from sale of depreciating assets	I, J	¶17-630	
	royalties	I, J	¶10-510	
	insurance recoveries	I, J	¶10-170, ¶10-270	
	subsidies and assessable non-government assistance	I, J	¶10-160	
	employee fringe benefit contributions	I, J	¶35-135	
	foreign exchange gains	I, J	¶23-075	
	Business expenses			P8 expenses
	opening stock	K	¶9-180	

BUSINESS AND PROFESSIONAL ITEMS

Return form item		**Return form label**	**Explanation**	**Link to online instructions**
	purchases and other costs	L	¶9-200, ¶9-210	
	closing stock	M	¶9-180	
	foreign resident withholding expenses		¶26-265	
	contractors and commissions		¶16-152	
	superannuation		¶13-710	
	bad debts		¶16-580	
	lease expenses		¶16-159, ¶16-060	
	rent		¶16-640	
	interest within Australia		¶16-740	
	overseas interest		¶22-700	
	depreciation		¶7-250, ¶17-005	
	motor vehicles		¶16-310	
	repairs and maintenance		¶16-700	
	other expenses generally		¶16-152	
	wages		¶16-520	
	accounting and professional fees		¶16-842	
	advertising		¶16-152	
	office supplies			
	foreign exchange losses		¶23-075	
	loss on the sale of a depreciating asset		¶17-630	
	business gifts and donations		¶16-940	
	managing the tax affairs of the business		¶16-850	
	home office		¶16-480	
	Reconciliation items			P8 reconciliation
	business-related capital costs (s 40-880)		¶16-156	
	pooled project expenditure		¶19-050	
	landcare, water facilities		¶18-100, ¶18-080	
	adjustments			
	disposal of depreciating assets		¶17-630	
	exempt income		¶10-600	
	prepayments		¶16-045	
	accounting adjustments		¶9-000	
	leased luxury cars		¶17-220	

BUSINESS AND PROFESSIONAL ITEMS

Return form item		Return form label	Explanation	Link to online instructions
	hire purchase		¶23-250	
	limited recourse debt		¶23-260	
	Deferred non-commercial business losses	D, E	¶16-020	
P9	Business loss activity details	D–U	¶16-880	P9
P10	Small business entity depreciating assets	A, B	¶7-250	P10
Other business and professional items				
P11	Trade debtors	E	¶9-050	P11
P12	Trade creditors	F	¶16-040	P12
P13	Total salary and wages expenses	G	¶16-520	P13
P14	Payments to associated persons	H	¶16-530	P14
P15	Intangible depreciating assets first deducted	I	¶17-280	P15
P16	Other depreciating assets first deducted	J	¶17-015	P16
P17	Termination value of intangible depreciating assets	D	¶17-640	P17
P18	Termination value of other depreciating assets	K	¶17-640	P18
P19	Trading stock election	P	¶9-245	P19

¶44-020 Instructions: Company tax return 2020

These instructions enable you to find explanations of each item in the Company Tax Return 2020. They also direct you to the relevant explanations in the ATO *Company tax return instructions*. ATO business industry codes can be found on the ATO website.

For lodgment requirements, see ¶24-010.

Return form item		Return form label	Explanation	Link to online instructions
	Substituted accounting period		¶9-010	
Company information				
	Tax file number		¶33-000	
	Australian business number		¶33-100	
3	Status of company			3
	Residence	C1	¶21-040	
	Permanent establishment	C2, C3	¶22-150	
	Cooperative	D1	¶3-420	
	Non-profit	D3	¶10-604	
	Strata title	D4	¶3-550	
	Pooled development fund	D5	¶3-555	

Return form item		Return form label	Explanation	Link to online instructions
	Limited partnership	D6	¶3-475	
	Corporate unit trust	D7		
	Public trading trust	D8	¶6-320	
	Private	D9	¶3-015	
	Public	D10	¶3-015	
	Business status	E1–E3		
	Small business entity	F1	¶7-050	
	Base rate entity	F2	¶3-055	
	Significant global entity	G1	¶30-200	
	Country by country reporting entity	G2	¶22-630	
	Consolidated head company	Z1	¶8-000	
	Consolidated subsidiary member	Z2	¶8-000	
4	Interposed entity election status	L	¶6-266	4
5	Country by country reporting entity	A, B	¶22-630	5
	Information statement			
6	Calculation of total profit or loss			
	Income			
	Gross payments subject to foreign resident withholding	B	¶26-265	6 B
	Gross payments where ABN not quoted	A	¶26-220, ¶33-130	6 A
	Other sales of goods and services	C	¶10-110	6 C
	Gross distribution from partnerships	D	¶5-130	6 D
	Gross distribution from trusts	E	¶6-110	6 E
	Forestry managed investment scheme income	X	¶18-020	6 X
	Gross interest	F	¶10-470	6 F
	Gross rent and other leasing and hiring income	G	¶10-500, ¶16-650	6 G
	Total dividends	H	¶4-100, ¶4-200	6 H
	Fringe benefit employee contributions	I	¶35-135	6 I
	Assessable government industry payments	Q	¶10-160	6 Q
	Unrealised gains on revaluation of assets to fair value	J	¶23-040	6 J
	Other gross income	R	¶10-110	6 R
	Expenses			
	Foreign resident withholding expenses	B	¶26-265	6 B

Return form item		Return form label	Explanation	Link to online instructions
	Cost of sales	A	¶9-160	6 A
	Contractor, sub-contractor and commission expenses	C	¶39-022, ¶16-520	6 C
	Superannuation expenses	D	¶13-710	6 D
	Bad debts	E	¶16-580	6 E
	Lease expenses	F, I	¶16-159, ¶16-060	6 F, I
	Rent expenses	H	¶16-640	6 H
	Interest expenses	V, J	¶16-740	6 V, J
	Royalty expenses	U, W	¶16-727	6 U, W
	Depreciation expenses	X	¶17-005	6 X
	Motor vehicle expenses	Y	¶16-310	6 Y
	Repairs and maintenance	Z	¶16-700	6 Z
	Unrealised losses on revaluation of assets to fair value	G	¶23-040	6 G
	All other expenses	S	¶16-152, ¶16-520, ¶17-630	6 S
7	Reconciliation to taxable income or loss			
	CGT event	G	¶11-240	7 G
	CGT exemption	M	¶11-640 – ¶11-900	7 M
	CGT rollover	M	¶12-035 – ¶12-555	7 M
	Net capital gain	A	¶11-030	7 A
	Non-deductible exempt income expenditure	U	¶16-880	7 U
	Franking credits	J	¶4-710	7 J
	Australian franking credits from a New Zealand company	C	¶4-490	7 C
	TOFA income from financial arrangements not included in item 6	E	¶23-020	7 E
	Other assessable income	B	¶10-005	7 B
	Assessable foreign exchange gains	B	¶23-075	
	Assessable balancing adjustments	B	¶17-630	
	Non-deductible expenses	W	¶16-005	7 W
	Accounting expenditure in item 6 subject to R&D tax incentive	D	¶20-150	7 D
	Section 46FA deductions for flow-on dividends	C	¶3-540	7 C
	Deduction for decline in value of depreciating assets	F	¶17-000	7 F

Return form item		Return form label	Explanation	Link to online instructions
	Forestry managed investment scheme deduction	U	¶18-125	7 U
	Immediate deduction for capital expenditure	E	¶19-010	7 E
	Deduction for project pool	H	¶19-050	7 H
	Capital works deductions	I	¶20-470	7 I
	Section 40-880 deduction	Z	¶16-156	7 Z
	Landcare operations and deduction for decline in value of water facility	N	¶18-100, ¶18-080	7 N
	Deduction for environmental protection expenses	O	¶19-110	7 O
	Offshore banking unit adjustment	P	¶21-080	7 P
	Exempt income	V	¶10-600	7 V
	Other income not included in assessable income	Q	¶10-005	7 Q
	TOFA deductions from financial arrangements not included in item 6	W	¶23-020	7 W
	Other deductible expenses	X	¶16-005	7 X
	Tax losses deducted	R	¶16-895	7 R
	Tax losses transferred in (from or to a foreign bank branch or a PE of a foreign financial entity)	S	¶3-090	7 S
8	Financial and other information			
	Functional currency translation rate	N	¶23-070	8 N
	Functional currency chosen	O	¶23-070	8 O
	Opening stock	A	¶9-170	8 A
	Purchases and other costs	S	¶9-160	8 S
	Closing stock	B	¶9-170	8 B
	Trading stock election		¶9-245	
	Trade debtors	C	¶9-050	8 C
	All current assets	D		8 D
	Total assets	E		8 E
	Trade creditors	F	¶16-040	8 F
	All current liabilities	G		8 G
	Total liabilities	H		8 H
	Total debt	J		8 J
	Commercial debt forgiveness	K	¶16-910	8 K
	Franked dividends paid	J	¶4-600	8 J
	Unfranked dividends paid	K	¶4-600	8 K
	Franking account balance	M	¶4-730	8 M
	Excess franking offsets	H	¶3-075	8 H

Return form item		Return form label	Explanation	Link to online instructions
	Loans to shareholders and their associates	N	¶4-200	8 N
	Total salary and wage expenses	D	¶16-520	8 D
	Payments to associated persons	Q	¶16-530	8 Q
	Gross foreign income	G	¶21-070	8 G
	Net foreign income	R	¶21-070	8 R
	Attributed foreign income			
	Listed country	B	¶21-200	8 B
	Unlisted country	U	¶21-200	8 U
	Transferor trust	V	¶21-300	8 V
	Total TOFA gains	T	¶23-035	8 T
	Total TOFA losses	U	¶23-035	8 U
	TOFA gains from unrealised movements in the value of financial arrangements	S	¶23-040	8 S
9	Capital allowances			
	Depreciating assets first deducted			
	Intangible depreciating assets first deducted	A	¶17-280	9 A
	Other depreciating assets first deducted	B	¶17-015	9 B
	Have you self-assessed the effective life of any of these assets?	C	¶17-270	9 C
	For all depreciating assets			
	Did you recalculate the effective life for any of your assets this income year?	D	¶17-270	9 D
	Total adjustable values at end of income year	E	¶17-485	9 E
	Assessable balancing adjustments on the disposal of intangible depreciating assets	F	¶17-630	9 F
	Deductible balancing adjustments on the disposal of intangible depreciating assets	G	¶17-630	9 G
	Termination value of intangible depreciating assets	H	¶17-640	9 H
	Termination value of other depreciating assets	I	¶17-640	9 I
	For entities connected with mining operations, exploration or prospecting			

Return form item		Return form label	Explanation	Link to online instructions
	Total mining capital expenditure and/or transport capital that you allocated to a project pool and for which you can claim a deduction this income year	J	¶19-010	9 J
	Total deduction for decline in value of intangible depreciating assets used in exploration or prospecting	K	¶19-010	9 K
	Total deduction for decline in value of other depreciating assets used in exploration or prospecting	L	¶19-010	9 L
10	Small business entity simplified depreciation			
	Deduction for certain assets	A	¶7-250	10 A
	Deduction for general small business pool	B	¶7-250	10 B
11	Consolidation deductions relating to rights to future income, consumable stores and work in progress			
	Pre-rules deductions	D	¶8-580	11 D
	Interim rules deductions	E	¶8-580	11 E
	Prospective rules deductions	F	¶8-580	11 F
12	National rental affordability scheme			
	National rental affordability scheme tax offset entitlement	J	¶20-600	12 J
13	Losses information			
	Tax losses carried forward to later income years	U	¶16-895, ¶3-060	13 U
	Net capital losses carried forward to later income years	V	¶11-040	13 V
14	Personal services income			
	Does your income include an individual's personal services income?	N	¶30-610	14 N
	Total amount of PSI included at item 6 income labels	A	¶30-610	14 A
	Total amount of deductions against PSI included at item 6 expense labels	B	¶30-630	14 B
	Did you satisfy the results test in respect of any individual?	C	¶30-665	14 C
	Do you hold a personal services business (PSB) determination in respect of any individual?	D	¶30-680	14 D
	Unrelated clients test	E1	¶30-670	14 E1

Return form item		Return form label	Explanation	Link to online instructions
	Employment test	E2	¶30-670	14 E2
	Business premises test	E3	¶30-670	14 E3
15	Licensed clubs only			
	Percentage of non-member income	A	¶3-820	15 A
16	Life insurance companies and friendly societies only			
	Complying superannuation class	B	¶3-515	16 B
	Net capital gain — complying superannuation class	C	¶11-038	16 C
	Net capital gain — ordinary class	D	¶11-030	16 D
	Assessable contributions	E	¶3-495	16 E
	Fees and charges	F	¶3-495	16 F
18	Pooled development funds			
	Small and medium-sized enterprises income	G	¶3-555	18 G
	Unregulated investment income	H	¶3-555	18 H
19	Retirement savings accounts (RSAs) providers only			
	No-TFN contributions income	U	¶3-530	19 U
	Income tax payable on no-TFN contributions income	X	¶3-530	19 X
	Net taxable income from RSAs	V	¶3-530	19 V
20	Foreign income tax offset	J	¶21-680	20 J
21	Research and development tax incentive			
	Non-refundable R&D tax offset	A	¶20-160	21 A
	Non-refundable R&D tax offset carried forward from previous year	B	¶20-160	21 B
	Non-refundable R&D tax offset to be utilised in current year	C	¶20-170	21 C
	Non-refundable R&D tax offset carried forward to next year	D	¶20-160	21 D
	Refundable R&D tax offset	U	¶20-160	21 U
	Feedstock adjustment — additional assessable income	W	¶20-180	21 W
22	Early stage venture capital limited partnership tax offset	L, P	¶5-040, ¶3-055	22 L, P
23	Early stage investor tax offset	M, R	¶20-700	23 M, R
25	Reportable tax position			
	Are you required to lodge a reportable tax position schedule?	B	¶3-045	25 B

Return form item		Return form label	Explanation	Link to online instructions
Overseas transactions or interests/thin capitalisation				
26	International related party dealings/ transfer pricing			
	Did you have any transactions or dealings with international related parties (irrespective of whether they were on revenue or capital account)?	X	¶22-580	26 X
27	Was the aggregate amount of the transactions or dealings with international related parties (including the value of property transferred or the balance outstanding on any loans) greater than $2 million?	Y	¶22-580	27 Y
28	Overseas interests			
	Did you have overseas branch operations or a direct or indirect interest in a foreign trust, foreign company, controlled foreign entity or transferor trust?	Z	¶21-105	28 Z
29	Thin capitalisation			
	Did the thin capitalisation provisions apply?	O	¶22-700	29 O
30	Transactions with specified countries			
	Did you directly or indirectly send to, or receive from, one of the countries specified in the instructions, any funds or property OR Do you have the ability or expectation to control, whether directly or indirectly, the disposition of any funds, property, assets or investments located in, or located elsewhere but controlled or managed from one of those countries?	I		30 I
Calculation statement				Calculation statement
	Taxable or net income	A	¶3-020	A
	Tax on taxable or net income	T1	¶3-055	T1
	R&D recoupment tax	M	¶20-180	M
	Gross tax	B		B
	Non-refundable non-carry forward tax offsets	C		C
	Subtotal 1	T2		T2

Return form item		Return form label	Explanation	Link to online instructions
	Non-refundable carry forward tax offsets	D		D
	Subtotal 2	T3		T3
	Refundable tax offsets	E		E
	Subtotal 3	T4		T4
	Franking deficit tax offset	F	¶4-780	F
	Tax payable	T5		T5
	Section 102AAM interest charge	G	¶6-130	G
	Credit for interest on early payments — amount of interest	H1	¶25-440	H1
	Credit for tax withheld — foreign resident withholding	H2	¶26-265	H2
	Credit for tax withheld where ABN is not quoted	H3	¶26-220	H3
	Tax withheld from interest or investments	H4	¶33-030	H4
	Credit for TFN amounts withheld from payments from closely held trusts	H5	¶26-200	H5
	Other credits	H7	¶6-120, ¶33-025	H7
	Credit for foreign resident capital gains withholding amounts	H8	¶26-269	H8
	Tax offset refunds (remainder of refundable tax offsets)	I		I
	PAYG instalments raised	K	¶27-100	K
	Amount due or refundable	S		S

¶44-040 Instructions: Partnership tax return 2020

These instructions enable you to find explanations of each item in the Partnership Tax Return 2020. They also direct you to the relevant explanations in the ATO *Partnership tax return instructions*. The ATO instructions are available online only; they are not available in print.

For lodgment requirements, see ¶24-010.

Return form item		Return form label	Explanation	Link to online instructions
Taxpayer details				
	Tax file number		¶33-000	
	Australian business number		¶33-100	
	Interposed entity election status		¶6-266	IEE status
1	Description of main business activity	A		1
2	Status of business	B1–B3, Z2		2

Return form item		Return form label	Explanation	Link to online instructions
	Significant global entity	G1	¶30-200	
	Country by country reporting entity	G2	¶22-630	
Income (excluding foreign income)				
5	Business income and expenses			
	Income			
	Gross payments where ABN not quoted	C, D	¶26-220, ¶33-130	5 C/D
	Gross payments subject to foreign resident withholding (excluding capital gains)	B	¶26-265	5 B
	Assessable government industry payments	E, F	¶10-160	5 E/F
	Other business income	G, H	¶10-110	5 G/H
	Expenses			
	Foreign resident withholding expenses (excluding capital gains)	P	¶26-265	5 P
	Contractor, sub-contractor and commission expenses	C	¶39-022, ¶16-520	5 C
	Superannuation expenses	D	¶13-710	5 D
	Cost of sales	E	¶9-160	5 E
	Bad debts	F	¶16-580	5 F
	Lease expenses	G	¶16-159, ¶16-060	5 G
	Rent expenses	H	¶16-640	5 H
	Total interest expenses	I	¶16-740, ¶22-700	5 I
	Total royalty expenses	J	¶16-727	5 J
	Depreciation expenses	K	¶17-005	5 K
	Motor vehicle expenses	L	¶16-310	5 L
	Repairs and maintenance	M	¶16-700	5 M
	All other expenses	N	¶16-152, ¶16-520, ¶17-630	5 N
	Reconciliation items			
	Income reconciliation adjustments	A		5 A
	Expense reconciliation adjustments	B		5 B
	Net small business income items	V		V
6	Tax withheld			
	Tax withheld where ABN not quoted	T	¶26-220	6 T

Return form item		Return form label	Explanation	Link to online instructions
	Credit for tax withheld — foreign resident withholding (excluding capital gains)	U	¶26-265	6 U
8	Partnerships and trusts			
	Primary production distribution from partnerships	A	¶5-130, ¶18-010, ¶18-200	8 A
	Primary production distribution from trusts	Z	¶6-110, ¶18-010, ¶18-200	8 Z
	Deductions relating to primary production income	S	¶5-130, ¶6-110	8 S
	Non-primary production distribution from partnerships	B	¶5-130	8 B
	Non-primary production distribution from trusts	R	¶6-110	8 R
	Deductions relating to non-primary production income	T	¶5-130, ¶6-110	8 T
	Franked distributions from trusts	F	¶4-860	8 F
	Deductions relating to franked distributions	G	¶4-860	8 G
	Credit for tax withheld where ABN not quoted	C	¶26-220	8 C
	Share of franking credits	D	¶4-860	8 D
	Share of credit for TFN amounts withheld from investment income	E	¶26-200	8 E
	Credit for TFN amounts withheld by closely held trusts	O	¶26-200	8 O
	Share of credit for tax withheld from foreign investment withholding	U	¶26-265	8 U
9	Rent	F	¶10-500	9
	Capital works deduction	X	¶20-470	
	Interest deductions and other rental	G, H	¶16-650	
10	Forestry managed investment scheme income	Q	¶18-125	10
11	Gross interest	I, J	¶10-470	11
12	Dividends	K, L, N	¶4-100, ¶4-200	12
	Franking credit	M	¶4-800	
14	Other Australian income	O		
	Gains on disposal of traditional securities		¶23-340	14-1
	Bonuses from life insurance companies and friendly societies		¶10-240	14-2

Return form item		Return form label	Explanation	Link to online instructions
	Bonuses credited from friendly society income bonds		¶3-470, ¶10-240	14-3
	Listed investment company capital gain		¶4-180	14-4
	Royalties		¶10-510	14-5
	Foreign exchange gains or losses		¶23-075	14-6
	TOFA amounts from financial arrangements		¶23-035	14-7
	Deductions			
16	Deductions relating to Australian investment income and franked distributions	P, R	¶16-660	16
17	Forestry managed investment scheme deductions	D	¶18-125	17
18	Other deductions	Q		
	Losses and outgoings		¶16-010	18-1
	Tax-related expenses		¶16-850	18-2
	Losses on disposal of traditional securities		¶23-340	18-3
	TOFA amounts from financial arrangements		¶23-035	18-4
	Payment of premiums to a non-resident insurer		¶22-110	18-5
	Gifts		¶16-940 and following	18-6
	Deductions for political contributions and gifts		¶16-950	18-7
	Subscriptions		¶16-430, ¶16-440	18-8
	Deductions for depreciating assets in a low-value pool		¶17-810	18-9
	Foreign income			
22	Attributed foreign income			22
	CFCs		¶21-200	
	Transferor trusts		¶21-300	
	Listed country	M	¶21-130	22 M
	Unlisted country	X	¶21-130	22 X
23	Other assessable foreign source income	B, V, Z, D	¶21-070	23
	Overseas transactions/thin capitalisation			
29	Overseas transactions	W, O, D, E, C	¶22-700, ¶22-580	29
	Personal services income			

Return form item		Return form label	Explanation	Link to online instructions
30	Personal services income	N, A–D, E1–E3	¶30-600	30
Taxation of financial arrangements				
31	Taxation of financial arrangements	L, M, N, O	¶23-035	31
32	Non-concessional MIT income			
	Business income	A–D	¶6-405, ¶26-267	32 A
	Partnerships and trusts	E–L		32 E
Key financial information				
33	All current assets	F		33
34	Total assets	G		34
35	All current liabilities	I		35
36	Total liabilities	J		36
Business and professional items				
37	Business name of main business			
38	Business address of main business			
39	Opening stock	C	¶9-170	39
40	Purchases and other costs	B	¶9-160	40
41	Closing stock	D	¶9-170	41
42	Trade debtors	E	¶9-050	42
43	Trade creditors	H	¶16-040	43
44	Total salary and wage expenses	L	¶16-520	44
45	Payments to associated persons	M	¶16-530	45
46	Fringe benefit employee contributions	T	¶35-135	46
47	Trading stock election		¶9-245	47
48	Capital allowances	A–K	¶17-015	48
49	Small business entity simplified depreciation	A, B	¶7-250	49
Miscellaneous				
50	National rental affordability scheme	F	¶20-600	50
51	Income tests	G, H	¶15-025	51
Statement of distribution				
52	Statement of distribution			
	Generally		¶5-070, ¶5-130 and following	52
	Uncontrolled partnership income		¶5-180 and following	52

¶44-060 Instructions: Trust tax return 2020

These instructions enable you to find explanations to each item in the Trust tax return 2020. They also direct you to the relevant explanations in the ATO *Trust tax return instructions 2020*. The instructions are available online only; they are not available in print.

For lodgment requirements, see ¶24-010.

Return form item		Return form label	Explanation	Link to online instructions
	Taxpayer details			
	Tax file number		¶33-000	
	Australian business number		¶33-100	
	Family trust election status		¶6-266	FTE status
	Interposed entity election status		¶6-266	IEE status
	Type of trust			Type of trust
	Also a charity?		¶10-605	Charity
	Managed investment trusts		¶6-400	MIT
	Is any tax payable by the trustee?		¶6-060	Tax payable
1	Description of main business activity	A		1
2	Status of business	B1–B3, Z2, G1, G2		2
	Income (excluding foreign income)			
5	Business income			
	gross payments where ABN not quoted	C, D	¶26-220, ¶33-130	5 C/D
	gross payments subject to foreign resident withholding (excluding capital gains)	B	¶26-265	5 B
	assessable government industry payments	E, F	¶10-160	5 E/F
	other business income	G, H	¶10-110	5 G/H
	Business expenses			
	foreign resident withholding expenses (excluding capital gains)	P	¶26-265	5 P
	contractor, sub-contractor and commission expenses	C	¶39-022, ¶16-520	5 C
	superannuation expenses	D	¶13-710	5 D
	cost of sales	E	¶9-160	5 E
	bad debts	F	¶16-580	5 F
	lease expenses	G	¶16-159, ¶16-060	5 G
	rent expenses	H	¶16-640	5 H
	total interest expenses	I	¶16-740, ¶22-700	5 I
	total royalty expenses	J	¶16-727	5 J

Return form item		Return form label	Explanation	Link to online instructions
	depreciation expenses	K	¶17-005	5 K
	motor vehicle expenses	L	¶16-310	5 L
	repairs and maintenance	M	¶16-700	5 M
	all other expenses	N	¶16-152, ¶16-520, ¶17-630	5 N
	Reconciliation items			
	income reconciliation adjustments	A		5 A
	expense reconciliation adjustments	B		5 B
	Net small business income	V		V
6	Tax withheld			
	tax withheld where ABN not quoted	T	¶26-220	6 T
	credit for tax withheld — foreign resident withholding (excluding capital gains)	U	¶26-265	6 U
7	Credit for interest on early payments — amount of interest	W	¶25-440	7
8	Partnerships and trusts			
	primary production — distribution from partnerships	A	¶5-130, ¶18-010, ¶18-200	8 A
	primary production — share of net income from trusts	Z	¶6-110, ¶18-010, ¶18-200	8 Z
	deductions relating to primary production income	S	¶5-130, ¶6-110	8 S
	non-primary production — distribution from partnerships	B	¶5-130	8 B
	non-primary production — share of net income from trusts	R	¶6-110	8 R
	deductions relating to non-primary production income	T	¶5-130, ¶6-110	8 T
	franked distributions from trusts	F	¶4-860	8 F
	deductions relating to franked distributions	G	¶4-860	8 G
	credit for tax withheld where ABN not quoted	C	¶26-220	8 C
	share of franking credits	D	¶4-860	8 D
	share of credit for TFN amounts withheld from investment income	E	¶26-200	8 E
	credit for TFN amounts withheld from payments from closely held trusts	O	¶26-200	8 O

Return form item		Return form label	Explanation	Link to online instructions
	share of credit for tax withheld from foreign resident withholding	U	¶26-265	8 U
9	Rent	F	¶10-500	9
	Capital works deduction	X	¶20-470	9 X
	Interest deductions and Other rental deductions	G, H	¶16-650	9 G
10	Forestry managed investment scheme income	Q	¶18-125	10
11	Gross interest	I, J	¶10-470	11
12	Dividends	K, L, N	¶4-100, ¶4-200	12
	Franking credit	M	¶4-800	
13	Superannuation lump sums and employment termination payments			
	superannuation death benefits	V, W	¶14-280, ¶14-270	13 V/W
	death benefit employment termination payments	X, Y	¶14-680	13 X/Y
14	Other Australian income	O		
	gains on disposal of traditional securities		¶23-340	14-1
	bonuses from life insurance companies and friendly societies		¶10-240	14-2
	bonuses credited from friendly society income bonds		¶3-470, ¶10-240	14-3
	listed investment company capital gain		¶4-180	14-4
	royalties		¶10-510	14-5
	foreign exchange gains or losses		¶23-075	14-6
	excepted net income		¶2-210	14-7
	TOFA amounts from financial arrangements		¶23-035	14-8
	Deductions			
16	Deductions relating to Australian investment income and franked distributions	P, R	¶16-660	16
17	Forestry managed investment scheme deductions	D	¶18-125	17
18	Other deductions	Q		
	losses and outgoings		¶16-010	18-1
	interest expenses		¶16-742	18-2
	tax-related expenses		¶16-850	18-3
	losses on disposal of traditional securities		¶23-340	18-4
	TOFA amounts from financial arrangements		¶23-035	18-5

Return form item		Return form label	Explanation	Link to online instructions
	payment of premiums to a non-resident insurer		¶22-110	18-6
	gifts		¶16-940 and following	18-7
	deductions for political contributions and gifts		¶16-950	18-8
	subscriptions		¶16-430, ¶16-440	18-9
	deductions for depreciating assets in a low-value pool		¶17-810	18-10
	film industry incentives		¶20-330	18-11
Capital gains				
21	Capital gains	G, M, A, B	¶11-000, ¶26-265	21
Foreign income				
22	Attributed foreign income			
	CFCs	S	¶21-200	22 S
	transferor trusts	S	¶21-300	22 S
	listed country	M	¶21-130	22 M
	unlisted country	X	¶21-130	22 X
23	Other assessable foreign source income	B, V, Z, D	¶21-070	23
Losses				
25	Tax losses deducted	C	¶6-262, ¶16-880	25
27	Losses information (income tax)	U	¶16-895	27 U
	Losses information (net capital losses)	V	¶11-040	27 V
Tax offsets				
28	Landcare and water facility tax offset	G	¶18-100, ¶18-080	28
Overseas transactions/thin capitalisation				
29	Overseas transactions	W, O, D, E, A, C	¶22-700, ¶22-580	29
Personal services income				
30	Personal services income	N, A–D, E1–E3	¶30-600	30
Taxation of financial arrangements				
31	Taxation of financial arrangements	M–N	¶23-035	31
32	Non-concessional MIT income			
	Business income	A–D	¶6-405, ¶26-267	32 A

Return form item		Return form label	Explanation	Link to online instructions
	Partnerships and trusts	E–L		32 E
	Capital gains	X, Z		32 X
	Key financial information			
33	All current assets	F		33
34	Total assets	G		34
35	All current liabilities	I		35
36	Total liabilities	J		36
	Business and professional items			
37	Business name of main business			
38	Business address of main business			
39	Opening stock	C	¶9-170	39
40	Purchases and other costs	B	¶9-160	40
41	Closing stock	D	¶9-170	41
42	Trade debtors	E	¶9-050	42
43	Trade creditors	H	¶16-040	43
44	Total salary and wage expenses	L	¶16-520	44
45	Payments to associated persons	M	¶16-530	45
46	Fringe benefit employee contributions	T	¶35-135	46
47	Unpaid present entitlement to a private company	Y	¶4-246	47
48	Trading stock election		¶9-245	48
49	Capital allowances	A–L	¶17-015	49
50	Small business entity simplified depreciation	A, B	¶7-250	50
	Miscellaneous			
51	National rental affordability scheme tax offset	F	¶20-600	51
52	Other refundable tax offsets (exploration credit tax offset)	G	¶19-010	52
53	Non-refundable carry-forward tax offsets			
	Early stage venture capital limited partnership	H	¶5-040	53 H
	Early stage investor tax offset	I	¶20-700	53 I
54	Medicare levy reduction or exemption	A–D	¶6-250	54
55	Income of the trust estate	A	¶6-085	55
	Statement of distribution			
56	Statement of distribution			
	generally		¶6-110 and following	56
	small business income tax offset information	Y	¶7-210	56 Y
	non-resident beneficiary additional information	J, K	¶6-220	56 J/K

Return form item		Return form label	Explanation	Link to online instructions
	trustee beneficiary statement information	P, Q	¶6-275	56 P/Q
	annual trustee payment report information	S, T	¶26-200	56 S/T
57	Choice for resident trustee to be assessed on capital gains	X, Y	¶11-060	57
58	Beneficiary under legal disability who is presently entitled to income from another trust		¶6-120	58
59	Non-resident trust		¶6-075	59

¶44-100 Tax records checklist

This checklist, based on information published by the ATO, shows the principal types of tax records that may commonly need to be kept by individual taxpayers, together with cross-references to further explanation in the Guide. The tax record keeping requirements are discussed at ¶9-045.

(1) Payments received as income

Salary, wages and allowances

To confirm amounts received and tax withheld:

- PAYG payment summary (¶26-640)
- employment income statement (under Single Touch Payroll), or
- signed letter or statement from employer.

Recipients of JobKeeper payments will have those payments included in the payment summary (or income statement) from their employers including any PAYG tax withheld.

Income from interest, dividends, managed funds and rental properties

To confirm amount and type of income received:

- statement, passbook or other documentation from financial institution showing interest received (¶10-470)
- statement from company, etc, showing amount of franked and unfranked dividends, amount of imputation credits and any TFN amounts withheld from unfranked dividends (¶4-400)
- statement or advice from managed fund showing amount of distribution, including primary production and non-primary production components, capital gains or losses, foreign income and share of credits such as imputation credits, or
- record of rent received, eg statement from property agent, rent book or bank statements showing rent transferred into taxpayer's account, and records of bond money retained in lieu of rent (¶10-500).

Benefits, pensions and annuities

To confirm amounts received and tax withheld:

- PAYG payment summary (or employment income statement) (¶26-640), or
- signed letter or statement from paying agency or fund.

(2) Car and travel expenses

Cents per kilometre method (¶16-370)

- Records showing calculation of business kilometres travelled and the amount of the claim, eg diary entries and documents to show the engine capacity of the car.

Logbook method (¶16-350)

- Odometer readings for the start and end of the period being claimed.
- Business usage percentage based on the logbook.
- Receipts for fuel and oil expenses or a reasonable estimate based on odometer readings.
- Receipts or other documents showing other expenses related to the car, eg registration, insurance, lease payments, services, tyres, repairs, interest charges.

For the logbook to be valid it must cover at least 12 continuous weeks and show:

- when the logbook period begins and ends
- the car's odometer readings at the start and end of the logbook period
- the total kilometres travelled in the logbook period
- the kilometres travelled for work activities based on journeys recorded in the logbook. In recording the journeys you need the start and finishing dates of the journey, the odometer readings at the start and end of the journey; kilometres travelled and the reason for the journey
- the business use percentage for the logbook period.

The logbook is valid for five years, unless specific rules require a new logbook to be kept earlier. For the year ending 30 June 2021, the logbook must begin on or after 1 July 2016.

Travel expenses (¶16-300, ¶16-210)

These records may include:

- a travel diary showing the dates, places, times and duration of your activities and travel
- written evidence of your travel expenses, eg receipts, invoices and travel allowance details
- in relation to award transport payments (¶16-210) — if you claim up to the value of the award that was in force on 29 October 1986, no written evidence is required. If you choose to claim more than this amount, written evidence is required for the whole of the amount claimed
- receipts for actual costs incurred for using a car owned or leased by someone else, eg petrol and oil
- receipts or other documents showing the amount and date of the expenditure in relation to vehicles other than cars, eg motor cycles, utilities or panel vans with a carrying capacity of one tonne or more, or any other vehicle with a carrying capacity of nine or more passengers
- receipts or other documents (diary entries) for air, bus, train, tram and taxi fares, bridge and road tolls, parking and car hire fees.

The documentation required for travel depends on the length of stay and whether a travel allowance has been received. Where a travel allowance is received, and you restrict your claim to the Commissioner's reasonable amount, you do not need to keep written evidence of the expenses incurred (¶16-210).

(3) Other expenses relating to business or work

Clothing, uniforms, sun protection

- Receipts for uniforms, occupation-specific and protective clothing.
- Basis for claim for laundry costs if less than $150; diary entries or receipts for claims greater than $150.
- Receipts for dry cleaning costs.
- Receipts for sun protection items (¶16-180, ¶16-210).

Self-education

- Receipts for expenses such as course fees, textbooks, stationery, decline in value of (and repairs to) depreciating assets (¶16-450).
- Receipts, documents or diary entries relating to travel expenses (¶16-300).

Other work-related expenses

- Receipts, other documents or diary entries recording expenses, eg diary maintained over representative period to support apportionment of computer, home office expenses (¶16-480).
- Taxpayers claiming the COVID-19 ''shortcut rate'' of 80 cents per hour are required to keep a record of the specific hours they worked at home in order to claim the higher rate (¶16-480).
- Receipts for expenses related to decline in value of depreciating assets.
- PAYG payment summaries (or employment income statement) showing union dues, overtime meal allowances, etc (¶26-640).

Rental expenses

- Documents such as bank statements showing interest charged on money borrowed on rental property.
- Receipts or other documents showing other property expenses, eg advertising, bank charges, council rates, gardening, property agent fees, repairs, maintenance.
- Documents showing details of expenses related to decline in value of depreciating assets or any capital work expenses, eg structural improvements (¶16-650).

(4) Acquisitions and disposals

For CGT purposes (¶11-180; ¶11-920):

- Documents showing dates of acquisition of asset and the date the CGT event occurred, eg contract for purchase or sale, dividend reinvestment statement.
- Document showing amount and date of expenditure in relation to asset, eg council rate notices for vacant block of land.
- Records of net capital losses from previous years.

(5) Gifts

To claim a concessional deduction for gifts (¶16-942):

- receipts for donations or contributions

- where donations made through your pay, PAYG payment summary (or employment income statement) or signed letter from donee organisation.

¶44-103 Employers' tax checklist

This checklist, prepared with the assistance of information from www.ato.gov.au, sets out the main tax-related obligations of employers in relation to their employees.

Pay As You Go (PAYG)

- Register for PAYG withholding (¶26-600).
- Determine whether relationship is that of employer/employee for PAYG purposes (¶26-150).
- Where employee provides a TFN declaration, complete and forward the original to the ATO within 14 days (¶26-350). An optional arrangement can be made using the Commissioner's online service from 1 January 2017.
- Ensure employer is using Single Touch Payroll software to pay employees and report to ATO. Prior to 1 July 2019, Single Touch Payroll was necessary only for employers of 20 or more staff (¶26-630).
- For each employee payment period, withhold appropriate PAYG amounts from payments to employees (¶26-130). This includes payments made to employees where the employer will be reimbursed for JobKeeper periods.
- For each ATO reporting period, report and pay amounts withheld to the ATO (¶26-620, ¶27-170, ¶27-200). Failure to do so may result in PAYG and salaries being non-deductible (¶26-620).
- By 14 July each year, provide a payment summary to each employee (¶26-640). For employers using Single Touch Payroll there is no longer an obligation to supply payment summaries to employees as amounts are disclosed to ATO.
- By 14 August each year, provide an annual report to the ATO (¶26-620).
- Keep the necessary records (¶26-720).

Superannuation guarantee

- Determine if the employee is eligible for superannuation support under the superannuation guarantee scheme (¶39-020).
- Ensure compliance with choice of fund rules (¶39-260).
- For each quarter, calculate required level of superannuation support for employee, based on ordinary time earnings (¶39-200, ¶39-230).
- Superannuation guarantee is only required for employee's on JobKeeper payment where it relates to the actual performance of work by the employee (¶39-030).
- Superannuation guarantee is not required for an employee if an employer shortfall exemption certificate is received for an applicable quarter (¶39-030). This applies in limited circumstances. Ensure superannuation guarantee is not reduced because of an employee's salary sacrifice (¶39-240).
- Pay appropriate superannuation contributions for employee within 28 days of end of quarter (¶39-240).
- Pass on employee's tax file number to fund (¶33-025).
- Where there is a shortfall in the contributions made, lodge a superannuation guarantee statement by the 28th day of the second month after the quarter, and pay the relevant amount of the superannuation guarantee charge (¶39-500).

- Claim appropriate deduction for SG contributions (not the SG charge) (¶13-710).
- Check whether there is an obligation to notify employee of contribution which arises under award or workplace relations law (¶39-240).
- Keep the necessary records (¶39-510).

Fringe benefits tax

- Determine if there is a benefit to be provided to an employee or employee's associate (¶35-060).
- Determine if the benefit is a taxable fringe benefit (¶35-060 – ¶35-120).
- Where there is a salary sacrifice arrangement, check effectiveness under ATO requirements (¶31-120).
- Pay FBT instalments, if applicable, for the quarters ending 30 June, 30 September, 31 December and 31 March (¶35-050).
- Lodge annual FBT return with the ATO and pay balance of FBT by 21 May each year (¶35-030, ¶35-050).
- Include reportable fringe benefits in employee's annual payment summary (¶35-055).
- Keep the necessary records (¶35-690).

Payroll tax

- Determine whether relationship is that of employer/employee for payroll tax purposes (¶36-010).
- Determine whether an exemption applies (¶36-060).
- Register within appropriate time (¶36-020).
- Comply with "group" requirements where relevant (¶36-110).
- Determine what payments constitute wages (¶36-050).
- Determine whether wages exceed threshold, where relevant (¶36-030).
- Pay payroll tax as required (¶36-010).

Extra requirements on cessation of employment

- Include the details of any final payments made to the employee in the PAYG payment summary (or employment income statement) (¶26-640).
- Forward payment summary to the employee by 14 July, or earlier if requested (¶26-640).
- Calculate and pay any final SG contributions (¶39-240).
- Determine whether there is an employment termination payment (ETP), and the amount to be withheld (¶14-610, ¶26-130, ¶26-180).
- Provide a "PAYG payment summary — employment termination payment" to the employee within 14 days of the ETP being paid to the employee (¶26-640). This requirement is not necessary if you are using Single Touch Payroll software as an employment income statement is provided directly to an employee.
- Include ETP details in the annual report to the Commissioner (¶26-620).

¶44-105 Small business tax concessions checklist

The checklist below identifies special tax exemptions and concessions that apply to small businesses, and provides cross-references to further detail.

Income tax

- Small business companies are taxed at a lower corporate rate of 27.5% from 2016–17. The aggregated turnover thresholds for the lower tax rate are $10 million in 2016–17, $25 million for 2017–18 and $50 million for 2018–19 (¶3-055). Lower rate of tax only applies if company has less than 20% of assessable income from passive sources (¶42-025).
- The lower tax rates for base rate entities has been moved forward to 26% for 2020–21 and 25% for 2021–22 onwards.
- Individual taxpayers with business income from an unincorporated business that has an aggregated turnover of less than $5 million will receive an 8% tax discount from the 2016–17 income year (¶7-210). This will increase to 13% for 2020–21 and 16% for 2021–22.
- Prepayments made by small business entities are entitled to concessional treatment (¶16-045). The small business entity threshold for prepayments has moved from $10 million to $50 million from 1 July 2020.
- An immediate write-off is available for assets costing less than $150,000 first used or installed ready for use from 12 March 2020 to 31 December 2020. Subsequently, assets of any value may be immediately written-off if held and first used or installed ready for use from 6 October 2020 (7:30 pm AEDT) to 30 June 2022 under full expensing rules. Various other limits apply for time periods before 12 March 2020 (¶7-050, ¶7-250).
- Accelerated deductions are available for pooled assets costing over $150,000 and purchased and first used or installed ready for use from 12 March 2020 to 31 December 2020. The deduction in the first year is 57.5% (¶7-050, ¶7-250). Small businesses also have the option to write-off the entire balance of the pool during the full expensing regime.
- Entities with aggregated turnover less than $50 million (¶7-050) with trading stock of less than $5,000 need not bring their stock to account, and any change in the value of trading stock need not be brought to account until the change exceeds $5,000 (¶7-050, ¶7-260).
- An entity with less than $50 million in aggregated turnover (¶7-050) will generally be eligible for a two-year amendment period for tax assessments (instead of four years) (¶25-310, ¶25-310).

Capital gains tax

- The basic conditions for eligibility for small business CGT concessions is to satisfy the $6 million net asset value test (¶7-130) or the $2 million aggregated turnover test (¶7-050) for the income year (¶7-120).
- CGT may not be payable by small businesses on capital gains from assets held for at least 15 years (¶7-165).
- CGT is discounted by 50% for small business active assets (¶7-175).
- Capital gains from small business assets may be exempt from CGT if the proceeds are used in connection with retirement (¶7-185).
- Capital gains from small business assets may be rolled over for two years or more if replacement assets are acquired (¶7-195).

- To qualify for CGT concessions, the asset sold by the small business must be an active asset (¶7-145).

- The CGT small business roll-over allows a restructure from one type of entity to another as long as ultimate economic ownership is maintained (¶12-380).

Goods and services tax

- Small business entities (¶7-050) and non-business entities with GST turnovers not exceeding $2 million can elect to lodge returns annually and pay GST by quarterly instalments (¶34-150, ¶34-150).

- Small business (¶7-050) and non-profit entities that are voluntarily registered for GST have the option of reporting and paying their GST on an annual basis (¶34-150).

- Registration is not compulsory for businesses with a GST turnover of less than $75,000 (¶34-100).

- Monthly tax periods are optional for businesses with a GST turnover of less than $20 million (¶34-120).

- The cash basis of accounting may be used by small business entities (¶7-050) and non-business entities with GST turnovers not exceeding $2 million (¶34-130, ¶34-130).

- A small business entity (¶7-050) can apportion GST input tax credits on an annual basis (¶34-270).

- Electronic lodgment and payment is not compulsory for businesses with a GST turnover of less than $20 million (¶34-150).

- Simplified accounting methods apply to small food retailers and certain other businesses with aggregated turnover less than $50 million (¶34-165).

- Input tax credits can be claimed on certain acquisitions related to making financial supplies if the credits do not exceed a specified threshold (¶34-190).

PAYG

- Entities with aggregated turnover less than $50 million are eligible to pay PAYG instalments based on GDP-adjusted notional tax (¶27-220, ¶27-470).

Fringe benefits tax

- Employers with aggregated turnover less than $50 million may provide car parking to employees and have an exemption from FBT (¶35-254, ¶35-254).

Payroll tax

- Employers with average wage bills below specified thresholds, varying from state to state, are not liable for payroll tax (¶36-030).

¶44-106 Online business tax checklist

- The timing of a contract made online may affect issues such as when income is derived (¶9-050) or deductions incurred (¶16-040), the date of acquisition and disposal of assets for CGT purposes (¶11-440) and year end tax planning (¶31-700).

- The place where an online contract is made is generally the place where the last act necessary for conclusion of the contract is performed. This may affect the source of the income (¶21-070).

- The ATO considers that a non-resident does not have a permanent establishment in Australia solely as a result of selling trading stock through an internet website hosted by an Australian resident internet service provider (¶22-150).
- Expenditure on computer maintenance, testing, code reviews, minor alterations and modifications, and remedying defects, may be deductible (¶16-725).
- Ongoing operating expenses of commercial websites are deductible in the year in which they are incurred as a recurrent cost of business. To the extent that the expenditure is on software (¶17-370), the cost may be depreciable, although immediate deductions for software are available in limited situations (¶16-725).
- The cost of computer hardware may be depreciable (¶16-725).
- Copyright in a computer program is a depreciating asset (¶17-015).
- Depending on the circumstances, payments for computer software from overseas suppliers may either be considered to be royalties (and therefore subject to withholding tax), or payments for goods (¶10-510).
- Where a software licence agreement covers both distribution rights as well as intellectual property rights, it may need to be determined whether withholding tax can be limited to the component relating to intellectual property rights (¶22-030).
- An FBT exemption applies to certain work-related internet access (¶35-645).

Enforcement and administration

- Existing problems of tax enforcement in relation to undeclared cash dealings (the ''black economy'') may be increased by the development of electronic payments systems and currency, such as ''bitcoin'' (¶30-005).
- The international nature of much online business may give rise to issues under the transfer pricing rules (¶22-580).
- Records must be kept of all tax-relevant electronic transactions (¶9-045).
- Sales suppression tools are illegal for use in electronic record keeping (¶29-310, ¶30-005).
- Guidelines on electronic tax records have been issued on security, encryption and access issues (¶9-045).
- The ATO conducts an ''online selling data matching program'' which examines tax compliance by individuals and businesses that sell goods and services through online selling sites (¶25-200).
- The government and the ATO are attempting to improve their methods for detecting identity fraud (¶25-200).

GST issues

For a more comprehensive GST checklist see the Australian Master GST Guide.

- As online business transactions often cross national borders, questions may arise about whether there is a sufficient connection with Australia to authorise the application of GST (¶34-105).
- GST generally applies to imported goods with a customs value of no more than $1,000 (¶34-250).
- The ''reverse charge'' rules may apply where there are acquisitions from overseas, for example where computer services are accessed from overseas by an Australian financial institution (¶34-250).

- A GST exemption applies to exports (¶34-165).

- Tax invoices and adjustment notes may be issued and stored electronically (¶34-140, ¶34-145).

¶44-107 Rental properties checklist

Acquiring and selling a rental property

- Travel and other expenses (such as agents' fees or the cost of newspapers) incurred during the process of searching for a suitable rental property to purchase are normally not deductible, and do not form part of the cost base of the property for CGT purposes (¶11-550, ¶16-650).

- Where a rental property is purchased as a long-term rental investment, the cost is normally not deductible, but it may form part of the cost base for CGT purposes (¶16-650). Any gain arising on the eventual sale will normally not be assessable as income, but CGT may apply, assuming that the property was not pre-CGT (¶10-340, ¶11-250).

- If the purpose of purchasing a rental property is to make a one-off speculative profit on buying and selling the property within a relatively short time-frame, any gain on that sale will be assessable and any loss deductible (¶10-340). Although the CGT provisions will also apply, any assessable capital gain would be reduced by the income amount otherwise included in the taxpayer's assessable income (¶11-690).

- Interest on funds borrowed to purchase a rental property is normally deductible. If the taxpayer constructs a new rental property, from 1 July 2019 a deduction **is not** available for interest incurred during the construction of the property (¶16-740, ¶16-650).

- If the taxpayer constructs a new rental property, it may be treated as a separate CGT asset from the land if the land is pre-CGT or a balancing adjustment applies. If the taxpayer makes a capital improvement to a pre-CGT building, the building and the improvement may be treated as separate assets if the improvement is ''substantial'' (¶11-410).

- If the taxpayer constructs a new rental property, certain costs will qualify for capital allowance at an annual rate of 2.5% (¶20-470).

- Stamp duty on the transfer of a property forms part of the property's CGT cost base (¶11-550).

- Certain expenditure incurred in connection with the continuing ownership of the property may be added to the third element of the cost base (¶11-550). This includes costs of ownership where the property is not being used for income-producing purposes.

- The initial expenses associated with borrowing money to purchase a rental property may be written off over a period of years (¶16-800).

- A deduction is available for the expense of discharging a mortgage over a property that has been used solely for the purpose of earning assessable income (¶16-800).

- If a rental property is owned by an individual taxpayer and has at some stage also been used as the taxpayer's ''main residence'', the taxpayer may be entitled to a partial CGT exemption (¶11-760). However, this exemption is not available if the individual is a non-resident at the time of sale (¶11-750).

- An additional CGT discount of up to 10% is available for individuals who invest in affordable housing from 1 January 2018 (¶11-036). Generally, the property is required to be rented to affordable housing tenants for an aggregate period of three years.

Assessability of rent

- The mere receipt of a bond by a taxpayer does not constitute assessable income. However, to the extent that the bond is actually retained in lieu of unpaid rent, the amount retained may be assessable income (¶10-020). Bond moneys retained to pay for deductible repairs may be offset against the deduction (¶16-700). Amounts received from the lessee for non-compliance with a lease obligation to repair business premises are assessable (¶10-500).
- Rental income is assessable to the lessor (¶10-500).
- The ownership of an investment property does not of itself constitute a business and, therefore, a taxpayer will only be assessable on rent that is actually received in the year of income (¶9-050).
- If a taxpayer's entitlement to retain prepaid rental amounts is irrevocable, the prepayment is assessable in the year of receipt. If the entitlement to retain the prepayment is conditional, it may be that the prepayment can be apportioned (¶9-090).
- A genuine lease premium is a capital receipt, and not assessable as income (¶10-500).

Deductibility of expenses

- Interest on funds borrowed to purchase a rental property is normally deductible. However, if the taxpayer constructs a new rental property, a deduction is not available for interest incurred until the construction of the property is completed, and the property is genuinely available for rent (¶16-740, ¶16-650).
- A taxpayer may claim a deduction for interest on money borrowed to purchase items for a rental property, such as furniture, and to pay expenses associated with repairing, maintaining or upgrading a property (¶16-740).
- In appropriate circumstances, negative gearing can provide tax benefits (¶16-740, ¶31-170). A taxpayer may also be able to apply for reduced levels of PAYG instalments to reflect the reduction in taxable income resulting from the accruing rental loss (¶26-130).
- Expenses incurred by a taxpayer for the purpose of deriving assessable rental income are normally deductible. These include documentation and legal expenses, advertising, agents' fees and administrative expenses, insurance, council and water rates, land tax and strata body corporate contributions but not travel expenses to collect rent or to inspect the property from 1 July 2017 (¶16-650).
- A deduction is available for expenses incurred on repairs to a property and depreciating assets associated with the property. The deduction does not apply if the repairs are of a capital nature, eg where they make the property or asset functionally superior to its previous condition or where the damage was present at the time the property was purchased (¶16-700).
- Amounts paid by the lessee for non-compliance with a lease obligation to repair business premises are deductible (and assessable to the lessor) (¶10-500, ¶16-640).
- When a property is not held solely for the purpose of earning assessable income, a taxpayer must apportion expenses between the income-producing activities and other activities (¶16-070).

Capital allowances

- If the taxpayer constructs a new rental property, certain costs will qualify for capital allowance at an annual rate of 2.5% (¶20-470).
- A taxpayer can claim a deduction for the decline in value (formerly ''depreciation'') of furniture and fittings in the rental property but for furniture and fittings purchased after 9 May 2017, only the original purchaser will be entitled to the deduction (¶17-040, ¶16-650).
- A ''balancing adjustment'' may be required when the taxpayer stops holding a depreciating asset. The adjustment is generally based on the difference between the value of the asset when the taxpayer stops holding it and its adjustable value (¶17-630).

Special holding structures

- When a rental property is held by two or more people jointly, each partner accounts for their share of the net partnership income or loss according to their ownership interests in the property. If the rental property forms part of a wider business activity carried on in partnership, then the net income or loss from the property may be distributed in accordance with the terms of the partnership agreement (¶31-520).
- Special tax considerations may apply where a rental property is held by a company (¶31-530), a family trust (¶31-540) or a unit trust (¶31-560).
- A refundable tax offset may be available where the investor participates in the National Rental Affordability Scheme (¶20-605).

¶44-108 Family home tax checklist

See also the checklists for Rental Properties (¶44-107) and Death of a Taxpayer (¶44-170).

Acquiring the home

- If the home is acquired in the name of a company, the CGT main residence exemption and the CGT discount will not apply on its subsequent disposal (¶11-033, ¶11-730).
- If the home is acquired in the name of an ordinary trust, the CGT main residence exemption does not apply and special rules will apply in determining the CGT discount on its subsequent disposal (¶11-060, ¶11-730).
- Interest on a loan used to finance the purchase of a home would generally not be deductible except to the extent that the home also serves as a place of business (¶16-740).
- Duty on the conveyance is payable by the purchaser, though in some cases reduced rates or other concessions may apply, eg for first home buyers (¶37-020).
- Special land-rich entity rules may apply to prevent exploitation (¶37-030).
- When purchasing the home, the vendor is required to provide a clearance certificate to ensure that no foreign resident CGT withholding applies (¶26-269).

Using the home for work or investment

- Rent derived by the owner where all or part of the home is rented out is assessable, though this may not apply to certain domestic arrangements (¶10-500).
- Relevant expenses incurred in deriving assessable rent are deductible (¶16-650).

- Where the home is also a place of business, eg where a doctor uses part of the home as a surgery, appropriate deductions may be claimed for expenses such as running costs and mortgage interest (¶16-480).
- Where the home is also a place of business, travel between it and other places of the taxpayer's business may be deductible. Otherwise, travel between home and work is normally not deductible, though there are some exceptions (¶16-220, ¶16-230).
- Where the home is simply used as a ''home office'' to do some work, as distinct from being a place of business, appropriate deductions may be claimed for expenses such as running costs (¶16-480). A special rate applies during the COVID-19 pandemic for individuals working from home.
- Land tax generally does not apply to land used as the owner's principal residence, though a proportional liability may apply where the home is used partly for carrying on a business (eg ¶38-010).
- A person's interest in their principal home is exempt from the social security assets test that is used for determining eligibility for certain government pensions and entitlements (www.humanservices.gov.au/individuals/centrelink).

Selling the home

- The sale of a home is exempt from CGT where it qualifies as the taxpayer's main residence, or where the taxpayer acquired it before 20 September 1985 (¶11-000, ¶11-730).
- The main residence exemption may apply where the taxpayer is an individual, or in certain situations where the taxpayer is the trustee of a special disability trust or a deceased estate (¶11-730, ¶11-770).
- The main residence exemption (full or partial) is not available to individuals who are non-residents at the time of sale (¶11-330, ¶11-750). However, grandfathering rules apply for properties purchased before 9 May 2017 and sold before 30 June 2020.
- The main residence exemption extends to certain adjacent land (¶11-730).
- Special rules apply to periods of absence, changing main residences, replacement main residences and building a main residence (¶11-740).
- In certain circumstances, the main residence exemption can apply to moneys received from a forfeited deposit if the contract for sale falls through (¶11-730).
- A pro rata exemption may apply where the home is used partly for income-producing activities (¶11-760).
- Where a deceased taxpayer's main residence is inherited, the exemption may apply to a subsequent sale where it takes place within two years of the date of death or in certain other circumstances (¶11-770).
- Roll-over relief may apply where there is a transfer as part of a settlement pursuant to a marriage or relationship breakdown (¶12-460).

GST implications

- GST generally would not apply on the sale of a family home, as the sale would not normally be in the course of an enterprise, or would be input taxed. However, GST may apply where, for example, a new home is sold by a GST-registered builder (¶34-100, ¶34-230).
- GST would not apply to the letting of a home as this is an input taxed supply (¶34-100).

- Where GST is payable on the sale, a (registered) purchaser may be able to claim partial input tax credits where part of the house is to be used for business purposes, though not where they are simply intending to let out the house (¶34-100).
- Where the sale is taxable, exposure to GST may be limited by adoption of the margin scheme (¶34-100, ¶34-230).

¶44-110 Motor vehicles checklist

Acquisition, financing and disposal

- Under a simple lease, the lessor is assessable on the lease payments and can claim depreciation on the vehicle. The lessee can claim deductions for the lease payments to the extent the vehicle is used for income producing purposes (¶10-500, ¶16-640).
- If the lessee has the right or obligation to purchase the vehicle, the arrangement will normally be treated as a hire purchase arrangement. Rental payment may be treated as part purchase payments where there are unreal residual values in the lease (¶16-310, ¶23-250).
- There are tax implications where a lease is fully or partly novated (¶16-310).
- There are tax implications where there is a sale and leaseback arrangement (¶23-240).
- Special rules apply to leases of luxury cars (¶17-220).
- Capital gains and losses on cars, motor cycles and similar vehicles are disregarded. The same applies where compensation is received for the loss of the car (¶11-640).
- Capital gains and losses are also generally disregarded on the disposal of depreciable business vehicles, or vehicles that are trading stock (¶11-700).
- A vehicle that is not used in business and is not a GST-exempt motor car, motor cycle or similar vehicle would generally be treated as a ‘‘personal use’’ asset for CGT purposes (¶11-400).
- A motor vehicle can qualify as an active asset for the purpose determining eligibility for the small business CGT roll-over (¶7-195).
- Where the lessee of a car that was used for income-producing purposes subsequently purchases the car, and then disposes of it, the lessee is assessable if a profit is made on the disposal (¶10-380).
- In certain situations, profits made on the trade-in of a previously leased vehicle may be assessable as income under ordinary concepts, or may give rise to depreciation balancing adjustments or capital gains (¶10-422).
- Special rules are designed to ensure that a lessor is assessable on all forms of consideration received from disposing of leased assets, including vehicles (¶23-230).

Trading stock

- Where a dealer acquires vehicles for the purpose of sale or exchange in the course of its business, the vehicles are treated as non-depreciable trading stock. This extends to vehicles acquired under a floor plan financing arrangement (¶9-150).
- For valuation purposes, the cost of a vehicle includes dealer delivery and other charges (¶9-190).
- Guidelines apply in determining the replacement value of a trade-in or demonstrator (¶9-225).

- Special considerations apply to trade incentives and warranties (¶9-050).
- If a business taxpayer trades-in a vehicle with a dealer, and does not quote an ABN, the dealer may be required to withhold tax from the payment for the trade-in (¶26-220).

Depreciation

- The depreciable cost of cars is capped (¶17-200) and special rules apply where these cars are disposed of (¶17-210, ¶17-640).
- Simplified depreciation rules may apply to a small business which purchases a vehicle (¶7-250). However, taxpayers who are subject to the alienation of personal services income provisions (¶30-600) cannot allocate more than one vehicle with a private use component to a small business pool (¶7-250).
- Depreciation is not calculated separately if the taxpayer has used the cents per kilometre method for calculating car expense deductions (¶17-030).
- Special rules apply for calculating balancing adjustments where the taxpayer has used any of the car expense substantiation methods (¶17-665).
- Depreciation on leased luxury cars is allowed to the lessee, not the lessor (¶17-220).
- Limited effective lives apply to certain vehicles (¶43-105).

Expenses

- In general, travel expenses incurred as part of a business are deductible as normal business expenses. This includes various costs relating to vehicles (¶16-220, ¶16-310).
- Special considerations may apply to travel between workplaces, to or from home, and self-education travel (¶16-220, ¶16-450).
- Deductions need to be apportioned where there is a mixed private and business use (¶16-280, ¶16-290).
- Travel allowances are generally assessable, but their payment does not necessarily mean that the recipient is entitled to a deduction for related expenses (¶16-240).
- Domestic car expenses of individuals must be substantiated or calculated in one of two ways — the logbook method or the cents per kilometre method (¶16-320).
- Overseas vehicle expenses of individuals must be substantiated as work expenses if incurred by an employee, or as business travel expenses if incurred by a self-employed person (¶16-300).
- Travel-related meals, accommodation and incidental travel may be eligible for concessional substantiation treatment (¶16-210, ¶16-320).

FBT and salary packaging

- Tax benefits can be achieved through salary packaging (¶35-057, ¶31-120).
- Special FBT rules apply to the provision of cars, or the reimbursement/payment of car expenses by employers (¶35-170, ¶35-330).
- FBT concessions apply to car parking (¶35-252).

GST and luxury car tax

- GST may apply where a motor vehicle is sold or leased as part of a business (¶34-220).

- GST is normally calculated as 10% of the sale price, or 10% of the amount of the lease payments (¶34-100).
- GST on *importations* is payable by the importer (¶34-250).
- Subject to some important exceptions, an additional tax (luxury car tax) applies where the GST-inclusive market value of a car exceeds a certain threshold (¶34-220).
- In accordance with the normal rules, the input tax credit on the acquisition of a vehicle is apportioned where the vehicle is acquired only partly for business purposes. Special apportionment methods may apply (¶34-110).
- Subject to various exceptions, the input tax credit that applies where a car is purchased for business purposes is limited where its GST-inclusive market value exceeds the car limit (¶34-220).
- If you supply taxi travel as part of your business, you are required to be registered for GST, irrespective of turnover (¶34-220).
- Supplies of cars to disabled veterans and other disabled persons may be GST-free in certain circumstances, and a rebate may apply to motor cycles (¶34-220).
- Special GST rules apply to insurance claims (¶34-210).
- Dealers may be able to claim an input tax credit on second-hand vehicles acquired from non-registered sellers. They may also be entitled to use a global method of accounting (¶34-260).
- The discounted transfer of a vehicle to an associate may be treated as being made for market value unless the associate would have been entitled to a full input tax credit (¶34-270).
- Deposits are not subject to GST when they are initially paid, but attract GST once they are applied towards the payment for the vehicle, or if they are forfeited (¶34-270).

Other taxes and duties

- Businesses can claim fuel tax credits for fuel used in heavy vehicles used on public roads and vehicles used in off-road business activities. The rate varies according to the type of vehicle and the use to which the fuel is put (¶40-200).
- Duty is imposed by the states and territories where new vehicles are being registered for the first time, or registration is being transferred to another person (¶37-020).

¶44-120 Company directors' checklist

Remuneration and benefits

- Directors' fees, bonuses and similar payments are deductible to the company and assessable to the director (¶10-050, ¶16-040, ¶16-520).
- Deferred directors' fees may qualify for the arrears-of-income rebate (¶15-340).
- Directors' remuneration is subject to PAYG instalments, but special rules may apply if the remuneration is passed on to a professional partnership (¶5-090, ¶26-150).
- Retirement or termination allowances are deductible to the company if their payment is in the future interests of the business. If not, a more limited deduction is available if they are paid in good faith for the past employee services of the director. A capital loss may arise when a director's covenant expires (¶16-540).

- Retirement or termination allowances received by directors generally qualify for concessional tax treatment as employment termination payments (¶14-620).
- An amount received by a retiring director in return for giving a restrictive covenant not to compete will not normally be assessable as ordinary income, but may be assessable as a capital gain. If the amount is received for a covenant which operates during the course of the director's employment, the ATO will generally seek to assess it as income (¶10-050, ¶11-280).
- Where remuneration or retiring allowances paid by private companies are excessive, the excess is not deductible and will generally be treated as an assessable dividend to the director (¶4-220).
- Amounts paid, lent or forgiven by private companies to associated persons (such as directors/shareholders) may be presumed to be assessable, non-frankable dividends unless it can be shown that the transaction is on commercial terms or satisfies various other conditions (¶4-200).
- An ''at call'' loan made by a director to the company is treated as equity rather than debt (¶23-115).
- Directors may be treated as employees who are subject to the employee share scheme rules (¶10-085).
- In certain limited cases, an Australian tax exemption applies to foreign earnings derived by a resident director during a continuous period of foreign service of at least 91 days. Exemptions may also be available under Double Tax Agreements (¶10-860).
- The source of a director's income will be important where the director is a non-resident (¶21-070).
- A director is generally classed as an employee for the purposes of the superannuation guarantee scheme and accordingly must be provided with the relevant level of superannuation support (¶39-020, ¶39-024).
- Contributions by an employer to a complying superannuation fund, to provide for superannuation benefits for a director may be deductible (¶13-710).
- The ATO does not regard it as acceptable for a non-professional to be a director of a practice company unless it is allowed by the relevant laws and there is no diversion of income to that person (¶31-570).
- A director may be an affiliate of a company under the turnover test for determining whether the company qualifies for tax concessions as a small business entity (¶7-050).
- Remuneration of non-working directors may be exempt from payroll tax (¶36-140).
- Directors' benefits are generally subject to FBT. However, FBT will not apply where the benefits are provided to a director in the capacity of shareholder or beneficiary of a trust. Miscellaneous exemption for certain work-related items may also apply (¶35-080, ¶35-120, ¶35-645).
- A company that allows its directors to make cash drawings for personal expenses is not necessarily providing loan fringe benefits under the FBT rules (¶35-270).

Insurance and guarantees

- Premiums paid by a director for professional liability insurance would normally be deductible (¶16-550).

- Fees paid to a director for guaranteeing the repayment of a debt by the company would normally be assessable to the director and deductible to the company. Special rules apply in determining the tax consequences where insurance policies are taken out to cover the director's potential liability. There may also be CGT consequences where the debt is repaid or the director is called on to make a payment under the guarantee (¶10-110, ¶11-270, ¶11-400, ¶16-060, ¶16-152).

- Premiums paid by a director on a sickness/accident insurance policy are deductible, and the benefits are assessable. This does not apply to trauma insurance taken out by the director (¶10-220, ¶16-560).

- If trauma insurance is taken out by the company in respect of a director, premiums will be deductible and proceeds assessable if the purpose is to protect the company from loss of profits (¶10-220, ¶16-570).

- Premiums paid by a company under a key person life and endowment policy are generally not deductible, and the proceeds are not income. However, in the case of an accident or term policy, the proceeds will be assessable (and the premiums deductible) if the purpose of the insurance was to replace profits lost through the loss of the key person's services (¶10-220, ¶16-570).

Deductions

- A company is entitled to a deduction for directors' fees for the income year in which it has definitively committed itself to the payment (¶16-040, ¶16-520).

- A company may claim a deduction for losses of money arising from theft or misappropriation by a director, but not if the "loss" is caused by a board of directors acting as the mind and will of the company itself. Alternatively, a deduction may be available where the loss is a natural incident of the business (¶16-590).

- Claims for legal expenses by companies in relation to actions of their directors may be successful where they are incurred as part of the ongoing business. Claims for legal expenses personally incurred by directors tend to be less successful, as they are sometimes treated as private outgoings or expenses of protecting a capital asset (¶16-830 – ¶16-845).

- The cost of providing morning tea to directors in an "in-house dining facility" is deductible (¶16-390).

- Where a partnership makes a payment to a director of a private company that is a member of the partnership, the deduction may be limited to what is reasonable (¶5-100).

- Particular care is necessary where directors claim deductions for expenses which they personally incur on behalf of the company (¶16-160).

- Interest on funds on-lent to the company may be deductible in certain circumstances (¶16-740).

- A person who is an active director of a number of companies may be regarded as carrying on the business of being a director, and may claim deductions accordingly. However, there may be GST implications (¶16-550, ¶34-110).

- Directors can claim deductions, in accordance with the normal rules, for the usual range of work expenses such as conferences, business travel, home offices and self-education (¶16-160).

Liabilities and offences

- It is the duty of directors to ensure that the company does not pay excessive tax. Judgments about tax compliance may need to be part of the corporate governance process (¶25-220, ¶31-000).
- Directors must ensure that, where the company has made PAYG deductions (eg from employees' wages), become liable for superannuation guarantee charge or has a liability for GST for a particular period, the company remits the instalments or SGC to the ATO within the prescribed time or make alternative arrangements. In default, each director becomes personally liable for a penalty equal to the unpaid amount (¶25-560). Directors should also ensure payments are made for PAYG withholding to the ATO to ensure tax deductions are available for the company's salary and wages (¶26-620).
- A director may be personally liable for a special "PAYG withholding non-compliance tax" where the company has withheld PAYG amounts from payments made to the director, but failed to pay its total withheld amounts to the Commissioner. Corresponding rules may also apply to associates of directors in certain circumstances (¶25-560).
- Where an offence is committed by the company, the directors may also be liable for a range of associated offences, including aiding and abetting, inciting or urging the commission of an offence, or conspiracy to defraud (¶29-700).
- Where a "taxation offence" is committed by the company, directors will also be treated as having committed the offence unless they can show that they were not involved with it. The court may also make reparation orders against the directors (¶29-710).
- A director who is appointed as the public officer of the company is responsible for the performance by the company of its tax obligations, and also bears personal liability in certain circumstances. Even if the director is not the public officer, the Commissioner may serve a notice on the director requiring him/her to ensure that the relevant company obligations are carried out (¶3-030).
- In the absence of a tax sharing arrangement, directors of a company which is part of a consolidated group may find that the company may be liable for the tax liabilities of other companies in the group (¶8-000).
- Directors may be liable under the "bottom of the harbour" legislation, and for a range of other offences such as making false and misleading statements, or hindering taxation officers (¶29-700).
- The state of mind of a company will normally be taken to be the state of mind of its directors and managers. In the case of taxation offences, the intentions of the employees who commit the relevant acts may be attributed to the company (¶29-710).
- For the purpose of assessing penalty tax, a disclosure made by a director of a private company after the ATO has already made contact with the company will not be regarded as a voluntary disclosure (¶29-710).

¶44-130 Natural disasters tax checklist

Loss or damage: general

- Premiums paid for insurance cover for business losses are normally deductible (¶16-550).
- Insurance payouts for loss of profits are assessable (¶10-170).

- Destroyed trading stock can be valued at nil. Payouts for loss of trading stock are assessable (¶9-240, ¶10-170).
- Payouts for loss of depreciating assets normally give rise to balancing adjustments, but a roll-over may be available where a replacement asset is acquired (¶17-720).
- Special depreciation rules apply on the loss of business cars (¶17-665).
- Where capital works are destroyed, there may be a balancing deduction based on the amount of undeducted construction expenditure. Payouts for loss of capital improvements reduce the balancing deduction otherwise arising (¶20-530).

Loss or damage: CGT

- CGT exclusions apply to the loss of trading stock and depreciating assets (¶11-700).
- Capital losses on collectibles acquired for $500 or less are disregarded (¶11-390, ¶11-640).
- Capital losses on personal use assets are disregarded (¶11-400, ¶11-640).
- Capital losses on cars or motor cycles are disregarded (¶11-640).
- The loss or destruction of an individual's main residence does not give rise to a capital loss. Special rules apply where there is a subsequent sale of the property (¶11-730).
- If an asset or part of an asset is totally lost or destroyed, and an exemption does not apply, CGT may apply but certain gains may be rolled-over (¶11-250, ¶12-260).
- If an asset is permanently damaged, CGT does not apply but insurance proceeds may reduce the cost base (¶11-550).

Repairs, prevention and other costs

- The cost of repairs to business property is deductible (¶16-700). If the expenditure is on capital improvements, it will instead be taken into account for the purpose of determining the cost under the depreciation (¶17-105), capital works (¶20-510) or CGT rules (¶11-550).
- Demolition costs would normally be capital (¶16-060).
- A three-year write-off applies for capital expenditure on a wide range of water facilities for the purpose of conserving or conveying water. This would include the cost of installing an extra pump for an in-ground swimming pool where the pump is to be used solely for fire fighting purposes (¶18-080).
- Rural businesses can claim an outright deduction for capital expenditure on landcare operations (¶18-100).
- Rural businesses can claim an outright deduction on construction and installation of fodder storage assets for their own business livestock (¶18-085).
- An outright deduction can be claimed for expenditure on business-related environmental protection activity (¶19-110).
- An outright deduction is allowable for expenditure on rehabilitation of mining sites (¶19-100).
- The cost of replacing plants in an existing plantation because of storm damage would normally be deductible outright (¶18-070).
- A deduction is allowed for capital business expenditure on the establishment of trees in ''carbon sink'' forests established for the purpose of sequestering carbon from the atmosphere (¶19-120).

- Expenses of closing down a business would normally not be deductible, but may qualify for a write-off over five years (¶16-156).

Other special rules for primary producers

- A concessional rule applies where drought, fire or flood causes there to be an advanced shearing by a primary producer carrying on a sheep grazing business (¶18-140).
- If the taxpayer's assessable income would otherwise include a disaster-related insurance recovery for the loss of livestock, the taxpayer can elect to spread the amount of the recovery in equal instalments over five years. The same applies to insurance recoveries for the loss of trees by fire (¶18-150).
- Special concessions apply if there has been a forced sale or death of livestock due to destruction of pasture or fodder due to drought, fire or flood (¶18-160).
- Averaging rules may apply where there are fluctuations of primary production income from year to year (¶18-200).
- Withdrawals of Farm Management Deposits may be made without tax penalty even though they occur within 12 months, provided that there are exceptional circumstances (¶18-290).

Grants and assistance

- One-off governmental grants to assist with living expenses may be tax free, but some grants made to businesses may be assessable (¶10-195, ¶10-197).
- Gifts to charitable funds to assist persons in necessitous circumstances are deductible, and payments from such funds would not normally be assessable (¶10-070, ¶16-950).
- Donations to disaster relief funds may be deductible (¶16-950).
- Gifts of goods and services by businesses to victims of disasters may be deductible as marketing expenses (¶16-152).
- Income earned from employment in the operations of a developing country relief fund or a public disaster relief fund qualifies under the exemption for foreign employment income (¶10-860).
- Primary producers affected by the North Queensland floods in January and February 2019 are not required to declare government grants in tax returns as they are non-assessable non-exempt income.
- Government support payments made to volunteer firefighters during the 2019–20 Australian summer bushfires are non-assessable non-exempt income (¶10-070, ¶10-895).
- Relief and recovery payments made to individuals or businesses from Australian government departments in relation to the 2019–20 Australian summer bushfires are non-assessable non-exempt income (¶10-895).
- Economic relief payments in relation to the COVID-19 pandemic are available for individuals who have lost their employment. Simplified qualification for JobSeeker Payment and Coronavirus Supplement payment exists (¶2-133, ¶10-895).
- COVID-19 tax-exempt relief payments to individuals already receiving social security is available (¶10-040).

Records and substantiation

- Concessional rules apply where substantiation records of work and travel claims have been lost as a result of circumstances outside the taxpayer's control (¶16-340).
- Bank fees for replacing business records are deductible (¶16-152).
- The ATO may be able to assist in reconstructing destroyed tax records (¶9-045).

Other hardship concessions

- An exception to the non-commercial loss rules may apply where there are special circumstances, including natural disasters (¶16-020).
- Early release of superannuation benefits may be possible in cases of severe financial hardship (¶13-025).
- Hardship resulting from natural disasters may be a factor in obtaining an extension of time to pay tax or lodge returns, a release from payment, relief from interest or penalties, and fast tracking of refunds (¶25-450, ¶29-400, ¶29-530).
- The financial effects of a natural disaster may be taken into account in determining whether an entity satisfies the ''small business entity'' income tests for obtaining tax concessions (¶7-050).

GST aspects

- A natural disaster may mean that a business is no longer a ''going concern'' that is eligible for GST-free status on sale (¶34-240).
- Charities can elect to have fundraising events treated as input taxed (¶34-170).
- The prospect of factors such as drought or fire may be taken into account in determining whether a business satisfies the income test for the ''small business entity'' GST concessions (¶34-270).
- An input tax credit on business items that you have acquired is not affected if the items are subsequently destroyed (¶34-100).
- If the business is reimbursed for its losses under an insurance policy, the settlement will not be subject to GST, provided that the insurance company was notified of the input tax credit entitlement for the premium (¶34-210).
- GST does not apply where unconditional gifts are made to victims of natural disasters (¶34-160).
- The Commissioner can waive or modify the formal requirements for tax invoices or adjustment notes in special circumstances such as natural disasters (¶34-140).

¶44-140 Students' tax checklist

Remuneration and benefits

- Commonwealth government education or training payments made for students aged 16 or over, such as Austudy, ABSTUDY or youth allowance, are generally assessable, though exemptions apply to certain supplementary payments (¶10-195, ¶10-700).
- Payments for students under Commonwealth assistance schemes for secondary education, or for education of isolated children, are exempt (¶10-700).
- A Commonwealth Trade Learning Scholarship is exempt (¶10-700).
- Certain apprenticeship bonus payments are wholly or partly exempt (¶10-700).

- Other scholarships, bursaries or other educational allowances derived by a student of any age receiving full-time education at a school, college or university are exempt, unless otherwise specified (¶10-740).
- Concessional tax treatment may apply to certain educational scholarship plans offered by friendly societies (¶3-470).
- A university does not have an obligation to make superannuation guarantee contributions in relation to scholarship payments made to students where the scholarship is funded by an industry-based organisation (¶39-024).
- An ordinary allowance received by a student from his or her parents would not normally be assessable unless it is a distribution from a family trust or is a wage received as a salaried employee (¶10-010).
- Payments received by visiting students from overseas for their maintenance, education or training are typically exempt from Australian tax where they're visiting solely for educational or training purposes and a Double Tax Agreement is in force (¶22-150).
- Certain international scholarships are exempt (¶10-700).
- Benefits relating to placement in an approved student exchange program may be exempt from FBT (¶35-645).
- A death benefit termination payment or superannuation death benefit paid to a financially dependant student may be eligible for concessional tax treatment (¶14-270, ¶14-680).

HELP and Financial Supplement repayments

- The Higher Education Loan Programme (HELP) offers loans to assist students to pay their higher education fees and to study overseas. The obligation to make repayments of HELP debt apply once repayment income reaches a minimum level. This is extended to debtors living overseas from 1 July 2017 (¶2-380).
- The PAYG rules apply to debts due under HELP and debts still due under the former Financial Supplement (FS) scheme. Variation of PAYG instalments may be appropriate once the debt is repaid (¶27-100, ¶27-280).
- Certain superannuation contributions may be treated as income for the purpose of determining liability to make HELP or FS repayments (¶13-730).

Deductions and offsets

- Education expenses may be deductible where they have the required connection with the production of assessable income. The expenses may include tuition fees, textbooks, student union fees, student services and amenities fees and travel and living expenses incurred in attending conferences, seminars and educational institutions. However, self-education expenses are no longer deductible against government assistance payments (¶16-450).

Liability, rates and thresholds

- An international student who is a non-resident of Australia is not eligible for the tax-free threshold, and must lodge an Australian tax return if they derive any Australian assessable income in the income year. However, students who are studying a course in Australia of a greater duration than six months may be treated as residents for tax purposes. In years in which they are residents for only part of the income year, the tax-free threshold will be apportioned. A short term vocational experience student would not normally be a resident (¶2-130, ¶21-010).

- Students under 18 years may be subject to the special tax rates applying under the minors' income rules (¶2-170).
- A person who is in full-time education at a school, college or university and is under 25 years can qualify as a dependant for the purpose of calculating a taxpayer's liability or exemption from the Medicare levy or the Medicare levy surcharge (¶2-310).

Other aspects

- Quotation of a TFN may be a precondition to enrolling in a higher education institution or in an Open Learning course (¶33-000).
- Secondary school students may use a simplified method of obtaining a Tax File Number by applying under the ATO's Secondary Schools TFN program (¶33-000). Overseas students whose course of study is six months or longer can apply online.
- Most educational services are GST-free (¶34-165).

¶44-145 Indigenous taxpayers tax checklist

This checklist sets out those tax-related measures that specifically apply to indigenous taxpayers or that may be particularly relevant to them.

- Aboriginal housing associations and land councils may qualify as public benevolent institutions, so gifts to them may be tax deductible (¶16-950) and payroll tax exemptions may apply (¶36-060).
- Mining payments made to Aboriginal people and distributing groups relating to the use of Aboriginal land for mining and exploration are subject to mining withholding tax, but are otherwise tax-exempt (¶10-895, ¶19-006).
- PAYG withholding may be required when making payments to indigenous artists where that artist is in business and does not quote an ABN. However, rates may be varied to nil where there is a payment for artistic works where the artist qualifies for a special Zone A rebate and does not quote an ABN (¶26-220).
- PAYG withholding may apply to Commonwealth supported payments for tutorial services provided to improve the education of indigenous people and specified interpretation and translation services (¶26-150).
- Retrospective tax exemption may apply to native title benefits accruing to indigenous people and associated bodies (¶19-006).
- Payments under the ABSTUDY scheme are assessable if made to students aged 16 or over (¶10-700), but may qualify for the beneficiary rebate (¶15-315). Supplementary amounts are exempt (¶10-700, ¶10-885).
- A special ''Application for TFN'' form (¶3-000) is available for Aboriginal or Torres Strait Islanders, with an expanded range of persons able to provide proof of identity.
- A beneficiary tax rebate applies to a range of assessable social security benefits and allowances, including ABSTUDY, the Assistance for Isolated Children Scheme and Community Development Employment Projects (¶15-315).
- Specified payments made to students awarded an Indigenous Training and Recruitment Initiatives (INTRAIN) Scholarship are tax exempt (CR 2011/37).
- A tax offset applies to investors providing low cost housing under the National Rental Affordability Scheme (¶20-605).
- Resale royalty payments received by an artist under the Resale Royalty Right for Visual Artists scheme are normally assessable (¶10-510).

- Assistance in preparation of tax returns may be available under the ATO's Tax Help program or from the ATO Indigenous Helpline (phone: 13 10 30).
- Tax offsets (''zone rebates'') are available for individuals who are residents of specified isolated areas (¶15-160).
- Various FBT concessions apply for fringe benefits provided to employees working in remote areas (¶35-650).

¶44-150 Sickness, injury and disability tax checklist

Medical expenses

- Medical expenses are normally not tax deductible (or depreciable) unless there is something peculiar to the taxpayer's income-earning activities that requires the expenditure to be incurred (¶16-175, ¶16-190, ¶17-010).
- A deduction is available for the cost of protective clothing. Sun protection equipment may also be deductible for outdoor workers (¶16-180).
- The cost of repairs made to control health risks may be deductible as environmental protection expenditure (¶19-110).
- An employer may be able to claim a deduction for medical expenses incurred in connection with its employees, provided that the necessary connection with the interests of the business can be shown (¶16-520).
- Providing benefits to employees by paying or reimbursing their expenses may expose the employer to fringe benefits tax (FBT). However, there are a number of medical and health-related FBT exemptions (¶35-645).
- Most supplies of health and medical services are GST-free (¶34-165).
- Supplies of cars to disabled veterans and other disabled persons may be GST-free (¶34-220).

Insurance, compensation and social security

- Lump sum compensation payments for personal injuries are assessable if they are solely for loss of earnings, but not if they are for loss of earning capacity (¶10-185).
- Certain annuities and lump sums provided to personal injury victims under ''structured settlements'' are tax exempt (¶10-185).
- Periodical payments for loss of wages, such as workers compensation, are assessable (¶10-180).
- A capital gains tax exemption applies to various personal injury compensation awards (¶11-650).
- Periodical payments under a personal accident, income protection or disability insurance policy would normally be assessable, and premiums deductible, where the payments take the place of lost earnings (¶10-210, ¶16-560).
- Ordinary health insurance contributions would normally not be deductible, but a tax offset may be available in some situations (¶15-330).
- Various social security and related benefits may be payable where a person is sick or disabled (¶10-195).
- Tax and CGT exemptions apply to certain foreign wounds and disability pensions, persecution compensation and military injury payments (¶10-200 – ¶10-204, ¶10-780, ¶11-650).

Superannuation and termination payments

- In certain cases, people can get early access to their superannuation benefits on medical grounds (¶13-025).
- Individuals who have been affected by the COVID-19 pandemic are able to get early access to superannuation on compassionate grounds. The maximum available is $10,000 per year for the 2019–20 and 2020–21 income years, and is non-assessable non-exempt income (¶13-810, ¶14-130).
- Certain carers or care recipients qualify as ''dependants'' who may be eligible to receive superannuation death benefits (¶14-270).
- Where a superannuation lump sum payment includes a disability benefit, a portion of the payment may be tax-free (¶14-130, ¶14-220).
- Where a lump sum employment termination payment includes a disability benefit, a portion of the payment may be tax-free (¶14-640).
- Certain personal injury contributions are excluded from the non-concessional contributions cap (¶13-780).
- A person entitled to a disability pension from a superannuation fund may qualify for a tax offset (¶14-220).
- The legal personal representative of a mentally incapacitated member of a self managed superannuation fund may take the member's place as a trustee (¶13-060).

Other exemptions, concessions and special rules

- Exemptions from the penal ''minors' tax'' apply where the minor is disabled (¶2-170).
- Periods of sick leave do not affect a person's continuity of foreign employment for the purpose of determining eligibility for the limited exemption on the foreign earnings (¶10-860).
- Full or partial exemption from the Medicare levy may apply to people entitled to concessional medical treatment (¶2-340).
- An individual who is permanently incapacitated may qualify for the small business 15-year asset CGT exemption (¶7-165).
- Ill-health may sometimes be taken into account in applying for deferment of payment or relief from various tax penalties (¶29-400).
- The illness of a director may constitute a defence against personal liability for the company's failure to account for PAYG instalments (¶25-560).
- The illness of a taxpayer may constitute special circumstances that enable the taxpayer to avoid the application of the non-commercial business rules (¶16-020).
- The Commissioner may release a taxpayer from tax liabilities where collection of the tax will cause serious hardship (¶25-450).
- A taxpayer may be able to claim a dependant (invalid and carer) offset in certain circumstances (¶15-100).
- Gifts to public funds established for the relief of persons in necessitous circumstances are tax deductible. So are gifts to certain bodies for public health purposes (¶16-950).

- Where the only source of income of a presently entitled but mentally incapacitated trust beneficiary is a distribution from that trust, the beneficiary is not required to lodge a tax return (¶6-120).

¶44-155 Marriage breakdown tax checklist

Disposals and transactions

- CGT consequences may arise where there is a division of assets or property between the spouses as a result of a marriage breakdown (¶11-000).
- Amounts paid as part of a settlement on the breakdown of a marriage or relationship may be exempt (¶11-670).
- In certain circumstances, a CGT roll-over applies where assets are transferred between spouses as a result of the breakdown of a marriage or relationship (¶12-460).
- The roll-over also applies where the assets are transferred by a company or trust. Special rules apply where the roll-over involves a CFC or certain non-resident trusts (¶12-470).
- Where the roll-over applies, balancing adjustment relief is also allowed for depreciation purposes (¶7-250, ¶17-710).
- Where the roll-over applies, eligibility for the main residence exemption is based on the way in which both spouses used the dwelling during their combined period of ownership (¶11-750).
- Where the roll-over applies, the 12-month period for determining eligibility for discounted capital gains is based on the combined period of ownership of each spouse (¶11-033).
- In determining eligibility for the CGT exemption applying to the disposal of a main residence, special attention should be paid to: (1) the rule requiring that the vendor be a natural person; (2) the rules governing the situation where spouses have different residences at the same time; and (3) the rules applying where one party leaves the former residence to live elsewhere (¶11-730, ¶11-740, ¶11-750).
- CGT roll-over relief is available where as a result of a marriage breakdown there is an "in specie" transfer of assets from a small superannuation fund to another complying superannuation fund (¶12-480).
- A marriage breakdown roll-over need not prevent compliance with the 15 years continuous ownership test for the purpose of the small business CGT exemption (¶7-165).
- The CGT provisions do not apply if the original beneficial owner of a life policy disposes of it. Similarly, a transferee who receives it as part of a settlement, and who provides no consideration, will be exempt from CGT on a subsequent disposal (¶11-880).
- Concessions apply to certain divisions of superannuation on a marriage breakdown (¶11-880).
- Special CGT consequences may arise where a debt is forgiven (¶11-270).
- If a loan to a spouse is forgiven by a family company, the Commissioner may seek to treat it as a deemed dividend. Failing that, if the spouse is an employee of the company, the forgiveness could potentially be treated as a debt waiver fringe benefit under the FBT rules (¶4-200, ¶35-310).

- Depreciation balancing adjustments may be rolled over in certain circumstances (¶17-710).
- Trading stock is not normally subject to the CGT rules. However, if the transferor spouse is in business and an item of trading stock is transferred as part of a property settlement, the value of that asset must be included in the transferor's assessable income. Correspondingly, the transferee spouse is taken to have purchased the asset for the same value (¶9-290, ¶11-700).
- Special considerations may apply where the asset is trading stock of a spousal partnership (¶9-295).
- A capital loss may arise if assets are sold or misappropriated by an estranged spouse without the taxpayer's consent (¶11-270).
- Where there is a change in the ownership of shares in a private company, this may affect the ability of the company to recoup prior year tax losses under the "continuity of ownership" test. It may also result in the value of the shares being treated as an assessable dividend (¶4-200, ¶11-350, ¶12-870).
- Trust distributions to former spouses, and to widows or widowers of family group members with new spouses, may be exempt from family trust distribution tax (¶6-266).

Maintenance

- Maintenance payments may be tax exempt (¶10-855).
- Maintenance payments would normally not be tax deductible as no connection with income earning activities could be shown (¶16-520).
- The higher rates applicable to the unearned income of minors do not apply to income derived by the minor from the investment of property transferred to the minor as a result of a family breakdown (¶2-180).
- The Commissioner may elect not to impose tax at punitive rates on trusts consisting of property received in certain family breakdown situations, even though there is no beneficiary presently entitled (¶6-230).

Costs and other matters

- Legal and accounting fees relating to a divorce or property settlement would generally not be tax deductible, except insofar as they are paid for tax advice. However, the fees relating to property matters, whether those matters are disputed or not, may form part of the costs of acquisition and disposal for CGT purposes (¶11-550, ¶16-840).
- Non-capital expenses relating to the management of a taxpayer's tax affairs or compliance with tax obligations may be tax deductible (¶16-850).
- Admissions made in affidavits as to a taxpayer's assets and income given in Family Court proceedings may be open to inspection by the ATO. They may therefore be used as the basis for a default tax assessment and can be presented as evidence in court proceedings involving that assessment (¶25-220).
- Marriage breakdown may alter a spouse's treatment as an affiliate in determining whether the small business concessions turnover or asset tests have been satisfied (¶7-050).
- A person required to attend and give evidence to the Commissioner cannot refuse to answer questions about their partner on the grounds of a claimed "spousal privilege" (¶25-240).

- GST considerations would not normally arise on asset disposals as a result of marriage breakdown as the vendor will not normally be registered, and the disposal will not normally be in the course of carrying on an enterprise (¶34-100).
- General professional fees for work done in relation to family court proceedings are subject to GST (¶34-105).
- Various duty exemptions or concessions apply to transactions associated with marriage breakdown (¶37-020).

¶44-160 Age thresholds tax checklist

This checklist sets out, in chronological order, the respective ages at which various tax concessions, restrictions or other rules start or cease to apply.

When a person is born:

- the person becomes a potential taxpayer (or dependant)
- the birth may entitle the eligible care giver to claim the tax-free Family Tax Benefit and/or the assessable parental leave payment (¶2-133)
- if the person is a dependant of the taxpayer, this may entitle the taxpayer's entitlement to a higher threshold for the Medicare levy (¶2-330). It may also affect the taxpayer's liability for the Medicare levy surcharge (¶2-335) and, if the taxpayer is a prescribed person, their entitlement to levy exemption (¶2-340)
- the person becomes subject to the minors' income rules (¶2-170)
- the person becomes a potential recipient of diverted income (¶30-900)
- the person becomes a potential eligible recipient of tax-free superannuation death benefit (¶14-270)
- for FBT purposes, the determination of a taxpayer's reasonable living-away-from-home allowance (¶35-470) or the taxable value of a board benefit (¶35-630) may be affected.

When a person turns 4:

- if the person is a child of the taxpayer, this may affect the taxpayer's calculation of standard values of goods taken from trading stock (¶9-245).

When a person turns 12:

- a higher amount may apply in determining the reasonable living-away-from-home food allowance for FBT purposes (¶35-470)
- a higher amount may apply in determining the taxable value of a board benefit for FBT purposes (¶35-630).

When a person turns 16:

- the person may qualify as an eligible dependant, enabling a dependant (invalid and carer) rebate to be claimed (¶15-100)
- the restriction on a taxpayer's entitlement to a deduction for maintenance of the person ceases (¶16-520)
- the person may become assessable on certain Commonwealth education and training payments paid to students (¶10-195, ¶10-700)
- the person may lose their exemption from quoting a TFN (¶26-350)
- if the person is a child of the taxpayer, this may affect the taxpayer's calculation of standard values of goods taken from trading stock (¶9-245).

When person turns 18:

- if the birthday is before the end of the income year, the minors' income rules cease to apply for that year (¶2-170, ¶2-250) and standard thresholds for lodgment of returns apply (¶24-010)
- the person is not affected by the restriction on claiming the low income tax offset in relation to ''unearned'' income (¶15-300)
- the person can qualify as public officer for tax purposes (¶3-030)
- the person can register as a tax agent (¶32-020)
- if the birthday is before the end of the income year, and the person is a partner, the uncontrolled partnership rules may apply for that year (¶5-180)
- a lower threshold for exemption from ABN quotation applies (¶33-130)
- the person ceases to be under the ''legal disability'' of infancy and, if a beneficiary of a trust, may become assessable on the share of net trust income to which it is presently entitled (¶6-210, ¶42-030)
- the person may lose their eligibility as a ''death benefits dependant'' (¶14-270). This may mean that they lose their entitlement to concessional treatment of superannuation death benefits (¶14-280) or death benefit termination payments received on the death of their parent (¶14-680)
- if the birthday is before the end of the income year, the person may become eligible for a deduction for personal superannuation contributions irrespective of requirement for employment or business income (¶13-730)
- the person may qualify for compulsory employer superannuation contributions even though their employment is only part-time (¶39-030).

When person turns 21:

- if a non-student, the person loses dependant status for purposes of the Medicare levy (¶2-310). This may affect the low income earner's levy exemption (¶2-330) and, if the taxpayer is a prescribed person, their entitlement to levy exemption (¶2-340), but means the person no longer has to be covered for parent to avoid levy surcharge (¶2-335).

When person turns 25:

- if a student, the person loses dependant status for purposes of Medicare levy (¶2-310). This may affect the low income earner's levy exemption (¶2-330) and, if the taxpayer is a prescribed person, their entitlement to levy exemption (¶2-340), but means the person no longer has to be covered for parent to avoid levy surcharge (¶2-335)
- if the person is a child of an overseas employee, the FBT exemption for education expenses is lost (¶35-655)
- if receiving a death benefit superannuation income stream, the person may be required to have commuted the stream to a lump sum by the date of the birthday (¶14-310)
- the person would normally lose their entitlement to exemption on a superannuation lump sum that has been commuted from a superannuation income stream in specified circumstances (¶14-310).

When a person turns 55:

- the person may become entitled to the CGT small business 15-year exemption (¶7-165)
- certain contribution preconditions to claiming the CGT retirement exemption cease to apply (¶7-185)
- if the person is a non-resident and not working primarily in Australia, they may become entitled to make withdrawals from their SHASA account (¶39-650)
- if born before 1 July 1960, the person reaches their superannuation "preservation age".

When a person turns 60:

- the person qualifies as an "elderly person" for FBT purposes, eg the exemption for residential care workers or for live-in help (¶35-380, ¶35-630)
- the person reaches "veteran pension age" and, if otherwise eligible for an age pension, may qualify for the low income aged persons rebate (¶15-310)
- the person reaches their superannuation "preservation age". This means that they may access preserved superannuation benefits on retirement (¶13-800) or may access their superannuation as a non-commutable income stream without having to retire (¶13-025). They may be entitled to concessional tax offsets on superannuation benefits that they receive (¶14-220, ¶14-240) and may also be entitled to a concessional offset in determining tax on employment termination payments (¶14-620). For persons born before 30 June 1964, see ¶42-250 for transitional rules
- superannuation benefits received from taxed funds are normally tax-free (¶14-220)
- superannuation benefits received from untaxed funds are normally assessable, but the person can claim certain tax offsets (¶14-240)
- the taxation of a superannuation death benefit income stream will be affected where the person is either the deceased or the recipient (¶14-280).

When a person turns 65:

- if the person is the oldest person covered by the policy, the private health insurance offset increases (¶15-330)
- limitations apply to the contributions that may be made to a regulated superannuation fund (¶13-700)
- an individual may make downsizer contributions from the proceeds of the sale of a dwelling that was the person's main residence, applicable to the proceeds from contracts entered into on or after 1 July 2018 (¶13-795)
- the person becomes entitled to access superannuation benefits without restriction (¶13-025, ¶13-800)
- the person becomes entitled to make withdrawals from their SHASA account (¶39-650)
- if born before 1 January 1954, the person reaches "age pension age" and if otherwise eligible may qualify for the low income aged persons rebate (¶15-310)
- the person will continue to be entitled to concessional treatment for genuine redundancy payments (¶14-700) or early retirement scheme payments (¶14-710). Recent legislation extends concessional treatment for genuine redundancies up to the age an individual reaches "age pension age", which is rising to age 67 by 1 July 2023 (see below)

- the minimum annual drawdown from a superannuation income stream increases, according to the person's age on 1 July in the year of payment or on commencement of stream (¶14-125).

When a person turns 66, $66^1/2$ or 67:

- depending on the relevant birth dates as set out below, the person reaches ''age pension age'' and may qualify for the low income aged persons rebate (¶15-310):

Date of birth	Age pension age	Date on which ''age pension age'' changes
Born between 1 January 1954 and 30 June 1955	66 years	1 July 2019
Born between 1 July 1955 and 31 December 1956	$66^1/2$ years	1 July 2021
Born from 1 January 1957 onwards	67 years	1 July 2023

- a work test starts to apply in determining eligibility to claim the superannuation spouse offset for contributions made for the person's benefit (¶13-700, ¶13-770)
- the special ''bring forward'' transitional rule for determining the taxpayer's non-concessional contributions cap does not apply unless the taxpayer is under 65 in the income year (¶13-780).

When a person turns 70:

- if the person is the oldest person covered by the policy, the private health insurance offset increases (¶15-330)
- further limitations apply to the contributions that may be made to a regulated superannuation fund (¶13-700).

When a person turns 71:

- if the birthday occurs during the income year, the person loses their eligibility for the government co-contribution to superannuation (¶13-760).

When a person turns 75:

- personal superannuation contributions are deductible only if made within 28 days after the month of their birthday (¶13-730)
- superannuation contributions by the person's employer are deductible only if made within 28 days after the month of the person's birthday, with some exceptions (¶13-710)
- the minimum annual drawdown from a superannuation income stream increases, according to the person's age on 1 July in year of payment or on commencement of stream (¶14-125)
- the superannuation spouse offset ceases to apply for contributions made for the person's benefit (¶13-700, ¶13-770).

When a person turns 80:

- the minimum annual drawdown from a superannuation income stream increases, according to the person's age on 1 July in the year of payment or on commencement of stream (¶14-125).

When a person turns 85:

- the minimum annual drawdown from a superannuation income stream increases, according to the person's age on 1 July in the year of payment or on commencement of stream (¶14-125).

When a person turns 90:

- the minimum annual drawdown from a superannuation income stream increases, according to the person's age on 1 July in the year of payment or on commencement of stream (¶14-125).

When a person turns 95:

- the minimum annual drawdown from a superannuation income stream increases, according to the person's age on 1 July in the year of payment or on commencement of stream (¶14-125).

¶44-170 Death of taxpayer tax checklist

Income to date of death

- The trustee of the deceased estate, administrator or legal personal representative (together ''LPR'') of a deceased is generally required to lodge a final, ''date of death'' individual tax return of the deceased's income covering the period from the beginning of the financial year up to the date of death, and any other outstanding returns (¶2-080, ¶25-530).
- If an assessment had been served on the taxpayer but remained unpaid at the time of death, the amount payable is a liability of the deceased's estate. The same applies where the LPR receives an assessment in respect of a return lodged by the deceased before the date of death (¶25-530).
- In the date of death return, the deceased is entitled to the normal tax-free threshold even though the return only relates to part of the year (¶2-080).
- In the date of death return, expenditure incurred by the LPR in relation to the income tax affairs of the deceased is deductible against the deceased's income (¶16-850, ¶6-030).
- A taxpayer's accrued losses can be offset against their income in the date of death tax return. Similarly, the taxpayer's capital losses can be offset against their capital gains in order to determine the taxpayer's net capital gain or loss for that return. However, in either case, unrecouped losses cannot generally be carried forward to the estate or the beneficiaries (¶12-570).
- Tax payable on the basis of the deceased's date of death return, or in relation to any earlier year for which the LPR lodges a return, is a liability of the estate once a notice of assessment is served on the LPR (¶25-530).
- The LPR may be able to obtain a release from payment of tax where payment would cause serious hardship to the beneficiaries (¶25-450).
- The LPR may be personally liable for tax payable by the estate if they have failed to set aside sufficient assets from the estate to pay it (¶6-040, ¶25-530).

During period of administration

- The LPR is required to lodge trust returns for income derived or received by the deceased estate after the date of death. The trust returns must be lodged for the period from the date of death up to the end of the financial year, and thereafter for each financial year until the estate is fully administered (¶6-030).
- Income derived by the estate during the period of administration is normally assessable to the estate, not to the beneficiaries, as they are not ''presently entitled'' (¶6-190).
- Generally, an estate in course of administration is subject to normal marginal rates for the period from the date of death up to the end of the financial year and for the following two financial years (¶42-030). Thereafter, the estate will be taxed at s 99 rates (¶6-190).

- The Commissioner may make an arbitrary assessment of the tax payable where the LPR fails to furnish a return, or probate is not taken out within a certain period (¶25-530).
- The LPR may be personally liable for tax payable by the estate if they have failed to set aside sufficient assets from the estate to pay it (¶6-040, ¶25-530).

After period of administration

- Where income is derived after the estate has been fully administered, the income will be assessable to any beneficiaries that are presently entitled and are not minors. Otherwise it is assessable to the estate (¶6-190).
- The Commissioner's right to recover unpaid taxes of the deceased from the beneficiaries is limited (¶25-510).
- The ATO may accept an appropriate apportionment of income between the LPR and beneficiaries for the income year in which an estate becomes fully administered (¶6-190).

Capital gains tax

- Generally, where a taxpayer dies, there are no CGT implications where the asset passes to the LPR or beneficiary, but CGT may apply when that asset is subsequently disposed of (¶12-570 – ¶12-590).
- Assets forming part of the estate are deemed to have been acquired by the LPR or beneficiary at the date of death of the deceased (¶12-580).
- Pre-CGT assets are deemed to have been acquired for a consideration equal to their market price at the date of death (¶12-580).
- Post-CGT assets are generally deemed to have been acquired for a consideration equal to the amount that would have been their cost base to the deceased at the date of death (¶12-580).
- As an exception, the deceased's main residence is generally deemed to have been acquired for a consideration equal to its market value at the date of death (¶12-580).
- As a further exception, trading stock is brought to account at its market value or, at the representative's election, at certain other values (¶9-300).
- Eligible costs incurred in relation to an asset after the date of death may also enter into the calculation of the cost price (¶12-580).
- Assets acquired subsequent to the date of death are subject to the normal CGT rules relating to the date and cost of acquisition (¶12-580).
- CGT generally does not apply where an estate asset is transferred by the LPR to a beneficiary (¶12-570 – ¶12-590).
- Where an asset passes to a remainder beneficiary on the subsequent death of a life tenant, the remainder beneficiary is taken to have acquired the asset when the original deceased owner died (¶12-580).
- Special cost base rules apply where the surviving joint tenant acquires the interest of a deceased joint tenant in the asset (¶12-580).
- Where the deceased would have been entitled to the small business CGT concessions, the LPR, beneficiary or surviving joint tenant may claim that entitlement in relation to CGT events occurring within a certain period (generally two years) after the date of death (¶7-160).

- An asset that was a personal-use asset of the deceased is treated as a personal-use asset of the representative or beneficiary, and is therefore subject to the special provisions applying to those assets on disposal. A corresponding rule applies to collectables (¶12-580).
- CGT generally does not apply on the subsequent sale of the deceased's main residence where it is sold within two years of the date of death or in certain other circumstances (¶11-770). However, where the deceased was an ''excluded foreign resident'' at the time of death, the main residence exemption does not apply (¶11-750).
- Where a taxpayer makes a post-CGT improvement to a pre-CGT asset and the improved asset is inherited by a beneficiary on the taxpayer's subsequent death, the improvement and the asset are treated as one asset when acquired by the beneficiary (¶11-410).
- A deceased's capital losses can be offset against their capital gains in order to determine their net capital gain or loss for the period up to the date of death. However, any unrecouped loss cannot be carried forward to the estate or the beneficiaries (¶12-570).
- Special rules apply where an asset passes to a beneficiary that is an exempt entity (¶11-350), a non-resident (¶12-720) or the trustee of a complying superannuation fund (¶12-580).

Termination, superannuation and insurance

- Special tax treatment applies to payments received after death in consequence of the deceased's termination of employment, with special concessions applying where the beneficiary was an eligible dependant (¶14-680).
- Payments for unused annual leave and long service leave made to the LPR or beneficiary on an employee's death are tax-free (¶14-720, ¶14-730).
- The taxation of superannuation death benefits varies depending on whether the payment is in a lump sum or income stream and on whether the beneficiary is an eligible dependant (¶14-270, ¶14-280).
- Lump sum life insurance proceeds are not assessable as income, and CGT does not apply where the recipient was the original owner or acquired the policy for no consideration (¶10-230, ¶11-880).

Specific assets, income and expenses

- Bequests of an asset or sum of money are normally not assessable income, unless related to performance of executorial duties (¶10-840). For CGT implications in the case of assets, see above.
- Funeral policy proceeds paid directly to a funeral director are fully assessable (¶3-470).
- Where funeral policy proceeds are paid to the trustee of the policyholder's estate, the trustee is liable on the investment return at the time of receipt. However, the proceeds may be exempt if the policy was issued before 1 January 2003 (¶3-470).
- Income of a deceased estate is exempt from the special rules applying to minors' unearned income. The same applies to benefits received on the death of another person such as life assurance or superannuation (¶2-180). However, concessional tax treatment only applies to minors on income derived directly from assets originally transferred from a deceased estate after 1 July 2019.
- Interest on money borrowed to satisfy a Supreme Court order under testator family maintenance provisions was not deductible (¶16-740).

- Dividends declared on shares owned by a deceased estate, but not paid over until after the production of probate, are not assessable until actually paid over (¶4-120).
- A deductible gift cannot be made by will, though testamentary gifts of property are CGT-exempt (¶11-670, ¶16-942).
- Where a primary producer dies and the LPR continues the business, there is a new taxpayer and a new averaging calculation applies for the LPR (¶18-200).
- Where the deceased held depreciating assets, a balancing adjustment may arise on death (¶17-640).
- A taxpayer who dies while on service in a qualifying overseas locality is entitled to the full amount of the overseas defence forces rebate, irrespective of the time served (¶15-180).
- The estate of a deceased Defence Force member may be entitled to be released from any unpaid tax liability relating to their pay or allowances (¶10-750).
- Compensation paid for death resulting from the service of specified personnel contributed by Australia to an armed force of the United Nations overseas is exempt (¶10-780).
- Maintenance payments made to a surviving child or spouse of the deceased would not normally be tax exempt when paid from the deceased's estate (¶10-855).

State duties, land tax and other considerations

- There are no state death duties imposed on the value of the deceased estate.
- Duty may apply where assets are transferred to LPR or to beneficiaries under the estate but, if so, this will typically be at a nominal rate. Other transfers may be subject to duty at full rates (¶37-020).
- Land tax exemptions for a deceased's principal place of residence may continue for a period after the deceased's death (eg ¶38-010).
- The possible impact on the deceased beneficiaries' social security entitlements may need to be taken into account.

¶44-300 Other checklists

Other checklists located elsewhere in the Guide are as follows:

- Checklist of tax changes taking effect in 2019–20 (¶2).
- Checklist of taxable and non-taxable items (¶10-005).
- Checklist of non-assessable non-exempt income (¶10-895).
- Checklist of CGT taxable and non-taxable events (¶11-005).
- Tax offset finding table (¶15-005).
- Deductions checklist (¶16-005).
- Checklist of Australia's DTAs (¶22-160).
- Checklist: methods of reducing tax liability (¶31-080).
- Table of payroll tax assessable and exempt items (¶36-140).
- Year end tax strategies checklist (¶31-700).

Chapter 45 Tax Calendar

¶45-100 Key tax dates

The Tax Calendar shows the key tax dates for satisfying various taxation obligations such as paying tax, filing returns and lodging activity statements (¶24-200). The dates for lodgment and payment generally apply to **taxpayers that balance at 30 June**. Special rules apply to companies and superannuation funds with substituted accounting periods (¶24-060).

Further, the ATO may grant extensions of time during the year which may not be reflected in these dates.

Where the due date for lodgment or payment falls on a Saturday, Sunday or public holiday, it may be done on the next business day.

DUE DATES IN 2021

JANUARY 2021

15th Due date for lodgment of 2019–20 returns by large/medium companies and superannuation funds, unless required earlier (¶24-060).

Payment for large/medium entities with a 15 January due date is:
- 1 December 2020 — for companies and super funds
- for trusts — as stated on their notice of assessment.

Due date for lodgment of 2019–20 returns by the taxable head company of a consolidated group (including a new registrant) that has a member who has been deemed a large/medium entity in the latest year lodged, unless the return was required earlier. Payment was due 1 December 2020.

21st Due date for lodgment of activity statements (¶24-200) for reporting and payment of:

- GST, wine equalisation tax and luxury car tax by monthly GST reporters (¶34-150)
- PAYG amounts withheld from payments during October to December 2020 by small PAYG withholders that are not deferred BAS payers (¶26-550)
- PAYG instalment for December 2020 by monthly PAYG instalment payers that are not deferred BAS payers (¶27-170, ¶27-200)
- the second PAYG instalment for the 2020–21 year by quarterly PAYG instalment payers that are not deferred BAS payers (¶27-200), and
- the third instalment of FBT for the year ending 31 March 2021 for employers that are not deferred BAS payers (¶35-050).

Lodge and pay quarter 2, 2020–21 PAYG instalment activity statement for head companies of consolidated groups.

28th Due date for superannuation guarantee contributions for October to December 2020 quarter (¶39-240). Employers who do not pay minimum super contributions for quarter 2 by this date must pay the super guarantee charge and lodge a superannuation guarantee charge statement — quarterly by 28 February 2021.

31st Due date for investment bodies to lodge TFN reports for investments made during December 2020 quarter where TFN quoted (¶26-620).

DUE DATES IN 2021

FEBRUARY 2021

21st Due date for lodgment of activity statements (¶24-200) for reporting and payment of:

- GST, wine equalisation tax and luxury car tax by monthly GST reporters (¶34-150)
- PAYG instalment for January 2019 by monthly PAYG instalment payers (¶27-170, ¶27-200), and
- PAYG amounts withheld from payments during January 2021 by medium PAYG withholders (¶26-550).

Lodge and pay January 2021 monthly business activity statement.

28th Due date for lodgment of activity statements (¶24-200) for reporting and payment of:

- GST, wine equalisation tax and luxury car tax by quarterly GST reporters (¶34-150)
- PAYG amounts withheld from payments during October to December 2020 by small PAYG withholders that are deferred BAS payers (¶26-550)
- PAYG amounts withheld from payments during December 2020 by medium PAYG withholders that are deferred BAS payers (¶26-550)
- PAYG instalment for December 2020 by monthly PAYG instalment payers that are deferred BAS payers (¶27-170, ¶27-200)
- the second PAYG instalment for the 2020–21 year by quarterly PAYG instalment payers that are deferred BAS payers (¶27-200), and
- the third FBT instalment for the year ending 31 March 2021 for employers that are deferred BAS payers (¶35-050).

Pay quarter 2, 2020–21 instalment notice. Lodge the notice only if the instalment amount is varied.

Due date for lodgment of annual GST return or Annual Information Report for certain GST payers if annual tax return not required to be lodged (¶34-150).

Due date for lodgment and payment of 2019–20 returns for all companies and superannuation funds (including SMSFs) that were not required to lodge earlier, including new registrations (¶24-060).

Due date for lodgment of superannuation guarantee statement and payment of superannuation guarantee charge for October to December 2020 quarter (¶39-500).

MARCH 2021

21st Due date for lodgment of activity statements (¶24-200) for reporting and payment of:

- GST, wine equalisation tax and luxury car tax by monthly GST reporters (¶34-150)
- PAYG instalment for February 2021 by monthly PAYG instalment payers (¶27-200), and
- PAYG amounts withheld from payments during February 2021 by medium PAYG withholders (¶26-550).

31st End of FBT year (¶35-000).

Lodge tax return for companies and super funds with total income of more than $2m in the latest year lodged (excluding large/medium taxpayers), unless the return was due earlier. Payment for companies and super funds in this category is also due by this date.

DUE DATES IN 2021

Lodge tax return for the head company of a consolidated group (excluding large/medium), with a member who had a total income in excess of $2m in their latest year lodged, unless the return was due earlier. Payment for companies in this category is also due by this date.

Lodge tax return for individuals and trusts whose latest return resulted in a tax liability of $20,000 or more, excluding large/medium trusts. Payment for individuals and trusts in this category is due as advised on their notice of assessment.

APRIL 2021

21st Due date for lodgment of activity statements (¶24-200) for reporting and payment of:

- GST, wine equalisation tax and luxury car tax by monthly GST reporters (¶34-150)
- PAYG instalment for March 2021 by monthly PAYG instalment payers that are not deferred BAS payers (¶27-200)
- PAYG amounts withheld from payments during January to March 2021 by small PAYG withholders that are not deferred BAS payers (¶26-550)
- PAYG amounts withheld from payments during March 2021 by medium PAYG withholders that are not deferred BAS payers (¶26-550)
- the third PAYG instalment for the 2020–21 year by quarterly PAYG instalment payers that are not deferred BAS payers (¶27-200), and
- the fourth FBT instalment for the year ending 31 March 2021 for employers that are not deferred BAS payers (¶35-050).

Lodge and pay quarter 3, 2020–21 PAYG instalment activity statement for head companies of consolidated groups.

28th Due date for lodgment of activity statements (¶24-200) for reporting and payment of:

- GST, wine equalisation tax and luxury car tax by quarterly GST reporters (¶34-150)
- PAYG amounts withheld from payments during January to March 2021 by small PAYG withholders that are deferred BAS payers (¶26-550)
- PAYG amounts withheld from payments during March 2021 by medium PAYG withholders that are deferred BAS payers (¶26-550)
- PAYG instalment for March 2021 by monthly PAYG instalment payers that are deferred BAS payers (¶27-170, ¶27-200)
- the third PAYG instalment for the 2020–21 year by quarterly PAYG instalment payers that are deferred BAS payers (¶27-200), and
- the fourth FBT instalment for the year ending 31 March 2021 for employers that are deferred BAS payers (¶35-050).

Lodge and pay quarter 3, 2020–21 PAYG instalment activity statement for head companies of consolidated groups.

Due date for superannuation guarantee contributions for January to March 2021 quarter (¶39-240).

30th Due date for investment bodies to lodge TFN reports for investments made during the March 2021 quarter where TFN quoted (¶26-620).

Due date for reporting lost members information, reporting and payment of unclaimed superannuation money, and reporting and payment of small or insoluble lost member accounts, for the period 1 July to 31 December 2020 (¶13-850).

DUE DATES IN 2021

MAY 2021

15th Lodge 2020 tax returns for all entities that did not have to lodge earlier (including all remaining consolidated groups), and are not eligible for the 5 June concession. Due date for companies and super funds to pay if required.

21st Due date for lodgment of activity statements (¶24-200) for reporting and payment of:

- GST, wine equalisation tax and luxury car tax by monthly GST reporters (¶34-150)
- PAYG instalment for April 2021 by monthly PAYG instalment payers (¶27-170, ¶27-200)
- PAYG amounts withheld from payments during April 2021 by medium PAYG withholders (¶26-550), and
- FBT return for the year ended 31 March 2021 to be lodged, together with payment of FBT (as reduced by the amount of any instalments already paid) (¶35-030, ¶35-050).

Final date to add new FBT clients to your client list to ensure they receive the lodgment and payment concessions for their fringe benefits tax returns. Lodge and pay fringe benefits tax annual return if lodging by paper.

26th Lodge and pay eligible quarter 3, 2020–21 activity statements if you or your client have elected to receive and lodge electronically.

28th Due date for lodgment of superannuation guarantee statement and payment of superannuation guarantee charge for January to March 2021 quarter (¶39-500).

Pay fringe benefits tax annual return if lodging electronically.

JUNE 2021

21st Due date for lodgment of activity statements (¶24-200) for reporting and payment of:

- GST, wine equalisation tax and luxury car tax by monthly GST reporters (¶34-150)
- PAYG instalment for May 2021 by monthly PAYG instalment payers (¶27-170, ¶27-200), and
- PAYG amounts withheld from payments during May 2021 by medium PAYG withholders (¶26-550).

25th Lodge 2021 fringe benefits tax annual return for tax agents if lodging electronically. Payment (if required) is due 28 May.

30th End of financial year.

Super guarantee contributions must be paid by this date to qualify for a tax deduction in the 2020–21 financial year.

If any client receives Child Care Subsidy and Family Tax Benefit payments, the client and their partners must lodge their 2019–20 tax return by 30 June 2021, regardless of any deferrals in place.

JULY 2021

21st Due date for lodgment of activity statements (¶24-200) for reporting and payment of:

- GST, wine equalisation tax and luxury car tax by monthly GST reporters (¶34-150)

DUE DATES IN 2021

	• PAYG withheld from employee share scheme amounts for the year ended 30 June 2021 where the employee did not quote his/her TFN or ABN (¶26-320)
	• PAYG instalment for June 2021 by monthly PAYG instalment payers that are not deferred BAS payers (¶27-170, ¶27-200)
	• PAYG amounts withheld from payments during April to June 2021 by small PAYG withholders that are not deferred BAS payers (¶26-550)
	• PAYG amounts withheld from payments during June 2021 by medium PAYG withholders that are not deferred BAS payers (¶26-550)
	• the fourth PAYG instalment for the 2020–21 year by quarterly PAYG instalment payers that are not deferred BAS payers (¶27-200), and
	• the first FBT instalment for the year ending 31 March 2022 for employers that are not deferred BAS payers (¶35-050).
	Lodge and pay quarter 4, 2020–21 PAYG instalment activity statement for head companies of consolidated groups.
28th	Due date for superannuation guarantee contributions for April to June 2021 quarter (¶39-240).
	Due date for lodgment of activity statements (¶24-200) for reporting and payment of:
	• GST, wine equalisation tax and luxury car tax by quarterly GST reporters (¶34-150)
	• PAYG amounts withheld from payments during April to June 2021 by small PAYG withholders that are deferred BAS payers (¶26-550)
	• PAYG amounts withheld from payments during June 2021 by medium PAYG withholders that are deferred BAS payers (¶26-500)
	• PAYG instalment for June 2021 by monthly PAYG instalment payers that are deferred BAS payers (¶27-170, ¶27-200)
	• the fourth PAYG instalment for the 2020–21 year by quarterly PAYG instalment payers that are deferred BAS payers (¶27-200), and
	• the first FBT instalment for the year ending 31 March 2022 for employers that are deferred BAS payers (¶35-050).
	Lodge and pay quarter 4, 2020–21 activity statement if electing to receive and lodge by paper and not an active STP reporter.
	Pay quarter 4, 2020–21 instalment notice. Lodge the notice only if the instalment amount is varied.
31st	Due date for investment bodies to lodge TFN reports for investments made during the June 2021 quarter where TFN quoted (¶26-620).
	Due date for most companies to pay 2020–21 franking tax and lodge franking account return, if required (¶4-980).
	Lodge venture capital deficit tax return for June balancers.
	Lodge early stage innovation company report.

AUGUST 2021

14th	Due date for entities subject to PAYG withholding to forward annual report relating to: (a) work or services payments; (b) retirement payments and annuities or pensions; (c) benefit and compensation payments; (d) alienated personal services payments; (e) non-cash benefits; or (f) reportable fringe benefits (¶26-620).

DUE DATES IN 2021

21st	Due date for lodgment of activity statements (¶24-200) for reporting and payment of: • GST, wine equalisation tax and luxury car tax by monthly GST reporters (¶34-150) • PAYG instalment for July 2021 by monthly PAYG instalment payers (¶27-170, ¶27-200), and • PAYG amounts withheld from payments during July 2021 by medium PAYG withholders (¶26-550).
25th	Lodge and pay quarter 4, 2020–21 activity statement if lodging electronically.
28th	Due date for lodgment of superannuation guarantee statement and payment of superannuation guarantee charge for April to June 2021 quarter (¶39-500). Due date for taxpayers in the building and construction, courier, cleaning, road freight, information technology (IT) and security, investigation or surveillance industries who pay contractors in these industries to lodge taxable payments annual report (¶33-200).

SEPTEMBER 2021

21st	Due date for lodgment of activity statements (¶24-200) for reporting and payment of: • GST, wine equalisation tax and luxury car tax by monthly GST reporters (¶34-150) • PAYG instalment for August 2021 by monthly PAYG instalment payers (¶27-170, ¶27-200), and • PAYG amounts withheld from payments during August 2021 by medium PAYG withholders (¶26-550).
30th	Final day for lodgment of annual TFN withholding report for closely held trusts where a trustee has been required to withhold amounts from payments to beneficiaries during the previous financial year (¶26-620). Lodge PAYG withholding payment summary annual report if prepared by a BAS agent or tax agent.

OCTOBER 2021

21st	Due date for lodgment of activity statements (¶24-200) for reporting and payment of: • GST, wine equalisation tax and luxury car tax by monthly GST reporters (¶34-150) • PAYG instalment for September 2021 by monthly PAYG instalment payers (¶27-170, ¶27-200) • PAYG amounts withheld from payments during July to September 2021 by small PAYG withholders that are not deferred BAS payers (¶26-550) • PAYG amounts withheld from payments during August 2021 by medium PAYG withholders (¶26-550) • the first PAYG instalment for the 2020–21 year by quarterly PAYG instalment payers that are not deferred BAS payers (¶27-200), and • the second FBT instalment for the year ending 31 March 2022 for employers that are not deferred BAS payers (¶35-050).

DUE DATES IN 2021

Due date for payment of annual PAYG instalment for 2020–21 (¶27-200). Lodge only if instalment amount varied or the rate method to calculate the instalment is used.

Lodge and pay quarter 1, 2021–22 PAYG instalment activity statement for head companies of consolidated groups.

28th Due date for lodgment of activity statements (¶24-200) for reporting and payment of:

- GST, wine equalisation tax and luxury car tax by monthly GST reporters (¶34-150)
- PAYG amounts withheld from payments during July to September 2021 by small PAYG withholders that are not deferred BAS payers (¶26-550)
- PAYG amounts withheld from payments during September 2021 by medium PAYG withholders that are deferred BAS payers (¶26-550)
- PAYG instalment for September 2021 by monthly PAYG instalment payers that are deferred BAS payers (¶27-170, ¶27-200)
- the first PAYG instalment for the 2020–21 year by quarterly PAYG instalment payers that are not deferred BAS payers (¶27-200), and
- the second FBT instalment for the year ending 31 March 2022 for employers that are not deferred BAS payers (¶35-050).

Lodge and pay quarter 1, 2021–22 activity statement if electing to receive and lodge by paper and not an active STP reporter. Pay quarter 1, 2021–22 instalment notice (form R, S or T). Lodge the notice only if the instalment amount varied.

Due date for superannuation guarantee contributions for July to September 2021 quarter (¶39-240).

Lodge and pay annual activity statement for TFN withholding for closely held trusts where a trustee withheld amounts from payments to beneficiaries during the 2020–21 income year.

31st Due date for entities subject to PAYG withholding to forward annual report relating to: (a) payments for a supply where the recipient does not quote an ABN; (b) dividend, interest and royalty payments; (c) payments to foreign residents; (d) departing Australia superannuation payments; (e) the seasonal labour mobility program; or (f) mining payments (¶26-620).

Due date for investment bodies to lodge annual investment income reports, together with a reconciliation statement, relating to the 2020–21 year under TFN arrangements (¶26-620).

Due date for investment bodies to lodge TFN reports for investments made during the September quarter where TFN quoted (¶26-620).

Due date for lodgment of 2020–21 returns by individuals, trusts and partnerships (¶24-060). Special extension arrangements apply to returns for individuals, trusts and partnerships lodged by tax agents. Due date for lodgment of 2020–21 returns by companies and superannuation funds with one or more prior year returns outstanding (¶24-060).

Due date for lodgment of annual 2020–21 GST return for instalment payers who are required to lodge tax returns by 31 October 2020 (¶34-150).

Due date for most private companies to provide distribution statements to shareholders for 2020–21 (¶4-690).

Due date for lodgment of member contributions statements by superannuation funds (non-SMSF) (¶39-530).

DUE DATES IN 2021

	Due date for reporting lost members information, reporting and payment of unclaimed superannuation money and reporting and payment of small or insoluble lost member accounts, for the period 1 January to 30 June 2021 (¶13-850).
	Due date for lodgment of statements and payment of former temporary residents' unclaimed superannuation (¶14-390).
	Final date to add new clients to your client list to ensure their 2021 tax return is covered by the lodgment program.
	Lodge tax returns for all entities if one or more prior year returns were outstanding as at 30 June 2021. If all outstanding prior year returns have been lodged by 31 October 2021, the lodgment program due dates will apply to the 2021 tax return. SMSFs in this category must lodge their complete self-managed superannuation fund annual return by this date.
	Lodge and pay self-managed superannuation fund annual return for (taxable and non-taxable) new registrant SMSF if we have advised the SMSF that the first year return has a 31 October 2021 due date.
	Lodge tax returns for all entities prosecuted for non-lodgment of prior year returns and advised of a lodgment due date of 31 October 2021.
	Some prosecuted clients may have a different lodgment due date — refer to the letter you received for the applicable due date.
	Payment (if required) for individuals and trusts in this category is due as advised in their notice of assessment.
	Payment (if required) for companies and super funds in this category is due on 1 December 2021.
	SMSFs in this category must lodge their complete self-managed superannuation fund annual return by this date.
	Lodge franking account tax return when the return is a disclosure only (no amount payable) and the taxpayer is a 30 June balancer.

NOVEMBER 2021

21st	Due date for lodgment of activity statements (¶24-200) for reporting and payment of: • GST, wine equalisation tax and luxury car tax by monthly GST reporters (¶34-150) • PAYG instalment for October 2021 by monthly PAYG instalment payers (¶27-170, ¶27-200), and • PAYG amounts withheld from payments during October 2021 by medium PAYG withholders (¶26-550).
25th	Due date for lodgment of activity statements (¶24-200) for July to September 2021 quarter if lodged electronically.
28th	Due date for lodgment of superannuation guarantee statement and payment of superannuation guarantee charge for July to September 2021 quarter (¶39-500).

DECEMBER 2021

1st	Due date for payment for large/medium companies and superannuation funds (¶24-060). Lodgment of return is due 15 January 2022.
	Due date for payment for the taxable head company of a consolidated group with a member deemed to be a large/medium taxpayer in the latest year lodged. Lodgment of return is due 15 January 2022.

DUE DATES IN 2021	
	Due date for payment for companies and super funds when lodgment of the tax return was due 31 October 2021.
21st	Due date for lodgment of activity statements (¶24-200) for reporting and payment of: • GST, wine equalisation tax and luxury car tax by monthly GST reporters (¶34-150) • PAYG instalment for November 2021 by monthly PAYG instalment payers (¶27-170, ¶27-200), and • PAYG amounts withheld from payments during November 2021 by medium PAYG withholders (¶26-550).

¶45-200 Contingent tax calendar

Objections and appeals

Objection against assessment	must be received by ATO within 2 years (4 years for some taxpayers: ¶25-300) after taxpayer is served with notice of assessment (¶28-020).
Objection against amended assessment ..	must be received within later of 2 years (4 years for some taxpayers: ¶25-300) after taxpayer is served with notice of original assessment that has been amended or 60 days after taxpayer is served with notice of amended assessment (¶28-020).
Objection against private ruling	must be received by ATO within later of 60 days after applicant is served with notice of ruling or 2 years (4 years for some taxpayers: ¶25-310) after last day for lodgment of rulee's return for income year to which ruling relates (¶24-560).
Application to AAT for review of disallowed objection	must be lodged (together with an application fee, subject to exemptions) within 60 days of service of notice of disallowance or partial disallowance of objection (¶28-090). (The AAT can grant an extension of time: ¶28-100.)
Appeal to Federal Court against disallowed objection	must be lodged (together with a filing fee, subject to exemptions) within 60 days of service of notice of disallowance or partial disallowance of objection (a setting down fee and hearing fee are also payable, subject to exemptions) (¶28-110). (Note that an extension of time cannot be granted.)
Appeal to Federal Court against decision of AAT	must be lodged (together with a filing fee, subject to exemptions) within 28 days of AAT's decision being furnished (a setting down fee and hearing fee are also payable, subject to exemptions) (¶28-120). (The court can grant an extension of time: ¶28-120.)

PAYG withholding

Deductions made by large remitters on a Saturday or Sunday	must be remitted by the second Monday after that day (¶26-550).
Deductions made by large remitters on a Monday or Tuesday	must be remitted by the first Monday after that day (¶26-550).
Deductions made by large remitters on a Wednesday	must be remitted by the second Thursday after that day (¶26-550).
Deductions made by large remitters on a Thursday or Friday	must be remitted by the first Thursday after that day (¶26-550).

TFN declaration received by employer from employee	must be forwarded to Commissioner within 14 days of receipt (¶26-350).
Amounts withheld, alienated personal services payments or payments in respect of non-cash benefits	must be notified to Commissioner on or before the day the amount is due to be paid (¶26-620).
Notification of a payee entitled to receive payment for work or services, retirement payment, annuity or pension, benefit or compensation	must be given to Commissioner within 14 days of the payer entering into the relationship with the payee (unless a TFN declaration is in force) (¶26-620).

Consolidation

Notification of choice to consolidate a consolidatable group as at a particular date	must be given to Commissioner by the date that the first consolidated income tax return is lodged (¶8-000).
Choice overriding entry history rule or exit history rule	must generally be made by the head company or leaving entity within 90 days after the joining time or leaving time (¶8-020).
Choice to continue consolidated group where shelf company interposed between head company and its shareholders	must be made within 28 days after completion time (¶8-500).
Notification of change of provisional head company of MEC group	must be given to Commissioner within 28 days of the change (¶8-610).

Corporate losses

Notification of choice as to amount of corporate loss from prior years to be deducted in current year	must be given to Commissioner in entity's tax return for the relevant income year (¶3-060).

Imputation

Shareholder distribution statement	must be given by non-private company to shareholder before or at the time the dividend is paid; or by private company within 4 months after end of income year (¶4-690).
Payment of untainting tax	must be made within 21 days after the end of the franking period in which the untainting choice was made (¶4-950).
Payment of franking deficit tax and lodgment of further return in respect of tax refund received within 3 months after year end	generally must be made within 14 days after the refund is received (¶4-980).

Life insurance companies

Transfer of excess assets out of the complying superannuation/FHSA asset pool or out of segregated exempt assets .	must be done within 30 days after completion of the relevant valuations (¶3-515, ¶3-520).

R&D

Registration with Innovation Australia ..	must be made within 10 months of the end of the year of income (¶20-190).

Case Table

This is a complete list of all cases referred to in the commentary. All references are to **numbered paragraphs**.

Cases involving the Federal Commissioner of Taxation or other taxation authorities are listed alphabetically according to the name of the taxpayer. The same applies to cases involving the Crown, the state, the Commonwealth, or the Attorney-General of any state.

The ''named'' AAT cases have been integrated into the alphabetical table of cases. The ''numbered'' Boards and AAT cases are listed separately at the end of the alphabetical table of cases.

Paragraph

A

Paragraph

Paragraph

Paragraph

G

M

Paragraph

Paragraph

Paragraph

Shail v FC of T 2007 ATC 4511 25-540
Shail Superannuation Fund v FC of T 2011 ATC ¶10-228 .... 13-100; 13-150
Sharp v FC of T [2010] AATA 1023 29-530
Sharp & Anor v DFC of T & Ors 88 ATC 4259; 89 ATC 4059 25-220
Sharpcan Pty Ltd; FC of T v 2019 ATC ¶20-715 16-060
Shaw v Director of Housing & Anor (No 2) 2001 ATC 4054 34-270
Shaw v Director of Housing and State of Tasmania (No 2) 2001 ATC 4054 34-105
Sheil v C of T 87 ATC 4430 16-010
Shepherd v FC of T 75 ATC 4244 10-430
Shepherd v FC of T (1965) 113 CLR 385 30-900
Sherritt Gordon Mines Ltd; FC of T v 77 ATC 4365 10-510
Shields; FC of T v 99 ATC 4783 16-665
Sills v FC of T Pitcher, 2010 ATC ¶10-164 14-640
Silverbrook v DFC of T; Lee v DFC of T 2020 ATC ¶20-747 .... 25-560; 26-710
Simionato Holdings Pty Ltd v FC of T (No 2) 95 ATC 4720 25-220
Simons v FC of T 81 ATC 4280 25-140
Sinclair v FC of T 2001 ATC 2092 16-420
Sinclair v FC of T 2010 ATC ¶10-163 .... 16-740; 29-160
Sinclair v FC of T 2012 ATC ¶10-275 14-300
Sinclair (HR) and Son Pty Ltd v FC of T (1966) 114 CLR 537; 14 ATD 194 10-260
Single v FC of T (1964) 13 ATD 284 6-180
Sisely v FC of T 2014 ATC ¶10-368 13-785
Skase v FC of T 92 ATC 4001 25-550
Skiba v FC of T 2007 ATC 2467 30-665
Skourmallas v FC of T 2019 ATC ¶10-514 34-110
Slade Bloodstock Pty Ltd v FC of T 2007 ATC 5276 35-120
Slater Holdings Ltd; FC of T v (No 2) 84 ATC 4883 4-140
Sleight; FC of T v 2004 ATC 4477 .... 18-020; 30-160; 30-170
Smiles v FC of T & Ors 92 ATC 4475 28-180
Smith v FC of T [2010] AATA 576; 2010 ATC ¶10-146 16-665
Smith v FC of T 2011 ATC ¶10-197 14-300
Smith (Darcy Peter); FC of T v 81 ATC 4114 .... 10-020; 10-210; 16-560
Smith; FC of T v 78 ATC 4157 16-450
Smithkline Beecham Laboratories (Australia) Ltd v FC of T 93 ATC 4629 16-844
Smorgon & Ors v FC of T & Ors 79 ATC 4039 25-240
Snaidr v FC of T 98 ATC 2048 16-340
Sneddon v FC of T 2012 ATC ¶10-264 21-010
Snell v DFC of T 2020 ATC ¶20-734 .... 25-560; 26-710
Snowden & Willson Pty Ltd; FC of T v (1958) 99 CLR 431; 11 ATD 463 16-840
Sobczuk v FC of T 2003 ATC 2235 16-844
Sobel Investments Pty Ltd v FC of T 2012 ATC ¶10-243 16-660
Social Credit Savings & Loan Society v FC of T 71 ATC 4232 3-810
Softwood Pulp & Paper Ltd v FC of T 76 ATC 4439 16-154
Solling; FC of T v 85 ATC 4518 18-020
Solomon; DFC of T v; DFC of T v MURIWAI 2003 ATC 4474 25-560
Sommer v FC of T 2002 ATC 4815 10-210
Sonntag v FC of T 2008 ATC ¶10-000 29-400
Soubra v FC of T 2009 ATC ¶10-113 4-490
South Australian Battery Makers Pty Ltd; FC of T v 78 ATC 4412 16-060
South Steyne Hotel Pty Ltd & Ors v FC of T 2009 ATC ¶20-145 34-230
South Sydney Junior Rugby League Club Ltd v FC of T 2006 ATC 2150 10-605
Southern Farmers Group Ltd v DFC of T & Ors 90 ATC 4056 28-180
Southwell-Keely v FC of T [2008] AATA 606 16-450
Spargo's case; Harmony & Montague Tin & Copper Mining Co, Re (1873) 8 Ch App 407 16-540
Sparks and FC of T, Re [2000] AATA 28; (2000) 43 ATR 1324 29-160
Spassked Pty Ltd v FC of T 2003 ATC 5099 .... 16-010; 16-740
Spassked v FC of T 2007 ATC 5406 16-740

Paragraph

Paragraph

W

Decisions of Boards of Review and AAT

Paragraph

Paragraph

1980 ATC

1981 ATC

1982 ATC

1983 ATC

1984 ATC

1985 ATC

Paragraph

2010 ATC

2011 ATC

2012 ATC

2013 ATC

2014 ATC

2015 ATC

2016 ATC

2018 ATC

Section Finding List

This Section Finding List enables the reader to locate commentary on specific legislative provisions. Opposite each provision listed you will find references to the **paragraph(s)** in the text at which the relevant commentary appears.

Pending Legislation is listed at the end of the Section Finding List.

INCOME TAX ASSESSMENT ACT 1997

Chapter 1 — Introduction and Core Provisions

Part 1-1 – Preliminary

Part 1-3 – Core Provisions

Part 1-4 – Checklists

Chapter 2 — Liability Rules of General Application

Part 2-1 – Assessable Income

Part 2-5 – Rules about Deductibility of Particular Kinds of Amounts

Part 2-5 – Rules about Deductibility of Particular Kinds of Amounts—continued

Part 2-10 – Capital Allowances

Part 2-15 – Non-assessable Income

Part 2-15 – Non-assessable Income—continued

Part 2-20 – Tax Offsets

Part 2-25 – Trading Stock

Chapter 3 — Specialist Liability Rules

Part 3-1 – Capital Gains and Losses: General Topics—continued

Part 3-3 – Capital Gains and Losses: Special Topics

Part 3-3 – Capital Gains and Losses: Special Topics—continued

Part 3-5 – Corporate Taxpayers and Corporate Distributions—continued

Part 3-6 – The Imputation System

Part 3-10 – Financial Transactions

Part 3-10 – Financial Transactions—continued

Part 3-30 – Superannuation

Part 3-32 – Co-operatives and mutual entities

Part 3-35 – Insurance Business

Part 3-80 – Roll-Overs Applying to Assets Generally

Part 3-90 – Consolidated Groups

Part 3-95 – Value Shifting

Chapter 4 — International Aspects of Income Tax

Part 4-5 – General

Chapter 5 — Administration

Part 5-30 – Record-keeping and Other Obligations

Part 5-35 – Miscellaneous

Chapter 6 — The Dictionary

Part 6-1 – Concepts and Topics

INCOME TAX ASSESSMENT REGULATIONS 1997

INCOME TAX ASSESSMENT ACT 1936

INCOME TAX ASSESSMENT (1936 ACT) REGULATION 2015

INCOME TAX (TRANSITIONAL PROVISIONS) ACT 1997

ADMINISTRATIVE APPEALS TRIBUNAL ACT 1975

A NEW TAX SYSTEM (GOODS AND SERVICES TAX) ACT 1999

A NEW TAX SYSTEM (GOODS AND SERVICES TAX) REGULATIONS 2019

FRINGE BENEFITS TAX ASSESSMENT ACT 1986

FRINGE BENEFITS TAX ASSESSMENT REGULATIONS 2018

INCOME TAX RATES ACT 1986

INTERNATIONAL TAX AGREEMENTS ACT 1953

MEDICARE LEVY ACT 1986

RETIREMENT SAVINGS ACCOUNTS REGULATIONS 1997

SUPERANNUATION GUARANTEE (ADMINISTRATION) ACT 1992

SUPERANNUATION GUARANTEE (ADMINISTRATION) REGULATIONS 2018

SUPERANNUATION (EXCESS TRANSFER BALANCE TAX) IMPOSITION ACT 2016

SUPERANNUATION (GOVERNMENT CO-CONTRIBUTION FOR LOW INCOME EARNERS) ACT 2003

SUPERANNUATION INDUSTRY (SUPERVISION) ACT 1993

SUPERANNUATION INDUSTRY (SUPERVISION) REGULATIONS 1994

SUPERANNUATION (UNCLAIMED MONEY AND LOST MEMBERS) ACT 1999

SUPERANNUATION (UNCLAIMED MONEY AND LOST MEMBERS) REGULATIONS 2019

TAXATION ADMINISTRATION ACT 1953

TAXATION ADMINISTRATION REGULATIONS 1976

TAXATION ADMINISTRATION REGULATIONS 2017

TAXATION (INTEREST ON OVERPAYMENTS AND EARLY PAYMENTS) ACT 1983

OTHER LEGISLATION

PENDING LEGISLATION

Rulings Finding List

This list shows details of the paragraphs where you will find specific rulings, determinations and other ATO statements in the text. The list is arranged into three categories:

- **Income Tax Rulings and Determinations**, covering both draft and final rulings in the TR, IT and TD series
- **Other Rulings and Determinations**, incorporating rulings on GST, superannuation and other areas
- **ATO Statements and Interpretative Decisions (ID)**, containing non-binding statements of the Commissioner's views.

For a list of rulings by subject matter, see the Index under the heading "Taxation Rulings".

INCOME TAX RULINGS AND DETERMINATIONS

Taxation Rulings

Taxation Rulings—continued

Draft Rulings

Income Tax Rulings

Taxation Determinations

Taxation Determinations—continued

Determination	Paragraph
TD 97/14	16-040; 16-550
TD 97/19	16-340
TD 97/24	17-015
TD 97/25	10-260
TD 98/4	6-320
TD 98/19	11-550
TD 98/20	21-180
TD 98/23	11-250; 11-270; 11-550; 12-680
TD 98/24	11-410; 17-640; 31-300
TD 1999/6	13-150
TD 1999/7	10-605; 22-150
TD 1999/8–TD 1999/26	22-022
TD 1999/34	10-030
TD 1999/35	16-010
TD 1999/38	3-820
TD 1999/40	11-390
TD 1999/42	16-740
TD 1999/43	11-740
TD 1999/45	16-430
TD 1999/47–TD 1999/61	12-460
TD 1999/62	16-180
TD 1999/63	16-635
TD 1999/66	11-760
TD 1999/67–TD 1999/69	11-730
TD 1999/70	11-770
TD 1999/71	11-760
TD 1999/73	11-750
TD 1999/74	11-770
TD 1999/76	11-270; 11-510
TD 1999/77	11-280
TD 1999/79	11-270
TD 1999/80	11-280
TD 1999/81	11-280
TD 1999/84	11-510
TD 2000/2	11-310
TD 2000/3	11-550; 12-600
TD 2000/5	4-300
TD 2000/6	12-580
TD 2000/7	11-270
TD 2000/8	12-870
TD 2000/9	22-160
TD 2000/10	11-250; 11-570; 12-330
TD 2000/11	12-580
TD 2000/12	10-865; 21-710
TD 2000/13	11-740
TD 2000/14	11-740
TD 2000/15	11-730
TD 2000/17	16-430
TD 2000/24	5-070; 16-856
TD 2000/31	11-380; 11-410
TD 2000/32	11-380
TD 2000/33	11-380
TD 2000/34	11-380
TD 2000/35	11-640
TD 2000/36	12-260
TD 2000/37	12-260
TD 2000/38	12-270
TD 2000/39	12-270
TD 2000/40	12-270
TD 2000/42	12-270
TD 2000/43	12-270
TD 2000/45	12-290
TD 2000/46	14-510
TD 2000/48	26-220
TD 2000/49	26-220
TD 2000/50	12-325
TD 2000/51	12-325
TD 2000/52	11-310
TD 2000/53	27-200
TD 2000/54	27-200
TD 2001/2	4-205
TD 2001/3	22-022
TD 2001/9	11-570; 12-290
TD 2001/13	11-560
TD 2001/14	4-300; 11-270; 11-310
TD 2001/19	22-020
TD 2001/21–TD 2001/24	10-885; 22-150
TD 2001/26	11-270
TD 2001/27	4-300; 11-270; 11-310
TD 2002/1	16-850
TD 2002/4	11-550; 12-325
TD 2002/10	11-033
TD 2002/18	18-030
TD 2002/22	12-325
TD 2002/23	16-152; 30-170
TD 2002/24	5-010; 30-170
TD 2002/25	11-380
TD 2003/1	11-550
TD 2003/3	30-170
TD 2003/9	16-060; 30-170
TD 2003/10	8-280; 16-850
TD 2003/11	8-280; 16-850
TD 2003/12	18-125
TD 2003/15	16-060; 23-240
TD 2003/16	23-250
TD 2003/17	23-250
TD 2003/20	16-040
TD 2003/27	21-097
TD 2003/28	11-290
TD 2003/32	16-660; 23-380
TD 2004/1	13-150; 16-010; 16-660
TD 2004/3	12-590
TD 2004/5	10-010
TD 2004/7	16-950
TD 2004/13	11-290
TD 2004/17	16-910
TD 2004/20	35-000
TD 2004/21	35-030
TD 2004/22	3-170
TD 2004/23	16-962
TD 2004/26	16-650
TD 2004/31	21-160
TD 2004/32	17-015
TD 2004/33	8-920
TD 2004/34	8-920
TD 2004/35	8-920
TD 2004/36	8-010; 16-740
TD 2004/40	8-010
TD 2004/42	8-010
TD 2004/47	8-010
TD 2004/50	8-010
TD 2004/51	8-010
TD 2004/53	8-210
TD 2004/55	8-210
TD 2004/57–TD 2004/60	8-210
TD 2004/62	8-210
TD 2004/68	8-010
TD 2004/70	8-210
TD 2004/72	8-210
TD 2004/74	8-210
TD 2004/75	10-010
TD 2004/76	8-010
TD 2004/79	8-010; 8-210; 8-920
TD 2004/80	8-920
TD 2004/81	8-920
TD 2004/82	8-010; 8-920
TD 2004/84	23-320
TD 2004/85	23-320
TD 2005/1	17-015; 17-710
TD 2005/2	22-150

Taxation Determinations—continued

Draft Determinations

OTHER RULINGS AND DETERMINATIONS

Class Rulings

Class Rulings—continued

Fuel Tax Rulings

Fuel Tax Determinations

GST Rulings

Draft GST Rulings

GST Determinations

ATO STATEMENTS AND INTERPRETATIVE DECISIONS

Statements

Statement	Paragraph
PS LA 2010/4	4-215; 4-246
PS LA 2011/2	29-400
PS LA 2011/12	29-530
PS LA 2011/14	25-410; 25-500
PS LA 2011/17	25-450
PS LA 2011/18	25-540
PS LA 2011/19	29-400
PS LA 2011/20	4-710
PS LA 2011/22	24-380
PS LA 2011/23	13-180; 13-755; 13-850
PS LA 2011/25	16-210
PS LA 2011/27	24-620
PS LA 2011/29	4-200
PS LA 2011/30	29-300
PS LA 2012/2	25-500
PS LA 2012/4	29-140; 29-400; 34-360
PS LA 2012/5	29-400; 34-360
PS LA 2012/6	24-380
PS LA 2013/3	25-210
PS LA 2013/4	1-710
PS LA 2013/5	8-000
PS LA 2014/1	16-962
PS LA 2014/2	22-630
PS LA 2014/3	22-630
PS LA 2014/4	29-140
PS LA 2015/1	25-210
PS LA 2015/2	6-230
PS LA 2015/3	22-610
PS LA 2015/4	22-650
PS LA 2016/3	33-120
PS LA 2016/4	33-110
PS LA 2016/5	33-110
PS LA 2016/6	22-165
PS LA 2017/1	19-003
PS LA 2017/2	30-205
PS LA 2020/3	13-800; 29-310
PS LA 2020/4	39-550

2001 Decisions

Decision	Paragraph
ID 2001/3	14-510
ID 2001/42	16-590
ID 2001/253	35-120
ID 2001/255	35-252
ID 2001/313	35-580
ID 2001/329	16-270
ID 2001/331	16-270
ID 2001/332	35-100
ID 2001/333	35-070
ID 2001/381	10-500
ID 2001/532	35-330
ID 2001/549	16-842
ID 2001/615	16-270
ID 2001/618	14-510
ID 2001/748	16-520
ID 2001/758	35-590
ID 2001/761	35-430
ID 2001/803	35-340

2002 Decisions

Decision	Paragraph
ID 2002/102	35-170
ID 2002/110	18-100
ID 2002/122	4-940
ID 2002/180	17-270
ID 2002/232	35-460
ID 2002/291	16-700
ID 2002/292	16-700
ID 2002/309	39-400
ID 2002/319	16-175
ID 2002/330	16-700
ID 2002/412	35-430
ID 2002/463	16-450
ID 2002/484	16-440
ID 2002/517	16-452
ID 2002/573	16-650
ID 2002/604	4-940
ID 2002/614	35-330
ID 2002/625	9-295
ID 2002/691	11-730
ID 2002/755	17-015
ID 2002/773	18-030
ID 2002/775	16-175
ID 2002/780	18-160
ID 2002/782	17-720
ID 2002/784	18-030
ID 2002/788	4-682
ID 2002/794	23-115
ID 2002/810–ID 2002/811	17-015
ID 2002/818	17-100
ID 2002/822	10-050
ID 2002/848	35-080
ID 2002/915	17-100
ID 2002/919	16-640
ID 2002/925	35-240
ID 2002/933	17-640
ID 2002/935	16-840
ID 2002/942	22-730
ID 2002/955	12-395
ID 2002/963	35-645
ID 2002/997	17-630
ID 2002/1004	16-310
ID 2002/1016	17-640
ID 2002/1017	17-640
ID 2002/1037	17-020
ID 2002/1083	17-020
ID 2002/1091	16-010
ID 2002/1092	16-010

2003 Decisions

Decision	Paragraph
ID 2003/25	35-254
ID 2003/40	35-100
ID 2003/48 (former)	13-220
ID 2003/80	17-330
ID 2003/84	16-452
ID 2003/110–ID 2003/112	17-630
ID 2003/111	17-640
ID 2003/128	12-700
ID 2003/140	14-510
ID 2003/157–ID 2003/160	35-650
ID 2003/180	14-510
ID 2003/185	17-630
ID 2003/186	17-630
ID 2003/206–ID 2003/208	19-060
ID 2003/218–ID 2003/221	17-630
ID 2003/229	20-470
ID 2003/261	23-320
ID 2003/315	35-270
ID 2003/316	35-120; 35-310
ID 2003/317	35-310
ID 2003/325–ID 2003/327	23-115
ID 2003/340	12-395
ID 2003/341	12-395
ID 2003/347	35-270
ID 2003/359	18-200
ID 2003/374	16-020

2003 Decisions—continued

2004 Decisions

Decision	Paragraph
ID 2004/657	16-152
ID 2004/659	16-842
ID 2004/685	3-060
ID 2004/714	18-100
ID 2004/718	16-060
ID 2004/721	17-015
ID 2004/731	11-440
ID 2004/757	10-605
ID 2004/760	3-015
ID 2004/768	16-060
ID 2004/795–ID 2004/797	19-070
ID 2004/796	19-070
ID 2004/798	3-430
ID 2004/810	16-895
ID 2004/811	3-800; 16-895
ID 2004/825	20-470
ID 2004/847	16-010
ID 2004/848	16-740
ID 2004/852	35-150
ID 2004/854	23-070
ID 2004/856	23-070
ID 2004/858	17-015
ID 2004/860–ID 2004/862	20-530
ID 2004/873	4-660
ID 2004/882	11-770
ID 2004/885	23-340
ID 2004/935	35-254
ID 2004/939	8-100
ID 2004/940	17-810
ID 2004/949	3-105
ID 2004/955	5-070
ID 2004/957	17-020
ID 2004/958	17-010
ID 2004/959	8-100
ID 2004/960	8-100
ID 2004/967	4-225
ID 2004/968	13-150; 16-010; 16-660
ID 2004/978	12-870
ID 2004/981	16-910
ID 2004/982	17-015

2005 Decisions

Decision	Paragraph
ID 2005/8	3-105
ID 2005/12	16-910
ID 2005/13	16-910
ID 2005/20	23-320
ID 2005/21	17-030
ID 2005/26	16-450
ID 2005/27	16-450
ID 2005/30	16-910
ID 2005/33	39-024
ID 2005/42	16-742
ID 2005/58	4-246
ID 2005/60	8-610
ID 2005/63	8-000
ID 2005/64	4-690
ID 2005/65	4-640; 4-690
ID 2005/67	4-660
ID 2005/69	16-450
ID 2005/99	16-858
ID 2005/109	35-500
ID 2005/141	39-260
ID 2005/143	14-270
ID 2005/146	35-617
ID 2005/156	35-430
ID 2005/157	19-050
ID 2005/158	35-380; 35-650
ID 2005/164	11-270
ID 2005/166	35-060
ID 2005/190	17-630
ID 2005/195	35-110
ID 2005/197	17-100; 17-200; 17-630
ID 2005/210	35-190; 35-210
ID 2005/216	11-260
ID 2005/244	16-910
ID 2005/246	16-310
ID 2005/252	22-730
ID 2005/260	22-020
ID 2005/263	23-250
ID 2005/275	18-135
ID 2005/281	23-340
ID 2005/284	16-152
ID 2005/297	4-249
ID 2005/299	4-246
ID 2005/314	35-460
ID 2005/318	23-075
ID 2005/320	23-075
ID 2005/321	23-075
ID 2005/323	23-075
ID 2005/344	23-350
ID 2005/348	10-605
ID 2005/366	35-645

2006 Decisions

Decision	Paragraph
ID 2006/6	39-500
ID 2006/17	21-098
ID 2006/18	5-050
ID 2006/31	4-940
ID 2006/34	11-770
ID 2006/35	3-105
ID 2006/52	35-655
ID 2006/72	10-260
ID 2006/93	35-252
ID 2006/102	16-740; 23-105
ID 2006/103	23-110
ID 2006/125	23-105
ID 2006/130	8-400
ID 2006/149	3-475
ID 2006/151	17-010
ID 2006/152	3-135
ID 2006/155	10-605
ID 2006/157	3-105
ID 2006/159	35-080
ID 2006/161–ID 2006/162	22-125
ID 2006/167	17-640
ID 2006/168	17-630
ID 2006/169	17-015
ID 2006/170	8-400
ID 2006/171	8-400
ID 2006/179	11-550
ID 2006/181	21-098
ID 2006/188	4-682
ID 2006/196	35-110
ID 2006/197	35-350
ID 2006/200	17-670
ID 2006/201	8-020
ID 2006/206	8-550
ID 2006/214	23-340
ID 2006/217	16-748
ID 2006/218	16-045
ID 2006/222	11-320
ID 2006/230	23-105
ID 2006/235	20-510
ID 2006/244	23-380
ID 2006/253	35-190; 35-230
ID 2006/258	3-120

2006 Decisions—continued

2007 Decisions

2008 Decisions

2009 Decisions

2012 Decisions—continued

2013 Decisions

2014 Decisions

2015 Decisions

2016 Decisions

2018 Decisions

Taxpayer Alerts

Index

All references are to paragraph numbers. Entries marked with a bullet (●) refer to overview commentary or to other general reference points such as checklists or tables.

Paragraph